FAMILY LAW:
CASES, TEXT, PROBLEMS

FAMILY LAW: CASES, TEXT, PROBLEMS

Fifth Edition

Ira Mark Ellman
Willard Pedrick Distinguished Research Scholar and Professor of Law
Arizona State University

Paul M. Kurtz
Associate Dean and J. Alton Hosch Professor of Law
University of Georgia

Lois A. Weithorn
Professor of Law
University of California, Hastings College of the Law

Brian H. Bix
Frederick W. Thomas Professor of Law and Philosophy
University of Minnesota

Karen Czapanskiy
Professor of Law
University of Maryland

Maxine Eichner
Professor of Law
University of North Carolina

Library of Congress Cataloging-in-Publication Data

Family law : cases, text, problems / Ira Mark Ellman . . . [et al.]. -- 5th ed.
    p. cm.
Includes index.
ISBN 978-1-4224-7663-5 (hardbound)
1. Domestic relations--United States--Cases. I. Ellman, Ira Mark.
    KF505.F344 2010
    346.7301'5--dc22

    2010021532

NOTE TO USERS

To ensure that you are using the latest materials available in this area, please be sure to periodically check the LexisNexis Law School web site for downloadable updates and supplements at www.lexisnexis.com/lawschool.

Editorial Offices
121 Chanlon Rd., New Providence, NJ 07974 (908) 464-6800
201 Mission St., San Francisco, CA 94105-1831 (415) 908-3200
www.lexisnexis.com

MATTHEW◆BENDER

(2010–Pub.3056)

DEDICATION

When I remember bygone days
I think how evening follows morn;
So many I loved were not yet dead,
So many I love were not yet born.

Ogden Nash, *The Middle*.

In memory of the lives of Edward Ellman and Larry Spector, and in awe of my marvelous luck 42 years ago when I married Tara.

I.M.E.

To Mom and Dad, who taught me the meaning of family and who I miss every day; to my loving sisters who have taught me over the years that geography is no impediment to closeness; and, most especially to the incredible Carol and our son, Benji, and to Claire who has made our family complete.

P.M.K.

To Zachary and Cara (the lights of my life), and in memory of my mother Corinne (a woman for all seasons).

L.A.W.

To Karen and David.

B.B.

To Dana, Cecily, Jake, Max and Nathan, who teach me something new about family every day.

K.C.

To Eric, and to Hannah, Abe, and Eli, who simultaneously delayed this project and gave it meaning.

M.E.

PREFACE

Twenty-five years ago, Ira Ellman carefully taped up a very large and very heavy box, preparing it for shipment to a publishing company called Michie. The box contained many hundreds of pages of typescript, and of Xerox copies of cases and articles that had been edited by cutting them up with scissors and pasting them with tape. The product of countless months of work by both Ellman and Paul Kurtz, the contents would become the first edition of *Family Law*. It was among the earliest law school casebooks published by Michie, which had recently acquired the casebook business previously owned by the Bobbs-Merrill Company — a company better known for having been the original publisher of the most popular American cookbook ever written, *The Joy of Cooking*, as well as the first American fairy tale, *The Wonderful Wizard of Oz*. *Family Law* never sold as well as they both did, although it has not done badly for a casebook. But it did get off to a rocky start. Unprepared for the potential heft of a law school casebook, Michie, which had its own printing plant, discovered that its factory's binding machines could not accommodate a book as large as *Family Law*'s first edition. The crisis was abated when the factory manager thought to place the unbound pages in large stacks under heavy weights, forcing out the air and compressing the pages just enough to allow them to be bound.

A lot has changed since the first edition appeared in 1986. Neither Bobbs-Merrill nor Michie any longer exist, and no publisher would allow an author to submit his work in the form of an actual physical *manuscript*. Nor do many publishers manufacture books themselves, and indeed we seem to be in sight of the day when no one will, when electronic distribution will entirely replace printed copies.

And of course the law continues to change. This new edition reflects those changes through the time when the electronic "manuscript" was submitted to the editor in November of 2009. We have omitted, in statutory citations, any references to a year, because statutory language is no longer checked against printed volumes and pocket parts with publication year, but against electronic research services. Such a check was made on all statutory citations at the time of the manuscript's preparation during 2009, and the citations were current as of that time.

Finally, the authors of *Family Law* continue to change. Successful collaborations create bonds that are one of the great pleasures of authorship. Ira Ellman and Paul Kurtz experienced that in the first edition, as we both remember, back before the age of email, the special pleasure we took in meeting one another for our very first face-to-face conversation some months *after* the first edition's publication. In the years since, we have been very fortunate in the additional partners we have been able to enlist to work with us, beginning with Kate Bartlett in the second edition, and Elizabeth Scott in the third and the fourth, and our friendship with each of them happily continues even though they have both gone on to focus on other endeavors. Ira and Paul are delighted that Lois Weithorn and Brian Bix, who joined for the fourth edition, have continued to contribute to this one, and all four of us have been very pleased to welcome Maxine Eichner and Karen Czapanskiy to the endeavor. Adding new authors adds new perspectives and new ideas, to the benefit of the entire enterprise, and their impact will undoubtedly grow in the future. We have nonetheless adhered to two features that were distinctive among family law casebooks in the first edition: extensive text along with cases and excerpts from the

PREFACE

scholarly literature, and Problems. The goal is to minimize the time the teacher must spend on making clear what the law is so that class time can instead focus on complications in the law's application, and on the policy issues presented by its formulation.

We all have people to thank, among the colleagues, librarians, staff, and students in our respective institutions, for invaluable assistance in this project and others. They know who they are, and they know that we do also.

I.M.E.
P.M.K.
L.A.W.
B.H.B
M.E.
K.C.

November 6, 2009

ACKNOWLEDGMENTS

Excerpted material appearing in this book is reprinted by permission as listed below.

Altman, Scott, *Lurking in the Shadow*, 68 S. CAL. L. REV. 493 (1995). Copyright © 1995. Reprinted by permission of the author.

AMERICAN LAW INSTITUTE, PRINCIPLES OF THE LAW OF FAMILY DISSOLUTION: ANALYSIS AND RECOMMENDATIONS (2002). Copyright © 2002 by The American Law Institute. Reprinted by permission.

Anderson, Elizabeth S., *Is Women's Labor a Commodity?*, 19 PHIL. & PUB. AFF. 71 (1988). Copyright © 1988. Reprinted by permission of the author.

Atwood, Barbara Ann, *Achieving Permanency for American Indian and Alaskan Children: Lessons From Tribal Traditions*, 37 CAP. U. L. REV. 243 (2008). Copyright © 2008. Reprinted by permission of the author.

Barrett, Paul M., *Wendt Divorce Dissects Job of Corporate Wife*, WALL ST. J., Dec. 6, 1996 at B. Copyright © 1996 Dow Jones & Company, Inc. Reprinted by permission.

Barth, Richard, Fred Wulczyn & Tom Crea, *From Anticipation to Evidence: Research on the Adoption and Safe Families Act*, 12 VA. J. SOC. POL'Y & L. 371 (2005). Copyright © 2005. Reprinted by permission

BIANCHI, SUZANNE M., JOHN P. ROBINSON & MELISSA A. MILKIE, CHANGING RHYTHMS OF AMERICAN FAMILY LIFE (2006). Copyright © 2006 American Sociological Association/Russell Sage Foundation, 112 East 64th Street, New York, NY 10065. Reprinted with permission.

Cahn, Naomi, *The Moral Complexities of Family Law*, 50 STAN. L. REV. 225 (1997). Copyright © 1997 by Stanford Law Review. Reprinted by permission of Stanford Law Review.

Case, Mary Anne, *How High the Apple Pie? A Few Troubling Questions About Where, Why and How the Burden of Care for Children Should be Shifted*, 76 CHI.-KENT L. REV. 1753 (2001). Copyright © 2001. Reprinted by permission.

CERE, DAN, REPORT FROM THE COUNCIL ON FAMILY LAW, THE FUTURE OF FAMILY LAW: LAW AND MARRIAGE CRISIS IN NORTH AMERICA (2005). Copyright © 2005. Reprinted by permission of the Institute for American Values.

CHERLIN, ANDREW J., MARRIAGE, DIVORCE, REMARRIAGE (rev. & enl. ed. 1992). Copyright © 1981, 1992 by the President and Fellows of Harvard College. Reprinted by permission of the author.

Coontz, Stephanie, Op-Ed., *Too Close for Comfort*, THE N.Y. TIMES, Nov. 7, 2006 at 21. Copyright © 2006 The New York Times. All rights reserved. Used by permission and protected by the Copyright Laws of the United States. The printing, copying, redistribution, or retransmission of the Material without express written permission is prohibited.

CRITTENDEN, ANN, THE PRICE OF MOTHERHOOD — WHY THE MOST IMPORTANT JOB IN THE WORLD IS STILL THE LEAST VALUED (2001). Copyright © 2001 by Ann Crittenden. Reprinted by arrangement with Henry Holt and Company, LLC.

Eichner, Maxine, *Dependency and the Liberal Polity: On Martha Fineman's The*

ACKNOWLEDGMENTS

Autonomy Myth, 93 CAL. L. REV. 1285 (2005). Copyright © 2005 by the California Law Review, Inc. Reprinted by permission of the California Law Review, Inc.

Ellman, Ira Mark, *"Contract Thinking" Was Marvin's Fatal Flaw*, 76 N.D. L. REV. 1365 (2001). Copyright © 2001. Reprinted by permission of the Author.

Ellman, *Divorce Rates, Marriage Rates, and the Problematic Persistence of Traditional Marital Roles*, 34 FAM. L.Q. 1 (2000). Copyright © 2000. Reprinted by permission of the author.

Ellman, *Fudging Failure: The Economic Analysis Used to Construct Child Support Guidelines*, 2004 U. CHI. L. FORUM 167. Copyright © 2004. Reprinted by permission of the author.

Ellman, *The Future of Marriage: Marital Roles and Declining Marriage Rates*, 41 FAM. L.Q. 455 (2007). Copyright © 2007. Reprinted by permission of the author.

Ellman, *The Misguided Movement to Revive Fault Divorce*, 11 INT'L J.L. POL'Y & FAM. 216 (1997). Copyright © 1997. Reprinted by permission of the author.

Ellman, *The Place of Fault in a Modern Divorce Law*, 28 ARIZ. ST. L.J. 773 (1996). Copyright © 1996. Reprinted by permission of the author.

Ellman, *The Theory of Alimony*, 77 CAL. L. REV. 1 (1989). Copyright © 1989. Reprinted by permission of the author.

Ellman, *Thinking About Custody and Support in Ambiguous-Father Families*, 36 FAM. L.Q. 499 (2002). Copyright © 2002. Reprinted by permission of the author.

Ellman, *Why Making Family Law is Hard*, 35 ARIZ. ST. L.J. 699 (2003). Copyright © 2003. Reprinted by permission of the author.

Ellman & Tara O'Toole Ellman, *The Theory of Child Support*, 45 HARV. J. LEG. 107 (2008). Copyright © 2008. Reprinted by permission of author Ira Mark Ellman.

Ellman & Stephen D. Sugarman, *Spousal Emotional Abuse as a Tort?*, 55 MD. L. REV. 1268 (1996). Copyright © 1996. Reprinted by permission of author Ellman.

Elster, Jon, *Solomonic Judgments: Against the Best Interest of the Child*, 54 U. CHI. L. REV. 1 (1987). Copyright © 1987 University of Chicago Law School. Reprinted by permission.

Estin, Ann Laquer, *Unmarried Partners and the Legacy of* Marvin v. Marvin: *Ordinary Cohabitation*, 76 N.D. L. REV. 1381 (2001). Copyright © 2001. Reprinted by permission of the author.

Fellmeth, Aaron Xavier, *State Regulation of Sexuality in International Human Rights Law and Theory*, 50 WM. & MARY L. REV. 797 (2008). Copyright © 2008. Reprinted by permission.

FINEMAN, MARTHA ALBERTSON, THE AUTONOMY MYTH: A THEORY OF DEPENDENCY (2004). Copyright © 2004. Reprinted by permission of The New Press. www.thenewpress.com.

Freundlich, Madelyn, *Expediting Termination of Parental Rights: Solving a Problem or Sowing the Seeds of a New Predicament?*, 28 CAP. U. L. REV. 97 (1999). Copyright © 1999. Reprinted by permission of the author.

FRIEDMAN, LAWRENCE M., AMERICAN LAW IN THE TWENTIETH CENTURY (2002). Copyright © 2002 by Yale University Press. Reprinted by permission.

ACKNOWLEDGMENTS

FRIEDMAN, A HISTORY OF AMERICAN LAW (3d ed. 2005). Copyright © 2001 by Lawrence M. Friedman. Reprinted by permission of the author

Galston, William A., *Public Morality and Public Policy: The Case of Children and Family Policy*, 36 SANTA CLARA L. REV. 313 (1996). Copyright © 1996. Reprinted by permission of The Santa Clara Law Review.

GLENDON, MARY ANN, THE TRANSFORMATION OF FAMILY LAW (1989). Copyright © 1989 by Mary Ann Glendon. Reprinted by permission of the author.

Grady, Denise, *Few Risks Seen to the Children of First Cousins*, THE N.Y. TIMES, Apr. 4, 2002 at A1. Copyright © 2006 The New York Times. All rights reserved. Used by permission and protected by the Copyright Laws of the United States. The printing, copying, redistribution, or retransmission of the Material without express written permission is prohibited.

GORNICK, JANET C. & MARCIA K. MEYERS, FAMILIES THAT WORK: POLICIES FOR RECONCILING PARENTHOOD AND EMPLOYMENT (2003). Copyright © 2003 Russell Sage Foundation, 112 East 64th Street, New York, NY 10065. Reprinted with permission.

Hadock, David D. & Daniel D. Polsby, *Family as a Rational Classification*, 74 WASH. U. L.Q. 15 (1996). Copyright © 1996. Reprinted by permission.

HARTOG, HENDRICK A., MAN AND WIFE IN AMERICA: A HISTORY (2000). Copyright © 2000 by the President and Fellows of Harvard College. Reprinted by permission Harvard University Press.

Hasday, Jill, *The Cannon of Family Law*, 57 STAN. L. REV. 825 (2004). Copyright © 2004. Reprinted by permission.

Hetherington, E. Mavis, Margaret Stanley-Hagan & Edward R. Anderson, *Marital Transitions: A Child's Perspective*, 44 AM. PSYCH. 303 (1989). Copyright © 1989. Reprinted by permission.

Landes, Elizabeth M. & Richard A. Posner, *The Economics of the Baby Shortage*, 7 J. LEGAL STUDIES 323 (1978). Copyright © 1978 by the University of Chicago Press. Reprinted by permission.

Legler, Paul K., *The Coming Revolution in Child Support Policy: Implications of the 1996 Welfare Act*, 30 FAM. L.Q. 519 (1996). Copyright © 1996 by The American Bar Association. Reprinted with permission. This information or any portion thereof may not be copied or disseminated in any form or by any means or stored in an electronic database or retrieval system without the express written consent of the American Bar Association.

Levy, Robert J., *Comment on the Pearson-Thoennes Study of Mediation*, 17 FAM. L.Q. 525 (1984). Copyright © 1984. Reprinted by permission of the author.

Malin, Martin, *Fathers and Parental Leave*, 72 TEX. L. REV. 1047 (1994). Copyright © 1994. Reprinted by permission of the author.

McLanahan, Sara et al., *The Fragile Families and Child Wellbeing Study Baseline Report*, http://www.fragilefamilies.princeton.edu/. Copyright © Center for Research on Child Wellbeing. Reprinted by permission. The Fragile Families and Child Wellbeing study is funded by the National Institutes of Health, National Science Foundation, and a consortium of private foundations.

Mnookin, Robert H. & Eleanor MacCoby, *Facing the Dilemmas of Child Custody*, 10

ACKNOWLEDGMENTS

VA. J. SOC. POL'Y & L. 54 (2002). Copyright © 2002. Reprinted by permission.

National Conference of Commissioners on Uniform State Laws, *Model Marriage and Divorce Act* (2002). Copyright © 2002 by NCCUSL. Reprinted by permission.

National Conference of Commissioners on Uniform State Laws, *Uniform Child Custody Jurisdiction and Enforcement Act* (1997). Copyright © 1997 by NCCUSL. Reprinted by permission.

National Conference of Commissioners on Uniform State Laws, *Uniform Interstate Family Support Act* (2001). Copyright © 2001 by NCCUSL. Reprinted by permission.

National Conference of Commissioners on Uniform State Laws, *Uniform Parentage Act* (1973, 2002). Copyright © 1973, 2002 by NCCUSL. Reprinted by permission.

National Conference of Commissioners on Uniform State Laws, *Uniform Premarital Agreement Act* (1983). Copyright © 1983 by NCCUSL. Reprinted by permission.

National Conference of Commissioners on Uniform State Laws, *Uniform Representation of Children in Abuse, Neglect, and Custody Proceedings Act* (2007). Copyright © 2007 by NCCUSL. Reprinted by permission.

Note, *Collusive and Consensual Divorce and The New York Anomaly*, 36 COLUM. L. REV. 1121 (1936). Copyright © 1936 Columbia Law Review Association. Reprinted by permission.

POLIKOFF, NANCY D., BEYOND (STRAIGHT AND GAY) MARRIAGE (2008). Copyright © 2008 by Nancy D. Polikoff. Reprinted by permission of Beacon Press, Boston.

Radin, Margaret Jane, *Market Inalienability*, 100 HARV. L. REV. 1849 (1987). Copyright © 1987. Reprinted by permission of the author.

Raeder, Myrna, *Comments on Child Abuse Litigation in a Testimonial World: The Intersection of Compency, Hearsay and Confrontation*, 82 IND. L. REV. 1009 (2007). Copyright © 2007. Reprinted by permission of the author.

REGAN JR., MILTON C., FAMILY LAW AND THE PURSUIT OF INTIMACY (1993). Copyright © 1993. Reprinted by permission of NYU Press.

RHEINSTEIN, MAX, MARRIAGE STABILITY, DIVORCE AND THE LAW (1972). Copyright © 1972 by The University of Chicago Press. Reprinted by permission.

Rivera, Ray, *Agency Lags in Protecting Children, Report Says*, THE N.Y. TIMES, Aug. 10, 2007 at City Weekly Section. Copyright © 2007 The New York Times. All rights reserved. Used by permission and protected by the Copyright Laws of the United States. The printing, copying, redistribution, or retransmission of the Material without express written permission is prohibited.

Sampson, John J., *Uniform Family Laws and Models Act*, 42 FAM. L.Q. 673 (2008). Copyright © 2008 by The American Bar Association. Reprinted with permission. This information or any portion thereof may not be copied or disseminated in any form or by any means or stored in an electronic database or retrieval system without the express written consent of the American Bar Association.

Sampson & Paul M. Kurtz, *UIFSA: An Interstate Support Act for the 21st Century*, 27 FAM. L.Q. 1 (1993). Copyright © 1993 by The American Bar Association. Reprinted with permission. This information or any portion thereof may not be copied or disseminated in any form or by any means or stored in an electronic database or retrieval

ACKNOWLEDGMENTS

TABLE OF CONTENTS

TABLE OF CONTENTS

TABLE OF CONTENTS

TABLE OF CONTENTS

TABLE OF CONTENTS

TABLE OF CONTENTS

TABLE OF CONTENTS

TABLE OF CONTENTS

TABLE OF CONTENTS

TABLE OF CONTENTS

TABLE OF CONTENTS

doesn't cite me (handwritten annotation)

TABLE OF CONTENTS

TABLE OF CONTENTS

TABLE OF CONTENTS

TABLE OF CONTENTS

TABLE OF CONTENTS

TABLE OF CONTENTS

TABLE OF CONTENTS

TABLE OF CONTENTS

Part I

INTRODUCTION

Chapter 1

INTRODUCTION

A generation ago, most family law casebooks began with a discussion of marriage and divorce. During the last generation, however, fundamental changes in the ways in which Americans organize their family lives have spurred questions about what were once basic presuppositions of family law. Critics have challenged the notion of what it means to be a family, and have contested the idea that the marital family should be at the core of family law. Some have even questioned the notion that the state should privilege any relationships, and have argued that the state should get out of the business of family law entirely, leaving relationships among adults to private contracts. This section seeks to give readers a sense of the many issues that are on the table in the contemporary study of family law, and the many themes that arise in considering the role that the state should play with respect to families. These themes will be explored further in the chapters to come.

A. THE THEMES OF FAMILY AND FAMILY LAW

[1] The Revolution in Families and The Direction of Family Law

JUDITH STACEY, IN THE NAME OF THE FAMILY: RETHINKING FAMILY
VALUES IN THE POSTMODERN AGE
6, 9, 11 (1997)

The past half-century of postindustrial social and economic transformations in the United States and Europe have rung down the historic curtain on the modern family regime. In 1950, three-fifths of U.S. households contained a male breadwinner and a full-time female homemaker, whether children resided with the couple or not. Now, more than three-fifths of married women with dependent children are in the labor force, as well as a majority of mothers of infants, while there are more than twice as many single-mother families as married, homemaker-mom families. By the middle of the 1970s, moreover, divorce had outstripped death as the key source of marital dissolutions, generating in its wake a complex array of new kinship ties and tribulations. While . . . the United States leads most of the globe, the same demographic and social trends pervade the postindustrial world. The diversity of our contemporary kinship relationships undermines Tolstoy's famous contrast between happy and unhappy families: even happy families no longer are all alike. No longer is there a single culturally dominant family pattern, like the "modern" one, to which a majority of citizens conform and most of the rest aspire. Instead, postindustrial conditions have compelled and encouraged us to craft a wide array of family arrangements which we inhabit uneasily and reconstitute frequently as our occupational and personal circumstances shift.

. . . .

[P]ostmodern changes in work, family, and sexual opportunities for women and men do open the prospect of introducing greater democracy, equality and choice than ever before into our most intimate relationships, especially for women and members of sexual minorities. However, . . . this democratic potential carries a big-ticket price tag of endemic instability and uncertainty. . . .

It is unsurprising, therefore, that so many today indulge fantasies of "escaping" from freedom and succumb to the alluring certainties of family-values pieties. But there are also elements of bad faith in popular nostalgia for modern, breadwinner-homemaker nuclear family life. If we judge mainstream family values more by what people do than by what they say about their family lives, we will find little evidence that most Americans genuinely wish to return to the gender order that those domestic sitcom families of the 1950s like "Ozzie and Harriet," have come to symbolize. Voting with their hearts and deeds rather than their words and creeds, the vast majority of Americans have been actively remaking their family lives, and their expectations about family life as well. For example, by a ratio of three to one, people surveyed in a 1990 *Newsweek* poll defined the family as "a group of people who love and care for each other" (quite a postmodern definition), rather than by the legalistic definition of "a group of people related by blood, marriage, or adoption." And while a majority of those surveyed gave negative ratings to the quality of American family life in general, 71 percent declared themselves "at least very satisfied" with their own family lives. Moreover, a *New York Times* survey in 1989 found that more than two-thirds of women, including a majority of those living in "traditional" (that is to say "modern") male breadwinner-female homemaker households, as well as a majority of men agreed that, "the United States continues to need a strong women's movement to push for changes that benefit women."

. . . .

More to the point, perhaps, whatever our "real" family values may actually be, we cannot rewind the historical reel in a quest to escape postmodern family life, however much some might wish to do so. "This is what is going on now," as single mother and author Shoshana Alexander sensibly reminds us. "This is what our families are like now." Therefore, we have only two real choices. Either we can come to grips with the postmodern family condition by accepting the end of a singular ideal family and begin to promote better living and spiritual conditions for the diverse array of real families we actually inhabit and desire. Or we can continue to engage in denial, resistance, displacement, and bad faith, by cleaving to a moralistic ideology of *the family* at the same time that we fail to provide social and economic conditions that make life for the modern family or any other kind of family viable, let alone dignified and secure.

DAN CERE, REPORT FROM THE COUNCIL ON FAMILY LAW, THE FUTURE OF FAMILY LAW: LAW AND THE MARRIAGE CRISIS IN NORTH AMERICA 5–8 (2005)

Family Law is on the front pages of our newspapers and is implicated in some of our deepest cultural conflicts, from no-fault divorce, to the status of cohabitation to, most recently, same-sex marriage.

At their core, these ongoing disputes are fueled by competing visions of marriage and of the role of the state in making family law.

This report on the current state of family law holds up for clear public view the underlying, dramatically different models of marriage that are contributing to deep public clashes over the law of marriage, cohabitation, and parenthood. Obtaining conceptual clarity about marriage and its meanings will allow family law experts, scholars from other disciplines, judges, legislators, and the general public to make more informed choices among completing legal proposals now being advanced in the United States. . . .

Two Recent Reports

Recently two highly influential reports have been published by legal scholars, one in the United States and one in Canada. Both reports are deeply influenced by a new vision of marriage. Both reports have potentially profound and far-reaching consequences for social attitudes and practices concerning marriage, parenthood, and children.

The first report is the *Principles of the Law of Family Dissolution*, published in 2002 by the American Law Institute (ALI). This report moves away from the idea that there can be public standards guiding marriage and parenthood. Instead, it says that the central purpose of the family law should be to protect and promote family diversity. The report sidelines what it calls "traditional marriage," viewing marriage as merely one of many possible and equally valid family forms. In the process the report denies the central place of biological parenthood in family law and focuses instead on the newer idea of "functional parenthood."

The second report is *Beyond Conjugality: Recognizing and Supporting Close Personal Adult Relationships*, published in 2001 by the Law Commission of Canada. This report proposes a fundamental reconstitution of contemporary family law. It argues that the law must go "beyond conjugality" and focus on the "substance of relationships," rather than giving legal recognition to any specific arrangements such as marriage. It recommends that the traditional conjugal idea of marriage be put on a level playing field with all other kinds of relationships. It also argues for redefinition of marriage and its extension to same-sex couples.

The Current Directions of Family Law

These recent reports indicate that family law is headed in . . . troubling directions. Some of these changes have already been implemented in some jurisdictions in the United States and Canada. . . . What is missing in new proposals in family law is any real understanding of the central role of marriage as a social institution in protecting the well-being of children.

Marriage organizes and helps to secure the basic birthright of children, when possible, to know and be raised by their own mother and father. It attempts to forge a strong connection between men and women and the children resulting from their bonds. These new marriage proposals call for a fundamental reevaluation of the relationships between children and their parents. These new reports make clear that eliminating the notion of biology as the basis of parenthood, and allowing parenthood to fragment into its plural and varied forms, is necessary if courts are to make family diversity a legal and cultural reality.

The vision outlined in these two reports frees adults to live as they choose. But social science data strongly suggest that not all adult constructions of parenthood are equally child-friendly. Further fragmentation of parenthood means further fragmented lives for a new generation of children who will be jostled around by increasingly complex adult claims. This vision also requires more systematic intrusion into the family and adjudication of its internal life by the state and its courts.

. . . .

Conclusion

If the proposed changes are put in place, there are likely to be important negative impacts on the lives of everyday people. A "close relationship" culture fails to acknowledge fundamental facets of human life: the fact of sexual difference; the enormous tide of heterosexual desire in human life; the procreativity of male-female bonding; the unique social ecology of parenting which offers children bonds with their biological parents; and the rich genealogical nature of family ties and the web of intergenerational supports for family members that they provide.

These core dimensions of conjugal life are not small issues. Yet at this crucial moment for marriage and parenthood in North America, there is no serious intellectual platform from which to launch a meaningful discussion about these elemental features of human existence. This report on the state of family law seeks to open that debate.

[2]   Does the State Have a Legitimate Interest in Privileging (Particular) Families?

MICHAEL WARNER, THE TROUBLE WITH NORMAL: SEX, POLITICS, AND THE ETHICS OF QUEER LIFE
111–112 (1999)

[Proponents of same-sex marriage] see marriage as an engine for social change and the state as the proper instrument of moral judgment. These deep assumptions about the social welfare and the state's role are almost never challenged in the current debate. Even allegedly liberal writers, such as the editors of the *New York Times*, typically endorse the idea that the state's business is "to foster stable, long-term" coupling. But this kind of social engineering is questionable. It brings the machinery of administration to bear on the realm of pleasures and intimate relations, aiming to stifle variety among ways of living. It authorizes the state to make one form of life — *already normative* — even more privileged. The state's administrative penetration into contemporary life may have numbed us to the deep coerciveness of this way of thinking. We take it for granted. Yet it is blind majoritarianism, armed not only with an impressive battery of prohibitions and punishments, but with an equally impressive battery of economistic incentives and disincentives, all designed to manipulate not just the economic choices of the populace, but people's substantive and normative vision of the good life.

The ability to imagine and cultivate forms of the good life that do not conform to the dominant pattern would seem to be at least as fundamental as any putative "right to marry." If so, then the role of the state should be to protect *against* the abuses of majoritarianism. The claim that the state has an interest in fostering long-term coupling is profoundly antidemocratic. When the state imposes a majoritarian view of the good life, it cannot claim to act on the basis of a neutral consideration of the possibilities; it acts to prevent such consideration.

MARTHA FINEMAN, THE AUTONOMY MYTH: A THEORY OF DEPENDENCY
34–35, 48–49 (2004)

[In the] traditional "separate spheres" understanding of society within legal discourse . . . the family is positioned as a unique and private arena. I argue that this is an incorrect and unsustainable conception. The family is contained within the larger society, and its contours are defined as an institution by law. Far from being separate and private, the family interacts with and is acted upon by other societal institutions. I suggest the relationship is not one of separation, but of symbiosis. It is very important to understand the roles assigned to the family in society — roles that otherwise might have to be played by other institutions, such as the market or the state.

. . . [A] state of dependency is a natural part of the human condition and is developmental in nature. . . . It is the family, not the state or the market, that assumes responsibility for inevitable dependency. In this regard, the institution of the family frees the market to act without consideration or accommodation for dependency. . . .

Individual dependency needs must be met if we, as individuals, are to survive, and our aggregate or collective dependency needs must be met if our society is to survive and perpetuate itself. The mandate that the state . . . respond to dependency, therefore, is not a matter of altruism or empathy . . . , but is a matter that is primary and essential because such a response is fundamentally society preserving.

Society-preserving tasks, such as dependency work, are commonly delegated. The delegation is accomplished through the establishment and maintenance of social institutions. For example, the armed services are established to attend to the collective need for self defense. . . . Certain members of society may volunteer, be recruited, or even be drafted for service, but they have a right to be compensated for their services from collective resources. They also have right to the necessary tools to perform their assigned tasks and to guarantees that they will be protected by rules and policies that facilitate their performance. Caretakers should have the same right to have their society-preserving labor supported and facilitated. Provision of the means for their task should be considered the responsibility of the collective society.

LINDA McCLAIN, THE PLACE OF FAMILIES: FOSTERING CAPACITY, EQUALITY, AND RESPONSIBILITY
3, 8 (2006)

Despite sustained concern over the state of families, the question of the place of families in our constitutional and political order has received insufficient attention. . . . I argue that underlying the common impulse to link the state of families to the state of the nation is an important idea: families have a place in the project of forming persons into capable, responsible, self-governing citizens. . . . [¶] . . . I contend that government properly takes an interest in families in light of the goods associated with families, the functions that families serve, and the political values at stake in the institution of the family.

Lynn Wardle, *The Bonds of Matrimony and the Bonds of Constitutional Democracy*
32 HOFSTRA L. REV. 349, 372–373 (2003)

I suggest that society has an interest in promoting individual happiness, and in encouraging social stability, and in fostering good citizenship, and in preventing the explosion of social problems, and that these interests gives it a direct interest in fostering secure, happy, marriage-based families. . . . The normative nature and structure of marriage and family are closely tied to the model of state authority. "[The family has a] critical role in raising good citizens. . . . The localist theory of family law affirms the vital role that families play in preserving the fundamental liberal values underlying the constitutional structure." . . . Marriage structures that underscore public commitment are an important foundation for self-government because such marriages are as much for the community as for the individuals. Couples say their vows for the community who gather to witness them pledge their troth to each other. Their marriage reaffirms a community value, the identity of the community and of the couple.

[3]   The Centrality of Marriage in Family Law

During the last few years, a vigorous and complex debate has been waged among legal theorists and social critics over the legitimacy of the scope, and even the existence, of civil marriage. Some argue that the state should continue to privilege only traditional marriage, others argue that the state should open marriage up to same-sex couples, and still others argue that a broad variety of families should receive privileges or, alternatively, that the state should terminate civil marriage entirely. What follows are a variety of entries in this debate:

Martha Fineman, The Autonomy Myth: A Theory of Dependency
xvii, 123 (2004)

Marriage is considered central to the concept of family, and family is perceived of as the foundation of society. Civil societarians argue for policies that promote marriage, a position that is increasingly popular among diverse sets of groups. The most telling aspects of these theories is what is left out — the growing inequality in access to resources that has characterized American society over the past several decades. Blaming the plight of children on their parents' marital status without seriously considering how governmental and employer actions (or lack thereof) contribute to and compound the plight is just bad policy analysis. . . . [I]n a diverse and secular society, it is impermissible for the state to privilege one form of sexual affiliation over others, and thus to make marriage the core connection in the institution of the family.

[F]or all relevant and appropriate societal purposes, we do not need marriage and we should abolish it as a legal category. . . . [W]e should transfer the social and economic subsidies and privilege that marriage now receives to a new family core connection — that of the caretaker-dependent [since these relationships deal with the inevitable dependency of the human condition, which the state has a duty to support]. In making his proposal, I want to be very clear about two things. First, to state that we do not need legal marriage to accomplish many societal objectives is not the same thing as saying we do not need a family to do so for some. However, family as a social and legal category should not be dependent on having marriage as its core relationship. Nor is family synonymous with marriage.

Family affiliations are expressed in different kinds of acts, only some of which are recognized by the law. Some affiliations are sexually based, as with marriage. Some are forged biologically, as with parenthood, although this tie can also be created legally through adoption. Other affiliations are more relational in nature, such as those based on nurturing or caretaking or those developed through affection and acceptance of interdependence.

Second, even if we conclude we don't need marriage as a legal category, this does not mean that marriage as a societal institution would disappear. The symbolic dimension of marriage — the coming-together of two individuals with vows of love and commitment — would most likely continue to exist as a social, cultural, and/or religious construct. Without legal status, however, marriage would no longer be the privileged mechanism whereby the state distributes certain social goods.

Lynn Wardle, *The Bonds of Matrimony and the Bonds of Constitutional Democracy*
32 Hofstra L. Rev. 349, 374–75 (2003)

The concept of marriage is founded on the factual reality that the union of two persons of different genders creates something unique, a special relationship of unique potential strengths and inimitable potential value to society. The integration of the universe of gender differences (profound and subtle, biological and cultural, psychological and genetic) associated with sexual identity constitutes the core and essence of marriage. The heterosexual dimensions of the relationship are at the very core of what makes "marriage" what it is, and why it is so valuable to individuals and to society.

The relationship between two persons of the same sex is fundamentally different from heterosexual "marriage" because men and women are fundamentally different. Marriage is unique. No other companionate sexual relationship provides the same great potential for benefiting individuals and society as the life-time covenant union of a man and a woman.

. . . On the basis of history and common experience across cultures, advocates of preserving marriage exclusively for male-female couples may reasonably assert that committed heterosexual unions we call marriages make unique and important contributions to achieving these public and social purposes of marriage. Committed heterosexual unions of marriage seem to provide the best setting for the safest and most beneficial expression of sexual intimacy. Heterosexual marriage also appears to provide the best environment into which children can be born. Heterosexual marriage likely provides the most advantageous environment in which children can be reared, providing profound benefits of dual-gender parenting to model inter-gender relations and show children how to relate to persons of their own and the opposite gender. Heterosexual marriage arguably provides the most enriching and liberating relationship to facilitate human adults to personally develop and achieve their fullest potential. Heterosexual marriage historically has provided the best security for those who take the greatest risks and invest the greatest personal effort in establishing and maintaining families, especially wives and mothers. Heterosexual marriage seems to provide the strongest and most stable companionate unit of society, and the most secure setting for intergenerational transmission of social knowledge and skills, and reflects the understanding of marriage that has been constant across cultures and throughout history.

Marriage is of such profound importance to society that there is great danger if its meaning and definition become ambiguous. It could be said that changing the meanings of marriage would be like moving the furniture in the house of a person who is blind.

Nancy Polikoff, Beyond (Straight and Gay) Marriage: Valuing All Families Under the Law
2–5 (2008)

The most contested issue in contemporary family policy is whether married-couple families should have "special rights" not available to other family forms. Excluded families include unmarried couples of any sexual orientation, single-parent households, extended-family units, and any other constellation of individuals who form relationships of emotional and economic interdependence that do not conform to the one-size-fits-all marriage model. No other Western country, including those that allow same-sex couples to marry, creates the rigid dividing line between the law for the married and the law for the unmarried that exists in the United States.

. . . .

I propose family law reform that would recognize all families' worth. Marriage as a family form is not more important or valuable than other forms of family, so the law should not give it more value. Couples should have the choice to marry based on the spiritual, cultural, or religious meaning of marriage in their lives; they should never *have to* marry to reap specific and unique legal benefits. I support the right to marry for same-sex couples as a matter of civil rights law . . . and I advocate solutions to the needs all families have for economic well-being, legal recognition, emotional peace of mind, and community respect.

Daniel A. Crane, *Abolishing Civil Marriage: A "Judeo-Christian" Argument for Privatizing Marriage*
27 Cardozo L. Rev. 1221, 1222 (2006)

[T]he traditions of Judaism and Christianity understand marriage as an institution whose legitimacy derives not from the state but from the sanction of religious communities. As such, marriage is the province of religious communities, and not the state, and empowering the state to define marriage uniformly not only profanes a holy institution but threatens the ultimate autonomy and authority of religious communities with respect to marriage.

Elizabeth S. Scott, *The Public and Private Faces of Family Law: Article: Marriage, Cohabitation and Collective Responsibility for Dependency*
2004 U. Chi. Legal F. 225 (2004)

[T]he special treatment of marriage can be justified, even if one has no nostalgic fondness for traditional family roles and rejects the moral superiority of marriage over other family forms. Through marriage, the government can delegate to the family some of society's collective responsibility for dependency. Retaining the privileged legal status of marriage in a contemporary setting can (and should) constitute part of a comprehensive policy of family support that acknowledges the pluralism of modern families.

[T]he government is justified in channeling intimate relationships into marriage because formal unions function as a useful means of providing care in a family setting. The availability of legal marriage allows couples to declare their commitment and choose a formal status with a package of clearly defined and enforceable legal rights, privileges, and obligations that embody that commitment. Even in an era of high divorce rates, marriage represents a relatively stable family form, partly because of its formal status and partly because it is regulated by a powerful set of social norms that reinforce commitment. Moreover, within a properly structured legal framework, even marriages that end in divorce can serve quite effectively to provide a measure of financial security for dependent family members. Informal unions, in contrast, are a less reliable family form because the behavioral expectations and financial obligations between the parties are uncertain and legal enforcement is difficult.

WILLIAM ESKRIDGE, THE CASE FOR SAME-SEX MARRIAGE: FROM SEXUAL LIBERTY TO CIVILIZED COMMITMENT
9 (1996)

Recognizing same-sex marriages would contribute to the integration of gay lives and the larger culture, to a nonlegal form of civilizing gays. Marriage would contribute to this integration because same-sex couples would be able to participate openly in this long-standing cultural institution.

Human history repeatedly testifies to the attractiveness of domestication born of interpersonal commitment, a signature of married life.

William A. Galston, *Public Morality and Public Policy: The Case of Children and Family Policy*
36 SANTA CLARA L. REV. 313, 314, 322 (1996)

With regard to what is called "family policy," here is my question: What would we do if we really want to create a society that puts children first, that allows every child the maximum feasible scope for the development or actualization of talents and personal relationships and the ability to make use of those developed talents and relationships in a way that is personally gratifying as well as socially beneficial?

Marriage . . . is not a panacea, but it is a vital part of the solution. In at least a majority of cases, marriage can make a positive contribution, not only to the well-being of children, but also to the well-being of their parents.

Does this represent nostalgia? Does it imply the reaffirmation of patriarchy? On the contrary: it means the simple recognition that for economic, emotional and developmental reasons, marriage is the most promising institution yet devised for raising children and forming caring, competent, responsible adults. . . . I am deeply skeptical that the abolition of marriage, with all of its imperfections, can possibly yield better lives, or a better society for our children.

Stephanie Coontz, *Too Close For Comfort*
N.Y. TIMES, Nov. 7, 2006, at A21

Ever since the Census Bureau released figures last month showing that married-couple households are now a minority, my phone has been ringing off the hook with calls from people asking: "How can we save marriage? How can we make Americans understand that marriage is the most significant emotional connection they will ever make, the one place to find social support and personal fulfillment?"

I think these are the wrong questions — indeed, such questions would have been almost unimaginable through most of history. It has only been in the last century that Americans have put all their emotional eggs in the basket of coupled love. Because of this change, many of us have found joys in marriage our great-great-grandparents never did. But we have also neglected our other relationships, placing too many burdens on a fragile institution and making social life poorer in the process.

A study released this year showed just how dependent we've become on marriage. Three sociologists at the University of Arizona and Duke University found that from 1985 to 2004 Americans reported a marked decline in the number of people with whom they discussed meaningful matters. People reported fewer close relationships with co-workers, extended family members, neighbors and friends. The only close relationship where more people said they discussed important matters in 2004 than in 1985 was marriage.

The solution to this isolation is not to ramp up our emotional dependence on marriage. Until 100 years ago, most societies agreed that it was dangerously antisocial, even pathologically self-absorbed, to elevate marital affection and nuclear-family ties above commitments to neighbors, extended kin, civic duty and religion. . . .

By the early 20th century, though, the sea change in the culture wrought by the industrial economy had loosened social obligations to neighbors and kin, giving rise to the idea that individuals could meet their deepest needs only through romantic love, culminating in marriage . . .

The insistence that marriage and parenthood could satisfy all an individual's needs reached a peak in the cult of "togetherness" among middle-class suburban Americans in the 1950s. Women were told that marriage and motherhood offered them complete fulfillment. Men were encouraged to let their wives take care of their social lives.

But many men and women found these prescriptions stifling. Women who entered the work force in the 1960s joyfully rediscovered social contacts and friendships outside the home. . . .

So why do we seem to be slipping back in this regard? . . . [I]t's the expansion of the post-industrial economy that seems to be driving us back to a new dependence on marriage. According to the researchers Kathleen Gerson and Jerry Jacobs, 60 percent of American married couples have both partners in the work force, up from 36 percent in 1970, and the average two-earner couple now works 82 hours a week.

This is probably why the time Americans spend socializing with others off the job has declined by almost 25 percent since 1965. Their free hours are spent with spouses, and as a study by Suzanne Bianchi of the University of Maryland released last month showed, with their children — mothers and fathers today spend even more time with their youngsters than parents did 40 years ago.

As Americans lose the wider face-to-face ties that build social trust, they become more dependent on romantic relationships for intimacy and deep communication, and more vulnerable to isolation if a relationship breaks down. In some cases we even cause the breakdown by loading the relationship with too many expectations. Marriage is generally based on more equality and deeper friendship than in the past, but even so, it is hard for it to compensate for the way that work has devoured time once spent cultivating friendships.

The solution is not to revive the failed marital experiment of the 1950s, as so many commentators noting the decline in married-couple households seem to want.

Nor is it to lower our expectations that we'll find fulfillment and friendship in marriage. . . . [¶] Instead, we should raise our expectations for, and commitment to, other relationships, especially since so many people now live so much of their lives outside marriage. . . . That indeed would be a return to marital tradition — not the 1950s model, but the pre-20th-century model that has a much more enduring pedigree.

[4] The Purposes and Limits of Family Law

Ira Ellman, *Why Making Family Law is Hard*
35 Ariz. St. L.J. 699, 699–702 (2003)

Most Americans believe that our choice of family law rules matters. . . . It is this widespread belief that . . . I want to examine here. My conclusion is that the outcome of many family law debates does not matter nearly so much as the debaters usually assume, and that when it does matter, it is often for reasons entirely different from those offered by the debaters.

For Americans, using the law to shape family behavior presents special problems because of our long legal tradition of family privacy, which has both common law and constitutional components. And because so much family law is statutory, rather than judge-made, citizens engage the political system to obtain family law rules that reflect their views. The American tradition of family privacy is thus in constant tension with a shifting majority's desire for rules that advance its vision of family. Regulation may triumph in one domain of family law while privacy advances in another, and regulation may advance and recede within domains, reflecting changes in the majority's balance of these competing values.

This particularly American tension between the privacy tradition and the regulatory impulse is rich because in every such dispute, both camps proceed from the conviction that family life is fundamental — to individual happiness and to societal success. So we honor a deeply entrenched family privacy doctrine meant to allow each of us our own route to private happiness, while we also want public policies that will strengthen the family — policies which must presuppose a shared vision of family.

A second problem is that the law probably cannot achieve the goal anyway, because in the entire scheme of things, the law is a minor actor among all the factors that influence people in their intimate behavior. My colleague, Owen Jones, has proposed a principle he calls "the law of law's leverage," which says that some domains of human behavior are so affected by our biological heritage that they are less responsive than other domains to the kinds of incentives the law can provide. That rule could explain, for example, why it may be easier to persuade college students to use contraceptives than to persuade them to be celibate. But whether one sees nature or culture at work, what seems clear is that law is a less important causal agent in family relations than one might think from the heated debates over its content. . . . [S]ocial forces may be more likely to change family law rules, than the other way around.

Mary Ann Glendon, The Transformation of Family Law
5–10 (1989)

[I]t will be useful to distinguish for analytical purposes between what a particular legal system may classify as "families" or "marriages" and the conduct which an anthropologist or sociologist is likely to describe as family or marriage behavior. . . .

The Tinker's Wedding

In John Synge's play, *The Tinker's Wedding*, the principal characters, Michael Byrne and Sarah Casey, are tinkers — traveling menders of metal household utensils. Their association began one day at Rathvanna, when Michael hit Sarah "a great clout in the lug," after which she came along with him "quiet and easy . . . from that hour to this present day." By the time we meet them, Sarah has been "going beside [him] a great while, and rearing a lot of them." The action of the play is set in motion by Sarah's sudden demand, backed up by a threat of leaving, that she and Michael be married. We can infer from their spirited and affectionate banter that Sarah's demand is not a symptom of any serious trouble that has arisen between Michael and herself. Except for this one point, she seems generally happy, "thriving, and getting [her] good health by the grace of the Almighty God." As the play opens, Michael has already agreed to go along with Sarah's desire for a wedding, although he does not understand it, and he is putting the finishing touches on her home-made wedding ring. All that remains to be done is to find a priest to do the job.

But things are not so easily arranged. The local priest comes walking along the road by the tinkers' camp, but he rejects as preposterous Sarah's request that he perform a wedding ceremony for them for no fee and give them a bit of silver into the bargain "to pay for the ring." After some discussion, he says he could see his way clear to offer the tinkers a special reduced price of one pound. But Michael and Sarah do not have a pound. Finally, after prolonged bargaining, the priest agrees to marry the couple for ten shillings and a gallon can which Michael has almost finished making — such a little sum "as wouldn't marry a child." The priest is not moved by Sarah's claim of poverty, unkindly pointing out that the tinkers are well known to steal "east and west in Wicklow and Wexford and the County Meath."

After the deal is struck, the wedding is set for the next day. But alas, during the night, Michael's old mother, Mary, is overcome by the temptation to take the newly made can and to sell it at the local pub in order to get a "pint for her sleep." To put off the moment of reckoning with Sarah, she sneaks a couple of empty bottles into the sack which had contained the can. Naturally, when the priest opens the sack the next day and finds only the bottles, he thinks that Michael and Sarah have tried to deceive him. He indignantly refuses to marry them for ten shillings without the can. After increasingly harsh words are exchanged, Sarah's disappointment turns to anger and the play ends with the priest trussed and thrown into a ditch. As the tinkers leave him, Sarah places her wedding ring on his finger to remind him of the promise he has made — under duress — not to tell the police he has been roughed up.

This little tale poses a number of interesting questions. It is Sarah's desire to get "married" that precipitates the action. But are not Michael and Sarah already married? A sociologist would probably consider that Michael and Sarah had been married for some time according to the long-standing customs of the subculture of the traveling people of Ireland. In the play, all indications are that Michael and Sarah intended that their union would be of some duration, and it is clear from the text that they held themselves out to the community of tinkers as belonging together. Furthermore, Michael's account of how he "got" Sarah at Rathvanna is reminiscent of descriptions by anthropologists of "marriage by capture," which is not really a kind of marriage, but rather a form of *wedding*. Thus, from a sociologist's or anthropologist's point of view, the "tinker's wedding" may well have taken place when Michael hit Sarah in the lug and carried her off.[10]

If the union of Michael and Sarah constituted behavior which a sociologist would call "marriage," is that the only sense in which they are married? In Ireland at the turn of the century, when Synge's play takes place, a couple validly married under the law of the Church was also married under the law of the state. Now, there is little doubt that Michael and Sarah would have been considered married under canon law as it stood until the Council of Trent made the presence of a priest at weddings mandatory in 1563. Prior to that time, Christians, like other people, could form marriages simply by exchanging consents and cohabiting. But [the rule] was expressly limited to marriages of baptized persons. The priest in Synge's play repeatedly alludes to the "heathen" state of the tinkers. This does not seem to be a mere epithet. At one point the priest speculates, "I'm thinking you were never christened, Sarah Casey," and remarks, "It would be a queer job to go dealing Christian sacraments unto the like of you."

If, in fact, Michael and Sarah were unbaptized persons, their marital status under canon law is unaffected by the marriage legislation of Trent. Under canon law, marriages between unbaptized persons are presumptively valid, provided the crucial element of consent exists. Furthermore, even if Michael and Sarah were baptized persons, and the Tridentine formalities were in principle required, the Church does not always insist on the priest's presence if compliance with this requirement would present "grave inconvenience." Grave inconvenience, it has been said, can arise from poverty.

Why then, if Michael and Sarah are already married in one or more senses of the word, should it be important to the state, to the Church, or to the parties, that a "wedding" should take place or that they should be "married" in another sense? If we ask this question from the point of view of the state and the Church, we fall upon a point of great significance for our inquiry into the changing relationship of

---

[10] The formation of marriage, in simple societies, is often better understood as a process rather than an event, with the "wedding" relatively minor importance. Customary marriages may be initiated by negotiation between families or by a ceremony of some sort, but often they merely involve living together, having a child, and gradually becoming accepted as a couple by relatives and neighbors. This is the case today, for example, for most New Guineans. See Owen Jessep and John Luluaki, PRINCIPLES OF FAMILY LAW IN PAPUA NEW GUINEA (Waigani: University of Papua New Guinea Press, 1985), 17–28. The marriages of as many as a fifth of the English population as late as the eighteenth century could also be characterized as having come into being in this way. See Stephen Parker, "*The Marriage Act 1753: A Case Study in Family Law-Making*," 1 INTERNATIONAL JOURNAL OF LAW AND THE FAMILY 133, 139 (1987).

family law to family life. In the case of Michael and Sarah, poor itinerants in Ireland at the turn of the century, it is fairly clear that neither the state nor the Church had much interest in their marital status. They belonged to what Max Rheinstein called the "neglected groups" of society and the law. By that he meant that, historically, family law paid little attention to the concerns of the poor, or of such ethnic minority groups as the Indians of North and South America or the Afro-Americans of the United States. Prior to the twentieth century, propertyless individuals came to the attention of the legal system chiefly as subjects of the criminal law. As Rheinstein observed, one of the great trends presently transforming the law of the family is precisely that of paying increasing attention to the needs and demands of hitherto neglected groups.

But we are running ahead of our story. Suffice it to say that Synge's priest repeatedly makes it plain that he considers tinkers to be outside the normal scope of his sphere of action and interest. He regards Michael and Sarah as different from "my own pairs living here in the place." He is, in fact, as puzzled about why Sarah wants to get married as are Michael and Michael's mother. When, during their haggling over the price of the wedding, Sarah begins to cry at the thought that she may never get married, the priest exclaims in surprise, "It's a queer woman you are to be crying at the like of that, and you your whole life walking the roads."

When we turn to the question of why Sarah, a member of a neglected group, with its own customary way of marrying, seeks nevertheless to be married in another way, we have a number of theories from which to choose. Yet those apt to come to mind first today can be ruled out. The playwright gives us no reason to believe that Sarah is motivated by any thought of improving her economic position or "legitimizing"[16] her children through bringing herself within the framework of legal rights and duties attaching to marriage. Nor does Synge give us the slightest hint that Sarah thought marriage by a priest was somehow related to the salvation of her immortal soul. Rather, it seems that she is concerned about the social approval of groups other than tinkers. After she is married, she thinks, "there will be no one have a right to call me a dirty name and I selling cans in Wicklow or Wexford or the city of Dublin itself."

But why should a hastily performed ritual make such a difference? For the purposes of our inquiry, this question opens up the subject of how imaginative representations in the law can sometimes affect the way people perceive and experience the reality of something as central to our lives as marriage. We are accustomed to viewing law as importantly shaped by beliefs and behavior, but we frequently overlook the reflexive and continuous nature of the interaction among laws, ideas, feelings, and conduct. Often mesmerized by the coercive power of law, we tend to minimize its persuasive and constitutive aspects.

---

[16] Note that the legal classification of children born outside legal marriage as "illegitimate" may or may not correspond to social concepts of legitimacy. The legal definition of legitimacy is a function of the definition of legal marriage, whereas a sociologist's definition of legitimacy has to take into consideration other cultural norms besides legal ones. Note, too, that the legal category of "illegitimacy" may include children who are living in families with both of their parents, while the set of "legitimate" children includes many who are living with only one parent.

In Synge's play, it is Mary Byrne who has the last word (inspired no doubt by the necessity of putting the best possible light on the situation which her own great thirst has brought about). To Michael, still fearful about Sarah's earlier threat to leave him if he doesn't marry her, she says: "And you're thinking it's paying gold to his reverence would make a woman stop when she's a mind to go?" With Sarah, whose hopes of marriage have been dashed, the rough, boozy old woman for the first time adopts a gentle tone: "It's as good a right you have surely, Sarah Casey, but what good will it do? Is it putting that ring on your finger will keep you from getting an aged woman and losing the fine face you have, or be easing your pain?" Feeling a little guilty about what has happened — but not too guilty — Mary affirms the folkways of the traveling people: "[I]t's a long time we are going our own ways — father and son and his son after him, or mother and daughter and her own daughter again — and it's little need we ever had of going up into a church and swearing."

And so, in the end, Sarah's notion of getting married is left in the ditch with the priest and the wedding ring. Why would a poor tinker, married and wedded in custom and the eyes of God, want in addition to be married by an official? It may, suggests Mary, have been the "changing of the moon." But, at the turn of the century, Ireland was changing too. And as part of that change, people like Sarah all over the world were beginning to associate legitimacy with legality.

HENDRIK HARTOG: MAN AND WIFE IN AMERICA: A HISTORY
23–27 (2002)

[Historically, American family law rested on] the assumption that marriage was a legally constituted private relationship between one man and one woman. It was not a marriage if it was not legally recognized. But if it was so recognized, then the marriage — the entity, the household, the couple — gained the privileges of private freedom, including some sense of security from the prying eyes of communities and the state.

Everything about the last paragraph can easily be reduced to absurdity. . . . [S]ome legal and political theorists had long recognized that marriage was not a private institution. At the very beginning of the eighteenth century, the English writer Mary Astell had already identified marriage as a political institution, signaled by the public power of husbands. . . . Public power constituted the private sphere.

And yet, despite contradictions and incoherence, the opening description retains its validity as a historical understanding. A marriage was both legally constituted and private. Law was not everything in a marriage. Love, lust, hatred, duty, friendship, respect, affection, abandonment, commitment, greed, and self-sacrifice, all the feelings and practices that made up a nineteenth-century marriage, were not primarily legal. But law was always there as well. Law was there when a marriage began; it was there when it ended. And in between: law was there when a husband and wife struggled or negotiated over the terms of power between them; law was there when a married couple constructed or reconstructed a relationship with a world of others — including children, parents, and third party creditors; law was there when husbands or wives thought about themselves as husbands or wives;

law was also there when those same husbands or wives denied or repressed their identities as husbands and wives.

In an ordinary legal consciousness, . . . the law of marriage would have appeared in two guises. The first would have been as the constitutive structure for beginnings and endings. About those, within the ongoing marriage, little more need be said. To marry, you usually needed a legal form and a little law. When your spouse died, you needed a legal form and a little law. If you divorced, you needed a lot of law. For the rest, law usually appeared as public interventions into a private relationship. Like private property, marriage was a realm of private choice and freedom, except when the public good required regulation. Government needed strong public reasons to justify entering that private sphere. . . .

[For many] men and some women, the law appeared as a friendly visitor, occasionally as a facilitative resource, sometimes as an invading army. But it always remained distinct from the marriage itself, which was private, distinctively so, more so than other relationships.

. . . .

That law, the law defined by public power and coercion, sometimes carried within it the conventional moral philosophy of an era and its cultural commitments. It always involved the landscape of institutions that lawyers and their clients explored. . . . Lawyers ordinarily looked to doctrine as a body of materials useful as predictions without regard to moral or ideological content. . . . Lawyers' predictions led husbands and wives to assume identities recognizable in the law, to make themselves into legal subjects.

Jill Hasday, *The Canon of Family Law*
57 STAN. L. REV. 825, 832 (2004)

The family law canon treats family law and welfare law as wholly separate categories. When legal authorities identify a statute or situation as part of welfare law, they assume for that reason that the statute or situation cannot be part of family law at the same time. The exclusion of welfare law from the family law canon has allowed legal authorities to avoid explaining why the law applies very different rules to govern familial rights and responsibilities in poor families. The Personal Responsibility and Work Opportunity Reconciliation Act of 1996, for example, structures familial rights and responsibilities in poor families in many ways that are directly contrary to the law's regulation of wealthier households. The Personal Responsibility Act is highly interventionist, while the family law applied to more affluent families is often reluctant to intervene into decisions about childbearing or the structure of family living arrangements. Yet the Congress that enacted the Personal Responsibility Act, and the courts that have upheld the act's provisions, have never felt the need to acknowledge that the Personal Responsibility Act applies different rules to govern the familial rights and responsibilities of the poor, much less to explain why this should be so. Challenging the construction of the family law canon reveals that many statutes, like the Personal Responsibility Act, and situations now classified exclusively within welfare law are actually forms of family law as well. It makes clear that poor families are subject to a different family law and that the difference must be explained or eliminated.

GARY S. BECKER, A TREATISE ON THE FAMILY
363 (rev. ed. 1991)

We believe that a surprising number of state interventions mimic the agreements that would occur if children were capable of arranging for their own care. Stated differently, our belief is that many regulations of the family improve the efficiency of family activities. To be sure, these regulations raise the welfare of children, but they also raise the welfare of parents, or at least they raise the combined welfare of parents and children.

[5] The Relationship Between Family Law And Morality: Is Moral Discourse in Family Law Waning — or Transforming?

MARY ANN GLENDON, ABORTION AND DIVORCE IN WESTERN LAW
10 (1987)

. . . Much of family law is no more — and no less — than the symbolic expression of certain cultural ideals. The older continental European civil codes told wives that they should obey their husbands, and children of all ages that they should honor and respect their parents. Today, modernized versions of the same codes tell husbands and wives that they are equal partners in running a household, and a recent Swedish law tells parents that they should not punish by spanking or otherwise humiliating their children. Probably no other area of law is so replete with legal norms that communicate ideas about proper behavior but that have no direct sanctions.

MILTON C. REGAN, JR., FAMILY LAW AND THE PURSUIT OF INTIMACY
1–4 (1993)

Family life in the last decade of the twentieth century . . . seems to provoke both longing and disillusionment, an acute sense that the intimacy we pursue too often eludes us. . . . [M]uch of modern family law reinforces this condition. This is because the premise of family law increasingly is that the vessel of family shouldn't be filled with substantive moral content, but should be left empty so that individuals can use it for their own purposes. On this view, family law, like other modern liberal institutions, should remain neutral among visions of the good life, intervening only when necessary to prevent one individual from harming another.

The expression of this outlook in family law is rejection of status in favor of contract as the governing legal principle of family life. While status purports to bestow standard rights and obligations on all who have legal identities, such as husband, wife, or parent, contract insists that individuals themselves should determine the terms of their intimate relationships. A contractual approach is skeptical of the notion that the family should be regarded as a social institution amenable to being shaped by collective ends. Instead, it asserts that the family is fundamentally a zone of private choice, in which the individual seeks to cultivate an authentic sense of self through intimacy with others. On this view, contract is the rule; "harm" is the only exception that justifies collective nullification of private choices. The result is that consent, rather than communal expectation, becomes the touchstone of obligation within the family.

. . .

The promise of the modernist vision therefore is that family life will be a haven of genuine intimacy among authentic individuals. Yet there is a reason to question whether this vision is being realized. A recent review of research on the family, for instance, describes "a renewed and growing concern, perhaps even a greater sense of urgency" in the last decade that marriage and family are being "severely weakened and threatened under the press of accelerated and pervasive social change." . . . [C]ontemporary life seems particularly haunted by a sense that the family is less and less able to offer a safe harbor from the relentless tides of social fragmentation.

One response is to insist that the modernist project is incomplete — that true intimacy will be achieved only when we are fully liberated from the collective demands that constrain our individuality. On this view, commitment to contract in family law is a vehicle for eliminating what may be the last obstacle to the modernist dream of individual emancipation. I will argue, however, that a better response is to question the premises of the modernist project. Those premises, I argue, ignore the social context in which individual identity emerges and in which intimacy is sustained. They foster the view that "private" life is preeminently the domain of the individual, who may draw upon intimate relationships as a resource in pursuing a genuine self, but whose authentic identity depends upon never being defined in terms of any given relationship.

Carl E. Schneider, *Moral Discourse and the Transformation of American Family Law*
83 MICH. L. REV. 1803, 1807–08, 1827–28, 1835–39, 1847–48 (1985)

[F]orces . . . that have shaped modern family law . . . have occasioned a crucial change: a diminution of the law's discourse in moral terms about the relations between family members, and the transfer of many moral decisions from the law to the people the law once regulated. I do not mean that this change is complete or will ever be completed. I do not suppose that it is occurring in every aspect of family law, or everywhere in the country with equal speed. I emphasize that there are other trends, and that there is a considered and considerable reaction to the trend impelled by a revived conservatism and a politicized fundamentalism. But I do suggest that the change is widespread jurisdictionally, institutionally, and doctrinally; that it is deep-seated; and that it is transforming family law.

. . . [L]egal actors and those they govern distinguish between decisions made on moral grounds and decisions made on social, economic, psychological, or "legal" grounds. . . .

The differences between these kinds of decisions may be illustrated by the various rationales for prohibiting incest. A decision made on moral grounds turns on whether particular conduct is "right" or "wrong," whether it accords with the obligations owed other people or oneself. Incest might be prohibited on moral grounds because it is with coercion or because it violates natural or divine law which prescribes standards of right and wrong. A decision made on psychological grounds turns on whether particular conduct promotes psychological health. Incest might be prohibited on psychological grounds because the prohibition eases resolution of the Oedipal conflict. A decision made on social grounds turns on whether particular conduct promotes the effective functioning of society as a whole. Incest might be prohibited on social grounds because "the prohibition of incest establishes a mutual dependency between families, compelling them, in order to perpetuate themselves, to give rise to new families." A decision made on economic grounds turns on whether particular conduct promotes economic efficiency. Incest might be prohibited on economic grounds because such a prohibition, by discouraging endogamy, encourages capital formation. A decision made on "legal grounds" turns on whether particular conduct is required in order to comply with authoritatively promulgated principles. A court might enforce a prohibition against incest quite apart from its own beliefs about the wisdom of such a prohibition because it believed that the legislature intended that such a prohibition be enforced and that the decision to prohibit such conduct was constitutionally confided in the legislature.

In each of these different situations, the governmental actor will consult a different rationale and will speak a different language; and the people acted upon will understand what has happened in different ways. It is, of course, always possible to reach a given result through several rationales and with varying language. But in analyzing legal problems, we legitimately test the merits of the rationales offered for a result, and we properly remember that the way we talk about problems can change the way we think about them. In this paper I direct attention to changes in the way we talk about and justify modern family law because those changes change the way we think about it and act on it. . . .

Perhaps the oldest impediment to moral discourse in family law is the legal tradition of noninterference in the family. That tradition rests in large measure on the practical difficulties of enforcing family law and the practical consequences of trying to do so. Because of this tradition, the moral problems associated with many kinds of family disputes do not enter legal discourse. The tradition is an old one, has telling rationales, and may be growing in appeal.

The strength of the tradition of noninterference is attested to by its age,[120] by the extreme circumstances in which the law has heeded it, and by the multiplicity of reasons for it. Each of these testimonies may be illumined by examining the unusually direct, eloquent, and provocative opinion in *State v. Rhodes*, an 1868 criminal prosecution of a husband for the assault and battery of his wife. The court condemned the evil the husband had done and expressly denied he had any "right" to do it. Nevertheless, the court forbade intervention in the absence of "permanent or malicious injury" or "intolerable" conditions, since each family has a "domestic

---

[120] As family law traditions go, this one, because it dates at least to the mid-nineteenth century, is quite old. But it is worth recalling that the view of the family as a haven and regard for family privacy and autonomy are primarily products of the nineteenth century. Earlier centuries did not perceive clear boundaries between the family and society, and were willing to intervene directly in families and to use families to carry out the policies of the state. See generally L. Stone, THE FAMILY, SEX AND MARRIAGE IN ENGLAND 1500–1800 (1977).

government . . . formed for themselves, suited to their own peculiar conditions, and . . . supreme, and from [which] there is no appeal except in cases of great importance requiring the strong arm of the law. . . ."

Several fears underlay the court's holding. First, the court feared the burden of dealing with "every trifling family broil." Second, it feared the complexities of deciding "what would be the standard?"

> "Suppose a case coming up to us from a hovel, where neither delicacy of sentiment nor refinement of manners is appreciated or known. The parties themselves would be amazed, if they were to be held responsible for rudeness or trifling violence. . . . Take a case from the middle class, where modesty and purity have their abode but nevertheless have not immunity from the frailties of nature, and are sometimes moved by the mysteries of passion. . . . Or take a case from the higher ranks, where education and culture have so refined nature, that a look cuts like a knife, and a word strikes like a hammer; where the most delicate attention gives pleasure, and the slightest neglect pain; where an indignity is disgrace and exposure is ruin. Bring all these cases into court side by side, with the same offense charged and the same proof made; and what conceivable charge of the court to the jury would be alike appropriate to all the cases. . . ."

Third, the court feared that, once in court, each family member would endeavor "to justify himself or herself by criminating the other, [and] that which ought to be forgotten in a day, will be remembered for life." Finally, the court feared "the evils which would result from raising the curtain, and exposing to public curiosity and criticism, the nursery and the bed chamber."

Each of these rationales applies in substance, if not in language or in particulars, today. Indeed, although a modern court would be unlikely to use them to dismiss a criminal prosecution for assault, they are regularly used in discussions of how police and prosecutors should handle spousal-assault complaints. And, to take an example from the civil side, courts commonly use them in declining to intervene in family disputes even where a husband and wife have by prenuptial agreement solicited intervention.

The law not only suspects that intervention will do harm; it doubts that intervention will do good: in family law as in few other areas of the law, the enforcement problems are ubiquitous and severe. . . .

Enforcement difficulties arise first because much of what family law seeks to regulate — from child and spouse abuse to fornication — occurs in private. The distastefulness of investigating private life is sharp enough to have been used to justify the doctrine of constitutional privacy and to have contributed to the rise of no-fault divorce. Family privacy is often hard to breach because the parties all participated in the violation of law, because they wish to protect those who did participate, or because they are ashamed to have people know about the incident in which the state is interested. . . .

Family law's second enforcement problem is that the person enforced against is often specially able to injure the very person the law intervened to protect. The spouse who wishes to resist divorce, the abused child or spouse, the pregnant woman, and her fetus are all vulnerable in this way. Legal intervention in these situations thus may be fruitless, or, worse, might provoke the person enforced against to retaliate against the person the law wants to protect. Because the person to be protected often depends on the person enforced against, even legal punishment itself can injure the person to be protected by depriving him or her of the presence or affection of the other.

The third enforcement difficulty arises from the fact that, in many critical areas of family law, the people the law wishes to regulate live in emotional settings and under psychological pressures which make them little susceptible to the law's persuasion or even coercion. . . .

In short, the law has long avoided many of the moral issues facing families under the authority of the tradition of "nonintervention."

Bruce C. Hafen, *Individualism and Autonomy in Family Law: The Waning of Belonging*
1991 B.Y.U. L. Rev. 1, 31–34

[M]any perceive the legal system as having become less judgmental of what people should expect of one another. This creates an impression that family law has lost its normative expectation that family members should feel a sense of personal responsibility to uphold their commitments. Thus, it is easy to assume that the law no longer seeks to restrain our almost unwilling self-indulgence. The very absence of demands by the law now seems to confirm our spreading fear that long-term, loving relationships are impossible to find anymore.

Naomi Cahn, *The Moral Complexities of Family Law*
50 Stan. L. Rev. 225, 228–9 (1997)

[It is true, as some commentators have argued,] that there has been a diminution in one type of moral discourse within family law: that relating to fault, sexuality, and patriarchal privileges. . . . However, . . . there has not been an overall decrease in moral discourse about the family. Instead, moral discourse about the family has shifted, not disappeared. Newly developing concerns about fairness, equity, and caregiving — which arise within the context of single-parent families, as well as within most other areas of family law — fit within the conventional definition of "moral" concerns.

The new ideology is based on fairness and equality both within and among families rather than on concepts of fairness and equality for the head of the family hiding within the language of family solidarity and interdependence. . . . [T]he new fairness/equality standard is better able to recognize and consider the dependencies within the family than is a fault-based standard. Emphasizing the interrelationships and caregiving that occur within the family provides a solid basis for this new morality. Instead of using a particular family form as the symbol for health, the new morality focuses on nurturing relationships. It is concerned about the rights of individuals, but only in the context of the family.

B.   THE "FAMILY" AS A REGULATORY CLASSIFICATION

The issues of determining which groupings constitute a family for the purpose of law, and whether there are any limits on the state's determination of which groupings constitute a family, raise difficult questions in family law. As this section makes clear, there are a variety of different positions that states and local governments, as well as courts, take on these issues.

[1]   Zoning Rules

VILLAGE OF BELLE TERRE v. BORAAS
United States Supreme Court
416 U.S. 1 (1974)

MR. JUSTICE DOUGLAS delivered the opinion of the Court.

Belle Terre is a village on Long Island's north shore of about 220 homes inhabited by 700 people. Its total land area is less than one square mile. It has restricted land use to one-family dwellings excluding lodging houses, boarding houses, fraternity houses, or multiple-dwelling houses. The word "family" as used in the ordinance means,

> "one or more persons related by blood, adoption, or marriage, living and cooking together as a single housekeeping unit, exclusive of household servants. A number of persons but not exceeding two (2) living and cooking together as a single housekeeping unit though not related by blood, adoption, or marriage shall be deemed to constitute a family."

Appellees, the Dickmans, are owners of a house in the village and leased it in December 1971 for a term of 18 months to Michael Truman. Later Bruce Boraas became a co-lessee. Then Anne Parish moved into the house along with three others. These six are students at nearby State University at Stony Brook and none is related to the other by blood, adoption, or marriage. When the village served the Dickmans with an "Order to Remedy Violations" of the ordinance, the owners plus three tenants thereupon brought this action for an injunction and a judgment declaring the ordinance unconstitutional.

. . . .

The present ordinance is challenged on several grounds: that it interferes with a person's right to travel; that it interferes with the right to migrate to and settle within a State; that it bars people who are uncongenial to the present residents; that it expresses the social preferences of the residents for groups that will be congenial to them; that social homogeneity is not a legitimate interest of government; that the restriction of those whom the neighbors do not like trenches on the newcomers' rights of privacy; that it is of no rightful concern to villagers whether the residents are married or unmarried; that the ordinance is antithetical to the Nation's experience, ideology, and self-perception as an open, egalitarian, and integrated society.

We find none of these reasons in the record before us. It is not aimed at transients. It involves no procedural disparity inflicted on some but not on others. It involves no "fundamental" right guaranteed by the Constitution, such as . . . the right of association, the right of access to the courts . . . or any rights of privacy. We deal with economic and social legislation where legislatures have historically drawn lines which we respect against the charge of violation of the Equal Protection Clause if the law . . . bears "a rational relationship to a [permissible] state objective." *Reed v. Reed*, 404 U.S. 71, 76 [(1971)].

It is said, however, that if two unmarried people can constitute a "family," there is no reason why three or four may not. But every line drawn by a legislature leaves some out that might well have been included. That exercise of discretion, however, is a legislative, not a judicial, function.

It is said that the Belle Terre ordinance reeks with an animosity to unmarried couples who live together.[6] There is no evidence to support it; and the provision of the ordinance bringing within the definition of a "family" two unmarried people belies the charge.

The ordinance places no ban on other forms of association, for a "family" may, so far as the ordinance is concerned, entertain whomever it likes.

The regimes of boarding houses, fraternity houses, and the like present urban problems. More people occupy a given space; more cars rather continuously pass by; more cars are parked; noise travels with crowds.

A quiet place where yards are wide, people few, and motor vehicles restricted are legitimate guidelines in a land-use project addressed to family needs. This goal is a permissible one. The police power is not confined to elimination of filth, stench, and unhealthy places. It is ample to lay out zones where family values, youth values, and the blessings of quiet seclusion and clean air make the area a sanctuary for people.

. . . .

Reversed.

MR. JUSTICE MARSHALL, dissenting.

. . . .

My disagreement with the Court today is based upon my view that the ordinance in this case unnecessarily burdens appellees' First Amendment freedom of association and their constitutionally guaranteed right to privacy. Our decisions establish that the First and Fourteenth Amendments protect the freedom to choose one's associates. Constitutional protection is extended, not only to modes of association that are political in the usual sense, but also to those that pertain to the social and economic benefit of the members. The selection of one's living companions involves similar choices as to the emotional, social, or economic benefits to be derived from alternative living arrangements.

---

[6] *Department of Agriculture v. Moreno*, 413 U.S. 528 [(1973)], is therefore inapt as there a household containing anyone unrelated to the rest was denied food stamps.

The freedom of association is often inextricably entwined with the constitutionally guaranteed right of privacy. The choice of household companions — of whether a person's "intellectual and emotional needs" are best met by living with family, friends, professional associates, or others — involves deeply personal considerations as to the kind and quality of intimate relationships within the home. That decision surely falls within the ambit of the right to privacy protected by the Constitution.

The instant ordinance discriminates on the basis of just such a personal lifestyle choice as to household companions. It permits any number of persons related by blood or marriage, be it two or twenty, to live in a single household, but it limits to two the number of unrelated persons bound by profession, love, friendship, religious or political affiliation, or mere economics who can occupy a single home. Belle Terre imposes upon those who deviate from the community norm in their choice of living companions significantly greater restrictions than are applied to residential groups who are related by blood or marriage, and compose the established order within the community. The village has, in effect, acted to fence out those individuals whose choice of lifestyle differs from that of its current residents.

[A]s a general proposition, I see no constitutional infirmity in a town's limiting the density of use in residential areas by zoning regulations which do not discriminate on the basis of constitutionally suspect criteria. This ordinance, however, limits the density of occupancy of only those homes occupied by unrelated persons. It thus reaches beyond control of the use of land or the density of population, and undertakes to regulate the way people choose to associate with each other within the privacy of their own homes.

. . . .

Because I believe that this zoning ordinance creates a classification which impinges upon fundamental personal rights, it can withstand constitutional scrutiny only upon a clear showing that the burden imposed is necessary to protect a compelling and substantial governmental interest. And, once it be determined that a burden has been placed upon a constitutional right, the onus of demonstrating that no less intrusive means will adequately protect the compelling state interest and that the challenged statute is sufficiently narrowly drawn, is upon the party seeking to justify the burden.

. . . It is claimed that the ordinance controls population density, prevents noise, traffic and parking problems, and preserves the rent structure of the community and its attractiveness to families. As I noted earlier, these are all legitimate and substantial interests of government. But I think it clear that the means chosen to accomplish these purposes are both overinclusive and underinclusive, and that the asserted goals could be as effectively achieved by means of an ordinance that did not discriminate on the basis of constitutionally protected choices of lifestyle. The ordinance imposes no restriction whatsoever on the number of persons who may live in a house, as long as they are related by marital or sanguinary bonds — presumably no matter how distant their relationship. Nor does the ordinance restrict the number of income earners who may contribute to rent in such a household, or the number of automobiles that may be maintained by its occupants. In that sense the ordinance is underinclusive. On the other hand, the statute restricts the number of unrelated persons who may live in a home to no more than two. It would therefore prevent three unrelated people from occupying a dwelling even if among them they had but one income and no vehicles. While an extended family of a dozen or more might live in a small bungalow, three elderly and retired persons could not occupy the large manor house next door. Thus the statute is also grossly overinclusive to accomplish its intended purposes.

. . . .

. . . [The village could address population density] problems by limiting each household to a specified number of adults, two or three perhaps, without limitation on the number of dependent children. The burden of such an ordinance would fall equally upon all segments of the community. It would surely be better tailored to the goals asserted by the village than the ordinance before us today, for it would more realistically restrict population density and growth and their attendant environmental costs. Various other statutory mechanisms also suggest themselves as solutions to Belle Terre's problems — rent control, limits on the number of vehicles per household, and so forth, but, of course, such schemes are matters of legislative judgment and not for this Court. Appellants also refer to the necessity of maintaining the family character of the village. There is not a shred of evidence in the record indicating that if Belle Terre permitted a limited number of unrelated persons to live together, the residential, familial character of the community would be fundamentally affected.

. . . .

NOTES

1. *Prior Case on Regulatory Definitions of Family.* Shortly before *Belle Terre*, the Supreme Court considered a case raising similar issues. In *Department of Agriculture v. Moreno*, 413 U.S. 528 (1973), the Court struck down a provision of the Food Stamp Act that denied assistance to households containing any unrelated individuals. The *Moreno* plaintiffs were an appealing group: most were traditional family units that had taken in unrelated individuals either as a charitable gesture, or to ease difficult financial problems by sharing expenses. Moreover, the household restriction had no apparent connection with the Act's stated purposes of stimulating the agricultural economy and assisting the poor with their nutritional needs. The actual motivation behind the provision was congressional hostility to some of the alternative lifestyle communes that had arisen in the 1960s, even though, as *Moreno* itself showed, the statutory language cast a broader net. The Court's opinion addressed the congressional motivation directly, observing that the legislative history revealed

> . . . that that amendment was intended to prevent so-called "hippies" and "hippie communes" from participating in the food stamp program. . . . The challenged classification clearly cannot be sustained by reference to this congressional purpose. For if the constitutional conception of "equal protection of the laws" means anything, it must at the very least mean that a bare congressional desire to harm a politically unpopular group cannot constitute a legitimate governmental interest. As a result, "[a] purpose to

discriminate against hippies cannot, in and of itself and without reference to [some independent] considerations in the public interest, justify the 1971 amendment."

Id. at 534. Such language would suggest that the "bare desire" to exclude communes or cohabitants could not sustain any classification. Such a broad reading of *Moreno* appears to be foreclosed, however, by *Belle Terre*. As you have read, *Belle Terre* made little effort to distinguish *Moreno*, with the exception of a footnote noting that the challenged ordinance, unlike the statute in *Moreno*, did not operate against an unmarried couple, since it included two "unrelated" individuals within the definition of family. This may suggest that the Court would strike down a zoning ordinance excluding unmarried couples entirely.

2. *The Majority's Position: Privileging the Traditional Family.* Consider this defense of the majority's view that zoning ordinances should be able to privilege traditional families:

> . . . Does a legislative preference for "family" amount to an irrational classification? [¶] The question was squarely raised in *Santa Barbara v. Adamson.* According to the California Supreme Court, the city violated the state's constitution by pegging its residential land use regulations to the subsistence of a "family" (as traditionally and legally constituted).[8]
>
> The court characterized the city's legislative purpose as preventing the moral hazards that communes pose to traditional families and their children. However, the court stated that to pursue such objectives by means of a flat ban amounts to erecting an "irrebuttable presumption" that communal life is immoral or socially corrosive. The city's legitimate goals — to head off the damage and misconduct that communards may (but do not always) do — and that traditional family members sometimes also do (if less frequently) — can be less-restrictively brought about by zeroing in on how the property is used rather than by whom it is used. Using family as an operational surrogate in a statutory plan aimed at assuring the stability of a neighborhood is overbroad because it thereby rules out many legitimate associations that would not introduce neighborhood instability. Additionally, family is underinclusive in that it allows many arrangements that would undermine neighborhood stability.
>
> . . . .
>
> [W]hy should organized society care, one way or another, about the family? If most people want to live in families, fine; if others do not, so what? [¶] . . . From ancient times, it has been widely recognized that there exists an essential connection between families and the larger societies that contain them. It is not only that families are the schools of first instance, in which children learn to embrace their deepest and most primitive assumptions about life and other people. It is also, as Confucius, Plato, and

---

[8] . . . "Family" is defined in the Santa Barbara city ordinance as, "1. An individual, or two (2) or more persons related by blood, marriage or legal adoption living together as a single housekeeping unit in a dwelling unit. 2. A group of not to exceed five (5) persons, excluding servants living together as a single housekeeping unit in a dwelling unit."

probably a hundred of their forerunners recognized, that the family is a sort of molecule, the very stuff of which the larger society is composed, so that the welfare of the one and the other are indissolubly coherent. As we should say in the patois of modern policy wonk-speak, families generate positive externalities for society relative to other living arrangements. One might suppose that so rooted an intuition would attract little skepticism. But a good deal of modern family law appears to accept the subtly inconsistent premise that how a person chooses to live, and with whom, is essentially a private matter into which the community intrudes as a hostile and officious stranger. According to our argument, that premise is specious. A matter, even a sensitively intimate one like a person's domestic living arrangements, can hardly be "private" if seen as threatening to result in important external harm.

. . . .

What is the basis for the fireside induction that "families" behave differently from a demographically matched group of non-family members? The answer is largely one of the stability of relationships, and the costs that members of any relational group will ordinarily encounter when they try to control the behavior of other group members. [¶] [T]he relative probabilities of exit, emotional as well as physical, from the household [is different for families]. The ease or difficulty of exit carries implications for the ability of the domestic unit to acquire and preserve reputational capital, which in turn affects the stake that household members have in investing in the household's "brand name."

. . . .

There [are] then, not only . . . anecdotes, but also a rather familiar theory which tells us that Santa Barbara was right: Communes, hippie or otherwise, can be expected to behave differently from families, even if one holds the demographic characteristics of their memberships constant, because communes and families expectationally have different time horizons, and thus different behavioral incentives. Like any other law, that "prediction" is overinclusive and underinclusive and contains a "conclusive presumption" (i.e., that deviation from the formal requirement of the law will tend to produce, though it may not always produce, the harm sought to be avoided). A highway speed limit is also over- and underinclusive, in addition to being a "conclusive presumption." So what? Nothing follows.

[Consider] the court's suggestion that the city attempt to enforce its interest behaviorally rather than structurally. . . . [This method of regulation would be costly to enforce, and] awkward for the state to scrutinize [in that it requires access to] the confidential dealings of families. Regulation, if it is required, must operate in domains that are accessible at reasonable cost. [A bright-line rule, such as those excluding certain family structures,] applies to easy-to-see conduct.

David D. Hadock & Daniel D. Polsby, *Family as a Rational Classification*, 74 WASH. U. L.Q. 15, 16–17, 22–24, 30 (1996).

3. *Justice Marshall's dissent.*   Would a broader definition of family than that used in the ordinance satisfy Justice Marshall? If not, what kind of zoning legislation by the village would he deem constitutional? The New Jersey Supreme Court adopted an approach that bears some resemblance to that laid out in Marshall's dissent in a similar zoning case, *Borough of Glassboro v. Vallorosi*, 568 A.2d 888 (N.J. 1990). In that case, ten college students challenged a New Jersey ordinance that defined the family as follows: "one or more persons occupying a dwelling unit as a single non-profit housekeeping unit, who are living together as a stable and permanent living unit, being a traditional family unit or the functional equivalency thereof." The New Jersey Supreme Court declared that "[r]estrictions based upon legal or biological relationships . . . impact only remotely upon [overcrowding and congestion] and hence cannot withstand judicial scrutiny" (quoting *State v. Baker*, 405 A.2d 368, 373 (N.J. 1979)). According to the court, although the state has the power to regulate for the general welfare, it must do so directly as opposed to indirectly through defining what constitutes a family.

4. *State Courts Use of* **Belle Terre.**   State courts have been split in their willingness to follow *Belle Terre*. Some adopt the Supreme Court's reasoning, applying a deferential standard to zoning ordinances excluding unrelated persons from single-family homes. *See, e.g., Ames Rental Prop. Ass'n v. City of Ames*, 736 N.W.2d 255, 260 (Iowa 2007); *Dinan v. Bd. of Zoning Appeals*, 595 A.2d 864 (Conn. 1991); *State v. Champoux*, 555 N.W.2d 69 (Neb. App. 1996); *Worcester v. Bonaventura*, 775 N.E.2d 795 (Mass. App. 2002); *Dvorak v. City of Bloomington*, 796 N.E.2d 236 (Ind. 2003); *Fischer v. N.H. State Bldg. Code Review Bd.*, 914 A.2d 1234 (N.H. 2006). Other state courts have relied on state constitutional provisions to reach a contrary result, including the California Supreme Court in *Santa Barbara v. Adamson*, 610 P.2d 436 (Cal. 1980), discussed in Haddock and Polsby's excerpt *supra*. *See also Charter Twp. of Delta v. Dinolfo*, 351 N.W.2d 831 (Mich. 1984); *State v. Baker*, 405 A.2d 368 (N.J. 1979; *Borough of Glassboro v. Vallorosi*, *supra*.

MOORE v. CITY OF EAST CLEVELAND
United States Supreme Court
431 U.S. 494 (1977)

MR. JUSTICE POWELL announced the judgment of the Court, and delivered an opinion in which MR. JUSTICE BRENNAN, MR. JUSTICE MARSHALL, and MR. JUSTICE BLACKMUN joined.

East Cleveland's housing ordinance, like many throughout the country, limits occupancy of a dwelling unit to members of a single family. § 1351.02. But the ordinance contains an unusual and complicated definitional section that recognizes as a "family" only a few categories of related individuals. § 1341.08.[2]

---

[2] Section 1341.08 provides:

  " 'Family' " means a number of individuals related to the nominal head of the household or to the spouse of the nominal head of the household living as a single housekeeping unit in a single dwelling unit, but limited to the following:

  "(a) Husband or wife of the nominal head of the household.

Because her family, living together in her home, fits none of those categories, appellant stands convicted of a criminal offense. The question . . . is whether the ordinance violates the Due Process Clause of the Fourteenth Amendment.

Appellant, Mrs. Inez Moore, lives in her East Cleveland home together with her son, Dale Moore, Sr., and her two grandsons, Dale, Jr., and John Moore, Jr. The two boys are first cousins rather than brothers; . . . John came to live with his grandmother and with the elder and younger Dale Moores after his mother's death.

In early 1973, Mrs. Moore received a notice of violation from the city, stating that John was an "illegal occupant" and directing her to comply with the ordinance. When she failed to remove him from her home, the city filed a criminal charge. Mrs. Moore moved to dismiss, claiming that the ordinance was constitutionally invalid on its face. Her motion was overruled, and upon conviction she was sentenced to five days in jail and a $25 fine. The Ohio Court of Appeals affirmed after giving full consideration to her constitutional claims, and the Ohio Supreme Court denied review. . . .

The city argues that our decision in *Village of Belle Terre v. Boraas*, 416 U.S. 1 (1974), requires us to sustain the ordinance attacked here. *Belle Terre*, like *East Cleveland*, imposed limits on the types of groups that could occupy a single dwelling unit. Applying the constitutional standard announced in this Court's leading land-use case, *Euclid v. Ambler Realty Co.*, 272 U.S. 365 (1926), we sustained the *Belle Terre* ordinance on the ground that it bore a rational relationship to permissible state objectives.

But one overriding factor sets this case apart from *Belle Terre*. The ordinance there affected only unrelated individuals. It expressly allowed all who were related by "blood, adoption, or marriage" to live together, and in sustaining the ordinance we were careful to note that it promoted "family needs" and "family values." 416 U.S., at 9. East Cleveland, in contrast, has chosen to regulate the occupancy of its housing by slicing deeply into the family itself. This is no mere incidental result of the ordinance. On its face it selects certain categories of relatives who may live together and declares that others may not. In particular, it makes a crime of a grandmother's choice to live with her grandson in circumstances like those presented here.

When a city undertakes such intrusive regulation of the family, neither *Belle Terre* nor *Euclid* governs; the usual judicial deference to the legislature is

---

"(b) Unmarried children of the nominal head of the household or of the spouse of the nominal head of the household, provided, however, that such unmarried children have no children residing with them.

"(c) Father or mother of the nominal head of the household or of the spouse of the nominal head of the household.

"(d) Notwithstanding the provisions of subsection (b) hereof, a family may include not more than one dependent married or unmarried child of the nominal head of the household or of the spouse of the nominal head of the household and the spouse and dependent children of such dependent child. For the purpose of this subsection, a dependent person is one who has more than fifty percent of his total support furnished for him by the nominal head of the household and the spouse of the nominal head of the household.

"(e) A family may consist of one individual."

inappropriate. "This Court has long recognized that freedom of personal choice in matters of marriage and family life is one of the liberties protected by the Due Process Clause of the Fourteenth Amendment." *Cleveland [Bd. of Educ.] v. LaFleur*, 414 U.S. 632, 639–40 (1974). A host of cases, tracing their lineage to *Meyer v. Nebraska*, 262 U.S. 390, 399–401 (1923), and *Pierce v. Society of Sisters*, 268 U.S. 510, 534–35 (1925), have consistently acknowledged a "private realm of family life which the state cannot enter." *Prince v. Massachusetts*, 321 U.S. 158, 166 (1944). . . .

When thus examined, this ordinance cannot survive. The city seeks to justify it as a means of preventing overcrowding, minimizing traffic and parking congestion, and avoiding an undue financial burden on East Cleveland's school system. Although these are legitimate goals, the ordinance before us serves them marginally, at best. For example, the ordinance permits any family consisting only of husband, wife, and unmarried children to live together, even if the family contains a half dozen licensed drivers, each with his or her own car. At the same time it forbids an adult brother and sister to share a household, even if both faithfully use public transportation. The ordinance would permit a grandmother to live with a single dependent son and children, even if his school-age children number a dozen, yet it forces Mrs. Moore to find another dwelling for her grandson John, simply because of the presence of his uncle and cousin in the same household. We need not labor the point. Section 1341.08 has but a tenuous relation to alleviation of the conditions mentioned by the city.

The city would distinguish the cases based on *Meyer* and *Pierce*. It points out that none of them "gives grandmothers any fundamental rights with respect to grandsons," and suggests that any constitutional right to live together as a family extends only to the nuclear family — essentially a couple and their dependent children.

To be sure, these cases did not expressly consider the family relationship presented here. They were immediately concerned with freedom of choice with respect to childbearing, *e.g.*, *LaFleur, Roe v. Wade* [410 U.S. 113 (1973)], *Griswold* [*v. Connecticut*, 381 U.S. 479 (1965)] *supra*, or with the rights of parents to the custody and companionship of their own children, *Stanley v. Illinois* [405 U.S. 645 (1972)], *supra*, or with traditional parental authority in matters of child rearing and education. [*Wisconsin v. Yoder*, 406 U.S. 205, 231–233 (1972); *Ginsberg v. New York*, 390 U.S. 629, 639 (1968)]; *Pierce, Meyer, supra*. But unless we close our eyes to the basic reasons why certain rights associated with the family have been accorded shelter under the Fourteenth Amendment's Due Process Clause, we cannot avoid applying the force and rationale of these precedents to the family choice involved in this case.

. . .

Substantive due process has at times been a treacherous field for this Court. . . .

[But a]ppropriate limits on substantive due process come not from drawing arbitrary lines but rather from careful "respect for the teachings of history [and] solid recognition of the basic values that underlie our society." *Griswold v.*

Connecticut, 381 U.S., at 501 (HARLAN, J., concurring). Our decisions establish that the Constitution protects the sanctity of the family precisely because the institution of the family is deeply rooted in this Nation's history and tradition. It is through the family that we inculcate and pass down many of our most cherished values, moral and cultural.

Ours is by no means a tradition limited to respect for the bonds uniting the members of the nuclear family. The tradition of uncles, aunts, cousins, and especially grandparents sharing a household along with parents and children has roots equally venerable and equally deserving of constitutional recognition. Over the years millions of our citizens have grown up in just such an environment, and most, surely, have profited from it. Even if conditions of modern society have brought about a decline in extended family households, they have not erased the accumulated wisdom of civilization, gained over the centuries and honored throughout our history, that supports a larger conception of the family. Out of choice, necessity, or a sense of family responsibility, it has been common for close relatives to draw together and participate in the duties and the satisfactions of a common home. Decisions concerning child rearing, which *Yoder, Meyer, Pierce* and other cases have recognized as entitled to constitutional protection, long have been shared with grandparents or other relatives who occupy the same household — indeed who may take on major responsibility for the rearing of the children. Especially in times of adversity, such as the death of a spouse or economic need, the broader family has tended to come together for mutual sustenance and to maintain or rebuild a secure home life. This is apparently what happened here.

Whether or not such a household is established because of personal tragedy, the choice of relatives in this degree of kinship to live together may not lightly be denied by the State. *Pierce* struck down an Oregon law requiring all children to attend the State's public schools, holding that the Constitution "excludes any general power of the State to standardize its children by forcing them to accept instruction from public teachers only." 268 U.S., at 535. By the same token the Constitution prevents East Cleveland from standardizing its children — and its adults — by forcing all to live in certain narrowly defined family patterns

Reversed.

[JUSTICE STEVENS concurred in the judgment, finding the challenged zoning regulation an unconstitutional "taking" of appellant's property because the city "failed totally" to explain the need for a rule allowing a homeowner to have grandchildren live with her if they are brothers but not if they are cousins. The other four Justices dissented.]

NOTES

1. ***Defining the Family.*** The definitional problem wrestled with in *Moore* — what constitutes a "family" — arises in other regulatory schemes as well. *See, e.g., Hann v. Housing Auth. of Easton*, 709 F. Supp. 605 (E.D. Pa. 1989) (holding that categorical exclusion of unmarried couples from eligibility under low-income housing programs violates United States Housing Act of 1937); *Dorado v. Gonzales*, 202 Fed. Appx. 898 (6th Cir. 2006) (upholding decision of Board of

Immigration Appeals, which was considering whether to remove the petitioner from the country, to allow hardship testimony from petitioner's two biological sons but to disallow testimony from petitioner's girlfriend's son); *Hartford Ins. Co. v. Cline*, 190 Fed. Appx. 650 (10th Cir. 2006) (affirming district court decision that "family member" in car insurance policy did not include a domestic partner).

2. *Distinguishing* Moore *and* Belle Terre.   The Court reconciles *Moore* and *Belle Terre* by emphasizing that the purpose of the *Belle Terre* ordinance was to promote "family values," while the *Moore* rule actually required the separation of families. This analysis therefore assumes a definition of family broad enough to encompass the extended family of *Moore* and narrow enough to exclude communes or groups of roommates, as in *Belle Terre*. As such, in determining which collections of individuals constitute a family whose privacy falls within the protection of the Due Process Clause of the Fourteenth Amendment, the Court stays within the parameters of the familiar formal categories of relation (blood, marriage, or adoption), although extending the boundaries beyond the nuclear family. Some commentators view *Belle Terre* "as simply excluding unrelated college students from single-family neighborhoods and not reaching the question of whether an alternative [functional] family can be excluded from the same neighborhoods." *E.g.*, Barbara J. Cox, *Alternative Families: Obtaining Traditional Family Benefits Through Litigation, Legislation and Collective Bargaining*, 15 WIS. WOMEN'S L.J. 93, 106 (2000).

Are there other ways to distinguish the households in *Moore* and *Belle Terre*? Consider, for example, the various "factors" set forth in *Braschi v. Stahl Associates Co*, 543 N.E.2d 49 (N.Y. 1989), *infra* at Section B[2], and apply them to the *Moore* and *Belle Terre* "families." Professors Haddock and Polsby assert that one key distinction between "families" and groups of "non-family members" is the stability of their relationships. How should stability be measured? In *Braschi, infra*, the court refers to "longevity." Are the two synonymous in this context? If not, what distinguishes them? How do the *Moore* and *Belle Terre* households compare with respect to either the stability or longevity of the relationships? Stability is only one part of what Haddock and Polsby see as the critical distinction. They also say that it is more difficult for persons to exit a family unit, both emotionally and physically, and that the "ease or difficulty of exit carries implications for the ability of the domestic unit to acquire and preserve reputational capital, which in turn affects the stake that household members have in investing in the household's 'brand name'." They believe this is the key feature of families that makes them more likely than other groups to conform to social norms, and thus the rationale for treating them more favorably in some regulatory schemes. Consider what implication this argument has for how such regulatory schemes should define families.

3. *Marshall's* Belle Terre *Dissent Versus the Plurality Opinion in* Moore.   Justice Marshall, who dissented in *Belle Terre* on the ground that the Constitution protects an individual's right to choose their familial or living arrangement, joined the plurality opinion written by Justice Powell in *Moore*. Is the position taken by Justice Powell in that opinion the same that Marshall presents in the *Belle Terre* dissent? The answer is probably not.

4. *Zoning Ordinances and Subtexts Relating to Race, Class, and Other*

Distinctions. In his concurring opinion in *Moore*, Justice Brennan notes that the family type excluded by the East Cleveland ordinance is one that is more prevalent in African-American families, an issue the plurality opinion by Justice Powell did not acknowledge. *Moore*, 431 U.S. at 509 (BRENNAN, J., concurring). Justice Stewart pointed out, in a footnote to his dissenting opinion, that "East Cleveland is a predominantly Negro community, with a Negro City Manager and City Commission." Professor Robert Burt suggests the following interpretation, noting that while the *Moore*

> plurality viewed the ordinance as directed against "overcrowding, minimizing traffic and parking congestion, and avoiding an undue financial burden on [the] school system" and observed that these "legitimate goals" could be pursued by other means, [it] did not consider that the purpose of the ordinance was quite straightforward: to exclude from a middle-class, predominantly black community, that saw itself as socially and economically upwardly mobile, other black families most characteristic of lower-class ghetto life.

The Constitution of the Family, 1979 SUP. CT. REV. 329, 388–89. However one views the motives of the East Cleveland city officials (and the Court's lack of deference to their judgment), Professor Burt's comments highlight the reality that zoning ordinances may exclude particular racial, ethnic, socioeconomic groups, whether or not that is the intent of the particular local government. Recent social science data suggest that what had been identified as a pattern of lower-class blacks at the time *Moore* was issued, was actually a trend that was becoming more prominent in lower income families more generally. *See* Frank F. Furstenberg, *If Moynihan Had Only Known: Race, Class, and Family Change in the Late Twentieth Century*, 621 ANNALS AM. ACAD. POL. & SOC. SCI. 94 (2009). For further discussion of some of the issues and subtexts relating to race and class in residential zoning and city planning policies, see, e.g., David Dante Troutt, *Ghettoes Made Easy: The Metamarket/ Antimarket Dichotomy and the Legal Challenges of Inner-City Economic Development*, 35 HARV. C.R.-C.L. L. REV. 427, 441–47 (2000); Richard Thompson Ford, *The Boundaries of Race: Political Geography in Legal Analysis*, 107 HARV. L. REV. 1841 (1994); James J. Harnett, *Affordable Housing, Exclusionary Zoning, and American Apartheid: Using Title VIII to Foster Statewide Racial Integration*, 68 N.Y.U. L. REV. 89 (1993); Jennifer C. Johnson, *Race-Based Housing Importunities: The Disparate Impact of Realistic Group Conflict*, 8 LOY. J. PUB. INT. L. 97 (2007); Benjamin Rajotte, *Environmental Justice in New Orleans: A New Lease on Life for Title VIII?*, 21 TUL. ENVTL. L.J. 51 (2007); *see also* C. Quince Hopkins, *The Supreme Court's Family Law Doctrine Revisited: Insights from Social Science on Family Structures and Kinship Change in the United States*, 13 CORNELL J.L. & PUB. POL'Y 431, 434 (2004).

    5. *Foster Families and Group Homes.* Many of these zoning battles involve foster families or group homes. For example, in *Children's Home of Easton v. City of Easton*, 417 A.2d 830, 830 (Pa. Commw. Ct. 1980), the court held that the definition of family in a city zoning ordinance was unconstitutional in its exclusion of a foster family headed by a married couple who had two of their own children and custody of three foster children. Distinguishing the proposed household from the "six unrelated college students" in *Belle Terre*, the court concluded that "the foster family proposed [is akin] in all respects . . . to a 'natural' family. There would be no professional counselors involved, nor any 'days off', for the foster parents. The 'hope' would be that the foster children would remain in the home until graduation from high school. The foster parents would be expected to provide all the services that would have been expected from natural parents. They would serve in a 'nurturing, supervisory and caring role.' In sum, the foster family in this instance would be the functional equivalent of a biologically related family." *See also Saunders v. Clark County Zoning Dep't*, 421 N.E.2d 152 (Ohio 1981) (holding that a household consisting of a minister, his wife and five children, and up to nine foster children who had been adjudicated as juvenile delinquents, constituted a "family" under the relevant zoning ordinance, asserting that "definitions of 'family,' [should not be] encrust[ed] with the barnacles of one's own notions and prejudices of what [constitutes a] 'family' "). A municipality in Colorado tried to limit the number of sex offenders in a neighborhood by defining "family" to include only one sex offender per household. Foster parents challenged this, when three of their foster children were forced to register, thereby violating the zoning ordinance. The state supreme court found that the municipality had overstepped its bounds under the state constitution and violated public policy by not allowing such juvenile offenders to live in rehabilitative foster homes together. *City of Northglenn v. Ibarra*, 62 P.3d 151 (Colo. 2003).

Not all courts have viewed foster homes as functional families, however. *See, e.g., Metro. Dev. Comm'n of Marion Cty. v. Vills., Inc.*, 464 N.E.2d 367 (Ind. App. 1984) (holding that the undefined term "family" in the zoning ordinance did not encompass a married couple caring for up to ten foster children placed there by child protective services, noting that those states that have construed the term "family" to encompass such groups have "exceed[ed] the constitutional requirements set forth in *Belle Terre* [and] *Moore*"). The Tenth Circuit found that a concern for safety of a neighborhood was a legitimate concern in restricting the size and make-up of foster homes and upheld a restrictive definition of family. The court refused to recognize a functional family and allow an exception to the local definition. *Keys Youth Servs. v. City of Olathe*, 248 F.3d 1267 (10th Cir. 2001).

Cases involving group homes housing children or adults with special needs, such as the mentally disabled or mentally ill, have been more complicated. The cases we have discussed thus far have been decided on the question of whether the household constitutes a "family" for the purposes of a zoning ordinance and, if not, whether the definition is unconstitutional in its exclusion of such household groups. Another group of cases has been decided on equal protection grounds. *See Cleburne v. Cleburne Living Center, Inc.*, 473 U.S. 432 (1985) (holding that the city's requirement of a special use permit for a group home for mentally-retarded residences, while not requiring such a permit for certain other uses, was irrational in light of the city's stated zoning goals). Assisted by 1988 Amendments to the Fair Housing Act, which prohibit discrimination in housing on the basis of an individual's "handicap," those who seek to establish group homes for a range of special populations have relied on various theories in challenging the ordinance's exclusion with mixed success. *See e.g., Albert v. Zoning Hearing Bd.*, 854 A.2d 401 (Pa. 2004) (holding that a halfway house was not stable enough to conform to the definition of a family); *Hill v. Cmty. of Damien of Molokai*, 911 P.2d 861 (N.M.

1996) (holding four unrelated individuals with AIDS using home restricted to use as single-family residence did not violate the covenant). For a discussion on how the right to privacy may affect foster homes and group homes, see Sara L. Dunski, Note, *Make Way for the New Kid on the Block: The Possible Zoning Implications* Lawrence v. Texas, 2005 U. ILL. L. REV. 847.

PROBLEMS

Problem 1-1. Two married couples, the Rademans and the Beravers, are each unable to afford a home of their own. As they are good friends, they decide to pool their resources and jointly purchase a single home which they will share. The home is in an area zoned for single family residences. The city zoning administrator brings an action against them for violation of the zoning laws, contending they do not constitute a single family. What result? What should be the result?

Problem 1-2. Opus Dei is an organization of Roman Catholic laymen, recognized by the Roman Catholic Church. The Opus Dei Center of St. Louis consists of seven laymen and a Roman Catholic priest. While continuing to work in their secular occupations, the seven men are fully committed to a single life so that they are completely available to carry out the spiritual and educational mission of Opus Dei. The Center acquires a home for the group to live in. The home is in an area zoned single-family, and the town denies Opus Dei an occupancy permit because it does not constitute a family. The zoning law defines family as "one or more persons living as a single housekeeping unit, all of whom or all but two of whom are related to each other by birth, adoption or marriage, as distinguished from a group occupying a boarding house or hotel." Opus Dei seeks judicial review of the zoning board's decision. What result? What should be the result?

Problem 1-3. Alice and Tom are both divorced. They begin living together but decide to postpone any marriage plans, preferring instead their oral understanding that they would share all income and expenses while together, but would have no obligations to each other if either decides to separate. They each have two children by their earlier marriage, and each has custody. Their housekeeping unit therefore includes six people. They rent a home in a single-family zone. The city zoning law defines a family as a single housekeeping unit that includes no more than two "unrelated" individuals. The city brings an action against them for violation of the zoning law. What result? What should be the result?

Problem 1-4. You are the city attorney of Familytown. The council has decided to do everything it can to suppress unconventional living arrangements, in order to preserve the family character of the town from the influences of the nearby city and its university. It wants to suppress communes, unmarried cohabitation and groups of roommates, but not "genuine" extended families.

The Council realizes that there may be constitutional restrictions, but wants to go as far as it can. It is willing to enact a law which might get challenged, so long as the chance of ultimately prevailing on appeal is reasonably good. It is not interested in enacting an ordinance that is likely to be struck down.

Draft a law for the council to consider. Assume that state law allows the city all authority you might need for criminal provisions, land-use regulations or other appropriate provisions.

[2]   Rent Control Regulation

BRASCHI v. STAHL ASSOCIATES CO.
New York Court of Appeals
543 N.E.2d 49 (1989)

TITONE, J.

. . . .

Appellant, Miguel Braschi, was living with Leslie Blanchard in a rent-controlled apartment . . . from the summer of 1975 until Blanchard's death in September of 1986. In November of 1986, respondent, Stahl Associates Company, the owner of the apartment building, served a notice to cure on appellant contending that he was a mere licensee with no right to occupy the apartment since only Blanchard was the tenant of record. In December of 1986 respondent served appellant with a notice to terminate informing appellant that he had one month to vacate the apartment and that, if the apartment was not vacated, respondent would commence summary proceedings to evict him.

[Braschi] initiated an action seeking a permanent injunction and a declaration of entitlement to occupy the apartment. [He] then moved for a preliminary injunction, pendente lite, enjoining respondent from evicting him until a court could determine whether he was a member of Blanchard's family within the meaning of 9 N.Y.C. [Rent and Eviction Regulations] R. § 2204.6(d). After examining the nature of the relationship between the two men, Supreme Court concluded that [Braschi] was a "family member" within the meaning of the regulation . . . and, accordingly, that a preliminary injunction should be issued. The court based this decision on its finding that the long-term interdependent nature of the 10-year relationship between [Braschi] and Blanchard "fulfills any definitional criteria of the term 'family.' "

The Appellate Division reversed, concluding that section § 2204.6 (d) provides non-eviction protection only to "family members within traditional, legally recognized familial relationships." Since [Braschi's] and Blanchard's relationship was not one given formal recognition by the law, the court held that appellant could not seek the protection of the noneviction ordinance. . . . We now reverse.

. . . .

The present dispute arises because the term "family" is not defined in the rent-control code and the legislative history is devoid of any specific reference to the noneviction provision.

. . . .

. . . [S]ection 2204.6 of the New York City Rent and Eviction Regulations (9 N.Y.C.R.R. § 2204.6), which authorizes . . . the eviction of persons occupying a rent-controlled apartment after the death of the named tenant, provides, in subdivision (d), noneviction protection to those occupants who are either the "surviving spouse of the deceased tenant or some other member of the deceased tenant's family who has been living with the tenant [of record]." The manifest intent of this section is to restrict the landowners' ability to evict a narrow class of occupants other than the tenant of record. The question presented here concerns the scope of the protections provided. Juxtaposed against this intent favoring the protection of tenants, is the over-all objective of a gradual "transition from regulation to a normal market of free bargaining between landlord and tenant". . . .

Emphasizing the latter objective, [landlord] argues that the term "family member" as used in 9 N.Y.C.R.R. § 2204.6(d) should be construed, consistent with this State's intestacy laws, to mean relationships of blood, consanguinity and adoption in order to effectuate the over-all goal of orderly succession to real property. Under this interpretation, only those entitled to inherit under the laws of intestacy would be afforded noneviction protection. Further, [landlord argues] that since the relationship between [Braschi] and Blanchard has not been accorded legal status by the Legislature, it is not entitled to the protections of section § 2204.6 (d). . . .

. . . [W]e conclude that the term family, as used in 9 N.Y.C.R.R. § 2204.6(d), should not be rigidly restricted to those people who have formalized their relationship by obtaining, for instance, a marriage certificate or an adoption order. The intended protection against sudden eviction should not rest on fictitious legal distinctions or genetic history, but instead should find its foundation in the reality of family life. In the context of eviction, a more realistic, and certainly equally valid, view of a family includes two adult lifetime partners whose relationship is long term and characterized by an emotional and financial commitment and interdependence. This view comports both with our society's traditional concept of "family" and with the expectations of individuals who live in such nuclear units. *See* BALLANTINE'S LAW DICTIONARY 456 (3d ed. 1969) ("family" defined as "(p)rimarily, the collective body of persons who live in one house and under one head or management"). . . . Hence, it is reasonable to conclude that, in using the term "family," the Legislature intended to extend protection to those who reside in households having all of the normal familial characteristics. Appellant Braschi should therefore be afforded the opportunity to prove that he and Blanchard had such a household.

This definition of "family" is consistent with both of the competing purposes of the rent-control laws: the protection of individuals from sudden dislocation and the gradual transition to a free market system. Family members, whether or not related by blood or law, who have always treated the apartment as their family home will be protected against the hardship of eviction following the death of the named tenant, thereby furthering the Legislature's goals of preventing dislocation and preserving family units which might otherwise be broken apart upon eviction. This approach will foster the transition from rent control to rent stabilization by drawing a distinction between those individuals who are, in fact, genuine family members, and those who are mere roommates or newly discovered relatives hoping to inherit the rent-controlled apartment after the existing tenant's death.

The determination as to whether an individual is entitled to noneviction protection should be based upon an objective examination of the relationship of the parties. In making this assessment, the lower courts of this State have looked to a number of factors, including the exclusivity and longevity of the relationship, the level of emotional and financial commitment, the manner in which the parties have conducted their everyday lives and held themselves out to society, and the reliance placed upon one another for daily family services. These factors are most helpful, although it should be emphasized that the presence or absence of one or more of them is not dispositive since it is the totality of the relationship as evidenced by the dedication, caring and self-sacrifice of the parties which should, in the final analysis, control. [Braschi's] situation provides an example of how the rule should be applied.

[Braschi] and Blanchard lived together as permanent life partners for more than 10 years. They regarded one another, and were regarded by friends and family, as spouses. The two men's families were aware of the nature of the relationship, and they regularly visited each other's families and attended family functions together, as a couple. Even today, [Braschi] continues to maintain a relationship with Blanchard's niece, who considers him an uncle.

In addition to their interwoven social lives, [Braschi] clearly considered the apartment his home. He lists the apartment as his address on his driver's license and passport, and receives all his mail at the apartment address. Moreover, [his] tenancy was known to the building's superintendent and doormen, who viewed the two men as a couple.

Financially, the two men shared all obligations including a household budget. The two were authorized signatories of three safe-deposit boxes, they maintained joint checking and savings accounts, and joint credit cards. In fact, rent was often paid with a check from their joint checking account. Additionally, Blanchard executed a power of attorney in [Braschi's] favor so that [Braschi] could make necessary decisions — financial, medical and personal — for him during his illness. Finally, [Braschi] was the named beneficiary of Blanchard's life insurance policy, as well as the primary legatee and coexecutor of Blanchard's estate. Hence, a court examining these facts could reasonably conclude that these men were much more than mere roommates.

Accordingly, the order of the Appellate Division should be reversed and the case remitted to that court for a consideration of undetermined questions.

NOTES

1. *A Postscript to* Braschi.   After *Braschi*, a lower appellate court held that the provision protecting family members under the Rent Stabilization Code also applied to a gay couple, using a functional definition of family. *E. Tenth St. Assoc. v. Goldstein*, 552 N.Y.S.2d 257 (App. Div. 1990). Unlike the rent control law at issue in *Braschi*, the rent stabilization statute defines "family members" quite specifically to include twenty-four enumerated relationships (husband, wife, son, daughter, stepson, stepdaughter, father, mother, sister, nephew, niece, son-in-law, etc.), but the definition does not include gay partners. Nonetheless, the court held

that *Braschi* was controlling because the two regulatory schemes have a similar underlying purpose.

In 1990, the Division of Housing and Community Renewal (DHCR) issued regulations defining "family members" entitled to succeed to a rent-regulated apartment on the death or departure of a tenant under both the rent-control and rent-stabilization laws. 9 N.Y.C.R.R. §§ 2401.6, 2204.6. "Family member" under the regulations includes "any other person residing with the tenant . . . in the housing accommodation as a primary . . . residence, who can prove emotional and financial commitment and interdependence between such person and the tenant." The regulations list several factors to be considered, emphasizing that no single factor is determinative. *Id.* The regulations were upheld against a constitutional challenge by a landlord group, who argued that the regulations effected an unconstitutional taking of property without just compensation. *See Rent Stabilization Ass'n v. Higgins*, 630 N.E.2d 626 (N.Y. 1993).

In practice, although both same-sex and heterosexual couples in long-term committed relationships may qualify as family members, individuals in relationships without sexual intimacy may have a harder time. For example, a woman who claimed a sibling-like relationship to the tenant was found to be more like a "good friend and roommate." *Seminole Realty Co. v. Greenbaum*, 619 N.Y.S.2d 5 (App. Div. 1994). The court implied that a real sibling-like relationship might qualify for functional family status, but it would seem that a constructive adult sibling relationship probably would fall short.

2. *Functional Definitions of Family.* The court in *Braschi* abandoned the traditional bases for defining family as a legal category — blood, marriage, and adoption — for an approach that focuses on "the reality of family life." Some family law scholars call such an analysis a "functional" approach to defining family. *See, e.g.*, Susan Frelich Appleton, *Parents by the Numbers*, 37 HOFSTRA L. REV. 11 (2008) (discussing rise of functional tests for parenthood); Joanna Radbord, *Lesbian Love Stories: How We Won Equal Marriage in Canada*, 17 YALE J.L. & FEMINISM 99 (2005) (discussing functional approaches to family law); Madeline Howard, *Subsidized Housing Policy: Defining the Family*, 22 BERKELEY J. GENDER L. & JUST. 97 (2007) (discussing functional approach to defining family).

3. *Functional Definitions of Family in the Law.* Advocates who seek to move the law away from traditional, formal definitions of family, and claim rights and privileges based on functional definitions have had limited success in courts. Their success has varied according to the particular right or benefit asserted. As for property rights after the breakup of a cohabitant relationship, Washington State alone provides for distribution of assets under a property theory between unmarried cohabitant couples in a marital-like relationship. This law is discussed *infra* Chapter 9. One of the most important contexts in which parties have successfully made claims based on functional family relationships is on issues of child custody, visitation, and adoption. In several jurisdictions, individuals who have formed parent-like relationships with children may acquire custodial or, more often, visitation rights with respect to the child. These "psychological parent" or "de facto parent" doctrines are discussed in more detail *infra* Chapter 6. Claims based on functional family relationships also arise in cases involving economic claims against third parties, such as wrongful death and worker's compensation benefits. These claims are also discussed *infra* Chapter 9.

4. *Comparative Perspective.* Many countries have gone much further than the United States in providing benefits to families that fall outside of traditional definitions, rather than to the marital family. *See* Nancy D. Polikoff, Beyond Straight and Gay: Valuing All Families Under the Law 119-120 (2008). For example, in Canada, federal law begins to treat both same- and different-sex couples as spouses after they have lived together for three years; entering into marriage at that point does not have a significant impact on their legal status. Further, in 2002 the province of Alberta passed the Adult Interdependent Relationships Act (AIP), under which unmarried adult couples share many of the same legal benefits and consequences as married couples. Adult Interdependent Relationships Act, SA 2002, c. A-4.5.

In keeping with a functional family approach, this act gives couples with children by either birth or adoption more leeway in determining their status, treating them as spouses if their relationship is "of some permanence," without regard for the three-year period that applies to other couples. Australia approaches unmarried heterosexual couples in a similar way, extending rights almost identical to those of married couples even without a minimum period of cohabitation, and describing these couples as "de facto spouses" living together "on a genuine domestic basis." *See, e.g., Commonwealth Powers (De Facto Relationships) Act 2003* (NSW); *Commonwealth Powers (De Facto Relationships) Act 2003* (Qld); *Commonwealth Powers (De Facto Relationships) Act 2004* (Vic); *De Facto Relationships (Northern Territory Request) Act 2004* (NT). Australian law limits marriage to different-sex couples, but has begun to offer "de facto relationship" status to same-sex partners in some states. Polikoff, *supra*, at 116–17. New Zealand, meanwhile, accommodates the wide range of couples in functional families by banning discrimination on the basis of either sexual orientation or marital status, which includes de facto couples. Polikoff, *supra*, at 118.

These statuses allow couples in functional families access to many more services and benefits than are available to similar couples in the United States. Under Canada's AIP status, couples can share healthcare benefits, inherit as a spouse would, and sue for ongoing support should the relationship end. Polikoff, *supra*, at 115. In Sweden, the law provides a limited set of rights that mainly concern tenancy and property, and applies equally to cohabiting and unmarried same-sex and different-sex couples. Sambolag "The Cohabitation Act" (2003:376). Unmarried cohabitants in many European countries have the right to make health care decisions as the next of kin and to sue for wrongful death, again regardless of registration. Polikoff, *supra*, at 119. For further discussion of other countries' adoption of a functional family model, see e.g., Jenni Millbank, *The Limits of Functional Family: Lesbian Mother Litigation in the Era of the Eternal Biological Family*, 22 Int'l J. L. Pol'y & Fam. 149 (2008); Jenni Millbank, *The Role of "Functional Family" in Same-Sex Family Recognition Trends*, 20 Child & Family L. Q. 1 3 (2008); Reg Graycar & Jenni Millbank, *From Functional Family to Spinster Sisters: Australia's Distinctive Path to Relationship Recognition*, 24 J.L. & Pol'y 121 (2007).

5. *Evaluating Formal vs. Functional Definitions of Family.* Same-sex partners have a particularly compelling claim to recognition of their status as functional family members, because they are prohibited from marrying in most states (*see* Chapter 2), and alternative formal statuses are only available to them in a few states as well. (*See* Chapter 9). Adopting a functional definition of family permits the extension of legal protection to non-traditional family relationships. By cutting the legal definition of family loose from its traditional moorings, however, the *Braschi* court has raised many questions.

For example, if the legal test for family, which heretofore was a bright line rule, is transformed into a broad, indeterminate standard, judges acquire broad discretion to determine which characteristics are important in defining family relationships. In addition, the relevant parties cannot be sure if special rights and protections exist until a determination is made by a court, which may take years. Furthermore, these determinations invite what may be intrusive inquiries into family life. For example, a landlord may be motivated to observe the activities of tenants and their visitors to acquire evidence that a couple is *not* in a family relationship. The risks of a functional standard, and the advantages of formal categories are suggested by a case involving an unsuccessful effort by a landlord to argue that a married couple was not a "family" under *Braschi*, based on evidence that the husband was gay and the couple had separate bank accounts. *John C. v. Martha A.*, 592 N.Y.S. 2d 229 (Civ. Ct. 1992). The court declined to "peer behind the marriage, into the parties' sexual and economic relationship," an inquiry that may be necessary under a functional test.

For perceptive criticism of functional tests to define family, see Martha Minow, *Redefining Families: Who's In and Who's Out?*, 62 U. COLO. L. REV. 269 (1991). For a thoughtful discussion of the context-specificity of definitions of family, and distinctions between those components of definitions that focus on "associations of choice," from "kinships of responsibility," see Barbara Bennett Woodhouse, *"It all Depends on What you Mean by Home": Toward a Communitarian Theory of the "Nontraditional" Family*, 1996 UTAH. L. REV. 569. For further discussion of *Braschi* and its contribution to the functional models of family definition, see Paris R. Baldacci, *Protecting Gay and Lesbian Families From Eviction From Their Homes: The Quest for Equality for Gay and Lesbian Families in* Braschi v. Stahl Associates, 13 TEX. WESLEYAN L. REV. 619 (2007); Lucille M. Ponte & Jennifer L. Gillan, *From Our Family to Yours: Rethinking the "Beneficial Family" and Marriage-Centric Corporate Benefit Programs*, 14 COLUM. J. GENDER & L. 1 (2005); Ryan E. Mensing, Note, *A New York State of Mind: Reconciling Legislative Incrementalism with Sexual Orientation Jurisprudence*, 69 BROOK. L. REV. 1159 (2004).

C. FAMILIES AND THE CONSTITUTIONAL RIGHT TO PRIVACY

Traditionally, domestic relations were regarded as virtually the exclusive province of the states. *Sosna v. Iowa*, 419 U.S. 393, 404 (1975). During the course of the last century, however, and particularly in the last few generations, the Supreme Court has crafted a doctrine of privacy that has profound relevance for family law.

In Justice Brennan's words, "[w]hile the outer limits of this aspect of privacy have not been marked by the Court, it is clear that among the decisions that an individual may make without unjustified government interference are personal decisions 'relating to marriage, procreation, contraception, family relationships, and child rearing and education.' " *Carey v. Population Servs. Int'l*, 431 U.S. 678, 684–85 (1977) (internal citations omitted). Constitutional doctrine therefore serves an important role in delineating the contours of permissible state regulation of families. The following decisions explore the scope of the constitutional doctrine of privacy and its relationship to families and the individuals who compose them.

[1]   **Evolution of the Right of Privacy**

Families' constitutional right to protection from state action dates at least as far back as a pair of U.S. Supreme Court cases concerning children's education that were decided in the 1920s, *Meyer v. Nebraska*, 262 U.S. 390 (1923), and *Pierce v. Society of Sisters*, 268 U.S. 510 (1925). In *Meyer*, the Supreme Court first suggested that liberty, as guaranteed by the Constitution, includes "not merely freedom from bodily restraint but also the right of the individual to . . . marry, establish a home and bring up children." 262 U.S. 390, 399. In that case, the Court struck down a statute that prohibited teaching German to children below the eighth grade. The Court stated that parents have a right to make decisions about the education of their children and that "the right of parents to engage [a teacher] so to instruct their children [in the German language] . . . are within the liberty of the [Fourteenth] Amendment." *Id.* at 400. Two years later, in *Pierce v. Society of Sisters*, the Court struck down an Oregon statute requiring children between the ages of eight and sixteen to attend public (rather than private) school, holding that "[t]he Act . . . unreasonably interfere[d] with the liberty of parents . . . to direct the upbringing and education of [their] children . . ." 268 U.S. at 534. In language that appeared to celebrate the Constitution as the protector of pluralism and diversity, *Pierce* concluded that: "The fundamental theory of liberty . . . excludes any general power of the state to standardize its children. . . . The child is not the mere creature of the state; those who nurture him and direct his destiny have the right, coupled with the high duty, to recognize and prepare him for additional obligations." *Id.* at 535.

Two decades later, the Court addressed the limits of parental autonomy in childrearing in a third decision, *Prince v. Massachusetts*, 321 U.S. 158, 166 (1944). The Court counseled that "the custody, care and nurture of the child reside first in the parents," and that its decisions "have respected the private realm of family life which the state cannot enter." It noted, however, that "the family is not beyond regulation in the public interest." *Id.* Subsequent cases have continued to explore the extent to which the State may regulate the lives of private individuals and families for the public's benefit. These cases rely on these earlier building blocks to develop what has come to be known as the constitutional right to privacy.

GRISWOLD v. CONNECTICUT
United States Supreme Court
381 U.S. 479 (1965)

MR. JUSTICE DOUGLAS delivered the opinion of the Court.

Appellant Griswold is Executive Director of the Planned Parenthood League of Connecticut. Appellant Buxton is a licensed physician and a professor at the Yale Medical School who served as Medical Director for the League at its Center in New Haven — a center open and operating from November 1 to November 10, 1961, when appellants were arrested. [Appellants were arrested and charged with giving information, instruction, and medical advice to married persons regarding the means of preventing conception, as well as of prescribing contraceptive devices or materials, in violation of the General Statutes of Connecticut §§ 53-32 and 54–196 (1958 rev.)].

. . . .

The appellants were found guilty as accessories and fined $100 each, against the claim that the accessory statute as so applied violated the Fourteenth Amendment. . . .

. . . [W]e are met with a wide range of questions that implicate the Due Process Clause of the Fourteenth Amendment. Overtones of some arguments suggest that *Lochner v. New York*, 198 U.S. 45 [(1905)], should be our guide. But we decline that invitation. . . . We do not sit as a super-legislature to determine the wisdom, need, and propriety of laws that touch economic problems, business affairs, or social conditions. This law, however, operates directly on an intimate relation of husband and wife and their physician's role in one aspect of that relation.

The association of people is not mentioned in the Constitution nor in the Bill of Rights. The right to educate a child in a school of the parents' choice — whether public or private or parochial — is also not mentioned. Nor is the right to study any particular subject or any foreign language. Yet the First Amendment has been construed to include certain of those rights.

By *Pierce v. Society of Sisters*[, 268 U.S. 510 (1925)], the right to educate one's children as one chooses is made applicable to the States by the force of the First and Fourteenth Amendments. By *Meyer v. Nebraska*, [262 U.S. 390 (1923)], the same dignity is given the right to study the German language in a private school. In other words, the State may not, consistently with the spirit of the First Amendment, contract the spectrum of available knowledge. The right of freedom of speech and press includes not only the right to utter or to print, but the right to distribute, the right to receive, the right to read . . . and freedom of inquiry, freedom of thought, and freedom to teach . . . — indeed the freedom of the entire university community. . . . Without those peripheral rights the specific rights would be less secure. And so we reaffirm the principle of the *Pierce* and the *Meyer* cases.

In *NAACP v. Alabama*, 357 U.S. 449, 462 [(1958)], we protected the "freedom to associate and privacy in one's associations," noting that freedom of association was a peripheral First Amendment right. . . . In other words, the First Amendment has a penumbra where privacy is protected from governmental intrusion. In like context, we have protected forms of "association" that are not political in the customary sense but pertain to the social, legal, and economic benefit of the members. *NAACP v. Button*, 371 U.S. 415, 430–431 [(1963)]. . . .

. . . The right of "association," like the right of belief, *Board of Education v. Barnette*, 319 U.S. 624 [(1943)], is more than the right to attend a meeting; it includes the right to express one's attitudes or philosophies by membership in a group or by affiliation with it or by other lawful means. Association in that context is a form of expression of opinion; and while it is not expressly included in the First Amendment its existence is necessary in making the express guarantees fully meaningful.

The foregoing cases suggest that specific guarantees in the Bill of Rights have penumbras, formed by emanations from those guarantees that help give them life and substance. . . . Various guarantees create zones of privacy. The right of association contained in the penumbra of the First Amendment is one, as we have seen. The Third Amendment in its prohibition against the quartering of soldiers "in any house" in time of peace without the consent of the owner is another facet of that privacy. The Fourth Amendment explicitly affirms the "right of the people to be secure in their persons, houses, papers, and effects, against unreasonable searches and seizures." The Fifth Amendment in its Self-Incrimination Clause enables the citizen to create a zone of privacy which government may not force him to surrender to his detriment. The Ninth Amendment provides: "The enumeration in the Constitution, of certain rights, shall not be construed to deny or disparage others retained by the people."

. . . .

We have had many controversies over these penumbral rights of "privacy and repose." . . . These cases bear witness that the right of privacy which presses for recognition here is a legitimate one.

The present case, then, concerns a relationship lying within the zone of privacy created by several fundamental constitutional guarantees. And it concerns a law which, in forbidding the *use* of contraceptives rather than regulating their manufacture or sale, seeks to achieve its goals by means having a maximum destructive impact upon that relationship. Such a law cannot stand in light of the familiar principle, so often applied by this Court, that a "governmental purpose to control or prevent activities constitutionally subject to state regulation may not be achieved by means which sweep unnecessarily broadly and thereby invade the area of protected freedoms." *NAACP v. Alabama*, 377 U.S. 288, 307 [(1964)]. Would we allow the police to search the sacred precincts of marital bedrooms for telltale signs of the use of contraceptives? The very idea is repulsive to the notions of privacy surrounding the marriage relationship.

We deal with a right of privacy older than the Bill of Rights — older than our political parties, older than our school system. Marriage is a coming together for better or for worse, hopefully enduring, and intimate to the degree of being sacred. It is an association that promotes a way of life, not causes; a harmony in living, not political faiths; a bilateral loyalty, not commercial or social projects. Yet it is an association for as noble a purpose as any involved in our prior decisions.

Reversed.

MR. JUSTICE GOLDBERG, whom THE CHIEF JUSTICE and MR. JUSTICE BRENNAN join, concurring.

I agree with the Court that Connecticut's birth-control law unconstitutionally intrudes upon the right of marital privacy, and I join in its opinion and judgment. Although I have not accepted the view that "due process" as used in the Fourteenth Amendment includes all of the first eight Amendments . . . , I do agree that the concept of liberty protects those personal rights that are fundamental, and is not confined to the specific terms of the Bill of Rights. . . . I add these words to emphasize the relevance of [the Ninth] Amendment to the Court's holding.

. . . .

This Court, in a series of decisions, has held that the Fourteenth Amendment absorbs and applies to the States those specifics of the first eight amendments which express fundamental personal rights. The language and history of the Ninth Amendment reveal that the Framers of the Constitution believed that there are additional fundamental rights, protected from governmental infringement, which exist alongside those fundamental rights specifically mentioned in the first eight constitutional amendments.

The Ninth Amendment reads, "The enumeration in the Constitution, of certain rights, shall not be construed to deny or disparage others retained by the people." . . . It was proffered to quiet expressed fears that a bill of specifically enumerated rights could not be sufficiently broad to cover all essential rights and that the specific mention of certain rights would be interpreted as a denial that others were protected.

. . . .

. . . To hold that a right so basic and fundamental and so deep-rooted in our society as the right of privacy in marriage may be infringed because that right is not guaranteed in so many words by the first eight amendments to the Constitution is to ignore the Ninth Amendment and to give it no effect whatsoever. . . .

. . . .

In determining which rights are fundamental, judges are not left at large to decide cases in light of their personal and private notions. Rather, they must look to the "traditions and [collective] conscience of our people" to determine whether a principle is "so rooted [there] . . . as to be ranked as fundamental." *Snyder v. Massachusetts*, 291 U.S. 97, 105 [(1934)]. The inquiry is whether a right involved "is of such a character that it cannot be denied without violating those 'fundamental principles of liberty and justice which lie at the base of all our civil and political institutions'. . . ." *Powell v. Alabama*, 287 U.S. 45, 67 [(1932)]. . . .

I agree fully with the Court that, applying these tests, the right of privacy is a fundamental personal right. . . .

. . . .

The Connecticut statutes here involved deal with a particularly important and sensitive area of privacy — that of the marital relation and the marital home. [Justice Goldberg here cites *Meyer*, *Pierce*, and *Prince*.]

I agree with MR. JUSTICE HARLAN's statement in his dissenting opinion in *Poe v. Ullman*, 367 U.S. 497, 551–552 [(1961)]: ". . . The home derives its pre-eminence as the seat of family life. And the integrity of that life is something so fundamental that it has been found to draw to its protection the principles of more than one explicitly granted Constitutional right. . . . Of this whole 'private realm of family life' it is difficult to imagine what is more private or more intimate than a husband and wife's marital relations."

. . . .

MR. JUSTICE HARLAN, concurring in the judgment.

. . . .

In my view, the proper constitutional inquiry in this case is whether this Connecticut statute infringes the Due Process Clause of the Fourteenth Amendment because the enactment violates basic values "implicit in the concept of ordered liberty," *Palko v. Connecticut*, 302 U.S. 319, 325. For reasons stated at length in my dissenting opinion in *Poe v. Ullman*, [367 U.S. 497, 522 (1961)], I believe that it does. While the relevant inquiry may be aided by resort to one or more of the provisions of the Bill of Rights, it is not dependent on them or any of their radiations. The Due Process Clause of the Fourteenth Amendment stands, in my opinion, on its own bottom.

A further observation seems in order respecting the justification of my Brothers BLACK and STEWART for their "incorporation" approach to this case. Their approach . . . [rests] on the thesis that by limiting the content of the Due Process Clause of the Fourteenth Amendment to the protection of rights which can be found elsewhere in the Constitution, in this instance in the Bill of Rights, judges will thus be confined to "interpretation" of specific constitutional provisions, and will thereby be restrained from introducing their own notions of constitutional right and wrong into the "vague contours of the Due Process Clause." . . .

While I could not more heartily agree that judicial "self restraint" is an indispensable ingredient of sound constitutional adjudication, I do submit that the formula suggested for achieving it is more hollow than real. "Specific" provisions of the Constitution, no less than "due process," lend themselves as readily to "personal" interpretations by judges whose constitutional outlook is simply to keep the Constitution in supposed "tune with the times." . . .

Judicial self-restraint . . . will be achieved in this area, as in other constitutional areas, only by continual insistence upon respect for the teachings of history, solid recognition of the basic values that underlie our society, and wise appreciation of the great roles that the doctrines of federalism and separation of powers have played in establishing and preserving American freedoms. . . . Adherence to these principles will not, of course, obviate all constitutional differences of opinion among judges, nor should it. Their continued recognition will, however, go farther toward keeping most judges from roaming at large in the constitutional field than will the interpolation into the Constitution of an artificial and largely illusory restriction on the content of the Due Process Clause.

. . . .

MR. JUSTICE STEWART, whom MR. JUSTICE BLACK joins, dissenting.

. . . I think this is an uncommonly silly law. But we are not asked in this case to say whether we think this law is unwise, or even asinine. We are asked to hold that it violates the United States Constitution. And that I cannot do.

. . . .

What provision of the Constitution . . . make[s] this state law invalid? The Court says it is the right of privacy "created by several fundamental constitutional guarantees." With all deference, I can find no such general right of privacy in the Bill of Rights, in any other part of the Constitution, or in any case ever before decided by this Court.

At the oral argument in this case we were told that the Connecticut law does not "conform to current community standards." But it is not the function of this Court to decide cases on the basis of community standards. We are here to decide cases "agreeably to the Constitution and laws of the United States." It is the essence of judicial duty to subordinate our own personal views, our own ideas of what legislation is wise and what is not. . . .

NOTES

1. *Strategic Litigation.* The legal struggle to repeal Connecticut's 1879 anti-contraceptives law began in the late 1950s. By that time, Connecticut was the only state that had a complete ban on contraceptive devices, with no exception even when the pregnancy threatened the life of the mother. Repeated attempts to repeal the statute had failed. In 1957, Estelle Griswold, the executive director of the Planned Parenthood League of Connecticut, along with C. Lee Buxton, a professor and chair of the Department of Obstetrics and Gynecology at the Yale University School of Medicine, and Fowler Harper, a family law professor at Yale Law School, hatched a plan to challenge the statute. They decided that suit should be brought by Dr. Buxton and some of his married patients. Among them was a woman who had suffered a stroke during pregnancy that resulted in a stillborn baby and the mother's permanent partial paralysis; Dr. Buxton believed that the woman could not survive another pregnancy. However, the cases, *Poe v. Ullman* and *Buxton v. Ullman*, were eventually dismissed by the Supreme Court because there had been no prosecutions under the statute and the plaintiffs faced no real threat of its enforcement. 367 U.S. 497 (1961).

It therefore became clear that only an actual arrest would allow Planned Parenthood to challenge the constitutionality of the statute. To secure this, the organization opened a clinic in New Haven and, after serving ten clients on the first day, issued a press release contending that the Supreme Court had been right that the statute was no longer enforceable. Griswold, the executive director of the clinic, and Buxton, its physician, were arrested ten days later. They turned themselves in peacefully, declining a police offer of a public bust to draw media attention. All parties involved understood that this had all been staged in order to bring a new constitutional challenge.

The arguments made to challenge the statute in the round of litigation that had been dismissed earlier focused on the statute's intrusion on the plaintiffs' right to life and liberty, health, and to happy marital relationships. The discussion was not framed in terms of the right to privacy. The Supreme Court's dismissal of the earlier actions, however, contained vigorous dissents by Justices Douglas and Harlan, both of which argued that the statute violated a right to privacy. As a result, in the litigation after the arrests, the statute's challengers added arguments about privacy. For a complete discussion of the background of the case, see JOHN W. JOHNSON, *GRISWOLD V. CONNECTICUT*: BIRTH CONTROL AND THE CONSTITUTIONAL RIGHT OF PRIVACY 21–96 (2005); Catherine G. Roraback, Griswold v. Connecticut: *A Brief Case History*, 16 OHIO N.U. L. REV. 395 (1989).

2. *Relationships Entitled to Constitutional Protection.* In delineating the parameters of the constitutional right to privacy, the Court has been confronted with the question of *which* relationships fall within the protected zone, and in particular, whether the definition of "family" extends to relationships outside of the nuclear marital family. Justice Douglas's majority opinion in *Griswold* emphasized the special status of the marital family. This focus picks up on a view that he expressed in *Skinner v. Oklahoma*, 316 U.S. 535, 541 (1942), that "[m]arriage . . . [is] fundamental to the very existence and survival of the race." Douglas's willingness to allow special protection for the marital family resurfaced in his later decision in *Belle Terre v. Boraas*, 416 U.S. 1 (1973), excerpted earlier in this chapter, in which the Court upheld a zoning statute that distinguished between marital families and other groupings. *See supra* at Section B[1].

As discussed in Section B earlier in this chapter, however, other Supreme Court decisions extend constitutional protection to groupings beyond the marital family. For example, in *Moore v. East Cleveland*, 431 U.S 494 (1977), reproduced *supra* at Section B[1], the Court struck down an East Cleveland zoning ordinance that precluded a grandmother from living in a single-family home with her son, his son and his nephew (her two grandchildren) on the ground that it "sliced deeply into the family itself." *Id.* at 498–99; *see also U.S. Dep't of Agric. v. Moreno*, 413 U.S. 528 (1973) (holding unconstitutional a statute treating parties living in a household with unrelated persons as ineligible for food stamps); *Stanley v. Illinois*, 405 U.S. 645 (1972) (stating that unmarried fathers have certain constitutionally-protected rights regarding their biological children).

EISENSTADT v. BAIRD
United States Supreme Court
405 U.S. 438 (1972)

MR. JUSTICE BRENNAN delivered the opinion of the Court.

Appellee William Baird was convicted at a bench trial . . . under Massachusetts General Laws Ann., c. 272, § 21, first, for exhibiting contraceptive articles in the course of delivering a lecture on contraception to a group of students at Boston University and, second, for giving a young woman a package of Emko vaginal foam at the close of his address. The Massachusetts Supreme Judicial Court unanimously set aside the conviction for exhibiting contraceptives on the ground that it violated Baird's First Amendment rights, but by a four-to-three vote sustained the conviction for giving away the foam. Baird subsequently filed a petition for a federal writ of habeas corpus. . . .

Massachusetts General Laws Ann., c. 272, § 21, under which Baird was convicted, provides a maximum five-year term of imprisonment for "whoever . . . gives away . . . any drug, medicine, instrument or article whatever for the prevention of conception," except as authorized in § 21A. Under § 21A, "[a] registered physician may administer to or prescribe for any married person drugs or articles intended for the prevention of pregnancy or conception. [A] registered pharmacist actually engaged in the business of pharmacy may furnish such drugs or articles to any married person presenting a prescription from a registered physician." As interpreted by the State Supreme Judicial Court, these provisions make it a felony for anyone, other than a registered physician or pharmacist acting in accordance with the terms of § 21A, to dispense any article with the intention that it be used for the prevention of conception. The statutory scheme distinguishes among . . . distinct classes of distributees — . . . married persons may obtain contraceptives to prevent pregnancy, but only from doctors or druggists on prescription; . . . single persons may not obtain contraceptives from anyone to prevent pregnancy. . . .

. . . .

The question for our determination in this case is whether there is some ground of difference that rationally explains the different treatment accorded married and unmarried persons under Massachusetts General Laws Ann., c. 272, §§ 21 and 21A. For the reasons that follow, we conclude that no such ground exists. . . .

First. [T]he Massachusetts Supreme Judicial Court explained [in *Commonwealth v. Allison*, 227 Mass. 57, 72 (1917)] that the object of the legislation is to discourage premarital sexual intercourse. Conceding that the State could, consistently with the Equal Protection Clause, regard the problems of extramarital and premarital sexual relations as "evils . . . of different dimensions and proportions, requiring different remedies," *Williamson v. Lee Optical Co.*, 348 U.S. 483, 489 (1955), we cannot agree that the deterrence of premarital sex may reasonably be regarded as the purpose of the Massachusetts law.

. . . Like Connecticut's laws, §§ 21 and 21A do not at all regulate the distribution of contraceptives when they are to be used to prevent, not pregnancy, but the spread of disease. . . . Nor, in making contraceptives available to married persons without regard to their intended use, does Massachusetts attempt to deter married persons from engaging in illicit sexual relations with unmarried persons. Even on the assumption that the fear of pregnancy operates as a deterrent to fornication, the Massachusetts statute is thus so riddled with exceptions that deterrence of premarital sex cannot reasonably be regarded as its aim.

. . . .

Second. . . . The Supreme Judicial Court in *Commonwealth v. Baird*, 355 Mass. 746, 247 N. E. 2d 574 (1969), held that the purpose of the amendment was to serve the health needs of the community by regulating the distribution of potentially harmful articles. It is plain that Massachusetts had no such purpose in mind before the enactment of § 21A. As the Court of Appeals remarked, "Consistent with the fact that the statute was contained in a chapter dealing with 'Crimes Against Chastity, Morality, Decency and Good Order,' it was cast only in terms of morals. A physician was forbidden to prescribe contraceptives even when needed for the protection of health." . . .

. . . Furthermore, we must join the Court of Appeals in noting that not all contraceptives are potentially dangerous. . . .

Third. If the Massachusetts statute cannot be upheld as a deterrent to fornication or as a health measure, may it, nevertheless, be sustained simply as a prohibition on contraception? . . .

. . . .

We need not and do not, however, decide that important question in this case because, whatever the rights of the individual to access to contraceptives may be, the rights must be the same for the unmarried and the married alike.

If under *Griswold* the distribution of contraceptives to married persons cannot be prohibited, a ban on distribution to unmarried persons would be equally impermissible. It is true that in *Griswold* the right of privacy in question inhered in the marital relationship. Yet the marital couple is not an independent entity with a mind and heart of its own, but an association of two individuals each with a separate intellectual and emotional makeup. If the right of privacy means anything, it is the right of the *individual*, married or single, to be free from unwarranted governmental intrusion into matters so fundamentally affecting a person as the decision whether to bear or beget a child. . . . On the other hand, if *Griswold* is no bar to a prohibition on the distribution of contraceptives, the State could not, consistently with the Equal Protection Clause, outlaw distribution to unmarried but not to married persons. . . .

Affirmed.

NOTES

1. ***Another Staged Litigation.*** Like the litigation in *Griswold*, the litigation in *Eisenstadt* was planned to challenge state restrictions on contraception. The challenge was initiated by 679 students at Boston University who, two years after the *Griswold* decision, invited birth-control activist Bill Baird to campus to test the constitutionality of the Massachusetts statute. On April 6, 1967, Baird delivered a lecture on birth control and abortion before an audience of 2,000 students, and a number of police officers who were waiting to arrest him. At the end of his lecture, during which he had exhibited various forms of birth control to the audience, he handed a student a single condom and package of foam. Seven police officers then climbed on the stage and, as expected, he was arrested. Bill Baird, *The People*

Versus Bill Baird: Struggling for Your Right to Privacy, 57(2) THE HUMANIST 39 (1997).

The *Eisenstadt* story differs from the *Griswold* story, however, in that Baird's actions were not part of an agenda by national groups pressing for birth control reform. After his arrest, Planned Parenthood, which had sought to reform the challenged laws legislatively, dissociated itself from Baird's arrest. The ACLU, after initially agreeing to represent Baird, changed its mind. The National Organization for Women also declined to aid him. As a result, Baird had difficulty finding counsel.

Baird also had a long struggle to get his case to the Supreme Court. After the state supreme court upheld his conviction, Baird was required to serve three months time in the Charles Street Jail, in conditions that he asserts were deplorable. He petitioned the U.S. Supreme Court for certiorari and this was surprisingly denied. *Baird v. Massachusetts*, 396 U.S. 1029 (1970). Baird then filed a writ of habeas corpus in federal court challenging the constitutionality of the statute. The writ was denied by the district court. On appeal, the First Circuit overruled the district court, and Massachusetts immediately sought review by the U.S. Supreme Court. *See* Roy Lucas, *New Historical Insights on the Curious Case of* Baird v. Eisenstadt, 9 ROGER WILLIAMS U.L. REV. 9, 15–35 (2003); Bill Baird, *The Politics of God, Government, and Sex: A Thirty-One-Year Crusade*, 13 ST. LOUIS U. PUB. L. REV. 139 (1993); *Symposium: A Celebration of Reproductive Rights: Twenty-Five Years of* Roe v. Wade, 19 WOMEN'S RTS. L. REP. 247 (1998). Years later, Planned Parenthood Federation of America president Loraine Campbell called Baird "a thorn in our flesh for years." She added "every social change and every forward step in history requires its nuts." DAVID J. GARROW, LIBERTY AND SEXUALITY: THE RIGHT TO PRIVACY AND THE MAKING OF *ROE V. WADE* 322–23 (updated ed. 1998).

2. Eisenstadt *and Marital Privileges.* Many constitutional scholars readily admit that *Eisenstadt*'s poor reasoning limited the application of the opinion in subsequent cases. Professor Dolgin, among others, asserts that the argument based in Equal Protection is incongruous with other Supreme Court holdings, both before and after *Eisenstadt*. *See* Janet L. Dolgin, *The Family in Transition: From* Griswold *to* Eisenstadt *and Beyond*, 82 GEO. L.J. 1519, 1544–45 (1994). As you will see throughout this book, the law extends many privileges and benefits to married couples that are unavailable to unmarried persons; these privileges are generally accepted as constitutional.

3. *From Family Privacy to Individual Autonomy.* In spite of the tenuous logic of the *Eisenstadt* decision, it is clear that the Court determined that the right to privacy protects more than the married couple as a unit, it protects certain decision-making by individuals. This holding has been confirmed in later cases. *See, e.g.*, *Roe v. Wade*, 410 U.S. 113 (1973) (extending bodily autonomy and personal integrity to a woman's right to terminate a pregnancy); *Carey v. Population Servs. Int'l*, 431 U.S. 678 (1977) (extending the right to access to contraceptives to minors); *Lawrence v. Texas*, 539 U.S. 558 (2003) (extending a right to sexual privacy to same-sex consenting adults). Professor Dolgin argues that, viewed in historical context, the holding in *Eisenstadt* was more ground-breaking than the result in *Griswold* a few years earlier:

The *Eisenstadt* Court's reference to a married couple as an "association of two individuals" and its language affirming the right of the "individual" to privacy seem familiar in a world largely defined through, and deeply dependent on, notions of the autonomous individual. In fact, it is revolutionary when applied to the family. Long after the last vestiges of the feudal order were replaced in the marketplace by notions of free contract and autonomous individuality, Western society continued to define spouses — and, even more particularly, parents and their children — as units of relationship with a reality apart from, and encompassing, that of the individuals involved. The Court's straightforward, unapologetic description in *Eisenstadt* of the "marital couple" as nothing other than two people associated together signals a fundamental alteration in the society's view of the sort of intimacy we have traditionally associated with families.

Janet L. Dolgin, *The Family in Transition: From* Griswold *to* Eisenstadt *and Beyond*, 82 Geo. L.J. 1519, 1522, 1545–46 (2004).

4. *The Breadth of the Right Enunciated in* Eisenstadt. Family privacy jurisprudence after *Eisenstadt* flourished in the 1970s. The Supreme Court broadened this doctrine of a privacy right inherent in an individual's person to strike down state prohibitions on abortion in *Roe v. Wade*, 410 U.S. 113 (1973), and to extend to minors the right to prevent conception in *Carey v. Population Services International*, 431 U.S. 678 (1977). It then used this line of cases to strike down legal obstacles to marriage in *Zablocki v. Redhail*, 434 U.S. 374 (1978) (striking down a statute that required a noncustodial parent to obtain the court's permission before obtaining a marriage license), and the right for extended families to live together without state zoning interference in *Moore v. East Cleveland*, 431 U.S. 494 (1977) (see excerpts and discussion of *Moore*, *supra*, at Section B[1]). Continuing the earliest line of privacy cases (*Meyer*, *Pierce*, and *Prince*, discussed, *supra*, at Section C[1]), the Court reaffirmed the rights of parents to make parenting decisions in *Wisconsin v. Yoder*, 406 U.S. 205 (1972) (striking down state law requiring children to attend school past the eighth grade, which conflicted with the religious beliefs of Amish parents and infringed upon the freedom of religion and the rights of parents to direct the upbringing of their children). Additionally, the Court looked at parenting rights in terms of the fundamental parenting rights of unmarried fathers in *Stanley v. Illinois*, 405 U.S. 645 (1972) (requiring states to consider the father for custody purposes before the state takes custody of the child after the death of the unwed mother) (see excerpts and discussion of *Stanley* at Chapter 9, Section B[2][a]). Citations in each new case cross-referenced the others, emphasizing that the right of privacy encompassed the right to make procreative decisions, the right to marry, and the right to exercise discretion in raising one's children.

Commentators and jurists disagreed as to whether there was a unitary conceptual thread linking all of the rights identified as falling within the protected ambit of privacy. One scholar suggested that the Court had substituted a "lengthy and undifferentiated string" of citations for a conceptual analysis of what constitutes the right of privacy. John Hart Ely, *Foreword: On Discovering Fundamental Values*, 92 Harv. L. Rev. 5, 11 n.40 (1978).

[2]   The Contemporary Right to Privacy

[a]   The Road to *Lawrence*

As of 1960, every state and the District of Columbia had some form of sodomy law. These laws appeared on the books as early as the colonial era as a way to discourage "sinful and threatening" behavior. Some merely prohibited homosexual non-procreative sex, some all non-procreative sex, whether hetero- and homosexual, while others merely prohibited certain sexual acts. The variation in the laws meant that in certain states only gay men were impacted, while in others lesbians and even some heterosexual couples were affected. *See* WILLIAM N. ESKRIDGE, JR. & NAN D. HUNTER, SEXUALITY, GENDER, AND THE LAW 44–45 (2nd ed. 2004). In the second half of the twentieth century, homosexuals began to have more of a presence in society. This social movement became a political movement when, early in the morning of Saturday, June 28, 1969, gay patrons of the Stonewall Inn in New York's Greenwich Village resisted a police raid and began to riot in the streets. VICKI L. EAKLOR, QUEER AMERICA: A GLBT HISTORY OF THE 20TH CENTURY 122 (2008). Almost overnight, the national gay rights movement was born and with it began efforts to have sodomy laws legislatively repealed. The introduction of the Model Penal Code and criminal law reform saw many sodomy laws repealed in the succeeding years. In the late 1970s and through the 1980s, litigation efforts by the American Civil Liberties Union and Lambda Legal Defense and Education Fund overturned additional sodomy laws, so that only twenty-five were still in force by the mid-1980s. Advocates for overturning sodomy laws, and state court judges who agreed with them, almost exclusively relied on the line of cases discussed above outlining a constitutional right to privacy, including *Griswold* and *Eisenstadt*, excerpted *supra*, as well as *Roe v. Wade. See, e.g., People v. Onofre*, 415 N.E.2d 936, 949–50 (N.Y. 1980); Brief for Respondent at 20–21, *Bowers v. Hardwick*, 478 U.S. 186 (1986). As the gay rights movement continued to grow and achieve certain successes, so too did opposition, especially from those who claimed that homosexuality was unnatural and contrary to strongly-held religious beliefs. Many anti-gay activists fought to block the efforts of the gay rights movement or pass legislation that discriminated against gay and lesbian individuals. With the beginning of the AIDS epidemic in the 1980s, some anti-gay activists believed they had found biological proof that the homosexual lifestyle was wrong and claimed that this was a "plague" sent to destroy the gay population.

It was in this setting that Michael Hardwick was arrested in Georgia in 1982. A warrant had been issued for Hardwick's arrest for drinking in public, after an officer saw Hardwick depositing a beer bottle in a public, outdoor trash receptacle. When the officer appeared at Hardwick's home to serve a summons, he entered with a warrant and discovered Hardwick engaged in mutual oral sex with another man in the bedroom of his home. *See* MARTHA CRAVEN NUSSBAUM, SEX & SOCIAL JUSTICE 193 (1999). Hardwick was charged with violating Georgia law by engaging in sodomy with another adult male. Although the charges against him were dropped, Hardwick brought suit challenging the constitutionality of the statute's criminalization of consensual sodomy. He "asserted that he was a practicing homosexual, that the Georgia sodomy statute, as administered by the defendants, placed him in imminent danger of arrest, and that the statute for several reasons violates the Federal Constitution." *Bowers v. Hardwick*, 478 U.S. at 188.

In a 5–4 decision, a majority of the Court rejected Hardwick's position that the Georgia statute violated the constitutional right to privacy. The Court narrowly framed the issue as "whether the Federal Constitution confers a fundamental right upon homosexuals to engage in sodomy and hence invalidates the laws of the many States that still make such conduct illegal and have done so for a very long time." *Id.* at 190. It concluded that it did not:

> [N]one of the rights announced in [our] cases bears any resemblance to the claimed constitutional right of homosexuals to engage in acts of sodomy. . . . No connection between family, marriage, or procreation on the one hand and homosexual activity on the other has been demonstrated. . . . Moreover, any claim that these cases nevertheless stand for the proposition that any kind of private sexual conduct between consenting adults is constitutionally insulated from state proscription is insupportable. . . . Precedent aside, however, respondent would have us announce . . . a fundamental right to engage in homosexual sodomy. This we are quite unwilling to do. . . .

Id. at 190–91. Justice Blackmun, in dissent (joined by Justices Brennan, Marshall and Stevens) roundly criticized the Court's narrow and highly specific characterization of the right in question, asserting that: "This case is [not] about 'a fundamental right to engage in homosexual sodomy,' as the Court purports to declare. . . . Rather, this case is about 'the most comprehensive of rights and the right most valued by civilized men,' namely, 'the right to be let alone.' " *Id.* at 199. Justice Blackmun argued that the Court's privacy precedents protected the "freedom an individual has to *choose* the form and nature of . . . personal bonds," stating that the majority's decision had "refused to recognize . . . the fundamental interest all individuals have in controlling the nature of their intimate associations with others." *Id.* at 206.

Bowers suggested that prohibitions against homosexuality would not be deemed to offend the U.S. Constitution, so those on both sides of the issue were surprised when, a decade later, in *Romer v. Evans*, the Supreme Court struck down an amendment to the Colorado Constitution that barred local governments and state agencies from adopting any non-discrimination clause protecting gay, lesbian or bisexuals. 517 U.S. 620, 624 (1996). In a majority opinion authored by Justice Kennedy, the Court held that the Colorado amendment violated the Equal Protection Clause of the U.S. Constitution. Applying rational basis analysis, the Court concluded that Colorado's passage of the amendment was "inexplicable by anything but animus toward the class that it affects" and that as such, "it lacks a rational relationship to legitimate state interests." *Id.* at 632. The majority further noted that the challenged amendment "classifies homosexuals not to further a proper legislative end but to make them unequal to everyone else. This Colorado cannot do. A State cannot so deem a class of persons a stranger to its laws. Amendment 2 violates the Equal Protection Clause. . . ." *Id.* at 635.

Justice Scalia, in a vociferous dissent joined by Chief Justice Rehnquist and Justice Thomas, noted that the majority had not mentioned *Bowers*. Justice Scalia claimed that *Romer*'s holding "that homosexuality cannot be singled out for disfavorable treatment. . . . contradicts a decision, unchallenged here, pronounced only 10 years ago . . ." *Id.* at 636. He asserted: "If it is constitutionally permissible for a State to make homosexual conduct criminal, surely it is constitutionally permissible for a State to enact other laws merely disfavoring homosexual conduct. . . . And *a fortiori* it is constitutionally permissible for a State to adopt a provision *not even* disfavoring homosexual conduct, but merely prohibiting all levels of state government from bestowing special *protections* upon homosexual conduct." *Id.* at 641. For the next several years, scholars debated the fundamental question of whether *Romer* impliedly overruled *Hardwick*. *Compare, e.g.*, Cass Sunstein, *Foreword: Leaving Things Undecided*, 110 HARV. L. REV. 4, 67–68 (1996) (arguing that the two cases can be distinguished), *with* Thomas Grey, Bowers v. Hardwick *Diminished*, 68 U. COLO. L. REV. 373, 373–74 (1997) (arguing that the cases cannot be reconciled). Until 2003, however, such commentary could only speculate about the Court's treatment of a post-*Romer* challenge to sodomy statutes.

LAWRENCE v. TEXAS
United States Supreme Court
539 U.S. 558 (2003)

JUSTICE KENNEDY delivered the opinion of the Court.

Liberty protects the person from unwarranted government intrusions into a dwelling or other private places. In our tradition the State is not omnipresent in the home. And there are other spheres of our lives and existence, outside the home, where the State should not be a dominant presence. Freedom extends beyond spatial bounds. Liberty presumes an autonomy of self that includes freedom of thought, belief, expression, and certain intimate conduct. The instant case involves liberty of the person both in its spatial and more transcendent dimensions.

I

The question before the Court is the validity of a Texas statute making it a crime for two persons of the same sex to engage in certain intimate sexual conduct.

In Houston, Texas, officers of the Harris County Police Department were dispatched to a private residence in response to a reported weapons disturbance. They entered an apartment where one of the petitioners, John Geddes Lawrence, resided. . . . The officers observed Lawrence and another man, Tyron Garner, engaging in a sexual act. The two petitioners were arrested, held in custody over night, and charged and convicted before a Justice of the Peace.

The complaints described their crime as "deviate sexual intercourse, namely anal sex, with a member of the same sex (man)." App. to Pet. for Cert. 127a, 139a. The applicable state law is Tex. Penal Code Ann. § 21.06(a) (2003). It provides: "A person commits an offense if he engages in deviate sexual intercourse with another individual of the same sex." The statute defines "deviate sexual intercourse" as follows:

"(A) any contact between any part of the genitals of one person and the mouth or anus of another person; or

"(B) the penetration of the genitals or the anus of another person with an object." § 21.01(1).

The petitioners. . . . challenged the statute as a violation of the Equal Protection Clause of the Fourteenth Amendment and of a like provision of the Texas Constitution. . . . Those contentions were rejected. . . . We granted certiorari to consider three questions:

"1. Whether Petitioners' criminal convictions under the Texas 'Homosexual Conduct' law — which criminalizes sexual intimacy by same-sex couples, but not identical behavior by different-sex couples — violate the Fourteenth Amendment guarantee of equal protection of laws?

"2. Whether Petitioners' criminal convictions for adult consensual sexual intimacy in the home violate their vital interests in liberty and privacy protected by the Due Process Clause of the Fourteenth Amendment?

"3. Whether *Bowers v. Hardwick*, 478 U.S. 186 (1986), should be overruled?"

II

. . . .

There are broad statements of the substantive reach of liberty under the Due Process Clause in earlier cases, including *Pierce v. Society of Sisters* and *Meyer v. Nebraska*; but the most pertinent beginning point is our decision in *Griswold v. Connecticut*.

In *Griswold* the Court invalidated a state law prohibiting the use of drugs or devices of contraception and counseling or aiding and abetting the use of contraceptives. The Court described the protected interest as a right to privacy and placed emphasis on the marriage relation and the protected space of the marital bedroom. *Id., at 485.*

After *Griswold* it was established that the right to make certain decisions regarding sexual conduct extends beyond the marital relationship. In *Eisenstadt v. Baird* the Court invalidated a law prohibiting the distribution of contraceptives to unmarried persons. . . . [It stated:]

"It is true that in *Griswold* the right of privacy in question inhered in the marital relationship. . . . If the right of privacy means anything, it is the right of the *individual*, married or single, to be free from unwarranted governmental intrusion into matters so fundamentally affecting a person as the decision whether to bear or beget a child." *Id.*, at 453.

The opinions in *Griswold* and *Eisenstadt* were part of the background for the decision in *Roe v. Wade*. . . . *Roe* recognized the right of a woman to make certain fundamental decisions affecting her destiny and confirmed once more that the protection of liberty under the Due Process Clause has a substantive dimension of fundamental significance in defining the rights of the person.

In *Carey v. Population Services Int'l*, 431 U.S. 678 (1977), the Court [struck down]a New York law forbidding sale or distribution of contraceptive devices to persons under 16 years of age. . . . Both *Eisenstadt* and *Carey*, as well as the holding and rationale in *Roe*, confirmed that the reasoning of *Griswold* could not be confined to the protection of rights of married adults. This was the state of the law with respect to some of the most relevant cases when the Court considered *Bowers v. Hardwick.*

. . . One difference between the two cases is that the Georgia statute prohibited the conduct whether or not the participants were of the same sex, while the Texas statute, as we have seen, applies only to participants of the same sex. . . .

The Court began its substantive discussion in *Bowers* as follows: "The issue presented is whether the Federal Constitution confers a fundamental right upon homosexuals to engage in sodomy and hence invalidates the laws of the many States that still make such conduct illegal and have done so for a very long time." That statement, we now conclude, discloses the Court's own failure to appreciate the extent of the liberty at stake. To say that the issue in *Bowers* was simply the right to engage in certain sexual conduct demeans the claim the individual put forward, just as it would demean a married couple were it to be said marriage is simply about the right to have sexual intercourse. The laws involved in *Bowers* and here are, to be sure, statutes that purport to do no more than prohibit a particular sexual act. Their penalties and purposes, though, have more far-reaching consequences, touching upon the most private human conduct, sexual behavior, and in the most private of places, the home. The statutes do seek to control a personal relationship that, whether or not entitled to formal recognition in the law, is within the liberty of persons to choose without being punished as criminals.

This, as a general rule, should counsel against attempts by the State, or a court, to define the meaning of the relationship or to set its boundaries absent injury to a person or abuse of an institution the law protects. It suffices for us to acknowledge that adults may choose to enter upon this relationship in the confines of their homes and their own private lives and still retain their dignity as free persons. When sexuality finds overt expression in intimate conduct with another person, the conduct can be but one element in a personal bond that is more enduring. The liberty protected by the Constitution allows homosexual persons the right to make this choice.

Having misapprehended the claim of liberty there presented to it, and thus stating the claim to be whether there is a fundamental right to engage in consensual sodomy, the *Bowers* Court said: "Proscriptions against that conduct have ancient roots." *Id.*, at 192. . . .

At the outset it should be noted that there is no longstanding history in this country of laws directed at homosexual conduct as a distinct matter. . . . [E]arly American sodomy laws were not directed at homosexuals as such but instead sought to prohibit nonprocreative sexual activity more generally.

. . . .

. . . The longstanding criminal prohibition of homosexual sodomy upon which the *Bowers* decision placed such reliance is as consistent with a general condemnation of nonprocreative sex as it is with an established tradition of prosecuting acts because of their homosexual character.

. . . [F]ar from possessing "ancient roots," *Bowers*, 478 U.S., at 192,, American laws targeting same-sex couples did not develop until the last third of the 20th century. . . .

. . . .

It must be acknowledged, of course, that . . . *Bowers* was making the broader point that for centuries there have been powerful voices to condemn homosexual conduct as immoral. The condemnation has been shaped by religious beliefs, conceptions of right and acceptable behavior, and respect for the traditional family. For many persons these are not trivial concerns but profound and deep convictions accepted as ethical and moral principles to which they aspire and which thus determine the course of their lives. These considerations do not answer the question before us, however. The issue is whether the majority may use the power of the State to enforce these views on the whole society through operation of the criminal law. "Our obligation is to define the liberty of all, not to mandate our own moral code." *Planned Parenthood of Southeastern Pa. v. Casey.*

. . . In all events we think that our laws and traditions in the past half century are of most relevance here. These references show an emerging awareness that liberty gives substantial protection to adult persons in deciding how to conduct their private lives in matters pertaining to sex. "History and tradition are the starting point but not in all cases the ending point of the substantive due process inquiry." *County of Sacramento v. Lewis*, 523 U.S. 833, 857 (1998) (KENNEDY, J., concurring).

This emerging recognition should have been apparent when *Bowers* was decided. In 1955 the American Law Institute promulgated the Model Penal Code and made clear that it did not recommend or provide for "criminal penalties for consensual sexual relations conducted in private." ALI, Model Penal Code § 213.2, Comment 2, p 372 (1980). . . .

. . . . Of even more importance, almost five years before *Bowers* was decided the European Court of Human Rights considered a case with parallels to *Bowers* and to today's case. . . . The court held that the laws proscribing the conduct were invalid under the European Convention on Human Rights. *Dudgeon v. United Kingdom*, 45 Eur. Ct. H. R. (1981) P 52. . . . In our own constitutional system the deficiencies in *Bowers* became even more apparent in the years following its announcement. The 25 States with laws prohibiting the relevant conduct referenced in the *Bowers* decision are reduced now to 13, of which 4 enforce their laws only against homosexual conduct. . . .

Two principal cases decided after *Bowers* cast its holding into even more doubt. . . . The *Casey* decision again confirmed that our laws and tradition afford constitutional protection to personal decisions relating to marriage, procreation, contraception, family relationships, child rearing, and education. *Id.*, at 851. In explaining the respect the Constitution demands for the autonomy of the person in making these choices, we stated as follows:

"These matters, involving the most intimate and personal choices a person may make in a lifetime, choices central to personal dignity and autonomy, are central to the liberty protected by the Fourteenth Amendment. At the heart of liberty is the right to define one's own concept of existence, of meaning, of the universe, and of the mystery of human life. Beliefs about these matters could not define the attributes of personhood were they formed under compulsion of the State." *Id.*

Persons in a homosexual relationship may seek autonomy for these purposes, just as heterosexual persons do. The decision in *Bowers* would deny them this right.

The second post-*Bowers* case of principal relevance is *Romer v. Evans*. There the Court struck down class-based legislation directed at homosexuals as a violation of the Equal Protection Clause. *Romer* invalidated an amendment to Colorado's constitution which named as a solitary class persons who were homosexuals, lesbians, or bisexual either by "orientation, conduct, practices or relationships," *id.*, at 624 (internal quotation marks omitted), and deprived them of protection under state antidiscrimination laws. We concluded that the provision was "born of animosity toward the class of persons affected" and further that it had no rational relation to a legitimate governmental purpose. *Id.*, at 634.

As an alternative argument in this case, counsel for the petitioners and some *amici* contend that *Romer* provides the basis for declaring the Texas statute invalid under the Equal Protection Clause. That is a tenable argument, but we conclude the instant case requires us to address whether *Bowers* itself has continuing validity. Were we to hold the statute invalid under the Equal Protection Clause some might question whether a prohibition would be valid if drawn differently, say, to prohibit the conduct both between same-sex and different-sex participants.

. . . The central holding of *Bowers* has been brought in question by this case, and it should be addressed. Its continuance as precedent demeans the lives of homosexual persons.

. . . .

The foundations of *Bowers* have sustained serious erosion from our recent decisions in *Casey* and *Romer*. When our precedent has been thus weakened, criticism from other sources is of greater significance. In the United States criticism of *Bowers* has been substantial and continuing, disapproving of its reasoning in all respects, not just as to its historical assumptions. . . .

To the extent *Bowers* relied on values we share with a wider civilization, it should be noted that the reasoning and holding in *Bowers* have been rejected. . . .

The rationale of *Bowers* does not withstand careful analysis. In his dissenting opinion in *Bowers* JUSTICE STEVENS came to these conclusions:

"Our prior cases make two propositions abundantly clear. First, the fact that the governing majority in a State has traditionally viewed a particular practice as immoral is not a sufficient reason for upholding a law prohibiting the practice; neither history nor tradition could save a law prohibiting miscegenation from constitutional attack. Second, individual decisions by married persons, concerning the intimacies of their physical relationship, even when not intended to produce offspring, are a form of "liberty" protected by the Due Process Clause of the Fourteenth Amendment. Moreover, this protection extends to intimate choices by unmarried as well as married persons." 478 U.S. at 216. . . .

JUSTICE STEVENS' analysis, in our view, should have been controlling in *Bowers* and should control here.

Bowers was not correct when it was decided, and it is not correct today. It ought not to remain binding precedent. *Bowers v. Hardwick* should be and now is overruled.

The present case does not involve minors. It does not involve persons who might be injured or coerced or who are situated in relationships where consent might not easily be refused. It does not involve public conduct or prostitution. It does not involve whether the government must give formal recognition to any relationship that homosexual persons seek to enter. The case does involve two adults who, with full and mutual consent from each other, engaged in sexual practices common to a homosexual lifestyle. The petitioners are entitled to respect for their private lives. The State cannot demean their existence or control their destiny by making their private sexual conduct a crime. Their right to liberty under the Due Process Clause gives them the full right to engage in their conduct without intervention of the government. "It is a promise of the Constitution that there is a realm of personal liberty which the government may not enter." *Casey, supra,* at 847. The Texas statute furthers no legitimate state interest which can justify its intrusion into the personal and private life of the individual.

Had those who drew and ratified the Due Process Clauses of the Fifth Amendment or the Fourteenth Amendment known the components of liberty in its manifold possibilities, they might have been more specific. They did not presume to have this insight. They knew times can blind us to certain truths and later generations can see that laws once thought necessary and proper in fact serve only to oppress. As the Constitution endures, persons in every generation can invoke its principles in their own search for greater freedom.

. . . .

JUSTICE O'CONNOR, concurring in the judgment.

The Court today overrules *Bowers v. Hardwick.* I joined *Bowers,* and do not join the Court in overruling it. Nevertheless, I agree with the Court that Texas' statute banning same-sex sodomy is unconstitutional. Rather than relying on the substantive component of the Fourteenth Amendment's Due Process Clause, as the Court does, I base my conclusion on the Fourteenth Amendment's Equal Protection Clause.

The Equal Protection Clause of the Fourteenth Amendment "is essentially a direction that all persons similarly situated should be treated alike." *Cleburne v. Cleburne Living Center, Inc.,* 473 U.S. 432, 439 (1985) . . . . Under our rational basis standard of review, "legislation is presumed to be valid and will be sustained if the classification drawn by the statute is rationally related to a legitimate state interest." *[Id.]* at 440; . . . We have consistently held, however, that some objectives, such as "a bare . . . desire to harm a politically unpopular group," are not legitimate state interests. *Dep't of Agric. v. Moreno, supra,* at 534. *See also Cleburne v. Cleburne Living Center, supra,* at 446–47; *Romer v. Evans, supra,* at 632. When a law exhibits such a desire to harm a politically unpopular group, we have applied a more searching form of rational basis review to strike down such laws under the Equal Protection Clause.

We have been most likely to apply rational basis review to hold a law unconstitutional under the Equal Protection Clause where, as here, the challenged legislation inhibits personal relationships.

. . . .

. . . Sodomy between opposite-sex partners . . . is not a crime in Texas. That is, Texas treats the same conduct differently based solely on the participants. . . .

The Texas statute makes homosexuals unequal in the eyes of the law by making particular conduct — and only that conduct — subject to criminal sanction.

. . . And the effect of Texas' sodomy law is not just limited to the threat of prosecution or consequence of conviction. Texas' sodomy law brands all homosexuals as criminals, thereby making it more difficult for homosexuals to be treated in the same manner as everyone else. . . .

. . . This case raises a different issue than *Bowers:* whether, under the Equal Protection Clause, moral disapproval is a legitimate state interest to justify by itself a statute that bans homosexual sodomy, but not heterosexual sodomy. It is not. Moral disapproval of this group, like a bare desire to harm the group, is an interest that is insufficient to satisfy rational basis review under the Equal Protection Clause. . . . Indeed, we have never held that moral disapproval, without any other asserted state interest, is a sufficient rationale under the Equal Protection Clause to justify a law that discriminates among groups of persons.

Moral disapproval of a group cannot be a legitimate governmental interest under the Equal Protection Clause because legal classifications must not be "drawn for the purpose of disadvantaging the group burdened by the law." *Id.,* at 633. Texas' invocation of moral disapproval as a legitimate state interest proves nothing more than Texas' desire to criminalize homosexual sodomy. But the Equal Protection Clause prevents a State from creating "a classification of persons undertaken for its own sake." *Id.,* at 635. And because Texas so rarely enforces its sodomy law as applied to private, consensual acts, the law serves more as a statement of dislike and disapproval against homosexuals than as a tool to stop criminal behavior. The Texas sodomy law "raises the inevitable inference that the disadvantage imposed is born of animosity toward the class of persons affected." *Id.,* at 634.

Texas argues, however, that the sodomy law does not discriminate against homosexual persons. Instead, the State maintains that the law discriminates only against homosexual conduct. While it is true that the law applies only to conduct, the conduct targeted by this law is conduct that is closely correlated with being homosexual. Under such circumstances, Texas' sodomy law is targeted at more than conduct. It is instead directed toward gay persons as a class. "After all, there can hardly be more palpable discrimination against a class than making the conduct that defines the class criminal." *Id.*, at 641 (SCALIA, J., dissenting) (internal quotation marks omitted). . . .

. . . A State can of course assign certain consequences to a violation of its criminal law. But the State cannot single out one identifiable class of citizens for punishment that does not apply to everyone else, with moral disapproval as the only asserted state interest for the law. The Texas sodomy statute subjects homosexuals to "a lifelong penalty and stigma. A legislative classification that threatens the creation of an underclass . . . cannot be reconciled with" the Equal Protection Clause. *Plyler v. Doe*, 457 U.S., at 239 (POWELL, J., concurring).

. . . .

A law branding one class of persons as criminal solely based on the State's moral disapproval of that class and the conduct associated with that class runs contrary to the values of the Constitution and the Equal Protection Clause, under any standard of review. I therefore concur in the Court's judgment that Texas' sodomy law banning "deviate sexual intercourse" between consenting adults of the same sex, but not between consenting adults of different sexes, is unconstitutional

JUSTICE SCALIA, with whom the CHIEF JUSTICE and JUSTICE THOMAS join, dissenting.

. . . .

Most of the rest of today's opinion has no relevance to its actual holding — that the Texas statute "furthers no legitimate state interest which can justify" its application to petitioners under rational-basis review. . . . Though there is discussion of "fundamental propositions," . . . and "fundamental decisions," . . . nowhere does the Court's opinion declare that homosexual sodomy is a "fundamental right" under the Due Process Clause; nor does it subject the Texas law to the standard of review that would be appropriate (strict scrutiny) if homosexual sodomy *were* a "fundamental right." Thus, while overruling the *outcome* of *Bowers*, the Court leaves strangely untouched its central legal conclusion: "Respondent would have us announce . . . a fundamental right to engage in homosexual sodomy. This we are quite unwilling to do." 478 U.S., at 191. Instead the Court simply describes petitioners' conduct as "an exercise of their liberty" — which it undoubtedly is — and proceeds to apply an unheard-of form of rational-basis review that will have far-reaching implications beyond this case. . . .

. . . .

II

. . . .

Our opinions applying the doctrine known as "substantive due process" hold that the Due Process Clause prohibits States from infringing *fundamental* liberty interests, unless the infringement is narrowly tailored to serve a compelling state interest. . . . We have held repeatedly, in cases the Court today does not overrule, that *only* fundamental rights qualify for this so-called "heightened scrutiny" protection — that is, rights which are " 'deeply rooted in this Nation's history and tradition' ". . . . All other liberty interests may be abridged or abrogated pursuant to a validly enacted state law if that law is rationally related to a legitimate state interest.

. . . .

After discussing the history of antisodomy laws, . . . the Court proclaims that, "it should be noted that there is no longstanding history in this country of laws directed at homosexual conduct as a distinct matter." This observation in no way casts into doubt the "definitive [historical] conclusion," *id.*, on which *Bowers* relied: that our Nation has a longstanding history of laws prohibiting *sodomy in general* — regardless of whether it was performed by same-sex or opposite-sex couples. . . . In any event, an "emerging awareness" is by definition not "deeply rooted in this Nation's history and traditions," as we have said "fundamental right" status requires. Constitutional entitlements do not spring into existence because some States choose to lessen or eliminate criminal sanctions on certain behavior. Much less do they spring into existence, as the Court seems to believe, because *foreign nations* decriminalize conduct. . . .

IV

I turn now to the ground on which the Court squarely rests its holding: the contention that there is no rational basis for the law here under attack. This proposition is so out of accord with our jurisprudence — indeed, with the jurisprudence of *any* society we know — that it requires little discussion.

The Texas statute undeniably seeks to further the belief of its citizens that certain forms of sexual behavior are "immoral and unacceptable," *Bowers, supra*, at 196, — the same interest furthered by criminal laws against fornication, bigamy, adultery, adult incest, bestiality, and obscenity. *Bowers* held that this *was* a legitimate state interest. The Court today reaches the opposite conclusion. . . . The Court embraces instead Justice Stevens' declaration in his *Bowers* dissent, that "the fact that the governing majority in a State has traditionally viewed a particular practice as immoral is not a sufficient reason for upholding a law prohibiting the practice." This effectively decrees the end of all morals legislation. If, as the Court asserts, the promotion of majoritarian sexual morality is not even a *legitimate* state interest, none of the above-mentioned laws can survive rational-basis review.

V

Finally, I turn to petitioners' equal-protection challenge, which no Member of the Court save Justice O'Connor . . . embraces: On its face § 21.06(a) applies equally to all persons. Men and women, heterosexuals and homosexuals, are all subject to its prohibition of deviate sexual intercourse with someone of the same sex. To be sure, § 21.06 does distinguish between the sexes insofar as concerns the partner with whom the sexual acts are performed: men can violate the law only with other men, and women only with other women. But this cannot itself be a denial of equal protection, since it is precisely the same distinction regarding partner that is drawn in state laws prohibiting marriage with someone of the same sex while permitting marriage with someone of the opposite sex.

. . . .

Justice O'Connor argues that the discrimination in this law which must be justified is not its discrimination with regard to the sex of the partner but its discrimination with regard to the sexual proclivity of the principal actor.

. . . .

[T]he same could be said of any law. A law against public nudity targets "the conduct that is closely correlated with being a nudist," and hence "is targeted at more than conduct"; it is "directed toward nudists as a class." But be that as it may. Even if the Texas law *does* deny equal protection to "homosexuals as a class," that denial *still* does not need to be justified by anything more than a rational basis, which our cases show is satisfied by the enforcement of traditional notions of sexual morality.

Justice O'Connor simply decrees application of "a more searching form of rational basis review" to the Texas statute. . . . The cases she cites do not recognize such a standard, and reach their conclusions only after finding, as required by conventional rational-basis analysis, that no conceivable legitimate state interest supports the classification at issue. . . . Nor does Justice O'Connor explain precisely what her "more searching form" of rational-basis review consists of. It must at least mean, however, that laws exhibiting " 'a . . . desire to harm a politically unpopular group,' " *ante*, at 156 L Ed 2d, at 527, are invalid *even though* there may be a conceivable rational basis to support them.

This reasoning leaves on pretty shaky grounds state laws limiting marriage to opposite-sex couples. Justice O'Connor seeks to preserve them by the conclusory statement that "preserving the traditional institution of marriage" is a legitimate state interest. . . . But "preserving the traditional institution of marriage" is just a kinder way of describing the State's *moral disapproval* of same-sex couples. Texas's interest in § 21.06 could be recast in similarly euphemistic terms: "preserving the traditional sexual mores of our society." In the jurisprudence Justice O'Connor has seemingly created, judges can validate laws by characterizing them as "preserving the traditions of society" (good); or invalidate them by characterizing them as "expressing moral disapproval" (bad).

. . . .

Today's opinion is the product of a Court, which is the product of a law-profession culture, that has largely signed on to the so-called homosexual agenda, by which I mean the agenda promoted by some homosexual activists directed at eliminating the moral opprobrium that has traditionally attached to homosexual conduct. . . .

One of the most revealing statements in today's opinion is the Court's grim warning that the criminalization of homosexual conduct is "an invitation to subject homosexual persons to discrimination both in the public and in the private spheres." . . . It is clear from this that the Court has taken sides in the culture war, departing from its role of assuring, as neutral observer, that the democratic rules of engagement are observed. Many Americans do not want persons who openly engage in homosexual conduct as partners in their business, as scoutmasters for their children, as teachers in their children's schools, or as boarders in their home.

They view this as protecting themselves and their families from a lifestyle that they believe to be immoral and destructive. . . .

Let me be clear that I have nothing against homosexuals, or any other group, promoting their agenda through normal democratic means. Social perceptions of sexual and other morality change over time, and every group has the right to persuade its fellow citizens that its view of such matters is the best. . . . But persuading one's fellow citizens is one thing, and imposing one's views in absence of democratic majority will is something else. I would no more *require* a State to criminalize homosexual acts — or, for that matter, display *any* moral disapprobation of them — than I would *forbid* it to do so. . . .

One of the benefits of leaving regulation of this matter to the people rather than to the courts is that the people, unlike judges, need not carry things to their logical conclusion. The people may feel that their disapprobation of homosexual conduct is strong enough to disallow homosexual marriage, but not strong enough to criminalize private homosexual acts — and may legislate accordingly. The Court today pretends that it possesses a similar freedom of action, so that we need not fear judicial imposition of homosexual marriage, as has recently occurred in Canada (in a decision that the Canadian Government has chosen not to appeal). *See Halpern v. Toronto*, 2003 WL 34950 (Ontario Ct. App.);. . . . At the end of its opinion — after having laid waste the foundations of our rational-basis jurisprudence — the Court says that the present case "does not involve whether the government must give formal recognition to any relationship that homosexual persons seek to enter." . . . Do not believe it. More illuminating than this bald, unreasoned disclaimer is the progression of thought displayed by an earlier passage in the Court's opinion, which notes the constitutional protections afforded to "personal decisions relating to *marriage*, procreation, contraception, family relationships, child rearing, and education," and then declares that "persons in a homosexual relationship may seek autonomy for these purposes, just as heterosexual persons do." . . . Today's opinion dismantles the structure of constitutional law that has permitted a distinction to be made between heterosexual and homosexual unions, insofar as formal recognition in marriage is concerned. If moral disapprobation of homosexual conduct is "no legitimate state interest" for purposes of proscribing that conduct, . . . ; and if, as the Court coos (casting aside all pretense of neutrality), "when sexuality finds overt expression in intimate conduct with another person, the conduct can be but one element in a personal bond that is more enduring," . . . ; what justification could there possibly be for denying the benefits of marriage to homosexual couples exercising "the liberty protected by the Constitution" . . . ? Surely not the encouragement of procreation, since the sterile and the elderly are allowed to marry. This case "does not involve" the issue of homosexual marriage only if one entertains the belief that principle and logic have nothing to do with the decisions of this Court. Many will hope that, as the Court comfortingly assures us, this is so.

. . . .

Justice THOMAS, dissenting.

I join Justice Scalia's dissenting opinion. I write separately to note that the law before the Court today "is . . . uncommonly silly." *Griswold v. Connecticut*, 381 U.S. 479, 527 (1965) (STEWART, J., dissenting). . . . Punishing someone for expressing his sexual preference through noncommercial consensual conduct with another adult does not appear to be a worthy way to expend valuable law enforcement resources.

Notwithstanding this, I recognize that as a member of this Court I am not empowered to help petitioners and others similarly situated. My duty, rather, is to "decide cases 'agreeably to the Constitution and laws of the United States.'" *Id.*, at 530. And, just like Justice Stewart, I "can find [neither in the Bill of Rights nor any other part of the Constitution a] general right of privacy," *id.*, or as the Court terms it today, the "liberty of the person both in its spatial and more transcendent dimensions," *ante*, at 156 L Ed 2d, at 515.

NOTES

1. *A Final Challenge to Sodomy Laws.* John Lawrence was engaging in sodomy when a neighbor reported a weapons disturbance at his home. As it turns out, the neighbor was in a romantic relationship with Lawrence's partner, Tyron Garner. It seems that his jealousy over Garner's relations with Lawrence led him to make this call and have both of the men arrested. The neighbor later pled guilty to filing a false police report and spent fifteen days in jail. *See* Dale Carpenter, *The Unknown Past of* Lawrence v. Texas, 102 Mich. L. Rev. 1464, 1478 (2004). However, the case presented what Lambda Legal saw as the perfect opportunity to challenge the constitutionality of the law before the U.S. Supreme Court. Lambda Legal was soon involved in this challenge, hoping that with only thirteen states still proscribing sodomy, a 2003 challenge would achieve what the ACLU was unable to achieve in 1986 in *Bowers.*

2. *What is the Essential Holding of* Lawrence? Most observers expected that the Texas statute would fail to survive the Court's review in *Lawrence.* Unlike the Georgia statute upheld in *Bowers v. Hardwick*, Texas' anti-sodomy law applied only to same-sex partners. Thus, the Court's striking of that law seemed a logical extension of the principles announced in *Romer.* Such an approach, laid out in Justice O'Connor's *Lawrence* concurrence, would have allowed the Court to invalidate the statute without directly overruling *Hardwick.* Given this Court's tendency toward moderation, few anticipated that a 5–4 majority would ground its ruling in the Due Process Clause, explicitly rejecting *Hardwick.*

Yet, it is not completely clear what aspects of *Hardwick* the *Lawrence* Court overruled, or even the standard of review the court applied. While the majority clearly reversed *Hardwick*'s holding that a state could constitutionally prohibit private, consensual, noncommercial sodomy between adult partners, Justice Kennedy's decision does not explicitly find a fundamental right to engage in such conduct. Was such a conclusion implicit in the Court's language? Justice Kennedy's reliance on precedents such as *Griswold, Eisenstadt*, and *Roe* certainly suggests that the interest at stake is a fundamental privacy right. Yet the majority opinion avoids the term "fundamental" and even the term "privacy" in defining this interest. Is this just a matter of semantics, or does this aspect of the Court's language portend limitations in *Lawrence's* reach as precedent? A number of scholars have offered a variety of opinions on this issue. *See, e.g.*, Erwin Chemerinsky, Constitutional Law: Principles and Policies 846 (3d ed. 2006) (asserting that *Lawrence* provides "a powerful affirmation of a right to privacy under the Constitution"); Laurence Tribe, Lawrence v. Texas: *The Fundamental Right That Dare Not Speak Its Name*, 117 HARV. L. REV. 1893, 1917 (2004) (Supreme Court's failure to explicitly deem the right at stake a "fundamental right" is of no consequence; the absence of these "magic words" is overcome by the Court's obvious invocation of a standard of review beyond mere rationality, and its reliance on cases such as *Roe v. Wade* and *Griswold v. Connecticut*); Nancy Marcus, *Beyond* Romer *and* Lawrence: *The Right to Privacy Comes Out of the Closet*, COLUM. J. GENDER & L. 355, 387 (2006) (*Lawrence* was based on fundamental rights values, despite not using these terms in the opinion, and Court recognized within Fourteenth Amendment's privacy and liberty protections, "an affirmative right to equal respect and autonomy in intimate relationships that transcends the spatial spheres of the home"); Joe Rollins, Lawrence, *Privacy, and the Marital Bedroom: A Few Telltale Signs of Ironic Worry, in* THE FUTURE OF GAY RIGHTS IN AMERICA 169 (H.N. Hirsch ed., 2005) (the semantics of *Lawrence* are a "double-edged sword" attempting to balance the huge constitutional significance of marriage with reference to sexual expression and privacy).

Justice Scalia is correct that nowhere does the *Lawrence* majority enunciate or apply the familiar language of strict scrutiny, the heightened level of review used by the Court when evaluating the constitutionality of statutes that infringe on fundamental rights such as privacy. In fact, the only language reminiscent of one of the tiers of constitutional review is Justice Kennedy's statement in *Lawrence* that "[t]he Texas statute furthers no legitimate state interest which can justify its intrusion into the personal and private life of the individual," suggesting that the Court was applying the lower court's rational basis level of review. Thus far, although several courts have granted relief to challengers based on *Lawrence*, no appellate court has accepted the argument that *Lawrence* announced a fundamental right. *See, e.g., Lofton v. Sec'y of the Dep't of Children & Family Servs.*, 377 F.3d 1275, 1289–90 (11th Cir. 2004) ("[A] closer and careful reading of *Lawrence* and other relevant precedents . . . indicate[s] that, even if *Lawrence*'s *dicta* did acknowledge a constitutional liberty interest in private sexual intimacy, this liberty interest does not rise to the level of a fundamental right nor does it necessarily trigger strict scrutiny."); *Muth v. Frank*, 412 F.3d 808, 817 (7th Cir. 2005) (finding that "*Lawrence*, whatever its ramifications, does not, in and of itself go so far" as to announce a fundamental right to private sexual intimacy). With that said, the Ninth Circuit Court of Appeals, in a recent challenge to the military's "Don't Ask, Don't Tell" policy, found that *Lawrence* applied a heightened level of scrutiny akin to intermediate scrutiny. *See Witt v. Department of the Air Force*, 527 F.3d 806, 816–17, 818 (9th Cir. 2008) ("[W]e conclude that the Supreme Court applied a heightened level of scrutiny in *Lawrence*."). In a similar challenge, the First Circuit Court of Appeals also held that *Lawrence* applied a standard of review that lay somewhere between strict scrutiny and rational basis scrutiny. *Cook v. Gates*, 528 F.3d 42 (1st Cir. 2008). In the court's words, "we are persuaded that *Lawrence* did indeed recognize a protected liberty interest for adults to engage in private, consensual sexual intimacy and applied a balancing of constitutional interests that defies either the strict scrutiny or rational basis label." *Id.* at 52.

3. *Framing of the Protected Right.* The majority opinion refers to the underlying interest in *Lawrence* as a form of "liberty" and avoids the term "privacy" in defining this interest. It then characterizes the liberty interest in several different ways, at different points framing it in terms of citizens' autonomy to live their own lives, their human dignity, their right to be free from unwarranted government intrusions in the home, their interest in consensual sexual activity, and the right to choose their own relationships. The scope of the right enunciated in *Lawrence* will be affected by how much weight is place on these various characterizations in upcoming cases. There has been much scholarly discussion on how the holding in *Lawrence* should be construed. *See, e.g.*, CHEMERINSKY, *supra*, at 846 ("*Lawrence*, more than any other case in American history, recognizes that sexual activity is a fundamental aspect of personhood and that it is entitled to constitutional protection."); Donald H.J. Hermann, *Pulling the Fig Leaf Off the Right of Privacy: Sex and the Constitution*, 54 DEPAUL L. REV. 909, 969 (2005) ("[T]he majority in *Lawrence* established a right to sexual intimacy on substantive due process grounds that should be recognized as a fundamental right"); Nan D. Hunter, *Living with* Lawrence, 88 MINN. L. REV. 1103 (2004) ("*Lawrence* marks the beginning of a substantive due process jurisprudence that examines negative liberty limits on state power before, or instead of, articulating a specific standard of review. . . ."); P. Landon Perkinson, *Sexual Privacy After* Lawrence v. Texas, 8 GEO. J. GENDER & L. 203 (2007) (discussing various possible readings of *Lawrence*); Note, *Unfixing* Lawrence, 118 HARV. L. REV. 2858, 2866 (2005) ("In one breath, the Court seemed to represent the protected liberty right as a form of privacy, emphasizing that '[l]iberty protects the person from unwarranted government intrusions into a *dwelling or other private places.*' But in the next breath, the Court channeled Justice Stevens's *Bowers* dissent, employing lofty rhetoric celebrating 'the right to define one's own concept of existence, of meaning, of the universe, and of the mystery of human life. . . .' ").

4. *Morality as a Justification for State Action.* *Lawrence* rejected, in no uncertain terms, the use of "morality" as the sole justification for state action. Can it be right about this? If so, how is it possible to ban cruelty to animals or cockfights? One possible view of what the *Lawrence* court must mean is that morality alone cannot justify a law that burdens an activity protected at some heightened scrutiny by the Constitution. Another possible view of the line that the Court is seeking to draw relates to what the political philosopher John Rawls referred to in his later work as "public reason." In Rawls' view, legitimate state action must be able to be justified in a manner that citizens with a broad range of world views can accept, rather than on private morality that only some citizens accept. This requirement of public reason represents a commitment to the principle that the state may not be used to impose any particular vision on its citizens based only on some citizens' personal philosophies. The requirement of public reason therefore posits that citizens have available to them a set of public ideals and principles — a sort of public morality — that alone must be used to justify state action. *See* JOHN RAWLS, POLITICAL LIBERALISM 218, 223 (1993). Is Justice Scalia correct that forbidding morality as a justification for state action would delegitimize criminal laws against fornication, bigamy, adultery, adult incest, bestiality, and obscenity? For one view of the implications of *Lawrence* for policy justifications relying on claims of morality, see Suzanne B. Goldberg, *Morals-Based*

Justifications for Lawmaking Before and After Lawrence v. Texas, 88 MINN. L. REV. 1233 (2004).

5. *Implications of* **Lawrence** *for Sexual Orientation Issues.* How will *Lawrence* affect other areas of family law in which gays and lesbians are disfavored? Will it open the door to same-sex marriage, facilitate gay and lesbian adoptions of children, or restrict consideration of a party's sexual orientation in child custody determinations? Justice Kennedy asserted in dicta that the *Lawrence* ruling "does not involve whether the government must give formal recognition to any relationship that homosexual persons seek to enter." However, some of the principles announced in *Lawrence*, would seem to bear on these issues. Is Justice Scalia correct that the majority opinion in *Lawrence* "dismantles the structure of constitutional law that has permitted a distinction to be made between heterosexual and homosexual unions. . . ."?

Whereas it is not necessarily as clear as Justice Scalia suggests that *Lawrence* leads directly to the conclusion that states *must* make marriage available to same-sex couples, several state courts have cited to the principles enunciated in the majority opinion in striking down same-sex marriage bans under their state constitutions. *See, e.g., Goodridge v. Dep't of Pub. Health*, 798 N.E.2d 941 (Mass. 2003); *Varnum v. Brien*, 763 N.W.2d 862 (Iowa 2009) (granting same-sex couples the right to marry based on the state constitution's Equal Protection Clause), discussed further in Chapter 2. Courts in other states, however, have also cited *Lawrence* in rejecting challenges to state bans on same-sex marriage. *See, e.g., Andersen v. King County*, 138 P.3d 963 (Wash. 2006) (distinguishing the liberty interest in private, adult consensual activities and the fundamental right to marry); *Hernandez v. Robles*, 855 N.E.2d 1 (N.Y. 2006) (finding that the legislature's definition of marriage as between one man and one woman does have a rational basis and holding it does not infringe upon a fundamental right).

Lawrence would also appear to bear on the question of whether and how homosexuality may be taken into account on issues of child custody and adoption. Presumably, in ensuring that the sexual practices of homosexuals cannot be criminalized, and by delegitimizing the view that the state can treat homosexuals less well simply because of private moral objections, *Lawrence* limits the extent that homosexuality can be used as a factor in these decisions. *See McGriff v. McGriff*, 99. P.3d 111, 117 (Idaho 2004) (*Lawrence* "has at least some bearing on the degree to which homosexuality may play a part in child custody proceedings."). Most states, however, already limit the extent to which private homosexual conduct can play a role in custody. See *infra* Chapter 6 for more discussion of this issue. However, a widely-publicized post-*Lawrence* challenge to the constitutionality of a Florida statute that barred homosexuals from adopting upheld the ban. The Eleventh Circuit declared that there was neither a fundamental right to adopt nor a fundamental right to homosexual intimacy under *Lawrence*, and further that homosexuals were not a suspect class. *Lofton v. Sec'y of the Dep't of Children & Family Servs.*, 358 F.3d 804 (11th Cir. 2004). In 2008, a Dade County Circuit Court judge found the ban unconstitutional in a case. *In re Adoption of Does*, 200WL5006172 (Fla. Cir. Ct., Nov. 25, 2008). As of this writing, an appeal is pending in the Florida District Court of Appeals. The issue of adoption by gays and lesbians is discussed further in Chapter 9. For an analysis of the potential effects of

Lawrence on child custody for gays and lesbians, see Matt Larsen, Note, Lawrence v. Texas *and Family Law: Gay Parents' Constitutional Rights in Child Custody Proceedings*, N.Y.U. ANN. SURV. AM. L. 53 (2004). For further discussion of the implications of *Lawrence* generally for the legal status of gays and lesbians, see *Symposium: Gay Rights after* Lawrence v. Texas, 88 MINN. L. REV. 1017 (2004).

[b]   Implications of *Lawrence* Beyond Sexual Orientation

[i]   Sodomy

After *Lawrence*, state sodomy laws clearly cannot be enforced against private consensual acts between adults, although public or commercial sexual acts can still be criminalized, as can sexual acts involving minors. *See, e.g.*, *Doe v. Pryor*, 344 F.3d 1282 (11th Cir. 2003) (referring to a "supplemental briefing" submitted to the court by the state's Attorney General concluding *Lawrence* rendered Alabama's sodomy statute unconstitutional). Unsurprisingly, prosecutors in several states where sodomy remains a crime dropped pending cases or changed their policies of enforcement of sodomy laws post-*Lawrence*. *See, e.g.*, Meredith Oakley, *Sex Ought to be Private*, ARK. DEMOCRAT GAZETTE, June 29, 2003 (noting that Missouri prosecutors dropped cases of "deviate sexual intercourse" against six men following *Lawrence*); Cristina C. Breen, *Sodomy Arrest Guidelines Revised*, CHARLOTTE OBSERVER, July 6, 2003, at 1B (describing revised guidelines for North Carolina police officers requiring that for arrests on suspicion of soliciting sodomy, the solicitation must be for a meeting in a public, rather than private, place). In one significant case, the Kansas Supreme Court reversed the Court of Appeals' rejection of a defendant's challenge to a Kansas statute that provides substantially harsher penalties for the crime of sodomy of a minor when the perpetrator and victim are of the same sex, as contrasted with when the two individuals are of the opposite sex. The Kansas Supreme Court held that the statutory scheme's application violated the equal protection guarantees of the U.S. and Kansas Constitutions, and affirmed the "holding of *Lawrence* that moral disapproval of a group cannot be a legitimate governmental interest." *Limon v. Kansas*, 122 P.3d 22, 43 (Kan. 2005).

[ii]   Fornication

To the extent that fornication laws, which proscribe sexual intercourse between unmarried adults, focus on private, consensual conduct between adults, *Lawrence* calls them into question. Virginia's fornication statute was held unconstitutional as applied to private, adult, consensual acts based on *Lawrence*. *See Martin v. Ziherl*, 607 S.E.2d 367 (Va. 2005). Similarly, the Georgia Supreme Court, although without citing to the *Lawrence* opinion, found its own fornication statute unconstitutional under a "right to privacy" analysis. *In re J.M.*, 575 S.E.2d 441 (Ga. 2003). With that said, fornication is still on the books as a crime in seven states. *See* ELIZABETH PRICE FOLEY, LIBERTY FOR ALL: RECLAIMING INDIVIDUAL PRIVACY IN A NEW ERA OF PUBLIC MORALITY 108 & 251 n.34 (2006).

[iii]   Cohabitation

While a single sexual act could, in principle, violate an anti-fornication statute, laws criminalizing cohabitation typically require more. At a minimum, "cohabitation" would appear to involve some form of living arrangement, and sharing a residence, with at least some regularity. Some states require that the cohabitation be "open and notorious" or "lewd and lascivious." *See, e.g.*, MICH. COMP. LAWS § 750.335 (2009); FLA. STAT. ANN. § 798.02 (2009). Anti-cohabitation statutes, in one form or another, remain on the books in several states: Florida, Massachusetts, Michigan, Mississippi, North Carolina, Virginia, and West Virginia. *See* ELIZABETH PRICE FOLEY, LIBERTY FOR ALL: RECLAIMING INDIVIDUAL PRIVACY IN A NEW ERA OF PUBLIC MORALITY 234 n.18 (2006). Prosecutions under these statutes are rare, however. *See Doe v. Duling*, 782 F.2d 1202 (4th Cir. 1986) (holding that a couple could not challenge Virginia's anti-cohabitation statute because there was no threat of prosecution, given that the last recorded conviction for private, consensual cohabitation occurred in 1883). For additional analysis of how *Lawrence* might further affect cohabitation laws, see Margaret M. Mahoney, *Forces Shaping the Law of Cohabitation for Opposite Sex Couples*, 7 J.L. & FAM. STUD. 135 (2005).

[iv]   Adultery

As of 2008, twenty states still had adultery laws on the books. Katherine M. Franke, *Longing for* Loving, 76 FORDHAM L. REV. 2685, 2694 n.42 (2008). After *Lawrence*, are adultery statutes likely to be sustained as constitutional? Whereas private consensual conduct between married partners or unmarried partners is clearly within the scope of *Lawrence's* holding, adultery which, by definition, involves a marital relationship may be distinguishable based on the harm it can cause to marriage and family. For thoughtful analysis of these issues, see Gabrielle Viator, Note, *The Validity of Criminal Adultery Prohibitions After* Lawrence v. Texas, 39 SUFFOLK L. REV. 837, 860 (2006).

[v]   Polygamy

Are there principled reasons that Justice Kennedy could give that would justify distinguishing the same-sex relationships that he protects from polygamous relationships? Currently, all states prohibit bigamous (and therefore also polygamous) marriages. *See* Mark Strasser, *Marriage, Free Exercise, and the Constitution*, 26 L. & INEQ. 59, 101–02 nn. 311–13 (2008). In *Utah v. Holm*, 552 137 P.3d 726 (Utah 2006), the Utah Supreme Court directly addressed the claim that *Lawrence* protects the practice of polygamy. In contrast to the proscribed conduct in *Lawrence*, the Utah court stated, "this case implicates the public institution of marriage, an institution the law protects, and also involves a minor. In other words, this case presents the exact conduct identified by the Supreme Court in *Lawrence* as outside the scope of its holding." *Id.* at 743. It is likely that defenders of criminal prohibitions on bigamy will be able to argue successfully in other cases that the practice is harmful either to the parties involved, or to the stability and welfare of the family as an institution. For further discussion on the constitutionality of polygamy in the wake of *Lawrence*, see Catherine Blake, Note, *I Pronounce You Husband and Wife and Wife and Wife: The Utah Supreme Court's Re-Affirmation of Anti-Polygamy Laws in* Utah v. Green, 7 J. L. & Fam. Stud. 405, 411 (2005); Joseph Bozzuti, *The Constitutionality of Polygamy Prohibitions after* Lawrence v. Texas: *Is Scalia a Punchline or a Prophet?*, 43 Cath. Law. 409, 419 n.88 (2004).

[vi]   Incest

Although Justice Scalia also predicted that *Lawrence* would give courts grounds to strike down bans on incest, courts have refused to do so in *Lawrence*'s wake. *See, e.g., State v. Freeman*, 801 N.E.2d 906 (Ohio Ct. App. 2003); *Muth v. Frank*, 412 F.3d 808 (7th Cir. 2005). Most courts have distinguished the unconstitutional proscription of sodomy from laws banning incest by finding a rational basis for such incest prohibitions, as did the Ohio Supreme Court, declaring that "*Lawrence* did not announce a fundamental right to all consensual adult sexual activity, let alone consensual sex with one's adult children or stepchildren" and holding that the incest prohibition "bears a rational relation to the legitimate interest in . . . protect[ing] the family unit." *State v. Lowe*, 861 N.E.2d 512 (Ohio 2007). *Accord People v. Scott*, 157 Cal. App. 4th 189 (2007). *See generally* Note, *Inbred Obscurity: Improving Incest Laws in the Shadow of the "Sexual Family,"* 119 Harv. L. Rev. 2464, 2465 (2006).

[vii]   "Sex Toys"

The ban on the sale of "sex toys" by several states has been litigated in several jurisdictions since *Lawrence*, with mixed results. In a heavily publicized case, the Eleventh Circuit in *Williams v. Attorney Gen. of Ala.*, 378 F.3d 1232 (11th Cir. 2004), reversed a district court's finding that an Alabama statute banning such sales was unconstitutional. The district court had applied strict scrutiny analysis. *Williams v. Pryor*, 220 F. Supp. 2d 1257, 1299 (N.D. Ala. 2002). On appeal, however, the Eleventh Circuit looked to *Lawrence* and found that it failed to announce a fundamental right to sexual privacy, and declined to find such a right on its own. It held that on remand the district court should apply only rational basis scrutiny in determining the constitutionality of the statute. On remand, the district court upheld the statute on public morality grounds. *Williams v. King*, 420 F. Supp. 2d 1224 (N.D. Ala. 2006), *aff'd, Williams v. Morgan*, 478 F.3d 1316 (11th Cir. 2007); *accord PHE, Inc. v. State*, 877 So. 2d 1244, 1248–50 (Miss. 2004).

However, in *Reliable Consultants v. Earle*, the Court of Appeals for the Fifth Circuit held that *Lawrence* required it to strike down Texas's ban on the sale of sex toys. 517 F.3d 738 (5th Cir. 2008). The court rejected the state's attempt to characterize the right at stake narrowly, as "the right to stimulate one's genitals for non-medical purposes unrelated to procreation or outside of an interpersonal relationship." *Id*. at 743. It stated that the characterization of the right in *Lawrence* must guide its decision: "The right the Court recognized was not simply a right to engage in the sexual act itself, but instead a right to be free from governmental intrusion regarding 'the most private human contact, sexual behavior.' " *Id*. at 744. The Fifth Circuit concluded that "[a]n individual who wants to legally use a safe sexual device during private intimate moments alone or with another is unable to legally purchase a device in Texas, which heavily burdens a constitutional right." *Id*. It then held that the state's justification for the statute, which was morality based, could not pass constitutional muster after *Lawrence*. *Id.* at 745–46.

PROBLEMS

Problem 1-5. After *Lawrence*, Joe, a former Army officer, filed a federal lawsuit challenging the military policy commonly referred to as: "Don't Ask, Don't Tell." This policy permits any branch of the armed forces to discharge its members for homosexual conduct or for "stat[ing] that he or she is a homosexual or bisexual," or words to that effect. 10 U.S.C. § 654(b) (2003). Joe's briefs state that "he was discharged in 1997, eight days shy of his 20-year retirement date [and is] seeking to recoup $1.1 million in lost pension benefits." His suit also challenges the military's criminal prohibition against "unnatural carnal copulation," set forth in Article 125 of the Uniform Code of Military Justice, even though he was not prosecuted under that provision. He argues that the military's criminal *investigation* of his case under Article 125 was a factor in his discharge. Several federal circuit courts decided challenges against Section 654(b) before *Lawrence*, and rejected equal protection and first amendment claims by service men and women. *See, e.g., Able v. United States*, 155 F.3d 628 (2d Cir. 1998); *Holmes v. Cal. Army Nat'l Guard*, 124 F.3d 1126 (9th Cir. 1997); *Steffan v. Perry*, 41 F.3d 677 (D.C. Cir. 1994). As attorney for Joe, how might you argue Joe's case after *Lawrence*? To what extent do you think that the traditional deference to military policies will affect the result?

Problem 1-6. Alice and Harry had been married for six years and had one child, Cathy. The two divorced when Alice indicated that she is a lesbian and planned to move in with another woman. Prior to *Lawrence*, Alice and Harry engaged in a bitter custody fight, and Harry succeeded in obtaining primary custody of Cathy on the basis that Alice's homosexuality rendered her an unfit mother. Alice now challenges the trial court's decision in light of *Lawrence*, and argues that the state's statute permitting consideration of the "morality" of parental conduct in the determination of a child's custody is unconstitutional after *Lawrence* if it is applied to exclude a parent based on her sexual orientation. What are the strongest arguments for and against Alice's claims? How, if at all, would your arguments differ if Justice O'Connor's concurrence in *Lawrence* had been adopted by the Court's majority?

D. FAMILY, WORK, AND GENDER

[1] Patterns Of Employment, Family Responsibilities, and Gender Roles

DAPHNE SPAIN & SUZANNE M. BIANCHI, BALANCING ACT: MOTHERHOOD, MARRIAGE, AND EMPLOYMENT AMONG AMERICAN WOMEN
77–78, 85, 167–69, 171–76, 195–99 (1996)

In a single generation, the lives of American women have undergone a remarkable transformation. Women who started families in the 1950s generally stayed home to raise their children; their daughters most often choose to work as they raise families. That such an enormous change in family lifestyle could occur in the span of a few decades testifies not only to changing attitudes about women's participation in the workforce but also to a labor market that has been able to attract and absorb women's labor.

Baby boom women have attended to the demands of jobs and babies simultaneously rather than sequentially for a variety of reasons [such as] later age at marriage, rising educational attainment, the high divorce rate and women's ensuing realization that they must be able to support themselves (and their children) financially, the women's movement and changing attitudes about the desirability of working outside the home, the contraceptive revolution and the increased control these women had over the timing of their fertility, [and] the stagnating wages of males after 1974 necessitating two-income families.

. . . .

Throughout the 1970s and 1980s, the group with the lowest rate of labor force participation historically — married women with young children — increased participation rapidly. In 1970, 44 percent of married women with young children worked during the year and only 10 percent worked full time, year round. By 1990, 68 percent of married women with young children worked outside the home and 28 percent worked full time, year round. By 1990, most married mothers of young children had some involvement in market work, although they typically were employed part time.

. . . .

The majority of American women have always been mothers, and now a majority of mothers are also employees. The dual responsibilities of child care and paid employment are particularly problematic for the growing number of single mothers. The economic realities of women's lives — that they earn less than men and are more likely to live in poverty — mean that the balancing act between motherhood and employment is less often a choice than a necessity. . . .

. . . .

Although the physical demands of housework are less strenuous for each generation of women, the total amount of housework to be done has remained fairly constant throughout this century. . . . In most households, women still bear the large brunt of housework. The persistence of employed wives' primary responsibility for child care and domestic tasks has been labeled the "stalled revolution" because of its seeming intransigence in the face of additional market work by women. . . .

171-76

. . . .

Given the increasing amount of time women spend in market work (men's traditional domain), it is reasonable to ask how much time men spend in housework and child care (women's traditional sphere). Over the past two decades, married mothers have experienced a sizable decline in their hours of housework (from about thirty hours to about twenty hours per week); married fathers, however, picked up only part of the slack, increasing their household work from about five hours a week to about ten hours. By 1985, married mothers performed about two-thirds of all housework compared with three-quarters in 1965. More recent data on time budgets corroborate the decline in hours that mothers spend on housework and the failure of fathers to compensate fully for mothers' increased market work . . . [¶] Household tasks continue to differ by gender . . .

        . . . .

Employed women and men face different dilemmas when juggling home and work responsibilities. Women's family roles tend to intrude on their work roles, whereas men's work roles tend to intrude on their family time. For example, when a child in day care becomes sick, the wife is more likely than the husband to leave work; when an overnight business trip is required, the husband is more likely than the wife to have the job that demands it. Husbands can "take work home" in ways that advance their careers, while taking "home to work" limits women's career development. As long as men have fewer family responsibilities and women have many more, the potential exists for women to choose or accept lower occupational status and earnings, which in turn affects their bargaining position within the marriage.

Academic researchers seem more troubled by the division of household labor than the women they interview, many of whom think their household arrangement is equitable. . . .

Women juggling home and employment adopt various adaptive strategies[.] . . . [¶]. . . . Women who work outside the home have fewer children than women who are not employed. In 1992, employed women aged eighteen to thirty-four had an average of 0.9 children compared with an average of 1.7 children for women not in the labor force. Employed women also are more likely to expect to remain childless: 11 percent in 1992 compared with 6 percent of women not in the labor force. . . . [¶][B]oth childbearing and employment create "hard choices" [for women] that must constantly be renegotiated throughout life. The ultimate reason for the negative correlation between fertility and employment — regardless of causation — is that the role of mother often contradicts that of a paid employee. Many women try to resolve this conflict by taking part-time jobs.

Ann Crittenden, The Price of Motherhood — Why the Most Important Job in the World Is Still the Least Valued
17–19, 26, 87–89, 91, 93–97 (2003)

Among married mothers with children under age eighteen, 28.4 percent of all those in the prime working years of twenty-five to fifty-four are not in the labor force, meaning that the only employment of these 6.9 million women is their home and children.

The persistence of traditional family patterns cuts across economic, class, and racial lines. Uneducated married mothers are the least likely to be employed, having the least to gain from a job. They calculate, quite correctly, that as long as there is one breadwinner in the family, their presence at home can create more value, and be more satisfying, than much of the (under)paid work they could find. But the United States also has one of the lowest labor force participation rates for college-educated women in the developed world; only in Turkey, Ireland,

Switzerland, and the Netherlands does a smaller proportion of female college graduates work for pay.

The college-educated stay-at-home mother is a fixture in American business and professional circles. With sixty-plus-hour work weeks the norm at the higher levels of the economy, a full-time "wife" is often the only thing that makes family life possible. A survey of chief financial officers in American corporations found that 80 percent were men with stay-at-home wives. Another survey of managerial employees revealed that 64 percent of the male executives with children under age thirteen had nonworking spouses. "The presence of a wife at home to care for family and personal matters is almost as much a requirement for success in business today as it was a generation ago," consultant Charles Rodgers told me, in an interview in his office in Cambridge, Massachusetts.

A second large group of wives and mothers — approximately 20 percent of married mothers with children under age eighteen — is officially classified as "working," but these women are employed part-time while their principal job is at home. The government classifies a person as "working" — that is, in the labor force — if he or she is employed for as little as one hour a week, is merely looking for paid work, or works unpaid for at least five hours a week in a family business. Thus a "working mother" can be the wife who lends a hand one afternoon a week in her husband's office; the mother who works a few evenings a week as a waitress after being home all day; or the consultant or editor who works out of a home-based office. . . . [A] substantial majority of working mothers appear to be reducing their work hours during the child-rearing years. In 1996, for example, married working mothers on average put 1,197 hours into their paying jobs, a mere half of the 2,132 hours averaged by married fathers.

Still, many mothers don't want or can't afford to put their jobs and careers on the back burner. Almost 18 million, roughly half of all women with children under eighteen, do work full-time; that is, at least thirty-five hours a week. And the tendency of mothers to work full-time is the long-term trend. Between 1994 and 1999 alone, nearly 1 million women a year moved from part-time to full-time employment, including a record number of mothers of even very young children.

. . . .

Despite the media's fondness for Mr. Mom, he remains an aberration. Of the 20.5 million American children under the age of five, only about 320,000 have fathers as their primary guardian — a minuscule 1.5 percent. . . .

[M]otherhood is now the single greatest obstacle left in the path to economic equality for women. . . . For most companies, the ideal worker is "unencumbered," that is, free of all ties other than those to his job. Anyone who can't devote all his or her energies to paid work is barred from the best jobs and has a permanently lower lifetime income. Not coincidentally, almost all the people in that category happen to be mothers.

The reduced earnings of mothers are, in effect, a heavy personal tax levied on people who care for children, or for any other dependent family members. This levy, a "mommy tax," is easily greater than $1 million [over a lifetime] in the case of a college-educated woman. For working-class women, there is increasing evidence both in the United States and worldwide that mothers' differential responsibility for children, rather than classic sex discrimination, is the most important factor disposing women to poverty.

. . . .

The much-publicized earnings gap between men and women narrowed dramatically in the 1980s and early 1990s. All a girl had to do was stay young and unencumbered. . . . But once a woman has a baby, the egalitarian office party is over. . . . Economist Shirley Burggraf has calculated that a husband and wife who earn a combined income of $81,500 per year and who are equally capable will lose $1.35 million if they have a child. Most of that lost income is the wages forgone by the primary parent. In a middle-income family, with one parent earning $30,000 per year as a sales representative and the other averaging $15,000 as a part-time computer consultant, the mommy tax will still be more than $600,000.

. . . .

The mommy tax is obviously highest for well-educated, high-income individuals and lowest for poorly educated people who have less potential income to lose. All else being equal, the younger the mother, and the more children she has, the higher her tax will be, which explains why women are having fewer children, later in life, almost everywhere.

. . . For fifty years, from about 1930 to 1980, the value of employed . . . full-time working women were only 60 percent of men's earnings. In the 1980s, that ratio began to change. By 1993, women working full-time were earning an average of seventy-seven cents for every dollar men earned. (In 1997, the gap widened again, as the median weekly earnings of full-time working women fell to 75 percent of men's earnings.)

But lo and behold, when we look closer, we find the same old sixty cents to a man's dollar. The usual way to measure the gender wage gap is by comparing the hourly earnings of men and women who work full-time year-round. But this compares only the women who work like men with men — a method that neatly excludes most women. As we have seen, only about half of the mothers of children under eighteen have full-time, year-round paying jobs.

To find the real difference between men's and women's earnings, one would have to compare the earnings of all male and female workers, both full- and part-time. And guess what one discovers? The average earnings of *all* female workers in 1999 were 59 percent of men's earnings.

. . . .

A good example is the experience of the 1974 female graduates of the University of Michigan Law School. During their first fifteen years after law school, these women spent an average of only 3.3 months out of the workplace, compared with virtually no time out for their male classmates. More than one-quarter of the women had worked part-time, for an average of 10.1 months over the fifteen years, compared with virtually no part-time work among the men. While working full-time, the women put in only 10 percent fewer hours than full-time men, again not a dramatic difference.

But the penalties for these slight distinctions between the men's and women's work patterns were strikingly harsh. Fifteen years after graduation, the women's average earnings were not 10 percent lower, or even 20 percent lower, than the men's, but almost 40 percent lower. Fewer than one-fifth of the women in law firms who had worked part-time for more than six months had made partner in their firms, while more than four-fifths of the mothers with little or no part-time work had made partner.

. . . .

The fact that many mothers work part-time also explains some of the difference between mothers' and comparable womens' hourly pay. (About 65 percent of part-time workers are women, most of whom are mothers.) Employers are not required to offer part-time employees equal pay and benefits for equal work. As a result, nonstandard workers earn on average about 40 percent less an hour than full-time workers. . . .

Suzanne M. Bianchi, John P. Robinson & Melissa A. Milkie, Changing Rhythms of American Family Life
1–2, 13, 16, 115–117, 137, 169–170, 175–178 (2006)

The cultural image of the American mother has changed from the cheery, doting homemaker to the frenzied, sleepless working mom. . . . [¶] Although family incomes have increased with higher maternal employment, social observers worry that this rise is offset by a decline in the quality of family life and in parental supervision and investment in their children. Concern about working mothers forced to endure a "second shift" of labor at home, and "latchkey kids" spending unsupervised time alone each day, sends shudders throughout American society.

However widely these viewpoints are believed, they are largely based on mass media images and familiar anecdotes. . . . Based on four decades of time-diary surveys in which representative samples describe a typical "day in the life of America," we are able to document more definitively the real changes that seem to have taken place in the American rhythms of time, work, and family.

As it turns out, our conclusions from this evidence stand in sharp contrast to the generally accepted story of modern parenting . . . [P]arents are spending as much — and perhaps more — time interacting with their children today than parents in 1965, the heyday of the stay-at-home mother. . . . By increasingly engaging in multitasking and incorporating their children in their own leisure activities, parents have deepened their time to circumvent the simple zero-sum trade-off between work and other areas of their lives. Mothers' time diaries contain about as much time for leisure and sleep as in earlier decades. The big difference is that today's mothers spend less time than their mothers doing housework, a deficit partially compensated for by husbands, who have increased the time they spend in domestic chores and fathering over the years.

[Further,] on balance, married mothers and fathers have about equal workloads. This may seem surprising to many, given the widespread perception that mothers' workloads are heftier than those of fathers. However, we make a simple but critical distinction: employed mothers do put in a long workweek but nonemployed mothers trail behind them. This heterogeneity among U.S. mothers has received too little attention and is the reason why some women are doing double duty, but average workloads are fairly even across the sexes. Even the mothers doing "double duty" because they are employed full-time have total workloads that are very similar to those of employed fathers.

. . . .

How Has the Gender Division of Labor in the Home Changed as a Result [of Women Working in the Labor Market]?

. . . [T]he gender differences in our time diaries in families with children show that men have increased the housework they do and that total workloads of men and women are actually remarkably similar. At the same time, the gender specialization of women into the unpaid work of family caregiving and of men into family providing via paid work remains very strong in families with children, particularly if young children are involved . . . . [I]t remains most common for couples to follow what is termed a neo-traditional model — with a wife's career and labor force participation taking a backseat to a husband's career advancement, especially when children are young.

. . . Although mothers now spend more time working outside of the home, we find that parents have adjusted to preserve the amount of time they spend with their children. . . . By all our measures, we find that parents are spending at least as much time, if not more, caring for their children in 2000 than in 1975. A large portion of this expansion is attributable to parents combining child care and leisure activities, indicating that either child care has become more oriented towards "fun" activities, or that parents are more frequently including children in their own leisure activities. In addition, we find that though married mothers still put in more time than married fathers, men have been closing the child care gap in recent decades.

. . . [When we focus] more explicitly on the issue of gender equality and the joint nature of mothers' and fathers' time allocation in families with children, . . . we find that total household work time [meaning the total paid and unpaid work performed by parents] is roughly equal for mothers and fathers, with fathers performing more paid work and mothers doing more household work. . . . We also find that increased market work for fathers is associated with increased child care time for mothers, but that the increased market work for women is not associated with greater child care by fathers.

. . . .

The Gender Gap in Weekly Workloads in Middle-Class Working Families

. . . Among all parents, the average total workload is almost equal, with married mothers averaging 65 hours and fathers 64 hours per week. These equal overall workloads are found despite marked gender difference in paid versus unpaid work, with fathers performing 34 percent of housework and 33 percent of child care, in contrast to their 64 percent of market work. In hourly terms, mothers average 19 fewer weekly hours of market work than fathers, but 13 hours more of housework and shopping and 6 hours more of child care.

In their one-day diaries, dual-earner, middle-class parents seem busier than all married parents, with mothers averaging total workloads of 71 hours per week and fathers averaging 67 hours (49 percent of the family's total workload). The figures derived from the weekly diaries indicate workloads to be relatively equal for mothers and fathers, but the figures for total workloads of mothers in the weekly diaries are 8 hours lower than the estimates from single-day diaries (63 hours per week) and similar to the one-day estimates for all married parents. Mothers in the weekly diary sample reported a little less market work, shopping, and child care (only about 75 percent of the average child care in one-day diaries multiplied by seven). Again, total workloads reported in the weekly diaries are similar for mothers and fathers, with fathers' 65 work hours per week averaging about 51 percent of the family's total workload. Gender specialization of fathers in market work and mothers in housework and child care are similar to the diary figures for all parents, with fathers doing about 60 percent of the paid work and mothers doing more than 60 percent of the unpaid work in the home.

. . . .

In middle-class families, when both the mother and father work full-time, the combined total workload is high — averaging 135 hours a week. However, the combined total workload in families where the wife works part-time is also high, at 129 hours per week, largely because these mothers do more nonmarket work than mothers who work full time. However, when these middle-class mothers work part-time, their total work remains significantly less than that of their counterparts working full-time (60 hours per week versus 68 hours) and of fathers (69 hours per week versus 60 hours per week for mothers). Although it is not necessarily leisurely to be a mother employed part-time in a middle-class, dual-earner family — mothers still log 60 hours a week of paid and unpaid work, it is a considerably lighter workload than for fathers and mothers who are employed full-time. Among couples where both are employed full-time, there is remarkable gender equality in total workloads, with mothers averaging 68 hours per week compared with 67 hours for fathers.

Gender and the Experience of Daily Time

Overall, 37 percent of parents in 2000 say they always feel rushed . . . Married men are the least likely to say this — 32 percent of married fathers versus 40 percent of married mother and 43 percent of single mothers. . . . Even after adding the objective diary measures (the number of activities and secondary activities per day), a significant gender difference remains between married fathers and all mothers. In brief, fathers are simply not as likely to always feel rushed.

Mothers' employment makes a difference, as we would expect. Fully 46 percent of employed mothers versus only 29 percent of homemakers report always feeling rushed. . . . It is employed mothers who are distinct from both homemakers and fathers in these feelings.

Conclusion

. . . If both market work and unpaid work count in what constitutes what we think of as good parenting — and we argue both should be included — fathers and mothers contribute equally. . . . In other words, fathers as well as mothers are burdened by a second shift.

There are several caveats to this claim of gender equality. First, mothers' greater subjective sense of time pressures may derive from their being the one who continues to orchestrate family life — a reality that is difficult to capture in time-diary data. Second, when children are reared outside a two-parent home, fathers are much less likely than mothers to shoulder the day-to-day responsibility of caregiving — that is, fathers remain more likely than mothers to drop the parental role altogether. At the same time, fathers who live with their children are working as much on behalf of their families as the mothers in those families. Third, women may not easily rebound from reducing paid work as they give their time over to unpaid labor. Lower pensions, forgone careers, and financial instability later in life (particularly in the case of divorce) can be a consequence of time away from full-time employment when children are young.

. . . .

Women and men are busy and, perhaps because time is at such a premium, fall into gender-specialized roles once a child arrives for at least two reasons. First, when couples try to decide about who should cut back on work, the gendered workplace structure encourages mothers to cut back because they are paid less and because family leaves are so incompatible with the demands of newborn care and breastfeeding. Second, given their own upbringing, in gender specialized homes, mothers may have been practicing traditionally female tasks and fathers so-called male tasks for a long time. When children are young, they may settle on a pattern of activities that becomes difficult to change or renegotiate when child care demands are no longer paramount. By then, everyone has grown accustomed to mothers who cook and run errands and to fathers who come home late from work . . .

NOTES

1. ***Changing Rates of Women's Labor Force Participation.*** Economists and demographers have observed that the "increase in the proportion of women who are working . . . has been one of the most significant social and economic trends in modern U.S. history." Howard V. Hayghe, *Developments in Women's Labor Force Participation*, Monthly Lab. Rev. 41 (Sept. 1997). The best measure of the impact of women's work force participation on family life is the dramatic change in the percentage of mothers in the labor force over time. This percentage nearly tripled between 1955 and 2008, rising from 27% to 71%. U.S. Dep't of Labor, Bureau of Labor Statistics, Employment Characteristics of Families 2 (2008), *available at* http://www.bls.gov/news.release/pdf/famee.pdf. Sixty-four percent of mothers with a child under six were in the labor force in 2008, compared with only 18.2% in 1955. *Id.* Breaking down these data by the age of the women's youngest child, in the year 2008, 56% of women had children under age 1, 64% of women had children under

age 6, and 77% of women had children between the ages of 6 and 17 years. *Id.* Mothers' labor force participation increased most dramatically (over 350%) for women with children under age 6, whose labor force participation in 1955 was only 18.2%. Not only have more mothers of minor children participated in the labor force in recent decades, but more of them have worked full-time and year-round. *Id.* at Table 5. In 2008, 71 percent of all employed women with minor children worked full time. *Id.* Of these, 70 percent of married women with minor children were in the labor force, and 71 percent of married working mothers worked full time. U.S. DEPARTMENT OF LABOR, *supra*, at Table 5. Mothers without husbands are even more likely to work full time. *Id.*

2. *The Second Shift.* In 1989, University of California sociologist Arlie Hochschild (with Anne Machung), coined the now-common phrase "second shift" to refer to the phenomenon in which mothers increasingly worked in the paid labor market, but still performed a disproportionate amount of work in the home. THE SECOND SHIFT: WORKING PARENTS AND THE REVOLUTION AT HOME (1989). Hochschild studied fifty families over an eight-year period, examining the ways in which these families managed their work and family responsibilities. Although both spouses in her sample worked full-time, most men in her study did not contribute equally to domestic chores. Both before and after work, mothers, but not fathers, routinely put in a "second shift" at home. Hochschild estimated that, on average, wives worked an extra month of twenty-four hour days each year compared to their husbands. However, recent time study data of Suzanne M. Bianchi, John P. Robinson, and Melissa A. Milkie, excerpted *supra*, suggest that the gap in total working hours between husbands and wives has almost disappeared if both paid and unpaid work are taken into account. Wives' time performing more of the housework, they conclude, is offset by husbands' time performing more paid work. *See* Suzanne M. Bianchi et al., *supra*.

3. *Women's Earnings and Future Trends.* "Equal pay for equal work" has been a rallying cry for the women's movement since the late 1960s. In the last decades, studies show a narrowing of the gender pay gap. Monthly Labor Review reports, "the women-to-men earnings ratio was 80 percent in 2003, up from 63 percent in 1979. The ratio of women-to-men earnings among 16-to 24-year-olds was 93.3 percent in 2003, compared with 78.5 percent in 1979; that for 25-to 34-year-olds was 87 percent in 2003, compared with 67.4 percent in 1979. Among 35-to 44-year-olds, women earned 76.2 percent as much as men in 2003 and 58.3 percent in 1979, while among 45-to 54-year-olds, women earned 73 percent as much as men in 2003 and 56.9 percent as much in 1979." *Women's Earnings*, 127 MONTHLY LAB. REV. 2, 2 (2004). Note that while this breakdown provides some support for the proposition that greater equality for women in the work force and in the home may accompany the entry of a new cohort of women with more progressive attitudes and different skills into the workplace, some of the closing of the gap between men and women in this breakdown come from the fact that fewer younger women have children now than they did in past years. Joan Williams and Nancy Segal have recently argued that workplace conditions that disfavor workers who combine their work with caregiving roles constitute a form of employment discrimination. *Beyond the Maternal Wall: Relief for Family Caregivers who are Discriminated Against on the Job*, 26 HARV. WOMEN'S L.J. 77 (2003). They cite a growing number of cases in which women and men have succeeded in challenging practices by employers, such as penalizing employees who request or return from maternity or paternity leaves, by giving them negative performance evaluations, passing them over for promotions, or assigning them inappropriate work.

4. *Comparative Perspective.* In a study that compares the regulatory approaches of different nations to conflicts between work and family, Janet Gornick and Marcia Meyers concluded that parents in the United States experience more serious conflicts between work and family than do parents in other nations, with negative consequences for both sex equality and children's welfare:

> American families are not alone in the demands they encounter on their time and energy. In all industrialized and industrializing countries, working families are at the epicenter of tensions arising from changing gender norms, social supports, and labor market opportunities. However, cross-national comparisons suggest that American families face heavier demands and receive less external support than do families in other equally rich industrialized countries. The characteristically American approach of expecting private forces to solve social problems has created especially pressing burdens in this country.

> On many indicators of family and child well-being, the problems confronting American families are more acute than elsewhere. American working parents are squeezed for time and pay a comparatively higher penalty for working reduced hours than do parents in our comparison countries [Nordic European countries: Denmark, Finland, Norway, and Sweden; Continental European countries: Belgium, France, Germany, Luxembourg, and the Netherlands; two English speaking-countries: Canada and the United Kingdom]. Relative to these other rich, high-employment countries, the United States has achieved only moderate levels of gender equality, especially among parents. And our families and children fare much worse than their counterparts in other countries on several other dimensions of well-being.

> American parents have good reason to feel that they are squeezed for time. Nearly all fathers and a substantial share of mothers in the United State are employed. Those who are employed are averaging long weekly hours in the workplace; and compared with their counterparts in other countries, many of them are spending extremely long hours at work. . . . The United States is exceptional, in comparative terms, with respect to the number of hours worked among those who are employed. According to the International Labour Organization (ILO 1999), the American workforce reports the longest annual hours of any in the industrialized world. American workers spend an average of 1,966 hours a year at work. Average annual work hours in the United States exceed those reported all across Europe; American "outwork" workers in Sweden (1,522), France (1,656), Germany (1,560) and the United Kingdom (1, 731 hours). American workers log nearly six more weeks of work a year than their Canadian counterparts (at 1,732 hours), and their hours exceed even those of the notoriously work-intensive Japanese (1,889 hours) (ILO 1999). . . .

American working parents spend exceptionally long hours each week in market work. American parents in dual-earner families spend an average of eighty hours a week at the workplace. Similar couples in the United Kingdom log almost nine fewer hours a week, and a typical Swedish working couple works for pay about eleven fewer hours each week.

What is even more remarkable about the working time of American couples with children are the high percentages logging very long hours. Nearly two-thirds of American dual-earner couples with children report joint workweeks of eighty hours or more. This is an exceptionally large share in comparative terms. Other than in Canada, no more than one-third of couples in our comparison countries spend this much time at the workplace. . . .

[W]omen in the United States who work part-time earn about 21 percent less an hour, on average, than their full-time counterparts . . . In contrast, women's part-time wage penalty is about half that magnitude in at least three other countries: Canada (12 percent), the United Kingdom (10 percent), and Germany (9 percent). Women who work part-time in Sweden earn about 3 percent more an hour, controlling for human-capital differences, than their full-time counterparts . . . Clearly, part-time work is particularly costly for women in the United States. . . .

American mothers are more likely than American fathers to leave the labor force because they have young children than are mothers in most of our comparison countries . . . American working mothers also lag behind mothers in some of our comparison countries when we consider gender equality in hourly wages . . . Mothers' share of family earnings lags behind that of fathers by a wide margin in all of our comparison countries . . . American mothers earn 28 percent of parents' total labor market earnings, which places the United States about in the middle of our group of countries. According to this composite measure, American mothers lag behind their counterparts in Canada and in six other countries, where mothers take home about 31 to 38 percent of parental labor market income. . . .

JANET C. GORNICK & MARCIA K. MEYERS, FAMILIES THAT WORK: POLICIES FOR RECONCILING PARENTHOOD AND EMPLOYMENT 36, 58–61, 63–64 (2003).

Gornick and Meyers suggest that the current system in the United States might best be described as "dual-earner-marketized-carer." In this system, both fathers and mothers are expected to be engaged fully in the workplace, and child care is largely left to the market. This system, they argue, has serious drawbacks: Parental time for care is limited. Further, leaving paid child care to the market exacerbates gender inequality because paid care work is so poorly remunerated. In addition, "the combination of unaffordable and poor-quality care forces many parents (in practice, mothers) to withdraw from the labor market more than they would otherwise prefer." Finally, subjecting children to low-quality care exposes children to worrisome risks. *Id.* at 93.

5. *Remedies   at   the   Termination   of   Marital   and   Cohabiting*

Relationships. Clearly, the allocation of gender roles during an intact family relationship bears on the circumstances in which the two parents find themselves if their relationship dissolves. Disproportionate contributions by one spouse or the other to market work versus domestic work may result in inequities at the dissolution of a marital or marriage-like cohabiting relationship, if not addressed in the financial remedies imposed at the termination of the relationship. For divorcing couples, the issues of fairness in the allocation of property, post-divorce income, and custodial responsibilities and opportunities become extremely important here, and are covered in Chapters 4, 5, and 6. Analogous questions relevant to unmarried parents are treated in Chapter 9.

[2] Regulatory Approaches to the Work-Family Conflict

If a principle explanation for women's relative disadvantage in the workplace is that they bear a greater share of the family's domestic responsibilities, how should policymakers respond to reduce the work-family conflict described above, whether it is experienced by women or by men? There are several different ways to conceptualize the problem here, and this conceptualization will affect the chosen solution. First, we can focus on the relative allocation of income-earning and home-based obligations between spouses. Second, we can focus on the way in which paid employment (and perhaps other institutions) are structured in our society. Third, we can focus on the availability (or not) of various governmental services, subsidies, or supports for working families, geared toward relieving the family's economic burdens or providing them with greater flexibility in choosing between various work and family commitments. The following readings approach the issue of the work-family conflict from a number of perspectives, and present very different solutions to what they see as the problem.

JOAN WILLIAMS, UNBENDING GENDER: WHY FAMILY AND WORK CONFLICT AND WHAT TO DO ABOUT IT
1–5 (2000)

"I decided to quit my job and stay home. But it was my choice; I have no regrets. I am going to start a part-time quilt business."

"Wouldn't you really rather be able to continue in your career, earning at your current salary rate, while being able to give your children the time you feel they need?"

"Well, of course, that's what I really want."

. . . Domesticity is a gender system comprised most centrally of the organization of market work and family work that arose around 1780, and the gender norms that justify, sustain, and reproduce that organization. Before then, market work and family work were not sharply separated in space or time. By the turn of the nineteenth century this way of life was changing, as domesticity set up the system of men working in factories and offices, while women (in theory) stayed behind to rear the children and tend the "home sweet home."

Domesticity remains the entrenched, almost unquestioned, American norm and practice. As a gender system it has two defining characteristics. The first is its organization of market work around the ideal of a worker who works full-time and overtime and takes little or no time off for childbearing or childrearing. Though this ideal-worker norm does not define all jobs today, it defines the good ones: full-time blue-collar jobs in the working-class context, and high level executive and professional jobs for the middle-class and above. When work is structured in this way, caregivers often cannot perform as ideal workers. Their inability to do so gives rise to domesticity's second defining characteristic: its system of providing for caregiving by marginalizing the caregivers, thereby cutting them off from most of the social roles that offer responsibility and authority.

. . . .

[M]arket work continues to be structured in ways that perpetuate the economic vulnerability of caregivers. Their vulnerability stems from the way we define the ideal worker, as someone who works at least forty hours a week year round. This ideal worker norm, framed around the traditional life patterns of men, excludes most mothers. . . . [¶] Moreover, full-time work is no guarantee of avoiding economic vulnerability: even mothers who work full-time often find themselves on the "mommy track." In addition, full-time workers who cannot work overtime often suffer economically because many of the best jobs now require substantial overtime. A rarely recognized, but extraordinarily important fact is that jobs requiring extensive overtime exclude *virtually all mothers* (93 percent).[¶] Our economy is divided into mothers and others. Having children has a very strong negative effect on women's income, an effect that actually increased in the 1980s despite the fact that women have become better educated.

. . . .

Domesticity takes a toll in a second way: by minimizing fathers' involvement. . . . [¶] Domesticity takes a toll on men by pressuring them to perform as ideal workers in an age when that often requires long hours of work: roughly one-third of fathers work forty-nine hours a week or more. The current fathers' rights and men's movements need to be seen not only as continued assertions of male privilege (which they are), but also as protests against the gender role domesticity assigns to men. That role includes both breadwinning and the narrow emotional range we associate with conventional masculinities. . . .

. . . .

. . . . My goal is not to advocate sameness or androgyny, but to deconstruct domesticity and encourage the development of new ways of organizing work as well as family, emotional, and political life. The guiding principles are that society needs not only market work but also family work, and that adults who do family work should not be marginalized.

. . . .

Eliminating the ideal-worker norm in market work requires restructuring work around the values people hold in family life, in particular around the norm of parental care. . . . Work/family activists have tried for twenty years to persuade companies to offer part-time jobs and other flexible policies by showing the productivity and other benefits to be gained by doing so. These attempts have had limited success. Their primary result is a pyrrhic victory: a set of mommy-track policies that offer flexibility at the price of work success. What we need is not a mommy track, but market work restructured to reflect the legitimate claims of family life. This requires a new legal theory that defines the current structuring of market work as discrimination against women. . . .

[T]he current design of work discriminates against mothers. This analysis starts from the fact that the current work ideal is someone who works full-time (and often overtime) and who can move if the job "requires it." This way of defining the ideal worker is not ungendered. It links the ability to be an ideal worker with the flow of family work and other privileges typically available only to men. [Professor Williams proceeds to review empirical data suggesting flexible, family-friendly and gender-neutral employment policies, such as job-sharing and caregiving leaves, would promote, rather than reduce, workplace efficiency and productivity. She reviews litigation strategies to challenge various aspects of the current system, ranging from salary inequities and promotion policies.]

Mary Anne Case, *How High the Apple Pie? A Few Troubling Questions About Where, Why, and How the Burden of Care for Children Should be Shifted*
76 CHI-KENT L. REV. 1753 (2001)

There is fairly widespread agreement among feminists that . . . "women (both as paid and unpaid caregivers) continue to bear the disproportionate burden for caregiving." Linda McClain, *Care as a Public Value: Linking Responsibility, Resources, and Republicanism*, 76 Chi-Kent L. Rev. 1673 (2001). Where to look in order to shift some of the burden of care for children is a subject for greater debate. . . . Unfortunately, a fact of our current American political culture often left unstated is that, fathers as a class having proven strongly resistant to accepting much more of the burden, paths of lesser resistance in this political culture at this particular moment seem to lie with employers or in the public sphere. In this Commentary, I want to put up some resistance, or at least begin to ask some preliminary, tough, critical questions about what it might mean, who might be benefited and who burdened, and how, if we looked in various alternative ways to employers or to the state to ease the burden of caring for children. . . .

Precisely because I do not think that children should be simply women's responsibility, I worry about localizing more of the responsibility for children, at least as a matter of law, at the level of the individual employer. . . . Working mothers unable or unwilling to shift more of the burden onto men have frequently been criticized for shifting some of it instead from one group of women to another — to nannies or underpaid daycare workers, to stay-at-home moms, to their own daughters or mothers. Adding their own and their husbands' childless female colleagues to the list is not a good solution. And this is part of what I fear might happen if more of the burden of care for children were localized at the level of the individual employer . . .

All women may be at increased risk for employment discrimination in a world in which women do all the childbearing and most of the childrearing if benefits, especially benefits required by law, for childbearing and childrearing come from the employer. Permanently childless women like me will be in a lose/lose situation — so long as we are potentially mothers, we are at risk for discrimination; so long as we are not actually mothers, we get no offsetting compensation from the increased childcare benefits. . . .

[I]f the premise of some parents's advocates really is one of strong equality of result (i.e., that parents should, in effect, be held harmless in time and money from their decision to have children; that their decision to have children should be made as close as possible to costless), then we really are talking, if not quite about a zero-sum game, then at least about a massive redistribution from nonparents to parents, one which, on grounds, inter alia, of inequity to people like myself, I would strongly oppose. . . . While there are, for example, good feminist arguments for reducing or eliminating the leisure gap between fathers and mothers, I can think of none comparably strong for similar opposition to a gap between parents and nonparents. . . .

[W]e need to get beyond the point of seeking more for parents from employers or the state and start asking, not only, "How much more?" but "To what end?" . . . On an economic level, if all we are looking for is a new generation of workers to pay my generation's social security, it may be cheaper to import them as adults than to raise them at home . . .

I realize that looking at childbearing and childrearing in cold-bloodedly economic terms may be disturbing, but it is some proponents of an increased shift of the burden of children to the state, not I, who introduce arguments sounding in economic rationality into the debate, for example, by insisting that children are a public good or that parents are entitled to compensation from the childless. All I am here urging we explore is what it might mean to take such arguments seriously. My sense is that such arguments are not only difficult to sustain, but they have nasty implications their proponents rarely face up to. Most notably, starting down the road of claims for compensation grounded in economic rationality invites case-by-case examination and analysis of precisely to what extent which children will produce positive externalities worthy of compensation. Consider, for example, the claim that children are a public good. First, to the extent they are a public good, the public is already paying a substantial percentage, by many estimates thirty-eight percent, of the cost of raising them. Some children may not produce positive externalities in excess of this; indeed, some will produce net negative externalities. To what extent should state subsidies take this into account and how? . . .

A further problem with arguments for subsidizing only reproduction at the level of demand is the distorting effect it might have: we may inflate the demand for reproduction relative to other activities. . . . That the opportunity cost of childrearing is rising for women cannot be seen as unmitigated bad news from a feminist perspective — it means, in part, that women are being offered a wider range of options for productive work. . . .

While subsidies are a great improvement on coercion into childrearing as a means of lowering the opportunity cost of childrearing to women, it is worth asking whether it makes sense to target childrearing specifically for greatly increased subsidy: what if a poor woman wants to write a book or start a business or get an advanced degree instead of raising a(nother) child? If money (whether in the form of a guaranteed income or a one-time grant) were provided without strings attached, it might have less of a distorting effect on preferences. . . .

In looking critically at incentive effects, we should not only consider the extent of available subsidy for childbearing and rearing in comparison to subsidies for other activities, but also the comparative costs imposed on those who do or do not have children. . . . Some fraction of those who choose to have no children personally . . . see the choice not to have children as a tradeoff: realizing that raising children takes a lot of time, money, and energy, they may, with some regret at an opportunity foregone, choose to spend their time, money, and energy in other ways. . . . If their time, money, or energy is taxed at a high level for the benefit of those with children (whether directly through government taxation and redistributive schemes or indirectly through, for example, workplace scheduling of the childless for all overtime, weekend, and out-of-town work), they may understandably feel that they have lost the benefit of their tradeoff, and may either rethink their decision whether to have children or become increasingly frustrated and resentful.

. . . .

I say . . . to prospective parents — if you insist that you are having children as a service to me for which I owe you big, do not do me any favors just yet.

Martin H. Malin, *Fathers and Parental Leave*
72 Tex. L. Rev. 1048–55, 1066–79 (1994)

The characterization of work-family conflicts as "women's issues" has also been necessary to a certain extent. The maternal role has had a substantial negative impact on the development of women's careers. Whereas the careers of single women without children tend to follow the male pattern, women with children often interrupt their careers, begin them later, or otherwise find that child-care responsibilities limit their career involvements. Recognition that the absence of adequate parental leave policies has inhibited women's roles in the workplace was a major reason for the enactment of the Family & Medical Leave Act (FMLA).

[Research on actual and anticipated use by fathers of paternal leave policies revealed that] only seven percent of male workers would take a twelve-week unpaid leave following the birth or adoption of a child whereas forty-three percent of working women would do so. Even liberal estimates place the participation rate of American fathers in parental leave programs at less than ten percent. [¶] Low paternal participation rates in parental leave programs are matched by low paternal participation rates in child-care tasks. . . .

. . .

Largely missing from the debate over maternal work-family conflicts is any discussion of paternal work-family conflicts. The two, however, are linked to a significant extent. Just as the absence of adequate maternal leave policies has been a barrier to women's roles in the workplace, the absence of adequate paternal leave policies has been a barrier to men's roles in the home. Furthermore, as long as parental leave remains de facto maternal leave, work-family conflicts will remain a significant barrier to women's employment and a significant source of discrimination against women.

. . .

Current practices in the division of family labor reinforce the stereotyped views concerning the relative competence of mothers and fathers in caring for young children. The threshold decision facing new parents is who will take leave from employment to care for the newborn baby. In the typical dual-worker family, the mother will take leave but the father will not. Consequently, the mother has much greater opportunity to participate and gains much more practice in child care than the father. This may lead to greater or more rapid development of the mother's parenting skills than the father's. [¶]. . . . Thus, when fathers do not take parental leave following the birth of their children, they rapidly fall behind their wives in gaining experience with the child and are perceived to be less competent. This results in marginalizing the father's role in child care and in placing the predominant burden on the mother.

If the absence of paternal leave fuels maternal domination of child-care responsibilities, one would expect that significant paternal use of parental leave would lead to a more equal division of child care between mothers and fathers. Evidence from Sweden suggests that it does.

. . . .

Unfortunately for men, their role as breadwinners interferes with their involvement with their children. Childbirth means substantial increases in household expenses and is often accompanied by a decrease in maternal contribution to household income. Fathers caught in this economic squeeze often respond by working more hours to enable the family to make ends meet. Feminists have rightly observed that many women who appear to have chosen to subordinate their careers to child-care responsibilities in reality have no choice. They often assert that men, in contrast, have the freedom to choose to have children without sacrificing their careers. Men's choices, however, are also limited. The father's primary role in providing economic security functions as a barrier to increased paternal involvement in the family. Fathers are often torn between their desires to provide financial security for their families and their desires to establish close relationships with their children. Indeed, fathers commonly express their desires to have more time with their children and to play a larger role in nurturing them.

. . . .

[M]ost men do take time off immediately following the births of their children. They do so by using accrued vacation and personal days. Fathers take this approach either because it is all they can get — that is, family leave as such is not available to them — or they believe it is all they can get away with — that is, taking a real family leave will jeopardize their careers because of employer hostility. These make-shift leaves are quite short . . . . [Most employers do not offer parental leave. And, even when they do, p]aid paternal leave policies are extremely rare. . . . [T]he absence of pay poses a major barrier to the father's ability to take leave.

[Furthermore, although e]mployer sensitivity to the need to accommodate workers' family responsibilities is increasing steadily[, many] employers' willingness to make such accommodations is limited to women workers. Men's accommodation requests are often met by, "Your wife should handle it." [¶] . . . It appears that many employers extend parental leave to fathers so that they can give the appearance of gender-neutral policies, but never intend for fathers to use it. [One research study revealed] glaring and pervasive employer hostility toward men taking parental leave. . . . [H]uman resource and other managers [have been] quite candid in their assessments that their companies would take a very negative view of fathers who might take leave to care for their children. . . . [¶] Employers are not the only source of workplace hostility. Co-worker hostility can generate powerful peer pressure. Such peer pressure can intimidate and deter fathers from taking leave. [¶] [T]here is anecdotal evidence in the United States that when an employer not only provides parental leave, but also sanctions its use, men actively participate in the program.

Maxine Eichner, *Dependency and the Liberal Polity*
93 Cal. L. Rev. 1285 (2005)

[Some feminists argue for] reordering the welfare state and the labor market so that access to societal goods and privileges are not precluded for those citizens with carework responsibilities. . . . [This] "public support" model . . . can be contrasted with two other models proposed by feminists for dealing with the issue of carework. The first of these other models, which I call the "parental parity" model, advocates policies that shift carework within families so that women no longer assume a disproportionate share relative to men's share. The second, the "anti-repronormativity" model, calls for policies that encourage women to consider other life options beside bearing and rearing children, since these tasks are so closely linked with sex inequality. Along with [the] public support model, these positions suggest very different routes for dealing with the inequality caused by women's disproportionate share of carework.

. . .

1. Parental Parity Model

The parental parity model seeks to solve the carework issue by adopting policies that would equalize the caretaking performed by men and women within families. . . . [This] position has a number of advantages. Achieving true equal distribution of carework between men and women would, of course, go a long way toward achieving sex equality. It would eliminate a large portion of the wage gap between the sexes, since the overwhelming portion of that gap comes from women's disproportionate performance of caretaking responsibilities. . . . Further, . . . it, at least theoretically, would not require changes to institutions outside of the family. . . .

Yet while such a limited version of parental parity, which demands no accommodation of institutions other than the family, is possible on a theoretical level, it fails on a practical level. Measures to persuade men to take on more caretaking will have little success without removing existing disincentives for men to perform this activity. Among the most potent of these is the substantial financial penalty that caregivers currently suffer in the labor market. . . .

Leaving aside the practical need to adjust other institutions in order to implement the parental parity model, how does the limited goal of parental parity fare in terms of achieving goods besides sex equality? Measured in terms of the welfare of children and others with significant dependency needs, the success of the parental parity model is questionable. Even if men were persuaded to assume half of the caretaking burden, they (along with their female counterparts) would still work in a labor market whose standards are constructed without reference to the needs of dependents. As a result, the value and prestige of caregiving, and the extent to which it is pursued in society, would continue to suffer. In addition, this model also leaves workers with significant caregiving responsibilities to rely on their own resources to locate and pay for substitute caregiving; the quality of substitute care that they can find and afford will, in many cases, not be adequate to meet their dependents' needs. Parental parity, moreover, would not lighten the heavy burden on the considerable numbers of single-mother families in which there is no man to share the workload.

Further, this system would continue to penalize workers with caregiving responsibilities to the extent that they cannot conform their caregiving to existing job structures. Those who have significant caretaking responsibilities will continue to be assigned to marginal positions in the workplace. For many, this will put them and their dependents in economic peril; some will be consigned to receiving means-tested welfare benefits which, in our work-oriented society, subjects them to stigmatization and exclusion. Given the inevitability and, often, the unpredictability of dependency, the failure to adapt the labor market to accommodate caretaking means that all workers are subjected to a system in which having a close family member become dependent can mean the sudden loss of many rights and privileges.

. . .

2. Anti-Repronormativity Model

[Mary Ann Case's] call to disrupt the persistent association of women with mothering adds an important, previously missing piece to the carework conversation. [Her] concern with challenging the vast array of cultural messages to women that suggest the only way to live a satisfying and productive life is through motherhood is vital to women's struggle for freedom and equality. . . . [¶] [H]owever, insofar as [she] argue[s] against state subsidization of childcare on these grounds, [she] translate[s] valuable insights into flawed public policy. . . . Roughly 80% of women become mothers at some time during their lives. [I]f having women bear large costs in terms of economic and social inequality would deter them from having children, humanity would already be threatened with extinction. . . .

Moreover, the anti-repronormativity position that both the state and private employers should not support caregiving ignores a central reality that . . .

feminists have long recognized: dependency is an unavoidable condition in human lives, rather than simply a product of women's choices. Even if women could be convinced that they do not want to become pregnant, sometimes dependency just happens. Parents or partners fall ill. Unplanned pregnancies occur. Public policy and the labor market could ignore the inevitability of dependency only because they were developed on the assumption that men had wives at home to deal with caretaking. While that model is now described in gender-neutral terms, the structures premised on these assumptions remain unchanged. And, it is these structures that anti-repronormativity advocates would allow to remain intact.

. . .

3. Public Support Model

And what about a public support model? . . . [T]here is little hope for achieving sex equality without public support for carework. So long as women bear an unequal share of caretaking responsibilities, they cannot attain equal status with men if societal prerogatives are denied based on these responsibilities. Moreover, as previously discussed with respect to the parental parity model, getting men to assume more responsibility for caretaking is unlikely in the absence of public support to eliminate the significant penalties incurred by caregivers.

Further, insofar as feminism seeks to transform society to truly accommodate both men and women, . . . it must transform public institutions that remain premised on traditionally male life patterns. The current system, in Nancy Fraser's words, "delivers the best outcomes to women whose lives most closely resemble the male half of the old family wage ideal couple. It is especially good to childless women and to women without other major domestic responsibilities." Because most women do not fall in this group, as a class they fare poorly. This standard, moreover, subjects people to a "dependency lottery" in which those who manage to go through life without having to take on caretaking responsibilities are awarded social prerogatives. Correspondingly, women who find themselves in caretaking roles are deprived not only of the salary and accompanying benefits of a job, they are also marginalized in a system that esteems the breadwinner, while it accords far less social value to the caretaker.

Toward a Unified Approach to the Carework Issue

. . . Even assuming that a public support model were to be completely implemented, the parental parity model's goal of an equal division of caretaking between the sexes [is] important to achieving sex equality. . . . Consequently, the goal of parental parity not only does not stand in tension with the public support model, it can and should be pursued as a complementary strategy.

In contrast, feminists should adopt a more cautious stance toward the measures advocated by anti-repronormativity theorists. . . . The project of deconstructing the reflexive association of women with motherhood by making alternative life courses visible and viable is a crucial counterpart to the public support approach. . . . In contrast, feminists should reject anti-repronormativity proposals to deny support for caretaking. No doubt some tension exists between public initiatives that support caregiving and anti-repronormativity proposals that emphasize the value of other life paths. But this tension, in my view, is both healthy and necessary, and can be mitigated by a more nuanced analysis than is usually offered. Such an analysis would make clear that neither childbearing nor childrearing is a woman's necessary or highest calling. Yet once children exist, caring for them, and caring for other dependents, is a critical responsibility that must be taken seriously by parents, other family members, and society. This analysis does not fetishize children, motherhood, or childrearing, yet it still recognizes the importance and dignity of carework.

. . .

NOTES

1. *What Would a "Restructured" Workplace Look Like?* What does Professor Williams mean when she says that "eliminating the ideal-worker norm in market work requires restructuring work around the values people hold in family life, in particular around the norm of parental care"? And how does her model compare with what has been labeled as the "Mommy Track"? The "Mommy Track" (taking its name from a 1989 article by Felice Schwartz in the *Harvard Business Review*) is an approach that allows parents in some higher-echelon jobs (such as law firms) to elect a less demanding work schedule with the goal of balancing career and family obligations. This approach has been applauded by many for permitting women to balance work and family, even though others, including Williams, decry it as relegating women to a second-class status. Williams argues these positions typically permit the worker flexibility, but "at the price of work success." For example, in law firms, part-time Mommy-Track workers have typically been placed outside of the partnership track. As Williams suggests in her other writings, these workers are "marginalized." Furthermore, workers on this type of track in many professions often are not paid in a manner commensurate with the proportion of a full-time schedule which they work, nor do they have access to benefits, progress toward seniority, and so on. Often they are passed over for preferable work assignments, even when such assignments could be successfully performed with their particular work schedule. Thus, the choice between being a full-time "ideal worker" versus a "Mommy Track" worker has often been a choice between achieving compensation, recognition, and progress appropriate to one's skills, actual efforts, and job performance *versus* forsaking all of the foregoing in order to obtain certain employer concessions to family obligations.

Is Professor Williams' vision of a restructured workplace truly feasible in our capitalistic system? She asserts that flexible, family-friendly and gender-neutral employment policies, such as job-sharing and caregiving leaves promote, rather than detract from, workplace efficiency and productivity. If her economic analysis is correct, wouldn't we expect at least some private employers to adopt her proposals voluntarily? Note that even if one concluded that Williams' proposals would yield some loss in productivity, one might believe the price (assuming you could calculate it) was worth paying because of gains in human welfare and sex equality. Consider whether the dominant European view is not in fact different than the American in just this dimension. Studies show that Americans work significantly longer hours than Europeans This difference in work ethic has been identified by economists as one important reason why the American economy has outperformed the European in recent decades. Responding to such an analysis, some European governments have recently sought reforms that would move their economy closer to the American model, in order to improve their global competitiveness, but such proposals have often met with fierce public opposition. This difference between Europe and the United States seems cultural as much as legal. Clearly, there is a choice to be made here, and the correct choice may not be as obvious as those on either side of this debate would claim. For an excellent comparison among work-family policies in the United States and other industrialized nations, see Janet C. Gornick & Marcia K. Meyers, *Families That Work: Policies for Reconciling Parenthood and Employment* (2003).

   2. *American Policy: The Family and Medical Leave Act.* The 1993 Family and Medical Leave Act ("FMLA"), 29 U.S.C. § 2601 et seq., constitutes the only federally-mandated parental leave policy in the United States. The Act was designed "to balance the demands of the workplace with the needs of families[;] to promote the stability and economic security of families[;] to promote national interests in preserving family integrity[;] to entitle employees to take reasonable leave for medical reasons, for the birth or adoption of a child, and for the care of a child, spouse, or parent who has a serious health condition"; and to do so in a manner that "accommodates the legitimate interests of employers" and "minimizes the potential for employment discrimination on the basis of sex." 29 U.S.C. § 2601(b). It applies to state employers, as well as certain private employers. *See Nevada Department of Human Resources v. Hibbs*, 538 U.S. 721 (2003). The legislation requires covered employers to provide eligible employees with a total of 12 weeks of leave during a 12-month period for any of several circumstances, including the birth or adoption of a child, or provision of care to a qualifying family member who suffers from a "serious health condition." 29 U.S.C. § 2612. Substantial litigation has ensued over the question of what constitutes a "serious health condition." Jessica Beckett-McWalter, Note, *The Definition of "Serious Health Condition" Under the Family Medical Leave Act*, 55 Hast. L.J. 451 (2003). The Act does not require or provide for employee compensation during the leave. The lack of an income during the leave renders the policy an impractical option for many employees in all but dire emergencies. Marc Mory & Lia Pistilli, Note, *The Failure of the Family and Medical Leave Act: Alternative Proposals for Contemporary American Families*, 18 Hofstra Lab. & Emp. L.J. 689 (2001). The primary benefit to employees under the FLMA is thus the right to reinstatement upon return to work. Some critics have argued that judicial interpretation of this provision has undercut the efficacy of even the reinstatement guarantee. *See, e.g.,* Stacey A. Hickox, *The Elusive Right to Reinstatement Under the Family Medical Leave Act*, 91 Ky. L. J. 477 (2002–03); Emily A. Hayes, *Bridging the Gap Between Work and Family: Accomplishing the Goals of the Family and Medical Leave Act of 1993*, 42 Wm. & Mary L. Rev. 1507 (2001).

   According to the 2007 "Work, Family, and Equity Index," out of 173 countries studied, the United States lags severely behind in the benefits and protections it offers to parenting. The report found that paid maternity leave is guaranteed in

169 countries, with over half these countries providing 14 or more weeks of paid leave. In contrast, the United States is one of only four countries that do not guarantee paid leave for mothers in any segment of the workforce in connection with childbearing; the other three countries are Liberia, Papua New Guinea, and Swaziland. Almost a third of the countries studied ensure that fathers receive paid parental or paternity leave, while the U.S. guarantees fathers neither type of paid leave. JODY HEYMANN ET AL., PROJECT ON GLOBAL WORKING FAMILIES, THE WORK, FAMILY, AND EQUITY INDEX: HOW DOES THE UNITED STATES MEASURE UP? (2007), *available at* http://www.mcgill.ca/files/ihsp/WFEI2007.pdf.

Three states have stepped in to fill the gap left by federal law, and have passed paid leave provisions in recent years. California's paid leave provision took effect in 2004; under it, workers are eligible for up to six weeks of partially paid leave if they take time off from work to: (1) bond with a newborn or adopted child, or (2) care for a seriously ill child, parent, spouse, or registered domestic partner. Washington then passed its paid leave provision in 2007. Finally, New Jersey passed paid leave in May 2008, which became effective in January 2009. *See* National Partnership for Women and Families, *New Jersey Becomes Third State to Adopt Paid Family Leave*, (May 2, 2008), *available at* http://www.nationalpartnership.org/site/Page Server?pagename =newsroom_pr_PressRelease_080502.

3. *American Policy: Childcare.* Affordable childcare is important to workers at all wage levels, but is of most pressing importance to lower-income earners, single-parents, and those returning to employment pursuant to reforms in federal and state welfare policies. Many commentators have criticized welfare reforms for failure to create and subsidize childcare resources, seen as an inextricable component to successful workforce reentry for parents with young children. *See, e.g.*, Martha Albertson Fineman, *The Inevitability of Dependency and the Politics of Subsidy*, 9 STAN. L. & POL'Y REV. 89 (1998); Kerri Harper, Note, *Stereotypes, Childcare, and Social Change: How the Failure to Provide Childcare Perpetuates the Public Perception of Welfare Mothers*, 4 N.Y.U. J. LEGIS. & SOC. POL'Y 387 (2000–2001); Peter Pitegoff, *Child Care Policy and the Welfare Reform Act*, 6 J. AFFORDABLE HOUSING & COMMUNITY DEV. L. 113 (1997). For further analysis and critique of American childcare policy, see Mildred Warner et al., *Addressing the Affordability Gap: Framing Child Care as Economic Development*, 12 J. AFFORDABLE HOUSING & COMMUNITY DEV. L. 294 (2003); Meghan Thompson, Comment, *The Role of Business and Government in the Provision of Child Care Assistance: A Comparative Analysis of the United States and Canada*, 17 U. PA. J. INT'L ECON. L. 1209 (1996).

4. *The Importance of Fathers.* Until relatively recently the role of fathers in childrearing was largely ignored by scholars as well as policymakers. That has changed. *See, e.g.*, THE ROLE OF THE FATHER IN CHILD DEVELOPMENT (Michael E. Lamb ed., 4th ed. 2003); William Marsiglio et al., *Scholarship on Fatherhood in the 1990s and Beyond, in* UNDERSTANDING FAMILIES IN THE NEW MILLENNIUM: A DECADE IN REVIEW 392 (R.M. Milardo ed., 2001); MEN IN FAMILIES (Alan Booth & Ann C. Crouter eds., 1998); R.P. Rohner & R.A. Veneziano, *The Importance of Father's Love: History and Contemporary Evidence*, 5 REV. OF GEN. PSYCH. 382–405 (2001). Scholars have increasingly concluded that an exclusive focus in developmental psychology and in the law on mothers' contributions to their children's well-being presents an inaccurate picture of developmental processes. *See, e.g.,* Catherine McBride-Chang et al., *Mother-Blaming, Psychology and the Law,* 1 S. CAL. REV. L. & WOMEN'S STUD. 69 (1992). Of course, studies showing the importance of a paternal role in child development typically rely on data collected from families in which the mothers are the primary caretaker of the children, since that arrangement continues to describe most families.

5. *Comparing the U.S. With Other Countries.* In a recent study comparing the United States with other countries, Professors Gornick and Meyers conclude that the United States' system of requiring American families to deal privately with a labor market that remains structured in a manner inconsistent with caretaking subjects them to a higher level of work-family conflict and to greater negative consequences. Gornick and Meyers contend that the American system requires families either to outsource significant amounts of caretaking to lightly regulated paid caretakers — often at high cost to children; to accept part-time or lower-paying jobs that accommodate caretaking, at a significant cost to the family's financial wellbeing and to sex equality; or to accept a job with non-standard hours, which often avoids the need for paid childcare, but at a high cost to children and the stability of marriages.

They note that,

> In several other industrialized countries — including those with male and female employment rates that are higher than those of the United States — employed parents spend less time in paid work and incur less-costly penalties for part-time work. In some other countries, gender inequality in the labor market is less pronounced, and men do a larger share of nonmarket work. In all of our eleven comparison countries, fewer parents work nonstandard hours, and families headed by employed parents are less likely to be poor. Children in many of these countries are also doing better on dimensions ranging from infant birth weight to adolescent childbearing.

Gornick & Meyers, *supra,* at 9.

Gornick and Meyers argue for a transformed society that they call a "dual-earner-dual-carer" society, which "recognizes the rights and obligations of women and men to engage in both market and care work and one that values children's need for intensive care and nurturance during their earliest years." *Id.* at 12. Among other things, they argue that this transformation in the U.S. would require a new and expanded role for government through publicly regulated and financed paid family leave, regulation of working time, and public early childhood education and care programs. *Id.* at 13.

6. *Further Reading.* For further discussion of workplace policies responsive to families, see Jane Waldfogel, *Family Friendly Policies for Families with Young Children,* 5 EMP. RTS. & EMP. POL'Y J. 273 (2001). For particular attention to the work-family conflicts experienced by lawyers and some of the responses by their employers, see Joan Williams & Cynthia Thomas Calvert, *Balanced Hours: Effective Part-Time Policies for Washington Law Firms: The Project for Attorney Retention: Final Report,* 8 WM. & MARY J. WOMEN & L. 357 (2002); Jacqueline

Slotkin, *Should I Have Learned to Cook? Interviews With Women Lawyers Juggling Multiple Roles*, 13 HASTINGS WOMEN'S L.J. 147 (2002); Deborah Rhode, *Balanced Lives for Lawyers*, 70 FORD. L. REV. 2207 (2002); Keith Cunningham, Note, *Father Time: Flexible Work Arrangements and the Law Firm's Failure of the Family*, 53 STAN. L. REV. 967 (2001); CYNTHIA FUCHS EPSTEIN ET AL., THE PART-TIME PARADOX: TIME NORMS, PROFESSIONAL LIVES, FAMILY, AND GENDER 5 (1999).

[3]   The Work-Family Conflict, Gender Roles, and Marriage Rates

Ira Mark Ellman, *The Future of Marriage: Marital Roles and Declining Marriage Rates*
41 FAM. L.Q. 455 (2007)

[M]arriage rates have been declining for some time, and by some measures, quite dramatically, as Table One shows.

Table One
Marriages Per 1000 Unmarried Women, 15 to 44 years old

Year	Marriages Per 1000
1969	149
1970	140
1974	128
1975	118
1978	109
1982	101
1988	91

Marriage rates continued to decline after 1988 but at a slower pace. . . . [¶]

Why marriage rates have declined is not entirely clear. Kathy Edin found [that poor] women in urban ghettos have a hard time finding men they want to marry. . . . Edin was surprised by the number who told her they had turned down marriage proposals. The problem, she concluded, is that these women did not believe they could trust the men around them to stay out of trouble, to not beat them, to remain faithful, and to stay employed and pay their share of the bills. They could have married if they wanted, but not to anyone they found acceptable. [¶] This finding is consistent with other evidence that declining marriage rates do not arise from any declining interest in being married. The percentage of Americans between 18 and 29 who tell interviewers that a "happy marriage" is part of the "good life" actually *increased* between 1991 and 1996, from 72% to 86%, while marriage rates were declining. . . . From what we know, Americans *want* to marry as much as they ever have; the problem is that they can't find suitable partners.

. . . The marriage rate decline is particularly steep among the poor, but it is not limited to them. [I]f you take a snapshot of all women between 40 and 44, and ask if they ever married, you find that the proportion who never did increases with education beyond one year of college. That marriage rate decline is not enormous — five percentage points as one goes from 13 to 19 years of education, for women in this age group in 2000 — but it is real. The finding is surprising because we would expect women who go to college to have less difficulty finding appealing men than do the women Kathy Edin talked with.

Of course such correlational data cannot tell us that work or education is the cause of the lower marriage rates for these women. It may be instead that those who do not marry are more likely to continue their education or their work, or that other factors affect both marriage and education or work. One possibility, however, is that some highly skilled women find appealing marriage prospects relatively scarce because they prefer men whose socio-economic status is at least as high, if not higher, than their own. Such a preference for "marrying up" is well-known in the social science literature, and would shrink the pool of appealing men as a woman's own socio-economic status increases. [A] preference for marrying up would seem most likely to persist among educated women who retained an interest in traditional marital roles, even if a modern, less rigid version of them, because only higher-earning men can offer them that choice in a palatable form.

I. The Possible Connection Between Marriage Rates and Marital Roles

A common claim in the social science literature is that the increase in women's labor market participation has contributed importantly to both declining marriage rates and increasing divorce rates. The claim is plausible if one believes that wives' employment reduces the attractiveness of marriage to some men or some women. The usual argument views women as the important actors, assuming that a woman's tolerance of a man's flaws declines when her earnings increase. This view is supported by studies that show declining marriage rates are associated with increased employment opportunities for women, and that women working outside the home are more likely to initiate divorce than are homemakers. . . .

[A] leading critic of this consensus view has observed [that] its widespread acceptance results in part from its compatibility with highly divergent ideologies. On one hand, feminists are comfortable with the idea that . . . as their economic choices broaden, more women would reject patriarchal marriage. On the other hand, economists see marital roles as but another example of the benefits of specialization: the wife with lower earning potential focuses on the family's domestic needs, the husband with higher earning potential focuses on producing income. . . . But if the earnings potential of women rises, the benefits of such specialization will decline, because women's focus on "domestic production" costs more in forgone market opportunities. . . . [¶]Both stories, however, are incomplete. They explain why traditional marital roles would become less appealing to women as their earnings potential increases, but not why the consequence wouldn't be a shift away from traditional marital roles, rather than a decline in marriage rates. . . . [N]either the feminist nor the economic perspective can explain why women's advancing market success leads to declining marriage rates without also assuming that gender-based marital roles will not change. Resistance to role-reversal marriages, or marriages in which the spouses share domestic tasks equally, must be strong enough to ensure that such marriages are too rare to absorb all the women with rising earning potential. Only then do declining marriage rates become likely.

So . . . the question of whether women's rising incomes leads to declining marriage rates becomes a question of whether marital roles are malleable. If they can change, but not fast enough to keep up with women's increasing market opportunities, then we would expect a temporary decline in marriage rates, until the transformation of marital gender roles catches up. . . . How fast have marital roles changed, and how likely are they to change more? We now turn to that question.

II. Marital Roles and Labor Force Participation

[N]o one denies the factual claim that on average, wives continue to shoulder a disproportionate share of domestic duties, whether or not they also work for pay. Explaining this fact is another matter. . . . One story focuses on men's preferences and assumes that few men will accept a financially dependent, domestic, marital role. . . . [¶] A different story, however, focuses on women's preferences, arguing that even highly skilled women want the opportunity to work less and spend more time caring for their children. But what kind of man will appeal to a high-potential, domestically inclined woman . . .? [T]he historical pattern suggests what many would intuit: they are less likely to find lower status men, with less earning potential than they have themselves, appealing. [They are] instead more likely to be attracted to men whose status and earning potential is at least as high as [theirs], and preferably higher.

Whether one focuses on men's preference to avoid the primary domestic role, or women's to seek it, one would predict that as women earn more they will have more trouble finding marriage partners. The two stories are not alternatives but complements, because both can be true. . . . Social scientists have long observed that men are more likely to marry "down" in socioeconomic status, and women more likely to marry "up." The result is a relative paucity of potential partners for low-status men and high-status women, each of whom suffer lower marriage rates. The result makes sense to the extent both genders prefer traditional marital roles. It does not seem to make sense if one assumes men and women are indifferent to marital roles.

. . . . [¶] While marriage rates obviously depend upon the preferences of both genders, my focus here is on women's. And I am more interested in identifying correctly the average preference of women, and how malleable it is, than in offering any particular argument for *why* it is what it is. . . . I need not attempt to resolve the question of the source of this common preference; it is enough that it in fact exists. [¶] But first one preliminary caution: it would surely be mistaken to think that any one story could capture the preferences of all women or all men, and nothing I say here is meant to suggest otherwise. . . . Overall marriage rates will be affected if these preferences are an important factor for many women, even though they are not the only thing that matters to most of them.

B. The Historical Data on Marital Roles

Everyone knows that a dramatic increase in the proportion of women in labor force was a major demographic story of the second half of the twentieth century. Has that translated into a change in proportion of marriages in which the wife is the dominant breadwinner? One way to look at that question is to ask about the proportion of marriages that conform to the traditional model, in which the husband engages in full time paid labor, and the wife does not at all, and the proportion that conform to a complete role-reversal, in which the wife engages in full time paid labor, and the husband does not at all. Figure 1 gives these proportions for the years 1978 to 2004, the most recent year for which we have data.

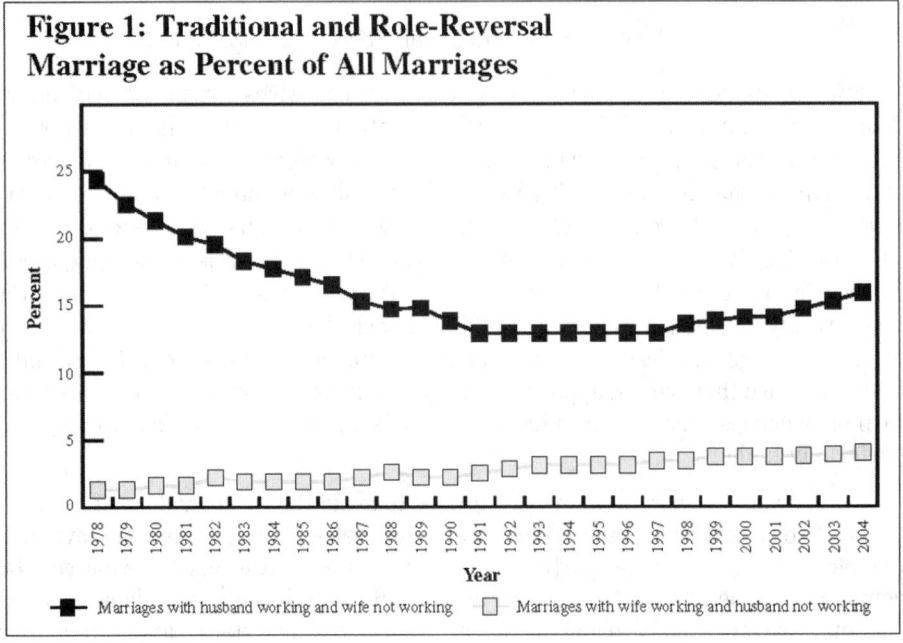

Figure 1: Traditional and Role-Reversal Marriage as Percent of All Marriages

Figure 1 confirms the conventional wisdom that the traditional marriage of breadwinner-husband and homemaker-wife has become less common. On the other hand, the role-reversal marriage remains as rare as it was three decades ago, remaining fixed at about one in twenty, and there is reason to think even this is an overestimate. Figure 1 also shows that the proportion of marriages in which the husband was the sole breadwinner has held steady since 1990, even increasing slightly. . . .

Figure 1 only addresses the 25% of marriages in which one spouse works and the other does not work at all. What about the larger number of marriages in which both work? The first set of figures in Table 2 examine them as well. The first line in this table tells the percentage of working husbands with a wife who earns more than he does. It tells us how often a working husband is the dominant financial partner in a marriage. However, some of these working husbands have wives who do not work at all. So the second line focuses on the 75% of marriages in which both spouses work. It tells us how often a working wife of a working husband earns more than he does. Comparing Lines 1 and 2 tells us, for example, in 1981 husbands who worked were the dominant financial partner in 90% of their marriages, but only 84% of the marriages in which the wife also worked (since their wives out-earned them in 10% and 16% of these marriages, respectively). The Table tells us that the proportion of marriages in which wives out-earned their working husbands jumped considerably between then and 1992, but in the 12 years after 1992 the change has been much less than during the eleven years before. This statistic thus tells a story of recent role stability that is similar to Figure 1.

Table 2
Relative Earnings of Husband and Wife, and of Men and Women
Five Selected Years

		1981	1992	1997	2001	2004
1.	Marriages in which Wife earns more than Husband,					
	As percent of all marriages in which husband works 10.0%	10.0%	16.5%	17.2%	17.9%	18.3%
	As percent of all marriages in which both work	15.9%	22.4%	22.7%	24.1%	25.5%
2.	Median earnings of Women Working Full Time,					
	As percent of male median, for					2005
	All men and women, 16 and older	64.5%	75.8%	74.5%	76.4%	81.0%
	Men and women 20 to 24 years old	80.7%	94.2%	90.6%	91.9%	94.0%
	Men and women 25 to 34 years old	70.4%	82.0%	82.9%	83.0%	89.1%

The second set of figures in Table 2 also illustrates a well-known phenomenon, that [t]he earnings gap [between men and women] increases as [they] age. As women become wives and mothers, they are more likely than single women to work part time. . . . Only forty-six percent of married women worked full time in 1997, compared to 83 percent of married men. [Moreover,] women working full time work fewer hours than men working full time, even when they have the same educational attainment and same profession. . . . Wives work [on average] fewer hours than their husbands, even when their hourly rate is higher. This difference in working hours almost surely arises from the impact, on the overall gender averages, of women with children . . . . [who] bear a larger share than their husbands of the responsibility for the family's domestic chores, even when they work full time . . . [T]his enhanced domestic labor necessarily limits the hours they have available for market labor. [Such earning capacity sacrifices by wives are] more reasonable to make if the husband, whose earning potential is not sacrificed, had a higher earning potential than the wife to start with. . . . [¶] But as more and more women enhance their earning potential, competition for higher-earning husbands grows. If men's earnings are not also rising — and in general they are not, as we shall see — then increasing numbers of women remain single, unless their preference in spousal attributes changes. We now go on to examine those preferences more closely.

C. Expressed Preferences and Economic Pressures

. . . Even though true role-reversal marriages remain rare, and economic equality between men and women has not yet been achieved, there *has* been a significant increase in the proportion of marriages in which the wife engages in both full-time as well as part-time work. The proportion of wives ages 25 to 54 who work full-time increased from 23 percent to 46 percent between 1969 and 1998. Surely this dramatic change is . . . evidence of a preference . . . for market work and, presumably, for a reduced domestic role. Survey data of ever-married women under 45 supports this inference. In 1970 80% of them told interviewers they agreed with the statement that "It is much better for everyone involved if the man is the achiever outside the home and the woman takes care of the home and the family"; by 1989 less than 30% agreed with that statement. In 1970, about half agreed that "A working mother can achieve just as warm a relationship with her children as a mother who does not work"; in 1989 about 78% agreed. These figures evidence a remarkably large change in attitude over a relatively short time. Maybe, then, we are in a transition period of changing preferences. Perhaps increasing numbers of women will be content to focus more on career and less on family. . . .

A change in attitude can of course be the product, as well as the cause, of a change in behavior. Women who worry about the impact of their working on their children or their marriage, but who felt constrained, by economic factors or otherwise, to work more hours, might be expected to resolve those doubts by changing their beliefs so that they were in less tension with their behavior. This follows from the classic psychological theory of *cognitive dissonance*. This observation does not suggest that the change in attitude is any less real, and indeed, it may then feed further changes in behavior. . . . [T]here is evidence to suggest that economic pressures played a large role in the trend toward wives' increased market hours. . . . The years during which wives increased their labor force participation were years during which many Americans experienced declining returns to each hour of market labor. . . . [A]ll married couples, except for those in the lowest ten percent of the income distribution, together worked more hours in 1997 than in 1979. [But only] families in the upper thirty percent of the income distribution experienced a growth in income per hour of labor. Moreover . . . the increase in wives' hours of labor was concentrated among the couples facing the greatest economic pressure. For this group of married couples, increased hours of labor were necessary to maintain their income, much less to enlarge it. . . .

. . . Another way to pursue this question is to see how wives' work choices are affected by their husband's income: Presumably, the higher her husband's income, the less economic pressure there will be on the wife to work. Figure 4, derived from unpublished data collected in the 1997 Current Population Survey shows the percentage of married mothers with minor children who work for pay full time. They are grouped by both their husband's income, and their own educational attainment. The data shows, as one might expect, that these married mothers are generally more likely to work full time when they have more education.

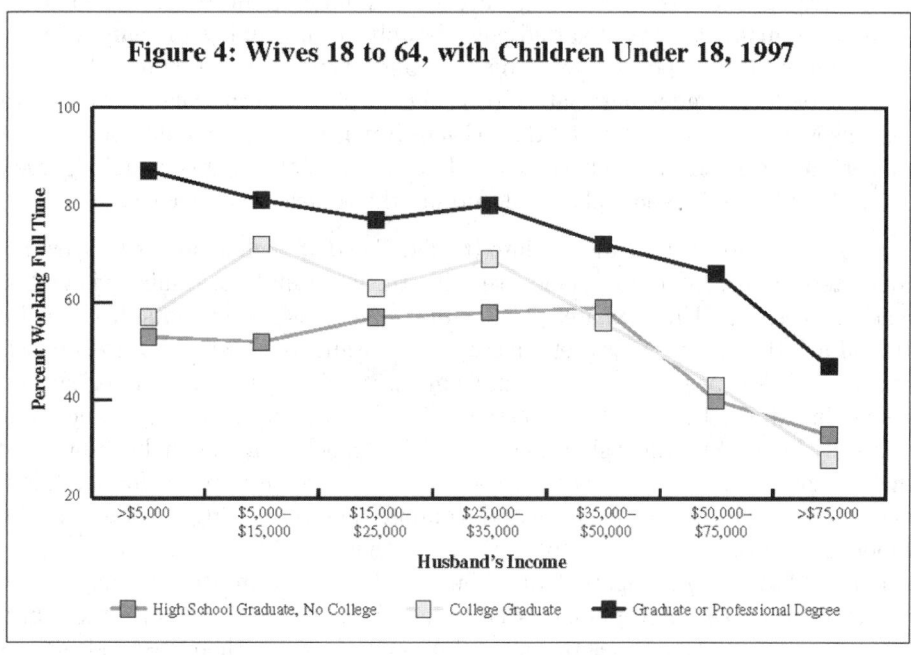

Figure 4: Wives 18 to 64, with Children Under 18, 1997

The opportunity cost of the wife's withdrawal from full time work obviously increases, on average, with her level of education. But no matter the mother's education, there seems to be a level of husband's income beyond which most choose to incur this opportunity cost. Even wives with graduate and professional degrees do not usually work full time if their husband's income exceeded $75,000. The majority of less well-educated wives withdraw from full-time work at lower levels of husband's income. Note as well that the proportion who work full time begins to decline at husband incomes between $25,000 and $35,000. The median income of husbands living with their wives was about $32,000 in 1997. The apparent message of this data is that as economic pressures decline, married American mothers increasingly choose to work part time rather than full time, regardless of their educational level. If that is their preference, then one would also expect most women to prefer potential spouses with an income potential sufficient to permit them to exercise it, which means that the income potential they will require in their prospective husband will rise along with their own.

D. Attitudes toward work and gender: some international comparisons

One way to examine the likelihood that the preferences of American men and women will change and converge is to look at the preference patterns in other countries: this can perhaps tell us how malleable the preferences are, under the impact of cultural forces. A 1996 cross-national Gallup survey seems to suggest that Americans persisted in preferring traditional family roles more than the residents of other developed countries. Two-thirds of Americans believe that one working parent is better for society than two, higher than in the UK (50%), France (56%), Spain (34%) or even Japan (52%). Gallup also asked whether the respondent favored *men* working with *women* taking care of the family. Interestingly, while the proportion answering "yes" varied considerably from country to country, within each country the responses given by men and women were remarkably similar . . . , a pattern suggesting that cultural forces play a large role in shaping the responses. [The survey revealed that 47% of American men and 49% of American women answered affirmatively.] [¶]. . . . Because the data suggest a high degree of cultural variation, it seems plausible to think the American view could shift.

One way to get further insight into the likelihood of such a shift is to learn how contented or discontented people are with their culture's prevailing view about marital roles. . . . Unfortunately, Gallup did not ask his respondents this question. He did ask them, however, whether they would want to be reborn as the opposite sex. . . . [Eight percent of American women, and four percent of American men responded affirmatively to this question..] By this measure, American women are relatively happy with their situation . . . [¶] The conclusion one might draw . . . is that American women . . . combine a relatively high preference for traditional marital roles with a very high level of contentment with being women. . . . The American data do not appear to be the stuff that a revolution in marital roles is made of. [¶] . . . The apparent durability of the American attitude may also be reflected in the repeated finding "that although dual-earner wives [in the United States] do two to three times the amount of domestic work their husbands do, less than one third of wives report the division of the daily family work as unfair." This finding has remained largely unchanged from the 1960s through today . . . .

. . . The apparent durability of the American attitude may also be reflected in the repeated finding "that although dual-earner wives [in the United States] do two to three times the amount of domestic work their husbands do, less than one third of wives report the division of the daily family work as unfair." This finding has remained largely unchanged from the 1960's through today (although there has been some change over that time period in the proportion of housework that wives say their husbands do, from about 1/4 in the earlier period to 1/3, more recently). Some may see this as self-delusion on wives' part, but a different interpretation is that many wives are content with an exchange in which their husbands have primary responsibility for earning money while they have primary responsibility for caring for their children. They are no more self-deluded, in other words, than are husbands in traditional marriages who believe it fair to support their wives.

. . . .

The Swedish experience may offer a lesson in the difficulty of changing gender role preferences through public policy. The sharing of family responsibilities between mothers and fathers is an explicit goal of Swedish law. Generous parental leaves are one element of this policy. Employed parents of newborns are allowed fifteen months leave, which may be taken any time up to the child's eighth birthday. A parent on leave receives benefits based on their earnings record during the 240 days preceding the birth. . . . Swedish scholars have observed that tying the benefit scale to earnings "has given young women strong incentives to establish themselves in the labour market before giving birth and even to postpone births until earnings are sufficiently high." . . . "For parents of children born in 1995 or later . . . , one of the 15 months is reserved for each parent — one mummy-month and one daddy-month — and cannot be transferred to the other parent." The reservation of a month for each parent was added to the law to force couples to allocate more leave time to the father than they had been doing. Combined with these generous parental leaves is a second element of Swedish policy: free child care provided by the government, once parents return to work. It is high quality care, costing as much as $11,900 per child.

On one level the Swedish policy appears very successful. The Swedish gender wage differential is much less than in the United States. Yet gender roles have not been much affected. Swedish women are more likely than American women to work part time, both absolutely, and relative to the proportion of men who work part-time. Sixty percent of employed mothers with children between 2 and 6 work only part-time, higher than in the U.S. By comparison, only about 5 percent of employed Swedish fathers with children between 2 and 6 work part-time. In 1999, fathers accounted for only 11.6% of all the leave benefit days claimed, a proportion that remained largely unchanged since the beginning of that decade. About half of all fathers never claim any leave at all. One survey picked a random week during the year and asked whether parents were absent from work that week to care for their children. Twenty-four percent of Swedish women with children below 7 were absent for the entire week, but only 2 percent of the men. Eighty-six percent of the women with children under a year of age were absent for a week, but only 6 percent of the men. While better educated Swedish women work more hours than the less-well educated, even those with a college education only work about 65% of the hours that men work, during the first ten years of their child's life — assuming that they have only one child. Those with more than one child work less, perhaps half the hours that men work. The most obvious explanation for this pattern is that Swedish women, freed by their nation's social programs from some of the economic pressures that force American women to work longer hours, choose home over full time in the market, just as American women do when they have husbands financially able to offer them the same choice.

One survey asked Swedish parents why their child's mother took more leave than the father. "Father's work situation" was the most frequent answer given by both mothers and fathers, suggesting perhaps that both parents see the father's market work as more important to protect than the mother's. But it is also true that fathers were more likely than mothers to report employer obstacles to parental leave-taking, while mothers were more likely than fathers to report positive responses from their employer. Perhaps employers who accept a woman's claim to domestic obligations at face value suspect that men who seek parental leave are really shirkers. Or perhaps employers give both men and women the impression that those taking parental leave will advance more slowly on the job, but men react to this message more negatively than do women.

But if employers were one source of resistance for fathers seeking leave, the fathers' partners were another. The researchers found that one important reason so many fathers took no leave at all is that half the mothers wanted it all for themselves. Fathers were more likely to take leave when the employed mother was highly educated; one might speculate that such mothers were more likely to have jobs they liked and thus to be among the half of mothers who did not seek all the leave-time for themselves. Fathers were more likely to take at least one month's leave for first-born children than for later-born children, as one would expect from other studies indicating that the division of parental labor becomes more gender-based with additional children. A Swedish researcher sympathetic to the announced Swedish policy, but frustrated by its apparent ineffectiveness in altering gender patterns in work and family behavior, concluded that it was inadequate to urge young women to choose "male" subjects in their education. "A second line of attack is to induce men to behave more like women in their career choices." But she had no ready strategy for achieving that goal either. Noting that local surveys found most Swedish women "quite content with their lot", she concluded with apparent resignation that "[p]erhaps we should avoid equating gender equality with 'sameness' and give more allowance for gender-specific personal fulfillment."

The Swedish data thus suggest that gender role preferences may be less malleable than some may hope. One might wonder whether their persistence in Sweden combines with Sweden's high male/female earnings ratio to explain the low Swedish marriage rate — half the American rate. . . .

III. Conclusion

If the declining marriage rate reflected no more than shifting American tastes about private matters, we might question whether the government should care. But the data suggests otherwise. First, the attitudinal data suggests that tastes have not shifted. The unmarried have not selected their situation, they have settled for it. Americans' preference for marriage also seems well-grounded in the facts. Compared to cohabitors, married couples are more likely to stay together, to pool their financial resources, to feel a sense of responsibility for one another, and to have the confidence in the durability of their relationship necessary to allow them to maximize its benefits by specializing in their contributions to it. . . . In short, a government concerned with improving the general welfare could reasonably desire to reverse the trend of declining marriage rates. But how?

One finding especially seems clearly established: marriage rates are higher when men's incomes are higher. The poor women Kathy Edin studied would have been more likely to marry if they had access to a pool of "marriageable" men — men with reasonable jobs as well as compatible dispositions. That suggests the surest path to raising marriage rates among the poor is to end their poverty: a worthy goal for many reasons, but hardly a simple one, politically or practically. . . . What we have learned here, however, suggests that to the extent more marriage is our goal, we need to fight poverty in a particular way. It is not just that we wish to lift the poor generally out of poverty, but also that we need to give a special boost to men. So long as marital gender roles persist, and women prefer to marry up, high marriage rates require not just the availability of men with jobs, but of men with jobs that are at least as good, if not better, than the jobs held by women.

. . .

The data suggest a version of this phenomenon extending beyond the poor, to highly skilled women. It is not that rising women's earnings alone suppress marriage rates, but that they do when men's earnings do not rise proportionately, because it is then more difficult for high-earning women to find potential mates with equal or greater earnings. While this social dynamic is of the same kind as that which explains low marriage rates among the poor, shifting the context helps bring home the importance of two more general difficulties in fashioning public policy in this area.

First, we must appreciate that we use the law for two different kinds of purposes. . . . Sometimes we use the law to create incentives or penalties for behaviors we want to encourage or discourage, such as marriage or divorce. But other times we use the law to achieve fairness, accepting the world as we find it, but seeking to rearrange things to make outcomes more fair (as when we accept divorce but require divorcing couples to share their property). Sometimes, of course, these purposes may combine. Penalties for gender discrimination seek to change people's behavior in order to bring about more fair results. Other times our social engineering goals and our fairness goals may conflict, and people may divide on which deserves priority. . . .

That is the kind of conflict that may arise in connection with our desire to raise marriage rates. . . . We want to ensure fair opportunities for women in the labor market, and for many the ultimate test of whether that goal is achieved is whether the actual average earnings of women and men are equal. Yet a world in which men and women have equal earnings may be a world with fewer marriages. I assume no one would suggest that the law ought to resist gender equality in the workplace for this reason, just as no one would suggest that fair treatment at divorce of financially dependent spouses should be abandoned because it may encourage them to seek divorce when mistreated. So at this level, the point is only to understand that our commitment to certain fairness norms, such as a belief in equal treatment in the workplace, may lead us to adopt some legal rules that may discourage choices we want people to make.

This point may also bear on the level of social engineering we may wish to undertake. While some fairness norms will trump concerns we otherwise might have with a rule's incentive effects, other fairness claims may be too contested to serve this role. Rules that free individuals from seemingly arbitrary limits on their range of choice typically enjoy wide support. Equal pay for equal work obviously falls in this category, as do many measures meant to protect women from being disadvantaged, as a general matter, by the simple fact that only they bear children. So do measures meant to keep employers from distinguishing between men and women in parental leave policies. Yet Sweden has taken all these steps but finds that gender roles survive nonetheless. Should government therefore embrace more direct efforts to alter the people's preferences, in the hope of reshaping them so that men and women on average make the same choices?

. . . . Just as the Swedes have been much less successful than many of them hoped in changing gender roles, we may also be wrong to attach too much causal impact of their policies on their marriage rates. The factors that influence social phenomena like divorce and marriage are in fact most often far too complex to predict. The potential spouses' relative earnings may be one factor affecting the inclination to marry, but it hardly seems likely that shifts in relative earnings will alone cause declines in the marriage rate without limit. Where economic values are extreme, as is the case for [poor urban neighborhoods in which there are many men who earn nothing] a powerful impact is plausible. Where values are less extreme, as in the social milieu of highly skilled women, who typically encounter many men whose earnings are at least close to theirs, the impact of their inclination to "marry up" will be more marginal. It may only push things a little bit one way or the other. So perhaps the Swedish effort to alter gender roles is not so important, because it will have much less impact on both the gender roles and on marriage rates, than opponents might fear or Swedes might hope.

NOTES

1. *Preferences and Choice.* Compare Professor Ellman's description of American women's and mothers' preferences with Susan Bianchi's description of mothers' preferences, which she draws from thousands of interviews her research team conducted with American parents:

> . . . [W]hy would mothers embrace market work, yet go to such great lengths to protect their time with their children? Put differently, why do mothers choose (or get pushed into) something in-between — not full-scale market equality with men, but not the stay-at-home path that also solved work-family balance in the past, as indeed, it did so for many of their mothers or grandmothers? As opportunities for women have expanded, being employed has become increasingly important to them. Employment provides resources but also meaning, a sense of worth, a definition of self and value, and a life outside the family. Moreover, many mothers cannot forgo employment, even if they wanted to . . . [¶] But neither can women easily give over the caregiving of their family members (particularly their children) to others in a world where being a good mother requires intensive involvement in all aspect of their children's lives . . . The two competing pulls on mother's time — one from the home, one form the marketplace — run parallel and add to societal ambivalence about maternal employment . . .

> So how do mothers respond? They seek compromise in struggling for the elusive balance between work and family. They relinquish the goal of equality with men in the workplace, in favor of more hours at home when their children are young. They emerge at age forty or fifty with employment histories that are more marginal, more part-time, more episodic than men's. They let go of activities and goals that are not seen as precious as the time they spend with their children. They live with less pristine and more disorganized homes. . . . They learn to live in a state of feeling time pressed — of feeling inadequate about the time they spend with their children, with their spouses, and on themselves.

SUZANNE M. BIANCHI ET AL., CHANGING RHYTHMS OF AMERICAN FAMILY LIFE 175–76 (2006). Is there any conflict between Professor Bianchi's view of women's preferences, and Professor Ellman's? How convincing is the data that Professor Ellman relies on to support his views on women's preferences? Would one expect Professors Bianchi and Ellman to favor the same policies on work-family conflict?

Feminist theorists have long argued that women's choices are not, by themselves, sufficient justification of an unequal status quo. They contend that women's preferences are the product of a society that sends both women and men strong messages about gender roles. Further, these choices are necessarily conditioned on the options available to them; in some cases, women may be choosing the best of a bad set of alternatives. . . . As Joan Williams has expressed this critique in the work-family context, "In the work/family context, the rhetoric of choice masks a gender system that defines childrearing and the accepted avenues of adult advancement as inconsistent and then allocates the resulting costs of child rearing to mothers." Joan Williams, *Gender Wars: Selfless Women in the Republic of Choice*, 66 N.Y.U. L. Rev. 1559, 1596 (1991).

Should mothers' choices to leave work to care for children be grounds for leaving the work-family division as it is if, as labor historian Alice Kessler-Harris argues, American law and social policy for much of the twentieth century encouraged employers to construct jobs on a model that made them incompatible with caretaking responsibilities? Alice Kessler-Harris, In Pursuit of Equity: Women, Men, and the Quest for Economic Citizenship in Twentieth-Century America (2001). If women's preferences to leave work to care for children indeed exist, should the fact that they were developed in a society marked by gender inequality be an argument against them serving as a justification of the status quo?

Professor Ellman's hypothesis for why women in well-paid jobs are less likely to marry combines a theory that a considerable number of these women prefer to be caregivers with a theory that these same women generally prefer to "marry up," which leaves them with a relatively small pool of available men from which to find a mate. He also suggests that they might have this preference because they hope to minimize the financial sacrifice they would make by assuming the primary caretaker role of their children. Notice that the two claims are not inevitably connected: a preference for marrying up would limit a high-earning women's pool of possible mates no matter how it came about. A preference for having children and staying at home with them, on the other hand, would make women more likely to settle for the mate who would be the best provider among the available contenders. How strong is Professor Ellman's evidence for each of these claims? To what extent does he support his hypothesis that the same explanation for why low-income women are not marrying also applies to high-income women? To what extent does the evidence show that that fall-off in marriage rates among high-earning women comes from women who want to marry up to have children, rather than for other reasons, such as that these women have somewhat less desire to marry than others, either because of less financial need or because they want to keep jobs that hinder family commitments?

Some recent research has found that as Western women achieve professional success and gain financial independence, their preference in a partner changes. Financially independent women are more likely to choose partners based on physical attractiveness than bank balance compared to lower-income women; in fact, these more independent women demonstrate preferences that look a lot like men's have historically. Fhionna Moore at al., *The Effects of Female Control of Resources on Sex Differentiated Mate Preferences*, 27 Evolution & Hum. Behaviour 193 (2006).

2. *Other Data on Women's and Men's Preferences.* There is evidence that suggests that most working mothers in the United States are not happy with the current gender division of labor. In the 1997 National Study of the Changing Workforce survey, 56 percent of employed mothers answered "more time," when asked the question "Do you wish your husband would spend more time (taking care of or) doing things with your child(ren), less time, or the same amount of time?" Interestingly, this appears to reflect a shift in the preferences of working mothers over time. Only 43 percent of working women answered "more time" to this question in 1977, a statistically significant difference. BIANCHI, *supra*, at 130.

In addition, other recent data suggests that fathers, too, are unhappy with the amount of time they can spend with their children in the current system. Fifty-four percent of married fathers compared with 37 percent of married mothers report spending too little time with their youngest child. Some 60 percent of married fathers and 53 percent of married mothers say that they do not have enough time to spend with their oldest child. *Id.* at 133. Do these figures suggest that *both* sexes would prefer that work be structured in a way that allows them more time with their children?

It is possible that surveys that consider the preferences of all American adults about their preferred division of childrearing, such as the Gallup survey included in Professor Ellman's excerpt, mask generational changes in views on parenting. When Suzanne Bianchi et al. asked three cohorts of adults — those born before World War II, Baby Boomers, and post-Baby Boomers — what the ideal division of labor was between mothers and fathers, earlier cohorts were much less likely than later cohorts to believe that both parents should share equally in caregiving, as shown below in her Figure 7.1.

128   Changing Rhythms of American Family Life

Figure 7.1   Percentage Who Believe that Both Parents Should be Equally Involved in Caregiving

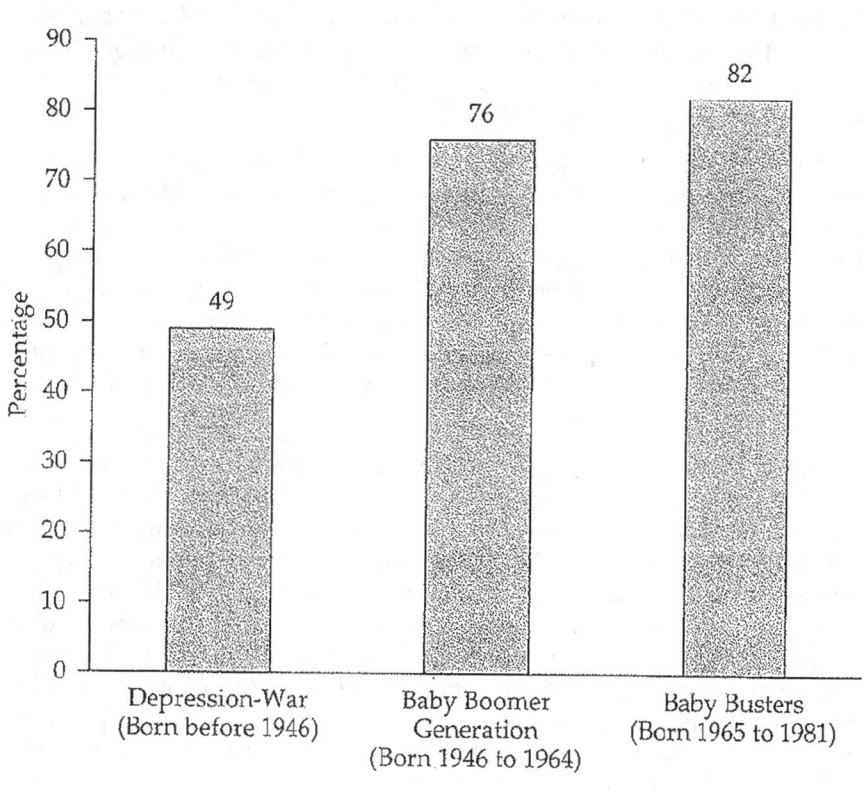

Source: Authors' calculations from the 1999 National Omnibus Survey, University of Maryland.
Note: Depression-War estimate statistically significantly different from Baby Boom and Baby Bust estimates, $p < 0.05$.

3. *How Much Behaviors Have Changed, and the Swedish Data.* Professor Ellman asks how much gender roles in actual parental *behavior*, as contrasted with the relatively large changes in self-reported *attitudes*. To discuss this issue, he presents data from Sweden, a country that has deliberately attempted to move toward equalizing fathers' and mothers' caretaking roles. While Professor Ellman observes that Sweden's work-family policies have not ended the gendered division of labor, Sweden can claim some movement. More than 75% of eligible Swedish fathers took some parental leave in their child's first year in 1994, up from 2% when the leave was first introduced in 1974, and nearly double the rate in the early 1980s. While this 1994 leave amounted to only 11.4 percent of all parental leave taken, on average, fathers were on leave for 44 days, a significant period of time. Sheila B. Kamerman, *Parental Leave Policies: An Essential Ingredient in Early Childhood*

Education and Care Policies, 14 Social Policy Report (2) 9–11 (2000). The 1995 introduction of the "use it or lose it" policy, reserving some leave time specifically for fathers, appears to have had a further impact. A full 90 percent of fathers of children born in 1998 took parental leave. Moreover, by 2005, the percent of leave taken by fathers had increased to 19.5 percent of all parental leave. Peter Moss & Margaret O'Brien, eds., *International Review of Leave Policies and Related Research*, Department of Trade and Industry, U.K., Employment Relations Research Series No. 57, 209–10 (2006), *available at* http://www.berr.gov.uk/files/file31948.pdf.

Professor Ellman makes no claim to explain why gender patterns persist, but whatever their source, it may not be surprising they are relatively slow to change. The complicated interaction of cultural and economic forces, and the simple biological reality that only women bear children, could combine to create powerful channeling pressures that shape behavior in ways that resist the impact of policies such as Sweden's. Perhaps, however, Swedish success in increasing use of parental leave time by fathers will have a bigger impact in the long-term by affecting the formative parenting experiences of men and women and through that, their sense of the possibility of role changes.

4. *Policy Prescriptions*. Professor Ellman suggests that Americans may be less willing than Swedes to adopt policies aimed at pushing couples to change the way they allocate work and domestic duties between them, as compared to policies that merely try to ensure they have the choice to adopt the allocation they prefer. He also observes that there may be a tension between policies aimed at achieving greater gender fairness, and the policies one might wish to adopt to promote marriage and reduce divorce rates. Perhaps most provocatively, he suggests that increasing the marriage rate (and thus reducing the rate of nonmarital births) among the poor might require a focus on improving the economic prospects of poor men, rather than the poor in general, because the high rates of nonmarital births currently found in lower-income communities arises from the difficulties that lower income women have in finding men they wish to marry. Do you agree that policymakers must choose between promoting gender fairness and promoting marriage? Does Professor Ellman make a persuasive case for this claim?

The alternative to using the law to channel people's choices about marriage and gender roles is the goal of legal neutrality: allow people to make their own choices, without pushing them in any direction. But are neutral government policies actually possible to craft? For example, if the availability of paid leaves strengthen women's attachment to the labor market, is it neutral to *not* provide paid leave? Or is simply a policy that weakens women's labor market attachment? What is the neutral policy in this case? The fact that different individuals have different preferences also complicates the task of formulating neutral policies. For example, a policy of providing paid parenting leave may seem neutral to women who seek more time with their children without having to give up their work, but not to women and men who are content with traditional parenting arrangements, especially because any policy involving subsidies, as for paid leave or free child care, inevitably involves some transfer from those who do not make a subsidized choice to those who do. Is any neutral government policy truly possible? If not, is it better to drop the pretense of neutrality, in favor of policies likely to encourage changes in behavior and marital roles that seem, in the long run, more fair? Of course, if "fair" means equal opportunity to pursue one's own preference, the dilemma repeats itself.

This dilemma is nicely illustrated by Neil Gilbert & Rebecca A. Van Voorhis in *The Paradox of Family Policy*, 40 Soc'y No. 6, 51–56 (Sept./October 2003). They compare the impact of the Swedish policy with the policy in Norway, which like Sweden provides paid leave and high quality child care to working parents, but which in 1998 began offering an additional option: those with children under three who did not enroll them in state-subsidized child care because they wished to care for their children themselves would receive a cash benefit. The purpose was to adopt a more "neutral" policy that did not provide a financial incentive to put for your children in others' care, rather than caring for them yourself. Finland has a program similar to Norway's, and both countries have higher marriage and fertility rates than Sweden. Gilbert and Van Voorhis suggest that the Swedish policy may be part of the reason why its fertility rate is 1.54, far below the replacement rate of 2.11or the American rate of 2.06. The "paradox" they suggest is that women have fewer children in the countries that make it easier for them to combine children with market work. Is it more neutral to prefer the Norwegian policy to the Swedish policy in order to encourage women to have more children?

If policy neutrality is an illusion, then what of Professor Ellman's suggestion that Americans are likely to be less willing than the Swedes to adopt policies overtly aimed at altering people's preferences for their conduct of their marriage, as compared to policies that seem on their face more neutral because they appear to do no more than ensure the availability of choices. Perhaps, that is, the difference between policies is not so much their actual neutrality, but how they are packaged and presented. Are there ways in which the government might seek to nudge couples toward a more equal division of family labor that might be acceptable to Americans?

Part II

MARRIAGE AND DIVORCE

Chapter 2

MARRIAGE

A. ENTERING MARRIAGE

[1] Formal Requirements

[a] Licensure and Solemnization

MODEL MARRIAGE AND DIVORCE ACT

§ 206. [*Solemnization and Registration*]

(a) A marriage may be solemnized by a judge of a court of record, by a public official whose powers include solemnization of marriages, or in accordance with any mode of solemnization recognized by any religious denomination, Indian Nation or Tribe, or Native Group. Either the person solemnizing the marriage, or, if no individual acting alone solemnized the marriage, a party to the marriage, shall complete the marriage certificate form and forward it to the [marriage license] clerk.

(b) If a party to a marriage is unable to be present at the solemnization, he may authorize in writing a third person to act as his proxy. If the person solemnizing the marriage is satisfied that the absent party is unable to be present and has consented to the marriage, he may solemnize the marriage by proxy. . . .

(c) Upon receipt of the marriage certificate, the [marriage license] clerk shall register the marriage.

(d) The solemnization of the marriage is not invalidated by the fact that the person solemnizing the marriage was not legally qualified to solemnize it, if either party to the marriage believed him to be so qualified.

NOTES

1. *Licensing Process.* All American states prescribe certain formalities for marriage entry. While details vary, regulations fall into two categories — licensure and solemnization. Contrary to popular belief, generally sexual intercourse is not required to solemnize a ceremonial marriage. *See In re Burnside*, 777 S.W.2d 660 (Mo. App. 1989).

All states have marriage license laws. Applicants provide certain information to a government official (usually a clerk) concerning age, existing relationship of the parties by blood or marriage, previous marriages, etc. This information helps in compiling vital statistics and could facilitate enforcement of substantive marriage regulations. For example, if the application revealed the bride and groom were siblings, the license would be denied under laws prohibiting incestuous marriages. In practice, the license law does little to restrain intentional violation of substantive regulations, because little effort is made to confirm the truth of the license application information.

Most states require a physical examination as a prerequisite for a marriage license.

> Most of the statutes require an examination for venereal disease alone. A few also require tests for tuberculosis, for mental incompetence, for rubella immunity and for sickle cell anemia. In all instances except the examination for rubella immunity and for sickle cell immunity, the physician's statement certifying freedom from the specified disease is required to be presented before the license may issue. There is usually provision in the statutes for waiver of the examination by a court upon proof of circumstances warranting such action.

HOMER CLARK, THE LAW OF DOMESTIC RELATIONS § 2.3 at 36–37 (2d ed. 1988).

Louisiana and Illinois experimented with requiring pre-marital AIDS testing requirements. Neither conditioned issuance of a license on "passing" the exam. Both statutes were quickly repealed. During the Illinois statute's first year, the issuance of marriage licenses dropped 25% from the prior year. Only 44 of the 221,000 people applying for a license tested positive for the HIV virus during the first 18 months. Health officials estimated about 12 were false positives and that the total cost of the testing was $5.4 million. Isabel Wilkerson, *Illinois Legislature Repeals Requirement for Prenuptial AIDS Tests*, N.Y. TIMES, June 25, 1989, at 12. It has been argued that mandatory pre-marital AIDS testing is unconstitutional. Michael Closen et al., *Mandatory Premarital HIV Testing: Political Exploitation of the AIDS Epidemic*, 69 TUL. L. REV. 71 (1994). A Utah statute declaring void any marriage in which either party was infected with AIDS, UTAH CODE ANN. § 30-1-2 (1995), was held to violate the Americans with Disability Act and the Rehabilitation Act of 1973. *T.E.P. v. Leavitt*, 840 F. Supp. 110 (D. Utah 1993).

Do the state interests served by physical exam requirements require denial of permission to marry or would they be satisfied by requiring both parties to be made aware of the exam results?

2. Waiting Period.   Many states impose a waiting period (of either 3 or 5 days), either between application and issuance of the license or between issuance and performance of the ceremony. Often the waiting period is waived under certain circumstances, e.g., where the woman is pregnant, where the parties are already the parents of a child, where both parties are adults or where one party is about to leave for an overseas military assignment. The waiting period requirement, as well as the entire licensing procedure, is explained as impressing upon the parties the seriousness of the entry into marriage. For a discussion of biases that can affect the pre-marital decisionmaking process and of how a waiting period can improve that process, see Elizabeth Scott, *Rational Decisionmaking About Marriage and Divorce*, 76 VA. L. REV. 9 (1990).

3. Ceremony and Registration. All states have statutes governing solemnization of marriage. While there is no explicit format for the marriage ceremony, some statutes require the couple to declare in the presence of the presiding official and the required witnesses that "they take each other as husband and wife." N.Y. DOM. REL. LAW § 12 (McKinney 1999). Each state has a statutory list of officials authorized to perform marriages, normally focusing on judges, justices of the peace and clergy.

Noting that the Universal Life Church permits all its members to become "ministers," a New York case found ministers of the Church not "clergymen" under the relevant statute and, thus, not authorized to perform weddings. *Ranieri v. Ranieri*, 539 N.Y.S.2d 382 (App. Div. 1989). *But see In re Blackwell*, 531 So. 2d 1193 (Miss. 1988) (upholding marriage performed by ULC minister). A 1997 Tennessee court remanded for a determination of whether Islamic law requires that a person have an official position in a mosque to be competent to perform a marriage ceremony. *Aghili v. Saadatnejadi*, 958 S.W.2d 784 (Tenn. App. 1997). Contrary to popular belief, there apparently are no statutes authorizing ship captains to perform ceremonies on the high seas.

Section 206(a) of the Model Act illustrates another common requirement — registration of a marriage certificate. This document, often printed on the reverse side of the license, is usually filed with a county or state official.

4. Proxy Marriage. Section 206(b) of the Model Act allows proxy marriages. While rare, marriage by proxy is necessary if one party cannot be present for the ceremony. While its most prominent use has been in wartime with one party on duty overseas, sometimes it is used by prisoners. *See Lyle Menendez Marries Girlfriend in Secret*, BUFFALO NEWS, Feb. 1, 1997, p. 5A (brother Erik served as best man during conference call ceremony held on the day the pair were sentenced to life in prison for killing their parents). Statutes requiring both parties's presence would appear to forbid proxy marriage, but there is some case law to the contrary. *See, e.g., State v. Anderson*, 396 P.2d 558 (Or. 1964) (permitting invocation of marital privilege).

STATE v. DENTON
Washington Court of Appeals
983 P.2d 693 (1999)

BECKER, J.

Mark Denton invoked the spousal privilege to prevent his wife from testifying against him. The trial court allowed her to testify, after finding the marriage invalid. . . . The ruling was in error. In Washington, failure to procure a [marriage] license does not invalidate a ceremonial marriage. Denton's conviction for theft is reversed. In 1986, Denton was active in the Bellevue Jaycees, a non-profit community service organization whose members were involved in various charitable fundraising projects. Denton set up and operated a Fourth of July fireworks stand to raise money for the Washington State Sudden Infant Death Syndrome (SIDS) Foundation. With three other officers of the Jaycees, he opened a bank account in Redmond in the name of Eastside Parents for SIDS. In 1989, the Bellevue Jaycees disbanded. . . . Denton continued to receive monthly statements. Bank records show the account remained inactive for seven years with a balance of over $2,000. In 1996, Denton withdrew the funds and used them for his own purposes.

His transaction came to the attention of the police through Jill Bowersox, an acquaintance of Denton's who became suspicious in the course of helping him withdraw the funds. . . . Denton told [Bowersox] in January 1996 he needed to close out an old account that had less than $100 remaining in it. He explained that the money belonged to the Bellevue Jaycees and he was going to send it to the SIDS Foundation. Denton told Bowersox that he needed her help . . . because he could not locate the former officers whose names were on the bank's signature card for the account. . . . Bowersox . . . agreed to assist Denton by adding her signature to the new card. The new card already bore the signatures of Denton, his 15-year-old daughter, and his wife. . . . According to the bank's policy, two of four signers were needed to authorize banking transactions. . . . Bowersox went to the bank with Denton to authorize the closing of the account. . . . Bank records show that Denton deposited a check for $2,610.38 into his own bank account [after the closing of the account]. . . . The State's theory was that Denton knew the money was not his but decided to convert the account to his own use when he encountered personal financial difficulty.

Before trial, Denton attempted to invoke the spousal testimonial privilege to prevent his wife, Leona Rosser, from testifying. The State argued that the Denton-Rosser marriage, though solemnized in a church wedding ceremony, was invalid because the couple did not procure a marriage license. The trial court . . . allowed Rosser to testify. Rosser, separated from Denton at the time of trial, testified that during the early years of their marriage, bank statements arrived at their home addressed to the Bellevue Jaycees. She said Denton told her he was going to send the money from the account to the State Jaycee organization. She also testified that in January or February 1996, she herself loaned Denton $2,000 to help him out with business debts. The jury convicted Denton as charged, and he appeals. Denton maintains his marriage to Rosser was valid and that the court erred in refusing to honor his exercise of the spousal privilege.

Washington's spousal privilege is provided by statute, in part: "A husband shall not be examined for or against his wife, without the consent of the wife, nor a wife for or against her husband without the consent of the husband; nor can either during marriage or afterward, be without the consent of the other, examined as to any communication made by one to the other during marriage." *RCW 5.60.060(1)*. The statute affording the spousal privilege contemplates legal marital status. . . . Denton and Rosser not only lived together and held themselves out as husband and wife for years, they . . . began their marriage relationship with a religious ceremony in which they promised to take each other to be husband and wife. The question is whether their ceremonial marriage was valid notwithstanding the lack of a license. . . . [T]he Court [in the earlier case] relied on the common law principle that a marriage without a license is universally held to be valid in the absence of an express declaration by the Legislature that such a marriage is void. [That] remains the rule today. In the eyes of the common law, marriage is a civil contract. As Blackstone put it, the law treats marriage "as it does all other contracts: allowing it to be good and valid in all cases, where the parties at the time of making it were, in the first place, willing to contract; secondly, able to contract; and, lastly, actually did contract, in the proper forms and solemnities required by law. *Picarella v. Picarella*, 316 A.2d 826, 832, n. 10 *(Md. App. 1974)*, quoting Blackstone, Commentaries, Book I, ch. 15, sec. 433 (Lewis's Ed.). The policy favoring valid marriages is strong. It justifies recognition of an unlicensed ceremony unless the licensing statute plainly makes an unlicensed marriage invalid. See e.g., *Carabetta v. Carabetta, 438 A.2d 109, 112–113 (Conn. 1980).* New Jersey's statute is an example of an express declaration making a marriage license necessary for a valid marriage; it provides that "no marriage . . . shall be valid unless the contracting parties shall have obtained a marriage license". Where such a statute exists, even a ceremonial marriage is invalid without a license. But where there is no such statute, a marriage license is not integral to the creation of a valid marriage. Washington has a statutory requirement for a marriage license. "Before any persons can be joined in marriage, they shall procure a license from a county auditor". *RCW 26.04.140*. But Washington does not have a statute plainly making an unlicensed marriage invalid. Therefore, the . . . license requirement is purely regulatory. The regulatory purpose cannot be enforced by "the radical process of rendering void and immoral a matrimonial union otherwise validly contracted and solemnized." *Feehley v. Feehley, 99 A. [663] at 665 [(Md. 1916)]*. Intentional failure to procure a license is punishable as a misdemeanor, *RCW 26.04.200*, but it does not render a marriage void or even voidable. See *RCW 26.04.130* (marriage voidable when party is unable to consent, or where consent obtained by force or fraud). The spousal privilege, although strictly construed, does apply when there is a valid, existing marriage. Because Denton and Rosser were parties willing and able to contract for marriage, and did contract for it in the solemnities required by law, their marriage was valid. We are aware of no authority for declaring a marriage to be valid for some purposes but not for others. The court erred in allowing Rosser to testify without Denton's consent.

[The court further determined that admission of the wife's testimony was reversible error because it materially affected the trial's likely outcome by casting significant doubt on defendant's defense of a good faith claim of title.]

NOTES

1. ***Violation of Formalities***.   *Denton* reflects the general rule that violations of formality requirements do not void the marriage. In the court's language, such rules are normally found "purely regulatory." *See also Accounts Management v. Litchfield*, 576 N.W. 2d 233 (S.D. 1998) (failure to record a marriage license does not invalidate marriage); *Fryar v. Roberts*, 57 S.W.3d 727 (Ark. 2001) (intentional burning of marriage license before filing did not invalidate marriage); *Yun v. Yun*, 908 S.W.2d 787 (Mo. App. 1995) (presumption of validity of marriage not rebutted by uncorroborated statement by "husband" that he did not obtain a license before ceremony); *Barbosa-Johnson v. Johnson*, 851 P.2d 866 (Ariz. App. 1993) (marriage performed in Puerto Rico with Arizona license not invalid for that reason). Lack of legal authority in the presiding official has also often been held not to make a marriage void. *See* Annot., *Validity of Marriage as Affected by Lack of Legal*

Authority of Person Solemnizing It, 13 A.L.R.4th 1323 (1982).

But in *Nelson v. Marshall*, 869 S.W.2d 132 (Mo. App. 1993), the court held the license requirement was designed to eliminate common law marriage and failure to obtain a license rendered the attempted marriage void even though there was a ceremony (on the day before decedent's death) following a 12-year relationship. *See also Yaghoubinejad v. Haghighi*, 894 A.2d 1173 (N.J. App. Div. 2006) (lack of license renders marriage void; "husband" not estopped); *Dire v. Dire-Blodgett*, 102 P.3d 1096 (Idaho 2004) (divorce petition properly dismissed where cohabiting couple purposely failed to obtain a marriage license; no marriage ever existed); *Estate of DePasse*, 97 Cal. App. 4th 92 (2002) (failure to obtain marriage license before deathbed ceremony fatal to claim of marriage).

Denton's facts illustrate the majority rule's rationale. According to the court, "Denton and Rosser not only lived together and held themselves out as husband and wife for years, they formally began their marriage relationship with a religious ceremony in which they promised to take each other to be husband and wife." Not only did they hold themselves out as a married couple, they obviously believed they were a married couple. This has led most courts to apply what Professor Clark calls the principle of "validation" to ratify the parties' intentions. *See* HOMER CLARK, LAW OF DOMESTIC RELATIONS § 2.7 (2nd ed. 1988). While this principle appears to leave the formality requirement with no sanction to enforce it, in fact most people comply anyway. Their compliance is not surprising; most people do not want ambiguity in their marital status.

Note that even where failure to comply with formality requirements does not affect the marriage's validity, other sanctions may apply. Those who knowingly perform a wedding ceremony in violation of the requirements may violate the criminal law. For example, in Georgia it is a misdemeanor for an official or clergyman to officiate at any unlicensed wedding or at any ceremony where "any disability of either of the parties . . . would render a contract of marriage improper and illegal. . . ." GA. CODE ANN. § 19-3-48. Similarly, some statutes punish the government official who illegally issues a license. *See, e.g.*, GA. CODE ANN. § 19-3-32 (misdemeanor to wrongfully issue a license). Additionally, the parties may commit perjury by fraudulently obtaining a license or, as in Washington according to *Denton*, the failure to obtain a license might be a crime. *See* Annot., *Perjury as Predicated upon Statements upon Application for Marriage License*, 101 A.L.R. 1263 (1936). Nonetheless, prosecutions under such laws are rare.

2. *Void Versus Voidable*. *Denton*, in rejecting the state's argument that the marriage was invalid, held that the parties were indeed married. It should be noted, however, that lack of validity would not necessarily mean that the marriage was void. Under the influence of English ecclesiastical law (the origin of much of our marriage law), cases and statutes have created a halfway house for some marriages — the "voidable" marriage.

A voidable marriage is neither valid nor void. It is not valid because a marriage regulation, either formal or substantive, has been violated. On the other hand, it is valid until a court decrees invalidity in an annulment action. The annulment, declaring the parties never were married, differs from a divorce, which terminates a marriage that once existed. Historically, the distinction between annulment and divorce was important because children born of later-annulled marriages were illegitimate and alimony or marital property claims were unavailable in annulments. Neither distinction is common today.

However, there are still theoretical reasons to inquire whether violation of a particular regulation renders the marriage void or voidable. First, a void marriage should need no judicial declaration of invalidity and be attackable in any collateral proceeding. (By contrast, a voidable marriage exists until annulment.) Second, a truly void marriage can be attacked (or ignored) by anybody, while voidable marriages usually can be attacked only by the parties, and sometimes only by one of the them. For example, usually an underage marriage can be attacked only by the underage party. *See* CLARK, *supra*, § 2.10 at 93; *Harris v. Harris*, 506 N.W.2d 3 (Mich. App. 1993) (knowing bigamist can assert bigamy as ground for annulment because such marriages are void). Third, a voidable marriage can be ratified, while a void marriage cannot. Fourth, there could be financial consequences. A New York case held division of marital property may validly take place in an annulment, but not when a marriage is declared void. *Rashkov v. Rashkov*, 522 N.Y.S.2d 782 (Sup. Ct. 1987).

The void/voidable distinction, however, often is ignored or confused. For example, some cases hold that while a particular marriage is statutorily "void" only a party can attack it. *See, e.g., Ragan v. Cox*, 194 S.W.2d 681 (Ark. 1946). Similarly, some statutes describe certain marriages as void, yet prescribe annulment as the means of terminating them. *See, e.g.,* GA. CODE ANN. § 19-3-5. Likewise, some cases permit ratification of statutorily "void" marriages. *See* CLARK, *supra*, § 2.10 at 96.

3. *The Marital Communication Privilege.* The communication privilege whose applicability was at issue in *Denton* was designed to encourage marital communication and frankness. Tracing its roots far back in English legal history, the rule has survived largely intact. Under UNIFORM RULES OF EVIDENCE § 504 (1974), a criminal defendant "has a privilege to prevent his spouse from testifying as to any confidential communication between the accused and the spouse." Most states apply the privilege in civil cases also. *See, e.g.,* MAINE RULES OF EVID. § 504; WIS. STAT. § 905.05. There are several exceptions, such as criminal prosecutions for a crime where a spouse is the victim of the other, actions against third parties for injury to the marital relation, divorce and litigation involving protection of a child. ROGER PARK, DAVID LEONARD & STEVEN GOLDBERG, EVIDENCE LAW 452 (2nd ed. 2004)

A recent case, focusing on the privilege's rationale, found admissible a wife's testimony about her husband's "boastful" confession that he had raped his stepdaughter (her biological daughter) and his specific plans to have sexual intercourse with their two daughters. *Commonwealth v. Spetzer*, 813 A.2d 707 (Pa. 2002). "It would be perverse, indeed," wrote the court, "to indulge a fiction of marital harmony to shield statements which prove the declarant spouse's utter contempt for, and abuse of, the marital union." The court found that, under these circumstances, the communications were not confidential.

[b]   Common Law Marriage: Exception to Formality Requirements

IN RE ESTATE OF HALL
Ohio Court of Appeals
67 Ohio App. 3d 715, 588 N.E.2d 203 (1990)

STEPHENSON, JUDGE: . . .

The following facts . . . , many . . . undisputed, appear in . . . a transcript of proceedings two hundred pages in length embodying the testimony of twenty-two witnesses and forty-nine documentary exhibits for [Denise] and three for [Burnworth].

. . . . In 1986 both Denise and decedent [Alan] were separated from their respective spouses and began living together in June. . . . Divorce actions were then pending. In August 1986, Denise was divorced from her husband and on January 23, 1987, decedent was divorced from his wife. Thereafter, Denise and decedent continued to reside together and had a close relationship, not only working together but also spending the non-working hours together in social and other activities.

At a family outing on July 4, 1988, tragically, decedent accidentally drowned while swimming. On July 13, 1988, Randall G. Burnworth was appointed administrator of the estate, the application not setting forth the name of a surviving spouse. On August 2, 1988, [Denise] filed an application to remove [Burnworth] and appoint her since she was the common-law spouse. . . .

. . . [T]he court . . . denied the removal motion. The decision, *inter alia*, set forth findings as follows:

"Decedent and Denise started cohabiting in June 1986. . . . They cohabited continuously until decedent's untimely death.

"At no time after decedent's divorce did the parties enter into a civil marriage contract. However, according to Denise, they did plan to participate in a civil marriage ceremony after they finished remodeling decedent's house on the west side of Marietta.

"During the time they lived together they shared expenses. They each had separate checking accounts. Denise at times paid financial obligations which were solely those of the decedent from her own account. Although Denise named the decedent as beneficiary on her individual retirement account, on her private life insurance policy and on her employment life insurance policy, decedent did not reciprocate.

"They were employed at the same job site. They spent a great deal of their work time, as well as their leisure time together. They took vacations together; and while in Florida they purchased a time share interest in a condominium for one week per year. However, they signed the purchase contract in their individual names, making no reference to their marital status.

"They attempted to borrow money in November/December 1987 from the Marietta Savings and Loan Company for the purpose of remodeling decedent's house on the west side of Marietta. In this application, the parties held themselves out as being unmarried.

"On their 1987 federal income tax returns decedent and Denise listed their marital status as 'single' and not as 'married filing singly.'

"In September 1988, Denise filed an application for death benefits as beneficiary of decedent with the Plumbers & Pipefitters Union. On the application she listed herself as beneficiary but did not list herself as decedent's spouse.

"At no time after his divorce . . . did the decedent change or attempt to change the name of the beneficiary on any of his life insurance policies or pensions into Denise's name. The decedent in fact is reported to have made statements very near to the time of his death that he would never marry Denise and that he had aspirations of some day reconciling with his former wife.

"Decedent and Denise acted in some respects similarly to the way a married couple would act. Although some of their acquaintances thought they were married, others did not think they were married.

"The court finds that Denise A. Chancellor has failed to prove by clear and convincing evidence that she and the decedent entered a mutual agreement of marriage in the present; that they cohabited as husband and wife; and that they were treated and received as husband and wife in the community in which they lived."

The law of Ohio respecting establishment of common-law marriage is succinctly summarized in . . . *Nestor v. Nestor* (1984):

"A common law marriage is the marital joinder of a man and a woman without the benefit of formal papers or procedures. Such marriages are not favored in Ohio, but have long been recognized as lawful if certain elements or circumstances are found to be present.

. . . .

"'An agreement of marriage in praesenti when made by parties competent to contract, accompanied and followed by cohabitation as husband and wife, they being so treated and reputed in the community and circle in which they move, establishes a valid marriage at common law . . .'

"The fundamental requirement . . . is a meeting of the minds between the parties who enter into a mutual contract to presently take each other as man and wife. The agreement to marry in praesenti is the essential element of a common law marriage. Its absence precludes the establishment of such a relationship. . . .

"The contract of marriage in praesenti may be proven either by way of direct evidence which establishes the agreement, or by way of proof of cohabitation, acts, declarations, and the conduct of the parties and their recognized status in the community in which they reside. However, all of the essential elements to a common law marriage must be established by clear and convincing evidence.

". . . [T]estimony regarding cohabitation and community reputation tends to raise an inference of the marriage. This inference is given more or less strength according to the circumstances of the particular case. The inference is generally strengthened with the lapse of time during which the parties are living together and cohabiting as man and wife."

No evidence was adduced by [Denise] of an express agreement. . . . [She] sought to establish her claim . . . based upon the nature and continuing relationship of the parties. There was evidence . . . tending to establish by inference a common-law marriage. While the lower court's factual findings are supported in the record, there was also evidence of open cohabitation, the intermingling of finances, the joint purchase of property and stock, recognition of at least part of decedent's family as to a common-law marriage, including placement of [Denise]'s name on the tombstone as wife, and on occasion the introduction of [Denise] by decedent as his wife.

The thrust of [Denise's] argument . . . is that the court below erred in evaluating the evidence by application of a burden of proof greater than that of clear and convincing evidence. . . .

. . . .

We are not . . . persuaded that the decision of the court below applied an incorrect standard. . . .

. . . [W]e also conclude that there is probative and substantial evidence to support the judgment below.

. . . .

Finally, this writer approves of the statement by Justice William B. Brown writing in dissent in *Nestor* . . . :

"Moreover, I call upon the legislature, in this last quarter of the Twentieth Century, to act to abolish the antiquated institution of common law marriage in Ohio. The days of the walking preacher and of the bishop on horseback are long gone. As was stated in *In re Estate of Maynard* (1962):

' "Is it not an amazing fact, that, in a matter which so profoundly affects the dignity and stability of a family institution, society should be slow to take enlightened action? Surely, no legislative reform is more needed than clear and positive statutes declaring such loosely contracted unions null and void." ' "

For the reasons above set forth, the assignment of error is overruled and the judgment affirmed.

GREY, Judge, concurring.

I concur . . . but . . . cannot agree with the suggestion that common-law marriages no longer be recognized. The ultimate philosophical question . . . is should we have laws which reflect the way we want people to behave, or should we have laws which reflect the way they actually behave? Some common-law marriages are of long duration, and have brought stability and happiness into the lives of the parties. Whatever the reason parties do not choose a ceremonial marriage, the unmistakable fact of life is that there are many long-term common-law marriages, which are real marriages in every sense of the word. Common-law marriages occasionally cause a problem for the courts which have to decide whether or not a common-law marriage, in fact, exists. This is not a major problem . . . , particularly in light of the clear standards for deciding such a case. . . .

If we refuse to recognize these kinds of marriages, we will often work a terrible injustice. A woman may have lived with a man for forty years, held herself out as his wife, borne his children, helped him through the bad times, celebrated the good times, and done everything a good and faithful wife might have done. But when he dies, we will ignore the fact of their life together, deny her survivor benefits, her right to share in his estate, even her right to bury him, for in the eyes of the law, this helpmate of a lifetime is only a legal stranger. . . .

The issue is not whether common-law marriages are antiquated, because we still get them regularly. The question is whether we will continue to have the common decency to recognize them.

. . . .

NOTES

1. ***Status as Marriage.*** A common law marriage where recognized is not simply "living together." It is a real marriage which requires capacity to marry under the same regulations applicable to ceremonial marriage. For example, where a same-sex couple cannot create a ceremonial marriage, they likewise cannot contract a valid common law marriage. *DeSanto v. Barnsley*, 476 A.2d 952 (Pa. Super. 1984). Likewise, a common law marriage is not created when one party is under the age of consent for marriage. *Mueggenborg v. Walling*, 836 P.2d 112 (Okla. 1992). *But see In re J.M.H.*, 143 P.3d 1116 (Col. App. 2006) (common law marriages in state are governed by common law and not statute; thus, marriage of 15-year old is valid). However, an existing marriage by either party prevents creation of a valid common law marriage. *In re Fisher*, 176 N.W.2d 801 (Iowa 1970). There is no concept of "common law divorce" to parallel "common law marriage." If there has been a marriage (whether ceremonial or common law), death or divorce must dissolve it to free either party to marry again. *See, e.g., In re Estate of Stodola*, 519 N.W.2d 97 (Iowa App. 1994).

While common law marriage claims often are made to establish a share in a decedent's estate as in *Hall*, it is not the only occasion. The case may involve establishment of jurisdiction on which to base a divorce, *Smith v. Smith*, 966 A.2d 109 (R.I. 2009), invocation of the evidentiary marital privilege, *Bowler v. United*

States, 480 A.2d 678 (D.C. App. 1984), a claim for insurance (life or health) benefits as a member of the insured's family, *Whyte v. Blair*, 885 P.2d 791 (Utah 1994), death benefits under a scheme of government entitlements, or appointment as representative of a decedent's estate, *In re Estate of Ober*, 62 P.3d 1114 (Mont. 2003).

   2. ***History of Common Law Marriage.***   Traditionally, the sole requirement for a so-called common law marriage was an agreement to be married. *See Davis v. Stouffer*, 112 S.W. 282 (Mo. App. 1908); Lawrence Stone, Uncertain Unions & Broken Lives 10–35 (1995). Some argue this doctrine was developed in England before American colonization, Frederick Pollack & Frederic Maitland, History of English Law 368 (1898); others believe the early American jurists who recognized the doctrine were misreading the English precedents. The doctrine was fairly widely utilized. Chief Justice Gibson, in *Rodebaugh v. Sanks*, 2 Watts 9, 11 (Pa. 1833), wrote: "a rigid execution of [the marriage laws requiring a ceremony] would bastardize a vast majority of the children which have been born within the state for half a century."

   As American conditions changed, so did acceptance of common law marriage. Critics claim the doctrine encourages fraudulent assertion of marriage after a party's death (note *Hall*'s facts), condones vice, frustrates state interests behind formality requirements and debases ceremonial marriage. Common law marriage is also described as unnecessary. As one court put it, "Cost is certainly not prohibitory, and a plethora of public and quasi-public officials are available to solemnize such an important and socially significant occasion." *Johnson v. Young*, 372 A.2d 992, 996 (D.C. 1977); *see also People v. Lucero*, 747 P.2d 660 (Colo. 1987) (public acknowledgment required to "guard against fraudulent claims"). It is also argued that abolition facilitates administrative efficiency and reduces litigation. That is, limitation of marriage to the formal, ceremonial marriage is alleged to serve the same purposes as the Statute of Frauds does in requiring certain important agreements to be written.

   Others defend the institution. In addition to justice-based arguments offered by the *Hall* concurrence, others assert fraud can be defeated by a heightened burden of proof and Dead Man's statutes limiting evidence about communications with people now dead. As for the promotion of vice, Clark argued that recognition of such relationships actually reduces vice by accepting its legitimacy. Clark, *supra*, § 2.4, at 60.

   A modern commentator has argued for the doctrine's return

> because it protects the interests of women, especially poor women and women of color, more effectively than any of the theories suggested to address the problems created by its absence. Most of the original reasons for abolishing common law marriage — fears of fraud, protection of morality and the family, racism, eugenics, and health-related reasons — do not withstand scrutiny; and other arguments, based on administrative convenience, are outweighed by more important values. [N]onrecognition . . . hurts most those women who are most vulnerable. . . .

Cynthia Bowman, *A Feminist Proposal to Bring Back Common Law Marriage*, 75 ORE. L. REV. 709, 779 (1996); *see also* Sonya Garza, *Common Law Marriage: A Proposal for the Revival of a Dying Doctrine*, 40 NEW ENG. L. REV. 541 (2006) (argues contract and "conscriptive" approaches which rely on agreements by the parties and imposition of rules on cohabitants by the state, respectively, are inadequate); Charlotte Goldberg, *The Schemes of Adventuresses: The Abolition and Revival of Common-Law Marriage*, 13 WM. & MARY J. OF WOMEN & L. 483 (2007) (asserts recognition of cohabitant rights, see Chapter ___. Section ___, has revived common law marriage in different form; concludes courts use "very traditional model for marriage for determining whether a cohabitant relationship is enough like marriage to provide . . . property rights"); John McCormack, *Title to Property, Title to Marriage: The Social Foundation of Adverse Possession and Common Law Marriage*, 42 VAL. U.L. REV. 461 (2008) (argues both property and family doctrines derive from a desire to protect parties' expectations and require communication of such an expectation).

Texas tries to avoid the marital status ambiguities which constitute an objection to common law marriage by allowing registration of the marriage. TEX. FAM. CODE ANN. §§ 2.402, 2.403, 2.404 (registering parties must swear that they agreed to be married, live together as husband and wife, and hold themselves out to others as married). Such registration is not required however; Texas also recognizes unregistered common law marriages. *See* TEX. FAM. CODE § 2.401(a)(2).

3. *Present Status.* Only 10 states and the District of Columbia currently clearly recognize common law marriages contracted within their borders (Alabama, Colorado, Iowa, Kansas, Montana, Oklahoma, Rhode Island, South Carolina, Texas and Utah). Ohio, where *Hall* was decided, has since taken the suggestion of the majority and abolished the doctrine. Pennsylvania is the most recent state to reject common law marriage via legislation effective January 1, 2005. 23 PA. C.S. § 1103. The legislative action came shortly after prodding from the state's Commonwealth Court, an intermediate court which prospectively abolished the doctrine. *PNC Bank Corp. v. Workers' Comp. Appeal Bd. (Stamos)*, 831 A.2d 1269 (Pa. Commw. 2003). All the states recently abolishing common law marriage preserve relationships created before abolition. *See* GA. CODE § 19-3-1.1; IDAHO CODE § 32-201; OHIO REVISED CODE ANNOT. § 3105.12. New Hampshire retains common law marriage but adds an additional requirement to the normal common law marriage rule: a three year period during which the couple cohabited and were reputed to be husband and wife. N.H. REV. STAT. 457:39 (a couple that has cohabited and acknowledged "each other as husband and wife, and [were] generally reputed to be such, for . . . 3 years" before the death of one of them, are "deemed to have been legally married").

By contrast, Utah relatively recently determined to accept common law marriage, in a 1987 statute. UTAH CODE ANN. § 30-1-4.5. The law requires official recognition by a court or agency, which can occur in the context of a suit predicated on the marriage's existence, such as litigation against an insurer claiming coverage as a family member of the insured. *See Whyte v. Blair*, 885 P.2d 791 (Utah 1994). One commentator believes the statute was aimed at eliminating welfare claims by mothers with *de facto* husbands they had never formally married. Ryan Tenney, Note, *Tom Green, Common-Law Marriage, and the Illegality of Putative*

Polygamy, 17 BYU J. Pub. l. 141, 148 (2002). For an encyclopedic treatment of the history (tracing back to Roman law) and jurisprudence of common law marriage, including international and comparative aspects, see Goran Lind, *Common Law Marriage: A Legal Institution for Cohabitation* (2008).

4. *Current Requirements.* *Hall* states the usual modern requirements in states that continue to allow common law marriage. While older cases required only an agreement to be married, *Hall* not only imposes a high evidentiary burden of proof on the proponent ("clear and convincing evidence"), but also adds to the substantive elements by requiring public declaration and continuous cohabitation. *See also Krier v. Krier,* 676 So. 2d 1335 (Ala. Civ. App. 1996); *Chandler v. Central Oil Corp.,* 853 P.2d 649 (Kan. 1993); *Winfield v. Renfro,* 821 S.W.2d 640 (Tex. App. 1991) (finding insufficient evidence of holding out to the community); *Copeland v. Richardson,* 551 So. 2d 353 (Ala. 1989). A few states are less stringent. *See Commonwealth v. Wilson,* 672 A.2d 293 (Pa. 1996) (requiring only agreement, with cohabitation and holding out raising presumption of agreement); *East v. East,* 536 A.2d 1103 (D.C. App. 1988) (rejecting requirement of clear and convincing evidence and adopting ordinary preponderance standard). Contrary to popular belief, however, no state but New Hampshire (see its newly-enacted rule, described in Note 3 above) prescribes a minimum cohabitation period.

A desire to thwart fraudulent claims causes courts to emphasize more "public" kind of evidence, such as cohabitation and representation of marriage to others, rather than the more easily fabricated claim that the parties agreed to be married. At least one court has held proof of cohabitation and holding out *eliminates* the need for agreement evidence. *Owens v. Owens,* 466 S.E.2d 373, 375 (S.C. App. 1995). Indeed, *Owens* refused to characterize the wife's testimony that "his mother would die and he knew it if he ever married me, but he said if he ever married anybody it would be me" as an express disavowal of agreement.

5. *Impediment Removal.* In *Hall,* plaintiff and decedent began their relationship when both were already married and, thus, ineligible to marry. Suppose they also had satisfied the objective requirements of a common law marriage (agreement, cohabitation and holding out to community) *before* they were both free to remarry on January 23, 1987 (when the second divorce was entered). Would a common law marriage have arisen between Denise and Alan immediately at the point of removal of the impediment to their marriage?

Treatment of such cases depends upon the parties' knowledge. If either party was ignorant of the impediment at the creation of the relationship, a marriage is created immediately upon the impediment's removal. *See, e.g., Bowlin v. Bowlin,* 285 S.E.2d 273 (N.C. App. 1981). On the other hand, if both knew of the impediment at the inception of their relationship, many courts require proof of a new agreement after the impediment's removal. *See, e.g., Johns v. Johns,* 420 S.E.2d 856 (S.C. App. 1992) ("A relationship illicit at its inception does not ripen into a common law marriage once the impediment . . . is removed. . . . [T]he parties must enter into a common law marriage after the impediment is removed."). Some courts, acknowledging the unlikelihood of a post-removal agreement, do not require a new agreement, finding marriage if the parties continue to cohabit and hold themselves out as married. *See, e.g., In re Estate of Alcorn*, 868 P.2d 629 (Mont. 1994).

6. *Conflict of Law and Common Law Marriage.* Common law marriage is more important than the short list of recognizing states in Note 2 might suggest because of the general conflicts rule that a marriage valid where contracted is recognized elsewhere.

Three basic fact patterns appear in the case law. In the first (the "circle" situation), two people agree to be married, cohabit and hold themselves out as married in a non-recognizing jurisdiction. Then, after spending time in a recognizing jurisdiction, they return home. At some later point (often the death of one "spouse"), the home state must decide if the couple was married.

In this situation, many courts find a marriage, often despite merely ephemeral connection to the common law marriage state. *See, e.g., Katebi v. Hooshiari*, 288 A.D.2d 188 (2001) (family vacations to common law marriage state are sufficient); *Carpenter v. Carpenter*, 617 N.Y.S.2d 903 (App. Div. 1994) (two visits of no more than a week each occurring 20 years apart); *Blaw-Knox Construction Equip. Co. v. Morris*, 596 A.2d 679 (Md. Spec. App. 1991) (two-day visit); *Renshaw v. Heckler*, 787 F.2d 50 (2d Cir. 1986) (eight two-day visits en route to vacations elsewhere); *Coney v. R.S.R. Corp.*, 563 N.Y.S.2d 211 (App. Div. 1990) (three-day visit). When a court in a non-common law marriage state finds a marriage, what is it saying about the forum's expressed policy against such relationships? Note that most cases recognizing marriage in these circumstances involve lengthy relationships and/or a particularly deep-pocketed defendant such as the government or an insurance company.

Some cases refusing to recognize marriage here frankly ground their analysis in what is described as a strong forum policy against common law marriage. *See, e.g., Lynch v. Bowen*, 681 F. Supp. 506 (N.D. Ill. 1988) (applying Illinois law); *Hesington v. Hesington*, 640 S.W.2d 824 (Mo. App. 1982). Other courts reject the marriage claim through application (and sometimes distortion) of the common law marriage state's law. *See Smith v. Anderson*, 821 So. 2d 323 (Fla. App. 2002) (finding insufficient connection to Georgia to support finding of common law marriage there); *In re Estate of Landolfi*, 283 App. Div. 2d 497 (2001) (rejecting alleged marriage created by brief visits to Pennsylvania for lack of agreement there); *Estate of Burroughs*, 486 N.W.2d 113 (Mich. App. 1992) (rejecting Texas common law marriage for lack of cohabitation); *Goldin v. Goldin*, 426 A.2d 410 (Md. Spec. App. 1981) (lack of intent to marry in common law state bars recognition).

Two other fact patterns ought to be noted. In contrast to the circular situation above, these scenarios can be described as "chains." In the first, a couple, having contracted a common law marriage in a recognizing state, moves to a non-recognizing state where the marriage's validity is litigated. Almost all courts recognize the marriage here, particularly if there was a significant connection to the common law state. *See Johnson v. Lincoln Square Properties*, 571 So. 2d 541 (Fla. App. 1990); *Delaney v. Delaney*, 405 A.2d 91 (Conn. Super. 1979); *Mission Ins. Co. v. Industrial Comm'n*, 559 P.2d 1085 (Ariz. 1976). In contrast, a recent Virginia decision rejected a claim of marriage where the couple stayed one night each in two common law marriage states during a trip. *Kelderhaus v. Kelderhaus*, 467 S.E.2d

303 (Va. App. 1996) (recognition here would "distort and trivialize" the doctrine recognized by common law marriage states).

The final pattern reverses the second one. In *Travers v. Reinhardt*, 205 U.S. 423 (1907), the couple lived together in several non-common law marriage states, then moved to New Jersey, then a recognizing state. There was no proof of any new agreement in New Jersey, but the Supreme Court found a marriage, based on an inferred continuing agreement. While *Travers* might simply reflect an earlier era when common law marriage enjoyed wider acceptance, more recent cases also adopt the *Travers* result. *See, e.g., Marriage of Winegard*, 257 N.W.2d 609 (Iowa 1977). *But see Callen v. Callen*, 620 S.E.2d 59 (S.C. 2005) (parties lived in several non-recognizing states before moving to recognizing forum, parties must reach new agreement to be married).

[c]   Putative Spouse Doctrine: Form over Substance or Substance over Form?

CALIFORNIA FAMILY CODE

§ 2251. If a determination is made that a marriage is void or voidable and the court finds that either party or both parties believed in good faith that the marriage was valid, the court shall:

(1) Declare the party or parties to have the status of a putative spouse.

(2) If the division of property is in issue, divide . . . that property acquired during the union which would have been community property or quasi-community property if the union had not been void or voidable. . . . This property is known as "quasi-marital property."

§ 2254. The court may, during the pendency of a proceeding for nullity of marriage or upon judgment of nullity of a marriage, order a party to pay for the support of the other party . . . if the party for whose benefit the order is made is found to be a putative spouse.

IN RE ESTATE OF VARGAS
California Court of Appeal
36 Cal. App. 3d 714, 111 Cal. Rptr. 779 (1974)

FLEMING, ASSOCIATE JUSTICE.

For 24 years Juan Vargas lived a double life as husband and father to two separate families, neither of which knew of the other's existence. This terrestrial paradise came to an end in 1969 when Juan died intestate in an automobile accident. In subsequent heirship proceedings the probate court divided his estate equally between the two wives. Juan's first wife Mildred appeals, contending that the evidence did not establish Juan's second wife Josephine as a putative spouse, and that even if Josephine were considered a putative spouse an equal division of the estate was erroneous.

Mildred . . . and Juan married in 1929, raised three children, and lived together continuously in Los Angeles until Juan's death in 1969. From 1945 . . . Juan never spent more than a week or 10 days away from home. They acquired no substantial assets until after 1945.

Josephine . . . met Juan in 1942 while employed in his exporting business. They married in Las Vegas in February 1945. . . . Josephine knew Juan had been previously married, but Juan assured her he had acquired a divorce. In July 1945 they moved into a home in West Los Angeles and there raised a family of four children. After 1949 Juan no longer spent his nights at home, explaining to Josephine that he spent the nights in Long Beach in order to be close to his business, but he and Josephine continued to engage in sexual relations until his death in 1969. He visited Josephine and their children every weekday for dinner, spent time with them weekends, supported the family, and exercised control over its affairs as husband and father. Throughout the years Josephine continued to perform secretarial work for Juan's business at home without pay.

The foregoing evidence amply supports the court's finding that Josephine was a putative spouse. An innocent participant who has duly solemnized a matrimonial union which is void because of some legal infirmity acquires the status of putative spouse. Although Josephine's marriage was void because Juan was still married to Mildred, Josephine, according to her testimony, married Juan in the good-faith belief he was divorced from his first wife. Her testimony was not inherently improbable; her credibility was a question for determination by the trial court; and court acceptance of her testimony established her status as a putative spouse.

The more difficult question involves the equal division of Juan's estate between Mildred and Josephine.

California courts have relied on at least two legal theories to justify the award of an interest in a decedent's estate to a putative spouse. The theory of "quasi-marital property" equates property rights acquired during a putative marriage with community property rights acquired during a legal marriage. Subsequent to the time of Juan's death this theory was codified in Civil Code section 4452: [quoted earlier in its renumbered form].

A second legal theory treats the putative marriage as a partnership: "In effect, the innocent putative spouse was in partnership or a joint enterprise with her spouse, contributing her services — and in this case, her earnings — to the common enterprise. Thus, their accumulated property was held in effect in tenancy-in-common in equal shares. Upon death of the husband, only his half interest is considered as community property, to which the rights of the lawful spouse attach." (*Sousa v. Freitas*)

In practice, these sometimes-conflicting theories have proved no more than convenient explanations to justify reasonable results, for when the theories do not fit the facts, courts have customarily resorted to general principles of equity. . . . For example, in *Brown v. Brown*, the court found that a legal wife's acquiescence in a putative wife's 28-year marriage equitably estopped the legal wife from claiming any interest in the community property.

. . . [T]he laws regulating succession and the disposition of marital property are not designed to cope with the extraordinary circumstance of purposeful bigamy at the expense of two innocent parties.[2]

The laws of marital succession . . . do not provide for contingencies arising during the course of felonious activity. For this reason resort to equitable principles becomes particularly appropriate here. . . . Equity need not wait upon precedent "but will assert itself in those situations where right and justice would be defeated but for its intervention.'. For example, in *Estate of Krone*, where the putative husband died intestate and there was no legal wife, the court awarded the entire quasi-marital estate to the putative wife, even though the putative wife had no legal claim to the husband's share of the quasi-marital estate.

In the present case, depending on which statute or legal theory is applied, both Mildred, as legal spouse, and Josephine, as putative spouse, have valid or plausible claims to at least half, perhaps three-quarters, possibly all, of Juan's estate. The court found that both wives contributed in indeterminable amounts and proportions to the accumulations of the community. Since statutes and judicial decisions provide no sure guidance for the resolution of the controversy, the probate court cut the Gordian knot of competing claims and divided the estate equally between the two wives, presumably on the theory that innocent wives of practicing bigamists are entitled to equal shares of property accumulated during the active phase of the bigamy. No injury has been visited upon third parties, and the wisdom of Solomon is not required to perceive the justice of the result.

The judgment is affirmed.

NOTES

1. **Vargas "II" (or "III"?).**   While *Vargas* reads like a law professor's dream hypothetical, news reports of such situations surface with some frequency. For example:

> The husband of a South Tampa divorce lawyer is headed to prison after pleading no contest to the bigamy charge she brought against him. But the women conned by George W. Dumstorf Jr. aren't happy about the terms of his punishment. . . . Dumstorf's sentence will run concurrent with the 27-month prison term he received on Oct. 31 after pleading guilty to a federal bank fraud charge. . . . He will serve the time in federal, not state, prison, which his victims and their families said amounts to no punishment at all for the bigamy charge.
>
> "He'll be in a country club for 27 months," said Valerie Gaines, whose mother, Judy Howell, was married to Dumstorf for 16 years. . . . For decades, he held himself out to be a high-level military and NASA man. But his three wives and a longtime girlfriend eventually learned that he was neither of those things, nor was he lawfully divorced from his first wife when he married two more times.

---

[2] "[I]n most, if not all, of the reported decisions involving a putative spouse, the supposed husband did in fact separate from his lawful wife" (Luther and Luther, [24 Hastings L.J.] at p. 318.)

Howell, Dumstorf's second wife, divorced him in 2000 after suspecting him of bigamy. He beat the accusation with the help of his divorce attorney, Martha-Irene Weed. Four years later, Weed herself married Dumstorf in Panama City Beach. Then she, too, accused him of bigamy after learning that he had been married since 1960 to another woman, the mother of his seven children.

Colleen Jenkins, *Bigamy Case Won't Go to Trial*, St. Petersburg Times (Florida), Nov. 19, 2008, p. 3B. In 1991, upon the death of Dr. Norman J. Lewiston, a prominent lung specialist at Stanford University, it was discovered that he had continuing relationships with three wives. His first spouse, who married him in 1960, lived in Palo Alto. He married a second spouse in 1985 and shared a house with her in the nearby town of Los Altos. A third spouse, who married him in 1989, had a home with him in San Diego. None of the spouses knew of the others before his death and each assumed that a very busy professional life, including travel, accounted for the doctor's failure to spend much time with her. His third wife, demonstrating some sense of perspective, commented, "The only thing I want to inherit is his frequent-flier miles." Rex Dalton, *Bigamy: Professor Led Full Life; Multiple Wives Kept Stanford's Medical Pioneer on the Move*, San Diego Union-Tribune, Oct. 8, 1991, p. A-1; *see also* Pete Donohue, *DA: Plumber With 2 Wives Wrenches Law*, N.Y. Daily News, Nov. 20, 1996 (defendant had one wife in Queens and another in Manhattan and allegedly "used the odd hours of a plumber on call to conceal a double life"); Bill Muller, *"I Still Have Feelings for Him, That's Why I Feel Betrayed"; Bigamist's First Wife Tries Hard to Forgive*, Ariz. Republic, Dec. 29, 1994, p. B1 (defendant "juggled" four wives in three states for several months; he "kept a log and took notes during conversations" to keep track of the stories he told each wife).

2. *Putative Spouse Doctrine.* The putative spouse doctrine exists primarily in states with a civil law tradition, protecting a party ignorant of an impediment to the marriage's validity. For other cases applying the doctrine, see *Williams v. Williams*, 97 P.3d 1124 (Nev. 2004) (court upheld division of property based on putative marriage, but held that a putative marriage generally will not support alimony); *Alfonso v. Gravois*, 739 So.2d 946 (La. App. 1999) (dealing with property division); *Xiong v. Xiong*, 648 N.W.2d 900 (Wis. 2002) (wrongful death); *Estate of DePasse*, 97 Cal. App. 4th 92 (2002) (court rejects claim of putative spousehood where both parties were aware their "marriage" ceremony lacked required license); *Kindle v. Kindle*, 629 So. 2d 176 (Fla. App. 1993) (permanent alimony); *Garduno v. Garduno*, 760 S.W.2d 735 (Tex. App. 1988) (property division). The Model Marriage and Divorce Act's optional putative spouse section (§ 209) creates property division and maintenance rights after termination of the relationship. Some non-community property states have adopted this provision. *See, e.g.,* Ill. Ann. Stat., ch. 750, § 5/305; Minn. Stat. Ann. § 518.055; Mont. Code Ann. § 40-1-404. The putative spouse is also protected under the Social Security statute. 42 U.S.C. § 416(h)(1)(B)(i).

Several states legislatively recognize putative spouse claims: in wrongful death actions, Cal. Civ. Proc. Code § 377.60(b); worker's compensation benefits, Cal. Labor Code § 3503; division of property in non-death termination of the relationship, La. Civ. Code art. 96; and alimony, Colo. Rev. Stat. § 14-2-111.

3. *Good Faith Belief.* Putative spousehood terminates upon a party's loss of good faith belief that he or she is married. *Welch v. State*, 83 Cal. App. 4th 1374 (2000). What *is* good faith? In *Marriage of Flores*, 252 Cal. Rptr. 687 (Ct. App. 1988), the parties were first cousins who had gone through a wedding ceremony 21 years earlier after being told by court personnel that such a marriage was prohibited. The court held there could be no good faith belief in the validity of the marriage, but affirmed an alimony order on an estoppel theory. In *In re Vryonis*, 248 Cal. Rptr. 807 (Ct. App. 1988), the court held that a belief that the couple had been married according to Islamic law in a "Muta" ceremony was insufficient. Holding good faith requires a belief in a legally-recognized marriage, the court held "(w)here there has been no attempted compliance with the procedural requirements of a valid marriage, and where the usual indicia of marriage and conduct consistent with a valid marriage are absent, a belief in the existence of a valid marriage, although sincerely held, would be unreasonable and therefore lacking in good faith." *Id.* at 813. For recent cases exploring the good faith requirement, see *Thomason v. Thomason*, 776 So. 2d 553 (La. App. 2000) (upholding claim of putative spousehood where parties obtained license and "went to a man" though there was no ceremony); *Kelderhaus v. Kelderhaus*, 467 S.E.2d 303 (Va. App. 1996) (rejecting claim of putative spousehood under California law). Several cases applying Louisiana law impose a duty to investigate when informed of a partner's prior marriage. *See Schaefer v. Schaefer*, 379 So. 2d 864 (La. App. 1980).

There is authority to support recognition of a putative common law marriage in a state which generally recognizes common law marriage. *Garduno v. Garduno*, 760 S.W.2d 735 (Tex. App. 1988) (finding, however, no good faith in instant case). *But see Welch v. State*, 83 Cal. App. 4th 1374 (2000) (despite 30-year relationship, appellant's "subjective belief that she was married, even if honestly held, does not constitute good faith" in non-common law marriage state).

4. *Putative Spousehood vs. Common Law Marriage.* A common law marriage is a marriage, while a putative marriage is not. Thus, common law marriage is impossible where the parties are ineligible for marriage, as in *Vargas*. On the other hand, divorce is unnecessary to terminate a putative marriage; a marriage by Josephine after "marrying" Juan in 1945 would have been valid. A recent case contrasted the two doctrines by noting that a common law spouse can invoke the marital testimonial privilege, while a putative spouse cannot. *Weaver v. State*, 855 S.W.2d 116 (Tex. App. 1993). Note also that the putative spouse doctrine would offer an alternative remedy for violations of the formality requirements (e.g., failure to obtain a marriage license).where the rule violation made the marriage void or voidable. An innocent "spouse" who believed in good faith that a valid marriage resulted from the ceremony would qualify as a putative spouse.

5. *Lawful vs. Putative Spouse.* Competing claims by a lawful and a putative spouse may arise in connection with an estate, as in *Vargas*, as well as in other circumstances. There may, for example, be competitive wrongful death actions, or life insurance claims. The equal division adopted in *Vargas*, while attractive on those facts, would not always be appropriate. Consider, for example, a case in which decedent's legal spouse split from decedent after 3 years, whereupon decedent moved in with the putative spouse and they lived together for 35 years until death. Section 209 of the MMDA, the model for most current statutes recognizing putative spousehood, provides:

> If there is a legal spouse or other putative spouses, rights acquired by a putative spouse do not supersede the rights of the legal spouse or those acquired by other putative spouses, but the court shall apportion property, maintenance, and support rights among the claimants as appropriate in the circumstances and in the interests of justice.

6. *The Presumption of the Validity of the Latest Marriage.* Although Josephine, Juan's second "wife" in *Vargas*, claimed putative spousehood, she might have argued her marriage was valid, utilizing a well-known evidentiary presumption — the presumption of the validity of the latest marriage. This presumption, along with such family law doctrines as the putative spouse concept and recognition of cohabitational contracts (*see* Chapter 9) operate in tension with the broadly-stated monogamy principle, limiting people to one spouse at a time. *See* Section A[2][c][iii], *infra*.

There are several recurring fact patterns in which this presumption is utilized. Common are situations where two individuals both seek: life insurance benefits, *Bailey-Mason v. Mason*, 122 S.W.3d 894 (Tex. App. 2003); retirement death benefits, *United States Steel & Carnegie Pension Fund v. Sneed*, 2007 U.S. Dist. LEXIS 3889 (N.D. Ind., Jan. 17, 2007); Social Security death benefits, *McKnight v. Schweiker*, 516 F. Supp. 1102 (D. Md. 1981); intestate succession rights, *Powell v. Estate of Fletcher*, 128 P.3d 670 (Wyo. 2006); or rights under a will, *Succession of Jones*, 6 So. 3d 331 (La. Ct. App. 2009) (court rejects presumption's existence). Occasionally, the second spouse seeks annulment, or defends a divorce suit, claiming the "marriage"was bigamous. *See, e.g., Callaway v. Callaway*, 739 So. 2d 1134 (Ala. Civ. App. 1999); *Loera v. Loera*, 815 S.W.2d 910 (Tex. App. 1991) (refusal to annul second marriage because of failure to rebut the presumption of legitimacy). In *Carr v. Carr*, 724 So. 2d 937 (Miss. App. 1998), a father asserted the presumption to defend his second marriage's validity in a custody action in which his first wife sought to limit visitation based on the second marriage's invalidity. The appellate court upheld a finding that the presumption had been rebutted, but also found that the father's non-marital status did not affect his visitation rights.

The presumption is said to be based on the principle that the "law presumes innocence, not criminality (bigamy); morality, not immorality; and marriage, not concubinage," *Sneed, supra; Grey v. Heckler*, 721 F.2d 41 (2d Cir. 1983), and requires the party attacking the later marriage to bear the burden of proof. Thus, the party asserting bigamy faces the difficult task of proving a negative: nondissolution of the first marriage. Given our society's mobility and the ease of divorce, this can be time-consuming and expensive. It is often made more difficult by judicial imposition of a heightened standard of proof: "to a moral certainty," *McKnight, supra;* "so cogent and conclusive as to fairly preclude any other result," *Smith v. Weir*, 387 So. 2d 761 (Miss. 1980); or "strong, distinct, satisfactory, and conclusive," *Johnson v. Young*, 372 A.2d 992 (D.C. 1977). The presumption has been described as "one of the strongest, if not the strongest, known to law," *Estate of Loveless*, 64 S.W. 3d 564 (Tex. App. 2001); *Powell v. Fletcher*, 128 P.3d 670 (Wyo. 2006), which increases as the length of the second marriage increases. *Lambertini v. Lambertini*, 655 So. 2d 142 (Fla. App. 1995); *Stokes v. Heckler*, 773 F.2d 990 (8th Cir. 1985).

For example, the presumption has been found unrebutted by testimony by Wife-1 that she had not filed for divorce and had received no notice of a divorce action. *In re Estate of Lucas*, 909 S.W.2d 365 (Mo. App. 1995). Likewise, failing to find a divorce record in the first marriage's domiciliary state has been found insufficient because there might have been a divorce in another state or country. *Croskey v. Ford Motor Co.*, 2002 U.S. Dist. LEXIS 8824 (S.D.N.Y., May 6, 2002) (applying Michigan law); *Brown v. Brown*, 57 S.W.3d 354 (Mo. App. 2001).

Some cases describe a weaker presumption. For example, in some states the introduction of any rebuttal evidence eliminates the presumption, making the question of which marriage is valid a simple fact question. *See, e.g., Hewitt v. Firestone Tire & Rubber Co.*, 490 F. Supp. 1358 (E.D. Va. 1980); *Claveria v. Claveria*, 615 S.W.2d 164 (Tex. 1981). In Georgia, the attacker need prove only that both parties to the first marriage were alive at the time of the second marriage; the defender of the second marriage must then prove dissolution. *See, e.g., Scott v. Jefferson*, 331 S.E.2d 1 (Ga. App. 1985). Courts sometimes acknowledge that appealing facts may weaken the presumption. Thus, in *In re O'Rourke*, 246 N.W.2d 461 (Minn. 1976), the court found the presumption inapplicable where the second marriage occurred only four months before the litigation and produced no children. At least one court has rejected the presumption altogether, writing "[w]here . . . both marriages have been lawfully solemnized and the record is silent as to whether there has been a divorce . . . there is a presumption that the status of the parties to the first marriage continues. . . ." *Estate of Bajurczak*, 742 N.E.2d 1191 (Ohio App. 2000).

Theoretically, the presumption would be available in any case, such as *Vargas*, where a person had contracted more than one marriage. The fact that courts (and apparently litigants) routinely ignore the presumption in such cases (*Vargas* omits any reference) suggests many trial courts ignore the "rule" of a strong presumption and apply a weaker version. Nevertheless, several recent cases (cited earlier in this Note) restate the strong version of the presumption.

For an article canvassing the cases in the area and discussing issues such as the rationale for the presumption, its relationship to other family law presumptions, the burden of proof and how it is carried, etc., see Peter Swisher & Melanie Jones, *The Last-in-Time Marriage Presumption*, 29 FAM. L.Q. 409 (1995).

PROBLEMS

Problem 2-1. In 1981, Harry married Clara in a church wedding. They split up in 1991, but because both abhorred the notion of divorce, neither obtained one. In 2007, Harry fell in love with next-door neighbor Wanda, an unmarried individual. During courtship, Harry told Wanda of the prior marriage. Wanda asked "Where is your former spouse." The reply was, "not, sure; I think Clara left town."

In early 2008, Harry and Wanda marry before a minister. They obtained a license as required by state law, but failed to wait the prescribed three days because they were in a hurry to get on with their honeymoon. On the way to the airport after the ceremony, Harry was killed in an accident. Wanda seeks advice as to the possible claims against Harry's estate. Harry died intestate but with 1,000 acres of prime farmland and investments worth $500,000. In your investigation, you discover all the above facts, plus the fact that Clara never left town after the separation from Harry. Your jurisdiction recognizes common law marriage and the putative spouse doctrine. What theories might you offer on Wanda's behalf? How do you think the court would respond to these theories?

Problem 2-2.   Alice and Bob were married ceremonially in 1989. In 1994, Alice filed for divorce. Bob signed a voluntary appearance in the law suit and signed a property settlement agreement. Notice of the hearing was mailed to Bob at the home address. Neither Bob nor anybody representing him appeared at the hearing where the divorce was granted. After the divorce, both parties lived together for another 14 years, holding themselves out as husband and wife with three children.

After splitting up in 2008, Bob comes to you as a client, seeking representation in a divorce action against Alice. Your research reveals the 1994 divorce. When you ask Bob about this, the response is "I signed some papers back then when we were having trouble. Alice, who is an attorney, handled all the business stuff in our marriage. After telling me of the divorce, Alice then told me it had been dismissed." Bob denies ever having received any notice of a divorce hearing, noting that because of Bob's strange working hours, Alice always retrieved the mail. You also discover that a large amount of property was obtained between 1994 and 2008. Alice earned considerably more money than Bob and virtually all property was titled in Alice's name. Your jurisdiction has the following statute, which was enacted in 1991:

> When the court finds that a party entered into the contract of marriage in good faith supposing the other to be capable of contracting, and the marriage is declared a nullity, such fact shall be entered in the decree and the court may order such innocent party compensated as in the case of dissolution of marriage, including an award for costs and attorney fees.

How will you argue on behalf of your client in seeking to claim a portion of the assets titled in Alice's name? What responses do you expect from the other side?

[2]   Substantive Requirements

[a]   Constitutional Restraints Upon Substantive Requirements

ZABLOCKI v. REDHAIL
United States Supreme Court
434 U.S. 374 (1978)

MR. JUSTICE MARSHALL delivered the opinion of the Court.

At issue . . . is the constitutionality of a Wisconsin statute . . . which provides that members of a certain class of Wisconsin residents may not marry . . . without first obtaining a court order granting permission to marry. The class is . . . any

"Wisconsin resident having minor issue not in his custody and which he is under obligation to support by any court order or judgment." . . . [C]ourt permission cannot be granted unless the marriage applicant submits proof of compliance with the support obligation and, in addition, demonstrates that the children covered by the support order "are not then and are not likely thereafter to become public charges." No marriage license may lawfully be issued in Wisconsin to a person covered by the statute, except upon court order; any marriage entered into [in violation of the statute] is declared void; and persons acquiring marriage licenses in violation of the section are subject to criminal penalties. . . .

[A 1972 judgment found Redhail father of a baby girl and ordered child support. In 1974, having failed to pay support for over two years, his marriage license application was denied for failure to satisfy the statute. It was stipulated that the child, who was on welfare, would have been "a public charge even if [Redhail] had been current in his support payments. . . ."]

[The trial court] analyzed the . . . statute under the Equal Protection Clause and concluded that "strict scrutiny" was required because the classification . . . infringed upon a fundamental right, the right to marry. The court then proceeded to evaluate the interests advanced by the State to justify the statute, and, finding that the classification was not necessary for the achievement of those interests, the court held the statute invalid. . . .

[The state] brought this direct appeal. . . . We agree . . . that the statute violates the Equal Protection Clause.

II

In evaluating [the statute] under the Equal Protection Clause, "we must first determine what burden of justification the classification created thereby must meet, by looking to the nature of the classification and the individual interests affected." *Memorial Hospital v. Maricopa County*. Since our past decisions make clear that the right to marry is of fundamental importance, and since the classification at issue here significantly interferes with the exercise of that right, we believe that "critical examination" of the state interests advanced in support of the classification is required.

The leading decision . . . on the right to marry is *Loving v. Virginia*, 388 U.S. 1 (1967). In that case, an interracial couple who had been convicted of violating Virginia's miscegenation laws challenged the statutory scheme on both equal protection and due process grounds. The Court's opinion could have rested solely on the ground that the statutes discriminated on the basis of race in violation of the Equal Protection Clause. But the Court went on to hold that the laws arbitrarily deprived the couple of a fundamental liberty protected by the Due Process Clause, the freedom to marry. The Court's language on the latter point bears repeating:

"The freedom to marry has long been recognized as one of the vital personal rights essential to the orderly pursuit of happiness by free men.

"Marriage is one of the 'basic civil rights of man,' fundamental to our very existence and survival." *Id.*, at 12, quoting *Skinner v. Oklahoma ex rel.*

Williamson, 316 U.S. 535, 541 (1942)."

[Justice Marshall here discussed prior Supreme Court authority dealing with privacy, procreative decisionmaking and family autonomy, discussed in Chapter 9, *infra.* No prior case squarely held there was a right to enter marriage, but there was some dicta to that effect.]

It is not surprising that the decision to marry has been placed on the same level of importance as decisions relating to procreation, childbirth, child rearing, and family relationships. As the facts of this case illustrate, it would make little sense to recognize a right of privacy with respect to other matters of family life and not with respect to the decision to enter the relationship that is the foundation of the family in our society. The woman [Redhail] desired to marry had a fundamental right to seek an abortion of their expected child, or to bring the child into life to suffer the myriad social, if not economic, disabilities that the status of illegitimacy brings. Surely, a decision to marry and raise the child in a traditional family setting must receive equivalent protection. And, [Redhail]'s right to procreate means anything at all, it must imply some right to enter the only relationship in which the State of Wisconsin allows sexual relations legally to take place.

[W]e do not mean to suggest that every state regulation which relates in any way to the incidents of or prerequisites for marriage must be subjected to rigorous scrutiny. To the contrary, reasonable regulations that do not significantly interfere with decisions to enter into the marital relationship may legitimately be imposed. The statutory classification at issue here, however, clearly does interfere directly and substantially with the right to marry.

Under the challenged statute, no Wisconsin resident in the affected class may marry in Wisconsin or elsewhere without a court order, and marriages contracted in violation of the statute are both void and punishable as criminal offenses. Some of those in the affected class, like [Redhail], will never be able to obtain the necessary court order, because they either lack the financial means to meet their support obligations or cannot prove that their children will not become public charges. These persons are absolutely prevented from getting married. Many others, able in theory to satisfy the statute's requirements, will be sufficiently burdened by having to do so that they will in effect be coerced into forgoing their right to marry. And even those who can be persuaded to meet the statute's requirements suffer a serious intrusion into their freedom of choice in an area in which we have held such freedom to be fundamental.

III

When a statutory classification significantly interferes with the exercise of a fundamental right, it cannot be upheld unless it is supported by sufficiently important state interests and is closely tailored to effectuate only those interests. [The state] asserts that two interests are served by the challenged statute: the permission-to-marry proceeding furnishes an opportunity to counsel the applicant as to the necessity of fulfilling his prior support obligations; and the welfare of the out-of-custody children is protected. We may accept for present purposes that these are legitimate and substantial interests, but, since the means selected by the State for achieving these interests unnecessarily impinge on the right to marry, the statute cannot be sustained.

There is evidence that the challenged statute, as originally introduced in the Wisconsin Legislature, was intended merely to establish a mechanism whereby persons with support obligations to children from prior marriages could be counseled before they entered into new marital relationships and incurred further support obligations. Court permission to marry . . . was automatically to be granted after counseling was completed. The statute actually enacted, however, does not expressly require or provide for any counseling whatsoever, nor for any automatic granting of permission to marry by the court, and thus it can hardly be justified as a means for ensuring counseling. . . .

With regard to safeguarding the welfare of the out-of-custody children, . . . [the state]'s counsel suggested that, since permission to marry cannot be granted unless the applicant shows that he has satisfied his court-determined support obligations to the prior children and that those children will not become public charges, the statute provides incentive for the applicant to make support payments to his children. This "collection device" rationale cannot justify the statute's broad infringement on the right to marry.

First, with respect to individuals who are unable to meet the statutory requirements, the statute merely prevents the applicant from getting married, without delivering any money at all into the hands of the applicant's prior children. More importantly, regardless of the applicant's ability or willingness to meet the statutory requirements, the State already has numerous other means for exacting compliance with support obligations, means that are at least as effective as the instant statute's and yet do not impinge upon the right to marry. . . . [C]ourt-determined support obligations may be enforced directly via wage assignments, civil contempt proceedings, and criminal penalties. And, if the State believes that parents of children out of their custody should be responsible for ensuring that those children do not become public charges, this interest can be achieved by adjusting the criteria used for determining the amounts to be paid under their support orders.

There is also some suggestion that [the statute] protects the ability of marriage applicants to meet support obligations to prior children by preventing the applicants from incurring new support obligations. But the challenged provisions . . . are grossly underinclusive with respect to this purpose, since they do not limit in any way new financial commitments . . . other than those arising out of the contemplated marriage. The statutory classification is substantially overinclusive as well: Given the possibility that the new spouse will actually better the applicant's financial situation, by contributing income from a job or otherwise, the statute in many cases may prevent affected individuals from improving their ability to satisfy their prior support obligations. And, although it is true that the applicant will incur support obligations to any children born during the contemplated marriage, preventing the marriage may only result in the children being born out of wedlock, as in fact occurred in [Redhail]'s case. Since the support obligation is the same whether the child is born in or out of wedlock, the net result of preventing the marriage is simply more illegitimate children.

The statutory classification . . . thus cannot be justified by the interests advanced in support of it. The judgment of the District Court is, accordingly,

Affirmed.

MR. JUSTICE STEWART, concurring in the judgment.

[While agreeing the statute was unconstitutional, Justice Stewart concluded this was not an equal protection case, but rather, a substantive due process case.]

I do not agree . . . that there is a "right to marry" in the constitutional sense. That right, or more accurately that privilege, is under our federal system peculiarly one to be defined and limited by state law. A State may not only "significantly interfere with decisions to enter into the marital relationship," but may in many circumstances absolutely prohibit it. Surely, for example, a State may legitimately say that no one can marry his or her sibling, that no one can marry who is not at least 14 years old, that no one can marry without first passing an examination for venereal disease, or that no one can marry who has a living husband or wife. But, just as surely, in regulating the intimate human relationship of marriage, there is a limit beyond which a State may not constitutionally go.

. . . [I]t is settled that the "liberty" protected by the Due Process Clause of the Fourteenth Amendment embraces more than those freedoms expressly enumerated in the Bill of Rights. And the decisions of this Court have made clear that freedom of personal choice in matters of marriage and family life is one of the liberties so protected.

It is evident that the Wisconsin law now before us directly abridges that freedom. The question is whether the state interests that support the abridgment can overcome the substantive protections of the Constitution.

[Justice Stewart found state concerns on behalf of collection of support for existing obligees and the prospective family's economic well-being were legitimate, but the "State's legitimate concern with the financial soundness of prospective marriages must stop short of telling people they may not marry because they are too poor or because they might persist in their financial irresponsibility. The invasion of constitutionally protected liberty and the chance of erroneous prediction are simply too great."]

MR. JUSTICE POWELL, concurring in the judgment.

. . . . I write separately because the majority's rationale sweeps too broadly in an area which traditionally has been subject to pervasive state regulation. The Court apparently would subject all state regulation which "directly and substantially" interferes with the decision to marry in a traditional family setting to "critical examination" or "compelling state interest" analysis. Presumably, "reasonable regulations that do not significantly interfere with decisions to enter into the marital relationship may legitimately be imposed." The Court does not present, however, any principled means for distinguishing between the two types of regulations. Since state regulation in this area typically takes the form of a prerequisite or barrier to marriage or divorce, the degree of "direct" interference with the decision to marry or to divorce is unlikely to provide either guidance for state legislatures or a basis for judicial oversight. [Justice Powell here repeated the discussion of prior privacy cases, concluding that "the Court has yet to hold that all regulation touching upon marriage implicates a 'fundamental right' triggering the most exacting judicial scrutiny.[1]"]

. . . Although *Loving* speaks of the "freedom to marry" as "one of the vital personal rights essential to the orderly pursuit of happiness by free men," the Court focused on the miscegenation statute before it. . . . [which denied] a "fundamental freedom' on a wholly unsupportable basis — the use of classifications "directly subversive of the principle of equality at the heart of the Fourteenth Amendment . . . It does not speak to the level of judicial scrutiny of, or governmental justification for, "supportable" restrictions on the "fundamental freedom" of individuals to marry or divorce.

In my view, analysis must start from the recognition of domestic relations as "an area that has long been regarded as a virtually exclusive province of the States" *Sosna v. Iowa.* . . . The State, representing the collective expression of moral aspirations, has an undeniable interest in ensuring that its rules of domestic relations reflect the widely held values of its people. . . . State regulation has included bans on incest, bigamy, and homosexuality, as well as various preconditions to marriage, such as blood tests. Likewise, a showing of fault on the part of one of the partners traditionally has been a prerequisite to the dissolution of an unsuccessful union. A "compelling state purpose" inquiry would cast doubt on the network of restrictions that the States have fashioned to govern marriage and divorce.

II

State power over domestic relations is not without constitutional limits. The Due Process Clause requires a showing of justification "when the government intrudes on choices concerning family living arrangements" in a manner which is contrary to deeply rooted traditions. *Moore v. East Cleveland* (plurality opinion). Due process constraints also limit the extent to which the State may monopolize the process of ordering certain human relationships while excluding the truly indigent from that process. . . .

Th[is statute] does not pass muster under either due process or equal protection standards. . . . The . . . Court amply demonstrates that the asserted counseling objective bears no relation to this statute. . . .

The so-called "collection device" rationale presents a somewhat more difficult question. I do not agree with the suggestion in the Court's opinion that a State may never condition the right to marry on satisfaction of existing support obligations simply because the State has alternative methods of compelling such payments. To

---

[1] Although the cases [indicate] that there is a sphere of privacy or autonomy surrounding an existing marital relationship into which the State may not lightly intrude, they do not necessarily suggest that the same barrier of justification blocks regulation of the conditions of entry into or the dissolution of the marital bond. See generally Henkin, *Privacy and Autonomy*, 74 COLUM. L. REV. 1410, 1429–1432 (1974).

the extent this restriction applies to persons who are able to make the required support payments but simply wish to shirk their moral and legal obligation, the Constitution interposes no bar to this additional collection mechanism. The vice inheres, not in the collection concept, but in the failure to make provision for those without the means to comply with child-support obligations. [Justice Powell here cited *Boddie v. Connecticut* which struck down filing fees for divorce actions as applied to those unable to pay]. The monopolization [here] is total, for Wisconsin will not recognize foreign marriages that [violate the statute].

The third justification . . . is that the statute preserves the ability of marriage applicants to support their prior issue by preventing them from incurring new obligations. The challenged provisions . . . are so grossly underinclusive with respect to this objective, given the many ways that additional financial obligations may be incurred [aside] from a contemplated marriage, that the classification "does not bear a fair and substantial relation to the object of the legislation."

. . . . This statute does more than simply "fail to alleviate the consequences of differences in economic circumstances that exist wholly apart from any state action." *Griffin v. Illinois* (Harlan, J., dissenting). It tells the truly indigent, whether they have met their support obligations or not, that they may not marry so long as their children are public charges or there is a danger that their children might go on public assistance in the future. Apparently, no other jurisdiction has embraced this approach. . . . Because the State has not established a justification for this [bar to marriage for many citizens based on poverty], I concur in the judgment. . . .

[Justice Stevens concurred, finding denial of permission to those whose children were public charges "either futile or perverse insofar as it applies to childless couples, couples who will have illegitimate children if they are forbidden to marry, couples whose economic status will be improved by marriage, and couples who are so poor that the marriage will have no impact on the welfare status of their children. . . ." Justice Rehnquist dissented. Applying rational relationship scrutiny, he found the statute within a state's "power to regulate family life and to assure the support of minor children, despite its possible imprecision in the extreme cases envisioned in the concurring opinions."]

NOTES

1. *Scope of* Zablocki. After establishing that marriage is "a right of fundamental importance," the majority rejects rigorous scrutiny for laws which "do not significantly interfere with decisions to enter into the marital relationship." Justice Marshall notes the *Zablocki* regulation "clearly does interfere directly and substantially with the right to marry" and, therefore, applies searching scrutiny. How are regulations which "significantly interfere" with marriage to be distinguished from those which do not? As you study the various marriage regulations, consider which level of scrutiny is appropriate under *Zablocki*. Professor Cass Sunstein has argued that the right to marry is more properly conceived as deriving from the Equal Protection clause rather than as a substantive Due Process case. *See* Sunstein, *The Right to Marry*, 26 CARDOZO L. REV. 2081 (2005).

2. *Importance of Poverty to* Zablocki's *Holding.* Consider the following statute: "All those in arrears on court-ordered child support cannot enter into a marital relationship until those arrearages are eliminated; provided, those financially unable to pay these arrearages can marry." Justice Marshall presumably would find this version of the statute equally objectionable, but it would appear to satisfy Justice Powell.

3. *What Is* Zablocki *Protecting?* One might ask what precisely is protected by a "right to marry." The Court states, e.g., "marriage is the only relationship in which the state . . . allows sexual relations legally to take place." Would the statute be equally defective if extramarital sexual relations were permitted?

What constitutionally protected interest would the marriage restriction deny a couple who may cohabit legally? It could be access to alimony or property division claims on divorce. Yet many states today allow cohabitants to create binding contractual obligations to one another (*see* Chapter 9 at Section ___), which might eliminate this concern. Is *Zablocki* acting to protect any future children from the burden of non-marital status? Not likely. The couple may not have children and, anyway, non-marital status rarely is relevant, under modern law, in the child's claims for support, intestate succession, etc. (*See* Chapter 9 at Section ___.) Then, is a right to marry designed to protect couples so they can file joint tax returns, inherit intestate, sue for wrongful death, or obtain the family rate at a local country club?

In sum, is *Zablocki* about the practical benefits of marriage or is it instead protecting access to the symbolic status of marriage? Do people choose to marry rather than cohabit because of practical consequences, or because of custom, psychic need, symbolic significance or religious belief? If *Zablocki* is providing constitutional protection of access to a symbolic act, it must be an extraordinarily important symbol.

While people can claim they are married even though the state refused them a license, the state has a practical "monopoly" over access to the marriage label. Most people probably believe state approval, obtained by adherence to state rules, is necessary to create a legitimate marriage. Access to legally recognized marriage is thus usually essential to social recognition of it and this is more important than any legal consequences which are likely never to have been considered. The couple wants to be married not only in their own eyes, but also in the perception of others.

Thus, the significant state power over marriage which is the subject of *Zablocki* is a very strange power: it is a power over a symbol, enforced by social convention. This is good to keep in mind in considering substantive restrictions on entering marriage.

4. *A Dissent on the Right to Marry.* Not all commentators accept the Supreme Court's right to marry jurisprudence uncritically. Professor Earl Maltz argues "the case law dealing with the . . . right to marry is far more ambiguous than is often assumed." Maltz, *Right to Marry: A Dissenting View*, 60 GEO. WASH. L. REV. 949, 954 (1992). He asserts:

> [G]overnment . . . plays a different role in *Loving* and *Redhail* than in many other cases involving claims of a fundamental right. Assertions of . . .

free speech, for example, rest on the view that the government should not be allowed to interfere . . . [R]ather than a right to be free from state interference, [however],the right to marry can only be conceptualized as the right to place the power of the state behind previously agreed-to, consensual arrangements. . . .

Id. at 955. The author identifies four aspects of the marital relationship which have been claimed to justify strict scrutiny of regulation (the "emotional support and public commitment provided by a marriage, the economic benefits derived from the marital relationship, the sexual relationship . . . and the relationship between the husband, wife, and offspring of the marriage") and finds each wanting as a basis upon which to find a fundamental right to marry. *Id.* at 956–67. *See also* Joseph Pull, *Questioning the Right to Marry*, 90 MARQ. L. REV. 21 (2006) (urging reinterpretation of "right to marry" as a negative liberty — "a claim of individual autonomy against the encroaching hand of the state — rather than a positive right that obligates the state to provide all persons a particular set of options under the heading 'marriage' ").

PROBLEMS

Problem 2-3.   Randy was employed by a company which assisted the police department in processing insurance claims of current and former police officers and, in that capacity, had access to files containing confidential information about the officers. Randy became romantically involved with an incarcerated felon and planned marriage. When Randy's supervisor learned of this plan, Randy was told to either end the relationship or leave the job. Randy resigned and now has come to you wanting to file a lawsuit seeking damages or to get back the job. Without regard to the appropriate remedy, how will you argue the case and what kind of response do you expect from the other side?

Problem 2-4.   Olaf is a citizen of Norway and has been in the United States for 6 years. He is here, however, without permission. He has fallen in love with Maria, an American citizen with whom he works at the car wash. When they went to the Probate Judge's office to obtain a marriage license they were refused. The clerk was adamant: "If you are here illegally according to federal law, you shouldn't be able to get married here." He comes to you for advice. What can you tell him about any action you might take and what response you might expect from the city?

Problem 2-5.   Jan is a state prison inmate serving a life sentence who has fallen in love with Barry, an old friend from high school. They've known each other for 30 years, each having been divorced for over 10 years. Following state statutory rules, each wrote a letter to the prison administrator seeking permission to marry. The matter was referred to the prison's marriage committee which, after separately interviewing the parties, denied permission to marry. The committee's memorandum stated "this marriage would not be in the best interest of either party or the institution. Both parties are unrealistic about the length of Jan's sentence and both seem to believe it will be reduced. Jan will not be eligible for parole under current rules for 21 years. Barry spoke of building a log cabin for the couple to live in after her release. While both spoke of a lengthy relationship, they were very vague about its details and, except for the last six months when contact was re-established, the relationship could not be documented. Jan was nervous during the interview. B was very sarcastic. Each stated that the other was 'pushing' to get married." The administrator accepted the committee's recommendation and Jan has filed suit to overturn the refusal to grant permission to marry. As law clerk to the judge hearing the suit, review the relevant Supreme Court authority and outline the arguments you expect from both sides.

[b]   Same-Sex Prohibitions

VARNUM v. BRIEN
Iowa Supreme Court
763 N.W.2d 862 (2009)

CADY, JUSTICE.

. . . [W]e must decide if our state statute limiting civil marriage to a union between a man and a woman violates the Iowa Constitution. . . . On our review, we hold the . . . statute violates the equal protection clause of the Iowa Constitution. Therefore, we affirm. . . .

I. Background Facts and Proceedings.

This . . . is a civil rights action by twelve individuals. . . . Like most Iowans, they are responsible, caring, and productive. . . . They include a nurse, business manager, insurance analyst, bank agent, stay-at-home parent, church organist and piano teacher, museum director, federal employee, social worker, teacher, and two retired teachers. Like many Iowans, some have children and others hope to have children. Some are foster parents. Like all Iowans, they prize their liberties and [have] the expectation that their rights will be maintained and protected . . .

Despite the commonality shared with other Iowans, the twelve plaintiffs are different from most in one way. . . . The twelve plaintiffs comprise six same-sex couples who live in committed relationships. Each maintains a hope of getting married one day, an aspiration shared by many throughout Iowa.

Unlike opposite-sex couples in Iowa, same-sex couples are not permitted to marry in Iowa. The Iowa legislature amended the marriage statute in 1998 to define marriage as a union between only a man and a woman. Despite this law, the six same-sex couples in this litigation asked the . . . recorder to issue marriage licenses to them. The recorder . . . refused to issue the licenses, and the six couples have been unable to be married in this state. Except for the statutory restriction . . . , the twelve plaintiffs met the legal requirements to marry in Iowa.

[The plaintiffs] seek to declare the marriage statute unconstitutional so they can obtain the array of benefits of marriage enjoyed by heterosexual couples, protect themselves and their children, and demonstrate to one another and to society their mutual commitment. . . . They claimed the statutory same-sex marriage ban violates . . . the fundamental right to marry, as well as rights to privacy and familial association [under the state constitution]. Additionally, plaintiffs claimed the legislative and the executive actions unconstitutionally discriminated against them on several bases, including sexual orientation.

The . . . record [below on a motion for summary judgment] included an explanation by some of the plaintiffs of the disadvantages and fears they face each day due to the inability to obtain a civil marriage in Iowa [including] the legal inability to make many life and death decisions affecting their partner, including decisions related to health care, burial arrangements, autopsy, and disposition of remains following death. Various plaintiffs told of the inability to share in their partners' state-provided health insurance, public-employee pension benefits, and many private-employer-provided benefits. . . . They also explained how several tax benefits are denied. Adoption proceedings are also more cumbersome and expensive for unmarried partners. Other obstacles . . . include numerous nongovernmental benefits of marriage that are so common in daily life they often go unnoticed, such as something so simple as spousal health club memberships. Yet, perhaps the ultimate disadvantage expressed . . . is the inability to obtain for themselves and for their children the personal and public affirmation that accompanies marriage.

The parties also explored the reasons for defining marriage in a way that denies these benefits to same-sex couples. The County offered five primary interests . . . in support of the legislature's exclusive definition of marriage. The first three interests are broadly related to the advancement of child rearing. . . . promoting procreation, promoting child rearing by a mother and a father within a marriage, and promoting stability in an opposite-sex relationship to raise and nurture children. The fourth interest . . . addressed the conservation of state resources, while the final reason [was] promoting the concept and integrity of the traditional notion of marriage.

Much of the testimony presented by the County was in the form of opinions by various individuals that same-sex marriage would harm the institution of marriage and . . . children raised in same-sex marriages. Two college professors testified that a heterosexual marriage is, overall, the optimal forum in which to raise children. A retired pediatrician challenged the accuracy of some of the medical research [finding] no significant difference between children raised by same-sex couples and opposite-sex couples. A clinical psychologist testified sexual orientation is not as defined and stable as race and gender and can change over time. He acknowledged, however, it is difficult to change a person's sexual orientation, and efforts to do so can be harmful to the person.

The plaintiffs produced evidence to demonstrate sexual orientation and gender have no effect on children raised by same-sex couples, and same-sex couples can raise children as well as opposite-sex couples. They also submitted evidence to show that most scientific research has repudiated the commonly assumed notion that children need opposite-sex parents or biological parents to grow into well-adjusted adults. Many leading organizations, including the American Academy of Pediatrics, the American Psychiatric Association, the American Psychological Association, the National Association of Social Workers, and the Child Welfare League of America, weighed the available research and supported the conclusion that gay and lesbian parents are as effective as heterosexual parents in raising children. For example, . . . the American Psychological Association declares, "There is no scientific evidence that parenting effectiveness is related to parental sexual orientation: Lesbian and gay parents are as likely as heterosexual parents to provide supportive and healthy environments for children." Almost every professional group that has studied the issue indicates children are not harmed when raised by same-sex couples, but to the contrary, benefit from them. In Iowa, agencies that license foster parents have found same-sex couples to be good and acceptable parents. It is estimated that more than 5800 same-sex couples live throughout Iowa, and over one-third of these couples are raising children.

The district court concluded the statute was unconstitutional under the due process and equal protection clauses of the Iowa Constitution and granted summary judgment to the plaintiffs.

. . . .

. . . . Like the United States Constitution, the Iowa Constitution . . . establishes three separate, but equal, branches of government and delineates the limited roles and powers of each branch. Among other basic principles essential to our form of government, the constitution defines certain individual rights upon which the government may not infringe. Equal protection of the law is one of the guaranteed rights. *See* Iowa Const. art. I, § 6. . . .

This case, as with most other civil rights actions before it, implicates these broad constitutional principles of governing. The legislature . . . enacted a law that effectively excludes gay and lesbian people from . . . civil marriage. The executive branch of government, in carrying out its role to execute the law, enforced this statute through a county official who refused to issue marriage licenses to six same-sex couples. These Iowans, believing that the law is inconsistent with certain constitutional mandates, exercised their constitutional right to petition the courts for redress of their grievance. This court, consistent with its role to interpret the law and resolve disputes, now has the responsibility to determine if the law . . . violates the Iowa Constitution.

. . . .

Our responsibility . . . is to protect constitutional rights of individuals from legislative enactments that have denied those rights, even when the rights have not yet been broadly accepted, were at one time unimagined, or challenge a deeply ingrained practice or law viewed to be impervious to the passage of time. The framers of the Iowa Constitution knew, as did the drafters of the United States Constitution, that "times can blind us to certain truths and later generations can see that laws once thought necessary and proper in fact serve only to oppress," and as our constitution "endures, persons in every generation can invoke its principles in their own search for greater freedom" and equality. *See Lawrence v. Texas*, 539 U.S. 558, 578–79 (2003) (acknowledging intent of framers of Federal Constitution that Constitution endure and be interpreted by future generations); *Callender v. Skiles*, 591 N.W.2d 182, 190 (Iowa 1999) ("Our constitution is not merely tied to tradition, but recognizes the changing nature of society.").

When individuals invoke the Iowa Constitution's guarantees of freedom and equality, courts are bound to interpret those guarantees.

. . . .

IV. Equal Protection.

A. Background Principles. The primary constitutional principle at the heart of this case is the doctrine of equal protection. . . .

The process of defining equal protection . . . begins by classifying people into groups. A classification persists until a new understanding of equal protection is achieved. The point in time when the standard of equal protection finally takes a new form is a product of the conviction of one, or many, individuals that a particular grouping results in inequality and the ability of the judicial system to perform its constitutional role. . . .

In the first reported case of the Supreme Court of the Territory of Iowa, *In re Ralph*, (Iowa 1839), we refused to treat a human being as property to enforce a contract for slavery and held our laws must extend equal protection to persons of all races and conditions. This decision was seventeen years before the United States Supreme Court infamously decided *Dred Scott v. Sandford*. . . . Similarly, in *Clark v. Board of Directors* (1868) and *Coger v. North West. Union Packet Co.* (1873), we struck blows to the concept of segregation long before the United States Supreme Court's decision in *Brown v. Board of Education*. Iowa was also the first state in the nation to admit a woman to the practice of law, doing so in 1869. *Admission of Women to the Bar*, 1 Chicago Law Times 76, 76 (1887). Her admission occurred three years before the United States Supreme Court affirmed the State of Illinois' decision to *deny* women admission to the practice of law and twenty-five years before the United States Supreme Court affirmed the refusal of the Commonwealth of Virginia to admit women into the practice of law. In each of those instances, our state approached a fork in the road toward fulfillment of our constitution's ideals and reaffirmed the "absolute equality of all" persons before the law as "the very foundation principle of our government." *See Coger*, 37 Iowa at 153.

So, today, this court again faces an important issue that hinges on our definition of equal protection. This issue comes to us with the same importance as our landmark cases of the past. The same-sex-marriage debate waged in this case is part of a strong national dialogue centered on a fundamental, deep-seated, traditional institution that has excluded, by state action, a particular class of Iowans. This class of people asks a simple and direct question: How can a state premised on the constitutional principle of equal protection justify exclusion of a class of Iowans from civil marriage?

. . . . Plaintiffs argue sexual-orientation-based statutes should be subject to the most searching scrutiny. The County asserts Iowa's marriage statute may be reviewed, at most, according to an intermediate level of scrutiny. Because we conclude [the] statute cannot withstand intermediate scrutiny, we need not decide whether classifications based on sexual orientation are subject to a higher level of scrutiny. Thus, we turn to a discussion of the intermediate scrutiny standard.

1. *Intermediate scrutiny standard.* [Quoting cases from the United States Supreme Court, the court determined the standard required "important" state

objectives and a scheme "substantially related" to those objectives.]

2. *Statutory classification: exclusion of gay and lesbian people from civil marriage.*. . . . [T]he issue presented . . . is whether the state has "exceedingly persuasive" reasons for denying civil marriage to same-sex couples. . . . Thus, the question we must answer is whether excluding gay and lesbian people from civil marriage is substantially related to any important governmental objective.

3. *Governmental objectives.* The County has proffered a number of objectives supporting the marriage statute. These objectives include support for the "traditional" institution of marriage, the optimal procreation and rearing of children, and financial considerations.[24]

The first step in scrutinizing a statutory classification [is] to determine whether the objectives purportedly advanced by the classification are important. "The burden of justification is demanding and it rests entirely on the State." Where we find, or can assume, the proffered governmental interests are sufficiently weighty to be called "important," the critical inquiry is whether these governmental objectives can fairly be said to be advanced by the legislative classification. . . .

a. *Maintaining traditional marriage.* First, the County argues the same-sex marriage ban promotes the "integrity of traditional marriage" by "maintaining the historical and traditional marriage norm ([as] one between a man and a woman)." This argument is straightforward and has superficial appeal. A specific tradition sought to be maintained cannot be an important governmental objective for equal protection purposes, however, when the tradition is nothing more than the historical classification currently expressed in the statute being challenged. When a certain tradition is used as both the governmental objective and the classification to further that objective, the equal protection analysis is transformed into the circular question of whether the classification accomplishes the governmental objective, which objective is to maintain the classification. . . .

This precise situation is presented by the County's claim that the statute in this case exists to preserve the traditional understanding of marriage. The governmental objective identified by the County — to maintain the traditional understanding of marriage — is simply another way of saying the governmental objective is to limit civil marriage to opposite-sex couples. . . .

. . . . [S]ome underlying reason other than the preservation of tradition must be identified.[25] Because the County offers no particular *governmental* reason

---

[24] Other jurisdictions considering the validity of legislative exclusion of gay and lesbian people from civil marriage have considered alternative justifications. *See, e.g., Kerrigan*, 957 A.2d at 476 [*90] (uniformity with laws of other jurisdictions); *id.* at 518 (Zarella, J., dissenting) (regulation of heterosexual procreation); *Hernandez v. Robles*, 7 N.Y.3d 338, 821 N.Y.S.2d 770, 855 N.E.2d 1, 32–34 (N.Y. 2006) (Kaye, C.J., dissenting) (moral disapproval, uniformity with other jurisdictions); *Andersen*, 138 P.3d at 982 (avoid "the need to resolve the sometimes conflicting rights and obligations of the same-sex couple and the necessary third party in relation to a child"). We need not independently analyze these alternative justifications as they are not offered to support the Iowa statute.

[25] The preservation of traditional marriage could only be a legitimate reason for the classification if expanding marriage to include others in its definition would undermine the traditional institution. The County has simply failed to explain how the traditional institution of *civil* marriage would suffer if

underlying the tradition of limiting civil marriage to heterosexual couples, we . . . consider other plausible reasons for the legislative classification.

    b. Promotion of optimal environment to raise children. Another governmental objective proffered . . . is the promotion of "child rearing by a father and a mother in a marital relationship which social scientists say with confidence is the optimal milieu for child rearing." This . . . implicates the broader governmental interest to promote the best interests of children. The "best interests of children" is, undeniably, an important governmental objective. Yet, we first examine the underlying premise . . . that the optimal environment for children is to be raised within a marriage of both a mother and a father.

    Plaintiffs presented an abundance of evidence and research, confirmed by our independent research, supporting the proposition that the interests of children are served equally by same-sex parents and opposite-sex parents. On the other hand, we acknowledge the existence of reasoned opinions that dual-gender parenting is the optimal environment for children. These opinions, while thoughtful and sincere, were largely unsupported by reliable scientific studies.

    Even assuming there may be a rational basis . . . to believe the legislative classification advances a legitimate government interest, this . . . would not be sufficient to survive the equal protection analysis applicable in this case. In order to ensure this classification based on sexual orientation is not borne of prejudice and stereotype, intermediate scrutiny demands a closer relationship between the . . . classification and [its] purpose . . . than mere rationality. Under intermediate scrutiny, the relationship between the . . . goal and the classification . . . must be "substantial." In order to evaluate that relationship, it is helpful to consider whether the legislation is over-inclusive or under-inclusive.

    A statute is under-inclusive when the classification made in the statute "does not include all who are similarly situated with respect to the purpose of the law." An under-inclusive statute means all people included in the statutory classification have the trait that is relevant to the aim of the statute, but other people with the trait are not included in the classification. . . . An over-inclusive statute "imposes a burden upon a wider range of individuals than are included in the class of those" with the trait relevant to the aim of the law. As the degree to which a statutory classification is shown to be over-inclusive or under-inclusive increases, so does the difficulty in demonstrating the classification substantially furthers the legislative goal.

    We begin with the County's argument that the goal of the same-sex marriage ban is to ensure children will be raised only in the optimal milieu. In pursuit of this objective, the statutory exclusion of gay and lesbian people is both under-inclusive and over-inclusive. The civil marriage statute is under-inclusive because it does not exclude from marriage other groups of parents — such as child abusers, sexual predators, parents neglecting to provide child support, and violent felons — that

---

same-sex civil marriage were allowed. There is no legitimate notion that a more inclusive definition of marriage will transform civil marriage into something less than it presently is for heterosexuals. Benjamin G. Ledsham, Note, *Means to Legitimate Ends: Same-Sex Marriage through the Lens of Illegitimacy-Based Discrimination*, 28 Cardozo L. Rev. 2373, 2388 (2007).

are undeniably less than optimal parents. Such under-inclusion tends to demonstrate that the sexual-orientation-based classification is grounded in prejudice or "overbroad generalizations about the different talents, capacities, or preferences" of gay and lesbian people, rather than having a substantial relationship to some important objective.

Of course, "[r]eform may take one step at a time, addressing itself to the phase of the problem which seems most acute to the legislative mind." *Knepper v. Monticello State Bank*, 450 N.W.2d 833, 837 (Iowa 1990). . . . While a statute does not automatically violate equal protection merely by being under-inclusive, the degree of under-inclusion nonetheless indicates the substantiality of the relationship between the legislative means and end.

As applied [here], it could be argued the same-sex marriage ban is just one . . . step toward ensuring the optimal environment for raising children. Under this argument, the governmental objective is slightly more modest. It seeks to reduce the number of same-sex parent households, nudging our state a step closer to providing the asserted optimal milieu for children. Even evaluated in light of this narrower objective, however, the ban on same-sex marriage is flawed.

The ban on same-sex marriage is substantially over-inclusive because not all same-sex couples choose to raise children. Yet, the marriage statute denies civil marriage to all gay and lesbian people. . . . In doing so, the legislature includes a consequential number of "individuals within the statute's purview who are not afflicted with the evil the statute seeks to remedy." *Conaway*, 932 A.2d at 649 (Raker, J., concurring in part and dissenting).

At the same time, the exclusion of gay and lesbian people from marriage is under-inclusive, even in relation to the narrower goal of improving child rearing by limiting same-sex parenting. Quite obviously, the statute does not prohibit same-sex couples from raising children. Same-sex couples currently raise children in Iowa, even while being excluded from civil marriage, and such couples will undoubtedly continue to do so. Recognition of this under-inclusion puts in perspective just how minimally the same-sex marriage ban actually advances the purported legislative goal. A law so simultaneously over-inclusive and under-inclusive is not substantially related to the government's objective. In the end, a careful analysis of the over- and under-inclusiveness of the statute reveals it is less about using marriage to achieve an optimal environment for children and more about merely precluding gay and lesbian people from civil marriage.

If the statute was truly about the best interest of children, some benefit to children derived from the ban on same-sex civil marriages would be observable. Yet, the germane analysis does not show how the best interests of children of gay and lesbian parents, who are denied an environment supported by the benefits of marriage under the statute, are served by the ban. Likewise, the exclusion of gays and lesbians from marriage does not benefit the interests of . . . children of heterosexual parents, who are able to enjoy the environment supported by marriage with or without the inclusion of same-sex couples.

The ban on same-sex civil marriage can only logically be justified as a means to ensure the asserted optimal environment for raising children if fewer children will be raised within same-sex relationships or more children will be raised in dual-gender marriages. Yet, the same-sex-marriage ban will accomplish these outcomes only when people in same-sex relationships choose not to raise children without the benefit of marriage or when children are adopted by dual-gender couples who would have been adopted by same-sex couples but for the same-sex civil marriage ban. We discern no substantial support for this proposition. . . . Consequently, a classification that limits civil marriage to opposite-sex couples is simply not substantially related to the objective of promoting the optimal environment to raise children. This conclusion suggests stereotype and prejudice, or some other unarticulated reason, could be present to explain the real objectives of the statute.

c. *Promotion of procreation.* The County also proposes that government endorsement of traditional civil marriage will result in more procreation. It points out that procreation is important to the continuation of the human race, and opposite-sex couples accomplish this objective because procreation occurs naturally within this group. In contrast, the County points out, same-sex couples can procreate only through assisted reproductive techniques, and some same-sex couples may choose not to procreate. While heterosexual marriage does lead to procreation, the argument by the County fails to address the real issue in our required analysis of the objective: whether *exclusion* of gay and lesbian individuals from the institution of civil marriage will result in *more* procreation? If procreation is the true objective, then the proffered classification must work to achieve that objective.

Conceptually, the promotion of procreation as an objective of marriage is compatible with the inclusion of gays and lesbians within the definition of marriage. Gay and lesbian persons are capable of procreation. Thus, the sole conceivable avenue by which exclusion of gay and lesbian people from civil marriage could promote more procreation is if the unavailability of civil marriage for same-sex partners caused homosexual individuals to "become" heterosexual in order to procreate within the present traditional institution of civil marriage. The briefs, the record, our research, and common sense do not suggest such an outcome. Even if possibly true . . . the statute is significantly under-inclusive with respect to the objective of increasing procreation because it does not include a variety of groups that do not procreate for reasons such as age, physical disability, or choice. In other words, the classification is not substantially related to the asserted legislative purpose.

d. *Promoting stability in opposite-sex relationships.* A fourth suggested rationale supporting the marriage statute is "promoting stability in opposite sex relationships." While the institution of civil marriage likely encourages stability in opposite-sex relationships, we must evaluate whether *excluding* gay and lesbian people from civil marriage encourages stability in opposite-sex relationships. The County offers no reasons that it does, and we can find none. . . .

e. *Conservation of resources.* The conservation of state resources is another objective arguably furthered by excluding gay and lesbian persons from civil marriage. The argument is based on a simple premise: couples who are married enjoy numerous governmental benefits, so the state's fiscal burden associated with civil marriage is reduced if less people are allowed to marry. . . . By way of example, the County hypothesizes that, due to our laws granting tax benefits to married couples, the State . . . would reap less tax revenue if individual taxpaying gay and lesbian people were allowed to obtain a civil marriage. Certainly, Iowa's marriage statute causes numerous government benefits . . . to be withheld from plaintiffs.[28] Thus, the ban on same-sex marriages may conserve some state resources. Excluding any group from civil marriage — African-Americans, illegitimates, aliens, even red-haired individuals — would conserve state resources in an equally "rational" way. Yet, such classifications so obviously offend our . . . collective sense of equality that courts have not hesitated to provide added protections against such inequalities.

One primary requirement of the equal protection clause is a more substantial relationship between the legislative goal and the means used to attain the goal. When heightened scrutiny is applicable, the means must substantially further the legislative end. Consequently, in this case, the sexual-orientation-based classification must substantially further the conservation-of-resources objective.

As observed in our [earlier] analysis . . . , significant degrees of over-inclusion and under-inclusion shed light on the true relationship between exclusion of gay and lesbian people from civil marriage and the goal of conserving governmental resources. Exclusion of all same-sex couples is an extremely blunt instrument for conserving state resources through limiting access to civil marriage. In other words, the exclusion of same-sex couples is over-inclusive because many same-sex couples, if allowed to marry, would not use more state resources than they currently consume as unmarried couples. To reference the County's example, while many heterosexual couples who have obtained a civil marriage do not file joint tax returns — or experience any other tax benefit from marital status — many same-sex couples may not file a joint tax return either. The two classes created by the statute — opposite-sex couples and same-sex couples — may use the same amount of state resources. Thus, the two classes are similarly situated for the purpose of conserving state resources, yet the classes are treated differently by the law. In this way, sexual orientation is a flawed indicator of resource usage.

---

[28] Plaintiffs identify over two hundred Iowa statutes affected by civil-marriage status. *See, e.g.*, Iowa Code § 85.31 (dependent surviving spouse receives benefits when spouse death caused by work injury); *id.* § 135J.1(4) (hospice patient's family includes spouse); *id.* § 142C.4 (spouse has power to make decision concerning anatomical gifts); *id.* § 144A.7 (patient's spouse determines application of life-sustaining procedures in absence of declaration); *id.* § 144C.5 (surviving spouse controls disposition of decedent's remains in absence of declaration); *id.* § 252A.3(1) (spouse liable for support of other spouse); *id.* § 252A.3(4) (children of married parents legitimate); *id.* § 422.7 (spouses may file joint tax return); *id.* § 422.9(1) (optional standard deduction for married taxpayers); *id.* § 422.12(1)(b) (spouses eligible for personal exemption credit); *id.* § 450.3 (inheritance rights of surviving spouses); *id.* § 450.9 (surviving spouse exempt from inheritance tax on property passed from decedent spouse); *id.* § 450.10(6) (spousal allowance for surviving spouse); *id.* § 523I.309 (surviving spouse must consent to decedent spouse's interment); *id.* § 613.15 (spouse may recover value of services and support of decedent spouse for wrongful death or negligent injury); *id.* § 622.9 (restriction of testimony of communication between husband and wife); *id.* § 633.211(1) (surviving spouse receives decedent spouse's entire estate in intestacy); *id.* § 633.236 (surviving spouse has right to elective share); *id.* § 633.272 (surviving spouse takes under partial intestacy if elective share not exercised); *id.* § 633.336 (damages for wrongful death). The Government Accounting Office, as of 2005, had identified more than 1000 federal legal rights and responsibilities derived from marriage. Isaak, 10 U. Pa. J. Const. L. at 607 n.6.

Just as exclusion of same-sex couples from marriage is a blunt instrument, however, it is also significantly undersized if the true goal is to conserve state resources. That is to say, the classification is under-inclusive. The goal of conservation of state resources would be equally served by excluding any similar-sized group from civil marriage. Indeed, under the County's logic, more state resources would be conserved by excluding groups more numerous than Iowa's estimated 5800 same-sex couples (for example, persons marrying for a second or subsequent time). Importantly, there is also no suggestion same-sex couples would use *more* state resources if allowed to obtain a civil marriage than heterosexual couples who obtain a civil marriage.

Such over-inclusion and under-inclusion demonstrates the trait of sexual orientation is a poor proxy for regulating aspiring spouses' usage of state resources. This tenuous relationship between the classification and its purpose demonstrates many people who are similarly situated with respect to the purpose of the law are treated differently. As a result, the sexual-orientation-based classification does not substantially further the suggested governmental interest, as required by intermediate scrutiny.

4. *Conclusion.* Having examined each proffered governmental objective through the appropriate lens of intermediate scrutiny, we conclude the sexual-orientation-based classification under the marriage statute does not substantially further any of the objectives. While the objectives asserted may be important . . . , none are furthered in a substantial way by the exclusion of same-sex couples from civil marriage. Our equal protection clause requires more than has been offered to justify the continued existence of the same-sex marriage ban under the statute.

. . . . Now that we have addressed and rejected each specific interest advanced by the County to justify the classification drawn under the statute, we consider the reason for the exclusion of gay and lesbian couples from civil marriage left unspoken by the County: religious opposition to same-sex marriage. The County's silence reflects, we believe, its understanding this reason cannot, under our Iowa Constitution, be used to justify a ban on same-sex marriage.

While unexpressed, religious sentiment most likely motivates many, if not most, opponents of same-sex civil marriage and perhaps even shapes the views of those people who may accept gay and lesbian unions but find the notion of same-sex marriage unsettling.[29] Consequently, we address the religious undercurrent propelling the same-sex marriage debate as a means to fully explain our rationale for rejecting the dual-gender requirement of the marriage statute.

---

[29] A survey in the *Des Moines Register* in 2008 found 28.1% of individuals surveyed supported same-sex marriage, 30.2% opposed same-sex marriage but supported civil unions, and thirty-two percent of respondents opposed both same-sex marriage and civil unions. Erin Jordan, *About 6 in 10 Iowans back same-sex unions, poll finds, Des Moines Register*, Nov. 26, 2008, at 4B. The *Des Moines Register* survey is consistent with a national survey by the PEW Research Center in 2003. This PEW survey found that fifty-nine percent of Americans oppose same-sex marriage, and thirty-two percent favor same-sex marriage. Schuman, 96 Geo. L.J. at 2108. However, opposition to same-sex marriage jumped to eighty percent for people "with a high level of religious commitment," with only twelve percent of such people in favor of same-sex marriage. *Id.*

It is quite understandable that religiously motivated opposition to same-sex civil marriage shapes the basis for legal opposition to same-sex marriage, even if only indirectly. Religious objections to same-sex marriage are supported by thousands of years of tradition and biblical interpretation. The belief that the "sanctity of marriage" would be undermined by the inclusion of gay and lesbian couples bears a striking conceptual resemblance to the expressed secular rationale for maintaining the tradition of marriage as a union between dual-gender couples, but better identifies the source of the opposition. Whether expressly or impliedly, much of society rejects same-sex marriage due to sincere, deeply ingrained — even fundamental — religious belief.

Yet, such views are not the only religious views of marriage. As demonstrated by amicus groups, other equally sincere groups and people in Iowa and around the nation have strong religious views that yield the opposite conclusion.

This contrast of opinions in our society largely explains the absence of any religion-based rationale to test the constitutionality of Iowa's same-sex marriage ban. Our constitution does not permit any branch of government to resolve these types of religious debates and entrusts to courts the task of ensuring government *avoids* them. *See* Iowa Const. art. I, § 3 ("The general assembly shall make no law respecting an establishment of religion. . . ."). The statute . . . does not prescribe a definition of marriage for religious institutions. Instead, [it] declares, "Marriage is a civil contract" and then regulates that civil contract. Thus . . . we proceed as civil judges, far removed from the theological debate of religious clerics, and focus only on the concept of civil marriage and the state licensing system. . . .

. . . .

[C]ivil marriage must be judged under our constitutional standards of equal protection and not under religious doctrines or the religious views of individuals. This approach does not disrespect or denigrate the religious views of many Iowans who may strongly believe in marriage as a dual-gender union, but considers, as we must, only the constitutional rights of all people. . . .

. . . .

In the final analysis, we give respect to the views of all Iowans on the issue of same-sex marriage — religious or otherwise — by giving respect to our constitutional principles. These principles require that the state recognize both opposite-sex and same-sex civil marriage. Religious doctrine and views contrary to this principle of law are unaffected, and people can continue to associate with the religion that best reflects their views. A religious denomination can still define marriage as a union between a man and a woman, and a marriage ceremony performed by a minister, priest, rabbi, or other person ordained or designated as a leader of the person's religious faith does not lose its meaning as a sacrament or other religious institution. The sanctity of all religious marriages celebrated in the future will have the same meaning as those celebrated in the past. The only difference is *civil* marriage will now take on a new meaning that reflects a more complete understanding of equal protection of the law. . . .

. . . . We are firmly convinced the exclusion of gay and lesbian people from the institution of civil marriage does not substantially further any important governmental objective. The legislature has excluded a historically disfavored class of persons from a supremely important civil institution without a constitutionally sufficient justification. There is no material fact, genuinely in dispute, that can affect this determination.

We have a constitutional duty to ensure equal protection of the law. Faithfulness to that duty requires us to hold Iowa's marriage statute violates the Iowa Constitution. . . . If gay and lesbian people must submit to different treatment without an exceedingly persuasive justification, they are deprived of the benefits of the principle of equal protection upon which the rule of law is founded.

. . . .

[W]e must decide how to best remedy the constitutional violation. The sole remedy requested by plaintiffs is admission into the institution of civil marriage. The County does not suggest an alternative remedy. The high courts of other jurisdictions have remedied constitutionally invalid bans on same-sex marriage in two ways. Some courts have ordered gay and lesbian people to be allowed to access the institution of civil marriage. *See In re Marriage Cases*, 183 P.3d at 453 [California]; *Kerrigan*, 957 A.2d at 480 [Connecticut]; *Opinions of the Justices to the Senate*, 802 N.E.2d 565, 571 (Mass. 2004). Other courts have allowed their state legislatures to create parallel civil institutions for same-sex couples. *See Lewis v. Harris*, 908 A.2d 196 (N.J. 2006); *Baker v. State*, 744 A.2d 864, 887 (Vt. 1999).

[Our statute] is unconstitutional because the County has been unable to identify a constitutionally adequate justification. . . . A new distinction based on sexual orientation would be equally suspect and difficult to square with the fundamental principles of equal protection embodied in our constitution. This record, our independent research, and the appropriate equal protection analysis do not suggest the existence of a justification for such a legislative classification that substantially furthers any governmental objective. Consequently, the language in [the statute] limiting civil marriage to a man and a woman must be stricken . . . and the remaining statutory language must be interpreted and applied in a manner allowing gay and lesbian people full access to the institution of civil marriage.

. . . .

The district court properly granted summary judgment to plaintiffs.

AFFIRMED.

All justices concur.

NOTES

1. *Status of Same-Sex Marriage Bans.* Since the late 1970s, litigants have argued that exclusion of same-sex couples from marriage is unconstitutional. No federal constitutional attack has yet been successful. *See, e.g., Citizens for Equal Protection v. Bruning*, 455 F.3d 859 (8th Cir. 2006) (upholding Nebraska's limitation of marriage to opposite-sex couples; valid purpose of "steering heterosexual procreation into marriage" insulates state constitutional provision against attack under First Amendment, Equal Protection Clause and the Bill of

Attainder prohibition); *Dean v. District of Columbia*, 653 A.2d 307 (D.C. App. 1995); *Adams v. Howerton*, 486 F. Supp. 1119 (C.D. Cal. 1980), *aff'd*, 673 F.2d 1036 (9th Cir. 1982); *cf. Shahar v. Bowers*, 836 F. Supp. 859 (N.D. Ga. 1993), *aff'd*, 114 F.3d 1097 (11th Cir. 1997) (termination of state employment after public marriage ceremony with same-sex partner did not violate employee's constitutional rights). Especially between 1986 (when the U.S. Supreme Court decided *Bowers v. Hardwick*) and 2003 (when it decided *Lawrence v. Texas*) (*Bowers* and *Lawrence* are discussed *supra* at Chapter 1, Section ___), a federal constitutional claim seemed futile. Litigants therefore focused their strategy on state constitutions.

Varnum is the most recent successful such attack, though it was preceded by similar decisions in *Kerrigan v. Commissioner*, 957 A.2d 407 (Conn. 2008), *In re Marriage Cases*, 183 P.3d 384 (Cal. 2008), and *Goodridge v. Dep't of Pub. Health*, 798 N.E.2d 941 (Mass. 2003). *See also Baehr v. Lewin*, 852 P.2d 44 (Hawaii 1993) (holding state constitution required strict scrutiny of same-sex marriage ban; state constitution amended to permit same-sex marriage ban before final decision in the litigation); *Baker v. State*, 744 A.2d 864 (Vt. 1999) (under state constitution same-sex couples "may not be deprived of the statutory benefits and protections afforded persons of the opposite sex who choose to marry") *Baker*, however, held the constitution would be satisfied if there was "an alternative legal status to marriage for same-sex couples, [with] similar formal requirements and limitations, . . . a parallel licensing or registration scheme, and . . . all or most of the same rights and obligations provided by the law to married partners." *See also Lewis v. Harris*, 908 A.2d 196 (N.J. 2006). The initial legislative response was a civil union statute conferring on same-sex partners essentially all the attributes of a married couple regarding state law issues, including, e.g., a "marital" property system. In 2009, however, Vermont, along with Maine and New Hampshire, enacted legislation legalizing same sex marriages. *See* Chris Garofolo, *Gay Marriage Passes*, BRATTLEBORO REFORMER, Apr. 8, 2009, at 1; Dennis Hoey, *State Finalizes Wording for Gay Marriage Ballot*, PORTLAND PRESS HERALD, May 20, 2009 at A1; Abby Goodnough, *New Hampshire Approves Same-Sex Marriage*, NEW YORK TIMES, June 4, 2009, at 19; *see also* discussion in Note 7, *infra*.

After *Goodridge*, a drive was launched to overrule it by amending the state constitution (as had been done in Hawaii in response to *Baehr*. This campaign was halted, however, by the refusal of the Massachusetts legislature to place the amendment before the voters in 2008. Frank Phillips & Andrea Estes, *Right of Gays to Marry Set for Years to Come — Vote Keeps Proposed Ban Off 2008 Ballot*, BOSTON GLOBE, June 15, 2007 at A1. The legislature's action insured that the constitution could not be amended before 2012.

A number of cases have rejected state constitutional attacks on same-sex marriage bans. *See, e.g., Conaway v. Deane*, 932 A.2d 571 (Md. 2007) (statute rationally related to state interest in procreation; no violation of state ERA or Substantive Due Process); *Hernandez v. Robles*, 855 N.E.2d 1 (N.Y. 2006) (rejecting claims under state constitution's equal protection and due process clauses); *Hebel v. West*, 803 N.Y.S.2d 242 (App. Div. 2005) (village mayor properly enjoined from solemnizing marriages in violation of state same-sex marriage ban); *Andersen v. King County*, 138 P.3d 963 (Wash. 2006) (same-sex marriage ban did not violate state constitution's equal protection, due process or privileges and immunities clauses); *Morrison v. Sadler*, 821 N.E.2d 15 (Ind. App. 2005) ("responsible procreation" sufficient state interest to justify state statute prohibiting same-sex marriage).

2. *Constitutional Overview of Same-Sex Marriage Prohibitions.*

a. *Sex discrimination?* While virtually all courts have rejected such a claim, the *Baehr v. Levin* court, *supra* Note 1, found sex discrimination under a state constitutional provision. The argument for it depends upon what might be a wooden understanding of a classic racial discrimination case, *Loving v. Virginia*, 388 U.S. 1 (1967). In that case, the Court struck down a statute barring interracial marriage, ignoring a state argument that the law was not racially discriminatory because it treated blacks and whites alike: each could marry members of their own racial group and neither could marry members of the other group. The claim that a same-sex marriage ban is sex discrimination assumes that the only defense against such an assertion is one analogous to this rejected Virginia argument: that it is not gender discrimination because men and women suffer the same legal disability under this rule. If this defense is no good, the argument goes, then this is sex discrimination.

Loving clearly was correct in seeing the racial animus behind the Virginia statute, despite the fact that the rule satisfied a literal test of equality. The very opposite is equally clear, however, regarding the same-sex marriage ban. While Virginia's purpose was to maintain the social segregation of African-Americans, it is equally obvious that the purpose of the same-sex marriage ban is *not* to maintain the social segregation of men or women. It is rather to make clear that gay relationships — male or female — are different from, and less favored than, heterosexual relationships. While after *Lawrence v. Texas*, discussed below, that may also be a constitutionally suspect goal, it is not sex discrimination, but discrimination based upon one's sexual orientation.

For an article analogizing treatment of mixed-race and same-sex marriages, see Josephine Ross, *The Sexualization of Difference: A Comparison of Mixed-Race and Same-Gender Marriage*, 37 HARV. CIV. R. CIV. LIB. L. REV. 255 (2002). Professor Ross argues that same-sex marriages have been "sexualized" by society just as mixed-race marriages were sexualized in the past. "Sexualization" means the relationships are "viewed as essentially sexual and . . . not about commitment, communication or love." Ross argues that "sexualization is a cause as well as a symptom of disempowerment" for both kinds of relationships.

b. *Fundamental right to marry?* *Zablocki* establishes that access to marriage is of fundamental federal constitutional importance. One can also argue, however, that the very definition of marriage inherent in this constitutional status assumes heterosexual unions only. The Hawaii Supreme Court in *Baehr*, *supra* Note 1, adopted this position, though the court accepted state constitutional arguments separate from the fundamental right approach. While *Goodridge*, *supra* Note 1, did not address the question of whether heightened scrutiny was appropriate because of interference with the fundamental right to marry, it did, as part of the remedy in the case reinterpret the concept of marriage "to mean the voluntary union of two persons as spouses, to the exclusion of all others."

c. General substantive due process. The possibility of a substantive due process argument prevailing against the same-sex marriage ban became far more plausible after the Supreme Court's decision in *Lawrence v. Texas*, 539 U.S. 558 (2003) (reprinted and discussed more fully in Chapter 1). *Lawrence* overruled *Bowers v. Hardwick*, 478 U.S. 186 (1986), in which the Court had upheld the constitutionality of a criminal prosecution of two adult men for violation of Georgia's sodomy statute. *Bowers* defined the question before it as whether the Constitution conferred on homosexuals a fundamental right to engage in sodomy. *Lawrence* is important because it redefined the question:

> To say that the issue in *Bowers* was simply the right to engage in certain sexual conduct demeans the claim . . . , just as it would demean a married couple were it to be said marriage is simply about the right to have sexual intercourse. The laws involved in *Bowers* and here are, to be sure, statutes that purport to do no more than prohibit a particular sexual act. Their penalties and purposes, though, have more far-reaching consequences, touching upon the most private human conduct, sexual behavior, and in the most private of places, the home. The statutes . . . seek to control a personal relationship that, whether or not entitled to formal recognition in the law, is within the liberty of persons to choose without being punished as criminals.

> . . .

> When homosexual conduct is made criminal . . . , that declaration in and of itself is an invitation to subject homosexual persons to discrimination both in the public and in the private spheres. . . . *Bowers'*. . . . continuance as precedent demeans the lives of homosexual persons. [ ]. . . . The [criminal defendants] are entitled to respect for their private lives. The State cannot demean their existence or control their destiny by making their private sexual conduct a crime. Their right to liberty under the Due Process Clause gives them the full right to engage in their conduct without intervention of the government. "It is a promise of the Constitution that there is a realm of personal liberty which the government may not enter." [Quoting *Casey*]. The Texas statute furthers no legitimate state interest which can justify its intrusion into the personal and private life of the individual.

539 U.S. at 567, 575, 578.

Does the ban on same-sex marriage demean the existence of homosexuals and deprive them of respect for their private lives? If so, does it further a legitimate state interest sufficiently important to justify the ban? Analysis of these questions must surely be informed by *Zablocki* which teaches marriage is a core part of an individual's private life protected from unjustified state regulation. The combination of *Zablocki* and *Lawrence* could suggest that government may not justify a ban on same-sex marriage with the goal of demeaning, discouraging or controlling the private lives of homosexuals. It must offer some other purpose for excluding their relationships from the advantages sought by persons who marry. What is the other purpose and is it adequate?

Despite the apparently powerful arguments available in any challenge to the same-sex marriage ban, most commentators would be surprised if the Court accepted them, at least in the near future. Indeed, dissension within the pro-same-sex marriage community precisely along that line erupted when a federal court action was filed seeking a declaration that California's Proposition 8 (state constitutional amendment overturning the California Supreme Court's ruling *The Marriage Cases, supra,* Note 1, violated the Federal Constitution. *See* Jesse McKinley, Bush v. Gore *Foes Join to Fight California Gay Marriage Ban,* N.Y. Times, May 28, 2009, at A1. Some critics of the lawsuit asserted that the time was not yet right to take this issue to the High Court and described it as "risky" and "dangerous."

Justice O'Connor, concurring in *Lawrence,* made clear she would distinguish and reject a constitutional challenge to the gay marriage ban. Justice Kennedy, speaking for the other five Justices in the majority, was more circumspect. He wrote only that *Lawrence* "does not involve whether the government must give formal recognition to any relationship that homosexual persons seek to enter." The matter, in other words, was reserved, not decided. The majority thus made clear it was not committed to finding homosexuals have a right to marry and, by going out of its way to announce this, might have been hinting that the decision, when made, will be against same-sex marriage. Alternatively, this language may simply express political prudence. Writing for the *Lawrence* dissenters, Justice Scalia argued the majority's

> reasoning leaves on pretty shaky grounds state laws limiting marriage to opposite-sex couples. Justice OConnor seeks to preserve them by the conclusory statement that "preserving the traditional institution of marriage" is a legitimate state interest. But "preserving the traditional institution of marriage" is just a kinder way of describing the State's *moral disapproval* of same-sex couples. Texas' interest in [eliminating homosexual sodomy] could be recast in similarly euphemistic terms: "preserving the traditional sexual mores of our society." (emphasis in original).

539 U.S. 601–02. Might there be state interests insufficient to justify criminal punishment, but sufficient to validate refusal of a state to offer its symbol of legitimacy to a relationship it didn't approve of?

3. ***More on the Interests of Gay Couples.***   As discussed in the notes following *Zablocki,* marriage is surely a symbol. Persons enter marriage to symbolize love and commitment to one another and they usually want others, including the state, to accept and acknowledge their marriage. One might therefore argue that the couple's most important interest is the symbolic one of state recognition, especially because the alternative rule — a ban on same-sex marriage — is not merely neutral, but an affirmative denigration of the relationship, at least in comparison with heterosexual families. Symbolic interests may seem unimportant to some, yet in human relationships they are often crucial. As the *Zablocki* notes point out, they seem to be an important part of the fundamental right recognized in that case. To the extent the symbolic issue is key, the *Baker* solution — the marriage alternative — falls short by continuing to affirm that same-sex relationships are different from, and in some sense less than, heterosexual relationships. As the *Varnum* court phrased it: the "ultimate disadvantage [asserted by the attackers of the same-sex marriage ban] . . . is the inability to obtain for themselves and for their children the personal and public affirmation that accompanies marriage." Of course, symbolic interests are not the entire story. In *What If? The Legal Consequences of Marriage and the Legal Needs of Lesbian and Gay Male Couples*, 95 MICH. L. REV. 447 (1996), Professor David Chambers concludes:

> the laws assigning consequences to marriage today [largely fall] within three sorts of regulation; . . . each of these . . . sorts of regulation would, as a whole, fit the needs of long-term gay male and lesbian couples; . . . while the law has changed in recent years to recognize nonmarital relationships in a variety of contexts, the number of significant distinctions resting on marital status remains large and durable; . . . in some significant respects the remaining distinctive laws of marriage are better suited to the life situations of same-sex couples than they are to those of the opposite-sex couples for whom they were devised; and . . . the package of rules relating to marriage, while problematic in some details and unduly exclusive in some regards, are a just response by the state to the circumstances of persons who live together in enduring, emotionally based attachments. Legal marriage, somewhat surprisingly to a person long dubious of the state's regulation of nonviolent private relationships, has much to be said for it.

Id. at 447–48. Professor Chambers' three categories are: (1) "regulations that recognize emotional attachments" (including those giving spouses decisionmaking authority for an incapacitated person, intestacy laws, family leave laws); (2) "regulations dealing with parenting" (laws dealing with stepparent status, surrogacy and the new technology of reproduction and adoption and foster care); (3) "laws regulating the economic relationships of couples or between the couple and the state" (including tax laws, property division and maintenance laws, forced share statutes).

4. *More on the State's Interests.* Professor Lynn Wardle, who opposes recognizing same-sex relationships, has offered this summary of "'important public interests in and social purposes' supporting that position":

> . . . . These include (1) safe sexual relations; (2) responsible procreation; (3) optimal child rearing; (4) healthy human development; (5) protecting those who undertake the most vulnerable family roles for the benefit of society, especially wives and mothers; (6) securing the stability and integrity of the basic unit of society; (7) fostering civic virtue, democracy, and social order; and (8) facilitating interjurisdictional compatibility.
>
> On the basis of history and common experience across cultures, advocates of preserving marriage exclusively for male-female couples may reasonably assert that committed heterosexual unions we call marriages make unique and important contributions to achieving the public and social purposes of marriage. [H]eterosexual . . . marriage seem[s] to provide the best setting for the safest and most beneficial expression of sexual intimacy. [It] also appears to provide the best environment into which children can be

born. Heterosexual marriage reasonably may be assumed to provide the most advantageous environment in which children can be reared, providing profound benefits of dual gender parenting to model intergender relations and show children how to relate to persons of their own and the opposite gender. [It] has been believed to provide the most enriching and liberating relationship to facilitate human adults to personally develop and achieve their fullest potential. . . . [I]t has long been believed that heterosexual marriage provides the best security for those who take the greatest risks and invest the greatest personal effort in establishing and maintaining families, especially wives and mothers. [It] appears to provide the strongest and most stable companionate unit of society, and the most secure setting for intergenerational transmission of social knowledge and skills, and reflects the understanding of marriage that has been constant across cultures and throughout history.

Wardle, *"Multiply and Replenish": Considering Same-Sex Marriage in Light of State Interests in Marital Procreation*, 24 HARV. J. L. & PUB. POL'Y 771 (2001).

Review Wardle's list carefully. Many of the interests he identifies assume certain facts. Do you think there is in fact agreement on the facts he assumes? (For example, would a gay person agree that for him or her, a heterosexual union would "provide the most enriching and liberating relationship to facilitate human adults to personally develop and achieve their fullest potential"? Or, assuming it is true that heterosexual marriages are a more stable "companionate unit" than same-sex relationships, is it possible that this is a *consequence* of our refusal to recognize same-sex relationships, rather than a *reason* for refusing?). Perhaps even more importantly, a state interest is relevant to the constitutional analysis only if recognition of same-sex marriage would somehow place it in jeopardy. Opponents of same-sex marriage seem to assume that its recognition would necessarily burden heterosexual marriage. But does that necessarily follow? Could it possibly follow? It may not be possible to offer any arguments in response to these questions, on either side, that many on the other side would credit. The final question is how much deference should then be given to the legislature's answer.

5. *Conflict Within the Gay/Lesbian Community.* The gay and lesbian community is not united in its view of same-sex marriage. Professor William Eskridge has stated

same-sex marriage is good for gay people and good for America and for the same reason: it civilizes gays and it civilizes America. . . . For most of the twentieth century, lesbians, gay men, and bisexuals have been outlaws. The law relevant to us was the criminal code. . . . The law relevant to us today is found in the civil code. . . . Virtually no one in the gay and lesbian community would deny that this "civilizing" shift in the law reflects enormous progress and that such progress is incomplete until gay people enjoy the same rights and responsibilities as straight people. Marriage is the most important right the state has to offer. . . . As a formal matter, law's civilizing movement will not be complete until the same-sex married couple replaces the outlawed sodomite. . . . [Additionally], [t]his country would be edified — civilized, if you will — if it would end all vestiges of legal discrimination against its homosexual population. Essential to this project is the adoption of laws guaranteeing rights for lesbian and gay couples.

ESKRIDGE, THE CASE FOR SAME-SEX MARRIAGE 8, 10 (1996); *see also* Evan Wolfson, *Crossing the Threshhold: Equal Marriage Rights for Lesbians and Gay Men and the Intra-Community Critique*, 21 N.Y.U. REV. L. & SOC. CHANGE 567 (1994) (supporting litigation attacking state marriage entry regulations). Others prefer to oppose the institution of marriage altogether:

> For lesbians, the abolition of marriage would mean that our relationships would not be in a different legal category from other legal relationships. . . . [T]he state would not relate to its citizens on the basis of their intimate relations. . . . Abolishing marriage would also mean that a nation could not resort to formalistic legal relations to determine the rights of its citizens.

RUTHANN ROBSON, SAPPHO GOES TO LAW SCHOOL 146, 149–50 (1998); *see also* Michael Warner, *Normal and Normaller: Beyond Gay Marriage*, 5 GLQ: a JOURNAL OF LESBIAN AND GAY STUDIES 119, 121 (1999) ("If reform of marriage was the goal [of those seeking legalization of same-sex marriage], the tactics of legal advocacy have not worked; in some way they have made the problem worse. . . . [N]ow that the ship has run aground, we might ask whether it was headed in the right direction.") Nancy Polikoff, *We Will Get What We Ask For: Why Legalizing Gay and Lesbian Marriage Will Not "Dismantle the Legal Structure of Gender in Every Marriage,"* 79 VA. L. REV. 1535, 1536 (1993) ("the desire to marry in the lesbian and gay community is an attempt to mimic the worst of mainstream society, an effort to fit into an inherently problematic institution that betrays the promise of both lesbian and gay liberation and radical feminism"); Steven Homer, Note, *Against Marriage*, 29 HARV. CIV. R.-CIV. LIB. L. REV. 507, 530 (1994) ("[m]arriage is not the same thing as love. . . . [H]eterosexuals have shown us what marriage is worth and how long it lasts. . . . [W]e have learned from our outlaw status a great deal about love — what it is worth, and how long it lasts. Rather than accept the narrowness under which heterosexuals themselves chafe, why not invite them to share in what we know . . .?").

6. *Changing Religious Views on Same-Sex Marriage?* Beginning in the mid-1980s a number of religious groups have endorsed the concept of same-sex relationships, either in marriage or quasi-marriage. For example, in 1996, the Unitarian Universalist Association General Assembly adopted a position in support of same sex marriages. *See* http://www.uua.org/socialjustice/socialjustice/statements/14251.shtml. The Pew Forum on Religion & Public Life summarizes the position of Judaism as follows:

> Both the Reform and Reconstructionist movements support gay and lesbian rights, including the right of same-sex couples to wed. The Conservative movement does not sanctify gay marriage but does grant rabbis the autonomy to choose whether or not to perform same-sex marriage ceremonies. Leaders in Orthodox Judaism have defined marriage as an institution between man and woman and therefore do not allow for same-sex marriage.

http://pewforum.org/docs/?DocID=291. The United Church of Christ, at its 25th Synod, voted to recognize and advocate for same-sex marriage. *Id.* Similarly, the Christian Church (Disciples of Christ) has "voted to allow same-sex unions." *Disciples D.C. Church Oks Same-Sex Unions*, CHRISTIAN CENTURY, Dec. 18-31, 2002, at 16. A major American Buddhist group, Soka Gakkai, which claims 300,000 followers in the United States also has decided to "support the [same-sex] couple in expressing their commitment" and the head monk at a California Buddhist Meditation Center reported having performed ten same-sex weddings even before the formal acceptance of the concept by the organization. John Dart, *For Buddhists, Gay Marriage is as Holy as Any Other Kind*, L.A. TIMES, July 1, 1995, at B11. The Metropolitan Community Churches, whose membership is predominantly gay and lesbian, report performing approximately 6,000 same-sex marriages annually. Barbara Whitaker, *Gay Couples Pop Big Question, But the States' Reply is the Same*, N.Y. TIMES, Feb. 15, 2003, at 15. An article in 2004 reported that clergy are "seeing a growing number of religiously observant gay couples who are sidestepping the debate over legal rights and seeking to consecrate their unions in churches and synagogues." Laurie Goodstein, *Gay Couples Seek Unions in God's Eyes*, N.Y. TIMES, Jan. 30, 2004, at A1. As one participant stated, "[w]e didn't want it to be like going to a justice of the peace or anything. We would be more concerned about breaking vows we'd promised to God than to some guy in a suit." Of course, a number of religions oppose same-sex marriage. *See* http://pewforum.org/docs/?DocID=291 (citing Mormonism, Catholicism, Islam, Lutheran Church-Missouri Synod, Southern Baptist Convention and the United Methodist Church as opposed).

However, it has been asserted that "clerical sympathy for same-sex marriage exists in denominations that have most fervently opposed same-sex unions." ESKRIDGE, THE CASE FOR SAME-SEX MARRIAGE 102 (1996) (identifying fundamentalist and Roman Catholic clergy who officiate at same-sex weddings); *see also* Gabriel Rotello, *To Have and to Hold: The Case for Gay Marriage*, THE NATION, June 24, 1996, at 11 (reporting "religious groups have been faster on the draw [than liberal political groups]).

7. *Public Opinion on Same-Sex Unions.* Public opinion on the question has undergone enormous change in recent decades. In 1977, The Gallup Organization first asked a national sample whether "homosexual relations between consenting adults should or should not be legal?" Americans were evenly split, with 43% on each side of the question and 14% undecided. By May 2003 (a month before *Lawrence* was decided by the Supreme Court), 60% of the sample favored legalization with 35% opposed and 5% undecided. Frank Newport, *Six in Ten Americans Agree That Gay Sex Should Be Legal*, THE GALLUP POLL NEWS RELEASES (June 27, 2003). Not only is acceptance broadening in the general population, but much of the support is concentrated on the younger generation. In the 2003 survey, 66% of 18- to 29-year-olds and 65% of those between 30 and 49 favored legalization. *Id.* Perhaps not surprisingly, support for legalization varied across different regions of the country. Only 49% of respondents in the South favored legalization, while support in the West was 73%. Debbie Howlett, *Attitudes on Gay Relations Tied to Demographics*, USA TODAY, June 27, 2003, at 6A. Legalization was favored by college graduates (71%), those earning more than $75,000 (72%) and those reporting they seldom attend religious services (76%). *Id.*

Attitudes toward same-sex marriage, however, have been and are less accepting. A 1994 poll reported almost 40% of the American public believe "homosexuals should have equal rights to marry one another." A USA Today/Gallup Poll report of polling done in May 2009 concluded 40% of Americans support legalization of same-sex marriage. http://www.pollingreport.com/civil.htm. It is interesting to contrast public support for same-sex marriage to public support of marriage between blacks and whites. In June 1968, approximately a year *after* the Supreme Court's decision in *Loving v. Virginia*, only 20% of Americans polled by Gallup approved of interracial marriage. Joseph Carroll, *Most Americans Approve of Interracial Marriages*, Aug. 16, 2007, http://gallup.com/poll/28417/most-americans-approve-interracial-marriages.aspx (collecting historical polling data on anti-miscegenous marriage bans). Thus, support for same-sex marriage was twice as strong in 2009 as support for interracial marriage was in 1968. It should be noted that, as late as 1994, less than half of those polled approved of marriage between blacks and whites. *Id.*

Undoubtedly, however, because of the greater support for same-sex marriage in the younger age cohorts over the years, support for the concept is growing. Nate Silver, whose web site is designed to "accumulate and analyze polling and political data in way that is informed, accurate and attractive," reported the following in the spring of 2009, immediately after *Varnum* was decided:

I looked at the 30 instances in which a state has attempted to pass a constitutional ban on gay marriage by voter initiative. The list includes Arizona twice, which voted on different versions of such an amendment in 2006 and 2008, and excludes Hawaii, which voted to permit the legislature to ban gay marriage but did not actually alter the state's constitution. I then built a regression model that looked at a series of political and demographic variables in each of these states and attempted to predict the percentage of the vote that the marriage ban would receive.

It turns out that you can build a very effective model by including just three variables:

1. The year in which the amendment was voted upon;

2. The percentage of adults in 2008 Gallup tracking surveys who said that religion was an important part of their daily lives;

3. The percentage of white evangelicals in the state.

These variables collectively account for about three-quarters of the variance in the performance of marriage bans in different states. The model predicts, for example, that a marriage ban in California in 2008 would have passed with 52.1 percent of the vote, almost exactly the fraction actually received by Proposition 8.

Unsurprisingly, there is a very strong correspondence between the religiosity of a state and its propensity to ban gay marriage, with a particular "bonus" effect depending on the number of white evangelicals in the state.

Marriage bans, however, are losing ground at a rate of slightly less than 2 points per year. So, for example, we'd project that a state in which a marriage ban passed with 60 percent of the vote last year would only have 58 percent of its voters approve the ban this year.

All of the other variables that I looked at — race, education levels, party registration, etc. — either did not appear to matter at all, or became redundant once we accounted for religiosity. Nor does it appear to make a significant difference whether the ban affected marriage only, or both marriage and civil unions.

www.fivethirtyeight.com/2009/04/will-iowans-uphold-gay-marriage.html.

There apparently has been a dramatic shift in Americans' understanding of whether homosexuality is "something a person is born with or . . . due to factors such as upbringing or environment." "In 1977, when the question was first asked in a Gallup poll, 56% of the public said that homosexuality was environmental, while only 13% said it was genetic" Frank Newport, *Some Change Over Time in American Attitudes Toward Homosexuality, But Negativity Remains*, THE GALLUP POLL MONTHLY, Mar. 1999, at 28. In the May 2007 survey, 42% of the respondents saw homosexuality is something one is "born with," and only 35% saw it as the product of upbringing and environment. Lydia Saad, *Tolerance for Gay Rights at High Water Mark*, http://www.gallup.com/poll/27694/Tolerance-Gay-Rights-HighWater-Mark.aspx Perhaps the more the public comes to believe homosexuality is genetically-determined, the more unfair it might find the exclusion of same-sex couples from the institution of marriage.

8. *Same-Sex Unions in Other Countries.* In the wake of court decisions in three provinces (Quebec Superior Court, the British Columbia Court of Appeal and the Ontario Court of Appeal) declaring the national same-sex marriage ban unconstitutional under the federal Charter of Rights and Freedoms, the Canadian Parliament legalized same-sex marriage in July, 2005. *See* Kathleen Harris, *Gay Canucks Can Now Say "I Do,"* TORONTO SUN, July 21, 2005, at 23; *Halpern v. Canada (Attorney General)*, 2003 Ont. Rep. LEXIS 153 (Ct. App., June 10, 2003); *EGALE Canada Inc. v. Canada (Attorney General)*, 2003 BCCA 251 (May 1); *Quebec Gays Hail Court Ruling*, TORONTO STAR, Sept. 7, 2002, at A9. Because there is no residency requirement for a Canadian marriage license, a number of same-sex couples from the United States have traveled north to marry. The legal efficacy of such marriages in the United States is considered below in the Notes on Conflict of Law and Marriage Regulation.

In the spring of 2009, Sweden became the fifth European country to authorize same-sex marriage, joining Belgium, the Netherlands, Norway and Spain. *Sweden: Same-Sex Marriage Now Legal*, N.Y. TIMES, Apr. 2, 2009, at A6. Many other countries have adopted domestic partnership or civil union legislation under which same-sex couples may gain most of the legal rights of married couples. Such legislation has been enacted in Denmark, Iceland, Finland, Hungary, France, Germany and Portugal. *See* YUVAL MERIN, EQUALITY FOR SAME-SEX COUPLES: THE LEGAL RECOGNITION OF GAY PARTNERSHIPS IN EUROPE AND THE UNITED STATES (2002); LEGAL RECOGNITION OF SAME-SEX PARTNERSHIPS (Robert Wintemute & Mads Andenaes eds., 2001); Note, *Developments — The Law of Marriage and Family,*

116 HARV. L. REV. 1996, 2004–27 (2003). In early March 2010, Mexico City became the first jurisdiction in Latin America to legalize same-sex marriage. While opposed by the president of Mexico, the reform was adopted by the federal district of Mexico City's Legislative Assembly, which is controlled by the center-left Democratic Revolution Party. Anne-Marie O'Connor, *With Same-Sex Marriage Law, Mexico City Becomes Battleground in Culture Wars*, WASHINGTON POST, Mar. 3, 2010, at A8.

9. ***Literature on Same-Sex Marriage.*** A rich and growing literature deals with same-sex marriage from many different perspectives. In a provocative application of economic analysis, Professor Jennifer Brown argued that New Mexico and Vermont both had strong incentives to become "first movers." Based on assumptions about the country's gay and lesbian population, expected wedding-related expenditures and the marriage rate among the gay population, in 1995 she estimated the "present value of the revenue to be generated by the first state than legalizes same-sex marriage is at least $3 billion to $4 billion." Brown, *Competitive Federalism and the Legislative Incentives to Recognize Same-Sex Marriage*, 68 S. CAL. L. REV. 745 (1995). In 2009, Vermont became the fourth state (and the first to do so legislatively) to legalize same sex marriage. For recent articles on the subject, see Gerald Bradley, *Three Liberal-But Mistaken-Arguments for Same-Sex Marriage*, 50 S. TEX. L. REV. 45 (2008) (rejecting three standard arguments made in support of same-sex marriage and challenging supporters to come up with others); Jesse Choper & John Yoo, *Can the Government Prohibit Gay Marriage?*, 50 S. TEX. L. REV. 15 (2008) (concluding there is possible federal power to prohibit gay marriage and probably not an individual right to gay marriage, but "without persuasive evidence about the direct harms caused by gay marriage, we would not choose a policy to ban it"); Dale Carpenter, *A Traditionalist Case for Gay Marriage*, 50 S. TEX. L. REV. 93 (2008) (arguing that "[s]ometimes it seems that gay people are practically the last people in the country who still believe in marriage, who are reaffirming its importance in their lives. . . . They are saying 'yes' to a traditionalizing institution. . . . [T]he question for conservatives . . . is why can't they take 'yes' for an answer?"); Michael Perry, *The Fourteenth Amendment, Same-Sex Unions, and the Supreme Court*, 38 LOY. U. CHI. L.J. 215 (2007) (arguing that while "state refusals to recognize same-sex unions violate the Fourteenth Amendment . . . it does not follow that we should want the Court, just yet, to so rule"); Mark Strasser, Lawrence *and Same-Sex Marriage Bans*, 69 BROOKLYN L. REV. 1003 (2004) (claims "although same-sex marriage bans violate both equal protection and due process guarantees, it is at best unclear whether this Court will recognize what the Constitution requires . . . or whether . . . that recognition will not take place until sometime in the perhaps distant future"); Amy Wax, *Untangling the Issues and Consequences: Traditionalism, Pluralism, and Same-Sex Marriage*, 59 RUTGERS L. REV. 377 (2007) (asserts that because of increasing ambivalence with traditionalist assumptions "same-sex marriage is likely to be adopted in the future through the democratic process"); Eugene Volokh, *Same-Sex Marriage and Slippery Slopes*, 33 HOFSTRA L. REV. 1155 (2005) (assesses different kinds of slippery slope arguments made against recognition of same-sex marriage; concludes that "on balance . . . the potential slippery-slope harms caused . . . while plausible and potentially significant, are not very likely; their costs, discounted by their improbability, are thus exceeded by the more direct benefits").

10. *Marriage Involving a Transsexual.* In *M.T. v. J.T.*, 355 A.2d 204 (N.J. App. 1976), the court held valid a marriage in which the wife had been born with male sex organs, but had them surgically removed and replaced with a vagina and labia "adequate for sexual intercourse." The husband was aware of (and funded) the surgery, so fraud was not an issue. The court held the transsexual had "become physically and psychologically unified and fully capable of sexual activity consistent with her reconciled sexual attributes of gender and anatomy." *But see Kantaras v. Kantaras*, 884 So. 2d 155 (Fla. Ct. App. 2004) ("common meaning" of gender as used in the marriage statutes refers to "immutable traits determined at birth" and, thus, post-operative female-to-male transsexual could not marry female), *pet. for rev. denied*, 898 So.2d 80 (Fla. 2005); *In re Simmons*, 825 N.E.2d 303 (Ill. App. Ct. 2005) (marriage between female and a female-to-male transexual who had not completed sex reassignment surgery was invalid same-sex marriage); *In re Application for a Marriage License*, 2003 Ohio App. LEXIS 6513 (Dec. 31, 2003) (refusing to recognize amended Massachusetts birth certificate of transsexual under public policy exception to Full Faith and Credit clause; upholding refusal to permit post-surgery male to marry female); *In re Estate of Gardiner*, 42 P.3d 120 (Kan. 2002) (court held sex reassignment surgery four years prior to marriage to decedent was legally ineffective to change sex; petitioner did not "fit the common meaning of female);. *See* Briana Morgan, Note, *The Use of Rules and Standards to Define Transsexual's Sex for the Purpose of Marriage: An Argument for a Hybrid Approach*, 55 HASTINGS L.J. 1329 (2004) (describes split in case law as reflective of traditional jurisprudential rules/standards debate; proposes multi-factor approach along with presumption in favor of a person's congruent sex as identified by physician); Leslie Pearlman, Comment, *Transsexualism as Metaphor: The Collision of Sex and Gender*, 43 BUFF. L. REV. 835 (1995).

NOTES ON CONFLICT OF LAW AND MARRIAGE REGULATION

1. *General Rule.* In a mobile society with 50 states, each able to enact marriage entry regulations, conflict of law questions often arise regarding a marriage's validity. As noted in the common law marriage materials, generally a "marriage is valid everywhere if valid under the law of the state where the marriage takes place." SCOLES & HAY, CONFLICT OF LAWS § 13.5 (2nd ed. 1992); RESTATEMENT (SECOND) CONFLICT OF LAWS § 283(2) (1971). It is often said, however, that there is a public policy exception to this rule, allowing a state that would not have allowed the marriage to refuse to recognize it, despite its validity in the state of celebration, if a state has the most significant relationship with the couple and finds the marriage offensive to a deeply-held forum public policy. *See* Anthony D'Amato, *Conflict of Laws Rules and the Interstate Recognition of Same-Sex Marriages*, 1995 U. ILL. L. REV. 911; RESTATEMENT (SECOND) CONFLICTS OF LAWS § 283(2); *New York v. Ezeonu*, 588 N.Y.S.2d 116 (Sup. Ct. 1992) (refusing to recognize Nigerian polygamous marriage). *But see Mason v. Mason*, 775 N.E. 2d 706 (Ind. App. 2002) (rejecting claim that Tennessee marriage between cousins violated Indiana public policy); *Leszinske v. Poole*, 798 P.2d 1049 (N.M. App. 1990) (recognizing a woman's Costa Rican marriage to her uncle; local law voiding such a marriage found not to express strong public policy). A second exception to the *lex* *loci* rule applies when a domiciliary marries in another state to avoid a rule disallowing the marriage in his home State. R. WEINTRAUB, COMMENTARY ON THE CONFLICT OF LAWS § 5.1A (4th ed. 2001). *See* ARIZ. REV. STATS. § 25-112(C); GA. CODE § 19-3-43; *In re Estate of Toutant*, 633 N.W.2d 692 (Wis. App. 2001) (applying statute refusing to recognize any marriage contracted in or out of state within 6 months of divorce). A 1912 codification of this exception by the National Conference of Commissioners on Uniform State Laws (the Uniform Marriage Evasion Act), was withdrawn by the Conference in 1943. Joseph Hovermill, *A Conflict of Laws and Morals: The Choice of Law Implications of Hawaii's Recognition of Same-Sex Marriages*, 53 MD. L. REV. 450, 455–56 (1994). Few states adopted this exception, which meant that most honored such marriages (an example is the underage couple, or first cousins, who cross state lines to marry in a state where their age or relationship is not a bar). Some states have statutes refusing marriage licenses to persons who are not entitled to marry in their domiciliary state. Massachusetts repealed such a statute after recognizing same-sex marriage, so that it would not deny same sex couples from other states the opportunity to marry in Massachusetts. MASS. GEN. LAWS ANN., Ch. 207, §§ 11, 12 (repealed). Michael Levenson, *Same-Sex Couples Applaud Repeal; Mass. Opens Doors for Out-of-State Gays to Marry*, BOSTON GLOBE, Aug. 1, 2008, at B1.

2. *Marriage Invalid Where Performed.* What if the marriage is invalid where performed but valid in the domiciliary state? Some cases hold such a marriage invalid under the *lex loci* rule. *See, e.g., Hudson Trail Outfitters v. Dep't of Employment Services*, 801 A.2d 987 (D.C. App. 2002) (ignoring Nicaragua wedding not registered according to law); *Police & Firemen's Disability and Pension Fund v. Redding*, 2002 Ohio App. LEXIS 4114 (Aug. 1, 2002) (rejecting asserted common law marriage contracted in non-recognizing state); *Farah v. Farah*, 429 S.E.2d 626 (Va. App. 1993) (rejecting proxy marriage which would be void in England where performed). The *Restatement (Second) of Conflicts*, § 283, Comment *l*, however, suggests the "fact that a marriage does not comply with the requirements of the state where it was contracted should not therefore inevitably lead to the conclusion that the marriage is invalid." Instead, the *Restatement* argues the marriage should be recognized "unless the intensity of the interest of the state where the marriage was contracted in having its invalidating rule applied outweighs the policy of protecting the expectations of the parties . . . and the interest of the other state with the validating rule." While the place of performance is probably most interested in the formalities of marriage, the *Restatement* continues:

> The state [of performance] . . . will probably have no similar interest in the application to a marriage between non-residents of such of its marriage rules as do not relate to formalities. So . . . there would seem to be little reason to invalidate a marriage between first cousins by application of a rule of the state where the marriage was contracted if such a marriage would be valid under the local law of the state where the parties were domiciled both before and immediately following their marriage. . . .

See also McPeek v. McCardle, 888 N.E.2d 171 (Ind. 2008) (using *Restatement* approach, recognizing marriage of Indiana residents in Ohio with Indiana marriage license, though voidable in Ohio); *Donlann v. Macgurn*, 55 P. 3d 74 (Ariz. App. 2002) (recognizing Mexican marriage performed by unauthorized person; domestic law would recognize the marriage); *In re Estate of Banks*, 629 N.E.2d 1223 (Ill. App. 1994) (upholding bigamous marriage contracted in Arkansas after removal of impediment, even though removal would not validate the marriage there).

3. *Choice of Law and Same-Sex Marriage.* With a number of states having recognized same-sex marriages over the past decade, the question of the interstate impact of such marriages is inevitable. While litigation in the area is not yet plentiful, Professor Andrew Koppelman, in *Same Sex, Different States: When Same-Sex Marriages Cross State Lines* (2006), has identified and analyzed four different situations which might arise, suggesting appropriate choice of law rules for each. *Id.* Ch. VII, pp. 97–113.

Evasive Marriages — In this situation, a couple domiciled in a non-recognizing state travels to a state recognizing same-sex marriage and marry. They then return to their home state. At some later time, their marital status is at issue in their home state. Professor Koppelman suggests that, while such marriages generally would not be recognized (under the rule explained in Note 1, *supra*), there should be exceptions for "cases in which the state policy underlying the specific incident of marriage . . . would be promoted by the recognition of the marriage, and in which there is no possibility that the marriage will continue to exist within the [forum] state's borders." *Id.* at 105–06. Thus, e.g., if a same-sex spouse died intestate, by applying the rules of intestate succession in favor of the surviving spouse, the state could further its interest in effectuating the likely preferences of the decedent without having to acknowledge or tolerate a continuing marriage. He also argues non-recognizing states ought to recognize such marriages for the limited purpose of entertaining divorce or annulment proceedings.

Visitor Marriages — Suppose two Iowa men validly married in that state take a vacation in Minneapolis. While one of them is crossing the street there, an intoxicated driver kills him. The survivor brings a wrongful death action in Minnesota, the jurisdictionally proper forum for this tort claim. Should Minnesota recognize their marriage for the limited purpose of allowing the wrongful death claim (which can only be brought by a surviving spouse, child, or parent of the person fatally injured)? What if Minnesota is the only state with jurisdiction over the defendant for the purpose of adjudicating this claim? Professor Koppelman argues Minnesota should allow the action, and even that the constitutional right to travel should be seen as requiring the forum to recognize the marriage. *Id.* at 111–12. He points to authority dating to 1879 when a federal court declared that parties to an interracial marriage would "have a right of stoppage, and of transit . . . through Virginia and of temporary carrying on any business here not requiring residence." *Id.* at 48 (citing *Ex parte Kinney*).

Extraterritorial Marriages — In this situation, the couple's only connection to the forum state is the presence of property there. *Id.* at 112. For example if a partner in a same-sex Connecticut marriage dies intestate in Connecticut, leaving real property in Georgia, the Georgia probate court, according to Koppelman, should recognize the marriage. Koppelman reports that the case law on this issue unanimously supports this result. The prior cases, *id.* at 39–41, all involved interracial marriages in Southern forums. "All deemed it dispositive that their states' laws were not intended to have any extraterritorial application." *Id.* at 39;

see Miller v. Lucks, 36 So.2d 140 (Miss. 1948) (recognizing an interracial marriage where the couple had never lived in the state, despite state constitutional provision describing such marriages as "unlawful and void").

Migratory Marriages — Here a same-sex couple is married in, e.g., Iowa, and migrates five years after their wedding to a non-recognizing state and the validity of their marriage becomes an issue in their new state. Professor Koppelman describes these as "hard cases." *Id.* at 106. While the general choice of law rule for marriage is that a marriage valid where and when created is always valid, the non-recognizing state (especially ones with "mini-DOMA's" (*see supra* Note 5)), might well argue an interest in not permitting same-sex cohabitation under the "marriage banner" as well as an interest in not creating two "classes of same-sex couples: longtime residents who cannot be in same-sex marriages, and recent arrivals who can." *Id.* at 107. On the other hand, the couple can argue from the Constitutional right to travel and migrate. Interestingly, Professor Koppelman notes that during the Jim Crow era there was a split in authority among Southern states whether to recognize migratory interracial marriages from other states. *See id.* at 43–47. Professor Koppelman's suggested rule in this situation would be to recognize such marriages "to the extent of being impediments to a subsequent marriage," *id.* at 110, so that a partner to the hypothetical Iowa marriage above could not marry again unless and until that marriage was legally dissolved. Further, it is suggested that "(a)ny right or obligation of marriage that can be recharacterized as a nonmarital right — such as a right to contract, or a parent-child relation, or an obligation created by a judicial judgment — should be recognized." *Id.*

4. *Defense of Marriage Act.* Article IV, § 1 of the United States Constitution provides:

> Full Faith and Credit shall be given in each State to the public Acts, Records, and judicial Proceedings of every other State. And the Congress may by general Laws prescribe the Manner in which such Acts, Records and Proceedings shall be proved, and the Effect thereof.

In 1996, responding to speculation that the Clause's first sentence might require all states to recognize a same-sex marriage legally contracted in one state (at that time, Hawaii seemed about to legalize such marriages), Congress passed the Defense of Marriage Act (DOMA), relying on its authority under the Clause's second sentence. The first of DOMA's two substantive provisions, codified at 28 U.S.C. § 1738C (2000), provides:

> No State . . . shall be required to give effect to any public act, record or judicial proceeding of any other State . . . respecting a relationship between persons of the same sex that is treated as a marriage under the laws of such other State . . . or a right or claim arising from such relationship.

This legislation was designed to retroactively authorize a wave of then-recent state legislation which refused recognition of any legal same-sex marriages. *See, e.g.*, ALASKA STAT. § 25.05.013 ("A marriage entered into by persons of the same sex . . . that is recognized by another state . . . is void in this state, and contractual rights granted by virtue of the marriage, including its termination, are unenforceable in this state"); IDAHO CODE § 32-209 ("[Marriages valid where performed are valid in this state] unless they violate the public policy of this state. Marriages that violate the public policy of this state include, but are not limited to, same-sex marriages. . . .").

As of 2009, 45 states had enacted either a statute or constitutional provision limiting marriage to opposite gendered couples. http://www.domawatch.org/stateissues/index.html Three of those states (Vermont, Maine, and New Hampshire) subsequently repealed their provisions and authorized same-sex marriage. In two other states (Iowa and Connecticut), the mini-DOMA was found unconstitutional. For an analysis of the various types of state DOMA's, see Brodie Butland, Note, *The Categorical Imperative: Romer as the Groundwork for Challenging State "Defense of Marriage" Amendments*, 68 OHIO ST. L.J. 1419 (2007) (identifies four different categories of state DOMA provisions; concludes some types are likely unconstitutional, while others are valid); *see also* Koppelman, *supra*, Chapter IX, pp. 137–48. In 2009, the District of Columbia Council passed what could be described as an anti-DOMA; the legislation declared that same sex marriages performed where such are legal would be recognized by the District. Brian Westley, *D.C. Council Passes Gay Marriage Bill*, p. 11, BOSTON GLOBE, May 6, 2009; *see also Martinez v. Monroe*, 50 A.D.3d 189 (N.Y. App. Div. 2008) (recognizing a same-sex Canadian marriage for purposes of state employee's health insurance coverage).

Many scholars conclude that the Full Faith and Credit Clause (FFCC) does not require a state to accept the validity of a marriage celebrated in another state, because it is not a judgment of a court but only a "record." In this view, the Clause, when applied to records as opposed to judgments, requires no more than that the second state accept the first state's record — here, the marriage certificate — as proper evidence of the fact it asserts. That means that, in this case, the second state must accept the fact that the parties were indeed married in a ceremony valid in the state of celebration. But that is different than accepting their marriage as valid in the second state as well. Under this view, DOMA's provision allowing states to decline to recognize same-sex marriages from other state is superfluous, because the FFCC would not require recognition even if Congress had not acted. On the other hand, if one believes that the FFCC does require one state to honor a marriage validly entered in another state, it is not clear that Congress would have the authority to override that requirement. Under this view, the same DOMA provision is unconstitutional. Either way, this portion of DOMA would seem to have no effect. *See* Patrick Borchers, *The Essential Irrelevance of the Full Faith and Credit Clause to the Same-Sex Marriage Debate*, 38 CREIGHTON L. REV. 353 (2005) (the claim that the Clause would require a second state to recognize a same-sex marriage in a recognizing jurisdiction is "very dubious"); Ralph Whitten, *Full Faith and Credit for Dummies*, 38 CREIGHTON L. REV. 465 (2005) (explaining the difference between the "public acts" portion of the Clause and the "judicial proceedings" portion). By contrast, it is widely agreed that the FFCC does require one state to honor and enforce a judgment of the court of another state, so long as that court had jurisdiction to enter the judgment. There is no "public policy" exception to the "judicial proceedings" section of the FFCC. *See Baker v. GMC*, 522 U.S. 222 (1998) (rejecting the notion of any public policy exception to the "judicial proceedings" portion of the Clause); Larry Kramer, *Same-Sex Marriage, Conflict of Laws, and the Unconstitutional Public Policy Exception*, 106 YALE L.J. 1965 (1997). Thus, while the issue has not been widely litigated, a Minnesota court would be bound to honor and enforce a jurisdictionally valid wrongful death judgment that a surviving Iowa same-sex spouse obtained in Iowa against a party who is now in Minnesota. There is also considerable doubt that Congress has the authority to relieve states of this FFCC requirement, as it appears to do under DOMA. Apart from any arguments that may be available about the extent of Congressional authority under the FFCC itself, there is also the argument that under *Lawrence v. Texas* (discussed *supra* at Chapter 1, Section C[1]) and *Romer v. Evans*, 517 U.S. 620 (1996) (discussed *infra* at Chapter ___, Section ___) a state may not single out such judgments as uniquely vulnerable to decisions by other states to ignore them. *See* Koppelman, *supra*, at 126.

To sample literature on the Act's constitutionality and related issues, see Mark Rosen, *Why the Defense of Marriage Act is Not (Yet?) Unconstitutional:* Lawrence, *Full Faith and Credit, and the Many Societal Actors That Determine What the Constitution Requires*, 90 MINN. L. REV. 915 (2006) (concluding *Lawrence* has not overruled DOMA and Congress acted within the scope of its power in enacting statute); Note, *Litigating the Defense of Marriage Act: The Next Battleground for Same-Sex Marriage*, 117 HARV. L. REV. 2684 (2004) (asserts statute is inconsistent with constitutionally protected liberty and motivated by animus against gays); Ralph Whitten, *Exporting and Importing Domestic Partnerships: Some Conflict-of-Laws Questions and Concerns*, 2001 BYU L. REV. 1235; Ann Estin, *When* Baehr *Meets* Romer: *Family Law Issues After Amendment 2*, 68 U. COL. L. REV. 349, 370 (1997). Several courts have rejected constitutional attacks on the federal DOMA. *See Wilson v. Ake*, 354 F. Supp. 2d 1298 (M.D. Fla. 2005) (rejecting claims that Congress had exceeded its power under the Full Faith and Credit, Equal Protection and Substantive Due Process clauses); *In re Kandu*, 315 B.R. 123 (W.D. Wash. 2004) (lesbian couple married in Canada sought right to file for bankruptcy as a couple; Federal DOMA upheld against claim of unconstitutionality under 10th Amendment; comity rejected because "court must prefer its own laws" to Canadian policy).

What about same-sex marriages validly contracted in a foreign country? (*See* Note 8 following *Varnum, supra*). The Full Faith and Credit Clause is clearly irrelevant here. Applicable instead is the principle of "comity," which the Supreme Court has defined as "the recognition which one nation allows within its territory to the legislative, executive or judicial acts of another nation, having due regard both to international duty and convenience, and to the rights of its own citizens or of other persons who are under the protection of its laws. *Hilton v. Guyot*, 159 U.S. 113, 164 (1895); *see also* Hessel Yntema, *The Comity Doctrine*, 65 MICH. L. REV. 9 (1966) (tracing comity to the 17th century in the Netherlands). It would seem that a state without a DOMA provision would be more likely to extend comity to a valid foreign same-sex marriage than a state in which a public policy against such marriages had been expressed legislatively.

The federal DOMA's second provision, codified at 1 U.S.C. § 7, defines "marriage" and "spouse" for purposes of federal legislation, administrative rulings and regulations as follows: "the word "marriage" means only a legal union between one man and one woman as husband and wife, and the word "spouse" refers only to a person of the opposite sex who is a husband or a wife." While Congress would seem to be able to define particular words as it chooses, this portion of the legislation might also be subject to attack on the ground that *Lawrence* prohibits a definition of marriage which excludes same-sex marriages. Professor Koppelman, after cataloguing the broad impact of the definitional section and noting an innocent explanation available to justify the definitional section (reflection of the "tradition of restricting marriage to one man and one woman"), believes that the entire statute is unconstitutional and the definitional section is not severable. Koppelman, *supra*, at 129–36. Assuming its constitutionality, this provision would be an obstacle to an American citizen, having contracted a legal same-sex marriage in another country, obtaining immediate relative treatment for his or her spouse. *See* Clifford Krauss, *Married Gay Canadian Couple Barred from U.S.*, N.Y. Times, Sept. 19, 2003, at A4 (married gay couple denied permission to enter the U.S. as a single family, though they would be permitted to do so as two individuals). A commentator has urged the Immigration and Naturalization Service to "end its policy of discrimination by granting immigration benefits to lawful same-sex spouses." Cynthia Reed, *When Love, Comity, and Justice Conquer Borders: INS Recognition of Same-Sex Marriage*, 28 Colum. Human Rights L. Rev. 97 (1996) (arguing DOMA's definition of marriage is unconstitutional).

In the wake of the Massachusetts decision in *Goodridge* (see Note 1 following *Varnum, supra*), a number of federal constitutional amendments on the subject of same-sex marriage were introduced in Congress. Most of these would, at the least, constitutionalize DOMA's definition of marriage in § 2 and expand it to all states. One read as follows:

> Marriage in the United States shall consist only of the union of a man and a woman. Neither this Constitution or the Constitution of any state, nor state or federal law, shall be construed to require that marital status or the legal incidents thereof be conferred upon unmarried couples or groups.

Richard Stevenson, *Bush Expected to Endorse Amendment on Marriage*, N.Y. Times, Feb. 5, 2004, at A27. Under this proposal, would a state legislature be able to permit same-sex marriage? Would it make a civil union statute which providing all the benefits and burdens of marriage to the partners unconstitutional? For a sampling of the scholarly debate over the proposed amendments, see Lynn Wardle, *Federal Constitutional Protection for Marriage: Why and How*, 20 BYU J. Pub. L. 439 (2006) (argues issue apparently will be decided on federal level); Christopher Wolfe, *Why the Federal Marriage Amendment is Necessary*, 42 San Diego L. Rev. 895 (2005) (claims such an Amendment would provide "structural response" to overreaching exercise of judicial power and "judicial exaltation of sexual autonomy"); Thomas Colby, *The Federal Marriage Amendment and the False Promise of Originalism*, 108 Colum. L. Rev. 529 (2008) (argues ambiguity of Amendment's impact on civil unions illustrates problem with originalism in constitutional law — the fact that often there "is no public meaning" of a constitutional provision); John Yoo & AntiimVulchev, *A Conservative Critique of the Federal Marriage Amendment*, 32 Hastings Const. L.Q. 725 (2004) (attacks Amendment as undermining benefits of federalism).

PROBLEMS

Problem 2-6. Beth and Donna, both of whom were born in Canada, were married in Ottawa at a time when same sex marriages were permitted. They now have moved to New York, where they have lived for a year and a half. They are having marital trouble and Beth is considering divorce and is seeking your advice. New York has no Defense of Marriage Act. Its highest court, however, has held that its statutes do not permit same-sex marriage and the statute is constitutionally acceptable. What will be the arguments in any action seeking a divorce? Would your analysis change if Beth and Donna were lifelong New Yorkers who went to Canada one weekend to get married?

Problem 2-7. Bill and Sam are residents of Nebraska. They want to marry, but cannot do so in their home state. They travel to Iowa, where same sex marriage is permissible. They marry and spend the rest of the summer vacation (they are college students) in Iowa, feeling they are more welcome there than at home. During the summer, they are both offered jobs after graduation in Iowa City as civil engineers. They are thrilled to be able to build a life in a state which recognizes their relationship as a valid one. At the end of the summer, however, they have to return for their senior year at the University of Nebraska. Soon thereafter things become rocky and, by Christmas, they are ready to break up. Sam comes to you, a Nebraska lawyer, seeking assistance. You discover an Iowa statute which says, "no marriage shall be contracted . . . by a party residing and intending to continue to reside in another jurisdiction if such marriage would be void if contracted in such other jurisdiction." What is your advice?

Problem 2-8. Lisa and Janet were residents of Vermont at a time when the state permitted same sex civil unions, but not marriage. They contracted such a civil union and soon after arranged for Lisa to bear their child through artificial insemination. About two years after the child was born, Lisa and Janet had a big argument; Lisa went with the child to Virginia, where Lisa had grown up and her parents continue to reside. Soon thereafter, Lisa filed a suit in Vermont seeking a dissolution of the civil union. The Vermont court granted the dissolution, along with custody of the child to Lisa and visitation rights for Janet. After returning to Virginia with the child, Lisa refused Janet's request to exercise her visitation rights. Soon thereafter the Vermont court (which continued to have jurisdiction of the dissolution action and the custody order under state law) found Lisa in contempt for failing to honor the original visitation order. Lisa has now asked a Virginia court for a declaration that she is the only parent of the child and that Janet has no rights in the child. You are representing Janet in the Virginia action. You have discovered a federal statute, the PKPA, which provides that, except in special circumstances not relevant here, no state "shall modify any custody . . . or visitation determination made consistently with the provisions of this statute by a court of another state." You determine that the Vermont decree was made consistently with the PKPA. What argument do you expect Lisa's attorney to make and how will you respond?

[c]   Other Restrictions on Available Marital Partners

[i]   Age

NOTES

1. *Age Regulations.*   Four types of age restrictions in American marriage law exist: 1) the age of consent when a person may choose to marry without consultation or permission of anyone; 2) an age when marriage is permitted with approval of a parent or parent-substitute; 3) age below the age of parental permission at which, in exceptional circumstances, marriage is authorized; 4) age of marriage capacity establishing the minimum "age of marriageability." Lynn Wardle, *Rethinking Marital Age Restrictions*, 22 J. FAM. l. 1 (1983–84). As of that time, the age of consent was 18 in virtually all states and all states had a parental permission period before 18. Most commonly, parental consent is required for older minors and both parental and judicial permission is required for younger children or in "other exceptional circumstances" such as the bride's pregnancy. Very few states have a true minimum age of marriageability which would void a marriage in violation of it.

A parental permission requirement was upheld against a *Zablocki*-based constitutional attack. *Moe v. Dinkins*, 669 F.2d 67 (2d Cir. 1982). In *Phelps v. Bing*, 316 N.E.2d 775 (Ill. 1974), the court struck down a statute which created different age requirements for men and women. The state offered no justification for the gender restrictions and the court found none. *Cf. Stanton v. Stanton*, 421 U.S. 7 (1975) (rejecting assertion that woman's intended role of wife and mother justified state law providing different ages of majority for men and women).

The Supreme Court of Nevada sustained a statute permitting a 15-year-old to marry with permission of only one parent and trial court approval, *Kirkpatrick v. Eight Judicial District Court*, 64 P.3d 1056 (Nev. 2003), rejecting the non-consenting parent's claim that this deprived him of his fundamental right to the parent-child relationship. The court held that the "statute strikes a balance between an arbitrary rule of age for marriage and accommodation of individual differences and circumstances."

2. *Rationale.*   The standard justification for age restrictions has been the claim that "[m]arriages involving teenagers are more unstable than other marriages and are more likely to end in divorce than other marriages." Wardle, *supra*, at 26. A positive correlation between youthful marriage and subsequent marital instability has been established. *See, e.g.*, Gary Lee, *Age at Marriage and Marital Satisfaction: A Multivariate Analysis with Implications for Marital Stability*, 39 J. MARRIAGE & FAM. 493 (1977). It is unclear, however, that the participants' youth is what causes their marital failure. Indeed one author suggested that the relationship between age at marriage and marital instability is caused by those marrying young: (1) being attracted to others who share a tendency toward rash decisionmaking or antisocial behavior or (2) having "been driven out of an abusive or combative family of origin whose values are inimical to marital stability." Thus, "both values [are] being determined by some common social or psychological antecedent." Scott South, *Do You Need to Shop Around-Age at Marriage, Spousal Alternatives, and Marital Dissolution*, 16 J. FAM. ISSUES 432 (1995). Many studies point to non-age related factors as important predictors of marital failure. Ironically, premarital pregnancy, often a statutory exception to age requirements, is a significant predictor of divorce. *See, e.g.,* Larry Bumpuss & James Sweet, *Differentials in Marital Instability, 1970*, 37 AM. SOC. REV. 754, 759 (1972).

In a recent case, a 14-year old became pregnant by her 22-year old boyfriend. In order to avoid a statutory rape charge, the couple (with their parents' blessing) went from their home state (Nebraska) where their marriage would not be permitted to Kansas where they could marry. Upon their return to Nebraska, he was convicted of statutory rape and sentenced to 18 to 30 months' imprisonment. *See* Melissa Murray, *Strange Bedfellows: Criminal Law, Family Law and the Legal Construction of Intimate Life*, http://papers.ssrn.com/sol3/papers.cfm?abstract_id=1340803 The case, *State v. Koso*, is unreported.

PROBLEM

Problem 2-9. Tom's a 17-year-old high school senior who recently married his long-time girlfriend, Rhoda, age 15. Soon after the wedding, Rhoda gave birth to their child. The relevant state statutes set the age of individual consent at 18, permit those between 16 and 18 to marry with parental permission and are silent regarding those under 16. Tom's parents gave their permission, but Rhoda falsely gave her age as 17 and forged her parents' signatures. Tom, who has competed for three years in football, basketball and baseball, learned after the wedding of the state high school athletic association rule providing: "Students who are or have ever been married are ineligible for interscholastic athletic competition." This has caused anger and frustration within the Tom's home. Tom asks if you can find a way to "help me play baseball this spring." What do you advise?

[ii]   Non-Relation

MODEL MARRIAGE AND DIVORCE ACT

§ 207. [Prohibited Marriages.]

(a) The following marriages are prohibited: . . .

    (2) a marriage between an ancestor and a descendant, or between a brother and a sister, whether the relationship is by the half or the whole blood, or by adoption;

    (3) a marriage between an uncle and a niece or between an aunt and a nephew, whether the relationship is by the half or the whole blood, except as to marriages permitted by the established customs of aboriginal cultures.

The American Law Institute's Model Penal Code (§ 230.2) criminalizes sexual intercourse and marriage within certain degrees of consanguinity. The Commentary identifies at least five different explanations for the "continuation of a criminal prohibition against incest." In addition to the religious rationale, the ALI asserted

> the laws against incest may . . . serve the civil and utilitarian function of preventing such inbreeding as would result in defective offspring. . . . [C]lose kinsmen are more likely to be genetically similar than are persons randomly selected from the population. Inbreeding therefore yields an increased . . . chance that the offspring will receive an identical genetic contribution from each parent. If the pedigree contains a recessive abnormality — a genetic defect that does not appear in an individual unless both parents transmit the appropriate determinant — the increased probability of homozygosity in the first generation of offspring may have tragic consequences.

The Institute acknowledged, however, that standard incest laws are typically overbroad in prohibiting more than child-bearing. Overbreadth is also reflected in those statutes barring marriages or sexual intercourse of those who are not blood relations. Moving on to consanguineous mating, the Commentary reports

> . . . [g]eneticists are not agreed in their assessments of the relative dangers posed by inbreeding, and the number of serious genetic disorders related to inbreeding is quite limited. More importantly, some have argued that any decrease in the number of first-generation defectives resulting from the prevention of consanguineous marriages will be balanced by an increase in later generations, as the dispersal of unfavorable genes among the general population through exogamous matings raises the frequency with which the marriage of unrelated persons produces the unfavorable characteristic. . . .

The ALI also noted

> various social objectives that the incest prohibition might serve. Perhaps the most persuasive theory is that social strictures against incest promote the solidarity of the nuclear family. . . . A critical component of [socialization of children within the nuclear family] is the channeling of the individual's erotic impulses into socially acceptable patterns. The incest prohibition regulates erotic desire in two ways that contribute to preservation of the nuclear family. First, the prohibition controls sex rivalries and jealousies within the family unit. . . . Second, by ensuring suitable role models, the incest restriction prepares the individual for assumption of familial responsibility as an adult. . . .

The final goals of such statutes identified by the Commentary are the reinforcement of community norms and prevention of "sexual imposition." In connection with the latter rationale, the Commentary states

> [t]he actual incidence of prosecution for incest suggests that such laws have operated primarily against a kind of imposition on young and dependent females. A study of 30 appellate decisions on incest in the United States from 1846 to 1954 disclosed that all prosecutions were against males and that in 28 of the 30 cases the other party was the daughter or stepdaughter of the defendant. . . .

Denise Grady, *Few Risks Seen to the Children of First Cousins*
N.Y. Times, Apr. 4, 2002, at A1

Contrary to widely held beliefs and longstanding taboos in America, first cousins can have children together without a great risk of birth defects or genetic disease, scientists are reporting today. They say there is no biological reason to discourage cousins from marrying.

First cousins are somewhat more likely than unrelated parents to have a child with a serious birth defect, mental retardation or genetic disease, but their increased risk is nowhere near as large as most people think, the scientists said.

In the general population, the risk that a child will be born with a serious problem like spina bifida or cystic fibrosis is 3 percent to 4 percent; to that background risk, first cousins must add another 1.7 to 2.8 percentage points, the report said.

Although the increase represents a near doubling of the risk, the result is still not considered large enough to discourage cousins from having children, said Dr. Arno Motulsky [of] the University of Washington. . . .

"In terms of general risks in life it's not very high," Dr. Motulsky said. Even at its worst, 7 percent, he said, "93 percent of the time, nothing is going to happen."

. . .

He and his colleagues said no one questioned the right of people with genetic disorders to have children, even though some have far higher levels of risk than first cousins. For example, people with Huntington's disease, a severe neurological disorder that comes on in adulthood, have a 50 percent chance of passing the disease to their children.

The researchers, a panel convened by the National Society of Genetic Counselors, based their conclusions on a review of six major studies conducted from 1965 to August 2000, involving many thousands of births.

. . .

. . . . [N]o countries in Europe have such prohibitions, and in parts of the Middle East, Africa and Asia, marriages between cousins are considered preferable.

. . . .

Dr. Motulsky said . . . some of the revulsion [against cousin marriages] might have stemmed from the eugenics movement, which intended to improve the human race by deciding who should be allowed to breed. The movement flourished in this country early in the 20th century.

It is not known how many cousins marry or live together. Estimates of marriages between related people, which include first cousins and more distant ones, range from less than 0.1 percent of the general population to 1.5 percent. In the past, small studies have found much higher rates in some areas. A survey in 1942 found 18.7 percent in a small town in Kentucky and a 1980 study found 33 percent in a Mennonite community in Kansas.

The report made a point of saying that the term "incest" should not be applied to cousins but only to sexual relations between siblings or between parents and children. Babies who result from those unions are thought to be at significantly higher risk of genetic problems, the report said, but there is not enough data to be sure.

. . . .

The small increase in risk is thought to occur because related people may be carrying some of the same disease-causing genes, inherited from common ancestors. The problems arise from recessive genes, which have no effect on people who carry single copies, but can cause disease in a person who inherits two copies of the gene, one from each parent. When two carriers of a recessive gene have a child, the child has a one-in-four chance of inheriting two copies of that gene. When that happens, disease can result. Cystic fibrosis and the fatal Tay-Sachs disease, for example, are caused by recessive genes. Unrelated people share fewer genes and so their risk of illness caused by recessive genes is a bit lower.

Keith T., 30, said he married his cousin seven years ago and in 1998, frustrated by the lack of information for cousins who wanted to marry, he started a Web site, cousincouples.com. It is full of postings from people who say they have married their cousins or want to do so.

The site highlights famous people who married their first cousins, including Charles Darwin, who, with Emma Wedgwood, had 10 children, all healthy, some brilliant. Mr. T. asked that his full name not be used because he said he did business in a small town and feared that he would lose customers if they found out his wife was also his cousin.

. . . .

NOTES

1. *Consanguinity Prohibition.* A 1984 survey reported that virtually every state describes at least some consanguineous marriages (between parties who share at least one common ancestor) as invalid or void. The only exception is Alabama, which, however, criminalizes incestuous marriage. ALA. CODE § 13A-13-3 and criminalizes any person who performs an wedding ceremony for an incestuous couple. ALA. CODE § 30-1-6. All states ban marriages between siblings, between parent and child, and between grandparents and grandchildren. The web site referred to toward the end of the *New York Times* excerpt above currently reports that approximately one-half the states permit marriage between first cousins. For a current compilation of incest laws, see Dennis Leiter, *National Survey of State Law* 301-12 (2nd ed. 1997).

Most jurisdictions include within their consanguinity prohibitions those related either by the whole blood (two common parents) or the half blood (one common parent). Several recent cases find half-blood relationships covered by statutes silent on the question. *See Tapscott v. State*, 684 A.2d 439 (Md. App. 1996) (upholding incest conviction of a man who had intercourse with his niece by the half-blood); *see also Singh v. Singh*, 569 A.2d 1112 (Conn. 1990); Annot., *Sexual*

Intercourse Between Persons Related by Half Blood as Incest, 34 A.L.R.5th 723 (1995). A recent article explores the issue of "accidental incest," defined as "intra-familial sexual behavior" between those whose "relationships [were] created through reproductive technology . . ." Naomi Cahn, *Accidental Incest: Drawing the Line — or the Curtain? — for Reproductive Technology*, 32 HARV. J.L. & GENDER 59 (2009). Professor Cahn notes that "most of the traditional incest prohibition do not apply in the reprotech context when it comes to restrictions on gamete provision." She argues that the "higher risks of genetic defects" could provide "a partial foundation" for banning genetically related individuals resulting from third party use of gametes, but

> the law could permit half-siblings raised apart from each other or donors and their offspring to engage in sexual relationships while continuing to ban these relationships between individuals who spent time together in the same family, this may be a difficult distinction to maintain

Id. at 107.

2. *Affinity Prohibition.* Those related by virtue of a marriage are said to be related by affinity. The classic affinity relationships are step-relationships and in-law relationships. According to Bratt, *supra*, fifteen states forbid certain marriages between affinial relations. What state interests are furthered by prohibiting such marriages? For an article attacking the legitimacy of statutes banning affinial marriages, see Christine Metteer, *Some "Incest" is Harmless Incest: Determining the Fundamental Right to Marry of Adults Related by Affinity Without Resorting to State Incest Statutes*, 10 KAN. J. L.& PUB. POL'Y 262 (2000).

Does an affinity relationship outlive the marriage upon which it is based? For example, in a state banning marriage between a woman and her son-in-law could the couple marry after the son-in-law's divorce? Some statutes make clear that affinity prohibitions "continue notwithstanding the dissolution, by death or divorce, of the marriage by which the affinity was created." MASS. ANN. LAWS, Ch. 207, § 3. By contrast, some cases hold such relationships cease with the end of the relationship-creating marriage. *See, e.g., Gish v. State*, 352 S.E.2d 800 (Ga. App. 1987); *Henderson v. State*, 157 So. 884 (Ala. App. 1934).

3. *Adoption and Incest.* While adoption statutes often require treatment of an adopted child as if she were the adoptive parents' natural child (*see* Chapter 11, Section B), several marriage cases raise doubts that these statutes mean what they say. For example, in *State ex rel. Miesner v. Geile*, 747 S.W.2d 757 (Mo. App. 1988), the court permitted an uncle and his niece-by-adoption to marry. The court relied on statutory silence regarding adoptive relationships. *See also Bagnardi v. Hartnett*, 366 N.Y.S.2d 89 (Sup. Ct. 1975) (approving marriage between adoptive father and daughter); *State v. Bale*, 512 N.W.2d 164 (S.D. 1994) (sexual intercourse with adopted child is not criminal incest; "adoption statute cannot erase lineal consanguinity and then create a new lineal consanguinity").

In *Israel v. Allen*, 577 P.2d 762 (Colo. 1978), the court struck down a statute prohibiting marriage between siblings related by adoption (groom's father had adopted bride). The court rejected the asserted state interest in family harmony, finding the law "illogical" and unconstitutional. The *Israel* couple never lived in the same household after adoption. Would the result have been different had they lived with their parents after the parental marriage? *See In re MEW & MLB*, 4 Pa. D. & C. 3d 51 (C.P. Allegheny 1977) (parties lived in same household "for a short period" and marriage license was denied, at least partly because of fear of encouragement of sexual rivalry within the household). Relatedly, the Indiana Supreme Court has upheld an incest conviction of a father who impregnated his natural daughter who was another man's adoptive daughter. *Bohall v. State*, 546 N.E.2d 1214 (Ind. 1989).

4. *Effect of Incestuous Marriage.* "The great majority of states . . . pronounce those marriages void which violate the incest statute. The meaning of 'void' in this context seems to be that the purported marriage is an absolute nullity, which cannot be ratified by the parties, and which may be attacked at any time, either collaterally or directly, either before or after the death of a party." HOMER CLARK, THE LAW OF DOMESTIC RELATIONS § 2.9, 85 (2nd ed. 1988). Thus, in *Weeks v. Weeks*, 654 So. 2d 33 (Miss. 1995), the court held that, because it was void, an uncle-niece marriage could not support a suit for separate maintenance upon separation after nine years. The court rejected plaintiff's assertion of equitable estoppel, concluding both parties were in *pari delicto*. *See Adams v. Adams*, 604 P.2d 332 (Mont. 1979) (rejecting equitable estoppel claim in case of void first cousin marriage); *Catalano v. Catalano*, 170 A.2d 726 (Conn. 1961) (rejecting widow's allowance in void uncle-niece marriage). *But see May's Estate*, 114 N.E.2d 4 (N.Y. 1953).

[iii]   Monogamy

All states prohibit marriages where either partner is already married. Any such attempted marriage is void and, in most states, a criminal act.

NOTES

1. *First Amendment and Polygamy.* The Supreme Court of the United States has consistently rejected assertions that religious freedom protects the practice of polygamy. *See Reynolds v. United States*, 98 U.S. 145 (1878); *Cleveland v. United States*, 329 U.S. 14 (1946) (upholding criminal conviction of polygamous Mormon fundamentalists travelling interstate). *Zablocki* has not changed the view of the lower federal courts. In *Potter v. Murray City*, 585 F. Supp. 1126 (D. Utah 1984), the court upheld the firing of a policeman for violating the criminal prohibition of polygamy. The court cited Justice Powell's *Zablocki* concurrence for its recognition of a state interest in "ensuring that its rules of domestic relations reflect the widely held values of its people" and rejected plaintiff's contention that this interest could be effectuated by a judicially-created exemption for those with plural marriages based upon "sincere religious belief." The court found *Zablocki* added nothing to the strength of plaintiff's case. *See also State v. Holm*, 137 P.3d 726 (Utah 2006) (criminal bigamy conviction affirmed over state constitutional objections; federal constitutional claim under *Lawrence v. Texas* likewise rejected); *State v. Green*, 98 P.3d 820 (Utah 2004) (in affirming bigamy conviction, court relies both on *Reynolds* and current Free Exercise jurisprudence, finding statute a neutral one of general applicability and not aimed at religious practice); *Bronson v.*

Swensen, 394 F. Supp. 2d 1329 (D. Utah 2005) (state bigamy statute upheld in face of claim based on *Lawrence*), *aff'd for lack of standing*, 500 F.3d 1099 (10th Cir. 2007); *Lukich v. Lukich*, 666 S.E.2d 906 (S.C. 2008) (wife's annulment of her earlier marriage, filed after marriage to second husband no defense to second husband's motion to annul second marriage because of bigamy; despite general relation back of annulment, state's overwhelming policy against bigamy must vindicated); *Guzman v. Alvares*, 205 S.W.3d 375 (Tenn. 2006) ("marriage by estoppel" not available to validate a bigamous marriage because such marriage is void).

Perhaps because polygamy is part of the slippery slope argument made by same-sex marriage opponents, a spate of scholarship concerning monogamy has recently appeared. See, for example, the debate between Professors Cheshire Calhoun and Samuel Rickless. Cheshire, *Who's Afraid of Polygamous Marriage? Lessons for Same-Sex Marriage Advocacy from the History of Polygamy*, 42 SAN DIEGO L. REV. 1023 (2004) (arguing that because legal bars to polygamous and same-sex marriages have not prevented proliferation of such relationships the central issue is "not whether the state should permit [such] marriages, but whether the state should support [such] marriages by assigning them the legal status of civil marriage;" asserts "it is not clear that legal recognition of polygamous marriage is incompatible with a liberal, democratic, and egalitarian society"); Rickless, *Polygamy and Same-Sex Marriage: A Response to Calhoun*, 42 SAN DIEGO L. REV. 1043 (2004) (polygamy "has certainly not achieved . . . the status of anything approaching monogamy in cultural signficance," that "[e]ven within a liberal political society, there is nothing sacrosanct about private contracts per se" and such contracts are often prohibited, and that "there are reasons to believe that polygamy is essentially problematic and unstable"). Shayna Sigman, *Everything Lawyers Know About Polygamy is Wrong*, 16 CORNELL J. L. & PUB. POL'Y 101 (2006) (urges rethinking criminalization of polygamy; after detailed history of legal regulation of polygamy, argues "the gap between American legal policy regulating polygamy and the root causes and likely effects of it has resulted in over-enforcement of anti-polygamy statutes, under-enforcement of other criminal provisions, [and] state persecution of men, women and children"); Elizabeth Emens, *Compulsory Monogamy and Polyamorous Existence*, 29 N.Y.U. REV. L. & SOC. CHANGE 277 (2004) (examines why "at a time of serious debate about the different-sex requirement of marriage . . . eliminating the numerosity requirement . . . is so widely agreed to be undesirable;" explains polyamory "which in principle eschews hierarchy and which encompasses various models of intimate relationships"); Maura Strassberg, *The Challenge of Post-Modern Polygamy: Considering Polyamory*, 31 CAPITAL UNIV. L. REV. 439 (2003) ("[t]he possibility that polyamory might threaten . . . fundamental aspects of the modern liberal state suggests that polyamory may be more of a Pandora's Box than many realize" and "advocates for same-sex monogamous marriage, [which] is compatible with modern liberal democracy, might justifiably choose not to endorse claims for a legal institution of polyamorous marriage"); Emily Duncan, Note, *The Positive Effects of Legalizing Polygamy: "Love is a Many Splendored Thing,"* 15 DUKE J. GEND. L. & POL'Y 315 (2008) (arguing "[p]ublic policy need not be constrained by an overriding, universally held, moral conclusion" and "legalizing polygamy could positively affect polygynist women and children" who have been harmed by driving the practice underground).

2. *Polygamy in the United States.* Polygamy prohibitions have not been completely effective in eliminating the practice. A recent article estimated that between 30,000 and 60,000 currently practice polygamy in this country. Ryan Tenney, Note, *Tom Green, Common-Law Marriage, and the Illegality of Putative Polygamy*, 17 BYU J. Pub. L. 141 (2002). The most well-publicized stronghold of the practice is in a community straddling the Arizona-Utah border (Hildale, Utah and Colorado City, Arizona) which is populated almost exclusively by members of the Fundamentalist Church of the Latter Day Saints. Other areas in which the FLDS has groups of adherents are Colorado, Texas, South Dakota and British Columbia. The group's separation from the mainline Mormon Church dates from the latter's acceptance of *Reynolds, supra,* in 1890. For a brief history of the separatist movement, see John Dougherty, *Polygamy's Odyssey*, Phoenix New Times, Mar. 13, 2003, at News Section.

In 2001, Tom Green, a prominent polygamist, was successfully prosecuted for bigamy. While he had never been married ceremonially to more than one person at a time, the prosecution convinced a jury that his continuing cohabitation with his wife after their legal divorce was a common law marriage under Utah law. Thus, his cohabitation with his other four "spiritual wives" constituted four counts of bigamy under the statute punishing married individuals who "cohabit with another person. Utah Code Ann. § 76-7-101. For an account of the prosecution and a critique of the prosecutorial theory accepted by the court, see the Note, *supra*.

Since 2002, under the initial leadership of then-Attorney General of Arizona (now-United States Secretary of Homeland Security) Janet Napolitano, Arizona and Utah have been investigating alleged criminal activity in the Colorado City area, including child abuse, misuse of state money and bigamy. *See* Robbie Sherwood & Dennis Wagner, *Polygamy Investigators Defend Work*, Ariz. Repub., Oct. 11, 2002, at B6; Dennis Wagner, *Bigamy Sex Charges Filed vs. Lawman*, Ariz. Repub., Oct. 8, 2002, at A1 (deputy marshal charged for marrying his sister-in-law while still married to his wife; also charged with unlawful sex with a minor);. John Dougherty, *Bound by Fear: Polygamy in Arizona*, Phoenix New Times, Mar. 13, 2003, at News Section. The recent campaign follows many prior efforts in the same vein. In 1953, Arizona state officials raided Short Creek (Colorado City's original name), arresting many residents for polygamy. After the raid, then-Governor Howard Pyle credited the officers with "quelling a rebellion that endangered "the lives and futures of 263 children, the products and the victims of the foulest conspiracy you could imagine.'" No convictions were obtained. *See also* Martha Bradley, Kidnapped from that Land: The Government Raids on the Short Creek Polygamists (1993); Krakauer, Under the Banner of Heaven (2003); Judd Slivka, *Polygamous Sect Persists Despite "Persecutions Past and Present*, Ariz. Repub., Oct. 11, 2002, at A1.

An FLDS compound (Yearning for Zion Ranch) outside Eldorado, Texas was raided in the spring of 2008 and the state took custody of 450 of the group's children as charges of child abuse and sexual assault were investigated. (See *In re Texas Dept. of Fam. & Protect. Services*, a principal case in Chapter 10, Section C.1.). David Fahrenthold, *An Unusual Prosecution of a Way of Life; Texas Will Attempt to Show That Polygamist Culture Itself Harms Children*, Washington Post, Apr. 27, 2008, at A3. The Texas Supreme Court eventually ruled that the children had to be returned to their families because the judicial order authorizing the raid was too broad, covering children who were not shown to be at risk. Lisa Sandberg & Terry Langford, *Court Sides with Sect*, SAN ANTONIO EXPRESS-NEWS, May 23, 2008, at 1A. The leader of the FLDS, Warren Jeffs, was convicted of being an accomplice to child rape in Utah in 2007 for ordering a 14-year old follower to marry her 19-year old first cousin. John Gibeaut, *Violation or Salvation?: Prosecutors Say It is a Sex Crime. Polygamist Leader Warren Jeffs Says It's Counseling His Flock*, 93 ABA J. 26 (2007). He subsequently was charged in Arizona on similar charges and in Texas on charges of bigamy. Sandberg, *Polygamist Leader Jeffs, 2 Other FLDS Men Charged with Bigamy*, SAN ANTONIO EXPRESS-NEWS, Aug. 23, 2008, at 2B.

For a discussion of empirical research on family relationships in the contemporary Mormon fundamentalist community conducted by an academic psychologist, see Irwin Altman, *Polygamous Family Life: The Case of Contemporary Mormon Fundamentalists*, 1996 UTAH L. REV. 367.

3. *Polygamy in Other Countries.* Polygamy is practiced in many cultures. Even in those societies, however, the practice is not without controversy. The Koran allows a man to take as many as four wives simultaneously. A 1979 Egyptian statute required a man to officially inform his first wife that he was taking a second. The first could then obtain a divorce, receive alimony immediately, retain custody of any marital children and either retain the marital abode or obtain a new residence to be provided by the husband. This women's rights law was heavily criticized by Islamic fundamentalists.

A 1985 Egyptian Supreme Court decision struck down the statute, reinstating earlier provisions under which a woman need not be informed of a divorce or a taking of a second wife. "No longer is a second marriage automatically grounds for divorce; a woman must . . . prove in court that the second marriage has harmed her." Judith Miller, *Egypt Divided by Court's Abolition of Law Guarding Rights of First Wives*, N.Y. TIMES, June 10, 1985, at A4.

4. *Enoch Arden Situation.* A classic problem raising polygamy concerns arises when one spouse is absent without explanation for a lengthy period, during which the other spouse remarries. Does the absent spouse's return render the second marriage void and/or criminal? This has been called the Enoch Arden situation, after the Tennyson poem in which the seaman returns after a 10-year absence (due to shipwreck) to find his wife remarried.

Most criminal bigamy statutes do not punish the second marriage in this situation. *See, E.g.*, ILL. REV. STAT. ch. 720, § 5/11-12(b)(3) (creating "affirmative defense . . . that the prior spouse had been continually absent for a period of five years during which time the accused did not know the prior spouse to be alive"). Under some statutes the deserted spouse can dissolve the first marriage using a presumption of death. *See, e.g.*, PA. STAT. tit. 23, § 1701(b), (c) (seven years' absence sufficient for finding of death and "[t]he fact that an absentee was exposed to a specific peril of death may be a sufficient ground for finding that he died less than seven years after he was last heard from"). With no statute, the deserted spouse would be wise to seek divorce before remarrying. While no case law has tested the proposition, absence for an extended period would seem to authorize a no-fault divorce on grounds of, e.g., "irretrievable breakdown" or a fault divorce based on abandonment.

PROBLEM

Problem 2-10.   Sean is seeking to immigrate to the United States from Canada. He has lived his entire life there and in 2002 he married his childhood sweetheart, Monique. Their marriage seemed doomed from the start and, by 2007, they were living in different cities. In 2009, with same-sex marriage legal in Canada and Sean having come to understand that he was gay, Sean married Bill. Now they are seeking to become resident aliens in the United States. A federal form asked "Have you ever been married to more than one person at the same time?" He has been charged with lying in answering this question "No." The federal statute under which he is being prosecuted (18 U.S.C. § 1015(a)) provides in part: "Whoever knowingly makes any false statement under oath in any case, proceeding or matter relating to naturalization, citizenship, or registry of aliens shall be fined or imprisoned to no more than five years in prison or both . . ." He consults you and tells you that he had been told by a good friend that living separate and apart from one's spouse for five years constituted a "common law divorce." If you represent him, what will the basis of your defense and what information do you need to proceed?

[d]   Consent Requirements

GEORGIA CODE

§ 19-3-2. To be able to contract marriage, a person must:

(1) Be of sound mind. . . .

§ 19-3-4. To constitute an actual contract of marriage, the parties must consent thereto voluntarily without any fraud practiced upon either. Drunkenness at the time of marriage, brought about by art or contrivance to induce consent, shall be held as fraud.

NOTES

1. *Capacity to Consent.* As Ga. Code Ann. § 19-3-4 indicates, a valid marriage requires both parties' consent. Such consent necessarily includes capacity to consent. GA. CODE ANN. § 19-3-2 defines this capacity in terms of each party being "of sound mind." *See also* PA. STAT. tit. 23, § 1304(c) (prohibiting license for the "weak minded, insane" or those "of unsound mind"). The cases interpreting such requirements define the mental competence standard fairly minimally. It is often defined as the ability to comprehend the nature of marriage and the duties and responsibilities attendant thereto. *See In re Hendrickson*, 805 P.2d 20 (Kan. 1991); *Pape v. Byrd*, 582 N.E.2d 164 (Ill. 1991). A recent case, however, annulled a marriage for lack of capacity where an 86-year old suffered from Alzheimer's disease. *Moss v. Davis*, 794 A.2d 1288 (Del. Fam. Ct. 2001); *see also* Terry Turnipseed, *How Do I Love Thee, Let Me Count the Days: Deathbed Marriages in America*, 96 KY. L.J. 275 (2007) (offers theoretical framework for model act designed protect heirs and beneficiaries from deathbed marriages on mental capacity grounds; argues that without such a statute a "greedy potential spouse has every incentive to find a minister or officer of the law willing" to perform a ceremony of marriage between him/her and a wealthy sick person "and no legal incentives not to try it"). Little, if anything, is done to screen out those without capacity in the licensing process. If incompetence is ever raised, it is in a suit for annulment or in probate litigation.

2. *Fraudulently Induced Consent.* Assuming both parties *could* consent, the next question is *did* they consent. There are two groups of cases in which lack of consent is alleged. In one, the claimant asserts fraudulent inducement. While fraudulently induced marriages generally are voidable, courts are very reluctant to find fraud. Rather than applying contracts doctrine, which defines fraud as merely a material misrepresentation causing consent, annulment courts traditionally require a misrepresentation concerning the "essentials" of marriage.

Tracing back to an old Massachusetts case, *Reynolds v. Reynolds*, 3 Allen 605 (1862), this test made clear that misrepresentations concerning wealth, temper or character ordinarily were not grounds for annulment. By contrast, misrepresentation about a party's fertility, or willingness or ability to engage in sexual relations, has traditionally been found to go to the "essentials." Many courts continue to apply the traditional essentials test. *See, e.g., Janda v. Janda*, 984 So. 2d 434 (Ala. App. Ct. 2007) (American woman granted annulment from Czech husband who had "unstated intent . . . to utterly refuse to engage in a sexual relationship" with wife); *Maegher v. Maleki*, 131 Cal. App. 4th 1 (2005) (annulment inappropriate where husband misrepresented his financial status and fraudulently induced wife to invest in business venture in attempt to gain control of her assets); *Blair v. Blair*, 147 S.W.3d 882 (Mo. App. 2004) (denial of annulment appropriate where, after 23 years of marriage, husband claimed fraud in wife's false representation that he was father of child born to her during her prior marriage); *Patel v. Navitlal*, 627 A.2d 683 (N.J. Super. 1993) (Indian bride's failure to reveal her mother had lived with a person of a different caste during a marital separation insufficient for annulment). Some decisions define marital "essentials" using a subjective approach. *See, e.g., Mayo v. Mayo*, 617 S.E.2d 672 (N.C. App. Ct. 2005) (applying law of Georgia where marriage took place, annulment affirmed where wife indicated on her marriage license that she had been married twice before when, in truth, she had been married seven times before); *Bilowit v. Dolitsky*, 304 A.2d 774 (N.J. Super. Ct. 1973) (false self-description as Orthodox Jew sufficient). In fact, some cases appear to go so far as to adopt a materiality test for fraud. *See, e.g., Charley v. Fant*, 892 S.W.2d 811 (Mo. App. Ct. 1995); *Kober v. Kober*, 211 N.E.2d 817 (N.Y. 1965).

A recent commentator reports:

> there is great variation in the way courts delineate . . . the essentials standard. Some courts have specified that it covers only frauds affecting sexual relations between the parties. Others take the view that the "essentials" cannot be definitively listed and will be determined on a case-by-case basis. . . . [T]he recurring themes are sex and procreation.

Lawrence Borten, Note, *Sex, Procreation and the State Interest in Marriage*, 102 COLUM. L. REV. 1089, 1097 (2002). The widespread availability of no-fault divorce has largely removed the incentive to seek annulment, leading to a decline in the number of cases addressing these questions and in judicial inclination to expand the grounds. For collections of cases on particular grounds for fraud annulments, see David Perlmutter, Annot., *Incapacity for Sexual Intercourse as Ground for Annulment*, 52 A.L.R.3d 589 (1973); Jeffrey Ghent, Annot., *Religion: Concealment or Misrepresentation Relating to Religion as Ground for Annulment*, 44 A.L.R.3d 972 (1972); Jay Zitter, Annot., *Homosexuality, Transvestism, and Similar Sexual Practices as Grounds for Annulment of Marriage*, 68 A.L.R.4th 1069 (1989).

3. *Duress-Induced Consent.* The other type of case raising questions about apparent consent involves claims of duress. A marriage in which the consent of one party has been obtained by duress is voidable. There are relatively few such modern cases. But in *Marriage of Weintraub*, 213 Cal. Rptr. 159 (Ct. App. 1985), an annulment was awarded where a woman was abducted "by force, physical beatings, and threat of physical harm and taken [to another state] where . . . against her will and as the result of coercion, physical beatings, intimidation and threats upon the safety of her family, [she] went through a marriage ceremony." *See also Clark v. Foust-Graham*, 615 S.E.2d 398 (N.C. Ct. App. 2005) (an 80-year old whose consent to marry his 40-year old wife was "obtained by undue influence" was "incapable of contracting from want of will"; annulment granted to husband's executrix). Many old cases find a threat of prosecution for criminal seduction or bastardy to be insufficient to prove duress. A recent commentator urges that adult arranged marriages in South Asia "merit a 'margin of appreciation' " when being measured by international human rights documents requiring "free and full" consent to marriage. Prashina Gagoomal, Note, *A "Margin of Appreciation" for "Marriages of Appreciation": Reconciling South Asian Adult Arranged Marriages with the Matrimonial Consent Requirement in International Human Rights Law*, 97 GEO. L.J. 589 (2009).

4. *Limited Purpose Marriage.* Fraud, duress and incapacity are theories alleging that the consent, though proper in form, lacks the required substance. Other cases do not challenge the *fact* of consent, but its *scope*, claiming that no genuine marriage was intended, but that the consent was for a marriage of limited purpose. Unlike claims of fraud, duress and incapacity, this attack ordinarily is brought by the government rather than a marriage party because the alleged limited purpose often is obtaining a government benefit available only upon marriage — most often, favorable immigration status for an alien married to a citizen. For a case dealing with a serviceman relying on a sham marriage to obtain a favorable housing allowance, see *United States v. Bolden*, 28 MIL. J. REP. 127 (Ct. Mil. App. 1989).

Typically the government denies the benefit, asserting a sham marriage. The facts usually suggest the parties married, at least in part, to obtain the benefit. Is that motivation sufficient to permit the court to ignore the marriage, or is more needed?

While some cases suggest a motivation inquiry, *see Ryan v. Ryan*, 281 N.Y.S. 709 (Sup. Ct. 1935) (annulment where party married solely for money), this cannot be the test because there is no societal consensus on appropriate motivations for marriage. Is love required (and, if it is, how do we define love?) or may one marry for money or status or lust? Instead, courts in the immigration area have focused on intent. For example, in *Bark v. INS*, 511 F.2d 1200, 1202 (9th Cir. 1975), the court asked if the parties intended "to establish a life together." This changes the issue from *why* the marriage occurred to what *type* of marriage was intended.

But this reformed inquiry also has difficulties. First, it is subjective: the question is what the parties meant, not what they did. Thus, in *Bark*, the INS rejected the marriage because of the couple's quick post-wedding separation. In reversing, the court wrote, "(c)onduct of the parties after marriage is relevant only to the extent that it bears upon their subjective state of mind at the time they were married." *Id.* at 1202. Because many couples who intend a "real" marriage nonetheless soon separate, the quick separation was not conclusive on whether a "life together" had been intended. *See also Dabaghian v. Civiletti*, 607 F.2d 868 (9th Cir. 1979) (divorce filed four months after marriage immediately after grant of favorable immigration status not dispositive).

Establishing subjective intent obviously is difficult. While the law sometimes inquires into subjective intent (e.g., in criminal mens rea), the limited purpose marriage inquiry is peculiar because of the murkiness of the intent required for a valid marriage. In determining whether the parties intended a "real" marriage, the court necessarily must have some concept of a "real marriage." At a time when many marriages fail despite "good" intentions and many others depart from traditional patterns, this is very difficult. As *Bark* pointed out, "[a]liens cannot be required to have more conventional or more successful marriages than citizens."

Not only is application of a rule requiring intent to create a "real marriage" difficult, there is also a certain irony in such a rule. As discussed earlier, most persons entering a "normal" marriage do not first study its legal consequences: their purpose usually has more to do with emotions and symbols. Their indifference (even opposition) to the legal consequences of marriage is irrelevant to its validity. By rejecting limited purpose marriage, the law would be punishing parties who often have studied at least some of the legal consequences and intend them and rejecting the marriage because they were indifferent to matrimony's emotional and symbolic aspects. While perhaps ironic, this approach is consistent with the understanding of legal marriage suggested *supra*, in the post-*Zablocki* notes: marriage's constitutional importance apparently derives not from its legal consequences, but its social and symbolic significance. Indeed, it is quite possible that these non-legal aspects of marriage are what prompted Congress to give alien spouses of citizens special consideration in immigration law. Most courts hold that state family law and federal immigration law can reach different conclusions as to a marriage's validity. *See, e.g., Villanueva v. Brown*, 1997 U.S. Dist. LEXIS 23759 (S.D. Ohio, Mar. 17, 1997); *Ponce-Gonzalez v. INS*, 775 F.2d 1342 (5th Cir. 1985); *Skelly v. INS*, 630 F.2d 1375 (10th Cir. 1980). Thus, even if the marriage is void for purposes of federal immigration law, it might be merely voidable or even valid under state law. *See Kunz v. Kunz*, 136 P.3d 1278 (Utah Ct. App. 2006) (after canvassing the varying positions attributed to different states by different federal courts, concluding that Utah law renders an immigration marriage voidable and, thus, not subject to attack after the death of one of the parties).

5. *More on "Immigration Marriages."*   During the 1980s, it was claimed that many aliens were contracting marriages with American citizens "fraudulently" for the purpose of gaining permanent residence here. According to a 1985 article, 111,653 foreigners were granted permanent American residency via marriage in 1984, twice as many as in 1974. Andree Brooks, *Marriage Fraud Aimed at Single Mothers*, N.Y. TIMES, June 13, 1985, at 19. The article reported an "epidemic increase in "illegal" marriages. In a common pattern, a foreigner might pay a citizen a fee to marry, with final payment deferred until the grant of permanent residency status. *See* John Wade, *Limited Purpose Marriages*, 45 MOD. L. REV. 159, 161 (1982) (claiming lax divorce laws and lessening stigma of divorce contributes to rise in such marriages).

Problems can arise, however. The *Times* article quoted an immigration official's estimate that 2/3 of the suspicious marriages investigated involved single mothers, who are often financially pressed. Some women are never paid as promised and many are unaware that a marriage valid under state law may support valid divorce claims on their assets by their husbands. Likewise, a valid marriage could terminate alimony payments from a prior husband. Of course, state law may reject the marriage's validity. *See, e.g., Faustin v. Lewis*, 427 A.2d 1105 (N.J. 1981) ("immigration marriage" annulled; no "meaningful" marital relationship intended). In 2003, four "career brides" who had applied for multiple marriage licenses were arrested by New York police who asserted each charged $1,000 for becoming a "bride." One woman had applied for 27 licenses in 19 years. Susan Saulny, *Here Comes the Bride, Again, and Again . . .*, N.Y. TIMES, July 10, 2003, at A1.

At least partially in response to assertions of a wave of fraudulent marriages, the federal Immigration Marriage Fraud Amendments, 8 U.S.C. §§ 1154(h), 1255(e), were passed in 1986. A study presented to Congress by the Immigration and Naturalization Service asserted 30% of marriage-based visa petitions involved sham marriages. In later litigation attacking the Act's constitutionality, an INS official acknowledged "this figure had no statistical basis." Hilary Sheard, *Ethical Issues in Immigration Proceedings*, 9 GEO. IMMIGR. L.J. 719, 737 (1995); Charles Gordon, *The Marriage Fraud Act of 1986*, 4 GEO. IMMIGR. L.J. 183 (1990). One analysis asserts the law was produced by "misinformation and anti-alien sentiment fueled by groups lobbying to restrict, if not close altogether, our borders to aliens." Mary Sfasciotti & Luanne Redmond, *Marriage, Divorce, and the Immigration Laws*, 81 ILL. B.J. 644, 645 (1993).

Under the amendments, an alien married to a citizen for less than two years is granted conditional status with reexamination of the marriage's bona fides and continuance after two years when permanent resident status may be granted upon petition of both spouses. If the marriage, however, takes place during deportation or exclusion proceedings, generally the alien must leave the United States for two years *before* obtaining conditional resident status.

Citing the Supreme Court's traditional reluctance to disturb Congressional action on immigration, *Fiallo v. Bell*, 430 U.S. 787 (1977), several courts have rejected equal protection and due process attacks on the Amendments. *See Azizi v. Thornburgh*, 908 F.2d 1130 (2d Cir. 1990); *Bright v. Parra*, 919 F.2d 31 (5th Cir. 1990); *Gomez-Arauz v. McNary*, 746 F. Supp. 1071 (W.D. Okla. 1990). *Anetekhai v.*

INS, 876 F.2d 1218 (5th Cir. 1989); *Almario v. Attorney General*, 872 F.2d 147 (6th Cir. 1989). One court, however, found unconstitutional the two-year exclusion after marriage during deportation, finding a procedural due process violation. *Escobar v. INS*, 896 F.2d 564 (D.C. Cir. 1990) (distinguishing *Fiallo* as recognition of plenary Congressional power in *substantive*, not procedural, aspects of immigration policy), but the opinion was later withdrawn on mootness grounds. *See* 925 F.2d 488 (D.C. Cir. 1991).

Further amendments in 1990 make it somewhat easier for an alien who marries a citizen during deportation or exclusion proceedings to remain here and expand the exceptions to the rule requiring a petition by both spouses to establish a marriage's bona fides after two years of conditional residency. For a discussion of the 1990 amendments, see Sfasciotti & Redmond, *supra*, at 648.

The legislative attention and judicial resources expended on the issue may not have made a major difference in the flow of immigrants married to American citizens. The number of spouses being admitted as an immediate relative of citizens continues to increase significantly. In 1984, 111,653 spouses of American citizens entered the country. By 2007, this number had more than doubled (274,358). *Compare* STATISTICAL YEARBOOK OF THE IMMIGRATION AND NATURALIZATION SERVICE 1984 12, *with* 2007 YEARBOOK OF IMMIGRATION STATISTICS 18. The overwhelming number of petitions for permanent resident status after the two-year waiting period are approved. Hiroshi Motomura, *The Family and Immigration: A Roadmap for the Ruritanian Lawmaker*, 43 AM. J. COMP. L. 511, 531 (1995) (reporting over 80,000 applications were granted of the 90,000 cases eligible for such a grant in 1993). In 1994, the parallel totals were 90,243 of 96,033 cases (94%). STATISTICAL YEARBOOK OF THE IMMIGRATION AND NATURALIZATION SERVICE 1994 70.

Some marriages of citizens and non-citizens result from the "mail-order bride" industry in which brokers, using catalogs describing and often picturing available mates, arrange marriages between women from foreign countries and American men. One commentator has asserted such international marriage brokers "have existed in various forms for over two hundred years." Karen Morgan, Note, *Here Comes the Mail-Order Bride: Three Methods of Regulation in the United States, the Phillipines, and Russia*, 39 GEO. WASH. INT'L L. REV. 423, 446 (2007). Another commentator reports that the industry "resurfaced in the 1970's when men discontented with the Women's Movement in the United States began looking overseas for wives with 'old-fashioned' values." Christine Chun, Comment, *The Mail-Order Bride Industry: The Perpetuation of Transnational Economic Inequalities and Stereotypes*, 17 U. PA. J. INT'L ECON. L. 1155, 1160 (1996). A 1999 report to Congress estimated between 4,000 and 6,000 marriages arranged by the industry each year. Linda Kelly, *Marriage for Sale: The Mail-Order Bride Industry and the Changing Value of Marriage*, 5 J. GENDER RACE & JUST. 175 (2001) (detailing allegations of rampant domestic abuse and fraud in mail-order marriages). More recently, another commentator has estimated that brokers "annually match between 9,500 and 14,000 foreign women with American men." Kirsten Lindee, *Love, Honor or Control: Domestic Violence, Trafficking, and the Question of How to Regulate the Mail-Order Bride Industry*, 16 COLUM. J. GENDER & L. 551, 552 (2007).

Because of widespread perception that the international mail-order bride industry facilitates domestic violence, trafficking and marriage fraud, Congress in 1996 enacted legislation requiring marriage brokers to provide information on American immigration law to potential brides. 8 U.S.C. § 1375(b)(1). In 2005, a much broader piece of legislation, the International Marriage Broker Regulation Act of 2005 was enacted. *See* 8 U.S.C. § 1375a. In addition to providing potential brides with extensive information (including information about, e.g., domestic violence and sexual assault laws, services for victims of domestic violence, the rights of immigrant victims of abuse, marriage fraud and the penalties for committing such fraud and the obligation), the Act prohibits brokers from providing information to prospective brides under the age of 18, and mandates research on the prospective husbands (dealing with criminal records, civil protection orders, arrests and restraining orders) and provision of that research to the prospective brides. *See also* Suzanne Jackson, *Marriages of Convenience: International Marriage Brokers, "Mail-Order Brides," and Domestic Servitude*, 38 U. Tol. L. Rev. 895 (2007); Erin Pleasant, Recent Development, *The International Marriage Broker Regulation Act: Protecting Foreign Women or Punishing American Men*, 29 Campbell L. Rev. 311 (2007). The Act was upheld against claims of unconstitutionality under freedom of speech and equal protection principles. *European Connections & Tours v. Gonzales*, 480 F. Supp. 2d 1355 (N.D. Ga. 2007).

PROBLEMS

Problem 2-11. (a) Mona and Stan had a long-standing sexual relationship. When Mona informed Stan she was pregnant, he proposed marriage, saying that while he really didn't want to be married, he didn't believe in abortions or non-marital children. He made no attempt to verify her pregnancy. The couple married and Stan later discovered that Mona was not and never had been pregnant and had never believed she was. He is outraged and comes to you anxious to "get rid of her." What is your advice?

(b) Assume Mona had actually been pregnant, but when she spoke to Stan she knew Harvey was really the child's father. Would this change your advice?

Problem 2-12. Ed and Corinne are first cousins and were born in England. Corinne emigrated to Arizona and became an American citizen. Later, Corinne invited Ed to share an apartment in Arizona. They soon fell in love and decided to marry. Because Arizona law would bar their marriage, they married in California which permits such marriaget. They immediately returned to Tempe, where they both are Arizona State University law professors. Ed now seeks to stay in Arizona, claiming to be entitled to permanent resident status as an American citizen's spouse. The federal government, however, rejects her application, asserting Ed is not married to Corinne. You are the federal judge before whom this dispute has been brought. How do you decide the case? What difference, if any, would the presence or absence of a marriage evasion statute make?

[3]   Breach of Promise to Marry: "A Change Of Heart"

NOTES

1. *"Pure" Breach of Promise Action.*   The common law recognized an action for breach of the promise to marry. While formally a contract action, the damages recoverable are tort-like in that plaintiff "may recover for loss to reputation, mental anguish, injury to health . . . expenditures made in preparation for the marriage and loss of the pecuniary and social advantages which the promised marriage offered." *Stanard v. Bolin*, 565 P.2d 94 (Wash. 1977). *Stanard* summarized the widespread criticism of the action:

> (1) [it] is used as an instrument of . . . blackmail; (2) engaged persons should be allowed to correct their mistakes without fear of publicity and legal compulsion; (3) [it] is subject to great abuse [by] juries; (4) it is wrong to allow under the guise of contract an action that is essentially tortious and penal . . . (5) the measure of damages is unjust because damages are allowed for loss of social and economic position, whereas most persons marry for reasons of mutual love and affection.

Id. at 96.

Stanard is one of the relatively few recent cases continuing to recognize the action based solely on emotional injury, failed expectations and compensation for pre-wedding expenditures. Defendant had told plaintiff he was worth in excess of $2 million, would soon retire, and that plaintiff would not have to work again. After she quit her job, sold most of her furniture, put her house on the market, and arranged for the ceremony and reception, defendant cancelled the wedding with one month's notice. The appellate court overturned a dismissal of plaintiff's action, writing that it did "not feel these injuries should go unanswered merely because the breach-of-promise-to-marry action may be subject to abuses. . . ." *Id.* at 97. The court refused, however, to permit recovery for damages of loss of expected financial and social position.

Is the court's distinction between damages for mental anguish (permissible) and loss of social position or financial advantage (impermissible) a sensible one? While the court's statement that most people do not marry for such material reasons is likely correct, what if that *was* an important motivation in a particular case? Should the law define the *proper* reason for marriage?

In *Hoffman v. Boyd*, 698 So. 2d 346 (Fla. App. 1997), a *written* contract provided for liquidated damages, requiring open-ended support of the plaintiff if defendant did not marry her within 12 months. Her suit for breach was rejected by both trial and appellate courts, both because of the state's Heart Balm statute (for details of such statutes, see *infra* Section C.3) abolishing breach of promise actions and because both parties were married to others at the time of the contract which, thus, promoted divorce. The court rejected plaintiff's assertion of estoppel, finding the agreement void.

While retaining the action, some states have legislatively modified it. For example, Illinois imposes a one-year statute of limitations, restricting recovery to actual damages. ILL. ANN. STAT. ch. 740, §§ 5/6, 15/2; *see Wildey v. Springs*, 840 F. Supp. 1259 (N.D. Ill. 1994), *rev'd on other grounds*, 47 F.3d 1475 (7th Cir. 1995) (according to diversity court, pain and suffering included within "actual damages"). A Tennessee plaintiff must either have written proof of the contract or testimony by two disinterested witnesses. Plaintiffs over 60 may recover only actual damages. TENN. CODE ANN. § 36-3-401; *see Rivkin v. Postal*, 2001 Tenn. App. LEXIS 682 (Sept. 14, 20010) (rejecting plaintiff's parents as disinterested witnesses).

2. *The Engagement Ring and Other Conditional Gifts.* Akin to breach of promise is a suit brought (usually by a jilted groom) to get back property (usually the engagement ring) after cancellation of wedding plans. This typically is not seen as a breach of promise action, but instead a quantum meruit action which survives enactment of a Heart Balm statute. *Aronow v. Silver*, 538 A.2d 851 (N.J. Super. 1987); *Brown v. Thomas*, 379 N.W.2d 868 (Wis. App. 1985). At least one court, however, refused to carve out a Heart Balm exception which it perceived as gender-biased in favor of men. In *Albinger v. Harris*, 48 P.3d 711 (Mont. 2002), the court held an engagement ring is not a conditional gift and need not be returned upon the breakup. Finding the Heart Balm statute often deprives women, who "often still assume the bulk of pre-wedding costs," of a cause of action, *Albinger* held that "[i]f this court were to fashion a special exception for engagement ring actions . . . , we would perpetuate the gender bias attendant upon the Legislature's decision to [reject] all actions for breach of antenuptial promises" *See* Rebecca Tushnet, Note, *Rules of Engagement*, 107 YALE L.J. 2583 (1998) (criticizes "particularly gendered effects of current doctrine, which requires the return of engagement gifts while allowing no redress for pre-wedding expenses borne mainly by women"); Brooke Blecher, *Broken Engagements: Who is Entitled to the Engagement Ring?*, 34 FAM. L.Q. 579 (2000).

Some Heart Balm laws explicitly preserve such actions. *See, e.g.*, N.Y. CIVIL RIGHTS LAW § 80-b; *Bruno v. Guerra*, 549 N.Y.S.2d 925 (Sup. Ct. 1990). *But see Dastugue v. Fernan*, 662 So. 2d 538 (La. App. 1995) (no recovery where plaintiff gave engagement ring to wife before marriage and returned it to her after divorce).

Other gifts conditioned on marriage have been ordered returned. In *Fanning v. Iversen*, 535 N.W.2d 770 (S.D. 1995), plaintiff recovered the value of a half-interest in a real estate investment made in contemplation of marriage. The court held plaintiff was "not asking for damages for loss of marriage or humiliation. Rather, he seeks to assert his equitable common-law right to recover property for which he paid and solely owns because the condition precedent . . . was not fulfilled." *Id.* at 774. *See also Volodarsky v. Malamud*, N.Y.L.J., Oct. 1, 1996 (Civ. Ct. Queens) (granting restitution of payment of defendant's pre-marital debts intended as gift conditioned on marriage).

The cases are divided on fault's role in such suits. Many courts limit recovery to "innocent" plaintiffs. In *Curtis v. Anderson*, 106 S.W.3d 251 (Tex. App. 2003), the court relied on prior law requiring the ring's return by a defendant at fault to find that the plaintiff who had broken the engagement for "vague reasons" was not entitled to the ring's return. *See also Clippard v. Pfefferkorn*, 168 S.W.3d 616 (Mo. App. 2005) (applying fault-based approach, court holds ring need not be returned to fiancé who broke engagement); RESTATEMENT OF RESTITUTION § 58, cmt. c (1937).

Most of the more recent cases, however, return property regardless of fault, likely influenced by the no-fault divorce regime. *See Fowler v. Perry*, 830 N.E.2d 97 (Ind. App. 2005) (donor entitled to return of ring without regard to reason for the failure of the marriage to occur); *see also Benassi v. Back & Neck Pain Clinic*, 629 N.W.2d 475 (Minn. App. 2001); *Meyer v. Mitnick*, 625 N.W. 2d 136 (Mich. App. 2000); *Vigil v. Haber*, 888 P.2d 455 (N.M. 1995). *See generally* Elaine Tomko, Annot., *Rights in Respect of Engagement and Courtship Presents When Marriage Does Not Ensue*, 44 A.L.R.5th 1 (1996). Some cases turn on whether a particular ring was an engagement ring or, e.g., a birthday present. *See Busse v. Lambert*, 773 So. 2d 182 (La. App. 2000).

After the wedding, who owns the engagement ring? In *Winer v. Winer*, 575 A.2d 518 (N.J. App. 1990), during the engagement the bride-to-be was given a 4-carat ring which throughout the seven-year marriage was kept in a safe-deposit box and worn only on special occasions. On divorce, husband argued that because the conditional gift became absolute at the wedding it then became marital property. The court rejected the argument, finding an engagement ring is intended to become wife's separate property. *See also Ward v. Ward*, 585 N.W.2d 551 (Neb. App. 1998); *Hanover v. Hanover*, 775 S.W.2d 612 (Tenn. App. 1989).

3. *Fraudulent Promises.*   Breach of promise actions assume defendant broke a genuine promise. What should a court do, in a state with a Heart Balm statute, where plaintiff alleges defendant never intended to marry, making the promise fraudulent at the outset? Courts facing this question have split on whether to permit such a suit. *See, e.g., Waddell v. Briggs*, 381 A.2d 1132 (Me. 1978) (dicta barring such an action as inconsistent with rejection of heart balm actions); *Piccininni v. Hajus*, 429 A.2d 886 (Conn. 1980) (entertaining deceit action). *See* Jeffrey Kobar, Note, *Heartbalm Statutes and Deceit Actions*, 83 MICH. L. REV. 1770 (1985) (arguing such actions, if "carefully construed and managed by courts, are outside the statutory bar of the heartbalm statutes and are not subject to the grave abuses once feared").

Some defendants conceal a matter other than an intention not to marry and the fraud is not discovered until long after marriage. For example, in *Askew v. Askew*, 22 Cal. App. 4th 942 (1994), the jury found against defendant who defrauded her prospective husband by claimed "lust," "passion" and "sexual desire" for him at the time of their wedding 13 years earlier. Plaintiff alleged these false statements led to his transfer of separate property to defendant. Terming this a breach of promise action "gussied up as a fraud action," the appellate court reversed the verdict, concluding "words of love, passion and sexual desire are simply unsuited to the cumbersome strictures of common law fraud and deceit." *See also Yang v. Lee*, , 163 F. Supp. 2d 554 (D. Md. 2001) (holding Maryland law prohibited suit by defrauded wife and her parents for defendant's misrepresentations concerning his sexual identity and history); *M.N. v. D.S.*, 616 N.W.2d 284 (Minn. App. 2000) ("if no cause of action can exist in tort for a fraudulent promise to marry, then . . . no cause of action can exist for a fraudulent promise by a married man to leave his wife and impregnate a woman who is not his wife"); *Charley v. Fant*, 892 S.W.2d 811 (Mo. App. 1995) (affirming dismissal of fraud action based on pre-marital concealment of prior marriage).

Despite the trend toward abolition of causes of action where questions of sexual behavior and misbehavior are central to the litigation, a commentator has argued forcefully for recognition of a "sexual fraud" action. Jane Larson, *Women Understand So Little, They Call My Good Nature "Deceit": A Feminist Rethinking of Seduction*, 93 COLUM. L. REV. 374 (1993). The author urges liability for one "who fraudulently makes a misrepresentation . . . for the purpose of inducing another to consent to sexual relations in reliance upon it." Recovery would be awarded for "serious physical, pecuniary, and emotional loss. . . ."

PROBLEMS

Problem 2-13. Charlene was 18 when she married Frank, a Navy captain who was often at sea. After 15 years, while Frank was at sea, a married girlfriend invited Charlene to dinner. Without her knowledge, her friend had invited a dinner date for her, Dante, another married naval officer. Charlene and Dante began to date and commenced a sexual relationship. After four months, they decided to marry and divorced their spouses.

Preparing for their wedding, the couple ordered wedding bands and arranged for the church, organist, caterer, florist and baker. Charlene purchased a wedding dress, a silk bouquet, shoes and a nightgown for the wedding night and bought Dante a desk set inscribed with the wedding date. The day before the ceremony Dante developed doubts. On the wedding day after the 150 guests had gathered, he arrived a half hour late and had a long talk with Charlene, eventually confessing "there's somebody else and I can't marry you." The wedding was cancelled. Dante soon married a high school sweetheart.

At the trial of her breach of promise suit, Charlene testifies she was "humiliated, devastated, nauseated and, from time to time, suicidal and undergone $3,000 worth of psychiatric treatment." She has also testified: "I am very upset about the loss of Frank. I could have lived with him forever. He makes a good living and always treated me very well. The marriage would have lasted had it not been for Dante." Charlene is working at a local bookstore. She makes little and survives on her divorce settlement. F has remarried.

Charlene obtains a jury verdict of $60,000. Dante seeks your representation on appeal. Your state recognizes breach of promise, but has never discussed the elements of damages. There is no statutory authorization and the most recent appellate case was decided in 1951. What will you argue on appeal?

Problem 2-14. Assume the same facts as above, except that the minister talked Dante into proceeding with the wedding. Three weeks later, however, certain that it was a mistake, he filed for divorce. A no-fault divorce was quickly granted and, given the short marriage and absence of children, Charlene got no alimony or property division. Her three-week marriage, however, ended her monthly alimony payments from Frank, which had supplemented her bookstore income, making subsistence into a comfortable life. Does she have a claim against Dante for breach of promise? For some other tort? Should she?

B. LAW OF THE INTACT MARRIAGE

[1]   Duty to Support

McGUIRE v. McGUIRE
Nebraska Supreme Court
59 N.W.2d 336 (Neb. 1953)

MESSMORE, JUSTICE.

. . . [Plaintiff's suit for separate maintenance was successful at trial, in which a decree was entered to require defendant to "pay for certain items in the nature of improvements and repairs, furniture, and appliances . . . ; . . . purchase a new automobile with an effective heater within 30 days; . . . pay travel expenses of the plaintiff for a visit to each of her daughters at least once a year; . . . [provide] a personal allowance . . . of $50 a month. . . . As an alternative to house improvements, defendant could "purchase a modern home elsewhere. . . ."]

. . . [P]laintiff and defendant were married . . . on August 11, 1919. . . . [D]efendant was a bachelor 46 or 47 years of age and had a reputation for more than ordinary frugality, of which the plaintiff was aware. She had . . . known him for about 3 years prior. . . . The plaintiff had been previously married. Her first husband died . . . leaving . . . plaintiff and two daughters [each a one-third interest in] 80 acres of land. . . . At the time . . . plaintiff's daughters were 9 and 11 years of age. . . .

At the time of trial plaintiff was 66 years of age and the defendant nearly 80 years of age. No children were born to these parties. The defendant had no dependents except the plaintiff.

The plaintiff . . . was a dutiful and obedient wife, worked and saved, and cohabited with the defendant until the last 2 or 3 years. She worked in the fields, did outside chores, cooked, and attended to her household duties such as cleaning the house and doing the washing. For a number of years she raised as high as 300 chickens, sold poultry and eggs, and used the money to buy clothing, things she wanted, and groceries. She . . . testified . . . defendant was the boss of the house and his word was law; that he would not tolerate any charge accounts and would not inform her as to his finances or business; and that he was a poor companion. The defendant did not complain of her work, but left the impression . . . that she had not done enough. On several occasions the plaintiff asked the defendant for money. He would give her very small amounts, and for the last 3 or 4 years he had not given her any money nor provided her with clothing, except a coat about 4 years previous. The defendant had purchased the groceries the last 3 or 4 years, and permitted her to buy groceries, but he paid for them by check. There is apparently no complaint about the groceries. . . . The defendant had not taken her to a motion picture show during the past 12 years. They did not belong to any organizations or charitable institutions, nor did he give her money to make contributions to any charitable institutions. The defendant belongs to the Pleasant Valley Church which occupies about 2 acres of his farm land. At the time of trial there was no minister for this church so there were no services. For the past 4 years or more, the defendant had not given the plaintiff money to purchase furniture. . . . Three years ago he did purchase an electric, wood-and-cob combination stove which was installed in the kitchen, also linoleum floor covering for the kitchen. [T]he house is not equipped with a bathroom, bathing facilities, or inside toilet. . . . She does not have a kitchen sink. Hard and soft water is obtained from a well and cistern. She has a mechanical . . . refrigerator, and the house is equipped with electricity. There is a pipeless furnace which she testified had not been in good working order for 5 or 6 years, and she testified she was tired of scooping coal and ashes. [Defendant refused to buy a new furnace.] She related that the furniture was old and she would like to replenish it, at least to be comparable with some of her neighbors; that her silverware and dishes were old and were primarily gifts, outside of what she purchased; that one of her daughters [gave her] at least a dress a year, or sometimes two; that the defendant owns a 1929 Ford coupe equipped with a heater which is not efficient, and on the average of every 2 weeks he drives the plaintiff to . . . visit her mother; and that he also owns a 1927 Chevrolet pickup. . . . The plaintiff was privileged to use . . . the rent money . . . from the 80-acre farm, and when she goes to see her daughters . . . she uses part of the rent money for that purpose, the defendant providing no funds for such use. . . . At the present time the plaintiff is not able to raise chickens and sell eggs. . . . The plaintiff has had three abdominal operations for which the defendant has paid. . . . The plaintiff further testified . . . use of the telephone was restricted, indicating that defendant did not desire that she make long distance calls, otherwise she had free access to the telephone.

. . . [D]efendant owns 398 acres of land with 2 acres deeded to a church, the land [valued at] $83,960; . . . he has bank deposits . . . of $12,786.81 and government bonds [worth] $104,500; and . . . his income . . . is $8,000 or $9,000 a year. . . .

. . . .

[The court noted prior state case law permitting maintenance actions where the parties had been separated and cases in other states allowing support actions where, while living in the same house, the parties had separate bedrooms, were not communicating and were generally leading separate lives.]

[T]here are no [Nebraska] cases cited by the plaintiff . . . that will sustain the action such as she has instituted in the instant case.

. . . .

[T]he marital relation has continued for more than 33 years, and the wife has been supported in the same manner during this time without complaint on her part. The parties have not been separated or living apart from each other at any time. In the light of the cited cases it is clear . . . that to maintain an action such as the one at bar, the parties must be separated or living apart from each other.

The living standards of a family are a matter of concern to the household, and not for the courts to determine, even though the husband's attitude toward his wife, according to his wealth and circumstances, leaves little to be said in his behalf. As long as the home is maintained and the parties are living as husband and wife it may be said that the husband is legally supporting his wife and the purpose of the marriage relation is being carried out. Public policy requires such a holding. It appears that the plaintiff is not devoid of money in her own right. She has a fair-sized bank account and is entitled to use the rent from the 80 acres of land. . . .

Reversed and remanded with directions to dismiss.

YEAGER, Justice (dissenting). . . .

. . . . [I]f this plaintiff were living apart from the defendant she could in equity and on the facts . . . be awarded appropriate relief. . . .

In the light of . . . the basis of the right to maintain an action for support, is there any less reason for extending the right to a wife who is denied the right to maintenance in a home occupied with her husband than to one who has chosen to occupy a separate abode?

If [separation is required] equity and effective justice would be denied where a wealthy husband refused proper support . . . to a wife physically or mentally incapable of putting herself in a position [to separate from her husband].

. . . .

In *Earle v. Earle*, it was said: "The question is, whether . . . plaintiff shall be compelled to resort to a proceeding for a divorce, which she does not desire to do, and which probably she is unwilling to do, from conscientious convictions, or, in failing to do so, shall be deprived of [appropriate] support. . . ."

NOTES

1. ***Common Law Duty of Support.*** As part of the legal fiction that the wife had no separate existence apart from the husband, the common law obligated him to provide for her in return for which she was obligated to render "services." *See Manby v. Scott*, 86 Eng. Rep. 781 (1659). Curiously, this gender-based reciprocal relationship survived the 19th century recognition of wives' independent status by enactment of Married Women's Property Acts in most American states. *See* Joan Krauskopf & Rhonda Thomas, *Partnership Marriage: The Solution to an Ineffective and Inequitable Law of Support*, 35 OHIO ST. L.J. 558, 560–62 (1974). Recent statutes codify spousal obligations in gender-neutral terms (*see, e.g.*, CAL. FAMILY CODE § 720) (spouses "contract toward each other obligations of mutual respect, fidelity, and support").

2. ***Refusal to Interfere.*** What explains the courts' general refusal to provide a direct remedy for the neglected spouse where spouses live together? With no direct remedy to effectuate a "right" to support, it can be argued no right actually exists.

> A very technical explanation at common law was that the wife had no legal existence. . . . A more likely explanation was the judicial reflection that the husband's authority in the home was not to be questioned and the belief that if the wife could live with him surely she could influence him to provide adequately for her. . . . The thought was that by ordering [support], the court would render the wife capable of leaving the husband.

Krauskopf & Thomas, *supra*, at 566.

A separate rationale underlying the *McGuire* rule is judicial fear of a heavy caseload or a regime requiring courts to decide issues such as whether a new set of furniture was needed, etc. As one court put it, courts refused to become "a sounding board for domestic financial disagreements, nor a board of arbitration to determine the extent to which a husband is required to recognize the budget suggested by the wife. . . ." *Commonwealth v. George*, 56 A.2d 228, 231 (Pa. 1948).

A commentator sees *McGuire* as adopting an "entity" approach under which "the family is regarded as a freestanding thing, or phenomenon, or group . . . distinct from . . . the state, and must be given some decisional space. By marrying, Mr. and Mrs. McGuire formed a precinct that stands apart from and is ordinarily closed to state authority." Lee Teitelbaum, *The Family as a System: A Preliminary Sketch*, 1996 UTAH L. REV. 537, 542. Dean Teitelbaum contrasts the entity view with a view of the family as an aggregation of individuals "who define for themselves the relationship into which they enter. *Id.* at 544. As a third perspective, he describes a "systems" approach in which a system is a network that 'integrate[s] parts into a whole.' " *Id.* at 549.

Divorce courts do inquire into the marriage's financial aspects and one might argue there is, thus, little reason to refuse involvement here. In divorce, of course, the courts have practically no choice — the marriage is effectively over and, in order to free the parties to remarry a final financial accounting must be made. The only practicable way for courts to minimize this kind of judicial "business," is to follow *McGuire* and refuse to hear disputes within the intact marriage. Is it not possible, however, that some marriages might be "saved" by providing a direct action *during* marriage to resolve some financial disagreements?

3. *Marital Autonomy.* Cases like *McGuire* can be characterized as establishing a common law family autonomy zone into which the state rarely intrudes. This same notion resurfaces in the constitutional law decisions dealt with in Chapters 9 and 10. This refusal to adjudicate spousal rights in the ongoing marriage is not universal. For example, Switzerland provides for "judicial adjustment of disputes about questions of family life in general." Max Rheinstein & Mary Ann Glendon, *Interspousal Relations*, IV INTERNATIONAL ENCYCLOPEDIA OF COMPARATIVE LAW 12 (Chloros ed. 1980). In Spain, a spousal disagreement over location of the family's place of residence should be can be resolved in court, if the parties have children. *Id.* at 12–13. Consider also the following statutes:

> Art. 168. — The husband and the wife shall . . . resolve by common agreement all that is conducive to managing the home, to the upbringing and education of the children and to the administration of the property appertaining thereto. In case of disagreement, the judge . . . shall resolve what is proper.

> Art. 169. — The spouses may have whatever employment activity they wish except that which harms the morale of the family or its structure. Either of them can oppose the other's employment activity, and the judge . . . shall resolve the disagreement.

THE MEXICAN CIVIL CODE 42 (Michael Gordon trans. 1980).

4. *Fault and Action for Support.* At one time, marital misconduct was "highly relevant" in separate maintenance suits. CLARK, LAW OF DOMESTIC RELATIONS 184 (1968). Thus, defendant could defeat the support claim by showing plaintiff's abandonment or adultery. Cases also generally exonerated the husband where the wife's "intolerable" behavior caused him to leave and sometimes required plaintiff to prove defendant's fault as an element of the suit for support.

In recent years, though, just as no-fault divorce has become the norm (*see* Chapter 3), fault has been eliminated in most support actions. *See* MMDA 308. Some statutes retain fault as a relevant issue in support actions. *See, e.g.,* GEORGIA CODE ANN. §§ 19-6-1, 19-6-4; NEV. REV. STATS. § 123.100.

FORSYTH MEMORIAL HOSPITAL v. CHISHOLM
North Carolina Supreme Court
467 S.E.2d 88 (N.C. 1996)

MITCHELL, CHIEF JUSTICE.

Shirley B. Chisholm and Melvin Chisholm were married in . . . 1953. They were separated in January of 1990. . . . Ms. Chisholm then moved to Winston-Salem [where she has remained]. Mr. Chisholm remained in Boone [the marital home] until his death. . . .

On 31 July 1992, Mr. Chisholm was . . . admitted by Ms. Chisholm [to the plaintiff hospital]. . . . [A]t the time of Mr. Chisholm's admission, he and Ms. Chisholm were married. . . . The hospital rendered medical services to Mr. Chisholm . . . until his death on 14 August 1992, which resulted in unpaid medical bills of $45,110.07.

After the hospital attempted to obtain payment from Mr. Chisholm's insurance company, it learned that the insurance company had sent a check to Mr. Chisholm's estate for payment of his medical bills. However, the estate had been administered and closed without payment having been made to the hospital.

The hospital then filed this action seeking to recover the unpaid hospital bills from Ms. Chisholm under the doctrine of necessaries. Ms. Chisholm served an answer denying liability . . . on the ground that at the time the bills were incurred, she and Mr. Chisholm were married but living separate and apart. The trial court granted summary judgment in favor of Ms. Chisholm, and the Court of Appeals affirmed the trial court.

The issue presented on appeal is whether Ms. Chisholm is entitled to benefit from any "separation exception" to the necessaries doctrine. We hold that she is not and reverse the decision of the Court of Appeals.

The necessaries doctrine arose from the common law duty of the husband to provide for the necessary expenses of his wife. The doctrine is now applied equally, holding a wife liable for the necessary expenses of her husband. *N.C. Baptist Hosp., Inc. v. Harris*, 354 S.E.2d 471 (N.C. 1987). [T]o establish a prima facie case against one spouse for the value of necessary medical services provided to the other spouse, the health-care provider must show that (1) medical services were provided to the receiving spouse, (2) the medical services were necessary for the health and well-being of the receiving spouse, (3) the person against whom the action is brought was married to the receiving spouse . . . and (4) payment for the necessaries has not been made.

[I]t is undisputed that the pleadings and affidavits . . . establish the applicability of the necessaries doctrine: Medical services were provided to Mr. Chisholm; the medical services were necessary for the well-being of Mr. Chisholm . . . ; Ms. Chisholm was married to Mr. Chisholm . . . ; payment has not been made. . . . Therefore, unless defendant can establish some exception to the necessaries doctrine, she must be held liable to the hospital for the necessary services it provided her husband.

The sole reason urged by defendant for denying her obligation under the necessaries doctrine is the . . . fact that she had been separated from Mr. Chisholm for over two years at the time the medical services were provided. This Court applied what is now known as the "separation exception" to the necessaries doctrine in *Pool v. Everton* (1858). [T]his Court reasoned that under the common law, "if a wife leaves the 'bed and board' of the husband without good cause," the husband would no longer be responsible for the wife's necessaries. This common law rule as applied by this Court in 1858 was based upon the ground that "it is wrong to harbor the wife by doing any act which will make it more easy for her to continue in the violation of her conjugal duties." The husband's right to his wife's conjugal services was so absolute that the common law gave him a cause of action for damages against "any person who administers to her wants and supplies her with necessaries."

This Court has not had occasion to reconsider or apply the separation exception since [1858]. However, the separation exception was applied in *Cole v. Adams*, 289 S.E.2d 918 (S.C. App. 1982), where the Court of Appeals . . . followed [*Pool*, holding] that in order to hold a husband liable for services furnished to his wife from whom he was separated, the provider . . . had the burden of proving that the separation was due to the fault of the husband. In the present case, the Court of Appeals simply followed . . . *Cole*.

When the necessaries doctrine and the separation exception were first established, the property of a woman vested in her husband at the point of marriage. Therefore, even if the parties separated, all of the property of both spouses was subject to the control of the husband. Any creditor bringing a suit against the wife was required to join the husband because the wife was considered incompetent and could not be sued without the joinder of her husband. Under current North Carolina law, assets acquired by either spouse during the course of the marriage continue to be owned jointly by the marital unit until or unless a separation agreement divides the property or the marriage is dissolved in divorce. There is also now a statutory presumption that all marital property be equally divided upon divorce or a claim for equitable distribution.

The modern marital relationship is viewed by the law as a partnership of equality, an evolution from the nineteenth century relationship of dominance by a husband and submission by a wife who had little standing as an individual person or legal entity. This Court has rejected such antiquated and obsolete notions concerning women by modernizing the common law necessaries doctrine to impose liability on a gender-neutral basis and, thereby, making either spouse responsible for the necessary services provided to the other. *See Harris, [supra]*

. . . . Because the historical purposes underlying the separation exception to the necessaries doctrine are incompatible with current mores and laws governing modern marital relationships in North Carolina, we conclude that the separation exception as previously applied in the courts of this State is "obsolete" within the meaning of [the statute directing courts to apply English common law unless it was, among other things, obsolete]. Being obsolete, that exception has no place in the common law and must be modified.

The Court of Appeals' decision in this case determined that "it is irrelevant whether the hospital had notice of the parties [sic] separation at the time the services were rendered." We disagree. Under this expansion of the separation exception by the Court of Appeals, in order to completely evade liability for one's spouse's medical expenses, one need only show that he or she was separated at the time services were provided. This would make separated spouses immune from liability under the necessaries doctrine even where they had presented themselves together at the hospital as an intact couple, one spouse had admitted the other spouse to the hospital, and the admitting spouse had expressly requested the medical care for the spouse receiving such care. The Court of Appeals' decision places the unreasonable burden on the health-care provider to determine before providing necessary services whether the couple has separated and, if so, whether the separation is due to the fault of the supporting spouse. Answers to these questions are within the knowledge of the spouses, but not the health-care provider.

The interpretation of the separation exception by the Court of Appeals . . . does not reflect modern societal values, sound public policy, or this Court's recent reconsideration and expansion of the necessaries doctrine in *Harris*. Therefore, we must modify the separation exception as applied by the Court of Appeals by rejecting that court's allocation of the burden of proof with regard to the exception. We conclude, instead, that the spouse seeking to benefit from the separation exception to the necessaries doctrine must show that the provider of necessary services had actual notice of the separation at the time the services were rendered. Furthermore, "fault" for the separation is not a factor to be considered in applying the separation exception.

In this case, it is clear . . . the . . . hospital had no reason to know that the Chisholms were separated at the time. . . . The defendant carried her husband to the hospital and admitted him. She did not put the hospital on notice of their separation. . . . It was not until the hospital had been frustrated in its efforts to collect the medical bills . . . that Ms. Chisholm first informed the hospital [of the separation].

As the hospital did not have actual notice of [the] separation . . . , the trial court erred in applying the separation exception to the necessaries doctrine and in entering summary judgment for the defendant. . . . Instead, the trial court was required to enter summary judgment in favor of the plaintiff. . . . The decision of the Court of Appeals affirming the order of the trial court must be and is reversed, and this case is remanded to the Court of Appeals for its further remand to the District Court, Forsyth County, for entry of summary judgment for the plaintiff.

NOTES

1. *Necessaries Doctrine.*   The common law necessaries doctrine provided an indirect remedy for husband's failure to fulfill his support obligations. Merchants could sue him for the cost of necessaries provided to wife. Thus, for example, Mrs. McGuire could have obtained the "new automobile with an effective heater" which she needed and the car dealer could seek payment from Mr. McGuire.

This doctrine was not tremendously effective in providing support for the needy spouse. First, merchants might not extend credit without husband's signature on a contract. Additionally, because the doctrine only covered "necessaries," the merchant had to prove necessity in the family's circumstances. For example, the *McGuire* issue would be whether the "new car with a heater" was necessary in that particular marriage. Also, husband generally would not be liable if he had already provided wife the necessaries or money to purchase them. *See Hubbard v. Suniland Furn. Co.*, 302 S.W.2d 688 (Tex. Civ. App. 1957). In some courts, husband's failure to provide was an element of plaintiff's case. *See* Jay Zitter, Annot., *Necessity, in Action Against Husband for Necessaries Furnished Wife, of Proving Husband's Failure to Provide Necessaries*, 19 A.L.R.4th 432 (1983).

Finally, the necessaries doctrine was tied to the fault-based divorce law. Thus, many courts held husband not liable if wife had wrongfully left him. *See Holiday Hosp. Ass'n v. Schwarz*, 166 So. 2d 493 (Fla. App. 1964). The merchant had to determine whether the cause of any separation. (This doctrine explains newspaper legal column items announcing "I am no longer liable for the debts of. . . .") Unlike in *Chisolm*, the fault-based nature of the necessaries doctrine has survived the move to no-fault divorce in some states. *See, e.g., Bartrom v. Adjustment Bureau, Inc.*, 618 N.E.2d 1 (Ind. 1993). For recent applications of the necessaries doctrine, see *Francis v. Francis*, 2001 Tenn App. LEXIS 434 (June 18, 2001) (doctrine covers funeral expenses); *North Shore Community Bank & Trust Co. v. Kollar*, 710 N.E.2d 106 (Ill. App. 1999) (refusing to apply codification of the necessaries doctrine to decedent-spouse's promissory note); *Dubois, Sheehan, Hamilton and Dubois v. Delarm*, 578 A.2d 1250 (N.J. Super. 1990) (spouse's legal expenses are covered by doctrine).

2. *The Necessaries Doctrine in a Gender-Neutral World.*   Despite the hazards to the creditor, the necessaries doctrine is utilized surprisingly often, particularly in cases like *Chisolm*, where necessary medical care is provided.

The major task facing modern courts has been reconciling the traditional doctrine with current marketplace realities and the abandonment of gendered conceptions of family roles. A rule holding men, but not women, liable for a spouse's debts would appear to violate the Supreme Court's modern interpretation of the Equal Protection Clause. *See* Margaret Mahoney, *Economic Sharing During Marriage: Equal Protection, Spousal Support and the Doctrine of Necessaries*, 22 J. FAM. L. 221, 237 (1983). Since 1986, the only courts affirming the gendered common law doctrine found the constitutional issue not before the court. *Davis v.*

Baxter Cty. Region. Hosp., 855 S.W.2d 303 (Ark. 1993); *Shands Teaching Hosp. v. Smith*, 497 So. 2d 644 (Fla. 1986). There are two obvious gender-neutral schemes: abolition of the doctrine altogether or a mirror-image expansion making wives liable in the same way husbands have been liable. For courts abolishing the doctrine, either for policy or constitutional reasons, leaving the creditor to ordinary contract relief, see *North Ottawa Comm. Hosp. v. Kieft*, 578 N.W.2d 267 (Mich. 1998); *Med. Ctr. Hosp. v. Lorrain*, 675 A.2d 326 (Vt. 1996); *Southwest Fla. Reg. Med. Center v. Connor*, 668 So. 2d 175 (Fla. 1995). For courts adopting the mirror-image expansion, see *Harris* (cited in *Chisolm*) and *Queen's Med. Ctr. v. Kagawa*, 967 P.2d 686 (Hawaii App. 1998).

A third alternative was adopted in New Jersey, in *Jersey Shore Medical Center-Fitkin Hospital v. Baum's Estate*, 417 A.2d 1003 (N.J. 1980), under which the creditor can sue the spouse only after failing in a suit against the spouse who obtained the goods or services. This rule is easily administered from the creditor's perspective and is gender-neutral. This alternative may be the emerging trend. *See, e.g., Cheshire Med. Ctr. v. Holbrook*, 663 A.2d 1344 (N.H. 1995); *Landmark Med. Ctr. v. Gauthier*, 635 A.2d 1145 (R.I. 1994); *Bartrom v. Adjustment Bureau, Inc.* 618 N.E.2d 1 (Ind. 1993); *St. Francis Reg. Med. Ctr. v. Bowles*, 836 P.2d 1123 (Kan. 1992). However, Professor Mahoney argues that this approach prejudices the wife in a traditional family where the homemaker "makes the purchases for the day to day operation of the household. . . ."

In *Marshfield Clinic v. Discher*, 314 N.W.2d 326 (Wis. 1982), the court held that, in a society where women generally earn less than men, husbands are always primarily liable for debts of either spouse. The court found this rule "lets a creditor know how to proceed in collecting for necessary expenses incurred by either spouse. The creditor does not have to delve into a family's financial background in order to ascertain from which spouse it can collect. . . . Such a fixed rule is essential in the commercial world." The court held its rule satisfied the intermediate Equal Protection scrutiny appropriate for analysis of gender discrimination. *See also Swidzinski v. Schultz*, 493 A.2d 93 (Pa. Super. 1985); *Borgess Medical Center v. Smith*, 386 N.W.2d 684 (Mich. App. 1986) (wife liable where husband's estate is insolvent).

A final alternative would be a case-by-case approach with liability based on the parties' respective financial resources with each spouse's responsibility based on a pro rata share of total spousal resources. *Discher* found this constitutionally acceptable, but concluded such a rule would "destroy any certainty on the part of providers. . . . How is the seller of goods to know which spouse possesses the greatest financial resources in any individual situation?"

Professor Mahoney endorses this approach and would require suit against both parties, directing the court to determine the compensation due from each party. She argues this would rarely be a significant burden for the creditor. "An exception could be made . . . where one spouse is outside the state or for some other compelling reason cannot be brought within the court's jurisdiction. . . . A discretionary power in the court to consider the respective circumstances of husband and wife in rendering judgment against one or both of them would provide a basis for equitable allocation of necessaries obligations and protection of dependent spouses." Mahoney, *supra*, at 259–60.

The case-by-case approach would also avoid any question of contribution which is raised under most other gender-neutral schemes. Under traditional law, the only person who could be sued was the husband who ultimately had sole financial responsibility. Where the duty of support is not gender-specific, a defendant-spouse successfully sued by a family creditor might seek contribution in a separate suit from the non-paying spouse.

3. *The Necessaries Doctrine in a No-Fault World.* *Chisolm*, in abandoning the fault inquiry in necessaries suits, reflects the modern trend in divorce law to reject a requirement of an assessment of fault in the determination of whether the marriage should be terminated and in financial issues (*see* Chapters 3, 4). *But see Bartrom v. Adjustment Bureau, Inc.*, 618 N.E.2d 1 (Ind. 1993) (introduction of no-fault divorce statute has no bearing on common law rules governing necessaries doctrine). The *Chisolm* court, in imposing a requirement in the separation defense that the defendant have given notice to the creditor actual notice of the separation at the time of the provision of goods or services, stated "interpretation of the separation exception by the Court of Appeals . . . does not reflect modern societal values, sound public policy, or this Court's recent reconsideration and expansion of the necessaries doctrine in *Harris*." Why does sound public policy and/or modern societal values require protection of the creditor unless he or she has "actual notice" of separation of the spouses?

4. *Criminal Non-Support.* Another indirect means of effectuating the support obligation is criminal prosecution for non-support. Virtually all states have statutes punishing willful non-support. This is generally held to require proof of financial ability to provide support. *See State v. Mehaffey*, 534 S.W.2d 563 (Mo. App. 1976). Interestingly, though, there is authority for the proposition that the state can place the burden of persuasion regarding ability to pay on the defendant. *See, e.g., Cooper v. State*, 760 N.E.2d 660 (Ind. App. 2001); *State v. Mays*, 1995 Ohio App. LEXIS 556 (Feb. 14, 1995). This state court authority is premised on a finding that ability to pay is *not* an element of the crime of non-support. If it were an element, the burden on the issue could not constitutionally be placed on the criminal defendant.

[2] Spousal Control Over Earnings and Property

Traditionally, marriage under the common law gave overriding financial power to the husband. His usual role of breadwinner was important because marriage did not alter his sole authority over his earnings and all property held in his name. As the prior section illustrates, the wife had no claim upon the husband's assets except the limited right to purchase necessaries on his credit and to seek support directly if the parties were separated. Indeed, the older rules gave him control over her earnings and property as well. For a discussion of the married woman's limited rights at common law, see H. Clark, *The Law of Domestic Relations* 286–89 (2nd ed. 1988).

In the middle and late 19th century, all states enacted what were known as Married Women's Property Acts, which were designed to ameliorate the married woman's position. Generally these statutes gave wives the right to acquire, own and transfer property without their husbands' participation, the right to make contracts and keep their own earnings, the right to make a will, the right to sue and be sued individually and the ability to testify in court. *See generally* HENDRIK HARTOG, MAN AND WIFE IN AMERICA: A HISTORY (2000) (providing interesting history of marital property reform). The reforms gave the wife no control or management rights over property titled in her husband's name and, thus, gave no assistance to the wife who lacked significant resources of her own.

Providing an apparent contrast to the status of wives under the common law was the community property system, which governed spousal property rights in the eight states whose marriage law has French or Spanish roots: Arizona, California, Idaho, Louisiana, New Mexico, Nevada, Texas and Washington. While details vary, community property typically includes all "property acquired by either husband or wife during the marriage . . . except for property that is . . . [a]cquired by gift, devise or descent." ARIZ. REV. STAT. § 25-211 (A)(1). This broad definition means every dollar acquired during marriage by *either* party, including all earnings, belongs to *both* husband and wife. There are, of course, further details in the community property law's classification rules; *e.g.*, acquisitions during marriage traceable to separate property typically retain their separate character, in contrast to earnings during marriage from either spouse's labor, which are community property. These details are explored further in Chapter 4's discussion of property division at divorce. Here we explore treatment of community property during marriage.

Under the original American community property system, the wife was hardly better off during marriage than in a common law state, because the husband had sole management authority over all community property. The wife could claim her share of the community upon divorce or her husband's death, but during marriage her interest in the community was described as a "mere expectancy." *Van Maren v. Johnson*, 15 Cal. 308, 311 (1860). *See* Susan Prager, *The Persistence of Separate Property Concepts in California's Community Property System, 1849-1975*, 24 UCLA L. REV. 1, 35–39, 47–52 (1976). For example, in *Wilcox v. Wilcox*, 98 Cal. Rptr. 319, 320 (Ct. App. 1971), the husband complained that his wife had "secreted" $30,000 of community funds and the appellate court recognized his claim:

> By statute a husband "has the management and control of the community personal property, with like absolute power of disposition, other than testamentary, as he has of his separate estate," subject to certain [irrelevant] exceptions. . . . The right of the husband . . . is invaded . . . when [wife] deprives him thereof by taking, secreting and exercising exclusive control over community funds.

The court recognized a cause of action without specific statutory authority.

Wilcox was a last hurrah for male management prerogatives. The 1970s saw a wave of reform in community property states which replaced "husband as manager" provisions with various forms of dual or coequal management. Louisiana was the last holdout. Its husband-dominated management system was struck down in *Kirchberg v. Feenstra*, 450 U.S. 55 (1981). Although again details vary, no community property state has male management provisions today. What does "equal management" of the community mean? Consider the relatively straightforward Arizona statute:

> A. Each spouse has the sole management, control and disposition rights of each spouse's separate property.
>
> B. The spouses have equal management, control and disposition rights over their community property and have equal power to bind the community.
>
> C. Either spouse separately may acquire, manage, control or dispose of community property or bind the community, except that joinder of both spouses is required in any of the following cases:
>
>> 1. Any transaction for the acquisition, disposition or encumbrance of an interest in real property other than an unpatented mining claim or a lease of less than one year.
>>
>> 2. Any transaction of guaranty, indemnity or suretyship. . . .

ARIZ. REV. STAT. § 25-214.

Note that the statute states both a default rule allowing either spouse to bind the community, and exceptions requiring agreement of both spouses. Federal law adds to this list of exceptions, with respect to plans covered under ERISA, the federal law that regulates tax-qualified pension plans. Pension plans typically offer retiring employees a choice between a pension that continues until the employee's death ("Life"), or one that continues until both the employee and the employee's spouse have died ("Joint Life"). Because the expected term of payments will be greater, the monthly payout is less with the joint-life plan. Because a pension is a community asset to the extent that it was earned by employment during marriage, the choice of plan is a community property management decision. Under general management rules such as those in the Arizona statute, either spouse could bind the community to a choice, although before ERISA pension plan administrators would ask only the employee. Employees choosing higher payouts that ended with their death left disappointed survivors who sometimes challenged the decision, but under applicable community property principles they usually lost. *Brown v. Boeing Co.*, 622 P.2d 1313 (Wash. App. 1980) (decedent-husband's choice of Life plan binding even though she objected to husband during his life). Under the Retirement Equity Act of 1984 (29 U.S.C. § 1055), ERISA now requires pension plans to obtain the non-employee spouse's written consent to selection of an annuity with no survivor benefits. This requirement applies to all covered pension plans (which is most plans); the spouse's consent is thus required in both common law and community property jurisdictions.

NOTES

1. Analogous Management Choices. Choice of pension plan is hardly the only management decision that may prove important to both spouses even though made only by one. It is common, *e.g.*, for one spouse alone to make decisions about investment accounts with community funds. For another everyday example, consider *Johnson v. Farmers Insurance Company*, 817 P.2d 841 (Wash. 1991), involving a choice of auto insurance coverage. After separation, a couple's daughter was injured in an accident in which the responsible third-party was uninsured. Her claim under their policy's Uninsured Motorist (UIM) coverage was limited by the father's unilateral pre-divorce decision waiving full coverage (in exchange for a reduced premium). The mother lost her challenge to the waiver. The court explained:

> As one spouse manages community affairs with the effect of binding or benefiting the community, then the other spouse enjoys the same benefits and incurs the same obligations. The . . . burden both [spouses] incurred under the insurance contract once they waived full UIM coverage was the burden of having to take affirmative steps with their insurer if they later desired to reacquire full UIM coverage.
>
> [E]ither spouse is authorized to act in management of community affairs. . . . Either [spouse] could have bound the other by individually executing a valid waiver, with that waiver surviving the termination of the marriage. Such a construction is consistent with the equal management authority principle.

2. *Three Kinds of Gender-Neutral Management.* *Brown v. Boeing* and *Johnson* illustrate the traps that exist when either spouse can bind the other. Particularly because third parties may rely upon the directions of either spouse, the first spouse to act often will prevail. The husband's purchase of a new car with community funds cannot be undone by wife; if the wife buys a certificate of deposit, the husband cannot avoid the early withdrawal penalty by asserting his lack of consent. At least for most day-to-day transactions, however, there does not seem to be any alternative. A rule requiring both spouses' consent to every management transaction would get very tedious. For example, it would mean both spouses would have to sign every credit card transaction. No community property state employs this rule. Instead, the Washington rule applied in *Brown* and *Johnson* is the most common formulation.

There is also a pattern to the statutory exceptions under which particular kinds of transactions require the consent of both spouses. The sale or encumbrance of real estate, identified by the Arizona statute quoted above, is such a common exception. *Droeger v. Friedman, Sloan & Ross*, 812 P.2d 931 (Cal. 1991) (wife's unilateral encumbrance of community real estate, in violation of statute requiring both spouses' consent to such transactions, voidable by husband by timely objection).

On the other hand, for some transactions, state law may give one spouse, selected on a gender-neutral basis, exclusive management authority. For example, some states give the entrepreneur-spouse sole management authority over a community property business "to assure the smooth functioning of the concern, on the assumption that joint decision-making is potentially divisive in a way that would be destructive of the community's ultimate interest in the business' success." Carol Bruch, *Management Powers and Duties Under California's Community Property Laws: Recommendations for Reform*, 34 HASTINGS L.J. 227, 274 (1982);

see, e.g., CAL. FAM. CODE § 1100(d) ("a spouse who is operating or managing a business . . . that is . . . community . . . property has the primary management and control of the business or interest. Primary management and control means that the managing spouse may act alone in all transactions but shall give prior written notice to the other spouse of any sale, lease . . . or other disposition of . . . substantially all of the . . . property used in the operation of the business . . . whether or not title to that property is held in the name of only one Spouse"); LA. CIV. CODE art. 2352 (spouse who is a partner has "exclusive right" to manage partnership Interest); NEV. REV. STATS. § 123.230(6) (where one spouse "participates in the management" of a business, that spouse may take actions "in the ordinary course of business" without consent "of the nonparticipating spouse"). In sum, gender-neutral management means: (1) often either spouse can act alone and bind the other, (2) sometimes both must consent, and (3) sometimes sole management authority is allocated to one spouse on a gender-neutral basis.

Finally, one cannot ignore the reality that factors unrelated to marital property law may give one spouse effective sole management authority over at least some community property. For example, commercial relations in a community property state lacking any "entrepreneur-spouse" exception as described in the preceding paragraph may effectively ensure the same result. In fact, sole management may be the effective rule for some assets outside the entrepreneur-spouse rule:

> As a practical matter, if stocks are registered in the name of one spouse, only that spouse can sell. True, the stock may be community property despite the paper title in the name of one spouse, and theoretically the non-titled spouse has "equal" power to manage; but the broker will transfer only on the signature of the registered owner. If one spouse manages an unincorporated business, the commercial world [normally] will deal only with that spouse. . . . If one spouse is a partner with third persons, partnership law gives the other spouse no power to act for the partnership. In short, "equal" management is fine in theory but is unrealistic in practice. It is probably harmless, however, to leave equal management statutory provisions as they are.

Richard Effland, *Arizona Community Property Law, Time for Review and Revision,* 1982 ARIZ. ST. L.J. 1, 15.

3. *Open Questions.* Does one spouse have an enforceable right to an accounting of community assets concealed by the other? Does one spouse have a claim against the other for negligent mismanagement of the assets? Where either can act alone for the community, can one spouse prevent the other from acting by informing the third party of his or her opposition? (For example, can husband prevent wife's sale of their boat by informing a prospective buyer that he has decided not to sell?)

Not all these questions have been answered in each community property state. California imposes on each spouse a fiduciary duty to the other when managing community assets. This duty includes "the obligation to make full disclosure to the other spouse of . . . the existence . . . of all assets in which the community has . . . an interest and debts for which the community . . . may be liable, . . . upon request. . . ." CAL. FAM. CODE § 1100(e). Either spouse may bring an action for an accounting to "determine the rights of ownership in, the beneficial enjoyment of, or access to, community property, and the classification of all property of the parties to a marriage," or an action for "any breach of the fiduciary duty that results in impairment to the claimant spouse's present undivided one-half interest in the community estate, including, but not limited to, a single transaction or a pattern or series of transactions, which . . . have caused or will cause a detrimental impact to the claimant spouses undivided one-half interest. . . . CAL. FAM. CODE § 1101. *See* Carol Bruch, *Protecting the Rights of Spouses in Intact Marriages: The 1987 California Community Property Reform and Why It Was So Hard to Get*, 1990 WIS. L. REV. 731 (recounting history of these provisions).

Two community property states have somewhat different management systems which avoid or deal with some of these questions. Texas unique system makes each spouse sole manager of community property "that the spouse would have owned if single." TEX. FAM. CODE ANN. § 3.102. This gives each spouse sole control over his or her earnings, although the manager cannot "unfairly dispose of the other spouse's one-half interest in the community." *Mazique v. Mazique*, 742 S.W.2d 805 (Tex. App. 1987). New Mexico provides, in effect, that written title to personal community property determines whether management control is in both spouses or one spouse. Control is given to the party or parties "named in a document evidencing ownership." N.M. STAT. ANN. § 40-3-14. In a unique provision, New Mexico permits a spouse to claim sole management authority by entering into a written agreement with a third party which designates that spouse as having that authority. *Id.* The apparent purpose is to protect merchants who enter into agreements with one spouse. *See* Anne Bingaman, *The Community Property Act of 1973: A Commentary and Quasi-Legislative History*, 5 N. MEX. L. REV. 1 (1974).

4. *Common Law Applications.* The Uniform Marital Property Act (UMPA), promulgated in 1983 by the National Conference of Commissioners on Uniform State Laws, largely follows community property principles while shunning community property labels, perhaps to make the proposal more palatable to traditionalists in common law states. Property obtained during marriage is "marital," not "community" property. Property brought into the marriage is "individual" not "separate." Wisconsin is the only state to have adopted UMPA to date. WIS. STAT. ANN. §§ 766.001 to.097 (2003). The state had considered adopting a community property system in earlier years, and, in opting for UMPA, the legislature understood it was moving toward a community property system. William Reppy, *The Uniform Marital Property Act: Some Suggested Revisions for a Basically Sound Act*, 21 HOUS. L. REV. 679, 686–87 (1984).

In many ways UMPA's management provisions follow New Mexico's title principle. Section 5 gives each spouse management authority over most untitled marital property (real and personal) with certain exceptions, including property held in one spouse's name, which may be managed by that spouse only. Both spouses must concur in management of property if their names appear on the title joined by an "and"; either can act alone if their names are joined by an "or." Section 15 establishes remedies for one spouse against another arising from the spouse's interest in marital property. The complete text of UMPA, as well as extensive commentary, may be found in *Uniform Marital Property Act Symposium*, 21 HOUS. L. REV. 595 (1984).

[3]   Varying the Marriage "Contract"

NOTES

1. *Traditional Rule on Enforcement of Marital Contracts.* As reflected in cases such as *Graham v. Graham*, 33 F. Supp. 936 (E.D. Mich. 1940), traditionally marriage was conceived as a tri-lateral contract between husband, wife and state. While individuals had virtually free choice of whether to marry, when to marry and whom to marry, once the marriage occurred the state mandated its own "standard-form" contract which defined the husband as head of household (and entitled to determine marital domicile) and supporter of his wife. Thus, *Graham* refused to enforce an agreement under which a man gave up his job and his right to determine marital domicile in exchange for his wife's support. In explanation, the court wrote:

> The [traditional rule forbidding private alteration of the marital con-tract] is based on sound foundations of public policy. If they were permitted to . . . contract [about] where the parties are to live and whether the husband is to work or be supported by his wife, there would . . . be no reason why married persons could not contract as to the allowance the husband or wife may receive, the number of dresses she may have, the places where they will spend their evenings and vacations, [etc.]. Such right would . . . would destroy the element of flexibility needed in making adjustments. . . . [Voluntary behavior along these lines is acceptable.] . . . It would be unfortunate if in making . . . adjustments . . . the parties should find their hands tied. . . .

Id. at 939.

Thus, while the state is quite reluctant to intervene to require marital partners to conform to *state*-created expectations (*see McGuire*), it also refuses to enforce any *private* agreements which vary those expectations.

A recent court reiterated the traditional approach. In *Diosdado v. Diosdado*, 97 Cal. App. 4th 470 (2002), a married couple contracted after the husband's extra-marital affair had caused a separation, committing both parties to "emotional and sexual fidelity." A breach was defined as "any [voluntary] kissing on the mouth or touching in any sexual manner of any person outside of said marital relationship, as determined by a trier of fact." A liquidated damages clause provided for payment of $50,000. The trial court dismissed the wife's suit for an alleged breach by husband by kissing another woman. The appellate court affirmed, holding enforcement of the agreement inconsistent with no-fault divorce regime.

2. *Modern   Developments.* Resistance to allowing marital partners contractual autonomy recently has softened in other areas of family law. Both prenuptial and separation agreements defining the financial consequences of a divorce are likely to be enforced by modern courts. *See* Chapter 8. Likewise, unmarried cohabitants are increasingly permitted to contract with each other. (*See* Chapter 9, Section A[2]). Though the contracts in most of the cohabitation cases deal with financial issues like those addressed by prenuptial or separation

agreements, the contract principles applied in them would seem to reach other matters as well.

Marriage contract advocates argue that refusal to extend contractual freedom to married couples encourages those who want flexibility in their relationships to stay outside of marriage. A number of commentators have urged enforcement of agreements between marital partners creating specific obligations and rights in various aspects of the marriage. For example, Professor Lenore Weitzman suggests parties might want provisions defining: the duration of the marriage, the decision-making process to be used concerning jobs and education, the classification of property obtained by either partner during marriage, living arrangements, responsibility for household tasks, surname(s) to be used, the nature of sexual relations, religious commitments, relationships with friends and family, intent to bear children and childrearing philosophies. WEITZMAN, THE MARRIAGE CONTRACT (1981). Professor Weitzman's book includes five actual contracts. In one, David, a first-year medical student, and Nancy, an aspiring dancer, agreed that she would turn down a two-year fellowship in Paris and the ensuing career she had always aspired to in exchange for the "usual benefits of being a doctor's wife (i.e., a beautiful home and summer home, expensive clothing, vacations in Europe, child care and private schools for her children, and a full-time housekeeper). "The contract also included provisions by which "the parties recognize that although Nancy's contribution to the partnership will be less tangible financially, her financial support during school, her home and child care afterwards, and her continuing emotional and psychological nurturance are of equal worth to the partnership" and "the location of the family domicile will be decided by David; the main consideration in making such a decision will be the best interest of David's career" and "both parties will use David's surname" and "Nancy agrees to further David's career by maintaining appropriate social relationships with other doctors and their wives" and "David agrees to accompany Nancy to the ballet at least once a month and agrees to schedule at least two two-week vacations with her each year, at least one of them in Europe." *Id.* at 295–98. *See also* Andrew Blair-Stanek, Comment, *Defaults and Choices in the Marriage Contract: How to Increase Autonomy, Encourage Discussion, and Circumvent Constitutional Constraints*, 24 TOURO L. REV. 31 (2008) (argues "policymakers have long recognized the value of optional terms and well-crafted defaults in other contractual regimes . . . [but] have barely begun to explore the possibilities . . . in the marriage contract").

3. *Enforcement of Non-financial Matters in Marriage Contracts.* Should courts enforce provisions of marital contracts such as Nancy's obligation to maintain "appropriate relationships with other doctors and their wives" or David's agreement on scheduling vacations? There are obvious enforcement difficulties with such provisions. One may question whether there is any point to a marriage which requires such an agreement. Would creation of a new court that would issue decrees of rebuke or condemnation to violators help facilitate recognition of marital contracting? Would such decrees be effective? Would such a process be more acceptable than traditional legal remedies? Perhaps a court would not be required to provide such remedies — a private agency might suffice. Enforcement might thus not require injunctive relief or even judicial appraisal of damages for such a breach. Is that enough to make enforcement likely or desirable?

Perhaps resistance to enforcement is related to resistance to recognizing a limited purpose marriage as "real" (discussed earlier). That is, while we are increasingly willing to allow couples to modify the financial consequences of marriage, we reject enforcement (and resulting legal legitimacy) of their contracts about the personal and symbolic aspects of marriage — the same aspects which courts, in other contexts, have treated as indicators of whether a marriage is real. Perhaps these personal matters, rather than marriage = s financial aspects, are now the "essentials" which cannot be modified.

One commentator contrasted judicial willingness to enforce interspousal agreements dealing with property division and alimony with the refusal to enforce "nonmonetary" contractual provisions such as those in Note 2 *supra*. Katharine Silbaugh, *Marriage Contracts and the Family Economy*, 93 Nw. U. L. Rev. 65 (1998). Asserting that the "rule of selective enforcement disproportionately benefits those who bring more money to a marriage, who are more likely to be men than women," Professor Silbaugh urges that, because the "nonmonetary aspects of marriage" cannot be meaningfully enforced, "equity dictates that we should at least have a presumption against the enforcement of monetary contracts."

4. *Ramifications of Marriage Contracting.* Some defend the legitimacy and efficacy of enforcement of marital contracts. One commentator argues that "[s]ince the new function of marriage is happiness and fulfillment of the individuals, it also follows that personal preferences as to the substance of the marriage should be honored. Our society is based on . . . tolerance of . . . diversity. If marriage has truly become a personal rather than a social institution, we would defer to personal private ordering. . . . " Gregg Temple, *Freedom of Contract and Intimate Relationships*, 8 Harv. J. L. & Pub. Pol'y 121 (1985); *see also* Marjorie Shultz, *Contractual Ordering of Marriage: A New Model for State Policy*, 70 Cal. L. Rev. 204 (1982). Temple asserts bargaining is not inimical to intimate relationships, nor inherently hostile or adversary. Problems such as overreaching by one party and change of circumstances can be dealt with by ordinary contract principles. While conceding judicial dispute resolution concerning such contracts might be problematic, Temple urges use of alternative dispute resolution methods, such as mediation, arbitration or conciliation courts. As for remedies, Temple argues money damages sometimes would be appropriate, but also suggests the possibility of specific performance in some situations and liquidated damages clauses.

A critic argues contract enforceability might produce unintended consequences such as increasingly intrusive notions of unconscionability and overreaching, a shift in general contract law damages from money damage to specific performance or divorce restrictions based on standard form church-drafted marriage contracts. Richard Helmholz, *Comment: Recurrent Patterns of Family Law*, 8 Harv. J.L. & Pub. Pol'y. 175, 181–83 (1985).

C. CONSEQUENCES OF MARITAL STATUS

[1] Names

IN RE NATALE

Missouri Court of Appeals

527 S.W.2d 402 (1975)

Dowd, Judge.

[Judith appealed denial of a name change petition. An attorney, she sought to change her name because she wanted to list her home phone number in telephone directories. Her husband (who joined her petition), a school administrator, did not want his phone number to be connected to his name in directories. She asserted the change would not defraud creditors. She sought to use the name "Montage" which was not her pre-marriage name. In her pre-marriage life, she had been known by three different surnames due to her mother's remarriage and her adoption.]

. . . [T]he court [denied] the Petition . . . on the ground that "[Judith] is lawfully married and resides with her legal spouse" and "that under such circumstances the granting of said petition could be detrimental to others in the future." . . . [A]t the hearing, the court had commented, "Where a married couple who do have and in the future are likely to have many obligations for which they are liable, I can see circumstances that would be detrimental. . . ." [Thus,] the . . . court found that the fact of a woman's ongoing marriage is prima facie evidence of detriment to creditors sufficient to deny her petition for change of name.

. . . [P]etitioner's first argument is that she has the right at common law to change her name, regardless of her marital status. . . .

Surnames arose as descriptive terms applied to individuals to differentiate between parties with the same baptismal name, eventually becoming a required part of a person's legal name. Even so, names could be adopted and abandoned at will, and all members of a family, including the husband and wife, were not necessarily known by the same surname. Gradually, the custom that all members of the family bear the same, fixed surname developed as surnames lost their character as descriptions of particular individuals. Since the husband and wife customarily adopted the name of the spouse with the most property and since men typically held more property than women, most women took the husband's name. However, the custom never became law. The English common law view was that a woman's surname was not bound to her marital status and arose only through her use of a name.

The law of England . . . recognized the right to change names by the nonfraudulent use of another. The right was never limited to males; indeed, it was through this common law method that a woman changed her surname to that of her husband after marriage. . . . [M]arried women in Missouri are free to adopt another name by the common law method if this right has not been invalidated by constitutional or statutory mandate.

This court is unaware of any constitutional or statutory provision which abrogates the English common law right to change names through usage. . . .

Policy argues in favor of acknowledging that a woman may exercise the common law right to change names. The custom of restricting a married woman's right to use a surname other than her husband's is an outgrowth of societal compulsion and economic coercion[3] inconsistent with developments granting women equal legal rights. The concept that the husband and wife are one, the "one" being the husband, has been abandoned. Insistence that a married couple use one name, the husband's, is equally outmoded.

[We have found] no appellate decision in any state which affirmed . . . denial of a married woman's name change petition on the ground of an ongoing marriage.

We are persuaded that the trial court abused its discretion in denying [Judith] her requested name change. . . .

In view of Judith's common law right to change her name, the requested name change is proper. . . . The law will not keep a wife under her husband's thumb by compelling her to keep his name. . . . The record . . . is devoid of evidence of harm to third parties. Since Judith's husband joined in her petition, no harm to her husband can be presumed, and possible harm to children born to the marriage in the future is too speculative. No harm to the state is shown . . . since Judith did not request a name which is bizarre, obscene, offensive, or of a governmental body.

. . . The damage to the couple's creditors is no greater than that to the creditor of any person whose name has been changed, yet creditors have not complained of undue harm when women have assumed their husband's name upon marriage or changed their names following divorce. . . . Given the notice provided creditors by [the name change statutes], it is at least as possible to defraud a creditor by nondisclosure of the existence of a spouse with the same name as the existence of a spouse with a different name. In addition, it does not seem difficult or uncommon to include the spouse's name, whether it be the same or different, whenever marital status is requested by creditors.

. . . [A] wife's property is not automatically subject to the debts of her husband and . . . a wife is deemed a feme sole for most purposes. It is difficult to imagine prima facie harm to creditors under these circumstances. Both spouses will be known when they seek credit together. The husband's creditors have no automatic right to proceed against the wife's property. The wife's creditors gain an

---

[3] It is not difficult to understand a married woman's assumption of her husband's name given the disabilities and privileges afforded a married woman under the common law. . . .

[Judith] chose to petition for a court ordered change of name . . . rather than use the common law method to change her name. . . . [The name change statutes] do not abrogate . . . the common law method of name change.

Under the common law, the change of name is accomplished by usage or habit. . . . The primary difference between the two methods is, therefore, the speed and certainty of the change of name under the statutory procedure. . . .

unexpected advantage if they have extended credit to a woman believed to be single who is married and whose husband is found to be obligated for the particular debt involved. In times past, the management of a woman was "given" to the woman's husband by her father in the marriage ceremony. The woman was symbolically, if not literally, traded from father to husband like a chattel. Today, a woman is under new management, her own. . . .

The judgment is reversed. . . .

NOTES

1. *Marriage as a Name Change.* The *Natale* petitioner came to be known by her husband's surname in the same way as most women who change their name upon marriage by using what can best be described as self-help through consistent, non-fraudulent use of her husband's surname. But *Natale* makes clear, as almost all modern courts have, that marriage itself does not change the wife's surname. Most such litigation involves a wife seeking to use a name other than husband's for purposes of voting, *Keltch v. Alfalfa County Election Bd.*, 737 P.2d 908 (Okla. 1987); *State v. Taylor*, 415 So. 2d 1043 (Ala. 1982); car registration, *Davis v. Roos*, 326 So. 2d 226 (Fla. App. 1976), getting a driver's license, *Traugott v. Petit*, 404 A.2d 77 (R.I. 1979), filing a dissolution action, *Malone v. Sullivan*, 605 P.2d 447 (Ariz. 1980), and the registration of vital statistics, *Secretary v. City Clerk of Lowell*, 366 N.E.2d 717 (Mass. 1977). Other married women, like the *Natale* petitioner, seek a court order changing her name. In all these cases, non-cooperation by the appropriate government official was overturned by an appellate court reaching the same conclusion as the *Natale* appellate court.

In 13th and 14th century England, a researcher asserts, it was "not unusual for a married heiress to retain her father's family name. Rosalyn Daum, *The Right of Married Women to Assert Their Own Surnames*, 8 J.L. REFORM 64, 67 (1974). One commentator concluded it was more common, in fact, for both spouses to be known by the wife's, not the husband's, surname. L.G. PINE, THE STORY OF SURNAMES 23 (1966). A recent commentator reports a trend in this country of men adopting their wives' surnames upon marriage. Michael Rosensaft, *Comment: The Right of Men to Change Their Names Upon Marriage*, 5 U. PA. J. CONST. L. 186 (2002) (asserting making it easier for women to change their name on marriage than men is unconstitutional). Dicta in an 1881 New York case declared that "[f]or several centuries, by the common law among all English speaking people, a woman, upon her marriage, takes her husband's surname." *Chapman v. Phoenix National Bank*, 85 N.Y. 437, 449 (1881). As recently as 1971, a federal in Alabama upheld against constitutional attack what it found to be a common law rule in Alabama automatically changing a woman's surname to that of her husband. *Forbush v. Wallace*, 341 F. Supp. 217 (M.D. Ala. 1971). In that same year, the U.S. State Department is reported to have written to a married woman requesting a passport that "the legal name of a married woman is her husband's surname [and] the wife at marriage loses her maiden name. . . ." UNA STANNARD, MRS. MAN 256 (Germainbooks 1977) (quoting letter without further attribution); *see also* Elizabeth Emens, *Changing Name Changing: Framing Rules and the Future of Marital Names*, 74 U. CHI. L. REV. 761 (2007) (urges state-created incentives for adoption of egalitarian choices for marital names; analyzes why names matter in general and at marriage, and evaluates different possible default rules for marriage names); Kif Augustine-Adams, *The Beginning of Wisdom is to Call Things by Their Right Names*, 7 S. CAL. REV. L. & WOMEN'S STUD. 1 (1998) (surveying history of naming practices in the U.S. and "naming practices and concomitant social meanings across . . . cultures"and other countries).

2. *Can More Than One Name Be Used?* May a married woman continue using her birth name professionally, but be known as Mrs. _____ socially? The cases do not address this issue explicitly, but a judge complained when a court apparently foreclosed the two-name option. In *Kruzel v. Podell*, 226 N.W.2d 458 (Wis. 1975), the dissent argued that the majority, by finding the only way a married woman acquires her husband's surname is to "habitually use" it, had forced her to elect one or the other. In the dissent's words, "[i]f she blurs the situation by using both her maiden name and her married name, she will be hard put to qualify as an 'habitual user' under the [majority's] test." A recent Ohio court wrote "[a] person may change his name at any time or *even use several different names*, so long as he does not do so for a fraudulent purpose." *State v. Hayes*, 774 N.E.2d 807 (Ohio Mun. Ct. 2002) (reversing conviction for displaying a fictitious identification designating driver as Santa Claus; court noted defendant had used this name, along with his given name, for approximately 20 years and no fraud was involved).

Should the law accommodate the wishes of women who want to use different names for different purposes? Would *Natale's* assurance of minimal risk to creditors be relevant in this context?

3. *Election of Remedies.* As illustrated in *Natale*, in addition to common law self-help, most states have a judicial name change procedure. The existence of this procedure, however, does not usually displace the self-help method. *But see In re Bobrowich*, 2003 N.Y. Misc. LEXIS 52 (N.Y.C. Civ. Ct., Jan. 6, 2003) (suggesting self-help's availability implies judicial discretion to refuse to authorize name change). At least one state, however, requires use of the statutory mechanism. *See* OKLA. STAT. tit. 12, § 1637 (exceptions for those who change their names after marriage, divorce or adoption). Eliminating self-help may be an acknowledgment of its ineffectiveness. One commentator describes the common law method as "practically meaningless. The realities of contemporary society require a state-sponsored corroboration to establish our identity. . . . It is doubtful whether a credit card company will issue new cards to someone calling up and declaring a common law name change." Michael Rosensaft, *Comment: The Right of Men to Change Their Names Upon Marriage*, 5 U. PA. J. CONST. L. 186, 206 (2002). *See also* 83 Op. Att'y Gen. Cal. No. 00-205 (2000) ("inability to establish one's name for purposes of life's daily transactions, although perhaps only occasionally resulting when sole reliance is placed on the common law method, can be a substantial inconvenience when it occurs"). The availability of self-help was cited by a court who rejected a man's attempt to force a woman to stop using his surname after the annulment of their marriage. *Smithers v. Smithers*, 804 So. 2d 489 (Fla. App. 2001) (no fraud involved and plaintiff lacked standing to seek to change another person's name).

A third method of changing names is available in some states in which divorce court judges can restore the wife's maiden name upon divorce. Some statutes make grant of the request mandatory, if requested. *See, e.g.,* GA. CODE ANN. § 19-5-16 ("If a divorce is granted, the judgment . . . shall . . . restore to the party the name [sought] in the pleadings."). Indeed, the Georgia statute speaks in terms of "restoration of a maiden or prior name," thus making clear that a divorcing husband who had adopted his wife's name upon marriage could return to his pre-marital surname. While divorce courts routinely grant such requests even without such mandatory language, some trial courts have expressed reluctance to grant the ex-wife/mother's name change request. *See Miller v. Miller,* 670 S.W.2d 591 (Mo. App. 1984) (reversing trial court's requirement that applicant prove no detriment to children).

4. *Limits on Freedom to Change Names.* There apparently are some limits on the ability to change one's name. Thus, it has been written that a person may be known by any name "in the absence of fraud, misrepresentation or interference with the rights of others. *In re Linda Ann A.,* 480 N.Y.S.2d 996 (Sup. Ct. 1984). Note the additional restraints suggested by *Natale* ("bizarre, obscene, offensive, or of a governmental body"). Another court wrote:

> A [denial of a name change is warranted] when there is factual proof of an "unworthy motive, the possibility of fraud on the public, or the choice of a name that is bizarre, unduly lengthy, ridiculous or offensive to common decency and good taste."

In re Porter, 31 P. 3d 519 (Utah 2001); *see also In re Petition for Change of Name,* 190 P.3d 354 (N.M. App. 2008) (state cannot interfere with the common law method of name change, but refusal to grant statutory name change to "Fuck Censorship" is neither violative of the First Amendment nor an abuse of discretion); *In re Bobrowich, supra,* (denial appropriate for "obscene, pornographic, or offensive" names or those which "violate . . . public policy or morals").

Thus, most courts will grant the petition of the married woman (or anybody else) so long as there is no evidence of fraud or misrepresentation, but some cases and statutes seem to require a justification. In *In re Mohlman,* 216 S.E.2d 147 (N.C. App. 1975), the court affirmed refusal of name changes for several married women who asserted only "personal and professional reasons" for the change. The court held that a statute permitting a change "for good cause shown and for good and sufficient reasons" (N.C. GEN. STAT. § 101-2) required something more. Perhaps understandably, the court did not detail what such good reasons might be. More recently, appellate courts have suggested a change from a male to a female name was inappropriate for a male with a history of "significant periods of gender confusion" without sex-change surgery, *In re DeWeese,* 772 N.E.2d 692 (Ohio App. 2002), and inappropriate where a person wanted to change his name to "Steffi Owned Slave." *In re Bobrowich, supra.*

Natale rejects the claim that children suffer sufficient harm when the parent(s) they live with don't share their name to justify rejection of a proposed name change. For further discussion of this claim, see Chapter 6, Section D[2].

5. *What Names are Being Used?* A 1993 survey conducted for *American Demographics* concluded only 10% of married women in this country use something other than their husband's last name. Joan Brightman, *Why Hillary Chooses Rodham Clinton*, AMERICAN DEMOGRAPHICS, March, 1994, at 9. The survey reported half of the 10% using non-traditional names use hyphenated surnames which include their birth name and their husband's. Twenty percent use their own birth name exclusively, while 30% "use other alternatives," including use of their birth name as a middle name.

Education, income and age were found to be important variables correlated to women's use of non-traditional names. For example, 21% of women with a post-graduate education do not use their husband's name as compared to 5% of women whose education stopped after high school. Fourteen percent of those under 30 use non-traditional names and only 5% of those over 60. Household income, however, does not present as neat a picture. Thirteen percent of women in households with $60,000 or more are in the non-traditional category, as compared to 7% of those whose income is between $12,500 and $39,999. One tenth of those below $12,500, however, use non-traditional names.

A more recent article describes a national survey of 2,000 married women in the United States reporting that 95% took their husband's names. Patricia Wen, *Tradition in Name Only*, BOSTON GLOBE, Mar. 17, 2001, at A1. The same article quoted a Danish academic who asserted that in her native country women went from taking their husbands' names to retaining their names "within one generation in the 1970s." She speculated that "the United States may have a more romantic notion of marriage, which keeps the name issue associated with emotional love, rather than a reminder of an old system in which a woman was the property of her husband."

The most ambitious study of surname retention used three complementary sources — *New York Times* wedding announcements, Harvard alumni records and Massachusetts birth records covering the period from 1975 to 2001 — to track changing patterns. Claudia Goldin & Maria Shim, *Making a Name: Women's Surnames at Marriage and Beyond*, 18 J. ECON. PERSP. 143 (2004). Focusing solely on women who had graduated from college, the study concludes "the fraction of all U.S. college graduate women who kept their surnames upon marriage rose from about 2 to 4 percent around 1975 to just below 20 percent in 2001. It seems likely that the fraction of women 'keeping' their maiden name rose sharply in the 1970s and 1980s, but declined slightly in the 1990s." The authors assert that the availability of "the Pill — the female oral contraceptive . . . was one important cause of the increase in surname retention" because it increased the age at first marriage and allowed more women to continue with their education. Statistically significant correlation was found between name retention and age at marriage, graduation from an Ivy League or top-25 liberal arts college, advanced college degrees (except for the M.B.A.) and with occupations in the arts, writing and the media. A religious wedding ceremony is correlated to a lower rate of surname retention.

[2]   Liability for Spousal Violence

Reva Siegel, *"The Rule of Love": Wife Beating as Prerogative and Privacy*
105 YALE L.J. 2117, 2118 (1996)

The . . . common law originally provided that a husband, as master of his household, could subject his wife to corporal punishment or "chastisement" so long as he did not inflict permanent injury. . . . During the nineteenth century, an era of feminist agitation for reform . . . , authorities in England and the United States declared that a husband no longer had the right to chastise his wife. Yet, for a century after . . . , the American legal system continued to treat wife beating differently from other cases of assault and battery. . . . [A]uthorities . . . intervened only intermittently in cases of marital violence: Men who assaulted their wives were often granted formal and informal immunities from prosecution, in order to protect the privacy of the family and to promote "domestic harmony." In the late 1970s, the feminist movement began to challenge the concept of family privacy [and] it has secured many reforms designed to protect women from marital violence. Yet violence in the household persists. The U.S. Surgeon General recently found that "battering of women by husbands, ex-husbands or lovers '[is] the single largest cause of injury to women in the United States.' "[5] "[T]hirty-one percent of all women murdered in America are killed by their husbands, ex-husbands, or lovers." [The author asserts "repudiation of chastisement precipitated a shift in the rules and rhetoric of laws regulating interspousal violence — giving rise to a new doctrinal regime couched in discourses of affective privacy that preserved, to a significant degree, the marital prerogative that chastisement rules once protected" This was reflected in both criminal and tort law through the early 20th century. While criminal courts explicitly rejected chastisement, they often refused to entertain prosecutions of husbands for wife-beating on grounds of family privacy. "If no permanent injury has been inflicted, nor malice, cruelty nor dangerous violence shown . . . , it is better to draw the curtain, shut out the public gaze, and leave the parties to forget and forgive. *State v. Oliver*, 70 N.C. 60 (1874). The tort interspousal immunity doctrine, based on marital privacy, barred assault and battery claims by wives.]

By the beginning of the twentieth century, [marital privacy] . . . found institutional expression in the criminal justice system. . . . [C]ities began to establish special domestic relations courts staffed by social workers to handle complaints of marital violence. . . . The family court system sought to decriminalize marital violence. [A] New York City judge explained . . . "domestic trouble cases are not criminal in a legal sense."

Rather than punish those who assaulted their partners, the judges and social workers urged couples to reconcile. . . . Battered wives were discouraged from filing criminal charges against their husbands, urged to accept responsibility for

---

[5] Zorza, The Criminal Law of Misdemeanor Domestic Violence, 1970-1990, 83 J. CRIM. L. & CRIMINOLOGY 46, 46 (1992) (quoting Hightower & McManus, Limits of State Constitutional Guarantees: Lesson from Efforts to Implement Domestic Violence Policies, 49 PUB. ADMIN. REV. 269 (1989)).

their role in provoking the violence, and encouraged to remain in the relationship and rebuild it. . . . The police adjusted their arrest procedures to accord with the new philosophy. . . .

The criminal justice system regulated marital violence in this "therapeutic" framework for much of the twentieth century. . . . [T]he criminal justice system developed a set of formal procedures for handling marital violence . . . that [often] provided informal immunity. . . . In the 1960s, for example, the training bulletin of the international association of chiefs of police offered the following instructions for handling "family disturbances."

> For the most part these disputes are personal matters requiring no direct police action. . . . Once inside the home, the officer's sole purpose is to preserve the peace . . . attempt to soothe feelings, pacify parties . . . [and] suggest parties refer their problem to a church or a community agency. . . . In dealing with family disputes . . . arrest should be [used] as a last resort. The officer should never create a police problem when there is only a family problem existing."

Until the last decade, this set of instructions was quite typical. . . .

. . . . Today, after numerous protest activities and law suits, there are shelters for battered women and their children, new arrest procedures for police departments across the country, and even federal legislation making gender-motivated assaults a civil rights violation. . . .

Because statistics on domestic violence document chastisement's continuing legacy in a different narrative mode, it is worth considering the recent figures in a bit more detail. As of 1995, justice department statistics show that:

- About three-quarters of all lone-offender violence against women was perpetrated by an offender whom the victim knew.

- In 29% of all violence against women by a lone offender, the perpetrator was a husband, ex-husband, boyfriend, or ex-boyfriend — an intimate.

- Female victims of violent incidents were more likely to be injured when the perpetrator was an intimate than when the assailant was a stranger.

The gender asymmetry of violence between intimates remains dramatic. The Justice Department has estimated that 90% to 95% of domestic violence victims are women. Compared to men, women were about six times more likely to experience violence committed by an intimate. Female homicide victims were more than nine times more likely to have been killed by a husband, ex-husband, or boyfriend than male homicide victims were to have been killed by their wife, ex-wife, or girlfriend. In 1992 approximately 28% of female victims of homicide were known to have been killed by their husband, ex-husband, or boyfriend; in contrast, just over 3% of male homicide victims were known to have been killed by their wife, ex-wife, or girlfriend. . . .

As the statistics on homicide of women by intimates suggest, assaults between intimates can involve significant amounts of violence. The Justice Department estimates that one-third of domestic violence attacks, if reported, would be classified as felony rapes, robberies, or aggravated assaults. The rest would be classified as simple assaults, though many of them involved "bodily injury at least as serious as the injury inflicted in 90 percent of all robberies and aggravated assaults." And the [AMA] reports that "over 80% of all assaults against spouses and ex-spouses result in injuries, compared with 54% of the victims of stranger violence; victims of marital violence also have the highest rates of internal injuries and unconsciousness." (In a 1985 survey of intact couples, nearly one of every eight husbands had carried out an act of physical aggression against hisfemale partner. "Over one-third of these assaults involved severe aggression such as punching, kicking, choking, beating up, or using a knife or a gun.)

Finally, domestic violence remains widespread. The [AMA Journal] reports that approximately four million women are believed to be battered every year by their partners, and estimates that at least one-fifth of all women will be physically assaulted by a partner or ex-partner during their lifetime. The 1985 National Family Violence Survey found that "154 out of every 1000 pregnant women were assaulted by their mates during the first four months of pregnancy, and 170 per 1000 women were assaulted during the fifth through the ninth months" of pregnancy. Women who are assaulted by their male partners are more likely to be repeatedly attacked, raped, injured, or killed than are women assaulted by other types of assailants.

As these statistics suggest, marital violence persists, notwithstanding profound changes in the laws and mores of marriage since [1900]. And, despite the contemporary feminist movement's efforts to pierce the veil of privacy talk . . . , Americans still reason about marital violence in the discourse of affective privacy. O.J. Simpson invoked this tradition in 1989 when he shouted at police who had responded to his wife's call for help: "The police have been out here eight times before, and now you're going to arrest me for this? This is a family matter. Why do you want to make a big deal out of it when we can handle it?". . . .

More recently, the Chief Justice of the United States invoked this discourse of the private when he objected to provisions in the new Violence Against Women Act that create a federal cause of action for gender-motivated violence. The bill's "broad definition of criminal conduct is so open-ended, and the new private right of action so sweeping," Chief Justice Rehnquist complained, "that the legislation could involve the federal courts in a whole host of domestic relations disputes.

NOTES

1. *Estimates of Family Violence.* Before examining the data presented in this and the following notes (as well as "facts" cited in the popular media), one should note the caution sounded by Dr. Richard Gelles, Dean of the School of Social Policy at the University of Pennsylvania, a major figure in family violence research. In *The Politics of Research: The Use, Abuse, and Misuse of Social Science Data — The Cases of Intimate Partner Violence*, 45 FAM. CT. REV. 42 (2007), Dean Gelles asserts family violence "policy and practice [are] more influenced by ideologies and political values than actual research and evidence." He urges the establishment of a "firewall" between "advocacy statistics" and "social science evidence," and expresses the hope that courts will be "both willing and able to draw only on the

latter to render judicial findings." Dean Gelles also identifies a number of what describes as "factoids" used by advocates, some of which are as yet unproven and others of which are exaggerations or misstatements of research data.

A summary of the various estimates of family violence (including their own) in the United States was published by then-Professor Gelles and Murray Straus. Using a definition of violent acts which included: throwing an object at another person, pushing, grabbing, shoving, slapping, spanking, kicking, biting, punching, choking, threatening with a knife or gun or using a knife or gun, they they estimated 8.7 million victims of spousal violence in 1985 (involving 16.1% of couples). They estimated 3.4 million (6.3%) victims of "severe violence" (kicking, biting, punching, beating up, choking, use or threatened use of a weapon). In summarizing other studies, they reported estimates of spousal violence ranging from 12.1% to 51%. Murray Straus & Richard Gelles, *How Violent Are American Families? Estimates from the National Family Violence Resurvey and Other Studies, in* FAMILY ABUSE AND ITS CONSEQUENCES: NEW DIRECTIONS IN RESEARCH (Gerald Hotaling, et al., eds. 1988). According to Straus and Gelles, the rate of spousal violence reported in the National Crime Survey (NCS) is less than 3%, as compared to their estimate of 16.1% from the National Family Violence Survey.

> The most likely reason for the tremendous discrepancy lies in differences between the context of the NCS versus the other studies. The NCS is presented to respondents as a study of crime, whereas the others are presented as studies of family problems. The difficulty with a "crime survey" . . . is that most people think of being kicked by their spouses as wrong, but not a "crime". . . . Thus [very few] assaults by spouses are reported in the National Crime Survey.

Id. at 20. A 1997 New York City Department of Health study reported "more women in New York City are killed by their husbands or boyfriends than in robberies, disputes, sexual assaults, drug violence, random attacks or any other crime in cases where the motive for murder is known." Pam Belluck, *A Woman's Killer is Likely to be Her Partner, a Study Finds*, N.y. TIMES, Mar. 31, 1997, at A12. Of the women killed in the city between 1990 and 1994 for whom a cause of death could be identified, nearly half "were killed by current or former husbands or boy-friends. . . ." *Id.* Nationally, FBI statistics show that approximately one-third of female murder victims between 1975 and 2005 were killed by an intimate. http://ojp.usdoj.gov/bjs/homicide/intimates.htm#intimates.

A 2003 study by the Centers for Disease Control based on data from the National Violence Against Women Survey in 1995 estimated over 5 million victimizations of women each year resulting in over 2 million injuries, more than 550,000 of which require medical attention. DEPARTMENT OF HEALTH AND HUMAN SERVICES, COSTS OF INTIMATE PARTNER VIOLENCE AGAINST WOMEN IN THE UNITED STATES 1 (2003). The same study estimates that women victims of intimate partner violence lose nearly 8 million days of paid work and 5.6 million days of household productivity traceable to the violence, *Id.*, and that the costs of intimate family violence against women costs approximately $5.8 million annually and that this estimate is likely to underestimate the cost because of several gaps in data. *Id.* at 2. The 2005 Behavioral Risk Factor Surveillance System survey, reported by the CDC, estimates that approximately 26% of women and 16% of men (adults over the age of 18) had experienced at least one intimate partner victimization during his or her lifetime. *See* http://www.cdc.gov/mmwr/preview/mmwrhtml/mm5705a1.htm. The same report indicates that, in households with total annual income of less than $25,000, over 30% of women and about 20% of men report having been victimized.

Research also suggests a link between violence inside and outside the family. A 1989 article, using two national household surveys and a student survey asserts domestic violence victims and perpetrators are more likely than others to perpetrate aggression outside the family. Gerald Hotaling et al, *Intrafamily Violence, and Crime and Violence Outside the Family*, 11 CRIME & JUSTICE 315 (1989). These links remain when controlling for socioeconomic status, gender and severity of family violence and is inconsistent with the notion that family violence is fundamentally different from "ordinary" violence or "crime in the streets." The breadth of family violence across a broad spectrum of socioeconomic strata is reflected by a recent spate of disciplinary actions against attorneys for domestic abuse. *See, e.g., In re Enna*, 971 A.2d 110 (Del. 2009) (disbarring attorney for, among other things, violating a domestic abuse order); *In re Grella*, 777 N.E.2d 167 (Mass. 2002) (suspending attorney for two months for assault and battery committed against wife while their four children were in the home).

Domestic violence often has a direct impact on victims outside the family. It has been reported that "more police die in connection with domestic violence encounters than during any other aspect of their work." Constance Fain, *Conjugal Violence: Legal and Psychosociological Remedies*, 32 SYRACUSE. L. REV. 497, 504 (1981) (reporting 22.2% of all police homicides occur during domestic violence calls). FBI statistics showed that 30% of the more than 57,000 assaults on police officers occurred during domestic disturbance calls. The next ranking category had only 16% of the total. http://nleomf.org/media/press/domesticviolence07.htm. This sometimes results from feuding spouses joining against the officer as a common enemy and at least partly explains the police manual language quoted by Professor Siegel.

2. *Men as Victims of Spousal Abuse.* Professor Siegel asserts women are more often the victims of spousal abuse than men. In fact, data based on The National Crime Victimization Survey suggests husbands commit spousal violence more than 10 times more often than wives do. National Family Violence Survey data, however, paints a very different picture. According to the 1985 Survey (utilizing a nationally representative sample of 6,002 married and cohabiting couples), women commit slightly more minor assaults than men on their mates and men are slightly more often guilty of severe assaults on their mates than women. Murray Straus, *Physical Assaults by Women Partners: A Major Social Problem in* WOMEN, MEN AND GENDER: ONGOING DEBATES 210 (M. R. Walsh, ed. 1997) (hereinafter "WOMEN, MEN AND GENDER"). Professor Straus suggests the difference between the Justice Department and Family Violence Survey data is caused by the fact that "in the context of a crime survey, people tend to report attacks only when they have been experienced as 'real crimes' — because they resulted in injury or were perpetrated by former partners." *Id.* at 212. Professor Straus asserts that every study that is not "self-selective . . . has found a rate of assault by women on male partners that is about the same as the rate of assault by men on female partners." *Id.* at 211.

Even if Straus' claim that women commit severe attacks almost as often as men do are true, female domestic violence victims clearly sustain greater injuries than males. For example, 3% of female victims in the Violence Survey needed medical treatment for their injuries, while only 0.4% of male victims required such attention. Jan Stets & Murray Straus, *Gender Differences in Reporting Marital Violence and Its Medical and Psychological Consequences in* PHYSICAL VIOLENCE IN AMERICAN FAMILIES: RISK FACTORS AND ADAPTATIONS TO VIOLENCE IN 8,145 FAMILIES 157 (Straus & Gelles eds. 1990) (hereinafter "PHYSICAL VIOLENCE IN AMERICAN FAMILIES"). Also, it is generally assumed that a significant portion of female-to-male violence is in self-defense, though Straus finds the evidence ambiguous. He cites studies claiming at least "25–30 percent of violent relationships are violent solely because of attacks by the woman." WOMEN, MEN AND GENDER at 214.

He argues further that even if female violence can be explained as self-defense, it nevertheless must be dealt with by society because the "moral justification of assault implicit when she slaps or throws something at him for something reinforces his moral justifications for slapping her when *she* is doing something outrageous — or when she is obstinate, nasty, or 'not listening to reason' as he sees it" (emphasis in original). *Id.* at 217. For other work on men as victims of spouse abuse, see Amanda Schmesser, Note, *Real Men May Not Cry, But They are Victims of Domestic Violence: Bias in the Application of Domestic Violence Laws*, 58 SYRACUSE L. REV. 171 (2007) (reviews empirical studies through 2007 demonstrating men are the victims of domestic violence at least as often as women); Linda Kelly, *Disabusing the Definition of Domestic Abuse: How Women Batter Men and Role of the Feminist State*, 30 FLA. ST. L. REV. 791 (2003) (asserting female violence presents a threat to feminist theory and the practice of domestic violence law and "today's myopic understanding of domestic violence has serious implications"); Alexander Detschelt, *Recognizing Domestic Violence Directed Towards Men: Overcoming Societal Perceptions, Conducting Accurate Studies, and Enacting Responsible Legislation*, 12 KAN. J. L.& PUB. POL'Y 249 (2003) (asserting "domestic violence against men is . . . a serious social issue that must be fully addressed" and suggesting gender-neutralization of domestic violence statutes); Todd Migliaccio, *Abused Husbands: A Narrative Analysis*, 23 J. FAM. ISSUES 26 (2002) (reporting on interviews with male victims of domestic violence); PHILIP COOK, ABUSED MEN: THE HIDDEN SIDE OF DOMESTIC VIOLENCE (1997).

3. *Criminally Prosecuting Family Violence.* The crimes of assault and battery can be used to prosecute spousal violence. "Not a single jurisdiction has chosen to exempt domestic assaults from the ambit of the criminal law. Maria Marcus, *Conjugal Violence: The Law of Force and the Force of Law*, 69 CAL. L. REV. 1657, 1662 (1981). As indicated in Professor Siegel's article, though, police and prosecutors traditionally have treated domestic violence differently from other similar incidents.

> Discriminatory enforcement policies . . . can be found in official state-
> ments as well as individual cases. . . . Victims are told that courts are not
> in session and that no judge is available. These [policies fail] to predicate
> arrest on relevant criteria such as seriousness of the injury, use of weapons,
> acts of violence committed in the officer's presence or outstanding orders of

> protection indicating repeated prior attacks. Prosecutors have required
> extra elements before proceeding . . . , including witnesses other than the
> victim and children, a record of prior attacks, a police report already on file
> and serious visible injuries. Even when [such] criteria are met, such cases
> may be rejected automatically on the theory that securing a conviction is
> more difficult than in nonfamilial cases. . . .

Id. at 1688–91. Empirical studies demonstrate relatively few arrests are made in
domestic violence incidents. *See* Eve Buzawa, *Responding to Crimes of Violence
Against Women: Gender Differences Versus Organizational Imperatives*, 41 CRIME
& DELINQ. 443 (1995); Sarah Buel, Note, *Mandatory Arrest for Domestic Violence*,
11 HARV. WOMEN'S L.J. 213, 217 (1988) (citing surveys showing arrest rates from 3%
to 10% and a Philadelphia study finding arrests in only 13% of the cases in which
police observed injuries to victim).

It has been argued that current criminal statutes do not fully cover domestic
abuse in its complete sense. *See* Deborah Tuerkheimer, *Recognizing and Remedying the Harm of Battering: A Call to Criminalize Domestic Violence*, 94 J. CRIM. L.
& CRIMINOLOGY 959 (2004) (claiming criminal law's coverage is incomplete because
"non-physical manifestations of the abuser's effort to dominate his victim" go
unpunished and, thus, "deep and pervasive suffering by battered women is not
redressed"); *see also* Alafair Burke, *Domestic Violence as a Crime of Pattern and
Intent: An Alternative Reconceptualization*, 75 GEO. WASH. L. REV. 552 (2007).

**4. *Civil Rights Actions Claiming Failure to Enforce Laws Against Domestic
Violence.*** A series of cases in the 1980s recognized a federal § 1983 civil rights
cause of action on behalf of abused spouses against municipalities failing to respond
to domestic violence reports or applied special arrest policies in such cases. *See,
e.g., Hynson v. City of Chester*, 864 F.2d 1026 (3d Cir. 1988); *Watson v. Kansas
City*, 857 F.2d 690 (10th Cir. 1988); *Balistreri v. Pacifica Police Dep't*, 855 F.2d 1421
(9th Cir. 1988); *Thurman v. City of Torrington*, 595 F. Supp. 1521 (D. Conn. 1984);
Bartalone v. Berrian Cty., 643 F. Supp. 574 (E.D. Mich. 1986). The *Thurman*
plaintiff was awarded $2.3 million by a jury. Amy Eppler, *Battered Women and the
Equal Protection Clause: Will the Constitution Help Them When the Police
Won't?*, 95 YALE L.J. 788, 795 at n. 31 (1986).

The efficacy of § 1983 in such cases, however, was limited by *DeShaney v.
Winnebago Cty. Dep't of Social Servs.*, 489 U.S. 189 (1989) (generally "State's
failure to protect an individual against private violence simply does not constitute a
violation of the Due Process Clause"). In *Town of Castle Rock v. Gonzales*, 545 U.S.
748 (2007), the Court held that what appeared to be a mandatory arrest statute (*see*
Note 5) created no " 'entitlement' to receive protective services in accordance with
the terms of [a family violence protective order statute]. The Court cast doubt on
whether even had such an entitlement to enforcement been created it could
"constitute a 'property' interest for purposes of the Due Process Clause."

Claims of a § 1983 violation based on gender discrimination may remain a viable
theory in seeking damages against a police department. *See Fajardo v. Los Angeles
County*, 179 F.3d 698 (9th Cir. 1999) (remanding for determination whether
domestic 911 calls were given lower priority than others and, if so, whether such a
policy survived rational relationship Equal Protection review). *See also* Susanne

Browne, Note, *Due Process and Equal Protection Challenges to the Inadequate Response of the Police in Domestic Violence Situations*, 68 S. CAL. L. REV. 1295 (1995) (detailing avenues available to civil rights plaintiffs); Laura Harper, Note, *Battered Women Suing Police for Failure to Intervene: Viable Legal Avenues After* DeShaney v. Winnebago Department of Social Services, 75 CORNELL L. REV. 1393 (1990).

5. *Mandatory Criminal Arrest and Prosecution.* A 2008 survey identified 22 states and the District of Columbia requiring arrest when the law enforcement official discovers domestic violence. David Hirschel, *Domestic Violence Cases: What Research Shows About Arrest and Dual Arrest Rates*, Table 1, National Institute for Justice Website: http://www.ojp.usdoj.gov/nij/publications/dv-dual-arrest-222679/welcome.htm; *see also* Deborah Epstein, *Procedural Justice: Tempering the State's Response to Domestic Violence*, 43 WM. & MARY L. REV. 1843 (2002) (noting 24 states with statutes mandating arrest on probable cause that a protective order has been violated); CONN. GEN. STAT. ANN. § 46b-38b (requiring arrest where officer "determines on speedy information that a family violence crime . . . has been committed within his jurisdiction"); OR. REV. STAT. § 133.055 (family violence exception to general policy permitting citation in lieu of arrest); *Campbell v. Campbell*, 682 A.2d 272 (N.J. Super. 1996) (approving action against police officer for negligent failure to abide by mandatory arrest statute). *See* Hirschel, et al., *Criminology: Domestic Violence and Mandatory Arrest Laws: To What Extent Do They Influence Police Arrest Decisions?*, 98 J. CRIM. L. & CRIMINOLOGY 255 (2007) (empirical study in 2819 police departments in 19 states concludes that mandatory and preferred arrest statutes have increased arrest rates not only in domestic violence cases, but also in acquaintance and stranger cases). Studies of jurisdictions with mandatory arrest statutes have found that arrests of women increase under a mandatory arrest regime. Kohn, *The Justice System and Domestic Violence: Engaging the Case But Divorcing the Victim*, 32 N.Y.U. REV. L. & SOC. CHANGE 191, 218 (2008) (collecting information on several studies).

It is not clear, however, that mandatory arrest statutes actually reduce domestic violence. A leading researcher concludes such policies "may be doing more harm than good." LAWRENCE SHERMAN, POLICING DOMESTIC VIOLENCE 1 (1993). In the early 1980s, Professor Sherman's "Minnesota experiment" tested arrest's effectiveness. He concluded "arrest and a night in jail for the suspect cut in half the risk of repeat violence against the same victim over a six-month follow-up period, from about 20% to 10%" *Id.* at 2. This study was used by many to justify mandatory arrest policies. But, in a later 5-city study, Professor Sherman reported evidence in three cities (Milwaukee, Charlotte and Omaha) that arrest *increases* the frequency of future domestic violence. By contrast, in addition to Minneapolis (the original test site), Colorado Springs and Miami data suggest arrest works. The distinction is in the "racial composition of the samples. On average, the proportion of black victims and suspects is substantially lower in the 'arrest deters' cities, and higher in the 'arrest backfires' cities." *Id.* at 3. *See also* Radha Iyengar, *Does the Certainty of Arrest Reduce Domestic Violence? Evidence from Mandatory and Recommended Arrest Laws*, 93 J. PUB. ECON. 85 (2009) (concluding mandatory arrest laws "actually increased partner homicides;" speculating this could either be due to reduced victim reporting or increase in reprisals). The methodology of the follow-up studies of the Minnesota experiment has been criticized, see Johanna Niemi-Kiesilainen, *The Deterrent Effect of Arrest in Domestic Violence: Differerentiating Between Victim and Perpetrator Response*, 12 HAST. WOMEN'S L.J. 283 (2001) (urging focus on impact of arrest on victim's future behavior, including willingness to report; theorizes that "arrest deters violence *and* encourages victims to call the police"); Marion Wanless, Note, *Mandatory Arrest: A Step Toward Eradicating Domestic Violence, But is It Enough?*, 1996 ILL. L. REV. 533, 555–57 (asserting mandatory arrest is important part of a comprehensive criminal justice policy); Joan Zorza, *Must We Stop Arresting Batterers? Analysis and Policy Implications of New Police Domestic Violence Studies*, 28 NEW ENG. L. REV. 929 (1994), while others have used the follow-up to argue for a flexible policy on arrest. Donna Welch, Comment, *Mandatory Arrest of Domestic Abusers: Panacea or Perpetuation of the Problem of Abuse?*, 43 DePAUL L. REV. 1133 (1994).

Reviewing several experiments on the impact of arrest on family violence, one commentator concluded:

> The lesson of these studies is that formal (legal) sanctions are effective when reinforced by informal social controls. . . . [T]he deterrent effects of arrest will be greater for batterers who perceive higher social costs associated with . . . violence and . . . arrest [including] loss of job, relationship and children, social status in the neighborhood, and whatever substantive punishment they receive.

JEFFREY FAGAN, THE CRIMINALIZATION OF DOMESTIC VIOLENCE: PROMISES AND LIMITS 22 (1996). For an annotated bibliography on police response to spouse abuse, see Egan, *The Police Response to Spouse Abuse: A Selective, Annotated Bibliography*, 91 L. LIB. J. 499 (1999); *see also* Nancy Fedders, *Lobbying for Mandatory-Arrest Policies: Race, Class, and the Politics of the Battered Women's Movement*, 23 N.Y.U. REV. L. & SOC. CHANGE 281 (1997) (asserting "mandatory-arrest advocates are from a limited demographic base [and] ascribe to a narrow theoretical framework. . . .").

Similar issues are raised by "no-drop" policies under which "the state pursues cases regardless of the victim's wishes." Cheryl Hanna, *No Right to Choose: Mandated Victim Participation in Domestic Violence Prosecutions*, 109 HARV. L. REV. 1849, 1852 (1996) (arguing such policies would make ineffective any attempt to pressure victim and impress on the community "that the state takes domestic violence cases seriously and that prosecution is consistent, not arbitrary"). Professor Epstein's article, *supra*, cites a survey indicating 2/3 of "prosecutor's offices in major urban centers . . . had adopted such policies." Under such a policy, victims may be subpoenaed to testify and face jail time for contempt for refusal to testify. Professor Hanna recognizes the risks posed by such a policy for victims, but asserts more "aggressive domestic violence policies" by prosecutors can "reduce the likelihood that the victim will ever have to take the stand." *Id.* at 1857. Such policies include putting more effort into gathering physical and medical evidence by creating "specific evidence-gathering and arrest protocols to ensure that the arrest of the batterer leads to prosecution and not to case dismissal." *Id.* at 1901. Professor Hanna, who formerly prosecuted such cases, argues "prosecutors have both a responsibility and a duty to present evidence that communicates that the harm of domestic violence extends beyond the victim's home and produces consequences for the whole community." *Id.* at 1908; *see also* Angela Corsilles, Note, *No-Drop Policies in the Prosecution of Domestic Violence Cases: Guarantee to Action or Dangerous Solution?*, 63 FORDHAM. L. REV. 853 (1994); Thomas Kirsch, *Problems in Domestic Violence: Should Victims Be Forced to Participate in the Prosecution of Their Abusers?*, 7 WM. & MARY J. WOMEN & L. 383(2001) (reporting empirical study of one prosecutor's office in Indiana; assesses costs and benefits of no-drop policies); Kalyani Robbins, *No-Drop Prosecution of Domestic Violence: Just Good Policy, or Equal Protection Mandate*, 52 STAN. L. REV. 205 (1999) (advocating adoption of no-drop policy along with "careful *ad hoc* consideration of victim safety" as best way to insure compliance with the Constitution).

For a critique of a range of mandatory policies, including those requiring arrest, prosecution and reporting by medical personnel, see Linda Mills, *Killing Her Softly: Intimate Abuse and the Violence of State Intervention*, 113 HARV. L. REV. 550 (1999) (social work professor argues "state interventions designed to eradicate the intimate abuse in battered women's lives all too often reproduce the emotional abuse of the battering relationship"); *see also* Donna Coker, *Crime Control and Feminist Law Reform in Domestic Violence Law: A Critical Review*, 4 BUFF. CRIM. L. REV. 801 (2001) (asserting mandatory policies "may further state control of women"); Erin Han, Note, *Mandatory Arrest and No-Drop Policies: Victim Empowerment in Domestic Violence Cases*, 23 B.C. THIRD WORLD L.J. 159 (2003) (urging arrest and prosecution policies be considered separately and arguing an "important component of a victim-centered approach to justice is the recognition that mandatory policies are problematic").

Even if a domestic violence case is prosecuted, the state may have difficulty convicting the defendant if the victim refuses to cooperate. For a discussion of recent Supreme Court jurisprudence which establishes constitutional issues with the admission of out of court statements by the victim and others in family violence cases, see Michael Baxter, Note, *The Impact of* Davis v. *Washington on Domestic Violence Prosecutions*, 29 WOMEN'S RIGHTS L. REP. 213 (2008); Deborah Tuerkheimer, Crawford's *Trial: Domestic Violence and the Right of Confrontation*, 85 N.C. L. REV. 1 (2006); *see also* R. Michael Cassidy, Note, *Reconsidering Spousal Privileges After* Crawford, 33 AM. J. CR. L. 339 (2006). Beyond any evidentiary problems, judges and juries may treat domestic violence differently from other types of violence. *See* David Faigman, Note, *The Battered Woman Syndrome and Self-Defense*, 72 VA. L. REV. 619 (1986); Mary Combo, Comment, *Wife Beating: Law and Society Confront the Castle Door*, 15 GONZAGA L. REV. 171, 197 (1979). Also, the jury may acquit despite overwhelming evidence of guilt. Jury nullification has been defended, in another context, as introducing into law enforcement the "mollifying influence of current ethical [standards]." *United States ex rel. McCann v. Adams*, 126 F.2d 774, 775 (2d Cir. 1942) (Hand, J.).

6. *Declining Intimate Violence.* Efforts by the legal system to condemn and punish domestic violence, to provide shelters for victims and provide alternative such as restraining orders (*see* Note 7) seem to be having an effect on the rates of domestic violence. Straus & Kaufman Kantor, *Paper Presented at the 13th World Congress of Sociology, Bielefeld, Germany*, July 19, 1994 (on file with Professor Kurtz). Using the National Family Violence Surveys of 1975 and 1985 and the 1992

National Alcohol and Family Violence Survey (all focused on couples who were either married or cohabiting), the authors find a constant decrease in the rate of severe assaultive behavior by men in the domestic context. It should be noted, however, that during this time there also has been a general decline in crime rates. While acknowledging the decline in male domestic violence may be based merely on increasing reluctance by men to report having assaulted their partner, rather than an actual decline in wife-beating, the authors argue that "even if the entire decrease (in male violence) reflects differences in willingness to report, that would still be an important achievement because it indicates a heightened sensitivity . . . and . . . awareness that hitting one's wife is condemned by society." *Id.*

By contrast, the authors found both the 1985 and 1992 surveys reflect no change in the rate of assaults by wives, as compared to the 1975 baseline. They conclude "part of the reason may be that there has been no effort to condemn assault by wives parallel to the effort to condemn assaults by husbands." *Id.*

As for cultural norms concerning domestic violence, Straus and Kaufman Kantor report four national surveys between 1968 and 1994 reflect a constantly declining percentage of approval of the statement, "Are there any situations that you can imagine in which you would approve of a husband slapping his wife's face?" Approval of slapping by husbands went from 20% in 1968 to 10% in 1994. Approval by both men and women of slapping by wives, however, "has not changed significantly." Straus & Kaufman Kantor, *Change in Cultural Norms Approving Marital Violence, in* OUT OF THE DARKNESS: CONTEMPORARY RESEARCH PERSPECTIVES ON FAMILY VIOLENCE (Glenda Kaufman Kantor & Jana Jasinski, eds., 1997) (reporting 21% approval of slapping by wives in 1968 and 22% in 1994).

More current data from the Department of Justice's Bureau of Justice Statistics (based on data from the FBI and local law enforcement agencies), reports a precipitous decline in intimate partner violence from 1993 to 2005. In the former year, there were 5.8 intimates victimized per 1,000 persons age 12 or over, while in the latter year 2.3 intimates were victimized. Similarly, the Bureau, using the same sources, reported that intimate homicide fell from a total of 1,891 in 1976 to a total of 1,410 in 2005. The decline in male victims (1,304 to 329) was much more pronounced than the decline in female victims (1,587 to 1,181). *See* http://www.ojp.usdoj.gov/bjs/intimate/overview.htm.

7. *Non-Criminal Response to Spousal Abuse.* Virtually every state has legislation providing for "civil orders of protection" for domestic violence victims. Such statutes often broadly define family, so as to protect victims unrelated by blood or marriage to their attackers. For example, the Minnesota Domestic Abuse Act provides for protection orders for violence between "family or household members" and defines the term as

> spouses and former spouses; parents and children; persons related by blood; persons who are presently residing together or who have resided together in the past; persons who have a child in common regardless of whether they have been married or have lived together at any time; a man and a woman if the woman is pregnant and the man is alleged to be the father . . . ; and persons involved in a significant romantic or sexual relationship.

MINN. STATS. ANN. § 518B.01, subd. 2(b). The statute's breadth would seem to include, for example, a cohabiting or formerly cohabiting same-sex couple. A commentator has identified 48 state statutes protecting cohabitors from domestic violence, while 6 such statutes explicitly exclude same-sex couples. Nancy Murphy, Note, *Queer Justice: Equal Protection for Victims of Same-Sex Domestic Violence*, 30 VAL. L. REV. 335, 345 (1995); *see also Ireland v. Davis*, 957 S.W.2d 310 (Ky. App. 1997) (finding the word "couple" in a domestic violence statute includes homosexual relationship); *State v. Carswell*, 871 N.E.2d 547 (Ohio 2007) (domestic violence criminal provision extending coverage to victim "living as a spouse" with abuser does not violate state constitutional provision denying recognition of "a legal status for relationships of unmarried individuals"); *see also* Shannon Little, *Challenging Changing Legal Definitions of Family in Same-Sex Domestic Violence*, 19 HASTINGS WOMEN'S L.J. 259 (2008) (asserting some statutory language designed to include same-sex domestic violence has been ineffective and offering better language); Mary Beth Collins, Note, *Same-Sex Domestic Violence: Addressing the Issues for the Proper Protection of Victims*, 4 J.L. SOC'Y 99 (2002). For recent articles urging broader family violence statutes, see Ruth Colker, *Marriage Mimicry: The Law of Domestic Violence*, 47 WM. & MARY L. REV. 1841 (2006) (because it privileges only those in marital or marriage-like relationships, law has underprotected many victims of domestic violence; urges more "functional" approach not limited to those in intimate relationships); Judith Smith, *Battered Non-Wives and Unequal Protection-Order Coverage: A Call for Reform*, 23 YALE L. & POL'Y REV. 93 (2005) (analysis of New York statute, noting gaps in coverage, both in terms of the individuals protected as well as the types of behavior which can serve as predicate for an order).

Does coverage of violence between those "who have resided together in the past," in the language of the Minnesota statute, last indefinitely? New Jersey's statute, covering "former household members" has triggered much litigation. Recent cases rejected jurisdiction where the litigants were middle-aged brothers who had not lived together for over 20 years, *Jutchenko v. Jutchenko*, 660 A.2d 1267 (N.J. Super. Ct. App. Div. 1995), and where a cohabitational relationship had ended over four years before with one intervening telephone call. *Sperling v. Teplitsky*, 683 A.2d 244 (N.J. Super. Ct. Ch. Div. 1996). By contrast, more recently a protective order was approved where the parties had not lived under the same roof for 19 years, *Storch v. Sauerhoff*, 757 A.2d 836 (N.J. Super. Ct. Ch. Div. 2000) (noting target was petitioner's stepmother and parties had lived on same street for 11 years), and where a dating relationship had ended four years earlier. *Tribuzio v. Roder*, 813 A.2d 1210 (N.J. Super. Ct. App. Div. 2003) (noting frequent attempted contact by defendant after break-up). Another New Jersey case held college dormitory suitemates members of the same household. *Hamilton v. Ali*, 795 A.2d 929 (N.J. Super. Ct. Ch. Div. 2002). For other cases dealing with coverage under domestic violence statutes, see *State v. Montoya*, 104 P.3d 540 (N. Mex. Ct. App. 2005) (man who attacked estranged adult married son covered despite fact that parties did not live in the same household); *Katherine B.T. v. Jackson*, 640 S.E.2d 569 (W. Va. 2006) (minor child can seek order against his mother); *Scott v. Shay*, 928 A.2d 312 (Pa. Super. Ct. 2007) (where statute protects parties to a "sexual relationship" protective order inappropriate when victim had been sexually assaulted as a youth 18 years earlier by target of order); *Corwell v. Corwell*, 179 P.3d 821 (Utah Ct. App. 2008) (protective order inappropriate where marriage of victim and defendant had been annulled; statute requires parties are or have been married and pre-abuse annulment meant the parties had never been married).

Generally short-term protective orders are obtained *ex parte* and may order the abuser's eviction, temporary child support and custody arrangements and, in some situations, mandatory counseling. After a hearing where both parties can be present, such orders may be made "permanent." Some statutes criminalize violation of protection orders. Because they are non-criminal, protection proceedings use a civil standard of proof (preponderance of the evidence) and focus on prevention of future anti-social conduct, rather than punishing prior behavior. Addressing the protective order's advantages and disadvantages, one commentator has written:

> Civil protection orders provide the only remedy for abuse that is not yet criminal. . . . Civil protection orders alone can provide victims with relief when the victim does not want the batterer charged criminally. . . . Due to fear of retaliation, many women do not want their partner arrested. In addition, if he were given a criminal record or jailed, he might lose his job and be unable to support the woman and their children. Moreover, the children might turn against their mother for "throwing dad in jail." Furthermore, most women are interested in stopping the battering, not punishing their partner. . . .

Peter Finn, *Statutory Authority in the Use and Enforcement of Civil Protection Orders Against Domestic Abuse*, 23 FAM. L.Q. 43, 44–45 (1989); *see also* Carolyn Ko, Note, *Civil Restraining Orders for Domestic Violence: The Unresolved Question of Efficacy*, 11 S. CAL. INTERDISC. L.J. 361 (2002) (reviewing empirical studies of effectiveness of orders, both from victim's perspective and objectively; finds impact much more positive from former perspective); Beverly Balos & Katie Trotzky, *Enforcement of the Domestic Abuse Act in Minnesota: A Preliminary Study*, 6 LAW & INEQUALITY 83 (1988) (concluding orders usually eliminate violence).

For a relatively current 50-state survey of protective order statutes, including statutory citations, salient provisions, etc., see http://www.abanet.org/domviol/docs/StalkingHarassmentCPOChartJune07.pdf.

Is personal jurisdiction over a defendant required for issuance of a protective order? An Iowa court analogized domestic violence litigation to divorce litigation where courts have power over the marital status even without personal jurisdiction over defendant and upheld an order against a Colorado resident sought by his former wife who had returned to her home state. *Bartsch v. Bartsch*, 636 N.W.2d 3 (Iowa 2001). Similarly, the New Jersey Supreme Court held that it did not need personal jurisdiction over a foreign defendant for entry of an order prohibiting him from doing certain things. *Shah v. Shah*, 875 A.2d 931 (N.J. 2005); *see also Caplan v. Donovan*, 879 N.E.2d 117 (Mass. 2008); *Spencer v. Spencer*, 191 S.W.3d 14 (Ky. Ct. App. 2006). For a decision requiring and finding personal jurisdiction, see *McNair v. McNair*, 856 A.2d 5 (N.H. 2004) (threatening phone calls from out of state sufficient to invoke long arm statute). *See also Dobos v. Dobos*, 901 N.E.2d 248 (Ohio Ct. App. 2008) (holding long-arm jurisdiction over defendant who repeatedly called individuals in Ohio from his home in Hungary might be appropriate). *But see Anderson v. Deas*, 615 S.E.2d 859 (Ga. Ct. App. 2005) (phone calls from out of state abuser insufficient to invoke state long arm jurisdiction).

Several recent commentators have questioned whether mandatory provisions and open-ended protection orders are appropriate. Professor Tamara Kuennan asserts that many judges refuse to comply with the requests of petitioners to vacate existing protective orders. Kuennan, *"No Drop" Civil Protection Orders: Exploring the Bounds of Judicial Intervention in the Lives of Domestic Violence Victims*, 16 UCLA WOMEN'S L.J. 39 (2007). Noting the many valid reasons a petitioner might have to seek to extinguish a protective order she originally sought, she asserts "neither public policy nor the public's interest requires judges to maintain Civil Protection Orders against the wishes of the victim. . . . [D]oing so may even be contrary to both." Professor Kuennan notes that most statutes do not even deal with the termination of civil orders of protection and many existing statutes provide enormous discretion to the judge. Similar to Professor Kuennan's argument for victim autonomy, Professor Sally Goldfarb, in *Reconceiving Civil Protection Orders for Domestic Violence: Can Law Help End the Abuse Without Ending the Relationship?*, 29 CARDOZO L. REV. 1487 (2008), asserts in some situations stay-away provisions are inappropriate and suggests "providing battered women with the option to obtain a protection order that authorizes a continuing relationship between the parties but forbids . . . further abuse." A recent commentator asserted "civil protection regimes should provide relief for non-physical, oppressive coercion." Jeffrey Baker, *Enjoining Coercion: Squaring Civil Protection Orders with the Reality of Domestic Abuse*, 11 J.L. FAM. STUD. 35 (2008).

Pioneered by the state of Washington, address confidentiality programs are available in many states to protect abuse victims fleeing from their abusers. Under such a program, the victim is given a "substitute address" to list for purposes of mail, employment, health care, etc. and all correspondence to that address is forwarded to the actual address. For a description of this program and recommendations for similar non-criminal responses to violence (including new name change laws and exceptions to public records acts), see Kristen Driskell, Note, *Identity Confidentiality for Women Fleeing Domestic Violence*, 20 HASTINGS WOMEN'S L.J. 129 (2008).

8. *Federal Response to Domestic Violence.* While not limited to domestic violence, the Violence Against Women Act of 1994 (VAWA) was a major entry into the field by the federal government. The Act (renewed in 2000 and 2006) created a national, toll-free hotline for domestic violence victims, and authorized grants for: battered women's shelters, implementation of mandatory domestic violence arrest policies and judicial and youth education about domestic violence. The Act criminalized interstate travel resulting in bodily injury to the actor's "spouse or intimate partner." *See United States v. Bailey*, 112 F.3d 758 (4th Cir. 1997) (rejecting constitutional attack). The Act also requires states to recognize protective orders issued in other states. *See* Emily Sack, *Domestic Violence Across State Lines: The Full Faith and Credit Clause, Congressional Power, and Interstate Enforcement of Protection Orders*, 98 NW. L. REV. 827 (2004) (examining VAWA mandate and analyzing scope of Congressional authority under the Full Faith and Credit clause); *see also* UNIFORM INTERSTATE ENFORCEMENT OF DOMESTIC-VIOLENCE PROTECTION ORDERS ACT, promulgated in 2002 by the National Conference of Commissioners on Uniform State Laws. Designed to put the interstate recognition mandate of VAWA into statutory form for state enactment, the Uniform Act has been adopted (as of summer 2009) in 16 states, plus the District of Columbia and the U.S. Virgin Islands.

VAWA's most controversial provision guaranteed "all persons within the United States . . . the right to be free from crimes of violence motivated by gender . . . ," creating a federal cause of action (including compensatory and punitive damages) for victims of such crimes. *See* 42 U.S.C. § 13981. The legislation claimed Congressional authority both under the Commerce Clause and § 5 of the Fourteenth Amendment. But in 2000 the Supreme Court held, in a 5-4 decision in *United States v. Morrison*, 529 U.S. 598 (2000), that creation of the private cause of action exceeded Congressional power. In affirming the Fourth Circuit's *en banc* decision, the Court rejected both Commerce Clause and Fourteenth Amendment assertions of power. Applying *United States v. Lopez*, 514 U.S. 549 (1995), the Court found "[g]ender-motivated crimes of violence are not . . . economic activity." It also found no "jurisdictional element" tying the cause of action to interstate commerce and found insufficient the Congressional findings of an impact on interstate commerce by domestic violence. Section 5 of the Fourteenth Amendment was rejected as a source of authority for lack of state action. Two dissenting opinions were filed. For critical commentary, see Judith Resnik, *The Programmatic Judiciary: Lobbying, Judging, and Invalidating the Violence Against Women Act*, 74 S. CAL. L. REV. 269 (2000); Michelle Anderson, *Women Do Not Report the Violence They Suffer: Violence Against Women and the State Action Doctrine*, 46 VILL. L. REV. 907 (2001).

Other VAWA provisions have withstood constitutional attack in the lower courts. *See, e.g., United States v. Al-Zubaidy*, 283 F.3d 804 (6th Cir. 2002) (upholding Act's interstate stalking provision against Commerce Clause attack); *United States v. Gluzman*, 154 F.3d 49 (2d Cir. 1998) (upholding criminalization of committing or attempting a crime of violence on a "spouse or intimate partner" after traveling in interstate commerce with that purpose); *United States v. Von Foelkel*, 136 F.3d 339 (2d Cir. 1998) (rejecting constitutional attack on provision criminalizing crossing of state lines with intent to violate a protective order).

Two federal gun crimes have been created by VAWA. Under 18 U.S.C. § 922(g)(8), it is a crime for the subject of certain domestic violence protection orders to possess a gun. The order must have been obtained after notice was given to the defendant and the order must restrain the respondent from harassing, stalking or threatening an intimate partner or a child of the intimate partner. Finally, the order must either find a "credible threat" to the safety of the intimate partner or child or must explicitly prohibit the use, attempted or threatened use of physical force. *See Weissenburger v. Iowa District Ct.*, 740 N.W.2d 431 (Iowa 2007) (rejecting trial court's attempt to permit the target of a domestic violence order to possess a gun for hunting purposes; court held federal law controlled issue). *But see* Lisa May, *The Backfiring of the Domestic Violence Firearms Ban*, 14 COLUM. J. GENDER & L. 1 (2001) (asserts trial court judges are inappropriately "denying orders of protection and throwing out misdemeanor domestic violence pleas" in order to permit batterers to continue owning and using firearms despite federal statutes; asserts some such actions are based on desire to protect batterer's ability to hunt). This provision, which was an amendment to the Gun Control Act of 1968, is subject to the general "public service" provision of that Act, which exempts law enforcement and military personnel and, thus, permits them to possess a gun while on duty. 18 U.S.C. § 925(a)(1).

In 1996, the Lautenberg Amendment created a separate gun crime punishing anyone "who has been convicted . . . of a misdemeanor crime of domestic violence" which included the "use or attempted use of physical force" to ship, possess or receive "any firearm or ammunition" in interstate or foreign commerce. 18 U.S.C. § 922(g)(9). The "physical force" provision has been heavily litigated, with one commentator finding three separate interpretations: "(1) that de minimis offensive contact qualifies . . . (2) that . . . offensive contact must be more than de minimis but need not rise to the level of "violent" physical force, and (3) that the statute requires 'violent' physical force." Adam Kersey, *Misdemeanants, Firearms, and Discretion: The Practical Impact of the Debate Over "Physical Force" and 18 U.S.C. § 922(g)(9)*, 49 WM & MARY L. REV. 1901 (2008) (collecting cases); *see also* John Skakun, Comment, *Violence and Contact: Interpreting "Physical Force" in the Lautenberg Amendment*, 75 U. CHI. L. REV. 1833 (2008). The Amendment has also been controversial because it specifically rejects the general "public service" exception to the federal gun laws and, thus, severely limits the ability of domestic violence abusers to serve in law enforcement or the military. For commentary on this legislation, see Emily Sack, *Courts Responding to Domestic Violence: Confronting the Issue of Gun Seizure in Domestic Violence Cases*, 6 J. CENTER FOR FAM. CHILD. & CTS. 3 (2005); Alison Nathan, Note, *At the Intersection of Domestic Violence and Guns: The Public Interest Exception and the Lautenberg Amendment*, 85 CORNELL L. REV. 822 (2000); Jodi Nelson, Note, *The Lautenberg Amendment: An Essential Tool for Combating Domestic Violence*, 75 N. DAK. L. Rev. 365 (1999). In 2009, the United States Supreme Court, in *United States v. Hayes*, 129 S. Ct. 1079 (2009), held that a "misdemeanor crime of domestic violence" includes a generic battery conviction where the victim is "a spouse or other domestic victim."

9. *Domestic Violence in the Workplace.* Domestic violence presents increasing problems in the workplace. It has been estimated that annually domestic violence committed in the workplace causes 175,000 days of missed employment. Jennifer Gaines, Comment, *Employer Liability for Domestic Violence in the Workplace: Are Employers Walking a Tightrope Without a Safety Net?*, 31 TEX. TECH. L. REV. 139, 143 (2000). In addition to its impact on the safety and productivity of the workplace, domestic violence may create liability for an employer who fails to provide protection to victims from their domestic abusers. *See id.; see also* Nicole Porter, *Victimizing the Abused: Is Termination the Solution When Domestic Violence Comes to Work?*, 12 MICH. J. GENDER & L. 275 (2006); Nina Tarr, *Employment and Economic Security for Victims of Domestic Abuse*, 16 S. CAL. REV. L. & SOC. JUST. 371 (2007). While workers' compensation coverage normally provides the exclusive remedy for employees injured on the job, exceptions to this exclusivity have been established in a number of jurisdictions. One such exception is recovery for damages caused by "injuries connected to inherently private relationships." Gaines, *supra*, at 146 (detailing unreported Louisiana case permitting suit against employer where plaintiff was shot during work hours by spouse). *See Temple v. Denali Princess Lodge*, 21 P.3d 813 (Alaska

2001) (denying compensation where employee's live-in girlfriend's former boyfriend came to the place of business and assaulted employee); *see also* Stephen Beaver, Comment, *Beyond the Exclusivity Rule: Employer's Liability for Workplace Violence*, 81 MARQ. L. REV. 103 (1997). While being outside the worker's comp system would leave open the possibility of a tort suit against the employer, the same factors which would make the incident not work-related would make it difficult to prove negligence by the employer.

The past decade has seen a flurry of legislative activity designed to prevent domestic violence victims from additional harm in the workplace. Deborah Widiss, *Domestic Violence and the Workplace: The Explosion of State Legislation and the Need for a Comprehensive Strategy*, 35 FLA. ST. L. REV. 669 (2008). Professor Widiss identifies several types of legislation. The most broadly-adopted model (law in 11 states and the District of Columbia covering approximately 25% of employees in the United States) provides for "domestic violence leave" during which a victim can, *e.g.*, consult with attorneys, obtain restraining orders, seek medical attention, change residences, etc. The D.C. legislation (enacted in 2008) provides that such leave should be paid. Other types of statutes collected and analyzed by Professor Widiss make discrimination against domestic violence victims illegal, require employers to make reasonable accommodations for domestic violence victims, define leaving a job because of domestic violence as "good cause" for purposes of unemployment compensation and enable employers to obtain domestic violence restraining orders against the abusers of employees. In *Green v. Bryant*, 887 F. Supp. 798 (E.D. Pa. 1995), the court rejected plaintiff's wrongful discharge claim based on her firing after being beaten and raped by her ex-husband. The court, however, suggested a claim would be recognized if "plaintiff alleged that she was discharged because she had applied for victim compensation or had sought a protective order." *See* Sandra Park, Note, *Working Towards Freedom From Abuse: Recognizing a "Public Policy" Exception to Employment-at-Will for Domestic Violence Victims*, 59 N.Y.U. ANN. SURV. AM. L. 121 (2003) (urging recognition of cause of action for victims dismissed because of any "reason directly stemming from intimate partner abuse").

10. *Marital Rape Exemption.* A particularly egregious form of domestic violence is the rape of a woman by her husband. The common law, however, did not criminally punish such behavior. In 1984, the New York Court of Appeals summarized the history and rationale for the common law position:

> The assumption . . . is traceable to a statement made by the 17th century English jurist Lord Hale, who wrote: "[T]he husband cannot be guilty of a rape committed by himself upon his lawful wife, for by their mutual matrimonial consent and contract the wife hath given up herself in this kind unto her husband, which she cannot retract" (1 Hale, HISTORY OF PLEAS OF THE CROWN, p. 629). Although Hale cited no authority for his statement it was relied on by State Legislatures . . . and by courts. . . . [An 1857 Massachussetts opinion] stated in dictum that it would always be a defense to rape to show marriage to the victim. . . . Decisions to the same effect . . . followed, usually with no rationale or authority cited other than Hale's implied consent view. . . .

. . . .

. . . . Any argument based on a supposed consent, however, is unten-able. Rape is not simply a sexual act to which one party does not consent. Rather, it is a degrading, violent act which violates the bodily integrity of the victim and frequently causes severe, long-lasting physical and psychic harm. To ever imply consent to such an act is irrational and absurd. Other than in the context of rape statutes, marriage has never been viewed as giving a husband the right to coerced intercourse on demand. Certainly, then, a marriage license should not be viewed as a license for a husband to forcibly rape his wife with impunity. A married woman has the same right to control her own body as does an unmarried woman. If a husband feels "aggrieved" by his wife's refusal to engage in sexual intercourse, he should seek [a divorce, but should not engage] in "violent or forceful self-help" (*State v. Smith*, 85 N.J. 193, 206).

The other traditional justifications . . . were the common law doctrines that a woman was the property of her husband and that the legal existence of the woman was "incorporated and consolidated into that of the husband" Both these doctrines, of course, have long been rejected in this State. . . .

People v. Liberta, 474 N.E.2d 567, 572–73 (N.Y. 1984); *see also* Jill Hasday, *Contest and Consent: A Legal History of Marital Rape*, 88 CAL. L. REV. 1373 (2000).

In finding the marital exemption unconstitutional, the *Liberta* court found that only consensual acts were protected by the marital privacy doctrine. Likewise, it dismissed arguments that this would be a difficult crime to prove and that "vindictive" wives would likely fabricate rape charges. The court noted rape is always a difficult crime to prove and found wives to be no more likely than unmarried women to falsify rape charges, noting the criminal justice system's ability to weed out false complaints. *Liberta* was later applied to New York's marital exemption for third degree sexual abuse. *People v. Naylor*, 609 N.Y.S.2d 954, 956 (App. Div. 1994); *see also People v. M.D.*, 595 N.E.2d 702 (Ill. App. Ct. 1992) (citing *Liberta*, while striking down scheme of marital exemptions for lesser crimes of sexual abuse, but no exemption for aggravated sexual assault).

11. ***Model Penal Code Position.*** The Model Penal Code includes a marital exemption, applying it to "persons living as man and wife, regardless of the legal status of their relationship" until entry of a judicial separation decree. *See* § 213.1, 213.6(2). The 1980 commentary explains:

[Certainly a woman] may marry without surrendering to sex on demand. If on occasion she refuses, the husband has no right to compel her to submit. If he does so by force or physical menace, he may be guilty of assault. . . . Liability for rape is another matter. Rape may consist of wholly non-violent conduct, but where force is used, rape carries sanctions more severe than . . . assault. . . . [A] prior and continuing relation of intimacy . . . is not irrelevant. . . .

First, marriage . . . does imply a kind of generalized consent that distinguishes some versions of . . . rape from parallel behavior by a husband. . . . At a minimum, therefore, husbands must be exempt from those categories of liability based . . . on a presumed incapacity . . . to consent [such as sexual intercourse with a person who is unconscious] at least unless there are aggravating circumstances. . . . Plainly there must also be some form of spousal exclusion applicable to . . . statutory rape. . . .

[As for rape committed by force or threat,] in many such situations . . . the law of rape . . . would thrust the prospect of criminal sanctions into the ongoing process of adjustment in the . . . relationship. Section 213.1, for example, defines as gross sexual imposition intercourse coerced "by any threat that would prevent resistance by a woman of ordinary resolution." [Perhaps] a woman of ordinary resolution would be prevented from resisting by her husband's threat to expose a secret to her mother, for example. Behavior of this sort . . . is no doubt unattractive, but it is a risky business for the law to intervene by threatening criminal sanctions. . . .

[As for sex] coerced by force or threat of physical harm, . . . the law already authorizes a penalty for assault. If the actor causes serious bodily injury, the punishment is quite severe. The issue is whether the still more drastic sanctions of rape should apply. The answer depends on whether the injury caused by forcible intercourse by a husband is equivalent to that inflicted by someone else. The gravity of the crime . . . derives not merely from its violent character but also from its achievement of a particularly degrading kind of unwanted intimacy. Where the attacker stands in an ongoing relation of sexual intimacy, that evil . . . may well be thought qualitatively different. . . . That, in any event, is the conclusion long endorsed by the law of rape and carried forward in the Model Code provision.

MODEL PENAL CODE & COMMENTARIES, Part II, Vol. 1, 344–46 (1980).

The Commentary posits a "generalized consent" to justify exonerating a husband who has sex with his unconscious wife. While echoing Lord Hale's view that marriage deprives women of the power to say no to sex, this provision seems sensible. While a husband who has sex with his unconscious wife has done something wrong, he certainly hasn't raped her.

But the Code exempts many more cases from its rape statute. For example, the cohabiting husband whose threats force his wife into sex would not be a rapist. Why not? Is it clear that "the voluntary association of husband and wife" changes the nature of the harm imposed by unwanted intercourse? One study reports more victims of marital rape suffer severe long-term effects than victims of stranger Rape. DIANA RUSSELL, RAPE IN MARRIAGE 192–93 (1982). On the other hand, consider: A married couple regularly has sex twice weekly (Monday and Wednesday). If the husband forces his wife to have sex on a Saturday morning, is she harmed in the same way as if a stranger had broken into the house and done the same acts?

Why is it "risky business for the law to intervene" where a wife is threatened by her husband with exposure of a secret? Is it any riskier, e.g., than when a co-worker threatens to "tell the boss"? Even if one accepts the Commentary's rationale, it does not support an exemption until legal separation. The "ongoing relation of sexual intimacy," asserted by the Commentary to justify the spousal exemption, often is over long before a legal separation is obtained.

12. *Current Status of the Marital Rape Exemption.* By 2003, it was reported that 24 states and the District of Columbia had completed removed the marital rape exemption. Michelle Anderson, *Marital Immunity, Intimate Relationships, and Improper References: A New Law on Sexual Offenses by Intimates*, 54 HASTINGS L.J. 1465 (2003). A 2007 Note, however, reported:

> . . . legal distinctions . . . still exist in states that continue to grant immunity to spouses for sex offenses other than forcible rape. Twenty states currently grant or imply spousal immunity from sexual offense charges if the spouse-victim is mentally incapacitated or physically help-less. [In Oklahoma, Ohio, and South Carolina, husbands cannot be con-victed of rape when they incapacitate their wives through drugs or other intoxicants.] Additionally, twelve states continue to grant spousal immunity for various nonconsensual sexual offenses such as gross sexual imposition, sexual abuse, sexual battery, sexual contact, and sexual misconduct. . . . These laws are examples of the failure to recognize that rape is a violent and serious offense regardless of one's marital status, and consent to any unwanted sexual contact should never be implied.

> . . . As of 2003, six states had amended their statutes to include a specific spousal rape section[. Four of the six states originally provided lesser penalties for marital, as opposed to non-marital rape, but three of those provisions have been repealed.] Mississippi still provides a marital exemption for sexual battery if the spouses are living together at the time of the incident unless use of force and lack of consent can be shown.

> . . . .

> In addition to establishing the elements of non-marital rape, proving marital sexual offenses in several states has additional requirements. [Such restrictions include a time limit for reporting, requirements of legal separation, corroboration, and additional showings of force or violence.]

Morgan Lee Woolley, Note, *Marital Rape: A Unique Blend of Domestic Violence and Non-Marital Rape Issues*, 18 HASTINGS WOMEN'S L.J. 269 (2007).

A counter-trend in the mid-1980s expanded the marital rape exemption. "[N]early one-quarter of the states have recently expanded the marital rape exemption to cover unmarried cohabitators and 'voluntary social companions.' " Note, *To Have and to Hold: The Marital Rape Exemption and the Fourteenth Amendment*, 99 HARV. L. REV. 1255 (1986) (criticizing trend as "modern version of Hale's theory that women who enter into relationships with men give an implied consent to sexual intercourse or that those who consent to intercourse once are forever bound"). While many of those statutes have been repealed since 1986, at least some remain. *E.g.*, Connecticut grants an affirmative defense to a number of sexual offenses where "defendant and the alleged victim were, at the time of the alleged defense, living together by mutual consent in a relationship of cohabitation, regardless of the legal status of their relationship." CONN. GEN. STAT. ANN. § 53a-67(b).

PROBLEMS

Problem 2-15. Martina and Boris have a tumultuous marriage. The police have been called a number of times to their apartment to settle domestic disputes. Last week, Boris moved out, yelling at Martina, "you haven't seen the end of me; I am going to be back at some point and finish this once and for all." The rental agent for the apartment overhears this and, the following day, after receiving calls from a number of worried neighbors who are afraid that there will be further violence which might involve them, tells Martina that she will have to leave after the end of her current lease. She has always paid her rent on time. She seeks your advice on whether she is in any way protected against this eviction. Would your opinion change if this were public housing?

Problem 2-16. Peter and Mary's 10-year marriage was a stormy one. After four years they separated, but reconciled after four months. In the tenth year, however, they agreed to a trial separation to "see if we want to divorce or not."

They saw each other occasionally but had no intimacies. After five months, they impulsively decided to have dinner together, after leaving an appointment with their lawyer. After a good dinner which included some wine, Peter escorted Mary back to her apartment, which they had formerly shared. Rather than leaving, he made some affectionate approaches. Mary felt ambivalent. She knew she did not wish to engage in sexual intercourse, but she also felt somewhat affectionate toward Peter, because of the warmth of the evening which revived memories of the good times in their marriage. Her attempts to be firm, but kind, were apparently too subtle for Peter.

As she got more definite he got more aggressive. He finally got angry when he realized she really meant to reject him. He pushed her onto the bed, pulled off her clothes while holding her and achieved sexual penetration. She yelled at him and clearly resisted, but couldn't rouse the neighbors. While Peter did not hit or bruise her during the attack, her clothes were ripped and she had numerous scratches. This was the first violent incident in their relationship.

Two days later Mary files a rape complaint. The state has recently abolished the marital rape exemption entirely. Forcible rape is a felony under state law punishable by a minimum of 20 years in prison. Aggravated assault (an assault with a deadly weapon) is a lesser felony with maximum punishment set at 15 years' imprisonment. Simple assault is a class-one misdemeanor, punishable by up to 2 years' imprisonment. You represent the state. What, if anything, would you charge Peter with? What penalty would you ask for?

Problem 2-17. Bree and Josiah had a violent marriage which eventually ended after 10 years in divorce. Soon after the divorce, Bree obtained a protective order against Josiah because of repeated abusive and threatening episodes. According to the terms of the protective order, "Josiah shall not have any contact with Bree and will remain at least 100 yards away from her at all times." The order was to last 1 year. Six months after entry of the order, Bree invited Josiah to her home for their 3-year old's birthday celebration. During the party, the couple consumed much alcohol which led to a physical altercation in which Josiah seriously injured Bree. He was charged with the crime of violation of the protective order and Bree is charged with being an accomplice. The state code makes it a crime "to intentionally or recklessly violate the terms of a protective order" and includes a complicity provision stating "no person, acting with the kind of culpability required for the commission of an offense shall aid, abet, assist, encourage or facilitate another in committing the offense." Bree's lawyer has filed a motion to dismiss the charges. As clerk to the presiding judge, prepare a memo outlining both sides' likely arguments.

Problem 2-18.   Horace and Shari have been married 15 years and have an active and mutually satisfactory sexual relationship. One evening they return home from a party both having had too much to drink. By the time they get to bed, Shari is nearly passed out. Horace had been looking forward to sexual intercourse and proceeds despite her semi-conscious state. At breakfast the next morning, Shari reports no recollection of the episode. Moreover, she expresses irritation when she learns about it, particularly because no contraception was used. She would have objected to had she been able to. Fortunately, Shari does not become pregnant.

Eight months later, the couple is having marital difficulties. When Horace discovers Shari's affair with a co-worker, he announces he wants a divorce. Shari learns, after consulting an attorney, that her state's divorce courts can consider marital misconduct in allocating marital property and awarding alimony. She files a rape charge against Horace with the police. State law provides that first degree rape includes intercourse with a person who is incapacitated from consenting. There is no marital rape exemption of any kind.

Should the d.a. prosecute? Assume she does proceed and the jury convicts under appropriate instructions. Should the appellate court affirm? Should the legislature change the law? If so, to what? Do your answers to any of the questions change if the incident recited above had happened more than once, despite S's objection, and her rape charge was filed immediately after the most recent such incident?

[3]   Evidence, Torts and Criminal Responsibility

EVIDENTIARY CONSEQUENCES OF MARRIAGE

The common law construct of spousal unity fostered several special evidentiary rules applicable solely to married couples. In addition to the marital communication privilege discussed in Note 3 after *Denton* at Section A[1][a], the spousal disqualification rule ruled out testimony for or against a spouse in civil or criminal proceedings. Wigmore identified several rationales for this rule beyond the legal unity fiction: (1) identity of interest — both spouses had the same interest in the outcome of any suit; because a party could not testify, likewise a party's spouse was ineligible; (2) pro-spouse testimony would likely reflect bias; and (3) adverse spousal testimony would interfere with the marital relationship. *See* WIGMORE, EVIDENCE § 2227 (McNaughton rev. 1961). Currently, a "spouse is now everywhere a competent witness for his or her spouse in criminal and civil cases." RONALD CARLSON, ET AL., EVIDENCE: TEACHING MATERIALS FOR AN AGE OF SCIENCE & STATUTES 173 (5th ed. 2002).

The states are split, however, concerning adverse testimony. In civil cases, most states define spouses as competent to testify against a spouse, while only a few jurisdictions grant a privilege to refuse to so testify. *Id.* At least one statute permits a spouse to exclude adverse testimony by his spouse. *See* Colo. Rev. Stat. § 13-90-107(1)(a)(I) (requiring consent, with some exceptions, of both spouses when either testifies); *In re Bozarth*, 779 P.2d 1346 (Colo. 1989) (custodial mother can exclude second husband's testimony in custody modification action filed by first husband).

The situation in criminal cases is more complicated. In 1980, the Supreme Court identified four positions with regard to the spousal disqualification rule in criminal cases: (1) the common law rule of ineligibility (8 states); (2) privilege against adverse spousal testimony vested either in defendant, or in witness and defendant (16 states); (3) privilege against adverse testimony vested solely in witness (9 states); (4) total abolition of the common law rule, thus rendering adverse spousal testimony competent and compellable (17 states). *See Trammel v. United States*, 445 U.S. 40, 48–49 n. 9 (1980). Where it exists, the privilege applies to any adverse testimony, not only to communications. Thus, it can bar adverse eyewitness testimony by a spouse. In a recent case where the privilege was vested in defendant, the Minnesota Supreme Court refused to find a marriage was a sham designed to take advantage of the privilege. The court also rejected a joint participant exception making the privilege unavailable when the spouses had both participated in a crime. *State v. Gianakos*, 644 N.W.2d 409 (Minn. 2002).

In interpreting Federal Rules of Evidence Rule 501, *Trammel* chose the third position, granting the witness the right to refuse to testify. It held this rule "furthers the important public interest in marital harmony without unduly burdening legitimate law enforcement needs." *Id.* at 53. Does the state interest in preserving marital harmony justify exempting a witness-spouse from the ordinary obligation to assist law enforcement? A commentator criticized the privilege's continued existence, particularly noting the problem posed in domestic violence cases:

> Courts and commentators may declare loudly that domestic violence is no longer tolerated . . . and that married women have the right to feel secure in their homes, but such rights, with little way to prove entitlement to the rights, echo emptily. [States in which the prosecutor cannot compel testimony in domestic violence cases as in other criminal cases] send an obvious message: When a man beats his wife it is not a crime that offends the state — it is simply a private matter. . . .

Malinda Seymore, *Isn't It a Crime: Feminist Perspectives on Spousal Immunity and Spousal Violence*, 90 Nw. L. Rev. 1032, 1035–36 (1996); *see Commonwealth v. Kirkner*, 805 A. 2d 514 (Pa. 2002) (spousal testimony compellable in cases where defendant is charged with domestic violence against witness).

By contrast, others urge a broadened *Trammel* privilege: "[*Trammel*] sanctioned attempts by the government to induce, if not coerce, the defendant's spouse to testify. . . . This . . . rewrote an ancient social contract, striking a new balance between the social importance of law enforcement and the family. . . ." Michael Mullane, Trammell v. United States: *Bad History, Bad Policy and Bad Law*, 47 Me. L. Rev. 105, 109,162 (1995); *see also* Roger Park, David Leonard & Steven Goldberg, Evidence Law 447 (2nd ed. 2004) (spouse may be willing to testify not because marital harmony has evaporated, but because "the government has threatened to prosecute the witness . . . on the underlying crime I f the privilege is claimed"); Steven Gofman, Note, *"Honey, the Judge Says We're History": Abrogating the Marital Privileges Via Modern Doctrines of Marital Worthiness*, 77 CORNELL. L. REV. 843 (1992) (arguing *Trammel* is one of several judicial doctrines showing "disrespect for both the purposes of the privileges and for state prerogatives in domestic relations law"). Another common law evidentiary rule linked to marriage was Lord Mansfield's Rule, under which spouses "shall not be permitted to say after marriage that they have had no connection and therefore that the offspring is spurious." *Goodright v. Moss*, 98 Eng. Rep. 1257 (1777). Some states still apply this rule, *see, e.g., In re Ellis V.N.*, 2008 Conn. Super. LEXIS 1229 (May 20, 2008), despite severe criticism of it. See cases in Maurice Brunner, Annot., *Rule as Regards Competency of Husband or Wife to Testify as to Nonaccess*, 49 A.L.R.3d 212 (1973).

PROBLEM

Problem 2-19. Tom and Juan were partners in a stormy marriage. After many fights and separations, Tom began an adulterous relationship with Bill. One night while waiting outside Tom and Juan's home, Bill witnessed a particularly violent and nasty argument between them. During the altercation, Tom shot Juan, who died from the injuries. In pretrial proceedings for murder in the first degree, he asserted self-defense. The morning of trial, with Bill under subpoena as a witness in the trial and Tom out on bond, they marry. At trial, Tom sought to exclude Bill's testimony under the spousal testimonial privilege, which the relevant jurisdiction vests in both witness and defendant. At the hearing on the motion to quash Bill's testimony, the next-door neighbor testifies Tom had told her "Yeah, I really put one over on that damned DA. I married Bill and that means that no eyewitness testimony against me. That's why we got married."

As judge in the case, will you require Bill to testify to what he saw on the night of the killing?

NOTES ON TORTS AND THE MARRIED COUPLE

1. *Interspousal Immunity.* Like the law of evidence, tort law has grown beyond special treatment for married people. Interspousal immunity long insulated spouses from tort claims, but during the past 100 years there has been a significant trend toward its abolition. A leading hornbook announced in 2000 that a majority of states now permit litigation between spouses, at least in some circumstances. DOBBS, LAW OF TORTS 752 (2000). The simultaneous demise of interspousal immunity and rise of no-fault divorce has led some litigants to file tort actions, alleging intentional infliction of emotional distress or assault, as part of divorce actions. These actions are discussed in Chapter 4.

For cases abolishing interspousal immunity, see *Bozman v. Bozman*, 830 A.2d 450 (Md. 2003); *Waite v. Waite*, 618 So. 2d 1360 (Fla. 1993); 630 A.2d 1096 (Del. Super. Ct. 1993); *Burns v. Burns*, 518 So. 2d 1205 (Miss. 1988); *Heino v. Harper*, 759 P.2d 253 (Or. 1988); *Moran v. Beyer*, 734 F.2d 1245 (7th Cir. 1984) (finding immunity unconstitutional). *But see Gates v. Gates*, 587 S.E.2d 32 (Ga. 2003) (applying the immunity to a cause of action arising *before* the marriage). *Burns* and

Harper include state-by-state analysis of the doctrine's status, listing 39 states which have abolished it and 8 others which have significantly restricted it. For a comprehensive treatment of the current status of interspousal tort immunity, see Laura Wanamaker, Case Comment, Waite v. Waite: *The Florida Supreme Court Abrogates the Doctrine of Interspousal Immunity*, 45 MERCER L. REV. 903, 906–07 (1994) (footnotes comprehensively list cases and citation); Carl Tobias, *Interspousal Tort Immunity in America*, 23 GA. L. REV. 359 (1989) (doctrine "one of the truly 'sick men' of American tort jurisprudence for whom the requiem may soon play").

Interspousal immunity's current poor reputation was underscored in *Boone v. Boone*, 546 S.E.2d 191 (S.C. 2001). Wife sued husband for her injuries suffered as a passenger in a car he was driving. While the site of the accident (Georgia) would have applied interspousal immunity, the South Carolina court invoked the public policy exception to ordinary choice of law rules in refusing to apply Georgia law, describing immunity as contrary to "natural justice, and its supporting rationales "simply not justified in the twenty-first century."

   2. Marriage-Related Torts. The common law simultaneously created several marriage-related torts. First, a husband could recover from third-party tortfeasors who deprived him of his wife's services due to injuries. Wives had no parallel action for loss of a husband's consortium because he did not owe her any services. The recovery in contemporary tort law is, of course, gender-neutral. DOBBS, *supra*, at 842.

   Two related torts, criminal conversation and alienation of affections, helped compensate the cuckolded husband. Criminal conversation required proof of defendant's sexual intercourse with plaintiff's wife (with or without her consent). DOBBS, *supra*, at 1246. Rather than address the obvious constitutional issue concerning gender-based discrimination, most states have abolished this tort. *See Saunders v. Alford*, 607 So. 2d 1214 (Miss. 1992); *Thomas v. Siddiqui*, 869 S.W.2d 740 (Mo. 1994); *Norton v. Macfarlane*, 818 P.2d 8 (Utah 1991) (noting plaintiff's spouse might be just as much at fault as defendant); *but see Nunn v. Allen*, 574 S.E.2d 35 (N.C. App. 2002) (rejecting opportunity to abolish criminal conversation; affirming verdict including punitive damages); *Oddo v. Presser*, 581 S.E.2d 123 (N.C. App. 2003) (upholding verdicts for criminal conversation and alienation of affections and delineating appropriate elements of damages, including punitives); *Neal v. Neal*, 873 P.2d 871 (Idaho 1994). In jurisdictions maintaining the action, it appears to be assumed that it is no longer gender-specific and either spouse may be a plaintiff.

   Many jurisdictions also have abolished the tort of alienation of affections. "The gist of the tort is not sexual intimacy but an interference with the marital relation that changes one spouse's mental attitude toward the other" KEETON, PROSSER & KEETON ON TORTS 918 (5th ed. 1984). While judicial abolition is relatively rare, several courts have done so. *See Russo v. Sutton*, 422 S.E.2d 750 (S.C. 1992); *Hoye v. Hoye*, 824 S.W.2d 422 (Ky. 1992) (abolishing tort of intentional interference with the marital relation, a combination of criminal conversation and alienation of affections); *O'Neil v. Schuckardt*, 733 P.2d 693 (Idaho 1986) (asserting 28 jurisdictions have either abolished or severely restricted the action). Even states retaining the action have severely modified it by, *e.g.*, eliminating money damages, apparently permitting only an action for injunction. *See, e.g.*, ALA. CODE § 6-5-331; VT. STAT. ANN. tit. 15, § 1001.

Some courts, however, continue to accept the tort. In *Fitch v. Valentine*, 959 So. 2d 1012 (Miss. 2007), the court "decline[d] the invitation to abolish the common law tort of alienation of affections. . . . Alienation of affections is the only available avenue to provide redress for a spouse who has suffered loss and injury to his or her marital relationship against the third party who, through persuasion, enticement, or inducement, caused or contributed to the abandonment of the marriage and/or the loss of affections by active interference." For other recent alienation of affection cases, see *State Farm v. Harbert*, 741 N.W.2d 228 (S.D. 2007) (holding insurance company had no obligation to defend alienation of affections suit under the intentional tort exclusion in policy); *Jones v. Skelley*, 673 S.E.2d 385 (N.C. Ct. App. 2009) (in addition to keeping alive the alienation action, granting summary judgment to plaintiff where commission of sexual intercourse was not disputed); *Dowling v. Bullen*, 94 P.3d 915 (Utah 2004); *Hutelmyer v. Cox*, 514 S.E.2d 554 (N.C. App. 1999) (upholding $1 million jury verdict).

Heart Balm statutes in many states abolish these marital torts along with eliminating the breach of promise action discussed at Section A[3]. Such statutes are consistent with the modern view of sexual autonomy and a distaste for public airing of "dirty linen" (see Chapter 3's discussion of divorce reform). For a commentary seeking reversal of the abolition trend arguing for punishment of "intentional interference with the husband-wife relationship and the violation of accepted canons of social conduct," see William Corbett, *A Somewhat Modest Proposal to Prevent Adultery and Save Families: Two Old Torts Looking for a New Career*, 33 ARIZ. ST. L.J. 985 (2001).

Recent imaginative litigants have used, with mixed success, the intentional infliction of emotional distress label for claims formerly made in the abolished marriage-related torts. In *Quinn v. Walsh*, 732 N.E.2d 330 (Mass. Ct. App. 2000), the court affirmed dismissal of a suit by a man and his son against the wife/mother's alleged lover. It rejected assertions that the injury's intentional infliction and the plaintiffs' emotional harm differentiated this case from traditional alienation of affection and criminal conversation actions. *See also Jones v. Henderson*, 2004 Tenn. App. LEXIS 567 (Aug. 30, 2004) (outrageous conduct suit by woman's husband and adult son based on discovery of a naked man in woman's closet properly dismissed; this was disguised action for either alienation of affections or criminal conversation, both of which had been abolished).

By contrast, in *Bailey v. Searles-Bailey*, 746 N.E.2d 1159 (Ohio Ct. App. 2000), the court held an intentional infliction of emotional distress claim by a husband whose wife and lover concealed the parentage of her child born during marriage survived an assertion that it was merely a disguised abolished marital tort. The court held the suit was based on plaintiff's emotional trauma upon discovery that his wife's child was not his. Judgment for plaintiff, however, was reversed for lack of outrageousness. *See also Williams v. Jeffs*, 57 P.3d 232 (Utah Ct. App. 2002) (requisite outrageousness not demonstrated); *Rosenthal v. Erven*, 17 P.3d 558 (Ore. Ct. App. 2001) (affair with wife not "so far beyond the bounds of social toleration that it should be actionable . . ."); Merle Weiner, *Domestic Violence and the Per Se Standard of Outrage*, 54 MD. L. REV. 183 (1995) (analyzing use of intentional infliction as remedy for domestic violence victims, urging per se standard of outrage which would be met by proof of violation of protective order).

A number of tort claims have been brought against clergy for sexual relationships with plaintiff's spouse. In *Osborne v. Payne*, 31 S.W.3d 911 (Ky. 2000), the court reversed summary judgment against plaintiff who alleged defendant priest's adulterous relationship with plaintiff's wife during counseling. The court held irrelevant the abolition of the amatory torts, finding the alleged conduct would constitute outrageous conduct sufficient for recovery for intentional infliction of emotional distress. *See also Odenthal v. Minnesota Conference of Seventh-Day Adventists*, 649 N.W.2d 426 (Minn. 2002) (rejecting claim that First Amendment bars negligent counseling claim based on relationship between pastor and plaintiff's wife during counseling); *but see Bailey v. Faulkner*, 940 So. 2d 247 (Ala. 2006) (negligence claim against pastor actually a claim for alienation of affections, a tort abolished in the state).

Osborne, however, affirmed dismissal of the church as a defendant under vicarious liability, concluding that while the priest's counseling was well within his job, his employment responsibilities did not include commission of adultery. *See also Mercier v. Daniels*, 533 S.E.2d 877 (N.C. Ct. App. 2000) (rejecting vicarious liability of employer for alienation of affections); *Thornburg v. Federal Express Corporation*, 62 S.W.3d 421 (Mo. Ct. App. 2001) (respondeat superior dismissed for failure to allege any wrongful action by any employee of defendant).

For analysis and criticism of the marital torts, see Robert Spector, *All in the Family — Tort Litigation Comes of Age*, 28 FAM. L.Q. 363–67 (1994).

Chapter 3

DISSOLVING THE MARITAL STATUS

INTRODUCTION

This chapter deals with the rules governing the termination of the marital status itself, as distinct from the financial and child custody issues raised by the termination. In 1970, California became the first state to eliminate *all* fault-based divorce provisions. While previously a few states granted divorce on the basis of "incompatibility," a ground focusing primarily on the breakdown of the marital relationship, rather than the "fault" of one or both parties, those incompatibility grounds existed alongside fault-based provisions in the statutes of these states. California's repeal of all fault provisions was a more dramatic departure from fault-based termination. Many states followed California's example but many others did not, instead just adding a no-fault alternative to their fault-divorce provisions. But one way or the other, all states eventually adopted no-fault grounds and the variations among states will be discussed below. For now, however, we note that the idea that parties should be able to end their marriage without proof of fault "spread like prairie fire. By 1974, . . . forty-five states already possessed a no-fault procedure." Herbert Jacob, Silent Revolution: The Transformation of Divorce Law in the United States 80 (1988). In the subsequent decade, the final five states joined the rest, with South Dakota as the last in 1985. *Id.* Many states retained fault as a consideration in marital property distributions or awards of spousal support. While the transition to no-fault divorce was one of the most dramatic changes in 20th century American family law, the foundation for these developments was laid gradually throughout the century It appears that the battle over the rules governing the termination of marital status is largely over, although not too many years ago some no-fault opponents succeeded in restoring fault alternatives to no-fault divorce in three states, under the rubric of "covenant marriage." We will discuss that later in this chapter, at Section C[3].

In this chapter, we examine the history of divorce law in the United States and analyze the various transitions that characterized the law on the books and the law in action throughout the last century and into the present one. What policies drove the no-fault reforms? How do no-fault and fault-based grounds function, side-by-side? Are the results of the no-fault "revolution" what the reformers expected? How will attempts to "reform the reforms" change modern divorce law?

A. THE ORIGINS AND HISTORY OF AMERICAN DIVORCE LAW

A culture's beliefs about marriage are reflected in its rules for divorce. Between the 16th and 18th centuries, there was a gradual change in Europe from a conception of marriage as an economic alliance between families to a conception of it as a romantic bond between individuals — what has been called "companionate" marriage. MARY ANN GLENDON, THE NEW FAMILY AND THE NEW PROPERTY 13–17, 23 (1981). The French Civil Code of 1804 (valid until 1965) reflected the older conception, providing for the title in land to remain in the blood family of each spouse. Alterations in this rule were permissible only by agreement *before* (and not after) marriage. Depending upon the role marriage plays in a particular society, the personal preferences of the marital partners may have more or less importance in determining whether the marriage will continue. The shift to a companionate marriage model ultimately was accompanied by the increasing centrality of the marital partners in determining whether and when the marriage dissolves. While the American history of divorce law is somewhat different from the European, the basic trends are essentially the same, as the following selection indicates.

[1] Early American Divorce

LAWRENCE M. FRIEDMAN, A HISTORY OF AMERICAN LAW
142–46, 377–81 (3rd ed. 2005)

England [was] a "divorceless society," and remained that way until 1857. . . . The very wealthy might squeeze a rare private bill of divorce out of Parliament. Between 1800 and 1836 there were, on the average, three . . . a year. For the rest, unhappy husbands and wives had to be satisfied with annulment (no easy matter) or divorce from bed and board (*a mensa et thoro*), a form of legal separation. Separated couples had no right to remarry. . . .

[During the American] colonial period, the South was generally faithful to English tradition. Absolute divorce was unknown, divorce from bed and board very rare. In New England, however, courts and legislatures occasionally granted a divorce. In Pennsylvania, Penn's laws of 1682 gave the right to a "Bill of Divorcement" to a spouse whose partner was convicted of adultery. Later, the governor or lieutenant governor was empowered to dissolve marriages on grounds of incest, adultery, bigamy, or homosexuality. There is . . . no evidence that the governor ever used this power.

After Independence . . . regional differences remained quite strong. In the South, divorce continued to be unusual. The extreme case was South Carolina. Henry William Desaussure, writing in 1817, stated flatly that South Carolina had never granted a single divorce. . . . There was no such thing as absolute divorce in South Carolina throughout the nineteenth century. In other southern states, legislatures dissolved marriages by passing private divorce laws. The Georgia constitution of 1798 allowed legislative divorce on a two-thirds vote of each branch of the legislature. . . . Between 1798 and 1835, there were 291 legislative divorces in Georgia. The frequency curve rose toward the end of the period. . . .

North of the Mason-Dixon line, courtroom divorce replaced legislative divorce. Pennsylvania passed a general divorce law in 1785, Massachusetts one year later. Every New England state had a divorce law before 1800, along with New York, New Jersey, and Tennessee. In these states, divorce took the form of an ordinary lawsuit. An innocent spouse sued for divorce, which had to be based on legally acceptable "grounds." . . . New York's law of 1787 permitted absolute divorce only for adultery. Vermont, on the other hand, allowed divorce for impotence, adultery, intolerable severity, three years' willful desertion, and long absence with presumption of death (1798). Rhode Island allowed divorce for "gross misbehaviour and wickedness in either of the parties, repugnant to and in violation of the marriage covenant." In New Hampshire, it was grounds for divorce if a spouse joined the Shaker sect B not an unreasonable rule, since the Shakers did not believe in sexual intercourse.

. . . More marriages seemed to be cracking under the strains of nineteenth-century life. . . . As the demand for divorce grew, private divorce bills became a nuisance B a pointless drain on the legislature's time. . . . [By the end of the 19th] century, private divorce laws had become extinct. . . .

. . . Where did the growing demand for easy (or at least easier) divorce come from? The rate of divorce in the nineteenth century was the merest trickle compared to rates in later times. But it was noticeable. To many devout and respectable people, it was an alarming fire bell in the night, a symptom of moral dry rot and a cause in itself of further moral decay. President Timothy Dwight of Yale, in 1816, called the rise in divorces "dreadful beyond conception." It was a form of "stalking, barefaced pollution"; if things went on as they appeared to be going, Connecticut would become "one vast Brothel; one great province of the World of Perdition." The "whole community," he warned, could be thrown "into a general prostitution."

. . .

. . . Easy divorce laws reflected changes in the nature of marriage; but they also grew out of the needs to the middle-class mass. The smallholder had to have some way to stabilize and legitimize relationships, to settle doubts about ownership of family property. It was the same general impulse that lay behind the common-law marriage. Divorce was simplest to obtain and divorce laws most advanced in those parts of the country B the West especially B least stratified by class. . . .

Divorce, . . . had genuinely popular roots. . . .

. . . Divorce laws were a kind of compromise. In general, the law never recognized full, free consensual divorce. It became simpler . . . but divorce was not routine or automatic. . . . [D]ivorce was in form an adversary proceeding. . . . Later, the collusive or friendly divorce came to dominate the field. What went on in court was a show, a charade, an afterthought. . . .

. . . The divorce statues varied from state to state. . . . From about 1850 to 1870, a few states adopted rather loose divorce laws. Connecticut at one point made any "misconduct" grounds for divorce, if it "permanently destroys the happiness of the petitioner and defeats the purposes of the marriage relation." In Maine, a supreme court justice could grant a divorce if he deemed it "reasonable and proper, conducive to peace and harmony, and consistent with the peace and morality of society." Divorce laws in states as different as North Carolina, Indiana, and Rhode Island were also quite permissive. Some states that did not go as far as Maine or Connecticut broadened their statutes considerably; they added to the traditional list of grounds for divorce (adultery, desertion, and impotence, for example) new and vaguer ones such as "cruelty." In the Tennessee Code of 1858, for example, divorce was available on grounds of impotence, bigamy, adultery, desertion, felony conviction, plus the following: attempting to take a spouse's life by poison; concealing a pregnancy by another man at the time of marriage; and nonsupport. In addition, the court might, in its "discretion," free a woman from the bonds of matrimony if her husband had "abandoned her, or turned her out of doors," if he was guilty of cruel and inhuman treatment, or if he had "offered such indignities to her person as to render her condition intolerable and force her to withdraw."

After 1870, the tide began to turn. Influential moral leaders had never stopped attacking loose divorce laws. Horace Greeley thought that "easy divorce" had made the Roman Empire rot. America could suffer a similar fate, "blasted by the mildew of unchaste mothers and dissolute homes." Theodore D. Woolsey, president of Yale University, wrote a book in 1869 denouncing the divorce laws of Connecticut as immoral and unscriptural. If laws against adultery were not vigorously enforced, the public sense of sin would be dulled. Moreover, adultery should be the only legal grounds for divorce. In Woolsey's view, "petitions for divorce become more numerous with the ease of obtaining them." Lax divorce laws could disintegrate the family, the backbone of American life. . . .

Militant feminists, on the other hand, took up the cudgels for permissive divorce. A furious debate raged in New York. Robert Dale Owen, son of the Utopian reformer, went into battle against Horace Greeley. Owen, . . . felt that strict divorce laws, not lax ones, led to adultery. . . . One thing was certain. The divorce rate was rising. In the period 1867–1871, 53,574 divorces were granted; in 1877–1881, 89,284. in every part of the country, but especially in the West, divorce rates rose faster than the population: By 1900, there were 39 divorces per 100,000 population In the North Atlantic states, and 131 per 100,000 in the Western states.

What accounts for the rising demand for divorce? There are various possibilities. One is that dry rot had affected family life . . . But perhaps a larger number of people simply wanted *formal* acceptance of the fact that their marriages were dead. Just as more of the middle class wanted, and needed, their deeds recorded, their wills made out, their marriages solemnized, so they wanted the honesty and convenience of divorce, the right to remarry in bourgeois style, to have legitimate children with their second wife (or husband), and the right to decent, honest disposition of their worldly goods. Only divorce could provide this.

. . . .

The migratory divorce, for people with money and the urge to travel, was another detour around strict enforcement of divorce law. To attract the "tourist trade," a state needed easy laws and a short residence period. Indiana was one of these states, before the 1870s. [I]n 1873, the legislature passed a stricter law that shut the divorce mill down. South and North Dakota, too, had their day. Finally, in the twentieth century, Nevada became *the* place. . . . Its career as national divorce mill proved to be quite durable . . .

For another history of divorce in the 19th century in the United States focusing on the "narratives presented at divorce trials, focusing on the stories told about men, women, marriage and fault," see Naomi Cahn, *Faithless Wives and Lazy Husbands: Gender Norms in Nineteenth-Century Divorce Law*, 2002 U. ILL. L. REV. 651; *see also* HENDRIK HARTOG, SEPARATED SPOUSES: MAN AND WIFE IN AMERICA: A HISTORY (2000), reviewed in Joanna Grossman, *Book Review*, 53 STAN. L. REV. 1613 (2001).

[2]   American Divorce in the Twentieth Century

The late 19th century law of divorce, described by Professor Friedman as a "hodgepodge," remained largely unchanged until the 1970s. The law of every state assumed an adversary proceeding in which the plaintiff had to prove the defendant's "fault." Just what sort of "fault" was necessary depended upon the state's particular statutory language. All states recognized adultery as a ground for divorce (until 1967, adultery was the *only* permissible ground for divorce in New York) and most states recognized desertion or abandonment. Plaintiffs claiming desertion were required to show that the defendant had abandoned all marital duties and that, for a minimum period of time (often specified by statute), the parties had not cohabited. A few jurisdictions granted divorce on desertion grounds even though the parties remained together, if the defendant had refused performance of marital duties, most commonly sexual relations, for the minimum statutory period. Because of the underlying fault premise, the defendant could defeat a desertion-based divorce action by showing plaintiff's consented to defendant's absence, or that plaintiff's conduct justified defendant's departure. Precisely what conduct could be offered in justification varied from state to state. A third common ground permitted under the traditional divorce laws was "cruelty." The law of many states required plaintiff here to show bodily harm resulting from defendant's actions, although mental suffering was accepted in some states.

The fault-based logic permeating the system was further exemplified by traditional divorce law's defenses. The most notorious defense was "recrimination" — a showing that plaintiff was also guilty of conduct which the law recognized as a ground for divorce. If both plaintiff and defendant proved the other's fault, neither was granted a divorce because divorce was a remedy available only to an innocent spouse.

Most divorces were uncontested and thus undefended. An uncontested divorce case, however, was a rather peculiar legal animal. Divorce by mutual consent was not formally available. Thus, the court could not issue the decree simply because the spouses agreed that it should. Some statutory ground for divorce still had to be proven in court. In form, an adversary proceeding was required, even if the parties were not, in fact, adversaries. Particularly where the jurisdiction had relatively restrictive rules on grounds for divorce, the official divorce law of the books often bore no relation to the law in action Several practices arose in response to the disconnect between formal legal notions of marital breakup and the circumstances that, in reality, led couples to seek dissolution of their marriage. In some jurisdictions, the courts granted divorces on facts far short of the standards articulated in the case law. For example, in his 1968 family law treatise, Professor Homer Clark observed that his discussion of the ground of cruelty was confined to "the law of the statutes and reported cases," which he underscored was "by no means the same as the law in action," explaining:

> [I]n uncontested cases . . . [c]ruelty . . . has proven to be capable of nearly limitless expansion, in the face of pronouncements by appellate courts which would lead one to think that the definition of cruelty had not changed much for one hundred and fifty years. In many states, especially in the West, a divorce for cruelty may be had for the asking, providing it is uncontested. Whether this condition be labeled hypocritical or sophisticated, it . . . is the means by which divorce has become easy in most of the United States without the necessity for enlarging the statutory grounds.

HOMER CLARK, LAW OF DOMESTIC RELATIONS 341 (1968).

In states with more restrictive divorce grounds, the challenges for a couple seeking a consensual divorce were greater. Wealthier residents of states with restrictive divorce laws often established an allegedly-permanent domicile in a state with more relaxed grounds for divorce, such as Nevada, in order to avail themselves of the more lenient divorce statutes. Chapter 7 examines the special jurisdictional rules governing domestic relations matters, many of which arose during this "migratory divorce" era. In situations where a domiciliary of a state with restrictive divorce statutes lacked either resources or desire to migrate in order to obtain a divorce, he or she theoretically had to prove specific behavior demonstrating defendant's faults. As the following excerpts reveal, these requirements invited collusion between the parties to manufacture the "evidence" necessary to prove the required statutory ground.

Note, *Collusive and Consensual Divorce and the New York Anomaly*
36 COLUM. L. REV. 1121–33 (1936)

. . . [C]ollusion [is] an agreement between husband and wife for (1) the commission of an offense for the purpose of obtaining a divorce, or (2) the introduction of false evidence of an offense not actually committed, or (3) the suppression of a valid defense. . . .

. . . [P]rocedural, as well as substantive rules have been evolved to prevent the practice. Thus, five states require the complainant to take a special oath that his petition is not founded on collusion. And generally a divorce will not be granted on default; the facts must thereafter be proved to the satisfaction of the court. Corroboration will be required to bolster the confessions or admissions of the parties, and the mutual corroboration of the spouses will not suffice. A higher standard of proof than that ordinarily required in civil cases may even be demanded. Direct sanctions against attorneys in the form of disbarment or contempt of court, and the inability of an attorney to represent both sides with their consent in a divorce suit, as well as a variety of other procedural regulations, have also sought the same objective. But "hotel evidence,"[33] which has lost some of its probative force in England, is still sufficient to create a *prima facie* case in most American jurisdictions.

. . . .

[I]n spite of the vast array of substantive and procedural weapons that have been utilized, no satisfactory method of eliminating collusion has been devised. [The author cites judges and lawyers who assert that collusive divorce is rampant, ranging from 75% to 100% of all cases, according to some.]

Factual Evidence of Collusion in New York. . . . Prominent . . . is the huge number of cases which are uncontested on the merits . . .[60] Similarly persuasive are the large percentage of co-respondents who remain unnamed, the surprising state of undress in which the defendant and co-respondent are generally found,[65] and the close relationships generally existing between the defendant and witnesses for the complainant. And the unusually short period commonly intervening between the alleged adultery and the service of process would constitute at least a suspicious circumstance. . . .

Conclusion. That the law relating to collusion is not serving its purpose is abundantly clear. Moreover, positive evils have grown up in its wake. Perjury arises to aid in the creation of legal farces, attorneys resort to degrading tactics, [and] the profession of co-respondents makes an appearance . . .[70]

LAWRENCE M. FRIEDMAN, AMERICAN LAW IN THE TWENTIETH CENTURY 434–38 (2002)

. . . . Marriage (in legal theory) was a contract between man and wife; but unlike most contracts, once the two were in it, it was devilishly hard to get out. A contract to buy a horse can be called off if both buyer and seller want to call it off;

---

[33] In England this normally consisted of a hotel bill being sent home by the husband, and witnesses testifying that he stayed at the hotel and occupied a bedroom with a woman not his wife. . . .

[60] In the Special Term for Trials in New York County, matrimonial actions disposed of were:

	1931	1932	1933	1934
Defended Matrimonials	188	239	188	196
Undefended Matrimonials Referred to Official Referees	1341	1186	1250	1417

The figures include matrimonials of all types. . . .

[65] [P]eople do not ordinarily open a door . . . to permit someone to enter unless they are more suitably clothed than the cases indicate. . . . As tabulated by Jackson, the cases show:

For the male, absolutely nude, 21; wrapped in towel, 2; wrapper, 1; nightgown, 8; B.V.D. or underwear, 119; bathrobe or dressing gown, 101; pajamas, 227; kimono, 4.

For the female: absolutely nude, 55; brassiere, 2; bloomers, 2; negligee, 67; slip, 5; wrapper, 1; chemise, 24; underwear, 26; lingerie, 5; nightgown, 126; pajamas, 73; bathrobe or dressing gown, 32; combination, 2; kimono, 68.

[70] See, *e.g.*, Jarvis, *I Was the Unknown Blonde in 100 New York Divorces*, SUNDAY MIRROR MAGAZINE, March 11, 1934. After performing their services at the "chosen hotel room . . . these divorce aiders receive their $50 (now often reduced to $25) and go home."

but a marriage contract is not like buying a horse. Only a court could dissolve a marriage, and only when one party, herself quite innocent, could prove the other guilty of an offense against the marriage — the so-called grounds for divorce.

Admissible grounds varied from state to state. In South Carolina absolute divorce was not available at all [until] 1948. In the other states, the common grounds were adultery, desertion, and cruelty; but there were all sorts of state idiosyncrasies. Drunkenness, failure to provide, imprisonment, and impotence were grounds in some states. Leprosy was grounds for divorce in Hawaii; in Virginia a husband could divorce his wife if he discovered she had been a prostitute. Cruelty became the grounds of choice in the twentieth century; it overtook adultery in 1922, and in 1950 accounted for almost three-fifths of all divorces. Most states recognized cruelty as a valid reason for divorce — New York was a prominent exception.

What accounts for this outbreak of marital cruelty? Nothing. It was, in fact, an outbreak of collusion. Most "cruelty" cases were uncontested. The plaintiff (usually the wife) filed for divorce. The husband made no defense. Divorce was granted, by default. Collusive divorce had become common in the late nineteenth century; in the twentieth century, it was absolutely pervasive. In legal theory, a collusive divorce was void. Husband and wife had no right to agree to split. In practice, collusion was the rule, not the exception; and the judges all knew it. . . .

The precise form of collusion did vary from state to state. It mirrored the state statute; it was, in a sense, "cheating in the shadow of the law." In California, as in most states, cruelty was the courtroom favorite. In case after case after case, the wife complained that her husband cursed her and hit her, and made her life miserable. . . .

In New York divorce was available, practically speaking, only for adultery. This was an extreme situation; but any and all attempts to amend the law ended in shipwreck in the legislature. The demand for divorce, however, was as strong in New York as it was elsewhere. . . .

New York also developed a weird form of collusive adultery — one might even call it soft-core adultery. A man would check into a hotel, a woman (usually a blonde) would appear, together with a photographer; the photographer would take pictures of the couple, in pajamas or underwear or even naked; the woman would get her fifty-dollar fee; and lo and behold! here was evidence of adultery. . . .

Collusion was by far the most popular, and practical, detour around tough divorce laws. But the federal system opened another door: the migratory divorce. There had been a number of divorce "mills" in the nineteenth century: states that attracted birds of passage with easy divorce laws. The clergy and respectable people usually objected to this rather tawdry business; and most divorce mills . . . were soon closed down. . . .

. . . . Divorce had become a classic example of what one might call a dual system — a system with a radical . . . gap between the official system and the living law. Of course, official law and living law are never perfectly congruent; but in a true dual system, the two systems are entirely separate, operating almost in two different worlds. [¶] . . . Dual systems arise from a number of causes. Divorce was kind of a stalemate. The forces that opposed it were powerful. Divorce was absolutely forbidden to Roman Catholics; other religions tolerated it, but barely. It carried a stigma. Yet, the demand for divorce continued to rise; and it proved impossible to confine it within the narrow channels of the official law. An irresistible force (the popular desire for divorce) had met an immovable object (the opposition to easy divorce).

. . . .

There were, of course, costs to the dual system. It was tawdry and unpopular; it was expensive; it degraded everybody who took part in it. Yet there was no easy way for the system to change. It was rotting from within; but the constant calls for reform made little headway. . . .

NOTES

1. ***Evading Divorce Restrictions with Annulments.***   In the face of restrictive divorce laws, parties wanting out of their marriages often sought annulments. In 1963, for example, 36% of all New York decrees ending marriages were annulments, not divorces. National Center for Health Statistics, *Divorce Statistics Analysis 1963*, at 10. New York annulments were available on a showing that one of the parties was fraudulently persuaded to enter the marriage. It is estimated that more than 150 types of fraud were recognized by New York courts. Richard H. Wels, *New York: The Poor Man's Reno*, 35 Cornell L.Q. 303, 319–20 (1950). With the advent of no-fault divorce, the importance of annulment declined. In fact, the California Governor's Commission (discussed *infra* at Section A[3]) recommended abolishing annulments entirely, although its recommendation was not adopted.

Professor Mary Ann Glendon observed a parallel phenomenon within the Roman Catholic Church, which recognizes annulment but not divorce. The New Family and the New Property 35, 122 (1981). In the United States,

> where Roman Catholics divorce in roughly the same proportion as the rest of the population, annulment law has been developing in a pattern reminiscent of the [the liberalized practice prevalent under the] old-fashioned fault-based secular divorce laws.
>
> . . . The Church's version of migratory divorce [means] many couples seek to find a ground for jurisdiction in a diocese where the tribunals are known to be more lenient in granting annulments. (In 1977, a mere 14 of 147 dioceses handed down 43 per cent of the annulment decisions.) [¶ How] can a tribunal declare that the marriage of a couple who had children and who lived together for many years, at least some of the time harmoniously, never existed? The answer is, quite easily. Lack of consent, capacity, or consummation, the [leading] grounds for annulment, have all undergone sea-changes in the case law of the marital tribunals. Thus, consent may have been rendered defective not only by fraud and duress, but by emotional immaturity. A person may be incapable if she is the sort who cannot live up to her marital obligations. The long marriage may not really have been consummated (despite the two children) if the spouses have not attained a spiritual and emotional, as well as physical, union. Here we see

the same legal mind that was at work adapting the old cruelty grounds to the rising demand for secular divorce in the late 1950s and the 1960s.

Id. at 122–24. Despite revisions of canon law that were expected to restrain the trend toward increased availability of annulments, *Pope Set to Issue New Church Laws*, N.Y. TIMES, Jan. 23, 1983, at A1, church annulments continue and are criticized by some. *See, e.g.*, Peter Steinfels, *Beliefs*, N.Y. TIMES, May 17, 1997 at A11 (citing the 1996 book, *Shattered Faith*, by Sheila Rauch Kennedy, former wife of Representative Joseph Kennedy II of Massachusetts, which criticized church policy that authorized annulment of her marriage, arguing the church's "current criteria and procedures for deciding [annulment issues] have opened the door to widespread manipulation and hypocrisy"). In recent years, the number of annulments has declined precipitously. While it was estimated in the late 1990s that the American church annually granted 60,000 annulments, *id.*, the most recent data from the Vatican shows that, in 2005, a total of 24,434 were granted by churches in the United States of a total of 40,549 worldwide. STATISTICAL YEARBOOK OF THE CHURCH 2005 443, 450 (Libreria Editrice Vaticana 2007). It was announced in 2007 that the Vatican's Romana Rota court had reversed the annulment granted to Joseph Kennedy. Andrea Estes, *Vatican Reverses Kennedy Ruling; Ex-Congressman's Annulment Voided*, BOSTON GLOBE, June 21, 2007 at B1.

2. *Additional Reading.* For further discussion of 20th century divorce law and the mechanisms and customs employed to avoid the law's harsh effects, see Lawrence M. Friedman, *A Dead Language: Divorce Law and Practice Before No-Fault*, 86 VA. L. REV. 1497 (2000) [hereinafter "Friedman, *A Dead Language*"]. For an analysis of these issues with particular attention to the changing status of women during the 20th century, see Herma Hill Kay, *From Second Sex to the Joint Venture: An Overview of Women's Rights and Family Law in the United States During the Twentieth Century*, 88 CAL. L. REV. 2017 (2000) [hereinafter "Kay, *From Second Sex to Joint Venture*"].

[3] The Development of the No-Fault Approach

Even before California's elimination of its fault-based grounds for divorce in 1970, some states had a no-fault divorce ground. For example, in 1933, New Mexico added the statutory ground of "incompatibility." Friedman, *A Dead Language, supra*, at 1527. In 1968, Professor Clark identified four jurisdictions that accepted "incompatibility" as a ground for divorce. CLARK, *supra*, at 350. He observed, however, that "the courts seem to be so strongly conditioned to the idea that divorce [requires] a showing of fault by the defendant that they have had great difficulty in dealing with the fact that incompatibility statutes contain no mention of fault." For a detailed account of the difficulties of dealing with an apparently no-fault ground like incompatibility in the context of a fault-based law, see Walter Wadlington, *Divorce Without Fault Without Perjury*, 52 VA. L. REV. 32 (1966). Yet, by the 1970s, most states were ready to embrace some version of no-fault divorce provisions.

MAX RHEINSTEIN, MARRIAGE STABILITY, DIVORCE AND THE LAW
373–81 (1972)

In 1963, the movement to modify the divorce law of California started as an effort not to turn the tide of conservative resistance to divorce but to stem the rising tide of divorce, to lessen the very high divorce rate of the state as a whole and of some counties in particular.

. . . [T]he governor, on 11 May 1966, established the Governor's Commission on the Family. . . .

[T]he California commission recommended the abandonment of the principle of matrimonial offense. The reasons were: commission of a matrimonial offense constitutes guilt in a formalistic sense only; guilt in the true sense almost always lies with both parties; the commission of a matrimonial offense does not by itself indicate that the marriage is no longer viable; the necessity of alleging a matrimonial offense creates an atmosphere of hostility in which it is difficult to settle . . . child custody and support, . . . property settlement and alimony; the commission of an offense can be feigned so that insincerity and perjury may be induced to the detriment of the respect for the law and the courts. The commission added another ground, the incompatibility of the principle of offense with the function of a family court as envisaged by the commission. While it would thus no longer be necessary or sufficient to prove adultery, desertion, cruelty, or any other of the matrimonial offenses enumerated in the existing law of California, it should be possible to obtain a divorce upon the initiative of either party. The proceedings could be assumed normally to last about eight months. . . .

The commission's extreme liberality in stating the grounds for divorce was counterbalanced by the proposal of an elaborate system of family courts. It is hard to say whether this proposal was meant as a serious check or as window dressing. . . . [¶] A family court . . . was to have comprehensive jurisdiction in all matters of family law. . . . The judges, it was hoped, would be interested and experienced in family matters. They were to be aided by a staff of professionals trained in counseling. This staff was to go to work when a petition of inquiry had been filed. . . . It was . . . to proceed . . . to explore whether and in what ways a reconciliation might be possible, to help the parties, through efforts of its own or through recommendation of an outside counselor or agency, and, if it appeared that the parties would not decide to be reconciled, consult with them "for the purpose of working out a settlement of the circumstances attendant upon the dissolution of the marriage including the problems of child custody and visitation." The counselor would then submit a report to the judge. [Additional steps were then provided.]

The plan of the . . . commission was a compromise. [T]he commission sought to bring together the essentially conservative family court plan and a divorce law of the books that in effect was to be more liberal than even the existing California law in action. While the former tendency was emphasized, the latter required some scrutiny to be discovered.

[T]he report did not meet with a friendly reception by the bar. . . . [which may] [¶] have been primarily responsible for the elimination from California divorce reform of the family court plan. Helped by taxpayers' desire for economy and the difficulty of finding sufficient numbers of trained personnel, tendencies to broaden the existing scheme of conciliation courts were also stopped. . . .

Elimination from the proceedings of allegation of misconduct and wrangling about guilt is one of the principal aims of the new California law. This desire has found expression not only in the substitution of the objective ground of breakdown for the former misconduct grounds, but also in what constitutes the most far-reaching innovation of the new scheme, the elimination of guilt as a determinant in the decision about property settlement, alimony, and child custody.

In 1970, the Commissioners on Uniform State Laws approved what was then termed a Uniform Marriage and Divorce Act [since been re-labeled a Model Act by the Commissioners], heavily influenced by the California developments. Section 302 . . . provided for entry of a dissolution decree if the court "finds that the marriage is irretrievably broken." Because this proposal sparked intense opposition in the Family Law Section of the American Bar Association, the ABA originally declined to approve it. The chairman of the Family Law Section later explained:

> [The Family Law Section] has opposed the draft . . . because that Act provides for no-fault divorce even against the wishes of one of the spouses, without regard to the fact that the marriage may have been of long duration and without an adequate cooling-off period or other delay. The FLS further opposes the Uniform Act as it contains no adequate provisions available for reconciliation and conciliation inquiries. . . . The FLS therefore proposed amendments . . . which will provide for an adequate delay before a divorce, together with necessary reconciliation inquiry and conciliation processes, where advisable.

> This writer answers those who seek to achieve a system of divorce on demand . . . that such a step will lead to the destruction of marriage and the family unit as social institutions and ultimately of society in general. A dead marriage . . . should be buried, but not so long as there is the slightest breath of life still left in it. The best test of whether the marriage is dead is a suitable period of living apart for at least one year prior to commencement of a divorce action; this separation should be coupled with an attempt at reconciliation. This then, should be the basis for establishing that the marriage is irretrievably broken and constitutes the ground for a no-fault divorce, not just a speedy and easy divorce. . . .

> The FLS revision . . . clearly defines irretrievable breakdown to be "(a) that the parties have lived separate and apart for a period of more than one year next preceding the commencement of this proceeding or, (b) that such serious marital misconduct has occurred which has so adversely affected the physical or mental health of the petitioning party as to make it impossible for the parties to continue the marital relation, and that reconciliation is improbable." This definition of irretrievable breakdown removes what the FLS understands to be the practice in many courts, where breakdown is the ground, of accepting a mere statement by the

petitioning party that the marriage is irretrievably broken as sufficient to warrant dissolution. . . .

Hon. Ralph J. Podell, *The Case for Revision of the Uniform Marriage and Divorce Act*, 18 S.D. L. REV. 601, 603 (1973). For a sample of the debate as it was then waged, *see also* Robert J. Levy, *Introduction to a Symposium on the Uniform Marriage and Divorce Act*, 18 S.D. L. REV. 531 (1973); Henry H. Foster, Jr., *Divorce Reform and the Uniform Act*, 18 S.D. L. REV. 572 (1973). The prospect of two competing Uniform Acts was averted when the ABA accepted an amended version of the Commissioners' draft. That version, still current, is reprinted below, at Section B[1]. (To read how this version was developed, see Harvey L. Zuckman, *The A.B.A. Family Law Section v. NCCUSL*, 24 CATH. U.l. REV. 61 (1974)).

Divorce reform percolated rapidly through the various state legislatures. In *Silent Revolution: The Transformation of Divorce Law in the United States*, Herbert Jacob explores how such an immense change could take place with so little public debate. By 1985, every state in the union had adopted some form of no-fault provision. There remained, and still remains, substantial variability in the wording of the statutes and in the extent to which the no-fault provisions coexist with fault-based provisions. Section B *infra*, examines the nature and variability of current divorce statutes, and how they work in practice. At least one commentator asserts that the "no fault revolution" simply reflects a return to earlier approaches to divorce. *See* Shaakirrah Sanders, *The Cyclical Nature of Divorce in the Western Legal Tradition*, 50 LOY. L. REV. 407 (2004) (tracing history of divorce in Western tradition to classical Roman times; traces cycles of grounds for divorce).

NOTES ON COMPARATIVE LAW OF DIVORCE

1. ***English Marriage and Divorce Law.*** LAWRENCE STONE, ROAD TO DIVORCE: ENGLAND 1530–1987 (1990), provides a comprehensive history of English marriage and divorce law. Two companion volumes offer collections of case studies, many quite colorful. *See, e.g.*, LAWRENCE STONE, UNCERTAIN UNIONS: MARRIAGE IN ENGLAND 1660–1753 (1992) (discussing marriage laws sufficiently ambiguous "that very large numbers of perfectly respectable people . . . could never be sure whether they were married . . ." N.Y. REV. BOOKS, Nov. 4, 1993); LAWRENCE STONE, BROKEN LIVES: SEPARATION AND DIVORCE IN ENGLAND 1660–1857 (1993) (addressing difficulties of ending unsatisfactory marriages).

European divorce reform was afoot during the same time that it occurred here. The Archbishop of Canterbury appointed a committee whose 1966 report, *Putting Asunder: A Divorce Law for Contemporary Society*, influenced American as well as British developments in its support of marital breakdown as the exclusive ground for divorce. In Britain, as in so many American states, compromise was necessary to achieve enactment and reforms were hedged. An uncontested no-fault divorce required a two-year separation, while a unilateral no-fault divorce required a five-year separation. Because of the lengthy separation requirements, approximately 70% of divorces in England proceed under fault-based provisions which permit a speedier dissolution of the marriage. D. MARIANNE BLAIR & MERLE H. WEINER, FAMILY LAW IN THE WORLD COMMUNITY 264 (2003). In response to proposals to eliminate fault-based grounds completely from the statutes and to reduce the waiting period to one year, Parliament passed the Family Law Act of 1996, which incorporated such provisions. Yet, controversy surrounding the Act led to delays of implementation, the addition of various amendments designed to save marriages, and several years of "pilot" projects to examine the effects of the law and the amendments. *Id.* at 265–66. Ultimately, the law was repealed in 2001, never having gone into effect nationwide. For further discussion of the struggles over divorce law in 20th century England, see Carol Smart, *Divorce in England 1950–2000: A Moral Tale?*, *in* CROSS CURRENTS: FAMILY LAW AND POLICY IN THE US AND ENGLAND 363 (S.N. Katz, J. Eekelaar & M. MacLean, eds., 2000).

2. *Divorce Reform in Europe.* Mary Ann Glendon noted that "[b]etween 1969 and 1985 divorce law in nearly every Western country was profoundly altered. Among the most dramatic changes was the introduction of civil divorce in the predominantly Catholic countries of Italy and Spain, and its extension to Catholic marriages in Portugal." ABORTION AND DIVORCE IN WESTERN LAW 66 (1987). The particulars of the new laws varied, with some jurisdictions following a path similar to that of California in eliminating fault-based grounds completely, others retaining fault grounds while adding no-fault grounds, and still others regulating divorces fairly restrictively (*e.g.*, by requiring lengthy waiting periods or providing courts with discretion to deny unilateral divorces). *Id.* at 67–69. See Mary Ann Glendon, *The Transformation of Family Law* 159–82 (1989), for an in-depth discussion of French and West German divorce reforms, which occurred at the same time as the transition to no-fault in the United States.

The Scandinavian countries followed a different path, introducing some form of no-fault divorce early in the 1900s. For example, Sweden has permitted divorce on the basis of marital breakdown since 1915, though it further liberalized its law in 1973. Denmark, Finland, and Iceland followed Sweden's lead within a few years thereafter. Glendon, THE TRANSFORMATION OF FAMILY LAW, *supra*, at 182–88.

Marching to a different drummer than every other state in Western Europe, Ireland barred divorce altogether until 1995. For accounts of the debate over varying reform proposals, See MICHELLE DILLON, DEBATING DIVORCE: MORAL CONFLICT IN IRELAND (1993); BLAIR & WEINER, *supra*, at 268–75. In a 1995 referendum, Ireland voted by a narrow margin (0.6%) to lift its constitutional ban on divorce. *Id.* at 270. The new Irish law allows divorce if the couple has lived apart for at least four of the preceding five years, there is no reasonable prospect of reconciliation, and proper provision has been made for the spouses and children. Ireland thus went directly from a bar on divorce to allowing unilateral no-fault divorce with a very long waiting period. *See* Lindsay Abbate, Comment, *What God Has Joined "Let" Man Put Asunder: Ireland's Struggle Between Canon and Common Law Relating to Divorce*, 16 EMORY INT'L L. REV. 583 (2002) (reviews case law under the new divorce law and predicts future of Irish divorce law "and its relationship with the Catholic Church"); Christine P. James, *Cead Mile Failte? Ireland Welcomes Divorce: The 1995 Irish Divorce Referendum and the Family (Divorce) Act of 1996*, 8 DUKE J. COMP. & INT'L L. 175 (1997) (discussing the historical and cultural context of the referendum); Jennifer A. Carter, Note, *Breaking the Bonds and Splitting the Assets: Women and Divorce in Ireland*, 15 B.U. INT'L L.J. 511 (1997) (analyzing the operation of the new divorce laws and their economic consequences for women). For a comprehensive country-by-country analysis of European divorce law, see EUROPEAN FAMILY LAW IN ACTION, Vol. I (GROUNDS FOR DIVORCE) (Katharina Boele-Woelki, Bente Braat & Ian Summer, eds., 2003).

3. *Divorce in Non-European Nations.* For a discussion of divorce laws and reform movements in Asian, African, and Middle Eastern countries, see BLAIR & WEINER, *supra*, at 281–87, 298–306. Chile was the last country in the Americas to establish a divorce procedure. Under the law, which became effective in 2004, a mutual consent divorce requires one year's separation; a unilateral no-fault divorce is available after three years of separation. Jen Ross, *Separate Ways: Divorce to Become Legal*, WASHINGTON POST, Mar. 30, 2004 at C1. Reportedly, before the establishment of divorce, 15% of all marriages in Chile ended in legal separation and another 10% were annulled. *Id.; see also* Robert M. Gordon, *The Limits of Limits on Divorce*, 1007 YALE L.J. 1435 (1998) (citing estimates that "nearly half of all married adults [in Chile] have separated unofficially"). Only a handful of countries in the world, including Malta and the Philippines, now lack a divorce law.

B.   THE MODERN LAW IN ACTION

[1]   Pure No-Fault Systems

MODEL MARRIAGE AND DIVORCE ACT

§ 302. [Dissolution of Marriage; Legal Separation]

(a) The [_____] court shall enter a decree of dissolution of marriage if:

. . . .

    (2) the court finds that the marriage is irretrievably broken, if the finding is supported by evidence that (i) the parties have lived separate and apart for a period of more than 180 days next preceding the commencement of the proceeding, or (ii) there is serious marital discord adversely affecting the attitude of one or both of the parties toward the marriage;

    (3) the court finds that the conciliation provisions of Section 305 either do not apply or have been met;

    (4) to the extent it has jurisdiction to do so, the court has considered, approved, or provided for child custody, the support of any child entitled to support, the maintenance of either spouse, and the disposition of property; or has provided for a separate later hearing to complete these matters.

(b) If a party requests a decree of legal separation rather than a decree of dissolution of marriage, the court shall grant the decree in that form unless the other party objects.

§ 305. [Irretrievable Breakdown]

(a) If both of the parties by petition or otherwise have stated under oath or affirmation that the marriage is irretrievably broken, or one of the parties has so stated and the other has not denied it, the court, after hearing, shall make a finding whether the marriage is irretrievably broken.

(b) If one of the parties has denied under oath or affirmation that the marriage is irretrievably broken, the court shall consider all relevant factors, including the circumstances that gave rise to filing the petition and the prospect of reconciliation, and shall:

(1) make a finding whether the marriage is irretrievably broken; or

(2) continue the matter for further hearing not fewer than 30 nor more than 60 days later, or as soon thereafter as the matter may be reached on the court's calendar, and may suggest to the parties that they seek counseling. The court, at the request of either party shall, or on its own motion may, order a conciliation conference. At the adjourned hearing the court shall make a finding whether the marriage is irretrievably broken.

(c) A finding of irretrievable breakdown is a determination that there is no reasonable prospect of reconciliation.

NOTES

1. *No-Fault Statutes in the U.S.* The MMDA, a product of the compromise between the Uniform Laws Commissioners and the ABA Family Law Section, described above, authorizes a court to find a marriage "irretrievably broken" if the parties have lived apart for 180 days. But even this half-year waiting period may be avoided if the court finds "serious marital discord adversely affecting the attitude of one or both of the parties toward the marriage." A party thus need not wait at all if he or she can show that the marriage is no longer viable, without regard to *why* it isn't or whose "fault" the lack of viability is. The Model Act is thus a "pure" no-fault statute, because it makes dissolution available to either party by a "no-fault" showing of marital failure. The parallel provision of the pioneering California law which inspired the MMDA requires a court finding of "irreconcilable differences," a formulation which some other states have also chosen.

By 1985 every state in the nation had added a no-fault provision to its divorce statutes. Some states, like California, repealed the fault-based grounds and thus, like the MMDA, may be characterized as pure no-fault systems, while other jurisdictions added no-fault grounds to the existing statutes. In these latter jurisdictions with "limited" no-fault systems, one or more no-fault grounds exist together with fault grounds. Section B.2, *infra*, examines some of the issues involved in resolution of cases in limited no-fault jurisdictions.

A 1987 survey found sixteen states with pure no-fault laws: Arizona, California, Colorado, Delaware, Florida, Hawaii, Iowa, Kentucky, Michigan, Minnesota, Montana, Nebraska, Oregon, Washington, Wisconsin and Wyoming. Herma Hill Kay, *Equality and Difference: A Perspective on No-Fault Divorce and Its Aftermath*, 56 U. CIN. L. REV. 1, 5–6 (1987) (hereinafter "Kay, *Equality and Difference*"). Only slight changes occurred with respect to this category in the next fifteen years. Most notably, the District of Columbia's fault-based grounds were repealed, moving the District from the limited no-fault to pure no-fault group. D.C.

CODE § 16-904. One pure no-fault state, Arizona, adopted "covenant marriage" as an optional alternative to standard marriage, which reintroduces fault-based divorce provisions. ARIZ. REV. ST. § 25-901 *et seq.* (See discussion of covenant marriage, *infra*, at Section C[3].) The remaining thirty-five states simply added a modern no-fault ground to their traditional fault grounds.

No-fault provisions, whether in pure or limited no-fault jurisdictions, can be grouped into two categories: (1) descriptive standards and (2) objective rules. The descriptive standards, adopted by over two-thirds of the states, require a finding that the marriage is "irretrievably" broken (e.g., GA. CODE ANN. § 19-5-3(13)); or that the spouses' relationship is characterized by "incompatibility" *(e.g.*, 43 OKLA. ST. § 101 (7)), "insupportability" (e.g., TEX. FAM. CODE § 6.001), or by "irreconcilable differences" (e.g., S.D. CODIFIED LAWS § 25-4-2(7)). The MMDA's influence is apparent; most states taking this approach adopt its terminology of irretrievable or irremediable breakdown. Like the MMDA, most states do not provide that irretrievable breakdown is automatically demonstrated by the proof of certain facts. Theoretically, under both the MMDA and the ordinary descriptive standard the proof of facts such as separation for 180 days or "marital discord," in the language of the MMDA, would constitute probative evidence that the marriage is "irretrievably" broken or the parties are "incompatible", but determination of whether the standard has been met remain theoretically in the hands of the trial court judge (*but see* Note 4, *infra*).

The "objective rules" provisions grant divorces upon a finding that the couple has lived "separate and apart" for a specified period of time. There is substantial variability in the length of separation required, ranging from six months in Vermont, 15 VT. ST. ANN. § 551, and Montana, MT. CODE ANN. § 40-4-104(1), to three years in Rhode Island, R.I. GEN. LAWS § 15-5-3(a), and Utah, UTAH CODE ANN. § 30-3-1-(3)(j). Other states require periods of one year, eighteen months, or two years. A handful of states, such as Hawaii and Texas, offer alternative no-fault grounds of marital breakdown and a period of separation. *See, e.g.*, HAW. REV. STAT. § 580-41 (permitting a decree of divorce upon a finding of either irretrievable breakdown or two year's separation); TEX. FAM. CODE §§ 6.001, 6.006 (permitting divorce upon finding that marriage is insupportable or a three years of separation without cohabitation). Many laws in this last group actually predated the California no-fault reform, although some of these states shortened their required periods of separation after the reform movement took hold. Despite the apparent no-fault divorce "revolution," much of the old divorce law remains remarkably intact in some states. This is especially true in states in which the only no-fault ground is a lengthy separation period. Depending upon the parties' situations, in such states proceeding on fault grounds may be preferable for to waiting several years.

2. *Can a No-Fault Petition Be Resisted Successfully?* An early California no-fault case suggested courts might require a meaningful showing that there were, indeed, irreconcilable differences between the parties. In *McKim v. McKim*, 493 P.2d 868, 890, n.3 (1972), the wife-petitioner did not personally appear. The husband filed no responsive pleading to the wife's petition, but appeared at the hearing as her witness:

Q. Mr. McKim, you are the respondent in this case; is that correct? A. Right.

Q. At the time the petition in this matter was filed, was it your belief that there were irreconcilable differences between you and your wife? A. Right.

Q. Since that time, have you and your wife attempted to resolve these differences? A. Yes.

Q. In fact, you reconciled for a period of time; is that correct? A. Yes.

Q. That reconciliation did not work out? A. No.

Q. Is it your opinion that at the present time there are irreconcilable differences? A. Right.

Q. Is it your opinion that any further waiting period or conciliation would assist in saving this marriage? A. No.

Q. As far as you are concerned, there is no longer a marriage? A. No.

Although this *pro forma* showing of "breakdown" has since become typical (albeit usually with the testimony coming from the petitioner, not the respondent), in 1972 the California Supreme Court did not accept it. It affirmed the trial court's refusal to grant the divorce:

> [T]he wife urges that collusion precluding the granting of a judgment of dissolution cannot exist [in no-fault divorce] because any agreement by the spouses that their marriage should be dissolved establishes . . . the breakdown of their marriage.
>
> . . . [A] traditional justification of the collusion doctrine . . . is the state's interest in preserving the institution of marriage. . . . Under the Family Law Act the court, not the parties, must decide whether the evidence adduced supports findings that irreconcilable differences do exist and that the marriage has broken down irremediably and should be dissolved.

Id. at 872.

But it soon became clear that courts would not probe into the facts of the parties' relationship. *McKim* is probably the last case in California denying an unopposed dissolution petition. *See* Elayne Carol Berg, Note, *Irreconcilable Differences: California Courts Respond to No Fault Dissolutions*, 7 Loy. L.A. L. Rev. 453 (1974). "No fault" divorce thus quickly became the vehicle for acceptance of divorce by mutual consent. Iowa adopted a no-fault law soon after California, and a 1973 study found dissolution hearings in uncontested cases averaged 15 to 20 minutes. Stephen L. Sass, *The Iowa No Fault Dissolution of Marriage Law in Action*, 18 S.D. L. Rev. 629, 650 (1973). Similar results were reported by a 1978 study of Nebraska's no-fault law. Alan H. Frank, et al., *No Fault Divorce and the Divorce Rate: The Nebraska Experience — An Interrupted Time Series Analysis and Commentary*, 58 Neb. L. Rev. 1, 61–65 (1978). An Iowa Supreme Court decision proved a better signal than *McKim* of how no-fault laws would be implemented, including in California:

The requirement for corroboration is almost repugnant to the concept of "no-fault" dissolution of marriage. . . . Corroborative evidence is required mainly to prevent collusion between the parties. . . . In truth, if it were demonstrated that the parties were in collusion to bring about a termination of the marriage . . . , it would . . . evidence the fact of the marriage breakdown.

In re Marriage of Collins, 200 N.W.2d 886, 890 (Iowa 1972); *see also McCoy v. McCoy*, 642 S.E.2d 18 (Ga. 2007) (fact that parties cohabited and had sexual relations after final hearing but before entry of decree was not grounds to vacate no-fault divorce decree finding irretrievable breakdown).

3. *Summary Proceedings.* In fact, California and other states soon adopted summary dissolution procedures designed to achieve a convenient divorce by mutual consent — precisely the goal thwarted by *McKim.* Summary dispositions typically dispense with a hearing altogether. They are usually available only for childless marriages, or those with no minor children, and require as well that the parties submit affidavits or other sworn statements demonstrating agreement upon the disposition of any marital property and waiver of any claim for support. California additionally sets a ceiling on the marital assets which a couple seeking a summary dissolution may have. CAL. FAM. CODE § 2400 *et seq.* Washington and Colorado allow summary dissolutions even if minor children are involved. WASH. REV. CODE ANN. § 26.09.030; COLO. REV. STAT. ANN. § 14-10-120.3. For other summary dissolution procedures, see CONN. GEN. STAT. ANN. § 46b-51(a); FLA. FAM. L.R. PROC. § 12.105; HAW. REV. STAT. § 580-42; 750 ILL. COMP. STAT. ANN. § 5/451 *et seq.*; IND. CODE ANN. § 31-15-2-13; MINN. STAT. § 518.195; MONT. CODE ANN. § 40-4-130; NEV. REV. STAT. ANN. § 125.181; OR. REV. STAT. § 107.485.

4. *Unilateral Divorce.* Studies in California, Iowa, and Nebraska revealed no-fault opponents were correct in forecasting that these reforms would ultimately permit unilateral divorce. Berg, *supra* (California); Sass, *supra* (Iowa); Frank, et al., *supra* (Nebraska). In Iowa, petitions were granted in each of 211 contested divorce cases. The Nebraska "survey of 10,000 dissolution cases failed to reveal a single instance in which it could be said with certainty that a divorce which was desired by even one of the spouses was ultimately refused." Frank, et al., *supra*, at 66–67. As the Nebraska investigators observed:

it is difficult to imagine what evidence a respondent spouse could introduce to counter the impressive demonstration of marital breakdown . . . exhibited when one of the parties . . . steadfastly insists that the relationship has come to an end. The strained and hostile atmosphere and the ugly courtroom confrontation that would attend a contest over whether marital breakdown has occurred would only further evidence the fact that it had.

Very few state laws recognize this reality officially. Washington is an exception. If one party denies that the marriage is irretrievably broken, "the court shall consider all relevant factors, including the circumstances that gave rise to the filing of the petition and the prospects for reconciliation and shall" either "make a finding that the marriage is irretrievably broken and enter a decree of dissolution" or order counseling in the hopes of inspiring reconciliation. If such a request is granted, the court must still order the dissolution within 60 days if the parties are not reconciled and "either party continues to allege that the marriage is irretrievably broken." WASH. REV. CODE ANN. § 26.09.030. But while Washington's official recognition of unilateral divorce may be rare, few disagree that unilateral divorce is, in practice, the rule in most jurisdictions. Thus, there remains a dual law of divorce, but the nature of the duality has changed. Today, while the law in the books does not recognize unilateral divorce, in most states the law in action does.

5. *Requiring Counseling as Part of the Divorce Process.* California never adopted the elaborate proposal for "family courts" that the Governor's Commission originally recommended, but more modest versions of the same idea were enacted in many states, often under the label of "conciliation courts." The Commission's recommendation reflects the hope that some divorces could be avoided by equipping domestic relations courts with marriage counselors and empowering domestic relations judges to order counseling. Yet, data were discouraging with respect to the effectiveness of conciliations courts. Frank, et al., *supra*, at 82–90. The recent trend has been to shift from marriage counseling to divorce counseling. The goal is not to preserve the marriage, but rather to assist the divorcing couple in reaching a divorce settlement, and (for those with minor children) working out a post-decree relationship supportive of the child's needs.

6. *Constitutional Right of Access to Divorce and to Block the Effect of No-Fault Reforms.* It is not clear whether the Constitution protects a fundamental right to divorce. In *Boddie v. Connecticut*, 401 U.S. 371 (1971), the Supreme Court struck down the application of filing fee requirements to indigent divorce petitioners. It held the state could not constitutionally deny indigents access to the only legally available means for terminating their marriage. In *United States v. Kras*, 409 U.S. 434 (1973), the Court distinguished *Boddie* in holding that filing fees could be imposed on indigents seeking bankruptcy. The only way to reconcile the cases is by attaching a special constitutional significance to divorce, although *Kras* conceded only that *Boddie* relied in part on "the marital relationship and the associated interests that surround it." *Id.* at 444. Yet, in *Sosna v. Iowa*, 419 U.S. 393 (1975), the Court applied only a rational basis test in rejecting a challenge to a durational residency requirement imposed on divorce petitioners. Several years later, in 1978, the Court, in *Zablocki v. Redhail* (reprinted in Chapter 2, Section A[2][a]), found a fundamental right to marry. Does this right to marry necessarily implicate a right to divorce, because impediments to divorce burden the right to remarry? Perhaps if the Court decided *Zablocki* first, *Sosna* might have arrived at a different result.

Some no-fault opponents have claimed unsuccessfully that certain no-fault divorce policies are unconstitutional. *See, e.g., Waite v. Waite*, 64 S.W.3d 217 (Tex. App. 2001) (no-fault does not violate Federal Establishment or Free Exercise Clauses or various state constitutional provisions); *Richter v. Richter*, 625 N.W.2d 490 (Minn. App. 2001) (marriage is not a "contract" within meaning of Contracts Clause of state or federal constitutions).

[2] Limited No-Fault Systems

MISSOURI ANNOTATED STATUTES

§ 452.320. Finding that marriage is irretrievably broken, when — notice — denial by a party, effect of — alternate findings

1. If both of the parties by petition or otherwise have stated under oath or affirmation that the marriage is irretrievably broken, or one of the parties has so stated and the other has not denied it, the court, after considering the aforesaid petition or statement, and after a hearing thereon shall make a finding whether or not the marriage is irretrievably broken and shall enter an order of dissolution or dismissal accordingly.

2. If one of the parties has denied under oath or affirmation that the marriage is irretrievably broken, the court shall consider all relevant factors, including the circumstances that gave rise to the filing of the petition and the prospect of reconciliation, and after hearing the evidence shall

(1) Make a finding whether or not the marriage is irretrievably broken, and in order for the court to find that the marriage is irretrievably broken, the petitioner shall satisfy the court of one or more of the following facts:

(a) That the respondent has committed adultery and the petitioner finds it intolerable to live with the respondent;

(b) That the respondent has behaved in such a way that the petitioner cannot reasonably be expected to live with the respondent;

(c) That the respondent has abandoned the petitioner for a continuous period of at least six months preceding the presentation of the petition;

(d) That the parties to the marriage have lived separate and apart by mutual consent for a continuous period of twelve months immediately preceding the filing of the petition;

(e) That the parties to the marriage have lived separate and apart for a continuous period of at least twenty-four months preceding the filing of the petition; or

(2) Continue the matter for further hearing not less than thirty days or more than six months later, or as soon thereafter as the matter may be reached on the court's calendar, and may suggest to the parties that they seek counseling. No court shall require counseling as a condition precedent to a decree, nor shall any employee of any court, or of the state or any political subdivision of the state, be utilized as a marriage counselor. At the adjourned hearing, the court shall make a finding whether the marriage is irretrievably broken as set forth in subdivision (1) above and shall enter an order of dissolution or dismissal accordingly.

KOON v. KOON
Missouri Court of Appeals
969 S.W.2d 828 (1998)

SHRUM, JUDGE

This case concerns two appeals arising from the dissolution of the marriage of Mary Elizabeth Koon (Wife) and Merle Richard Koon (Husband). . . . Husband's claim that the trial court erred in finding irretrievable breakdown of the marriage has merit; consequently, we must reverse this judgment.

. . . .

Husband and Wife were married August 1, 1970. Four children were born of the marriage. At the time of trial, two children, ages 13 and 10, remained unemancipated.

[Wife's divorce petition alleged that the couple "separated on March 19, 1996" and that ". . . [Husband] has behaved during the marriage in such a way that [Wife] cannot reasonably be expected to live with him."]

. . . .

At trial, Wife testified that Husband tried to control everything she did and that they often argued over how and where money should be spent. She told the court that Husband "fought [her] most of the way" as she pursued a college education. Wife also recounted that while Husband was working on a job in Virginia for fifteen months she was much happier without Husband around. In Wife's opinion, there was no hope for reconciliation with Husband. Contrarily, Husband testified that he did not believe the marriage was irretrievably broken and that he did not want the court to dissolve the marriage.

In rendering judgment, the trial court found that the parties' marriage was irretrievably broken; yet, the court also specifically stated it did "*not* find that [Husband] has behaved in such a way that [Wife] could not reasonably be expected to live with him." [The trial court terminated the marriage and provided for custody, child support and marital property.]

Husband . . . challenges the trial court's finding that the marriage . . . was irretrievably broken. Husband contends Wife did not prove irretrievable breakdown because the [court] declined to find that husband behaved during the marriage in such a way that Wife could not reasonably be expected to live with him.

Because Husband . . . testified under affirmation that he did not believe the marriage was irretrievably broken, § 452.320.2(1) is implicated. Specifically, when one party alleges under oath that a marriage is not irretrievably broken, a trial court is required . . . to find whether the marriage is irretrievably broken. . . . "[T]here must be factual support found in one or more of the five factors [enumerated in 425.320.2(1)(a)–(e)] when one party denies the marriage is irretrievably broken." A trial court's finding that a marriage is irretrievably broken must be supported by substantial evidence. . . .

Attempting to meet her burden to establish irretrievable breakdown, Wife . . . adduced evidence that Husband's behavior was such that she could not reasonably be expected to live with him. Yet, the trial court [held] it did *"not find"* such behavior by Husband. . . . Wife has not challenged this finding and, therefore, any question about its correctness is not before this court. Thus, § 425.315.2(1)(b) was eliminated as a basis for finding irretrievable breakdown.

Mindful that we are to affirm a dissolution decree if the result was correct on any tenable basis, we examine the record to see if one or more of the other four fact situations exist that will support the trial court's finding of irretrievable breakdown.

First, there is no evidence in the record that Husband committed adultery. Thus, § 452.320.2(1)(a) is not implicated.

Second, there is no evidence that Husband abandoned Wife for a period of six months or more before the petition was filed. . . . Here, Husband spent fifteen months in Virginia just before Wife filed for dissolution, yet the evidence at trial did not establish that this separation amounted to an abandonment of Wife. Significantly, Wife never pled abandonment, nor did she offer evidence to support such a finding. To the contrary, Wife herself testified Husband went to Virginia with the intention of working there three months, but ended up working fifteen months. Husband extended his stay in Virginia because work was available and his wages were much greater than Husband had ever earned. Husband immediately returned to Missouri "with all of his stuff" once he learned of Wife's intent to file for dissolution.

The actions of Husband and Wife belie a finding of abandonment. There is simply no evidence that Husband was in Virginia "without good cause" or that he was a "deserter." Consequently, § 452.320.2(1)(c) cannot be the basis for the trial court's finding of irretrievable breakdown.

Third, we consider whether Husband's absence from Wife while working in Virginia constituted living separate and apart by mutual consent as contemplated by § 452.320.2(1)(d). . . . *Uhls* . . . indicates that the phrase "separate and apart" . . . "means separate lives." Wife's pleadings and evidence preclude any finding of "separate lives" or that all interaction between Husband and her ceased once he went to work in Virginia.

Specifically, Wife pled that she and Husband separated March 19, 1996, just ten days before she filed her initial petition. At trial, Wife testified that she and Husband separated "on March 19th of 1996." The trial court stated in its judgment that Husband and Wife separated on March 19, 1996, and Wife has not challenged that finding on appeal.

The only reasonable inference that can be drawn from this record is that Husband's job in Virginia was only provisional or temporary and neither party perceived himself or herself as living "separate lives" until March 1996. Since there is no evidence that the parties' arrangement while Husband worked in Virginia was truly one of living separate and apart by mutual agreement, § 452.320.2(1)(d) is not a basis for the trial court's finding of irretrievable breakdown.

Finally, the twenty-four month separation requirement of § 452.320.2(1)(e) cannot be the basis for the trial court's finding of irretrievable breakdown. . . .

. . . . We hold that the record does not provide substantial evidence that the marriage of the parties was irretrievably broken under § 452.320.2(1)(a,c,d,e) and that the decree of the trial court was against the weight of the evidence.

. . . [W]e do not ignore Wife's arguments against Husband's first point. . . . First, Wife cites us to *Burns v. Burns*, 872 S.W.2d 628 (Mo.App. 1994) [where] husband denied his marriage was irretrievably broken and the wife conceded that "there was no evidence to support a finding of any of the circumstances set forth in [§ 452.320.2(1)]."

. . . [¶] *Burns* is not authority for the proposition that we must affirm a judgment that is unsupported by competent evidence where Husband did not in his pleadings request the only other relief possible, i.e., a continuance. At most, *Burns* might support a reversal and remand of the case for [a continuance]. Yet, we have already found that Wife could not prove the circumstances in § 452.320.2(1)(c-e) at any subsequent hearing because they contain time frames that are based on the date of the filing of the petition.

Moreover, the facts in *Burns* distinguish it from this case. Here, Wife never conceded a lack of evidence to support her claim. She pled and adduced evidence that Husband had behaved in such a way that she could not reasonably be expected to live with him. Yet, the trial court apparently disbelieved that part of Wife's testimony, as it was entitled to do.

. . . .

. . . . Contrary to Wife's argument, no irreconcilable conflict exists between the trial court's finding that Husband's behavior was not the cause of the marriage breakdown and the judgment that the marriage was irretrievably broken. Under § 452.320.2(1), four additional, specific, and individual grounds were available to the court for finding irretrievable breakdown, *provided* there was competent evidence to support one or more of them. Apparently, the trial court disbelieved Wife's evidence about Husband's conduct but dissolved the marriage based on one or more of the other four grounds. [While] [t]he trial court did not have to state why it concluded that the marriage was irretrievably broken . . . , the trial court's finding . . . had to be supported by substantial evidence. Having concluded that there was no evidence to support a finding of any of the other circumstances set forth in the statute, the judgment must be reversed. . . . [3]

The judgment of the trial court is reversed.

---

[3] The comments of *In re Marriage of Mitchell*, 545 S.W.2d 313 (Mo.App. 1976) are apropos here:

This marriage may well be beyond saving, and in holding as we do that there is not sufficient evidence in this record to support the finding of the trial court that this marriage is irretrievably broken within the terms of § 452.320.2(1) we are but delaying the inevitable; nevertheless, we as an appellate court, construe and apply the law, we do not make it.

NOTES

1. *The Missouri Statute.* The Missouri statute provides that where defendant contests the assertion of an irretrievably broken marriage, the court can grant the divorce only if one of five grounds are proven. The first three are traditional fault grounds and the latter two are no-fault grounds requiring either a year of separation by mutual consent or two years of separation without mutual consent. As the Missouri Court of Appeals in *In re Mitchell*, cited in fn. 3 by *Koon*, wrote:

> Unlike other states which have adopted the "no fault" concept of divorce reform laws . . . Missouri clearly did not enact a total "no fault" dissolution law. Rather, our General Assembly adopted a "modified no fault" dissolution law. In those jurisdictions where the true "no fault" dissolution law is in effect all that needs to be shown to authorize the entry of a decree of dissolution is that the marriage is "irretrievably broken." In most "no fault" laws the term "irretrievably broken" is left undefined and no definitive standards or guidelines are given to control the dissolution process and consideration is given to each case individually. . . .
>
> However, . . . the Missouri General Assembly . . . intended that a spouse, who by his or her actions makes the life of the other spouse intolerable or whose behavior makes it unreasonable for the marriage to be expected to continue, should not profit by his or her own wrongdoing and thereby obtain a dissolution of the marriage over the objection of the other perhaps innocent spouse. This intention is evidenced, we think, by the establishment of guidelines within the Law itself for trial courts . . .

545 S.W.2d 313, 318–19 (Mo. Ct. App. 1976).

In *Mitchell*, the facts showed a deteriorating marriage which included a separation, arguments, marriage counseling, an adulterous relationship during the separation, and a statement by plaintiff that he could no longer live in this marriage. The court found, however, that none of the three fault grounds had been proven and the separation of the parties was not long enough to qualify under the fifth ground. Five months after the case was decided, the husband again filed for dissolution, claiming 24 months of separation. When the trial court granted the husband's decree, the wife again appealed, contending that in reckoning the period of separation, the trial court should not have counted the portion of their separation which had occurred before the previous appellate decision. The court rejected this claim and ordered the dissolution. 581 S.W.2d 442 (Mo. Ct. App. 1978).

2. *Other Interpretations of Missouri Statute.* Contrast *Mitchell* and *Koon* with another Missouri opinion interpreting the same statute. In *Gummels v. Gummels*, 561 S.W.2d 442 (Mo. Ct. App. 1978), in rejecting defendant's arguments that the marriage was not "irretrievably broken," the court wrote:

> Defendant . . . appeals, contending only that . . . the evidence did not warrant a finding . . . that he had behaved in such a way that his wife cannot reasonably be expected to live with him. . . .

Defendant's only cited case on the merits is . . . *Mitchell.* There, . . . the plaintiff . . . 's sole reason for his inability to live with his wife . . . was his bald statement he no longer loved her. That case is distinguishable.

Here, there was evidence of the parties' deteriorating relationship and the waning of their affections for several years. . . . She testified that only she disciplined their two children; that defendant usually consoled them and would not "back her up." Plaintiff also testified she and defendant were "unable to communicate"; that they could not "iron out our differences"; they couldn't live together, and she "needed some peace of mind." Plaintiff testified . . . she no longer loved him and believed there was no likelihood the marriage could be preserved.

. . .

. . . [W]e find no reversible error in the court's conclusion that there remains no reasonable likelihood the marriage can be preserved and is irretrievably broken.

Id. at 443–44.

A perusal of Missouri cases suggests that *Gummels* presents a more accurate picture of how Missouri's law usually works in practice than in *Koon* and *Mitchell.* But the spirit of *Koon* and *Mitchell* can still be seen in some cases. *Compare Nieters v. Nieters*, 815 S.W.2d 124 (Mo. App. 1991) (adulterous husband denied divorce over wife's opposition where the evidence in support of marital breakdown was husband's testimony that parties were sometimes "unable to get along," disagreed on financial and child-raising matters and were sometimes mutually violent; court held this did not establish he could not reasonably be expected to live with wife; court concedes it is "but delaying the inevitable" but is bound by statute), *with Welsh v. Welsh*, 869 S.W.2d 802 (Mo. App. 1994) (deferring to trial court's judgment that wife could not reasonably be expected to live with husband where she believed he was "not compassionate or considerate" and testified to several specific incidents, contested by him, to support that conclusion).

3. *What Is "Living Apart"?* For statutes requiring lengthy periods of *de facto* separation to establish no-fault divorce eligibility, questions can arise as to what constitutes "living apart." Missouri and Illinois courts have held, for example, that parties have "lived apart" under these statutes even though they lived in the same home, where they did not share a bedroom, did not communicate with each other and in general led "separate lives." *In re Marriage of Kenik*, 536 N.E.2d 982 (Ill. App. Ct. 1989); *In re Marriage of Uhls*, 549 S.W.2d 107 (Mo. Ct. App. 1977) (cited in *Koon*). A North Carolina court held a couple had not begun living apart when the husband had taken a job in Boston, so long as he flew home to North Carolina for the holidays and a public posture of an intact marriage was maintained. *Hall v. Hall*, 363 S.E.2d 189 (N.C. Ct. App. 1987).

4. *Requiring Mutual Consent.* A few states go beyond requiring long waiting periods for unilateral divorce: they bar it altogether. New York, among the most reluctant converts to no-fault, recognizes only one ground for a no-fault divorce: living apart for the requisite period of time. But in New York (unlike Missouri and most other limited no-fault states), "living apart" requires proof of either a written

separation agreement (and thus mutual consent) or a judgment of legal separation, N.Y. Dom. Rel. Law § 170. Legal separation in turn can be obtained only on fault grounds, N.Y. Dom. Rel. L. § 200. Thus, in New York, a spouse who cannot be shown "at fault" can effectively block a divorce by refusing to enter into a written separation agreement. In a 1996 report, a task force appointed by the New York State Bar to review the state's family law statutes recommended repeal of the restrictive rules and adoption of unilateral no-fault divorce. Ira M. Ellman & Sharon Lohr, *Marriage as Contract, Opportunist Violence, and Other Bad Arguments for Fault Divorce*, 1997 U. Ill. L. Rev. 719, 723 n.8. A commission appointed by the Chief Judge of the state's Court of Appeals recommended a move to no-fault divorce in early 2006, but no reform has occurred. *See* Danny Hakim, *Panel Asks New York to Join the Era of No-Fault Divorce*, N.Y. Times, Feb. 7, 2006, at 1; Gabriella L. Zborovsky, Note, *Baby Steps to "Grown-Up" Divorce: The Introduction of the Collaborative Family Law Center and the Continued Need for True No-Fault Divorce in New York*, 10 Cardozo J. Confl. Resol. 305 (2008); J. Herbie DiFonzo & Ruth Stern, *Addicted to Fault: Why Divorce Reform Has Lagged in New York*, 27 Pace L. Rev. 559 (2007) ("achieving true no-fault divorce . . . is dependent on further reform of divorce finances, particularly a more equitable determination of spousal maintenance").

Mississippi and Tennessee follow a similar approach, although in those states the no-fault ground requiring agreement by the parties is "irreconcilable differences." Miss. Code Ann. §§ 93-5-1, 93-5-2; Tenn. Stat. Ann. §§ 36-4-101 (14), 36-4-103(b). Rules that require mutual consent as the only alternative to proof of fault are subject to the same concerns raised with respect to long waiting periods for unilateral divorce. For discussion of these problems, see the excerpt of Professor Ellman's article, at Section C[3], *infra*.

5. *Continued Use of Fault Grounds.*   There are several reasons why a spouse might claim fault grounds in a state that provides both fault and no-fault divorce: (1) A fault ground might not be subject to a lengthy delay imposed by a particular state's no-fault grounds and, thus, be chosen by a couple who had reached an agreement to divorce; (2) Where there is no settlement, a fault divorce may provide one party an advantage in settling the divorce's financial aspects. In about half the states marital misconduct can be considered in deciding upon alimony awards, and a smaller group allows its consideration in allocating marital property. *See* Chapter 4. In some such states, only a spouse who obtains a fault divorce can introduce fault on such issues. Thus, even today some cases read like classic fault-based litigation. *See, e.g., In re Guy*, 969 A.2d 373 (N.H. 2009) (plaintiff's discovery of "sexually suggestive" emails from defendant to a lover insufficient to prove defendant had behaved "so seriously as to injure. . . . health or endanger . . . reason"); *Bacon v. Bacon*, 351 S.E.2d 37 (Va.. Ct. App. 1986) (decree based on one year's separation reversed because trial court must consider wife's claim for divorce based on husband's desertion, since such grounds may be relevant in determining alimony); *Hughes v. Hughes*, 531 S.E.2d 645 (Va. App. 2000) (trial judge erred in granting divorce on adultery grounds because wife's cohabitation in same home with the man she intended to marry was insufficient proof of adultery, given their separate bedrooms; even "highly suspicious circumstances" are insufficient as proof of adultery; remand to consider divorce on grounds of one year's separation).

In the few states that bar unilateral no-fault divorce, such as Tennessee and Mississippi, there is an incentive to assert fault grounds. *See, e.g., Simpson v. Simpson,* 716 S.W.2d 27 (Tenn. 1986) (considering whether insanity is a defense to fault divorce based on cruel and inhumane treatment); *Earls v. Earls,* 42 S.W.2d 877 (Tenn. Ct. App. 2000) (reversing trial court's refusal to grant divorce on "inappropriate marital conduct" grounds). In *Morris v. Morris,* 783 So. 2d 681 (Miss. 2001), the court affirmed a grant of divorce for reasons of "habitual cruel and inhuman treatment" based on an open relationship between defendant and a same-sex partner. *See also Bowen v. Bowen,* 688 So. 2d 1374 (Miss. 1997) (divorce denied to both parties because neither had made sufficient showing of "habitual cruel and inhuman treatment," despite testimony from couple's children concerning couple's physical altercations); *Harmon v. Harmon,* 757 So.2d 305 (Miss. App. 2000) (neither condonation or recrimination defenses barred wife's divorce action grounded on husband's adultery). For recent commentary defending the co-existence of fault and no-fault divorce, see Karen Boyd, *The Tale of Two Systems: How Integrated Divorce Can Remedy the Unintended Effects of Pure No-Fault Divorce,* 12 Cardozo J.L. & Gender 609 (2006); Peter Swisher, *Marriage and Some Troubling Issues with No-Fault Divorce,* 17 Regent U. L. Rev. 243 (2004).

6. *The Perceptions of Parties in Limited No-Fault Jurisdictions.* English law is similar to Missouri's in its combination of fault and no-fault grounds for divorce. A study concluded that this version of no-fault divorce did not succeed in shifting the parties' perception of the divorce process from one based on a "fault" principle to one based on a no-fault "breakdown" principle.

> The law tells the parties, on one hand, that the sole ground for divorce is irretrievable breakdown, and on the other hand, that unless they are able to wait for at least two years after separation, a divorce can only be obtained by proving fault. Not surprisingly, the subtlety that the facts are not ground for divorce, but merely evidence of breakdown, is seldom grasped.

British Law Commission, *Facing the Future: A Discussion Paper on the Ground for Divorce,* 17 Law Com. 170 (1988). Another British study found presentation of evidence to demonstrate fault "facts" generates the same kind of hostility that prior fault-based regimes produced, and which the no-fault reforms were supposed to lessen. G. Davis & M. Murch, Grounds for Divorce (1988). A 1996 English statute eliminated fault entirely from the divorce process while requiring a 12-month procedure (18 months if the parties had a child under 17) to finalize a divorce. A pilot project using the procedures under the new law indicated less than 10% of the litigants attending "marriage-support" meetings required by the act believed, after the session, that divorce was then less likely. The Government then decided not to implement the new law, thus restoring the pre-reform rule requiring a two-year wait for a no-fault divorce. *See* N.V. Lowe & G. Douglas, Bromley's Family Law 287–301 (10th ed. 2007) (discussing the 1996 legislation and the pilot projects).

C.   REPRISE: RE-EVALUATING NO-FAULT, FAULT, AND THE LAW'S ROLE IN PROMOTING MARITAL STABILITY

In the past 15 years, critics have argued that no-fault divorce reforms need to be modified. Two basic arguments are offered to support this critique. The first is that no-fault divorce (especially the unilateral version) has made divorce too easy and therefore increased the number of divorces. The increased divorce rate is bad, the argument continues, because the children of divorced parents are harmed by their parents' separation, and because it undermines an important social norm, that marriage is a life-long commitment. *See, e.g.*, Linda J. Waite & Maggie Gallagher, THE CASE FOR MARRIAGE: WHY MARRIED PEOPLE ARE HAPPIER, HEALTHIER AND BETTER OFF FINANCIALLY 195–99 (2000); Elizabeth Scott, *Social Norms and the Legal Regulation of Marriage*, 86 VA. L. REV. 1901 (2000). The norm is important, even apart from the harm divorce causes to individual children and their parents, because, the argument goes, marriage is a core building block of our society. *See* Kay, *From Second Sex to Joint Venture, supra*, at 2068–69 (citing White House Working Group on the Family, THE FAMILY: PRESERVING AMERICA'S FUTURE 6 (1986)). In Section C.1, *infra*, we consider the data and alternative interpretive arguments surrounding the relationship between no-fault divorce and the divorce rate. Section C.2 examines relevant social science evidence and some conclusions suggested by recent studies on the effects of divorce on children. This discussion continues in Chapter 6.

The second argument against no-fault divorce claims that allowing either spouse to decide unilaterally to end the marriage increases the likelihood of injustice. Yet, the precise nature and extent of the gender discrepancies is the subject of significant debate. *See* Note on Debate Over Differences in the Financial Impact of Divorce on Men and Women, *infra* at Chapter 4, Section D[1]. At this point, it is enough to note that most scholars have concluded that, to the extent that divorce impoverishes women and children after divorce, this is caused by current legal policies governing characterization and distribution of marital property and post-dissolution spousal and child support, not the no-fault divorce laws. *See, e.g.*, AMERICAN LAW INSTITUTE, PRINCIPLES OF THE LAW OF FAMILY DISSOLUTION: ANALYSIS AND RECOMMENDATIONS (2000) (proposing reforms of property distribution and support provisions in divorce law); DIVORCE REFORM AT THE CROSSROADS (Stephen D. Sugarman & Herma Hill Kay, eds., 1990) (reviewing, with several essays, alternative approaches to improving economic well-being of women and children following divorce). Chapter 4 examines this subject in greater depth.

Proceeding from these goals of reducing the divorce rate and making the process of divorce fairer to women and children, commentators in the past 10–15 years have offered a series of proposals to "reform the reform." Most, if not all, of these proposals seek at least a partial return to a fault regime. These proposals are discussed and evaluated in Section C[3], *infra*.

[1]   The Data on Marriage and Divorce Rates

[a]   What Are the Trends?

There is more than one way to calculate divorce rates. The best measure is the number of divorces per 1,000 existing marriages. Figure 1-5 reports annual measures of these statistics, and reflects "the particular social and economic conditions of each year." ANDREW CHERLIN, MARRIAGE, DIVORCE, REMARRIAGE 20–21 (rev. and enlarged ed. 1992).

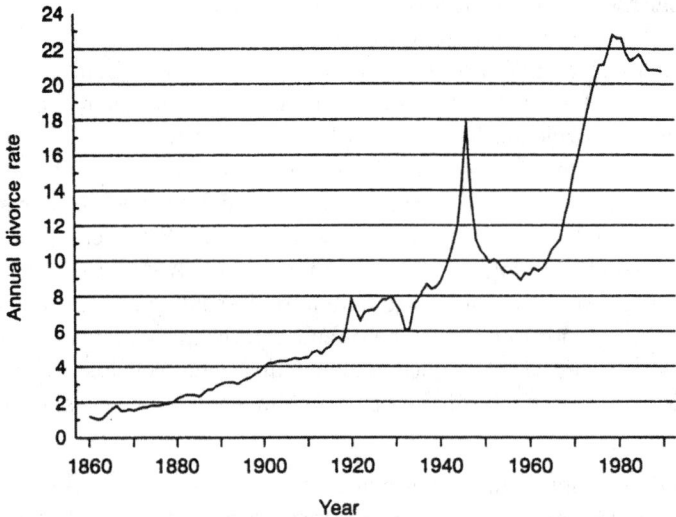

Figure 1-5 Annual divorce rates, United States. For 1920-1988: divorces per 1,000 married women aged 15 and over; for 1860-1920: divorces per 1,000 existing marriages.

Professor Cherlin notes the rise of divorce rates after major wars (e.g., Civil War, World Wars I and II) and the lowering of these rates during the Depression. The rates in the period from 1950 to 1960 depart from the pattern of long-term rise. *Id.* at 21–22. Following this sharp drop is a correspondingly sharp rise, with a peak around 1979, and a subsequent decline. Many of those who posit a causal relationship between changes in divorce laws in the 1970s and subsequent rates of marriage view a truncated version of these figures, comparing the annual rates from 1960s with those following the divorce law reforms in the 1970s and 1980s. These observers therefore, miss the big picture of rising divorce rates throughout the 20th century and the latter portion of the 19th century.

Professor Cherlin provides another, more revealing, picture of the pattern in divorce rates throughout this same period of time. Figure 1-6 charts the "proportion of all marriages begun in every year between 1867 and 1985 which will have ended, or will end, in divorce before one of the spouses dies." *Id.* at 22–23. The dots in the chart indicate actual data; the smooth line is the curve that most closely fits the pattern revealed by these dots and which therefore suggests the long-term trend. One value of the second chart, Cherlin explains, is that it gives us a better picture of the general trends. "We can see from the dotted line that the proportion of all marriages in a given year that eventually end in divorce has increased at a faster and faster rate since the mid-nineteenth century. Moreover, the increase has been relatively steady, without the large fluctuations which the annual rates show in times of war or depression." *Id.* at 23.

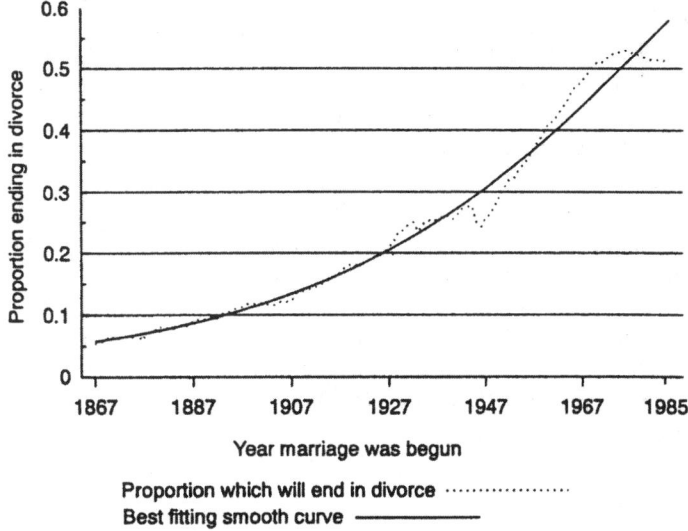

Figure 1-6   Proportion of marriages begun in each year that will end in divorce, 1867 to 1985.

Divorce rates are most commonly calculated as divorces per 1,000 people, and, although it is not as good a measure, these are the only data available presently for the 1990s and early 2000s.[1] The American divorce rate peaked, at 5.3 divorces per 1,000 people in 1979 and 1981 (it was 5.2 in 1980). The rate then declined to 5.0 in 1982, and remained there until the decline resumed in 1986. The rate has dropped steadily since. It was 4.7 in 1990, 4.2 in 2000, and 3.6 in 2005. U.S. Census Bureau, Statistical Abstract of the United States: 2008, Table No. 121, at 50. This latter figure reflects a decrease of more than 30% from the 1979/1981 peaks. Presently the rate of divorce per 1,000 in the population is at the lowest level in the United States since 1970.[2]

---

[1] The difficulty with measuring divorces as a proportion of 1,000 people, rather than 1000 marriages, is that a reduction in the number of people who are married will yield an apparent reduction in the divorce rates, even if there is no actual change in the proportion of marriages that are dissolved in any year. And in fact American marriage rates have declined. While it seems likely that this marriage rate decline accounts for a portion of the reduction in divorce rates measured per 1,000 people, it is hard to tell what proportion. The task is further complicated by the fact that the collection method for the reported national statistics on divorces per 1,000 people changed in 1996, in a way that may cause those numbers to be somewhat inflated, and if that is true the current divorce rate is lower than the reported numbers suggest. *See* note 5 [[**Note 5 of what?**]].

[2] The 2005 figure reported for divorces per 1000 people is probably higher than good data would show. The problem is that no national divorce statistics have been systematically collected since January 1996.

One study, using 1988 data, estimated that 43% — a figure somewhat lower than the frequently-cited one-half — of all marriages in the United States fail. Robert Schoen & Robin M. Weinick, *The Slowing Metabolism of Marriage: Figures from 1988 U.S. Marital Status Life Tables*, 30 DEMOGRAPHY 737, 742 (1993). More recently, researchers report disruption of approximately 20% of first-time marriages by separation or divorce within the first five years, one-third within ten years, and 43% by the fifteen-year mark. Matthew D. Bramlett & William D. Mosher, *First Marriage Dissolution, Divorce, and Remarriage: United States*, ADVANCE DATA No. 323, May 31, 2001. The percentage of marriages that end in formal divorce is, of course, somewhat lower than those ending in divorce or separation, although about 75% of the separations lead to divorce within about two years, and 90% within five years. The researchers examined some of the variables that relate to the likelihood a marriage will terminate early. In particular, if the wife was a teenager (even 18–19), her marriage was significantly more likely to dissolve early than were marriages of women age 20 and older. The relationship between marriages of persons under age 20 and higher rates of divorce is a frequently-cited finding. *See, e.g.*, The National Marriage Project, THE STATE OF OUR UNIONS 2002 21, *available at* www.marriage.rutgers.edu/Publications/SOOU/SOOU2002.pdf. Furthermore, racial factors were also relevant to the likelihood that a marriage would terminate within the first fifteen years. Bramlett and Mosher examined the marital patterns from the perspective of the women partners, and found that Asian-American women had the lowest rate of marital dissolution, African-American women had the highest, and Caucasian and Hispanic women fell between the two extremes.

Rates of marriage have also dropped in the second half of the 20th century, although not following a linear course. The rate of marriage, measured as the number per 1,000 in the population, was 11.1 in 1950, 8.5 in 1960, and 10.6 in 1970. It spiked briefly to 10.9 in 1972, dropped to 10.6 in 1980, to 9.8 in 1990, to 8.9 in 1995, and to 7.5 in 2005, well below the 1960 rate. U.S. Census Bureau, STATISTICAL ABSTRACT OF THE UNITED STATES: 2008, Table No. 121, at 50. Does the decline in marriage rates arise from a declining interest in marriage? A 1996 Roper survey found that 86% of Americans between the ages of 18 and 29 say a happy marriage is "part of the good life" — a 14% *increase* over the percentage who so answered that question in 1991. *The Big Picture*, AMERICAN DEMOGRAPHICS, Aug. 1997, at 35. Not only do Americans believe that a happy marriage is important to them, but most Americans think they have one. A 2002 Gallup Poll reported 68% of

---

Change in the Reporting of Marriage and Divorce Statistics, *Notice: Changes in Marriage and Divorce Data Available from the Center for Health Statistics*, 60 Fed. Reg. 64437–64438 (1995). According to the Centers for Disease Control, the parent of the National Center for Health Statistics, the suspension was triggered by "[l]imitations in the information collected by the States as well as budgetary consider-ations. . . ." Since that time, only "provisional" data have been collected. These data differ from the "final data collected prior to this change, in that they are incomplete and do not include data from counties or perhaps even states that have not reported at the time the data are compiled. While the editors are not aware of any studies that have made systematic comparisons between such provisional data and the final data that were previously collected, casual inspection of provisional and final data collected before 1996 suggests that provisional data systematically overestimated divorce rates as reported in the final data. One must therefore exercise caution in comparing divorce statistics from before 1996 with the provisional statistics available for later years, as this more recent data may also overestimate post-1995 divorce rates.

Americans (as compared to only 59% in 1996) gave their own marriage a grade of A. GEORGE GALLUP, JR., THE GALLUP POLL: PUBLIC OPINION 2002 239; *see also Poll Finds Religion Underscores Sense of Well-Being: Some Lifestyles Correlate to Greater Sense of Happiness*, GRAND RAPIDS PRESS, Apr. 15, 2006 at D7 (reporting 60% of all married people in Scripps Howard/Ohio University poll describe themselves as "very happy" as compared to only 41% of singles); *Are We Happy Yet?*, PEW SOCIAL & DEMOGRAPHIC TRENDS, Feb. 13, 2006, www.pewsocial trends.org/pubs/301/ (reporting 43% of marrieds are very happy, as compared to 24% of unmarrieds).

Average marital duration is affected by death as well as divorce, and mortality rates declined this century while divorce rates were rising. As a result, the aggregate dissolution rate — the number of marriages ending by either divorce or death, per 1,000 existing marriages — actually remained quite stable between 1860 and 1970. At the beginning of that period, the combined rate was 33.2 dissolutions per 1,000 marriages, while in 1970 the combined rate was 34.5. At least one scholar has therefore speculated that divorce may merely be a functional substitute for death, made necessary by increasing longevity. L. STONE, THE FAMILY, SEX AND MARRIAGE IN ENGLAND 1500–1800 56 (1977). Stone observed that as a result of the mortality rates "one very firm conclusion about the pre-modern family . . . was [that it was], statistically speaking, a transient and temporary association both of husband and wife and of parents and children." *Id.* at 55. The steep rise in divorce rates in the 1970s far exceeded mortality reductions, however, pushing the aggregate dissolution rates to 40.5 dissolutions per 1,000 marriages in 1978. Indeed, by the mid-1970s, for the first time in American history, more marriages ended every year in divorce than in death.

Estimates of remarriage rates vary, although it is clear that the remarriage rate declines with age, particularly for women. Bramlett & Mosher, *supra* at 9–10, found that 75% of divorced women remarry within ten years of their divorce, and that remarriage rates are significantly higher for women who are younger at divorce. *See also* Peter Uhlenberg, Teresa Cooney & Robert Boyd, *Divorce for Women After Midlife*, 45 J. GERONTOLOGY S3, S5 (1990) (measuring remarriages per 1,000 divorced women and reporting 1985 rates of 264 per 1,000 for women under 25, 184 per 1,000 for women 25 to 29, 80 per 1,000 for women 35 to 44, and 29 per 1,000 for women 45–64). Men are more likely to remarry than are women. THE STATE OF OUR UNIONS, *supra* at 20–21. Consistent with the gender differences in remarriage rates across the lifespan, older men remarry more often than older women. For example, ten percent of divorced men aged 45 to 54 married in 1988, compared to five percent of divorced women of that age. Dewitt, *supra*.

[b]   Did No-Fault Divorce Laws Cause More Divorce and, If Not, What Did?

Social scientists frequently remind us that "correlation does not imply causation." In other words, the fact that two variables or trends appear to be associated, such as a change in divorce laws and a rise in the divorce rates, does not demonstrate that one *caused* the other. *See e.g.*, Maire Ni Bhrolchain, *"Divorce Effects and Causality in the Social Sciences*, 17 EUROPEAN SOCIOL. REV. 33, 44–53

(2001); CAUSALITY IN CRISIS? (V.R. McKim & S.P. Turner, eds. 1997). Two sets of changes may be unrelated, both sets might be caused by a third variable, or the direction of causality may be the reverse of that postulated by observers. Frequently, with complex social phenomena like divorce rates, a combination of multiple-interacting factors may explain observed changes. We examine the patterns of change in divorce rates in relation to the passage of no-fault statutes below, together with other social and cultural shifts, analyzing what factors may have contributed to the observed increases in divorce rates.

Look again at Figure 1-5, *supra*. Putting aside the one-time spike associated with the return of soldiers from World War II, the picture divides into three clear segments: a long-term gradual upward trend in divorce rates from the year when data first became available, 1860, through the early 1960s; a dramatically accelerated upward trend between the early 1960s and 1979; then a leveling off and decline. Most of the shift to no-fault laws occurred between the early 1970s and 1980 — *after* the largest increases in divorce rates had already occurred.

This aggregate picture is replicated when one looks at the relative timing of rises in divorce rates and transition to no-fault laws in the individual states. In fact, state-by-state analyses bring the trends into even starker relief than do aggregate national data, because each state adopted no-fault reforms at different times during the fifteen year period between 1970 and 1985. In Arizona, for example, the divorce rate rose from 5.0 per thousand population in 1961 to 7.9 in 1971 under a regime of fault divorce. No-fault divorce was adopted in 1973. Only once between 1973 and 1979 — in 1976 — did the divorce rate exceed the 1971 fault-divorce level. The Arizona divorce rate peaked in 1979 at 8.2, but by 1994 had declined nearly 30 %, to 5.8. This decline occurred entirely under the state's new no-fault divorce law. Similar patterns are observed in most states, where divorce rate increases preceded no-fault reforms. For a detailed analysis of the state-by-state data, see Ira Mark Ellman & Sharon L. Lohr, *Dissolving the Relationship Between Divorce Rates and Divorce Laws*, 18 INT'L REV. L. & ECON. 341 (1998) (hereinafter "Ellman & Lohr, *Dissolving the Relationship*").

This makes clear that the no-fault statutes *followed*, rather than preceded, the rise in divorce rates. To the extent one ventures hypotheses as whether the legal changes and rising divorce rates are causally related to each other, no-fault laws were more likely a *result* of the increasing divorce rate, rather than its cause. Recall the discussion in Section A of the costs of the fault-based regime to the participants and the legal system. "When divorce rates began a steep rise in the late 1960s, an increasing proportion of the population began experiencing this charade [of colluding to manufacture and testify to 'evidence' sufficient to allow for a fault-based divorce adjudication]. More lawyer time was spent producing it, and more judge time was spent listening to it. In that way the rising divorce rate . . . enlarged the constituency for divorce law reform." Ira Mark Ellman, *Divorce Rates, Marriage Rates, and the Problematic Persistence of Traditional Marital Roles*, 34 FAM. L.Q. 1, 5 (2000) (hereinafter "Ellman, *Divorce Rates*").

Furthermore, there is much historical and sociological evidence indicating the increase in divorce rates and the transition to no-fault statutes were *both* caused by a plethora of sociocultural changes which dramatically affected American family life in the latter decades of the 20th century. The most commonly-cited factor affecting the divorce rate is the entrance of women into the labor market. *See, e.g.*, Cherlin, *supra* at 51 ("[A]lmost every well-known scholar who has addressed [the rise in divorce and separation] in the twentieth century has cited the importance of the increase in the employment of women."); HERBERT JACOB, SILENT REVOLUTION: THE TRANSFORMATION OF DIVORCE LAW IN THE UNITED STATES 17–18 (1988) (after 1940, married women's participation in workforce "exploded" with a rise of 10% per decade; by 1985, 54.3% of all married women were in the labor force, including a majority of married mothers with children under age three). The relationships between women's employment and divorce are complex, but many researchers agree that the decreasing economic dependence of employed women on their husbands made it easier to end an unhappy marriage. Cherlin, *supra* at 53; Jacob, *supra* at 18–19; *see* Ellman, *Divorce Rates, supra*, at 13–14 & n.33, for a discussion of the role that wives' employment played in the rise of divorce rates and a summary and analysis of empirical research on the subject.

Furthermore, as discussed in Chapter 1, women's increasing participation in the labor market was not accompanied by commensurate reductions in their responsibilities in the home. Children and households still needed as much care as before, and husbands did not take over a significant portion of the load. *See, e.g.*, Jacob, *supra* at 19; SUZANNE M. BIANCHI & DAPHNE SPAIN, AMERICAN WOMEN IN TRANSITION 160 (1986). In addition, few workplaces responded flexibly to familial demands on their female employees. JOAN WILLIAMS, UNBENDING GENDER: WHY FAMILY AND WORK CONFLICT AND WHAT TO DO ABOUT IT (2000). Women struggled, and continue to struggle, with balancing their obligations to the workplace and home, a fact that often contributes to marital stress and Dissatisfaction. ARLIE HOCHSCHILD & ANNE MACHUNG, THE SECOND SHIFT (1989).

Concurrent with these changes were the ideological shifts triggered by the women's movement. "Although only a small minority of American women ever openly declared themselves to be feminists, . . . the arguments of the women's movement dramatically altered women's attitudes toward family roles, marital relationships, femininity, and housework." STEVEN MINTZ & SUSAN KELLOGG, DOMESTIC REVOLUTIONS: A SOCIAL HISTORY OF AMERICAN FAMILY LIFE 208 (1988). The women's movement in the United States followed on the heels of the struggle for racial equality, focusing initially on gender discrimination in the workplace. As the movement progressed, the agenda expanded and came to embrace the goal of women's equality more broadly. Ultimately, feminism advanced a new way of thinking of marital relationships. "Talk of marriage as a contract between equals became more common and undermined the traditional view of marriage as a . . . relationship in which the husband dominated by natural right." Jacob, *supra*, at 23. Although coverture of married women had, in theory, ended a century earlier, most American families did not internalize the view of women as equal partners of husbands until the latter decades of the 20th century.

Thus, a range of factors relating to women's entry into the labor market, their attempts to juggle family and workplace obligations, and shifting perceptions of women's place in the family led to transitions in marital roles and relationships. In many cases, partners had married with expectations that each would play more traditional marital roles, and these sociocultural changes crept up on them unexpectedly, altering the expectations of at least one of the partners. Some marriages adapted, others did not.

Expectations for marriage as a source of personal satisfaction also soared during the 1960s and 1970s: "[I]n addition to its traditional functions of caring for children, providing economic security, and meeting is members' emotional needs, the family has become the focus of the new expectations for sexual fulfillment, intimacy, and companionship." Mintz & Kellogg, *supra*, at 205; *see also* PAUL R. AMATO & ALAN BOOTH, A GENERATION AT RISK: GROWING UP IN AN ERA OF FAMILY UPHEAVAL 12 (1997) (hereinafter "Amato & Booth, 1997"). Reflecting the continuation of this trend, a study of young adults reports that an overwhelming majority (94%) are searching for a marital partner who will be a "soul mate," that is, someone with whom they can share a "deep emotional and spiritual connection, and with whom they can communicate about their deepest feelings." Barbara Dafoe Whitehead & David Popenoe, *Who Wants to Marry a Soul Mate? New Survey Findings on Young Adults' Attitudes about Love and Marriage*, in THE STATE OF OUR UNIONS: 2001 at 6, 8 (2001), *available at* www.marriage.rutgers.edu/ Publications/SOOU/NMPAR2001.pdf. Whereas higher expectations of personal satisfaction from one's marriage may, in some instances, propel a couple to a more rewarding relationship, in other cases it can lead to disappointment in the marriage. In fact, survey data reveal that the percentage of people who reported their marriages as "very happy," gradually declined between 1973 and 1988. Norval D. Glenn, *The Recent Trend in Marital Success in the United States*, 53 J. MARRIAGE & FAM. 261 (1991). *See* Amato & Booth, 1997, *supra*, at 11 (summarizing studies). Furthermore, while research in prior decades revealed that married people reported being happier with their lives than did single people, the gap between the groups has narrowed; never-married men and women in the 1980s reported higher levels of personal happiness than they did in the 1970s, and young married women's reports of personal happiness declined between these two decades. *Id.* The lengthening of Americans' lifespans and the attendant lengthening of the lifespans of marriages created circumstances in which "marriages which are not companionate [could be experienced as] intolerable. Intolerable marriages more frequently lead to divorce. . . ." Jacob, *supra* at 26.

Scholars also cite other critical attitudinal changes that occurred in the latter half of the 20th century as contributing both to the rise in divorce rates and the move to no-fault divorce. The trend toward enhanced "commitment to individual choice and private ordering" was one such change. Michael Grossberg, *Balancing Acts: Crisis, Change, and Continuity in American Family Law*, 28 IND. L. REV. 273, 295 (1995). "Before no-fault divorce, the law retained for itself much of the responsibility for the moral choice whether to divorce; after no-fault, most of that responsibility was transferred to the husband and wife." Carl E. Schneider, *Moral Discourse and the Transformation of American Family Law*, 83 MICH. L. REV. 1803, 1809–10 (1985). Other beliefs about marriage and divorce had changed as well. The notion that marriages fail primarily because one spouse was wronged by the other no longer meshed with popular beliefs. Divorce and those who obtained it became less stigmatized because people had stopped believing the message fault-based divorce laws were sending. People also rejected the premise that the state should be in the business of enforcing the aspiration that marriages should last a lifetime. Schneider, *supra*, at 1809.

The language used by the U.S. Supreme Court in *Boddie v. Connecticut*, a 1971 case holding unconstitutional a Connecticut statute that required divorce petitioners to pay a filing fee (*see* Note 6, *supra* at Section B[1]) reveals how dramatically public attitudes toward divorce had changed. The *Boddie* Court referred to divorce as an "adjustment of a fundamental human relationship," and divorce procedures as the method by which "two consenting adults may divorce and mutually liberate themselves from the constraints of legal obligations that go with marriage, and more fundamentally the prohibition against remarriage." *Id.* at 383, 376; *see* Grossberg, *supra*, at 296. To the extent that the Court's language serves as a barometer of public attitudes, it is noteworthy that in 1971, eight justices agreed that the state must not put onerous obstacles in the path of couples who seek a divorce. *Boddie* preceded no-fault divorce reforms in most states by several years. Although *Boddie* concerned exclusion of economically-disadvantaged parties from access to divorce, the language used reveals acceptance of divorce and remarriage as facts of life in America.

The list of explanations for the rise in divorce rates and transition to no-fault statutes set forth above is not exhaustive. *See, e.g.*, Ellman, *Divorce Rates, supra*, at 7–13 (discussing relationship between mobility and divorce). In the final analysis, the relationship between divorce rates and divorce law reform may be characterized as one of reciprocal influence, much like the relationship between law and social change more generally:

> [M]ajor social change begins outside the legal system . . . in society. . . . When we look at [the complete transformation of Western legal systems since the Middle Ages,] it is clear that the legal system has been carried along by great waves of social force. . . . Social forces in the larger society create [law], shape it, twist it and turn it, pull it and push on it. But these forces produce a system that becomes itself part of social life; once in place, the system works its own influence on society, on how we live, how we think, how we feel.

LAWRENCE M. FRIEDMAN, AMERICAN LAW: AN INTRODUCTION 254–276 (1984). Thus, once no-fault divorce became a fixture in America's legal landscape, it no doubt had an effect on social attitudes. "Law is a . . . thing that is shaped by culture, and in turn shapes the culture." Carol Weisbrod, *On the Expressive Functions of Family Law*, 22 U.C. DAVIS L. REV. 991, 991–93 (1989). The empirical data, however, simply do not support the conclusion that the passage of no-fault divorce statutes is responsible for the *long-term* increase in divorce rates reported above. Although there appear to have been short-term increases in divorce rates in some jurisdictions immediately after the enactment of no-fault statutes, no long-term effect has been demonstrated. *See, e.g.*, Justin Wolfers, *Did Unilateral Divorce Laws Raise Divorce Rates? A Reconciliation and New Results* (2003), www.papers.ssrn.com/paper.taf?abstract_id=444620.

For articles concluding no-fault statutes played a causative role in the rise in divorce rates, see, e.g., Margaret F. Brinig & F.H. Buckley, *No-Fault Laws and At-Fault People*, 18 INT'L J. L. POL'Y & FAM. 225 (1997); Leora Friedberg, *Did*

Unilateral Divorce Raise Divorce Rates?, 88 Am. Econ. Rev. 608 (1998). For analyses disputing a causal role of no-fault reforms in stimulating a long-term rise in divorce rates, see Cherlin, *supra* at 48; Ira Mark Ellman, *The Misguided Movement to Revive Fault Divorce*, 11 Int'l J. L. Pol'y & Fam. 216 (1997); Ellman, *Divorce Rates, supra* at n.7; Ellman & Lohr, *Dissolving the Relationship, supra*; Norval D. Glenn, *A Reconsideration of the Effect of No-Fault Divorce on Divorce Rates*, 59 J. Marriage & Fam. 1023 (1997); Norval D. Glenn, *Further Discussion of the Effects of No-Fault Divorce on Divorce Rates*, 361 J. Marr. & Fam. 800 (1999); Wolfers, *supra*; *see also* Ian Smith, *European Divorce Laws, Divorce Rates, and Their Consequences*, *in* The Law and Economics of Marriage 212, 226–27 (A.W. Dnes & R. Rowthorn, eds. 2002) (concluding the move to no-fault divorce laws in European nations was not responsible for the rise in divorce rates, and that both trends were likely "jointly determined" by social, cultural, and economic forces). It is noteworthy, however, that even those authors who attribute some of the rise in divorce rates to passage of no-fault statutes assert only a relatively small causative effect. For summaries and critiques of the various studies, and in-depth discussion of their methodologies, see Wolfers, *supra*; Ellman, *Divorce Rates, supra*, at n.7; Ellman & Lohr, *Dissolving the Relationship, supra*.

Given that the enactment of no-fault statutes does not explain the long-term rise in divorce rates, it is unlikely that repeal of no-fault laws would lead to a substantial reduction in divorce. As in the pre-no-fault era, parties seeking divorces would likely resort to whatever path to divorce provided the least resistance, whether it be proceeding on fault grounds or obtaining a dissolution in a more divorce-friendly jurisdiction. It should be emphasized, in conclusion, that divorce rates have declined steadily since they peaked in 1979 and 1981, and are now at their lowest since 1970, when the "no-fault revolution" began in California. Thus, the no-fault era has coincided with only period in United States history during which divorce rates have declined consistently for a quarter century.

[2] The Effects of Divorce on Children

Few subjects relating either to family law or to children have garnered as much attention from the media and the general public as has the topic of the effects of divorce on children. It is therefore not surprising that discourse about these effects would be dominated by overly-simplified "soundbites" highlighted by exaggerated claims. These soundbites mask the complexities in the data and obscure the important messages that the data could transmit to policymakers, lawyers, mental health professionals, and parents.

The release of Judith Wallerstein and Joan Kelly's 1980 Book, *Surviving the Breakup: How Children Actually Cope with Divorce*, stimulated concerns about the psychological consequences of divorce for children. Painting a bleak picture, and widely quoted in the popular press, Wallerstein and Kelly's report garnered the attention of policymakers and others, and etched into the American consciousness the notion that divorce is uniformly and irreversibly damaging to children. *See also* Judith S. Wallerstein, Julia M. Lewis & Sandra Blakeslee, The Unexpected Legacy of Divorce (2000). Social scientists from a range of disciplines, however, severely criticized Wallerstein's work because of methodological shortcomings, such as the absence of control groups, and the use of a sample drawn from families seeking psychological services (i.e., families that were already encountering emotional difficulties). Wallerstein's work has been so discredited by researchers and scholars that it does not even appear in the reference list of the important summaries and analyses of empirical studies (unless the author's purpose is to criticize the study). *See, e.g.*, Paul R. Amato & Bruce Keith, *Parental Divorce and the Well-Being of Children: A Meta-Analysis*, 110 PSYCHOL. BULL. 26 (1991); ROBERT E. EMERY, MARRIAGE, DIVORCE, AND CHILDREN'S ADJUSTMENT (2nd ed. 1999) (hereinafter "EMERY, MARRIAGE, DIVORCE & CHILDREN'S ADJUSTMENT"); E. Mavis Hetherington, Margaret Bridges, & Glendessa M. Insabella, *What Matters? What Does Not? Five Perspectives on the Association Between Marital Transitions and Children's Adjustment*, 53 AM. PSYCHOLOGIST 167 (1998).

Contrary to various assertions, parental divorce is neither a destructive force rendering most children who encounter it maladjusted, nor is it irrelevant to children's well-being. One meta-analysis concluded, "Divorce benefits some individuals, leads others to experience temporary decrements in well-being that improve over time, and forces others on a downward cycle from which they might never fully recover." Paul Amato, *The Consequences of Divorce for Adults and Children*, 62 J. MARRIAGE & FAM. 1269, 1282 (2000). Parental divorce is an experience that might best be thought of as introducing certain stressors into a child's life. Robert E. Emery, *Postdivorce Family Life for Children: An Overview of Research and Some Implications for Policy, in* THE POSTDIVORCE FAMILY: CHILDREN, PARENTING, AND SOCIETY 3 (R.A. Thompson & P.R. Amato, eds. 1999) (hereinafter "Emery, *Postdivorce Family Life*"). For example, divorce changes living arrangements, leads to periods of separation from one or both parents, and brings economic hardships to many families. These factors and others accompanying divorce place psychological challenges in the path of children. Yet, researchers repeatedly emphasize that "despite the increase in risk, *resilience* is the normative outcome of divorce for children, that is, most children from divorced families function as well as children from married families on various commonly used indices of their adjustment." *Id.* at 4. In other words, most children who experience parental divorce negotiate those stressors quite well, and emerge without notable long-term difficulties. *Id.* Many exhibit short-term adjustment difficulties, and most report experiencing sadness, anxiety, or other unpleasant emotions during the transitions associated with marital dissolution. Yet most children cope with the challenges successfully, and end up as relatively well-adjusted adults, enjoying "satisfying social and intimate relationships." *See, e.g.*, E. MAVIS HETHERINGTON & JOHN KELLY, FOR BETTER OR FOR WORSE: DIVORCE RECONSIDERED 252 (2002).

Despite these general findings, however, some children who experience parental divorce encounter greater difficulties coping and reveal longer-term adjustment difficulties. One recent meta-analysis revealed "that children of divorced parents, as a group, continue to fare more poorly than children with continuously married parents," demonstrating less adaptive academic, behavioral, emotional, and interpersonal functioning. Paul R. Amato, *Children and Divorce in the 1990s: An Update of the Amato and Keith (1991) Meta-Analysis*, 15 J. FAM. PSYCHOL. 355, 366

(2001); *see also* Hetherington, Bridges & Insabella, *supra*, at 169–70. These differences remain, even into early adulthood. *See, e.g,* Paul R. Amato & Bruce Keith, *Parental Divorce and Adult Well-Being: A Meta-Analysis*, 53 J. MARRIAGE & FAM. 43 (1991); Hetherington, Bridges & Insabella, *supra*, at 169–70. Indeed, there is evidence that divorce in one generation can have a negative impact on the grandchildren's generation. Paul Amato & Jacob Cheadle, *The Long Reach of Divorce: Divorce and Child Well-Being Across Three Generations*, 67 J. MARRIAGE & FAM. 191 (2005). And, although the *magnitude* of the differences between the divorced-parent and married-parent groups is generally reported to be small, *see, e.g.*, Emery, *Postdivorce Family Life, supra*, at 13, researchers sensibly are turning their attention to identifying which variables predict adaptive versus maladaptive postdivorce outcomes for children. The findings that emerge from this latter endeavor offer the promise of promoting development of strategies to minimize the likelihood that children will experience such difficulties.

A handful of research teams have studied large samples of children and families over several-decade time periods, using sophisticated methodologies and increasingly sensitive analyses of a wide range of variables and their interactions. *See, e.g,* Andrew Cherlin, P. Lindsay Chase-Lansdale & Christine McRae, *Effects of Parental Divorce on Mental Health Throughout the Life Course*, 63 AM. SOCIOL. REV. 239 (1998); Hetherington & Kelly, *supra*; Paul R. Amato & Alan Booth, a GENERATION AT RISK: GROWING UP IN AN ERA OF FAMILY UPHEAVAL (1997). Although many questions are yet unanswered, several important themes emerge. First, we are reminded to be cautious in reaching conclusions about causal connections between two associated variables, such as divorce and children's adjustment. Many writers have incorrectly assumed that a direct causal relationship exists between parental divorce and any problems in children's postdivorce adjustment. The data does not support this. For a discussion of these issues, see Maire Ni Bhrolchain, *"Divorce Effects" and Causality in the Social Sciences*, 17 EUR. SOCIOL. REV. 33, 44–53 (2001); Maire Ni Bhrolchain, et al., *Parental Divorce and Outcomes for Children: Evidence and Interpretation*, 16 SOCIOL. REV. 67 (2002). To the contrary, recent studies make clear that children whose parents divorce reveal adjustment difficulties in social, emotional, and academic realms *well before* (sometimes as far ahead as five to ten years) a divorce occurs. Andrew J. Cherlin, *Going to Extremes: Family Structure, Children's Well-Being, and Social Science*, 36 DEMOGRAPHY 421 (1999). Given the convergent findings of several studies published in the 1990s, Cherlin concludes that "the evidence that precursors of the difficulties associated with divorce are visible to some extent in children years before the break-up. . . . is now a well-established finding." *Id.* at 435. Thus, it is important to keep in mind that any differences in psychological, social, academic, or occupational functioning observed between individuals who experienced parental divorce as children and those who did not is subject to these interpretive limitations regarding causality. The focus on predivorce factors and their possible impact on children's well-being has led to a reformulation of divorce as an occurrence that is not "a discrete event" marked by the occurrence of the formal legal marital dissolution,

> But . . . part of a series of family transitions and changes in family relationships. The response to any family transition will depend both on what precedes and follows it. The response to divorce and life in a

single-parent household will be influenced by individual adjustment and the quality of family relationships before the divorce as well as circumstances surrounding and following the divorce.

E. Mavis Hetherington, Tracey C. Law & Thomas G. O'Connor, *Divorce: Challenges, Changes, and New Chances, in* FAMILY IN TRANSITION 176, 177 (A.S. Skolnick & J.H. Skolnick eds., 9th ed. 1997). "[M]arital disruption [is] a multistage process that may begin long before families dissolve and extend many years after divorce or separation." Yongmin Sun, *Family Environment and Adolescents' Well-Being Before and After Parents' Marital Disruption: A Longitudinal Analysis,* 63 J. MARRIAGE & FAM. 697, 699 (2001).

The understanding of the role of postdivorce factors creates an opportunity to interrupt potentially negative effects of divorce on children. In some families, postdivorce family relationships and patterns perpetuate predivorce problems and do not promote children's positive adjustment to the changes brought by the divorce. Yet, in other families, divorce creates the opportunity for positive change in any of several domains. Professor Robert Emery explains:

> Many differences [in the psychological adjustment of children following parental divorce] are attributable to postdivorce family relationships, especially: (a) the quality of the children's relationship with their residential parent, (b) the degree and manner in which conflict is expressed between the parents, (c) the family's economic standing, and (d) the children's contact and relationship with the nonresidential parent.

Emery, *Postdivorce Family Life, supra,* at 4. Thus, perhaps the most important conclusion that can be drawn from current research is that *the effects of divorce on children are not irrevocably predetermined* by virtue of their parents' decisions to dissolve the marriage. Adjustment to life stressors is a dynamic process that does not occur in one moment in time. The growing body of knowledge about children's response to life stressors makes clear that environmental factors, particularly healthy supportive relationships with caring adults, can do much to mitigate the ill effects of challenging life circumstances. *See generally* E. MAVIS HETHERINGTON, ED., COPING WITH DIVORCE, SINGLE PARENTING, AND REMARRIAGE: A RISK AND RESILIENCY PERSPECTIVE (1999); ROBERT J. HAGGERTY, ET AL., STRESS, RISK, AND RESILIENCE IN CHILDREN AND ADOLESCENTS: PROCESSES, MECHANISMS, AND INTERVENTIONS (1996).

How should policymakers respond to these findings? Some have advocated a return to fault grounds, asserting divorce is deleterious to children's well-being, and that exit from marriage should be limited to those situations where a spouse has violated one of certain limited statutory grounds. The argument here is that keeping the non-qualifying marriages together will be in the best interest of children in those families. Others argue that rather than returning to fault-based divorce across the board, exit from marriage ought to be made more difficult when marriages involve children. Thus, for example, some recommend longer waiting periods for divorce by couples with minor children. *See, e.g.,* Waite & Gallagher, *supra,* at 195–96 (citing with approval pre-no-fault waiting periods of two to three years in the United States and five-to-seven years in Europe); Elizabeth S. Scott, *Divorce, Children's Welfare, and the Culture Wars,* 9 VA. J. SOC. POL'Y & L. 95, 105 (2001) (suggesting couples entering marriage, particularly couples with children, be permitted to commit voluntarily to a legally-enforceable period, such as two years, to serve as a waiting period prior to marital termination). These reformers assert that such a waiting period would serve as a barrier to divorce, requiring parties to deliberate and reconsider the decision to divorce and perhaps to work harder toward the success of the marriage. Waite & Gallagher, *supra*, at 195; *see also* Scott, *supra*, at 105–06. Furthermore, these authors suggest that such policies would send the proper messages to the populace about the marriage as a life-long commitment.

There is, of course, another side to the debate about whether making marital exit more difficult will promote children's well-being. Opponents of policies to restrict access to divorce would first reject the premise that making divorce harder to obtain will result in fewer divorces or reductions in the deleterious effects associated with growing up in a family disrupted by divorce. Ellman, *The Misguided Movement to Revive Fault Divorce*, *infra*. Second, given evidence that much of children's postdivorce adjustment problems can be tied to *predivorce* factors, critics of this set of proposals would assert that restrictive divorce laws merely maintain the *de jure* marital status of dysfunctional families, while forcing them to remain together. Some proposals would force them to live separately during a several-year waiting period. Yet, long waiting periods risk "freezing" family processes at the height of crisis, placing children in an extended period of "limbo" — living with parental separation and the specter of an impending divorce. Particularly problematic for these children is the uncertainty as to whether, when, and how a divorce will change their lives. Living quarters may be temporary, other facets of everyday life make-shift and unsettled, and family relationship issues unresolved. Such circumstances are highly unlikely to promote children's well-being.

Furthermore, as shown in the first half of this chapter, couples still find ways to divorce under a fault-based system or a system with long waiting periods. Couples manufacture fault grounds where none exist, seek annulments, or take advantage of friendlier policies in other jurisdictions. Additionally, and of even greater concern, the obstacles placed in the paths of unhappy couples may well exacerbate interparental conflict (by requiring an adversarial determination of fault) and to tax the families' financial resources (by requiring hefty outlays of funds for legal fees). As such, proposals imposing substantial barriers to divorce may even *enhance* the likelihood that children will be exposed to risk factors known to have deleterious effects on children such as parental conflict and economic hardship.

Recently a variation on the proposal to deal with families with minor children has appeared. This approach distinguishes between those couples with minor children appropriate for a "fast track" (i.e., easy access to divorce), and those couples with minor children appropriate for a "slow track" (i.e., more difficult access to divorce). The "fast track" would be reserved for those parents whose divorces involving fault on the part of one spouse, mutual consent between spouses, or a high degree of interparental conflict. *See, e.g.*, William A. Galston, *The Law of Marriage and Divorce: Options for Reform*, *in* MARRIAGE IN AMERICA: A COMMUNITARIAN PERSPECTIVE 179, 185 (M.K. Whyte, ed. 2000). The couples assigned to the "slow track" would be required to wait for "years rather than months" to obtain a divorce. Judges would retain discretion to determine which track is most appropriate for any particular couple. The diversion of high-conflict divorces onto a fast track is based on the findings of one study which noted that, while divorce seemed to lead to a net "loss" in the prospects for adjustment for children whose parents' marriages were characterized by *low* levels of conflict, divorce seemed to *improve* the prospects for adjustment for children whose parents' marriages were characterized by *high* levels of conflict, *See* Alan Booth & Paul R. Amato, *Parental Predivorce Relations and Offspring Postdivorce Well-Being*, 63 J. MARRIAGE & FAM. 197 (2001). This finding surprised the researchers, who interpret it as relating, in part, to the following:

> Children in households where parents engage in a long-term process of overt, unresolved conflict are at risk for a variety of developmental and emotional problems. . . . When a divorce occurs, these children are freed from a dysfunctional home environment and may genuinely welcome the shift to a calmer single-parent household. Under these circumstances, children's conflict-related symptoms are likely to improve over time. By contrast, children in households in which parents engage in relatively little overt conflict are at low risk for developmental and emotional problems. [These children] are likely to view divorce under these circumstances as an unexpected, unwelcome, and uncontrollable event, an event that sets into motion a series of stressful circumstances (a decline in standard of living, loss of contact with one parent, and moving) with no compensating advantages. Under these circumstances, children may exhibit a variety of stress-related symptoms. . . .

Id. at 199. Further research is needed to replicate and better understand this particular finding. For the moment, however, advocates who wish to make divorce more difficult for parents with minor children now argue that this study supports placement of barriers to marital exit in the paths of those parents whose relationships fall into the "low conflict" group.

The obvious response to such a proposal emphasizes that conditioning access to a "fast track," or quicker, divorce upon these factors creates perverse incentives. Given what we know about the lengths to which unhappy marital partners will go to obtain a divorce, some may be motivated to create (or falsify) a higher level of spousal conflict so that the couple will "qualify" for the fast track. Such policies would thus either promote precisely the types of family interaction patterns we know are most damaging to children's well-being or encourage perjury.

While providing parents whose unhappy marriages are not characterized by the high levels of conflict with various support services seems sensible, *forcing* such couples to stay together is a very different proposition. Sociologist Paul Amato, the study's author and the chief proponent of providing assistance to parents in "good enough marriages," flatly rejects the notion that legal policies should be crafted to make divorce less accessible for these couples. Paul R. Amato, *Good Enough Marriages: Parental Discord, Divorce, and Children's Long-Term Well-Being*, 9 VA. J. SOC. POL'Y & L. 71, 92–94 (2001). Professor Amato's point echoes assertions made by other scholars. They argue that it would make more sense to focus on interventions that could preserve marriages *in fact* as well as *in form*, and might promote healthier relationships within marital families. Professor Andrew Cherlin and colleagues argue that society could better improve the welfare of children by working to prevent the increasingly-predictable downward spiral from family dysfunction to divorce, paying "[a]t least as much attention . . . to the processes that occur in troubled, intact families" as is now paid to children's postdivorce functioning. Andrew Cherlin, et al., *Longitudinal Studies of Effects of Divorce on Children in Great Britain and the United States*, 252 SCIENCE 1386, 1388 (1991).

While the rules of termination cannot reduce the incidence of family breakup, during the last several decades there have been attempts to reduce the negative impact of divorce on children by focusing on the known risk factors summarized above by Emery. Thus, there has been an emphasis on child custody mediation as an alternative to litigation. Mediation proponents hoped that this would benefit the children of divorce by reducing their exposure to the conflict surrounding custody disputes. While it is not clear that children have been directly benefitted by custody mediation, evaluation studies reveal that it has increased participant satisfaction with the legal process, reduced relitigation of custody orders, increased compliance with these orders, and has been an economically-efficient alternative to courtroom adjudication. Joan B. Kelly, *Psychological and Legal Interventions for Parents and Children in Custody and Access Disputes: Current Research and Practice*, 10 VA. J. SOC. POL'Y & L. 129, (2002); *see also* Connie J.A. Beck & Bruce D. Sales, *A Critical Reappraisal of Divorce Mediation Research and Policy*, 6 PSYCHOL. PUB. POL'Y & L. 898 (2000).

Many jurisdictions have adopted policies or funded pilot projects requiring divorcing parents to attend "divorce education" classes, the main purpose of which is to instruct the parents on how to minimize the negative effects of their divorce on their children. While these studies have not yet reported long-term results in reducing postdivorce difficulties in children, preliminary indications are that such efforts may have benefits. *See, e.g.*, Brenda L. Bacon & Brad McKenzie, *Parent Education After Separation/Divorce*, 42 FAM. CT. REV. 85 (2004); *see also* Kelly, *supra*, at 133–37 (summarizing types of programs and initial research findings); Sanford L. Braver, Melanie C. Smith & Stephanie R. DeLuse, *Methodological Considerations in Evaluating Family Court Programs*, 35 FAM. & CONCILIATION CTS. REV. 9 (1997) (critiquing absence of formal evaluations of court-based intervention programs). Furthermore, divorce education programs for *children*, "designed to help children develop a better understanding of their parents' divorces and skills for coping with them" have developed nationwide, and are currently undergoing empirical evaluation. Kelly, *supra*, at 136–37.

Given research findings demonstrating that the quality of parent-child relationships is highly predictive of children's postdivorce adjustment, availability of low-cost psychological intervention programs geared toward improving postdivorce parenting and parent-child relationships might be particularly helpful to children's welfare. In light of the role that reduced standards of living and economic opportunities play in hindering children's adaptive postdivorce adjustment, legal policies that promote adequate support for the child and custodial parent are essential. For example, Professor Glendon proposes a "children first" policy in divorce cases. MARY ANN GLENDON, ABORTION AND DIVORCE IN WESTERN LAW 94–99 (1987). In other words, "the judge's main task would be to piece together, from property and income and inkind personal care, the best possible package to meet the needs of the children and their physical custodian"; property distribution and spousal support awards would be governed by this principle, relegating other rationales and formulas for distribution as secondary.

On the substantive side of divorce, joint custody has been adopted as an option (and sometimes a preferred option) in many states. One of the primary goals of this doctrine is the prevention or reduction of "father drift," the gradual disengagement of noncustodial parents from their relationships with their children. The details of the joint custody debate and jurisprudence is left for Chapter 6.

[3]   Reform Proposals and Analysis

Elizabeth Scott, *Marriage as Precommitment* *in* MARRIAGE IN AMERICA: A COMMUNITARIAN PERSPECTIVE 161–171 (M.K. Whyte, ed. 2000)

A different approach to promoting marital stability is one in which the law's role is to assist couples to achieve their goal of lasting marriage. Most people enter marriage aspiring to a lifelong relationship, and view the success of their marriage as important to a good life. . . . [¶] As divorce statistics reveal, for many people the commitment and optimism with which they enter marriage does not last. Life presents stresses and temptations, and decisions are made that weaken or destroy the bond between spouses. Gradually (or suddenly), the marriage succumbs. The original commitment is "nonbinding" under the current no-fault divorce regime and can be readily set aside. Not only are there few legal restraints to provide disincentive to divorce, but under current law, the couple may not be permitted to voluntarily undertake a more binding commitment through restrictions on divorce.

I . . . argue . . . that divorce law should build on the aspirations with which many people enter marriage, by providing couples with the means to reinforce their commitment to the . . . relationships that they are undertaking. From an ex ante perspective, the voluntary reinforcement of the marital commitment through restriction on divorce serves two important functions. First, the restrictions can serve as precommitment mechanisms, which discourage each spouse from pursuing transitory preferences that are inconsistent with the couple's self-defined long term interest in lasting marriage. Second, each spouse, knowing that the other's commitment is enforceable, receives assurance that his or her investment in the relationship will be protected. If marriage is a relationship that can be easily terminated at any time by either party, trust will be impaired and investment will be tentative. Allowing couples . . . to undertake a greater commitment to the relationship than the law currently encourages or allows would have a direct effect on the decision to divorce and indirect effects on attitude toward and behavior in marriage. [¶]. . . . [C]urrent divorce law undermines commitment, by assuming that commitment is antithetical to personal freedom. To the contrary, basic contract principles demonstrate that freedom to commit extends our ability to fulfill our ends. . . .

. . . .

[Sometimes marriages fail because t]he long-term rewards of the relationship . . . seem remote and incompatible with immediate desires and preferences. In most marriages, even successful ones, both spouses will be tempted to engage in selfish or uncooperative behavior, which reflects current preferences that may be transitory but which undermine the stability of the relationship. There are obvious examples: immersion in career at the expense of family, pursuit of other relationships, disputes over family finances and children, withdrawal, boredom; etc. A pattern of uncooperative behavior can cause retaliation, estrangement, erosion of the marital commitment and ultimately can lead to the breakdown of the relationship.

. . . . Described in this way, the failure of marriage is analogous to other situations in life in which individuals make choices based on transitory preferences that temporarily dominate and undermine the fulfillment of their long term goals. A commitment to a healthy diet to lose weight, moderate use of alcohol, completion of a project, or saving money for a new home can involve sacrificing pleasures that, at a particular moment may represent the more compelling choice than adherence to the long term goal. . . . A familiar corrective . . . involves the use of precommitment mechanisms. Precommitments are self-management strategies designed to penalize the short term choice that the decisionmaker wants to avoid (eating the cake) or to reward adherence to her long term goal (losing 10 pounds). Through the use of enforceable penalties or rewards, she reinforces her initial commitment to her goal and reduces the likelihood that she will be diverted by temporarily attractive temptations. . . .

. . . Suppose, for example, that the couple agrees before marriage to a three year mandatory waiting period before divorce. This barrier imposes a substantial cost on the decision to exit the marriage, and thus reduces the likelihood that divorce will take place unless the costs of remaining in the marriage are substantial (or the benefits minimal). In other words, as the unhappy spouse makes a choice between continued marriage and divorce, the precommitment shifts the calculus in favor of remaining in the marriage. Predictably, decisions to divorce will be less common and more carefully made.

More subtly but perhaps more importantly, precommitments that impose restrictions on divorce can promote stability in marriage by influencing the couple's attitude about the kind of relationship that they have undertaken, which in turn may affect their behavior in marriage. The decision by the couple to undertake a binding commitment signals the seriousness with which each enters the marriage. Moreover, at least indirectly, knowledge that exit will not be easy can encourage cooperation and assist each spouse to resist the temptation to pursue her short term self interest. In a marriage bounded by precommitment, the original cooperative intentions may be less likely to be forgotten because the relationship cannot be readily abandoned if it becomes unsatisfactory. This may influence the parties to protect the marriage by avoiding behavior that could lead them to confront the costly decision to divorce. Such a conception of marriage might be expressed as follows: "We have made a commitment to this marriage and we're not getting out of it easily. Since we're in for the duration, we might as well make the best of it."

. . . .

. . . . By restricting her or his own freedom, each spouse gains greater assurance of the commitment of the other, and confidence that the relationship will endure through good and bad times. This sense of security promotes a level of trust in the partner that fosters substantial investment in the marriage, in terms of time, energy, emotions and resources. Indeed the kind of interdependence that is often associated with a successful marriage may only be possible with the level of trust that is conditioned on a binding commitment. . . .

. . . .

Courts have been lukewarm toward premarital contracts in which the couple seeks to reinforce their commitment to one another by restricting divorce, a response that is curiously inconsistent with the liberal premises of modern regulation of marriage. . . . [¶] Individuals who are about to marry may tend to be influenced by emotional and cognitive biases that could distort decision-making. . . . [¶] The effect of these cognitive biases on decision-making about marital precommitment is not easy to predict. Optimism could lead some couples to see no need for precommitment [i.e., "undercommitment"]. Other couples may . . . reject the possibility that their own marriage will fail. [¶] The upshot of this latter response may be "overcommitment," a more onerous restriction on divorce than most observers would conclude was rational under the circumstances. Thus, the couple might agree never to divorce or create a prohibitive fine to be imposed on the spouse who ends the marriage. . . . Thus, legal regulation is necessary to ensure that precommitments impose only moderate obstacles to divorce.

Sometimes, precommitments that are moderate in most cases may be unacceptable because of the conduct of one spouse and the resulting vulnerability of the other. In cases of spousal abuse, for example, obstacles to divorce may increase the harm to the victims, and exemption should be readily available. In general, any precommitment that insists on continued cohabitation or even direct association is risky and should be unenforceable. Procedures should be readily available to expedite spousal and child support upon separation in cases involving dependent spouses and minor children. That is not to say that mandatory delay before final divorce or remarriage cannot be prescribed, under conditions in which financial support for a dependent is provided.

Caution is required on other grounds as well. A precommitment that is likely to have a differential impact on the spouses because of different marital roles is undesirable. Thus, monetary penalties — includ[ing] those affecting spousal support — are problematic unless the spouses have equal assets and earning capacity, which in most marriages will not be the case. . . . . Furthermore, since the ultimate policy goal of promoting marital stability is to enhance the welfare of children, only precommitments that serve that objective are acceptable. Thus, precommitments withholding access to visitation or child support, or otherwise undermining children's security, should not be enforced.

. . . .

A mandatory waiting period of some substantial duration before divorce (perhaps two or three years) is the optimal precommitment . . . because it serves several functions. First, a mandatory period of delay serves well the standard precommitment purposes. It creates a barrier to divorce that makes leaving the marriage more costly, and at the same time it defines the relationship as one that is not easily set aside, subtly influencing the spouses' attitudes and behavior. Beyond this, an extended waiting period promotes better decisionmaking. The spouse who is unhappy in the marriage can more accurately assess whether her decision reflects her long term interest or transitory intense preferences. In general, time is a good tool for making better decisions and avoiding cognitive errors. Finally, a waiting period undermines the ability of a spouse quickly to establish a new family, a step that dilutes interest in children of an earlier marriage.

Fault-based divorce laws served a little noticed precommitment function that was sacrificed in the movement toward no-fault divorce. . . . Should fault be reintroduced as a precommitment? [¶] In some regards, fault would seem to serve quite well as a precommitment. . . . It may . . . influence marital behavior in a direction that stabilizes the relationship. Fault grounds certainly create barriers and restrict divorce. [¶] In many regards, however, fault grounds do not function well as precommitments. . . . The proving of fault [before no-fault reforms] undermined the integrity of the judicial process and surely undermined the parties' future relationship, an important concern if the objective is to promote the welfare of the children. . . . In general, I would hesitate to reintroduce fault as a precommitment.

Ira Mark Ellman, *The Misguided Movement to Revive Fault Divorce*
11 INT'L J. LAW, POLICY, AND THE FAMILY 216, 221–37 (1997)

. . . [Consider the imposition of waiting periods on mutual consent divorces.] Proponents . . . apparently believe that couples made to wait might change their minds and reunite, and live happily — or at least functionally — ever after. They apparently think that many couples with children divorce casually . . . and that they therefore will stay together if we just make them think about it some more. [This seems unlikely. Consider too that] a waiting period for divorce is really a waiting period for remarriage, for remarriage is the only thing that is truly delayed [since the parties will still separate physically, and a court may still grant a legal separation with custody and support provisions]. Do we want [to delay remarriage]? For what purpose? Do waiting period proponents want the [divorced] to avoid establishing new relationships, or to cohabit without marrying?

. . .

. . . [J]urisdictions with lengthy waiting periods typically apply them only to no-fault divorces. . . . The result . . . is that couples who agree on divorce also quickly agree on some fault ground that they can present to the court so as to avoid the waiting period. [¶]Consider, for example, some recent data from England, which requires two years' separation before a mutual consent no-fault divorce can be granted (and five years' separation before a unilateral no-fault divorce is ordered). The result: there are very few no-fault mutual consent divorces. Where wives are the petitioner, 76% of divorces were granted on grounds of adultery or "unreasonable behavior"; only 19% on two years' mutual separation and 5 percent on five years' unilateral separation. Among the 30 percent of divorces in which the husband was the petitioner, fault grounds were less dominant, but still accounted for a clear majority of all decrees. Similar patterns are found in the American statistics as well as in other British data. . . . [Thus] the primary consequence of imposing waiting periods for no-fault divorces is the revival of the sham "fault" proceedings that were common under the old fault regimes, in which the spouses collude in presenting the fault grounds necessary to obtain the quicker decree.

There is a further detail in this recent British data that is even more interesting: both husbands and wives were even less likely to wait . . . if they had children under 16: the percentage who instead relied upon fault grounds increased 6% among petitioning wives, and 11% among petitioning husbands (46% of whom charged their wives with adultery). Indeed, the younger that the youngest child was, at the time of divorce, the more likely were the parents to avoid the waiting periods and petition instead on fault grounds. The parents apparently knew something that the law's draftsmen did not: that once a marriage fails, prolonging the divorce process is unlikely to be good for the children, particularly if the divorce is likely to exacerbate parental conflict.

. . .

. . . [W]hat then of a common companion proposal, an even longer waiting period — five years has been suggested — before a unilateral no-fault divorce is allowed. . . . [¶] Imagine [*Marriage of Mitchell*, Section B[2], *supra*] decided under [that] regime. . . . Mr. Mitchell, after moving out for the last time, must wait five more years for divorce — while Mrs. Mitchell presumably waits for him to return. Will denying Mr. Mitchell the right to remarry during this time drive him back to Mrs. Mitchell? No one . . . could think that likely, nor would they believe it necessarily the best result for Mrs. Mitchell or her children. And surely a five year wait followed by divorce would not help them. Mrs. Mitchell needs to rebuild her life, and sooner is better than later, especially for her children.

. . . [And] while the law can keep Mr. Mitchell from remarrying, it is unlikely to keep him celibate. What then happens when he develops a close relationship with Mrs. Smith? The enforced wait means he cannot legally commit himself to her and her child. Perhaps they will cohabit in any event — and perhaps produce a nonmarital child during that time. While that is surely not the result that waiting period proponents intend, it may be the result they achieve. Their effort to protect Mrs. Mitchell will thus burden Mrs. Smith.

And [c]onsider Mrs. Mitchell's sister, Mrs. Jones. She is unhappy in her marriage because Mr. Jones is an insensitive, domineering bully who psychologically mistreats both her and their child. Mr. Smith would be a far better husband for her and they would like to marry. But Mr. Jones, who has no immediate interest in remarrying, gets in his last licks at Mrs. Jones by refusing to cooperate with her in obtaining a consensual divorce. So now the only way Mrs. Jones can avoid waiting five years before marrying Mr. Smith is to assume the burden of proving Mr. Jones' fault. But his nasty, demeaning conduct, though real enough, is not so simple to prove in a contested proceeding — and perhaps Mrs. Jones also worries that he might defend with proof of an adulterous act between her and Mr. Smith. Surely adultery is also misconduct under the fault law, and would be an effective defense under classic fault regimes.

So Mrs. Jones has a dilemma. Should she incur the cost of a contest over his fault, in the hope she can prevail — and prevail soon enough to make the effort worthwhile? Or should she perhaps try to induce Mr. Jones' agreement to a quicker consensual no-fault divorce, by offering to accept a reduced share of their marital property? This is probably not the scenario that waiting period proponents have in mind, but it is surely one that their proposals are likely to produce. Fans of fault often make the mistake of thinking that fault laws protect the innocent. They do not. They protect the person who does not care about delaying the divorce, at the expense of the person who does — and who may have very good reasons for wanting out. That is why the "bargaining chip" rationale for these rules doesn't work: no matter how we design them, it is inevitable that in many cases they will give bargaining leverage to the wrong spouse. We can achieve the goal of protecting the financially vulnerable spouse far more effectively by the direct strategy of reforming the law of alimony than by the indirect one of hoping that the imposition of a waiting period will allow the financially vulnerable spouse to negotiate a better deal.

NOTES

1. *Existing Laws on Mandatory Waiting Periods.* As *Koon* illustrates, some states never permitted unilateral no-fault divorce without long waiting periods. *Koon* required 2 years. The original MMDA "compromise" draft required that "marital breakdown" be "shown" by evidence of 180 days' separation. Missouri effectively imposes delay on unilateral divorces only, since parties who agree may present the court with fault grounds that require no wait. That is in fact what many do, as the English data cited by Ellman, *supra*, illustrate. One can instead impose delay on all divorces, in one of two ways: by requiring that the initial divorce decree be interlocutory, with a "final" divorce decree issued after an additional delay, or by imposing a statutory delay following service of process in a divorce suit. Prior to 1989, Nebraska employed both techniques, requiring a sixty-day wait following service of process, and another six months once the judge enters the decree of divorce. A 1978 study found that about 25% of Nebraska divorce actions are in fact dropped during these waiting periods. Frank, Berman & Mazur-Hart, *No Fault Divorce and the Divorce Rate: The Nebraska Experience — An Interrupted Time Series Analysis and Commentary*, 58 NEB. L. REV. 1, 78, 80 n.329. But, whether any lasting reconciliation has occurred in these cases is not known, and if so, whether these reconciliations were the result of delay imposed by the process, or would have occurred without it. For example, about 10% of currently-married American couples have experienced a separation and reconciliation in their marriage, and about one-third of women who attempted a reconciliation were still married to their husband more than one year afterward. See the sources cited in Howard Wineberg, *The Resolutions of Separation: Are Marital Reconciliations Attempted?*, 15 POPULATION RES. & POL'Y REV. 297 (1996).

2. *Premarital and Separation Agreements Limiting or Expanding Available Grounds for Termination Beyond Those Set Forth by*

Statute. Professor Scott observes that courts have been "lukewarm" toward premarital agreements restricting divorce. There are few cases on point. In *Penhallow v. Penhallow*, 649 A.2d 1016 (R.I. 1994), a court enforced a premarital agreement penalizing the spouse who initiated a divorce action in the allocation of marital property. In *Massar v. Massar*, 652 A.2d 219 (N.J. App. Div. 1995), a court enforced a separation agreement in which the husband promised to vacate the marital home in exchange for the wife's agreement not to seek divorce on a fault-based ground. Given New Jersey's statutes required 18 months' separation for a unilateral no-fault divorce, the agreement required the wife to incur this waiting period rather than seek a quicker fault-based divorce. When the wife petitioned six months later on grounds of extreme cruelty, the court enforced the agreement, rejecting the claim that it violated public policy. Yet, the court's language suggested that it might not be willing to enforce a *premarital* agreement limiting the parties' access to a fault-based divorce. It noted that in the instant case, the parties had "full knowledge of the conduct of each during the marriage which could form the basis for a cause of action for divorce. We do not suggest that the parties could enter an agreement which would preclude seeking . . . divorce on [fault grounds arising from] conduct which occurred after the execution of the agreement." *Id.* at 223. *But see P.B. v. L.B.*, 855 N.Y.S.2d 836 (Sup. Ct. 2008) (court refuses to enforce separation agreement provision under which husband (but not wife) was precluded from seeking divorce, for any reason, for five years, without wife's written consent; court held provision violated public policy for foreclosing no-fault ground of divorce, and because of one-sidedness).

A court's willingness to enforce a premarital agreement stipulating the grounds on which a divorce can proceed, or how evidence of "fault" will affect property distribution and support, may depend, in part, on whether the agreement's substantive provisions conflict with the state's public policy. California, for example, has thoroughly rejected fault-based divorce and its vestiges, in both the enumeration of grounds for divorce and the principles set forth for property division and support orders. Thus, not surprisingly, an appellate court refused to enforce a premarital contract provision requiring an adulterous spouse to pay "liquidated damages" as part of a divorce action, concluding the provision which would require examination of "fault in dissolving the marriage, dividing property, or ordering support" violated the public policy expressed in the no-fault divorce laws in 1969. *Diosdado v. Diosdado*, 97 Cal. App. 4th 470, 473, 118 Cal. Rptr. 2d 494, 496 (2002).

For discussion of the enforcement of obligations set forth in contracts entered into as part of religious traditions, see *Avitzur v. Avitzur*, 58 N.Y.2d 572, 459 N.Y.S.2d 572 (App. Div. 1983) (enforcing provision in Jewish marriage contract, i.e., a "Ketubah," permitting a religious court to summon the parties for marital counseling). See also *Akileh v. Elchahal*, 666 So. 2d 246 (Fla. Ct. App. 1996), described in Chapter 8, Section A[4] (addressing an Islamic marriage contract).

3. *Working Justice Between Divorcing Spouses?* Have no-fault divorce laws transformed marriage into a contract with no remedy for breach by one party? Whereas Professor Scott relies on a contract analogy to argue for a precommitment strategy for strengthening marital bonds, thus focusing on the notion of parties' agreeing in advance to the terms governing *termination* of their marriage, a different version of the contract argument focuses on the parties' terms for *conducting* the marriage. Professors Brinig and Crafton and Professor Ellman have debated the applicability of the contract analogy in this context:

> While marriage has many of the characteristics of relational contracting, it has become in many places a kind of unenforceable, illusory contract; it is splendid as long as both spouses are committed to the relationship but ethereal once one spouse decides to take advantage of the other. [T]he terms . . . are, to a great extent, the expectations of the parties as to the allowable parameters of marital behavior. . . . [Legal] changes . . . that make marital promises unenforceable . . . allow opportunistic behavior [and that is what is done by] the enactment in many states of no-fault divorce with the simultaneous removal of fault (breach) as a consideration in grants of spousal support and property division. A marriage is, as are many business relationships, now terminable at will, *but* without penalties for breach of other conditions.

Margaret F. Brinig & Steven M. Crafton, *Marriage and Opportunism*, 23 J. Legal Studies 869, 871–72 (1994). Professor Ellman rejects this model, arguing that, unlike commercial contracts, the ordinary marital "contract" is insufficiently specific enough to allow a court to determine when there has been a breach:

> The most fundamental requirement of contract is the ability to identify when there is a breach: a contract's terms must be sufficiently clear to permit this. What are the terms of the marriage contract . . .? [Brinig and Crafton suggest that] the words of the typical wedding ceremony — that the parties take each other "for richer or poorer, in sickness and in health . . . as long as life shall last" and will "love and cherish" one another — are intended to create contractual obligations, rather than to express by well-known ritual the parties' feelings of mutual love and commitment. . . . But neither contract theory nor existing law would treat such statements of intent as unconditional commitments to "care for," "live with," or "cherish" the other spouse, no matter what. Everyone understands that this is not what the parties really mean. [T]he wife who later ceases to love or cherish her husband is [not] always in breach. Even the most fault-regarding of divorce regimes would want to know the reason for her change of heart. Did she cease to love him because he turned out to be a poor provider or a bad father, or because she later decided she did not want to be the housewife that both of them initially expected her to be, or because she found she felt more passion for the neighbor across the street, or because as she matured and changed she concluded he was not worth her affection?

> The "contract" terms derivable from the wedding ceremony itself are . . . inadequate to tell us whether the answers to such questions matter. [Brinig and Crafton] suggest . . . that . . . the "terms of the marriage contract are the expectations of the parties as to the allowable parameters of marital behavior." But [they themselves] concede . . . that "the parties [are] incapable of reducing important terms of the arrangement to well-defined obligations." How then can this be contract? . . . [Because of the absence of such terms] judgments purportedly based on the parties'

. . . values will in reality be based on the judge's, which means that thinking of such an alimony remedy in contract terms obscures rather than reveals what is actually happening.

Ira Mark Ellman & Sharon Lohr, *Marriage as Contract, Opportunistic Violence, and Other Bad Arguments for Fault Divorce*, 1997 ILL. L. REV. 719, 746. Some critics of no-fault reform express concern that fault-based divorce policies are needed to protect an innocent spouse. Such protection could take any of several forms. If the "guilty" spouse cannot easily obtain a divorce over the objections of the "innocent" spouse, the "innocent" spouse has a bargaining chip in the negotiations regarding the financial aspects of the dissolution not available under no-fault. Furthermore, about half of the states still permit the consideration of marital misconduct in alimony awards, and a smaller group in the allocation of property. Professor Ellman argues that a rule awarding money at divorce on the premise that one spouse has caused the other harm has more in common with tort than with contract. Ira Mark Ellman, *The Place of Fault in a Modern Divorce Law*, 28 ARIZ. ST. L.J. 773 (1996). He states that such a rule is based on the defendant's violation of a duty to the person harmed, rather than on breach of promise. For a discussion of the special difficulties involved in using tort ideas to compensate individuals for marital misconduct, see Ira Mark Ellman & Stephen Sugarman, *Spousal Emotional Abuse As a Tort?*, 55 MD. L. REV. 1268 (1996). For a discussion of the use of fault rules to protect the innocent spouse from a feminist perspective, see Barbara Bennett Woodhouse & Katherine Bartlett, *Sex, Lies, and Dissipation: The Discourse of Fault in a No-Fault Era*, 82 GEORGETOWN L.J. 2525 (1994). The question of tort claims between divorcing spouses is treated more fully in Chapter 4.

What if dissolution will cause one spouse far more harm than the other, in ways that cannot be remedied by the divorce court? The British no-fault reforms gave judges discretion to deny a divorce, regardless of whether adequate grounds exist, where one party has shown that dissolution "will result in grave financial or other hardship to him and that it would in all circumstances be wrong to dissolve the marriage." Divorce Reform Act, 1969, C. 55, § 4(2)(6). An Indiana case, *Abney v. Abney*, 374 N.E.2d 264 (Ind. App. 1978), provides an example of what the drafters may have had in mind. James Abney had been denied a divorce in Tennessee, where Dorothy Abney lived after their separation. He was paying support to her under a Tennessee separation decree, and the Tennessee courts had ordered Abney not to seek dissolution in Indiana. Indiana declined to honor this Tennessee order:

> Dorothy. . . . argues . . . the . . . court should have exercised equitable discretion to deny the dissolution, notwithstanding its finding that the marriage was irretrievably broken. . . . [¶] . . . When . . . the marriage is . . . irretrievably broken . . . the Act directs the . . . court to grant dissolution. . . . [¶] The . . . court [has] no alternative.

> We are not insensitive to [her] ultimate concern. . . . She suffers from severe rheumatoid arthritis which requires costly medical treatment. [T]he assistance she has been receiving through [James'] military benefits terminates upon dissolution. . . . [she] claims these benefits are her "life

blood" and respectfully asserts that the equities compel us to reverse the dissolution decree.

> . . . Admittedly, the . . . court found that James . . . is economically unable to . . . offset the loss of the . . . benefits. Yet we are without authority to reverse a dissolution decree . . . solely because the . . . dissolution will . . . terminate benefits . . . advantageous to one of the parties.

Abney, 374 N.E.2d at 269–70. For other installments of the saga, see *Abney v. Abney*, 360 N.E.2d 1044 (Ind. App. 1977); 456 S.W.2d 364 (Tenn. App. 1970), and 433 S.W.2d 847 (Tenn. 1968). *See also Bartz v. Bartz*, 452 N.W.2d 160 (Wis. App. 1989) (trial court may not refuse divorce even though loss of husband's health insurance would impose financial hardship for wife).

The British considered repeal of their "hardship" provision, *Facing the Future: A Discussion Paper on the Ground for Divorce, (supra)*, but decided against it, British Law Comm., *The Ground for Divorce* (Law Com. No. 192, 1990). It only applies to divorces sought on the basis of five years' separation, less than 6 % of all British divorces, and has been successfully invoked in only two reported cases, both involving lost pensions. Ingman, *Reform of the Ground for Divorce, in* FAMILY LAW 94 (1989). French law has a similar provision, allowing a judge to dismiss a petition for a no-fault divorce (available only after six years' separation) if the divorce would entail "material or moral consequences of exceptional hardship" for the unwilling spouse or their children. French courts have applied this provision in cases to deny divorce where the court concludes that the nonconsenting spouse's physical or mental health would be deleteriously affected, as where the wife "who suffers already from having been abandoned by her husband, would be subject to reproach" in her Catholic community. MARY ANN GLENDON, ABORTION AND DIVORCE IN WESTERN LAW 72–74 (1987).

4. *Covenant Marriage.* In 1997, Louisiana created a two-track divorce system via the establishment of "covenant marriage." Leaving intact its "standard" no-fault divorce provisions, which allow divorce after a six-month period of separation, LA. CIV. CODE art. 102, the legislature created different rules for exit from covenant marriage. LA. REV. ST. §§ 9:272 to 9:275, 9:307 to 9:309. Since August 15, 1997, those marrying in Louisiana have had the option of choosing between standard marriage or covenant marriage, and already-married couples have been permitted to "convert" their existing marriages into covenant marriages. Parties must recite words expressing the following:

> We do solemnly declare that marriage is a covenant between a man and a woman who agree to live together as husband and wife for so long as they both may live. We have chosen each other carefully and disclosed to one another everything which could adversely affect the decision to enter into this marriage. We have received premarital counseling on the nature, purposes, and responsibilities of marriage. We have read the Covenant Marriage Act, and we understand that a Covenant Marriage is for life. If we experience marital difficulties, we commit ourselves to take all reasonable efforts to preserve our marriage, including marital counseling.

LA. ST. REV. § 9:273. Prior to the ceremony, the parties must submit evidence of premarital counseling and an understanding of the terms and provisions of the covenant marriage statutes. Section 9:307 governs dissolutions of covenant marriages, and lists several fault grounds (i.e., proof of adultery, sentence of death or imprisonment at hard labor for conviction of a felony, abandonment of the marital domicile for one year and refusing to return, physical or sexual abuse of the petitioner or a child of one of them), and also permits divorce upon a period of two years' separation without reconciliation. The statute also permits dissolution if the parties, having no minor children, have been separated for one year without reconciliation after a judgment of separation. If the parties have a minor child or children, 18 months of separation is required unless there has been domestic violence or child abuse, in which case one year is sufficient. LA. ST. REV. § 9:307A(6)(a)&(b). Judgments of separation are available on the same grounds as dissolution plus an additional ground: "habitual intemperance of the other spouse, or . . . cruel treatment or outrages of the other spouse . . . that render their living together insupportable." LA. ST. REV. § 307B(6).

The provisions governing dissolution of covenant marriage in Louisiana are not, in substance, highly unusual. After all, several states require a period of separation of two years or more before granting a no-fault divorce (e.g., Maryland, New Hampshire, Pennsylvania, Rhode Island), and in these states, the separation period exists as an alternative to fault grounds. What makes Louisiana's enactment of covenant marriage unique is that it was the first state to adopt a statute that makes divorce *harder* to obtain since no-fault swept the country between 1970 and 1985. Covenant marriage appeared after several years of completely unsuccessful attempts by no-fault opponents in a handful of states to repeal no-fault reforms. *See, e.g.,* Laura Bradford, Note, *The Counterrevolution: A Critique of Recent Proposals to Reform No-Fault Divorce Laws,* 49 STAN. L. REV. 607, 617–620 (1996). No-fault opponents, having come to understand that legislatures were unwilling to roll back no-fault reforms, saw covenant marriage as a compromise means by which to reintroduce fault, while leaving no-fault statutes intact. Its advocates argue that it is a form of private ordering, allowing couples to choose the marital regime most congruent with their values and goals. From this vantage point, one can analogize covenant marriage to a premarital contract with predetermined nonwaivable terms.

Professor Elizabeth Scott characterizes covenant marriage as introducing a type of precommitment mechanism. *Marriage as Precommitment, supra,* at 172. Although she believes the fault-based provisions of covenant marriage regimes detract from their virtues, she believes such statutes are a "first step toward an approach to reform of no-fault divorce law that [treats] restriction on divorce as precommitment undertaken by the couple entering marriage, to assist them to achieve their goals for a lasting relationship." Obviously, within this framework, allowing spouses to modify or rescind the terms of the exit provisions would undercut the goals of covenant marriage. Covenant marriage proponents assert marriage will be strengthened by premarital counseling requirements, provisions for resolving marital problems through "reasonable efforts to preserve the marriage," and creation of barriers to marital exit. Furthermore, proponents assert that covenant marriage conveys to marrying partners the concept of marriage as a life-long commitment. Other advantages include the invitation to religious and other community organizations to help support marriages, and the asserted restoration of "some power and some protection to the 'innocent' spouse who desires to continue the marriage." Katherine Shaw Spaht, *Louisiana's Covenant Marriage: Social Analysis and Legal Implications*, 59 LA. L. REV. 63, 74–78 (1998).

What is the other side of the covenant marriage argument? The first criticism is that there is no evidence that making divorce harder to obtain reduces the divorce rate or makes marriage stronger or more stable. A corollary criticism asserts that the same objections lodged against fault-based divorce can be lodged against covenant marriage. *See, e.g.*, Amy L. Stewart, Note, *Covenant Marriage: Legislating Family Values*, 32 IND. L. REV. 509, 522–23, 535 (1999) (referring to covenant marriage as "the ghost of a system that was declared dead three decades ago"); *see also* Heather K. McShain, *For Better or Worse: A Closer Look at Two Implications of Covenant Marriage*, 32 FAM. L.Q. 629 (1998). For example, unhappy spouses may replicate the patterns of their predecessors who engaged in collusion and evasion to avoid restrictive divorce laws. As noted in Section C2, *supra*, long pre-divorce waiting periods may be particularly difficult for children to weather. Furthermore, victims of psychologically-abusive relationships, who lack a fault-based remedy under Louisiana's covenant marriage divorce statute, may be prevented from escaping such marriages in a timely manner, subjecting them, and possibly their children, to sustained emotional harm.

Given the voluntary nature of covenant marriage, however, proponents view its availability as a positive manifestation of pluralism in marital choice. From this perspective, the existence of covenant marriage raises the basic questions suggested by enforcement of premarital contracts more generally. That is, to what extent should people entering marriage be permitted to bind themselves before marriage to terms governing marital exit? This question is the subject of debate with respect to premarital contracts generally and are discussed in Chapter 8. Note also that if a state does not allow parties to a covenant marriage to divorce by mutual consent (Arizona does), then the covenant marriage is not properly described as a contract, because it lacks the normal feature of any contract that the parties to it can always revise or rescind it by their later agreement. The fact that the statutes typically make no provision for the parties to agree on converting *from* covenant marriage to standard marriage has been criticized as binding couples to an arrangement even if upon reflection, they now believe the "choice . . . was ill-conceived or ill-advised." Chauncey E. Brummer, *The Shackles of Covenant Marriage: Who Holds the Keys to Wedlock?* 25 U. ARK. LITTLE ROCK L. REV. 261, 289 (2003). For a thoughtful analysis of the potential impact of covenant marriage, examining arguments on both sides, see Jean Louise Carriere, *"It's Deja Vu All Over Again": The Covenant Marriage Act in Popular Cultural Perception and Legal Reality*, 72 TUL. L. REV. 1701 (1998).

5. *The Future of Covenant Marriage.* While Lousiana got considerable attention when it adopted covenant marriage, the idea has not swept the country. While many legislatures have considered similar statutes, Lynne Marie Kohm, *A Comparative Survey of Covenant Marriage Proposals in the United States*, 12 REGENT U.l. REV. 31 (1999–2000) (reviewing state proposals), only two have joined Louisiana in enacting them, ARIZ. REV. ST. § 25-901 *et seq.* (adopted in 1998); ARK. CODE §§ 9-11-802 *et seq.* (adopted in 2001). While similar in principle, these statutes differ slightly. For example, Arizona permits covenant marriage spouses to avoid the fault grounds and the two-year waiting period by mutual consent. ARIZ. REV. ST. § 25-903.8.

It may be that covenant marriage is an idea whose time has come and gone. Florida, the site of the first covenant marriage proposal (in 1990), failed repeatedly to pass the bill and the attempts appear to have ended.. The number of state legislatures considering covenant marriage proposals has dropped annually. In 2003, proposals were introduced in the legislatures of Indiana, Iowa, Mississippi, Missouri, Oklahoma, Texas, Utah, and Virginia. The bills never emerged from committees in some states. In other states, the proposals failed to pass one or both legislative houses. In an interesting follow-up to Louisiana's enactment of its covenant marriage statutes, in 1998 the state legislature asked the Louisiana State Law Institute to make recommendations as to the merits of reinstating fault as a prerequisite to *all* Louisiana divorces. In 2002, the Institute strongly recommended against such a move. Kenneth Rigby, *Report and Recommendations of the Louisiana State Law Institute to the House Civil Law Committee of the Louisiana Legislature Relative to the Reinstatement of Fault as a Prerequisite of Divorce*, 62 LA. L. REV. 561 (2002) (concluding return to fault would not improve quality of marriage and would promote animosity between spouses).

Not only have state legislatures failed to embrace the covenant marriage concept, but very few marrying couples in the covenant marriage states have chosen to avail themselves of the option. For example, data obtained from the Louisiana State Center for Health Statistics reveal that in 1998, 1999, and 2000 respectively, covenant marriages constituted 1.54%, 1.21%, and 1.16% of the annual number of new marriages. State Center for Health Statistics, Office of Public Health, State of Louisiana, Vital Statistics Data Tables, www.oph.dhh.state.la.us/recordsstatistics/statistics;page0cda.html?page=117 (visited 2004).[3]The number of covenant marriages in this three-year period totaled 1,577. (Louisiana's published statistics do not indicate how many existing marriages converted to covenant marriages, and what proportion of divorces were covenant marriage divorces.) For a review of the early Louisiana experience by the author of the statute, see Katherine Shaw Spaht, *Covenant Marriage Seven Years Later*, 65 LA. L. REV. 605 (2005) (concludes court clerks and the clergy "have failed in different ways to embrace the [covenant marriage] option"). Arizona statistics likewise demonstrate only minimal interest in the institution by the public. During the period from enactment (1998) through January 2000, the Maricopa County (Phoenix) Recorder issued 316 licenses for covenant marriages as compared with 16,168 ordinary marriage licenses (thus, covenant marriages constituted 1.95% of the new marriages). *Covenant Marriages Haven't Exactly Caught On In State*, THE ARIZONA REPUBLIC, Feb. 18, 2001, at A12. Finally, statistics from Arkansas are remarkably similar to those from the other two covenant marriage states. According to data compiled by the Arkansas Department of Health for the years 2002 (the first full year covenant marriage was available) through 2007 (made

---

[3] The website at this URL is no longer active and a search for information concerning covenant marriages in Louisianna for 1998 through 2000 has been fruitless. Professor Kurtz recorded this information from that website for the Fourth Edition of this casebook.

available to Professor Kurtz in an email), the yearly total of covenant marriages ranged from 185 (2004) to 318 (2005). The yearly total for the number of marriages performed in the state ranged from 35,077 (2006) to 38,816 (2002). During the six years, 1,358 covenant marriages were performed out of 218,757. While no precise statistics are available concerning the conversion of "regular" to "covenant" marriages, the Department estimates that 1,349 marriages were converted during the six-year period, with 1,162 occurring in 2005, the year then-Governor Mike Huckabee and his wife converted their 30-year marriage to a covenant marriage on Valentine's Day before a crowd of 5,000. Rick Lyman, *Trying to Strengthen an "I Do" With a More Binding Legal Tie*, N.Y. TIMES, Feb. 15, 2005, at A5.

Especially given the very small proportion of newlyweds who choose covenant marriage, there is no way to tell whether it reduces divorce. The problem is that those who choose it are almost certainly different in important respects than the great majority who do not. Comparisons between them and the rest of the population will therefore tell us less about the effects of covenant marriage than it will about the characteristics of those who chose it. One report found that the groups differ on both demographic and attitudinal variables, such as their levels of religious involvement, whether they cohabited prior to marriage, and whether they favor more egalitarian or more traditional gender roles in marriage. Steven L. Nock, et al., *Covenant Marriage Turns Five Years Old*, 10 MICH. J. GENDER & L. 169 (2003). These findings are consistent with earlier attitudinal surveys revealing that persons who hold more conservative gender-role ideologies and are more active in their religious institutions are more likely to endorse the concept of covenant marriage. *See, e.g.*, Alan J. Hawkins et al., *Attitudes About Covenant Marriage and Divorce: Policy Implications From a Three-State Comparison*, 51 FAM. RELATIONS 166 (2002); Laura Sanchez, et al., *Setting the Clock Forward or Back? Covenant Marriage and the "Divorce Revolution,"* 23 J. FAM. ISSUES 91 (2002).

Some argue that whatever the virtues of covenant marriage itself, the proposal has been valuable for the debate that it has generated about the appropriate legal response to changing domestic life. STEVEN NOCK, LAURA SANCHEZ & JAMES WRIGHT, COVENANT MARRIAGE: THE MOVEMENT TO RECLAIM TRADITION IN AMERICA (2008).

6. *The Interstate Effect of a Covenant Marriage.* Does a covenant marriage really bind the parties? Almost certainly not if they are willing to travel. As detailed below in Chapter 7 on Jurisdiction, American courts always apply their own law in deciding whether to terminate a marriage. In the era when most states had restrictive divorce laws, this led to "migratory divorce" in which one of the spouses would acquire domicile in a state with more relaxed divorce laws, giving its courts jurisdiction to grant a divorce. The Supreme Court ultimately held that other states were bound, under the Full Faith and Credit Clause, to honor such a divorce decree. There is no reason why the same principle would not apply to a divorce a no-fault state granted to one of the spouses to a covenant marriage. Peter Hay, *The American "Covenant Marriage" in the Conflict of Laws*, 64 LA. L. REV. 43 (2003) (in light of traditional choice of law in divorce and trends in marriage and divorce law in foreign countries "the legal efficacy of covenant marriages is basically restricted to the state in which they are contracted when the issue arises there"); *see also* Brian H. Bix, *Choice of Law and Marriage: A Proposal*, 36 FAM.

L.Q. 255, 260 (2002); Brian H. Bix, *State of the Union: The States' Interest in the Marital Status of their Citizens*, 55 U. MIAMI L. REV. 1, 21 (2000). One writer who concedes that this is the American law suggests Canadian courts might apply the law of the state in which the spouses entered marriage. Lily Ng, *Covenant Marriage and the Conflict of Laws*, 44 ALBERTA L. REV. 815 (2007).

7. *Other Proposals to Strengthen Marriage.*   Other initiatives seek to reduce divorce by strengthening marriage and can be usefully divided into two groups: those seeking to encourage forethought regarding decisions to enter marriage, and those seeking to strengthen existing marriages. These approaches differ from legal policies regulating divorce in that they seek to prevent dysfunctional marriages from coming into being, and to ameliorate marital problems, rather than simply restricting unhappy couples' access to divorce. For example, approaches seeking to improve the quality of couples' decisions to marry include statutes providing minor incentives (such as reductions in the marital license fee) for couples' participation in a premarital counseling program. *See e.g.*, 43 OKLA. ST. § 5-B-2. Florida, Maryland, and Minnesota also have similar initiatives. National Conference of State Legislatures, *State Trends in Marriage and Divorce Legislation*, www.ncsl.org/programs/cyf/marriagefact.htm. Some states encourage applicants for marriage licenses to attend a premarital education course. *See, E.g.*, TEX. FAM. CODE § 2.013. Under Florida's Marriage Preparation and Preservation Act, those seeking marriage licenses are given a marriage preparation handbook. Furthermore, graduation from high school in Florida now requires a course relating to relationship skills.

Approaches geared toward improving the quality of existing marriages include those in Oklahoma (Oklahoma Marriage Initiative, bringing together policymakers, social scientists, community and religious leaders to develop strategies to strengthen marriage;); New Hampshire (creating a committee to develop a marriage education and enhancement program); and Arizona (creating an advisory Marriage and Communication Skills Commission in 2000). For a summary and description of marital promotion and support policies and proposals across the states, see Karen N. Gardiner, et al., *State Policies to Promote Marriage* (2002), http://aspe.hhs.gov/hsp/marriage02f/.

In a parallel movement, private community efforts to promote and support marriages have become increasingly popular. Most such efforts have been organized by religious institutions, with explicit goals of encouraging better decisions regarding marital entry and providing support and counseling to those couples who marry. As of early 2006, clergy in approximately 200 cities nationwide had adopted the Community Marriage Policies. *See* www.marriagesavers.org/sitems/News/News060124LasCruces.htm. Founded in Modesto, California in 1986, this movement encourages the clergy of a community to agree not to perform a wedding unless certain conditions are met. While each community group writes its own policy, an illustrative policy in Tallahassee, Florida requires a one-year courtship, five counseling sessions, trained married couple/mentors for young marrieds, and clergy-sponsored couples' retreats. Kristina Zurcher, Note, *"I Do" or "I Don't"? Covenant Marriage After Six Years*, 18 N.D. J.L. ETHICS & PUB. POL'Y 273, 297 (2004); *see also, e.g., Across our Nation*, INDIANAPOLIS NEWS/INDIANAPOLIS STAR, Dec. 6, 2003 (describing signing of the

Covenant by 50 clergy leaders in Indianapolis); Deidre Erin Murphy, *To Have and To Hold*, PORTLAND PRESS HERALD, June 7, 2003 (describing similar movement in Portland, Maine).

PROBLEMS

Consider the statutory proposals set forth in the following problems and explain (a) how they would change the law of your state, or why they would not change the law of your state; (b) why they would or would not be good policy; and (c) what changes or amendments you would suggest.

Problem 3-1. Upon the joint verified petition of any husband and wife, filed with the clerk of the superior court, the clerk shall issue a decree of divorce terminating their marital status. If the petition provides for the custody of any minor children, the support obligations of either of the spouses, or the division of the spouses' property, the decree shall incorporate the provisions. If the petition does not provide for these matters, the spouses may later submit a joint sworn petition which does, and the clerk shall cause the original decree to be amended to incorporate the provisions of the second petition. Either spouse may separately petition the court to seek an order covering matters not dealt with in a decree issued pursuant to a joint sworn petition, or to modify an order for support or custody incorporated in such a decree. Such a separate petition shall be dealt with according to the ordinary rules for handling post-decree matters in domestic relations cases.

Problem 3-2. The clerk of the superior court shall issue a decree terminating a marriage on the 91st day following the filing of a sworn request for such a decree by either spouse. Notice of the request shall be given to the non-moving spouse within 10 days of its filing, by first class, certified, or registered mail. If before the issuance of the order the clerk receives a sworn statement of both spouses providing for the division of their property, their support obligations, or the custody of their children, the decree terminating the marriage shall incorporate these provisions. Either spouse may separately petition the court for an order covering such matters, if not dealt with by a joint sworn statement, or to modify an order for support or custody based upon such a statement. Such a separate petition shall be dealt with according to the ordinary rules for handling post-decree matters in domestic relations cases.

Problem 3-3. No decree of divorce shall be issued in any marriage in which there are minor children, except when the following conditions have been met:

(a) at least one year has passed since a petition for divorce has been filed, and

(b) for a period of at least one year, both spouses have regularly met with a licensed marriage counselor in an effort to effect a reconciliation, and

(c) the court finds that there are no realistic prospects for reconciliation, and

(d) there is clear and convincing evidence that termination of the marriage is consistent with the best interests of the minor children.

Problem 3-4.   When applying for a marriage license, each couple shall file with the county clerk a notarized statement, signed by each, setting forth the grounds upon which their marriage may be terminated. In particular, the statement may indicate:

(a) that either spouse shall have the right to terminate the marriage without cause, and, if so, any required notice period before such termination is effective;

(b) that cause shall be required for termination on the petition of either spouse, and, if so, what cause shall be sufficient;

(c) that the marriage may not be terminated for any reason, including the mutual consent of the spouses, either for a specified period after its solemnization, or at all;

(d) that the marriage be terminated solely upon the mutual consent of the spouses; or

(e) that the marriage may be terminated only in accordance with the religious principles of a specified faith, provided that the statement specifies a religious authority which shall rule on any divorce petition that may be filed.

Any marriage for which such a statement has been filed may not be terminated except in accordance with its terms. If no such statement has been filed, a marriage may be terminated by either spouse, without cause and upon 90 days' notice.

Chapter 4

PROPERTY DIVISION AND ALIMONY UPON DIVORCE

INTRODUCTION

In most divorce cases, a large portion of the lawyer's efforts focus on the financial issues: property division, alimony (or as it is increasingly called, spousal support or maintenance) and child support. In this chapter, we deal with the first two. The introductory materials place the doctrinal discussions of property division and alimony in a larger practical context. Of course, most divorces are settled, so that litigated alimony and property disputes, like litigated child support and custody disputes, are uncommon. But, as in all fields, settlement terms are affected by the legal rules a judge would apply in litigation. They are also affected by the tax laws, which treat alimony, but not property allocations, as income to the recipient with a corresponding deduction for the obligor. (Child support is also not income to the recipient and not deductible for the obligor; dispositions of property may or may not trigger capital gains taxes depending on how they are arranged.) Tax laws as well as family law rules are thus important considerations to attorneys fashioning an agreement.

THE RELATION OF PROPERTY DIVISION TO ALIMONY

Although we defer consideration of alimony until after exploring property division, their relationship to each other must be acknowledged at the outset. Because they are both simply awards of resources, in judging the fairness of the divorce's financial result it is necessary to look at both the property division and the alimony award, which constitute a single economic package. Both property awards and alimony can be structured either as lump sum payments or as periodic payments (though it is more usual for alimony to be periodic); and periodic payments for a specified period of time are financially equivalent to a lump-sum payment. In the course of negotiating the terms of dissolution, there are a variety of reasons for preferring a property award over an alimony obligation, or vice versa. Some of these reasons have to do with current ability to pay, a preference for the certainty of current payment over a future obligation, or the desire to prevent modification of the obligation. For many couples, the most important reasons for choosing one over the other are the different treatments of property division and alimony under tax law and bankruptcy.

RULES OF MARITAL PROPERTY

AMERICAN LAW INSTITUTE, PRINCIPLES OF THE LAW OF FAMILY DISSOLUTION
21–23 (2002)

The common-law treated property owned by the spouses during their marriage as the individual property of one of them unless, as to a particular piece of property, they had acted to create joint ownership. The title in which property was held was critical. The usual effect was to vest ownership in the spouse who earned the money with which the property was purchased, although that owner could make a gift to the other spouse by shifting property to joint title, or sole title in the other spouse's name. At divorce each spouse was allocated his or her property. The result in most cases was to allocate the bulk of the property to the husband. Alimony was therefore often the only financial remedy available to meet claims the divorced wife might have on her own behalf, as contrasted with claims of child support she might make on behalf of her children.

Community-property law begins with the contrary presumption: all earnings from spousal labor during the marriage are the property of the marital "community" in which each spouse has an undivided one-half interest. Property acquired with spousal earnings is therefore ["community property"] owned equally by the spouses, regardless of whether purchased with funds earned by the husband, the wife, or both, unless the parties change the character of the property by agreement or gift. In three community-property states [California, Louisiana, and New Mexico], all community property is divided at divorce into spousal shares equal in value, although not necessarily identical in kind. Alimony (renamed as "spousal support" or "maintenance" in most jurisdictions) may also be allowed, as determined on a case-by-case basis.

This sharp dichotomy between common-law and community-property traditions no longer prevails in the United States. All the common-law states now allow the divorce court to distribute ["marital property," which includes all property derived from earnings during marriage] between [the divorcing spouses,] on a basis other than common-law principles of ownership, under a doctrine known generally as "equitable distribution." Five of the eight community property states also instruct their divorce courts to divide the community-property between the spouses "equitably" (rather than "equally"). Equitable distribution is the dominant rule today, followed everywhere but in the three "equal division" community-property states.

The consensus, however, is not so great as first appears. In community property states, the concept of joint ownership is pervasive, applicable not only at dissolution but also at death and during the intact marriage. The common-law states, in contrast, generally retain their traditional separate-ownership principles in all matters other than the system of equitable distribution they apply at divorce. These different starting points in the basic underlying concepts of ownership may yield differences in the application of equitable-distribution rules that are similar in form. The two most critical features of any law of equitable distribution are its rules for identifying the pool available for allocation on equitable grounds, and its default or presumptive allocation rule. The trend in equitable division states has favored a presumption, whether formal or in practice, that an equitable division of property is an equal division, but not all states follow this pattern, and its strength varies among those that do. Such differences in the default allocation rule are sometimes related to differences in the definition of property available for allocation. Strong presumptions of equal division are more common among states that limit the pool of allocable property by excluding inherited property, or property owned by the spouses individually before their marriage. States that put all property owned by either spouse into the allocable pool tend to employ more discretionary rules of allocation. California is a leading example of the first kind; it requires equal division in all cases, but has detailed and comprehensive rules distinguishing the equally divided community property from each spouse's "separate property," which the court cannot reallocate to the other spouse.

Looking behind these differences nonetheless reveals some common substantive themes. For example, even in those states that do not require or strongly presume equal division, property acquired with marital labor (that is, labor by a spouse during marriage) is often divided equally at dissolution. At the same time, courts in states that in principle allow the court to allocate all property owned by the spouses, in fact tend nonetheless to treat property inherited by one spouse during the marriage differently than property acquired through marital labor. Important distinctions among the states thus emerge primarily at the next level of detail: when is a case not "ordinary," so that an equal-division presumption should not apply? When, if ever, should the court be allowed to divide property that one of the spouses inherited or owned before the marriage?

One helpful overview of property division issues was given by Robert J. Levy, Reporter for the Model Marriage and Divorce Act. Levy states that a family lawyer facing a property division question should ask four questions regarding any item potentially subject to division:

(1)   is an item property?

(2)   is it marital or separate property?

(3)   how much is it worth (valuation)?

(4)   what is the basis/standard for division/distribution?

Robert J. Levy, *An Introduction to Divorce-Property Issues*, 23 FAM. L.Q. 147, 147 (1989).

All of these questions and distinctions will be revisited in the coming sections.

A. PROPERTY DIVISION: GENERAL PRINCIPLES

[1]   The Classic Common Law Title Rule

As already mentioned, prior to their adoption of equitable division as the principle of property division at divorce, common law states divided property at divorce according to who owned title. This usually produced a one-sided division in the husband's favor, as (1) many women did not work outside the home; (2) those who did work outside the home usually made far less than their husbands did; and (3) in those times and jurisdictions where the traditional rule of "coverture" applied, whatever property the wife brought to the marriage automatically became the property of the husband.

The harshness of the classic common law title approach is exemplified by *Saff v. Saff*, 61 A.D.2d 452, 402 N.Y.S.2d 690 (1978), *appeal dismissed*, 46 N.Y.2d 969, 415 N.Y.S.2d 829, 389 N.E.2d 142 (1979). Mr. and Mrs. Saff were married in 1936. Both worked at various jobs and held the accumulated funds jointly. In 1946, Mr. Saff and a partner founded Jamestown Fabricated Steel; each invested $2000. Mr. Saff's contribution came from the Saffs' joint funds; however, Mrs. Saff never had an express legal interest in the business. At the time of divorce, the company was estimated to have a net worth exceeding $500,000. The court stated:

> A minority of the court would grant [Mrs. Saff] relief by imposing a constructive trust. . . .

> Before the court may declare that [Mr. Saff] holds his separately owned property as a trustee for [Mrs. Saff]'s benefit, [Mrs. Saff] must prove that there was (1) a promise by him — express or implied, (2) which caused her to transfer property to him relying on the promise, (3) that a confidential relationship existed between the parties and (4) that [Mr. Saff] has been unjustly enriched at her expense by his conduct.

> Marriage is a confidential relationship, of course, and there was a transfer of funds and labor by [Mrs. Saff] to [Mr. Saff]. The remedy of constructive trust, however, requires more. There must be proof that the transfer was made in reliance on a promise that the property transferred would be held for the benefit of [Mrs. Saff], and that [Mr. Saff] was enriched unjustly by retaining the fruits of the transfer.

> We find no express promise by [Mr. Saff]. [Mrs. Saff] testified that from 1946 to 1960, apparently after the purchase of the business, [Mr. Saff] told her on various occasions, "Baby girl, what is mine is yours; you're my wife. It's always all half yours, you're my wife." Such representations undoubtedly reflected the emotions of a happier time but they most assuredly did not constitute a promise by [Mr. Saff] that he held one-half of his corporate stock as trustee for [Mrs. Saff]. The statements meant precisely what most people would interpret them to mean — not that [Mrs. Saff] had a proprietary interest in every personal belonging of [Mr. Saff], be it clothing or corporate stock, but rather that the parties would share their successes equally in raising their family and enjoying their life together.

61 A.D.2d at 455–56.

The court found no implied promise, adding: "The remedy of constructive trust may not be applied randomly to adjust general equities between spouses or as a punitive measure to divvy up a husband's separately owned property because of his past indiscretion." *Id.* at 456.

After noting that Mrs. Saff had been compensated, by salary, for some of her work for the company, the court commented:

> There was no unjust enrichment of [Mr. Saff]. [Mrs. Saff] has been more than adequately compensated for her efforts and in ways fully to be expected in a marriage. [Mr. Saff] has kept the couple happily circumstanced for 30 years. All of his earnings from the company were deposited in the couple's joint accounts and were used to support [Mrs. Saff]. Generous purchases of property and investments were made from these funds for her. The income has been sufficient to enable her to travel, to enjoy the satisfying social and athletic life which she described in her testimony as the routine of "the most beautiful marriage in the world." [Mrs. Saff] will continue to enjoy the support available through [Mr. Saff]'s efforts, by the separately owned property accumulated for her or, if her needs require it, by [Mr. Saff]'s income for as long as he is able to do so. There is no need for a division of [Mr. Saff]'s capital. . . .

> [Mrs. Saff] is not penniless. She came to this marriage with few material assets but she has lived a financially secure life for over 30 years since then. The Trial Court granted her exclusive, tax free use of the marital residence and the extensive furnishings in it. She has joint ownership in $100,000 in stocks, several thousand dollars of various stocks in her own name, $15,200 in savings and ownership of a sizeable insurance policy on her husband's life. In addition to this, she receives $12,500 a year income from her part-time employment at Jamestown Steel and she has dividend income of $3,600 per year. Neither the Trial Court nor the majority of this court find alimony justified on these facts.

> .   This case is a vivid illustration of the dangers of creating a judicial version of a community property law. A businessman or businesswoman ought to be able to determine whether his or her spouse is a partner in business, a partner in marriage, or both, without obtaining a judicial decree, after the fact, based upon nebulous and subjective concepts of what is equitable. The result sought by [Mrs. Saff] here would foist an unwanted business partner on [Mr. Saff and his partner], a business partner who may be motivated by considerations unrelated to the best interests of Jamestown Steel, those who own it and those who are employed by it. It is one thing to make an equitable adjustment of real and personal property of divorced spouses. It is quite another thing for a court of equity to trifle with corporate enterprises involving the vital interests of innocent third parties.

Id. at 458–59.

The common law title system effectively employed a narrow "contribution" principle: property is allocated between the spouses in proportion to their direct financial contribution to the marriage. The traditional homemaker earned nothing and was therefore entitled to nothing: to obtain a portion of the accumulated property, she had to show that she earned part of it herself by "direct business services of the type which an employee or partner" would contribute. *Patterson v. Patterson*, 277 S.E.2d 708, 712 (W. Va. 1981). The "constructive trust" doctrine was the only escape from the title system under the traditional common law, and it had limited utility. Constructive trust is an equitable remedy available to the party who can show that he or she is the true owner of property held by another, which most wives could not do under traditional common law principles (the dissenters in *Saff* supported the application of "constructive trust" in that case, but, as seen, the majority rejected that approach).

Some common-law courts avoided the harsher results of the traditional title system by applying the constructive trust doctrine more flexibly to aid wives who had participated directly in their husbands' businesses. Some courts also divided property under the guise of "alimony" awards giving the wife, for example, the family car and a life estate in the family residence. *Patterson v. Patterson, supra,* at 709. Such tactics often achieved a more equitable result, but did not approach either the generosity of the community property system or the flexibility of an equitable distribution system.

[2]   Equal Division

The historic American alternative to the common law title system was the community property system. Essential to that system is the distinction between community property and separate property briefly explained in the introductory section's excerpt from the *ALI Principles*. Each spouse took his or her separate property at the marriage's conclusion, but community property is divided at divorce between the spouses. Today, the common law states use a largely analogous set of rules that distinguish what they call "marital property" from separate property. Income earned during the marriage is community or marital property, while property received during the marriage by gift or inheritance is separate. Property acquired by either spouse before the marriage is also separate. As a general matter, property acquired in exchange for other property assumes the character of the property traded for it. Thus, if a spouse buys shares of stock with funds earned during the marriage, the shares are community or marital. If the same spouse owned stock before the marriage, sells it during the marriage, and buys new stock with the proceeds, the new stock is separate property (as were the predecessor shares). This rule can require tracing assets the spouses hold at divorce back to their source. A spouse cannot change community property into separate property by unilateral action. For example, a car purchased with earnings during marriage is community property even though the spouse who bought it had title placed in his or her name alone. Common law states usually follow the same rule with respect to marital property. The foregoing sets forth the basics; complications can and do arise, and Section B below examines the classification rules in more detail. In this section, we begin our examination of the allocation rule itself: how is marital (or community) property divided at divorce?

Most states employ a rule of "equitable" distribution, detailed in the next section, which allows the trial court some discretion in deciding upon the fair division of the marital or community property between the spouses. A smaller group, however, employs a rule of equal division. Three community property states require strict equal division in all cases, including, most importantly, California, CAL. FAM. CODE § 2550. Louisiana has a similar provision, LA. REV. STAT. ANN. § 9:2801(A)(4)(b) ("court shall divide the community assets and liabilities so that each spouse receives property of an equal net value"), and New Mexico has reached the same result by judicial decision. *Ruggles v. Ruggles*, 860 P.2d 182, 188 (N.M. 1993) ("property attributable to community earnings must be divided equally when the community is dissolved"). The remaining community property states (Arizona, Idaho, Nevada, Texas and Washington) follow a rule of "equitable distribution." However, some of those states create a strong *presumption* of equal division. *See, e.g.,* IDAHO CODE § 32-712(1)(A) ("Unless there are compelling reasons otherwise, there shall be a substantially equal division in value, considering debts, between the spouses."); NEV. REV. STAT. § 125.150(1)(b) (requiring "an equal disposition of the community property of the parties" unless "the court finds a compelling reason" to make an unequal distribution and "sets forth in writing the reasons for making the unequal disposition.").

While no common law property state has a rule *mandating* equal division, some have presumptions similar to the Nevada rule, that marital property should be divided equally in the absence of identified countervailing considerations, e.g., *Brown v. Brown*, 914 P.2d 206 (Alaska 1996); ARK. CODE ANN. § 9-12-315(a)(1)(A) ("All marital property shall be distributed one-half (½) to each party unless the court finds such a division to be inequitable."); N.C. GEN. STAT. ANN. § 50-20(c) ("There shall be an equal division by using net value of marital property and net value of divisible property unless the court determines that an equal division is not equitable."); W. VA. CODE §§ 84-7-101, 84-7-103 (presumption of equal division); or find equal division to be an appropriate place from which to start the analysis, e.g., *Cherry v. Cherry*, 421 N.E.2d 1293 (Ohio 1981).

The distinction between community and separate property is obviously more critical when the allocation rules governing each are more disparate. They are most disparate in the three community property states with strict equal division rules. As one might therefore expect, California has a rich trove of statutory and caselaw plumbing the distinction between community and separate property. Common law equitable distribution states, on the other hand, have no reason to distinguish marital and separate property apart from divorce, and even then precise accuracy in characterizing property may seem less essential, particularly among states with a tendency to treat all difficult-to-characterize items as marital property on the assumption that one can then rely on the court's discretion to allocate them in some reasonable fashion. Ten or so common law states go very far down this road, making no distinction at all between marital and separate property, instead allowing their courts to take the property's origin into account in its equitable judgment as to how to divide it. This substitution of judicial discretion for clear rules that identify the property's character has drawbacks as well as advantages, as we shall see further below.

Compliance with an equal division rule requires accurate valuations of every item that is not itself divided in half, and it is the rare divorce that does not include at least some such items. Careful valuations (like careful characterization of property as community or separate) may be more easily foregone under an equitable distribution system. Even though one would think that accurate valuation of the marital property is necessary to know whether any particular allocation of property is fair or equitable, some equitable distribution jurisdictions simply rely on the trial court's instincts and discretion. The need to obtain accurate valuations can be viewed as either an advantage or a disadvantage of the equal division rule. On one hand, valuations may be time consuming or expensive. On the other hand, because they are necessary only when the parties cannot agree on the division of their property the need for careful valuation may impose a useful discipline on the court, avoiding a kind of "rough justice" approach which may be unfair to one party. Of course, equitable distribution states can also require careful valuations if they choose to do so.

When careful valuation is required in a contested proceeding, one spouse may need to compel discovery of information held by the other, especially in the case of business assets. *E.g., In re Petition of B & F Towing & Salvage*, 551 A.2d 45 (Del. 1989) (wife entitled to discovery of financial records of three corporations in which the husband held an interest). In a community property state a spouse can claim access not only under normal discovery rules, but also as a co-owner of the property. *Schnabel v. Superior Ct.*, 5 Cal. 4th 704, 21 Cal. Rptr. 2d 200, 854 P.2d 1117 (1993) (close corporation that employed husband, who owned 30% of shares, must comply with the wife's subpoena for production of financial records, including corporate tax returns); *Fountain v. Knebel*, 45 S.W.3d 736 (Tex. App.-Dallas, 2001) (compelled discovery justified to determine valuation of husband's interest in law firm).

Spouses may agree upon one of several methods to divide their assets, of which the most familiar is the "piece of cake" approach, in which one spouse divides the property into two lists of items and the other chooses which list he or she wants. Devising a truly equitable method, however, is not without its difficulties, particularly where the assets are not fungible and the parties attach different values to them. A mathematician and political scientist jointly developed a version of the "one values, the other chooses" method said to ensure an equitable and "envy-free" division (in the sense that neither party would be willing to exchange his/her share for the other's share). *See* Peterson, *Formulas for Fairness*, 149 SCIENCE NEWS 284 (1996).

PROBLEM

Problem 4-1. Joan and Fred have been married ten years. During that time, Fred has been a full-time homemaker and Joan has operated a business. Upon divorce their assets include:

a. the business (a closely-held corporation in which all stock is held by Joan);

b. Joan's vested interest in a pension;

c. a home titled in both their names;

d. two cars, one titled in each of their names;

e. a large interest in a mutual fund, purchased with Fred's inheritance from his father and held solely in his name;

f. two joint bank accounts.

Except for the mutual fund, which is only a small part of the entire value of the property, all assets were acquired with funds earned by Joan during the marriage. How would each asset be divided on divorce in California (a community property state following an equal division property rule) and how would it likely be divided in a common law equitable division state?

[3]   Equitable Division

"Equitable Distribution" is today the dominant form of property distribution on divorce. But many different practices are packaged under that label. Two samples follow: the first from a common law state, the second from a community property state.

MICHAEL v. MICHAEL
Missouri Court of Appeals
791 S.W.2d 772 (1990)

Pudlowski, Presiding Judge.

This is an appeal from a judgment and decree of dissolution which awarded respondent [Deborah Michael] the majority of marital property and awarded appellant [Dennis Michael] . . . no maintenance.

[Dennis] and [Deborah] . . . married in August 1972 and separated in April 1987. There were no children. . . . Both [Dennis] and [Deborah] are well educated. [Dennis] holds a baccalaureate degree in political science and a master's degree in journalism. [Deborah] holds a baccalaureate degree in journalism and a master's degree in public administration.

[T]he day following the parties' marriage, the couple moved to Little Rock, Arkansas where [Deborah] was going to work for Southwestern Bell Corporation. While . . . in Little Rock, [Dennis] was employed as a reporter for a local newspaper.

In June 1974, [Deborah] received a promotion and was transferred back to St. Louis. In St. Louis, [Dennis] worked for APC Skills Company and then for Maritz, Inc. In 1978, [Dennis] was fired from Maritz, Inc. [T]he couple [then] agreed that [Dennis] would not seek outside employment but instead would devote time to writing fiction. In that same year [Deborah] received another transfer and the couple moved to Oklahoma City.

While living in Oklahoma, [Dennis] . . . abandoned [his writing career] without ever having written a chapter. . . . [He then] worked briefly in a food store and spent 8–9 months working free-lance public relations. When [Dennis] was not employed outside of the home, the couple agreed that [he] would be responsible for the general upkeep of the house and . . . the preparation of the evening meal. [He] spent several hours a day preparing the couple's dinner. [Deborah] claimed that [Dennis]'s other domestic chores were very lax. For two years while the couple was living in Oklahoma [Dennis] drove [Deborah] to and from work. However, for the rest of the mornings, [Dennis] slept until 10 or 11:00 a.m. [¶] In 1984 [Deborah] was again transferred to St. Louis. [Dennis] continued to cook the couple's dinner [and] periodically took [Deborah] to work but did not seek outside employment.

Throughout the marriage, the couple's lifestyle improved and they had a significant amount of disposable income. They were able to purchase homes whenever [Deborah] accepted a job transfer and the couple took many trips including visits to Europe. In addition, [Deborah] . . . provided her mother annually with support . . . of $5,000.

At the time of trial, [Deborah] had been working for Southwestern Bell for more than 15 years and was earning over $70,000 per year. [Deborah also had] vested pension benefits through the Southwestern Bell Corporation Management Pension Plan equal to $1,169.58 monthly payable at age sixty-five (65), as of March 1, 1988. [Dennis has] no income from employment, however he receives $75 per month in interest, and his share of the gross income on the previous year's Federal Income Tax Return was $1200.

[C]ertainly the sex of the parties should have no bearing on the division of marital property or on the allowance or prohibition of maintenance.

The trial court allocated $51,347 or 75.5% of the parties' marital property to [Deborah] and $14,128 or 21.5% to [Dennis]. The court granted [Dennis] no maintenance. . . . [¶] [Dennis] claims that the trial court abused its discretion by its distribution of the parties' marital property [and] by awarding [him] no maintenance. . . .

. . .

Section 452.330 RSMo 1988 directs the trial court to divide the marital property in a just manner, after considering all relevant factors including . . .

(1) The economic circumstances of each spouse at the time the division of property is to become effective. . . .

(2) The contribution of each spouse to the acquisition of the marital property, including the contribution of a spouse as a homemaker;

(3) The value of the non-marital property set apart to each spouse;

(4) The conduct of the parties during the marriage; and

(5) Custodial arrangements for minor children.

There are two guiding principles inherent in § 452.330: "[F]irst property division should reflect the concept of marriage as a shared enterprise similar to a partnership; and, second property division should be utilized as a means of providing future support for an economically dependent spouse." Krauskopf, *A Theory for "Just" Division of Marital Property in Missouri*, 41 Mo. L. Rev. 165

(1976).

[A]pplying these guiding principles . . . we find that the trial court abused its discretion. . . . Throughout the course of the marriage, [Dennis] has become economically dependent on [Deborah]. At . . . dissolution . . . [Dennis] was unemployed, had not been employed in his chosen field of journalism for fifteen years, and had not been employed full-time since 1978. Conversely, at . . . dissolution . . . [Deborah] had elevated herself within the Southwestern Bell organization to a position directing press relations.

With regard to the second statutory factor, the trial court found that . . . the funds used to acquire the marital property had been earned almost solely by [Deborah]. Also, the court found that [Dennis] made no substantial contribution to the marriage as a homemaker because he showed a marked disinclination to undertake the normal domestic duties of a homemaker, engaging only in those duties, such as cooking the evening meal, which he found fulfilling, stimulating and interesting.

. . . While [Dennis]'s performance of traditional domestic chores was often times lax, he did prepare dinner. We are not finding that [Dennis]'s contributions entitled him to an equal division of the marital property, however, we do hold that the trial court's division of property is against the weight of the evidence and therefore an abuse of discretion.

[Dennis] claims . . . the trial court . . . abused its discretion in awarding no maintenance to [him]. [Dennis] argues that although he is educated and possesses a degree in journalism and public administration, the fact that he is 40 years old and has not held employment in either of these fields for the past fifteen (15) years will have a negative effect on his ability to . . . support himself. [He] does not claim that he is completely unable to support himself. However . . . he requires a period of rehabilitative maintenance. [Dennis] argues that he would require an additional two and one half or three years of education to take course work that would enable him to be self-supporting as a journalist.

We have said that maintenance is awarded when one spouse has detrimentally relied on the other spouse to provide the monetary support during the marriage. If the relying spouse's withdrawal from the marketplace so injures his/her marketable skills that he/she is unable to provide for his/her reasonable needs maintenance may be awarded. "Rehabilitative maintenance" should be awarded for a term reasonably sufficient to receive job training. Rehabilitative maintenance is appropriate where there is substantial evidence that the party seeking maintenance will or should become self-supporting. [¶] We . . . find that the trial court did . . . abuse its discretion. . . .

. . .

. . . Our disposition of the issues of marital property and maintenance is consistent with the generally accepted principles . . . , that marriage is a shared enterprise and that maintenance should be utilized as a means of providing support for an economically dependent spouse until said spouse is self-reliant. [¶] . . . This matter is remanded for further proceedings consistent with this opinion.

Crandall, Judge, dissenting. I believe the trial court acted within its discretion. [¶] If we accept the concept of marriage as a shared enterprise similar to a partnership, husband had a negative impact on that partnership. Husband did not sacrifice his career for wife, rather he was a hindrance to her progress. On the issue of maintenance, husband has simply shown that he is unwilling, rather than unable, to support himself through appropriate employment. [¶] . . . I would affirm. . . .

TOTH v. TOTH
Supreme Court of Arizona
946 P.2d 900 (1997)

MARTONE, JUSTICE.

We granted review to decide whether an equitable distribution of marital joint property upon dissolution under A.R.S. § 25-318(A) requires an equal distribution of the assets in this case. We conclude that it does not. We also hold that joint tenancy property and community property should be treated alike under A.R.S. § 25-318(A).

I. Introduction

Anthony Toth and Gloria Snyder Toth met at a senior citizens dance in Mesa in 1992. Anthony was 87 and Gloria was 66. They married a year later on December 13, 1993. The following day, Anthony used $140,000 of his sole and separate funds to buy a house for the couple. They took title as joint tenants with the right of survivorship. About two weeks later, Anthony moved out of the marital bedroom, and on January 10, 1994, he filed for an annulment. The court ultimately entered a final decree of dissolution on September 19, 1995. The house was the only property to be divided. The court awarded Gloria $15,000 as her share. She appealed.

The court of appeals decided that A.R.S. § 25-318(A)[1] requires a substantially equal division of joint property, absent sound reason to the contrary. The court indicated that sound reason is limited to the statutory factors of fraud, excessive or abnormal expenditures, destruction, or concealment. It then held that the trial court had abused its discretion in ordering a substantially unequal division of the property and reversed. Judge Kleinschmidt dissented, believing that "equitable" had a broader meaning than the majority gave it. Believing that an important issue of law had been decided incorrectly, we granted Anthony's petition for review.

---

[1] . . . In a proceeding for dissolution of the marriage, or for legal separation . . . the court shall assign each spouse's sole and separate property to such spouse. It shall also divide the community, joint tenancy and other property held in common equitably, though not necessarily in kind, without regard to marital misconduct. . . . Nothing in this section shall prevent the court from considering excessive or abnormal expenditures, destruction, concealment or fraudulent disposition of community, joint tenancy and other property held in common.

II. Analysis

A. Treatment of joint tenancy property under A.R.S. § 25-318

Gloria argues that the gifted portion of the property is her sole and separate property and, therefore, the court must award her half its value under A.R.S. § 25-318(A).

Section 25-318(A) provides that "the court shall assign each spouse's sole and separate property to such spouse." It then provides that the court shall "divide the community, joint tenancy and other property held in common equitably, though not necessarily in kind, without regard to marital misconduct."

Joint tenancy property is separate, not community, property. Although joint tenancy property is considered separate property, section 25-318(A) treats it in two ways-first by stating that separate property is assigned to the owner spouse, then by directing that joint tenancy property be divided equitably.

Before 1973, section 25-318(A) did not include joint tenancy property in the equitable (then "just and right") division, and, as now, prohibited divesting either spouse of separate property upon dissolution. From that, we concluded that joint tenancy property could not be divided equitably. The statute now expressly lists joint tenancy property as part of the property to be equitably divided. In *Wayt v. Wayt*, 123 Ariz. 444, 445, 600 P.2d 748, 749 (1979), we held that the modification of section 25-318 allowed joint tenancy property to be divided upon dissolution "in the same manner as . . . property held by the community or in common." We did not address the potential anomaly in treating separate property as community property upon dissolution.

From the 1973 modification, one could argue that the legislature abrogated the rule that joint tenancy property is separate property. But whether property is treated as separate or community has consequences beyond dissolution, particularly with respect to tax liability and the rights of creditors. *See* Charles Marshall Smith, *Arizona Community Property Law* §§ 4:4, 4:5 (1995). The statute does not provide that marital joint tenancy property is now, in all respects, community property. It only allows it to be treated as community property upon dissolution. Joint tenancy property remains separate property, but is excepted from the requirement that separate property be assigned to each spouse separately upon dissolution. . . .

Thus, under the statute, joint tenancy property and community property are to be treated alike only for dissolution purposes. For that purpose, the court should divide all such property equitably. We thus reject Gloria's argument that we must treat her share of property held in joint tenancy as separate property upon dissolution.

Gloria also argues that because her share of the property is designated as a "gift" from Anthony, it should be considered irrevocable under the law of gifts. Ordinarily, when property is purchased in the name of one person with money furnished by another, a resulting trust arises in favor of the person furnishing the purchase money. But in the marital context, the presumption changes.

When one spouse buys property with separate funds and places it in joint tenancy, there is a presumption that the spouse intended to make a gift to his spouse of one-half of the property. But gifts of joint tenancy property are not irrevocable inter vivos transfers. They are made in expectation of a permanent relationship, but if cut short, fully subject to equitable divestment under the statute. Since marital joint tenancy property is subject to equitable division upon dissolution generally, if we treated "gifted" joint tenancy as requiring an equal, not equitable, division, we would be giving greater property rights to a non-contributing spouse than to a contributing one. Instead, the "gift" in the non-purchasing spouse of joint tenancy property is an equitable right in the property, not an irrevocably gifted interest in half. Under A.R.S. § 25-318, all marital joint tenancy property, "gifted" or otherwise, is to be divided equitably.

B. Meaning of equitable division under A.R.S. § 25-318

Although A.R.S. § 25-318(A) requires an equitable division of joint property, it also provides that nothing shall prevent the court from considering "excessive or abnormal expenditures, destruction, concealment or fraudulent disposition" of the property in making that equitable division. Gloria argues that the statute requires an equal division of joint property absent exceptional circumstances. She contends that those circumstances are limited to the parties' relationship to the property, rather than to each other. She characterizes other factors, such as the duration of the marriage, as inquiring into fault, which the statute prohibits.

We disagree for two reasons. First, the legislature's intent that the division be equitable, not equal, is clearly evidenced by the legislative history of the dissolution statute. In 1973, a proposed version of the statute required an equal division of all common assets. Senator O'Connor then moved to replace "equally" with "equitably," to be defined as "equally absent compelling reasons to the contrary." The version eventually adopted states only that the court shall make an "equitable" division. The legislature clearly contemplated that the trial court should not be bound by any per se rule of equality, but rather intended the court to have discretion to decide what is equitable in each case.

Second, the statute does not limit the inquiry to conduct regarding the property. Instead, it expressly instructs the court to divide the marital property equitably. Although the statute forecloses an argument that the listed factors are not relevant, it does not purport to define the universe of relevance. "Equitable" means just that — t is a concept of fairness dependent upon the facts of particular cases.

This is not a departure from the general principle that all marital joint property should be divided substantially equally unless sound reason exists to divide the property otherwise. That approach simply reflects the principle that community property implies equal ownership. William Q. de Funiak & Michael J. Vaughn, *Principles of Community Property*, 1-3 (2d ed.1971). In most cases, therefore, an equal distribution of joint property will be the most equitable.

However, there may be sound reason to divide the property otherwise. The trial court has discretion in this decision. The trial judge in this case found sound reason to divide the Toths' property unequally, and we agree.

In this case, equal is not equitable. Community property rests on the assumption that the two spouses worked together to accumulate property for the community, each contributing in pecuniary or other ways. Anthony paid for this property entirely from his separate funds. Gloria made no contribution — pecuniary or otherwise — to the purchase of the house. The marriage lasted two weeks, allowing no time for a marital relationship to develop, or for other equities to come into play. This is not a determination of fault; why the marriage dissolved is irrelevant. This unusual case is one of those "rare occasions when the circumstances and facts are such that, in all fairness to the parties, the property should not be characterized as community and should, instead, be awarded [in large measure] to one spouse accordingly." Barbara J. Torrez, Comment, *Arizona Property Division Upon Marital Dissolution*, 1979 Ariz. St. L.J. 411, 437.

The court of appeals found that the trial judge's division in this case was contrary to *Whitmore v. Mitchell*, 152 Ariz. 425, 733 P.2d 310 (App.1987) and *Valladee v. Valladee*, 149 Ariz. 304, 718 P.2d 206 (App.1986). In those cases, the court of appeals found that the trial judge had abused his discretion by ordering an unequal division of joint tenancy property solely to reimburse the purchasing spouse. But in *Valladee*, the parties had been married for sixteen years and had four children. And in *Whitmore*, the parties had been married over a year, and had a prenuptial agreement regarding their property, which the trial judge ignored. In both cases, as is likely in any real marriage of any significant duration, other equities made a division based solely on reimbursement clearly inappropriate. The facts here, of course, are vastly different. This is not a case in which an equitable division is based "solely" on reimbursement. Source of funds can be a factor in determining what is equitable. *Wayt*, 123 Ariz. at 446, 600 P.2d at 750. The "marriage" lasted two weeks. Every judge who has reviewed this case saw that equal was not equitable. The trial judge so found. The majority of the court of appeals said it seemed "somewhat unfair" for Gloria to receive half the value of the house in these circumstances, but thought the law required that result. The dissenting judge thought equitable was broader than equal. We agree that an equal distribution here is not equitable. Indeed, if this is not a case in which "equitable" means something other than "equal," we would be hard pressed to imagine one.

C. Consideration of marital misconduct

Gloria argues that the trial court made a finding of fault when it stated that she had not made a "good faith effort to create a viable marriage." While the statement does connote fault, it is unclear whether the trial court relied on it in dividing the property. The statement is part of the court's description of the facts of the case. But in its findings, the court noted only that the marriage was of extremely short duration, and that the husband had paid the entire purchase price of the house, as well as subsequent maintenance costs, solely from his separate property. We note that the court received evidence on the parties' ages, needs, health, income and personal situations. It heard evidence that Gloria sold her house, that Anthony continued to pay household expenses after he moved out and that Gloria lived in the house for 1 1/2 years thereafter. The court found that Gloria should not receive an equal portion of the residence, and allocated $15,000 as her equitable share.

Thus, it may be that the court did not use the "good faith" finding in dividing the property. But we cannot be sure.

III. Conclusion

We vacate the memorandum decision of the court of appeals and remand to the superior court for further consideration of the evidence in light of today's opinion. The court may allocate equitably rather than equally and the court may consider source of funds. The court may consider other equitable factors as they may bear on the outcome, but the court may not consider fault. . . .

JONES, V.C.J., and FELDMAN, J., concur.

MOELLER, Justice, Dissenting.

I respectfully dissent. I do so because I believe the trial court's unequal division of the home is contrary to Arizona case law, to Arizona statutory law, and to basic principles of fairness and equity. In my view, the court of appeals correctly held that the case should be remanded with instructions for a substantially equal distribution. Mr. Toth chose to make a gift of one-half of the house to Mrs. Toth.[1] Having chosen to make a gift, Mr. Toth seeks the help of the domestic relations court to compel Mrs. Toth to give it back. The majority opinion permits the trial court to order her to give it back despite established Arizona law prohibiting an unequal division for any of the reasons relied upon by the trial court.

A.R.S. § 25-318(A) ("the statute") does permit the trial court to divide joint tenancy property "equitably" rather than "equally." If the legislature intended by this statute to permit courts to order the disgorgement of gifts, it did not say so. Doubtless, the 1973 enactment of the statute permitting equitable division of jointly held property was in recognition of the fact that married couples commonly use community funds to acquire joint tenancy property. In dissolution actions prior to enactment of the statute in 1973, courts could not order the parties to divest themselves of title to their separate property, and their interest in joint tenancy property was separate property. The statute was intended to alleviate some practical problems by permitting joint tenancy property to be divided equitably, but not necessarily in kind. As the *Valladee* case, *infra*, makes clear, the statute was never intended to convert property held in joint tenancy into community property. The statute only contemplates a significantly unequal distribution in cases of "excessive or abnormal expenditures, destruction, concealment or fraudulent disposition" of the property. A.R.S. § 25-318(A). None of the statutory elements permitting an unequal division are present here. What then justifies an unequal division? The trial court supported its unequal division of the property with the following findings:

---

[1] Arizona law establishes that when Mr. Toth used his separate funds to purchase the home in joint tenancy, he presumptively made a gift of one-half of the home to Mrs. Toth. In the trial court, Mr. Toth made an unsuccessful attempt to rebut the presumption. In this court, Mr. Toth frankly admitted that he intended to make a gift to Mrs. Toth.

All the money used to purchase the residence located at 2303 North 76th Street was the sole and separate property of the Petitioner/Husband, Anthony Toth. The Respondent/Wife, Gloria Toth, did not contribute any money toward the purchase of the residence. The Respondent/Wife, Gloria Toth, did sell her former residence and is now receiving monthly payments from said sale.

* * *

The parties lived together as husband and wife for only two weeks. For one additional week, Petitioner/Husband, Anthony Toth, lived in a separate room in the marital residence. After approximately three weeks, Petitioner/Husband moved out of the marital residence and has lived in a separate residence since that time.

* * *

Petitioner/Husband, Anthony Toth, expected that the parties would each make a good faith effort to live together as husband and wife for the rest of their lives. No evidence has been presented that Respondent/Wife, Gloria Toth, made a good faith effort to create a viable marriage.

THE COURT FINDS that the facts and circumstances of this case indicate that this was a marriage of extremely short duration. Respondent/Wife contributed nothing economically either toward the purchase of the marital residence or toward the necessary expenses of utilities and taxes on the residence since its purchase, even though she has remained in the residence since January of 1994. . . .

THE COURT FURTHER FINDS it would be unjust enrichment and a windfall to Respondent/Wife to award her an equal disposition of the value of the marital residence. While this Court may not set aside a transaction merely because one of the parties to a marriage contract may have been imprudent or made a poor bargain, nonetheless, the Court must make an equitable disposition pursuant to A.R.S. sec. 25-318(A).

Any reasonable reading of these findings compels the conclusion that the trial judge made the unequal division because of some perceived fault on Mrs. Toth's part and to reimburse Mr. Toth because he paid for the house out of his separate funds. Under Arizona law, neither reason authorizes an unequal division of the joint tenancy property.

In *Valladee v. Valladee*, 149 Ariz. 304, 306–07, 718 P.2d 206, 208–09 (App.1986), the trial court ordered a substantially unequal distribution of jointly held property to reimburse the husband for the expenditure of his separate funds in acquiring the properties. The court of appeals, Division One, overturned the unequal distribution, finding it inequitable as a matter of law for two reasons. It first discussed the concept of joint tenancy:

First, while § 25-318(A) makes jointly held property susceptible to the same equitable division as community property, we do not believe it eliminates the distinctions between the two forms of ownership. Arizona has long recognized that the general rules of joint tenancy apply between husband and wife. Thus, some consideration must be given to the general principles of joint tenancy law when dividing jointly held property under § 25-318(A).

Under joint tenancy rules, "the legal consequence of holding property jointly is that each spouse takes an undivided *separate property* interest in one-half of the property." *Id.* (citation omitted). Additionally, although a tenant has a right to contribution from the co-tenants for expenditures and obligations of the property, that right does not begin until the properties are held in joint tenancy. Therefore, under the law of joint tenancy, one spouse has no right of contribution from the other spouse for the funds he or she expended before the property was held in joint tenancy.

The *Valladee* court next focused on the gift aspect of the case, which was identical to the situation here. It held that the trial court's reimbursement scheme conflicted with the presumption of a gift. "The gift to the wife of an interest in the property clearly encompasses any monies spent in the past by husband to acquire it. Thus, to award husband reimbursement here for the sole reason that he used his own funds to acquire the joint properties is, without more, inconsistent and inequitable." *Id.* at 310, 718 P.2d at 212 (footnote omitted).

Joint tenancy property is not identical to community property. Community property "rests on the assumption that the two spouses worked together to accumulate property for the community, each contributing in pecuniary or other ways." Joint tenancy property, however, rests on no such assumption. In a marriage, when joint tenancy property is purchased with the separate funds of one spouse, one-half of the property is a presumed gift. In the instant case, we have more than a presumed gift: we have an acknowledged intended, completed gift. Division Two of the court of appeals in *Whitmore v. Mitchell*, 152 Ariz. 425, 427, 733 P.2d 310, 312 (App.1987), like Division One in *Valladee*, also held that jointly held property may not be unequally divided for the purpose of reimbursing the party who supplied the purchase price.

I am unpersuaded by the majority's effort to distinguish *Valladee* and *Whitmore* on the ground that in those cases the unequal division was based "solely" on principles of reimbursement. It is true that the courts used the word "solely" because in those cases the desire to reimburse the gifting party was the only reason advanced in support of the unequal division. But I read those cases as holding that reimbursement is an improper consideration and will not support an unequal distribution. Reimbursement clearly motivated the trial court here to unequally divide the property and that inequitable division should not be permitted to stand.

It is also clear from the trial court's findings that the unequal division was based, in part, on the trial court's perception that Mrs. Toth was more at fault than Mr. Toth for the failure of the marriage. I find nothing in the record that supports that view, but even if it is well-founded, it is not a permissible reason for an unequal division. The statute upon which the majority relies to support the unequal division expressly precludes consideration of fault. . . . Similarly, Arizona case law precludes consideration of fault in making a property allocation. Indeed, consideration of fault in the division of marital property is precluded on [state] constitutional grounds.

The majority readily acknowledges that fault, even if it exists, cannot support an unequal division. The majority also acknowledges that the trial court used language indicating fault, but the majority concludes that it is "unclear" whether the trial court relied upon its finding of fault in dividing the property and concludes that "it may be that the [trial] court did not use" the finding. *Id.* The majority refers to other evidence before the trial court that it believes might justify the trial court's disparate distribution. I fail to find the trial court's comments concerning Mrs. Toth's fault to be as antiseptic as does the majority. . . .

The trial court also found and relied upon the obvious: that this was a short marriage. The trial court obviously blamed Mrs. Toth for the brevity of the marriage. I find no authority for the proposition that a spouse must remain married for a certain number of years before her right to retain a gift vests, nor has the majority or Mr. Toth cited any. The marriage was as short for Mrs. Toth as it was for Mr. Toth. Because fault cannot be considered, I find no relevance to the length of the marriage.

Under Arizona case law, equitable division has been interpreted to mean a substantially equal division "unless some sound reason exists for a contrary result." Length of marriage has never been held to constitute a "sound reason" to divide joint tenancy property other than substantially equally. Cases in which our courts have upheld unequal distributions have dealt with the factors given in A.R.S. § 25-318 that the court may legitimately consider. *See Martin v. Martin*, 156 Ariz. 452, 454–55, 457–58, 752 P.2d 1038, 1040–41, 1043–44 (1988) (court upheld giving wife sum of money to reimburse her for improper dissipation of community assets by husband); *Hrudka v. Hrudka*, 186 Ariz. 84, 93–94, 919 P.2d 179, 188–89 (App.1995) (court upheld husband receiving more assets than wife because trial court found waste on wife's part where wife transferred, concealed, and sold substantial assets in violation of a trial court order); *Kosidlo v. Kosidlo*, 125 Ariz. 32, 607 P.2d 15 (App.1979), *disapproved on other grounds*, 125 Ariz. 18, 607 P.2d 1 (trial court justified in concluding that equity favored distributing greater share of community assets to wife where husband refused to use checking account, insisted on cash transactions, secreted large amounts of cash, and evaded questions about community assets); *Lindsay v. Lindsay*, 115 Ariz. 322, 565 P.2d 199 (App.1977) (court directed trial court to award sum of money to wife representing her share of community's interest in an aircraft where her husband secretly sold aircraft during dissolution proceedings and lost the proceeds in gambling).

Factors permitting unequal distribution of joint tenancy property should be limited to those enumerated in A.R.S. § 25-318(A), which should not be expanded to include perceptions of fault or evaluations of the length of the marriage. No § 25-318 factor exists here. Under the majority's length-of-marriage test, how long is long enough? The majority opinion states that gifts of joint tenancy property "are made in expectation of a permanent relationship, but if cut short, fully subject to equitable divestment under the statute." Under this approach, joint tenancy property can always be divided unequally in any dissolution because the relationship, by definition, turned out not to be permanent. Such a result is totally at variance with Arizona law as it has existed to date. There are very few valid reasons to divide joint tenancy property unequally, because each spouse has a vested separate property interest in one-half of the property and A.R.S. § 25-318 does not change that well-established tenet.

In summary, no proper reason supports an order requiring Mrs. Toth to return the gift Mr. Toth chose to make. The court of appeals correctly concluded that a substantially equal division should have been ordered. The remand should be limited to ordering an equal division.

ZLAKET, C.J., concurs.

NOTES AND QUESTIONS

1. *What Does "Equitable" Distribution Mean?* Consider the summary contained in § 4.09, Comment *a* of the *ALI Principles:*

> [In the] dominant . . . "equitable distribution [model]," . . . the govern-ing statute provides a list of "factors" that the trial judge is authorized or directed to consider in deciding the fairest allocation of the property. These statutes typically provide the judge no guidance in weighing the relative importance of the various factors. Although these lists often include eight or 10 factors, most of the factors are specific examples of two basic but conflicting principles: Property should be allocated in proportion to the spousal contributions to its acquisition, and property should be allocated according to relative spousal need.

For an example of a state law's list of eleven factors, based on the Model Marriage and Divorce Act, see the excerpt from the Pennsylvania law at Note 3, *infra*. One factor commonly listed in such statutes, and emphasized in court decisions, is length of the marriage. However, it is difficult to see how marital duration can operate as an independent factor, as it is generally the same for both parties. It is perhaps intended to affect the application of the primary factors of contribution (which perhaps lessens in importance with increasing duration) and need (which perhaps increases in importance with increasing duration). It has been noted, however, that an equal division rule will in most cases automatically adjust the impact of need and contribution by duration in just this way: the longer the parties have been married, the more marital or community property they will usually accumulate — so that more property is shifted from the spouse whose market labor earned it to the other spouse. Mary Ann Glendon, *Family Law Reform in the 1980's*, 44 LA. L. REV. 1553, 1561–62 (1984).

"Equitable" is merely a four-syllable word for "fair." As any group of schoolchil-dren dividing a bag of candy know, the default meaning of fair is "equal." Anyone proposing an unequal allocation must provide persuasive arguments for that position. In the case of "equitable distribution," what might those arguments be? Any effort to answer that question must begin by analyzing how the parties' relative need, or their relative contribution to the acquisition of property, are relevant to the allocation of the property.

2. *Need as a Factor in Equitable Distribution and the Award's Relationship*

With Alimony.   While financial need is one of the two most commonly cited factors to consider in allocating property under equitable distribution, it is also the most dominant factor offered to justify awards of alimony. Because income flows and capital assets can be substituted for one another and valued on a common scale, an enhanced share of marital property may in principle always substitute for a fixed-term alimony award. This was in fact the premise sometimes relied upon early in the no-fault reform era by those who hoped equitable distribution reforms, by recognizing the wife's property claims, would replace alimony. Those hopes were frustrated in practice. Few divorcing couples have capital assets sufficiently large to provide an adequate substitute for any but the most modest of alimony awards. Nonetheless, need remains a critical factor in most equitable distribution statutes, often in language that duplicates the language of the state's alimony provisions. The overlap arises because the policy basis for awarding alimony is largely indistinguishable from the basis for allowing one spouse an enhanced share of the marital property. "Need" is the most common rationale for both under existing law. Whatever "need" might mean, there is no reason it should mean different things in these two contexts.

The question of how to handle need-based claims will be largely postponed until we examine alimony. There are, nonetheless, some points that should be previewed now.

   a. *The appropriateness of a property allocation to meet need.* How would a court in California (a mandatory equal division state) deal with a fact situation where one of the former spouses has a significant claim based on need (e.g., based on a physical disability, see *Provinzano v. Provinzano*, 570 P.2d 513 (Ariz. App. 1977) (unequal division of property justified by combination of husband's disabilities and wife's greater earning capacity))? In equitable division states, the courts can deal with one spouse's need through a property division rather than through alimony, while in a mandatory equal division state like California alimony is the only option. From the perspective of the needy spouse, what are the advantages and disadvantages of property versus alimony? What about from the perspective of the more financially secure payor spouse? Note that even in California, the spouses can *agree* to an unequal division of property in their separation agreement, perhaps by way of a tradeoff against a foregone alimony claim.

   b. *Do courts now allocate property on the basis of need?* The language of most equitable distribution statutes makes possible need-based claims to an enhanced share of the property. *E.g., Schwartz v. Linders*, 426 N.W.2d 97 (Wis. App. 1988) (noting that four of its state's typical list of "factors" relate to spousal needs). One commentator concludes, however, that allocations under equitable distribution laws in common law states have focused more heavily on spousal contributions than on relative spousal needs. Suzanne Reynolds, *The Relationship of Property Division and Alimony: The Division of Property to Address Need*, 56 FORDHAM L. REV. 827 (1988). If need were the *preeminent* consideration (and if "need" were understood, as it frequently is, to mean something like a right to a standard of living close to that experienced during the marriage), the spouse with less earning capacity would receive a more than equal (often much more than equal) share of the accumulated property, even if his or her contribution to its acquisition was less. Many courts, however, have rejected such distributions as inequitable. For example, in both *Sattari v. Sattari*, 503 A.2d 125 (R.I. 1986) and *Schnarr v. Schnarr*, 491 N.E.2d 561 (Ind. App. 1986), awards of virtually all of the assets to the wife, premised on the husband's greater earning capacity, were overturned on appeal. Courts have split on whether less extremely disparate allocations are defensible on grounds of the favored spouse's lower earning capacity. *Compare, e.g., In re Marriage of Agazim*, 530 N.E.2d 1110 (Ill. App. 1988) (wife, with limited earning potential, entitled to 76% of property, after 11-year marriage in which husband was principal wage-earner) and *Goller v. Goller*, 758 S.W.2d 505 (Mo. App. 1988) (trial court award to homemaker wife of 36% of $2.3 million estate too low because she needed the property as means of providing future support), *with Longo v. Longo*, 533 So. 2d 791 (Fla. App. 1988) (wife's lower earning capacity and more modest separate assets did not justify giving her nearly two-thirds of the marital property). Community property equitable distribution states may be more willing than their common law counterparts to favor a needy spouse in allocating the property. *See, e.g., McNabney v. McNabney*, 782 P.2d 1291 (Nev. 1989) ("preeminent example" of case in which unequal allocation is equitable "is that of the wife and mother in a long-term marriage who has given up career opportunities to devote herself to her family" because in such cases equity might require giving the wife more than half).

c. *Need and the marital home.* Where there are minor children of the marriage, it may seem sensible to award the marital home to the custodial parent. In many cases, however, the marital home is so large a portion of the community assets that it is impossible to offset it with an equal award to the noncustodial spouse. Under a rule of equitable division the court may conclude it is not necessary to do so, at least if the needs of the custodial spouse and children are thought proper considerations in applying the rule of equity. *See, e.g.*, N.C. GEN. STAT. § 50-20(c)(4). One common order defers sale of the home while giving the custodial spouse exclusive use of it during this deferral period. An equitable division state may conclude this is appropriate even where the noncustodial spouse receives no offsetting benefit in exchange for deferring realization of his or her share of the equity. *E.g., Cenci v. Cenci*, 16 FAM. L. REP. 1069 (N.Y. Sup. Ct. 1989) (rent-controlled apartment leased in husband's name awarded to wife/custodial parent).

Because its purpose is to serve the children's interests, the cost of a deferred sale can be thought of as a form of child support, *In re Marriage of Herrmann*, 84 Cal. App. 3d 361, 148 Cal. Rptr. 550 (1978), thereby providing a rationale for departing from equal division in states which require it. At sale, the former spouses divide the proceeds equally, perhaps with adjustments for expenditures on the home in the interim. Carol Bruch, *The Definition and Division of Marital Property in California: Towards Parity and Simplicity*, 33 HASTINGS L.J. 769, 848–50 (1982); *Marriage of Duke*, 101 Cal. App. 3d 152, 161 Cal. Rptr. 444, 446 (1980) ("immediate loss of a long established family home" would result in "adverse economic, emotional and social impacts on minor children" with roots in the "school and social milieu of their neighborhood"). Deferral may be problematic, however, if the effect is to deny the non-custodial spouse access to his principal asset for many years. *In re Marriage of Horowitz*, 159 Cal. App. 3d 368, 205 Cal. Rptr. 874, 879 n.6 (1984) (*Duke* should apply only where children are old enough that sale will occur in two or three years); *In re Marriage of Stallworth*, 192 Cal. App. 3d 742, 237 Cal. Rptr. 829 (1987) (where home equity is major community asset, deferring sale until son reached 18 improper where no evidence showing sale of home would yield an adverse impact on the minor child; very young child's emotional attachment to home is minimal, and in any event a sale could occur at natural transition point, as when child changes schools, rather than await child's majority). California has now codified its rules for dealing with the marital home at CAL. FAM. CODE §§ 3800–3810.

3. *The Contribution Rationale and the Residual Effects of Title.* While no common law state still divides property strictly according to title, the effects of the old title-based approach can still be seen. For example, the Pennsylvania law, 23 PA. CONS. STAT. ANN. § 3502, adopts most of the language of § 307 of the Model Marriage and Divorce Act. It uses typical language in empowering the court to

> . . . equitably divide, distribute or assign, in kind or otherwise, the marital property . . . without regard to marital misconduct in such proportions and in such manner as the court deems just after considering all relevant factors . . . [which] include the following:

> (1) The length of the marriage.

> (2) Any prior marriage of either party.

> (3) The age, health, station, amount and sources of income, vocational skills, employability, estate, liabilities and needs of each of the parties.

> (4) The contribution by one party to the education, training, or increased earning power of the other party.

> (5) The opportunity of each party for future acquisitions of capital assets and income.

> (6) The sources of income of both parties, including but not limited to medical, retirement, insurance or other benefits.

> (7) The contribution or dissipation of each party in the acquisition, preservation, depreciation or appreciation of the marital property, including the contribution of a party as homemaker.

> (8) The value of the property set apart to each party.

> (9) The standard of living of the parties established during the marriage.

> (10) The economic circumstances of each party, including Federal, State and local tax ramifications, at the time the division of property is to become effective.

> (10.1) The Federal, State and local tax ramifications associated with each asset to be divided, distributed or assigned, which ramifications need not be immediate and certain.

> (10.2) The expense of sale, transfer or liquidation associated with a particular asset, which expense need not be immediate and certain.

> (11) Whether the party will be serving as the custodian of any dependent minor children.

Some Pennsylvania courts held that property should be divided equally under this authority unless the listed factors or some other important equitable consideration required otherwise. *E.g., Paul W. v. Margaret W.,* 130 PITTSBURGH L.J. 6 (Ct. C.P. Allegheny County 1981) ("property division based on the concept of marriage as a shared enterprise [must initially assume] that the contributions of both parties were sufficiently significant that the parties shall be deemed equal partners of the marital assets"). But to other judges the idea of "marriage as a shared enterprise" sounded more like a community property concept than they believed the Pennsylvania legislature intended. *E.g., Fratangelo v. Fratangelo,* 520 A.2d 1195 (Pa. App. 1987):

> . . . *Paul W.* ['s adoption of] a starting point of fifty-fifty distribution . . . simply ignores the legislative mandate and adopts the easiest solution which, in keeping with human nature, will be the only solution.

> Once the fifty-fifty starting point is universal, lip service will be paid to equitable distribution and we will, in fact, if not in word, be distributing property in the manner of community property regimes. . . . [the] automatic bestowal of the separate property of one spouse upon the other, as is the law in community property states, . . . is unconstitutional as a deprivation of property in violation of due process. . . . In Perlberger, *Pennsylvania Divorce Code,* 1980, § 5.2 The Concept of Equitable Distribution, it is stated: "[W]hile many factors go into the formula for post-divorce division, it is important to note that record ownership of assets remains significant and the court must find that equity requires a transfer of ownership from one party to the other. . . ." Marital property is not property that is thrown into the pot to be divided equally as in community property states, but property impressed with equitable consideration which must be evaluated before apportionment is considered. We cannot, therefore, approve a starting point of fifty-fifty without consideration of section 401(d) factors.

Id. at 1200.

 The continuing influence of the title approach is obvious in *Fratangelo.* The idea that the property really "belongs" to the spouse who earned it reflects the schizophrenic character of the common law marital property system: during the intact marriage and at death the spouses in fact have no ownership interest in one another's earnings. The concept of marital property thus appears only at divorce, making it seem more natural for the divorce court to assign property to the spouse who earned it unless "equitable" factors make it fair to *transfer* ownership of some portion to the other spouse. In a community property state, of course, notions of "transferring" ownership could arise only when one did *not* divide the property equally. Common law and community property judges may thus approach equitable division with very different attitudes.

The lingering impact of the common law title system can also be seen in the limits some states place on the authority of divorce courts to allocate property under their "equitable division" regime. For example, one common law state does not allow courts to transfer ownership of real or personal property from one spouse to the other, even though it can grant a monetary award in accordance with the "equities and rights of the parties." MD. ANN. CODE FAM. LAW §§ 8-202; 8-205. Others get around the strictures of the title system by defining alimony to include the transfer of property from one spouse to another, e.g., N.C. GEN. STAT. § 50-16.7(a). Another halfway measure engrafted upon the title system in some states was a doctrine allowing transfer of property only to spouses who have shown "special equity." See, e.g., Wilson v. Wilson, 241 S.E.2d 566, 569 (S.C. 1978); Morris v. Morris, 232 S.E.2d 326, 327 (S.C. 1977); Canakaris v. Canakaris, 382 So. 2d 1197, 1200 (Fla. 1980). These partial fixes have gradually been replaced with full-fledged equitable distribution systems, e.g., FLA. STAT. ANN. § 61.075.

Note that contribution is not relevant under the community property system. Spousal labor is pooled, and it does not matter which spouse's labor accounts for the asset's acquisition — it is community property. What of property acquired through no labor at all, but sheer luck, such as a winning lottery ticket? In community property states, if the ticket was purchased from community property, such as current earnings, as it almost always is, then the winnings are also community property. See, e.g., In re Marriage of Rossi, 90 Cal. App. 4th 34, 108 Cal. Rptr. 2d 270 (2001) (wife's lottery winnings were community property, and her efforts to hide them during the divorce proceedings constituted fraud, justifying the award of those winnings entirely to the husband); Lynch v. Lynch, 791 P.2d 653 (Ariz. App. 1990) (husband's $2 million lottery winnings treated as community property, even though received during the course of the divorce action and two years after the couple physically separated). Regarding the division of lottery proceeds in common law equitable division states, Thomas v. Thomas, 579 S.E.2d 310 (S.C. 2003) summarizes the two main approaches: an automatic 50/50 split (citing Ullah v. Ullah, 555 N.Y.S.2d 834 (App. Div. 1990)), because it is a "fortuitous circumstance" for which the spouses' "contributions" hold little significance; or an approach applying all the usual "equitable factors." The Thomas court chose the second approach, but nonetheless affirmed a 50/50 split.

4. Broadening the Contribution Principle with Homemaker Provisions. Concerned that the common law contribution principle might be particularly burdensome to the traditional homemaker, many common law states added "homemaker" provisions to their equitable distribution states. Homemaker provisions would be superfluous in community property equitable distribution states, as the homemaker spouse owned half of all the property attributable to the other spouse's earnings during marriage. The typical provision adds a spouse's contributions as a homemaker to the list of factors the court may or should consider in allocating marital property. Yet some of these provisions allow consideration of homemaker services only to the extent they contributed to "the acquisition, preservation and maintenance, or increase in value of marital property." W. VA. CODE § 48-7-103(2)(A).

If that requirement were applied as written, the homemaker would not often do well. While it may be easy to show that the homemaker wife contributed greatly to her husband's comfort or happiness, it is less easy to show that her services yielded a significant contribution to "the acquisition, preservation and maintenance, or increase in value of marital property." Married men do earn more, on average, than do bachelors, but that is not necessarily because having a wife increases a man's earning potential. One can just as plausibly hypothesize that men with better earnings prospects have more success in attracting a wife, or that certain traits help a man both in courting women and in earning money. *See, e.g.,* Yinon Cohen & Yitchak Haberfeld, *Why Do Married Men Earn More than Unmarried Men?*, 20 Soc. Sci. Res. 29 (1991).

It thus matters greatly whether a "homemaker" statute is read to create an irrebuttable presumption that the homemaker's economic contribution is equal, or merely to create an opportunity for the homemaker to try to show how her services contributed to the parties' assets. *Compare Axtell v. Axtell*, 482 A.2d 1261, 1264 (Me. 1984) (husband's financial contributions to 23-year marriage held "responsible for by far the greater portion of the value of the increase in the marital assets" as compared to contribution of homemaker wife) *with Ferguson v. Ferguson*, 357 N.W.2d 104 (Minn. App. 1984) (statutory presumption that homemaker's contributions are equal to earner's conclusive in allocating property of ten-year marriage). Note also that the homemaker spouse might not be much aided by demonstrating the market value of her services, rather than her financial contribution to creation of the parties' property, because housecleaning and child care are invariably low-paid occupations. At the typical hourly wage for this work, the homemaker spouses married to a physician, attorney or successful corporate executive could not come close to showing an equal market value for their labor, even if, as is usually the case, the homemakers worked very long hours.

The foregoing may suggest only that it is misleading to rest the claim for equal division of property accumulated during a marriage on a homemaker's *financial* contributions. Indeed, one might even argue that insisting on such a narrow vision of that spouse's contribution trivializes rather than recognizes her role. In thinking about the appropriate way to treat the contribution of the spouse who is not the primary breadwinner, consider *Michael*. Should Dennis Michael share equally in the parties' accumulated assets? If you believe so, is it because of his contribution as a homemaker? If you believe not, is it because he did not do such a great job as a homemaker?

5. *Different Rule for High Asset Divorces?* Where the community or marital property estate is very large, common law states are far more likely than community property states to order an unequal division favoring the primary breadwinner. In these cases the differing property heritage of the two groups of states has a very clear impact. The estate's size has no effect on the foundational premise of equal ownership from which community property courts reason. The common law states, by contrast, have great difficulty justifying the transfer of so much property, for they cannot conclude that the homemaker's contribution was worth that much no matter how fine the homemaking job. *See* Barrett, *Wendt Divorce Dissects Job of "Corporate Wife,"* Wall St. J., Dec. 6, 1996, at B1:

> Gary Wendt has had a stellar 20-year career at General Electric Co. and now, at the age of 54, is one of its top executives. His wife, Lorna, 53, has been behind him every step of the way — giving advice on job applicants, making small talk with foreign dignitaries, even minding the offspring of colleagues. [¶] . . . Mr. Wendt, chief executive of GE's giant and hugely profitable GE Capital unit, says the [marital] estate is . . . $52 million. . . .

He is offering [Mrs. Wendt] $8 million, plus $250,000 a year in alimony indefinitely, Mrs. Wendt's lawyers say.

. . .

[In cases with such large marital estates, few divorce courts in common law states give the wife half.] Knowing [that], lawyers for women often persuade them to settle for less than half. . . . [¶] [But] Mrs. Wendt has decided to take her chances in court. In testimony . . . , she said that the question wasn't what she "needed" but what she deserved after decades of organizing GE dinner parties and trips abroad, giving other "GE wives" tips on shopping and entertaining and generally being "the ultimate hostess." "I took my job very seriously," she testified . . .

. . .

By the time Mr. Wendt had taken over the GE subsidiary that generates 36% of the parent's profits, Mrs. Wendt testified, she was orchestrating black-tie dinners for 90 at their luxurious Stamford home. . . .

Testifying in the drab, tiny Fairfield County courtroom, a stylishly dressed Mrs. Wendt spoke alternately with affection and resentment in her voice. "He loved to entertain," she said of her husband. "He just didn't see that it was a lot of work." Mrs. Wendt wasn't compensated by GE. Her husband earns roughly $2 million a year in salary and bonus. . . .

. . .

Mr. Wendt, a famously tough corporate negotiator, asserted in his deposition that it was he who had worked hard and sacrificed and therefore deserved to keep a much larger share of the couple's assets. "There is no attempt at meanness, but there is an understanding of how hard I've worked and what I've accomplished and the stress I put myself under and what the rest of my life might in fact be like because of that." . . . [¶] "My rewards were financial, and I think her rewards were perhaps emotional," specifically, "the satisfaction of being with the children". . . .

Should Mrs. Wendt have received half of the $52 million marital estate? *See* June Carbone, From Partners to Parents 147–51 (2000) (discussing the *Wendt* case and mentioning that the trial court in that case awarded Mrs. Wendt $20 million). From 1998 to 2006, Lorna Jorgenson Wendt ran the "Equality in Marriage Institute," to help others "maintain equality" during and after marriage. http://www.equalityinmarriage.org/d/News/headlines.html. On the plight of corporate spouses in divorce, see Geraldine Fabrikant, "Divorce, Corporate American Style," N.Y. Times, Aug. 14, 2005.

Wendt is hardly alone. From reported cases and other anecdotal evidence, many of the cases involving a large disparity in income or assets (*e.g.*, where one of the spouses is a corporate executive, successful athlete, celebrity actor, or the like) result in a division of property that deviates significantly from an equal split. *See* Carbone, at 147–53. It is not easy either to explain or to justify why the division in high-asset, high-differential divorces should be so much more one-sided than the division in marriages with a more modest or more equal level of assets. In some recent Australian cases, the courts have awarded rich corporate executives significantly unequal shares of marital property under the rubric of "special contributions." *See* Patrick Parkinson, *The Yardstick of Equality: Assessing Contributions in Australia and England*," 19 INTERNAT'L J. L. POL'Y & FAM. 163 (2005).

One possible explanation implied by the court's conclusion in such cases is that the high-income spouse simply "contributed" more than the other spouse, even when the lower-income spouse's contributions to the marriage are considered. While that point might seem plausible in one sense — how much can domestic services be worth? — it might seem clear that the courts themselves don't really adopt that view, or they would not conclude that the homemaking services of a woman like Mrs. Wendt be worth $20 million (while spouses who gave comparable homemaking services in other marriages are awarded a small fraction of that). So their award to Mrs. Wendt must be grounded on something other than their estimates of the market value of her services — and, if so, what is it, and why is it capped at $20 million?

If the basic idea of marriage is that the spouses are "in it together," for better and for worse, then a presumption of equal division is the logical starting point (the *ALI Principles* recommends a strong presumption of equal division, § 4.09), and an exceptional ability to earn money is no more a justification for deviation than a particular facility at raising children. *See, e.g. Arneault v. Arneault*, 639 S.E.2d 720 (W. Va. 2006) (corporate executive's "intelligence and financial prowess" does not warrant deviation from 50/50 presumptive split). Any deviation from rough equality would seem to require justification, though, as the next Note discusses, the criteria the legislatures require courts to consider often end up increasing discretion (and lack of accountability) rather than offering any sort of structure for decision.

6. *A Discretionary System?* Appellate courts in equitable distribution states that do not follow a clear presumption of equal division typically emphasize the trial judge's discretion whenever the property allocation is challenged on appeal. "While the trial court must consider the delineated statutory criteria, no single criterion is preferred over the others, and the court is accorded wide latitude in varying the weight placed upon each item under the peculiar circumstances of each case." *Sunbury v. Sunbury*, 553 A.2d 612 (Conn. 1989). Can there be meaningful appellate review under such a system? One Indiana judge observed that the trial court's range of choice in equitable distribution "is virtually limitless and [appellate] review little more than pretense." *Baker v. Baker*, 488 N.E.2d 361, 366 (Ind. App. 1986) (Young, J., concurring). *See also* Mary Ann Glendon, *Family Law Reform in the 1980's*, 44 LA. L. REV. 1553, 1556 (1984) (movement to equitable distribution more aptly described as a movement to "discretionary distribution, since what consistently distinguishes [it] from [its] predecessors is not that [it is] more equitable, but that [it is] more unpredictable"). A classic article points out that unpredictability in judicial decision puts a negotiating burden on the risk-averse spouse. While it makes that point in the context of child custody disputes, much of its analysis applies equally to property division. Robert H. Mnookin & Lewis Kornhauser, *Bargaining in the Shadow of the Law: The Case of Divorce*, 88 YALE L.J. 950 (1979). But despite all the criticisms of a discretionary allocation system, many jurisdictions continue to resist the move towards an equal division presumption. In 1992, the Hawaii Supreme Court disapproved property allocation

guidelines developed by its intermediate appellate courts because they improperly deprived trial judges of discretion. *Gussin v. Gussin*, 836 P.2d 484 (Haw. 1992).

7. *Rebutting an Equal Division Presumption.* Common law states using a rebuttable presumption of equal division struggle with the question of what it takes to rebut it. For example, Oregon law directs the court to make a "just and proper" division of the property, and to consider homemaker contributions, and then concludes that "[t]here is a rebuttable presumption that both spouses have contributed equally to the acquisition of property during the marriage, whether such property is jointly or separately held." O.R.S. § 107.105(1)(f). In *Marriage of Stice*, 779 P.2d 1020 (Or. 1989), husband and wife both worked for Teledyne during their 25-year marriage, had nearly equal incomes, and had separate bank accounts. They had agreed to an equal division of their property, with the exception of certain stock.

> The disputed stock [was] acquired by wife in her sole name . . . through monthly payroll deductions to Teledyne's employee stock plan. In all, she paid $10,296 for the stock, which . . . is now valued at over $400,000. Husband holds in his name about $72,000 in Teledyne and related stock he received . . . as bonuses. Husband also purchased other stocks, which, in the words of the trial court, "didn't pan out." . . .
>
> The trial court found that the "wife has always been the saver and purchaser throughout the marriage. She saved from her earnings and purchased the furniture the parties have from those savings. When they originally bought a beach house in Waldport, it was purchased from her savings. [Husband] has generally been a spender, and he has used most of his income above that needed for the monthly expenses for his enjoyment and hobbies. The Court is satisfied that the [disputed] Teledyne and related stocks were accumulated through [wife's] industry and frugality. It was her interest and perseverance that allowed the parties to obtain the . . . property that is being awarded to [husband]. I am satisfied, however, that [wife] was able to do this with her income, because of the financial support she received from [husband] in paying the monthly bills."

Id. at 1022, 1024. On the basis of these findings the trial court awarded most of the stock to the wife. The Oregon Supreme Court reversed:

> In a long-term marriage in which the parties' properties were acquired during the marriage, the parties should separate on as equal a basis as possible. In *Jenks*, . . . we explained:
>
> > "When couples enter marriage, they ordinarily commit themselves to an indefinite shared future of which shared finances are a part. Acquisitions are made, foregone or replaced for the good of the family unit rather than for the financial interests of either spouse. Property is bought, sold, enhanced, diminished, intermixed and used without regard to ease of division upon termination of the marriage. . . . [B]y the nature of the marital relationship, couples ordinarily pledge their troth for better or worse until death parts them and their financial affairs are conducted accordingly.

"If the marriage is terminated before the parties' financial affairs become commingled or committed to the needs of children to the point that the parties cannot readily be restored to their premarital situations, then property division is a relatively simple task in the nature of a rescission. With each common financial act or decision, however, extrication upon dissolution becomes increasingly difficult. The origin of each item becomes less significant in making a property division which is 'just and proper in all the circumstances.'"

Id. at 1026–27.

As to the wife's claim that she had performed the major share of the homemaking services, as well as contributing equally if not more to the marriage's finances, the court said:

We do not find the ORS 107.105(1)(f) "homemaker" provision relevant. . . . The provision primarily was intended to recognize that "non-earning spouses who maintain the home, do the cooking and cleaning and raise the children, also contribute to the acquisition of property in a tangible way." The provision effectively places the homemaker-spouse's non-economic contributions on a par with the breadwinner-spouse's direct economic contribution to the acquisition of property.

We find no legislative intent, however, that a spouse [who] works outside the home and, additionally, performs "homemaker" duties, should be able to rely upon the homemaker provision to establish that she or he contributed more than 50 percent to the acquisition of property.

Id. at 1027–28. In *Arneault v. Arneault*, 639 S.E.2d 720 (W. Va. 2006), the West Virginia Supreme Court rejected an argument (which had been accepted by the trial court in the case, in making a 65/35 split of marital property) that a husband's "intelligence and financial prowess" in becoming a high-paid corporate executive "is . . . sufficient justification for straying from the presumption of a 50/50 split." *Id.* at 729.

In *Kelly v. Kelly*, 9 P.3d 1046 (Ariz. 2000), a federal statute prevented the wife's social security benefits from being divided, while the husband's retirement benefits were not similarly excluded. The court concluded that this imbalance created a justification for deviating from an equal division, but that the solution was declaring the husband's retirement benefits to be his separate property (as the wife's social security benefits were effectively her separate property, for the purpose of property division), regardless of whether that amount was greater than, less than, or equal to the wife's benefits.

8. *Are Homemaker Provisions Obsolete?* Although much of the discussion of marital property regimes assumes a homemaker wife, she is becoming uncommon. In 1940, only one of seven married women (with their husband present) was working outside the home or looking for work. By 1979, it was one of two. Hayghe, *Two-Income Families*, Am. Demographics 35–36 (Sept. 1981). Government data shows that in recent years the number of "traditional households" (in which the husband was the sole breadwinner) has hovered at slightly under 20%. *See* Ira Mark Ellman, *Marital Roles and Declining Marriage Rates*, 41 Fam. L.Q. 455

(2007) (summarizing and discussing the data). It may therefore seem that modern marital property law should not assume a traditional family organization.

One writer, anticipating these developments, suggested that as women come to participate fully and equally in the workplace, separate property regimes would protect their interests more than community property, or reformed common law equitable distribution systems. Mary Ann Glendon, *Is There a Future for Separate Property?*, 8 FAM. L.Q. 315 (1974). But a closer look at the data reveals some important realities: many wives do not work full-time, and even most of those who do earn less than their husband. *E.g.*, Hayghe and Bianchi found that in 1992 only 43 percent of married mothers with children between ages 6 and 17 worked *full-time* for the whole year, and only 31 percent of married mothers with children under six did so. Howard V. Hayghe & Suzanne M. Bianchi, *Married Mothers' Work Pattern: The Job-Family Compromise*, MONTHLY LABOR REVIEW, June 1994, at 24–30. In short, about half the working mothers worked less than full time. This contrasts with the experience of married men, who are *more* likely to work, and to work full time, if they have children. The emergence of the "working wife" is thus not the same as the demise of the homemaker wife. As a factual matter, most working wives still base their employment decisions on the assumption that they bear the primary responsibility for household tasks and child rearing, and this constraint has been estimated to account for 70% of the difference in earnings between married men and women. Riche, *All About Working Women*, AM. DEMOGRAPHICS 6 (Oct. 1981). Even where both spouses work, they are unlikely to make career decisions on the same basis as if they were not married. Most couples are likely to pool their resources on the assumption, perhaps unspoken, that they are partners in a sharing relationship. Susan Prager, *Sharing Principles and the Future of Marital Property Law*, 25 UCLA L. REV. 1, 7–11, 13 (1977). This reality argues strongly for "sharing principles" as a foundation of marital property regimes, on the simple premise that it would be unfair to allocate to one spouse all of the financial benefits of the preferred career. And as a matter of social policy, Prager said, we may wish to encourage "sharing principles" by our marital property law:

> A separate property system encourages each person to function as an earner by refusing to compensate a spouse who remains in the home for some significant period. [¶] But if many couples . . . make decisions with the special exigencies of the marital relationship in mind, a system of property law which assumes decisions ought to be made on an individual basis may produce two quite different ill effects. First, one spouse may ultimately be treated unfairly if the couple does not alter its behavior to conform to the individualistic . . . model. Second, if behavior is indeed responsive to a legal structure which dictates putting oneself first, other social values will suffer. By dictating that a married person behave as if unmarried with respect to certain choices or suffer the consequences of subsequent property disadvantage for not doing so, the individually oriented model works to reward self-interested choices which can be detrimental to the continuation of the marriage. At the same time it punishes conduct of accommodation and compromise so important to furthering and preserving the relationship. From a social engineering

standpoint, an individualistic property system will begin to produce behavior that is at cross-purposes with other values, such as stability and cooperation in marital relationships.

Id. at 12.

9. *Marital Misconduct as a Factor in Equitable Distribution.* A full examination of whether marital misconduct should influence the financial terms of a divorce is deferred until Section G of this chapter. But note that even states that permit its consideration in alimony awards often allocate property on a no-fault basis. The Model Marriage and Divorce Act, provides in § 307 that property is allocated by the court "without regard to marital misconduct." Under the old common law there was little opportunity to consider marital misconduct in allocating property because property allocation involved no equitable judgment. Property was simply allocated to the spouse who held title to it. Before the no-fault revolution, some community property states did consider marital fault in allocating community property upon divorce. Equitable distribution came to the common law states at about the same time as no-fault divorce, and most followed the MMDA's lead. But fifteen states permit their courts broad authority to consider marital misconduct when allocating property at divorce: Alabama, Connecticut, Georgia, Maryland, Massachusetts, Michigan, Mississippi, Missouri, New Hampshire, North Dakota, Rhode Island, South Carolina, Texas, Vermont, and Wyoming. *ALI Principles*, at 43–49, 68, 77–82.

In these fifteen states misconduct claims are a wild card with unpredictable results that vary with the trial judge. As the *ALI Principles* explain:

> The problem of creating standards by which to determine the dollar consequences of a fault finding is particularly intractable. Appellate decisions in fault states sometimes caution that fault is only one factor relevant to the allocation of property or granting of alimony, and should not be given disproportionate weight. *E.g., Sparks v. Sparks*, 485 N.W.2d 893 (Mich. 1992). But the meaning of such cautionary language is at best obscure. For example, in *Sparks* itself, the trial court had awarded the husband 75 percent of the marital property after finding that the wife's adultery was the principal cause of the marital failure. The Michigan Supreme Court held that the trial court had given the wife's fault disproportionate weight in this disposition, but was unable to state any rule [to] determine the proportionate weight to accord such misconduct. . . .
>
> In a number of fault states, appellate courts have attempted to establish rules . . . , but such guidelines do not seem to create effective bounds on trial-court discretion. For example, Missouri opinions specify that "the conduct factor becomes important . . . when the conduct of one party to the marriage is such that it throws upon the other party marital burdens beyond the norms to be expected in the marital relationship." *Burtscher v. Burtscher*, 563 S.W.2d 526, 527 (Mo. App. 1978). Even in laying down this rule, the court observed that "it is unnecessary and probably impossible to lay down any precise guidelines for the weight to be given to the conduct factor." So in *Burtscher* itself the appeals court declined to reverse the trial court's conclusion that husband's adultery was counterbalanced by his

wife's insistence on playing bingo four nights a week over the husband's objection.

ALI Principles at 83. The *ALI Principles* themselves endorse a no-fault approach to property allocation. Early in the no-fault divorce era, the New Jersey Supreme Court explained its adoption of a no-fault rule with two salient observations:

> First of all, . . . marriage is such an intricate relationship that often it is difficult, if not impossible, to ascertain upon whom the real responsibility for the marital breakup rests.
>
> . . .
>
> Second, . . . equitable distribution is merely the recognition that each spouse contributes something to the marital estate. The concept of fault is not relevant to such distribution since all that is being effected is the allocation to each party of what really belongs to him or her.

Chalmers v. Chalmers, 320 A.2d 478, 482–83 (N.J. 1974). Note *Chalmers'* emphasis on equitable distribution as simply allocating each spouse "what really belongs to him or her." Misconduct then seems less relevant in dividing property than it would if the process is instead framed as deciding whether equitable considerations require awarding one spouse property that belongs to the other. It is therefore not surprising that only one community property state permits consideration of marital misconduct. It may also be true that the common law states most inclined to divide property equally upon divorce are also those least likely to consider marital misconduct.

New York occupies something of a middle ground between the fifteen states that consider fault and the majority that do not. Marital fault is excluded from consideration in equitable distribution except for "egregious cases that shock the conscience." *O'Brien v. O'Brien*, 66 N.Y.S.2d 576, 489 N.E.2d 712, 498 N.Y.S.2d 743, 750 (1985) (except for such extreme cases, misconduct is not a "just and proper" consideration as it is inconsistent with the premise of economic partnership). It appears that only serious felonies meet this standard. "[V]erbal harassment, threats and several acts of minor domestic violence" are not egregious misconduct, *Kellerman v. Kellerman*, 187 A.D.2d 906, 590 N.Y.S.2d 570, 571 (1992), nor is a refusal to have children in violation of an explicit promise, *McCann v. McCann*, 156 Misc. 2d 540, 593 N.Y.S.2d 917 (Sup. Ct. 1993) (discussing the rule at length), nor the combination of the wife's open adultery, physical abuse (scratching, biting, and pulling hair of husband), verbal abuse (repeatedly berating him in front of coworkers and friends), and wounding of her husband with a knife while breaking into his locked briefcase, *Stevens v. Stevens*, 107 A.D.2d 987, 484 N.Y.S.2d 708 (1985), nor necessarily the husband's verbal and physical abuse of wife, which may not be sufficiently extreme or outrageous to allow reduction in his share of marital property, *Orofino v. Orofino*, 215 A.D.2d 997, 627 N.Y.S.2d 460 (1995). Attempted murder is egregious misconduct, *Brancoveanu v. Brancoveanu*, 145 A.D.2d 395, 535 N.Y.S.2d 86 (1988) and *Wenzel v. Wenzel*, 122 Misc. 2d 1001, 472 N.Y.S.2d 830 (Sup. Ct. 1984); as is rape, *Thompson v. Thompson*, N.Y. L.J., Jan. 5, 1990, at 28 (rape of wife's daughter by husband-stepfather); and repeated physical abuse in which, over a 20-year period, the husband: slapped defendant's face weekly; broke her foot by stamping on it; broke her finger, leaving it permanently deformed; pushed her, causing a broken arm with a permanent 40 percent loss of use, and punched her so that she sustained dental damage requiring caps and root canal work. *Debeny v. Debeny*, N.Y. L.J., Jan. 24, 1991, at 29.

10. *Financial Misconduct*. All states permit the dissolution court to consider, in allocating marital property, misconduct directly affecting the amount or value of the property available for allocation. Even a pure no-fault system committed to equal division of community property must take account of misconduct by one spouse that deprives a spouse of a true half-share. In many states the rule often is statutory, though the statutes are of varying formulation. *E.g.*, ARIZ. REV. STAT. ANN. § 25-318(C) (court may consider, in allocating property, a spouse's "abnormal expenditures, destruction, concealment or fraudulent disposition" of assets); CAL. FAM. CODE § 2602 (court may deduct from a spouse's share of community property an "amount the court determines to have been deliberately misappropriated by the party to the exclusion of the interest of the other party in the community estate"); KAN. STAT. ANN. § 60-1610(b)(1) (court may consider a spouse's "dissipation" of assets).

Excluding claims of marital misconduct is not inconsistent with allowing claims of financial misconduct, as analogy to a business partnership's dissolution makes clear. A court allocating a dissolving partnership's assets among the business partners may consider a claim that one partner fraudulently conveyed partnership assets to a confederate and has therefore already realized much or all of his share. But it would be inappropriate for the court to consider one partner's claim that another's nasty conduct caused the complainant great emotional distress or that another partner had committed a battery. Resolution of a fraudulent conveyance claim is necessarily part of any complete accounting of the dissolving partnership's assets, while the battery or emotional distress claim is a collateral matter to be decided under tort law. Note too that the intractable problem of establishing standards by which to gauge the financial value of a marital misconduct claim does not arise in most cases of financial misconduct.

But the term "financial misconduct" is sufficiently broad and vague to raise some difficult questions. Consider the rule of Kansas and others allowing the court dividing marital property to consider a spouse's "dissipation" of marital assets. As the *ALI Principles* observe, "[w]hile the term ['dissipation'] communicates the conclusion that a particular use of the assets was improper, it provides no criteria for distinguishing improper uses from the many unfortunate but lawful ways in which funds may be lost, including poor judgment." § 4.10, Comment *a*.

Gambling losses are frequently held to constitute dissipation, but not investment losses, even where the investment was of high risk — at least if it was not inconsistent with the general investment pattern within the marriage. *Compare Harrison v. Harrison*, 787 S.W.2d 738 (Mo. App. 1989) (dissipation found where wife lost joint access funds in 12-hour gambling spree), *and Booth v. Booth*, 371 S.E.2d 569 (Va. App. 1988) (wife "wasted" $60,000 lost in a speculative stock market investment), *with Hauge v. Hauge*, 427 N.W.2d 154 (Wis. App. 1988) (investment in Arabian horses not dissipation), *and Marriage of Drummond*, 509 N.E.2d 707 (Ill.

App. 1987) (commodities trading not dissipation where trader had experience with it).

What if a spouse's gambling losses are part of the long-term marital pattern? Can a spouse who has apparently tolerated them — perhaps even participating at times in the gambling activities — suddenly disavow the losses at dissolution? In *Marriage of Williams*, 927 P.2d 679 (Wash. App. 1996), the court concluded that the wife's $12,000 gambling losses were not dissipation because her gambling activities were legal under state law and were essentially entertainment costs indistinguishable from other expenditures on entertainment that either spouse might make. The court noted that her husband was aware of the wife's gambling activities. The court presumably felt that his failure to object, or at least the willingness to continue the marriage despite the objectionable behavior, suggests that he accepted this behavior as part of an overall marital arrangement. Having done so, the spouse cannot later disfavor just those parts of the marital relationship he or she did not like. Note that this principle would not apply to alleged acts of dissipation that occurred once the marital relationship had effectively ended. In apparent reliance on such reasoning, some courts limit dissipation claims to losses that occurred in the "waning days" of the marriage, or after its "breakdown." *Siegel v. Siegel*, 574 A.2d 54 (N.J. Super. Ct. Ch. Div. 1990) (husband's gambling losses of $227,000 treated as dissipation where incurred after marriage was "irreparably fractured"). This restriction has been held crucial to prevent spouses from using the dissolution action to question every spending decision made during the marriage and thereby requiring courts to "become auditing agencies for every marriage that falters." *In re Marriage of Getautas*, 544 N.E.2d 1284, 1288 (Ill. App. 1989). *See also Panhorst v. Panhorst*, 390 S.E.2d 376, 379 (S.C. App. 1990) ("One spouse . . . may have spent marital funds foolishly or selfishly or may have invested them unprofitably. The statute wisely prevents the other spouse from resurrecting these transactions at the end of the marriage to gain an advantage in the equitable distribution.")

While there is a certain logic to this approach, the experience of Illinois, a principal proponent of it, suggests that the uncertainty of a test framed in terms of whether the dissipation occurred after the marital breakdown may invite litigation. *See, e.g., Marriage of Harding*, 545 N.E.2d 459, 467 (Ill. App. 1989) (appellate court reverses finding that breakdown occurred, for purpose of judging validity of dissipation claim, when wife stopped cooking for husband; "no evidence of an irreconcilable breakdown of the marriage until the point at which petitioner filed for dissolution . . ."). An alternative to the breakdown standard that still attempts to vindicate the logic of the approach is to employ a more objective indicator of the marital termination, such as the parties' separation. *See, e.g.,* N.C. GEN. STAT. § 50-20(c)(11a), allowing the court to consider, in making an equitable distribution, "[a]cts of either party to . . . waste, neglect, devalue or convert the marital property . . . during the period after separation of the parties and before the time of distribution." But fixing the time of separation may also be subject to dispute. Thus, *ALI Principles* § 4.10 takes this approach a step further, limiting most dissipation claims to a fixed period of time prior to service of the dissolution petition.

In *Finan v. Finan*, 949 A.2d 468 (Conn. 2008), the Connecticut Supreme Court followed the majority rule allowing consideration of financial dissipation of assets even if these occur prior to the physical separation of the couple. Additionally, though, it held (following a number of other states) that the dissipation must occur when divorce is imminent, or, at least the marriage is clearly in trouble. This rule discourages parties from second-guessing all financial decisions made during the marriage. The same court clarified that a very bad investment would not constitute financial dissipation; dissipation only occurs where there has been a harmful or selfish expenditure for a "nonmarital purpose." *Gershman v. Gershman*, 943 A.2d 1091 (Conn. 2008).

The Massachusetts Supreme Judicial Court, in *Kittredge v. Kittredge*, 803 N.E.2d 206 (Mass. 2004), similarly held that for expenditures to be "dissipation," they must be for that party's own personal enjoyment at a time that the marriage seemed to be ending. *Id.* at 313–314 (citing and quoting from the *American Law Institute Principles of the Law of Family Dissolution*).

Note that while the line between financial misconduct and marital misconduct is real, it is also permeable. Gifts to paramours are a frequent fact pattern in dissipation claims, *e.g., Marriage of Charles*, 672 N.E.2d 57 (Ill. App. 1996) (trial court reversed for failing to consider whether husband's purchase of house and furniture for his mistress after parties' separation was dissipation); *Zeigler v. Zeigler*, 530 A.2d 445 (Pa. Super. 1987) (reimbursement ordered where husband used marital funds toward down-payment on home titled in girlfriend's name), as are expenditures on adulterous relationships, *e.g., Noll v. Noll*, 375 S.E.2d 338 (S.C. App. 1988) (reimbursement required where wife spent $2,000 of joint funds on cruise with boyfriend). Judicial willingness to treat such expenditures as dissipation is undoubtedly influenced by disapproval of the financed conduct. But note as well that a dissipation claim is necessarily limited to recovering the lost marital funds, so that its contours are far more well-defined than a general claim in a true fault system for an enlarged property award as compensation for the other spouse's adultery.

Some state statutes speak of a spouse causing a "diminution of assets" rather than a "dissipation of assets," and at least one court has held that the choice of "diminution" means that wrongful action need not be proven, and that there is no timing requirement. *In re Martel*, 944 A.2d 575 (N.H. 2008).

For more on the doctrine of dissipation, and the way it has developed differently in community property and equitable distribution jurisdictions, see J. Thomas Oldham, *"Romance Without Finance Ain't Got No Chance": Development of The Doctrine of Dissipation in Equitable Distribution States*, 21 J. AM. ACADEMY MATRIMONIAL LAW. 501 (2008).

PROBLEMS

Problem 4-2. Alice and Jerry marry in 1995. During the marriage, Alice attends schools, pursues hobbies and keeps house, while Jerry works for a computer software company. In the evenings, Jerry works at home designing computer programs, and in 2004 he comes up with a new program which he markets himself through Softsell, a company he creates for this purpose. Jerry is the sole proprietor of Softsell, which he started with savings accumulated since 1996. The program is an immense success, and by 2005, Softsell is worth $4 million. In 2006, it is worth $20 million. Also in 2006, Alice files for divorce, complaining Jerry is spending too much time with the computer and not enough with her. Alice has never been interested in computers and has never participated in Softsell in any way. How would the Softsell Company be treated on divorce, in community property and common law equitable distribution states?

a. Would it matter if during the pending divorce proceedings, Alice inherited $2 million when her father passed away? Should it?

b. Suppose Alice, miffed that Jerry is spending many evenings working on the computer rather than spending time with her, begins seeing other men. Unbeknownst to Jerry, by the end of 2004, she has a regular boyfriend named Vincent. Unfortunately, Vincent is an aspiring painter of questionable talent who cannot provide Alice with many material goods. By 2006, however, Alice decides she can no longer put up with Jerry's nerdish ways and commences divorce proceedings. She assures Vincent that with her share of Softsell (which she has found out is now worth $20 million), they will both be able to live comfortably while Vincent paints. Is she right? Should she be?

c. Would it matter whether the capital Jerry put into Softsell came from a gift from his mother, rather than savings accumulated during the marriage? Should it?

Problem 4-3. During their 12-year marriage, H and W attended jai-alai matches every Saturday, at which H placed regular bets. At the dissolution of the marriage, W seeks to have her share of the marital property augmented to reflect the losses from those bets. W alleges that she did not participate in the betting and objected to H's gambling. H alleges that W enjoyed the gambling and shared eagerly in the winnings. Is it necessary to resolve their factual dispute to decide this case? What is the appropriate resolution?

B. PROPERTY DIVISION: CLASSIFICATION PROBLEMS

[1]   The Basics

ALI PRINCIPLES (2002)

§ 4.03 Definition of Marital and Separate Property

(1) Property acquired during marriage is marital property, except as otherwise expressly provided in this Chapter.

(2) Inheritances, including bequests and devises, and gifts from third parties, are the separate property of the acquiring spouse even if acquired during marriage.

(3) Property received in exchange for separate property is separate property even if acquired during marriage.

(4) Property acquired during marriage but after the parties have commenced living apart pursuant to either a written separation agreement or a judicial decree, is the separate property of the acquiring spouse unless the agreement or decree specifies otherwise.

(5) For the purpose of this section "during marriage" means after the commencement of marriage and before the filing and service of a petition for dissolution (if that petition ultimately results in a decree dissolving the marriage), unless there are facts, set forth in written findings of the trial court . . . , establishing that use of another date is necessary to avoid a substantial injustice.

———

The old Model Marriage and Divorce Act (MMDA) recommended that common law states adopt a version of equitable distribution that authorized courts to allocate all the spouses' property, rather than limiting the allocation to marital property. MMDA § 307. This has been called the "hotchpot" (or "kitchen sink") system. Most common law states did not follow the MMDA, however. They instead adopted a system in which the divorce court has equitable authority to distribute only marital property. A recent commentator lists 14 states as "hotchpot": Connecticut, Hawaii, Indiana, Kansas, Massachusetts, Michigan, Mississippi, Montana, New Hampshire, North Dakota, South Dakota, Vermont, Washington, and Wyoming. J. THOMAS OLDHAM, DIVORCE, SEPARATION, AND THE DISTRIBUTION OF PROPERTY § 3.03[2] n.3 (Law Journal Press, 1987 & Supp. 2009). Washington is the only community property state in that group. The same source gives an (overlapping) list of Alabama, Alaska, Arkansas, Hawaii, Iowa, Minnesota, Ohio, Oregon and Wisconsin, as examples of "hybrid" states where separate property may be divided, in circumstances where division of only marital property would lead to an unfair outcome. *Id.*, § 3.03[4] & n. 21; *see, e.g.*, MINN. STAT. § 518.58, subd. 2 (if the court finds the division of marital property alone would "work an unfair hardship," up to one half of the separate property may be apportioned).

Even for states on the pure "hotchpot" list, one must consider nuances in the application of the rules that could make the "hotchpot" designation at least partly misleading. *See ALI Principles* § 4.03, Reporters Notes, Comment *a*. Many cases in the purported "hotchpot" states show the court in fact *not* ignoring the distinction between marital and separate property, finding "the fact that property subject to distribution was acquired by one of the parties prior to the marriage is a consideration weighing in favor of that party," *Fraase v. Fraase*, 315 N.W.2d 271, 274 (N.D. 1982), and that inherited property should ordinarily go to the spouse who inherited it, *Bonelli v. Bonelli*, 576 A.2d 587 (Conn. App. 1990); *see also* J. Thomas Oldham, *Tracing, Commingling, and Transmutation*, 23 FAM. L.Q. 219, 220 n.5 (1989); Robert J. Levy, *An Introduction to Divorce Property Issues*, 23 FAM. L.Q. 147, 151–56 (1989). Examination of appellate cases in "hotchpot" states suggests that they are most likely to give one spouse a share of the other's "separate" property (as other states would call it) in long-term marriages where the spouses' financial capacity would otherwise be very disparate, an outcome similar to that authorized in the "hybrid" states. *See, e.g.*, *Zeh v. Zeh*, 618 N.E.2d 1376 (Mass. App. 1993) (at dissolution of 24-year marriage, trial court required to include within the "hotchpot" the husband's $420,000 inheritance, which dwarfed the parties' other assets). The *ALI Principles* come to a similar outcome, albeit in less discretionary form, by adopting the distinction between marital and separate property, but also providing that a very gradual re-characterization of each spouse's separate property into marital property as their marriage lengthens, if the parties have not taken steps to provide otherwise. *ALI Principles* § 4.18.

NOTES

1. *When Does the Marital Community Begin and End?* While the marriage ceremony provides a convenient bright line for the beginning of the marriage, difficulties arise where the parties acquire some significant asset during a period of nonmarital cohabitation preceding marriage. While the acquisition is clearly not "during the marriage" in the literal sense, some courts permit the inclusion of such assets in the marital estate. *E.g., Marriage of Dubnicay*, 830 P.2d 608 (Or. App. 1992) (relying in part on the fact that parties commingled their assets during this period); *Northrop v. Northrop*, 622 N.W.2d 219 (N.D. 2001) (in a case involving the division of a pension earned partly during the seven-year cohabitation that preceded a marriage of less than two years, court reaffirms that courts may consider premarital cohabitation). Other courts allow separate actions to enforce claims based on premarital cohabitation, following *Marvin v. Marvin*, 18 Cal. 3d 660, 134 Cal. Rptr. 815, 557 P.2d 106 (1976) (*see* Chapter 9), but reject claims that such cohabitation should affect the division of marital property. *Rolle v. Rolle*, 530 A.2d 847 (N.J. Super. Ch. Div. 1987); *Marriage of Leversee*, 156 Cal. App. 3d 891, 203 Cal. Rptr. 481 (1984). A third group not only hold the premarital cohabitation period irrelevant to the division of marital property but also reject any *Marvin* claims based upon it, either because the court rejects *Marvin* in general, *Marriage of Crouch*, 410 N.E.2d 580 (Ill. App. 1980), or rejects its application in this context, *Mangone v. Mangone*, 495 A.2d 469, 471 (N.J. Super. Ch. Div. 1985) (property acquired during premarital cohabitation not subject to equitable distribution, and any contract rights that wife may once have had arising from the cohabitation "merged into the greater contract of marriage"); *see also Stoner v. Stoner*, 2001 Tenn. App. LEXIS 30 (Jan. 18, 2001) (refusing to treat as marital property husband's stock accounts accumulated during cohabitation of nearly 20 years that preceded the short-lived marriage).

Several possibilities exist for the termination of (the creation of) marital or community property. Some jurisdictions choose the date upon which the divorce petition is filed, which might be called the "petition rule." *See, e.g., Painter v. Painter*, 320 A.2d 484 (N.J. 1974). *ALI Principles* § 4.03(5) endorses the petition rule as the presumptive termination date, but allows the court to substitute a different date in order to avoid a substantial injustice. Such a case might arise, for example, if the parties move to separate cities and commence leading entirely separate lives years before either seeks a legal termination of their marriage. In *Warner v. Warner*, 859 So. 2d 146 (La. App. 2003), both husband and wife filed for divorce, the wife filing first, but the eventual divorce was granted on the husband's petition. The trial court's decision, that the community property regime ended at the filing of the petition on which the divorce judgment was granted, not the first divorce petition filed, was affirmed.

Another group of states choose the date of the final divorce decree, holding that all earnings and acquisitions prior to that moment to be "during the marriage." *Friedman v. Friedman*, 384 S.E.2d 641 (Ga. 1989); *Alston v. Alston*, 629 A.2d 70 (Md. 1993); *Giha v. Giha*, 609 A.2d 945 (R.I. 1992) ($2.4 million lottery prize is marital property when won six months after entry of the interlocutory divorce decree but before entry of final decree). This "decree rule" often gives bargaining leverage to the lower-earning spouse, who may purposely delay settlement, because these delays permit her to continue sharing in the other spouse's accumulations of property, such as pension benefits. Ohio follows the decree rule, but like the *ALI Principles* allows the court to depart from it in exceptional cases to avoid injustice. Ohio Rev. Code Ann. § 3105.171(A)(2)(b).

California uses a third rule, under which spousal earnings acquired while the spouses live "separate and apart" are separate property, Cal. Fam. Code § 771(a). The case by case determinations that this rule requires — asking in each case precisely when the parties separated — would seem a likely source of difficulty, particularly as couples often go through one or more physical separations over several years before deciding definitely to end their marriage. California, however, has applied the rule so strictly, requiring a "complete and final break," *Marriage of Von Der Nuell*, 23 Cal. App. 4th 730, 28 Cal. Rptr. 2d 447 (1994), that the time of separation would not often be much before the time of the petition. *See also Marriage of Hardin*, 38 Cal. App. 4th 448, 45 Cal. Rptr. 2d 308 (1995). For discussion of the inherent problems in applying the California rule, see Carol S. Bruch, *The Legal Import of Informal Separations: A Survey of California Law and a Call for Change*, 65 Cal. L. Rev. 1015, 1021–24 (1977). Washington is the only other community property state following the California rule, Wash. Rev. Code § 26.16.140. Under a fourth approach, there is no rule at all, but instead the matter is within trial court discretion. This is the Alaska approach. *Schanck v. Schanck*, 717 P.2d 1, 3 (Alaska 1986) (each "case must be judged on its facts to determine when the marriage has terminated as a joint enterprise").

2. *As of What Date Is Marital Property Valued?* Note 1 discusses the alternative rules for determining the "closing date" of the marital community. The "valuation date" is a separate question. Assume marital acquisitions cease as of January 1, when the divorce petition is filed, and that the court actually divides the property on the following July 1, when it formulates its decree. At that later time it must assess the value of the various assets in order to make an equitable or equal distribution. But the value as of which date: January 1, July 1, or something in between? See *ALI Principles* § 4.03, Comment *f*:

> As a general matter a court should always use the most recent valuation date practical, even though marital property acquisitions cease on an earlier date. Use of the most recent date helps ensure that the parties are affected equally by market fluctuations, during the pendency of a divorce proceeding, in the value of their marital property. A different rule is appropriate, however, where the value of marital property is altered by the labor of either spouse after the cut-off date for marital acquisitions.

See Quinn v. Quinn, 575 A.2d 764 (Md. App. 1990) (trial court erroneously failed to consider whether husband's post-separation labor increased the value of marital property). Under CAL. FAM. CODE § 2552, courts are directed to value community assets "as near as practicable to the time of trial," but, according to subsection (b) of the statute, the trial court has discretion to set another date, if there is good cause for doing so. In *In re Marriage of Nelson*, 139 Cal. App. 4th 1546, 44 Cal. Rptr. 3d 52 (2006), the court found good cause for a different date of valuation when the wife's bad record-keeping precluded a valuation later than the date of separation. See generally Toni Hendricks, *Valuation Date in Divorces: What a Difference a Day Makes*, 21 J. AM. ACADEMY MATRIMONIAL LAW. 747 (2008)

[2]   Some Special Problems

While state statutes or judicial decisions may set bright lines for determining when a marriage has begun and ended for the purpose of determining which property is subject to division at divorce, there are recurrent complicating issues that arise in situations when efforts during the period of the marriage lead to property acquired after — sometimes, long after — the end of the marriage. This section explores general principles for such property; one important sub-category, pensions, will be covered in the next section.

NIROO v. NIROO
Maryland Court of Appeals
545 A.2d 35 (1988)

MURPHY, CHIEF JUDGE.

The question . . . is whether anticipated renewal commissions on insurance policies sold by a spouse during marriage but accruing after dissolution of the marriage are "marital property" [under state law which] defines "marital property" as

> "property, however titled, acquired by 1 or both parties during the marriage.
>
> (2) 'Marital property' does not include property:
>
> > (i) acquired before the marriage;
> >
> > (ii) acquired by inheritance or gift from a third party;
> >
> > (iii) excluded by valid agreement; or
> >
> > (iv) directly traceable to any of these sources."

I

The appellant, David Niroo (the husband) . . . challenges the determination of the trial judge that future renewal commissions accruing on insurance policies sold by him or his agents during the marriage were marital property.

The couple was married in 1977. In 1978, the husband began work as an insurance salesman for Pennsylvania Life Insurance Company (Penn Life) [and] received commissions on individual policies sold. In 1980, he became a branch manager and entered into agency manager agreements with Penn Life. . . . Under these agreements, the husband shared in the profits (and the losses) of the company as determined by specific "office codes," or blocks of insurance, assigned to agents under him and for whom he was responsible. The husband was entitled under the agreements to receive income derived from net profits generated if and when insurance policies coming under his office codes were renewed, provided that certain conditions . . . were satisfied [including,] inter alia, a covenant not to compete, an exclusivity clause, and a required renewal volume. . . .

At trial, both parties presented expert testimony as to the present day [sic] value of these renewal commissions after expenses were deducted, i.e., what the husband could expect to receive from the renewal policies. This valuation was based on industry "persistency rates," explained by the husband's expert witness as "the portion of the premiums that are in force in one year that renew and hence are paid and are still in force in the following year." This expert included only those renewal commission profits on policies sold during the marriage.

The trial judge determined that the husband's interest in the renewal income constituted marital property. He . . . found the present discounted profit value of the renewal commissions to be $410,000. The court also took into account various "advances" made to the husband by the insurance companies which were chargeable against renewal commissions. Under the agreements, these advances were considered as loans, repayable on demand. At the time of trial, the husband was indebted to the companies in the amount of $267,000. . . . [T]he trial judge determined that although the renewal income was marital property, the husband's $267,000 debt was not marital debt, but instead was to be taken into account as an "economic circumstance." The court arrived at a final monetary award of $200,000; in doing so, it considered various statutory factors, including the economic circumstances of the parties.

The husband appealed. We granted certiorari. . . .

II

In 1978 . . . the General Assembly enacted the Property Disposition in Divorce and Annulment Act, which significantly changed traditional notions as to property rights between spouses upon dissolution. . . . Enacted to remedy the inequities inherent under the previous [title] system . . . , the Act . . . does not authorize the court to transfer title, nor require that all property be evenly divided, [but] does allow . . . a monetary adjustment to more . . . equitably allocate the various property interests between the divorcing spouses. . . .

[T]he statute imposes a three-step process whereby the trial judge first determines what property is marital property . . . ; then assigns a value to it . . . ; and thereafter may grant a monetary award to whichever spouse would not otherwise receive his or her fair share of the marital assets. . . . In determining the proper amount and method of payment of this award, the court must consider the following factors provided under [the statute]:

"(1) the contributions, monetary and nonmonetary, of each party to the well-being of the family;

(2) the value of all property interests of each party;

(3) the economic circumstances of each party at the time the award is to be made;

(4) the circumstances that contributed to the estrangement of the parties;

(5) the duration of the marriage;

(6) the age of each party;

(7) the physical and mental condition of each party;

(8) how and when specific marital property was acquired, including the effort expended by each party in accumulating the marital property;

(9) any award of alimony and any award or other provision that the court has made with respect to family use personal property or the family home; and

(10) any other factor that the court considers necessary or appropriate to consider in order to arrive at a fair and equitable monetary award."

III

The husband. . . . asserts that due to the speculative and contingent nature of [the renewal] commissions, they are not within the definition of marital property [under] § 8-201(e). Furthermore, he argues that as it is necessary for him to "work" and nurture these accounts through activities performed after the marriage was dissolved, the income thereby derived is not "acquired" during the marriage. Thus, he contends, classification of renewal commissions as marital property would improperly give his former wife the fruits of his future efforts and would penalize him if the renewal commissions were not actually realized.

. . . [W]e have repeatedly noted that the meaning of property within the statutory definition of "marital property" . . . " 'embraces everything which has exchangeable value or goes to make up a man's wealth — every interest or estate which the law regards of sufficient value for judicial recognition.' " [¶] Under this broad concept . . . we have found that marital property includes: that portion of a husband's workers' compensation award for permanent partial disability which compensated for wages lost during the marriage; pension rights accumulated during the marriage; and a work-related contributory disability pension plan. On the other hand, we have found the following interests not includable as marital property: an inchoate personal injury claim arising from an accident occurring during the marriage, and a medical degree or license.

[We have] found that the right to pension benefits accumulated during marriage was a contractual right and therefore enforceable as a property right rather than as a mere conditional expectation. [W]e said that the proper analysis . . . was, first, to decide whether the property right was acquired during the marriage and secondly, whether it is equitable to include it as marital property, without regard to whether the right is vested or not. Moreover, we noted that the fact that the right to the pension benefit may be contingent upon continued employment did not matter, as such contingent future interests constituted property. Finally, it was clear that both spouses were relying on the pension benefits to provide for their future, so that an equitable distribution of the benefits was indeed proper. [¶] [We have also found the portion of any worker's compensation award] which compensated for the loss of earning capacity during the marriage was marital property, while his loss of future earning capacity arising after dissolution of the marriage was not marital property, [and that] a personal injury claim arising from an injury which occurred while the injured spouse was married was so uniquely personal that it could not be considered marital property "acquired" during the marriage, as required by the statute. . . .

When analyzed under the principles set forth in our cases, . . . contractually vested rights in renewal commissions are . . . marital property. . . . [A]n insurance agent has a vested right in commissions on renewal premiums when provided for by contract. . . . This contractual right . . . cannot be terminated unilaterally by the company, but instead would require an affirmative surrender by the agent to forfeit the future commissions due. [T]he agency contract provided that should the husband die or become disabled, his right to receive the renewal commissions, as well as his heirs' right thereto, would not be affected. [The agency contract also made] the husband's right to the renewal commission . . . assignable with the prior written consent of the company . . . [T]he husband's right amounts to more than a "mere expectancy," or a "mere historical possibility of gain" as he alternatively characterizes it.

The husband claims that after the dissolution . . . , he must continue to "service" his accounts after their initial procurement if he is to realize the renewal commissions. He thereby seeks to distinguish his situation from that involving pension benefits. We are not persuaded by his argument. The husband's primary effort was expended in acquiring the original policies. Evidence at trial showed that on a national average, 72% of the existing policies will be automatically renewed after the first year; 82% will be renewed after the second year; and 88% will be renewed thereafter. The husband nevertheless maintains that he must satisfy certain conditions not present with pension benefits, thus rendering his right to the commissions only a tenuous property interest. Specifically, he refers to the covenant in the agency agreements not to compete and to certain requirements as to renewal volume, the violation or nonattainment of which could result in forfeiture or diminishment of his commissions. He also asserts that uncertainties inherent in renewals, such as customer preferences, economic conditions, and agency turnover, render the renewal commissions too speculative for valuation. While we recognize these concerns, we do not find these conditions so onerous, and the contingencies so uncertain, as to make the contractual right to renewal commissions beyond valuation, particularly when the insurance industry itself assigns a value to them based on statistical persistency rates.

Courts in other jurisdictions have reached like conclusions. . . .

These cases support the view that the claim to renewal commissions is not the type of right that is uniquely personal to the holder, as in a personal injury claim or a professional degree. Instead, it is . . . part of the compensation package developed during the marriage by one of the spouses that each could have justifiably relied upon to provide for their economic future. [I]t is a . . . valuable asset not separable from the original policies sold during the marriage, and thus properly a part of the couple's shared assets during marriage. This determination, we think, is consistent with the declared policy of the Marital Property Act, . . . , "that marriage is a union between a man and a woman having equal rights under the law." Plainly, this policy recognizes the nonmonetary contributions made by the wife in this case in accumulating the assets. . . .

IV

The husband next argues that the advances received by him as a loan from Penn Life should have reduced the present value of the future commissions in valuing marital property. [T]he husband asserts that he borrowed the money against the profits from the anticipated renewal commissions to finance his agency operation; and that the debt therefore was an encumbrance upon the renewal income to be paid to him in the future. The wife . . . argues that the husband did not use the advances for the purpose of acquiring renewal commissions but rather for family expenses, including high personal expenditures of his own to support a lavish life style. The wife suggests that the husband's annual income, particularly in the later years of his agency business, was sufficiently high that no need existed to borrow money from Penn Life to meet the expenses of his branch manager operation.

The trial judge [found] that the loans . . . were used for family living expenses and that a sufficient nexus had not been established between the debt and the renewal income for it to be considered marital debt. . . . The trial judge considered the debt . . . a nonmarital "economic circumstance" of the husband under § 8-205(a)(3), to be taken into account in determining the amount and the method of payment of the monetary award to the wife. In doing so, the court recognized that no renewal commissions may have been available had the advances not been taken by the husband; nevertheless, it found that "the real use of those monies was not to purchase renewal commissions" but was for family living expenses.

On the record before us, we think the trial judge was wrong. In *Schweizer v. Schweizer*, 301 Md. 626, 484 A.2d 627 (1984), we said:

> "[A] 'marital debt' is a debt which is directly traceable to the acquisition of marital property. Conversely, 'nonmarital debt' is a debt which is not directly traceable to the acquisition of marital property. That part of marital property which is represented by an outstanding marital debt has not been 'acquired' for the purpose of an equitable distribution by way of a monetary award. Therefore, the value of that marital property is adjusted downward by the amount of the marital debt."

In considering the legal effect . . . of the advances drawn by the husband against future commissions, the trial judge seemingly applied the second sentence quoted above without regard to the context in which that sentence was written.

Schweizer presented the question . . . of whether debt incurred by the husband during the marriage which was not secured by marital property could be used to reduce the value of unencumbered marital property. Because none of the husband's debt was secured by marital property, the wife submitted that the husband's total debt was . . . only . . . an economic circumstance [the court could consider] . . .

when [it set] the amount of any monetary award. The husband in *Schweizer*, on the other hand, contended that all of his liabilities should be deducted from marital property, . . . which under the facts in *Schweizer* would have resulted in a negative valuation of marital property.

We rejected both contentions. The wife's contention was too narrow and the husband's contention was too broad. [W]e said that a debt which could be traced to the acquisition of marital property reduced the value of the marital property and that a debt which could not be so traced did not reduce the value of marital property. We remanded for the trial court to determine what portion, if any, of the husband's indebtedness was "marital debt."

Nothing . . . in *Schweizer* contradicted that part of the wife's contention which recognized that encumbrances on marital property reduce its value. In effect, the value of encumbered marital property is ordinarily the value of its equity. . . .

In the instant matter the advances drawn by Mr. Niroo against future insurance commissions are repayable on demand. If called, the debt can be set off by Penn Life against future commissions. The debt, in economic effect, is an encumbrance on the future commissions which reduces their present value. The trial judge therefore erred in not subtracting the debt of $267,000 from the value of the renewal income.

. . .

JUDGMENT AFFIRMED IN PART AND REVERSED IN PART. . . .

NOTES

1. Niroo *as Exemplifying the Maturing Marital Property System.* Common law courts asked to resolve the more difficult questions of marital property law find a plentiful selection of relevant precedent in the community property states, and many seem more willing than they were years ago to take guidance from the community property states' greater experience with what are now essentially identical property classification issues. That is not to say that no differences remain between the two systems. Note, for example, that the Maryland law applied in *Niroo* does not permit the court to transfer title to property, but only to make a monetary judgment. Title thus retains a significance in Maryland, and in some other common law states, that it does not have under community property regimes.

Niroo touches on many different issues in its discussion, including the treatment of pensions, personal injury claims, degrees, and debts, and the husband's claim that some portion of the property in question derives its value from post-dissolution labor. We return to the question of degrees, and of the treatment of spousal labor as property, in Section C of this chapter, which addresses a number of issues that intersect both property and alimony concepts. We explore the other issues now in the following notes.

2. *The Case of Deferred Compensation: In General.* The applicable principle is simple to state: income earned during the marriage is classified as marital property even though its receipt is deferred until after divorce. The renewal commissions at issue in *Niroo* are treated as marital property because they were earned during the marriage. This is the usual result. *See Marriage of Skaden*, 19 Cal. 3d 679, 139 Cal. Rptr. 615, 566 P.2d 249 (1977); *Marriage of Wade*, 923 S.W.2d 735 (Tex. App. 1996); *Bigbie v. Bigbie*, 898 P.2d 1271 (Okla. 1995) (relying on *Niroo*). *But see Lawyer v. Lawyer*, 702 S.W.2d 790 (Ark. 1986) (possible future termination payments, used to compensate for lost commissions, too speculative to be marital property). Pensions are the most prominent example of this principle's application, involved in a high percentage of divorces, and the special complications they raise are discussed in Section B[3], *infra*. Royalties paid out after divorce on work completed during marriage is another example. *E.g.*, *Heinze v. Heinze*, 631 N.E.2d 728 (Ill. App. 1994) (books); *Marriage of Worth*, 195 Cal. App. 3d 768, 241 Cal. Rptr. 135 (1987) (books as one type of artistic work); *Dunn v. Dunn*, 802 P.2d 1314 (Utah App. 1990) (royalties from invention of surgical instrument). Accounts receivable — as-yet-unpaid invoices owed to either spouse at divorce, for work that spouse performed during the marriage — are another common example. But while the principle is clear, its application to particular cases can raise knotty problems.

a. *Allocation issues*. Questions sometimes arise as to whether a particular post-dissolution income stream is the product of marital labor or of post-divorce labor. Mr. Niroo claimed, for example, that the renewal commissions were the result, at least in part, of his labors in servicing the renewing accounts — labors that would continue after divorce. The claim is at least plausible. Clients of Mr. Niroo's whose business was sought by competing agents might be tempted to switch — and thus cancel their policies with him — if they believed he was not responding adequately to their requests for assistance or information. The commission penalty he would incur if his renewals fell below specified percentages would seem aimed at providing him with additional incentives to maintain good relationships with his clients so as to encourage their renewals, suggesting that the insurance company itself agrees that renewals are at least partly dependent on the agent's continuing efforts.

The court nonetheless rejected Mr. Niroo's claim with two observations. It first notes that over 70 percent of policies are renewed. This is a non-sequitur. The fact that most people renew does not suggest that agents are not working to make sure of that result. More important is the court's second point, that "the husband's primary effort was expended in acquiring the original policies." The question is what to do with that plausible factual conclusion. One could theoretically allocate the income between marital and separate property components in proportion to one's estimate of the relative contributions that the pre- and post-divorce labor provide towards acquiring it. That estimate might be difficult to devise, both in principle (how does one measure the relative contribution? are hours an adequate measure, or are some hours more crucial than others?) and in fact (how accurately can one forecast the future labor required to maintain the accounts?). Perhaps because of these practical difficulties, many courts avoid such allocations, remaining content to treat as marital property any income attributable primarily to marital labor. *See, e.g.*, *Skaden, supra* (rejecting husband's claim that a portion of his agent's "termination payments," based primarily on renewal commissions, should be treated as separate property because attributable to his post-dissolution labor). This practice can work in both directions. Consider, for example, a major league baseball player who performs superbly during the 2009 season, and then goes on the free agent market in which he obtains a very lucrative contract for the next three seasons. He is divorced after signing the contract but before the 2010 season commences. Is any portion of the post-dissolution pay he will earn under this contract marital property? The conventional answer in such cases is no, yet surely much of the 2010 pay could be attributed to his labor during 2009. *See Chambers v. Chambers*, 840 P.2d 841 (Utah App. 1992) (wife's marital property claim on husband's post-divorce income under remaining three years of his five-year basketball contract with the Phoenix Suns rejected, because the income would derive from his post-marital labor, "rather than from some past effort or a product produced during the marriage").

Other courts do make such allocations, however. For example, one large and important group of cases in which courts routinely unravel the relative contributions of marital and nonmarital labor to post-marital payments are pension allocations, where the stakes are relatively high for a relatively large proportion of divorcing couples. It is also the case with pensions that extensive experience with the matter in many states has given rise to well-accepted methods for approximating, if not calculating, an appropriate allocation. *See* Section B.3., *infra*; *see also Heinze, supra* (husband awarded only 25% of royalties received after marriage on books wife wrote during marriage because future book sales were attributable in part to wife's post-marital promotional labors); *Dunn, supra* (value of time spent by husband after dissolution in generating royalty income deducted from wife's otherwise equal share in royalties).

b. ***Estimating future income flows.*** How could *Niroo* award the wife a share in the renewal commissions the husband would receive in the future when he had not received them? This problem will arise, of course, in any award of marital income to be realized in the future. Where the future compensation, or its amount, is uncertain, a court, generally, has three options: it can set now the shares each spouse will obtain if and when there are such payments; it can reserve jurisdiction to make an appropriate order when the payments are actually received or their amount established with relative certainty; and it can make an immediate lump sum payment, as occurred in *Niroo*.

In order to make an immediate lump sum distribution to the wife, the *Niroo* court had to fix a value for the future income. It relied upon expert witnesses who estimated the future income, based upon industry data on the average renewal rate, and then calculated a present value for this estimated future income flow. *See also Quinn v. Quinn*, 575 A.2d 764 (Md. App. 1990) (urging division at divorce, despite the valuation difficulties). On the other hand, where the amount of future income is uncertain, courts sometimes refuse to allocate it at all, because its receipt is too "speculative." *Marriage of Teitz*, 605 N.E.2d 670 (Ill. App. 1992) (speculative nature of attorney's contingent fees, where case has not yet reached final conclusion, distinguishes them from accounts receivable); *Beasley v. Beasley*, 518 A.2d 545, 554 (Pa. Super. 1986) (contingent fees excluded where assigning value at time of dissolution would be "tenuous and risky"). This approach denies the other spouse any share in the contingent fees even though most of the labor performed to earn them occurred during marriage. Other courts (and the *ALI Principles*, § 4.08) conclude that in such situations jurisdiction should be reserved. *E.g., Garrett v. Garrett*, 683 P.2d 1166 (Ariz. App. 1984) (jurisdiction reserved for the purpose of dividing contingent fees when they are in fact received by the law firm); *Marriage of Weiss*, 365 N.W.2d 608 (Wis. App. 1985) (same).

3. *Personal Injury and Worker's Compensation Awards.* Generally, personal injury recoveries and workers' compensation claims are marital property to the extent they compensate for the loss of a marital asset, of which the most important example is the loss of income that the injured spouse would otherwise have earned during the marriage. Because post-divorce income is separate property, compensation for its loss is separate as well. *Niroo* quotes a prior case that follows this rule with respect to workers' compensation benefits. Most courts classify compensation for pain and suffering, typically available in tort awards but not in workers' compensation claims, as separate property, leaving the portion of the tort award intended to replace marital earnings as the main marital property component. Because tort awards are typically undifferentiated, the divorce court often must examine the circumstances to make the allocation itself. *See, e.g., Ramsey v. Ramsey*, 682 So. 2d 797 (La. App. 1996) (affirming trial court allocation of undifferentiated award between community property portion compensating for lost wages, and separate property portion compensating for pain and suffering); *Bandow v. Bandow*, 794 P.2d 1346 (Alaska 1990) (similar); *Landwehr v. Landwehr*, 545 A.2d 738 (N.J. 1988) (similar). Some courts avoid the allocation issue by following a mechanical approach under which tort recoveries are classified entirely according to the timing of their receipt rather than according to the losses for which they provide compensation.

The majority approach to the division of worker's compensation awards is to treat benefits received up to the time of separation or dissolution (and not yet spent) as marital property subject to equitable division, but benefits received after divorce are treated as separate property. *E.g., In re Marriage of Schriner*, 695 N.W.2d 493 (Iowa 2005). However, a minority of jurisdictions take different approaches, either focusing on when the award was given or accrued (if during the marriage, then it is marital property, even if the benefits extend beyond dissolution, and even if the award is intended to cover diminished future earning capacity), *e.g., Drake v. Drake*, 725 A.2d 717 (Pa. 1999), or treating all such awards as separate property, *e.g., Goria B.S. v. Richard G.S.*, 458 A.2d 707 (Del. Fam. Ct. 1983). The *ALI Principles*, § 4.08(2)(b), suggest characterizing disability pay and worker's compensation payments according to the nature of the wages they replace, and this approach has been adopted by at least one jurisdiction. *Holman v. Holman*, 84 S.W.3d 903 (Ky. 2002) (citing the *Principles* in an application to disability retirement benefits).

4. *Dividing Debts.* Courts have struggled with devising a sensible rule allocating debts and *Niroo*'s treatment is characteristically incomplete. State statutes typically contain no definition of a marital debt. *See Marriage of Welch*, 795 S.W.2d 640 (Mo. App. 1990). There is nonetheless little difficulty in dealing with an encumbered asset such as the mortgaged marital home; as *Niroo* suggests, one simply takes the debt into account in valuing the asset. That is effectively how the court dealt with Mr. Niroo's renewal commissions, which apparently served as security for his debt to the company. So long as the debt and the asset are both marital rather than separate, this is clearly correct. Because Mr. Niroo is alone legally responsible for debt properly characterized as marital debt, then an equal division requires that he be allocated an offsetting amount of marital property. The court therefore netted the debt against the asset, giving Mrs. Niroo a share of the excess only. Note that the parties differed over the characterization of the debt: was it separate or marital? The importance of that dispute should be clear: if the debt was Mr. Niroo's separate obligation rather than the spouses' joint obligation, then his liability for it would not justify allocating him an offsetting share of the marital property. The characterization of debts as separate or marital, while therefore important, is an issue which many courts have found difficult.

In equitable division states, the statutory provisions dealing with division of property either refer directly to the division of debts (*e.g.*, referring to the distribution of "marital assets *and liabilities*"), e.g. FLA. STAT. ANN. § 61.075(2); HAW. REV. STAT. § 580-47(a)(4); or they expressly or implicitly authorize courts to consider debt as a factor in making an equitable division of property. E.g., MINN. STAT. ANN. § 518.58(1)–(2); S.C. CODE ANN. § 20-7-472. In community property states, the division of debts is usually governed by statute. Generally, any debt acquired for the benefit of the community is community debt, even if only one spouse contracted for the debt, e.g., CAL. FAM. CODE § 1102(a). (Either spouse can usually incur debt for the community, though there are statutory exceptions — often including real property and certain forms of guaranty or surety. E.g. ARIZ. REV. STAT. § 25-214(C); CAL. FAM. CODE § 1102(a).) However, one party cannot incur debts for the community after a petition for divorce has been filed (unless that petition is later dismissed), and any debt incurred during the marriage will be presumed to be a community obligation.

Generally, debts incurred during the marriage, like assets obtained during the marriage, are presumed to be marital debts. While courts sometimes say that the characterization test is whether the debt was incurred for "the joint benefit of the parties," this is probably not a good description of the test the courts are actually applying or should apply. Inevitably, many expenditures within a marriage will inure primarily to the benefit to one spouse or the other. It is only when debts support activities that will have ongoing benefits to one spouse only — the paradigmatic case being educational loans — that the courts tend to characterize such debts as "separate" rather than "marital." *See ALI Principles*, § 4.09, Comment h.

Some jurisdictions also expressly allow an unequal division of marital debts where there is sharply disparate income or wealth (and thus ability to repay the debts), or where other factors might make an unequal division "equitable." CAL. FAM. CODE § 2622 (where parties' debts exceed their assets, the general equal division rule does not apply; court shall instead divide debts equitably after giving due consideration to relative incomes and other unspecified factors); *see also ALI Principles*, § 4.09(2)(c).

5. *Appreciation of Separate Property During Marriage.* As for appreciation of separate property during marriage, community property states distinguish appreciation attributable to either spouse's labors from the property's "natural increase" in value. In every community property state, the "natural increase" is also separate. If a spouse enters marriage owning 100 shares of Acme Corporation, which double in value during marriage, the increase as well as the original 100 shares remain separate property. On the other hand, any increase in value of separate property attributable to either spouse's labor during marriage is community property, following the general rule that the community owns the fruits of marital labors. Many common law states today apply the same rule. *Merriken v. Merriken*, 590 A.2d 566, 575 (Md. Spec. App. 1991) (wife had claim on appreciation of husband's separate real property because its appreciation was largely traceable to his marital labor); *Knowles v. Knowles*, 588 A.2d 315, 317 (Me. 1991) (wife had interest in appreciation of husband's separate property business resulting from his labor); *Baker v. Baker*, 753 N.W.2d 644 (Minn. 2008) (appreciation of value of husband's separate property in investment portfolio separate property; his potential control over investments insufficient to make appreciation marital property); KY. REV. STAT. ANN. § 403.190(2) (separate property appreciation resulting from spousal labor is marital); Mo. ANN. STAT. § 452.330(2)(5); ILL. ANN. STAT. ch. 750, para. 5/503; VA. CODE. ANN. § 20-107.3(A)(3); OHIO REV. CODE ANN. § 3105.171(A)(6)(a) ("passive" appreciation is separate, implying appreciation resulting from spousal labor is marital). It is difficult, however, to characterize comprehensively current law in the common law states on this question because in many cases the governing authority is sparse or unclear. Some statutes provide only that the appreciation of separate property remains separate, without more. *E.g.*, ARK. CODE ANN. § 9-12-315(b) (though Arkansas is also a state that allows recourse to separate property if necessary for an equitable division of property, *id.* at § 9-12-315(a)(2)). A few states treat all appreciation as marital property. *See* COLO. REV. STAT. § 14-10-113(4); 23 PA. CONS. STAT. ANN. DOM. REL. § 3501. Other states will treat the appreciation as marital property (entirely or partially) if the appreciation was due in large part to marital funds or the efforts of the spouse who was not the property's owner. *See, e.g., Innerbichler v. Innerbichler*, 752 A.2d 291 (Md. 2000); *Godley v. Godley*, 429 S.E.2d 382 (N.C. Ct. App. 1993).

Under the community property rule, apportionment will be necessary in many cases because the property has increased in value due both to "natural" reasons and spousal labor. One common example arises when one spouse begins a business before marriage, with separate property capital, but continues to operate it during marriage. If the business is worth more at divorce than at the time of marriage, the increase must be allocated between the original capital and its natural increase (separate property) and the fruits of the spousal labor (community or marital property). No neutral, established accounting principles exist to make such an apportionment and courts have developed different, and conflicting, rules. One line of cases finds no community property component in the incremental value where the entrepreneur spouse took compensation from the business during marriage which was reasonable in light of market standards for that kind of work. This approach (called *Van Camp* after the case that first announced it) seems mistaken in excluding the possibility that this spouse's labor was more valuable than the norm: the marital community owns all the returns to his labor, including unusually lucrative ones. The *Van Camp* approach, thus, sometimes attributes implausibly high returns to the initial separate-property capital stake. The competing *Pereira* line of authority attributes an ordinary rate of return to the separate property capital, and allocates all the return above this amount to spousal labor. *See Marriage of Dekker*, 17 Cal. App. 4th 842, 21 Cal. Rptr. 2d 642 (1993) (reviewing both lines of authority). Section 4.05 of the *ALI Principles*, which adopts the basic community property rule, generally favors the *Pereira* rule. *See also* J. Thomas Oldham, *Separate Property Businesses That Increase in Value During Marriage*, 1990 WIS. L. REV. 585; Sandra Lynn Perkins, *Appreciation of the Separately Owned, Closely Held Business*, 14(3) COMM. PROP. J. 62 (1987); Paul E. Messinger, *Unification of the Pereira and Van Camp Rules: The Economics Underlying the Division of a Business Between Separate and Community Property in California Divorce Proceedings*, 9 COMM. PROP. J. 286 (1982).

Common-law states addressing the apportionment problem have divided. Some follow *Van Camp. Meservey v. Meservey*, 841 S.W.2d 240 (Mo. App. 1992) (increase in value of H's family farm entirely separate because W did not prove H had received inadequate compensation from the farm); *Marriage of Werries*, 616 N.E.2d 1379 (Ill. App. 1993); *Huger v. Huger*, 433 S.E.2d 255 (Va. App. 1993) (evidence failed to show increased value of stock in spousal business was due to uncompensated spousal efforts, and was therefore separate). Two decisions in common law states are more consistent with *Dekker* and *Pereira. Schorer v. Schorer*, 501 N.W.2d 916 (Wis. App. 1993) (appreciation of company stock marital property where husband's labor largely responsible for business's increased value; irrelevant whether owning spouse "fairly" compensated); *Knowles v. Knowles*, 588 A.2d 315 (Me. 1991) (described *supra*). Other common law states do not apportion the appreciation of separate property between marital and separate property components, but instead treat the characterization as requiring an all or nothing resolution. TENN. CODE ANN. § 36-4-121(b)(1)(B) (all appreciation is marital if nontitled spouse contributed to it); *Zelnick v. Zelnick*, 169 A.D.2d 317, 573 N.Y.S.2d 261 (1991) ("wife is entitled to an award based upon the appreciation of the property unless the appreciation was completely unrelated to any effort expended by her and due solely to the fluctuations of the real estate market"); *Bowen v. Bowen*, 543 So. 2d 1284 (Fla. App. 1989) (orange grove worked by husband is entirely marital property even though premarital assets were used to acquire option to purchase it and to make down payment).

In many common law states, of course, placing all of the appreciation in the marital property pot merely permits the court to exercise discretion in its allocation. The other spouse's claim to share it thus becomes an appeal to equity, in contrast with the community property view that the spousal interest is a property right with precise contours that the court is required to identify.

6. *Income Realized During Marriage from Separate Property.* While many states have express statutory language regarding the appreciation of separate property during the marriage, relatively few have statutes dealing directly with income (e.g., rents, bank account interest, stock dividends, offspring of livestock) from separate property. Among common law property states, when legislation does provide for categorization, it is usually to define them as separate property. E.g., ARK. STAT. ANN. § 9-12-315; 750 ILL. COMP. STAT. § 5/503; N.C. GEN. STAT. § 50-20. Where there is no such express statutory language, some courts label such income as marital property under the general principle that any property acquired during the marriage and not expressly labeled as "separate property" by legislation should be treated as marital property. E.g., *Wilhelm v. Wilhelm*, 688 S.W.2d 381 (Mo. App. 1985). In a number of jurisdictions, such income will be treated as marital property if its acquisition required substantial efforts by one of the spouses. J. Thomas Oldham, Divorce, Separation and The Distribution of Property § 6.05[3] (Law Journal Press, 2009). Most community property states treat all income from separate property as separate; a smaller number take the opposite view ("the Spanish rule"), treating all such income as community property. Idaho Code § 32-906 (adopting the Spanish rule); La. Civ. Code, art. 2339 (same). In general, income from separate property is less likely than its appreciation to give rise to significant disputes at divorce. There are few marriages with significant separate property income, and any income that the parties do realize is often consumed during marriage, leaving no opportunity to dispute its allocation at divorce.

7. *Assets Acquired With a Blend of Separate and Marital Capital.* This problem arises most frequently in connection with the marital home. If one party owns a home before the marriage, it is that party's separate property, but mortgage payments may be made from marital earnings. Or the marital home may be purchased with a down payment made from the separate property of one spouse, such as a gift to that spouse from his or her parents, but the mortgage paid from marital earnings. Or the mortgage may be paid off with a separate property inheritance, while all prior mortgage payments were from marital property. At divorce the court must allocate the property's value between marital and separate property components.

The allocation may be made in one of two ways. The choice between them becomes significant principally when the property has appreciated so that its value at divorce is higher than the value of the two contributions (marital and separate) combined. One approach allocates the value according to the relative proportions of the marital and separate contributions. *E.g.*, *Thomas v. Thomas*, 377 S.E.2d 666 (Ga. 1989) (proceeds from house sale divided between separate and marital property in proportion to the contributions of the spouses, both jointly and separately, to its purchase). The other approach characterizes the property as entirely marital or entirely separate, often by applying an "inception" rule under which the house retains the characterization it had at the moment of its acquisition. Under this approach, for example, a house purchased with a separate property down payment would remain entirely separate even though subsequent mortgage payments and improvements were financed from marital property sources. Courts applying such a rule often also find, however, that in such cases the marital estate must be reimbursed for the marital property contributions. One can see that the marital community does less well under the reimbursement approach, than under the shared equity approach, if the property has appreciated in value, but it may do better in a declining market. Note finally that some common law states reject both allocation methods but instead, as in other areas, choose to rely on the trial court to do "equity" by taking these facts into account in making the allocation. *E.g.*, *Yeldell v. Yeldell*, 551 A.2d 832 (D.C. 1988) (husband's payment of mortgage on home owned by the wife before the marriage establishes an equitable interest in it).

There are additional complications as well, including the handling generally of assets acquired on credit. For much more on this topic, and more generally on the treatment of assets acquired with a blend of marital and separate funds, see § 4.06 of the *ALI Principles.* See also Peter M. Moldave, Comment, *The Division of the*

Family Residence Acquired with a Mixture of Separate and Community Funds, 70 CAL. L. REV. 1263 (1982).

8. ***Transmutation of Property.*** Separate property can become marital or community property ("transmutation") through a number of means: a gift from one spouse to the marital estate (a gift from one spouse to the other maintains the "separate property" designation, but changes the owner); changing the record title of real property from individual to joint title; and commingling of funds or other property. Additionally, in some jurisdictions it is sufficient that the couple use separate property "in support of the marriage." See S.C. CODE ANN. § 20-3-630(A)(1); *Edwards v. Edwards*, 682 S.E.2d 37 (S.C. Ct. App. 2009) (husband's separate property life estate in produce business transmuted into marital property through joint efforts working there and use of its income to provide for family). However, it should be noted that some jurisdictions create a high burden of proof before they will find transmutation, including a requirement of proof of the intention of the separate property owner, so even these actions may be held insufficient. *See, e.g.*, *Krize v. Krize*, 145 P.3d 481 (Alaska 2006) (recognizing the possibility of transmutation, but holding that the husband's depositing of lease proceeds into a joint account was insufficient evidence that he intended to transmute those proceeds from separate property to marital property); *cf. Sexton v. Sexton*, 125 S.W.3d 258, 270–271 (Ky. 2004) (rejecting the doctrine of transmutation through use of separate funds to take title in joint tenancy, as inconsistent with the state's other family law rules and principles). A number of states — primarily community property states — have legislation authorizing the transmutation of community or marital property to separate property, or in the other direction, by express agreement. *See, e.g.*, TEX. FAM. CODE §§ 4.101 to 4.106 ("partition agreements" changing community property to separate property), §§ 4.201 to 4.206 ("conversion agreements" changing separate property to community property). The *ALI Principles* proposes that a portion of separate property should automatically be re-characterized as marital property at divorce in long-term marriages. *Principles* § 4.12.

9. ***Bankruptcy.*** It is estimated that about a quarter of all bankruptcy filings are caused by divorce, so the question of whether divorce-related obligations can be discharged in bankruptcy is crucial (and determining which sorts of debts can be discharged would also naturally affect parties' approaches to the negotiation of separation agreements). The federal Bankruptcy Abuse Prevention and Consumer Protection Act of 2005 (BAPCPA) has made it significantly harder for ex-spouses to use bankruptcy procedures to avoid divorce-related obligations. Even prior to the 2005 reforms, almost all support obligations (both child support and alimony) were non-dischargeable in bankruptcy; allowing bankruptcy discharge only for a small subset of division of property obligations.

BAPCPA makes it much more difficult for consumers to discharge debt in Chapter 7 (liquidation); it creates a means test, such that those who have means to repay a significant portion of their debt are forced into a repayment plan under Chapter 13 (reorganization). However, if a consumer is in Chapter 7, both support and non-support debts arising from a divorce or separation are non-dischargeable. BAPCPA has created a new broad category of "domestic support obligation," that includes not only child and spousal support obligations arising from a divorce, but also obligations of unmarried parents to their children, and also applies (as had not been the case under the earlier bankruptcy law) to debts that accrue after the bankruptcy filing. These provisions have been construed very broadly. *E.g., In re Busch*, 369 B.R. 614 (B.A.P. 10th Cir. 2007), upheld a trial court decision that concluded that an ex-husband's obligation to pay off a 2nd mortgage was "in the nature of support," and thus non-dischargeable, because the effect of it was to allow the wife and their child to remain in the marital residence.

BAPCPA also removed two defenses to non-dischargeability that had been present under the previous (1994) bankruptcy reform for Chapter 7 filings: one relating to debtor inability to pay, and one relating to a balance of the equities between creditor hardship and debtor's "fresh start"; both of those defenses are now gone. Thus, bankruptcy discharge for divorce-related obligations is now only allowed for debts relating to a property division and only if the debtor enters a Chapter 13 repayment plan. On the intersection of bankruptcy and divorce law, see generally SHAYNA M. STEINFELD & BRUCE R. STEINFELD, THE FAMILY LAWYER'S GUIDE TO BANKRUPTCY (2nd ed. 2008); and Janet Leach Richards, *A Guide to Spousal Support and Property Division Claims Under the Bankruptcy Abuse Prevention and Consumer Protection Act of 2005*, 41 FAM. L.Q. 227 (2007).

PROBLEMS

Problem 4-4. Sam, a movie producer, is the CEO and sole shareholder of a closely owned corporation, Sam's Productions Inc (or SP), through which he produces his movies. He marries Sophie, and during the marriage SP agrees to produce a new movie, *The British Patient*. SP employs Sam in this endeavor. *British Patient* is a smash hit, and the various contractual rights owned by SP become enormously valuable. Sam and Sophie divorce. Sophie claims a share in the increased value of SP. Sam says SP, having been created before the marriage, is his separate property. He concedes, of course, that the salary SP paid him during the marriage is marital property. Does Sophie also have a marital property interest in SP's enhanced value?

Problem 4-5. After filing her petition to dissolve her 15-year marriage with Ronald, Rhonda learns that she is among a group of employees to be released in a corporate downsizing. The company provides released employees severance pay equal to one month's salary for each year of employment at the company. Rhonda therefore receives ten months' salary, or $80,000. Rhonda, a hard worker, had also accumulated a month's worth of unused vacation time during her years of employment, worth another $8,000. Ronald claims all $88,000 is marital property, Rhonda claims it is all separate property. What is the correct result?

Problem 4-6. Joan, a trial attorney, wins a $1,000,000 verdict for her client in a contingent fee case in which she is entitled to 35% of any recovery. The defendant has filed an appeal which is scheduled to be heard in six months. Joan will handle the appeal for the plaintiff. Her husband has now filed a divorce petition. He claims that Joan's contingent fee is marital property. Is he right?

Problem 4-7. Tom's prized Alfa Romeo, bought with his own funds before his marriage to Tonya, is his separate property. In January of 2006, Tom, testing the Alfa's limits on a back country road, has a serious accident. In consequence his Alfa is totaled, and he suffers chronic injuries leaving him too disabled to continue his prior employment. In June of 2006, Tom and Tonya file for divorce. Among their assets are: a) a check for $90,000 from the Acme Insurance Company, for the total loss of the Alfa; b) monthly payments of $10,000 from the Acyou Insurance Co., on a disability insurance policy the company had previously issued on Tom, and which will continue until Tom ceases to be disabled; and c) a term life insurance policy issued by the Acwe Insurance Co, expiring in October of each year, which is automatically renewable. Because of Tom's current medical condition, he would not otherwise be able to purchase life insurance. The premiums on all three policies were made from Tom's earnings during marriage. Which of these are marital assets? Which separate? Are any not property at all?

[3]   Applying Marital Property Rules To Pensions

In many marriages, the pension or other retirement benefits earned by one or both spouses during the marriage may be the only significant asset available for division. Therefore, the rules and procedures regarding the division of this asset are central to much divorce practice.

[a]   State Law Issues

NOTES

All states treat pensions as marital property divisible on divorce. There are a number of issues that arise in working out the details, however:

1. *Should the Court Divide Unvested Pension Rights?*   Pension benefits are typically funded, at least in part, by the employer's contributions. While these contributions are made in each pay period, the employee typically does not acquire a right to receive them upon retirement until she has worked for the employer a specified period of time. At that moment, the employee's pension rights are said to "vest." An early California case found no community interest in unvested pension rights, but this rule was later reversed, *In re Marriage of Brown*, 15 Cal. 3d 838, 126 Cal. Rptr. 633, 544 P.2d 561 (1976), *overruling French v. French*, 17 Cal. 2d 775, 112 P.2d 235 (1941). Nearly all states now treat unvested pensions as marital property. Grace G. Blumberg, *Marital Property Treatment of Pensions, Disability Pay, Workers' Compensation, and Other Wage Substitutes: An Insurance, Or Replacement, Analysis*, 33 UCLA L. REV. 1250, 1263 (1986). Recent cases so holding include *Stotler v. Wood*, 687 A.2d 636 (Me. 1996); *Cohen v. Cohen*, 937 S.W.2d 823 (Tenn. 1996); *Burns v. Burns*, 84 N.Y.2d 369, 618 N.Y.S.2d 761, 643 N.E.2d 80 (1994). Two apparently still valid authorities, however, excluding unvested pension plans from the marital property pot are *Charles v. Charles*, 713 P.2d 1048 (Okla. App. 1986) and *Skirvin v. Skirvin*, 560 N.E.2d 1263 (Ind. App. 1990) (pension vesting 32 days after divorce decree not marital property).

There are basically two options when treating unvested pensions. First, a court could defer the pension's distribution until vesting, when its value becomes more certain. *See Laing v. Laing*, 741 P.2d 649 (Alaska 1987) (concluding immediate distribution of unvested pension benefit would unfairly place full risk of forfeiture on employee-spouse); *see also ALI Principles* § 4.08(3) & Comment d. Alternatively, the value of the pension can be discounted to reflect the risk of nonvesting and distributed immediately. Especially where the amounts are small and the time of vesting is some time off, this may be more convenient for the parties. *See Lowry v. Lowry*, 544 A.2d 972, 983 (Pa. Super. 1988) (finding that unvested pension can be distributed immediately to the nonemployee spouse by discounting its value).

2. *Deferred vs. Immediate Distribution of Pension Benefits.* A court can fix each spouse's share of future annuity payments when the employee spouse retires. If there are sufficient assets, the court can permit the employee-spouse to receive the entire pension, with the non-employee spouse allocated an enhanced share of the remaining property as an offset. Such an immediate distribution requires establishing the current value of the pension so that the amount of the required offset can be determined. One can see that immediate and deferred distributions each have advantages and difficulties whose importance varies with the facts of each case. When the parties are relatively young, their accumulated pension entitlements are usually small, and their retirement is far in the future — a combination of facts that suggests that immediate distribution makes the most sense. When the parties are older and on the verge of retirement, pension values are usually high, and it usually makes more sense to fix the spouses' respective shares of the annuity payments as they are made, typically monthly.

Decisions favoring an immediate lump-sum distribution of the pension rights emphasize that it completes the property arrangements, thus reducing the need for the former spouses to remain in contact with each other ("clean break"), and also eliminates potential problems in ensuring that the nonemployee spouse receives his share of each pension payment when made. *Koelsch v. Koelsch*, 713 P.2d 1234 (Ariz. 1986); *Dewan v. Dewan*, 506 N.E.2d 879 (Mass. 1987); *Moore v. Moore*, 553 A.2d 20 (N.J. 1989); *Cross v. Cross*, 363 S.E.2d 449 (W. Va. 1987). Where it is not feasible for one spouse to buy out the other with one lump-sum payment, these courts sometimes permit a schedule of payments over a relatively short period of time. *E.g., Moore, supra*, at 29 (trial court decision giving husband two years to buy out wife's pension rights "defensible" where resources lacking for immediate, full payment); *Cross, supra*, at 445 (where lump-sum buy-out is not feasible the next-best solution is to require monthly payments for a term of years by which the employee spouse pays out the present value of pension rights, with interest).

Decisions favoring the deferred distribution method emphasize the hardship of a buyout on the employee-spouse when the value of currently available assets is small relative to the pension entitlement, as well as the difficulties in calculating at divorce the value of an unvested pension or the present value for the annuity provided by a defined benefit plan. *Marriage of Nelson*, 746 P.2d 1346 (Colo. 1987); *Marriage of Hobbs*, 442 N.E.2d 629 (Ill. App. 1982); *Rask v. Rask*, 445 N.W.2d 849 (Minn. App. 1989); *Hodgins v. Hodgins*, 497 A.2d 1187 (N.H. 1985); *Bailey v. Bailey*, 745 P.2d 830 (Utah App. 1987). Deferred distributions pose a problem if the employee-spouse chose to work beyond the date on which she was eligible to retire, thus delaying receipt of the pension. While the delay would provide compensating benefit to the employee whose pension account was thereby enlarged, it provided no benefit to the other spouse, who has no claim on the increment in the pension benefit earned by post-marital labor, and who therefore can only lose by the additional delay in receipt of the pension benefits. Some courts once held that the employee could not postpone the former spouse's realization of her share of the pension by delaying retirement. Where the employee cannot afford to buy out the former spouse or to fund equivalent substitute payments himself, such decisions effectively require the employee to retire early and forego potentially important benefits. *Gillmore v. Gillmore*, 29 Cal. 3d 418, 174 Cal. Rptr. 493, 629 P.2d 1 (1981); *Koelsch v. Koelsch*, 713 P.2d 1234, 1243 (Ariz. 1986).

Today, however, the conflict between the spouses as to the employee's choice of when to retire is not an important consideration in most cases. Governing law usually allows the dissolution court to "bifurcate" the pension and require the pension plan administrator to make monthly payments directly to each spouse of his or her share of the pension. The timing of the employee spouse's retirement becomes irrelevant under such a bifurcation, because the court can require the pension plan to begin payments to the nonemployee spouse at the employee's earliest retirement eligibility date, even if the employee does not choose to then retire. The plan administrator will make payments to the nonemployee spouse that are equal to her share of the payments that *would* have been due the employee *if* the employee-spouse had then retired. The pension plan funds these payments to the nonemployee-spouse with compensating reductions in the payments eventually made to the employee-spouse at his actual retirement.

The most important source of law allowing the dissolution court to order such bifurcations is the federal Employee Retirement Income Security Act (ERISA), 29 U.S.C. § 1001 *et seq*. The Act defines a Qualified Domestic Relations Order (QDRO) as including a state court judgment pursuant to state domestic relations or community property law that meets certain formal requirements and assigns to an "alternate payee" (that is, a payee other than the pension beneficiary) the right to "receive all or a portion of the benefits payable" to a participant in a covered pension plan. *Id.* at § 1056(d)(3). Covered pension plans are required to "establish reasonable procedures . . . to administer distributions under such qualified orders," *Id.* At § 1056(d)(3)(G)(ii). The Act specifies that a QDRO may "require[] the payment of benefits . . . to the alternate payee" prior to the employee's actual retirement, so long as the order, among other things, provides that benefits are payable to the alternative payee "as if the participant had retired on the date on which such payment is to begin under such order (but taking into account only the present value of benefits actually accrued and not taking into account the present value of any employer subsidy for early retirement)," *id.* at § 1056(d)(3)(E). Not every pension plan is covered by ERISA, however. Most importantly, the Act excludes public pension plans from coverage. Some states have enacted analogous provisions, however, to cover various state and local employees. *See, e.g.*, GRACE G. BLUMBERG, COMMUNITY PROPERTY IN CALIFORNIA 341 (2d ed. 1993) (describing CAL. GOV'T CODE § 21215 *et seq.* and CAL. EDUC. CODE § 22650, et seq.); *Grieve v. Mankey*, 679 A.2d 814 (Pa. Super. 1996) (discussing Pennsylvania statute that authorizes QDROs for public school employee pensions). But many gaps remain. *See, e.g.*, *Bryant v. Employees Retirement System of Georgia*, 455 S.E.2d 839 (Ga. App. 1995) (while husband's retirement benefits are marital property subject to division, trial court had no authority under state or federal law to order state retirement system to make payments directly to wife).

3. *Valuation of Pensions.* As explained in Note 2, fashioning an appropriate order at dissolution often requires establishing a value for the pension that has been earned during the marriage. The approach taken to this valuation usually depends upon whether the pension plan is a "defined benefit" or "defined contribution" plan. While attorneys commonly hire experts to make such valuations, it is important for the attorney to understand what the expert is doing. See *ALI Principles* § 4.08, Comment *e*:

> In a defined-contribution plan, contributions to a pension fund are made on the employee's behalf during employment. The accumulated contributions and the investment income derived from them are then available to fund the employee's retirement, often by the purchase of an annuity. At any point up to that time, the amount accumulated on the employee's behalf can in principle be determined. On this basis a determination can be made of the marital-property share, which equals the accumulations during the marriage plus the investment return attributable to them. Difficulties can sometimes arise when accurate values are, as a practical matter, unavailable for the particular assets allocable to the employee.

> "Defined-benefit" plans create a contractual obligation of the employer to provide an annuity fixed by a formula that has no necessary connection to any amounts nominally set aside to fund it. It is thus inappropriate to value it by reference to such nominal contributions. An alternative method used to value some defined-benefit pensions calculates a present value for the annuity entitlement earned as of the time the valuation is made. Defined-benefit plans, for example, may set the annuity payment by multiplying the employee's average salary during his final working years by a particular percentage and by the total years of service. One could apply the formula to the employee spouse at divorce, whether or not the spouse is then eligible to retire, and then calculate a present value for that flow of payments . . . by assuming a retirement date and a life expectancy. In a variation of this approach, one could calculate the present value of the annuity to which the employee would be entitled at retirement, assuming the additional years of post-marriage service remaining to that time, and then reduce the resulting value in proportion to the nonmarital years of service assumed in its calculation. Other possibilities emerge from the particular characteristics of the pension plan in question.

> Any such calculation of course requires an assumption about the employee-spouse's life expectancy, to project the number of years over which payments will be made, but in most cases a projection based upon standard actuarial tables will permit an adequate valuation of the payment flow. The uncertainties of projecting the employee's life span are alone usually surmountable.

An individual may begin employment before marriage, continue it during his marriage, and remain at it after the marriage ends. That individual's spouse is entitled to share in only the portion of the pension entitlement earned during the marriage. How is this apportionment between marital and non-marital portions made? See *ALI Principles* § 4.08, Comment *f*:

> The apportionment formulas used are generally variants of either of two basic methods, which can be called the relative-value rule and the relative-time rule. The relative-value rule in principle provides an accurate apportionment method for defined contribution plans. It takes the total contributions that were made during the marriage, combined with the investment gains (or losses) derived from those contributions, and classifies this total as marital property for the purpose of calculating a lump-sum distribution. If a deferred distribution is made one can then determine, at the time of retirement, the ratio of this marital-property share to the total of all accumulated contributions and investment returns. This same proportion of each annuity payment, when made, is considered marital property. Accuracy requires identifying the actual investment results on the marital- and separate-property contributions, rather than assuming they are proportional to the relative value of the contributions themselves. This adjustment is necessary because returns on contributions made in the early years of employment will ordinarily be proportionately greater than the returns from more recent years, which will have been invested for less time. While in principle the relative-value rule provides the most accurate method for apportioning a defined-contribution pension, it may be difficult in some cases to obtain the information necessary to apply it.
>
> . . .
>
> . . . The relative-time rule apportions the pension between its marital- and separate-property components by assuming that all years of labor contribute equally to the pension entitlement. It thus classifies as marital property the same proportion of the pension as the marital years of labor bear to the total years of labor. It may be implemented by establishing a fraction (sometimes called the "coverture factor") in which the numerator is the period of employment during the marriage and the denominator is the total period of employment (considering, of course, only employment giving rise to the pension entitlement at issue).

For a recent case upholding the use of the relative-time rule in a community property state, see *Hunt v. Hunt*, 43 P.3d 777 (Idaho 2002).

4. *Other Retirement Benefits.* It has become common for employers to offer special incentives to persuade employees to retire early. When the early retirement for one ex-spouse occurs after the marriage has ended, should such payments be considered part of the couple's marital or community property, or should it be considered as post-marital income, and thus separate property of the employee spouse? While there is not much case-law on this issue as of yet, it seems clear that such payments are grounded in the employee's years of prior work, and thus would be marital or community property just as pensions earned during the marriage are. *See, e.g., Simon v. Simon*, 770 N.W.2d 683 (Neb. Ct. App. 2009).

[b]   Federal Preemption of State Law

A series of Supreme Court decisions affects the inclusion of federal pension rights within the community and marital property pot. *Hisquierdo v. Hisquierdo*, 439 U.S. 572 (1979), involved a husband's Railroad Retirement Act pension. The California court had held the wife entitled to share in the pension, but the Supreme Court reversed. The Court found Railroad Retirement pensions resembled social welfare benefits more than private contractual rights, because Congress can alter or eliminate them at any time. Moreover, the social welfare scheme contained a number of provisions which arguably evidenced a considered decision to exclude Mrs. Hisquierdo's claim. One section barred assignment, garnishment or attachment of the benefits, except to satisfy a child support or alimony obligation, while another section defined "alimony" for this purpose as "excluding any payment . . . in compliance with any community property settlement, equitable distribution of property, or other division of property between spouses or former spouses." *Id.* at 577. Relying upon these provisions, the Court found that Congress had intended to exclude community property claims to these pension rights. Under the Supremacy Clause, California community property law was therefore preempted by the federal pension law. The Court held further that California was barred from frustrating this "federal policy" by giving the wife an offsetting award from presently available community assets, to compensate her for the denial of pension rights.

Hisquierdo was noteworthy because of the Court's willingness to find a federal preemption in an area traditionally reserved for state law. The Court itself quoted earlier decisions holding that a preemption of state family law requires a finding that the state law would impose "major damage" on "clear and substantial federal interests" and that "Congress has positively required by direct enactment" that the state law be preempted. *Id.* at 581.

The Court's approach was similar in its next case in the area, *McCarty v. McCarty*, 453 U.S. 210 (1981). *McCarty* involved military retired pay. Such pay was arguably compensation for current services rather than deferred compensation, and in fact lower courts had divided on that question. Only if it were deferred compensation for services rendered during the marriage would it be community property in which the former wife had an interest. The Supreme Court declined to decide, however, "whether federal law prohibits a State from characterizing retired pay as deferred compensation," 543 U.S. at 233, because the Court concluded that here, as in *Hisquierdo*, federal law preempted state marital property rules.

Implicit in the Court's reasoning was an assumption that a congressional failure to acknowledge a spouse's interest in the other's pay was equivalent to a considered decision to override that interest. A much more plausible conclusion from the evidence was that Congress, in designing military retired pay as well as the compensation schemes for other federal employees, never thought much at all about the impact of state marital property law. That conclusion would not support preemption under established rules, as the dissent vigorously pointed out. Nonetheless, the Court made no attempt to show why active duty pay would not come within its holding, and even "reserved" the question, suggesting the possibility of a much broader net, in fact reaching all earnings of most federal employees. 453 U.S. at 225, n.17.

McCarty itself was overruled by Congress in September 1982, by the Uniformed Services Former Spouses Protection Act, 966 Stat. 730, codified in part at 10 U.S.C. § 1408, which provides, subject to certain limitations, that a court "may treat disposable retired pay . . . either as property solely of the member or as property of the member and his spouse in accordance with the law of the jurisdiction of such court." The statute is prospective only, and does not permit reopening of pension rights settled before it became effective. It contains certain procedural devices to assist the claimant. A former spouse in a marriage of at least 10 years entitled to share in the monthly payments under a state court order may receive the payments directly from the government. 10 U.S.C. § 1408(d). State courts may also divide pension rights arising in shorter marriages, although in such cases direct payments from the government will not be available. *E.g., Konzen v. Konzen*, 693 P.2d 97 (Wash. 1985).

While the Former Spouses' Protection Act applies only to the military, and does not deal generally with deferred (or present) compensation of federal employees, it was hoped that its enactment would limit judicial extension of *McCarty* to other federal workers or compensation programs. But in *Mansell v. Mansell*, 490 U.S. 581 (1989), the Court refused to accept that Congress really meant to overrule *McCarty* in the Uniformed Services Former Spouses' Protection Act. *Mansell* dealt with a federal rule allowing a military pensioner also eligible for disability pay, to collect it only to the extent he waives an equivalent amount of pension rights; the rule is intended to prevent double-dipping. Waiving the retirement pay in favor of the disability pay is nonetheless advantageous to the veteran because disability benefits are exempt from federal and local income taxes. After *Mansell*, it has the additional advantage of shielding the payments from a former wife's claims, since the Court found that the federal law barred a state from treating as divisible marital property the disability pay taken in lieu of the divisible retirement pay.

The Court dealt with the intersection of ERISA and community property law (in this case, from Louisiana) again in *Boggs v. Boggs*, 520 U.S. 833 (1997). *Boggs* dealt with a conflict between the decedent's second wife and his sons by his first wife, who had predeceased him. The first wife had bequeathed the sons her community property share of their father's retirement benefits, which included a monthly annuity, an individual retirement account, and shares in an employee stock ownership plan. At the time of her death he had not yet retired. The Court held that her bequest of the IRA and ESOP (Employee Stock Ownership Plan) shares was an "assignment" or "alienation" barred by the Act, both in the transfer of the interest from her husband to her, and in her testamentary transfer of it to her sons. Note that this reasoning does not apply to QDRO's issued by divorce courts, which Congress, in the Retirement Equity Act of 1984, specifically excepted from these anti-alienation provisions. One might hope that attention will at some point be paid to Justice Breyer's dissent in which, in a portion joined by O'Connor, Rehnquist, and Ginsberg, he argued against the Court's application of the anti-alienation and assignment provisions to the first wife's possession of the retirement benefits:

"[The first wife's] interest arose not through assignment or alienation, but through the operation of Louisiana's community property law itself. Thus, [the second wife's] claim must be that community property law's grant of an undivided one-half interest in retirement benefits to a nonparticipant wife or husband itself violates some congressional purpose. But what purpose could that be? Congress has recognized that community property law, like any other kind of property law, can create various property interests for nonparticipant spouses. See 29 U.S.C. § 1056(d)(3)(B)(ii)(II). Community property law, like other property law, can provide an appropriate legal framework for resolving disputes about who owns what. § 1056(d)(3). The anti-alienation provision is designed to prevent plan beneficiaries from prematurely divesting themselves of the funds they will need for retirement, not to prevent application of the property laws that define the legal interest in those funds. One cannot find frustration of an "anti-alienation" purpose simply in the state law's definition of property."

In *Egelhoff v. Egelhoff*, 532 U.S. 141 (2001), the Court dealt with the interaction of a Washington statute and ERISA. While Washington is a community property state, the issue is relevant in all states. ERISA specifies that it "shall supersede any and all State laws insofar as they may now or hereafter relate to any employee benefit plan" covered by it. The husband had designated his wife as the beneficiary of his employer-provided pension and life insurance plans, both of which were covered by ERISA. He was then divorced, and died unexpectedly two months later, intestate and unmarried, and without having removed his wife as the beneficiary. Under Washington law, as that of many other states, her beneficiary status was revoked automatically by the divorce. If the Washington law prevailed, the husband's children from a prior marriage would succeed to the assets. ERISA directs the plan administrator to make payments to a beneficiary "in accordance with the documents and instruments governing the plan." 29 U.S.C. § 1104(a)(1)(D). The majority held that this language effectively required that payment be made to the wife despite the Washington law, thus preempting it. This result makes little sense. The wife had already been allocated her fair share of the community property, including the pension, in the divorce proceeding itself (in which she received certain stock and business assets as a setoff against her share of the pension, which was allocated entirely to the husband). Under this decision she now receives the pension as an add-on to her divorce settlement. It is difficult to believe that Congress intended by its general language to override state laws designed to avoid just this sort of result. These points were made by Justice Breyer, in a dissent joined by Justice Stevens (the dissent also urged that there was in fact no direct conflict or contradiction between the Washington statute and the plan documents at issue when the two are read carefully).

PROBLEMS

Problem 4-8.   You handled Gloria's divorce action, which was completed in 2004 with a separation agreement. The parties had been married since 1981, and during that entire time, her husband George worked for a small private corporation owned entirely by Edward. George had been Edward's right-hand man, but retired in 2008.

Shortly afterward, Gloria comes to you to say that she has heard that Edward recently gave George a large interest in a ranch, worth something like $600,000. She wants to know if she can get a share of it.

Problem 4-9. W has worked for 20 years for the police force. She is eligible to retire and receive her now-vested pension benefits. She wants to continue working, however, in order to reach the rank of a sergeant and to make herself eligible for the greater pension available after 30 years of service. The couple has few other assets and H has no pension of his own. You represent the husband. What is your problem and how might you solve it?

Problem 4-10. Robert began working for Acme in 1980. In 2003, when he was 55, he married Roberta. In 2010 they divorce. Under his defined benefit retirement plan Robert, who has risen high in the company, is eligible, in 2010, to retire with an annual annuity payments totaling $140,000. Had he retired in 2003, he would have received only $60,000 under the benefit plan formula. Roberta argues that the marital share of Robert's pension is an annuity of $80,000 — the difference between what he would receive if he retired now, at the time of divorce, and what he would have received had he retired at the time of marriage. She wants an award of her share now, even if Robert wishes to continue working until his late 60s. What is she entitled to?

C. SHOULD EARNING CAPACITY, PROFESSIONAL CREDENTIALS, OR GOODWILL BE TREATED AS MARITAL PROPERTY?

[1] Earning Capacity and Professional Credentials

The traditional and still dominant rule is that earning capacity is not property. That rule is no longer always followed, however. A handful of jurisdictions have departed from it overtly; more do so covertly, or perhaps even inadvertently. The following decision by the New York Court of Appeals is by far the most important one overtly treating earning capacity as property, although it does so only in the limited context of professional licenses. No other state high court has followed its lead, and many have rejected it. Why?

O'BRIEN v. O'BRIEN
New York Court of Appeals
489 N.E.2d 712 (1985)

Simons, Judge.

In this divorce action, the parties' only asset of any consequence is the husband's newly acquired license to practice medicine. . . . [¶] We . . . hold that [husband]'s medical license constitutes "marital property" within the meaning of Domestic Relations Law § 236(B)(1)(c) and . . . is . . . subject to equitable distribution. . . .

I

[Husband] and [wife] married on April 3, 1971. At the time both were employed as teachers at the same private school. [Wife] had a bachelor's degree but required 18 months of postgraduate classes at an approximate cost of $3,000, excluding living expenses, to obtain permanent certification in New York. The trial court found she had relinquished the opportunity to obtain permanent certification while [husband] pursued his education. At the time of the marriage, [husband] had completed only three and one-half years of college but shortly afterward he returned to school at night to earn his bachelor's degree. In September 1973 the parties moved to Guadalajara, Mexico, where [husband] became a full-time medical student. While he pursued his studies [wife] held several teaching and tutorial positions and contributed her earnings to their joint expenses. The parties returned to New York in December 1976 so that [husband] could complete the last two semesters of medical school and internship training here. [Wife] resumed her former teaching position and remained in it at the time this action was commenced. [Husband] was licensed to practice medicine in October 1980. He commenced this action for divorce two months later. At the time of trial, he was a resident in general surgery.

During the marriage both parties contributed to the living and educational expenses and they received additional help from both . . . families. [I]n addition to performing household work and managing the family finances [wife] was gainfully employed throughout the marriage. . . . The trial court found that she had contributed 76% of the parties' income exclusive of a $10,000 student loan obtained by [wife (sic)]. Finding that [husband]'s medical degree and license are marital property, the court received evidence of its value and ordered a distributive award to [wife]. [Wife] presented expert testimony that the present value of [husband]'s medical license was $472,000. Her expert . . . arrived at this figure by comparing the average income of a college graduate and that of a general surgeon between 1985, when [husband]'s residency would end, and 2012, when he would reach age 65. After considering Federal income taxes, an inflation rate of 10% and a real interest rate of 3% he capitalized the difference in average earnings and reduced the amount to present value. . . .

The court, after considering the life-style that [husband] would enjoy from the enhanced earning potential his medical license would bring and [wife]'s contributions and efforts toward attainment of it, made a distributive award to her of $188,800, representing 40% of the value of the license, and ordered it paid in 11 annual installments of various amounts. . . . The court also directed [husband] to maintain a life insurance policy on his life for [wife]'s benefit for the unpaid balance of the award. . . . It did not award [wife] maintenance. [¶] A divided Appellate Division . . . concluded that a professional license acquired during marriage is not marital property subject to distribution. . . .

II

The Equitable Distribution Law contemplates only two classes of property: marital . . . and separate property. . . . The former, which is subject to equitable distribution, is defined broadly as "all property acquired by either or both spouses during the marriage and before the execution of a separation agreement or the commencement of a matrimonial action, *regardless of the form in which title is held*" (Domestic Relations Law § 236[B][1][c] [emphasis added]). [Husband] does not contend that his license is excluded from distribution because it is separate property; rather, he claims that it is not property at all but represents a personal attainment in acquiring knowledge. He rests his argument on decisions in similar cases from other jurisdictions and on his view that a license does not satisfy common law concepts of property. Neither contention is controlling because decisions in other States rely principally on their own statutes, and the legislative history underlying them, and because the New York Legislature deliberately went beyond traditional property concepts. Instead, our statute recognizes that spouses have an equitable claim to things of value arising out of the marital relationship and classifies them [according to] the marital status of the parties at the time of acquisition. Those things acquired during marriage and subject to distribution have been classified as "marital property" although . . . they hardly fall within the traditional property concepts because there is no common law property interest remotely resembling marital property. Having classified the "property" subject to distribution, the Legislature did not attempt to go further and define it but left it to the courts to determine what interests come within the terms of section 236(B)(1)(c).

. . . .

Section 236 provides that in making an equitable distribution of marital property, "the court shall consider: . . . (6) any equitable claim to, interest in, or direct or indirect contribution made to the acquisition of such marital property by the party not having title, including joint efforts or expenditures and contributions and services as a spouse, parent, wage earner and homemaker, and *to the career or career potential* of the other party [and] . . . (9) the impossibility or difficulty of evaluating any component asset or any interest in a business, corporation or *profession*" [emphasis added]. . . . Where equitable distribution of marital property is appropriate but "the distribution of an interest in a business, corporation or profession would be contrary to law" the court shall make a distributive award in lieu of an actual distribution of the property. . . . The words mean exactly what they say: that an interest in a profession or professional career potential is marital property which may be represented by direct or indirect contributions of the non-title-holding spouse, including financial contributions and nonfinancial contributions made by caring for the home and family.

The history which preceded enactment of the statute confirms this interpretation. . . . [E]xperience had proven that application of the traditional common law title theory of property had caused inequities. . . . The Legislature replaced the existing system with equitable distribution of marital property, an entirely new theory which considered all the circumstances of the case and of the respective parties to the marriage. . . . Equitable distribution was based on the premise that a marriage is, among other things, an economic partnership to which both parties contribute as spouse, parent, wage earner or homemaker. . . .

The determination that a professional license is marital property is also consistent with the conceptual base upon which the statute rests. As this case demonstrates, few undertakings during a marriage better qualify as the type of joint effort that the statute's economic partnership theory is intended to address than contributions toward one spouse's acquisition of a professional license. Working spouses are often required to contribute substantial income as wage earners, sacrifice their own educational or career goals and opportunities for child rearing, perform the bulk of household duties and responsibilities and forego the acquisition of marital assets that could have been accumulated if the professional spouse had been employed rather than occupied with the study and training necessary to acquire a professional license. In this case, nearly all of the parties' nine-year marriage was devoted to the acquisition of [husband]'s medical license and [wife] played a major role in that project. She worked continuously during the marriage and contributed all of her earnings to their joint effort, she sacrificed her own educational and career opportunities, and she traveled with [husband] to Mexico for three and one-half years while he attended medical school there. The Legislature has decided, by its explicit reference in the statute to the contributions of one spouse to the other's profession or career, . . . that these contributions represent investments in the economic partnership of the marriage and that the product of the parties' joint efforts, the professional license, should be considered marital property.

. . . .

[Husband]'s principal argument . . . is that a professional license does not fit within the traditional view of property as something which has an exchange value on the open market and is capable of sale, assignment or transfer. The position does not withstand analysis. . . . First, . . . it ignores the fact that whether a professional license constitutes marital property is to be judged by the language of the statute which created this new species of property. . . . Thus, whether the license fits within traditional property concepts is of no consequence. Second, it is an overstatement to assert that a professional license could not be considered property even outside the context of section 236(B). A professional license is a valuable property right, reflected in the money, effort and lost opportunity for employment expended in its acquisition, and also in the enhanced earning capacity it affords its holder, which may not be revoked without due process of law. That a professional license has no market value is irrelevant. Obviously, a license may not be alienated as may other property and for that reason the working spouse's interest in it is limited. The Legislature has recognized that limitation, however, and has provided for an award in lieu of its actual distribution.

[I]t has been suggested that even if a professional license is considered marital property, the working spouse is entitled only to reimbursement of his or her direct financial contributions. By parity of reasoning, a spouse's down payment on real estate or contribution to the purchase of securities would be limited to the money contributed, without any remuneration for any incremental value in the asset because of price appreciation. Such a result is completely at odds with the statute's requirement that the court give full consideration to both direct and indirect contributions "made to the acquisition of such marital property by the party not having title, including joint *efforts* or expenditures and *contributions and services as a spouse, parent, wage earner and homemaker*" . . . [emphasis added]. If the license is marital property, then the working spouse is entitled to an equitable portion of it, not a return of funds advanced. Its value is the enhanced earning capacity . . . and although fixing the present value of that enhanced earning capacity may present problems, the problems are not insurmountable. Certainly they are no more difficult than computing tort damages for wrongful death or diminished earning capacity resulting from injury and they differ only in degree from the problems presented when valuing a professional practice for purposes of a distributive award, something the courts have not hesitated to do. The trial court retains the flexibility and discretion to structure the distributive award equitably, taking into consideration factors such as the working spouse's need for immediate payment, the licensed spouse's current ability to pay and the income tax consequences of prolonging the period of payment. . . .

MEYER, Judge (concurring). I . . . write separately to point up for consideration by the Legislature the potential for unfairness involved in distributive awards based upon a license of a professional still in training. An equity court normally has power to "change its decrees where there has been a change of circumstances". . . . [H]owever . . . a distributive award . . . is not subject to change. Yet a professional in training who is not finally committed to a career choice when the distributive award is made may be locked into a particular kind of practice simply because the monetary obligations imposed by the distributive award made on the basis of the trial judge's conclusion (prophecy may be a better word) as to what the career choice will be leaves him or her no alternative.

The present case points up the problem. . . . Here it is undisputed that [husband] was in a residency for general surgery at the time of the trial, but had the previous year done a residency in internal medicine. [Wife]'s expert based his opinion on the difference between the average income of a general surgeon and that of a college graduate of [husband]'s age and life expectancy, which the trial judge utilized, impliedly finding that [husband] would engage in a surgical practice despite [husband]'s testimony that he was dissatisfied with the general surgery program he was in and was attempting to return to the internal medicine training. . . . The trial judge had the right, of course, to discredit that testimony, but the point is that equitable distribution was not intended to permit a judge to make a career decision for a licensed spouse still in training. Yet the degree of speculation involved in the award made is emphasized by the testimony of the expert on which it was based. Asked whether his assumptions and calculations were in any way speculative, he replied: "Yes. They're speculative to the extent of, will Dr. O'Brien practice medicine? Will Dr. O'Brien earn more or less than the average surgeon earns? Will Dr. O'Brien live to age sixty-five? Will Dr. O'Brien have a heart attack or will he be injured in an automobile accident? Will he be disabled? I mean, there is a degree of speculation. That speculative aspect is no more to be taken into account, cannot be taken into account, and it's a question, again, Mr. Emanuelli, not for the expert but for the courts to decide. It's not my function nor could it be."

The equitable distribution provisions of the Domestic Relations Law were intended to provide flexibility. . . . But if the assumption as to career choice on which a distributive award payable over a number of years is based turns out not to be the fact (as, for example, should a general surgery trainee accidentally lose the use of his hand), it should be possible for the court to revise the distributive award to conform to the fact. . . .

POSTEMA v. POSTEMA
Michigan Court of Appeals
471 N.W.2d 912 (1991)

Maher, J.:

[Both parties challenge] the property distribution provisions of a . . . judgment of divorce. The primary issue concerns the valuation of defendant's law degree and whether the trial court erred in finding the law degree to be a marital asset. We affirm in part and remand.

Plaintiff and defendant were married on August 11, 1984. At the time of their marriage, defendant was employed as a cost accountant and plaintiff was working as a licensed practical nurse and attending school in pursuit of an associate's degree in nursing so that she could become a registered nurse. It was the plan of the parties when they married that defendant would enroll in law school and that plaintiff would postpone her schooling and work full-time to support them while defendant attended school. Accordingly, shortly after the marriage, the parties moved from Grand Rapids to the Detroit area, where they stayed from September 1984 until May 1987 while defendant attended Wayne State University Law School. In furtherance of the parties' plan, plaintiff obtained a full-time job at an area hospital, earning approximately $53,000 during the period defendant was in law school. Plaintiff also assumed the primary responsibility of maintaining the household, doing all cooking and cleaning, and running all errands. Though defendant did not work at all during his first year in law school, he later worked as a law clerk, full-time during the summers following his first and second years in law school and then part-time during his second and part of his third years. In all, defendant earned approximately $12,000 from clerking. The parties' earnings were used primarily for their support, while defendant's education was financed mostly through student loans totaling $15,000.

Defendant proved to be a successful law student and wrote for the school's law review. After defendant graduated in May 1987, the parties moved back to the Grand Rapids area, where defendant accepted a position as an associate attorney with a local law firm at a starting annual salary of $41,000. The following September, plaintiff resumed classes in pursuit of her associate's degree in nursing. In November 1987, however, the parties separated. Despite the separation, plaintiff continued her classes and eventually received her associate's degree in May 1988, although she had to support herself during that period by working full-time at a local hospital.

Plaintiff testified that marital problems developed early in the marriage. She said defendant would often complain that she was overweight, saying it embarrassed him, and that he would start many verbal fights, usually over things that were insignificant. She claimed the situation got to the point where her whole life revolved around trying not to agitate defendant. Defendant testified that he often asked plaintiff to leave, complained that she was a "fanatic" about cleaning, and admitted that he once presented her with a list of things for her to remember to do so that she wouldn't "irritate" him. Although defendant agreed that he was sometimes difficult to live with and that he treated plaintiff badly from time to time, he blamed it on the stress of law school. According to plaintiff, defendant would often apologize the day after a fight, sometimes verbally and sometimes in a letter. The parties finally separated . . . after defendant informed plaintiff that he had met another woman and had gone out with her a couple of times while plaintiff was working.

The trial court found that the breakdown of the marriage was primarily the fault of defendant, and announced it had considered this fact in its property distribution. After awarding each of the parties their respective automobiles, the trial court awarded plaintiff specific household goods and bank funds totaling $5,000, while awarding defendant specific goods and funds totaling $3,000. Defendant was also held solely responsible for repayment of $14,000 in student loans. Finally, the trial court determined that defendant's law degree was a marital asset subject to distribution. The court valued the degree at $80,000, and awarded plaintiff, as her share of the degree, $32,000 on the basis that this amount would equalize the parties' respective distributive shares. The court ordered this obligation to be paid off in monthly installments of $371.55 or more, at seven percent interest, until fully paid. The court did not award either party alimony.

[D]efendant challenges various aspects of the . . . property distribution, with his primary objection being the court's inclusion of his law degree in the marital estate and the resultant valuation of that degree. On cross appeal, plaintiff also challenges the trial court's valuation of the law degree. . . .

The goal . . . with respect to the division of the marital estate is a fair and equitable distribution under all of the circumstances. The division is not governed by any rigid rules or mathematical formula and need not be equal. . . . The primary question is what is fair.

Panels of this Court have expressed different views concerning the treatment, characterization, and valuation of an advanced degree. . . . Nevertheless, most panels have agreed that fairness dictates that a spouse who did not earn an advanced degree be compensated whenever the advanced degree is the end product of a concerted family effort involving mutual sacrifice and effort by both spouses. [W]e will begin by first discussing the rationale behind the recognition that a nonstudent spouse must be compensated whenever a concerted family effort is involved in obtaining an advanced degree, which discussion will include an application of the concept "concerted family effort" to the facts of the instant case. Secondly, we will discuss what we believe to be the appropriate and preferable means of characterizing a claim for compensation involving an advanced degree. Finally, we will address the factors and methods that we believe are relevant in valuing such a claim upon divorce.

. . . The relevancy of fairness is that, in Michigan, equitable considerations form the underlying basis for recognizing a claim for compensation involving an advanced degree, and that the ultimate goal in every divorce case is to do what is necessary to accord complete equity. . . . Second, the concept "concerted family effort" stresses the fact that it is not the . . . degree itself that gives rise to an equitable claim for compensation, but rather the fact of the degree being the end product of the mutual sacrifice, effort, and contribution of both parties as part of a larger, long-range plan intended to benefit the family as a whole. The concept is premised, in part, on the fact that the attainment of an advanced degree is a prolonged undertaking involving considerable expenditure of time, effort, and money, as well as other sacrifices. Where such an undertaking is pursued as part of a concerted family effort, both spouses expect to be compensated for their respective sacrifices, efforts, and contributions by eventually sharing in the fruits of the degree. Where, however, the parties' relationship ends in divorce, such a sharing is impossible. Although the degree holder will always have the degree to show for the efforts, the nonstudent spouse is left with nothing. Therefore, a remedy consistent with fairness and equity requires that an attempt be made to at least return financially to the nonstudent spouse the value of what that spouse contributed toward attainment of the degree.

Generally, the existence of a concerted family effort will be reflected in many ways[, such as] through a spouse's tangible efforts and financial contributions associated with working and supporting the mate while the mate pursues the advanced degree, [and] through other intangible, nonpecuniary efforts and contributions, such as where a spouse increases the share of the daily tasks, child-rearing responsibilities, or other details of household and family management undertaken in order to provide the mate with the necessary time and energy to study and attend classes. A concerted family effort is also exemplified by the fact that both spouses typically share in the emotional and psychological burdens of the educational experience. For the nonstudent spouse, these burdens may be experienced either directly, such as through the presence of increased tension within the household, or indirectly, such as where the spouse shares vicariously in the stress of the educational experience. Finally, the attainment of an advanced degree during marriage is usually accompanied by considerable sacrifice on the part of both spouses. For the nonstudent spouse, such sacrifice may be reflected by a change in life style during the educational process, the availability of less time to pursue personal interests, or even a decision to either give up or temporarily postpone one's own educational or career pursuits as part of the larger, long-range plan designed to benefit the family as a whole.

[P]laintiff temporarily postponed her pursuit of an associate's degree in nursing, moved with defendant to the Detroit area so that he could attend law school, and then worked full-time to support [them while he] attended classes. This was all done as part of a larger plan to benefit both parties as a whole. Plaintiff, in addition to being the primary financial provider while defendant attended school, wherein she accounted for approximately eighty percent of the parties' total financial support, also bore primary responsibility for the daily household tasks. Moreover, the stress of the law school experience was certainly experienced by both parties, as reflected by the fact that defendant repeatedly blamed his inappropriate behavior toward plaintiff on the stress of law school, and by plaintiff's testimony explaining that her whole life revolved around her trying not to agitate defendant.

We conclude, therefore, that defendant's law degree was clearly the end product of a concerted family effort giving rise to an equitable claim for compensation in favor of plaintiff. . . .

. . . [Our] panels are in disagreement over the appropriate manner in which a claim for compensation should be considered. While some panels have characterized an advanced degree as a marital asset subject to property division, other panels have held that an advanced degree is more properly considered as a factor in awarding alimony.

After reviewing the various decisions addressing the issue and taking into consideration the underlying principles upon which an award of compensation for an advanced degree is premised, we reject the view holding that an advanced degree is more properly considered as a factor in awarding alimony.

The cases adhering to the alimony view, have stated that a degree is simply not "property" for the reasons expressed in *Graham v Graham*, 194 Colo. 429, 432; 574 P.2d 75 (1978):

> An educational degree . . . , is simply not encompassed even by the broad views of the concept of "property." It does not have an exchange value or any objective transferable value on an open market. It is personal to the holder. It terminates on death of the holder and is not inheritable. It cannot be assigned, sold, transferred, conveyed or pledged. An advanced degree is a cumulative product of many years of previous education, combined with diligence and hard work. It may not be acquired by the mere expenditure of money. It is simply an intellectual achievement that may potentially assist in the future acquisition of property. In our view, it has none of the attributes of property in the usual sense of that term.

In rejecting the alimony approach, we first recognize that the basic purpose of paying alimony is to assist in the other spouse's support. Unlike alimony, however, the principles underlying an award of compensation based on the attainment of an advanced degree are neither rooted in nor based on notions of support. . . . [W]here a concerted family effort is involved, a spouse's entitlement to compensation constitutes a recognized right; it is not dependent upon factors related to the need for support. . . .

Moreover . . . an award in terms of alimony may unfairly jeopardize a spouse's recognized right to compensation because a trial court has broad discretion in deciding whether to grant alimony, because an award of alimony is dependent on factors different from those related to the division of marital property, and because . . . alimony may be terminated if the spouse receiving it remarries. Regarding this latter observation, we agree with the panel in [*Lewis v Lewis*, 181 Mich. App. 1, 6; 448 N.W.2d 735 (1989)], which stated: "Because the value of an advanced degree does not 'evaporate' upon the nondegree-earning spouse's remarriage, we do not find an award of alimony a satisfactory method of recognizing that spouse's efforts toward earning the degree." Furthermore, we note that it is often the case that a nonstudent spouse will already have demonstrated the ability of self-support by virtue of having supported the degree-earning spouse through graduate school. While such fact would ordinarily militate against an award of alimony, we do not believe it should operate to deprive the nonstudent spouse of a recognized right to be compensated for unrewarded sacrifices, efforts, and contributions toward attainment of the degree.

Finally, . . . we do not believe that the consideration of an advanced degree when making the property distribution would be improper merely because a degree cannot be characterized as "property" in the classic sense. Rather, we agree with [*Woodworth v. Woodworth*, 126 Mich. App. 258, 263; 337 N.W.2d 332 (1983)], that "whether or not an advanced degree can physically or metaphysically be defined as 'property' is beside the point[;] [c]ourts must instead focus on the most equitable solution to dissolving the marriage and dividing among the respective parties what they have." Furthermore, as I stated in my concurring opinion in Olah [*Olah v. Olah*, 135 Mich. App. 404, 412, 354 N.W.2d 359 (1984)]: "This is an equitable distribution jurisdiction, in which classification of an item as either property or non-property is not decisive in determining the best division of the parties' holdings on divorce." Finally, in *Lewis, supra*, p. 6, this Court added: "[T]he fundamental question in cases involving advanced degrees is not whether a degree is property, but rather 'whether the facts in the case give rise to an equitable claim regarding the degree so that a property division can be considered fair and equitable between the parties.' "

We conclude, therefore, that [in a case like this], there arises a "marital asset" subject to distribution, wherein the interest of the nonstudent spouse consists of an "equitable claim" regarding the degree.

Having found that a marital asset giving rise to an "equitable claim" subject to distribution exists . . . , we will now discuss the appropriate factors and considerations relative to an evaluation of such a claim for purposes of distributing property. *Woodworth, supra*, pp. 268–269, discussed two methods of compensating a nonstudent spouse . . . : (1) awarding a percentage share of the present value of the future earnings attributable to the degree, or (2) restitution. The first method focuses on the degree's present value by attempting to estimate what the person holding the degree is likely to make in a particular job market and subtracting therefrom what that person would probably have earned without the degree. *Id.*

[The court here recounts the steps taken by the trial court to value the wife's share of the degree. Dissatisfied, the court said:]

Accordingly, we conclude that the appropriate remedy . . . is to remand . . . for revaluation of plaintiff's "equitable claim" in light of this opinion. On remand, we do not believe that the present value method . . . is an appropriate means by which to evaluate plaintiff's equitable claim. . . . Such a method emphasizes the notion that a nonstudent spouse possesses some sort of pecuniary interest in the degree itself. We believe such a notion misconstrues the underlying premise upon which an award of compensation involving an advanced degree is based. As we have attempted to explain throughout this opinion, an award of compensation is premised upon equitable considerations, wherein the goal is to attempt to financially return to the nonstudent spouse what that spouse contributed toward attainment of the degree. Because such an award is not premised upon the notion that a nonstudent spouse possesses an interest in the degree itself, we do not believe the actual value of the degree is a relevant consideration.

Among the arguments advanced by defendant in support of his contention that an advanced degree should not be considered when dividing the marital estate are: (1) that marriage is not a commercial venture, (2) that the value of an advanced degree cannot be ascertained with reasonable certainty, and (3) that consideration of a degree as part of the property division would be akin to involuntary servitude. Inherent in each of these arguments, however, is the notion that a nonstudent spouse possesses some type of pecuniary interest in a degree or is entitled to be compensated for a portion of the so-called "value" of the degree, views we specifically reject. Again, we emphasize that the focus of an award involving an advanced degree is not to reimburse the nonstudent spouse for "loss of expectations" over what the degree might potentially have produced, but to reimburse that spouse for unrewarded sacrifices, efforts, and contributions toward attainment of the degree on the ground that it would be equitable to do so in view of the fact that that spouse will not be sharing in the fruits of the degree.

[The] Appellate Division of the Superior Court of New Jersey in *Mahoney v Mahoney*, 182 N.J. Super. 598; 442 A.2d 1062 (1982) [stated]:

> The termination of the marriage represents, if nothing else, the disappointment of expectations, financial and nonfinancial, which were hoped to be achieved by and during the continuation of the relationship. It does not, however, in our view, represent a commercial investment loss. Recompense for the disappointed expectations resulting from the failure of the marital entity to survive cannot, therefore, be made to the spouses on a strictly commercial basis. . . .

> * * *

> If the plan fails by reason of the termination of the marriage, we do not regard the supporting spouse's consequent loss of expectations by itself as any more compensable or demanding of solicitude than the loss of expectations of any other spouse who, in the hope and anticipation of the endurance of the relationship and its commitments, has invested a portion of his or her life, youth, energy and labor in a failed marriage.

In our view, any valuation of a nonstudent spouse's equitable claim involving an advanced degree involves a two-step analysis. First, an examination of the sacrifices, efforts, and contributions of the nonstudent spouse toward attainment of the degree. Second, given such sacrifices, efforts, and contributions, a determination of what remedy or means of compensation would most equitably compensate the nonstudent spouse under the facts of the case. In this regard, . . . the length of the marriage after the degree was obtained, the sources and extent of financial support given to the degree holder during the years in school, and the overall division of the parties' marital property are all relevant considerations. . . .

. . .

[A]n equitable remedy may be exemplified in different ways. For example, as this Court recognized in [*Krause v Krause*, 441 N.W.2d 66 (1989)]: "[I]f [the nonstudent spouse] wishes to pursue [an] education or take other similar steps to improve . . . employability or income earning potential, it is reasonable and equitable to require the [degree-holding spouse] to assist . . . in those endeavors." Thus, in this type of situation, an award consistent with fairness and equity would be one which requires the degree-earning spouse to provide assistance, in the form of financial support, equivalent to that provided by the nonstudent spouse during the marriage.

Where, however, a nonstudent spouse does not wish to further pursue an education, then perhaps equity would best be served by an award reimbursing the spouse for the amount of financial assistance provided toward attainment of the degree, while also recognizing the other intangible, nonpecuniary sacrifices made and efforts expended.

. . .

We note . . . the parties separated shortly after defendant attained his law degree. Thus, plaintiff received little reward, if any, for her sacrifices, efforts, and contributions toward defendant's degree. Further, while defendant did contribute some financial support during the degree-earning period, it was plaintiff who accounted for the vast majority of it, approximately eighty percent. Moreover, while defendant certainly worked hard in obtaining his degree, it is abundantly clear from the record that plaintiff's nonpecuniary efforts and contributions toward the degree were indeed significant also, and that she certainly endured many hardships and sacrifices as a result of her participation in the law school experience. We also note that while plaintiff did ultimately further her own career objectives in the manner she chose, she was required to do so on her own and did not have nearly the same benefits, financial or otherwise, that defendant had while he attended school. Defendant was, however, primarily responsible for the actual cost of his education, which was financed mostly through student loans for which he remains solely responsible. These are just some of the factors which were not discussed by the trial court, but yet are relevant to the valuation of plaintiff's equitable claim involving the degree. Therefore, these factors shall be considered by the trial court on remand.

After valuing plaintiff's equitable claim, the trial court may order that the amount determined to be due be payable in monthly installments over a fixed period of time. . . .

. . .

Affirmed in part and remanded for proceedings consistent with this opinion regarding the valuation of plaintiff's equitable claim involving defendant's law degree. We do not retain jurisdiction.

ALI PRINCIPLES OF THE LAW OF FAMILY DISSOLUTION

§ 4.07 Earning Capacity and Goodwill

(1) Spousal earning capacity, spousal skills, and earnings from post-dissolution spousal labor are not marital property.

(2) Occupational licenses and educational degrees are not marital property.

(3) Business and professional goodwill earned during marriage are marital property to the extent they have value apart from the value of spousal earning capacity, spousal skills, or post-dissolution spousal labor.

(a) Evidence of an increment during marriage in the market value of business or professional goodwill establishes the existence of divisible marital property in that amount except to the extent that market value includes the value of post-dissolution spousal labor.

(b) Business or professional goodwill that is not marketable is nevertheless marital property to the extent a value can be established for it that does not include the value of spousal earning capacity, spousal skills, or post-dissolution spousal labor.

Comment:

a. Earning capacity and the relation between property and compensatory payments. . . .[¶] "Earning capacity" has no meaning or existence independent of the method used to measure it. It is generally measured by finding a present value for . . . the individual's future earnings, and is thus no more than a shorthand term for that present value. A rule characterizing earning capacity as marital property is a rule treating future earnings as marital property, which in operation requires that those earnings be estimated at divorce so that their present value can then be fixed and allocated between the spouses.

Traditionally, however, spousal claims on post-divorce earnings were made under the rubric of alimony. . . . A major purpose of Chapter 5 [of *The Principles*] is to reconceive alimony in a form that provides a more reliable and consistent remedy, in cases of disparate earning capacity, than is offered by the existing law. It is likely that the historical unreliability of the alimony remedy is an important reason why some potential alimony claimants recast their claim on post-marital earnings into property terms. The ease with which any income flow can be described as a property interest of equivalent value facilitates this strategy. . . . [¶] While property and alimony remedies are financially fungible, they have different procedural and substantive traditions that bear on the kind of claims best treated under each. These traditions explain why courts that confront the question directly usually decline to treat earning capacity as property. . . .

Procedurally, alimony awards are exercises of continuing equitable authority and typically remain modifiable, while a division of marital property is an ordinary civil judgment and therefore final and nonmodifiable. The finality and nonmodifiability that are critical to adjudications of property ownership make these judgments poor instruments by which to allocate future spousal earnings. Not only may the earnings of the former spouses vary in unpredictable ways, but also spousal claims on one another's post-dissolution income are properly affected by some post-dissolution events, such as the obligee's remarriage. . . .

The traditional procedural differences between alimony and property are related to their divergent substantive heritage. An alimony obligee's improved living standard after divorce can provide substantive grounds for terminating the alimony award, while it would violate substantive norms to require a newly fortunate spouse to return some of the marital property he or she was allocated at dissolution. Increased prosperity does not compromise previously established property rights. . . . [A] regime that treats earning capacity acquired during marriage as marital property approaches the cases according to property rules designed to serve other policies, rather than according to the equitable considerations with which the law of alimony has traditionally been concerned. The treatment of earning capacity as property would therefore deny relief to many deserving spouses while allowing it to others with no equitable claim.

. . .

The preceding observations relate to a broader theme from which the differences between property and alimony in part emerge. The law has treated alimony as appropriate in only a subset of divorces in which there are circumstances, sometimes temporary, that justify equitable adjustments in post-marriage income between former spouses. In contrast, marital-property claims are normally viewed as property entitlements created by the marriage alone, even if subject to equitable adjustment. The principle underlying this difference is that marriage creates property entitlements to certain *things* acquired during it, but does not create property entitlements against the *person* of the other spouse. Marriage does not create a lifetime claim by one spouse on the other's talents and labor, even though a long-term or even permanent claim on a former spouse's post-marriage earnings does result from the combination of marriage with other factors of the kind traditionally considered under the rubric of alimony and addressed in Chapter 5. . . . Section 4.07(1) therefore reflects the law's longstanding distinction between claims on things and claims on another's personal attributes.

. . .

c. Educational degrees and occupational licenses. Paragraph (2) [of § 4.07] bars marital property claims on educational degrees and occupational licenses. This bar is an application of the more fundamental principle stated in Paragraph (1). Any value assigned to degrees or licenses is necessarily a valuation of spousal earning capacity. Degrees and licenses are not marketable nor is there any market data on which their valuation can be based. The few decisions that recognize a marital property interest in a degree or license value them by projecting the probable difference, over the holder's lifetime, between the earnings of an individual with the license or degree and the earnings of one without it. Under this formulation, the credential's value is simply the average increment in income earned by its holders. Other skills or entitlements that increase average earnings cannot be distinguished, even if their acquisition is not recognized in a formal document such as a degree. The principle that treats degrees or licenses as marital property would necessarily extend, for example, to job seniority and promotions.

Some cases rejecting property claims on degrees rely entirely on the fact that degrees are not marketable. That explanation sweeps too broadly, however, for nonmarketable assets are routinely and properly treated as marital property. Pension rights, which are typically nontransferable, perhaps provide the most common example. The principle on which this section relies is not marketability and it therefore does not exclude property claims on spousal pensions. Pensions differ from degrees because, even though pensions are not saleable, market data can establish a value for them that does not include the value of "spousal earning capacity, spousal skills, and post-marital spousal labor". . . .

Marital-property claims to degrees and licenses are often made by persons who supported their spouse in school or in training. The decisions rejecting such property claims often allow instead an alimony claim based upon these facts.

NOTES

1. *The* O'Brien *Case.* As with many other famous cases, the reality of the O'Brien divorce is only imperfectly and misleadingly presented in the reported decision. Among other additional facts: Michael O'Brien claimed that Loretta O'Brien refused to have sex with him throughout their marriage (his initial filing for divorce had claimed "constructive abandonment"); Michael never became a surgeon, a future that had been assumed for him in the valuation of his medical degree; during the pendency of the appeal, Loretta remarried, which might be why she held out for a property division award (that would not terminate on remarriage, as an alimony award would); and the judgment was never paid to Loretta, as she instead accepted a lesser amount offered in settlement after the Court of Appeals decision. Ira Mark Ellman, O'Brien v. O'Brien: *A Failed Reform, Unlikely Reformers*, in FAMILY LAW STORIES 269–94 (Carol Sanger, ed., Foundation, 2008). The discussion also points out the misunderstandings of marital property that pervaded the trial: e.g., how the calculation of the value of Michael's medical license assumed the additional income that he would obtain if he continued on his training to become a surgeon, but that training was to occur, if at all, only after the marriage was over, and so it could not properly be included in the marital property that was to be divided. *Id.* at 280.

2. **O'Brien 's *Logic, and Other Cases on Licenses and Degrees.*** *Marriage of Graham*, 574 P.2d 75 (Colo. 1978), quoted in *Postema*, preceded the New York decision in *O'Brien*, and read the Colorado law, based upon the Model Marriage and Divorce Act, quite differently than *O'Brien* read the New York law.

Graham has proven far more influential than *O'Brien*. *O'Brien* itself conceded that other states have reached the opposite result. A 1987 National Law Journal survey, found New York was then the only state with surviving authority for classifying a professional degree as property. State high court cases decided since then uniformly favor *Graham*. These include *Guy v. Guy*, 736 So.2d 1042 (Miss. 1999); *Simmons v. Simmons*, 708 A.2d 949 (Conn. 1998); *Becker v. Perkins-Becker*, 669 A.2d 524 (R.I. 1996); *Downs v. Downs*, 574 A.2d 156 (Vt. 1990); *Hodge v. Hodge*, 520 A.2d 15 (Pa. 1986); *Marriage of Francis*, 442 N.W.2d 59 (Iowa 1989); *Drapek v. Drapek*, 503 N.E.2d 946 (Mass. 1987); *Sweeney v. Sweeney*, 534 A.2d 1290 (Me. 1987); *Stevens v. Stevens*, 492 N.E.2d 131 (Ohio 1986); *Nelson v. Nelson*, 736 P.2d 1145 (Alaska 1987); *Hoak v. Hoak*, 370 S.E.2d 473 (W. Va. 1988); and *Archer v. Archer*, 493 A.2d 1074 (Md. 1985); *see generally Simmons*, *supra*, at 955 n.7 (listing cases from each state). Most cases rejecting degree-as-property claims conclude that other remedies can be found to reimburse one spouse for the support provided the other for schooling, sometimes by way of alimony and sometimes by creating restitutionary remedies designed just for this purpose. For more on these alternative remedies, see Notes 3 and 4, *infra*. The *ALI Principles* similarly reject *O'Brien* in favor of the majority rule.

O'Brien emphasizes a phrase in the New York statute defining marital property as all property acquired after the marriage "regardless of the form in which title is held," as if that phrase were unusually dramatic. In fact, variants of this phrase can be found in nearly all modern equitable distribution statutes, including § 307 of the Model Marriage and Divorce Act (permitting division of property "whether title thereto is in the name of the husband or wife or both") upon which the Colorado statute construed in *Graham* is based. The intent of such language likely was to make clear the reformers' purpose of overruling the common law's traditional emphasis on title in allocating property on divorce, and thereby ensure that the title's form would not bar the court from allocating it. In making the title to property irrelevant it did not alter common understandings of what was property. One can make similar observations about the New York statute's list of factors relevant to the allocation of marital property, also mentioned in *O'Brien*. New York's inclusion, as one factor on this list, of one spouse's contributions to the other's career is entirely typical, as we saw above in Section A[1], and offers no basis for suggesting that New York's law is unusual. And of course the list of factors is meant to guide the courts in *dividing* property, not in *defining* it.

O'Brien was reaffirmed and actually expanded by *McSparron v. McSparron*, 87 N.Y.2d 275, 639 N.Y.S.2d 265, 662 N.E.2d 745 (1995). The court there wrote: "Contrary to plaintiff's contentions, nothing that has occurred in the 10 years since *O'Brien* was decided suggests a reason to overrule it. The 'chaos' and 'confusion' that plaintiff perceives are really nothing more than reflections of how difficult it is to achieve true fairness in the division of a married couple's tangible and intangible assets." *Id.* at 281, 639 N.Y.S.2d at 268, 662 N.E.2d at 748. *McSparron* reviewed a series of decisions by lower New York courts that had declined to apply *O'Brien* to a degree held by a spouse who had subsequently established a successful professional practice that was also subject to division. These lower courts had found that the degree or license had "merged" into the practice and need not be divided separately from it. Many expected the court to overrule *O'Brien*, but the contrary occurred. *McSparron* disapproved these lower court decisions and suggested that ensuring the separate treatment of the license as marital property is necessary in order to *avoid* introducing "nettlesome legal fictions" in the law.

The New York courts continue to affirm and apply *O'Brien v. O'Brien* in license and degree cases. See, e.g., *Holterman v. Holterman*, 3 N.Y.3d 1, 781 N.Y.S.2d 458, 814 N.E.2d 765 (2004) (affirming award of 35% of value of husband's enhanced earning capacity, adjudged to be $612,000, based on his medical degree; the court added: "In the 19 years since we adopted the *O'Brien* rule, we have adhered to the principle that both parties in a matrimonial action are entitled to fundamental fairness in the allocation of marital assets, and that the economic and noneconomic contributions of each spouse are to be taken into account.").

3. Applying O'Brien. One New York lower court concluded early on that advances during marriage in the wife's acting career were marital property. *Golub v. Golub*, 527 N.Y.S.2d 946 (Sup. 1988):

> Plaintiff . . . contends that her celebrity status is neither "professional" nor a "license" and hence not an "investment in human capital subject to equitable distribution." Moreover, plaintiff argues that because a career in

show business is subject to substantial fluctuation, it should not be considered. In *O'Brien*, the fact that the professional license itself had no market value was irrelevant. It is the enhanced earning capacity that the license affords the holder that is of value. In this respect, all sources of enhanced earning capacity become indistinguishable.

. . . *O'Brien* is the law. If it is to remain as good law, the rule should be uniformly applied. There seems to be no rational basis upon which to distinguish between a degree, a license, or any other special skill that generates substantial income.

See also Elkus v. Elkus, 169 A.D.2d 134, 572 N.Y.S.2d 901 (1991) (husband's claim to wife's successful career as an opera singer); *Allocco v. Allocco*, 152 Misc.2d 529, 578 N.Y.S.2d 995 (Sup. 1991) (husband's successful completion of civil service examinations for police lieutenant is divisible property which his wife should share because she contributed to his success); *but see McAlpine v. McAlpine*, 176 A.D.2d 285, 574 N.Y.S.2d 385 (1991) (even if husband's successful completion of last five actuary examinations during marriage had added to his earning capacity, wife had no claim because husband performed most household duties during marriage and wife did not contribute to his examination success or sacrifice her own career prospects to further it). While this effort to limit *O'Brien*'s reach is understandable, any serious requirement that the claimant show a direct causal link between his or her contributions and the spouse's career success would probably doom most claims.

For other applications of *O'Brien*, see *Morrongiello v. Paulsen*, 195 A.D.2d 594, 601 N.Y.S.2d 121 (1993) (where marriage occurred after husband finished one year of law school, two-thirds of his degree, equal to $189,474, is marital property); *Finocchio v. Finocchio*, 162 A.D.2d 1044, 556 N.Y.S.2d 1007 (1990) (license to practice law); *Di Caprio v. Di Caprio*, 162 A.D.2d 944, 556 N.Y.S.2d 1011 (1990) (master's degree and permanent certification in school administration); *Holihan v. Holihan*, 159 A.D.2d 685, 553 N.Y.S.2d 434 (1990) (guidance counselor license); *Morimando v. Morimando*, 145 A.D.2d 609, 536 N.Y.S.2d 701 (1988) (physician's assistant certification); *McGowan v. McGowan*, 142 A.D.2d 355, 535 N.Y.S.2d 990 (1988) (master's degree); *Anderson v. Anderson*, 153 A.D.2d 823, 545 N.Y.S.2d 335 (1989) (master's degrees in health care administration and labor and industrial relations, nursing home administrator license).

Some lower courts have developed rules of equity under which the degree, while treated as marital property, should not be divided between the spouses, or at least not in anything approaching an equal division. In *Gandhi v. Gandhi*, 283 A.D.2d 782, 724 N.Y.S.2d 541 (2001), the court said that neither the husband's accounting degree, earned partially before marriage, nor the wife's paralegal degree, earned partially after the marriage, should be allocated. In justification, the court observed (among other things) that the husband's CPA license was attributable in part to his intelligence and hard work. In *Brough v. Brough*, 285 A.D.2d 913, 727 N.Y.S.2d 555 (2001), the court granted the husband only 10% of the wife's enhanced earnings arising from the B.A., M.A., and teacher's certificate she earned during their 20-year marriage, reasoning that even though the husband fully supported the wife during her education, and gave her personal assistance with her studies, the degrees and licenses were primarily the result of her own abilities and efforts. *Corasanti v. Corasanti*, 296 A.D.2d 831, 744 N.Y.S.2d 614 (2002), similarly granted the wife only 30% of the husband's medical degree, because "while [the wife's] efforts certainly contributed to the ability of [the husband] to obtain his medical license and advanced degrees, those achievements were accomplished primarily through [his] own ability and Herculean effort as well as his own capacity for hard work" (citing *Brough*). Of course, similar claims could have been made for the license-holding spouse in *O'Brien* and in most of the cases that have followed. While requiring the court to decide on the relative importance of the contributions of the degree-holding spouse and the supporting spouse to the holder's achievement may avoid some of the absurd results *O'Brien* seems to entail, wildly inconsistent results appear inevitable. Their one "reliable" common feature is that as property rather than alimony awards, their allocations of post-divorce income will not be modifiable to correct the erroneous projections of the degree-holder's future economic circumstances that courts will inevitably make in some cases.

4. *Alternative Remedies I*: Postema, etc. As *Postema* indicates, there are alternatives to *O'Brien*'s treatment of licenses as marital property. First, one could find the license or degree obtained during the course of the marriage irrelevant to the financial terms of divorce, but consider the greater earning power the license or degree may have brought relevant, particularly in alimony decisions (treated in Note 4 and Section D, *infra*). The advantage of alimony over *O'Brien*'s property treatment is that it does not require the court to hazard a guess of the value of the license or degree — which, if wrong, could create a windfall for the non-degree-holding spouse at the degree-holding spouse's expense. At the least, a high evaluation of the value of the license or degree could unjustly constrain the degree-holding spouse's career options (*e.g.*, forcing a lawyer to choose corporate law firm work over public interest or public sector work). An alimony award can be modified over time, as it becomes clearer whether and to what extent obtaining a license or degree has increased its holder's earning capacity.

An additional advantage of alimony becomes clear when one notes that the same degree or license may be acquired in a marriage of three years' duration or during the first three years of a thirty-year marriage. The *O'Brien* rule does not distinguish these cases: in both, the degree's entire value is marital property. Within a long-term marriage, (1) as *Postema* points out, the non-degree-owning spouse will likely have benefited significantly, if indirectly, from the license and the increased earning power it brought; and (2) if the marriage ends with a significant difference in earning potential between the two spouses, most courts allow the lower earner (usually the non-degree-holder) a share in the other spouse's earnings through an alimony award.

The disadvantages of a traditional alimony award are: (1) as *Postema* points out, that it implies that the payments are at the discretion of the court, and perhaps based on "need" or "status," rather than any sort of entitlement; and (2) in many jurisdictions, alimony is subject to modification based on the obligor's ability to pay, and it is terminated on the death of either former spouse or the remarriage of the recipient (all three factors reflecting the view of alimony as discretionary rather than an entitlement). *Postema* sought a middle ground that would avoid the problems of both property treatments of degrees and alimony awards. However,

Postema's compromise does not seem successful; its decision proclaims a quasi-property entitlement which leaves trial courts with little guidance and a great deal of discretion. The solution may be not much better than (and not much different from) the problems it was seeking to remedy.

Often support for a spouse's education becomes just another factor being considered in determining an "equitable" division of property. According to a recent survey, 28 states expressly require courts to take contribution to a spouse's education into account in dividing property at divorce. Linda D. Elrod & Robert G. Spector, *A Review of the Year in Family Law 2007–2008: Federalization and Nationalization Continue*, 42 FAM. L.Q. 713, 762 (2009) (Chart 5).

One obvious alternative response to a situation where property is inappropriate and alimony inadequate, is to fix the alimony option — to make it more of an entitlement, and less discretionary and unpredictable. As is discussed in the following Note, a number of jurisdictions, and the *ALI Principles*, have taken that path.

5. *Alternative Remedies II: Reimbursement Alimony.* While the discussion of alimony is left to Section D, brief mention should be made here of the way alimony is commonly used to respond to marriages where one spouse has supported the other in obtaining a degree (with the marriage ending during the degree program or shortly after the degree is attained). Many statutes expressly authorize the award of alimony to the spouse who "[c]ontributed to the educational opportunities of the other spouse," without regard to need, or to whether the claimant intended to return to school herself. ARIZ. REV. STAT. § 25-319(A)(3). In other states, courts have relied upon more flexible statutory language to create a remedy called "reimbursement alimony," available to the supporting spouse without regard to that spouse's educational plans. For example, in *DeLa Rosa v. DeLa Rosa*, 309 N.W.2d 755 (Minn. 1981), Pedro and Elena married in 1972, when Pedro was beginning his undergraduate education. By agreement, she supported him through his undergraduate education and in his medical school training. Pedro filed for divorce during his second year of medical education.

> Prior to their separation, [Elena] was the primary source of financial income, thus permitting her husband to focus his energies upon obtaining an undergraduate degree, entering and attending medical school. The trial court found that [she] earned approximately $41,000 during coverture which was used for the parties' joint living expenses. [Pedro's] contributions were nominal; he earned $2,300 and received Veterans' educational benefits . . . of $9,031. He also received a grant to attend medical school . . . of $5,680. [Pedro] had incurred student loans of approximately $10,000 at the time of separation. The record reveals that tuition for [Pedro's] under-graduate and medical educations during the parties' marriage was roughly $8,811.

Id. at 757. The trial court concluded (and the Minnesota Supreme Court agreed) that Elena was not entitled to alimony under the Minnesota statute, due to her ability to support herself through appropriate employment. However, the trial court awarded Elena $29,669 for contributions she made to [Pedro's] education. The Minnesota Supreme Court commented:

The trial court's award was grounded in equity and represented restitution of the financial support [she] provided to [him] during the time he was attending college and medical school.

[Elena] had a reasonable expectation that she would be rewarded for her efforts by a higher standard of living when [Pedro] began practicing medicine. We find that the trial court did not abuse its discretion in making an equitable award to [Elena] for the financial support she provided . . . during his schooling in light of the facts and circumstances of this case.

Id. at 758. However, the court modified the original award (reducing it to $11,400) based on the following reasoning:

It is this Court's view that the award should have been limited to the monies expended by [Elena] for [Pedro]'s living expenses and any contributions made toward [his] direct educational costs. To achieve this result, we subtract from [her] earnings her own living expenses. This has the effect of imputing one-half of the living expenses and all the educational expenses to the student spouse. The formula subtracts from [her] contributions one-half of the couple's living expenses, that amount being the contributions of the two parties which were not used for direct educational costs: Working spouse's financial contributions to joint living expenses and educational costs of student spouse *less* 1/2 (working spouse's financial contributions *plus* student spouse's financial contributions less cost of education) *equals* equitable award to working spouse.

Id. at 759. *DeLa Rosa*'s approach to measuring reimbursement alimony is consistent with the bulk of existing authority — *e.g.*, *Mahoney v. Mahoney*, 453 A.2d 527 (N.J. 1982); *Hubbard v. Hubbard*, 603 P.2d 747, 750–53 (Okla. 1979); *Hoak v. Hoak*, 370 S.E.2d 473 (W.Va. 1988); *Geer v. Geer*, 353 S.E.2d 427 (N.C. App. 1987); *Donahue v. Donahue*, 384 S.E.2d 741 (S.C. 1989) — and also with *ALI Principles* § 5.12.

California requires "reimbursement" upon divorce to the marital community "for community contributions to education or training of a party that substantially enhances the earning capacity of the party." CAL. FAM. CODE § 2641(b)(1). The statute distinguishes between long- and short-term marriages by authorizing departures from the required reimbursement when the education or training had occurred so long ago that "the community has substantially benefited" from it already. The statute creates a rebuttable presumption that such benefit has accrued where the education occurred more than ten years before divorce. While thus excluded from reimbursement, the long-term spouse may benefit from an alimony award based on the degree holder's larger earnings.

Some authorities that authorize reimbursement alimony do not allow recovery for living expenses, as compared with the direct costs of the other spouse's education. *Bold v. Bold*, 574 A.2d 552 (Pa. 1990); CAL. FAM. CODE § 2641; IND. CODE ANN. § 31-15-7-6. Some statutes and cases make support for the other spouse's education a relevant factor in considering an alimony claim without providing any specific guidance for calculating the entitlement. *E.g.*, N.H. REV. STAT. ANN. § 458:16-a(II)(h) (one factor in determining an equitable division of the property is "direct or indirect contribution made by one party to help educate or develop the career . . . of the other"); ARIZ. REV. STAT. § 25-319(A)(3) (a basis for alimony); N.C. GEN. STAT. §§ 50-20(b)(2), (c)(7) (to be considered in alimony; degrees not considered marital property); TENN. CODE ANN. § 36-4-121 (a factor in allocating marital property, but degrees are not themselves property); *Schmitz v. Schmitz*, 801 S.W.2d 333, 336 (Ky. App. 1991) (there is no "set formula" for reimbursement alimony); *Downs v. Downs*, 574 A.2d 156 (Vt. 1990). California statutes allow both property and alimony remedies, although presumably not in the same case. See *Watt v. Watt*, 214 Cal. App. 3d 340, 262 Cal. Rptr. 783 (1989) (finding the wife ineligible for property award but entitled to alimony).

Comment *a* of *ALI Principles* § 5.12 explains the reimbursement award for educational expenses as a limited exception to the usual rule rejecting claims based on inequities in the allocation of financial resources during the marriage — an exception justified by two factors:

> First, arrangements under which one spouse supports the other through school are often seen as separable from other spousal arrangements. . . . Second, the equities favoring a remedy are thought particularly strong when the educated spouse leaves the marriage with an advantage in earning capacity achieved with the other's uncompensated assistance.

However, matters change with a longer marriage:

> [C]ompensation is available only when the divorce occurs reasonably soon after completion of the education or training. With the passage of time the spousal arrangements for support of the education can no longer be treated as a distinct transaction to be evaluated independently from the rest of the marital give and take. Spouses still married 10 years after one of them has completed an education with the other's support will normally have both enjoyed benefits . . . from the earning capacity enhancement it brought, and will share as well in marital property purchased with those incremental earnings.

Id.; *see also Pyeatte v. Pyeatte*, 661 P.2d 196, 204 (Ariz. Ct. App. 1983) (in the ordinary case the value of each spouse's labor during marriage "is consumed by the community in the on-going relationship and forms no basis for a claim"); *Mahoney v. Mahoney*, 453 A.2d 527, 533 (N.J. 1982) (marriage cannot be treated as "a business arrangement in which the parties keep track of debits and credits, their accounts to be settled upon divorce").

Does a claim for reimbursement alimony require that the claimant spent money directly on his spouse's *education*? In *Bold* the wife provided much of her husband's living expenses through school, but made no direct contribution to his educational expenses, which he paid from loans and grants. The lower court held she therefore had no reimbursement claim, because she had merely satisfied her ordinary duty of support in the marriage. In reversing and sustaining an award, the Pennsylvania Supreme Court allowed her a claim for all support she paid in excess of the "bare minimum" she was legally obliged to provide. *Bold v. Bold*, 574 A.2d 552 (Pa. 1990). Does a reimbursement claim require that the claimant herself suffered a loss from having supported her spouse, as by foregoing one's own education in order to support one's spouse? Minnesota seemed to require this element in the *DeLa Rosa* sequel of *Ellesmere v. Ellesmere*, 359 N.W.2d 48 (Minn. App. 1984). The wife earned three advanced degrees during the marriage while the husband, a physician, supported her. Relying on *DeLa Rosa*, he sought on divorce to recover his expenditures on her education, but was rebuffed in part because he incurred no "sacrifice and foregoing of the enjoyment of earned income significant enough to fit within the *DeLa Rosa* principle." What then of a schoolteacher who continues her teaching career unhampered after a divorce from her physician husband? A later Minnesota case, citing *DeLa Rosa* without further explanation, allowed restitution under just such facts for the teacher's support of her periodontist husband's education, despite a dissent citing *Ellesmere*. *Wilson v. Wilson*, 388 N.W.2d 432 (Minn. App. 1986).

6. *Equity, Entitlement, and Sympathy.* One might wonder whether the courts' evaluations of the equities in *O'Brien*, *Postema*, and *DeLa Rosa*, were affected by unarticulated assumptions concerning marital fault. The stereotypic facts that many assume in these sorts of claims involves a husband who leaves his wife for another woman after she has supported him through school. Would we be as sympathetic to Mrs. O'Brien's claim for half of her former husband's lifetime earnings as a physician if she instead had left him for their impecunious next-door neighbor, the two of them planning to live comfortably ever after on half of Mr. O'Brien's future earnings? Would we think differently about the reimbursement of expenses for Mrs. Postema and Mrs. DeLa Rosa if the reason for their marriage's ending was their cruel treatment or adultery? If we do not wish to introduce fault into marital property allocations, then we need rules which are equitable without regard to whose actions caused the breakup. That is one argument that might be offered for allowing short-term spouses only reimbursement of their outlays, while allowing longer-term spouses a share in the other's post-dissolution income, when it is much greater than the claimant's.

[2]   Goodwill

Definitions of goodwill found in the cases often quote Justice Story's classic description in COMMENTARIES ON THE LAW OF PARTNERSHIPS, § 99, at 170 (6th ed. 1868), which has even found its way into statute, CAL. BUS. & PROF. CODE § 14100 ("The 'good will' of a business is the expectation of continued public patronage."). But if we really want to know what goodwill means, this statement is of little help. It is better to ask: how is goodwill measured? And, indeed, if we put aside their testimony in lawsuits, and look instead at how accountants measure goodwill in their actual practice, there are some well-established conventions. Those conventions assume a sale, which is ordinarily the only occasion, apart from lawsuits, on which goodwill is measured. When a business is sold, values may be assigned to its various components to establish their basis for subsequent tax treatment. Standard accounting principles applicable to publicly traded corporations specify that the value of goodwill is the excess of a business's market value — what it sells for — over its asset value — the sum of the value of each of the firm's identifiable assets. RALPH L. BENKE, JR., BUSINESS COMBINATIONS: GOODWILL AND OTHER INTANGIBLE ASSETS (2006); DONALD E. KIESO, JERRY J. WEYGANDT & TERRY D. WARFIELD, INTERMEDIATE ACCOUNTING 580–84 (12th ed., 2007).

The value of the goodwill thus depends upon the firm's market value, as the *ALI Principles* observe in § 4.07, Comment *d*:

> Standard accounting practice . . . give[s] goodwill a purely operational definition: it is no more (and no less) than the amount by which the market value of a going concern exceeds the total value of its tangible assets. . . . [¶] . . . One may speculate that this additional value arises from factors such as the business's reputation or location but such speculations have no relevance in accounting for the sale: the difference between sale price and asset value is entered as goodwill on the buyer's balance sheet, without regard to the explanation for it. . . . [B]uyers are willing to pay more than simple asset value for an operating business when they believe the business will generate an income, in their hands, that justifies the enhanced price. The greater the income expectation, the greater a premium over asset value buyers will be willing to pay, and the greater will be the goodwill component that accountants will assign to the purchase price. But this relationship between income expectations and goodwill is essentially circular, with no meaning apart from the definitional conventions employed by accountants. . . . Goodwill is not some "thing" which is the source of the income flow, and which is therefore marital property if acquired during marriage. Goodwill is simply the label placed on the price that a buyer is willing to pay for the income flow. . . .

Thus, once the market sets a value for the business as a whole, the definitional conventions employed by accountants yield a value for its goodwill. Before the market value for the business is established, the accountant cannot tell whether the business has any goodwill value at all; after it is established, the accountant cannot tell why the goodwill value is X rather than Y.

Why should domestic relations lawyers care how much of the market value of a business is accounted for by goodwill? Ordinarily, they don't. If Sally creates a business during her marriage to John, using marital capital, then the entire value of the business is marital property. And if we know what the business would sell for, we ordinarily know its value; ordinarily, the market value of a business is its value for marital property purposes as well. It matters not whether a buyer's accountant, after the sale, would conclude that goodwill accounted for fifty percent, ten percent, or zero percent of the purchase price; the entire purchase price is marital property in all three cases. For the ordinary saleable business, for which a market price can be established, there is thus no occasion for disputes over the value of goodwill.

The occasion for such disputes arises instead when the business is not saleable, or when it is claimed that the market price does not reflect the full value of the business for marital property purposes. The most common example is the professional practice. Regulatory rules may bar or restrict the sale of a professional practice, so that it has no market price, or a depressed market price that the professional's spouse believes is less than its marital property value. The question then is: What benchmark other than the market price can be used to fix the practice's value? One common approach seeks a market value for each component of the business (books, furniture, office equipment, and the like), as well as the goodwill. In such a case then, the usual accountant's convention is turned on its head: a value is offered for the goodwill (as well as the other components) in order to establish the full value of the business or practice, rather than the market value being used to determine the value, if any, of the goodwill. While ordinarily goodwill cannot be employed to calculate that market value, in this case it is not the market value that the evaluator seeks to establish. The whole point is to have a valuation that reflects the belief that, for marital property purposes, the business has a value that is something more than the market value. This observation identifies the problem but not the solution, which necessarily requires developing a method for valuing the goodwill (and thus the business) that differs from and does not depend upon knowing its market value.

Once one accepts the proposition that the value of an asset for marital property purposes is something other than its market value, the opportunities for contention over the valuation method become considerably enriched. There are no substitutes for market value that experts or courts agree upon. Ordinary appraisal methods seek to estimate the market price of an object, and that market value serves as a benchmark against which to judge the accuracy of an appraiser or his methods. What is the benchmark if market value is rejected? And what then is goodwill? These are the questions that many goodwill cases wrestle with, and all necessarily resolve, knowingly or not. The problem is particularly difficult because the purported experts in valuation relied upon in such cases do not always understand that their choice for the meaning of value, or of goodwill, should be driven by marital property rules and the policies that underlie them. In the midst of such confusion the opportunities for creative lawyering multiply. Indeed, if nonmarket meanings of value or goodwill are acceptable, why should they be limited to the case in which regulatory rules restrict or eliminate the market? Perhaps the true meaning of an asset for marital property purposes is different than its market value even where there is a market value.

While the conflicting authorities over the treatment of goodwill therefore spill over into a number of areas, the cases of professional practices remain the dominant arena. In contrast to professional licenses, and earning capacity itself, most courts agree that professional goodwill is divisible property. They differ, however, on the rules they adopt with respect to evidence of its existence and value. As one might expect from the preceding discussion, these measurement differences are more than technicalities. Not only can they yield dramatically different dollar amounts; they reflect fundamentally different conceptions of what constitutes divisible property. In some cases the measurement method used or adopted effectively includes earning capacity. It is therefore not possible to understand the policy at issue in the goodwill cases without mastering the valuation basics. Such mastery is also necessary for competent representation of a client in a case in which the marital property includes potentially valuable business or professional assets. The valuation evidence typically is offered by an expert witness who is an accountant or a business appraiser, but a lawyer who wants to persuade the court to accept one expert's valuation rather than another's must understand what the experts have done. The following case, *Hanson v. Hanson*, involves two divorces in which two different valuation methods were used. One method relies upon establishment of a market value; the other is more mysterious.

HANSON v. HANSON
Missouri Supreme Court
738 S.W.2d 429 (1987)

ROBERTSON, JUDGE.

These are consolidated appeals arising out of decrees of dissolution of marriage. . . . The husbands . . . are the sole partners in an oral surgery partnership. *In Hanson*, . . . the Circuit Court of Boone County valued the partnership at $324,862, including $233,727, an amount characterized as "goodwill" by the parties. In *Graham*, [another] Circuit Court . . . hearing virtually identical evidence, valued the same partnership at $90,280. . . .

We granted transfer to determine whether our dissolution of marriage laws recognize the existence of goodwill in a professional practice as a marital asset and to determine the extent to which those laws permit the division of such goodwill upon dissolution of marriage. . . .

I.

The Oral Surgery Partnership

Drs. Graham and Hanson formed their partnership for the practice of oral surgery in Jefferson City . . . in July, 1973. At trial, both Mrs. Hanson and Mrs. Graham employed Stephen Smith, a C.P.A., as an expert witness. Smith valued the oral surgery partnership as follows:

$39,750.00	equipment
$51,385.00	accounts receivable
$351,077.00	going concern value
$442,212.00	Total Value

Smith defined "going concern value" as the "opportunity to walk into a successful situation and to start work and earn money without having to build the practice." Smith further testified that going concern value represented the ability of the buyer to trade on the past reputation of the seller. [The court later concludes that "going concern value," as defined here, is equivalent to goodwill.]

Smith applied an 85 percent capitalization rate to the previous year's gross receipts to determine the value of the partnership. This capitalization rate was the product of Smith's assessment of the partnership's "monopolistic" position in the Jefferson City market, its expenses, the degree of risk attendant to the practice, and the reputation of the practice and the practitioners in the community. From these factors, Smith fashioned a tentative going concern value for the partnership. He compared his tentative conclusions to the national average sales price for oral surgery practices, for gross production per oral surgeon, and for average revenues and expenses for oral surgery partnerships containing five or fewer oral surgeons. From these considerations Smith reached his conclusion as to the appropriate capitalization factor to apply to the Graham and Hanson partnership. . . .

Both Dr. Hanson and Dr. Graham produced Elmer Evers, C.P.A. as an expert for purposes of valuing their partnership interests. Evers valued the partnership at $91,000, the approximate value of equipment, cash on hand and accounts receivable. Evers compared sales of professional practices in the area served by the partnership, the nature of the partnership's patronage, and the reputation of the partners to determine that neither goodwill nor going concern value existed in the partnership.

Dr. Thomas Coyle, an oral surgeon practicing in Columbia, . . . testified on behalf of Dr. Hanson. Dr. Coyle bought into a partnership . . . in Columbia in 1975. He testified that his purchase price included neither an amount for goodwill nor for the going concern value. . . . Upon the retirement of Dr. Coyle's partner, Dr. Coyle bought his partner's interest in the partnership; again, Dr. Coyle paid nothing for goodwill or going concern value.

Drs. Graham and Hanson introduced their partnership agreement in their respective cases. Paragraph eight of that agreement provided:

> The value of the interest of a withdrawing partner shall be the sum of: (a) One-half of the reasonable market value of the fixtures, equipment and contents of the office partnership; (b) His proportionate share of the accrued net profits; (c) One-half of all accounts receivable as of the date of dissolution which can be reasonably expected to be collected in the first six months following the date of dissolution; (d) No value for goodwill or firm name shall be included in any computations of a partner's interest; (e) If a net loss has been incurred to the date of dissolution, his share of such loss shall be deducted.

Dr. Hanson testified that profits were drawn from the partnership account twice monthly; there were no accrued net profits.

The Hanson Marriage

Dr. and Mrs. Hanson married on March 20, 1974. By the time of the marriage, Dr. Hanson had already completed his oral surgery training, had retired all but $1,000 of the debt he incurred to finance his education and had opened the oral surgery practice with Dr. Graham. Mrs. Hanson [had] a nursing degree. Following the marriage, Mrs. Hanson continued to pursue her nursing career. She earned a Master's Degree in nursing in December, 1981. At the time of the trial, Dr. Hanson earned approximately $120,000 per year in his oral surgery practice; Mrs. Hanson earned approximately $7,000 per year. There were no children.

The Boone County Circuit Court valued the partnership at $324,862.00, an amount which included the fair market value of the partnership's equipment ($39,750), the accounts receivable ($51,385) and the partnership's ordinary income for 1984 ($233,727). . . .

Dr. Hanson appeals the valuation of his partnership interest. . . .

The Graham Marriage

Dr. and Mrs. Graham married on May 24, 1969. The marriage produced two children. By the time of the marriage, Dr. Graham had completed his dental studies; he finished his oral surgery training during the marriage. Mrs. Graham completed registered nurse training prior to the marriage. In 1978, the Grahams began investing in real estate. The couple accumulated several parcels of improved real estate[.] Mrs. Graham managed the couple's properties. In 1980, she obtained a real estate license and began selling real estate on a full-time basis. In 1983, Mrs. Graham grossed approximately $27,000 as a real estate salesperson. After the couple's separation in 1983, her income declined to $5,000 in 1984. Dr. Graham earned approximately $120,000 per year at the time of the trial.

The Circuit Court of Cole County dissolved the marriage, valued Dr. Graham's interest in the partnership at $45,140, divided the marital property equally between the parties, awarded Mrs. Graham permanent maintenance of $500 per month to continue until remarriage, death or modification by court order. . . .

Both parties appealed the trial court's order. Mrs. Graham assigns error to the court's valuation of Dr. Graham's interest in the oral surgery partnership. . . .

II.

Section 452.330.1, RSMo 1986, authorizes the court to "set apart to each spouse his property and . . . divide the marital property in such proportions as the court deems just. . . ."

A.

Is goodwill property? Our courts have long recognized that "the goodwill of a business is property. . . ." Goodwill produced in a professional setting is no less property than that arising from a commercial setting.

[G]oodwill which can be sold, and is therefore property, attaches not to an individual but to a business entity. Goodwill has no separate existence; it has value only as an incident of a continuing business.

B.

In addressing the question of the existence and value of goodwill in a professional context as marital property, the courts have not spoken with a uniform voice.

1.

In *Dugan v. Dugan*, 92 N.J. 423, 457 A.2d 1 (1983), the New Jersey Supreme Court found that goodwill in the law practice of a sole practitioner is property subject to distribution in a dissolution action. The court recognized that reputation is "at the core" of any consideration of professional goodwill. While acknowledging that future earning capacity is not *per se* goodwill, the New Jersey justices noted that when "future earning capacity has been enhanced because reputation leads to probable future patronage from existing and potential clients, goodwill may exist and have value." *Id. Dugan* has been criticized, and properly so in our view, for its failure to distinguish between the reputation of the professional as an individual and the reputation of the professional practice as a business entity. Allen Parkman, *The Treatment of Professional Goodwill in Divorce Proceedings*, 18 Fam. L.Q., 213, 219 (Summer 1984).

In *In the Matter of the Marriage of Fleege*, 91 Wash. 2d 324, 588 P.2d 1136 (banc 1979), the Washington Supreme Court defined the critical question as "not whether the goodwill of the practice could be sold . . . but whether it [the goodwill] has value to [the practitioner]." 588 P.2d at 1138–9. In determining the value of the such [*sic*] goodwill, *Fleege* outlined several factors for consideration: "[T]he practitioner's age, health, past earning power, reputation in the community for judgment, skill and knowledge, and his comparative professional success." 588 P.2d at 1138. Each of these factors is, in our view, directly attributable to the professional as a person. For this reason, we find that the *Fleege* analysis is mired in the same mixture of personal reputation and entity reputation as is found in *Dugan*.

2.

Several courts have refused to acknowledge professional goodwill as property. A leading case is *Holbrook v. Holbrook*, 103 Wis. 2d 327, 309 N.W.2d 343 (App. 1981). There the court refused to follow "the twisted and illogical path that other jurisdictions have made in dealing with the concept [of professional goodwill] in the context of divorce." The court continued, "[t]he concept of professional goodwill evanesces when one attempts to distinguish it from future earning capacity. . . . The goodwill or reputation of such a business accrues to the benefit of the owners only through increased salary." 309 N.W.2d at 354. . . .

3.

Between the opposing results reached in *Dugan* and *Holbrook*, several courts have attempted to chart a course which recognizes that goodwill is marital property, but only insofar as it exists independently of the individual professional's reputation. Characteristic of these cases is *Taylor v. Taylor*, 222 Neb. 721, 386 N.W.2d 851 (1986). There the Nebraska Supreme Court concluded that "goodwill must be a business asset with value independent of the presence or reputation of a particular individual, an asset which may be sold, transferred, conveyed, or pledged. . . ." *Taylor*, 386 N.W.2d at 858–9. . . .

C.

As we have said, goodwill is recognized as property in this state. . . . Goodwill may exist in both commercial and professional entities. Irrespective of the setting . . . , the meaning of goodwill does not change. It is property which attaches to and is dependent upon an existing business entity; the reputation and skill of an individual entrepreneur — be he a professional or a traditional businessman — is not a component of the intangible asset we identify generally as goodwill.

With the caveats which follow, we hold that goodwill in a professional practice acquired during a marriage is marital property subject to division. . . . We define goodwill within a professional setting to mean the value of the practice which exceeds its tangible assets and which is the result of the tendency of clients/patients to return to and recommend the practice irrespective of the reputation of the individual practitioner. Our understanding of goodwill is thus consistent with and no broader than the economic, accounting and legal definition which existed prior to the advent of *Dugan, Fleege* and cases reaching similar results.

Goodwill is not dependent, however, on the manner in which the professional practice is organized nor the size of the practice itself. We recognize . . . that goodwill will more likely exist in larger professional practices than in the offices of sole practitioners. This is so because reliance by patients/clients on the reputation and skill of the individual practitioner is, in most cases, inversely related to the number of practitioners in the practice. However, to the extent that, for instance, competent evidence exists that clients/patients will return to the place of the practice — or recommend it to acquaintances who have not yet patronized it — irrespective of the presence of the individual professional, goodwill exists in the solo practice.

Professional goodwill may not be confused with future earning capacity. We have not declared future earning capacity to be marital property. We do not now do so. Instead, we leave to the trial court broad discretion in striking an appropriate balance between husband and wife in the division of property and any award of maintenance. . . .

D.

1.

Proof of the existence of goodwill is particularly troublesome in a professional context [because] the reputation of the individual practitioner and the goodwill of his enterprise are often inextricably interwoven. Because of the difficulties inherent in separating the reputation of the professional from that of his enterprise, evidence that other professionals are willing to pay for goodwill when acquiring a practice is, in our view, the only acceptable evidence of the existence of goodwill. Thus, as a matter of proof, the existence of goodwill is shown only when there is evidence of a recent actual sale of a similarly situated professional practice, an offer to purchase such a practice, or expert testimony and testimony of members of the subject profession as to the existence of goodwill in a similar practice in the relevant geographic and professional market. Absent such evidence, one can only speculate as to the existence of goodwill.[1]

----

[1] Courts which have employed capitalization formulae, see discussion, *infra*, often appear to mix concepts of value with concepts of proof. See, *e.g., In re Marriage of Hall*, 692 P.2d at 175. Expert testimony concerning the value of goodwill based on capitalization formulae is not tantamount to proof of the existence of goodwill. An expert can simply assume the existence of goodwill and, using a capitalization formula, produce a value.

Divisions of marital property may not be based on speculation as to the very existence of the property being divided.

2.

As to the issue of valuation, *In re the Marriage of Hall*, 103 Wash. 2d 236, 692 P.2d 175, 179–80 (1984), outlines five major formulae for establishing goodwill value. Of these, three are accounting formulae. The first utilizes a straight capitalization method. The average net profits of the professional are capitalized. The result is the total value of the business including tangible and intangible assets. Book value of the assets is subtracted to determine goodwill value.

The second formula is the capitalization of excess earnings method. The annual salary of the average employee practitioner is subtracted from the average net income of the practice. The remaining amount is multiplied by a capitalization rate to determine goodwill value.

The third method is the Internal Revenue Service variation of capitalized excess earnings. Under this formula, a reasonable rate of return based on the business' average net tangible assets is subtracted from the average net income of the business for the last five years. From this amount a comparable net salary is subtracted. A capitalization rate is applied to determine goodwill value.

The fourth *Hall* formula focuses on fair market value. The value of goodwill, if any, is determined by the price the practice would bring were it sold on the open, relevant market to a qualified professional.

The fifth valuation method is based on a buy-sell agreement. The value established in a partnership agreement, for example, determines the value of any goodwill in the practice.

Of the suggested formulae, we state our strong preference for the fair market value approach. First, the fair market value approach "does not take explicitly into consideration the future earning capacity of the professional goodwill or the post-dissolution efforts of the professional spouse." Comment, *Professional Goodwill in Louisiana: An Analysis of Its Classification, Valuation and Partition*, 43 La. L. Rev. 139, 142 (1982). As we have previously said, in Missouri, the future earning capacity of one of the marital partners is not *per se* property. . . .

Second, fair market value evidence appears to us to be the most equitable and accurate measure of both the existence and true value of the goodwill of an enterprise. Evidence of a recent actual sale of a similarly situated practice, an offer to purchase the subject or a similar practice, or expert testimony and testimony of members of the subject profession as to the present value of goodwill of a similar practice in the open, relevant, geographical and professional market is the best evidence of value.

Third, the fair market value method is most likely to avoid the "disturbing inequity in compelling a professional practitioner to pay a spouse a share of intangible assets at a judicially determined value that could not be realized by a sale or another method of liquidating value." *Holbrook*, 309 N.W.2d at 355. We therefore reject the notion advanced by some courts that goodwill may exist and be subject to division in a dissolution proceeding even though it may not be sold. See, *e.g.*, *In re Marriage of Freedman*, 23 Wash. App. 27, 592 P.2d 1124 (1979); *Hall*, 692 P.2d at 175.

Under certain circumstances, the buy-sell agreement method for determining goodwill value may be appropriate. We believe the trial court is best suited to determine when a buy-sell agreement constitutes competent evidence of goodwill value, *In re Marriage of Morris*, 588 S.W.2d 39, 43–4 (Mo. App. 1979), recognizing that "the professional spouse may be influenced by many factors other than fair market value in negotiating the terms of the agreement. . . ." *Hall*, 692 P.2d at 180.

We reject the use of capitalization formulae as a substitute for fair market value evidence of the value of goodwill in a professional practice.[2] The very purpose of capitalization formulae is to place a present value on the future earnings of the business entity being valued. *Beasley* [*v. Beasley*, 518 A.2d 545] at 552 [(Pa. Super. 1986)]. The formulae draw no distinction between the future earning capacity of the individual and that of the entity in which he or she practices. And as we have said previously, the future earning capacity of the individual professional is not, *per se*, an item of marital property subject to division in a dissolution proceeding. . . .

Hanson v. Hanson

Dr. Thomas Coyle stated that he paid nothing for either goodwill or going concern value when he joined an established oral surgeon in a partnership in Columbia or when he purchased his partner's interest in the practice upon the partner's retirement. The husbands' [Graham and Hanson's] expert, Mr. Evers, testified that in his experience similar practices were sold in the geographic area of the partnership without payment for goodwill or going concern value. He concluded that there was no going concern value or goodwill in the partnership. Mr. Smith, the wives' expert, provided no fair market value evidence for goodwill or going concern value in the relevant geographical market, relying instead on a capitalization formula we have rejected. . . .

The Circuit Court of Boone County valued the partnership at $324,862. This included $233,727, the partnership's ordinary income for 1984. Ostensibly, the trial court based its valuation on paragraph eight of the partnership agreement. We find no support for the trial court's conclusion in either that document or in the evidence. . . . The fair market value evidence in the record indicates no goodwill value in the partnership. . . . [W]e therefore remand the case to the Circuit Court . . . with directions to assign a value to Dr. Hanson's share in the oral surgery partnership which does not reflect either goodwill or accrued net profits. . . .

---

[2] We recognize that evidence of the fair market value of the goodwill of an entity may reveal that such value is the product of the application of a capitalization rate to the gross receipts or net income of the entity. To the extent that fair market value as shown by the evidence includes such a product, we obviously do not reject it.

Graham v. Graham

The only evidence of fair market value before the trial court in the *Graham* case consisted of the testimony of Elmer Evers, Dr. Graham's expert. As he did in the *Hanson* case, Mr. Evers stated that in his experience in the relevant market, practices similar to that of the Graham and Hanson oral surgery partnership are sold without payment for goodwill or going concern value. The court heard no contrary fair market value evidence. We must, therefore, affirm the trial court's valuation of the oral surgery partnership. . . .

BILLINGS, C.J., BLACKMAR, DONNELLY, RENDLEN, HIGGINS, J.J., and PREWITT, Special Judge, concur.

WELLIVER, J., not sitting.

NOTES

1. *Capitalization of Income Flows: the Basics.*   Although the opinion does not make clear precisely what calculations Expert Smith performed, one can in general describe the "capitalization" method he employed. While that method is rejected by *Hanson*, it has been accepted by more than a few other courts. Perhaps the leading authority favoring a capitalization approach is *Dugan*, which endorses the method described by *Hanson* as "capitalization of excess earnings." This method is employed by most experts asked to do such a valuation of nonmarketable goodwill. *Dugan* explains it this way:

> Goodwill is to be differentiated from earning capacity. It reflects not simply a possibility of future earnings, but a probability based on existing circumstances. Enhanced earnings reflected in goodwill are to be distinguished from a license to practice a profession and an educational degree. In that situation the enhanced future earnings are so remote and speculative that the license and degree have not been deemed to be property.

> . . . An individual practitioner's inability to sell a law practice does not eliminate existence of goodwill. . . . [D]ifficulty in fixing its value does not justify ignoring its existence. Goodwill should be valued with great care, for the individual practitioner will be forced to pay the ex-spouse "tangible" dollars for an intangible asset at a value concededly arrived at on the basis of some uncertain elements. For purposes of valuing the goodwill of a law practice, the true enhancement to be evaluated is the likelihood of repeat patronage and a certain degree of immunity from competition. Identification of goodwill in this fashion differs from that utilized in evaluating goodwill in businesses where an identification of a return on tangible assets is made.

> . . .

> One appropriate [measure] of goodwill of a law practice [is] the amount by which the attorney's earnings exceed that which would have been earned

as an employee by a person with similar qualifications of education, experience and capability. . . . An attorney who earns $35,000 per year as an employee would, as any employee, not have goodwill properly ascribable to his employment. The same attorney earning a net income of the same amount from his individual practice should likewise not be considered to have property consisting of goodwill in ascertaining the value of his practice.

The court should first ascertain what an attorney of comparable experience, expertise, education and age would be earning as an employee in the same general locale. The effort that the practitioner expends on his law practice should not be overlooked when comparing his income to that of the hypothetical employee. A sole practitioner who, for example, works a regular sixty-hour week may have a significantly greater income than an employee who regularly works a forty-hour week, and the income may be due to greater productivity rather than the realization of income on the sole practitioner's goodwill. Next, the attorney's net income before federal and state income taxes for a period of years, preferably five, should be determined and averaged. The actual average should then be compared with the employee norm. If the attorney's actual average realistically exceeds the total of (1) the employee norm and (2) a return on the investment in the physical assets, the excess would be the basis for evaluating goodwill.

This excess is subject to a capitalization factor. The capitalization factor is generally perceived as the number of years of excess earnings a purchaser would be willing to pay for in advance in order to acquire the goodwill. 2 J. Bonbright, VALUATION OF PROPERTY 731 (1937). The minimum capitalization factor is zero. The precise capitalization factor would depend on other evidence. Such evidence could consist of a comparison of capitalization factors used to measure goodwill in other professions, such as medicine or dentistry, adjusted, however, for ingredients peculiar to law, such as the inability to sell the practice and nonavailability of a restrictive covenant. The age of a lawyer may be particularly important because a sole practitioner's goodwill would probably terminate upon death, contrary to that of a doctor.

. . . .

[The expert who testified at trial on the value of the attorney's goodwill] used a [capitalization] factor of five. . . . No evidence supported capitalization at that figure. Our New Jersey inheritance practice indicates a frequent use of three in evaluating goodwill in close corporations or partnerships and Bonbright points out that in New York three is the factor regarded as least in need of justification. See 2 J. Bonbright, *supra*, at 731. When calculating the value of an attorney's goodwill, the court should also consider the risks and competitiveness of the practice. A string of recent successes in contingent fee cases, for example, may lead to overestimating expected income, although averaging over a number of years will correct for many . . . such distortions. Even a properly adjusted estimate may reflect a portion of income attributable to return on risk-taking by the attorney, rather than on his reputation. Similarly, a practice in a highly competitive field might reduce the estimated value of an attorney's goodwill. If consideration is given to plaintiff's work life expectancy, to his inability to sell the practice, to his inability to grant a restrictive covenant, and to the competitiveness and risks of the practice, a factor of five is inordinately high. . . .

457 A.2d 1, 6, 7, 9–10, 11–12.

Note that the method endorsed by *Dugan* has two steps, each of which depends upon certain assumptions. The first step involves identifying that portion of the lawyer's income attributable to "goodwill." The apportionment is necessary because, as even *Dugan* and *Hanson* agree, the lawyer's entire potential income is not divisible property. Rather, *Dugan* treats as divisible property only that portion of the income attributable to the practice's (not the lawyer's) "goodwill." Under *Hanson*, if there is no market for the goodwill then it doesn't exist; if there is a market, then it is worth what it would sell for, as with any other marital asset. By contrast, *Dugan* holds goodwill often exists even if it is nonsaleable, and so *Dugan* must offer a method for identifying and valuing it. To establish the existence of such nonsaleable goodwill, *Dugan's* first step asks whether the lawyer has "excess earnings" — earnings that derive from this nonmarketable professional goodwill. We return in Note 2 to examining the criteria *Dugan* employs for determining what portion of the lawyer's future expected income is "excess." For now we proceed to the second step, which is placing a value on those excess earnings.

Mathematically, this second step is rather straightforward. There is a standard formula for establishing the current value of a future income flow. This is sometimes called "capitalizing" the income flow, and is sometimes called figuring its "present value." The process is mathematically equivalent to calculating a mortgage, but from the bank's perspective rather than the borrower's. One can think of a bank as buying an income flow — the mortgage payments it will receive over the loan's life, which might last 30 years into the future — with a lump sum it has to pay out right now: the amount of money it lends to the borrower. The equation that solves the calculation has four key values: the principal amount of the mortgage, the interest rate, the term of the mortgage in years, and the monthly payments. Once you know three of these values, the fourth is determined.

The same calculation applies to capitalizing, or figuring the present value of, an income flow. To calculate what a future income flow is worth in current dollars, one must have two other facts: the number of years over which this income will flow, and the prevailing interest rate, sometimes also called the "discount rate." The interest rate is presumably taken from prevailing market rates at the time the calculation is made. Finding a benchmark for the term of years is a bit trickier (called the "capitalization factor" by *Dugan*). For the ordinary income producing asset — a bond, a patent, a franchise, a business — this number would be fixed by the market: how many years of income is a buyer willing to pay for? Some income is so far in the future that it has little or no current value. Income not so far in the future may also have little value; if potential buyers believe there is a substantial risk it will not be realized. This perception of risk will vary with the asset. The market will employ shorter capitalization factors for assets viewed as riskier, longer ones for less risky assets. But of course in the case of attorney income addressed by *Dugan*, there is no market. Establishment of the "capitalization factor" is thus rather arbitrary. Perhaps for this reason, *Dugan* takes a fairly conservative approach, finding a factor of five "inordinately high" and suggesting three as more appropriate. (*Stolow v. Stolow*, 540 N.Y.S.2d 484 (N.Y. A.D. 1989), and *Chandler v. Chandler*, 32 P.3d 140 (Idaho 2001), both approved a rate of 5, while *Eslami v. Eslami*, 591 A.2d 411 (Conn. 1991), approved a rate of 2.)

Once one has all the terms — the amount of excess income per year, the interest rate, and the number of years — the calculation is done by employing the same formula used to calculate a mortgage. The income flow is the equivalent of the mortgage payments, the period of years over which the income is capitalized is equivalent to the term of the mortgage, and of course, the interest rate serves the same function in both cases. The "capitalized" amount of the income flow which the expert offers as the present value of the goodwill is equivalent to the principal amount of the mortgage loan. Looking at a mortgage from the bank's perspective, one can see that the process is the same, since for the bank the question is: how much money will we give the borrower for this secured promise to provide us with an income flow over the next X years?

Dugan relies on the ethical principle, then followed in most jurisdictions, that law practices could not be sold. This has since been changed, in all, or nearly all, jurisdictions. See AMERICAN BAR ASSOCIATION, MODEL RULES OF PROFESSIONAL CONDUCT RULE 1.17 & Comments (Sale of Law Practice: permitting sale, as long as clients are informed in writing of their right to retain other counsel). It may be that much of the force of the *Dugan* approach has diminished with that change.

2. *Identifying Excess Earnings in the Nonmarket Valuation Method.* Now we return to the more fundamental question. Anyone with a business calculator can perform a present value calculation for an income flow which provided the numbers described in Note 1. But how does one determine the amount of income, monthly or annual, to be plugged into the formula? This is the key question of the entire valuation enterprise. In the case of a lawyer's practice, *Dugan* uses "the amount by which the attorney's earnings exceed that which would have been earned as an employee by a person with similar qualifications of education, experience and capability" — otherwise known as the attorney's "excess earnings." Yet the key question is *why* the attorney has such "excess earnings." Most jurisdictions do not recognize the attorney's personal attributes or skills as marital property, an important basis for their rejection of *O'Brien*. Also, the returns on post-dissolution labor are not marital property anywhere. These "excess earnings" therefore cannot be properly treated as marital property unless one identifies them as arising from some source other than the professional's personal skills or post-dissolution labor (for example, if the cause is the business' location, which the owner acquired with marital assets, this "goodwill" should clearly be considered a marital asset). *ALI Principles* § 4.07, Comment d, adds:

> Some authorities, apparently concerned that the division of professional goodwill is necessarily a mechanism for treating earning capacity as property, suggest that it is never divisible property. However, in many

professions, a practice is saleable, and its market value will exceed the value of its tangible assets. The price paid for a medical practice, for example, may reflect income expectations resulting from receipt of the seller's medical records, a list of the patients, office location, and a letter from the seller to his patients recommending the buyer's services. A market value that reflects these components is properly treated as marital property. As with businesses, however, care must be taken to exclude value attributable to the seller's post-divorce labors or personal skills. For example, the sale of a medical practice might include the seller's agreement to remain at the office for a transitional period in which patient loyalties were gradually transferred to the buyer. This is a payment for the seller's labor, and if the labor is post-divorce then it is not marital property.

3. _Current State of the Law._   The question of whether a professional practice has goodwill is a mixed question of fact and doctrine. Under any plausible doctrinal treatment, some law practices will have goodwill, and others will not. A successful major big city law firm almost certainly has goodwill: it has a brand name that brings business to its partners that they would not get if they left to practice on their own. Other law firms, especially small ones, may get very little business on the basis of institutional reputation, even though the individual attorneys may attract clients on the basis of their personal skills and reputation. Indeed, even within any one law firm, the appropriate result may differ from attorney to attorney. The institutional goodwill may provide no additional income to the firm's major rainmaker, even though it does for his or her partners.

There has been a gradual increase in the sophistication with which courts have handled goodwill questions. Cases from the early and mid-1980's tended to treat the question of professional goodwill as exclusively one of doctrine, and one commentator writing at that time observed, with respect to valuation of nonmarketable goodwill, that "there appear to be almost as many formulas as there are accountants." Carol Bruch, _The Definition and Division of Marital Property in California: Towards Parity and Simplicity_, 33 Hastings L.J. 769, 811 (1982). Especially in an equal distribution state like California, some may have found advantage in having a marital asset with no objectively determinable value, because it gave courts the freedom to use it as a fudge term allowing them to reach an overall result they think equitable. The same commentator observed that many attorneys have remarked "we know how much the goodwill is worth; it's worth the equity in the house." Bruch, _supra_, at 812. More recent cases generally sort themselves according to whether, like _Hanson_, they will accept only market evidence of goodwill, or whether, like _Dugan_, they will accept evidence based on capitalization of some portion of the professional's earnings. Cases that follow _Hanson_ typically do not consider the possibility that there may be nonmarketable goodwill that nonetheless reflects something other than the professional's personal attributes, while cases that follow _Dugan_ typically do not acknowledge that the methods for valuing goodwill which they allow are likely to treat post-dissolution income arising from the professional's personal attributes or post-dissolution labor as part of goodwill.

Cases adopting _Dugan_'s valuation approach include _Marriage of Hull_, 712 P.2d 1317 (Mont. 1986) (uses same method to determine goodwill of anesthesiology practice); *Marriage of Watts*, 171 Cal. App. 3d 366, 217 Cal. Rptr. 301, 305 (1985) ("the mere fact that a professional practice cannot be sold . . . will not justify a finding that the practice has no goodwill nor that the . . . goodwill has no value"; its value is found by capitalizing the "excess earnings"); *Marriage of Brooks*, 756 P.2d 161, 166 n.10 (Wash. App. 1988) (goodwill of husband's law practice found by capitalizing difference between "reasonable average income" and his income without regard to partnership agreement fixing lower price at which partner can be bought out); *Clark v. Clark*, 782 S.W.2d 56 (Ky. App. 1990) (following *Dugan*); *Porter v. Porter*, 526 N.E.2d 219 (Ind. App. 1988) (medical practice had goodwill despite lack of marketability and partnership agreement excluding goodwill from purchase price); *Molloy v. Molloy*, 761 P.2d 138 (Ariz. App. 1988) (same, with regard to lawyer's practice); *Ford v. Ford*, 782 P.2d 1304 (Nev. 1989) (explicitly rejects *Hanson* and endorses *Dugan*).

Cases which, like *Hanson*, are skeptical of goodwill claims in the absence of saleability include *Thompson v. Thompson*, 576 So. 2d 267, 270 (Fla. 1991) (goodwill is marital property only if it is "separate and distinct from the presence and reputation of the individual attorney"; fair market value is the preferred valuation method); *McCabe v. McCabe*, 575 A.2d 87, 89 (Pa. 1990) ("future income is not marital property because it has not been acquired during the marriage"); *Mocnik v. Mocnik*, 838 P.2d 500, 504 (Okla. 1992) (same); *Depner v. Depner*, 478 So. 2d 532 (La. App. 1985); *Smith v. Smith*, 709 S.W.2d 588 (Tenn. App. 1985); *Taylor v. Taylor*, 386 N.W.2d 851 (Neb. 1986); *Prahinski v. Prahinski*, 540 A.2d 833 (Md. App. 1988); *Antolik v. Harvey*, 761 P.2d 305 (Haw. App. 1988); *Richmond v. Richmond*, 779 P.2d 1211 (Alaska 1989); *Theilen v. Theilen*, 847 S.W.2d 116 (Mo. App. 1992) (husband's dental practice had no goodwill value where the only evidence of value was the capitalization method).

Even courts following *Hanson*, and considering only market data, are sometimes offered wildly varying valuations, presumably because available market data is sparse. *E.g.*, in *Makowski v. Makowski*, 613 So. 2d 924 (Fla. Dist. Ct. App. 1993), the wife's and husband's experts estimates of the market value of the husband's surveying practice were, respectively, $190,000 and $24,197 (the trial court evaluation of $60,000 was affirmed). The scarcity of real data may blur the line between honest efforts at a difficult evaluation, and entirely dishonest ones. *Cf. Carden v. Getzoff*, 190 Cal. App. 3d 907, 235 Cal. Rptr. 698 (1987) (tort claim alleging expert fabricated "comparable" medical practices used to establish value of plaintiff's practice). Perhaps concerned with the scarcity of good data, some courts go further than *Hanson* and hold that professional goodwill is always indistinguishable from earning capacity and is therefore never marital property, in the absence of a sale. *Marriage of Zells*, 572 N.E.2d 944, 945–56 (Ill. 1991) (treating goodwill as divisible marital asset "results in gross inequity"; goodwill is merely "income potential" which is already reflected in support award, rendering further consideration of it "duplicative and improper"); *Powell v. Powell*, 648 P.2d 218, 223 (Kan. 1982) ("[t]he practice is personal to the practitioner"); *Nail v. Nail*, 486 S.W.2d 761, 764 (Tex. 1972) (practice of ophthalmologist is "no more than an expectancy wholly dependent upon the continuation of existing circumstances" and not a marital asset). Even these states recognize, of course, that saleable business goodwill is property. Illinois, for example, has distinguished between "personal goodwill," which is not marital property, and "enterprise goodwill," which is. *Marriage of Talty*, 652 N.E.2d 330, 333 (Ill. 1995) (car dealership may have "enterprise goodwill," but valuation must distinguish that from "personal goodwill" which is not divisible under *Zells*); *Yoon v. Yoon*, 711 N.E.2d 1265 (Ind. 1999); *Solomon v. Solomon*, 611 A.2d 686 (Pa. 1992); *Howell v. Howell*, 523 S.E.2d 514 (Va. Ct. App. 2000); *Moretti v. Moretti*, 766 A.2d 925 (R.I. 2001).

Zells emphasizes, in explaining why it does not treat personal goodwill as property, that double counting would result: because a spouse's future earnings are a primary consideration in fashioning an alimony award, they should not also be treated as property under the rubric of a goodwill measure that reduces future earnings to a present value. *See also Peerenboom v. Peerenboom*, 433 N.W.2d 282, 284 (Wis. Ct. App. 1988) (only marketable goodwill may be divided to ensure its distinction from earning capacity). But another court following the *Dugan* approach rejected this argument against dividing nonmarketable goodwill because "the capitalization of excess earnings method used to value goodwill examines appellant's past earnings, not his future earnings. Thus, there was no double recovery. . . ." *Clark v. Clark*, 782 S.W.2d 56 (Ky. App. 1990). Is this response persuasive? What if one is dealing with a jurisdiction where alimony is rarely awarded (or usually only awarded at modest levels and for a short duration)?

In recent years, courts have continued to be sharply split in their treatment of professional goodwill. *See* J. Thomas Oldham, Divorce Separation and the Distribution of Property 10.03[3] & nn. 59, 107 (2009) (noting that it is no longer clear which view is the majority view). For example, in *Baker v. Baker*, 861 A.2d 298 (Pa. Super. Ct. 2004), the court held that goodwill attributable to the location or customer lists of an established veterinary practice is marital property subject to division; any goodwill attributable to the attributes and skills of the vet was not. By contrast, in *In re Marriage of Schneider*, 824 N.E.2d 177 (Ill. 2005), the Illinois Supreme Court clarified its holding in *Zells* (above) to direct that personal goodwill was *never* to be included in the valuation of a professional practice, as this would be duplicative of the factors the judge should already consider in making an equitable division of property and any award of alimony. *See also Held v. Held*, 912 So. 2d 637 (Fla. Dist. Ct. App. 2005) (following *Hanson* and emphasizing the distinction between "enterprise goodwill," which is subject to equitable distribution, and personal goodwill, which is not); *cf.* Watson v. Watson, 882 So. 2d 95 (Miss. 2004) (distinguishing personal goodwill and enterprise goodwill, but concluding that they are too interwoven in the case of a solo professional practice, and neither should be used in its valuation).

4. *Implications of Allowing Recovery for Professional Goodwill.* If an attorney has "goodwill" value in a practice even though he cannot sell it, what of an author or an artist? Would Agatha Christie have goodwill in her book writing business, or Pablo Picasso in his painting business, that is distinct from earning capacity and thus divisible? While the suggestion may seem amusing, it was not to comedian Joe Piscopo, who was told by a New Jersey appellate court that his talents had created divisible goodwill:

> The trial judge in this case analogized the celebrity goodwill of plaintiff to the professional goodwill of *Dugan*. Plaintiff's record of past earning was

undisputed. It was also undisputed that whatever plaintiff had achieved as a celebrity had taken place during the marriage. While the trial judge recognized that it would be difficult to value plaintiff's celebrity goodwill, that difficulty would not affect its includability in the marital estate.

Piscopo v. Piscopo, 557 A.2d 1040 (N.J. App. Div. 1989). Is there a principled distinction between *Dugan* and *Piscopo*? If not, are they both right or both wrong? For some criticisms of *Piscopo*, see Donahue & Skoloff, *Court Views Celebrity Good Will as Part of Assets in Divorce Case*, NAT'L L.J., Aug. 14, 1989, at 18.

PROBLEMS

Problem 4-11. *W* has a successful business manufacturing a specialty product for the electronics industry. *W* invented the product and her personal reputation makes the product saleable. The business was started with capital that came in part from *H's* parents; the remainder came from funds which *W* had saved out of her salary as an engineer, earned during the first years of the marriage. *H* worked in the business during its early years, as a bookkeeper. He did much of the work at home while also tending the couple's children and keeping house. He never received compensation from the business for this work. For the last several years, a professional bookkeeper has worked for the business.

The couple has been married 20 years. Their children are now 16, 17 and 19. *H* has never held regular employment since their marriage, but he is a high school graduate. *W* reported $130,000 in income last year, but they appear to live at a higher level than that, with frequent traveling, four cars, and a nicely furnished, expensive home. The children have always had summer jobs in the business. You represent *H*. What is your approach?

Problem 4-12. Harry owns and operates a car dealership, which is entirely marital property. At his divorce his wife's expert testifies that the value of the dealership is $2.8 million. Harry's expert testifies to a value of $1.6 million. The difference between them is due entirely to the inclusion by the wife's expert of a value for goodwill of $1.2 million. Harry's annual income from the car dealership varies between $800,000 and $1.2 million. You are representing one of the parties to the divorce. What additional facts do you wish to develop and what arguments can you make concerning valuation of the dealership?

Problem 4-13. Shortly after marrying Joan, John is hired as an Administrative Assistant to the Governor, specializing in legislative liaison. Five years later, he files for divorce and resigns his post. At the time of his resignation, his annual salary is $100,000. After his resignation, he opens a law practice and solicits business as a lobbyist. In his first year as a self-employed lobbyist, he earns $200,000. His new success is known before the divorce decree is entered, and Joan seeks to share in his new wealth. She claims a portion of the goodwill value of John's practice. What is her best argument? What is his best argument? Assume they are in a state in which the accumulation of "marital" or "community" property ends when the divorce petition is filed.

Problem 4-14. Dentist Bridge signs a contract to sell his dental practice. The sales contract specifies a payment to Bridge of $120,000 for the practice itself, and

$450,000 for Bridge's "covenant not to compete," under which he promised to never open a competing dental practice in the same metropolitan area. At the time of the sale Bridge also files for divorce. His wife claims the dental practice as a marital asset, since it was begun during the marriage using only marital funds. What is the value of the practice for marital property purposes?

Problem 4-15. Lawyer Loretta has had a very successful solo practice in the small suburban town where she lives with her husband, earning $400,000 annually, on average. But she's now had enough, and wishes to work less. She hires Associate Alice, an ambitious young lawyer whose work for opposing firms has impressed Loretta. Their understanding is that Loretta will gradually reduce her workload to part-time, as Alice assumes the major share of the lawyering work. A year later Loretta is working half time, and Alice is working long weeks, and both are earning about $250,000 annually. Loretta suggests to Alice that if she continues, Loretta will eventually retire and leave the entire practice to her. With her new found free time, Loretta acquires a boyfriend and files for divorce. Loretta's law practice is marital property. Her husband claims that its value includes an important component of goodwill. What is the appropriate valuation method?

D.   ALIMONY

[1]   History and Historical Justifications

ALI, Principles of the Law of Family Dissolution
23–25 (2002)

Alimony was originally a remedy of the English ecclesiastical courts developed at a time when complete divorce was available only by special legislative action, and gender roles in marriage were rigid and unquestioned. The husband had a legal and customary duty to support his wife. This duty continued after divorce because there was no divorce in the modern sense, but only legal separation. When judicial divorce became available in the 18th and 19th centuries, alimony remained a remedy even though its initial justification — the duty of the husband to support his wife-no longer applied. One explanation was that the duty to support his wife could not be extinguished by the husband's own misconduct. Following that rationale, some jurisdictions allowed alimony claims only by "innocent" wives divorcing "guilty" husbands. Other jurisdictions, focusing on women's financial dependency, in theory allowed claims by guilty wives as well. This view was eventually adopted by the English ecclesiastical courts from their concern that the wife might otherwise "be turned out destitute on the streets or led into temptation," the assumption being that women were limited to domestic skills and could not support themselves by employment. The traditional explanation for alimony was weakened considerably once absolute divorce was allowed, and was undermined completely by modern reforms removing fault from divorce and rejecting gender roles. Yet the financial dependency of wives continued in most marriages. On a practical level a doctrine such as alimony was thus necessary even though the law had no theory to explain it.

Unease over the continuing validity of the traditional rationale for alimony affected decisions early in the modern regime of no-fault divorce. These decisions granted only limited-duration alimony to women who had been homemakers in long-term marriages, and expressed the view that alimony's principal purpose was to provide short-term transitional assistance to such women. The inability to articulate any basis for an indefinite continuation of the husband's support obligation, and the conviction that where possible divorce should effect a "clean break" between the marital partners, combined to push the courts in this direction. The result was buttressed by the expectation that the homemaker would develop marketable skills sufficient to afford her an acceptable living standard, at least when combined with her share in the equitable distribution of their accumulated property, an entitlement which was then relatively new in many common-law states.

But these expectations were often frustrated, and this vision of alimony does not describe the law that one finds today in most appellate opinions. At least in long-term marriages one instead finds a widespread view that marital dissolution should not dissolve all financial ties between the former spouses if the result would be a significant disparity in the spouses' post-dissolution financial standing. However this apparent consensus exists only in very general terms, and has produced no dominant theory to explain the alimony award. The prevailing statutory formulation allows the court to grant alimony (now usually called "spousal support" or "maintenance") to the spouse who is in need. Neither the statutes nor the cases, however, explain why a needy person's former spouse should be liable for his or her support rather than the needy person's parents, children, or society as a whole. The result is that the meaning of "need" — the most fundamental issue created by such statutes — is hopelessly confused. Some opinions find an alimony claimant in "need" only if unable to provide for her basic necessities; others find need if the claimant is unable to support himself at a moderate middle-class level; and still others find need when the claimant is unable to sustain the living standard enjoyed during the marriage even if it was lavish. There can be no principled basis for choosing among these definitions of need without an explanation for imposing the obligation to meet it. In fact, "need" is often used in the law as a conclusory term whose only meaning is that a court has found the spouse entitled to an award of alimony.

It is therefore not surprising that research studies find that trial court decisions on alimony vary widely, even within the same jurisdiction. Some decisional variation would be expected in even a perfect system, because trial courts must have discretion in these matters to deal appropriately with factual variations that no statute can comprehensively anticipate. But it seems clear that the variation arises at least in part because trial courts apply different principles as often as they face different facts. As a consequence, decisions are very difficult to predict. This unpredictability affects the negotiations that settle the great majority of cases.

NOTES

1. *Stereotype Reinforcement.* In *Orr v. Orr*, 440 U.S. 268 (1979), the United States Supreme Court held that Alabama's divorce law, which allowed alimony awards for divorced wives, but not divorced husbands, violated the Equal Protection Clause. Because the alimony applicant had to show "need" in any event (not all divorced wives qualified), Alabama's claim that gender served as a proxy for need could not explain the law. More importantly, the Court rejected Alabama's argument that its public policy of encouraging the traditional family could justify the gender classification. The Court agreed that some permissible purposes could justify gender classifications "substantially related" to them, but held that encouraging traditional family forms was not among them. *Orr* made clear that that the law cannot fashion rules with the purpose of disfavoring couples who choose non-traditional marital roles. The "tender years" doctrine, an older and once common rule for deciding child custody disputes, raises some of the same issues. *See* Chapter 6.

2. *Traditional Statutes.* The Alabama statute invalidated in *Orr* was a typical traditional enactment: it allowed an alimony award to the wife who obtained a divorce based on "the misconduct of the husband" and specified that such an award "must be as liberal as the estate of the husband will permit." On the other hand, it also allowed the court to make no award, and gave the court discretion to make an award to the wife divorced for her own misconduct in an amount "regulated by the ability of the husband and the nature of the misconduct of the wife." The combination of the fault provisions and the general language gave the court wide discretion to make an award of almost any amount or no amount at all.

One traditional consideration, the standard of living during the marriage, remains a common statutory criterion for setting the amount of the award, sometimes as one factor among others, *e.g.*, Model Marriage and Divorce Act § 308, 9A (Part I) U.L.A. 159, 446 (1998 & Supp. 2009), other times as a more fundamental but not invariable benchmark, *e.g.*, Cal. Fam. Code § 4320 (in determining amount of award, court must consider "[t]he extent to which the earning capacity of each party is sufficient to maintain the standard of living established during the marriage"). There are many examples of modern cases that employ this traditional standard in long-term marriages. *Heim v. Heim*, 763 P.2d 678, 683 (Nev. 1988) (35-year marriage; wife allowed more alimony than the $1,500 monthly she asked for, since she is "entitled . . . to live as nearly as fairly possible to the station in life that she enjoyed before the divorce"); *Simmons v. Simmons*, 409 N.E.2d 321, 326–29 (Ill. App. 1980) (court applying statutory language identical to Model Marriage and Divorce Act orders maintenance to childless wife earning $1,750 monthly to allow her to approach marital living standard); *Rosenberg v. Rosenberg*, 595 N.E.2d 792, 793 (Mass. App. 1992) (29-year marriage; in affirming alimony award of $2,000 weekly to wife allocated $5.38 million in property division, court notes "the central objective of alimony is, subject to the availability of resources, maintenance of the more dependent spouse in an economic style close to which the spouse had become accustomed during the marriage"). Clearly, unless the parties have more income after their divorce than they had during their marriage, it will not be possible for both to enjoy the marital living standard once their single household becomes two. In *Marriage of LaRocque*, 406 N.W.2d 736

(Wis. 1987), the court held that the marital living standard is the "goal" of maintenance, and even where beyond reach is a relevant benchmark justifying reversal of smaller awards to the extent the obligor's income allows. Nonetheless, the historic reality is that most alimony awards fall well short of permitting the obligee to maintain the marital living standard. Does that reality reflect an intuition that a different standard is in fact more appropriate? We pursue that question further below.

   3. _Frequency._   One thing to keep in mind in considering the issues relating to alimony is that alimony is awarded in this country infrequently, relative to the number of divorces. It appears that this was equally true during the fault divorce era and since the advent of no-fault. _See, e.g._, BUREAU OF THE CENSUS, CHILD SUPPORT AND ALIMONY: 1985 14 (1987) (nation-wide figure of 14.6%); LENORE J. WEITZMAN, THE DIVORCE REVOLUTION 169 (1985) (in a study of California divorces, the percentage of wives receiving alimony was 18.8% during the fault regime of 1968, 12.9% during the no-fault year of 1972, and 16.5% in 1977).

   It is hard to get current accurate numbers of the current frequency with which alimony is awarded, but one can get some sense of its rarity from the Current Population Survey, http://www.census.gov/hhes/www/income/incomestats.html. In 2006, there were 9,621,000 divorced women, 18 years or older (Table PINC-02, Part 49). However, among individuals (male or female) 15 years or older, only 382,000 were receiving alimony income (PINC-08, Part 190).

   In considering this data, one must, of course, take into account the mismatch in the groups (though there are probably not a large number of 15–17 year-olds receiving alimony, and men get only a trivial percentage of the alimony granted — the 1998 Census showed 8,000 men receiving alimony income to 158,000 women), as well as the fact that some alimony obligors may not be paying (thus not creating alimony income), that the recipients' self-reporting of alimony income might be inaccurate, and, of course, a significant percentage of alimony obligations are temporary (thus terminating after a term of years), or, even if "permanent," may have terminated due to remarriage of the recipient, significant reduction in the obligor's means or significant increase in the means of the recipient.

   On the other hand, the low figures for frequency of alimony may be misleading in a quite different way. On the approaches recommended by many commentators and applied by most courts, alimony is not appropriate where the marriage was short-lived (Texas precludes alimony, in all but exceptional circumstances, where the marriage did not last 10 years, TEX. FAM. CODE § 8.051(2)), where neither partner has significant assets or income, or whether both partners have comparable levels of assets and income. As indicated by later discussions, the rate of alimony is inevitably higher for longer marriages and marriages with children. (It is also important to note that where the financial provisions are determined by party agreement, as occurs in the vast majority of divorces, a spouse might "trade off" alimony for a larger share of the property or higher child support payments.) Perhaps alimony is awarded in a significant portion of the divorce situations where it is "appropriate," given general criteria, but these are only a small fraction of divorces filed every year.

[2] The Struggle for a Modern Rationale

MODEL MARRIAGE AND DIVORCE ACT

§ 308. [Maintenance.]

(a) In a proceeding for dissolution of marriage, legal separation, or maintenance following a decree of dissolution of the marriage by a court which lacked personal jurisdiction over the absent spouse, the court may grant a maintenance order for either spouse only if it finds that the spouse seeking maintenance:

(1) lacks sufficient property to provide for his reasonable needs; and

(2) is unable to support himself through appropriate employment or is the custodian of a child whose condition or circumstances make it appropriate that the custodian not be required to seek employment outside the home.

(b) The maintenance order shall be in amounts and for periods of time the court deems just, without regard to marital misconduct, and after considering all relevant factors including:

(1) the financial resources of the party seeking maintenance, including marital property apportioned to him, his ability to meet his needs independently, and the extent to which a provision for support of a child living with the party includes a sum for that party as custodian;

(2) the time necessary to acquire sufficient education or training to enable the party seeking maintenance to find appropriate employment;

(3) the standard of living established during the marriage;

(4) the duration of the marriage;

(5) the age and the physical and emotional condition of the spouse seeking maintenance; and

(6) the ability of the spouse from whom maintenance is sought to meet his needs while meeting those of the spouse seeking maintenance.

NOTE: GENDER PATTERNS IN ALIMONY CLAIMS

Although all modern alimony statutes are gender-neutral, alimony awards go disproportionately to women, at least in part because wives make alimony claims far more often than husbands. That is hardly surprising in light of the fact that women remain far more likely to be economically dependent on their spouse. ("According to the U.S. Census Bureau's March 2002 Current Population Survey, among two-parent households, there were 189,000 children with stay-at-home dads [compared with] 11 million children with stay-at-home moms. . . ." Kemba J. Dunham, *Stay-at-Home Dads Fight Stigma*, WALL ST. J., Aug. 26, 2003.) Nonetheless, the picture is gradually changing. The extent of the change is summarized in the articles and notes given in Chapter 1, Section C.

The gendered factual background of alimony claims undoubtedly affects the way men and women think about the appropriate rules. Men are much more likely to think of themselves as potential obligors; women as potential obligees. It may also suggest that the formal gender neutrality of the governing law may mask possibly relevant facts. Consider: if we react differently to claims by men than by women, is that because we are making different assumptions about the stories that lie behind their claims? If so, those assumptions need be made more overt, and their relevance assessed.

One thing that is clear is that, on average, divorce affects men and women differently. What are the differences in financial impact? The next note explores that question.

NOTE: THE DEBATE OVER DIFFERENCES IN THE FINANCIAL IMPACT OF DIVORCE ON MEN AND WOMEN

Do modern divorce laws leave women worse off financially than men? The perception that they do is largely traceable to the extraordinary impact of a book, Lenore Weitzman's 1985 publication, THE DIVORCE REVOLUTION. Her thesis was that the shift to no-fault divorce robbed financially dependent women of bargaining leverage with husbands who abandoned them. In making this case, she captured attention largely through data showing dramatic differences between the post-divorce standard of living of men and women. We defer until Section G the specific question of whether *no-fault rules* are the source of any inequity, as that section addresses more generally the question of whether courts should consider marital misconduct in alimony and property adjudications. Here we look at two more fundamental questions: a) what do we know about the post-divorce finances of men and women, and b) are the disparities that surely exist a consequence of inequitable *divorce laws* (as compared to other possible sources of inequity). Men and women historically entered marriage with different earnings histories and different earnings prospects. They usually leave marriage the same way. Divorce laws may or may not enlarge or contribute to that result, and to observe a difference is not necessarily to establish that it is inequitable. Just what financial arrangements the law should require at divorce is of course the central question of this entire chapter. So while this note raises some important questions of equity, it does not conclude them. We continue to address them throughout this chapter and into others, such as Chapter Five's discussion of the appropriate levels of child support. But we turn first to the facts, and to the controversy over Weitzman's data.

[a]   The Weitzman Data on the Gender Impact of Divorce

Weitzman's dramatic claims were first made in her 1981 article, *The Economics of Divorce: Social and Economic Consequences of Property, Alimony and Child Support Awards*, 28 UCLA L. REV. 1181, 1249–53 (1981) (reprinted in THE DIVORCE REVOLUTION, at 337–43). She claimed that data from a sample of divorced California families showed that one year after divorce men experienced a 42% improvement in their post-divorce standard of living, while women experienced a 73% loss. This bleak picture was widely reported. Weitzman's percentages on the spouses' relative standard of living was quoted often in publications ranging from serious academic articles to Dear Abby, often with erroneous attribution to official government studies which had themselves merely quoted Weitzman. However, after years of challenge by other researchers, Weitzman ultimately conceded that her published data were wrong, as explained below.

In fact, there were many other studies of this question both before and after Weitzman's, and all found a significant gender gap in the financial consequences of divorce. However, those studies all found that wives' post-divorce decline in living standard was about 30%, rather than the 73% Weitzman claimed. Greg J. Duncan & Saul D. Hoffman, *A Reconsideration of the Economic Consequences of Divorce*, 22 DEMOGRAPHY 485 (1985); Robert S. Weiss, *The Impact of Marital Dissolution on Income and Consumption in Single-Parent Households*, 46 J. MARRIAGE & FAMILY 115 (1984). These other studies received much less attention than Weitzman's, undoubtedly because their numbers and conclusions were less dramatic, but are today regarded as more accurate. The debate that led to this conclusion is worth review here, both because the truth of the matter is important to family law policy, and because it provides an important lesson in why those interested in family law policy must be sophisticated consumers of the social science data often offered in these policy debates.

The first step in understanding this debate is to be clear that the effect that all researchers sought to measure was the change after divorce in the spouses' standard of living, not in their income. The two are not the same. Weitzman never claimed, for example, that the average husband's income increased by 42% in the year after divorce, nor would such a figure be plausible. His standard of living would increase, however, if his income remained relatively constant while his needs declined. Why might needs decline? The most obvious reason would be a decline in family size. In fact, the needs of both husbands' and wives' *households* typically decline after divorce, if they do not remarry, because their household size declines. If, for example, we assume that the pre-divorce family consisted of husband, wife and two minor children, then the post-divorce family size of a noncustodial husband is one, a reduction of three, and the post-divorce family size of a custodial wife is three, a reduction of one. Either post-divorce family can maintain the same standard of living that it enjoyed pre-divorce with a lower income than the pre-divorce family had, although of course the family of three will need more to maintain that standard than would a family of one. If the incomes of custodial mothers and their former husbands are, say, equal after taking account of alimony and child support payments, their standards of living will not be. It is this reality which Weitzman and other researchers seek to capture by comparing standards of living rather than income. There are a variety of methods for comparing the living standards of households of different size, and opinions vary among economists about their relative virtues; all have flaws. We will look at some of the problems below. But this was not the reason why Weitzman's figures were different than that of others, because her choice of method was not different than theirs. The problem with her published results appeared to be logistical rather than conceptual: as ultimately demonstrated by Richard Peterson, one simply could not derive her published results from her raw data. Richard D. Peterson, *A Revolution of the Economic Consequences of Divorce*, 61 AM. SOC. REV. 528 (1996). The explanation for this discrepancy is still not known for certain, but in response to Peterson,

Weitzman conceded the problem, and blamed errors by her computer staff. Weitzman, *The Economic Consequences of Divorce Are Still Unequal: Comment On Peterson*, 61 AM. SOC. REV. 537 (1996). Peterson's own analysis of Weitzman's raw data showed a 27% drop in wives' post-divorce living standards, very close to the figure obtained by the other researchers, and a ten percent average increase in their husband's living standards, also consistent with other sources.

There are some general lessons to be learned from this small bit of social science history. Perhaps the most important is that the attention social scientists receive for their work is often more proportional to the dramatic impact of its claims than to the soundness of its methodology. The fame of a piece of research cannot be taken as a proxy for its quality. Any serious effort to look to social science sources for policy guidance requires a reasonably comprehensive and methodologically informed review of the relevant literature.

[b]   Beyond Weitzman: Assessing the Gender Impact of Divorce

As Peterson says, nearly all researchers in the field find an average post-divorce decline of about 30 % in wives' living standards. He also suggests that the ten percent average increase in husbands' living standard shown by a correct analysis of Weitzman's data is consistent with other sources. Let us assume these figures are correct. Are not these results sufficiently disparate to suggest an important inequity?

Perhaps. Whatever the raw figures, their policy implications require some interpretation: Do the figures capture the full financial picture of the spouses? Is the financial picture they paint long-term or merely transitional? Are there nonfinancial factors that also must be taken into account in assessing the relative fairness of the outcome? To what extent is the divorce law a cause of the disparate financial picture? These are important questions to ask if one wants to move from the data to the making of legal policy. In fact, much of the literature attacked Weitzman's conclusions on these grounds, rather than attacking the figures themselves. *See, e.g.*, Herbert Jacob, *Faulting No-Fault*, 1986 A.B.F. RES. J. 773; Herbert Jacob, *Another Look at No-Fault Divorce and the Post Divorce Finances of Women*, 23 LAW & SOC. REV. 95 (1989); Jed H. Abraham, *"The Divorce Revolution" Revisited: A Counter-Revolutionary Critique*, 9 N. ILL. U.L. REV. 251 (1989). Some of the most interesting criticisms, from a policy standpoint, are made in Stephen D. Sugarman, *Dividing Financial Interests at Divorce*, in S. Sugarman & H. Kay, eds., DIVORCE REFORM AT THE CROSSROADS 130–259 (1990). While Weitzman's own numbers are no longer on the table, the points made in this literature are still important to consider.

1. Do the Cost of Living Figures Reflect the Parties' Complete Financial Situation? A problem could arise if the calculations were based upon assessments of what is required to maintain a particular standard of living that left out or undercounted expenses that did not affect men and women equally. There is at least one possible example of importance: taxes. Researchers in this area generally base their assessments of comparative living standards on the parties' gross income (before taxes). If the parties are paying roughly equivalent portions of their income in taxes, then the choice between gross and net income does not matter. But several tax rules combine to suggest that noncustodial fathers pay a higher proportion of their income in taxes than do custodial mothers. The child support obligor must typically pay taxes on the portion of his income that is paid out in child support, while the obligee does not count child support received as part of taxable income. (This point does not matter, of course, to the obligee who in fact receives no child support. But to the extent one wishes to use this data in choosing a policy for deciding upon the appropriate size of child support or other required spousal income transfers, the point is quite relevant.) The custodial parent may also benefit from child care credits, the lower tax rate accorded heads of households, and the tax credit for low earners. One researcher has tentatively concluded that these and other tax factors compress the standard of living differences between the typical custodial mother and non-custodial father sufficiently to eliminate most of them. Sanford L. Braver, *The Gender Gap in Standard of Living After Divorce: Vanishingly Small?*, 33 FAM. L.Q. 111 (1999). Difficult methodological issues, however, ensure that this study is not the final word.

2. What is the Long-Term Financial Situation of Men and Women After Divorce? At what point should the comparison be made? Weitzman took a single snapshot at one year after divorce. Compare a study by Duncan and Hoffman that looked at the economic situation five years after divorce. By then divorced wives who were still single had a living standard that was on average about 94% of the standard they enjoyed in the year before divorce — a 6% decline in living standard, rather than the 30% decline that nearly all researchers find after one year. Greg J. Duncan & Saul D. Hoffman, *Economic Consequences of Marital Instability*, in M. David & T. Smeeding, HORIZONTAL EQUITY, UNCERTAINTY, AND ECONOMIC WELL-BEING 427, 437 (1985). Similar conclusions are suggested by the 1992–93 National Survey of Families and Households, which asked women who had split from their husband since the prior survey, taken in 1987–88, how their finances compared to their situation during the marriage. Forty-three percent said their finances were better than during their marriage, while only 40% said they were worse. Frank Furstenberg, *The Future of Marriage*, AMERICAN DEMOGRAPHICS, June 1996, at 36–37. Perhaps, then, the problem uncovered by the one-year data is more a problem of transition, requiring different remedies than would be required to correct a long-term difficulty.

3. Should We Consider Remarriage? The parties' post-divorce economic status will be affected by whether they remarry; remarriage may be the most important change that is captured by extending the comparison past the first year after divorce. Only four to six percent of the women in Weitzman's sample had remarried in the year after divorce, Weitzman, *supra*, at 328, 333. Andrew Cherlin's important study concludes that about two-thirds of divorced women eventually remarry, and that a significant portion of the remainder enter a nonmarital union. A. CHERLIN, MARRIAGE, DIVORCE, REMARRIAGE 28 (revised ed., 1992). Duncan and Hoffman's five year followup study, noted above, found that divorced women who had remarried on average enjoyed a living standard five years after divorce that was 25% *greater* than in the last year of their prior marriage. Duncan & Hoffman, *supra*, at 437.

4. Should the Gender Comparison Include Non-Financial Factors? Some argue that if non-financial factors are weighed in the balance, a different impression is given of the comparative outcomes for men and women. Weitzman herself found that women as well as men report a rise in "competence and self esteem" in the first year after divorce. Weitzman, *supra*, at 345. Indeed, in most of the non-financial post-divorce measures she took, women fare better than men; a larger percentage "feel better about themselves," consider themselves "more competent in their work," feel "more physically attractive" and "possessed of better parenting skills" than during the marriage. *Id.* at 345–46. Data from the 1992–93 National Survey of Families and Households suggest the same result. The survey asked women who had split from their husband since the 1987–88 survey to compare their situation in several non-financial respects: Seventy-seven percent said they were happier than during their marriage, 65% said their home life had improved, 57% said their social life had improved, and 55% said their parenting had improved. Frank Furstenberg, *The Future of Marriage*, AMERICAN DEMOGRAPHICS, June 1996, at 36–37. Sugarman argues that custodial arrangements are the most important omitted consideration: "[W]here women have physical custody of the children and men feel that they have, as a result, lost something terribly important to them, it is deeply troubling to compare the former spouses' living standards in terms that treat the children solely as a liability." Sugarman, *supra*, at 151. (Children are a "liability" in standard of living comparisons because their presence in the household increases "need," and thus results in a lower percentage of "need" being met at a given level of income.)

These points perhaps explain why, despite women's relatively worse financial situation, a 1985 poll found that 85% of divorced or separated women say that they are happier since the dissolution of their marriage, while only 58% of men so report. Harper's Index, HARPER'S MAGAZINE, Nov. 1985 at 15 (reporting on poll conducted for USA TODAY). It may also explain why, roughly two thirds of the time, it is the wife who instigates the separation or divorce. Braver, Whitley, & Ng, *Who Divorced Whom? Methodological and Theoretical Issues*, 20 J. DIVORCE & REMARRIAGE 1 (1993); *cf.* Margaret F. Brinig & Douglas W. Allen, *"These Boots are Made for Walking": Why Most Divorce Filers are Women*, 2 AM. J. L. & ECON. 126 (2000) (arguing higher filing rates for wives is due to desire to obtain child custody). Of course, the fact that women are happier after divorce does not of itself demonstrate that the divorce process treated them fairly. If their marriage was oppressive enough, then even an unfair divorce settlement could be an improvement in their lives. Another approach to getting at the question is to ask divorcing parties whether they believe they were treated fairly in the divorce process. Such inquiries give mixed results. A study of couples divorcing in Maricopa County (Phoenix) in 1986, with at least one child fifteen or less, found that one year after divorce wives reported themselves significantly more satisfied than did husbands with the custody, visitation, property division, and "other financial provisions" of their divorce decree (defined as everything other than child support and property division). But interviewed again three years after divorce, the wives now were significantly less satisfied than their former husbands with the financial terms of the divorce, while their greater satisfaction than men with the custody and visitation terms remained — and indeed, the satisfaction gap between them on this measure had increased. V. L. Sheets & S. L. Braver, *Gender Differences in Satisfaction with Divorce Settlements*, 45 FAMILY RELATIONS 336–342

(1996). While such data certainly suggest that a different picture is painted if one looks at the entire situation rather than at the financial issues alone, it does not resolve the more difficult policy question of deciding upon the significance of this comparison.

This discussion can hardly resolve the question of whether existing divorce law or practice contains a systematic gender bias. It does provide a background against which to consider the principal question addressed in the remainder of this chapter: what constitutes a fair law of alimony?

NOTE: THE ALIMONY PUZZLE

The Model Marriage and Divorce Act sought to establish the convention, as the no-fault era began, that alimony would be a short-term remedy, based on "need," and awarded without regard to fault. There is currently a fairly wide consensus that it is appropriate to impose an alimony obligation of some length at the dissolution of a long-term marriage when the parties would otherwise have very disparate living standards. The basis of that obligation remains unclear, however, with the consequence that the consensus rapidly disappears as the facts vary or more detailed questions are put. (How much of the disparity should be eliminated? For how long should the award continue?) In fact, if alimony cannot be based on gender roles, nor limited to cases in which it can be justified by the obligor's fault for ending the marriage, it is not so easy to explain its basis. That is the modern alimony puzzle to which we now turn.

People often develop a view on alimony with some particular fact pattern in mind. That is not necessarily a bad way to start, but any set of principles must deal with many fact patterns. To test your own intuitions on this difficult problem, you might want to keep in mind the following hypotheticals, and ask yourself: should there be an alimony award in this case? Why or why not? What principle am I following, and is it consistent with my treatment of the other hypotheticals? And you might do the mind experiment of posing these same questions to the authors of materials excerpted below, as you read them.

a. *The classic case.* Alice and Barry (both 48) divorce after 23 years of marriage. Alice has been a homemaker and also worked part time. Their children are now grown and Alice is available for full time work although she has not done it since she was much younger and would not have planned on returning to full time work but for the divorce. Barry, who always worked full time during the marriage, earns $90,000 annually. Alice's current earning potential as a retail clerk, her best prospect for full time work, is about $40,000 annually. The parties' net assets at divorce, about $80,000 in home equity and savings, have been divided equally.

b. *The classic case, professional version.* Lionel and Anne met in law school, and married in their third year. They both obtained desirable law firm jobs after graduation. After their first child was born in the fourth year of their marriage, Anne took a year's maternity leave. She returned to the firm on a part time "mommy track." When their second child was born two years later, she left the firm altogether. After their younger child turned four, Anne began regular volunteer work with a local public interest firm. By the time the children were both in school, her volunteer work turned into a half time position. After fifteen years of marriage, the parties seek divorce. The children are eleven and eight. Anne earns $30,000 annually in her half-time position, which the public interest firm has offered to convert to full time at twice the pay. She likes the work and has no desire to seek more lucrative employment at private firms, although she probably could obtain such work because of her litigation experience. Lionel remained at his original firm, made partner, and at divorce is earning $300,000 annually.

c. *The role reversal case.* Carl and Denise are in the same situation as Alice and Barry, except that Carl was the homemaker and Denise earns $90,000 annually. This was not the couple's original plan when they married. Carl had dreams of becoming a novelist, and wrote while also doing odd jobs to generate some income. Denise, who had no similar aspirations, began work as an administrative assistant in a business office, thinking that this would be a suitable temporary post until Carl's career developed. Over time, however, Denise's quiet competence and reliability won her promotions to her current executive position. Over the same period, Carl's writing ambitions, repeatedly frustrated by publisher's rejections, faded. So the parties slid into a pattern in which Denise was the primary breadwinner while Carl was the homemaker, who stayed home with the couple's two children, who are now grown.

d. *The classic case with further facts, No. 1.* Alice and Barry grew apart over the last ten years of their marriage. Barry developed a friendship with a coworker which eventually developed into a romantic relationship. Once the children were grown, he decided it was time to end the marriage so that he could begin a new life with a new spouse. Alice was not surprised at this development, as she was fully aware that the mutual affection she and Barry once had for one another had left their marriage. But while she is not emotionally crushed by this development, neither is she happy about it, as she has no potential new mate.

e. *The classic case with further facts, No. 2.* Same as Version D, except that it is Alice rather than Barry who develops a new relationship, with an attorney for whom she did some part time office work. She therefore initiates divorce proceedings. During those proceedings, however, Alice and the attorney end their relationship. With no plans to remarry after the divorce, Alice requests alimony.

f. *The role reversal case with further facts, No. 1.* Over the last ten years of their marriage, Denise has become increasingly impatient with Carl, whom she realizes is a loser. She contrasts her own ability to develop job skills and ambition, as the circumstances required, with Carl's inability to reorient and develop another useful and remunerative skill once it became clear his writing career would not work out. She feels Carl, a college graduate, could have done more to develop his life once the children were older and more independent. When she begins to develop an enjoyable social relationship with an executive at another firm with whom she deals, she concludes her marriage is empty and should be ended. She therefore files for divorce.

g. *The role reversal case with further facts, No. 2.* Carl, feeling unappreciated by Denise and insecure in his own self-image, takes refuge in a relationship he develops with a woman neighbor who is usually home during the day. With her encouragement, he starts writing again. Feeling he can begin his life over with her, he files for divorce. Knowing that the neighbor's earning capacity is limited and that his own earning prospects from writing are speculative at best, Carl seeks an alimony award.

[3]   Why do we have Alimony?

CLAPP v. CLAPP
Vermont Supreme Court
653 A.2d 72 (1994)

DOOLEY, JUSTICE.

Michael Clapp appeals a decision . . . in the divorce action between him and his former wife, Elizabeth Clapp, challenging both property and maintenance orders contained therein. . . .

The parties were married in 1967 following [Michael]'s first year of law school. When [Michael] graduated in 1969, the parties returned to Vermont and he began his legal practice that continues. . . . The parties' son was born in 1970 and their daughter in 1972. [Elizabeth] remained home to care for the children full time until 1975, at which time she began pursuing her master's degree in education. In 1977, having received her degree, [Elizabeth] began work as a junior high school guidance counselor. In 1981, she became a high school guidance counselor and has continued in that job. . . . In 1987, after twenty years of marriage, the parties separated. [Elizabeth] filed for divorce in 1989. In 1991, her annual income before taxes was $45,237; [Michael]'s annual income before taxes was $137,600.

The parties were divorced by final order . . . entered in February 1993. At that time, both parties were forty-eight years old. The court found that the parties' assets totaled $1,257,577, and their liabilities $498,773. Finding that the merits of the situation favored [Elizabeth] wife slightly, the court ordered the parties' assets to be split 60% to wife and 40% to husband. In so decreeing, the court awarded each spouse the respective homes, but required that both homes be sold and the equity divided 60/40.

The court ordered [Michael] to pay maintenance and set the amount temporarily at $2,000 per month. Thereafter, it required a calculation of maintenance based on an equalization of the parties' after-tax income from June 1987 to the date of the divorce. This maintenance amount had not been calculated at the time of the appeal, and the parties had widely divergent claims about the result of the calculation. [Elizabeth claimed the correct amount was $4,333.33 per month; Michael claimed it was either $2,460 or $2,720 per month.] Once calculated, the base maintenance amount would be adjusted annually based on . . . the Consumer Price Index.

. . . .

[Michael] argues any maintenance award cannot exceed the amount necessary to enable the obligee to meet her reasonable needs. [He argues that the family court improperly exceeded this amount] in order to compensate [Elizabeth] for past contributions as a homemaker [but that] the statute does not allow for restitutionary or compensatory awards.

Much of [Michael]'s argument is based on the statutory language, which provides:

§ 752. Maintenance

(a) In an action under this chapter, the court may order either spouse to make maintenance payments, either rehabilitative or permanent in nature, to the other spouse if it finds that the spouse seeking maintenance:

(1) lacks sufficient income, property, or both, including property apportioned . . . , to provide for his or her reasonable needs, and

(2) is unable to support himself or herself through appropriate employment at the standard of living established during the marriage or is the custodian of a child of the parties.

The argument specifically emphasizes § 752(a)(1) which requires a threshold finding that the prospective obligee lacks income or property to meet "reasonable needs." In [Michael]'s view, the court must first determine reasonable need without regard to the income available during the marriage, or the obligor's current income, and award maintenance only if this need is not met by the obligee's nonmaintenance income and property. [¶] [Michael]'s argument involves an overly narrow reading of § 752(a)(1). The statute is based on a concept of relative, not absolute, need. [The] court can award maintenance even though the wife is meeting her needs through employment where [a] vast inequality in [the] parties' financial position remains. [R]easonable need is not to be judged in relation to subsistence [but] "in light of the standard of living established during the marriage." [T]he term "reasonable needs" allow[s] the court "to balance equities whenever the financial contributions of one spouse enable the other spouse to enhance his or her future earning capacity." [O]ne purpose of maintenance under § 752(a) is to compensate a homemaker for contributions to family well-being not otherwise recognized in the property distribution.

We do not have to plunge deeply into the detail of [Elizabeth]'s post-separation needs to affirm the award of maintenance in this case. According to the findings, the parties were living on an after-tax income of approximately $130,000 per year and spending most of it. Of this, about $33,000 is attributable to [Elizabeth]. Both parties had attained maximum vocational skills and employability. [Michael]'s earning capacity should, however, grow at a faster rate as he approaches retirement. [¶] [Elizabeth] would not maintain the standard of living realized during the marriage on her share of the marital income. . . . In light of the standard of living of the parties, the court acted within its discretion in awarding maintenance in this case.

[Michael] attacks the amount of maintenance awarded. [T]he court found that the deficit in [Elizabeth]'s income to pay expenses amounted to about $1,000 per month. It also recognized that [Elizabeth] had made a significant nonmonetary contribution to the marriage as a homemaker, and had reduced her earnings over the years because of this contribution. For the dual purpose of avoiding "an adverse economic impact upon [Elizabeth]" and compensating her for her nonmonetary contributions during the marriage, the court ordered such permanent maintenance as would equalize after-tax income, as calculated over the period from the date of separation to the date of divorce. . . . The amount is not adjusted on a regular basis because of changes in either party's income, although it is adjusted for inflation.

[T]he family court has broad discretion in determining the amount of maintenance, and we will reverse only if there is no reasonable basis to support the award. In determining the amount of maintenance to award, the court must consider all relevant factors, including seven statutory factors. [Similar to Section 308(b) of the Model Act, excerpted above.] Most of the statutory factors figured into the family court's decision, including the ability of the obligee to meet her needs without maintenance, the standard of living established during the marriage, the duration of the marriage, the age and physical and emotional condition of each spouse, and the ability of the obligor to meet reasonable needs while paying maintenance. The award was tailored to maintain for [Elizabeth] the standard of living during the marriage. This objective was supported by the length of the marriage, twenty-five years. It is also supported in this lengthy marriage by the need to compensate [Elizabeth] for homemaker contributions to family well-being not otherwise recognized in the financial awards.

It is important to recognize the difference between the income equalization approach of this award and the approach we rejected in *Delozier*. In *Delozier*, the income equalization award was prospective and permanent so each spouse was to receive half of their joint income for the remainder of their lives. On facts somewhat similar to those here, . . . we held that permanent income equalization may "wind up being punitive rather than compensatory." *Delozier*, 640 A.2d at 60.

Here, income equalization was used as a method to calculate an appropriate monthly maintenance award, but the amount of the award will not change in the future because of changes in the income of either of the parties. In light of the court's conclusion that the gap between the income of the parties would grow over time, this award equalized income for only a year, with [Michael] keeping an increasing share of the combined income in the future. We believe the award equalized income for "an appropriate period of time". . . .

Need here should also be viewed in relation to the standard of living established during the marriage, another statutory factor. The main objective of the award was to maintain that standard of living for [Elizabeth].

[Also] restitution for past homemaker contributions is a basis [for alimony we] explicitly recognized in *Klein*, 555 A.2d at 387. We see no reason to abandon that recognition here. [Michael] claims that consideration of this factor was not warranted because there was no evidence of the extent of the contribution. The court found that [Elizabeth] delayed her education and entry into the job market in order to raise the parties' children while they were infants. Thereafter, the parties jointly decided that [Elizabeth] should work in a school system, rather than in other employment with higher remuneration, in order to care for the children and manage the home. This also enabled her to stay in the home during the summer. In comparison, [Michael] consistently put in night and weekend hours at his law office.

Homemaker contributions are, by their nature, nonmonetary so they cannot be quantified or put into a monetary formula to specify their impact on the ultimate maintenance award. The court's characterization of these contributions as "significant . . . over many years" is probably as specific as is possible. . . . [¶] [T]he family court acted within its discretion in awarding permanent maintenance to [Elizabeth], and the amount is also within its discretion.

[The trial court had also ordered Michael to sell a lakefront home he had purchased as his separate property for $415,000, because his mortgage payments made it impossible for him to meet his maintenance payments. Michael argued that the court could not order sale of property in which there was no marital equity.] In our view, this is a distinction without a controlling difference. Just as the house in which [Elizabeth] resides is being sold to give [Michael] his interest in it, [Michael]'s house is being sold to give [Elizabeth] her interest in his income, an interest that cannot realistically exist as long as so much of the income is diverted to a house payment.[4]

. . . .

MARRIAGE OF WILSON
California Court of Appeal
247 Cal. Rptr. 522 (1988)

HADEN, J.

Elma Wilson appeals an order terminating her spousal support after 58 months following a 70 month marriage. Having found her permanently disabled and her former husband able to pay continued support, the trial court weighed the length and nature of the marriage, and the duration of spousal support payments and ruled husband no longer had the legal obligation to support his former spouse. We affirm.

Factual and Procedural Background

Thomas and Elma Wilson (Tom and Elma) were married in May 1976 and separated in March 1982, after 70 months. Elma was injured in a fall two years before separation. As a result of her injuries or subsequent infection following dental work, she could no longer work as a bartender. In 1983 her doctor believed her neurologic deficit would remain permanent but recommended some rehabilitation to enable her to pursue work which would not require verbalization. A clinical psychologist opined Elma suffered brain damage which left her "lacking in social judgment, common sense, and social intelligence." The psychologist felt Elma would probably not succeed where she had to make decisions using common sense.

---

[4] After the divorce, [Michael] can, of course, purchase any property he desires, and the new property will not fall within the jurisdiction of the family court under 15 V.S.A. § 751(a). Any new mortgage lender will, however, be aware of [Michael]'s outstanding obligation to pay maintenance in determining whether [Michael]'s income is adequate to meet his mortgage payments.

In the November 1983 stipulated interlocutory judgment, Tom received, inter alia, his Navy pension and a Volkswagen while Elma took the house, a Jaguar automobile, and spousal support of $500 per month for two years plus medical insurance coverage for the same period.

In September 1985 Elma sought continued spousal support. She anticipated further brain surgery in one to two years. The same clinical psychologist reexamined her and concluded "[i]t appears unlikely that Mrs. Wilson could succeed in today's competitive job market. . . . [S]he would have difficulty with any job that required an intellectual component that was above the mildly mentally retarded level." The psychologist further stated, "[I]t appears doubtful that Mrs. Wilson is able to profit from training that could lead to employment." In December 1985 the trial court extended the $500 per month spousal support for one year. After considering Elma's serious physical problems, the court went on to explain this was not a lengthy marriage, there were no children born of the marriage, and the ages of the parties at the time of the marriage indicated they had established their lives before they married. In April 1986 the court temporarily reduced support to $350 per month when Tom was unemployed.

In September 1986 Elma once again sought continuing spousal support, claiming she was still unemployed and neither rehabilitated nor capable of rehabilitation. She continued to receive $436 per month in social security benefits. She noted her daughter and son-in-law had been living with her since May 1986 and he began earning $5.00 per hour in September 1986 but was unemployed by the December 1986 hearing. Her daughter was in rehabilitation for injuries suffered in an automobile accident. In October 1986 Tom declared he earned over $2,200 per month in salary plus over $1,000 in Navy retirement.

At a hearing on the support issue in December 1986 Tom argued Elma should not be entitled to lifetime support from him based on a 70-month marriage. The court found Tom, age 46, had the earning capacity to continue to make support payments and Elma, age 48, had a need for such payments because she was both disabled and could not regain her previous income earning status. The court considered the length of the marriage (70 months) and the length of the spousal support period (58 months). The court then stated, "My question . . . that I'm faced with is at what point in time does the obligation to assist Mrs. Wilson become one of society's as distinguished from an obligation that is Mr. Wilson's, and I find that it is society's at this point in time." The court continued support for four months and then terminated it.

Discussion

I

A promise to "love, honor and cherish as long as we both shall live" is in fact easily and frequently revocable today. It is lamentable that many decide to live together without benefit of such vows and many who take them soon forget them. However, we are concerned here with legal, not moral, obligations. We are asked to decide whether following a childless marriage of short duration it was an abuse of discretion to terminate spousal support even though the supported spouse was permanently disabled.

II

Civil Code section 4801 provides for spousal support in any amount and for any period just and reasonable, provided the trial court in making the award considers all of the [eight factors specified]. . . . The record reflects the trial court weighed each of these eight factors before exercising discretion to terminate support. Tom had the earning capacity to continue to make support payments. Elma had virtually no marketable skills and could not regain her previous income. This was not a marriage in which Elma's earning capacity was impaired by unemployment incurred to permit her to attend to domestic duties. The parties were in their forties when they married and, the court noted, had already established their lives. There were no children of this marriage. There was no evidence Elma had contributed to the attainment of Tom's career. His military career must have been completed or substantially completed when the couple married. Elma had a need for support because she was disabled, the court balanced the equities and decided under these circumstances the obligation to assist Elma should shift from Tom to society.

. . . .

Elma contends it was an abuse of discretion to terminate spousal support where there was no present evidence of her ability to be self-supporting. . . . Specifically, Elma argues the trial court failed to comply with *In re Marriage of Morrison* (1978) 20 Cal. 3d 437 [143 Cal. Rptr. 139, 573 P.2d 41]. . . . *Morrison*, however, concerned a lengthy marriage of 28 years during which wife at husband's insistence devoted her time principally to maintaining the home and raising two children. In this context a trial court should . . . retain jurisdiction over support unless the record indicates the supported spouse will be able adequately to meet his or her financial needs at the time of termination. [But] *Morrison* need not apply here.

. . . .

The order is affirmed.

Todd, Acting P. J., and Benke, J., concurred.

NOTES

1. *Problematic Rationales for Alimony: Need.* The wife in *Clapp* leaves the marriage at the age of 48 with no dependents (the parties' children being grown), a share of the marital property worth about $455,000 (60% of the total marital equity), and an apparently secure job paying $45,000 annually. The court concludes that she also qualifies for a substantial and permanent alimony award, with automatic adjustments for inflation. The wife in *Wilson* leaves her marriage substantially disabled and dependent for her basic needs upon charity or public assistance. The court concludes that her modest alimony award must expire after a fixed-term of around five years. *Clapp* was decided under a statute whose basic

terms closely track the Model Marriage and Divorce Act — an Act that established "need" as the announced basis for alimony in the no-fault era. But the *Clapp* court is quite straightforward in rejecting need as the principal touchstone for alimony awards, treating it as just one of several relevant factors. Need is thus not a necessary condition for an alimony award. *Wilson* teaches that it is also insufficient — that need alone, without more, is inadequate. *Clapp* and *Wilson* are not atypical in their rejection of need as the dispositive consideration in alimony awards, although they may be somewhat atypical in the overtness with which they reach this result. Because many statutes still follow the M.M.D.A.'s lead in appearing to establish need as the primary consideration, some courts are more reluctant than *Clapp* to state otherwise. Nor is obfuscation in this matter difficult. Need can easily be thought of as varying with the obligee — some "need" to enjoy a higher standard of living more than others. In the end, need becomes, as the *ALI Principles* observe, a conclusion rather than an explanation. The difficulties with need as an underlying concept for alimony have been understood for some time. *See* Ira Mark Ellman, *The Theory of Alimony*, 77 CAL. L. REV. 1, 5 (1989).

Divorced spouses even more comfortable than Elizabeth Clapp have been awarded alimony. *See, e.g., Johnston v. Johnston*, 649 N.E.2d 799 (Mass. App. 1995) (weekly alimony of $1250 for wife who also received $3 million distribution of marital property, "not excessive"); *Wrobleski v. Wrobleski*, 653 A.2d 732 (R.I. 1995) (sustaining five-year alimony award of $5000 monthly, and $2000 monthly thereafter, to wife awarded $1.3 million in marital assets). In *Marriage of McNaughton*, 145 Cal. App. 3d 845, 194 Cal. Rptr. 176, 179 (1983), the court sustained a maintenance award of $3,500 monthly to wife with $3 million in property, at the conclusion of a 32-year childless marriage, saying "[a]rguments that a spouse could live with less are properly addressed to the trial court. The award may seem excessive, but given the lavish lifestyle of the parties, the financial needs of Wife, and the Husband's ability to pay, another judge could reasonably make the same order under the same circumstances." Those who try to force such results into the rubric of need sometimes appeal to notions of "social need," that women accustomed to the life of "the highest and most prosperous socioeconomic group" by virtue of their husband's income require such awards because otherwise "the moorings of their identification with a certain social class, and with it the core of their self-esteem — formerly exclusively determined by the husband's education, occupation, and income — [would otherwise be] shaken loose." J. WALLERSTEIN & J. KELLY, SURVIVING THE BREAKUP 23 (1980).

Cases like *Wilson* are perhaps less common. In *Marriage of Heistermann*, 234 Cal. App. 3d 1195, 286 Cal. Rptr. 127 (1991), where the facts were otherwise similar, the initial decree, unlike *Wilson*, provided permanent alimony, and the court declined to modify it because there were no new circumstances. In *Marriage of Biderman*, 5 Cal. App. 4th 409, 6 Cal. Rptr. 2d 791 (1992), the parties had separated in 1984 after 20 years of marriage, and each was awarded about $350,000 in property. The husband was also awarded $650 monthly in spousal support for one year. Seeking an extension, he claimed he was still disabled by depression and unable to support himself. The trial court granted the extension but the appeals court reversed, concluding that even if he was disabled, his assets could provide sufficient support to make alimony unnecessary.

Does "need" in high-income divorces include savings? In *Drapeau v. Drapeau*, 93 Cal. App. 4th 1086, 114 Cal. Rptr. 2d 6 (2001), the husband earned $1 million annually. The wife argued that the trial court's $12,206 monthly alimony award was too low because it would not allow her to save at the same rate as the parties saved during the marriage ($15,000 monthly). The appeals court remanded with directions to the trial court to consider this savings history, although it did not require an award that would allow the wife to duplicate it. The Florida Supreme Court took precisely the opposite view in *Mallard v. Mallard*, 771 So.2d 1138 (Fla. 2000). The *Mallard* parties lived modestly despite their high income, allowing them to save at least 25% of their income and amassing considerable assets. Lower courts had allowed the wife an alimony award based upon that income rather than their life style, intentionally allowing her to continue the savings pattern. The Florida Supreme Court held, however, that amassing savings was not part of the purpose of an alimony award and therefore could not be considered in setting its amount. In *Kampf v. Kampf*, 732 N.W.2d 630 (Minn. App. 2007), the court held it proper to include savings in the calculation of alimony, on the basis that the parties' savings and retirement planning had been a central part of the couple's standard of living while they were married.

2. Problematic Rationales for Alimony: Contract. Can one simply infer a contract between the parties whose terms explain the alimony obligation? The *ALI Principles* conclude not. Comment b of § 5.05 explains:

> Contract analogies are sometimes relied upon to explain alimony awards to the long-time homemaker. . . . [A] conventional contract rationale would require describing the spousal relation in exchange terms that seem inapt because the parties define their relation by its nonfinancial aspects even though financial sharing is an important part of it. Spouses pool their financial affairs as part of a more general expectation of a shared life in which they have emotional and personal obligations as well as financial ones. At dissolution, no compensation is provided either spouse for loss of these non-financial aspects of their marriage. Nor is compensation provided for the loss of the nonfinancial services, such as homemaking, or home maintenance, which spouses typically provide each other during their marriage. Even if marriage as a whole were susceptible to being understood strictly in contract terms, a contract rationale could not explain why the financial obligations of marriage should alone survive dissolution when the larger relationship upon which those obligations depended does not.

Note as well that if alimony is viewed as roughly analogous to damages for breach of contract, then it would be available only to claimant who could show that it was their spouse, and not them, who breached the agreement — which is close to making alimony turn on marital "fault." Few commentators or courts would find such a rule desirable, *and* it is not the law anywhere today. For more on the contract rationale for alimony and the difficulties with it, see Ira Mark Ellman, *Why Family Law is Hard*, 35 ARIZ. ST. L.J. 699, 709–14 (2003), and Ira Mark Ellman & Sharon Lohr, *Opportunistic Violence, Marriage as Contract, and Other Bad Arguments for Fault Divorce*, 1997 U. ILL. L. REV. 719. For commentators more favorably inclined toward the contract approach, see June Carbone, *Economics, Feminism, and the Reinvention of Alimony: A Reply to Ira Ellman*, 43 VAND. L. REV. 1463 (1990); Allen

M. Parkman, *Reform of the Divorce Provisions of the Marriage Contract*, 8 B.Y.U. J. Pub. L. 91 (1994); Cynthia Starnes, *Application of a Contemporary Partnership Model for Divorce*, 8 B.Y.U. J. Pub. L. 107 (1993). Some commentators employ contract concepts more metaphorically, and their conclusions are not necessarily inconsistent with the ALI's approach. *E.g.*, Elizabeth Scott, *Rehabilitating Liberalism in Modern Divorce Law*, 1994 Utah L. Rev. 687; Carol Weisbrod, *The Way We Live: A New Discussion of Contracts and Domestic Arrangements*, 1994 Utah L. Rev. 777.

3. *Problematic Rationales for Alimony: Restitution.* If no contract can be inferred, perhaps relief can be premised upon a quasi-contract doctrine like unjust enrichment, or restitution — an approach sometimes used in other contexts to work justice when the formal requirements of contract cannot be met. The husband in *Clapp* argued that the trial court improperly based its award "on a theory of restitution for past homemaker services," but the Vermont Supreme Court held that alimony can be granted on this basis even though not mentioned in the governing statute. But *Clapp* makes no formal inquiry into whether that doctrine's requirements were in fact met. What if it had? *See Pyeatte v. Pyeatte*, 661 P.2d 196 (Ariz. App. 1983), an unusual case because both parties conceded the existence of an agreement under which the spouses would take turns attending school and rely upon the support of the other. They divorced after the husband completed his schooling but before the wife began hers, and she sued. The court rejected her contract claim because the husband's reciprocal obligations under the agreement could not be established with sufficient specificity to enforce. But it did allow her restitution of the support she had provided. Yet the very success of the *Pyeatte* restitution claim points out the doctrine's limits as a broadly applicable rationale for alimony. See Ellman, *The Theory of Alimony*, 77 Cal. L. Rev. 1, 25–28 (1989):

> There are three elements to a restitution claim in modern law: First, the defendant must have received a cognizable benefit; second, the benefit must have been conferred at the plaintiff's expense; and third, the defendant's retention of the benefit must be unjust. There is ordinarily no difficulty in cases like *Pyeatte* in establishing the first two elements of restitution, that the defendant benefitted at the plaintiff's expense. The only real question becomes whether the defendant's gratuitous retention of the benefit is "unjust." The general rule is that there is no unjustness where the benefit was originally conferred with "donative intent." Conversely, retention of a benefit is unjust where there was "an expectation of payment or compensation for services at the time they were rendered." The existence of a contract, even one that fails for indefiniteness, suggests that both parties understood that some compensation would be due — that the benefit was not conferred as a gift. Precisely this reasoning led the court in *Pyeatte* to conclude that the requirement of unjustness was met. Thus *Pyeatte's* precedential force is limited: Even though it provides a remedy without requiring a breach of contract, it necessarily relies heavily on the incomplete agreement whose existence was conceded by both parties.
>
> Because other claimants are unlikely to have an agreement to rely upon, they will have considerably more difficulty showing that the other spouse's

retention of the benefit is unjust. In *Pyeatte* the agreement dealt with a specific and rather limited aspect of the marriage, the immediate educational plans of each party. While all of the terms were not spelled out in detail, there was no difficulty establishing what benefit had been conferred on the husband (support during school), and the nature of the compensation both parties agreed upon in return. We know both that the wife's intent was not donative and that she did not receive the expected compensation. We could therefore conclude that the husband's retention of his benefit without some payment to the wife was unjust.

It is harder to find nonpayment in the case of the long-term homemaker. The benefit she conferred is presumably her many years of companionship and homemaking service. Perhaps the parties expected the wife to receive lifetime support in return, even if the marriage dissolved. In that case, the wife remains without full compensation, so that the husband has been unjustly enriched. Yet just as plausibly, the quid pro quo might have been the companionship and financial support that she has *already* received over the years in which they lived together. Or perhaps the parties had no defined expectations, but simply gave to each other out of love — that is, with a donative intent rather than with an expectation of repayment. If a court can determine which set of motivations accurately describes the particular case before it, then it can determine whether one spouse "unjustly" retains a benefit conferred by the other. In many cases, however, the court will find no unjustness using traditional criteria, and in many others the facts simply will not be clear enough to allow any conclusion. In the end, . . . the court attempting a restitution analysis will inevitably be drawn to its own understanding of the marital relation to test whether there was "unjust" enrichment. The parties' own expectations or understandings, having been expressed unclearly (or else they would have a valid contract) will be less important.

This can be seen from the *Pyeatte* case itself. The court took pains to distinguish the facts before it from the kind of homemaker case we have just been discussing: "Where both spouses perform the usual and incidental activities of the marital relationship, upon dissolution there can be no restitution for performance of these activities." Restitution, the court felt, is appropriate only where "the facts demonstrate an agreement between the spouses and an extraordinary or unilateral effort by one spouse which inures solely to the benefit of the other by the time of dissolution." Traditional marital roles cannot constitute such "extraordinary or unilateral effort."

Some will agree with the *Pyeatte* court's description of the marital relation; others will undoubtedly find it too narrow or unrealistic. But it is precisely this debate that ultimately dooms restitution as a workable solution to the problem of alimony, for it demonstrates that a court can resolve a restitution claim only by referring to its own unguided conception of marriage. In the end, restitution principles do no more than direct the court to order repayment where it feels that to do otherwise would be "unjust." Since directives from the parties themselves are absent, the court can only employ its own sense of the marital obligations and claims necessarily flowing from marriage in deciding what justice requires.

The doctrine of restitution thus offers no conceptual framework that explains generally why post-marriage payments are appropriate in some cases but not in others. Before the doctrine can be applied coherently, one must first have an established understanding of the social and economic conventions that ordinarily govern the relationship between the parties, against which to test claims that there has been an "unjust" enrichment. In the business and employment relations in which the doctrine is ordinarily applied, such conventions exist. In marriage they once did, but do not any longer. The doctrine of unjust enrichment cannot replace these conventions, because its application requires their prior existence. . . .

What conception of marriage must one have to ground the *Clapp* award on the idea of restitution? It is perhaps suggested by the court's observation that the wife took employment that "enabled her to stay at home during the summer" while in contrast, the husband "consistently put in night and weekend hours at his law office." But is this necessarily an argument for the wife, as the court seems to think, or could it also be offered as an argument for the husband? Could he have a restitution claim for the excess support he provided during the marriage? Which spouse, if either, made contributions that exceeded "the usual and incidental activities of the marital relationship"? If neither made such contributions, how can a restitution claim succeed?

4. *Problematic Rationales for Alimony: Contribution.* Courts like *Clapp*, as well as some governing statutes, often refer to a spouse's contributions to the marriage as a basis for alimony without tying the contributions to some doctrinal explanation for an award, such as contract or restitution. This contribution argument is often connected with the observation that the contributing spouse gave up other opportunities. *Marriage of LaRocque*, 406 N.W.2d 736 (Wis. 1987) (because parties did not accumulate a great deal of property during marriage, alimony rather than property distribution must be relied upon to "compensate" the homemaker wife for her contribution and her loss of a stream of income); *McNamara v. McNamara*, 443 N.W.2d 511, 516 (Mich. App. 1989) (24-year marriage in which homemaker wife said to "contribute significantly" to lawyer-husband's success "by not pursuing her own career opportunities and by providing the comfort and support, financial and otherwise, needed for defendant's well-being while he was climbing a professional and financial ladder."); *Rosenberg v. Rosenberg*, 155 A.D.2d 428, 547 N.Y.S.2d 90, 92 (1989) ("wife had contributed to the economic partnership as a parent and homemaker"). In that sense the claim may be just a less explicit version of unjust enrichment. But putting aside the problems we have already seen with unjust enrichment, we might ask how such contributions could be taken into account.

In offering the contribution argument itself, *Clapp* says that "homemaker contributions are, by their nature, nonmonetary so that they cannot be quantified or put into a monetary formula to specify their impact on the ultimate maintenance award." Of course, housekeeping and child care services can be purchased, and their monetary value thus established. The court's point makes sense, however, if one assumes a broader view of homemaking functions that includes intangible factors like emotional support, or spousal and parental love. These items are not available in market transactions and are therefore not easily valued in dollar amounts. But if Mrs. Clapp's intangible contributions to the marriage are considered, surely Mr. Clapp also made contributions. Perhaps the alimony claimant should be required to present evidence of the spouses' respective intangible contributions, to establish that she contributed more than her share. If courts should neither make assumptions about the spouses' relative contributions, nor require evidence on the question, then how can such contributions be made relevant to the alimony decision?

There is another version of the contribution argument: the claim is that compensation is due for the homemaker's contributions to the breadwinner's career success, whether on an unjust enrichment rationale or on some more general claim of equity. If that is the rationale, should obligors be able to defend the claim by showing, if they can, that they would have done as well financially without their spouses? (Recall *Michael v. Michael*, Section A[3], *supra*.) Or do we mean instead to explain alimony by reference to a more general proposition that homemakers typically "contribute" to their spouse's success, and thereby justify a general remedy for homemakers that is available without regard to the particular facts of their case. The problem with that view is that it is actually quite uncertain whether, as a general matter, husbands earn more than bachelors *because* of their wives' homemaking contributions. It is at least equally plausible that married men earn more because women are more likely to choose financially successful men for husbands, or because many of the attributes that make a man more likely to enjoy financial success also make him more able to attract a wife. *See* Yinon Cohen & Yitchak Haberfeld, *Why Do Married Men Earn More Than Unmarried Men?*, 20 Soc. Sci. Res. 29 (1991).

Yet another version of the contribution argument is that a homemaker spouse's support makes the breadwinner spouse more comfortable or more happy. Clearly true in many marriages, it may be less often true in precisely those marriages that end in divorce. In any event, the converse is equally plausible, that the homemaker is more comfortable or more happy during marriage by virtue of sharing in the financial rewards of the other spouse's market efforts. The point, of course, is that at dissolution each spouse loses the benefits conferred by the other spouse in an intact marriage, and therefore a claim of compensation requires more explanation than the simple recognition of that loss (or we would end up allowing remedies to both spouses).

5. *The Importance of Marital Duration.* One obvious difference between *Clapp* and *Wilson* is the length of the respective marriages. Marital duration appears to be a critical factor for nearly every court asked to make an award of "support alimony" — alimony with no definite termination date that is intended to provide the obligee with a more comfortable living standard. For example, see Rosalyn B. Bell, *Alimony and the Financially Dependent Spouse in Montgomery County, Maryland*, 22 Fam. L.Q. 225, 253 (1988) (survey of appellate decisions concludes that, excluding cases involving minor children, permanent alimony rarely awarded in marriages of less than 30 years duration). Studies of trial court decisions suggest the same result, *id.* at 288 (median marital duration in contested cases in which fixed-term alimony awards were granted was 14 years; median marital duration for contested cases in which awards of indefinite term were granted was 27 years).

Why should the length of the marriage matter? One might distinguish between two kinds of cases. The first group are those for which we believe the spouse's "need" in some sense arises from the marriage. *Clapp* seems to make this point in noting that the wife delayed her education and entry into the job market in order to take primary responsibility for raising the marital children. The longer the marriage, the more plausible is the claim that the homemaker has lost significant earning capacity, and the more plausible is the intuition that the potential obligor in fact benefitted from the homemaking labors that now give rise to the need asserted by the obligee. For this group of claims, then, we may look to the length of marriage as a rough indication of the extent to which the former spouse should be liable for current needs, because the length of marriage will be correlated with the factors that justify imposing the obligation in the first place.

Wilson, however, illustrates a second kind of case, in which the need does not arise *from* the marriage, even though it arises *during the* marriage. *Wilson* concludes that where one has an inadvertent accident or illness, one's spouse does not necessarily incur a lifetime obligation to provide the financial assistance which is thereby made necessary, but it suggests it would be more receptive to such a claim if the marriage had been of longer duration. But why? If the marital commitment is "revocable," as *Wilson* suggests, then we might think it is just as revocable after 20 years as after two years.

There is no accepted answer to this question, but the *Wilson* court's instinct that the length of the marriage matters in both kinds of cases is widely shared. Some might argue there is rough justice in the claim that "I've given you the best x years of my life and if you want to leave me now, when things aren't going so well, for somebody else, you ought to pay for it in spades." That argument cannot carry the day, however, because it assumes the obligor is at fault for leaving: what if the potential obligee ends the marriage? Or what if things have never gone well, and one spouse finally decides to call it off? Should a long-term award be allowed in that case? *See, e.g., Andersen v. Andersen,* 16 Fam. L. Rep. 1345 (N.Y. Sup. Ct. 1990) (wife who supported her alcoholic husband during their 27-year marriage ordered to pay $3,000 per month in rehabilitative alimony for set term of three years). If we want to answer "yes" without relying upon assumptions of fault, the rationale needs to be set out more clearly than it is in most cases. Perhaps we believe that as the spouses age, their reliance on the marital commitment increases because one's life course becomes harder to change and the prospects of finding a new spouse decline.

6. *The ALI Approach.* For many of the reasons just surveyed, the *ALI Principles* conclude that neither need nor contribution provides a satisfactory explanation of alimony. The *Principles* observe that alimony has historically been a residual category encompassing any financial claim at divorce that was not a property or child support claim, and that several different kinds of claims have in fact been allowed, each with its own rationale. The *Principles* separates these threads more clearly into separate claims, with set criteria for each, which when met create a presumption of entitlement to an award of a specified amount. An individual may qualify for more than one kind of claim. Another significant change is the *Principles*' reconceptualization of alimony as compensation for losses, rather than the meeting of needs. Thus, each claim recognized under the *Principles* asserts a different kind of loss. Comment *a* to § 5.02 of the *Principles* lays out the basic approach:

> The principal conceptual innovation of this Chapter is . . . to recharacterize the remedy it provides as compensation for loss rather than relief for need. A spouse frequently seems in need at the conclusion of a marriage because its dissolution imposes a particularly severe loss on him or her. The intuition that the former spouse has an obligation to meet that need arises from the perception that the need results from the unfair allocation of the financial losses arising from the marital failure. This perception explains why . . . all alimony claims cannot be adjudicated by reference to a single standard of need. If the payment's justification is not relief of need but the equitable reallocation of the losses arising from the marital failure, then need is not an appropriate eligibility requirement for the award. While many persons who have suffered an inequitable financial loss will be in need, others will not, and the remainder will vary in their degree of need. At the same time, some formerly married individuals may find themselves in need for reasons unrelated to the marriage and its subsequent dissolution. In that case, there may be no basis for imposing a special obligation to meet that need on their former spouses.
>
> . . . [F]ocusing on loss permits more coherent definition of the cases qualifying for compensatory payments [the term used instead of "alimony" or "maintenance"] than is possible in a system judging all claims on the single but ill-defined goal of relieving need. The shift in analysis from need to loss thus facilitates more precise rules of adjudication, with a correspondingly reduced disparity of result. . . .
>
> Equally important, recharacterizing the award's purpose from the relief of need to the equitable allocation of loss transforms the claimant's petition from a plea for help to a claim of entitlement. Although conceptual confusion over the grounds of alimony has undoubtedly contributed to mistaken judgments in both directions, inadequate or missing awards have been the more frequent problem. This failure of alimony has created pressure to expand the relief available through the division of property so as to reach claims for which that remedy is ill-suited. Reconceptualizing alimony as compensatory payments for losses arising from the marriage and its failure establishes it as an entitlement providing a more reliable remedy for the divorce-related financial claims.

Section 5.03 lists the "compensable losses" — the losses for which claims arise. As explained in § 5.02, these are limited to financial losses; there are no claims, for example, for emotional damage (although the *Principles* do not preclude tort claims). Claims are also limited to financial losses arising from the marriage's dissolution, as compared to claims for financial inequities during the marriage. Some of the claims (such as reimbursement for support during school-discussed in

Section C, *supra*.) arise only at the dissolution of short-term marriages. By far the most important of the claims recognized by the *Principles* are the two that would replace, in existing law, the traditional claim of "support alimony" — potentially long-term awards meant to assist the obligee in maintaining a level of support. Section 5.03 describes those two losses this way:

(a) In a marriage of significant duration, the loss in living standard experienced at dissolution by the spouse who has less wealth or earning capacity. . . .

(b) An earning-capacity loss incurred during marriage but continuing after dissolution and arising from one spouse's disproportionate share, during marriage, of the care of the marital children or of the children of either spouse. . . .

Homemakers in long-term marriages with children will typically qualify for both awards. As for the second award, its basic rationale is that because care for marital children is a joint obligation of both spouses, financial losses which arise from marital child care and which endure after the marriage ends ought also to be shared. The *Principles* provides that the size of the award increases with the duration of the child care period. The *Principles* offers the following rationale for the first award, compensation for the loss of living standard:

§ 5.04, Comment *c*:

[T]he cases reflect an enduring intuition that the homemaker in a long-term marriage has some claim on her spouse's post-divorce income. That intuition does not depend on any assumption that the parties made explicit promises to one another, but on the belief that the relationship itself gives rise to obligations. Anglo-American legal traditions, individualistic as they are, recognize duties between relative strangers that arise from even fleeting interactions in which one person's behavior affects another. Further duties may be owed those with whom one has a more established relationship. The relationship of employer and employee, landlord and tenant, and shareholder and corporate officer, all give rise to legal duties. Some may be waivable by contract and some not, but few are dependent upon contract to establish their existence. They emerge from entry into the relationship itself, whether or not the parties expressly adopt them. The relationship of husband and wife is of this kind, but more so. Its effects may accrete slowly, but with great impact as the spouses' lives become entwined over time.

In understanding the nature of the obligation that arises in the long-term marriage, it is useful to think first about the traditional homemaker wife, as perhaps the clearest case. . . . That wife has more at risk, financially, from the dissolution of a long-term marriage than does her breadwinner spouse. The observation is not limited to full-time homemakers but applies equally to anyone economically dependent on his or her spouse. . . . The marital dissolution may leave both spouses financially less well off, but whenever the spouses have significantly different earning capacities, the loss for the lower-earning spouse will be much greater than for the other. Under this section, when there is such an income differential, and the marriage exceeds some minimum duration, there will usually be a remedy in favor of the lower-earning spouse . . . proportional to both the income differential and the marital duration.

The remedy is proportional to the marital duration because the obligations recognized under this section do not arise from the marriage ceremony alone, but develop over time as the parties' lives become entwined. . . . To leave the financially dependent spouse in a long marriage without a remedy would facilitate exploitation of the trusting spouse and discourage investment by the nervous one.

The *Principles*, in §§ 5.04 and 5.05, provide in effect guidelines that set a presumptive award amount, once the entitlement criteria have been shown. The awards equal a percentage of the difference between the two spouse's incomes, with that percentage gradually increasing with either marital duration or the duration of the child care. The combined value of the two awards is capped (the suggested cap is 40% of the income difference). The emphasis on duration can be understood on two grounds. First, duration provides a rough measure of the size of the claimant's loss: a longer child care period will usually entail a greater loss of earning capacity; also the longer the marriage, the greater is the dependent spouse's sense of the marriage's more affluent living standard as the benchmark against which to compare her post-divorce situation. Second, duration provides a rough measure of the obligor-spouse's duty to share the other spouse's loss, as the parties' obligations to one another increase the longer they are married. For a view critical of the *ALI Principles*' approach to alimony, see Cynthia Lee Starnes, *Mothers as Suckers: Pity, Partnership, and Divorce Discourse*, 90 IOWA L. REV. 1513 (2005) (arguing that the *Principles* portrays mothers as gullible people "economically incapacitated by their unpaid labor"; advocating instead for a business partnership model of marriage, which would justify income-sharing while children are in the household).

7. *Alimony Guidelines.* As will be discussed in Chapter 5, child support guidelines, creating (for better or for worse) relatively predictable results for child support cases within a jurisdiction, now rule that area of post-divorce financial obligations. In most such cases, the presumptive amount of support to be ordered is determined by a formula that uses the income of the obligor parent or the income of both parents. While there has been significant debate about the merits of such guidelines, there is little doubt that they have made child support determinations more consistent and more predictable. As discussed in the previous note, the *ALI Principles*' treatment of alimony seeks a similar predictability in the results for alimony. Additionally, according to one review, at least 12 states have experimented, either at a state-wide level, or at the county level, with guidelines for setting alimony, or alimony *pendente lite*. *See* Virginia R. Dugan & Jon A. Feder, *Alimony Guidelines: Do They Work?*, 25(4) FAMILY ADVOCATE 20 (2003). However, these guidelines tend to give only rough or "rule of thumb" guidance as to whether to order alimony, or at what level. They tend to set a minimum duration of the marriage before alimony can be awarded, a preference for rehabilitative or permanent alimony, and, occasionally, some formula for determining the level of support. One barrier for alimony guidelines is that the varied purposes for alimony affects perceptions of the appropriate amount. For this reason, any suggested set of guidelines is unlikely to seem appropriate across the full range of cases. It remains to be seen whether the ALI's recommendations will have any impact on the process of establishing alimony guidelines. The Family Court of Maricopa County, Arizona (Phoenix) has adopted guidelines that are in some respects similar to the ALI recommendations, although considerably less comprehensive. *See* Ira Mark Ellman, *The Maturing Law of Divorce Finances: Toward Rules and Guidelines*, 33 Fam. L.Q. 801 (1999); *Cullum v. Cullum*, 160 P.3d 231 (Ariz. App. Div. 1 2007) (approving use of county-wide spousal maintenance guidelines in Maricopa County, Arizona).

For a discussion of recent use of alimony "guidelines," see Twila Larkin, *Guidelines for Alimony: The New Mexico Experiment*, 38 Fam. L.Q. 29, 38–49 (2004). A Commission of the American Academy of Matrimonial Lawyers has developed its own guidelines in 2007, listed and discussed in Mary Kay Kisthardt, *Rethinking Alimony: The AAML's Considerations for Calculating Alimony, Spousal Support or Maintenance*, 21 J. Am. Acad. Matrimonial Law. 61 (2008).

8. *Ex Ante vs. Ex Post Considerations.* A standard tension in the analysis, and in lawmaking in general, is rules which do justice between the parties (looking back on the facts of their case ("ex post")) may not create the best incentives for other people's behavior in the future ("ex ante"). Sometimes this distinction is put in terms of considerations of fairness versus considerations of (economic) efficiency. In any event, such tensions potentially arise in connection with the rules of alimony. Some feminist theorists have argued against rules that compensate spouses who sacrifice for the sake of the marital household, on the basis that such rules, though perhaps offering just compensation for those sacrifices, improperly encourage women to (continue to) make economically disabling choices, perpetuating their financial dependence on men and their inequality in society. June Carbone, *Economics, Feminism, and the Reinvention of Alimony*, 43 Vand. L. Rev. 1463 (1990). Of course, whether incentives created by the laws of divorce in fact have any effect on people's choices in their domestic lives is itself a matter of dispute. For those who believe that there are such effects, a choice may be necessary between doing justice between the parties and encouraging changes in the way marriages are conducted in the future.

PROBLEM

Problem 4-16. Suppose the disability in *Wilson* developed just after the spouses separated, rather than just before. Should the husband have any obligation in that case, for even a short period of assistance? What if the marriage were of 16 years' duration, rather than 6?

[4]   Size and Duration of Awards Following a Long-Term Marriage

RAINWATER v. RAINWATER
Arizona Court of Appeals
869 P.2d 176 (1993)

FIDEL, CHIEF JUDGE.

Sam Rainwater ("husband") appeals from the trial court's award of spousal maintenance to Barbara Rainwater ("wife") until her death or remarriage. He argues that unless the receiving spouse, through age, disability, or lack of earning capacity, is permanently unable to become self-sustaining, Arizona law permits spousal maintenance only for a finite, transitional, rehabilitative term. We find that husband's argument gives inadequate weight to marital standard of living as a factor in maintenance awards, and to the receiving spouse's contribution to the earning ability of the paying spouse. We conclude that the trial court did not exceed its discretion in awarding indefinite maintenance in this case.

I.

In June of 1988, wife petitioned . . . to dissolve the parties' twenty-two-year marriage. Resolving all other issues by stipulation, the parties went to trial on the . . . appropriate spousal maintenance for wife.

Wife through much of the parties' marriage worked full time outside the home. In the early years, she helped support husband while he worked toward an engineering degree. In later years, . . . she contributed socially and emotionally to husband's career. Additionally, wife maintained the home and was primary caretaker for the parties' two children, who now are grown. After husband received his degree, his income rose substantially. In the year of the divorce and for two years prior, husband's earnings exceeded $100,000.

At the time of dissolution, wife, a forty-one-year-old secretary, was working toward a Bachelor of Arts degree, but neither party showed the extent to which her earning capacity would be enhanced by that degree. Weighing wife's needs in the context of her marital standard of living, the trial court found that wife "would not be able to meet her reasonable needs . . . nor enjoy the standard of living established during the marriage based on reasonably anticipated income from her investments and her employment." Specifically, the trial court estimated wife's after-tax income from labor and pre-tax income from investments as $20,000 per year and her reasonable needs as $41,000 per year. Finding that husband's earnings exceeded his needs, the trial court awarded wife $1900 per month for three years or until one year after completion of her B.A. degree, whichever should first occur, and $1200 per month thereafter till her death or remarriage.

Although husband argued in the trial court that wife should receive no spousal maintenance, on appeal he challenges only the duration and amount of the award. Husband argues that the trial court erred by entering an award that would allow his able-bodied former wife "to live off his labors forever." He argues that, in the absence of evidence that wife is permanently unable to become self-sustaining, Arizona public policy permits only a fixed-term award to assist her in transition to an independent life. Wife responds that our maintenance law requires a case-by-case determination, that it is flexible enough to permit an indefinite award when justified by statutorily enumerated considerations, and that those considerations support indefinite maintenance in this case.

II.

Arizona law extends the trial court substantial discretion to set the amount and duration of spousal maintenance. The framework for that discretion is largely provided by Ariz. Rev. Stat. Ann. ("A.R.S.") section 25-319 (1991). First, to justify any award, the evidence must support a finding . . . that the receiving spouse lacks sufficient property and ability to meet reasonable living expenses. That finding is not contested in this case. Second, in deciding the duration and amount of maintenance, the trial court must balance the factors listed in section 25-319(B).[1]

To strike the proper balance, the trial court need not apply every factor listed. . . . In what is necessarily a case-by-case inquiry, some factors will not apply. The trial court may abuse its discretion, however, by neglecting an applicable factor.

We turn to husband's claim that the 25-319(B) balance is weighted by public policy in favor of maintenance that is transitional, rehabilitative, and limited in term. We agree up to a point. Citing *Schroeder v. Schroeder*, 778 P.2d 1212 (Ariz. 1989), husband emphasizes the supreme court's statement that

---

[1] The factors listed in section 25-319(B) are:

1. The standard of living established during the marriage.

2. The duration of the marriage.

3. The age, employment history, earning ability and the physical and emotional condition of the spouse seeking maintenance.

4. The ability of the spouse from whom maintenance is sought to meet his or her needs while meeting those of the spouse seeking maintenance.

5. The comparative financial resources of the spouses, including their comparative earning abilities in the labor market.

6. The contribution of the spouse seeking maintenance to the earning ability of the other spouse.

7. The extent to which the spouse seeking maintenance has reduced his or her income or career opportunities for the benefit of the other spouse.

8. The ability of both parties after the dissolution to contribute to the future educational costs of their mutual children.

9. The financial resources of the party seeking maintenance, including marital property apportioned to such party, and such party's ability to meet his or her needs independently.

10. The time necessary to acquire sufficient education or training to enable the party seeking maintenance to find appropriate employment and whether such education or training is readily available.

11. Excessive or abnormal expenditures, destruction, concealment or fraudulent disposition of community, joint tenancy and other property held in common.

the current aim [of spousal maintenance] is to achieve independence for both parties and to require an effort toward independence by the party requesting maintenance. The temporary award of maintenance in its present form reflects both of these values. In most cases of temporary maintenance, the key issue for the parties and the court will be whether that independence will be achieved by a good faith effort.

This general statement is best examined in the context of the facts.

In *Schroeder*, the trial court had initially awarded wife four years of spousal maintenance, but later extended maintenance until her death or remarriage or the further order of the court. The supreme court upheld the modified award. The court explained that maintenance awards are modifiable both in amount and in duration, unless the parties have expressly agreed to the contrary and the trial court has so ordered. The wife in *Schroeder* was fifty and had worked primarily as a homemaker before her twenty-eight-year marriage ended. Although the initial award of four years' duration was "intended to support [wife's] transitional growth of earning capacity," by the time of the petition for modification, wife had only found relatively unlucrative work as a filing clerk, and her expenses had increased to include chemotherapy treatment for cancer. Because time had disproved the trial court's apparent initial expectation that four years of transitional support would enable wife to become self-supporting, the supreme court concluded that the evidence now justified an indefinite maintenance award.

Schroeder indeed recognizes the transition toward independence as a principal objective of maintenance. . . . But *Schroeder* also reaffirms the trial court's discretion to award indefinite maintenance when it appears . . . that independence is unlikely. . . . Additionally, *Schroeder* shows that assessing the likelihood of a successful transition to independence requires a prediction that may vary not only from case to case, but from time to time within a case.

III.

It does not resolve this case to recognize that maintenance orders, whenever possible, should promote a transition toward financial independence. The crux of husband's argument is that indefinite maintenance can be awarded only to a spouse who is "permanently unable to be self-sustaining."

The principal flaw in this argument is husband's failure to define "self-sustaining" by reference to any standard of living. The evidence certainly suggests that wife can be self-sustaining beyond the minimal subsistence level. Yet the trial court expressly found that wife's "reasonably anticipated income" would not meet her "reasonable needs," when those needs were determined by reference to "the standard of living established during the marriage."

Marital standard of living has long been listed by our legislature among the factors pertinent to the duration and amount of spousal maintenance. And though Arizona courts have stated that public policy favors fixed-term maintenance as a means to promote a diligent effort to become self-sustaining, we have repeatedly cautioned that this goal "must be balanced with some realistic appraisal of the probabilities that the receiving spouse will in fact subsequently be able to support herself in some reasonable approximation of the standard of living established during the marriage." [¶] In 1987, when the legislature enacted the most recent amendments to section 25-319, it expanded subsection (B) by adding [factors 6, 7, and 8, as reprinted in footnote 2]. It is apparent from these changes that the legislature does not regard a 25-319(B) decision as exclusively an inquiry into the speed with which the receiving spouse might become self-supporting without maintenance. See *Elliott v. Elliott*, 796 P.2d at 938 (Factors 6 and 7 "differ from most of the other section 25-319(B) factors in that they are not based upon the parties' needs.").

We do not suggest that at the end of every marriage, the party of lesser earning capacity is entitled to enough support to maintain the standard of living achieved during the marriage. First of all, divorce often requires a lesser standard of living for both parties. The statute requires consideration of "[t]he ability of the spouse from whom maintenance is sought to meet his or her needs while meeting those of the spouse seeking maintenance." A.R.S. § 25-319(B)(4). Second, there will be case-to-case variance in the degree to which the marital standard of living may be seen as a product of the marriage. For this reason, such factors as length of the marriage, the receiving spouse's contributions to the education and earning capacity of the paying spouse, and the receiving spouse's reduction in income or career opportunities for the benefit of the family home and children bear heavily on the trial court's effort to establish an equitable award. . . .

In this case, the parties had a marriage of long duration, to which wife contributed financially and by assuming the role of primary caretaker for the family home and children. She contributed to husband's support as he worked toward an engineering degree, and she contributed socially and emotionally to his professional advancement once his formal education was complete. The parties had achieved a relatively high standard of living by the last years of their marriage, which the trial court properly regarded as a product of their sustained common efforts for 23 years. The trial court built an incentive toward independence into its maintenance award by reducing wife's monthly payment from $1900 to $1200 after the expiration of a reasonable period for getting her B.A. degree. But the trial court also concluded — and the evidence permits the conclusion — that wife could not foreseeably expect to maintain her standard of living without ongoing support from husband at a level reasonably within his ability to provide. Under all of these circumstances, we find that the trial court properly balanced the many relevant factors of 25-319(B), and we find no abuse of discretion in the trial court's award.

We add that our decision is strongly affected by the presumptive modifiability of spousal maintenance awards. Because maintenance awards are modifiable, an award of maintenance until death or remarriage does not lock long-term maintenance irrefutably into place. Rather, it places the burden on the paying spouse to prove a later change in circumstances sufficiently substantial to warrant shortening the duration of the award. A fixed-term award, by contrast, places the burden on the receiving spouse to prove a change in circumstances sufficiently substantial to warrant extending the award.

The allocation of the burden of seeking modification order represents a prediction of when independence will occur, and that the effects of changing circumstances should not be borne solely by the receiving spouse. [¶] An award until death or remarriage is a prediction that one spouse will never be able to independently approximate the standard of living established during marriage, and that the other spouse will remain financially able to contribute to the first spouse's support. When, as in this case, that finding is supported by the evidence, we find no inequity in placing the burden on the paying spouse to later prove that a substantial and continuing change of circumstances has occurred.

. . .

We affirm the trial court's order of spousal maintenance.

[The Arizona Supreme Court denied the husband's Petition for Review, but Justice Martone dissented:

"[T]his case decides an important issue of law. . . . There is no existing authority for the proposition that a spouse 'needs' to live forever in the style to which he or she has become accustomed. It can be argued that the allowance of lifetime maintenance at the standard of living established during marriage turns the institution of marriage into a lifetime annuity. This important issue warrants our consideration."

Rainwater v. Rainwater, 869 P.2d 175 (Ariz. 1994).]

HECKER v. HECKER
Minnesota Supreme Court
568 N.W.2d 705 (1997)

KEITH, CHIEF JUSTICE.

. . . [¶] Dennis and Sandra Hecker were married on February 23, 1973. . . . Dennis enjoyed considerable success in the auto sales business while Sandra engaged in traditional homemaking responsibilities, including caring for the parties' two children. . . . In August 1982, Dennis petitioned the district court to dissolve the marriage. [A] marital termination agreement . . . award[ed] Sandra sole physical custody of the parties' 5- and 8-year-old daughters, child support in the amount of $800 per month per child, certain real and personal property, and temporary spousal maintenance of $800 per month for 121 months until June 1, 1993. The [May 1983] judgment . . . incorporated the terms of this agreement.

[Sandra obtained modifications of the judgment in 1985 and again in 1986, which together gave her an additional $155,000 in a lump sum settlement of property claims, increased her child support to $900 per month per child, and increased spousal maintenance to $1,000 per month for a five-year period, after which it returned to the original $800 per month until its scheduled termination on June 1, 1993.]

On February 2, 1993, four months before her temporary spousal maintenance award was to expire, Sandra again [sought a modification] increasing her monthly maintenance to $2,000 and designating it as a permanent award. In support of her claim that changed circumstances rendered the original award unreasonable or unfair, Sandra stated that she was then 45 years old and, because of her responsibilities with regard to the children, she never completed vocational training as she had intended at the time of the marriage dissolution entered ten years earlier. She claimed that her monthly income from child support and maintenance was $3,196.92 and that her monthly expenses for herself and the youngest child were $3,107, but because the oldest child was to graduate from high school in June 1993, the loss of support for that child and that the expiration of the temporary maintenance period would leave her without sufficient means to provide for her own support. While Dennis acknowledged that he had sufficient income to support a modification, he opposed it based upon the parties' earlier agreements.

Sandra, who was 35 at the time of the marriage dissolution, apparently initially appreciated that, because of her stipulation for durational, not permanent maintenance, it was necessary for her to retrain or otherwise enter the labor market. Within a year of that dissolution in 1984, she obtained a part-time position at the YMCA, performing various tasks during her eight-year employment. She earned approximately $6 per hour during that employment period. She left the YMCA in October 1992 and, from December 1992 to February 1993, was employed as an interviewer for a temporary job service earning $7 to $7.50 per hour. During this time, she applied for several full-time positions, stating that she had initially preferred part-time employment so that she could retain flexibility and meet her children's needs.

The referee granted Sandra's motion for an increased and permanent award in its entirety, finding that she had failed to rehabilitate and that this failure constituted the requisite substantial change in circumstances that rendered the original award unreasonable and unfair. The referee's award of $2,000 per month was affirmed by the district court [but reversed by a divided appeals panel and remanded to the district court for further proceedings to address, *inter alia*, the reasons for her failure to rehabilitate]. [T]he appellate court appears to have suggested . . . that the reasons for Sandra's failure to rehabilitate must be ascertained because, at the time of the dissolution, the parties contemplated that she would be the primary custodian of the children and, as far as the record was developed, there existed no *changed* circumstances — that is, the fact that Sandra would devote considerable time to the care of the children was expected when the parties agreed to her sole physical custody.

On remand. . . . Dennis' . . . vocational expert [testified] that Sandra could expect entry-level earnings of $16,000 per year in retail management and, with three years' experience, could increase those earnings to $25,000 per year. The expert commented that during the time since the marriage was dissolved, Sandra was "minimally involved" in preparing for or pursuing a career and that she could have improved her earning capacity had she made a greater effort. The report was not rebutted.

The referee found that Sandra "chose not to make any serious effort at obtaining vocational training or work experience, but rather decided to rely upon the possibility that she would continue to receive spousal maintenance, despite the terms of the decree." The referee found no evidence to support Sandra's claim that her health problems, the health or needs of the children, the stress of divorce or the need to appear in court for periodic litigation restricted her achievement of better employment with greater income. Based upon Sandra's failure to make any reasonable effort toward rehabilitation, the referee [attributed] to her an annual income of $25,000 which, when coupled with annual investment income of $5,400 [based on the earlier $155,000 property settlement], would result in an approximate net monthly income of $1,825. Finding also that Sandra's reasonable monthly expenses are $3,200, the referee awarded her permanent monthly spousal maintenance of $1,375 — the difference between the monthly expenses and the total of investment and attributed income — to allow Sandra to meet her needs. The district court affirmed [the referee]. [¶] On Dennis' second appeal. . . . the court of appeals [affirmed,] holding that Sandra's willful failure to rehabilitate did not preclude her from receiving further maintenance if, after attributing to her the maximum earning capacity attainable by diligent efforts, she failed to become self-supporting.

. . . . Minn. Stat. § 518.64, subd. 2 (1996) . . . provides. . . .

> The terms of an order respecting maintenance or support may be modified upon a showing of one or more of the following: (1) substantially increased or decreased earnings of a party; (2) substantially increased or decreased need of a party * * *; (3) receipt of assistance * * *; (4) a change in the cost of living for either party * * *, any of which makes the terms unreasonable and unfair * * *.

That statute places a dual burden on the party seeking modification — first, to demonstrate that there has occurred a substantial change in one or more of the circumstances identified in the statute and second, to show that the substantial change has the effect of rendering the original award unreasonable and unfair.

Here, the parties originally stipulated to their respective rights and obligations, including that Sandra would receive temporary or durational spousal maintenance in presumed anticipation of her efforts to achieve some level of self-sufficiency. [It has] relevance in a modification context [as an] identification of the baseline circumstances against which claims of substantial change are evaluated. . . .

The referee implicitly concluded that the requisite substantial change in circumstances was . . . the frustration of the parties' expectations of [Sandra's] self-sufficiency. . . . [The trial court did not abuse its discretion accepting this finding and] recasting Dennis' obligation for spousal maintenance as permanent.

[T]he referee . . . fashioned an award which attributed to her the income that the unrefuted expert testimony demonstrated could have been produced by reasonable effort. . . . The result is . . . consistent with . . . the principle embodied in the statutory maintenance provision, which calls for a "just" award.

Affirmed.

[Justice Page's short concurring opinion not included.]

NOTES

1. ***The Size of Alimony Awards.*** Recall that *Clapp* approved an alimony award intended to equalize the parties' incomes, with annual inflation adjustments. The *Rainwater* award is considerably less generous, although it is difficult to make a precise calculation. We are told that the husband's earnings "exceed" $100,000 annually, presumably a pre-tax income figure, and that the wife's after-tax annual income is $20,000. The wife is allowed a transitional award of $1900 monthly, and a long-term award of $1,200 monthly, equivalent to annual amounts of $22,800 and $14,400, respectively. If we assume the husband's after-tax income is $80,000, then the parties respective after-tax annual incomes, after the alimony payments, would be $57,200 and $44,800, during the transitional period, and $65,600 and $34,400, once that period had ended. Of course, the alimony reduction after the transitional period is premised on the assumption that the wife will achieve greater earnings once she acquires her B.A. degree. If one assumes an after-tax income for her of $40,000 annually rather than $20,000, her post-transition income is $55,000, not so far below the husband's net of $65,600. But it is probably unrealistic to assume that her after-tax income will double while his stays constant. In any event it seems likely that some gap between their incomes will continue long into their future. Is that gap appropriate? What standard should the court adopt for setting the size of the alimony award?

Income equalization is an easily understood benchmark, but is rarely adopted by the courts. *Rainwater*, like many other courts, refers to the marital standard of living as an appropriate goal. It is obvious, however, that if the spouses' incomes are the same after divorce as during the marriage, they cannot both retain the marital living standard. For example, if the aggregate income of both Rainwater spouses was $120,000 during the marriage and also after it, then an income equalization rule would give each $60,000 after post-divorce alimony payments. However, it surely would require more than $60,000 for one person to have the same living standard as the two-person intact marital household had at $120,000. To provide Mrs. Rainwater with the marital living standard would thus require an award that *exceeded* income equalization, transferring more than half of Mr. Rainwater's income to his former wife, and driving his living standard considerably below hers. Not surprisingly, no court endorses that result. The marital living standard is thus an aspiration, not a rule, as *Rainwater* appreciates when it notes that "divorce often requires a lesser standard of living for both parties." When could divorce *not* require a reduction from the marital living standard, for at least one party? Only when the spouses' aggregate income after divorce is higher than during marriage. This does sometimes happen, either because a former homemaker devotes more hours to market labor after divorce, or because spousal incomes rise with the passage of time. If the obligor's income were to rise enough after divorce, he could make an alimony payment sufficient to provide his former spouse with the marital living standard while still retaining an even better standard for himself. (Imagine, for example, that Mr. Rainwater achieved an annual income of $200,000 after divorce.) In such atypical cases, an alimony award that falls *short* of income equalization could nonetheless provide the obligee with funds sufficient to maintain the marital living standard.

Rainwater's struggle with this problem reflects both the concerns and the confusion inherent in existing law. On one hand, cases often suggest that maintenance at the marital living standard is the appropriate goal of an alimony award, and is therefore required whenever the obligor can afford to provide it to a former spouse unable to achieve that standard on his own. *E.g., see Marriage of LaRocque*, 406 N.W.2d 736 (Wis. 1987). Courts sometimes go even a bit further. The same court that decided *LaRocque*, for example, later held that the maintenance claimant after a 20-year marriage with two children could seek the standard of living the parties "anticipated" as well as that which they actually experienced during their marriage, where the husband's income had increased from $88,000 at the time of filing to over $400,000 at the time of the decree. *Hefty v. Hefty*, 493 N.W.2d 33 (Wis. 1992). On the other hand, at least one state provides by statute that an indefinite alimony award is permitted only when the recipient cannot be "self-supporting" or the "respective standards of living of the parties will be unconscionably disparate." MD. CODE ANN., FAM. LAW, § 11-106(c), which also suggests that an award reducing the disparity to a level that is not "unconscionable" satisfies the statute.

Vermont, as *Clapp* suggests, has in at least some cases held it appropriate to allow an alimony award that equalizes the parties' post-divorce incomes, see *Guiel v. Guiel*, 682 A.2d 957 (Vt. 1996) (23-year marriage). Other courts reject the goal of income equalization, *Stone v. Stone*, 488 S.E.2d 15 (W. Va. 1997) (alimony award cannot be based on goal of equalizing parties' incomes); *Marriage of Barcroft*, 773 P.2d 21, 22 (Or. App. 1989) (spousal support need not equalize parties' earning capacity, so long as their standards of living are "not overly disproportionate to . . . [that] enjoyed during the marriage"). A commentator who supports post-divorce income-equalization concluded, after surveying the cases, that "none of [the reported cases] have divided all income equally. . . . Even judges who have expressed concern with the disparity of income capacity have typically kept women at income levels half that of their former husbands. Although spousal support statutes typically list a range of factors to be considered in setting support, not a single state suggests that equality should be the goal of post-divorce support." Jane Rutherford, *Duty in Divorce: Shared Income as a Path to Equality*, 58 FORDHAM L. REV. 539, 578–79 (1990).

   2. *Rehabilitation and An Alimony Award's Duration.*   Alimony awards tend to be either indefinite ("permanent alimony") or for a fixed term of years. (In Texas, permanent alimony is generally unavailable. Unless either the recipient or a child in the recipient's custody has a significant disability, alimony can be awarded for no longer than three years. TEX. FAM. CODE § 8.054.) Why should an alimony award ever have a fixed termination date? The *ALI Principles* offer two possible rationales for a fixed term, depending upon the facts of a particular case. They are a) expectation of rehabilitation, and b) limitations on the obligor's responsibility.

   a. *Expectation of rehabilitation.* Possibly the obligee will not "need" the award after an adequate period for rehabilitation. This presents a choice in framing the initial decree — a choice between alternatives exemplified by the lower courts in *Rainwater* and *Hecker*. The *Rainwater* trial court ordered alimony for an indefinite period, observing that the award could always be modified if the obligee later acquired additional resources or earning capacity, while in *Hecker* an initial award for a fixed term was later modified into a permanent award. Because alimony awards are modifiable, one might think that it matters little whether the initial decree is for an indefinite or fixed term: in either case the trial court's initial projection about the parties' future circumstances can be corrected if it turns out wrong. But as *Rainwater* aptly points out, the award's initial characterization determines which party will have the burden of persuasion in any modification proceeding. In addition, as the *ALI Principles* point out, the initial award also communicates the law's expectations. "A fixed-term award communicates the law's expectation that after its expiration the former spouses will no longer have financial obligations to or claims upon one another. This expectation encourages both spouses to plan their future accordingly." § 5.06, Comment *a*. That expectation is, in effect, given bite by the burden allocation that *Rainwater* notes.

The problem is that under some traditional procedural rules, the bite associated with the fixed term award may be too deep. Those rules often constrain the court's ability to extend a fixed-term alimony award past its initial termination date. In some states the court cannot extend it at all; in some it cannot do so unless its initial order expressly reserved jurisdiction for that purpose; in many it cannot in any event revive an alimony award that has expired. These rules encourage courts to issue more indefinite awards than they otherwise would, for fear that mistaken projections of obligee rehabilitation will be more difficult to correct than mistakes in the other direction. The trend is to abandon these procedural restrictions. *See, e.g., Milner v. Milner*, 672 A.2d 206 (N.J. App. 1996) (reversing trial court holding that "rehabilitative alimony may be modified but cannot be changed into permanent alimony"). California had such procedural constraints until it amended its law in 1987 to provide that in the absence of either a court order terminating spousal support, or of the parties' agreement to the contrary, the court retains jurisdiction over spousal maintenance awards "indefinitely" in marriages of long duration. CAL. FAM. CODE § 4336; *see Beck v. Beck*, 57 Cal. App. 4th 341, 67 Cal. Rptr. 2d 79 (1997) (finding no jurisdiction to reinstate support 16 years after it had expired under the original decree because marriage predated the amendment and was not governed by it).

Relaxation of these procedural rules has its origins in cases decided soon after the original no-fault reforms, in which long-term homemakers were given fixed-term awards on the basis of idealistic assumptions about their capacity to re-enter the job market at the age of 40 or 50. Lack of modifiability often resulted in injustice. In an important decision, the California Supreme Court held that "[a] trial court should not terminate jurisdiction to extend a future support order after a lengthy marriage, unless the record clearly indicates that the supported spouse will be able to adequately meet his or her financial needs. . . . In making its decision . . . the court must rely only on the evidence in the record. . . . It must not engage in speculation." *In re Marriage of Morrison*, 20 Cal. 3d 437, 143 Cal. Rptr. 139, 573 P.2d 41, 52 (1978). While the short term "rehabilitative award" was still the ideal, the court was to retain jurisdiction to extend the term, indefinitely if necessary, if the former homemaker turned out to be unable to secure employment that would allow her to be self-supporting at the middle class level reasonably similar to that to which she was accustomed.

b. *The limits of obligor responsibility.* Even if the obligee's loss or need is indefinite in duration, the obligor's responsibility to share it may not be. This is essentially the basis of *Wilson*, reprinted above, and is probably an important if silent rationale in other cases as well. *See, e.g., Marriage of Bevers*, 326 N.W.2d 896 (Iowa 1982) (college-educated homemaker wife allowed alimony for two years after termination of 11-year marriage). One is most likely to reach this conclusion in comparatively short marriages such as *Wilson*.

There are important implications to justifying a fixed term by limitations on the obligor's responsibility, rather than by optimistic projections of the obligee's future earning capacity. Equity requires that fixed terms based upon such projections of the obligee's future income remain modifiable in case they prove inaccurate. In contrast, the extent of the obligor's responsibility to share any financial shortfall of the obligee's, whatever it is, can be fully assessed at the time of the initial decree. While the size of the obligee's loss (to use the *ALI* terminology) may be affected by post-divorce developments, the extent of the obligor's responsibility for it cannot be. Thus, if the rationale for a fixed term is the extent of the obligor's responsibility, the term should not be modifiable.

3. *Policing Obligee's Rehabilitation Attempts.* *Hecker* confronts a recurring issue: Does the obligee's continuing income shortfall arise from the impact of the marriage on earning capacity or from a failure to make reasonable efforts to maximize earnings? *Hecker* is typical of many courts that apply some version of a "diligence" test. For example, the court may issue an order setting an alimony award with a termination date based upon the expectation that with reasonable diligence the obligee will by then have become self-supporting. *See, e.g., Marriage of Richmond*, 105 Cal. App. 3d 352, 164 Cal. Rptr. 381 (1980). The court can later extend the award beyond the cutoff date for the obligee who has not become self-supporting despite reasonable diligence. As in *Hecker*, the court must evaluate the particular facts to determine if adequate rehabilitation efforts have been made. *See, e.g., Berland v. Berland*, 215 Cal. App. 3d 1257, 264 Cal. Rptr. 210 (1989) (wife's unrealistic efforts to find employment as a paid fundraiser delayed her rehabilitation, justifying reduction of her alimony award); *see also* Or. Rev. Stat. § 107.412(2) ("if the . . . party receiving support has not made a reasonable effort during the previous ten years to become financially self-supporting and independent of the support provided under the decree, the court shall order that support terminated.").

PROBLEM

Problem 4-17. Husband and wife are married for 10 years. No children were born to the marriage, and at the time of divorce, wife is 47 years old. She is a college graduate, but her employment experience was limited to two years before the marriage as a social worker. During the marriage, the wife did not work, but accompanied her husband in business-related travel and helped to entertain business clients. Wife is a diabetic, suffers from a thyroid condition, and often does not feel well, but she does not claim that the illness is entirely disabling or that she is prevented from working at least part time. The parties agree to split the interest in the husband's business. Additionally, wife seeks permanent alimony, arguing that the property does not allow her to meet her reasonable living expenses. Husband argues that any alimony should be restricted to a fixed term, in order to give the wife an incentive to gain the employment she requires to meet her own needs. Is permanent or temporary alimony appropriate? What criteria should the trial court use to answer this question?

NOTE: EARNING CAPACITY LOSSES AND THEIR RECOVERY

While establishing the exact dollar value of the earning capacity loss incurred by any particular person, who, during a long marriage, foregoes the labor market, is difficult (because accurate calculation would require knowing, and projecting the consequences of, the different decisions that particular individual would have made if living a different life), some studies attempt to gauge the average effects, usually by comparing groups of women with varying work histories but similar in other relevant respects. These studies consistently find that a traditional domestic role has a significant negative impact on a women's earning capacity, although they differ on the precise size of the impact, whether the earning capacity can be restored, and on the length of time required to restore it. Many studies focus on the residual loss in earning capacity produced by a parent's temporary withdrawal from market labor. For an early example, see Mary E. Corcoran, *Work Experience, Labor Force Withdrawals, and Women's Wages: Empirical Results Using the 1976 Panel of Income Dynamics*, in WOMEN IN THE LABOR MARKET 216 (Cynthia B. Lloyd, Emily S. Andrews & Curtis L. Gilroy eds., 1979).

What of the duration of the earning capacity decline caused by leaving the workforce? Joyce P. Jacobsen and Laurence M. Levin, *The Effects of Intermittent Labor Force Attachment on Female Earnings*, 118 MONTHLY LABOR REV. 14 (Sept. 1995), looked at data from the mid-1980s. They defined "gappers" as women taking a break from work of six months or longer after attainment of their final educational degree. The average length of the most recent "gap" for such women in their study was 7.5 years. The gappers were on average less well-educated, older, and less productive than "non-gapper" women. In order to determine the effects of the gap itself, they compared two groups of women after correcting for these differences. They found that gappers reentering the workforce on average earned 14 percent less than the "non-gappers," but that 32 months after reentry the wage difference had declined to 10 percent. They conclude that the income effects of gaps clearly decline over time, but that some difference may persist after even 20 years.

A more optimistic view of the speed of wage recovery for gappers is found in Mincer & Ofek, *Interrupted Work Careers: Depreciation and Restoration of Human Capital*, 17 J. HUM. RESOURCES 3 (1982), although they also find a small permanent loss. They found that in the short run the average cost of a year's interruption was a wage reduction of between 3.3 and 7.6 percent, but that in the long run, this average cost declined to between 1.5 and 1.8 percent for each year away. Their data, however, includes women who withdrew from the labor force because of layoffs, ill health, or migration, and these groups experienced greater depreciation of their earning capacity per year away than did other women. They also found that the duration of the work interruption is inversely related to the worker's level of education.

Employment gaps are not the full story, however. The birth of children usually affects the earning capacity of women who continue to work full time as well as those who do not. See Joni Hersch, *The Impact of Nonmarket Work on Market Wages*, 81(2) AM. ECON. REV. 157 (1991), who found that, while the time spent on housework is positively correlated with the number of children for both men and women, the wages of married women, but not married men, are reduced by time spent on housework. (This difference probably results from the fact that married men consistently spend less than half the time of married women in housework. *Id.* at 158. With the range of time on housework so restricted for married men, variations within that range may have little effect on wages.) Hersch suggests that the effect of housework on women's wages results from either a reduction in the effort they put in their market labor, or their demand that employers accommodate their working conditions to their household role, which results in their lower wages. *Id.* at 160. In either case, a residual loss in earning capacity is likely.

A comprehensive study by a distinguished economist concludes that disproportionate responsibility for child care is by far the most important single factor explaining the difference in the earnings of men and women, swamping all other possible factors including discrimination by employers. VICTOR FUCHS, WOMEN'S QUEST FOR ECONOMIC EQUALITY (1988). For example, by looking at women aged 30 to 39 who worked at least 1,000 paid hours during the year, and controlling for both age and education, Fuchs found that women's relative wage declines in a nearly straight line with the number of children in the household, so that women in households with four or more children earn 70 percent of the hourly wage earned by women with no children. The identical result is obtained whether one looks at data from 1960 or 1986, despite the passage of anti-discrimination legislation during this period. *Id.* at 62. On the other hand, while women's wages as a percentage of men's was virtually unchanged between 1960 and 1980, they increased by an unprecedented seven percent between 1980 and 1986. There is no reason to believe that this increase resulted from increased vigor in enforcement of employment discrimination laws. Fuchs concludes that it was instead due largely to the increased proportion of women workers who were born after 1946 and had fewer children than their older sisters. *Id.* at 65–66. *See also* Gary S. Becker, *Human Capital, Effort, and the Sexual Division of Labor*, 3(1) J. LAB. ECON. 533 (Supp. 1985).

Average data will not accurately describe individual cases. Any general rule is thus necessarily a compromise. However, the difficulty of determining the correct length on a case-by-case basis requires use of a general rule if compensation is to be provided at all.

Should alimony awards seek to compensate homemakers in long-term marriages for the full value of their lost earning capacity? Only some portion of the value, so that their loss is shared by both spouses? Should such compensation be paid even to the obligee who can achieve a reasonably satisfactory income without it? Does it matter whether the obligor derived any *financial* benefit from the homemaker's efforts, or whether the obligor's earning capacity as the marriage's end is significantly higher than the obligee's? These are the kinds of questions any systematic approach to alimony must address.

PROBLEMS

Problem 4-18. Jim and Alice, two school teachers, divorce after 23 years of marriage. They have two grown children. Jim's income at divorce is $160,000, Alice's is $112,000. The income differential arises almost entirely from the ten-year leave from teaching that Alice took to care for the children when they were younger. Alice can live comfortably on $112,000, but not as well as Jim can live on $160,000. Alice seeks a permanent alimony award that would equalize the parties' post-dissolution incomes. Will she get it? Should she get it?

Problem 4-19. Fred and Mildred divorce after 18 years, and have no children. Mildred is a family practice physician and Fred a registered nurse. Two years before their divorce, however, Mildred commenced a specialty in hair transplants. This work is phenomenally successful, and Mildred's income has increased from $120,000 to $400,000 annually. Fred's fortunes are less favorable. He developed a debilitating immune system disorder. During the marriage, Fred introduced Mildred to a social acquaintance who, in their ensuing conversation, gave her the idea for the hair transplant business. Fred made no other contributions to the business's success. The spouses' marital assets at dissolution, worth $650,000, were mostly acquired through Mildred's new business venture. The court divides them equally. Fred also seeks permanent maintenance at a level based upon Mildred's newly enhanced income. Mildred objects. What will be the result? What should be the result?

Problem 4-20. During his marriage Pat, an actuary, regularly earned in excess of $300,000 annually by averaging 60-hour work weeks. Bill, her husband, was the primary caretaker of the couple's children and did not work outside the home. Subsequent to the parties' separation, Pat reduced her regular work week to 45 hours, with a corresponding reduction in her income. At divorce, Bill seeks an alimony award based upon the marital living standard. Pat seeks an award based upon her lower, post-separation income. What result? What should be the result?

Problem 4-21. Joan and Michael have one child. Joan is a schoolteacher. When the child was two years old, Michael lost his job in a corporate downsizing. After unsuccessfully seeking comparable work, he opened a consulting business. The business never did well, however, and Joan's income provided the majority of the family's support. Joan was also the primary caretaker of their child, performing the majority of domestic chores. When their child was 8, the parties filed for divorce. At this time Joan's income is $76,000 annually, while Michael income's is sporadic but averages between $20,000 and $40,000. Joan seeks spousal maintenance, arguing that her role as homemaker and primary caretaker has burdened her earning capacity, and she is entitled to payments from him to compensate her for that loss. She offers evidence that she had good prospects for advancement to a principal's post but could not apply because she could not commit herself to the job's additional hours away from home. What result? What should be the result? Why?

Problem 4-22. Jack and Jill married 20 years ago after Jack finished his medical training. After marriage, Jill went back to school and earned a credential as a special education teacher. She worked in this field throughout their marriage, and eventually became a district-wide administrator. Last year, however, the district consolidated its program with an adjoining school district, as a result of which Jill's job was eliminated. She could go back to being a classroom teacher, at lower pay, but has no interest in doing that. Jack and Jill have two children at home, ages 9 and 11, and Jill has been thinking that for now she would prefer to spend more time with them. She has been doing that for the past few months, but now she and Jack have agreed to divorce. Even with child support, she will need a substantial alimony award to maintain something close to the standard of living she has been accustomed to, unless she can find new employment that pays as well as her former job. Even then, she would need an alimony award to come close to the living standard that Jack will enjoy. The parties have agreed that Jill will have primary custody of their children.

a. Would Jill be able to get a long-term, substantial alimony award to allow her to be a full-time homemaker until her children are grown? Should she? Assume her best employment prospect is the classroom teaching job she very much does not want.

b. Assume Jill takes the classroom teaching job. Will she be able to get a permanent alimony award sufficient to bring her standard of living up to the same level as Jack's? Should she? Assume that Jack's annual income as a physician is $300,000, that her teaching job, with her seniority, would pay her $70,000, and that the alimony award necessary to achieve financial equivalence with Jack would be $4,000 per month (in addition to the $6,000 per month Jack will pay in child support).

c. Assume Jill decides she would like to go to law school. Because she also wants to spend time with her children, she feels it is feasible for her to return to school only if she does not have to work. She seeks an alimony award from Jack that will pay her educational costs and allow her to live at her accustomed living standard while she is in school. Will she get such an award? Should she?

E. RESCISSION AFTER THE SHORT-TERM MARRIAGE

ROSE v. ROSE
Alaska Supreme Court
755 P.2d 1121 (1988)

Burke, J.

Debra E. Rose and Duane A. Rose were married in Anchorage, Alaska, on November 17, 1984. They [separated] in May 1986. The marriage produced no children, but each partner had children from a previous marriage. Debra's two children, Victoria and Jonathan, lived with the couple throughout the marriage, as did Duane's daughter, Brandy.

The parties each brought assets into the marriage. Debra owned a condominium and Duane owned a house. The family used Duane's home as a residence during their marriage. Each party had an automobile. During their marriage, both parties were employed, Duane as a police officer, earning approximately $63,000 per year, and Debra as a service order clerk, earning approximately $27,000 per year. Both Duane and Debra have retirement plans through their employers. Likewise, each party has a vacation plan which allows them to accumulate leave time which may be converted to cash. During the marriage Duane accumulated 216 hours of leave time; Debra accumulated seventeen hours.

Shortly after the parties were married, Duane, who had substantial premarital savings, made a down payment on property in Kenai and took title in his own name. Thereafter, the family began using the Kenai property for recreational purposes. While there, the family stayed in a camper/trailer which Duane had purchased approximately two months prior to the parties' marriage. The family also enjoyed the use of a boat and motor purchased by Duane after the couple's marriage.

During the marriage, the parties maintained the separate checking and savings accounts they had established prior to the marriage. Their paychecks were directly deposited into their respective accounts. Debra made payments on her condominium and her automobile from her account, and Duane made his own house payments and the monthly payments on the Kenai lot from his account. The trailer, the boat and the motor were purchased by Duane using his separate funds. Both parties bought groceries and clothing for the family. The parties agree that Duane contributed approximately $47,500 to the mutual household expenditures during the course of the marriage, while Debra contributed approximately $20,000.

At trial, the parties stipulated to a number of facts, including the values and dispositions of some of the properties involved in this marriage. They agreed, for example, that the condominium that Debra brought into the marriage and the house that Duane brought into the marriage would be retained by the respective parties. They also agreed that each would retain the automobile in his or her possession at the time of separation. Consequently, the only items in dispute at the time of trial were the Kenai property, the boat and motor, the trailer, and Duane's accumulated leave time and pension assets.

. . . . Debra contended . . . that the Kenai property, though purchased with savings accumulated by Duane prior to the marriage, was marital property subject to division. She also contended that the trailer, . . . was a precoverture asset subject to division under *AS 25.24.160(a)(4)*.[8] Debra requested that the court award her one-half the value of the foregoing assets, as well as one-half the value of Duane's accumulated leave time and pension, and one-half the value of the boat and motor. Duane argued that the couple had never "come together" as an "economic marriage" and, hence, he should be entitled to keep 100% of the disputed items,

---

[8] *AS 25.24.160(a)(4)* provides:

In a judgment in an action for divorce or action declaring a marriage void or at any time after judgment, the court may provide

(4) for the division between the parties of their property, whether joint or separate, acquired only during coverture, in the manner as may be just, and without regard to which of the parties is in fault; however, the court, in making the division, may invade the property of either spouse acquired before marriage when the balancing of the equities between the parties requires it. . . ."

since they were acquired in his name and with his funds.

[The trial court] agreed with Duane, awarding him 100% of all of the disputed items of property. Debra appeals. . . .

We . . . will reverse the trial court's determination only where it is clearly unjust. Nonetheless, we have established . . . an accepted method of legal analysis to be followed in determining property dispositions under *AS 25.24.160(a)(4)*. The first step . . . is to determine the specific property available for distribution. Such property includes all assets acquired by the parties during marriage, plus any premarital property which the "balancing of equities" suggests should be divided. Second, the court must determine the value of all property available for distribution. Finally, the court must determine the most equitable allocation of the property between the parties, beginning [with a presumption of equality.] The principal factors the trial court must consider . . . are

> the respective ages of the parties; their earning ability; the duration and conduct of each during the marriage; their station in life; the circumstances and necessities of each; their health and physical condition; their financial circumstances, including the time and manner of acquisition of the property in question, its value at the time and its income producing capacity if any.

Merrill v. Merrill, 368 P.2d 546, 547–48 n.4 (Alaska 1962).

It is apparent, from an examination of the record in this case, that the court below did not strictly adhere to the [required] analysis. . . . The court made no determination in its findings as to whether the Kenai property and the trailer were items subject to distribution under *AS 25.24.160(a)(4)*. . . . Moreover, the record makes no mention of the *Merrill* factors and gives no indication that the court began with the "equal division" presumption. Although it might be divined from the record that the court considered some of the *Merrill* factors, *e.g.*, the duration of the marriage, the conduct of parties during marriage, and the time and manner in which the property at issue was acquired, the court gave no discernible consideration to the ages of the parties, their earning capacity, their station in life, their circumstances and necessities, their health, or their financial condition.

Instead, the court took an alternative approach [reasoning] as follows:

> Concerning the division of property, *this is a marriage of an extremely short duration. It's possible to untangle these parties' financial activities and to trace their respective contributions.* I also take into account their expectations, and what reasonable people expect under this type of circumstance, and what the community expects. When people have been together a number of years, there's an expectation that essentially what they have is theirs, but *when people are together a very short time, as these two people were, there's not that expectation*, nobody expects that, even though, of course, one's dreams and hopes are burst, *it's still economically not a unit and if tracing can be done, tracing should be done.*

(Emphasis added). [The court] further noted that both parties had contributed monetarily to the marital estate, in the form of food, clothing and other household expenses, and that neither party had been forced to "scrimp and save to make sure that the marital unit survived while the other party was building his own assets." In light of the short duration of this marriage and the fact that these parties, by their conduct, had indicated that they were "economically not a unit," the court concluded that the best course was to "leave the parties as [it found] them. Mr. Rose tak[ing] his property [and] Mrs. Rose tak[ing] hers." We must decide whether such an alternative analysis was justified . . .

[The court here cited two Oregon cases using the same reasoning as the trial court.]

We are persuaded by the reasoning of these decisions. . . . [T]he parties were married only eighteen months. During that period, they maintained completely separate economic identities, carrying on their individual fiscal affairs in the same manner as they had prior to their marriage. Neither party was forced to forego employment opportunities, and neither party withheld family contributions to the detriment of the other. Finally, none of the items in dispute here appreciated in value during the course of the marriage. We see no compelling reason why, under these circumstances, the trial court should have been bound to begin with an "equal division" presumption, or to engage in a painstaking analysis under the *Merrill* factors before concluding that assets Duane accrued or purchased with his separate, uncommingled funds were his to retain. We believe that the disposition arrived at by the trial court put the parties in, as nearly as possible, the financial position they would have occupied had no marriage taken place. Accordingly, we cannot say that the result reached was clearly unjust.

. . . [I]n marriages of short duration, where there has been no significant commingling of assets between the parties, the trial court may, without abusing its discretion, treat the property division as an action in the nature of rescission, aimed at placing the parties in, as closely as possible, the financial position they would have occupied had no marriage taken place. Our reading of the record . . . convinces us that the trial court recognized this principle and applied it appropriately. The judgment is therefore AFFIRMED.

[The dissenting opinion by Justice Compton is omitted.]

NOTES

1. ***Rescission.*** The idea of rescission comes primarily from the area of contract law, and its application to family law is not entirely comfortable. Even the few jurisdictions which have expressly endorsed the option of rescission have emphasized that this conclusion should be reached only in cases where the marriage has been short *and* there has been no significant commingling of funds *and* there are no other equitable factors pointing to a different sort of division. *See, e.g., Marriage of Massee*, 970 P.2d 1203 (Or. 1999) (all criteria must be met); *Bell v. Bell*, 794 P.2d 97 (Alaska 1990) (though marriage only 16 months long, rescission inappropriate because of significant commingling of funds).

2. ***ALI Principles.*** In dissolving short-term marriages, the *ALI Principles*, § 5.13, adopt the general principle that the divorce court should return the parties to the position they were in before they were married. The *Principles* also recognize, however, that there are facts other than commingling which could

render rescission inappropriate even in a very short marriage such as the kind of situation faced in *Lill v. Lill*, 520 N.W.2d 855 (N.D. 1994) (alimony award appropriate at termination of short marriage where claimant left employment because of marriage and at divorce could only find employment at "a significantly lower wage"; award's purpose is to "place the disadvantaged spouse in the position she could have been in if it were not for the marriage").

3. *Combined with Premarital Cohabitation.* Where the parties have lived together for an extended period of time prior to a short marriage, rescission will likely be inappropriate or difficult, as the parties' funds will likely have comingled significantly. Additionally, some courts have held that an extended period of premarital cohabitation should be treated as a factor in helping to determine whether alimony is appropriate. *E.g.*, *Sprouse v. Sprouse*, 678 S.E.2d 328 (Ga. 2009) (alimony granted though couple's marriage had lasted less than 2 years; including premarital cohabitation, couple had been together for 13 years); *Lind and Lind*, 139 P.3d 1032 (Or. App. 2006) (four-year premarital cohabitation properly considered in decision to award alimony after marriage that lasted less than five years).

F. MODIFICATION OF AWARDS: SOME SPECIAL PROBLEMS

[1]   Basic Rules

MODEL MARRIAGE AND DIVORCE ACT

§ 316.

(a) Except as otherwise provided in subsection (f) of Section 306 [pertaining to separation agreements] the provisions of any decree respecting maintenance or support may be modified only as to installments accruing subsequent to the motion for modification and only upon a showing of changed circumstances so substantial and continuing as to make the terms unconscionable. The provisions as to property disposition may not be revoked or modified, unless the court finds the existence of conditions that justify the reopening of a judgment under the laws of this state.

(b) Unless otherwise agreed in writing or expressly provided in the decree, the obligation to pay future maintenance is terminated upon the death of either party or the remarriage of the party receiving maintenance.

(c) Unless otherwise agreed in writing or expressly provided in the decree, provisions for the support of a child are terminated by emancipation of the child but not by the death of a parent obligated to support the child. When a parent obligated to pay support dies, the amount of support may be modified, revoked, or commuted to a lump sum payment, to the extent just and appropriate in the circumstances.

The MMDA provision is fairly straightforward, as well as typical in most of its results: property division is not modifiable, while maintenance and child support are; maintenance is presumed to terminate at the remarriage of the receiving spouse, while neither child support nor property settlement is so affected. Death of either party terminates maintenance obligations, but not claims based upon the allocation of marital property. These results have a certain logic which should make them relatively easy to keep in mind. If a property division award is based upon property rights, then a judgment regarding those property rights should be as final, and nonmodifiable, as any other civil judgment, and should survive the parties as assets or liabilities of their respective estates. Support judgments, on the other hand, were historically based upon current facts concerning the needs and resources of the parties, which may change. They are continuing obligations, and as with analogous forms of equitable relief, can be reevaluated if a change in circumstances warrants. Because of the historical basis of spousal support, it is not surprising that it would normally be presumed to terminate upon the receiving spouse's remarriage, but there is no similar basis for presuming that the custodial spouse's right to child support payments would also end, unless a new spouse undertakes legal responsibility for the children by adopting them.

Not all jurisdictions follow the MMDA rules. For example, contrary to subsection (c), most states provide that child support obligations die with the obligor, and many states require the modification petitioner to prove only that there has been a change in circumstances justifying the modification, and not that there has been a change "so substantial" as to make the existing order "unconscionable." Second, the MMDA rules do not always apply comfortably to some modern categories of award developed after these rules were written. For example, courts usually hold reimbursement awards are not modifiable and are unaffected by the obligee's remarriage, even if made under the rubric of "alimony." See Marriage of Francis, 442 N.W.2d 59 (Iowa 1989); Reiss v. Reiss, 490 A.2d 378 (N.J. Super. Ch. Div. 1984); Petersen v. Petersen, 737 P.2d 237 (Utah App. 1987). Likewise, conceiving of alimony as a form of compensation suggests a different treatment of obligee's remarriage than traditional law. We will examine that question further below.

Finally, although the modification rules differentiate among child support, alimony and property division, judicial decrees and separation agreements do not always explicitly distinguish the financial elements of an award. Poor drafting is not the only reason. The parties may have a tax incentive to treat periodic payments as alimony rather than child support (because the higher earning obligor can typically make more effective use of the tax deduction) and for similar reasons may wish to manipulate the alimony/property settlement characterization for tax purposes. An ambiguous agreement may result from the desire to have a particular element characterized one way for divorce law purposes and another for tax purposes. The form of the award is not necessarily dispositive. A division of property might be satisfied in periodic payments, either to make it look like an alimony award in order to achieve a certain tax result, or simply because the amount is too great for the obligor to pay in one lump sum. Whether such manipulations are effective under the tax law turns on the changing tax rules. Here our point is to make clear that for divorce law purposes it is the actual function and justification of the award, rather than the label attached to it, that normally determines how it is treated in divorce law for modification purposes.

Some examples will make the point. In *Zullo v. Zullo*, 613 A.2d 544 (Pa. 1992), the husband had been ordered to make payments to the wife for 48 months following divorce, as his contribution toward retiring the marital debt — a debt the wife had settled by mortgaging her house. Because the trial court labeled the payments alimony, another trial court terminated them upon her remarriage. Were they really alimony? Not if one considers the allocation of debts an aspect of property division, and the original order merely a tool by which this debt was equitably allocated. That is essentially what the Pennsylvania Supreme Court concluded in finding no termination upon remarriage. *See also Andrews v. Whitaker*, 453 S.E.2d 735 (Ga. 1995) (suggesting functional criteria for distinguishing alimony from property); *Wagoner v. Wagoner*, 648 A.2d 299 (Pa. 1994) (payments intended to approximate wife's share of husband's pension are property even though parties labeled them alimony); *Amos v. Amos*, 879 S.W.2d 856 (Tenn. App. 1994) (payments terminating on death or obligee's remarriage are not property but alimony); *Erickson v. Erickson*, 449 N.W.2d 173 (Minn. 1989) (payments labeled alimony for tax purposes are really child support, and should now be relabeled so that they can continue past recipient's remarriage); *Lieberman v. Lieberman*, 568 A.2d 1157 (Md. Sp. App. 1990) (payments unallocated for tax reasons are modifiable because they are in fact child support); *Schaffer v. Schaffer*, 643 P.2d 1300 (Or. App. 1982) (payment labeled "alimony" by agreement, for tax purposes, is really non-modifiable property settlement). In at least one case, the wife's property interest in her husband's federal pension was labeled "alimony" in order to preserve a garnishment remedy because of federal rules barring garnishment to enforce property division (but not alimony) obligations. When the wife remarried, the former husband sought termination of the payments, but the court held that these alimony payments could continue past remarriage since they substituted for property division. *McGhee v. McGhee*, 131 Cal. App. 3d 408, 182 Cal. Rptr. 456 (1982). The wife thus reaped the benefit of having the payment considered as alimony for purposes of federal law, while treated as property division under state law.

[2] Remarriage of the Obligee

When alimony reflected the law's acceptance of a gender-based support duty, it followed naturally that any claim would terminate upon the woman's remarriage:

> [I]t is against public policy that a woman should have support or its equivalent during the same period from each of two men. . . . Aside from positive unseemliness, it is illogical and unreasonable that she should have the equivalent of an obligation for support by way of alimony from a former husband and an obligation from a present husband for an adequate support at the same time.

Wolter v. Wolter, 158 N.W.2d 616, 619 (Neb. 1968), quoting *Bowman v. Bowman*, 79 N.W.2d 554 (Neb. 1956). But this rationale is undercut by the modern rule making alimony available to a needy spouse of either sex. If the alimony obligee's need continues after the remarriage, why should alimony terminate? The cases do not much address this question, even though they continue to enforce the rule ending alimony at remarriage. For example, in *Dunaway v. Dunaway*, 560 N.E.2d 171 (Ohio 1990), obligee remarried 10 years after divorce, but new husband's only income was his disability payments. Claiming continued need, she opposed termination of her alimony. In rejecting her claim, the Ohio Supreme Court said:

> . . . [W]hen parties marry they assume mutual obligations of maintenance and support. It is a conscious election to share life together, and this necessarily includes financial circumstances. To hold a first spouse responsible for continued support of a former spouse who has remarried is tantamount to imposing a legal obligation to support another couple's marriage. . . . [W]here a dependent divorced spouse remarries, the obligation of the first spouse to pay sustenance alimony terminates as a matter of law, unless . . . the parties have executed a separation agreement in contemplation of divorce that expressly provides for the continuation of sustenance alimony after the dependent party remarries. . . .

> Consequently, the fact that defendant chose to marry Barnard when his sources of income consisted of approximately $830 per month in Social Security benefits and $553 per month in retirement benefits in no way diminishes the choice she voluntarily made to share her living expenses with him. While Barnard may not be wholly able to support defendant, Ohio law recognizes defendant's obligation to assist in supporting her new husband.

Id. at 232.

In an opinion that provides a comprehensive review of authorities nationwide, the Massachusetts Supreme Court concluded that most states' statutes specify automatic termination of alimony upon the obligee's remarriage, and that most of the rest apply a judicially-created rule that remarriage terminates alimony in the absence of extraordinary circumstances. *Keller v. O'Brien*, 652 N.E.2d 589 (Mass. 1995); *see also* Annotation, *Alimony as Affected by Recipient Spouse's Remarriage in Absence of Controlling Specific Statute*, 47 A.L.R.5th 129 (1997). In adopting the extraordinary circumstance rule itself, *Keller* observed that such extraordinary circumstances are "rare." The court provided but one example of such a circumstance: where the obligee would otherwise become a public charge.

A small number of states take a contrary approach — treating marriage (as most states treat cohabitation — see the next section) as an event that *might* affect the recipient's level of need, but which will not cause an *automatic* termination. *See, e.g., Taylor v. Taylor*, 819 A.2d 684 (Vt. 2002); *Marriage of Jones and Jones*, 17 P.3d 491 (Ore. App. 2001); *Harris v. Harris*, 2009 Tenn. App. LEXIS 264 (Feb. 18, 2009). In *Maher v. Maher*, 90 P.3d 739 (Wyo. 2004), the Wyoming Supreme Court clarified that not only does alimony not terminate in that state upon remarriage, remarriage does not even create a legal or evidential presumption. The burden remains entirely on the party seeking modification of alimony to show that the remarriage created a substantial change of circumstances from the time of divorce.

Does the *Dunaway* analysis also apply if alimony is based not on need, but on a compensation rationale such as that adopted by the ALI? Perhaps. If an alimony obligee who remains in "need" despite her remarriage nonetheless loses her award under current law, then perhaps the obligee whose financial loss continues after remarriage may be denied further compensation. A useful overview of the arguments for and against the automatic termination of alimony upon remarriage appears in Cynthia Lee Starnes, *One More Time: Alimony, Intuition, and the Remarriage-Termination Rule*, 81 INDIANA L.J. 971 (2006).

One's rationale for ending alimony at the obligee's remarriage may have implications for how the law should treat nonmarital cohabitation by the obligee. It is often said that nonmarital cohabitation is relevant only insofar as it has an impact on the obligee's financial circumstances. That does not appear to be the principle applied to remarriage, which ends alimony nearly everywhere without regard to financial consequences for the obligee. Are any of the foregoing efforts successful at explaining that result? If so, one should perhaps reconsider them when we address cohabitation in the next section.

NOTES

1. ***Agreements to Make Alimony Non-modifiable.*** A number of jurisdictions will enforce separation agreement provisions that alter the usual rules of modification. Missouri is one jurisdiction that allows the parties to agree to a no-modification rule. MISSOURI STAT. ANN. § 452.325(6). The state's courts have taken this very seriously, to the point of continuing to enforce such a provision even after the wife (allegedly) tried to kill the husband. *Richardson v. Richardson*, 218 S.W.3d 426 (Mo. 2007).

2. ***Agreements to Continue Alimony Past Remarriage.*** Most states will enforce the parties' agreement to continue alimony beyond the obligee's remarriage. What if an agreement-based decree specifies events that will terminate maintenance, such as the obligee's death, but does not mention the obligee's remarriage? Some courts conclude such an omission is intentional and continue the alimony. *E.g.*, *In re Marriage of Sherman*, 162 Cal. App. 3d 1132, 208 Cal. Rptr. 832 (1984); *Raymond v. Raymond*, 447 A.2d 70 (Me. 1982); *Sprentall v. Sprentall*, 75 Misc. 2d 405, 347 N.Y.S.2d 659 (Sup. Ct. 1973). Other courts require explicit language for continuance of the alimony. *Gunderson v. Gunderson*, 408 N.W.2d 852 (Minn. 1987); *In re Williams*, 796 P.2d 421 (Wash. 1990); *In re Thornton*, 95 Cal. App. 4th 251, 115 Cal. Rptr. 2d 380 (2002); *Moore v. Jacobsen*, 817 A.2d 212 (Md. 2003). A California court held an agreement specifying that alimony "shall be nonmodifiable for any reason whatsoever" was insufficiently explicit to override the statutory presumption that alimony ends on the recipient's remarriage, since "nonmodifiable" is not the same as "nonterminable." *In re Marriage of Glasser*, 181 Cal. App. 3d 149, 226 Cal. Rptr. 229 (1986).

3. ***Agreements to Revive Alimony If Second Marriage Fails.*** Generally, alimony obligations terminated upon remarriage do not revive if the remarriage ends in divorce: the former obligee must seek relief from the second spouse. But of course alimony claims against the second spouse may fail if the second marriage is short. The remedy for the foresighted is an agreement that provides for the revival of the first spouse's alimony obligation in such a case. *See, for example, Diedrich v. Diedrich*, 424 N.W.2d 580 (Minn. App. 1988) (court enforces first husband's promise

to reinstate his maintenance payments if the wife's second marriage ended in divorce within five years). The first husband might make such an agreement to encourage his former wife to remarry, in the hope that the remarriage will last and thus end his obligation.

4. *The Annulled Second Marriage.* Because an annulment theoretically declares that a marriage never existed in the first place, arguably the obligee's annulled remarriage should not affect the obligor's alimony obligations. Although conceptually neat, this reasoning often leads to unreasonable results. Under the old fault-oriented divorce laws, spouses might have sought an annulment rather than divorce only because divorce was difficult to obtain. Under some modern statutes, the conceptual distinction may no longer be so clear, because there is no difference in the grounds for divorce and the grounds for annulment.

Although the annulment issue does not arise often, especially under modern divorce laws which have reduced the use of annulments, generally alimony obligations terminated on remarriage are not revived if the remarriage is held void. *In re Harris*, 560 N.E.2d 1138 (Ill. App. 1990); *Falk v. Falk*, 462 N.W.2d 547 (Wis. App. 1990). In *Hutton v. Hutton*, 118 S.W.3d 176 (Ky. 2003), overruling prior case law, the court held that no such revival is allowed: the recipient's remarriage terminates alimony, and the alimony is to stay terminated even if the remarriage is annulled. *See also Fredo v. Fredo*, 894 A.2d 399 (Conn. Super. 2005). Some courts reaching this result qualify it by saying that the annulled remarriage must be valid on its face in order to terminate the first spouse's alimony obligations. *Hodges v. Hodges*, 578 P.2d 1001 (Ariz. Ct. App. 1978); *Joye v. Yon*, 547 S.E.2d 888 (S.C. Ct. App. 2001) (wife's remarriage annulled because of would-be new husband's previous undissolved marriage; court reinstates alimony because wife's second marriage was "void" rather than "voidable").

A handful of states, however, hold that whether the annulment revives alimony should be decided on a case-by-case basis. *E.g., In re Marriage of Cargill and Rollins*, 843 P.2d 1335 (Colo. 1993); *cf. Marriage of Weintraub*, 167 Cal. App. 3d 420, 213 Cal. Rptr. 159 (1985) (wife could reclaim lost alimony payments after annulment upon proof that she had consented to annulled second marriage only because she had been abducted, beaten and threatened with harm to her family). In *In re Marriage of Campbell*, 38 Cal. Rptr. 3d 908 (Ct. App. 2006), the court construed a statute that required termination upon remarriage as *not* requiring termination of a *temporary* spousal support order when the recipient spouse remarries before her divorce is final (thus creating a void second marriage). A small number of jurisdictions seem to have a blanket rule refusing reinstatement of alimony after a second marriage, even if that marriage is annulled. *See Beebe v. Beebe*, 179 S.E.2d 758 (Ga. 1971) (emphasizing that annulled marriages could be revived later by subsequent events and proceedings); *In re Marriage of Kolb*, 425 N.E.2d 1301 (1981) (emphasizing that rule of termination on "remarriage" focuses on ceremony, not relationship).

PROBLEMS

Problem 4-23. Sam and Alice were married for 20 years when they divorced. Alice, a homemaker throughout their marriage, was awarded permanent alimony of $3,000 monthly. Six months later, Sam and Alice reconciled and remarried. Sadly, however, their new marriage lasted only three months, when they agreed they could no longer live together. They filed for divorce. It is virtually unheard of in this jurisdiction to obtain an alimony award in connection with the dissolution of a marriage of only three months' duration. Could Alice get her original alimony award reinstated? Should she be able to? Are there other arguments to be made on her behalf?

Problem 4-24. Alice was awarded $7,000 monthly alimony from George, who divorced her after a 20-year marriage. Their children are grown, so Alice has no custodial responsibilities and receives no child support. The alimony award was based on the fact that Alice had never worked during the marriage and could not now realistically expect to obtain employment that would maintain her at the economic level that she was accustomed to in her marriage with George. George is a successful businessman earning $500,000 annually.

Alice falls in love with Pablo and they marry. Pablo is a painter. He earns nothing now, although some say he shows promise. He might be able to obtain some kind of unskilled employment while still painting, but it would produce little income and interfere with his painting. He has no ability to earn much more than minimum wage in any event (unless his paintings start selling).

(a) George seeks to eliminate alimony payments based upon Alice's remarriage. What result? What should be the result? Assume that by the time the hearing on George's motion is held, Alice's marriage to Pablo had already failed, and divorce proceedings concluded. Does this alter the result? Should it?

(b) Suppose before remarriage, Alice had sought legal advice. What would you have advised her to do?

[3]   Obligee's Cohabitation

O'CONNOR BROTHERS ABALONE CO. v. BRANDO
California Court of Appeal
114 Cal. Rptr. 773 (1974)

Compton, Associate Justice.

In July of 1968, in connection with the annulment of their marriage, Marlon and Movita Brando executed a written agreement purporting to settle certain financial matters and child custody rights.

As a part of that agreement Marlon undertook to make monthly payments of $600 for the support of the minor children and monthly payments of $1400 for the support of Movita. Only the latter payments to Movita are at issue here. . . .

The resolution of this dispute turns on whether, under the terms of the agreement . . . , her conduct was such as to terminate Marlon's obligation to make further payments. The crucial provision . . . is as follows:

"(a) Defendant agrees to pay . . . Plaintiff, the amount of $1,400.00 per month . . . for a period of one-hundred fifty-six (156) months, *or until she remarries or dies, whichever occurs sooner. For the purposes of this Agreement, 'remarriage' shall include, without limitation, Plaintiff's appearing to maintain a marital relationship with any person, or any ceremonial marriage entered into by Plaintiff even though the same may later be annulled or otherwise terminated or rendered invalid.*" (Emphasis added.)

In reliance on this "remarriage" clause, Marlon ceased to make the payments in April 1971. He contends that in 1968, Movita entered into a relationship with one James Ford which . . . was within the provisions of the term "remarriage". . . .

The evidence . . . left little doubt that Movita and Ford enjoyed a relationship of substantial duration, which . . . bore the objective indicia of marriage. By their own admission they engaged in frequent sexual intercourse. Ford kept his clothes at [Movita's] residence in Coldwater Canyon, he ate meals there, many of which he prepared. Ford frequently purchased groceries for their meals by charging them to Movita's account at the market, he drove her cars and was authorized to use her charge account at one of the major department stores.

Additionally, Ford on significant occasions gave the Coldwater Canyon address as his own. He used that address in applying for a driver's license and in reporting to his probation officer. The two were often in company together and in company with Movita's children in public.

The trial court's finding that they "lived" together is well supported. The further finding that such relationship could not be reasonably interpreted as indicating that Ford and Movita were in fact married apparently flowed from the absence of any evidence that they told anyone they were married.

The parties' real dispute centers on whether the above described relationship is one contemplated by the Agreement . . .

O'Connor contends, and the trial court concluded, that the phrase "appearing to maintain a marital relationship" means a holding out by Movita that she was in fact married or conduct on her part that would imply a marriage in fact. According to this version, a meretricious relationship, no matter how intimate and enduring, would not terminate the obligation for support payments so long as it was made clear to the world that Movita and her paramour were *not* married. This interpretation would place a premium on the persistence with which Movita publicized the illicit nature of the relationship.

On the other hand, Marlon contends that the Agreement was designed to prevent Movita from maintaining a relationship with a male companion as a result of which the latter appeared to enjoy the usual rewards of marriage without assuming the obligations which flow from a ceremony of marriage. According to Marlon the Agreement means a "marital type" relationship and such interpretation is necessary to avoid what he sought to avoid, i.e., the possibility that Movita's male companion, in sharing Movita's shelter, bed and board, would also benefit from the support payments which Marlon was providing. . . .

Marlon testified his intent was ". . . that I was not to pay for any man that she might be living with through the support payments; that if she were going to live with somebody, then they would have to support her, and it would not fall to me, outside of the support for the children, . . . to pay for her continuing support." Movita testified that she understood that if she "lived" with another man the support payments would stop.

Mr. Garey, the attorney, testified that his client Marlon's and his intent were to provide for terminating the payments if Movita lived with another man who would benefit from the support payments and if the relationship would be demeaning to Marlon in the eyes of the public.

The final Agreement evolved from two previously written drafts. The first draft simply used the phrase "until she remarries" without further definition. To this Marlon objected. The second draft defined remarriage as "cohabitation by plaintiff with any person." To this Movita objected.

Mr. Garey testified that Movita's attorney indicated that the objection to "cohabitation" was based on a fear that the word might apply to so-called "one night stands." . . .

Clearly the purpose of the Agreement was not to circumscribe Movita's sexual activity per se as she was free to engage in sexual intercourse with other men. The Agreement sought to embrace actual ceremonial marriages on the one hand and on the other, relationships which were not marriages but which had the attributes of marriage such as companionship of substantial duration, the sharing of habitation, eating together and sexual intimacy. The characterization of such a relationship as "marital" does not depend on whether third persons are led to believe the existence of a ceremonial marriage. In fact, public belief that Movita and Ford were actually married would be less demeaning to Marlon than their conduct of "living" together while disavowing an actual marriage.

What is important here from the standpoint of the objectives of the Agreement is that such a relationship creates the strong probability that the male partner will derive benefit from the support payments. And that, in fact, is what occurred here. O'Connor contends in its brief that there was no common financial or economic relationship between Ford and Movita and that this detracts from the "marital" character of the relationship. Interestingly enough, however, in respondent's support of this argument it is admitted that Movita paid for the upkeep of her cars which Ford drove. She paid for the groceries which Ford charged, and she paid for the department store purchases which Ford charged. It appears without contradiction that Movita paid for the maintenance of the house in which they lived.

We interpret the phrase "appearing to maintain a marital relationship" as including the appearance of "living together" under circumstances such as existed here, whether or not there is the appearance of marriage in fact. This appears to us to be the only possible reasonable interpretation of the Agreement.

[Thus, O'Connor lost.]. . . .

LOVE v. LOVE
South Carolina Court of Appeals
626 S.E.2d 56 (2006)

WILLIAMS, J.:

Ann B. Love (Wife) appeals a family court order terminating her former husband's alimony obligation. We affirm.

Miller L. Love, Jr., (Husband) and Wife married in Florence, South Carolina, on June 3, 1962. In January 1990, Wife was granted a divorce on the ground of adultery. The final divorce order incorporated a separation agreement . . . [which] addressed all of the major issues arising from the marriage, including, but not limited to, custody, visitation, spousal support, and the division of marital property.

The parties agreed Husband would pay Wife $1,100 per month in alimony, an obligation which "shall end . . . upon the Wife's remarriage or death, whichever occurs first." With the exception of the provisions concerning the division of marital property, the agreement provides:

> The provisions of this Agreement . . . shall be subject to the approval, confirmation and adoption of the Court, such that it becomes the Order of the Court and enforceable and modifiable as such.

In 1995, Wife petitioned the family court for a modification of the alimony agreement. Prior to a hearing on the matter, the parties agreed Husband's alimony obligation would increase by $600 per month, making the total monthly payment $1,700.

In 1995, Wife began dating Otis Goodwin, who had recently divorced his first wife. Approximately a year and a half later, Wife moved in with Goodwin into the home they share today. Goodwin testified that Wife pays him $200 per week for rent and her share of the utilities. Over the course of their relationship, Goodwin loaned Wife $8,000, which was repaid, and a partially outstanding business loan of $25,000. Wife is also a cardholder on Goodwin's American Express Account, although each pays his or her own portion of the credit card bill. Mr. Goodwin has authority to write checks on Wife's business's checking account. In 1997, Goodwin transferred to Wife a parcel of land in Surfside, South Carolina worth approximately $40,000 for the consideration of "$5.00 love and affection." Goodwin routinely attends holiday celebrations and special occasions with Wife's family and Wife's grandchildren refer to him with terms of affection such as "Grandpa O." Although both Wife and Goodwin openly admit the romantic nature of their relationship, they are not formally married, nor do they express plans of marrying in the future.

In 2003, Husband filed the present action, petitioning the court for further modification of the alimony agreement. Specifically, Husband alleged Wife's amorous relationship and seven-year cohabitation with Goodwin constituted grounds for termination, or at least a substantial reduction, of his alimony obligation. Husband averred that 2002 amendments to South Carolina Code Section 20-3-130(B)(1)

(1976) prescribed this modification. Alternatively, he argued Wife's relationship was tantamount to marriage, warranting a termination of alimony as a significant change in circumstances under the common law of alimony.

The family court agreed with Husband and ordered the termination of alimony pursuant to both the recent statutory amendments and a determination that Wife's relationship is "tantamount to marriage.". . . .

Wife argues the family court erred in terminating Husband's alimony obligation because the family court lacked the authority to do so under both the law of this state and the terms of the agreement. We disagree.

In *Moseley v. Mosier*, 279 S.C. 348, 306 S.E.2d 624 (1983), our supreme court perspicuously held that the family court has the authority to modify alimony agreements "unless the agreement unambiguously denies the court jurisdiction" to do so. Not only does the present agreement fail to expressly deny the family court this authority, it definitively grants the court such in stating that its terms "shall be subject to the approval, confirmation and adoption of the Court, such that it becomes the Order of the Court and enforceable and modifiable as such." Accordingly, the family court had authority to modify the alimony in the present case.

Wife subtly concedes this point, a position due, no doubt, to the fact that she herself petitioned the court for an increase in alimony in 1995. Wife, however, would have us somehow distinguish between the power to *modify* alimony and the power to *terminate* alimony. We draw no such distinction. Parties to a separation agreement may either agree to make alimony unmodifiable, or leave the issue within the traditional oversight of the family court. Should the parties agree to the latter, the family court may modify alimony to the same extent permissible in court-awarded alimony, a scope of authority which certainly includes the power to terminate payments based on substantial changes in the parties' circumstances. *See* S.C. Code Ann. § 20-3-170 (1976); *Bryson v. Bryson*, 347 S.C. 221, 224, 553 S.E.2d 493, 495 (Ct.App.2001).

Having concluded the family court possessed the authority to terminate alimony, we move to the issue of whether this authority was properly exercised in the present case. As a ground for termination, the family court concluded Wife's relationship with Goodwin was tantamount to marriage, constituting a substantial change in circumstances which warranted alimony termination. We affirm the family court's termination of alimony on this ground.[1]

"The purpose of alimony is to provide the ex-spouse a substitute for the support which was incident to the former marital relationship." *Croom v. Croom*, 305 S.C. 158, 160, 406 S.E.2d 381, 382 (Ct.App.1991). "Living with another, whether it is with a live-in lover, a relative, or a platonic housemate, changes [a person's] circumstances and alters [his or] her required financial support." *Vance v. Vance*, 287 S.C. 615, 618, 340 S.E.2d 554, 555 (Ct.App.1986). Because the State has "a compelling

---

[1] Because we affirm the family court on the ground Wife's relationship constitutes a change of circumstance warranting alimony termination, we need not address the statutory grounds for the family court's termination of alimony.

interest in promoting marriage and discouraging meretricious relationships," a rule allowing alimony to continue when the supported spouse cohabits without marrying is "illogical and offensive to public policy." *Croom*, 305 S.C. at 160, 406 S.E.2d at 382. Accordingly, courts will treat the relationship between a supported spouse and a third party as "tantamount to marriage" and terminate alimony when the two cohabitate for an extended period of time and some degree of economic reliance between them is established.

Such a relationship is certainly established in the case at bar. Wife and Goodwin have cohabitated for over seven years. . . . [T]he record reflects the pair share a substantial amount of expenses, be it in the form of loans, reduced rent, or gifts. The record also reflects the romantic nature of the party's relationship and the unmistakable connection between Goodwin and Wife's family. We therefore affirm the family court's conclusion that Wife and Goodwin are in relationship that is tantamount to marriage. . . .

AFFIRMED.

STILWELL and KITTREDGE, JJ., concur.

NOTES

1. ***The Effect of Obligee's Cohabitation When Parties Have No Agreement.*** Both the cases deal with the application of the parties' separation agreement. What is the rule if there is no agreement concerning cohabitation? States vary.

a. ***The traditional rule.*** The traditional rule, surviving in many states and exemplified in *Love*, recognizes that the obligee's cohabitation can be a basis for modifying or terminating alimony, apart from its financial impact. *E.g.*, GA. CODE. ANN. § 19-6-19(b) (in addition to change in income or financial status, "the voluntary cohabitation of [the obligee] with a third party in a meretricious relationship shall also be grounds to modify . . . alimony"); NEW YORK DOM. REL. L. § 248 ("annulling" alimony orders for an ex-wife "habitually living with another man" if she "hold[s] herself out" as his wife); UTAH CODE ANN. § 30-3-5(10) ("Any [alimony] order . . . terminates upon establishment by the [obligor] that the former spouse is cohabitating with another person."); ILL. ST. CH. 750 § 5/510(c) ("Unless otherwise agreed by the parties in a written agreement set forth in the judgment or otherwise approved by the court, the obligation to pay future maintenance is terminated . . . if the party receiving maintenance cohabits with another person on a resident, continuing conjugal basis"); W.V. CODE § 48-5-707 (courts have authority to modify or terminate alimony if the recipient is in a "de facto marriage," based on the nature of that relationship and its economic effects).

In such statutes, particular care is necessary in defining the "cohabitation" that can trigger the provision. The principal difficulty, as illustrated by the *Brando* negotiations, is distinguishing between couples who share a household and those who do not even though they may see one another regularly. Courts are in fairly wide agreement that cohabitation means more than an intimate relationship, and even where the parties do live together, a minimum duration may be thought necessary to trigger a statutory rule. *See, e.g., Leming v. Leming*, 590 N.E.2d 1027

(Ill. App. 1992) (obligee's four-month cohabitation does not meet statutory test). At the same time, a longer sharing of a residence may be inadequate lacking other indicia of "cohabitation." *Marriage of Nolen*, 558 N.E.2d 781 (Ill. App. 1990) (alimony should not be terminated even though obligee's room and board were provided by the man in whose house she lived, in exchange for nursing and housekeeping services, where there was no de facto marriage between them). For a comprehensive review of the many different ways that cohabitation clauses have been phrased in agreements, see *Gordon v. Gordon*, 675 A.2d 540 (Md. 1996) (holding such agreements enforceable but concluding wife was not "cohabiting" within contractual meaning of that term). The Illinois Supreme Court held one alimony obligee to be cohabiting within the meaning of its statute even though her partner was impotent. *Marriage of Sappington*, 478 N.E.2d 376, 379 (Ill. 1985) ("[I]f to avoid the application of this section all that a person had to do was to claim impotency or deny any sexual relations, then the purpose of this statute could easily be defeated")

b. *The recent trend.* The trend appears to favor the financial impact rule: the obligee's cohabitation is relevant only insofar as it affects her need. Recent cases favoring this approach include *Lyon v. Lyon*, 728 A.2d 127 (Me. 1999) (cohabiting obligee's alimony should not have been reduced because the cohabitation did not change her financial circumstances sufficiently to justify the modification); *Ozolins v. Ozolins*, 705 A.2d 1230 (N.J. Super. 1998) (fact of cohabitation alone insufficient to justify termination of alimony; evidence of financial consequence of cohabitation in this case justified reduction, not termination); *Marriage of Chew*, 888 P.2d 428 (Mont. 1995) (trial court wrong to provide alimony would terminate if recipient cohabited, since test is financial need); *Hollowell v. Hollowell*, 369 S.E.2d 451 (Va. App. 1988) (cohabitation provides a basis for modification only when it results in a change in financial circumstances); *Ramsbottom v. Ramsbottom*, 542 A.2d 1098 (R.I. 1988) (same); *Gottsegen v. Gottsegen*, 492 N.E.2d 1133 (Mass. 1986) (same); *Bisig v. Bisig*, 469 A.2d 1348 (N.H. 1983) (same); *Myhre v. Myhre*, 296 N.W.2d 905 (S.D. 1980) (same); *Combs v. Combs*, 787 S.W.2d 260 (Ky. 1990) (same); *cf. Yarnell v. Yarnell*, 2006 Ohio App. LEXIS 3886 (July 31, 2006) (statute silent on effect of cohabitation, but courts choose to treat it as a factor potentially justifying modification of alimony). Courts sometimes say they follow a financial test when it appears they do not.

2. *The Validity of Contractual Terms on the Effect of Cohabitation.* At least one jurisdiction holds that the parties may not enter an enforceable agreement making the recipient's cohabitation relevant to alimony (either by way of automatic termination or automatic reduction of amount) where the default statutory rule would make cohabitation irrelevant. *See Ramsbottom v. Ramsbottom*, 542 A.2d 1098 (R.I. 1988). For precisely the contrary result, see *Bramson v. Bramson*, 404 N.E.2d 469 (Ill. App. 1980), in which the court held that the Illinois law described in Note 1 (making continuous cohabitation a ground for terminating alimony) is "mandatory" and cannot be "avoided" by the parties' agreement. Both approaches — refusing to allow party agreement to modify the state's default rule — are rare, and neither seems to make much sense. Separation agreements are ordinarily submitted to the court for approval, and could in any event be set aside for procedural unconscionability (*see* Chapter 8). The question here is whether an agreement that passes these process tests should be rejected because of public policy objections to its substantive content. Given the split among the states as to the appropriate rule on cohabitation, it seems remarkable for courts to decide that *either* choice is so far from reasonable that parties may not voluntarily adopt it.

3. Conceptual Difficulties With the Financial-Impact Rule.

Cases limiting consideration of cohabitation to its financial impact sometimes say that reduced need is the only financial impact that matters. That is, they purport to make cohabitation relevant only to the extent that the obligee is being supported by his or her cohabitant. However, when pushed, many courts concede that one may also consider whether the obligee is using alimony payments to pay the cohabitant's living expenses — the precise concern said to have motivated Brando. This concession poses two difficult problems for courts that adopt the financial-impact rule.

There is first the problem that it is nearly always true that when two people pool their resources to conduct a joint household, they both benefit financially — as is known by every unmarried person who has ever taken a roommate. (People may see personal burdens in taking a roommate — but they often do so despite them because of the economic advantages.) So it would seem that the financial-impact requirement will be met in nearly every case of true cohabitation, if the court concedes that support of the obligee's cohabitant satisfies the requirement.

Second, there is a more fundamental conceptual problem, for the concession comes back to bite the very argument that is offered for the financial-impact rule: the argument that the financial impact of cohabitation is the only aspect of it that is the obligor's business. However, why is it the obligor's business whether the obligee spends her income to support a paramour? The only answer is that this is a special kind of expenditure. For surely any court would agree that the obligor cannot normally complain about how the obligee chooses to spend her funds — nice clothes or vacation, or whatever (unless her choices demonstrate that she has more resources than the court was led to believe when the amount of obligation was established, an entirely different matter). In short, it is difficult to see how courts can have it both ways; if they really believe the obligee's living arrangements are of no legitimate interest to the obligor, then they cannot concede that the obligors have any legitimate complaint when the obligee uses her alimony to support her paramour as well as herself. In this sense, the usual financial impact rule seems too broad when it reaches the case in which the obligee provides financial benefit to her cohabiting partner.

Yet in another way, the usual rule is also too narrow. Consider, for example, Cal. Fam. Code § 4323, which offers one typical statement of the test:

> (a)(1) Except as otherwise agreed to by the parties in writing, there is a rebuttable presumption, affecting the burden of proof, of decreased need for spousal support if the supported party is cohabiting with a person of the opposite sex. Upon a determination that circumstances have changed, the court may modify or terminate the spousal support . . .

(2) Holding oneself out to be the husband or wife of the person with whom one is cohabiting is not necessary to constitute cohabitation as the term is used in this subdivision.

The presumption of decreased need only applies under this rule when the "supported party" cohabits "with a person of the opposite sex." Why so limit the presumption? Doesn't *any* pooling of resources permit the supported party a higher living standard, thus reducing her "need"? One explanation for the "opposite sex" requirement is, of course, that the obligee's decision to economize on her housing arrangements by taking a roommate (perhaps so that she may have more funds for other purposes) does not ordinarily give rise to a presumption of decreased need because *ordinarily* an obligee's particular preference in allocating her resources remains her choice alone — unless a new intimate relationship is involved. The presumption thus requires not only the economy of a joint household, but the existence of an intimate relationship. *See, e.g., Marriage of Thweatt*, 96 Cal. App. 3d 530, 157 Cal. Rptr. 826 (1979) (wife is not "cohabiting" within the meaning of this section where there was no evidence of a sexual relationship, a romantic involvement, or even a homemaker-companion relationship between her and either of her two male boarders). Of course, an intimate relationship between same-sex partners is also possible. In *Van Dyck v. Van Dyck*, 425 S.E.2d 853 (Ga. 1993), the court held Georgia's cohabitation statute (see Note 1, above) applied only to heterosexual relationships. *Van Dyck* was subsequently overruled by the legislature, which made clear that its concern was with intimate relationships with partners of either gender. *See* GA. CODE ANN. § 19-6-19(b) ("cohabitation means dwelling together continuously and openly in a meretricious relationship with another person regardless of the sex of the other person"). But whether the requirement of an intimate relationship is met by a homosexual relationship or not, the main point is unaffected: A true financial impact rule cannot exclude non-intimate cohabitees, it would seem.

So why not replace the prevalent approach to cohabitation with a true, pure financial impact rule to avoid these conceptual problems? Consider a case that did so, *Van Dyke v. Steinle*, 902 P.2d 1372 (Ariz. App. 1995). The wife was awarded alimony of $13,000 monthly. Her fiancée moved into her home six months after the divorce decree, and they planned a large wedding a year later. But the wife cancelled the wedding ceremony a month before its scheduled date, when she realized her remarriage would terminate her alimony. The "newlyweds" nonetheless went forward with the wedding party and honeymoon, and continued an apparently permanent cohabitation in her home (the sale of which would have also terminated her alimony under the decree, apparently because of her substantial equity in it). Because the fiancée paid her no rent, and provided her with no other financial support that her former husband could establish as altering her economic circumstances, the court — applying a pure financial-impact rule — denied him any modification of his alimony obligation.

The problem is obvious: Given that we terminate alimony upon remarriage without regard to its financial impact on the obligee, it is difficult to explain why we do not do so when the obligee enters a *de facto* marriage. In an earlier era in which social mores sharply distinguished between marital and nonmarital cohabitation, this point would be less important. But if the law makes such a distinction at a time when social mores do not, strategic behavior is invited. There is, to be sure, one difference that often exists between the marital and non-marital relationships: the law may recognize no alimony or marital property claim at the termination of the nonmarital relationship. Is that difference sufficient to justify the distinction? Some courts think so. *See Marriage of Sasson*, 129 Cal. App. 3d 140, 180 Cal. Rptr. 815, 819–20 (1982). But even this distinction may be evaporating. Courts today increasingly recognize financial claims at the termination of a long-term cohabiting relationship (*see* Chapter 9). Nonetheless, where the cohabiting parties make no explicit agreement to share property, or for the payment of support at the termination of their relationship, many courts will deny such relief. One could fashion a test terminating alimony on the obligee's cohabitation if, and only if, that cohabitation also satisfies whatever requirements the court would apply before granting remedies when *that* relationship ends. Is this a satisfactory resolution?

4. *Administrative Difficulties with the Pure Financial Impact Rule.* What if the wife's new partner in *Van Dyke* (*see* Note 3, *supra*) had substantial resources, but made no apparent contribution to the joint household? Should a court applying a pure financial impact test look at the partner's *capacity* to assist the alimony obligee and thus reduce her need, or is it only concerned with whether he or she in fact does so? Most courts assume the latter, a plausible position given that the cohabitants have no legal obligation of mutual support. But what then of "under the table" transfers? In a case under the California statute, the wife attempted to rebut the presumption of decreased need with evidence that she collected no rent from her cohabiting partner. But he did make repairs and improvements to the house and had given her a $4,200 diamond ring. The court held the cohabiting wife cannot "evade [the new statute's] strictures by accepting 'gifts' in lieu of monetary reimbursement for joint household expenses, and thereby create a situation of apparent continuing need." *In re Marriage of Schroeder*, 192 Cal. App. 3d 1154, 238 Cal. Rptr. 12, 17 (1987). Wisconsin faced a similar issue in *Van Gorder v. Van Gorder*, 327 N.W.2d 674 (Wis. 1983). The former wife sought to retain her alimony award of $700 monthly, which by its own terms continued only so long as her income did not exceed $8,000 per year. She worked as a typist and earned about $600 a month, but then began cohabiting with a man whose net monthly income was $2,250. She claimed he made no contribution to the rent, utilities or any of her personal expenses, but paid only for his share of the meals and for the couple's entertainment. She thus argued that her financial needs had not changed. The trial court had terminated the alimony, but the Wisconsin Supreme Court held that before termination the trial court must find that he was in fact supporting her. Appreciating the strategic possibilities made available by such a rule, however, the court also held the parties were not free to "fashion their relationship and finances in a manner that is intended solely to prevent the modification of maintenance payments." The meaning of these instructions is difficult to fathom. Suppose the trial court believes the wife's testimony that she receives no rent, utilities or personal support from her companion, but finds that in the absence of her alimony income he would offer such support, and she would accept it. Is this sufficient evidence that they have "fashioned their relationship" with an eye toward the maintenance payments? How important is the word "solely" in the court's instructions? The *Van Gorder* opinion itself is not especially helpful on these points.

PROBLEM

Problem 4-25. Mabel and Ernest divorce after 20 years of marriage and two children. Mabel, who is 39, receives an alimony award of indefinite duration that reflects the fact that, as the primary caretaker of the couple's children, she gave up educational and career opportunities that now make it unlikely she will ever come close to matching Ernest's substantial income as an attorney. A year after the divorce she begins a serious relationship with Fernando. Fernando, 30 years old, is an aspiring novelist. He has supported himself as a waiter, but works fewer hours after moving in with Mabel so that he can devote more time to his writing. He tells Mabel he does not want to marry until he feels he can make a more substantial financial contribution to their relationship. A year later Ernest moves to terminate the alimony award of $3000 a month. Mabel earns $1500 a month taking telephone orders for a mail-order retailer. Fernando once earned $2000 a month as a waiter, but with his reduced hours brings in only $500. Fernando and Mabel plan to continue to live together. The parties' separation agreement does not address the effect of Mabel's nonmarital cohabitation. State law ends alimony automatically upon the obligee's remarriage. Should Ernest's motion be granted? Will it?

[4]   Economic Changes

[a]   Increase in Obligor's Income

An increase in alimony can generally not be grounded solely on an increase in the obligor's income, given that the measure of the alimony recipient's needs is ordinarily based on the marital standard of living. *See, e.g., Cole v. Cole,* 409 A.2d 734 (Md. App. 1979). The exception is where the original award was set too low (because of the obligor's temporary inability to pay more), and the obligor's increased income allows a modification that merely raises the award to where it should have been originally. *See Marriage of Hopwood,* 214 Cal. App. 3d 1604, 263 Cal. Rptr. 401 (1989); *Marriage of Smith,* 225 Cal. App. 3d 469, 274 Cal. Rptr. 911, 926 (1990). Yet, where the obligor's income increases dramatically after the marriage has ended, it seems inevitable that the court will hear the recipient's claims more sympathetically. It should be noted that some states, by case-law, statute, or some combination of the two, expressly allow modification of alimony grounded solely on the obligor's increased income. *Bedell v. Bedell,* 583 So.2d 1005, 1007 (Fla. 1991) (holding that "a substantial increase in the financial ability of the paying spouse, standing alone, may justify but does not require an order of increased alimony"); *cf.* MINN. STAT. § 518A.39, subd. 2(a)(1) ("The terms of an order respecting maintenance or support may be modified upon a showing of . . . substantially increased or decreased gross income of an obligor or obligee").

Note that there is a better argument for increasing child support on account of post-marriage increases in the obligor's income. The children, unlike the former spouse, are ordinarily thought entitled to share in the post-marital prosperity of their parents. "Parental relationships and obligations continue after the parents divorce each other. The children are not thereby divorced from either parent. They have a right to expect the same support and care they would have reasonably expected if their parents had remained married." *Colizoli v. Colizoli,* 474 N.E.2d

280, 283 (Ohio 1984) (allowing increase in child support award but not in alimony award).

[b]   The Obligor's Retirement or Change in Employment

Any spousal support or child support proceeding contains the potential issue of whether the actual earnings of either party are a fair indicator of what they could or should earn. We consider here the case in which a party's income *declines* after the initial award is set, perhaps because of a later retirement or loss of employment. In deciding whether the income change justifies a modification of the award, the court frequently must decide whether the party whose earning capacity is at issue has acted reasonably.

The obligor's voluntary retirement may be complete, or may involve a change to less lucrative employment. Should an alimony award be reduced to reflect the obligor's reduced earnings? Where the retirement occurs at a typical retirement age, the answer almost always is "yes." *See Sylvan v. Sylvan*, 632 A.2d 528 (N.J. App. Div. 1993) (while retirement at 65 does not justify an automatic reduction in alimony, obligor is entitled to hearing on whether changed circumstances justify reduction). *But see Hemmingsen v. Hemmingsen*, 767 N.W.2d 711 (Minn. App. 2009) (obligor's retirement at customary retirement age of 65 does not preclude finding that retirement was in bad faith, made with the intention of reducing the alimony obligation). When retirement occurs early, the case is more difficult. *Ellis v. Ellis*, 262 N.W.2d 265 (Iowa 1978), is a classic example. The obligor, a veterinarian, had a high-level Department of Agriculture position in Iowa at the time of divorce. But a few years later, at age 62, he sought to retire from this position and move to Florida with his new wife, their small child, and his mother-in-law. He testified that work had become "too much for him" and a warmer climate would "be a lot better for my upper respiratory tract." He provided no medical evidence to support a need to move away from winter, and did not claim to be unable to work in his field. He bought a house in Florida for cash and owned a sailboat, and his new wife intended to attend school there. The court denied his modification petition:

> We do not dispute the sincerity of his wish to leave his employment and move to a warmer climate. We do not doubt his desire to see his present wife continue her education. Nor do we question his devotion to their child and his mother-in-law. Although . . . his health problems are not as serious as he makes them out to be, we do not think they are imaginary. However, he is not free to plan his future without regard to his obligation to his first wife. He cannot arbitrarily freeze her out of his future. Similar obligations in and apart from family life compel many persons to maintain employment which may be difficult, undesirable and even physically or mentally painful.

See also Marriage of Sinks, 204 Cal. App. 3d 586, 251 Cal. Rptr. 379 (1988) (refusing to reduce alimony obligation of 62-year-old husband so that he could take advantage of chance to retire with full pension benefits); *Barbarine v. Barbarine*, 925 S.W.2d 831 (Ky. App. 1996) (modification denied to husband seeking to retire at 62 because advantages to him did not substantially outweigh disadvantage to former spouse). For a more sympathetic treatment of a retiring obligor, see *Burns v. Burns*, 331

A.2d 768 (Pa. Super. 1975) (husband retiring in response to his son's death and his own failing health; court added, "even if he and his wife were living together there could be no complaint [by] the wife that her income would be reduced."); *Reeves v. Reeves*, 803 S.W.2d 52 (Mo. App. 1990) (59-year-old husband allowed to reduce alimony upon retirement where wife had increased her income); *Bogan v. Bogan*, 60 S.W.2d 721 (Tenn. 2001) (establishing principle that "when an obligor's retirement is objectively reasonable, it does constitute a substantial and material change in circumstances — irrespective of whether the retirement was foreseeable and voluntary — so as to permit modification of the support obligation"). For a broad overview of cases, *see* Jane Massey Draper, Annot., *Retirement of Husband as Change of Circumstances Warranting Modification of Divorce Decree — Early Retirement*, 36 A.L.R. 6th 1 (2008).

Many reasons other than retirement may motivate an obligor to reduce his income. In one group of cases the obligor seeks to return to school. In *Stiltz v. Stiltz*, 223 S.E.2d 689 (Ga. 1976), the husband sought relief from his $150 per month alimony obligation when he quit work to attend a seminary. The court held it had "no authority to relieve appellant of his obligations even for the worthy purpose of entering the ministry." Similarly, in *Goldberger v. Goldberger*, 624 A.2d 1328 (Md. App. 1993), both parents were Orthodox Jews, and they had six children. The father had never worked, having always intended, in the Orthodox tradition, to be a permanent Torah and Talmud student. The court held that the father's study plans amounted to voluntary impoverishment justifying a support award set according to his earning capacity. Left for the trial court to figure out was the earning capacity of an unemployed Talmud student who had never had a job. But in *Meegan v. Meegan*, 11 Cal. App. 4th 156, 13 Cal. Rptr. 2d 799 (1992), the court reduced the former husband's spousal support obligations to zero when he quit his employment to enter a monastery with the goal of entering the priesthood. The change was permanent because the husband's plans included taking a vow of poverty.

Courts are sometimes more favorably inclined when the obligor's educational plans seem likely to enhance his earning capacity, to the eventual economic benefit of his dependents. *E.g.*, *Arce v. Arce*, 566 So. 2d 1308 (Fla. App. 1990) (physician allowed to reduce alimony and child support obligations while completing 3-year cardiology fellowship). *But see Ilas v. Ilas*, 12 Cal. App. 4th 1630, 16 Cal. Rptr. 2d 345 (1993) (pharmacist who quit to attend medical school was told that his spousal and child support obligations would be measured by earning capacity rather than earnings).

When an obligor caught up in a corporate downsizing accepts his company's severance offer, how should the courts respond to requests for alimony modification? The cases tend to be highly fact-sensitive, and may turn on how sympathetic the parties are, or the general inclinations of the judges. In one case, the obligor, a 59-year old supervisor at Otis Elevator in San Diego, accepted the company's offer of 8.5 months' salary as a severance pay bonus for accepting early retirement. The court found his decision reasonable because the only alternative was to risk involuntary layoff with no similar accompanying severance pay. But it also required that alimony continue at pre-layoff levels during the 8.5 month severance pay period. The decision of whether to reduce it then was deferred to permit the court to assess his earning capacity under the economic circumstances prevailing when the severance pay period ran out. *Marriage of Stephenson*, 39 Cal. App. 4th 71, 46 Cal. Rptr. 2d 8 (1995). In another case, an obligor, reassigned from his supervisory position at Johnson Wax and told that further advancement was unlikely, accepted the company's buyout package to purchase a video rental franchise. Upon his separation he prepaid a year's worth of child support, signed over to his former wife her interest in his separation benefits, and later sought an order suspending further child support and maintenance payments until he had his new business sufficiently well-established to draw an income from it. The court found that while the father's income reduction was well intended it fell within the state's "shirking" rule because it was unreasonable in light of the father's child support obligations. Because the court felt the father should have kept his Johnson Wax job, it continued his support obligations as if he had. *Van Offeren v. Van Offeren*, 496 N.W.2d 660 (Wis. Ct. App. 1992).

Often, of course, termination of employment is not voluntary (though it may still come with severance payments). In *Pettinato v. Pettinato*, 2008 Tenn. App. LEXIS 687 (Nov. 24, 2008), the appellate court ruled a provision of a separation agreement enforceable, under which the husband's alimony obligation would end entirely if he were involuntarily terminated without severance, and would terminate at the end of the severance payments if any were granted (as they had been in the case). Where there is no prior agreement, involuntary termination still usually justifies downward modification, and perhaps termination, of alimony. *See, e.g., Rosen v. Rosen*, 2002 Conn. Super. LEXIS 3319 (Sept. 20, 2002) (obligor terminated involuntarily from high-paying job, but specialized skills meant that the next job he found paid significantly less; alimony reduced from $4600/month to $1000/month, though this was declared to be temporary, until obligor found better-paying work).

Courts have held that the obligor's reduction in earnings were not voluntary and therefore did justify reducing the alimony award, where the income loss arose from alcoholism, *Haas v. Haas*, 552 So. 2d 252 (Fla. App. 1989), and participation in a strike, *Reep v. Reep*, 565 So. 2d 814 (Fla. App. 1990). For a comprehensive overview of the area, and a proposal for reform, see Lewis Becker, *Spousal and Child Support and the "Voluntary Reduction of Income Doctrine,"* 29 Conn. L. Rev. 647 (1997).

[c]   Voluntary Employment Changes by the Obligee

Most litigation on the obligee's earning capacity involves competing claims regarding the obligee who is returning to the labor market, or whose rehabilitative award is about to end. These cases are treated above, at Section D[4]. The same issue could arise if an obligee leaves lucrative employment for a less well-paying position. Such cases are unusual because alimony obligees ordinarily are not well-employed, since the very fact of their lucrative employment would typically defeat their alimony claim. The issue does arise in the context of child support, however.

[d]   Inflation

In the 1970s modifications based upon inflation were an important consideration in alimony awards, due to the high rate of inflation at that time. The issue has subsided in importance with changing economic conditions, but of course economic cycles come and go. It is sometimes said in passing that inflation does not justify a modification of a support award, since it equally affects both parties. *Baker v. Baker*, 332 S.E.2d 550, 552 (S.C. App. 1985); *Fakouri v. Perkins*, 322 So. 2d 401 (La. 1975); *Binder v. Binder*, 390 N.E.2d 260 (Mass. App. 1979). Such a statement oversimplifies the problem considerably. To the extent the obligee relies upon a fixed award, inflation surely reduces her standard of living, while the obligor's income typically rises over time. The problem with a claim based only on general indicators of inflation is that modifications are supposed to be based on changes in the circumstances of the particular party subject to the original order, not on general societal indicators. In any particular case, the obligor may not have a rising income or the obligee may benefit from increases in her own resources. Other courts acknowledge this. *Goldberg v. Goldberg*, 332 N.E.2d 710 (Ill. App. 1975); *Edelstein v. Edelstein*, 28 A.D.2d 979, 283 N.Y.S.2d 658 (1967); *cf. Hillier v. Iglesias*, 901 So.2d 947 (Fla. App. 2005) (inflation alone is not sufficient to ground an increase in alimony; petitioner must at least show that inflation has affected the recipient's ability to support himself or herself). An increase in the obligor's earnings combined with inflation-created erosion in the obligee's standard of living should be enough to justify an increase in the award. *See, e.g., Pope v. Pope*, 342 So. 2d 1000 (Fla. App. 1977); *Alexander v. Alexander*, 540 P.2d 457 (Wash. Ct. App. 1975). *But see Nichols v. Nichols*, 236 S.E.2d 36 (W. Va. 1977) (court reversed increase in support despite such a showing, after concluding increase in obligor's earnings was contemplated at outset). Some jurisdictions respond to the problem by ordering that orders for alimony or child support include automatic adjustments for changes in cost of living. *See, e.g.,* MINN. STAT. § 518A.75, subd. 1 ("biennial adjustment in the amount to be paid based on a change in the cost of living" as determined by an index such as the consumer price index).

PROBLEMS

Problem 4-26.   Joan and Larry were married for 20 years at divorce. Larry operated a service station and earned about $40,000 annually. Joan had worked at a meat packing plant for ten years, by the end of which she was earning $15.00 per hour. She quit two years before their divorce, when her pension partially vested, to help Larry with the service station business. When they later divorced, she went to work at a popcorn packing plant, earning $8.00 an hour. She could have resumed her old job in the meat packing plant, although it would pay only $10.00 because she had now lost her seniority. Joan contends that she is entitled to an award of alimony based upon her current earnings at the popcorn plant; Larry contends that the court should give her a lower award, based on her earning capacity at the meat packing plant. Joan does not want to return to the meat packing plant because the job there is grueling and she is concerned about its effects on her health. What is the appropriate result?

Problem 4-27.   The divorce decree requires Richard to pay Sally $800 monthly in spousal maintenance and $1,200 monthly in child support. It also provides that the payments should be increased annually in proportion to any increases in Richard's income. Richard has a bachelor's degree and is employed as a bookkeeper by a large corporation. He decides to go to law school, with the thought that he will become a tax lawyer, increasing his earnings substantially. When school begins he shifts to part time work for his former employer, reducing his income from $60,000 annually to $36,000. He adjusts his payments to Sally accordingly. Sally seeks enforcement of the original amount. What result? What should be the result?

G.   SHOULD COURTS CONSIDER CLAIMS OF MARITAL MISCONDUCT?

[1]   As a Factor in Alimony or Marital Property Adjudications?

Until the no-fault divorce revolution, claims of marital misconduct were central to divorce litigation, as the usual (sometimes exclusive) grounds for divorce. They were also central to divorce's financial issues. Many states would not allow the award of alimony to a wife who had committed adultery (a rule still in force in a few states). This was at a time when alimony was likely to be the only money a wife could take out of a dissolved marriage. Alimony, like the dissolution itself, was a reward to "an innocent and victimized" wife and unavailable to a "guilty" wife.

The grounds for divorce have changed significantly in recent decades, as have the rules of property division after marriage and the principles governing the grant of alimony. While fault plays a far smaller role than it once did as a ground of divorce, some jurisdictions continue to give it a role in the financial terms of divorce. According to a recent survey, 27 states and the District of Columbia are listed as allowing the consideration of fault in alimony claims. Linda Elrod & Robert Spector, *A Review of the Year in Family Law 2007–08*, 42 Fam. L.Q. 713, 757 (2009) (Chart 1).

Ellman, *The Place of Fault in a Modern Divorce Law*
28 Ariz. St. L.J. 773 (1996)

Prior to 1968, consideration of marital misconduct, or "fault," was almost universally allowed. The two decades that followed saw considerable change in the law. The Uniform Marriage and Divorce Act (UMDA), initially approved in 1970, provides unambiguously that both allocation of marital property and determinations of spousal support or maintenance (the new terms for "alimony") be made "without regard to marital misconduct". [¶] . . . Published surveys typically report that approximately half the states now share the Uniform Act's position. Yet two categories — fault and no-fault — are inadequate to describe the major variations in state policy. The tables that follow place states in one of five categories. Some preliminary comments are necessary to explain these classifications.

There are two senses in which marital misconduct affects property disposition and alimony orders in even the most thoroughly no-fault jurisdictions. One might call them the "financial cost" exceptions to the no-fault principle. First, it appears that all states recognize the power of dissolution courts to consider, in allocating marital property, misconduct that has affected directly the amount of property available for allocation. Second . . . misconduct affects both alimony and property allocations to the extent it enlarges either spouse's need. . . . [as] when domestic violence leaves one spouse with increased medical costs or a reduced earning capacity. Because existing law in no-fault states emphasizes that disparities in post-dissolution living standards are the primary basis for alimony awards, it can respond to such facts without explicit consideration of the misconduct that has altered the disparity. . . .

Categorization of fault states is complicated by the variation . . . in the definition of both the relevant misconduct and the financial issues to which it applies. Some allow consideration of only specified forms of misconduct; some leave the matter to trial court discretion; and some leave the matter to trial court discretion but attempt to contain its exercise through rules that in general terms limit the kind of conduct that may be considered.

. . .

1. Pure no-fault (20 states). These states exclude consideration of marital misconduct entirely, subject to the two universal "financial cost" exceptions. Many employ the language of the Uniform Marriage and Divorce Act in their statutes, stating clearly that both property allocations and spousal maintenance adjudications are made "without regard to marital misconduct."

2. Pure no-fault property, almost pure no-fault alimony (5 states). The states in this category all adopt a pure no-fault position with regard to property, but may allow some very limited consideration of misconduct with respect to alimony. In one state in this group, it appears that the state supreme court is gradually retreating from a 1973 decision allowing consideration of fault with respect to alimony, and in 1995 came within one vote of excluding it altogether. In the second there is caselaw that allows consideration of misconduct in alimony adjudications but few reported decisions that actually do so. In the third a 1990 amendment deleted the requirement that alimony claimants be free from fault, establishing instead need and ability to pay as the primary basis for the awards; it is not yet clear whether any consideration of fault survives this amendment. In the fourth there are a handful of twenty-year-old cases from intermediate appellate courts considering fault in fixing alimony awards. While these have never been formally overruled, more recent practice seems identical to states in Category 1. In the fifth very recent legislation allows but does not require courts to consider fault in alimony adjudications. While established case law in that state strongly suggests that its courts will not embrace this invitation, there is not yet an authoritative interpretation of the new provision.

3. Almost pure no-fault (3 states). These states seem very much like those in Category 1, but the slight possibility of considering fault that exists under their law applies to both alimony and property allocation. Two of the three could easily be placed in Category 1: In one the governing state supreme court decision establishes a no-fault rule with language that is nearly absolute, and in fact there have been no reported decisions in that state allowing consideration of misconduct since that case was decided. In the second there is a single decision of the state supreme court that allowed an exception (to the state's otherwise complete no-fault approach) in a case of murder. The third state in this group has an apparently unique rule that in practice excludes fault from consideration except in cases of serious violent assault.

4. No-fault property, fault in alimony (7 states). These states have a pure no-fault position with regard to marital property allocations, but give their trial courts considerable discretion to consider fault in alimony awards.

5. Full-fault (15 states). These are true fault states. They give their courts discretion to consider the parties' marital misconduct in both alimony adjudications and property allocations. In some, authoritative appellate opinions have on occasion attempted to describe the range of misconduct that trial courts should consider, or suggest restraint in the weight to be accorded misconduct. These states are nonetheless classified as "full-fault" because their appellate opinions also embrace the importance of trial judge discretion, and the pattern of reported cases suggests that the hortatory language in the more cautious fault opinions has little impact on the decisions in others.

. . .

The *[ALI] Principles* . . . reconceptualize alimony claims as compensation for the disproportionate share of the financial losses that the obligee spouse incurs at the dissolution of the marriage. . . . [¶] [This] understanding of alimony's function helps define the question presented by the fault debate. . . . Assessments of misconduct have no logical connection to the factual foundation upon which [the *Principles'*] presumptions of entitlement are based. Such misconduct would not itself cast doubt on the existence and size of the loss recognized by the presumptions, or on their basis for asserting joint responsibility for losses: the duration of the parties' relationship and of the period of foregone employment opportunity.

In that case fault can be relevant only to vindicate interests not addressed by the basic alimony award — interests that in a given case require a concurrent financial award which can be added to, or offset against, the award based upon the compensatory payment rationale. An examination of the policy question must therefore begin by identifying these other interests to determine whether they should in fact be considered in the dissolution action.

III. The Possible Functions of Fault

. . .

A. A Fault Rule as An Agent of Morality: Rewarding Virtue and Punishing Sin.

Punishing the wrongdoer has been a persistent but troubled theme in the law of fault states. Punishment is more usually the function of the criminal law. [E]ven in fault states, punitive [alimony] awards are ordinarily condemned — when they are recognized as such. On the other hand, many fault states apply rules that cannot be explained as anything but punitive. The clearest example is the rule that inflexibly bars alimony awards to every adulterous spouse, without regard to any other facts of the case.[30] The caselaw's oft-stated rejection of punitive awards[31] seems preferable to these silent impositions of them.

. . .

Some courts appeal to a rationale that seems at first to avoid the punitive nature of a fault award by casting it as compensation for the financial costs of splitting one household in two, costs that necessarily arise in most dissolutions. These courts argue that a fault-based award is justified because it allocates more of those costs to the spouse whose conduct caused them, by causing the dissolution. Framing the rule this way thus casts it as compensation rather than punishment even though no losses are identified beyond the financial consequences present in nearly every dissolution.

Closer examination suggests, however, that this principle . . . necessarily relies on sleight of hand in application. The problem is the principle's reliance on being able to establish which spouse "caused" the dissolution. Inquiring into the cause of marital dissolution is different from inquiring into the cause of chicken pox, or of a plumbing failure. The fundamental problem is that the inquiry is ultimately one of morality, not science. Some individuals tolerate their spouse's drunkenness or adultery and remain in their marriage. Others may seek divorce if their spouse grows fat, or spends long hours at the office. Is the divorce caused by one spouse's offensive conduct or the other's unreasonable intolerance? In deciding that question the court is assessing the parties' relative moral failings, not the relationship between independent and dependent variables. And the complexity of marital

---

[30] The potential recipient's adultery is a complete bar to alimony, without regard to any other facts of the case, in Georgia, North Carolina, South Carolina, and West Virginia. In Virginia it is a complete bar unless the court finds that its denial "would constitute a manifest injustice based upon the respective degrees of fault during the marriage and the relative economic circumstances of the parties." In Mississippi it is generally a bar, but not after a long marriage if the adulterous spouse would otherwise be "destitute," in which case a reduced award may be allowed. The Mississippi rule was applied to limit the alimony that would otherwise have been allowed the wife in the dissolution of a 25-year marriage, even though the husband in that case also committed adultery. Adultery is an "appropriate consideration" in many other fault states; decisions sustaining its consideration without any apparent important limitation on the trial court's discretion include Alabama (trial court reversed for failing to consider H's adultery in allocating marital property); Connecticut; Kentucky (W's adultery may reduce alimony award, but H's adultery cannot be the basis for increasing it); Louisiana; South Dakota (H's adultery may also be considered); Maryland (trial court reversed for refusing to hear testimony of W's adultery); New Hampshire; North Dakota (trial court properly allocated 83 percent of property to H after 19-year marriage, where W guilty of adultery); Tennessee; Texas; and Vermont . . .

[31] This sentiment is expressed even in full-fault states, Young v. Young, 609 S.W.2d 758 (Texas 1980) (court should use fault to make "a just and right division" of the community property, not to "punish" the guilty spouse); *Paul v. Paul*, 616 P.2d 707, 712 (Wy. 1980) (court should not use its discretion to reward one party and punish the other).

relations of course confounds the inquiry. The fading of affective ties makes spouses less tolerant of one another. So of course the decisionmaker inquiring into "cause" should ask about the reason for the loss of affection in order, for example, to determine whether it is the complainant's apparently unreasonable intolerance that is the cause of the marital failure, rather than conduct of the other spouse that prompted the complainant's loss of affection (and which in turn encouraged the intolerance). Perhaps courts in fault states sometimes engage in such tracing, although surely many do not. But in either case the inquiry is not really about cause in the true sense of that term. It is not about the conduct that caused the dissolution, but about the misconduct that can be assigned the blame for it. Was the marital breakdown in Marriage One caused by one spouse's adultery or the other's emotional insensitivity? In Marriage Two, by the first's adultery or the second's failure to keep fit? The court's answer tells us which conduct it finds more blameworthy, not which [caused] the other.

This analysis does not suggest, of course, that it is wrong to assign the costs of dissolution to the spouse whose conduct was more blameworthy. It only reveals that this is what the court is in fact doing. Once that is revealed, however, a problem is uncovered: by dressing up its conclusion in the neutral language of causation, the court can assign such blame without identifying the standards under which it does so. Much mischief can result from allowing courts to assign liability to non-tortious conduct by application of unarticulated — and effectively unreviewable — standards of blameworthiness. Nor is such a rule necessary to reach serious misconduct. Offensive conduct in marriage that does violate norms of tort or criminal law will normally be actionable whether or not it is the "cause" of the actor's marital dissolution.

In sum, courts that purport to allocate the unavoidable costs of dissolution by assessing the cause of the marital failure are in fact rewarding virtue and punishing sin. They are not compensating one spouse for a harm "caused" by the other. . . .

B. Fault Law as a Source of Compensation for Harms Caused by Wrongful Conduct.

Compensation is a more palatable rationale than punishment for fault-based adjustments in alimony awards. . . . But just what kind of loss would the fault-based rule provide compensation for? No-fault principles already recognize financial losses traceable to spousal misconduct, under the two [financial cost exceptions to no-fault identified above]. . . . What additional losses would a fault system recognize, beyond these losses of property and earning capacity? The answer is non-financial losses.

That is, a compensation-based rationale for considering marital misconduct is, in its essence, an argument to provide compensation at dissolution for non-financial losses. This seems true even though existing law in fault states probably does not now provide such compensation . . . reliably, simply because existing fault law includes no standard for setting the dollar consequences that should flow from a finding of fault.[36] It is hardly an exaggeration to say that the existing law in fault states leaves the dollar consequence of a fault finding largely to the whim of the trial court judge. But the argument for considering fault must rest on this rationale of compensating for non-financial losses, even if current practice does not implement it. Could a reformed law implement this principle more effectively? This question seems central to examining any proposal to consider marital misconduct at dissolution. The first step is to identify more precisely just what these additional non-financial losses are. There are in principle two possibilities, each of which has a tort analog:

1. Compensation for emotional losses arising from the other spouse's misconduct. (Intentional or negligent infliction of emotional distress.)

2. Compensation for the pain and suffering arising from the other's misconduct. (General damages in battery or assault actions.)

In short, a fault rule would serve compensation functions that may already be served by the tort law. Such duplication is inadvisable. There is no reason to reinvent compensation principles under the rubric of fault adjudications, nor to incorporate tort principles into divorce adjudications. A jurisdiction that wants concurrent consideration of tort claims and dissolution remedies may permit their joinder. . . .

In comparing the virtues of recognizing certain interspousal claims in tort or in dissolution, it might seem natural to assume that their incorporation into dissolution law would have the advantage of facilitating such claims by lowering the procedural or transactional hurdles that confront them. But whether a fault-regarding dissolution law would actually have this effect, as compared to a rule allowing the joinder of the dissolution and tort actions, is hardly clear. Even more importantly, however, one cannot in fact assume that sound policy favors such encouragement of tort claims. Most acts that meet the formal elements of battery, or of intentional infliction of emotional distress, do not lead to tort claims. Both inside and outside the family, people do not sue over every shove, punch, or outrageously mean and hurtful act. Their reticence is usually regarded as a good thing, not as a problem to be solved. There is no general enthusiasm abroad for encouraging more tort suits by finding ways that people can conveniently add their claims to the end of forms they must file anyway for other reasons. Interspousal tort claims present no reason for a different view. To the contrary, an effective strategy to encourage spousal tort claims could easily, if unintentionally, tap the anger and bitterness often present at

---

[36] Courts in full-fault states do sometimes describe their consideration of fault as serving this compensation function. *E.g., Robinson v. Robinson*, 444 A.2d 234, 234–35 (Conn. 1982) (in considering the "gravity" of the wife's adultery as it applies to the allocation of property, the court may consider the "humiliation and mental anguish" that it imposed on the husband). And it seems clear that in exercising the wide discretion typically allowed them in full-fault jurisdictions, trial judges often think of themselves as awarding damages in the guise of alimony or property allocations. Whether those damages are compensatory or punitive in nature is typically difficult to ascertain, however, because of the fault law's disinclination to acknowledge either purpose overtly. For a telling illustration, see *Martone v. Martone*, 611 A.2d 896, 901 (Conn. App. 1992) (trial judge initially refers to award of $15,000 to W as "damages" for H's conduct in "brutally causing the breakup of this marriage," *id.* at 899, but subsequently recharacterizes it as alimony; award affirmed on appeal since fault is valid factor in alimony and court's "later characterization" of its award should control).

divorce, yielding additional tort suits that are disproportionately of the sort that should not be brought. Some tort claims might be made for tactical advantage in the divorce settlement negotiations. A conclusion that more claims would be brought, were it possible to easily add them to the dissolution petition, would be cause for caution. The question is not whether incorporating the tort law into dissolution action would yield more claims. It is rather whether the tort law provides an adequate opportunity to obtain a remedy for worthy claims that should be brought. If it does, then inviting additional claims in the dissolution action is a problem, not a solution.

NOTES

1. *State Law Variations.* The Ellman article contains appendices that describe the law of every state, with supporting authorities; a similar break-down is given in JOHN DEWITT GREGORY, JANET LEACH RICHARDS & SHERYL WOLF, PROPERTY DIVISION IN DIVORCE PROCEEDINGS: A FIFTY STATE GUIDE § 12.04 (2006). As a logical matter, there are three possible ways for considering fault: it may be an eligibility requirement (the claimant must prove his spouse at fault in order to receive alimony); it may be a bar (the claimant otherwise eligible for alimony is disqualified if at fault); or it may be a factor affecting the amount of alimony, rather than entitlement to it. In South Carolina, adultery creates a bar to the award of alimony. *See Brown v. Brown,* 665 S.E.2d 174 (S.C. 2008) (*S.C. Code Ann.* § 20-3-130 creates a blanket ban on awarding alimony to spouse who commits adultery).

Until recently, North Carolina treated fault as an eligibility requirement, but it no longer does so, and it appears that no other state now does. Footnote 30 in Ellman, *supra,* identifies states that treat the obligee's adultery as a bar. Note that these possibilities may be combined. For example, before its recent amendment North Carolina treated fault as a bar as well as an eligibility requirement. It can also be both a bar and a factor, so that the claimant free from fault may point to the obligor's fault to enhance the amount of the award. In fact, all the states that consider fault treat it as a factor, whether or not they also consider it a bar.

While many states maintain a strict standard of not considering fault in the award of alimony, e.g., *Mani v. Mani,* 869 A.2d 904 (N.J. 2005) (husband's adultery and cruelty cannot be used to justify reduction in the alimony he receives); *Calbi v. Calbi,* 935 A.2d 796 (N.J. Super. Ct. App. Div. 2007) (ex-husband could not terminate alimony based on wife's killing of their son), other states will allow consideration of marital misconduct at least if it has financial consequences. *Dykman v. Dykman,* 253 S.W.3d 23 (Ark. Ct. App. 2007) (husband's spending large amount of money on mistresses and forging wife's signature on second mortgage could be considered in award of alimony; the fact of his infidelity and his placing a snake in the wife's driveway with a threatening note could not).

With property division, a few states will consider fault, but usually only in extreme cases. *See, e.g., Havell v. Islam,* 301 A.D.2d 339, 751 N.Y.S.2d 449 (N.Y. A.D. 1 Dept. 2002) (marital misconduct may be taken into account in dividing property if it is egregious). In *Havell,* the trial court's award to the wife of 95% of the marital property was upheld in a case of extreme violence of the husband against the wife that amounted to attempted murder. By contrast, the same court held that the wife's infidelity and alleged concealment of a child's parentage were not sufficient grounds for altering the division of property. *Howard S. v. Lillian S.*, 62 A.D.3d 187, 876 N.Y.S.2d 351 (N.Y. App. Div. 2009).

2. *Do Wives Do Better Under Fault Laws?* One of Professor Lenore Weitzman's most important claims (Section D[2], *supra*) was that no-fault divorce contributed to the relative poverty of divorced women — that women were better off under the predecessor fault system. The argument that the change of available grounds for divorce made divorced women financially worse off than before the reform focused on the bargaining process:

> The fault rules gave great bargaining leverage to the spouse who felt no urgency to end the marriage, especially if it would be difficult to prove that spouse guilty of "fault." Knowing the difficulty of obtaining a divorce in a truly contested proceeding in which her fault would have to be shown, such an innocent spouse might offer to cooperate with a "consent" decree only if certain financial demands were met. So, for example, the older married man who abandoned his long-term wife for a younger woman could not obtain his "freedom" to remarry her without buying it from his first wife. In such a system the laws governing property division and alimony often didn't matter, since in many cases the wife had great [bargaining] leverage regardless of their content. This is not to say that the system necessarily produced equitable results. While it protected the marital investment of an "innocent" spouse, or one whose "fault" would be tricky to prove, it failed entirely to protect the "guilty" spouse who had invested a great deal in her marriage, while giving bargaining leverage to the innocent spouse who had invested very little.

> No-fault reform created a sea-change in this legal environment. Although motivated in large part by a desire to end the charade of perjured testimony and falsified residency that permeated consent divorces under the fault system, its effects went considerably further. The no-fault reform effectively recognized unilateral divorce. The man who wants to end his marriage now simply files a petition alleging that it is irretrievably broken; there is no defense against such an allegation. The wife seeking alimony, property division, or child support has no leverage to demand such compensation as the price of her husband's "freedom," but must rely instead on the substantive law governing these issues. Thus, the law of alimony and property division now count in a way neither did before.

Ira Mark Ellman, *The Theory of Alimony*, 77 CAL. L. REV. 1, 7–8 (1989).

It thus seemed plausible to think that the no-fault reforms adversely affected the financial outcome of divorce for women. And perhaps as well, the typically concomitant change in many states from fault-regarding alimony rules to no-fault alimony rules, somehow also had the unintended effect of burdening women. These are ultimately empirical propositions, not theoretical ones, and it turns out the evidence is at best uncertain whether women fare worse under no-fault divorce. One might note that if women want out of their marriage as often as men, then no-fault reforms that remove the bargaining lever previously held by the party resisting divorce would burden women as often as men. In fact, available evidence suggests that, at least today, women are *more* likely than men to be the instigators of their divorce. Braver, Whitley & Ng, *Who Divorced Whom? Methodological and Theoretical Issues*, 20 J. DIVORCE & REMARRIAGE 1 (1993); Margaret F. Brinig & Douglas W. Allen, *"These Boots Are Made for Walking": Why Most Divorce Filers Are Women*, 2 AM L. & ECON. REV. 126 (2000). Finally, if one believes women do less well than justice requires in the financial remedies at divorce, one must consider whether one is better off reforming the substantive law of alimony and property division, or restoring fault in the hope it will give bargaining leverage to the right party.

On the basic empirical question — did women in fact do less well in California after its adoption of no-fault divorce? — Weitzman's conclusions drew some criticism even before the fundamental flaws in her data analysis were exposed. The critics were of two kinds. Some, looking at other data, concluded that no-fault had little impact, *e.g.*, Jacob, *Another Look at No-Fault Divorce and the Post-Divorce Finances of Women*, 23 LAW & SOC. REV. 95, 112–13 (1989). Others, examining Weitzman's own published data, concluded that she had misinterpreted it. *See especially* Sugarman, *Dividing Financial Interests at Divorce*, in S. SUGARMAN & H. KAY, DIVORCE REFORM AT THE CROSSROADS 130, 132–34 (1990). More recently, it has been pointed out that while Weitzman focused on California divorces, in the common law states the ascendancy of no-fault divorce occurred during much the same period as the transition to equitable distribution, making it likely that women's situations might well have improved over this period. Ellman, *The Misguided Movement to Revive Fault Divorce*, 11 INT'L J. LAW, POLICY, & THE FAMILY 216, 242 n.45 (1997). For an examination of the interaction of different marital property rules and fault divorce, see Gray, *The Economic Impact of Divorce Law Reform*, 15 POP. RES. & POLICY REV. 275 (1996). Despite its theoretical plausibility, the claim that no-fault divorce adversely affected divorced women is, at best, unproven.

[2]   As the Basis of an Interspousal Tort Claim?

The prospect of tort suits for marital misconduct is made possible by the gradual abandonment, in most states, of the doctrine of interspousal tort immunity, for both personal injury and intentional torts. Ironically enough, this movement took place at the same time as the movement to eliminate fault adjudications in divorce actions. By 1994, 39 jurisdictions had totally abrogated interspousal immunity and 10 states had partially nullified it. Laura H. Wanamaker, Waite v. Waite: *The Florida Supreme Court Abrogates the Doctrine of Interspousal Immunity*, 45 MERCER L. REV. 903, 906–07 (1994) (footnotes give a comprehensive list of case and statutory citations). Only Hawaii, *Peters v. Peters*, 634 P.2d 586 (Haw. 1981), and Louisiana, LA. REV. STAT. ANN. § 9:291, appear to retain full interspousal tort immunity. The trend to abrogate the immunity has been endorsed by commentators as well as by the AMERICAN LAW INSTITUTE, RESTATEMENT (SECOND) OF TORTS § 895F and Comment *f* (1979). These authorities agree that allowing such suits seems particularly plausible after divorce, where there is little domestic harmony to undermine. It should be noted that courts that have abandoned absolute interspousal tort immunity may still employ special rules restricting recovery to a specified class of interspousal torts. *See* 1 DAN B. DOBBS, THE LAW OF TORTS § 279, at 751 (2001 & Supp. 2008).

The movement to abolish interspousal tort immunity was motivated largely by the perception that the principal consequence of the immunity doctrine was to deny someone injured by his spouse's negligence the ability to recover compensation from the spouse's insurance carrier, and by the conclusion that any concern that the spouses might collude with one another on fraudulent insurance claims could be met by a response less drastic than complete immunity. But, of course, insurance coverage is not a factor in intentional torts, so that concerns over fraudulent claims could never provide an adequate explanation for immunity as to them. Is there some other rationale for caution in recognizing claims of intentional torts between spouses? With the general abolition of interspousal tort immunity, that question has now been put. Consider the following:

[a]   Ordinary Battery Claims

It is difficult to think of plausible policy arguments that could be offered to justify a rule disallowing battery claims between separated, divorcing or divorced spouses. The arguments for no-fault divorce have no application to such a battery suit. Without revisiting all the arguments here, recall one in particular: that making the outcome of a divorce action turn on assessments of blame for the breakup of the marriage will not work because allocating such blame is often beyond the court's ken. (Is the wife who leaves her husband "at fault"? Surely that must depend upon why she left. If she left because he treated her cruelly, then he must be at fault. If because she went to live with her lover, then she is at fault. But what if he treated her cruelly and she went to live with her lover? Is it then critical which occurred first? But what occurred before that?) Reformers found this kind of inquiry pointless and unproductive. But no such inquiry is necessary to resolve a battery suit between former spouses. Because physical violence is an actionable wrong without regard to whether we think the perpetrator had good reason to be angry with the victim, the court need not attempt to determine whether it believes he did.

If battery claims are generally allowed, and if spousal violence is not rare, why aren't battery claims common among divorcing spouses? Consider the speculations in Ira Mark Ellman & Stephen D. Sugarman, *Spousal Emotional Abuse As a Tort?*, 55 MD. L. REV. 1268, 1291–92 (1996):

> It is not entirely clear to us why spousal battering victims so rarely seek special financial redress. Because we do not know the actual explanation, we can only consider the various possibilities. . . .

> One explanation that seems likely is that neither the battery victim nor her lawyer even considers the tort suit possibility. A common pattern, we imagine, involves battery incidents that leave the victim with no permanent physical loss, even though they are painful and humiliating when they occur. Perhaps the victim initially responds to these experiences by trying to avoid events or situations that might provoke the batterer, or by staying out of his way at those times. When these strategies fail, the victim eventually leaves the marital home, and at some point then consults a divorce lawyer. Especially if the victim has no permanent physical injury, it might not occur to a divorce lawyer — who may have never handled a

personal injury case, and who does not think of himself as a personal injury lawyer — that a tort claim is a possibility, even though the lawyer would understand, if the matter were raised, that it is doctrinally clear that a battery has been committed. But the victim may never raise the question because the goal foremost in her mind when she consults the lawyer is ending her relationship with the batterer. She is also likely to be concerned about the custody and support of her children, and perhaps about leaving with a fair share of accumulated property. Again, however, these concerns translate much more easily into traditional divorce rather than tort claims.

Even if the tort possibility is raised, we can imagine more than a few reasons why the battery victim and her lawyer would decide not to pursue it, especially in the case in which there is no remaining physical injury. In the basic pattern we imagined, the victim's avoidance efforts may have been successful in reducing the frequency of incidents considerably — and claims resting on some, or even all, of the physical strikings may now be barred by the statute of limitations. The price of having acted in ways designed to forestall further battering may, of course, have been great stress for the victim, but that stress does not itself present a battery claim. With only few recent incidents of physical attack, the victim and her lawyer might believe there is little prospect for obtaining an award large enough to warrant the additional lawyer time. Indeed, they may foresee that a battery claim will provoke some retaliatory legal strategy that will further increase the cost and hassle of the divorce process.

Other spousal battering victims may pursue no legal remedy against their abusers because they may fear further and more serious postseparation physical abuse. Others may find the psychological price of such a claim too high. They may feel personal shame in having been abused, leaving them either unwilling to reveal it in a public process, or believing it too painful to relive the abuse by testifying to it in a legal proceeding. Finally, whether warranted or not, many may doubt that their claims will be sympathetically received. They may worry that the court will dismiss their charges as manufactured, especially if they suffered abuse for some time and have no witnesses or physical evidence to offer. Some battering victims may assume that because of their own conduct judges and juries will not be sympathetic. Suppose the victim is a drug addict, or a drinker, or an adulterer, or a whiner and complainer. While . . . none of this remotely entitles the other spouse to engage in physical abuse, the victim may nonetheless fear that if she takes the matter to court she will be thought to have earned the beating.

Ellman and Sugarman note that battery claims brought at the marriage's end might be time-barred under the ordinary statute of limitations. Courts have developed doctrines under which the statute of limitations may be waived in some such cases, however. *See, e.g., Giovine v. Giovine*, 663 A.2d 109 (N.J. App. Div. 1995) (allowing wife to include claims for battering incidents that would ordinarily be time-barred, if she was victim of "battered woman's syndrome" and rendered incapable of bringing earlier action). *But see Mustilli v. Mustilli*, 671 A.2d 650, 651 (N.J. Super. Ct., Ch. Div., 1995) ("psychological paralysis" argument accepted in

Giovine may only be made by a woman).

[b]   Emotional Distress Claims Based Upon Adultery

In *Ruprecht v. Ruprecht*, 599 A.2d 604 (N.J. Super. Ct. Ch. Div. 1991), the parties' marriage appeared stable from its commencement in 1960 to about 1980, when the wife returned to work after the children had grown. Over the next decade there were several separations and during these years the husband repeatedly asked his wife whether she was having an affair with her boss, which she consistently denied. But soon after filing for divorce in 1990 the husband learned that she had maintained an adulterous relationship with her employer during her entire period of employment. He then added a claim for intentional infliction of emotional distress (IIED) to his divorce action. The New Jersey court decided that while interspousal IIED claims would be allowed in principle, these facts did not meet the "outrageousness" requirement which is part of such causes of action.

Ruprecht seems typical of the general pattern: IIED claims based upon adultery fail, the court holding either that there are general policy reasons for rejecting interspousal IIED claims altogether, or that in any event claims of unfaithfulness are insufficient to satisfy the tort's outrageousness requirement. *See, e.g., Whittington v. Whittington*, 766 S.W.2d 73, 74 (Ky. Ct. App. 1989) (holding conduct not outrageous); *Browning v. Browning*, 584 S.W.2d 406, 408 (Ky. Ct. App. 1979) (public policy bars emotional distress claim against wife for "openly consorting" with another man); *Alexander v. Inman*, 825 S.W.2d 102, 105 (Tenn. App. 1991) (holding extramarital affair is not sufficiently extreme or outrageous to support claim); *Perkins v. Dean*, 570 So. 2d 1217, 1219 (Ala. 1990) (extramarital affair may be morally or socially repugnant, but does not normally constitute outrageous conduct); *Weicker v. Weicker*, 22 N.Y.2d 8, 290 N.Y.S.2d 732, 237 N.E.2d 876 (1968) (rejecting IIED claims in marital context for policy reasons); *Pickering v. Pickering*, 434 N.W.2d 758, 761 (S.D. 1989) (holding IIED unavailable in divorce action for public policy reasons). Similar results have followed in claims for IIED or fraud arising from husband's discovery that wife had misled him over the paternity of a child born during the marriage. *See Nagy v. Nagy*, 210 Cal. App.3d 1262, 258 Cal. Rptr. 787 (1989) (allowing IIED claim based on misrepresentation of paternity would be contrary to public policy).

[c]   Other Interspousal Claims for Outrageous Infliction of Emotional Distress

Emotional distress claims have often been allowed when the distress is said to arise from the defendant's battery and the IIED and battery claims are joined, *Noble v. Noble*, 761 P.2d 1369 (Utah 1988); *Stuart v. Stuart*, 421 N.W.2d 505 (Wis. 1988); *McCoy v. Cooke*, 419 N.W.2d 44 (Mich. App. 1988).

If one allows battery actions between divorcing or former spouses, there seems little reason to exclude companion emotional distress claims based upon the battering conduct. But the IIED claim adds little, because the damages available to the successful battery plaintiff in any event include compensation for severe emotional distress resulting from the battery. The more difficult question is how to treat the IIED claim that is for the most part based upon conduct that does *not* constitute assault or battery. Many courts have held that for such claims to be recognized in the marital setting, the threshold of "outrageousness" to be proven must be set very high. *See, e.g., Hakkila v. Hakkila*, 812 P.2d 1320 (N.M. App. 1991) (husband's insults, outbursts, minor assaults, and refraining from sexual intercourse insufficient to ground claim). The *Hakkila* court expressed concern that such claims become a basis for a public investigation into all aspects of a marriage. One might similarly worry that if allowed, tort claims for emotional distress might be routinely added to divorce petitions filed by bitter or spiteful spouses, perhaps as a strategy to increase their bargaining leverage in the property and spousal maintenance negotiations. Yet no similar phenomenon seems to have happened with battery claims. Is there reason to think the experience might be different?

Another possible concern is that there is no satisfactory standard of liability to apply to spousal claims for emotional distress. One scholar has observed that successful emotional distress claims arise almost entirely where there is some established relationship between the parties, such as landlord and tenant or debtor and creditor, that gives the court sufficient context for establishing limits of decency by which to judge whether the defendant's conduct was adequately outrageous. Daniel Givelber, *The Right to Minimum Social Decency and the Limits of Evanhandedness: Intentional Infliction of Emotional Distress by Outrageous Conduct*, 82 COLUM. L. REV. 42, 46–50 (1982). Can we articulate analogous "limits of decency" for conduct within marriage? Surely there are some things that can quickly be identified as beyond the pale — physical violence being the most obvious. But are there objective standards when one gets beyond physical mistreatment covered by the criminal law, to accusations of unacceptable emotional mistreatment? For claims of that sort, an objective standard may be hard to discern, and it may be equally difficult to extract one from the couple's own relationship. *See* Ellman & Sugarman, *supra*, 1318, *et seq.* Ellman and Sugarman suggest later in their article that interspousal tort claims should be permitted when the tortious conduct is also a criminal violation, but not otherwise. So, for example, battery and false imprisonment would be actionable, but outrage as well as many forms of invasion of privacy would not be. Does this solution make sense?

[d]   Criminal Conversation and Related Tort Actions

Among the traditional common law causes of action that once potentially applied to the break-up of a marriage were *criminal conversation* (an action by one spouse against someone who had committed adultery with his or her spouse) and *alienation of affection* (intentional interference with a marriage by a third party — usually involving an outside lover, but actual adultery need not be proven; and cases could also, in principle, be brought against friends and relatives who tried to break up a marriage). Most states, by statute or case-law, have abolished these "heart balm" actions (along with other related actions, including "breach of promise to marry" and "seduction" (brought by a parent against a man who had enticed a daughter of chaste character to have sex)). *See, e.g., Helsel v. Noellsch*, 107 S.W.3d 231 (Mo. 2003) (abolishing alienation of affection tort); MINN. STAT. § 553.01 (2002) (abolishing causes of action of breach of promise to marry, seduction, alienation of affection, and criminal conversation). While only a handful of states still recognize causes of action for alienation of affection or criminal conversation, one can still find a few large verdicts being returned on such actions. *E.g.*, *Veeder v. Kennedy*, 589 N.W.2d 610 (S.D. 1999) (upholding a $265,000 judgment for alienation of affection); *Hutelmyer v. Cox*, 514 S.E.2d 554 (N.C. App. 1999) (upholding a judgment of one million dollars for criminal conversation and alienation of affection); *Jones v. Swanson*, 341 F.3d 723 (8th Cir. 2003) (affirming a large alienation of affection judgment subject to acceptance of a remittitur, which would reduce a judgment of $450,000 in compensatory damages and $500,000 in punitive damages to $150,000 compensatory and $250,000 punitive). The Mississippi Supreme Court recently refused an invitation to get rid of the state's cause of action for alienation of affection. *Fitch v. Valentine*, 959 So.2d 1012 (Miss. 2007), cert denied, 552 U.S. 1100 (2008) (upholding a $750,000 judgment for alienation of affection). According to Eugene Volokh (in a August 11, 2009 posting on "The Volokh Conspiracy" blog, volokh.com), in "fiscal years 2000–2007, there were an average of 230 filings [of alienation of affection lawsuits] per year — a bit over 0.5% of the number of all divorces, but about twice the number of product liability lawsuits. . . ." (The history and current law relating to the causes of actions discussed in this Note are discussed at greater length in Chapter 2.)

PROBLEMS

Problem 4-28. At marriage, Faith and Hubert are devout members of an orthodox religious congregation which understands its sacred texts to treat both homosexuality and adultery as an outrage. Ten years after their marriage Faith realizes, finding herself in love with another woman, that she is a lesbian. When she tells Hubert of her new self-understanding and of her new relationship, he not only seeks divorce but sues for intentional infliction of emotional distress. He claims that in the context of their marriage, her adulterous lesbian affair is outrageous conduct. What result? What should be the result?

Problem 4-29. Joan repeatedly tells her husband John that she prefers privacy while dressing. After he nonetheless enters their bedroom without knocking on several occasions, she files a tort claim for invasion of privacy. Assume that the claim would clearly be good if the parties were strangers. What result here? What should be the result?

Problem 4-30. Henrietta and Horace have a stormy relationship, caused in part by Henrietta's temper and impulsive behavior. After a bout of yelling and screaming when Horace refused to apologize for making plans with his family for Thanksgiving, rather than hers, Henrietta called the local police and filed a formal complaint accusing Horace of beating her. The report was entirely false, as Horace had never attacked her physically nor had he ever threatened to do so. Horace nonetheless spent 24 hours in jail until his lawyer obtained his release, and he was not exonerated for another two months, during which Henrietta made repeated phone calls to other members of his accounting firm, accusing him of domestic violence. As a result of her behavior, Horace had to resign from the firm. In his subsequent divorce action against Henrietta, he joins tort claims for damages for false imprisonment and intentional infliction of emotional distress, as well as compensation for his lost employment. What result? What should be the result?

Problem 4-31.   Unbeknownst to Chastity, her husband Clyde sets up a digital camera in their bedroom which takes pictures of their lovemaking, posting them on the Internet. She discovers this when a coworker tells her he enjoyed viewing them and asks her out to lunch. She files for divorce and adds a tort claim for invasion of privacy. What result? What should be the result? Does it matter whether the pictures are legally obscene? What if Clyde had been provoked by anger at learning that Chastity has performed a striptease at the office Christmas party?

Chapter 5

CHILD SUPPORT

INTRODUCTION

All American jurisdictions recognize a parental duty to support minor children. In the household where the child lives with two legal parents, the state intervenes only in the rare case where support is so inadequate as to constitute child neglect. When the child lives with only one of the parents or is in the care of a third party, however, the state is empowered to set and enforce child support owed by a noncustodial parent to the child's household. These orders are the subject of this chapter.

At one time, the support duty was paternal rather than parental. The mother's lack of financial responsibility was explained by the wife's common law disabilities and the natural differences between the sexes. Any duty imposed on the mother was secondary to the father's obligation. Today, the law imposes an equal duty of support on mothers and fathers, a regime generally believed mandated by the Fourteenth Amendment or by state equal rights provisions. *See Rand v. Rand*, 374 A.2d 900 (Md. 1977); *Cotton v. Municipal Court*, 130 Cal. Rptr. 876 (App. 1976); Sonja A. Soehnel, Annot., *Constitutionality of Gender-Based Classifications in Criminal Laws Proscribing Nonsupport of Spouse or Child*, 14 A.L.R.4th 717 (1982).

The support duty is not based upon the obligor's consent to sexual relations, much less intent to conceive a child. For example, in *State ex rel. Hermesmann v. Seyer*, 847 P.2d 1273 (Kan. 1993), the defendant, a 12-year old, had a sexual relationship with his 16-year-old babysitter. After a child was born, the defendant argued in a support action that, because he was protected by the statutory rape law, he was legally incapable of giving consent to the intercourse which produced the child. The court found his age irrelevant, concluding that, "as a father he has a common-law duty, as well as a statutory duty, to support his child." *See also Dubay v. Wells*, 506 F.3d 422 (6th Cir. 2007) (imposing a child support obligation on a man who was hoodwinked by his partner into believing she was infertile does not violate the 14th Amendment's equal protection clause); *Jacob v. Shultz-Jacob*, 923 A.2d 473 (Pa. Super. Ct. 2007) (sperm donor who actively engaged with and supported the two resulting children was an indispensable party in the support action by the children's biological mother against the mother's former lesbian partner); *see* Laura W. Morgan, *Child Support Fifty Years Later*, 42 Fam. L. Q. 365 (2008).

The precise rationale for imposing the duty to support children on their parents is rarely discussed or articulated. *See* Scott Altman, *A Theory of Child Support*, 17 Int. J. L., Pol'y & Fam. 173 (2003) (arguing private child support duties should be viewed "primarily as remedies for parental wrongs," a theory which "has specific consequences for issues of support allocation, including who should be declared a parent, and how much child support parents owe"); Leslie Joan Harris, *The Basis for Legal Parentage and the Clash between Custody and Child Support*, 42 IND. L. REV. 611 (2009) (practice of assigning child support obligation based solely on biological relationship reflects a public family law system that threatens to unbalance the private family law system in which parenthood often has been defined based on functional relationships for custody and visitation purposes); Jane C. Murphy, *Legal Images of Fatherhood: Welfare Reform, Child Support Enforcement, and Fatherless Children*, 81 NOTRE DAME L. REV. 325 (2005) (arguing that increasing reliance on biology to define fatherhood is an unintended and largely negative consequence of using child support to reimburse states for welfare expenditures).

Section A of this chapter outlines the contours of the duty of support. Section B covers reduction of the legal obligation to a specific amount of support. Section C discusses enforcement of support orders. Section D focuses on interstate support issues.

A. DUTY OF SUPPORT

[1]   Duration

[a]   General Rule

At the very least, parents must support their children during the child's minority or, in some states, until graduation from high school. *See, e.g.*, KAN. STAT. ANN. § 60-1610(a) (duty lasts through high school); *Carr v. Carr*, 834 P.2d 970 (Okla. 1992) (statute extends duty to 19th birthday for high school students); *Walworth v. Klauder*, 615 So. 2d 219 (Fla. App. 1993) (same); *Freyer v. Freyer*, 427 N.W.2d 348 (N.D. 1988) (duty lasts through high school); *Paaso v. Paaso*, 428 N.W.2d 724 (Mich. App. 1988) (reduction of age of majority to 18 not intended to cut off support of high school students); *Bornemann v. Bornemann*, 931 A.2d 1154 (Md. Ct. App. 2007) (retroactively applying statutory amendment extending child support to the later of a child's 18th birthday or graduation from secondary school).

Some states once ended the obligation to support daughters earlier than the obligation to support sons, on the assumption that women were ready for their life's work — housewifery — sooner than men, who needed more education for their tasks. This distinction was held to violate the Equal Protection Clause. *Stanton v. Stanton*, 421 U.S. 7 (1975).

Despite the general rule, some circumstances may extend the support obligation into the child's majority and other circumstances may extinguish the obligation before the child reaches majority.

[b]   Post-Majority Support for Disabled Children

The disabled child incapable of self-support is a widely recognized exception to the general rule terminating the support obligation at the child's majority. *See, e.g.,* ARIZ. REV. STAT. ANN. § 25-320 E; HAWAII REV. STAT. § 580-47(a); TEX. FAM. CODE ANN. § 154.001(a)(4); Katherine Ellis Reeves, Note, *Post-Majority Child Support Awards for Disabled Children: A Fifty State Survey*, 8 WHITTIER J. CHILD & FAM. ADVOC. 109 (2008); *but see Pierce v. Pierce*, 770 A.2d 867 (R.I. 2001) (discussing statute which overruled judicial precedent authorizing extended support for disabled children); *In re Thurmond*, 715 N.E. 2d 814 (Ill. App. Ct. 1999) (overturning extended support order for "slow learner" who had graduated from high school, had a job and been accepted to college).

States recognizing a duty to support disabled children split on whether the disability must exist before the child reaches majority. *Compare Towery v. Towery*, 685 S.W.2d 155 (Ark. 1985) (no duty when crippling injury occurred after majority), *with Racherbaumer v. Racherbaumer*, 844 S.W.2d 502 (Mo. Ct. App. 1992) (duty exists where disabled child is adult at time of divorce) and *Riggs v. Riggs*, 578 S.E.2d 3 (S.C. 2003) (support can be ordered where genetic degenerative disease did not reveal itself until adulthood, 8 years after divorce).

[c]   Post-Majority Support for Higher Education

DONARSKI v. DONARSKI
North Dakota Supreme Court
581 N.W.2d 130 (1998)

NEUMANN, J.

[The trial court granted a divorce and ordered the former husband to provide post-minority support to the couple's daughter BethAnn for college.]

Kenneth and Janet Donarski were married in 1974. Janet's daughter from a prior marriage, Amy, age 27, was adopted by Kenneth after he and Janet married. Kenneth and Janet also have two children of this marriage, Nathan, age 21, and BethAnn, age 16.

Kenneth graduated from the University of North Dakota in 1975 with a bachelor's degree in social work . . . Kenneth worked first as a housing rehabilitation specialist and then as Director of the Grand Forks Housing Authority . . . [before] Kenneth accepted the position of Director of the Fargo Housing Authority, and the family moved to Fargo. After receiving her high school diploma, Janet received one year of medical technical training and an additional year of junior college. Throughout the marriage Janet assumed various minimum wage part-time jobs while she was the primary homemaker and caregiver for the children.

. . . The trial court ordered Kenneth to pay . . . "one-half of BethAnn's reasonable college education expenses, including books, tuition and housing. Reasonable expenses are those incurred in pursuing a four year degree in consecutive years upon graduation from high school." Kenneth asserts these orders are clearly erroneous, because the trial court has no authority to order a parent to pay support for an adult child.

In a divorce action, the court has authority to order payment of post-minority support, including college expenses, under appropriate circumstances. *See Zarrett v. Zarrett*, 574 N.W.2d 855 (N.D. 1998); *see also* N.D.C.C. 14-09-08.2(4) . . .

We caution that a trial court's authority to award post-minority support to a child of a divorce is limited, and must be based upon full consideration of the particular circumstances of the case. The Supreme Court of New Jersey in *Newburgh v. Arrigo*, 443 A.2d 1031, 1038–1039 (1982), aptly describes the factors a court must consider in directing a parent to pay for costs of a child's college education:

> In evaluating the claim for contribution toward the cost of higher education, courts should consider all relevant factors, including (1) whether the parent, if still living with the child, would have contributed toward the costs of the requested higher education; (2) the effect of the background, values and goals of the parent on the reasonableness of the expectation of the child for higher education; (3) The amount of the contribution sought by the child for the cost of higher education; (4) the ability of the parent to pay that cost; (5) the relationship of the requested contribution to the kind of school or course of study sought by the child; (6) the financial resources of both parents; (7) the commitment to and aptitude of the child for the requested education; (8) the financial resources of the child, including assets owned individually or held in custodianship or trust; (9) the ability of the child to earn income during the school year or on vacation; (10) the availability of financial aid in the form of college grants and loans; (11) the child's relationship to the paying parent, including mutual affection and shared goals as well as responsiveness to parental advice and guidance; and (12) the relationship of the education requested to any prior training and to the overall long-range goals of the child.

Of these factors, the parent's ability to pay is most significant, and a parent cannot be compelled to contribute to an adult child's college expenses if the parent's financial resources are lacking . . . The court must consider all relevant factors in deciding whether to award post-minority support . . . It is essential the court consider evidence pertaining to the amount required for college costs, including books, tuition, room and board, and to determine the amount that a parent can contribute without experiencing undue hardship . . .

The Supreme Court of Alabama emphasizes in *Ex Parte Bayliss*, 550 So. 2d 986, 987 (Ala. 1989), the relevant factors the trial court must consider in awarding post-minority support:

> [A] trial court may award sums of money out of the property and income of either or both parents for the post-minority education of a child of that dissolved marriage. . . . In doing so, the trial court shall consider all relevant factors that shall appear reasonable and necessary, including primarily the financial resources of the parents and the child and the child's

commitment to, and aptitude for, the requested education. The trial court may consider, also, the standard of living that the child would have enjoyed if the marriage had not been dissolved and the family unit had been preserved and the child's relationship with his parents and responsiveness to parental advice and guidance.

Here the trial court found Kenneth "helped the older children, Amy and Nathan, by providing funds toward a college education." The court also found "Kenneth has the ability to provide for and pay a portion of BethAnn's college expenses." Other than these conclusory statements, the court made no specific findings of the relevant factors and circumstances the court needed to consider in awarding BethAnn post-minority support for college and medical expenses. The court placed no limit on the amount of Kenneth's obligation to BethAnn. While the court did attempt to define college expenses, and did impose a limit as to time, it said nothing as to the cost or quality of the education to be financed. While setting an exact dollar amount for such an obligation will not always be desirable or even possible in many cases, fairness and equity require that obligors not be subjected to court-ordered obligations that are unlimited.

We conclude the trial court's award of post-minority support is not adequately supported by specific findings of fact, and is insufficiently bound by reasonable limitations. We, therefore, reverse the award of post-minority medical and college expenses and remand for additional findings of fact and reconsideration of the issue.

. . .

SANDSTROM, JUSTICE, . . . dissenting in part.

Because the majority's opinion affirming the district court's order that Kenneth Donarski contribute to the college education of his adult child is contrary to law and public policy, I respectfully dissent from [the affirmation of the order to provide for the college education expenses].

The parties conceded at oral argument that absent a statute to the contrary, parents generally have no duty to support their adult children. Under our statutes, parents' duty to support their child will generally terminate when the child is age 18 . . . But the majority boldly states . . . "In a divorce action, the court has authority to order payment of post-minority support, including college expenses, under appropriate circumstances" . . . [citing] *Zarrett v. Zarrett* . . . *Zarrett* involved a stipulation-something not present here . . . [The legislative history and context of N.D.C.C. § 14-09-08.2(4) does not support the majority's conclusion that courts are authorized by the legislature to order support.]

. . .

Under the majority's analysis, post-minority support is not limited to college expenses; there is no age limit on adult children eligible for support; there is no requirement a child be mentally or physically disabled; there is no requirement of a specific statutory authorization for a particular purpose. Under the majority's analysis, except for college expenses, apparently all that is required is the court determine the support to be "appropriate."

Under the majority's analysis, a trial court in a divorce case could apparently order one or both parents to provide an allowance to their mentally and physically able middle-aged adult children as long as the court determines the support to be "appropriate." And a trial court could order divorcing parents to treat all their adult children the same, by providing the same support for all, or equalizing for previous gifts as long as the court determines the support to be "appropriate." Such decisions have previously belonged exclusively to the parents . . . Unfortunately, this clearly established law is apparently irrelevant under the majority analysis.

I would reverse the district court's order of support for an adult child.

NOTES

1. ***Legislative Sequel.*** Immediately following the court's decision in *Donarski*, the child support statute was amended. The new language was interpreted as precluding a court from ordering a noncustodial parent to pay for the college education of a child over the age of 18. *Larson v. Larson*, 694 N.W.2d 13 (ND 2005). If you had been in the North Dakota legislature, would you have voted to maintain the authority of a court to order a parent to provide support for college under the terms of *Donarski*, or would you have voted to eliminate the court's authority? For an overview of support for college education, see Abraham Kuhl, *Post-Majority Educational Support for Children in the Twenty-First Century*, 21 J. AM. ACAD. MATRIM. LAW. 763 (2008).

2. ***The Remand.*** The appeals court criticized the court below for offering only "conclusory statements" without "specific findings of the relevant factors and circumstances the court needed to consider in awarding BethAnn post-minority support for college and medical expenses. The court placed no limit on the amount of Kenneth's obligation to BethAnn." Imagine you are the trial judge asked to reconsider the judgment on remand on the basis of additional factual findings. What factual circumstances should be relevant? Just how should the court define the nature and extent of the support obligation, assuming it concludes there should be one? Should all students who can gain admission to a college be treated identically in their claims for support? Should a student who gains admission to a prestigious and expensive private college have a claim for more support than a student admitted to a much less expensive local public university? Community college? It is clear that a rule allowing courts to award support for college must have principles by which to answer such questions.

3. ***Authority to Award Post-Majority Educational Support.*** Even when the age of majority in most states was 21, a college education often was found to be outside the parental child support obligation. *See* Glen A. Smith, Note, *Educational Support Obligations of Noncustodial Parents*, 36 RUTGERS. L. REV. 588, 593–603 (1984). By contrast, many current statutes specifically authorize the award of post-majority parental support for higher education. *See, e.g.*, COLO. REV. STAT. ANN. § 14-10-115 (15)(c)(I) ("if the court finds it appropriate for the parents to contribute to the costs of a program of postsecondary education"); HAW. REV. STAT. § 580-47(a); ILL. REV. STAT. ch. 750, § 5/513; IND. CODE ANN. § 31-16-6-2; MO. ANN. STAT. § 452.340(5); N.Y. DOM. REL. LAW § 240(1-b) (b)(2) (support may include amounts for the "education of any unemancipated child under the age of twenty-

one years"); Or. Rev. Stat. § 107.108; Wash. Rev. Code Ch. 26.19, Child Support Schedule Appendix, *Postsecondary Education Standards*; W. Va. Code § 48-13-702. *See Snow v. Rincker*, 823 N.E.2d 1234, 1237 (Ind. App. 2005) ("although a parent is under no absolute legal duty to provide a college education for his children, a court may nevertheless order a parent to pay part or all of such costs when appropriate"); *Eppler v. Eppler*, 837 N.E.2d 167, 177 (Ind. App. 2005) (disparity between father's annual income of $280,000 and mother's of $20,800, coupled with facts that mother earned little or no income after first child was born and, if parties had remained married, father would have been sole contributor to children's college expenses, warranted ordering father to pay 100% of children's college expenses). Awards for post-majority educational support are not necessarily limited to undergraduate school. *See, e.g., Ross v. Ross*, 400 A.2d 1233 (N.J. Super. 1979) (law school); *Kopp v. Turley*, 518 A.2d 588 (Pa. Super. 1986)(commercial art school). *But see In re Holderrieth*, 536 N.E.2d 946 (Ill. App.1989)(no support for trade school); *cf. delCastillo v. delCastillo*, 617 A.2d 26 (Pa. Super. 1992) (agreement to fund education "beyond high school" excludes graduate school expenses). However, some courts have been very careful to separate educational costs from general support. *See, e.g., In re: Gilmore*, 803 A.2d 601 (N.H. 2002) (transportation, clothing, medical and dental coverage not properly included in "educational expenses"); *Meek v. Warren*, 726 So.2d 1292 (Miss. App. 1998). College expense statutes often require the child to inform the non-custodial parent of academic progress and to enroll and complete a minimum amount of credits to continue eligibility. *See Mandel v. Eagleton*, 90 S.W.3d 527 (Mo. App. 2002) (failure to enroll in statutory minimum of college credits is an emancipation, rendering child ineligible for future support).

Some courts refuse to authorize post-majority support for educational purposes, relying "on the argument that if the marriage had continued, the parents would have been free to decide not to send their child to college, and that divorce should not deprive them of that discretion." Clark, the law of domestic relations, § 17.1 at 718 (2d ed. 1988); Kuhl, *supra*; *see, e.g., In re Plummer*, 735 P.2d 165 (Colo. 1987); *Grapin v. Grapin*, 450 So. 2d 853 (Fla. 1984); *Cariseo v. Cariseo*, 459 A.2d 523 (Conn. 1983). That argument, however, seems weak because parents in intact families are generally free to choose any level of support above the minimal threshold needed to avoid liability for neglect, while child support awards always exceed this minimum if parental resources permit.

Divorced parents have argued that requiring support for a college education is unconstitutional, claiming an equal protection violation because married parents are not similarly obligated. Most courts reject such arguments, usually citing state interests in educating its youth and in ameliorating the particular hardships for children of divorce. *See, e.g. In re Crocker*, 22 P.3d 759 (Or. 2001); *Kohring v. Snodgrass*, 999 S.W.2d 228 (Mo. 1999); *LeClair v. LeClair*, 624 A.2d 1350 (N.H. 1993) (rational to conclude that "absent judicial involvement, children of divorce may be less likely than children of intact families to receive college financial support from both . . . parents"); *Ex Parte Bayliss*, 550 So. 2d 986 (Ala. 1989); *but see Curtis v. Kline*, 666 A.2d 265 (Pa. 1995) (holding legislation authorizing post-majority educational support violates federal Equal Protection Clause). At least one state allows courts to order post-majority support for children of divorce but not for non-marital children. This law was sustained over an Equal Protection challenge in *Johnson v. Louis*, 654 N.W.2d 886 (Iowa 2002).

4. *Educational Support by Agreement.* Regardless of whether a court may order post-majority support for education, parents can agree to provide the support. Their agreement, if incorporated into a decree, is an enforceable obligation. *See, e.g.*, Cal. Fam. Code § 3587 (". . . the court has the authority to approve a stipulated agreement . . . for the support of an adult child or for the continuation of child support after [age 18] and to make a support order to effectuate the agreement"); Vt. Stat. Ann. tit. 15, § 659(b) ("If the parties agree, the court may include . . . an additional amount designated for the purpose of providing for postsecondary education"); *Hayward v. Lawrence*, 312 S.E.2d 609 (Ga. 1984) (father in contempt for failing to comply with incorporated agreement); *Acrey v. Acrey*, 356 S.E.2d 437 (S.C. App. 1987). Alternatively, the court may decline to incorporate a parental agreement into the divorce decree, but enforce it as a contract. *See Solomon v. Findley*, 808 P.2d 294 (Ariz.1991); *Madson v. Madson*, 636 So. 2d 759 (Fla. App.1994)(separation agreement announcing father's "moral obligation" and "intention" to support children through college is unenforceable).

5. *Can An Obligor Condition Support on Student's Behavior?* In *Mayes v. Fisher*, 854 S.W.2d 430 (Mo. App. 1993), the court rejected the obligor's claim that his daughter's enrollment in a single community college course was a "sham" created solely to extend his support obligation. The court found the daughter's financial circumstances did not permit her to enroll in more courses and the limited nature of her course load did not justify termination of the support obligation. In *In re Sandlin*, 831 P.2d 64 (Ore. App. 1992), the obligor sought to eliminate support payments to his college-student daughter who was living with her boyfriend. Finding the statutory eligibility requirements had been met, the court found the daughter's lifestyle irrelevant to the support issue.

Other obligors have been treated more sympathetically. In *Moss v. Nedas*, 674 A.2d 174 (N.J. Super. App. Div. 1996), the court found daughter had treated obligor solely as a "wallet" when, in violation of prior court orders, the father was denied input into her selection of a college and information on her performance at school. The appellate court found the "obstructive behavior" justified terminating the support obligation. *See also McKay v. McKay*, 644 N.E.2d 164 (Ind. App. 1994) (college student's refusal to have any relationship with father relieves obligor of duty of support).

6. *The ALI Approach.* Because so many parents attempt to save money for the college expenses of their children, parents might assume that some money for college saving is included in the basic support obligation. However, if state law does not require a divorced parent to support his child in college, then a court generally cannot include savings for such a college nest egg in its calculation of the support order. Even in states that do allow support for college, the basic order set by the support guidelines all states now use (those guidelines are explored in detail below) will not include provision for it.

The ALI Principles § 3.12 subsume postsecondary education in the category of "life opportunities." The commentary explains that in deciding whether to order support for post-secondary education under this standard, the trier of fact must first decide whether the parent would provide the opportunity if the child were residing with the parent. If there are no objective indicia of what the parent would do (such as educational support for another child), then "the parent should be assumed to do what residential parents of similar wealth and background ordinarily do." The second question (reached only if one concludes that post-secondary education would have been provided in the intact family) is whether the parents can now contribute to it without undue hardship to themselves or their other dependents. If they can, then the court may require support in college.

7. *Value of Post-Secondary Education.* The importance of a college education to financial success over a lifetime is hard to overstate. According to the Census Bureau, on an annual basis, "High school graduates earn about $27,000, while those with a bachelor's degree earned about $47,000." Sarah R. Crissey, *Current Population Reports, Educational Attainment in the United States: 2007,* U.S. Dep't of Commerce, Census Bureau P20-560 (Jan. 2009), http:// www.census.gov/prod/2009pubs/p20-560.pdf. The cost of obtaining a college education, however, is substantial. Parental contributions average approximately one-quarter of the cost, or about $5,000 a year. Students pay another quarter, on average, and public support or institutional assistance account for the rest. Nancy Folbre, Valuing Children: Rethinking the Economics of the Family (2008). Although children of divorced parents are less likely to receive parental support for college, many financial aid sources require all parents to file financial aid forms, and financial aid is often based on an assessment of the parent's ability to pay rather than the parent's willingness to pay. *Id.*

PROBLEMS

Problem 5-1. Karen Miller relates the following: After 22 years of marriage, she and David separated in December of their son Caleb's final year in high school. Caleb (then 18) remained in the marital home with Karen. Soon after, however, she and Caleb began having problems. He violated his curfew, refused to study and neglected household chores. Several violent arguments ensued, during which Caleb shoved her and spat in her face. In March, he moved in with his father and ceased communication with her.

After graduating from high school, Caleb entered the University of Richmond, earning a 3.0 grade point average as a freshman. His father paid all educational expenses and Caleb returned to his father's home during vacations. After his freshman year, he transferred to Occidental College in California. Before enrolling there, Caleb (through his father) filed a support action seeking $5,000 toward his college expenses. Karen and David are both fairly well-off financially. Karen tells you, "I can afford it, but I don't think I need to pay." Caleb wants no communication with his mother. The parents are not divorced.

In David and Karen's jurisdiction, a divorce court has power to order post-majority support for educational purposes. The leading appellate case directs trial courts to consider two factors in deciding whether to order support: "the child's desire and ability to successfully pursue post-secondary education and the parents' ability to contribute to that effort without undue hardship." Lower court cases have additionally considered the child's independent financial resources, whether private school is appropriate for the child and parental educational background. The jurisdiction has a no-fault divorce statute.

How would you argue on behalf of Karen and what arguments would you expect to hear from opposing counsel?

Problem 5-2. Jerry and Mary's divorce decree incorporated the following provision from their separation agreement: "Mary will pay all of the children's college expenses, including room, board, tuition, reasonable transportation expenses, school supplies and similar costs. She will have a say in the choice of college for each child and will have the right to approve or disapprove a particular college but will exercise that right in a reasonable fashion." Three years after the divorce, Mary filed a motion to terminate her support obligation for the couple's second child, Oren. The motion alleged that Oren had turned 18, graduated from high school and was not attending college. The relevant age of majority was 18. At a pre-trial conference, Mary learned for the first time that Oren had indeed been enrolled in community college for a semester and was in the middle of his second semester. She was unaware of these developments because she had not exercised any visitation with Oren or communicated with him in the three years since the divorce. She now insists that she need not provide college support because the divorce provision has been violated. How should the court rule on her claim?

Problem 5-3. Fred and Ethel were divorced in Georgia in 2001, when their daughter, Michelle, was 12. The decree ordered weekly support payments by Fred. The decree was silent about support beyond the age of 18, Georgia's age of majority, at which time all support obligations stop. Ethel and Michelle moved to Columbia, South Carolina, while Fred remains in Georgia in a border town from which he commutes daily to his job as a physician in South Carolina. He has paid his support regularly and exercises his visitation rights. Michelle has done fairly well academically in high school. South Carolina law is clear that an order for post-majority support for educational purposes is within judicial discretion, upon consideration of factors such as parental ability to so provide, the child's ability to succeed and the advantages which might be obtained by such an education. Michelle has been accepted at a private college and her mother has retained you to represent them. What are the issues and how would you argue on behalf of your client?

Problem 5-4. Sam and Janet were divorced when their daughter Ilene was 15. Ilene had been diagnosed with an autism-related chronic condition (Asperger's syndrome) for which she had begun receiving treatment when she was 9. Janet obtained custody of Ilene and Sam was ordered to pay support until Ilene turned 21. Now, 35 years later, Ilene is 50, having lived with her mother since the divorce. Janet has just died and Ilene comes to your office wondering if she might be able to obtain support from Sam, who is now very wealthy. Ilene has never worked and is unable to do so. She had been supported by Janet alone since the support order terminated on her 21st birthday. What do you advise her?

Problem 5-5. Casey and Drew have three children, all teenagers at the time of the divorce. Both Casey and Drew earned bachelor degrees at a highly-selective private university, and both then attended medical school. Each has inherited property worth between $500,000 and $750,000. Casey earns over $150,000 a year in fulltime private practice, while Drew earns $75,000 a year in a part-time practice.

They live in a state where the court is empowered to order parents to provide support for the college education of their children. Neither opposes the entry of such an order, but Casey wants the amount capped at the cost of the local public university. Drew argues that the children should be able to attend colleges of the same sort as the parents attended, assuming they are admitted. How should the court rule?

[d]   Pre-Majority Termination of Support

Many states adhere to the common law rule terminating the support obligation with the obligor's death. *See, e.g.*, *Benson v. Patterson*, 830 A.2d 966 (Pa. 2003) (reviewing case law, declaring common law rule to be the majority rule); *Hirst v. Dugan*, 611 A.2d 616 (N.H. 1992) (duty to marital and non-marital children terminated); Tex. Fam. Code Ann. § 154.006 (2002). This is said to be consistent with the "generally accepted view in American law that a parent may disinherit his minor children if he wishes. . . ." Homer H. Clark, The Law of Domestic Relations § 17.2 at 733 (2d ed. 1988). Even in states following this rule, the parties may agree that support shall survive the obligor's death. *See, e.g.*, *In re North Carolina Inheritance Taxes*, 277 S.E.2d 403 (N.C. 1981). This is often accomplished by requiring the obligor to maintain life insurance naming the child as beneficiary.

In contrast, the Model Marriage and Divorce Act § 316(c) provides that, on the obligor's death, "the amount of support may be modified, revoked, or commuted to a lump sum payment, to the extent just and appropriate. . . ." At least six states have adopted the language of the MMDA. *See* Ariz. Rev. Stat. § 25-327(c); Col. Rev. Stat. Ann. §§ 14-10-122, Ill. Rev. Stat. ch. 750, Ky. Rev. Stat. § 403.213(3); Minn Stat. § 518A.39 Subd. 4; Mont. Code. Anno. § 40-4-208(5). In rejecting an automatic cutoff, states adopting this view may recognize that "disinherited children are in fact protected where the marriage does not end in divorce, since in most states the surviving spouse is given a statutory forced share of the decedent's estate which can then be subjected to the child's claim for support." Clark, *supra; see Kujawinski v. Kujawinski*, 376 N.E.2d 1382 (Ill. 1978). Some courts find power to order post-death support where the statute is silent. *See, e.g.*, *Knowles v. Thompson*, 697 A.2d 335 (Vt. 1997) (court can order obligor to purchase life insurance with children as beneficiaries because "it is reasonable to assume that [obligor] would have provided for his children in his will"); *Scott v. Wagoner*, 400 S.E.2d 556 (W. Va. 1990) (post-death support can be ordered if "compelling equitable considerations" exist); *Koidl v. Schreiber*, 520 A.2d 759 (N.J. Super. 1986); Susan L. Thomas, Annot., *Death of Parent as Affecting Decree for Support of Child*, 14 A.L.R.5th 557 (1993); John Michalik, Annot., *Divorce: Provision in Decree That One Party Obtain or Maintain Life Insurance for Benefit of Other Party or Child*, 59 A.L.R.3d 9 (1974).

Another event terminating the support obligation before majority is emancipation. At common law, the minor child's marriage or entry into the military service terminated or suspended the parental support obligation. *See Bishop v. Bishop*, 671 A.2d 644 (N.J. Super. Ch. Div. 1995) (child enrolled at United States Military Academy is, by definition, emancipated); *Porath v. McVey*, 884 S.W.2d 692 (Mo. App. 1994) (same); Sanford N. Katz, William A. Schroeder & Lawrence R. Sidman, *Emancipating Our Children — Coming of Legal Age in America*, 7 Fam.

L.Q. 211 (1973). Many current statutes establish procedures for judicial emancipation at the behest of the child or, sometimes, the parent. They vary widely on the standard for and the scope of an emancipation. There are cases finding a child emancipated because of his or her behavior. *See, e.g., Caldwell v. Caldwell*, 823 So. 2d 1216 (Miss. App. 2002) (emancipation where daughter had non-marital child, quit school, chose not to seek employment and accepted child support from child's father); *P.K. v. M.K.*, 19 FAM. L. REP. 1362 (N.Y. Fam. Ct. 1993) (child's unreasonable refusal to permit visitation justifies suspension of support); *Hunter v. Hulgan*, 609 So.2d 5 (Ala. Civ. App. 1992) (support termination justified by 16-year-old's marriage and fatherhood of child). A child's gainful employment has been held to constitute emancipation. In *Ware v. Ware*, 391 S.E.2d 887 (Va. App. 1990), the divorce decree obligated the father to support the children until majority or until they "married, died, or become otherwise emancipated." The court held a 17-year-old daughter earning over $15,000 annually in a full-time job while living with her mother was emancipated. The court held the parties contemplated emancipation when the child "earned sufficient funds to fully provide for herself."

While some cases declare emancipation on extreme facts, generally courts are reluctant to terminate support obligations based on the child's behavior. *See, e.g., In re Schoby*, 4 P.3d 604 (Kan. 2000) (16-year-old boy's marriage did not automatically terminate support obligation; divorce decree incorporating agreement that support would be terminated by marriage not dispositive); *Dunson v. Dunson*, 769 N.E.2d 1120 (Ind. 2002) (child living outside home not emancipated because he was not self-supporting); *Carroll v. Carroll*, 593 So. 2d 1131 (Fla. App. 1992) (support continued where child had successfully petitioned to terminate obligor's visitation rights); *Allison C. v. Susan C.*, 598 N.Y.S.2d 970 (App. Div. 1993) (lack of parent-child contact was obligor's fault); *Wulff v. Wulff*, 500 N.W.2d 845 (Neb. 1993) (emancipation rescinded where child who had left home and given birth returned to the parental home); *In re Brown*, 597 N.E.2d 1297 (Ind. App. 1992) (17-year-old's refusal to visit non-custodial parent does not justify finding of emancipation); *Trosky v. Mann*, 581 A.2d 177 (Pa. Super. 1990) (imposing obligation where 16-year-old said he "wanted absolutely nothing" from his parents after leaving home; court found child incapable of self-support and unwelcome in his parents' home).

[2]   Support of Step-Children

Step-relationships are established by the remarriage of a widowed or divorced parent. Questions concerning whether stepparents owe any obligation of support to a child arise most commonly when the child lives in the same household as the stepparent. Questions about whether a stepparent's resources should affect the child support obligation of either a custodial or a noncustodial parent are discussed later, in Section B.

How many children are in step-relationships with one or two adults? The best information exists concerning children who reside in a household with a custodial parent and that person's marital partner. In 2004, of the 51 million children who lived with two parents, 87% (44.5 million) lived with their biological mother and biological father. An additional 10% (5.3 million) lived with a biological parent and a stepparent, usually with a biological mother and a stepfather (4.1 million). U.S. Dept't of Commerce, Bureau of the Census, *Living Arrangements of Children: 2004* (Feb. 2008), http://www.census.gov/prod/2008pubs/p70-114.pdf. Less certainty exists concerning children in informal stepparent relationships. "[The Census Bureau's] percentage would be even greater and would include more families from marginalized groups if the broader definition of stepfamilies (including unmarried couples) were used." Sarah H. Ramsey, *Constructing Parenthood for Stepparents: Parents by Estoppel and De Facto Parents under the American Law Institute's Principles of the Law of Family Dissolution,* 8 DUKE J. GENDER L. & POL'Y 285 (2001). The Census Bureau also does not provide data on how many children in the care of one parent have a stepparent in the household of the other parent.

[a]   General Rule of Non-Liability

At common law, the step-relationship itself imposed no legally enforceable support obligation. Some courts held that accepting a step-child into one's home established an obligation to support because the step-parent was acting *in loco parentis,* but this "obligation" was terminable at will by the step-parent. Today, similar rules are usually provided by statute. *See, e.g.,* DEL. CODE ANN. tit. 13, § 501(b) (expanding duty to include cohabitors if natural parent is not supporting child); MONT. CODE ANN. § 40-6-217; N.D. CENT. CODE § 14-09-09, or MO. REV. CODE § 453.400 (stepparent duty to stepchildren identical with duty to natural or adoptive child so long as stepchild is coresident); VT. STAT. ANN. § 296 (stepparent's duty exists during coresidency with stepchild or duration of marriage with child's parent, and duty contingent on financial resources of the natural or adoptive parents being insufficient). This traditional rule creates step-parent obligations that are illusory at best. No support can be ordered at divorce or separation and, during the marriage between parent and step-parent, the obligation — like all support obligations in the intact family — is satisfied by minimal support. Practically, of course, a step-parent in fact does support the child by virtue of sharing the same household.

[b]   Imposing Liability on Step-Parents

An exception to the limited support liability of step-parents is found in family expense statutes which protect creditors who provide goods and services to family members, including step-children. WASH. REV. CODE ANN. § 26.16.205. Of potentially greater significance is the occasional imposition of step-parent support obligations through equitable estoppel. In *Miller v. Miller,* 478 A.2d 351 (N.J. 1984), the court estopped a divorcing step-parent from denying a post-divorce obligation to support his step-children. During the marriage, defendant tore up support checks from the natural father, who was serving a prison term for narcotics offenses, because defendant did not want to be connected to narcotics activities. *See also W. v. W.,* 779 A.2d 716 (Conn. 2001) (defendant had represented himself as father for 12 years, interfered with relationship with natural father and caused detrimental reliance by child); Laura W. Morgan, *Child Support Fifty Years Later,* 42 FAM. L. Q. 365 (2008).

Contracts between a parent and stepparent for support of a stepchild have been enforced. *See Dewey v. Dewey*, 886 P.2d 623 (Alaska 1994); *Duffey v. Duffey*, 438 S.E.2d 445 (N.C. App. 1994) (enforcing separation agreement, but finding stepparent secondarily liable to biological parents); *In re Marriage of Dawley*, 551 P.2d 323 (Cal. 1976) (enforcing antenuptial agreement to support wife's child for 14 months, a period longer than the marriage lasted); *L. v. L.*, 497 S.W.2d 840 (Mo. App. 1973) (enforcing pre-marital promise to "treat the child as his" during and after marriage). In a related fact pattern, courts have acknowledged that grandparents might have a support obligation, either through contract, *Mooney v. Mooney*, 538 S.E.2d 864 (Ga. App. 2000), or the doctrine of equitable adoption. *Johnson v. Johnson*, 617 N.W.2d 97 (N.D. 2000). Guardianship status alone, without a support agreement, has been held not to create a support obligation. *Favrow v. Vargas*, 647 A.2d 731 (Conn. 1994); *Tilley v. Tilley*, 489 N.W.2d 185 (Mich. App. 1992). *See generally*, David B. Sweet, Annot., *Stepparent's Postdivorce Duty to Support Stepchild*, 44 A.L.R.4th 520 (1986).

For discussions of the obligations of step-parents, see Mary-Lynne Fisher, *Stepparent Responsibility for Child Support in California's Community Property System*, 22 LOYOLA L. REV. 73 (1988); Margaret M. Mahoney, *Stepfamilies in the Federal Law*, 48 PITT. L. REV. 491 (1987) (focusing on Social Security programs and immigration); Katharine T. Bartlett, *Rethinking Parenthood as an Exclusive Status: The Need for Legal Alternatives When the Premise of the Nuclear Family Has Failed*, 70 VA. L. REV. 879, 912 *et seq.* (1984) (discussing support, custody and visitation). For an article urging expansion of the duty to support beyond biological parenthood, see Lawrence C. Nolan, *Legal Strangers and the Duty of Support: Beyond the Biological Tie — But How Far Beyond the Marital Tie?*, 41 SANTA CLARA L. REV. 1 (2000) (argues duty should extend to legal strangers "to the extent that their own actions and conduct would bind them under the principles of *in loco parentis*, contract law, or equitable estoppel").

[c]   Same-Sex Partners as Step-Parents?

The relationship of a same-sex partner to the child of a biological parent, which could be analogized to the stepparent relationship, is treated in Chapter 9, Section B[4][a][i].

[3]   Relationship Between Visitation and Support Obligations

Visitation and support are often intertwined in the minds of divorced parents. A support obligor may feel he need not pay child support when the custodial parent has interfered with his access to the child, and a custodial parent may feel justified in limiting or denying access to a non-custodial parent who is in arrears. Conversely, studies have routinely found positive correlations between consistent payment of child support and regular contact of the payor parent with the child. *See* Paul R. Amato, Catherine E. Meyers & Robert E. Emery, *Changes in Nonresident Father-Child Contact From 1976 to 2002*, 58 FAM. REL. 41 (2009).

Most states treat child support and visitation as independent obligations. This means one parent cannot defend a failure to pay support or allow visitation with evidence of the other parent's failure to comply with the court order. This ban on "self-help" does not necessarily bar a *court* from linking the obligations, however, as a tool of enforcement — an approach on which the states are split. Under § 315 of the Model Marriage and Divorce Act (MMDA), a party's failure to comply with the decree does not affect "the obligation of the other party to make payments for support or maintenance or to permit visitation . . . ; but he may move the court to grant an appropriate order." The MMDA thus allows a wronged parent to seek a judicial order conditioning support on visitation, or visitation on support. *See also* Minn. Stat. Ann. § 518.612. By contrast, under the Uniform Interstate Family Support Act § 305(d) the court "may not condition the payment of a support order . . . upon compliance . . . with provisions for visitation."

Some state statutes specifically authorize decrees linking visitation and support obligations. *See, e.g.,* Or. Rev. Stat. § 107.431. A New York statute permitting suspension of alimony or cancellation of arrears for the withholding of visitation rights was applied to child support, *Vigo v. Vigo*, 467 N.Y.S.2d 436 (App. 1983); *but see* N.Y. Dom. Rel. Law § 241 (making clear that any suspension must be prospective and not retroactive); *Smith v. Bombard*, 741 N.Y.S.2d 336 (App. Div. 2002). For more on this topic, see Ira Ellman, *Should Visitation Denial Affect the Obligation to Pay Support?*, in The Law and Economics of Child Support Payments (William Comanor, ed. 2004), *reprinted in* 36 Ariz. St. L.J. 661 (2004); Karen Czapanskiy, *Child Support and Visitation, Rethinking the Connections*, 20 Rutgers L.J. 619 (1989).

A support obligor who engages in self-help and ceases payments when the other parent refuses to permit visitation may also find that the rule against retroactive modification of support arrearages bars consideration of his claim on the merits. *See* Section B[7][b] of this chapter.

PROBLEMS

Problem 5-6. Ward and June's marriage produced two sons, Wallace and Theodore. The couple divorced after ten years and June was ordered to pay Ward, the custodial parent, $250 monthly in support. Two years later, Ward married a wealthy nightclub entertainer, Margaret Anderson. Euphoria, where all relevant events occurred, has a law requiring step-parents who "accept children of their spouse into their home" to support them while they are in the home.

Ward and Margaret moved with the boys to an expensive home. June, who was earning $25,000 annually when she and Ward divorced, now earns $30,000 annually. She asks you whether, in light of the boys' new living situation, she can seek a reduction in her child support payments. What is your response?

Problem 5-7. Your client Bill is involved in a bitter divorce with Camilla. The couple has two children, a 13-year-old girl and a 16-year-old boy. In the divorce decree, the judge has ordered maintenance, property division, and $500 monthly support for the two children. Additionally, because the parents are well-educated and Bill's financial resources are ample, he's been ordered to buy $150,000 of life insurance with the two children as beneficiaries.

The order provides that if Bill dies while either child is in college or under the age of 19, the insurance proceeds shall be put in a trust fund to be used for costs at their chosen undergraduate school and "graduate education if appropriate." They are to split any funds remaining when the younger turns 30. Bill wants to appeal the insurance portion of the order. What will you need to know about your state's law, and how will you argue the case?

Problem 5-8. Alex and Bailey's divorce agreement provided for sharing the care of the child as well as the costs and gave Alex custody on alternate weekends during the year and a month during the summer. Two years later, Bailey comes to you complaining that Alex has never exercised the summer custody rights and often cancels weekend visitation, sometimes on short notice. What do you advise?

B. ESTABLISHING THE AMOUNT OF SUPPORT: FROM DISCRETION TO GUIDELINES

[1]   Structure Of Guidelines

Ira Mark Ellman, Sanford Braver & Robert J. Maccoun, *Intuitive Lawmaking: The Example of Child Support*
6 J. EMPIRICAL LEG. STUDIES 69, 70–77 (2009)

At one time, child support amounts were decided case by case, with individual judges exercising broad discretion. This changed, however, with the legal reforms adopted to improve enforcement. Since 1989, the federal Department of Health and Human Services has required all states to have child support guidelines "based on specific descriptive and numeric criteria" that lead to the computation of a specific child support award in each case. 45 CFR § 302.56(a)(2). One important purpose of the guideline requirement was to make it easier and less costly for a custodial parent to obtain a support order by simplifying the process through which the amount of a child support award is determined. Support amounts were to be set in a way that facilitates justice on a "wholesale" rather than customized "retail" basis. To achieve this goal, the federal law also requires the states to enact legal rules requiring their judges to set child support awards at the exact dollar amount yielded by application of the required guideline, unless the judge writes an opinion explaining why the guideline amount would be "inappropriate or unjust" in the particular case. Even the parents' agreement to a support amount different than that specified by the guidelines does not, as a formal matter, alone justify departing from the guideline, although judges ordinarily accept such parental determinations and issue the required statement explaining their order. But in any event, parental agreements are, of course, themselves formed "in the shadow of" the guideline rules. It is therefore not surprising that support orders conform to the amount specified in the formulaic guidelines in about 85 percent or more of support cases. Child support policy is thus made by those assigned the task of drafting a state's support guidelines, not by judges deciding individual cases.

One benefit sought by guideline proponents, greater consistency in support awards, was certainly achieved, but only if one focuses on support awards *within* each state. Federal law imposes no national substantive standards on state guidelines. States are free to set child support amounts at whatever level they believe appropriate. This allows for substantial variation *across* states, and such variation in fact exists. One state's guidelines may call for twice the support amount specified in the adjoining state's schedule in what seems the identical case. Of course, such inconsistency could be intentional, the result of different policy choices by the policymakers of each state. But is it? Not necessarily. Much of the variation in fact comes from differing choices of the method used to generate the numbers found in any particular set of guidelines, methodological choices that may be made by consultants without full appreciation by state officials of their policy implications. . . .

The great majority of state guidelines rely on a method referred to in the literature as "income shares," while a minority employ an alternative system often called POOI, an acronym for "percentage of obligor income." The POOI system's great advantage is simplicity: the obligor is required to pay a support amount equal to a specified percentage of his income. For example, Wisconsin, an early champion of the POOI system, specifies that the obligor must pay in support 17 percent of his gross income for one child, 25 percent of his gross income for two children, 29 percent for three children, 31 percent for four children, or 34 percent for five or more children. [The court may use somewhat lower percentages for any portion of the obligor's income that exceeds $84,000 annually, as specified in a second set of guidelines, and a somewhat lower percentage yet (as set forth in a third set of guidelines) potentially applicable to any portion of the obligor's income exceeding $150,000.] The *custodial* parent's income has no effect on the support amount; it simply does not enter into the child support calculation at all.

This exclusion of the custodial parent's income from the computation strikes many as unfair: their intuition is that the obligee's income should count, too. The POOI calculation also suffers from the unintended public relations implication that the obligor appears responsible for *all* the child's support: if the custodial parent is supposed to be responsible to provide at least some of the child's financial support, why isn't her income included in the calculation? Indeed, [two studies] that explored the POOI system found opposition from the public on just this point. A 1985 telephone survey of Wisconsin residents asked for the child support amounts they would recommend in various parental income situations. For any given paternal income, mean support amounts declined as maternal incomes rose. More recently, the Australian Institute of Family Studies conducted a survey of Australian attitudes toward child support rules. The vast majority of respondents said they preferred a child support system that based support amounts on both parents' incomes, rather than on the obligor's income alone. These perceived shortcomings have led most states to reject POOI in favor of income shares. . . .

In [contrast, an] income shares guideline starts with a table that specifies a *joint* parental support obligation in dollars, for any given combination of their *combined* parental income with number of children. That joint parental obligation, based on both parents' incomes, is then allocated between the parents in proportion to their incomes. Suppose, for example, that the obligor's monthly income is $4,000 and the custodial parent's is $3,000, and the state income shares guideline sets their joint parental obligation at $1,132. The custodial parent is deemed to pay her share of that support obligation (3/7 of $1,132 = $485) automatically by virtue of the child's presence in her household, while the noncustodial parent is required to pay his share (4/7 of $1,132 = $648) to the custodial parent in cash.

A moment's reflection reveals that there is no inherent reason why an income shares guideline would produce a different support obligation for the noncustodial parent than a POOI guideline. For example, if both systems required the parents to pay 0.17 of their gross income for one child, as does Wisconsin, then both systems would yield the same ultimate support obligation. The POOI guideline would achieve this more directly by simply taking 0.17 of the obligor's income. The income shares guidelines would add intermediate steps by first taking 0.17 of the sum of the two parents' incomes, and then making a proportional allocation of the resulting amount — the arithmetic equivalent of applying the 0.17 to the obligor's share of the total income in the first place.[1] So why then does it matter which guideline approach is used? The reason is that incomes shares guidelines do *not* employ the same set of percentages that POOI guidelines use. It is their different rate structures, more than the focus on one versus two incomes, which primarily explains why POOI states and income shares states achieve different results. Income shares guidelines, in contrast to POOI, apply a declining percentage to the combined parental income in their initial calculation of the total parental support obligation that they then allocate proportionately between the parents. Figure 1 shows how this works in Arizona, an income shares state.

---

[1] An example may help. If Mom earns $1,000 and Dad earns $2,000, then a POOI system would require Dad to pay 0.17 of his income of $2,000 or $340. An incomes shares system would require him to pay his proportionate share of the total support obligation. [The total obligation] is 0.17 times 3,000 = 510. [H]is proportionate share is two-thirds; two-thirds of 510 is 340 and so the ultimate obligation is identical.

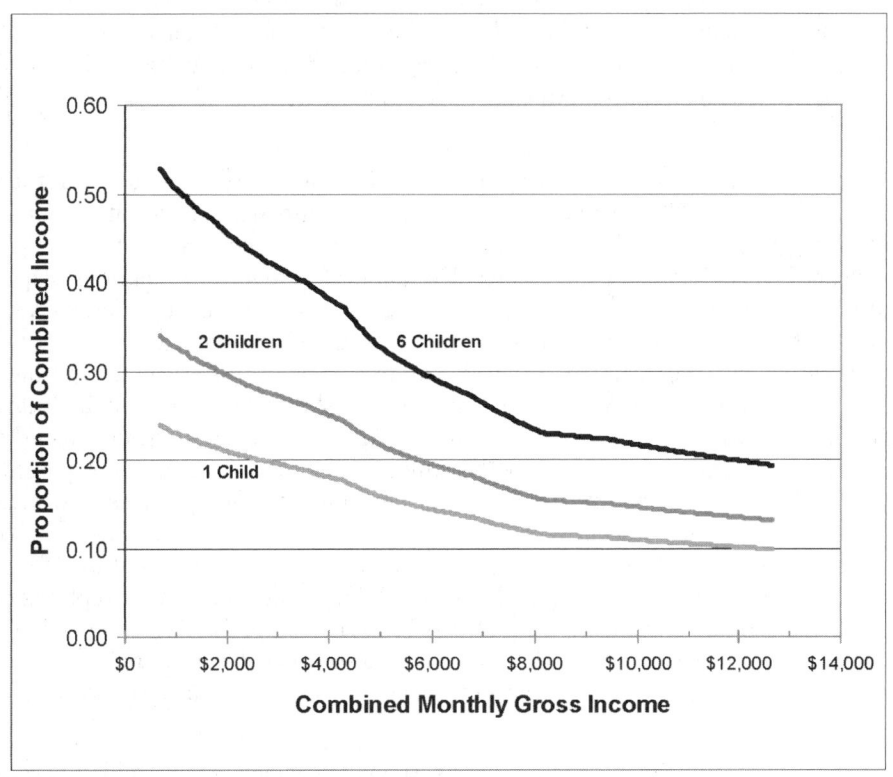

Figure 1. Combined parental support obligation
(custodial and noncustodial parent), as a proportion of combined parental income,
under 2005 Arizona guidelines.

Arizona's guidelines set support obligations by reference to the gross incomes of
the parents, as does the Wisconsin guideline previously provided as an example of
a POOI state. . . . One can see that Arizona rates start very high for low-income
parents — considerably higher than the corresponding Wisconsin figures — but
drop steeply as parental income increases. For one child, for example, the Arizona
rate begins at 0.25 for the lowest income parents, much higher than Wisconsin's 0.17
rate for a single child. But by the time *combined* parental income reaches $5,000
monthly, or $60,000 a year, the applicable rate has fallen below 0.17, while Wisconsin
continues to require 0.17 of the obligor's income. The Arizona rate eventually drops
to 0.10. When there is more than one child, the Arizona rates start even higher,
relative to Wisconsin rates, but drop even more steeply. This pattern of sharply
declining rates is typical of income shares guidelines.

Declining rates means that increases in obligor income do not produce proportional increases in the support obligation. This has particular impact on low-earning
custodial parents. Consider, for example, a custodial parent of one child with a
monthly gross income of only $1,000, formerly married to a support obligor who
grosses $2,500. His support obligation in Arizona will be $471, or 0.19 of his gross
income. Now consider her sister, identically situated except that her former

husband earns $6,000 instead. His support obligation would be $781 or 0.13 of his gross income, yielding a precipitous decline for both mother and child from the solid middle-class living standard of her formerly intact family. Her former husband's higher earnings do not give her nearly the advantage over her sister that one might expect.

One might reasonably ask why rates in income shares states exhibit this declining pattern. Ellman (2004) shows that this rate pattern results from the methodological choices of the consultants on whom income shares states rely to construct and update their guidelines. The applicable federal regulations require states to consider "economic data on the cost of raising children." However, one cannot estimate what children "cost" without first deciding what to buy for them. Appreciating that the question "What do children cost?" is insufficiently specific to allow an answer, consultants preparing income shares guidelines substitute a different question: What do parents in intact families on average in fact *spend* on their children? Once they establish this amount, they then set the joint parental support obligation at the average amount spent on children by parents in intact families with household incomes comparable to those of the combined income of the separated parents before the court. Income shares may appeal to state officials because it seems to provide them with a method that is value neutral. It replaces the need to choose an appropriate tradeoff between the competing resource claims of the two parental households with a technical exercise that can be delegated to a consultant — ascertaining what parents in intact families in fact spend on their children.

Nonetheless, as Ellman (2004) explains, the value choice is not avoided because tabulating how much parents spend on their children requires deciding what to count as an expenditure on the child. For example, if one counts any expenditure that confers benefit on the child, one arrives at a different number than if one counts only the marginal expenditures made necessary by the child's presence. [Ed. note: The *marginal expenditures* on children, as defined operationally by the consultants who devise income shares tables, are the *additional* expenditures that a childless couple would have to make to maintain the same living standard when children are added to their household, such as the *additional* rental cost of an apartment with one more bedroom, or the *additional* food purchases. Expenditures that are not additional, such as the rest of the rent, or the utility bills, or the unchanged costs of car ownership, are not counted, even though the child may benefit from those expenditures.] So anyone employing this method to construct support guidelines makes a methodological decision that reflects his or her choice about what to count, and different choices yield different tradeoffs. This point was recognized by the economist whose work is most frequently relied on by consultants implementing this method. This insight from the academic literature does not appear, however, to have come to the attention of policymakers, for whom the difficult trade-off choices remain hidden in the method employed to measure "expenditures on children." . . .

[Many state child support statutes include language suggesting that support guidelines should seek to provide] the child the same living standard the child would have had if the parents remained together[. This goal] is laudable, but probably unobtainable: in the usual case it would require imposing a considerable living standard decline on the support obligor. An income shares guideline that grounds support amounts on the *marginal* expenditures of children in intact families (which is the norm), is unlikely to have that result in the common case in which the custodial parent earns less than the noncustodial parent. The custodial parent's receipt of the other parent's share of the *marginal* expenditures still leaves the low-income custodial household without the base to which that margin must be added to recapture the living standard of the intact household. But state officials might easily (and incorrectly) conclude that the method for constructing their income shares guidelines was indeed based on a value-neutral technical exercise that avoided any need to think about tradeoffs in the resources available to the two parental households.

NOTES

1. ***Expenditures, Not Costs, and the Tradeoff in Living Standard.*** As the preceding excerpt notes, it is misleading to think of current child support guidelines as reflecting estimates of the costs of raising children. A classic work on this subject, relied on by those who originally developed the system consultants now use for devising support guidelines, observed that asking what a child costs is like asking what a car costs: you can't answer the question until you decide just what kind of car you mean to buy. THOMAS J. ESPENSHADE, INVESTING IN CHILDREN: NEW ESTIMATES OF PARENTAL EXPENDITURES 1-6 (1984). Similarly, the children of wealthier parents do not cost more than the children of less wealthy parents — they cost exactly the same, for any given living standard you wish to buy for them. But wealthier parents normally *do* spend more on their children because they *do* buy a higher living standard for them, and it is this reality — this difference in parental expenditures — that support guidelines reflect when they increase the support level as parental incomes go up. In this sense the guidelines reflect a policy that child support statutes seem to embrace, and which the pre-guideline law shared: that children are entitled to share — at least to some degree — in the living standard their parents are capable of providing, and which they probably would have provided the child if the family were intact.

That said, it is also important to note that this policy does not necessarily mean that children are entitled to have the *same* living standard they would have enjoyed if the family were intact. Indeed, that goal, as the excerpt points out, is necessarily impractical in most cases because the parties do not have sufficient income to maintain both households at the intact family living standard. In the usual case, then, a support payment that allowed the custodial household to continue the intact family living standard would reduce the support obligor's living standard far below it — a demand on the support obligor that few courts require. This observation illustrates that the setting of child support payments unavoidably requires tradeoffs among the parties. The required tradeoffs are complicated by the fact that all the members of a household normally share a living standard, so that any increase in the child's living standard also increases the living standard of the parent who lives with that child, just as the reduction in the obligor's living standard also necessarily has an impact on those living with him. Setting child support amounts therefore requires deciding on tradeoffs among at least three parties: the claim of the child (or children) to support, the claims of the custodial parent to have the other parent contribute a fair share of the support, and claim of the support obligor to keep his own earnings and not be forced to use them — under the rubric of child support — to contribute to the custodial parent's living standard. For more on how to think about these tradeoffs, see Ira Mark Ellman & Tara O'Toole Ellman, *The Theory of Child Support*, 45 HARV. J. LEG. 107 (2008). The American Law Institute recommendations face this question directly, see American Law Institute PRINCIPLES OF THE LAW OF FAMILY DISSOLUTION: ANALYSIS AND RECOMMENDATIONS 423–38, 570–85, 586–644 (2002). Its analysis focuses on the competing interests of the parties; for further discussion of its approach, see Grace Ganz Blumberg, *Balancing the Interests: The American Law Institute's Treatment of Child Support*, 33 FAM. L. Q. 39 (1999).

2. *The Expenditure Estimates: Where They Come From, and Why They Matter.* As the preceding excerpt explains, existing child support guidelines are based on data showing the expenditures that parents of different income levels make on their children. That data is used to generate the percentages that determine support amounts in both the Income Shares and POOI systems. The basis for the relatively flat percentages employed by Wisconsin and some other POOI states is a study by Jacques van der Gaag, *On Measuring the Cost of Children*, 4 Children and Youth Services Review No. 1/2 (1982). The basis for the declining percentages that Incomes Shares states employ are series of unpublished studies by David Betson, which he provides to the consultants who advise state guideline committees. Some of these studies are available on his website, http://www.nd.edu/~dbetson/research/ChildSupport.htm.

The earlier work on this topic by Thomas Espenshade, cited above, found that the percentage of parental *expenditures* that are devoted to children is unaffected by parental income. Betson's most recent study, done for the state of Oregon in 2006, reaches the same conclusion. (The study is available for download from Betson's website.) Why then do Income Shares guidelines end up with percentages that decline as income rises? The reason is almost entirely the relationship between income and expenditures. Most people would expect that as income reaches higher levels, the percentage of income that is spent *in total* will decline — because higher income individuals have a greater ability to save and invest some of their income, as compared to lower income individuals. In that case, expenditures on children, just like expenditures on everything else, will decline as a percentage of *income*, as income increases, even if they remain steady as a percentage of *expenditures*. And because child support guidelines set support amounts for different parental incomes, not different parental expenditure levels, declining percentages seem plausible.

The difficulty, however, is in the pattern of the decline these guidelines exhibit. Look again at Figure 1, describing Arizona's (quite typical) 2005 Income Shares guidelines. There is a steep decline from the lowest income levels up to $8,000 in gross monthly income. After $8,000, the line flattens, indicating that the underlying data found that the percentages of income spent on children remains relatively unchanged as income increases above this level. Yet one might expect the opposite pattern. Savings rates were low, for the years in which the data on these guidelines are based were collected, for middle class families. Because middle income people in fact spend nearly *all* their income, the percent of their income spent on children should be about the same as the percent of their expenditures devoted to children.

Indeed, what we might expect is a pattern in which the percentage of income spent on children is quite flat until one gets to upper middle class income levels, as which time it would begin to decline because at that point savings rates really would increase. Yet the pattern exhibited by these guidelines is the opposite. All the decline in percentage of income spent on children takes place *below* the upper middle class incomes; by the time one reaches those higher incomes the line becomes nearly flat.

What accounts for this odd pattern? Almost certainly, flaws in the data on which the income shares guidelines are based, compounded by the consultants' treatment of those flaws. The expenditure-by-income data that consultants use to generate the support guidelines come from interviews with consumers conducted for the federal government's Consumer Expenditure Survey. While the data is accurate enough for the purpose for which the federal government collects it, it has systematic errors that distort the detailed expenditure-by-income results the guideline consultants rely on. People in the interview panels make mistakes in their recall or reporting of their income and expenditures, such that income is systematically underreported among lower-income respondents, and expenditures are systematically underreported among the higher-income respondents. The income underreporting yields data that seem to show the lower 40 percent of the income distribution routinely spending more than they earn, while the expenditure underreporting yields data that seem to show the upper third routinely spend remarkably little of what they earn. To some large but not precisely known degree, the rapidly declining percentages of the typical Income Shares guideline are thus the result of the impact these data errors have on the complex methods the consultants use to estimate parental expenditures from them. For a full account of the problem, see Ira Mark Ellman, *Fudging Failure: The Economic Analysis Used to Construct Child Support Guidelines*, 2004 U. CHI. LEG. FORUM 162. The bottom line, however, is that the shape of the support function in the typical income shares guideline is heavily affected by this problem in the data, yielding lower support amounts for the upper half of the income distribution, and higher amounts for the lower half, than accurate data would justify.

3. *The Importance of the Choice of Marginal Expenditures.* As explained in the article excerpt above, what the consultants seek to estimate are the *marginal* expenditures on children by their parents. As the consultants define it, this means the additional amount a couple must spend when their intact family adds children, if they wish to maintain the same living standard that they had when childless. (Observe that to make this calculation, one must have some way of measuring when families of different composition have the same living standard — one assumes the larger family needs more money, but how much more? This calculation, which relies on something called an "equivalence scale", also presents a problem, addressed below in Note 4.) As noted in that excerpt, the parents' marginal expenditures on children is a very different measure than all parental expenditures that confer a benefit on their children. An example will help to see the difference.

Consider a childless couple who live in a one-bedroom apartment they rent for $1,000. They now have a child. To maintain the equivalent housing standard, they could rent a two-bedroom apartment in the same complex for $1,300. (Assume for this purpose that the rent includes utilities.) The *marginal* expenditures on the child for housing is thus $300. Similarly, if the childless couple already own two cars, and continue to own only two cars after they have a child, there may be no marginal expenditures on children for transportation (unless perhaps more miles are driven). While the consultants attempt to measure marginal expenditures on children globally (comparing total expenditures required by couples with and without children, to maintain an equivalent living standard), rather than item by item, these examples communicate its fundamental logic. But note, then, that this measure excludes the many joint consumption items in every household: *all* its members benefit from the living room, the kitchen, the heating system, and the cars, and it is obvious that a child's welfare depends upon sharing the expenditures that provide the family with these joint consumption items. But expenditures on joint consumption items are largely excluded systematically from the accounting of child expenditures. Child support amounts based on marginal expenditure estimates will therefore only allocate those marginal expenditures between the parents.

The policy implications of choosing a marginal expenditure measure are typically not considered by state lawmakers or committees who approve their guidelines, because it is often regarded as a value-neutral technical question best resolved by economic consultants. In fact, it is a very important child support policy choice. Its significance is explored further in the following excerpt. Note that this excerpt makes use of the official federal government poverty threshold to assess the living standard of families. This is a useful device for comparisons at the lower end of the income distribution. A family is said to be at 100% of the poverty threshold if its income is at precisely the dollar amount needed to avoid poverty according to this official federal statistic. The poverty threshold is set at different levels depending on the family's composition: a single person needs less income to avoid poverty than a couple with two children. In 2009 the poverty threshold for a single person was $903 per month; officially, a single person earning more than that is not "in poverty."[1]

The official poverty threshold is based on a formula, first devised more than fifty years ago, that assumes a relationship between the cost of food and the cost of other necessities. That assumed relationship is now outdated (because food is cheaper, relative to housing and other necessities, than it was fifty years ago). The result is that the official poverty threshold is lower than most economists believe it should be. Because many government programs set eligibility requirements with reference to it, changes in the poverty threshold have budgetary implications which make it politically difficult to update or revise. The consequence is that rather than reform the poverty measure itself, most means-tested federal programs to assist the poor include people with incomes above the official poverty threshold. For example, a household is eligible for food stamps so long as the gross income of

---

[1] For a basic understanding of the poverty threshold, prepared by the Census Bureau, see http://www.census.gov/hhes/www/poverty/povdef.html. For a broad overview of the history and issues with the poverty threshold, see the HHS account at http://aspe.hhs.gov/poverty/contacts.shtml. For a description of efforts to update the measure, undertaken by a panel of the National Academy of Sciences at the direction of the Census Bureau, see http://www.cbpp.org/cms/index.cfm?fa=view&id=1385. For a summary of the recommendations of that panel prepared by the Rapporteur, *see* http://www.nap.edu/catalog.php?record_id=11166.

household members does not exceed 130% of the poverty threshold, while the maximum income allowed to be eligible for WIC (The Special Supplemental Nutrition Program for Women, Infants, and Children) is 185% of the poverty threshold. (States are permitted to set a lower income level.) Some programs do not use the official poverty threshold at all, but rely instead on other measures for the eligibility rules. *See* http://aspe.hhs.gov/poverty/faq.shtml#programs.

Ira Mark Ellman & Tara O'Toole Ellman, *The Theory of Child Support*
45 Harv. J. On Leg. 107, 116–121 (2008)

Some courts and state officials . . . apparently believ[e] that the [incomes shares] method gives children the same living standard they would have if their family were intact — that the same amount of money will be spent on them as would have been spent had their parents remained together. As a Maryland court put it, "[t]he conceptual underpinning [of Maryland's child support guidelines] is that a child should receive the same proportion of parental income, and thereby enjoy the standard of living, he or she would have experienced had the child's parents remained together."[35]

But unless their two incomes rise, the two post-separation households cannot both achieve the same living standard as the single pre-separation household. To ensure that the custodial household suffers no living-standard decline at all, state guidelines would have to impose a severe living standard decline on the support obligor, but (as we shall see) that is not in fact what they do. Nor does it seem likely that policymakers would want to do this. How then can policymakers and judges be under the illusion that existing guidelines preserve the child's pre-separation living standard?

The sleight of hand takes place in the course of measuring expenditures on the child. To conclude the child will receive "the same proportion of parental income" after parental separation as before requires having previously established a definition of "parental expenditures on the child" that distinguishes them from other parental expenditures, as well as a method for measuring the proportions of parental income spent on the child and on other things. The definition one would necessarily have to employ for support guidelines to do what the Maryland court believed its guidelines did, is to count all pre-separation expenditures that conferred a benefit on the child, and thus contributed to the child's living standard, as an expenditure on the child. Only if expenditures are defined in this way could one say that ensuring equal expenditures ("same proportion of total parental income") on the child before and after separation will also ensure equal living standards for the child at these two times. But while this might be the definition implicitly assumed by the Maryland court (and by others who share their belief), it is not the definition of expenditures on the child actually used in the conventional methodology, and that is why the usual state guidelines do not in fact yield the

---

[35] *Voishan v. Palma*, 609 A.2d 319, 322 (Md. 1992); *see also K. v. K.*, 373 N.Y.S.2d 486, 494 (N.Y. Fam. Ct. 1975) (stating that the objective of a child support order is to emulate the standard of living of the intact family) . . .

result that the Maryland court assumes they do. Understanding how the conventional method in fact defines and estimates child expenditures is thus central to understanding why it produces the kind of guidelines that it does.

Essential to the illusion that the conventional method is value-neutral is the assumption that the task of estimating the average expenditures of intact families on their children is just a technical exercise that requires no policy choices. [But the] definitional choice is a matter of child support policy, not something one looks up in a technical manual on economic statistics. Which definition of child expenditure is appropriate depends on the policy purpose for which one is measuring it. . . . What parents spend on their children cannot be tallied without first deciding what counts as a child expenditure, and more than arithmetic is involved.

Consider, for instance, a couple that spends the same amount on rent and utilities after having a child as they did when childless. Now they separate, and we want to know what they spent on their child when together. If we wish to capture any expenditure that conferred benefit on the child, then a large portion of the rent and utilities should be included. Indeed, we might even say that all of it should be included, because we might believe the child benefitted from all of it. Of course, other family members also benefitted from having a place to live and from having lights and heat, but the benefit to them does not reduce the benefit to the child. If less is spent on these items, all family members experience a decline in living standard. There really is no inherently correct way to allocate the cost of such joint consumption items among the joint consumers. The allocation rule one employs must be based on the policy purpose for which one is making the allocation. If the policy purpose is, for example, to ensure the economic well-being of children in constructing child support guidelines, then one will likely want to consider most of these expenditures to be expenditures on the child.

Unfortunately, consultants who prepare the estimates of child expenditures — used to construct the support guidelines they recommend — do not bring this definitional question to the attention of child support policymakers. Instead, as we shall explain further below, the conventional method simply assumes that "child expenditures" is best defined as the *marginal* expenditures on the child. That is, how much more did the couple spend on rent and utilities after they had their child? In our example, the answer would be zero. None of the pre-separation parental expenditures on rent and utilities would count as an expenditure on the child. A guideline based on that estimate of parental expenditures is going to produce a very different result than one based on whether an expenditure conferred a benefit on the child. Though marginal analysis yields powerful insights in many areas, a marginal analysis of child expenditures marginalizes children.

[Income shares guidelines effectively] allocate responsibility for those marginal expenditures between the two parents in proportion to their incomes. The noncustodial parent pays his share to the custodial parent as the support order. This income-proportional allocation of child expenditures between the parents seems appropriate, but an appropriate allocation of a mistaken estimate of child expenditures yields an inappropriate result. Items not counted as child expenditures are not part of the estimate and thus are not allocated between the parents. Thus, applying the income shares model to our hypothetical would require the support obligor to pay the custodial parent very little for rent and utilities if the custodial parents do not spend much more on those items due to the child's presence. But if the custodial parent does not have sufficient income of her own to pay for rent and utilities expenses — the cost were she by herself — then she and the child may both end up out on the street.

Building on this insight, the following section looks more carefully at what actually happens under current support guidelines.

B. Support Levels Called for Under Current Guidelines

[One can examine the consequences of basing support amounts on marginal expenditures by] examining the child support amounts that it yields in selected cases. Consider Table 1, which sets out three cases, each involving a custodial parent ("CP") who lives with the couple's one child and earns $1,000 monthly. The cases differ only in the income earned by the non-custodial parent ("NCP"), who lives alone and who earns either $500 monthly (Case 1), $2,500 monthly (Case 2), or $6,000 monthly (Case 3). Table 1 uses the Arizona support schedule,[43] but . . . Arizona is not atypical. It is an income shares state with guidelines based on the conventional methodology, and it revised its guidelines in 2004. The overall message of Table 1 does not depend on which state's guidelines are used.

Table 1 shows the NCP's required monthly child support payment, both in dollars and as a percentage of the NCP's income. The last two columns of the table report the incomes of the custodial and noncustodial households after the child support payment is made, shown as a percentage of the federal government's poverty threshold for a household of that composition. For ease of exposition, we refer to the custodial parent in these examples as the mother, and the noncustodial parent as the father, an assumption that conforms to the actual facts in the great majority of such cases.

---

[43] Arizona Child Support Guidelines, ARIZ. REV. STAT. ANN. § 25-320 (2006). Arizona normally reduces the support award to reflect the time a child spends with the support obligor under the visitation schedule. *Id.* at § 11. Table 1 does not include a visitation adjustment.

Table 1: Low-income Custodial Parent in Three Cases
(In Each Case, CP Lives with One Child and Earns $1000 Monthly Before Child Support)

Case Number	NCP's Monthly Income (Before Paying Child Support)	Monthly Child Support Amount (Under 2005 Arizona Guidelines)	Child Support Amount as Percent of NCP's Income	CP's Income After Child Support Payment, % of Poverty Threshold	NCP's Income After Child Support Payment, % of Poverty Threshold
1	$ 500	$110	22%	107%	50%
2	$2,500	$471	19%	142%	260%
3	$6,000	$781	13%	173%	668%
Table 1 Notes: 1. Income is gross income (before taxes). 2. Poverty threshold calculations are based on 2002 data.[48]					

Case 1 represents the all too common situation in which both parents are poor and the father earns even less than the mother. Their combined monthly income of $1,500 does not and cannot possibly support two households above the poverty line. The fifth column shows that after the child support payment of $110, the child's total household income of $1,100 barely exceeds the official federal estimate of the amount a household of this composition requires to avoid poverty — the household's income is only 107% of the poverty threshold. The first child's household is thus in relatively desperate straits. The father is even worse off, however, as the $390 left after he pays the support payment leaves him with an income that is half the poverty threshold for a single individual. In fact, Arizona would probably excuse this father from making more than a nominal support payment. Like most states, the Arizona guidelines provide for a "self-support reserve." The details of these provisions vary among the states, but their general purpose is to shield obligors from support orders that would impoverish them. In Arizona, a trial court is authorized to reduce the support payment to zero if the obligor has less than $775 in monthly gross income. This father qualifies for that reduction, which may be granted at the court's discretion.

. . . . A competing method for estimating expenditures on children is adopted by the Agricultural Department, which issues its estimates annually. *See, e.g.*, Mark Lino, *Expenditures on Children by Families: 2001 Annual Report*, U.S. Department of Agriculture, Center for Nutrition Policy and Promotion, Miscellaneous Publication No. 1528-2001 (2002). This approach allocates some expenditures, such as housing, on a per capita basis, while allocating others on marginal expenditure basis. The Agriculture Department's estimates of expenditures on children are

---

[48] Arizona Child Support Guidelines, Ariz. Rev. Stat. Ann. § 25-320 (2006). The 2004 Arizona Child Support Guidelines are based on an economic consultant's report dated February 2003. The 2002 poverty threshold figures are contemporaneous with the economic data relied upon by the consultant that developed the guidelines. Jane C. Venohr & Tracy E. Griffith, *Economic Basis for Updated Child Support Schedule, State of Arizona* 3 (2003), available at http://www.supreme.state.az.us/dr/Pdf/psi1.pdf.

typically higher than the estimates of guideline consultants, and the author of its reports argues its estimates would provide a better basis for guidelines. . . .

NOTES

1. ***Disparate Incomes and Marginal Expenditures***.   To consider the general question of the effect on the two households of allocating only marginal expenditures through the child support order, examine the figure below, also taken from the article excerpted above.

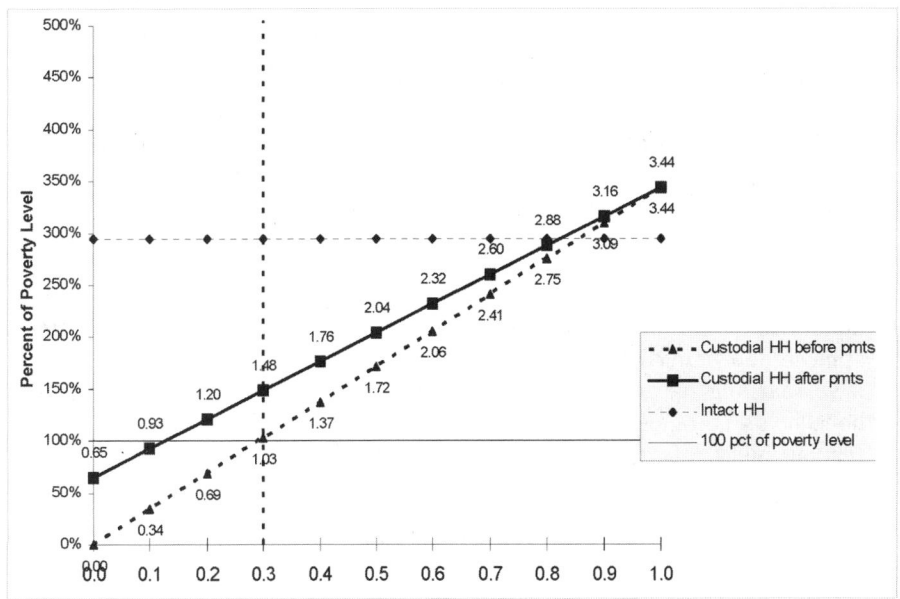

Figure 2. Custodial household income, as a percentage of federal poverty level, for one-child family with a combined parental income of $3,500

The figure describes the financial circumstances of a couple with one child before and after separation. The couple earns $3500 monthly, approximately the median American household income. What changes from case to case is the proportion of this total parental income that is earned by the custodial parent. The horizontal axis tells you the proportion earned by the custodial parent, from zero, on the left, to all of it, on the right. The vertical axis tells you the how the family is doing financially, by describing its income as a percentage of the official federal poverty threshold for a family of that composition. (A family of three needs a higher income to avoid poverty than does a family of one or two.) The straight horizontal line, at just below 300% of poverty level, shows the financial situation of the intact family household containing both parents and the child. The line is horizontal because *the intact family* remains at about 300 percent of the poverty threshold whether the parents are equal earners, or one parent earns most of their total income and the other parent earns very little. Now look at the two diagonal lines. They show you the financial situation of the custodial household, one parent and the child, after separation. There are two lines because the higher, solid one shows the custodial household living standard *after* receipt of the child support payment called for under the 2005 Arizona income shares guideline, while the lower dashed diagonal shows the custodial household living standard *before* receipt of the child support payment. Both lines rise as they go to the right because after separation, the higher the proportion of the total parental income is earned by the custodial parent, the higher is the living standard of the custodial household. A committee appointed by the Arizona Supreme Court to examine its state guidelines concluded, in 2006, that this graph revealed a problematic pattern. As explained by that committee:

> 1. The child's financial well-being depends primarily upon the income of the custodial parent, and relatively little on the income of the support obligor. If the custodial parent is poor, the custodial household remains poor even when the support obligor's income is high. This feature of existing guidelines is the direct result of basing support amounts on marginal child expenditures in intact families.

> 2. Children whose parents earn, in the aggregate, the same income, can nonetheless find themselves in dramatically different financial circumstances depending upon whether they live primarily with the higher or lower earning parent. This financial disparity between the two parents' households becomes even more pronounced as the allocation of custodial responsibility between them approaches equality.

> 3. Low-income obligors are expected to pay unreasonably high support amounts to high-income custodial parents, given that in these cases the child enjoys a much higher living standard than the obligor even before any support is paid.

You can see the basis for the committee's concern by comparing, as an example, the case in which the custodial parent earns thirty percent of the total parental income of $3550 (about $1000) with the case in which she earns 70 percent (about $2485). The graph tells you that when the custodial parent earns 30 percent (0.3) of the total parental income, that parent and the child live at 103% of the federal poverty threshold before they receive any child support. The child support payment mandated by the Arizona guideline brings them up to 148% of the poverty threshold. This is an enormous drop from the 300% of poverty that the child enjoyed before the separation-low enough to qualify for food stamps in most states. By contrast, the child who lives with the parent earning 70% (0.7) of the total parental income enjoys a living standard at 241% of poverty before receiving the payment, and 260% afterward. A child could be in the custody of either parent, of course. Depending on whether the 30% parent or the 70% parent has custody, two children who enjoyed identical living standards before their parents separated end up in dramatically different situations after the separation, depending upon whether they live with the high or the low income custodial parent, even after payment of child support. To appreciate the basis of the committee's third concern, note the case in which the custodial parent earns 90 percent of the parental income. Even before *any* child support payment, the custodial household is better off than was the intact family. The reason is fairly obvious: the departure of the other parent is a financial benefit, because the added cost of that other parent was more than that parent earned. We may still wish to require this low-earning noncustodial parent to make some nominal child support payment, as a symbolic gesture that recognizes the parental status, but we should not think that the child's financial welfare depends in any important way on the payment, and we may therefore wish to avoid requiring more than a nominal amount form this low-income obligor.

For all these reasons, the Interim Committee recommended replacing the traditional Income Shares method for generating Arizona's support guidelines with a new system that was not based on estimates of marginal expenditures in intact families, but was instead based on a direct examination of the relative financial outcomes for the two post-separation households. As of this writing, its proposal was still under consideration. The committee's conclusions should be of interest to other states because Arizona's income shares guidelines are not atypical. One should note, however, that the problem uncovered by the Arizona committee arises principally when parental incomes are disparate. The custodial household in our example certainly does not end up in financial comfort when the parental incomes are equal (Figure 2 shows it at 200% of poverty after receipt of support). But the committee concluded the payment was appropriate because in that case the support payment based on a marginal expenditure calculation leaves the two households in very similar financial circumstances, which seems appropriate when the parents are equal earners.

2. *What Child Support Arrangements Do People Think Fair?* The article by Ellman, Braver and MacCoun excerpted at the beginning of this section reported on an empirical study of the views of Arizona citizens about appropriate child support guidelines. The study asked for the child support amount the respondent thought appropriate for a series of cases in which the only variable that changed were the incomes of the parents. As one might expect, it found considerable variation in the absolute amounts that people favored. On the other hand, it found very little variation among the respondents in their view of how the child support amount should change in response to changes in parental income. The respondents consistently adjusted their support amounts to changes in the custodial parent's income far more than do existing income shares guidelines, much less POOI guidelines: For low income custodial parents, the respondents favored higher support amounts than do most income shares guidelines, while for high-income custodial parents, they favored lower amounts. Translating their dollar support amounts into percentages of the obligor's income, one could see that the lower the custodial parent's income, the greater was the support amount *as a percentage of* the obligor's income. By contrast, the respondents did not respond nearly as much as do current income shares guidelines to changes in the obligor's income; for any given custodial parent income, the respondents favored support amounts that were a relatively consistent percentage of the noncustodial parent's income even as the dollar amount of that income changed. Men and women agreed on this basic rate pattern, even though women consistently favored somewhat higher support amounts than did men. The study also found that men who reported having been ordered to pay child support favored the lowest support amounts, while women who reported being the beneficiaries of a child support order favored the highest

support amounts. (Men and women with no experience in the child support system were closer to one another in their favored amounts, although in this case men also favored lower amounts than did women.) There were too few cases of female obligors, or male obligees, to provide statistically useful results.

   3. *Prevailing Systems Other than POOI and Income Shares.*   A 2009 report found that three states (Montana, Delaware, and Hawaii) currently use what has been called the Melson Formula for their support guidelines. Jane C. Venohr & Tracy E. Griffith, *Economic Basis for Updated Child Support Schedule, State of Arizona* 3 (2003), http://www.supreme.state.az.us/dr/Pdf/psi1.pdf. A variant of Income Shares, it was originally adopted by the Delaware Family Court in 1979. Its distinguishing feature is a special form of the self-support reserve. (Most incomes shares states have some kind of self support reserve meant to shield very low income obligor's from paying support amounts that would drive them below some measure of poverty, but these states generally follow a normal income shares schedule once that reserve amount is exceeded.)

   The 2002 version in Delaware can provide an example. It incorporates a monthly self-support reserve of $850 for each parent and then requires the parents to contribute 100% of net income until the children have been provided a minimal "primary support allowance." Each adult self-support reserve is intended to meet the parent's minimum needs living alone, but the child's reserve will suffice only if the custodial parent actually has the $850 base. For one child, that amount is $350. If the custodial parent lacks the full $850 for self-support, the $350 child support allowance will not save the child from poverty. Once all self-support requirements are satisfied, the formula applies a rate of 16% to the non-custodial parent's additional net income. The total primary support allowance increases with the number of children ($650 for two children, $920 for 3 children, $1170 for 4 children, and each additional child is allocated $220) and the child support percentage of the parent's additional net income also increases (26% for two children, 33% for three, 39% for four and 4% for each additional child). For examples of cases applying the Melson Formula, see *T.E.N. v. T.J.C.*, 2003 Del. Fam. Ct. LEXIS 117 (Aug. 20, 2003); *In re D.J.D., Jr. v. K.L.D.*, 2003 Del. Fam. Ct. LEXIS 151 (Aug. 7, 2003); *In re Marriage of Eugene J.R. & Gail M.R.*, 1996 Del. Fam. Ct. LEXIS 99 (Aug. 1, 1996) (including detailed worksheet demonstrating Melson Formula in operation).

   The Melson reserves have little effect when the incomes of both parents are relatively equal and exceed the amounts of the self-support reserves. If, for example, each parent of an only child has monthly income of $1025 ($850 + ($350/2)), all self-support reserves will be satisfied. The child's primary support allowance, $350, is 17% of $2,050, the combined amount of parent income. Sixteen percent is the percentage that the formula applies to net earnings beyond the amount necessary to satisfy the self support reserves. Thus, so long as each parent has net income of at least $1025 monthly, it makes little difference whether one applies the self-support reserves or a simple 17% of net income. Yet the self-support reserve does have real bite when the custodial parent has little or no income. Then the support obligor, who may also have low income, must provide most or all of the child's self-support reserve.

Although the Massachusetts system seems formally similar to an income shares guideline, it provides for support amounts that are much higher than the typical income shares guideline, especially for cases in which the custodial parent income is low and the obligor income is higher. Its guideline figures are thus similar to (although sometimes higher than) those being proposed for consideration in Arizona by the committee charged with re-examining its income shares guideline. In its Principles of the Law of Family Dissolution, the American Law Institute endorsed a similar approach. For a description of it by the Reporter primarily responsible for devising it, see Grace Ganz Blumberg, *Balancing the Interests: The American Law Institute's Treatment of Child Support*, 33 FAM. L.Q. 39 (1999).

4. *Comparing Living Standards.* One reason the guideline amounts adopted by different income shares diverge is they use different methods for estimating marginal expenditures on children. Historically, the "Engel" method yields consistently higher support amounts than the Rothbarth method. Both methods derive estimates of marginal expenditures by estimating the additional income a couple must spend to maintain the same living standard when children are added to their household. The difficult question is determining the incomes at which the childless household and the household with children have the same living standard (one knows that the larger household requires more money, but how much more?) The Engel method assumes that households have the same living standard if they spend the same proportion of their income on groceries. The Rothbarth method assumes they have the same living standard if they spend the same dollar amount on alcohol, tobacco, and adult clothing. There is no way to settle empirically which method is more accurate because to do so, one would have to have a third method of known accuracy against which to compare them — in which case, one would just employ that method rather than either Engel or Rothbarth. The consequence is that the choice between the two methods is usually based on little more than intuition as to which yields the more plausible support amounts. In addition, both methods rely on the problematic data from the Consumer Expenditure Survey — especially problematic for the Rothbarth method because of its great sensitivity to mistaken estimates of the amount spent on adult clothing. For a full examination of all these difficulties, see Ira Ellman, *Fudging Failure: The Economic Analysis Used to Construct Child Support Guidelines*, 2004 U. CHI. L. FORUM 162.

Nearly all incomes-shares guidelines in force today are based on either the Engel or Rothbarth methods, although according to Venohr, *supra*, Minnesota's guidelines are based on the expenditure estimates prepared for the Department of Agriculture. *See* Mark Lino & Andrea Carlson, Andrea, *Expenditures on Children by Families, 2008*, U.S. Department of Agriculture, Center for Nutrition Policy and Promotion, Miscellaneous Publication No. 1528-2008 (2009). This approach allocates some expenditures, such as housing, on a per capita basis, while allocating others on marginal expenditure basis. The Agriculture Department's estimates of expenditures on children are typically higher than the estimates of guideline consultants.

5. *Visitation Discount.* In the view of some, another reason that guideline amounts in income shares states differ from one another is the possible impact of a "visitation discount." In Wisconsin, the first state to adopt child support guidelines, the framers included a visitation discount. That is, the amount the obligor was required to pay was less than the full amount of the obligor's proportional share of the child's marginal expenditures, because it was expected that the obligor would spend some money on the child when exercising his or her right to visitation. Irwin Garfinkel, Sara McLanahan & Judith Wallerstein, *Visitation and Child Support Guidelines*, 42 FAM. CT. REV. 342, 347 (2004). Whether a visitation discount is a feature of the guidelines of other states is a matter of dispute. *Compare* Garfinkel, *supra*, *and* Marygold S. Melli, *Guideline Review: Child Support and Time Sharing by Parents*, 33 FAM. L. Q. 219 (1999), *and* Karen Czapanskiy, *Child Support, Visitation, Shared Custody, and Split Custody in* CHILD SUPPORT GUIDELINES: THE NEXT GENERATION 43–50 (Margaret C. Haynes, ed. 1994), *with* William V. Fabricius & Sanford L. Braver, *Expenditures On Children And Visitation Time: A Reply to Garfinkel, McLanahan, and Wallerstein*, 42 FAM. CT. REV. 350 (2004), William V. Fabricius & Sanford L. Braver, *Non-Child Support Expenditures on Children by Nonresidential Divorced Fathers*, 41 FAM. CT. REV. 321 (2003), *and* Jane C. Venohr & Robert G. Williams, *The implementation and periodic review of state child support guidelines*, 33 FAM. L. Q. 7 (1999). Resolving the dispute would be helpful to child support commissions, because they need full information about the component parts of the guidelines under consideration. In cases of sole physical custody, a visitation discount reallocates to the visiting parent some of the resources that would be spent on the child if the child and both parents lived together. If the visiting parent is not exercising his or her visitation rights, the money is lost to the child. Even if the parent is exercising his or her visitation rights, the child's primary household lacks some of the funds that theoretically it should have. In states that provide a child support adjustment for shared physical custody, a visitation discount may mean that the some days the child spends in the non-primary household are counted twice, so the resources available to the child in the primary household are reduced below the theoretically proper amount.

PROBLEMS

Before considering these problems, review the specific child support guidelines of your state or of a state specified by your professor.

Problem 5-9. Under the guidelines statute you reviewed, what do you need to know before you can identify the presumptively correct child support obligation of each parent in a simple case that is subject to the guidelines? What would you need to know under a discretionary regime?

Problem 5-10. Use the guideline you reviewed to calculate support amounts for five cases involving one child in which the parents' total monthly gross income is $5,000: one case in which the obligor earns the entire $5,000 and the custodial parent is not employed, and four more in which the custodial parent earns $1,000, $2,000, $3,000, and $4,000 of the $5,000 total. If your state guidelines provide for an adjustment to the support amount based on the allocation of parenting time, consider variations in which the support obligor has the child for 15%, 25%, and 35% of the time. Does your state seem to have a result like that illustrated by Figure 2 above, in which children who start out at the same living standard in an intact family come out very differently depending upon which parent they live with? Would you suggest changes to your state's guidelines to address this? If so, what changes?

Problem 5-11. The custodial parent has monthly income of $2,000. The noncustodial parent has monthly income of $2,000. They have one child. Under a POOI guideline, is there a presumptively correct child support obligation of the custodial parent? Under an Income Shares guideline?

Problem 5-12. The child's custodial parent believes the child should eat expensive food and wear expensive clothing, compared with other children in the neighborhood. Before the parents separated when the child was 13, they agreed to spend more than the average amount on food and clothing for the child. When they separated, the income of each parent was $3,000 a month, and the noncustodial parent was order to pay $387 a month under the guidelines. The custodial parent wants to continue the same pattern of spending on the child's food and clothing but finds that the household has insufficient money to do so. The custodial parent asks the noncustodial parent to agree to an increase in child support. The noncustodial parent refuses and predicts that the court will refuse as well. Who is right under the statute you reviewed?

Problem 5-13. Both parents graduated from high school and college, and both work in professional jobs. They expect the child will attend college after finishing high school. The parents separate when the child is 3 years old, and each has a monthly income of $3,000. After the child support order is entered, the custodial parent learns from a financial advisor that parents who expect their children to attend college should be saving approximately $400 a month from the time the child turns 3. The custodial parent asks the noncustodial parent to put $200 a month into a savings program for the child's college expenses, and promises to do the same. The noncustodial parent refuses on the basis that the custodial parent should be able to save $400, given that the noncustodial parent is paying the full amount of child support required under the statute. Who is right?

Problem 5-14. Each parent has an adjusted actual income of $5,000 a month, for a combined parental income of $10,000. Assume that, under a typical income shares guideline, the basic child support obligation is $1040, which is 10.4% of $10,000. If each parent earned $3,000 a month, each would be required to spend 25.8% of their combined income on child support under the same typical income share guideline. Why is the obligation higher as a percentage of parental income where the parental income is lower? Should it be?

Problem 5-15. Your state is about to undertake its federally-mandated quadrennial review of its child support guidelines. You have been appointed to the Commission as a member of the bar. The Commission also includes a lawyer who specializes in family law, two judges, the administrator of the state's child support enforcement program, a father's rights advocate, a PTA official and an advocate from a women's rights organization. The official web page of your state's child support enforcement agency says that the current guideline is designed "to give children the same standard of living they would have if their parents were together." It also says that "The guideline was put in the law to make sure that people pay an amount for support that is actually close to what it costs to care for a child." The consultant to the commission four years ago described the guidelines as producing "awards roughly in line with the accepted standard of requiring the noncustodial parent to pay in support what he or she would have contributed to the children in an intact family." Are these three contemporary descriptions of the same state guidelines consistent with one another? Assuming the guidelines were created with the dominant marginal expenditure method, are any of these descriptions accurate? What do you think the current Commission should set as its primary goal? What, if any, information do you want the Commission to obtain before considering whether to recommend changes to the state's guidelines? What, if any changes to your state's guideline do you want the Commission to consider? What are your best arguments for your position? What counter-arguments do you anticipate?

[2]   Aspects of Support not Included Within the Ordinary Guideline

[a]   Expenditure for Child Care Required by the Custodial Parent's Gainful Employment

The treatment of child care required for employment may matter greatly to the employed custodial parent. Child care expenditures are generally not covered by the basic incomes shares support schedule, but are instead treated as an add-on. One reason for this approach is that the expenditures on child care are highly variable: there may be no costs if another family member cares for the children without charge, or the costs may be quite high for a lucratively employed custodial parent who secures the most expensive child care arrangements. For these and other reasons, most income shares guidelines provide that the cost of child care required by a parent's gainful employment should be shared by the child's parents, either equally or in proportion to their relative incomes. *See, e.g.*, CAL. FAM. CODE §§ 4061, 4062. The minority POOI (obligor income only) jurisdictions usually make no provision for child care required by the custodial parent's employment, effectively imposing all such costs on the custodial parent. Note also that the noncustodial parent may also incur child care costs if there is overlap between his work schedule and his parenting time schedule. States that allow an adjustment for child care for the custodial parent often also allow an analogous adjustment for the noncustodial parent in this situation.

[b]   Expenditure for Health Insurance and for Uninsured Health Care Costs

Like child care required by the custodial parent's employment, health care expenditure is highly variable, as is parent access to reasonable or inexpensive health insurance. Federal law requires that state guidelines take health care costs into account. Under federal law,

(1) all orders enforced by the state child support enforcement agency must include a provision for medical support; (2) the state may look to either or both parents to provide such support; and (3) the state child support agency may enforce a medical support order against both custodial and non-custodial parents. In addition, [federal law] contains a definition of "medical support" which includes both health insurance and payment for medical expenses incurred on behalf of a child. As a result, if health insurance coverage is available to either parent, states will be required to establish an

order requiring that the children be placed on such coverage with appropriate cost sharing. States will also be able to enforce such orders against both custodial and noncustodial parents. If health insurance coverage is not available, states can pursue cost-sharing of the expenses associated with the child's medical expenses.

Paula Roberts, *Enacted and Proposed Changes to the Child Support Program: An Overview of the Provisions of the 2006 Federal Budget and the 2007 Budget Proposal*, Center for Law and Social Policy (2/9/06); *see* 42 USC §§ 652(f), 666(a)(19); 42 CFR §§ 302.56 and 303.31.

In practice, the same guidelines apply to orders enforced by the state child support enforcement agency as well as to other cases, so all new child support orders should now provide for medical support.

[3] Determining the Obligor's Resources

Regardless of whether the amount of child support is determined under a guidelines or a discretionary regime, the first step is to determine the resources of the obligor parent or, in the case of an income-sharing guidelines, the resources of both parents. As the next case demonstrates, determining resources is not a straightforward exercise when a parent works in something other than a routine, wage-based employment situation. The same problem occurs where a parent earns money "under the table" or generates no income in the market, such as when a parent leaves paid work to care for a newborn or a child with a serious disabling condition or chronic illness.

IN RE MARRIAGE OF DENNIS
Wisconsin Supreme Court
344 N.W.2d 128 (1984)

STEINMETZ, JUSTICE.

The issue . . . is whether the circuit court may . . . require this divorced father to make a search for other employment to increase or to add to his limited income.

. . . .

[In a divorce action, defendant was ordered to pay $35 weekly for temporary "family maintenance."]

On February 25, 1980, Dennis appeared [at a contempt hearing where] the court reduced his support obligation to $15 per month, which was $5 per child per month, and ordered payment of $5 monthly toward arrearages of $560.

[At the final hearing on March 24, 1981], the court ordered:

> . . . that the respondent should pay $300.00 per month for child support. It appears that respondent does not have the present ability to do so. . . . That he should look for additional or alternative work because it appears that he has never made over $3,500.00 per year in his past endeavors. That respondent . . . use his good faith efforts to apply for other work at least

in ten places per month. . . . that he is to . . . report . . . any additional or alternative employment obtained. . . ."

. . . Dennis filed a motion for reconsideration . . . asking the court to reconsider the "seek-work" order [because] such an order constituted an abuse of discretion.

At the hearing . . . the court again took notice of the fact that Dennis had never earned over $3,500 per year and then stated that this income was insufficient to permit reimbursement of the AFDC payments for his family. The court reasoned that Dennis's earning history strongly suggested that in the future he would not earn enough to meet the AFDC payments. . . .

On July 20, 1981 . . . Dennis introduced into evidence a list of 30 separate employers he had contacted regarding employment. He testified that he had called each . . . , inquiring as to whether they were accepting employment applications. He stated that in many cases, the employers were not taking applications and so he did not drive to those places. . . .

The court renewed its order at the . . . hearing. . . . This renewed order again required Dennis to apply for work with ten separate employers per month, and the judge [additionally required] Dennis to apply to both Polk County and Barron County Job Services, and to follow all leads suggested by such Job Services. The court ordered Dennis to appear again . . . on September 14, 1981 . . . to demonstrate compliance. . . .

. . . [T]he court ordered Dennis to appear on October 22, 1981 [at which time he] testified that he had not kept a list of employers to whom he had submitted applications. However, he stated he had talked to several people in an effort to seek work and named three specific persons and that he had talked to "quite a few people" with no success. He stated he had not been to either county Job Service, but had watched the "help wanted" section of the newspaper.

. . . Dennis . . . had been in the car repair business off and on for 20 years, although steadily for ten years, but had operated his present automobile garage business at its present location for only about a year. His business gross receipts averaged $500 to $700 monthly with his take-home pay at about $300 monthly. His personal monthly expenses included $200 for food, part of which went to feed his three children who spent some weekends with him. As part of the property division . . . , Dennis mortgaged his trailerhouse for half its value, and thereby paid his wife $2,000. His monthly payment toward that mortgage was $105. His monthly gasoline expenses . . . were $160 which included driving to and from work and driving to auto parts suppliers to obtain parts for his work. He deducted his gasoline expenses from his gross receipts. His other monthly business expenses were telephone charges of $15 to $20, gas and oxygen charges for welding purposes of $40 to $50, electricity charges of $20 to $25, and rental of the building for which he did mechanical work for the landlord as payment.

Dennis testified that because of his limited income and monthly expenses, he could not afford to comply with the court's order that he apply for ten different jobs per month. Nor could he afford to drive weekly to both Polk and Barron County Job Services and to follow up leads those services might suggest. At the time of the hearing, he had nothing in his checking account and did not have any savings [and] still owed nearly the entire $2,000 [mortgage].

Dennis indicated he worked six days per week and worked between 8:00 a.m. and 6:00 p.m. He testified he never passed up nor avoided any work unless it was unlikely that he would be paid for his services. There was no direct evidence at any hearing that Dennis intentionally shirked or avoided work. Mrs. Dennis testified that he had always been a hard and steady worker. . . .

. . . [T]he court found Dennis in willful contempt of court. Dennis was sentenced to 60 days in the Barron county jail under the work release program and was allowed to purge the contempt by payment of $800. . . . The court found him in contempt on two bases:

1. For failing to make application for work as ordered, and

2. For failing to make child support payments of $15 per month or $5 per month on the arrears as ordered.

The court of appeals affirmed the . . . holding that the court had the inherent power to order Dennis to look for other work. The court held Dennis's testimony incredible which led . . . to the "inescapable conclusion" that Dennis had undisclosed income. The trial court had not made such a finding. The court of appeals found the holding of contempt sustained by the evidence and that the purge . . . was within Dennis's ability to meet by borrowing on his remaining equity in the lot and mobile home.

. . . What is before this court is the order which required the defendant to "seek work" other than or in addition to his present business. . . . The defendant also contests the trial court's authority to retain jurisdiction over him . . . after the final divorce hearing for the purpose of enforcing the "seek-work" order.

The trial court did not order the defendant to take another or different job, but only to seek other work. The rule of *Balaam v. Balaam*, therefore is not controlling. In *Balaam*, we held:

> A divorced husband should be allowed a fair choice of a means of livelihood and to pursue what he honestly feels are his best opportunities even though he might for the present, at least, be working for a lesser financial return. This rule is, of course, subject to reasonableness commensurate with his obligations to his children and his former wife.

Id. at 867.

The *Balaam* rule is not an absolute prohibition against . . . requiring a divorced supporting spouse to consider a change in livelihood, especially where as here Dennis's income as a mechanic has never exceeded $3,500 per year . . . and it has not increased since he has become a garage operator. Not present in *Balaam* was the supporting father's claimed inability to pay $5 per month per child and $5 per month toward arrearage pursuant to the trial court's order as in this case. If ever there was a minuscule support order recognizing the party's lack of present earnings, this is it. It shows great respect and restraint by the trial judge . . . and in no way reflects that the trial court was insisting that the defendant repay the AFDC payments his family was receiving.

Edwards v. Edwards, dealt with the issue of consideration of . . . father's potential earning capacity rather than . . . actual earnings at . . . divorce. . . .

However, until the trial court requires the defendant to "seek work" . . . , there can be no accurate and informed finding as to [his] ability to earn. . . . Until that is known, the court has no way of testing the person's economic worth,. . . . It is to the defendant's benefit to learn his own value, and . . . perhaps to be better able to meet his financial responsibilities. . . . [D]efendant should be interested in supporting his children the best he can and not be satisfied with society supporting them minimally on AFDC. He was not ordered to earn enough to repay AFDC but rather to seek work to investigate whether he is complacent by continuing in . . . non-productive work just so he can feed, house and clothe himself.

Until the defendant and the judge know what other work and income is available, there is no way the judge can determine . . . that the defendant can do no better and there is no way, except by way of inference, to determine that the defendant is satisfied with his own lot in life and is willing to allow society to support his children. To obtain definite and meaningful information, the order of the trial court is reasonable. . . . Telephone calls at random to possible employers do not appear to be a sincere nor effective means of seeking work information. The defendant . . . has not been ordered to abandon his occupation. . . . He was ordered to seek work and report to the court. The trial court read *Edwards* correctly, since in *Edwards* we held: "While a $3,200 a year income is obviously low, no attempt was made to ascertain whether better barbering jobs were available . . . and, if so, how much he could be expected to earn in such a job." The *Edwards* court thereby informed trial courts to have the supportive parent seek other work to learn whether his lot was improvable. . . .

The "seek-work" order was not an abuse of discretion.

. . . .

ABRAHAMSON, JUSTICE (Concurring). . . .

This case presents issues somewhat different from other child support cases, since both the husband and the wife are subsisting below the poverty line. In this case the supporting parent . . . earned very little per month, both before and after the divorce. Before the divorce proceedings, [his] income apparently was sufficient to support the family without government assistance; after the divorce proceedings began, the same income was insufficient to support two family units without government assistance for one unit. . . . While I concur in the court's decision, I have . . . reservations about the court's analysis of the issues. . . .

I am uneasy with the majority's characterization of the circuit court's order as a "seek-work order" issued for the purpose of enabling the trial court "to make an accurate and informed finding as to the defendant's ability to earn and what his worth is economically." . . . I agree that under the *Edwards* dictum the trial court may issue a reasonable seek-work order to gather information about the income of the supporting parent. . . . But I am concerned that this . . . order does not comport with . . . *Edwards* . . . in several respects.

Edwards speaks about examining job opportunities in the same profession in which the parent is trained. Yet the order in this case requires the father to seek employment generally. An order designed to help the trial court ascertain whether the father was fulfilling his earning capacity through diligent work in his chosen trade should have been more narrowly drawn. . . .

Edwards speaks in terms of giving a parent a fair choice of a means of livelihood subject to reasonableness commensurate with obligations. The order in this case was not specifically designed to determine "fair choice" or "reasonableness." Prior to issuing the order, it appears that the trial court may have concluded that the father had had enough time to make a "go" of work in the car repair field and that his fair choice had been used up. . . .

If the trial court's order were interpreted as not merely information gathering but as requiring the father to get another job, the order may not be within the trial court's discretion under the rules set forth [in our prior cases].

Under these rules, the support order must be based on the actual earnings of $300 per month, unless the trial court finds that the father was not fairly or diligently working at an occupation for which he is best suited or that he has willfully accepted employment and lowered compensation in order to reduce the ability to pay child support. There is no evidence in this record to support such a finding. . . . [T]he record indicates that the father was diligent, that he was working at the job for which he was trained, and that his income in his chosen trade has remained stable over many years. Under these circumstances the . . . court appropriately based its support order on the father's actual income. For the trial court . . . to order the father to change his trade so as to increase his income so that the . . . court can increase the support order may be a clear abuse of discretion. . . .

As a matter of constitutional law, strict standards must be met before the highly protected freedom from compulsory work can be infringed. Without a finding of willfulness or lack of diligence an order directing the supporting parent to take alternative employment raises questions of due process, equal protection, and involuntary servitude. . . .

As to the reasonableness of such an order, I wonder whether a man in this father's situation is likely to find a much better-paying job. . . . He is 43 years old; he does not have a high school diploma; he has had 20 years' experience in the car repair business and has had no other job experience; he is accustomed to operating his own business; his compensation has been at the same level for a number of years; and he is earning $3,600 a year, the most he has ever earned. And even if he is successful in finding a job, I wonder what the prospects for job stability are, considering his employment history and his being forced to work at a job he does not want. With these reservations, I concur in the holding.

CECI, JUSTICE (dissenting).

I dissent . . . because a clear reading of the entire record indicates to me a defendant who clearly does not wish to exert himself in any respect for purposes of supporting his children.

. . . .

The record indicates that during this period of nearly zero effort by this defendant, he was able to trade off repair work for a membership in the golf country club, which was valued at $100. Had the defendant truly been making any effort to support his . . . children, he could have used the $100 [to] pay . . . the support the court had ordered for a period of five months and all of the amounts ordered to be paid on the arrearages for a period of five months. Instead, this defendant chose to trade off his labor and efforts so that he could go golfing.

[T]he entire record indicates . . . this defendant was totally satisfied that the taxpayers were supporting his . . . children. My reading . . . indicates an individual who just did not care to comply with the court's orders. I would affirm.

NOTES

1. *Establishing Obligor's Ability to Pay.* Ordinarily a court or guideline looks to the parent's income in setting the amount of the child support obligation. What should be done when the actual earnings are much less than earning capacity? A court might use earning capacity rather than the actual earnings to set the award, thus leaving the parent to deal with the problem, presumably by finding new work. This is often described as imputing income to the parent. When the court is not certain that the parent has an earning capacity greater than his current income, a "seek-work" order might be an apt solution. By requiring a search for more lucrative work, the court will presumably find out if, in fact, that parent can obtain it. That is the problem addressed by the *Dennis* trial court and the solution it adopted.

While the seek-work order may seem attractive, the *Dennis* opinions suggest the conflicting policies at work here. On the one hand, obligees (and the state which is paying welfare benefits) argue that obligors ought to support their children to the extent permitted by their earning capacity. On the other hand, the obligor parent argues for the same right other people have to choose employment free from state coercion, particularly where his income, which was relatively constant, was sufficient to support the family during the marriage. Certainly, both support of children and freedom to work at one's chosen profession are policies worthy of recognition and support. In dealing with these conflicting policies, most appellate courts direct trial courts to follow some version of the rules set out in Justice Abrahamson's concurrence. That is, the trial courts have discretion to resolve conflicts between the interests of the obligee parent and the obligor parent on a case-by-case basis.

A seek-work order is no help in the case of the incarcerated parent. The California courts have held that no income should be imputed to a prisoner-obligor unless there is an opportunity to work for pay while in prison. *Oregon v. Vargas*, 83 Cal.Rptr.2d 229 (5th Dist. 1999); *see Adkins v. Adkins*, 656 S.E.2d 47 (W.Va. 2007) (while imprisonment does not extinguish child support obligation, income of imprisoned parent is his or her currently available income, not imputed based on pre-incarceration income); *Glenn v. Glenn*, 848 P.2d 819 (Wyo. 1993) (obliging father to pay support, but on basis of his prison income). A later California court, in dealing with a modification case raising the same issue, refused to create a "public policy exception" to *Vargas* where the incarcerated obligors had been convicted of offenses such as child molestation and child pornography. *Smith v. Smith*, 108 Cal. Rptr. 2d 537 (5th Dist. 2001). Understandably, courts are particularly reluctant to permit an incarcerated obligor to reduce or eliminate a support obligation where the incarceration results from conviction for failure to support the child. *See, e.g., Commissioner of Human Resources v. Bridgeforth*, 604 A.2d 836 (Conn. 1992).

Some other jurisdictions have refused to exempt prisoners from the imputation of income or have simply included incarceration as one factor to be considered. *See, e.g., Richardson v. Ballard*, 681 N.E.2d 507 (Ohio App. 1996) (incarceration is a voluntary lowering of income which is foreseeable result of criminal behavior); *Mooney v. Brennan*, 848 P.2d 1020 (Mont. 1993) (same); *In re Marriage of Burbridge*, 738 N.E.2d 979 (Ill. App. 2000) (incarceration is one factor to be considered); *Thomasson v. Johnson*, 903 P.2d 254 (New. Mex. 1995) (same). For an article asserting incarcerated parents are often overlooked as a source of child support, see Karen Rothschild Cavanaugh & Daniel Pollack, *Child Support Obligations of Incarcerated Parents*, 7 Cornell J. L. & Pub. Pol'y 531 (1998). *See also* Catherine Moseley Clark, Comment, *Imputing Parental Income in Child Support Determinations: What Price for a Child's Best Interests?*, 49 Cath. U. L. Rev. 167 (1999) (discussing imputation of income in general).

2. *Seek-Work Orders.* The *Dennis* trial court, rather than litigating the question of ability to pay in a vacuum, ordered the defendant to explore other employment possibilities. While this order was approved by the appellate court, such orders are rarely issued. But in a post-*Dennis* case, the trial court was criticized for *failure* to issue a seek-work order. In *In re Marriage of Wallen*, 407 N.W.2d 293 (Wis. App. 1987), the father, who was laid off from a factory job paying almost $30,000 annually, immediately took a minimum wage job at a theme park. The court ordered substantial child support (his entire salary plus $25 weekly) because it believed parent "has taken a very low paying job . . . when he could have sought and obtained employment that was higher paying. . . ." The appellate court found no evidence of shirking. Citing *Dennis*, the court held "use of a seek-work order here would have put the trial court in a much better position to determine . . . whether [the father] was shirking his obligations by refusing, or failing to seek, suitable employment."

3. *Calculating Imputed Income.* Trial courts and administrative agencies commonly seem to avoid deciding how much a parent has the ability to pay by routinely imputing income equal to a fulltime job paying minimum wage and calculating child support based on this potential income. While this is authorized under some statutes, the more common statutory provisions concerning imputed or potential income require evidence that the parent has the education, experience and opportunity in the local employment market sufficient to earn the imputed income. *See* Elaine Sorensen, Liliana Sousa & Simon Schaner, Assessing Child Support Arrears in Nine Large States and the Nation 73 (2007), *available at* http://aspe.hhs.gov/bsp/07/assessing-CS-debt (while imputation of income common where parent reported no income, only 3 of the 8 study states had statutes requiring imputation of full-time minimum wage income). *Compare* Correne Saunders, Danielle Young, Pamela Caudill Ovwigho & Catherine E. born,

MARYLAND CHILD SUPPORT GUIDELINES: CASE-LEVEL REVIEW 21(2008) (found that one in seven (15.2%) of randomly-selected child support cases reflected a noncustodial parent income within a few dollars of full-time minimum wage; concluded that courts and child support agency may be routinely attributing income without evidence in individual cases), *with* MD. FAM. L. CODE § 12-201(j) ("Potential income" means income attributed to a parent determined by the parent's employment potential and probable earnings level based on, but not limited to, recent work history, occupational qualifications, prevailing job opportunities, and earning levels in the community). In *Bardzik v. Bardzik*, 83 Cal. Rptr. 3d 72 (Cal. App. 2008), the court reversed the imputation of income to the obligee parent in an income shares state where the obligor parent had failed to satisfy the burden of proof regarding the obligee parent's ability and opportunity to earn the imputed income. According to the court, "[w]ithout evidence of ability or opportunity to earn money, the power to impute income would easily devolve into a trial judge's power to arbitrarily establish a support order at any given level, plucked from mid-air, just as long as it is over the level otherwise required by the payor parent's actual, taxable income." *Cf. Turner v. Turner*, 785 N.E.2d 259 (Ind. 2003) (upholding imputation based on evidence of obligor parent's skills and income history). Some statutes allow imputation only where a parent is deliberately failing to maximize market activity specifically to avoid the child support obligation. *See Gilpin v. Gilpin*, 664 N.E.2d 766, 768 (Ind. Ct. App. 1996).

PROBLEMS

Problem 5-16. Tammy and Jim are divorcing after a 15-year marriage with three children, now aged 11, 5 and 3. For most of the marriage, Jim was a trial lawyer in a major firm. After seven years, he was made a partner and earned approximately $150,000 annually for the next seven years. About a year ago, when the marriage began to crumble, Jim quit and entered a seminary to train to be a clergyman. During the last year, the family has lived on savings and Jim's part-time job at a local supermarket where he grossed about $275 per week. Tammy, who has a high school education, is a secretary and grosses about $17,000 per year. Tammy seeks your advice on what child support she can expect to receive. All events take place in Georgia.

Problem 5-17. Patricia and Joseph are divorcing. Your client, Joseph, owns real estate appraised at approximately $1.5 million. The property is not income-producing and consists of a vineyard, two dilapidated commercial buildings (currently being renovated) and two pieces of undeveloped land. During the marriage, Joseph was not gainfully employed and used his investment income from stocks and bonds to support the family. The trial court has awarded support to Patricia for the couple's two children, basing his calculation of Joseph's income, in part, on an imputation of a 6% return on the value of his real estate. What is your response on appeal?

[4]   Customizing a Child Support Order

As indicated above, the Family Support Act of 1988 requires all support guidelines to identify a presumptive amount of child support. After this baseline is calculated, either obligor or obligee can attempt to convince the court that the particular circumstances render an award at this level inappropriate. Of course, the number of variations in this situation are almost infinite. Consider the following cases.

DONOHUE v. GETMAN
South Dakota Supreme Court
432 N.W.2d 281 (1988)

MILLER, JUSTICE.

Virginia Getman Donohue appeals from an order which set Richard Getman's child support payments at $120 per month. We reverse.

Richard and Virginia were divorced in 1982 [and] Richard received physical custody of their three children. Both parties subsequently remarried, and their new spouses either have custody of or pay child support for children from prior marriages.

In 1986 the trial court . . . awarded sole . . . custody of the parties' three children to Virginia. The court denied Virginia's request for child support, finding that Richard did not have the means or ability to make support payments.

Shortly thereafter, Virginia petitioned the trial court for child support based on the guidelines set forth in SDCL 25-7-7, since Richard was receiving worker's compensation and social security disability benefits totaling $1,405.33 per month. The trial court found that Richard is totally disabled within the meaning of worker's compensation and social security law. Richard has a severe degenerative condition of the spine and a herniated disc; as a result, he suffers pain, has occasional blackouts, and is experiencing atrophy of his arms. Richard has undergone surgery at least four times due to these problems, and his present wife cannot work because she must stay at home to take care of him. The trial court also found that the children of Richard's new spouse are experiencing medical problems which will require surgery, and Richard will be obligated to pay those medical bills. The trial court concluded that even though the statutory guidelines would require Richard to pay between $539 and $578 per month . . . , he should pay only $120 per month. The trial court gave the following reasons for its deviation . . . : Richard's medical condition and total disability; his monthly expenses and large indebtedness; his future medical expenses; his inability to hold any kind of gainful employment; and the medical condition of his step-children, which will require further expenditures of money.

Did the trial court abuse its discretion by deviating from the child support guidelines . . . ?

This court will not disturb an award . . . unless it clearly appears that the trial court abused its discretion. Virginia argues that the trial court abused its discretion when it failed to enter findings with regard to all five factors listed in SDCL 25-7-7 before deviating from the guidelines. Virginia also contends that it was an abuse of discretion to allow expenses from Richard's second family to [justify] deviation from the guidelines. We agree.

SDCL 25-7-7 states in part:

These guidelines shall be used in setting child support. *Deviation from the guidelines may be made only upon the entry of specific findings based upon the following factors:*

1. Financial condition of the parents, including . . . income of a new spouse or contribution of a third party to the income or expenses of that parent;

2. The standard of living of the child;

3. The age and special needs of the child;

4. The effect of provisions relating to custody and visitation; or

5. Child care. (emphasis added)

Very recently, in *Bruning v. Jeffries*, we addressed the guidelines set forth in SDCL 25-7-7 and stated:

"As the above quoted portion of SDCL 25-7-7 indicates, *there may be no deviation from the guidelines unless there is an entry of specific findings regarding the five listed factors.* The question becomes whether Secretary (and hearing examiner) must consider these factors in every case he hears. We conclude . . . that *the legislature intended that these factors be considered in each proceeding* (emphasis added)."

422 N.W.2d at 580.

Here, the trial court entered findings regarding the financial condition of Richard and his second family, but none on the financial condition of Virginia or the other four [statutory] factors. . . . [T]he failure of the trial court to address these factors constitutes an abuse of discretion. The trial courts of this state must consider the totality of both parents' financial condition and the needs of the children, . . . before deviating from the statutory guidelines.

Furthermore, it is well settled that a parent's responsibility to support his children is paramount; other debts are secondary. This includes obligations resulting from remarriage. *Brunick v. Brunick.* In this case the trial court failed to address the financial needs of Richard's natural children, while focusing on the needs of Richard's step-children by his second marriage and his other debts. The trial court then used the step-children's needs as a basis for reducing Richard's support for his natural children. This is contrary to our holdings . . . and constitutes a further abuse of the trial court's discretion.

We therefore reverse . . . and remand for reconsideration. . . .

NOTES

1. *Variation from Guideline Amount.*   Federal law specifies that the guideline amount may be rebutted only by a "written finding or specific finding on the record that the application of the guidelines would be unjust or inappropriate in a particular case, as determined under criteria established by the state . . .", 42 U.S.C. § 667(b), and this requirement is reflected in the typical state statute. Some cases, however, accept fairly flimsy "specific findings." *See, e.g., Manzanares v. Manzanares*, 769 P.2d 156 (Okla. 1989) (trial court varied amount "based on the equities of the case"). South Dakota's statute is like many in defining the information relevant to deciding whether to order less or more than the guideline amount. Some statutes provide less guidance to the court. Other statutes are very detailed, mentioning parental financial resources, relative standards of living, child's resources, tax consequences, disparity between parental incomes, step-children of the obligor and in-kind contributions by each parent. *See, e.g.,* GA. CODE ANN. § 19-6-15(c) (15 specific factors); N.Y. DOM. REL. L. § 240, 1-b, (f) (nine factors). Listed factors often are described as illustrative and not exhaustive.

A constitutional attack on child support guidelines by a group of support obligors, asserting they constituted an improper "irrebutable presumption" because courts would not consider arguments that a particular child's needs were below the guideline amount, was rejected in *Parents Opposed to Punitive Support (POPS) v. Gardner*, 998 F.2d 764 (9th Cir. 1993). The court held that even if the statutory amount was irrebutable, it was constitutionally acceptable as a substantive legislative judgment that "divorcing parents will be required to sustain their children at a certain standard of living determined by the parents' income." A state constitutional attack based on an alleged violation of separation of powers doctrine was rejected in *Gallaher v. Elam*, 104 S.W.3d 455 (Tenn. 2003) (legislative delegation to executive agency of power to promulgate guidelines was acceptable because appropriate standards for guidelines were provided). *See also Row v. Row (Deese)*, 650 S.E.2d 1 (N.C. App. 2007) (child support guidelines found constitutional against obligor's claims that guidelines offend supremacy, equal protection and due process clauses of U.S. Constitution).

What if the parties reach an agreement on child support which specifies an amount different from that which the guidelines would provide? Is the agreement itself a reason to award a non-guideline amount? Blackletter law has always provided that "an agreement of the parties cannot usurp the authority of the court to ultimately determine the child support award." LAURA W. MORGAN, CHILD SUPPORT GUIDELINES: INTERPRETATION AND APPLICATION p. 4-78. Many states, however, either via statute or case law, identify an agreement as a relevant circumstance which is appropriate to consider in determining whether to vary from the guideline level of support. *Id.* at pp. 4-81, 4-82; *see Marriage of Rosenthal*, 903 P.2d 1174 (Col. App. 1995).

2. *Obligor's Second Family as Justifying Deviation.*   Courts often must deal with the financial demands of the obligor's new family when the obligor seeks to *reduce* existing child support obligations. *See* Section B[7][a], *infra. Donohue*, however, faced the issue in *establishing* a support order. The same establishment issue might arise where a married obligor was asked to support a non-marital child

or an obligor was separated from the child's parent and cohabiting with a new family.

While *Donohue* (and the South Dakota statute) recognize the relevance of such financial demands, note the court's signal as to the appropriate weight of this factor. The court notes "a parent's responsibility to support his children is paramount; other debts are secondary. This includes obligations from remarriage." A trial judge on remand might have difficulty operationalizing this mandate. Must the second family subsidize the obligor's marital child? If the marital child doesn't get all the support otherwise due, is he subsidizing the second family? Recall the Wisconsin statute found unconstitutional in *Zablocki v. Redhail* in Chapter 2. Would your answer depend on whether the children of the second marriage were the obligor's step-children (and whether state law required stepparental support) or were the obligor's "natural" children? The South Dakota court later rejected an Equal Protection clause attack on the preference for the first family. *Feltman v. Feltman*, 434 N.W.2d 590 (S.D. 1989). Similarly, the Tennessee Supreme Court upheld the constitutionality of support guidelines under which other dependents of the obligor can be considered only where such dependents are beneficiaries of a court order. *See Gallaher, supra* (rejecting Equal Protection and Due Process attacks, noting statute permits consideration of other dependents without a decree in "extreme circumstances").

In *Betty v. Betty*, 552 S.E.2d 846 (Ga. 2001), the Georgia Supreme Court noted that obligations to prior children justified variance under the state statute only where an existing order requires support of those children. While obligor had legal custody of his older child, the child was living with obligor's mother, he was not under any order to support that child and no evidence suggested he was doing so. In this context, the court found no reason to consider the fact that obligor had legal custody of his prior child in setting support in the current divorce case.

3. *Guidelines Versus Discretion.* Allowing deviations from the presumptively correct guidelines amount only upon written justification is designed to limit opportunities for courts to return to the former discretionary regime, under which child support amount were considered too low and the variation from case to case too great. What effect has the introduction of guidelines had on the level of awards? An early (1989) study in three states with different models (Hawaii — Melson Formula; Colorado — Income Shares; Illinois — Percentage of Obligor's Income) reported a modest closing of the asserted adequacy gap between the amount needed and the amount ordered in the pre-guideline discretion era, with support ordered in the three states (as a group) increasing by 15%. The study offered reasons for the relatively modest increase in awards. "The picture we have generated may be only temporary, with full impact requiring a longer implementation phase. The most dramatic effects of guidelines may only be realized when they are applied to the modification of previously established orders." Jessica Pearson, Nancy Thoennes & Patricia Tjaden, *Legislating Adequacy: The Impact of Child Support Guidelines*, 23 LAW & SOC. REV. 569, 586–87 (1989). An examination of data about families collected between 1979 and 1993 showed that "guidelines have not increased child-support awards among divorced or separated women, but there is evidence that awards for the nonmarital birth sample may be substantially higher when guidelines are present." Laura M.

Argys, H. Elizabeth Peters, Donald M. Waldman, *Can the Family Support Act Put Some Life Back into Deadbeat Dads?: An Analysis of Child Support Guidelines, Award Rates, and Levels*, 36 J. HUMAN RESOURCES 226 (2001). Perhaps the most important point, however, is that only with the adoption of guidelines can there be any systematic discussion of the appropriate level of child support.

The other major impetus behind the guideline movement has been a sense that guidelines will make support awards more consistent. The sparse empirical research on actual awards suggests the pre-guideline system resulted in wide disparity in the amount of support ordered in similar circumstances. For example, a Denver study in the 1970s reported non-custodial parents were ordered to make payments ranging from 6% to 33.3% of their incomes to support one child and 5.6% to 40% of their incomes to support two children. Lucy Yee, *What Really Happens in Child Support Award Cases: An Empirical Study of Establishment and Enforcement of Child Support Orders in the Denver District Court*, 57 DEN. L.J. 21, 38–42 (1979); *see also* Kenneth R. White & Thomas R. Stone, *A Study of Alimony and Child Support Rulings with Some Recommendations*, 10 FAM. L.Q. 75, 83 (1976). The Pearson, Thoennes & Tjaden study cited above reports a reduction in variability of the level of support awards in the three states studied. 23 LAW & SOC. REV. at 577. On the other hand, a commentator in 1998 found existing empirical data suggest that the goals of increased award levels and decreased award variability have not been met by the enactment of guidelines. Marsha Garrison, *An Evaluation of Two Models of Parental Obligation*, 86 CALIF. L. REV. 41 (1998) (urging adoption of Equal Living Standards guidelines as exemplifying author's "Community Model" of support); *see also* Tim Graves, *Comparing Child Support Guidelines*, 34 FAM. L.Q. 149 (2000); J. Thomas Oldham, *Child Support Symposium*, 33 FAM. L.Q. 1 (1999). The study by Argys et al. cited above found that

> more than half of the child-support awards differ from the guideline formula by more than 30 percent. These differences are almost evenly split between awards that exceed the guideline and those that are below the guideline (33 percent and 37 percent respectively) . . . [A]ctual awards differ from the guideline amounts in response to various characteristics of the father. For example, a family in which the father is highly educated deviate upward from the guideline amount . . . Actual awards are higher than the guideline awards for fathers who have infrequent contact with their children . . . In contrast, as father's income rises, the actual award falls relative to the guideline award . . . [A]t earnings below $18,100 actual awards are above guideline awards, and as income increases above this amount, awards fall further and further below the guideline amounts.

[5]   High Income Parents

ISAACSON v. ISAACSON
New Jersey Superior Court, Appellate Division
792 A.2d 525 (2002)

CARCHMAN, J.A.D.

[Joel Scott Isaacson and Lily Isaacson divorced in 1996. With the agreement of the parents, the court placed legal custody of their two children, then ages 7 and 9, in both parents, with primary residential custody in Lily. On divorce, Joel agreed to pay $1200 monthly as support for each child, pay for the children's unreimbursed medical expenses and pay for their summer camp. He also agreed to make additional payments of $800 a month for the 1996 and 1997 school years to be applied to the girls' private school tuition, with tuition for subsequent years to be negotiated. Joel's annual income in 1996 was approximately $180,000; Lily's income was zero except for short-term alimony in the amount of $2,600 a month. Two years later, when Lily sought a modification of child support shortly before the termination of alimony, Joel's annual income was more than $550,000 per year, while Lily, now employed, was earning $50,000 a year.]

The [trial] judge ordered . . . father to pay total child support . . . of $3,500 per month or $42,000 per year, tax free, allocated equally between the two girls. The judge rejected mother's argument that because father's income had tripled, his child support obligation should triple. The judge instead considered the maturation of the children and the standard of living and economic circumstances of both spouses. Mother, in particular, was more financially self-sufficient than she had been at the time of the divorce, and the total amount of money now available to her was almost equal to what she had before she earned any money on her own. The judge maintained father's responsibility for private school tuition at 79% because father would be absorbing greater educational expenses for the children as they matured . . .

The judge also noted that the maximum amount of child support set forth in the guidelines was $650 per week for two children, or $34,000 per year, and that this figure was based on net family income of $2,900 per week, or $225,000 of gross income per year. Here, however, without even considering mother's income of $50,000, the judge had ordered father to pay $8,000 per year more than the maximum in the guidelines. He stated that child support awards were never intended to "pyramid all the way out" just because a father earned several times more than the maximum set forth in the guidelines. He made the award retroactive to the termination of alimony — December 1999 . . .

Two issues dominate in these consolidated appeals . . . The second issue concerns the modification of child-support where a parent has received a substantial increase in income, can be classified as a "high-income earner" whose income level exceeds the scope of the Child Support Guidelines and who does not dispute the ability to pay any reasonable amount of child support.

We particularly focus on the standards to be applied in considering a modified award [and] the supporting parent's obligation to provide additional benefits to the children . . . We conclude that the increased award of child support was supported by the record, but the father should provide increased private school costs . . .

We have generally recognized that where the parties have the financial wherewithal to provide for their children, the children are entitled to the benefit of financial advantages available to them. We have characterized such circumstances as reflecting a parent's "good fortune" and have held that children are entitled to have their needs accord with the current standard of living of both parents, which may reflect an increase in parental good fortune. Children are entitled to not only bare necessities, but a supporting parent has the obligation to share with his children the benefit of his financial achievement.

We need not define the parameters of "good fortune," except to observe that recent economic prosperity has spawned parents whose income far exceeds the norm and who can be characterized as "high earners." For the purposes of our inquiry, we include in such category those earners whose wage level substantially exceeds the child support guidelines and who . . . can . . . afford any rationally based award of increased child support. . . .

Where our attention is focused on the unique circumstances of the high-income earner whose ability to pay increased child support is not in issue, the dominant guideline for consideration is the reasonable needs of the children, which must be addressed in the context of the standard of living of the parties. The needs of the children must be the centerpiece of any relevant analysis. Other economic-dependant factors are of less significance, as the high earner's concession of ability to pay has essentially limited the consideration of such economic-dependent issues. However, any consideration of needs must factor in the age and health of the children, as well as the other assets or income of the children, including any debts. Obviously, when considering the age factor, the needs of an infant child are distinctly different from the needs of teenage children, as is the case here.

Determining a child's needs in these unusual financial circumstances presents unique problems. First, a balance must be struck between reasonable needs, which reflect lifestyle opportunities, while at the same time precluding an inappropriate windfall to the child or even in some cases infringing on the legitimate right of either parent to determine the appropriate lifestyle of a child . . . This latter consideration involves a careful balancing of interests reflecting that a child's entitlement to share in a parent's good fortune does not deprive either parent of the right to participate in the development of an appropriate value system for a child. This is a critical tension that may develop between competing parents. Ultimately, the needs of a child in such circumstances also calls to the fore the best interests of a child.

We have suggested that " 'needs' accord with the current standard of living of both parents, which may reflect an increase in parental good fortune." We have also recognized that after basic needs are met and a parent's income permits, children are entitled to other non-essential items that are reasonable and in the child's best interest. We have expounded on examples of sharing in a parent's good fortune . . . . :

In the future, where, as here, the children are entitled to share in a parent's good fortune, the custodial parent's budget should be broken down into two parts: the reality-based component dictated by his or her income and the added projections which will, in fact, allow the children to share in the other parent's financial gain. This could include, by way of example, private school tuition, private tutoring, summer camps, music or art lessons, sports clinics, vacations, study abroad, and the provision of transportation for a child who drives, to mention only a few possibilities. It could also include help to make the family home more presentable, assistance with the cost of a family car, or a larger amount of money for a teenager's clothing and incidentals. As we have said, these are only examples.

The examples . . . do not provide an exhaustive list of opportunities for a child to share in a parent's good fortune. Yet, the promulgation of such "needs" is not an open-ended opportunity for a parent to develop a "wish-list" for a child that does not comport with the child's best interests; "needs" is a relative factor in appropriate upbringing of a child and a reflection of the lifestyle of the parents. By way of example, the fact that a parent may be driving a luxury automobile does not mean that a child of driving age will be entitled to a similar luxury automobile, but the supporting parent's financial wherewithal may enable a child with a need for an automobile to enjoy the luxury of an automobile, suitable and appropriate for a teen-age driver and sufficient to meet the child's transportation needs. Judges must be vigilant in providing for "needs" consistent with lifestyle without overindulgence. As one court observed in dealing with high income support, "[p]ractitioners dealing with situations such as this sometimes refer to the 'Three Pony Rule.' That is, no child, no matter how wealthy the parents, needs to be provided more than three ponies." . . .

We also recognize, as we have done in the past, that the law is not offended if there is some incidental benefit to the custodial parent from increased child support payments. As we noted . . .

> In short, we see no reason why, because of their mother's impecuniousness, these children of a very successful father should be required to live in a house which is in a state of disrepair, be transported in an old or unreliable vehicle or go without a necessary new furnace. Their father's income entitles them to better, and the fact that their mother may benefit incidentally from the component for which the father pays is of no moment.

This, too, requires the judge to balance the needs of the child. Incidental benefit is not offensive, but overreaching in the name of benefitting a child is. . . . [W]e can easily perceive different considerations of incidental benefit applying where an application for increased child support including repairs to a home is made when the child is approaching majority, as opposed to such an application where the child or children are younger. A custodial parent seeking an increase in child support to provide for adequate transportation for children when the children are young and not of driving age is decidedly different than an application made when the child is seventeen years old. These, too, are factors which must be considered by the judge. Judges, of course, must be conscious that in balancing the award with the incidental benefit to the custodial parent, the lifestyle of the supporting and custodial parent may be so disparate that a disconnect between financial resources available to a child and the lack of similar resources available to a custodial parent may generate other issues. We need not address this issue here, as the difference in lifestyle between the plaintiff and defendant is not so disparate so as to crystalize the issue.

. . . [W]e reverse that part of the order of February 16, 2000, allocating 79% of the private school costs to father and remand for the entry of an order allocating 100% of such costs to father . . . ; in all other respects the order is affirmed.

NOTES

1. *High Income Obligors.*   Different methods of dealing with high-income parents have been developed. Within the percentage-of-obligor-income model, some guidelines establish a maximum guideline amount and make the obligor's high income a factor upon which an upward deviation may be based. Others set no maximum guideline amount, though the court can consider factors such as obligor's unusually high income as a factor justifying an award lower than the otherwise applicable percentage. *Compare* Tex. Fam. Code § 154.126 (child support capped at amount applicable to obligor with income of $7500 unless obligee demonstrates that child's needs exceed that amount and parental income sufficient), *with* Wis. St. Ann. § 767.511(1m) (court may reduce child support below applicable percentage of obligor's income if presumptive award would be unfair to obligor). While both states thus allow consideration of an obligor's high income, they frame the issue quite differently. In a state with a cap, the obligee parent must prove that the maximum guideline amount is inadequate. In a state with no cap, the obligor parent bears the burden of showing that the presumptively correct amount is inordinately high. One can therefore imagine quite different results. *See also Ford v. Ford*, 600 A.2d 25 (Del. 1993) (under Melson Formula, defendant obligor must rebut presumption that the Formula calculation is appropriate).

The *ALI Principles* point in a different direction. The Principles reject the approach of setting a cap on the amount of obligor income subject to the formula and agree that unusually high income enters the analysis only as a rebuttal factor offered by the obligor. Yet, the *Principles* argue, the ultimate issue in high income cases is not the amount of obligor income, but achievement of child well-being. Section 3.07 of the *Principles* thus provide that departures from the support amount resulting from application of its required formula may be allowed upon:

> proof that, taking into account the interests of the child, the amount determined by the child-support formula would be unjust or inappropriate, under the particular circumstances of the case, for one or more of the following reasons:

> (a) the support obligor has extraordinarily high income and the amount determined under the formula exceeds an amount necessary to insure that (i) the child enjoys a standard of living that is both adequate and not grossly inferior to that of either parent and (ii) the child's . . . life opportunities are adequately secured . . .

> Comment:

. . .

c. When the support obligor has extraordinarily high income. The principle that a parent should share income with a child seeks to ensure that the child enjoys economic adequacy and a standard of living not grossly inferior to that of either parent, and that the child is not deprived of important life opportunities that would have been available had the child resided with that parent. . . . When the amount of child support generated by application of the formula is sufficient to accomplish all these objectives, the rationale for continued sharing of income loses much of its force, although the court may still require that some percentage of additional income be shared with the child on the unqualified principle that a parent should share income with a child.

The exception for support obligors with extraordinarily high income should be treated as a rebuttal factor, rather than as a general limitation on the amount of income subject to the formula. Some states have unwisely taken the latter path, often cutting off application of the formula at inappropriately low limits of obligor or total parent income. That a nonresidential parent enjoys a high income does not imply that a child support obligation expressed as a *percentage* of this income will provide similarly or even adequately for the child. It is only when the income of an obligor is extraordinarily high that this result is certain to occur. With the illustrative ALI formula, such cases are likely to involve only support obligors whose annual net income exceeds $200,000 and such cases are in any event likely to require individualized treatment by the trier of fact.

ALI, Principles, pp. 477–79 (2002).

Some Income Shares states provide that if the combined parental income exceeds the highest amount listed on the chart, the court should exercise discretion in determining the basic support obligation (which is then divided proportionately between the parents). *See* N.Y. Dom. Rel. L. § 240(1-b)(c)(3) (for combined annual net income above $80,000, court shall consider list of factors and/or standard percentage establishing basic child support obligation); Colo. Rev. Stats. § 14-10-115(10)(a)(II)(E) (court may exercise "discretion where combined monthly gross income exceeds $15,000" but support must be at least the amount appropriate where combined monthly income was $15,000); Md. Fam. Law Code § 12-204(d) (discretion where income exceeds guideline maximum of $10,000 joint monthly adjusted). *See also Downing v. Downing*, 45 S.W.3d 449 (Ky. App. 2001) (above-chart income should be considered on case-by-case basis; rejecting mechanical extrapolation from chart requiring 4% of all beyond-chart income as support).

Must a high-income obligor reveal the exact amount of his income? In *Hubner v. Hubner*, 114 Cal.Rptr.2d 646 (App. 2001), the father asserted that so long as he stipulated that he could afford to pay whatever support was ordered he had a right to keep the amount of his income private. The appellate court held that the need for sufficient information to "properly assess the child's needs" outweighed any privacy interest. Noting that both obligor and obligee had complained about the support order, the fact that it was based on "fictional gross income assumptions" left the court "unable to assess whether either party is correct." A remand to develop accurate information was ordered. An issue arising with some frequency in cases involving high income obligors is the appropriate treatment of stock options. *See In re Cheriton*, 111 Cal. Rptr. 2d 755 (App. 2001); *Murray v. Murray*, 716 N.E.2d 288 (Ohio App. 1999); Susan Isard, *Stock Options and Child Support: The Price of Accuracy*, 14 Hast. Women's L.J. 215 (2003).

2. *Disparity Between Parental Incomes in Nonmarital Support Cases.* In *Isaacson*, one parent earned ten times more than the other parent. Some cases involve an even greater discrepancy. *See State v. Hall*, 418 N.W.2d 187 (Minn. App. 1988), where the singer Daryl Hall had a monthly income of $116,000, while the obligee mother had so little income she qualified for welfare. Such a situation forces the court to confront head-on the tension between the idea that the obligor should share income with his child and the reality that the custodial parent — to whom the obligor may have no legal duty — will also benefit from the award of child support. The *Hall* trial court noted the mother's proposed budget did not indicate "the actual monthly expenses of the minor child." It was concerned she would use the child support for her own needs, concluding "it would be inappropriate to use a child support obligation to upgrade (mother's) standard of living." The mother's budget proposed the purchase of an $80,000 home by the mother, who apparently was living on welfare, food stamps and child support for her other child. *Hall's* reasoning suggests that, if the mother were better off, the support order would be higher. Some statutes identify disparity of parental income as a factor in deciding whether to vary the guideline amount. *See, e.g.*, Nev. Rev. Stats. § 125B.080(9)(l) ("relative income of both parents"); N.Y. Dom. Rel. L. § 240(1-b)(f)(7).

Can this dilemma be resolved without penalizing either the child or the non-custodial obligor? The *Isaacson* court says that "incidental" benefits to the custodial parents are inevitable and should not change the outcome if it is in the best interests of the child. *See In re Marriage of Catalano*, 251 Cal. Rptr. 370 (App. 1988) ("where the supporting parent enjoys a lifestyle that far exceeds that of the custodial parent, child support must to some degree reflect the more opulent lifestyle even though this may . . . produce a benefit for the custodial parent"). One appellate court, reversing an award it found too low in a case involving great disparity, suggested the court could order the support paid directly to the provider of specific services for the child. *In re Marriage of Hubner*, 252 Cal. Rptr. 428 (App. 1988). In a recent Arizona case involving a baseball player making approximately $10,000,000 a year, the trial court decision not to exceed the guidelines cap of $1560 a month was reversed. The appellate court, relying on language in the guidelines statute requiring consideration of the standard of living the child would have enjoyed if the parents were living together, held that the nonmarital status of the parents was irrelevant. *East v. Matthews*, 213P.3d 248 (Ariz. App. 2009).

3. *Low Income Support Obligor Cases.* "About a third of states impose a mandatory minimum monthly award, usually between $20 and $50." Laura W. Morgan, Child Support Guidelines: Interpretation and Application 4-64 to 4-67 (1996 & Supp.) (hereinafter "Morgan"); *see, e.g.*, Colo. Rev. Stats. § 14-10-115(10)(b) ($50 minimum). In *Rose ex rel. Clancy v. Moody*, 629 N.E.2d 378 (N.Y. 1993), however, the court struck down a $25 monthly minimum for all obligors. The court found this pre-empted by the federal requirement of "rebuttable" guidelines.

See also Hunt v. Hunt, 648 A.2d 843 (Vt. 1994) (Dooley, dissenting) (no federal requirement of at least nominal support in all cases). The *Moody* dissenter argued that the federal statute did not prohibit imposition of a minimum support obligation and that such a minimum, rather than conflicting with federal interests, actually furthered the interest in strengthening the support enforcement program. The dissent also noted state law protection of the obligor, a mother with custody of two of her three children whose sole income was welfare benefits, from actual enforcement of the $25 monthly obligation. Some courts have discretion to award a lesser amount than the "minimum" on a finding of inability to pay. *See, e.g.*, NEV. REV. STATS. § 125B.080(4).

4. *Other Factors Justifying Variance.* A myriad of factors are listed in various statutes as relevant to the question of variance from guideline amounts. These factors include joint custody arrangements, extraordinary medical or educational expenses for the child, unusual expenses of the obligor or obligee, transportation for visitation, age of the child, in-kind contributions of either parent and custodial parent's income (in POOI states).

Should the child's income be considered? In *In re Emerson*, 850 P.2d 942 (Kan. App. 1993), the court refused to consider the fact that the child received Supplemental Security Income (SSI) benefits based on the child's disability. Describing the benefits as a "gratuity from a governmental agency," the court noted such benefits are available only for the disabled who have inadequate income from other sources. Thus, these payments are designed to *supplement*, not *replace* child support payments. In fact, the SSI payments might be reduced or eliminated after the award and receipt of child support. *See also Paton v. Paton*, 742 N.E.2d 619 (Ohio 2001) (adopting same rule in context of modification motion); *Nelson v. Nelson*, 454 N.W.2d 533 (S.D. 1990).

Emerson distinguished the situation where the child received Social Security benefits as a dependent of a disabled obligor. In that situation, the benefits are designed to replace the obligor's income and are based on contributions made by the obligor. Courts regularly credit such payments to the disabled obligor's support obligation. *See Ford v. Ford*, 816 So. 2d 1193 (Fla. App. 2002); *Brooks v. Brooks*, 881 P.2d 955 (Utah App. 1994); *In re Henry*, 622 N.E.2d 803 (Ill. 1993). Similar treatment is accorded Social Security payments to the child based on the obligor's retirement. *In re: Marriage of Belger*, 654 N.W.2d 902 (Iowa 2002); *In re Allsup*, 926 S.W.2d 323 (Tex. App. 1996).

[6] Non-Judicial Processes for Establishing Support

Support orders have traditionally been entered by courts, but, as a result of the Child Support Enforcement Amendments of 1984, which required "expedited processes" to establish support orders in cases handled by the state's child support enforcement agency, many states have adopted administrative or quasi-judicial processes. 42 U.S.C. § 666(a)(2); 45 C.F.R. § 303.101. (State child support enforcement agencies, more fully described in Section C, *infra*, were established to collect support due obligees receiving welfare assistance. They are known as IV-D agencies after the title of the Social Security Act mandating their creation, 42 U.S.C. § 654(3), and now are used also by non-welfare obligees.) The expedited process must assure that, in most categories of establishment cases, an order is entered within a year of the time of filing by the agency. 45 C.F.R. § 303.101(b)(2). A waiver of the expedited process requirement is available to a state whose judicial system is equally efficacious. 42 U.S.C. § 666(d).

In response to this federal mandate, some states have chosen to offer these expedited processes to all support obligees, not simply those served by the child support enforcement agency. In about half the states, these processes involve quasi-judicial officials such as masters, referees or commissioners who either enter an order subject to review by a judge or recommend an order to the judge.

Other states use an administrative process to establish support obligations. In such a system, an executive agency (*e.g.*, department of social services) has the power to determine support duties and to enter orders. Administrative adjudication is similar to judicial process. A parent may be represented by a lawyer. There is notice, a right to a hearing, and judicial review. In practice, this administrative process has had minimal participation by attorneys. Proponents argue the administrative approach is cheaper and quicker because it avoids court calendar problems. Judges have higher salaries and larger staffs and decide fewer cases per day.

The federally-mandated guidelines apply in both judicial and non-judicial proceedings. Appeals are available from administrative proceedings, though the states are split on whether this review is de novo or on the record. In Maine, an administrative process state, only one percent of agency decisions were appealed to the judicial system in 1987. Jeffrey Ball, *Administrative Process, in* INTERSTATE CHILD SUPPORT REMEDIES 125 (Haynes, ed. 1989). Some states authorize agencies to modify support decrees as well as establish them initially. The Montana Supreme Court found such a scheme violated the state constitution's separation of powers provisions. *Seubert v. Seubert*, 13 P. 3d 365 (Mont. 2000). The court noted that, unlike statutory provisions in other states, in Montana there was no automatic judicial review of the agency determination. *See also Hilburn v. Staeden*, 91 S.W.3d 607 (Mo. 2002) (rejecting constitutional attack on administrative proceeding requiring payment of support); *State ex rel. Allee v. Gocha*, 555 N.W.2d 683 (Iowa 1996) (rejecting state constitutional attack on administrative modification).

For an overview of the use of the administrative process to establish child support, see Ball, *supra* (especially Appendix V-2, indicating range of treatment of recurring issues); P. COOPER, ET AL., A GUIDE FOR DESIGNING AND IMPLEMENTING AN ADMINISTRATIVE PROCESS FOR CHILD SUPPORT ENFORCEMENT (1985); Paula Roberts, *Expedited Processes and Child Support Enforcement: A Delicate Balance, Parts I and II*, 19 CLEARING. REV. 483, 620 (1985); FRED SILVESTER & DENNIS C. COOPER, THE ADMINISTRATIVE ADJUDICATION OF CHILD SUPPORT OBLIGATIONS (1981).

[7]   Modification of Child Support Awards

Like alimony awards, child support judgments are based upon current facts concerning the parties' needs and resources, which may change. As continuous obligations, they can be reevaluated if warranted by a change in circumstances. Either obligor or obligee can seek modification. The traditional rule permitted modification upon a "material change in circumstances," sometimes with the additional requirement that the change be "substantial and continuing." Some statutes imposed a more stringent burden on the movant. The Model Marriage and Divorce Act § 316(a) requires that the change of circumstances be "so substantial and continuing as to make the terms [of the original award] unconscionable." The drafters designed this provision to "discourage repeated or insubstantial motions for modification." *Commentary*, MMDA § 316. Some courts explicitly require proof that the change of circumstances was unforeseen and unforeseeable at the time of the original order. *See, e.g., In re Marriage of Feustel*, 467 N.W.2d 261 (Iowa 1990); *Miller v. Miller*, 384 S.E.2d 715 (S.C. 1989).

At one time, a party seeking an increase in child support had to show increased needs of the child as well as an increase in available obligor resources. *See* MORGAN, *supra*, at 5-4; *Kerby v. Kerby*, 60 P.3d 1038 (Okla. 2002) (four-fold increase in obligor income is cause to review support award, but "trial court . . . must consider all the relevant factors including the needs of the children . . . and the parents' income"); *Yeatman v. Gortney*, 562 So. 2d 258 (Ala. Civ. App. 1990); *Wexelman v. Donnelly*, 782 S.W.2d 72 (Mo. App. 1989). Such a requirement, though, is inconsistent with the modern approach to setting the initial award, which abandons the unhelpful "needs" formulation and instead focuses upon parental income. Under a principle that the child is entitled to share in post-divorce increases in the parent's prosperity, just as the child typically would in an intact family, higher obligor income is sufficient by itself to justify an increase in the child support award. *Miller v. Schou*, 616 So. 2d 436 (Fla. 1993) ("child is . . . entitled to share in the good fortune of his parent consistent with an appropriate life-style"); *Graham v. Graham*, 597 A.2d 355 (D.C. 1991) (doubling of obligor's income justifies increase).

Federal regulations permit a state to provide that an "inconsistency" between the original award and the guideline amount under the current facts is sufficient to justify modification without inquiry into the child's "needs." 45 C.F.R. § 303.8(c). While the regulations apply only to Title IV-D cases, most states apply the federal rule to all cases. MORGAN, *supra*, at 5-10. Under the rule, states are permitted to establish a "reasonable, quantitative" standard by which to determine whether the necessary "inconsistency" is shown. 45 C.F.R. § 303.8(c)(2002). Most states have identified a certain percentage of variance as their quantified standard (ranging from 10% to 30%). MORGAN, *supra*, at 5-12 & 5-13. It would seem that if the inconsistency between the guidelines and the current guideline amount stems from a variance or rebuttal of the guideline amount in the original action, the moving party should be obligated to prove that changed circumstances nullify the original variance. *See Smith v. Collins*, 667 N.E.2d 1236 (Ohio App. 1995).

The traditional modification process left awards unchanged unless a party initiated legal action to change them. The transaction costs involved deterred modifications and likely resulted in many support awards becoming inadequate over time. *See generally* J. Thomas Oldham, *Abating the Feminization of Poverty: Changing the Rules Governing Post-Decree Modification of Child Support Obligations*, 1994 BYU L. REV. 841; Sarah K. Funke, Note, *Preserving the Purchasing Power of Child Support Awards: Can the Use of Escalator Clauses Be Justified After the Family Support Act?*, 69 IND. L.J. 921 (1994). Since 1988, federal law has required routinized periodic review and modification of certain support orders without demonstration of a substantial change of circumstances. As of 2007, states must conduct triennial reviews in all TANF cases and in any non-TANF cases in which a parent requests a review. 42 U.S.C. § 666(a)(10)(A)(i); 45 C.F.R. § 303.8.

Another approach requires all support decrees to include a cost of living adjustment. *See, e.g.*, MINN. STAT. ANN. § 518A.75 (unless court accepts contrary agreement, every support award "shall provide for a biennial adjustment in the amount to be paid based on a change in the cost of living"). The obligee must notify the obligor of an intention to claim the adjustment, giving the latter an opportunity to seek judicial elimination or reduction of the COLA on the ground that any increase in the obligor's income has not matched inflation. MINN. STAT. ANN. § 518.641(2). Courts in other states have endorsed similar decrees. *See, e.g., Cochran v. Rodenbarger*, 736 N.E.2d 1279 (Ind. App. 2000) (approving agreement-based self-modifying order, even though court could not enter similar order outside of parental agreement); *Roya v. Roya*, 494 A.2d 132 (Vt. 1985); *H.P.A. v. S.C.A.*, 704 P.2d 205 (Alaska 1985).

The *ALI Principles* propose a system similar to the federal law, requiring review of all awards at least every three years, to be carried out by a state agency designated either by the court or legislature. *ALI, Principles* § 3.19 (2002). The designated agency would be empowered to gather, either from the parties or from others, such as employers, any information necessary for the calculation of the appropriate award. The parties could avoid such a review by reaching an agreement, either rejecting review or agreeing on a new level of support. The *Principles* also recommend that "whenever practicable," child support awards be self-modifying by their own terms, "automatically and continuously . . . as all relevant income changes." *Id.* at § 3.18(1). The *Principles* suggest that compliance with this requirement could be achieved by expressing support orders as a percentage of obligor's income, which would account for post-divorce decreases in income as well as increases. The Commentary acknowledges, however, that such an automatic modification system may be inconsistent with current federal regulations.

NOTES

1. ***Voluntary Reductions in Income: Some Special Cases.*** Many obligors seek a downward modification based on a return to school or a new job or career. Results vary. *See Marriage of Meegan*, 13 Cal. Rptr. 2d 799 (App. 1992) (reducing support to zero when obligor entered priesthood). *But see Putz v. Putz*, 645 N.W.2d 343 (Minn. 2002), (rejecting downward notification proposed by postal employee who quit job to attend school for computer science in absence of evidence that education would enhance earning capacity and obligor in arrears when he quit his job); *Goldberger v. Goldberger*, 624 A.2d 1328 (Md. Sp. App. 1993) (father's plans to be permanent Torah and Talmud student amount to voluntary impoverishment, even though he had done this throughout the marriage and had never had a paying job).

PROBLEM

Problem 5-18. You are a Legal Aid attorney who works with prisoners. Fred Felon reports he was divorced from Sally three years ago and ordered to pay $50 per week support for their child. Last month, he was convicted of theft and incarcerated for a term of six-to-ten years. The earliest he will be eligible for release is in three years. He earns approximately $24 a week in prison. He wants relief from his obligations during his imprisonment. What counter-arguments do you expect from Sally? Is it relevant that Fred was current on his obligations upon entering prison? Is it relevant that he had been awarded one-half the equity in the parties' marital home (the only marital asset) at the time of divorce?

[a]   Serial Families

Most of the discussion of child support guidelines thus far examines the paradigmatic question of how much support is owed by each parent of a child with two parents. But what happens when one or both parents have additional children in a second family? And what if one or both parents enter into a subsequent partnership with someone who has a child from an earlier relationship? Each of these facts can affect the establishment and modification of the child support obligation. Four questions occur most frequently. First, should the financial resources and obligations of a new partner of a parent affect the parent's child support obligation when the parent's own income does not change? Second, should the answer change if the parent's economic situation improves because he or she can depend on the income of the new partner? Third, should an obligor parent's child support decrease because the child's standard of living improves due to the household's access to the new partner's financial resources? Fourth, if it is relevant to consider the financial resources of the partner of a child's parent, should the consideration vary depending on whether the parent is custodial or noncustodial?

In the case of *Donohue v. Getman, supra*, the court stressed what is considered the usual rule, that a stepparent owes no duty of support to stepchildren, so the fact that the obligor has stepchildren should be irrelevant to the question of how much support the parent owes his or her own children. Similarly, the fact that an obligee lives in a household with a partner who has substantial financial resources should not reduce the obligor's child support duty to his or her children, because the partner has no duty of support to the obligor's child. As Section A of this Chapter suggests, however, the rule of non-liability has limited applicability when the child resides with the stepparent. One can understand *Donohue*, therefore, as more a statement of policy than a fully accurate statement of law. What are the policy considerations that might lead a court to make such a generalization, and do all courts agree with *Donohue* about the irrelevancy of a parent's other resources and obligations?

KESTNER v. CLARK

Alaska Supreme Court

182 P.3d 1117 (2008)

FABE, C.J.

[Diane and Christopher had one son, Nathan, born in 1990. Nathan was in Diane's custody until he turned 14, when Christopher was granted school-year custody. In the child support proceeding which followed, Diane, now the non-custodial parent, sought a downward deviation from the presumptively correct guidelines amount to $50/month based on her lack of income. Diane had stopped working for pay in 2001, when she had the first of her two children with her second spouse. She had previously earned about $21,000 a year. She had another child soon after, so she was caring for 3 children, including Nathan, for three years. She estimated that child care costs would be between $9,000 and $10,000/year, making her paid employment uneconomic. At the time of the child support hearing, Diane's spouse had an annual adjusted gross income of nearly $64,000, and the family had a net worth exceeding $450,000. The court refused discovery of the income of Christopher's co-resident fiancé, but Diane testified that Christopher and his fiancé had a combined household income of between $90,000 and $100,000, and the only child in the household was Nathan. The trial court imputed income of $25,000 to Diane, with a resultant child support order of $299 a month.]

Diane appeals the superior court's order . . . While she concedes that her decision to leave the work force to care for her three children was voluntary, she challenges the superior court's finding that it was unreasonable. She emphasizes the permissive language in [the] Rule . . . "the court may calculate child support based on a determination of the potential income of a parent who voluntarily and unreasonably is unemployed or underemployed" — and contends that because of her economic circumstances, her decision to stay at home to care for her children is both practical and reasonable. As Diane correctly contends, "[the Rule] does not rigorously command pursuit of maximum earnings." She points to the language of [the Rule], which forbids imputation of income to a parent "who is caring for a child under two years of age to whom the parents owe a joint legal responsibility." And while she concedes that the children for whom she provides care are not from the original marriage, she argues that "the superior court certainly should be able to consider the young age of siblings in determining the reasonableness of the decision." Diane points to the benefits that Nathan received from her staying at home when he lived with her and emphasizes Christopher's acknowledgment that he does not need her financial contribution in order to provide for their son.

Christopher responds that while Diane's decision to stay at home may be subjectively reasonable for her new family, it is objectively unreasonable as a matter of law given her legal duty to support Nathan. Christopher acknowledges that he can afford to provide for Nathan but maintains that regardless of his financial situation, Diane's income should be imputed so that she can properly fulfill her obligation as the non-custodial parent.

Although in most cases, the superior court considers an obligor's actual income in initially determining or later re-calculating a child support award, in some cases it may be appropriate to use an obligor's potential income . . . When deciding whether to impute income, the superior court should consider the totality of the circumstances . . . Parents have a paramount duty to support their children. New obligations incurred after the birth of the parent's first child do not diminish that duty. As the Mississippi Supreme Court put it, a rule relieving a parent of his obligation to support a prior child because of the birth of a subsequent child would "quite literally allow[ ] the non-custodial parent to sire himself out of his child support obligation." Because of the significance of a parent's duty to meet his or her child support obligations, we prioritize fulfillment of that duty over even "legitimate" decisions to be voluntarily unemployed or underemployed. As we have repeatedly recognized, a parent should not be relieved of the obligation to support his or her children except under the most extreme circumstances.

[The] Rule provide[s] for limited exceptions to this general principle, none of which apply to Diane in this case . . . Diane analogizes her situation to the one anticipated in [the] Rule . . . , which forbids imputation of income to a parent who is caring for very young children "of the marriage," and argues that the superior court erred in failing to give adequate weight to the young age of her children in evaluating the reasonableness of her decision to leave the work force. But the rule goes no further than to except obligor parents who care for children "under two years of age" who are "of the marriage" and "to whom the parents owe a joint legal responsibility" from strict adherence to the rule's guidelines. By negative implication, income can be imputed to parents who stay home with children of a subsequent marriage. Because we conclude that the superior court did not err in finding Diane's voluntary unemployment to be unreasonable, we uphold the imputation of income to Diane . . .

Diane maintains that the superior court erred by permitting discovery of her husband's finances but prohibiting discovery of information about Christopher's fiancée's finances. In explaining her ruling on these discovery motions, Judge Collins stated that while information about Diane and Terry, as the heads of the obligor household, was "either relevant or likely to lead to discovery of relevant evidence," information about Nicole's finances did not have "the same potential for relevance."

Diane argues that affirming these discovery orders would have negative policy consequences. She contends that any discovery of economic information should have been reciprocal because the economic information of both parents was equally relevant to the child support determination. But this argument reflects a misunderstanding of the procedural stance of her case: when one parent has primary physical custody, the question . . . is what amount of child support must be paid by the non-custodial parent — the obligor — to support his or her child while that child is not in his or her custody. In other words, the process is naturally one-sided, focusing on the economic circumstances of the obligor parent. When the obligor has remarried, the income of the obligor parent's new spouse may be discoverable if the obligor is seeking a variance from . . . schedule based on financial hardship or where, as here, the obligor is a stay-at-home parent who does not work because of the income of the new spouse. However, the income of the obligor's spouse will not normally be relied upon when calculating the obligor's child support payment . . . Given the procedural stance of this case, the superior court correctly determined that the Kestners' income information was discoverable and Christopher's fiancée's financial information was not.

NOTES

1. *Serial Families and Theories about Child Support.* Compare *Kestner* court's analysis to the following excerpt. If the court had accepted this approach, what, if anything, would it have done differently?

Existing child support guidelines in most states exclude from consideration the income of a custodial parent's new spouse. . . . The logic of the stepparent-income exclusion is straightforward. The new spouse, it is said, has no legal obligation to provide for stepchildren. To assume the new spouse's income is available to his stepchildren, and on this basis reduce the child support obligation of the children's noncustodial legal parent would, in effect, improperly require a stepparent to support a legal parent's children. Yet this doctrinal logic is in tension with the realities of household finances. Most custodial parents are mothers. When they remarry, their new husbands usually earn at least as much as they do and most often more. The new husband's income thus typically improves the living standard of the custodial household. Regardless of whether the law requires the new husband to support his new wife's children, the addition of his income to the custodial household has that effect. . . .

[Even if states routinely imposed on stepfathers an enforceable obligation to support his or her stepchildren, in general, people] do not believe the existence of a stepfather excuses the legal father from his support obligations. This tells us that the reason for the usual child support rule that excludes the income of a stepparent probably has less to do with our view of the stepparent obligations than it does with ensuring that the legal father is not let off the hook. Might we reasonably compromise by allowing consideration of stepfather income to reduce but not replace the legal father's support obligation? States sometimes do this, although they do not always characterize their actions in this way. One example arises in the application of income-imputation rules. When calculating support, virtually all states will impute income to a parent regarded as shirking employment, but not to a parent whose decision to reduce working hours is considered reasonable in light of all the circumstances (as where reduced employment is thought necessary to care for a young or disabled child). What then of the case in which a remarried custodial mother, for example, reduces her working hours, perhaps to zero, because she can now rely on her new husband's income? In calculating the father's support obligation, should the court impute a full-time equivalent income to the mother (thus reducing the father's support obligation) or should it accept her actual reduced income as her income (thus increasing the father's support obligation)? Some states . . . impute a full-time income to this mother . . . [based on a conclusion that] her reasonable decision to reduce her income does not, in this case, justify an increase in the father's support payments. This conclusion necessarily accepts the stepfather's contribution to the children's support as an appropriate factor to consider in fixing the father's support obligation. Such rules acknowledge the reality that the new family is one economic unit. . . .

It is fair, then, to conclude that despite the general understanding that stepparent income is excluded from support calculations, many states make exceptions and qualifications, reflecting ambivalence about the basic rule. This ambivalence mirrors popular views. . . . There are several possible explanations for these views. The fact that most support guidelines aim to allocate the support obligation between parents in proportion to their incomes may reflect an intuition that this achieves effective equality by equalizing the parental sacrifice. But if the custodial parent benefits financially from her remarriage, then her relative "sacrifice" is less than before. That point becomes especially salient where the custodial parent's new spouse earns more money than the support obligor, because people are not entirely comfortable with a rule that transfers money from a lower income household to a higher income household, especially when the lower income household also has children, as it often does. This example also illustrates another possible explanation of people's reactions: the perception that when the custodial parent's new spouse has a good income, the child's well-being may no longer depend as much upon the support payments. . . .

A sense of symmetry might lead one to assume that the same rules should govern the remarriage of the support obligor as govern the remarriage of the custodial parent. But in the usual situation in which the child lives primarily in one of the parental households, symmetrical treatment is inappropriate. The support obligor's remarriage has no direct impact on the financial well-being of the child who is the intended beneficiary of the support order, and the obligor's new spouse has no obligation to the child. In most cases this provides sufficient basis to conclude that the remarriage has no effect on the support order. A possible exception arises when the obligor was excused from more than nominal support because of his very low income, but now marries someone with an ample income. Especially where the custodial household income is well below the well-being maximum, an upward revision of the support award may be appropriate.

Ira Mark Ellman & Tara O'Toole Ellman, *The Theory of Child Support*, 45 Harv. J. Leg. 107, 153–59 (2008).

Relying on a subsequent spouse for support occurs in cases like *Kestner*, where the custodial parent has additional children with the subsequent spouse and reduced her income from employment. A discussed above, a typical child support statute allows the court to impute income to the parent. *See, e.g.*, Md. Fam. Law. Art. §§ 12-201(h)(2), 12-202(a)(2)(iv). Reliance on a subsequent spouse also occurs when a custodial parent with a new partner is caring for a child with a disabling condition or chronic illness. While many courts sympathize with custodial parents who reduce or terminate paid employment because of the caregiving requirements of these children, the majority of states allow imputation, even when the child is the child of the obligor and not of the subsequent spouse. *See* Karen Syma Czapanskiy, *Chalimony*, ___ NYU J. Law & Soc. Change ___ (forthcoming 2010); *Dunlap v. Fiorenza*, 738 A.2d 312 (1999) (annual income of $50,000 a year imputed to custodial parent who terminated paid work, in part, due to caregiving requirements of child with severe ADHD).

2. *Priority of One Family over Another.* New families lead to new children as well as new spouses with income or needs. Can a support obligor obtain a reduction in the order's amount to enable him to spend more on his new children? Many states apply a firm rule of "first in time, first in right" and reject downward modification motions in this case. *See, e.g., In re Marriage of Vucic*, 576 N.E.2d 406 (1991) (new family obligation does not lessen duty to support children from prior marriage); *Feltman v. Feltman*, 434 N.W.2d 590 (S.D. 1989) (obligor who becomes responsible for supporting new children does so knowing of continuing responsibility to existing children). *Feltman* rejected a constitutional attack on the statutory preference for the first family, finding the classification rational. If the second relationship also ends, so that a court is now asked to set a support order for the second set of children, the most commonly applied rule reduces the obligor's income by the amount of the first support order in calculating the guideline amount for support of the second set of children. Laura w. Morgan, Child Support Guidelines: Interpretation and Application 3-45 (collecting citations to relevant state guidelines).

The "first" family may be the one reaching court first, rather than the one with the obligor's oldest child. Some states give these families priority by counting all of the obligor's income as available for supporting the child, even where the obligor is supporting other children in his or her household. *See, e.g.,* Md. Fam. Law. Art. § 12-202(a)(2)(iii) & (iv) (presence of child in parent's household pertinent to whether to deviate from guidelines); *Gallaher v. Elam*, 104 S.W.3d 455 (Tenn. 2003) (no constitutional barrier to calculating child support obligation for first child to sue without regard to obligor's duty of support to obligor's older co-resident children).

Favoring first children, however defined, has a procedural appeal, because of the difficulties inherent in getting all the parties to court simultaneously to establish or modify a child support order. Some states resolve the procedural issues by creating a hypothetical order taking into account all of the children owed support by the same parent and then allocating the appropriate portion to the children affected by the litigation. *See, e.g.,* N.D. Admin. Code § 75-02-04.1-06.1; Tex. Fam. Code Ann. §§ 154.128-129. Others provide a formulaic adjustment where a parent is owes a duty to another child in his or her home. D.C. Code § 16-916.01(d)(5).

Despite the procedural complications, a minority of states reject the rules favoring the children of the first family. *See, e.g., Martinez v. Martinez*, 660 A.2d 13 (N.J. Ch. Div. 1995) (subsequent child's right to adequate support not dependent on timing of birth); *Rohr v. Rohr*, 911 P.2d 133 (Idaho 1996) (remarriage and new child states claim for downward modification); *In re Marriage of Paulin*, 54 Cal. Rptr. 2d 314 (App. 1996) ("hardship deduction" available for obligor seeking downward modification who has twins with new wife). Many states take an intermediate position. Some admit facts about the new family as part of the exercise of the trial court's discretion. Another way to handle the issue is to "provide that the consideration of subsequent children may only be used 'defensively' and not 'offensively.' This means that an obligor may not . . . seek a modification on the support obligation on the grounds that he or she has new children. . . . The obligor may, however, defend a motion for an upward modification . . . on the grounds that he or she has new children. . . ." MORGAN, supra, at 3-51; *see also Taylor v. McGlothlin*, 919 P.2d 1349 (Alaska 1996) (trial court did not abuse discretion in setting support for prior children less than guideline level after considering obligor's subsequent children); *Molstad v. Molstad*, 535 N.W.2d 63 (Wis. Ct. App. 1995) (trial court properly considered needs of subsequent children in addressing modification petition brought by mother of children of first marriage).

For an argument for changing the preference favoring existing families, see Adrienne Lockie, *Multiple Families, Multiple Goals, Multiple Failures*, 32 HARV. J. L.& GENDER 109 (2009)(proposes replacing "first family first" child support approach with limited equalization approach resulting in more equality of treatment of all the children of a particular parent; argues that change more consistent with family composition, more beneficial to children in poorer families, and produces greater gender equity).

PROBLEM

Problem 5-19.   John and Alice each earn $40,000 at the time of their divorce. Under their state's income shares guideline, Alice, who has custody of their 6 year old son Donald, and John each have a child support obligation of $519 a month. Five years later, both John and Alice have remarried. Each has a new child with the new spouse. John's new spouse, who had worked as a school secretary, moves to part time work after their child is born. She would prefer to stop work altogether, but she and John cannot afford that on John's annual salary of $40,000. Alice quits work entirely after her child is born. Her new spouse is an attorney who earns $175,000 annually, and they are able to live comfortably with Alice home tending both Donald and their new child. Under the state's support guidelines, Alice is entitled to an increase in child support to $644 if her income has declined to nothing. She seeks an increase, saying that it is reasonable for her to quit work with a newborn. Assume that the local practice is not to attribute income to a parent who stays home to care for a very young child. Should this case be treated differently? Suppose John seeks a reduction in child support. He simply wants to have more money to provide a better environment for his new family. He argues that even if he paid no support — which is not what he asks — Donald would still live better than John and his new family, because of income of Alice's new husband. How much of a reduction, if any, should be granted?

[b]   Retroactive Modification

PRICE v. PRICE
Kentucky Supreme Court
912 S.W.2d 44 (1995)

STEPHENS, C.J.

This appeal arises from an order of the . . . Circuit Court relieving [David's] obligation to pay child support arrearages which accrued from October 31, 1990, until February 14, 1992. The Court of Appeals affirmed this decision. We do not agree.

David . . . (hereinafter Father) and Janet Price (hereinafter Mother) were divorced in 1987. [T]he couple had one minor son (hereinafter Child). . . . Mother was awarded custody . . . Father was ordered to pay $1400 per month in . . . support. . . .

In an attempt to correct some behavioral problems, the parents agreed to change Child's residence, from Mother to Father. The change occurred on October 31, 1990. The Child remains in Father's home. Father stopped all payment . . . as of [that date]. Mother filed a motion to compel Father to pay . . . arrearages on February 14, 1992. Father [then] filed for modification of the child support decree and a legal change of custody. Thereafter . . . Mother and Father entered into an agreed order changing custody from Mother to Father.

. . . Father maintains that because he was in physical custody of Child and providing for all necessities of Child that he was not obligated to pay Mother child support between October 31, 1990 and [the date of the order changing custody in 1992]. [¶] It is undisputed that . . . legal custody of Child was not changed from Mother until the agreed order of April 27, 1992.

The trial court found that . . . "it would be unfair to require that child support be paid" by Father after October 31, 1990. The Court of Appeals . . . found no abuse of discretion. . . . This Court finds that the trial judge had no power to relieve Father of his . . . obligations which became due between the time Child changed residences and the filing of the motion for a modification of that order.

. . . KRS § 403.213 . . . explicitly states that "the provisions of any decree respecting child support may be modified only as to installments accruing subsequent to the filing of a motion for modification . . ." [No] motion for modification was made to the court prior to Father's motion [in] 1992. . . . There is no ambiguity in the wording of this statute.

This statute is in place to avoid litigation when one parent decides what is best for the child, much like the case before us now. Once a court has issued an order for . . . child support, neither parent can unilaterally decide upon a different course of action. In issuing this order, the court, along with the legislature, has made a determination as to what is best for the child. It is unfortunate that divorcing parents are often unable to make these decisions, but divorce by its nature is a time of conflict. We have recognized that many parents do agree, without the aid of the courts, as to modifications of custody and child support. In those instances, a court has the power to recognize the modification of the child support obligation and reduce the arrearages accordingly.

A court will enforce a private agreement . . . if it meets certain requirements. If the agreement is oral it must be proven with reasonable certainty and the court must find "that the agreement is fair and equitable under the circumstances." *Whicker v. Whicker*. Moreover, the agreement, once proven, will only be enforced if the "modification might reasonably have been granted, had a proper motion to modify been brought." *Id.*

Furthermore, . . . *Whicker* reinforces the fundamental concept that child support can only be modified prospectively. This Court has long understood "that unpaid periodical payments for maintenance of children, . . . become vested when due." *Dalton v. Dalton*. As a result and "as a matter of fact, each installment of child support becomes a lump sum judgment, unchangeable by the trial court when it becomes due and is unpaid." *Stewart v. Raikes*. Accordingly, "the courts are without authority to 'forgive' vested rights in accrued maintenance." *Mauk*. In the case before us, . . . there was no agreement . . . as to a modification. . . . We will not reach into this dispute and find an implicit agreement.

Appellee urges that equitable principles require [relief] . . . because he, in fact, supported his child while Child lived in Father's home. We understand that "equity provides relief where the law does not furnish a remedy." *Heisley v. Heisley*. Here, appellee's recourse was at law, by the filing of a motion for modification or at least coming to an agreement with the custodial parent when circumstances warranted. Moreover, appellee took his child into his home in an attempt to correct some problems Child was having. The support given, while admirable, is the support of a parent. That does not impact the court ordered child support. As we stated long ago:

> . . . If a party wishes to contribute to the support of his children in some manner other than that in which a court has directed, the court is always open to a timely application for modification. If he does it without such permission it is not incumbent on the court to give him any credit for it.

Tucker v. Tucker, Ky., 398 S.W.2d 238, 239 (1965)

. . . [T]he trial court abused its discretion in relieving appellee's child support arrearages. Under the circumstances, the trial court did not . . . have the power to do so. Accordingly, the Court of Appeals is reversed and this case is remanded for proceedings in conformity with this opinion.

WINTERSHEIMER, Justice, Dissenting.

. . . [T]he oral agreement between the parties satisfied any . . . obligation. The change in actual custody and the ending of child support payments constituted a complete acquiescence by the wife to the oral modification of the custody agreement. Equity prevents the wife from receiving . . . payments for the period that the husband provided all the support for the son.

The parties may modify child support by oral agreement. Such agreements are enforceable prospectively if they can be proven with reasonable certainty and they are fair and equitable and if the modification is on the same terms as might reasonably been granted [by the court]. This Court has recognized that many parents can agree without the aid of the legal system to a modification of custody and child support. Clearly, a court [can] recognize the modification . . . and . . . reduce the arrearage accordingly.

The situation presented here is highly inequitable. The mother waived her right to child support by surrendering physical custody of the child for almost two years. . . . There is no equitable reason to provide a windfall. . . . The trial judge was acting with proper discretion. . . . The Court of Appeals . . . properly found no abuse of discretion. . . . Now a majority of this Court "finds" that the trial judge had no power to relieve the father of his . . . obligations. This is clearly an invasion of the fact finding authority of the trial judge. Neither the law nor equity supports such a substitution of findings.

This case teaches a very harsh lesson to . . . litigants in a domestic relations matter. . . . [I]t is always necessary to obtain such modification in writing and with the specific approval of the circuit court. It is a primary but hard lesson that voluntary payments and even beneficial conduct are simply that, only voluntary, and clearly have no legal support.

NOTE

Rule Against Retroactive Modification. *Price* is a particularly harsh application of the rule, required by federal law, 42 U.S.C. § 666(a)(9)(C), barring retroactive modification of child support payments. The act, familiarly known as the Bradley Amendment, mandates that every "payment or installment of support under any child support order . . . is (on and after the date it is due) . . . not subject to retroactive modification" in any state. There are no exceptions, although a court may modify a support obligation as of the date on which the modification petition itself was filed. *See* 45 C.F.R. §§ 302.70(a), 303.106.

The federal law was well-motivated. At one time, support obligors who believed themselves entitled to a reduction in their obligation commonly would simply pay less, forcing the obligee to seek enforcement of the full award. If such enforcement was sought, the obligor would counterclaim for retroactive modification. The obligor thus had little to lose by the self-help tactic of reducing his payments, and he might benefit inappropriately if the obligee left his reduction unchallenged for any period of time — as she might if she were financially unable to incur the cost of an enforcement, especially one that was made more complex by a counterclaim for modification. There is now an emerging consensus, however, that the wooden and inflexible federal rule has itself led to serious injustices. *Price* offers a good example: One parent recovers substantial child support for a lengthy period of time during which the child, by parental agreement, was in the other parent's custody. This fact pattern is not rare. *See also Houser v. Houser*, 535 N.W.2d 882 (S.D. 1995) (father ordered to pay $32,000 in arrearages accrued during a ten-year period when two of the couple's three children were living with him). In Maryland, the court refused to modify arrearages owed by the father of four children then in his custody, although he was currently supporting not only those children but also an extended household on wages of $10.96 an hour as a landscaper. The father testified that the arrearage debt adversely affected "his credit rating, prevented him from purchasing or financing a home, and undermined his ability to pay and save for his children's education." *Harvey v. Marshall*, 884 A.2d 1171 (Md. 2005); *see* Daniel L. Hatcher, *Child Support Harming Children: Subordinating the Best Interests of Children to the Fiscal Interests of the State*, 42 WAKE FOREST L. REV. 1029 (2007) (criticizing outcome as ignoring usual test of whether child support award serves the best interests of the child).

The retroactive modification ban also can combine with the rule refusing credit for nonconforming payments to produce inequitable results. In *Niemi v. Fisher*, 547 N.W.2d 801 (Wisc. Ct. App. 1996), obligor paid the custodial parent directly, rather than through the court clerk; the obligee then obtained a judgment for "unpaid" arrearages, plus interest. The appeals court, affirming, wrote:

> We confess that the results . . . are troublesome because . . . [obligor] made direct payments. Because [the relevant statutes] preclude recognition of these payments, [obligee] is unfairly enriched by double payments. This is a public policy decision made by the legislature, apparently on the belief that the public interest in addressing the problem of nonpayment of child support is best served by limiting payments to those made in accordance with the divorce judgment. This policy fixes arrearages with certainty and facilitates the determination as to who owes arrearages and what amount.

Id. at 815; *see also In re: Marriage of Lehr*, 740 N.E.2d 417 (Ill. App. 2000) (rejecting reimbursement for voluntary overpayment of support because it would constitute retroactive modification).

Despite the rule against modification, some courts rely on doctrines of equity to estop obligees from seeking arrearages in some situations. *See, e.g., Nill v. Martin*, 666 N.E.2d 936 (Ind. App. 1996) (no arrearage recovery where parents agreed to reduce support when one of three children died, even though award itself specified a gross amount rather than an amount per child); *Bowens v. Bowens*, 668 A.2d 90 (N.J. App. 1995) (permitting retroactive modification to date of child's attainment of majority or emancipation); *Brakke v. Brakke*, 525 N.W.2d 687 (N.D. 1994) (permitting retroactive modification where child changed residence and lived with obligor); *Ours v. Glocke*, 514 N.W.2d 724 (Wisc. Ct. App. 1993) (obligee estopped from seeking arrearages for six-year period during which children lived with obligor); *Johnston v. Johnston*, 552 N.E.2d 93 (Ill. App. 1990) (mother estopped from collecting arrearages accruing while child lived with father, when she had told him he need not pay). In one kind of case, the support obligor cannot make current support payments that will reach the child because the custodial parent has concealed herself and the child. When the custodial parent reappears, can she now collect arrearages covering the concealment period? Courts have divided. *See, e.g., In re Shorten*, 967 P.2d 797 (Mont. 1998) (concealment of child for 8 years by custodial parent leads to an estoppel); *In re Marriage of Damico*, 872 P.2d 126 (Cal. 1994) (mother estopped from seeking arrearages where she actively concealed child from obligor). *But see In re Vroenen*, 94 Cal. App. 4th 1176 (Cal. App. 2001) (rejecting concealment as basis for estoppel where concealment ended before child reached majority). For more on these cases, see Ira Ellman, *Should Visitation Denial Affect the Obligation to Pay Support?, in* THE LAW AND ECONOMICS OF CHILD SUPPORT PAYMENTS (Comanor, ed. 2004), reprinted in 36 ARIZ. ST. L.J. 661 (2004).

A Massachusetts court rejected a former prisoner's suit for rescission of child support debts accrued during his imprisonment. *D'Avella v. McGonigle*, 711 N.E. 2d 882 (Mass. 1999). The court noted the lack of explicit exceptions to the statutory ban on retroactive modification of child support debts. A similar situation with an egregious twist was reported more recently. Clarence Brandley, a Texas school janitor, was released from prison in 1992 on a finding by a state appeals court that he had been wrongfully convicted of murder. In 1993, however, his wages were garnished for about $35 weekly for support arrearages which accrued during his nine years of wrongful imprisonment. Brandley described the situation as a "double insult," and asserted the state ought to forgive or pay his arrears because it had wrongfully placed him on death row for nine years. A spokesman for the Attorney General's office, acknowledging "special circumstances," said the "obligation for child support does not go away." An attorney who represented Brandley in a support arrearage action in 1993 noted the action was begun "shortly after Brandley filed a $120 million civil rights lawsuit against an array of state agencies" which was later dismissed on the basis of sovereign immunity. Rice, *"It's Like a Double Insult": Free From Prison, Brandley Baffled by Order to Pay Back Child Support*, HOUST. CHRON., Apr. 27, 2002, at 1.

C. ENFORCEMENT OF SUPPORT ORDERS

[1]   Traditional Difficulties in Collecting Support

According to reports from custodial parents, in surveys conducted by the Census Bureau, a significant proportion of children do not receive support from an absent parent. Non-marital fathers are disproportionately represented in the group of non-supporters. It seems the usual problem is not that a support order is ignored but that no order has been obtained. In the 2004 survey, only 60% of the nearly 14 million parents living with children under 21 whose other parent was not living in the household reported having either a decree or an agreement for child support. U.S. Department of Commerce, Bureau of the Census, *Custodial Mothers and Fathers and Their Child Support: 2003, Current Population Reports, Consumer Income*, Series P60-230 (July 2006) (hereinafter *"2004 Data"*).

Several types of explanations were offered by parents without an award or agreement. Perhaps surprisingly, of the 5.9 million such parents, only about 15.6% claimed to be unable to locate the absent parent. *Id.* at Fig. 3. More than 32% reported they "did not feel the need to make (support arrangements) legal." More than half indicated that the other parent provided what he or she could provide or could not afford more. A total of over 35% reported either that they "did not want the other parent to pay" (19%) or that they did "not want to have contact with the other parent" (16.2%). *Id.* While 64.2% of female custodial parents had obtained an award or agreement for child support, only 39.8% of male custodial parents reported agreements or awards imposing a support obligation on non-custodial mothers. *Id.*

What would explain a refusal to seek support? Some custodial parents, because of their partner's attitude or meager resources, conclude a support suit would be futile. Others want to minimize or eliminate further interaction with the absent parent. Some fear that former partners will use violence against them or their children if they pursue child support. *See* Naomi Stern, *Battered By The System: How Advocates Against Domestic Violence Have Improved Victims' Access to Child Support and TANF*, 14 HASTINGS WOMEN'S L.J. 47 (2003); Susan Notar & Vicki Turetsky, *Models for Safe Child Support Enforcement*, 8 AM. U. J. GENDER, SOC. POL'Y & L. 657 (2000). The phenomenon of custodial parents entitled to, yet not seeking, support may be a particular example of the common situation in which a right-holder fails to enforce his or her rights either in court or elsewhere. But, of course, here the custodial parent is failing to enforce his or her child's or children's support rights.

In those same surveys, custodial parents who do have awards or support agreements often report that they did not receive payments that were due. Of custodial parents to whom child support was owed in 2003, only 45.3% reported receiving the full amount due, 31.1% reported partial payment, and 23.6% received none of the expected support. *2004 Data* at Fig. 4. From other studies, it seems certain that comparable surveys of noncustodial parents would produce reports of greater compliance. Unfortunately it is not possible to be certain of the actual facts. A study in the late 1980's of 378 divorcing families in Maricopa County, Arizona (Phoenix) found a higher compliance rate regarding child support obligations than that found by the Census Bureau surveys, with only 16% of divorced custodial mothers reporting no child support payments as opposed to approximately 25% in the Census Bureau data. Custodial mothers reported 71% of all court-awarded support paid, compared to the Census data which, during that time period using a different methodology than currently used, reported full receipt in the 60–65% range. The difference can be traced in part to the fact that the Arizona study was limited to divorcing families, while the Census data includes never-married custodial mothers. Such a finding is consistent with the popular perception of non-marital fathers being less involved with their children than the fathers of in-wedlock children.

The Arizona study also tested the Census Bureau's methodology by asking support *obligors* how much support had been paid. Not surprisingly, the reports were not identical. Obligors reported having paid 93% of their obligations. Fully 2/3 of obligors reported having paid at least 100% of their support obligations during the preceding 12 months (11% reported having paid more than the required amount). By contrast, only 45% of custodial parents reported their ex-spouse was current in support payments. *See* Sanford Braver, Pamela J. Fitzpatrick & R. Curtis Bay, *Noncustodial Parent's Report of Child Support Payments*, 40 FAM. REL. 180 (1991). The authors did not speculate on whether the custodial or noncustodial parents were being more truthful.

The increased efforts at enforcement detailed in the rest of this Chapter seem to be having a positive impact on the effectiveness of child support collection. Between 1993 (when the Census Bureau changed its methodology and thus rendered earlier data non-comparable) and 2004, the percentage of custodial parents reporting full payment of owed support rose from 36.9% of those who were owed support to 45.3

in 2003. *2004 Data* at Fig. 4. Comparison of the Census data in 1993 and 2004 also makes clear that while more custodial parents reported receiving all support due in 2003, the percentage reporting partial receipt declined from 38.9% in the earlier year to 31.1% in the latter year. *2004 Data* at Fig. 4.

It has long been asserted that there is a linkage between contact with the child and the payment of child support. The 2004 data supports the existence of such a link. At least some child support was reported paid in approximately 79.2% of the cases in which the obligor had either joint custody or visitation privileges, as compared to only 62.5% of the cases lacking any legally-mandated access to the child. *2004 Data* at 8.

The average child support payments reported received in 2005 was $4,717, U.S. Department of Commerce, Bureau of the Census, *The 2009 Statistical Abstract*, Table 549. While approximately 77% of all custodial parents who were due money actually received some during 2005, only 46% reported receiving the full amount and 23% reported receiving none of the child support that was due. *Id.*

What explains non-collection of support orders? The most important impediment is the fact that such orders usually require multiple periodic payments. Obviously there is a greater risk of non-compliance when compliance requires performance of a series of acts over a long period of time. Enforcing support judgments, therefore, requires enforcement mechanisms such as the threat of jail or garnishment of wages. Some courts, however, are reluctant to jail non-paying obligors. Another factor contributing to under-enforcement is difficulty in identifying and locating obligors (particularly those living far from the child) or the obligor's assets. Another difficulty is that the obligor may have inadequate financial resources. A study of child support debtors in California found that many child support orders are too high relative to the incomes of the low and moderate-income obligors, with some ordered to pay twice their income; that only half of child support obligors with arrearage debts were employed; and that their average earnings were below those of other workers. Elaine Sorensen, Heather Koball, Kate Pomper & Chava Zibman, *Examining Child Support Arrears in California: The Collectability Study* (Urban Institute, Mar. 2003). There is no easy solution where parents of limited financial means incur more obligations than they can fulfill. (Recall Wisconsin's unsuccessful attempt to deny marriage licenses to obligors delinquent in existing support obligations in *Zablocki*, reprinted in Chapter 2.) Finally, in the past, enforcement was left to the custodial parent, who had to initiate the necessary legal proceedings. The need to pursue the non-paying parent often presented a financial or emotional obstacle for a custodial parent not anxious for contact with the absent parent. Incomplete records concerning payments often make such litigation difficult. Such problems have contributed to increasing government involvement in the enforcement of support.

[2]   Governmental Involvement in Support Enforcement

Paul K. Legler, *The Coming Revolution in Child Support Policy: Implications of the 1996 Welfare Act*
30 Fam. L.Q. 519, 520–24 (1996)

We have seen the American family undergo dramatic structural changes in the last thirty years. The skyrocketing increase in . . . out-of-wedlock births coupled with the high rate of divorce means that more and more families are single parent families. The custodial parent . . . is often the sole source of financial support, and since that parent is often a mother with low income, millions . . . are subject to a childhood of poverty. Efforts to reduce poverty for children in single parent families will require a broad, comprehensive strategy. One part of that comprehensive strategy . . . is the need for increased child support collections through better child support enforcement.

Efforts to increase child support enforcement are not new. Congress first passed an amendment to the Social Security Act in 1975 which required each state to develop its own child support enforcement program, commonly known as the "IV-D" program. It established the child support system as a joint federal and state effort with the federal government providing partial funding for IV-D programs and providing oversight and technical assistance. The federal government also operates the Federal Parent Locator Service (FPLS). States operate their own IV-D programs with substantial discretion but with certain program requirements imposed by federal law.

The original legislation creating the IV-D program has been . . . expanded several times. State IV-D programs must currently provide child support services to all cases where the custodial parent receives AFDC or Medicaid. These individuals must assign their right to receive child support to the state. State agencies must also serve any other individual custodial parent who requests services. . . . It is estimated that 60 percent or more of all child support cases are now in this public IV-D collection system. Non-IV-D cases . . . are handled through private arrangements. . . .

Yet, despite some successes, . . . we still have a long way to go. A . . . report issued in 1994 by the Urban Institute showed just how far the current child support system falls short.[24]

The report showed an immense gap between what is currently collected in child support and what could theoretically be collected. According to the findings, if child support orders, reflecting current ability to pay, were to be established for all children with a living noncustodial father, and these orders were fully enforced, aggregate child support payments would have been as high as $48.2 billion dollars in 1990. Only $14.4 billion was actually received. Thus, there is a gap between what

---

[24] Elaine Sorenson, Noncustodial Fathers: Can They Afford to Pay More Child Support? (Urban Institute 1994) (hereinafter "Urban Institute").

is currently received and what could theoretically be collected of $33.8 billion dollars per year. . . .[25]

Three facts that emerge . . . are striking. First, the total picture the reports show is bleak — millions of children are not receiving the support they deserve. Second, the gap from the inadequacy of awards ($7.0 billion) is as large as from the failure to collect what is owed ($7.2 billion). Third, and perhaps most importantly, the largest part of the gap ($19.6 billion) is due to the failure to obtain child support awards. Because the lack of paternity establishment is the chief reason for a lack of awards, improving paternity establishment is crucial to closing the collection gap.

NOTE ON FEDERAL INVOLVEMENT IN SUPPORT ENFORCEMENT

As noted by Legler, Congress in the past three decades has mandated many improvements and expansion of state techniques of enforcing child support. "Quietly — almost without notice — Congress has spent the last 15 years altering the nature of America's family law system." PAULA ROBERTS, TURNING PROMISES INTO REALITIES: A GUIDE TO IMPLEMENTING THE CHILD SUPPORT PROVISIONS OF THE FAMILY SUPPORT ACT OF 1988 1 (Center for Law and Social Policy 1989). The IV-D child support enforcement agency described in the excerpt was designed to "help locate absent parents, establish paternity, obtain support orders and enforce those orders." Id.

In some states, the IV-D agency is located within the human services or welfare department. In other states, the local contact is affiliated with the county attorney's office or as an administrative branch of the courts. The trend is toward incorporating the IV-D agency responsibilities within a state government agency with other significant law enforcement responsibilities, such as the Attorney General's Office or the State Department of Revenue.

Historically, most IV-D "clients" have been welfare recipients. Services to welfare families were pursued more vigorously by the states because of their taxpayers' pocketbook interest in seeking reimbursement and elimination of AFDC awards. See Daniel L. Hatcher, Child Support Harming Children: Subordinating the Best Interests of Children to the Fiscal Interests of the State, 42 WAKE FOREST L. REV. 1029 (2007) (describes history and present workings of welfare cost recovery process through assignment of child support; concludes that program does not serve the best interests of children and is a failure).

Federal law makes clear that non-welfare families must have equal access to IV-D services. In re Marriage of Lappe, 680 N.E.2d 380 (Ill. 1997) (state provision of such services is mandated by Federal statutes and not violative of state constitutional provision limiting expenditure of public funds to "public purposes");

---

[25] According to the study, 21% of the $33.8 billion, or $7.2 billion, is due to a failure to collect what is ordered; another 21%, or $7.0 billion, is due to inadequate awards; and 58%, $19.6 billion, is due to the fact that many potentially eligible custodial parents do not have a legal child support award or order. Some caution must be taken in using the numbers from this study. The collection gap of $34 billion dollars represents what could "theoretically" be collected, not court ordered child support that was not paid.

Cabinet for Human Resources v. Houck, 908 S.W.2d 673 (Ky. 1995) (same). While ordinarily obligees are served by the support agency, obligors may also use the agency in various matters such as the establishment of parenthood, petition for a downward modification, etc.

In fact, a substantial number of IV-D cases do not involve "welfare" clients. By 2002, because of the late 1990's welfare reform limiting access to TANF, the vast majority of IV-D child support collection cases involved obligees who were not currently receiving government assistance. According to the federal Office of Child Support Enforcement, only 2.8 million of the 16 million IV-D cases were welfare cases in 2002 (because of changes in methodology the 2002 data is not directly comparable to earlier data). www.acf.hhs.gov/programs/cse/pubs/2003/ reports/prelim_datareport/Table 1.

States are required to charge custodial parents who have never received TANF-funded assistance an annual fee of $25 if the state collects at least $500 in support. 42 USC § 666(a)(10)(A)(i). Retained counsel may use IV-D services such as the parent locator service. Once the absent parent is located, legal procedures to obtain or enforce an order can be instituted, either by the agency or by private counsel.

The 1984 Child Support Amendments (Pub. L. 98-378) used the conditional spending power to encourage states to enact a number of specific remedies and procedures designed to improve support enforcement and to equalize treatment of welfare and non-welfare families. States, for example, were required to create expedited processes for establishment of support orders in IV-D cases. Additional requirements applicable to all child support cases (not just IV-D cases) included automatic wage withholding for obligors in arrears and allowing establishment of paternity at any time until the child's 18th birthday. The 1988 Family Support Act (Pub. L. 100-485) and the Personal Responsibility and Work Opportunity Reconciliation Act of 1996 (Pub. L. 104-193) (hereinafter "PRWORA") imposed additional requirements concerning enforcement. As one court described the changes under PRWORA:

> The PRWORA, also known as "welfare reform," made sweeping changes in social policy relating to low-income people. It replaced the Aid to Families with Dependent Children (AFDC) program with the Temporary Assistance to Needy Families (TANF) program. The new program consists of federal block grants that are distributed to states, which then use the money to provide cash assistance and other supportive services to low-income families within their borders. Although this funding structure gives the states greater flexibility in designing their own public assistance programs, they are required to work toward program goals, satisfy a maintenance-of-effort requirement for the expenditure of state funds, and abide by federal regulations.

> Title III of the PRWORA amended the Child Support Enforcement Program (IV-D), which provides federal money to assist states in collecting child support from absent parents. *See* 42 U.S.C. §§ 651–669. State IV-D programs must currently provide child support services to all cases in which the custodial parent either receives temporary assistance under TANF or Medicaid, or requests IV-D assistance.

The PRWORA imposes greater federal oversight and control over the states' participation in the IV-D program in an effort to increase efficiency in child support enforcement, particularly in interstate cases, through information sharing, mass case processing, and uniformity. Among other things, the states must establish a Case Registry which contains all child support orders within the state, *see id.* § 653a, and a Directory of New Hires, *see id.* § 654a. These databases are regularly matched against one another and against a Federal Case Registry and National Directory of New Hires, which function as part of the existing Federal Parent Locator Service. *See id.* § 653.

The PRWORA also requires states to adopt the Uniform Interstate Family Support Act. *See id.* § 666(f). This act, which has been passed by the legislatures of all fifty states, allows state agencies to send income-withholding orders across state lines directly to employers. In addition, the PRWORA requires states to pass laws facilitating genetic testing and paternity establishment, *see id.* § 666(a)(5), and authorizing state child support agencies to take expedited enforcement action against non-paying noncustodial parents, *see id.* § 666(c). When a parent fails to pay child support, the PRWORA requires states to revoke passports, suspend professional and other licenses, place liens on property, and notify consumer credit reporting agencies, *see id.* §§ 652(k), 666(a)(1)–(4), (6)–(7), (16).

Kansas v. United States, 214 F. 3d 1196 (10th Cir. 2000); *see* Stacy L. Brustin, *The Intersection Between Welfare Reform and Child Support Enforcement*, 52 Cath. U.L. Rev. 621 (2003); Linda Elrod, *Child Support Reassessed: Federalization of Enforcement Nears Completion*, 1997 U. Ill. L. Rev. 695 (predicts improvement of support enforcement alone will not solve problem of child poverty and argues current law reduces public support for families by focusing on support enforcement rather than assistance to needy families); Ann Laquer Estin, *Federalism and Child Support*, 5 Va. J. of Soc. Pol'y & l. 541 (1998) (discusses use of Commerce and Spending Power to promulgate federal support legislation; argues "boundaries between national and state power are worth preserving in family law and . . . Congress and the courts have important roles to play in helping to preserve the balance").

While responsibility for support enforcement remains with the states, considerable federal resources are available to initiate and finance state programs. States meeting the minimum standards established by OCSE receive substantial federal funding for the administrative costs of collection programs.

How successful has the effort to increase support collection been? Collections by the state IV-D agencies continue to increase every year. Support collection of current year's support went from $6 billion in FY 1990 to $9.5 billion in FY 1998 to $19 billion in FY 2008. U.S. Department of Health and Human Services, Office of Child Support Enforcement, *Thirteenth Annual Report to Congress* 6-7 (1990); U.S. Department of Health and Human Services, Office of Child Support Enforcement, *FY 2008 Preliminary Report* (2009), http://www.acf.hhs.gov/programs/cse/pubs/2009/reports/preliminary_report_fy2008.

Understood as a percentage of the support owed, collection also has become more successful in the past two decades. For FY 1986, the states collected 45.8% of the amount of current support owed. For FY 1994, they collected 53% of the current support owed. By FY 2008, the comparable percentage was 62%.

While the IV-D program has become progressively more effective in collecting support, a significant part of the improvement stems from the movement of non-welfare cases into the IV-D collection machinery. "Enforcement trends show that non-TANF collections have grown much faster than collections for the purpose of reimbursing welfare costs. From 2002 to 2006, total distributed . . . TANF collections decreased from $2.9 to $2.1 billion, whereas total distributed . . . non-TANF collections increased from $17.2 to $21.8 billion. Thus, . . . non-TANF collections now account for over ninety-one percent of all child support collections. Daniel L. Hatcher, *Child Support Harming Children: Subordinating the Best Interests of Children to the Fiscal Interests of the State*, 42 WAKE FOREST L. REV. 1029 (2007).

[3]   Enforcement Remedies

[a]   Income Withholding

Traditionally, wage garnishment was rarely employed to enforce child support awards. State and federal law often barred garnishment for certain categories of workers. Even where available, garnishment could be obtained only where an obligor was in arrears and required a new action by the obligee ordering payment of a specific amount of money. Because future payments were not yet debts (before becoming due), no garnishment order could be obtained to secure their payment. Thus, a garnishment order would expire upon satisfaction of the arrearage. Meanwhile, the obligor might have missed current payments, creating a new arrearage which required reduction to judgment for a new garnishment order. Another difficulty under traditional rules was the inability to gain jurisdiction over an obligor's out-of-state employer. *Champion Int'l Corp. v. Ayars*, 587 F. Supp. 1274 (D. Conn. 1984). Thus, at one time that main successful enforcement technique was imprisonment for contempt rather than garnishment as shown in a famous study by Professor David Chambers detailed in Section C.3.b, *infra*.

Today this has all changed. Largely because of federal requirements imposed during the 1980s, wage garnishment (now known as income withholding) has become the most important and effective tool for enforcement of support awards. Income withholding orders require the obligor's employer to deduct the employee's obligation from the paycheck, much like income tax withholding. While distribution formerly could be made either directly to the obligee or to a governmental collection and disbursement agency, the PRWOA (§ 312) generally requires all withholding be collected by a governmental agency and disbursed to the obligee within two business days. Income withholding orders today are not limited to arrearages.

In fact, the success of this technique led Congress — in the Family Support Act — to require all child support orders to include an income withholding order unless the court finds "good cause" for not ordering it or the parties agree in writing to an alternative payment plan. The Child Support Enforcement Amendments of 1984 separately require such income withholding provisions where the obligor is one month in arrears and the "good cause" exception is unavailable in cases of arrearage. The most recent data from the federal Office of Child Support Enforcement reports that approximately 68% percent of payments were collected via income withholding. U.S. Department of Health and Human Services, Office of Child Support Enforcement, *FY 2008 Preliminary Report* (2009), http://www.acf.hhs.gov/programs/cse/pubs/2009/reports/preliminary_report_fy2008. This reflects a quantum leap from the data reported at the beginning of the decade, when the parallel percentage was 56% of the collections or $6.1 billion. U.S. Department of Health and Human Services, Office of Child Support Enforcement, *Twenty-Third Annual Report to Congress*, at p. 31 (2000). States also must make their income withholding procedures available for interstate collection of support. 42 U.S.C. § 666(b)(9); *see* 45 C.F.R. § 303.100(f). PRWORA (§ 321) requires states to adopt the Uniform Interstate Family Support Act which requires employers to comply with income withholding orders of another state (§ 501). *See* Section D, *infra*, for more information.

While enormously helpful, income withholding is not a panacea. Until enactment of the PRWORA (§ 314) in 1996, federal law required only wage withholding and not all obligors earn wages. There are many forms of income other than wages, such as, *e.g.*, a partnership draw in a law firm, patent or book royalties or periodic payments under a mortgage. The Welfare Reform Act required states to enact an expanded definition of accessible resources. Under 42 U.S.C. § 666(b)(8), "income" means "any periodic form of payment due to an individual, regardless of source, including wages, salaries, commissions, bonuses, workers' compensation, disability, payments pursuant to a pension of retirement program, and interest."

While an expanded definition of income certainly helps obligees, there may be practical difficulties in identifying the obligor's non-wage sources of income. Even if the obligor earns income under the state definition, a change of jobs requires transfer of the withholding order to the new employer. Additionally, while federal law now requires states to accommodate interstate withholding, a move by the obligor to a new state may create difficulties in locating the obligor and his or her sources of income. Also, the federal Consumer Credit Protection Act, 15 U.S.C. § 1673(b), limits the amount which can be withheld from an employee's pay check and states may enact lower ceilings. *See, e.g., Wilcox v. Wilcox*, 575 A.2d 127 (Pa. Super. Ct. 1990) (applying state limit of 50% instead of federal ceiling of 65%); Wyo. Stats. § 20-6-210 (limiting withholding to 35% of obligor's disposable income rather than the CCPA's 50%–65% ceiling). Due process requirements, most importantly allowing the obligor to correct mistakes of fact, must be satisfied by the withholding statute and by the procedures utilized in the individual case. For litigation addressing the adequacy of state withholding procedures, see *State ex rel. Sheppard v. Money*, 529 N.E.2d 542 (Ill. 1988) (applying *Mathews v. Eldridge*, 424 U.S. 319 (1976)); *State ex rel. Keasling v. Keasling*, 442 N.W.2d 118 (Iowa 1989) (upholding statute permitting child support agency to order wage attachment).

[b]   Contempt

Prior to the routine use of income withholding, imprisonment for contempt of court was perhaps the most commonly used remedy for recalcitrant support obligors. While perhaps relatively less common today, it is still available in difficult cases.

NOTES

1. *Civil Versus Criminal Contempt.*   One traditional enforcement tool is a contempt action for failure to abide by a child support order. A contempt action may be civil or criminal in nature. While a jail sentence or fine is usually authorized under state law for either type of contempt, the sanctions have different purposes. *Hicks v. Feiock*, 485 U.S. 624 (1985). Criminal contempt results in a fine or jail sentence of definite amount or duration imposed as punishment for violation of a court order and the usual constitutional rules protecting criminal defendants must be followed.

By contrast, the purpose of civil contempt is to coerce compliance with the court order, and it normally results in placing the defendant in jail until he complies by paying. Some contempt proceedings result in a finding of both civil and criminal contempt. Thus, the obligor may be sentenced to a precise term, with the further condition that he will not be released until he purges himself of the contempt by paying his debts. Where incarceration is possible, certain procedures may be mandated. *See Arrington v. Department of Human Resources*, 935 A.2d 432 (Md. 2007) (under Maryland rules and caselaw, if court anticipates prospect of incarceration in a civil attempt action, it must determine whether defendant has the current ability to meet the purge). While *Hicks* holds federal constitutional rights afforded criminal defendants inapplicable in civil contempt, state constitutional or statutory law often grant such rights. Thus, some states provide a jury trial in civil contempt. *See, e.g., Mead v. Batchlor*, 460 N.W.2d 493 (Mich. 1990); *Johansen v. State*, 491 P.2d 759 (Alaska 1971). Likewise, several cases hold that the possibility of any jail sentence (whether civil or criminal contempt) guarantees an indigent defendant appointed counsel. *See, e.g., Black v. Div. of Child Supp. Enforcement*, 686 A.2d 164 (Del. 1996)(jail time impermissible without right to counsel); *Santa Clara Cty. v. Superior Court (Rodriguez)*, 2 Cal. App. 4th 1686 (1992) (appointment of counsel mandated by legislative authorization for governmental payment for indigents' counsel); *Cox v. Slama*, 355 N.W.2d 401 (Minn.1984); *In re Stahira*, 509 N.E.2d 1117 (Ind. App. 1987); *see also* Jack W. Shaw, Jr., Annot., *Right to Counsel in Contempt Proceedings*, 52 A.L.R.3d 1002 (1973). *Hicks* also makes clear that the classification of a particular proceeding as civil or criminal contempt is itself a question of federal constitutional law.

For a study examining the effect of the presence of counsel on time spent in jail by civil contemnors, see Michele Hermann & Shannon Donahue, *Fathers Behind Bars: The Right to Counsel in Civil Contempt Proceedings*, 14 N. MEX. L. REV. 275 (1984). The authors found unrepresented (72%) defendants spent an average of 14 days in jail, while represented defendants spent an average of three days in jail.

2. *Incarceration and Compliance.* An extensive study in Michigan by Professor David Chambers makes clear that jail for contempt is effective in improving support collections. CHAMBERS, MAKING FATHERS PAY (1979); David L. Chambers, *Men Who Know They Are Watched: Some Benefits and Costs of Jailing for Nonpayment of Support*, 75 MICH. L. REV. 900 (1977).

Created in 1917, the Michigan Friend of Court is a support enforcement agency in each county. Support payments are made to the agency, which forwards them to the obligee. The agency can investigate nonpayment, issue warnings and initiate actions to secure payment, such as contempt proceedings. In his study of 28 counties, Chambers found jail sentences served both as a specific and general deterrent. Not only did those jailed pay more often after their imprisonment, but compliance among those never jailed was higher in areas of well-organized enforcement. The most important factors in explaining the level of support collection were: a) whether the Friend of Court acted on its own in seeking contempt or awaited a complaint by the obligee; b) the frequency of jail sentences (not their length); and c) county size (smaller counties consistently collected a higher percentage of support owed).

Chambers also found that a "credible threat of jail improves the payment record of every identifiable group of men — whether classified by age, type of employment, race, income or events following divorces." The study also refutes claims that aggressive collection techniques are "not worth the expenditures, because you spend more than you collect." For example, it concludes that a "generous" estimate of costs of the enforcement program in one county was $400,000 as compared to almost $3.5 million in support collected. MAKING FATHERS PAY, at 101.

Although his data shows its effectiveness, Chambers is philosophically opposed to jailing people for nonpayment, in part because he believes the sanction is applied unequally. *Id.* at 253. He suggests many who are incarcerated are less blameworthy than those who are not. He found unskilled blue collar workers and men with employment difficulties or alcohol problems overrepresented in jail and managers and professionals underrepresented. *Id.* at 201–16.

He also discredits the notion that attorneys are unnecessary in civil contempt because the defendant has "the jailhouse keys in his pocket." He reports courts did not inquire whether defendant had money available to pay the portion of arrearages required as the price of release. MAKING FATHERS PAY, at 187. Although more than half the jailed men in the study paid enough to be released from jail, Chambers cautions against concluding that this proves that a man is capable of making regular support payments, because the source of the "release" money may be someone other than the jailed man himself. *Id.* at 218–20.

In 1983, Michigan revised its civil contempt procedures to designate jail as the last resort for support violations. Commitment is limited to 45 days for the first contempt order and 90 days for any subsequent order. While incarcerated for contempt, a person may have the privilege of released time to seek or continue work. *See* MICH. COMP. L. §§ 552.633, 552.637. Repeat offenders may also be prosecuted for criminal non-support. *See People v. Parker*, 738 N.W.2d 257 (Mich. Ct. App. 2007).

In an attempt to handle nonsupport cases efficiently and to deter nonpayment, roundups of parents accused of not paying child support are not uncommon. They are often scheduled close to Christmas and Father's Day. *See, e.g.,* Ryan Dezember, *Deputies Hunt for Dead Beat Parents* MOBILE PRESS-REGISTER, June 21, 2009, at B1; *Child-Support Roundup Nets $122,000,* BATON ROUGE ADVOCATE, Dec. 16, 2008; John Appezzato, *N.J. Collects Nearly $300,000 in Child Support Sweep,* Dec. 6, 2008, http://www.nj.com/news/index.ssf/2008/12/nj_collects_nearly_300000_in_ c.html. A Florida roundup involving 480 civil contempt cases heard by a single judge over four days drew some criticism for "the total absence of oaths, court reporters, witnesses, and rules of evidence. *Robbins v. Robbins,* 429 So. 2d 424 (Fla. App. 1983).

3. *Imprisonment for Debt?* Jail terms for contempt in support cases do not violate state constitutional prohibitions on imprisonment for debt because child support is generally held not a debt within the meaning of the prohibition. *In re Pettit,* 626 N.E.2d 444 (Ind. 1993); *Gould v. Gould,* 823 S.W.2d 890 (Ark. 1992); *Ex parte Wilbanks,* 722 S.W.2d 221 (Tex. App. 1986); *Marriage of Lenger,* 336 N.W.2d 191 (Iowa 1983). In fact, some state constitutional provisions prohibiting imprisonment for debt explicitly exempt support debts. *See* MD. CONST. ART. III, § 38.

PROBLEM

Problem 5-20. David has fathered nine children by four different women over the past 15 years. He has been ordered to pay child support for each child, but has not been regular in his payments. He has been convicted of criminal non-support of one child and the trial judge has sentenced him to three years in prison followed by five years of probation. One of the probation conditions is that "David cannot have any more children unless he demonstrates the ability to support new children and that he is supporting his existing children." In the non-jury trial, the judge found that David had the ability to support his existing children, but refused to work. You are law clerk to a judge on the appellate court which will hear David's appeal. What are the issues and how should they be resolved?

[c] Other Enforcement Techniques

[i] Criminal Prosecution

All states criminally punish nonsupport (or abandonment or desertion) of children. About half of these statutes are patterned after the Uniform Desertion and Nonsupport Act. Promulgated in 1910, it read:

> Any . . . parent who shall without lawful excuse, desert or willfully neglect or refuse to provide for the support and maintenance of his or her child or children under the age of sixteen . . . in destitute or necessitous circumstances, shall be guilty of a crime.

10 UNIFORM LAWS ANN. § 1 (1922); *see* VA. CODE § 20-61; WYO. CODE § 20-3-101. A more modern model act adopted in several states is Model Penal Code § 230.5 (MPC) which provides:

A person commits a misdemeanor if he persistently fails to provide support which he can provide and which he knows he is legally obliged to provide to a spouse, child or other dependent.

See Ala. Code § 13A-13-4(a); Neb. Rev. Stats. § 28-706 (excluding failure to pay for abortion if parent wasn't consulted or abortion was not therapeutic); Ky. Rev. Stats. § 530.050(1).

Nonsupport is criminal under the Uniform Act only if the child is left without basic necessities, while the MPC punishes any failure to meet the defendant's "legal" obligation. By incorporating the general standards of child support, the MPC requires more than mere subsistence support. *See, e.g., State v. Davis*, 469 S.W.2d 1 (Mo. 1971) (interpreting MPC-type provision to require support "reasonably suitable to the condition in life and commensurate with the defendant's ability").

While statutes rarely include specific language dealing with mens rea, most courts, because of a reluctance to impose criminal strict liability unless such is clearly statutorily provided, require proof of at least recklessness. *See State v. Collins*, 733 N.E.2d 1118 (Ohio 2000) (lacking evidence of mistake or misdirected payments, failure to pay over a number of years provides sufficient evidence from which recklessness or even intent can be found beyond a reasonable doubt).

Most states treat nonsupport as a misdemeanor, and the remainder usually set the maximum incarceration at three years. Clark, Law of Domestic Relations 269–70 (2d ed. 1988). At least one state varies the punishment based on the amount of arrearages. *See* Nev. Rev. Stats. § 201.020(1)(a). Some states punish defendants more severely if they have left the state. *See* Ga. Code § 19-10-1(b); Okla. Code tit. 21, § 852. The United States Supreme Court has upheld such a statute against a constitutional attack based on the right to interstate migration. *Jones v. Helms*, 452 U. S. 412 (1981). Many statutes explicitly authorize intermittent or suspended sentences to allow defendants to maintain jobs. *See, e.g.,* Ga. Code § 19-10-1(j).

Does prior conviction for criminal contempt provide a double jeopardy defense in a criminal non-support prosecution? No, according to *Iowa v. Rater*, 568 N.W.2d 655 (Iowa 1997). Defendant had been convicted of criminal contempt for failure to support between December, 1992 and September, 1993. In a prosecution alleging non-support in a later period, he asserted non-support was a single continuous offense and, therefore, any criminal prosecution would constitute double jeopardy. The court rejected this claim, finding each failure to make a monthly payment a separate offense.

Criminal prosecutions for non-support are relatively rare, because similar penalties are obtained more easily through contempt proceedings. The crime may be charged in egregious circumstances where there is no existing support order, however, because most criminal statutes do not require a prior support order. The states are split on whether the state or the defense has the burden of proof on defendant's ability to pay. *See* Marygold S. Melli, *Remedies in Child Support Enforcement, in* 2 Alimony, Child Support & Counsel Fees — Award Modification & Enforcement 15-31 & 15-32 (Melli & Stanton eds. 1989); *see also State v. Burg*, 648 N.W.2d 673 (Minn. 2002) (Due Process requires proof of absence of lawful excuse for non-payment, an element of criminal non-support under the statute); *State v. Stamm*, 664 S.E.2d 161 (W.Va. 2008) (unconstitutional to shift to defendant accused of criminal nonsupport the burden of providing inability to pay).

The Federal Child Support Recovery Act of 1992 criminalized failure to pay support for a child in another state. *See* 18 U.S.C. § 228. Subsection (a) punishes the defendant who "willfully fails to pay a past due support obligation with respect to a child who resides in another State. . . ." A past due support obligation is defined as one which has been unpaid for at least a year or is more than $5,000. The statute authorizes imprisonment for 6 months for a first offense and up to 2 years for subsequent offenses. Restitution in the amount of the unpaid support is required. The Act (since renamed the Deadbeat Parents Punishment Act as part of a 1998 stiffening of punishment levels) has survived a number of constitutional attacks based on *United States v. Morrison*, 529 U.S. 598 (2000) (striking down a portion of the Violence Against Women Act), claiming it exceeded Congressional Commerce Clause authority. *See United States v. Kukafka*, 478 F.3d 531 (3d Cir. 2007); *United States v. Klinzing*, 315 F.3d 803 (7th Cir. 2003); *United States v. Monts*, 311 F.3d 993 (10th Cir. 2002); *United States v. King*, 276 F.3d 109 (2d Cir. 2002); *United States v. Lewko*, 269 F.3d 64 (1st Cir. 2001); *United States v. Faasse*, 265 F.3d 475 (6th Cir. 2001); *cf. United States v. Ballek*, 170 F.3d 871 (9th Cir. 1999) (rejecting 13th Amendment attack in a case where defendant had refused to work in order to avoid support obligations).

In addition to the consideration of constitutional attacks, the federal courts have been busy interpreting the Act. For example, courts have not allowed defendants to collaterally attack the order establishing the support obligation. *See, e.g., United States v. Kukafka, supra* (support obligation not invalidated by presence of questionable provision in divorce decree concerning obligation by obligor to get a Get); *U.S. v. Brand*, 163 F.3d 1268 (11th Cir. 1998). Nor have courts agreed with defense arguments that the government bears the burden of proving the defendant's ability to pay the support obligation. *See United States v. Mattice*, 186 F.3d 219 (2d Cir. 1999); *United States v. Kukafka, supra*. The definition of the word "child" in the phrase "child support" was at issue in *United States v. Molak*, 276 F.3d 45 (10th Cir. 2002), where the trial court had ordered defendant to pay restitution of money attributable to post-majority support for higher education. While acknowledging that the Act does not define "child," the court deferred to the state court decree in which post-majority support was included as part of the parent's "support obligation." According to the court, federal courts "should accept state-court support orders as they are written and avoid relitigating matters already decided in the family courts." *See also United States v. Gill*, 264 F.3d 929 (9th Cir. 2001) (restitution award appropriately included both principal and interest); *United States v. Craig*, 181 F.3d 1124 (9th Cir. 1999) (arrearage award can appropriately include all arrearages, not simply amount accruing during period specified in the indictment). For venue purposes, the crime defined by the CSRA occurs in both the place where the obligor is and the place where the children live. *See United States v. Muench*, 153 F.3d 1298 (11th Cir. 1998). In *United States v. Fields*, 500 F.3d 1327 (11th Cir. 2007), the court held that the Act was not violated where the obligor did not know the child lived out of state. Another recent case is *Giordano v. Giordano*, 913 A.2d 146 (N.J. App. Div 2007). Rejecting the defendant's claim that the federal court had continuing jurisdiction over the enforcement of his child support duty once he was convicted of violating the CRSA, the court held that the law does not preempt state law or otherwise bar a state court from enforcing the underlying obligation.

U.S. Attorneys, responsible for prosecutions under the Act, "usually only accept cases when all reasonable available state remedies have first been exhausted and . . . any additional efforts would most likely prove to be futile. Other considerations include a pattern of flight from state to state, a pattern of deception to avoid payment, the defendant's being held in contempt by state courts, in a case where the child has special needs, such as when a child is handicapped or when the custodial family is facing a potential homeless situation. U.S. Attorneys are also urged to pursue cases where the children are still minors and require current support." Michael J Pimpinelli, *Deadbeat Parents Are Subject to Federal Criminal Law: Preventing Child Support Obligors from Avoiding Their Responsibility*, 193 N.J.L.J. 348 (Aug. 11, 2008).

[ii]   Civil Remedies

The 1984 Child Support Enforcement Amendments require states to provide several additional enforcement devices including: (1) income tax refund offsets, (2) security and (3) liens. The availability of these procedures depends upon such factors as obligor's payment record and availability of other remedies. Federal income tax refund intercepts (under which the obligor's refund is sent, in full or in part, to the obligee) are available through IV-D agencies for collection of support arrearages (but not current child support or any spousal support). 42 U.S.C. § 664(a); 45 C.F.R. § 303.72. States with income taxes must allow intercepts of refunds in IV-D cases. 42 U.S.C. § 666(a)(3). Such intercepts are not subject to the limits of the Consumer Credit Protection Act. *See Kokoszka v. Belford*, 417 U.S. 642 (1974); *Usery v. First Nat'l Bank of Arizona*, 586 F.2d 107 (9th Cir. 1978). In *Sorenson v. Secretary of Treasury of U.S.*, 475 U.S. 851 (1986), the Court approved the interception of a "refund" payable to the taxpayers only because their income was low enough for them to qualify for the Earned Income Tax Credit, a work-support program for low-income workers with dependent children. *See* Jennifer E. Spreng, *When "Welfare" Becomes "Work Support": Exempting Earned Income Tax Credit Payments in Consumer Bankruptcy*, 78 Am. Bankr. L.J. 279 (2004) ("EITC functions as a public benefit delivered through the tax system. Eligibility is limited to comparatively low-income persons who work and is targeted to single parents with children; more than nineteen million families have received the credit each year since 1994"). In *Sorenson*, only the wife had taxable earnings and the child support debt was owed by the husband, but they had filed a joint return.

Due process guarantees entitle obligors to advance notice of and a chance to contest an intercept. Defenses are limited to challenging: (1) jurisdiction of the court entering the support order, (2) the determination that arrearages exist and (3) the amount owed. For federal litigation concerning the precise requirements of due process in the Tax Refund Intercept Program, see *Anderson v. White*, 888 F.2d 985 (3d Cir. 1989); *McClelland v. Massinga*, 786 F.2d 1205 (4th Cir. 1986); *Nelson v. Regan*, 731 F.2d 105 (2d Cir. 1984). *See also* Diana Gribbon Motz & Andrew H.

Baida, *The Due Process Rights of Post-judgment Debtors and Child Support Obligors*, 45 MD. L. REV. 61 (1986).

Federal law requires states to provide in all support cases a procedure by which the court can require obligor to give security, post a bond, or otherwise guarantee payment of overdue support. 42 U.S.C. § 666(a)(6). A guarantee need not be required in every case. The use of a security, bond or other guarantee is most appropriate where obligor is self-employed or has income not easily reached by other means or is likely to leave the state. If required payments are not forthcoming, the court may (after notice and hearing) declare the security forfeited.

Each state must provide a procedure, available in all support cases, for the creation of a lien on obligor's real or personal property for support arrearages. 42 U.S.C. § 666(a)(4). As a practical matter, an existing lien prevents sale or transfer of the property until it has been satisfied. Some statutes permit a support decree itself (with recordation in the appropriate office) to operate as a lien. *See, e.g.*, NEB. REV. STAT. § 42-371 (liens "upon real property and any personal property registered with any county office. . . ."); IND. CODE ANN. § 12-17-2-33 (automatic lien on motor vehicle titles). Some states had required arrearages to be reduced to judgment before creation of a lien, but the PRWORA, requires (§ 368) that all states create liens on real and personal property by operation of law, without reduction to a specific money judgment of an arrearage, and interstate recognition of such liens. Recordation may still be required. While ordinarily there are statutory exemptions from liens, either in terms of a type of asset or a particular value of obligor's assets, some states permit support obligees to overcome such exemptions. *See, e.g.*, 42 PA. STATS. § 8123(b); IDAHO CODE § 11-607(1); *Redick v. O'Brien*, 468 A.2d 735 (N.J. Super. 1983).

Finally, while the prior collection devices derive from state law (albeit with the federal government's "encouragement"), a purely federal enforcement technique also is available. The Internal Revenue Service can collect a support arrearage "as it would attempt to collect federal taxes." Diane Dodson, *IRS Full Collection Procedure and Use of Federal Courts*, *in* INTERSTATE CHILD SUPPORT REMEDIES at 159 (Margaret Haynes & Diane Dodson eds. 1989); *see* 26 U.S.C. § 6305. The state IV-D agency must certify the amount of arrearages to the Office of Child Support Enforcement, which requests IRS help. *See* 42 U.S.C. § 652(b); 45 C.F.R. § 303.71. There must be at least $750 in arrearages and reasonable attempts to use other collection techniques must have been made. *Id.*

[iii]   Revocation or Denial of Privileges

Common enforcement techniques for the collection of child support include license revocation programs under which obligors with outstanding support debts may lose their driver's or professional licenses. *See* Drew A. Swank, *The National Child Non-Support Epidemic*, 2003 MICH. ST. DCL L. REV. 357 ("driver's license suspension clearly improved child support compliance, increasing payments in cases in which it was effective by an average of fifty-one percent six months after the suspension. Compared with merely sending a warning letter, an actual suspension was eight percent more likely to result in payments, and the amount of the payments on average were thirteen percent higher than those associated with a warning letter alone"); Mark R. Fondacaro & Dennis P. Stolle, *Revoking Motor Vehicle and Professional Licenses for Purposes of Child Support Enforcement: Constitutional Challenges and Policy Implications*, 5 CORN. J.L. & PUB. POL'Y 355, 358 (1996). While attorneys are not subject to most license revocation statutes, some attorneys have been subjected to professional discipline for failure to pay child support. *See Disciplinary Counsel v. Geer*, 858 N.E.2d 388 (Ohio 2006); *Disciplinary Counsel v. Curry*, 858 N.E.2d 392 (Ohio 2006) (one-year suspension imposed where attorneys failed to pay their child support and ignored questions on matter from disciplinary counsel).

The PRWORA (§ 369) requires license suspension laws for obligors who are delinquent or fail to respond to a warrant. The licenses covered include driver's, occupational and recreational licenses. Passports also can be denied or revoked for obligors owing more than $2,500 in support. 42 USC §§ 652(k)(1), 654(31). In addition, a 1996 Presidential Executive Order makes it more difficult for support obligors in arrears to obtain federal loans. Exec. Order No. 13019, 61 Fed. Reg. 51763 (Sept. 28, 1996).

In *Berntson v. Indiana Div. of Fam. & Child Support*, 737 N.E.2d 1208 (Ind. Ct. App. 2000), the court rejected obligor's assertion that an earlier finding of contempt of a support order precluded revocation of his license as a certified public accountant. While conceding that inability to pay would be a valid defense in a license revocation action, the court found the claim had been raised and rejected on factual grounds at trial. *See Office of Child Support, ex rel. Stanzione v. Stanzione*, 910 A.2d 882 (Vt. 2006) (obligor properly found to have ability to pay based on pro rata share of income of religious community in which she lived and worked); *Dep't of Revenue v. Beans*, 965 P.2d 725 (Alaska 1998) (obligor has constitutional right to assert and prove inability to pay defense in driver's license revocation proceeding).

Constitutional challenges to privilege revocation enforcement techniques generally have been unsuccessful. *See* Fondacaro & Stolle, *supra*. In *Eunique v. Powell*, 281 F.3d 940 (9th Cir. 2002), the court rejected an attack by a child support debtor denied a passport based on the right to travel. The court noted the right to travel internationally is merely part of the liberty protected by the Due Process Clause and, as such, is significantly narrower than the separately-guaranteed right to interstate travel. Applying rational relationship scrutiny, the majority found the scheme related to special concerns about the problems of enforcement where obligor has left the jurisdiction. The dissent applied intermediate scrutiny and found the statute wanting. *See also Weinstein v. Albright*, 261 F.3d 127 (2d Cir. 2001) (rejecting Procedural Due Process and Equal Protection attacks on same provision); Jeffrey T. Walter, Annot., *Validity and Application of Statute or Regulation Authorizing Revocation or Suspension of Driver's License for Reasons Unrelated to Use of, or Ability to Operate, Motor Vehicle*, 18 A.L.R. 5th 542 (1994).

[iv]   Termination of Parental Rights

The ultimate sanction for failure to support is termination of parental rights. Of course, termination of parental rights and obligations, including the support obligation, is of dubious value to the child in need of financial support. Termination actually relieves the chronically delinquent obligor of the legal duty to support and could leave a child with no parent obligated to provide support. Therefore, termination of parental rights for nonsupport is rarely pursued unless adoption seems likely.

[4] Defenses to Actions to Collect Arrearages

When the obligee seeks to collect unpaid arrearages, res judicata generally precludes any attempt to raise substantive objections to the order's existence or amount. While historically some states allowed such defenses under the rubric of "retroactive modifications," federal law, described above, now severely limits the availability of such modification. However, other defenses are sometimes raised. Some are obvious, if unusual, as where defendant claims mistaken identity or asserts the order was for less than the obligee claims. Other defenses are more common and include:

[a] Prior Payment

The obligor may claim to have already made the payments in question. This happens most often where the payments were made in a different manner than that prescribed in the order. The discrepancy can be "technical," as where the obligor made direct payments to the obligee rather than through the court as provided by the order. Obligors sometimes argue that credit should be given for "in kind" payments of toys, clothing, entertainment or allowance. The usual rule is that support must be rendered according to the order's provisions and nonconforming payments do not count. *Palagi v. Palagi*, 627 N.W.2d 765 (Neb. App. 2001) (voluntary payment of college expenses not recoverable); *Stringer v. Sheffield*, 451 So. 2d 109 (Ala. Civ. App. 1984) (no credit for purchases of clothing and sports and automotive equipment); *Glover v. Glover*, 598 S.W.2d 736 (Ark. 1980); Robert A. Brazener, Annot., *Right to Credit on Accrued Support Payments for Time Child is in Father's Custody or for Other Voluntary Expenditures*, 47 A.L.R.3d 1031 (1973). Crediting non-conforming payments erodes the custodial parent's authority to determine the details of the child's upbringing. *Williams v. Budke*, 606 P.2d 515 (Mont. 1980).

However, equitable considerations may require crediting non-conforming payments. For example, in *Payson v. Payson*, 442 N.E.2d 1123 (Ind. App. 1982), support was payable to the court clerk, but obligor had paid directly to obligee's landlord with obligee's consent. The court granted credit in an action for contempt and declaration of arrearages. *See also Kinsey v. Kinsey*, 425 So. 2d 483 (Ala. App. 1983) (direct payments to child which were used for tuition).

[b] Custodial Changes

Unless the decree provides otherwise, the noncustodial parent generally is not entitled to a support payment deduction for visitation periods. *See, e.g., Peak v. Peak*, 772 P.2d 775 (Kan. 1989); *Marriage of Eagen*, 640 P.2d 1019 (Or. 1982). Visitation periods are ordinarily contemplated in the decree and, in any event, most expenses for children do not decline during a temporary absence from home. *Escott v. Escott*, 325 N.E.2d 395 (Ill. App. 1975). Sometimes the parents informally change the child's primary residence without modifying the decree. In such cases, obligors often find the de facto custodial change is no defense to non-payment of support, even though it may provide grounds for prospective changes in the support award.

[c] Delay

Some support defendants assert the equitable defense of laches, arguing obligee's failure to pursue support for a lengthy period excuses non-payment. Courts are relatively hostile to such defense claims, often summarily dismissing the defense for lack of demonstrated prejudice. *See, e.g., State ex rel. Bennett v. Peterson*, 657 N.W.2d 698 (S.D. 2003) (12-year delay in bringing suit on behalf of non-marital child did not prejudice defendant or any other parties, such as new family); *Myers v. Myers*, 768 N.E.2d 1201 (Ohio Ct. App. 2002) ("length of delay [28 years] alone is insufficient to constitute material prejudice. The mere inconvenience of having to meet an existing obligation imposed by an earlier order . . . cannot be called material prejudice"); *In re Marriage of Capetillo and Kivett*, 932 P.2d 691 (Wash. Ct. App. 1997) (10-year delay insufficient; "defendant cannot prove damage simply by showing he is having to do now what he has been legally obligated to do for years"); *LeMaster v. LeMaster*, 596 So. 2d 1117 (Fla. Ct. App. 1992) (10-year period of concealment of child does not justify imposition of laches); *Connin v. Bailey*, 472 N.E.2d 328 (Ohio 1984) (no prejudice where obligee waited 35 years and obligor was now dead); *but see In re Hilborn*, 58 P.3d 905 (Wash. Ct. App. 2002) (18-year delay in bringing paternity action deprived defendant of chance for relationship and court-ordered visitation); *Davis v. Davis*, 689 So. 2d 433 (Fla. Ct. App. 1997) (15-year delay which "denied [obligor] the opportunity to share in the upbringing of his child" sufficient, especially where obligor has no property and more expenses than income); *Pyne v. Black*, 650 So. 2d 1073 (Fla. Ct. App. 1995) (12-year lapse and loss of opportunity to maintain parent-child relationship because of denial of visitation sufficient to show legal prejudice); *Kerrigan v. Kerrigan*, 642 A. 2d 1324 (D.C. Ct. App. 1994) (8-year delay and obligor's change of position in reliance on obligee's failure to seek enforcement, along with his expenditure of large amounts on child, including wedding expenses, sufficient to present prima facie case of laches). Rather than examining prejudice to the defendant in applying laches, some courts categorically reject laches in support cases, usually concluding the custodial parent cannot forfeit the child's rights through mere inaction. *See, e.g., Hammond v. Hammond*, 14 P. 3d 199 (Wyo. 2000) (finding arrearages to be an action at law, while laches is an equitable defense); *Lamon v. Hamm*, 702 So. 2d 449 (Ala. 1997); *Rodgers v. Woodin*, 672 A.2d 814 (Pa. Super. 1996). *See generally* John C. Williams, Annot., *Laches or Acquiescence as Defense, So As to Bar Recovery of Arrearages of Permanent Alimony or Child Support*, 5 A.L.R. 4th 1015 (1981).

Closely related is a statute of limitations defense. While there may be a relevant statute, it may begin to run only when the child reaches majority. *See Marriage of Wight*, 264 Cal. Rptr. 508 (App. 1989) (five-year statute begins at majority); *Harvey v. McGuire*, 635 S.W.2d 8 (Ky. 1982). The length of statutes of limitations to enforce child support varies considerably. *Valley v. Selfridge*, 639 P.2d 225 (Wash. App. 1982) (six years); *Huff v. Huff*, 634 S.W.2d 5 (Tex. Civ. App. 1982) (ten years);

Kroeger v. Kroeger, 353 N.W.2d 60 (Wis. 1984) (20 years).

The same fact pattern that may suggest a laches or statute of limitations defense has also given rise to an argument that arrearages should not be collectible because the child is now an adult, but that argument is generally rejected. *See Cramer v. Petrie*, 637 N.E.2d 882 (Ohio 1994).

[d] Estoppel

In a variety of situations, defendant may claim the custodial parent is estopped from seeking to enforce a support order. While a major element of most such cases will be the delay involved, often there are other factors, such as a parental agreement or the custodial parent's wrongful hiding of the child. In *Hendrickson v. State*, 72 S.W. 3d 124 (Ark. Ct. App. 2002), the trial court was directed to consider whether equitable estoppel was a defense in an arrearage action. The obligor had asserted an oral agreement with obligee to split custody 50/50 and eliminate all support obligations. The trial court should not have relied on a "mistaken understanding that unless the agreement of the parties was incorporated in a modification to the divorce decree, the agreement was not enforceable." See also Chapter 8's discussion of separation agreement provisions waiving support.

[e] Nature of Obligor's Resources

Defendants sometimes argue that their only resources are privileged against the particular enforcement device. For example, in *Rose v. Rose*, 481 U.S. 619 (1987), the obligor argued that his main source of income, VA disability benefits, were paid under a federal statute providing that benefits "shall not be liable to attachment, levy, or seizure by or under any legal or equitable process whatever, either before or after receipt by the beneficiary." Interpreting the federal statute as creating the benefits for the assistance of both obligor and his family, *Rose* rejected defendant's claim, finding no preemption. *But see Ridgway v. Ridgway*, 454 U.S. 46 (1981) (finding preemption in allocation of military insurance proceeds).

Several cases have held Social Security disability benefits subject to garnishment. *See, e.g., Mariche v. Mariche*, 758 P.2d 745 (Kan. 1988); *Marriage of Schonts*, 345 N.W.2d 145 (Iowa Ct. App. 1983); *Barbour v. Barbour*, 642 S.W.2d 904 (Ky. App. 1982). On the other hand, benefits paid under the means-tested program for people with disabilities, Supplemental Security Income (SSI), have been held exempt from garnishment. *See Department of Human Servs. ex rel. Young v. Young*, 802 S.W.2d 594 (Tenn. 1990) (distinguishing Supplemental Security Income (SSI) payments, finding them protected). State entitlements also may be protected from particular types of enforcement. *See, e.g., Lapeer Cty. v. Harris*, 453 N.W.2d 272 (Mich. Ct. App. 1990) (state general assistance benefits immune from wage withholding); Angela F. Epps, *To Pay or Not to Pay, That is the Question: Should SSI Recipients Be Exempt From Child Support Obligations*, 34 RUTG. L. REV. 63 (2002) (arguing disabled obligors should be exempt from making support payments and urging creation of an alternative "monthly benefit to the children involved, to ensure that they have a minimum level of income").

[f]   Bankruptcy

The federal Bankruptcy Code precludes a debtor from discharging debts "to a spouse, former spouse, or child of the debtor, for alimony to, maintenance for, or support of such spouse or child, in connection with a separation agreement, divorce decree or other order of a court." 11 U.S.C. § 523(a)(5). Discharge is also unavailable where the child support has been assigned to the state. 42 U.S.C. § 656(b).

[5]   Special Procedures in Enforcement of Support for Indigent Families

The child support collections process for indigent families typically begins when the custodial parent applies for benefits from the state Temporary Assistance to Needy Families agency, which entitles parent to support enforcement services without charge. As a condition of eligibility for TANF, a parent must cooperate with the support enforcement agency in identifying and seeking support from the absent parent and assign the right to support to the agency, making the debt due directly to the state. 42 U.S.C. § 608(a)(2), (3); *see* Daniel L. Hatcher, *Child Support Harming Children: Subordinating the Best Interests of Children to the Fiscal Interests of the State*, 42 WAKE FOREST L. REV. 1029 (2007) (describing history and present workings of welfare cost recovery process through assignment of child support). Generally the obligor will be liable to the state only up to the amount he is obligated to pay under a support order. *See, e.g.,* ALASKA STATS. § 25.27.120. Because of the state's right to reimbursement, it is entitled to notice of any proceeding to modify the support obligation. *See Marriage of Mena*, 260 Cal. Rptr. 314 (Ct. App. 1989) (agency indispensable party to modification proceeding).

An applicant refusing to cooperate with the agency may be denied between 25% and 100% of the grant. 42 U.S.C. § 608(a)(2). There is a "good cause" exception to the duty to cooperate in securing support payments, applicable if there is reasonable likelihood of physical or emotional harm to applicant or child. 42 U.S.C. § 654(29); 45 C.F.R. §§ 260.52, 264.30; *see* Susan Notar & Vicki Turetsky, *Models for Safe Child Support Enforcement*, 8 AM. U. J. GENDER, SOC. POL'Y & L. 657 (2000) (analyzing appropriate balance between protecting against abuse and collecting support). There is no exception to the assignment requirement.

The TANF agency must make all relevant records available to the IV-D enforcement agency. An attempt to recover support is begun regardless of whether there was ever a marriage, a support judgment, or paternity action or acknowledgment. All support is paid to and disbursed by the enforcement agency. Former law provided that the first $50 of any support payment went directly to the family; the rest was devoted to reimbursing the state and federal governments for past payments to the family. 42 U.S.C. § 602(a)(8)(A)(vi). This is no longer mandated by the federal government. PRWORA § 302. As of 2008, however, states can pass through up to $100 for one child and $200 for two children without reimbursing the federal government a share of the payments, and the federal government will share in the costs of states that are more generous to TANF families. *See* Laura Wheaton & Elaine Sorensen, *The Potential Impact of Increasing Child Support Payments to TANF Families* (The Urban Institute,

Brief 5, Dec. 2007), http://www.urban.org/UploadedPDF/411595_child_support.pdf. Few states exercised their option to pass through child support after the passage of TANF, however, preferring instead to use welfare cost recovery funds as a source of general revenue, so it is not yet clear how many will exercise the more generous options now available. *See* Daniel L. Hatcher, *Child Support Harming Children: Subordinating the Best Interests of Children to the Fiscal Interests of the State* 42 WAKE FOREST L. REV. 1029 (2007).

PROBLEMS

Problem 5-21. Dick and Jane had two children. Their divorce decree ordered Dick to "pay support for the two minor children at the rate of $400 monthly." Six years later, the couple's older child, Sam, has entered the Navy, at age 17. That was six months ago. The younger child, Sally, is now 14. When Dick heard Sam had enlisted, he immediately reduced his monthly check to $200. Jane thinks this entirely inadequate and seeks your advice. The age of majority in your jurisdiction is 18. What options do you have?

Problem 5-22. Jeffrey and Polly were divorced three years ago. She has custody of the couple's two children and he was ordered to pay $350 per month support. Six months ago, without notice, he stopped paying. Representing Polly, you have learned that Jeffrey has joined a religious organization called the "Bride of Christ," which forbids members from having separate earnings or supporting non-members. The members are supported by a church business. How do you advise Polly? How would Jeffrey respond to your actions?

Problem 5-23. Raymond and Christi were divorced two years ago. Christi got custody of their three children and Raymond was ordered to pay $50 monthly support for each child. Soon afterward, Raymond was declared totally disabled and awarded Social Security disability benefits of $700 monthly. Each child was awarded $89 monthly in "child's insurance benefits" under the Social Security Act. Christi was named representative payee for the children. Raymond now seeks to end his support obligations. As judge, how will you decide the case?

Problem 5-24. Rodney was ordered to pay child support in his divorce from Patricia. He ceased payments about three years ago. The support agency has been unable to obtain wage assignments because he works as a carpenter on many different jobs. Each time the agency tracks him down, he has gone to a different job. Rodney's union refuses to inform the agency of his jobs.

In response to these problems, the agency has asked the court to join the union (whose hiring hall refers its members to various jobs) as a party to the continuing divorce action. An order requiring the union to inform the agency when it sends Rodney out on a job (along with the employer's name, address and telephone number) also has been sought. What arguments do you expect from the union and how would you decide the case?

Problem 5-25. Edward was ordered to pay $300 monthly support for his daughter, Michelle. He has complied fully. He complains, however, that often when Michelle, now 15, visits she is so ill-clothed he must purchase clothes for her. He also reports she is usually hungry when he sees her. Edward suspects his ex-wife is spending the support money on herself rather than on Michelle. He does not mind spending money for the child's well-being, but is generally upset about his daughter's condition. What options does he have?

Problem 5-26. Lois and Clark were divorced after a 15-year marriage which produced three children. Clark was awarded custody and Lois was ordered to pay support, but never complied. Three years later, the couple remarried. Support arrearages of over $12,000 had accrued at the time. In discussions at the time of the remarriage, they laughed about the arrearages and Clark said, "That's okay, I got along well enough as it was." Unfortunately, the second marriage didn't last very long. After eight months, Clark walked out on Lois. Clark seeks your advice concerning the arrearages and future support payments. How do you respond? Would the analysis differ if the order was for their non-marital child?

Problem 5-27. (a) Jennifer, wanting nothing to do with her soon-to-be ex-husband Michael, agrees to forego maintenance and support in return for his promise to leave her and their children alone. She expects to rely on her family's help to get by on her income of $28,000. Michael earns $45,000 annually at a local factory. Should the court accept such an agreement?

(b) The court accepted the agreement in (a), dividing the marital property but awarding no maintenance or support. Two years later, Jennifer has lost her job and is on welfare. As required by law, she assigned her rights to the welfare agency which has now sought reimbursement from Michael for benefits provided his children. State law provides: "An obligor is liable to the state in the amount of assistance granted to a child whom the obligor owes a duty of support except that if a support order has been entered, the obligor's liability may not exceed the amount of support provided for in the support order." You are the judge. What will the arguments of the parties be and how will you decide the case?

D.   INTERSTATE SUPPORT LITIGATION

Even before the statutory developments outlined below, which were designed to make interstate litigation more accessible, at least one-fourth of all child support litigation involved obligors and obligees residing in different states. U.S. GENERAL ACCOUNTING OFFICE, INTERSTATE CHILD SUPPORT: MOTHERS REPORT RECEIVING LESS SUPPORT FROM OUT-OF-STATE FATHERS 3 (1992). A study of California child support collection issues found that, in a fifth of cases with arrearages, the obligor parent lived outside of California. Elaine Sorensen, et al., *Examining Child Support Arrears in California: The Collectability Study* (The Urban Institute, Mar. 2003). In Fiscal Year 2008, 952,787 of the 15.7 million cases in the IV-D system involved interstate claims. Collections occurred in 64.3% of the cases, up from 58.6% only 4 years earlier. US Dep't Health & Human Services, Office of Child Support Enforcement, *FY 2008 Preliminary Report* (2009), http://www.acf.hhs.gov/ programs/cse/pubs/2009/reports/preliminary_report_fy2008.

Interstate support disputes may involve either initial support awards or petitions to modify or enforce them. The issues are the same whether or not the parties were ever married. A different kind of interstate dispute occurs when the interstate movement of one or both parties occurs *after* a support order is issued in a divorce or paternity action and one party seeks to enforce or modify the decree. In many interstate cases, the moving party (obligor or obligee) could obtain long-arm jurisdiction over the respondent in petitioner's state of residence, under the jurisdictional rules discussed in Chapter 7. Alternatively, the petitioner can file in the respondent's state. There are difficulties, however, with both choices. Sometimes the petitioner cannot obtain jurisdiction in her own state, while litigating in the courts of the respondent's state may be difficult and expensive.

This section considers a third alternative. Its basic structure was established in 1950 by the Uniform Reciprocal Enforcement of Support Act (URESA) promulgated by the National Conference of Commissioners on Uniform State Laws (NCCUSL) and eventually adopted, in some form, by all states. In this "two-state" litigation, the petitioner remains in his or her state and the respondent need not leave his or her state. URESA was eventually replaced by the Uniform Interstate Family Support Act (UIFSA), now the law in all states.

John J. Sampson & Paul M. Kurtz, *UIFSA: An Interstate Support Act for the 21st Century*
27 FAM. L. Q. 85, 85–89 (1993)

. . . . The National Conference of Commissioners on Uniform State Laws [hereinafter NCCUSL or the Conference] has been dealing with the subject of interstate support for most of this century. Its major effort, however, began in 1950 with the promulgation of the Uniform Reciprocal Enforcement of Support Act [hereinafter URESA]. That act was amended in 1952 and again in 1958. By 1968, enough experience had been gathered to lead to an even more extensive revision; in fact, the amendments were so sweeping that the new act was retitled the Revised Uniform Reciprocal Enforcement of Support Act [hereinafter RURESA]. [By 1992, all states and the District of Columbia had enacted some version of URESA or RURESA.]

By 1988 it had become apparent . . . that the time had come for another version of URESA. During the ensuing process . . . , the focus shifted from revision . . . to a complete overhaul of the URESA system and the establishment of a new approach. Four years of effort culminated [in 1992], when the . . . Conference voted unanimously to replace RURESA with the Uniform Interstate Family Support Act [hereinafter UIFSA].

. . . .

[F]or its time URESA was a . . . breakthrough in legal thought by providing a means to establish and enforce . . . support obligations . . . across state lines . . . without requiring the custodial parent to travel to any distant forum in which the obligor might reside. Rather, the obligee was represented on both ends of the lawsuit by a governmental attorney. The process of filing a petition in State A . . . forwarding it to State B, . . . where the noncustodial parent resides or owns property, and establishing or enforcing a support order in that distant forum is a complex task. . . . Part of the difficulty is caused by the inevitable problems of "lost paper" endemic to bureaucratic structures. When time and distance are added to the equation, along with certain structural defects in URESA itself, the difficulty . . . is readily apparent.

The Family Support Act of 1988 established the U.S. Commission on Interstate Child Support, . . . charged with the task of identifying ways to improve interstate child support enforcement and report its findings and recommendations to Congress. The Commission was specifically directed to work with NCCUSL in an effort to improve URESA. . . . UIFSA provides a new beginning.

How does the new Act differ from URESA?. . . . Probably the most significant improvement offered by UIFSA is the elimination of the multiple-order system. . . . Orders entered under URESA have been defined as additional to, and not replacements of, prior support orders. Thus, at any particular time, two or more orders covering the same child might exist with different levels of support set by each one. When combined with the general family law rule permitting modifications of existing child support orders on the basis of changed circumstances, the resultant chaos and confusion is certainly understandable.

By contrast, UIFSA adopts the concept of continuing, exclusive jurisdiction to establish and modify the levels of child support due to a particular child. Thus, once a court or administrative agency enters a support decree with jurisdiction, it is the only body entitled to modify it so long as it retains continuing, exclusive jurisdiction under the Act. Another state, while required by UIFSA to enforce the existing decree, has no power . . . to modify the original decree or enter a support order at a different level.

UIFSA also recognizes, for the first time in a uniform act, the role of each state's support enforcement agency. . . . Likewise, the Act recognizes that some states have elected to have support orders entered by administrative agencies, rather than courts, and extends recognition to such awards in the interstate context.

Efficiency in the interstate support context is an explicit goal. . . . The Act recognizes certain situations in which interstate . . . enforcement can be sought directly by an obligee without utilization of courts or agencies in his or her own state. Thus, an obligee with an existing order may have it sent directly to the obligor's employer or to a support enforcement agency in the obligor's state. Alternatively, the obligee can file the case in . . . the obligor's state without the intervention of any support enforcement agency.

. . . .

The Act includes several rules designed to speed up the processing of interstate cases. Federal forms presently in use in only certain cases are mandated for all cases in order to ensure complete information; authority is given for transmission of information and documents through modern technology; interstate telephone conferencing is authorized; and tribunals and state enforcement agencies are required to keep parties informed of the progress of their interstate cases. Visitation issues are explicitly severed from support issues to eliminate delay in the establishment and enforcement of support obligations.

John J. Sampson, *Uniform Family Laws and Model Acts*
42 Fam. L. Q. 673, 680 (2008)

. . . . By the summer of 1996, thirty-five states had enacted UIFSA (1992). This was followed that same summer by federal legislation that tied the federal subsidy for child support enforcement to enactment of UIFSA (1996). Not surprisingly, all states met the federal "request" for uniformity by the target date of 1998; to do otherwise would have cost states millions of federal dollars. As of 2008, all states have either UIFSA (1996) or UIFSA (2001) on their books.

In 2001, additional amendments to UIFSA were made following another review and analysis. Some of the 2001 amendments are procedural, while others are substantive. However, none are fundamental changes in UIFSA policies and procedures. UIFSA (2001) continues to serve the basic principle of one order from one state that will be enforced in other states. The amendments are meant to enhance that basic objective.

Finally, a new version was approved by NCCUSL in 2008 to accommodate a new Hague Convention on the International Recovery of Child Support and Other Forms of Family Maintenance, which is anticipated to come into force in the United States in the future. . . .

[1] Establishing a Support Decree Through Uniform Interstate Family Support Act of 2008

§ 102. Definitions

. . . .

(8) "Home state" means the state . . . in which a child lived with a parent or person acting as parent for at least six consecutive months immediately preceding the time of filing of a [petition] . . . and, if a child is less than six months old, the state . . . in which the child lived from birth with any of them. A period of temporary absence of any of them is counted as part of the six-month . . . period.

. . . .

§ 203. Initiating and Responding Tribunal of this State

Under this [act], a tribunal of this state may serve as an initiating tribunal to forward proceedings to another state and as a responding tribunal for proceedings initiated in another state . . .

§ 204. Simultaneous Proceedings

(a) A tribunal of this state may exercise jurisdiction to establish a support order if the [petition] . . . is filed after a [petition] . . . is filed in another state . . . only if:

(1) the [petition] in this state . . . is filed before the expiration of the time allowed in the other state . . . for filing a responsive pleading challenging the exercise of jurisdiction by the other state;

(2) the contesting party timely challenges the exercise of jurisdiction in the other state . . . ; and

(3) . . . this state is the home state of the child.

(b) A tribunal of this state may not exercise jurisdiction to establish a support order if the [petition] . . . is filed before a [petition] . . . is filed in another state . . . if:

(1) the [petition] . . . in the other state is filed before the expiration of the time allowed in this state . . . for filing a responsive pleading challenging the exercise of jurisdiction by this state;

(2) the contesting party timely challenges the exercise of jurisdiction in this state; and

(3) . . . the other state . . . is the home state of the child.

§ 301. Proceedings under This [Act]

. . .

(b) An individual . . . or a support enforcement agency may initiate a proceeding authorized under this [act] by filing a [petition] in an initiating tribunal for forwarding to a responding tribunal or by filing a [petition] . . . directly in a tribunal of another state . . . which has or can obtain personal jurisdiction over the [respondent].

§ 303. Application of Law of this State

Except as otherwise provided in this [act], a responding tribunal of this state shall:

(1) apply the procedural and substantive law generally applicable to similar proceedings originating in this state and may exercise all powers and provide all remedies available in those proceedings; and

(2) determine the duty of support and the amount payable in accordance with the law and support guidelines of this state.

§ 304. Duties of Initiating Tribunal

(a) Upon the filing of a [petition] . . . , an initiating tribunal of this state shall forward the [petition] and its accompanying documents:

(1) to the responding tribunal or appropriate support enforcement agency in the responding state; or

(2) . . . to the state information agency of the responding state with a request that they be forwarded to the appropriate tribunal. . . .

. . . .

§ 305. Duties and Powers of Responding Tribunal

(a) When a responding tribunal of this state receives a [petition] . . . from an initiating tribunal or directly pursuant to Section 301(b), it shall cause the [petition] . . . to be filed and notify the [petitioner]. . . .

(b) A responding tribunal of this state, to the extent not prohibited by other law, may . . . :

(1) establish . . . a support order . . . or determine parentage of a child;

(2) order an obligor to comply with a support order, specifying the amount and the manner of compliance;

(3) order income withholding;

(4) determine the amount of any arrearages . . . ;

. . . .

(8) order an obligor to keep the tribunal informed of the obligor's current residential address, electronic mail address, telephone number, employer, address of employment, and telephone number at the place of employment;

(9) issue a [bench warrant; capias] for an obligor who has failed after proper notice to appear at a hearing . . . ;

(10) order the obligor to seek appropriate employment by specified methods;

(11) award reasonable attorney's fees and other fees and costs; and

(12) grant any other available remedy.

(c) A responding tribunal of this state shall include in a support order . . . the calculations on which the support order is based.

(d) A responding tribunal of this state may not condition the payment of a support order issued under this [act] upon compliance by a party with provisions for visitation.

. . . .

§ 316. Special Rules of Evidence and Procedure

(a) The physical presence of a nonresident party . . . in a tribunal of this state is not required for the establishment . . . of a support order or the rendition of a judgment determining parentage of a child.

. . . .

(e) Documentary evidence transmitted from outside this state . . . by telephone, telecopier, or other electronic means that do not provide an original record may not be excluded from evidence on an objection based on the means of transmission.

(f) In a proceeding under this [act], a tribunal of this state shall permit a party or witness residing outside this state to be deposed or to testify by telephone, audiovisual means, or other electronic means. . . .

(g) If a party called to testify at a civil hearing refuses to answer on the ground that the testimony may be self-incriminating, the trier of fact may draw an adverse inference from the refusal.

(h) A privilege against disclosure of communications between spouses does not apply in a proceeding under this [act].

(i) The defense of immunity based on the relationship of husband and wife or parent and child does not apply in a proceeding under this [act].

(j) A voluntary acknowledgment of paternity, certified as a true copy, is admissible to establish parentage of the child.

§ 317. Communications Between Tribunals

A tribunal of this state may communicate with a tribunal outside this state or foreign country . . . in a record, electronic mail, or by telephone or other means, to obtain information concerning the laws, the legal effect of a judgment, decree, or order of that tribunal, and the status of a proceeding in the other state or foreign country. . . . A tribunal of this state may furnish similar information by similar means. . . .

§ 401. [Petition] to Establish Support Order

(a) If a support order entitled to recognition under this [act] has not been issued, a responding tribunal of this state with personal jurisdiction over the parties may issue a support order if:

(1) the individual seeking the order resides outside this state; or

(2) the support enforcement agency seeking the order is located outside this state.

(b) The tribunal may issue a temporary child support order if the tribunal determines that such an order is appropriate and the individual ordered to pay is:

(1) a presumed father of the child;

(2) petitioning to have his paternity adjudicated;

(3) identified as the father of the child through genetic testing;

(4) an alleged father who has declined to submit to genetic testing;

(5) shown by clear and convincing evidence to be the father of the child;

(6) an acknowledged father as provided by [applicable state law];

(7) the mother of the child; or

(8) an individual who has been ordered to pay child support in a previous proceeding and the order has not been reversed or vacated.

(c) Upon finding, after notice and opportunity to be heard, that an obligor owes a duty of support, the tribunal shall issue a[n] order directed to the obligor and may issue other orders pursuant to Section 305.

NOTES

1. *Establishing a Support Order Under the Uniform Interstate Family Support Act.* The statutory provisions reprinted above are from the 2008 version of the Uniform Act. Individual states, of course, may have slightly different versions.

As explained in the Sampson & Kurtz excerpt above, UIFSA makes several dramatic changes in the area of interstate child support litigation but maintains the basic structure of URESA's two-state suit. That is, under § 401, a petitioner-obligee or the support enforcement agency (the IV-D agency mentioned in the Enforcement materials above) may file a petition to establish an obligation if "a support order entitled to recognition . . . has not been issued." The latter language is designed to establish one of the main differences between the old and new Uniform Acts. Under URESA, courts would routinely enter new orders involving children for whom orders had already been entered in other states. At the heart of the "one-order" world of UIFSA is the proposition that once an order covering a particular child has been issued, no other court ("tribunal" in the Act's language to account for the fact that some states empower administrative agencies to order support) can issue an order for the support of the same child unless the Act's restrictive rules concerning modification (discussed below) are satisfied.

The mechanics of filing a suit to establish support are summarized in § 301, which authorizes the filing of a petition in an initiating tribunal for forwarding to the responding tribunal where the respondent resides. While URESA permitted only this method of initiating an interstate action, UIFSA also permits petitioner to contact the IV-D agency in his or her home state who can forward the information to the IV-D agency in the respondent's state. Other alternatives include the use of private attorneys (specifically authorized under § 309) or direct contact by the petitioner with the IV-D agency in the respondent's state. Section 307 empowers the support enforcement agency in the responding state to "take all steps necessary to enable an appropriate tribunal . . . to obtain jurisdiction over the respondent." Most petitioners using UIFSA use the services of a IV-D agency.

Once personal jurisdiction over the respondent is obtained, the responding tribunal is directed by § 303(1) to treat the case as it would a purely domestic suit. For example, the parties would be notified of any hearing, responsive pleadings would be permitted, etc. The special nature of two-state litigation with the parties in different states is dealt with by § 316 which makes clear, among other things, that the presence of the non-resident party is not required in the responding state and that any restrictions imposed by the hearsay rule are trumped by use of federally-mandated forms. Section 401 authorizes issuance of a temporary support order in certain circumstances, while § 305 authorizes the responding tribunal to issue a permanent order.

As detailed in Chapter 7, UIFSA contains a long-arm provision which can be used by petitioner where the parties live in different states to force respondent to litigate, not in a two-state format, but instead in "one-state litigation" in the petitioner's state. URESA had no similar provision and, thus, during the URESA era there was a wide range of provisions, with many states having no specific family law long-arm statute. For material generally comparing the two acts and their provisions, see Robert E. Oliphant, *Is Sweeping Change Possible? Minnesota Adopts the Uniform Interstate Family Support Act*, 21 WM. MITCHELL L. REV. 989 (1996); Janelle T. Calhoun, Note, *Interstate Child Support Enforcement System: Juggernaut of Bureaucracy*, 46 MERCER L. REV. 921 (1995); Tina M. Fielding, Note, *The Uniform Interstate Family Support Act: The New URESA*, 20 DAYT. L. REV. 425 (1994). *See also* Kurtis A. Kemper, Annot., *Construction and Application of the Uniform Interstate Family Support Act*, 90 A.L.R.5th 1 (originally published 2001).

2. *Choice of Law Under UIFSA.* The fact that in the two-state litigation the petitioner (and usually the child) are in one jurisdiction and the respondent (usually the obligor) is elsewhere raises the question of which state's law should be applied. Under UIFSA § 303, the responding tribunal generally applies its own law (substantive, procedural, and choice of law), with a specific direction in subsection (b) to apply its own state's support guidelines. While other plausible policy choices existed (*e.g.*, apply the law of the jurisdiction where the child is or apply whichever law best promotes the child's interest), the section's Official Comment explains § 303 as an attempt to insure efficiency in interstate litigation. As the drafters put it, "it is vital that decision-makers apply familiar rules of substantive and procedural law. . . ."

In *Department of Human Services v. Frye*, 754 A.2d 1000 (Me. 2000), respondent argued for application of Florida law (where his son was living) which would restrict any retroactive award to 24 months' worth of support and mandate imputation of income to the child's mother who had chosen not to work. The court held that even if Maine choice of law rules would provide for application of Florida law, § 301(b) mandated application of the Maine rules concerning these issues. The court concluded that "[t]here is good reason for this position, to [among other reasons] assure ease of calculation. . . ." *See also State v. Frisard*, 694 So. 2d 1032 (La. App.1997); John J. Sampson, *Uniform Interstate Family Support Act (1996) (with More Unofficial Annotations by John J. Sampson)*, 32 FAM. L.Q. 390, 451 (1998).

Several of the act's provisions create rules for the conduct of interstate litigation which are exceptions to the general local law rule. Section 316 includes various evidentiary rules, § 312 permits the sealing of identifying information where a party's or child's health or safety might be threatened if disclosed to another party, authority is granted by § 313 to award fees and costs, including attorney's fees, and immunity from service or the exercise of personal jurisdiction in other actions is provided by § 314. Notice, also, that the preface to § 305(b)'s laundry list of powers of a responding tribunal specifically grants such power "to the extent not prohibited by other law." This provision grants power to the responding court in interstate cases that it might not have in domestic cases.

3. *Simultaneous Proceedings.* As part of UIFSA's commitment to a one order system, it imposes self-restraint on a state in exercising jurisdiction where more than one action concerning support of a particular child has been filed. Section § 204(a) is directed to a State 2 tribunal considering a petition to establish a support order when such a petition already is pending in State 1. State 2 can entertain an action only if: (a) the second action is filed before the expiration of the time for challenging State 1's exercise of jurisdiction; (b) a timely challenge to State 1's exercise of jurisdiction is filed; and (c) State 2 is the child's "home state" under 102(4). The latter concept was borrowed from the Uniform Child Custody Jurisdiction Enforcement Act and the Federal Parental Kidnapping Prevention Act. Subsection (b) of § 204 speaks to the State 1 court in the above scenario.

The act's preference for application of forum law could, without § 204, encourage forum shopping and competition between states in the exercise of support jurisdiction. For example, consider a situation where a married couple (X and Y) lives with their young child in Jurisdiction A, near its border with Jurisdiction B. Y moves alone to Jurisdiction B, whose support laws are less congenial to the obligor than A (*e.g.*, higher levels of support and a longer duration of support). Given the choice of law rule of § 303, X would prefer to litigate the support issues in Jurisdiction B, while Y would rather litigate in Jurisdiction A. If each filed a lawsuit to establish the support obligation in their preferred jurisdiction, § 204's rules would be used to decide which suit could proceed. Under the facts as outlined, so long as Y challenged B's exercise of jurisdiction in a timely fashion, the litigation would occur in Jurisdiction A, the child's home state.

4. *Establishment of Parentage Under UIFSA.* Because of ambiguous URESA language, pre-UIFSA courts were split on whether to permit interstate litigation to establish parentage of a child. A federal commission charged in the late 1980s with proposing improvements to the interstate support system reported that, "[s]ome responding courts will not resolve parentage in a contested case unless the out-of-state petitioner physically appears and participates in the hearing. If the petitioner . . . lacks the resources to make the trip, the URESA case remains in limbo until parentage is determined elsewhere." U.S. COMMISSION ON INTERSTATE CHILD SUPPORT, SUPPORTING OUR CHILDREN: A BLUEPRINT FOR REFORM 232 (1992); *see, e.g., Packard v. Cargile*, 546 N.E.2d 301, 302 (Ind. 1989) ("[o]ne does not have a duty to support because of allegations of one's paternity"). Likely, this interpretation of URESA was bolstered by a sense that a respondent-alleged father would be prejudiced by his inability to subject the testimony against him to cross-examination. *Cf. State ex rel. T.L.R. v. R.W.T.*, 737 So. 2d 688 (La. 1999) (rejecting respondent's claim that finding of paternity in such a context was unconstitutional).

In the 2001 version of UIFSA, § 701 makes clear that a determination of parentage can be made in the interstate litigation itself. The 2008 amendments to UIFSA provide for the determination of parentage in §§ 704 and 705, depending on whether the action is initiated by an individual or by a government agency.

[2] Uniform Interstate Family Support Act Litigation of 2008 When an Order Exists

§ 205. Continuing, Exclusive Jurisdiction

(a) A tribunal . . . that has issued a child-support order consistent with the law of this state has and shall exercise continuing, exclusive jurisdiction to modify its child-support order if the order is the controlling order and:

(1) at the time of the filing of a request for modification this state is the residence of the obligor, the individual obligee, or the child . . . ; or

(2) . . . the parties consent . . . that the tribunal of this state may continue to exercise jurisdiction to modify its order.

(b) A tribunal . . . may not exercise continuing, exclusive jurisdiction to modify the order if:

(1) all of the parties who are individuals file consent . . . with the tribunal of this state that a tribunal of another state . . . may modify the order and assume continuing, exclusive jurisdiction. . . .

(c) If a tribunal of another state has issued a child-support order pursuant to the [Uniform Interstate Family Support Act] . . . which modifies a child-support order of a tribunal of this state, tribunals of this state shall recognize the continuing, exclusive jurisdiction of the tribunal of the other state.

(d) A tribunal of this state [lacking modification jurisdiction] may serve as an initiating tribunal to request a tribunal of another state to modify a support order issued in that state.

(e) A temporary support order issued ex parte or pending resolution of a jurisdictional conflict does not create continuing, exclusive jurisdiction. . . .

§ 206. Continuing Jurisdiction to Enforce Child-Support Order

(a) A tribunal . . . that has issued a child-support order consistent with the law of this state may serve as an initiating tribunal to request a tribunal of another state to enforce:

(1) the order if the order is the controlling order and has not been modified [pursuant to UIFSA]; or

(2) a money judgment for arrears . . . on the order accrued before a determination that an order of another state is the controlling order.

. . . .

§ 207. Determination of Controlling Child-Support Order

(a) If a proceeding is brought under this [act] and only one tribunal has issued a child-support order, the order of that tribunal controls and must be so recognized.

(b) If a proceeding is brought under this [act], and two or more child-support orders have been issued . . . with regard to the same obligor and same child, a tribunal of this state . . . shall apply the following rules and by order shall determine which order controls and must be recognized:

(1) If only one of the tribunals would have continuing, exclusive jurisdiction under this [act], the order of that tribunal controls.

(2) If more than one of the tribunals would have continuing, exclusive jurisdiction under this [act]:

(A) an order issued by a tribunal in the current home state of the child controls; but

(B) if an order has not been issued in the current home state of the child, the order most recently issued controls.

(3) If none of the tribunals would have continuing, exclusive jurisdiction under this [act], the tribunal of this state shall issue a child-support order, which controls.

(c) If two or more child-support orders have been issued for the same obligor and same child, upon request of a party . . . , a tribunal of this state having personal jurisdiction over both the obligor and the obligee. . . . shall determine which order controls . . .

. . . .

(e) The tribunal that issued the controlling order under subsection (a), (b), or (c) has continuing jurisdiction to the extent provided in Section 205 or 206.

. . . .

(g) Within [30] days after issuance of an order determining the controlling order, the party obtaining the order shall file a certified copy of it in each tribunal that issued or registered an earlier order. . . . The failure to file does not affect the validity or enforceability of the controlling order.

. . . .

§ 315. Nonparentage as a Defense

A party whose parentage of a child has been previously determined by or pursuant to law may not plead nonparentage as a defense to a proceeding under this [act].

§ 501. Employer's Receipt of Income-Withholding Order of Another State

An income-withholding order issued in another state may be sent . . . to the . . . obligor's employer . . . without first filing a [petition] . . . or registering the order with a tribunal. . . .

§ 502. Employer's Compliance with Income-Withholding Order of Another State

(a) Upon receipt of an income-withholding order, the obligor's employer shall immediately provide a copy of the order to the obligor.

(b) The employer shall treat an income-withholding order issued in another state which appears regular on its face as if it had been issued by a tribunal of this state.

(c) Except as otherwise provided in subsection (d) and § 503, the employer shall withhold and distribute the funds as directed in the withholding order by complying with terms of the order which specify:

(1) the duration and amount of periodic payments of current child-support
. . . ;

(2) the person designated to receive payments . . . ;

(3) medical support, whether in the form of periodic cash payment, stated as a sum certain, or ordering the obligor to provide health insurance coverage for the child under a policy available through the obligor's employment;

(4) . . . fees and costs for a support enforcement agency, the issuing tribunal, and the obligee's attorney, stated as sums certain; and

(5) . . . arrearages and interest on arrearages, stated as sums certain.

(d) An employer shall comply with the law of the state of the obligor's principal place of employment for withholding from income with respect to:

(1) the employer's fee for processing an income-withholding order;

(2) the maximum amount permitted to be withheld . . . ; and

(3) the times within which the employer must implement the withholding order and forward the child-support payment.

§ 504. Immunity From Civil Liability

An employer that complies with an income-withholding order [in compliance] with this article is not subject to civil liability . . . with regard to the employer's withholding of child support from the obligor's income.

§ 506. Contest by Obligor

(a) An obligor may contest the validity or enforcement of an income-withholding order issued in another state and received directly by an employer in this state by registering the order in a tribunal of this state and filing a contest to that order as provided in Article 6, or otherwise contesting the order . . . as if [it] had been issued by a tribunal of this state.

. . . .

§ 507. Administrative Enforcement of Orders

(a) A party or support enforcement agency seeking to enforce a support order or an income-withholding order, or both, issued by a tribunal of another state . . . may send the documents required for registering the order to a support enforcement agency of this state.

(b) . . . [T]he support enforcement agency . . . shall consider and, if appropriate, use any administrative procedure authorized by the law of this state to enforce a support order or an income-withholding order, or both. If the obligor does not contest administrative enforcement, the order need not be registered. If the obligor contests the validity or administrative enforcement of the order, the support enforcement agency shall register the order pursuant to this [act].

§ 601. Registration of Order for Enforcement

A support order or income-withholding order issued in another state . . . may be registered in this state for enforcement.

§ 602. Procedure to Register Order for Enforcement

(a) . . . [a] support order or income-withholding order of another state . . . may be registered in this state by sending the following . . . to the [appropriate tribunal] in this state:

(1) a letter of transmittal . . . requesting registration and enforcement;

(2) two copies, including one certified copy, of the order to be registered, including any modification of the order;

(3) a sworn statement by [petitioner] or a certified statement by the custodian of the records showing the amount of any arrearage;

(4) [identifying information about the obligor an any of the obligor's property in the state not exempt from execution]

(5) except as otherwise provided in § 312, the name and address of the obligee and, if applicable, the person to whom support payments are to be remitted.

(b) On receipt . . . , the registering tribunal shall cause the order to be filed as an order of anther state . . .

. . .

(d) If two or more orders are in effect, the [petitioner] shall:

(1) furnish . . . a copy of every support order asserted to be in effect in addition to the documents specified in this section;

(2) specify the order alleged to be the controlling order, if any; and

(3) specify the amount of consolidated arrears, if any.

(e) A request for a determination of which is the controlling order may be filed separately or with a request for registration and enforcement or for registration and modification. . . .

§ 603. Effect of Registration for Enforcement

(a) A support order or income-withholding order issued in another state . . . is registered when the order is filed in the registering tribunal of this state.

(b) A registered support order issued in another state is enforceable in the same manner and is subject to the same procedures as an order issued by a tribunal of this state.

(c) Except as otherwise provided in this article, a tribunal of this state shall recognize and enforce, but may not modify, a registered support order if the issuing tribunal had jurisdiction.

§ 604. Choice of Law

(a) . . . [T]he law of the issuing state . . . governs:

(1) the nature, extent, amount, and duration of current payments under a registered support order;

(2) the computation and payment of arrearages and accrual of interest on the arrearages under the support order; and

(3) the existence and satisfaction of other obligations under the support order.

(b) In a proceeding for arrears under a registered support order, the statute of limitation of this state or of the issuing state . . . , whichever is longer, applies.

(c) A responding tribunal of this state shall apply the procedures and remedies of this state to enforce current support and collect arrears and interest due on a support order of another state . . . registered in this state.

. . . .

§ 605. Notice of Registration of Order

(a) When a[n] order . . . issued in another state . . . is registered, the registering tribunal of this state shall notify the nonregistering party. . . .

(b) A notice must inform the nonregistering party:

(1) that a registered order is enforceable as of the date of registration in the same manner as an order issued by a tribunal of this state . . . ;

(2) that a hearing to contest the validity or enforcement of the registered order must be requested within [20] days after notice;

(3) that failure to contest the validity or enforcement of the registered order in a timely manner will result in confirmation of the order and enforcement of the order and the alleged arrearages; and

(4) of the amount of any alleged arrearages.

(c) If the registering party asserts that two or more orders are in effect, a notice must also:

(1) identify the two or more orders and the order alleged by the registering person to be the controlling order and the consolidated arrears, if any;

(2) notify the nonregistering party of the right to a determination of which is the controlling order;

(3) state that the procedures provided in subsection (b) apply to the determination of which is the controlling order; and

(4) state that failure to contest the validity or enforcement of the order alleged to be the controlling order in a timely manner may result in confirmation that the order is the controlling order.

(d) Upon registration of an income-withholding order for enforcement, the support enforcement agency or the registering tribunal shall notify the obligor's employer pursuant to [the income-withholding law of this state].

§ 606. Procedure to Contest Validity or Enforcement of Registered Order

(a) A nonregistering party seeking to contest the validity or enforcement of a registered order in this state shall request a hearing within the time required by section 605. The nonregistering party may seek to vacate the registration, to assert any defense to an allegation of noncompliance . . . , or to contest the remedies being sought or the amount of any alleged arrearages pursuant to § 607.

(b) If the nonregistering party fails to contest the validity or enforcement of the registered support order in a timely manner, the order is confirmed by operation of law.

(c) If a nonregistering party requests a hearing . . . , the registering tribunal shall [set a] hearing and give notice to the parties. . . .

§ 607. Contest of Registration or Enforcement

(a) A party contesting the validity or enforcement of a registered support order or seeking to vacate the registration [must prove] . . . :

(1) the issuing tribunal lacked personal jurisdiction over the contesting party;

(2) the order was obtained by fraud;

(3) the order has been vacated, suspended, or modified by a later order;

(4) the issuing tribunal has stayed the order pending appeal;

(5) there is a defense under the law of this state to the remedy sought;

(6) full or partial payment has been made;

(7) the statute of limitation under § 604 precludes enforcement . . . ; or

(8) the alleged controlling order is not the controlling order.

(b) If a party presents evidence establishing a full or partial defense . . . , a tribunal may stay enforcement of a registered support order, continue the proceeding to permit production of additional relevant evidence, and issue other appropriate orders. . . .

(c) If the contesting party does not establish a defense under subsection (a). . . . , the registering tribunal shall issue an order confirming the order.

§ 608. Confirmed Order

Confirmation of a registered support order, whether by operation of law or after notice and hearing, precludes further contest of the order with respect to any matter that could have been asserted at the time of registration.

§ 609. Procedure to Register Child-Support Order of Another State for Modification

A party . . . seeking to modify . . . a child-support order issued in another state shall register that order in this state in the same manner provided in [the earlier registration provisions] if the order has not been registered. A [petition] for modification may be filed at the same time as a request for registration, or later [and] must specify the grounds for modification.

§ 610. Effect of Registration for Modification

A tribunal of this state may enforce a child-support order of another state registered for purposes of modification, in the same manner as if the order had been issued by a tribunal of this state, but the registered support order may be modified only if the requirements of § 611 or § 613 have been met.

§ 611. Modification of Child-Support Order of Another State

(a) If § 613 does not apply, . . . upon [petition] a tribunal of this state may modify a child-support order issued in another state which is registered in this state if, after notice and hearing, the tribunal finds that:

(1) the following requirements are met:

(A) [no party] resides in the issuing state;

(B) a [petitioner] who is a nonresident of this state seeks modification; and

(C) the [respondent] is subject to the personal jurisdiction of the tribunal of this state; or

(2) this state is the state of residence of the child, or a party who is an individual is subject to the personal jurisdiction of the tribunal of this state, and all of the parties who are individuals have filed consents . . . in the issuing tribunal for a tribunal of this state to modify . . . and assume continuing, exclusive jurisdiction [over the order].

(b) Modification of a registered child-support order is subject to the same requirements, procedures, and defenses that apply to the modification of an order issued by a tribunal of this state and the order may be enforced and satisfied in the same manner.

(c) A tribunal of this state may not modify any aspect of a child-support order that may not be modified under the law of the issuing state, including the duration of the obligation of support. If two or more tribunals have issued child-support orders for the same obligor and same child, the order that controls and must be so recognized under § 207 establishes the aspects of the support order which are nonmodifiable.

(d) In a proceeding to modify . . . , the law of the state that is determined to have issued the initial controlling order governs the duration of the obligation of support. The obligor's fulfillment of the duty of support established by that order precludes imposition of a further obligation of support by a tribunal of this state.

(e) On the issuance of an order [of modification] by a tribunal of this state . . . , the tribunal of this state [obtains] continuing, exclusive jurisdiction.

(f) Notwithstanding subsections (a) through (e) and Section 201(b), a tribunal of this state retains jurisdiction to modify an order issued by a tribunal of this state if:

(1) one party resides in another state; and

(2) the other party resides outside the United States.

§ 612. Recognition of Order Modified in Another State

If a child-support order issued by a tribunal of this state is modified by a tribunal of another state [under UIFSA], a tribunal of this state:

(1) may enforce its order that was modified only as to arrears and interest accruing before the modification;

(2) may provide appropriate relief for violations of its order which occurred before the effective date of the modification; and

(3) shall recognize the modifying order of the other state, upon registration, for the purpose of enforcement.

§ 613. Jurisdiction to Modify Child-Support Order of Another state When Individual Parties Reside in This State

(a) If all of the parties who are individuals reside in this state and the child does not reside in the issuing state, a tribunal of this state has jurisdiction to enforce and to modify the issuing state's child-support order in a proceeding to register that order.

. . . .

HARBISON v. JOHNSTON
New Mexico Court of Appeals
28 P.3d 1136 (2001)

SUTIN, JUDGE.

. . . . (Mother) appeals the district court's order dismissing . . . her motion to modify and enforce the child support provisions of a Texas support and visitation judgment. Mother raises two issues: (1) whether . . . (Father) submitted to personal jurisdiction . . . when he initiated proceedings to enforce the visitation provisions of the Texas judgment, and (2) whether the district court had subject matter jurisdiction to modify or enforce the child support provisions of the same judgment. . . .

. . . . Mother and Father are parents of a child . . . born in El Paso, Texas, in May 1995. When Child was one year old, Father filed an action in Texas . . . to establish paternity. [In]1996, the . . . court entered a judgment . . . adjudicating Father as parent, granting Mother permanent custody, awarding Father visitation rights, and ordering Father to pay child support.

For about two years, Father exercised his visitation rights. . . . In July 1998 Mother and Child moved from El Paso to Las Cruces, New Mexico, so Mother could finish [college]. In August 1998 Father moved to California to perform temporary work on a reservoir construction project, whereupon his visitation with Child ceased, except for one week . . . when Child visited him in California. After . . . approximately nine months, Father returned to El Paso and tried, unsuccessfully, to resume visitation with Child, who continued to live with Mother in Las Cruces.

In November 1999 Father filed a petition in New Mexico . . . , requesting that it recognize and enforce the visitation provisions . . . in the Texas judgment and hold Mother in contempt for violating its requirements. Mother . . . filed a countermotion to modify and enforce the child support provisions . . . in the Texas judgment. . . . Father [moved] to dismiss the child support action. Father argued that the New Mexico court had neither personal jurisdiction nor subject matter jurisdiction to modify and enforce the Texas support order and that Texas had continuing, exclusive jurisdiction over the support order.

Following an evidentiary hearing . . . , the district court entered an order giving full faith and credit to the Texas judgment, modifying its visitation provisions. . . . Following a later hearing, the district court dismissed Mother's motion . . . regarding child support. The district court determined New Mexico lacked both subject matter jurisdiction and personal jurisdiction over Father, and concluded Texas retained exclusive jurisdiction over the support order. Mother appeals. . . .

. . . .

[The court determined the trial court had personal jurisdiction over Father for purposes of the support action, holding that under the state long-arm statute, patterned after UIFSA § 201 (*see* Chapter 7), Father had submitted to jurisdiction by entering a general appearance in New Mexico seeking enforcement of the Texas visitation order. "Once Father invoked and submitted himself to the jurisdiction of New Mexico, he could not then attempt to limit his appearance solely to attacking the personal jurisdiction of the court in the support portion of the proceedings." The court acknowledged that the *Texas* child custody jurisdiction statute [based on § 109 of the Uniform Child Custody Jurisdiction Enforcement Act] would provide a petitioner immunity from personal service in another action when pursuing a custody action under it, but there was no parallel immunity under New Mexico law.]

Mother contends the district court erred in determining that it did not have [subject matter] jurisdiction to consider her motion to modify and enforce the Texas support order. The crux of her argument appears to be that because Father [sought] enforcement of the Texas visitation order, the district court also acquired jurisdiction to hear her motion to modify and enforce the Texas support order.

Two statutory acts govern: the Child Custody Jurisdiction Act (CCJA) and the UIFSA. Jurisdiction over . . . visitation is governed by the CCJA. Jurisdiction over the modification and enforcement of another state's child support order is governed by UIFSA. The standards under each act are different and assign jurisdiction independently. A court's jurisdiction to hear a custody or visitation dispute under the CCJA does not confer jurisdiction . . . to determine issues of child support under the UIFSA. Similarly child support jurisdiction under UIFSA does not confer jurisdiction [over]custody or visitation. We hold the district court's jurisdiction over the visitation proceeding did not confer subject matter jurisdiction to modify and enforce the Texas support order.

Under the UIFSA, a New Mexico court "shall recognize the continuing, exclusive jurisdiction of a tribunal of another state which has issued a child-support order pursuant to a law substantially similar to the Uniform Interstate Family Support Act." [Ed.'s Note: this is the language of UIFSA § 205(d) as it was promulgated in 1992. While this precise language no longer exists in the current version of the Uniform Act, it still accurately describes the position taken by UIFSA] Texas . . . has adopted the UIFSA. Therefore, the two acts are "substantially similar." Under its continuing jurisdiction provision, identical to [New Mexico's], Texas, as the state that issued the child support order, still has continuing, exclusive jurisdiction to modify the order because Father continues to reside in Texas, and the parties have not mutually agreed to confer jurisdiction to New Mexico.

A New Mexico court's power to modify another state's child support order is specifically governed by [UIFSA § 611(a). Ed.'s Note: again, this is the 1992 version, the substance of which remains the law under the 2008 version]. That provision states in pertinent part:

> After a child support order issued in another state has been registered in this state, the responding tribunal of this state may modify the order only . . . after notice and hearing the tribunal finds that:
>
> (1) the following requirements are met:
>
>> (A) the child, the individual obligee, and the obligor do not reside in the issuing state;
>>
>> (B) a petitioner who is a nonresident of this state seeks modification; and
>>
>> (C) the respondent is subject to the personal jurisdiction of the tribunal of this state; or
>
> (2) the child, or a party who is an individual, is subject to the personal jurisdiction of the tribunal of this state and all of the parties who are individuals have filed . . . written consents for a tribunal of this state to modify the support order and assume continuing, exclusive jurisdiction over the order[.]

As a threshold matter, we determine that the Texas judgment . . . was "registered" in New Mexico when Father filed it in the district court for purposes of enforcing its visitation provision.

We conclude, however, that the other statutory prerequisites for New Mexico district court modification of the support order were not met in this case. First, Father still resided in . . . Texas. Second, Mother and Father did not consent in writing for New Mexico to assume continuing, exclusive jurisdiction over the support order. Finally, Mother was a New Mexico resident and thus did not meet the requirement that the party seeking modification be a non-resident of the forum state. Therefore, the district court did not have jurisdiction to modify the Texas support order.

Mother nevertheless argues that the district court had jurisdiction to modify the support order under the federal Full Faith and Credit for Child Support Orders Act (FFCCSOA), 28 U.S.C. § 1738B. Although Mother did not raise [this] below, we address her argument . . . because the FFCCSOA governs subject matter jurisdiction and full faith and credit for support orders and, thus, may be considered for the first time on appeal.

The FFCCSOA . . . is intended to work in tandem with the UIFSA and essentially mirrors its jurisdictional concepts. *See Gentzel v. Williams*, 965 P.2d 855, 860 (Kan. App. 1998) ("FFCCSOA is similar to UIFSA both in . . . structure and intent."); *see generally* Patricia Wick Hatamyar, *Critical Applications and Proposals for Improvement of the Uniform Interstate Family Support Act and the Full Faith and Credit for Child Support Orders Act*, 71 St. John's L. Rev. 1 (1997).

According to subsections (a) and (c) of § 1738B, if a child support order is made by a court that had jurisdiction and gave the parties notice and an opportunity to be heard, a court of another state cannot modify the order except as provided. That is, the FFCCSOA allows modification of a valid order only if (1) neither the child nor any of the parties remain in the issuing state, and the forum state has jurisdiction over the parties; or (2) all parties have consented to the jurisdiction of the forum state to modify the order. 28 U.S.C. § 1738B(e). Because Father remains a resident of Texas and the parties have not consented to a change in jurisdiction, Texas retains continuing, exclusive jurisdiction over modification of the support order under the FFCCSOA. We do not find Section 205(d) of the UIFSA to be in direct conflict with the FFCCSOA and the full faith and credit clause of the United States Constitution, as Mother suggests.

Mother also asked the district court to enforce certain provisions of the Texas support order. In particular, Mother sought employment and financial information as required by the order and a determination of the amount of past child support owed by Father. . . .

We conclude the district court incorrectly concluded it did not have jurisdiction to enforce the support order. Under the UIFSA, if a child support order of another state is properly registered, the registering state is obligated to enforce the order in the same manner as if it had issued the order, even though it remains an order of the issuing state for purposes of modification. [See UIFSA § 603(c) ("Except as otherwise provided in this article, a tribunal of this state shall recognize and enforce, but may not modify, a registered order if the issuing tribunal had jurisdiction.")]

The FFCCSOA similarly obligates states to give full faith and credit to child support orders properly issued by other states and to refrain from modifying such orders unless the limited conditions of the act are met. 28 U.S.C. § 1738B(a), (e). The intended purpose and effect of the enforcement provisions in the UIFSA and the FFCCSOA are to facilitate the enforcement of child support orders among the states. *See generally* Patricia Wick Hatamyar, *Interstate Establishment, Enforcement, and Modification of Child Support Orders,* 25 Okla. City U. L. Rev. 511, 541–43.

We hold the district court had personal jurisdiction over Father regarding the Texas judgment he registered in New Mexico and subject matter jurisdiction to enforce, but not modify, the child support order in that judgment.

NOTES

1. *Restriction of Modification of Child Support Orders Under UIFSA.* As noted in the Sampson & Kurtz excerpt above, under URESA courts would often, in an interstate action, enter a support order for a particular child with terms that differed from the terms of a previously-existing support order. Usually the second, or URESA, order would be for a lesser amount. Generally this second order was not conceived of as a modification of the existing order. *See, e.g., Jefferson County Child Support Enforcement Unit v. Hollands,* 939 S.W.2d 302 (Ark. 1997); *Alaska v. Valdez,* 941 P.2d 144 (Alas. 1997); *In re Kramer,* 625 N.E.2d 808 (Ill. App. 1993) (URESA decree which set lower payments than divorce decree did not stop accumulation of arrearages under the latter); *Dep't of Health & Rehab. Servs. v. Franklin,* 630 So. 2d 661 (Fla. App. 1994); Andrea G. Nadel, Annot., *Construction and Effect of Provision of Uniform Reciprocal Enforcement of Support Act That No Support Order Shall Supersede or Nullify Any Other Order,* 31 A.L.R.4th 347 (1984). Indeed URESA § 31, the so-called anti-supersession clause, stated that a URESA order did not "nullify" any prior order "unless otherwise specifically provided by the [URESA] court. . . ." Courts would rarely even attempt to take advantage of the final proviso, likely because of the awkwardness of a court purporting to change the terms of an order of another state. Instead, most URESA courts likely imagined themselves as merely "enforcing" the prior order, even if only partially, by entering an order for the same or a lesser amount of support than had previously been ordered.

UIFSA's drafters set out to establish a system under which, rather than multiple orders possibly setting different levels of support for the same child, at any one time there would be only one support order for any child. Section 205 of UIFSA is designed to carry out this intent by providing that the court which issued the original order shall have "continuing, *exclusive* jurisdiction" [CEJ] to modify it unless certain conditions are met. While UIFSA does not explicitly define "modify," the federal Full Faith and Credit for Child Support Orders Act (FFCCSOA), 28 U.S.C. § 1738B (referred to in *Harbison* and discussed at Note 7, *infra*) provides a very broad definition of the concept which, when combined with UIFSA § 205, means a UIFSA court lacking modification jurisdiction can do very little where a support order already exists. Under FFCCSOA (which, as federal law, controls in determining when and in what ways full faith and credit must be given to existing support orders), modification is defined as "a change in a child support order that affects the amount, scope, or duration of the order and modifies, replaces, supersedes or *otherwise is made subsequent to the child support order.*" § 1738B(b) (emphasis added).

Under UIFSA § 205, no other court can gain jurisdiction to modify an existing order if one party currently lives in the jurisdiction which issued the original decree. Thus, because the father in *Harbison* was living in Texas, which had issued the original decree, New Mexico lacked subject matter jurisdiction to modify that order. Originally, UIFSA provided that the issuing state would retain continuing, exclusive jurisdiction to modify "*as long as [it] remains*" the residence of one of the parties. In 2001, the language was changed to make explicit that the issuing state would regain CEJ if a party (such as the *Harbison* father) left the issuing state, but returned before any modification had been issued. *Harbison* (and the statute) distinguish between personal and subject matter jurisdiction, making clear that both are required and that the presence of the former does not guarantee the existence of the latter.

Now that New Mexico has told the mother in *Harbison* that it has no jurisdiction to modify the original support order, what would you advise her to do?

2. *Jurisdiction to Modify Under UIFSA.* While the UIFSA rules for modification are much more restrictive than the URESA regime, there are some narrow situations in which a second state can modify another state's support order and assume CEJ to make any future modifications. Two sections deal with modification of an order issued by another state. Under § 611, there must be a finding that either: (1) all the parties have left the issuing state, and the petitioner is a non-resident of the forum and the respondent is subject to the forum's personal jurisdiction *or* (2) all parties have agreed to a modification determination in the forum, so long as the forum is either child's residence or has personal jurisdiction over a party. Thus, *e.g.*, if an Idaho decree was entered when all parties lived there, but now the obligor lives in Iowa and the obligee lives with the child in Maine, Iowa could be a forum under UIFSA for a modification action brought by the obligee. Similarly, Maine would be able to issue a modification order in an action brought by the obligor. Any court which issued such a modification would become the CEJ court with power to deal with any future modifications. Alternatively under § 611, the parties can agree to give a new state the power to modify an existing order so long as it has connection to the litigation by either having personal jurisdiction over a party or being the child's residence. Under § 613, if all parties reside in the forum state and the child has left the issuing state, there is modification jurisdiction.

3. *Enforcing an Existing Support Order Under UIFSA.* The UIFSA approach to enforcement of existing orders is very different from its approach to modification. The statute (§ 603) makes clear that any state can and, indeed, must recognize and enforce the support decrees of other states. Thus, the *Harbison* appellate court held that the trial court had UIFSA jurisdiction to order Father to turn over employment and financial information required under the Texas order and the ability to determine arrearages owed under the Texas decree. Note the breadth of the court's enforcement powers under § 305 reprinted above. It could, *e.g.*, "specify a method of payment" of any arrearages it had determined to exist, it could "enforce orders by civil or criminal contempt," it could "order income withholding," etc.

Of course, not only could the appropriate New Mexico court enforce the order against Father, but Texas, as the issuing state, could also enforce its order so long as Father remained subject to its jurisdiction. In fact, even if another state eventually modified the Texas order under modification jurisdiction obtained under § 611 or § 613, the issuing tribunal in Texas, under § 612(1), could enforce its order to the extent that "arrears and interest" had accrued before the modification.

4. ***The Mechanics of Modifying or Enforcing an Existing Order.*** Article Six of UIFSA outlines the details of the process of modifying or enforcing an existing order. While registration is required as a pre-requisite to modification in the new state, there are situations (*see* Note 6, *infra*) in which enforcement in a non-issuing state can be accomplished without registration. The UIFSA rules for registering an existing order are set out in § 602 which, although titled as a procedure "for enforcement" is made applicable to the modification proceeding by § 609. Note that *Harbison* held that the Texas decree had been properly registered for purposes of UIFSA.

The filing of the foreign order under § 602 constitutes registration under § 603 and the order thereby becomes enforceable in the registering state. The Commentary to §§ 602 and 603 makes clear that the registering of a foreign order in State 2 does not convert a State 1 order into an order of the new state. Instead, as stated in the Commentary to § 603, "the registering tribunal must bear in mind that the enforcement procedures taken, whether to enforce current support or to assist collecting . . . arrears are made on behalf of the issuing State, and are not to be viewed as modifications of the . . . order."

Sections 605 through 608 explain registration contests by the non-registering party. Under § 605, the latter is informed that he or she has 20 days in which to contest the registered order. The respondent may, according to § 606(a), "seek to vacate the registration, to assert any defense to an allegation of noncompliance . . . or to contest the remedies being sought or the amount of any alleged arrearages . . . ." The grounds for contesting the validity or enforcement of a registered order are detailed in § 607(a). If no contest is filed or if no defense is proven under § 607(a), the order is confirmed which, under § 608, precludes the respondent from raising any claim that "could have been asserted at the time of registration."

5. ***Choice of Law in Enforcement of Existing Orders.*** As noted earlier, UIFSA's general choice of law rule (§ 303) directs the forum tribunal to apply the law of its own state. Based on a policy of allowing a forum court to apply familiar rules, § 303 acknowledges that other UIFSA provisions make exceptions to the general rule. The most important such provision is § 604, which deals with the enforcement of an existing decree in another state. It states that the law of the issuing state will control "the nature, extent, amount, and duration of current payments" where the support order is being enforced in a second state. Similarly, if the support order in the issuing state terminates support when the child turns 18, a new order cannot thereafter be entered by a different state where child support is available for an older child, because that would be the equivalent to allowing multiple orders for one child, in contravention of UIFSA's basic approach. *In re Spencer v. Spencer*, 882 N.E.2d 886 (N.Y. 2008); *see Marshak v. Weser*, 915 A.2d 613 (N.J. App. Div. 2007). Thus, for example, if State A's order provides for support "until adulthood," which is defined in State A as the age of 21, and it is registered in State B, which has an 18-year-old age of majority, the latter state will be obligated to enforce the order until the age of 21. *See, e.g., Robdau v. Va. Dept. Soc. Servs.*, 543 S.E.2d 602 (Va. Ct. App. 2001); *State ex rel. Harnes v. Lawrence*, 538 S.E.2d 223 (N.C. Ct. App. 2000). The rationale for this rule is explained by the Drafters as deriving from the Act's insistence that the second state is not creating a new order, but simply assisting in the enforcement of the first state's order. Thus, the law of the issuing state determines the meaning of the terms of the order.

A different choice of law rule is provided in subsection (b) for the statute of limitations for collection of arrearages. This provision directs the court to the law of either the forum or the issuing state, whichever is longer. *See Attorney General v. Litten*, 999 S.W.2d 74 (Tex. App. 1999). According to the Commentary, this rule ensures that "the obligor should not gain an undue benefit from the choice of residence if the forum State has a shorter statute of limitations. . . ." The Drafters assert that if the forum state's statute provides for a longer period of recoverability than the issuing state's the obligor cannot justly complain about being treated the same as all other obligors in the forum state. While not mentioned by the Commentary, this rule might be even more persuasively justified by its child-centered nature. Local law governs, under § 604(c), in determining the procedures available for enforcement. Thus, the enforcement court could, *e.g.*, rely on its license revocation statute even if the issuing state did not have a similar law.

6. *Direct Enforcement of Child Support Orders and Wage Withholding Orders.* One of UIFSA's major innovations is direct enforcement of existing orders in a second state without involvement by any tribunal in the second state. Under § 501, a wage withholding order issued by State X can be sent to the obligor's employer in State Y "without first filing a [petition] . . . or registering the order with a tribunal. . . ." Under § 502(b), upon receipt of such an order, the employer must treat it "as if it had been issued by a tribunal" of State Y and, under subsection (c), comply with the order's terms concerning the duration and amount of periodic payments, medical support, fees and costs of attorneys and child support agencies and arrearages. Subsection (d) provides, however, that the law of the obligor's state shall govern limits on the amount the employer can charge for processing, the maximum amount which can be withheld from the obligor's income and time limits on employer compliance. Failure to comply with a foreign income withholding order subjects the employer, under § 505, to any penalties applicable to the failure to withhold under an in-state order. Under § 506, an obligor seeking to contest the validity of enforcement of an out-of-state order received by his or her employer must register the order and then file a contest under §§ 605–608 (Note 4, *supra*).

A separate provision of the statute, § 507, deals with administrative enforcement of a support order by the support enforcement agency of the obligor's state, again without involvement of a tribunal. Under subsection (a), a party or agency in the obligee's state can send a copy of the order to the agency in obligor's state. That agency is authorized, under subsection (b), to use any administrative procedures available for domestic orders to enforce the out-of-state order. As the Commentary to § 507 states, "[f]or example, if the administrative hearing procedure must be exhausted for an intrastate order before a contesting party may seek relief in a tribunal, the same rule applies to an interstate order received for administrative enforcement."

7. *The Federal Full Faith and Credit for Child Support Orders Act of 1994.* Between the initial promulgation of UIFSA in 1992 and the passage of the federal mandate to the states to enact UIFSA (in the 1996 Welfare Reform Act), Congress passed the Full Faith and Credit for Child Support Orders Act of 1994 (FFCCSOA, codified at 28 U.S.C. § 1738B) which, like UIFSA, was designed to replace the multiple orders of URESA with a "one-order" regime. The rationale for enacting the Federal law merely two years after the Uniform Act had been proposed has been described as "somewhat elusive." Patricia Wick Hatamyar, *Critical Applications and Proposals for Improvement of the Uniform Interstate Family Support Act and the Full Faith and Credit for Child Support Orders Act*, 71 St. John's L. Rev. 1 (1997). Professor Hatamyar reports, however, that

> [s]ome child support advocates . . . worried that piecemeal, state-by-state adoption of UIFSA would delay receipt of the intended benefits by interstate obligees. In addition, given the states' patchwork adoption of variants of URESA . . . UIFSA supporters believed that the "uniform law" would become anything but uniform.

Id. at 6; *see also* Patricia Wick Hatamyar, *Interstate Establishment, Enforcement, and Modification of Child Support*, 25 Okla. City U.L. Rev. 511(2000).

Under the statute, states must enforce support orders of other states so long as the original order was entered consistently with the provisions of § 1738B(c). The latter subsection in turn requires that the original order be entered with jurisdiction (both personal and subject matter) and consistent with due process requirements of notice.

The federal statute, like UIFSA, restricts a second state's ability to modify an existing support order. According to § 1738B(e), modification is allowed only when there is no longer a court with continuing, exclusive jurisdiction or all parties have agreed to transfer continuing, exclusive jurisdiction to a new state. Critically, the federal law does not permit a second state to use the URESA-era charade that it was not modifying a prior support order but merely issuing an independent order. As mentioned in Note 1, *supra*, the Act defines modification as "a change in a child support order that affects the amount, scope, or duration of the order and modifies, replaces, supersedes or *otherwise is made subsequent to the child support order.*" § 1738B(b) (emphasis added). *See Isabel M. v. Thomas M.*, 624 N.Y.S.2d 356 (Fam. Ct. 1995) (finding italicized phrase prohibits action filed under New York's version of URESA where another state has continuing, exclusive jurisdiction over existing order).

The federal act has been upheld against constitutional attack. *Kilroy v. Superior Court*, 63 Cal. Rptr. 2d 390 (App. 1997). In addressing petitioner's argument that the Act exceeded Congressional power under the Commerce Clause, the court distinguished *United States v. Lopez*, 514 U.S. 549 (1995), in which the Gun-Free School Zone Act of 1990 was found unconstitutional. The court found "payments between parents in different states substantially affects interstate commerce," 63 Cal. Rptr. 2d at 400, noting extensive Congressional findings identifying the particular problems faced by children and custodial parents in interstate litigation. *Kilroy* also rejected petitioner's Tenth Amendment attack, noting express Congressional authority under the Full Faith and Credit Clause, Art. IV, § 1, to provide for the proof of the acts of other states and "prescribe . . . the effect thereof."

For other cases interpreting FFCCSOA, see Kurtis A. Kemper, *Validity, Construction, and Application of Full Faith and Credit for Child Support Orders Act (FFCCSOA), 28 U.S.C.A. § 1738B — State Cases*, 18 A.L.R.6th 97 (2006).

8. *Sorting Through Multiple Orders.* Despite UIFSA's determination to move from a world of multiple orders to one in which there is only one effective order at any time, the possibility of more than one existing support order for a particular child remains. For example, a prior order under URESA might exist, or a court in a UIFSA case might have erroneously entered an order without jurisdiction or a modification order might have been entered without jurisdiction in a default proceeding. In *P.A.N. v. R.N.*, 1996 Del. Fam. Ct. LEXIS 139 (Nov. 8, 1996), the court found a pre-UIFSA Delaware decree to be a nullity. The decree, entered under URESA, ordered payment of the same amount of support ordered by a prior New York divorce. The declaration of nullity was based upon UIFSA § 207(a)(2) (now § 207(b)(1)), which provides that where multiple support orders for the same child exist and only one of the issuing courts would have continuing exclusive jurisdiction under the Act that the latter was the order entitled to recognition. In *P.A.N.*, the obligee and the child remained in New York which, thus, retained continuing exclusive modification jurisdiction.

Section 207's rules designed to guide a court in determining what order is the UIFSA "one-order" will be especially important in the transition period as the country moves from the URESA multiple order regime to the UIFSA world with only one binding order at any time. As the Official Comment to the section states,

> [E]ven assuming universal enactment of UIFSA, many years will pass before its one-order system will be completely in place. . . . [This provision] is designed to span the gulf between the one-order system and the multiple order system in place under RURESA. . . . [M]ultiple orders issued under RURESA number in the tens of thousands; it can be reasonably anticipated that those orders . . . will continue in effect far into the future.

PROBLEMS

Problem 5-28. Morris and Kitty, a married couple with two children, live in Nevada. Morris leaves one morning "for work" and does not communicate with Kitty any further. She discovers that he now lives in Maine. She would like to be rid of Morris and get support for their children, a 6-year-old and a 4-year old. Assume both states have enacted UIFSA. What do you advise? Which state's law will govern the duration of any child support order she might obtain? Which state's guidelines govern?

Problem 5-29. George and Martha divorce and he is awarded custody of their only child, Denzel. Martha is ordered to pay $250 monthly child support. She moves to another state. After three years, George reports Martha hasn't paid support in two years and also has obtained a new job which pays a lot more money. George would like to collect the arrearages and seek an upward modification. Both states have enacted UIFSA. What are his options?

Problem 5-30.   Rebecca and Dan's New Jersey divorce decree ordered Dan to pay $300 monthly in support for their children. Three years later, with all parties having moved to Florida, a court there ordered Dan to pay off his $8,000 in arrearages at a rate of $150 per month in addition to the $300 monthly support. Two years after that, when Dan moved back to New Jersey, Rebecca sought an order from the original divorce court, ordering him to pay arrearages at a rate of $300 monthly. Neither Rebecca in her petition nor Dan in his response mentioned the Florida decree. The judge granted Rebecca's petition changing the arrearage payment schedule. Now Dan has sought a rehearing claiming a violation of UIFSA and FFCCSOA. As clerk to the judge who will decide the case, outline your analysis of the issues, the best arguments on both sides and your recommended resolution.

Problem 5-31.   John and Betsy are divorced in State A. Though they have three children, their divorce decree omits mention of support, but does provide for alimony, property division and custody. John subsequently moves to State B. The duty to support in State A extends to age 18, while State B requires support until age 21. Betsy has filed a UIFSA action in State A which is forwarded to State B. In this action, she seeks support for the children until age 21. Personal jurisdiction over John has been obtained. What are the issues and the parties' likely arguments? Would your answer change if the State A divorce decree, instead of ignoring child support had said that it "reserves the question of support until John is released from his current jail sentence"?

Problem 5-32.   Eduardo and Helga are married, have two children and live in Tennessee. On a business trip to Illinois, Eduardo meets Natasha, with whom he falls madly in love. When Helga finds out, she divorces Eduardo in Tennessee. The decree orders Eduardo to pay $250 monthly child support. Subsequently, Eduardo loses his job in Tennessee and moves to Illinois to live with Natasha. Because he has not been paying his support, Helga files a UIFSA petition in Tennessee which is forwarded to Illinois. After obtaining personal jurisdiction over Eduardo, the Illinois court enters an order for $300 monthly in support, failing to address arrearages, which were not mentioned in the pleadings. After futile attempts to find gainful employment in Illinois, Eduardo is kicked out of their home by Natasha and moves to Wyoming. Helga moves to Illinois with the children to live with her parents and files an action in Wyoming seeking to register the Illinois decree providing for prospective payment of $300 monthly and seeks arrearages in Wyoming under the Tennessee divorce decree. Is she entitled to such relief?

Chapter 6

CHILD CUSTODY

A. INTRODUCTION

Custody of a minor child ordinarily encompasses a broad set of rights, including the right to live with the child in a shared residence and decision-making authority with respect to such matters as discipline, the child's name, where the child lives, who visits the child, and the child's education, earnings, medical treatment, and religious training. With these rights comes the duty to provide the child protection and support. But when a divorce court allocates custody between the parents, one or the other parent may lose some of these rights. Nonetheless, even when one parent is awarded primary custody, the other usually retains visitation rights, support duties, and the right to make certain decisions, particularly when the child is temporarily with that parent. In joint custody awards, courts often divide the broad concept of "custody" into legal custody, which refers to authority to make important decisions for the child such as those relating to education and medical care, and physical custody, which refers to rights to physical care and control.

Custody disputes between separating parents should be distinguished from child abuse proceedings, in which the state may deprive either or both parents of some or all parental rights, including physical custody, temporarily or permanently. These proceedings are addressed in Chapter 10. While in abuse proceedings the state must justify the limitation of parental rights as necessary to protect the child from harm, showings of harm are not required in private custody proceedings. Custody disputes can arise between two loving and entirely adequate parents: although in such a case neither parent could show that the other's custody risked harm to the child, the court must still resolve the parents" custody dispute. Harm can be at issue in custody proceedings, of course, and a showing of harm is normally necessary before one of the separating parents can be deprived of all contact with the child. This chapter addresses custody disputes between parents and between parents and third parties. Issues concerning whether a person enjoys legal status as a parent are addressed in Chapter 9.

[1] Brief History of Inter-Parental Custody Disputes

"The power of a parent by our English laws is much more moderate [than the practically absolute power of the father in laws of ancient Rome]; but still sufficient to keep the child in order and obedience." 1 BLACKSTONE, COMMENTARIES 452. Blackstone wrote that "a mother, as such, is entitled to no power, but only to reverence and respect." *Id.* at 453. In the oft-cited case of *Rex v. DeManneville*, 102 Eng. Rep. 1054 (K.B. 1804), the court ordered an eight-month-old nursing infant removed from the mother and returned to the father, despite the mother's uncontested allegations that the parental separation was due to the father's extreme cruelty. Applicable only to married fathers, the broadly-stated paternal preference rule of English law never gained a significant foothold in the United States, at least after colonial times. June Carbone, From Partners to Parents 180–81 (2000) While some early 19th century American courts approvingly cited the English rule, *see, e.g.*, *Commonwealth v. Briggs*, 16 Pick. 203 (Mass. 1834), the American rule quickly became the "best interests of the child." Many rules of thumb have been used to apply this standard. One mid-19th century commentator suggested that in divorce disputes, most courts followed the general rule that "children will be best taken care of and instructed by the innocent party." Bishop, Commentaries on the Laws of Marriage and Divorce 520 (1852). Although this principle today is outdated, remnants of the fault notion persist. Mary Ann Mason, From Father's Property to Children's Rights 63–64 (1994) ("Courts were so offended by adulterous mothers that they most often denied them visitation rights and cut off all obligations for support by the husband.")

The "tender years" doctrine, under which the mother was deemed to be the more suitable custodian for young children, was developed in the 19th century. In 1813, the Pennsylvania Supreme Court reasoned: "[C]onsidering [the children's] tender age, they stand in need of that kind of assistance which can be afforded by none so well as a mother." *Commonwealth v. Addicks*, 5 Binn. 520 (Pa. 1813). The presumption favoring mothers was justified both by the assumed biological superiority of mothers as parents and by social custom, which assigned responsibility for parenting to mothers. Early defenses of this doctrine glorified maternal love. *See, e.g. Krieger v. Krieger*, 81 P.2d 1081, 1083 (Idaho 1938) (the maternal preference "needs no argument to support it because it arises out of the very nature and instincts of motherhood; nature has ordained it"); *Tuter v. Tuter*, 120 S.W.2d 203, 205 (Mo. Ct. App. 1938) ("[t]here is but a twilight zone between a mother's love and the atmosphere of heaven.")

The tender years presumption was the dominant rule for resolving custody disputes between married parents through much of the twentieth century. It eroded in the 1970s and has been formally abolished in virtually all states. *See* Mary Ann Mason, From Father's Property to Children's Rights 124–27 (1994). The decline of the presumption can be attributed in part to a rejection by courts of the sharply differentiated gender roles. Although in actual practice roles are changing slowly, courts and legislatures are reluctant to assume that maternal custody is in the child's best interest. Courts in the 1980s described the tender years presumption as based on "outdated stereotypes." *Pusey v. Pusey*, 728 P.2d 117 (Utah 1986). The decline of the legal preference for mothers in custody disputes was hastened by a series of constitutional challenges. The United States Supreme Court has never addressed the constitutionality of a gender preference rule in divorce custody cases, but many lower courts have struck down such a rule, either on constitutional grounds or under the best interests principle. *See, e.g.*, *Ex parte Devine*, 398 So. 2d 686 (Ala. 1981) (unconstitutional); *Bazemore v. Davis*, 394 A.2d 1377 (D.C. 1977) (violates best interests principle); *State ex rel. Watts*, 350 N.Y.S.2d 285 (1973) (both); *see also Commonwealth ex rel. Spriggs v. Carson*, 368 A.2d 635 (Pa. 1977) (doctrine of questionable constitutionality). At least one court has found it violative of a state Equal Rights Amendment. *People ex rel. Irby v. Dubois*, 354 N.E.2d 562 (Ill. App. Ct. 1976).

In contrast to the early power of the married father and the expansion of authority in the married mother, parental rights were slow to develop in other large groups of parents. Until emancipation, the right to custody of the children of slaves resided solely in the child's owner, who could separate the child from the mother and father at any time. "Indignation against . . . violations of the parental bond was a central rallying cry of the antislavery movement" and one of the motivations for the enactment of the Thirteenth and Fourteenth Amendments. PEGGY COOPER DAVIS, NEGLECTED STORIES: THE CONSTITUTION AND FAMILY VALUES 105, 112–17 (1997). At common law, the child of unmarried parents was the legal child of neither, "filius nullius." In the middle to late nineteenth century, state laws began to recognize mothers as legal parents of their nonmarital children and proper custodians even against the claims of adjudicated fathers, who, nonetheless, were obligated to provide support. *See* MARY ANN MASON, FROM FATHER'S PROPERTY TO CHILDREN'S RIGHTS 68–73 (1994). In many states, nonmarital fathers had no claim to the custody of their children against the mother or the state until the 1972 Supreme Court decision in *Stanley v. Illinois*, 405 U.S. 645 (1972). *Id.* at 145–48.

[2] Children and Divorce: Perspectives from Social Science

The impact of family dissolution on children has been a subject of considerable interest to social scientists. While experts tend to agree on the importance of the child's need for continuity, there is variation of opinion about what type of continuity is most important. Three well-known psychoanalysts, Joseph Goldstein, Anna Freud, and Albert Solnit emphasize the child's need for an undisturbed bond with a psychological parent, who has unconditional parental authority. This focus, which derives from psychological attachment theory, holds that the child's healthy psychological development is only possible if this critical parent-child bond is protected. This emphasis, in the divorce context, leads these authors to favor giving the primary caregiver sole authority and to permit only so much visitation with others as that parent deems appropriate. JOSEPH GOLDSTEIN, ANNA FREUD & ALBERT J. SOLNIT, BEYOND THE BEST INTERESTS OF THE CHILD 38 (1973).

Other experts have emphasized that continued, meaningful contact with both parents after divorce is important to a child's well-being. Beginning in the 1970s, research on children's relationships with their fathers confirmed that fathers can play an important role in children's development. *See generally* Michael E. Lamb & Charlie Lewis, *The Development and Significance of Father-Child Relationships in Two-Parent Families, in* THE ROLE OF THE FATHER IN CHILD DEVELOPMENT 272 (Michael E. Lamb, ed., 4th ed. 2004); Paul R. Amato & Julie M. Sobolewski, *The Effects of Divorce on Fathers and Children: Nonresidential Fathers and Stepfathers, id.* at 341. Although social scientists agree that exposure to intense conflict between their parents is harmful to children, in most families, maintaining parent-child relationships with both parents is now viewed by many psychologists as important for children's adjustment. The post-divorce family must be restructured, but family relationships should be maintained. ROBERT E. EMERY, RENEGOTIATING FAMILY RELATIONSHIPS: DIVORCE, CHILD CUSTODY, AND MEDIATION

184–93 (1994). Studies addressing continuing contact with both parents in the context of joint custody are discussed in Note 5, Section C[1], *infra*.

Another issue on which expert opinion varies is on the impact of divorce on children. Most psychologists emphasize the harmful impact to children of divorce, but some researchers have stressed the diversity of children's responses, noting that some children even gain maturity during their parents' divorce. In general, long-term predictions about the impact of divorce or what arrangement is best for children may be problematic.

E. Mavis Hetherington, Margaret Stanley-Hagan & Edward R. Anderson, *Marital Transitions: A Child's Perspective*
1989 AM. PSYCH. 303, 303–10

There is great diversity in children's responses to their parents' marital transitions . . .

Following the initial responses to the crisis period in their parents' divorce and remarriage, some children exhibit remarkable resiliency and in the long term may actually be enhanced by coping with these transitions; others suffer sustained developmental delays or disruptions; still others appear to adapt well in the early stages of family reorganization but show delayed effects that emerge at a later time, especially adolescence . . . The most commonly reported problem behaviors found in children from divorced and remarried families are aggressive, noncompliant, and acting-out behaviors; decrements in prosocial behavior; problems in academic achievement and school adjustment; and disruptions in peer and heterosexual relations. . . . Although there are some reports of greater depression or internalizing disorders in these children when they reach adolescence . . . these findings are less well substantiated and less consistently found than those citing externalizing problems. . . . Researchers consistently find that children adapt better in a well-functioning single-parent or step-parent family than in a conflict-ridden family of origin. . . .

Temperamentally difficult children have been found to be less adaptable to change and more vulnerable to adversity than are temperamentally easy children. . . . Other individual attributes such as intelligence, independence, internal locus of control, and self-esteem also are related to children's adaptability in the face of stressful life experiences. . . .

The adaptation of children to family transitions also varies with their developmental status. . . . [T]he type of behavior problems and coping mechanisms differ for children of different ages. Although nothing is known about the effects of divorce on infants, young children's responses are mediated by their limited cognitive and social competencies, their dependency on their parents, and their restriction to the home. During the interval immediately following divorce, preschool children are less able to appraise accurately the divorce situation, the motives and feelings of their parents, their own role in the divorce, and possible outcomes. Thus young children may blame themselves for the divorce, may fear abandonment by both parents, may misperceive parents' emotions, needs, and behaviors, and may harbor fantasies of reconciliation. . . .

The cognitive immaturity that creates profound anxieties for the child who is young at the time of [the] parents' divorce may prove beneficial over time. Ten years after divorce these children have fewer memories of either parental conflict [or] their own earlier fears and suffering . . . and they typically have developed a close relationship with the custodial parent. . . . In contrast, those who had been adolescents and who retain memories of the conflict and stress associated with the divorce may be more consciously troubled. . . .

. . . [Older children] are better able to accurately assign responsibility for the divorce, to resolve loyalty conflicts, and to assess and cope with additional stresses such as economic changes and new family role definitions. The older child also is able to take advantage of extra-familial support systems. Adolescents may show remarkable maturity as they assume greater responsibilities . . . but many experience premature detachment from their families. It is estimated that one-third of older children and adolescents become disengaged from their families. If this disengagement leads to greater involvement in a prosocial peer group, school attainment, or nurturant, constructive relationships outside of the family, this can be an adaptive, positive coping mechanism. If, however, it is associated with involvement in antisocial groups and activities with little adult concern [or] monitoring, the outcomes can be disastrous. . . .

The deleterious effects of marital discord, divorce and life in a single-parent family in which the mother has custody are more pervasive for boys than for girls. . . . [B]oys . . . show a higher rate of behavior disorders and problems in interpersonal relations both in the home and in the school with teachers and peers. Boys also are more likely to show more sustained noncompliant, aggressive behavior even two to three years after divorce. . . . Disturbances in social and emotional adjustment in girls living with their mothers have largely disappeared by two years after divorce; however, problems may reemerge at adolescence in the form of precocious sexual behavior and disruptions in heterosexual relations. . . . There is some evidence that school-aged children adapt better in the custody of a parent of the same sex. . . .

The balance between conflict and cooperation and the conflict resolution strategies used by divorced parents seem to play an especially important role in the adjustment of children. . . . Although parents may feel angry or resentful, if they are able to control their anger, cooperate in parenting, negotiate differences, and not directly expose their children to quarrels or violence, children show fewer emotional and social problems. Most children wish to maintain relations with both parents, and continued positive relations with both parents has been shown to be an important factor in children's successful adjustment to family transitions. . . .

In single-parent families, the well-being of the custodial parent and the quality of the parent-child relationship become central to the adjustment of the child. Yet the stress of separation and divorce places both men and women at risk for psychological and physical dysfunction. . . . Alcoholism, drug abuse, depression, psychosomatic problems, and accidents are more common among divorced than non-divorced adults. . . .

. . . The significance of these . . . changes is that children are encountering an altered parent at a time when they need stability. . . . Furthermore, parents and children may exacerbate each other's problems. A physically ill, emotionally disturbed, or preoccupied parent and a distressed, demanding, noncompliant child may have difficulty giving each other support or solace.

In 2002, Mavis Hetherington and Joan Kelly published a comprehensive reflection on the impact of divorce on children, drawing on Hetherington's 30 years of research. E. MAVIS HETHERINGTON & JOAN B. KELLY, FOR BETTER OR FOR WORSE: DIVORCE RECONSIDERED (2002); *see also* ROBERT E. EMERY, MARRIAGE, DIVORCE, AND CHILDREN'S ADJUSTMENT (2d ed. 1999) (summarizing current research evidence on children and divorce); ROBERT E. EMERY, RENEGOTIATING FAMILY RELATIONSHIPS: DIVORCE, CHILD CUSTODY, AND MEDIATION 184–93 (1994). In an important longitudinal study, Paul Amato and Alan Booth compared the adjustment and well being of young adults whose parents divorced during the 20 years of the study with those whose families remained intact. PAUL R. AMATO & ALAN BOOTH, A GENERATION AT RISK: GROWING UP IN AN ERA OF FAMILY UPHEAVAL (1997). These researchers found that children who were exposed to serious conflict in their parents' marriages were better off when the conflict was reduced by divorce. Children whose parents' marriages involved low to moderate conflict (perhaps a majority of divorces), however, experienced negative consequences when their parents divorced, as compared to a similar group whose parents remained married.

B. THE BEST INTEREST OF THE CHILD STANDARD

[1]   Introduction

In most states today, the best interest of the child standard is the legal rule applied to child custody decisions. In considering this rule, it is important to recognize that custody determinations under the best interest standard differ in significant ways from most other forms of adjudication.

1. *Child custody determinations are "person-oriented" disputes.* Most legal rules require a determination of the facts relating to some event and are thus "act-oriented." Child custody determinations under the best interest standard, in contrast, are "person-oriented," making relevant "the attitudes, dispositions, capacities, and shortcomings of each parent." Robert H. Mnookin, *Child-Custody Adjudication: Judicial Functions in the Face of Indeterminacy*, 39 LAW & CONTEMP. PROBS. 226, 250–51 (1975). Indeed, because each parent's goal is to persuade the judge that the child's welfare will be promoted by giving that parent custody, each is motivated to present evidence about his or her strengths and about the other parent's deficiencies. It is not surprising that pursuit of this goal generates a great deal of acrimony between parents, an unfortunate outcome since they will continue to have a relationship, the quality of which may affect their child's welfare.

2. *Custody determinations involve predictions about the future.* Most adjudication "requires determination of *past* acts and facts. Child custody determinations under the best interests standard, on the other hand, require individualized predictions: with whom will this child be better off in the years to

come? Proof of what happened in the past is relevant only insofar as it enables the court to decide what is likely to happen in the future." *Id.* at 251–52.

3. *Future behaviors of many persons, including the loser's, may be relevant.* The predictions about the future necessary in child custody determinations under a best-interest standard depend in part on the future behavior of the parties. Even the "loser's" future behavior — how cooperative a parent will he be in a particular visitation arrangement, for example — may be an important factor in determining what result will be best for the child. How the best interests of the child rule is applied may create incentives for certain kinds of behavior and disincentives for others. *Id.* at 252–53.

4. *Trial courts have wide discretion and appellate review is difficult.* Statutory versions of the best interest standard are either simply a reiteration of the policy objective (to make the decision that reflects the child's best interest) or a list of factors to be considered by the court, with no direction about rank ordering or about the weight that should be attached to any particular factor. (The Minnesota statute below is a good example). Thus, a court resolving a custody dispute is free to consider anything that seems relevant under the circumstances to the child's interest, and to weigh the evidence as the judge sees fit — unless it is excluded under the statute or on constitutional grounds. (*See Palmore v. Sidoti, infra*). As a broad discretionary standard, the best interest test does little to constrain judges who might be inclined to base the custody decision on their personal moral and social values. One effect is that the outcome of adjudication is less predictable than it would be under a bright line rule. In the face of this uncertainty, a risk-averse parent for whom having custody is important may be inclined to make concessions to the other spouse in negotiations in order to secure custody by agreement, rather than leave the decision to a court. Moreover, because the standard allows so much discretion, "[p]rior reported cases . . . provide little basis for controlling or predicting the outcome of a particular case." This fact makes appellate review very difficult, and results in wide discretion for trial courts. Mnookin, *supra* at 253–54. *See also* Elizabeth S. Scott, *Pluralism, Parental Preference and Child Custody*, 80 Cal. L. Rev. 615 (1992), (discussion of the shortcomings of the best interest standard).

5. *Adjudication is rare.* The final point is that actual adjudication is relatively rare, in part, as suggested above, because risk-averse parents, faced with an uncertain outcome, favor agreement. Parties often agree about who should have custody. *See* Robert H. Mnookin & Eleanor E. Maccoby, *Private Ordering Revisited: What Custodial Arrangements Are Parents Negotiating?*, in Divorce Reform at the Crossroads 52 (S. Sugarman & H. Kay, eds. 1990) (parents agree from the beginning in 78.1% of divorce cases). Even when they initially disagree, parents often settle their disagreements before going to court. Litigation involving parents who are in deep conflict, however, can take substantial time and resources, both for the family and the court. "Parents in chronic custody disputes often distrust each other, are afraid, angry, project blame onto the ex-partner, refuse to cooperate and communicate, make allegations of abuse, and sabotage each other's parenting. Many high conflict cases pose an even greater threat to children because there are additional problems of violence, substance abuse, mental illness or threats of abduction." Linda D. Elrod, *Reforming the System to Protect Children*

in High Conflict Custody Cases, 28 Wm. Mitchell L. Rev. 495 (2001). In some states, mandatory mediation and court-ordered custody evaluations may reduce the necessity of adjudication. These topics are considered in Chapter 8, Section B (mediation) and Section D of this chapter.

STATUTORY FRAMEWORKS

MINNESOTA STATUTES ANNOTATED

§ 518.17

Subdivision 1. The best interests of the child.

(a) "The best interests of the child" means all relevant factors to be considered and evaluated by the court including:

(1) the wishes of the child's parent or parents as to custody;

(2) the reasonable preference of the child, if the court deems the child to be of sufficient age to express preference;

(3) the child's primary caretaker;

(4) the intimacy of the relationship between each parent and the child;

(5) the interaction and interrelationship of the child with a parent or parents, siblings, and any other person who may significantly affect the child's best interests;

(6) the child's adjustment to his home, school, and community;

(7) the length of time the child has lived in a stable, satisfactory environment and the desirability of maintaining continuity;

(8) the permanence, as a family unit, of the existing or proposed custodial home;

(9) the mental and physical health of all individuals involved except that a disability . . . of a proposed custodian of a child shall not be determinative of the custody of the child, unless the proposed custodial arrangement is not in the best interest of the child;

(10) the capacity and disposition of the parties to give the child love, affection, and guidance, and to continue educating and raising the child in the child's culture and religion or creed, if any;

(11) the child's cultural background;

(12) the effect on the child of the actions of an abuser, if related to domestic abuse . . . that has occurred between the parents;

(13) except in cases in which a finding of domestic abuse . . . has been made, the disposition of each parent to encourage and permit frequent and continuing contact by the other parent with the child.

The court may not use one factor to the exclusion of all others. The primary caretaker may not be used as a presumption in determining the best interests of the child. The courts must make detailed findings on each of the factors and explain how the factors led to its conclusions and to the determination of the best interests of the child.

(b) The court shall not consider conduct of a proposed custodian that does not affect the custodian's relationship to the child.

MODEL MARRIAGE AND DIVORCE ACT (as amended 1973)

§ 402. [Best Interest of Child].

The court shall determine custody in accordance with the best interest of the child. The court shall consider all relevant factors including:

(1) the wishes of the child's parent or parents as to his custody;

(2) the wishes of the child as to his custodian;

(3) the interaction and interrelationship of the child with his parent or parents, his siblings, and any other person who may significantly affect the child's best interest;

(4) the child's adjustment to his home, school, and community; and

(5) the mental and physical health of all individuals involved.

The court shall not consider conduct of a proposed custodian that does not affect his relationship to the child.

[2]   Determining the Child's Best Interests

[a]   Gender and Caretaking Roles

BURCHARD v. GARAY
California Supreme Court
229 Cal. Rptr. 800 (1986)

BROUSSARD, J.

This case concerns the custody of William Garay, Jr., age two and one-half at the date of trial. Ana Burchard, his mother, appeals from an order . . . awarding custody to the father, William Garay.

As a result of a brief liaison between Ana and William, Ana became pregnant. Early in her term she told William that she was pregnant with his child, but he refused to believe that he was the father. . . .

. . . Ana undertook the difficult task of caring for her child, with the help of her father and others, while working at two jobs and continuing her training to become a registered nurse. William continued to deny paternity, and did not visit the child or provide any support.

. . . Ana [subsequently] brought a paternity and support action. After court-ordered blood tests established that William was the father, he stipulated to paternity and to support in the amount of $200 a month. Judgment was entered accordingly on November 24, 1980. In December . . . William visited his son for the first time. In the next month he moved in with Ana and the child in an attempt to live together as a family; the attempt failed and six weeks later he moved out.

William asked for visitation rights; Ana refused and [sought] exclusive custody. William responded, seeking exclusive custody himself. . . .

. . . Applying the "best interests" test, [the court] awarded custody to William. Its decision appears to be based upon three considerations. The first is that William is financially better off — he has greater job stability, owns his own home, and is "better equipped economically . . . to give constant care to the minor child and cope with his continuing needs." The second is that William has remarried, and he "and the stepmother can provide constant care for the minor child and keep him on a regular schedule without resorting to other caretakers"; Ana, on the other hand, must rely upon babysitters and day care centers while she works and studies. Finally, the court referred to William providing the mother with visitation, an indirect reference to Ana's unwillingness to permit William visitation.

Pursuant to the court order William took custody of the child on August 15, 1982. Ana appealed from the order . . . and William, Jr., remained in his father's custody pending this appeal . . .

[W]e conclude that the trial court erred in applying [the best interests] standard. . . .

The trial court's decision referred to William's better economic position, and to matters such as homeownership and ability to provide a more "wholesome environment" which reflect economic advantage. But comparative income or economic advantage is not a permissible basis for a custody award. . . . If in fact the custodial parent's income is insufficient to provide proper care for the child, the remedy is to award child support, not to take away custody.

The court also referred to the fact that Ana worked and had to place the child in day care, while William's new wife could care for the child in their home. But in an era when over 50 percent of mothers and almost 80 percent of divorced mothers work, the courts must not presume that a working mother is a less satisfactory parent or less fully committed to the care of her child. A custody determination must be based upon a true assessment of the emotional bonds between parent and child. . . . It must reflect also a factual determination of how best to provide continuity of attention, nurturing, and care. It cannot be based on an assumption, unsupported by scientific evidence, that a working mother cannot provide such care — an assumption particularly unfair when, as here, the mother has in fact been the primary caregiver. . . .

All of [the grounds relied on by the trial court] . . . are insignificant compared to the fact that Ana has been the primary caretaker for the child from birth to the date of the trial court hearing, that no serious deficiency in her care has been proven, and that William, Jr., under her care, has become a happy, healthy, well-adjusted child. We have frequently stressed . . . the importance of stability and continuity in the life of a child, and the harm that may result from disruption of established patterns of care and emotional bonds. The showing made in this case is, we believe, wholly insufficient to justify taking the custody of a child from the mother who has raised him from birth, successfully coping with the many difficulties encountered by single working mothers. . . .

The order is reversed.

BIRD, C. J., Concurring.

I write separately to underscore that the trial court's ruling was an abuse of discretion not only in its failure to give due weight to the importance of continuity and stability in custody arrangements but in its assumption that there is a negative relation between a woman's lack of wealth or her need or desire to work and the quality of her parenting. As this case so aptly demonstrates, outmoded notions such as these result in harsh judgments which unfairly penalize working mothers . . .

When the record contains no evidence as to which parent does provide [the greatest] care, clearly the "working mother" factor operates as a negative presumption. Even more clearly, this factor operates unfairly when the record indicates that the mother has in fact been the primary caregiver. The use of such a presumption as a basis for a custody award is of dubious constitutionality.

Furthermore, the presumption is inappropriate because the relationship between maternal employment and the "presumed facts" about the child's best interests is not supported by reason or experience. Typically, it is the mother who provides most day-to-day care, whether or not she works outside the home. . . . A presumption which ignores this fact is likely to lead to erroneous and unfair decisions.

Moreover, there is no accepted body of expert opinion that maternal employment per se has a detrimental effect on a child. . . .

The burden of the trial court's reasoning would certainly fall most heavily on women. In those cases where the father contests custody, he is the parent likely to have superior economic resources. . . . This alone would give him an advantage under the trial court's reasoning. Further, such resources may well include the ability to support a nonworking spouse. Conversely, the mother is likely to have no choice about working, particularly if she does not remarry. . . . In the 25 to 44 age range, the remarriage rate of divorced men is almost double that of divorced women. . . .

Yet, under the trial court's rationale, it is the mother — and not the father — who would be penalized for working out of the home. She and she alone would be placed in this Catch-22 situation. If she did not work, she could not possibly hope to compete with the father in providing material advantages for the child. She would risk losing custody to a father who could provide a larger home, a better neighborhood, or other material goods and benefits . . .[5]

If she did work, she would face the prejudicial view that a working mother is by definition inadequate, dissatisfied with her role, or more concerned with her own needs than with those of her child. This view rests on outmoded notions of a woman's role in our society. Again, this presumption is seldom, if ever, applied even-handedly to fathers. The result — no one would take an unbiased look at the amount and quality of parental attention which the child was receiving from each parent. . . .

The double standard appears again when, as here, the father is permitted to rely on the care which someone else will give to the child. It is not uncommon for courts to award custody to a father when care will actually be provided by a relative, second wife, or even a babysitter. . . . However, the implicit assumption that such care is the equivalent of that which a nonworking mother would provide "comes dangerously close to implying that mothers are fungible — that one woman will do just as well as another in rearing any particular children." ([Nancy D.] Polikoff, *Why Are Mothers Losing?* 7 WOMEN'S RIGHTS L. REP. 235, 241 (1982)). This is scarcely consistent with any enlightened ideas of childrearing. . . .

NOTES

1. *Past Caretaking as a Consideration in Custody Decisions.* The *Burchard* court, in ordering maternal custody, emphasized the mother's experience as the child's primary caretaker. In general, this is a key consideration in custody determinations. Under the tender years presumption, maternal custody was presumed to be in the child's best interest because mothers were primarily responsible for their children's care. Although that presumption has been abandoned, the parents' past caretaking roles continue to be an important consideration in custody determinations. Under the best interest standard, of course, courts can consider many other factors — the focus of our inquiry in this section. This should not be taken to mean that parents' childrearing roles in the intact family no longer are central to custody determinations, both as a legal and as a practical matter. Indeed, it is fair to say that a fundamental debate in custody law and policy focuses on how much weight should be given to past caretaking in deciding future custodial arrangements.

Some courts and legislatures have concluded that custody should be decided primarily on the basis of past caretaking roles. In the past generation, a few states have adopted a primary caretaker preference. *See Garska v. McCoy*, 278 S.E.2d 357 (W. Va. 1981). Recently, the American Law Institute has modernized the primary caretaker preference, adopting a standard that allocates custody in proportion to each parents' fulfillment of caretaking responsibilities during

---

[5] For example, in *Porter v. Porter* (N.D. 1979), 274 N.W.2d 235, the reviewing court affirmed a custody award to a working father because "he is in a position to lend more stability and guidance to nurturing the development of the children during those periods of time in which he would not be actually pursuing his employment. . . ." As the wife had forsaken a career during marriage to care for the children, the husband's earning capacity was substantially greater than hers. It was this greater earning capacity which apparently was the source of his "stability and guidance."

marriage. AMERICAN LAW INSTITUTE, PRINCIPLES OF THE LAW OF FAMILY DISSOLUTION §§ 2.08–2.09 (2002). Reforms of the best interest standard that base the custody determination on parents' past caretaking will be explored at length in Section C[2], *infra*. *See* Elizabeth S. Scott, *Pluralism, Parental Preference and Child Custody*, 80 CAL. L. REV. 615 (1992).

As *Burchard* suggests, under the best interest standard, each parent's past role in caring for the child has an uncertain status. For this reason, feminists and others have argued that mothers are seriously disadvantaged under the best interest standard in ways that are fundamentally unfair.

2. Gender Roles. Chief Justice Bird's concurrence emphasizes the disadvantages divorced women would face in custody cases if a parent's economic advantage and/or remarriage to a stay-at-home spouse were factors a court could take into account. Remarriage of a parent, of course, offers the child a two-parent home, which may be beneficial for some children, although not for all, as discussed below in Note 3. Similarly, economic stability is, generally speaking, good for children. Granting that these factors should not outweigh other, more important, factors, is it consistent with the child's best interest to disregard them altogether?

Some courts have concluded that favoring the parent who can provide home care for the child disadvantages women since most mothers work after divorce and divorced men are more likely to remarry spouses who are not employed outside the home. *See e.g., West v. West*, 21 P.3d 838 (Alaska 2001) (reversing trial court's custody award to father, whose fiancé-nurse (with whom the child had little relationship) would care for child; the father was in Coast Guard and was subject to deployment, while the working mother lived near her parents who could help with child care); *Ireland v. Smith*, 547 N.W.2d 686 (Mich. 1996) (reversing trial court's transfer of custody to father on the ground that mother was a college student and child was in day care); *Linda R. v. Richard E.*, 561 N.Y.S. 2d 29 (App. Div. 1990) (reversing custody award to father where trial court expected mother, but not father, to give priority to child over career). However, some courts may continue to apply different "baselines" to mothers and fathers, crediting fathers who are more involved than traditional fathers (perhaps coaching a team or performing some child care functions), because he is being measured against the role of traditional father, while deeming the working or student mother deficient because she is measured against the performance of a traditional mother.

For a feminist critique of courts for treating mothers like "draftees" (taking for granted their responsibility for children), and fathers like "volunteers," whose efforts are encouraged and appreciated, see Karen Czapanskiy, *Volunteers and Draftees: The Struggle for Parental Equality*, 38 UCLA L. REV. 1415 (1991).

Fairness to mothers may not be the only reason for courts to disregard or limit the salience of economic factors when applying the best interests test. According to Carolyn Frantz, "Wealth allows the distorting influence of socioeconomic biases and cognitive errors, obscures the importance of child support as a means of meeting children's financial needs, and creates harmful incentives for parental behavior in divorce litigation." She argues that courts should consider wealth only "when minimal subsistence is implicated." Carolyn J. Frantz, Note, *Eliminating*

Consideration of Parental Wealth in Post-Divorce Child Custody Disputes, 99 MICH. L. REV. 216 (2000).

3. Serial Partners. In *Bouchard*, the father persuaded the trial court that having a new partner was advantageous for the child. For some children, however, living with the serial partners of a parent may put them at risk for poor outcomes. See ANDREW CHERLIN, THE MARRIAGE-GO-ROUND 190 (2009):

> "Those [children] who experience a series of parental partnerships seem to be more likely to act out, be delinquent, or have a baby . . . Perhaps children find it difficult to adjust to repeated changes in the caregivers and partners of caregivers in their households. Perhaps some short-term boyfriends preoccupy their mothers while providing little support to the children. Or perhaps it's just too hard to cope with complex households in which each child may have different parents and parents have children living elsewhere. What may matter for children, then, is not simply the kind of family they live in but how stable that family is."

4. Parental Interests. As the title of the test says, a child's custody turns on the best interests of the child. In her concurrence in *Bouchard*, however, Justice Bird is arguing that the court must consider a parent's interest in being treated fairly regardless of gender. Fairness to parents arises in other cases as well, such as where the parent has a disabling condition, holds unpopular views or participates in an unusual lifestyle and, as in *Bouchard*, fairness to a parent is sometimes the basis of the custody decision. What is rarely articulated, however, is whether and how parental interests should be taken into account. Professor Jon Elster has argued that

> Barring siblings, a custody case involves three persons, all of whom have a strong interest in the decision. Yet according to the best interest principle, the child's welfare is the dominant consideration. The law does not take any account of the needs and rights of the parents, except to the extent that it admits the child's interest to be the "first and paramount" rather than the "sole" criterion. . . . Even when the consideration of the child's best interest yields a determinate preference for one parent, parental interests ought also to be considered. Some of these derive from the rights of parents, and others from their needs . . . [I]f one parent, usually the mother, has devoted crucial years to child care and perhaps given up her career to do so, it seems prima facie right that she should get custody . . . Another rights-based principle is that custody should not be given to a parent who has used illegal tactics of abduction or procrastination to create a fait accompli in order to benefit from the status quo presumption . . . Considerations of parental needs or welfare also may be relevant . . . The custody decision [however] should not be made on utilitarian principles, with the goal of maximizing the total welfare of the family members. The child needs special protection. That protection should not, however, extend to small gains in the child's welfare achieved at the expense of large losses in parental welfare. Assume, for instance, that the parents are equally fit except that one of them earns twenty percent more than the other. The child can be expected to be somewhat better off with the parent with the

higher income, yet one might feel justified in giving custody to the other parent if having custody means much more to him.

Jon Elster, *Solomonic Judgments: Against the Best Interest of the Child*, 54 U. Chi. L. Rev. 1, 16–20 (1987).

Professor Chambers argues that parental interests are a legitimate basis for preferring the child's primary custodian in a custody dispute. As he notes, parental interests are the driving force behind visitation rules and in some relocation disputes. The problem is how to contain consideration of parental interests:

> While legitimating rules for custody that openly take into account adult needs may have the valuable effect of creating more honest and open legislative debate on the separate interests of adults and children, it also runs the risk, in a world ruled by adults, that legislatures will forget that children, not adults, are the most vulnerable participants in the divorce process . . . I regard these risks as serious. Adults cannot be trusted to keep their own needs in check. We live in a particularly self-indulgent era. At the same time, I continue to believe that, if primary caretakers do in fact typically suffer more than secondary caretakers upon loss of custody, their claims are compelling enough to justify the risks.

David L. Chambers, *Rethinking the Substantive Rules for Custody Disputes in Divorce*, 83 Mich. L. Rev. 477, 503 (1984).

In a recent study of public opinion about child custody, "respondents weigh parental equities along with, and perhaps more heavily than, the children's interests." Sanford L. Braver, et al., *Public Opinion About Child Custody* (2009), http://ssrn.com/abstract=1435043. According to the study's authors, "It may well make sense for the law to acknowledge more openly the relevance of fairness concerns in custody disputes" because debates could then take place openly about the role of fairness to parents on such contentious issues as whether a parent should be allowed to relocate with the child when relocation would impose an emotional and financial burden on the other parent or whether joint legal custody should be awarded to symbolically enhance the noncustodial parent's sense of involvement with the child.

5. Who Wins Custody Contests? Despite the elimination of explicit gender preferences in most jurisdictions, most divorces still conclude with the mother as the primary custodial parent. Although the research is a little dated, many studies have put the figure at about 90%. Robert Mnookin and Eleanor Maccoby, in a study of divorce custody cases in two California counties in the mid-1980s, found that only 10% of families had an arrangement in which fathers had custody and mothers visitation. In 70%, mothers had sole custody and in 20% custody was shared. Eleanor E. Maccoby & Robert H. Mnookin, Dividing the Child: Social and Legal Dilemmas of Custody (1992). A study of a representative sample of cases filed in Maryland during fiscal year 2003 shows a different pattern. "Mothers received primary physical custody in 65 percent of the cases (sole custody plus joint legal with physical to mother) and fathers received primary physical custody in 13 percent of the cases (sole custody plus joint legal with physical to father)." The Women's Law Center of Maryland, Inc., *Families In Transition: A Follow-Up*

Study Exploring Family Law Issues In Maryland (2006), http://www.wlcmd.org/pdf/FamiliesInTransition.pdf. Joint legal and physical custody was ordered in 15% of the cases. *Id.* More than half the cases included joint legal custody. *Id.* Interestingly, the physical custody orders tracked the pattern of the children's residences at the time of filing for custody or divorce, with children living with mothers in 64 percent of cases, with fathers in 11 percent. *Id.* In Wisconsin, "[i]n 1980–81 physical placement with the mother was the post-divorce parenting arrangement in 86% of the cases; with the father in 8% of the cases; shared placement in 2% of the cases; and other arrangements in 2% of the cases . . . [In] . . . 2001 . . . mother placement has decreased to 59%; father placement has remained about the same at 7%; shared placement has increased to 32%; and other arrangements remain at about 2%. Marygold S. Melli & Patricia R. Brown, *Exploring a New Family Form — The Shared Time Family*, 22 INT'L J. LAW, POL'Y & FAM. 231 (2008).

Many fathers who express a desire for sole or joint custody do not actually petition for custody. Maccoby and Mnookin found that only 30% of fathers expressed a preference for maternal custody. The authors suggest that fathers may voice desires for custody but that their preferences are weaker than those of mothers. Also, some fathers may realize that they might desire custody, but are not prepared to assume the responsibilities of child rearing, a role with which they have little experience. *Id.* at 100–03.

Feminist authors continue to question whether the best interest standard, as applied, is gender-neutral. *See, e.g.,* Penelope E. Byran, *Reasking the Woman Question at Divorce*, 75 CHI.-KENT L. REV. 713 (2000) (discussing how gender stereotypes disadvantage women in custody proceedings, and examining feminism's relevance to these problems); Martha Albertson Fineman, *Fatherhood, Feminism and Family Law*, 32 McGEORGE L. REV. 1031 (2001) (arguing that the movement for gender-neutrality in custody proceedings focuses too much on achieving egalitarian results, ignoring important differences between the sexes and ultimately doing mothers a disservice); Katharine T. Bartlett, *Comparing Race and Sex Discrimination in Custody Cases*, 28 HOFSTRA L. REV. 877 (2000) (arguing that the similarities between race and sex discrimination support the categorical ban on all types of discrimination in the *ALI Principles*); Mary Becker, *Judicial Discretion in Child Custody: The Wisdom of Solomon?*, 81 ILL. B.J. 650 (1993) (arguing that highly discretionary aspects of best interests test allow judges to discriminate against women who work for pay, engage in sexual activity, or have less financial resources than the father). Others argue that the test is biased against men. *See, e.g.,* Cynthia A. McNeely, *Lagging Behind the Times: Parenthood, Custody, and Gender Bias in the Family Court*, 25 FLA. ST. U. L. REV. 891 (1998) (arguing that persistence of stereotypes about women as caregivers and men as breadwinners result in persistence of bias against fathers in application of best interest test in custody disputes); Matthew B. Firing, *In Whose Best Interests? Courts' Failure to Apply State Custodial Laws Equally amongst Spouses and its Constitutional Implications*, 20 QUINNIPIAC PROB. L.J. 223 (2007) (arguing that prevalence of custody awards to mothers indicates that courts are engaging in unconstitutional sex discrimination).

6. *Preference for Sex-Matching Parent and Child.*   Another gender-based rule is the preference in custody disputes involving older children for the parent of the same sex. The psychological data demonstrating the importance to adolescent and pre-adolescent children of close relationships with the same-sex parent — both boys and girls — is collected in E. Mavis Hetherington, Margaret Stanley Hagan & Edward R. Anderson, *Marital Transitions: A Child's Perspective*, 1989 AM. PSYCH. 303, 306, and Judith S. Wallerstein, *Child of Divorce: An Overview*, 4 BEHAVIORAL SCIENCE & THE LAW 105, 113 (1986). Professor David Chambers concluded that the research does not justify a preference for sex-matching in custody disputes. David L. Chambers, *Rethinking the Substantive Rules for Custody Disputes in Divorce*, 83 MICH. L. REV. 477 (1984). Nonetheless, some courts have concluded that a child's best interest requires custody with the same-sex parent, at least at certain ages. *See, e.g., Warner v. Warner*, 534 N.E.2d 752 (Ind. Ct. App. 1989) (upholding custody award to father based in part on psychologist's testimony that as child gets older, identification with same-sex parent is important); *Matter of Marriage of Clement*, 627 P.2d 1263 (Or. App. 1981) (stressing importance of mother as role model for five-year-old girl). *But see Giffin v. Crane*, 716 A.2d 1029 (Md. 1998) (citing Maryland's Equal Rights Amendment, court rejects trial court's custody award to mother on ground that teen-age daughter "needs a female hand"); *Tresnak v. Tresnak*, 297 N.W.2d 109 (Iowa 1980) (rejecting "a *priori* notion of parental fitness . . . based on the sex of parent or child").

PROBLEM

Problem 6-1. Emma was born to Jane and Eric, who were 19 years old and unmarried. They separated before Emma was born. Eric got a job in a neighboring town and lived with his mother, while Jane stayed in Somerville and cared for Emma. Eric visited his daughter every two weeks or so and contributed sporadically to her support. When Emma was a year old, Jane became a full-time student at Somerville College, working part-time and getting some financial help from her parents. About a year later, Eric petitioned for custody, on the ground that Emma would be better cared for by his mother, Emma's grandmother, than by "strangers" in the day care center where Emma spent several hours a day while Jane worked, studied and went to classes. Also, he presented evidence that Jane had lived in two different student family housing units since she started school and argued that Emma would be better off in the stable quiet neighborhood where his mother lived. He claimed, and Jane did not dispute, that Jane would be involved in her studies for many years because she planned to go on to law school after graduating from college. Who should be awarded custody if this case is decided under the Minnesota statute?

NOTE ON DOMESTIC VIOLENCE AS A FACTOR IN CUSTODY DECISIONS

A parent's abusive conduct toward a child will be central (probably dispositive) in a custody decision. What about abusive conduct toward the other parent? In an earlier era, domestic violence by one parent against the other may have been considered tangential to consideration of the child's interest. However, in the past decade or so, this has changed; almost every state today considers whether a parent has engaged in domestic violence in the custody analysis.

This trend is a response to heightened concern generally about domestic violence and to the growing recognition that children may experience harm from violence directed at another family member. First, the parent who is violent toward his spouse may also abuse his children. Studies show a correlation between spousal or partner abuse and child abuse. Robert B. Strauss, *Supervised Visitation and Family Violence*, 29 FAM. L.Q. 229, 237–8 (1995). The parent who is violent to his partner has revealed a capacity for violence that may create a risk for the child, even if he has not yet engaged in child abuse. Moreover, even if the child has not suffered physical injury, the likelihood that he has experienced psychological harm is substantial. Children exposed to domestic violence experience anxiety and other adjustment problems. H.M. Hughes, *Impact of Spousal Abuse on Children of Battered Women*, 2(12) VIOLENCE UPDATE (1992). Further, these children are more likely than others to engage in domestic abuse themselves when they become adults. *See generally* Stephanie Holt & SadhbhWhelan, *The Impact Of Exposure to Domestic Violence on Children and Young People: A Review of the Literature.* 32 CHILD ABUSE AND NEGLECT 797 (2008). The impact of domestic violence is not limited to the child or the family of the child. A recent study demonstrated that "children from troubled families [defined as families in which a charge of domestic violence had been filed in local courts] significantly decrease their peers' reading and math test scores and increase misbehavior in the classroom." Scott Carrell & Mark Hoekstra, *Externalities in the Classroom: How Children Exposed to Domestic Violence Affect Everyone's Kids* (2009), http://www.econ.ucdavis.edu/faculty/scarrell/domesticviolence.pdf.

The clear statutory trend is toward a rebuttable presumption against awarding custody to a parent who has engaged in domestic violence, although there is considerable variation among jurisdictions. Linda D. Elrod & Milford D. Dale, *Paradigm Shifts And Pendulum Swings In Child Custody: The Interests Of Children In The Balance*, 42 FAM. L. Q. 381 (2008) (in all states, evidence of violence against one parent by the other is relevant in custody disputes and 24 states have rebuttable presumption against custody in the abusive partner); Katharine T. Bartlett, *U.S. Custody Law and Trends in the Context of the ALI Principles of the Law of Family Dissolution*, 10 VA. J. Soc. POL'Y & L. 5 (2002) ("most significant development in custody law in the past five to ten years is an increasing legal protection for parents and their children from domestic violence"). Some statutes take a narrow approach, applying the presumption only in cases where there has been a substantial history of domestic violence. *See, e.g.*, MASS. GEN. LAWS ch. 209A, § 3 (requiring a pattern or serious incident); TEX. FAM. CODE ANN. § 153.004 ("history or pattern"). Sometimes conviction of a felony is required for the presumption to operate. FLA. STAT. ANN. § 61.13(2)(b)(2) (Supp.). Courts sometimes also have narrowed the construction of statutes. A grandmother who alleged that the mother had assaulted her was found to lack standing as a non-parent to petition for custody under the domestic violence statute. *J.M.R. v. S.T.R.*, 15 P.3d 253 (Alaska 2001). Other states, in contrast, have been willing to apply the presumption without limiting it to recurring or egregious incidents of abuse. OR. REV. STAT. § 107.137(2). California does not require a pattern or serious incident, but does require that the incident of domestic violence have occurred within five years of the custody dispute before the presumption will be applied. CAL. FAM. CODE § 3044 (Supp); *see also Tulintseff v. Jacobsen*, 615 N.W.2d 129 (N.D. 2000) (statutory presumption does not apply where abuse occurred long before custody proceeding). In other states, this factor must be considered, although there is no presumption.

Even where the legal standard is clear, however, credibility issues remain a concern. One can be sure some claims of abuse made in the course of divorce are factually justified and some are not, but it is difficult to say just what the proportions are of each. No matter what estimates one believes correct, however, there are surely enough factually justified claims of abuse that it would be wrong for courts and counsel to treat them less than seriously and fail to engage in adequate investigation. The child's interests cannot be protected without knowing if the charge is true. If the charge is false, the erroneously (or perhaps falsely) accused parent deserves vindication. Sometimes, a serious investigation may reassure a charging parent who may have overreacted to some objective fact.

Many courts emphasize the potential link between domestic violence and parenting capacity, and assume that custody in a parent who has abused his spouse will likely have harmful effects on the child. *See, e.g., Acevedo v. Acevedo*, 606 N.Y.S.2d 307 (Sup. Ct. App. Div. 1994) (father's physical abuse of mother "reveals that [he] possesses a character that is manifestly ill-suited to the difficult task of providing young children with moral and intellectual guidance"); *Rohan v. Rohan*, 623 N.Y.S.2d 390 (Sup. Ct. App. Div. 1995) (reversing custody award to father who committed "egregious acts of spousal abuse," which the trial court weighed insufficiently; the appellate court suggested that "it [was] possible that [the child] at some future point might become the victim of petitioner's explosive emotions and may also develop a pattern of abuse, thereby becoming an abuser himself when he matures"). In the notorious dispute between O.J. Simpson and the parents of his murdered wife, Nicole, the appellate court reversed the trial court rulings excluding evidence of domestic violence and evidence that Simpson had killed his wife. *Guardianship of Simpson*, 79 Cal. Rptr. 2d 389 (Cal. Ct. App. 1999).

Joint custody is viewed as problematic in families with a history of domestic violence. *See* Peter G. Jaffe, et al., *Custody Disputes Involving Allegations of Domestic Violence: Toward a Differentiated Approach To Parenting Plans*, 46 FAM. CT. REV. 500 (2008) (coparenting involving either joint decisionmaking or joint caretaking not appropriate in cases involving domestic violence generally). Joint custody requires more contact and cooperation between the parents than sole custody, and even non-violent conflict can be harmful to the children. Moreover, the parent who was a victim of marital violence may be subject to intimidation. A number of custody statutes include a prohibition or a rebuttable presumption against joint custody in this situation. *See e.g.*, ARIZ. REV. STAT. ANN. § 25-403.03(A) (Supp.) ("joint custody shall not be awarded if the court makes a finding of the existence of significant domestic violence"); IOWA CODE ANN. § 598.41 (1)(b) (rebuttable presumption); *see also Caven v. Caven*, 966 P.2d 1247 (Wash. 1998) (mutual decision-making power under parenting plan prohibited where there is history of domestic violence).

In recent years experts in the field increasingly have come to believe it is wrong to treat all domestic violence as having the same potential relevance to custody decisions. Many if not most now distinguish between two basic patterns of violence revealed in the empirical literature. The pattern most relevant to custody decisions involves the batterer who uses violence or the threat of violence to control his or her partner. The threat of violence is a central feature of the intimate relationships involving this pattern, and there is wide agreement that this pattern has negative effects on children. On the other hand, it is also the case that partners in relationships without a history of violence often engage in mutual violent acts for the first time as their relationship deteriorates. In this case, the violence is not part of an historic and ongoing pattern of control but is rather an unmanaged expression of anger that may be more situation-specific. This "common couple" violence, limited in time and perhaps in severity, and not central in the larger relationship, is thought less relevant in custody decisions. For an influential review of this work, see Nancy Ver Steegh, *Differentiating Types of Domestic Violence: Implications for Child Custody*, 65 LA. L. REV. 1379 (2005). For reports from a recent conference of domestic violence experts considering this work and other developments, see the collection of articles in the Special Issue on Domestic Violence, 46 Fam. Ct. Rev. 431–570 (2008).

A statutory presumption against awarding custody to a parent who has engaged in domestic violence may give rise to special difficulties where both parents have engaged in abusive conduct toward the other. *See Gietzen v. Gabel*, 718 N.W.2d 552 (S.D. 2007). The majority and dissent in *Gietzen* identified possible approaches. Under an earlier South Dakota case, the court could compare the degree of violence each parent has committed and apply the presumption only against the one who has committed greater harm or committed more frequent acts of violence. *Krank v. Krank*, 529 N.W.2d 844 (N.D.1995). Alternatively, the presumption might arise against both parents and, unless one can demonstrate that the presumption can be overcome by other evidence, the court might be required to place the child in the custody of a third party. *See Gietzen, supra* (dissenting opinion of Justice Maring).

A parent who is the victim of domestic violence may leave the home to escape. This may put her in a vulnerable position in a custody dispute, particularly if she does not take the children with her. If the woman goes to a shelter or moves in with family or friends, her living arrangements are likely to be temporary and the home that she offers the child may seem less "stable" than that of the father who remains in the family home. Uncertainty about the effect of her circumstances on the custody decision may lead the victim to return to the abuser. Statutory provisions that require courts to consider one parent's acts of domestic violence against the other can partially offset the disadvantage created by the victim's circumstances. Further, some custody statutes address this concern directly by providing that abandonment of the home by a victim of abuse cannot be considered in determining the best interest of the child. COLO. REV. STAT. § 14-10-124(1.5)(b)(V)(4); IOWA CODE ANN. § 598.41 (1)(d).

[b]   Sexual Conduct and Moral Unfitness

VAN DRIEL v. VAN DRIEL
South Dakota Supreme Court
525 N.W.2d 37 (S.D. 1994)

MILLER, CHIEF JUSTICE.

Appellant James Mark Van Driel (James) appeals the trial court's award of primary physical custody of his minor children to their mother, appellee Lori Ann Van Driel (Lori), citing their mother's lesbian relationship and the parties' status as joint legal custodians as grounds for reversal . . . We affirm. . . .

James and Lori were married on May 23, 1981. In 1989 or 1990, the couple separated. During this period of separation, Lori became involved in a lesbian relationship and began sharing a residence with her lesbian partner.

James and Lori divorced on January 3, 1991. Pursuant to a settlement agreement, James and Lori shared joint legal and physical custody of their two children, an eight-year-old daughter and a five-year-old son. Under this arrangement, the children lived with each parent on an alternating weekly basis.

Approximately three weeks after the finalization of her divorce, Lori "exchanged vows" with her lesbian partner, with the intent to enter into a permanent and monogamous relationship. Considering Lori's lesbian relationship, James objected to Lori having custody, fearing the children would be ridiculed by their peers and would react negatively in the future to their mother's sexual orientation. Therefore, in August 1991, James petitioned the court for a modification of custody. . . . In a memorandum opinion, the trial court awarded primary physical custody to Lori, subject to reasonable and liberal visitation with James. . . .

James argues that Lori's cohabitation with a woman in a lesbian relationship was *per se* not in the best interests of the children, and the trial court's designation of Lori as the primary custodial parent constituted an abuse of discretion for this reason. We disagree. . . .

The trial court found that both James and Lori were loving and caring parents who had the best interests of their children at heart. Although James suggests that Lori's relationship with another woman is immoral *per se*, "immoral conduct by one parent does not automatically render that parent unfit to have custody of the children and require an award of custody to the other parent." *Shoop v. Shoop*, 460 N.W.2d 721, 724 (S.D.1990) (citing *Williams*, 425 N.W.2d 390). The parent's conduct must be shown to have had some harmful effect on the children. *Id.* at 724–25. . . . Furthermore, the issue properly before us is whether the trial court abused its discretion in awarding primary custody of these children to their mother. We are called upon to make a judicial review of the trial court's decision rather than a moral evaluation of the parties' conduct. . . . James mistakenly relies on *Chicoine*, 479 N.W.2d 891, to bolster his argument that Lori's lesbian relationship automatically disqualifies her as a custodial parent. The facts in this case and those in *Chicoine* are so wholly dissimilar as to render *Chicoine* irrelevant. In *Chicoine*, this Court held that the trial court abused its discretion in awarding unsupervised overnight visitation to a lesbian mother without first ordering a home study and enforcement measures to ensure compliance with restrictions on visitation. This Court's ruling was triggered by evidence that the mother had experienced a myriad of psychological problems, had taken the children to gay bars, had allowed the children to sleep with her and her partner while the mother was unclothed, had kissed and caressed her partner in front of the children despite protests by her oldest son, and had continued a sexual encounter rather than comfort her child after the child had discovered her engaged in sexual activity. *Id.* at 893–94.

In contrast, there is no evidence of this type of behavior in this case. The record indicates that both Lori and her partner are affectionate and attentive toward the children, while being discreet about the sexual aspects of their own relationship. Contrary to James' fears, there was no evidence that the children were ridiculed by classmates or the larger community because of their mother's sexual orientation or that the children were repulsed or embarrassed by, or otherwise showed adverse reactions to, their mother's living arrangement. Indeed, the children's own statements, as reported by the clinical psychologist, indicated that they would prefer living with their mother. Finally, a custody evaluation issued by a clinical psychologist who was retained by both parties recommended that the court award physical custody of the children to Lori. This recommendation was based on a wealth of information, including interviews, psychological tests, and clinical observations of the parties and the children, collateral contacts with the parties' friends and family, and psychological literature concerning the effect of gay or lesbian parents on child development. In light of all of this evidence, this Court cannot conclude that the trial court's custody decision was an abuse of discretion.

NOTES

1. Rationales for Considering a Parent's Sexual Behavior. Both heterosexual and homosexual behavior by parents may be brought into evidence in litigated custody disputes. One rationale for considering the behavior is that the parent's immoral or even illegal conduct will influence a child's conduct, and that it is detrimental to a child for his parent to set a "bad example." This rationale, however, raises many difficulties. Children will not necessarily be aware of their parent's sexual conduct, and even if they are, little is known about the circumstances under which they will emulate that conduct. Some custody statutes specifically address the issue of morality. The Alabama custody statute, for example, directs courts to consider "the moral character and prudence of the parents," ALA. CODE § 30-3-1. *See also* MICH. COMP. LAWS ANN. § 722.23(f) ("moral fitness of the parties involved" is factor to be considered by court deciding custody); UTAH CODE ANN. § 30-3-10(1)(a) (Supp.) ("the court shall consider . . . the past conduct and demonstrated moral standards of each of the parties"). The Minnesota statute, in contrast, precludes consideration of "conduct of a proposed custodian that does not affect his relationship to the child." MINN. STAT. ANN. § 518.17(13)(b). This general language could encompass a whole range of parental conduct, of which sexual behavior is just one example. The majority rule with respect to non-marital, heterosexual behavior, however, is that such conduct alone cannot justify denial of custody to a parent, unless adverse effects on the child are shown. *See, e.g.*, *Fletcher v. Fletcher*, 504 N.W.2d 684 (Mich. Ct. App. 1993) (mother's extramarital affairs insufficient reason to award custody to father where children may not have been aware of the affairs and, even if they had been aware, adultery alone is insufficient for a finding of immorality); *Lackey v. Fuller*, 755 So. 2d 1083 (Miss. 2000) (mother's pre-divorce extra-marital affair could not be the basis of custody award to father); *Judith R. v. Hey*, 405 S.E.2d 447 (W.Va. 1991) (reversing trial court order requiring a custodial mother who was cohabiting with a man to either marry him within 30 days or lose custody to former husband). Few recent appellate court opinions have reviewed custody decisions in which a parents' heterosexual conduct was an issue, suggesting the declining importance of this issue.

The movement away from considering parental sexual conduct as a morality issue affecting child custody is not uniform across the country. *See* June Carbone & Naomi Cahn, *Judging Families*, 77 UMKC L. REV. 267, 290 (2008) ("The states with the lowest average ages of marriage, all of which are in the South, the mountain west, or the border between the North-South border, have been slower to move away from policing the morality of the litigants before them, and they remain more likely to reaffirm traditional moral values as part of their decisions. The states with the highest average ages of marriage, in contrast, have been much more eager to review lower court decisions to insure equality and fairness for gay and lesbian parents. Nonetheless, the decisions in both groups of states have evolved in a much less polarized fashion than might be expected from voting patterns.")

   2. *Gay and Lesbian Parents*. The District of Columbia is the only jurisdiction with a statute which directly speaks to whether a parent's sexual orientation is relevant to child custody and visitation. D.C. CODE ANN. § 16-914(a) ("with respect to matters of custody and visitation . . . sexual orientation, in and of itself, of a party shall not be a conclusive consideration"). Traditionally, courts have tended to be harder on parents involved in same sex relationships, perhaps because of a view that the child will experience stigma and that her sexual identity will be affected. *See Pulliam v. Smith*, 501 S.E.2d 898 (N.C. 1998) (order upheld changing custody to mother after father's male partner moved in, despite no showing of an adverse impact on the children); *Tucker v. Tucker*, 910 P.2d 1209 (Utah 1996) (custody award to father reinstated, because mother's lesbian cohabitating relationship before and after divorce demonstrated "lack of moral example"); *In re H.H.*, 830 S.2d 21 (Ala. 2002) (concurring opinion) ("Homosexual conduct by its very nature is immoral"); *Roe v. Roe*, 324 S.E.2d 691 (Va. 1985) (custody changed from father to mother and visitation at father's home prohibited where father living with male lover).

Although, as the *Van Driel* decision indicates, the traditional hostility to gay and lesbian parents is declining, an analysis of reported family law opinions concludes that gay and lesbian parents are subjected to gender-influenced stereotypes in custody and visitation cases — stereotypes that are influenced by the parent's gender, the child's gender, and the judge's gender. Specifically, the author found that gay fathers are stereotyped as HIV agents and child molesters more often than lesbian mothers, that parents of sons are stereotyped as recruiters and role models more often than the parents of daughters, and that male judges are more likely than female judges to accept gender-influenced stereotypes about gay and lesbian parents. *See* Clifford J. Rosky, *Like Father, Like Son: Homosexuality, Parenthood, and the Gender of Homophobia*, 20 YALE J.L. & FEMINISM 257 (2009).

The belief that gay and lesbian people act differently as parents when compared with heterosexual people is not accepted by every court. For example, In *Varnum v. Brien*, 763 N.W.2d 862, 899 (2009), the Iowa Supreme Court rejected the state's argument that promoting child-rearing by a married mother and father is an important governmental objective supporting a same-sex marriage ban on the basis that:

> Plaintiffs presented an abundance of evidence and research, confirmed by our independent research, supporting the proposition that the interests of children are served equally by same-sex parents and opposite-sex parents. On the other hand, we acknowledge the existence of reasoned opinions that dual-gender parenting is the optimal environment for children. These opinions, while thoughtful and sincere, were largely unsupported by reliable scientific studies.

Cf. Goodridge v. Department of Public Health, 440 Mass. 309, 798 N.E.2d 941 (Mass. 2003) (dissenting opinion of Justice Cordy: [necessary to assume that legislature] "would be familiar with many recent studies that variously support the proposition that children raised in intact families headed by same-sex couples fare as well on many measures as children raised in similar families headed by opposite-sex couples; support the proposition that children of same-sex couples fare worse on some measures; or reveal notable differences between the two groups of children that warrant further study".)

Empirical research on whether children have different outcomes depending on the sexual orientation of their parents is more nuanced than the assertions expressed by the court in *Varnum*. In general, researchers have found no differences. *See* Jennifer L. Wainright & Charlotte J. Patterson, *Peer Relations Among Adolescents With Female Same-Sex Parents*, 44 DEV. PSYCH. 117 (2008) (no identifiable difference in development of sexual identity between children residing with lesbian mothers and those residing with heterosexual parents); Am. Psychological Ass'n Council of Representatives, Am. Psychological Ass'n, *Resolution on Sexual Orientation, Parents, and Children* (2004) ("There is no scientific evidence that parenting effectiveness is related to parental sexual orientation: Lesbian and gay parents are as likely as heterosexual parents to provide supportive and healthy environments for children."). In a major review of the literature, however, Professors Stacey and Biblarz concluded that, while child outcomes were equivalent regardless of the sexual orientation of the parents in most areas of child wellbeing, statistically significant differences existed in the areas of sexual and gender development. Judith Stacey & Timothy J. Biblarz, *(How) Does the Sexual Orientation of Parents Matter?*, 66 AM. SOC. REV. 159, 161 (2001).

The Supreme Court's decision in *Lawrence v. Texas*, 539 U.S. 558 (2003), discussed more fully in Chapter 1, Section C[2], may reduce the salience of evidence of a parents' sexual orientation in a custody action unless there is evidence of actual harm to the child. In *Lawrence*, the Court struck down a Texas sodomy law that criminalized consensual sexual relations between same sex partners and denounced in strong language the stigma and intrusiveness of such laws. In *A.O.V. v. J.R.V.*, 2007 Va. App. LEXIS 64 (Feb. 27, 2007), the court upheld an award of joint custody over the mother's claim that the father's homosexuality rendered him unfit. The court noted that, particularly in light of *Lawrence*, which casts doubt on the constitutionality of the state's criminal fornication prohibition, allowing a parent's sexual orientation to impact the custody decision is improper in the absence of evidence that child is affected. The court nonetheless upheld restrictions on the father's expressing affection for partner in presence of the children. Other courts disagree. *See McGriff v. McGriff*, 99 P.3d 111, 117 (Idaho 2004) (*Lawrence* requires no change in state's rule that sexual orientation of a parent is relevant to custody if it causes harm to the child); *Page v. Page*, 2008 Ohio App. LEXIS 2506 (June 20, 2008) (*Lawrence* limited to criminal prohibitions and requires no changes to custody law; but even if *Lawrence* makes morality of same-sex relationship irrelevant, custody decision here was valid because based on the problems children experienced in relationship with custodial parent's same-sex partner, not on a morality claim about the relationship).

In addition to the article by Rosky, *supra*, thoughtful articles on issues surrounding child custody and gay and lesbian parents include Bruce D. Gill, *Best Interest of the Child? A Critique of Judicially Sanctioned Arguments Denying Child Custody to Gays and Lesbians*, 68 Tenn. L. Rev. 361 (2001); David L. Chambers & Nancy Polikoff, *Family Law and Gay and Lesbian Family Issues in the Twentieth Century*, 33 Fam. L.Q. 523 (1999); Julie Shapiro, *Custody and Conduct: How the Law Fails Lesbian and Gay Parents and their Children*, 71 Ind. L.J. 623 (1996).

3. *Transgendered Parents and Children.* Transgendered status presents relatively new issues in custody litigation, and it can involve both the parent and the child. *See In re Marriage of Magnuson*, 170 P.3d 65 (Wash. Ct. App. 2007) (custody award to mother upheld over dissent arguing that trial court's bias against transgendered father entered into its decision; majority and dissent agreed that father's transgendered status is not a valid ground for deciding against father unless adverse impact on child is shown, which it was not in this case). *See also Smith v. Smith*, 2007 Ohio App. LEXIS 1282 (Mar. 23, 2007) (custody changed from mother to father when mother treated son as having Gender Identity Disorder without medical diagnosis, child expressed suicidal ideation because of his gender issues and mother not compliant with prior judicial orders about how to care for child).

4. *Commentaries.* The *ALI Principles* prohibit consideration of both sexual orientation and of extramarital sexual conduct unless shown to have an adverse impact on the child. § 2.12(1)(d) & (e).

PROBLEM

Problem 6-2. Theresa has custody of her three daughters, ages 12, 10 and 7. Because of her unsatisfying marriage, Theresa has sworn off men altogether, and has remained celibate since her divorce. She has told her daughters that men are not worth the trouble. She has also told them that if a woman decides to get involved with a man, she should live with him for a long time before marriage, in order to be sure that they are sexually compatible. The girls' father, Donald, strongly objects to this advice, which he considers both immoral and a violation of the criminal statute against contributing to the delinquency of a minor. Does Donald have adequate grounds for a modification of custody in his favor? Advise him.

[c] Race

PALMORE v. SIDOTI
United States Supreme Court
466 U.S. 429 (1984)

CHIEF JUSTICE BURGER delivered the opinion of the Court.

We granted certiorari to review a judgment of a state court divesting a natural mother of the custody of her infant child because of her remarriage to a person of a different race.

When petitioner Linda Sidoti Palmore and respondent Anthony J. Sidoti, both Caucasians, were divorced in May 1980 in Florida, the mother was awarded custody of their three-year-old daughter.

In September 1981 the father sought custody of the child by filing a petition to modify the prior judgment because of changed conditions. The change was that the child's mother was then cohabiting with a Negro, Clarence Palmore, Jr., whom she married two months later. . . .

After hearing testimony from both parties and considering a court counselor's investigative report, the court. . . . made a finding that "there is no issue as to either party's devotion to the child, adequacy of housing facilities, or respect[a]bility of the new spouse of either parent." . . .

The court then addressed the recommendations of the court counselor . . . for a change in custody because "[t]he wife [petitioner] has chosen for herself and for her child, a life-style unacceptable to her father and to society . . . The child . . . is, or at school age will be, subject to environmental pressures not of choice."

The court then concluded that the best interests of the child would be served by awarding custody to the father. The court's rationale is contained in the following:

> The father's evident resentment of the mother's choice of a black partner is not sufficient to wrest custody from the mother. It is of some significance, however, that the mother did see fit to bring a man into her home and carry on a sexual relationship with him without being married to him. Such action tended to place gratification of her own desires ahead of her concern for the child's future welfare. This Court feels that despite the strides that have been made in bettering relations between the races in this country, it is inevitable that Melanie will, if allowed to remain in her present situation and attains school age and thus more vulnerable to peer pressures, suffer from the social stigmatization that is sure to come. . . .

The judgment of a state court determining or reviewing a child custody decision is not ordinarily a likely candidate for review by this Court. However, the court's opinion, after stating that the "father's evident resentment of the mother's choice of a black partner is not sufficient" to deprive her of custody, then turns to what it regarded as the damaging impact on the child from remaining in a racially-mixed household. . . . This raises important federal concerns arising from the Constitution's commitment to eradicating discrimination based on race.

The Florida court did not focus directly on the parental qualifications of the natural mother or her present husband, or indeed on the father's qualifications to have custody of the child. The court found that "there is no issue as to either party's devotion to the child, adequacy of housing facilities, or respect[a]bility of the new spouse of either parent." . . . This, taken with the absence of any negative finding as to the quality of the care provided by the mother, constitutes a rejection of any claim of petitioner's unfitness to continue the custody of her child.

The court correctly stated that the child's welfare was the controlling factor. But that court was entirely candid and made no effort to place its holding on any ground other than race. Taking the court's findings and rationale at face value, it is clear that the outcome would have been different had petitioner married a Caucasian male of similar respectability.

A core purpose of the Fourteenth Amendment was to do away with all governmentally-imposed discrimination based on race. . . . Such classifications are subject to the most exacting scrutiny; to pass constitutional muster, they must be justified by a compelling governmental interest and must be "necessary . . . to the accomplishment" of its legitimate purpose, *McLaughlin v. Florida*, 379 U.S. 184 (1964).

The State, of course, has a duty of the highest order to protect the interests of minor children, particularly those of tender years. In common with most states, Florida law mandates that custody determinations be made in the best interests of the children involved. The goal of granting custody based on the best interests of the child is indisputably a substantial governmental interest for purposes of the Equal Protection Clause.

It would ignore reality to suggest that racial and ethnic prejudices do not exist or that all manifestations of those prejudices have been eliminated. There is a risk that a child living with a step-parent of a different race may be subject to a variety of pressures and stresses not present if the child were living with parents of the same racial or ethnic origin.

The question, however, is whether the reality of private biases and the possible injury they might inflict are permissible considerations for removal of an infant child from the custody of its natural mother. We have little difficulty concluding that they are not. The Constitution cannot control such prejudices but neither can it tolerate them. Private biases may be outside the reach of the law, but the law cannot, directly or indirectly, give them effect. "Public officials sworn to uphold the Constitution may not avoid a constitutional duty by bowing to the hypothetical effects of private racial prejudice that they assume to be both widely and deeply held. *Palmer v. Thompson*, 403 U.S. 217, 260–261 (1971). (WHITE, J., dissenting).

This is by no means the first time that acknowledged racial prejudice has been invoked to justify racial classifications. In *Buchanan v. Warley*, 245 U.S. 60 (1917), for example, this Court invalidated a Kentucky law forbidding Negroes from buying homes in white neighborhoods.

> It is urged that this proposed segregation will promote the public peace by preventing race conflicts. Desirable as this is, and important as is the preservation of the public peace, this aim cannot be accomplished by laws or ordinances which deny rights created or protected by the Federal Constitution.

Id., at 81.

Whatever problems racially-mixed households may pose for children in 1984 can no more support a denial of constitutional rights than could the stresses that residential integration was thought to entail in 1917. The effects of racial prejudice, however real, cannot justify a racial classification removing an infant child from the custody of its natural mother found to be an appropriate person to have such custody.

The judgment . . . is reversed.

NOTES

1. ***The Limits of* Sidoti?** The Court in *Sidoti* concedes that "a child living with a stepparent of a different race may be subject to a variety of pressures and stresses not present if the child were living with parents of the same racial or ethnic origin," but concludes that these pressures and stresses are not "permissible considerations" in a custody dispute. Is there a limit to the amount or severity of "pressures" and "stresses" a child should have to sustain in order that the law not give effect to private biases? One student notewriter suggests that where a child has actually sustained harm from a difficult racial situation, *Sidoti* does not preclude consideration of that harm in custody determinations. *See* Eileen M. Blackwood, Note, *Race as a Factor in Custody and Adoption Proceedings*, 71 CORNELL L. REV. 209 (1985). At least one court has hinted in dictum that it agreed. *Holt v. Chenault*, 722 S.W.2d 897 (Ky. 1987) (child's reaction might be taken into account if it is significant and severe). For a comprehensive and critical analysis of the use of race in custody decisions, see Twila L. Perry, *Race and Child Placement: The Best Interests Test and the Cost of Discretion*, 29 J. FAM. L. 51 (1990–91). *See also* Katharine T. Bartlett, *Comparing Race and Sex Discrimination in Custody Cases*, 28 HOFSTRA L. REV. 877 (2000) (arguing that the similarities between race and sex discrimination support the categorical ban on all types of discrimination in the *ALI Principles*).

2. ***Custody of Biracial Children.*** Can race be taken into account as a positive factor if one parent is more likely to contribute to the child's minority racial identity? Would this be allowed under the Minnesota custody statute, *supra*, which provides for considering the "child's cultural background" and the capacity of the parent to "continue educating the child in the child's culture"? Some courts have found such consideration to be precluded by *Palmore*. *See In re Marriage of Brown*, 480 N.E.2d 246, 248 (Ind. Ct. App. 1985). Other courts have found that the

special needs of bi-racial children justify taking race into account. In *Ebirim v. Ebirim*, a Nebraska court concluded that race was one factor among many to be considered in the custody decision, but upheld an award to the white mother. 620 N.W.2d 117 (Neb. App. 2000). The Nigerian-born father argued that he was better able to raise the child to appreciate his biracial heritage, pointing out that there were no other black children in the town where the mother lived, and that some members of the mother's family had made racist comments in the past. The court posited that when individuals of different races have a child, neither gains priority on grounds of race alone. *But see Jones v. Jones*, 542 N.W.2d 119 (S.D. 1996) (awarding custody of a bi-racial child to a Native American father, as more likely than mother to expose the child to his racial heritage).

The *ALI Principles* prohibit consideration of race or ethnicity as a factor in the custody decision. § 2.12 (1)(a). The Reporter's comments acknowledge the importance of children having a positive racial identity, but reject the notion that a bi-racial child shares his race with only one parent, and that, on that basis, custody should be awarded to the parent of the stigmatized race. The *Principles* allow consideration of the parents' capacity to nurture self esteem, including positive racial identity. Professor Randall Kennedy argues that race should be excluded as a consideration in both custody and adoption cases. RANDALL KENNEDY, INTERRACIAL INTIMACIES: SEX, MARRIAGE, IDENTITY AND ADOPTION (2003). In Kennedy's view, racial identity should not be socially ascribed, but instead, chosen by individuals.

For a comparison of judicial treatment of race and religious practice as considerations in the custody decision, see the Notes following *Leppert, infra.*

PROBLEM

Problem 6-3. Billy, aged 11, is the son of Mary, who is white and John, who is African American. During their marriage, Mary and John adopted traditional roles. Mary was a homemaker and Billy's primary caretaker, and John was a busy history professor. Most of Billy's friends were African American and he identified himself as African American, although he was very close to his mother and there is no evidence that his racial identity has interfered with his relationship with her. Mary and John separate and both parents seek custody of Billy. The judge appoints you as Billy's guardian *ad litem* to investigate the family situation and to advise in making the custody decision. Do you have an opinion about which parent should get custody? What information should you seek to assist the judge?

NOTE ON CUSTODY AND HEALTH

Difficult questions arise when a parent's ability to function is affected by physical or mental disability, conditions that are beyond the parent's control. The Model Marriage and Divorce Act, *supra*, and many statutes permit consideration of factors such as "the mental and physical health of all individuals involved." *See, e.g.*, COLO. REV. STAT. § 14-10-124(1.5)(a)(V); MINN. STAT. ANN. § 518.17(a)(9). Although a physical condition might sometimes be relevant to the custody determination, courts try to weigh carefully how much the condition actually impairs important parenting functions, and to avoid decisions based on prejudiced assumptions about the incapacities of disabled persons. *See, e.g., Bednarski v. Bednarski*, 366 N.W.2d

69 (Mich. Ct. App. 1985) (reversing trial court award of custody of child to grandparents because, although mother was deaf, the children had adequate alternatives for learning verbal and oral communication skills). In recent years, both federal and state governments have pursued policies of full integration into society of disabled persons through laws that prohibit discrimination in employment, education, housing, transportation and public access. *See, e.g.* Americans with Disabilities Act and the ADA Amendments Act of 2008, 42 U.S.C. §§ 12101 *et seq.* Although these laws have not focused on child custody decisions, courts have recognized that full integration encompasses fulfillment of family roles to the extent possible. *In re Carney*, 598 P.2d 36 (Cal. 1979). Where the disability seriously affects the parent's ability to care for the child, however, it will be considered. In a South Dakota case, the Court reiterated that a physical disability was not *per se* an impediment to custody, but then upheld a custody award of a three-year-old to her mother, where the father suffered from cerebral palsy and had an attendant. *Arneson v. Arneson*, 670 N.W.2d 904 (S.D. 2003). The trial court based its decision largely on the opinion of an evaluator who concluded that, although the father could care for the child, he might have difficulty responding to emergencies until she was older.

The child's health is also a consideration, particularly when one parent or other proposed custodian has more experience caring for the child's special needs or lives in a situation better suited to the child's situation. For example, in *In re Marriage of Dafoe*, 754 N.E.2d 419 (Ill. App. Ct. 2001), the child's grandparents were awarded custody over the objection of the child's father, because the grandparents, who had cared for the child for most of his ten years, understood how to address the child's multiple problems, including attention deficit disorder and developmental delays. They obtained educational and therapeutic services for the child beginning when he was a toddler. The grandmother was deeply involved in the child's school and was employed there while the child attended school. In *Burns v. Burns*, 737 N.W.2d 243 (N.D. 2007), the father was awarded custody of a son with autism, despite his having used inappropriate physical discipline on the child and his older sister in the past. A major factor was that the father's home was in a school district where the child's special needs had been addressed successfully.

PROBLEM

Problem 6-4. Tom Card lived in California with his two sons and his partner, Marie, who acted as a stepmother. Tom had custody of the boys under a separation agreement with his wife, who had moved to New York after the divorce. Five years later, Tom was injured in a car accident that left him quadriplegic. Tom's former wife sued for a change in custody. Should she prevail?

[d]   Religion

LEPPERT v. LEPPERT
North Dakota Supreme Court
519 N.W.2d 287 (1994)

NEUMANN, JUSTICE.

Joel Leppert appeals from a divorce judgment awarding physical custody of his three youngest children to their mother, Quinta Leppert. We reverse and remand to the district court.

Joel and Quinta were married June 18, 1984. Five children were born of this marriage . . . On January 14, 1992, Judge Mikal Simonson issued an . . . order granting temporary physical custody of the three youngest children to Quinta, with the physical custody of the two older children alternating between the parents on a bimonthly basis. . . .

The guardian recommended custody of all five of the children should be with Joel, allowing for limited periods of visitation with Quinta. Concluding his report, the guardian stated "Quinta, despite her many admirable traits, is likely to provide parenting that is in several crucial respects, extremely dangerous to the children's psychological and emotional health, personality and characterological development, their physical well being and even their life."

One of the guardian's primary concerns was the harmful impact of Quinta's beliefs and resulting actions. Specifically, Quinta is a devout follower of the teachings of her father, Gordon Winrod (Winrod). Her father is the supreme leader of his own religious sect known as Our Savior's Church. . . . His church is not affiliated with any religious denomination, but purports to follow the teachings of the Bible.

Winrod and his followers believe there are only two types of people in the world: God's enemies, and those who are obedient to God. Those who do not follow Winrod's teachings are not obedient to God, and they are consequently evil, and are to be hated as God's enemies.

Testimony at trial stated Winrod teaches lying to God's enemies, stealing from God's enemies, and violent behavior toward God's enemies. He also rejects the authority of governments, and his followers therefore refuse to pay taxes, refuse to register with selective service, ignore hunting and fishing regulations, and refuse to buy liability insurance on their vehicles as required by law. Quinta believes she has a duty to raise her children to follow Winrod. She insists that her children adopt all of his teachings and beliefs.

Joel was at one time a follower of Winrod, but has since stopped following his teachings. Since the marital separation, Quinta has moved to live with her father and several of his followers in a commune-like residence in Gainesville, Missouri. Joel has continued to live and work on the Leppert family farm in Dickey, North Dakota.

Prior to the separation, Quinta home-schooled the two oldest children. Since the separation, Joel enrolled the two oldest children in public school in Jud, North Dakota. When the children enrolled in classes, evaluation assessments showed James' reading and writing skills were significantly below the norm for his age. The children's social skills lagged far behind those of their classmates.

Testimony was introduced at trial that supported Joel's contention that Quinta was attempting to poison the children's relationship with Joel and his family. Tape recorded telephone conversations between Quinta and the two oldest children, James and Stephanie, include statements by Quinta, such as:

> ". . . [Y]our daddy's such a pin head . . . , birds of a feather flock together so do pigs and swine, that's the way your father is, he's a pig and he's a swine. . . .

> ". . . You know I thought some day maybe he [Joel] would grow up so I waited for seven years but all he did was grow hideous . . . his heart rotted out till he's an evil man now, just evil . . .

> ". . . [Delores Leppert is] wicked and evil, and I'm gonna talk like that and your daddy can hear it whether he likes it or not. She's evil and she's made him evil, and your Uncle Tim is evil and Danny's evil and they're evil there."

Joel also testified that the younger children started to exhibit behavior that suggests Quinta is poisoning them against Joel as well.

Home studies were conducted both in Quinta's home in Missouri, and Joel's home in North Dakota. The results of the studies were that both households would be adequate for raising the five children . . .

Child custody determinations are findings of fact. N.D.R.Civ.P. Rule 52(a); *e.g.*, *Weber v. Weber*, 512 N.W.2d 723, 726 (N.D.1994). On appeal, findings of fact are not disturbed unless clearly erroneous.

Joel argues that the trial court clearly made a mistake when it awarded custody of the three youngest children to Quinta. Specifically, he argues the court erred when it refused to consider the harmful impact of Quinta's beliefs when determining the best interests of the children. We agree.

In its memorandum opinion, the trial court clearly addressed each of the enumerated factors of our best interests statute. NDCC § 14-09-06.2. Subsection (f) of the best interests statute is entitled "moral fitness of the parents." Addressing this subsection, quoting *Hanson v. Hanson*, 404 N.W.2d 460 (N.D.1987), the district court stated "that physical and [sic] emotional harm must be clearly shown, before religious beliefs may become a determining factor" in the best interests of the child analysis, but went on to find that there was not a clear showing of physical and emotional harm to the children from Quinta's practices and beliefs. We cannot agree. The guardian's report unequivocally stated that Quinta's parenting, because of her beliefs, constituted an extreme danger to the children, both physically and emotionally. Based upon such a record, the district court's finding is clearly erroneous.

Although we agree with the district court that Quinta must not be discounted from consideration as a custodial parent simply because of her religious beliefs, this does not mean her religiously motivated actions, which are emotionally and physically harmful to the children, should be ignored when determining the children's best interests. Such a holding would immunize from consideration all religiously motivated acts, no matter what their impact on the children. Carl E. Schneider, *Religion and Child Custody*, 25 U. Mich. J.L. Ref. 879, 888 (1992). Almost all of the behavior of members of "other-worldly" sects would be excluded from consideration. *Id.* Not only would we be ignoring the best interests of the child, but the "worldly" parent would be comparatively disadvantaged. Schneider, *supra*, at 888.

Consideration of the harmful impact of a parent's beliefs when determining the best interests of the child is in no way intended to punish parents. . . . Schneider, *supra*, at 883. To the contrary, the goal in custody determinations is to foster the health and well-being of the child, not to punish either of the parents.

The only reason for any consideration of religious beliefs when determining the best interests of the child is to take into account any harmful impact the belief system may have on the child. The best interests factors enumerated in § 14-09-06.2 are secular in nature, and the courts' functions do not include determining the road to salvation. Although secular courts have no place deciding one religion is better than another, they do have the duty of objectively determining whether a belief system's secular effects are likely to cause physical or emotional harm to children. We acknowledge that, ultimately, secular courts may not fully accommodate the desires of those who wholly reject secular standards. Remedying a conflict such as that, however, is beyond the scope of this appeal.

There are factors the trial court appeared to ignore in the best interests analysis because they were religiously motivated. Applying the correct standard for considering the adverse impact that Quinta's beliefs are likely to have on the children, it is in the best interests of all five children that their physical custody be with Joel. . . .

NOTES

1. *Background on the Winrod Family.* Gordon Winrod was the son of Rev. Gerald B. Winrod of Kansas, "a notorious anti-Semite whose pro-German activities during World War II earned his the title 'Jayhawk Nazi.' The father was charged with sedition." *Supremacist Pastor Ready To Go on Trial*, Associated Press, Jan. 28, 2001. Winrod, according to his former son-in-law, "considers white Christians superior to nonwhites and Jews . . . Winrod sent out thousands of newsletters around the country each year, often calling for the killing of Jews." *Id.* Not long after the custody decision in *Leppert*, Quinta Leppert, her father, Gordon Winrod, and her sister kidnapped Quinta's children and the sister's children from their fathers, who happened to be brothers. Winrod and the daughters were convicted of the kidnapping or associated crimes after six children were recovered from Winrod's farm in 2000. Two of the children were hospitalized for psychiatric treatment after being recovered. According to prosecutors, "The teachings of their grandfather were deeply instilled in the children . . . Following [Winrod's] arrest, his grandchildren, ages 9 to 16, barricaded themselves on the farm for four days." *Pastor Convicted of Kidnapping Grandchildren*, Associated Press, Feb. 1, 2001. In a civil suit brought by the fathers and some of the children, Winrod was ordered to pay $26 million for the pain and suffering experienced by the plaintiffs, including subjecting the children to mind-altering techniques, keeping them isolated and whipping them to change their attitudes. *Jurors Order Pastor to Pay $26 Million*, Associated Press, May 2, 2002.

2. When Can Religious Practice be Considered in the Custody Decision? Although parents' religious beliefs *per se* are not considered in custody cases, religious practices may be taken into account under some circumstances. Courts have used various tests to determine whether parents' religious practices are relevant to the decision. Some courts apply a general best interest test, allowing courts to consider such evidence "to the extent that such views or practices are demonstrated to bear upon the physical or emotional welfare of the child." *Bienenfeld v. Bennett-White*, 605 A.2d 172, 182 (Md. Ct. Spec. App. 1992); *see also Burnham v. Burnham*, 304 N.W.2d. 58 (Neb. 1981) (early and much-cited case awarding custody to father where mother's church taught anti-Semitism and advocated cessation of communication with non-believers, beliefs that could have a "deleterious effect upon the well being of the child herself"). Other courts allow consideration of religious beliefs and practices if there is a reasonable likelihood that the practice will jeopardize the child's physical safety or mental health.

The Colorado Supreme Court requires a showing of substantial or reasonable likelihood of present or future harm. *In re Short*, 698 P.2d 1310 (Colo. 1985); *see also Hadeen v. Hadeen*, 619 P.2d 374 (Wash. Ct. App. 1980) (religious practices can be considered to the extent that they create likelihood of "immediate or future impairment"). A stricter test requires a showing that the religious practice poses an imminent danger to the child. The Maine Supreme Court applied a variation of the strict test, in rejecting the claim of a father that the Jehovah's Witness mother should be denied custody because she could not authorize a blood transfusion for her child under any circumstances. *Osier v. Osier*, 410 A.2d 1027 (Me. 1980). Because the child was normal and healthy and did not need a blood transfusion, the court found that custody in the mother did not constitute endangerment.

The strictest standard requires that actual harm from the religious practice be demonstrated. *Quiner v. Quiner*, 59 Cal. Rptr. 503 (Cal. Ct. App. 1967). Under the *Quiner* test, impairment of physical, emotional and mental well-being is necessary and evidence offered by psychologists and psychiatrists of the projected effect of a parent's religious practices on the child is excluded. The *ALI Principles* adopt a test that strictly limits the admissibility of evidence of religious practice to situations where the practice threatens severe and almost certain harm. § 2.12 (1)(c). *Leppert* stresses the need to show that the mother's religious practices have a "harmful impact" on the child, which sounds like the strict *Quiner* test, but it then concludes that the mother's beliefs and practices are in fact causing harm to her children, without offering any clear evidence that this is the case.

In some sense, *Osier* presents an "easy" case; the religious practice of refusing blood transfusions is discrete, and the potential impact simple to evaluate — and not likely to affect the child's life. Much harder are cases like *Leppert*, in which the parent's religious practice defines her life on a day-to-day basis — and will shape the children's lives if she has custody. When the parent's religious belief and practice have a range of important secular effects on how the parent rears her children, can those effects be excluded from consideration by the court choosing between the parents in a custody dispute? Will the Leppert children be affected by the mother's isolation from society and hostility toward outsiders, including the father, and by her attitude toward education? In *Johnson v. Johnson*, 564 P.2d 71 (Alaska 1977), the mother was a Jehovah's Witness who did not believe that secular education was important, did not teach the children to count money or wash themselves, opposed celebration of holidays and birthdays, and believed that her former husband (who had been "disfellowshipped" by the church) was subject to satanic control. The father proposed to offer the children "exposure to the usual experiences of children their age," *id.* at 74, and planned to send them to college. In such a cases, if evidence of the mother's religious practice is excluded from consideration, how can the parents be compared to determine which parents' custody promotes the children's welfare?

As courts recognize, however, consideration of evidence of parents' religious practice raises serious concerns. Not only are the parents' Free Exercise rights implicated, but a court's preference for one religious view over another would raise Establishment Clause concerns. It is not surprising that courts have struggled to limit consideration of this kind of evidence, while still focusing on the welfare of the children who are the subject of the dispute.

Carl Schneider offers a thoughtful treatment of these issues, in an article heavily relied upon by the *Leppert* court. *See* Carl Schneider, *Religion and Child Custody*, 25 U. MICH. J.L. REF. 879 (1992). Schneider argues that focusing on whether parents' religious practices have secular effects that are harmful to the child is legitimate and, indeed, that any other policy would immunize all religiously motivated behavior. James Dwyer challenges the position that parents have a right to inculcate their children in their religious beliefs and argues that religious practices that are contrary to children's temporal interest are not protected. *See* James G. Dwyer, *Parents' Religion and Children's Welfare: Debunking the Doctrine of Parents' Rights*, 82 CAL. L. REV. 1371 (1994). In a similar vein, see Jerry Bergman, *Dealing with Jehovah's Witness Custody Cases*, 29 CREIGHT. L. REV. 1483 (1996). This author contends the child-rearing practices of Jehovah's Witnesses are "not conducive to achieving the goals that most deem important for their children. These goals include being socially involved in school, attending college, pursuing a career, utilizing appropriate medical treatment, and developing tolerance toward persons of a variety of religious faiths and orientation." Eugene Volokh argues, on the other hand, that denying a parent custody based on the parent's religious views or limiting that parent's expression of religious views "are generally unconstitutional, except when [the restrictions are] narrowly focused on preventing one parent from undermining the child's relationship with the other." In his view, protection of the parent's expression is necessary "not primarily because of their self-expression rights, or their children's interests in hearing the parents' views. Rather, the main reason to protect parental speech rights is that today's child listeners will grow up into the next generation's adult speakers." Eugene

Volokh, *Parent-Child Speech and Child Custody Speech Restrictions*, 81 N.Y.U. L. REV. 631(2006).

3. *Custody and the Child's Prior Religious Upbringing.* Ordinarily the custodial parent will determine the child's religious training. This may result in a child being raised after the divorce in a different religion than the one in which he or she was earlier raised. Some courts have allowed consideration of the child's prior religious training and practice to be weighed in the custody decision, often in response to statutory guidelines directing that courts making custody determinations consider the child's "religious needs." *See Bonjour v. Bonjour*, 592 P.2d 1233 (Alaska 1979) (under statute requiring consideration of child's religious needs, court can consider which parent is better situated to meet those needs); *see also Boylan v. Boylan*, 577 A.2d. 218 (Pa. Super. Ct. 1990) (children's religious faith favors same faith parent, but is not determinative). The ALI standard allows consideration of the parents' and child's religious practice where necessary to protect the child's ability to practice a religion that has been a significant part of her life. *See* § 212(1)(c) *supra.*

4. *Parental Religious Conflicts and Visitation.* Just as denying a parent custody based on the parent's religious expression has been upheld in limited circumstances, court have also approved limits on what a parent may do or say about religion while exercising the parent's visitation rights or custodial responsibility. In *In re Marriage of McSoud*, 131 P.3d 1208 (Colo. Ct. App. 2006), the trial court allocated decision-making with respect to religion to the father, who is a Catholic, and ordered the mother, a Protestant, not to take the children to her church during her parenting time unless she "supports the religion chosen by [the] father." On appeal, the first order was upheld, while the second was reversed as an unconstitutional infringement on the mother's rights under the First Amendment. The court said, "absent a clear showing of substantial harm to the child, a parent who does not have decision-making authority with respect to religion nevertheless retains a constitutional right to educate the child in that parent's religion" Exposing the child to more than one religion, according to the court, would not generally constitute substantial harm.

In *Zummo v. Zummo*, 574 A.2d 1130 (Pa. Super. 1990), the parents and children, before the separation, "participated fully in the life of the Jewish faith and community." After the separation, the father, a Roman Catholic, refused to take the children to scheduled Jewish religious or educational activities during his visitation time and announced his intention to take the children, on occasion, to Roman Catholic religious and family events. The trial court ordered the father to take the children to their synagogue's Sunday school during his visitation time and not to take them to non-Jewish religious services except those involving the celebration of family events in the father's family. "The trial court concluded that, 'to expose the children to a competing religion after so assiduously grounding them in the tenets of Judaism would unfairly confuse and disorient them and quite possibly vitiate the benefits flowing from either religion.' " *Id.* at 1154. No other harm to the children was found.

Applying the same test as in *McSoud, supra*, the appellate court reversed the restraints on the father's exercise of his religion with the children. The court found the evidence demonstrated insufficient harm to the children to justify infringing on the parent's right to engage in religious practices and to involve his children in those religious practices. According to the court,

> For children of divorce in general, and children of intermarriage and divorce especially, exposure to parents' conflicting values, lifestyles, and religious beliefs may indeed cause doubts and stress. However, stress is not always harmful, nor is it always to be avoided and protected against. The key . . . is not whether the child experiences stress, but whether the stress experienced is unproductively severe.

Id. at 1155. The court upheld the requirement that the father take the children to the synagogue's Sunday school because the mother had the legal authority to decide about the children's religious education. The father's periods of visitation with the children were extended at other times during the week.

Restrictions on religious practice have been upheld where the custodial parent shows some actual harm to the children. The Vermont Supreme Court upheld a trial court order prohibiting a non-custodial father from taking his children to Jehovah's Witness religious meetings or inculcating them as Jehovah's Witnesses, where conflict between the religious beliefs of the mother and father was causing extreme confusion and anxiety in the children. *Meyer v. Meyer*, 789 A.2d 921 (Vt. 2001). The court found no First Amendment Establishment Clause violation, noting that it was not interfering with the father's ability to practice his religious faith or favoring one parent's religion over the other, but merely giving effect to the mother's decision as the custodial parent charged with the legal responsibility for the children. *See also Kendall v. Kendall*, 687 N.E.2d 1228 (Mass. 1997) (restriction upheld based on clear evidence that exposure to the father's Christian fundamentalist religion caused substantial harm to the children; father's beliefs included conviction that those not of his religion were damned to go to hell; beliefs distressed the children by interfering with their Jewish identities, alienating them from their mother, and forcing them to choose between their parents); *Sagar v. Sagar*, 781 N.E.2d 54 (Mass. App. Ct. 2003) (father prohibited from initiating child in Hindu religious ceremony, absent agreement of both parents); *Baker v. Baker*, 1997 Tenn. App. LEXIS 837 (Nov. 25, 2007) (father's inculcation efforts in his Jehovah's Witness faith caused children's confusion and withdrawal, which the court found to be clear and affirmative harm as a result of exposure to their parents' conflicting religious beliefs).

PROBLEMS

Problem 6-5. George seeks your advice about whether he can protect his children from the bizarre religious practices of his former wife, Karen, who has custody. Karen is a devoted and loving mother, but she has become increasingly committed to a religious sect that teaches near-total separation from non-church members, who are deemed "unclean." Karen instructs the children to associate only with church members at school, and prohibits them from participating in any school or after-school activities, including sports, Boy or Girl Scouts, drama, and clubs. She also prohibits them from listening to the radio, watching T.V., playing with video games or reading books unless she first approves them. The children have also been taught that adults in their sect do not vote or participate in any civic, political or governmental activities. George travels a great deal in his job and does not want to seek custody himself. Should he be able to obtain a court order placing conditions on Karen's continued custody, such as that she permit the children to socialize with other children? That she refrain from teaching her children that non-church-members (including their father) are "unclean"?

Problem 6-6.   What if Karen's teachings and rules, described above, are based not upon religious convictions, but upon her personal views that present-day society is corrupt and immoral, and that the less her children have to do with it, the better? Does this improve George's position?

[e]   Alienation of the Child's Affections

RENAUD v. RENAUD
Vermont Supreme Court
721 A.2d 463 (1998)

The parties were married in October 1989. They had one child, a son, born in January 1994. In May 1996, the parties separated following father's disclosure that he was having an affair with a co-worker and wanted a divorce. At the time of trial in April and May of 1997, mother was living with the three-year-old child in the marital home, and father was living with the co-worker and her children. . . .

Both parties worked full time in supervisory positions for the federal government. Before the separation, both shared in attending to the minor's childcare needs. Mother arranged her work schedule to have Fridays off to spend with the child. Father took the child to daycare in the morning, visited him there during the day, and brought him home at night. Mother generally took time off from work when the child was sick, purchased his clothes, and did his laundry. The court found that both parents provided the child with love, discipline, structure, and guidance, and that either would be fit to serve as the custodial parent.

Following the separation, father voluntarily moved out, and mother and child continued to reside in the family home. Almost immediately [after the separation], mother began to impede father's contact with the child, forcing father to file a number of motions to establish an emergency visitation schedule. Following a hearing in July 1996, the court established a temporary visitation schedule. Thereafter, mother filed a succession of relief-from-abuse petitions, alleging that father had physically and sexually abused the minor. The allegations ranged from evidence of diaper rash, to sunburn, cuts and bruises, and inappropriate touching. . . .

None of the abuse allegations was substantiated, and all . . . were ultimately dismissed. Indeed, the court found that father had never abused the minor, that the factual support for the "excessive number of motions and petitions" was "weak at best". . . . The court further found that mother's actions were the result of a heightened distrust of father because of his marital unfaithfulness, and that her "baseless suspicions ha[d] adversely affected [the minor] in that he is no longer as loving towards [father] as he once was." A team of psychiatric experts appointed by the court observed that the child interacted well with each parent, but noted that mother's repeated accusations had damaged the child's relationship with father, and warned that if such accusations continued they could seriously compromise the father-child relationship. . . .

In light of the court's express findings that mother had undermined the child's relationship with father by filing excessive and baseless abuse allegations, father contends that the court's decision to award mother sole parental rights and responsibilities was a patent abuse of discretion. Like the trial court here, we are reluctant to condone any conduct by a parent that tends to diminish the child's relationship with the other parent. Indeed, in awarding parental rights and responsibilities, the court is statutorily required to consider "the ability and disposition of each parent to foster a positive relationship and frequent and continuing contact with the other parent, including physical contact, except where contact will result in harm to the child or to a parent." 15 V.S.A. § 665(b)(5). Across the country, the great weight of authority holds that conduct by one parent that tends to alienate the child's affections from the other is so inimical to the child's welfare as to be grounds for a denial of custody to, or a change of custody from, the parent guilty of such conduct.

The paramount consideration in any custody decision, however, is the best interests of the child. Children are not responsible for the misconduct of their parents toward each other, and will not be uprooted from their home merely to punish a wayward parent. Nevertheless, a child's best interests are plainly furthered by nurturing the child's relationship with both parents, and a sustained course of conduct by one parent designed to interfere in the child's relationship with the other casts serious doubt upon the fitness of the offending party to be the custodial parent. See *Young v. Young*, 628 N.Y.S.2d 957, 958 (1995) (interference with relationship between child and non-custodial parent raises "'a strong probability that the offending party is unfit to act as a custodial parent'") (quoting *Maloney v. Maloney*, 617 N.Y.S.2d 190, 191 (1994)).

This is not to say that evidence of alienation of affection automatically precludes the offending parent from obtaining custody. . . . Courts should be wary, however, of over-reliance on such otherwise significant considerations as the child's emotional attachment to, or expressed preference for, the offending parent, or on such factors as stability and continuity. For as one court has observed, "The desires of young children, capable of distortive manipulation by a bitter, or perhaps even well-meaning, parent, do not always reflect the long-term best interest of the children." *Nehra v. Uhlar*, 372 N.E.2d 4, 7 (N.Y.1977). And although stability is undoubtedly important, the short-term disruption occasioned by a change of custody may be more than compensated by the long-term benefits of a healthy relationship with both parents.

Thus, where the evidence discloses a continual and unmitigated course of conduct by a parent designed to poison a child's relationship with the other parent, a change of custody from the offending parent may well be in the child's long-term best interests. . . .

A more subtle, but no less invidious, form of interference in parent-child relations may take the form of persistent allegations of physical or sexual abuse. In

Young, for example, the court reversed an award of custody to the mother where the trial court had inexplicably ignored uncontradicted evidence that the mother had filed numerous false accusations of sexual abuse by the father. As the court observed, "[t]hese repeated uncorroborated and unfounded allegations of sexual abuse brought by the mother against the father cast serious doubt upon her fitness to be the custodial parent." 628 N.Y.S.2d at 962.

. . . . The situation is more difficult where the allegations of abuse, although ultimately found to be baseless, may initially be in doubt. Society has a strong interest in encouraging parents to take action if they suspect that their child is being abused. Accordingly, courts should infer an ulterior motive in the filing of such charges only where a parent knew, or reasonably should have known, that they were groundless. . . .

The record mitigates in favor of mother in this regard. The evidence showed that she did not act precipitously in filing the petitions, but consulted with the child's pediatrician and therapist, as well as her own therapist, about her suspicions. The child's pediatrician . . . informed her that the child's physical condition did not necessarily suggest abuse or neglect, [but]he also told her that if the child's sunburns continued he would "be quite alarmed," and would feel that the "caregiver [father] is not able to protect [the child] from an obvious source of harm". . . .

Mother also expressed her concerns to the child's therapist. She was particularly anxious about statements by the child suggesting that father had manipulated the child's penis. The therapist recalled . . . that mother "chiefly wanted guidance." Although he ultimately concluded that it was unlikely the child had been abused, he was sufficiently concerned to contact Social and Rehabilitation Services. . . . Although the court again found the allegations of abuse to be groundless, it stressed that it was "not at all suggesting that the mother's reaction wasn't appropriate. She was obviously concerned. . . ."

Thus, the record evidence does not support a finding that mother's purpose was to alienate the child from his father, or that her concerns were wholly unreasonable. It is particularly significant in this regard that mother repeatedly sought expert guidance before acting and received ambiguous messages, suggesting on the one hand that the physical evidence of abuse was weak, but on the other hand that her concerns were not entirely unfounded and certainly warranted investigation.

. . . . Although there was conflicting evidence on this point, substantial credible expert evidence supported the conclusion that mother's actions were a transient reaction to a highly volatile emotional situation, and that she had progressed to the point where she could within a reasonable period of time cooperate with father and foster a healthy relationship with the child. We note that the child's tender years may facilitate the healing process envisioned by the court, whereas an older child might not be so amenable to change.

Indeed, the evidence and the findings here contrast sharply with those in another case decided today, *Begins*. There, the family court awarded the father parental rights and responsibilities for two teenage boys, notwithstanding its express finding that the father had willfully poisoned the mother's relationship with the boys and had demonstrated no inclination to act otherwise. The court had also found that the mother had been the children's primary care provider before the separation, and was the custodian of choice in all other significant respects. We thus concluded that an award to the father in these circumstances would seriously impede the mother's opportunity to reestablish a healthy relationship with her sons in the future, and that reversal of the judgment was compelled. *Id.* Here, in contrast, the court expressly found that mother's actions were transitory, unlikely to be repeated, and subject to cure.

Finally, we note that the court awarded father extremely liberal visitation, resulting in a nearly equal sharing of time with the child. This fact, coupled with the court's finding that a change of custody would be highly detrimental to the minor, and that mother would be able to foster a healthy relationship with father within a reasonable period of time, leads us to conclude that the court did not abuse its discretion in awarding parental rights and responsibilities to mother. We hasten to remind the parties, however, that the court's ruling is subject to future modification, and underscore the court's specific admonishment to mother to encourage a warm and loving relationship between father and child. . . .

Affirmed.

NOTE

In recent years, courts deciding custody have focused increasingly on the extent to which each parent is supportive of the other's relationship with the child. An important goal of modern custody law is to promote continued contact between the child and both parents, and some statutes direct courts to consider which parent is more likely to support the child's relationship with the other parent. Many statutes include provisions directing the court deciding between the parents to consider "[t]he ability of the parties to encourage the sharing of love, affection, and contact between the child and the other party." *See* COLO. REV. STAT. § 14-10-124 (1.5)(a)(VI). Such "friendly parent" provisions are designed to discourage the parents from letting their hostility toward one another affect their children. *See* ILL. STAT. ANN. Sect. 750 para. 5/602(a)(8); *see Morehouse v. Morehouse*, 452 S.E.2d 632 (S.C. App. 1995) (father awarded custody because he encouraged good relationship between child and mother, though mother claimed he had engaged in "almost every kind of misconduct"); *Garrett v. Garrett*, 527 N.W.2d 213 (Neb. 1995) (Jehovah's Witness mother awarded custody despite depression, because father tried to alienate children); *In re Marriage of Quirk-Edwards*, 509 N.W.2d 476 (Iowa 1993) (refusal of one parent to provide opportunity for other parent to have meaningful contact with child without just cause shall be considered harmful to the child's interest).

Courts and commentators have focused on a variation of this theme where one parent claims that the other has purposely alienated the child's affections. *See Begins v. Begins*, 721 A.2d at 473 (Vt. 1998) (custody transferred to mother where father poisoned the sons' relationship with the mother, who had been the primary caretaker). In a dispute described as the "worst case of parental alienation syndrome . . . in the history of the United States," a North Dakota trial court not only ordered that custody be changed from the mother to the father, but also denied the mother visitation for a year. *Hendrickson v. Hendrickson*, 603 N.W.2d 896 (N.D. 2000). The Supreme Court ordered supervised visitation, but upheld the change in custody due to the mother's frustration of visitation and poisoning of the relationship between the children and their father. In a juvenile court proceeding initiated because of the children's "unruly" behavior while in the father's custody, however, the children were returned to their mother's custody by the department of social services. *In re C.H.*, 622 N.W.2d 720 (N.D. 2001).

The claim of alienation has gained some notoriety due to the argument by some that it should be recognized as a clinical pathology. The main proponent of this view has been child psychiatrist Richard Gardner, who coined the term "parental alienation syndrome" (PAS) to describe the case in which one parent "brainwashes" the child to hate and fear the other parent, and parent and child become enmeshed in a *folie a deux*. RICHARD GARDNER, THE PARENTAL ALIENATION SYNDROME (2d ed. 1998). Gardner argues that the syndrome is implicated in many false allegations of child sexual abuse in custody disputes, as well as in other situations. Separation of the child and the offending parent is often indicated, in Gardner's view, a conclusion that, if accepted, would have important implications for custody decisions.

Despite Gardner's arguments, no such "syndrome" is recognized by the Diagnostic and Statistical Manual of Mental Disorders (DSM-IV), the official inventory of psychiatric diagnoses published by the American Psychiatric Association. Gardner's critics find no empirical support for the existence of such a psychiatric diagnosis. Janet R. Johnston, *Children of Divorce Who Reject a Parent and Refuse Visitation: Recent Research and Social Policy Implications for the Alienated Child*, 38 Fam. L.Q. 757 (2005). Identifying a child as suffering from PAS, further, does not necessarily help a court resolve a custody or visitation disputes. As Johnston points out, many different factors may combine to cause a child to be alienated from a parent, so that an exclusive focus on the actions or behavior of the other parent as the cause is typically unhelpful in understanding how the alienation came about. Among those factors can be the conduct or inept parenting by the parent from whom the child is distant. *See* Barbara Jo Fidler & Nicholas Bala, *Children Resisting Post-Separation Contact with a Parent: Concepts, Controversies and Conundrums*, 48 FAM. CT. REV. 10 (2010) ("Child alienation needs to be differentiated from a 'realistic estrangement', where the child's resistance or refusal may result from the trauma of witnessing domestic violence or from experiencing physical abuse, sexual abuse, or significantly inept or neglectful parenting by the rejected parent.") According to Johnston,

> [T]he label 'PAS' does not add any information that would enlighten the court, the clinician, or their clients, all of whom would be better served by a more specific description of the child's behavior in the context of his family . . .". It therefore seems likely that the dispute over the existence of PAS is really a distraction from the main issue that properly concerns courts, which is to make a disposition, if possible, that allows a child to maintain a good relationship with both parents. A court need not appeal to question-able psychiatric diagnoses to take account of behavior by either or both parents, when it is shown by the evidence, that is intended to undermine

the other parent's relationship with their common child . . .

[f]   Child's Preference: The Role of Child Preferences in Custody Decisions

Statutes in most jurisdictions identify the child's preference as a factor to be considered in determining custody. Some statutes make the preferences of older children virtually dispositive. For example, the Georgia law provides that a child of 14 "shall have the right to select the parent with whom he or she desires to live. The child's selection for purposes of custody shall be presumptive unless the parent so selected is determined not to be in the best interests of the child." GA. CODE 19-9-3(a)(5) (Supp.). Under such a standard, the parent not selected must prove the selected parent's unfitness. *See also* W.VA. CODE § 44-10-4 (minor over 14 years can nominate parent to serve as custodian who shall be approved by the court unless unfit).

Most states give courts more discretion, providing that the child's preference be considered and given weight if it reflects a level of mature judgment. For example, the Florida statute provides that the best interests determination includes the "reasonable preference of the child, if the court deems the child to be of sufficient intelligence, understanding, and experience to express a preference." FLA. STAT. ANN. § 61.13(3)(i). What is a "reasonable preference?" Many courts will evaluate the reasons given for the preference and discount it if convinced there is an illegitimate basis for the child's choice, or if one parent has put undue pressure on the child. *See, e.g., Marriage of Black*, 837 P.2d 407 (Mont. 1992) (upholding trial court's denial of father's petition for custody modification, where court concluded that children's preference for father was based in part on fact that he took them more places, bought them more things and did not make them work around the house); *Leo v. Leo*, 213 N.W.2d 495 (Iowa 1973) (child preferred father because he permitted him to drink alcoholic beverages and play pool in father's nightclub where boy could regularly view "go-go girls who at times engaged in lewd acts with customers"). Sometimes courts reject the importance of reasons given by the child that seem legitimate. For example a North Dakota court chided children for trying to "hold on to the past" where their preference for their father was based on a desire to stay in the same town and school. *Gould v. Miller*, 488 N.W. 2d 42, 44 (N.D. 1992). Of course, the determination of the maturity of a preference provides opportunity for the judge to inject value-laden opinions into the decision.

There is conflicting evidence about how much weight judges actually give to the child's preferences, although it seems likely that older children's preferences are considered carefully. A Virginia study established a clear correlation between the child's age and the degree to which the child's preference is considered. *See* Elizabeth S. Scott, N. Dickon Reppucci & Mark Aber, *Children's Preference in Adjudicated Custody Decisions*, 22 GA. L. REV. 1035 (1988). Although the Virginia custody statute does not make the child's preference a factor, nearly 90% of judges surveyed reported that the preferences of children age 14 and older were either "dispositive . . . or extremely important," the preferences of children age 10–13 were given somewhat less weight; the preferences of younger children were "discounted significantly." Somewhat different results were found in a survey of

Arizona judges. *See* Barbara A. Atwood, *The Child's Voice in Custody Litigation: An Empirical Survey and Suggestions for Reform*, 45 ARIZ. L. REV. 629 (2003) (80% consider the preferences of older teenagers to be "very or extremely significant;" about 40% "ascribe that same weight to the views of children aged eleven to thirteen years;" about half thought the preferences of children aged three to five were possibly significant, as did about half as to children aged six to ten).

Is it clear a child's preference should be solicited and considered in a custody proceeding? Consider the following:

> Having the child choose has much to commend it. The child, after all, is the focus [of] social concern. Moreover, in the face of indeterminacy, why not have the child's values inform the choice? The child, better than the judge, may have an intuitive sense of the parent's love, devotion, and capacity. But particularly for infants, this standard is little more than a random process, and for the younger child, what would this standard mean? Would the child be able to express a preference? If so, would the child's choice be pressured or corrupted by the prelitigation behavior of one parent? Is it desirable or fair to ask the child to choose? This rule might make the child, in the parents' eyes, responsible for the choice. This might often be a very great burden for the child. Furthermore, if the child were made responsible, the child's relationship with the nonchosen parent might be substantially injured.

Robert H. Mnookin, *Child-Custody Adjudication: Judicial Functions in the Face of Indeterminacy*, 39 LAW & CONTEMP. PROBS. 226, 285 (1975).

How should the child's preference be obtained? Children rarely testify in court in divorce custody proceedings, although the Virginia study found that many judges felt obligated to allow such testimony if one parent insisted. More common are *in camera* interviews of the child by the judge. What rules apply to such interviews? Some courts allow no one else to be present, raising the concern that parties may be disabled from responding to important evidence offered by the child. Scott, et al., *Children's Preference in Adjudicated Custody Decisions*, *supra*. Some statutory procedures deal with this concern. Consider a Minnesota statute:

> The court may interview the child in chambers to ascertain the child's reasonable preference as to custodian, if the court deems the child to be of sufficient age to express preference. The court shall permit counsel to be present at the interview and shall permit counsel to propound reasonable questions to the child either directly or through the court. The court shall cause a record of the interview to be made and to be made part of the record in the case unless waived by the parties.

MINN. STAT. § 518.166.

This statute is intended to provide a way for the child to give useful information to the judge, while giving parents the ability to question child witnesses. A record of the interview makes meaningful review of trial court decisionmaking possible. Such statutory protections in favor of parents have been strictly enforced. *See, e.g., Smith v. Smith*, 425 N.W.2d 854 (Minn. 1988); *Williams v. Cole*, 590 S.W.2d 908 (Mo. 1979). A few states even require that evidence of the child's preference be given in open court. *See, e.g., Stevens v. Stevens*, 215 S.E.2d 991 (N.C. Ct. App. 1975); *Jethrow v. Jethrow*, 571 So. 2d 270 (Miss. 1990) (parent has right to call child as witness in divorce action).

The child's preference seems to have increased in importance in recent years. Some courts have found the failure to consider the preferences of quite young children to be reversible error. *See, e.g., Hensgens v. Hensgens*, 653 So. 2d 48 (La. Ct. App. 1995) (court should have considered the preferences of mature, intelligent children aged eight and ten); *Ellison v. Ellison*, 628 So. 2d 855 (Ala. Civ. App. 1995) (reversible error for court to refuse to allow testimony of mentally retarded ten-year-old); *Bowers v. Bowers*, 475 N.W.2d 394 (Mich. Ct. App. 1991) (reversible error not to interview 6- and 9-year-old children).

NOTE ON THE ROLE OF THE CHILD'S ATTORNEY

If the child's preference is an important consideration in the custody dispute, should children have a right to representation by an attorney who will advocate for the outcome favored by her client? Guardians *ad litem* are often appointed by courts in litigated custody disputes to represent the child's interests, but views vary widely about their appropriate role. Should a guardian ad litem treat the child like any other client? Many observers support this position, but it may not be feasible (or advisable) with younger children.

In a famous Note, Kim Landsman and Martha Minow reported their study in which they interviewed attorneys and found two competing models of legal representation of children in custody disputes — advocates and fact finders. Kim Landsman & Martha Minow, *Lawyering for the Child: Principles of Representation in Custody and Visitation Disputes arising from Divorce*, 87 YALE L.J. 1126 (1978). Advocates generally urged conferral of party status on the child and argue that the attorney's role is to advocate for the child's preference. Under the fact-finder model, the principal role of the attorney is that of impartial investigator; to "insure that all considerations regarding the best interests of the child will have been brought to the Court's attention." Landsman and Minow argue that both of these models offers a limited conception of legal representation, because neither addresses the needs of a child during the period of litigation. They urge a more flexible approach and propose guidelines for attorneys representing children:

(1) The attorney should invite the child to participate and should provide explanation to the extent of the child's desire and capacity. He should also respect a child's desire not to participate. . . .

(2) The attorney should be wary of opposing the child's preference; there may be good reasons for the preference that are not readily observable.

(3) The attorney should act to enhance existing parent-child relationships; this requires a duty to the parents greater than avoiding the infliction of needless harm.

(4) The attorney should take advantage of his unique opportunity to act as mediator and arbitrator in a manner consistent with the child's interests.

The authors also discourage attorneys from relying on investigative agencies or experts, and from seeking psychological evaluations, which are deemed intrusive.

In 2007, a Uniform Law was proposed concerning the representation of children in custody and other civil judicial proceedings involving children. According to the National Conference of Commissioners,

> The Act provides for two categories of lawyers for children — the child's attorney and the best interests attorney — and does not endorse the hybrid category of attorney/guardian ad litem.[26]. . . .
>
> The child's attorney is in a traditional attorney-client relationship with the child and is therefore bound by ordinary ethical obligations governing that relationship. Under the Act, the child's attorney is a client-directed representative and should function within that role rather than advocating for what the lawyer believes to be in the child's best interests. The Act authorizes, however, a limited exercise of substituted judgment by the child's attorney in taking positions in the proceeding . . . [W]hen the child is incapable of directing or refuses to direct representation as to a particular issue, the child's attorney may take a position that is in the child's best interests so long as the position is not in conflict with the child's expressed objectives. The child's attorney may also request appointment of a best interests advocate [a person acting as a non-lawyer "whose role is to assist the court in determining the child's best interests] or a best interests attorney. In contrast, if a child's expressed goals would put the child at risk of substantial harm and the child persists in that position despite the attorney's advice and counsel, the attorney *must* request a best interests advocate or best interests attorney for the child or withdraw from representation and request the appointment of a best interests attorney. Thus, the Act provides mechanisms to protect the attorney-client relationship while still ensuring that evidence of potential harm to the child will be brought to the attention of the court.
>
> The best interests attorney is also in an attorney-client relationship with the child but, in contrast with the child's attorney, is not bound by the child's expressed wishes in determining what to advocate. Instead, the best interests attorney has the substantive responsibility of advocating for the child's best interests based on an objective assessment of the available evidence, including the circumstances and needs of the child, and according to applicable legal principles. Often the best interests attorney's position and the child's stated position will coincide, particularly in light of the attorney's duty to take the child's expressed wishes into account in

---

[26] The Act rejects the hybrid category because it has given rise to a blurring of professional roles where, for example, the same individual functions both as an attorney for the child and a witness in the proceeding. *See* American Bar Association Model Rules of Professional Conduct 3.7 (2004) (generally prohibiting attorney from acting as advocate and witness in same proceeding). In addition, problems have arisen with the dual role approach because of ethical constraints that are inherent in the attorney/client relationship, including in particular the confidentiality of client communications. For judicial recognition of the tensions inherent in the hybrid attorney/guardian ad litem, see *Jacobsen v. Thomas*, 100 P.3d 106 (Mont. 2004); *Clark v. Alexander*, 953 P.2d 145 (Wyo. 1998).

determining what to advocate and to present the child's wishes to the court if the child so desires. Moreover, the availability of a best interests model of representation is particularly important for those children who are unable or unwilling to direct counsel.

The practical tasks facing a best interests attorney will vary according to context. In contested custody cases, judges generally must resolve access and visitation disputes under a discretionary best interests standard . . . [T]he parties' presentations in an adversarial setting may not be adequate to provide the court with necessary information. Because of the potential impact of these proceedings on the lives of children, many courts want the participation of a best interests lawyer to ensure that they receive an independent presentation of evidence and legal argument that includes but is not limited to the child's stated objectives . . . [T]he Act directs the best interests attorney to advocate for a resolution of the proceeding that is consistent with the child's best interests "according to criteria established by law and based on the circumstances and needs of the child and other facts relevant to the proceeding." In other words, the best interests attorney is not free to rely on subjective bias but should adhere to recognized legal standards, such as those found in statutes, case law, and procedural rules, and should develop a position that reflects the child's unique circumstances. Unlike the child's attorney, the best interests attorney is not bound by the client's expressed objectives, but neither should the best interests attorney disregard the child's preferences. Instead, the best interests attorney has an explicit duty to take into account the child's objectives and the reasoning underlying those objectives, in light of the child's developmental level, in determining what to advocate . . .

Significantly, in other respects the best interests attorney serves as a traditional lawyer, and the ethical precepts governing a lawyer-client relationship apply to the best interests attorney's relationship with the child . . . [T]he best interests attorney, like the child's attorney, must counsel the child about the consequences of the child's choices and must keep the child informed of the status of the proceedings. Similarly, the best interests attorney must present the child's expressed objectives to the court if the child so desires. Moreover, the best interests attorney may not disclose the child's confidential communications unless otherwise permitted to do so under applicable ethical standards. The best interests attorney, however, may use the child's confidences for purposes of the representation.

NATIONAL CONFERENCE OF COMMISSIONERS ON UNIFORM STATE LAWS, UNIFORM REPRE-SENTATION OF CHILDREN IN ABUSE, NEGLECT, AND CUSTODY PROCEEDINGS ACT (2007). For a collection of state laws governing representation of children in custody cases, see Linda D. Elrod, *Raising the Bar for Lawyers Who Represent Children: ABA Standards of Practice for Custody Cases*, 37 FAM. L. Q. 105, 126 (2003) (Appendix).

Courts have had a mixed response to requests by children for independent representation in custody disputes. An Arizona court held that the trial court abused its discretion in rejecting the request of a 7-year-old boy for independent counsel in his parents' divorce proceedings. The court noted that state statutes provided discretion to the trial court, but found that where the divorce involved allegations of mistreatment by each parent and the child was able to articulate his feelings well, counsel should have been appointed. *J.A.R. v. Superior Ct.*, 877 P.2d 1323 (Ariz. 1994); *see also G.S. v. T.S.*, 582 A.2d 467 (Conn. App. 1990) (same, in case involving allegation of sexual abuse). A Maryland court, however, followed what is probably the majority rule, in denying the request of the children, ages 12 and 14, to intervene in their parents' custody proceeding through their own attorney. *Auclair v. Auclair*, 730 A.2d 1260 (Md. Ct. Spec. App. 1999). The children argued that their guardian *ad litem* failed to communicate their preferences forcefully to the court. The trial court replaced the first guardian *ad litem* with a second (with whom the children refused to meet), but rejected the petition to intervene through their chosen attorney, and further ordered the attorney not to speak with them. The appellate court held that the children were not entitled to independent representation because they were not parties to the proceeding. Moreover, the court noted that, where attorneys have been allowed, they are appointed by the court and not chosen by the children, to assure competence and independence from either parent. [Here, the mother had chosen the attorney.] In rejecting the children's right to independent representation, the court pointed to the added burden of time and expense that would be incurred. However, the lower court was found to have erred in prohibiting the children from consulting with counsel of their choice. Since the primary task of the guardian *ad litem* is to investigate and obtain information from the children, private counsel could play an important role in providing the children with information and legal advice on effective formulation of their preferences.

The role of counsel for parents is discussed in Section G, *infra*.

PROBLEM

Problem 6-7. You have been appointed to represent a twelve-year-old child, Sarah, in a bitterly contested custody fight. In your discussion with Sarah, she states firmly and consistently that she wants to live with her mother, Hannah, because "Mommy has always taken care of me, and I take care of her too." After conducting a full investigation of the case, you learn that the mother has a history of rather serious emotional problems and was hospitalized for depression last year. You also learn that Hannah has had a secret problem with alcohol abuse over the past decade; she admits that in the past she has been intoxicated around Sarah occasionally. Although Hannah insists that her drinking problem is under control, you are concerned that under stress, she may start drinking again. Sarah's father, Mike, is a stable and affectionate parent, although he is a busy lawyer and has always left Sarah's care to Hannah. Although Sarah is not as close to him as she is to her mother, you are convinced that in the long run, she will receive better care and greater stability with her father. From your discussions with the father and with his attorney, it is clear that neither knows of the mother's drinking problem.

In the custody proceedings, do you advocate the position that corresponds to Sarah's preferences, or the position that you believe is in her long-term best interests? What alternative courses of action do you have? Do you tell the father's attorney or the court about the mother's alcohol problems?

C. ALTERNATIVE CUSTODY DECISION RULES

The best interest of the child standard has been criticized over the years on the ground that it provides little guidance to courts about what factors should be given priority in the custody decision. See the discussion in Section B[1], *supra*. Indeed, it might be said that the best interest standard hardly qualifies as a legal rule at all; more accurately, it simply describes the court's goal in determining custody — to decide the child's custodial arrangements according to her best interests. As the preceding section demonstrates, most doctrinal developments have focused on whether certain controversial factors (race, religion, gender, sexual behavior) should be *excluded* from consideration under the best interest standard. The best interest standard gives courts vast discretion, allowing judges' subjective values and biases to influence the custodial choice. Moreover, adjudication of custody disputes under this standard, which effectively invites each parent to marshal evidence about the other's deficiencies, is likely to have a particularly damaging impact on the parties' future relationship. To the extent that parents' cooperation in the post-dissolution period serves their children's interests, the best interest standard paradoxically may undermine children's interests.

Many observers have argued that the best interest of the child standard should be replaced with a more determinate decision rule that narrows the discretion of courts. We will consider the two most important alternatives to emerge in the past generation. The first approach is for parents to share responsibility and authority for their children under an order for joint physical or legal custody. The rationale for joint custody is that it promotes the child's welfare by preserving her relationships with both parents after separation. Although joint physical custody has not gained the popularity that advocates predicted in the 1980s, joint legal custody is routinely ordered in many states. The second approach focuses on the parents' caretaking role in the child's life before the family broke down. Until recently, the dominant version of this approach was the primary caretaker preference, under which custody was awarded to the parent who assumed primary responsibility for the child's care before dissolution. *See Garska v. McCoy*, 278 S.E.2d 357 (W. Va. 1981). This rule was essentially a gender-neutral version of the tender years presumption; it assumed that the child had only one primary caretaker, but that either parent might fill the role. Recently, this approach has been adapted to recognize both parents' caretaking roles. Under the A.L.I. standard, custodial responsibility is allocated between the parents so as to approximate each parent's caretaking role before separation. Sect. 2.08-2.09.

[1] Joint Custody

Courts have an option today that was not available in most states until the 1980s of awarding legal or physical custody to both parents. This approach to custody, mostly accomplished through statutory reform, reflects an underlying policy of encouraging both parents to maintain post-divorce relationships with the child. Although the overriding policy goal of joint custody is clear, the term is used in a confusing way because it includes two types of legal arrangements. Joint physical custody involves a relatively equal sharing by the parents of physical care of the child; the term refers to the child's residential placement. Joint legal custody involves sharing by the parents of the authority to make important decisions affecting the child's welfare — decisions relating to education, medical care and religious training and practice. Although advocates of joint custody generally seek to promote joint physical custody, commentators, courts and even legislatures formulating statutes tend to be unclear about which form is intended. The following case addresses the distinctions between joint physical and joint legal custody.

In the last section, the focus was on factors affecting the best interests of the child in cases where a parent is seeking sole physical and legal custody. The same best interests factors inform the court where a parent is seeking joint legal or physical custody. Where joint legal and physical custody is at issue, however, the court must also consider whether the parents can cooperate sufficiently to serve the child's best interests.

McCARTY v. McCARTY
Maryland Court of Special Appeals
807 A.2d 1211 (2002)

MOYLAN, JUDGE.

This case concerns the award of joint legal custody to the estranged parents of three-year-old Jessica McCarty. The appellant, Carol Marie McCarty (the Mother), and the appellee, Douglas Neal McCarty (the Father), were married on January 31, 1998. Jessica was born on August 8, 1999. The parties separated on November 17, 2000. The Father filed a motion in the Circuit Court for Montgomery County, asking for both joint legal custody and joint physical custody of his daughter. The Mother filed a counter-complaint in the same court, asking for a limited divorce and for sole custody, both legal and physical, of her daughter. [The trial court] awarded sole physical custody to the Mother but joint legal custody to the Mother and Father. The Mother has taken this appeal from that award of joint legal custody.

Initially, it will be helpful to contrast joint legal custody and joint physical custody. Although the landmark case of *Taylor v. Taylor*, 508 A.2d 964 (Md. 1986), discusses both forms of joint custody, it is careful to distinguish the two from each other. . . .

[A] distinction must be made between sharing parental responsibility in major decision-making matters and sharing responsibility for providing a home for the child. Embraced within the meaning of "custody" are the concepts of "legal" and "physical" custody. Legal custody carries with it the right and obligation to make long range decisions involving education, religious training, discipline, medical care, and other matters of major significance concerning the child's life and welfare. Joint legal custody means that both parents have an equal voice in making those decisions, and neither parent's rights are superior to the other. . . .

Physical custody, on the other hand, means the right and obligation to provide a home for the child and to make the day-to-day decisions required during the time the child is actually with the parent having such custody. Joint physical custody is in reality "shared" or "divided" custody. Shared physical custody may, but need not, be on a 50/50 basis, and in fact most commonly will involve custody by one parent during the school year and by the other during summer vacation months, or division between weekdays and weekends, or between days and nights. . . .

Proper practice in any case involving joint custody dictates that the parties and the trial judge separately consider the issues involved in both joint legal custody and joint physical custody, and that the trial judge state specifically the decision made as to each.

The only issue before us in this case is joint legal custody, and not joint physical custody. . . .

The Mother points to two factors to support her claim that Judge Sundt was guilty of a clear abuse of discretion in awarding joint legal custody. One is her own reluctance to share legal custody. . . . This is a factor that self-evidently applies to joint legal custody and joint physical custody alike. "Generally, the parents should be willing to undertake joint custody or it should not be ordered." 508 A.2d 964.

. . . . [T]he Court of Appeals rejected the proposition "that a trial judge may never order joint legal custody over the objection of one parent." *Id.* It was unwilling to grant either parent "veto power" over such a possibility.

> A caring parent, believing that sole custody is in the best interest of the child, may forcefully advance that position throughout the litigation but be willing and able to fully participate in a joint custody arrangement if that is the considered decision of the court. 508 A2d 964.

The Mother's reluctance to share legal custody, moreover, does not come across to us as an adamantine or Shermanesque refusal to participate in the event that such an arrangement were to be ordered by the court. She had moved, after all, for sole legal custody in herself and her position on joint custody, expressed in her brief, simply supports that position.

A mere reluctance to participate in an arrangement is not tantamount to a refusal to participate and should not be given the same weight as the judge assesses the prospects for a successful resolution.

The other factor cited by the Mother as a contraindication of joint legal custody is the inability of the Mother and Father to communicate effectively with each other. This is a . . . factor that is particularly pertinent to joint legal custody.

> This is clearly the most important factor in the determination of whether an award of joint legal custody is appropriate, and is relevant as well to a consideration of shared physical custody. Rarely, if ever, should joint legal custody be awarded in the absence of a record of mature conduct on the part of the parents evidencing an ability to effectively communicate with each other concerning the best interest of the child, and then only when it is possible to make a finding of a strong potential for such conduct in the future.

508 A.2d 964.

It is that "rarely, if ever . . ." dictum . . . on which the appellant essentially hinges this appeal. The trial judge would obviously need a substantial basis for looking beyond the surface appearance of poor communication.

In this case, the actual "track record" of the Mother and Father for effective communication had been, to be sure, abysmal. Indeed, on September 7, 2001, Judge Sundt deferred making a final decision on joint legal custody for six months and ordered both the Mother and the Father to "work with a parent coordinator, Dr. Linda Gordon," whose "primary purpose shall be to facilitate communication between the parties, to reduce the conflict between the parties."

It was the relative optimism of Dr. Gordon, six months later, based on improvements in the attitude of both parties, that persuaded Judge Sundt to award joint legal custody. Ordinarily the best evidence of compatibility with this criterion will be the past conduct or "track record" of the parties. We recognize, however, that the tensions of separation and litigation will sometimes produce bitterness and lack of ability to cooperate or agree. The trial judge will have to evaluate whether this is a temporary condition, very likely to abate upon resolution of the issues, or whether it is more permanent in nature. . . .

Admittedly, tensions and disagreements between the parties have escalated. Nevertheless, after hearing the testimony, and judging the credibility and demeanor of the witnesses, the trial court concluded that the parties could resolve their differences and act together in [the child's] best interest.

. . . . Judge Sundt found that, after six months of the parties' working with Dr. Gordon, there had been "enormous improvement" in their ability and willingness to communicate with each other. Linda Gordon talked about the successes first, the fact that there had been sharing of information, and the way the she had institutionalized that was through faxes on a weekly basis, so that the parties could communicate as to what was going on with Jessica.

She talked about the reduction of conflict and strategies that she had been working with the parties on, even small language strategies, so that Mrs. McCarty, who has demonstrated, by both experts' testimony, real learning skills in handing off Jessica — even there, in small nuances of language, could turn a phrase so that it might appear more positive than pejorative as she is getting Jessica ready to go on visits — and certainly with Mr. McCarty, who had a longer road to travel, doing whatever he could to, if not mask his hostility toward his wife, at least put on a civil face and address her and in a tone of voice that would not be threatening or would not be perceived as frightening.

In a case in which there is not an established "track record" of good communication, . . . the trial court must articulate the bases for any optimistic expectation on its part that the situation will improve.

In this case, Judge Sundt did just that. She pointed to 1) the fact that the tensions of litigation were subsiding and 2) the continuing help of a third party. . . .

In terms of that third-party help, part of Judge Sundt's final order, moreover, was her firm directive that both parties must continue, at their own mutual expense, to work with Dr. Gordon for an additional six months in the effort to improve their communicative skills. Judge Sundt was emphatic:

Neither one of you is to make a major decision without consulting the other, and, as I said, if you run into an impasse, that is the time you meet with Dr. Gordon. I want you to meet with her no fewer than 10 times over these six months. So, that is roughly every other week.

I think you can do legal custody. . . . [T]he primary factor in joint legal custody has to do with valuing and respecting each other so that you can actually confer and consult.

But I am relying on Linda Gordon in this respect. Her sense was that to the extent that . . . the conflict is situational, and to the extent that you have been able to move past that and that there are ways of communicating without having to do it face-to-face and certainly not in Jessica's presence, it will come.

And I tend to adopt her view that the alternative is worse — that a period of time right now for one of you to be making the decisions without the other's input will be perceived as such disrespect and such disregard that the conflict will not abate — that the only way that conflict is going to abate is with your having to be civil, courteous, and respectful.

We cannot say that Judge Sundt's decision constituted a clear abuse of discretion.

NOTES

1. *The Dual Meaning of Joint Custody.* The *McCarty* court describes the difference between joint physical custody and joint legal custody and emphasizes that only joint legal custody is at issue in this case in which the mother is awarded primary physical custody. Other courts are far less clear, and even statutes can be ambiguous. For example, the Iowa statute creates a preference favoring joint custody. Iowa Code § 598.41. Iowa judicial opinions clarify, however, that the preference applies only to joint *legal* custody, and even conclude that joint physical custody is to be awarded only in exceptional circumstances — a conclusion that the statute itself certainly does not indicate. *See In re Marriage of Will*, 489 N.W.2d 394 (Iowa 1992). The Maryland court in *McCarty* suggests that the factors to be considered in deciding whether joint physical custody is appropriate differ from those that would be considered in a decision about joint legal custody. Other than logistical factors such as the proximity to one another of the parties' homes, how would the inquiry be different? The ability of the parties to communicate with one another would be important both in joint legal and physical custody — probably more important when physical custody is shared. Would a court considering joint physical custody have found these parents' communication to be adequate?

One effect of the confusion about the meaning of "joint custody" is that it is hard to evaluate the prevalence of joint custody and the impact of the trend. The most comprehensive study of joint custody to date is the California study conducted by Eleanor Maccoby and Robert Mnookin, described earlier. E. Maccoby & R. Mnookin, Dividing the Child: Social and Legal Dilemmas of Custody (1992). These researchers found that joint legal custody (awarded in 79% of cases) is much more common than joint physical custody (19.6% of cases). Moreover, in about 45% of the families with joint physical custody, a "drift" took place over the next three years, and the arrangements became *de facto* sole custody arrangements, with children living with their mother. Complicating the issue further is the fact that what distinguishes joint and sole physical custody is the amount of time the child spends with each parent, and it may not be clear where the line between sole and joint physical custody lies. The *McCarty* court emphasizes that a 50\50 division of time is not necessary. Do parents have joint custody when the child spends two days a week with one parent (and five with the other)? Three days with one and four with the other?

2. *The Current Law.* While precedential authority for joint custody awards dates from early in the last century, *see, e.g., Baer v. Baer,* 51 S.W.2d 873 (Mo. App. 1932), the modern availability of joint custody as an alternative to traditional sole custody has been described as a "small revolution . . . in child custody law." Elizabeth Scott & Andre Derdeyn, *Rethinking Joint Custody,* 45 Ohio St. L.J. 455, 455 (1984). Beginning in the late 1970s, many courts have authorized joint custody without express statutory support. *See, e.g., Taylor v Taylor,* 508 A.2d 964 (Md. 1986) (discussed in *McCarty*); *Beck v. Beck,* 432 A.2d 63 (N.J. 1981); *Daniel v. Daniel,* 238 S.E.2d 108 (Ga. 1977). The 1980s saw a flood of legislation, such that a 1989 article found 34 states with joint custody statutes of one sort or another. Doris Jonas Freed & Timothy B. Walker, *Family Law in the 50 States,* 22 Fam. L.Q. 367, 467 (1989). A few were enacted in the 1990s. *See* D.C. Code Ann. § 16-911, 16-914.

The momentum behind joint custody legislation has come in part from the political efforts of fathers' groups. Fathers who are involved with their children have been frustrated by traditional sole custody arrangements, under which their access to their child and parental status generally is quite limited. Mel Roman & William Haddad, The Disposable Parent (1978). The receptiveness to joint custody and the legal reforms that have resulted may be attributed, in part, to a belief that fathers with joint custody will maintain their relationship with their children, and thus will be more likely to continue to provide financial support. The continued involvement of both parents in their children's lives after divorce is expressed as a policy goal under many custody laws.

3. *State Law Variations.* State statutes reveal a wide range of policies with respect to joint custody. Consider the following state statutes:

CALIFORNIA FAMILY CODE

§ 3040. Order of preference in granting custody

(a) Custody should be awarded in the following order of preference according to the best interests of the child. . . . :

> (1) To both parents jointly . . . or to either parent. In making an order for custody to either parent, the court shall consider, among other factors, which parent is more likely to allow the child or children frequent and continuing contact with the noncustodial parent, . . .

(b) This section establishes neither a preference nor a presumption for or against joint legal custody, joint physical custody, or sole custody. . . .

§ 3080. Presumption for joint custody where parents agree to joint custody

There is a presumption, affecting the burden of proof, that joint custody is in the best interests of a minor child where the parents have agreed to an award of joint custody or so agree in open court. . . .

§ 3081. Grant of joint custody absent agreement of parents

On the application of either parent, joint custody may be ordered in the discretion of the court. . . .

FLORIDA STATUTES ANNOTATED

§ 61.13. Support of children; parenting and time-sharing; powers of court

(2)(b)2. The court shall order that the parental responsibility for a minor child be shared by both parents unless the court finds that shared parental responsibility would be detrimental to the child. . . .

> a. In ordering shared parental responsibility, the court may consider the expressed desires of the parents and may grant to one party the ultimate responsibility over specific aspects of the child's welfare or may divide those responsibilities between the parties based on the best interests of the child. Areas of responsibility may include primary residence, education, medical and dental care, and any other responsibilities which the court finds unique to a particular family.

> b. The court shall order sole parental responsibility, with or without visitation rights, to the other parent when it is in the best interests of the minor child.

The statutes show considerable variation. Some create a preference for joint custody and direct courts to consider several factors to determine whether this arrangement is appropriate. These factors include whether each parent would be a suitable custodian; whether the parents can communicate with each other regarding the child's needs; whether both parents have actively cared for the child before and since the separation; and whether each parent can support the other parent's relationship with the child. Some states require joint custody to be considered if one parent petitions, while others simply authorize joint custody. A few states, like California, *supra* create a preference in favor of joint custody that only applies if both parents agree. *See* CONN. GEN. STAT. ANN. § 46b-56b. In others, the preference is overcome by a showing that another award is in the child's best interests. *See* MICH. COMP. LAWS ANN. § 722.26a(1). A few statutes prohibit an award of joint custody unless the parents agree. *See* OR. REV. STAT. § 107.169(3); VT. STAT. ANN tit. 15 § 665(a).

Some courts have tended to interpret joint custody statutes restrictively. In Nebraska, a judicially-created rule requires a hearing to determine whether joint physical custody is in the best interest of the child, even when the parents agree to it. *Hildebrand v. Hildebrand*, 477 N.W.2d 1, 4 (1991). *See* Note 1, *supra*.

4. *Joint Custody Over Parental Objection.* Most joint custody statutes at least implicitly allow courts to order joint custody over the objection of one parent, and many permit a joint custody order even if neither parent seeks this arrangement. (Some statutes require parental agreement, and others have been interpreted in this way.) As the *McCarty* court suggests, a parent's opposition to joint custody is usually treated as simply one of the several factors weighed by the court when the other parent has requested joint custody. *See, e.g., Squires v. Squires,* 854 S.W.2d 765 (Ky. 1993) (a requirement of agreement would give one parent a veto that could be exercised in bad faith). As *McCarty* suggests, this view assumes (and some social scientists agree) that some parents who have been hostile to one another can set aside their disagreements and cooperate in a joint custody arrangement, if ordered to do so by a court. *See, e.g.,* R. McKinnon & Judith S. Wallerstein, *Joint Custody and the Preschool Child,* 4 BEHAV. SCI. & L. 169, 177 (1986); Geoffrey L. Greif, *Fathers, Children, and Joint Custody,* 49 AM. J. ORTHOPSYCHIATRY 311, 318 (1979).

A few courts have ordered joint custody *because* one (or both) parent is hostile and seeks to alienate the child from the other parent. In *Barton v. Hirshberg,* a Maryland court upheld an award of joint legal custody, based on a diagnosis of Parental Alienation Syndrome, caused by the mother's hostility toward the father. 767 A2d 874 (Md. Ct. App. 2000). The court justified the order (along with increased visitation) on the ground that the mother's alienating behavior could result in the child being "distanced from his father . . . and . . . impede his emotional maturation." The court concluded (optimistically) that the parents would be able to communicate adequately after the tensions surrounding the legal proceedings abated. *See also Scott v. Scott,* 579 S.E.2d 620 (S.C. 2003) (joint physical custody ordered where both parents seek to alienate the child from the other; either parent with sole custody would compromise the child's relationship with the other). Are these courts elevating the importance of maintaining the child's relationship with both parents over every other consideration? Is this a consideration in *McCarty*? In considering that question, the following additional facts about the McCarty family are important. First, Mrs. McCarty testified to two incidents involving Mr. McCarty screaming at her and shoving her, once in front of the child. Mr. McCarty denied significant aspects of Mrs. McCarty's account. The trial court decided it was unimportant to determine what actually happened. Second, about a year after the appeal was decided, the father moved to modify the access schedule and for sole legal custody. The mother opposed both changes and moved for sole legal custody in her. After a two-day trial, the court refused to modify the joint legal custody, made the access schedule more specific, and ordered changes with regard to the child's mental health treatment. After the parties filed additional motions to modify access and legal custody, further changes were made in 2008, this time with the consent of the parties, with respect to access over the summer and during vacations and with respect to mental health treatment for the child, who was then eight years old.

By contrast, some courts are unwilling to coerce parents into a joint custody arrangement, reasoning that there is no reasonable hope of post-divorce cooperation in such an arrangement unless the parents are committed to it. *See, e.g., Emerick v. Emerick,* 502 A.2d 933 (Conn. App. Ct. 1985); *Frey v. Wagner,* 433

So. 2d 60 (Fla. App. 1983). This view is also supported by some research indicating that court-ordered joint custody does not promote cooperative parenting. *See* Susan Steinman, *Joint Custody: What We Know, What We Have Yet to Learn, and the Judicial and Legislative Implications*, 16 U.C. DAVIS L. REV. 739, 759 (1983). Consider again the situation in McCarty, where the undisputed evidence showed a history of conflict between the parents, a father who had to learn to communicate civilly with the mother without demonstrating his hostility or being threatening, and a mother who had to learn to be "more positive" and less pejorative. Once the court, over the mother's objection, enters a joint legal custody order, does the father continue to have an incentive to learn to work more cooperatively with the mother?

5. ***Well-Being of the Children.*** Advocates of joint physical custody argue that children need continuing contact with both parents. Empirical research to date, while limited in various ways, bears out parts of the claim while offering significant caveats. One recent summary of the research states, "In all, it appears joint physical custody does not increase conflict among parents, as some have feared, and that it either has no effect or a modest positive effect on children's psychosocial well-being if parents' relationships are not characterized by conflict." Robert F. Kelly & Shawn Ward, *Social Science Research and The American Law Institute's Approximation Rule*, 40 FAM. CT. REV. 350 (2002). The researchers were careful to note that the studies they summarized were likely to have included few cases in which joint custody was mandated by a court over a parental objection. *Id.* More recently, Professor Margaret Brinig examined data from the National Longitudinal Study of Adolescent Health and determined that, while children in maternal custody who spent time with both parents generally did better than children who visited their fathers infrequently, there was "no increase in custodial time that made a statistically significant difference." Margaret F. Brinig, *Does Parental Autonomy Require Equal Custody at Divorce?*, 65 LA. L. REV. 1345 (2005). In other words, children can benefit from contact with the noncustodial parent even if it occurs several times a month rather than half the time. She also found, in a study of Oregon cases, that joint physical custody was associated with statistically significant decreases in the amount of child support provided to the child's primary household. In addition, "[the children] may live the life of peripatetic suitcase-dwellers, and even worse, may be shuttled between parents who actively seek to undermine each other." *Id.* Substantial psychological research supports the proposition that exposure to conflict between their parents has a destructive impact on children after divorce (or in an intact family, for that matter), an impact that may be more harmful than reduced contact with a parent. See the research summarized in Scott and Derdeyn, *Rethinking Joint Custody*, Note 1, *supra*; Christy M. Buchanan & Parissa L. Jahromi, *A Psychological Perspective on Shared Custody Arrangements*, 43 WAKE FOREST L. REV. 419 (2008). Thus, coercing a continued relationship (through a joint custody arrangement) between parents who are extremely hostile toward one another may be more disruptive to the child than a sole custody arrangement.

6. ***Logistical Complications of Physical Joint Custody Arrangements.*** As the Mnookin and Maccoby study suggests, even in California, only a small proportion of divorced couples share physical custody. Robert H. Mnookin &

Maccoby, *Facing the Dilemmas of Child Custody*, 10 Va. J. Soc. Pol'y & L. 54 (2002). One constraint on joint physical custody is mobility. Many people relocate after divorce and sharing in the child's care becomes impractical. Relocation is discussed in Section E[2], *infra*. Moreover, courts are resistant to complicated and constantly shifting residential arrangements. *See, e.g.*, *Lukens v. Lukens*, 587 N.W. 2d 141 (N.D. 1998) (court rejects award rotating custody on a monthly basis); *Evans v. Lungrin*, 708 So. 2d 731 (La. 1998) (trial court abused discretion in ordering custody to alternate in four month blocks between Louisiana father and Washington mother); *Peek v. Berning*, 622 N.W.2d 186 (N.D. 2001) (reversing joint physical custody order where child would move from one parent's home to the other every 28 days before child starts kindergarten, after which custody would alternate on a monthly basis and where court made no finding that parents could cooperate adequately; trial court justified order on basis that child's best interests involve spending as much time as possible with each parent).

7. *Resolving Disputes Between Parents with Joint Custody.* As a general matter, conflicts between parents over their custodial arrangements after divorce are in fact uncommon, and when they arise they normally are resolved without resort to legal proceedings. Maccoby and Mnookin found that less than two percent of their sample of cases required legal proceedings to resolve a parental conflict. Robert H. Mnookin & Eleanor Maccoby, *Facing the Dilemmas of Child Custody*, 10 Va. J. Soc. Pol'y & L. 54, 60 (2002). Nonetheless, the potential for conflict over everyday matters of scheduling, discipline, etc., is greater in joint physical custody arrangements. Substantial parental conflict which detrimentally affects the child can result in modification to a sole custody arrangement. Parents with joint legal custody may disagree about the decisions that are the subject of shared authority. Many courts will resolve the dispute by deciding the matter itself, while some will designate the parent with decisionmaking authority. An example of the latter approach is *Hight v. McKinney*, 627 N.Y.S.2d 271 (Fam. Ct. 1995), in which the court gave the mother the authority to decide whether the child should attend sex education classes to which the father objected. In *In re Debenham*, 896 P.2d 1098 (Kans. App. 1995), joint custodial parents had deadlocked over where to send their child to school. The appellate court affirmed the order directing the child's continued attendance at the private school chosen by the primary physical custodian, but emphasized it was not adopting a *per se* rule in favoring the primary physical custodian's decision and stressed that the other parent could return to court to renew his request for a different educational plan for the child. The court acknowledged that this solution, with its built-in invitation for continued litigation, was not very satisfactory. However, it blamed the legislature for "declar[ing] joint custody and equal decisional rights as the public policy of this state." *Id.* at 1101. *See also Sotnick v. Sotnick*, 650 So. 2d 157 (Fla. App. 1995) (court resolves issue of where child should attend school when parents with shared responsibility deadlock). In a recent Maryland study, the categories of custody cases involving the highest rates of subsequent litigation were "joint legal with physical custody to father" and "joint legal and physical custody" — 27 percent and 19 percent, respectively — where the original order had been resolved through judicial intervention. The Women's Law Center of Maryland, Inc., Families In Transition: A Follow-Up Study Exploring Family Law Issues In Maryland 56 (2006), http://www.wlcmd.org/pdf/FamiliesInTransition.pdf; *cf.* Robert E. Emery &

Kimberly C. Emery, *Should Courts or Parents Make Child-Rearing Decisions?: Married Parents as a Paradigm for Parents Who Live Apart*, 43 WAKE FOREST L. REV. 365 (2008) (proposing that courts should usually treat divorced parents the same as married parents and abstain from intervening in most disputes).

8. *"Friendly Parent" Provisions and Joint Custody.* The California statute, *supra*, includes a "friendly parent" provision directing the court to consider "which parent is more likely to allow the child . . . frequent . . . contact with the non-custodial parent" if it decides to award sole, rather than joint, custody. Such provisions can present a formidable obstacle to the parent who opposes a joint custody petition by the other. Consider one court's statement: "[A] court may properly consider that a parent's unreasonable or obdurate resistance to joint custody is a factor which can weigh in favor of awarding sole custody to the other parent." *In re Marriage of Weidner*, 338 N.W.2d 351 (Iowa 1983). Critics of "friendly parent" provisions argue these provisions discourage well-intentioned parents from opposing joint custody, for fear that this might be used to label the complainer as a non-friendly parent and, therefore, an inappropriate candidate for a sole custody award. *See* Joanne Schulman & Valerie Pitt, *Second Thoughts on Joint Child Custody: Analysis of Legislation and Its Implications for Women and Children*, 12 GOLDEN GATE U.L. REV. 538, 554–55 (1982). *Weidner* and other cases have emphasized, however, that a parent's good faith opposition to joint custody should not penalize her request for sole custody. *See, e.g., Rolde v. Rolde*, 425 N.E.2d 388 (Mass. App. 1981); *In re Marriage of Heinel and Kessel*, 637 P.2d 1313 (Or. 1981). Nonetheless, seeking to prove good faith opposition carries some risk.

9. *The Feminist Critique of Joint Custody.* Pointing out that the joint custody movement has been dominated by fathers' rights groups, some feminists argue that the reforms are detrimental to women. They assert that laws favoring joint custody give fathers additional leverage, which is used to exact concessions from mothers during divorce negotiations, or to manipulate or harass women after the divorce. Moreover, awarding custody rights to fathers who have had minimal involvement with their children is unfair to primary caretaking mothers. As Martha Fineman has argued:

> In most marriages, one parent, normally the mother, assumes day-to-day primary care. Shared parenting in these situations seldom means equally divided responsibility and control: typically one parent sacrifices more than the other in order to care for the child. The sense of sharing in this context is not based on the actual assumption of divided responsibilities by the parents. . . . Yet an unrealistic and idealized vision of shared parenting *independent* of the relationship is now imposed on couples after divorce. . . . [T]his amounts to furthering the interests of non-caretaking fathers over the objections and against the interests of caretaking mothers.

Martha Fineman, *Dominant Discourse, Professional Language and Legal Change in Child Custody Decisionmaking*, 101 HARV. L. REV. 727, 768 (1988). *See also* Scott & Derdeyn, *Rethinking Joint Custody, supra;* Schulman & Pitt, *supra;* Jana B. Singer & William B. Reynolds, *A Dissent on Joint Custody*, 47 MD. L. REV. 497 (1988). Some feminists acknowledge the deficiencies of joint custody, but defend this arrangement, arguing that it expresses egalitarian parenting roles, which ultimately serve women's interests as well as those of men. *See* Katharine T. Bartlett & Carol B. Stack, *Joint Custody, Feminism and the Dependency Dilemma*, 2 BERKLEY WOMEN'S L.J. 9 (1985).

A response to Fineman's critique is that a party in a legal dispute always has more leverage in negotiations when the legal rule favors that party. So just as a joint custody presumption gives fathers leverage, a primary caretaker presumption gives mothers leverage. Where the wellbeing of children is involved, the key question should not be whether one party or the other benefits from a legal rule, but rather whether the rule allocates those benefits appropriately as a matter of public policy. Fineman and others argue that a joint custody rule does not, because it favors the parent who has not exercised responsibility for the child comparable to the other parent when the family was intact. Certainly a presumption favoring joint custody might have this effect. Supporters, however, argue that by promoting the involvement of both parents, joint custody benefits children. Andrew Schepard, *Taking Children Seriously: Promoting Cooperative Custody After Divorce*, 64 TEX. L. REV. 687 (1985). Whether that point is well taken is discussed in Note 5, *supra*.

Another criticism of joint custody is that women may be required to "cooperate" with their physically abusive former spouses. States have taken the critique seriously and most have enacted statutes that reduce the likelihood that joint custody will be ordered where one parent has engaged in acts of domestic violence against the child or other parent. Many states have a rebuttable presumption against joint custody where domestic violence is shown. *See, e.g.*, WIS. STAT. ANN. § 767.41; CAL. FAM. CODE § 3011; ALASKA STAT. § 25.20.090(8); ARIZ. REV. STAT. ANN. § 25-403.03; LA. STAT. ANN.-REV. § 9:364. Courts also have addressed this issue. *See, e.g., Hurd v. Hurd*, 219 P.3d 258 (Ariz. Ct. App. 2009) (upholding award of sole custody to mother where evidence showed substantial history of domestic violence by father against mother and children and father did not overcome presumption against award of joint custody); *Bishop v. Bishop*, 457 So. 2d 264 (La. Ct. App. 1984) (rejecting joint custody because of impact of physical abuse and extreme antagonism between parents on child); *In re Marriage of Hickey*, 689 P.2d 1222 (Mont. 1984) (reversing joint custody decree because of father's history of violent temper and threats against wife); *Headrick v. Headrick*, 916 So. 2d 610 (Ala. Civ. App. 2005) (finding statutory presumption against joint custody overcome where both parents had abused the other; neither had abused or posed threat to the child; and neither was a better parent than the other).

10. *High Conflict Parents.* Joint legal and physical custody orders are sometimes entered when the parents have engaged in highly conflictual litigation. Sometimes, as in *McCarty*, litigation conflict and domestic violence may occur in the same case. While joint custody orders in such situations are somewhat unexpected, they may occur because of the sometimes perplexing characteristics of parents who engage in highly conflictual litigation. As described by Mnookin and Maccoby,

> It may well be that the attitudes and behavior of fathers, more than those of mothers, will provide the key to understanding better how families with high legal conflict differ. We saw that the two variables most significantly related to legal conflict were the father's concern over the

child's well-being in the mother's household and the father's hostility toward the mother. In addition, parents involved in high levels of legal conflict often had been involved in the children's lives before the separation. When fathers believed they had been substantially involved, they were more likely to press for their rights to time with the child, while mothers who thought that fathers had not been substantially involved were more likely to resist such demands. The roots of legal conflict may often lie in psychological aspects of the spousal relationship that existed long before the separation — factors which we made no attempt to assess . . . Our most disturbing finding with respect to legal conflict concerns the frequency with which joint physical custody decrees are being used by high-conflict families to resolve disputes. About a third of the 166 cases in our study in which the decree provided for joint custody involved substantial or intense legal conflict. In about half of these cases, the children in fact resided with the mother — the legal label did not reflect the social reality. Nevertheless, we did find some 25 joint physical custody cases in which the children were in fact dividing their residential time fairly equally between parents who had substantial legal conflict. Moreover, we found a strong relationship between the intensity of legal conflict and the ability of parents to develop cooperative co-parental relations following the divorce: a much higher proportion of those families with substantial or intense legal conflict had conflicted co-parenting styles, and many fewer were able to develop cooperative co-parenting relationships. Legal conflict was not related, however, to how well the father subsequently abided by his support obligations.

Robert H. Mnookin & Eleanor Maccoby, *Facing the Dilemmas of Child Custody*, 10 VA. J. SOC. POL'Y & L. 54, 61 (2002); *see also* Suzanne Reynolds, Catherine T. Harris & Ralph A. Peeples, *Back To The Future: An Empirical Study of Child Custody Outcomes*, 85 N.C. L. Rev. 1629 (2007).

PROBLEMS

Problem 6-8.   Pat and Al have one child, Jennie, now age 5. When Pat and Al separated, they agreed to share physical custody of Jennie, alternating weeks. Pat then moved to a neighboring state because of a work transfer. Pat and Al are relatively amicable, and both want what's best for Jennie, which each believes in sole custody. When it became clear that the trial court was likely to award sole custody to Al, Pat proposed a joint physical custody arrangement in which Jennie would alternate school years and spend half of each summer vacation with each parent on a rotating week-by-week basis. The trial court is empowered to award joint physical custody if it is in the best interests of the child. You are counsel to Al. What evidence will you introduce to prove that it is in Jennie's best interest to spend first grade with Al, second grade with Pat, third grade with Al, and so forth?

Problem 6-9.   Your client, Jane, is divorcing her husband Fred, who has left her for a young associate in his law firm. Jane tells you that Fred is a decent parent who loves his children, Mary and Liza, ages 5 and 7. However, because of his busy professional life, he has played a small role in their upbringing. Fred is seeking joint physical custody of the children. Jane tells you that she is adamantly opposed to joint custody and wants sole custody. She does not believe that Fred is capable of caring for the children and she does not believe that they can cooperate — in part, because she is so angry with him about his treatment of her. Assume that your jurisdiction has adopted a statute similar to Florida's, and a friendly parent provision. What do you advise Jane?

[2] Past Parental Caretaking Roles

The role of each parent in caring for the child before separation has long been an important consideration in deciding custody under the best interest of the child standard. Feminists and others who are dissatisfied with the best interest standard have argued that awarding custody to the primary caretaker is the best means to promote the child's best interests. *See, e.g.*, Martha Fineman, *Dominant Discourse, Professional Language, and Legal Change in Child Custody Decisionmaking*, 101 HARV. L. REV. 727 (1988). In the 1980s a few states adopted this approach and, in others, custody statutes gave priority to this factor. Recently, a new custody standard based on past parenting roles has been proposed. Rather than awarding sole custody to the primary caretaker, the *ALI Principles'* approximation standard allocates custodial responsibility *between* the parents in proportion to their caretaking roles in the intact family. This standard, which has been adopted by West Virginia (a former primary caretaker state), is responsive to many of the criticisms that have been directed toward other custody standards.

[a] Primary Caretaker Preference

The primary caretaker presumption takes one factor under the best interest standard and designates it as the most important in choosing the custodial parent. In *Garska v. McCoy*, 278 S.E.2d 357 (W. Va. 1981), the West Virginia Supreme Court adopted what might be called a strong version of the presumption; the primary caretaker is awarded custody unless she is unfit. A weaker form would give the other parent the burden of proving that the child's interest is not served by custody in the primary caregiver. The presumption could also serve as a tie-breaker rule under the best interest standard. Indeed, it seems quite likely that courts applying the best interest standard often informally utilize the weaker variations of the presumption, because of the widespread acceptance of the importance to the child of the relationship with her primary caretaker.

Garska offered the following guidelines for determining the primary caretaker:

> In establishing which . . . parent is the primary caretaker, the trial court shall determine which parent has taken primary responsibility for, *inter alia*, the performance of the following caring and nurturing duties of a parent: (1) preparing and planning of meals; (2) bathing, grooming and dressing; 3) purchasing, cleaning, and care of clothes; (4) medical care, including nursing and trips to physicians; (5) arranging for social interaction among peers after school, *i.e.*, transporting to friends' houses or, for example, to girl or boy scout meetings; (6) arranging alternative care, *i.e.*, babysitting, day-care, etc.; (7) putting child to bed at night, attending to child in the middle of the night, waking child in the morning; (8) disciplining, *i.e.*, teaching general manners and toilet training; (9) educat-

ing, *i.e.*, religious, cultural, social, etc.; and, (10) teaching elementary skills, i.e., reading, writing and arithmetic.

Id. at 363.

As compared with the best interest standard, the primary caretaker presumption substantially narrows the judicial inquiry. It shifts the court's task from predicting the future (with whom will the child be better off?) to deciding historical facts (who was the child's primary caretaker?). This rule also discourages qualitative inquiry about which parent will function more effectively to meet the child's needs. Neither parent's deficiencies (either past or future) are relevant to the decision — unless they are of such severity as to render the parent unfit to have custody. Because qualitative evidence is excluded, a parent has less incentive to focus on the failings of the spouse, an effect that may reduce acrimony in the litigation. It is clear that, in theory at least, a primary caretaker presumption is more determinate than the best interest standard and can be more easily applied by courts. Moreover, because the parties can better predict the outcome of adjudication, the presumption may also discourage strategic bargaining and generally reduce the costs of negotiation. For a discussion of the impact of different custody decision rules on divorce bargaining, see Elizabeth Scott, *Pluralism, Parental Preference and Child Custody*, 80 CAL. L. REV. 615, 635 (1992).

Whether the presumption results in custody decisions that promote the child's best interest depends on whether the underlying premise is correct: that nothing is more important to the child's future welfare after family dissolution than undisturbed continuity of her relationship with her primary caregiver. Many child development experts agree with this premise, at least as to younger children. It derives from attachment theory, which posits that the child forms a critical attachment to the adult who cares for his needs from infancy, and that healthy psychological development (emotional security, self esteem and the ability to form relationships later in life) is based on the stability and continuity of the child's relationship with that person. When attachment theory was developed, that relationship was presumed to be the mother-child bond, but today it is described in gender-neutral terms. *See, e.g.*, GOLDSTEIN, FREUD & SOLNIT, *supra*.

A primary caretaker rule can also be justified on fairness grounds. *See* David L. Chambers, *Rethinking the Substantive Rules for Custody Disputes in Divorce*, 83 MICH. L. REV. 477, 499–503 (1984); Jon Elster, *Solomonic Judgments: Against the Best Interests of the Child*, 54 U. CHI. L. REV. 1, 16–21 (1987). On this view, if the spouses implicitly divided roles in marriage, the primary caretaker has invested most of her efforts in her parenting role. Continuing to fulfill that role after divorce is likely to be extremely important to her, and the loss of custody may be devastating. Presumably, she has made sacrifices, having foregone the opportunity to have a career (and the earning capacity that goes with it). The breadwinner, on the other hand, has invested in his career and his role in rearing his children has been a more limited one. He will leave the marriage with a valuable asset — his earning capacity developed over years of work. If he also gets custody when the couple divorces, the primary caretaker leaves the marriage with little to show for her efforts. On the other hand, what if the secondary parent wanted to be the primary caretaker, but sacrificed his or her preferences in order to be the family breadwinner?

Although the primary caretaker preference has generated support among feminist and other academics, few states have formally adopted this legal standard in place of the best interest standard. The Minnesota Supreme Court adopted the presumption only to have it abolished by the legislature several years later. *Pikula v. Pikula*, 374 N.W.2d 705 (Minn. 1985) (*see* Minnesota statute, *supra*). For an analysis of the Minnesota experience, see Gary Crippen, *Stumbling Beyond Best Interest of the Child: Reexamining Child Custody Standard Setting in the Wake of Minnesota's Four Year Experiment with the Primary Caretaker Preference*, 75 MINN. L. REV. 427 (1990) (attributing failure of preference to broad exceptions allowed and to introduction of fault). The West Virginia legislature recently abolished the presumption, replacing it with the ALI standard, outlined below. A few states rank past parental care as the most important consideration in the custody decision without creating a formal presumption. The Washington statute directs courts making "residential provisions" to give "greatest weight" to "[t]he relative strength, nature and stability of the child's relationship with each parent, including whether a parent has taken greater responsibility for performing parenting functions relating to the daily needs of the child." WASH. REV. CODE ANN. § 26.09.187(3)(a)(iii). This statute also provides that the best interest of the child is ordinarily served when the existing pattern of interaction between a parent and child is altered only to the extent necessitated by the changed relationship of the parents or as required to protect the child from physical, mental, or emotional harm. The Washington Supreme Court, however, rejected a lower court holding that this provision creates a primary caretaker presumption. *Kovacs v. Kovacs*, 854 P.2d 629, 632 (Wash. 1993). The court recounted the legislative history of the statute — and the explicit rejection by the legislature of such a presumption — in reaching this conclusion. Other states such as South Carolina, through judicial opinion, have recognized the importance of this factor, without creating a presumption. *See, e.g., Parris v. Parris*, 460 S.E.2d 571 (S.C. 1996) (father wins as primary caregiver); *see also Lamb v. Wenning*, 600 N.E.2d 96 (Ind. 1992); *Harris v. Harris*, 546 A.2d 208 (Vt. 1988) (rejecting primary caretaker rule, but concluding that relationship should be given great weight).

Why have courts and legislatures not embraced the primary caretaker preference as a custody rule with many advantages over the best interest standard? Some suggests this presumption is simply a re-creation of the tender years presumption. Although the primary caretaker test is ostensibly gender neutral, the vast majority of primary caretakers of young children are women, and most advocates are motivated to protect mothers, who, they believe, are disadvantaged under the best interest standard. Alternatively, in a world of changing gender roles, one might question whether the primary caretaker presumption is a very useful aid in child custody determinations. As women enter the work force and men become more involved in rearing their children, fewer parents may have performed traditional roles of primary caretaker and breadwinner. At present, most married mothers who work continue to perform the bulk of child rearing responsibilities. If this pattern were to change so that many parents substantially shared child care responsibilities in the future, the primary caretaker preference would become obsolete.

If these criticisms have some merit, but maintaining the stability of the child's relationships is critical to her welfare, then perhaps what is needed is a custody rule that bases custody on past parental roles, but does not presume that one parent is the primary caretaker. This is the approach of the ALI custody standard, below.

[b]   The ALI Standard — Approximation of Past Parental Roles

WEST VIRGINIA CODE ANNOTATED

§ 48-9-206. Allocation of custodial responsibility.

(a) Unless otherwise resolved by agreement of the parents . . . or unless manifestly harmful to the child, the court shall allocate custodial responsibility so that the proportion of custodial time the child spends with each parent approximates the proportion of time each parent spent performing caretaking functions for the child prior to the parents' separation or, if the parents never lived together, before the filing of the action, except to the extent . . . necessary to achieve any of the following objectives:

(1) To permit the child to have a relationship with each parent who has performed a reasonable share of parenting functions [including caretaking; "economic support; decision-making regarding the child's welfare; maintenance or improvement of the family residence . . . ; financial planning and . . . tasks supporting the consumption and savings needs of the family . . . W. VA. CODE ANN. § 48-1-235.2];

(2) To accommodate the firm and reasonable preferences of a child who is fourteen years of age or older, and with regard to a child under fourteen years of age, but sufficiently matured that he or she can intelligently express a voluntary preference for one parent, to give that preference such weight as circumstances warrant;

(3) To keep siblings together when the court finds that doing so is necessary to their welfare;

(4) To protect the child's welfare when, under an otherwise appropriate allocation, the child would be harmed because of a gross disparity in the quality of the emotional attachments between each parent and the child or in each parent's demonstrated ability or availability to meet a child's needs;. . . .

(6) To avoid an allocation of custodial responsibility that would be extremely impractical or that would interfere substantially with the child's need for stability in light of economic, physical or other circumstances, including the distance between the parents' residences, the cost and difficulty of transporting the child, the parents' and child's daily schedules, and the ability of the parents to cooperate in the arrangement. . . .

(b) In determining the proportion of caretaking functions each parent previously performed for the child under subsection (a) of this section, the court shall not consider the divisions of functions arising from temporary arrangements after separation, whether those arrangements are consensual or by court order. The court may take into account information relating to the temporary arrangements in determining other issues under this section.

(c) If the court is unable to allocate custodial responsibility under subsection (a) of this section because the allocation under that subsection would be manifestly harmful to the child, or because there is no history of past performance of caretaking functions, as in the case of a newborn, or because the history does not establish a pattern of caretaking sufficiently dispositive of the issues of the case, the court shall allocate custodial responsibility based on the child's best interest . . . preserving to the extent possible this section's priority on the share of past caretaking functions each parent performed. . . .

§ 48-9-207. Allocation of significant decision-making responsibility.

(a) Unless otherwise resolved by agreement of the parents . . . , the court shall allocate responsibility for making significant life decisions on behalf of the child, including the child's education and health care, to one parent or to two parents jointly, in accordance with the child's best interest, in light of:

(1) The allocation of custodial responsibility under section 9-206 of this article;

(2) The level of each parent's participation in past decision-making on behalf of the child;

(3) The wishes of the parents;

(4) The level of ability and cooperation the parents have demonstrated in decision-making on behalf of the child;

. . . .

(b) If each of the child's legal parents has been exercising a reasonable share of parenting functions for the child, the court shall presume that an allocation of decision-making responsibility to both parents jointly is in the child's best interests. The presumption is overcome if there is a history of domestic abuse, or by a showing that joint allocation of decision-making responsibility is not in the child's best interest.

(c) Unless otherwise provided or agreed by the parents, each parent who is exercising custodial responsibility shall be given sole responsibility for day-to-day decisions for the child, while the child is in that parent's care and control, including emergency decisions affecting the health and safety of the child.

The West Virginia legislature adopted this statute, based on the ALI custody standard, in 1999, and repealed the state's primary caretaker preference. The statute appears to have been a legislative compromise of sorts, in response to intense pressure both from groups advocating the adoption of a joint physical custody presumption and from supporters of retaining the primary caretaker preference. A key supporter of the ALI standard in the legislature argued that both of these alternative rules encouraged parents to raise allegations of unfitness against one another. Karin Fischer, *Changes in Custody Law Concern Some; Predictability of Primary Caregiver Positive, Negative*, CHARLESTON DAILY MAIL, May 5, 1999; John D. Athey, *The Ramifications of West Virginia's Codified Child Custody Law: A Departure from* Garska v. McCoy, 106 W. VA. L. REV. 389 (2004).

Like the primary caretaker preference, the ALI standard directs courts to allocate custodial responsibility after divorce on the basis of parents' roles in caring for the child in the intact family. Relevant evidence would include the same tasks and duties described by the West Virginia court in *Garska*. This standard differs from the primary caretaker preference, however, in recognizing that many parents divide childrearing responsibilities in ways that do not follow the primary caretaker model. For each family, the ALI standard allocates custody after divorce to quantitatively approximate the parents' pre-divorce division of responsibility. Thus, a court applying this standard might order a custodial arrangement that is similar to joint physical custody, but only if the parents both spent a substantial amount of time caring for the child when the family was intact. On the other hand, if one parent was the primary caretaker, that parent will be awarded a greater proportion of custodial time after divorce. Moreover, under the ALI formulation, "parenting functions" are defined somewhat more broadly than caretaking, such that a traditional father who supports his children, but does little caretaking, will qualify for a minimum custody allocation. The standard also creates a rebuttable presumption that decision-making responsibility should be shared jointly, on the assumption that this is the understanding in most intact families. For a feminist defense of this standard, see Margaret Brinig, *Feminism and Child Custody Under Chapter Two of the American Law Institute's Principles of the Law of Family Dissolution*, 8 DUKE J. GENDER & L. POL. 301 (2001).

Professor Elizabeth Scott, who first proposed the approximation standard adopted by the ALI, argues that this rule effectively promotes the child's best interests. Her analysis also supports the intuition of the West Virginia legislator, *supra*, that allegations of parental unfitness may be less common under the new standard.

Elizabeth Scott, *Pluralism, Parental Preference and Child Custody*
80 Cal. L. Rev. 615 (1992)

[T]he inquiry regarding future custody arrangements should focus on the past relationship of each parent to the child and do so in a more precise and individualized way than either the best interests standard or the reform alternatives require. The custody decision is an announcement and prescription of the future part each parent will play in the child's life over the years of her minority. There is . . . no sounder basis for this prescription than past relationships. Therefore, in most cases the law's goal should be to approximate, to the extent possible, the predivorce role of each parent in the child's life. . . .

Divorce, which by any measure is a period of upheaval in a child's life, should not be treated as an opportunity for restructuring parent-child relationships. Child development experts emphasize the harmful impact of the disruption associated with divorce, and the link between continuity of the parent-child relationship and healthy child development. Custody law can minimize disruption of the child's habitual routines and relationships after divorce by perpetuating patterns of parental care established in the intact family. A rule that preserves the continuity of family relationships would seem to reflect the best interests of the child as accurately as this elusive concept permits.

The approximation approach . . . accommodates two strands of child development research and theory that have been drawn into the policy debate over custody and are currently treated as irreconcilable. The first strand, . . . [a]ttachment theory would support the assertion that the gravest deficiency of the best interests standard is the risk of disrupting the relationship between the child and her primary caretaker. More recently, however, other researchers have suggested that the role of fathers in their children's lives has been undervalued and that attachment theory exaggerates the uniqueness and exclusiveness of the primary caretaker-child bond. Some observers argue that this research supports a stronger claim for father custody or, at least, weakens the viability of a primary caretaker preference. Taken together, these two psychological perspectives point to a legal response that does not choose between parents or split custody of the child but rather seeks to gauge the strength of existing bonds and to perpetuate them through the custody arrangement. Thus, for example, if both parents have been active caretakers, the child should not have to suffer from the disruptive effects of relegating one parent's status to that of visitor. On the other hand, if one parent's involvement and care for the child has been dominant, that strong bond should not be disturbed. The secondary role of the other parent, however, should also be recognized.

Structuring future custody [in this way] could also mitigate the observed tension between two goals of custody law: encouraging the participation of both parents after divorce and avoiding exposure of the child to excessive interparental conflict. The joint custody debate demonstrates this tension, with advocates stressing the harm of lost parental contact while opponents emphasize the detriment to the child from exposure to interparental conflict. It is plausible to assume that basing custody roles on past patterns of caretaking would provide optimal parental involvement with minimal conflict. Joint physical custody, which provides the greatest opportunity for conflict, will be ordered under this approach only if it replicates the pattern of childrearing that occurred during the marriage. In such a situation, the couple's prior experience of shared responsibility increases the likelihood of mutual commitment, competency, and respect. Thus, the prospect of a cooperative adjustment is better than it would be were new roles thrust upon parents. The resentment of joint custody by primary caretaker mothers and the potential conflict that it could generate might be reduced if custody is formulated on the basis of past roles. . . .

[The] contention that parents are generally inclined to track predivorce roles is consistent with the growing body of empirical research on custody. Children of divorce in single-parent homes are overwhelmingly in the custody of their mothers, an arrangement that is closer to patterns of parent-child relationships in most intact families than is the alternative of exclusive paternal custody. When the menu of custody arrangements expands to include joint custody, the importance of predivorce roles seems even clearer. Joint legal custody, which . . . reflects typical role allocation more accurately than does sole custody, has been accepted by both mothers and fathers and is now the prevailing norm in some jurisdictions. In comparison, parents have been less receptive to joint physical custody, suggesting that parents resist radically altering patterns of care and authority established in the intact family. Moreover, researchers in California have found that, even in custody arrangements that began as joint physical custody, children of divorce tended over time to live primarily with their mothers. This trend suggests that parents might be revealing their true preferences through their conduct, "drifting" toward arrangements that may reflect predivorce patterns of care. Parental resistance to the transformation of established roles might also contribute to the poor adjustment and high relitigation rates associated with court-ordered joint custody in which one party, usually the mother, resists the arrangement. In general, the experience with joint custody is consistent with [the] hypothesis that parents tend to accept and adapt to this innovation to the extent that it comports with past roles.

Implicit in this analysis is the conclusion that a rule that reflects parents' preferences for custody is also in the best interests of the child. . . . Parents adopt roles and functions in the family according to complex sets of values and preferences and with little legal supervision. The law can look to these family patterns as the best reflection of the parents' true preferences and the best predictor of the future stability of custody arrangements. . . .

NOTES

1. *The ALI Standard as a Decision Rule.* As a legal decision rule, the ALI standard shares many advantages with the primary caretaker preference. It is far more determinate than the best interest standard and thus should yield more predictable results. Adjudication should be easier because the inquiry is narrower and focuses on concrete facts about each parent's care of the child. As the Comment to § 208 explains:

> . . . [The standard] requires factfinding that is less likely than the traditional best-interests test to require expert testimony about such matters as the child's emotional state or developmental needs, the parents' relative abilities and the strength of their emotional relationships to the child. Avoiding expert testimony is desirable because such testimony, within an adversarial context, tends to focus on the weaknesses of each parent and thus undermines the spirit of cooperation and compromise necessary to successful post-divorce custodial arrangements. . . .

> Some parents will disagree over how caretaking roles were previously divided, making the past division of caretaking functions itself a litigation issue. The difficulties in applying the standard, however, must be evaluated in light of the available alternatives. While each parent's share of past caretaking will in some cases be disputed, these functions encompass

specific tasks and responsibilities about which concrete evidence is available and thus offer greater determinacy than more qualitative standards, such as parental competence, the strength of the parent-child emotional bond or . . . the child's best interests. These qualitative criteria are future oriented and highly subjective, whereas how the parents divided caretaking responsibilities in the past is a concrete question of historical fact, like other questions courts are accustomed to resolving.

A.L.I. PRINCIPLES § 2.08 cmt.

Although focusing on past parenting roles will simplify fact finding in custody adjudication, it is unlikely to be error-proof. In a recent Vermont case, the court accepted the trial court conclusion that the father has "a slightly more active engagement in the children's lives," while the dissent argued persuasively that uncontested evidence suggested that the mother spent twice as many waking hours with the children as did the father. *Hoover (Letourneau) v. Hoover*, 764 A.2d 1192 (Vt. 2000).

2. Comparison with Alternative Rules. The ALI approximation rule amounts to a primary caretaker presumption when one parent has been exercising a substantial majority of the past caretaking, and it amounts to a joint custody presumption when past caretaking has been shared equally in the past. Professor Melli argues the rule responds to all variations and combinations of past caretaking patterns between those two poles, declining to impose some average, idealized family form on all families and instead favoring solutions that roughly approximate the caretaking shares each parent assumed before the divorce or before the custody issue arose. Marygold S. Melli, *The American Law Institute Principles of Family Dissolution, the Approximation Rule and Shared-Parenting*, 25 N. ILL. U. L. REV. 347 (2005). The major exception to using past caretaking as the basis for assigning residential responsibility is the case of a parent who specialized in economic support of the family and spent little time in direct contact with the child. The Principles ensure that a parent who performed "parenting functions," including breadwinning, has sufficient time with the child to have a relationship. W. VA. CODE ANN. § 48-9-206(a)(1), *supra*.

As discussed earlier, shared custody may be problematic if one of the parents has been violent to other family members. *See* Note on Domestic Violence, *supra*. Under the *ALI Principles*, the approximation rule should not govern if the outcome would be "manifestly harmful to the child." W. VA. CODE ANN. § 48-9-206. Whether the manifest harm standard will provide adequate protection is unclear and, in the view of Professor Melli, the issue was given insufficient attention by the ALI. *See* Melli, *supra*.

3. Rejection of the "Custody/Visitation" Distinction. The second major innovative feature of the ALI Standard (besides narrowing the custody inquiry to parents' past caretaking roles) is that it abolishes the categories of custody and visitation, and instead simply directs the allocation of custodial responsibility between the parents. In part, this is a matter of terminology. A parent who played little role in childrearing when the family was together may receive an allocation of custodial time that is similar to a standard visitation award. However, the abolition of the hierarchical categories of custody and visitation has important symbolic meaning. Neither parent is relegated to the inferior status of "visitor," and the custody award is less likely to be characterized as the prize in a zero sum game. Further, as Professor Scott puts it, by rejecting traditional categories and "recognizing the role allocation that each couple has adopted, this framework removes barriers to the evolution of parental roles erected by legal rules that give exclusive custody to one parent." Scott, *supra* at 672.

4. *The Presumption of Shared Decisionmaking Authority.* The ALI Custody Principles (W. VA. CODE § 48-9-207(b)) create a rebuttable presumption that the parents will share decisionmaking authority (legal custody) if both have been reasonably involved in rearing the child. ALI CUSTODY PRINCIPLES § 2.09. The presumption shifts the burden of proof on this issue to the parent opposed to joint decision-making to show that it is not in the child's best interests or that it is inappropriate because of a history of domestic violence. Factors relevant to this best interest determination include the past involvement of each parent in decisionmaking, and the parents' ability to cooperate. Each parent, under § 209, also has authority over day-to-day decisions while the child is in that parent's custodial care. Thus, even if the vegetarian mother has been awarded sole decisionmaking, the meat-eating father can feed the children hamburgers when they are with him. *See id.*, cmt.

This approach reflects a move toward shared decisionmaking. See the discussion of joint legal custody, Section C[1], *supra*. Some commentators have argued that parents who are denied decisionmaking authority may feel disenfranchised as parents and that this may undermine their commitment to their parental role. *See* Elizabeth Scott, *Parental Autonomy and Children's Welfare*, 11 WM. & MARY BILL OF RIGHTS J. 1071 (2003). A study by Professor Judith Selzer found that joint legal custody had a positive correlation with increased visits by parents, but not with better compliance with child support orders. Judith Selzer, *Father by Law: Effects of Joint Legal Custody on Non-Resident Fathers Involvement with Children*, 35 DEMOGRAPHY 135 (May 1998).

PROBLEM

Problem 6-10. Elaine and Vic were married in 1990. In 1995, their son Jay was born and Elaine quit her job as a web page designer. From 1995 to 1999, Elaine remained at home caring for Jay, while Vic supported the family with his job as a college professor. In 1999, Elaine got a part-time job in a graphic design firm. Vic arranged his schedule so that he could be home in the afternoons three days a week while Elaine worked. When Jay started school in 2000, Vic met the school bus in the afternoons and stayed with Jay until Elaine arrived home at 6:00. During this time, Elaine continued to get Jay up and ready for school; she also prepared his meals, arranged play dates and doctors' appointments, bought his clothes and bathed him and put him to bed. In October 2002, Vic moved out, but he continued to meet the bus and stay with Jay until Elaine got home from work. In 2003, Elaine filed for divorce. Both parties sought custody. You are a trial judge in a jurisdiction that has adopted the ALI custody standard. How should custodial responsibility be allocated? Which parent should get custody in a jurisdiction that has adopted the primary caretaker presumption?

D. RIGHTS OF THE NONCUSTODIAL PARENT

[1] Visitation Rights

Although joint legal custody is becoming the norm in some states, most child custody decrees today give sole physical custody to one parent and "visitation rights" to the other. Access by both parents is strongly favored in the law and visitation will be granted unless the custodial parent shows that visitation is likely to lead to some serious harm or detriment to the child. *See* CAL. FAM. CODE § 3100(a) (visitation refused only if shown to be "detrimental to the best interests of the child"). Courts take this admonition seriously. In *Smith v. Smith*, 869 S.W.2d 55 (Ky. 1994), for example, the Kentucky Supreme Court reversed a trial court that denied visitation to a father incarcerated for murder, robbery and kidnapping, because there had been no hearing, and thus no finding that visitation would endanger the child. While courts rarely address constitutional considerations, the noncustodial parent's right to have access to his or her child is generally considered to be constitutionally grounded. *See also Damiani v. Damiani*, 2002 Fla. App. LEXIS 17138 (Nov. 20, 2002) (court order conditioning mother's visitation on $100,000 bond was abuse of discretion, despite her non-compliance with previous court orders to produce the child, as it would effectively eliminate visitation). *See Zummo v. Zummo, supra; see also* Chapter 9 (discussing constitutional protection of unmarried father's access to his children); Chapter 10 (discussing parental authority generally).

The strong presumption favoring visitation can be overcome, of course, in dire situations. For example, a Rhode Island court upheld a denial of visitation where the father, a convicted murderer serving a life sentence without parole, made accusations against the mother and child and evidenced "distorted thinking." *Laurence v. Nelson*, 785 A.2d 519 (R.I. 2001). Standard fact patterns for denial of visitation include violence or the threat of violence, *In re D.M.*, 771 A.2d 360 (D.C. App. 2001); drug addiction, *Soltis v. Soltis*, 470 So. 2d 1250 (Ala. App. 1985); sexual abuse, *Nelson v. Jones*, 781 P.2d 964 (Alaska 1989); severe conflict between parents, *In re Jones*, 462 P.2d 680 (Or. App. 1978); and absolute refusal by the child to cooperate, *In re Two Minor Children*, 249 A.2d 743 (Del. 1969).

In general, rights to visitation or access are accepted as minimally fair recognition of parents who have lost full parental status. Moreover, in general, it is assumed that visitation benefits the child and is not simply a right of the non-custodial parent.

NOTES

1. ***Religion and Visitation.*** Where parents follow different religions, or where one parent is religious and the other is not, issues can arise about whether a parent, in the exercise of parental decisionmaking rights with respect to decision, can require the other parent to conform his or her conduct with the children and whether a parent exercising visitation or parental responsibility rights, can expose a child to that parent's religious views and practices. Both issues are discussed in Note 4, Section B[2][d], *supra*.

2. *Visitation and Parents' Sexual Activities.* Another often-litigated issue involves efforts by custodial parents to restrict non-custodial parents' sexual activities during overnight visitation. A typical case involves the custodial mother's objection when the father's girlfriend spends the night while the children are visiting. Today, courts generally are reluctant to intervene where heterosexual non-marital sexual activities are involved, unless it is shown that the parent's sexual activities are detrimental to the child. *See Kelly v. Kelly*, 524 A.2d 1330 (N.J. Super. Ct. Ch. Div. 1986). In *Kelly*, the court rejected the mother's petition to prohibit visitation "in the presence of an unrelated person of the opposite sex." She had argued that, in light of the family's Catholic faith, the father's activities violated their agreement not to do anything that would have an adverse effect on the children's moral welfare. Based on the testimony of a psychologist, the court concluded that denial of visitation would be harmful to the children's development. Where the parent, as in *Kelly*, is "managing" his or her visitation activities under circumstances that appear to be sensitive to the emotional needs of the children, and where the children do not appear to be harmed, overnight visits usually will not be limited. *See, e.g., Jones v. Haraway*, 537 So. 2d 946 (Ala. Civ. App. 1988); *Nowicki v. Nowicki*, 393 N.W.2d 797 (Wis. App. 1986).

Courts have been more willing to intervene in cases involving parents in same-sex relationships. *See, e.g., J.P. v. P.W.*, 772 S.W.2d 786 (Mo. Ct. App. 1989) (trial court order banning lover from house during visitation remanded for further visitation restrictions, including supervision and no overnight visits); *A.O.V. v. J.R.V.*, 2007 Va. App. LEXIS 64 (Feb. 27, 2007) (although granted joint legal custody of children, father's partner could not stay overnight during visitation or engage in displays of affection in the children's presence).

Some courts have gone even further, directing that the children should not be around the mother's partner during the visitation period or be exposed to a "gay lifestyle." In *Ex Parte D.W.W.*, 717 So. 2d 793 (Ala. 1998), the court concluded that any exposure could greatly traumatize the children, because the mother's conduct was immoral and criminal. *See also Marlow v. Marlow*, 702 N.E.2d 733 (Ind. Ct. App. 1998) (upholding order prohibiting gay non-custodial father from involving the children in social, religious or educational activities that were "sponsored by or otherwise promote the homosexual lifestyle"). In *Marlow*, the court justified the restrictions on the ground that the children's mother continued to raise them as fundamentalist Christians, and they were too young to understand or resolve the conflicts between their mother's and father's lifestyles. The court rejected the father's constitutional challenge, based on *Palmore v. Sidoti, supra*, that the restriction was based on private bias against homosexuality, and thus was a violation of his Equal Protection rights. Instead, the court concluded, it was based on concern for the welfare of the children.

Increasingly, courts take a different view, finding these restrictions impermissible absent a finding that the child was physically or emotionally harmed by the experiences. Thus, for example, in *Dorworth v. Dorworth*, 33 P.3d 1260 (Colo. Ct. App. 2001), a trial court order prohibiting the father from having overnight visitors during visitation (and from taking his daughter to his gay church) was reversed on appeal. The court pointed out that under Colorado's statutory provision, parenting time could not be restricted on the basis of sexual orientation, and observed that no evidence was presented that the child was physically or emotionally harmed. One court, accepting the analogy to *Palmore v. Sidoti*, rejected the argument that the child's embarrassment about others' reactions to his mother's lesbian relationship was a sufficient reason to bar visitation in the presence of the mother's lover. *Blew v. Verta*, 617 A.2d 31 (Pa. Super. Ct. 1992); *see also Eldridge v. Eldridge*, 42 S.W.3d 82 (Tenn. 2001) (upholding trial court order authorizing unrestricted overnight visitation for a lesbian mother who lived with her partner where no evidence showed that the child had been, or would be, subject to physical or emotional harm).

Many courts seem inclined to ignore or tolerate parental behavior in the visitation context that might get more attention in a custody decision. A showing of real risk of harm, of course, may result in restriction or prohibition. *See, e.g., Bacon v. Goff*, 20 FAM. L. REP. 1012 (S.C., Rich. Cty. Fam. Ct., Oct., 8, 1993) (non-custodial mother ordered not to smoke around her asthmatic son). However, sexual conduct by parents (particularly same-sex conduct) that might be deemed important in choosing between parents in a custody dispute may not be restricted in visitation. Perhaps this is because the noncustodial parent has such a limited protected interest in his relationship with his child that courts are reluctant to burden it further. There also may be a concern that the parent might choose his sexual partner over his children if he is not permitted to continue to associate with them together. In *Kelly*, above, for example, the court did not consider ordering the father not to have his girlfriend present during visitation. It considered only the options of permitting her presence or sacrificing the children's relationship with their father. Encouraging noncustodial parents to continue to stay involved with their children is an important goal of legal regulation in this area.

3. Child's Wishes in Visitation. How important should the child's wishes be in resolving conflicts between parents over visitation? We saw that courts often give considerable weight to the preferences of children, especially older children, in deciding which parent will get custody. Generally, courts give less weight to the child's preference in visitation matters than in custodial determinations. For example, in *Roberts v. Roberts*, 371 A.2d 689 (Md. App. 1977), the court held the opposition of a 14-year-old to visitation by her mother should be given only slight consideration, if any. By comparison, a teenager's preference normally would be accorded great weight in choosing a custodian.

NOTE ON THE ENFORCEMENT OF VISITATION ORDERS

Complaints about compliance with visitation orders are not uncommon. Studies have found that one-fifth of custodial parents concede that have at some time denied the other parent access to their common child. One-third of the noncustodial parents claim they have been so denied. Jessica Pearson & Nancy Thoennes, *Programs to Increase Father's Access to the Children, in* FATHERS UNDER FIRE 220, 221 (Irwin Garfinkel, et al., eds. 1998). A custodial parent may remove the child from the custodial home at visitation time, report (truthfully or otherwise) that the child does not want visitation, or simply refuse to permit entry into the custodial home to pick up the child. In theory, the court can issue orders to coerce compliance. *See* Margaret M. Mahoney, *The Enforcement of Child Custody*

Orders by Contempt Remedies, 68 U. PITT. L. REV. 835 (2007) (reviewing civil and criminal contempt remedies available to enforce custody and visitation orders and distinguishing such remedies from injunctive remedies used outside of family law context).

Yet the enforcement of visitation orders presents the law with special difficulties. Despite the law's historic failure to enforce child support obligations, substantial progress was made once policymakers acquired the will to enforce them, because collecting money is a familiar legal task for which the law can employ familiar remedies such as wage assignment. The enforcement of visitation orders, on the other hand, requires using the law to coerce changes in behavior, and there may be a conflict between the desire to employ a remedy with sufficient coercive power to effect behavioral change and the desire to avoid the use of remedies which might harm children. Especially knotty problems arise if the problem is the child's refusal to participate in the visitation called for by the decree. In one infamous case, a frustrated trial judge found two children in direct contempt for refusing to visit their father in North Carolina, and put the older (12-year-old) child in a juvenile detention facility until she agreed to go. While the appellate court upheld the finding of contempt, it reversed the sanctions as inappropriate without further consideration of alternative measures — although the only alternative the appellate court specifically noted was to hold the children's mother in contempt, and presumably threaten her with incarceration if the children did not visit with their father. *Marriage of Marshall*, 663 N.E.2d 1113 (Ill. App. Ct. 1996). We do not know what happened subsequently in this case, but in a different case in which the trial court imprisoned the father for contempt when his daughter refused to visit with the mother, the appellate court reversed, holding that he could not be punished for his daughter's violation of the visitation order. *Shellhouse v. Bentley*, 690 S.2d 401 (Ala. Civ. App. 1997). Part of the difficulty, of course, in cases such as these comes from ambiguity about just where fault for the non-visitation lies. Is a child's resistance the result of problematic behavior by the parent the child refuses to see, by actions of the custodial parent that undermine the other parent, neither, or both? Fashioning an appropriate remedy require answering such a question. By contrast, analogous questions do not normally arise in disputes over the payment of support.

Even when the court is clear about the reason for the failure of visitation, designing an appropriate remedy may be difficult. In *Hendrickson v. Hendrickson*, 603 N.W.2d 896 (N.D. 2000), for example, the court considered (for the third time) a long and bitter dispute in which the mother seemed to work relentlessly to frustrate the father's visitation efforts and to alienate the children from him. The trial court found the mother in contempt, but was reluctant to put her in jail for fear that would harm the children. It chose instead to order transfer custody to the father, denying the mother all visitation for a year. The appellate court upheld the transfer of custody, finding that the mother's interference with visitation constituted the required changed circumstance, but reversed the visitation denial, ordering instead that the mother be allowed supervised visitation.

An alternative remedy may be to suspend the support obligation of the noncustodial parent whose visitation rights are frustrated by the other parent's improper conduct. While it is clear that the support obligor cannot justify his

unilateral decision to stop paying support by claims that the other parent denied him access to the child, he can ask the court to impose such a remedy. Court have been divided on whether such a remedy can be justified, although most have not allowed it for fear that any cutoff in support will harm the child. One commentator argues, however, that there are at least a subset of cases in which such fears are not justified, such as cases involving a custodial parent who has hidden with the child (frustrating her receipt of support as well as visitation), but later reappears to seek arrearages, or cases in which the custodial parent has independent resources with which to provide for the child. He argues that in such cases, denying the arrearage claim, or reducing or eliminating current support obligations, may be justified. Ira Ellman, *Should Visitation Denial Affect The Obligation to Pay Support?, in* THE LAW AND ECONOMICS OF CHILD SUPPORT PAYMENTS (W. Comanor, ed. 2003). This topic is treated more extensively in Chapter 5, which deals with child support.

An innovative remedy for parents wrongfully denied visitation rights is authorized by MICH. COMP. LAWS ANN. § 552.642 (Supp.). Under this statute, the "friend of the court" (a court official who has the responsibility for investigating custody disputes and supervising compliance with custody decrees) is authorized to formulate a makeup visitation policy. Under such a policy, a wrongfully denied visitation day can be made up at a time chosen by the noncustodial parent within one year after the wrongful denial. The makeup day shall be "the same type and duration of parenting time as the parenting time that was denied. . . ." *Id.* § 552.642(1)(a). The statute provides for a referee or trial judge to determine whether there has been a wrongful denial of visitation. What kind of conduct on the part of the custodial parent should qualify?

The Non-Visiting Parent. What of the situation, not infrequent, where the noncustodial parent fails to exercise visitation rights? Instead of defining the noncustodial parent's access to the child as a right, should there be an enforceable duty to maintain the relationship with the child? An unusual Arizona statute authorizes courts to sanction defaulting parents by holding them in contempt, ordering compliance with visitation orders, requiring education or counseling or imposing fines (up to $100 per violation). ARIZ. REV. STAT. ANN. § 25-414. Courts have generally declined to find such a duty (or to find that the child has a right to visitation). *See In re Mitchell*, 745 N.E.2d 167 (Ill. App. Ct. 2001). One scholar has argued that courts ought to order noncustodial parents to visit their children on a regular basis. Carol Bruch, *Making Visitation Work: Dual Parenting Orders*, 1 FAM. ADVOCATE 22, 26 (1978). Given the recognized goal of maintaining post-divorce relationships between both parents and the child, why do you think this has not happened? Perhaps enforcement costs would be too high. What sanction would be appropriate? Professor Bruch suggests that recalcitrant noncustodial parents be required to pay the custodial parent an increased amount of child support to cover "the costs of increased child care requirements" imposed by the failure to visit. *Id.* at 42. In *Mitchell*, the court acknowledged that the purpose of the custody statute was to promote a close relationship between the child and the non-custodial parent, but questioned whether forcing visitation between the child and a reluctant parent would truly be in the child's best interest.

PROBLEMS

Problem 6-11.   Lou, the custodial father, is very health conscious, and is very concerned about recent news reports of the dangers of "passive" smoking. Lily, the non-custodial mother, and Lily's parents, with whom she lives, all are smokers. Can Lou obtain a modification of Lily's visitation privileges to prevent Lily from smoking while visiting with their 6-year-old daughter, Jill? Can he get a court order requiring that all visitations occur in a smoke-free environment, even if that means overnight visitations can occur only in a hotel (which Lily cannot afford)?

Problem 6-12.   Bill's favorite activity during his biweekly weekend visitations with his 8-year-old son, Eddy, is to ride mini-trail bikes around the hills and woods in a nearby state park. It is an activity which Eddy also enjoys immensely, and which gives him a great sense of accomplishment and camaraderie with his dad. Eddy's custodial mother, June, has researched the safety of the mini-bikes and found the accident rate for children Eddy's age is 20 times greater than the accident rate on normal bicycles. June has spoken with Bill about her concern for Eddy's safety, but Bill insists that it is a safe sport, that he and Eddy are careful, and that he should decide the visitation activities. June wants a court order forbidding mini-bike riding during Bill's visitation periods. Should she be successful? What should June have to prove?

Problem 6-13.   Stan and Dianne are the divorced parents of a 4-year-old daughter, Nicole. Under the terms of the divorce decree, Stan has custody of Nicole and Dianne has visitation rights each summer for two weeks and every other weekend throughout the year. Nicole is enrolled in nursery school during the week. The formal program ends at 3 p.m., but Stan has made arrangements with the school to provide day care from 3 p.m. until 5 p.m. when he picks up Nicole on his way home from the office. Dianne has come to school and asked Nicole's teacher to permit her access to the child from 3 to 5 every afternoon. She has not told Stan about this. The teacher's impression is that the divorce was bitter and hard-fought. The teacher asks your advice. What is your response?

NOTE ON CUSTODY AGREEMENTS AND PARENTING PLANS

As divorce has become commonplace in the past generation or so, many commentators have advocated that children's welfare is promoted if parents assume responsibility for making decisions about their children's future custody. *See* Elizabeth S. Scott, *Parental Autonomy and Children's Welfare*, 11 Wm. & M. Bill of Rights J. 1071 (2003). The past generation has seen a trend toward private ordering of custody disputes and encouragement of parents to plan for their children's future. This trend, perhaps most evident in the enthusiasm for mediation, *see* Chapter 8, reflects the view that when parents can reach agreement about custody arrangements, the resulting plan may be more likely to prove satisfactory over time than one imposed by a court over the objection of one or both parents. Parents know more about their children's needs and their own preferences than a court is likely to learn in an adversary proceeding. In general, enforcement costs over the post divorce period are likely to be lower when parents participate in and agree to the custody plan. *See* MACCOBY & MNOOKIN, *supra*, at 41-42; Elizabeth E. Scott & Robert S. Scott, *Parents as Fiduciaries*, 81 VA. L. REV. 2401 (1995).

Traditionally, courts had considerable formal authority to review parents' custody agreements (although it seems unlikely that courts ever made a practice of routinely overriding parents' agreements). Even today, statutes direct courts to review agreements concerning custody and child support to determine whether the child's best interest is promoted. *See, e.g.*, ALASKA STAT. § 25.24.220(h), (i) (court shall review agreement to determine whether it furthers child's best interests). Such review is deemed justified on the ground that parents in the midst of divorce cannot be relied on to act to promote their children's welfare. Children's rights advocates, who are generally skeptical of parental authority, see a fundamental conflict of interest between parent and child in this context that justifies active judicial oversight of parents' agreements. *See* Janet Leach Richards, *Redefining Parenthood: Parental Rights Verses Children's Rights*, 40 WAYNE L. REV. 1227 (1994). Moreover, judicial oversight of agreements may be justified because mothers may sacrifice property and support to secure custody. *See In re Rife*, 878 N.E.2d 775 (Ill. App. Ct. 2007) (clause in a couple's marital settlement agreement under which the mother would forfeit ownership of the IRA established by the father for child support purposes if she sought judicial modification of the agreement's custody, visitation or support provisions is against public policy protecting the children's best interests).

Although most states continue to recognize the *parens patriae* authority of courts to review custody agreements, the evidence suggests that parents' custody agreements rarely are set aside, suggesting that courts view arrangements agreed upon by the parents to be more likely to be successful than those imposed by a court. *See* MACCOBY & MNOOKIN, *supra*, at 41. Beyond this, some modern statutes limit judicial freedom in this area. In many states today, courts are directed by statute to approve parents' agreements unless they are found to be contrary to the child's best interest. N.J. STAT. ANN. § 9:2-4(d). Under some statutes, the court must explain why it has declined to enter a custody order based on the parents' agreement. *See* PA. CONS. STAT. ANN. § 5307 (court must state on the record the reasons for declining to base its order on the parents' agreement). A higher standard of proof is required to override parental agreements in some states. *See* MICH. COMP. LAWS ANN. § 722.27a(2) (court must determine by clear and convincing evidence that agreement is not in child's best interest to override). Joint custody agreements are given special deference under some statutes, probably because legislatures assume courts may be more likely to set them aside. California, for example, creates a rebuttable presumption that such agreements are in the best interests of the child. CAL. FAM. CODE § 3080; *see also* CONN. GEN. STAT. § 46b-56a(b)(same); Robert E. Emery & Kimberly C. Emery, *Should Courts or Parents Make Child-Rearing Decisions?: Married Parents as a Paradigm for Parents Who Live Apart*, 43 WAKE FOREST L. REV. 365 (2008) (advocating deference to parental agreements with the claim that excluding judicial oversight of them will encourage even parents with high-conflict cases to take responsibility and work together).

The *ALI Principles* are strongly deferential toward parental custody agreements, directing courts to order custody on the basis of a knowing, voluntary custody agreement unless it is harmful to the child. § 2.06. The Comments justify this approach on the ground that courts have neither the time nor resources to review agreements meaningfully. Moreover, an arrangement based on parental agreement is more likely to be successful than one imposed on unwilling and objecting parents. *Id.* at cmt. *a.*

The last two decades have seen many states adopt statutes that require the adoption of "parenting plans," which are more detailed and specific than traditional custody orders. (In the extreme, the traditional order would just award primary custody to one parent and "reasonable visitation" to the other.) Typical parenting plans include provisions for each parent's rights and responsibilities for the care of the child and for educational and health care decisions, a schedule for the child's living arrangements, including holidays and vacations, and procedures for communication and dispute resolution between parents. WASH. REV. CODE ANN. § 26.09.181; VT. STAT. ANN. tit. 15, § 666 (plan to include (1) physical living arrangements, (2) parent-child contact, (3) education (4) medical, dental and health care, (5) travel arrangements, (6) procedures for communicating about the child's welfare, and (7) procedures for resolving disputes).

Psychologists advocate comprehensive planning at the time of divorce as a means to promote future cooperation between parents by reducing the potential for uncertainty and misunderstandings that can lead to later conflict. ROBERT E. EMERY, RENEGOTIATING FAMILY RELATIONSHIPS: DIVORCE, CHILD CUSTODY AND MEDIATION (1994). Ideally, the process of creating a parenting plan involves both parents working together to make decisions about the child's future, and commits both to the agreements they reach. Legislative drafters of the Washington law, the first statute mandating parenting plans, described its goals along these lines — to encourage parents to take responsibility for creating a plan that reflects their individualized needs, rather than having families subject to court-devised formulas; to encourage continued participation of both parents in their children's lives through shared parenting; to focus parents on their future parental responsibilities; and to reduce conflict. *See* Jane W. Ellis, *Plans, Protections and Professional Interventions: Innovations in Divorce Custody Reform and the Role of Legal Professionals*, 24 U. MICH. J.L. REFORM 65, 80–94 (1990).

States vary in the extent to which parenting plans are required in custody cases. The Washington Parenting Act requires a parenting plan in every custody case. WASH. REV. CODE ANN. § 26.09.181 et seq. More typically, plans are required when parents plan to share physical custody. ILL. ANN. STAT. ch. 750, para. 5\602.1(b); MASS. GEN. LAWS ch. 208, § 31. In some states, courts have discretion to order parents to submit a parenting plan. CAL. FAM. CODE § 3040 (a)(1); MICH. COMP. LAWS § 722.27a(8).

The *ALI Principles* require all parents seeking custody to submit parenting plans to the court, and, indeed, describes the parenting plan as "the core concept" of custody regulation. § 2.05, cmt. *a.* The requirement encourages parents to cooperate because plans to which parents agree generally must be adopted by the court. Moreover, the parenting plan concept recognizes the diversity of parenting arrangements and encourages parents to tailor their plans to accommodate their family needs. *Id.* Like many statutory provisions, the *Principles* require parents to include provisions for dispute resolution and to establish remedies in order to discourage relitigation. § 2.05(5)(c).

[2] Naming the Child

The issue of children's surnames arises typically when a custodial mother wants to change the child's surname to her own "maiden" or remarried name after divorce, when an unmarried father seeks to have the child adopt his surname and when the custodial mother wants the child to bear the name of the child's father. There is some traditional authority for the view that a father has a protectable interest in having his children bear his surname. *See, e.g., In re Harris*, 236 S.E.2d 426, 429 (W. Va. App. 1977), but the modern trend is to resolve disputes over the child's name under a best interest standard. *See In re Marriage of Gulsvig*, 498 N.W.2d 725 (Iowa 1993) (presuming that child should bear father's surname is "outdated"). In *In re Willhite*, 706 N.E.2d 778 (Ohio 1999), the court adopted the best interests standard and directed the trial court to consider several factors: the effect of the change on the child's relationship with each parent, the identification of the child as part of a family unit, the length of time the child has had the surname, the preference of a child with sufficient maturity, and whether the child's surname is different from the residential parent's and any embarrassment that might cause. Additional factors that may affect a child's best interest include whether it is convenient for the child to have the same name or a different name from the custodial parent, whether the mother seeking the name change provides assurances that she will not change her name if she marries, whether the noncustodial parent has consistently paid support and maintained contact with the child, the degree of community respect associated with the present or new name, and whether a parent seeks the name change to alienate the child from the other parent. *See Montgomery v. Wells*, 708 N.W.2d 704 (Iowa Ct. App. 2005).

Courts increasingly have allowed name changes where the mother offers a plausible justification, despite the father's objections. *See, e.g., In re Douglass*, 205 Cal. App. 3d 1046 (1988) (granting mother's petition for name change based upon desire to avoid embarrassment to the children of having last name different from other family members). Modern courts tend to respond less positively to claims that the father's future relationship with the child will be undermined if the child does not bear his name. *See, e.g., In re Marriage of McManamy*, 18 Cal. Rptr. 2d 216 (1993) ("Kate's understanding of her father's role in her life will not be based solely on her surname, but will develop in light of his conduct and attitudes, particularly his active involvement in her life").

Courts have responded to name change disputes arising between parents who were never married by favoring the custodial mother. The New Jersey Supreme Court has announced a "strong presumption" that the custodial parent has the right to choose the child's surname. In *Gubernat v. Deremer*, 657 A.2d 856 (N.J. 1995), the court concluded that the traditional presumption favoring the father's surname was grounded in a patriarchal legal regime and that it should not be applied today. The presumption favoring the custodial parent is rebuttable upon a demonstration by the noncustodial parent that another surname served the child's interests (for example, when the child had carried the noncustodial parent's surname for some period of time and would be confused or embarrassed by a change). *See also Workman v. Olszewski*, 993 P.2d 667 (Mont. 1999) (upholding a lower court's decision that the child should retain his mother's surname — and acknowledging preference for the father's surname in its earlier decisions); *Huffman v. Fisher*, 987 S.W.2d 269 (Ark. 1999) (rejecting decision to change surname of a child of unmarried parents to the father's name, and directing a best interest inquiry).

The best interests test has also been applied where the custodial mother wanted the child to bear the father's surname, and the father objected that the use of his surname would harm his relationship with his family. *Scoggins v. Trevino*, 200 S.W.3d 832 (Tex. App. 2006). The father was married when he and the custodial mother had a "clandestine" relationship resulting in her pregnancy. The court rejected the father's argument as self-serving, rather than based on "harm to the child," and the other factors affecting the child's best interests were either neutral or favored changing the child's name to that of the father.

PROBLEM

Problem 6-14.   Mary Dolan and Bill Williams were not married and separated shortly after Sarah was born. Sarah, who is now 5 years old, has used her father's surname since she was born. Mary recently married Brad Grady, who has two children living with him. Mary (now Mary Grady) would like to change Sarah's name to Grady. Bill objects to the name change. Although he only sees Sarah 2 or 3 times a year, he provides modest financial support on a regular basis. Should the court order a name change?

E. MODIFICATION OF CUSTODY

[1]   General Principles

BURCHARD v. GARAY
California Supreme Court
724 P.2d 486 (1986)

[The facts and the court's analysis of the merits of the modification petition are set forth in Section B[2][a], *supra*. The court reversed the trial court award of custody to the father.]

. . . [W]e first consider the function of the changed-circumstance rule in child custody proceedings. In deciding between competing parental claims to custody, the court must make an award "according to the best interests of the child." . . . This test, established by statute, governs all custody proceedings. . . . The changed-circumstance rule is not a different test, devised to supplant the statutory test, but an adjunct to the best-interest test. It provides, in essence, that once it has been established that a particular custodial arrangement is in the best interests of the child, the court need not reexamine that question. Instead, it should preserve the established mode of custody unless some significant change in circumstances indicates that a different arrangement would be in the child's best interest. The rule thus fosters the dual goals of judicial economy and protecting stable custody arrangements. . . .

"The change of circumstances standard is based on principles of *res judicata*." ([Sally Burnett] Sharp, *Modification of Agreement-Based Custody Decrees: Unitary or Dual Standard?* (1982) 68 VA. L. REV. 1263, 1264, fn. 9.) The rule established in a majority of jurisdictions, which we here endorse, applies [the changed circumstances] standard whenever custody has been established by judicial decree. A minority of states . . . [apply] it only when custody was determined through an adversarial hearing. No state, so far as we have ascertained, applies the changed-circumstance standard when there has been no prior judicial determination of custody.

Ana [the child's mother] argues that the trial court erred in failing to apply the changed circumstance rule [on the grounds that, although there was no prior custody determination, she has had custody for a significant period. Thus, she argues, the father] should have the burden of persuading the court that a change in custody is essential or expedient for the welfare of the child. We agree in substance with this argument: in view of the child's interest in stable custodial and emotional ties, custody lawfully acquired and maintained for a significant period will have the effect of compelling the noncustodial parent to assume the burden of persuading the trier of fact that a change is in the child's best interest. That effect, however, is different from the changed-circumstance rule, which not only changes the burden of persuasion but also limits the evidence cognizable by the court . . .

The contrary [rule that the changed-circumstance standard protects a "de facto" custody arrangement][3] is in our opinion unsound, unworkable, and potentially harmful. It is unsound because, absent some prior determination of the child's best interests as of some past date, the courts have no warrant to disregard facts bearing upon that issue merely because such facts do not constitute changed circumstances. It is unworkable because . . . absent such a prior determination the courts have no established basis on which they can assess the significance of any change. And it is potentially harmful because it could compel the court to make an award inconsistent with the child's best interest.[5]

. . . . In most cases, of course, the changed-circumstance rule and the best interest test produce the same result. When custody continues over a significant period, the child's need for continuity and stability assumes an increasingly important role. That need will often dictate the conclusion that maintenance of the current arrangement would be in the best interests of that child. But there will be occasional cases where it makes a difference. Consider, for example, a case in which a couple separate, and in the emotional turmoil of the separation the less suitable spouse takes custody of the child. In a later custody proceeding, the noncustodial parent may be able to prove that the custodial parent is unable to provide proper

---

[3] The parties use the term "de facto custody" to refer to custody established without a court order. Strictly speaking, Ana's custody of William, Jr., was "de jure," since under Civil Code section 197 as a matter of law an unmarried woman acquires sole custody of her child at birth when there is no presumed father.

[5] The risk of harm to the child would be reduced, but not eliminated, by requiring a rather long period of custody before it becomes "significant" enough to invoke the changed-circumstances rule . . .

care, but not that his or her ability to do so has deteriorated since the separation. In such a case the changed-circumstance rule might require the court to confirm a custody not in the best interest of the child. Or, to take another example, a child may be born out of wedlock to a woman who for some reason is not able to give it suitable care. The changed-circumstance rule would require the father, when he seeks custody, to prove not only that the mother is unsuitable, but that she has become more so since the baby's birth. In this example, the changed-circumstance rule again might require the court to endorse a custodial arrangement harmful to the child.[7]

. . . . We conclude that custody in the present case should be decided on the basis of the best interests of the child without requiring William to prove in addition that changed circumstances render it essential that he receive custody. . . .

[The trial court abused its discretion.]

MOSK, J., concurring.

I concur in the reversal . . . but strongly disagree with the manner in which the majority reach that result.

. . . [T]he limited application of the changed-circumstances rule that the majority adopt is in conflict with the primary purpose of the rule. The child whose custody was established by means other than judicial decree has the same need for and right to stability and continuity — and accordingly the same entitlement to the protection the rule is intended to provide — as the child whose custody was established by judicial decree. Because it is not unreasonable to assume that the children of two-parent and relatively more affluent families are disproportionately represented in the class of children whose custody was originally established by judicial decree, the majority's holding, I fear, will effectively deny needed protection disproportionately to children of single-parent and less affluent families. . . .

The [majority states that absent a prior determination of the child's best interests], "courts have no established basis on which they can assess the significance of any change." But "[i]dentification of a base line against which to measure a subsequent change of conditions is not as difficult as the [majority] suggest. The simple fact is that a demonstration of changed conditions does not normally require a preexisting record of all the facts that prevailed at the time [custody was originally established]. . . .

---

[7] To avoid the danger that the changed circumstances rule might dictate a result harmful to the child's best interests, Justice Mosk's concurring opinion suggests two possible ways to modify that rule. The first is that "when the noncustodial parent shows that custody has remained unchanged but inadequate since its inception, he need prove only that a change is essential or at least expedient for the welfare of the child in order to obtain custody." We assume that "welfare of the child" is equivalent to "best interests of the child." If so, this proposal would permit the noncustodial parent to prevail by showing that a change in custody would promote the best interests of the child as demonstrated by either changed or unchanged circumstances. So modified, the changed-circumstances test is identical to the statutory best-interests test.

NOTES

1. **The Changed-Circumstances Rule.** "The traditional custody modification standard allows modification of an initial custody decree if the court determines that a subsequent, substantial change of circumstances warrants a change of custody in order to promote the best interests of the child." Joan G. Wexler, *Rethinking the Modification of Child Custody Decrees*, 94 YALE L.J. 757, 761 (1985). As it is usually described, the rule requires that the changed circumstances must have occurred since the degree was entered and have been unanticipated by the parties. *Lizzio v. Jackson*, 640 N.Y.S.2d 330 (N.Y. Sup. Ct. App. Div. 1996) (asthmatic child's allergic reaction to custodial mother's smoking is not a changed circumstance, since mother smoked at time of divorce). While this rule is well-grounded in the principle of *res judicata* and also comports with the widely held view that a child's interest is best served by stable custody orders, courts vary a great deal in their conclusions about what constitutes a sufficient change of circumstance to warrant a change of custody. For some, the threshold is quite low. *See, e.g., Marriage of Richardson*, 622 N.E.2d 178 (Ind. 1993) (age change from 8 to 12 and increased interest in athletics was sufficient change of circumstance to modify custody); *Butland v. Butland*, 1996 Ohio App. LEXIS 2773 (June 27, 1996) (children's preference together with their desire to participate in extracurricular activities were changed circumstances). Others apply a stricter test. *See, e.g., Pierce v. Pierce*, 620 N.E.2d 726 (Ind. Ct. App. 1993) (significant improvement in mother's depression is not a change of circumstances). Remarriage (or marriage, in the case of unmarried parents) of either the custodial and noncustodial parent is sometimes viewed as a changed circumstance, but generally remarriage alone will not warrant a change of custody. *Porter v. Porter*, 298 S.E.2d 130 (W.Va. 1982) (custodial mother's remarriage is changed circumstance warranting custody reconsideration, but alone creates no presumption that change of custody is warranted); *Seeley v. Jaramillo*, 727 P.2d 91 (N.M. Ct. App. 1986). The modification rules in the *ALI Principles* follow this approach. § 2.15(3)(b).

2. **The Exceptions.** Some jurisdictions apply a relaxed standard when the original custody award was based upon a settlement agreement or a default judgment, allowing facts that occurred before the custody order to be considered, because they were never formally adjudicated. *See, e.g., Wetch v. Wetch*, 539 N.W.2d 309 (N.D. 1995) (when original custody is based on settlement agreement or default judgment, it was error not to consider pre-divorce conduct); *Hill v. Hill*, 620 P.2d 1114 (Kan. 1980) (default judgment); *see also* DEL. CODE ANN. tit. 13, § 729 (order based on parties' consent may be modified under best interest standard; order entered after full hearing on the merits may not be modified within two years, absent endangerment or emotional impairment). Given that more than 90% of custody arrangements are based on parental agreement, *see* MACCOBY & MNOOKIN, *supra*, at 137, this exception has the effect of severely undercutting the rule. Justice Mosk, in his *Burchard* concurrence, rejects this approach:

> . . . [T]he fact remains that even when custody is not adjudicated. . . . , we may nevertheless presume that such custody is in the child's best interest and as a result require the noncustodial parent to show that a material change of circumstances has subsequently occurred.

> Such a presumption is justified when custody is established by agreement. "First, most parents genuinely love their children, and it is reasonable to assume that the children's welfare is a vital consideration in the parents' decision to resolve their dispute by agreement. . . . Second, parents have a better informational base upon which to make a decision about custody. The adversarial process is an inadequate means to assemble sufficient 'facts' to resolve custodial disputes satisfactorily. Third, it is difficult to protect a child from the painful pull of divided loyalties when his parents fail to agree. Parental agreements help to preserve an atmosphere of at least superficial peace between parents and thereby facilitate a much easier and more meaningful future relationship between the child and the non-custodial parent." (Sharp, [*Modification of Agreement-Based Custody Decrees: Unitary or Dual Standard?* (1982), 68 Va. L. Rev. 1263, 1280] . . .)

724 P.2d at 498.

The California Supreme Court has revisited and somewhat qualified the *Burchard* approach, holding that the modification of an initial custody order is subject to the changed circumstances rule only if the parties clearly intended that the stipulated order was a final judgment. *Montenegro v. Diaz*, 27 P.3d 289 (Cal. 2001). The court upheld the trial court's application of the best interest standard to a father's request that the earlier stipulated order be modified to provide for joint physical custody, because it was not clear that the parties had intended that the stipulated order be final. In the court's view, stipulated orders are often meant to be temporary, and parties would be wary of entering such orders if they were treated as final judgments.

Some courts simply abandon any rule of *res judicata* when the facts of the individual case seem compelling enough. The usual justification is that, in the end, the best interests of the child must always be the predominant consideration. *See, e.g.*, *Elmer v. Elmer*, 776 P.2d 599 (Utah 1989) ("the *res judicata* aspect of the rule must always be subservient to the best interests of the child").

3. *De Facto Custody Arrangements.* *Burchard* holds that the changed-circumstances rule should apply only to court-ordered, not to de facto, custody arrangements. Other courts treat both situations alike, as Justice Mosk urges in his concurrence, requiring proof of changed circumstances in both situations.

> First, as between the parent who undertakes to provide care and the parent who fails or refuses to do so, custody with the former must be deemed to serve the child's best interests. Thus, it is altogether reasonable to require the latter to demonstrate changed circumstances should he subsequently attempt to obtain custody. Second, as Dr. Andrew Watson, psychiatrist and professor of law, has observed, stability is "practically the principal element in raising children" and "a child can handle almost anything better than he can handle instability.

724 P.2d at 498.

What if the *de facto* arrangement arises because the custodial parent, a reservist, placed the child with the other parent when she was about to be deployed. If the deployment lasts for a year or more, should the deployment be considered a change in circumstances? If a change in custody is allowed, what effect will there be on parents who consider joining the reserves or remaining in the military? *See* 50 App. U.S.C.A. § 521 (as amended in 2008, provides protection from default judgments in civil actions, including child custody proceeding, where a party is in the military and was "materially affected by reason of that military service in making a defense to the action"); Christopher Missick, *Child Custody Protections in the Servicemembers Civil Relief Act: Congress Acts to Protect Parents Serving in the Armed Forces*, 29 WHITTIER L. REV. 857 (2008) (criticizing 2008 amendments as not going far enough to protect service members from losing custody because of military service).

For consistency, should a jurisdiction use the same approach for *de facto* arrangements as for settlement agreements? Montana, for example, which applies the changed-circumstances rule to orders based upon a settlement agreement or a default judgment, *see In re Marriage of Hay*, 786 P.2d 1195 (Mont. 1990), also applied the rule to a *de facto* custody arrangement, on the theory that stability in such an arrangement was as important as stability of court-ordered arrangements. *See Andre v. Bobson (McAllister)*, 761 P.2d 809 (Mont. 1988).

4. *Future-Oriented Provisions in Custody Orders Based on Agreements.* Custody orders and agreements sometimes include provisions directing that custody arrangements be changed in the future. The question sometimes arises whether such provisions should be enforced or are subject to the modification rule. Particularly in jurisdictions that require parenting plans, this issue may arise, because parenting plans frequently include provisions for future modifications of the plans. *See* Jane W. Ellis, *Plans, Protections, and Professional Interventions: Innovations in Divorce Custody Reform and the Role of Legal Professionals* 24 U. MICH. J. L. REF. 65, 144 (1990) (finding 23 % of plans in King Co., Wash. include future modification provisions). The *ALI Principles* note this development and takes the position that provisions in a parenting plan that deal with future changes in custodial arrangements under certain conditions should be treated as implementations and not modifications of the plan. § 2.15, cmt. *b*. For example, provisions in the plan directing a change of custody when the child reaches a certain age or when a custodial parent relocates should not be subject to the changed circumstances rule. This stance is compatible with the general deference to parental agreements. *See ALI Principles* § 2.06 (directing courts to adopt parents' agreements, unless harmful to the child).

Some courts reject *in futuro* provisions in agreements and court orders. The North Dakota Supreme Court refused to enforce a provision in the custody agreement of two Air Force personnel (and included in the divorce judgment) that custody would be transferred to the father if the custodial mother accepted an assignment to be transferred out of state. *Zeller v. Zeller*, 640 N.W.2d 53 (N.D. 2002). When the mother was assigned to Fort Leonard Wood, Mo., she petitioned to relocate and the father sought to enforce the custody-change provision. The appellate court rejected the trial court's order changing custody to the father, finding the stipulation to change custody to be unenforceable as against public policy. The trial court, instead, should have applied the standard for considering a petition by the custodial parent to relocate. *See also Frauenshuh v. Giese*, 599 N.W.2d 153 (Minn. 1999) (rejecting stipulation in divorce agreement that best interest standard be applied to modification; holding parties must apply state standard based on endangerment). Court orders directing future custody changes have also been rejected. A Maryland court reversed a Solomonic custody order awarding custody of the two-year-old child to his mother until 30 days following the completion of the fifth grade, at which time custody was to go to the father, who would have custody until the child was eighteen years old. *Schaefer v. Cusack*, 722 A.2d 73 (Md. Ct. App. 1998). The appellate court held that modification of custody must be based on a contemporaneous assessment of whether substantial changed circumstances exist that warrant the change. "We have not the faintest idea of what the situation of the parents may be at the time when this child finishes the fifth grade . . . [or] what effect a change of custody might have on the child." 722 A.2d at 78. Would such a provision in an agreement between the parents be enforceable under the *Principles*?

5. *Time Limitations on Modification Actions.* Many statutes prohibit modification petitions made within a short time after the initial custody decree. A typical period is two years after the most recent court order, although some statutes have shorter periods. *See* COLO. REV. STAT. § 14-10-131(1) (two years after most recent decree); WIS. STAT. ANN. § 767.451 (1) (two years after initial order unless necessary for the child's physical or emotional well-being). These provisions seek to promote stability in the custodial arrangements and to deter petitions by disgruntled non-custodial parents. Exceptions to these rules are often allowed where the child's health or emotional well-being is endangered, or where the custodial parent can no longer care for the child. *See e.g.*, the Arizona provision ARIZ. REV. STAT. ANN. § 25-411(T) (modification allowed if court believes current environment may endanger child's "physical, mental, moral or emotional health"); *Naylor v. Kindred*, 620 N.E.2d 520 (Ill. App. Ct. 1993) (custodial mother incarcerated).

6. *Modification Actions Affecting Joint Custody.* Should the rule for modification of joint custody awards be different from other awards? Some states have abandoned the changed circumstances rule in this context, based on an implicit (and sometimes explicit) concern that joint custody arrangements may be undesirable if cooperation between the parents breaks down, but that this may not be seen as a basis for modification. A few courts have resolved the problem by explicitly holding that the parents' inability to cooperate is a material changed circumstance, warranting modification. *See, e.g.*, *Word v. Remick*, 58 S.W.3d 422 (Ark. Ct. App. 2001). Other courts have held that the changed circumstance rule does not apply to joint custody arrangements, and that petitions to modify joint custody should be considered under the best interest standard. *In re Pasquale*, 777 A.2d 877 (N.H. 2001). In this case, both parents agreed that the joint custody arrangement was not working, but the mother, after losing custody, challenged the use of the best interest standard. *See Lewis v. Lewis*, 557 S.E.2d 40 (Ga. Ct. App. 2001); *Weigle v. Weigle*, 43 P.3d 740 (Colo. Ct. App. 2002); *Russell (Bichsel) v. Russell*, 210 S.W.3d 191 (Mo. 2007) (custody modification courts should not apply the substantial change in circumstances test when the requested modification merely rearranges the parties' joint physical custody schedule, as opposed to modification of a sole custody and visitation order where modification would result in a drastic change for the child). *See* UTAH CODE ANN. § 30-3-10.4(1)(a) (joint legal custody order can be modified if unworkable or inappropriate under the circumstances).

Jurisdictions that favor joint custody, on the other hand, have made modification of sole custody to joint custody easier than other modifications. *See, e.g. In re Marriage of Wall*, 868 P.2d 387 (Colo. 1994) (joint custody statute requires best interests standard, rather than a change of circumstance standard for modification from sole custody to joint custody); *Karis v. Karis*, 544 A.2d 1328 (Pa. 1988). A few courts have held that to modify a joint custody award, a higher standard is appropriate. *See, e.g., In re Burke*, 541 N.E.2d 245 (Ill. App. Ct. 1989) (change from joint custody requires "clear and convincing evidence" of changed circumstances, even where parents have agreed to change).

PROBLEM

Problem 6-15. Elwyn consults you about obtaining a modification of a court order issued two years ago giving custody of his children to his former wife Mary. Two weeks after the decree, Elwyn remarried. He and his wife have had a child, and Elwyn's wife stays at home to care for the child. Also since the decree, Mary has gone back to work and sought psychotherapy for periodic depression. The children are now ages 9 and 14.

Would any of these factors be relevant to Elwyn's attempt to obtain a modification order? Should they be sufficient to justify modification if the court concluded that it was in the best interests of the children? What if Elwyn simply wants a modification to give him joint legal custody and increase his visitation time?

[2]   The Problem of Relocation

MARRIAGE OF LAMUSGA
California Supreme Court
88 P.3d 81 (2004)

MORENO, J.

In *In re Marriage of Burgess*, 913 P.2d 473 (1996), we held that a parent seeking to relocate after dissolution of marriage is not required to establish that the move is "necessary" in order to be awarded physical custody of a minor child. Similarly, a parent who has been awarded physical custody of a child under an existing custody order also is not required to show that a proposed move is "necessary" and instead " 'has the right to change the residence of the child, subject to the power of the court to restrain a removal that would prejudice the rights or welfare of the child.' (Fam.Code, § 7501.)" . . .

In the present case, the superior court ordered that primary physical custody of two minor children would be transferred from their mother to their father if their mother moved to Ohio. The Court of Appeal reversed, holding that if the custodial parent "has a good faith reason to move . . . the custodial parent cannot be prevented, directly or indirectly, from exercising his or her right to change the child's residence" unless the noncustodial parent makes a "substantial showing" that a change of custody is "essential" to prevent detriment to the children. We granted review to determine whether the Court of Appeal in the present case misapplied our holding in *Burgess*. We conclude that it did and reverse its judgment.

. . . [W]e conclude that just as a custodial parent does not have to establish that a planned move is "necessary," neither does the noncustodial parent have to establish that a change of custody is "essential" to prevent detriment to the children from the planned move. Rather, the noncustodial parent bears the initial burden of showing that the proposed relocation of the children's residence would cause detriment to the children, requiring a reevaluation of the children's custody. The likely impact of the proposed move on the noncustodial parent's relationship with the children is a relevant factor in determining whether the move would cause detriment to the children and, when considered in light of all of the relevant factors, may be sufficient to justify a change in custody. If the noncustodial parent makes such an initial showing of detriment, the court must perform the delicate and difficult task of determining whether a change in custody is in the best interests of the children.

The father in the present case satisfied his initial burden of showing that the mother's planned move would cause detriment to the children, requiring a reevaluation of the children's custody. The superior court properly considered the relevant factors and did not abuse its discretion in deciding that a change in primary custody from the mother to the father would be in the best interests of the children if the mother moves to Ohio. . . .

Susan LaMusga . . . filed [a] petition for dissolution of marriage on May 10, 1996, and requested sole physical custody of the children [Garrett, age 4 and Devlen, age 2], who were living with her in the family residence. The father objected and requested joint legal and physical custody. . . .

[T]he superior court awarded the parties joint legal custody of the children, with the mother having "primary physical custody". . . .

The mother subsequently married Todd Navarro and, on September 16, 1999, gave birth to a daughter. The father also remarried. His wife, Karin, has a daughter from her prior marriage.

On February 13, 2001, the mother filed an order to show cause to modify the visitation order to permit her to relocate with the children to Cleveland, Ohio. She alleged that she had family in the Cleveland area and her husband had received an offer for a more lucrative job there. . . .

The father objected to the mother's plan to move the children to Ohio and asked that primary custody of the children be transferred to him if the mother moved to Ohio. The father declared that the mother had attempted to alienate him from their sons since their separation and feared that moving the boys to Ohio would result in his "being lost as their father."

. . . . The court . . . [appointed] Dr. Stahl "to [evaluate] whether the relocation of the parties' two minor children is in the best interest of said children."

Dr. Stahl's . . . report notes that the mother has wanted to move ever since the divorce. . . . The move would improve her family's "economic standard of living, and . . . inherent quality of life. . . ." The mother "believes that she will have no difficulty supporting the boys in their relationship with their dad," asserting ". . . . that she is not a contributor to any alienation that the boys might feel. . . ."

Dr. Stahl was concerned "that the boys might not maintain any positive relationship with their dad if they move," noting that such a loss "would be significant." But he added that this "must be balanced with the potential losses that the boys might experience if their mother moves, and they stay," observing: "They have been in the primary care of their mother since the parents' divorce and they will likely have a significant loss [if] she moves without them. They also have a very close relationship with their sister Aisley, as well as Todd, and they will feel those losses as well. Third, they have their own desire to move. . . . If they don't move, they're likely to feel that their wishes aren't being heard." Dr. Stahl also observed that forcing the children to remain in California could cause them to further reject their father. . . .

Although the mother stated that she wanted to move to Ohio because that "is where she is originally from and where she has family support," Dr. Stahl suggested an additional motive: "Underneath, however, it has always appeared that [the mother] has wanted to move so that she can remove herself and the boys from the day-to-day interactions with [the father]. She has difficulty dealing with him and prefers to have as little communication with him as possible." . . .

Dr. Stahl [recommended that . . . the mother should not be permitted to move the children to Ohio, stating: "[T]here is no evidence that . . . [the mother] will really do what she said she will do . . . [i]n terms of being supportive of the boys' relationship with their father. . . . [I]t is still a tenuous relationship . . . [that could] get worse if the move is allowed."

Dr. Stahl acknowledged that the father also bore some of the responsibility for his strained relationship with his sons. . . . [H]e contributes to the children's alienation to the extent he perpetuates his conflict with the mother . . .

The [superior] court acknowledged that the mother is not purposely trying to alienate the children from their father, but noted that the mother's inability to "let go" of her anger toward the father caused her to project those feelings onto their children and to reinforce the children when they expressed negative feelings toward their father. . . . The court also acknowledged that this was not "a bad faith move away. I don't think this is an instance where [the mother is] attempting to relocate with the children for the specific purpose of limiting their contact or relationship with their father". . . .

"The primary importance, it seems to me at this point, is to be able to reinforce what is now a tenuous and somewhat detached relationship with the boys and their father . . . [A] relocation of the children out of . . . California . . . would inevitably under these circumstances be detrimental to their welfare. . . . If [the mother] wishes to relocate to the state of Ohio, certainly she is entitled to do that. Should she choose to do so, then I [order] primary physical custody of the children, at least during the school year, to Mr. LaMusga. . . . [I]f [the mother] decides not to relocate, then the existing custodial arrangement will remain."

The mother appealed and the Court of Appeal reversed the judgment. . . . The Court of Appeal concluded that the superior court "neither proceeded from the presumption that Mother had a right to change the residence of the children, nor took into account this paramount need for stability and continuity in the existing custodial arrangement. Instead, it placed undue emphasis on the detriment that would be caused to the children's relationship with Father if they moved." We granted review. . . .

In *In re Marriage of Burgess, supra*, [w]e observed that "[i]n an initial custody determination, the trial court has 'the widest discretion to choose a parenting plan that is in the best interest of the child.' (Fam.Code, § 3040, subd. (b).)." . . . Citing Family Code section 7501, which states that "[a] parent entitled to custody of a child has a right to change the residence of the child, subject to the power of the court to restrain a removal that would prejudice the rights or welfare of the child," we noted that the court must also consider "the presumptive right of a custodial parent to change the residence of the minor children, so long as the removal would not be prejudicial to their rights or welfare." . . .

We rejected the Court of Appeal's holding that the mother was required to show that it was "necessary" for her to move. . . .

Although *Burgess* involved an initial determination of custody, we held that "the same conclusion applies when a parent who has sole physical custody under an *existing* judicial custody order seeks to relocate:". . . . But we recognized that, as with any allegation that "changed circumstances" warrant a modification of an existing custody order, the noncustodial parent has a substantial burden to show that " 'some significant change in circumstances indicates that a different arrangement would be in the child's best interest.'. . . ." In a 'move-away' case, a change of custody is not justified simply because the custodial parent has chosen, for any sound good faith reason, to reside in a different location, but only if, as a result of relocation with that parent, the child will suffer detriment rendering it "essential or expedient for the welfare of the child that there be a change."

We were quick to emphasize, however, that "bright line rules in this area are inappropriate: each case must be evaluated on its own unique facts. Although the interests of a minor child in the continuity and permanency of custodial placement with the primary caretaker will most often prevail, the trial court, in assessing 'prejudice' to the child's welfare as a result of relocating even a distance of 40 or 50 miles, may take into consideration the nature of the child's existing contact with both parents . . . and the child's age, community ties, and health and educational needs. Where appropriate, it must also take into account the preferences of the child. . . .

Recently, the Legislature codified our decision in *Burgess* by amending Family Code section 7501 to add subdivision (b), which reads: "It is the intent of the Legislature to declare[*Burgess*] to be the public policy and law of this state."

[The Court then reviewed several cases applying *Burgess*, most of which upheld decisions by lower courts permitting relocation, including two cases permitting relocation to Australia and Israel, the custodial mothers' homes. The Court emphasized the broad discretion allowed lower courts. In one of the few cases in which an appellate court reversed the superior court's granting permission to relocate, the trial court considered only whether the custodial parent was acting in bad faith and failed to consider whether 'as a result of relocation with [the custodial] parent, the child will suffer detriment rendering it " 'essential or expedient for the welfare of the child that there be a change.' "

The Court of Appeal in the present case held that the superior court abused its discretion [because it] "neither proceeded from the presumption that Mother had a right to change the residence of the children, nor took into account this paramount need for stability and continuity in the existing custodial arrangement. Instead, it placed undue emphasis on the detriment that would be caused to the children's relationship with Father if they moved." We disagree.

We reaffirm our statement in *Burgess* that "the paramount need for continuity and stability in custody arrangements — and the harm that may result from disruption of established patterns of care and emotional bonds with the primary caretaker — weigh heavily in favor of maintaining ongoing custody arrangements." But there is nothing in the record before us that indicates that the superior court failed to consider the children's "interest in stable custodial and emotional ties" with their mother. . . . The court placed "primary importance" on the effect the proposed move would have on "what is now a tenuous and somewhat detached relationship with the boys and their father," concluding that the proposed move would be "extremely detrimental" to the children's welfare because it would disrupt the progress being made by the children's therapist in promoting this relationship. . . . In future cases, courts would do well to state on the record that they have considered this interest in stability, but the lack of such a statement does not constitute error and does not indicate that the court failed to properly discharge its duties.

. . . [T]he superior court's function in determining custody is not to reward or punish the parents for their past conduct. . . . But this does not mean that the court may not consider the past conduct of the parents in determining what future arrangement will be best for the children. . . . There is nothing in the record before us that indicates the superior court acted out of a desire to punish or reward either parent. But the mother's past conduct indicated that it was unlikely that she would follow through on her promises to encourage the children's relationship with their father if they moved to Ohio. . . .

The superior court did misspeak, however, in stating that the mother might have had a presumptive right to relocate with the children if the parents had coparented cooperatively. The mother-as the parent with primary physical custody of the children-had a presumptive right to change the children's residence unless the proposed move "would result in 'prejudice' to [the children's] 'rights or welfare.' " . . . The court was correct that the situation might have been far different had the parents shown a history of cooperative parenting. If that had been the case, it might have appeared more likely that the detrimental effects of the proposed move on the children's relationship with their father could have been ameliorated by the mother's efforts to foster and encourage frequent, positive contact between the children and their father. . . . [T]he court concluded that the mother's past conduct made it unlikely that she would facilitate the difficult task of maintaining the father's long-distance relationship with the boys.

The Court of Appeal was concerned about the superior court's reliance upon the detriment to the children's relationship with their father that would be caused by the proposed move, because "[t]here is inevitably a significant detriment to the relationship between the child and the noncustodial parent" whenever the custodial parent relocates with the children. . . . We do not suggest that a showing that a proposed move will cause detriment to the relationship between the children and the noncustodial parent *mandates* a change in custody. But it is within the wide discretion of the superior court to order a change of custody based upon such detriment, if such a change is in the best interests of the children in light of all the relevant factors. . . .

. . . . [T]he Court of Appeal in [*In re Marriage of Edlund & Hales*] may have inadvertently generated some confusion when it stated as a general conclusion: "The showing of 'changed circumstances' required of the noncustodial parent must consist of more than the fact of the proposed move". . . .

. . . . [S]ome courts have mistakenly interpreted [this] statement . . . to mean that the likely consequences of a proposed move can never constitute changed circumstances that justify a reevaluation of an existing custody order . . . This is incorrect. The likely consequences of a proposed change in the residence of a child, when considered in the light of all the relevant factors, may constitute a change of circumstances that warrants a change in custody, and the detriment to the child's relationship with the noncustodial parent that will be caused by the proposed move, when considered in light of all the relevant factors, may warrant denying a request to change the child's residence or changing custody. . . .

The Court of Appeal in the present case held that the father bore the burden of showing "that modification of custody is essential for the child's welfare". . . . In doing so, the Court of Appeal placed too great a burden on the noncustodial parent in a move-away case.

. . . . A change in custody is "essential or expedient" within the meaning of *Burgess* . . . if it is in the best interests of the child.

The Court of Appeal in the present case further concluded that the superior court improperly used its conditional order transferring primary physical custody to the father as a device to restrain the mother from relocating. We agree that a court must not issue such a conditional order for the purpose of coercing the custodial parent into abandoning plans to relocate. . . . There is nothing to indicate that the order transferring primary physical custody of the children to the father if the mother relocated was issued to coerce the mother into abandoning her plans to move.

The mother places great emphasis on the superior court's finding that she was not acting in "bad faith.". . . .

. . . . In . . . [*Burgess*], we observed that ". . . . Once the trial court determined that the mother did not relocate in order to frustrate the father's contact with the minor children, but did so for sound 'good faith' reasons, it was not required to inquire further into the wisdom of her inherently subjective decisionmaking.". . . .

In *In re Marriage of Bryant*, 91 Cal. App. 4th 789, . . . the Court of Appeal . . . overstate[d] the importance of the superior court's finding that the mother was not acting in bad faith, holding that once the superior court found that the mother was not acting in bad faith, "[n]o further inquiry [into the reasons for the proposed move] was necessary or appropriate.". . . .

This is not what we said in *Burgess*. . . . [W]e did not say that the reasons for a proposed move are irrelevant if the custodial parent is acting in good faith. . . .

Even if the custodial parent has legitimate reasons for the proposed change in the child's residence and is not acting simply to frustrate the noncustodial parent's contact with the child, the court still may consider whether one reason for the move is to lessen the child's contact with the noncustodial parent and whether that indicates, when considered in light of all the relevant factors, that a change in custody would be in the child's best interests.

. . . . [T]his area of law is not amenable to inflexible rules. Rather, we must permit our superior court judges — guided by statute and the principles we announced in *Burgess* and affirm in the present case — to exercise their discretion to fashion orders that best serve the interests of the children in the cases before them. Among the factors that the court ordinarily should consider when deciding whether to modify a custody order in light of the custodial parent's proposal to change the residence of the child are the following: the children's interest in stability and continuity in the custodial arrangement; the distance of the move; the age of the children; the children's relationship with both parents; the relationship between the parents including, but not limited to, their ability to communicate and cooperate effectively and their willingness to put the interests of the children above their individual interests; the wishes of the children if they are mature enough for such an inquiry to be appropriate; the reasons for the proposed move; and the extent to which the parents currently are sharing custody. . . .

The judgment of the Court of Appeal is reversed and the matter is remanded to that court with directions to affirm the superior court's post-judgment order transferring custody of the children to the father if the mother moves to Ohio. . . .

Dissenting Opinion by KENNARD, J.

A mother who had been the primary caretaker of her two children since their birth, and who had never violated the trial court's visitation orders, wanted to provide a better life for her children by moving with them to another state where she had relatives and where her new husband had accepted a better-paying job. Concerned that his tenuous relationship with the children would be weakened, the children's father objected. After a hearing, the trial court ordered that custody of the children be transferred to the father in the event the mother moved. The majority holds the trial court did not abuse its discretion in so ruling. I disagree.

When it explained its ruling, the trial court said that moving the children to another state could damage the children's relationship with their father, but the court never mentioned the potential harm to the children from losing their mother as their primary caretaker, despite undisputed evidence that this harm would be significant. The majority acknowledges that the trial court was required to consider this detriment — indeed it acknowledges " 'the paramount need for continuity and stability in custody arrangements' " — but it assumes the trial court adequately considered this point.

In a matter of this importance, involving the custody and welfare of minor children, a reviewing court should not make such a speculative assumption. . . .

A parent with custody of minor children has a "presumptive right" to change the children's residence. (*In re Marriage of Burgess* (1996) 913 P.2d 473; see also Fam.Code, § 7501.) A noncustodial parent opposing such a change of residence bears the initial burden of showing that the move will cause some detriment to the children. Once this showing of detriment has been made, the trial court must then weigh the likely effects on the child's welfare from moving with the custodial parent, against the likely effects from a change in custody. Only if the child's interests are better served by changing custody than by relocating with the custodial parent may a court order custody transferred to the other parent.

Here, the trial court's explanation for its ruling shows that it properly considered how relocation to Ohio might detrimentally affect the children — including the impact on their tenuous relationship with their father. But the trial court was also required to weigh this detriment against the detriment that would result from removing the boys from the mother's custody. This the court did not do. In its statement of reasons, the court said: ". . . . *The issue is the effect on these children of relocating, and the effect of the relationship with their father if they are permitted to relocate.*" (Italics added.) But the effect of the relocation on the children's relationship with the father . . . just one of the potential detriments shown by the evidence that the trial court was required to consider. Equally important was the potential detriment from disrupting the existing custodial arrangement by transferring custody from the mother to the father.

This court has stressed that the "paramount need for continuity and stability in custody arrangements — and the harm that may result from disruption of established patterns of care and emotional bonds with the primary caretaker — weigh heavily in favor of maintaining ongoing custody arrangements." (*In re Marriage of Burgess, supra,* 13 Cal. 4th at pp. 32–33.) Here, the trial court's explanation for its ruling provides no assurance that the trial court gave any weight to the importance of continuity and stability in custody arrangements.

. . . . [A] trial court abuses its discretion whenever it applies the wrong legal standard to the issue at hand. . . .

. . . . [N]othing in the record indicates that the court [considered the children's 'interest in stable custodial and emotional ties' with their mother]. . . . In the absence of such a statement, or some other evidence in the record showing that the trial court affirmatively considered and weighed the required factors, I cannot conclude that the trial court properly exercised its discretion.

NOTES

1. *The Dilemma of Relocation.* Almost one half of Americans move in a five year period, according to the U.S. Bureau of the Census statistics. Thus the legal response to a custodial parent's desire to relocate is a very important issue. These cases "present some of the knottiest and most disturbing problems" that courts face. *See Tropea v. Tropea*, 642 N.Y.S.2d 575 (1996), pitting the custodial parent's wish to better her circumstances by moving to a place where presumably she can have a better life against the noncustodial parent's desire to continue to have a relationship with his child that involves frequent contact.

The custodial parent's claim may be compelling. If she was the homemaker in the marriage, she may have moved to the location where the family has lived only because of her husband's employment, and she may have strong ties to another locale. Sometimes, the custodial parent may seek to move because of a job or a new marriage, or to return to home and family, reasons that courts usually find to be legitimate. In *LaMusga*, the custodial mother had family in Ohio and her new husband had a better job there. Why did the court reject her petition? If relocation is strongly deterred by the legal response, the custodial parent may be "forced" to continue to reside in a particular community where she has few opportunities or ties, only because it suits the interest of her former spouse to live there. Thus, a restrictive relocation policy may be extremely burdensome to the primary caregiver. Moreover, some courts have suggested that the primary custodian and children make up a new family unit after divorce, all of whose members may benefit from the move. *Ireland v. Ireland*, 717 A.2d 676 (Conn. 1998). Courts cite social science evidence suggesting that "in general, what is good for the custodial parent, is good for the child." Judith Wallerstein & Tony J. Tanke, *To Move or Not to Move: Psychological and Legal Considerations in the Relocation of Children Following Divorce*," 30 FAM. L.Q. 305, 315 (1996); *Baures v. Lewis*, 770 A.2d 214 (N.J. 2001) (citing this claim).

On the other hand, relocation of the custodial parent and child to a distant locale can inflict considerable costs on both the noncustodial parent and the child if they have had a close relationship. In *LaMusga*, the court weighed heavily the harm to even a tenuous relationship between the father and children, should the children move to Ohio. Moreover, a rule that creates no barriers to relocation by the custodial parent may encourage her to move for frivolous or spiteful reasons; at a minimum, it makes it less likely that she will weigh the cost to the relationship between the noncustodial parent and child in her decision. Such a rule gives her a weapon to use against the noncustodial parent in the not uncommon situation in which she finds proximity to him distasteful. Was this a consideration in *LaMusga*? Finally, many social scientists disagree with the views of Wallerstein and Tanke, above. *See* Joan B. Kelly & Michael Lamb, *Developmental Issues in Relocation Cases Involving Young Children: When, Whether, and How?*, 17 J. FAM. PSYCHOLOGY 193 (2003); Richard A. Warshak, *Social Science and Children's Interest in Relocation Cases: Burgess Revisited*, 34 FAM. L. Q. 83 (2000) (criticizing the research support for the benefits of relocation). One recent study indicates that college students who experienced a parent's relocation showed negative effects as compared to those whose parents did not move. Sanford L. Braver, Ira Ellman & William V. Fabricus, *Relocation After Divorce and Children's Best Interests: New*

Evidence and Legal Considerations, 17 J. Fam. Psychology 206 (2003).

Relocation disputes are perhaps among the more dramatic of many illustrations of why the idea of a "clean break" has little sensible application to divorces in which there are minor children of the marriage. Because the custodial parent's move can affect the other parent's access to the children, it can affect the other parent, but a rule that restricts a custodial parent's move to protect the other parent can adversely affect the custodial parent. Divorce cannot mean a clean break from the perspective of a noncustodial parent legally obligated to continue to pay support despite any relocation, even if the other parent takes the child so far away that his parental relationship is effectively broken. At the same time, there is also no clean break for the custodial parent denied an opportunity to move to protect the child's relationship with the other parent. Unavoidably, each parent's plans after divorce continue to have an important impact on the other parent. As Professor Glennon demonstrates in her review of relocation caselaw, courts attempt to be attentive to the emotional harms that parents may suffer because of a relocation, but no attempt is made to address the economic harm. *See* Theresa Glennon, *Still Partners? Examining the Consequences of Post-Dissolution Parenting*, 41 Fam. L. Q. 105 (2007). In her examination of all 602 relocation cases decided between 2001 and 2006 and appearing in a Westlaw search, Professor Glennon found that, for both custodial fathers and custodial mothers, but especially the fathers, the single most common reason given for the desired move was employment related. Another large group, and especially the mothers, sought to relocate on account of remarriage, or to accommodate a new spouse's job. *Id.* For both custodial mothers and custodial fathers, the move was allowed a bit less than half the time. *Id.* at 127–28.

Some courts and commentators find that a restrictive relocation rule that effectively ties the custodial parent to a particular geographic area interferes with that parent's constitutional right to travel. The Wyoming Supreme Court found that the right to travel "carries with it the right of a custodial parent to have the children move with that parent," and that it could only be impaired upon a clear showing that a change of circumstances exists and that the move would have a detrimental effect on the child. *Watt v. Watt*, 971 P.2d 608, 616 (Wyo. 1999); *see also In re D.M.G.*, 951 P.2d 1377 (Mont. 1998) (rejecting a trial court directive that the mother return to Montana from Oregon or relinquish custody, and holding that interference with the right to travel justified only where the party seeking the restriction demonstrates it is in the child's best interest); *Jaramillo v. Jaramillo*, 823 P.2d 299, 305 (N.M. 1991) (placing the burden of proof on the custodial parent is an unconstitutional impairment of the parent's right to travel); *Holder v. Polanski*, 544 A.2d 852, 856 (N.J. 1988) (allowing relocation unless adverse to child's best interests avoids the unconstitutional burden on parent's right to travel). *But see Bartosz v. Jones*, 197 P.3d 310, 315 (Idaho 2008) (restricting right to travel of custodial parent allowed where that parent has failed to demonstrate that moving from Idaho to Hawaii in child's best interests, and best interests of the child is a compelling governmental interest). There is no question that this interest is burdened if continued custody is contingent on remaining in the jurisdiction. *See* Wis. Stat. Ann. § 767.481 (Supp. 2002). However, the noncustodial parent also has a constitutionally protected interest in his relationship with his child, which is impaired if the custodial parent is free to move to a distant location. Although courts do not tend to focus on this interest (perhaps because parental rights are inherently restricted for noncustodial parents), either outcome will burden a constitutional interest of one parent. *See* Arthur LaFrance, *Child Custody and Relocation: A Constitutional Perspective*, 34 U. LOUISVILLE J. FAM. L. 1 (1996).

A threshold consideration in many relocation cases is the good faith of either the relocating custodial parent or of the noncustodial parent who is seeking to block the child's relocation. Courts want to discourage spiteful and strategic behavior by either parent. Thus, for example, it is not surprising that courts have paid attention to the actual extent of involvement of the noncustodial parent with the child (and not just the contact allowed under the custody/visitation order). *Taylor v. Taylor*, 849 S.W.2d 319 (Tenn. 1993) (court reversed order prohibiting mother's move, emphasizing that father failed to visit as scheduled on 20 or more occasions). The underlying premise is that a parent who has not been significantly involved with the child has little legitimate basis for objecting to the move. *See* Merle H. Weiner, *Inertia and Inequality: Reconceptualizing Disputes Over Parental Relocation*, 40 U. C. DAVIS L. REV. 1747 (2007) (arguing that missing element in relocation disputes is consideration of the noncustodial parent's mobility; including that element would improve outcomes for some children, would counter gendered assumptions about "who must accommodate whom," and would treat parents as partners after divorce by emphasizing responsibility of both parents to act in best interests of child, rather than allowing either to act solely out of self-interest).

Of course, the good faith of the relocating parent is also important. Even under liberal relocation laws, the custodial parent must offer a reasonable good faith basis for the relocation. In some states this fulfills her obligation to justify the move. In New Jersey, for example, "any sincere, good-faith reason will suffice," even though the relocating parent can not show a "real advantage" to the move. *Holder v. Polanski*, 544 A.2d 852, 56 (N.J. 1988). In others, the burden then shifts to the noncustodial parent to demonstrate that relocation is not in the child's interest. *Ireland v. Ireland, supra. LaMusga* suggests that some California courts misinterpreted *Burgess* to require only good faith on the part of the relocating parent. Instead, the Court says *Burgess* treats the relocating parent's good faith as simply a threshold requirement.

Most cases, however, do not involve bad faith on the part of either parent, but rather a conflict between two parents, each with legitimate interests. This may explain why courts have struggled with this issue, such that the legal response has been varied and unstable (*see* Note 3, *infra*).

2. Relocation and the Modification Standard. The fact that one parent wants to relocate is sometimes considered in the initial custody decision. More often the issue arises later, perhaps because the parent who wants to move is reluctant to have this factor weighed in the initial decision. Thus, often an important question is whether the planned move by the custodial parent constitutes a "changed circumstance" so as to trigger a reconsideration of custody under the modification standard. Some courts hold the custodial parent's move does not justify reexamination of the basic custody decision. *See, e.g., Taylor v. Taylor, supra; Pitt v. Olds*, 511 S.E.2d 60 (S.C. 1999). Other courts treat the relocation itself as a changed circumstance, justifying a new inquiry and decision about custody. *See Rowland v. Kingman*, 629 A.2d 613 (Me. 1993) (relocation constitutes a substantial change of circumstances); *Rice v. Shepard*, 877 S.W.2d 229 (Mo. App. 1994) ("residential change of the custodial parent to a distant location away from the non-custodial parent is a change of circumstances"); *Domingues v. Johnson*, 593 A.2d 1133 (Md. 1991) (same). *LaMusga* suggests that, under recent California law, while the move is not *per se* a changed circumstance, under some circumstances, it may be treated as such.

A related issue involves orders that condition the custodial parent's continued right to custody on remaining in the jurisdiction, (and automatically transfer custody to the other parent if she moves), with no separate determination that a change of custody is warranted. Some courts have upheld conditional orders with automatic transfer provisions. *See Lozinak v. Lozinak*, 569 A.2d 353 (Pa. Super. Ct. 1990) (upholding order transferring custody to the father if mother left Pennsylvania); *Maeda v. Maeda*, 794 P.2d 268 (Haw. App. 1990) (upholding conditional order). These conditional orders are often transparently designed to discourage the custodial parent from relocating. Courts may conclude that they lead to the best outcome; *i.e.*, the custodial parent stays in the jurisdiction and retains custody. This is suggested by a New York opinion in which the court conditioned the mother's custody on her not moving, after concluding that the child's best interest would not be served by a transfer of custody to the father. *Sullivan v. Sullivan*, 594 N.Y.S.2d 276 (Sup. Ct. App. Div. 1993). *LaMusga* somewhat disingenuously rejects the argument that the conditional order was designed to deter the mother.

Other courts reject an automatic transfer of custody upon relocation, and require instead that the change of custody must be justified under legal modification standards. In *Korn v. Korn*, 867 So. 2d 338 (Ala. Civ. App. 2003), the appellate court concluded that the trial court abused its discretion in holding that custody would automatically switch to the father if the mother, who was from Israel, left the United States. The court emphasized that custody could not be changed on the basis of a parent's relocation unless the non-custodial parent met the standard for modification of custody which required him to demonstrate that the relocation amounts to a material change of circumstances, that the change of custody will promote the child's best interests, and that the benefits of changing custody outweigh the disruption. *See also Moeller-Prokosch v. Prokosch*, 53 P.3d 152 (Alaska 2002) (order giving mother custody as long as she stayed within reasonable distance of father's school choice for child was reversed; trial court instructed to determine whether mother's reasons for moving were legitimate and whether mother's or father's custody was in child's interest).

Whether relocation results in a change of primary custody, it usually will result in some modification of the custody arrangements. Thus, it is useful to think of most relocation cases as belonging to a unique category of modification cases, which in most states are subject to special rules. For example, the *ALI Principles* treat relocation as a substantial changed circumstance when it impairs either parent's ability to continue to exercise custodial responsibilities. § 2.17 (1). The court is then directed to modify the parenting plan in accordance with the child's best interests. However, where one parent has had primary custodial responsibility, she will be allowed to relocate if she demonstrates a valid purpose and good faith, and the location is reasonable in light of the purpose. *See Hayes v. Gallacher*, 972 P.2d 1138 (Nev. 1999) (adopting ALI relocation standard); *see also* Note 3, *infra*.

3. ***The Contemporary Legal Trend.***   Generalizations about the legal response to moves by custodial parents are dangerous, although the current trend appears to be toward a rule that allows greater freedom to relocate by a parent with primary custody. Relatively restrictive rules that placed the burden of justifying the move on the custodial parent seeking to relocate with the child have been supplanted in many states by rules that direct a more neutral multi-factored inquiry, or that place the burden of demonstrating harm to the child on the parent seeking to block the move. The trend has certainly not been linear, however.

California law, and particularly *LaMusga*, demonstrate the unpredictability of doctrine in this area. Before *Marriage of Burgess*, 913 P.2d 473 (Cal. 1996), discussed at length in *LaMusga*, lower appellate courts in California responded inconsistently to relocation cases. Some courts favored the relocating parent while others placed the burden on that parent to prove that the move was in the child's best interest. In *Burgess*, the state supreme court interpreted the statute, which had not changed in a century, to require that the non-custodial parent challenging relocation must meet the modification test; he must prove that a change of custody is "essential or expedient for the welfare of the child." Until *LaMusga*, most courts and commentators interpreted *Burgess* to afford the custodial parent substantial freedom to relocate. In 2003, with *LaMusga* pending, the legislature adopted a statute that provided that "a parent entitled to custody of a child has a right to change residence of the child [unless the removal would] prejudice the rights or welfare of the child." CAL. FAM. CODE § 7501. The statute also expressly affirmed *Burgess* as "the public policy and law of the state." *LaMusga* upholds the trial court's rejection of the mother's petition to relocate, despite the fact that the trial court seems to have based its decision mostly on the cost of relocation to the noncustodial father's relationship with his children. Although *LaMusga* seeks to align its conclusion with *Burgess* by noting repeatedly that *Burgess* emphasized the importance of deference to trial court discretion, without question, *LaMusga* has seriously undermined *Burgess*. After *LaMusga*, no clear legal standard would seem to govern relocation cases in California. For the time being, trial courts are left to decide these cases, virtually without restraint.

Until recently, New York may have had the most restrictive relocation standard of any state, putting the burden on the relocating parent to demonstrate "exceptional" or "compelling" circumstances relating to the child's best interests. *See Daghir v. Daghir*, 439 N.E.2d 324 (N.Y. 1982) (test not met where mother moved with her husband when he was transferred to France). More recently, however, the New York "exceptional circumstances" test has been interpreted to allow a custodial parent to move with the child even in very unexceptional circumstances. *See, e.g., Aldrich v. Aldrich*, 516 N.Y.S.2d 328 (Sup. Ct. App. Div. 1987) (mother allowed to move from New York to California where her husband resided). In *Tropea v. Tropea*, Note 1, *supra*, the Court of Appeals officially abandoned the "exceptional circumstances" test in favor of a balancing test that requires that all relevant facts and circumstances be evaluated. Under the new test, important considerations include the impact of the move on the relationship between the child and the non-custodial parent, the reasons for the move, the feasibility and desirability of a change of custody, the quality of the lifestyle the child will experience in the new location, each parent's good faith, and the possibility of developing a visitation schedule that will enable the child and non-custodial parent to maintain their relationship. This test, although it gives courts discretion to weigh the non-custodial parent's interest in preventing the move, is far more favorable to relocation than the former "exceptional circumstances" test. *See Ireland v. Ireland*, 717 A.2d 676 (Conn. 1998) (adopting *Tropea* factors under test in which non-custodial parent must demonstrate that move is not in child's best interest).

Several other states have established burdens of proof or presumptions that require the noncustodial parent to demonstrate that the proposed relocation is not in the best interests of the child. *See Ireland, supra*; *Sefkow v. Sefkow*, 427 N.W.2d 203, 214 (Minn. 1988) (removal allowed absent showing by noncustodial parent that such action is not in child's best interests and would endanger child's well-being); *Lane v. Schenck*, 614 A.2d 786 (Vt. 1992) (relocation must be allowed unless noncustodial parent proves that best interests of child would be "so undermined by a relocation . . . that a transfer of custody is necessary"); *Harrison v. Morgan*, 191 P.3d 617 (Okla. Civ. App. 2008) (once relocating parent demonstrates good faith, burden on objecting parent to show that relocation not in child's best interests). The Colorado Supreme Court interpreted its amended statute as removing the presumption in favor of the relocating parent and placing an equal burden on both parents to demonstrate whether or not the relocation would be in the best interests of the child. *In re Marriage of Ciesluk*, 113 P.3d 135 (Colo. 2005). In that case, the mother sought to modify the parenting time order so she could move to a state where she had family and could be employed by the company that had laid her off after seven years. The trial court denied her petition on the basis that it is generally in the best interests of the child for parents to remain in close proximity to the child. The decision was reversed on the basis that the court's generalization acted as a presumption against relocation and, as a result, placed the burden of proof solely on the mother.

Some courts continue to disfavor relocation. *See, e.g., Rowland v. Kingman*, 629 A.2d 613 (Me. 1993) (relocation constitutes a substantial change of circumstances). Others put the burden of proof on the relocating parent to demonstrate that relocation is in the child's best interest. *Brown v. Brown*, 621 N.W.2d 70 (Neb. 2000) (same); *Stout v. Stout*, 560 N.W.2d 903, 913 (N.D.1997) (same). Illinois puts the burden of proof on the relocating parent by statute. ILL. STAT. ANN. ch. 750 para. 5/ 609. In *In re Marriage of Collingbourne* 791 N.E.2d 532 (Ill. 2003), the Illinois Supreme Court upheld the trial court's grant of the mother's petition to relocate, emphasizing that the court should weigh benefits of the relocation to the custodial parents that indirectly benefited the child.

Some states address part of the issue procedurally by imposing notification requirements on a custodial parent who is contemplating a move. *See, e.g.,* MD. CODE ANN., FAM. L. ART. § 9-106 (allowing court to require advance notification of 90 days or more where a custodial parent plans to move, except where parent or child had been subject to abuse by other parent or for other good cause); ME. REV. STAT.

ANN., title 19-A, § 1653(14) (notice of relocation by one parent with child must be provided to other parent no less than 30 days prior to move, unless relocation to occur in less than 30 days; partial exception permissible if notice may cause danger to relocating parent or child).

The *ALI Principles* allow parents with primary custody freedom to relocate if they act in good faith and for a valid purpose; this stance is described as consistent with the "modern view" that a "primary purpose" of divorce is "to allow each party to go his or her way." *Principles* § 2.17, cmt. The *Principles* direct that courts should recognize the following as valid purposes: To be closer to family; to address health problems; to protect the child or other family members from harm; to pursue an employment or educational opportunity; to be with a spouse or domestic partner; or to significantly improve the family's quality of life. The relocating parent must prove that other purposes are valid.

4. *Joint Custody and Relocation.* Not surprisingly, parents with joint physical custody are generally subject to a restrictive relocation rule. Thus, under the *ALI Principles*, where neither parent has been exercising a clear majority of custodial responsibility, the court simply resolves the relocation dispute under the best interest standard, considering all relevant factors including the benefits and disruptive effects of the relocation. § 2.17(4)(c). Similarly, a de novo determination of custody is required for California couples with joint physical custody where one parent plans to relocate. *Niko v. Foreman*, 50 Cal. Rptr. 3d 398 (App. Ct. 2006); CAL. FAM. CODE § 30887. Other states also distinguish sole and joint custody cases. In allocating the burden of proof, for example, the Wisconsin statute distinguishes circumstances in which the relocating parent has custody "for the greater period of time" (burden on party resisting move) from circumstances in which the parents have "substantially equal periods of physical" custody (burden of proof on party seeking move). *See* WIS. STAT. ANN. § 767.481 (Supp.). In Tennessee, where parents spend "substantially equal" amounts of time with the child, relocation is determined based on the best interests of the child; otherwise, relocation petitions are to be granted in most cases. Tenn. Code Ann. §§ 36-6-108(c) & (d). In Nevada, a joint custody order is not a bar to relocation; instead, the usual relocation factors apply (the extent to which relocation improved the quality of life for parent and child, the motives of each parent, opportunities for reasonable visitation, etc.). *McGuinness v. McGuinness*, 970 P.2d 1074 (Nev. 1998). The court in *McGuiness* chided trial courts for "chain[ing] custodial parents, most often women, to the state of Nevada." *Id.* at 1079. The dissenting justice pointed out that the court's holding was in tension with its previously announced preference for joint custody. Whether each parent is exercising the parenting time awarded by the court may be an issue. The Maccoby-Mnookin study of divorced California families found that in about half of those families with joint physical custody orders, one parent (usually the mother) had primary *de facto* custody. *See* Section A[2], *supra*.

5. *High Conflict Families.* The parents in *LaMusga* engaged in frequent litigation over custody, visitation and relocation, expressed substantial anger toward one another, and had a history of pushing and shoving one another. They continue to litigate to this day about visitation. *See* Case MSD95-01136, Contra County, CA, Superior Court, http://icms.cc-courts.org. Relocation in a family that is in high conflict both from a litigation and a personal perspective, may be beneficial for the child. *See* Note 10, Section C[1], *supra* Is the test adopted in *LaMusga* likely to lead to relocation being approved in other high conflict families?

6. *Critiques and Alternatives.* A large literature has examined relocation issues, much of it sympathetic to relocating parents. *See, e.g.*, Carol S. Bruch & Janet M. Bowermaster, *The Relocation of Children and Custodial Parents: Public Policy Past and Present*, 30 FAM L. Q. 245 (1996). These authors provide a comprehensive description of the legal trend toward liberalized relocation rules and argue that this trend is justified because the relationship between the child and the custodial parent is central to the child's well-being. They view restrictive rules as providing "inappropriate opportunities for abuses of power by former partners" and "doing a great disservice to children and their primary caretakers." *Id.* at 246. Because custodial parents are most often women, some critics have been concerned about how restrictive relocation rules have a disparate impact upon women. For example, Professor Glennon, argues that the economic consequences of doctrines restricting relocation are particularly harsh on custodial mothers, whose economic situation is typically worse than that of fathers, often in large measure because of their larger share of parental responsibility during and after the marriage. Nonetheless, while courts attempt to be attentive to the emotional harms that parents may suffer because of a relocation, no attempt is made to address the economic harm. Theresa Glennon, *Still Partners? Examining the Consequences of Post-Dissolution Parenting*, 41 Fam. L. Q. 105 (2007). Professor Weiner argues that the interests of mothers are subordinated to those of fathers when, in relocation disputes, courts fail to consider whether the noncustodial parent could move to the child's new location. Merle H. Weiner, *Inertia and Inequality: Reconceptualizing Disputes Over Parental Relocation*, 40 U. C. DAVIS L. REV. 1747 (2007). Still other commentators opposed to restrictive relocation rules have focused on the right-to-travel issue. *See, e.g.*, Paula M. Raines, *Joint Custody and the Right to Travel: Legal and Psychological Implications*, 24 J. FAM. L. 625 (1985–86). Some observers argue for more a restrictive relocation policy, or at least one that allows greater consideration of the child's interest in unchanged relationships with both parents. *See, e.g.*, Warshak, Note 1, *supra*; Braver, Ellman & Fabricus, Note 1, *supra*; Frank G. Adams, *Child Custody and Parent Relocations: Loving Your Children From a Distance*, 33 DUQ. L. REV. 143 (1994) (arguing greater weight should be given to the importance of the noncustodial parent-child relationship).

F. DISPUTES BETWEEN PARENTS AND NON-PARENTS

[1] Grandparent Visitation

TROXEL v. GRANVILLE
United States Supreme Court
530 U.S. 57 (2000)

JUSTICE O'CONNOR announced the judgment of the Court and delivered an opinion, in which THE CHIEF JUSTICE, JUSTICE GINSBURG, and JUSTICE BREYER join.

. . .

Tommie Granville and Brad Troxel shared a relationship that ended in June 1991. The two never married, but they had two daughters, Isabelle and Natalie. Jenifer and Gary Troxel are Brad's parents, and thus the paternal grandparents of Isabelle and Natalie. After Tommie and Brad separated in 1991, Brad lived with his parents and regularly brought his daughters to his parents' home for weekend visitation. Brad committed suicide in May 1993. Although the Troxels at first continued to see Isabelle and Natalie on a regular basis after their son's death, Tommie Granville informed the Troxels in October 1993 that she wished to limit their visitation with her daughters to one short visit per month.

In December 1993, the Troxels commenced the present action by filing . . . a petition to obtain visitation rights with Isabelle and Natalie. The Troxels filed their petition under . . . Wash. Rev. Code 26.10.160(3) (1994) . . . Section 26.10.160(3) provides: "Any person may petition the court for visitation rights at any time including, but not limited to, custody proceedings. The court may order visitation rights for any person when visitation may serve the best interest of the child whether or not there has been any change of circumstances." At trial, the Troxels requested two weekends of overnight visitation per month and two weeks of visitation each summer. Granville did not oppose visitation altogether, but instead asked the court to order one day of visitation per month with no overnight stay. In 1995, the Superior Court issued an oral ruling and entered a visitation decree ordering visitation one weekend per month, one week during the summer, and four hours on both of the petitioning grandparents' birthdays. . . .

[The Washington Court of Appeals reversed the visitation order and dismissed the Troxels' petition on statutory grounds. 940 P.2d 698 (Wash. Ct. App. 1997). The Washington Supreme Court affirmed, 969 P.2d 21 (Wash. 1998), rejecting the statutory ground, but agreeing with the lower court that the Troxels could not obtain visitation. During the appeal process, Granville married and her husband adopted the children.]

The [Washington Supreme] [C]ourt rested its decision on the Federal Constitution, holding that § 26.10.160(3) unconstitutionally infringes on the fundamental right of parents to rear their children. . . .

We granted certiorari, and now affirm the judgment. . . .

The demographic changes of the past century make it difficult to speak of an average American family. . . . While many children may have two married parents and grandparents who visit regularly, many other children are raised in single-parent households. In 1996, children living with only one parent accounted for 28 percent of all children under age 18 in the United States. . . . Understandably, in these single-parent households, persons outside the nuclear family are called upon with increasing frequency to assist in the everyday tasks of child rearing. In many cases, grandparents play an important role. . . .

The nationwide enactment of nonparental visitation statutes is assuredly due, in some part, to the States' recognition of these changing realities of the American family. Because grandparents and other relatives undertake duties of a parental nature in many households, States have sought to ensure the welfare of the children therein by protecting the relationships those children form with such third parties. The States' nonparental visitation statutes are further supported by a recognition . . . that children should have the opportunity to benefit from relationships with . . . their grandparents. The extension of statutory rights in this area to persons other than a child's parents, however, comes with an obvious cost. For example, the State's recognition of an independent third-party interest in a child can place a substantial burden on the traditional parent-child relationship. . . .

The Fourteenth Amendment provides that no State shall "deprive any person of life, liberty, or property, without due process of law." . . . The Clause . . . includes a substantive component that "provides heightened protection against government interference with certain fundamental rights and liberty interests."

The liberty interest at issue in this case — the interest of parents in the care, custody, and control of their children — is perhaps the oldest of the fundamental liberty interests recognized by this Court. . . . *Meyer v. Nebraska*, 262 U.S. 390 (1923) . . . *Pierce v. Society of Sisters*, . . . *Stanley v. Illinois*, . . . *Wisconsin v. Yoder*, . . . *Quilloin v. Walcott*, . . . *Parham v. J. R.*, . . . *Santosky v. Kramer*. . . .

Section 26.10.160(3), as applied to Granville and her family in this case, unconstitutionally infringes on that fundamental parental right. The Washington nonparental visitation statute is breathtakingly broad. According to the statute's text, "*[a]ny person* may petition the court for visitation rights *at any time*," and the court may grant such visitation rights whenever "visitation may serve *the best interest of the child*." § 26.10.160(3) (emphases added). That language effectively permits any third party seeking visitation to subject any decision by a parent concerning visitation of the parent's children to state-court review . . . [in which] a parent's decision that visitation would not be in the child's best interest is accorded no deference. Section 26.10.160(3) contains no requirement that a court accord the parent's decision any presumption of validity or any weight whatsoever. . . . Should the judge disagree with the parent's estimation of the child's best interests, the judge's view necessarily prevails. Thus, in practical effect, in the State of Washington a court can disregard and overturn any decision by a fit custodial parent concerning visitation whenever a third party affected by the decision files a visitation petition, based solely on the judge's determination of the child's best interests. The Washington Supreme Court had the opportunity to give § 26.10.160(3) a narrower reading, but it declined to do so. . . .

Turning to the facts of this case, the record reveals that the Superior Court's order was based on precisely the type of mere disagreement we have just described and nothing more. The Superior Court's order was not founded on any special factors that might justify the State's interference with Granville's fundamental right to make decisions concerning the rearing of her two daughters. . . . [T]he combination of several factors here compels our conclusion that Sect. 26.10160(3), as applied, exceeded the demands of the Due Process Clause. . . .

First, the Troxels did not allege, and no court has found, that Granville was an unfit parent. That aspect of the case is important, for there is a presumption that fit parents act in the best interests of their children. As this Court explained in Parham:

> "[O]ur constitutional system long ago rejected any notion that a child is the mere creature of the State and, on the contrary, asserted that parents generally have the right, coupled with the high duty, to recognize and prepare [their children] for additional obligations. . . . [I]t has recognized that natural bonds of affection lead parents to act in the best interests of their children." 442 U.S., at 602.

Accordingly, so long as a parent adequately cares for his or her children (*i.e.*, is fit), there will normally be no reason for the State to inject itself into the private realm of the family to further question the ability of that parent to make the best decisions concerning the rearing of that parent's children. . . .

The problem here is not that the Washington Superior Court intervened, but that when it did so, it gave no special weight at all to Granville's determination of her daughters' best interests. More importantly, it appears that the Superior Court applied exactly the opposite presumption. . . .

The judge's comments suggest that he presumed the grandparents' request should be granted unless the children would be "impact[ed] adversely." In effect, the judge placed on Granville, the fit custodial parent, the burden of *disproving* that visitation would be in the best interest of her daughters. . . .

The decisional framework employed by the Superior Court directly contravened the traditional presumption that a fit parent will act in the best interest of his or her child. In that respect, the court's presumption failed to provide any protection for Granville's fundamental constitutional right to make decisions concerning the rearing of her own daughters. . . . In an ideal world, parents might always seek to cultivate the bonds between grandparents and their grandchildren. Needless to say, however, our world is far from perfect, and in it the decision whether such an intergenerational relationship would be beneficial in any specific case is for the parent to make in the first instance. And, if a fit parent's decision of the kind at issue here becomes subject to judicial review, the court must accord at least some special weight to the parent's own determination. Finally, we note that there is no allegation that Granville ever sought to cut off visitation entirely. . . . Granville did not oppose visitation but instead asked that the duration of any visitation order be shorter than that requested by the Troxels. . . . The Superior Court gave no weight to Granville's having assented to visitation even before the filing of any visitation petition or subsequent court intervention. . . . Significantly, many other States expressly provide by statute that courts may not award visitation unless a parent has denied (or unreasonably denied) visitation to the concerned third party. *See, e.g.* . . . ORE. REV. STAT. § 109.121(1)(a)(B) (court may award visitation if the "custodian of the child has denied the grandparent reasonable opportunity to visit the child"). . . .

Considered together with the Superior Court's reasons for awarding visitation to the Troxels, the combination of these factors demonstrates that the visitation order in this case was an unconstitutional infringement on Granville's fundamental right to make decisions concerning the care, custody, and control of her two daughters. The Washington Superior Court failed to accord the determination of Granville, a fit custodial parent, any material weight. In fact, the Superior Court made only two formal findings in support of its visitation order. First, the Troxels "are part of a large, central, loving family, all located in this area, and the [Troxels] can provide opportunities for the children in the areas of cousins and music." App. 70a. Second, "[t]he children would be benefitted from spending quality time with the [Troxels], provided that that time is balanced with time with the childrens' [sic] nuclear family." *Ibid.* These slender findings . . . show that this case involves nothing more than a simple disagreement between the Washington Superior Court and Granville concerning her children's best interests. . . . As we have explained, the Due Process Clause does not permit a State to infringe on the fundamental right of parents to make childrearing decisions simply because a state judge believes a "better" decision could be made. . . . Accordingly, we hold that § 26.10.160(3), as applied in this case, is unconstitutional.

Because we rest our decision on the sweeping breadth of § 26.10.160(3) and the application of that broad, unlimited power in this case, we do not consider the primary constitutional question passed on by the Washington Supreme Court — whether the Due Process Clause requires all nonparental visitation statutes to include a showing of harm or potential harm to the child as a condition precedent to granting visitation. We do not, and need not, define today the precise scope of the parental due process right in the visitation context. . . . Because much state-court adjudication in this context occurs on a case-by-case basis, we would be hesitant to hold that specific nonparental visitation statutes violate the Due Process Clause as a *per se* matter. . . .

There is . . . no reason to remand the case for further proceedings in the Washington Supreme Court. . . . [I]t is apparent that the entry of the visitation order in this case violated the Constitution. We should say so now, without forcing the parties into additional litigation that would further burden Granville's parental right. We therefore hold that the application of § 26.10.160(3) to Granville and her family violated her due process right to make decisions concerning the care, custody, and control of her daughters.

Accordingly, the judgment of the Washington Supreme Court is affirmed.

JUSTICE SOUTER, concurring in the judgment.

I concur in the judgment affirming the decision of the Supreme Court of Washington, whose facial invalidation of its own state statute is consistent with this Court's prior cases addressing the substantive interests at stake. I would say no more. . . .

[T]he state court authoritatively read [the statutory] provision as placing hardly any limit on a court's discretion to award visitation rights. As the court understood it, the specific best-interests provision in the statute would allow a court to award visitation whenever it thought it could make a better decision than a child's parent had done. . . .

JUSTICE THOMAS, concurring in the judgment.

 . . . . [I] agree with the plurality that this Court's recognition of a fundamental right of parents to direct the upbringing of their children resolves this case. . . . The opinions of the plurality, Justice KENNEDY, and Justice SOUTER recognize such a right, but curiously none of them articulates the appropriate standard of review. I would apply strict scrutiny to infringements of fundamental rights. Here, the State of Washington lacks even a legitimate governmental interest — to say nothing of a compelling one — in second-guessing a fit parent's decision regarding visitation with third parties. On this basis, I would affirm the judgment below.

JUSTICE STEVENS, dissenting.

 . . . . The second key aspect of the Washington Supreme Court's holding — that the Federal Constitution requires a showing of actual or potential "harm" to the child before a court may order visitation continued over a parent's objections — finds no support in this Court's case law. While, as the Court recognizes, the Federal Constitution certainly protects the parent-child relationship from arbitrary impairment by the State, we have never held that the parent's liberty interest in this relationship is so inflexible as to establish a rigid constitutional shield, protecting every arbitrary parental decision from any challenge absent a threshold finding of harm. The presumption that parental decisions generally serve the best interests of their children is sound, and clearly in the normal case the parent's interest is paramount. But even a fit parent is capable of treating a child like a mere possession.

Cases like this do not present a bipolar struggle between the parents and the State over who has final authority to determine what is in a child's best interests. There is at a minimum a third individual, whose interests are implicated in every case to which the statute applies — the child.

 . . . .

A parent's rights with respect to her child have thus never been regarded as absolute, but rather are limited by the existence of an actual, developed relationship with a child, and are tied to the presence or absence of some embodiment of family. These limitations have arisen, not simply out of the definition of parenthood itself, but because of this Court's assumption that a parent's interests in a child must be balanced against the State's long-recognized interests as *parens patriae*, see, *e.g.*, . . . *Prince v. Massachusetts*, 321 U.S. 158, 166 (1944), and, critically, the child's own complementary interest in preserving relationships that serve her welfare and protection, *Santosky*, 455 U.S., at 760.

While this Court has not yet had occasion to elucidate the nature of a child's liberty interests in preserving established familial or family-like bonds, it seems to me extremely likely that, to the extent parents and families have fundamental liberty interests in preserving such intimate relationships, so, too, do children have these interests, and so, too, must their interests be balanced in the equation. At a minimum, our prior cases recognizing that children are, generally speaking, constitutionally protected actors require that this Court reject any suggestion that when it comes to parental rights, children are so much chattel. The constitutional protection against arbitrary state interference with parental rights should not be extended to prevent the States from protecting children against the arbitrary exercise of parental authority that is not in fact motivated by an interest in the welfare of the child.

This is not, of course, to suggest that a child's liberty interest in maintaining contact with a particular individual is to be treated invariably as on a par with that child's parents' contrary interests. Because our substantive due process case law includes a strong presumption that a parent will act in the best interest of her child, it would be necessary, were the state appellate courts actually to confront a challenge to the statute as applied, to consider whether the trial court's assessment of the "best interest of the child" incorporated that presumption. Neither would I decide whether the trial court applied Washington's statute in a constitutional way in this case. . . . For the purpose of a facial challenge like this, I think it safe to assume that trial judges usually give great deference to parents' wishes, and I am not persuaded otherwise here.

But presumptions notwithstanding, we should recognize that there may be circumstances in which a child has a stronger interest at stake than mere protection from serious harm caused by the termination of visitation by a "person" other than a parent. The almost infinite variety of family relationships that pervade our ever-changing society strongly counsel against the creation by this Court of a constitutional rule that treats a biological parent's liberty interest in the care and supervision of her child as an isolated right that may be exercised arbitrarily. It is indisputably the business of the States, rather than a federal court employing a national standard, to assess in the first instance the relative importance of the conflicting interests that give rise to disputes such as this. Far from guaranteeing that parents' interests will be trammeled in the sweep of cases arising under the statute, the Washington law merely gives an individual — with whom a child may have an established relationship — the procedural right to ask the State to act as arbiter, through the entirely well-known best-interests standard, between the parent's protected interests and the child's. It seems clear to me that the Due Process Clause of the Fourteenth Amendment leaves room for States to consider the impact on a child of possibly arbitrary parental decisions that neither serve nor are motivated by the best interests of the child. . . .

Justice SCALIA, dissenting.

. . . . Only three holdings of this Court rest in whole or in part upon a substantive constitutional right of parents to direct the upbringing of their children — two of them from an era rich in substantive due process holdings that have since been repudiated. *See Meyer v. Nebraska.* . . . ; *Pierce v. Society of Sisters*; *Wisconsin v. Yoder,*. . . . The sheer diversity of today's opinions persuades me that the theory of unenumerated parental rights underlying these three cases has small claim to *stare decisis* protection. . . . While I would not now overrule those earlier cases (that has not been urged), neither would I extend the theory upon which they rested to this new context. . . .

[Dissenting opinion by Justice KENNEDY omitted.]

NOTES

1. ***Grandparents Visitation Rights — The Background.*** In the years before the Supreme Court decided *Troxel*, most states enacted statutes giving grandparents and, to a lesser extent, other non-parents, standing to petition for visitation, over the objection of custodial parents. The traditional common-law rule gave grandparents no legal right to continue their relationship with their grandchildren when their own child (the grandchild's parent) died, divorced, or had her parental rights terminated. This position was compatible with the general stance that the custodial parent is entitled to exclusive custody against the entire world, a right which includes the authority to decide who (including relatives) can associate with the child. *See, e.g., Thomas v. Pickard*, 195 S.E.2d 339 (N.C. App. 1973); *Odell v. Lutz*, 78 Cal. App. 2d 104, 177 P.2d 628 (1947). Largely through lobbying efforts by grandparent groups, state legislatures across the country enacted statutes authorizing courts to order grandparent visitation under some circumstances. In part, this sweeping legal reform was likely driven by a view that both children and grandparents have a special interest in this unique relationship that justifies trumping parental authority. Moreover, legislatures, to some extent, were responding to particularly compelling claims by grandparents who had cared for their grandchildren as *de facto* parents, or those whose relationships with grandchildren were threatened when their own children died (as happened in *Troxel*) or lost parental rights. Some statutes were limited to these compelling cases. *See e.g.* MINN. STAT. ANN. § 257C.08 (subd. 3) (only grandparent who lived with child for more than 12 months had standing). The sweeping Washington statute at issue in *Troxel*, of course, contained none of these limits, allowing the trial judge to order visitation in favor any third party. Subsequent to *Troxel*, courts generally upheld narrower statutes and some legislatures revised and limited standing along these lines. For a survey of the judicial and legislative response to *Troxel*, see Notes 2 and 3, *infra*.

Grandparent visitation has always had its critics, despite its popularity in the period before *Troxel*. Many observers have challenged the wisdom of courts' overriding the decisions of responsible custodial parents who may have good reasons not to allow the contact. The issue, of course, is not whether it is generally beneficial to children to have contact with their grandparents, but whether courts or parents should make that decision. Moreover, this kind of intervention can also be challenged on fairness grounds. Unlike non-custodial parents, most grandparents (like the Troxels) have never lived with the children or taken responsibility for their upbringing — and they have no support obligation. *See* Elizabeth S. Scott, *Parental Autonomy and Children's Welfare*, 11 Wm & M. Bill of Rights J. 1071 (2003); Karen Czapanskiy, *Grandparents, Parents and Grandchildren: Making a Case for Interdependency in Law*, 26 U. Conn. L. Rev. 1315 (1994).

Even before *Troxel*, some lower courts either limited or overturned broadly written grandparent visitation statutes, and some found that even narrower formulations violated parental autonomy. Particularly, courts found statutory provisions authorizing visitation over the objection of parents in an intact family (including the grandparent's own child) to be unconstitutional, or they simply refused to apply general statutory authorization of grandparent visitation to this kind of case. *See, e.g., Brooks v. Parkerson*, 454 S.E.2d 769 (Ga. 1995) (holding statute permitting visitation in intact families to be unconstitutional state interference in family autonomy, unless harm to child is shown). In 1996, the Georgia legislature amended the statute to require that visitation be ordered only where denial resulted in harm to the child. *See* Ga. Code Ann. § 19-7-3; *see also Herbst v. Sayre*, 971 P.2d 395 (Okla. 1998) (statute unconstitutional as applied to parents in an intact family, absent demonstrable harm to the child or parental unfitness); *Williams v. Williams*, 501 S.E.2d 417 (Va. 1998) (same).

2. Troxel *and its Aftermath* — *The Judicial Response.*   The broadly written Washington statute gave trial court authority to grant visitation to any third party whenever doing so was in the child's best interests. Yet Justice O'Connor's plurality opinion did not find the statute to be unconstitutional *on its face*, but only as applied in the *Troxel* case itself. Given the extraordinary breadth of the Washington statute, it would seem that every contemporary statute would pass facial constitutional muster. It is therefore surprising perhaps that, after *Troxel* a number of lower courts have ruled various state provisions facially unconstitutional. Michigan's highest court did so by announcing that the Supreme Court in fact had found the Washington statute to be unconstitutional despite the failure of the O'Connor plurality to acknowledge this directly. *DeRose v. DeRose*, 666 N.W.2d 636 (Mich. 2003). Because the Michigan statute also failed to require deference to a fit parent's objection to visitation, the state court found it facially unconstitutional. The Illinois Supreme Court struck down that state's statute because it put non-parent and parent on equal footing, and contravened the presumption that parents are fit and act in the best interest of their children. In language far broader than *Troxel*, the court stated, "A fit parent's constitutionally protected liberty interest to direct the care, custody and control of his or her children mandates that parents — not judges — should be the ones to decide with whom their children will and will not associate." *Wickham v. Byrne*, 769 N.E.2d 1 (Ill. 2002); *see also Marriage of Howard*, 661 N.W.3d 183 (Iowa 2003) (provision permitting visitation petition by grandparent only when parents are divorced is unconstitutional on face); *Doe v. Doe*, 172 P.3d 1067 (Haw. 2007) (applying a strict scrutiny standard, court found that, in the absence of a "harm to the child" standard, the grandparent visitation statute, which allowed visitation order in best interests of the child, was unconstitutional on its face); *cf. Linder v. Linder*, 72 S.W.3d 841 (Ark. 2002) (statute authorizing visitation over parents' objection categorically unconstitutional as applied to fit parents; but not as applied to an entity (such as state agency) without fundamental interest). *Linder* and *Doe* applied strict scrutiny, a position advocated only by Justice Thomas in *Troxel*, and found grandparent visitation to be a major intrusion on the fundamental right of parents to rear their children.

The O'Connor plurality expressly left undecided the question of whether the Constitution required a showing that denial of visitation was harmful to the child before the court could justify ordering visitation. The Connecticut Supreme Court prescribed such a harm requirement. *Roth v. Weston*, 789 A.2d 431 (Conn. 2002) (party seeking visitation must have a parent-like relationship with the child and demonstrate by clear and convincing evidence that denial of visitation would cause significant harm to the child, of a kind that is contemplated by the neglect/dependency statute); *see also Neal v. Lee* 14 P.3d 547 (Okla. 2000) (unless parent is unfit, court should order grandparent visitation only on the basis of clear and convincing evidence that children would suffer harm without visitation); *Scott v. Scott*, 80 S.W.3d 447 (Ky. Ct. App. 2002).

Other courts have explicitly rejected the claim that a showing of harm to the child was constitutionally required before visitation can be ordered over a parent's objections. *Kan. Dep't of Soc. and Rehab. Serv. v. Paillet*, 16 P.3d 962 (Kan. 2001) (petitioner must rebut presumption that a fit parent acts in child's best interest, by showing that visitation is in child's best interest); *Zeman v. Stanford*, 789 So. 2d 798 (Miss. 2001) (best interest of child is paramount); *State ex. rel. Brandon L. v. Moats*, 551 S.E.2d 674 (W. Va. 2001) (court must find visitation is in child's best interest and that it represents no substantial interference with parental authority); *Rideout v. Riendeau*, 761 A.2d 291 (Me. 2000) (showing of parent-like relationship with child or harm from denial of visitation are alternative means of showing compelling state interest).

Would the trial judge's order in *Troxel* have been constitutional if made pursuant to a more narrow statute? For example, a statute that allows the court to grant visitation only to grandparents, and only those whose own child had died, would be much narrower than the Washington statute. However, unless the judge gave some special deference to the parental decision, under Justice O'Connor's analysis the constitutional flaw would remain. The plurality opinion, however, offers little guidance about acceptable statutory formulations. Justice O'Connor recognizes that allowing the parent's decision to be overruled only if harm to the child is shown would be sufficient, but does not tell us whether this formulation is necessary.

In the face of this these ambiguities, state courts have wrestled, post-*Troxel*, with custody decisions rendered under narrower statutes. These statutes are interpreted to give special weight to the parents' decision and/or restrict visitation that substantially interferes with the parent-child relationship. Thus, in a case involving a grandmother who had been a *de facto* parent to the child, the Supreme Court of Maine upheld a visitation order under a statute that includes a threshold standing requirement that the grandparent must have a sufficient existing relationship with the child; the statute then directs the court to consider the parent's objection and order visitation only if it does not significantly interfere with the parent-child relationship. *Rideout v. Riendeau, supra.* Some grandparent visitation statutes have been upheld on the basis of narrowing interpretations, although trial courts are left with considerable discretion. The Mississippi Supreme Court approved a statute that restricts petitioners seeking visitation to grandparents (unlike *Troxel*), but gives courts rather broad authority to order visitation. *Zeman v. Stanford*, 789 So. 2d. 798 (Miss. 2001). The court emphasized that the statute had been interpreted earlier to require courts to analyze numerous factors in deciding whether visitation is in the child's best interest, including that the grandparent would not interfere with the parents' child rearing. The court minimized the burden to parents' interests imposed by court-ordered grandparent visitation, and stressed that the child's best interest is paramount. *See also Galjour v. Harris*, 795 So. 2d 350 (La. 2001) (statute applying best interest standard upheld because it was limited to a narrow category of petitioners [parents of deceased, absent or noncustodial parents]); *Kan. Dep't of Soc. and Rehab. Serv. v. Paillet*, *supra* (statute that requires "substantial relationship" and places burden on petitioner to demonstrate that visitation is in the child's best interest is upheld, although unconstitutionally applied); *State ex. rel. Brandon L. v. Moats*, *supra* (statute upheld; requires finding that visitation does not substantially interfere with the parent-child relationship; best interest standard identifies twelve factors to guide court); *Blixt v. Blixt*, 774 N.E.2d 1052 (Mass. 2002) (statute limiting grandparent visitation to families in which parents do not reside together upheld against facial equal protection challenge); *Koshko v. Haining*, 921 A.2d 171 (Md. 2007) (upholding grandparent visitation statute as constitutional on its face, once statute construed as requiring a presumption that parental decision regarding visitation is correct; finding statute as applied unconstitutional where married parents opposed visitation by maternal grandparents and no threshold finding of parental unfitness or exceptional circumstances was made); *E.S. v. P.D.*, 863 N.E.2d 100 (N.Y. 2007) (upholding grandparent visitation statute as constitutional on its face, as construed to include safeguards protecting parental rights; finding statute constitutional as applied where grandparent, with approval of parent, lived in home of parents and child and cared for the child before and after the death of the child's other parent).

3. *Post*-Troxel *Statutory Reform.* In response to *Troxel*, many state legislatures reexamined their grandparent visitation statutes, and narrowed judicial authority to order visitation over parental objection. *See, e.g.*, Ore. Rev. Stat. § 109.119 (permitting any person having a parent-child relationship with a child to be awarded custody, guardianship, or rights of visitation if it is in the child's best interests, but requiring the petitioning party to overcome by clear and convincing evidence the presumption that the legal parent acts in the best interest of the child); S.D. Codified Laws § 25-4-52 (permitting grandparent visitation if it would be in the best interests of the child, and either the visitation would not significantly interfere with the parent-child relationship, or the parent or custodian of the child has unreasonably denied the grandparent reasonable opportunity to visit the child); Tenn. Code Ann. § 36-6-306 (identifying conditions which necessitate a hearing when a grandparent petitions for visitation, and providing that grandparent visitation may be ordered upon a finding of danger of substantial harm to the child of denial, and a finding that such visitation would be in the child's best interests); Utah Code Ann. § 30-5-2 (creating a rebuttable presumption that the parent's decision as to grandparent visitation is in the best interests of the child, and permitting courts to consider the child's wishes in regard to visitation). *See generally* Michael K. Goldberg, *A Survey of the Fifty States' Grandparent Visitation Statutes*, 10 MARQ. ELDER'S ADVISOR 245 (2009) (reviewing grandparent visitation under statutes adopted or amended since *Troxel*).

Under the *ALI Principles*, grandparents would have standing to seek a portion of custodial responsibility only if they qualify as *de facto* parents or parents by estoppel, *i.e.*, they must have resided with the child and performed many parenting functions with the parent's acquiescence. § 2.03(1). Because the *Principles* abolish the conventional "visitation" category, and limit custodial access to adults who have lived with and cared for the child, most grandparents would lack standing.

4. ***Commentary on* Troxel.** Much has been written about *Troxel* and its implications. *See, e.g.*, Emily Buss, *Adrift in the Middle: Parental Rights After* Troxel v. Granville, 2000 SUP. CT. REV. 279 (2000); Stephen G. Gilles, *Parental (and Grandparental) Rights after* Troxel, 9 SUP. CT. ECON. REV. 69 (2001); Emily Buss, *"Parental" Rights*, 88 VA. L. REV. 635 (2002) (criticizing grandparent visitation, arguing that the Constitution grants strong protection to parental child rearing rights, but weaker protection to any individual's claim to parental identity); Janet L. Dolgin, *The Constitution as Family Arbiter: A Moral in the Mess?*, 102 COLUM. L. REV. 337 (2002) (arguing that constitutional jurisprudence is inadequate to the task of determining the proper scope of familial relationships, because constitutional law presumes individual autonomy); Solangel Maldonado, *When Father (or Mother) Doesn't Know Best: Quasi-Parents and Parental Deference After* Troxel v. Granville, 88 IOWA L. REV. 865 (2003) (arguing that "quasi-parents" should have greater rights to third-party visitation over parental objection than other third parties, including grandparents; category includes parties who have established a significant emotional bond with the child and participated in the rearing of the child). A symposium on *Troxel* in 32 RUTGERS LAW JOURNAL 695 (2001) includes articles by Earl M. Maltz, David Meyer, Margaret Brinig, Sally Goldfarb, and Nancy Polikoff.

PROBLEM

Problem 6-16. Sam and Ilsa Jameson, who lived in San Francisco, were very fond of their grandchildren, Ann and Lois, who lived in Canton, Ohio, with the Jameson's daughter Ariel, and her husband Mark. The Jamesons saw the family twice a year at Christmas and in the summer. The visits were memorable experiences for both grandparents and grandchildren. The children loved being with their grandparents; Sam and Ilsa took them to museums, theater performances and did other special things with them. As the children got older, they developed a close bond with their grandparents. However, the visits were always a little stressful because Sam and Ilsa were quite critical of Ariel and Mark's parenting. They felt that Mark particularly let the children do whatever they wanted to do, never disciplined them, and allowed them to live on junk food. Although Sam and Ilsa tried to keep their views to themselves, they sometimes could not restrain themselves from expressing their concern. In 2000, when Ann was 10 years old and Lois was 8, Ariel died in a car accident. After her death, Mark was less than eager for the Jamesons to visit with their grandchildren. During one tense visit in 2001, the Jamesons had an argument with Mark over how much unmonitored TV the children were watching. Mark said he thought it would be better for the children if they didn't see their grandparents. The next time the Jamesons suggested a visit, Mark refused. Sam and Ilsa petition for visitation with the children. How should the court respond?

[2]   Custody Disputes Between Legal and De Facto Parents

V.C. v. M.J.B.
New Jersey Supreme Court
748 A.2d 539 (2000)

LONG, J.

In this case, we are called on to determine what legal standard applies to a third party's claim to joint custody and visitation of her former domestic partner's biological children, with whom she lived in a familial setting and in respect of whom she claims to have functioned as a psychological parent. Although the case arises in the context of a lesbian couple, the standard we enunciate is applicable to all persons who have willingly, and with the approval of the legal parent, undertaken the duties of a parent to a child not related by blood or adoption.

V.C. and M.J.B., who are lesbians, met in 1992 and began dating on July 4, 1993. On July 9, 1993, M.J.B. went to see a fertility specialist to begin artificial insemination procedures. . . .

According to V.C., early in their relationship, the two discussed having children. However, V.C. did not become aware of M.J.B.'s visits with the specialist and her decision to have a baby by artificial insemination until September 1993. . . .

During M.J.B.'s pregnancy, both M.J.B. and V.C. prepared for the birth of the twins by attending pre-natal and Lamaze classes. . . .

The children were born on September 29, 1994. V.C. took M.J.B. to the hospital and she was present in the delivery room at the birth of the children. . . . After the children were born, M.J.B. took a three-month maternity leave and V.C. took a three-week vacation.

The parties opened joint bank accounts for their household expenses, and prepared wills, powers of attorney, and named each other as the beneficiary for their respective life insurance policies. At some point, [they] also opened savings accounts for the children, and named V.C. as custodian for one account and M.J.B. as custodian for the other.

The parties also decided to have the children call M.J.B. "Mommy" and V.C. "Meema." M.J.B. conceded that she referred to V.C. as a "mother" of the children. . . . M.J.B. encouraged a relationship between V.C. and the children and sought to create a "happy, cohesive environment for the children." M.J.B. admitted that, when the parties' relationship was intact, she sometimes thought of the four of them as a family. However, although M.J.B. sometimes considered the children "theirs," other times she considered them "hers".

M.J.B. agreed that both parties cared for the children but insisted that she made substantive decisions regarding their lives. . . . V.C. countered that she was equally involved in all decision-making regarding the children. Specifically, V.C. claimed that she participated in choosing a day care center for the children, and it is clear that M.J.B. brought V.C. to visit the center she selected prior to making a final decision.

M.J.B. acknowledged that V.C. assumed substantial responsibility for the children, but maintained that V.C. was a mere helper and not a co-parent. However, according to V.C., she acted as a co-parent to the children and had equal parenting responsibility. Indeed, M.J.B. listed V.C. as the "other mother" on the children's pediatrician and day care registration forms. M.J.B. also gave V.C. medical power of attorney over the children.

Together the parties purchased a home in February 1995. Later that year, . . . [they] held a commitment ceremony where they were "married."

. . . . V.C., M.J.B. and the twins attended family functions, holidays, and birthdays. . . . V.C. claimed that the children were very close to V.C.'s family. Apparently, the children referred to S.D. [V.C.'s mother] as "Grandma," and to V.C.'s grandmother, as "great-grandma."

. . . . M.J.B. testified that the parties considered adoption and in June 1996 consulted an attorney on the subject. M.J.B. paid a two thousand dollar retainer, and the attorney advised the parties to get letters from family and friends indicating that the parties and the twins functioned as a family. The parties never actually attempted to get the letters or proceed with the adoption. . . .

Just two months later, in August 1996, M.J.B. ended the relationship. The parties then took turns living in the house with the children until November 1996. In December 1996, V.C. moved out. M.J.B. permitted V.C. to visit with the children until May 1997. During that time, V.C. spent approximately every other weekend with the children, and contributed money toward the household expenses.

In May 1997, M.J.B. went away on business and left the children with V.C. for two weeks. However, later that month, M.J.B. refused to continue V.C.'s visitation with the children, and at some point, M.J.B. stopped accepting V.C.'s money. . . . Eventually, V.C. filed this complaint for joint legal custody. . . .

The trial court denied V.C.'s applications for joint legal custody and visitation. . . .

M.J.B. contends that there is no legal precedent for this action by V.C. She asserts, correctly, that a legal parent has a fundamental right to the care, custody and nurturance of his or her child. . . . According to M.J.B., that right entitles her to absolute preference over V.C. in connection with custody and visitation of the twins. She argues that V.C., a stranger, has no standing to bring this action. We disagree. . . .

According to M.J.B., because there is no allegation by V.C. of unfitness, abandonment or gross misconduct, there is no reason advanced to interfere with any of her constitutional prerogatives. What she elides from consideration, however, is the "exceptional circumstances" category . . . that has been recognized as an alternative basis for a third party to seek custody and visitation of another person's child. . . .

Subsumed within that category is the subset known as the psychological parent cases in which a third party has stepped in to assume the role of the legal parent who has been unable or unwilling to undertake the obligations of parenthood.

At the heart of the psychological parent cases is a recognition that children have a strong interest in maintaining the ties that connect them to adults who love and provide for them. That interest, for constitutional as well as social purposes, lies in the emotional bonds that develop between family members as a result of shared daily life. That point was emphasized in *Lehr v. Robertson*, 463 *U.S.* 248, 261, (1983), where the Supreme Court held that a stepfather's *actual* relationship with a child was the determining factor when considering the degree of protection that the parent-child link must be afforded. . . .

To be sure, prior cases in New Jersey have arisen in the context of a third party taking over the role of an unwilling, absent or incapacitated parent. The question presented here is different; V.C. did not step into M.J.B.'s shoes, but labored alongside her in their family. However, because we view this issue as falling broadly within the contours we have previously described, and because V.C. invokes the "exceptional circumstances" doctrine based on her claim to be a psychological parent to the twins, she has standing to maintain this action separate and apart from the statute. . . .

The next issue we confront is how a party may establish that he or she has, in fact, become a psychological parent to the child of a fit and involved legal parent. . . . The most thoughtful and inclusive definition of *de facto* parenthood is the test enunciated in *Custody of H.S.H.-K.*, 533 N.W. 2d 419, 421 (Wis.1995). . . . Under that test,

> [t]o demonstrate the existence of the petitioner's parent-like relationship with the child, the petitioner must prove four elements: (1) that the biological or adoptive parent consented to, and fostered, the petitioner's formation and establishment of a parent-like relationship with the child; (2) that the petitioner and the child lived together in the same household; (3) that the petitioner assumed the obligations of parenthood by taking significant responsibility for the child's care, education and development, including contributing towards the child's support, without expectation of financial compensation [a petitioner's contribution to a child's support need not be monetary]; and (4) that the petitioner has been in a parental role for a length of time sufficient to have established with the child a bonded, dependent relationship parental in nature.

[*Custody of H.S.H.-K., supra*, 533 N.W. 2d at 421. . . .]

. . . . We are satisfied that that test provides a good framework for determining psychological parenthood in cases where the third party has lived for a substantial period with the legal parent and her child.

Prong one is critical because it makes the biological or adoptive parent a participant in the creation of the psychological parent's relationship with the child.

Without such a requirement, a paid nanny or babysitter could theoretically qualify for parental status. To avoid that result, in order for a third party to be deemed a psychological parent, the legal parent must have fostered the formation of the parental relationship between the third party and the child. By fostered it is meant that the legal parent ceded over to the third party a measure of parental authority and autonomy and granted to that third party rights and duties vis-à-vis the child that the third party's status would not otherwise warrant. . . .

The requirement of cooperation by the legal parent is critical because it places control within his or her hands. That parent has the absolute ability to maintain a zone of autonomous privacy for herself and her child. However, if she wishes to maintain that zone of privacy she cannot invite a third party to function as a parent to her child and cannot cede over to that third party parental authority the exercise of which may create a profound bond with the child.

Two further points concerning the consent requirement need to be clarified. First, a psychological parent-child relationship that is voluntarily created by the legally recognized parent may not be unilaterally terminated after the relationship between the adults ends. Although the intent of the legally recognized parent is critical to the psychological parent analysis, the focus is on that party's intent during the formation and pendency of the parent-child relationship. The reason is that the ending of the relationship between the legal parent and the third party does not end the bond that the legal parent fostered and that actually developed between the child and the psychological parent. . . .

In practice, that may mean protecting those relationships despite the later, contrary wishes of the legal parent in order to advance the interests of the child. As long as the legal parent consents to the continuation of the relationship between another adult who is a psychological parent and the child after the termination of the adult parties' relationship, the courts need not be involved. Only when that consent is withdrawn are courts called on to protect the child's relationship with the psychological parent.

The second issue that needs to be clarified is that participation in the decision to have a child is not a prerequisite to a finding that one has become a psychological parent to the child. . . .

The third prong, a finding that a third party assumed the obligations of parenthood, is not contingent on financial contributions made by the third party. . . . Obviously, as we have indicated, the assumption of a parental role is much more complex than mere financial support. It is determined by the nature, quality, and extent of the functions undertaken by the third party and the response of the child to that nurturance.

Indeed, we can conceive of a case in which the third party is the stay-at-home mother or father who undertakes all of the daily domestic and child care activities in a household with preschool children while the legal parent is the breadwinner engaged in her occupation or profession. . . .

It bears repeating that the fourth prong is most important because it requires the existence of a parent-child bond. A necessary corollary is that the third party must have functioned as a parent for a long enough time that such a bond has developed. What is crucial here is not the amount of time but the nature of the relationship. How much time is necessary will turn on the facts of each case including an assessment of exactly what functions the putative parent performed, as well as at what period and stage of the child's life and development such actions were taken. Most importantly, a determination will have to be made about the actuality and strength of the parent-child bond. Generally, that will require expert testimony . . .

This opinion should not be viewed as an incursion on the general right of a fit legal parent to raise his or her child without outside interference. What we have addressed here is a specific set of circumstances involving the volitional choice of a legal parent to cede a measure of parental authority to a third party; to allow that party to function as a parent in the day-to-day life of the child; and to foster the forging of a parental bond between the third party and the child. In such circumstances, the legal parent has created a family with the third party and the child, and has invited the third party into the otherwise inviolable realm of family privacy. By virtue of her own actions, the legal parent's expectation of autonomous privacy in her relationship with her child is necessarily reduced from that which would have been the case had she never invited the third party into their lives. Most important, where that invitation and its consequences have altered her child's life by essentially giving him or her another parent, the legal parent's options are constrained. It is the child's best interest that is preeminent as it would be if two legal parents were in a conflict over custody and visitation. . . . .

Once a third party has been determined to be a psychological parent to a child, under the previously described standards, he or she stands in parity with the legal parent. Custody and visitation issues between them are to be determined on a best interests standard giving weight to the factors set forth in [the New Jersey custody statute]. . . .

That is not to suggest that a person's status as a legal parent does not play a part in custody or visitation proceedings in those circumstances. . . . The legal parent's status is a significant weight in the best interests balance because eventually, in the search for self-knowledge, the child's interest in his or her roots will emerge. Thus, under ordinary circumstances when the evidence concerning the child's best interests (as between a legal parent and psychological parent) is in equipoise, custody will be awarded to the legal parent.

Visitation, however, will be the presumptive rule, . . . as would be the case if two natural parents were in conflict. . . . [V]isitation rights are almost "invariably" granted to the non-custodial parent. [T]he denial of visitation rights . . . should be invoked only . . . where . . . the granting of visitation will cause physical or emotional harm to the children or where it is demonstrated that the parent is unfit. . . .

[The court concluded that remand was unnecessary, because V.C. was clearly a psychological parent to the twins. It ordered visitation but declined to order joint legal custody because V.C. had not been involved in making decisions for the children for nearly four years due to the pendency of the proceedings.].

NOTES

1. **Sequels.** Later cases applying a *de facto* parent doctrine take the requirements of *V.C. v. M.J.* seriously, and deny the claim when they are not met. A post-*V.C.* New Jersey court denied *de facto* parent status to the mother's romantic partner, who lived with the mother and was very involved with the child, but was not held out to the child or to others as the child's parent by the mother. *A.F. v. D.L.P.*, 771 A.2d 692 (N.J. Super. Ct. App. Div. 2001). The court reasoned that this requirement was essential to afford constitutional protection to the parent-child relationship. *See also Swiss v. Cabinet for Families and Children*, 43 S.W.3d 796 (Ky. Ct. App. 2001) (foster parents were not *de facto* parents because agency provided financial support); *Boone v. Ballinger*, 228 S.W.3d 1 (Ky. Ct. App. 2007) (de facto parent status not proven where person provided care with the parent; only where person provided care in place of the parent).

2. **Parent-Non-Parent Custody Disputes In General.** Custody and visitation disputes between parents and non-parents can arise in many contexts in addition to those involving grandparent visitation discussed above. For example, the parent who seeks the return of a child from a non-parent who has cared for the child may be met with *de facto* parent claim. A Massachusetts court awarded visitation to an aunt who had cared for the child for 11 years, in a contest with the father, who was taking the child to his home in Georgia. Citing the ALI *Principles*, the court held that the aunt was the child's *de facto* parent. *Youmans v. Ramos*, 711 N.E.2d 165 (Mass. 1998). Or a non-parent may seek to take custody from a parent on the ground that the parent is not providing adequate care. Another type of dispute pits a step-parent who has been living with the child and the custodial parent against the noncustodial parent, when the custodial parent dies or becomes unable to care for the child. *See* John DeWitt Gregory, *Defining the Family in the Millennium: The* Troxel *Follies*, 32 U. Mem. L. Rev. 687, 690–91 (2002) (describing statutes that expressly or implicitly authorize step-parent visitation). Finally, in cases like *V. C. v. M.J.B.*, a same-sex partner or step-parent living with the custodial parent and the child may seek custody or visitation on dissolution of the relationship. This last group of cases has received a great deal of attention in recent years and we focus on it Note 4, below. We consider here more general questions applicable to all these cases.

Many states continue to apply to all these cases the traditional rule that a parent prevails against a non-parent in a dispute over custody, unless the parent is shown to be unfit or to have abandoned his or her rights. *See, e.g.*, Wis. Stat. Ann. § 767.41(3)(a) (Supp.) (custody may be awarded to a relative if "neither parent is able to care for the child adequately or . . . neither parent is fit and proper to have the care and custody of the child"). For example, the North Dakota Supreme Court relied on the parental preference in affirming award of custody of a 9-year-old to her non-custodial mother over the claims of the custodial father's widow. The daughter had lived with father and his second wife for eight years, but the court noted the strong bond between mother and child and the lack of evidence that maternal custody would be detrimental to the child. *Simons v. Gisvold*, 519 N.W.2d 585 (N.D. 1994). The Supreme Court of Missouri reversed a custody award to the older half-sister of the children on the death of the mother, finding that even though the father had little previous involvement with the children, and had failed to pay child support, he was nonetheless entitled to custody under the Missouri statute unless he was unfit, unwilling, or unable to assume responsibility for the children, even if their welfare would be detrimentally affected. *Cotton v. Wise*, 977 S.W.2d 263 (Mo. 1998); *see also Ex Parte S.T.S.*, 806 So. 2d 336 (Ala. 2001) (father wins custody over grandmother, absent unfitness or voluntary relinquishment).

In most jurisdictions, however, the parental preference is somewhat weaker, allowing a grant of custody to a nonparent not only when the parent is unfit, but also when parental custody is found likely to cause substantial harm to the child. This is still a demanding test; courts make clear that the nonparent challenger cannot meet it by merely showing that their custody is in the child's best interest. Thus in *Custody of Anderson*, 890 P.2d 525, 526 (Wash. App. 1995), the court awarded custody to the child's mother rather than the aunt and uncle who had cared for the child for two years and "could offer her a superior home environment and a greater opportunity for optimum growth and development." *See also Lewis v. Donoho*, 993 S.W.2d 1 (Tenn. 1999) (mother awarded custody over non-parent, with whom eight-year-old child had lived almost since birth, absent showing of "substantial harm"); *Kinnard v. Kinnard*, 43 P.3d 150 (Alaska 2002) (upholding shared custody based on stepmother's demonstration that she was psychological parent of child and that severing bond would be detrimental to child); *Froelich v. Clark*, 745 N.E.2d 222 (Ind. Ct. App. 2001) (*de facto* custodian with whom child lived for 8 years must overcome presumption favoring parental custody to retain custody).

California, by statute, applies a similar rule. *See* CAL. FAM. CODE § 3041 (nonparent may be awarded custody if "granting custody to a parent would be detrimental to the child and granting custody to the nonparent is required to serve the best interest of the child"). In the highly publicized custody dispute between O.J. Simpson, the former football star, and his deceased wife's parents, Louis and Juditha Brown, the trial court applying this statute granted Simpson custody, but the appellate court reversed, finding that evidence of Simpson's involvement in his wife's murder (based on the verdict against him in the civil action) must be admitted in the custody determination. *Simpson v. Brown*, 79 Cal. Rptr. 2d 389 (Ct. App. 1998). However, the Browns subsequently agreed to relinquish physical custody to Simpson. *O.J. Getting the Kids/In-laws Will Let Them Go to Fla.*, L.A. Times, Aug. 7, 2000, at A8.

New York permits a non-parent to win custody against a fit parent only if "extraordinary circumstances" can be proved. *Bennett v. Jeffreys*, 356 N.E.2d 277 (N.Y. 1976) (non-parent had cared for child for long period of time). This creates a substantial hurdle for non-parents, as the Court of Appeals demonstrated in *In re Michael B.*, 590 N.Y.S.2d 60 (N.Y. 1992). The court reversed a grant of custody to foster parents who had been custodians of the child for five years (characterized by the court as "temporary foster care"). The father sought custody of the child, who had been voluntarily placed in state-sponsored foster care by his mother. The court emphasized that there had been no finding of parental unfitness, and distinguished *Bennett v. Jeffreys*, which involved a private unsupervised placement with the non-parent, rather than a state placement. In Connecticut, an order granting the paternal aunt of a child joint custody with the child's father was reversed where the aunt, when she sought to intervene in the custody proceeding, failed "to prove by a fair preponderance of the evidence that she has a relationship with the child akin to that of a parent, that parental custody clearly would be detrimental to the child and, upon a finding of detriment, that third party custody would be in the child's best interest." *Fish v. Fish*, 939 A.2d 1040 (Conn. 2008.) As the court in *V.C.* explains, *de facto* parents in New Jersey can also invoke the "extraordinary circumstances" doctrine. However, for other nonparent claimants, New Jersey courts have narrowly construed this basis of rebutting the parental presumption. *See, e.g., Watkins v. Nelson*, 748 A.2d 558 (N.J. 2000) (affirming strong parental presumption emphasizing narrowness of exceptions).

The Model Marriage and Divorce Act § 401 (1987), gives non-parents standing to contest custody but only where the child "is not in the physical custody of one of his parents." This approach has been adopted in a number of states. *See, e.g.,* ILL. ANN. STAT. ch. 750, para. 5/601(b)(2) (Supp.); WASH. REV. CODE ANN. § 26.10.030 (Supp.). A similar approach is used in some jurisdictions that apply the best interest standard applied to parent-nonparent custody disputes when the child has lived with the nonparent who functions in a parental role for some significant length of time, and the parent has not had custody. *See, e.g., Price v. Howard*, 484 S.E.2d 528 (N.C. 1998) (where parent voluntarily relinquished child to non-parent, with whom child has lived for substantial period, best interest test applies). Some apply the changed circumstances modification rule to parents reclaiming their children from custodial nonparents. For example, in *C.R.B. v. C.C.*, 959 P.2d 375 (Alaska 1998), the grandparents had been awarded custody when their divorced daughter became unable to care for the children due to her cocaine addiction. When the father, after almost three years without contact, sought custody from them, the court turned him down, applying the principle that the father must show some changed circumstance that cast new doubt on the current custodial parents. rejecting his argument that the changed circumstance standard should be relaxed when a parent seeks modification of custody in a non-parent. *See also Blair v. Badenhope*, 77 S.W.3d 137 (Tenn. 2002).

   3. *The Concept of Psychological Parenthood.* The concept of "psychological parenthood" has been influential in the weakening of the parental rights approach in parent-third party disputes. Under one well-known proposal, the legally favored parent would be the adult who has actually functioned as the child's primary caregiver, and whom the child identifies, psychologically, as the parent. *See* JOSEPH GOLDSTEIN, ANNA FREUD & ALBERT J. SOLNIT, BEYOND THE BEST INTERESTS OF THE CHILD (1973). These authors approach the custody decision from a psychoanalytic perspective. Their argument that the psychological parent should be favored in custody disputes rests on attachment theory, which holds that the child's healthy psychological development depends on the security of the bond with her attachment figure, the adult who cares for her basic needs from infancy. Thus, in the custody determination, little weight would be given to one party's status as biological parent.

Although few courts weigh psychological parenthood as heavily as the authors advocate, the concept has had an important influence in disputes between parents and non-parents and is at the heart of the rationale for recognizing claims by *de facto* parents. In another context, the Colorado Supreme Court, in *C.R.S. v. T.A.M.*, 892 P.2d 246 (Colo. 1995), awarded custody to prospective adoptive parents in a failed adoption case, on the ground that they were psychological parents. Emphasizing that the foster parents had raised the child since birth and fulfilled his psychological needs, the court concluded that disrupting the emotional bond that had formed between them (by awarding custody to the mother) "would likely prove devastating to the child." Continuation of that relationship was "presumed to be in the child's best interests." Oregon has recognized the psychological parenthood concept statutorily, by allowing anyone who has "established emotional ties creating a child-parent relationship . . . with a child" to petition for custody or visitation. OR. REV. STAT. § 109.119 (Supp.). The statute defines child-parent relationship as:

> . . . a relationship that exists or did exist . . . and in which relationship a person having physical custody of a child or residing in the same household as the child supplied, or otherwise made available to the child, food, clothing, shelter and incidental necessaries and provided the child with necessary care, education and discipline, and which relationship continued on a day-to-day basis, through interaction, companionship, interplay and mutuality, that fulfilled the child's psychological needs for a parent as well as the child's physical needs.

Id. at 109.119(10)(a).

4. *Custody and Visitation Claims by De Facto Parents.* Custody disputes such as *M.J. v. V.C.*, between former same-sex partners, can present the most compelling nonparent claims. Many of these contests involve lesbian couples who created a child through the artificial insemination of one partner, after which both partners function fully as parents and share childrearing responsibilities. The same scenario can arise where a gay couple uses the sperm of one partner to inseminate a surrogate mother. In some jurisdictions, the partner who is not the biological parent can legally adopt the child. *See* Chapter 11. In many states, however, this route to recognized parental status is foreclosed. When the relationship of the partners ends, the *de facto* parent may seek custody or visitation. In doing so, *de facto* parents assert their interest in a continued parental relationship with children with whom they have lived in a family unit — often since the child's birth.

This is an area in which legal doctrine is evolving as courts respond to social change. Traditionally, courts have been hostile to custody or visitation claims by same-sex *de facto* parents. In *Alison D. v. Virginia M.*, 572 N.E.2d 27 (NY 1991), for example, the court rejected the *de facto* parent's visitation petition, declining to recognize her parental status under the doctrine of *in loco parentis*, even though she had shared fully with the biological parent in planning and caring for the child. *See also Titchenal v. Dexter*, 693 A.2d 682 (Vt. 1997) (lesbian partner of adoptive mother could have adopted child, but court has no statutory or equitable authority to adjudicate visitation petition). In recent years, as *V. C.* suggests, courts have begun to respond positively to these claims and to develop legal standards for determining when claimants have parental status.

The test announced by the New Jersey Supreme Court in *M.J. v. V.C.* is close to that adopted by the *ALI Principles*, which provide that courts can allocate residential responsibility to an individual who has resided with the child for a significant period and has performed many parenting functions without financial compensation. *Id.* §§ 2.03(1)(c), 2.18. Like the New Jersey test, the ALI standard emphasizes the acquiescence of the legal parent to the development of the parent-child relationship between the *de facto* parent and the child (or the complete default of any legal parent). Unlike the New Jersey test, under which the amount of time that the claimant has functioned in a parental role is not crucial, the *ALI Principles* set a minimum two-year time period. The latter approach seems likely to reduce litigation.

Other courts have recognized the visitation claims of *de facto* parents, often citing with approval the *ALI Principles* or the New Jersey test. *See Rubano v. DiCenzo*, 759 A.2d 959 (R.I. 2000) (enforcing a written visitation agreement after determining that the domestic partner was the child's *de facto* parent); *E.L.O. v. L.M.M*, 711 N.E.2d 886 (Mass. 1999) (upholding recognition of lesbian domestic partner as *de facto* parent, citing the ALI standard, and awarding visitation); *Mason v. Dwinnell*, 660 S.E.2d 58 (N.C. 2008) (former same-sex partner of birth parent granted joint legal and physical custody of child where the partners had entered into a parenting agreement, had lived together with the child for 3 years and shared physical caretaking for another 3 years after separation, shared financial responsibilities for the child, held child out to family and community as their child, etc.; court applied rule that the best interests test applies in custody conflict with nonparent where a natural parent's conduct has not been consistent with his or her constitutional status and cites and quotes from *V.C.*); *cf. Estroff v. Chatterjee*, 660 S.E.2d 73 (N.C. App. 2008) (joint custody claim of former domestic partner of natural parent dismissed where natural parent had not acted inconsistently with constitutionally-protected status as parent; while the partners lived together during the pregnancy and early years of the lives of the twin children and both cared for and financially supported the children, the birth mother never agreed to the partner's identifying herself as a coparent, never entered into a formal coparenting agreement, moved to a separate home when twins were 18 months old, and thereafter allowed the twins to spend half of each week with the partner for over a year before reducing visitation to one night a week).

Despite the trend toward accepting claims for custody and visitation by same sex partners of legal parents, some courts have decided in recent years to reject the *de facto* parent doctrine. For example, the New York Court of Appeals recently affirmed its holding in *Alison D.*, *supra*, in *Debra H. v. Janice R.*, 2010 N.Y. LEXIS 620 (May 4, 2010). The court rejected the *de facto* parent doctrine, stating that the proper way for the plaintiff to have received parental status was through second-parent adoption. *See also Stadter v. Siperko*, 661 S.E.2d 494 (Va. App. 2008) (rejects de facto parent doctrine; finds that interests of former same-sex partner of child's parent to continuing relationship with child adequately protected by statute permitting court to award visitation to persons with a "legitimate interest" in the child over the objection of the child's parent where petitioner demonstrates by clear and convincing evidence that visitation is in the best interests of the child); *Janice M. v. Margaret K.*, 948 A.2d 73 (Md. 2008) (rejecting de facto parent doctrine; visitation may be granted to former same-sex partner of child's adoptive parent over objection of that parent only where court finds exceptional circumstances or parental unfitness); *Jones v. Barlow*, 154 P.3d 808 (Utah 2007) (declining to adopt the *de facto* parent doctrine to avoid usurping legislative authority, court denies visitation to former same-sex partner of child's mother, even though she and the parent had entered into a Vermont civil union and even though she had been named the child's co-guardian with the child's parent).

Although *V.C.* holds that *de facto* parents stand in parity with legal parents (and thus the best interest standard applies to their disputes), it recognizes that usually these claimants will be awarded visitation rights and not custody. How does the court reach this conclusion? Many courts have held explicitly, under the general parental preference rule, that if the legal parent is both a fit parent and has had custody of the child, *de facto* parents can only seek visitation. *In re Custody of H.S.H.-K.,supra.* (*de facto* parent has no standing to sue under custody statute absent showing of unfitness);. *Kazmierazak v. Query*, 736 So. 2d. 106 (Fla. App. 1999) (same). The ALI approach provides that the *de facto* parent should not get the majority of custodial responsibility. *See* § 2.18.

Much commentary has focused on the legal treatment of de facto parents and on the ALI approach to this issue. *See* Emily Buss, *Parental Rights*, 88 Va. L. Rev. 635 (2002) (critiquing the ALI *de facto* parent status as interfering with legal parent's rights); Gregory A. Loken, *The New Extended Family: "De Facto" Parenthood and Standing Under Chapter 2*, 2001 BYU L. Rev. 1045 (arguing that the costs to biological parents of the ALI standard exceed any possible gains); Barbara Bennett Woodhouse, *Horton Looks at the ALI Principles*, 4 J.L. & Fam. Stud. 151 (2002) (criticizing *Principles'* treatment of *de facto* parenthood for ignoring children's developmental needs); *see also* Nancy D. Polikoff, *This Child Does Have Two Mothers: Redefining Parenthood to Meet the Needs of Children in Lesbian-Mother and Other Nontraditional Families*, 78 Geo. L.J. 459 (1990) (arguing that all functional parental relationships formed with the cooperation and consent of the biological parent should be legally recognized, in both custody and visitation cases).

For further discussion of the issue of the legal response to same-sex families, see Chapter 9. For further discussion of the judicial response to a parent's homosexuality in custody and visitation matters, see Sections B and D, *supra*.

5. *Doctrinal Alternatives to De Facto Parent.* Some courts use other doctrinal paths to protect the relationships of children and *de facto* parents. The Pennsylvania Supreme Court, for example, invoked the common law doctrine of *in loco parentis* in awarding visitation to the mother's domestic partner, who lived with the child until she was almost three years old. *T.B. v. L.R.M.*, 786 A.2d 913 (Pa. 2001). The doctrine of equitable estoppel, developed in the context of conventional families, can also be applied to these disputes. That doctrine has been used most often to treat the mother's husband as the legal father of her child despite another man's biological paternity, where both parents have treated him as the father during their marriage. At divorce the husband may seek to avoid child support, or the wife may seek to cut off his custody claims, by denying his paternity. The doctrine of equitable estoppel, when applied, disallows either nonpaternity claim. As a common law doctrine, its details vary among courts that apply it. It has often been applied to deny the husband's claim of nonpaternity when he has treated the child as his for years even though he knew that biologically it was not. It has also been applied to deny the wife's claim of her husband's nonpaternity when she allowed him to believe the child was his despite her knowledge that her pregnancy probably arose from an extramarital liaison. See the equitable estoppel cases collected in Chapter 9. The *ALI Principles* recognize the estoppel doctrine, but also broaden it in defining a category called a "parent by estoppel." In addition to the kinds of facts recognized in the traditional cases, the Principles would also treat as a parent by estoppel a person who "lived with the child since the child's birth, holding out and accepting full and permanent responsibilities as parent, as part of a prior co-parenting agreement with the child's legal parent (or, if there are two legal parents, both parents) to raise a child together each with full parental rights and responsibilities, when the court finds that recognition of the individual as a parent is in the child's best interests." § 2.03(1)(b)(iii). An important difference between a parent by estoppel, in the traditional sense or the sense used by the Principles, and a de facto parent as understood in cases like *V.C. v.M.J.*, is that a parent by estoppel is in fact treated as a legal parent, and not merely as a third party who may have special, but nonetheless limited, rights. For example, a parent by estoppel, under both the traditional cases and the A.L.I. Principles, is liable for child support whether or not he seeks a share of parenting time.

6. *Constitutional Questions with De Facto Parenthood Claims.* Does *Troxel v. Granville*, 530 U.S. 57 (2000), reprinted above, cast doubt on rules allowing visitation by *de facto* parents? Key to *Troxel* was the trial court's failure to give proper deference to the parent's decisions about allowing contact with the grandparents. If courts applying the *de facto* parent doctrine accord the parent's decision proper respect, *Troxel* may be satisfied. Notice that, in *V.C. v. M.J.B.*, the New Jersey court makes parental consent to the development of the parent-like relationship between the child and the third party a prerequisite for a finding that the third party is eligible for custody. The *ALI Principles* follow the same path. Whether this prerequisite is an adequate response to *Troxel* is explored in a recent article by Professor June Carbone. Professor Carbone demonstrates that, in a series of cases extending parental status to stepparents, same-sex partners and other third parties, the California appellate courts have found a way to avoid *Troxel* issues attendant on claims by non-parents for custody and visitation. She argues that California courts have gone too far, from a constitutional perspective, in recognizing parental status in those third parties whose relationship with the child is not grounded in an agreement with the existing legal parent or parents. June Carbone, *From Partners to Parents Revisited: How Will Ideas of Partnership Influence the Emerging Definition of California Parenthood?*, 7 WHITTIER J. CHILD & FAM. ADVOC. 3 (2007).

7. *Other Non-Parent Visitation.* Note that under the Washington statute considered in *Troxel, supra,* "any person" could petition for visitation. Aside from grandparents, most non-parent visitation petitions involve *de facto* parents discussed above or step-parents who resided with the child. *See* John DeWitt Gregory, *Defining the Family in the Millennium: The* Troxel *Follies*, 32 U. MEM. L. REV. 687 (2002) (discussing statutes authorizing stepparent visitation after *Troxel.)* Some states have adopted statutes allowing others to seek visitation. *See, e.g.*, OR. REV. STAT. § 109.119(6)(d) (any person who "has maintained an ongoing personal relationship with substantial continuity for at least one year, through interaction, companionship, interplay and mutuality" may petition for visitation). Some statutes specifically authorize sibling visitation, *see, e.g.*, N.J. Stat. Ann. § 9:2-7.1 (Supp.), and some courts have ordered sibling visitation without express statutory authority. In *State v. Ken W.*, 529 N.W.2d 548 (Neb. App. 1995), the court upheld a sibling visitation order sought by a boy who was in state custody because he was uncontrollable. The court, in granting the boy visitation with his two-year-old sister over their parents' objection, concluded that siblings (unlike grandparents) have a direct right of access. On the facts of the case, the court found that visitation would benefit the brother while there was "no evidence that the supervised sibling visitation would have a negative impact" on his sister.

PROBLEMS

Problem 6-17. In 1998, Jessica moved in with Marie and her five-year-old daughter, Sarah. Jessica was an English professor, whose schedule is flexible, while Marie often worked evenings and weekends as a manager of a local department store. Jessica took care of Sarah on weekends when Marie worked and usually picked her up after school and gave her dinner. As Sarah got older, Jessica often helped her with homework, took her to soccer practice, and to play dates and birthday parties. The couple pooled their financial resources; they had joint checking and savings accounts. Marie made all important decisions affecting Sarah, including medical and educational decisions, and important disciplinary decisions. Usually she went to teachers' conferences, although occasionally Jessica performed this function. After five years, when Sarah was 10 years old, the couple split up. You represent Jessica in her effort to get custody or visitation. Is she likely to be recognized as a *de facto* parent? What other information might be important? The court has ordered a psychological evaluation of all parties. What should be the focus of the psychologist's evaluation?

Problem 6-18. Julie and Mark hired Dasha as a live-in nanny for their children when their first child was three months old. They now have three children, ages 6, 8, and 10, and have decided to terminate Dasha to save money and retrieve some of their privacy. Dasha is extremely attached to the children, and wants to continue to see them on a regular basis. Julie and Mark believe it would be better for the children to make a clean break with Dasha.

As a matter of policy, should Dasha have standing to petition a court for visitation? Is she a *de facto* parent under the New Jersey test? Under the ALI approach?

Problem 6-19. Jane and Jim of Tacoma, Washington, are the aunt and uncle of Sam, age 23, a young man with serious emotional problems. In 1998, Sam and his girl friend, Ellie, had a child, Michael. Jane and Jim became involved with the young family, spending time with them, giving advice, and buying clothes, books, and toys for Michael. They had raised three children, loved kids, and wanted to bring stability and support to Michael's life. Ellie was a loving mother, but she was immature and somewhat erratic and she managed to care for Michael only with much difficulty. In 2000, Sam and Ellie split up and Ellie took off for Alaska with Michael. She moved from place to place, getting jobs that allowed Michael to be with her and living in whatever accommodations she could find. Jane and Jim traveled to

Alaska and persuaded Ellie to let them take Michael home to Washington. A few months later, having earned enough money to travel, Ellie returned to Washington and asked that Michael be returned to her. Jane and Jim refuse and petition for custody of Michael. Will they be successful?

G.   THE ROLE OF THE ATTORNEY IN CUSTODY CASES

Lawyers representing parents in custody disputes may be constrained in their role because, although the attorney is responsible primarily to her client, the purpose of the proceeding is to promote the best interest of the child. For example, although attorneys are prohibited under the attorney-client privilege from disclosing confidential communications from their clients, an attorney may be required to disclose her client's whereabouts where the client has taken the child out of the jurisdiction in violation of a court order. *See Bersani v. Bersani*, 565 A.2d 1368 (Conn. Super. 1989). Similarly, it may be advisable and ethical for an attorney to disclose information concerning a client or former client's where the lawyer "reasonably believes [disclosure is] necessary to prevent substantial physical or sexual abuse of a child." American Academy of Matrimonial Lawyers, *Bounds of Advocacy: Children*, Standard   6.5   (2000),   http://www.aaml.org/go/library/publications/bounds-of-advocacy. Attorneys advising their clients must explain the limits of the privilege.

Attorneys for the parents in custody disputes have been subject to substantial criticism because they have traditionally understood their role to be that of zealous advocate for their client's interest, even if the child's interest is sacrificed. As part of a larger effort to define the ethical obligations of divorce attorneys under a model that deemphasizes the "zealous advocate" role, the American Academy of Matrimonial Lawyers, a reform group, has promulgated standards that encourage attorneys to consider the interest of the child in representing the parent. *The Bounds of Advocacy, Standards of Conduct*, http://www.aaml.org/go/library/publications/bounds-of-advocacy (2000). The introduction to the section of the standard regarding the representation of parents describes the basis of the obligation of parent's attorney to consider the welfare of the children:

> One of the most troubling issues in family law is determining a lawyer's obligations to children. The lawyer must competently represent the interests of the client, but not at the expense of the children. The parents' fiduciary obligations for the well being of a child provide a basis for the attorney's consideration of the child's best interests consistent with traditional advocacy and client loyalty principles. It is accepted doctrine that the attorney for a trustee or other fiduciary has an ethical obligation to the beneficiaries to whom the fiduciary's obligations run. Statutory and decisional law in most jurisdictions imposes a fiduciary duty on parents to act in their child's best interests.

Id. at Standard 6.

The standards direct the parent's attorney to consider the welfare of the children (Standard 6.1). The attorney is also prohibited from contesting custody for financial leverage or vindictiveness, and is directed to seek to withdraw if the client persists in such strategic pursuits (Standard 6.2 and Comment). *See also* Lewis Becker, *Ethical Concerns in Negotiating Family Law Agreements*, 30 FAM. L.Q. 587 (1996). Becker suggests that, under the ABA Model Rules of Professional Conduct, the attorney should counsel a parent against pursuing a course that is detrimental to the child. Rule 2.1; William J. Howe & Hugh McIsaac, *Finding The Balance: Ethical Challenges And Best Practices For Lawyers Representing Parents When The Interests Of Children Are At Stake*, 46 FAM. CT. REV. 78 (2008) (asserting that adversary model of representation of parents in custody disputes is being replaced with alternatives, including collaborative, therapeutic and restorative justice models of representation).

PROBLEM

Problem 6-20. (a) Alix is Devin's attorney in his divorce action against Sidney. Devin seeks custody of the three children. Alix's investigation of the case reveals that Devin is not a very good father. He often leaves the family for days at a time, has a poor relationship with his children, and often refuses, for no apparent reason, to allow his children to play with their neighborhood friends. Sidney, on the other hand, is an excellent parent and Alix therefore believes she ought to be awarded custody of the children. What can Alix do, consistent with the ethical obligations of an attorney?

(b) Suppose Alix has learned, from a discussion with the children, that Devin has molested his daughter. Sidney appears to be ignorant of this fact; in any event, it is clear that Sidney has not told her attorney. What are Alix's obligations?

H.   INTERNATIONAL CUSTODY DISPUTES

In times of increasing migration across international borders, child custody disputes may involve parents who live in different countries. Resolving these disputes quickly and efficiently requires countries to cooperate in terms of exercising jurisdiction, which is a primary purpose of the 1980 Hague Convention on Child Abduction. The United States became a contracting party in 1988. The International Child Abduction Remedies Act, 42 U.S.C. § 11601 et seq., is the implementing legislation. As of the middle of 2009, there were 81 contracting states. *See* Hague Convention Web Site, www.hcch.net.

The Convention applies to children under 16 "habitually resident in a contracting state" immediately before any breach of custody or access rights. Lacking criminal sanctions or extradition provisions, it provides a civil remedy under which a party's access to or custody of his or her children can be restored. A taking of a child is wrongful if it violates custody rights, as determined by the law of the child's habitual residence. A custody decree is not a pre-requisite; thus, pre-decree removal of the child by a parent can violate the other parent's access rights. Moreover, the wrongdoer's obtaining of a favorable custody decree in the asylum State does not affect rights under the Act, although a court may consider the reasons underlying such a decree when asked to apply the Convention. Every contracting state must establish a Central Authority to receive claims under the Convention by citizens of that state or from any other contracting state. The United States' Central Authority is the Department of State's Office of Citizen's Consular Services. Raymond R.

Norko, *Mandatory Implementation of the Hague Convention on International Child Abduction: An Open Letter to President William Clinton*, 8 Conn. J. Int. L. 575, 577 (1993).

Under Article 13, there are three exceptions to the general obligation to defer to the "habitual residence" of the child: (1) the objecting party was not actually exercising custody or consented to such removal or retention; (2) the child would be exposed to "physical or emotional harm" or other intolerable situation upon return; and (3) a mature child objects to the return. The second exception's scope was at issue in *Tahan v. Duquette*, 613 A.2d 486 (N.J. App. Div. 1992). The father opposing his child's return to Canada was not allowed to present evidence about alleged possible psychological harm caused by returning the child to live with mother. The appellate court affirmed the trial court's refusal to admit the evidence, holding

> . . . [T]the Article 13b inquiry was not intended to deal with issues or factual questions . . . appropriate for consideration in a plenary custody proceeding. Psychological profiles, detailed evaluations of parental fitness, evidence concerning lifestyle and the nature and quality of relationships all bear upon the ultimate issue.

Id. at 489.

The court did note that trial courts must be permitted to "evaluate the surroundings to which the child is to be sent and the basic personal qualities of those located there." In another Article 13 case, the appellate court affirmed a trial court finding that respondent-grandparents had wrongfully taken two children from their father in Mexico. *March v. Levine*, 249 F.3d 462 (6th Cir. 2001). Believing their daughter to have been murdered by their son-in-law, the grandparents had obtained an Illinois visitation order which a Mexican court enforced. They refused to return the children at the end of the visit, triggering father's petition. The court rejected the claim that petitioner should be "disentitled from bringing the action because of unclean hands." Noting that the Convention mandates proof by clear and convincing evidence of an Article 13 exception, the court upheld summary judgment in favor of petitioner. *See also Kufner v. Kufner*, 519 F.3d 33 (1st Cir. 2008) (order to return children to Germany affirmed where mother failed to establish grave risk of harm; grave risk standard of Convention is not violative of the Constitution); *Mendez-Lynch v. Pizzutello*, 2008 U.S. Dist. LEXIS 10507 (N.D. Ga., Feb. 13, 2008) (children's adamant opposition to returning to Argentina not equivalent to a grave risk of physical or emotional abuse); *Danaipour v. McLarey*, 386 F.3d 289 (1st Cir. 2004) (Convention does not require inquiry in every case concerning remedies against alleged risk available in country of habitual residence).

For litigation dealing with habitual residence under the Convention, see *Clarke v. Clarke*, 2008 US Dist. LEXIS 41600 (E.D. Pa., May 27, 2008) (applies shared parental intent approach to determine Pennsylvania was not children's habitual residence and, thus, they must be returned to the habitual residence in Australia); *Mikovic v. Mikovic*, 541 F. Supp. 2d 1264 (M.D. Fla. 2007) (court determines appropriate approach in determining shared parental intent is to look at larger context of how particular activities of the couple fit in to the "bigger picture of the history of this couple and their child"); *Robert v. Tesson*, 507 F.3d 981(6th Cir. 2007) (court rejects shared parental intent approach to determination of habitual residence and instead holds that "habitual residence is the nation where, at the time of . . . removal, the child has been present long enough to allow acclimatization, and where this presence has a 'degree of settled purpose from the child's perspective' "); *Alonzo v. Claudino*, 2007 U.S. Dist. LEXIS 9656 (M.D.N.C., Feb. 9, 2007) (mother's claim that U.S. is child's place of habitual residence undercut by mother's status as illegal alien; mother had also prevented removal of child to Honduras by theft of passports of father and child); *Kijowska v. Haines*, 431 F. Supp. 2d 873 (N.D. Ill. 2006) (while mother took child from U.S. to Poland without knowledge or consent of father, court finds Poland became child's habitual residence); *Samholt v. Samholt*, 2006 U.S. Dist. LEXIS 51649 (M.D.N.C., July 26, 2006) (father's acquiescence in the relocation of his daughter to North Carolina where she would be spending most of the year and all of the school year indicated he intended that for the foreseeable future the child would be habitually resident in U.S.); *Humphrey v. Humphrey*, 434 F.3d 243 (4th Cir. 2006) (burden of proof for party alleging particular country was child's habitual residence is preponderance, not "beyond a reasonable doubt" as required by trial court); *Gitter v. Gitter*, 396 F.3d 124 (2d Cir. 2005) (while parental shared intent is appropriate first step in determining habitual residence, court must also inquire into whether child has acclimatized to new location; courts, however, should be slow to find acclimatization has trumped shared parental intent); *Ruiz v. Tenorio*, 392 F.3d 1247 (11th Cir. 2004) (stay of 34 months in Mexico with father did not change children's habitual residence; parental intention is crucial factor, but cannot alone transform habitual residence). *See also* Stephen Schwartz, Note and Comment, *The Myth of Habitual Residence: Why American Courts Should Adopt the Delvoye Standard for Habitual Residence under the Hague Convention on the Civil Aspects of Child Abduction*, 10 Cardozo Women's L.J. 691 (2004) (urges adoption of Third Circuit's test for determining child's habitual residence; test makes age and maturity of child threshold question and uses different factors depending on how advanced child is).

For litigation dealing with a mature child's objection, see *Yang v. Tsui*, 499 F.3d 259 (3d Cir. 2007) (trial court order to return wrongfully retained child's return to mother in Canada affirmed despite 10-year old's generalized desire to remain in this country); *de Silva v. Pitts*, 481 F.3d 1279 (10th Cir. 2007) ("considered decision" by 13-year old to stay with father in Oklahoma rather than return to Canada is appropriate basis on which to reject mother's Hague petition); *Gonzalez Locicero v. Nazor Lurashi*, 321 F. Supp. 2d 295 (D.P.R. 2004) (preference of 13-year old boy to remain in Puerto Rico rather than return to his mother in Argentina pursuant to her Hague Convention petition insufficient to qualify for Article 13 exception). *See also Diallo v. Bekemeyer*, 2007 U.S. Dist. LEXIS 94948 (E.D. Mo., Dec. 28, 2007) (federal legislation implementing Convention mandates recognition of decisions of foreign countries on Convention litigation; Netherlands court determination that New Zealand was child's habitual resident binding on U.S. court); *Wasniewski v. Grzelak-Johannsen*, 2007 U.S. Dist. LEXIS 62929 (N.D. Ohio, Aug. 27, 2007) (Convention's one-year filing period for petitions for return of child tolled where child is being concealed wrongfully; mother's claim that child has become "settled" here during two years of wrongful concealment is rejected; court describes outcome as having "basis in fairness and respect for the intent of the Convention"); *Hanley v. Roy*, 485 F.3d 641 (11th Cir. 2007) (testamentary guardianship satisfied requirement for "right of custody" under Convention; court orders return of children to

Ireland to their grandparents after they were wrongfully taken to Florida by their father); *Escaf v. Rodriquez*, 200 F. Supp. 2d 603 (E.D. Va. 2002) (return of child to Colombia required).

The remedies by the Convention are not exclusive. Thus, a litigant claiming wrongful taking or retention of a child might sue under state custody law or, alternatively, seek a return order under the Convention. It has been held, however, that utilization of state law may waive rights under the Convention. *See, e.g., Holder v. Holder*, 2002 Cal. App. Unpub. LEXIS 2898 (Mar. 20, 2002); *see also Journe v. Journe*, 911 F. Supp. 43 (D.P.R. 1995) (failure to win custody in French courts prevents later use of Convention to relitigate same issues). If state litigation is pending, federal court abstention may be appropriate. *Barzilay v. Barzilay*, 536 F.3d 844 (8th Cir. 2008) (abstention inappropriate where neither party raised Hague issue in state court proceedings); *Small v. Clark*, 2006 U.S. Dist. LEXIS 27638 (M.D. Fla., May 9, 2006) (abstention inappropriate solely because state court proceeding is pending; abstention in such situations "is the exception, not the rule"); *see* Ion Hasskikostas, Note, *Federal Court Abstention and the Hague Child Abduction Convention*, 79 NYU L. REV. 421 (2004) (after analyzing different strands of abstention doctrine, "attempts to establish a scheme for classifying the various types of 'parallel proceedings' [in state and federal courts] that may arise under" federal statute implementing the Convention; urges use of Colorado River abstention analysis "with a focus aimed at guarding against forum shopping").

For other relevant secondary authority, see Merle Weiner, *Intolerable Situations and Counsel for Children: Following Switzerland's Example in Hague Abduction Cases*, 58 AM. U.L. REV. 335 (2008); Dana Beth Finkey, Note, The *Hague Convention on the Civil Aspects of International Child Abduction: Where are We and Where Do We Go From Here?*, 30 HASTINGS INT'L & COMP. L. REV. 505 (2007) (argues Violence Against Women Act should be used as a model to help "rectify the Convention's unintended impact on victims of domestic violence . . ."); Radoslaw Pawlowski, Note, *Alternative Dispute Resolution for Hague Convention Child Custody Disputes*, 45 FAM. CT. REV. 302 (2007) (explains why ADR is often more suitable than Hague litigation; urges ADR protocol for the Convention); Smita Aiyar, Comment, *International Child Abductions Involving Non-Hague Convention States: The Need for a Uniform Approach*, 21 EMORY INT'L L. REV. 277 (2007) (offers amendment to Convention to provide for uniform approach for dealing with non-signatory nations); Carshae Davis, *Development, The* Gitter *Standard: Creating a Uniform Definition of Habitual Residence under the Hague Convention on the Civil Aspects of International Child Abduction*, 7 CHI. J. INT'L L. 321 (2006) (explains Second Circuit standard in Convention cases, asserting that it "is the most comprehensive standard that thoroughly contemplates the acclimatization of the child"); Linda Silberman, *Interpreting the Hague Abduction Convention in Search of a Global Jurisprudence*, 38 U.C. DAVIS L. REV. 1049 (2005) (in 2004 Bodenheimer Lecture, author provides overview of the Convention and identifies tools available achieving a global jurisprudence of Convention); Merle Weiner, *Strengthening Article 20*, 38 U.S.F.L. REV. 701 (2004) (focuses on human rights provision of the Convention, concluding that, while it has had "minimal doctrinal significance," it should be strengthened to "make the . . . Convention operate more justly for those domestic violence victims who flee transnationally with their children as part of their effort to escape from domestic violence"); Merle Weiner, *Navigating the Road between Uniformity and Progress: The Need for Purposive Analysis of the Hague Convention on the Civil Aspects of International Child Abductions*, 33 COLUM. HUM. RTS. L. REV. 275 (2002) (analyzing federal court activism in interpreting Convention, especially in cases involving domestic violence victims who flee transnationally with children); Symposium, *The Past and Promise of the 1980 Hague Convention on the Civil Aspects of International Child Abduction*, 33 NYU J. INTL. L. & POL'Y 1 (2000); Jeanine Lewis, Comment, *The Hague Convention on the Civil Aspects of International Child Abduction: When Domestic Violence and Child Abuse Impact the Goal of Comity*, 13 TRANSNAT'L LAW. 391 (2000); Susan Kreston, *Prosecuting International Parental Kidnapping*, 15 NOTRE DAME J. L. ETHICS & PUB. POL'Y 533 (2001); Note, *Due Process Rights of Parents and Children in International Child Abductions: An Examination of the Hague Convention and Its Exceptions*, 26 VAND. J. TRANSNAT. L. 865 (1993).

The most recent Hague Convention dealing with international custody disputes is the 1996 Convention on Jurisdiction, Applicable Law, Recognition, Enforcement and Cooperation in Respect of Parental Responsibility and Measures for the Protection of Children. An American law professor who was one of three U.S. delegates negotiating the Convention described its main purpose as the "establish-[ment of] international standards of jurisdiction and enforcement of judgments for custody cases." Linda Silberman, *The 1996 Hague Convention on the Protection of Children: Should the United States Join?*, 34 FAM. L.Q. 239 (2000). As of the middle of 2009, 16 countries have contracted to the Convention and two have acceded to it. *See* Hague Convention website, www.hcch.net.

Chapter 7

DIVORCE JURISDICTION

A. TERMINATION OF MARITAL STATUS

SOSNA v. IOWA
United States Supreme Court
419 U.S. 393 (1974)

Mr. Justice Rehnquist delivered the opinion of the Court.

[Carol Sosna filed a divorce petition in Iowa within a month of her arrival in the state. Her husband, who had remained in New York after the separation, was served during a trip to Iowa to visit his children. The trial court dismissed for lack of jurisdiction because Carol had not been, as required by statute, "for the last year a resident of the state." The District Court rejected Carol's constitutional challenge to the statute.] [We] . . . hold that the Iowa durational residency requirement for divorce does not offend the United States Constitution.

I

[The Court rejected a mootness claim.]

II

The durational residency requirement . . . is a part of Iowa's comprehensive statutory regulation of domestic relations, an area . . . long . . . regarded as a virtually exclusive province of the States. . . . In *Barber v. Barber* (1859), the Court said: "We disclaim altogether any jurisdiction in the courts of the United States upon the subject of divorce. . . ." In *Pennoyer v. Neff* (1878), the Court said: "The State . . . has absolute right to prescribe the conditions upon which the marriage relation between its own citizens shall be created, and the causes for which it may be dissolved."

The statutory scheme in Iowa, like those in other States, sets forth . . . the grounds upon which a marriage may be dissolved and the circumstances in which a divorce may be obtained. Jurisdiction . . . is . . . in "the county where either party resides" and the Iowa courts have construed the term "resident" to have much the same meaning as is ordinarily associated with the concept of domicile. . . .

The imposition of a durational residency requirement for divorce is scarcely unique . . . , since 48 States impose such a requirement. . . . [ranging] from six weeks to two years. The one-year period selected by Iowa is the most common length of time prescribed.

[Carol] contends that the Iowa requirement . . . is unconstitutional for two separate reasons: *first*, because it establishes two classes of persons and discriminates against those who have recently exercised their right to travel to Iowa, thereby contravening the Court's holdings in *Shapiro v. Thompson*; *Dunn v. Blumstein*; and *Memorial Hospital v. Maricopa County*; and, *second*, because it denies a litigant the opportunity to make an individualized showing of bona fide residence and therefore denies such residents access to the only method of legally dissolving their marriage. *Vlandis v. Kline*; *Boddie v. Connecticut*.

State statutes imposing durational residency requirements were, of course, invalidated when imposed by States as a qualification for welfare payments, *Shapiro*; for voting, *Dunn*; and for medical care, *Maricopa County*. But none of those cases intimated that the States might never impose durational residency requirements, and such a proposition was in fact expressly disclaimed. . . . [T]he durational residency requirements they struck down were justified [by] budgetary or recordkeeping considerations which were held insufficient to outweigh the constitutional claims of the individuals. But Iowa's divorce residency requirement is of a different stripe. [Carol] was not irretrievably foreclosed from obtaining some part of what she sought, as was the case with the welfare recipients in *Shapiro*, the voters in *Dunn*, or the indigent patient in *Maricopa County*. She would eventually qualify for the same sort of adjudication which she demanded virtually upon her arrival in the State. Iowa's requirement [only] delayed her access to the courts. . . .

Iowa's residency requirement may reasonably be justified on grounds other than purely budgetary considerations or administrative convenience. A decree of divorce is not a matter in which the only interested parties are the State as a sort of "grantor," and a divorce petitioner such as [Carol] in the role of "grantee." Both spouses are obviously interested in the proceedings, since it will affect their marital status and very likely their property rights. Where a married couple has minor children, a decree of divorce would usually include provisions for their custody and support. With consequences of such moment riding on a divorce decree . . . , Iowa may insist that one seeking to initiate such a proceeding have the modicum of attachment to the State required here.

Such a requirement additionally furthers the State's parallel interests both in avoiding officious intermeddling in matters in which another State has a paramount interest, and in minimizing the susceptibility of its own divorce decrees to collateral attack. A State . . . may quite reasonably decide that it does not wish to become a divorce mill. . . . Until . . . Iowa is convinced that [Carol] intends to remain in the State, it lacks the "nexus between person and place of such permanence as to control the creation of legal relations and responsibilities of the utmost significance." *Williams v. North Carolina*, (1945). Perhaps even more important, Iowa's interests extend beyond its borders and include the recognition of its divorce decrees by other States under the Full Faith and Credit Clause of the Constitution. For that purpose, this Court has often stated that "judicial power to grant a divorce — jurisdiction, strictly speaking — is founded on domicile."

Williams, supra. Where a divorce decree is entered after a finding of domicile in *ex parte* proceedings, this Court has held that the finding of domicile is not binding upon another State and may be disregarded in the face of "cogent evidence" to the contrary. . . . The State's decision to exact a one-year residency requirement . . . is therefore buttressed by a quite permissible inference that this requirement . . . provides a greater safeguard against successful collateral attack than would a requirement of bona fide residence alone. This is precisely the sort of determination that a State in the exercise of its domestic relations jurisdiction is entitled to make.

We therefore hold that the state interest in requiring that those who seek a divorce from its courts be genuinely attached to the State, as well as a desire to insulate divorce decrees from the likelihood of collateral attack, requires a different resolution of the constitutional issue presented than . . . in *Shapiro, Dunn* and *Maricopa County.*

. . .

In *Boddie, supra,* this Court held that Connecticut might not deny access to divorce courts to those persons who could not afford to pay the required fee. Because of the exclusive role played by the State in the termination of marriages, it was held that indigents could not be denied an opportunity to be heard "absent a countervailing state interest of overriding significance." But the gravamen of [Carol's] claim is not total deprivation . . . but only delay. The operation of the filing fee . . . served to exclude forever a certain segment of the population from obtaining a divorce. . . . No similar total deprivation is present in appellant's case. . . .

Affirmed.

NOTES ON DIVORCE JURISDICTION

1. *Domicile as Basis of Jurisdiction to Terminate.* The idea that termination of a marriage may have special jurisdictional rules has a long history. *Pennoyer,* which established federal constitutional boundaries for state court jurisdiction, lumped "cases affecting the personal status of the plaintiff" with "*in rem*" cases for purposes of jurisdictional rules. Because marital status is such a personal status, jurisdiction to terminate marriage is determined by *in rem,* not *in personam* rules. Under the usual *in rem* analysis, the presence of the affected res "before the court" is both necessary and sufficient for jurisdiction. For jurisdiction over a status, all that is required is that the person whose status is being adjudicated is a forum domiciliary.

The special jurisdictional rule for divorce was addressed in *Williams v. North Carolina,* 317 U.S. 287 (1942) (*Williams I*) and *Williams v. North Carolina,* 325 U.S. 226 (1945) (*Williams II*), which both arose during the fault divorce era. The jurisdiction issue then was of immense practical importance, in part because of an established choice of law rule under which the forum applied its own divorce law. For example, it was critically important for New York residents to know the circumstances under which one could escape their state's restrictive substantive divorce rules (limiting divorce to cases of adultery) by seeking divorce elsewhere, such as Nevada.

The *Williams I* issue was whether North Carolina had to honor Nevada divorces granted to two domiciliaries who had traveled to Las Vegas, stayed for the six weeks required under Nevada law, served their spouses by mail or delivery, obtained divorce decrees, and then remarried (each other). On their return to North Carolina, they faced bigamy prosecutions. Because the divorce proceedings contained no contrary evidence, the Supreme Court held North Carolina bound by the Nevada court's finding that the couple were Nevada domiciliaries and held the Full Faith and Credit Clause required the divorces' recognition. *Wiilliams I* thus established the principle relied upon in *Sosna*: either party's domicile supports jurisdiction to terminate a marriage.

2. *Is There an Acceptable Jurisdictional Substitute for Domicile?* While *Williams I* held domicile *sufficient* for jurisdiction, it did not decide whether it was *necessary*. That is, it left open the question of whether a state could end a marriage on a jurisdictional basis other than domicile. Suppose, *e.g.*, a court had personal jurisdiction over two non-domiciliary spouses. Because the Supreme Court has never been presented with this question, it has not answered it.

Nonetheless, states have fashioned their laws on the assumption that divorce jurisdiction requires domicile and state courts routinely interpret statutes as if domicile of at least one party is a constitutional necessity. For example, in *Fletcher v. Fletcher*, 619 A.2d 561 (Md. Spec. App. 1993), no statute explicitly required domicile and, in fact, a procedural rule appeared to permit divorce if one party merely did business in the state. Nevertheless, describing the rule requiring domicile of a party for divorce jurisdiction as one which "has a Constitutional underpinning and remains firmly intact," the appellate court, citing *Sosna* and several state court decisions, required domicile of at least one party. *See also Carr v. Carr*, 724 So. 2d 937 (Miss. 1998) (citing *Williams II* for proposition that domicile is cornerstone of divorce jurisdiction).

3. *Divorces Involving Military Personnel.* While there is no direct Supreme Court authority upholding any non-domiciliary assertion of jurisdiction, one standard exception to the domicile requirement seems to stand on the proposition that personal jurisdiction under traditional presence standards can substitute for domicile in at least one situation. Military personnel often present special jurisdictional issues in divorce cases. They typically are not domiciled where they are stationed because they are there involuntarily and do not wish to establish a new domicile. They are thus domiciled in a state where they may have not actually lived for some years, where their spouse may have no contact, and where a divorce action may be inconvenient. To solve these practical problems, the typical statute asserts divorce jurisdiction where a spouse who serves in the armed forces is a resident. *See, e.g.*, M.M.D.A. § 302(a)(1) (asserting jurisdiction if, at commencement of the action, either party "was stationed in this State while a member of the armed forces" and such "military presence" was maintained for 90 days).

While most divorce jurisdictional issues involving military respondents are raised in the state of respondent's residence, suit may also be filed in respondent's domicile. In *Wamsley v. Wamsley*, 635 A.2d 1322 (Md. 1994), a divorce petitioner sued in a jurisdiction where respondent had not lived during his 11 years of naval service. Citing cases from other courts as authority, the court upheld jurisdiction, noting respondent had a Maryland driver's license, was registered to vote there and paid state income taxes.

4. *When Does a Finding of Domicile Bind Other Courts?* *Williams I* and *II*, particularly dicta suggesting domicile was necessary for jurisdiction as well as sufficient, created issues which were addressed in a series of cases.

a. *Can State-2 re-examine a divorce court's finding of domicile?* This issue was reserved in *Williams I*, because the record did not raise the bona fides of the spouses' Nevada domicile. That is, *Williams I* held only that domicile conferred jurisdiction; it did not address proof of domicile or the circumstances under which it can be challenged. On remand from *Williams I*, the state court rejected Nevada's finding that the parties had been Nevada domiciliaries when the divorces were granted. When the case returned to Supreme Court of the United States, the Court, in *Williams II*, found North Carolina not bound by Nevada's decision on domiciliary status.

Williams II held that, while North Carolina was bound to "respect" the Nevada finding, it could reach its own judgment on whether the Nevada divorce petitioners were domiciliaries because it was not party to the Nevada litigation. Thus, the Court permitted North Carolina's challenge, apparently because as the original domiciliary state it had an adequate interest in the divorce decision. The result is that for *ex parte* divorces such as the Nevada decree in *Williams*, the finding of domicile had to be persuasive enough to withstand scrutiny by the court of the original domiciliary state. This rule underlies *Sosna*'s observation that by requiring a year's residence, Iowa was furthering a valid state interest in ensuring its divorce decrees would be honored elsewhere. Of course, a state is not *compelled* to impose a durational residency requirement. For example, Alaska has no durational residency requirement, though residence is required. *Perito v. Perito*, 756 P.2d 895 (Alaska 1988) (upholding finding of residence when suit was filed the day after petitioner's arrival).

b. *Can State-1's jurisdiction be collaterally attacked where both spouses participated in the divorce proceedings, acknowledging domicile and jurisdiction?* The Supreme Court held that it could not, *Sherrer v. Sherrer*, 334 U.S. 343 (1948), not even by some third parties. *Johnson v. Muelberger*, 340 U.S. 581 (1951). Although no direct authority exists, the prevailing view is that the original domiciliary state is also bound, thus limiting it to "protection of the stay-at-home spouse against unilateral (*ex parte*) actions by the other [spouse] in a distant forum." Scoles, Hay, Borchers & Symeonides, Conflict of Laws § 15.11, 640 (4th ed. 2004). In combination with *Williams II*, this meant that, while a spouse could not unilaterally evade his state's restrictive divorce laws by obtaining a Nevada decree based upon sham residence there because another state could redetermine the validity of Nevada domicile, if the spouses cooperated they *could* evade their state law through a joint appearance in Nevada, insulating their divorce decree from collateral attack.

5. *"Sham" Domicile and Lack of Contact by Respondent.* Because one party's domicile suffices for divorce jurisdiction, a party can unilaterally grant a state jurisdiction over termination by establishing domicile there. What if this move is made for a "bad" reason or to a state with which the other party has no contact? The cases are clear that the reason for changing domicile is irrelevant. In *Fletcher* (Note 2, *supra*), the court observed:

> The [trial] court . . . seemed concerned that Louis had moved here solely to take advantage of . . . more favorable divorce law. That may well be so, and if it is so, it is unfortunate. But jurisdiction does not hinge on why he moved here, only whether he moved here . . . and whether, at present, he intends to remain here for the foreseeable future, which it appears he does. . . .

619 A.2d at 566. Note, however, that the petitioner's domicile does not alone establish jurisdiction over the respondent for any purpose other than terminating the marital status. *See* Sections B & C, *infra*. Domicile does not require citizenship. *Padron v. Padron*, 641 S.E.2d 542 (Ga. 2008); *Weber v. Weber*, 929 So. 2d 1165 (Fla. Ct. App. 2006) (nonimmigrant alien may establish domicile for purposes of divorce jurisdiction; nonimmigrant status is factor in determining presence of bona fide intent to remain in state indefinitely); *Cho v. Jeong*, 1997 Tenn. App. LEXIS 407 (June 6, 1997) (petitioner with student spouse visa); *Kimura v. Kimura*, 471 N.W.2d 869 (Iowa 1991) (permanent resident alien).

6. *Foreign Divorces.* Recognition of a foreign divorce is not governed by the Full Faith and Credit Clause. As a matter of comity, American states generally recognize divorces granted by foreign countries if one party was domiciled in that country. *Mori v. Mori*, 931 P.2d 854 (Utah 1997); *Atassi v. Atassi*, 451 S.E.2d 371 (N.C. App. 1995). *But see Aleem v. Aleem*, 947 A.2d 489 (Md. 2008) (refusing to recognize under the rules of comity a Pakistani *talaq* divorce under which the defendant was neither given notice or an opportunity to appear); *Banu v. Saheb*, 2009 Mich. App. LEXIS 733 (Apr. 7, 2009) (same, noting absence of due process in the Muslim law of *talaq*). During the fault divorce era, Americans sometimes sought foreign divorces to avoid restrictive local rules, but such divorces were usually held invalid when neither spouse actually lived abroad. For cases reviewing this law, see *Carr v. Carr*, 724 So. 2d 937 (Miss. 1998); Annot., *Domestic Recognition of Divorce Decree Obtained in Foreign Country and Attacked for Lack of Domicil or Jurisdiction of Parties*, 13 A.L.R.3d 1419 (1965). In a rule adopted during the era of very limited divorce grounds, New York recognizes foreign divorces even with no domiciliary attachment to the foreign country if both parties were before the foreign court. *Rosenstiel v. Rosenstiel*, 16 N.Y.2d 64, 209 N.E.2d 709 (1965) (recognizing Mexican divorce; while the parties were only there very briefly, "Nevada gets no closer to the real public concern with the marriage than Chihuahua").

7. *Modern Relevance of Domicile Rule.* The problem of divorce jurisdiction is quite different today than when the above-discussed cases were decided, though one scholar has argued that the Supreme Court's divorce cases of the 1940s and 1950s "fundamentally altered state power to set the normative boundaries of family life by extending to individual citizens the ability to choose which jurisdiction would control their marital status" and "seem to anticipate the more extensive infusion of constitutional principles into family law that occupied the Court during the decades that followed." Ann Lacquer Estin, *Family Law Federalism: Divorce and the Constitution*, 16 WM. & MARY BILL OF RTS. J. 381 (2007). In practical terms, however, the dominance of no-fault divorce has reduced the incentives for seeking a traditional divorce haven like Nevada and a home state's incentives to restrict its residents' ability to seek divorce elsewhere. At the same time, people are increasingly mobile, so that while a move to Nevada to establish a sham domicile is less likely, an individual may in fact move to Nevada or Iowa or Maine, before or after the termination of the marital status. In that case, which state court should divide their property, decide child custody and determine the level of child or spousal support? As a commentator has observed, the problem today is not so much migratory divorce as migratory people. Helen Garfield, *The Transitory Divorce Action: Jurisdiction in the No-Fault Era*, 58 TEX. L. REV. 501, 504 (1980). We now turn to these jurisdictional problems.

B.   JURISDICTION TO ISSUE SUPPORT ORDERS AND DIVIDE PROPERTY

In addition to terminating the marital status, a divorce decree usually fixes rights to support, custody, and property. The rules in the preceding section do not establish jurisdiction over these issues, which today form the most important part of any divorce action. This difference in jurisdictional rules creates the possibility of "divisible divorce"; while the marital status can always be terminated by a spouse's domiciliary state, it cannot bind an absent spouse to determinations of property and alimony without personal jurisdiction over him. *Estin v. Estin*, 334 U.S. 541 (1948); *Vanderbilt v. Vanderbilt*, 354 U.S. 416 (1957). The termination of the marital status by the domiciliary state thus "divides" the divorce issues with the financial and custody issues left for determination elsewhere. *See, e.g., Von Schack v. Von Schack*, 893 A.2d 1004 (Me. 2006) (jurisdiction existed to terminate marriage, but not to decide property or custody issues); *Ellithorp v. Ellithorp*, 575 S.E.2d 94 (W. Va. 2002) (Texas had jurisdiction to issue divorce, but only West Virginia had jurisdiction over financial and custody issues); *Muckle v. Muckle*, 102 Cal. App. 4th 218 (2002) (jurisdiction to terminate marriage present in California, but property issues must be litigated in Georgia); *Snider v. Snider*, 551 S.E.2d 693 (W. Va. 2001) (Illinois decree terminating marriage does not deprive West Virginia court of jurisdiction over property division or alimony issues); *Poston v. Poston*, 624 A.2d 853 (Vt. 1993) (rejecting Texas decree purporting to extinguish party's right to maintenance without personal jurisdiction).

In requiring personal jurisdiction over respondent to adjudicate the financial issues, *Estin* did not focus so much upon the absent spouse's Due Process rights as upon permitting each state to decide the matters of its "dominant" concern. In *Estin*, Nevada could adjudicate the marital status of its domiciliary, the husband; New York could adjudicate the support rights of its domiciliary, the wife. While the Court would reach the same result today, it would be based more explicitly upon the non-resident's Due Process rights; as in any other civil action, the Constitution requires personal jurisdiction over an individual in order to fix his or her rights or obligations regarding property or support. The following case applies this rule.

KULKO v. SUPERIOR COURT OF CALIFORNIA
United States Supreme Court
436 U.S. 84 (1978)

Mr. Justice Marshall.

. . . The issue before us is whether, in this action for child support, the California state courts may exercise *in personam* jurisdiction over a nonresident, nondomiciliary parent of minor children domiciled within the State. . . . [W]e hold that the exercise of such jurisdiction would violate the Due Process Clause of the Fourteenth Amendment.

I

. . . Ezra . . . married . . . Sharon . . . in 1959, during [Ezra's] three-day stopover in California en route . . . to a tour of duty in Korea. At the time of this marriage, both parties were domiciled in . . . New York State. Immediately following the marriage, Sharon . . . returned to New York, as did [Ezra] after his tour of duty. [The couple's two children were born in New York.] The [family] resided together . . . in New York City continuously until March 1972, when the Kulkos separated.

Following the separation, Sharon . . . moved to San Francisco. . . . A written separation agreement was drawn up in New York; in September 1972, Sharon . . . flew to New York City in order to sign this agreement. The agreement provided, *inter alia*, that the children would remain with their father during the school year but would spend their Christmas, Easter, and summer vacations with their mother. . . . Ezra . . . agreed to pay his wife $3,000 per year in child support for the periods when the children were in her care, custody, and control. Immediately after execution of the separation agreement, Sharon . . . flew to Haiti and procured a divorce there; the divorce decree incorporated the terms of the agreement. She then returned to California. . . .

[Both parties complied with the agreement] until December 1973. At this time, just before Ilsa was to leave New York to spend Christmas vacation with her mother, she told her father that she wanted to remain in California after her vacation. Ezra bought his daughter a one-way plane ticket, and Ilsa [began] living in California with her mother during the school year and spending vacations with her father. In January 1976, appellant's other child, Darwin, called Sharon from New York and advised her that he wanted to live with her in California. Unbeknownst to Ezra, Sharon sent a plane ticket to her son, which he used to fly to California where he took up residence with his mother and sister.

Less than one month after Darwin's arrival . . . , [Sharon] commenced this action . . . in the California Superior Court. She sought to establish the Haitian divorce decree as a California judgment; to modify the judgment so as to award her full custody of the children; and to increase [Ezra's] child-support obligations. [Ezra attacked personal jurisdiction for lack of "minimum contacts" under *International Shoe*.]

The trial court summarily denied the motion to quash, and [Ezra] sought review in the California Court of Appeal [which] affirmed the denial of [Ezra's] motion to quash, reasoning that, by consenting to his children's living in California, appellant had "caused an effect in th[e] state". . . .

The California Supreme Court . . . sustained the rulings of the lower state courts. It noted first that the California Code of Civil Procedure demonstrated an intent that the courts of California utilize all bases of *in personam* jurisdiction "not inconsistent with the Constitution." . . . [T]he Supreme Court stated that, where a nonresident defendant has caused an effect in the State . . . , personal jurisdiction . . . in causes arising from that effect may be exercised whenever "reasonable." It went on to hold that such an exercise was "reasonable" in this case because [Ezra] had "purposely availed himself of the benefits and protections of the laws of California" by sending Ilsa to live with her mother. . . . — [T]he court concluded that it was "fair and reasonable for [Ezra] to be subject to personal jurisdiction for the support of both children, where he has committed acts with respect to one child which confers [sic] personal jurisdiction and has consented to the permanent residence of the other child in California."

II

The Due Process Clause . . . operates as a limitation on the jurisdiction of state courts to enter judgments affecting rights or interests of nonresident defendants. See *Shaffer v. Heitner*, 433 U.S. 186 (1977). . . . [A] valid judgment imposing a personal obligation or duty . . . may be entered only by a court having jurisdiction over the person of the defendant. . . . The existence of personal jurisdiction, in turn, depends upon the presence of reasonable notice . . . , and a sufficient connection between the defendant and the forum State to make it fair to require defense of the action in the forum. . . . In this case, [Ezra] does not dispute the adequacy of the notice . . . , but contends that his connection with . . . California is too attenuated. . . .

. . . [T]he constitutional standard for determining whether the State may enter a binding judgment against [Ezra] here is that set forth in this Court's opinion in *International Shoe Co.*: that a defendant "have certain minimum contacts with [the forum State] such that the maintenance of the suit does not offend 'traditional notions of fair play and substantial justice.' " While the interests of the forum State and of the plaintiff in proceeding with the cause in the plaintiff's forum of choice are, of course, to be considered, . . . , an essential criterion in all cases is whether the "quality and nature" of the defendant's activity is such that it is "reasonable" and "fair" to require him to conduct his defense in that State. . . .

. . . [T]he "minimum contacts" test of *International Shoe* is not susceptible of mechanical application; rather, the facts of each case must be weighed. . . .

A

. . . [T]he California Supreme Court did not rely on [Ezra's] glancing presence in the State some 13 years before the events that led to this controversy, nor could it have. [Ezra] has been in California on only two occasions [on stopovers to and from service in Korea.]. To hold such temporary visits to a State a basis for the assertion of *in personam* jurisdiction over unrelated actions arising in the future would make a mockery of the limitations on state jurisdiction. . . . Nor did the California court rely on the fact that [Ezra] was actually married in California. . . . We agree that where two New York domiciliaries, for reasons of convenience, marry in the State of California and thereafter spend their entire married life in New York, . . . their California marriage by itself cannot support a California court's exercise of jurisdiction over a spouse who remains a New York resident in an action relating to child support.

Finally, . . . the court below carefully disclaimed reliance on the fact that [Ezra] had agreed at the time of separation to allow his children to live with their mother three months a year and that he had sent them to California each year pursuant to this agreement. . . . [T]o find personal jurisdiction in a State on this basis . . . would discourage parents from entering into reasonable visitation agreements. Moreover, it could arbitrarily subject one parent to suit in any State of the Union where the other parent chose to spend time while having custody of their offspring pursuant to a separation agreement. As we have emphasized:

> "The unilateral activity of those who claim some relationship with a nonresident defendant cannot satisfy the requirement of contact with the forum State. . . ." *Hanson v. Denckla, supra,* at 253.

The "purposeful act" that the California Supreme Court believed did warrant the exercise of personal jurisdiction over [Ezra] . . . was his "actively and fully consent[ing] to Ilsa living in California for the school year . . . and . . . sen[ding] her to California for that purpose." We cannot accept the proposition that [Ezra's] acquiescence in Ilsa's desire to live with her mother conferred jurisdiction. . . . A father who agrees, in the interests of family harmony and his children's preferences, to allow them to spend more time in California than was required under a separation agreement can hardly be said to have "purposefully availed himself" of the "benefits and protections" of California's laws. . . .

Nor can we agree with the assertion . . . that the exercise of *in personam* jurisdiction here was warranted by the financial benefit [Ezra] derived from his daughter's presence in California for nine months of the year. This argument rests on the premise that, while [Ezra's] liability for support payments remained unchanged, his yearly expenses for supporting the child in New York decreased. But this circumstance, even if true, does not support California's assertion of jurisdiction here. Any diminution in [Ezra's] household costs resulted, not from the child's presence in California, but rather from her absence from [Ezra's] home. Moreover, an action by [Sharon] to increase support payments could now be brought, and could have been brought when Ilsa first moved to California, in the State of New York. . . . Any ultimate financial advantage to [Ezra] thus results not from the child's presence in California, but from [Sharon's] failure earlier to seek an increase. . . .

B

In light of our conclusion that [Ezra] did not purposefully derive benefit from any activities relating to the State of California, it is apparent that the California Supreme Court's reliance on [Ezra's] having caused an "effect" in California was misplaced.

The circumstances [here] clearly render "unreasonable" California's assertion of personal jurisdiction. There is no claim that [Ezra] has visited physical injury on either property or persons within . . . California. The cause of action herein asserted arises, not from the defendant's commercial transactions in interstate commerce, but rather from his personal, domestic relations. . . . [Ezra's] activities cannot fairly be analogized to an insurer's sending an insurance contract and premium notices into the State to an insured resident of the State. Furthermore, the controversy . . . arises from a separation that occurred in . . . New York; [Sharon] seeks modification of a contract that was negotiated in New York and that she flew to New York to sign. As in *Hanson*, the instant action involves an agreement . . . with virtually no connection with the forum State.

Finally, basic considerations of fairness point decisively in favor of [Ezra's] . . . domicile as the proper forum for adjudication. . . . It is [Ezra] who has remained in the State of the marital domicile, whereas . . . [Sharon] . . . has moved across the continent. . . . As noted above, [Ezra] did no more than acquiesce in the stated preference of one of his children to live with her mother in California. This single act is surely not one that a reasonable parent would expect to result in the substantial financial burden and personal strain of litigating a child-support suit in a forum 3,000 miles away, and we therefore see no basis on which it can be said that [Ezra] could reasonably have anticipated being "haled before a [California] court," *Shaffer*. To make jurisdiction . . . turn on whether [Ezra] bought his daughter her ticket or instead unsuccessfully sought to prevent her departure would impose an unreasonable burden on family relations, and one wholly unjustified by the "quality and nature" of appellant's activities in or relating to the State of California. . . .

III

. . . [Sharon] argues that California has substantial interests in protecting the welfare of its minor residents and in . . . a healthy and supportive family environment. . . . These interests are unquestionably important. But . . . the fact that California may be the "center of gravity" for choice-of-law purposes does not mean that California has personal jurisdiction over the defendant. And California has not attempted to assert any particularized interest in trying such cases in its courts by, *e.g.*, enacting a special jurisdictional statute.

California's legitimate interest in ensuring the support of children resident in California without unduly disrupting the children's lives, moreover, is already being served by the State's participation in the Revised Uniform Reciprocal Enforcement of Support Act of 1968. . . .

Accordingly, we conclude that [Ezra's] motion to quash service . . . was erroneously denied. . . . The judgment . . . is, therefore,

Reversed.

NOTES

1. *Variations.* *Kulko* applies, in the divorce context, the general rule requiring personal jurisdiction over respondent (along with the constitutional minimum contacts analysis) as a pre-requisite to a determination of financial rights and obligations. While directly covering only modification of child support, the principle also covers establishment of child support, establishment or modification of spousal maintenance and property division. The case's central point is made in part II's last paragraph: fairness principles require the traveling party, not the one who has remained in the state of the marital home, to bear the burden of litigating in another state. This principle will decide many (if not most) disputes over the application of long-arm jurisdiction in domestic relations cases. For a case applying *Kulko*, see *In re Crew*, 549 N.W.2d 527 (Iowa 1996) (payment of child support in state, communication via letter and telephone and sending children back to state to custodial parent insufficient for personal jurisdiction for support modification).

In many marriages, of course, the parties have lived in more than one state, so that more than one state could assert jurisdiction. Consider, *e.g.*, the couple who spends ten years of married life in State *A*, and then relocates to State *B*. After a year, they divorce and custodial parent returns to *A* with the couple's children. Both State *A* and State *B* could obtain personal jurisdiction over the defendant in the child support action, under ordinary jurisdiction rules, for defendant has strong contacts with State *A* related to the dispute and lives in State *B*.

Nonetheless, the passage of time alone may cause a state to lose sufficient contact to sustain jurisdiction. For example, in *Garrett v. Garrett*, 668 So. 2d 991 (Fla. 1996), the court found no jurisdiction over a non-resident who had fathered a child in the state, lived there with his family for 12 years and periodically returned to visit. Noting the state had been abandoned (by both parties) as the marital domicile eight years before the suit and that they had lived for five of the intervening years in Texas, the court found an exercise of jurisdiction here "would empower the Florida courts to exercise jurisdiction over any party to a dissolution proceeding if the couple had ever lived in the state, for however brief a time. This would clearly violate the Due Process Clause of the United States Constitution." *See also Morris v. Morris*, 672 So. 2d 622 (Fla. App. 1996) (applying *Garrett*). *But see Panganiban v. Panganiban*, 736 A.2d 190 (Conn. App. Ct. 1999) (extending jurisdiction over defendant absent from state for 11 years after living there with wife for 6 years).

Of course, as *Kulko* suggests, availability to the obligee of an interstate enforcement mechanism, such as the Revised Uniform Reciprocal Enforcement of Support Act of 1968 (since replaced by the Uniform Interstate Family Support Act) removes some pressure to stretch jurisdictional rules to allow such actions, at least to the extent one believes the interstate statute effective. (UIFSA is discussed in Chapter 5). No such action was available to the wife in *Khan v. Superior Ct.*, 251 Cal. Rptr. 815 (Ct. App. 1988), whose husband had divorced her in a Saudi Arabian court by repeating "I divorce you" three times. The couple had lived in California an aggregate of nine years during their thirty-year marriage, most of the remaining 21 years having been spent in various Middle Eastern locales. But they maintained California contacts even during foreign stays, including ownership of two California homes. Despite the husband's presence in Saudi Arabia since 1974, the court found sufficient contact with California to distinguish *Kulko* and find jurisdiction over maintenance and marital property claims. The court may have been relying on plaintiff's lack of other forums, a factor considered in long-arm jurisdiction cases in ordinary civil suits.

As in other civil actions, personal jurisdiction over the divorce respondent can be established by serving respondent with process while in the forum state, even if there is no other contact with the state. *Burnham v. Superior Court*, 495 U.S. 604 (1990) (in personam jurisdiction over father in mother's divorce action established by service on him while he was in state visiting his children); *see also In re Peterson*, 843 P.2d 1107 (Wash. App. 1993) (finding *Burnham* precludes respondent's minimum contacts argument against in-state personal service); *In re Craze*, 2006 Wash. App. LEXIS 1279 (June 19, 2006) (rejecting claim that D had been tricked into coming into the state where he was served).

2. *Long-arm Statutes.* California's broad long-arm statute provided simply jurisdiction "on any basis not inconsistent with the Constitution. . . .", making it easier for the *Kulko* petitioner to argue that the state intended to exercise jurisdiction over her former husband. States with less-sweeping language in their long-arm statutes require the petitioner to fit the support or property division claim within a much narrower provision and this can be difficult. Courts have held, *e.g.*, that support claims normally cannot be brought under the "transacts any business" portion of the typical long-arm statute, while the negotiation and execution of a separation agreement within the state may qualify as the conduct of "business" within the statute. *Warren v. Warren*, 287 S.E.2d 524 (Ga. 1982); *but see Poindexter v. Poindexter*, 594 N.W.2d 76 (Mich. Ct. App. 1999) (finding support jurisdiction against defendant who had been out of state for 22 years; fathering child creates quasi-contractual obligation under long-arm provision covering those contracting with state citizens).

To avoid such problems, many states have enacted special domestic relations provisions in their long-arm statutes. In fact, since 1998 states have been required as a condition of their receipt of federal welfare funding (*see* 42 U.S.C. § 666(f)), to have enacted the Uniform Interstate Family Support Act, which includes a long-arm provision for child and spousal support claims. The Uniform Act provides:

SECTION 201. BASES FOR JURISDICTION. . . . In a proceeding to establish, enforce, or modify a support order or to determine parentage, a [court] may exercise personal jurisdiction over a nonresident . . . if:

(1) the individual is personally served . . . within this State;

(2) the individual submits to the jurisdiction of this State by consent . . . ;

(3) the individual resided with the child in this State;

(4) the individual resided in this State and provided prenatal expenses or support for the child;

(5) the child resides in this State as a result of the acts or directives of the individual;

(6) the individual engaged in sexual intercourse in this State and the child may have been conceived by that act of intercourse;

. . . or

(8) there is any other basis consistent with the constitutions of this State and the United States for the exercise of personal jurisdiction.

Given the inclusion of the California-style subsection (8), the earlier subsections might seem superfluous. The drafters may have included the specific provisions in hopes that reliance on a narrowly-drafted provision might satisfy any notice requirements implicit in the Due Process clause. Alternatively, the inclusion of such specific language might express the drafters' opinion that any of the facts in the subsections would satisfy minimum contacts requirements. If so, are they right? What if, *e.g.*, the respondent's only connection with the forum state was residence there with the child which had ended ten years earlier? *See Levy v. Levy*, 592 N.Y.S.2d 480 (App. Div. 1993) (Constitution not violated by application of long-arm where forum marital domicile had ended ten years earlier). Similarly, would brief marital residency in the forum confer jurisdiction on a defendant who had been absent for 20 years? *See Strickland v. Strickland*, 534 S.E.2d 74 (Ga. 2000) (finding exercise of jurisdiction in such a situation unconstitutional); *Senhart v. Senhart*, 782 N.Y.S.2d 576 (Sup. Ct. 2004) (absence of defendant from jurisdiction for 13 years rendered exercise of long-arm jurisdiction unconstitutional). For a recent application of a specific family law long-arm statute, see *Miller v. Miller*, 861 N.E.2d 393 (Mass. 2007) (personal jurisdiction appropriate where couple had numerous conversations within forum, to which wife had fled with couple's children because of health problems; noting long-arm provision covers acts "giving rise to [the divorce] claim" within state, court concludes conversations in forum gave rise to action; minimum contacts to satisfy Due Process were also present).

Another explanation for subsection (8) is hinted at in a North Carolina case which noted that most of UIFSA's provisions define jurisdiction in child support litigation. Other than personal service or consent (in subsections 1 and 2, respectively), the only ground for exercise of jurisdiction over in non-support situations is subsection (8). *Butler v. Butler*, 566 S.E.2d 707 (N.C. Ct. App. 2002). It upheld jurisdiction under subsection (8) where defendant had jointly purchased a home in the forum, decided to move his wife and children to the state because of the good schools and visited them (from his home in the Bahamas) several days each month over a two-year period.

3. *Continuing Jurisdiction.* The usual rule is that personal jurisdiction, once established in a case, is not lost through subsequent events. Courts of equity claim continuing jurisdiction to enforce or modify their orders even if the parties move. This principle generally applies in support actions. *See, e.g., Bailey v. Bailey*, 867 P.2d 1267 (Okla. 1994) (constitutional attack based on lack of minimum contacts rejected in support modification where neither parent nor children remained in forum); *see also Hall v. Hall*, 524 So. 2d 370 (Ala. Civ. App. 1988); Annot., *Necessity of Personal Service within State Upon Nonresident Spouse as Prerequisite of*

Court's Power to Modify Its Decree as to Alimony or Child Support in Matrimonial Action, 62 A.L.R.2d 544 (1958). Importantly, however, a state could choose to statutorily abandon modification jurisdiction when, *e.g.*, the child support obligor, obligee and child all have left the state. This is, in fact, the result mandated by § 205 of the Uniform Interstate Family Support Act, currently the law in all states. *See In re Abplanalp*, 7 P.3d 1269 (Kan. App. 2000). Modification jurisdiction under UIFSA is discussed in detail in Chapter 5. Even outside of the child support context reflected in UIFSA, in light of *Kulko*'s emphasis on fairness to an absent defendant, is it possible that at some point the exercise of continuing jurisdiction might violate the minimum contacts doctrine? For example, what if both parties had left the forum immediately after the decree 10 years before, neither was a forum domiciliary when modification of the alimony award was sought and the respondent had not set foot in the forum since the decree was rendered. Could modification jurisdiction be exercised constitutionally?

4. *Modification by Another State.* In general, of course, a final judgment made by a court with jurisdiction is entitled to full faith and credit in sister states. While this principle theoretically applies to judgments for alimony and maintenance, the result is a bit different than with ordinary civil judgments because the Constitution requires recognition only of final decrees and, to the extent family law decrees are modifiable, there is no mandate for recognition. *Aldrich v. Aldrich*, 378 U.S. 540 (1964); *Barber v. Barber*, 323 U.S. 77 (1944); *Sistare v. Sistare*, 218 U.S. 1 (1910). Thus, if an existing decree for child support or alimony is modifiable in the rendering state, a second state need not enter its own decree ordering future payments of child support or maintenance. While a state is not *bound* to honor modifiable decrees, it may *choose* to adopt (or domesticate) the existing decree and rendering a new judgment of its own. *Griffin v. Griffin*, 327 U.S. 220 (1946). After adopting the decree, the second state may modify it. *Norwood v. Craig*, 658 So. 2d 212 (La. App. 1995); *Watson v. Blakely*, 748 P.2d 984 (N.M. App. 1987); *Walzer v. Walzer*, 376 A.2d 414 (Conn. 1977). Of course, to modify the new order the second state will need personal jurisdiction over the respondent. *Laney v. Nigro*, 905 S.W.2d 902 (Mo. App. 1995); *Scott (Anderson) v. Scott*, 492 N.W.2d 831 (Minn. App. 1992). Two Uniform Acts each provide mechanisms for the domestication of one state's judgment in another state. *See* UNIFORM ENFORCEMENT OF FOREIGN JUDGMENTS ACT, http://www.law.upenn.edu/bll/archives/ulc/fnact99/1920_69/ruefja64.htm; UNIFORM INTERSTATE FAMILY SUPPORT ACT, http://nccusl.org/nccusl/ActSearchResults.aspx. To reduce relitigation in multiple jurisdictions over the appropriate level of child support, Congress has restricted states' ability to exercise modification jurisdiction. *See* Full Faith and Credit for Child Support Orders Act, 28 U.S.C. § 1738B (2000) (discussed in Chapter 5).

5. *Real Property Outside the Forum State.* A complicating factor in divorce jurisdiction arises where divisible real property is located outside the forum. Traditionally, only the state where real property is located has power to affect title to it. *Buchanan v. Weber*, 567 S.E.2d 413 (N.C. App. 2002); SCOLES, HAY, BORCHERS & SYMEONIDES, CONFLICT OF LAWS § 24.10, 1276 (4th ed. 2004). This would bar a change in title by a non-situs state, even one with personal jurisdiction over the owner. Over 100 years ago the Supreme Court applied this rule in the divorce context, affirming Nebraska's refusal to recognize a Washington decree awarding wife title to Nebraska realty. *Fall v. Eastin*, 215 U.S. 1 (1909). Despite the fact that some applications of this rule would appear inconsistent with modern jurisdictional standards, it survives, though not without serious questioning. *See* Russell Weintraub, *An Inquiry into the Utility of "Situs as a Concept in Conflict Analysis*, 52 CORN. L.Q. 1 (1966).

As a practical matter, the rule is unworkable for a divorce court making an equitable division of property. Only the court settling the parties' entire financial arrangement can determine the proper disposition of their real property, and in any event that court's law will govern the division of property upon divorce, not the law of the situs. Thus, despite the absence of constitutional compulsion, situs states typically recognize decrees of non-situs divorce courts fixing spousal property rights. Usually, the divorce court avoids any attempt to affect directly the title and instead orders the spouses to make an appropriate conveyance to effectuate the property disposition. *TWE Retirement Fund Trust v. Ream*, 8 P.3d 1182 (Ariz. Ct. App. 2000) (Nevada court with personal jurisdiction over defendant could order specific performance of a contract to convey Arizona land); *In re Marriage of Day*, 904 P.2d 171 (Ore. Ct. App. 1995) (directing distribution of equity of California property); *Eckard v. Eckard*, 636 A.2d 455 (Md. 1994) (upholding order to ex-wife to authorize ex-husband to sell Florida land). Orders issued with personal jurisdiction over the defendant ordinarily will be recognized and enforced by the situs state. Some states do this as a matter of comity, while others assert Full Faith and Credit compulsion, distinguishing such orders from those directly affecting title to land. *In re Marriage of Hanley*, 245 Cal. Rptr. 441 (Ct. App. 1988) (recognizing efficacy of Washington decree requiring conveyance of California property). A court with personal jurisdiction over owner-spouse can hold him in contempt for refusing to comply with its order to convey non-situs real property. *Collins v. Collins*, 898 P.2d 1316 (Okla. Ct. App. 1995).

6. *Jurisdiction Based on Marital Property?* In *Abernathy v. Abernathy*, 482 S.E.2d 265 (Ga. 1997), the divorcing couple had never lived in Georgia and apparently the wife had never been within the state. After their separation in Louisiana, however, the husband moved to Georgia and established domicile. He brought some marital property with him and also earned marital property in Georgia before filing for divorce. He sought division of the marital property, both real and personal, located in Georgia.

The Georgia Supreme Court affirmed the trial court's exercise of jurisdiction to divide the property, finding it to be consistent with *Shaffer v. Heitner*. The majority relied on the following language in *Shaffer* which suggested that in some cases the mere presence of property in the forum necessarily would satisfy the required *International Shoe* minimum contacts analysis:

> [W]hen claims to the property itself are the source of the underlying controversy between the plaintiff and the defendant, it would be unusual for the State where the property is located not to have jurisdiction. In such cases, the defendant's claim to property located in the State would normally indicate that he expected to benefit from the State's protection of his interest. . . . The State's strong interests in assuring the marketability of property within its borders and in providing a procedure for peaceful

resolution of disputes about the . . . property would also support jurisdiction, as would the likelihood that important records and witnesses will be found in the State.

Id. at 272, 268. This is not the *quasi in rem* jurisdiction disallowed in *Shaffer* because the court's jurisdiction was limited to adjudicating interests in the property before it. However, whether it is consistent with the constitutional requirements for limited jurisdiction may be disputed. For example, an *Abernathy* dissenter noted the wife "has never lived here and . . . did not participate in the decision . . . to acquire property in this state. . . . Forcing the wife to litigate her interests . . . wherever her husband happens to relocate violates 'traditional notions of fair play and substantial justice.'" *See Hoffman v. Hoffman*, 821 S.W.2d 3 (Tex. App. 1992) (citing *Shaffer* for proposition that court may "lack jurisdiction to divide property within the [forum] state").

7. Military Pensions. The federal Uniformed Services Former Spouses Protection Act (summarized in Chapter 4's discussion of pension division), bars a divorce court from exercising jurisdiction over a spouse's military pension using the ordinary minimum-contacts analysis usually used in property claims. The Act requires that the pensioned spouse be resident or domiciled in the forum state, or consent to jurisdiction. *Blackson v. Blackson*, 579 S.E.2d 704 (Va. Ct. App. 2003) (filing of a cross-claim in a divorce action constituted consent to jurisdiction under federal statute); *Peters v. Haley*, 762 So. 2d 695 (La. Ct. App. 2000) (finding domicile of retired service member to be in forum state); *In re Atkins*, 932 P.2d 863 (Colo. Ct. App. 1997) (holding that the federal statutory requirements establish subject matter jurisdiction rules).

PROBLEMS

Problem 7-1. Harvey and Wilhelmina marry in California, where they live together for ten years. They then separate, and Harvey moves to Oregon with his new girlfriend. Wilhelmina, who remains behind in California, files an action for divorce there. What may the California court adjudicate?

Problem 7-2. Assume the same facts as in Problem 7-1, except that instead of remaining in California, Wilhelmina moves to New York where her family lives and seeks to bring a divorce action which will include claims for property division, alimony and child support. Can a unitary action addressing all matters be brought by her in New York? In Oregon? In California?

Problem 7-3. Suppose, in Problem 7-2, Wilhelmina could not bring a unitary action in Oregon because state law required a divorce petitioner to be a domiciliary. In a constitutional challenge to this requirement, would *Sosna* control?

Problem 7-4. Harry and Sally were married in the State of Bliss which was where her parents had moved when she left the original family home in Oregon. Immediately after the wedding, they left Bliss and spent the next 16 years traveling around the world where each had assignments as journalists. The only time during this period in which they were in the United States for more than a week was when they spent 6 months in Georgia in the mid-90s. During the marriage, all federal income tax forms and returns were sent to Harry and Sally at her parents' home in

Bliss. From 1991 to 1997 Harry had his salary direct deposited into a Bliss bank account. From 1989 to 2000, Harry had a Bliss driver's license. Harry's will named his parents-in-law co-executors of his estate. Harry and Sally had an investment account in Bliss for the last 7 years of their marriage. After their separation in 2003, Sally returned to Bliss to live with her parents. She has filed for divorce there, seeking alimony. State law provides for personal jurisdiction over the parties in any case "that arises out of the marital relationship within this State, notwithstanding subsequent departure from the State, if the other party to the marital relationship continues to reside in this state." Is the statute satisfied and is the Constitution satisfied?

Problem 7-5. Beverly and James were married in Massachusetts. After living there for 7 years, the childless couple moved to Florida. Eleven years later, pregnant with their first child, Beverly left her husband to move back to Massachusetts, where the child was born. Several years later, she filed for divorce in Massachusetts, claiming cruel and abusive treatment by James throughout their marriage and seeking child support. Her affidavit asserts the only way she could support herself and her child after her separation was to live in her parents' home in Massachusetts. James has never owned any real estate in the state, has transacted no business there in over 15 years and has visited the state only once since Beverly moved there to see his daughter perform in her third grade play. The state statute authorizes the exercise of personal jurisdiction over any person:

> (1) who acts directly or by an agent, as to a cause of action arising from the person's maintaining a domicile in this commonwealth while a party to a personal or marital relationship out of which arises a claim for divorce, alimony, property settlement, parentage of a child, child support or child custody; or the commission of any act giving rise to such a claim; . . . . 6) where the claim is for child support and the child resides in this Commonwealth as a result of the acts of the defendant. . . .

Is the statute satisfied? Is the Constitution satisfied?

C. JURISDICTION TO ADJUDICATE CUSTODY DISPUTES

[1]   Constitutional Framework

Section B applied ordinary personal jurisdiction rules to cases adjudicating the financial incidents of divorce, noting that generally the minimum contacts principle determines whether judicial power over the respondent exists. Does this rule also apply to child custody adjudications? Surprisingly, the Supreme Court's most recent opinion on this point, now almost 60 years old, leaves this question unanswered. In *May v. Anderson*, 345 U.S. 528 (1953), the wife left her husband in Wisconsin and moved to Ohio with their children. Soon after, the husband commenced a Wisconsin divorce action. The wife failed to appear, though she was served in Ohio. Wisconsin's grant of custody to father was unchallenged for four years, until mother refused to surrender the children after her summer visitation period.

In the father's *habeas corpus* action, the Ohio courts held the Constitution's Full Faith and Credit Clause required recognition of the Wisconsin order, accepting father's claim that the children remained Wisconsin domiciliaries despite their physical presence in Ohio and Wisconsin retained jurisdiction over them. The Supreme Court, however, held Ohio was not bound by the Wisconsin decree, finding the children's domicile irrelevant, because "that does not give Wisconsin . . . the personal jurisdiction . . . it must have in order to deprive their mother of . . . their immediate possession." *Id.* at 534.

The case reads oddly today because of its restrictive notions of personal jurisdiction. The modern Court likely would uphold Wisconsin's exercise of personal jurisdiction over wife where (a) it had long been the marital home, (b) the father remained there, and (c) the wife had been personally served soon after departing.

In any event, *May* is less important than one might expect. While it rejected any obligation to honor custody decrees rendered without personal jurisdiction over the respondent spouse, in practice there always had been little application of full faith and credit to custody decrees anyway. The Clause has been held to require only that a second state give a judgment the same effect as it has in the rendering state. Because all states permit modification of custody upon changed circumstances, almost all custody decrees have been considered reviewable by a second state, at least for changed circumstances. *See Ford v. Ford*, 371 U.S. 187 (1962); *Kovacs v. Brewer*, 356 U.S. 604 (1958).

May would have mattered more had it found that due process requires personal jurisdiction over respondent spouse for a binding custody decision, but the Court never quite said that. To the modern ear, any distinction between the dictates of due process, and of full faith and credit, may sound strange. The current assumption is that full faith and credit is required for all decrees obtained with jurisdiction, thus making due process and full faith and credit coextensive. But in a concurring opinion, Justice Frankfurter, the fifth member of the five-justice *May* majority, found that while personal jurisdiction over the respondent spouse was required for full faith and credit, a decree in the absence of such jurisdiction would not offend the Due Process Clause. That is, "one-state jurisdiction" not requiring interstate respect was possible; a state constitutionally could render a custody decree enforceable only within its borders.

The remaining members of the majority never spoke to this question, however, and it remains uncertain whether personal jurisdiction over respondent spouse is required under due process as well as under the Full Faith and Credit Clause. One explanation for the Frankfurter view is that custody, like termination of the marriage, is an adjudication of "status," to which the personal jurisdiction requirements of due process do not apply. Even many years after *May*, when the Court extended the personal-jurisdiction principles of *International Shoe* to *quasi-in-rem* actions, the Court reiterated the status rules. *Shaffer v. Heitner*, 433 U.S. 186, 208 n.30 (1977).

All states and Congress consistently have acted to authorize custody jurisdiction without personal jurisdiction over the respondent parent. Thus, the traditional state law rule based custody jurisdiction solely on the presence of the subject child.

This was analogized to state power to adjudicate marital status based solely on one spouse's presence even without personal jurisdiction over respondent. Such traditional rules would be valid only if Frankfurter's understanding of *May* were adopted.

Today traditional state law rules governing custody jurisdiction have been supplanted by new statutes — the Uniform Child Custody Jurisdiction and Enforcement Act (UCCJEA) and the Parental Kidnapping Prevention Act (PKPA) — considered at length below. The *May* issue survives, however, because these statutes sometimes assert jurisdiction without personal jurisdiction over an absent parent. Some lower courts have ignored Frankfurter's concurrence, reading *May* as holding due process forbids enforcement of custody decrees in such cases. *Pasqualone v. Pasqualone*, 406 N.E.2d 1121 (Ohio 1980); *In re Dean*, 447 So. 2d 733 (Ala. 1984). However, most courts and commentators conclude that a custody decree complying with the UCCJEA (or its predecessor, the UCCJA) is constitutionally acceptable, even without satisfaction of the minimum contacts test. *See, e.g., In re Thomas J.R.*, 663 N.W.2d 734 (Wisc. 2003) (termination of parental rights under UCCJA despite lack of minimum contacts); *Balestrieri v. Maliska*, 622 So. 2d 561 (Fla. Ct. App. 1993) (finding custody within *Shaffer v. Heitner*'s "status exception"); Russell Coombs, *Interstate Child Custody: Jurisdiction, Recognition, Enforcement*, 66 MINN. L. REV. 711 (1982). Professor Atwood agrees that personal jurisdiction over the absent parent is not and ought not be required. Instead, she proposes requiring "territorial jurisdiction" to be determined through analysis of "child-centered contacts with the forum state." Barbara Atwood, *Child Custody Jurisdiction and Territoriality*, 52 OHIO ST. L.J. 369, 372–73 (1991).

[2] The Modern Statutory Framework

Frankfurter's approach left each state free to devise its own custody jurisdiction rules, because due process imposed no threshold for permissible assertions. When most custody disputes remained within one state, interstate divisions over appropriate jurisdictional rules did not matter much, but custody disputes became increasingly multi-state. A parent dissatisfied with a custody decision often would seek a new one elsewhere. To the extent a second state was willing to render a new decree, enforceable so long as the child was physically within the jurisdiction, child snatching was encouraged. This unfortunate situation became a target of reform, resulting in successive uniform laws and a federal statute. In 1968, the National Conference of Commissioners on Uniform Laws proposed the Uniform Child Custody Jurisdiction Act (UCCJA). While eventually adopted in each state, before its universal adoption (and likely in an effort to encourage the remaining states to adopt it), Congress in 1980 passed the Parental Kidnapping Prevention Act (PKPA), which defines the jurisdictional bases for custody decrees commanding respect by other states. While the two acts were similar, there were critical differences between them concerning the appropriate bases for jurisdiction. Because of those differences and also because of widely varying interpretations of the UCCJA over the prior 29 years, in 1997 the Uniform Law Commissioners, with the endorsement of the American Bar Association, proposed a replacement, the Uniform Child Custody Jurisdiction and Enforcement Act (UCCJEA). By spring, 2009, this Act had been passed in 46 states, plus the District of Columbia. The remaining jurisdictions retain their version of the UCCJA. For the history of the Uniform and federal legislation, see Patricia Hoff, *The ABC's of the UCCJEA*, 32 FAM. L.Q. 267 (1998); Russell Coombs, *Child Custody and Visitation by Non-Parents Under the New Uniform Child Custody Jurisdiction and Enforcement Act: A Rerun of Seize-and-Run*, 16 J. AM. ACAD. MATRIMONIAL LAW. 1 (1999); Stoner, *The Uniform Child Custody Jurisdiction and Enforcement Act (UCCJEA) — A Metamorphosis of the Uniform Child Custody Jurisdiction Act (UCCJA)*, 75 N. DAK. L. REV. 301 (1999); *see also* Minneman, Annotation, *Construction and Operation of Uniform Child Custody Jurisdiction and Enforcement Act*, 100 A.L.R.5th 1 (2003).

UNIFORM CHILD CUSTODY JURISDICTION AND ENFORCEMENT ACT

§ 102. DEFINITIONS.

In this [Act]:

. . .

(3) "Child-custody determination" means a judgment, decree, or other order of a court providing for the legal custody, physical custody, or visitation with respect to a child. The term includes a permanent, temporary, initial, and modification order. . . .

(4) "Child-custody proceeding" means a proceeding in which legal custody, physical custody, or visitation with respect to a child is an issue. The term includes a proceeding for divorce, separation, neglect, abuse, dependency, guardianship, paternity, termination of parental rights, and protection from domestic violence, in which the issue may appear. The term does not include a proceeding involving juvenile delinquency, contractual emancipation, or enforcement. . . .

. . .

(7) "Home State" means the State in which a child lived with a parent or a person acting as a parent for at least six consecutive months immediately before the commencement of a child-custody proceeding. In the case of a child less than six months of age, the term means the State in which the child lived from birth with any of the persons mentioned. A period of temporary absence of any of the mentioned persons is part of the period.

(8) "Initial determination" means the first child-custody determination concerning a particular child.

. . .

(11) "Modification" means a child-custody determination that changes, replaces, supersedes, or is otherwise made after a previous determination concerning the same child, whether or not it is made by the court that made the previous determination.

. . .

(13) "Person acting as a parent" means a person, other than a parent, who:

(A) has physical custody of the child or has had physical custody for a period of six consecutive months, including any temporary absence, within one year immediately before the commencement of a child-custody proceeding; and

(B) has been awarded legal custody by a court or claims a right to legal custody under the law of this State.

. . . .

§ 103. PROCEEDINGS GOVERNED BY OTHER LAW.

This [Act] does not govern an adoption proceeding. . . .

. . . .

§ 105. INTERNATIONAL APPLICATION OF [ACT].

(a) A court of this State shall treat a foreign country as if it were a State. . . .

. . .

(c) A court of this State need not apply this [Act] if the child custody law of a foreign country violates fundamental principles of human rights.

§ 106. EFFECT OF CHILD-CUSTODY DETERMINATION.

A child-custody determination made by a court of this State that had jurisdiction under this [Act] binds all persons who have been served in accordance with the laws of this State or notified in accordance with [the laws of this state or of the state in which service is made] or who have submitted to the jurisdiction of the court, and who have been given an opportunity to be heard. As to those persons, the determination is conclusive as to all decided issues of law and fact except to the extent the determination is modified.

. . .

§ 110. COMMUNICATION BETWEEN COURTS.

(a) A court of this State may communicate with a court in another State concerning a proceeding arising under this [Act].

(b) The court may allow the parties to participate in the communication. If the parties are not able to participate . . . , they must be given the opportunity to present facts and legal arguments before a decision on jurisdiction is made.

. . . .

§ 201. INITIAL CHILD-CUSTODY JURISDICTION.

(a) Except as otherwise provided in § 204, a court of this State has jurisdiction to make an initial child-custody determination only if:

(1) this State is the home State of the child [at] the commencement of the proceeding, or was the home State . . . within six months before the

commencement of the proceeding and the child is absent from this State but a parent or person acting as a parent continues to live in this State;

(2) a court of another State does not have jurisdiction under paragraph (1), or . . . the home State of the child has declined to exercise jurisdiction on the ground that this State is the more appropriate forum under § 207 or § 208, and:

(A) the child and the child's parents, or the child and at least one parent or a person acting as a parent, have a significant connection with this State other than mere physical presence; and

(B) substantial evidence is available in this State concerning the child's care, protection, training, and personal relationships;

(3) all courts having jurisdiction under paragraph (1) or (2) have declined to exercise jurisdiction on the ground that a court of this State is the more appropriate forum. . . . ; or

(4) no court of any other State would have jurisdiction under the criteria specified in paragraph (1), (2), or (3).

(b) Subsection (a) is the exclusive jurisdictional basis for making a child-custody determination by a court of this State.

(c) Physical presence of, or personal jurisdiction over, a party or a child is not necessary or sufficient to make a child-custody determination.

§ 202. EXCLUSIVE, CONTINUING JURISDICTION.

(a) Except as otherwise provided in § 204, a court of this State which has made a child-custody determination consistent with § 201 or § 203 has exclusive, continuing jurisdiction over the determination until:

(1) a court of this State determines that neither the child, nor the child and one parent, nor the child and a person acting as a parent have a significant connection with this State and that substantial evidence is no longer available in this State concerning the child's care, protection, training, and personal relationships; or

(2) a court of this State or a court of another State determines that the child, the child's parents, and any person acting as a parent do not presently reside in this State.

. . . .

§ 203. JURISDICTION TO MODIFY DETERMINATION.

Except as otherwise provided in § 204, a court of this State may not modify a child-custody determination made by . . . another State unless a court of this State has jurisdiction to make an initial determination under § 201(a)(1) or (2) and:

(1) the court of the other State determines it no longer has exclusive, continuing jurisdiction under § 202 or that a court of this State would be a more convenient forum under § 207; or

(2) a court of this State or a court of the other State determines that the child, the child's parents, and any person acting as a parent do not presently reside in the other State.

. . . .

§ 204. TEMPORARY EMERGENCY JURISDICTION.

(a) A court of this State has temporary emergency jurisdiction if the child is present in this State and the child has been abandoned or it is necessary . . . to protect the child because the child, or a sibling or parent of the child, is subjected to or threatened with mistreatment or abuse.

(b) [If there is no existing order or ongoing litigation elsewhere], a child-custody determination made under this section remains in effect until an order is obtained from a court of a State having jurisdiction under [the Act]. If a child-custody proceeding has not been or is not commenced in a court of a State having jurisdiction under [the Act], a child-custody determination made under this section becomes a final determination, if it so provides and this State becomes the home State of the child.

(c) If there is a previous child-custody determination that is entitled to be enforced under this [Act], or a child-custody proceeding has been commenced in a court of a State having jurisdiction under [the Act, the emergency jurisdiction shall] specify in the order a period [during which petitioner must obtain an order from the court which issued the prior order]. The order issued in this State remains in effect until [such]an order is obtained . . . within the period specified or the period expires.

. . . .

§ 206. SIMULTANEOUS PROCEEDINGS.

(a) Except as otherwise provided in § 204, a court of this State may not exercise its jurisdiction under this [article] if, at the time of the commencement of the proceeding, a proceeding concerning the custody of the child has been commenced in a court of another State having jurisdiction substantially in conformity with this [Act], unless the proceeding has been terminated or is stayed by the court of the other State because a court of this State is a more convenient forum under § 207.

(b). . . . If the court determines that a child-custody proceeding has been commenced in a court in another State having jurisdiction substantially in accordance with this [Act], the court of this State shall stay its proceeding and communicate with the court of the other State. If the court of the State having jurisdiction substantially in accordance with this [Act] does not determine that the court of this State is a more appropriate forum, the court of this State shall dismiss the proceeding.

. . . .

§ 207. INCONVENIENT FORUM.

(a) A court of this State which has jurisdiction under this [Act] to make a child-custody determination may decline to exercise its jurisdiction at any time if it determines that it is an inconvenient forum under the circumstances and that a court of another State is a more appropriate forum. The issue of inconvenient forum may be raised upon motion of a party, the court's own motion, or request of another court.

(b) Before determining whether it is an inconvenient forum, a court . . . shall consider whether it is appropriate for a court of another State to exercise jurisdiction. . . . [T]he court shall allow the parties to submit information and shall consider all relevant factors, including:

(1) whether domestic violence has occurred and is likely to continue in the future and which State could best protect the parties and the child;

(2) the length of time the child has resided outside this State;

(3) the distance between the court in this State and the court in the State that would assume jurisdiction;

(4) the relative financial circumstances of the parties;

(5) any agreement of the parties as to which State should assume jurisdiction;

(6) the nature and location of the evidence required to resolve the pending litigation, including testimony of the child;

(7) the ability of the court of each State to decide the issue expeditiously and the procedures necessary to present the evidence; and

(8) the familiarity of the court of each State with the facts and issues in the pending litigation.

(c) If a court of this State determines that it is an inconvenient forum and that a court of another State is a more appropriate forum, it shall stay the proceedings upon condition that a child-custody proceeding be promptly commenced in another designated State and may impose any other condition the court considers just and proper.

(d) A court of this State may decline to exercise its jurisdiction under this [Act] if a child-custody determination is incidental to an action for divorce or another proceeding while still retaining jurisdiction over the divorce or other proceeding.

§ 208. JURISDICTION DECLINED BY REASON OF CONDUCT.

(a) Except as otherwise provided in § 204 [or by other law of this State], if a court of this State has jurisdiction under this [Act] because a person seeking to invoke its jurisdiction has engaged in unjustifiable conduct, the court shall decline to exercise its jurisdiction unless:

(1) the parents and all persons acting as parents have acquiesced in the exercise of jurisdiction;

(2) a court of the State otherwise having jurisdiction under §§ 201 through 203 determines that this State is a more appropriate forum under § 207; or

(3) no court of any other State would have jurisdiction under the criteria specified in §§ 201 through 203.

(b) If a court of this State declines to exercise its jurisdiction pursuant to subsection (a), it may fashion an appropriate remedy to ensure the safety of the child and prevent a repetition of the unjustifiable conduct, including staying the proceeding until a child-custody proceeding is commenced in a court having jurisdiction under §§ 201 through 203.

(c) If a court dismisses a petition or stays a proceeding because it declines to exercise its jurisdiction pursuant to subsection (a), it shall assess against the party seeking to invoke its jurisdiction necessary and reasonable expenses. . . .

PARENTAL KIDNAPPING PREVENTION ACT

28 U.S.C. § 1738A

(a) The appropriate authorities of every State shall enforce according to its terms, and shall not modify except as provided in subsections (f), (g), and (h) of this section, any custody . . . or visitation determination made consistently with the provisions of this section by a court of another State.

(b) As used in this section, the term —

(1) "child" means a person under the age of eighteen;

(2) "contestant" means a person, including a parent or grandparent, who claims a right to custody or visitation of a child;

(3) "custody determination" means a judgment, decree, or other order of a court providing for the custody of a child, and includes permanent and temporary orders, and initial orders and modifications;

(4) "home State" means the State in which, immediately preceding the time involved, the child lived with his parents, a parent, or a person acting as parent, for at least six consecutive months, and in the case of a child less than six months old, the State in which the child lived from birth with any of such persons. Periods of temporary absence of any of such persons are counted as part of the six-month or other period;

(5) "modification" and "modify" refer to a custody or visitation determination which modifies, replaces, supersedes, or otherwise is made subsequent to, a prior custody or visitation determination concerning the same child, whether made by the same court or not;

(6) "person acting as a parent" means a person, other than a parent, who has physical custody of a child and who has either been awarded custody by a court or claims a right to custody;

(7) "physical custody" means actual possession and control of a child;

(8) "State" means a State of the United States, the District of Columbia, the Commonwealth of Puerto Rico, or a territory ·or possession of the United States; and

(9) "visitation determination" means a judgment, decree, or other order of a court providing for the visitation of a child and includes permanent and temporary orders and initial orders and modifications.

(c) A child custody or visitation determination made by a court of a State is consistent with the provisions of this section only if —

(1) such court has jurisdiction under the law of such State; and

(2) one of the following conditions is met:

(A) such State (i) is the home State of the child on the date of the commencement of the proceeding, or (ii) had been the child's home State within six months before the date of the commencement of the proceeding and the child is absent from such State because of his removal or retention by a contestant or for other reasons, and a contestant continues to live in such State;

(B) (i) it appears that no other State would have jurisdiction under subparagraph (A), and (ii) it is in the best interest of the child that a court of such State assume jurisdiction because (I) the child and his parents, or the child and at least one contestant, have a significant connection with such State other than mere physical presence in such State, and (II) there is available in such State substantial evidence concerning the child's present or future care, protection, training, and personal relationships;

(C) the child is physically present in such State and (i) the child has been abandoned, or (ii) it is necessary in an emergency to protect the child because the child, a sibling, or parent of the child has been subjected to or threatened with mistreatment or abuse;

(D) (i) it appears that no other State would have jurisdiction under subparagraph (A), (B), (C), or (E), or another State has declined to exercise jurisdiction on the ground that the State whose jurisdiction is in issue is the more appropriate forum to determine the custody or visitation of the child, and (ii) it is in the best interest of the child that such court assume jurisdiction; or

(E) the court has continuing jurisdiction pursuant to subsection (d) of this section.

(d) The jurisdiction of a court of a State which has made a. . . . determination consistently with the provisions of this section continues as long as the requirement of subsection (c)(1) of this section continues to be met and such State remains the residence of the child or of any contestant.

(e) Before a . . . determination is made, reasonable notice and opportunity to be heard shall be given to the contestants, any parent whose parental rights have not been previously terminated and any person who has physical custody of a child.

(f) A court of a State may modify a determination of the custody of the same child made by a court of another State, if —

(1) it has jurisdiction to make such a child custody determination; and

(2) the court of the other State no longer has jurisdiction, or it has declined to exercise such jurisdiction to modify such determination.

(g) A court of a State shall not exercise jurisdiction in any proceeding . . . commenced during the pendency of a proceeding in a court of another State where such court of that other State is exercising jurisdiction consistently with the provisions of this section to make a custody determination.

(h) A court of a State may not modify a visitation determination made by a court of another State unless the court of the other State no longer has jurisdiction to modify such determination or has declined to exercise jurisdiction to modify such determination.

[a]　　Jurisdiction to Render Initial Custody Decree

WELCH-DODEN v. ROBERTS
Arizona Court of Appeals
42 P.3d 1166 (2002)

BARKER, JUDGE

This opinion resolves a statutory conflict in the meaning of "home state" as that phrase is used to determine initial jurisdiction between competing states in child custody disputes under Arizona's . . . Uniform Child Custody Jurisdiction and Enforcement Act ("UCCJEA"). . . .

[Mother and Father married in Arizona in 1996. After moving to Oklahoma, their child was born there in April, 1999. Subsequently, mother and child moved several times between the two states to permit mother to research job opportunities in Arizona. The child was in Oklahoma for the first 7 1/2 months of life. Mother and child then were in Arizona for 3 months, Oklahoma for 6 months and then Arizona for four months when Mother filed there for divorce, seeking custody. Immediately thereafter father, still in Oklahoma, filed there. He contested jurisdiction in Arizona and the trial court, finding Oklahoma the child's home state, dismissed for lack of jurisdiction. Mother appealed this dismissal.]

. . . .

. . . . The question of "home state" jurisdiction under the UCCJEA is of first impression, has statewide importance, and is likely to recur. . . .

. . . .

We consider several issues: First, does the UCCJEA provide that home state jurisdiction is based on a child residing in a state (a) for a six-month period *immediately prior* to the filing of a custody petition, or (b) for a six-month period that is completed *at any time within* six months of the filing?

Second, if a state has home state jurisdiction, does home state jurisdiction then become pre-eminent, thereby precluding a court without home state jurisdiction from considering the child's best interests for jurisdictional purposes?

And finally, does a state with home state jurisdiction have jurisdictional priority when a petition in another state was filed first-in-time?

. . . .

[UCCJEA § 201] is the statutory starting place for determining initial jurisdiction. . . . Subsection (a), paragraph (1) provides for Arizona to have jurisdiction when Arizona qualifies as a home state. If a state is the "home state" under this paragraph, it has jurisdiction. There is no further factual inquiry on the *jurisdictional* issue. Paragraphs (2)–(4) . . . provide the circumstances whereby Arizona may have jurisdiction when it does *not* qualify as the home state. Paragraph 2, in particular, requires the court to consider whether the child has a significant connection to the state (as well as other factors) before jurisdiction may be found. Subsection (c) clarifies that the presence of the child is neither necessary nor sufficient to establish jurisdiction.

In considering [§ 201] . . . , we must . . . take into account [that] [Section 102(7)] defines "home state" as follows:

> . . . The state in which a child lived with a parent or a person acting as a parent for *at least six consecutive months immediately before the commencement of a child custody proceeding*, including any period during which that person is temporarily absent from that state.

. . . [T]he application of this definition of "home state" to [§ 201] . . . creates a statutory conflict. [Under § 201(a)(1)] a state has jurisdiction if [it]

> is the [1] home state of the child *on the date of the commencement of the proceeding*, or [2] was the home state of the child *within six months before the commencement* of the proceeding and the child is absent from this state but a parent or person acting as a parent continues to live in this state.

The definition of "home state" . . . provides, however, that a state is a "home state" *only* when "a child lived with a parent . . . for at least six consecutive months *immediately before* the commencement of a child custody proceeding." (Emphasis added.)

Thus, applying literally the definition of "home state" from [§ 102] to element one of [§ 201(a)(1)] renders superfluous the language . . . that says jurisdiction lies when a state is the home state "on the date of the commencement of the proceeding." That latter phrase merely restates what is already required by the definition of "home state". . . .

Element two of [§ 201(a)(1)] poses a more significant problem in statutory construction when the home state definition . . . is applied: the two statutes directly conflict. Element two . . . provides that a state has jurisdiction if it is the "home state . . . *within six months before*" the commencement of the child custody proceeding. Section [102(7)] requires that in order to be a "home state" . . . , a child must have lived in a state for six consecutive months "immediately before" the child custody proceeding. Thus, if a child's home state two months before a proceeding was commenced is different from the state to which a child has permanently moved (and in which the proceeding was commenced), [§ 102] would indicate there is no home state at all. Initial jurisdiction would then be determined based on substantial connections to the state and other factors under [§ 201]. On the other hand, under the same facts, element two of [§ 201(a)(1)] would declare the *prior state* the home state because it was the home state *within* six months of the filing. Initial jurisdiction would then be in the prior state regardless of any significant connections to the state in which the filing was made.

The statutory conflict . . . is directly at issue here. The child lived in Oklahoma for six consecutive months ending in September 2000. The child then resided in Arizona for the next four months, immediately before the petition was filed in January 2001. Thus, under father's (and the trial judge's) reading of the statute, Oklahoma is the home state . . . under element two of [§ 201(a)(1)]. Oklahoma, under this view, was the home state (from March to September 2000) *within* six months of the filing of the petition in January 2001 and thus has initial jurisdiction.

Under mother's reading of the statute, however, neither Oklahoma nor Arizona is the home state as neither state meets the requirement of [§ 102(7)]. . . . Under that scenario, Oklahoma does not have initial jurisdiction. The trial court would be required to . . . determine whether there were significant connections with Arizona and other factors per [§ 201(a)(2)], to determine whether Arizona should have initial jurisdiction. . . .

. . . .

To appropriately resolve the conflict here, it is critical to examine the stated purposes behind the changes in home state jurisdiction brought about by the UCCJEA.

. . . .

The precursor to the UCCJEA was the . . . [UCCJA]. The stated purposes of the UCCJA were to avoid jurisdictional competition and conflict, promote cooperation between states, discourage the use of the interstate system to continue custody controversies, deter abductions, avoid relitigation in different states, and facilitate enforcement of custody decrees between states.

All fifty states, the District of Columbia and the Virgin Islands adopted the UCCJA. However, many states departed from its original text, and subsequent litigation produced substantial inconsistencies in interpretation among state courts — defeating the goals of a uniform interstate jurisdictional act.

. . . .

In particular, . . . the UCCJA provided four separate bases to take initial jurisdiction in child custody disputes. Those bases included (1) domicile or home state, (2) significant connections to the state and a consideration of the child's relationships, training, care and protection, (3) the child's best interests, and (4) emergency.

The . . . drafters of the UCCJA had assumed that home state jurisdiction was the most appropriate factor in demonstrating the best interests of the child. They also thought that a state should be able to proceed without delay and, therefore, should find jurisdiction on any acceptable basis. Thus, the drafters included the four separate bases for jurisdiction. However, state courts were split as to whether the four bases were equal or whether home state was preferred. These conflicts created an unworkable and non-uniform interstate act.

Additionally, . . . a significant federal statute was passed by the United States Congress. That statute, the [PKPA] was aimed at interstate custody problems that continued to exist after the adoption of the UCCJA. It mandated states to apply full faith and credit to interstate custody decisions. Importantly, it did not allow for full faith and credit on the four bases as set forth in the UCCJA. Instead, enforceability under the PKPA was based on the priority of home-state jurisdiction:

[The court here cited (c)(2) of the PKPA.]

In 1997, [the UCCJEA was promulgated]. As the drafters . . . noted, lack of uniformity between jurisdictions "increases the costs of the enforcement action; it decreases the lack of certainty of outcome; and it often turns enforcement of a child custody or visitation order into a long and drawn out process." The National Conference of Commissioners on Uniform State Laws, *Uniform Child Custody Jurisdiction and Enforcement Act* (2001). Arizona adopted the UCCJEA effective January 1, 2001.

The UCCJEA drafters dealt specifically with the conflict created by differing jurisdictions taking contrary views of the four bases of jurisdiction. They reconciled the jurisdictional provisions of the UCCJA with the PKPA:

> The UCCJA, however, specifically authorizes four independent bases of jurisdiction without prioritization. Under the UCCJA, a significant connection custody determination may have to be enforced even if it would be denied enforcement under the PKPA [which prioritizes home state jurisdiction]. *The UCCJEA prioritizes home state jurisdiction*[.]

9 U.L.A. 650–51 (emphasis added). The drafters made it clear that the new act was to give priority to a finding of home state jurisdiction over any other jurisdictional provisions.

Furthermore, the UCCJEA completely eliminates a determination of "best interests" of a child from the jurisdictional inquiry. These changes advance a more efficient and "bright line" jurisdictional rule consistent with the UCCJEA's purpose. The UCCJEA specifically seeks to avoid a judicial analysis of substantive issues in the determination of jurisdiction. . . . [A]s noted above, the statutory text of [§ 201] allows consideration of other substantive factors *only* if no state qualifies as a "home state."

It is clear from the drafters' intent that the UCCJEA should be construed to [avoid] the jurisdictional competition and conflict that flows from hearings in competing states when each state substantively reviews subjective factors (such as "best interests") for purposes of determining initial jurisdiction. With this fundamental purpose in mind, when there is a statutory conflict in the application of home state jurisdiction, the conflict should be resolved to strengthen (rather than dilute) the certainty of home state jurisdiction . . . . . .

. . . .

Given the fundamental purpose of the UCCJEA to establish the certainty of home state jurisdiction, it is clear to us that [§ 201(a)(1)] acts to enlarge and modify the definition of home state. . . . We hold that "home state" for purposes of determining initial jurisdiction under [§ 201(a)(1)] is not limited to the time period of "six consecutive months immediately before the commencement of a child custody proceeding[.]" Instead, the applicable time period to determine "home state" in such circumstances is "within six months before the commencement of the [child custody] proceeding." [§ 201]. This interpretation promotes the priority of home state jurisdiction. . . . [Mother's theory] would increase the number of potentially conflicting jurisdictional disputes in competing jurisdictions. This is contrary to the UCCJEA's purpose.

Even though the UCCJEA is a uniform act, which has been adopted by twenty-seven states and introduced in nine states, we have found no cases that construe the statutory conflict at issue. While not discussing the conflict, other states have ruled in a manner that is consistent with the interpretation we adopt here. *E.g., In re McCoy*, 52 S.W.3d 297, 303–304 (Tex. App. 2001) (finding that Texas was not the children's home state at any time during the six months prior to the filing of the suit); *Nesa v. Baten*, 290 A.D.2d 663, 736 N.Y.S.2d 173, 174 (N.Y.A.D. 2002) ("New York had not been the children's home state at the time of commencement of the custody proceeding or within the preceding six months.").

. . . .

Thus, we conclude that the trial court did not err in rejecting mother's position and concluding that Oklahoma had home state jurisdiction.

. . . .

Mother also contends that even if Oklahoma is the home state . . . , the trial judge still erred in not conducting a hearing to determine if jurisdiction was in the child's best interests. Mother puts forth two reasons: (1) Arizona's version of UCCJEA requires it, and (2) it would be inequitable and unfair not to consider the child's best interests in a determination of initial jurisdiction. We address each argument in turn.

First, in contending that Arizona's version of the UCCJEA requires a "best interests" hearing even though home state jurisdiction is found elsewhere, mother relies on the prefatory phrase in [§ 201(a)]: "[A] court of this State has jurisdiction to make an initial child custody determination only if *any of the following is true*." Mother argues the phrase "if any of the following is true" allows courts to choose between the four bases of jurisdiction . . . much as courts chose between the four bases of jurisdiction provided under the UCCJA. This argument is directly contrary to the express language of the statute.

. . . .

Second, mother argues that the equitable issues presented in a case such as this one (child having always been with mother; mother and child having significant connections in Arizona; mother and child having lived in Arizona for the four months prior to filing) or in a hypothetical case (child lives five months and 29 days in one state, but the prior six months in another resulting in home state jurisdiction in the prior case) require a hearing to consider the child's best interests. Mother's argument does not consider that the UCCJEA expressly provides for a factual hearing *in the home state . . .* which . . . may decline to exercise its jurisdiction and allow another jurisdiction to proceed. [§ 207]. This hearing may include a "best interests" determination.

The drafters . . . expressly recognized — and sought to eliminate — the jurisdictional disputes that resulted when "best interests" was used to determine initial jurisdiction. That language and inquiry, present in the previously enacted UCCJA, was intentionally omitted from the newly-drafted UCCJEA. The drafters stated:

> The *"best interest language* in the jurisdictional sections of the UCCJA was *not intended to be an invitation to address the merits of the custody dispute in the jurisdictional determination* or to otherwise provide that "best interests" considerations should override jurisdictional determinations or provide an additional jurisdictional basis.

> *[This draft] eliminates the term "best interests in order to clearly distinguish between the jurisdictional standards and the substantive standards relating to custody and visitation of children.*

9 U.L.A. at 651–652 (emphasis added).

Thus, the "best interests" analysis does not take place in determining jurisdiction. "Best interests" may be fully explored and considered in the context of a request under [§ 207]. . . .

The issue of an inconvenient forum "may be raised on motion of a party, the court's own motion or request of another court." Any such request, however, must be pursued in Oklahoma rather than Arizona, as Oklahoma has home state jurisdiction. . . . This is critical: To allow the state without home state jurisdiction to conduct the hearing would lead to the jurisdictional competition the drafters sought to avoid. Thus the equitable arguments that mother wishes to pursue are not eliminated, but are merely re-directed to the home state. . . . [M]other can ask the Oklahoma court to relinquish jurisdiction.

Accordingly, mother's argument that the trial judge erred in not considering the "best interests" of the child . . . is wrong. The trial judge correctly determined that this was an issue for the Oklahoma court.

. . . .

Mother also argues, relying on [§ 206(a)], that Arizona should have jurisdiction as her filing was first-in-time. This argument fails as well. . . .

Mother's argument is that this provision mandates jurisdiction in Arizona as the filing was first-in-time. What mother ignores is that the first-in-time filing must be in a state "having jurisdiction substantially in conformity with this chapter." [§ 206(a)]. Because Oklahoma had home state jurisdiction, Arizona did not have jurisdiction "substantially in conformity with this chapter." *Id.* Thus, the first-in-time filing granted mother no rights. . . .

. . . .

NOTES

1. ***Priority of Home State Jurisdiction.*** The UCCJA § 3 identified four different bases for jurisdiction to issue a custody decree, the most important of which were home state and significant connection. Because they were listed as alternatives, the natural reading of the statute gave no jurisdictional priority to the home state as compared with a state with significant connection to the child and a parent. *See, e.g., Weinstein v. Weinstein,* 408 N.E.2d 952 (Ill. App. 1980); Foster, *Child Custody Jurisdiction: UCCJA and PKPA,* 28 N.Y.L. SCH. L. REV. 297 (1981). Such priority for the home state was favored, however, by Professor Bodenheimer. As Reporter for the UCCJA, she had been unable to get approval for statutory language explicitly giving priority to the home state, but she argued this result was the necessary implication of the organization of § 3, which placed home state jurisdiction first on the list of alternative jurisdictional bases. Bodenheimer, *Interstate Custody: Initial Jurisdiction and Continuing Jurisdiction Under the UCCJA,* 14 FAM. L.Q. 203 (1981). Before the UCCJEA's promulgation, some states had modified the UCCJA to give priority to home state jurisdiction. *See, e.g.,* TENN. FAM. CODE ANN. § 36-6-203(a)(1) & (2) (1996); TEX. FAM. CODE § 11.53 (1) & (2) (1996). Of course, piecemeal amendment of the Uniform Act was ineffective. For example, any state which had enacted the UCCJA as promulgated could exercise significant interest jurisdiction even though Texas was the home state, while Texas law would not require it to recognize that other state's decree (because it had not been rendered under jurisdictional rules substantially the same as Texas).

At the same time, subsection (c)(2)(B) of the federal Parental Kidnapping Prevention Act (PKPA) required full faith and credit for home state decrees, but not for a decree based upon significant connection jurisdiction if a home state existed at the time it was issued. While nothing in the PKPA *barred* the exercise of significant connection jurisdiction when another state was the home state, some courts have mistakenly so held. *See, e.g., Rogers v. Rogers,* 907 P.2d 469 (Alaska 1995); *Michael P. v. Diana G.,* 553 N.Y.S.2d 689 (App. Div. 1995).

As noted in *Welch-Doden,* the major difference between the UCCJEA and its predecessor is the clear statement of priority for home state jurisdiction announced in subsections (a)(2), (a)(3) and (a)(4) of § 201. The "significant connection" jurisdiction of (a)(2) can be exercised only if there is no home state or the home state has declined to exercise jurisdiction under § 207 (forum non conveniens) or § 208 (unclean hands). Likewise, (a)(3) jurisdiction cannot be exercised unless all courts with home state or significant connection jurisdiction have deferred to the forum and, finally, (a)(4) jurisdiction can be exercised only if there is no court with jurisdiction under any of the other three grounds. For a sampling of recent litigation dealing with establishing home state jurisdiction, see *Duwyenie v. Moran,* 207 P.3d 754 (Ariz. App. 2009) (child's abduction by party did not deprive forum of home state status); *Carter v. Carter*, 758 N.W.2d 1 (Neb. 2008) (rejecting assertion by father who left state for posting in Japan when child was 10 days old that the family's 2 ½ years in Japan was "temporary absence"); *Waltenburg v. Waltenburg*, 270 S.W.3d 308 (Tex. Ct. App. 2008) (pre-birth filing of suit for custody does not make forum home state under statute); *A.K. v. N.B.*, 2008 Ala. Civ. App. LEXIS 316 (May 23, 2008) (forum court lacked home state jurisdiction in dispute regarding child born in California when mother filed suit one month after arriving in Alabama with child); *Miller-Jenkins v. Miller-Jenkins*, 637 S.E.2d 330 (Va. Ct. App. 2006) (Virginia court had no jurisdiction to decide custody dispute between same-sex couple when Vermont had already entered a dissolution decree determining custody and visitation issues); *In re Kalbes (Hatch v. Hatch)*, 733 N.W.2d 648 (Wis. Ct. App. 2007) (home state custody jurisdiction present where child was born in forum after father had sued mother for divorce in a different state; under Act, home state of child of less than 6 months of age is state where child has lived with a parent since birth; child had never lived in state where divorce was filed); *Thrapp v. Thrapp*, 2007 Tenn. App. LEXIS 124 (Mar. 8, 2007) (physical removal of child after lawsuit's filing did not deprive forum of home state jurisdiction); *In re D.S. (People v. Hollis)*, 840 N.E.2d 1212 (Ill. 2005) (home state jurisdiction found concerning child born in Indiana to Illinois woman who left the state to avoid adjudication of neglect; temporary hospital stay in Indiana did not deprive Illinois of home state jurisdiction; child had lived in Illinois with her mother since birth, except for the temporary, purposeful absence).

2. *"Conflict" Between Definition of Home State and Description of Home State Jurisdiction?* The *Welch-Doden* court resolved what it characterized as a conflict between the definition of home state in § 102 and the description of § 201(a)(1) home state jurisdiction. It is not clear that there is actually a conflict between the two sections. While Oklahoma was clearly not the home state at the time of the beginning of the Arizona litigation, it is equally clear that, under § 201(a)(1), home state *jurisdiction* is a broader concept than that of home state and it can be exercised for six months after a jurisdiction's status as home state has been lost, if a parent or a person acting as a parent remains in the state. The purpose of this provision, which has its roots in UCCJA § 3(a)(1) and the PKPA, is to discourage self-help by a parent designed to deprive a home state of custody jurisdiction. The new provision is slightly different from both the prior Uniform Act and the PKPA. As explained in the UCCJEA commentary:

> The UCCJA provided that home state jurisdiction continued for six months when the child had been removed by a person seeking the child's custody or for other reasons and a parent or a person acting as a parent continues to reside in the home State. Under this Act, it is no longer necessary to determine why the child has been removed. . . . This change provides a slightly more refined home state standard than the UCCJA or the PKPA [(c)(2)(A)], which also requires a determination that the child has been removed "by a contestant or for other reasons." The scope of the PKPA's provision is theoretically narrower than this Act. However, the phrase "or for other reasons" covers most fact situations where the child is not in the home State and, therefore, the difference has no substantive effect.

9 U.L.A. Part IA, p. 672 (1997).

The PKPA home state jurisdiction provision extends jurisdiction for six months so long as a "contestant" remains in the home state. Under subsection (b), the federal statute defines "contestant" as any person "including a parent or grandparent, who claims a right to custody or visitation." The UCCJEA, by contrast, extends jurisdiction only if a parent or a person acting as a parent remains in the former home state. As the UCCJEA commentary states,

> This eliminates the undesirable jurisdictional determinations which would occur as a result of differing state substantive laws on visitation involving grandparents and others. For example, if State A's law provided that grandparents could obtain visitation with a child after the death of one of the parents, then the grandparents, who would be considered "contestants" under the PKPA, could file a proceeding within six months after the remaining parent moved and have the case heard in State A.

Id. While the UCCJEA commentary finds the result under the PKPA definition "undesirable,"according to Professor Russell Coombs, a drafter of the PKPA, the UCCJEA result where only a grandparent (and not the child or any parent) remains in the home state is the inappropriate one. He argues the UCCJEA provisions are "cause for grave concern among grandparents and numerous other non-parents who visit minor children or sometimes have their custody." Coombs, *Child Custody and Visitation by Non-Parents Under the New Uniform Child Custody Jurisdiction and Enforcement Act: A Rerun of Seize-and-Run*, 16 J. AM. ACAD. MATRIMONIAL LAW. 1, 3 (1999). He notes, however, that a UCCJA state that issued the initial decree would retain jurisdiction under its own law so long as a grandparent with visitation rights under that decree remained in that state — even if the parents and children moved to a UCCJEA state. He further asserts that the PKPA would require full faith and credit for the initial decree in the parents' new state. While Professor Combs views this as illustrating a problem with the UCCJEA, others would argue the problem is with statutes that make parents and children subject to jurisdiction in a distant state to which only grandparents retain a connection. Professor Coombs criticizes other aspects of the UCCJEA as well, including its provisions on notice and joinder, modification and its interaction with other federal statutes. He speculates that, at least in some situations, it may be unconstitutional. *Id.* at pp. 78–91.

In a case similar to *Welch-Doden* where litigation was brought in the child's original home state, the Alaska Supreme Court held, in *Atkins v. Vigil*, 59 P.3d 255 (Alaska 2002), that "extended home state jurisdiction" was satisfied even though the action was filed six months and a week after the child had left the state for California to be with his maternal grandparents. The court held that, under the PKPA and UCCJEA definitions of home state, a period of temporary absence constitutes presence in the determination of home state. Because the child's original departure to California was intended to be temporary, Alaska had been the home state within six months and could exercise extended home state jurisdiction at the time of the father's filing. *See also Rosen v. Celebrezze*, 883 N.E.2d 420 (Ohio 2008) (recognizing that, because West Virginia retained "extended home state jurisdiction" when child moved to Ohio four months previously but father had remained in West Virginia, trial court erred by entertaining mother's custody suit; fact that it was filed before father's West Virginia action irrelevant because Ohio lacked jurisdiction); *In re Oliver v. Oliver*, 61 Va. Cir. 88 (Cir. Ct. Fairfax Cty. 2003) (home state jurisdiction found on basis of six months' presence followed by four-year series of temporary absences in various countries because of father's State Department work assignments). *But see In re Calderon-Garza*, 81 S.W.3d 899 (Tex. Ct. App. 2002) (even if mother, a Mexican domiciliary, was in Texas "temporarily" when child was born, Texas is still child's home state; child cannot be temporarily away from a place she had never been).

3. *Significant Connection Jurisdiction.* While the UCCJEA and the PKPA both require deference to a child's home state in making an initial custody award, sometimes there is no home state. For example, in *In re Amberley D.*, 775 A.2d 1158 (Me. 2001), the 14-year-old child had lived with her mother in New Hampshire for several months, but then ran away to Maine to live with her stepfather's parents who soon thereafter filed a guardianship petition. The child's mother asserted New Hampshire was the home state, but the Maine court held there was no home state (because the child had not been in New Hampshire for six months when the petition was filed in Maine) and that Maine could claim jurisdiction as a state with a "significant connection" to the child in which a person acting as a parent lived. Also required under both statutes is substantial evidence, in the words of the UCCJEA, "concerning the child's care, protection, training and personal relationships," within the forum. The court found this present because the child previously had visited the petitioners often and had attended school in Maine for six years earlier in her childhood. *See also Christine L. v. Jason L.*, 874 N.Y.S.2d 794 (Fam. Ct. 2009) (significant connection jurisdiction appropriate where children have lived all but five months of their lives in the state and extended maternal and paternal family live within same county); *In re Diaz*, 845 N.E.2d 935 (Ill. App. 2006) (significant connection jurisdiction appropriate where child has no home state, was born in forum, mother and maternal grandmother live in state and substantial evidence of child's health care, protection, training and personal relationships existed in forum); *In re Brilliant*, 86 S.W.3d 680 (Tex. Ct. App. 2002) (finding jurisdiction where grandfather had lived in state for over 25 years and assisted in raising of child, child had much interaction with extended family and child's medical records were in state).

4. *Forum Non Conveniens Under UCCJEA § 207.* The Act identifies several situations in which a court with § 201 jurisdiction might decline (or in some situations be barred from exercising) that jurisdiction. Section 207 (reprinted above) outlines the Act's "inconvenient forum" doctrine under which the forum would defer to another state. According to the Commentary, this section is based on UCCJA § 7 and "authorizes courts to decide that another state is in a better position to make the custody determination, taking into consideration the relative circumstances of the parties." 9 U.L.A. Part IA, p. 683. For example, in *Welch-Doden*, the Oklahoma court might later on decide to defer to Arizona after all, in light of the mother and child's presence there. While not intended to be exhaustive of the possibly relevant factors, subsection (b) suggests considering any history of domestic violence and the ability of both courts to protect the victim from further violence. A recent Montana case offers an example. *Stoneman v. Drollinger*, 64 P.3d 997 (Mont. 2003). The court noted the UCCJEA's rejection of the UCCJA's explicit focus on the child's best interests in the inconvenient forum determination.

The court held trial courts should "give priority to the safety of victims of domestic violence when considering jurisdictional issues under the UCCJEA." It found the victim-mother felt safer in Washington "where she is surrounded by extended family and where [abuser-father] does not know her address or daily pattern of activities," and, after analyzing the relevance of the other factors in § 207(b), reversed the lower court's refusal to defer to Washington. *See also McNabb v. McNabb*, 65 P.3d 1068 (Kan. App. 2003) (abuse allegations appropriately considered by Virginia court in deciding to withdraw its deference to Kansas and, thus, Kansas custody proceeding inappropriate); *Griffith v. Tressel*, 925 A.2d 702 (N.J. Ct. App. 2007) (while continuing exclusive jurisdiction was retained by forum, trial court should have declined to exercise jurisdiction where child attends school, consults counselor and spends 80% of her time with Maryland mother; court noted Maryland would better be able to provide protection of child if alleged abuse by father was proven); *S. W. v. D.P.*, 860 N.E.2d 42 (Mass. App. Ct. 2007) (trial court properly declined to exercise continuing exclusive jurisdiction to modify its order where child had lived for most of his life with mother in Canada; court noted while the uniform law might be inapplicable, general *forum non conveniens* principle is applicable either under or outside of Act); *Doss v. Doss*, 2005 Tenn App LEXIS 238 (Apr. 25, 2005) (where neither forum nor Illinois had home state or extended home state jurisdiction, but mother and children had lived in Illinois for two years and both states'courts had issued orders giving her legal custody; court held "it certainly makes sense . . . for a court in the state where the primary residential parent lives to decide custody"); *Van Wechel v. Mueller*, 662 N.W.2d 371 (Iowa Ct. App. 2003) (refusal to find inconvenient forum affirmed where recent evidence concerning child was in Iowa where the parties lived at time of filing of modification suit).

A determination that another forum would be more convenient results in a stay of forum proceedings upon condition that a proceeding be instituted "promptly" in the other jurisdiction. Other conditions might be imposed and temporary orders issued to govern until the other state issues a decree. The order can also specify that jurisdiction would be resumed if the other state declines to hear the case.

Section 207 expressly applies to all situations in which the forum court has UCCJEA jurisdiction. This has been held to include a situation where the court has continuing, exclusive modification jurisdiction under § 202 (discussed more fully in the following subsection on modification jurisdiction). *Lord v. Lord*, 2001 Conn. Super. LEXIS 2646 (Sept. 14, 2001) (while Connecticut had § 202 modification jurisdiction, child had lived in New York for four years after living in forum for only 9 months and most relevant evidence concerning her was located in New York). The *Lord* court stayed the proceedings on the condition that a modification action was filed in New York within 45 days.

5. *Unclean Hands Under UCCJEA § 208.* Even in a UCCJEA world in which ordinarily there is only one state with jurisdiction over custody at any point, the equitable clean hands doctrine (which also was recognized in UCCJA § 8) sometimes will still be relevant. For example, a parent may abduct a child and establish a new home state which, after expiration of the 6 months of "extended home state jurisdiction" in § 201(a)(1), theoretically would have priority over any other state attempting to exercise jurisdiction. Under § 208, however, if the court in the new home state concludes that its jurisdiction exists "because a person seeking to invoke" it "has engaged in unjustifiable conduct" the court must reject the exercise of such jurisdiction. In attempting to define the concept of "unjustifiability," the UCCJEA's Reporter has written that the "focus on unjustifiable conduct represents a continuation of the balancing process [of the UCCJA]. The court should balance the wrongfulness of the conduct of the parent that establishes jurisdiction against the reasons for the parent's conduct." Robert Spector, *Uniform Child-Custody Jurisdiction and Enforcement Act (with Prefatory Note and Comments by Robert G. Spector)*, 32 FAM. L.Q. 303, 359, n.124.(1998); *see also* Deborah Goelman, *Shelter from the Storm: Using Jurisdictional Statutes to Protect Victims of Domestic Violence after the Violence Against Women Act of 2000*, 13 COLUM. J. GENDER & L. 101 (2004) (focuses on § 208 and analyzes methods by which batterers attempt to use custody litigation to control their victims; urges training and education which could "lead to . . . cultural change").

Focusing on the behavior of domestic violence victims in fleeing such violence with the child, the Commentary to § 208 warns courts not to characterize "technically illegal conduct as "unjustifiable." ". . . [I]f a parent flees with a child to escape domestic violence and in the process violates a joint custody decree, the case should not be automatically dismissed. . . . An inquiry must be made into whether the flight was justified under the circumstances. . . . However, an abusive parent who seizes the child and flees to another State to establish jurisdiction has engaged in unjustifiable conduct and the new State must decline to exercise jurisdiction under this section." *Id.* at p. 685.

6. *Simultaneous Proceedings Under UCCJEA § 206.* Simultaneous custody proceedings in more than one state can arise under the UCCJEA if there is no home state, there is no existing decree and more than one state is able to assert significant connection jurisdiction. Under the UCCJEA, however, the priority of home state jurisdiction expressed in § 201 should handle the vast majority of disputes. The effectiveness of the home state prioritization in solving the problem of simultaneous proceedings is reflected in *Welch-Doden*. While the Arizona litigation had been filed first, the appellate court ordered deference to the later-filed Oklahoma suit. The court recognized Arizona was not the home state and that Oklahoma could exercise "extended home state" jurisdiction, preferred under § 201 to Arizona's significant connection jurisdiction. UCCJEA § 206 deals with the problem of "dueling proceedings" where neither state can exercise home state jurisdiction by adopting a first in time rule, though subsection (b) orders communication with the court of another state where prior litigation was filed, and deference on inconvenient forum grounds is authorized.

7. *Tribal Jurisdiction.* The Indian Child Welfare Act of 1978, 92 Stat. 3069, largely codified at 25 U.S.C. § 1901 *et seq.*, provides for exclusive tribal court jurisdiction over adoptive or foster care placement of Indian children in certain classes of cases, but specifically excludes from its jurisdictional provisions "an award, in a divorce proceeding, of custody to one of the parents." 25 U.S.C. § 1903. It has been held that the exclusion "demonstrates a recognition by Congress of the concurrent jurisdiction of state and tribal courts in such cases. . . ." *Kelly v. Kelly*, 759 N.W.2d 721 (N.D. 2009). Much litigation and commentary has addressed the appropriate factors in determining the ICWA's applicability in a particular case. *See, e.g., In re Vincent M.*, 59 Cal. Rptr. 3d 321 (Ct. App. 2007) (rejecting the assertion that the "existing Indian family exception" is constitutionally mandated); *Baby Boy C. v. Tohono O'odham Nation*, 805 N.Y.S.2d 313 (Sup. Ct. App. Div. 2005) (judicially-created "existing family exception" finding ICWA inapplicable where child is not a member of an existing Indian family is rejected; concludes exception is contrary to ICWA's language and purpose); *In re J.L.*, 654 N.W.2d 786 (S.D. 2002) (forum non conveniens analysis appropriate in determining whether to transfer case to tribal court); Cheyanna Jaffke, *The "Existing Indian Family" Exception to the Indian Child Welfare Act: The States' Attempt to Slaughter Tribal Interests in Indian Children*, 66 LA. L. REV. 733 (2006); Jerry Foxhoven, *The Iowa Indian Child Welfare Act: Clarification and Enhancement of the Federal Act*, 54 DRAKE L. REV. 53 (2005); Barbara Atwood, *Fighting Over Indian Children: The Uses and Abuses of Jurisdictional Ambiguity*, 36 UCLA L. REV. 1051 (1989). Substantively, the Act's provisions favor the child's extended family, other members of the child's tribe and other Indians. *See generally* Annot., *Construction and Application of Indian Child Welfare Act of 1978 Upon Child Custody Determinations*, 89 A.L.R.5th 195 (2001).

PROBLEMS

Problem 7-6. Mary is a resident of Florida who was pregnant with her sixth child when she left the state to go to Arkansas after learning that termination proceedings were about to be filed with regard to her new child as soon as she was born. Child neglect proceedings were pending on each of her five older children (who remained in Florida with relatives) at the time she left Florida. Three months after the birth of Mary's daughter, Cheyenne, the Arkansas child welfare agency received a "pick up order" issued by a Florida trial court directing that Cheyenne be taken to Florida. The Florida court based its order on its understanding of state law that the filing of termination of parental rights regarding the five older children would automatically include the new child at birth. As soon as Cheyenne was picked up in Arkansas by the child welfare authorities, the child's maternal grandmother (who had been housing Mary and Cheyenne) filed a guardianship proceeding and sought an order halting the child's removal. Arkansas has adopted the UCCJEA. What arguments do you foresee being made by both sides and what result?

Problem 7-7. Wilton and Marsha are the grandparents of Johnny, whose parents are Sybil and Tyrone. All the parties are residents of Confusion. After Sybil's death, however, Tyrone moves with Johnny to Nirvana. Under the law of Confusion, while grandparents cannot seek visitation during an intact marriage, they can seek court-ordered visitation within six months of the death of a parent. Wilton and Marsha come to your office three weeks after Tyrone and Johnny have left for Nirvana, seeking to file a Confusion visitation action. Both Confusion and Nirvana have adopted the UCCJEA. What will be your advice and why?

Problem 7-8. Mary Jo and Frank are the parents of a child. They have separated, however, and Frank has moved with their child to a different state. After eight months in his new state, he files for divorce and seeks a determination that he is entitled to be the primary custodian of the child. Mary Jo has remained in the original marital home and has never been to Frank's state. Does Frank's state have jurisdiction under the UCCJEA to determine custody? Does Frank's state have jurisdiction to determine child support?

Problem 7-9.   Steve and Beth are husband and wife, but their marriage is a stormy one. One night after an especially traumatic episode of spousal abuse in which she received physical injuries, Beth takes the couple's 6-year old child and flies to a distant state, where her parents live. The morning after she arrives, her mother suggests that a protective order ought to be obtained from the court in the new state. No protective orders were ever sought or issued in the original marital home state. Assuming the UCCJEA has been enacted in the new state, what jurisdictional issue(s) are raised by Beth's action?

Problem 7-10.   Sandra and Larry met when Larry was on temporary assignment in Sandra's home state of New Mexico. During his three months' sojourn there, a close personal relationship arose and Sandra became pregnant, though she did not tell Larry of her pregnancy until the birth of their child, Benjamin. By that time Larry was back in his home state of Connecticut. When he learned of Benjamin's birth, Larry began to urge Sandra to bring the child and live as a family with him in his home. After four months of his entreaties, Sandra moved to Connecticut. She did not, however, want to move in with Larry, saying she was not sure about their relationship or about living so far away from her parents in New Mexico. Instead, she signed a one-year lease at a condominium in the next town from Larry, who paid 50% of the rent. The entire rent was prepaid (Sandra used an inheritance she had been left by her Aunt Viola). She enrolled Benjamin in day care and began work for a company which places secretaries as temporary employees. After about five and a half months of this, she left Connecticut with Benjamin without notifying Larry or her landlord. Three days later, Larry comes to your office anxious to file a law suit seeking custody of Benjamin or at least visitation rights. Connecticut is a UCCJEA state. What are the issues and what is your advice?

[b]   Jurisdiction to Modify an Existing Decree

SNOW v. SNOW
Oregon Court of Appeals
74 P.3d 1137 (2003)

HASELTON, P. J.

    . . . . Respondents . . . (father) and . . . (mother) are the parents of "S" who is now nine years old. Petitioner is . . . S's paternal grandmother. [Grandmother] acted as S's primary caregiver from mid-1995 until June 2001.

[Father was granted custody of S in a 1995 North Dakota divorce which gave Mother "reasonable visitation rights." Father soon moved to Oregon, leaving S with Grandmother in North Dakota. In 1997, Grandmother and S rejoined Father in Oregon. Mother has remained in North Dakota. In June 2001, Grandmother, suspecting abuse of S by Father, had an altercation with Father, whereupon he removed S to California and then to England, where S lives with Father's half-sister.]

In July 2001, [Grandmother] filed a petition . . . seeking custody of S. That petition, which named only father as a respondent, asserted . . . that (1) mother "has had no contact with [S] for over six years and her whereabouts are unknown"; (2) "Oregon is [S's] home state * * * and it appears that no other state would have jurisdiction"; and (3) [Grandmother] should be awarded sole custody of S [with supervised visitation by Father].

. . . [Grandmother] amended her petition to name mother as an additional respondent [acknowledging that Mother was a North Dakota resident] and that the . . . dissolution . . . decree [granted Father custody and Mother visitation. [Grandmother] also acknowledged both parents should be permitted visitation.] Both respondents appeared and opposed the amended petition.

. . . [Grandmother] argued . . . that Oregon had jurisdiction under the UCCJEA because it was "the home state of [S], father, and grandmother for the past four years" and because it was "the most convenient forum" in that "most evidence concerning the child's formative years and relationships is in Oregon."

Father responded that Oregon lacked jurisdiction . . . because mother continued to live in North Dakota, "which is the state which made the initial determination regarding custody." Father asserted . . . North Dakota had neither . . . determined that "it does not have exclusive, continuing jurisdiction" nor that Oregon was "the most convenient forum."

The trial court dismissed the petition, concluding that Oregon "does not have subject matter jurisdiction" . . . and that "continuing jurisdiction" resides in North Dakota. . . . [Grandmother appeals.]

On appeal, the parties dispute the applicability and operation of various UCCJEA provisions, including [§§ 202, 203, 206] . . . [W]e conclude that [§ 203] is dispositive and, consequently, we do not address the potential applicability of other UCCJEA provisions that might also preclude subject matter jurisdiction.

. . . .

The application of [§ 203] . . . depends on the resolution of two questions. First, did the . . . petition here seek to "modify a child custody determination made by a court of another state"? Second, if so, were the requisites of modification jurisdiction . . . satisfied in this case?

[Section 102] of the UCCJEA defines both "modification" and "child custody determination." [The court here recited the Oregon definitions which are virtually identical to the UCCJEA language in § 102.]

Applying those definitions [here], the petition . . . seeks to "modify" the "child custody determination" rendered in the . . . North Dakota . . . decree of dissolution.

[Grandmother] seeks sole custody of S. A judgment granting such relief would, necessarily, "change," "replace," or "supersede" the North Dakota court's prior award of sole custody to father. The plain language of [§ 203] read in conjunction with [§ 102] is conclusive. . . . [Grandmother] argues, nevertheless, that subjecting her petition to the jurisdictional strictures of [§ 203] cannot be reconciled with our analysis and holding in *Fenimore v. Smith*, 930 P.2d 892 (1996). We disagree. In *Fenimore*, the petitioner was the stepfather of a 12-year-old child. [A California divorce decree had granted the parents joint legal custody of their then-3-year old child and gave mother physical custody.] After the divorce, the mother married the stepfather, and the child grew up in their home in California. When the child was 11, she moved with her mother and stepfather to Oregon. A few months later, her mother died. The father and the stepfather disputed custody, and the stepfather filed a petition [here] seeking custody. . . . The trial court dismissed . . . for lack of jurisdiction under . . . the [UCCJA].

On appeal, we reversed that dismissal. In so holding, we observed:

> *It is important to keep in mind that this is an initial action seeking custody.* . . .

> However, under the UCCJA even if there is a jurisdictional basis . . . for this child custody proceeding, Oregon would be barred from exercising that jurisdiction . . . if a modification of another state's custody decree was sought and that state retained and had not declined jurisdiction. . . . *The modification bar of the UCCJA is . . . inapplicable as this is an initial custody proceeding between stepfather and father, not the modification of the divorce decree between mother and father.*

145 Ore. App. at 506 (emphasis added; footnote omitted). Petitioner invokes the emphasized language as compelling the conclusion that her . . . petition cannot be deemed to seek "modification". . . .

Fenimore is substantively distinguishable, and noncontrolling, because it was decided under a different statute, the UCCJA, not the UCCJEA, and the pertinent statutory provisions are materially different. The UCCJA's "modification jurisdiction" provision read as follows:

> If a court of another state has made a custody decree, a court of this state shall not modify that decree unless it appears . . . that the court which rendered the decree does not now have jurisdiction under jurisdictional prerequisites substantially in accordance with [the UCCJA] or has declined to assume jurisdiction to modify the decree and the court of this state has jurisdiction.

The UCCJA included no definition of "modify" or "modification" but did define "modification decree" as:

> [A] custody decree which modifies or replaces a prior decree, whether made by the court which rendered the prior decree or by another court.

ORS 109.710(7) (1995).

Thus, under the UCCJA, "modification" connoted alteration or replacement of the prior decree. Conversely, under the UCCJEA, "modification" seems much more broadly to encompass any child custody determination that "changes, replaces, [or] supersedes" any "previous determination concerning the same child." Given that distinction, while [the UCCJA provision] could be narrowly construed (as in

Fenimore) to apply only to literal modification of the same judgment or decree, [the UCCJEA provision] is not plausibly susceptible to such a construction.[5] Under [§ 203], it is irrelevant whether modification is sought in a continuation of the original proceeding or in a new proceeding, or even whether the party seeking custody was a party to the original proceeding — so long as the petition seeks to change, replace, or supersede the prior award of custody, it seeks "modification" and must satisfy the statute's jurisdictional requisites.

We thus conclude that the petition here is subject to [§ 203]. Under the statute, the court can exercise modification jurisdiction only if two cumulative conditions are satisfied. First, the Oregon court must have jurisdiction to make an initial determination under [§ 201]. And, second, *either* (1) the court of the other state must determine that it no longer has "exclusive, continuing jurisdiction," as described in [§ 202] or that the Oregon court would be a "more convenient forum," [§ 207]; *or* (2) either the Oregon court or the court of the other state must determine that "the child's parents and any person acting as a parent do not presently reside in the other state."

We need not address, and decide, whether the first of those two cumulative conditions is satisfied, because the second is not. In particular, the North Dakota court has not determined that it no longer has "exclusive, continuing jurisdiction" or that Oregon would be a "more convenient forum." Further, because mother continues to live in North Dakota, no court could render the necessary determination [that none of the parents or persons acting as parents still live in North Dakota.] In sum, [§ 203] precludes subject matter jurisdiction. . . .

. . . .

Affirmed.

NOTES

1. *Continuing Exclusive Jurisdiction. Snow* illustrates a major change made by the UCCJEA. Sections 202 and 203 were added to remedy what the drafters described as a "failure of the UCCJA to clearly enunciate that the decree-granting State retains exclusive continuing jurisdiction to modify a decree. . . ." UCCJEA Prefatory Note, 9 U.L.A. Part IA, p. 651 (1997). While the idea that a court, having issued a custody decree, continued to have jurisdiction to modify it was generally recognized, the UCCJA failed to articulate rules defining the duration of such jurisdiction. This created a chaotic situation with many conflicting custody decrees. As the UCCJEA drafters described the situation under the UCCJA,

> States . . . have different interpretations as to how long continuing jurisdiction lasts. Some courts have held that [it] continues until the last contestant leaves the State, regardless of how many years the child has

---

[5] We note one final consideration that may have underlay our analysis in *Fenimore*: There, the mother, who had been awarded physical custody, had died; consequently, the stepfather's petition did not seek to divest the custodial parent of custody, effectively nullifying the prior judgment. Here, however, that is precisely the relief that petitioner seeks. . . .

lived outside the State or how tenuous the child's connections to the State. . . . Other courts have held that continuing modification jurisdiction ends as soon as the child has established a new home State, regardless of how significant the child's connections to the decree State remain. Still other States distinguish between custody orders and visitation orders. . . ."

Id. This murky situation was further complicated by the PKPA provision requiring states to give full faith and credit to decree modifications made under continuing jurisdiction so long as the issuing state had jurisdiction under its own law and the child or any contestant still lived there. § 1738A(d).

UCCJEA §§ 202 and 203 aim to create clarity and uniformity to reduce the number of conflicting custody decrees. Under § 202, a state which has issued a custody decree is the only state (with an exception described in Note 2 below) which can modify that determination until one of two events occurs. One such event is the departure of the child, the parents, and anyone "acting as a parent" from the issuing state. (§ 202(a)(2)). The second appears in § 202(a)(1), which is not a model of drafting clarity. According to the Commentary, this provision provides that even though a parent or person acting as a parent remains in the issuing state, continuing jurisdiction is ended when the decree state no longer has "the general requisites of the 'substantial connection' jurisdiction provisions of § 201. . . . If the relationship between the child and the person remaining in the [original] State. . . . becomes so attenuated that the court could no longer find significant connections and substantial evidence, jurisdiction would no longer exist." *Id.* at p. 674. Thus, the decree state might well retain exclusive jurisdiction to modify the original decree long after another state had become the child's home state. For example, in *In re Bellamy*, 67 S.W.3d 482 (Tex. App. 2002), the child had lived with her mother in Louisiana for well more than six months. Her father remained in Texas, however, and she still attended school in Texas (using her grandparents' home address as her residence for attendance purposes) and stayed with her father for six weeks each year, plus some holidays and weekends. The court held Texas retained exclusive modification jurisdiction. *See also Bearden v. Mauldin*, 2008 Ky App. LEXIS 163 (trial court retained jurisdiction over mother's visitation petition even after child had left state to live with grandparents who were adopting child, despite child's new home state); *Kelso v. Decker*, 262 S.W.3d 307 (Tenn. Ct. App. 2008) (modification of Ohio decree in Tennessee inappropriate where Ohio remained the residence of father, even though mother and child had moved to Tennessee); *Thomas v. Avant*, 260 S.W.3d 266 (Ark. 2007) (fact that child had not lived in forum for 7 years does not deprive it of modification jurisdiction where parent remains in forum which issued decree); *Wallace v. Wallace*, 224 S.W.3d 587 (Ky. App. 2006) (forum retained continuing exclusive jurisdiction over custody issues involving all three children, even though two lived in Tennessee with their mother); *Watson v. Watson*, 724 N.W.2d 24 (Neb. 2006) (forum court with continuing exclusive jurisdiction should not have relinquished such jurisdiction solely because its order had been registered in Maryland where custodial parent and children lived; remanded for determination of *forum non conveniens* issue); *In re Forlenza*, 140 S.W.3d 373 (Tex. 2004) (children's absence from state for 5 ½ years did not deprive issuing court of modification jurisdiction where significant connection remains and substantial evidence is available in forum); *but see Graham v. Graham*, 2009 Tenn. App. LEXIS 18 (decree state renounces continuing jurisdiction due to lack of significant connection and lack of substantial evidence within state); *In re M.B. II*, 756 N.Y.S.2d 710 (Nassau Fam. Ct. 2002) (same).

At this point, a review of the requirements of "significant connection" jurisdiction under § 201(a)(2) might be helpful. Have the goals of clarity and uniformity been met by extending exclusive modification jurisdiction until a court concludes the parties no longer have "significant connection with [a] state other than mere physical presence" and that "substantial evidence is available in [the forum] state concerning the child's care, protection, training, and personal relationships"? While reasonable minds might disagree on whether the jurisdiction-terminating facts exist, under UCCJEA § 202(a)(1) only the issuing state can make the decision. Thus, *e.g.*, in *Bellamy, supra*, only Texas (not Louisiana) could decide that continuing exclusive modification jurisdiction under § 202(a)(1) had been lost by Texas for lack of significant connection jurisdiction. By contrast, Louisiana would be authorized, under § 202(a)(2), to make the more objective determination that all of the relevant parties had left Texas. Section 203 defines modification jurisdiction from the perspective of the claimed modification state and, as such, was the provision applied by *Snow*. This companion to § 202 states that, with the exception of emergency jurisdiction described in Note 2, a court lacks power to modify another state's custody determination unless one of three events have occurred: 1) the issuing court has decided it no longer has continuing jurisdiction; 2) the issuing court has deferred under forum non conveniens under § 207; or 3) all the relevant parties have abandoned the issuing state. If one of those conditions exists, the court can modify if it has jurisdiction under § 201.

The UCCJEA's continuing exclusive jurisdiction provisions are narrower than the PKPA's parallel provisions. Subsection (d) of the federal statute mandates full faith and credit to modification decrees issued by a state in which any "contestant" continues to reside and the latter word encompasses anybody, including grandparents or other third parties, who claims a right to custody or visitation. § 1738A(b)(2). While the "contestants" category obviously is broader than the parties referred to in § 202(a)(2), there is no conflict between the federal and the uniform statute because subsection (d) also requires that the issuing state have continuing jurisdiction under its own law. In a UCCJEA state, the state would be claiming, under § 202, less continuing jurisdiction than the PKPA would recognize. The UCCJEA drafters decided that the continued presence of a third party, such as a grandparent, who might be claiming only a right to visitation, was an inadequate basis for continuing modification jurisdiction. During the transition to nationwide adoption of the new Uniform Act, however, "some states may continue to base continuing jurisdiction on the continued presence of a contestant. . . . The PKPA will require that such decisions be enforced. The problem will disappear as states adopt [the UCCJEA] to replace the UCCJA." UCCJEA, § 202, cmt., 9 U.L.A., Part IA, p. 675.

2. *Emergency Jurisdiction.* Section 204 provides an exceptional type of jurisdiction. Based on the child's presence in the state, jurisdiction is premised on the child being abandoned or in need of protection "because the child, or a sibling or parent of the child, is subjected to or threatened with mistreatment or abuse."

§ 204(a). The use of "mistreatment or abuse" as triggering conditions was designed to harmonize subsection (a) with the parallel PKPA provision. Protective order proceedings to deal with family violence (discussed in Chapter 2) often deal with custody and visitation questions. So long as the child is present in the state, jurisdiction to handle custody and visitation matters would exist under § 204.

In one of the few cases under § 204, in *P.E.K. v. J.M.*, 52 S.W.3d 653 (Tenn. Ct. App. 2001), the trial court issued a custody decree concerning a child outside the state who was in need because of threatened or actual abuse, apparently viewing the statute as providing two alternative jurisdictional predicates (abandoned in the state OR in need of protection because of abuse, actual or threatened). After examining the prior UCCJA provision, the appellate court rejected this interpretation of § 204, finding "no indication that the legislature intended to involve the courts of this state in emergencies existing in other states. *See also Hearld v. Hearld*, 278 S.W.3d 162 (Ky. App. 2009) (deployment of custodial father to Iraq does not constitute an emergency); *Button v. Waite*, 208 S.W.3d 366 (Tenn. 2006) (trial court erred in exercising emergency jurisdiction on a finding of "threat of immediate mistreatment or abuse to the child" by Hawaii court's "selection of an alternate therapist for the child. . . .").

Unlike its predecessor, the new statute's emergency jurisdiction is explicitly temporary, though it may become a final order if the conditions of subsection (b) are satisfied. Emergency jurisdiction may be exercised whether or not there is an existing order and even if there is ongoing custody litigation elsewhere. If there is an existing order or ongoing litigation, the statute requires that the emergency order provide a specific amount of time in which petitioner is to obtain an order from the appropriate other court. § 204(c). Subsection (d) of the statute requires "emergency jurisdiction" courts and "regular jurisdiction" courts to communicate with each other "to resolve the emergency, protect the safety of the parties and the child, and determine a period for the duration of the temporary order."

3. *Other UCCJEA Innovations.* The new act makes many other changes to the UCCJA regime. It explicitly defines the types of proceedings qualifying as custody proceedings (§ 102(4) which notably excludes adoption proceedings, jurisdiction of which is covered by the Uniform Adoption Act). As *Welch-Doden* acknowledged, the Act omits any reference to the child's best interests to emphasize that the substantive custody decision is to be decided only *after* the existence of jurisdiction is clear. The Act, in Article 3, also deals with the enforcement of other states' custody and visitation orders. As noted in the Prefatory Note to the UCCJEA,

> . . . [S]tate borders have become one of the biggest obstacles to enforce-ment of custody and visitation orders. If either parent leaves the State where the custody determination was made, the other parent faces considerable difficulty in enforcing the . . . decree. Locating the child, making service of process, and preventing adverse modification in a new forum all present problems.

> There is currently no uniform method of enforcing custody and visitation orders validly entered in another State. . . . [D]espite the fact that both the UCCJA and the PKPA direct the enforcement of visitation and custody

orders entered in accordance with mandated jurisdictional prerequisites and due process, neither act provides enforcement procedures or remedies.

. . . [T]he lack of specificity in enforcement procedures has resulted in the law of enforcement evolving differently in different jurisdictions. In one State, [one might] file a Motion to Enforce or a Motion to Grant Full Faith and Credit to initiate an enforcement proceeding. In another State, a Writ of Habeas Corpus or a Citation for Contempt might be commonly used. In some States, Mandamus and Prohibition also may be utilized. . . . While many States tend to limit considerations in enforcement proceedings to whether the court which issued the decree had jurisdiction to make the custody determination, others broaden the considerations to scrutiny of whether enforcement would be in the best interests of the child.

Lack of uniformity complicates the enforcement process in several ways: (1) It increases the costs of the enforcement action. . . . ; (2) It decreases the certainty of outcome; (3) It can turn enforcement into a long and drawn out procedure. . . ."

UCCJEA Prefatory Comment, 9 U.L.A. Part IA, p. 652 (1997).

PROBLEMS

Problem 7-11. Janet and Sammy were Texas residents whose marriage produced one child, Melissa. The couple separated in June, 2001 and Sammy filed for divorce the next month in Texas. Temporary orders were entered naming the couple joint legal custodians and granting Sammy primary physical custody. Janet immediately moved to New York City. In January 2002, Sammy died, while the divorce suit was still pending. Rather than uproot Melissa immediately, Janet allowed her to stay in Texas with her maternal grandparents. After four months of this arrangement, Janet brought Melissa to New York. In September, 2002, Sammy's parents filed suit under a Texas statute which allows a court to order visitation of a grandchild within one year of the death of a child's parent. Texas is a UCCJEA state. State law also provides that the death of a parent with legal custody terminates the custody order. You are law clerk to the judge in whose court the lawsuit has been filed. Write a memorandum outlining the issues and your proposed resolution of Janet's motion to dismiss for lack of jurisdiction.

Problem 7-12. Timothy was born to Sara and John (who were never married to each other) in California. Sara is a drug addict, has a lengthy criminal record and has been investigated numerous times on charges of abusing her other five children. When Timothy was four months old, he was removed from Sara's care and placed with his paternal grandmother (Laura) who was appointed his guardian in a court proceeding. The guardianship order directed John and Sara to stay away from the child. Five years later, with her health failing, Laura sent Timothy to Alaska to live with Lynne, John's former wife who was the mother of Timothy's two half-siblings. After writing a notarized letter purporting to transfer guardianship of Timothy to Lynne, Laura died. For the past five years Timothy has lived with Lynne and his half-siblings in Alaska. The Alaska child welfare agency has filed suit to terminate Sara's parental rights on the grounds that she has not seen the child in five years. Alaska is a UCCJEA state. You are a law clerk to the judge hearing the case. What jurisdictional issues do you see in this case and what do you think you need to know about California law to resolve them?

Problem 7-13.   Weldon and Mary Ann have a troubled marriage. After years of physical and emotional abuse, she obtains a domestic violence protective order in Minnesota (their home state) which prohibits him from seeing her and requires him to undertake anger management counseling for 8 months. Weldon completes his required counseling and seems to have turned over a new leaf. In the intervening period, however, Mary Ann has left for Hawaii with the couple's child, Joshua. She and the child have been in Hawaii for seven months and she has told Weldon by phone "I have no intention of ever living anywhere within 100 miles of you and I don't have any intention of having Joshua being exposed to your evil ways and miserable temper." Weldon comes to you in your Minnesota law office wanting to file a suit to obtain joint custody of Joshua with visitation rights. You know Minnesota is a UCCJEA state. What else will you need to know before you know whether you will be able to obtain jurisdiction?

Problem 7-14.   Dennis and Sheila were divorced in New York in 1999. The decree provided for joint legal custody of their child, Jacob, with primary physical custody in the father. Sheila was given reasonable visitation. Since 2002, however, Jacob has lived with Sheila in her new residence in the Virgin Islands with the permission of Dennis. You are clerking in the New York court which entered the original decree and in which Sheila has moved for a modification (in 2004) to grant her sole legal custody and child support. You know that New York enacted the UCCJEA in 2001 and enacted the UIFSA in 1998. What issues do you foresee and how would you expect them to be resolved?

Problem 7-15.   Lola and Cosmo were divorced in South Dakota in 2007. Cosmo received custody of their child, Fritz. Cosmo and Fritz immediately moved to Maine. Lola, having decided that Cosmo's post-divorce life is not healthy for Fritz, files for a modification of custody in Maine. Soon after the suit is filed, Lola's attorney dies. She comes to you for advice. Will she likely get a judgment on the merits of her suit in Maine? If not, can you recommend an alternative route for her?

Problem 7-16.   Melissa had a child, Mark, at the age of 14. The father, to whom she was not married, soon died. Because of her youth and her mistreatment at the hands of her parents, Melissa's parents' parental rights were terminated about 7 months after Mark's birth. Temporary custody of Melissa and Mark was awarded to the state of Montana (where Mark had been born), which arranged to place them both in foster care with the Smiths, a married couple in their 50's, living in Butte. During the following 3 ½ years, Melissa and Mark lived with the Smiths. When Melissa obtained her GED certificate and completed a course for nurse's aide certification, the state's temporary custody of both Melissa and Mark was terminated, along with the foster care placement with the Smiths. Melissa and Mark immediately moved to Washington state. Three months later, the Smiths filed an action in Washington alleging the Melissa was an unfit mother whose parental rights and custody should be terminated. You are law clerk to the judge in whose court this petition was filed. Write a memorandum explaining to your judge what you see as the issues in this case.

DOMESTIC RELATIONS JURISDICTION AND FEDERALISM

Federal courts consistently have refused to hear domestic relations cases that would otherwise qualify for diversity jurisdiction. This domestic relations "exception" to federal jurisdiction excludes, *e.g.*, a petition to modify an existing custody decree, even though the contestants live in different states. The exception traces from United States Supreme Court dicta in *Barber v. Barber*, 21 How. 582 (1859). In its most recent analysis of the issue, the Court found the exception statutory rather than constitutional. *Ankenbrandt v. Richards*, 504 U.S. 689 (1992). *Ankenbrandt* held that the Judiciary Act of 1789, in providing for federal diversity jurisdiction of "all suits of a civil nature at common law or in equity," did not reach those domestic relations issues not within the jurisdiction of the English Chancery Court. Finding Congressional failure to overrule *Barber's* dicta constituted approval of it, *Ankenbrandt* held that actions for divorce or alimony fell within the exception and noted that it had added custody decrees to the exception in *In re Burrus*, 136 U.S. 586 (1890). On the *Ankenbrandt* facts, the Court permitted litigation of a mother's tort claim based upon assertions of physical and sexual abuse by her ex-husband and his female companion.

A number of lower courts have approved the exercise of jurisdiction, finding the domestic relations exception inapplicable. In *Dunn v. Cometa*, 238 F.3d 38 (1st Cir. 2001), a diversity plaintiff sued on behalf of his disabled son and himself, alleging financial misfeasance by his former daughter-in-law during the waning days of the marriage. Discovery into these matters in the divorce action had been abandoned. The divorce judge found "not a shred of evidence to support a finding of economic misconduct or fraud." Soon after the divorce, the federal action was filed. While conceding the alleged economic misconduct could have had an impact on the level of alimony, the appellate court found federal jurisdiction, noting that sometimes events can simultaneously have relevance to different types of relationships. *See also Matusow v. Trans-County Title Agency*, 545 F.3d 241 (3d Cir. 2008) (suit by divorced woman claiming improper sale of her former marital home not within exception); *Norton v. McOsker*, 407 F.3d 501 (1st Cir. 2005) (paramour's suit against married boyfriend for promissory estoppel and intentional infliction of emotional distress not within exception); *Hildebrand v. Lewis*, 281 F. Supp. 2d 837 (E.D. Va. 2003) (suit for breaches of fiduciary duty and conversion by plaintiff against former husband concerning their business interests which were divided by a separation agreement incorporated in their divorce decree not within the exception); *Rash v. Rash*, 173 F.3d 1376 (11th Cir. 1999)(entertaining suit seeking declaratory judgment as to which of two divorce decrees was valid); *Shelar v. Shelar*, 910 F. Supp. 1307 (N.D. Ohio 1995) (suit against former spouse for intentional infliction of emotional distress for concealing or misapplying marital property during divorce proceeding); *Strasen v. Strasen*, 897 F. Supp. 1179 (E.D. Wisc. 1995) (conspiracy, fraudulent misrepresentation by divorcing spouse); *Rubin v. Smith*, 817 F. Supp. 987 (D.N.H. 1993) (exception inapplicable in federal question litigation based on childnapping by father and policemen); *but see Weiss v. Weiss*, 375 F. Supp. 2d 10 (D. Conn. 2005) (while framed as asserting contract and tort claims, action sought interpretation of separation agreement and thus was within domestic relations exception); *McLaughlin v. Cotner*, 193 F.3d 410 (6th Cir. 1999) (upholding dismissal of diversity suit alleging breach of separation agreement); *Bidwell v. Baker*, 2001 U.S. Dist. LEXIS

12503 (D. Ore., Aug. 16, 2001) (dismissing suit alleging violation of a post-judgment oral agreement to modify result of a divorce action); *Johnson v. Rodrigues*, 226 F.3d 1103 (10th Cir. 2000) (dismissing action seeking return of child to biological father because of alleged constitutional invalidity of adoption notification procedure); *Mazur v. Woodson*, 932 F. Supp. 144 (E.D. Va. 1996) (dismissing action challenging appointment of guardian of allegedly incompetent person). For post-*Ankenbrandt* commentary on the domestic relations exception, see Emily Sack, *The Domestic Relations Exception, Domestic Violence, and Equal Access to Federal Courts*, 84 WASH. U. L. REV. 1441 (2006) (details history of exception, arguing it may well derive from the principles of coverture and that a primary cause of the creation of the exception is "the belief that family law is a 'woman's issue' that is not deserving of the attention of the federal courts"); Michael Stein, *The Domestic Relations Exception to Federal Jurisdiction: Rethinking an Unsettled Federal Courts Doctrine*, 36 BOST. COLL. L. REV. 669 (1995).

Some lower federal courts had held the PKPA created an implied federal cause of action to resolve custody jurisdictional conflicts between state courts, but the Supreme Court found to the contrary, noting state courts can themselves implement the statute's purpose of applying full faith and credit principles to custody decisions. *Thompson v. Thompson*, 484 U.S. 174 (1988). For recent commentary suggesting that later Supreme Court jurisprudence in related areas suggests the possibility of a limited federal forum "to decide jurisdictional deadlocks," see Christine Jones, *The Parental Kidnaping Prevention Act: Is There New Hope for a (Limited) Federal Forum?*, 18 TEMP. POL. & CIV. RTS. L. REV. 141 (2008).

The same emphasis on state primacy over domestic relations cases which keeps most family law cases out of federal court animates a body of law holding that domestic relations litigation involving foreign diplomats based in the United States can be litigated in state courts. Thus, in *Ohio ex rel. Popovici v. Agler*, 280 U.S. 379 (1930), the Supreme Court upheld Ohio jurisdiction in a diplomat-defendant's divorce action despite Constitutional and federal legislative provisions establishing diplomatic immunity in state courts. *See also Salvatierra v. Calderon*, 836 So. 2d 149 (La. App. 2002) (diplomatic status did not prevent establishment of state domicile by diplomat's spouse or exercise of personal jurisdiction over diplomat-defendant); *Duran-Ballen v. Duran-Ballen*, 40 N.Y.S.2d 617 (Sup. Ct. 1943) (state could obtain jurisdiction over diplomat in declaratory judgment action dealing with validity of his foreign divorce).

Chapter 8

FIXING THE CONSEQUENCES OF DIVORCE BY AGREEMENT OF THE PARTIES

INTRODUCTION

As this chapter will show, American family law has a decidedly mixed view of agreements between partners married or about to be married: relatively encouraging and supportive for separation agreements, grudgingly accepting of some premarital agreements, and uncertain and occasionally hostile to comparable agreements entered in the middle of a marriage. (The ambivalence to agreements in the domestic context extends to agreements having no direct relation to marriage — surrogacy agreements, open adoption agreements, co-parenting agreements, etc. — some of which are dealt with elsewhere in this book. For a general overview, see Brian Bix, *Domestic Agreements*, 35 Hofstra L. Rev. 1753 (2007).)

This chapter deals with premarital agreements and separation agreements. A separation agreement fixes the terms of the couple's separation and, usually, their divorce; it is also often called a settlement agreement. A premarital (or "antenuptial") agreement may also fix the consequences of the marriage's dissolution, but is made before the parties enter the marriage rather than after they have decided to end it. The traditional premarital agreement applied only when the marriage ended by the death of a spouse, because the traditional law did not allow enforcement of agreements "contemplating" divorce. That limitation has now been widely abandoned, leaving timing as the major difference between premarital and separation agreements. The difference in timing leads to other process differences, however. For example, premarital agreements, like other contracts, are extrajudicial when made; courts see them for the first time when their enforcement is sought, which may be years after their execution. In contrast, divorce settlement agreements ordinarily are presented to the divorce court for approval soon after they are made, because the parties usually want their terms incorporated in the divorce decree. Perhaps because of this difference, it is unusual for settlement agreements to be upset later, while successful attacks on the validity of premarital agreements were historically common. This chapter's treatment of premarital agreements therefore focuses on the rules that govern their enforceability, while its treatment of settlement agreements gives more attention to the negotiating process and the role of lawyers in that process. Sometimes spouses who are not planning a separation make an agreement during their marriage. Such "during-marriage" agreements, sometimes called marital agreements, function much like premarital agreements and are covered in the premarital agreement section of this chapter. While largely similar, they may present special procedural problems, and are sometimes subject to different requirements.

A. PREMARITAL AGREEMENTS

[1]   Introduction

Why do parties seek premarital agreements? In the reported cases and in the media, one tends to hear one of two narratives. The more sympathetic narrative is about protecting children from a prior marriage from competing financial claims by the new spouse, and the keeping of family businesses and family heirlooms within the family. The somewhat less sympathetic story is about a richer partner's desire not to have to give significant funds to a spouse should the upcoming marriage fail. In many of the reported cases, the partner who presents (insists upon) the premarital agreement has been through (at least) one divorce, and may be trying to avoid what that partner considered to be an unjust financial outcome in that divorce. In both kinds of cases, one can see the relevance of the growing number of second (and third, and later) marriages. In 1988, in 46% of the marriages, at least one of the newlyweds had been married before, Paula Mergenhag DeWitt, *The Second Time Around*, American Demographics, November, 1992, at 60, 63. Cautious but wealthy individuals marrying for the first time and without children may also seek a premarital agreement to limit any financial claims their new spouse might have if the marriage fails. One can also imagine premarital agreements that deal with nonfinancial issues, such as custody arrangements in the event of divorce, or with the conduct of the marriage rather than the consequences of its dissolution. Terms concerning such nonfinancial issues are typically not binding, however, see Section A[4] below.

The possible impact of a premarital agreement on property arrangements will vary with local law. In a "hotchpot" system in which all property is normally before a divorce court, the agreement could exclude premarital acquisitions from the divorce court's reach. In the majority of states in which divorce courts divide only community or marital property, the agreement could opt out of the community property or marital property regime entirely, reserving to each spouse all property earned by that spouse during the marriage. The parties might agree to exclude from divisible property the appreciation, during the marriage, of any separate assets, which some states otherwise would reach. This could be important where one spouse enters the marriage with an operating business he expects will prosper. The agreement might also avoid rules transforming separate property into marital property when assets are commingled. Finally, the agreement could affect the availability or size of an alimony award although, as we shall see, there are occasional restrictions on provisions limiting alimony that do not apply to parallel property provisions.

NOTES

1. *Echoes of the Traditional Rule.* The traditional rule barring agreements that "contemplated divorce" was consistent with the prevailing law of the fault-divorce era: given that the law barred divorce by mutual consent, one would expect it to also look skeptically on premarital agreements setting forth divorce terms. As no-fault divorce was widely adopted during the 1970s and 1980s, this limitation on premarital agreements gradually disappeared as well. *Scherer v. Scherer*, 292 S.E.2d 662 (Ga. 1982) was typical of this transition. The Scherer agreement, executed in 1976, required the husband to maintain life insurance policies that would pay the wife death benefits of about half a million dollars, if the parties were married at the time of his death, but provided that the wife would otherwise have no claims on his sizeable stock holdings in a family business. A second provision stated simply that "in the event of the termination of marriage other than by death, the intent and provisions hereof shall be considered and applied to the extent permitted by law." The agreement's language thus carefully avoided even mentioning the word "divorce," for fear of putting the entire agreement in legal jeopardy. When husband sought a divorce in 1980, the question was whether the agreement applied. In holding that it did, Scherer quoted approvingly language from *Volid v. Volid*, 286 N.E.2d 42, 46–47 (Ill. App. 1972), that "Public policy is not violated by permitting these persons . . . to anticipate the possibility of divorce and to establish their rights by contract in such an event as long as the contract is entered with full knowledge and without fraud, duress or coercion."

Scherer and *Volid* reflect the current prevailing view; *see also Gentry v. Gentry*, 798 S.W.2d 928 (Ky. 1990). This trend was strengthened by Uniform Premarital Agreement Act (UPAA) § 3 which authorizes spouses to contract about their rights with respect to the "property of either or both of them whenever and wherever acquired or located." That Act has been adopted in 25 states and the District of Columbia, although, as explained below in Note 1 following *Bonds* and *Simeone*, other provisions of it have proven controversial and adoption has slowed.

2. *Requirement of a Writing.* As a general matter, most states require a writing for a valid premarital agreements. E.g., CAL. FAM. CODE § 1611; MINN. STAT. § 519.11, subd. 2. Section 2 of the Uniform Premarital Agreement Act requires a writing, as does the American Law Institute's *Principles of the Law of Family Dissolution*, § 7.04(1). Some jurisdictions have held that an oral agreement otherwise barred by a Statute of Frauds may be enforceable if one of the parties has performed in reliance upon it. On rare occasion, one can find an oral premarital agreement enforced on that basis. *See, e.g., Snyder v. Snyder*, 558 A.2d 412 (Md. App. 1989) (husband's oral premarital agreement to transfer title from himself to his spouse and him together might in principle be enforceable due to part performance).

3. *Agreements "Encouraging" Divorce.* Modern courts still occasionally say they will not enforce agreements "encouraging" divorce, but no one appears to know precisely what this means. *Marriage of Noghrey*, 215 Cal. Rptr. 153 (App. 1985), relied on this principle in refusing to enforce a provision in a *ketubah*, the traditional Jewish marriage contract. The *ketubah* typically requires a payment from the husband to the wife in the event of divorce. In modern Jewish weddings the specified payment is usually small and symbolic, but the disputed provision in *Noghrey* required the husband to pay the wife $500,000. The court held the provision void because it was not meant to adjust property rights arising from the marriage, and created an incentive for the wife to seek divorce. The parties were Iranians, and the wife had claimed the payment was meant to compensate her for the difficulty she would have in finding a new Iranian husband when she was no longer a virgin. An analogous provision in a Jordanian marriage contract was involved in *Marriage of Dajani*, 251 Cal. Rptr. 871 (App. 1988), and the court relied on *Noghrey* in refusing to enforce it, even though here the required payment was only 5,000 Jordanian dinars, about $1,600 at the time. More recently, in *Bellio v. Bellio*, 129 Cal. Rptr. 2d 556 (App. 2003), the court considered a provision allowing the wife a lump sum payment of $100,000 if the marriage ended by either divorce or the husband's death; the agreement otherwise provided that the spouse's respective earnings would remain separate. The wife was 48 and the husband 71 at the time of the marriage; the husband, a multimillionaire, had asked wife to agree that all accumulations during the marriage would remain separate, and the wife had insisted on the lump-sum provision in exchange. Her earnings were modest and she depended upon alimony payments from her first husband, which would terminate with this second marriage, and she was therefore concerned that at the end of the second marriage she would be left in precarious financial circumstances. The trial court had nonetheless held the provision invalid under *Noghrey* and *Dajani*, but the appeals court reversed and enforced it. It distinguished *Noghrey* as involving a bonus payment so large as to induce the divorce, and said that *Dajani* was wrongly decided because the payment there was too small to have that effect. Is $100,000 large enough to induce divorce? It might seem so. But the court sensibly explained its enforcement of the provision by reference to a different principle: the payment involved no more than reasonable financial planning that would assure the wife that the marriage could not make her worse off than before. Although the court did not note it, the provision was also surely a reasonable — indeed, modest — *quid* for the *quo* of her waiving any community property claims that would otherwise have arisen during the marriage — putting the provision in a very different light than those involved in the earlier cases.

Consider whether such decisions cast doubt upon the premarital agreement entered into by Donald Trump and Marla Maples, who announced in May of 1997 that they would divorce "as friends" after "a long relationship and a three-and-a-half year marriage." According to reports from "a person familiar with Mr. Trump's portfolio and marital situation," the separation was his idea and "was happening now for reasons of economy." This source reported that the parties' premarital agreement "which would pay Ms. Maples $1 million to $5 million in the event of divorce, is to expire within 11 months, after which she would be entitled to a settlement based on a percentage of Mr. Trump's net worth. [¶] If he's really worth $2.5 billion, 'even . . . a small percentage is a lot of money,' the person said." According to this person there was no third party involved in the divorce, which occurred because Mr. Trump "has been forced economically to act. . . . Unless you're married to someone you have 1000 percent surety in, you just can't do [otherwise]." *Donald and Marla Headed for Divestiture*, N.Y. Times, May 3, 1997, at 20.

Note that the cases just described all involve provisions in which the payments in question did *not* depend upon who sought the divorce. Provisions that create penalties for the party seeking divorce raise different issues. See the *Penhallow* case discussed in the notes in Section A[3] below.

[2]   Should Courts Ensure the Procedural or Substantive Fairness of Premarital Agreements?

Should courts scrutinize premarital agreements more carefully than commercial contracts, before enforcing them? The traditional law contemplated such heightened scrutiny. But the Uniform Premarital Agreement Act, adopted by the Commissioners in 1983, treated premarital agreements more like commercial contracts, with very limited judicial review for substantive or procedural fairness, and in the fifteen years that followed this seemed to be the trend in the law. But adoptions of the UPAA have slowed, and the more recent recommendations of the American Law Institute seek instead to clarify and systemize the traditional approach of heightened scrutiny. Which policy is best? We examine examples of both.

[a]   The Traditional Rule of Heightened Scrutiny

WISCONSIN STATUTES

§ 767.61(3)

The court shall presume that all [marital] property . . . is to be divided equally between the parties, but may alter this distribution without regard to marital misconduct after considering all of the following:

. . .

(L) Any written agreement made by the parties before or during the marriage concerning any arrangement for property distribution; such agreements shall be binding upon the court except that no such agreement shall be binding where the terms of the agreement are inequitable as to either party. The court shall presume any such agreement to be equitable as to both parties.

BUTTON v. BUTTON
Wisconsin Supreme Court
388 N.W.2d 546 (1986)

SHIRLEY S. ABRAHAMSON, JUSTICE.

This is an appeal from a judgment . . . dividing property upon divorce in accordance with the terms of a written property agreement which the circuit court found binding under § 767.255. . . .

[1. The Facts]

. . . The parties married on September 12, 1969, having known each other for approximately five years. . . . Both . . . had been married previously; Mrs. Button had one adult child . . . and Mr. Button had three adult children. When they were married, Mrs. Button was 50 years old, and Mr. Button 61 years old. Mrs. Button began the divorce action in 1983.

Prior to the marriage, Mrs. Button had acquired some personal property and other assets with a total worth of no more than $3,000 and a life insurance policy on the life of her former husband in the amount of $12,000. Mr. Button had an upholstery business, a stock portfolio, personal property and real estate upon which a duplex residence and the business were located. He had inherited a substantial part of this property and, under sec. 767.255, inherited property is considered separate property not generally subject to division upon divorce.

The parties entered into a written prenuptial agreement on August 15, 1969. While this prenuptial agreement is not the agreement in issue here, the facts relating to the execution of the 1969 agreement may bear on the determination of whether the 1974 agreement is inequitable.

Mrs. Button testified that there was no discussion of Mr. Button's finances prior to their marriage, although she was aware that he owned a duplex house, an upholstery business, a car, and a snowmobile. Mrs. Button also testified that Mr. Button's attorney told her that "if [you] wanted to take it to another attorney [you] could, but if [you] did that then you would say that you didn't trust Charles and Charlie said that's right. . . ." Mrs. Button also stated that she did not read the agreement before signing it. Mr. Button's attorney testified that he believed that both parties understood the agreement, although he has no record of any financial disclosures being made between the parties. Mr. Button testified that he did not make any financial disclosures to Mrs. Button. Neither Mrs. Button nor Mr. Button's attorney had any recollection of Mrs. Button's being advised of the rights she was surrendering by signing the agreement.

. . .

In June 1974, after Mr. Button sold his upholstery business to his son for $85,000, the parties signed a postnuptial agreement which expressly rescinded and terminated the 1969 prenuptial agreement. Mr. Button's assets had appreciated in value during the marriage to approximately $110,000. Mrs. Button's assets were essentially the same as before marriage. . . .

The 1974 agreement was drafted by Mr. Button's attorney. Mrs. Button did not have independent counsel. She testified that the agreement was never explained to her and that no financial disclosures were made. Mrs. Button also testified, however, that she was generally aware of Mr. Button's property, that they filed joint tax returns and that she had access to copies of the returns. She also testified that she was unfamiliar with tax returns, having never prepared one herself. Furthermore, Mr. Button acknowledged that the full extent of his financial holdings could not be discerned from his tax returns.

The 1974 postnuptial agreement provided that in the event of a divorce all property owned by either party prior to marriage would remain the separate property of that party and that all property acquired after the marriage would be deemed the separate property of the party acquiring the property. In the event of divorce, Mrs. Button was to accept as full property settlement her own articles of personal property, her own separate property and one-half of all properties acquired jointly by the parties.

At the time of divorce Mrs. Button was in ill health, confined to a skilled care nursing home receiving public assistance. In addition to receiving $255,103 in property, Mr. Button was working part-time after the divorce.

[At the dissolution of this 14-year marriage . . . the circuit court awarded Mrs. Button assets valued at $7,882.10 and awarded Mr. Button assets valued at $255,103.99. Florence S. Button appeals only from that part of the judgment directing a division of property pursuant to the 1974 written agreement. The circuit court's entire finding relating to the division of property . . . is as follows:

> . . . Mrs. Button was 54 years of age when she signed the June 19, 1974 agreement, some five years after the initial agreement and the marriage of the parties. . . . [S]he had already given her daughter $12,000 from funds brought to the marriage by her from funds she received at the time of the death of her first husband. She clearly wanted to be able to dispose of her own property as she saw fit and it is reasonable to assume she understood that Mr. Button would be able to do the same thing as a result of this agreement. In light of the entire record, the Court is convinced that Mrs. Button was well aware of the consequences of the June 19, 1974 agreement and it is enforceable as written with regard to the distribution of the property.]

[2. The Court's Analysis]

[2a. In general]

We now turn to the question of what is an inequitable agreement for purposes of § 767.255. The statute does not define inequitable. . . . [¶] The legislature has recognized that prenuptial and postnuptial agreements dividing property . . . allow parties to structure their financial affairs to suit their needs and values and to achieve certainty. This certainty may encourage marriage and may be conducive to marital tranquility by protecting the financial expectations of the parties. The right to enter into an agreement regulating financial affairs in a marriage is important to a large number of citizens.

Section 767.255 however, sets forth a competing public policy when it empowers a divorce court to override the parties' agreement if the agreement is inequitable. This latter policy reflects the unique role of the marriage contract in society. Marriage is not simply a contract between two parties. Marriage is a legal status in which the state has a special interest. Certain rights and obligations dictated by the state flow from marriage, and the legislature requires a divorce court to scrutinize an agreement between the spouses carefully. The parties are free to contract, but they contract in the shadow of the court's obligation to review the agreement on divorce to protect the spouses' financial interests on divorce.

[We conclude that an agreement is inequitable under § 767.255 if it fails to satisfy any one of the following requirements: each spouse has made fair and reasonable disclosure to the other of his or her financial status; each spouse has entered into the agreement voluntarily and freely; and the substantive provisions of the agreement dividing the property upon divorce are fair to each spouse. The first two requirements must be assessed as of the time of the execution of the agreement. As we shall explain, the third requirement is assessed as of the time of the execution of the agreement and, if circumstances significantly changed since the agreement, then also at the divorce.]

[3b. Procedural Fairness]

Fairness in procurement depends on two factors: whether each spouse makes fair and reasonable disclosure . . . of his or her financial status, and whether each spouse enters into the agreement voluntarily and freely. Obviously these two factors are determined as of the date of the execution of the contract. If the parties fail to satisfy either of these factors, the agreement is inequitable. . . .

An agreement is inequitable if either spouse has not made fair and reasonable disclosure to the other of his or her assets, liabilities and debts. A party might not have entered into the agreement had she or he known the facts. Where it can be shown that a spouse had independent knowledge of the opposing spouse's financial status, this independent knowledge serves as a substitute for disclosure. This case does not raise the question of whether a spouse may waive disclosure and we do not decide that issue. . . . Married persons and persons about to marry stand in a confidential relationship and must deal fairly with each other. Fair and reasonable disclosure of financial status is a significant aspect of the duty of fair dealing.

An agreement is also inequitable if it is not entered into voluntarily and freely. In determining [this], the relevant inquiry is whether each spouse had a meaningful choice. Some factors a circuit court should consider are whether each party was represented by independent counsel, whether each party had adequate time to review the agreement, whether the parties understood the terms of the agreement and their effect, and whether the parties understood their financial rights in the absence of an agreement. If the agreement was not entered into voluntarily and freely, the agreement is inequitable. . . .

[3c. Substantive Fairness]

. . . The third requirement is an issue of "substantive fairness." Substantive fairness is an amorphous concept. We can set forth general principles, but the courts must determine substantive fairness on a case by case basis.

An agreement need not approximate a division a circuit court might make under § 767.255 to meet the requirement of substantive fairness. If the parties are permitted to do only that which a circuit court would do under § 767.255, the parties would not have a meaningful right to contract or to divide their property as they wish. [To meet the requirement of substantive fairness, an agreement should, in some manner appropriate to the circumstances of the parties, take into account that each spouse contributes to the prosperity of the marriage by his or her efforts.]

In framing the agreement the parties should consider the circumstances existing at the execution of the agreement and those reasonably foreseeable. The parties should consider that the duration of the marriage is unknown and that they wish the agreement to govern their financial arrangements whether the marriage lasts a short time or for many years. The parties should consider such factors as the objectives of the parties in executing an agreement, the economic circumstances of the parties, the property brought to the marriage by each party, each spouse's family relationships and obligations to persons other than to the spouse, the earning capacity of each person, the anticipated contribution by one party to the education, training or increased earning power of the other, the future needs of the respective spouses, the age and physical and emotional health of the parties, and the expected contribution of each party to the marriage, giving appropriate economic value to each party's contribution in homemaking and child care services.

In assessing the fairness of the substantive terms of the agreement, a circuit court considers these factors and evaluates the terms of the agreement from the perspective of the parties at the execution of the agreement. We conclude that the court should look at the substantive fairness of the agreement as of the time it was made if the court is to give effect to the parties' freedom to contract. At execution the parties know their property and other relevant circumstances and are able to make reasonable predictions about the future; they should then be able to draft a fair agreement considering these factors.

Clearly an agreement fair at execution is not unfair at divorce just because the application of the agreement at divorce results in a property division which is not equal between the parties or which a court might not order under § 767.255. If, however, there are significantly changed circumstances after the execution of an agreement and the agreement as applied at divorce no longer comports with the reasonable expectations of the parties, an agreement which is fair at execution may be unfair to the parties at divorce. [¶] . . . This approach protects the parties' freedom to contract and the parties' financial interests at divorce.

[Conclusion]

. . . [¶] Because the circuit court has not considered this agreement in this case under the three-part test we have set forth, we remand the cause to the circuit court to exercise its discretion under the test set forth herein. . . .

GANT v. GANT
West Virginia Supreme Court of Appeals
329 S.E.2d 106 (1985)

[The middle-aged parties, both previously married, entered into a premarital agreement the day before their 1979 wedding, under which the wife waived all her rights to post-divorce alimony. They separated in 1981 and, after an apparent reconciliation failed, the wife brought a divorce action in 1982. The husband, a physician, though impaired by mental problems, apparently had more earning capacity than the wife, a licensed realtor and vocational nurse. In upholding the agreement, the trial court said:]

Many courts supervise prenuptial agreements by inquiring into their "fairness," either at the time they were entered into, or at the time of divorce, or at both times. We have no problem accepting . . . that prenuptial agreements must be voluntarily and knowledgeably entered and validly procured, but we are loath to apply a vague and entirely subjective standard of "fairness." Throughout all of contract law there is the recurring problem of disparity of bargaining power; thus if mere disparate bargaining power alone is grounds for invalidating contracts, contracts between rich and poor or between strong and weak will always be of questionable validity. Such, however, is not the rule elsewhere in contract law, and we see no policy reasons to make it so in the law of prenuptial agreements.

The term "fair," without some further elaboration, gives no guidance whatsoever concerning which agreements will be binding and which agreements will be struck down. Furthermore, candor compels us to raise to a conscious level the fact that, as in this case, prenuptial agreements will almost always be entered into between people with property or an income potential to protect on one side and people who are impecunious on the other. Measuring an agreement by an undefined judicial standard of fairness is an invitation to the very wealth redistribution that these agreements are designed to prevent.

. . . [W]hen courts talk about "fairness" in the setting of a prenuptial agreement, they are usually not talking about an entirely subjective, open-ended concept that allows judges to renegotiate contracts and substitute their own judgment for the agreement of the parties. Rather, what other courts are really concerned about is "foreseeability." [¶] In the case of Larry and Elana Gant there is no reason not to honor the parties' prenuptial agreement because circumstances have transpired exactly as the parties foresaw that they might transpire at the time the prenuptial agreement was made. Basically, things did not work out romantically between two middle-aged adults, and that was the exact eventuality about which they had bargained and contracted.

But what . . . if Elana and Larry had had an idyllic relationship for five years and had decided to have three children? Certainly that was not a foreseen event, and if ten years after entering into this prenuptial agreement, with three hypothetical children aged four, three, and one, Larry had decided to divorce, these hypothetical, unforeseen, intervening events would compel us to think very hard about whether to honor the prenuptial agreement's waiver of alimony. Elana would need support for herself so that she could care for the children, but neither party had contemplated having children at the time they entered into the agreement. . . .

Accordingly, we hold today that. . . . the burden of demonstrating the invalidity of a prenuptial agreement is upon the person who would have it held invalid. Although advice of independent counsel at the time parties enter into a prenuptial agreement helps demonstrate that there has not been fraud, duress, or misrepresentation, and that the agreement was entered into knowledgeably and voluntarily, such independent advice is not a prerequisite to enforceability when the terms of the agreement are understandable to a reasonably intelligent adult, as long as both parties had the opportunity to consult with independent counsel.

Unless a prenuptial agreement is so outrageous as to come within unconscionability principles as developed in commercial contract law, West Virginia courts will not evaluate the substantive fairness of prenuptial agreements. . . . Nonetheless, prenuptial agreements will be enforced in their explicit terms only to the extent that circumstances at the time the marriage ends are roughly what the parties foresaw at the time they entered into the prenuptial agreement. In this regard the passage of time, a change of position based upon reasonable reliance on the permanence of the marriage, and the birth of children are relevant factors, among others, for a court to consider.

In [this] case we find nothing unreasonable about Elana's waiver of alimony. . . . Both parties were middle-aged, both had been married before, and the divorce occurred sufficiently close in time (5 years) to the signing of the prenuptial agreement that this divorce was an event that was contemplated and foreseen at the time the agreement was entered into.

[b]   The Contractual Model

UNIFORM PREMARITAL AGREEMENT ACT

§ 1. Definitions

As used in this Act:

(1) "Premarital agreement" means an agreement between prospective spouses made in contemplation of marriage and to be effective upon marriage.

(2) "Property" means an interest, present or future, legal or equitable, vested or contingent, in real or personal property, including income and earnings.

§ 2. Formalities

A premarital agreement must be in writing and signed by both parties. It is enforceable without consideration.

§ 3. Content

(a) Parties to a premarital agreement may contract with respect to:

(1) the rights and obligations of each of the parties in any of the property of either or both of them whenever and wherever acquired or located;

(2) the right to buy, sell, use, transfer, exchange, abandon, lease, consume, expend, assign, create a security interest in, mortgage, encumber, dispose of, or otherwise manage and control property;

(3) the disposition of property upon separation, marital dissolution, death, or the occurrence or nonoccurrence of any other event;

(4) the modification or elimination of spousal support;

(5) the making of a will, trust, or other arrangement to carry out the provisions of the agreement;

(6) the ownership rights in and disposition of the death benefit from a life insurance policy;

(7) the choice of law governing the construction of the agreement; and

(8) any other matter, including their personal rights and obligations, not in violation of public policy or a statute imposing a criminal penalty.

(b) The right of a child to support may not be adversely affected by a premarital agreement.

§ 4. Effect of Marriage

A premarital agreement becomes effective upon marriage.

§ 5. Amendment, Revocation

After marriage, a premarital agreement may be amended or revoked only by a written agreement signed by the parties. The amended agreement or the revocation is enforceable without consideration.

§ 6. Enforcement

(a) A premarital agreement is not enforceable if the party against whom enforcement is sought proves that:

(1) that party did not execute the agreement voluntarily; or

(2) the agreement was unconscionable when it was executed and, before execution of the agreement, that party:

(i) was not provided a fair and reasonable disclosure of the property or financial obligations of the other party;

(ii) did not voluntarily and expressly waive, in writing, any right to disclosure of the property or financial obligations of the other party beyond the disclosure provided; and

(iii) did not have, or reasonably could not have had, an adequate knowledge of the property or financial obligations of the other party.

(b) If a provision of a premarital agreement modifies or eliminates spousal support and that modification or elimination causes one party to the agreement to be eligible for support under a program of public assistance at the time of separation or marital dissolution, a court, notwithstanding the terms of the agreement, may require the other party to provide support to the extent necessary to avoid that eligibility.

(c) An issue of unconscionability of a premarital agreement shall be decided by the court as a matter of law.

§ 7. Enforcement: Void Marriage

If a marriage is determined to be void, an agreement that would otherwise have been a premarital agreement is enforceable only to the extent necessary to avoid an inequitable result.

§ 8. Limitation of Actions

Any statute of limitations applicable to an action asserting a claim for relief under a premarital agreement is tolled during the marriage of the parties to the agreement. However, equitable defenses limiting the time for enforcement, including laches and estoppel, are available to either party.

§ 9. Application and Construction

This [Act] shall be applied and construed to effectuate its general purpose to make uniform the law with respect to the subject of this [Act] among states enacting it.

MARRIAGE OF BONDS
California Supreme Court
5 P.3d 815 (2000)

GEORGE, CHIEF JUSTICE.

In this case we consider whether appellant Susann (known as Sun) Margreth Bonds voluntarily entered into a premarital agreement with respondent Barry Lamar Bonds. We conclude that the Court of Appeal erred [when it concluded] that because Sun, unlike Barry, was not represented by independent counsel when she entered into the agreement, the voluntariness of the agreement must be subjected to strict scrutiny. Instead, we determine that the circumstance that one of the parties was not represented by independent counsel is only one of several factors that must be considered in determining whether a premarital agreement was entered into voluntarily. Further, as we shall explain, we conclude that substantial evidence supports the determination of the trial court that the agreement in the present case was entered into voluntarily.

I

Sun and Barry met in Montreal in the summer of 1987. . . . In November 1987, Sun moved to Phoenix to take up residence with Barry and, one week later, the two became engaged. . . . [T]hey decided to marry before the commencement of professional baseball's spring training. On February 5, 1988, in Phoenix, the parties entered into a written premarital agreement in which each party waived any interest in the earnings and acquisitions of the other party during marriage. That same day, they flew to Las Vegas, and were married the following day.

Each of the parties then was 23 years of age. Barry, who had attended college for three years and who had begun his career in professional baseball in 1985, had a contract to play for the Pittsburgh Pirates. His annual salary at the time of the marriage ceremony was approximately $ 106,000. Sun had emigrated to Canada from Sweden in 1985, had worked as a waitress and bartender, and had undertaken some training as a cosmetologist, having expressed an interest in embarking upon a career as a makeup artist for celebrity clients. Although her native language was Swedish, she had used both French and English in her employment, education, and personal relationships when she lived in Canada. She was unemployed at the time she entered into the premarital agreement.

Barry petitioned for legal separation [later amended to divorce] on May 27, 1994, in California, the parties then being California residents. Sun requested custody of the parties' two children, then three and four years of age. In addition, she sought child and spousal support, attorney fees, and a determination of property rights. . . . Child support was awarded in the amount of $ 10,000 per month per child. Spousal support was awarded in the amount of $ 10,000 per month, to terminate December 30, 1998. Only the . . . validity of the premarital agreement is before this court.

Barry testified that he was aware of teammates and other persons who had undergone bitter marital dissolution proceedings involving the division of property, and recalled that from the beginning of his relationship with Sun he told her that he believed his earnings and acquisitions during marriage should be his own. He informed her he would not marry without a premarital agreement, and she had no objection. He also recalled that from the beginning of the relationship, Sun agreed that their earnings and acquisitions should be separate, saying "what's mine is mine, what's yours is yours." Indeed, she informed him that this was the practice with respect to marital property in Sweden. She stated that she planned to pursue a career and wished to be financially independent. Sun knew that Barry did not anticipate that she would shoulder her living expenses while she was not employed. She was not, in fact, employed during the marriage. Barry testified that he and Sun had no difficulty communicating.

Although Barry testified that he had previous experience working with lawyers in the course of baseball contract negotiations and the purchase of real property, his testimony at trial did not demonstrate an understanding of the legal fine points of the agreement.

Sun's testimony at trial differed from Barry's in material respects. She testified that her English language skills in 1987 and 1988 were limited. Out of pride, she did not disclose to Barry that she often did not understand him. She testified that she and Barry never discussed money or property during the relationship that preceded their marriage. She agreed that she had expressed interest in a career as a cosmetologist and had said she wished to be financially independent. She had very few assets when she took up residence with Barry, and he paid for all their needs. Their wedding arrangements were very informal, with no written invitations or caterer, and only Barry's parents and a couple of friends, including Barry's godfather Willie Mays, were invited to attend. No marriage license or venue had been arranged in advance of their arrival in Las Vegas. . . .

Sun testified that on the evening before the premarital agreement was signed, Barry first informed her that they needed to go the following day to the offices of his lawyers. . . . She was uncertain, however, whether Barry made any reference to a premarital agreement. She testified that only at the parking lot of the law office where the agreement was to be entered into did she learn, from Barry's financial adviser, Mel Wilcox, that Barry would not marry her unless she signed a premarital agreement. She was not upset. She was surprised, however, because Barry never had said that signing the agreement was a precondition to marriage.

She did not question Barry or anyone else on this point. She was under the impression that Barry wished to retain separate ownership of property he owned before the marriage, and that this was the sole object of the premarital agreement. She was unaware the agreement would affect her future and was not concerned about the matter, because she was nervous and excited about getting married and trusted Barry. Wilcox's statement had little effect on her, because she had no question but that she and Barry were to be married the following day.

Sun recalled having to hurry to arrive at the lawyers' office in time both to accomplish their business there and make the scheduled departure of the airplane to Las Vegas so that she and Barry could marry the next day. Sun recalled that once they arrived at the lawyers' office on February 5, 1988, she, her friend Margareta Forsberg, Barry, and . . . Mel Wilcox were present in a conference room. She did not recall asking questions or her friend asking questions, nor did she recall that any changes were made to the agreement. She declared that her English language skills were limited at the time and she did not understand the agreement, but she did not ask questions of anyone other than Margareta Forsberg or ask for more time, because she did not want to miss her flight and she was focused on the forthcoming marriage ceremony. She did not believe that Barry understood the agreement either. Forsberg was unable to assist her. Sun did not recall the lawyers telling her that she should retain her own lawyer, that they were representing Barry and not her, that the applicable community property law provided that a spouse has an interest in the earnings and in acquisitions of the other spouse during marriage, or that she would be waiving this right if she signed the agreement. The lawyers may have mentioned the possibility of her being represented by her own lawyer, but she did not believe she needed one. She did not inform anyone at the meeting that she was concerned about the agreement; the meeting and discussion were not cut short, and no one forced her to sign the agreement.

Forsberg . . . confirmed that she was present when [Barry's attorneys] Brown and Megwa explained the agreement, that Wilcox also was present, that no changes to the agreement were made at Sun's or Forsberg's request, and that she had been unable to answer Sun's questions or explain to Sun the terminology used in the agreement. She confirmed that Sun's English was limited, that the lawyers had explained the agreement, and that Sun never stated that she was considering not signing the agreement, that she did not understand it, or that she was not signing of her own free will. Sun never said that Barry threatened her or forced her to sign, that she wanted to consult independent counsel concerning the agreement, or that she felt pressured. Forsberg understood that Brown and Megwa were Barry's attorneys, not Sun's. She testified that when the attorneys explained the agreement, she did not recall any discussion of Sun's community property rights.

Barry and other witnesses offered a different picture. . . . Barry and his attorney, Brown, recalled that approximately two weeks before the parties signed the formal agreement, they discussed with Sun the drafting of an agreement to keep earnings and acquisitions separate. Brown testified that he told Sun at this meeting that he represented Barry and that it might be in her best interest to obtain independent counsel.

Barry, Brown, and Megwa testified that . . . the attorneys informed Sun of her right to independent counsel. All three recalled that Sun stated she did not want her own counsel, and Megwa recalled explaining that he and Brown did not represent her. Additionally, all three recalled that the attorneys read the agreement to her paragraph by paragraph and explained it as they went through it, also informing her of a spouse's basic community property rights in earnings and acquisitions and that Sun would be waiving these rights. Megwa recalled it was clearly explained that Barry's income and acquisitions during the marriage would remain Barry's separate property, and he recalled that Sun stated that such arrangements were the practice in Sweden. Furthermore, Barry and the two attorneys each confirmed that Sun and Forsberg asked questions during the meeting and were left alone on several occasions to discuss its terms, that Sun did not exhibit any confusion, and that Sun indicated she understood the agreement. They also testified that changes were made to the agreement at Sun's behest. Brown and Megwa experienced no difficulty in communicating with Sun, found her confident and happy, and had no indication that she was nervous or confused, intimidated, or pressured. No threat was uttered that unless she signed the agreement, the wedding would be cancelled, nor did they hear her express any reservations about signing the agreement. Additionally, legal secretary Illa Washington recalled that Wilcox waited in another room while the agreement was discussed, that Sun asked questions and that changes were made to the agreement at her behest, that Sun was informed she could secure independent counsel, that Sun said she understood the contract and did not want to consult another attorney, and that she appeared to understand the discussions and to feel comfortable and confident.

The trial court observed that the case turned upon the credibility of the witnesses [and determined] that Sun entered into the agreement voluntarily, "free from the taint of fraud, coercion and undue influence . . . with full knowledge of the property involved and her rights therein". . . . [¶] The court also determined that Barry and Sun were not in a confidential relationship at the time the agreement was executed. The trial court also declared that pursuant to a pretrial stipulation the burden of proof rested upon Sun, but that even if the court were to place the burden of proof upon Barry, Barry had demonstrated by clear and convincing evidence "that the agreement and its execution [were] free from the taint of fraud, coercion or undue influence" and that Sun "entered the agreement with full knowledge of the property involved and her rights therein." . . .

The Court of Appeal in a split decision reversed the judgment rendered by the trial court and directed a retrial on the issue of voluntariness. The majority stressed that Sun lacked independent counsel, determined that she had not waived counsel effectively, and concluded that under such circumstances the evidence must be subjected to strict judicial scrutiny to determine whether the agreement was voluntary. The majority asserted that Attorneys Brown and Megwa failed to explain that Sun's interests conflicted with Barry's, failed to urge her to retain separate counsel, and may have led Sun to believe they actually represented her interests as they explained the agreement paragraph by paragraph. . . . [¶] We granted Barry's petition for review.

II

. . . We [first] conclude [the court of appeals] erred in holding that a premarital agreement in which one party is not represented by independent counsel should be subjected to strict scrutiny for voluntariness. Such a holding is inconsistent with Family Code § 1615, which governs the enforceability of premarital agreements.

A

From the inception of its statehood, California has retained the community property law that predated its admission to the Union and consistently has provided as a general rule that property acquired by spouses during marriage, including earnings, is community property. [¶] At the same time, applicable statutes recognized the power of parties contemplating a marriage to reach an agreement containing terms at variance with community property law. Thus in 1850, the Legislature provided that community property principles shall govern the rights of the parties "unless there is a marriage contract, containing stipulations contrary thereto." [¶] . . . In order to encourage enforcement of [premarital] agreements on a more certain and uniform basis, while, according to the drafters of the act, retaining some "flexibility," the Uniform Premarital Agreement Act (hereafter sometimes referred to as the Uniform Act) was promulgated in 1983. [¶] In 1985, the California Legislature adopted most of the provisions of the Uniform Act. . . .

B

The California enactment, like the Uniform Act, . . . provides in pertinent part:

(a) A premarital agreement is not enforceable if the party against whom enforcement is sought proves either of the following:

(1) That party did not execute the agreement voluntarily.

(2) The agreement was unconscionable when it was executed and, before execution of the agreement, all of the following applied to that party:

(A) That party was not provided a fair and reasonable disclosure of the property or financial obligations of the other party.

(B) That party did not voluntarily and expressly waive, in writing, any right to disclosure of the property or financial obligations of the other party beyond the disclosure provided.

(C) That party did not have, or reasonably could not have had, an adequate knowledge of the property or financial obligations of the other party.

Pursuant to [this excerpt from] Family Code § 1615, a premarital agreement will be enforced unless the party resisting enforcement of the agreement can demonstrate either (1) that he or she did not enter into the contract voluntarily, or (2) that the contract was unconscionable when entered into *and* that he or she did not have actual or constructive knowledge of the assets and obligations of the other party and did not voluntarily waive knowledge of such assets and obligations. In the present case, the trial court found no lack of knowledge regarding the nature of the parties' assets, a necessary predicate to considering the issue of unconscionability, and the Court of Appeal accepted the trial court's determination on this point. We do not reconsider this factual determination, and thus the question of unconscionability is not before us. . . . Thus, the only issue we face concerns the trial court's determination that Sun entered into the agreement voluntarily.

Neither the article of the Family Code in which section 1615 is located, nor the Uniform Act, defines the term "voluntarily." . . . [¶] To the extent it is unclear on the face of the statute what was intended by the Legislature in employing the term "voluntarily," we consult the history of the statute and consider its general intent. . . .

The debate that preceded the adoption of the Uniform Act indicated a basic disagreement between those commissioners at the National Conference of Commissioners on Uniform State Laws who placed the highest value on certainty in enforcement of premarital agreements and the vocal minority of commissioners who urged that such contracts routinely should be evaluated for substantive fairness at the time of enforcement. Indeed, over sharp and repeated objection from commissioners of the minority view, eventually it was settled that the party against whom enforcement of a premarital agreement was sought only could raise the issue of unconscionability, that is, the substantive unfairness of an agreement, if he or she also could demonstrate lack of disclosure of assets, lack of waiver of disclosure, *and* lack of imputed knowledge of assets. The language adopted was intended to *enhance* the enforceability of premarital agreements and to convey the sense that an agreement voluntarily entered into would be enforced without regard to the apparent unfairness of its terms, as long as the objecting party knew or should have known of the other party's assets, or voluntarily had waived disclosure. The commissioners, however, did not supply a definition of the term "voluntarily," nor was there much discussion of the term.

We find an indication of the commissioners' understanding of the term in their official comment to the enforcement provision of the Uniform Act, stating that the conditions to enforcement "are comparable to concepts which are expressed in the statutory and decisional law of many jurisdictions." (9B West's U. Laws Ann., *supra*, Uniform Act, com. to § 6, p. 376.) In support of this statement, the comment cites cases from various jurisdictions examining the voluntariness of premarital agreements. . . . In the majority of these cases . . . the question is viewed as one involving such ordinary contract defenses as fraud, undue influence, or duress, along with some examination of the parties' knowledge of the rights being waived, or at least knowledge of the intent of the agreement.

These cases demonstrate the commissioners' belief that a number of factors are relevant to the issue of voluntariness. In considering defenses proffered against enforcement of a premarital agreement, the court should consider whether the evidence indicates coercion or lack of knowledge. . . . Specifically, the cases . . . direct consideration of the impact upon the parties of . . . the coercion that may arise from the proximity of execution of the agreement to the wedding, or from surprise in the presentation of the agreement; the presence or absence of independent counsel or of an opportunity to consult independent counsel; inequality of bargaining power — in some cases indicated by the relative age and sophistication of the parties; whether there was full disclosure of assets; and the parties' understanding of the rights being waived under the agreement or at least their awareness of the intent of the agreement.

The cases cited in the comment to the enforcement provision of the Uniform Act indicate that the commissioners considered that . . . voluntariness . . . may turn in part upon whether the agreement was entered into knowingly, in the sense that the parties understood the terms or basic effect of the agreement. . . . [These cases also] indicate that the parties' general understanding of the effect of the agreement constitutes a factor for the court to consider in determining whether the parties entered into the agreement voluntarily.

The commissioners' debate over the problem of unconscionability throws further light on their view of the voluntariness requirement, which, as noted, did not receive much explicit discussion. Those taking the minority view noted with concern that the proposed Uniform Act would enforce agreements that might be declared void as unconscionable under the Uniform Commercial Code, because the Uniform Act precluded consideration of the substantive fairness of the agreement unless the party challenging the agreement also could prove lack of notice of the other party's assets and obligations. Commissioners who valued substantive fairness over certainty of enforcement urged, for example, that if a premarital agreement waiving property rights is entered into between a pregnant teenager — who wishes to ensure the legitimacy of her child — and an older man, the agreement should be subject to searching scrutiny for unconscionability; those taking the majority position countered that the requirement that the contract be entered into voluntarily provided adequate protection to the weaker party. In addition, it was clear from their discussion that the commissioners anticipated that such defenses as lack of capacity, fraud, duress, and undue influence would apply in determining the voluntariness of the agreement.

In sum, it is clear from the cases cited in the comment to the enforcement section of the Uniform Act and from the record of the proceedings of the National Conference of Commissioners on Uniform State Laws that the commissioners intended that the party seeking to avoid a premarital agreement may prevail by establishing that the agreement was involuntary, and that evidence of lack of capacity, duress, fraud, and undue influence, as demonstrated by a number of factors uniquely probative of coercion in the premarital context, would be relevant in establishing the involuntariness of the agreement.

Not only did the commissioners intend that the above factors be considered in determining whether a premarital agreement was entered into voluntarily, but the same intention safely may be attributed to the California Legislature, because an examination of the history of the enactment of Family Code § 1615 in California indicates that the Legislature adopted the views of the commissioners in all respects relevant to the present discussion.

. . . .

We have considered the range of factors that may be relevant . . . in order to consider whether the Court of Appeal erred in according such great weight to one factor — the presence or absence of independent counsel for each party. . . .

It is clear . . . that the commissioners rejected the view that independent counsel was essential. . . . Although the proposed Uniform Act initially contained a proviso stating that premarital agreements were presumptively valid unless the party against whom enforcement was sought was not represented by independent legal counsel or there was not full disclosure, the commissioners eventually removed any reference to independent counsel. A commissioner explained the action of the executive committee in removing the proviso: "We feel that, certainly, that representation would be a *factor* in determining whether the party acted voluntarily and knowingly. We do not believe, however, that legal representation alone would be a desirable basis for enforcement." An amendment was proposed to restore the omitted provision, but it was rejected . . . (Proceedings, Uniform Act, *supra*, pp. 61–62.)

. . .

Finally, and perhaps most significantly, the rule created by the Court of Appeal would have the effect of shifting the burden of proof on the question of voluntariness to the party seeking enforcement of the premarital agreement, even though the statute expressly places the burden upon the party challenging the voluntariness of the agreement. . . . [¶] We conclude that although the ability of the party challenging the agreement to obtain independent counsel is an important factor in determining whether that party entered into the agreement voluntarily, the Court of Appeal majority erred in directing trial courts to subject premarital agreements to strict scrutiny where the less sophisticated party does not have independent counsel and has not waived counsel according to exacting waiver requirements.

C

[Despite our conclusions concerning] independent counsel . . . we . . . agree with the Court of Appeal majority that considerations applicable in commercial contexts do not necessarily govern the determination whether a premarital agreement was entered into voluntarily.

. . . Even apart from the circumstance that there is no statutory requirement that commercial contracts be entered into voluntarily as that term is used in Family Code § 1615, we observe some significant distinctions between the two types of contracts. A commercial contract most frequently constitutes a private regulatory agreement intended to ensure the successful outcome of the business between the contracting parties — in essence, to guide their relationship so that the object of the contract may be achieved. Normally, the execution of the contract ushers in the applicability of the regulatory scheme contemplated by the contract and the endeavor that is the object of the contract. As for a premarital agreement (or clause of such an agreement) providing solely for the division of property upon marital dissolution, the parties generally enter into the agreement anticipating that it never will be invoked, and the agreement, far from regulating the relationship of the contracting parties and providing the method for attaining their joint objectives, exists to provide for eventualities that will arise only if the relationship founders, possibly in the distant future under greatly changed and unforeseeable circumstances.

Furthermore, marriage itself is a highly regulated institution of undisputed social value, and there are many limitations on the ability of persons to contract with respect to it, or to vary its statutory terms, that have nothing to do with maximizing the satisfaction of the parties or carrying out their intent. Such limitations are inconsistent with the freedom-of-contract analysis espoused, for example, by the Pennsylvania Supreme Court. (See *Simeone v. Simeone*, 581 A.2d 162, 165–166.) We refer to rules establishing a duty of mutual financial support during the marriage and prohibiting agreements in derogation of the duty to support a child of the marriage; the unenforceability of a promise to marry; the circumstance that a party may abandon the marriage unilaterally under this state's no-fault laws; and the pervasive state involvement in the dissolution of marital status, the marriage contract, and the arrangements to be made for the children of the marriage — even without consideration of the circumstance that marriage normally lacks a predominantly commercial object. We also observe that a premarital agreement to raise children in a particular religion is not enforceable. We note, too, that there is authority — as conceded by the commissioners who considered the Uniform Act — to the effect that a contract to pay a spouse for personal services such as nursing cannot be enforced, despite the undoubted economic value of the services. These limitations demonstrate further that freedom of contract with respect to marital arrangements is tempered with statutory requirements and case law expressing social policy with respect to marriage.

There also are obvious differences between the remedies that realistically may be awarded with respect to commercial contracts and premarital agreements. Although a party seeking rescission of a commercial contract, for example, may be required to restore the status quo ante by restoring the consideration received, and a party in breach may be required to pay damages, the status quo ante for spouses cannot be restored to either party, nor are damages contemplated for breach of the marital contract. In any event, the suggestion that commercial contracts are strictly enforced without regard to the fairness or oppressiveness of the terms or the inequality of the bargaining power of the parties is anachronistic and inaccurate, in that claims such as duress, unconscionability, and undue influence turn upon the specific context in which the contract is formed. (See Bix, *Bargaining in the Shadow of Love: The Enforcement of Premarital Agreements and How We Think About Marriage* (1998) 40 Wm. & Mary L. Rev. 145, 163, 182, 188, 205; see also Atwood, *Ten Years Later: Lingering Concerns About the Uniform Premarital Agreement Act* (1993) 19 J. Legis. 127, 146.)

We also have explained generally that we believe the reference to voluntariness in the Uniform Act was intended to convey an element of knowing waiver that is not a consistent feature of commercial contract enforcement. Further, although the Uniform Act contemplated that contract defenses should apply, in the sense that an agreement should be free from fraud (including constructive fraud), duress, or undue influence, it is clear from the debate of the commissioners who adopted the Uniform Act and the cases cited in support of the enforcement provision of the Uniform Act that subtle coercion that would not be considered in challenges to ordinary commercial contracts may be considered in the context of the premarital agreement. The obvious distinctions between premarital agreements and ordinary commercial contracts lead us to conclude that factual circumstances relating to contract defenses that would not necessarily support the rescission of a commercial contract may suffice to render a premarital agreement unenforceable. The question of voluntariness must be examined in the unique context of the marital relationship.

On the other hand, we do not agree with Sun and the Court of Appeal majority that a *premarital* agreement should be interpreted and enforced under the same standards applicable to *marital* settlement agreements. First, although persons, once they are married, are in a fiduciary relationship to one another (*Fam. Code,* § 721, subd. (b)), so that whenever the parties enter into an agreement in which one party gains an advantage, the advantaged party bears the burden of demonstrating that the agreement was not obtained through undue influence, a different burden applies under the Uniform Act in the premarital setting. Even when the premarital agreement clearly advantages one of the parties, the party challenging the agreement bears the burden of demonstrating that the agreement was not entered into voluntarily. Further, under the Uniform Act, even when there has been a failure of disclosure, the statute still places the burden upon the party challenging the agreement to prove that the terms of the agreement were unconscionable when executed, rather than placing the burden on the advantaged party to demonstrate that the agreement was not unconscionable. Thus the terms of the act itself do not support the Court of Appeal's conclusion that the Legislature intended that premarital agreements should be interpreted in the same manner as agreements entered into during marriage.

In particular, we believe that both the Court of Appeal majority and Sun err to the extent they suggest that the Uniform Act or its California analog established that persons who enter into premarital agreements must be presumed to be in a confidential relationship, a status that would give rise to the fiduciary duties between spouses expressly established by § 721 of the Family Code. California law prior to the enactment of the Uniform Act was to the contrary, and we discern nothing in the Uniform Act suggesting that its adoption in California was intended to overrule our earlier decision.

The primary consequences of designating a relationship as fiduciary in nature are that the parties owe a duty of full disclosure, and that a presumption arises that a party who owes a fiduciary duty, and who secures a benefit through an agreement, has done so through undue influence. For example, a transaction in which an attorney gains an advantage over his or her client "is presumptively invalid, and the attorney must show not only that it was fair, but that the client was fully informed of all facts necessary to enable him to deal at arm's length." (1 Witkin, Summary of Cal. Law, *supra*, Contracts, § 425, pp. 381–382, italics omitted.) It long has been the rule that "[w]hen an interspousal transaction advantages one spouse, '[t]he law, from considerations of public policy, presumes such transactions to have been induced by undue influence.'" (*In re Marriage of Haines, supra*, 33 Cal. App. 4th at p. 293, quoting *Brison v. Brison* (1888) 75 Cal. 525, 529 [17 P. 689].)

. . .

Because the Uniform Act was intended to enhance the enforceability of premarital agreements, because it expressly places the burden of proof upon the person challenging the agreement, and finally because the California statute imposing fiduciary duties in the family law setting applies only to spouses, we do not believe that the commissioners or our Legislature contemplated that the voluntariness of a premarital agreement would be examined in light of the strict fiduciary duties imposed on persons such as lawyers, or imposed expressly by statute upon persons who are married. Although we certainly agree that persons contemplating marriage morally owe each other a duty of fair dealing and obviously are not embarking upon a purely commercial contract, we do not believe that these circumstances permit us to interpret our statute as imposing a *presumption* of undue influence or as requiring the kind of strict scrutiny that is conducted when a lawyer or other fiduciary engages in self-dealing. On the contrary, it is evident that the Uniform Act was intended to *enhance* the enforceability of premarital agreements, a goal that would be undermined by presuming the existence of a confidential or fiduciary relationship.

. . .

III

Finally, we conclude that the trial court's determination that Sun voluntarily entered into the premarital agreement in the present case is supported by substantial evidence. . . . [¶] The trial court made specific findings of fact regarding the factors we have identified as relevant to the determination of voluntariness. These findings . . . should have been accepted by the Court of Appeal majority. . . .

. . .

[A]lthough Sun lacked legal counsel, the trial court determined that she had a reasonable opportunity to obtain counsel. The trial court stated: ". . . . Respondent was advised at a meeting with Attorney Brown at least one week prior to execution of the Agreement that she had the right to have an attorney represent her and that Attorneys Brown and Megwa represented Petitioner, not Respondent. On at least two occasions during the February 5, 1988, meeting, Respondent was told that she could have separate counsel if she chose. Respondent declined. Respondent was capable of understanding this admonition."

. . . . [¶] The Court of Appeal majority surmised that Sun did not have a reasonable opportunity to consult counsel because a copy of the agreement was not provided in advance of the February 5, 1988, meeting, and because Sun had insufficient funds to retain counsel and was not informed that Barry would pay for independent counsel's services. Again, this determination is contradicted by the conclusion of the trial court that Sun had "an adequate and reasonable opportunity to obtain independent counsel prior to execution of the Agreement." . . . Additionally, there was evidence supporting the inference that she declined counsel because she understood and agreed with the terms of the agreement, and not because she had insufficient funds to employ counsel. [T]he Court of Appeal . . . majority's opinion departed from the appropriate standard of review in this respect. . . .

IV

The judgment of the Court of Appeal is reversed to the extent that it reversed the judgment of the trial court on the issue of the voluntariness of the premarital agreement. . . .

MOSK, J., KENNARD, J., BAXTER, J., WERDEGAR, J., CHIN, J., and BROWN, J., concurred.

SIMEONE v. SIMEONE
Pennsylvania Supreme Court
581 A.2d 162 (1990)

At issue in this appeal is the validity of a prenuptial agreement executed between the appellant, Catherine E. Walsh Simeone, and the appellee, Frederick A. Simeone. At the time of their marriage, in 1975, [Catherine] was a twenty-three year old nurse and [Frederick] was a thirty-nine year old neurosurgeon. [Frederick] had an income of approximately $90,000 per year, and [Catherine] was unemployed. [Frederick] also had assets worth approximately $300,000. On the eve of the parties' wedding, [Frederick]'s attorney presented [Catherine] with a prenuptial agreement to be signed. [Catherine], without the benefit of counsel, signed the agreement. [Frederick]'s attorney had not advised [Catherine] regarding any legal rights that the agreement surrendered. The parties are in disagreement as to whether [Catherine] knew in advance of that date that such an agreement would be presented for signature. [Catherine] denies having had such knowledge and claims to have signed under adverse circumstances, which, she contends, provide a basis for declaring it void.

The agreement limited [Catherine] to support payments of $200 per week in the event of separation or divorce, subject to a maximum total payment of $25,000. . . . The Superior Court [upheld the agreement and enforced this limit].

. . . . There is no longer validity in [the] implicit presumption [of earlier cases] that . . . spouses are of unequal status and that women are not knowledgeable enough to understand the nature of contracts that they enter. Society has advanced . . . to the point where women are no longer regarded as the "weaker" party in marriage, or in society generally. Indeed, the stereotype that women serve as homemakers while men work as breadwinners is no longer viable. . . . Nor is there viability in the presumption that women are uninformed, uneducated, and readily subjected to unfair advantage in marital agreements. . . . [¶] . . . [T]he standards governing prenuptial agreements [in earlier cases] reflected a paternalistic approach that is now insupportable.

. . . Prenuptial agreements are contracts, and, as such, should be evaluated under the same criteria as are applicable to other types of contracts. . . . Absent fraud, misrepresentation, or duress, spouses should be bound by the terms of their agreements. [¶] Contracting parties are normally bound by their agreements, without regard to whether the terms thereof were read and fully understood and irrespective of whether the agreements embodied reasonable or good bargains. [T]he present prenuptial agreement must be . . . binding, without regard to whether the terms were fully understood by [Catherine]. *Ignorantia non excusat.*

Accordingly, we find no merit in a contention raised by [Catherine] that the agreement should be declared void on the ground that she did not consult with independent legal counsel. . . . [¶] Further, the reasonableness of a prenuptial bargain is not a proper subject for judicial review. . . . [¶] [E]veryone who enters a long-term agreement knows that circumstances can change during its term, so that what initially appeared desirable might prove to be an unfavorable bargain. Such are the risks that contracting parties routinely assume. Certainly, the possibilities of illness, birth of children, reliance upon a spouse, numerous other events that can occur in the course of a marriage cannot be regarded as unforeseeable. If parties choose not to address such matters in their prenuptial agreements, they must be regarded as having contracted to bear the risk of events that alter the value of their bargains.

[c]   Current Trends and the ALI's Proposals

1. *The Overview.* One may police premarital agreements by imposing special procedural requirements, or by imposing special tests of substantive fairness. *Button* does both. It allows enforcement only if: 1) the parties had knowledge of each other's assets, either independently or through disclosure; *and* 2) the agreement was "voluntary," meaning that the parties had a "meaningful choice"; *and* 3) its terms were fair at the time of execution; *and* 4) it is fair to apply it at the time of divorce. The third and fourth are obviously requirements of substantive fairness, and the first is a procedural fairness requirement. As we shall see below in Note 2, the "voluntariness" requirement becomes procedural as well, once one tries to give it meaning. All four of these requirements go well beyond what courts ordinarily demand before enforcing a commercial contract. At the other end of the spectrum is *Simeone*, which largely adopts normal contractual rules (Rhode Island's law on premarital agreements is now almost as pro-enforcement as *Simeone*; see R.I. GEN. LAWS 1956, § 15-17-6; *Marsocci v. Marsocci*, 911 A.2d 690 (R.I. 2006)).

In between the endpoints of *Button* and *Simeone* lie *Gant, Bonds*, and the UPAA, in approximately that order. As explained further below, the recommendations of the American Law Institute's *Principles* adopt *Gant's* foreseeability test for substantive fairness, while also imposing some procedural fairness requirements that are more carefully defined than the test of voluntariness found in both *Button* and the UPAA. Following the decision in *Bonds*, the California legislature amended that state's version of the UPAA in several respects, overruling *Bonds* and adopting some provisions that follow the ALI's recommendations. *See* Notes 4 and 5, *infra*.

The UPAA has been criticized for its relative willingness to enforce premarital agreements in circumstances that the commentators believe inappropriate. *See* Barbara Atwood, *Ten Years Later: Lingering Concerns about the Uniform Premarital Agreement Act*, 19 J. LEGIS. 127, 128 (1993) ("Despite the representations of N.C.C.U.S.L., the U.P.A.A. departs, sometimes dramatically, from the common law of many states"); Katharine Silbaugh, *Marriage Contracts and the Family Economy*, 93 Nw. U. L. REV. 65 (1998) (critical of the trend toward enforcement of agreements, noting that accepted arguments against enforcement of some nonmonetary terms may apply to monetary terms as well); Gail F. Brod,

Premarital Agreements and Gender Justice, 6 YALE J.L. & FEMINISM 229, 295 (1994) (arguing that the UPAA fails to give adequate weight to policies other than freedom of contract and personal autonomy, such as the "attainment of economic justice for the economically vulnerable spouse at the end of marriage"). Twenty-five States and the District of Columbia have adopted the UPAA (and a 26th state, Wisconsin, adopted core provisions of the UPAA when it became the only state to enact the Uniform Marital Property Act), but about half the adopting states have varied from the official text in some important respect (most, but not all, in the direction of greater protection of parties and less enforcement of agreements); some of these departures are noted below.

2. *The Voluntariness Requirement: A Form of Procedural Fairness.* The UPAA, as well as all the preceding cases but *Simeone*, make special note that agreements must be "voluntary" to be enforceable. Much of the *Bonds* opinion is an exploration of the meaning of this requirement, which the UPAA itself leaves undefined. As *Bonds* notes, the narrow majority of Uniform Act commissioners who favored the UPAA's severe limits on the unconscionability doctrine (more on this below in Note 4) defended their position in the Uniform Act debates with assurances that the requirement of voluntariness would prevent the enforcement of questionable contracts. *E.g.*, the drafting committee was asked why it deleted language making an agreement's enforcement dependent upon the parties having "understood [its] effect" ("[W]as it that the 'voluntary' carries the freight . . . or you don't care whether they understood it or not?"). The committee's spokesman responded "We think the 'voluntary' covers it." National Conference of Commissioners on Uniform State Laws, Proceedings in the Committee of the Whole, Uniform Premarital Agreements Act, at p. 63 (July 23, 25, and 26, 1983). And as *Bonds* notes, when concern was raised over the case of a young pregnant girl, asked to sign a one-sided agreement as a condition of marriage to the father, the draft's defenders said that agreement would be unenforceable as involuntary because that doctrine would reach cases of "oppression," *id.* at 72–73. But these hints are all we have of the intended meaning of "voluntary," and the act itself does not define the term. Courts thus have wide latitude in its construction. But the legislative history of the Uniform Commissioners' deliberations, as well as earlier case law using the term, strongly suggests that it is meant to add *something* to the usual requirements for enforcing a contract. This seems to be agreed upon by all the other authorities other than *Simeone*.

Those usual contract principles deny enforcement of agreements entered into under "duress," a seeming close cousin of "involuntary." But in fact contract law's traditional duress requirement has a very limited reach, leaving plenty of room for the additional requirement of voluntariness to add real meaning. *E.g.*, the duress rule offers no basis for voiding an agreement just because the disfavored party did not understand its effect. Consider as well that in the commercial contract context, courts have held that a defense of economic duress usually requires a showing that the promisor's dire circumstances were the result of the promisee's acts. JOHN EDWARD MURRAY, JR., MURRAY ON CONTRACTS § 93, at 528 (4th ed., 2001). Could an analogous showing be made in the debated case of the pregnant teenage bride, thus sustaining a duress defense to such an agreement? Not necessarily. In *Hamilton v. Hamilton*, 591 A.2d 720, 722 (Pa. Super. 1991), the wife was 18, unemployed, and three months pregnant (by the husband) when the parties married. The husband had conditioned marriage on the wife's agreement to waive all alimony claims; the wife's counsel had advised her against signing but she signed anyway. The court enforced the waiver, concluding that "[w]here a party has been free to consult counsel before signing an agreement, the courts have uniformly rejected duress as a defense to the agreement." *See also Lebeck v. Lebeck*, 881 P.2d 727 (N.M. App. 1994) (duress not shown by wife with independent counsel, who signed agreement demanded by her attorney-husband because she wished to legitimate their daughter; "a threat to do that which the demanding party has the right to demand is not sufficient to support a claim of duress.") By contrast, compare *Williams v. Williams*, 617 So. 2d 1032 (Ala. 1992), which evaluates such claims by reference to ideas of voluntariness rather than duress. It found that under a rule requiring "that the agreement was entered into freely and voluntarily," the lower court must decide whether, as a question of fact, "the father's conditioning the marriage on the pregnant mother's signing the antenuptial agreement, joined with the mother's moral objection to abortion and the importance of legitimacy in a small town, created a coercive atmosphere in which the mother had no viable alternative to accepting the father's condition for marriage. . . ."

So the concept of "voluntariness" must go beyond conventional ideas of "duress" in order to deny enforcement of contracts that the enforcement-oriented commissioners conceded were problematic. But how far beyond, and to where? *Button*'s definition of voluntary — did the actor have a "meaningful choice" — does not help very much to answer this question. Any choice in which one has a lot at stake may seem meaningful. *Bonds* tries to discern the UPAA's understanding of "voluntary" by looking at the fact patterns that recur in the cases cited by the UPAA commentary, and concludes "that the voluntariness of a premarital agreement may turn in part upon whether the agreement was entered into knowingly, in the sense that the parties understood the terms or basic effect of the agreement." Yet it is of course difficult to know what someone really understood. This requirement therefore tends to get redefined into procedural safeguards to make sure the party had every chance to understand it: *e.g.*, was the party advised by independent counsel, were assets disclosed, and was an adequate explanation of the agreement's significance provided? A second thread *Bonds* finds in the voluntariness cases reflects the view of some drafting Commissioners that the voluntariness requirement deals with cases of "oppression." What does voluntary mean in this context? A rule of voluntariness cannot require looking into the soul of each party to the contract to determine whether his or her free will is intact. The victim of the armed robber makes a choice when told "your money or your life," and he probably would rather have that choice, than not. We nonetheless call the choice "involuntary" because threatening to kill people is an improper bargaining tactic, and we do not bind people to choices made in response to such threats. So we say that one party's improper — "oppressive" — bargaining tactics denies the other party a "voluntary" choice. But it is our condemnation of the bargaining tactic, not the psyche of its victim, that is key.

In both conventional contract law and in moral philosophy, there are efforts to understand "coercive proposals" as extending beyond "unacceptable bargaining tactics," though the analyses tend to be notoriously difficult (and more than occasionally unconvincing). Generally, the discussion of whether B is coerced by A's proposal covers some combination of (1) whether A's proposal to B is within A's moral or legal right to make, (2) whether A is threatening to make B's situation significantly worse from B's status quo if B does not accept the proposal, (3) whether A is knowingly exploiting some vulnerability or desperate need in B's circumstances, and (4) whether B has reasonable alternatives to accepting A's proposal. *See* E. ALLAN FARNSWORTH, CONTRACTS 255–263 (4th ed. 2004) (doctrine of duress in contract law); ALAN WERTHEIMER, COERCION (1987) (moral analysis of when coercion occurs).

To assess whether bargaining tactics are improper in premarital agreement cases, and whether there are reasonable alternatives to signing the agreement, courts must make some subtle distinctions. On one hand, for example, an agreement is not involuntary merely because one party insisted upon it as a condition of marriage, because the "threat of a refusal to marry is not wrongful in the eyes of the law." *Liebelt v. Liebelt*, 801 P.2d 52, 55 (Idaho App. 1990); *accord, Gardner v. Gardner*, 527 N.W.2d 701, 706 (Wis. App. 1994); *Howell v. Landry*, 386 S.E.2d 610, 617–18 (N.C. App. 1989); *Taylor v. Taylor*, 832 P.2d 429, 431 (Okla. App. 1992). But on the other hand, one party's insistence on conditioning the marriage to the other's consent to an agreement may be regarded as improper if the demand is made, for the first time, on the eve of the wedding. "The presentation of an agreement a very short time before the wedding ceremony will create a presumption of overreaching or coercion if . . . the postponement of the wedding would cause significant hardship, embarrassment or emotional stress . . . [¶] The meaningfulness of the opportunity of the nonproponent party to seek counsel before executing an antenuptial agreement is . . . [significant in determining] whether coercion or overreaching occurred." *Fletcher v. Fletcher*, 628 N.E.2d 1343 (Ohio 1994) (but upholding the agreement before it because the wedding's postponement would not have caused hardship or embarrassment). Similarly, conditioning marriage on an agreement may be thought improper in pregnant-bride cases like *Williams, supra*, if the groom is seen as exploiting the bride's vulnerability, to gain an unfair advantage. To the extent that the idea of voluntariness captures this exploitation concern, it protects the vulnerable party in situations in which courts might otherwise rely upon the unconscionability doctrine to reach the same result. *See* Note 6, *infra*.

Recent state court decisions have varied greatly (even by the same court from case to case) on the connected issues of voluntariness and duress. *See, e.g., Francavilla v. Francavilla*, 969 So.2d 522 (Fla. App., 2007) (duress argument rejected, though agreement not signed until an hour before the wedding, and the bride was 7 months pregnant; court noted that the agreement had been negotiated for months, and the woman had left the man twice before); *In re Marriage of Shirilla*, 89 P.3d 1 (Mont. 2004) (agreement invalidated for lack of voluntariness, where wife did not understand agreement due to poor knowledge of English, and where her ability to stay in the country depended on marriage); *Peters-Riemers v. Riemers*, 644 N.W.2d 197 (N.D. 2002) (agreement invalidated for lack of voluntariness, where presented three days before the marriage, with inadequate financial disclosure and insufficient opportunity to consult independent counsel);

Binek v. Binek, 673 N.W.2d 594 (N.D. 2004) (voluntariness challenge rejected despite presentation two days before the marriage and some question about adequacy of financial disclosure and lack of representation); *In re Yannalfo*, 794 A.2d 795 (N.H. 2002) (duress argument rejected despite presentation day before wedding, threat marriage would not take place, wife unrepresented); *In re Estate of Hollett*, 834 A.2d 348 (N.H. 2003) (agreement invalidated on voluntariness grounds, due in part to imbalance in power and resources and apparent bad faith by husband, and presentation of agreement only days before the wedding); *Azarova v. Schmitt*, 2007 Ohio App. LEXIS 586 (Feb. 16, 2007) (agreement invalidated on "overreaching," coercion, and duress when "mail order bride" presented agreement shortly before visa was to expire, wife had limited knowledge of English, no knowledge of state property division law, and no practical opportunity to consult a lawyer).

3. The ALI Principles' Approach to the Voluntariness Requirement. The *ALI Principles* follow the analysis of the prior note and avoid any use at all of the term "voluntary." "The best understanding of the frequently stated voluntariness requirement is that it expresses the law's heightened sensitivity to duress and coercion concerns in the context of premarital agreements. . . . Consent is involuntary when it is elicited by . . . problematic bargaining tactics." *ALI Principles* § 7.04, Comment *b*. The ALI recommends special procedural requirements as a more effective and more certain alternative to reliance upon the vague requirement of "voluntariness." It requires the party seeking to enforce the agreement to show that the other party's consent was informed and not obtained under duress. Section 7.04(3) then gives the agreement's proponent the benefit of a presumption (rebuttable) that this burden has been met, if the proponent shows that:

(a) [the agreement] was executed at least 30 days before the parties' marriage;

(b) both parties were advised to obtain independent legal counsel, and had reasonable opportunity to do so, before the agreement's execution; and,

(c) in the case of agreements concluded without the assistance of independent legal counsel for each party, the agreement states, in language easily understandable by an adult of ordinary intelligence with no legal training,

(i) the nature of any rights or claims otherwise arising at dissolution that are altered by the contract, and the nature of that alteration, and

(ii) that the interests of the spouses with respect to the agreement may be adverse.

Section 7.04 thus deals directly with the principal issues that recur under the rubric of voluntariness: the parties' understanding of the agreement's terms and its significance, reasonable opportunity to consult independent counsel, and last minute demands for an agreement. The agreement's proponent may prevail even if these requirements are not met, but only by carrying the burden of proving that "the other party's consent was informed and not obtained under duress."

The requirement of execution at least 30 days prior to the wedding is not generally found in prevailing American law. The *Principles* explain:

> [T]he late insistence on an agreement places the offeree in a dilemma. [It] may give the offeree doubts about the marriage. Yet, by this time, the parties have already agreed to marry, and perhaps publicly announced their commitment. The newly created doubts, even if worrisome, may come too late to reverse the momentum of the existing marital plans, or to overcome the offeree's preexisting emotional commitment to the marriage, as well as the offeree's naturally optimistic expectations of married life with the offeror. So the agreement is signed.

> Because no one is ever obliged to marry, people are generally free to insist on an agreement as a condition for entering marriage. The difficulty in these cases is the late hour at which this insistence is expressed — often some time after the parties had decided to marry, and after they have acted on that decision in both their public and private behavior. In this context, the proffered premarital agreement resembles new terms that one party insists upon adding to an agreement to marry that had already been reached and partially executed. . . . [¶] Premarital agreements are rarely proposed on impulse. They are usually planned. The party who wants the agreement typically hires a lawyer to draft it. There is usually no reason why this process cannot begin early enough to be completed a month before the wedding.

In § 7.04(5), the *Principles* also require the disclosure of a party's assets and income for the enforcement of any provision limiting the other party's financial claims at divorce, or proof that the other party knew the first party's assets and income, at least approximately.

4. *Disclosure of Assets and Unconscionability in Premarital Agreements.* Disclosure is probably the most universal of the heightened procedural requirements applied to premarital agreements, required under pre-UPAA law as well as the *ALI Principles.* Even *Simeone*, in a passage not included in the excerpt above, holds that absent a "full and fair disclosure of the financial positions of the parties . . . material misrepresentation in the inducement for entering a prenuptial agreement may be asserted." Mandatory disclosure is of course one way to vindicate a concern that consent to an agreement is "knowledgeable," an important part of the "voluntariness" rubric. One might also argue that concealment of one's assets is precisely the kind of bargaining tactic barred under the rubric of voluntariness. The Uniform Premarital Agreement Act's treatment of the disclosure requirement is therefore puzzling. Under § 6(a)(2), disclosure is important only if the agreement is also unconscionable, as the failure to disclose does not alone affect the agreement's validity. The UPAA would therefore enforce an unfair agreement the disadvantaged party would not have signed if disclosure had been made, unless it is so unfair as to be unconscionable.

Note that the reverse problem is also possible under the UPAA; an agreement is immune from attack as unconscionable, if either disclosure was made, or the disadvantaged party had knowledge of the other party's assets. *Bonds* relies on this very point in concluding that the issue of unconscionability is not before the court because the parties had agreed that Sun had knowledge of Barry's assets.

Moreover, § 6(a)(2)(ii) of the UPAA allows a party to waive disclosure, creating the stunning possibility that an unconscionably unfair agreement could be enforced against an uninformed party who waived disclosure. Three states that have otherwise adopted the UPAA changed its language to avoid the implication that disclosure can be waived. *See* Conn. Gen. Stat. Ann. § 46b-36g(a)(3); Iowa Code Ann. § 596.7(2)(c); N.J. Stat. Ann. § 37:2-38(c)(1). There may be reason to wonder whether the Commissioners really intended the result apparently called for under this UPAA language. Perhaps the drafters expected the Act's vague requirement of voluntariness to protect parties who would have unconscionability claims but for the Act's unique provisions. But in the end it is difficult to be confident of what the UPAA drafters had in mind. The official UPAA commentary to § 6 cites with approval the case of *Del Vecchio v. Del Vecchio*, 143 So. 2d 17 (Fla. 1962), but that case is inconsistent with these UPAA provisions. It requires disclosure and disallows its waiver, and does not treat disclosure as "cleansing" an otherwise unconscionable agreement so as to allow its enforcement. *See* the Reporter's Notes to Comment *g* of § 7.04 of the *ALI Principles.*

Generally courts have not required that disclosure be entire and precise, but egregious failures of disclosure will lead to the invalidation of the agreement. *Compare, e.g., Blige v. Blige*, 656 S.E.2d 822 (Ga. 2008) (premarital agreement not enforceable due to husband's failure to disclose $150,000 in cash; wife had no "duty of inquiry") *and In re State of Schinn*, 925 A.2d 88 (N.J. App. 2007) (significant failure of disclosure requires invalidation of wife's waiver of spousal share of estate) *with Friezo v. Friezo*, 914 A.2d 533 (Conn. 2007) (fair and reasonable disclosure sufficient for state version of UPAA).

5. More on Independent Counsel. Recall that under the *ALI Principles* the agreement's proponent will benefit from a presumption that the other party's consent was informed and free from duress only if, among other requirements, "both parties were advised to obtain independent legal counsel, and had reasonable opportunity to do so, before the agreement's execution." If there in fact was no independent counsel, there is the additional requirement set forth in § 7.04(3)(c), reprinted above in Note 3, that the agreement contain a plain language explanation of both its significance, and that the parties' interests may be adverse. In this respect (as others, see Note 7 below) the *ALI Principles* follow *Gant*, which also requires either independent counsel or an agreement reasonably understandable to the layman. Most authorities are not as explicit on the counsel requirement, however. As *Bonds* point out, for example, there is no mention of independent counsel in the UPAA, an omission that was apparently intentional. On the other hand, as *Bonds* also points out, the presence or absence of independent counsel, and the availability of an understandable explanation of the agreement's terms and significance, are factors that can be weighed in assessing whether consent was "voluntary," even though their absence does not shift the burden of proof, as it effectively does under the *ALI Principles.* In fact, after *Bonds* was decided, the California legislature amended its statute to adopt provisions very similar to the *ALI Principles'* recommendations. Subsequently-enacted Cal. Fam. Code § 1615(c) provides that an agreement is not voluntary unless two conditions are met:

(1) The party against whom enforcement is sought was represented by independent legal counsel at the time of signing the agreement or, after

being advised to seek independent legal counsel, expressly waived, in a separate writing, representation by independent legal counsel.

(2) The party against whom enforcement is sought had not less than seven calendar days between the time that party was first presented with the agreement and advised to seek independent legal counsel and the time the agreement was signed.

It is thus apparent that the *Bonds* agreement itself would not be enforceable under current California law.

Did Sun Bonds have a "reasonable opportunity" to obtain counsel, as required in § 7.04(3) of the *ALI Principles*? One question is whether Sun Bonds could *afford* independent counsel. In commentary, the *ALI Principles* conclude that a party does *not* have "reasonable opportunity" to consult independent counsel if that party cannot afford to pay counsel. *See* § 7.04, Comment *e*. Thus, to obtain the benefit of the presumption of validity under the *ALI Principles*, Barry would have had to have offered to pay for independent counsel for Sun, if she did not have adequate funds of her own. The court of appeals believed she did not, an important factor contributing to its conclusion that her agreement was not voluntary. In reversing, the California Supreme Court relied on the trial court's finding that Sun had reasonable opportunity to obtain counsel, but there is no indication that the trial court considered Sun's ability to pay counsel as bearing on its conclusion. Nor do the general provisions ultimately adopted by the legislature in § 1615(c) address this question (is the waiver allowed under § 1615(c)(1) valid, when executed by a party who could not pay for counsel?). Note that California now applies a special requirement for counsel applicable to provisions waiving spousal support. *See* Note 6, *infra*.

6. *Special Rules With Respect to Provisions Limiting Alimony*. Note that Sun in fact received a large alimony award, and there was apparently no provision in their agreement — or at least none that Barry sought to enforce — which limited her spousal support claim. Historically, some courts and legislatures have been more resistant to enforcing waivers of alimony than waivers of marital property rights, and this resistance lingers. Indiana added language to its version of the UPAA allowing its courts to require spousal maintenance, despite contract terms to the contrary, when a spouse would otherwise suffer "extreme hardship under circumstances not reasonably foreseeable at the time of the execution of the agreement." *See Rider v. Rider*, 669 N.E.2d 160, 163–64 (Ind. 1996). Illinois has adopted the same language, 750 ILL. COMP. STAT. 10/7 § 7(b). Four other UPAA states (California, Iowa, New Mexico, and South Dakota) removed "spousal maintenance" from the list of subjects that a valid agreement may address. In a decision handed down with *Bonds*, the California Supreme Court held that this omission was not intended to bar agreements on maintenance, *Pendleton v. Fireman*, 5 P.3d 839 (Cal. 2000). In response, the California legislature then barred enforcement of agreements waiving spousal support if they are "unconscionable at the time of enforcement" or if the waiving party was not represented by independent counsel at the time of the waiver. CAL. FAM. CODE § 1612(c). Even where agreements to waive alimony are not forbidden across the board, they may be struck down on the particular facts of a case. See, e.g., *Lane v. Lane*, 202 S.W.3d

577 (Ky. 2006) (agreement to waive alimony unconscionable at time of enforcement, where husband became a millionaire, in part because wife devoted herself to being a homemaker). For a good overview of the topic, see Susan Wolfson, *Premarital Waiver of Alimony*, 38 Fam. L.Q. 141 (2004).

7. Substantive Fairness, the Doctrine of Unconscionability, and the ALI's Proposals. Section 208 of Restatement (Second) of Contracts states the classic rule:

> If a contract or term thereof is unconscionable at the time the contract is made a court may refuse to enforce the contract, or may enforce the remainder of the contract without the unconscionable term, or may so limit the application of any unconscionable term as to avoid any unconscionable result.

The Restatement does not attempt to define unconscionability with any further precision. It is not inadvertent, however, that § 208 specifies that the question is whether an agreement is unconscionable "at the time the contract is made," not at some later time when its enforcement is sought. This feature of the unconscionability principle is inherent in its rationale. As explained in Comment *d* of § 7.01 of the *ALI Principles*,

> The doctrine goes primarily to defects in the bargaining process, including unfairness in the negotiating tactics used to obtain agreement. Along with procedural defects, however, the law has also recognized substantive unconscionability, or a gross one-sidedness in terms. The two often go hand in hand, for one may tend to prove the other. A grossly one-sided agreement may corroborate unconscionable bargaining tactics, while unfair bargaining tactics may most often be employed to obtain a one-sided agreement.

In other words, one would not usually expect a competent adult to agree to contract terms that are oppressive — substantively unconscionable — at the time of the agreement, unless there was a defect in the bargaining process. That process defect might be of the sort contemplated by other contract doctrines, such as misrepresentation or duress. But it might not, and then the unconscionability doctrine is important. An example is the unfair exploitation, by one party, of the other's special vulnerability. *See* Melvin Aron Eisenberg, *The Bargain Principle and Its Limits*, 95 Harv. L. Rev. 741 (1982) (explaining how the unconscionability doctrine is necessary to deny enforcement of the stranded desert traveler's promise to pay a million dollars for a jug of water). Substantive unconscionability thus suggests the likelihood of procedural unconscionability, and can be said to depend upon that likelihood as part of its rationale for denying enforcement of an unconscionable agreement. But procedural unconscionability is not suggested by terms that seemed fair at the time of execution, even if they may be very unfair under the facts prevailing at some later time when enforcement is sought. We still may wish, of course, to deny enforcement of terms that, as things turn out, are enormously one-sided. But doing so requires the development of a different doctrine, for while substantive unconscionability exists as a legal concept, it is not entirely independent from concerns with procedural unconscionability. *See, e.g., In re Marriage of Smith*, 115 S.W.3d 126 (Tex. App. 2003) (unconscionability under state's adoption of UPAA to be tested at time agreement executed, not at time of enforcement).

That need for a different doctrine is obscured by courts and statutes which deny enforcement of an agreement if it is unconscionable at the time of enforcement. Some UPAA states have modified it to add such language. *E.g.*, CONN. GEN. STAT. ANN. § 46b-36g(a)(2) (agreement is unenforceable if "unconscionable when it was executed or when enforcement is sought"); N.J. STAT. ANN. 37:2-32(c)(3) (defining as unconscionable any agreement that "would provide a standard of living far below that which was enjoyed before the marriage"); CAL. FAM. CODE § 1612(c) (with respect to spousal support terms only). It may seem that asking whether an agreement is "unconscionable" at the time of enforcement merely applies an established doctrine to a new situation, but the temporal shift robs the doctrine of much of its rationale. *Button* avoids the word "unconscionable," simply holding that an agreement can be reviewed for "fairness" as of the time of enforcement. This may not be entirely satisfactory either, for it seems inconsistent with basic ideas of contract law to allow courts to reject any agreement they find "unfair." Indeed, concern with just such freewheeling judicial scrutiny is what appears to have motivated the Uniform Commissioners to circumscribe the unconscionability doctrine in the UPAA. The challenge, then, is to develop a doctrine dealing with agreements that seem wrong to enforce because of circumstances prevailing at the time of enforcement, while doing so in a way that is more limited than just allowing courts to refuse enforcement of any contract they believe very unfair.

Gant takes up this challenge. It is probably correct in concluding that when courts talk about unfairness at the time of *enforcement*, they are really talking about the unforeseeability, at the time of *execution*, of the circumstances under which enforcement is sought. This is not a problem of unconscionability in the classic sense, because neither party has necessarily imposed unfairly on the other. It may even be a case in which *neither* party really foresaw, at the time of execution, the impact of enforcing its terms later. Other jurisdictions have established a similar fairness inquiry focused on whether circumstances have changed (by the time of enforcement) relative to what was reasonably expected at the time of execution. *See, e.g.*, *McKee-Johnson v. Johnson*, 444 N.W.2d 259, 267 (Minn. 1989); *Reed v. Reed*, 693 N.W.2d 825, 834 (Mich. App. 2005).

In adopting *Gant's* general approach, the *ALI Principles* necessarily must fill in some details. These are found in § 7.05:

ALI PRINCIPLES

§ 7.05 When Enforcement Would Work a Substantial Injustice

(1) A court should not enforce a term in an agreement if, pursuant to Paragraphs (2) and (3) of this section,

(a) the circumstances require it to consider if enforcement would work a substantial injustice; and

(b) the court finds that enforcement would work a substantial injustice.

(2) A court should consider whether enforcement of an agreement would work a substantial injustice if, and only if, the party resisting its enforce-

ment shows that one or more of the following have occurred since the time of the agreement's execution:

(a) more than a fixed number of years have passed, that number being set in a rule of statewide application;

(b) a child was born to, or adopted by, the parties, who at the time of execution had no children in common;

(c) there has been a change in circumstances that has a substantial impact on the parties or their children, but when they executed the agreement the parties probably did not anticipate either the change, or its impact.

Comment:. . . .

b. . . . . [N]early all premarital agreements involve special difficulties arising from unrealistic optimism about marital success, the human tendency to treat low probabilities as zero probabilities, the excessive discounting of future benefits, and the inclination to overweigh the importance of the immediate and certain consequences of agreement — the marriage — as against its contingent and future consequences. Paragraph (2), however, does not call for the court's examination at divorce of all premarital agreements, but only a subset in which these difficulties are particularly likely. Paragraph (2)(a) identifies contracts made more than a fixed period of years before enforcement is sought, that period having been set in a uniform rule of statewide application. A period of about 10 years would ensure scrutiny of agreements whose enforcement is particularly likely to be problematic, while leaving a clear majority of divorces unaffected (because most divorces occur after fewer years of marriage). Paragraph (2)(b) identifies for scrutiny those cases in which the parties had no children in common at the time of the agreement, but do so at the time that its enforcement is sought. Even childless parties who anticipate having children are often unable to anticipate the impact that children will have on their values and life plans. Once they are parents, the effect of the terms they earlier agreed upon are therefore likely to seem quite different than they expected when childless. Note that, when the parties have children, there are policy issues as well. See Comment *c.*

Most of the fact patterns justifying a substantial-injustice inquiry when enforcement is sought will be captured by Paragraphs (2)(a) and (2)(b), but not all. There are additional cases in which the cognitive difficulties are particularly severe, but which are not easily identified by the simple objective indicators employed in Paragraphs (2)(a) and (2)(b). Paragraph (2)(c) states a more general standard under which at least some of these problem cases may be reached. It requires the party resisting enforcement to show a change in life circumstances that was probably unanticipated by the parties but that has a substantial impact on them or their children. To meet this burden, the party resisting enforcement need not show the nature of the parties' deliberations and their cognitive capacities at the time of execution, which may have been many years earlier. As an initial matter, the resisting party may satisfy this burden by showing that normal, competent individuals would not usually anticipate either the circumstances at the time of divorce, or the change in the impact of the agreement's terms under those new circumstances. The party seeking to enforce the agreement may rebut such a showing, however, with evidence that the particular parties were in fact likely to have anticipated the new circumstances and to have considered the impact that enforcement of the agreement would have on them if those circumstances arose.

The ALI thus offers an approach to fairness that is more limited than *Button* because it permits the inquiry in only a subset of premarital agreement cases. Another subsection not reprinted above lists the considerations that bear upon whether an agreement works a substantial injustice. This subsection, informed by the discussion of it in the accompanying commentary, guides the substantial injustice inquiry. The limitation in the circumstances under which the inquiry can be made at all remains, however, the most important reason why the *ALI Principles* do not in fact allow the kind of open-ended review of an agreement's fairness that the Uniform Commissioners also wished to avoid.

Whether a state speaks of "[substantive] fairness" or "unconscionability," a great deal of discretion is left to judges to invalidate provisions perceived to be unfair as written or as applied. In *Kessler v. Kessler*, 33 A.D.3d 42, 818 N.Y.S.2d 571 (2006), the court refused enforcement on unconscionability grounds of provisions in a premarital agreement that waived the spouses' rights to seek award of attorney fees for claims relating to the equitable division of property. *See also In re Marriage of Ikeler*, 161 P.3d 663 (Colo. 2007) (waiver of attorney's fees subject to unconscionability review despite state marital agreement statute that appears to allow such review only for waiver of alimony). On the other hand, one commentator has found that between 2000 and February 2007, "only one of the states' highest courts has invalidated an agreement on the basis of substantive unfairness." Judith T. Younger, *Lovers' Contracts in the Courts: Forsaking the Minimum Decencies*, 13 WILLIAM & MARY J. WOMEN & L. 349, 358 n. 83 (2007).

8. More on the Rationale for Heightened Scrutiny. Why impose special process requirements on premarital agreements, and why allow courts ever to inquire into the fairness of enforcing them? The *ALI Principles* summarizes the arguments it relies upon, in Comment *c* of § 7.02:

> While there are good reasons to respect contracts relating to the consequences of family dissolution, the family context requires some departure from the rules that govern the commercial arena. First, the relationship between contracting parties who are married, or about to marry, is different than the usual commercial relationship in ways that matter to the law's treatment of their agreements. Persons planning to marry usually assume that they share with their intended spouse a mutual and deep concern for one another's welfare. Business people negotiating a commercial agreement do not usually have that expectation of one another. . . . These distinctive expectations that persons planning to marry usually have about one another can disarm their capacity for self-protective judgment, or their inclination to exercise it, as compared to parties

negotiating commercial agreements. This difference justifies legal rules designed to strengthen the parties' ability and inclination to consider how a proposed agreement affects their own interest, such as rules that require transparency in the agreement's language and that encourage parties to seek independent legal counsel.

Second, even though the terms of agreements made before, or during, an ongoing family relationship address the consequences of its dissolution, the parties ordinarily do not expect the family unit to dissolve. Even if the possibility of dissolution is considered, it is necessarily imagined as arising at some indefinite time in the future. The remoteness of dissolution in both likelihood and timing, as well as the difficulty of anticipating other life changes that might occur during the course of the marriage, further impedes the ability of persons to evaluate the impact that the contract terms will have on them in the future when its enforcement is sought. . . .

The two concerns just identified describe distinctive limits on the cognitive capacity with which persons may enter family contracts, as contrasted with commercial agreements. There is, in addition, the point that the rights and obligations that parties might seek to waive through private agreements are designed to protect the interests of persons who enter into family relationships, and the interests of their children. Enforcement of agreements about the consequences of family dissolution therefore present a different policy question than enforcement of commercial agreements between persons who otherwise have no claims on one another's property or income. Family contracts set aside otherwise applicable public policies while commercial agreements do not. Two implications of this difference are noted here. First, when a contract departs from otherwise applicable public policies that are designed to protect parties, the law can reasonably require greater assurance that the parties understand and appreciate what they are doing, than when the contract does not. Second, vindication of the public policies may require rules that limit the enforcement of private agreements that significantly infringe upon them. These policy concerns thus suggest a rationale for special rules for family contracts that is additional to the rationale based upon the cognitive limitations that are likely to impinge upon persons entering into family contracts. . . . [¶] Indeed, the cases in which the parties are most likely to make errors of cognition overlap considerably with those in which significant public policies are most likely implicated: long marriages and marriages producing children. . . .

The Institute thus offers two complementary explanations for treating premarital agreements differently than ordinary commercial contracts: a cognitive rationale, and a policy rationale. The cognitive rationale, as the Institute later explains, arises from the fact that "[c]ontract law is . . . based not only upon a philosophical commitment to individual autonomy, but also upon a factual assumption about the abilities of contracting parties." In this respect, the Institute relies on modern studies from behavioral economics which suggest that the cognitive capacities necessary for the kind of assessment of self-interest assumed by contract doctrine are more likely to be deficient in the premarital agreement context than in the commercial context, and particularly so in the case of long marriages and marriages with after-born children. The policy rationale notes that the obligations arising from family relationships are not based upon contract in the first place, and thus not necessarily waivable by contract either. This point seems obvious with respect to the obligations of parents to their children, but applies as well, the Institute argues, to duties arising between spouses in a long-term relationship. While obligations imposed by law cannot always be waived by contract, the law may allow their partial waiver, or their waiver under specified conditions — which is the approach taken by the *ALI Principles*. A more complete explanation for the Institute's recommendation for a limited time-of-enforcement fairness review can be found in Comments *b* and *c* of § 7.05 of the *ALI Principles*. For further development of the argument that obligations between spouses in a long-term relationship are not based upon contract ideas, see Ira Mark Ellman, *Contract Thinking Was Marvin's Fatal Flaw*, 76 NOTRE DAME L. REV. 1365 (2001).

As regards cognitive biases or other aspects of bounded rationality as a justification for limits on the enforcement of premarital agreements, it is undoubtedly true that many people, when they are about to marry, and are deeply in love, find it difficult to think clearly about a possible divorce, and what financial effects it might bring. This is similar to the way that someone who is starting a new job, and on good terms with her boss, is unlikely to be able to think clearly about the post-termination provisions of her contract. On the other hand, being presented with a premarital agreement puts one on notice in a way that a normal employment contract does not: the only purpose of a premarital agreement is for one party (or both parties) to waive rights, so people presented with such proposed agreements might be more likely to reflect on that waiver. At the same time, the cognitive biases that have been shown to accompany any consideration of the long-term, especially long-term risks (here the "risk" that the marriage will end in divorce), remain present, and may justify some level of protective regulation.

Much of the justification of fairness review tied to the time of enforcement is based on the unforeseen changes in circumstances that a long-term marriage can bring to one or both partners. *See, e.g., McKee-Johnson v. Johnson*, 444 N.W.2d 259 (Minn. 1989) (enforcement may be denied to a premarital agreement fair at its inception "if the premises upon which [the contract was] originally based have so drastically changed that enforcement would not comport with the [original] reasonable expectations of the parties . . . to such an extent that . . . enforcement would be unconscionable."). In response to the unforeseen way that children can affect one's life, Maine modified its version of the UPAA to make premarital agreements void 18 months after the couple become biological or adoptive parents unless the couple enters a written agreement during those 18 months reaffirming or altering the agreement. ME. REV. STAT. ANN. titl. 19, § 606. For a different perspective, consider the final paragraph of the excerpt from *Simeone*, reprinted above: "the possibilities of illness, birth of children, reliance upon a spouse, career change, financial gain or loss, and numerous other events that can occur in the course of a marriage cannot be regarded as unforeseeable. If parties choose not to address such matters in their prenuptial agreements, they must be regarded as having contracted to bear the risk of events that alter the value of their bargains." Is the issue whether parties anticipate having children, or anticipate all the changes in their life that the presence of children may bring? *See* Melvin Aron Eisenberg, *The Limits of Cognition and the Limits of Contract*, 47 Stan. L. Rev. 211, 254–58 (1995) ("It is almost impossible to predict the impact that a prenuptial agreement will have if it does come into play. Personal income may increase or decrease; job skills may be acquired or lost; family obligations may vary in regard to both the other spouse and children; personal expectations may change. Change in the course of marriage is foreseeable, but the specifics of the change are not. The limits of cognition therefore provide a strong justification for a second-look approach to prenuptial agreements.").

9. *"Fiduciary Relationships".* *Bonds* says that while *spouses* are in a fiduciary or "confidential" relationship with one another, those just planning their marriage to one another are not. A "fiduciary relationship" most typically arises when parties are in a position of trust, such that one can presume that the other party has one's best interests in mind. For example, a lawyer might be in a fiduciary relationship with his or her client. In lawyer-client dealings (and similar contexts), the "fiduciary relationship" label carries with it heavy duties for contractual dealings: the person in the position of trust (e.g., the lawyer) has the duty to prove to the court that the terms are substantively fair. *Bonds* reads the UPAA as rejecting the view that parties about to marry should be seen as being in a "fiduciary relationship."

Other courts have reached a different conclusion. The court in *Friedlander v. Friedlander*, 494 P.2d 208 (Wash. 1972), said: "[A]n engagement to marry creates a confidential relationship. Parties to a pre-nuptial agreement do not deal with each other at arm's length. Their relationship is one of mutual confidence and trust which calls for the exercise of good faith, candor and sincerity in all matters bearing upon the proposed agreement." *See also Friezo v. Friezo*, 914 A.2d 533 (Conn. 2007) (follows majority rule that parties to premarital agreement in confidential relationship); *Cannon v. Cannon*, 865 A.2d 563 (Md. 2005) (prospective spouses in a confidential relationship as a matter of law; also, agreement must thus meet test of substantive unfairness at time of execution). However, one can find occasional cases coming out the other way. *E.g.*, *Mallen v. Mallen*, 622 S.E.2d 812 (Ga. 2005) (prospective spouses not in a confidential relationship as a matter of law). It should be noted, however, that the courts that do conclude that parties about to marry are in a "fiduciary relationship," usually take this conclusion as grounding only a duty of financial disclosure prior to entering a premarital agreement, rather than the more substantial duties (e.g. a burden of proving substantive fairness) that are imposed on tradition fiduciary dealings, like those between lawyers and clients. *See, e.g., Friezo*, 914 A.2d at 547–549 (fiduciary relationship between parties about to marry requires financial disclosure).

10. *Amendment by Conduct.* While the law is generally clear that a writing is required to establish a premarital agreement, courts have occasionally held that the parties' conduct during their marriage negated an earlier written agreement. *E.g.*, in *Baxter v. Baxter*, 911 P.2d 343 (Ore. App. 1996), the parties had kept their finances separate during the first half of their 13-year marriage, but during the second half the wife left her own employment and worked without pay as manager of the husband's golf course, and applied some of her separate assets to the business's debts. The court found that this conduct "demonstrated mutual intent to rescind" their agreement to retain separate ownership of their assets. See the compilation of such cases in Annotation, *Antenuptial Contracts: Parties' Behavior During Marriage as Abandonment, Estoppel, or Waiver Regarding Contractual Rights*, 56 A.L.R.4th 999 (1987). The UPAA has been criticized for appearing to bar such modifications of agreements by later conduct. Barbara Atwood, *Ten Years Later: Lingering Concerns about the Uniform Premarital Agreement Act*, 19 J. LEGIS. 127, 147 (1993).

It is important that *Baxter* and like cases involve more than a claim of an oral agreement to modify the earlier writing: They claim as well (or instead) that the parties have in fact conducted their lives differently than they had contemplated at the time of the agreement. One can therefore understand these cases as an application of the rule that partial performance takes a contract out of the Statute of Frauds (in this case, a contract being one to modify to the original agreement), or instead as an instance of an equitable doctrine (most plausibly, estoppel) serving its traditional purpose of providing relief from an injustice that would otherwise result from the application of technical legal rules. The latter approach is of course most easily adopted in jurisdictions that permit their courts broad equitable authority to decline to enforce premarital agreements. *E.g., Krejci v. Krejci*, 667 N.W.2d 780 (Wisc. Ct. App. 2003) (concluding it would be inequitable to enforce an agreement that excluded the appreciated value of resort hotel from marital property division where, during their 18-year marriage, the parties combined their resources, including inheritances, savings, and incomes, operated the resort as a partnership, and generally ignored the agreement, which no longer comported with their expectations).

One must distinguish claims that parties mutually agreed to amend or rescind their agreement, from claims that one party's marital misconduct should allow the other to avoid it. The latter claim is not ordinarily allowed. *E.g., Perkinson v. Perkinson*, 802 S.W.2d 600 (Tenn. 1990) (wealthy widow had signed agreement providing husband with $150,000 in full satisfaction of any claim he might have on her separate property; provision cannot be avoided by wife's allegation, in divorce action, of cruel and inhumane treatment). To be distinguished, also, are claims that partial performance make enforceable an oral premarital agreement that otherwise would be unenforceable due to a writing requirement. Courts are split on the application of this doctrine. *Compare Hall v. Hall*, 271 Cal. Rptr. 773 (App. 1990) (applying the partial performance exception), *and DewBerry v. George*, 62 P.3d 525 (Wash. 2003) (same), *with Dunagan v. Dunagan*, 213 P.3d 384, 2009 Idaho LEXIS 91 (Idaho) (refusing application of the exception).

11. *Same-Sex Unions.* Though there is no case law (at the time of writing), it is reasonably to be assumed that state premarital agreement rules would apply equally to same-sex marriages (in those states which recognize them) as opposite-sex marriages. What of those states that grant some status like marriage, but under another rubric? Both New Jersey and the District of Columbia have expressly modified their versions of the UPAA to indicate that it applies to such unions. N.J. STAT. §§ 37:2-32 to 37:2-34; D.C. STAT § 46-501.

12. *Choice of Laws and Conflict of Laws.* Generally, the conflict of laws rules for contracts is that agreements are to be interpreted according to the laws of the state where the agreement was entered, unless those laws are contrary to a strong public policy of the forum state. However, there are indications that with premarital agreements that courts may sometimes apply their own law even to agreements entered in another jurisdiction. For example, in the *Bonds* case, the court appears to apply California law to an agreement entered in Arizona, without any detailed consideration for the conflict of laws issue. (The matter is complicated in the *Bonds* case, and in the area of premarital agreements generally. For a more detailed discussion, see Ira Mark Ellman, *Marital Agreements and Private Autonomy in the United States, in* MARITAL AGREEMENTS AND PRIVATE AUTONOMY IN A COMPARATIVE PERSPECTIVE (Jans M. Scherpe ed., forthcoming, Hart Publishing 2011)).

Similarly, parties to a premarital agreement, like parties to other agreements, can usually opt, through an express choice of law provision, to have the premarital agreement subject to a law of a designated state, and that choice of law provision will usually be upheld unless, or to the extent that, it involves the application of rules strongly against the forum state's public policy. *See, e.g., Bradley v. Bradley,* 164 P.3d 537 (Wyo. 2007) (couple's premarital agreement had choice of law provision designating Minnesota law; effort to modify the agreement after marriage void because it did not comply with the requirements of Minnesota law).

13. *General Sources.* For recent discussions of the law of premarital agreements, offering a variety of different perspectives, see, e.g., Judith T. Younger, *Lovers' Contracts in the Courts: Forsaking the Minimum Decencies,* 13 WILLIAM & MARY J. WOMEN & LAW 349 (2007); Brian Bix, *The ALI Principles and Agreements: Seeking a Balance Between Status and Contract, in* RECONCEIVING THE FAMILY: CRITICAL REFLECTIONS ON THE AMERICAN LAW INSTITUTE'S *PRINCIPLES OF THE LAW OF FAMILY DISSOLUTION* 272–291 (Robin Fretwell Wilson ed., Cambridge, 2006); Jeffrey Sherman, *Prenuptial Agreements: A New Reason to Revive an Old Rule,* 53 CLEVELAND STATE L. REV. 539 (2005); Developments in the Law, *Marriage as Contract and Marriage as Partnership: The Future of Antenuptial Agreement Law,* 116 HARV. L. REV. 2075 (2003); Judith T. Younger, *Antenuptial Agreements,* 28 WILLIAM MITCHELL L. REV. 697 (2001); Brian H. Bix, *Bargaining in the Shadow of Love: Premarital Agreements and How We Think About Marriage,* 40 WILLIAM & MARY L. REV. 145 (1998); Allison A. Marston, *Planning for Love: The Politics of Prenuptial Agreements,* 49 STANFORD L. REV. 887 (1997). For a comparative law perspective, see MARITAL AGREEMENTS AND PRIVATE AUTONOMY IN A COMPARATIVE PERSPECTIVE (Jens M. Scherpe ed., forthcoming, Hart Publishing, 2011).

PROBLEMS

Problem 8-1. Jean and Julius meet at a class reunion when they are both 60. Both have grown children from an earlier marriage that ended with the death of their respective spouses. Jean and Julius begin dating, and eventually acquire a common primary residence. After living together four years, they decide to marry so that Jean will be covered under Julius' health insurance policy. Julius has been employed for 30 years by the same bank, where he is now a regional manager. He has his secretary type up a premarital agreement for them to sign, based upon a form provided him by a friend who is an attorney. The agreement specifies that each party gives up any claims he or she might have to marital property, in the event of their divorce, as well as any claims to the surviving spouse's share to which they would otherwise be entitled under their state's probate law, in the event of the other's death. The agreement specifies that the parties disclosed their assets to one another in attached schedules, which in fact they do. The parties sign the agreement before a notary, and marry the next day. Six months later, they both consult an attorney Jean knows, to prepare their wills. Jean's will leaves all of her property to her son, and Julius's will leaves all of his property to his two children. Julius assets' total about $1,500,000; Jean's, about $600,000.

The parties divorce after three years of marriage. Under otherwise applicable law, property acquired during the four years they lived together, as well as that acquired during their marriage, is marital property that is ordinarily divided equally. The effect of the agreement is to exclude these acquisitions from such a division. Julius seeks to enforce it. Should it be enforced?

Problem 8-2. After Paul and Helen decide to marry, Paul asks his attorney, Delores, to draft a premarital agreement. Delores arranges for Helen to meet separately with another attorney, Frank, whose office was down the hall from hers. Delores supplies Frank and Helen with a copy of the proposed agreement just as Frank and Helen meet for the first time. But the copy lacks the attachments referred to in the agreement, detailing Paul's financial situation. Helen's meeting with Frank was interrupted after a half-hour by Paul, who arrived unannounced to inquire "what was taking so long." The wedding was then canceled, but the parties reconciled a few weeks later and married hurriedly so that they could take the honeymoon arranged in connection with their original wedding plans. The agreement was signed the day before the wedding at Delores's office, with no further meetings between Helen and Frank. The attachments were included in the signed copies. The parties divorce ten years later. The agreement denies Helen any share in property acquired by Paul during the marriage and limits her alimony claims to a two-year rehabilitative award. It allows her a lump sum of $100,000 in lieu of any further alimony or property claim. The couple has no children. Paul has substantial assets that would be marital property but for the agreement, and a healthy annual income. Helen is an R.N. and can obtain reasonable employment. She has few assets. Should this agreement be enforced?

Problem 8-3. Eugene and Delores enter into an agreement before they marry under which all their property will remain separate and neither will have a claim for spousal support. At the time they enter this agreement, they are both employed full time, have comparable incomes, and have no children. They have lived together for four years, and feel they know each other well. Both enjoy their work as well as their time together. They sign the agreement after jointly consulting an attorney they both know. He suggested that they may wish to have separate attorneys, but they assure him it is unnecessary because the agreement is their mutual idea. They both believe this kind of arrangement is fair and "eliminates problems." They each have a very good idea of the other's income and assets, given their four years of living together. They feel they are equals, and wish a marital arrangement that reflects that. They do not plan to have children, but when questioned by their attorney they say that if they do, they will share child care duties equally and make equal adjustments in their work schedules.

They file for divorce 15 years later. They now have two children, seven and 11. Delores has been the children's primary caretaker since their birth, and her income potential, at the time of divorce, is considerably less than Eugene's. When their first child was born they planned alternate leaves from work, but Delores was much more comfortable with taking a leave than was Eugene. Eugene would have hired a live-in nanny to allow both of them to keep working, but Delores was uneasy with that arrangement, preferring less hired child care and more care by her. This is therefore the arrangement they came to. Both agree that Delores will continue to be the primary residential parent after their divorce. Under the law applicable but for their agreement, she would have a substantial claim for spousal support, and an equal share in the property accumulated with Eugene's much greater earnings. Under the agreement she has neither. Eugene seeks to enforce the agreement, while Delores seeks the support and property awards allowed under otherwise applicable law.

Should the agreement be enforced? Would it be enforced under the UPAA, the *ALI Principles*, *Bonds*, and *Button*?

[3]   Limitations on Subjects Governed by Premarital Agreements

DIOSDADO v. DIOSDADO
California Court of Appeal
118 Cal. Rptr. 2d 494 (2002)

Epstein, Acting P. J.

In this case we conclude that a contract entered into between a husband and wife, providing for payment of liquidated damages in the event one of them is sexually unfaithful to the other, is unenforceable. [¶] For the purpose of reviewing this grant of judgment on the pleadings, we take as true the allegations of the complaint and the facts presented to the trial court in an offer of proof.

Donna and Manuel Diosdado were married in November 1988. In 1993, Manuel had an affair with another woman. When Donna learned of this, the parties separated but did not divorce. Instead, they entered into a written "Marital Settlement Agreement" (hereafter the agreement) intended to "preserve, protect and assure the longevity and integrity of an amicable and beneficial marital relationship between them."

Section 1 of the agreement provides that if either party expresses concern that the goals of the marriage are not being met, they agree to seek counseling and make a good faith effort to resolve their problems to preserve the relationship.

Section 2 is labeled "Obligation of Fidelity," and provides: "It is further acknowledged that the parties' marriage is intended to be an exclusive relationship between Husband and Wife that is premised upon the values of emotional and sexual fidelity, and mutual trust. The parties hereto are subject to a legal obligation of emotional and sexual fidelity to the other. It shall be considered a breach of such obligation of fidelity to volitionally engage in any act of kissing on the mouth or touching in any sexual manner of any person outside of said marital relationship, as determined by a trier of fact. The parties acknowledge their mutual understanding that any such breach of fidelity by one party hereto may cause serious emotional, physical and financial injury to the other."

Section 3 is labeled "Liquidated Damages." It provides:

> In the event it is shown by a preponderance of the evidence in a court of competent jurisdiction that either party has engaged in any breach of the obligation of sexual fidelity as defined hereinabove . . . and, additionally, that election is made by one or both parties to commence an action to terminate the marriage by divorce because of said breach, the following terms and conditions shall become effective:
>
> (a) The party shown to have committed the breach shall vacate the family residence immediately upon the completion of a showing of breach as defined above;
>
> (b) The party shown to have committed the breach will be solely responsible for all attorney fees and court costs incurred as a result of or in connection with the litigation of any issue surrounding or relating to said breach;
>
> (c) The party shown to have committed the breach will pay the other party (hereinafter, the 'recipient') liquidated damages for said breach in the sum of $ 50,000, said sum to be paid over and above, and irrespective of, any property settlement and/or support obligation imposed by law as a result of said divorce proceeding. Said damages shall be due and payable on a date that is no later than six (6) months following entry of judgment of dissolution of marriage by a court of competent jurisdiction. Said damages shall become the sole and separate property of the recipient, except that, should said recipient remarry at any time following such payment, said damages shall be fully and completely refunded to the party shown to have committed the breach. Said refund shall be due and payable on a date no later than six (6) months following the date of the recipient's remarriage;
>
> (d) Both parties shall cooperate in the negotiation and execution of a reasonable property settlement and support agreement for the resolution of said divorce proceeding so as to minimize the emotional and financial expense of said litigation.

The agreement was drafted by Manuel's attorney, and both Donna and Manuel signed it voluntarily in December 1993. They resumed living together. [¶] In 1998, Manuel again had an affair with another woman. When Donna learned of it, she confronted Manuel, who denied it. Donna obtained independent verification from a witness who saw Manuel kissing this other woman. The parties separated in August 1998, and thereafter divorced. [¶] Donna then brought this action for breach of contract in February 2000, seeking to enforce the liquidated damages clause of the agreement. On the first day of trial, the trial court, on its own motion, granted a judgment on the pleadings in favor of Manuel. Donna appeals from the judgment.

The only question before this court is whether the agreement is enforceable. The trial court found that it was not because it was contrary to the public policy underlying California's no-fault divorce laws. That reasoning is sound.

In 1969, California enacted [legislation authorizing] dissolution of marriage based on irreconcilable differences which have caused the irremediable breakdown of the marriage. This change was explained in *Marriage of Walton* (1972) 28 Cal. App. 3d 108, 119 [104 Cal. Rptr. 472]: "After thorough study, the Legislature, for reasons of social policy deemed compelling, has seen fit to change the grounds for termination of marriage from a fault basis to a marriage breakdown basis."

With certain exceptions (such as child custody matters or restraining orders), "evidence of specific acts of misconduct is improper and inadmissible" in a pleading or proceeding for dissolution of marriage. Fault is simply not a relevant consideration in the legal process by which a marriage is dissolved. Recovery in no-fault dissolution proceedings "is basically limited to half the community property and appropriate support and attorney fee orders — no hefty premiums for emotional angst." (*Askew v. Askew*, 28 Cal. Rptr. 2d 284 (1994).)

Contrary to the public policy underlying California's no-fault divorce laws, the agreement between Donna and Manuel attempts to impose just such a premium for the "emotional angst" caused by Manuel's breach of his promise of sexual fidelity. . . . [¶] The family law court may not look to fault in dissolving the marriage, dividing property, or ordering support. Yet this agreement attempts to penalize the party who is at fault for having breached the obligation of sexual fidelity, and whose breach provided the basis for terminating the marriage. This penalty is in direct contravention of the public policy underlying no-fault divorce.

To be enforceable, a contract must have a "lawful object." (Civ. Code, § 1550, subd. 3.) A contract is unlawful if it is contrary to an express provision of law, contrary to the policy of express law, or otherwise contrary to good morals. (Civ. Code, § 1667.) Here, where the agreement attempts to impose a penalty on one of the parties as a result of that party's "fault" during the marriage, it is contrary to the public policy underlying the no-fault provisions for dissolution of marriage. For that reason, the agreement is unenforceable.

Donna claims a different result is required, by [*Marriage of Bonds.*] [¶] In *Bonds*, the court addressed the enforceability of a premarital agreement. . . . [¶] What is informative in *Bonds* is the distinction the court drew between the freedom of contract found in ordinary commercial contracts and the existence of limitations in marital agreements. The court recognized that "marriage itself is a highly regulated institution of undisputed social value, and there are many limitations on the ability of persons to contract with respect to it, or to vary its statutory terms, that have nothing to do with maximizing the satisfaction of the parties or carrying out their intent. . . . These limitations demonstrate further that freedom of contract with respect to marital arrangements is tempered with statutory requirements and case law expressing social policy with respect to marriage." *Bonds* does not support Donna's position.

Judgment on the pleadings was properly granted in this case. [¶] The judgment is affirmed.

HASTINGS, J., and CURRY, J., concurred.

NOTES AND QUESTIONS

1. *Can a Premarital Agreement Establish Fault Standards for Alimony and Property?* *Diosdado* was followed in *Marriage of Dargan*, 13 Cal. Rptr. 3d 522 (App. 2004), which held unenforceable the husband's agreement to grant the wife his interest in specified items of community property if he used drugs. The position taken in *Diosdado* is also consistent with *Atkinson v. Evans*, 787 A.2d 1033 (Pa. Super. 2001), in which the parties separated after 21 years of marriage when the husband discovered the wife's affair with Evans. They then reconciled, pursuant to an agreement under which the wife promised to terminate her relationship with Evans and to not engage "in any other adulterous relationship." When her affair with Evans apparently later resumed, the husband brought an action against him for interference with a contractual relationship — claiming Evans had induced the wife to break her agreement. The court sustained a general demurrer, viewing the claim as an attempted end-run around the state's abolition of the tort of alienation of affections. These cases are also consistent with § 7.08 of the *ALI Principles*, which states:

> A term in an agreement is not enforceable if
>
> (1) it limits or enlarges the grounds for divorce otherwise available under state law;
>
> (2) it would require or forbid a court to evaluate marital conduct in allocating marital property or awarding compensatory payments, except as the term incorporates principles of state law that so provide; or
>
> (3) by its terms, it penalizes a party for initiating the legal action leading to a decree of divorce or legal separation.

The *Principles* go on to explain:

> . . . While there have been significant changes during the second half of the 20th century in the state law governing the grounds for divorce, there has been little change in the principle that this law reflects a fundamental policy choice not subject to alteration by the parties. The rationale for this principle may be somewhat different under modern no-fault statutes than it was under the older fault-oriented divorce laws. Classic fault-based divorce laws did not accept mutual consent as a ground for divorce, and it is nearly tautological to observe that it would be inconsistent with this policy to permit parties to avoid it by agreement. Modern no-fault divorce laws reflect, among other things, a policy of limiting the role of legal institutions in monitoring and policing the details of intimate relationships, and it would defeat that purpose if parties were permitted, by their own agreement, to require courts to decide if either of them was at fault for their relationship's decline.
>
> In principle, a state could adopt laws that allowed parties to choose, at the time of their marriage, the rules that would govern its potential dissolution. This section neither endorses nor opposes this possibility.

Parties may agree to any set of rules permitted by state law. Historically, however, state law has offered no such choice, and even recent legislative proposals contemplate a choice between only two alternatives. This section reflects the view that such state-law rules articulate public-policy choices binding upon individual parties. In the United States, the state has always been the exclusive source of the legal rules by which the status of marriage is created and dissolved.

By contrast, consider the case of *Penhallow v. Penhallow*, 649 A.2d 1016 (R.I. 1994), in which the parties' agreement made the financial consequence of divorce turn upon which party first filed: Susan would keep half John's property if he divorced her, but not if she divorced him. He was 78, and she 50, at the time of their marriage. About four years after their marriage, the parties had a conflict, the details of which were not resolved by the court, but which led to the husband being served with a "protection from abuse" order requiring him to leave the marital home. The following month he petitioned for divorce. He claimed that their dispute arose from the wife's refusal to return his bankbooks, which she had taken without his consent; the wife claimed it arose from the husband's spending "excessive" amounts of time with a younger woman who was a tenant on his farm. The court held the agreement enforceable under Rhode Island's recently adopted version of the UPAA, but remanded to the lower court for a determination of whether the wife's having filed for the order of protection was in effect an initiation of a divorce under the agreement. On remand, the trial court held it was, and this interpretation was affirmed on appeal, *Penhallow v. Penhallow*, 725 A.2d 896 (1998), thus denying the wife any share of the property. The court's willingness to enforce the agreement under these facts seems surprising, but the court apparently felt compelled to reach this result under the governing statute. The Rhode Island legislature had altered the UPAA in several respects before adopting it, and all of its changes had the effect of making it more difficult to deny enforcement of a premarital agreement.

The court's interpretation of the agreement is more difficult to explain. The wife argued that since she was not the one to file the divorce complaint, she did not "initiate" the divorce within the meaning of the agreement, but the court gave a different meaning to the term "initiate," apparently treating it as a synonym for "precipitate." The issue, then, as the court read the agreement, was which spouse's conduct was the cause of the divorce. Or at least that would appear to be the court's construction, although it never addressed this point explicitly. It relied instead on the trial court's resolution of the question on remand, which in turn emphasized the wife's poor impression as witness. The case may perhaps be best offered as a fine example of why most states abolished fault divorce law in the first place. *Penhallow* is explicitly rejected by the *ALI Principles*, which observe in Comment c of § 7.08: "A provision that by its terms disfavors a party because that party initiates the divorce action . . . effectively imposes a penalty upon a party's invocation of the state's rules governing the availability of divorce. The imposition of such a burden restricts the legally available grounds for divorce and violates the policy underlying § 7.08(1). It is therefore barred by [§ 7.08(3)]."

As will be discussed in Section A[4] below, some interpretations of Islamic *Mahr* premarital agreements condition payments on party fault. In *Akileh v. Elchahal*, 666 So. 2d 246 (Fla. App. 1996), the question was whether the $50,000 *Mahr* payment was forfeited if the wife sought the divorce (as the husband believed) or only if she had been sexually unfaithful (as the wife believed). Both parties thus believed that the agreement incorporated some form of fault standard for determining whether the wife would collect the *mahr*; they simply differed on what that standard was. Florida is a no-fault state that does not normally consider marital misconduct in the allocation of property or the awarding of alimony, *Heilman v. Heilman*, 610 So. 2d 60 (Fla. App. 1992), but it enforced the *mahr* (sustaining the wife's interpretation of it). While Rhode Island law allows the court to consider the parties' conduct, its state supreme court has not encouraged placing much weight on fault considerations, see *Rochefort v. Rochefort*, 494 A.2d 92 (R.I. 1985) and *Fisk v. Fisk*, 477 A.2d 956 (R.I. 1984). Thus, both Florida and Rhode Island seem to accept agreements, at least in some circumstances, that are likely to alter the way in which fault considerations would otherwise affect the outcome under their state law.

At least one author has urged judicial recognition of this kind of agreement. *See* Theodore Haas, *The Rationality and Enforceability of Contractual Restrictions on Divorce*, 66 N. Car. L. Rev. 879 (1988); *see also* Jeffrey Evans Stake, *Mandatory Planning for Divorce*, 45 Vand. L. Rev. 397, 431–32 (1992), who would require parties to enter premarital agreement and recognizing that some might choose to include fault terms, and Elizabeth Scott, *Rational Decisionmaking About Marriage and Divorce*, 76 Va. L. Rev. 9 (1990), who offers a precommitment approach she believes will aid marital stability. Stake develops his views further in Eric Rasmussen and Jeffrey Evans Stake, *Lifting the Veil of Ignorance: Personalizing the Marriage Contract*, 73 Indiana L.J. 453 (1998).

Would you urge an agreement of the form that the *Akileh* wife thought she had? How would that agreement apply to the case in which both spouses had committed adultery? In short, are fault terms imposed by contract any less problematic than those imposed by law? Another court enforced the parties' agreement that neither could file an action for divorce on any grounds other than 18 months' continuous separation. *Massar v. Massar*, 652 A.2d 219 (N.J. App. Div., 1994). While New Jersey has both no-fault and fault grounds, in this case the wife's petition for divorce on grounds of extreme cruelty was dismissed as violative of the agreement.

2. *Terms Affecting Children.* The traditional rule is that a contract between prospective spouses cannot bind a court in deciding child support or child custody matters. Section 3(b) of the UPAA seems to continue this restriction with respect to child support. Arguably, however, the UPAA restriction operates in one direction only, and would not bar enforcement of a provision enlarging support, as, *e.g.*, by obliging a parent to support a child in college where the governing state law would not otherwise impose that duty. As to custody, the UPAA is silent. Custody is omitted from § 3's list of specific items that the agreement may address, but neither is it specifically barred by any other provision analogous to § 3(b)'s bar of any provision adversely affecting the right to child support. The question for a court in a UPAA state would therefore be whether a custody provision violated "public policy" under § 3(a)(8). Long tradition in the domestic relations area would seem to ensure, however, that courts would not consider themselves bound by custody provisions they believed injurious to the child's interest. The law of separation agreements in every state is explicit on that point, and there is no reason why premarital agreements would be treated differently. *See Combs v.*

Sherry-Combs, 865 P.2d 50 (Wyo. 1993) (provision in agreement executed one month after parties' marriage, providing that "any progeny resulting from this union, should this contract be terminated, shall remain in the custody of the parent of that progeny's sex," is not enforceable because state law forbids basing custody determinations solely on the gender of the parent).

Arbitration of support or custody disputes is arguably a different matter, and comes up more often in the context of separation agreements than with premarital agreements. *See* Section B[5] below. On one hand, one line of cases, exemplified by *Kelm v. Kelm*, 623 N.E.2d 39 (Ohio 1993), favors such agreements. *See* Annot., *Validity and Construction of Provisions for Arbitration of Disputes As to Alimony or Support Payments or Child Visitation or Custody Matters*, 38 A.L.R.5th 69 (1993). On the other hand, courts typically indicate some reservation of power to override the arbitrator's award where the interest of the child so requires, as *Kelm* also appears to do. Such a rule is inconsistent, however, with the usual understanding of arbitration, under which courts have no authority at all to reexamine the merits of the arbitrator's decision. Judicial review of arbitration is ordinarily limited to fundamental challenges to the arbitrator's authority, rather than to the substance of the decision — to matters such as whether the issue in question was in fact within the scope of the arbitration agreement, or whether the arbitrator's decision was based upon a bribe. This tension between recognition of the merits of arbitration, and the desire to preserve in the court some residual authority to protect the child's interest, remains largely unresolved. For recent commentary on this topic, see E. Gary Spitko, *Reclaiming the "Creatures of the State": Contracting for Child Custody Decisionmaking in the Best Interests of the Family*, 57 WASH. & LEE L. REV. 1139 (2000).

[4]   Religious Premarital Agreements

There is growing caselaw regarding two kinds of premarital agreements grounded in religious traditions: the Jewish *Ketubah* and the Islamic *Mahr.*

1. Ketubah: Within Orthodox Judaism, for a divorce to be effective, the husband must give the wife a religious divorce document ("*get*"). Without that document, she is not free under religious law to marry again (and any children of a subsequent civil marriage would be considered illegitimate within her religious community). Because only the husband can obtain the *get*, he has significant leverage in negotiating separation agreements (e.g., threatening to withhold the *get* unless his demands regarding property, alimony, or custody are met). The Jewish marriage contract, the *Ketubah*, contains a variety of promises, often including financial obligations. In recent decades, it has also often included promises by the groom to provide a *get* when seeking a civil divorce, or promises to go to religious arbitration, where such provision would be ordered.

The New York legislature has been active (with the cooperation of the local Orthodox Jewish community) in creating rules that might make divorce outcomes in the Orthodox Jewish community more fair. Under NEW YORK DOM. REL. § 253, those seeking a (civil) divorce or civil annulment must allege they have taken all steps solely in their power to remove barriers to partner's remarriage. This statute works if it is the husband who is seeking the divorce. To cover cases where the wife is seeking the divorce, NEW YORK DOM. REL. § 236 Part B(5)(h) allows courts to impose financial penalties on a spouse who has not removed barriers to a religious divorce. (Both statutes are couched in neutral terms, but clearly are targeted at Orthodox Jewish men.)

This sort of state intervention seems to raise obvious first amendment issues. However, the issue has not been frequently litigated. The New York courts have upheld judicial enforcement of terms of a religious premarital agreement (even if they involve requiring the parties to go to a religious arbitration entity). *Avitzur v. Avitzur*, 446 N.E.2d 136 (N.Y. 1983) (holding enforceable *ketubah* term requiring parties to appear before religious tribunal and accept its decision regarding a religious divorce). A New Jersey court came out the other way. *Aflalo v. Aflalo*, 685 A.2d 523 (N.J. Super. Ch. 1996) (holding that first amendment forbids any order to obtain a *get* or to appear before a religious tribunal). On the issue, see generally Kent Greenawalt, *Religious Law and Civil Law: Using Secular Law to Assure Observance of Practice with Religious Significance*, 71 S. CAL. L. REV. 781 (1998).

2. Mahr. The Islamic *Mahr* (also sometimes called "*sadaq*"), a kind of premarital agreement, involves the promise of payment of a certain sum to the wife. A small payment is usually made to the wife prior to the marriage with a much larger payment due after the termination of the marriage. One interpretation appears to be that this post-marriage payment should be above and beyond the civil law division of property; however, a different view argues that the *Mahr* payment is in lieu of any division of property. *E.g.*, *Chaudry v. Chaudry*, 388 A.2d 1000 (N.J. Super. Ct. App. Div. 1978) (*Mahr* interpreted as supplanting any other financial claims the wife has against the husband on divorce). This second interpretation, where accepted, could leave divorced wives significantly impoverished. (As discussed elsewhere in the chapter, courts already, as a matter of course, refuse to enforce premarital agreements to the extent that the financial terms will leave one spouse on state benefit.) There are also questions regarding what actions on the wife's part will lead to a forfeit of her *Mahr* payments. Some Islamic experts argue that the payment is forfeited if the wife initiates divorce, see *Dajani v. Dajani*, 204 Cal. App. 3d 1387, 1389, 151 Cal. Rptr. 871, 872 (1988). Others argue that the forfeit only occurs if the wife is at fault for the breakdown of the marriage. Recall *Akileh v. Elchahal*, 666 So. 2d 246 (Fla. App. 1996), discussed in Section A[3] above, in which the court was faced with two interpretations — that a $50,000 *Mahr* payment was forfeited if the wife sought the divorce (as the husband believed) or only if she had been sexually unfaithful (as the wife believed); the court sided with the wife's interpretation.

American courts have been inconsistent in their treatment of *Mahr*, and there have only been a handful of reported cases. Whether enforcing such agreements or refusing enforcement, the court analysis is usually under the usual criteria applied to premarital agreements. *E.g.*, *Aziz v. Aziz*, 488 N.Y.S.2d 123 (N.Y. Sup. Ct. 1985) (enforcing deferred *Mahr* payment of $5,000); *Odatalla v. Odatalla*, 810 A.2d 93 (N.J. Super. Ch. 2002) (enforcing *Mahr* of $10,000 delayed payment as enforceable premarital agreement); *Zawahiri v. Alwattar*, 2008 Ohio App. LEXIS 2928 (July 10, 2008) (refusing enforcement, based on the criteria for when premarital agreements are enforceable). *But see Ahmed v. Ahmed*, 261 S.W.3d 190 (Tex. App. 2008) (*Mahr* agreement should not be treated as premarital agreement, because it was part of a religious marriage ceremony that was entered six months after a civil marriage ceremony); *Mir v. Birjandi*, 2007 Ohio App. LEXIS 5517 (Nov. 21, 2007) (refusing to enforce a *Mahr* provision, in part because it was a religious provision, not a legal one; and in part because the provision was said not to have met the general requirements for enforceable premarital agreements).

On the issue generally, see, e.g., Lindsey Blenkhorn, Note, *Islamic Marriage Contracts in American Courts: Interpreting Mahr Agreements as Prenuptials and Their Effect on Moslem Women*, 76 S. Cal. L. Rev. 189 (2002); Ghada G. Qaisi, *Religious Marriage Contracts: Judicial Enforcement of Mahr Agreements in American Courts*, 15 J. L. & Religion 67 (2001).

[5]   Marital Agreements

Marital agreements (also called "postnuptial agreements" or "post-marital agreements") are agreements that fall (both chronologically and doctrinally) in between premarital agreements and separation agreements. They are agreements entered when the parties are already married (unlike premarital agreements), but when divorce is not imminent (unlike separation agreements).

The usual narratives of marital agreements tend to be distinctly different from premarital agreements. The relatively sympathetic story is of a "reconciliation agreement," where a marriage is on the brink of ending, and one spouse (usually the party more wronged) is willing to take the other spouse back in return for a promise of more property or alimony should things not work out. The less sympathetic story is analogous to the commercial law "hold up," where a party threatens divorce, mid-marriage, without any justification, unless he or she is promised more property or alimony. Thus, marital agreements pose the same problems for legislative or judicial regulation that commercial modification cases do: distinguishing good faith arrangements from bad faith coercion. If the main issues for premarital agreements are one-sided terms and unforeseen developments, the main issue for marital agreements is duress.

The authorities are divided on whether marital and premarital agreements should be governed by the same rules. Eleven states (Alabama, Florida, Hawaii, Indiana, Kentucky, Missouri, Pennsylvania, Utah, West Virginia, Washington, and Wisconsin) appear to apply the same rules to marital agreements as they do to premarital agreements — e.g., Wisconsin Statutes § 766.58; *Tibbs v. Anderson*, 580 So.2d 1337, 1339 (Ala. 1991); Stoner v. Stoner, 819 A.2d 529, 533 n.5 (Pa. 2003) — and the *ALI Principles* take the same position. American Law Institute, *Principles of the Law of Family Dissolution*, § 7.04(4). However, *The Principles* suggests that the unconscionability doctrine is more likely to have application in the context of marital agreements, while if premarital agreements are problematic it is more likely to be because of circumstances at the time of enforcement that the parties could not anticipate at the time of execution. *See ALI Principles*, § 7.01, Comment *e.* (British law, by contrast, appears to treat marital agreements more sympathetically than premarital agreements, as a variation of separation agreements, arguing that those desiring to marry might have their judgment clouded by that desire and give up their rights in a premarital agreement, while a spouse entering a marital agreement is seen as "a grown up and able to look after him — or herself." *MacLeod v. MacLeod* [2008] UKPC 64.)

Approximately half the American states still have no case-law or statutory language setting the standards for marital agreements. The remaining states have in some way distinguished the rules for marital agreements from the rules for premarital agreements. For example, under Minnesota law, marital agreements must meet certain requirements not imposed on premarital agreements: Each party must be represented by separate legal counsel, and an agreement will be presumed unenforceable if either party commences an action for legal separation or divorce within two years of its execution (unless the party seeking enforcement proves that the agreement is "fair and equitable"), MINN. STAT. § 519.11, subd 1a(2)(c), (2)(d). Louisiana requires marital agreements, but not premarital agreements, to be judicially approved, the judge being required to find that the agreement serves both parties' "best interests" and that both understood "the governing rules and principles." LA. CIV. CODE art. 2329. A New Jersey court concluded that it was inappropriate to treat a "mid-marriage" agreement similarly to a premarital agreement because "the dynamics and pressures" are different, and the court required fairness review of such agreements both relative to time of signing and to the time of enforcement. *Pacelli v. Pacelli*, 725 A.2d 56 (N.J. App. Div. 1999) At least one state, Ohio, refuses to enforce marital agreements at all. OHIO REV. CODE § 3103.06.

State courts may also raise consideration issues (with premarital agreements, even one-sided agreements have consideration, because the agreement to marry is the consideration); an agreement to remain married despite serious marital problems can be sufficient consideration in some jurisdictions. State courts seem inclined to enforce agreements when they are convinced that the agreement was motivated by a genuine desire to reconcile, and where the party subsequently seeking enforcement made a good-faith effort to follow through. See, e.g., *Garner v. Garner*, 848 N.Y.S.2d 741 (App. Div. 2007) (enforcing reconciliation agreement, and holding that wife's threat of divorce, after husband confessed adultery and drug addiction, was not duress invalidating agreement; husband had chance to consult independent counsel, and he made changes on some terms of drafted agreement; also, substantive terms were not far from statutory provisions and thus not unconscionable); *In re Marriage of Tabassum, Younis*, 881 N.E.2d 396 (Ill App. 2007) (enforcing reconciliation agreement assigning wife the house as non-marital property, where wife forebore filing for divorce for five months, and made good-faith efforts to make the marriage work, while husband did not); *In re Marriage of Burkle*, 139 Cal. App. 4th 712 (2006) (upholding a reconciliation agreement in a high-asset marriage, and deciding that the state statutory presumption of undue influence in interspousal agreements applies only where the terms were one-sided, which the agreement was not).

However, where one or more of those elements are not present, the agreement will not be enforced. *See, e.g., Grover v. Grover*, 276 S.W.3d 740 (Ark. App. 2008) (applying Florida law, affirming trial court conclusion that reconciliation agreement was one-sided and the product of duress, where husband presented agreement without warning, he threatened divorce if it were not signed, there was little to no financial disclosure relating to the terms, and the wife was not represented). Of course, where one of the parties is not legally competent, and the other party is aware of that, no agreement will be enforced, marital or otherwise. See RESTATEMENT (SECOND) OF CONTRACTS § 15 (lack of competency as defense to enforcement); *Bailey v. Bailey*, 677 S.E.2d 56 (Va. App. 2009) (refusing to enforce marital agreement where husband, a schizoaffective psychotic, on weekend furlough from a psychiatric ward, signed an agreement transferring all marital assets to wife and all marital debts to husband).

For a thoughtful piece that discusses some of the difficulties with contracts between persons already married, see Michael Trebilcock & Steven Elliott, *The Scope and Limits of Legal Paternalism: Altruism and Coercion in Family Financial Arrangements*, in THE THEORY OF CONTRACT LAW (Peter Benson ed., Cambridge University Press, 2001), and for a good overview of marital agreement law, see Sean Hannon Williams, *Postnuptial Agreements*, 2007 WIS. L. REV. 827, which also includes an appendix listing relevant statutes and case-law, *id.* at 881–87.

PROBLEMS

Problem 8-4.   Carol and Doug have been married for six years, and have two children, ages four and two. Doug is a physician earning a substantial income. Carol is an R.N. She works occasionally in order to maintain her job skills and her license, but has been the children's primary caretaker since the first child's birth. Doug is a doting father, and does all he can to make sure he has time with the children on weekday evenings, and on weekends when he is not out on call. Carol and Doug live in Sweet Lake, a small city near the Rocky Mountains, where Doug completed his medical training. He is affiliated with the University's medical school.

Carol has never liked Sweet Lake, and has long wanted to return to New York, where she grew up and where her family still lives. Her discontent has affected her marriage. Assured of support from her family, optimistic about her job prospects in New York when she is ready to return to work, and interested in renewing her relationship with an old boyfriend there, she tells Doug she intends to divorce him and return there with the children. Doug is devastated, not only about the demise of his marriage, but also about the loss of daily contact with his young children if Carol returns to New York. He consults a lawyer who advises him that, under applicable law, Carol, as the children's primary caretaker, is nearly certain to be awarded primary custody, and is likely to prevail if he were to oppose her relocation to New York with the children. He begs Carol to reconsider.

Carol agrees to remain in Sweet Lake with Doug for at least two more years, if Doug will agree that, if they later divorce, she will receive sixty percent of their marital property, and spousal support for a nonmodifiable term of at least 10 years, calculated on the assumption that she is unavailable for work, and to continue even if she remarries. Desperate to maintain daily contact with his children, and hopeful that in two years' time he can persuade Carol to remain in the marriage, Doug agrees. After two years, Carol files for divorce and seeks primary custody of the children, and their relocation, with her, to New York. Due to a current shortage of R.N.s, well-paying jobs with flexible hours are in fact available to Carol in N.Y., and under applicable law she would therefore receive a relatively small support award for a short term, which would end if she remarried. Carol, however, seeks enforcement of the parties' agreement: (a) a guaranteed 10-year term of compensatory payments, even if she remarries, and calculated on the basis that she has no income, even if she chooses to work; and (b) 60 percent of the parties' marital property, rather than the half she would receive under otherwise applicable law.

Should their agreement be enforced? Would it be enforced in California? In a jurisdiction following the *ALI Principles*? Does it matter that it is a marital rather than premarital agreement? How?

Problem 8-5. Susan Rose consults you for advice on a premarital agreement. She is an Orthodox Jew planning to marry. Her intended husband, David, is also Jewish but has not heretofore been completely faithful to traditional practices. He has agreed, however, to conduct himself according to Jewish law from now on. While satisfied of his sincerity, she seeks some assurance in a premarital agreement. Two points are especially important to her. The first is that their children be raised according to traditional Orthodox practice. She has no concern about their training during the marriage, since she will be the primary caretaker of the children, but wants to guarantee that if the marriage should end by divorce, or her death, that any children be raised in an Orthodox Jewish home. The second point concerns the authority of the Beth Din, or Jewish religious tribunal, over their marriage. In particular, she wants to be certain that if she and David did obtain a civil divorce, he would cooperate in also appearing before the Beth Din, so that she would be eligible to remarry under Jewish law as well.

What do you advise? How would you prepare an appropriate agreement?

Problem 8-6. Richard comes to consult you about a premarital agreement. He is 38-years-old, and a successful businessman. This is his second marriage. His first ended in divorce after seven years, when his wife left him for another man. He is still bitter, especially because the divorce court gave his first wife a major share of his business, allowing her and her new husband to live well as a result of his efforts. It rankles him that, as he sees it, she was allowed to profit by her adultery, even though he was faithful. He is determined to avoid a repetition of that experience.

He has heard that it is possible to agree in advance that his wife would not share in his property. While such an agreement is acceptable to him, it goes further than he would demand. If the marriage is successful, as he expects it to be, he would be happy for her to share in his financial successes. What he wants to be certain of, however, is that if his wife commits adultery, he can divorce her without paying her either alimony or a share in the property he is able to accumulate during their marriage. He is quite willing for the agreement to be reciprocal, although it is not clear to him how that would work, since she has relatively little prospect to earn significant sums herself. He suggests he might agree to pay her a liquidated sum, such as $200,000, in the event that he commits adultery.

He has mentioned the possibility of a premarital agreement to his fiancée once, in a general way. While they discussed it only briefly then, he had the feeling that she was not happy about it. He did not discuss particular terms with her. He has no children by his first marriage, and is not expecting any to result from this one.

What do you advise? Does it matter if you are in a community property state or common law property state? Does it matter if this is a state that allows fault to be taken into account when dividing property?

B. SEPARATION AGREEMENTS

The sense that courts and lawyers ought to promote settlement certainly transcends the field of divorce. One set of reasons typically given for preferring settlement focuses on the parties: settlement is said to give them more satisfaction than litigated outcomes, is more responsive to their needs, saves them time and money, and spares them from unwanted risk and emotional stress. Settlement is also said to yield outcomes that are superior because they are based upon superior knowledge of the parties' preferences, involve compromise (which is assumed to be superior), can be based upon a wider range of norms than permitted in litigation, can be more flexible and inventive in the solutions adopted, and are more likely to be complied with by the parties. Settlement is said to promote judicial efficiency, and even to change the parties for the better. Whether settlement in fact achieves all or any of these objectives may not be as certain as one might think, nor is the available evidence entirely favorable to settlement. *See* Marc Galanter & Mia Cahill, *"Most Cases Settle": Judicial Promotion and Regulation of Settlements*, 46 STAN. L. REV. 1339 (1994). But a full exploration of the settlement literature is beyond our charge. Most divorces, like most other lawsuits, are in fact resolved by a settlement agreement negotiated by the parties and their lawyers. In this section we examine that process as it operates in divorce, and consider as well alternative methods of achieving settlement — primarily, mediation.

[1]   Achieving an Agreement

[a]   The Traditional Bargaining Process

[i]   Factors Influencing Whether a Case is Settled

The vast majority of civil litigation results in settlement, even if the actual rates are far below the 90% or 95% often quoted. Theodore Eisenberg & Charlotte Lanvers, *What is the Settlement Rate and Why Should We Care?*, 6 J. EMPIRICAL LEG. STUD. 111 (2009) (showing settlement rates for civil litigation in two federal district courts to be 71.6% and 57.8%, with rates varying across types of civil litigation). Divorcing spouses generally expect to settle. Parties in one study of Wisconsin divorces "spent very little time weighing the costs of litigation against settlement because most — even those who were most reluctant — viewed settlement as the better solution." Marygold S. Melli, Howard S. Erlanger & Elizabeth Chambliss, *The Process of Negotiation: An Exploratory Investigation in the Context of No-Fault Divorce*, 40 RUTGERS L. REV. 1133, 1143 (1988). This expectation of settlement is shared by the lawyers as much as by the divorcing spouses themselves. Contrary to the claims one sometimes hears, lawyers usually push their clients toward settlement, not toward litigation. A study of 115 divorce cases in California and Massachusetts concluded: "Although some of our lawyers occasionally advised clients to ask for more than the client had originally contemplated or to refuse to concede on a major issue when the client was inclined to do so, most seemed to believe that it is generally better to settle than contest divorce disputes." Austin Sarat & William L. F. Felstiner, *Law and Strategy in the Divorce Lawyer's Office*, 20 Law & Soc'y Rev. 93, 109 (1986). Studies of British and Dutch lawyers reached the same conclusion. Richard Ingleby, *The Solicitor as Intermediary*, in R. Dingwall & J. Eekalaar, Divorce Mediation and the Legal Process 43, 44–45 (1988); John Griffiths, *What Do Dutch Lawyers Actually Do in Divorce Cases?*, 20 Law & Soc'y Rev. 135, 154 (1986).

Sarat and Felstiner describe in detail the lawyer-client discussions in one "typical" case. The client-wife felt keenly that an injustice had been done by the judge who granted her husband's *ex parte* request for an order restraining her from entering the marital home, and for that reason wanted to fight. Her lawyer agreed that the order was wrong, but urged her to focus on negotiating a favorable property settlement. He believed that contesting the restraining order would be unduly costly, and would interfere with the negotiations, and thus would not be in her interest, especially as she had already agreed to allow her husband to buy out her share in the home. Much of the discussion between the wife and her lawyer involved his efforts gently to bring her around to this view, while agreeing with her that the restraining order was indeed unjust. The lawyer, focusing on the practical and the long-term, pushed negotiation on a client who was reluctant because she was focusing on gaining vindication in a symbolic matter of short-term interest. The lawyer pushed settlement, even though he liked trial work, and went into a divorce practice in part because of the trial opportunities it offered. At one point in the discussions, he invoked the advice of the client's therapist in support of his advice to settle. *Id.* at 111–13. Sarat and Felstiner conclude that "it is clear that this lawyer, and most of those we observed, construct an image of the appropriate mode of disposition . . . that is at odds with the conventional view in which lawyers are alleged to induce competition and hostility, transform noncontentious clients into combatants, and promulgate a 'fight theory of justice.' " *Id.* at 113.

Why do lawyers prefer to settle divorce cases? Ingleby suggests that lawyers appreciate the fact that in divorce cases, goodwill and cooperation are necessary to perform the agreement, creating an advantage for non-adversarial bargaining over confrontational strategies. Ingleby, *supra*, at 47. He reports that a main thread in the reasoning of solicitors is the belief that the parties are more likely to observe an agreement they made themselves than a court-ordered one. Ingleby also notes that less contentious cases are less demanding on the lawyer, and that the additional burdens of litigation are not always accompanied by proportionately increased fees. Melli *et al.* note that in divorce, as in other areas, there is pressure from the court to settle, which often becomes explicit in judicial comments made at pretrial conferences. They also found many spouses anxious to settle to avoid the emotional costs associated with prolonging the divorce process, including the burdens they perceived this would impose upon their children. *Id.* at 1156. And of course, one cannot exclude the possibility that lawyers urge settlement at least in part because in most cases they see it as furthering their client's interests, as did the lawyer described above in the Sarat and Felstiner study.

It may be that matrimonial lawyers are more likely to encourage settlement than lawyers in some other fields. Gilson and Mnookin developed a game theory model of litigation that takes account of the fact that it is carried out by lawyer-agents on behalf of their clients, and distinguishes between the client, typically a one-time player in the litigation game, and the lawyer, a repeat player who has the opportunity to establish a reputation for either a cooperative or adversarial style. They show that the ordinary game theory model suggests that disputants in many legal conflicts find themselves in a classic "prisoner's dilemma" in which they have strong incentives to be contentious, but that the introduction of lawyer-agents makes it possible for disputants to overcome this dilemma by "selecting cooperative lawyers whose reputations credibly commit each party to a cooperative strategy." They hypothesize that matrimonial practice, as compared to commercial litigation, might have two structural characteristics that would make such a reputational market for cooperativeness more possible. First, divorce practice may be a non-zero sum game in which gains from cooperation may be more easily achieved. If both spouses care about their children, then arrangements that benefit the children produce gains to both. Because of differences in the parties' preferences, and in the relative values they attach to different assets or activities, value can be created through trades — an opportunity that cannot arise in a commercial dispute in which dollars are the only thing at issue. Second, because family law practice tends to be both localized and specialized, it is more possible than in some other fields for lawyers to develop and sustain reputations for cooperativeness. They also observe that while "the strong emotions attending divorce may pose a formidable barrier to collaborative rational problem solving," that barrier can be overcome by negotiation through lawyer-agents committed to cooperative strategies. Interviews conducted by the authors with California family law specialists seemed to confirm their analysis by suggesting that many lawyers did develop a reputation as cooperative problem solvers, that clients often sought attorneys with such reputations, and that such attorneys often turned away clients who sought a more adversarial approach. Ronald J. Gilson and Robert H. Mnookin, *Disputing Through Agents: Cooperation and Conflict Between Lawyers in Litigation*, 94 COLUM. L. REV. 509 (1994).

Of course, lawyers cannot decide whether a case is settled, or alone decide upon a bargaining strategy. Clients matter too. For an examination of how lawyers and clients manage their relationship in divorce cases, see William L. F. Felstiner & Austin Sarat, *Enactments of Power: Negotiating Reality and Responsibility in Lawyer-Client Interactions*, 77 CORNELL L. REV. 1447 (1992). One study using Mnookin and Maccoby's data set of California divorces involving minor children found three factors that reduced the likelihood a divorce would require adjudication: when the wife had more education, the time between separation and divorce was longer, or the parties owned a home. Settlement was less likely the higher the husband's income and when lawyers were present. Amy Farmer & Jill Tiefenthaler, *The Determinants of Pretrial Settlement*, 21 INT'L REV. L. & ECON. 157 (2001). Note that these correlations do not of course demonstrate cause. *E.g.*, parties who have more assets may be more likely to have lawyers and also more likely to litigate, or parties who are more likely to litigate in any event may for that reason also be more likely to have an attorney.

Just what percentage of divorces settle? Of 349 cases examined by Melli et al., *supra*, only 32 (about 9 percent) went to trial because the parties themselves could not reach agreement on the substantive issues. (Some others went to trial due to third-party objections by state agencies seeking reimbursement for welfare costs, or for other unrelated reasons.) Melli's data cannot tell us precisely why these particular cases did not settle, but she concluded from her interviews that the parties' attitude toward divorce is an important factor. Wisconsin, where she conducted this research, has a pure no-fault law in which irretrievable breakdown is the only ground for divorce, so that one spouse cannot block the other's decision to end the marriage. Apparently, such unilateral breakups are disproportionately represented among the unsettled cases, and the lawyers in her sample felt that this resulted from the inclination of the party who did not want the divorce to fight about whatever there was that could be fought over.

The fact that settlement is the norm does not mean that the legal rules governing divorce are irrelevant, for they obviously influence the negotiating process. Recall from Chapter 6 that encouragement of settlement is one argument made in support of deciding custody disputes by the more predictable primary-caretaker doctrine rather than by the vague best-interests test. This argument reflects the conventional wisdom that parties are more likely to settle when the outcome of litigation is easy to predict, because there is then little point to litigating. Griffiths confirmed this prediction in the Netherlands, where the alimony and child support rules are framed in a way that makes judicial decision highly predictable. Griffiths, *supra*, at 161 n.24. Surely lawyers who see defeat as certain are unlikely to urge their clients to litigate, and confident predictions of defeat are more likely when the decision rules are clear. Yet the American law of support, property division, and custody has historically ceded much to trial judge discretion, which makes outcomes difficult to predict. While the conventional wisdom concludes that this uncertainty reduces the probability of settlement, some argue that extreme unpredictability also creates pressure to settle, at least for risk-averse clients who then view the courtroom as a high-risk enterprise. Griffiths, *id.*, quoting Felstiner & Sarat. The same studies in which Felstiner and Sarat found that lawyers typically urge settlement also found that divorce lawyers frequently emphasize to clients that trial court decisions in divorce are arbitrary and depend more on the particular personnel involved than on any general rules of justice. Sarat & Felstiner, *supra*, and Austin Sarat & William L. F. Felstiner, *Lawyers and Legal Consciousness: Law Talk in the Divorce Lawyer's Office*, 98 YALE L.J. 1663 (1989).

For an excellent and more recent study, see LYNN MATHER, CRAIG MCEWEN, AND RICHARD MAIMAN, DIVORCE LAWYERS AT WORK: VARIETIES OF PROFESSIONALISM IN PRACTICE (2001).

[ii]   Factors Influencing the Terms of a Settlement

If the parties are more likely to settle when the legal rules are clear, it is because they have those rules in mind during the negotiations. The classic study of the effect of legal rules on negotiations is Robert H. Mnookin & Lewis Kornhauser, *Bargaining in the Shadow of the Law: The Case of Divorce*, 88 YALE L.J. 950 (1979), on which portions of this note are based. They point out (among other things) that rules that would favor a party at trial also give that party leverage during negotiations. But the relevant legal doctrine consists of more than the rules establishing each party's entitlements. On one hand, while the rules of property division, child support, and alimony are doctrinally separate, in many cases they will be at least partly fungible. Financially all can be reduced to a present value, and if there are not items of property that have important noneconomic value to one or the other spouse, then the labels property, child support, and alimony are merely names for essentially one thing: money. Of course, the parties' relative preference between money now (lump sum) and money later (as in payments over time) may differ, creating the possibility for trade-offs. Moreover, legal doctrine may be important in calculating how much money a particular award is really worth. For example, alimony is less valuable to the recipient than child support because it is taxable. If it is labeled alimony, it will probably terminate when the recipient remarries or becomes employable, while child support will last until the children reach majority. In part, negotiating a separation agreement will involve manipulating these labels to obtain an overall package that appeals to both parties, and some arrangements may produce more total value for the spouses (and less for the government). But to the extent the negotiations focus on maximizing each party's financial outcome, they are in principle no different than the negotiation of commercial disputes. The lawyer's skills can help to enlarge the pot, and to advise clients on how much of it they are likely to obtain in a contested proceeding.

As observed in the preceding section of this note, however, parties to a divorce are more likely than parties to a commercial dispute to have negotiating goals other than the maximization of financial gain. The sample case from Sarat and Felstiner illustrates one way in which symbolic or emotional issues peculiar to divorce may compete with purely financial motivations. Melli provides another example. One client told her "50 lawyers could tell me to go after more money and I wouldn't have. I just didn't want to buck [my husband]. . . . I just wanted it over." Melli et al., at 1156.

A variety of emotional attitudes can affect the negotiated terms substantially. Some spouses are driven to settle for less than they might otherwise have gotten because they feel guilty about ending the marriage, because they are genuinely concerned about their former spouse's welfare, because they simply want to "put this behind" them, or because they hope that amiability in the bargaining process may trigger a desired settlement. Others are driven to hard bargaining because they want to punish the other spouse for walking out on the marriage, because they want to protect the financial standing of the children, or because they believe that hard bargaining may force the other spouse to give up and return to the marriage. And of course, some have multiple emotions that push them in opposite directions.

Data that Melli gathered in a small sample of cases also suggest the importance of spousal attitudes toward the divorce. Examining cases involving minor children, she and her co-investigators looked at the amount of child support called for in the agreement, calculated as a percentage of the obligor's total income. From their interviews with clients and their lawyers, they also classified the parties' attitude as "impatient" to end the marriage, "reluctant" to end the marriage, or "accepting" of the marital termination. They found that "reluctant" obligors agreed to pay an average of 19% of their income in support, "accepting" obligors 24%, and "impatient" obligors 29%. The differences were even more striking when payments were classified according to the attitude of the obligee. Reluctant obligees received an average of 30% of the obligor's income in child support, accepting obligees 24%, and impatient obligees 19%. These data do not mean that legally relevant financial factors have no importance in the negotiation of support awards. To the contrary, Melli also found that 50 percent of the variation among cases in the amount of child support was accounted for by three clearly relevant factors: the number of children, the income of the obligor, and the couple's estimated net worth. Attitude toward divorce was an important additional factor that influenced the settlement amount when the parties negotiated, but it did not supplant these other factors.[1]

We have thus far focused exclusively on financial issues, but of course there is also often the question of child custody, which complicates the analysis considerably. The parts of the financial package are all fungible, but potential tradeoffs between money and custody are more difficult to evaluate. For many, obtaining primary custody will have overriding importance, so that the financial terms will be minor in comparison. Others, however, do not even want primary custody, and a few may even be indifferent to their visitation rights. A party indifferent to his custody rights may still use it as a bargaining lever; if the other parent has a strong preference for custody, the indifferent parent can threaten to contest it unless the other parent agrees to unfavorable financial terms. This kind of strategy has no ready analog in a commercial dispute in which money is the only issue, for the parties are not going to value money differently from one another, in the way that divorcing spouses may attach different values to custody.

This potential interaction between custody and the financial issues is, of course, affected by the jurisdiction's rule for deciding custody disputes. Consider that a party less willing than the other to risk litigation is at a bargaining disadvantage in settlement negotiations. This bargaining handicap is appropriately imposed upon a party who resists litigation because she is likely to lose under prevailing legal rules: that party settles for a "bad deal" in the negotiations because it is all she is entitled to under the law. But rules of divorce may lead a party to avoid litigation for other reasons that yield less defensible results. The outcome of custody disputes decided under a best-interests standard that invests the trial court with considerable discretion may be difficult to predict for even competent, experienced attorneys. In that case lawyers will advise their clients that custody litigation is chancy (as well as unpleasant or worse). Mnookin and Kornhauser point out that this advice gives the bargaining advantage to the parent more willing than the other to risk the litigation "lottery" as well as emotional stress and harm to the child. This is not necessarily the parent that a sensibly designed policy would favor. And as Solomon knew, the parent more anxious to spare his children the trauma of custody litigation is then put at a bargaining disadvantage — and may therefore agree to unfavorable financial terms in return for an agreement on custody. There are thus a variety of reasons why parties may settle on terms that appear unfair, and that is one reason why § 306 of the M.M.D.A., as the law of most states, requires some

---

[1] The small size of Melli's sample also counsels caution in interpreting her results. A temporary support order had been issued in one-third of the cases Melli examined, and in those cases it was a very important additional factor. In four of five such cases, the parties settled on exactly the same amount as that contained in the temporary order. Of course, the temporary order itself might have been the result of stipulation — of an agreement between the parties.

form of judicial review of separation agreements before they become incorporated in the divorce decree.

Is another solution to bar settlement agreement involving custody tradeoffs? Should a party be able to avoid an unfavorable financial settlement by showing that she agreed to it only to avoid such a custody contest? We address this question in Section B[2] below. We first complete this section, however, by examining a method for reaching an agreement that is an alternative to the traditional process of negotiations between lawyers: mediation.

[b]   Mediation as a Means of Achieving Agreement

Within the last generation, much attention has been paid to mediation as a route to agreement. "Mediation is a process in which an impartial third party — a mediator — facilitates the resolution of a dispute by promoting voluntary agreement (or 'self-determination') by the parties to the dispute." AMERICAN ARBITRATION ASSOCIATION, SOCIETY OF PROFESSIONALS IN DISPUTE RESOLUTION, AND THE AMERICAN BAR ASSOCIATION, THE STANDARDS OF CONDUCT FOR MEDIATORS 1 (1996). In contrast to an arbitrator, who decides for the parties, the mediator facilitates dispute settlement by the parties. It has been described as a "solution to overcrowded dockets and a way to rid judges of unsavory divorce cases. Moreover, . . . proponents tell divorce lawyers that mediation offers a 'better way' of resolving divorce disputes. In contrast with traditional lawyer representation, the informality of mediation, they explain, honors client autonomy and family privacy, preserves post-divorce family relationships, fosters greater compliance with final decrees, and permits idiosyncratic agreements unconstrained by the insensitive dictates of formal law." Penelope E. Bryan, *Reclaiming Professionalism: The Lawyer's Role in Divorce Mediation*, 28 FAM. L.Q. 177 (1994). For more on why some believe that meditation has important advantages over traditional negotiation, see Loeb, *New Forms of Resolving Disputes — ADR*, 33 FAM. L.Q. 581 (1999); Robert A. B. Bush, *"What Do We Need a Mediator For?": Mediation's "Value-Added" for Negotiators*, 12 OHIO ST. J. ON DISP. RES. 1 (1996).

In recent years, many mediation programs have been created through court-affiliated conciliation courts, which originally sought to reunite couples (see Chapter 3). Additionally, many private mediation centers have been created and a number of mediators have established practices on their own. A 1989 survey reported "divorce mediation has been implemented in one form or another in 36 states and the District of Columbia, with more than 120 programs operating in the states." S. Myers et al., *Court-sponsored Mediation of Divorce, Custody, Visitation, and Support: Resolving Policy Issues*, 13 STATE CT. J. 24 (Winter 1989); *but see* Carol J. King, *Burdening Access to Justice: The Cost of Divorce Mediation on the Cheap*, 73 ST. JOHN'S L. REV. 375 (1999) (arguing mandatory "party-paid . . . mediation presents jurisprudential as well as policy problems concerning fair access to justice which outweigh the benefit").

What does mediation look like?

> . . . [T]here are tremendous variations in the ways that the mediation process takes place . . . There may be one mediator, or a pair of co-mediators, or even a group of mediators who work together as a

panel. . . . The makeup of the mediation team may also neutralize potential power imbalances by providing specific gender, ethnicity, or other diverse representation. The mediators may meet alone with the disputants one at a time, or may never speak separately with any disputant. The process may be highly structured, or completely fluid. The mediators may truly leave the outcome in the parties' hands, or may take a strong role in encouraging, influencing, or even coercing settlement. The mediators may, or may not, suggest to the parties what they ought to do. The mediators may encourage, permit, or forbid attorneys to be present.

MARK D. BENNETT & MICHELLE S. G. HERMANN, THE ART OF MEDIATION 15 (NITA 1996). Mediation of family law disputes has its own distinctive features:

Because of the emotional issues involved and the nature of the disputes between the parties, many of the original divorce mediation practitioners felt that the mediation sessions should be broken down over a period of weeks. The parties need time to adjust to their renegotiated relationship and to think through major life changes. Consequently, divorce mediation sessions are often limited to approximately an hour, and take place once a week until all matters are settled.

KIMBERLEE K. KOVACH, MEDIATION: PRINCIPLES AND PRACTICES 35 (2000); *see also* COOGLER, STRUCTURED MEDIATION IN DIVORCE SETTLEMENT: A HANDBOOK FOR MARITAL MEDIATORS (1978).

NOTES

1. ***Who Are the Mediators?***   At least four basic patterns have emerged: (1) the mediator is a lawyer; (2) the mediator is a marriage counselor, child psychologist or social worker; (3) team mediation with lawyers and non-lawyers working together; (4) the mediator is a "pure" dispute resolution specialist who is neither an attorney nor a mental health or social welfare professional. Any of these kinds of mediators may also bring into the process specialists or consultants to help parties to assess particular aspects of their dispute (*e.g.* a financial planner to help parties assess the short and long-term costs of particular settlements.)

Those mediators with a legal background tend to emphasize divorce's legal consequences and the need to protect the parties' rights, while non-lawyers often emphasize divorce's trauma and the need to protect the parties' emotional interests. *Compare* B. W. Callner, *Boundaries of the Divorce Lawyer's Role*, 10 FAM. L.Q. 389 (1977), *with* John M. Haynes, DIVORCE MEDIATION: A PRACTICAL GUIDE FOR THERAPISTS AND COUNSELORS (1981). For an explanation of the advantages and disadvantages of the various patterns, see Nichol M. Schoenfeld, Note, *Turf Battles and Professional Biases: An Analysis of Mediator Qualifications in Child Custody Disputes*, 11 OHIO ST. J. DISP. RES. 469 (1996). The Note concludes that "empirical studies suggest no differences in user satisfaction rates" among them. *Id.* at p. 486. The most important variable linked to party satisfaction is the mediator's experience level rather than professional background. *Id.* In fact, the Note finds little difference in satisfaction rates when comparing professional to volunteer mediators. *Id.* at p. 487.

2. *Mediation Ordered by Law.* Some statutes impose mandatory mediation, at least in certain circumstances. The following statutory provisions, are taken from the CALIFORNIA FAM. CODE:

§ 3164. Qualifications of mediator

(a) The mediator may be a member of the professional staff of a family conciliation court, probation department, or mental health services agency, or may be any other person or agency designated by the court.

(b) The mediator shall meet the minimum qualifications required of a counselor of conciliation as provided in Section 1815 [which requires a master's degree in "psychology, social work, marriage, family and child counseling" or other relevant behavioral science, and, among other things, knowledge of the court system and knowledge of "child development, child abuse, clinical issues relating to children, the effects of divorce on children, the effects of domestic violence on children, and child custody research. . . ."].

§ 3170. Setting contested issues for mediation

(a) If it appears on the face of a petition . . . to obtain or modify a temporary or permanent custody or visitation order that custody, visitation, or both are contested, the court shall set the contested issues for mediation.

. . . .

§ 3177. Confidentiality of proceedings

Mediation proceedings . . . shall be held in private and shall be confidential. . . .

. . . .

§ 3181. Separate mediation following history of domestic violence

(a) . . . [W]here there has been a history of domestic violence between the parties or where a protective order . . . is in effect, at the request of the party alleging domestic violence in a written declaration under penalty of perjury or protected by the order, the mediator . . . shall meet with the parties separately and at separate times.

. . . .

§ 3182. Exclusion of counsel from participation

(a) The mediator has authority to exclude counsel from participation in the mediation proceedings . . . . if [it] is appropriate or necessary.

. . . .

§ 3183. Recommendations to court

(a) The mediator may . . . submit a recommendation to the court as to the custody of or visitation with the child.

(b) Where the parties have not reached agreement . . . , the mediator may recommend to the court that an investigation be conducted . . . or that other services be offered to assist the parties to effect a resolution of the controversy. . . .

(c) In appropriate cases, the mediator may recommend that restraining orders be issued . . . to protect the well-being of the child involved in the controversy.

Most statutes do not themselves mandate mediation but instead grant trial court judges the power to do so in appropriate situations. The Kansas statute, e.g., grants the court the power to appoint a mediator to help resolve any child custody or visitation issue. KAN. STAT. ANN. § 23-602(b). For a collection of statutes dealing with divorce mediation, see Carrie-Anne Tondo, Rinarisa Coronel & Bethany Drucker, *Mediation Trends: A Survey of the States*, 39 FAM. CT. REV. 431 (2001). This survey finds: 10 states that have statutes mandating mediation in divorce cases; 24 in which mediation is "discretionary"; 5 states that mandate mediation in particular circumstances (commonly in cases involving children); and 12 states with no statutes on point. The authors caution: "Findings to date show that mediation of family relations is not used in the precise [same] manner in any two states. . . . This finding in and of itself suggests the need for uniformity." *Id* at 433.

Where a party is ordered to mediate, what constitutes compliance with the order? Clearly, neither the court nor a statute can require an agreement. The test must instead be whether the party participated. An objective participation standard (did the party attend a mediation session?) seems the only practical test of compliance. *See* John Lande, *Using Dispute System Design Methods to Promote Good-faith Participation in Court-Connected Mediation Programs* 50 UCLA L. REV. 69 (2002) (concluding good faith requirements are unworkable and proposing pre-mediation information, limited attendance requirements, and protections against misrepresentation as more effective methods to assure participation); David S. Winston, Note, *Participation Standards in Mandatory Mediation Statutes: "You Can Lead a Horse to Water. . . .",* 11 OHIO ST. J. DISP. RES. 187 (1996).

3. ***Should Lawyers Participate in Mediation?*** One set of authors argues for a "lawyer-participant" model, their description of the pattern they say is used in Maine and other states. Craig A. McEwen, Nancy H. Rogers & Richard J. Maiman, *Bring in the Lawyers: Challenging the Dominant Approaches to Ensuring Fairness in Divorce Mediation*, 79 MINN. L. REV. 1317 (1995). Under this model, lawyers attend mediation sessions and, in Maine, "believe that their primary role in mediation is to provide a check on unfairness." *Id.* at p. 1360. On the basis of a Maine empirical study, the authors conclude lawyer participation does not reduce the number of settlements, does not create an adversarial atmosphere and does not result in the lawyers "taking over the process."

At the same time, lawyers increasingly are being advised on how to advocate effectively for their clients in mediation. For example, the National Institute for Trial Advocacy has published a manual for "Mediation Advocacy," including advice on "delineating the extent of the client's verbal participation," which includes: "the client should face the mediator when speaking . . . the client should state only facts . . . the client should never argue . . . the client should never ask difficult questions." JOHN W. COOLEY, MEDIATION ADVOCACY 85 — 104 (NITA 1996). Advice for the attorney includes how to make opening statements, how to gain tactical advantages through private caucuses with the mediator, and how to select conflict behaviors that maximizes a client's gains. *Id* at 103–123. *Compare* Kinberlee K. Kovach, *New Wine Requires New Wineskins: Transforming Lawyer Ethics for Effective Representation in a Non-adversarial Approach to Problem Solving: Mediation,* 28 FORDHAM URB. L.J. 935 (2001).

4. *Confidentiality of Mediation.* Note that § 3183 of the California Family Code, quoted in Note 2, permits local courts to hear a mediator's recommendations concerning custody disposition, presumably if the parties fail to reach agreement. After unsuccessful mediation, could a party or the court subpoena the mediator at trial? While mediation contracts often assure the parties of confidentiality, it is not at all clear that such provisions would survive a court order to produce the evidence. It has been held, for example, that contracts providing for suppression of evidence are contrary to public policy. *Simrin v. Simrin,* 43 Cal. Rptr. 376 (App. 1965). One commentator has stated flatly,

> [M]ediation programs habitually assert that the confidentiality of the process will be protected, even from court intrusion. This is inaccurate and, in New Jersey and elsewhere, the mediator may be called to court and questioned as to admissions made by either party. This would be true even though the "rules" ' governing the mediation provide to the contrary, in the absence of some statute or court rule which would assure such confidentiality.

Alan J. Cornblatt, *Matrimonial Mediation,* 23 J. FAM. L. 99, 102 (1984–85).

The ABA Standards of Practice for Lawyer Mediators in Family Disputes state:

> II. (A) At the outset of mediation, the parties should agree in writing not to require the mediator to disclose to any party any statements made in the course of mediation. The mediator shall inform the participants that the mediator will not voluntarily disclose . . . any of the information obtained through the mediation process, unless such disclosure is required by law, without the prior consent of the participants. The mediator also shall inform the parties of the limitations of confidentiality such as statutory or judicially mandated reporting.

> (B) If subpoenaed or otherwise noticed to testify, the mediator shall inform the participants immediately so as to afford them an opportunity to quash the process.

> (C) The mediator shall inform the participants of the mediator's inability to bind third parties to an agreement not to disclose information furnished during the mediation in the absence of any absolute privilege.

See also Standard V, MODEL STANDARDS OF CONDUCT FOR MEDIATORS (1996), which states, "The mediator shall not disclose any matter that a party expects to be confidential unless given permission by all parties or unless required by law or other public policy."

In 2001, the National Conference of Commissioners on Uniform State Laws promulgated a Uniform Mediation Act (UMA). The Act, which has been adopted in several states, creates a broad-based privilege for any "mediation communication," UMA §§ 4-8, which is defined as "a statement, whether oral or in a record or verbal or nonverbal, that occurs during a mediation or is made for purposes of considering, conducting, participating in, initiating, continuing, or reconvening a mediation or retaining a mediator." *Id* § 2(2). The privilege permits parties to prevent disclosures of any mediation communication. The mediator may prevent disclosure of any mediation communication "of the mediator." *Id* § 4(b)(1) & (2). The Act provides for waiver of the privilege and delineates a series of exceptions; it also limits the reports that a mediator may make to any tribunal which must later rule on the dispute. *Id* § 7. For debate on the Act's approach, see Scott H. Hughes, *The Uniform Mediation Act: to the Spoiled Go The Privileges*, 85 MARQ. L. REV. 9 (2001); and Ellen E. Deason, *The Quest for Uniformity in Mediation Confidentiality: Foolish Consistency or Crucial Predictability?* 85 MARQ. L. REV. 79 (2001).

The UMA emerged from what one commentator reported as a "profusion of mediation privilege statutes and rules." Alan Kirtley, *The Mediation Privilege's Transition from Theory to Implementation: Designing a Mediation Privilege Standard to Protect Mediation Participants, The Process and the Public Interest*, 1995 J. DISP. RES. 1. This survey reports the typical statute provides that all the mediator's work product, as well as any communication made in the course of mediation is "confidential" and "not subject to disclosure in any judicial or administrative proceeding." *See, e.g.*, MASS. GEN. LAWS, Ch. 233, § 23C; OKLA. STAT. ANN., tit. 12, § 1805. What interests favor confidentiality of mediation? Professor Kirtley observes that: "A principal purpose of the mediation privilege is to provide mediation parties protection against these downside risks of a failed mediation. Participation will diminish if perceptions of confidentiality are not matched by reality." 1995 J. DISP. RES. at pp. 9–10.

Not all commentators support a broadly-defined privilege, suggesting counter-vailing interests such as protection of individual rights and enforcement of the criminal law. *See* Kirtley, *supra* (citing need for consideration of exceptions dealing with "fraud, unconscionability, 'manifest injustice,' public health and safety issues, or violations of law"); C. H. Macturk, Note, *Confidentiality in Mediation: The Best Protection Has Exceptions*, 19 AM. J. TR. ADV. 411 (1995); Joshua P. Rosenberg, Note, *Keeping the Lid on Confidentiality: Mediation Privilege and Conflict of Laws*, 10 OHIO ST. J. DISP. RES. 157 (1994).

5. *Criticism and Limits of Mediation.* Mediation has not met with universal approval and even its advocates acknowledge it is not appropriate in every case. Many argue that the process requires trust between the parties and a willingness to reach a fair settlement. Those who would rather fight to "win" the divorce battle at any cost and those who are bitter or highly emotional are not likely to reach a mediated agreement. "Divorcing couples come to mediation with their personal and economic lives on the line. They come at a time when feelings of anger, guilt and failure run high. And they come with established patterns of reacting to each other." E. M. Brown, The Emotional Context of Divorce: Implications for Mediation 43 (1982). While some may be able to simultaneously handle their emotions and the mediation process, the capacity of others may be temporarily diminished by the emotional upheaval of divorce. To guard against emotional incapacity to bargain, a cooling-off period before an agreement would become enforceable, has been suggested. Robert H. Mnookin, *Divorce Bargaining: The Limits on Private Ordering, in* The Resolution of Family Conflict 364 (J. Eekelaar & S. Katz eds. 1984).

Perhaps the broadest criticism leveled at mediation is the feminist critique. Some fear that a system that requires parties to negotiate with each other directly, rather than through lawyer-agents, may advantage the more aggressive or dominant spouse. Martha A. Fineman, The Illusion of Equality: The Rhetoric and Reality of Divorce Reform 144–46 (1991) (contending women are hurt by mediation's bias toward joint custody); Trina Grillo, *The Mediation Alternative,* 100 Yale L.J. 1545 (1991); Penelope E. Bryan, *Killing Us Softly: Divorce Mediation and the Politics of Power,* 40 Buff. L. Rev. 441 (1992); Martha Shaffer, *Divorce Mediation: A Feminist Perspective,* 46 U. Toronto Fac. L. Rev. 163 (1988). *But see* Mary G. Marcus et al., *To Mediate or Not to Mediate: Financial Outcomes in Mediated Versus Adversarial Divorces,* 17 Mediation Q. 143 (1999) (reporting on Connecticut empirical study showing that the mediated cases resulted in women receiving more of the marital assets, longer periods of alimony and more child support than the litigated cases); Jessica Pearson, *Ten Myths About Family Law,* 27 Fam. L.Q. 279 (1993); Joshua D. Rosenberg, *In Defense of Mediation,* 33 Ariz. L. Rev. 467 (1991).

A separate non-gender-based critique asserts that mediation is inappropriate where there has been domestic violence or neglect, or where one party has serious psychological problems. Sarah Krieger, Note, *The Dangers of Mediation in Domestic Violence Cases,* 8 Cardozo Women's L.J. 235 (2002). Critics sometimes draw a distinction between court-mandated mediation and voluntary mediation. *See* Grillo, *supra,* (criticizing mandatory mediation); Laurel Wheeler, *Mandatory Family Mediation and Domestic Violence,* 26 S. Ill. U. L.J. 559 (2002). Within court-mandated mediation, the primary issues include whether to exempt domestic violence cases, how to screen for domestic violence, and how to respond when the fact of violence emerges in mediation. Rene L. Rimelspach, Note, *Mediating Family Disputes in a World with Domestic Violence: How to Devise a Safe and Effective Court-Connected Mediation Program,* 17 Ohio St. J. Disp. Resol. 95 (2001); Zylstram, *Mediation and Domestic Violence: a Practical Screening Method for Mediators and Mediation Program Administrators,* 2001 J. Disp. Resol. 253; Alison E. Gerenscer, *Family Mediation: Screening for Domestic Abuse,* 23 Fla. St. U. L. Rev. 43 (1995); Kara C. Utzig, *Entering the Debate on Spousal Abuse Divorce Mediation: Safely Managing Divorce Mediation When Domestic Violence Is Discovered,* 7 Buff. Women's L. J. 51 (2001). As for voluntary mediation, while some critics argue against any mediation of these cases, others advocate for the victim's right to choose mediation. Nancy Ver Steegh, *Yes, No, and Maybe: Informed Decision Making about Divorce Mediation in the Presence of Domestic*

Violence 9 WM. & MARY J. WOMEN & L. 145 (2003).

Others question some of the claims made by mediation enthusiasts about both mediation and the adversarial system. Consider the following:

> That mediation enthusiasts continually oversimplify the problem suggests . . . commitment to the institution and desire to enhance its image by distinguishing its process and values . . . from the "adversarial system."
>
> . . . [M]ediation literature usually implies (and often . . . contends) that mediators share a number of values as to process and outcomes which distinguish . . . their enterprise from . . . the "traditional adversarial approach." For example, such notions as shared post-divorce parenting responsibilities . . . ; more rapid processing; lower legal costs; maximized self-determination for the divorcing spouses; minimized interpersonal and legal conflict during and after the divorce.
>
> . . . [B]ut a great many nonmediator lawyers would like to lessen the legal costs of divorce. Many lawyers, whose clients have returned time and again to relitigate their divorces endlessly in one form or another, share mediators' concerns as to post-divorce "recidivism." Many lawyers and judges . . . believe that children are better off if their parents are satisfied with only one trial. Yet all such perspectives and policy choices are the products of values and hunches — anecdotal experiences sprinkled liberally with personal background factors and emotion. There is . . . very little known as to the relative utility of various possible treatments, and no consensus as to the values about the adjustment of divorced persons and their children which should inform choices.
>
> Consider our ignorance about the couples who endlessly relitigate. Some of them must be so full of interpersonal venom that: (a) they would never permit a professional to "mediate" their differences; (b) their relitigations are symbolic spousal batterings which [replace] physical assaults; or, (c) their children do "better" when the parents are litigating, because so long as they are fighting . . . in court they do not fight with the children at home. Continuing litigation may be, at least for some. . . , a "healthy adaptation."

Robert J. Levy, *Comment on the Pearson-Thoennes Study on Mediation*, 17 FAM. L.Q. 525, 531–33 (1984). *See also* Phyllis Gangel-Jacob, *Some Words of Caution About Divorce Mediation*, 23 HOFSTRA L. REV. 825 (1995). Justice Gangel-Jacob, a New York trial court judge, concluded:

> A civilized divorce may be an oxymoron, but it is less likely to be when there is economic justice. . . . [B]uzz words that connote fairness are "joint custody," "shared decision making power," "no fault divorce," and "mediation." What could be more civilized than a nice, mediated settlement which results in joint custody, few economic burdens on the monied spouse, and a quick divorce? I propose that far more civilized is a fair economic package that takes into consideration the children's economic and emotional needs and makes adequate provision for the non-monied spouse.

> . . . I appeal to . . . legislators, those who influence legislators, those who are academics . . . those who are judges and administrators . . . those who are lawyers . . . and those who are law students . . . not to cast matrimonial attorneys as the "villains" and mediators as the "saviors". . . .

Id. at pp. 835–36.

6. *Empirical Evidence.* A study reported in 1994 "found no differences in children's problems when children whose parents had used mediation were compared with those whose parents had used litigation to settle their child custody dispute one year earlier." Katherine Kitzmann & Robert E. Emery, *Child and Family Coping One Year After Mediated and Litigated Child Custody Disputes*, 8 J. OF FAM. PSYCHOLOGY 150 (1994). The study, however, was relatively small (involving fewer than 60 families) and the mediating couples each experienced 4 to 8 hours of mediation. The same study did document a dramatic reduction in post-divorce court hearings and an increase in party satisfaction and compliance with child support orders. Robert E. Emery, S. G. Matthews & Katherine Kitzmann, *Child Custody Mediation and Litigation: Parents' Satisfaction and Functioning One Year After Settlement*, 62 J. CONSULT. & CLIN. PSYCHOLOGY 124 (1994). A long-term study found that nine years after resolution of a custody dispute those who had mediated their case reported greater current contact with their children and greater involvement in current decisions. The mediating parents also reported more frequent communication with each other about the children during the post-resolution period. Peter A. Dillon & Robert E. Emery, *Divorce Mediation and Resolution of Child Custody Disputes: Long-Term Effects*, 66 AM. J. OF ORTHOPSYCHIATRY 131 (1996). In addition to the report of the specific study involved, the latter article surveys the empirical literature.

For other studies, see Robert E. Emery, *Easing the Pain of Divorce for Children: Children's Voices, Causes of Conflict and Mediation. Comments on Kelly's "Resolving Child Custody Disputes,"* 10 VA. J. SO. POL'Y & L. 164, 167 (2002); CONNIE J. A. BECK & BRUCE DENNIS SALES, FAMILY MEDIATION: FACTS MYTHS AND FUTURE PROSPECTS (2001); Judith Caprez & Micki A. Armstrong, *A Study of Domestic Mediation Outcomes with Indigent Parents*, 9 FAM. CT. REV. 415 (2001); Robert E. Emery, RENEGOTIATING FAMILY RELATIONSHIPS: DIVORCE, CHILD CUSTODY, AND MEDIATION (1994).

7. *Collaborative Law.* There has been a growing movement towards "collaborative law" in family law. Collaborative law involves efforts to resolve disputes where all the participants agree in advance not to resort to, or threaten to resort to, litigation while the collaborative process is underway. For an overview of this approach, its application to family law and separation agreements, and the distinctive legal ethics questions it raises, see Pauline H. Tesler, *Collaborative Family Law*, 4 PEPP. DISP. RESOL. L.J. 317 (2004); Gary L. Voegele, Linda K. Wray & Ronald D. Ousky, *Collaborative Law: A Useful Tool for the Family Law Practitioner to Promote Better Outcomes*, 33 WM. MITCHELL L. REV. 971 (2007); Ted Schneyer, *The Organized Bar and the Collaborative Law Movement: A Study in Professional Change*, 50 ARIZ. L. REV. 289 (2008). In July 2009, the Uniform Law Commission voted to adopt a Uniform Collaborative Law Act to guide practice in this area. This text can be accessed at http://www.law.upenn.edu/bll/archives/ulc/ucla/2009am_approved.htm.

[2] The Requirement That Divorce Settlements be Judicially Approved

[a] In General

Divorcing spouses are not done when they reach agreement on the terms of their marital dissolution, for they must still obtain a decree from the divorce court. Ordinarily, the divorce decree will reflect the terms of the parties' agreement. Nonetheless, a variety of issues may arise. A party may have a change of heart after reaching an agreement but prior to the decree's issuance, and may thus challenge the agreement's terms before the court asked to issue the decree based upon it. Or, a party may challenge the terms *after* the issuance of the decree, seeking a change in the judicial order on the grounds that there were defects in the agreement upon which it was based. Finally, a party may seek what would ordinarily be a permissible modification of a divorce decree, upon the grounds of changed circumstances, but be met with the claim that he or she is contractually bound by the agreement's provisions so that the decree also is not modifiable. In this section we examine each of these issues in turn.

MODEL MARRIAGE AND DIVORCE ACT

§ 306. Separation Agreement

(a) To promote amicable settlement of disputes between parties to a marriage attendant upon their separation or the dissolution of their marriage, the parties may enter into a written separation agreement containing provisions for disposition of any property owned by either of them, maintenance of either of them, and support, custody, and visitation of their children.

(b) In a proceeding for dissolution of marriage or for legal separation, the terms of the separation agreement, except those providing for the support, custody, and visitation of children, are binding upon the court unless it finds, after considering the economic circumstances of the parties and any other relevant evidence produced by the parties, on their own motion or on request of the court, that the separation agreement is unconscionable.

(c) If the court finds the separation agreement unconscionable, it may request the parties to submit a revised separation agreement or may make orders for the distribution of property, maintenance, and support.

(d) If the court finds that the separation agreement is not unconscionable as to disposition of property or maintenance, and not unsatisfactory as to support:

(1) unless the separation agreement provides to the contrary, its terms shall be set forth in the decree of dissolution or legal separation and the parties shall be ordered to perform them, or

(2) if the separation agreement provides that its terms shall not be set forth in the decree, the decree shall identify the separation agreement and state that the court has found the terms not unconscionable.

(e) Terms of the agreement set forth in the decree are enforceable by all remedies available for enforcement of a judgment, including contempt, and are enforceable as contract terms.

(f) Except for terms concerning the support, custody, or visitation of children, the decree may expressly preclude or limit modification of terms set forth in the decree if the separation agreement so provides. Otherwise, terms of a separation agreement set forth in the decree are automatically modified by modification of the decree.

WEBER v. WEBER
North Dakota Supreme Court
589 N.W.2d 358 (1999)

SANDSTROM, JUSTICE.

Ruby Moos appealed from the judgment of the district court vacating the property settlement agreement between her and Herbert Weber. The district court found the agreement unconscionable and set it aside in its entirety. We affirm, concluding the district court did not err in finding the agreement unconscionable.

I

Moos and Weber were married on September 13, 1995. Twenty-seven days later, Moos retained an attorney to begin a divorce action. Moos signed a property settlement agreement at a meeting with Weber on October 12, 1995. Weber was not represented by counsel. Moos was represented by attorney Thomas Bair, who advised Weber he represented only Moos and Weber should retain his own attorney. Weber declined to retain his own attorney and signed the document after reviewing it. The property settlement agreement was accompanied by a quitclaim deed giving Moos ownership of a condominium worth about $ 70,000 and owned by Weber prior to the marriage. [¶] The property settlement agreement was filed in . . . court on October 16, 1995. [On the same day,] Weber retained an attorney and moved the . . . court to set aside the . . . agreement, including the quitclaim deed executed in conjunction with it. On October 20, 1995, Weber filed a motion to repossess the condominium, and on October 24, 1995, Weber filed a motion of lis pendens with the . . . court.

In denying Weber's motions, the district court found Weber was able to act independently of the plaintiff and freely to protect his own interests. The district court also found no mistake, fraud, or undue duress. Weber appealed from the district court's judgment. [¶] In *Weber v. Weber*, 548 N.W.2d 781 (N.D. 1996), we remanded to the district court, saying its analysis and ruling were too narrow. In reviewing the property settlement agreement giving substantial property to Moos, the district court limited its review to the contractual capacity of the parties and to whether the contract was entered freely and knowingly, without fraud, duress, menace or undue influence, or genuine mistake of fact or law. We concluded the district court should have considered whether the property settlement agreement was unconscionable.

On remand, the district court addressed three issues for unconscionability. First, was the property settlement agreement "one-sided"? Second, did the agreement create a hardship on either party? And third, given the station in life of each of the parties, and considering the Ruff-Fischer guidelines for property division, was the agreement fair, just, and proper? Applying these, the district court found the October 12, 1995, property settlement agreement . . . unconscionable, and set it aside in its entirety. Moos appealed.

II

. . .

B

When a divorce is granted, N.D.C.C. § 14-05-24 requires a trial court to "make such equitable distribution of the real and personal property of the parties as may seem just and proper." In doing so, however, we have encouraged district courts to recognize valid agreements between divorcing parties. The public policy on divorce favors a "prompt and peaceful resolution of disputes." *Wolfe v. Wolfe*, 391 N.W.2d 617, 619 (N.D. 1986). "To the extent that competent parties have voluntarily stipulated to a particular disposition of their marital property, a court ordinarily should not decree a distribution of property that is inconsistent with the parties' contract." *Wolfe*, 391 N.W.2d at 619.

District courts should not, however, blindly accept property settlement agreements. See Principles of the Law of Family Dissolution: Analysis and Recommendations, Tentative Draft No. 2, A.L.I. § 4.01 comment (1996) (stating "agreements between spouses have traditionally been subject to various procedural and substantive rules beyond those which apply to contracts generally"). We have noted the district court's duty to make a just and proper distribution of property under N.D.C.C. § 14-05-24 includes the authority to rewrite a property settlement agreement for mistake, duress, menace, fraud, or undue influence under N.D.C.C. § 9-09-02(1). See *Wolfe*, 391 N.W.2d at 619.

We have also held a district court should not enforce an agreement if it is unconscionable. See also Uniform Marriage and Divorce Act, 9A U.L.A. 306(b) (1998) (stating "the terms of a separation agreement . . . are binding upon the court unless it finds, after considering the economic circumstances of the parties and any other relevant evidence produced by the parties, on their own motion or on request of the court, that the separation agreement is unconscionable"). Unconscionability is a doctrine by which courts may deny enforcement of a contract "because of procedural abuses arising out of the contract formation, or because of substantive abuses relating to terms of the contract." Black's Law Dictionary, 6th Ed., 1524.

Therefore, district courts should make two findings when considering whether a settlement agreement between divorcing parties should be enforced. The first inquiry is whether the agreement is free from mistake, duress, menace, fraud, or undue influence under N.D.C.C. § 9-09-02(1). On remand, the district court stated: "The Court has determined in its previous judgment that the parties and their resulting agreement did not occur as the result of fraud, deceit, misrepresentation, or mistake of law or fact. Further, that the Supreme Court decision herein did not reverse the Court's findings thereon. Accordingly, the trial court is left to determine whether or not the result of the property settlement agreement of the parties is unconscionable."

The district court did not err in finding the agreement free from mistake, duress, menace, fraud, or undue influence. The inquiry does not, however, end there.[¶] . . . The district court [also] found the result of the property settlement agreement . . . unconscionable. The court first found the agreement to be "one-sided," based on the brevity of the marriage, the additional assets of $ 75,000 Moos received during the brief marriage, the gifts given to Moos by Weber in this very short marriage, and Weber giving up his only residence.

Moos argues the district court was clearly erroneous in this finding. . . . [Moos] argues the agreement between her and Weber must be perceived as more than unfair or "one-sided," it must be "blatantly one-sided" and "rankly unfair," citing language from *Crawford*, 524 N.W.2d 833. [¶] Although the district court does not call the agreement between Moos and Weber "rankly unfair" or "blatantly one-sided," that does not mean it could not have been described as such. The agreement left Weber with far less than he brought into the one-month marriage. This appears to be the kind of agreement no rational, undeluded person would make, and no honest and fair person would accept. The district court did not err in finding the agreement one-sided. Whether it was characterized as "rankly" or "blatantly" one-sided is not important.

The district court's second finding on unconscionability was that the agreement created a greater hardship on Weber. Weber gave up his condominium and lost his household furnishings, and he would have had to expend a substantial portion of his retirement assets to replace the condominium. Moos, on the other hand, could resume renting an apartment comparable to her previous accommodations without reducing her assets. Moos argues the agreement allowed Weber to retain 73% of the marital estate. This argument fails, however, to consider Weber brought nearly 100% of the estate into the one-month marriage. The district court did not err in finding the agreement placed a greater hardship on Weber.

Finally, the district court applied the Ruff-Fischer guidelines and found the agreement "unfair and unjust under the circumstances with respect to [Weber]."[2]

---

[2] The Fuff-Fischer guidelines are applied to distribute property in a divorce in the absence of an ante or postnuptial agreement. Considered under the Ruff-Fischer guidelines are: " 'the respective ages of the parties, their earning ability, the duration of the marriage and conduct of the parties during the marriage, their station in life, the circumstances and necessities of each, their health and physical condition, their financial circumstances as shown by the property owned at the time, its value at the time, its income-producing capacity, if any, whether accumulated before or after the marriage, and such other matters as may be material." Weir v. Weir, 374 N.W.2d 858, 862 (N.D. 1985).

Traditionally, the Ruff-Fischer guidelines are applied in divorce cases to distribute property of divorcing spouses, absent an agreement. While Ruff-Fischer is not the standard in a domestic relations case to determine unconscionability of a settlement agreement of divorcing parties, it is appropriate for a district court to consider. The Ruff-Fischer guidelines are proper because a domestic relations agreement should not be scrutinized in the same way as a business contract. Thus, the district court did not err in applying Ruff-Fischer to determine unconscionability.

The haste with which the agreement was entered and the involvement of only one attorney is also troubling. The action by Weber to rescind immediately after having signed the agreement is also persuasive. As we said in *Peterson v. Peterson*, 555 N.W.2d 359, 362 (N.D. 1996), "a stipulation in a divorce proceeding which occurs this rapidly with the use of one attorney and under serious threats of harm to one of the parties should be viewed with great skepticism." Although there were no serious threats of physical harm, Weber was under strain from the threat of losing considerably more of his life's earnings if he did not sign the agreement. The skepticism we noted in *Peterson* was correctly applied to this agreement.

The district court did not err in finding the agreement unconscionable. The decision of the district court is affirmed.

ALI Principles
Chapter 1 Introduction
40–41(2002)

Separation agreements resolving the [divorcing parties' alimony and property division arrangements] are favored, both under existing law and these Principles. . . . In negotiating a separation agreement in the shadow of state default rules that set the standard for fairness, the parties can often settle their affairs more efficiently and more to their satisfaction than a court can. The greater favor shown to separation agreements than to premarital agreements may also reflect the different negotiating context. The parties to a premarital agreement are contracting about a speculative future event, dissolution, in a setting dominated by a quite different and immediate event, marriage. In contrast, at dissolution the parties are contracting for events that are already upon them. They are better able to comprehend the circumstances in which the agreement will be enforced and thus to grasp the significance of the terms of the agreement. Given the demise of their relationship, the parties may generally be expected to bargain at arm's length. Although parties making agreements before or during marriage may assume that the other party is acting for their common good, parties bargaining about the terms of an impending dissolution are more likely to appreciate that each party has individual interests to advance and safeguard.

Thus, the law should enforce separation agreements unless the rules of contract, viewed in the context of family dissolution, have been violated, or the terms of the agreement would frustrate some important policy of the law of family dissolution. . . . [¶] These Principles impose few formal requirements for the enforceability of separation agreements. Recognizing that parties may not settle until the hour of trial, separation agreements may either be in writing or stipulated by the parties before the court. The party seeking enforcement need only show the prima facie existence of an agreement, that is, a signed writing or a stipulation. The party resisting enforcement bears the burden of showing that the agreement should not be enforced.

. . . Judicial economy is better served by limiting court oversight to those relatively few cases in which a term of an agreement is ultimately contested than by requiring courts to examine all separation agreements, including those that are unproblematic or may never be contested. In any event, these Principles acknowledge the reality that most courts do not have the resources to exercise meaningful oversight of all separation agreements. Therefore the Principles do not require judicial approval of agreements regulating property disposition or compensatory payments, and instead require judicial inquiry only when one party objects to the terms of an agreement.

NOTES AND QUESTIONS

1. ***In General.***   While modern divorce law encourages negotiated settlement, it usually requires the parties to present their agreement to the court, which may in theory reject it. The MMDA instructs the court to approve the provisions concerning alimony and property division unless it finds them "unconscionable," but provides more vigorous review of terms on custody and child support. The purpose is to assure, through judicial supervision of the parties, that the interests of the children are not submerged in an effort to accommodate the spouses, while giving the spouses broad authority to set terms affecting only themselves. Most states have similar provisions for judicial review of separation agreements. The *ALI Principles* also require approval of custody and child support terms, which directly affect children, but conclude that routine review of the property or alimony portions of a separation agreement are usually unnecessary, and are unlikely to provide meaningful oversight in any event. While it therefore dispenses with the pretense of routine review, it does allow post-agreement challenges to the settlement's terms at the instance of a party, under standards described below.

2. ***Can Routine Judicial Review of All Agreements Really Work?***   Note that in *Weber* itself a careful review of the agreement occurred because one of the parties had a change of heart and objected to it by the time judicial approval was sought. But how can a requirement of routine review work in the usual case, where the parties remain in agreement so that the court cannot depend upon the adversarial process to bring out the critical facts? If the requirement were to be meaningful it would appear that the court would have to probe for the facts *sua sponte*, yet existing law generally does not put courts under any obligation to make such an unprompted investigation, *Dow v. Dow*, 732 S.W.2d 906 (Mo. 1987), and they rarely will. It is thus not surprising that there are few reported decisions rejecting an agreement endorsed by both husband and wife. Melli's study revealed the same pattern in the trial courts. The court rejected the parties' agreement in only one case of 349 she examined, and that case arose from an objection by the state child support agency, which pointed out that the custodial parent had agreed to the support terms only because additional funds were being provided through AFDC. Where judges made inquiries about the agreement, they asked only

whether the parties understood and supported it. Like the trial court in *Weber*, they never inquired into the agreement's substantive fairness; they limited themselves to verifying that it was voluntarily entered. Indeed, in three-fourths of Melli's cases, the file before the judge did not contain the financial information that would be necessary to make a substantive evaluation, and even financial disclosure forms required by state law were often missing or incomplete. Marygold S. Melli, Howard S. Erlanger & Elizabeth Chambliss, *The Process of Negotiation: An Exploratory Investigation in the Context of No-Fault Divorce*, 40 RUTGERS L. REV. 1133, 1145–47 (1988).[2]

The court's failure to give an agreement meaningful review will not normally provide a basis for later upsetting the decree which incorporates it. For example, in *Monroe v. Monroe*, 413 A.2d 819 (Conn. 1979), the former wife sought to vacate a divorce decree based upon a negotiated agreement. Among other grounds, she argued that she had not actually consented to the agreement, or to its submission to a court-appointed referee, who handled uncontested divorces. The referee's review of the agreement was so cursory that he made no effort even to verify that the wife consented to it. The Connecticut Supreme Court observed:

> The plaintiff claims that she was coerced by her attorney into agreeing to the order of reference and into appearing before the referee, but there are no findings of fact to support those allegations. The plaintiff's argument would have us impose upon the defendant, the burden of establishing that the plaintiff's relationship with her counsel was one of informed consent. This we are not prepared to do.

> Although the plaintiff . . . has not sustained her burden, the questions indirectly raised by her appeal are not trivial. Lawyers who represent clients in matrimonial dissolutions have a special responsibility for full and fair disclosure, for a searching dialogue, about all of the facts that materially affect the client's rights and interests. . . . It is . . . noteworthy that the referee who accepted the stipulated divorce settlement and incorporated it into his decree did so completely upon the representations of counsel. Although both parties — were present, the referee made no inquiry whatsoever to ascertain the parties' actual consent to the proposal before him. Because of the emotionally-laden circumstances under which negotiations about marital dissolutions necessarily take place, reasonable [inquiries] should be made to ensure, as far as possible, that reasonable settlements have been knowingly agreed upon. Nonetheless, even judicial failure to conduct a searching inquiry into the acceptability of a divorce settlement does not make the subsequent judgment of divorce vulnerable to collateral attack as a miscarriage of justice.

---

[2] Other studies support the impression left by Melli's data. See the authorities cited in Robert H. Mnookin & Lewis Kornhauser, *Bargaining in the Shadow of the Law*, 88 YALE L.J. 950, 954 (1979). A survey of Nebraska judges suggests that some scrutiny of provisions concerning children may take place, but even when such cases were counted the judges reported alteration of less than five percent of the agreements. A. H. Frank, J. J. Berman & S. F. Mazur-Hart, *No Fault Divorce and the Divorce Rate: The Nebraska Experience — An Interrupted Time Series Analysis and Commentary*, 58 NEB. L. REV. 1, 77 n. 311 (1978). *See also* Sally Burnett Sharp, *Modification of Agreement Based Custody Decrees: Unitary or Dual Standard?*, 68 VA. L. REV. 1263, 1279 n.69 (1982).

Monroe suggests both judges and attorneys may have a special obligation to protect the divorcing parties from settlements which are unfair or which do not in fact reflect the parties' desires. But the court still denied the wife's claim, saying that the husband need not prove her informed consent to the agreement. This combination of strong words with little action is typical. *See also Marriage of Manzo*, 659 P.2d 669, 674 (Colo. 1983).

How would a trial court proceed if it actually wanted to do the policing that most statutes seem in principle to require? In *Linnenburger v. Linnenburger*, 741 S.W.2d 872 (Mo. App. 1987), the court found the trial court had erred in setting its own amounts for child support and maintenance, even though it did not disagree with the trial court that the provisions in the parties' agreement were unconscionable. The agreement had waived maintenance and set support at only $35 per week; the trial judge had ordered support payments of $50 weekly and maintenance of $100 per month. The appeals court held that the trial judge should have either ordered the parties to submit a revised separation agreement, or held a separate evidentiary hearing. It also held that the trial court could not set aside the maintenance and support provisions while honoring the agreement's property terms; the agreement must stand or fall in its entirety.

3. *What Standards Should Govern Challenges to Agreements?* What standards should a court apply in cases like *Weber*, when a party asks a court to reject the agreement he had previously accepted but which has not yet been incorporated into the decree? *Weber* suggests that courts should subject these agreements to standards more demanding than would be imposed on commercial agreements, but the opinion does not make entirely clear what the more demanding standards consist of. "Mistake, duress, menace, fraud, [and] undue influence" are all terms identifying doctrines that apply to contracts generally, as does the unconscionability doctrine. The first group involves defects in process, while unconscionability may arise from substantive as well as process failures. (A recent example of a separation agreement not being enforced due primarily to procedural issues (lack of full disclosure) is *In re Marriage of Salby*, 126 P.3d 291 (Col. Ct. App. 2005).)

Note that unconscionability, with separation agreements as with contracts generally, is an evaluation of fairness relative to the time the agreement was entered, not the time at which enforcement is sought. Later changed circumstances cannot make a "conscionable" agreement unconscionable, though it may, of course, warrant a judicial modification of the agreement's child support or alimony terms. *Richardson v. Richardson*, 218 S.W.3d 426, 430 (Mo. 2007) (en banc).

In suggesting that it is appropriate for a court to compare the result under the agreement with the property allocation that a court might order under North Dakota law absent any agreement, however, the court implies that in this realm, as compared to commercial agreements, there are legally established substantive standards setting forth benchmarks of fairness and that agreements may be substantively unconscionable if they depart too dramatically from those standards. Other courts have also suggested a fuller substantive review of challenged divorce agreements than contract law alone would usually accept, sometimes relying upon statutory language. For example, in *Sharp v. Sharp*, 877 P.2d 304 (Ariz. App. 1994), the parties negotiated with each other directly and over the course of several weeks reached agreement on a divorce settlement. But the wife's attorney rejected the agreement after he was asked by both spouses to prepare the necessary papers to finalize the divorce, and the wife therefore opposed it when the husband filed. She offered several arguments based upon defects in the bargaining process that were rejected, but the trial court was reversed nevertheless for failure to determine whether the agreement was "fair" — the standard adopted (rather than unconscionability) in the state's version of MMDA § 306(b). The court held, in effect, that the wife's objections to the agreement created a factual dispute about its fairness that could not be resolved without an examination of the parties' financial particulars. As in *Weber*, the appellate court held that the trial court could not bypass the task by relying upon the parties' having agreed on the terms.

Process and substantive concerns are of course inevitably related; concerns about the negotiating process can motivate or justify a fuller substantive review. The process claims of the wife in *Sharp* were hardly implausible, even though rejected by the court. She was imprisoned in Hawaii on criminal charges while negotiating with her husband in Arizona. While conceding she may have been in distress due to "external circumstances," the court found that this distress did not transform her husband's "entreaties to sign the agreement" into "duress, coercion or undue influence," noting that he was not responsible for the charges against her. In *Weber* the objecting spouse was uncounseled and the process hurried; one might wonder whether the husband's initial willingness to proceed that way might have arisen from an overriding desire to bring a stressful episode to conclusion. Yet divorce is typically a stressful experience, and thus many settlements would become vulnerable to challenge if emotional turmoil alone were grounds for upsetting a divorce agreement. *See, e.g.*, *Beattie v. Beattie*, 368 N.E.2d 178 (Ill. App. 1977) (wife's claim of "anxiety neurosis" at the time of settlement insufficient to permit her to disavow the agreement). This seems to be the position taken by most courts, although there are exceptions. *E.g.*, in *Jenks v. Jenks*, 657 A.2d 1107 (Conn. 1995) (affirming trial court findings of duress arising from husband's threatening and intimidating behavior in divorce negotiations).

In *Morand v. Morand*, 767 N.Y.S.2d 523 (A.D. 2003), the court emphasized that separation agreements are held "to a higher standard of equity" than are other contracts, but refused the wife's claims of duress and unconscionability. The agreement was presented to her as she was going out for the night, her husband "made a scene" in front of the children, and threatened to prevent her from going out unless she signed; and wife claimed to have signed the agreement hastily without having had a chance to read the agreement. However, she also admitted to not having been fearful or stressed by her husband's behavior, she was aware of the basic terms of the agreement, and those terms were generally fair. By contrast, a separation agreement was set aside on unconscionability grounds in *Eberle v. Eberle*, 766 N.W.2d 477 (N.D. 2009), even though the challenge was brought nearly a year after the agreement was signed, filed with the court, and approved by the judge. In the case, the wife's decision to sign the agreement was rushed, she had been subject to pressure and overpersuasion, she was not represented by counsel, there had been little or no discussion of the terms, and the property and alimony terms were highly one-sided.

Nor is it uncommon for parties to settle on the eve of trial under what in retrospect might seem precipitous circumstances. For example, in *Marriage of Steadman*, 670 N.E.2d 1146 (Ill. App. 1996), the parties and their attorneys reached a comprehensive agreement during hallway negotiations conducted just before their scheduled hearing on the husband's motion to enjoin the wife from taking their children out of state, and their agreement was then presented to the court, which accepted it. But the wife challenged the agreement a month later, before the court actually entered a judgment based upon it. In rejecting her claim, the appeals court conceded that "the oral settlement agreement was contrived during two hours of negotiations," but emphasized that the parties "negotiated for two hours at arms length with the aid of counsel." While the court agreed "that the record demonstrates wife may have been unhappy with the settlement terms," as she claimed, she could still be held to her stipulation in open court that accepted them: "this unhappiness does not negate the fact that she stated under oath to counsel and the trial court that this was her agreement." For a similar result on similar facts, see *Richardson v. Richardson*, 392 S.E.2d 688 (Va. App. 1990).

Stookey v. Stookey, 554 S.E.2d 472 (Ga. 2001), would seem to go a step further. The wife's attorney negotiated a deal on her behalf in a telephone conversation with the husband's attorney, in which the wife also participated. Her attorney then informed the court that a scheduled hearing could be cancelled because settlement had been reached. But the wife refused to sign the agreement later prepared by the husband's attorney, denying she had authorized a settlement on those terms. Finding the wife bound by her attorney's representations because she had authorized him to settle on her behalf, the Georgia Supreme Court held that a binding agreement had in fact been entered. Note that the *ALI Principles* would distinguish between these cases: it accepts oral stipulations before a court as creating a binding agreement, but requires nonjudicial agreements to be in writing. See § 7.09. In contrast to both the *ALI Principles* and *Stookey* is the decision of the Virginia Supreme Court in *Flanary v. Milton*, 556 S.E.2d 767 (Va. 2002), which held unenforceable the wife's oral agreement, entered into before the court, to accept a lump-sum payment in settlement of her marital property claims. Virginia law includes a general statutory provision applying the state's version of the Uniform Premarital Agreement Act to agreements between spouses; the court held that the UPAA's requirement of a writing therefore applied to this agreement as well.

For more on this general topic, see Robert Mnookin, *Divorce Bargaining, The Limits of Private Ordering, in* J. EEKELAAR & S. KATZ, RESOLUTION OF FAMILY CONFLICTS: CONTEMPORARY LEGAL PERSPECTIVES 364 (1984), on which portions of the preceding note are based.

4. *Possible Reforms: Replacing Pro Forma Routine Review with Demanding But Focused Review.* On one hand, it appears that many courts are disinclined to allow parties to avoid agreements whenever they were made under emotional stress or pursuant to fast, high-pressure negotiations, because such rules would make too many agreements vulnerable. On the other hand, one commentator has argued that because such circumstances are in fact common appropriate rules would require fairness in the results of the agreement, going beyond ordinary contract doctrines that focus on the bargaining process and generally accept a wide range of results as conscionable. Sally Sharp, *Fairness Standards and Separation Agreements: A Word of Caution on Contractual Freedom*, 132 U. PA. L. REV. 1399 (1984). This may be the implied message of cases like *Weber* and *Sharp*, described above. It is also the approach taken by the American Law Institute. When an agreement is challenged by a party before it has been incorporated into the decree, the ALI would subject it to more searching substantive scrutiny than commercial contracts receive. The Institute's key recommendations are contained in the following excerpt from § 7.09 of the *ALI Principles*:

§ 7.09 The Enforceability of a Separation Agreement

(1) The terms of a separation agreement providing for the disposition of property or for compensatory payments are enforceable and, under § 7.10, are binding on the court if

(a) the agreement is in writing and signed by the parties, or is stipulated by the parties before the court;

(b) the agreement otherwise satisfies the requirements of an enforceable contract;

(c) prior to accepting the agreement, each party had full and fair opportunity to be informed of the existence and value of the parties' marital and separate assets, each party's current earnings and prospects for future earnings, and the significance of the terms of the agreement;

(d) the agreement satisfies any other requirements of state law specially applicable to separation agreements; and

(e) the terms of the agreement have not been found unenforceable under Paragraph (2).

(2) Except as provided in the last sentence of this Paragraph, the terms of a separation agreement providing for the disposition of property or for compensatory payments are unenforceable if they substantially limit or augment property rights or compensatory payments otherwise due under law, and enforcement of those terms would substantially impair the economic well-being of a party who has or will have

(a) primary or dual residential responsibility for a child or

(b) substantially fewer economic resources than the other party.

Nevertheless, the court may enforce such terms if it finds, under the particular circumstances of the case, that enforcement of the terms would not work an injustice.

(3) The party seeking enforcement of a separation agreement must demonstrate that it satisfies Paragraph (1)(a). The party opposing enforce-

ment must show that the separation agreement is unenforceable under another provision of Paragraph (1) or Paragraph (2).

These provisions set modest process requirements: disclosure, analogous to the typical requirements for an enforceable premarital agreement, is the only significant process requirement added to the usual prerequisites for any enforceable contract. But the court's authority to reject a substantively unfair agreement is also made clear in certain specified cases: where the disadvantaged party is a custodial parent, or has "substantially fewer economic resources" than the other party. In those cases, the agreement is unenforceable if it substantially limits the financial claims that party would otherwise have under applicable law, and yields results that "substantially impair the economic well-being" of that party, unless the court also finds that its unfavorable terms do not "work an injustice." Thus, the goal is to specify a subset of cases in which the judicial scrutiny will take place, but to ensure that in those cases the scrutiny is real rather than *pro forma*. The special focus is on children, and those who are financially much worse off than their former partner.

5. *Fiduciary Duties Between Spouses.* If one wished to impose heightened process requirements to separation agreements, one might argue that spouses have special duties to one another beyond those imposed on parties to a commercial agreement. And indeed, in separation agreements as in premarital agreements, courts sometimes say that. *Marriage of Smith*, 115 S.W.3d 126 (Tex. App. 2003) ("because of the confidential relationship between husband and wife, courts closely scrutinize property agreements made by spouses during marriage and have imposed the same duties of good faith and fair dealing on spouses as required of partners and other fiduciaries"); *Manes v. Manes*, 717 N.Y.S.2d 185 (App. Div. 2000) ("In view of the fiduciary relationship existing between spouses, separation agreements are more closely scrutinized by courts than ordinary contracts and may be set aside upon the demonstration of good cause, such as mistake, fraud, duress or overreaching or when found to be unconscionable."). These duties are said to require disclosure of assets, and in general to bar one marital partner from using his or her superior knowledge or influence over the other, to obtain some advantage to the other's detriment. But in many states, any confidential relation between spouses may cease to exist when a divorce petition is filed, separation occurs, or attorneys are hired, depending upon the law of the particular state. *E.g., Webb v. Webb*, 431 S.E.2d 55 (Va. App. 1993) ("if parties have separated, have employed independent counsel and are then negotiating agreement, it is an arms length transaction and their former fiduciary relationship is deemed to have ended"); *Sidden v. Mailman*, 529 S.E.2d 266 (N.C. App. 2000) (a fiduciary relationship exists between husband and wife unless they have become adversaries negotiating over the terms of a separation or property settlement agreement). In these states, the protective rules applying to confidential relations have no application to the typical separation agreement problem. *See* Sally Burnett Sharp, *Fairness Standards and Separation Agreements*, 132 U. Pa. L. Rev. 1399, 1414–23 (1984). In community property states, the spouses' fiduciary duty to one another in their handling of community assets continues while the community is intact. *See* Sharp at 1415; *Miller v. Bechtel Corp.*, 663 P.2d 177 (Cal. 1983) (fiduciary relationship between spouses continues to exist, even during separation, when one spouse controls community property); *Compton v. Compton*, 612 P.2d 1175, 1182

(Idaho 1980). Community property states divide on whether the community ends when the spouses commence living apart, or only at divorce. Where the rule is "living apart," there can obviously be some difficulties in construction.

6. *The Attorney's Obligations in Settlement.* An attorney may be held liable for negligently advising a client to settle. *Grayson v. Wofsey*, 646 A.2d 195 (Conn. 1994); *McWhirt v. Heavey*, 550 N.W.2d 327 (Neb. 1996). In these jurisdictions the attorney can be liable for negligence in the settlement process even though the agreement was approved by the court as fair and equitable. *E.g.*, in *Grayson* a $1.5 million judgment was upheld against an attorney charged with failing to adequately investigate and value the husband's estate and business interests, in consequence of which the wife accepted an agreement that gave her too little property and less alimony than she should have received. In *Heavey* the husband obtained a judgment of $91,000 against an attorney where he accepted a settlement offer after the attorney inaccurately advised him that his inherited property would be considered marital property under local law, and that his wife was likely to receive a long-term alimony award. In both cases there were also more general allegations, including inadequate trial preparation. No malpractice liability should arise from the attorney's exercise of judgment in advising the client with respect to the amount to accept or pay, as contrasted with mistaken advice about the law or about the impact of the agreement on the client's rights and obligations. *McMahon v. Shea*, 657 A.2d 938 (Pa. Super. Ct. 1995).

7. *Where There Are No Lawyers.* One way for the indigent or thrifty to obtain a divorce is for them to act as their own lawyers. With the advent of no-fault divorces — and especially summary divorce procedures — such pro se divorces have increased. One study found that 47 percent of the divorces obtained in the Superior Court in Phoenix, Ariz., during 1985 did not involve lawyers. Those most likely to obtain a divorce pro se were under 30, in a low-income job, married less than ten years, and without children. *Self Helpers on the Increase*, A.B.A. JOURNAL 40 (1988). By 1990 neither spouse had an attorney in 52 percent of the divorces filed in Phoenix, Bruce D. Sales, Connie J. Beck, and Richard K. Haan, *Is Self-Representation a Reasonable Alternative to Attorney Representation in Divorce Cases?*, 37 St. LOUIS U. L. REV. 553, 571 n.81 (1992), and more recent data from the court indicate even higher rates. The domestic relations court in Phoenix has had a "self-help" center that included automated access to forms and other legal assistance, a library of self-help materials, and limited access to consultations with volunteer lawyers. Similar efforts have been undertaken in other jurisdictions. *See* Robert B. Yegge, *Divorce Litigants Without Lawyers*, 28 FAM. L.Q. 407 (1994). Sales, et al., *supra*, includes an empirical study that confirms the earlier findings on the demographic characteristics of Phoenix pro se divorce litigants and some comparative data on pro se and attorney-represented litigants.

What happens if the party to a no-lawyer divorce later claims that the spousal agreement is tainted by a bargaining process that was inadequate or coercive? Probably because no-lawyer divorces usually involve parties with few assets, such claims seem uncommon. Consider, however, *Carsey v. Carsey*, 508 A.2d 533 (Md. App. 1986), in which an extraordinarily informal agreement was enforced. The husband, then president of a local community college, suddenly "chucked it all," leaving both his job and his wife of 14 years. He took all their liquid assets but left her two notes and a tape, all composed without counsel. One note "relinquished all claims" to their joint estate and disclaimed all responsibilities for their debts; the second told her of the physical and emotional mess he found himself in, and referred her to a tape with more information about the family finances. When she later filed for divorce, the court found that there was no marital property to divide because the husband's notes constituted an offer of all their joint property in exchange for assuming liability for their obligations, an offer which the wife accepted by her subsequent actions.

[b] Special Rules To Govern Bargaining Over Children

Consider *Marriage of Lawrence*, 642 P.2d 1043 (Mont. 1982), in which the parties' agreement allocated the wife property and support payments worth about $60,800, while estimates of the husband's share ranged from $227,000 to $422,500. The wife had been advised by her attorney that the agreement was unwise, and that she could probably do better if she went to trial, but, according to the attorney, she rejected this advice and gave no indication she felt coerced. Yet she later sought to set the agreement aside as unconscionable, saying she signed it because her husband had threatened he would otherwise contest custody with evidence of her adultery.

The court rejected her claim, concluding that "custody is frequently a bargaining chip in negotiations whether we like it or not," and declining to adopt a rule that would "encourage a challenge of negotiated property settlement agreements where custody rights have been settled on an arm's length basis as here." The court relied heavily upon her separate representation by competent counsel and her apparently knowing rejection of counsel's advice. The agreement involved no fraud, nor coercion as that term would be understood in policing commercial contracts: the husband's threat, after all, amounted to no more than a statement that if his wife did not agree to a provision with respect to one term in the agreement, he would press his legal rights with respect to another term. Or, to cast it in even more palatable terms, he offered to forgo a tenable legal claim he had to one item on the negotiating table, if the wife would forgo a claim she had to another. This is, of course, the ordinary stuff of negotiated agreements. Why, then, does this agreement leave us uneasy? There is at least one apparent explanation.

In commercial settlement negotiations, the threat to litigate a particular item has leverage primarily to the extent the party making the threat has a good claim on the merits, or at least, a claim that would be difficult to defeat. While parties desire to avoid litigation, this mutual preference gives neither side a negotiating advantage unless litigation would impose greater costs on one party than the other. Custody contests, however, have the unusual feature that heavy costs — perhaps the highest costs — are imposed on third parties (the children). A negotiating advantage thus lies with the party less concerned about the burden of litigation on the children. We may find a special kind of unfairness in allowing one spouse to achieve a negotiating advantage by exploiting the other's more responsible concern for the children's welfare. Good advice from independent counsel will not ameliorate this concern. Whether this is the reason or not, some courts, unlike *Lawrence,* have held that under appropriate facts a one-sided property agreement may be later upset on grounds of duress where a disfavored party shows that she agreed to it only in response to her spouse's threat to otherwise contest custody. *Brockman v. Brockman*, 240 Cal. Rptr. 96 (App. 1987) (wife gave up all claims to couple's substantial community property in exchange for husband's agreement to forfeit a $100,000 bond if he should ever contest the custody or support order; trial court must give wife opportunity to show that she was thereby coerced).

Yet there are of course also cases in which both parents are sincere in wanting a larger share of the custodial responsibilities than the other parent wishes to accept. If settlement of such conflicts is to be encouraged — and surely we do not wish to push them all to litigation — then musn't we allow agreements in which the parent who concedes more on custody obtains more on something else? The problem, in other words, may lie in distinguishing this kind of case from one in which a divorcing spouse threatens a custody claim for strategic advantage only, rather than from a genuine desire to undertake more residential responsibility for his or her children. Or is this the right distinction? One author tried to capture the difference between acceptable and problematic tradeoffs by comparing three hypotheticals:

1. Allan explicitly threatens to litigate custody if not given most of the marital property. He does not want custodial time. He is motivated by spite and self-interest. He settles for twenty percent custodial time and seventy-five percent of the marital property.

2. Bob makes no explicit threat. He simply proposes a settlement in which he has sixty percent custodial time and fifty percent of the marital property. He makes the proposal with the hope and belief that it will induce his wife to make a counter-proposal in which she gets eighty percent custody and twenty-five percent of the marital property. When she does, he accepts it.

[3. Charlie proposes a settlement identical to Bob's. He wants sixty percent custodial time because he thinks the children are best off spending time with him. After difficult negotiations he accepts twenty percent custody, and seventy-five percent of the marital property. His wife refused to compromise about time. So he accepted her terms to avoid litigation for the children's sake. He demanded the property because he felt taken advantage of if he did not get something in exchange for giving up time.]

I see no reason to judge Bob less harshly than Allan. If he would have given his wife eighty percent custody without extracting marital property had he not seen the chance to use custody as leverage, he has coerced his wife by depriving her of an important option. The use of this leverage was exploitative if he benefits financially because she cares for the children and perhaps because she cannot afford to fight for them.

Whether trades are less problematic if initiated by the person seeking more custodial time rather than by the person seeking more money is not obvious. Consider for example a mother who suggests receiving lower child support payments if the father does not seek primary custody. Perhaps her initiation indicates that she has reason to believe the father would actually have litigated had she not agreed to less child support. If so, the transaction was not coercive because it provides a benefit to both parents. However, payor initiation might indicate only that the mother fears litigation, which need not reflect actual likelihood of litigation.

Of course, not all trades of custodial terms for financial benefits coerce or exploit. . . . Because Charlie did not enter the negotiations demanding payment for something he would otherwise give for free, he has not coerced his wife. Nothing in the example suggests that he used his wife's desperation or attachment to the children to gain marital property.

Scott Altman, *Lurking in the Shadow*, 68 S. Cal. L. Rev. 493, 515–16 (1995). Do you find Altman's distinctions persuasive? Would it matter if Charlie, in Hypothetical 3, agreed to the tradeoff not because he felt the need to spare his children the custody fight, but because he thought his chance of winning the fight wasn't good enough to make persistence worthwhile?

Even if one agrees upon a principle that distinguishes proper from improper bargaining, it may still be difficult to develop a practical legal rule that reliably implements it. For example, would it be a practical rule that allowed subsequent attacks on settlement agreements only when they resulted from negotiations in which one party threatened to seek custody he or she did not really want? There is an obvious difficulty in trying to make such assessments of a party's motivations at some time in the past. One state attempted to address this problem by experimenting with bifurcated proceedings in contested divorces, in which adjudication of custody disputes did not take place until all other matters in the divorce had been decided. Ariz. Rev. Stat. § 25-328 (on request court can decide all other issues before deciding custody and parenting time issues). The goal was to eliminate custody contests that were actually the product of one party's hard bargaining for economic advantage. With the economic issues settled, there is no point to contesting custody unless one actually wants it. Perhaps the threat to contest custody is also less effective under such a rule, at least where the other spouse believes the threatener does not truly want custody, since the threat cannot be carried out until such time as it can achieve no purpose other than obtaining custody.

The *ALI Principles* conclude that "a distinction between good-faith and bad-faith threats of litigation is unworkable" even while also expressing concern that "the potential for oppressive bargaining is substantial." *ALI Principles* § 3.13, Comment *d*. In the context of considering when to approve agreements that call for "substantially less child support" than the court would otherwise award, perhaps as a trade-off to forestall a threatened custody claim, the *Principles* call for the court to reject the child support terms unless it determines that the agreement "as a whole" is "consistent with the interests of the child." *ALI Principles* § 3.13. When would lower child support amount satisfy this test? One relatively easy case suggested by Illustration 1 of § 3.13 involves an agreement under which the obligor provides other financial assistance to the custodial household that he might not otherwise be required to provide, and which confers benefits upon the child equivalent to the foregone support. More generally, the *Principles* observe that clear and appropriate custody allocation rules are perhaps the most effective way to suppress improper bargaining tactics over custody. Referring to the custody allocation rules that the *Principles* themselves adopt in its Chapter Two, Comment *d* to § 3.13 explains:

> The frequency of cases in which a custody challenge is threatened and then relinquished in exchange for a reduction of that parent's child-support obligation is a function of the bargaining positions of the parties, which derive in part from the rules regulating the allocation of custodial responsibility. The stronger a parent's claim to custodial responsibility, the less vulnerable the parent is to pressure to compromise child support in order to preserve that connection. In Chapter 2, these Principles base the allocation of custodial responsibility on past exercise of caretaking functions. Thus, the parent likely to have the stronger connection to the child should experience less pressure to compromise child support in order to preserve that connection. Similarly, the other parent's interest in access is guarded by a guarantee of access sufficient to maintain a strong relationship with the child even though that may be more contact than otherwise justified by that parent's preseparation caretaking role. Thus, Chapter 2 minimizes the extent to which either parent may be pressured to compromise child support in order [to] maintain an appropriate relationship with the child.

Does the problem of strategic threats to contest custody arise often enough to require a solution? Data on that point is hard to obtain, because of course one cannot easily establish the motivation for a threatened or actual custody contest. Altman surveyed members of the Family Law Section of the California Bar, and asked in what percentage of their prior year's family law cases involving minor children had "opposing counsel or their clients ever stated or clearly implied that they might litigate over custodial time if your client did not agree to a favorable financial settlement, [including proposals reported to you by your clients]." Forty percent said this had not happened in any of their cases; the mean response of all attorneys was 13 percent of the cases. Altman also reports data from several surveys in other states, but they use widely varying methods and obtain widely varying results.

It does not appear that standards of professional conduct would bar an attorney from tactical assertions of custody claim intended to obtain some other benefit for the client. *See* Lewis Becker, *Ethical Concerns in Negotiating Family Law Agreements*, 30 FAM. L.Q. 587, 628–29 (1996).

Note that the law generally imposes substantive limitations on custody and child support terms in separation agreements that do not arise from concerns over improper bargaining tactics. Most important is the general rule that such provisions always remain modifiable as necessary to protect the child's interest (the precise standard for modification varying among the states). Trade-offs of custody and support may also be vulnerable under such provisions. In that sense, the parties do not possess complete contractual freedom to specify by agreement the support and custody terms of their divorce. More consideration to these substantive limitations is given in Section B[5] below.

[3]   Where there is Only One Attorney

[a]   Joint Representation

It is common for separation agreements to be negotiated and executed by parties who are jointly assisted by a single attorney. The ethical obligations applicable to attorneys in these situations are addressed below in Notes 1 and 2. But the question of whether the resulting agreement is itself vulnerable to attack by an aggrieved party is in principle separate from the question of whether the lawyer complied with all applicable rules of professional conduct. In general, enforcement of the agreement cannot be resisted on this basis. In *Levine v. Levine*, 56 N.Y.2d 42, 451 N.Y.S.2d 26, 436 N.E.2d 476 (1982):

> The separation agreement was prepared by an attorney, related to the husband by marriage, who had previously represented the husband in connection with his business and who had known both parties for a number of years. The husband initially contacted the attorney and informed him that he had discussed the possibility of a separation agreement with his wife and that the couple had agreed on the essential terms. The attorney then arranged to meet with the wife at his office.
>
> At this meeting, the attorney told the wife that he was involved in the matter only because the basic terms of the agreement had already been settled by the parties and that the wife was free to seek the advice of another attorney. Based on conversations with both parties, the attorney prepared a draft agreement. Further negotiations and consultations followed, after which a final agreement was drawn up, thoroughly reviewed by plaintiff, and then signed by her. . . .

The court held that the fact that the same attorney represented both parties in the preparation of the agreement did not require its "automatic nullification."

> While the absence of independent representation is a significant factor to be taken into consideration when determining whether a separation agreement was freely and fairly entered into, the fact that each party retained the same attorney does not, in and of itself, provide a basis for rescission. . . . [W]here one attorney has represented both parties to the agreement, a question of overreaching on the part of the party who is the prime beneficiary of the attorney's assistance may arise. Nevertheless, as long as the attorney fairly advises the parties of both the salient issues and the consequences of joint representation, and the separation agreement arrived at was fair, rescission will not be granted. While the potential conflict of interests inherent in such joint representation suggests that the husband and wife should retain separate counsel, the parties have an absolute right to be represented by the same attorney provided "there has been full disclosure between the parties, not only of all relevant facts but also of their contextual significance, and there has been an absence of inequitable conduct or other infirmity which might vitiate the execution of the agreement."

In *Marriage of Egedi*, 105 Cal. Rptr. 2d 518 (App. 2001), the husband seeking to avoid enforcement of the settlement agreement claimed the attorney's disclosures were insufficient to permit his informed consent to the dual representation. While the trial court agreed with him, he lost on appeal. It may in fact be difficult to imagine what more the attorney could have done. He initially resisted the parties' request that he represent them both (he had previously represented each of them individually in unrelated matters), forcefully asserted his concern over a conflict of interest, and insisted on their signed acknowledgment that he advised them to seek independent counsel. After the parties reached an understanding and reduced it to writing without any participation by the attorney, he explained that his only role would be to type up their agreement after adding some "standard provisions." He thus obtained their consent to excluding any "advisory capacity" from his role, and he consistently refused to discuss the substance of the agreement's terms with either spouse. All this was applauded by the appeals court, which even observed that a "single attorney acting as a scrivener should not advise the parties of the pros and cons of their agreement so that they might 'unagree.' This would defeat the very purpose for which they sought assistance." *Id.* at 523.

What if the *Egedi* agreement contained terms that the attorney believed grossly one-sided? Is he supposed to remain silent in the face of such facts? Might not the parties, despite their understanding, assume from his silence that their agreement contained no unreasonable, unconscionable, or obviously unenforceable provisions, or provisions that, for example, subject them to avoidable tax liabilities? Recognizing this possibility the court observes in footnote that in such a case the attorney might "decline to act as a scrivener," but the court believed this case itself presented no such facts.

On one hand, the *Egedi* court seems right that the attorney was clear as could be about the limited nature of his role. On the other hand, is it appropriate for an attorney to agree to such a limited role? If the parties only want a scrivener, one might ask why they need an attorney at all. This court didn't ask, and that is surprising in light of an earlier California Case, *Ishmael v. Millington*, 241 Cal. App. 2d 520, 50 Cal. Rptr. 592 (1966). After discovering that in the divorce agreement she signed away most of her community property rights, the wife brought a malpractice action against the attorney who handled their divorce. His defense was that she had "sought no advice from the attorney and was given none," and that even in her deposition the wife conceded that "in signing the complaint and property settlement agreement she relied solely on her husband and did not rely on the attorney." The court observed:

> Divorces are frequently uncontested; the parties may make their financial arrangements peaceably and honestly; vestigial chivalry may impel them to display the wife as the injured plaintiff; the husband may then seek out and pay an attorney to escort the wife through the formalities of adjudication. We describe these facts of life without necessarily approving them. Even in that situation the attorney's professional obligations do not permit his descent to the level of a scrivener. . . . A husband and wife at the brink of division of their marital assets have an obvious divergence of interests. Representing the wife in an arm's length divorce, an attorney of ordinary professional skill would demand some verification of the husband's financial statement; or, at the minimum, inform the wife that the husband's

statement was unconfirmed, that wives may be cheated, that prudence called for investigation and verification. Deprived of such disclosure, the wife cannot make a free and intelligent choice. Representing both spouses in an uncontested divorce situation (whatever the ethical implications), the attorney's professional obligations demand no less. He may not set a shallow limit on the depth to which he will represent the wife.

The trial court's summary judgment in the attorney's favor was reversed, although the ultimate outcome of the malpractice action is not reported. *Egedi* and *Ishmael* could be reconciled by observing that a rule denying the cheated spouse the right to avoid the agreement need not also deny that spouse recovery for the loss against the attorney who failed to advise of the danger. Yet *Egedi* hardly invites that reading; to the contrary, it suggests that the attorney has a duty to avoid pointing out possibly unfair terms to the disadvantaged spouse, for fear of upsetting the agreement. If that is indeed the rule, then surely the attorney finding herself in that position ought to withdraw, as the *Egedi* court suggests she may. Consider, however, whether such a withdrawal might not inevitably suggest to the parties that the attorney believes the agreement problematic.

Intimately connected with the question of whether an attorney's conduct in joint representation constitutes malpractice is the question of whether it violates rules of professional conduct. The old A.B.A. Code of Professional Responsibility took a very skeptical approach toward joint representation. It provided in Disciplinary Rule 5-105(c) that

> a lawyer may represent multiple clients if it is obvious that he can adequately represent the interest of each and if each consents to the representation after full disclosure of the possible effect of such representation on the exercise of his independent professional judgment on behalf of each.

Under this language, even the consent of both clients may be insufficient to permit joint representation, since it may not be "obvious that [the lawyer] can adequately represent the interest of each" client if there is in fact a potential conflict between them.

Most states today follow the A.B.A.'s newer Model Rules of Professional Conduct, first promulgated in 1983. In its original form it had two provisions potentially applicable to the question of joint representation at divorce. Model Rule 1.7 stated the general rule dealing with conflicts of interest that can arise when a lawyer represents two persons whose interests may be adverse, while Rule 2.2 dealt with "intermediation," and was intended to apply to the case where the lawyer acted to facilitate such parties' reaching an agreement. The American Bar Association adopted major changes to the Model Rules in 2002; included among them was deletion of Rule 2.2 and the revision of Rule 1.7.

The language of new Rule 1.7 seems both more clear and less tolerant of multiple representation. Subdivision (a) states the basic rule ordinarily barring an attorney from representing two clients whenever "the representation of one client will be directly adverse to another client." Subsection (b) nonetheless creates a limited exception permitting such representation if

(1) the lawyer reasonably believes that the lawyer will be able to provide competent and diligent representation to each affected client;

(2) the representation is not prohibited by law;

(3) the representation does not involve the assertion of a claim by one client against another client represented by the lawyer in the same litigation or other proceeding before a tribunal; and

(4) each affected client gives informed consent, confirmed in writing.

Divorcing spouses must eventually become opposing parties in a lawsuit, at which point the Rule clearly bars joint representation under subsection (b)(3), even if both spouses consented. Nonetheless, lawyers often consult with both spouses up to the point of concluding their separation agreement, even though the lawyer can be counsel of record for only one of them in the divorce papers then filed before the court. Is that practice consistent with Rule 1.7? Paragraph 4's requirement of written informed consent means that it cannot be if the lawyer does not first obtain consent in writing from both spouses, after having explained to them the risks and dangers of such joint representation, including its effects on the attorney obligations of loyalty and confidentiality. Official Comment 19 to the Code suggests that clients may wish to weigh the added cost of securing a second attorney against such risks. Such added costs are of course a common concern in divorce proceedings. What seems clear from the Rule, however, is that it is for the client, and not the attorney, to make the judgment of whether the monetary savings justify the risks of joint representation. The client cannot weigh those risks properly if the attorney does not adequately describe them. An adequate description ought to include, one might think, more than abstractions. Specific illustrations of potential conflicts between the parties about the identification, classification, and valuation of property could, for example, bring home the nature of the risk to the naive client who might not otherwise appreciate it. On the other hand, such illustrations might have little meaning to some clients who have no significant property. The trick lies in assessing the kind of warnings most appropriate to particular clients in advance of undertaking their joint representation.

It is also important to keep in mind that consent is not sufficient in every case. Subsection (b)(1) bars joint representation if the lawyer does not "reasonably believe" that it is possible to provide "competent and diligent representation" to both of the spouses. This independent requirement is not avoided by client consent, even fully informed client consent. The trick here is to determine when a lawyer can "reasonably believe" these facts. This question is addressed through example in G. HAZARD & W. HODES, THE LAW OF LAWYERING §§ 11.4, 11.11, and 11.15, at 11–12, 11–28, and 11–46 (3d ed., 2009 Supp.)

The illustration involves a case in which both husband and wife come to the lawyer claiming to have worked out the details of their separation agreement, and ask him to "look over the figures" and then "represent them both in their 'amicable' divorce." The authors conclude that while the relationship between the parties is not antagonistic, it is "surely . . . directly adverse," so that Rule 1.7(a) applies. Thus the dispositive question is whether the clients can give effective consent. The authors point out that there is an unavoidable risk of as yet unknown magnitude that the lawyer cannot offer his best efforts on behalf of one client without materially limiting his representation of the other. Effective representation would be "extremely difficult," the authors conclude, if the attorney senses that the parties are not equally committed to the figures that they present, or would not equally welcome suggested revisions to their draft agreement. If the lawyer views the agreement as one-sided, as compared to agreements in comparable situations, the lawyer must feel free to express that view or he is not properly serving the interests of the disadvantaged client. Yet his duty to the advantaged client is to remain silent.

Is representation in this context "consentable," or must the reasonable lawyer conclude that competent and diligent representation cannot be provided simultaneously to both parties? The answer may require a deeper understanding of the clients' goals. Perhaps, for example, one is confident that both clients appreciate the possibility of such potential conflicts but consent anyway because both believe it best to settle on terms seen as fair by objective third parties. They thus affirmatively desire the attorney's assessment, even if the consequence would be a refashioning of the terms that altered the relative outcome. Persons who see themselves in a long-term relationship may well think in such terms, believing that any short-term advantage realized from a one-sided agreement would be offset by its longer-term costs to a relationship they wish to maintain. Divorcing parties could feel this way even though they are obviously ending their marital relationship, for any of a variety of reasons, such as their joint interest in maintaining a cooperative approach in their post-divorce parental roles. Assisting the parties to reach this kind of fair agreement is the kind of situation contemplated by the now abandoned Rule 2.2. At least some informed commentators, such as Hazard and Hodes, believe it may still be permissible under the revised Rule 1.7. But even they also caution that the lawyer must be alert to the possibility that the parties are not equally committed to such a vision of their task. If the lawyer does not have confidence that they are, then the common representation is not consentable because the lawyer cannot reasonably believe it possible to provide both clients with adequate representation. Making this judgment may be extremely difficult. The attitude of divorcing spouses may be more volatile than at first appears. Comment 29 to the revised Rule 1.7 cautions that the clients should be advised that common representation requires each client to assume greater responsibility for decisions than is necessary when they are separately represented with each lawyer free to pursue his own client's interest more vigorously.

It should not be assumed that separate representation is more likely to lead to a relationship of animosity. An attorney with clearly undivided loyalty to one spouse may be more effective in persuading that spouse that a less aggressive stance on short-term goals will be more effective in furthering his or her long-term interests, than would an attorney attempting to represent both parties. Common representation would seem unlikely to offer much advantage to the parties apart from the potential savings on attorney fees when it is successful. Yet those savings will be important to many divorcing spouses. For those with limited resources especially, the risk that common representation will leave one or both inadequately counseled may seem low enough to accept, given that less may be at stake in their allocation of property or the size of any support award. Ultimately, the ethical rules appear to reflect the uneasy tension between the ideal of separate representation and the reality for many divorcing couples of limited resources.

It must also be noted that the risk of common representation is greater where the attorney has a preexisting relationship with one of the spouses. The attorney may not be able to maintain his obligation of confidentiality with respect to information gained in that prior representation without compromising his obligations to the other spouse. If the spouse with the prior relationship is unwilling to waive the attorney's duty of confidentiality, common representation in the divorce would not be possible. *See* Comment 31 to Rule 1.7. Finally, the position of the American Academy of Matrimonial Lawyers is considerably less nuanced than the Model Rules on the question of joint representation. "An attorney should not represent both husband and wife even if they do not wish to obtain independent representation." American Academy of Matrimonial Lawyers, THE BOUNDS OF ADVOCACY § 2.20, at p. 25 (1991). While acknowledging that such common representation was permitted within the limitations of Model Rule 2.2 (which was still part of the Model Rules when the Academy's standards were adopted), the comment to this section concludes that "it is impossible for the attorney to provide impartial advice" to both husband and wife and that "even a seemingly amicable separation or divorce may result in bitter litigation over financial matters or custody." The Academy's standards do not have legal force but they do represent the collective judgment of this voluntary association.

[b]   Where Only One Party is Represented

The material in the preceding section considered the problems confronted by the attorney who attempts to service both husband and wife. One way to deal with the conflict, of course, is to define only one of the spouses as your client. The other is then unrepresented. While this approach eliminates the problem of conflict, it can raise its own difficulties. *Tenneboe v. Tenneboe*, 558 So. 2d 470 (Fla. Ct. App. 1990), provides a good example. The husband sought to set aside an agreement that obligated him to pay $700 monthly in alimony and child support against a net income of only $800 monthly, earned in a seven-day work week. The agreement also called for the husband to quit claim to the wife all his interest in the marital home, leaving her with the parties' full equity of $30,000. He assumed all their debts, and kept only a pension plan and credit union account worth approximately $10,500.

> The husband . . . was not represented by an attorney at the time of either the preparation or execution of the agreement, which was drafted in its entirety by the attorney representing the wife. He testified that when he signed the agreement at the wife's attorney's office, he protested that the payments were more than he "could handle," and inquired of the wife's attorney whether, by virtue of the agreement, the permanent alimony payments were set for the rest of his life. In response, the wife's attorney told him that he could return to court at a future time to have the payments modified, but according to the husband, the wife's attorney did not tell him that he would have to show a substantial change in circumstances or

financial ability in order to obtain such reduction. . . . The husband testified that he signed the agreement at that time in reliance on the attorney's representation, and that he would not have signed the agreement had he known that in order to prevail on a later request for modification, he would have to establish a change in circumstances or financial ability.

While the wife and her attorney disputed the precise content of the conversation, it was undisputed that her attorney had a conversation with the husband concerning his ability to pay the amounts called for in the agreement. The trial court nonetheless denied his motion to set aside the agreement, but the appeals court reversed.

If the wife's attorney told the husband that he could return to court later to have the payments reduced, without also explaining that he would have to establish a substantial change in circumstances or financial ability, he misinformed him. Indeed, the husband's efforts to obtain relief in the trial court met with resounding defeat, both at the hearing on the motion to set aside the agreement as well as at the final hearing of dissolution, which only served to confirm the intricacies inherent in successfully obtaining such relief. In any event, the advice given by the wife's attorney was, at best, an oversimplification. [¶] . . . [W]e conclude that the trial court abused its discretion in refusing to set aside the property settlement agreement. The husband's evidence on the matters of misrepresentation and overreaching was persuasive enough to steer the exercise of discretion in the direction of affording the husband relief from the rigorous provisions of the agreement.

Rule 4.3 of the Model Rules of Professional Conduct applies to a lawyer dealing with an unrepresented opposing person. It requires the lawyer to refrain from saying or implying that he is "disinterested," and requires the lawyer to correct any misunderstandings the unrepresented party may have as to the lawyer's role. *Tenneboe* quotes the comment to Rule 4.3 that the unrepresented party might think the lawyer is "a disinterested authority on the law even when the lawyer represents a client" and cautions that the "lawyer should not give advice to an unrepresented person other than the advice to obtain counsel." Revisions to the Rules after *Tenneboe* strengthen these points by moving them from the Comment to the Rule itself. The Comment now explains that the lawyer can negotiate with an unrepresented person on behalf of the client, by explaining the terms on which the client will settle a dispute and preparing the necessary papers for signature by the other person as well as the client. But it cautions that the lawyer can undertake such a role only after explaining that he or she represents the client only. The conduct of the *Tenneboe* attorney probably violated these guidelines, for both husband and wife agreed — and the attorney did not deny — that he discussed the alimony provision with the husband. Even if his explanation of it was accurate — a matter in dispute — he still appeared to give the husband legal advice on the substance of the agreement he had prepared as the wife's attorney. *See also* William J. Hazzard, Note, *Professional Responsibility: Duties Owed to An Unrepresented Party*, 44 FLA. L. REV. 489 (1992).

[4]   The Impact of the Decree on the Agreement: Of Merger and Modification

ALI PRINCIPLES

§ 7.10 Incorporation of the Terms of a Separation Agreement in a Decree

(1) Except as provided by Paragraph (3), if the court has not found the terms of a separation agreement unenforceable under § 7.09 and if the agreement does not provide otherwise, the court should incorporate the terms of the separation agreement in the decree of dissolution. . . .

(2) Unless otherwise agreed by the parties, terms of a separation agreement that are incorporated in a decree are merged in the decree.

(3) In those jurisdictions that do not allow a court to enforce decree terms that the court does not have the power to order on its own, terms of a separation agreement that a court does not have the power to enforce as decree terms, but that are otherwise enforceable as contract terms, are not incorporated in the decree and survive the decree as enforceable contract terms.

(4) Terms of a separation agreement incorporated in a decree are enforceable by all remedies available for the enforcement of judgments generally.

(5) Incorporated terms of a separation agreement that survive the decree as contract terms are automatically modified by modification of the decree.

NOTES

1. *Merger of the Agreement Into the Decree.*   Generalization on the subject of merger is difficult because of subtle variations among the states in the applicable procedural rules. Do the parties' intentions as expressed in their agreement determine whether merger occurs? Is there a particular form in which those intentions must be expressed to be effective? In the absence of any expression by the parties, does the agreement merge or not? In answering these sorts of questions, state law may vary enormously. Compare, for example, *Binder v. Binder*, 390 N.E.2d 260 (Mass. App. Ct. 1979), holding that merger is precluded if the agreement provides that it survives the decree, even if the decree incorporates the agreement by reference, with *Appels-Meehan v. Appels*, 805 P.2d 415 (Ariz. Ct. App. 1991), holding that there is merger unless the agreement contains language "unequivocally precluding merger," and *Walters v. Walters*, 298 S.E.2d 338 (N.C. 1983), holding that any separation agreement brought to the court for its approval merges into the decree, no matter what it says. *See* Sally Sharp, *Semantics as Jurisprudence: The Elevation of Form Over Substance in the Treatment of Separation Agreements in North Carolina*, 69 N.C. L. REV. 319 (1991).

Nonetheless, § 7.10 of the *ALI Principles* sets forth the basic framework as generally understood. The parties' agreement is normally but a prelude to the divorce decree that incorporates its terms. Whatever the necessary local procedure, the usual result is that the agreement is merged into the decree once it has been issued. One effect of merger is that the agreement no longer has independent status as a contract, and contract actions to enforce it therefore become unavailable. The contract terms are instead enforceable as terms of the decree. As a general matter, this is an enforcement advantage, because there are remedies available for enforcement of a decree that are not available in a contract action and which are usually more effective. For example, the spousal maintenance and child support portions of a decree (but not a contract) can be enforced by contempt, as well as periodic wage withholding or the diversion of tax refunds. *E.g., Ex Parte Hall*, 854 S.W.2d 656 (Tex. 1993) (contempt not available as remedy to enforce support and maintenance payments based upon premarital agreement rather than judicial decree). On the other hand, state law typically allows courts to modify the child support and alimony provisions of a decree, including decrees based upon agreements, while contract terms of course cannot normally be modified except by the agreement of both parties. Nonetheless, the modification of agreement-based decrees is itself a matter on which state law varies, and is addressed in more detail in Notes 3 and 4, and with respect to alimony, in Section A[5] below.

State law also varies as to the consequences of nonmerger. For example, in *Binder*, the court held that without merger, the separation agreement survives as a contract creating obligations independent of the decree, that the contract is enforceable by an ordinary contract action, and that the decree is enforceable like an ordinary decree. Needless to say, having two potential remedies for any nonpayment can be confusing, especially since the contract cannot ordinarily be modified but the decree can, and modification of the obligation established in the decree would not affect the parties' contractual obligations. A few cases hold that where the agreement specifies it shall be incorporated into the decree but not merged, the result is not only survival of the agreement as a contract, but also preclusion of any judicial modification of the decree or enforcement of it by contempt. E.g., *Riffenburg v. Riffenburg*, 585 A.2d 627 (R.I. 1991) (court lacked authority to modify alimony provision that was incorporated but not merged).

One reason the parties may wish to avoid merger is that they have agreed on a contract that includes terms that the divorce court could not order on its own. The most common example is an agreement to pay child support past the age of majority while the child attends college. Many states do not allow support orders for college students over age 18, even if the parties agree. In these states the only way such a term can be enforced is to ensure that it does not merge into the decree, but survives as a contract term enforceable in an action for breach. *Solomon v. Findley*, 808 P.2d 294 (Ariz. 1991). In other states, however, a provision in the agreement that the court could not order on its own can nonetheless be incorporated into the decree and enforced as any other provision; in these states merger is probably preferable. *See, e.g., Foltz v. Foltz*, 232 S.E.2d 66 (Ga. 1977) (provision obligating husband to support wife's child); *Peterson v. Leonard*, 622 A.2d 87 (Me. 1993) (same).

For a general treatment of the problem of merger, see Doris DelTosto Brogan, *Divorce Settlement Agreements: The Problem of Merger or Incorporation and the Status of the Agreement in Relation to the Decree*, 67 Neb. L. Rev. 235 (1988).

2. *Challenges to an Agreement After Merger.* In *Weber* and *Tennenboe*, objections to the agreement were raised before the decree had been issued or the terms approved under the jurisdiction's procedures for routine review of all agreements. But what if objection is first raised later, after the court presumably approved the agreement and merged it into the resulting decree? One basis for upsetting a decree already entered is fraud, and it is possible, for example, for an attorney's conduct with an unrepresented opposing party to cross that line. *See, e.g., Adkins v. Adkins*, 186 Cal. Rptr. 818 (Ct. App. 1982) (agreement held void as having been secured by fraud where wife's attorney secured the uneducated husband's consent by misleading him concerning his rights). Yet, the traditional fraud rule may not be adequate to deal with all cases of abuse. Part of the problem is the distinction between intrinsic and extrinsic fraud. The traditional rule requires "extrinsic" fraud to set aside a judgment. Some courts have abandoned this distinction, in part because it is so difficult to apply, *e.g., St. Pierre v. Edmonds*, 645 P.2d 615 (Utah 1982). Other courts continue to struggle with explaining the difference. *Stevenot v. Stevenot*, 202 Cal. Rptr. 116 (App. 1984), explains it this way:

> Fraud is extrinsic where the defrauded party was deprived of the opportunity to present his or her claim or defense to the court, that is, where he or she was kept in ignorance or in some manner, other than from his or her own conduct, fraudulently prevented from fully participating in the proceeding. . . .
>
> Any fraud is intrinsic if a party has been given notice of the action and has not been prevented from participating therein, that is, if he or she had the opportunity to present his or her case and to protect himself or herself from any mistake or fraud of his or her adversary, but unreasonably neglected to do so.

Under this approach, extrinsic fraud permits reopening the matter addressed by the decree, but intrinsic fraud does not. For example, in *Marriage of Alexander*, 261 Cal. Rptr. 9 (Ct. App. 1989), neither party had counsel; the husband prepared their *pro se* divorce papers based on his wife's waiver of any interest in his pension, their joint bank accounts or spousal support. But there was no extrinsic fraud because the wife "was not deliberately kept in ignorance of the proceeding or fraudulently prevented . . . from presenting her claims. Any failure was due to her own failure to act diligently." She was thus denied the chance to reopen the settlement agreed to 15 months earlier. Compare *Grissom v. Grissom*, 35 Cal. Rptr. 2d 530 (Ct. App. 1994), in which the husband told the wife that the papers he presented to her were needed to dismiss their pending divorce action. The papers in fact divided their property and allowed him to proceed with a divorce without notifying her. He filed the papers while continuing to live with the wife for ten years as if they were married — at which time the wife discovered they were not. Her motion to set aside both the dissolution and the marital settlement was allowed, the court finding extrinsic fraud.

One common claim is that one party intentionally misled the other as to the value of certain marital property assets; the defense will often be that the statement of value was an opinion rather than a fact, and cannot therefore constitute fraud. The cases divide. *E.g., Greger v. Greger*, 578 A.2d 162 (Conn. App. 1990) (constitutes fraud); *contra, Billington v. Billington,* 578 A.2d 674 (Conn. App. 1990) (*Greger* does not apply where fraud perpetrated only on party and not on the court, and where the party had not exercised diligence in protecting herself from the fraud). See also the cases collected in *Hresko v. Hresko,* 574 A.2d 24 (Md. Sp. App. 1990) and *Fraud and Duress — Relief from Judgment,* 12 EQUITABLE DIST. J. 73 (1995). Provisions in the separation agreement in which the parties each warrant that they have made full disclosure can provide a basis for later claims. *E.g., Hess v. Hess,* 580 A.2d 357 (Pa. Super. 1990) (wife allowed compensatory and punitive damages for fraud and breach of contract where husband concealed assets and agreement warranted that each party had made full disclosure). One court found extrinsic fraud where the husband and the wife's attorney were having an affair during the divorce proceedings. *Nobes v. Earhart,* 769 S.W.2d 868 (Tenn. App. 1988).

Some courts stretch traditional fraud doctrine to permit a post-judgment attack on egregious separation agreements. Professor Sharp suggests the law would be better served by a general rule requiring disclosure. Sharp, *Fairness Standards and Separation Agreements,* 132 U. PA. L. REV. 1399, 1410, 1426–27. See *Maranda v. Maranda,* 449 N.W.2d 158 (Minn. 1989) and the cases collected at 3 EQUITABLE DIST. J. 73–76, 154–55 (1986). Note that even with claims of fraud, statutes of limitation may bar later attack on the judgment.

The American Law Institute recommends abandoning reliance on the fraud doctrine in favor of a simpler approach, set out in § 7.11 of the *ALI Principles.* This provision generally allows the court to set aside any decree based upon an agreement that it would have rejected under § 7.09 (described above), had objection then been raised, if the "incorporated terms of the decree were substantially less favorable to the moving party than they would have been without the agreement." This power is subject to two limitations only: time limitations imposed by state law, and the rights of third parties. A typical source of time limitations under state law are provisions of state procedural rules modeled upon Rule 60 of the Federal Rules of Civil Procedure, which allows the court, on such terms as are just, to grant relief from judgment on diverse grounds, including: (1) mistake, inadvertence, surprise, or excusable neglect; (2) newly discovered evidence; (3) fraud (whether extrinsic or intrinsic), misrepresentation, or other misconduct of an adverse party; or (6) "any other reason justifying relief from the operation of the judgment." Rule 60 provides that the motion shall be made within a reasonable time and, for reasons (1), (2), and (3), not more than one year after entry of judgment. As for the rights of third parties, ordinary equity principles would usually bar compromising the claims of innocent third parties to property they purchased for value subsequent to its allocation under the challenged decree.

3. *Should Agreement-Based Custody and Support Terms Be More Modifiable Than Adjudication-Based Ones?* Some courts treat agreement-based decrees as *more easily* modifiable than custody decrees ordered by the court after litigation. Courts that apply such a "dual standard" to modification petitions may believe that judges can make better custody decisions than parents, perhaps because they are objective, or have the assistance of professionals such as social workers or psychologists, so that an initial custody decision made by a judge is entitled to more deference than one made by the parents. For a critical review of these cases, see Sally Sharp, *Modification of Agreement Based Custody Decrees:*

Unitary or Dual Standard?, 68 VA. L. REV. 1263, 1278–79 (1982).

If the custody terms of an agreement are more modifiable than those imposed by a judge, what of the agreement's child support terms? *Consider Thomas v. Thomas*, 120 Cal. App. 3d 33, 173 Cal. Rptr. 844 (1981). The husband sought a reduction in child support from $125 to $100 monthly. The original order had been entered in 1976 pursuant to the parties' agreement, and the record supporting the 1976 order contained no evidence of the circumstances at that time. (Such an empty record will be common in settled cases, as has been noted in other contexts as well, Owen Fiss, *Comment, Against Settlement*, 93 YALE L.J. 1073 (1984)). Over the wife's objection, the court concluded that the trial judge had discretion to revise the child support award on the basis of current circumstances alone, without considering whether the circumstances had changed:

> Our decision should not be construed as discouraging parties from entering into stipulated dispositions because of the concern they will later be upset without a showing of changed circumstances. Parties may either include in their stipulation the relevant circumstances on which it is based or, at either interlocutory time or on motion to modify, file a financial declaration or otherwise show his or her version of the circumstances. On motion to modify the resisting party may assert and show the lack of change as a bar to the motion. The record does not show any of these things was done in this case.

For a similar result, see *Essex v. Ayres*, 503 So. 2d 1365 (Fla. Ct. App. 1987). Does the problem of an empty record explain the lack of deference to the agreement's custody terms as well?

4. *Should Agreement Based Decrees Be Less Modifiable?* One might conclude they should, on the reasoning that a contract would not be modifiable without approval of both parties, and therefore the decree based upon it should be subject to the same rule. Because the court's obligations to protect the interests of children are regarded as paramount, this claim is not usually accepted with respect to child support or child custody — indeed, the opposite inclination is sometimes seen, as explained in Note 3. But alimony may be a different matter. Even though they are normally modifiable, one might regard it inappropriate to alter alimony terms in a decree based on an agreement, given the likelihood that they are part of an overall financial package that includes nonmodifiable provisions on property allocation. This conclusion might be strengthened if the agreement itself provided for such non-modifiability. These possibilities are all considered below in Section B[5][c], on the enforceability of no-modification clauses. The next section also gives fuller consideration to the enforceability of provisions concerning children.

[5]   Limitations on the Subject or Terms of Separation Agreements

[a]   Children

Almost any separation agreement ending a marriage with children will contain custody arrangements and child support terms. But in these areas courts assert a special role. Section 3.06 of the MMDA excludes terms "providing for the support, custody, and visitation of children" from the rule that otherwise makes provisions of a separation agreement binding on the court unless it finds them unconscionable. The same section also provides that these terms remain modifiable even if the agreement attempts to limit their modifiability. These rules are typical, and have the purpose of ensuring that the court can always revise the agreement, initially or through modification, as needed to protect the interests of the child.

Should courts retain such power to overrule parental decisions? The *ALI Principles* retain but limit that judicial authority, providing in § 206 that the court should order the custody terms agreed upon by the parents unless "the agreement is not knowing or voluntary, or would be harmful to the child." Thus, apart from defects in the bargaining process considered in the prior section, the court's power to overrule the parental arrangements may be exercised only when it finds such harm.

In *Ayo v. Ayo*, 235 Cal. Rptr. 458 (Ct. App. 1987), Patricia had a four year old son by a prior relationship at the time of her marriage to Larry. Larry adopted him within a year. The parties were divorced when the boy was 8; Patricia was awarded custody, and Larry was granted visitation and was ordered to pay child support. But almost immediately the parties had disputes over both the visitation and support arrangements. When the boy's biological father began to visit him a year after the divorce, the parties agreed to terminate Larry's visitation, and Patricia agreed to "hold Larry harmless from any claims" involving the boy. Their agreement was incorporated into the court's decree in 1979 when the boy was 9. But in 1985 Patricia sought current child support from Larry, who argued that even if he had to pay currently, he should have a right to eventual reimbursement from Patricia under their agreement. The court rejected this claim.

> [T]o uphold Larry's contention would mean that the broad powers of the courts regarding the support of minor children could be thwarted by the subterfuge of an indemnity provision in a contract between the parties. [U]nder such a provision a parent could find himself or herself allocating resources for indemnification that would otherwise be used to support the child, thereby harming the child's welfare. In sum, the 1979 agreement fails on public policy grounds. . . . [¶] [T]he rights of the contracting parties under agreements such as this one affecting children must yield to the welfare of the children. [¶] [T]he 1979 agreement was an attempt to completely obviate the clear and strong policy of this state that a parent must support his children. . . .

Saying it was "not without sympathy" for Larry, given the earlier judicial approval of the agreement and his reliance upon that, the court noted that Patricia had not sought support arrearages for the period between the 1979 agreement and her 1985 claim to renew Larry's support obligation, and observed that were she to seek such arrearages, "issues of waiver and estoppel would undoubtedly have to be addressed." In effect then, the *Ayo* court suggested that it would accept the agreement subject to the court's power to modify it as the child's needs required. But the case can also be read to suggest that the initial judicial approval of the agreement was mistaken, so that Larry should never have been allowed to avoid support obligations pursuant to it, even if the court was not prepared to penalize him now for the earlier court's mistake.

Was the original decision in *Ayo* to approve the agreement wrong? The *Ayo* fact pattern is not uncommon: an estranged father agrees to forego visitation in exchange for the custodial mother's agreement to forego child support. The deal may be struck, as in *Ayo*, after the divorce, when the father-child estrangement has occurred. Or it may be the parental arrangement from the outset. Such understandings seem particularly common between nonmarital parents. What is unusual about *Ayo* is that the parties formalized this arrangement in an agreement incorporated in a judicial decree. Because most courts would find such agreements not in the child's interests, they are rarely offered to courts and more rarely accepted. *Ayo* demonstrates they may not be enforceable even if approved, at least as to future support. Recall as well that most states hold that a spousal agreement does not alone justify a child support award that departs from prevailing guidelines. Such a rule clearly casts doubt on any no-visitation/no-support agreement, which by definition does not comply with support guidelines. *See DePalmo v. DePalmo*, 679 N.E.2d 266 (Ohio 1997) (holding husband's waiver of all support invalid, as the court has the obligation to test any proposal put forth by the parents against the support guidelines).

Sometimes the parties attempt to settle the child support obligation in a lump sum; the entire agreement may or may not include a visitation tradeoff as well. For example, in *Kelley v. Kelley*, 449 S.E.2d 55 (Va. 1994), the divorce decree incorporated the parties' agreement under which the husband relinquished to the wife his share of the equity in the marital home, valued at $40,000, in exchange for which "the husband shall never be responsible for payment of child support." The agreement also required the wife to indemnify the husband were he ever ordered to pay support. Six years later the husband petitioned "for definite periods of visitation" with the children, the wife counterclaimed for child support, and the husband replied with a motion asking the court to order the wife to reimburse him for any support he was required to pay. The court held the support provisions of the agreement, and the decree that incorporated them, void as a violation of the rule that "parents cannot contract away their children's right to support nor can a court be precluded by agreement from exercising its power to decree child support." It therefore affirmed the trial court order requiring support and barring the indemnification. For a similar result on similar facts, but with the genders reversed, see *Reimer v. Reimer*, 502 N.W.2d 231 (N.D. 1993).

The *ALI Principles* may be somewhat more willing to accept parental arrangements in these cases. *See* Illustration 3 of § 3.13 of the *Principles*:

Sandra and Richard are the parents of eight-year-old Charlene, who was born while Sandra was still in high school and living in her parents' home. Sandra and Richard have never lived together and Sandra has always been Charlene's residential parent. Richard, a low-wage earner who has been able to pay only small amounts of child support, has visited Charlene sporadically, generally arriving unannounced on major holidays, sometimes in a state of inebriation. Sandra married Bob three years ago. Bob, a pharmacist, earns good wages and he and Sandra have had a child together. Charlene is deeply attached to her little brother Billy and to Bob, who are equally attached to her. The entire family is disturbed by Richard's holiday visits. Charlene has become increasingly distressed during holiday periods and becomes visibly depressed and withdrawn during and after Richard's visits. Sandra proposed to Richard that she waive child support in return for his agreement not to visit Charlene until she feels differently about his visits. Richard agreed. The court should approve this agreement.

Some may be disturbed by this result because it seems to allow Richard to use his own irresponsible behavior as a bargaining chip allowing him to obtain an agreement that frees him from his financial responsibilities to his child. On the other hand, it seems clear that the relatively modest payments Richard would otherwise be required to make would probably provide little real financial benefit for the child, who is adequately provided for in any event. In light of that, it is plausible to think that on balance the child is better off with this agreement than without it. Under such circumstances, the *Principles* take the position that the court should defer to the parental judgment expressed in the agreement. Note that this example from the *Principles* does not address whether Richard should remain immune from any claim for future child support were Charlene's circumstances to change. Suppose, for example, Charlene and Bob were to divorce, placing Charlene in a financially less comfortable situation. Should Richard then be liable for current support if he were financially capable of providing it? Most courts would probably say yes, although depending upon the facts a plausible case could be made that the support obligation should then fall to Bob rather than Richard.

For a case that might seem consistent with the approach of the *Principles*, see *Albins v. Elovitz*, 791 P.2d 366 (Ariz. App. 1990). Although stating that such agreements were not "binding" where the child's interests were adversely affected, the court held that "a custodial parent can waive child support" and that the noncustodial parent, "in consideration of the waiver," can surrender visitation rights. The court nonetheless allowed the father to resume visitation, despite his agreement waiving it, although it also declined to enforce the contract's liquidated damages provision, which would have required the father to pay an amount equal to the past due support that would have been ordered but for the agreement. In short, *Albins* seems to endorse both the view that such agreements may be accepted and the caution that the court may still modify their application at a later time if the child's interests so require.

In general, courts seem far quicker to find unconscionability where the allegedly unfair terms involve children then when they involve only the financial terms between the adult former spouses. *E.g., Bright v. Freeman*, 808 N.Y.S.2d 359 (A.D. 2005) (though child support provisions of separation agreement did not violate

Child Support Standards Act, the distribution of child-related expenses was so one-sided in favor of husband that the agreement was unconscionable).

NOTE

Agreements concerning relocation. The relocation of a custodial parent to a distant location is one of the most contentious issues that can arise after divorce. *See* Chapter 6, Section E[5]. Some parties may anticipate the issue at the time of the initial decree and provide for it in their agreement. Should such an agreement be enforced? Consider *Bell v. Bell*, 572 So. 2d 841 (Miss. 1990), in which the parties provided that the children would live near Tupelo (the marital home) and that "neither husband nor the wife shall remove the children . . . without the express written consent of the other." These terms were incorporated in the 1986 divorce decree, but in 1988 the wife sought to move with the children from Tupelo to Jackson, over the husband's objection. The court conceded that the agreement barred the move, but held it unenforceable and evaluated the parties' conflict with the same kind of best interest analysis it would apply had there been no agreement (with the result that the mother was allowed to take one child with her, but not the other, a teenager who wished to remain with his father).

The decision in *Bell* appears typical; see the Reporter's Notes to Comment *h* of § 2.17 of the *ALI Principles* for a review of the cases. The *Principles* nonetheless recommend honoring such agreements unless the parent who seeks to relocate can make out a case for modifying the custody decree, which under the *Principles* requires a showing of an unanticipated and substantial change in circumstances. *See ALI Principles* § 2.17, Comment *h*. The comment points out that parties may find it easier to reach agreement on custodial arrangements initially if they can include provisions concerning such relocation. Suppose in *Bell* the husband had obtained his wife's agreement to the "no-move" provision in exchange for a financial settlement more generous to the wife than the court would ordinarily be expected to order: should that matter?

Recent cases show a continued resistance to enforcing agreements on relocation (both provisions allowing and refusing relocation in advance): *e.g.*, *Delamielleure v. Belote*, 704 N.W.2d 746 (Mich. Ct. App. 2005) (man's blanket waiver of right to challenge former wife's relocation does not bind the court; relocation of child governed by statute); *Helton v. Helton*, 2004 Tenn. App. LEXIS 20 (Jan. 13, 2004) (separation agreement in which wife promised not to relocate without husband's written permission is not binding on the court; parties cannot "bargain away the court's continuing jurisdiction over the care of the child"); *cf. Roberts v. Roberts*, 64 P.3d 327 (Idaho 2003) (wife had agreed in separation agreement not to relocate, but court's refusal of relocation request, and appellate court's affirmance, appeared to be on other grounds).

[b] Arbitration Clauses

Parties may provide in their settlement agreement for arbitration of disputes that may arise under it, or of petitions for its modification. The United States Supreme Court has recently been quite consistent and persistent in its support for the enforcement of arbitration provisions. E.g., *Preston v. Ferrer*, 128 S. Ct. 978 (2008); *Buckeye Check Cashing, Inc. v. Cardegna*, 546 U.S. 440 (2006). In the shadow of these decisions, it is not surprising that state courts will enforce arbitration agreements as a matter of course in separation agreements: both provisions for settling disputes arising out of the agreement, e.g. *Lauren S. v. Ira S.*, 811 N.Y.S.2d 1 (App. Div. 2006) (broad arbitration provision in separation agreement, requiring arbitration of "any claims or disputes arising out of or in connection with this Agreement or any breach thereof," not vitiated by boilerplate language in decree, that court retains jurisdiction to enforce); *Drysdale v. Drysdale*, 2006 Conn. Super. LEXIS 2607 (Aug. 24, 2006) (separation agreement provided for arbitration of any dispute about division of property; resulting arbitration award is subject to the deferential review set by state arbitration statute); and agreements of parties to have the property and alimony provisions of their separation agreement set by binding arbitration. *Vendittelli v. Vendittelli*, 2006 Mich. App. LEXIS 3280 (Nov. 7, 2006).

Some courts, however, still refuse to enforce arbitration awards concerning child custody. *Lipsius v. Lipsius*, 673 N.Y.S.2d 458 (App. Div. 1998) (holding disputes over custody and visitation are not subject to arbitration). In *Miller v. Miller*, 620 A.2d 1161 (Pa. Super. 1992), the mother sought to enforce a custody award by the arbitrator under the arbitration process created by the parties' separation agreement. Although holding that such an arbitration clause was not void as against public policy, and offering many kind words about the virtue of parental agreement and of arbitration, the court concluded:

> We cannot ignore our duty to protect the rights and interests of children once called upon to do so. Therefore, while arbitration proceedings in custody disputes are not void as against public policy, the question of the enforceability of arbitration awards in this context is a very different matter. [W]hile agreements entered into between parties are binding as between the parties, they may not bind the court once its jurisdiction is invoked. It follows necessarily that an award rendered by an arbitration panel would be subject to the supervisory power of the court in its parens patriae capacity in a proceeding to determine the best interests of the child. It has long been recognized by the courts that it is the Commonwealth who is charged with the duty of protecting the rights and interests of children.

Courts may be reluctant to enforce child custody arbitration provisions because the arbitrator is limited to deciding the dispute on the basis of the agreement of the parties, while courts consider the child's best interests in deciding custody disputes. Two commentators have offered the following illustrative example: In deciding whether a noncustodial father ought to be required to pay for a child's psychiatric care under a clause obligating him to pay medical expenses, an arbitrator would properly focus on what parties usually mean when they use this kind of language and whether that accepted meaning includes psychiatric care. By contrast, a judge might properly consider the child's interests and whether the father was in a position to pay for the care. Janet M. Spencer & Joseph P. Zammit, *Mediation and Arbitration: A Proposal for Private Resolution of Disputes Between Divorced or Separated Parents*, 1976 Duke L.J. 911, 921–22. It has been suggested that to assuage any such fears by the courts, properly drafted arbitration clauses could require the arbitrator to consider the child's best interests in making arbitration awards. Additionally, independent representation could be provided for the children in the arbitration. Melissa Douthart Philbrick, Note, *Agreements to Arbitrate Post-Divorce Custody Disputes*, 18 COLUM. J.L. & Soc. PROBS. 419, 452–59 (1985); Janet M. Spencer & Joseph P. Zammit, *Reflections on Arbitration Under the Family Dispute Services*, 32 ARB. J. 111 (1977).

There are indications, however, that courts are becoming more receptive to the use of arbitration even in child custody and parenting time (visitation) issues, when arbitration is used either for the construction of separation terms, or for the resolution of disputes arising out of an existing separation agreement. In *Fawzy v. Fawzy*, 973 A.2d 347 (N.J. 2009), the New Jersey Supreme Court held that it was within the "constitutionally protected sphere of parental autonomy" to use arbitration to resolve issues of custody and parenting time on the eve of divorce, as long as the agreement to arbitrate was in writing, and the parties knowingly waived their rights to a judicial determination. The court in *Fawzy* reserved only the normal limited judicial review of arbitration decisions under state (and federal) arbitration statutes, with an additional right to review the arbitration decision when a *prima facie* claim of harm to the child has been made out.

For recent commentary on this topic, see E. Gary Spitko, *Reclaiming the "Creatures of the State": Contracting for Child Custody Decisionmaking in the Best Interests of the Family*, 57 WASH. & LEE L. REV. 1139 (2000); Aaron E. Zurek, Note, *All the King's Horses and All the King's Men: The American Family after Troxel, the Parens Patriae Power of the State, A Mere Eggshell Against the Fundamental Right of Parents to Arbitrate Custody Disputes*, 27 HAMLINE J. PUB. L. & POL'Y 357 (2006).

[c] No-Modification Clauses

As explained above in Section B[4], once an agreement is merged into the divorce decree it is no longer enforceable as a contract but is instead enforceable as a decree. Alimony provisions in a decree are ordinarily modifiable. Is their modifiability for changed circumstances affected by the fact that they are based on the parties' agreement? On one hand, alimony, unlike child support, is not subject to the rule that the court must retain the power to modify the obligation as necessary to protect the child's interest. On the other, the alimony provisions may be part of an overall financial settlement that includes non-modifiable terms on property allocation, so that modifications of the alimony provisions alone may seem unfair to one party.

State laws vary considerably on this question. A number statutes expressly authorize no-modification provisions. *E.g.*, CONN. GEN. STAT. § 46b-86(a). It is common to find separation agreements that have language along the lines: "No modification or waiver of any of the terms of this agreement will be valid unless the same shall be in writing and executed with the same formality as this agreement." This language allows for modification, but precludes (claims of) oral modifications. *See, e.g., Sutherland v. Sutherland*, 944 A.2d 395, 402 (Conn. App. Ct. 2008).

Without express statutory guidance, a few courts take a contract approach and provide that the terms of a separation agreement, even though merged in the decree, are not modifiable unless the parties' agreement expressly permits modification. *Husband B. v. Wife H.*, 451 A.2d 1165 (Del. Super. 1982) (but court retains power to modify child support provision). Such a policy may even be extended, in part, to child support awards, *McInturff v. McInturff*, 644 S.W.2d 618 (Ark. App. 1983) (court retains power to modify child support awards only where the portion intended as child support can be determined; aggregate award which is partially child support is not modifiable). Other courts make agreement-based decrees subject to the same modification rules as judge-made decrees. *E.g., Lepis v. Lepis*, 416 A.2d 45 (N.J. 1980). One state with restrictive alimony rules manages to take both positions depending upon whether the alimony obligation in question could have been ordered by the court. *Voigt v. Voigt*, 670 N.E.2d 1271 (Ind. 1996) (state law allows only rehabilitative alimony limited to three years, unless the obligee is either physically or mentally incapacitated and therefore unable to support himself, or is unable to work because he must care for a child with a physical or mental incapacity; agreement-based alimony not modifiable by the court unless the facts were such that the court could have imposed the alimony award in question).

In a jurisdiction which ordinarily allows modification of agreement-based alimony orders, what if the agreement expressly bars or limits such modifications? Again, the states vary. One approach allows enforcement of "no-modification" clauses, but only if they meet strict requirements. California seems to take this approach. *Hufford v. Hufford*, 199 Cal. Rptr. 726 (App. 1984) (spousal support modifiable despite general language in agreement precluding alteration; effective no-modification clause must be in "specific, unequivocal language"); *In re Marriage of Benson*, 171 Cal. App. 3d 907, 217 Cal. Rptr. 589 (1985) (relies on *Hufford* in allowing extension of spousal support despite an agreement-based decree specifying support would terminate after eight years); *Marriage of Jones*, 222 Cal. App. 3d 505, 271 Cal. Rptr. 761 (1990) (similar). *Compare In re Marriage of Zlatnik*, 197 Cal. App. 3d 1284, 243 Cal. Rptr. 454 (1988) (agreement stating "in no event shall husband be obligated to pay spousal support after April 30, 1986" (seven years from the decree) sufficiently explicit to satisfy *Hufford* and effectively precludes an extension).

Other courts are less grudging in permitting enforcement of no-modification clauses, at least for alimony. In *Karon v. Karon*, 435 N.W.2d 501 (Minn. 1989), the parties' agreement called for spousal maintenance for ten years and contained a provision waiving "any right to maintenance except as provided therein" and divesting the court "of jurisdiction to alter the agreement or maintenance." Five years later, the wife sought an increase in maintenance because she had lost her job and her former husband was doing well. In a split decision, the court turned her down in language strongly suggesting this was largely a matter of contract: "[I]ntelligent adult women, especially when represented by counsel, must be expected to honor their contracts the same as anybody else." *Id.* at 504. The Wisconsin Supreme Court held that a father whose income had declined could not obtain a child support reduction because the agreement contained a no-modification provision which explicitly bound him "notwithstanding a reduction in his income." The court avoided the question of whether it would enforce an agreement limiting increases in child support. *Honore v. Honore*, 439 N.W.2d 827 (Wis. 1989).

No-modification clauses may render seemingly unreasonable results when events turn out in ways the parties did not anticipate. For example, in *Josic v. Josic*, 397 N.E.2d 204 (Ill. App. 1979), the parties' 1975 agreement provided that the husband's alimony obligations to the wife would be non-modifiable. He later had a stroke which he "alleged . . . rendered him permanently disabled and thus permanently unemployed and unable to make the payments." The court nonetheless enforced the agreement as permitted under state law. In *Toni v. Toni*, 636 N.W.2d 396 (N.D. 2001), the court enforced a provision in the parties' separation agreement barring modification of the alimony terms. At the 1999 dissolution of the parties' 28-year marriage the husband earned $14,000 monthly as a urologist while the wife earned only $1,000 as a bookstore clerk. Their agreement allowed her $5,000 monthly in alimony but terminated all payments at her remarriage or in April 2001, whichever occurred first. She agreed to this limited term because she expected soon to remarry. When her marital plans fell through she sought the extension which the court denied. Note that under § 7.12 (3) of the *ALI Principles*, an agreement to limit the modifiability of "compensatory payments" (the ALI's replacement for alimony) is not enforceable if "the court finds that modification is required to avoid a substantial injustice." Recall that the *Principles* allow courts to examine the substantive fairness of premarital agreements in specified categories of cases in which it seems particularly likely that the circumstances under which enforcement is sought were not anticipated by the parties; the concern is that enforcement should not be available where it would yield very unfair results under such unanticipated circumstances. The principle that the ALI applies here to separation agreements seems similar.

As a planning matter, the attorney drafting a separation agreement intended to govern the parties' relationship over a long period may well want to build some flexibility into it. Permitting petitions for judicial modification is the traditional answer, but may provide too much flexibility. Another approach is to establish by agreement both standards for modification and for the arbitration of disputes between the parties on the application of these standards.

PROBLEMS

Problem 8-7. *H* asks you to prepare a separation agreement for him and his wife. They have mutually agreed upon divorce and want to proceed with it amicably and simply. They have already produced their own rough draft without legal assistance and need you only to take care of the legal technicalities. You do not know *H* well, although a few years ago you reviewed a limited-partnership agreement for him in connection with an investment he was considering. The couple have been married for 15 years, and have two children. For the last ten years, *W* has not worked outside the home; *H* has been a plant manager for the American Can Company. *H* tells you he's agreed to give *W* custody of the children, reasonable child support (around $1,000 a month for the two of them), possession of the marital home, including the household furnishings, until the younger child (now 11) reaches 18, and one of their cars. *H* will make the mortgage and insurance payments on the home, and has already given *W* a lump-sum of $10,000, since she was interested in buying an ice-cream business. He also mentioned that he was putting aside $50,000 for each of the children, to be given them upon their graduation from high school, and that he had promised W that each child would receive at least one-fourth of his estate.

How do you proceed?

Problem 8-8. Attorney A calls to arrange your representation of W. He has prepared a separation agreement for the couple but feels that W should have her own counsel. When W arrives for an appointment the next day, she is accompanied by H. How do you proceed?

Problem 8-9. The Johnsons come to consult about a separation agreement. They present you with a rough draft working out most of the terms. You have represented H on some prior business dealings, from which you have a general idea of his financial standing. It seems to you the agreement gives W relatively little. Nonetheless, they do not seem interested in having you review the substance of their agreement, except for tax considerations or other "legal technicalities." When you suggest that W probably ought to have separate counsel, H makes it clear that he thinks that would be an unnecessary expense "since we've already worked everything out." W says nothing, but agrees with H when you ask her opinion. In explaining the agreement to you, H, who generally seems to dominate the discussion, emphasizes that it gives W sole custody of their two children, ages 8 and 6.

How do you proceed?

Problem 8-10. An agreement between H and W provided that W would sell their house, receiving the first $120,000 of net proceeds, while H would receive the rest. When the agreement was negotiated and signed, H was unrepresented. But he assumed that the agreement would result in net proceeds to him of about $100,000. In fact, the house did not sell at the original listing price, as a result of which W lowered it. She now expects to net a total of about $140,000 from a sale, leaving $20,000 for H. H seeks your advice, since he now wants to challenge the agreement, which has not yet been approved by the court. What do you advise?

Problem 8-11. H and W's separation agreement required H to provide 36% of his gross income in support, assist in the two children's medical expenses as well as the cost of the college education, and to share in the purchase of a home for W and the children. At the time the agreement was made, the children, then of preschool age, suffered severely from cystic fibrosis, and the parties assumed W would be needed in the home full-time to tend the children's medical needs. Nine years later, H seeks relief from the agreement. The children's condition has improved well beyond prior expectations so that they now lead essentially normal lives. W has received an inheritance of $200,000, and is employed at a salary of $28,500. H's annual salary of $72,000 produces a monthly net of $3,674, of which about $2,200 must be paid per month under the agreement.

Can he obtain an order modifying the agreement's provisions for child support?

Part III

NONTRADITIONAL FAMILIES

Chapter 9

NONTRADITIONAL FAMILIES

INTRODUCTION

United States Supreme Court Justice O'Connor noted that the "demographic changes of the past century make it difficult to speak of an average American family. The composition of families varies greatly from household to household." *Troxel v. Granville*, 530 U.S. 57, 63 (2000). These changes include increases in numbers of unmarried heterosexual couples living together and of children born and raised outside of marriage. Same-sex partners are more visible in American society, and many are raising children together. This Chapter examines the legal system's responses to these changing demographics. Courts and legislatures have varied greatly in the pace and manner with which they have recognized nontraditional family forms. The resulting mosaic of policies offers a fascinating study of how the law responds to social change. Section A examines legal treatment of nonmarital cohabitant relationships. Section B considers the legal status of nonmarital children and their relationships with their parents, with special attention to the obstacles that have faced gays and lesbians who seek to adopt children.

A. NONMARITAL COHABITATION

[1] The Demographics of Unmarried Cohabiting Couples in the United States

Between 1960 and 2006, the number of unmarried heterosexual couples living together increased more than ten-fold, while the number of married couples did not even double. *See* Table 9-1. During this same period, the ratio of unmarried heterosexual couples to married couples in the United States increased from 1.1 unmarried couples per 100 married couples in 1960 to 9.2 in 2006. Although most nonmarital cohabitants are in their 20s, 30s and 40s,[1] there has also been an increase in cohabitation among older Americans.[2] Most observers attribute this rise largely to the economic disincentives of marriage for elder couples, which may include loss of pension survivor benefits and reduction of pension assistance,

---

[1] Data from the year 2000 reveal that 47.4% of male and 42.2% of female unmarried cohabiting adults were ages thirty-five and older, that 37% of the men and 33.2% of the women were ages twenty-five to thirty-four years old, and that the remaining 15.6% and 24.5%, respectively, were ages twenty-four and younger. U.S. Census Bureau, *America's Families and Living Arrangements* (2000).

[2] One study reported an increase from 9,600 cohabitants age 60 and older in 1960 to 407,000 senior cohabitants in 1990. *See* Albert Chevan, *As Cheaply as One: Cohabitation in the Older Population*, 58 J. Marriage & Fam. 656, 660 (1996).

combined with the growing social acceptance of nonmarital cohabitation. Albert Chevan, *As Cheaply as One: Cohabitation in the Older Population*, 58 J. MARRIAGE & FAM. 656, 660 (1996).

Research reveals that heterosexual cohabiting relationships are less stable than marriages. Approximately half of such relationships last one year or less, one-sixth last about three years, and only one-tenth last five years or longer. Larry Bumpass & Hsien-Hen Lu, *Trends in Cohabitation and Implications for Children's Family Contexts in the United States*, 54 POPULATION STUDIES 29, 33 (2000). In addition, couples who cohabit before marriage are more likely to divorce than are couples who did not cohabit before marriage. *Id.* Although this phenomenon is not well understood, most sociologists suggest that couples who choose to cohabit before marriage differ from other married couples in ways including their values, attitudes, and relationship skills, and that this ultimately affects the durability of their marriages. *See, e.g.*, Judith A. Seltzer, *Families Formed Outside of Marriage*, 62 J. MARRIAGE. & FAM. 1247 (2000); Lee A. Lillard, Michael J. Brien & Linda J. Waite, *Premarital Cohabitation and Subsequent Marital Dissolution: A Matter of Self-Selection?* 32 DEMOGRAPHY 437 (1995).

Table 9-1
Unmarried Heterosexual Couple Households in the United States, by Presence of Children: 1960 to 2006[3]

Year	Total Married Couples	Total Unmarried Heterosexual Couples ("UHC")	Total UHC Without Children Under 15	Total UHC With Children Under 15	Ratio of Unmarried Couples per 100 Married Couples
2006	58,179,000	5,368,000	3,540,000	1,828,000	9.2
2005	57,975,000	5,214,000	3,475,000	1,738,000	9.0
2000	55,311,000	4,736,000	3,061,000	1,675,000	8.6
1995	53,858,000	3,668,000	2,349,000	1,319,000	6.8
1990	52,317,000	2,856,000	1,966,000	891,000	5.5
1980	49,112,000	1,589,000	1,159,000	431,000	3.2
1970	44,728,000	523,000	327,000	196,000	1.2
1960	39,254,000	439,000	242,000	197,000	1.1

Demographic data on same-sex cohabitating couples have been somewhat more difficult to obtain. The United States Census Bureau introduced a category for unmarried partners that allowed tracking for same-sex couples only in the 1990 decennial census, and repeated it in the 2000 census.[4] It also began tracking

---

[3] Table 9-1 was compiled and adapted from the following sources: U.S. Census Bureau, *Table HH-1. Households, by Type: 1940 to Present*, June 12, 2003, *available at* http://www.census.gov/population/ socdemo/hh-fam/hh1.xls; U.S. Census Bureau, *Table UC-1. Unmarried-Couple Households, by Presence of Children: 1960 to Present*, January 2009, *available at* http://www.census.gov/population/socdemo/hh-fam/uc1.xls. For additional information regarding data collection methods, see Statistical Note following this section.

[4] See Statistical Note following this section for a discussion of this category.

statistics regarding same-sex partners on an annual basis in the American Community Survey ("ACS"). As it turns out, however, difficulties in coding both the decennial censuses and the ACS before 2008 appear to have resulted in substantially overestimating the total number of same-sex partners in the United States. *See* Gary J. Gates, Williams Institute, "Same Sex Couples in the 2008 American Community Survey," (Sept. 2009), *available at* http://www.law.ucla.edu/williamsinstitute/pdf/ACS2008_WEBPOST_FINAL.pdf. The 2008 ACS appears to have corrected this flaw. Based on the 2008 ACS, there are approximately 564,743 same-sex couples in the United States, which comprise just under one percent (.9 percent) of all coupled households. U.S. Census Bureau, Families and Living Arrangements, *available at* http://www.census.gov/population/www/socdemo/hh-fam.html (scroll down to "Same Sex Couples," find the heading marked "Data from the American Community Survey," hit the tab for "2008 Tables). Determining the exact legal status of these same-sex couples is complicated, however. Of the 564,743 same-sex couples, 149,956 identified themselves as "husband/wife" and 414,787 identified themselves as "unmarried partner." *See* Martin O'Connell & Daphne Lofquist, U.S. Census Bureau, Changes to the American Community Survey between 2007 and 2008 and their Potential Effect on the Estimates of Same-Sex Couple Households, Table 1 (Sept. 2009), *available at* http://www.census.gov/population/www/socdemo/files/changes-to-acs-2007-to-2008.pdf. However, given the limited availability of same-sex marriage and the state data regarding the numbers of same-sex couples who have married thus far, it is clear that most of the same-sex couples who have identified themselves as spouses are not legally married under state law. (Some of these couples may have entered into a civil union or domestic partnership; there is no option on the ACS to report these statuses. In addition, other same-sex partners may have declared themselves as married because they have been wed in a religious ceremony, or because they consider themselves married despite not having the legal status.) The Williams Institute of UCLA, based on calculations from state data, estimates that as of the end of 2008, approximately 35,000 of these same-sex couples were legally married, and 86,000 couples (some of whom may also later have gotten married, and therefore are also counted in the same-sex marriage estimates) were in other legally-recognized relationships such as civil unions or registered domestic partnerships. *See* Gates, *supra*, at 2. Table 9-2 examines data obtained in the 2008 ACS.

Table 9-2
Same-Sex Partner Households in the United States, Compared with Married and Unmarried Heterosexual Partner Households: 2008[5]

Total House-holds	Total Coupled Households	Married Heterosexual Couple House-holds	Unmarried Heterosexual Couple House-holds	Same-Sex Partner Households
113,101,329	61,905,637	55,692,103	5,648,791	564,743

It is important to note, however, that the data presented thus far examine *household composition only*. That is, they do not tell us how many people identify themselves as gay or lesbian, or how many people are in gay or lesbian relationships, but *not* sharing a household. Many same-sex and opposite-sex unmarried couples may consider themselves to be in a committed relationship, perhaps even spending extended periods of time living together in one partner's home, while still maintaining separate legal residences. When confronted with a formal document such as a Census questionnaire, many such persons will not classify themselves as sharing a household. Furthermore, it is likely that in some cases, a survey respondent living with a same-sex partner may choose not to identify the unrelated person with whom she or he is lives as an "unmarried partner." Rather, some respondents may check the box for "housemate" or "roommate," as the Census form permits, either because of reluctance to reveal the nature of their intimate relationships on a governmental questionnaire or because at the time of the 1990 census many states still had sodomy laws which criminalized such relationships. The decision in *Lawrence v. Texas*, 539 U.S. 558 (2003), may reduce the deterrent effect of this second factor. One study suggested that approximately thirty-four percent of persons who identify as homosexual reported involvement in current same-sex partnerships. *See* Dan Black, et al., *Demographics of the Gay and Lesbian Population in the United States: Evidence from Available Systematic Data Sources*, 37 DEMOGRAPHY 139, 143 (2000) (indicating that 2.8% of men identify themselves as gay, and 1.4% of women identify themselves as lesbian). *See also* sources cited in David Chambers, *What If? The Legal Consequences of Marriage and the Legal Needs of Lesbian and Gay Male Couples*, 95 MICH. L. REV. 447, 449 (1996) (indicating that, at any given time, nearly half of persons identifying themselves as gay, and more than half of those identifying themselves as lesbians, report themselves "in a relationship with a primary partner," and many of these have exchanged rings or otherwise engaged in a commitment ceremony).

---

[5] Table 9-2 was compiled and adapted from the following sources: U.S. Census Bureau, American Factfinder, 2008 ACS Data Set, B11009 Unmarried-Partner Households By Sex Of Partner, *available at* http://factfinder.census.gov/servlet/DTTable?_bm=y&-geo_id=01000US&-ds_name=ACS_2008_1YR_G00_&-_lang=en&-redoLog=false&-mt_name=ACS_2008_1YR_G2000_B11009&-format=&-CONTEXT =dt; American Factfinder, 2008 ACS Data Set, B11001 Household Type (Including Living Alone), *available at* http://factfinder.census.gov/servlet/DTTable?_bm=y&-geo_id=01000US&-ds_name=ACS_2008_1YR_G00_&-_lang=en&-mt_name=ACS_2008_1YR_G2000_B11001&-format=&-CONTEXT=dt; U.S. Census Bureau, Families and Living Arrangements, *available at* http://www.census.gov/population/www/socdemo/hh-fam.html (scroll down to "Same Sex Couples," find the heading marked "Data from the American Community Survey," hit the tab for "2008 Tables").

STATISTICAL NOTE

A brief history of the Census Bureau's measurement of nonmarital cohabitation rates can assist in the interpretation of the statistics reported in this chapter. Prior to 1990, the United States Census Bureau did not have any category in the decennial census to that could accurately identify cohabitating couples. The decennial census tracks population data by sending questionnaires to every household in the country at the beginning of each decade. In 1990, the decennial census survey added a category called "unmarried partner" in the section that asks for a report of the nature of the relationship between the respondent and others with whom she or he lives.

The data reported in Table 9-1, above, which date back to 1960, do not derive from the decennial census. Rather, they derive from the Census Bureau's Current Population Surveys ("CPS") which obtain data via telephone interviews of a random sample of American households, and extrapolate from that data to obtain estimates for the national population. For several decades, the Census Bureau has used CPS results to estimate the number of unmarried cohabitant households, a category that it calls Partners of Opposite Sex Sharing Living Quarters ("POSSLQ"), which is the category referred to in Table 9-1 as "unmarried heterosexual couple households." This category counts those households containing an unrelated adult man and woman sharing a housing unit with each other, and with no other adults. In some unknown percentage of the cases, assumed to be relatively small, the man and woman do not have an intimate relationship, but are merely roommates. Furthermore, this category does not include the small percentage of nonmarital cohabiting heterosexual couples who are intimate partners, but happen to share a residence with other adults. The reason that these distinctions are important is that there are some discrepancies between the data collected by the CPS and reported in Table 9-1, and the more accurate data collected in 1990 and 2000 through the decennial census. Compare the 1990 and 2000 figures from Table 9-1, of 2.86 million and 4.74 million couples respectively with the 1990 and 2000 figures from the decennial census of 3.04 and 4.88 million couples respectively. In both instances, the decennial census indicates slightly higher figures. Despite these discrepancies, the Census Bureau represents the CPS data reported in Table 9-1 to provide a fairly good estimate of historical trends.[6]

The introduction of the American Community Survey (ACS), which was fully implemented nationwide in 2005, allowed for annual calculation of the number of same-sex-couple households through its category of "unmarried partners." Like the CPS, the APS samples a random sample of U.S. households, and extrapolates from that data to calculate estimates for the national population. Until 2008, the Census Bureau coded as "same-sex unmarried partners" all those who identified themselves as married who were coded as members of the same sex. It did this according to a coding process it introduced in the 2000 decennial census, when no state permitted same-sex marriage, and continued even after same-sex marriage became legal in some states on the assumption that these couples were not married

---

[6] Telephone conversation with Jason Fields, Family Demographer, Fertility and Family Statistics Branch, Population Division, U.S. Census Bureau (August 5, 2003).

under federal law because of the Defense of Marriage Act ("DOMA"), 1 U.S.C. § 7 (1997). *See* Martin O'Connell & Daphne Lofquist, U.S. Census Bureau, Counting Same-sex Couples: Official Estimates and Unofficial Guesses, http:// www.census.gov/population/www/socdemo/files/counting-paper.pdf. Unfortunately, this coding process resulted in the mistaken inclusion of a considerable number of heterosexual married couples who had mistakenly checked off the wrong box in identifying their sexes. Because of the dramatically larger number of married households in the survey, even very minimal rates of sex miscoding have the potential to swamp the actual same-sex population. As a result, the 2000 decennial census, and ACS surveys before 2008, likely substantially overestimated the actual number of same-sex couples. As of the 2008 ACS, this problem of miscoding heterosexual couples as same-sex couples appears to have been largely corrected. *See* Williams Institute, "Same Sex Couples in the 2008 American Community Survey," (Sept. 2009), *available at* http://www.law.ucla.edu/williamsinstitute/pdf/ACS2008_WEBPOST _FINAL.pdf. In addition, the Census Bureau has separately released data showing the breakdown of same-sex couples on the ACS between 2005 and 2008 who have identified themselves as spouses or unmarried partners. *See* U.S. Census Bureau, Families and Living Arrangements, *available at* http://www.census.gov/population/ www/socdemo/hh-fam.html (scroll down to "Same Sex Couples," find the heading marked "Data from the American Community Survey"). Although the 2010 decennial census will still count same-sex partners who mark their relationship status as "husband/wife" to be "unmarried partners" (albeit with checks on the kind of coding errors that resulted in past mistaken inclusion of married, heterosexual couples in this category), in late 2011, Census officials will for the first time release the state-by-state data on same-sex couples who identified their relationship status as spouses.

[2]   Enforcing Obligations Between Cohabitants

[a]   Contract-Based Remedies

MARVIN v. MARVIN
California Supreme Court
557 P.2d 106 (1976)

Tobriner, Justice.

During the past 15 years, there has been a substantial increase in the number of couples living together without marrying. Such nonmarital relationships lead to legal controversy when one partner dies or the couple separates. . . . We take this opportunity to . . . declare the principles which should govern distribution of property acquired in a nonmarital relationship.

We conclude: (1) The provisions of the Family Law Act do not govern the distribution of property acquired during a nonmarital relationship; such a relationship remains subject solely to judicial decision. (2) The courts should enforce express contracts between nonmarital partners except to the extent that the contract is explicitly founded on the consideration of meretricious sexual services. (3) In the absence of an express contract, the courts should inquire into the conduct of the parties to determine whether that conduct demonstrates an implied contract, agreement of partnership or joint venture, or some other tacit understanding between the parties. The courts may also employ the doctrine of *quantum meruit*, or equitable remedies such as constructive or resulting trusts, when warranted by the facts of the case.

[P]laintiff and defendant lived together for seven years without marrying; all property acquired during this period was taken in defendant's name. When plaintiff sued to enforce a contract under which she was entitled to half the property and to support payments, the trial court granted judgment on the pleadings for defendant, thus leaving him with all property accumulated by the couple during their relationship. Since the trial court denied plaintiff a trial on the merits of her claim, its decision conflicts with the principles stated above, and must be reversed.

1. The factual setting of this appeal

. . . .

Plaintiff avers that in October of 1964 she and defendant "entered into an oral agreement" that while "the parties lived together they would combine their efforts and earnings and would share equally any and all property accumulated as a result of their efforts whether individual or combined." Furthermore, they agreed to "hold themselves out to the general public as husband and wife" and that "plaintiff would further render her services as a companion, homemaker, housekeeper and cook to . . . defendant."

Shortly thereafter plaintiff agreed to "give up her lucrative career as an entertainer [and] singer" in order to "devote her full time to defendant . . . as a companion, homemaker, housekeeper and cook;" in return defendant agreed to "provide for all of plaintiff's financial support and needs for the rest of her life."

Plaintiff alleges that she lived with defendant from October of 1964 through May of 1970 and fulfilled her obligations under the agreement. During this period the parties as a result of their efforts and earnings acquired in defendant's name substantial real and personal property, including motion picture rights worth over $1 million. In May of 1970, however, defendant compelled plaintiff to leave his household. He continued to support plaintiff until November of 1971, but thereafter refused to provide further support.

On the basis of these allegations plaintiff asserts two causes of action. The first, for declaratory relief, asks the court to determine her contract and property rights; the second seeks to impose a constructive trust upon one half of the property acquired during the course of the relationship. . . .

2. Plaintiff's complaint states a cause of action for breach of an express contract

. . . Although [the trial] court did not specify the ground for its conclusion that plaintiff's contractual allegations stated no cause of action, defendant offers [several] theories to sustain the ruling. . . .

Defendant . . . relies on the contention that the alleged contract is so closely related to the supposed "immoral" character of the relationship. . . . that the enforcement of the contract would violate public policy. He points to cases asserting that a contract between nonmarital partners is unenforceable if it is "involved in" an illicit relationship, or made in "contemplation" of such a relationship. A review of the numerous California decisions concerning contracts between nonmarital partners, however, reveals that the courts have not employed such broad and uncertain standards to strike down contracts. The decisions instead disclose a narrower and more precise standard: a contract between nonmarital partners is unenforceable only *to the extent* that it *explicitly* rests upon the immoral and illicit consideration of meretricious sexual services.

. . . . Numerous other cases have upheld enforcement of agreements between nonmarital partners in factual settings essentially indistinguishable from the present case.[5] [¶] Although the past decisions hover over the issue in the somewhat wispy form of the figures of a Chagall painting, we can abstract from those decisions a clear and simple rule. The fact that a man and woman live together without marriage, and engage in a sexual relationship, does not in itself invalidate agreements between them relating to their earnings, property, or expenses. Neither is such an agreement invalid merely because the parties may have contemplated the creation or continuation of a nonmarital relationship when they entered into it. Agreements between nonmarital partners fail only to the extent that they rest upon a consideration of meretricious sexual services. Thus the rule asserted by defendant, that a contract fails if it is "involved in" or made "in contemplation" of a nonmarital relationship, cannot be reconciled with the decisions.

The . . . cases cited by defendant which have declined to enforce contracts between nonmarital partners involved consideration that *was* expressly founded upon . . . illicit sexual services. In *Hill v. Estate of Westbrook*, 95 Cal. App. 2d 599, 213 P.2d 727 (1952), the woman promised to keep house for the man, to live with him as man and wife, and to bear his children; the man promised to provide for her in his will, but died without doing so. Reversing a judgment for the woman based on the reasonable value of her services, the Court of Appeal stated that "the action is predicated upon a claim which seeks, among other things, the reasonable value of living with decedent in meretricious relationship and bearing him two children. . . . The law does not award compensation for living with a man as a concubine and bearing him children. . . . As the judgment is, at least in part, for the value of the claimed services for which recovery cannot be had, it must be reversed." (95 Cal. App. 2d at 603, 213 P.2d at 730.) Upon retrial, the trial court found that it could not sever the contract and place an independent value upon the legitimate services performed by claimant. We therefore affirmed a judgment for the estate. [¶] In . . . *Updeck v. Samuel*, 123 Cal. App. 2d 264, 266 P.2d 822 (1964),

---

[5] Defendant urges that all [but perhaps two of the cases cited by the court to support this proposition] can be distinguished on the ground that the partner seeking to enforce the contract contributed either property or services additional to ordinary homemaking services. No case, however, suggests that a pooling agreement in which one partner contributes only homemaking services is invalid. . . . A promise to perform homemaking services is, of course, a lawful and adequate consideration for a contract. . . .

the contract "was based on the consideration that the parties lived together as husband and wife." (123 Cal. App. 2d at 267, 266 P.2d at 824.) Viewing the contract as calling for adultery, the court held it illegal.

. . . *Hill* and *Updeck* . . . demonstrate that a contract . . . expressly made in contemplation of a common living arrangement is invalid only if sexual acts form an inseparable part of the consideration . . . even if sexual services are part of the contractual consideration, any *severable* portion of the contract supported by independent consideration will still be enforced.

The principle that a contract between nonmarital partners will be enforced unless expressly and inseparably based upon an illicit consideration of sexual services not only represents the distillation of the decisional law, but also offers a far more precise and workable standard than that advocated by defendant. . . . [¶] [A] standard which inquires whether an agreement is "involved" in or "contemplates" a nonmarital relationship is vague and unworkable. Virtually all agreements between nonmarital partners can be said to be "involved" in some sense in the fact of their mutual sexual relationship, or to "contemplate" the existence of that relationship. Thus defendant's proposed standards, if taken literally, might invalidate all agreements between nonmarital partners, a result no one favors. Moreover, those standards offer no basis to distinguish between valid and invalid agreements. By looking . . . only to the consideration underlying the agreement, we provide the parties and the courts with a practical guide to determine when an agreement between nonmarital partners should be enforced.

. . . [Defendant also] contends that enforcement of the oral agreement between plaintiff and himself is barred by Civil Code section 5134, which provides that "All contracts for marriage settlements must be in writing. . . ." A marriage settlement, however, is an agreement [relating to] marriage. . . . The contract at issue here does not conceivably fall within that definition, and thus is beyond the compass of section 5134.

. . . .

In summary, we base our opinion on the principle that adults who voluntarily live together and engage in sexual relations are nonetheless as competent as any other persons to contract respecting their earning and property rights. Of course, [cohabiting adults] cannot lawfully contract to pay for the performance of sexual services, for such a contract is, in essence, an agreement for prostitution and unlawful for that reason. But they may agree to pool their earnings and to hold all property acquired during the relationship in accord with the law governing community property; conversely they may agree that each partner's earnings and the property acquired from those earnings remains the separate property of the earning partner. So long as the agreement does not rest upon illicit meretricious consideration, the parties may order their economic affairs as they choose, and no policy precludes the courts from enforcing such agreements.

In the present instance, plaintiff alleges that the parties agreed to pool their earnings, that they contracted to share equally in all property acquired, and that defendant agreed to support plaintiff. The terms of the contract as alleged do not rest upon any unlawful consideration. . . . The trial court consequently erred in granting defendant's motion for judgment on the pleadings.

3. Plaintiff's complaint can be amended to state a cause of action founded upon theories of implied contract or equitable relief

. . . [B]oth causes of action in plaintiff's complaint allege an express contract; neither assert any basis for relief independent from the contract. In *Marriage of Cary*, 34 Cal. App. 3d 345, 109 Cal. Rptr. 862 (1973), however, the Court of Appeal held that, in view of the policy of the Family Law Act, [which requires equal division of community property when married partners divorce,] property accumulated by nonmarital partners in an actual family relationship should be divided equally. . . . Although our conclusion that plaintiff's complaint states a cause of action based on an express contract alone compels us to reverse the judgment for defendant, resolution of the *Cary* issue will . . . resolve a conflict . . . in published Court of Appeal decisions. . . .[11]

. . . .

[T]he cases prior to *Cary* exhibited a schizophrenic inconsistency. By enforcing an express contract between nonmarital partners unless it rested upon an unlawful consideration, the courts applied a common law principle as to contracts. Yet the courts disregarded the common law principle that holds that implied contracts can arise from the conduct of the parties. Refusing to enforce such contracts, the courts spoke of leaving the parties "in the position in which they had placed themselves" (*Oakley v. Oakley*, 82 Cal. App. 2d 188, 192, 185 P.2d 848, 850 (1947)), just as if they were guilty parties "*in pari delicto.*"

Justice Curtis noted this inconsistency in his dissenting opinion in *Vallera*, pointing out that "if an express agreement will be enforced, there is no legal or just reason why an implied agreement to share the property cannot be enforced." [*Vallera v. Vallera* 21 Cal. 2d 681, 686, 34 P.2d 761, 764 (Cal. 1943). [¶] Still another inconsistency in the prior cases arises from their treatment of property accumulated through joint effort. To the extent that a partner had contributed *funds* or *property*, the cases held that the partner obtains a proportionate share in the acquisition, despite the lack of legal standing of the relationship. Yet courts have refused to recognize just such an interest based upon the contribution of *services.* As Justice Curtis points out "Unless it can be argued that a woman's services as cook, housekeeper, and homemaker are valueless, it would seem logical

---

[11] We note that a deliberate decision to avoid the strictures of the community property system is not the only reason that couples live together without marriage. Some couples may wish to avoid the permanent commitment that marriage implies, yet be willing to share equally any property acquired during the relationship; others may fear the loss of pension, welfare, or tax benefits resulting from marriage. Others may engage in the relationship as a possible prelude to marriage. In lower socio-economic groups the difficulty and expense of dissolving a former marriage often leads couples to choose a nonmarital relationship; many unmarried couples may also incorrectly believe that the doctrine of common law marriage prevails in California, and thus that they are in fact married. Consequently we conclude that the mere fact that a couple have not participated in a valid marriage ceremony cannot serve as a basis for a court's inference that the couple intend to keep their earnings and property separate and independent; the parties' intention can only be ascertained by a more searching inquiry into the nature of their relationship.

that if, when she contributes money to the purchase of property, her interest will be protected, then when she contributes her services in the home, her interest in property accumulated should be protected" [*Vallera*, 21 Cal. 2d at 686–687, 134 P.2d at 764 (Curtis, J., dissenting opinion)].

. . . .

[A]lthough we reject the reasoning of *Cary* . . . we share the perception of the [*Cary* court] that the application of former precedent in [similar factual settings] would work an unfair distribution of the property accumulated. . . . [¶] The principal reason why the pre-*Cary* decisions result in an unfair distribution of property inheres in the court's refusal to permit a nonmarital partner to assert rights based upon accepted principles of implied contract and equity. We have examined the reasons advanced to justify this denial of relief, and find that none have merit.

First, we note that the cases denying relief do not rest their refusal upon any theory of "punishing" a "guilty" partner. Indeed, to the extent that denial of relief "punishes" one partner, it necessarily rewards the other by permitting him to retain a disproportionate amount of the property. Concepts of "guilt" thus cannot justify an unequal division of property between two equally "guilty" persons.

Other reasons advanced in the decisions fare no better. The principal argument seems to be that "[e]quitable considerations arising from the reasonable expectation of . . . benefits attending the status of marriage . . . are not present [in a nonmarital relationship]." (*Vallera v. Vallera, supra,* 21 Cal. 2d at 685, 134 P.2d at 763.) But, although parties to a nonmarital relationship obviously cannot have based any expectations upon the belief that they were married, other expectations and equitable considerations remain. The parties may well expect that property will be divided in accord with the parties' own tacit understanding and that in the absence of such understanding the courts will fairly apportion property accumulated through mutual effort. We need not treat nonmarital partners as putatively married persons in order to apply principles of implied contract, or extend equitable remedies; we need to treat them only as we do any other unmarried persons.[22]

The remaining arguments advanced from time to time to deny remedies to the nonmarital partners are of less moment. There is no more reason to presume that services are contributed as a gift than to presume that funds are contributed as a gift; in any event the better approach is to presume, as Justice Peters suggested, "that the parties intend to deal fairly with each other." (*Keene v. Keene, supra,* 57 Cal. 2d 657, 674, 371 P.2d 329, 339 (dissenting opn.))

The argument that granting remedies to the nonmarital partners would discourage marriage must fail; as *Cary* pointed out, "with equal or greater force the point might be made that the pre-1970 rule was calculated to cause the income-producing partner to avoid marriage and thus retain the benefit of all of his or her

---

[22] In some instances a confidential relationship may arise between nonmarital partners, and economic transactions between them should be governed by the principles applicable to such relationships.

accumulated earnings." (34 Cal. App. 3d at p. 353, 109 Cal. Rptr. at p. 866.) Although we recognize the well-established public policy to foster and promote the institution of marriage . . . , perpetuation of judicial rules which result in an inequitable distribution of property accumulated during a nonmarital relationship is neither a just nor an effective way of carrying out that policy.

In summary, we believe that the prevalence of nonmarital relationships in modern society and the social acceptance of them, marks this as a time when our courts should by no means apply the doctrine of the unlawfulness of the so-called meretricious relationship to the instant case. [T]he nonenforceability of agreements expressly providing for meretricious conduct rested upon the fact that such conduct . . . pertained to . . . prostitution. To equate the nonmarital relationship of today to such a subject matter is to do violence to an accepted and wholly different practice. . . .

The mores of the society have . . . changed so radically in regard to cohabitation that we cannot impose a standard based on alleged moral considerations that have apparently been so widely abandoned by so many. Lest we be misunderstood, however, we take this occasion to point out that the structure of society itself largely depends upon the institution of marriage, and nothing we have said in this opinion should be taken to derogate from that institution. The joining of the man and woman in marriage is at once the most socially productive and individually fulfilling relationship that one can enjoy in the course of a lifetime.

We conclude that the judicial barriers that may stand in the way of a policy based upon the fulfillment of the reasonable expectations of the parties to a nonmarital relationship should be removed. . . . We add that in the absence of an express agreement, the courts may look to a variety of other remedies in order to protect the parties' lawful expectations.[24]

The courts may inquire into the conduct of the parties to determine whether that conduct demonstrates an implied contract or implied agreement of partnership or joint venture or some other tacit understanding between the parties. The courts may, when appropriate, employ principles of constructive trust or resulting trust. Finally, a nonmarital partner may recover in *quantum meruit* for the reasonable value of household services rendered less the reasonable value of support received if he can show that he rendered services with the expectation of monetary reward.

. . .

The judgment is reversed and the cause remanded for further proceedings consistent with the views expressed herein.

---

[24] We do not seek to resurrect the doctrine of common law marriage, which was abolished in California by statute in 1895. Thus we do not hold that plaintiff and defendant were "married," . . . or putative spouses; we hold only that she has the same rights to enforce contracts and to assert her equitable interest in property acquired through her effort as does any other unmarried person.

HEWITT v. HEWITT
Illinois Supreme Court
394 N.E.2d 1204 (1979)

UNDERWOOD, JUSTICE.

The issue in this case is whether plaintiff Victoria Hewitt, whose complaint alleges she lived with defendant Robert Hewitt from 1960 to 1975 in an unmarried, family-like relationship to which three children have been born, may recover from him "an equal share of the profits and properties accumulated by the parties" during that period.

[The plaintiff's divorce action was dismissed because the parties had never married.] Plaintiff thereafter filed an amended complaint alleging . . . (1) that because defendant promised he would "share his life, his future, his earnings and his property" with her and all of defendant's property resulted from the parties' joint endeavors, plaintiff is entitled in equity to a one-half share; (2) that the conduct of the parties evinced an implied contract entitling plaintiff to one-half the property accumulated during their "family relationship"; (3) that because defendant fraudulently assured plaintiff she was his wife in order to secure her services, although he knew they were not legally married, defendant's property should be impressed with a trust for plaintiff's benefit; (4) that because plaintiff has relied to her detriment on defendant's promises and devoted her entire life to him, defendant has been unjustly enriched.

[She further alleged] that in June 1960, when she and defendant were students at Grinnell College in Iowa, [she] became pregnant; that defendant thereafter told her that they were husband and wife and would live as such, no formal ceremony being necessary, and that he would "share his life, his future, his earnings and his property" with her; that the parties immediately announced to their respective parents that they were married and thereafter held themselves out as husband and wife; that in reliance on defendant's promises she devoted her efforts to his professional education and his establishment in the practice of pedodontia, obtaining financial assistance from her parents for this purpose; that she assisted defendant in his career with her own special skills and although she was given payroll checks for these services she placed them in a common fund; that defendant, who was without funds at the time of the marriage, as a result of her efforts now earns over $80,000 a year and has accumulated large amounts of property, owned either jointly with her or separately; that she has given him every assistance a wife and mother could give, including social activities designed to enhance his social and professional reputation.

The amended complaint was also dismissed, the trial court finding that Illinois law and public policy require such claims to be based on a valid marriage. The appellate court reversed, stating that because the parties had outwardly lived a conventional married life, plaintiff's conduct had not "so affronted public policy that she should be denied any and all relief," and that plaintiff's complaint stated a cause of action on an express oral contract. . . .

The appellate court, in reversing, gave considerable weight to the fact that the parties had held themselves out as husband and wife for over 15 years. The court noted that they lived "a most conventional, respectable and ordinary family life" that did not openly flout accepted standards, the "single flaw" being the lack of a valid marriage. Indeed the appellate court went so far as to say that the parties had "lived within the legitimate boundaries of a marriage and family relationship of a most conventional sort," an assertion which that court cannot have intended to be taken literally. Noting that the Illinois Marriage and Dissolution of Marriage Act does not prohibit nonmarital cohabitation and that the Criminal Code of 1961 makes fornication an offense only if the behavior is open and notorious, the appellate court concluded that plaintiff should not be denied relief on public policy grounds.

In finding that plaintiff's complaint stated a cause of action on an express oral contract, the appellate court adopted the reasoning of the California Supreme Court in the widely publicized case of *Marvin v. Marvin*. . . .

The issue of whether property rights accrue to unmarried cohabitants cannot, however, be regarded realistically as merely a problem in the law of express contracts. Plaintiff argues that because her action is founded on an express contract, her recovery would in no way imply that unmarried cohabitants acquire property rights merely by cohabitation and subsequent separation. However, the *Marvin* court expressly recognized and the appellate court here seems to agree that if common law principles of express contract govern express agreements between unmarried cohabitants, common law principles of implied contract, equitable relief and constructive trust must govern the parties' relations in the absence of such an agreement. In all probability the latter case will be much the more common, since it is unlikely that most couples who live together will enter into express agreements regulating their property rights. The increasing incidence of nonmarital cohabitation referred to in *Marvin* and the variety of legal remedies therein sanctioned seem certain to result in substantial amounts of litigation, in which, whatever the allegations regarding an oral contract, the proof will necessarily involve details of the parties' living arrangements.

. . . We are aware, of course, of the increasing judicial attention given to claims of unmarried cohabitants to jointly accumulated property, and the fact that the majority of courts considering the question have recognized an equitable or contractual basis for implementing the reasonable expectations of the parties unless the sexual services were the explicit consideration. The issue of unmarried cohabitants' mutual property rights, however, as we earlier noted, cannot appropriately be characterized in terms of contract law, nor is it limited to considerations of equity or fairness as between the parties to such relationships. There are major public policy questions involved. . . . Of substantially greater importance than the rights of the immediate parties is the impact of such recognition upon our society and the institution of marriage. Will the fact that legal rights closely resembling those arising from conventional marriages can be acquired by those who deliberately choose to enter into what have heretofore been commonly referred to as "illicit" or "meretricious" relationships encourage formation of such relationships and weaken marriage as the foundation of our family-based society? In the event of death shall the survivor have the status of a surviving spouse for purposes of inheritance, wrongful death actions, workmen's compensation, etc.? And still more importantly: what of the children born of such relationships? What are their support and inheritance rights and by what standards are custody questions resolved? What of the sociological and psychological effects upon them of that type of environment? Does not the recognition of legally enforceable property and custody rights emanating from nonmarital cohabitation in practical effect equate with the legalization of common law marriage — at least in the circumstances of this case? And, in summary, have the increasing numbers of unmarried cohabitants and changing mores of our society reached the point at which the general welfare of the citizens of this State is best served by a return to something resembling the judicially created common law marriage our legislature outlawed in 1905?

     . . . .

It is true, of course, that cohabitation by the parties may not prevent them from forming valid contracts about . . . matters [independent of sexual services], for which it is said the sexual relations do not form part of the consideration. . . . [S]everal courts have reasoned that the rendition of housekeeping and homemaking services such as plaintiff alleges here could be regarded as the consideration for a separate contract between the parties, severable from the illegal contract founded on sexual relations. . . .

The real thrust of plaintiff's argument here is that we should abandon the rule of illegality because of certain changes in societal norms and attitudes. It is urged that social mores have changed radically in recent years, rendering this principle of law archaic. It is said that because there are so many unmarried cohabitants today the courts must confer a legal status on such relationships. . . . If this is to be the result, however, it would seem more candid to acknowledge the return of varying forms of common law marriage than to continue displaying the naiveté we believe involved in the assertion that there are involved in these relationships contracts separate and independent from the sexual activity, and the assumption that those contracts would have been entered into or would continue without that activity.

Even if we were to assume some modification of the rule of illegality is appropriate, we return to the fundamental question earlier alluded to: If resolution of this issue rests ultimately on grounds of public policy, by what body should that policy be determined? *Marvin*, viewing the issue as governed solely by contract law, found judicial policy-making appropriate. Its decision was facilitated by California precedent and that State's no-fault divorce law. In our view, however, the situation alleged here was not the kind of arm's length bargain envisioned by traditional contract principles, but an intimate arrangement of a fundamentally different kind. The issue, realistically, is whether it is appropriate for this court to grant a legal status to a private arrangement substituting for the institution of marriage sanctioned by the State. The question whether change is needed in the law governing the rights of parties in this delicate area of marriage-like relationships involves evaluations of sociological data and alternatives we believe best suited to the superior investigative and fact-finding facilities of the legislative branch in the exercise of its traditional authority to declare public policy in the domestic relations field. That belief is reinforced by the fact that judicial recognition of mutual property rights between unmarried cohabitants would, in our opinion, clearly violate the policy of our recently enacted Illinois Marriage and Dissolution of Marriage Act [which says that its purpose, *inter alia*, is to "strengthen and preserve the integrity of marriage and safeguard family relationships."]. Although the Act does not specifically address the subject of nonmarital cohabitation, we think the legislative policy quite evident from the statutory scheme.

. . . .

While the appellate court denied that its decision here served to rehabilitate the doctrine of common law marriage, we are not persuaded. Plaintiff's allegations disclose a relationship that clearly would have constituted a valid common law marriage in this State prior to 1905. . . . It is of course true, as plaintiff argues, that unlike a common law spouse she would not have full marital rights in that she could not, for example, claim her statutory one-third share of defendant's property on his death. The distinction appears unimpressive, however, if she can claim one-half of his property on a theory of express or implied contract.

. . . .

We accordingly hold that plaintiff's claims are unenforceable [because] they contravene the public policy, implicit in the statutory scheme of the Illinois Marriage and Dissolution of Marriage Act, disfavoring the grant of mutually enforceable property rights to knowingly unmarried cohabitants. The judgment of the appellate court is reversed. . . .

NOTES

1. *Michelle Triola Marvin's Recovery on Remand.* On remand the trial court found no contract between Lee and Michelle, but based on its equitable powers, awarded Michelle $104,000 for economic rehabilitation, so that she could become self-supporting. The court of appeals reversed:

> [T]he special findings in support of the challenged rehabilitative award merely established plaintiff's need therefore and defendant's ability to respond to that need. This is not enough. The award, being nonconsensual in nature, must be supported by some recognized underlying obligation in law or in equity. A court of equity admittedly has broad powers, but it may not create totally new substantive rights under the guise of doing equity.
>
> The trial court in its special conclusions of law addressed to this point attempted to state an underlying obligation by saying that plaintiff had a right to assistance from defendant until she became self-supporting. But this special conclusion obviously conflicts with the earlier, more general, finding of the court that defendant has never had and did not then have any obligation to provide plaintiff with a reasonable sum for her support and maintenance and, in view of the already-mentioned findings of no damage (but benefit instead), no unjust enrichment and no wrongful act on the part of defendant with respect to either the relationship or its termination, it is

clear that no basis whatsoever, either in equity or in law, exists for the challenged rehabilitative award. It therefore must be deleted from the judgment.

Marvin v. Marvin, 122 Cal. App. 3d 871, 876 (1981). Compare this approach to that traditionally taken upon the dissolution of marriage where "need" is deemed a sufficient reason to award spousal support. The sharp contrast between such applications of *Marvin* and the remedies available after marriage has led some to propose that long-term cohabiting relationships be treated like marriages upon dissolution. See discussion of status-based remedies below.

2. *State Recognition of* Marvin *Remedies.* The majority of states will recognize some contracts claims between unmarried cohabitants, as well as claims grounded in equity. *See, e.g., Doe v. Burkland*, 808 A.2d 1090 (R.I. 2002); *Salzman v. Bachrach*, 996 P.2d 1263, 1267, 1269 (Colo. 2000) (en banc); *Goode v. Goode*, 396 S.E.2d 430 (W. Va. 1990); *Boland v. Catalano*, 521 A.2d 142 (Conn. 1987); *Watts v. Watts*, 405 N.W.2d 303 (Wis. 1987); *see also* Margaret M. Mahoney, *Forces Shaping the Law of Cohabitation for Opposite Sex Couples*, 7 J.L. & Fam. Stud. 135, 159 (2005) ("In the decades since the Marvin case was decided, the courts and legislatures in almost all states have adopted some version of this contract doctrine."); Marsha Garrison, *Nonmarital Cohabitation: Social Revolution and Legal Regulation*, 42 Fam. L. Q. 309, 315–16 (2008) ("Appellate courts in at least twenty-six states and the District of Columbia have now approved some relational contract claims between cohabitants, although a few of these jurisdictions have disapproved recovery based on an implied contract.").

A few states have explicitly rejected allowing cohabitants to recover on implied contract claims, even where they would recognize express contracts. *See, e.g., Wilcox v. Trautz*, 693 N.E.2d 141, 146 (Mass. 1998); *Morone v. Morone*, 413 N.E.2d 1154 (N.Y. 1980); *Tapley v. Tapley*, 449 A.2d 1218 (N.H. 1982); *Merrill v. Davis*, 673 P.2d 1285 (N.M. 1983); *Sutton v. Valois*, 846 N.E.2d 1171, 1175 (Mass. App. Ct. 2006). The reasoning in the New York case of *Morone* is fairly typical of these decisions. In that case, a couple lived together for over 20 years, had two children, and held themselves out to the community as husband and wife. After their separation, plaintiff claimed that "she ha[d] performed domestic duties and business services at the request of defendant with the expectation that she would receive full compensation for them, and that defendant ha[d] always accepted her services knowing that she expected compensation for them." 413 N.E.2d at 1155. The New York court decisively refused to consider this claim. It reasoned that the task of finding an implied contract, as permitted in *Marvin*, is "conceptually so amorphous as practically to defy equitable enforcement." It continued:

> The major difficulty with implying a contract from the rendition of services for one another by persons living together is that it is not reasonable to infer an agreement to pay for the services rendered when the relationship of the parties makes it natural that the services were rendered gratuitously. As a matter of human experience personal services will frequently be rendered by two people living together because they value each other's company or because they find it a convenient or rewarding thing to do. . . . For courts to attempt through hindsight to sort out the intentions of the

parties and affix jural significance to conduct carried out within an essentially private and generally noncontractual relationship runs too great a risk of error. Absent an express agreement, there is no frame of reference against which to compare the testimony presented and the character of the evidence that can be presented becomes more evanescent. There is, therefore, substantially greater risk of emotion-laden afterthought, not to mention fraud, in attempting to ascertain by implication what services, if any, were rendered gratuitously and what compensation, if any, the parties intended to be paid.

413 N.E.2d 1154, 1154–55, 1158.

Only five states have explicitly disapproved of all forms of relief based on a cohabiting relationship. In addition to *Hewitt*, see *Davis v. Davis*, 643 So. 2d 931 (Miss. 1994); *Long v. Marino*, 441 S.E.2d 475 (Ga. Ct. App. 1994); *Schwegmann v. Schwegmann*, 441 So. 2d 316 (La. Ct. App. 1983); *Carnes v. Sheldon*, 311 N.W.2d 747 (Mich. Ct. App. 1981). Ohio appears to have taken this position as well, although its precedents are less clear. *See Lauper v. Harold*, 492 N.E.2d 472, 474, 170 (Ohio Ct. App. 1985); *Tarry v. Stewart*, 649 N.E.2d 1 (Ohio Ct. App. 1994). A recent Illinois case relied on *Hewitt* in denying equitable claims brought at the end of 24-year relationship; it rejected the plaintiff's argument that changes in society and public policy in the decades since *Hewitt* requiring softening its rule. *Costa v. Oliven*, 849 N.E.2d 122, 125 (Ill. App. 2006).

3. *Assessing the Impact of* **Marvin.** Commentators have noted that despite the wide judicial acceptance of *Marvin* in principle, there have been surprisingly few recoveries allowed by courts on cohabitation claims. Ann Estin writes:

> *Marvin v. Marvin* has been cited in approximately two hundred other court decisions, about half of which come from the California courts, and approximately three hundred law review articles. It is still a fixture of family law classes, appearing as a principal case in each of the eleven casebooks currently on the market. The term "palimony" has entered general usage, particularly in the context of entertainers, sports figures, and wealthy entrepreneurs.

> With all its celebrity, the *Marvin* decision stands more as a cultural icon than as a legal watershed. In the twenty-five years since Lee and Michelle hit the gossip columns, rates of unmarried cohabitation have climbed steadily, and courts have continued to confront the claims of unmarried partners at the end of their relationships. As living together without marriage has become less glamorous, less forbidden, and more ordinary among the middle class, there is more of this legal work for courts and lawyers to do. But the law governing nonmarital relationships remains largely an ad hoc affair, with tremendous variation between states and from case to case.

> At one end of the spectrum, courts in Illinois and Georgia have refused to embrace the Marvin principle and will not enforce even express written "relationship" contracts between unmarried cohabitants. At the other end of the spectrum, courts in Washington and Nevada have begun to apply

rules that treat some nonmarital opposite-sex couples as if they were married for purposes of property claims at the end of their cohabitation. In between these extremes, most states' courts routinely enforce express agreements and recognize various equitable claims between unmarried partners, particularly where they share a business or property.

. . . .

. . . It is clear from the legal and demographic literature that the social practices of cohabitation have shifted significantly over the past twenty-five years and that the transition is still continuing. The law, however, has not changed at the same rate. Remedies available to cohabitants are largely limited to untangling shared property interests and reimbursing extraordinary contributions made by one partner to the other's business or property interests. Under these rules, most cohabitants have no rights or obligations that arise by virtue of their shared life.

Ann Laquer Estin, *Unmarried Partners and the Legacy of* Marvin v. Marvin: *Ordinary Cohabitation*, 76 NOTRE DAME L. REV. 1381, 1382–85 (2001). *Accord*, Marsha Garrison, *Nonmarital Cohabitation: Social Revolution and Legal Regulation*, 42 FAM. L.Q. 309 (2008) ("Surveying the case law, I find that, although the California Supreme Court's widely cited decision in *Marvin v. Marvin* appeared to inaugurate a new era of expanding law and rights for nonmarital cohabitants, courts and legislatures — both within California and outside of it — have in fact responded to *Marvin* quite cautiously.").

Professor Ellman has argued that the reason for the limited impact of *Marvin* is that contract doctrine is in fact a conceptually inapt way to address the issues that arise in cohabitation cases, so that its doctrinally correct application is unlikely to yield a remedy even in cases that present equitably appealing facts to which the law should respond. See Ira Mark Ellman, *"Contract Thinking" Was Marvin's Fatal Flaw*, 76 Notre Dame L. Rev. 1365, 1365–1373 (2001):

> *Marvin v. Marvin* held that claims that unmarried partners might have against one another at the conclusion of their relationship would be governed primarily by principles of contract law. [¶] [¶] The main defect with contract as the conceptual underpinning for claims between intimate partners is that couples do not in fact think of their relationship in contract terms. [D]ecades of urging by contract enthusiasts have led few couples (married or unmarried) to make express contracts. . . . [C]ourts have no sensible rule to apply in dealing with end-of-relationship disputes between the typical unmarried partners who have no express agreement. Some courts hold that in the absence of an express agreement there can be no claim at all, but more seem to follow *Marvin* and ask whether an agreement between parties can be implied from their conduct. The difference between these two approaches may be more apparent than real, however. If couples do not in fact think of their relationship in contract terms, then a doctrine that directs courts to decide their disputes by looking for a contract is unlikely to find one. . . . Do we want courts to think broadly about the rules that yield a fair dissolution of an unmarried couple's relationship, or do we want to limit courts to searching the parties' conduct for evidence

that at some point in the past they agreed upon terms that should now govern their mutual obligations?

The contract inquiry is obviously the more narrow one, for contract focuses on one particular aspect of fairness, keeping one's promises. The very idea of contract is to bind parties now to terms that they agreed upon earlier, to require the later self to remain true to the earlier self's commitments . . . Yet, there is considerable social science evidence that perfectly competent adults lack the capacity to evaluate rationally the contractual commitments involved in an agreement about the consequences that should flow from the dissolution of their intimate relationships — a dissolution which they do not expect to occur and which may well occur, if it does occur, many years in the future when their lives are dramatically different. [See in particular Melvin A. Eisenberg, *The Limits of Cognition and the Limits of Contract*, 47 STAN. L. REV. 211, 254–58 (1995).] Relationships develop over time in ways that competent adults will often fail to anticipate and that may change their lives fundamentally. . . .

If such concerns over the ability of spouses to foresee the long-term consequences of premarital agreement require limits on their enforceability, then surely those same concerns also cast doubt on any rule that would decide claims between unmarried partners by reference to express contracts they made years earlier. Even more doubtful would be a rule directing the court, if there is no express contract, to decide the claim by attempting to plumb the intentions that the parties may have brought to the relationship years before their current dispute arose. Contracts bind parties forever to the terms they agreed upon at execution, and this static conception of obligation is unsuited to the realities of intimate relationships.

One need only look at some of the cases to see how far a contract rubric takes one from results that sensibly and fairly coordinate with actual human behavior. *Friedman v. Friedman*, [24 Cal. Rptr. 2d 892 (App. 1993)], a California case, was decided nearly twenty years after *Marvin*, but involved a couple (Terri and Elliott) who began living together in 1967, before *Marvin* had been decided. Children of the 1960s, they did not believe official marriage necessary for the lifetime commitment they intended and so vowed to be "partners in all respects 'without any sanction by the State.'" They purchased property in Alaska as "Husband and Wife," had two children together, and in the late 1970s moved to Berkeley where Elliott attended law school and prospered economically.

By 1982, their attitude about relationships had perhaps changed, because they made plans to marry. Yet when bad weather kept Elliott from returning from a business trip in time for the wedding, it was never rescheduled, suggesting perhaps that the interest in marriage was not entirely mutual. By the mid-1980s, Terri, who had performed the classic homemaking role throughout their relationship, became disabled with serious back problems. Their relationship apparently deteriorated with her back, and in 1992, Terri filed a legal complaint seeking equitable relief, including support. The trial court found the parties had an "implied contract" providing that if they separated Elliott would support Terri in the same manner as if they had married and, accordingly, ordered temporary support pending final determination of Terri's claim. The couple had no express agreement defining the obligations they would have to one another at their relationship's end, and the appeals court, plausibly enough, held the evidence of implied agreement also insufficient to sustain the trial court's order. Indeed, the parties' decision to live together "without any sanction by the State" was inconsistent, the court concluded, with Terri's claim that they agreed to be bound by the support rules applicable to marriage. As Elliot said of Terri's claim for post-relationship support: "That was not part of our life. It was not part of what we were doing. . . . [W]hen we split up, we split up."

Even those most sympathetic to Terri's claims must concede that Elliot's understanding of the couple's arrangement, at the time they decided to live together, was entirely plausible. Young persons in their twenties, with no children, few responsibilities, and many prospects in front of them, may see little reason to bind themselves to lifetime obligations that could outlast their mutual affection. But for Terri, 1967 is then; 1992 is now. Much of a lifetime has passed. Should the law really say that after twenty-five years together raising two children, Elliott can leave their relationship lucratively employed and with no obligations at all to Terri, who has become disabled, because she cannot show that at some earlier time he had entered into a contract agreeing to them? . . .

. . . . The *Marvin* doctrine does not [work justice at the dissolution of cohabiting relationships]. There are other cases like Elliott's and Terri's with similar results. There are also cases in which the court responds to similar facts by stretching contract doctrine beyond recognition in order to justify a remedy, as the dissenting judge urged in *Friedman* itself.[41]

Either response would seem to indicate a mismatch between the problem (what do people owe one another when it is over?) and the doctrine these courts employ to deal with it.

On the other hand, as Professor Estin suggests, straight out equitable claims grounded in the plaintiff cohabitant's provision of homemaker services, or in the relationship itself, are rare, although courts will generally provide equitable relief for business loans or the provision of market-type services. *Compare, e.g., Slocum v. Hammond,* 346 N.W.2d 485 (Iowa 1984) (rejecting unjust enrichment claim for equitable division of assets acquired during cohabitation), *with Shold v. Goro,* 449 N.W.2d 372 (Iowa 1989) (permitting recovery by a woman for repayment of funds advanced to cohabitant during their six-year relationship, despite absence of formal loan agreement). In short, most jurisdictions adopting *Marvin* agree that "an unmarried cohabitant does not have the type of claim to a share of the other partner's earnings that a spouse could make in a divorce proceeding[, nor does it] give rise to a presumption of shared property rights." Estin, *supra* at 1400. An

---

[41] "The result reached by the majority may be, in the eyes of some, good law; it is lousy justice." Friedman, 24 Cal. Rptr. 2d at 896 (Poche, J., dissenting).

exception is the approach taken in *Connell*, reprinted *infra*, which allows claims based on the existence of a marriage-like relationship, without requiring a showing of a contract. The American Law Institute, as well as several foreign jurisdictions including Canada and Australia, favor a similar approach over the contract analysis; that alternative is presented below.

For analyses of trends in state enforcement of contract-based claims between nonmarital cohabitants, see also *Symposium: Unmarried Partners and the Legacy of Marvin v. Marvin*, 76 NOTRE DAME L. REV. 1261 (2001), containing, in addition to the article by Professor Ellman excerpted above, articles by Grace Ganz Blumberg, Margaret F. Brinig, David L. Chambers, Ann Laquer Estin, J. Thomas Oldham, Milton C. Regan, Jr., and David Westfall. For further discussion and analysis of trends in state laws, *see also* George L. Blum, Annot., *Property Rights Arising from Relationship of Couple Cohabiting Without Marriage*, 69 A.L.R.5th 219 (1999); William A. Reppy, Jr., *Choice of Law Problems Arising When Unmarried Cohabitants Change Domicile*, 55 SMU L. REV. 273, 275–288 (2002); Mark Strasser, *A Small Step Forward: The ALI Domestic Partners Recommendation*, 2001 BYU L. REV. 1125, 1146–57.

4. *Comparing* Marvin *and* Hewitt — *Household Services Versus Market Labor and Economic Contributions.* In footnote 5, *Marvin* rejects the defendant's proffered distinctions between cases in which the plaintiff contributed directly to the acquisition of property (with material, labor or money) and those in which the plaintiff's claim is grounded in performance of household services. The distinction, however, is one that many pre-*Marvin* cases adopted, when they recognized a party's equitable interests in a joint *economic* venture independent of the partners' cohabitation. *Compare, e.g., Garza v. Fernandez*, 248 P.2d 869 (Ariz. 1952) (woman claimed business partnership with decedent; action for accounting allowed without regard to their cohabitation) *with Stevens v. Anderson*, 256 P.2d 712 (Ariz. 1953) (woman denied relief against decedent's estate after 30 years' cohabitation; *Garza* distinguished as not involving a contract for a meretricious relationship). Even courts that reject *Marvin* therefore will allow recovery where market labor or economic contributions are at stake. *See, e.g. Spafford v. Coats*, 455 N.E.2d 241 (Ill. App. 1983) (allowing recovery where it furnished money to buy several vehicles); *see also Crooke v. Gliden*, 414 S.E.2d 645 (Ga. 1992) (upholding written contract regarding real estate, which specified sharing of expenses and assets, relying on parol evidence rule to exclude evidence of "immoral [cohabiting] relationship" as irrelevant); *Spafford v. Coats*, 455 N.E.2d 241 (Ill. App. 1983) (imposing constructive trust with regard to vehicles jointly purchased because claims were independent of relationship). Claims like those in *Spafford* are based on conventional rules regarding property rights. By contrast, homemaker services provided within the context of an intimate relationship have not traditionally been viewed in terms of their economic productivity.

The distinctions between claims permitted and those not can be exceedingly fine, however. For example, while one Illinois court permitted a former cohabitant's claim for return of $47,188 that she had given him to pay off the mortgage on *his* home, *Kaiser v. Fleming*, 735 N.E.2d 144, 148–149 (Ill. App. 2000), another denied relief to a woman who made monetary contributions to the home in which she and cohabitant lived together for ten years. *Ayala v. Fox*, 564 N.E.2d 920, 922 (Ill. App.

1990). In distinguishing these cases, *Kaiser* construed the plaintiff's "lump sum" payoff of the mortgage on her boyfriend's home as a financial investment which he convinced her to make. By contrast, the monthly mortgage payments in *Ayala* seem to have been viewed as regular living expenses, and the relief sought as "akin to a marital relationship." For criticism of *Ayala*, arguing it extends *Hewitt*, see Jan Skelton, Hewitt *to* Ayala: *A Wrong Turn for Cohabitants' Rights*, 82 ILL. B.J. 364 (1994); *see also* Cynthia Grant Bowman, *Legal Treatment of Cohabitation in the United States*, 26 LAW & POL'Y 119 (2004).

5. *Requirements for* Marvin-*type Claims*.

a. *Are the provision of household services necessary for recovery?* Although most courts have held that the consideration in palimony claims are plaintiff's household services, one court has found such services are not necessary to maintain such a claim. In *In re Estate of Roccamonte*, the cohabitant's estate argued that because deceased had not required domestic services from plaintiff, the case should fail for lack of valid consideration, "because sexual favor as the sole consideration would render the palimony contract unenforceable as meretricious." 808 A.2d 838, 844 (N.J. 2002). The New Jersey Supreme Court rejected the estate's contention. In its words:

> That argument . . . misperceives the fundamental point of our palimony cases. The principle we recognized and accepted is that the formation of a marital-type relationship between unmarried persons may, legitimately and enforceably, rest upon a promise by one to support the other. A marital-type relationship is no more exclusively dependent upon one partner's providing maid service than it is upon sexual accommodation. It is, rather, the undertaking of a way of life in which two people commit to each other, foregoing other liaisons and opportunities, doing for each other whatever each is capable of doing, providing companionship, and fulfilling each other's needs, financial, emotional, physical, and social, as best as they are able. And each couple defines its way of life and each partner's expected contribution to it in its own way. Whatever other consideration may be involved, the entry into such a relationship and then conducting oneself in accordance with its unique character is consideration in full measure.

Id. at 844–45. On the facts, the court stated, there was "no doubt that plaintiff provided that consideration here until her obligation was discharged by Roccamonte's death." *Id.* at 845.

Roccamonte also addressed the estate's argument that because the plaintiff was employed for most of the relationship and therefore not entirely dependent on the deceased, no valid palimony agreement could exist. The court acknowledged that most of the prior cases did involve complete economic dependency, but stated "we see no reason why complete dependency is a sine qua non of a valid palimony agreement. The issue is, more pertinently, one of economic inequality, and the relevant question is whether the promisee is self-sufficient enough to provide for herself with a reasonable degree of economic comfort appropriate in the circumstances." *Id.* at 845.

b. *Were the services provided with the expectation of payment?* Although various approaches to property distribution and spousal support at divorce explicitly or implicitly incorporate notions of the economic value of non-wage services provided by spouses (see Chapter 4), contract-based approaches in the nonmarital cohabitation context must contend with the characterization of homemaker services as expressions of affection and caregiving, not as labor that contributes to the economic well-being of the couple. *See* Katharine Silbaugh, *Turning Labor into Love: Housework and the Law*, 91 Nw. U.L. REV. 1 (1996). For a discussion of the concept of homemaker services expressed in *Marvin* and its relevance for cohabitation and marriage, see Margaret F. Brinig, *The Influence of* Marvin v. Marvin *on Housework During Marriage*, 76 NOTRE DAME L. REV. 1311 (2001). For a general discussion of cohabitant property decisions arising after *Marvin*, see George L. Blum, Annot., *Property Rights Arising From Relationship of Couple Cohabitating Without Marriage*, 69 A.L.R. 5th 219 (Supp. 2004).

c. *The severability of the sexual relationship. Marvin* required that the sexual relationship between the cohabiting parties be *severable* from the rest of their agreement. Thus, the valid portion of the contract can be enforced, and recognition denied to any portion that rests explicitly on sexual services. Is this distinction tenable? The *Hewitt* majority observed that typically, cohabitation contracts would not be made in the absence of a sexual relationship between the parties. In this view, the sexual component of the relationship is integral and cannot be severed from the rest of the contract. Arguably the court in *Latham v. Latham*, 547 P.2d 144, 147 (Or. 1976), set out a more workable distinction for relationships in which recovery was warranted than the severability distinction set out by *Marvin*. In *Latham*, the Oregon Supreme Court did not require that the sexual relationship be severable, but rather that "the agreement contemplated all the burdens and amenities of married life" and was not *primarily* a contract for sexual services. 547 P.2d 144, 147 (Or. 1976); *see also Wilcox v. Trautz*, 427 Mass. 326 (1998) (agreement is "valid even if expressly made in contemplation of a common living arrangement, except to the extent that sexual services constitute the only, or dominant, consideration for the agreement. . . ."). For a discussion of courts' use of the severability doctrine in nonmarital relationships, see Jill Elaine Hasday, *Intimacy and Economic Exchange*, 119 HARV. L. REV. 491, 507–511 (2005).

d. *What constitutes cohabitation? And is cohabitation required for recovery?* Which living arrangements between nonmarital couples should be construed as "cohabitation"? Sociologists and demographers note that there is a broad spectrum of living arrangements that may or may not fit within various concepts of cohabitation. *See, e.g.,* Judith Teitler & Nancy E. Reichman, *Cohabitation: An Elusive Concept.* Center for Research on Child Wellbeing Working Paper #01-07-FF (2001), *available at* http://crcw.princeton.edu/workingpapers/WP01-07-FF-Teitler.pdf. Romantically-involved couples often do not spend every night together, and their relationship may not be sexually exclusive. *Id.* These issues were raised in *Cochran v. Cochran*, 106 Cal. Rptr. 2d 899 (Ct. App. 2001). Patricia Cochran claimed that her unmarried companion of 25 years, attorney Johnnie Cochran, had breached his agreement to provide her with lifetime support. The couple had lived together two to four days a week, in the home which Johnnie had purchased in their names as joint tenants. The couple also had a child together. During a portion of this relationship, they held themselves out to the world as husband and wife. (Johnnie was married to another woman during the first decade of their relationship.) Johnnie argued that he had never "cohabited" with Patricia in a manner consistent with the meaning of that term under *Marvin*. The court rejected Johnnie's position: "We save for another day the issue of whether consenting adults need cohabit at all in order to enter an enforceable agreement regarding their earnings and property. Assuming . . . that cohabitation is required, . . . the rationale of *Marvin* is satisfied . . . by a cohabitation arrangement that is less than full-time." *Cochran*, 106 Cal. Rptr. at 905. "Here, the parties shared a long-term, stable and significant relationship. In this context, evidence that they lived together two to four days a week . . . is sufficient to raise a triable issue of fact that they cohabited under *Marvin*." *Id.* at 906.

California courts before *Cochran* had suggested that at least some threshold level of cohabitation may be required in order to trigger remedies under *Marvin*. *See, e.g., Bergen v. Wood*, 18 Cal. Rptr. 2d 75 (Ct. App. 1993); *Taylor v. Fields* 224 Cal. Rptr. 186 (Ct. App.1986). However, recently, a New Jersey court held that cohabitation is not an essential requirement for a cause of action for palimony. *Devaney v. L'Esperance*, 949 A.2d 743, 744 (N.J. 2008). That court reasoned that "[i]t is the promise to support, expressed or implied, coupled with a marital-type relationship, that are the indispensable elements to support a valid claim for palimony." Such a relationship may exist, the court stated, despite circumstances such as "employment, military, or educational opportunities" which prevent the couple from cohabiting. *Id.* at 259. Consider what principles should guide line-drawing between those couples the law considers eligible for palimony claims and those it does not.

e. *Is a writing required?* The Statute of Frauds typically applies to agreements made "upon consideration of marriage," and therefore not to cohabitant agreements. Although the California Supreme Court explicitly declined to extend the statute of frauds to cohabitation, courts in Florida and North Dakota have held that cohabitation agreements fall within the statute. *See Posik v. Layton*, 695 So. 2d 759, 761 (Fla. App. 1997); *Kohler v. Flynn*, 493 N.W.2d 647 (N.D. 1992). In addition, the legislatures of two other states, Minnesota and Texas, have passed provisions requiring that cohabitation agreements must be in writing to be enforceable. *See* Minn. Stat. § 513.075 (2008); Tex. Fam. Code § 1.108 (2008). In practice, few cohabitants have written agreements today. *See* Jennifer Robbennolt & Monica Kirkpatrick Johnson, *Legal Planning for Unmarried Committed Partners: Empirical Lessons for a Therapeutic and Preventative Approach*, 41 Ariz. L. Rev. 417 (1999). Thus, the requirement of a writing is likely to result in denial of relief in many cases in states that adopt this requirement. *See, e.g., Roatch v. Puera*, 534 N.W.2d 560 (Minn. App. 1995).

f. *Relationship between implied-in-fact contracts and equitable claims.* When courts do not find an express agreement between the parties, *Marvin* leaves open the possibility that they can find an implied agreement or apply equitable principles. As courts have developed these two alternatives, they often look fairly similar to one another. *See* Ann Estin, *Ordinary Cohabitation*, at 1391. Courts that imply contracts look at the property accumulated jointly during the relationship and the couple's joint lives together, and assume that the couple intended to do what was fair and equitable by sharing property. *See, e.g., Watts v. Watts*, 405 N.W.2d 303, 313–14 (Wis. 1987); *Goode v. Goode*, 396 S.E.2d 430, 439 (W. Va. 1990). Similarly, when courts apply equitable principles, they look at the couple's joint lives and financial arrangements and apply principles of fairness. *See, e.g., Eaton v. Johnston*, 681 P.2d 606, 610–11 (Kan. 1984); *Pickens v. Pickens*, 490 So. 2d 872, 875–76 (Miss. 1986); *Shuraleff v. Donnelly*, 817 P.2d 764, 768–69 (Or. Ct. App. 1991). The only difference is that in the latter set of cases, equitable considerations are not necessarily presumed to have been implicitly agreed to by the couple during the relationship. Implied contracts are often called "implied-in-fact" contracts, whereas recovery on equitable claims is sometimes described as recovery in contract "implied in law" or "quasi contract."

The measure of damages for implied-in-fact contracts is quantum meruit. Recovery in quantum meruit is said to be based upon the "assent" of the parties and, is therefore deemed to be contractual in nature, Since specific terms in an implied contract are absent, the law supplies the missing contract price by determining the fair market value of the services rendered, a frequently disputed finding of fact which is left to the jury. *See* Judy Beckner Sloan, *Quantum Meruit: Residual Equity in Law*, 42 DePaul L. Rev. 399 (2000); 66 Am. Jur. 2d *Restitution and Implied Contracts* § 37 (2009). An obstacle to recovery in unmarried cohabitant cases, however, is that quantum meruit is unavailable for services that were rendered gratuitously. In family-like situations, courts often apply a presumption that services are conferred without expectation of payment, and in these cases plaintiffs must show evidence to overcome this presumption.

g. Requirements for equitable claims. Equitable doctrines that plaintiffs seek to invoke in the cohabitation context turn on the principle of unjust enrichment, that "[o]ne person should not be permitted unjustly to enrich himself at the expense of another, but should be required to make restitution of or for property or benefits received, retained, or appropriated, where it is just and equitable that such restitution be made. . . ." *Harman v. Rogers* 510 A.2d 161, 164 (Vt. 1986) (citing 66 Am. Jur. 2d *Restitution and Implied Contracts* §§ 1–3). In order for a cohabitant to make a claim of unjust enrichment, he or she must show that "(1) at plaintiff's expense (2) defendant received a benefit (3) under circumstances that would make it unjust for defendant to retain the benefit without paying." *Salzman v. Bachrach*, 996 P.2d 1263, 1265–66 (Colo. 2000). In practice, courts have been less reluctant to find unjust enrichment when one cohabitant enriches the other through giving them money or property, than when they have provided them unpaid household services.

The measure of damages for unjust enrichment is different than the measure of damages under the quantum meruit remedy for implied-in-fact contracts. Rather than focus on the reasonable value of the services provided, unjust enrichment focuses on the value of the benefit conferred upon the recipient. This may be the same as the market value of the services, but it need not be.

Courts may invoke a few other equitable remedies on finding a party has been unjustly enriched by the other party. These include constructive trusts and resulting trusts. To impose a constructive trust, courts must usually find 1) a confidential or fiduciary relationship; 2) a promise, express or implied, by the transferee; 3) a transfer of property in reliance on the promise; and 4) unjust enrichment of the transferee. Note, though, that courts apply these requirements somewhat loosely, generally using the remedy to prevent unjust enrichment. *See* JESSE DUKEMINIER & STANLEY M. JOHANSON, WILLS, TRUSTS, AND ESTATES 585 (6th ed. 2000). To impose a resulting trust, courts must find that the parties intended for the defendant to hold property on behalf of the plaintiff. Courts will then transfer title to the property on equitable grounds.

h. *Applying* Marvin *to same-sex couples.* Most courts have held that cohabitation agreements between same-sex partners are enforceable to the same extent as those between opposite-sex partners. *See, e.g., Posik v. Layton*, 695 So. 2d 759 (Fla. Dist. Ct. App. 1997) and cases cited therein; *see also Crooke v. Gilden*, 414 S.E.2d 645 (Ga. 1992); *Zaremba v. Cliburn*, 949 S.W.2d 822 (Tex. App. 1997); *Whorton v. Dillingham*, 248 Cal. Rptr. 405 (Cal. Ct. App. 1988). For further discussion of the legal treatment of same-sex cohabitants, see Amy D. Romer, *Homophobia: In the Closet and in the Coffin*, 21 L. & INEQUALITY. 65 (2003); Angie Smolka, Note, *That's the Ticket: A New Way of Defining Family*, 10 CORNELL J.L. & PUB. POL'Y 629 (2001).

6. *Does Recognition of Cohabitation Remedies Revive Common-Law Marriage?* *Hewitt* characterized recognition of legally-enforceable rights emanating from nonmarital cohabitation as tantamount to legalization of common law marriage. *Accord Carnes v. Sheldon*, 311 N.W.2d 747, 753 (Mich. Ct. App. 1981) ("recovery based on principles of contracts implied at law essentially would resurrect the old common-law marriage doctrine which was specifically abolished by the Legislature"); *Glidewell v. Glidewell*, 790 S.W.2d 925, 927 (Ky. Ct. App. 1990) (to imply that the "performance of domestic and household work produce[s] any rights analogous to those of a spouse . . . 'would be reinstituting by judicial fiat common law marriage' "). Yet, *Marvin*, in footnote 24, rejects this assertion. Which characterization is correct? Common law marriage, although effectuated by an informal agreement between the parties, is a legally-binding marriage in those states recognizing it, and it is accompanied by all of the legal rights and obligations of marriage. (*See supra*, Chapter 2.) Not only does the status of marriage create a wide range of legal rights and obligations between the parties, but also between the couple and third parties, including the state. *Marvin* does not create a marriage-like status between nonmarital cohabitants, nor does it enable the parties to create such a status for themselves. It does, however, allow nonmarital cohabitants to agree on certain financial implications arising out of their relationship. In many instances, the asserted financial arrangements, such as a particular distribution of property acquired during the life of the relationship, or promises of post-relationship support, are similar to the state-supplied terms that accompany marital dissolution. Yet, to the extent that the contracts enforced are express or implied-in-fact, the state's role is limited to private dispute settlement. By contrast, the state's role in the regulation of marriage extends well beyond this function, seeking to promote an institution to serve as the cornerstone or foundation of its society. *See, e.g., Maynard v. Hill*, 125 U.S. 190 (1887). For a detailed explication of the claim that *Marvin* principles essentially recapitulate principles of common law marriage, see Charlotte K. Goldberg, *The Schemes of Adventuresses: The Abolition and Revival of Common-Law Marriage*, 13 WM. & MARY J. WOMEN & L. 483 (2007).

7. *Separation Agreements for Cohabitants.* Even if state law is unsettled on a particular cohabitation claim, the cohabitation version of a separation agreement should still be enforceable as a contract, on the grounds that a contract to settle claims is valid without reference to the validity of the underlying claims. *See, e.g., Kinnison v. Kinnison*, 627 P.2d 594 (Wyo. 1981). Courts may be particularly inclined to honor such agreements as a device for avoiding potentially difficult claims of unjust enrichment or implied contract. *See, e.g., Silver v. Starrett*, 674 N.Y.S. 2d 915 (N.Y. Sup. Ct. 1998). These issues arise in regard to same-sex marriages even in states that do not recognize them, where courts are called upon to resolve disputes regarding the distribution of assets in these relationships. In these cases, there should be no impediment to enforcement of the parties' separation agreement insofar as it concerns their personal property and monetary obligations. *See e.g., Gonzalez v. Green*, 831 N.Y.S.2d 856, 859 (N.Y. Sup. Ct. 2006).

8. *Effect of Property Accumulated in Cohabitation on Property Distribution in Subsequent Marriage and Divorce.* If a couple lives together before marriage, should their cohabitation and the showing of *Marvin*-type agreements affect the division of their property upon divorce? Some states consider contributions made by one spouse to the others' "education, training, or increased earning power" during a preceding period of cohabitation in setting spousal support awards determined at marital dissolution. *Meyer v. Meyer*, 620 N.W.2d 382, 386 (Wis. 2000); *see also Nielsen v. Nielsen*, 446 N.W.2d 356 (Mich. Ct. App. 1989); *Nelson v. Nelson*, 384 N.W.2d 468 (Minn. Ct. App. 1986); *Chestnut v. Chestnut*, 499 N.E.2d 783 (Ind. Ct. App. 1986); *In re Marriage of Burton*, 758 P.2d 394 (Or. Ct. App. 1988); *Helbush v. Helbush*, 122 P.3d 288 (Haw. Ct. App. 2005). Other jurisdictions take a slightly different approach, dividing property acquired during a preceding period of cohabitation only if the property was acquired "in contemplation of marriage." *See, e.g., In re Marriage of Malters*, 478 N.E.2d 1068 (Ill. App. Ct. 1985); *Weiss v. Weiss*, 543 A.2d 1062 (N.J. Super. Ct. App. Div. 1988). *But see Wilen v. Wilen*, 486 A.2d 775 (Md. Ct. Spec. App. 1985) (holding that property acquired during a period of cohabitation prior to marriage is not marital property). California separates the claims related to divorce from those related to cohabitation, requiring that property claims arising from premarital cohabitation be brought in a separate *Marvin* action, *see Watkins v. Watkins*, 192 Cal. Rptr. 54 (Ct. App. 1983), although it may consolidate that action with the divorce proceedings. *See Bukaty v. Bukaty*, 225 Cal. Rptr. 492 (Ct. App. 1986).

[b]   The Status Alternative to Contract Remedies

In recognizing cohabitation agreements, *Marvin* responded to real and important changes in the way in which many people are living their lives and in social mores. Yet, "*Marvin* has been much criticized as unworkable, inapt, artificial, and inadequately responsive to a range of worthy claims." Grace Ganz Blumberg, *The Regularization of Nonmarital Cohabitation: Rights and Responsibilities in the American Welfare State*, 76 Notre Dame L. Rev. 1265, 1292 (2001). This section examines two status alternatives to *Marvin's* contract approach: the approach adopted by Washington State, and the approach proposed for nonmarital cohabitants by the American Law Institute in the *Principles of the Law of Family*

Dissolution (*ALI Principles*), which built upon the work of Professors Blumberg, Ellman, and others.

[i]   Washington State's Approach

In 1984, the Washington Supreme Court held that property accumulated during a nonmarital cohabitant relationship is subject to the same equitable division principles that guide disposition of property after divorce if the parties had a "stable, marital-like relationship where both parties cohabit[ed] with knowledge that a lawful marriage between them [did] not exist." *Marriage of Lindsey*, 678 P.2d 328, 330–31 (Wash. 1984). *Lindsey* established a doctrine that allows some unmarried cohabitants an interest in property received during the relationship, even in the absence of an express or implied contract and regardless of which partner holds title. In the following case, the Washington State Supreme Court examines the principles that should guide courts in these cases.

CONNELL v. FRANCISCO
Washington Supreme Court
898 P.2d 831 (1995) (en banc)

GUY, JUSTICE.

This case requires us to decide how property acquired during a meretricious relationship is distributed.[2]

BACKGROUND

Petitioner Richard Francisco and Respondent Shannon Connell met in Toronto, Canada, in June 1983. Connell was a dancer in a stage show produced by Francisco. She resided in New York, New York. She owned clothing and a leasehold interest in a New York apartment. Francisco resided in Las Vegas, Nevada. He owned personal property, real property, and several companies, including Prince Productions, Inc. and Las Vegas Talent, Ltd., which produced stage shows for hotels. Francisco's net worth was approximately $1,300,000 in February 1984.

Connell, at Francisco's invitation, moved to Las Vegas in November 1983. They cohabited in Francisco's Las Vegas home from November 1983 to June 1986. While living in Las Vegas, Connell worked as a paid dancer in several stage shows. She also assisted Francisco as needed with his various business enterprises. Francisco managed his companies and produced several profitable stage shows.

In November 1985, Prince Productions, Inc. purchased a bed and breakfast, the Whidbey Inn, on Whidbey Island, Washington. Connell moved to Whidbey Island in June 1986 to manage the Inn. Shortly thereafter Francisco moved to Whidbey Island to join her. Connell and Francisco resided and cohabited on Whidbey Island

---

[2] We recognize that historically, the term "meretricious" had a demeaning connotation. Today the word is a term of art and conveys a clear and specific legal meaning, and we will therefore continue to use it. . . .

until the relationship ended in March 1990.

While living on Whidbey Island, Connell and Francisco were viewed by many in the community as being married. Francisco acquiesced in Connell's use of his surname for business purposes. A last will and testament, dated December 11, 1987, left the corpus of Francisco's estate to Connell. Both Connell and Francisco had surgery to enhance their fertility. In the summer of 1986, Francisco gave Connell an engagement ring.

From June 1986 to September 1990 Connell continuously managed and worked at the Inn. She prepared breakfast, cleaned rooms, took reservations, laundered linens, paid bills, and maintained and repaired the Inn. Connell received no compensation for her services at the Inn from 1986 to 1988. From January 1989 to September 1990 she received $400 per week in salary.

Francisco produced another profitable stage show and acquired several pieces of real property during the period from June 1986 to September 1990. . . . Connell did not contribute financially toward the purchase of any of the properties, and title to the properties was held in Francisco's name individually or in the name of Prince Productions, Inc.

Connell and Francisco separated in March 1990. When the relationship ended Connell had $10,000 in savings, $10,000 in jewelry, her clothes, an automobile, and her leasehold interest in the New York apartment. . . . In contrast, Francisco's net worth was over $2,700,000, a net increase since February 1984 of almost $1,400,000. . . .

Connell filed a lawsuit against Francisco in December 1990 seeking a just and equitable distribution of the property acquired during the relationship. The Island County Superior Court determined Connell and Francisco's relationship was sufficiently long term and stable to require a just and equitable distribution. The Superior Court limited the property subject to distribution to the property that would have been community in character had they been married. The trial court held property owned by each party prior to the relationship could not be distributed. In addition, the Superior Court required Connell to prove by a preponderance of the evidence that the property acquired during their relationship would have been community property had they been married.

The only property characterized by the Superior Court as being property that would have been community in character had Connell and Francisco been married was the increased value of Francisco's pension plan. The increased value of the pension plan, $169,000, was divided equally, with $84,500 distributed to Connell. The Superior Court, concluding Connell did not satisfy her burden of proof with respect to the remaining property, distributed to Francisco the remainder of the pension plan and all real property.

The Court of Appeals reversed, holding both property owned by each prior to the relationship and property that would have been community in character had the parties been married may be distributed following a meretricious relationship. The Court of Appeals also ruled the analogous application of [Washington's equitable distribution statute] . . . to meretricious relationships would be meaningless without a community-property-like presumption attaching to all property acquired during the relationship. . . .

Francisco petitioned this court for discretionary review. He argues property owned by each party prior to the relationship may not be distributed following a meretricious relationship, and a community-property-like presumption is inapplicable when a trial court distributes property following a meretricious relationship. . . .

ANALYSIS

A meretricious relationship is a stable, marital-like relationship where both parties cohabit with knowledge that a lawful marriage between them does not exist.

Relevant factors establishing a meretricious relationship include, but are not limited to: continuous cohabitation, duration of the relationship, purpose of the relationship, pooling of resources and services for joint projects, and the intent of the parties.

In *Lindsey*, this court ruled a relationship need not be "long term" to be characterized as a meretricious relationship. While a "long term" relationship is not a threshold requirement, duration is a significant factor. A "short term" relationship may be characterized as meretricious, but a number of significant and substantial factors must be present. *See [In re] Marriage of Lindsey*, 678 P.2d at 331 (a less than 2-year meretricious relationship preceded marriage).

The Superior Court found Connell and Francisco were parties to a meretricious relationship. This finding is not contested.

Historically, property acquired during a meretricious relationship was presumed to belong to the person in whose name title to the property was placed. "[I]n the absence of any evidence to the contrary, it should be presumed *as a matter of law* that the parties intended to dispose of the property exactly as they did dispose of it." *Creasman v. Boyle*, 196 P.2d 835[, 841] (1948). This presumption is commonly referred to as "the *Creasman* presumption." . . .

In 1984, this court overruled *Creasman* [in *Lindsey*]. In its place, the court adopted a general rule requiring a just and equitable distribution of property following a meretricious relationship.

. . . .

In *Lindsey*, the parties cohabited for less than 2 years prior to marriage. When they subsequently divorced, the wife argued the increase in value of property acquired during the meretricious portion of their relationship was also subject to an equitable distribution as if the property were community in character. We agreed, citing [the Washington equitable distribution statute].

Francisco contends the Court of Appeals misinterpreted *Lindsey* when it applied all the principles contained in [the statute] to meretricious relationships. [Eds. note: Washington State's equitable distribution provision is an "all property" statute, which allows a judge to distribute both community and separate property in a divorce proceeding]. We agree. A meretricious relationship is not the same as a marriage. As such, the laws involving the distribution of marital property do not directly apply to the division of property following a meretricious relationship. Washington courts may look toward those laws for guidance.

Once a trial court determines the existence of a meretricious relationship, the trial court then: (1) evaluates the interest each party has in the property acquired during the relationship, and (2) makes a just and equitable distribution of the property. The critical focus is on property that would have been characterized as community property had the parties been married. This property is properly before a trial court and is subject to a just and equitable distribution.

While portions of [the statute] may apply by analogy to meretricious relationships, not all provisions of the statute should be applied. The parties to such a relationship have chosen not to get married and therefore the property owned by each party prior to the relationship should not be before the court for distribution at the end of the relationship. However, the property acquired during the relationship should be before the trial court so that one party is not unjustly enriched at the end of such a relationship. . . . Until the Legislature, as a matter of public policy, concludes meretricious relationships are the legal equivalent to marriages, we limit the distribution of property following a meretricious relationship to property that would have been characterized as community property had the parties been married. This will allow the trial court to justly divide property the couple has earned during the relationship through their efforts without creating a common law marriage or making a decision for a couple which they have declined to make for themselves. Any other interpretation equates cohabitation with marriage; ignores the conscious decision by many couples not to marry; confers benefits when few, if any, economic risks or legal obligations are assumed; and disregards the explicit intent of the Legislature that [the statute] apply to property distributions following a marriage.

. . . .

In a marital context, property acquired during marriage is presumptively community property. When no marriage exists there is, by definition, no community property. However, only by treating the property acquired in a meretricious relationship similarly can this court's reversal of "the *Creasman* presumption" be given effect. Failure to apply a community-property-like presumption to the *property acquired during a meretricious relationship* places the burden of proof on the non-acquiring partner. This would overrule *In re Marriage of Lindsey*, 678 P.2d 328 (1984) and reinstate the presumption expressed in *Creasman v. Boyle*, 196 P.2d 835 (1948). The Court of Appeals properly rejected the resurrection of "the *Creasman* presumption."

We hold income and property acquired during a meretricious relationship should be characterized in a similar manner as income and property acquired during marriage. Therefore, all property acquired during a meretricious relationship is presumed to be owned by both parties. This presumption can be rebutted.

. . . .

In the case before us, the majority of real property was purchased during Connell and Francisco's meretricious relationship. This real property is presumed to be owned by both parties, notwithstanding the fact the real property is not held in both parties' names.

CONCLUSION

In summary, we hold that property which would have been characterized as separate property had the couple been married is not before the trial court for division at the end of the relationship. The property that would have been characterized as community property had the couple been married is before the trial court for a just and equitable distribution. There is a rebuttable presumption that property acquired during the relationship is owned by both of the parties and is therefore before the court for a fair division.

We reverse the Court of Appeals in part, affirm in part, and remand the case to the Superior Court for a just and equitable distribution of property.

NOTES

1. ***Factors Indicating a Cohabiting Relationship Requiring Equitable Distribution.*** While the Washington Supreme Court used the term "meritricious relationships" in developing its status-based doctrine concerning unmarried cohabitants, it later substituted the term "committed intimate relationships" because of the negative connotations of the term "meritricious." *See Olver v. Fowler*, 168 P.2d 348, 348n.1 (Wash. 2007).

Connell used five factors to determine the existence of a relationship appropriate for equitable distribution of property: "continuous cohabitation, duration of the relationship, purpose of the relationship, pooling of resources and services for joint projects, and the intent of the parties." *Id.* at 831. The court in *Marriage of Pennington*, 14 P.3d 764 (Wash. 2000) (en banc), reiterated these factors, noting that "[these] characteristic factors are neither exclusive nor hypertechnical. Rather, these factors are meant to reach all relevant evidence helpful in establishing whether a meretricious relationship exists. Thus, whether relationships are properly characterized as meretricious depends upon the facts of each case." *Id.* at 770. The last three of these factors require some explanation.

In considering the "purpose" factor, *Pennington* stated that the relationship there had many purposes that could support a finding of a committed intimate relationship, which "included companionship, friendship, love, sex, and mutual support and caring." *Pennington*, 14 P.3d at 772. *Fenn v. Lockwood*, 2006 Wash. App. LEXIS 2715 (Dec. 12, 2006), expands on possible purposes, including "having a child, raising their daughter, participating in a community, to live like a marriage, but without state or religious involvement, to operate like — and present themselves to the world as — a family, and to share the joys and responsibility of parenting" and noting that even once the couple was informed of Washington's committed intimate relationships doctrine, they took no steps to avoid incurring that status. *Fenn*, 2006 Wash. App. LEXIS at *10.

With respect to "pooled resources," the *Pennington* Court held that shared living expenses (food, kitchen supplies, interior decorating) alone do not meet this criteria, but rather that "joint projects" are necessary. *Pennington*, 14 P.3d at 771. In *Fenn* the court added that "[t]he question is not simply whether they pooled their resources and services for joint projects; the question is whether they pooled and invested their time, effort, or financial resources enough to require an equitable distribution of property," and found that having worked for years to build a business together was sufficient pooling of resources. 2006 Wash. App. LEXIS, at *10.

In considering the "intent of the parties" factor, the *Pennington* court was dissuaded from finding sufficient intent by the fact that Pennington was married to another woman for the first several years of the relationship, and that even after his divorce he refused to marry Van Pevenage: "Pennington's refusal, coupled with Van Pevenage's insistence on marrying, belies the existence of the parties' mutual intent to live in a meretricious relationship. Furthermore, Van Pevenage's intent to live in a stable, longterm, cohabiting relationship is also negated by her own actions, particularly her repeated absences from the . . . home and her relationship with another man." *Pennington*, 14 P.3d at 771. *Vasquez v. Hawthorne*, 33 P.3d 735 (Wash. 2001).

2. *Comparing Washington's Unmarried Cohabitant Doctrine with Common Law Marriage.* The court in *Pennington* emphasized that the case-by-case analysis of whether a meretricious, or committed intimate, relationship exists distinguishes the doctrine from a renewed policy of common-law marriage. "The use of the term 'marital-like'" is a mere analogy because defining meretricious relationships as related to marriage would create a de facto common-law marriage, which this court has refused to do." *Pennington*, 14 P.3d at 770. It is interesting to note that despite the courts' assertion in both *Connell* and *Pennington* that these relationships are distinct from marriage, Pennington's refusal to marry Van Pevenage is used to demonstrate his lack of intent to enter a meretricious relationship.

Committed intimate relationships are also distinguished from common law marriage in that courts cannot find these relationships to have existed where a relationship is terminated by death, as noted in the concurrence in *Vasquez v. Hawthorne*:

> [W]e developed this equitable doctrine because the legislature has not provided a statutory means of resolving the property distribution issues that arise when unmarried persons, who have lived in a marital-like relationship and acquire what would have been community property had they been married, separate. On the other hand, the laws of intestacy . . . dictate how property is to be distributed when an individual dies without leaving a will. Accordingly, we have held that the meretricious relationship doctrine's analogy . . . does not apply when a relationship between unmarried cohabitants is terminated by death of one cohabitant.

33 P.3d 735, 738 (Wash. 2001) (Alexander, C.J., concurring). For examination of the doctrine's implications for relationships terminated by death, *see* John E. Wallace, Comment, *The Afterlife of the Meretricious Relationship Doctrine: Applying the*

Doctrine Post Mortem, 29 SEATTLE U. L. REV. 243 (2005).

3. ***Application of Washington's Unmarried Cohabitant Relationship Doctrine to Same-Sex Couples.***   In 2004, a court of appeals extended the committed intimate relationship doctrine to apply to a case involving a same-sex couple. *Gormley v. Robertson*, 83 P.3d 1042 (Wash. Ct. App. 2004). The court emphasized that, while the question of whether same-sex couples can marry is a matter for the legislature, the extension of certain marriage-like property rights and obligations to intimate unmarried couples lies within the court's equitable powers, and that there was no basis for distinguishing between unmarried opposite-sex and same-sex couples in applying this doctrine. *Gormley* stated that "it is of no consequence to the cohabiting couple, same-sex or otherwise, whether they can legally marry. Indeed, one of the key elements of a meretricious relationship is knowledge by the partners that a lawful marriage between them does not exist." *Gormley*, 83 P.3d at 1046. The decision in *Gormley* was consistent with the Washington Supreme Court's statement in *Vasquez v. Hawthorne* that, because the committed intimate relationship doctrine was an equitable doctrine, its application was "not dependent on the 'legality' of the relationship between the parties, nor . . . the gender or sexual orientation of the parties." *Vasquez*, 33 P.3d at 737.

4. ***Application of Status-Based Unmarried Cohabitant Relationship Doctrine in Other States.***   Except for Washington, no high courts in other states have permitted recovery based on the fact of cohabitation, without any showing of unjust enrichment or an express or implied agreement. *See* Marsha Garrison, *Nonmarital Cohabitation: Social Revolution and Legal Regulation*, 42 FAM. L.Q. 309, 319–320 (2008).

[ii]   The ALI Approach

As with the Washington State approach, the American Law Institute's ("ALI") *Principles of the Law of Family Dissolution* ("the *Principles*"), treats couples who are "domestic partners" almost identically to married couples with respect to property claims at dissolution. The ALI goes still further in putting unmarried cohabitants on the same footing as married couples: It also provides for post-dissolution income transfers (called "compensatory payments" rather than alimony in the ALI formulation) in some unmarried couples. The ALI permits domestic partners, like married couples, to enter into agreements before or during their relationship to alter the usual property or support rules that would otherwise apply at termination of their relationship. (See Chapter 8 for further discussion of approaches to enforcement of premarital agreements.) Absent such agreements, however, the ALI provisions apply. Note that the ALI's use of the term "domestic partners" must be distinguished from the use of that term to identify a *formal* status alternative available to nonmarital cohabitants requiring registration. The latter type of domestic partnership is discussed later in this chapter, Section A[4]. Like Washington State's approach, the ALI's recommendations apply equally to opposite-sex and same-sex couples. While the ALI's suggested rules for unmarried cohabitant relationships have not been adopted in any American state, they are very similar to the Washington State's rules that preceded them, and to the rules in several other common law countries, as we shall see.

ALI PRINCIPLES OF THE LAW OF FAMILY DISSOLUTION: ANALYSIS AND RECOMMENDATIONS
(2002)

§ 6.03 Determination That Persons Are Domestic Partners

(1)   For the purposes of defining relationships to which this Chapter applies, domestic partners are two persons of the same or opposite sex, not married to one another, who for a significant period of time share a primary residence and a life together as a couple.

(2)   Persons are domestic partners when they have maintained a common household, as defined in Paragraph (4), with their common child, as defined in Paragraph (5), for a continuous period that equals or exceeds a duration, called the *cohabitation parenting period*, set in a rule of statewide application.

(3)   Persons not related by blood or adoption are presumed to be domestic partners when they have maintained a common household . . . for a continuous period that equals or exceeds a duration, called the *cohabitation period*, set in a uniform rule of statewide application. The presumption is rebuttable by evidence that the parties did not share life together as a couple, as defined by Paragraph (7).

. . . .

(6)   When the requirements of Paragraphs (2) or (3) are not satisfied, a person asserting a claim under this Chapter bears the burden of proving that for a significant period of time the parties shared a primary residence and a life together as a couple, as defined in Paragraph (7). Whether a period of time is significant is determined in light of all the Paragraph (7) circumstances of the parties' relationship and, particularly, the extent to which the circumstances wrought change in the life of one or both parties.

(7)   Whether persons share a life together as a couple is determined by reference to all the circumstances including:

  (a)   the oral or written statements or promises made to one another, or representations jointly made to third parties, regarding their relationship;

  (b)   the extent to which the parties intermingled their finances;

  (c)   the extent to which their relationship fostered the parties' economic interdependence, or the economic dependence of one party upon the other;

  (d)   the extent to which the parties engaged in conduct and assumed specialized or collaborative roles in furtherance of their life together;

  (e)   the extent to which the relationship wrought change in the life of either or both parties;

(f)   the extent to which the parties acknowledged responsibilities to one another, as by naming one another the beneficiary of life insurance or of a testamentary instrument, or as eligible to receive benefits under an employee benefit plan;

(g)   the extent to which the parties' relationship was treated by the parties as qualitatively distinct from the relationship either party had with any other person;

(h)   the emotional or physical intimacy of the parties' relationship;

(i)   the parties' community reputation as a couple;

(j)   the parties' participation in some form of commitment ceremony or registration as a domestic partnership;

(k)   the parties' participation in a void or voidable marriage that, under applicable law, does not give rise to the economic incidents of marriage;

(l)   the parties' procreation of, adoption of, or joint assumption of parental functions toward a child;

(m)   the parties' maintenance of a common household. . . .

Comment:

b. . . .

This section . . . relies, as do the marriage laws, on a status classification: property claims and support obligations presumptively arise between persons who qualify as domestic partners, as they do between legal spouses, without inquiry into each couple's particular arrangement, except as the presumption is itself overcome by contract. This approach reflects a judgment that it is usually just to apply to both groups the property and support rules applicable to divorcing spouses, that individualized inquiries are usually impractical or unduly burdensome, and that it therefore makes more sense to require parties to contract out of these property and support rules than to contract into them. . . .

d. . . . [In order to qualify for "compensatory payments," the ALI's equivalent of alimony,] domestic partners under this section must . . . meet the [same Chapter 5] requirements [as a marital claimant]. [Because] Chapter 5 imposes its own durational thresholds for award eligibility [the] value of any award . . . is ordinarily proportional to the duration of the parties' cohabitation. The amount of the parties' property subject to division under § 6.05 will also, in the ordinary case, be proportional to the duration of the parties' cohabitation. *See* § 6.04. Thus, this section does not require long cohabitation periods to screen out inappropriate compensatory-payment or property-distribution awards [because other sections of the Principles accomplish that result].

The required durations do need to be long enough to make it likely that the parties have established a life together as a couple and that [this life together] has had some significant impact on the circumstances of one or both parties. . . . Cohabitation periods of two or three years have been used by Canadian provinces that have adopted an approach similar to Paragraph (3). The parties' procreation or adoption of a child with whom they share a household is itself sufficiently indicative of this likelihood that the duration required under Paragraph (2) need not be as long as that required under Paragraph (3). If a jurisdiction sets the Paragraph (3) cohabitation period at three years, a reasonable choice, a Paragraph (2) cohabitation parenting period of two years would be appropriate.

NOTES

1. *Understanding the ALI Proposal.* What is the non-contractual basis of cohabitor obligation upon which the ALI relies? As Professor Ellman observes:

> Relationships are themselves the source of legal duties, without the need for any assistance from contract. This is not a new idea. Landlords and tenants, employers and employees, neighbors, lawyers and clients, and doctors and patients all incur legally enforceable duties to one another arising from their relationships. They may have a contract which itself creates obligations, and we may think of their mutual decision to enter into the relationship as a kind of contract. But in all these cases, the law may impose duties upon them which are based upon the relationship itself, not upon any agreement between them. [¶] . . . [F]amily law provides perhaps the oldest examples of legal duties arising from relationships, whether as husband and wife, or parent and child. [¶] . . . A sensible legal rule for deciding when legal duties arise between unmarried cohabitants will not ask whether they had a contract, but whether their nonmarital relationship shares with marriage those qualities which lead us to impose legal duties as between husbands and wives.

Ira Mark Ellman, *"Contract Thinking" was* Marvin's *Fatal Flaw*, 76 NOTRE DAME L. REV. 1365, 1375–76 (2001). In the ALI's view, then, such relational duties arise between intimate partners who in fact "share a life together as a couple," whether or not they choose to formalize their relationship with a marriage ceremony. One can surely debate the precise nature of, and rationale for, relational duties, but their existence is widely acknowledged in the law as well as in popular understandings of moral obligation. For a sophisticated effort at exploring the basis of relational duties, see Samuel Sheffler, *Relationships and Responsibilities*, 26 PHILOS. & PUB. AFF. 189 (1997).

Of course, the law often allows parties to alter or eliminate relational duties it would otherwise impose, as does the ALI (which applies the same rules to contracts between domestic partners that it applies to premarital agreements). In that sense, one can see the ALI as doing no more than shifting the default rule for the longer relationships that qualify as domestic partners and give rise to significant support or property claims: rather than saying the partners have no claims arising from the relationship unless they had a contract that creates the claim, the ALI presumes that claims do arise from relationships in which persons share a life together over an extended period unless they have a contract that excludes those claims. Critics of the ALI's proposals, however, object that its rules on premarital agreements, which apply to domestic partners as well, set too demanding a standard for their enforceability. *See* Notes, *infra.* For more on agreements, see Chapter 8.

To avoid the need to decide on a case by case basis whether two individuals have "shared a life together as a couple," the Principles employ presumptions under which couples who share a primary residence together for more than the specified number of years may be treated as domestic partners without the need for such an inquiry. While the Principles leave the precise time periods up the choice of an adopting jurisdiction, they advise that the chosen period be "long enough to make it likely that the parties have established a life together as a couple and that [this life together] has had some significant impact on the circumstances of one or both parties." Because they had children and lived together for twenty years, it's clear, for example, that the ALI Principles would treat Terry and Elliott Friedman, whose case was described above in the excerpt from Ellman's article, as domestic partners.

A claimant like Michelle Marvin might also benefit from the ALI's approach, although the matter is less certain. Because Michelle and Lee shared a primary residence for six and a half years, a presumption would likely arise (unless the jurisdiction adopted an even longer durational requirement). But Lee, unlike Elliott, could rebut it if he could show that they had not "shared a life together as a couple," thus defeating Michelle's domestic partner claim entirely. Whether Lee would bother to attempt such a showing, however, might depend upon the jurisdiction's approach to financial claims at the dissolution of relatively short, childless marriages (because those same rules would apply to Lee and Marvin as domestic partners). Most states allow only modest claims in such cases — perhaps no more than the kind of transitional assistance that Lee provided Michelle voluntarily. (The *Marvin* opinion reports that he supported Michelle for a year and a half after she moved out.) It thus seems likely someone in Lee's place would have no reason to fight Michelle's domestic partner claim to avoid an alimony obligation, because he is prepared to pay more or less the modest amount that would be ordered in any event. The property claim, however, is another matter, and was undoubtedly the reason why both sides in *Marvin* itself believed their dispute worth fighting through two appellate levels and a retrial. California is a community property state with a strict equal division rule, under which Michelle would own half of all the property Lee accumulated during their relationship — property that she claimed included motion picture rights worth more than $1 million. Such a substantial property pot is obviously unusual, and many states would reject her claim to share equally in it even if they had married. Be that as it may, the ALI's position is that whatever rules the state finds appropriate to apply at the dissolution of a short-term childless marriage should apply as well to couples who live together in a true *de facto* marriage for the same time period. Of course, a high income person like Lee Marvin is just the kind of individual most likely and most able to obtain legal assistance in preparing a premarital, or pre-domestic-partner, agreement. An agreement limiting Michelle's claims if their childless relationship were to end after six years would be enforceable under the ALI's rules, as it is not "unconscionable" and would not even qualify for scrutiny of whether its enforcement would constitute a "substantial injustice." *See* Chapter 8.

As you consider whether the ALI's approach makes sense, it is of course useful to compare its likely resolution of cases like *Marvin* and *Friedman* with the likely resolution under other approaches. Of course, the California courts tell us that neither case gives rise to valid claim under *Marvin* itself.

2. *Critiques of the ALI.* Tentative drafts of the ALI proposals circulated for several years prior to the promulgation of the final version. During these years, the proposals generated substantial scholarly debate. *See, e.g., Symposium on the ALI Principles of the Law of Family Dissolution,* 2001 BYU L. REV. 857; *Symposium: Unmarried Partners and the Legacy of* Marvin v. Marvin, 76 NOTRE DAME L. REV. 1261 (2001). While some have greeted the unmarried cohabitant provisions with enthusiasm, *see, e.g.,* Mary Coombs, *Insiders and Outsiders: What the American Law Institute has Done for Gay and Lesbian Families,* 8 DUKE J. GENDER L. & POL'Y 87 (2001), others have been more critical. The critics have two principal contentions:

a. *The ALI proposals and the traditional family.* In voicing one of the more vehement objections to Chapter 6, Professor Lynn D. Wardle claims that the creation of an "official, alternative, concubinage-like status of domestic partnership," could "seriously weaken and undermine the institution of marriage." *Deconstructing Family: A Critique of the American Law Institute's "Domestic Partners" Proposal,* 2001 BYU L. REV. 1189, 1193, 1206. On this question, the ALI drafters assert that the domestic partner provisions are likely to have the reverse effect. "[T]o the extent that some individuals avoid marriage in order to avoid responsibilities to a partner, this Chapter reduces the incentive to avoid marriage because it diminishes the effectiveness of this strategy. . . . Nor are domestic partnerships likely to provide a satisfactory alternative to marriage for those otherwise inclined to marry, because informal domestic relationships are not generally recognized by third parties, including governments, which often make marriage advantageous under various regulatory and benefit schemes." Comment b, § 6.02, American Law Institute, *Principles of the Law of Family Dissolution: Analysis and Recommendations* (2002). For a view contrasting with that of Professor Wardle, see Lynne Marie Kohm, *How Will the Proliferation and Recognition of Domestic Partnerships Affect Marriage?,* 4 J. L. & FAM. STUD. 105 (2002); *see also* Steven L. Nock, *Marry Me, Bill: Should Cohabitation Be the (Legal) Default Option?,* 64 LA. L. REV. 403 (2004) (stating that cohabitation plays an increasingly important role in society, but that it does not supplant or subvert the role of marriage).

b. *The ALI proposals and private ordering.* Professor David Westfall argues that the provisions of Chapter 6 would "impos[e] marital obligations on parties in an informal relationship," which he views as "wholly at odds with some of the potentially liberating implications of the *Marvin* court's decision." *Forcing Incidents of Marriage on Unmarried Cohabitants: The American Law Institute's* Principles of Family Dissolution, 76 NOTRE DAME L. REV. 1467, 1470 (2001). Professor Westfall argues that the "*Principles*' recognition of domestic partners would substitute an emphasis on status, very similar to common-law marriage, for the powerful contemporary movement to recognize the parties' freedom to contract about the terms of their relationship. And it would inject a troubling degree of uncertainty into the determination of when domestic partnership status exists." *Id.* at 1479. Chapter 6 does permit couples to contract out of some or all of the legal consequences of the domestic partner status, just as married partners can contract out of a range of state-supplied terms governing the dissolution of their marriage. Professor Westfall expresses dissatisfaction with this option, however, arguing that the procedural and substantive requirements for an enforceable contract under the *Principles* (which are the same as the *Principles* recommend for premarital contracts) are quite strict, potentially invalidating many agreements and making Chapter 6's provisions difficult to escape.

Professor Marsha Garrison takes issue not just with the difficulty of constructing valid agreements, but also with the premise that couples choosing to cohabit are entering a relationship with the kind of commitment that should be treated as equivalent to marriage. *Is Consent Necessary? An Evaluation of the Emerging Law of Cohabitant Obligation*, 52 UCLA L. REV. 815, 896 (2005). For other discussions of the implications for private ordering of Chapter 6 of the *ALI Principles*, see Milton C. Regan, Jr., *Calibrated Commitment: The Legal Treatment of Marriage and Cohabitation*, 76 NOTRE DAME L. REV. 1435, 1446–1449 (2001); Margaret Brinig, *Domestic Partnership: Missing the Target?* 4 J. L. & FAM. STUD. 19 (2002).

3. *The Blending of Contract and Status Frameworks.* Several commentators, dissatisfied with both a status approach such as Connell's or the ALI's, and *Marvin*, have sought third ways that blend them. Consider, for example, Elizabeth Scott's proposal, in *Marriage, Cohabitation And Collective Responsibility For Dependency*, 2004 U. CHI. LEGAL F. 225, 255–63:

> [Despite the] legitimate preference that lawmakers have for formal marriage with its set of clear obligations. . . . courts should enforce agreements between cohabiting parties about property distribution and support under ordinary contract principles.
>
> Many courts have adopted this view in recent years and have been ready to enforce these contracts. . . . Often, however, no express agreement can be proved and the claimant must seek to demonstrate that the parties had a contract implied in fact based on conduct. [¶] Courts' responses to financial claims by cohabiting parties based on conduct rather than express promise have been mixed . . . [¶] In general, although claimants have sometimes prevailed, enforcement of implied contracts by cohabitants is an uncertain and costly business. . . .
>
> Some commentators have responded to these difficulties by concluding that the contractual framework is unsuitable for this context because the parties' understandings are too ambiguous. . . . [Professor] Ellman's (and the A.L.I.['s]) response is to substitute a non-consensual status as the mechanism to enforce financial obligations between intimate partners.
>
> [T]he A.L.I.'s abandonment of contract is undesirable. It is also unnecessary, in that contract law can provide efficient default rules to clarify the implied understandings about property and support obligations between parties in long-term intimate unions. The application of properly structured default rules can facilitate legal enforcement and simplify the judicial evaluation of these claims.
>
> [W]here a couple provide[s] clear evidence through . . . conduct that [the] relationship is marriage-like, [an] agreement to assume marital obligations can be inferred — and legally enforced. Where a couple lives

together for many years, sharing a life and financial resources, and holding themselves out as husband and wife, it is a sound presumption that they intend to share the property acquired during the relationship. Further, [partners] who assume traditional marital roles of wage earner and homemaker can be presumed to intend to provide the financially dependent partner with "insurance" in the form of support should the relationship dissolve. The default terms of the marriage contract represent mutual obligations that spouses incur whether or not they expressly agree; these obligations should also be incurred in marriage-like informal unions.

The challenge is to design clear criteria that separate marriage-like unions from those in which the parties are not married because they do not want marital commitment or obligations . . . [A] cohabitation period of substantial duration is the best available proxy for commitment, and the only practical means to avoid intrusive and error-prone inquiry in the effort to distinguish marriage-like relationships from more typical informal unions that involve less financial interdependency. A period of five years or more, for example, supports a presumption that the relationship was marriage-like and discourages opportunistic and marginal claims. At that point, the party challenging the contractual obligation can fairly be required to demonstrate that the parties' intent was not to undertake marital obligations and that the union was of a different kind. A five-year period will significantly limit the category of claimants, because most informal unions do not last this long. Thus, a presumption based on this duration promises to be a relatively accurate sorting mechanism for separating marriage-like unions from casual unions. To be sure, this means that some deserving parties will not receive the benefit of the default rule. However, dependent partners in unions of extended duration present the most compelling claims, and these parties will be protected.

The default rule framework represents a significant improvement over current law; today, many claims fail, although it seems likely either that the parties had some agreement (but what, exactly?) or that one partner misled or exploited the other. Default rules clarify that the conduct of parties in long term unions will be deemed promissory unless clear evidence is offered that it is not. . . . Where the default rule does not reflect both parties' expectations, it has a useful information-forcing function, putting the burden on the dissatisfied party to identify himself explicitly as a "non-committer." The proposed framework presents the primary wage earner with two options: he can . . . accept the legal obligations that follow from the application of the default rule as the cost of being in a long term intimate union, or he can disclose to his partner his intentions not to engage in financial sharing. At this point, she can make an informed choice about whether to end the union or to remain in a role that leaves her financially vulnerable. A jurisdiction that wants to offer additional legal protection to the dependent partner can do so by requiring a written agreement to opt out of the default rule. In any event, the default rule allows the parties to act upon more complete information about the financial terms of their relationship, reducing both misunderstanding and exploitation.

As compared with current doctrine, the default rule approach simplifies the judicial determination of financial obligations between cohabitants; it avoids an open-ended inquiry into the parties' expectations in every case. . . . [T]he framework provides a means to enforce the sometimes opaque financial understandings between cohabiting partners and does so by using familiar legal tools. The default framework offers far greater financial security than current law to vulnerable partners who may otherwise be exploited or misled — or who may simply have a different understanding of the relationship than the primary wage earning partner.

. . . .

Outcomes under my proposed framework will often be quite similar to those obtained under the A.L.I.'s Domestic Partnership status, which also imposes marriage-like obligations on cohabitants. The contract-based default framework has some advantages, however over the A.L.I. approach. . . .

[A] contractual framework is compatible with liberal values and thus has a normative appeal that the status-based approach adopted by the A.L.I. lacks. . . . Parties are free to contract out of default rules, and *imposing* a marriage-like status on cohabiting parties, as the A.L.I. Principles do, excludes an option for intimate affiliation that some parties might choose. The A.L.I. approach assumes that financially vulnerable partners would always choose no relationship over a relationship without financial security; in fact, some may prefer a shared life without financial sharing. Adults with full information should be free to make these choices. To be sure, sometimes the outcome under the default framework may result in inequity. However, the alternative of paternalistically imposing financial obligations on unchoosing (and even unwilling) parties after a certain period of cohabitation is even less satisfactory. Although an imposed status may sometimes beneficially deter exploitation of dependent partners, it sacrifices the freedom of individuals to order their intimate lives.

Is there any difference in substance, as opposed to nomenclature, between the ALI's rule and Scott's proposal that once a couple have lived together for five years, a "presumption" should arise that their "relationship was marriage-like" and therefore gives rise to marital obligations unless "the party challenging the contractual obligation can . . . demonstrate that the parties' intent was not to undertake marital obligations"? Scott calls this a contractual default rule, but consider whether it is in fact based on contractual notions of consent or on something much closer to the ALI's argument that relational obligations arise when parties conduct themselves in this way over a sufficient period of time. How would Scott deal, for example, with the case of Elliott and Terry Friedman: would Elliott be able to overcome Scott's presumption by showing that *he* never intended to commit himself to marriage-like obligations, or would he have to show that *both* he and Terry had agreed on that? Suppose he could show that Terry stayed with him after their children were born even though he reminded her, from time to time, that he did not mean to undertake marital obligations — does that establish her consent to a contract that rebuts Scott's "presumption" and "default rule"? There is certainly no contract, in such a case, to *impose* marriage-like obligations on the parties, but neither, most likely, is there sufficient basis to conclude they had a contract *to avoid them* (suppose in staying, for example, Terry always says, in response to Elliott's reminders, that she does not agree and believes he has committed himself.) If Scott means to require a true contract between Terry and Elliott to avoid the default rule presumption, then it would seem Elliott is bound, but can we explain binding him to the default rule on a contractual or consent basis in that case?

4. *Other Proposed Compromises Between the ALI and Contract Regimes.* Other commentators have proposed "compromises" between the ALI domestic partners proposal and the now-dominant contract-based regime. Concluding that the ALI proposals go too far in creating parity between married and unmarried couples, Professor Milton Regan would limit legal recognition of nonmarital cohabitant relationships in order to retain the "legally privileged" legal status of marriage. Regan, *supra*, at 1464. Yet, inter se claims between nonmarital cohabitants should be recognized, he argues, even in the absence of a contract, "when an individual is rendered vulnerable by virtue of her reliance on a nonmarital relationship," *id.* at 1465, and where a partner can demonstrate that "failure to honor the claim would impose undue hardship." *Id.* at 1452. Professor Regan asserts that where "a claimant can establish that the relationship involved financial and emotional interdependence," the law should recognize that "individuals may have responsibilities of care toward one another that arise not simply from consent but by virtue of a shared life, whatever legal form it takes." *Id.* at 1450–51. At the other end of the spectrum, Professor Bowman believes that in such relationships the ALI does not go far enough — that the law should treat such cohabitants as married for all purposes, not just for claims between the partners themselves. Cynthia Grant Bowman, *Social Science and Legal Policy: The Case of Heterosexual Cohabitation*, 9 J. L. & Fam. Studies 1 (2007). For other thoughtful discussions of the ALI regime and its alternatives, see J. Thomas Oldham, *Lessons From Jerry Hall v. Mick Jagger Regarding U.S. Regulation of Heterosexual Cohabitants Or, Can't Get No Satisfaction*, 76 NOTRE DAME L. REV. 1409, 1427 (2001); Daniel I. Weiner, *The Uncertain Future of Marriage and the Alternatives*, 16 UCLA WOMEN'S L.J. 97 (2007).

5. *Comparative Perspectives on Nonmarital Cohabitation.* While nonmarital cohabitants in most countries have few rights, several countries in Europe, as well as Canada, have accorded more status-based legal recognition to nonmarital cohabitants than is accorded in the United States. For example, Canada provides for parity in receipt of certain federal benefits among married couples and cohabiting couples (both opposite-sex and same-sex). *See* Nicholas Bala, *Alternatives for Extending Spousal Status in Canada*, 17 CAN. J. FAM. L. 169 (2000). It also has revised both tax and old-age pension rules so that the same standards apply to married and "common-law" partners. Individual Canadian provinces have gone still further: Ontario and British Columbia, have statutorily addressed support obligations of nonmarital cohabitants following relationship dissolution. *See* Grace Ganz Blumberg, *The Regularization of Nonmarital Cohabitation: Rights and Responsibilities in the American Welfare State*, 76 NOTRE DAME L. REV. 1265, 1300 (2001); Noel Semple, *In Sickness and in Health?*

Spousal Support and Unmarried Cohabitants, 24 CAN. J. FAM. L. 317 (2008). Ontario treats nonmarital partners as "spouses" for such purposes if the couple has cohabited consecutively for at least three years or "lived together in a relationship of some permanence, if they are the natural or adoptive parents of a child." British Columbia focuses on the existence of a "marriage-like relationship for a period of at least 2 years." *Id.* at 1300–01 (quoting Ontario Family Reform Act and Family Relations Act of British Columbia).

Several European nations have also accorded cohabitants significant rights and recognition. In France, nonmarital couples (opposite- and same-sex) can register as partners under *Le Pacte Civil de Solidarité et du Concubinage* (or "PACS"), a formal avenue for recognition. Eva Steiner, *The Spirit of the New French Registered Partnership Law — Promoting Autonomy and Pluralism or Weakening Marriage?* 12 CHILD & FAM. L. Q. 1 (2000); *see also* CLARE MCGLYNN, FAMILIES AND THE EUROPEAN UNION (2006). Couples who enter into a PACS have some financial rights similar to those associated with marriage, such as filing joint income taxes; and some rights of succession to protect surviving partners. *See* Claude Martin & Irene Thery, *The PACS and Marriage and Cohabitation in France*, 15 INT'L J. L. POL'Y & FAM. 135 (2001). However, since a 2006 amendment, property acquired after the creation of the PACS is no longer considered jointly held; instead, couples must affirmatively choose to hold property jointly.

Sweden also applies a status-based approach to nonmarital cohabitants. S.F.S. 2003:376 (Swed.) *available at* http://www.homo.se/o.o.i.s/1784. Under Swedish law, cohabitant couples' (whether opposite- or same-sex) joint dwellings and household goods are considered joint property to be divided equally upon dissolution. Sweden's protections for nonmarital cohabitants, however, do not extend beyond property rights. Cynthia Grant Bowman, *Social Science and Legal Policy: The Case of Heterosexual Cohabitation* 9 J. L. & FAM. STUD. 1, 42 (2007).

In Spain, the rights of cohabitants vary by region and are most prominent in Catalonia under the 1998 *Stable Couples Act.* The act applies to both same-sex and opposite-sex unmarried couples, and imposes joint liability for household costs and also for some kinds of debts. The *Act* applies to couples who have lived together for over two years, to opposite sex couples who have children together regardless of the duration of the relationship, and to couples who choose to opt in to the act prior to the two year period. Caroline Forder, *European Models of Domestic Partnership Laws: The Field of Choice*, 17 CAN. J. FAM. L. 371, 382. At the end of cohabitation, this act provides that a partner who has taken care of the household is entitled to compensation to prevent unfair enrichment of the other party. The act does not provide for inheritance rights for opposite-sex couples, but includes provisions for same sex-couples to inherit portions of their partners' estates. GÖRAN LIND, COMMON LAW MARRIAGE: A LEGAL INSTITUTION FOR COHABITATION 833–34 (2008).

The extension of rights to nonmarital cohabitants is not limited to Western European countries. In New Zealand, for example, beginning in 2001 nonmarital cohabitants who live together for three years have the same property rights as married couples under the Property (Relationships) Act. *See* Bill Akin, *The Challenge of Unmarried Cohabitation — The New Zealand Response*, 37 FAM. L.Q. 303 (2003). In addition, Croatia has extended to nonmarital partners certain rights to property and post-relationship support. *See, e.g.*, Dijana Jakovac-Lozic, *Croatia's New Family Act and its Implications on Marriage and Other Forms of Family Life*, 31 CAL. W. INT'L L. J. 83, 92–94 (2000). For a detailed discussion of other countries' treatment of cohabitant relationships, as well as an argument for more parity between cohabitant relationships and marital relationships in the United States, see Nancy D. Polikoff, BEYOND (STRAIGHT AND GAY) MARRIAGE: VALUING ALL FAMILIES UNDER THE LAW (2008), especially chapter 6.

6. *Interstate Recognition of Nonmarital Cohabitant Relationships.* For a thoughtful analysis of the special issues raised when nonmarital couples begin their relationship in one jurisdiction and one or both of them changes domiciles, see William A. Reppy, Jr., *Choice of Law Problems Arising When Unmarried Cohabitants Change Domicile*, 55 SMU L. REV. 273 (2002).

PROBLEMS

Consider how the following cases might be decided in a state following *Marvin, Hewitt, Connell*, the ALI proposal, or Elizabeth Scott's approach.

Problem 9-1. Cliff and Nancy lived together as a couple on and off during college. After college, from 1992 to 1997, they lived together continuously in one half of a duplex which Cliff had purchased in his own name, using his separate funds for a down payment. The other half of the duplex was rented out, and Nancy helped to maintain it by cleaning between tenants, painting, showing it to prospective tenants, and so forth. Nancy and Cliff had joint savings and checking accounts, into which the rental payments and their separate earnings were always deposited. Mortgage payments as well as household purchases were made from these funds. The parties kept no careful record of their respective earnings during this period of cohabitation, but it appears that Cliff earned significantly more than Nancy. In 1993, Nancy gave birth to a child, which Cliff admits is his. The parties owned a number of automobiles during the period, all of which were registered solely in Cliff's name. Some of their household items were gifts from their parents. Nancy had purchased a car in 1991, before they had begun living together, but when she stopped working after giving birth, she transferred title to Cliff, who took over the payments. Cliff later sold that car and used the proceeds to purchase a truck, in his own name.

At various times during their cohabitation, Nancy asked Cliff to put her name on the title to the duplex or the cars, but he always refused. She asked him to marry her on several occasions but he would not. She was hospitalized under his name on one occasion, and his health insurer paid her bills. Nancy claims Cliff assured her that if he died, all his property would go to her and the child.

(A) After their relationship terminates, Nancy brings an action for a declaration of her rights in the duplex, automobiles, household furnishings and other personal property. What result?

(B) Suppose Nancy had come to you for advice before the relationship terminated. Would you suggest preparing a *Marvin* agreement for the parties to sign?

(C) Suppose Cliff had come to you for advice, seeking an agreement to present to Nancy, which would ensure that she has no claims upon him if their relationship ends. He confides that a few years ago he came into a significant inheritance, which he invested in his brother's software company, and things have gone very well. Nancy doesn't know about these developments; he is reluctant to tell her for fear that she will pester him to spend money on things like a nicer home or better car, which he doesn't want to do. What do you advise?

Problem 9-2. Assume the facts of Problem 9-1, except that when Nancy became pregnant she came to seek your advice on whether it was important that she and Cliff marry. She knows Cliff wants the child, and probably would marry her if she insisted upon it as a condition of her completing the pregnancy to term. She wants to know how important it is that she do that, and exactly how it would matter if they were married. What do you tell her?

(A) What if Cliff insists upon a premarital agreement that upon divorce, neither party will have any obligation to the other? Is there any reason for Nancy to prefer marriage with such a premarital agreement to cohabitation with a *Marvin* agreement?

(B) Suppose Cliff says that while he is willing to sign a cohabitation agreement stating that he will be financially responsible for the child, he will insist on also including provisions which deny any financial obligations to Nancy?

Problem 9-3. Irma was a 48-year-old Polish immigrant, married with two children, with little knowledge of English, when she met Thaddeus. Thaddeus, a sophisticated and well-to-do Polish businessman, was 42, married and the father of two children. He urged Irma to live with him and she consented. She raised both of their children and otherwise performed normal housewifely duties while he supported her and the children. He originally promised to divorce his wife and marry her, and sought out her husband to arrange for a divorce for her. Irma was divorced, but Thaddeus never was. For some time he was evasive when questioned about marriage. In 1998, she left him after a serious argument. At this point, however, he made it clear that he would not marry her, but promised that he would "take care of her and provide for her for the rest of her life if she would only come back." She relented and returned. They continued living together until 2007, when Thaddeus became interested in another woman, 30 years younger. Irma left him, crushed and hurt, upon discovering he had finally begun divorce proceedings against his wife so he could marry this new love.

Irma now brings an action to enforce Thaddeus' promise to provide for her for the rest of her life. What result?

Problem 9-4. Mario Bruno hired Angela into his business in 1979, and began an affair with her in 1980. Mario was married and had one adopted child, but frequently expressed to Angela his desire to have a child "of his own." He promised Angela that if she had his child he would support them and provide for the child in his will. He also promised to divorce his wife and marry Angela. Angela finally consented, but despite their efforts, Angela did not become pregnant until 1993. Their son was named Mario Bruno, Junior. Mario paid for all hospital expenses, visited Angela daily, both in the hospital and afterward, paid Angela's rent, and provided her with $60 per week support. As the years progressed, he spent more time with his son and Angela, and frequently bought gifts for them in addition to his regular support payments.

Bruno died suddenly in 2009. His will made no provision for either Angela or Mario Junior. Angela brings this action to obtain specific performance of Mario's agreement to provide for them in his will. Assume that as a general matter, contracts to make a will are enforceable. Is this one?

Problem 9-5. Contrast Problem 9-4 with the case of Joseph and Celeste. The couple began dating regularly in 1998. During that year, Celeste gradually increased the time she spent "staying over" at Joseph's home. Later that year, Joseph asked Celeste to move in with him permanently. She initially resisted, asserting that she "did not want to move in unless we were going to have a long range permanent husband and wife type of relationship." She reports that the next year, she did move into Joseph's home and that two "started living together by mutual agreement as Husband and Wife," including spending most of their time with one another and planning for their future together. She states: "We agreed that we were thereafter building our future together — personal, family, social contacts, community activities, our joint assets, debts and everything else was thereafter being done as husband and wife — not for Joe, not for Celeste, but for our joint benefit." Celeste prepared meals and managed the home. Celeste alleged that, in consideration of her moving in and "living together . . . as Husband and Wife," the two agreed that "all property acquired [with either party's skills, efforts, labor or earnings] were to be treated as their joint property." An integral part of the basic agreement, Celeste acknowledged in the trial court, was a commitment to try to "have a family." "Joe wanted me to get pregnant and have his children, to stop using birth control." And, indeed, they did: Celeste became pregnant in, apparently, late 2000; their first child, Joseph, Jr., was born in August 2001. The parties married in April 2002 and two more children, twin girls, were born to them in November 2006. Celeste filed a dissolution action in January 2008. How is she likely to fare in a claim for a half of the property accumulated by either one of them during the several-year period of premarital cohabitation?

Problems 9-6. Ann and Mary lived together for 12 years in a marriage-like relationship. During that period they both worked outside of the home: Mary as a preschool teacher, and Ann as a vice president of a clothing company. Ann's income was over four times as high as Mary's. In their domestic relationship, Mary performed most of the housekeeping chores while Ann managed their finances, which included stock investments as well as real estate. They each contributed similar proportions of their income to the investments, which were generally held solely in Ann's name. When their relationship ended, Mary sought an equitable share in their accumulated property. She alleged an oral agreement "to commingle their resources and assets, to invest in real estate and other property, and to share the profits between themselves." Does she have a cause of action?

Problem 9-7. Phyllis and Robert begin an intimate relationship in 2001, around the time Phyllis decided to file for divorce from her husband. Phyllis completed the divorce in 2004, and the relationship continued until 2009. During much of this time, their affair was conducted clandestinely, and at no point did the parties actually cohabit. Beginning in 2004, Robert gave Phyllis the first of a series of payments intended to allow her to acquire and furnish a house, because Robert believed they would marry and the house would be their home. In fact, Phyllis later broke off the relationship. She refused to return the money, since "it was a gift for sexual services," and she "was prostituting herself for this home." Robert had purchased engagement and wedding rings in 2008; Phyllis wore the engagement ring for some time but then returned it. Robert wants to recover the monies he advanced for the home, totaling $21,000. What arguments does he have? Will he prevail?

[3] Legal Status Of Unmarried Partners Vis-à-Vis Third Parties

Nonmarital cohabitants have few rights arising out of their relationship against third parties (with the notable exception of couples who enter into formal status alternatives to marriage in those states that allow them, discussed *infra* Subsection [4]).

NOTES

1. *Torts Claims.* Unmarried partners have encountered substantial obstacles to recovery in tort for claims that require a court to recognize their relationship as analogous to a marriage. States that allow couples to enter into civil unions or "everything-but-the-word-'marriage'" domestic partnerships allow each partner spouse-like rights to recover in tort. However, it is unusual for such rights to extend beyond marriage in the remaining states and beyond civil unions and marriage in those states that allow both. The primary categories of tort claims that are grounded in the marital relationship include negligent infliction of emotional distress, loss of consortium, and wrongful death. Except in a small minority of states, courts have typically restricted the field of potential plaintiffs to spouses and other members deemed part of the immediate family; nonmarital cohabitants have generally not been included in this circle. Of the states that allow limited-right domestic partnerships, only Maryland permits partners to bring a wrongful death claim. MD. CODE REGS. 4.20.020 (2009).

The California Supreme Court in *Elden v. Sheldon*, 758 P.2d 582 (Cal. 1988), followed the majority rule in denying a man's claim for negligent infliction of emotional distress experienced upon witnessing the accidental death of his alleged "de facto spouse." It expressed concern that courts would be over-burdened if required to determine which relationships are equivalent to a marriage, and also cited the state's interests in promoting marriage. *Id. See also Chiesa v. Rowe*, 486 F. Supp. 236 (W.D. Mich. 1980); *Sawyer v. Bailey*, 413 A.2d 165 (Me. 1980); *Tremblay v. Carter*, 390 So. 2d 816 (Fla. Dist. Ct. App. 1980); *Sostock v. Reiss*, 415 N.E.2d 1094 (Ill. App. Ct. 1980). In contrast, the New Jersey Supreme Court diverged from the majority approach in allowing the decedent's fiancée cohabitant to bring a claim for negligent infliction of emotional distress in *Dunphy v. Gregor*, 642 A.2d 372 (N.J. 1994). Justice Handler, writing for the majority, asserted that courts could determine whether the relationship between the victim and bystander was sufficiently intimate and "familial" to permit an action to be brought, and concluded that the state's interest in marriage would not be harmed by extension of the eligible category of plaintiffs to include certain unmarried cohabitants. In 2003, the New Hampshire Supreme Court adopted *Dunphy's* reasoning, permitting the deceased's nonmarital cohabitant/fiancée to bring a claim for negligent infliction of emotional distress. *Graves v. Estabrook*, 818 A.2d 1255 (N.H. 2003). For a survey of cases addressing claims for negligent infliction of emotional distress by persons who stand in nontraditional family relationships to the victim, see Dale Joseph Gilsinger, Annot., *Relationship Between Victim and Plaintiff-Witness as Affecting Right to Recover Under State Law for Negligent Infliction of Emotional Distress Due to Witnessing Injury to Another Where Bystander Plaintiff Is Not Member of Victim's Immediate Family*, 98 A.L.R.5th 609 (2002).

Only rarely have courts permitted nonmarital cohabitants to bring loss of consortium actions. In 2003, the New Mexico Supreme Court became the first and only state supreme court to recognize a loss of consortium claim by an unmarried cohabitant. *Lozoya v. Sanchez*, 66 P.3d 948 (N.M. 2003). In this case, the couple had been together for over 30 years, and had three children together. Citing *Dunphy's* emphasis on the "realities, not simply of legalities of relationships," *Lozoya* concluded that courts could make reliable assessments of which plaintiffs should be permitted to sue, and rejected the assertion that to allow recovery would be to recognize common law marriage. *Id.* at 954–56.

Wrongful death actions generally are authorized by statute rather than judge-made law, and plaintiffs are therefore limited to those classes of persons enumerated in the statutory provisions, typically including persons with formal legal relationships with the decedent, such as spouse or child. Courts have generally been reluctant to extend such legislative designations to nonmarital cohabitants. *See, e.g., Raum v. Restaurant Assocs., Inc.*, 675 N.Y.S.2d 343 (App. Div. 1998); *Garcia v. Douglas Aircraft Co.*, 184 Cal. Rptr. 390 (Ct. App. 1982). In *Raum*, which involved a same-sex couple, the dissent argued that "precedent exists for preferring a functional over a literal interpretation of a statute whose purpose is to promote the public welfare, so that homosexual couples will not be disadvantaged by their inability to give their relationship a legal status." *Id.* at 345.

For further discussion of tort-related claims by nonmarital cohabitants, *see* Shannon Minter, *Expanding Wrongful Death Statutes and other Death Benefits to Same-Sex Partners*, 30 HUMAN RIGHTS MAGAZINE 6 (Summer 2003), *available at* http://www.abanet.org/irr/hr/summer03/expanding.html; Michael Jay Gorback, Note, *Negligent Infliction of Emotional Distress: Has the Legislative Response to Diane Whipple's Death Rendered the Hard-Line Stance of* Elden *and* Thing *Obsolete?*, 54 HASTINGS L. J. 273, 276 (2002); Angie Smolka, Note, *That's the Ticket: A New Way of Defining Family*, 10 CORNELL J. L. & PUB. POL'Y 629 (2001); John G. Culhane, *"Clanging Silence": Same-Sex Couples and Tort Law*, 89 KY. L. J. 911 (2000-01); Laura M. Raisty, Note, *Bystander Distress and Loss of Consortium: An Examination of the Relationship Requirements in Light of* Romer v. Evans, 65 FORDHAM L. REV. 2647 (1997); Alisha M. Carlile, *Like Family: Rights of Nonmarried Cohabitational Partners in Loss of Consortium Actions* 46 B.C. L. REV. 391 (2005); John G. Culhane, *Even More Wrongful Death: Statutes Divorced from Reality*, 32 FORDHAM URB. L.J. 171 (2005).

2. *Unemployment Compensation.* While unemployment compensation is ordinarily denied to persons who leave their employment voluntarily, California is among those states that compensates individuals if they leave their jobs for "good cause." CAL. UNEMP. INSUR. CODE § 1256 (2003). The governing statute sets forth certain rebuttable presumptions regarding the "good cause" requirement: "An individual may be deemed to have left his or her most recent work with good cause if he or she leaves employment to accompany his or her spouse or domestic partner to a place from which it is impractical to commute to the employment. For purposes of this section 'spouse' includes a person to whom marriage is imminent." *Id.* This language reflects a 2001 amendment which inserted the words "or domestic partner," as well as a 1988 amendment including persons for whom "marriage is imminent." Before the most recent amendment, the California Supreme Court had sustained the unemployment benefits of one claimant who moved to be with her nonmarital partner, *see MacGregor v. Unemployment Ins. Appeals Bd.*, 689 P.2d 453 (1984), but the year before on different facts had denied benefits to another. *Norman v. Unemployment Ins. Appeals Bd.*, 663 P.2d 904 (1983).

3. *Employee Benefits.* Social Security and worker's compensation benefits generally flow to surviving spouses, but not to surviving cohabitants. *See, e.g., Banegas v. State Indus. Ins. Sys.*, 19 P.3d 245 (Nev. 2001) (legislature did not intend to provide death benefits to dependents such as unmarried cohabitants lacking legally cognizable relationship with deceased worker). The Social Security rule was sustained against constitutional challenge in *Califano v. Boles*, 443 U.S. 282 (1979).

With that said, a minority of states provide worker's compensation benefits to cohabitants in some cases. For example, some allow benefits to surviving cohabitants who can show economic dependency on the deceased employee. *See, e.g., West v. Barton-Malow Co.*, 230 N.W.2d 545 (Mich. 1975) (decedent's unmarried cohabitant of thirteen years eligible as dependent, given that they lived as, and regarded each other as, husband and wife). Oregon treats unmarried cohabitants who have lived together for over a year as married for the purpose of the worker's compensation law. OR. REV. ST. § 656.226 (2003).

4. *Housing Discrimination.* Some states have laws prohibiting landlords from discriminating in rental of housing units based on marital status. In some cases, landlords have contested these laws as infringements on their first amendment rights of free exercise of religion and free speech. *See, e.g., Thomas v. Anchorage Equal Rights Comm'n*, 220 F.3d 1134 (9th Cir. 2000) (en banc). State courts have been mixed in their analyses of these cases. Alaska, Massachusetts, and California have rejected them. *See, e.g., Swanner v. Anchorage Equal Rights Comm'n*, 874 P.2d 274 (Alaska 1994); *Thomas v. Anchorage Equal Rights Comm'n*, 102 P.3d 937 (Alaska 2004); *Smith v. Fair Employment & Housing Comm'n*, 913 P.2d 909 (Cal. 1996); *Attorney Gen. v. Desilets*, 636 N.E.2d 233 (Mass. 1994). Those courts upholding the landlords' claims have gleaned support from the formal disapproval of nonmarital cohabitation and fornication reflected in the state's criminal statutes. As such, the validity of those holdings has been called into question by the United States Supreme Court's 2003 decision in *Lawrence v. Texas*.

Other landlords have successfully challenged charges that they violated non-discrimination prohibitions based on marital status by asserting the somewhat tenuous distinction that they refused to rent because cohabitation was criminal under state law rather than because of their status as married persons. *See, e.g., N.D. Fair Housing Council, Inc. v. Peterson*, 625 N.W.2d 551 (N.D. 2001). *See also*

Cooper v. French, 460 N.W.2d 2 (Minn. 1990), (upholding a landlord's refusal to rent to an unmarried couple because his religious convictions precluded him from renting to a couple who intended to violate the state's fornication statute). Such decisions, too, are called into question by *Lawrence.*

In several New York cases, the courts have determined whether unmarried cohabitants fall within various definitions of "family" set forth in certain housing policies. Most recently, the state's highest court rejected the claims of lesbian medical students who sued Yeshiva University. *Levin v. Yeshiva Univ.*, 754 N.E.2d 1099 (N.Y. 2001). The women challenged the university's policy of giving priority to married couples in school-owned housing, arguing that this preference constituted discrimination on the basis of marital status that had a disparate impact on gay and lesbian students in violation of the City Human Rights Act. The court held that the provision limiting housing "to only those in a legal, family relationship with the tenant" did not amount to marital discrimination. The court conceded that the plaintiffs might have a cause of action for disparate impact discrimination if they could demonstrate in further proceedings that the statute "disproportionately burdens lesbians and gay men." *Id.* at 1102, 1106.

For further discussion of the relationship between nonmarital cohabitation, state antidiscrimination laws, and landlords' "rights," see Erin P.B. Zasada, *Civil Rights — Rights Protected and Discrimination Prohibited: Living in Sin in North Dakota? Not Under my Lease*, 78 N.D. L. REV. 539 (2002); Scott A. Johnson, Note, *The Conflict Between Religious Exercise and Efforts to Eradicate Housing Discrimination Against Nontraditional Couples: Should Free Exercise Protect Landlord Bias?* 53 WASH. & LEE L. REV. 351 (1996); Kelly D. Eckel, Comment, *Legitimate Limitation of a Landlord's Rights — A New Dawn For Unmarried Cohabitants*, 68 TEMP. L. REV. 811 (1995).

5. *Employment Discrimination.* A few litigants have successfully used state anti-discrimination laws to challenge employer refusals to hire them or continue their employment because of a nonmarital relationship. *See, e.g., McClure v. Sports & Health Club*, 370 N.W.2d 844 (Minn. 1985). Government employees disciplined or dismissed for engaging in unmarried cohabitation have occasionally sought relief in the courts, with mixed results. In a case that resulted in *six* different opinions from a panel of federal judges, Robin Shahar lost her claim against the state of Georgia after a job offer from the Georgia Attorney General's office was withdrawn. *Shahar v. Bowers*, 114 F.3d 1097 (11th Cir. 1997). Ms. Shahar claimed that the state had violated her rights of intimate and expressive association, freedom of religion, equal protection, and substantive due process by retracting its job offer upon learning of her lesbian commitment ceremony. All of her claims were rejected. For a survey of relevant cases, *see* Annot., *Federal and State Constitutional Provisions as Prohibiting Discrimination in Employment on Basis of Gay, Lesbian, or Bisexual Sexual Orientation or Conduct*, 96 A.L.R.5th 391 (2002).

Employees have had more success challenging disciplinary actions based on unmarried procreation because of the well-established constitutional interest in procreative decisions. *See, e.g., Lewis v. Delaware State College*, 455 F. Supp. 239 (D. Del. 1978) (employer college enjoined to reinstate unmarried mother to her position as Director of Residence Halls for Women because of her right to bear a nonmarital child). *See also* Annot., *Discrimination Against Unwed Mothers or Unwed Pregnant Women as Prescribed Under Pregnancy Discrimination Act*, 91 A.L.R. FED. 178 (1990). Some employers have rules restricting the employment of spouses within the same employment setting. In *Espinoza v. Thoma*, 580 F.2d 346 (8th Cir. 1978), such a no-spouse rule was applied by analogy to deny employment to a woman cohabiting with another employee. The court sustained this application, finding that it followed logically from the purpose of the no-spouse rule.

6. *Probate.* In general, statutory rules that set forth intestate succession rights do not recognize cohabitants. *See* Mary Louise Fellows, Monica Kirkpatrick Johnson et al., *Committed Partners and Inheritance: An Empirical Study*, 16 LAW & INEQ. 1, 15 (1998). An implied contract claim against an estate by a decedent's cohabitant may be allowed, however, *see Byrne v. Laura*, 60 Cal. Rptr. 2d 908 (Ct. App. 1997); *In re Estate of Steffes*, 290 N.W.2d 697 (Wis. 1980), as may a claim in *quantum meruit, Green v. Richmond*, 337 N.E.2d 691 (Mass. 1975) (services were performed in reliance upon unenforceable oral agreement). Equal protection challenges to a state's inheritance and elective share statutes have failed. *See In re Estate of Cooper*, 592 N.Y.S.2d 797 (App. Div. 1993) (holding that "spousal-like" relationships do not give rise to spousal rights). Inheritance taxes typically treat surviving spouses more favorably than strangers, and a cohabitant taking under a will is a stranger under the tax law. *See, e.g., In re Estate of Edgett*, 168 Cal. Rptr. 686 (Ct. App. 1980) (rejecting claim by decedent's former wife that she should be treated as a surviving spouse for inheritance tax purposes where the couple had divorced after 33 years of marriage, subsequently resumed cohabitation, and the decedent left all of his assets to her). For a proposal urging reform of Uniform Probate Code to recognize unmarried cohabitants, *see* Marissa J. Holob, Note, *Respecting Commitment: A Proposal To Prevent Legal Barriers From Obstructing the Effectuation of Intestate Goals*, 85 CORNELL L. REV. 1492 (2000); *see also* Jennifer Seidman, *Functional Families and Dysfunctional Laws: Committed Partners and Intestate Succession*, 75 U. COLO. L. REV. 211 (2004).

7. *Spousal Violence.* Do statutory provisions criminalizing spousal violence apply as well to unmarried cohabitants? In recent years, as awareness of the prevalence and dynamics of domestic violence has grown, nonmarital cohabitants have increasingly been recognized as falling within the purview of spousal abuse statutes. This is particularly important in light of empirical research revealing that unmarried women may be at greater risk for assaults by intimate partners than are married women. *See* PATRICIA TJADEN & NANCY THOENNES, EXTENT, NATURE, AND CONSEQUENCES OF INTIMATE PARTNER VIOLENCE, FINDINGS FROM THE NATIONAL VIOLENCE AGAINST WOMEN SURVEY III (July 2000). Presently, most state statutes specifically refer to "partners" or "cohabitants" as well as spouses when delineating those categories of relationships that fall within the statutes' reach. *See, e.g.,* CAL. PENAL CODE § 273.5 (listing cohabitants and former cohabitants as two of the several categories of relationships falling within the statute's jurisdiction). In many of those that do not, courts still interpret the provisions to protect unmarried cohabitants.

Congress provided significant leadership in this regard in the Violence Against Women Act ("VAWA"), defining family violence to include acts "committed by a person against another individual . . . to whom such person is or was related by blood or marriage or otherwise legally related or with whom such person is or was lawfully residing." 42 U.S.C.A. § 10421. *See also* 18 U.S.C.A. § 921 (defining "intimate partner" to include "an individual who cohabits or has cohabited with the person" for purpose of special firearms provisions of federal criminal code). It is unclear whether same-sex cohabitants and intimate partners are included within this protection although the trend has been toward such inclusion. For further discussion of the reach of domestic violence statutes to same-sex relationships, *see* Marnie J. Franklin, *The Closet Becomes Darker for the Abused: A Perspective on Lesbian Partner Abuse*, 9 CARDOZO WOMEN'S L.J. 299 (2003); Krisana M. Hodges, *Trouble in Paradise: Barriers to Addressing Domestic Violence in Lesbian Relationships*, 9 L. & SEXUALITY 311 (1999–2000). *See also* Shannon Little, *Challenging Changing Legal Definitions of Family in Same-Sex Domestic Violence*, 19 HASTINGS WOMEN'S L.J. 259 (2008).

8. *Testimonial Privileges.* The testimonial privileges for marital communications and adverse testimony are generally statutory, and as such have not generally been judicially extended to cohabitants. *See, e.g., Badgett v. Lindsey*, 2004 U.S. Dist. LEXIS 7000 (N.D. Cal. 2004) (holding claimant failed to prove that he was partner to a valid marriage under Texas law, and, thus, marital communication privileges did not apply); *People v. Delph*, 156 Cal. Rptr. 422 (Ct. App. 1979) (the common law and statutory marital communication privileges do not extend to cohabitants in marriage-like relationships); Annot., *Communication Between Unmarried Couple Living Together as Privileged*, 4 A.L.R.4th 422 (1981). For a proposal to extend the testimonial privileges to same-sex couples, see Jennifer R. Brannen, *Unmarried with Privileges: Extending the Evidentiary Privileges to Same-Sex Couples*, 17 REV. LITIG. 311 (1998); *see also* Katherine M. Forbes, *Time for a New Privilege: Allowing Unmarried Cohabitating Couples to Claim the Spousal Testimony Privilege*, 17 REV. LITIG. 311 (2007).

9. *Guardianship and Health Care.* In most jurisdictions, adults can execute an "advanced directive" or a "health care power of attorney" in order to nominate any adult of her choosing to serve as proxy decision-makers if they become incompetent to make their own health care decisions. *See* NANCY M.P. KING, MAKING SENSE OF ADVANCED DIRECTIVES (rev. ed. 1996). Yet, most adults do not execute such documents, and in their absence, health care professionals must rely on the individuals identified by statute as default decision-makers. Few states recognize nonmarital partners as "default" decision-makers. *See* Rebecca K. Glatzer *Equality at the End: Amending State Surrogacy Statutes to Honor Same-Sex Couples' End-Of-Life Decisions*, 13 ELDER L.J. 255 (2005). *But see* Health Care Surrogate Act, 755 ILL. COMP. STAT. 40/25(a) (1998) (recognizing "close friend" as default decision-maker). *Id.*

The best-known case addressing a dispute between a patient's family and her nonmarital cohabitant is *In re Guardianship of Kowalski*, 478 N.W.2d 790 (Minn. Ct. App. 1991). In that case, Sharon Kowalski's same-sex partner, Karen Thompson, petitioned the court to become Sharon's guardian after Sharon suffered severe brain damage in an accident. Opposed by Sharon's family, Karen litigated for eight years until a Minnesota appellate court ultimately granted her petition. For a discussion of this case, see Angie Smolka, Note, *That's the Ticket: A New Way of Defining Family*, 10 CORNELL J. L. & PUB. POL'Y 629, 636–37 (2001). For surveys of state laws and proposals for including nonmarital partners as decision-makers, see Amy L. Brown, Note, *Broadening Anachronistic Notions of "Family" in Proxy Decisionmaking for Unmarried Adults*, 41 HASTINGS L.J. 1029 (1990); Jonathan Andrew Hein, *Caring for the Evolving Family: Cohabiting Partners and Employee Sponsored Health Care*, 30 N.M. L. REV. 19 (2000). Finally, for a discussion of the issues relating to post-mortem decisions by proxy decision-makers, see Jennifer E. Horan, Note, *"When Sleep at Last Has Come": Controlling the Disposition of Dead Bodies for Same-Sex Couples*, 2 J. GENDER RACE & JUST. 423, 449–51 (1999).

10. ***The Aftermath of 9/11.*** As reviewed in the preceding notes, nonmarital partners generally are not treated in a manner equivalent to spouses with respect to a range of legal rights and benefits. The losses experienced by nonmarital partners of victims of the September 11, 2001, terrorist attacks, however, captured the public's attention. Private relief agencies and the state and federal government faced the challenge of deciding whether spouse-like relationships would qualify survivors for benefits from the various victim compensation funds. The policies ultimately adopted reflect increasing recognition of the importance of nontraditional family relationships. For example, after some initial uncertainty, the American Red Cross determined that gay and lesbian partners of September 11th victims were eligible to receive survivor benefits. Cynthia Billhartz, *What is the Legal Status of Gay Unions?*, ST. LOUIS POST-DISPATCH, June 16, 2003, at E1. The New York State World Trade Center Relief Fund, which provided financial relief to surviving spouses, children, and parents, also extended eligibility for this benefit to domestic partners of either sex satisfying certain criteria. Pennsylvania's fund also permitted recovery by nonmarital partners. *See* Susan J. Becker, *Tumbling Towers as Turning Points: Will 9/11 Usher in a New Civil Rights Era for Gay Men and Lesbians in the United States?*, 9 WM. & MARY J. WOMEN & L. 207, 231–32 (2003). In contrast, Virginia denied compensation to surviving nonmarital partners of September 11th victims. *Id.* at 232. While it was initially unclear whether nonmarital partners of deceased victims could recover from the Federal September 11th Victim Compensation Fund of 2001, the Fund's benefits were not categorically denied to nonmarital partners. *See* Air Transportation Safety and System Stabilization Act of 2001, 49 U.S.C. §§ 40101, 44302–44306 (2001). *See generally* Erin G. Holt, Note, *The September 11th Victim Compensation Fund: Legislative Justice Sui Generis*, 59 N.Y.U. ANN. SURVEY AM. L. 513 (2004).

PROBLEMS

Problem 9-8. An employee group suggests that the employer extend benefits such as dependent health insurance to an employee's informal family. The employer asks for your advice on whether or how to make such changes. What do you advise?

Problem 9-9. The same-sex partner of a woman who was killed in a ferry accident seeks to be treated as a spouse in order to obtain tort remedies and to inherit from her deceased partner under the laws of intestate succession. What is her likelihood of success in various jurisdictions discussed *supra*?

[4]   Formal Status Alternatives to Marriage

In the past few decades, an increasing number of U.S. states and local jurisdictions, and some other nations have extended legal recognition to relationships between same-sex partners and, occasionally, to other non-marital relationships. The nature and type of recognition varies substantially. Some allow partners access to some or even all of a range of governmental entitlements and rights typically reserved for married couples. Other schemes give a limited range of privileges to same-sex partners, for example, by treating them as "close family members" for the purposes of hospital visitation, providing proxy consent for their partners' treatment, or making post-mortem decisions such as donation of their partners' organs. Still other status alternatives grant partners the right to designate their partners as qualifying family members for access to employee benefits, but no more. The many variations and permutations of these status alternatives reflect the widely-varying and rapidly-changing views on these issues in the United States. While an exhaustive treatment of the nature, diversity, and prevalence of the various forms of non-marital partnerships is beyond the scope of this book, it is clear that the trend toward extending legal recognition to non-marital partnerships is proceeding with substantial momentum.

HISTORY AND TRENDS

In the United States, formal status alternatives to marriage, referred to in various jurisdictions as domestic partnerships, civil unions, and reciprocal beneficiary relationships, began to emerge in the late 1980s. The creation and evolution of these partnerships followed one of two distinct (but often intersecting) paths. Grace Ganz Blumberg, *The Regularization of Nonmarital Cohabitation: Rights and Responsibilities in the American Welfare State*, 76 NOTRE DAME L. REV. 1265 (2001). In some jurisdictions, the creation of a new status was triggered by state supreme court judgments critical of the state's exclusion of same-sex couples from marriage or its legal incidents. In Hawaii and Vermont, for example, lawmakers created new legal statuses for same-sex couples to respond to judicial pronouncements that exclusion of same-sex couples from marriage or its benefits violated the state constitution (in Vermont) or was constitutionally suspect (in Hawaii). WILLIAM N. ESKRIDGE, JR., EQUALITY PRACTICE, 57–58, 22–23 (2002) (*see* Chapter 2, Section A[2][b], for further discussion of the legal challenges to those states' marriage restrictions and of the legal developments that followed). Hawaii ultimately amended its state constitution to nullify its supreme court's decision. At the same time, however, in 1995, the legislature created the status of "reciprocal beneficiaries," providing registering same-sex couples with a few of the rights and benefits enjoyed by marital partners. Similarly, in 2000, the Vermont legislature created "civil unions," and became the first state to create a status intended to be the legal equivalent of marriage in everything but name. *Id.* at 44. (Vermont's legislature has since allowed for same-sex marriage, breaking ground again by becoming the first state to enact a same-sex marriage law that was not the result of a judicial decree, on April 7, 2009. *See* Joanna L. Grossman, *The Vermont Legislature, Inventor of the "Civil Union," Grants Full Marriage Rights to Same-Sex Couples: Why It Decided Civil Unions Were Not Sufficient to Ensure*

Equality, FindLaw, April 13, 2009, http://writ.news.findlaw.com/grossman/20090413.html.)

In other jurisdictions, new legal statuses were created as a result of same-sex rights' advocates petitioning local city and county governments to enact domestic partner ordinances. William N. Eskridge, Jr., *Comparative Law and the Same-Sex Marriage Debate: A Step-by-Step Approach Toward State Recognition*, 31 McGeorge L. Rev. 641 (2000). Although these ordinances gave same-sex couples a mechanism to formally announce the partners' mutual commitment to the relationship, most provided few tangible benefits for registrants beyond the opportunity to designate one's partner as a beneficiary on health insurance and related benefit plans. Even the path to securing these limited benefits for same-sex partners was not without roadblocks. In a series of lawsuits, most of which were brought by taxpayers, state courts across the country adjudicated the authority of various local governments to offer benefits to its employees' same-sex partners. While some ordinances were struck down, most survived review relatively intact. *Compare, e.g., Ralph v. City of New Orleans*, 4 So. 3d 146 (La. Ct. App. 2009) (since city was not actually "governing" civil relationships but merely allowing the extension of health benefits, city domestic partnerships did not violate the state constitution), *Tyma v. Montgomery County*, 801 A.2d 148 (Md. Ct. App. 2002) (county ordinance did not infringe upon state's authority to regulate marriage and was within authority delegated to county), *and Heinsma v. City of Vancouver*, 29 P.3d 709 (Wa. 2001) (*en banc*) (city's defining "dependents" to include domestic partners in its employees benefit plans did not violate its authority under the state constitution), *with Nat'l Pride at Work, Inc. v. Governor of Mich.*, 748 N.W.2d 524 (Mich. 2008) (public employers and the City of Kalamazoo were not permitted to extend health benefits to partners within a domestic partnership because under Michigan's "Marriage Amendment," the union of a man and a woman is the only one that can be "recognized as similar to marriage for any purpose"), *and Arlington County v. White*, 528 S.E.2d 706 (Va. 2000) (county exceeded its authority in interpreting the term "dependents" in its health insurance plan to include domestic partners).

The following sections survey the many formal status alternatives to marriage that currently exist in the United States

[a] State Laws that Allow Partners the Same Rights and Benefits as Marriage — Civil Unions and Civil-Union-Like Domestic Partnerships

In recent years, a minority of states have passed legislation allowing couples to enter into civil unions or domestic partnerships that provide the same rights and benefits as marriage, but under a different name. Although some states, particularly on the east coast, call this form of relationship a "civil union," other states, mainly on the west coast, offer this "everything-but-the-word-'marriage'" status under the name of "domestic partnership." This nomenclature is particularly confusing because, as described below, several states use the term "domestic partnership" to describe a status that confers only a few of the rights of marriage. For clarity's sake, this chapter refers to all statuses that give couples the same rights and privileges as marriage without the name "marriage" as "civil unions."

Of the eight states that originally permitted them, civil unions continue to be performed in only five of these states: California (as of 2005); Nevada (2009); New Jersey (2006); Oregon (2007); and Washington (2008). *See* Freedom to Marry, *Where Can Gay Couples Get Married?*, http://www.freedomtomarry.org/states.php (dedicating a frequently updated page to each of the fifty states). This is because the other three — Connecticut, New Hampshire, and Vermont — have begun to allow same-sex marriage. In each of the latter group of states, legislation provided that no new civil unions were to be performed once the same-sex marriage law went into effect. 2009-0003 Vt. Adv. Legis. Serv. (LexisNexis) (repealing statutes permitting the issuance of civil union licenses); 2009–13 Conn. Legis. Serv. (West) (stating that all civil unions will automatically become marriages by given date); 2009-59 N.H. Rev. Stat. Ann. Adv. Legis. Serv. (LexisNexis) (same).

Typically, civil unions are not available to opposite-sex couples because of the concern that it would discourage such couples from marrying. However, California's domestic partnership status allows entry by heterosexual couples over the age of sixty-two, a gesture recognizing the financial losses often incurred by Social Security recipients upon marrying. Cal. Fam. Code § 297(b)(5)(B) (providing that "persons of opposite sexes may not constitute a domestic partnership unless one or both persons are over the age of 62" and satisfy specified Social Security eligibility requirements). Even more revolutionary is Nevada's new domestic partnership law, which allows same-sex and *any* opposite-sex couples who could otherwise marry to enter. *Nevada Legalizing Domestic Partnerships*, CNN.com, June 1, 2009, http://www.cnn.com/2009/POLITICS/05/31/nevada.domestic. partnerships/; Nev. Rev. Stat. § SB 283 (2009).

For those couples eligible to enter, the required formalities are identical to those for marriage for those statuses called "civil unions;" this means that a solemnization ceremony is required. However, "everything-but-the-word- 'marriage'" domestic partnerships generally do not require a solemnization ceremony. *See* Restore America, *A Rose By Any Other Name: Why Oregon's Domestic Partnership Law is Thinly Veiled Same-Sex Marriage* (2007), http://www.restoreamerica.org/pdf/Oregon%20DomesticPartnershipsComparedto Marriage.pdf; Lambda Legal, Civil Unions for Same-Sex Couples in New Jersey, FAQs (2007), http://www.lambdalegal.org/our-work/publications/facts-backgrounds/ page.jsp?itemID= 31975759.

Once entered, civil unions are engineered to function as similarly as possible to marriage, aside from the name. As can be seen from the passages of New Jersey's civil union statute excerpted below, rights and responsibilities of civil unions are identical to those for marriage. In fact, states that allow civil unions sometimes simply amend their existing marriage statutes to add the term "civil union" to them. *See, e.g.,* N.J. Stat. Ann. § 37:1–2; 1–17 (below). The parity to same-sex couples that state civil union status can confer, however, is limited by federal law's failure to recognize civil unions for the purpose of the many federal rights and benefits allowed to married couples. State statutes generally make provisions to address these inconsistencies in federal and state legal treatment. For instance, California's Family Code section 297.5(e) states that "to the extent that provisions of California law adopt, refer to, or rely upon, provisions of federal law in a way that otherwise would cause registered domestic partners to be treated differently than spouses, registered domestic partners shall be treated by California law as if federal law recognized a domestic partnership in the same manner as California law."

California's history with domestic partnership legislation deserves special mention. The California legislature originally created the status in 1994 as a state registry for same-sex couples, which would also extend benefits to partners of state employees. In subsequent years, the status was gradually expanded to grant more rights and protections to registering couples. *In re: Marriage Cases*, 183 P.3d 384, 413–14 (Cal. 2008). These extensions culminated with the passage of the California Domestic Partner Rights and Responsibilities Act of 2003, effective Jan. 1, 2005, which created parity between registered domestic partners and spouses with respect to the "rights, protections, and benefits" and "responsibilities, obligations, and duties under law, whether they derive from statutes, administrative regulations, court rules, government policies, common law, or any other provisions or sources of law, as are granted to and imposed upon spouses." CAL. FAM. CODE § 297.5(a). One of the most dramatic effects of this law was the extension of California's community property system to assets acquired by domestic partners during the partnership. In contrast to other states that have adopted same-sex marriage, the domestic partnership status continued to be available to couples even during the brief window of time that same-sex marriage was allowed in California, following the California Supreme Court's striking down of California's law banning same-sex marriage under the state constitution in *In re Marriage Cases*, 183 P.3d 384 (Cal. 2008). *See* California Secretary of State Debra Bowen, *Domestic Partners Registry Frequently Asked Questions*, http://www.sos.ca.gov/dpregistry/faqs.htm #question1 (assuring couples that "the Court's decision regarding same-sex marriage" — i.e. *In re Marriage Cases* — "did not invalidate or change any of the Family Code statutes relating to registered Domestic Partners."). After Proposition 8 was passed by voters in the 2008 election, which amended the state constitution to limit marriage to opposite-sex couples, domestic partnership is once again the only status available to same-sex couples in California (though a recent ruling confirmed that the nearly 18,000 couples who married in the interim remain legally married.) *Strauss v. Horton*, 46 Cal. 4th 364, 385, 474 (2009).

AN EXAMPLE — NEW JERSEY'S CIVIL UNION STATUTE

New Jersey's civil union statute is fairly typical of an "everything-but-the-word-'marriage'" statute. The legislation amended existing sections setting out the formalities to enter marriage to include civil unions in these requirements:

§ 37:1–2. Before a marriage or a civil union can be lawfully performed in this State, the persons intending to be married or to enter into a civil union shall obtain a marriage or civil union license from the licensing officer . . .

§ 37:1–17. . . . The person by whom or the religious society, institution, or organization by or before which, the marriage or civil union was solemnized, shall personally or by legally authorized agent subscribe where indicated on the form the date and place of the marriage or civil union.

Each certificate of marriage or civil union shall also contain the signature and residence of at least two witnesses who were present at the marriage or civil union ceremony.

Specifics of civil unions are set out in newly added sections, N.J. STAT. ANN. §§ 37:1–28 to 1–36. The legislation provides that:

§ 37:1–30. For two persons to establish a civil union in this State, it shall be necessary that they satisfy all of the following criteria: (a) Not be a party to another civil union, domestic partnership or marriage in this State; (b) Be of the same sex; and (c) Be at least 18 years of age . . .

§ 37:1–31. (a) Civil union couples shall have all of the same benefits, protections and responsibilities under law, whether they derive from statute, administrative or court rule, public policy, common law or any other source of civil law, as are granted to spouses in a marriage. (b) The dissolution of civil unions shall follow the same procedures and be subject to the same substantive rights and obligations that are involved in the dissolution of marriage. (c) The laws of domestic relations, including annulment, premarital agreements, separation, divorce, child custody and support, property division and maintenance, and post-relationship spousal support, shall apply to civil union couples. (d) Civil union couples may modify the terms, conditions or effects of their civil union in the same manner and to the same extent as married persons who execute an antenuptial agreement or other agreement recognized and enforceable under the law, setting forth particular understandings with respect to their union. (e) The rights of civil union couples with respect to a child of whom either becomes the parent during the term of the civil union, shall be the same as those of a married couple with respect to a child of whom either spouse or partner in a civil union couple becomes the parent during the marriage. (f) All contracts made between persons in contemplation of a civil union shall remain in full force after such civil union takes place. (g) A copy of the record of the civil union received from the local or State registrar shall be presumptive evidence of the civil union in all courts.

Furthermore, the statute sets forth an explicitly non-exclusive list of "benefits, protections and responsibilities of spouses [that] apply in like manner to civil union couples." N.J. STAT. ANN. § 37:1–32. That list includes:

(a) laws relating to title, tenure, descent and distribution, intestate succession, survivorship, or other incidents of the acquisition, ownership or transfer, inter vivos or at death, of real or personal property, including but not limited to eligibility to hold real and personal property as tenants by the entirety;

(b) causes of action related to or dependent upon spousal status, including an action for wrongful death, emotional distress, loss of consortium, or other torts or actions under contracts reciting, related to, or dependent upon spousal status;

(c) probate law and procedure, including nonprobate transfer;

(d) adoption law and procedures;

(e) laws relating to insurance, health and pension benefits;

(g) prohibitions against discrimination based upon marital status . . .

Id. Also included among the enumerated rights are a host of benefits relating to family leave, public assistance, testimonial privileges, hospital visitation privileges, end-of-life proxy decision-making, and state pay for military service.

Finally, the statute sets forth requirements for terminating the status:

§ 37:1-31(b). The dissolution of civil unions shall follow the same procedures and be subject to the same substantive rights and obligations that are involved in the dissolution of marriage.

[b]   State Laws that Provide Limited Privileges to Relationships — Domestic Partnerships and Reciprocal Beneficiaries

Other states have adopted statuses that give a limited range of privileges to nonmarried couples without giving them the full rights and benefits available to married couples. These include Hawaii, Vermont, Maine, Maryland, and Colorado. As with other formal statuses, the legal names of these relationships vary from state to state. Hawaii (1997) and Vermont (1999), for example, enacted "reciprocal beneficiary" statuses, while Washington, D.C. (2002), Maine (2004), and Maryland (2008) opted for "domestic partnerships," and Colorado, "designated beneficiaries" (2009). National Gay and Lesbian Task Force, *Relationship Recognition for Same-Sex Couples in the U.S.*, http://www.thetaskforce.org/downloads/reports/issue _maps/relationship_recognition_06_09_color.pdf. Maine and Vermont have since adopted full marriage equality, but both states' domestic partnership statuses are still available to two unmarried adults who are living together and responsible for the other's welfare. 22 ME. REV. STAT. ANN. § 2710; 15 VT. STAT. ANN. § 1301.) The specifics of each status also vary somewhat from state to state. For example, the Hawaii legislation extends to those who register as beneficiaries some of the third-party benefits available to married couples, such as eligibility for derivative health insurance coverage for family members, hospital visitation privileges, wrongful death and loss of consortium claims, family and funeral leave from employment, and state employee pension rights and death benefits. However, it does not provide for alimony or equitable distribution between the partners if either member of the party seeks to terminate the status. WILLIAM N. ESKRIDGE, JR., EQUALITY PRACTICE 24–25 (2002). Building on Hawaii's concept, Colorado passed a bill in 2009 that allows designated beneficiaries many of the same benefits, but within a "menu of options" that allow one or both people to opt out of certain ones. For example, if one person wants to leave her designated beneficiary her assets but would rather that someone else made end-of-life decisions for her, the Colorado reciprocal beneficiary form allows for such wishes. H.B. 1260, 67th Gen. Ass'y., Reg. Sess. (Colo. 2009); *see also* Posting of Nancy Polikoff to Beyond (Straight and Gay) Marriage blog, http://beyondstraightandgaymarriage.blogspot.com/2009/04/extraordinary-new-colorado-law.html (last visited Apr. 15, 2009).

In contrast to most civil unions, which recognize only romantic relationships, a majority of domestic partnerships are also available to people who are cohabitating blood relatives. For example, the Hawaii Reciprocal Beneficiaries statute allows registration by any two unmarried individuals legally prohibited from marrying each other under state law. The legislative findings refer to brothers and sisters, a widowed mother and her unmarried son, and, finally, "two individuals who are of the same gender," stating that, while "the people of Hawaii choose to preserve the tradition of marriage as a unique social institution based upon the committed union of one man and one woman . . . there are many individuals who have significant personal, emotional, and economic relationships with another individual yet are prohibited . . . from marrying." HAW. REV. STAT. ANN. § 572C-2. Between passing civil union and same-sex marriage legislation, the Vermont legislature also extended limited rights to "two persons who are blood-relatives or related by adoption the opportunity to establish a consensual reciprocal beneficiaries relationship," providing for particular spouse-like rights such as hospital visitation, surrogate medical decision-making, and decision-making regarding anatomical gifts and disposition of remains. 15 VT. STAT. § 1301. On the other end of the spectrum is Maryland, which specifically forbids the domestic partnership status to those who are related by blood. MD. CODE ANN. HEALTH-GEN. § 6-101(a)(2).

In order to enter into such reciprocal beneficiary/domestic partnership statuses, states often require that the two parties provide proof that they meet statutory requirements; that they complete a notarized application; and that they pay a fee. District of Columbia Dep't of Health Vital Records Division, *Domestic Partnership FAQs*, http://doh.dc.gov (follow "Domestic Partnerships" hyperlink under "Services," then follow "Frequently Asked Questions" hyperlink); Hawaii Dep't of Health, *About Reciprocal Beneficiary Relationships*, http://hawaii.gov/health/vital-records/vital-records/reciprocal/index.html. As for exiting the statuses, in some states, one partner mailing in a signed and notarized form, along with a fee, is sufficient (as in Hawaii). *Id.* In other states, like Maine, both partners must either send in a signed, notarized form, or the partner who desires dissolution is required to notify the other partner before the dissolution can take place. *See* Office of Health Data and Program Management, *Domestic Partner Registry*, http://www.maine.gov/dhhs/bohodr/domstcprtnrspge.htm. Most of these statuses create no claims between the partners once the relationship is terminated, in contrast to married couples who have rights to alimony or equitable distribution. This omission is understandable for some of the types of relationships that may be covered by such statuses. For example, an unmarried person who has access to benefits may commendably wish to share them with a less fortunate blood relative. That unmarried person should be able to terminate the relationship to the less fortunate relative without continuing obligation. On the other hand, same-sex partners' relationships may include children as well as a much greater degree of financial interdependence than is likely in the case of reciprocal beneficiaries who are blood relatives. The failure to give rights similar to alimony or equitable distribution may not be fair in such cases. *See* Grace Ganz Blumberg, *The Regularization of Nonmarital Cohabitation: Rights and Responsibilities in the American Welfare State*, 76 NOTRE DAME L. REV. 1265, 1277–78 (2001).

[c]　Statuses Granting Employment Benefits to Domestic Partners of Government Employees

Finally, a rapidly-expanding number of jurisdictions have extended benefits to the partners of government employees. One advocacy organization cites more than 200 jurisdictions that provide such benefits, including twenty states and the District of Columbia. *See* Equality Maryland, *The Issues: Domestic Partner Benefits*, http://equalitymaryland.org/issues/domesticpartner.htm. Furthermore, in one of the first federal efforts to bring equality to same-sex couples, in May 2009, Secretary of State Hillary Clinton announced plans to extend benefits to partners of U.S. diplomats — who, unlike family pets, have not been eligible for such benefits as paid travel to and from international posts. *See* Glenn Kessler, *Clinton to Extend Benefits to Gay Partners*, WASH. POST, May 25, 2009, at A8. President Obama followed with an announcement the following month that he would extend some benefits to same-sex partners of federal employees, although he stopped short of pledging full health insurance coverage. *See* Jim Rutenberg, *Gay and Lesbian Leaders Say Federal Same-Sex Benefits Don't Go Far Enough*, N.Y. TIMES, June 18, 2009, at A18.

Although most domestic partner city and county ordinances are directed at same-sex couples, some also permit unmarried opposite-sex couples to register. *See, e.g.*, S.F., CAL., ADMIN. CODE § 62.2 (defining eligible parties as "two adults," without reference to gender). The constitutionality of domestic partner policies that exclude opposite-sex nonmarital partners has been upheld by a federal appellate court. See *Irizarry v. Bd. of Educ.*, 251 F.3d 604 (7th Cir. 2001) (upholding Chicago Board of Education's policy of providing health benefits to partners of employees in same-sex, but not opposite-sex, relationships). For an analysis of the issues concerning such differential treatment in the United States, see Terry S. Kogan, *Competing Approaches to Same-Sex Versus Opposite-Sex, Unmarried Couples in Domestic Partnership Laws and Ordinances*, 2001 BYU L. REV. 1023; Erin Cleary, Note, *New Jersey Domestic Partnership Act in the Aftermath of* Lewis v. Harris: *Should New Jersey Expand the Act to Include All Unmarried Cohabitants?*, 60 RUTGERS L. REV. 519 (2008).

Unquestionably, employment benefits have played a much more important role in the growing recognition of same-sex partnerships in the United States than in other nations because of the absence of a national health-care system. As a result, governmental endorsement of parity between spouses of married employees and domestic partners of gay or lesbian employees carries with it significant economic consequences for couples. For further discussion of the history, evolution, and issues raised by domestic partner ordinances and statutes, see Nancy J. Knauer, *Domestic Partnership and Same-Sex Relationships: A Marketplace Innovation and A Less than Perfect Institutional Choice*, 7 TEMP. POL. & CIV. RTS. L. REV. 337 (1998); Jennifer A. Drobac & Antony Page, *A Uniform Domestic Partnership Act: Marrying Business Partnership and Family Law*, 41 GA. L. REV. 349 (2007); William B. Turner, *The Perils Of Marriage as Transcendent Ontology:* National Pride at Work v. Governor Of Michigan, 9 GEO. J. GENDER & L. 279 (2008).

In a bold move, San Francisco distinguished itself from the other cities and counties with domestic partnership laws by adopting the Equal Benefits

Ordinance, effective 1997. This enactment prohibits the city from contracting with any businesses that do not provide parity in benefits to their employees with domestic partners. *See* S.F., CAL., ADMIN. CODE §§ 12B.1, 12B.4. Because all companies doing business at San Francisco's International Airport fell within the reach of the nondiscrimination provision, not surprisingly the city was promptly sued by the trade association representing the airlines and by other affected employers. Although some components of the San Francisco scheme were found preempted by the federal Employee Retirement Income Security Act ("ERISA"), 29 U.S.C. § 1002, in which "self-insured" companies are not required to recognize same-sex marriages under the federal Defense of Marriage Act ("DOMA"), 1 U.S.C. § 7 (1997), most survived. *See Air Transp. Ass'n of Am. v. San Francisco*, 992 F. Supp. 1149 (N.D. Cal. 1998); *aff'd* 266 F.3d 1064 (9th Cir. 2001); *see also S.D. Myers v. San Francisco*, 336 F.3d 1174 (2003). Other jurisdictions have adopted or attempted to adopt similar provisions. For the most current listing of these ordinances, *see* Human Rights Campaign, *Equal Benefits Ordinances*, http://www.hrc.org/issues/equal_benefits_ordinances.htm (listing the State of California; Miami Beach, Florida; Minneapolis, Minnesota; and Olympia, Washington, among others). For a discussion of a recent legal challenge overturning a proposed ordinance granting equal benefits to same-sex couples in New York City, see Bradley A. Benedict, Note, *Upsetting the Balance: Ignoring the Separation of Powers Doctrine in* Council of New York v. Bloomberg, 72 BROOK. L. REV. 1261 (2007).

NOTES

1. ***The Demographics of Those Who Enter Civil Unions.*** In 2000, the first year that Vermont offered civil unions, 2,479 couples entered into that status. Greg Johnson, *In Praise of Civil Unions*, 39 CAP. U. L. REV. 315, 334 (2002). Most of the couples (approximately three-quarters) were from out-of-state (hailing from forty-six different states) or other nations. *Id.* By June, 2008, 8,711 couples, including 7,221 from out-of-state, had entered into a Vermont civil union. Vermont Secretary of State Deborah L. Markowitz, *The Vermont Guide to Civil Unions*, http://www.sec.state.vt.us/otherprg/civilunions/civilunions.html.

As of 2003, about two-thirds of the couples were female, and most were college graduates with above-average incomes. Patricia Wen, *A Civil Tradition: Data Show Same-Sex Unions in Vt. Draw a Privileged Group*, BOSTON GLOBE, June 29, 2003, at B.1. In addition, over ninety percent of those who entered into civil unions in Vermont were of European descent. Esther D. Rothblum, Kimberly F. Balsam & Sondra E. Solomon, *Comparison of Same-Sex Couples Who Were Married in Massachusetts, Had Domestic Partnerships in California, or Had Civil Unions in Vermont*, 29 JOURNAL OF FAM. ISSUES 48, 71 (2008). On average, the couples had been together for about 11 to 12 years prior to entering the formal union. Rona Marech, *Gay Couples Can be as Stable as Straights, Evidence Suggests*, SAN FRANCISCO CHRONICLE, Feb. 27, 2004, A19.

2. ***Challenges to the Civil Union Statutes.*** Shortly before Vermont's governor signed the civil union law, "a group comprised of Vermont taxpayers, members of the Vermont House of Representatives, and three Vermont town

clerks" filed various suits to enjoin its implementation. *Brady v. Dean*, 790 A.2d 428, 429 (Vt. 2000). In one action, taxpayers and legislators joined to challenge the validity of the legislation on the basis that "fourteen members of the House . . . participated in a 'dollar-a-guess' betting pool in connection with a preliminary vote on the civil unions bill." *Id.* Citing the independence of the legislature from judicial scrutiny of certain actions, the Vermont Supreme Court dismissed the action as a nonjusticiable political question. *Id.* at 545–46. The court also rejected the claims of several town clerks that their obligation to issue civil union licenses violated their free exercise of religion. *Id.* at 433–35. In contrast to the events in Hawaii, a state constitutional amendment that would have nullified the Vermont Supreme Court's decision in *Baker* was easily defeated in the state senate, 21 to 9. MICHAEL MELLO, LEGALIZING GAY MARRIAGE 111 (2004).

A legal challenge to California's 2003 Domestic Partner Rights and Responsibility Act, which provided same-sex couples the same rights and benefits as marriage, was also unsuccessful. Following the passage of that act, two conservative groups sued to block its enforcement, on the ground that it conflicted with Proposition 22, a proposition that had been passed by voters in 2000, which limited marriage to a union between one man and one woman. The California Court of Appeals, however, found that since Proposition 22 had not mentioned domestic partnerships, it did not limit the legislature's authority to regulate such unions. *Knight v. Superior Court*, 128 Cal. App. 4th 14 (2005).

As of July 2009, nineteen states have amended their constitutions not only to designate marriage as strictly between one man and one woman, but also to proactively forbid civil unions — and sometimes also domestic partnerships, reciprocal beneficiary status, and any other form of same-sex partner recognition. These states include Alabama, Arkansas, Florida, Georgia, Idaho, Kansas, Kentucky, Louisiana, Michigan, Nebraska, North Dakota, Ohio, Oklahoma, South Carolina, South Dakota, Texas, Utah, Virginia, and Wisconsin. National Gay and Lesbian Task Force, *Anti-Gay Marriage Measures in the U.S.* (2009), http://www.thetaskforce.org/downloads/reports/issue_maps/GayMarriage_05_09.pdf.

3. *Interstate Recognition of Civil Unions.* Substantial scholarly commentary, summarized in Chapter 2, Section A[2][d] (Notes at the end of the section), has been devoted to the question of whether states are required to recognize same-sex marriages performed elsewhere. These choice of law issues are further complicated when parties seek recognition of a non-marital status such as a civil union. Although civil unions are legally identical to marriage within the state, they are not called *marriages*. It is therefore possible for states to conclude that the rules for recognition of an out-of-state marriage are inapplicable. Alternatively, a court may reason by analogy that they are applicable. Moreover, while normal choice of law rules call for a state to recognize a marriage that was valid in the state in which it was entered (recall Chapter 2's discussion of common law marriage and choice of law), some states and the federal government have enacted special rules (in the federal Defense of Marriage Act, sometimes called "DOMA," and state statutes precluding recognition of same-sex marriages, sometimes called "mini-DOMA") denying recognition of same-sex marriages. So in deciding how to deal with civil unions, should states look to the marriage rules with respect to both normal choice of law and DOMA, to neither, or should it apply by analogy the choice of law rules with respect to marriage but not the DOMA rules? The question is further complicated for a status such as a domestic partnership or a reciprocal beneficiary relationship that shares some but not all features in common with marriage.

At this point, it is in fact uncertain how the DOMA and mini-DOMA will treat civil unions, domestic partnerships, reciprocal beneficiary relationships, and any other alternative-to-marriage statuses states create. These alternative statuses may escape application of these Defense of Marriage statutes because they are not called marriages. Or judges may focus on the similarities between the status and marriage with respect to the provisions at issue in the case. On the other hand, even in unfriendly jurisdictions, plaintiffs seeking to enforce particular provisions of a same-sex status might argue that *inter se* claims should be enforced on contract grounds. Given most states' willingness to enforce express contracts between nonmarital cohabitants, contract theory might allow recognition of claims concerning partners' rights and obligations to each other, eliminating the need for the court to recognize the underlying status. For a discussion of the special issues relating to interstate recognition of civil unions, domestic partnerships, and reciprocal beneficiary relationships, see Andrew Koppelman, *Interstate Recognition of Same-Sex Marriages and Civil Unions: A Handbook for Judges*, 153 U. PA. L. REV. 2143 (2005).

A handful of state courts in which civil unions are not celebrated have been asked to recognize civil unions validly entered into in other states, with mixed results. In an opinion filed just as this casebook went to press, the New York Court of Appeals, in *Debra H. v. Janice R.*, 2010 N.Y. LEXIS 620 (May 4, 2010), held that the ex-partner of the biological mother of a child conceived through artificial insemination had parental rights that entitled her to sue for custody visitation because the child was born during her civil union with the biological mother. The court reasoned that under Vermont law, the biological mother's partner was a parent as a result of the child being born during the civil union. It then determined that no reason existed for it to deny recognition of the parentage created in Vermont based on the doctrine of comity. It state that the availability of second-parent adoption to same-sex couples under New York law "negates any suggestion that recognition of parentage based on a Vermont Civil Union would conflict with our state's public policy. *Id.* at *13. However, in an earlier case, the New York courts refused to allow the partner of a deceased man, with whom he had entered into a civil union in Vermont, to sue for wrongful death. In reaching this decision, in a divided opinion, the Appellate Division relied on the plain language of New York's wrongful death statute, noting that the Vermont Supreme Court had not equated civil unions with heterosexual marriage. *Langan v. St. Vincent's Hosp.*, 802 N.Y.S.2d 476 (N.Y. App. Div. 2d Dep't 2005).

In another case raising the issue of the treatment of civil unions, a Georgia court determined that a civil union is not a marriage for the purpose of construing a visitation order. *Burns v. Burns*, 560 S.E.2d 47 (Ga. Ct. App. 2002). In that case, the divorced mother of a child challenged her former husband's refusal to allow the children to visit her in the presence of her same-sex partner, with whom she had entered into a civil union in Vermont. The visitation order prohibited "visitation or residence by the children with either party during any time where such party cohabits with or has overnight stays with any adult to which such party is not legally married. . . ." *Id.* at 47. The court rejected the mother's claims that her relationship with her partner was analogous to that of a marriage.

Some states address the question of recognition of civil unions and other similar statuses by statute. For example, California's 2003 expansion of its domestic partner statute explicitly provided for recognition of similar statuses entered into in other states. CAL. FAM. CODE § 292.2 (2004). New Jersey also explicitly provides for recognition of other states' civil unions through statute. N.J. STAT. ANN. § 37: 1-34. By contrast, Texas and Ohio laws declare that the states will not recognize civil unions, or any status that provides for the specific statutory benefits of legal marriage to same-sex couples. TEX. FAM. CODE ANN. § 2.001(b) (2003); OHIO REV. CODE ANN. § 3101.01(C)(1)e (2004).

One commentator believes that choice-of-law issues regarding interstate recognition of same-sex relationships will play an important part in the next wave of advancement for LGBT rights. Even in light of DOMA, he asks, would a same-sex Massachusetts spouse who relocates to Tennessee to marry a new partner of the opposite sex truly elicit a non-response from Tennessee's courts? Or would a partner to a New Jersey civil union who escapes to North Carolina with all of her family's funds have escaped with impunity? *See* Andrew Koppelman, *The Limits of Strategic Litigation*, 17 TUL. J.L. & SEXUALITY 1, 4 (2008). Most states' courts have yet to consider these questions (*but see* Note 5, *infra)*, yet it seems inevitable that interstate recognition litigation will steadily increase as greater numbers of mobile couples enter into newly legally-recognized relationships. Consider the following theory for interstate recognition:

> It is a commonplace rule of statutory interpretation that when terminology has previously appeared in earlier statutes, and has been interpreted by courts to have a certain meaning, it should be understood to mean the same thing in a new statute. The language used by the mini-DOMAs was ubiquitous in the miscegenation statutes, which usually declared interracial marriages "void" and "prohibited." Yet the Southern courts usually recognized nonevasive interracial marriages [where parties do not immediately return home to a hostile jurisdiction after a ceremony in a legal jurisdiction]. If such language did not bar recognition in those cases, it should not do so now, either. In this context, "void" evidently means "void for residents of this state," not "void for anyone in the world whose marriage is in any way pertinent to litigation in our courts."

Id. at 4.

4. *Fiscal Implications of Civil Unions, Domestic Partnerships, and Reciprocal Beneficiary Relationships.* Some policymakers express concern that extension of marriage-like benefits to same-sex couples will place a financial strain on state budgets as increasing numbers of couples become eligible for various state benefits. Yet, the economic analyses performed to date have found or predicted the fiscal effects of legal recognition of same-sex relationships for state budgets to be positive or insignificant. The 2002 Report of the Civil Union Commission in the Office of the Legislative Council in Vermont concluded that civil unions had a positive financial impact on the couples entering them and no significant impact on the functioning of governmental agencies. VT. CIVIL UNION REVIEW COMM'N, FINAL CIVIL UNION REVIEW COMM'N REPORT FOR 2002, http://www.leg.state.vt.us/baker/Final%20CURC%20Report%20for%202002.htm. Furthermore, a prospective analysis of the implications for Oregon of its domestic partnership act predicted a gain of anywhere from $1.5 to 3.7 million biennially. M.V. LEE BADGETT, ET AL., THE IMPACT ON OREGON'S BUDGET OF INTRODUCING SAME-SEX DOMESTIC PARTNERSHIPS 1 (2008), http://www.law.ucla.edu/williamsinstitute/publications/OregonFiscalAnalysis.pdf. The authors of this policy study underscored reduced reliance on public benefits following the pooling of economic resources between partners and predicted that the majority of domestic partner couples, who would begin filing state income taxes jointly, would pay higher state taxes than they had when they were filing singly. *Id.* at 2, 7–8. Other studies suggest that the greatest economic benefits result when full marriage equality is granted, citing the dollars spent on greater numbers of ceremonies and the resulting tourism, taxes and fees. In Massachusetts, an additional $111 million in revenue was gained in spending on gay weddings during the first five years that it conducted same-sex marriage. And according to the U.S. Congressional Budget Office in 2004, an estimated $1 billion in yearly tax revenue would flow from same-sex marriage recognition by the federal government and the fifty states. Rachel F. Elson, *Gay-onomics and the Marriage Debate*, NEWSWEEK, June 3, 2009, *available at* http://www.newsweek.com/id/200365/.

5. *Dissolving a Civil Union or Domestic Partnership.* An important benefit of marriage is the divorce remedies available to spouses whose relationship ends. These remedies provide security and clarity regarding the couple's marriage status. Further, after years of economic interdependence, divorce proceedings allow for assets to be distributed equitably between the parties as they separate their lives. Since civil unions recognize the same kind of economic interdependence between two parties, they also provide the benefit of a statutory provision for equitable distribution. Difficult situations arise, however, when couples who obtained civil unions move to a jurisdiction that does not recognize their legal status. Just as with marriage, there are typically no residency requirements to enter into civil unions in those states that allow them, while residency usually is required to file under a state's procedures for dissolving a civil union. This is the case in both New Jersey and Vermont, which require at least one member of the union to be a resident of the State for one year before dissolution. N.J. STAT. ANN. § 2A: 34–38; 15 VT. STAT. ANN. § 1206. In addition, courts in the jurisdictions in which the parties reside may refuse to hear such dissolution cases if the forum state lacks civil union laws. For example, a Virginia judge refused to dissolve the Vermont civil union of a lesbian couple who lived in Virginia. In doing so, the court refused any remedy to a partner who claimed that the other had stolen money from her. "Vermont Civil Union Void, Roanoke County Judge Says," Posting to VLW Blog, http://www.valawyersweekly.com/vlwblog/2008/05/30/vermont-civil-union-void -roanoke-county-judge-says/ (May 30, 2008). To read more about the potential complications of dissolving a civil union that spans "ideological, biological, and state lines," see Lorraine Ali, *Mrs. Kramer vs. Mrs. Kramer*, NEWSWEEK, Dec. 15, 2008, at 32 (detailing the conflict in the case *Miller-Jenkins v. Miller-Jenkins*, 661 S.E.2d 822 (Va. 2008), in which an artificially-inseminated mother living in Virginia

attempted unsuccessfully to block a Vermont order awarding visitation rights to her former Vermont civil union partner); *see also* Deirdre M. Bowen, *The Parent Trap: Differential Familial Power in Same-Sex Families*, 15 WM. & MARY J. WOMEN & L. 1 (2008).

A few courts in states that do not otherwise recognize civil union status have granted dissolutions. For example, in Massachusetts, which does not provide for civil unions to be celebrated, a probate court judge dissolved a couple's civil union, relying on the state's high court's decision in *Goodridge v. Dep't of Public Health*, 798 N.E.2d 941 (Mass. 2003). The court reasoned that if the state constitution requires extension of marriage rights to same-sex couples, extension of the state's mechanisms for terminating relationships should be likewise available. Kathleen Burge, *Citing [Supreme Judicial Court] Ruling, Judge Dissolves Gay Civil Union*, BOSTON GLOBE, Mar. 25, 2004, *available at* http://www.boston.com/news/specials/gay_marriage/articles/2004/03/25/citing_sjc_ruling_judge_dissolves_gay_union/. This rationale, however, is obviously limited to those few states that allow same-sex marriage.

6. *Are Civil Unions Sufficiently Equal to Marriage?* When New Jersey instituted the status of civil unions in 2006, the legislature established a Review Commission to study the act and issue recommendations for its improvement or abolition. N.J. STAT. ANN. § 37:1–36. The Commission's final report, released in December, 2008, unanimously declared that civil unions were not sufficient legal equivalents to marriage. N.J. Civil Union Review Comm'n, *The Legal, Medical, Economic & Social Consequences of New Jersey's Civil Union Law* 7 (2008), http://www.nj.gov/oag/dcr/downloads/CURC-Final-Report-.pdf. It found that private companies can easily disallow civil union partner health benefits, because "the insurance provider does not recognize the civil union to be the equivalent of marriage." *Id.* at 13. It also contended that civil unions "perpetuate psychological harm" for adults and children in same-sex parent families who are implicitly told that their families are inferior. *Id.* at 15, 17. The Commission further found that since the term "civil union" remains widely misunderstood (and unknown to some), the status had to be explained repeatedly to health care professionals, causing great frustration in emergency situations. Many scholars agree with the conclusions of the New Jersey Civil Union Review Commission:

> If no message is conveyed by eschewing the word "marriage," and replacing it with "civil union," then why would the legislature be so "purposeful" in creating a new and different statutory structure solely for one group's committed relationships? . . . When government marks lesbian and gay individuals as inferior, it sets an example for others to treat them as inferior. . . .

David S. Buckel, Lewis v. Harris: *Essay on a Settled Question and an Open Question*, 59 RUTGERS LAW REVIEW 229–30 (2007).

In rejecting "everything-but-the-word-'marriage'" domestic partnerships as constitutionally inadequate, the California Supreme Court noted similar doubts that "separate" could truly be "equal":

[B]ecause of the long and celebrated history of the term "marriage" and the widespread understanding that this term describes a union unreservedly approved and favored by the community, there clearly is a considerable and undeniable symbolic importance to this designation. Thus, it is apparent that affording access to this designation exclusively to opposite-sex couples, while providing same-sex couples access to only a novel alternative designation, realistically must be viewed as constituting significantly unequal treatment to same-sex couples. In this regard, plaintiffs persuasively invoke by analogy the decisions of the United States Supreme Court finding inadequate a state's creation of a separate law school for Black students rather than granting such students access to the University of Texas Law School (Sweatt v. Painter (1950) 339 U.S. 629, 634) . . . and a state's founding of a separate military program for women rather than admitting women to the Virginia Military Institute (United States v. Virginia (1996) 518 U.S. 515, 555–556.) . . . Even when the state grants ostensibly equal benefits to a previously excluded class through the creation of a new institution, the intangible symbolic differences that remain often are constitutionally significant.

In Re Marriage Cases, 183 P.3d 384, 445 (2008).

Other commentators in favor of expanding gay rights believe that civil unions are useful stepping stones; they argue that a sudden windfall for gay marriage equality could actually prove counterproductive in the long run. They see an incremental strategy as the best way to ensure a lasting victory:

For the judiciary or the professoriate to tell traditionalist citizens that their time-tested family values count for *nothing* in the same-sex marriage debate is a time-tested path to political alienation or revolt. The genius of Vermont's equality practice is that the state insisted that traditional family values give way to the recognition of lesbian and gay rights — at the same time that the state insisted that lesbian and gay family values give way to accommodation of traditionalist anxieties for the time being. Once civil unions in action reveal to Vermonters that lesbian and gay relationships are serious and loving (and fraught with the same problems as marital unions), the state might be ripe for graduation from equality *practice* to equality *simpliciter*.

William N. Eskridge, Jr., Equality Practice: Civil Unions and the Future of Gay Rights 158 (2002).

NOTE ON FORMAL REGISTRATION SCHEMES OUTSIDE OF THE UNITED STATES

Western Europe and Canada

In Western European nations (and a number of other developed countries), the progress toward same-sex relationship recognition has tended to occur relatively rapidly, but in a piecemeal fashion. Decriminalization of homosexual sex occurs first, followed by the passage of anti-discrimination laws, followed by the legislative grant of legalized status. Kees Waaldijk, *Civil Developments: Patterns of Reform in the Legal Position of Same-Sex Partners in Europe*, 17 CAN. J. FAM. L. 62, 66 (2000). Denmark serves as a classic example: it fully decriminalized homosexual sex in the 1970s, passed anti-discrimination laws in 1987, and then become the first country in the world to unveil a same-sex partnership recognition status dubbed "registered partnerships" in 1989, which provided the same rights and responsibilities as marriage. *Id.* at 74–75, 80. Denmark's registered partnerships created the model for similar legislation in Norway (1993), Sweden (1995), and Finland (2002). The Scandinavian nations' more southerly neighbors continued the trend by passing their own (less comprehensive) legislation, starting with Hungary (1998), France (1999), Germany (2000), and Portugal (2001). *Developments In The Law: The Law Of Marriage And Family*, 116 HARV. L. REV. 1996, 2007–09 (2003). More than a dozen other European nations followed later, as well as Iceland (1996), New Zealand (2004), Argentina (2008), and a number of local governments in countries like Brazil and Australia. Aaron Xavier Fellmeth, *State Regulation of Sexuality in International Human Rights Law and Theory*, 50 WM. & MARY L. REV. 797, 854 (2008); *Timeline: Same-Sex Marriage Around the World*, CBC NEWS, June 3, 2009, http://www.cbc.ca/world/story/2009/05/26/f-same-sex-timeline.html.

These nations' registered partnerships and civil unions vary vastly in form and degree. At one end of the spectrum is the Danish "everything-but-the-word-'marriage'" registered partnership, with Hungary's partnerships permitting nearly every benefit except for the right to adopt a bit further down. *Id.* Toward the middle would be France's Pacte Civil de Solidarite (PaCS), which does not require sexual fidelity and does not result in automatic inheritance rights, parental privileges, or extension of French nationality to partners. Farther toward the opposite end would be nations such as Australia, which do not recognize same-sex partnerships *per se* but do extend some employment benefits and property rights to same-sex couples. Fellmeth, *supra*, at 858–61.

Outside of Europe

Same-sex relationship recognition laws are nonexistent in the vast majority of Central and South America, Asia, the Middle East, and Africa, and remain far from a political reality there. As one commentator summarized the situation:

> As of 2008, same-sex intercourse remains subject to criminal penalties in 41 of the 192 United Nations member states for women and in 81 states and 3 sub-state provinces for men, including almost all of Africa and the Middle East, and much of Asia. . . . Laws and policies in countries prohibiting homosexual intercourse directly or indirectly regulate the behavior of some 2.5 billion of the world's 6.7 billion people, more than a third of the world's population. . . . Fewer than two dozen states approving same-sex marriage or the rough equivalent on a national level hardly evidences an international custom. On the whole, opposition to such recognition remains overwhelming.

Fellmeth, *supra*, at 861.

For further discussion of legal recognition for same-sex partnerships from an international and comparative perspective, see YUVAL MERIN, EQUALITY FOR SAME-

SEX COUPLES, THE LEGAL RECOGNITION OF GAY PARTNERSHIPS IN EUROPE AND THE UNITED STATES (2002); LEGAL RECOGNITION OF SAME-SEX PARTNERSHIPS: A STUDY OF NATIONAL, EUROPEAN AND INTERNATIONAL LAW (R. Wintemute & M. Andenaes eds., 2001); Katharina Boele-Woelki, *Lessons for the United States? Family Law: The Legal Recognition of Same-Sex Relationships Within the European Union*, 82 TUL. L. REV. 1949 (2008).

B.   UNMARRIED PARENTS AND THEIR CHILDREN

Although the increase in rates of nonmarital births had begun to stabilize in the mid-1990s after a two-decade rise, since 2002 it has again begun to rise steeply. More than 1.6 million babies were born to unmarried mothers in 2006, the highest number ever recorded in the United States. The 2006 total (1,641,946 births) was nearly 8 percent greater than in 2005 (1,527,034) and a 20-percent increase from 2002 (1,365,966). Births to unmarried women, as a percent of all births, was up to 38.5% in 2006, up from 36.9 percent in 2005 and 34 percent in 2002. The birth rate for unmarried women increased 7 percent between 2005 and 2006, reaching 50.6 births per 1,000 unmarried women aged 15–44 years. Joyce A. Martin et al., *Births: Final Data for 2006*, NATIONAL VITAL STATISTICS REPORTS, VOL. 57, NO. 7 (2009), at 2, 11 (report for the U.S. Dept. of Health and Human Services, prepared by the Centers for Disease Control and Prevention, the National Center for Health Statistics, and the National Vital Statistics System). These increases followed a period of relative stability during the years 1998–2002. Table 9-6 expresses these data as a percentage, revealing particularly steep increases between 1970 and 1990, and since 2000.

Although nonmarital births were once viewed as occurring primarily within certain minority groups, they are becoming increasingly common across the population. For example, while the percentage of nonmarital births to Caucasian women more than tripled between 1970 and 2000, the percentage of nonmarital births to African-American women has not quite doubled during this same period. *See* Table 9-6. As a result, some social scientists assert that what once appeared to be a pattern of lower-class African-Americans was actually a trend that was becoming more prominent in lower-income families more generally. *See* Frank F. Furstenberg, *If Moynihan Had Only Known: Race, Class, and Family Change in the Late Twentieth Century*, 621 ANNALS AM. ACAD. POL. & SOC. SCI. 94 (2009). Rates increased for all population groups in 2006 by 4 to 6 percent each, to 25.9 per 1,000 Asian or Pacific Islander women, 32.0 for non-Hispanic white women, 71.5 for black women, and 106.1 for Hispanic women. Interestingly, the age distribution of nonmarital births has also changed. Whereas 4 in 10 nonmarital births were to teenagers in 1980, by 2006, this fraction had dropped by nearly one-half, to just over 2 in 10. *Births: Final Data for 2006, supra*, at 11.

The considerable numbers of nonmarital births mean that discussions about the possible consequences for children of growing up in a single-parent family cannot focus exclusively on divorce. As of 2008, never-married mothers (as compared to widowed, divorced or separated mothers), were 43.9% of all single-mother house-holds. U.S. Census Bureau, *Housing and Household Economic Statistics Division: 2008*, Table FG6, *available at* http://www.census.gov/population/www/socdemo/

hh-fam/cps2008.html. This number represents a sizeable increase from the 17% rate of never-married mothers compared to all single-parent households in 1976. *See* Elaine Sorenson & Ariel Halpern, *Child Support Enforcement Is Working Better Than We Think*, Urban Institute Report No. A-31 (March, 1999), available at http://newfederalism.urban.org/html/anf_31.html.

Table 9-6
Nonmarital Births as Percent of All Births in the
United States: 1970 to 2006

Year	Total	White	Black
2006	38.5	32	71.5
2005	36.9	31.6	69.4
2000	33.2	27.1	68.5
1990	28.0	20.1	65.2
1980	18.4	11.0	55.2
1970	10.7	5.7	37.6

Sources: Table 98, *Statistical Abstract of the United States: 1996*; Tables 74 & 75, *Statistical Abstract of the United States: 2002, Statistical Abstract of the United States: 2009*, Table 79 & 84, http://www.census.gov/compendia/ statab/tables/09s0079.pdf, http://www.census.gov/compendia/statab/tables/ 09s0084.pdf; Joyce A. Martin, Brady E. Hamilton, Paul D. Sutton, Stephanie J. Ventura, Fay Menacker; Sharon Kirmeyer, & T.J. Mathews., *Births: Final Data for 2006*, NATIONAL VITAL STATISTICS REPORTS, VOL. 57, No. 7 (2009), Table D (report for the U.S. Dept. of Health and Human Services, prepared by the Centers for Disease Control and Prevention, the National Center for Health Statistics, and the National Vital Statistics System).

What accounts for the increase in nonmarital births? While there is surely no simple answer to that question, some observations can be made. Any of the following, alone or in combination, would yield an increase in the proportion of births that are nonmarital: an increase in the proportion of pregnancies that are nonmarital; an increase in the proportion of nonmarital pregnancies that continue to term; and a decrease in the proportion of nonmarital pregnancies in which the mother marries before birth — what were once called "shotgun" marriages. One study, which defined a "shotgun marriage" as a marriage occurring within seven months prior to birth, calculated the shotgun marriage ratio, defined as the proportion of births conceived out of wedlock in which the mother marries before birth. It found that for whites, the shotgun marriage ratio declined from 0.61 in 1969 to 0.35 in 1988. The analogous decline for blacks was from 0.25 to 0.085. The authors then compared the nonmarital birth ratio during the four year period from 1965 to 1969 with the period from 1985 to 1989 and found that among whites, about three-fourths of the increase in nonmarital births between these two periods is accounted for by a decline in shotgun marriages, and about three-fifths of the increase among blacks. (They reach this conclusion by comparing the actual increase in nonmarital births to the increase that would have occurred if the same proportion of single pregnant women had married before their child's birth, in the late 1980s, as had done so in the late 1960s.) George A. Akerlof et al., *An Analysis of Out-of-Wedlock Childbearing in the United States*, 111 QUART. J. ECON. 277 (1996).

It thus seems that the increase in non-marital births has been due less to an increase in non-marital pregnancy and more to a decrease in shotgun marriages. Why are fewer unmarried parents marrying after the pregnancy is known? The authors speculate that the availability of legal abortion may reduce the social pressure on the fathers to marry the mothers, even mothers who do not themselves wish to abort. Another possibility is that the mothers are not interested in marrying the fathers, or that they believe that the fathers' circumstances keep them from being good providers. A large proportion of unmarried mothers live in a social and economic milieu in which men with good jobs, or sometimes any jobs, are scarce. These women may not marry because they cannot find appealing candidates. If this is the explanation, then the most effective strategy for reducing the rate of nonmarital birth is to reduce poverty levels. *See* Ira Mark Ellman, *Why Making Family Law is Hard*, 35 ARIZ. ST. L.J. 699 (2004).

What are the implications of birth into a nonmarital family? Children born to unmarried mothers, including those born to cohabiting parents, are more likely to experience certain disadvantages than are children born to married parents. Bumpass et al., *supra*; Smock, *supra*. Parental education and income levels are lower in nonmarital families, and as a result, children born outside of marriage are more likely to experience poverty. U.S. Census Bureau, *America's Families and Living Arrangements: 2008*, Table FG3 & UC3. Furthermore, the average duration of cohabiting relationships is significantly shorter than the average marital duration, which means that children living with cohabiting adults are more likely to experience the dissolution of their parents' relationship and separation from their fathers. *See* Sara McLanahan, *Fragile Families and the Marriage Agenda* (Lori Kowaleski-Jones & Nicholas Wolfinger eds., 2006). But these studies cannot tell us whether their parent's unmarried status is the cause of these disabilities, or whether these disabilities are due to the kind of parents who have children outside of marriage compared with the kinds of parents who marry.

In an important study led by Sara McLanahan of Princeton University, researchers are currently examining a birth cohort of approximately 5,000 non-marital children and their parents in twenty cities. An interim report from data on unmarried parents collected in sixteen cities from April 1998 through August 2000 concluded:

> One of the most striking findings is the high rate of cohabitation among unmarried parents. One-half of unmarried mothers are living with the father of their child at the time of the child's birth, and another one-third are romantically involved with the father but living apart. Eight percent are "just friends," and 10 percent have little or no contact with the father or report the father as unknown. . . .
>
> The majority of unmarried parents have high hopes for the future of their relationships. Seventy-four percent of the unmarried mothers believe that their chances of marrying the father are 50 percent or better. Ninety percent of fathers say their chances of marriage are "50-50" or better. In

addition, the majority of mothers and fathers believe marriage is beneficial for children. Two-thirds of mothers and three-quarters of fathers agree or strongly agree with the statement, "it is better for children if their parents are married." For unmarried couples in which both the mother and father were interviewed, the fathers are somewhat more positive than the mothers about marriage and its effects. . . .

. . .

In summary, unmarried parents have high hopes about their future together. The majority view marriage as a positive institution that benefits their children. Steady employment and emotional maturity are widely regarded by both the new mothers and fathers as essential prerequisites for good marital relations.

Sara McLanahan, et al., *The Fragile Families and Child Wellbeing Study Baseline Report* 3, 7 (2003), *available at* http://www.fragilefamilies.princeton.edu /documents/nationalreport.pdf).

The report also made interesting findings about the level of effort and involvement of nonmarital fathers:

[These findings] will surprise those who believe that unmarried fathers are indifferent to their children. Eighty-one percent of mothers and 92 percent of fathers indicate that the father contributed financially during the pregnancy, and 79 percent of mothers and 90 percent of fathers report that he contributed in other ways (such as provide transportation) during the pregnancy. In addition, 83 percent of mothers and 94 percent of fathers indicate that the father's name will be on the birth certificate and 78 percent of mothers and 89 percent of fathers report that their child will take the father's surname. Again, fathers' responses to these questions need to be viewed in light of the fact that the unmarried men who agreed to participate in our study are also more likely to be more committed to the mothers and children than the average unmarried father. Even so, the mothers' responses to these questions, which do not reflect a select group of unmarried mothers, indicate very high levels of intended father involvement.

Id. at 9.

The report concluded, however that:

Although they have high hopes for their families, most unmarried parents are poorly equipped to support themselves and their children. Among those who reported their employment history, 85 percent of mothers and 98 percent of fathers worked at some time during the past year. However, two of ten fathers were out of work in the week prior to the interview. In addition, the human capital of both parents is low: 43 percent of mothers and 38 percent of fathers lack a high school degree, and only 20 percent of mothers and 22 percent of fathers have more than a high school degree. Human capital and earnings are likely to play critical roles in the success or failure of these parents in maintaining stable families. In fact, a majority of respondents felt that steady employment of both partners is "very important" to a successful marriage.

Id. at 3.

The following section explores the legal issues surrounding nonmarital children. While children born to married mothers are usually also the biological, social, and legal child of her husband, the situation is often not so simple with children born to unmarried mothers. The legal questions that arise with respect to these children do not ordinarily involve their relationship to their mother, but to other adults — the biological father and the mother's husband or partners. The law's characterization of these relationships — as parental, stranger, or something in-between — turns on its assessment of the relative importance of biological and social links. It also forces attention to gender differences. Maternity is rarely uncertain, even temporarily, and most of these children live with their biological mothers. The social realities of maternity and paternity are thus different, and these differences led to differences in the rules the law historically applied to the recognition of legal maternity and paternity. But modern sensitivities to gender distinctions, as well as the advent of genetic testing, require reexamination of these differences.

Part 1 of this section reviews the law governing the establishment of parentage — primarily, paternity. This law has been affected enormously by scientific advances that allow the confident identification of a child's biological father, and by the increased proportion of cases, as compared to decades ago, in which an unmarried father seeks rather than avoids responsibility for his child. Part 2 focuses on constitutional and state law responses to the paternal claims of unwed fathers, and to the special issues affecting the paternity of a child born to a married woman. Part 3 summarizes other constitutional rules protecting nonmarital children from discriminatory treatment by government. Finally, Part 4 reviews the legal treatment of gay and lesbian couples or individuals who are parents or seek to become parents.

For further discussion of demographic, social, and economic factors associated with nonmarital cohabitation, childbearing, and childrearing, see Cynthia Osborne, et al., *Married and Cohabiting Parents' Relationship Stability: A Focus on Race and Ethnicity*, 69 J. MARR. & FAM. 5 (2007); Wendy D. Manning & Pamela J. Smock, *First Comes Cohabitation and then Comes Marriage?: A Research Note*, 23 J. FAM. ISSUES 1065 (2002); Laura Tach & Sarah Halpern-Meekin, *How Does Premarital Cohabitation Affect Trajectories of Marital Quality?*, 71 J. MARR. & FAM. 2 (2009); Karen B. Guzzo, *Marital Intentions and the Stability of First Cohabitations*, 30 J. FAM. ISSUES 179 (2009); Judith A. Seltzer, *Families Formed Outside of Marriage*, 62 J. MARR. & FAM. 4 (2004); Molly A. Martin, *Family Structure and Income Inequality in Families With Children, 1976 to 2000*, 43 DEMOGRAPHY 3 (2006); Susan L. Brown & Wendy D. Manning, *Family Boundary Ambiguity and the Measurement of Family Structure: The Significance of Cohabitation*, 46 DEMOGRAPHY 1 (2009).

[1]   Establishing Paternity

Until quite recently, the old saw was still largely true: maternity is a question of fact, while paternity is a matter of opinion. No more. Maternity remains clear in almost all cases, although baby-switching cases occasionally arise (*e.g.*, *Mays v. Twigg*, 543 So. 2d 241 (Fla. Dist. Ct. App. 1989), *on remand Twigg v. Mays*, 543 So. 2d 241 (Fla. Cir. Ct. 1993) (adjudicating request for parentage testing where two girls were allegedly switched in the hospital after birth)), and modern reproductive medicine offers new opportunities for such mistakes (*e.g.*, *Perry-Rogers v. Fasano*, 715 N.Y.S.2d 19 (App. Div. 2000) (adjudicating parentage of twins whose embryos had mistakenly been implanted in the wrong woman at a fertility clinic)). *See generally* Tara R. Crane, *Mistaken Baby Switches: An Analysis of Hospital Liability and Resulting Custody Issues*, 21 J. Leg. Med. 109 (2000). Proof of maternity could also be needed when a biological mother abandons her newborn, if their biological relationship becomes relevant in a later proceeding.

Paternal ambiguity was historically more common. It can arise from paternal abandonment, of both mother and child, as well as from maternal concealment of the child from the biological father. Not only have disputes over paternity always been more common than disputes over maternity, but the increased proportion of children born to unmarried mothers in recent years increases that gap. Yet the truly important change of the last several decades was the development of reliable scientific tests. Biological paternity has now also become, for the most part, a question of fact and not opinion. But biological paternity need not, and in fact is not, always the same thing as *legal* paternity, so that our increased confidence in establishing biological paternity creates as many legal issues as it solves, as we shall see below.

[a]   Methods of Proof

The classic paternity case was a maternal claim for support brought against a man alleged to be the child's father; proof of paternity was a prerequisite to a support order. But historically such proof was hard to make out. If the defendant denied sexual relations with the mother during the probable period of conception, one was left simply to choose between two stories. Direct corroboration of the plaintiff's testimony was rare, the relevant acts ordinarily having occurred in private. Perhaps in desperation, judges were sometimes known to permit exhibition of the child to the jurors, to resolve the conflict by assessing the child's resemblance to the putative father. Nor was the conduct of the case aided by a defense known as *exceptio plurium concubentium*, allowed in most jurisdictions, by which the defendant could escape liability, even if he had sexual relations with the mother during the period of conception, by showing that another man had also done so. Of course, were the other man then charged, he could use the same defense, relying upon the testimony of the initial defendant. The temptation to perjure oneself to help out a friend was too great for many to resist. In an often-cited Chicago study, an attempt was made to measure the incidence of perjury in paternity cases through the use of polygraph tests, but the tests (the accuracy of which are debatable) were not needed to make the point. Merely confronting witnesses with the machine elicited a startlingly high percentage of confessions.

Fifty-seven percent of the witnesses who had testified to intercourse with the complainant (for the purpose of establishing an *exceptio plurium* defense), admitted they had lied. On the other hand, 48% of the mothers were shown to have lied in denying intercourse with another man during the period of conception, and 88% of the defendants admitted having lied in court about the number of times they had had intercourse with the mother. Arthur and Reid, *Using the Lie Detector to Determine the Truth In Disputed Paternity Cases*, 45 J. CRIM. L., CRIMINOLOGY & POLICE SCI. 213 (1954). Some courts attempted to deal with these difficulties by imposing a higher standard of proof in paternity cases, such as "clear and convincing," or by requiring corroborating evidence of sexual acts despite the implausibility of obtaining it. But a higher standard of proof hardly solves the problem of reaching accurate results; it merely reduces the risk of one kind of error, mistaken verdicts for the plaintiff, at the price of increasing the risk of another kind of error, mistaken verdicts for the defendant. A requirement of corroborating evidence may just encourage more perjury.

At one time, Sweden recognized a standard of proof in paternity cases quite different from that in American jurisdictions. Any man identified by the mother as having had sexual relations with her at the relevant time was considered the father, unless there was evidence, such as a blood test, making that conclusion obviously wrong. The defense of *exceptio plurium* was not allowed, and indeed was considered against "Swedish public order." But when the law was changed to give the nonmarital child full inheritance rights from his father and his father's family, requirements for proof of paternity were also tightened, becoming more similar to American rules. *See* Ake Lodgberg, *The Reform of Family Law in the Scandinavian Countries*, in THE REFORM OF FAMILY LAW IN EUROPE 201, 213 (A. Chloros ed., 1978). Denmark adopted another solution, imposing an obligation of support upon all men who had intercourse with the woman during the relevant time, rendering an *exceptio plurium* defense irrelevant. Such offspring were called "company children." *Id.* at 217.

Given the difficulties in establishing the biological father using traditional evidence, a reliable scientific test for paternity would obviously provide welcome relief. For many years, blood tests had been available to exclude putative fathers, but as explained below, their value was limited by the small proportion of exclusions they yielded. During the 1970s, however, new biological tests became available that were much more powerful. But the establishment of reliable means to determine *biological* paternity does not necessarily settle the question of establishing *legal* paternity, as we consider in the next section.

[b]   Biological or Social Paternity? Of Procedures and Presumptions

Ira Mark Ellman, *Thinking About Custody And Support In Ambiguous-Father Families*
36 FAM. L. Q. 49, 50–55 (2002)

Typical family composition has changed greatly [since 1970,] when most children were born to traditional families. Our image of that traditional family includes a husband who also fulfills the role of father. He provides a major portion of the child's financial support, lives with the child, spends at least some time in direct care of the child, and shares with the mother at least the major decisions of parenthood. Both he and the child view him as father, and third parties do as well. We can call this man the child's social father. . . . [T]he focus of this essay is on two . . . kinds [of paternal ambiguity]. Both of them . . . are much more common now than they once were. In the first, there is no dispute about the child's social father, but there is ambiguity about the legal father because the social father is not the biological father, and no formal adoption has taken place to align the two. In the second, the child has no social father, and one may therefore question whether the biological father should be considered the legal father. The resolution of these ambiguities tells us something, I believe, about the relationship between support obligations and custody claims.

When a married woman bears a child, both social conventions and legal presumptions have long treated her husband as the father. That was once how the rights and responsibilities of legal fatherhood were established for nearly all children, with little cost, contention or complication. During the final quarter of the twentieth century, however, things became more complex. The complexity arose from three developments, two social and one scientific. The two social developments were the increasing proportion of children born out of wedlock, and the increasing determination of policymakers to collect child support from absent fathers. Because of the first, there were more children whose father was not identified by the social conventions and legal presumptions applicable to marital children. Because of the second, identifying the legal father (and thus, the man responsible to provide support) became more important. The scientific development was the ability to establish biological paternity through genetic tests. This scientific development seemed to provide an answer to the problem created by the social developments. Legal paternity could be established by biology. But a new set of problems have been created by the possibility of establishing legal paternity in the absence of, or even in opposition to, social indicators of paternity.

Prior to the development of modern tissue tests, it was usually impossible to determine biological paternity. In consequence the law usually relied upon presumptions that typically attributed legal paternity to the child's social father — most importantly, to the mother's husband. States had varying rules concerning the admissibility of evidence to rebut the presumption of the husband's paternity. Some restricted such evidence very severely, while others might allow it. But even when courts accepted such rebuttal evidence, it was not often persuasive. The primitive blood tests then available were unlikely to exclude a man as the child's biological father even when he in fact was not. [That is, even most husbands who in fact were not the biological father of their wife's child would not be excluded by the test then available.] Under these conditions, husbands were almost always identified as the legal father of their wife's children. Because as recently as 1970 about ninety percent of all children were born to married mothers, the "marital presumption," as it is called, settled the question of legal paternity in the vast majority of cases. The presumption also identified as the legal father a man who was nearly always their social father. He was probably their biological father as well, but if he was not, few knew, at least not for certain. In short, the law did not then often face a forced choice between social and biological paternity.

For the relatively small proportion of children then born to unmarried women, the absence of the marital presumption usually left the child with no legally established father. A paternity action could be brought, of course. But prior to the advent of modern genetic testing, the typical paternity case consisted of conflicting testimony over the alleged father's sexual "access" to the mother during the probable period of conception, and over whether the mother had sexual relations during the same time period with other men. . . . In these muddied waters, the mother seeking to establish paternity was unlikely to meet her burden of proof, and her claim would fail. Doubtless many unmarried mothers never brought a paternity claim in the first place, anticipating this result. It would seem that this state of affairs ill served nonmarital children, who were deprived of the financial support that a finding of paternity would promise. On the other hand, it might not have much mattered, because child support orders, and especially those obtained against unmarried fathers, rarely fulfilled that promise anyway. This was the era before child support enforcement became a national policy priority.

While the outcomes for children born to married and unmarried mothers were thus very different, they were also consistent in one important respect: in both cases the attribution of legal paternity paralleled the reality of social paternity. The husband was the legal and social father of the marital child. And while no one was the legal father of the nonmarital child, typically no one was the child's social father either. Indeed, a nonmarital biological father who was the social father of his children was thought sufficiently rare that the law did not need to consider the possibility of his existence. For example, single mothers could alone consent to the adoption of their child, a core parental right. It was 1972 before American constitutional law recognized that the nonmarital father had any parental rights at all. In that case, the Supreme Court came to the assistance of Mr. Stanley, a nonmarital father who, rather atypically, had lived with his children and their mother for years. . . . [See the discussion of *Stanley v. Illinois* in Section B[2][a] of this chapter.] [¶] The Court ultimately decided four more cases on this general topic of nonmarital fathers' rights. Between the first and the last of these five cases (from 1972 to 1989), a sea change occurred in the science of paternity testing (and it has advanced even further since). In later cases the Court therefore had to confront a question that *Stanley* never raised: whether the Constitutional rights it had recognized arose from social paternity, biological paternity, or both. Its later decisions suggest that the Constitution guarantees the biological father some opportunity to establish a social connection with his offspring, but does not guarantee full paternal rights to the man who declines that opportunity. And the

Court's decisions also suggest that state policymakers may treat a child's social father as the legal father, in preference to the biological father, although the Constitution does not require them to make this choice. So answers to the important questions were left largely to state policymakers.

Choosing the appropriate rule for assigning legal paternity becomes more difficult when social and biological paternity diverge. The newly-developed reliability in assessing biological paternity forces attention to this issue because it makes our knowledge of such divergence more likely. At the same time, the recent legislative determination to collect child support from absent fathers gives assignment of legal paternity enhanced importance in public policy. Moreover, a parent is not only obliged to provide support, but can also seek custody and is usually guaranteed at least some time with the child. Support duties and custody rights are in this way legally connected. Parents intuit the connection, and both custodial parents considering claims for support, and noncustodial parents considering claims for custody, sometimes forego their claim to avoid triggering the corresponding claim back from the other parent. The two also have a social connection: The biological father who has enjoyed a parental relationship with a child is more likely to pay support, and to want assured access, than the biological father who has not. So, in allowing the law to identify genetic fathers who have never known their child, modern science has given the law a challenge as well as a tool.

[i]   The Uniform Parentage Acts of 1973 and 2002

The Uniform Parentage Act, first drafted in 1973, was groundbreaking in its equal treatment of nonmarital children. The act was revised in 2000, to take into account advances in reproductive technology and genetic testing, and then amended again in 2002. The 2002 version of the act has been adopted in Alabama, Delaware, New Mexico, North Dakota, Oklahoma, Texas, Utah, Washington, and Wyoming, and was being considered in Colorado as of 2009. Provisions of the 1973 version of the statute, however, are still in effect in California, Colorado, Hawaii, Illinois, Kansas, Minnesota, Missouri, Montana, Nevada, New Jersey, Ohio, and Rhode Island, which causes the 1973 Act still to be important today. Below, we reprint key portions of both the 1973 and 2002 versions of the act.

[Comments to individual sections of UPA 2002 are reproduced below selectively, as are the sections of both UPA 1973 and UPA 2002. Omissions of sections or comments are not indicated individually.]

UNIFORM PARENTAGE ACT (1973)

Section 4. [*Presumption of Paternity.*]

(a) A man is presumed to be the natural father of a child if:

(1) he and the child's natural mother are or have been married to each other and the child is born during the marriage, or within 300 days after the marriage is terminated by death, annulment, declaration of invalidity, or divorce, or after a decree of separation is entered by a court;

(2) before the child's birth, he and the child's natural mother have attempted to marry each other by a marriage solemnized in apparent compliance with law, although the attempted marriage is or could be declared invalid, and

(i) if the attempted marriage could be declared invalid only by a court, the child is born during the attempted marriage, or within 300 days after its termination by death, annulment, declaration of invalidity, or divorce; or

(ii) if the attempted marriage is invalid without a court order, the child is born within 300 days after the termination of cohabitation;

(3) after the child's birth, he and the child's natural mother have married, or attempted to marry, each other by a marriage solemnized in apparent compliance with law, although the attempted marriage is or could be declared invalid, and

(i) he has acknowledged his paternity of the child in writing filed with the [appropriate court or Vital Statistics Bureau],

(ii) with his consent, he is named as the child's father on the child's birth certificate, or

(iii) he is obligated to support the child under a written voluntary promise or by court order;

(4) while the child is under the age of majority, he receives the child into his home and openly holds out the child as his natural child; or

(5) he acknowledges his paternity of the child in a writing filed with the [appropriate court or Vital Statistics Bureau], which shall promptly inform the mother of the filing of the acknowledgment, and she does not dispute the acknowledgment within a reasonable time after being informed thereof, in a writing filed with the [appropriate court or Vital Statistics Bureau]. If another man is presumed under this section to be the child's father, acknowledgment may be effected only with the written consent of the presumed father or after the presumption has been rebutted.

(b) A presumption under this section may be rebutted in an appropriate action only by clear and convincing evidence. If two or more presumptions arise which conflict with each other, the presumption which on the facts is founded on the weightier considerations of policy and logic controls. The presumption is rebutted by a court decree establishing paternity of the child by another man.

Section 6. [*Determination of Father and Child Relationship; Who May Bring Action; When Action May Be Brought.*]

(a) A child, his natural mother, or a man presumed to be his father under Paragraph (1), (2), or (3) of Section 4(a), may bring an action

(1) at any time for the purpose of declaring the existence of the father and child relationship presumed under Paragraph (1), (2), or (3) of Section 4(a); or

(2) for the purpose of declaring the non-existence of the father and child relationship presumed under Paragraph (1), (2), or (3) of Section 4(a) only if the action is brought within a reasonable time after obtaining knowledge of relevant facts, but in no event later than [5] years after the child's birth. After the presumption has been rebutted, paternity of the child by another man may be determined in the same action, if he has been made a party.

(b) Any interested party may bring an action at any time for the purpose of determining the existence or non-existence of the father and child relationship presumed under Paragraph (4) or (5) of Section 4(a).

(c) An action to determine the existence of the father and child relationship with respect to a child who has no presumed father under Section 4 may be brought by the child, the mother or personal representative of the child, the [appropriate state agency], the personal representative or a parent of the mother if the mother has died, a man alleged or alleging himself to be the father, or the personal representative or a parent of the alleged father if the alleged father has died or is a minor.

(d) Regardless of its terms, an agreement, other than an agreement approved by the court in accordance with Section 13(b), between an alleged or presumed father and the mother or child, does not bar an action under this section.

(e) If an action under this section is brought before the birth of the child, all proceedings shall be stayed until after the birth, except services of process and the taking of depositions to perpetuate testimony.

Section 7. [*Statute of Limitations.*]

An action to determine the existence of the father and child relationship as to a child who has no presumed father under Section 4 may not be brought later than [3] years after the birth of the child, or later than [3] years after the effective date of this Act, whichever is later. However, an action brought by or on behalf of a child whose paternity has not been determined is not barred until [3] years after the child reaches the age of majority. Sections 6 and 7 do not extend the time within which a right of inheritance or a right to a succession may be asserted beyond the time provided by law relating to distribution and closing of decedents' estates or to the determination of heirship, or otherwise.

UNIFORM PARENTAGE ACT (2002)

Article Two: Parent-Child Relationship

Section 201. Establishment of Parent-Child Relationship.

. . . .

(b) The father-child relationship is established between a man and a child by:

(1) an unrebutted presumption of the man's paternity of the child under Section 204;

(2) an effective acknowledgment of paternity by the man under [Article] 3, unless the acknowledgment has been rescinded or successfully challenged;

(3) an adjudication of the man's paternity;

(4) adoption of the child by the man;

(5) the man's having consented to assisted reproduction by a woman under [Article] 7 which resulted in the birth of the child; or

(6) an adjudication confirming the man as a parent of a child born to a gestational mother if the agreement was validated under [Article] 8 or is enforceable under other law.

Section 202. No Discrimination Based on Marital Status.

A child born to parents who are not married to each other has the same rights under the law as a child born to parents who are married to each other.

Section 203. Consequences of Establishment of Parentage.

Unless parental rights are terminated, a parent-child relationship established under this [Act] applies for all purposes, except as otherwise specifically provided by other law of this State.

Section 204. Presumption of Paternity.

(a) A man is presumed to be the father of a child if:

(1) he and the mother of the child are married to each other and the child is born during the marriage;

(2) he and the mother of the child were married to each other and the child is born within 300 days after the marriage is terminated by death, annulment, declaration of invalidity, or divorce [, or after a decree of separation];

(3) before the birth of the child, he and the mother of the child married each other in apparent compliance with law, even if the attempted marriage is or could be declared invalid, and the child is born during the invalid marriage or within 300 days after its termination by death, annulment, declaration of invalidity, or divorce [, or after a decree of separation];

(4) after the birth of the child, he and the mother of the child married each other in apparent compliance with law, whether or not the marriage is or could be declared invalid, and he voluntarily asserted his paternity of the child, and:

(A) the assertion is in a record filed with [state agency maintaining birth records];

(B) he agreed to be and is named as the child's father on the child's birth certificate; or

(C) he promised in a record to support the child as his own; or

(5) for the first two years of the child's life, he resided in the same household with the child and openly held out the child as his own.

(b) A presumption of paternity established under this section may be rebutted only by an adjudication under [Article] 6.

Article 3: Voluntary Acknowledgment of Paternity

Comment

. . . .

Voluntary acknowledgment of paternity has long been an alternative to a contested paternity suit. Under UPA (1973) § 4, the inclusion of a man's name on the child's birth certificate created a presumption of paternity, which could be rebutted. In order to improve the collection of child support, especially from unwed fathers, the U.S. Congress mandated a fundamental change in the acknowledgment procedure. The Personal Responsibility and Work Opportunity Reconciliation Act of 1996 (PRWORA, also known as the Welfare Reform Act) conditions receipt of federal child support enforcement funds on state enactment of laws that greatly strengthen the effect of a man's voluntary acknowledgment of paternity, 42 U.S.C. § 666(a)(5)(C). This statute. . . . provides that a valid, unrescinded, unchallenged acknowledgment of paternity is to be treated as equivalent to a judicial determination of paternity.

Because in many respects the federal act is nonspecific, the new UPA contains clear and comprehensive procedures to comply with the federal mandate. Primary among the factual circumstances that Congress did not take into account was that a married woman may consent to an acknowledgement of paternity by a man who may indeed be her child's genetic father, but is not her husband. Under the new UPA, the mother's husband is the presumed father of the child, *see* § 204, *supra*. By ignoring the real possibility that the child will have both an acknowledged father and a presumed father, Congress left it to the states to sort out which of the men should be recognized as the legal father.

. . . .

Sections 302–305 clarify that, if a child has a presumed father, that man must file a denial of paternity in conjunction with another man's acknowledgment of paternity in order for the acknowledgement to be valid. If the presumed father is unwilling to cooperate, or his whereabouts are unknown, a court proceeding is necessary to resolve the issue of parentage.

Congress also directed that the acknowledgment can be "rescinded" within a particular time frame, and subsequently can be "challenged" without stating a time frame. Those procedures are dealt with in §§ 307–309.

Finally, the related issue of issuance or revision of birth certificates is left to other state law.

Section 301. Acknowledgment of Paternity.

The mother of a child and a man claiming to be the genetic father of the child may sign an acknowledgment of paternity with intent to establish the man's paternity.

Comment

. . . .

PRWORA does not explicitly require that a man acknowledging parentage necessarily is asserting his genetic parentage of the child. In order to prevent circumvention of adoption laws, § 301 corrects this omission by requiring a sworn assertion of genetic parentage of the child. A 2002 amendment provides that a man who signs an acknowledgment of paternity declares that he is the genetic father of the child. Thus both the man and the mother acknowledge his paternity, under penalty of perjury, without requiring the parents to spell out the details of their sexual relations. Further, the amended language also takes into account a situation in which a man, who is unable to have sexual intercourse with his partner, may still have contributed to the conception of the child through the use of his own sperm. Henceforth, a man in that situation will be able to recognize legally his paternity through the voluntary acknowledgment procedure.

Section 302. Execution of Acknowledgment of Paternity.

(a) An acknowledgment of paternity must:

(1) be in a record;

(2) be signed, or otherwise authenticated, under penalty of perjury by the mother and by the man seeking to establish his paternity;

(3) state that the child whose paternity is being acknowledged:

(A) does not have a presumed father, or has a presumed father whose full name is stated; and

(B) does not have another acknowledged or adjudicated father;

(4) state whether there has been genetic testing and, if so, that the acknowledging man's claim of paternity is consistent with the results of the testing; and

(5) state that the signatories understand that the acknowledgment is the equivalent of a judicial adjudication of paternity of the child and that a challenge to the acknowledgment is permitted only under limited circumstances and is barred after two years.

(b) An acknowledgment of paternity is void if it:

(1) states that another man is a presumed father, unless a denial of paternity signed or otherwise authenticated by the presumed father is filed with the [agency maintaining birth records];

(2) states that another man is an acknowledged or adjudicated father; or

(3) falsely denies the existence of a presumed, acknowledged, or adjudicated father of the child.

(c) A presumed father may sign or otherwise authenticate an acknowledgment of paternity.

Comment

[Federal law requires states to establish] specific procedures for voluntary acknowledgment of paternity. This deceptively simple principle proved difficult to implement.

Problems most notably include . . . situations in which the mother is . . . married to someone other than the man who intends to acknowledge his paternity. With an acknowledgment the child would then have both an acknowledged father and a presumed father. To deal with this circumstance, many states have passed laws allowing the presumed father to sign a denial of paternity, which must be filed as part of the acknowledgment. This Act adopts this common sense solution; otherwise the acknowledgment would have no legal consequence because it cannot affect the legal rights of the presumed father.

At least two other provisions of this section warrant special emphasis. Subsection (a)(2) requires that the acknowledgment be "signed, or otherwise authenticated, under penalty of perjury," just as income tax returns and many other government documents require. Clearly, the potential punishment for false swearing is substantial, and the benefits from avoiding the complication of requiring witnesses and a notary are significant in this context. Mandating greater formality would greatly discourage the in-hospital signatures so earnestly desired in 42 U.S.C. § 666(a)(5)(C)(ii), *see* APPENDIX: FEDERAL IV-D STATUTE RELATING TO PARENTAGE, *infra*.

Similarly, in an attempt to ensure full disclosure and avoid false swearing, subsection (a)(4) requires that the results of genetic testing, if any, be reported along with confirmation that the acknowledgment is consistent with the results of that testing. This provision is also designed to avoid a possible subversion of the requirements for an adoption. A would-be "father" whose parentage of a child has been excluded by genetic testing may not validly sign an acknowledgment once that fact has been established.

Section 307. Proceeding for Rescission.

A signatory may rescind an acknowledgment of paternity or denial of paternity by commencing a proceeding to rescind before the earlier of:

(1) 60 days after the effective date of the acknowledgment or denial, as provided in Section 304; or

(2) the date of the first hearing, in a proceeding to which the signatory is a party, before a court to adjudicate an issue relating to the child, including a proceeding that establishes support.

Section 308. Challenge after Expiration of Period for Rescission.

(a) After the period for rescission under Section 307 has expired, a signatory of an acknowledgment of paternity or denial of paternity may commence a proceeding to challenge the acknowledgment or denial only:

(1) on the basis of fraud, duress, or material mistake of fact; and

(2) within two years after the acknowledgment or denial is filed with the [agency maintaining birth records].

(b) A party challenging an acknowledgment of paternity or denial of paternity has the burden of proof.

Comment

The federal statute also includes a provision for a "challenge" of an acknowledgment of paternity after the period for rescission of a voluntary acknowledgment of paternity has elapsed. Such a collateral attack is to be limited to a challenge based on alleged "fraud, duress, or material mistake of fact," and according to 42 U.S.C. § 666(a)(5)(c)(D)(iii), must be made "in court". . . .

Article 5: Genetic Testing

Section 505. Genetic Testing Results; Rebuttal.

(a) Under this [Act], a man is rebuttably identified as the father of a child if the genetic testing complies with this [article] and the results disclose that:

(1) the man has at least a 99 percent probability of paternity, using a prior probability of 0.50, as calculated by using the combined paternity index obtained in the testing; and

(2) a combined paternity index of at least 100 to 1.

(b) A man identified under subsection (a) as the father of the child may rebut the genetic testing results only by other genetic testing satisfying the requirements of this [article] which:

(1) excludes the man as a genetic father of the child; or

(2) identifies another man as the possible father of the child.

(c) Except as otherwise provided in Section 510, if more than one man is identified by genetic testing as the possible father of the child, the court shall order them to submit to further genetic testing to identify the genetic father.

Comment

The selection of a probability of paternity of 99.0% and a combined paternity index of 100 to 1 as the rebuttably identified man as father of the child is consistent with the year 2000 standard of practice in the genetic-testing community. Accrediting agencies require the reporting of both of these numbers. . . . [F]or several years the standard of practice in the scientific community has been 99.0%.

Therefore, raising the genetic presumption to the 99.0% level should have no impact on those states. . . .

Article 6: Proceedings to Adjudicate Parentage

Section 602. Standing to Maintain Proceeding.

Subject to [Article] 3 and Sections 607 and 609, a proceeding to adjudicate parentage may be maintained by:

(1) the child;

(2) the mother of the child;

(3) a man whose paternity of the child is to be adjudicated;

(4) the support-enforcement agency [or other governmental agency authorized by other law];

(5) an authorized adoption agency or licensed child-placing agency; [or]

(6) a representative authorized by law to act for an individual who would otherwise be entitled to maintain a proceeding but who is deceased, incapacitated, or a minor [; or

(7) an intended parent under [Article] 8].

Section 606. No Limitation: Child Having No Presumed, Acknowledged, or Adjudicated Father.

A proceeding to adjudicate the parentage of a child having no presumed, acknowledged, or adjudicated father may be commenced at any time, even after:

(1) the child becomes an adult, but only if the child initiates the proceeding; or

(2) an earlier proceeding to adjudicate paternity has been dismissed based on the application of a statute of limitation then in effect.

Comment

[Federal law requires states] to "permit the establishment of the paternity of a child at any time before the child attains 18 years of age." States have chosen a wide range of age options: age 18 (20 states), age 19 (6 states), age 20 (2 states), age 21 (10 states), age 22 (2 states), age 23 (2 states), and no limitation (9 states). Several states limit the establishment of parental rights to a shorter period. [¶] The new UPA directs that an individual whose parentage has not been determined has a civil right to determine his or her own parentage, which should not be subject to limitation except when an estate has been closed. . . .

Section 607. Limitation: Child Having Presumed Father.

(a) Except as otherwise provided in subsection (b), a proceeding brought by a presumed father, the mother, or another individual to adjudicate the parentage of a child having a presumed father must be commenced not later than two years after the birth of the child.

(b) A proceeding seeking to disprove the father-child relationship between a child and the child's presumed father may be maintained at any time if the court determines that:

(1) the presumed father and the mother of the child neither cohabited nor engaged in sexual intercourse with each other during the probable time of conception; and

(2) the presumed father never openly held out the child as his own.

Section 608. Authority to Deny Motion for Genetic Testing.

(a) In a proceeding to adjudicate the parentage of a child having a presumed father or to challenge the paternity of a child having an acknowledged father, the court may deny a motion seeking an order for genetic testing of the mother, the child, and the presumed or acknowledged father if the court determines that:

(1) the conduct of the mother or the presumed or acknowledged father estops that party from denying parentage; and

(2) it would be inequitable to disprove the father-child relationship between the child and the presumed or acknowledged father.

(b) In determining whether to deny a motion seeking an order for genetic testing under this section, the court shall consider the best interest of the child, including the following factors:

(1) the length of time between the proceeding to adjudicate parentage and the time that the presumed or acknowledged father was placed on notice that he might not be the genetic father;

(2) the length of time during which the presumed or acknowledged father has assumed the role of father of the child;

(3) the facts surrounding the presumed or acknowledged father's discovery of his possible nonpaternity;

(4) the nature of the relationship between the child and the presumed or acknowledged father;

(5) the age of the child;

(6) the harm that may result to the child if presumed or acknowledged paternity is successfully disproved;

(7) the nature of the relationship between the child and any alleged father;

(8) the extent to which the passage of time reduces the chances of establishing the paternity of another man and a child-support obligation in favor of the child; and

(9) other factors that may affect the equities arising from the disruption of the father-child relationship between the child and the presumed or acknowledged father or the chance of other harm to the child.

(c) In a proceeding involving the application of this section, a minor or incapacitated child must be represented by a guardian ad litem.

(d) Denial of a motion seeking an order for genetic testing must be based on clear and convincing evidence.

(e) If the court denies a motion seeking an order for genetic testing, it shall issue an order adjudicating the presumed or acknowledged father to be the father of the child.

Comment

This section incorporates the doctrine of paternity by estoppel, which extends equally to a child with a presumed father or an acknowledged father. In appropriate circumstances, the court may deny genetic testing and find the presumed or acknowledged father to be the father of the child. The most common situation in which estoppel should be applied arises when a man knows that a child is not, or may not be, his genetic child, but the man has affirmatively accepted his role as child's father and both the mother and the child have relied on that acceptance. Similarly, the man may have relied on the mother's acceptance of him as the child's father and the mother is then estopped to deny the man's presumed parentage. . . .

Section 609. Limitation: Child Having Acknowledged or Adjudicated Father.

(a) If a child has an acknowledged father, a signatory to the acknowledgment of paternity or denial of paternity may commence a proceeding seeking to rescind the acknowledgement or denial or challenge the paternity of the child only within the time allowed under Section 307 or 308.

(b) If a child has an acknowledged father or an adjudicated father, an individual, other than the child, who is neither a signatory to the acknowledgment of paternity nor a party to the adjudication and who seeks an adjudication of paternity of the child must commence a proceeding not later than two years after the effective date of the acknowledgment or adjudication.

(c) A proceeding under this section is subject to the application of the principles of estoppel established in Section 608.

Section 631. Rules for Adjudication of Paternity.

The court shall apply the following rules to adjudicate the paternity of a child:

(1) The paternity of a child having a presumed, acknowledged, or adjudicated father may be disproved only by admissible results of genetic testing excluding that man as the father of the child or identifying another man as the father of the child.

(2) Unless the results of genetic testing are admitted to rebut other results of genetic testing, a man identified as the father of a child under Section 505 must be adjudicated the father of the child.

(3) If the court finds that genetic testing under Section 505 neither identifies nor excludes a man as the father of a child, the court may not dismiss the proceeding. In that event, the results of genetic testing, and other evidence, are admissible to adjudicate the issue of paternity.

(4) Unless the results of genetic testing are admitted to rebut other results of genetic testing, a man excluded as the father of a child by genetic testing must be adjudicated not to be the father of the child.

NOTES

1. *Comparing the Statutory Rules.* Section 4 of UPA 1973 sets out the classic paternity rules applied in most jurisdictions. Much of the section is devoted to specifying the boundaries of the marital presumption, while subsection (a)(4) states the equivalent of the marital presumption for the man who was not married to the child's mother but is the child's social father. Subsection (b) requires clear and convincing evidence to overcome any of these statutory presumptions, a standard that would often have been difficult to meet prior to the development of modern paternity tests. Under Section (a)(5) acknowledgment can also establish a presumption of paternity, but only if the mother does not object after being informed, and only if no other man is presumed to be the child's father. Section 6 strengthens the marital presumption by setting clear time limits on any challenges to it; these limits do not apply to any of the nonmarital presumptions.

The need to accommodate modern scientific testing and new federal requirements led to a more complex set of rules under UPA 2002. Usually paternity will be established by a presumption arising under § 204, or an acknowledgment arising under § 301; in their absence it will be established, typically, by genetic evidence under § 505 (as provided under § 631). A key question is the extent to which paternity established by acknowledgment or presumption can be challenged. An acknowledgment under § 301 can be rescinded under § 307, but only within 60 days of the acknowledgment. After that, the acknowledgment can only be challenged under § 308, which has more demanding requirements as well as its own time limit of two years. Presumptions may be rebutted only as allowed under § 607 and § 608. As a general matter, challenges to presumed paternity are also barred more than two years after the child's birth; the only exception is if the challenger can persuade the court that the mother and presumed father neither cohabited, nor had sexual relations during the probable time of conception, nor did the presumed father hold himself out as the father. Moreover, challenges to acknowledged as well as presumed paternity must be based on genetic evidence (§ 631), and under § 608 a court may refuse to order genetic testing even where the child is less than two years old, if the challenger's conduct estops him from denying the presumed or acknowledged paternity and it would be inequitable to allow the challenge. One can thus see that while genetic evidence is very important under the Act, presumptions will still often prevail over any actual or potential genetic evidence to the contrary, either under estoppel or because the child is more than 2 years old. The Act thus makes clear that even though biological paternity and legal paternity are ordinarily the same, they need not be. In particular, the Act disallows genetic challenges to a child's social paternity — as reflected by the presumption and acknowledgment provisions — if brought too late. The Act establishes that more than two years after the child's birth is always too late, and provides that even earlier challenges may be too late if equity so requires.

The marital presumption initially established by UPA 1973 and strengthened by UPA 2002 thus reflects a public policy that the child's interests in maintaining settled social understandings about the child's parentage are more important than biological paternity. UPA 2002 thus resolves the possible conflict between social paternity and biological paternity, made so salient by modern scientific advances, in favor of social paternity. Where neither the biological father nor any other man is the social father, biological paternity will equal legal paternity. But where there is one social father who is not the biological father, UPA 2002 will usually identify that social father as the legal father. Sometimes, of course, there can be more than one man plausibly identified as the child's social father. These difficult cases are considered further below in connection with our review of *Michael H.* in Section B[2][b].

2. *The Traditional Marital Presumption and Its Allied Equitable Rules.* The marital presumption codified by both versions of the UPA has long been part of the law. Some states, like California, had their own statutory provisions that effectively anticipated UPA 2002: California law has long barred all challenges to a husband's paternity more than two years after the child's birth, and excluded even timely challenges by anyone other than the husband, the wife, or (in consequence of recent amendments) men who qualify as presumed fathers under § 4 of UPA 1973. We examine third-party challenges of a husband's paternity below, in Section B[2][b], in connection with the unsuccessful federal constitutional attack on California's exclusion of them in *Michael H.* Here, we review how the rule operates to bar attacks by the spouses themselves. Such challenges typically arise when either the husband challenges his paternity to avoid liability to support his wife's child, or the wife challenges his paternity in order to defeat his claims for custody of or visitation with the child.

Most states have had marital presumptions that are not as strong as California's or UPA 2002. The typical statutory law allows its rebuttal, and does not even impose the absolute five-year time limit on challenges contained in § 6(a)(2) of UPA 1973, much less a two-year limit. This is not to say that the presumption was, historically, easily overcome. It was protected by high evidentiary standards, once nearly impossible to meet. Consider, for example, the traditional Massachusetts formulation: "The presumption of legitimacy may not be rebutted, even in a civil case, 'except on facts which prove, beyond all reasonable doubt, that the husband could not have been the father.' [citing 1861 case] . . . [A] child *conceived* by a married woman is presumed to be the child of the man to whom the mother was then married even if the mother and the husband are divorced at the time of the child's birth. This holding fosters the important social policy of affording legitimacy to children whenever possible." *P.B.C. v. D.H.*, 483 N.E.2d 1094, 1096 (Mass. 1985). Moreover, the usual marital presumption was often buttressed by judicially created equitable doctrines that pre-existed the availability of genetic evidence, and which in light of scientific advances are now even more important. For example, in the pre-genetic-test case of *Watts v. Watts*, 337 A.2d 350 (N.H. 1975), the wife sought a divorce after 21 years of marriage. Four children were born during the marriage, but the husband sought to show the two youngest were not his. The court denied his request for blood tests, even though the usual rule allowed their use to rebut the marital presumption, because "those rules do not apply in a situation such as this one where the defendant has acknowledged the children as his own without challenge for over fifteen years. To allow defendant to escape liability for support by using blood tests would be to ignore his lengthy, voluntary acceptance of parental responsibilities." *Id.* at 352.

Note that *Watts* does not override blood test evidence; it rather denies a motion to obtain it. A possible difficulty with this approach is the implication that *if* scientific evidence of biological nonpaternity were available, the court would be obliged to follow it. By contrast, many other courts historically applied equitable rules that barred the claim itself, not just the gathering of evidence to support it. Some involved efforts by married mothers to defeat custody or visitation claims at divorce by husbands who had acted as the child's father during marriage. *E.g.*, *Atkinson v. Atkinson*, 408 N.W.2d 516, (Mich. App. 1987) (where husband had always treated the child as his during the marriage, was the only father the child had known, and now sought both the responsibilities and rights of fatherhood, he is treated as the child's "equitable parent" even though he is not the biological parent); *Pettinato v. Pettinato*, 582 A.2d 909 (R.I. 1990) (couple married 11 months after child's birth; mother who told husband he was father is estopped from challenging his paternity on divorce, six months later, in order to defeat his custody claim); *Seger v. Seger*, 547 A.2d 424 (Pa. Super. 1988) (husband could not be denied visitation for lack of biological parenthood where he had assumed parental duties during the marriage). There were similar results in cases involving married fathers who sought to deny support obligations for their wife's child. *E.g.*, *Johns v. Johns*, 443 N.W.2d 446 (Mich. App. 1989) ("Where, as in this case, a father rears a child as his own, he is estopped to deny the child is his"), and, more recently, *Miscovich v. Miscovich*, 688 A.2d 726 (Pa. App. 1997), *aff'd by an equally divided court*, 720 A.2d 764 (Pa. 1998) (husband could not disclaim legal paternity, despite DNA tests excluding biological fatherhood, in face of father-child relationship that had existed from the time of the child's birth); *W. v. W.*, 779 A.2d 716 (Conn. 2001) (husband estopped from denying his paternity of wife's child he had treated as his for 12 years, even after he located purported biological father, from whom support might instead be sought; court relies in part on husband's discouraging wife from seeking support from the biological father at the time of birth or otherwise involving him in the child's life) *C.C.A. v. J.M.A.*, 744 So. 2d 515 (Fla. App. 1999) (husband estopped from disavowing at divorce a child of his wife's by a man she had intentionally chosen as a "surrogate" biological father, in light of the husband's vasectomy and his earlier agreement to such an arrangement with a different man; husband had treated the child as his long enough to support estoppel).

While these estoppel doctrines may serve an important purpose, they are ultimately less satisfactory than a rule like California's, or UPA 2002, in serving the child's interests:

> The estoppel doctrine, unlike a simple two-year rule, necessarily requires a case-by-case examination of the facts, with far more variable results. Some courts apply the doctrine flexibly to bar either spouse from

denying the husband's paternity whenever they have both treated the children as the husband's over a significant time period, if the disavowal has the potential for causing the children harm. But other courts adhere to the doctrine's technical requirements and therefore focus on facts that are irrelevant to the child's interests, such as whether the husband knew he was not the children's biological father when he treated them as his own. A narrow technical analysis leads other courts to reject a claim that the husband is estopped from denying his paternity, no matter how long he treated the children as his, unless he is directly responsible for the biological father's unavailability as a source of support. For example, these courts treat the mother's husband as the children's father if she sought severance of the biological father's parental status in reliance upon her husband's promise to support them, but will allow the husband to deny paternity, despite having treated the children as his throughout their life, if the biological father is unavailable because he is dead or cannot be found. Overall, then, the estoppel doctrine is poorly equipped as a general approach to these cases, although it can serve as a useful stopgap when better statutory provisions are not available.

Ira Mark Ellman, *Thinking About Custody and Support in Ambiguous-Father Families*, 36 Fam. L.Q. 49, 61–62 (2002).

We do not yet know whether UPA 2002 will be successful in moving the statutory law of most states toward the social paternity model. There certainly are good reasons in support of its approach, reflected in much (but not all) of this traditional estoppel case law.

3. *Res Judicata Effect of Divorce Decree.* Where a child support order is entered as part of a marital dissolution, ordinary res judicata principles would bar both former spouses from subsequently contesting his paternity of the marital children, even if the marital presumption did not. As the rules governing modification of custody decrees illustrate (see Chapter 6), courts sometimes relax ordinary res judicata principles to permit reconsideration of prior orders where the child's interests appear to require it. Nonetheless, reconsideration of divorce decree provisions premised on the husband's paternity is not ordinarily possible, even in states that relax normal res judicata principles. "Whatever the interests of the presumed father in ascertaining the genetic 'truth' of a child's origins, they remain subsidiary to the interests of the state, the family, and the child in maintaining the continuity, financial support, and psychological security of an established parent-child relationship. Therefore, absent a clear and convincing showing that it would serve the best interests of the child, a prior adjudication of paternity is conclusive." *Godin v. Godin*, 725 A.2d 904, 910 (Vt. 1998). The *Godin* father had sought to set aside the support order for the girl he raised as his daughter for eight years during his marriage and six more years after his divorce. *See also Martin v. Pierce*, 257 S.W.3d 82 (Ark. 2007) (former husband barred); *Doe v. Doe*, 52 P.3d 255 (Haw. 2002) (former wife barred); *Marriage/Children of Betty L.W. v. William E.W.*, 569 S.E.2d 77 (W.Va. 2002) (same); *In the Interest of T.S.S.*, 61 S.W.3d 481 (Tex. App. 2001) (same); *Anderson v. Anderson*, 552 N.E.2d 546 (Mass. 1990) (same). Because prior judgments do not bind persons who were not parties to them, the divorce decree cannot bind the child, *Simcox v. Simcox*, 546

N.E.2d 609 (Ill. 1989) (child not represented in divorce action); *Gipson v. Enright*, 753 S.W.2d 122 (Mo. App. 1988) (same, allowing child to seek to establish paternity and thereby her right of inheritance).

There has been little retreat from this general rule despite the recent passage in some states of statutes permitting or requiring courts to reconsider paternity in the face of genetic test results contrary to the initial disposition. States apply these statutes directly to adjudicated *nonmarital* fathers but not usually to marital fathers' who seek to revisit their paternity as adjudicated in the divorce decrees. *See, e.g., Martin v. Pierce*, 257 S.W. 3d 82 (Ark. 2007) (holding state statute does not limit the res judicata effect of paternity as adjudicated by a divorce decree); *Gann v. Gann*, 705 So.2d 509 (Ala. App. 1997) (same).

4. The "Nonmarital Presumption." An important change in the 2002 amendments to the 2000 UPA is the preservation of what might be called a "nonmarital presumption" — a presumption of paternity arising from a *de facto* family relationship that establishes a presumed father of a child born to an unmarried mother. That presumption, arising under UPA 2002 § 204(a)(5), is the successor to § 4(a)(4) of UPA 1973. The new provision applies only to a nonmarital father who lived with the child during the first two years of the child's life, while under the 1973 provision presumed paternity could be established later as well. On the other hand, the 2002 version, like all the presumptions arising under that law, has much greater force, because it can only be challenged within two years of the child's birth. Here again, this statutory reform may be necessary to protect the interests of nonmarital children, given especially that many courts will not apply the estoppel doctrine in connection with them. Consider, for example, *Van v. Zahorik*, 597 N.W.2d 15, 23 (Mich. 1999). In that case, the mother cohabited with Van for five years, and continued to see him after that. She led him to believe he was the father of the two children born to her during their relationship, and Van treated them as his children. When the children were 7 and 3 the couple's relationship ended. The mother now denied Van all access to them. When he sought legal relief she alleged, for the first time, that he was not their biological father. Tests confirmed her claim. The court refused to apply estoppel to protect Van because he was not married to the mother. The court conceded that the case presented "tragic circumstances":

> [T]he children were suddenly separated from Mr. Van, the only father they had known; Mr. Van lost contact with the children whom he helped raise and support; and Ms. Zahorik only belatedly introduced the biological fathers into the picture. However, the current state of child custody law simply provides no means for Mr. Van, who is not related to the children . . . either biologically or by marriage, to pursue parental rights under . . . equitable estoppel. In short, he has no *legal right* to continue a relationship with the children."

See also Price v. Howard, 484 S.E.2d 528, 537 (N.C. 1997) (although man lived together with child's mother from the time of her birth, held himself out as the father, was her primary caretaker at the time of the action, mother had represented to the man and to others that he was the child's father, and the child believed that he was her father, parental rights doctrine requires award of sole custody to child's biological mother, absent a finding of her unfitness or that she engaged in conduct "inconsistent with the constitutionally protected status of a natural parent"); *Petition of Bruce*, 522 N.W.2d 67 (Iowa 1994) (similar). Is the *Price* court correct in believing that the mother's constitutionally protected parental rights bar the recognition of her partner, the child's social father, as the child's legal father? The difficulty with the court's position is that it assumes an answer to the question being put — it assumes that the child's social father is *not* the child's legal father. If that assumption is correct, then cases like *Troxel v. Granville*, 530 U.S. 57 (2000), reprinted *supra* in Chapter 6, indeed suggest that constitutional principles would limit a court's authority to require the mother to share her custodial rights with this "legal stranger" to the child. But of course the real question in this case is *whether* this man is a legal stranger to the child. Constitutional principles do *not* enshrine biological paternity as the ultimate or dispositive criterion of legal paternity, as will become more clear in the next section of this chapter. For a persuasive discussion of the importance of distinguishing constitutional rules protecting parental rights from rules for identifying the parents, see Emily Buss, *Parental Rights*, 88 VA. L. REV. 635 (2002).

PROBLEMS

Problem 9-10. Betty, unmarried, gives birth to daughter Joy. Just after the birth she is visited in the hospital by her boyfriend Ben. During the visit a hospital social worker asks for both their signatures on a form stating that Ben is Joy's father. They sign. The form states the parties' belief that Ben is Joy's father, and asserts that no other man is her presumed father or has acknowledged her paternity. Betty and Ben have in fact never lived together, although they have known one another for several years and have often been physically intimate during that time. They try living together after Betty leaves the hospital, but it does not go well, and six months later they are no longer seeing one another. When Betty seeks public assistance, the social welfare agency files a claim against Ben for child support. You are a legal services attorney advising Ben. He tells you that one of the reasons he broke up with Betty was her continuing relationship with Alan, an old boyfriend. At the time he signed the acknowledgment he thought it was possible that Alan was really Joy's father, but he had believed Betty when she told him that she had hardly seen Alan for over a year and wanted nothing to do with him anymore. Friends now tell him that Betty had been lying to him, and that she has told others she thought Alan was Joy's father. In fact, Ben just learned that Alan has moved in with Betty and Joy. Ben is angry with Betty, has no interest in Joy who he now thinks is not his daughter anyway, and certainly does not want to pay support to Betty while she is living with Alan. What defenses can be raised on Ben's behalf under UPA 2002? Under the law of your state, if it is different?

Problem 9-11. Assume the facts are the same as in Problem 9-10, except that Ben also tells you he has learned that Alan has just married Betty. Does this matter?

Problem 9-12. Assume the facts of Problem 9-10 except that Ben and Betty have an off and on relationship until they finally end their relationship permanently when Joy is two and a half years old, and shortly after that the welfare agency seeks support from Ben. Alan moves in with Betty when Joy is three.

Problem 9-13. Arzina and David are married with seven children. The sixth is Trudy. When Trudy is 15, Arzina tells her that her real father is not David, but Cornelius. Thereafter, Trudy visits Cornelius often, and he acknowledges her as his daughter in front of others. Trudy remains part of the Arzina-David household, however. When Trudy is 27, Cornelius dies with no marital children and is survived by two sisters, who nominate an executor for his estate. Trudy opposes their nomination and seeks appointment herself, as Cornelius' daughter. Her offer of proof includes not only Arzina's testimony, but also genetic evidence that she cannot be David's daughter. David has never been told of Arzina's claim, nor of this proceeding brought by Trudy. Should Trudy be permitted to prove her assertion? Would she be allowed to under UPA 2002?

Problem 9-14. Edward asked Robin to marry him. Robin told him that she was then pregnant by another man. Edward assured her that it was all right: "We will have this child and he will have a father and a name." He promised her that he would not deny the child was his, and they were married in June. In September the child was born. The couple named him Edward Jr., and Edward was named as the father on the birth certificate. He acted as the child's father for the early part of their marriage, but within 18 months, it fell apart. In the divorce action which followed, Edward denied paternity and sought to be relieved of any obligation of support. What result under UPA 2002? Suppose the marriage had broken up two months after the child was born? A month before?

NOTE ON ENFORCING PATERNAL SUPPORT OBLIGATIONS FOR NONMARITAL CHILDREN: SOME SPECIAL CONSIDERATIONS

The purpose of the traditional paternity action is to establish the defendant as the child's father so as to secure his support obligation. While Chapter 5's treatment of child support generally applies to both marital and nonmarital children, the establishment and collection of support for nonmarital children does raise additional problems. Collecting support from nonmarital fathers is an increasingly important social issue because nonmarital children account for an increasing share of the children on whose behalf support orders are issued.

a. Establishing paternity and collecting support. Child support collections have always been much lower for nonmarital children than for children whose parents divorce. Historically, the obvious difficulty in proving paternity provided the most obvious explanation. Today, however, that explanation will not do. Yet it remains the case that the most important reason fathers of nonmarital children do not pay support is that there is no support order. While child support orders are routinely made in divorce cases involving minor children, for nonmarital children the support obligation must be enforced on its own.

> The Census Bureau tells us that 6.6 million custodial parents in 1997 had no formal, legal agreement for support payments. When asked why, 32% said they "did not feel need to make legal" (as characterized by the Bureau's truncated descriptions of the parents' responses.) Perhaps the father was contributing informally to the child's support in amounts the mother

believed appropriate. . . . Another group said the other parent "provides what they can" (23%) or "could not afford to pay" (25%), and in fact researchers have estimated that thirty percent of the nonpaying fathers of nonmarital children are "poor" or "near-poor." Irwin Garfinkel, Sara McClanahan and Thomas Hanson, *A Patchwork Portrait of Nonresident Fathers*, in Irwin Garfinkel, Sara McLanahan, Daniel Meyer, and Judith Seltzer, eds. FATHERS UNDER FIRE: THE REVOLUTION IN CHILD SUPPORT ENFORCEMENT 31, 51 (1998). . . . [¶] Of greatest relevance, however, are the 19% who responded that they "did not want other parent to pay," and the 16% who said they "did not want to have contact with other parent." One imagines that this too is a diverse group. It must include some women who do not want contact with the father because they are afraid of him, including some who have been threatened explicitly with retaliation if a support order is sought. But it must also include others who simply prefer to live their lives free of the father's presence, and believe that they can get by well-enough without his financial assistance. Mothers receiving welfare benefits may be denied this choice by the relevant public agency, which will require their cooperation in locating the father unless persuaded the mother has "good cause" to refuse. But those not receiving welfare benefits will have more freedom of choice. They may be employed, have assistance from family members, or have established a relationship with another man who provides support.

Ellman, *Ambiguous-Father Families*, *supra*, at 69–70.

An important part of recent child support enforcement reforms have aimed directly at increasing the proportion of nonmarital children for whom a support order has been made. In 2005, the proportion of custodial never-married mothers who had either a child support agreement or award was 48% compared to 65% for divorced mothers. Meanwhile, 40% of never-married mothers reported receipt of all child support benefits for that year, compared to 53% of divorced mothers. Timothy S. Grall, *Custodial Mothers and Fathers and Their Child Support: 2005*, U.S. CENSUS BUREAU (2007), at Table 2. The 1996 federal welfare reform Act ("PRWORA," for Personal Responsibility and Work Opportunity Reconciliation Act) is focused especially on this group. It requires states, with narrow exceptions, to treat an acknowledgment of paternity signed by the mother and putative father as establishing legal paternity — as UPA 2002 does. Massachusetts pioneered this technique before 1996, obtaining such acknowledgments before the mother and child left the hospital in an astonishing 70% of all nonmarital births. Marilyn Rae Smith, *Child Support Reform in Action: New Strategies and New Frontiers in Massachusetts*, in MARRIAGE IN AMERICA: A COMMUNITARIAN PERSPECTIVE 269, 275 (Martin Whyte, editor 2000). Its success has apparently now been replicated elsewhere under the press of the federal law. (Paul Legler, President Clinton's Assistant Commissioner in the Office of Child Support Enforcement, reported "astounding success" in the initial results from the federal law. Paul Legler, *The Impact of Welfare Reform on the Child Support Enforcement System*, in CHILD SUPPORT: THE NEXT FRONTIER 46, 48 (Thomas Oldham & Marygold Melli, eds., 2000). But this program is, of course, dependent upon the father's knowledge that resistance is futile because genetic tests are available to establish paternity if needed. The 1996 welfare reform act requires states, with narrow exceptions, to authorize their child support enforcement agency to compel tests administratively if the agency receives a sworn statement of facts establishing "a reasonable possibility" of the requisite sexual contact. 42 U.S.C. § 666(a)(1)(B). While earlier reforms substantially improved the collection of child support for nonmarital children, the 1996 reforms promise much greater success.

Putative fathers may not appreciate the potentially dispositive and irreversible impact of a paternity acknowledgment, and most are probably unlikely to have legal counsel to caution them. Perhaps some will seek counsel once support enforcement has begun. As previously observed, under UPA 2002 § 308 they may usually rescind the acknowledgment if they act within 60 days, but after that the acknowledgment can only be challenged under § 307, which has more demanding requirements as well as its own time limit of two years.

b. The amount of support. Can a state apply different rules for calculating the amount of support owed by a noncustodial parent who was never married to the custodial parent, from the rules it applies to divorced parents? The answer is not entirely clear. In *Gomez v. Perez*, 409 U.S. 535 (1973), the Supreme Court held that Texas violated the Equal Protection Clause by denying nonmarital children any claim for paternal support, given that it recognized such claims on behalf of marital children. It would be a further step to conclude, however, that no distinction may be drawn in the *amount* of support for each. Nonetheless, the Court's evident concern about discriminatory treatment in the support law governing nonmarital children, not only in *Gomez* but also in other cases described in the material on statutes of limitation for paternity claims, has led most state courts to be skeptical of any such distinctions. For example, the Supreme Court of Connecticut recently held that a statute giving nonmarital children the right to support until they had completed the twelfth grade or reached the age of nineteen should be construed to be retroactive, since children of divorced parents had that same right to support. To construe the statute as only having a prospective effect would mean that Connecticut was in violation of equal protection law, according to the Court, a construction that the Court sought to avoid where the statute did not explicitly address the issue of retroactivity. *Walsh v. Jodoin*, 925 A.2d 1086 (Conn. 2007); *see also Doe v. Roe*, 504 N.E.2d 659 (Mass. App. 1987) (nonmarital child between 18 and 21 years of age was entitled to support while living at home and dependent upon a parent, because a marital child would be entitled to such support under state law).

The most important contrary authority arose in New York. In *Kathy G.J. v. Arnold D.*, 501 N.Y.S.2d 58 (App. Div. 1986), the court considered a support claim against a "world-famous entertainer" who had fathered a non-marital child with a woman on welfare. *Id.* at 65. New York (like many states) at that time had separate statutes governing child support for marital and nonmarital children, but the court found the only "potentially significant difference" between them was the former's reference to the "marital standard of living" as a relevant factor in fixing the support level. *Id.* at 63. "The reason for this distinction is an important, valid and constitutional one. Using the marital standard of living as a guidepost in determining a marital child's support decreases the possibility that such a child will have to face the additional trauma of adjusting to a new standard of living, while adjusting to all of the other changes engendered by the breakup of a marriage." *Id.* The court agreed that if a nonmarital child had lived with his parents and established a "nonmarital family," their standard of living would be relevant in setting support.

This New York court thus found that a permissible line could be drawn that placed both marital and "nonmarital" families in one group, while placing in the other nonmarital children who had never lived with both parents in a family setting. In focusing on the de facto rather than the de jure family status of the unit, the court took an approach quite similar to that of the U.S. Supreme Court in determining which nonmarital fathers have their relationship with their children protected by the Constitution. See the Notes discussing *Quilloin* in Section B[2][a], *infra. Kathy G.J.* may also reflect the fact that a generous child support award unavoidably confers benefit on all members of the custodial household, including the custodial parent to whom no legal duty may be owed by the *nonmarital* noncustodial parent. *See Edgar v. Johnson*, 731 P.2d 131 (Ariz. App. 1986), which suggests this argument.

Whatever the merits of the positions reflected in *Kathy G.J.* or *Edgar*, the continuing relevance of either case is in doubt. As the determination of child support obligations moved from a rule of judicial discretion to the application of guidelines, courts have increasingly concluded that no distinction ought to be made between marital and nonmarital children in the application of those guidelines. Whether or not the result is constitutionally compelled, courts typically find it required under state law establishing child support guidelines. *Ortiz v. Rappeport*, 820 P.2d 313, 314 (Ariz. App. 1991) ("The [child support] guidelines apply to all children whether they are born in or out of wedlock [and] . . . supersede any statements made in *Edgar*"); *Jones v. Reese*, 642 N.Y.S.2d 378 (App. Div. 1996) (rejecting *Kathy G.J.* on the basis that the child support guidelines are equally applicable to children born out of wedlock). *See also Shuba v. Reese*, 564 A.2d 1084 (Del. 1989) (rejecting nonmarital father's claim that Melson Formula's Standard of Living Adjustment should not be applied because parents had never cohabited). New York may nonetheless continue to follow *Kathy G.J.* in making child support determinations not governed by the guidelines. *See, e.g., Merithew v. Tuper*, 601 N.Y.S.2d 671 (Fam. Ct. 1993) (relying on *Kathy G.J.* in rejecting argument that nonmarital child cannot be denied an order directing father to name child as life insurance beneficiary, where such an order might be issued for marital child); *Orna S. v. Leonard G.*, 599 N.Y.S.2d 285 (App. Div.1993) (similar).

c. Time limits on bringing a support action. Are there time limits within which a paternity action against a putative father must be brought? At one time, many states had such limitations but they have been overriden by constitutional and statutory developments. First, *Gomez v. Perez*, 409 U.S. 535 (1979), held that Texas violated the Equal Protection Clause when it allowed marital but not nonmarital children to enforce a right to support. Then, *Mills v. Habluetzel*, 456 U.S. 91 (1982), and *Pickett v. Brown*, 462 U.S. 1 (1983), held respectively that both one- and four-year periods were too short to meet the state's constitutional obligation to allow "a reasonable opportunity" for a claim to be brought on the child's behalf. Finally, Justice O'Connor, writing for a unanimous Court, found unconstitutional a Pennsylvania rule barring most suits to establish the paternity of a nonmarital child brought more than six years after the child's birth. The Court relied on Equal Protection grounds, as the state allowed later actions on behalf of the children in certain situations, and allowed fathers to bring suits to establish their paternity without any statute of limitation. *Clark v. Jeter*, 486 U.S. 456 (1988).

Taken together, these opinions suggest that the Constitution requires allowing a paternity action to be brought at any time during child's minority. The constitutional question seems unlikely to present itself again, however, because after *Pickett*, Congress enacted the Child Support Enforcement Amendments of 1984, which effectively eliminate all statutes of limitation in paternity actions by requiring every state "to have procedures which permit the establishment of the paternity of any child at any time prior to such child's eighteenth birthday." 42 U.S.C.A. § 666(a)(5). The Family Support Act of 1988 further strengthened this provision by extending it to children whose earlier paternity action was dismissed because of a statute of limitations then in effect of less than 18 years. Using a carrot and stick, the Act also requires states to meet higher standards as to the percentage of out-of-wedlock children for whom paternity has been established (capping out at 50 percent). The Act also encourages states to set up a simple civil process for voluntary acknowledgment of paternity.

Long statutes of limitation are not without their complications, however. Especially troubling may be their interaction with the laws of some states that permit claims for support arrearages retroactive to the child's birth. Consider, for example, *Brad L. v. Lee D. (In re Brad L.)*, 564 N.W.2d 354 (Wisc. Ct. App. 1997). Brad Michael was born to Catherine in 1977; she was unmarried and never sought to establish paternity. She changed her mind in 1992, however, when Brad was fifteen, and she became concerned about paying for his college education. At that time, she wrote Lee asking for help. When he didn't reply she sought help from the county child support enforcement office, which obtained blood tests confirming Lee's paternity. All agreed that Lee never knew of Brad's existence before receiving Catherine's 1992 letter. Still, Lee, the court explained, was always liable for Brad's support; he just didn't know that he was. He was therefore ordered to pay retroactive support for the past fifteen years, as well as current support during the next three. During his fifteen years of ignorance, Lee had married, fathered two children, and ran a farm and logging business with his wife. Perhaps he had been setting aside college money for the two marital children he knew about; perhaps he would have made some life decisions differently during the past fifteen years if he had known he was responsible for a third child. But while expressing some sympathy for these concerns, the court concluded that Brad was nonetheless entitled to the money, for "the child cannot be held responsible . . . simply because the father was not aware of his child's birth." *Id.* at 359.

The UPA does not itself speak to child support issues such as the collection of arrearages. Consider, however, that UPA 2002 § 606 allows the *adult* child to bring a parentage action. Why would someone do that? The reason could be entirely nonfinancial, such as the desire to establish family lineage for emotional, social, or symbolic reasons. (Recall, for example, news accounts during 2003 concerning the belated public recognition of then-deceased Senator Strom Thurmond's nonmarital bi-racial daughter, by that time a middle-aged woman.) There could possibly be a claim in probate. But there could also be a claim for support arrearages akin to *Mitchell*. *Tedford v. Gregory*, 959 P.2d 540 (N.M. Ct. App. 1998), provides a perhaps bizarre example. After their 1975 divorce, Tedford paid Nina support for all four children born during their marriage, including Jeanne, the youngest, who was 14 months when the marriage ended. When Jeanne was 16, Nina told her that Gregory, not Tedford, was her biological father, a fact that neither Jeanne nor Tedford had known. When she was 20, Jeanne sought child support arrearages from Gregory. After genetic tests confirmed his biological paternity, he was ordered to pay 18 years' support. Left unresolved was whether Tedford could claim reimbursement from Jeanne for funds collected from Gregory.

Cases like *Tedford* and *Mitchell* are not unique. *See* Annotation, *Liability of Father for Retroactive Child Support on Judicial Determination of Paternity*, 87 A.L.R.5th 361 (2001). There are good arguments that the collection of arrearages in such circumstances is unlikely to serve any of the policy purposes that normally explain enforcement of the support obligation. See the discussion of these cases in Ira Mark Ellman, *Should Visitation Denial Affect the Obligation to Pay Support?*, *in* THE LAW AND ECONOMICS OF CHILD SUPPORT PAYMENTS (William Comanor ed., 2004), reprinted in 36 ARIZ. ST. L.J. 661 (2004). In fact, many states limit or disallow claims for arrearages arising before establishment of paternity. Ohio bars courts from ordering pre-decree arrearages when paternity is first established after the child's third birthday and the father "had no knowledge and had no reason to have knowledge of his alleged paternity of the child" before that initial paternity filing. OHIO REV. CODE ANN. § 3111.13(F)(3)(a)(ii) (West Supp. 2003). Maine limits arrearages to no more than six years prior to the decree. *Department of Human Services v. Bell*, 711 A.2d 1292 (Me. 1998) (applying statute). California bars pre-decree arrearages in their entirety in nearly all paternity cases. CAL. FAM. CODE § 4009 (West 1994 & Supp. 2004); *see also Marriage of Goosmann*, 31 Cal. Rptr. 2d 613, 616 (Cal. App. 1994).

d. Res judicata effect of paternity adjudications. When factual disputes over actual paternity were common, before the availability of modern scientific evidence, paternity actions might be settled for a lump sum amount. The mother might agree to compromise the potential dollar amount of the father's support obligation, in exchange for his concession of his liability. Does that judgment bind the child in a later action? In *Gerhardt v. Estate of Moore*, 441 N.W.2d 734 (Wisc. 1989), the mother had settled her paternity claim for a lump sum of $3,600 in 1971, a year after the child was born. In 1984, the child brought an action against her father's estate for past and present support. The Wisconsin Supreme Court held that since such lump sum settlements of child support claims are not allowed to bar future support actions for marital children, no such bar could apply to nonmarital children under the Equal Protection Clause. The child was therefore free to bring an action. For a similar result, see *Dones v. Thomas*, 534 N.W.2d 221 (Mich. App. 1995); *Willerton v. Basham*, 889 P.2d 823 (Nev. 1995); and *Caruthers v. Caruthers*, 37 Cal. Rptr. 2d 23 (Ct. App. 1995). Yet notice that while these cases allow reopening of the amount of support — the child can seek more than the lump sum the mother originally settled for — the fact of paternity cannot be reconsidered in light of the modern scientific evidence. The *Gerhardt* dissenters complained that it "is patently unfair and a violation of contract law principles to reopen, nineteen years later, one part of the bargain, the amount of child support, without reopening the other, the admission of paternity itself. But this is what the majority has done." *See Robert J. v. Leslie M.*, 59 Cal. Rptr. 2d 905 (App. 1997) (res judicata bars man who stipulated to judgment that he was the child's father from later challenging that judgment with blood test evidence excluding him); *Tandra S. v. Tyrone W.*, 648 A.2d 439 (Md. 1994) (similar, but reviewing authorities that allow reopening the judgment in such cases). The Michigan Supreme Court declined to follow *Gerhardt* in *Crego v. Coleman*, 615 N.W.2d 218 (Mich. 2000), sustaining the constitutionality of nonmodifiable support agreements.

Some state legislatures have responded to the application of res judicata principles in such cases with statutes expressly permitting the reopening of paternity adjudications. After the decision in *Tandra S., supra,* the legislature amended Maryland Code § 5-1038(a)(2)(i)2 to permit adjudicated fathers to present genetic evidence excluding their paternity, and in *Langston v. Riffe*, 754 A.2d 389 (Md. App. 2000), the court decided that the revisions statute should be applied retroactively, in light of the legislature's intent to "remedy the effect *Tandra S.* had on paternity decisions." 754 A.2d at 39. For similar statutory amendments, see ALA. CODE § 26-17A-1(a) (mandating reconsideration); ARK. CODE ANN. § 9-10-115 (2003) (same). Note that these provisions conflict with UPA 2002. Consider whether courts could still apply estoppel doctrines to bar at least some men from relying upon such statutory provisions to upset established paternity rulings.

e. Defense of Nonconsensual Paternity. Some paternity defendants concede biological paternity but argue that they should not incur child support obligations because their fatherhood was not consensual. They may claim the mother falsely said she was taking birth control pills at the time of intercourse, or that she had been sterilized. Such defenses have been consistently rejected, courts finding the father's failed expectations not relevant to his liability. *E.g., N.E. v. Hedges*, 391 F.3d 832 (6th Cir. 2004) (birth control pills); *Wallis v. Smith*, 22 P.3d 682 (N. Mex. Ct. App. 2001) (same); *Murphy v. Myers*, 560 N.W.2d 752 (Minn. App. 1997) (false claim of sterilization). *See also Straub v. B.M.T.*, 645 N.E.2d 597 (Ind. 1994) (refusing to enforce, as against public policy, the mother's agreement relieving defendant of prospective child support obligations, which he claimed she had signed to induce him to engage in unprotected intercourse with her); *Budnick v. Ct. of Appeal*, 805 So. 2d 1112 (Fla. Ct. App. 2002) (similar). One group of cases involves support claims brought against boys by older women convicted of their statutory rape; even here, courts have consistently refused the defense. *E.g., County of San Luis Obispo v. Nathaniel J.*, 57 Cal. Rptr. 2d 843 (App. 1996) (34-year-old woman, convicted of unlawful sexual intercourse with 15-year-old, entitled to child support judgment against him). These statutory rape cases were relied upon by the court in *S.F. v. T.M.*, 695 So. 2d 1186 (Ala. Ct. App. 1996), which found irrelevant the putative father's evidence that the mother had raped him while he was heavily intoxicated, including witnesses who testified the mother had bragged about having had intercourse with the defendant while he was passed out. It seems likely the evidence would have supported a conviction for rape of a woman analogously treated, but that did not matter given the court's conclusion that the child support claim would not be affected anyway. For an interesting and provocative feminist argument that permitting support claims in cases of nonconsensual paternity is inconsistent with feminist arguments justifying laws that give women exclusive control in deciding upon whether to abort, see Sally Sheldon, *"Sperm Bandits," Birth Control Fraud and the Battle of the Sexes*, 21 LEGAL STUD. 460 (2001).

PROBLEMS

Problem 9-15. JoAnn and Bubba were a couple during high school, but they split up when JoAnn's family moved to another state after their graduation. Neither JoAnn nor Bubba knew that JoAnn was pregnant at the time of her family's move. By the time she learned she was, she had a new home and a new boyfriend, Ben. JoAnn and Ben planned to marry, and JoAnn let him think that the child was his. But in the end that relationship did not work out either. With some help from her parents, JoAnn got by on her own after her son Butch was born, never seeking support from either Bubba or Ben. But after her father died, things became tough. JoAnn sought public assistance, and the local welfare agency asked her to name the child's father. She named Bubba. The agency brought a support enforcement action against him. By this time, Butch was 12 years old. JoAnn, who wanted to go back to school at her local community college, asked for arrearages as well, from the time of Butch's birth, believing that this lump sum would enable her to do that.

Bubba was surprised when served in this action, since he never saw JoAnn after she moved away and had no idea she had a child, much less his child. Bubba had since married and works in his father's auto repair business. He has two children with his wife, and had been trying to save money to pay for their college education. He cannot maintain his family at their current living standard and also pay the support sought without dipping into those savings. If he has to pay the arrearage claim also, his savings would be wiped out and he might have to borrow money. He concedes that he was still seeing JoAnn in June of 1992, just before she moved away, nine months prior to Butch's birth. However, even as a high school student Bubba was concerned about birth control. He had always used a condom in his relations with JoAnn. But during their last two weeks together, JoAnn told him that she had begun taking birth control pills. She explained that she wanted their time together during this last month before she moved to be special, and wanted Bubba to experience sex with her without a condom. In fact JoAnn was not taking birth control pills, but she didn't think she would get pregnant based on the timing of her menstrual cycle. She didn't tell that to Bubba, however, because she knew he would not be willing to skip the condom on that basis.

Assume UPA 2002 is in effect in your state. Does Bubba have any defense to the claim for current support, or to the support-arrearage claim? Should he?

Problem 9-16. (A) Suppose JoAnn in Problem 9-15 had married her new boyfriend, Ben, and Butch was born three months after the wedding. But Ben died when Butch was three. Would that affect the claim against Bubba?

(B) What if the marriage had instead ended in divorce when Butch was three, and Ben had been ordered to pay support for Butch? Assume that he paid until he died when Butch was five.

[2] Establishing Paternal Rights

[a] Constitutional Protection of the Unwed Father's Claim

Not so long ago, the law hardly considered the possibility that an unmarried father might seek to assert paternity rather than escape it, and procedures for such actions were often not available. This began to change with the decision in *Stanley v. Illinois*, 405 U.S. 645 (1972), the first of five Supreme Court cases over two decades that constitutionalized the law of paternal rights. Justice White, writing for the Court, explained:

> Joan Stanley lived with Peter Stanley intermittently for 18 years, during which time they had three children. When Joan Stanley died, Peter Stanley lost not only her but also his children. Under Illinois law, the children of unwed fathers become wards of the State upon the death of the mother. Accordingly, upon Joan Stanley's death, in a dependency proceeding instituted by the State of Illinois, Stanley's children were . . . placed with court-appointed guardians. Stanley appealed, claiming that he had never been shown to be an unfit parent and that since married fathers and unwed mothers could not be deprived of their children without such a showing, he had been deprived [his right to equal protection]. The Illinois Supreme Court accepted the fact that Stanley's own unfitness had not been established but rejected the equal protection claim, holding that Stanley could properly be separated from his children upon proof of the single fact that he and the dead mother had not been married. . . .
>
> . . . .
>
> The State's right — indeed, duty — to protect minor children through a judicial determination of their interests in a neglect proceeding is not challenged here. Rather, we are faced with a dependency statute that empowers state officials to circumvent neglect proceedings on the theory that an unwed father is not a "parent" whose existing relationship with his children must be considered. "Parents," says the State, "means the father and mother of a legitimate child, or the survivor of them, or the natural mother of an illegitimate child, and includes any adoptive parent," . . . but the term does not include unwed fathers.
>
> Under Illinois law, therefore, while the children of all parents can be taken from them in neglect proceedings, that is only after notice, hearing, and proof of such unfitness as a parent as amounts to neglect, an unwed father is uniquely subject to the more simplistic dependency proceeding. By use of this proceeding, the State . . . . need not prove unfitness in fact, because it is presumed at law. Thus, the unwed father's claim of parental qualification is avoided as "irrelevant."

The Court had granted certiorari "to determine whether this method of procedure by presumption could be allowed to stand in light of the fact that Illinois allows married fathers — whether divorced, widowed, or separated — and mothers — even if unwed — the benefit of the presumption that they are fit to raise their children." *Id.* at 647. There was of course no difficulty in the Court's acknowledging the legitimacy and importance of the state interest involved — protection of "the moral, emotional, mental, and physical welfare of the minor." *Id.* at 650. But as the Court noted, "the State registers no gain towards its declared goals when it separates children from the custody of fit parents. Indeed, if Stanley is a fit father, the State spites its own articulated goals when it needlessly separates him from his family." *Id.* at 652–53.

> It may be . . . that most unmarried fathers are unsuitable and neglectful parents. It may also be that Stanley is such a parent and that his children should be placed in other hands. But all unmarried fathers are not in this category; some are wholly suited to have custody of their children. . . . Given the opportunity to make his case, Stanley may have been seen to be deserving of custody of his offspring. Had this been so, the State's statutory policy would have been furthered by leaving custody in him.
>
> Procedure by presumption is always cheaper and easier than individualized determination. But when, as here, the procedure forecloses the determinative issues of competence and care, when it explicitly disdains present realities in deference to past formalities, it needlessly risks running roughshod over the important interests of both parent and child. It therefore cannot stand. . . . [¶]. . . .
>
> We have concluded that all Illinois parents are constitutionally entitled to a hearing on their fitness before their children are removed from their custody. It follows that denying such a hearing to Stanley and those like him while granting it to other Illinois parents is inescapably contrary to the Equal Protection Clause.

When *Stanley* was decided, many worried that requiring states to give all unwed fathers notice and hearing might put unreasonable burdens upon state adoption procedures. They were concerned that the rationale of *Stanley* would seem to require paternal consent, or a finding of paternal unfitness, before the unwed mother could give her child up for adoption. They feared that required involvement of the father could frustrate favorable placement for such children for no good reason, because most unwed fathers, unlike Stanley himself, were in fact uninterested in their children and were often difficult to locate. This tension between protecting the paternal rights of unwed fathers and facilitating favorable placement for their children might seem central to the analysis of these cases. In fact, however, none of the Supreme Court decisions has involved a case in which the mother sought simply to relinquish the child for adoption over the actual or potential objection of a recalcitrant or absent father. There have always been other complications.

In *Stanley* itself, the Court addressed the adoption problem only briefly, in footnote 9:

> We note in passing that the incremental cost of offering unwed fathers an opportunity for individualized hearings on fitness appears to be minimal. If unwed fathers, in the main, do not care about the disposition of their children, they will not appear to demand hearings. If they do care, under

the scheme here held invalid, Illinois would admittedly at some later time have to afford them a properly focused hearing in a custody or adoption proceeding.

Extending opportunity for hearing to unwed fathers who desire and claim competence to care for their children creates no constitutional or procedural obstacle to foreclosing those unwed fathers who are not so inclined. The Illinois law governing procedure in juvenile cases . . . provides for . . . notice by publication when personal or certified mail service cannot be had or when notice is directed to unknown respondents under the style of "All whom it may Concern." Unwed fathers who do not promptly respond cannot complain if their children are declared wards of the State. Those who do respond retain the burden of proving their fatherhood.

This footnote served as the guidepost for many states which amended their adoption procedures in light of *Stanley.*

Six years later the Court decided *Quilloin v. Walcott,* 434 U.S. 246 (1978). The mother in *Quilloin* married after giving birth — but her husband was not the child's father. She later sought to have the child adopted by her husband. By the time of the dispute, the child was 11. The father had never lived with the mother and child, and had never wanted custody. He had never been under a court order of support, and the mother did not encourage him to visit the child. He had in fact visited and supported the child, but only irregularly. He now wanted to veto the husband's adoption (because it would necessarily terminate his paternal rights), and he also sought a visitation order to insure access if the adoption were granted.

State law gave unwed fathers like Quilloin no claims to their children unless they had legitimated the child by marriage and acknowledgement, or by court order. Quilloin had done neither. Quilloin was permitted to appear at the adoption hearing, but the only issue at the hearing was whether the adoption was in the child's "best interests." The court concluded that it was, and effectively terminated Quilloin's rights by granting the adoption.

Quilloin argued that the Due Process Clause barred the termination of his parental rights without a finding of abandonment or unfitness. The state did require such a finding before terminating the rights of married fathers, as when a man's former wife, with custody, remarries, and wants her new husband to adopt her children. Quilloin also argued that this distinction between married and unmarried fathers violated the Equal Protection Clause.

The Supreme Court unanimously rejected both of Quilloin's claims. In doing so, the Court conceded that the Due Process Clause would probably require the state to show parental unfitness, before involuntarily separating a "natural family." But the Court found this principle inapplicable to Quilloin because he never "had, or sought, actual or legal custody of his child." *Id.* at 255. In other words, the non-custodial relationship between Quilloin and his child did not qualify as a constitutionally-protected "family" relationship. The Court buttressed this result by arguing that the disputed adoption merely recognized "a family unit already in existence" — the unit of mother, child and stepfather-husband. *Id.* at 254. It rejected the Equal Protection claim on similar reasoning, saying that Quilloin's interests were distinguishable from those of a married father, because "legal custody of children is . . . a central aspect of the marital relationship, and even a father whose marriage has broken apart will have borne full responsibility for the rearing of his children during the period of the marriage." *Id.*

What stands out in *Quilloin* is the Court's emphasis on the substance of the parent-child relation, rather than on the legal formalities surrounding it. The state law at issue in *Quilloin* did give the father paternal rights if he obtained a court order legitimating the child, which Quilloin had not done. The Court might have disposed of the case by holding that the state may constitutionally require the unwed father to go through such a formality to protect his paternal interest, but it did not. Nor did the Court, in explaining why a married father may be treated differently, rely solely upon the fact of marriage itself. The Court instead argued that the substance of the married father-child relationship is typically custodial and therefore adequate to justify the additional protections guaranteed by state law. In sum, Quilloin lost his case not just because he failed to legitimate his child or marry the mother, but because he also failed to act sufficiently like a concerned father (as the Court saw the facts). The implication that the extent of paternal rights turns on the nature of biological father's relationship with his child has reappeared in ensuing cases. Indeed, in *Caban v. Mohammed*, 441 U.S. 380 (1978), which followed *Quilloin* by less than a year, the court pointed to the father's much greater paternal role in distinguishing him from Mr. Quilloin.

Doctrinally, however, *Caban* dealt with an issue that *Quilloin* had left undecided. The New York law at issue in *Caban* was similar to the Georgia law under which Quilloin lost his child. While the unwed father was afforded notice of any hearing concerning the adoption of his child, the adoption could be allowed over his objection if the court found it was in the child's best interests. The unwed mother's objection to any adoption was dispositive, however, unless her parental rights were terminated, which would require findings of unfitness. For procedural reasons, the Court had declined to consider Quilloin's separate claim that this rule constituted an unconstitutional gender classification, but in *Caban*, it decided this "gender-based distinction" was not "required by any universal difference between maternal and paternal relations" and that by "discriminate[ing] against unwed fathers even when their identity is known and they have manifested a significant paternal interest in the child," the rule exemplified an "overbroad generalization" barred by the Equal Protection Clause. *Id.* at 389.

This last phrase's allusion to Mr. Caban's "significant paternal interest" was stressed by the Court in footnote 7, in which it characterized *Quilloin* as emphasizing "the importance of the appellant's failure to act as a father toward his children, noting that he 'has never exercised actual or legal custody over his child, and thus has never shouldered any significant responsibility with respect to the daily supervision, education, protection, or care of the child. . . . [I]ndeed, he does not even now seek custody of his child.' " *Id.* at 389. Mr. Caban certainly presented a far different picture. He had lived together with the mother and their two children for seven years in a de facto marital relationship, and consistently sought to maintain his relationship with the children after he and the mother separated. He apparently sought custody of them with his new wife, but lost in the New York proceeding at issue in the Supreme Court, which terminated his paternal rights in order to allow adoption of the children by the mother's new husband. Thus, while the Court decided in Caban's favor the issue it had reserved in *Quilloin*, it did so in a way which suggested that Mr. Quilloin himself might still have lost, or at least that the state could permissibly treat him differently than Mr. Caban because of the differences in their respective relationships with their children.

Finally, the Court also seemed undecided as to whether the state's interests in facilitating adoption might be more persuasive in justifying disparate treatment of unwed fathers in a statute limited to newborns, given the possibility of "special difficulties attendant upon locating and identifying unwed fathers at birth." *Id.* at 392. Presumably, the unwed father of the older child who has an established paternal relationship with the children, like Caban, can easily be found, while footnote 9 of *Stanley* made clear that no further account need be taken of the father with no relationship who cannot be found, if reasonable efforts were taken to give him notice. The unwed father of the newborn presents a possibly different problem, however, because there may have been no opportunity for him to develop a paternal relationship, and thus no basis for relying on his failure to do so to justify dispensing with his consent to adoption. In such a case, should he be accorded the constitutional rights of the de facto father, even though he is not yet one, or should he be treated like the man who didn't care, even though he has had no chance to care? This puzzle, not really addressed by *Caban* or its predecessors, also arises in the case of the older child, if the father has no relationship with the child because the mother has denied him access to it. Such a fact pattern came to the Court five years after *Caban*, in *Lehr v. Robertson*.

Justice Stevens' opinion for the Court in *Lehr*, which is reprinted below, was foreshadowed by his dissent in *Caban*. In *Caban*, he argued that the Court resolved the gender discrimination claim improperly:

> Men and women are different, and the difference is relevant to the question whether the mother may be given the exclusive right to consent to the adoption of a child born out of wedlock. Because most adoptions involve newborn infants or very young children, it is appropriate at the outset to focus on the significance of the difference in such cases.

> Both parents are equally responsible for the conception of the child out of wedlock. But from that point on through pregnancy and infancy, the differences between the male and the female have an important impact on the child's destiny. Only the mother carries the child; it is she who has the constitutional right to decide whether to bear it or not. In many cases, only the mother knows who sired the child, and it will often be within her power to withhold that fact, and even the fact of her pregnancy, from that person. If during pregnancy the mother should marry a different partner, the child will be legitimate when born, and the natural father may never even know that his "rights" have been affected. On the other hand, only if the natural mother agrees to marry the natural father during that period can the latter's actions have a positive impact on the status of the child; if he instead should marry a different partner during that time, the only effect on the child is negative, for the likelihood of legitimacy will be lessened.

These differences continue at birth and immediately thereafter. During that period, the mother and child are together. . . . The father, on the other hand, may or may not be present; his identity may be unknown to the world and may even be uncertain to the mother. These natural differences between unmarried fathers and mothers make it probable that the mother, and not the father or both parents, will have custody of the newborn infant.

In short, it is virtually inevitable that from conception through infancy the mother will constantly be faced with decisions about how best to care for the child, whereas it is much less certain that the father will be confronted with comparable problems. . . . [A]s a matter of equal protection analysis, it is perfectly obvious that at the time and immediately after a child is born out of wedlock, differences between men and women justify some differential treatment of the mother and father in the adoption process.

Most particularly, these differences justify a rule that gives the mother of the newborn infant the exclusive right to consent to its adoption. Such a rule gives the mother, in whose sole charge the infant is often placed anyway, the maximum flexibility in deciding how best to care for the child. It also gives the loving father an incentive to marry the mother, and has no adverse impact on the disinterested father. Finally, it facilitates the interests of the adoptive parents, the child, and the public at large by streamlining the often traumatic adoption process and allowing the prompt, complete, and reliable integration of the child into a satisfactory new home at as young an age as is feasible. Put most simply, it permits the maximum participation of interested natural parents without so burdening the adoption process that its attractiveness to potential adoptive parents is destroyed.

Later in his opinion, Stevens emphasized the distinction the *Caban* majority suggested it might draw between cases involving newborns and those involving older children, saying that the " 'procedure . . . in cases involving infants . . . in the custody of their mothers . . . is entirely unaffected by the Court's holding or by its reasoning." *Id.* at 416. He urged this narrow reading of the Court's opinion in part to avoid difficulties in the adoption process, which involves newborns disproportionately. Having concluded that the Court could not have intended to apply the *Caban* rule to newborns, he argued the rule was also inappropriate for older children unless a challenger can show "that its unjust applications are sufficiently numerous and serious to render it invalid." *Id.* at 410.

But Caban had "made no such showing," and Stevens doubted that cases like his were sufficiently numerous to warrant throwing out the general rule. For Stevens, the unwed father involved enough with his child to justify constitutional protection of their relationship was too unusual to provide the rationale for a constitutional principle that applies to all unwed fathers.

In sum, Justice Stevens' *Caban* dissent combines a number of arguments for a restrained view of the rights of unwed fathers: 1) according them rights will in most cases burden their children and their children's mothers, because it will frustrate the adoption process and the mother's freedom to deal with the adoption process, 2) the natural differences between men and women justify state rules which in general give unwed mothers more parental rights than unwed fathers, 3) only fathers with established relationships with their children (which necessarily means older children to whom they have had access) present a plausible case for constitutional protection, but they constitute too small a group to warrant imposing general rules protecting the interests of unwed fathers. Five years later, Justice Stevens had the opportunity to implement some of these views when he spoke for the Court in *Lehr*.

LEHR v. ROBERTSON
United States Supreme Court
463 U.S. 248 (1983)

Stevens, Justice.

The question presented is whether New York has sufficiently protected an unmarried father's inchoate relationship with a child whom he has never supported and rarely seen in the two years since her birth. The appellant, Jonathan Lehr, claims that the Due Process and Equal Protection Clauses . . . give him an absolute right to notice and an opportunity to be heard before the child may be adopted. We disagree.

Jessica M. was born out of wedlock on November 9, 1976. Her mother, Lorraine Robertson, married Richard Robertson eight months after Jessica's birth. On December 21, 1978, when Jessica was over two years old, the Robertsons filed an adoption petition in the Family Court of Ulster County, New York. The court heard their testimony and received a favorable report from the Ulster County Department of Social Services. On March 7, 1979, the court entered an order of adoption. In this proceeding, appellant contends that the adoption order is invalid because he, Jessica's putative father, was not given advance notice of the adoption proceeding. The State of New York maintains a "putative father registry." A man who files with that registry demonstrates his intent to claim paternity of a child born out of wedlock and is therefore entitled to receive notice of any proceeding to adopt that child. Before entering Jessica's adoption order, the Ulster County Family Court had the putative father registry examined. Although appellant claims to be Jessica's natural father, he had not entered his name in the registry.

In addition to the persons whose names are listed on the putative father registry, New York law requires that notice of an adoption proceeding be given to several other classes of possible fathers of children born out of wedlock — those who have been adjudicated to be the father, those who have been identified as the father on the child's birth certificate, those who live openly with the child and the child's mother and who hold themselves out to be the father, those who have been identified as the father by the mother in a sworn written statement, and those who were married to the child's mother before the child was six months old. Appellant admittedly was not a member of any of those classes. He had lived with appellee prior to Jessica's birth and visited her in the hospital when Jessica was born, but his name does not appear on Jessica's birth certificate. He did not live with appellee or Jessica after Jessica's birth, he has never provided them with any financial support, and he has never offered to marry appellee. Nevertheless, he contends that the following special circumstances gave him a constitutional right to notice and a hearing before Jessica was adopted.

On January 30, 1979, one month after the adoption proceeding was commenced in Ulster County, appellant filed a "visitation and paternity petition" in the Westchester County Family Court. In that petition, he asked for a determination of paternity, an order of support, and reasonable visitation privileges with Jessica. Notice of that proceeding was served on appellee on February 22, 1979. Four days later appellee's attorney informed the Ulster County Court that appellant had commenced a paternity proceeding in Westchester County; the Ulster County judge then entered an order staying appellant's paternity proceeding until he could rule on a motion to change the venue of that proceeding to Ulster County. On March 3, 1979, appellant received notice of the change of venue motion and, for the first time, learned that an adoption proceeding was pending in Ulster County.

On March 7, 1979, appellant's attorney telephoned the Ulster County judge to inform him that he planned to seek a stay of the adoption proceeding pending the determination of the paternity petition. In that telephone conversation, the judge advised the lawyer that he had already signed the adoption order earlier that day. According to appellant's attorney, the judge stated that he was aware of the pending paternity petition but did not believe he was required to give notice to appellant prior to the entry of the order of adoption.

Thereafter, the Family Court in Westchester County granted appellee's motion to dismiss the paternity petition, holding that the putative father's right to seek paternity ". . . must be deemed severed so long as an order of adoption exists." Appellant did not appeal from that dismissal.[6] On June 22, 1979, appellant filed a petition to vacate the order of adoption on the ground that it was obtained by fraud and in violation of his constitutional rights. The Ulster County Family Court received written and oral argument on the question whether it had "dropped the ball" by approving the adoption without giving appellant advance notice. [I]t denied the petition, explaining its decision in a thorough written opinion.

The Appellate Division of the Supreme Court affirmed. The majority held that appellant's commencement of a paternity action did not give him any right to receive notice of the adoption proceeding, that the notice provisions of the statute were constitutional, and that *Caban v. Mohammed* was not retroactive.[7]. . . . [¶] The New York Court of Appeals also affirmed by a divided vote. . . .

Appellant . . . offers two alternative grounds for holding the New York statutory scheme unconstitutional. First, he contends that a putative father's actual or potential relationship with a child born out of wedlock is an interest in liberty which may not be destroyed without due process of law; he argues therefore that he had a constitutional right to prior notice and an opportunity to be heard before he was deprived of that interest. Second, he contends that the gender-based classification in the statute, which both denied him the right to consent to Jessica's

---

[6] Without trying to intervene in the adoption proceeding, appellant had attempted to file an appeal from the adoption order. That appeal was dismissed.

[7] *Caban* was decided on April 24, 1979, about two months after the entry of the order of adoption.

adoption and accorded him fewer procedural rights than her mother, violated the Equal Protection Clause.

The Due Process Claim. . . .

[The Court here reviews *Stanley*, *Quilloin*, and *Caban*, emphasizing "the clear distinction between a mere biological relationship and an actual relationship of parental responsibility."]

The difference between the developed parent-child relationship that was implicated in *Stanley* and *Caban*, and the potential relationship involved in *Quilloin* and this case, is both clear and significant. When an unwed father demonstrates a full commitment to the responsibilities of parenthood by "com[ing] forward to participate in the rearing of his child," *Caban*, 441 U.S., at 392, his interest in personal contact with his child acquires substantial protection under the due process clause. At that point it may be said that he "act[s] as a father toward his children." *Id.*, at 389, n.7. But the mere existence of a biological link does not merit equivalent constitutional protection. The actions of judges neither create nor sever genetic bonds. "[T]he importance of the familial relationship, to the individuals involved and to the society, stems from the emotional attachments that derive from the intimacy of daily association, and from the role it plays in 'promot[ing] a way of life' through the instruction of children as well as from the fact of blood relationship." *Smith v. Organization of Foster Families for Equality and Reform*, 431 U.S. 816, 844 (1977) (quoting *Wisconsin v. Yoder*, 406 U.S. 205, 231–233 (1972)).

The significance of the biological connection is that it offers the natural father an opportunity that no other male possesses to develop a relationship with his offspring. If he grasps that opportunity and accepts some measure of responsibility for the child's future, he may enjoy the blessings of the parent-child relationship and make uniquely valuable contributions to the child's development.[18] If he fails to do so, the Federal Constitution will not automatically compel a state to listen to his opinion of where the child's best interests lie. In this case, we are not assessing the constitutional adequacy of New York's procedures for terminating a developed relationship. Appellant has never had any significant custodial, personal, or financial relationship with Jessica, and he did not seek to establish a legal tie until after she was two years old.[19] We are concerned only with whether New York has

---

[18] Of course, we need not take sides in the ongoing debate among family psychologists over the relative weight to be accorded biological ties and psychological ties, in order to recognize that a natural father who has played a substantial role in rearing his child has a greater claim to constitutional protection than a mere biological parent. New York's statutory scheme reflects these differences, guaranteeing notice to any putative father who is living openly with the child, and providing putative fathers who have never developed a relationship with the child the opportunity to receive notice simply by mailing a postcard to the putative father registry.

[19] This case happens to involve an adoption by the husband of the natural mother, but we do not believe the natural father has any greater right to object to such an adoption than to an adoption by two total strangers. If anything, the balance of equities tips the opposite way in a case such as this. In denying the putative father relief in *Quilloin*, we made an observation equally applicable here:

"Nor is this a case in which the proposed adoption would place the child with a new set of parents with

adequately protected his opportunity to form such a relationship.

The most effective protection of the putative father's opportunity to develop a relationship with his child is provided by the laws that authorize formal marriage and govern its consequences. But the availability of that protection is, of course, dependent on the will of both parents of the child. Thus, New York has adopted a special statutory scheme to protect the unmarried father's interest in assuming a responsible role in the future of his child.

After . . . *Stanley*, the New York Legislature . . . enacted a statutory adoption scheme that automatically provides notice to seven categories of putative fathers who are likely to have assumed some responsibility for the care of their natural children. If . . . qualification for notice were beyond the control of an interested putative father, it might be thought procedurally inadequate. Yet, . . . the right to receive notice was completely within appellant's control. By mailing a postcard to the putative father registry, he could have guaranteed that he would receive notice of any proceedings to adopt Jessica. The possibility that he may have failed to do so because of his ignorance of the law cannot be a sufficient reason for criticizing the law itself. The New York legislature concluded that a more open-ended notice requirement would merely complicate the adoption process, threaten the privacy interests of unwed mothers, create the risk of unnecessary controversy, and impair the desired finality of adoption decrees. Regardless of whether we would have done likewise if we were legislators instead of judges, we surely cannot characterize the state's conclusion as arbitrary.

Appellant argues, however, that . . . he was nevertheless entitled to special notice because the court and the mother knew that he had filed an affiliation proceeding in another court. . . . The Constitution does not require either a trial judge or a litigant to give special notice to nonparties who are presumptively capable of asserting and protecting their own rights. Since the New York statutes adequately protected appellant's inchoate interest in establishing a relationship with Jessica, we find no merit in the claim that his constitutional rights were offended because the family court strictly complied with the notice provisions of the statute.

The Equal Protection Claim. . . .

. . . [The New York law] guarantees to certain people the right to veto an adoption and the right to prior notice of any adoption proceeding. The mother of an illegitimate child is always within that favored class, but only certain putative fathers are included. Appellant contends that the gender-based distinction is invidious. . . . We have held that these statutes may not constitutionally be applied in that class of cases where the mother and father are in fact similarly situated with regard to their relationship with the child. In *Caban v. Mohammed*, the Court held that it violated the Equal Protection Clause to grant the mother a veto over the adoption of a four-year-old girl and a six-year-old boy, but not to grant a veto to

whom the child had never before lived. Rather, the result of the adoption in this case is to give full recognition to a family unit already in existence, a result desired by all concerned, except appellant. . . ." 434 U.S. at 255.

their father, who had admitted paternity and had participated in the rearing of the children. The Court made it clear, however, that if the father had not "come forward to participate in the rearing of his child, nothing in the Equal Protection Clause [would] preclude[] the State from withholding from him the privilege of vetoing the adoption of that child." 441 U.S., at 392.

Jessica's parents are not like the parents involved in *Caban.* Whereas appellee had a continuous custodial responsibility for Jessica, appellant never established any custodial, personal, or financial relationship with her. If one parent has an established custodial relationship with the child and the other parent has either abandoned or never established a relationship, the Equal Protection Clause does not prevent a state from according the two parents different legal rights.

The judgment of the New York Court of Appeals is *Affirmed.*

JUSTICE WHITE, with whom JUSTICE MARSHALL and JUSTICE BLACKMUN join, dissenting.

The question in this case is whether the State may, consistent with the Due Process Clause, deny notice and an opportunity to be heard in an adoption proceeding to a putative father when the State has actual notice of his existence, whereabouts, and interest in the child.

I

It is axiomatic that "[t]he fundamental requirement of due process is the opportunity to be heard 'at a meaningful time and in a meaningful manner.'" *Mathews v. Eldridge*, 424 U.S. 319, 333 (1976), quoting *Armstrong v. Manzo*, 380 U.S. 545, 552, (1965). As Jessica's biological father, Lehr either had an interest protected by the Constitution or he did not. If the entry of the adoption order in this case deprived Lehr of a constitutionally protected interest, he is entitled to notice and an opportunity to be heard before the order can be accorded finality.

According to Lehr, he and Jessica's mother met in 1971 and began living together in 1974. The couple cohabited for approximately 2 years, until Jessica's birth in 1976. Throughout the pregnancy and after the birth, Lorraine acknowledged to friends and relatives that Lehr was Jessica's father; Lorraine told Lehr that she had reported to the New York State Department of Social Services that he was the father.[2] Lehr visited Lorraine and Jessica in the hospital every day during Lorraine's confinement. According to Lehr, from the time Lorraine was discharged from the hospital until August, 1978, she concealed her whereabouts from him. During this time Lehr never ceased his efforts to locate Lorraine and Jessica and achieved sporadic success until August, 1977, after which time he was unable to locate them at all. On those occasions when he did determine Lorraine's location, he visited with her and her children to the extent she was willing to permit

---

[2] Under 18 NYCRR § 369.2(b), recipients of public assistance in the Aid to Families with Dependent Children program are required as a condition of eligibility to provide the name and address of the child's father. Lorraine apparently received public assistance after Jessica's birth; it is unclear whether she received public assistance after that regulation went into effect in 1977.

it. When Lehr, with the aid of a detective agency, located Lorraine and Jessica in August, 1978, Lorraine was already married to Mr. Robertson. Lehr asserts that at this time he offered to provide financial assistance and to set up a trust fund for Jessica, but that Lorraine refused. Lorraine threatened Lehr with arrest unless he stayed away and refused to permit him to see Jessica. Thereafter Lehr retained counsel who wrote to Lorraine in early December, 1978, requesting that she permit Lehr to visit Jessica and threatening legal action on Lehr's behalf. On December 21, 1978, perhaps as a response to Lehr's threatened legal action, appellees commenced the adoption action at issue here.

The majority posits that "[t]he intangible fibers that connect parent and child . . . are sufficiently vital to merit constitutional protection *in appropriate cases.*" . . . (emphasis added). It then purports to analyze the particular facts of this case to determine whether appellant has a constitutionally protected liberty interest. We have expressly rejected that approach. In *Board of Regents v. Roth*, 408 U.S. 564, 570–571 (1972), we stated that although "a weighing process has long been a part of any determination of the *form* of hearing required in particular situations, . . . to determine whether due process requirements apply in the first place, we must look not to the 'weight' but to the *nature* of the interest at stake . . . to see if the interest is within the Fourteenth Amendment's protection. . . ."

The "nature of the interest" at stake here is the interest that a natural parent has in his or her child, one that has long been recognized and accorded constitutional protection. We have frequently "stressed the importance of familial bonds, whether or not legitimized by marriage, and accorded them constitutional protection." *Little v. Streater*, 452 U.S. 1, 13 (1981). . . . It is beyond dispute that a formal order of adoption, no less than a formal termination proceeding, operates to permanently terminate parental rights.

Lehr's version of the "facts" paints a far different picture than that portrayed by the majority. . . . Appellant has never been afforded an opportunity to present his case. The legitimation proceeding he instituted was first stayed, and then dismissed, on appellees' motions. Nor could appellant establish his interest during the adoption proceedings, for it is the failure to provide Lehr notice and an opportunity to be heard there that is at issue here. We cannot fairly make a judgment based on the quality or substance of a relationship without a complete and developed factual record. This case requires us to assume that Lehr's allegations are true — that but for the actions of the child's mother there would have been the kind of significant relationship that the majority concedes is entitled to the full panoply of procedural due process protections.[3]

---

[3] In response to our decision in *Caban v. Mohammed*, the statute governing the persons whose consent is necessary to an adoption has been amended to include certain unwed fathers. The State has recognized that an unwed father's failure to maintain an actual relationship or to communicate with a child will not deprive him of his right to consent if he was "prevented from doing so by the person or authorized agency having lawful custody of the child." N.Y. Dom. Rel. Law § 111 (1) (d) (as amended by Chap. 575, L. 1980). Thus, even the State recognizes that before a lesser standard can be applied consistent with due process requirements, there must be a determination that there was no significant relationship and that the father was not prevented from forming such a relationship.

I reject the peculiar notion that the only significance of the biological connection between father and child is that "it offers the natural father an opportunity that no other male possesses to develop a relationship with his offspring." A "mere biological relationship" is not as unimportant in determining the nature of liberty interests as the majority suggests.

"[T]he usual understanding of 'family' implies biological relationships, and most decisions treating the relation between parent and child have stressed this element." *Smith v. Organization of Foster Families, supra*, 431 U.S., at 843. The "biological connection" is itself a relationship that creates a protected interest. Thus the "nature" of the interest is the parent-child relationship; how well-developed that relationship has become goes to its "weight," not its "nature."[4]

Whether Lehr's interest is entitled to constitutional protection does not entail a searching inquiry into the quality of the relationship but a simple determination of the fact that the relationship exists — a fact that even the majority agrees must be assumed to be established.

. . . Any analysis of the adequacy of the notice in this case must be conducted on the assumption that the interest involved here is as strong as that of *any* putative father. That is not to say that due process requires actual notice to every putative father or that adoptive parents or the State must conduct an exhaustive search of records or an intensive investigation before a final adoption order may be entered. The procedures adopted by the State, however, must at least represent a reasonable effort to determine the identity of the putative father and to give him adequate notice.

II

In this case, of course, there was no question about either the identity or the location of the putative father. . . . Lehr was entitled to due process, and the right to be heard is one of the fundamentals of that right. . . . [¶] The State concedes this much but insists that Lehr has had all the process that is due to him. It relies on § 111-a, which designates seven categories of unwed fathers to whom notice of adoption proceedings must be given, including any unwed father who has filed with the State a notice of his intent to claim paternity. The State submits that it need not give notice to anyone who has not filed his name, as he is permitted to do, and who is not otherwise within the designated categories, even if his identity and interest are known or are reasonably ascertainable by the State.

. . . .

The State asserts that any problem [with the inclusiveness of the categories] in this respect is overcome by the seventh category of putative fathers to whom notice must be given, namely, those fathers who have identified themselves in the putative father register maintained by the State. Since Lehr did not [identify himself in this

---

[4] The majority' citation of *Quilloin* and *Caban* as examples that the Constitution does not require the same procedural protections for the interests of all unwed fathers is disingenuous. Neither case involved notice and opportunity to be heard. In both, the unwed fathers were notified and participated as parties in the adoption proceedings.

manner] he was not entitled to notice and a hearing even though his identity, location and interest were known to the adoption court prior to entry of the adoption order. I have difficulty with this position. First, it represents a grudging and crabbed approach to due process. . . . It makes little sense to me to deny notice and hearing to a father who has not placed his name in the register but who has unmistakably identified himself by filing suit to establish his paternity and has notified the adoption court of his action and his interest. [It] is the sheerest formalism to deny him a hearing because he informed the State in the wrong manner.

. . . .

Because in my view the failure to provide Lehr with notice and an opportunity to be heard violated rights guaranteed him by the Due Process Clause, I need not address the question whether § 111-a violates the Equal Protection Clause by discriminating between categories of unwed fathers or by discriminating on the basis of gender.

Respectfully, I dissent.

NOTES

1. *The Due Process Claims in* Lehr.   Lehr asserted two grounds on which he asked the Court to declare New York's statutory scheme unconstitutional: due process and equal protection. The due process claim itself, however, has both procedural and substantive components. Lehr claimed that he had been deprived of "prior notice and an opportunity to be heard" on the matter of Jessica's adoption by Robertson. Thus, he argued that New York's statute violated his *procedural* due process rights. He necessarily grounded this argument, however, in the contention that the statute's operation infringed his *substantive* due process right to, or liberty interest in, a relationship with his biological daughter. Procedural due process rights are triggered by the deprivation of something in which one has a substantive liberty or property interest. *Mathews v. Eldridge*, 424 U.S. 319, 332 (1976) ("Procedural due process imposes constraints on governmental decisions which deprive individuals of 'liberty' or 'property' interests within the meaning of the Due Process Clause of the Fifth or Fourteenth Amendment.").

Does the court reject the proposition that Lehr has a constitutionally protected liberty interest at stake under these facts? On one hand, it seems not. The Court says "the New York statutes adequately protected appellant's inchoate interest in establishing a relationship with Jessica" by allowing him, through the registry, to ensure himself notice and an opportunity to be heard in any adoption proceeding. "If . . . qualification for notice were beyond the control of an interested putative father, it might be thought procedurally inadequate. Yet, . . . the right to receive notice was completely within appellant's control. By mailing a postcard to the putative father registry, he could have guaranteed that he would receive notice of any proceedings to adopt Jessica." The registry portion of New York's law is therefore important because the other methods it offers the unwed father to secure his procedural rights require the mother's cooperation; the registration alternative alone allows the unwed father to establish his claim by a *unilateral* act. Courts have read *Lehr* as requiring the state to afford the father at least one such unilateral method as the bare constitutional minimum. *See, e.g., B.G. v. H.S.*, 509 N.E.2d 214 (Ind. Ct. App. 1988) ("If Indiana law is to pass constitutional muster under *Lehr*, it must . . . provide some means by which fathers may unilaterally identify themselves as putative fathers and entitle themselves to notice of adoption proceedings."). This is an application of a more general understanding that the biological connection alone does in fact trigger some level of procedural due process protection. *See, e.g., In re Baby Boy*, 988 P.2d 1270, 1274 (Okla. 1999) (biological father had right to notice and opportunity to be heard prior to termination of his parental rights where biological mother had concealed her pregnancy from him, depriving him "of the chance to grasp his parental opportunity interest"); *Adoption of B.G.S.*, 556 So. 2d 545, 550 (La. 1990) ("We reject appellants' interpretation of the Supreme Court cases as holding that *only* an unwed father with a *developed* relationship with his child may have a constitutionally protected interest in his parenthood.").

So why then did Mr. *Lehr* himself lose? One might think of *Lehr* as applying a principle that while the state cannot deprive someone of a constitutionally protected liberty interest without procedural due process, it can require an individual to meet reasonable procedural requirements to avoid loss of these procedural rights. To take another example from the law of parent and child, a child support system may operate, as some now do, by imposing an automatic increase in the child support obligation on an individual who does not respond within a reasonable time to notice that such an increase is proposed. That failure to respond effectively waives that individual's right to a hearing on the factual assumptions offered to justify the increase. Registration is, by this way of thinking, an analogous and reasonable procedural requirement to impose on men like Lehr.

Yet at the same time, the Court makes clear that Lehr's constitutional claim is weaker than Stanley's or Caban's because he, unlike either of them, did not have an established relationship with his biological child. If he had, then the procedural claim he makes here might not have failed. Suppose, for example, the case were exactly the same except that Lehr had visited Jessica regularly, developed a warm relationship with her, and provided regular support to her during the first few years of her life, and only then lost contact with her because at this point (rather than earlier) Lorraine hid herself and the child from him. Even under these revised facts Lehr would not qualify for notice under the New York law at issue in the case, but its application to these circumstances would seem, given the Court's language, to call for a different result. In this portion of its opinion the Court deemphasizes the biological link between Lehr and Jessica, saying that biological paternity is important only because

> it offers the natural father an opportunity that no other male possesses to develop a relationship with his offspring. If he *grasps that opportunity* and accepts some measure of responsibility for the child's future, he may enjoy the blessings of the parent-child relationship and make uniquely valuable contributions to the child's development. If he fails to do so, the Federal Constitution will not automatically compel a state to listen to his opinion of where the child's best interests lie.

It is this weakened protection of Lehr's *procedural* rights to which Justice White objects in dissent. In one sense the majority's position seems almost circular because one cannot make the right to be heard depend upon factual conclusions concerning the *nature* of the relationship that can themselves be established only at a hearing. Justice White thus argues that whether "Lehr's interest is entitled to constitutional protection does not entail a searching inquiry into the quality of the relationship but a simple determination of the *fact* that the relationship exists-a fact that even the majority agrees must be assumed to be established." At least for the purpose of deciding procedural rights, the dissenters would not have a hierarchy of biological fathers arrayed according to the strength and nature of their parental relationship with the child. Of course, even Justice White's view depends upon the factual distinction between the likely biological father — the "putative father" — and the rest of the male population. Justice White would not impose on the state an unlimited obligation to find every plausible putative father and give him notice. But he concludes that the state's procedures "must at least represent a reasonable effort to determine the identity of the putative father and to give him adequate notice" — a standard which he believes New York's statute did not meet.

What if Lehr did appear at the adoption hearing — under what substantive standard could the trial court terminate his parental rights? This is a different substantive due process question, one the Court addressed in *Quilloin*. Recall the Court conceded in that case that the Due Process Clause would probably require the state to show parental unfitness, before involuntarily separating a "natural family." But the Court found this principle inapplicable to Mr. Quilloin because he never "had, or sought, actual or legal custody of his child." Mr. Lehr certainly never had custody of his child, and it is not clear he sought primary custody in any event. But his claims, which he never got to present in court, were that he sought regular access to the child so that he could maintain a parental relationship, and was prepared to provide financial support, and was prevented from doing either by the mother's having concealed herself from him. By his account, then, Mr. Lehr is what has been called a "thwarted" father — one who seeks to establish the relationship required by *Quilloin* but is prevented from doing so by the mother's resistance. The Court has never clearly established whether thwarted fathers are entitled to the same substantive constitutional protection that is accorded those who have succeeded in establishing a relationship. The language in *Quilloin* suggests they would be (since it notes that Mr. Quilloin never had "or sought" custody), but the Court has not had occasion to face that question squarely. Of course, in *Lehr* itself the Court seems unconcerned that it may have allowed the state to deny a hearing to a thwarted father, much less a favorable substantive ruling. But that is not dispositive either, given the Court's view that Lehr was offered a reasonable procedure under which he would have been granted a hearing, and lost only because he failed to take advantage of it.

For more on the problem of thwarted fathers, which has occupied the attention of a number of state supreme courts, see Note 5 below.

2. *The Equal Protection Claim in* Lehr.   Relying upon *Caban*, Lehr claimed that New York's failure to accord unwed fathers the same rights as unwed mothers to block their children's adoptions constituted a gender-based classification violating the Equal Protection Clause. There is no question the law distinguished parents on the basis of gender. The *Lehr* statute would require notice even to the mother who abandoned the child at birth to the father. Of course, such a mother would presumably lose on the merits of her objection, on the very ground of her abandonment. But the point is that the mother's rights to notice and hearing, and to have any petition to terminate her parental rights tested against the demanding standard of unfitness, do not depend on her having put her name on a registry or on having "participated in the rearing of the children," while the father's do. The Court nonetheless rejected the Equal Protection claim. It distinguished this case from *Caban* by pointing to the presence of a paternal relationship in that case and the absence of one in this case. "If one parent has an established custodial relationship with the child and the other parent has either abandoned or never established a relationship, the Equal Protection Clause does not prevent a state from according the two parents different legal rights." It is presumably necessary to the Court's treatment of this point that there was indeed no factual dispute about the absence of any relationship between Mr. Lehr and his daughter. If there were — if Lehr had claimed to have lived with the child for some time and to have provided support — it would then seem necessary to offer him the chance to prove his story. He would not be denied a hearing on the *assumption* that the facts are otherwise. By parity of reasoning, the Court clearly decided, albeit *sub silentio*, that Lehr's claim that he was a thwarted father was not relevant — that even if true, it would not entitle him to notice and a hearing.

To see the meaning of this last point, imagine two cases: the first is like *Lehr*, while in the second a father seeks to have his child adopted by his new wife, and claims no need to notify the child's mother of this potential termination of her rights because, he says, the mother never had any post-birth relationship with the child. Perhaps the mother concedes this fact, but claims that the reason is that father took the child shortly after birth and concealed himself and the child from her, thus denying her all contact with the child despite her considerable effort to find them. Or perhaps she has no such kidnapping claim and always knew where the father and child were, and never came by anyway. Either way, New York law would guarantee this mother notice and hearing before the adoption, even though she is at best in precisely the same situation as was Mr. Lehr. It is this differential treatment of mothers and fathers that the Court here necessarily says is permissible under the Equal Protection Clause. If one goes back to Justice Stevens' dissent in *Caban*, one can see how he would reach this result, because he believes that the biological differences in the roles of men and women in the procreative process lead to inevitable behavioral differences that the law of parent and child may constitutionally take into account. In *Lehr*, he speaks for the entire Court, which appears to have adopted his view.

That appearance was further confirmed in *Nguyen v. Immigration and Naturalization Service*, 533 U.S. 53 (2001), in which the issue came before the Court in the context of immigration law. Justice Kennedy wrote the opinion for the Court in *Nguyen*, joined not only by Stevens, but also Rehnquist, Scalia and Thomas. The non-marital son of a U.S. serviceman and a Vietnamese woman was denied citizenship because his American father had not complied with the law's requirement that the child be legitimated, or his citizen father's paternity adjudicated or acknowledged, before he was 18. (His father did cooperate in establishing his paternity after the son's 18th birthday, and joined in this action.) Nonmarital children of citizen mothers and noncitizen fathers could be recognized as citizens without their mother's meeting any analogous requirement to establish parentage prior to the child's 18th birthday. The Court held 5-4 that this distinction was constitutional because it reflected natural differences between mothers and fathers, differences with consequences the Court believed important to the statute's valid policy objectives of ensuring that there is an actual parental relationship between a child born overseas and the citizen parent:

> Fathers and mothers are not similarly situated with regard to the proof of biological parenthood. The imposition of a different set of rules for making that legal determination with respect to fathers and mothers is neither surprising nor troublesome from a constitutional perspective. Section 1409(a)(4)'s provision of three options . . . for a father seeking to establish paternity — legitimation, paternity oath, and court order of paternity — is designed to ensure an acceptable documentation of paternity.

Of course, this observation did not explain why the parentage of fathers, but not mothers, must be established before the child's 18th birthday to confer American citizenship. As the petitioners pointed out, modern DNA tests could establish biological paternity with confidence at any time. But biological parentage was not the government's sole interest, the Court explained:

> The second important governmental interest . . . is . . . to ensure that the child and the citizen parent have some demonstrated opportunity or potential to develop not just a relationship that is recognized, as a formal matter, by the law, but one that consists of the real, everyday ties that provide a connection between child and citizen parent and, in turn, the United States. In the case of a citizen mother and a child born overseas, the opportunity for a meaningful relationship between citizen parent and child inheres in the very event of birth, an event so often critical to our constitutional and statutory understandings of citizenship. The mother knows that the child is in being and is hers and has an initial point of contact with him. There is at least an opportunity for mother and child to develop a real, meaningful relationship.

> The same opportunity does not result from the event of birth, as a matter of biological inevitability, in the case of the unwed father. Given the 9-month interval between conception and birth, it is not always certain that a father will know that a child was conceived, nor is it always clear that even the mother will be sure of the father's identity. This fact takes on particular significance in the case of a child born overseas and out of wedlock. One concern in this context has always been with young people, men for the most part, who are on duty with the Armed Forces in foreign countries. Even if a father knows of the fact of conception, moreover, it does not follow that he will be present at the birth of the child. Thus, unlike the case of the mother, there is no assurance that the father and his biological child will ever meet. . . . [The law] takes the unremarkable step of ensuring that an opportunity [to develop a relationship], inherent in the event of birth as to the mother-child relationship, exists between father and child before

citizenship is conferred upon the latter.

The importance of the governmental interest at issue here is too profound to be satisfied merely by conducting a DNA test. The fact of paternity can be established even without the father's knowledge, not to say his presence. Paternity can be established by taking DNA samples even from a few strands of hair, years after the birth. Yet scientific proof of biological paternity does nothing, by itself, to ensure contact between father and child during the child's minority. . . .

. . . .

. . . There is nothing irrational or improper in the recognition that at the moment of birth . . . the mother's knowledge of the child and the fact of parenthood have been established in a way not guaranteed in the case of the unwed father. This is not a stereotype. See *United States v. Virginia*, 518 U.S. 515, 533 (1996). ("The heightened review standard our precedent establishes does not make sex a proscribed classification. . . . Physical differences between men and women . . . are enduring"). [¶] To fail to acknowledge even our most basic biological differences — such as the fact that a mother must be present at birth but the father need not be — risks making the guarantee of equal protection superficial, and so disserving it. . . . The distinction embodied in the statutory scheme here at issue is not marked by misconception and prejudice, nor does it show disrespect for either class. The difference between men and women in relation to the birth process is a real one, and the principle of equal protection does not forbid Congress to address the problem at hand in a manner specific to each gender.

Justice O'Connor's dissent, joined by Souter, Ginsberg, and Breyer, argued that the congressional purpose could be served without relying upon gender as a proxy for the presence of a parental relationship. She argued that the challenged law's reliance upon gender

finds support not in biological differences but instead in a stereotype — *i.e.*, "the generalization that mothers are significantly more likely than fathers . . . to develop caring relationships with their children." Such a claim relies on "the very stereotype the law condemns," "lends credibility" to the generalization, and helps to convert that "assumption" into "a self-fulfilling prophecy.". . . . "Indeed, contrary to this stereotype, Boulais has reared Nguyen, while Nguyen apparently has lacked a relationship with his mother." *Id.*

This statute, Justice O'Connor thundered, is "paradigmatic of a historic regime that left women with responsibility, and freed men from responsibility, for nonmarital children."

3. *More on Permitted Gender Distinctions in Parentage.* There are other examples of gender distinctions in legal rules about parents. Consider that the law makes important gender distinctions in the significance it attaches to the pre-birth behavior of the father as compared to the mother. No state accepts a mother's pre-birth relinquishment of her child to adoption (*see* Chapter 11, Section B[2], Note 2), and efforts to terminate maternal rights on the basis of a mothers' pre-birth behavior, such as drug abuse that harms her unborn child, are highly controversial (*see* Chapter 10, Section C[3][b]). Yet the father's uncaring or irresponsible pre-birth behavior can be relied upon in terminating his rights to his child. *See, e.g., Adoption of Michael H.*, 898 P.2d 891 (Cal. 1995), discussed below in Note 4. For an article devising an approach to paternal rights that seeks to walk the "fine line between adopting false gender-neutrality by treating men and women identically on the one hand, and reinforcing gender stereotypes on the other," see Mary Shanley, *Unwed Fathers' Rights, Adoption, and Sex Equality: Gender-Neutrality and the Perpetuation of Patriarchy*, 95 COLUM. L. REV. 60 (1995). For commentaries on the U.S. Supreme Court's decision in *Nguyen*, see Lica Tomizuka, *The Supreme Court's Blind Pursuit of Outdated Definitions of Familial Relationships in Upholding the Constitutionality of 8 U.S.C. 21 1409 in* Nguyen v. INS, 20 LAW & INEQ. 275 (2002); Erin Chlopak, Comment, *Mandatory Motherhood and Frustrated Fatherhood: The Supreme Court's Preservation of Gender Discrimination in American Citizenship Law*, 51 AM. U. L. REV. 967 (2002).

Well-established differences in the law governing paternal obligations, as compared with paternal rights, provide another example. Imagine the *Lehr* facts but the other way around. Suppose, that is, that Jessica's mother had filed a paternity action seeking Lehr's support of Jessica, rather than the adoption petition that cut off his rights. The absence of any developed father-child relationship between Lehr and Jessica would not matter. Yet if the state is not constitutionally required to provide Lehr notice of the adoption petition, how can it require him to pay child support? The Supreme Court has not ventured a view on this question. Of course, for many of these cases, there is a ready response: one can waive one's rights, but one cannot waive one's obligations. A biological father may therefore lose some or even all of his custodial and access rights to his children by failing to act responsibly with respect to them, but he cannot use his own irresponsible behavior as a defense in an action to enforce paternal obligations. Yet that response is not really satisfactory with respect to thwarted fathers, as Mr. Lehr appears to be. Indeed, even if the law did not necessarily allow the mother to defeat the *legal* claims of the biological father by concealing a child from him, a long-enough concealment period could obviously defeat his effort to establish an actual paternal relationship. In that case, should the law reduce or repeal his legal obligations as well? For a suggestion that in some of these cases it should, see Ira Mark Ellman, *Should Visitation Denial Affect the Obligation to Pay Support?*, in THE LAW AND ECONOMICS OF CHILD SUPPORT PAYMENTS (William Comanor ed., 2004), reprinted in 36 ARIZ. ST. L.J. 661 (2004).

4. *Newborns.* The rules considered by the Court in *Lehr* did not apply to nonmarital children under six months of age. For them, the applicable New York statute required the consent of the *mother only*, unless the father had: (1) lived with the mother for six consecutive months immediately preceding the child's placement; (2) openly acknowledged his paternity during this period; and (3) paid reasonable pregnancy and birth expenses in accordance with his means. These rules were challenged in *Raquel Marie X*, 76 N.Y.2d 387, 559 N.Y.S.2d 855, 559 N.E.2d 418, *cert. denied, sub nom. Robert C. v. Miguel T.*, 498 U.S. 984 (1990), *on remand*, 570 N.Y.S.2d 604 (App. Div. 1991), New York's highest court held the requirement that the father live with the mother unconstitutional, because it "cuts off their [a father's] interest by imposing as an absolute condition an obligation only tangentially related to the . . . relationship [between the father and the child] [¶] The 'living together' requirement . . . permits adoption despite the father's prompt objection, even when he wishes to form or actually has attempted to form a relationship with the infant that would satisfy the State as substantial, continuous and meaningful by any other standard." 599 N.E.2d at 426.

Raquel Marie is consistent with the principle that the father is entitled to a *unilateral* method for establishing his procedural rights in any proceeding concerning the placement of his child (*see* Note 1, *supra*). The court in *Raquel Marie* held that, in determining whether an unwed father of a newborn has a right to be heard regarding the child's adoption, he must have demonstrated "a willingness himself to assume full custody of the child not merely to block adoption by others, ... and the manifestation of [his] parental responsibility must be prompt." *Id.* at 428. Further, the court held that during the critical six-month period preceding adoptive placement, the father must demonstrate indicia of responsibility such as "public acknowledgement of paternity, payment of pregnancy and birth expenses, steps taken to establish his legal responsibility for the child, and other factors evincing a commitment to the child." *Id.* On remand, New York's mid-level appellate court concluded that the conduct of Raquel Marie's father fell below this standard, rendering his consent to the adoption unnecessary. *See also Adoption of Michael H.*, 10 Cal. 4th 1043, 1060, 898 P.2d 891 (1995) (holding unwed biological father who had failed to "promptly [come] forward and demonstrate[full] commitment to his parental responsibilities" could not block his child's adoption). Some states, however, require less of the father, accepting his willingness to share *financial* responsibility for the pregnancy, birth, and the child's subsequent needs as alone sufficient to trigger his rights; readiness to take on childrearing and custodial responsibilities are not also necessary. *See, e.g., Adoption of B.V.*, 33 P.3d 1083, 1087–88 (Utah App. 2001) (allowing unwed father of newborn to block adoption where he had agreed to be "legally responsible for" and made "reasonable efforts to contribute to medical and pregnancy related expenses"). Recall Justice Stevens' dissenting opinion in *Caban*, excerpted above in Section B[2][a], in which he argued that the majority's holding should not apply to newborns. While the matter is not free from doubt, it seems likely that nonmarital fathers of newborns have the same *procedural* due process rights to notice and hearing as do fathers of older children. Less clear is whether Justice Stevens has prevailed or would prevail in his view that the substantive standard applied to terminating the parental rights of a newborn's nonmarital father can be less demanding than the standard applied to the fathers of older children.

5. Unaware, Deceived, and Thwarted Fathers. *Lehr* tells us that a state may impose the registry requirement to the detriment of the father who failed to register through his own ignorance of the registration requirement, even if he took other steps that showed his interest in the child. But does that principle also apply to a father who does not register because he is ignorant of the fact that he has a child?

The father who does not know he has a child because he left the mother may not seem a particularly sympathetic figure. One court concluded that such a father is "on notice," given his sexual relationship with the mother, "that a pregnancy and an adoption proceeding regarding that child may occur" and therefore responsible "to protect his own rights of notice and consent." *Adoption of B.B.D.*, 984 P.2d 967, 971 (Utah 1999) (citing Utah Code § 78-30-4.13(1)). *See also, Paternity of Baby Doe*, 734 N.E.2d 281, 287 (Ind. App. 2000) (confirming adoption where mother had not notified father of her pregnancy, concluding "a child should . . . not be made to suffer when a putative father makes no inquiry regarding the possibility of a pregnancy after a sexual relationship with the mother"); *Matter of Adoption of S.J.B.*, 745 S.W.2d 606 (Ark. 1988) (same); *Baby Boy K.*, 546 N.W.2d 86 (S.D. 1996) (mother's failure to tell alleged father of pregnancy, and her misrepresentations to trial court concerning his identity, did not toll the statutory time period within which father had to assert paternity); *In re Karen A.B.*, 513 A.2d 770 (Del. 1986) (where mother refuses to disclose identity of unwed father, and states he was unaware of her pregnancy, would be unsuitable as a custodian, and might harass her if he learned of the child's existence, court may terminate his rights and permit adoption without notice to him). The mother's simple failure to tell the father of the pregnancy, or identify him to the court, is not, under this understanding, enough to allow his claim when he finds out about the child later.

This view was well-articulated by New York in *Robert O. v. Russell*, 590 N.Y.S.2d 37, 604 N.E.2d 99 (1992). The father had been engaged to the mother, and lived with her for two months, but they then separated, and the mother never told him she had become pregnant. She consented to their child's adoption by friends and certified to the court that no other person's consent was required under New York law. The certification was correct because the father did not qualify under any of the New York rules for newborns. The father received no notice of the adoption. Thirteen months after the child's birth the parents reconciled, and five months later — after they had married — the mother told the father of the child's existence. He immediately filed with New York's putative father registry and, with the mother's support, sought to vacate the adoption. The court, however, held that this father must lose because he failed to meet the test of *Raquel Marie*, described *supra* in Note 4. In reaching this result the court found the record supported the trial court's conclusion that there was no "deception or concealment" by the mother.

> Petitioner analogizes his situation to that of the father in *Baby Girl S.* [a companion case to *Raquel* in which the court found that the father preserved his paternal rights because he sought "full custodial responsibility virtually from the time he learned of [the mother's] pregnancy [and] did everything possible to manifest and establish his parental responsibility."] Petitioner correctly reads *Lehr* and *Raquel Marie* to stand for the proposition that an unwed father who has promptly done all that he could to protect his parental interest is entitled to constitutional protection. His argument falters, however, in its conclusion that he has met that standard.

> [W]e stressed in *Raquel Marie* that the period in which the biological father must manifest his parental interest is limited in duration: if the father's actions are untimely, the State can deny a right of consent. In *Raquel Marie* we limited the period in which the father must act to the six

continuing months immediately preceding the child's placement for adoption.

To conclude that petitioner acted promptly once he became aware of the child is to fundamentally misconstrue whose timetable is relevant. Promptness is measured in terms of the baby's life not by the onset of the father's awareness. The demand for prompt action by the father at the child's birth is neither arbitrary nor punitive, but instead a logical and necessary outgrowth of the State's legitimate interest in the child's need for early permanence and stability. The competing interests at stake in an adoption — and the complications presented by petitioner's position — are clearly illustrated here: nearly a year and a half after the baby went to live with the adoptive parents, and more than 10 months after they were told by the court that the baby was legally theirs, petitioner sought to rearrange those lives by initiating his present legal action.

. . . .

. . . No one, . . . let alone any State actor, prevented petitioner from finding out about Carol's pregnancy. His inaction . . . was solely attributable to him. Nothing in *Raquel Marie* or the Supreme Court decisions on which it rests suggests that the protections of constitutional due process must or should be extended to him under these circumstances.

What then of cases in which the mother has affirmatively "deceived" or "concealed"? Would New York or other states protect these men if they act promptly upon learning the truth, even if it is not soon after the child's birth? Such facts require a court to decide whether the state's "legitimate interest in the child's need for early permanence and stability" outweigh the father's paternal rights even when he is entirely blameless for his delay in asserting them.

Two well-publicized cases seem to suggest the Constitution requires protecting such fathers' paternal claims. In *Petition of Doe*, 638 N.E.2d 181 (Ill. 1994), the mother consented to adoption four days after birth but refused to reveal the father's name. In fact, she told the father the child had died. Suspicious, he investigated, learned the truth when the child was 57 days old, and immediately contested the adoption. The trial court found him unfit because he had failed to show "a reasonable degree of interest in the child in the first 30 days of life" as required by the Illinois Adoption Act. The Illinois Supreme Court eventually reversed, noting that there was no evidence to support the finding that the father had no early *interest* in the child. By the time of its decision the child was more than three years old, and had been with the adoptive parents throughout the appeals. But the court nonetheless ordered the child returned to the father, vindicating his paternal rights despite the disruption in the child's placement. In *B.G.C.*, 496 N.W.2d 239 (Iowa 1992), known popularly as the "Baby Jessica" case, the mother knowingly misrepresented her daughter's actual father in the adoption consent she gave two days after her birth. Ten days later she recanted and named the true father, who shortly thereafter intervened in the adoption case and filed his own paternity action seeking custody, and prevailed. Thus this case is in one sense not entirely on point because the father acted promptly, whether measured from the child's birth or from the time he learned of it. There was, however, considerable delay before he actually gained custody of the child, because the adoptive parents (the DeBoers) appealed, and retained custody of the child during those appeals. The appeals did not end until the little girl was two and a half, when the U.S. Supreme Court denied review of a decision of the Michigan Supreme Court, which had refused their plea to ignore the Iowa authorities and decide the matter anew. *In re Baby Girl Clausen*, 502 N.W. 2d 649 (Mich. 1993), *cert. denied sub nom, DeBoer v. DeBoer*, 509 U.S. 1301 (1993) (requiring the DeBoers' return of the child to the biological father (who by this time had married the biological mother) because the father's paternal rights "had not been terminated in accordance with Iowa law and therefore applicants were not entitled to adopt the child").

In both *Doe* and *Clausen* the considerable delay in effecting the child's final placement seemed disruptive to the child and prompted considerable, and unfavorable, attention in the popular media. Clearly, however, the father bore no responsibility for the delay in this case: it resulted instead from mistaken judicial decisions combined with the adoptive parents' recalcitrance. Perhaps significantly, however, given his views about the limited rights of nonmarital fathers with respect to newborns, Justice Stevens joined the denial of certiorari in *Clausen* with an opinion clearly rejecting the adoptive parents' claim. "Neither Iowa law, nor Michigan law, nor federal law authorizes unrelated persons to retain custody of a child whose natural parents have not been found to be unfit simply because they may be better able to provide for her future. [The DeBoers' claim that the child's interests require leaving her with them are grounded in part] on the relationship they have been able to develop with the child after it became clear that they were not entitled to adopt her." Both *Clausen* and *Doe* are also described in Chapter 11.

These cases present difficult conflicts between the child's interest in stability and the father's paternal rights. In *Clausen* and *Doe* the courts hold that the blameless father's paternal rights must prevail. But will they prevail no matter how long the delay before they are asserted? Consider what would happen if the mother in *Doe* had covered her tracks more effectively so that the father, despite his best efforts, did not learn the truth until the child was five years old? Ten years old? Perhaps at some point the result would shift. For further discussion of these issues, see Jeanette Mills, Comment, *Unwed Birthfathers and Infant Adoptions: Balancing a Father's Rights with the State's Need for a Timely Surrender Process*, 62 LA. L. REV. 615 (2002); Carol A. Gorenberg, *Fathers' Rights v. Children's Best Interests*, 31 FAM. L. Q. 169 (1997).

In an attempt to prevent unwed mothers from hiding their pregnancies from the biological fathers, and going forward with an adoption by third parties without the father's knowledge, Florida briefly required mothers who place their children for adoption to publish certain information. FLA. ST. §§ 63.087–63.088 (2002). The required information included details as to the persons with whom the mother had sexual relations that may have resulted in the child's conception. A Florida court struck down the statute as unconstitutional, in an action by four women who argued that the statute infringed on their right of privacy under the Florida Constitution. *G.P., C.M., C.H. and L.H. v. Florida*, 842 So. 2d 1059 (Fla. Ct. App. 2003). On a related note, some biological fathers have brought tort claims against the mothers or their attorneys whom they allege have intentionally concealed the child's birth or her plans to place the child for adoption. *See, e.g., Kessel v. Leavitt*, 511 S.E.2d 720

(W. Va. 1998) (affirming $7.85 million judgment for fraud against mother, her attorney, and mother's relatives; and tortious interference with custodial relationship against all except mother); *Smith v. Malouf*, 722 So. 2d 490 (Miss. 1998) (reversing trial court judgment dismissing father's claim against mother and her parents for civil conspiracy and emotional distress; father had constitutional right to be notified of or withhold his consent to the adoption of child).

6. *More On Putative Father Registries.* Undoubtedly influenced by the Court's decision in *Lehr*, the putative father registry has proven a popular method for states to ensure that their statutes will meet constitutional standards. However, state registry laws often seem designed more to defeat paternal claims than to protect them. *See, e.g., Friehe v. Schaad*, 545 N.W.2d 740 (Neb. 1996) (sustaining requirement that the putative father register within five days of the child's birth). Alabama created what appeared to be an absolute bar to adoption challenges by putative unwed fathers who do not file with its state registry within thirty days of the child's birth. *See* ALA. ST. § 26-10C-1 (2003). A divided Alabama Supreme Court held nonetheless that a man who had not filed with the registry, but had filed a legitimation and paternity action within fifteen days of child's birth, could pursue his paternity action. *S.C.W. v. C.B.*, 826 So. 2d 844 (2001). The legislature then amended the law to remove the ambiguity that the court had relied upon to avoid the registry requirement. ALA. ST. §§ 26-10C-1, 26-10A-7, 26-10C-9 (2003). For further discussion of these developments, see Shirley D. Howell, *The Putative Father Registry: Behold Now the Behemoth (A Cautionary Tale)*, 64 ALABAMA LAWYER 237 (2003). Some states that do not have registries have concluded that they do not need one because the provisions they do have satisfy *Lehr's* constitutional requirements. *See, e.g., B.G. v. H.S.*, 509 N.E.2d 214 (Ind. Ct. App. 1988) (holding that statutes entitling a man to notice if he has filed a paternity action are sufficient).

Recent decisions have suggested that the failure of unwed fathers to register with putative father registries will not always be fatal to claims of paternity. In *J.S.A. v. M.H.*, 863 N.E.2d 236 (Ill. 2007), the Illinois Supreme Court reversed a lower court's ruling that a putative father's failure to register with the state putative father registry within the time allotted by statute precluded his filing a parentage action for the child. Further, in *M.T. v. Lentz (In re N.L.B.)*, 212 S.W.3d 123 (Mo. 2007), the Missouri Supreme Court held that the biological father's failure to file with state putative father registry within the statutorily prescribed time should not, under the state's adoption statute, keep him from objecting to the adoption:

> To be sure, the clear implication from the statute is that written consent to an adoption need not be obtained by any father who is not presumed to be the father (under section 210.822) or who has not filed an action to establish his paternity or who has not filed with the putative father registry within 15 days of the child's birth. But the fact that consent from those fathers need not be obtained does not necessarily mean that they are deemed to have consented to the adoption. Nothing in the statute precludes these putative fathers from otherwise timely challenging the adoption and the termination of their parental rights incident to the adoption, and the fact that they were not required to give consent to the adoption because they failed to file an

action for paternity or to file with the putative father registry is but one factor to be considered as part of the challenge.

Id. at 127.

UNIFORM PARENTAGE ACT (2002)

Section 102. Definitions. In this [Act]:

(1) "Acknowledged father" means a man who has established a father-child relationship under [Article] 3.

(2) "Adjudicated father" means a man who has been adjudicated by a court of competent jurisdiction to be the father of a child.

(3) "Alleged father" means a man who alleges himself to be, or is alleged to be, the genetic father or a possible genetic father of a child, but whose paternity has not been determined. The term does not include:

(A) a presumed father;

(B) a man whose parental rights have been terminated or declared not to exist; or

(C) a male donor.

. . . .

(16) "Presumed father" means a man who, by operation of law under Section 204, is recognized as the father of a child until that status is rebutted or confirmed in a judicial proceeding.

Section 402. Registration for Notification.

(a) Except as otherwise provided in subsection (b) or Section 405, a man who desires to be notified of a proceeding for adoption of, or termination of parental rights regarding, a child that he may have fathered must register in the registry of paternity before the birth of the child or within 30 days after the birth.

(b) A man is not required to register if [:

(1)] a father-child relationship between the man and the child has been established under this [Act] or other law [; or

(2) the man commences a proceeding to adjudicate his paternity before the court has terminated his parental rights].

(c) A registrant shall promptly notify the registry in a record of any change in the information registered. The [agency maintaining the registry] shall incorporate all new information received into its records but need not affirmatively seek to obtain current information for incorporation in the registry.

Section 404. Termination of Parental Rights: Child under One Year of Age.

The parental rights of a man who may be the father of a child may be terminated without notice if:

(1) the child has not attained one year of age at the time of the termination of parental rights;

(2) the man did not register timely with the [agency maintaining the registry]; and

(3) the man is not exempt from registration under Section 402.

Section 405. Termination of Parental Rights: Child at Least One Year of Age.

(a) If a child has attained one year of age, notice of a proceeding for adoption of, or termination of parental rights regarding, the child must be given to every alleged father of the child, whether or not he has registered with the [agency maintaining the registry].

(b) Notice must be given in a manner prescribed for service of process in a civil action.

The way to understand a set of provisions like these is to ask which men are entitled under them to notice of an adoption or termination proceeding. The answer, where the child is under one year of age, is: a) those who have registered within 30 days of the child's birth; b) those who have already established their paternity of the child under the UPA or some other state law; and c) those who have initiated their own paternity action before the adoption or termination proceedings have become final. Where the child is at least one year old, notice must also be given to every alleged father, whether or not he has registered. One can immediately see that Mr. Lehr would have been entitled to notice under the UPA 2002 provisions because he had commenced his own paternity action prior to the entry of the adoption order. What is added by Section 405? If one understands "alleged father" to mean only a man who has been alleged to be the father in a legal proceeding of some kind, not very much, for the man who has brought a paternity action is entitled to notice even if the child is less than one. The intended meaning, however, is broader: any man whom the mother identifies as the likely or perhaps even possible father, either in response to an adoption agency's inquiries or in her adoption petition, is also an "alleged father" entitled to notice when the child is more than one year old, even if he has not put himself in the adoption registry.

Also key under these provisions is understanding when "a father-child relationship between the man and the child has been established" under the UPA, because such men are entitled to notice even if unregistered. First, a man who has signed an acknowledgment of paternity under § 302 has an established father-child relationship because, as § 305 provides, "a valid acknowledgment of paternity filed with the [agency maintaining birth records] is equivalent to an adjudication of paternity of a child and confers upon the acknowledged father all of the rights and duties of a parent." Recall that under current child support enforcement programs such acknowledgment is routinely sought from putative fathers at the time of birth, and is increasingly obtained. Second, consider a man (call him Joe) who has lived with the mother and her child since the child's birth, holding himself out as the child's father. Perhaps he did not register because he saw no need to. Joe and the mother have a falling out and they part. The mother marries another man, and seeks to have him adopt the child. Must notice be given to Joe? Joe may be in touch with the mother, and know of her new relationship, but that alone does not guarantee that he would know of the adoption petition the mother has filed. If he had lived with the mother and child for at least two years from the child's birth, he is a presumed father under § 204(a)(5). Moreover, under § 607, the paternity of such a presumed father cannot be challenged, even with genetic evidence, unless the challenger can show the presumed father never lived with the mother, never had sexual relations with her during the probable period of conception, and never held the child out as his own. Given that § 201 says that the "father-child relationship is established . . . by . . . an unrebutted presumption of the man's paternity . . . under Section 204," presumed fathers are established fathers entitled to notice. (This group includes husbands of the mother as well as men like Joe.)

By contrast, if Joe's falling out with the mother occurred when they had lived together only 20 months, he would not qualify as a presumed father. Nor would he if their period of cohabitation did not begin at the child's birth, even if it lasted more than two years. These "Joe-lights," so to speak, are not presumed fathers and are therefore not entitled to notice under §§ 402 or 405. To protect themselves, they must bring their own paternity action promptly after the falling out with the mother. If they do so prior to the entry of an adoption or termination order, they are guaranteed notice of any such action; otherwise they are not. What if the child is more than one year old at the time of the adoption proceeding, so that § 405 applies? This man will be entitled to notice even without filing such an action if the mother names him in the adoption petition as the likely father, because he is then an "alleged father" under that section. But what if she doesn't? Or more generally, what if an adoption order is entered without notice having been given to a man entitled to notice under the UPA? Adoption laws may allow the father to petition to annul the adoption. Adoption laws typically provide a time limit within which such an action must be brought. If the father acts within this limit he should be successful if he shows that he was indeed entitled to notice. Would our "Joe-light" succeed? If § 405 were read as written it would seem not, for even though the mother *should* have named him at the time of adoption she did not, and so he was not *then* an alleged father even though he should have been, and is now. Nonetheless, it seems likely that this provision will be read to vindicate such men on the ground that they would have been an alleged father at the time of adoption but for the mother's false statements to the adoption agency or in her adoption petition.

What happens under UPA 2002 with the deceived father (see Note 5 *supra*)? Consider, for example, the facts of *Petition of Doe*, described above in Note 5. Recall the mother told the father the child had died in childbirth. Suppose the father understandably does not register, and does not learn the truth until after the 30 day registration period has passed. Once again, his only recourse is to file his own paternity action, and hope he does so before entry of any adoption or termination order.

7. *The Substantive Criteria Applied in the Adoption Hearing.* If the unwed father receives notice of an adoption hearing and objects in a timely manner, what standard should be used to resolve the dispute between the father and those parties who wish the adoption to go forward? In *Quilloin*, the Supreme Court held that the state could approve an adoption over the father's objection on a best-interests standard. This standard, of course, gives strangers equal claims to the child as the nonmarital father, according him no deference. In reaching this result the Court emphasized that Mr. Quilloin did not have constitutionally-protected interests in a relationship with his child because he never "had, or sought, actual or legal custody of his child." *Quilloin*, 434 U.S. at 254. *Quilloin* involved an older child whose whereabouts the father had known, and so he had had years of opportunity in which to assert his paternal rights. In *Caban*, by contrast, the Court found that the same rule, if applied to unwed fathers, "even when their identity is known and they have manifested a significant paternal interest in the child," was a gender classification that violated the Equal Protection Clause (given that adoption could not be approved over the objection of the mother unless she was found unfit). *Caban*, 441 U.S. at 393. Left unresolved was whether the unwed father of the newborn, whose interest in the child could not yet have been acted upon, was to be treated like Mr. Quilloin or Mr. Caban. There have been a fair number of state supreme court decisions addressing this question, however.

In *Adoption of Kelsey S.*, 1 Cal. 4th 816, 823 P.2d 1216 (Cal. 1992), the California Supreme Court rejected the best interests standard. The biological father, Rickie M., brought an action to establish his paternity two days after the birth of his biological son, Kelsey. The mother, Kari S. had placed Kelsey with a prospective adoptive couple immediately after Kelsey's birth, and prevented Rickie from taking custody of the child, despite his statements to her that he wished to raise Kelsey. Rickie's action was consolidated with the adoption petition filed by that couple. The trial court terminated Rickie's rights on best interests grounds. Applying the UPA (1973), which California had adopted, the trial court construed the plain language of the statute to exclude him as a "presumed father" because he did not qualify under any of the provisions relating to marriage or attempted marriage to the mother, and he had not received the child into his home, holding the child out as his own. If he had been determined to be a presumed father, California law would have precluded the adoption unless he was found to be unfit. Thus, although Rickie was permitted to appear in the adoption action to object, the trial court allowed the adoption after applying the best interests standard.

The California Supreme Court agreed that Rickie was not a presumed father under the statute but held that federal constitutional principles required California to recognize his "reasonable and meaningful attempt to establish a relationship." 1 Cal. 4th at 837, 823 P.2d at 1228. Overriding his objection to the adoption on a best interests standard was therefore unconstitutional:

> [The California] statutory scheme violates the federal constitutional guarantees of equal protection and due process for unwed fathers *to the extent that* the statutes allow a mother unilaterally to preclude her child's biological father from becoming a presumed father and thereby allowing the state to terminate his parental rights on nothing more than a showing of the child's best interest. If an unwed father promptly comes forward and demonstrates a full commitment to his parental responsibilities — emotional, financial, and otherwise — his federal constitutional right to due process prohibits the termination of his parental relationship absent a showing of his unfitness as a parent. Similarly, when the father has come

forward to grasp his parental responsibilities, his parental rights are entitled to equal protection as those of the mother.

. . . . The father's conduct both *before and after* the child's birth must be considered. Once the father knows or reasonably should know of the pregnancy, he must promptly attempt to assume his parental responsibilities as fully as the mother will allow and his circumstances permit. In particular, the father must demonstrate "a willingness himself to assume full custody of the child — not merely to block adoption by others." [citing *Raquel Marie*]. A court should also consider the father's public acknowledgment of paternity, payment of pregnancy and birth expenses commensurate with his ability to do so, and prompt legal action to seek custody of the child.

1 Cal. 4th at 849, 823 P.2d at 1236–37 (emphasis in original).

The court emphasized further that "any finding of petitioner's unfitness must be supported by clear and convincing evidence. Absent such evidence, he shall be permitted to withhold his consent to the adoption." 1 Cal. 4th at 851, 823 P.2d at 1238. Finally, the court qualified that this standard applied solely to the question of whether the father can block the adoption. "Even if petitioner has a right to withhold his consent (and chooses to prevent the adoption), there will remain the question of the child's custody. That question is not before us, and we express no view on it." 1 Cal. 4th at 851, 823 P.2d at 1238. For a similar analysis, see *Baby Girl Eason*, 358 S.E.2d 459, 462–63 (Ga. 1987).

For more on this topic, see Katherine T. Bartlett, *Re-Expressing Parenthood*, 98 YALE L.J. 293 (1988), and Elizabeth Buchanan, *The Constitutional Rights of Unwed Fathers Before and After* Lehr v. Robertson, 45 OHIO ST. L.J. 313 (1984), on which *Eason* heavily relies.

PROBLEMS

Problem 9-17. (a) John and Mary have lived together for five years in a marriage-like relationship. They have a two-year-old child. They are now breaking up, and both want custody. State law provides that the unmarried mother should be given custody unless the father shows that maternal custody would be detrimental to the child. John loses the custody contest and challenges this standard. What result?

(b) John and Mary lived together for five years, but broke up when their child was six months old. In the year since then, John has visited the child irregularly and contributed occasionally to his support. Mary sought a formal order giving her custody and allowing her new husband to adopt the child. John opposed both. State law permits an adoption over the unmarried father's objection where it is in the best interests of the child. The law also prefers the mother for custody unless the father shows that maternal custody would be detrimental to the child. The mother prevails on both the custody and adoption petitions. John challenges the state law on appeal. What result?

(c) Suppose John and Mary had broken up during Mary's pregnancy. John has continually made efforts to see the child, but has been effectively stymied by Mary.

His offers of support have been refused. Mary now seeks to have her new husband adopt the year-old child, who has never seen John. She knows that John will object, and therefore prefers to go forward with the adoption without notifying him. State law allows unwed fathers to register their interest in the child, but John, who has never consulted counsel, is unaware of the law and has never registered. Under state law, only married fathers and registered putative fathers must be notified of adoption proceedings. The adoption is completed without notification to John. Will he prevail on a subsequent constitutional challenge to the procedure?

(d) Assume the same facts as in (c), but John learns of the hearing and appears to object. Do constitutional rules permit the adoption petition to be granted on a best-interests standard?

(e) Assume the same facts as (c), but Mary has not remarried. She seeks to place the child for adoption in the home of a couple known to her doctor. She knows that John would oppose the adoption and would seek custody himself, and therefore wants to proceed without notifying him. Is notice constitutionally compelled? Assume that John learns of the adoption hearing and appears to object and seek custody. May the court grant the adoption on a best-interest standard?

Problem 9-18.　Jonathan and Jessica have a child together while unmarried but cohabiting. They raise the child together for a year and half, but then their relationship ends. Their separation is relatively amicable. Jessica retains primary custody of the child but Jonathan see the child several times a week and often has the child overnight. When the child is four Jessica moves in with a new boyfriend, and she becomes a bit less cooperative with Jonathan. Jessica then marries the new boyfriend. Jonathan is nervous that Jessica may try to cut off his access, but he has heard that there is a putative father registry in his state. He places his name and his claim to paternity of Jessica's child on the registry. Jessica and her husband begin proceedings shortly after to have him adopt the child. No notice of the adoption petition is given to Jonathan, in reliance upon a state law which requires such notice only to men who register within 30 days of the child's birth. State law also requires notice to presumed fathers, and includes a definition of presumed paternity taken from UPA 2002. Jonathan is not a presumed father under this definition because he did not live with mother and child for at least two years from the child's birth. The adoption petition is granted in conformity with state law. Jonathan learns of this for the first time when Jessica denies him access to the child shortly after the adoption is finalized. Jonathan promptly files an action to annual the adoption alleging that it is void because he was denied constitutionally required notice of the proceedings. Evaluate his constitutional claim.

Problem 9-19.　Assume the facts of Problem 9-18 except that Jonathan and Jessica never live together because Jessica does not wish to live with Jonathan. Indeed, Jessica is uncooperative from the outset with Jonathan's attempts to see the child, and Jonathan begins to worry that she will give the child up for adoption. A friend tells him about the putative father registry and he files with it 45 days after the child's birth. Unbeknownst to him, an adoption proceeding has already been filed. The child is adopted by a couple Jessica has picked from the files of a local adoption lawyer. Jonathan challenges the adoption promptly claiming that he should have been given notice of the adoption proceeding. The failure to give him notice complied with state law because Jonathan had not registered within 30 days of the child's birth, had not filed a paternity action, and was not a presumed father under the state's UPA-inspired definition.

Problem 9-20.   Assume in Problem 9-19 Jonathan heard about the adoption proceeding even though he was not provided notice, and files an objection to the adoption. Jessica does not contest Jonathan's standing to object but argues that adoption is in the child's best interest. The court grants the adoption under that standard. State law is clear that an adoption over the objection of the mother can be allowed only if the court finds the mother has abandoned the child or is unfit. Jonathan appeals the adoption order on both substantive due process and equal protection grounds. Jonathan does not wish primary custody of the child himself, but objects to the adoption because it would cut off his access to the child completely. What result? Suppose Jonathan does seek primary custody of the child?

[b]   The Unwed Father vs. the Mother's Husband

Historically, cases in which unwed fathers claimed paternal rights with respect to a child born to a married women were rare. Does such an unwed father have a constitutional right to assert paternity that overrides state marital presumptions of paternity? Must states give such men the opportunity to rebut that presumption, or are there policies that justify, in such cases, ignoring biological paternity when assigning legal paternity? In 1989, the Supreme Court considered such a case.

MICHAEL H. v. GERALD D.
United States Supreme Court
491 U.S. 110 (1989)

JUSTICE SCALIA announced the judgment of the Court and delivered an opinion, in which THE CHIEF JUSTICE joins, and in all but note 6 of which JUSTICE O'CONNOR and JUSTICE KENNEDY join.

Under California law, a child born to a married woman living with her husband is presumed to be a child of the marriage. The presumption of legitimacy may be rebutted only by the husband or wife, and then only in limited circumstances. The instant appeal presents the claim that this presumption infringes upon the due process rights of a man who wishes to establish his paternity of a child born to the wife of another man, and the claim that it infringes upon the constitutional right of the child to maintain a relationship with her natural father.

The facts of this case are, we must hope, extraordinary. On May 9, 1976, in Las Vegas, Nevada, Carole D., an international model, and Gerald D., a top executive in a French oil company, were married. The couple established a home in Playa del Rey, California in which they resided as husband and wife when one or the other was not out of the country on business. In the summer of 1978, Carole became involved in an adulterous affair with a neighbor, Michael H. In September 1980, she conceived a child, Victoria D., who was born on May 11, 1981. Gerald was listed as father on the birth certificate and has always held Victoria out to the world as his daughter. Soon after delivery of the child, however, Carole informed Michael that she believed he might be the father.

In the first three years of her life, Victoria remained always with Carole, but found herself within a variety of quasi-family units. In October 1981, Gerald moved to New York City to pursue his business interests, but Carole chose to remain in California. The end of that month, Carole and Michael had blood tests of themselves and Victoria, which showed a 98.07% probability that Michael was Victoria's father. In January 1982, Carole visited Michael in St. Thomas, where his primary business interests were based. There Michael held Victoria out as his child. In March, however, Carole left Michael and returned to California, where she took up residence with yet another man, Scott K. Later that spring, and again in the summer, Carole and Victoria spent time with Gerald in New York City, as well as on vacation in Europe. In the fall, they returned to Scott in California.

In November 1982, rebuffed in his attempts to visit Victoria, Michael filed a filiation action in California Superior Court to establish his paternity and right to visitation. In March 1983, the court appointed an attorney and guardian ad litem to represent Victoria's interests. Victoria then filed a cross-complaint asserting that if she had more than one psychological or *de facto* father, she was entitled to maintain her filial relationship, with all of the attendant rights, duties, and obligations, with both. In May 1983, Carole filed a motion for summary judgment. During this period, from March through July of 1983, Carole was again living with Gerald in New York. In August, however, she returned to California, became involved once again with Michael, and instructed her attorneys to remove the summary judgment motion from the calendar.

For the ensuing eight months, when Michael was not in St. Thomas he lived with Carole and Victoria in Carole's apartment in Los Angeles, and held Victoria out as his daughter. In April 1984, Carole and Michael signed a stipulation that Michael was Victoria's natural father. Carole left Michael the next month, however, and instructed her attorneys not to file the stipulation. In June 1984, Carole reconciled with Gerald and joined him in New York, where they now live with Victoria and two other children since born into the marriage.

In May 1984, Michael and Victoria, through her guardian ad litem, sought visitation rights for Michael *pendente lite*. To assist in determining whether visitation would be in Victoria's best interests, the Superior Court appointed a psychologist to evaluate Victoria, Gerald, Michael, and Carole. The psychologist recommended that Carole retain sole custody, but that Michael be allowed continued contact with Victoria pursuant to a restricted visitation schedule. The court concurred and ordered that Michael be provided with limited visitation privileges *pendente lite*.

On October 19, 1984, Gerald, who had intervened in the action, moved for summary judgment on the ground that under Cal. Evid. Code § 621 there were no triable issues of fact as to Victoria's paternity. This law provides that "the issue of a wife cohabiting with her husband, who is not impotent or sterile, is conclusively presumed to be a child of the marriage." Cal. Evid. Code Ann. § 621(a) (Supp. 1989). The presumption may be rebutted by blood tests, but only if a motion for such tests is made, within two years from the date of the child's birth, either by the husband or, if the natural father has filed an affidavit acknowledging paternity, by the wife. §§ 621(c) and (d).

On January 28, 1985, having found that affidavits submitted by Carole and Gerald sufficed to demonstrate that the two were cohabiting at conception and birth and that . . . Gerald was neither sterile nor impotent, the Superior Court granted Gerald's motion for summary judgment, rejecting Michael's and Victoria's challenges to the constitutionality of § 621. The court also denied their motions for continued visitation pending the appeal. . . . [because] such visitation would "violat[e] the intention of the Legislature by impugning the integrity of the family unit."

On appeal, Michael asserted, *inter alia*, that the Superior Court's application of § 621 had violated his procedural and substantive due process rights. Victoria also raised a due process challenge to the statute, seeking to preserve her *de facto* relationship with Michael as well as with Gerald. She contended, in addition, that as § 621 allows the husband and, at least to a limited extent, the mother, but not the child, to rebut the presumption of legitimacy, it violates the child's right to equal protection. Finally, she asserted a right to continued visitation with Michael. . . . [T]he California Court of Appeal affirmed the judgment . . . and upheld the constitutionality of the statute. . . . It interpreted that judgment, moreover, as having denied permanent visitation rights . . . regarding that as the implication of the Superior Court's reliance upon § 621 and [other California authorities]. . . .

The . . . California Supreme Court denied discretionary review. . . . Before us, Michael and Victoria both raise equal protection and due process challenges. We do not reach Michael's equal protection claim, however, as it was neither raised nor passed upon below. (citations omitted)

II

The California statute that is the subject of this litigation is, in substance, more than a century old. . . . In their present form, the substantive provisions of the statute are as follows:

"§ 621. Child of the marriage; notice of motion for blood tests

"(a) Except as provided in subdivision (b), the issue of wife cohabiting with her husband, who is not impotent or sterile, is conclusively presumed to be a child of the marriage.

"(b) Notwithstanding the provisions of subdivision (a), if the court finds that the conclusions of all the experts, as disclosed by the evidence based upon blood tests performed pursuant to Chapter 2 (commencing with Section 890) of Division 7 are that the husband is not the father of the child, the question of paternity of the husband shall be resolved accordingly.

"(c) The notice of motion for blood tests under subdivision (b) may be raised by the husband not later than two years from the child's date of birth.

"(d) The notice of motion for blood tests under subdivision (b) may be raised by the mother of the child not later than two years from the child's date of birth if the child's biological father has filed an affidavit with the court acknowledging paternity of the child.

III

We address first the claims of Michael. . . . California law, like nature itself, makes no provision for dual fatherhood. Michael was seeking to be declared the father of Victoria. The immediate benefit he evidently sought to obtain from the status was visitation rights. See Cal. Civ. Code Ann. § 4601 (West 1983) (parent has statutory right to visitation "unless it is shown that such visitation would be detrimental to the best interests of the child"). But if Michael were successful in being declared the father, other rights would follow — most importantly, the right to be considered as the parent who should have custody. . . . All parental rights, including visitation, were automatically denied by denying Michael status as the father. . . . [since] California law denies visitation, against the wishes of the mother, to a putative father who has been prevented by § 621 from establishing his paternity.

Michael . . . [f]irst . . . asserts that requirements of procedural due process prevent the State from terminating his liberty interest in his relationship with his child without affording him an opportunity to demonstrate his paternity in an evidentiary hearing. We believe this claim derives from a fundamental misconception of the nature of the California statute. While § 621 is phrased in terms of a presumption, that rule of evidence is the implementation of a substantive rule of law. California declares it to be, except in limited circumstances, *irrelevant* for paternity purposes whether a child conceived during and born into an existing marriage was begotten by someone other than the husband and had a prior relationship with him. As the Court of Appeal phrased it:

> " 'The conclusive presumption is actually a substantive rule of law based upon a determination by the Legislature as a matter of overriding social policy, that given a certain relationship between the husband and wife, the husband is to be held responsible for the child, and that the integrity of the family unit should not be impugned.' " 191 Cal. App. 3d, at 1005, 236 Cal. Rptr., at 816, quoting *Vincent B. v. Joan R.*, 126 Cal. App. 3d, at 623, 179 Cal. Rptr. at 10.

Of course the conclusive presumption not only expresses the State's substantive policy but also furthers it, excluding inquiries into the child's paternity that would be destructive of family integrity and privacy.

This Court has struck down . . . certain "irrebuttable presumptions." Those holdings did not, however, rest upon procedural due process. . . . We therefore reject Michael's procedural due process challenge and proceed to his substantive claim.

Michael contends as a matter of substantive due process that because he has established a parental relationship with Victoria, protection of Gerald's and Carole's marital union is an insufficient state interest to support termination of that relationship. This argument is, of course, predicated on the assertion that Michael has a constitutionally protected liberty interest in his relationship with Victoria.

[T]he term "liberty" in the Due Process Clause extends beyond freedom from physical restraint. . . . [T]o limit and guide interpretation of the Clause, we have insisted not merely that the interest denominated as a "liberty" be "fundamental" (a concept that, in isolation, is hard to objectify), but also that it be an interest traditionally protected by our society.

. . . Michael reads the landmark case of *Stanley* and the subsequent cases of *Quilloin, Caban,* and *Lehr,* as establishing that a liberty interest is created by biological fatherhood plus an established parental relationship — factors that exist in the present case as well. We think that distorts the rationale of those cases. As we view them, they rest not upon such isolated factors but upon the historic respect — indeed, sanctity would not be too strong a term — traditionally accorded to the relationships that develop within the unitary family. In *Stanley,* for example, we forbade the destruction of such a family when, upon the death of the mother, the state had sought to remove children from the custody of a father who had lived with and supported them and their mother for 18 years. As Justice Powell stated for the plurality in *Moore v. East Cleveland:* "Our decisions establish that the Constitution protects the sanctity of the family precisely because the institution of the family is deeply rooted in this Nation's history and tradition."

Thus, the legal issue in the present case reduces to whether the relationship between persons in the situation of Michael and Victoria has been treated as a protected family unit under the historic practices of our society, or [otherwise] has been accorded special protection. We think, . . . quite to the contrary, our traditions have protected the marital family (Gerald, Carole, and the child they acknowledge to be theirs) against the sort of claim Michael asserts.

The presumption of legitimacy was a fundamental principle of the common law. Traditionally, that presumption could be rebutted only by proof that a husband was incapable of procreation or had had no access to his wife during the relevant period. . . . BLACKSTONE'S COMMENTARIES 456 (Chitty ed. 1826). . . . The primary policy rationale underlying . . . the common law's severe restrictions on rebuttal of the presumption appears to have been an aversion to declaring children illegitimate, thereby depriving them of rights of inheritance and succession, and likely making them wards of the state. A secondary policy concern was the interest in promoting the "peace and tranquility of States and families," . . . a goal that is obviously impaired by facilitating suits against husband and wife asserting that their children are illegitimate. . . . [¶] [E]ven in modern times — when, as we have noted, the rigid protection of the marital family has in other respects been relaxed — the ability of a person in Michael's position to claim paternity has not been generally acknowledged. . . .

. . . What Michael asserts here is a right to have himself declared the natural father *and thereby to obtain parental prerogatives.* What he must establish, therefore, is not that our society has traditionally allowed a natural father in his circumstances to establish paternity, but that it has traditionally accorded such a father parental rights, or at least has not traditionally denied them. . . . What counts is whether the States . . . award substantive parental rights to the natural father of a child conceived within and born into an extant marital union that wishes to embrace the child. We are not aware of a single case, old or new, that has done so. This is not the stuff of which fundamental rights qualifying as liberty interests are made.[6]

In *Lehr* . . . we observed that "[t]he significance of the biological connection is that it offers the natural father an opportunity that no other male possesses to develop a relationship with his offspring," and we assumed that the Constitution might require some protection of that opportunity. Where, however, the child is born into an extant marital family, the natural father's unique opportunity conflicts with the similarly unique opportunity of the husband of the marriage; and it is not unconstitutional for the State to give categorical preference to the latter. . . . In accord with our traditions, a limit is . . . imposed by the circumstance that the mother is, at the time of the child's conception and birth, married to and cohabiting with another man, both of whom wish to raise the child as the offspring of their union. It is a question of legislative policy and not constitutional law whether California will allow the presumed parenthood of a couple desiring to retain a child conceived within and born into their marriage to be rebutted.

We do not accept Justice BRENNAN's criticism that this result "squashes" the liberty that consists of "the freedom not to conform." [T]hat reflects the erroneous view that there is only one side to this controversy. . . . [B]ut to provide protection to an adulterous natural father is to *deny* protection to a marital father, and vice versa. If Michael has a "freedom not to conform" (whatever that means), Gerald must equivalently have a "freedom to conform." . . . Our disposition does not choose between these two "freedoms," but leaves that to the people of California. Justice BRENNAN's approach chooses one of them as the constitutional imperative, on no apparent basis except that the unconventional is to be preferred.

---

[6] Justice Brennan criticizes our methodology in using historical traditions specifically relating to the rights of an adulterous natural father, rather than inquiring more generally "whether parenthood is an interest that historically has received our attention and protection." There seems to us no basis for the contention that this methodology is "nove[l]," For example, in Bowers v. Hardwick, 478 U.S. 186 (1986), we noted that at the time the Fourteenth Amendment was ratified all but 5 of the 37 States had criminal sodomy laws, that all 50 of the States had such laws prior to 1961, and that 24 States and the District of Columbia continued to have them; and we concluded from that record, regarding that very specific aspect of sexual conduct, that "to claim that a right to engage in such conduct is 'deeply rooted in this Nation's history and tradition' or 'implicit in the concept of ordered liberty' is, at best, facetious." Id., at 194. In Roe v. Wade, 410 U.S. 113 (1973), we spent about a fifth of our opinion negating the proposition that there was a longstanding tradition of laws proscribing abortion. Id., at 129–141.

We do not understand why, having rejected our focus upon the societal tradition regarding the natural father's rights vis-a-vis a child whose mother is married to another man, Justice Brennan would choose to focus instead upon "parenthood." Why should the relevant category not be even more general — perhaps "family relationships"; or "personal relationships"; or even "emotional attachments in general"? Though the dissent has no basis for the level of generality it would select, we do: We refer to the most specific level at which a relevant tradition protecting, or denying protection to, the asserted right can be identified. If, for example, there were no societal tradition, either way, regarding the rights of the natural father of a child adulterously conceived, we would have to consult, and (if possible) reason from, the traditions regarding natural fathers in general. But there is such a more specific tradition, and it unqualifiedly denies protection to such a parent. . . .

IV

We have never had occasion to decide whether a child has a liberty interest symmetrical with that of her parent, in maintaining her filial relationship. We need not do so here because, even assuming that such a right exists, Victoria's claim must fail. Victoria's due process challenge is, if anything, weaker than Michael's. Her basic claim is not that California has erred in preventing her from establishing that Michael, not Gerald, should stand as her legal father. Rather, she claims a due process right to maintain filial relationships with both Michael and Gerald. This assertion merits little discussion, for, whatever the merits of the guardian ad litem's belief that such an arrangement can be of great psychological benefit to a child, the claim that a State must recognize multiple fatherhood has no support in the history or traditions of this country. Moreover, even if we were to construe Victoria's argument as forwarding the lesser proposition that, whatever her status vis-à-vis Gerald, she has a liberty interest in maintaining a filial relationship with her natural father, Michael, we find that, at best, her claim is the obverse of Michael's and fails for the same reasons.

Victoria claims in addition that her equal protection rights have been violated because, unlike her mother and presumed father, she had no opportunity to rebut the presumption of her legitimacy. We find this argument wholly without merit. We reject, at the outset, Victoria's suggestion that her equal protection challenge must be assessed under a standard of strict scrutiny because, in denying her the right to maintain a filial relationship with Michael, the State is discriminating against her on the basis of her illegitimacy. Illegitimacy is a legal construct, not a natural trait. Under California law, Victoria is not illegitimate, and she is treated in the same manner as all other legitimate children: she is entitled to maintain a filial relationship with her legal parents.

We apply, therefore, the ordinary "rational relationship" test to Victoria's equal protection challenge. The primary rationale underlying § 621's limitation on those who may rebut the presumption of legitimacy is a concern that allowing persons other than the husband or wife to do so may undermine the integrity of the marital union. When the husband or wife contests the legitimacy of their child, the stability of the marriage has already been shaken. In contrast, allowing a claim of illegitimacy to be pressed by the child — or, more accurately, by a court-appointed guardian ad litem — may well disrupt an otherwise peaceful union. Since it pursues a legitimate end by rational means, California's decision to treat Victoria differently from her parents is not a denial of equal protection.

The judgment of the California Court of Appeal is *Affirmed.*

JUSTICE O'CONNOR, with whom JUSTICE KENNEDY joins, concurring in part.

I concur in all but footnote 6 of JUSTICE SCALIA's opinion. This footnote sketches a mode of historical analysis to be used when identifying liberty interests protected by the Due Process Clause of the Fourteenth Amendment that may be somewhat inconsistent with our past decisions in this area. See *Griswold* and *Eisenstadt.* On occasion the Court has characterized relevant traditions protecting asserted rights at levels of generality that might not be "the most specific level" available. See

Loving v. Virginia, 388 U.S. 1, 12 (1967); *Turner v. Safley*, 482 U.S. 78, 94 (1987). I would not foreclose the unanticipated by the prior imposition of a single mode of historical analysis.

JUSTICE STEVENS, concurring in the judgment.

. . . .

. . . Michael was given a fair opportunity to show that he is Victoria's natural father, that he had developed a relationship with her, and that her interests would be served by granting him visitation rights. On the other hand, the record also shows that after its rather shaky start, the marriage between Carole and Gerald developed a stability that now provides Victoria with a loving and harmonious family home. In the circumstances of this case, I find nothing fundamentally unfair about the exercise of a judge's discretion that, in the end, allows the mother to decide whether her child's best interest would be served by allowing the natural father visitation privileges. Because I am convinced that the trial judge had the authority under state law both to hear Michael's plea for visitation rights and to grant him such rights if Victoria's best interests so warranted, I am satisfied that the California statutory scheme is consistent with the Due Process Clause of the Fourteenth Amendment.

I therefore concur in the Court's judgment of affirmance.

JUSTICE BRENNAN, with whom JUSTICE MARSHALL and JUSTICE BLACKMUN join, dissenting.

In a case that has yielded so many opinions as has this one, it is fruitful to begin by emphasizing the common ground shared by a majority of this Court. Five Members of the Court refuse to foreclose "the possibility that a natural father might ever have a constitutionally protected interest in his relationship with a child whose mother was married to and cohabiting with another man at the time of the child's conception and birth." (STEVENS, J., concurring in judgment.) Five Justices agree that the flaw inhering in a conclusive presumption that terminates a constitutionally protected interest without any hearing whatsoever is a *procedural* one. See *infra*, (WHITE, J., dissenting); *ante*, (STEVENS, J., concurring in judgment). Four Members of the Court agree that Michael H. has a liberty interest in his relationship with Victoria, see *infra*, (WHITE, J., dissenting), and one assumes for purposes of this case that he does, see *ante*, (STEVENS, J., concurring in judgment).

In contrast, only two Members of the Court fully endorse Justice SCALIA's view of the proper method of analyzing questions arising under the Due Process Clause. See *ante*, (O' CONNOR, J., concurring in part). Nevertheless, because the plurality opinion's exclusively historical analysis portends a significant and unfortunate departure from our prior cases and from sound constitutional decisionmaking, I devote a substantial portion of my discussion to it. [Most of this discussion is omitted. Eds.]

. . . .

Today's plurality . . . does not ask whether parenthood is an interest that historically has received our attention and protection; the answer to that question is too clear for dispute. Instead, the plurality asks whether the specific variety of parenthood under consideration — a natural father's relationship with a child whose mother is married to another man — has enjoyed such protection.

If we had looked to tradition with such specificity in past cases, many a decision would have reached a different result. Surely the use of contraceptives by unmarried couples, *Eisenstadt*, or even by married couples, *Griswold*; the freedom from corporal punishment in schools, *Ingraham v. Wright*, 430 U.S. 651 (1977); the freedom from an arbitrary transfer from a prison to a psychiatric institution, *Vitek v. Jones*, 445 U.S. 480 (1980); and even the right to raise one's natural but illegitimate children, *Stanley*, were not "interest[s] traditionally protected by our society," at the time of their consideration by this Court. If we had asked, therefore, in *Eisenstadt, Griswold, Ingraham, Vitek*, or *Stanley* itself whether the specific interest under consideration had been traditionally protected, the answer would have been a resounding "no." That we did not ask this question in those cases highlights the novelty of the interpretive method that the plurality opinion employs today.

. . . We are not an assimilative, homogeneous society, but a facilitative, pluralistic one, in which we must be willing to abide someone else's unfamiliar or even repellant practice because the same tolerant impulse protects our own idiosyncrasies. Even if we can agree, therefore, that "family" and "parenthood" are part of the good life, it is absurd to assume that we can agree on the content of those terms and destructive to pretend that we do. In a community such as ours, "liberty" must include the freedom not to conform. The plurality today squashes this freedom by requiring specific approval from history before protecting anything in the name of liberty.

II

. . . Where the interest under consideration is a parent-child relationship, we need not ask, over and over again, whether that interest is one that society traditionally protects. . . . The better approach . . . is to ask whether the specific parent-child relationship under consideration is close enough to the interests that we already have protected to be deemed an aspect of "liberty" as well. [T]herefore, the question is not what "level of generality" should be used to describe the relationship between Michael and Victoria, but whether the relationship under consideration is sufficiently substantial to qualify as a liberty interest under our prior cases.

On four prior occasions, we have considered whether unwed fathers have a constitutionally protected interest in their relationships with their children. [Citing *Stanley, Quilloin, Caban*, and *Lehr*.] . . . [T]hese cases have produced a unifying theme: although an unwed father's biological link to his child does not, in and of itself, guarantee him a constitutional stake in his relationship with that child, such a link combined with a substantial parent-child relationship will do so . . . This commitment is why Mr. Stanley and Mr. Caban won; why Mr. Quilloin and Mr. Lehr lost; and why Michael H. should prevail today. Michael H. is almost certainly

Victoria D.'s natural father, has lived with her as her father, has contributed to her support, and has from the beginning sought to strengthen and maintain his relationship with her.

Claiming that the intent of these cases was to protect the "unitary family," the plurality waves *Stanley, Quilloin, Caban,* and *Lehr* aside. In evaluating the plurality's dismissal of these precedents, it is essential to identify its conception of the "unitary family." . . . Though it pays lip service to the idea that marriage is not the crucial fact in denying constitutional protection to the relationship between Michael and Victoria, the plurality cannot mean what it says.

The evidence is undisputed that Michael, Victoria, and Carole did live together as a family; that is, they shared the same household, Victoria called Michael "Daddy," Michael contributed to Victoria's support, and he is eager to continue his relationship with her. Yet they are not, in the plurality's view, a "unitary family," whereas Gerald, Carole, and Victoria [are]. The only difference between these two sets of relationships, however, is the fact of marriage. . . . However, the very premise of *Stanley* and the cases following it is that the marriage is not decisive in answering the question whether the Constitution protects the parental relationship under consideration. . . . It is important to remember, moreover, that in *Quilloin, Caban,* and *Lehr,* the putative father's demands would have disrupted a "unitary family" as the plurality defines it; in each case, the husband of the child's mother sought to adopt the child over the objections of the natural father. Significantly, our decisions in those cases in no way relied on the need to protect the marital family. Hence the plurality's claim that *Stanley, Quilloin, Caban,* and *Lehr* were about the "unitary family," as that family is defined by today's plurality, is surprising indeed.

The plurality's focus on the "unitary family" . . . conflates the question whether a liberty interest exists with the question what procedures may be used to terminate or curtail it. It is no coincidence that we never before have looked at the relationship that the unwed father seeks to disrupt, rather than the one he seeks to preserve, in determining whether he has a liberty interest in his relationship with his child. To do otherwise is to allow the State's interest in terminating the relationship to play a role in defining the "liberty" that is protected by the Constitution. According to our established framework under the Due Process Clause, however, we first ask whether the person claiming constitutional protection has an interest that the Constitution recognizes; if we find that she does, we next consider the State's interest in limiting the extent of the procedures that will attend the deprivation of that interest. By stressing the need to preserve the "unitary family" and by focusing not just on the relationship between Michael and Victoria but on their "situation" as well, today's plurality opinion takes both of these steps at once.

The plurality's premature consideration of California's interest is evident from its careful limitation of its holding to those cases in which "the mother is, at the time of the child's conception and birth, married to and cohabiting with another man, *both of whom wish to raise the child as the offspring of their union.*" (emphasis added). . . . The highlighted language suggests that if Carole or Gerald alone wished to raise Victoria, or if both were dead and the State wished to raise her, Michael and Victoria might be found to have a liberty interest in their relationship with each other. But that would be to say that whether Michael and Victoria have a liberty interest varies with the State's interest in recognizing that interest, for it is the State's interest in protecting the marital family — and not Michael and Victoria's interest in their relationship with each other — that varies with the status of Carole and Gerald's relationship. . . .

III

[T]he effect of § 621 is to terminate the relationship between Michael and Victoria before affording any hearing whatsoever on the issue whether Michael is Victoria's father. This refusal to hold a hearing is properly analyzed under our procedural due process cases. . . . California's interest, minute in comparison with a father's interest in his relationship with his child, cannot justify its refusal to hear Michael out. . . .

A

We must first understand the nature of the challenged statute: it is a law that stubbornly insists that Gerald is Victoria's father, in the face of evidence showing a 98 percent probability that her father is Michael. What Michael wants is a chance to show that he is Victoria's father. By depriving him of this opportunity, California prevents Michael from taking advantage of the best-interest standard embodied in § 4601 of California's Civil Code, which directs that *parents* be given visitation rights unless "the visitation would be detrimental to the best interests of the child."

As interpreted by the California courts, however, § 621 not only deprives Michael of the benefits of the best-interest standard; it also deprives him of any chance of maintaining his relationship with the child he claims to be his own. When, as a result of § 621, a putative father may not establish his paternity, neither may he obtain discretionary visitation rights as a "nonparent" under § 4601. See *Vincent B.* Justice STEVENS' assertion to the contrary, *ante*, is mere wishful thinking. . . . The California appellate court's decision will not support Justice STEVENS' reading, as the court's reasoning applies to all putative fathers whom § 621 has denied the opportunity to show paternity. . . . Likewise, in the case before us, the court's finding that "the existence of two 'fathers' as male authority figures will confuse the child and be counterproductive to her best interests," is not an evaluation of the relationship between Michael and Victoria, but a restatement of the policies underlying § 621 itself. . . .

Section 621 as construed by the California courts thus cuts off the relationship between Michael and Victoria — a liberty interest protected by the Due Process Clause — without affording the least bit of process. This case, in other words, involves a conclusive presumption that is used to terminate a constitutionally protected interest — the kind of rule that our preoccupation with procedural fairness has caused us to condemn. . . .

. . . .

. . . Today's plurality [is] disturbing [in] its failure to recognize that the defect from which conclusive presumptions suffer is a procedural one: the State has declared a certain fact relevant, indeed controlling, yet has denied a particular class of litigants a hearing to establish that fact. This is precisely the kind of flaw that procedural due process is designed to correct.

. . . .

B

The question before us, therefore, is whether California has an interest so powerful that it justifies granting Michael no hearing before terminating his parental rights. . . .

. . . .

The purported state interests here . . . stem primarily from the State's antagonism to Michael and Victoria's constitutionally protected interest in their relationship with each other and not from any desire to streamline procedures. Gerald D. explains that § 621 promotes marriage, maintains the relationship between the child and presumed father, and protects the integrity and privacy of the matrimonial family. It is not, however, § 621, but the best-interest principle, that protects a stable marital relationship and maintains the relationship between the child and presumed father. . . .

. . . .

[T]o say that the State must provide Michael with a hearing to prove his paternity is not to express any opinion of the ultimate state of affairs between Michael and Victoria and Carole and Gerald. In order to change the current situation among these people, Michael first must convince a court that he is Victoria's father, and even if he is able to do this, he will be denied visitation rights if that would be in Victoria's best interests. See § 4601. . . .

The plurality's misunderstanding of Michael's claim leads to its assertion that "to provide protection to an adulterous natural father is to deny protection to a marital father." To allow Michael a chance to prove his paternity, however, in no way guarantees that Gerald's relationship with Victoria will be changed.

IV

The atmosphere surrounding today's decision is one of make-believe. Beginning with the suggestion that the situation confronting us here does not repeat itself every day in every corner of the country, moving on to the claim that it is tradition alone that supplies the details of the liberty that the Constitution protects, and passing finally to the notion that the Court always has recognized a cramped vision of "the family," today's decision lets stand California's pronouncement that Michael — whom blood tests show to a 98 percent probability to be Victoria's father — is not Victoria's father. When and if the Court awakes to reality, it will find a world very different from the one it expects.

Justice White, with whom Justice Brennan joins, dissenting.

California law, as the plurality describes it, tells us that, except in limited circumstances, California declares it to be "*irrelevant* for paternity purposes whether a child conceived during and born into a lawful marriage was begotten by someone other than the husband," (emphasis in original). This I do not accept, for the fact that Michael H. is the biological father of Victoria is to me highly relevant to whether he has rights, as a father or otherwise, with respect to the child. Because I believe that Michael H. has a liberty interest that cannot be denied without due process of the law, I must dissent.

I

Like Justices Brennan, Marshall, Blackmun and Stevens, I do not agree with the plurality opinion's conclusion that a natural father can never "have a constitutionally protected interest in his relationship with a child whose mother was married to and cohabiting with another man at the time of the child's conception and birth." (Stevens, J., concurring in judgment). Prior cases here have recognized the liberty interest of a father in his relationship with his child. In none of these cases did we indicate that the fathers' rights were dependent on the marital status of the mother or biological father. The basic principle enunciated in the Court's unwed father cases is that an unwed father who has demonstrated a sufficient commitment to his paternity by way of personal, financial, or custodial responsibilities has a protected liberty interest in a relationship with his child.

We have not before faced the question of a biological father's relationship with his child when the child was born while the mother was married to another man. . . .

. . . .

In the case now before us, Michael H. is not a father unwilling to assume his responsibilities as a parent. To the contrary, he is a father who has asserted his interests in raising and providing for his child since the very time of the child's birth. [Justice White here repeats the facts establishing the paternal relationship.] *Lehr* was predicated on the absence of a substantial relationship between the man and the child. . . . "When an unwed father demonstrates a full commitment to the responsibilities of parenthood . . . his interest in personal contact with his child acquires substantial protection under the Due Process Clause." *Lehr*, at 261. The facts in this case satisfy the *Lehr* criteria, which focused on the relationship between father and child, not on the relationship between father and mother. Under *Lehr* a "mere biological relationship" is not enough, but in light of Carole's vicissitudes, what more could Michael H. have done? . . . Michael H . . . has a liberty interest entitled to protection under the Due Process Clause. . . .

II

California plainly denies Michael this protection, by refusing him the opportunity to rebut the State's presumption that the mother's husband is the father of the child. . . . The grant of summary judgment against Michael H. was based on the conclusive presumption of § 621. The Court gives its blessing to § 621 by relying on the State's asserted interests in the integrity of the family (defined as Carole and Gerald) and in protecting Victoria from the stigma of illegitimacy and by balancing away Michael's interest in establishing that he is the father of the child.

The interest in protecting a child from the social stigma of illegitimacy lacks any real connection to the facts of a case where a father is seeking to establish, rather than repudiate, paternity. The "stigma of illegitimacy" argument harks back to ancient common law. . . . It may be true that a child conceived in an extra-marital relationship would be considered a "bastard" in the literal sense of the word, but whatever stigma remains in today's society is far less compelling in the context of a child of a married mother, especially when there is a father asserting paternity and seeking a relationship with his child. It is hardly rare in this world of divorce and remarriage for a child to live with the "father" to whom her mother is married, and still have a relationship with her biological father.

The State's professed interest in the preservation of the existing marital unit is a more significant concern. To be sure, the intrusion of an outsider asserting that he is the father of a child whom the husband believes to be his own would be disruptive to say the least. On the facts of this case, however, Gerald was well aware of the liaison between Carole and Michael. The conclusive presumption of evidentiary rule § 621 virtually eliminates the putative father's chances of succeeding in his effort to establish paternity, but it by no means prevents him from asserting the claim. It may serve as a deterrent to such claims but does not eliminate the threat. Further, the argument that the conclusive presumption preserved the sanctity of the marital unit had more sway in a time when the husband was similarly prevented from challenging paternity.

. . . .

As the Court has said: "The significance of the biological connection is that it offers the natural father an opportunity that no other male possesses to develop a relationship with his offspring. . . ." *Lehr*, 463 U.S., at 262. It is as if this passage was addressed to Michael H. Yet the plurality today recants. Michael H. eagerly grasped the opportunity to have a relationship with his daughter (he lived with her; he declared her to be his child; he provided financial support for her) and still, with today's opinion, his opportunity has vanished. He has been rendered a stranger to his child.

. . . I respectfully dissent.

NOTES

1. *Framing the Issue.* Justice Scalia asks whether "the relationship between persons in the situation of Michael and Victoria has been treated as a protected family unit under the historic practices of our society." This question arises, of course, from Justice Scalia's distinctive methodological approach to fundamental rights. He would fix the boundaries of the liberty protected by the Due Process Clause by asking whether the asserted interest is one that has historically or traditionally been protected by our society. This historical approach is not only rejected by the dissent but also by concurring Justices O'Connor and Kennedy. Justice Brennan's dissent also criticizes the *level of specificity* at which the

plurality characterizes the right in question. That is, Justice Scalia describes the issue as whether a man who had an adulterous affair with a married woman has a constitutionally-protected relationship with the resulting child. Compare that to Justice Brennan's and Justice White's broader characterization of the right at issue.

Justice Scalia concludes that Michael H. has no liberty interest in his relationship with Victoria in part because Victoria's mother and her mother's husband, who were married at her conception and birth, jointly wish to raise the child as their own. Justice Brennan argues that this way of framing the issue is inconsistent with preexisting case law because the Court has never made the father's liberty interest turn on an examination of "the relationship the unwed father seeks to disrupt, rather than . . . the one he seeks to preserve." And as Justice White argues, even if *Lehr* is read to recognize a liberty interest in the biological father only when he has a demonstrated paternal relationship with the child, Michael H. surely qualifies.

On the other hand, recognizing that Michael H. has a liberty interest in maintaining a relationship with his daughter does not end the inquiry, for California explains its rule as necessary to its interest in protecting the integrity of the marital family. The question, then, is whether the latter interest justifies the burden on Michael H.'s paternal claim. Justice Brennan points out that California permits the rebuttal of the "unrebuttable" presumption by biological evidence of the husband's nonpaternity, and suggests that these exceptions undercut California's stated policy rationale. Consider whether his opinion is persuasive on this point. The statutory exceptions only allowed paternity claims brought by the husband or wife, and only if brought within two years of the child's birth. Perhaps it is plausible for California to assume that the integrity of the family will not be much aided by denying standing to the *spouse* who seeks to challenge the child's status: the integrity of that family has already been undone, if that is a spouse's inclination, whether or not the law chooses to recognize it. And by limiting even spouses to acting within two years after birth, California evinces a policy of protecting the settled expectations of the other family members as to the husband's paternal rights and obligations, even if one spouse seeks to upset them. The spousal exception thus concedes nothing about the validity of the basic policy of California law: a husband and wife united in their desire to treat a child born *during* their marriage as a child *of* their marriage cannot be challenged by a third party. On this policy California has been steadfast, denying standing even to the child who sought to prove that her father was someone other than her mother's husband. *Estate of Cornelious*, 674 P.2d 245 (Cal. 1984).

Justice White, who would recognize a liberty interest in any biological father, also recognizes that the state's interest in the preservation of the existing marital unit "is a . . . significant concern," but would set it aside, at least on the facts of this case, since "Gerald was well aware of the liaison between Carole and Michael." Is this view persuasive? Or does it seem likely that allowing Michael to assert paternal claims of visitation, or perhaps even custody, would be "disruptive," to use Justice White's term, to this family unit as well? If so, then the real question presented by the case is whether California may constitutionally protect the marital unit from such disruption by denying Michael an opportunity to assert his paternity of Victoria. Or, to put it another way, may California declare that the biological paternity of the child born to a woman living with her husband is not relevant to the question of the child's *legal* paternity, when the mother and her husband decide to treat the child as their joint offspring? If so, then Michael H. can be denied a hearing in which to introduce his blood test evidence, because that evidence will not be relevant.

Justice Brennan frames the question as whether California can employ an irrebuttable presumption, suggesting the defect in its law is procedural rather than substantive. After that doctrine was first employed by the court in *Vlandis v. Kline*, 412 U.S. 441 (1973), it was heavily attacked by most commentators as a "confusion" of equal protection and procedural due process, Note, *The Irrebuttable Presumption Doctrine in the Supreme Court*, 87 HARV. L. REV. 1534 (1974), and as a "fundamentally misconceived" analysis, "logically equivalent to an equal protection argument" but "standardless" and "illusory" in application. Note, *Irrebuttable Presumptions: An Illusory Analysis*, 27 STAN. L. REV. 449 (1975). It was thought to have been killed by the Court just two years after its birth, in *Weinberger v. Salfi*, 422 U.S. 749, 770 (1975) (the doctrine is "a virtual engine of destruction for countless legislative judgments which have heretofore been thought wholly consistent with [the Constitution]."). Nonetheless, it "may survive for use where there are independent reasons for heightened scrutiny, as when 'fundamental interests' are protected." Gerald Gunther, *The Brief and Troubled Life of Irrebuttable Presumption Analysis*, in GUNTHER, INDIVIDUAL RIGHTS IN CONSTITUTIONAL LAW 519, 520 n.4 (1985).

California did not adopt the irrebuttable presumption as an administrative convenience. For example, it did *not* argue that the presumption is justified because most third parties asserting paternity of a married woman's child are not, in fact, the biological father, and that therefore it will save time and effort to assume their nonpaternity. It instead offered a policy of protecting the integrity of the marital family. The question then is the substantive one of whether this policy is a constitutionally adequate counterweight to the father's interest. The real issue, in other words, is not procedural but substantive: whether California has identified an interest that entitles it to treat a particular fact — biological paternity — as irrelevant to the question of legal paternity

2. ***The Husband's Versus the Putative Father's Interests.*** How important to the result in *Michael H.* was the paternity claim of the mother's husband? In evaluating the California policies at issue in this case, consider that he, like Michael H., also had a paternal relationship with Victoria. Is his paternal relationship with Victoria also entitled to constitutional protection? Although the dissenters chastise the majority for their "pinched" and traditional view of family, perhaps the dissenters have a pinched view as well, if they believe that biological paternity should swamp all other factors that one might consider in identifying the legal father. One can view this case as a contest between two men with equally plausible claims to being treated as the legal father, one on the basis of biological paternity, the other on the basis of his marital relationship with the mother, both of whom assumed responsibility for the child in the past and seek it now. Nothing in *Michael H.* bars a state from choosing to honor the biological father's claim. Or, like California, it could choose instead to protect the integrity of the traditional family unit — wife, husband, child — from all third parties who seek to disrupt it, even at the cost of denying the biological father any familial claims on his child. Or perhaps it could adopt a third approach, recognizing both father-child relationships. Plausible policy arguments might be offered for any of these approaches. Our experience with changing social conditions and our understanding of children's interests might all bear on the choice. But the question before the Court was of course not which policy is correct, but whether the Constitution compels the choice among them. For discussion of these issues, see Katharine Bartlett, *Rethinking Parenthood as an Exclusive Status: The Need for Legal Alternatives When the Premise of the Nuclear Family Has Failed*, 70 VA. L. REV. 879 (1984); Melanie B. Jacobs, *My Two Dads: Disaggregating Biological and Social Paternity*, 38 ARIZ. ST. L.J. 809, 851–52 (2006); Nancy E. Dowd, *Multiple Parents/Multiple Fathers*, 9 J. L. & FAM. STUD. 231 (2007); Laura Nicole Althouse, *Three's Company? How American Law Can Recognize a Third Social Parent in Same-Sex Headed Families*, 19 HASTINGS WOMEN'S L.J. 171 (2008); Susan Frelich Appleton, *Parents by the Numbers*, 37 HOFSTRA L. REV. 11 (2008).

   3. *Victoria's Due Process Claim.* In the plurality opinion, the Court notes that it "never had occasion to decide whether a child has a liberty interest symmetrical with that of her parent, in maintaining her filial relationship." But it deals with the issue by effectively reasoning back from its conclusion that California may constitutionally treat Gerald as the father to the further conclusion that therefore, even if Victoria had such reciprocal rights, they would protect her relationship with Gerald, not with Michael, and certainly not both men simultaneously because the law has not traditionally recognized "multiple fatherhood." For further discussion of this issue, see Justice Stevens' dissent in *Troxel v. Granville*, reprinted in Chapter 6, Section F[1], and also Emily Buss, *Children's Associational Rights? Why Less is More*, 11 WM. & MARY BILL RTS. J. 1101 (2003) (arguing that because children rely on adults to exercise rights on their behalf, affording children associational rights such as preservation of relationships with non-parents will not necessarily foster the children's independent interests).

   4. Michael H. *Epilogue.* Born in 1980, Victoria was nine years old when the Supreme Court decided the case of *Michael H. v. Gerald D.* After the litigation, Michael H. was not permitted further contact with Victoria. They did have a meeting, on Father's Day of 2001. Michael H. reported that it had been fifteen years since he had seen her last. According to Michael, the intervening years made it difficult for the two to re-establish a parent-child relationship, and he has not seen his daughter since that date. He said, however, that Victoria did develop a strong father-daughter bond with Gerald, which has endured. (Telephone conversation with Michael H., March 6, 2003.)

   5. *Revised California Law on Marital Presumption.* Following *Michael H.*, California amended its code to allow a "presumed father" who seeks to establish his own paternity to challenge the husband's paternity with a blood test before the child is two years old. California Family Code § 7541. Recall that the former statute described in *Michael H.* allowed only husbands or wives to challenge the husband's paternity in that time period. California also adopted a definition of "presumed father" taken from § 4 of UPA 1973. Because Michael H. is a "presumed father" under § 4(a)(4) of UPA 1973, he would have fallen within the class of persons who could have challenged Gerald's paternity within two years of birth. Yet his paternity claim was not lodged until Victoria's third year of life, and would therefore have been time barred. Could the challenge nonetheless be mounted with the blood test results that Gerald and the mother had apparently obtained previously on their own? Perhaps not, because § 7540(a) requires blood tests performed "pursuant to Chapter 2" of the Family Code, and it is not clear these would qualify. *See Rodney F. v. Karen M.*, 61 Cal. App. 4th 233, 71 Cal. Rptr. 2d 399 (1998) (blood tests erroneously ordered by court which indicated that husband was not the biological father of wife's child cannot be used to overcome the conclusive presumption of husband's paternity). What about a man who wants to be a presumed father within the meaning of UPA 1973 but is not because the mother does not choose to live with him? He loses because he is not a man who can challenge her husband's paternity under the statute. *See Dawn D. v. Superior Court*, 17 Cal. 4th 932, 72 Cal. Rptr. 2d 871, 952 P.2d 1139 (1998) (putative father of child whose mother moved back with her husband during the pregnancy does not have standing to obtain blood tests to challenge husband's paternity, even though the action is brought four months before the child's birth, because he is not a presumed father).

6. ***Extending California's Conclusive Presumption to Nonmarital Fathers.*** Should the paternal status of an unmarried "father" who has taken the child into his home, and who is thus a presumed father under UPA 1973 (which still applies in California), be subject to rebuttal by biological evidence? The California Supreme Court, in a significant decision, held not, at least in some circumstances, in *Nicholas H.*, 120 Cal. Rptr. 2d 146 (Cal. 2002). Nicholas was born to Kimberly in 1995, who was then living with Thomas, with whom she continued to live till the end of 1997, and for a nine-month period in 1999. The pregnancy had begun before Kimberly and Thomas had begun to live together, and the biological father could not be found. Kimberly and Thomas agreed to raise Nicholas as their child despite these facts. Kimberly herself was often homeless, usually unemployed, and used drugs. Thomas had some troubles of his own but did much better, and was "the constant" in Nicholas' life. After Thomas and Kimberly split up, Nicholas lived with Thomas pursuant to a January 2000 custody order, obtained after Kimberly had denied him access. The child preferred living with Thomas, according to the family services counselor's report to the court, because Kimberly "is mean to him, she hits and slaps him, and she smokes weed." Nonetheless, the intermediate appellate court held that while Nicholas was a presumed father under California's UPA, (having taken the child into his own home and held himself out as his natural father), that the presumption had been rebutted by his admission that he was not the child's biological father. The California Supreme Court reversed, relying on statutory language allowing for the rebuttal of a presumption of paternity in an "appropriate case." This was not an appropriate case, the court decided, emphasizing both the child's interests and the fact that "no other man claims parental rights."

What then if the biological father had appeared, or reappeared, in a case like this, and sought himself to rebut the presumption? In *Kiana A.*, 113 Cal. Rptr. 2d 669 (App. 2001), the child had a paternal relationship with Kevin, who was living with the mother when the child was born, although another man, Mario, appeared as the father on her birth certificate. Mario married the mother two years after the child's birth. Both men were presumed fathers under the UPA 1973 provisions that govern in California, Mario because of the birth certificate and marriage, Kevin because he had treated the child as his, lived with her, and taken responsibility for her (not perfectly, but much more clearly so than Mario). The child herself thought of Kevin, not Mario, as her father. The appeals court held Kevin the father, denied Mario's request for genetic testing as untimely and in any event inappropriate as it could disrupt an established parental relationship. *See also Steven W. v. Matthew S.*, 39 Cal. Rptr. 2d 535 (App. 1995). Note that *Kiana* actually applied the social paternity policy underlying California's strong marital presumption to *defeat* the paternity claim of the mother's husband in favor of the child's social father. It could do this because California's conclusive marital presumption did not arise under the *Kiana* facts, as at the time of the child's birth the mother was not yet married to, or cohabiting with, the husband, even though he was named on the child's birth certificate and was, apparently, the child's biological father. In sum, the court has clearly indicated its receptiveness to rules protecting as parental the relationship between children and their social (but not biological) fathers, sometimes even over an objecting biological father. This sense is further strengthened by the *Nicholas M.* court's favorable references to the appeals court's statutory analysis in *Raphael P.*, 118 Cal. Rptr. 2d 610 (App. 2002), which held that biological proof of nonpaternity did not necessarily preclude a man from presumed father status under UPA 1973, and indeed, decided that courts should not order genetic tests of presumed fathers. As the court explained, "where there is a man claiming presumed father status and no indication of another man asserting paternity, we question whether paternity can rightly be considered 'a relevant fact' [as required under the provision authorizing a court to order genetic testing]". *Raphel P.*, as quoted in *Nicholas H.*, 120 Cal. Rptr. 2d at 156.

7. *State Constitutional Claims.* A handful of state supreme courts have accepted state constitutional claims analogous to the federal one rejected in *Michael H.* The Texas Supreme Court struck down Texas' irrebuttable marital presumption in *J.W.T.*, 872 S.W.2d 189 (Tex. 1994), as violating the due process clause of its state constitution. However, the decision is limited, for it applies only where the biological father "assert[s] his interest near the time of the child's birth" and "both (1) acknowledges responsibility for child support or other care and maintenance, and (2) makes serious and continuous efforts to establish a relationship with the child." Thus, for example, the irrebuttable presumption contained in the UPA 2002 would appear to be constitutional under Texas law. A sharply divided Iowa court rendered a more sweeping decision in *Callender v. Skiles*, 591 N.W.2d 182 (Iowa 1999), in which the mother became pregnant by another man during a brief period of separation from her husband. It struck down on state constitutional grounds an Iowa law barring the biological father from asserting his paternity of the child, with whom he had never lived and did not know. The court denied that the state could constitutionally protect the child's interests in maintaining the integrity of his existing family, responding that the family's integrity "suffered at the time of the extramarital affair" — even though the husband and wife were reconciled and united in their opposition to the biological father's claims. The Iowa court may have had second thoughts: after visitation was ordered on remand, the court conceded that the arrangement had caused the parties "anguish." 623 N.W.2d 852, 855 (Iowa 2001). A year later, it affirmed a judgment in a different case in which the trial court dismissed the putative father's paternity action because it was not brought until seven years after the child's birth, during which time the mother and her husband (to whom she was married at the time of conception) raised the child as their own. *Huisman v. Miedema*, 644 N.W.2d 321 (Iowa 2002).

8. *Alternative State Rules on Third Party Challenges to the Marital Presumption.*   California's bar on challenges to the marital presumption by third parties is distinctive only because of its mechanical nature — the automatic exclusion of all third-party challenges other than from men who qualify as presumed fathers, and the automatic exclusion of all challenges after the child's second birthday. Many other states have rules that are more fact sensitive. In many, for example, the court's evaluation of the child's best interests plays an important role, although it emerges in various doctrinal forms. Some permit third-party paternity claims to children born of a married woman only where the challenger can show that the action will serve the child's interest. *See, e.g.*, *R.N. v. J.M.*, 61 S.W. 3d 149 (Ark. 2001) (putative father has standing to bring paternity action, but trial court has discretion to determine whether DNA testing is in the child's best interests); *Weidenbacher v. Duclos*, 661 A.2d 988 (Conn. 1995) (in determining whether putative father has standing to challenge marital presumption, court must find that his interests and the best interests of the child outweigh those of the marital family unit); *Ross v. Ross*, 783 P.2d 331 (Kan. 1990) (trial court abused its discretion in ordering paternity tests prior to determining whether doing so was in the best interests of children); *McDaniels v. Carlson*, 738 P.2d 254 (Wash. 1987) (trial court must make individualized determination as to whether paternity action is in child's best interests).

Massachusetts allows challenges to the husband's paternity only by men who have an established parental relationship with the child, in a judicially created version of the California rule allowing challenges only by "presumed fathers." The Massachusetts rule does not limit challenges to two years after the child's birth, however. *See, e.g.*, *Paternity of Cheryl*, 746 N.E.2d 488 (2001); *C.C. v. A.B.*, 550 N.E.2d 365, 372 (1990) ("the existence of a substantial parent-child relationship" is the "controlling factor in determining whether" an unwed father can challenge the marital presumption). *See also Allen v. Stone*, 474 S.E.2d 554, 566 (W.Va. 1996) (impact of putative father's paternity action on existing parent-child relationships "may be considered in both the standing and paternity determinations"). Some of these courts relied, in part, on the analysis urged in Note, *Rebutting the Marital Presumption: A Developed Relationship Test*, 88 COLUM. L. REV. 369 (1988). In an interesting twist on the typical constitutional argument, an Ohio court held in 1993 that the statute permitting an alleged biological father to challenge the mother's husband's paternity was unconstitutional in that it violated the marital family's fundamental rights to privacy. *Merkel v. Doe*, 635 N.E.2d 70 (Common Pleas 1993). The court held that the statute was not narrowly tailored, in that it granted *any* man standing to allege biological fatherhood of a married woman's child. Ultimately, however, the court's reasoning emphasized preservation of the father-child bond, indicating that the mother's husband is "the only father [the child] has ever known. [The mother's husband] is, at the very least, John Jr.'s psychological father. . . ." *Id.* at 75.

Increasingly, in response to the virtual certainty of biological paternity determinations, and a growing sense that legal paternity should reflect the biological "truth," some courts and legislatures have been "relaxing" the marital presumption. For example, Tennessee repealed its conclusive marital presumption, and now allows any man to file suit to prove paternity, without reference to the mother's marital status. See TENN. CODE ANN. § 36-2-304 (2003); *Cihlar v. Crawford*, 39 S.W.2d 172, 184 (Tenn. App. 2000). The statute does require paternity actions concerning a child born into a marriage to be brought within two years of the child's birth, however. TENN. CODE ANN. § 36-2-305 (2003). *See also Witso v. Overby*, 627 N.W.2d 63 (Minn. 2001) (interpreting Minnesota's statutes as permitting putative father seeking custody and visitation to litigate paternity of a child born into an intact marriage, despite unified objections from the mother and her husband); *K.S. v. R.S.*, 669 N.E.2d 399 (Ind. 1996) (permitting married woman's neighbor with whom she had had sexual relationship to bring paternity action based on statute, silent on marital status of mother, allowing "a man alleging that he is the child's biological father" to file a paternity action); *Doran v. Doran*, 820 A.2d 1279 (Pa. Super. 2003) (holding that former husband was not estopped from denying paternity of child that he held out as his own for ten years because he relied on his former wife's "fraudulent" assertions that the child was his).

Of course, if UPA 2002 becomes widely adopted, this variability will be reduced. UPA 2002 effectively adopts California's two-year limit on challenges to the husband's paternity, combined with recognition of equitable grounds for refusing even timely genetic challenges to the marital presumption.

9. *Multiple Parents — More Than Two.* One state, Louisiana, applies a concept of dual paternity. While any child born to a married woman is considered the "legitimate" child of the mother's husband, the mother can still establish the paternity and support obligation of the child's biological father. "Recognition of actual paternity, through filiation actions brought by the . . . child, the biological father, or the state, does not affect the child's . . . status as the legitimate offspring of [the mother's] husband." *Smith v. Cole*, 553 So. 2d 847 (La. 1989). Professor Mary Louise Fellows endorses this concept, indicating that it is the arrangement that "more clearly reflect[s] the realities of a child's complex life." *A Feminist Determination of the Law and Legitimacy*, 7 TEX. J. WOMEN & L. 195, 207 (1998). *See also* Nancy E. Dowd, *Multiple Parents, Multiple Fathers*, 9 J. L. FAM. STUD. 231 (2007). Theresa Glennon, *Erosion of the Marital Presumption*, at 602–03. The concept that a child can have more than two parents has also been recently endorsed in other circumstances, as well. In *Jacob v. Shultz-Jacob*, 923 A.2d 473 (Pa. Super. Ct. 2007), the Superior Court of Pennsylvania, the state's appellate court, ruled that a child could have three parents, all of whom are subject to parental rights and responsibilities. In that case, the court held that two lesbians who had jointly raised the children and the sperm donor who had been involved in the lives of the children could all be considered parents for purposes of child custody and child support.

PROBLEMS

Problem 9-21. Harry and Sally are married when Sally starts seeing Tom. When she becomes pregnant, she tells Tom the child is his, while also allowing Harry to think it is his. She divorces Harry two years later, receives custody, and then moves in with Tom. After five months, things don't work out and she moves out. Harry and Sally then remarry and deny Tom access to the child. A year later, Tom brings a paternity action to establish his parental rights. It is opposed by both Harry and Sally, although by this time they have filed for divorce again. The child calls the men "Daddy Harry" and "Daddy Tom," and both have a good paternal relationship with the child. Should the court allow Tom to proceed with his paternity action? Is its decision on this question constitutionally compelled?

Problem 9-22. Catherine became pregnant by Leslie during her short marriage to Gregory. She separated from Gregory in June of 1996, petitioned for dissolution of her marriage in October, gave birth in March of 1997, and obtained her final divorce decree in May. Neither Leslie nor Gregory knew of the child's existence until 2008, and in 2009 the district attorney sought child support from both. Blood tests excluded Gregory but showed Leslie the likely father. Who is the father under California's conclusive marital presumption? Under UPA 2002? Who should be the legal father? What should his child support obligations be?

[3]   The Constitutional Protection of Nonmarital Children From Discriminatory Treatment by Government

Traditionally, state and federal policies recognized a range of financial rights for marital or "legitimate" children that flow from the children's legal relationships with their parents. Many of these same rights were not available to nonmarital or "illegitimate" children, or were available only under certain limited circumstances or with particular restrictions or burdens that did not apply to children born into a legal marriage. In particular, children born out-of-wedlock did not have the same legally-enforceable rights as did marital children to parental support, to intestate succession, or to bring suits to recover for the wrongful death of a parent. Beginning in 1968, with the case of *Levy v. Louisiana*, 391 U.S. 68 (1968), the United States Supreme Court decided a series of cases addressing the extent to which the Equal Protection Clause precludes the government from employing classifications that distinguish between marital and nonmarital children. Although the standard of review was unclear in the earlier of these cases, in a pair of cases considered a year apart, *Trimble v. Gordon*, 430 U.S. 762 (1977), and *Lalli v. Lalli*, 439 U.S. 259 (1978), the Court made clear that the appropriate standard was intermediate review.

In *Trimble*, the Court considered a challenge to an Illinois law permitting nonmarital children to inherit by intestate succession only from their mothers, while marital children could inherit from either parent. Under that statute, despite the existence of a prior adjudication of the decedent's paternity, the petitioning nonmarital child received no share of his estate. Although refusing to adopt a strict scrutiny standard of review for classifications based on illegitimacy, the Court noted that, given that "illegitimacy is analogous in many respects to the personal characteristics that have been held to be suspect when used as the basis of statutory differentiations," the appropriate standard of review "is not a toothless one," as the rational basis standard so often was. 430 U.S. at 767. The Court went on to reject both of the state's justifications for its classification. The state's interest in promoting the marital family could not constitutionally be achieved by attempting "to influence the actions of men and women by imposing sanctions on the children born of their illegitimate relationships." 430 U.S. at 769. Furthermore, although the state did have a valid interest, the Court concluded, in establishing an accurate and efficient method of property disposition in probate, the Court held that the Illinois law was not "carefully tuned to alternative considerations" and failed "to consider the possibility of a middle ground between the extremes of complete exclusion and case by case determination of paternity." *Id.* at 770–72. Four members of the Court dissented.

The following year, in *Lalli*, the Court considered a challenge to New York's intestacy law. That law, unlike the law challenged in *Trimble*, allowed a nonmarital child to recover in at least some instances from their deceased father, if a court of competent jurisdiction had found during the decedent's lifetime that he was the father of the child. The Court for the first time explicitly applied the emerging "intermediate" standard of review: in order to be sustained, a statute that distinguishes between legitimate and illegitimate children must be "substantially related to the important state interests the statute is intended to promote." 439 U.S. at 275–76. However, the Court sustained the challenged statute in this case. In contrast to a blanket ban on inheritance of nonmarital children, the Court in this case found the restrictions justified based on the state's interest in "just and orderly disposition of property at death." *Id.* at 268, as well as the "peculiar problems of proof" that attended determining paternity, as contrasted with maternity, particularly when the alleged father is deceased. *Id.* at 268. Thus, while *Trimble* and earlier cases make it clear that the state cannot discriminate against nonmarital children in order to promote the marital family, there will sometimes be justification between marital and nonmarital children that can survive review.

[4]   Gay and Lesbian Parenthood

The "unitary family" described by Justice Scalia in *Michael H.*, Section B[2][b], above, is comprised of one mother and one father and makes "no provision for dual fatherhood" and presumably, no provision for dual motherhood. Thus, to the extent that states endorse this model of family, parenting dyads of two men or two women and the children they raise do not enjoy legal recognition. Despite this, households with children parented by same-sex couples are increasingly visible in American society. Making use of assisted reproductive technologies, some same-sex couples have planned and effected the conception of children biologically related to one of the partners. Others have jointly parented a child born to one of them in a previous heterosexual relationship. Others have adopted or sought to adopt children not related to either partner. These scenarios have set in motion a range of challenges to traditional family law doctrines.

Historically, American law has relied on biology, marriage, and adoption to establish legal parentage. With joint genetic procreation and marriage traditionally unavailable to same-sex couples, adoption law has become an increasingly important vehicle for legal recognition of the parent-like relationship that frequently exists between children and their biological parents' same-sex partners. Such "second-parent" adoptions have broken new legal ground in some states, while other states have refused to grant them. In the absence of a second-parent adoption, the relationship between a biological parent's same-sex partner and his or her child is on uncertain legal ground. Most states regard the child and partner as legal strangers, even if the partner has co-parented the child and participated fully in providing caregiving and support.

Until fairly recently, gays and lesbians were disfavored in child custody determinations following divorce, even in the absence of any adverse effects on the child's well-being. More recently, courts in most jurisdictions have rejected the traditional approach of viewing homosexual conduct as evidence of *per se* parental unfitness, and have focused instead on the question of whether the parent's sexual conduct affects the child deleteriously. Social disapproval of homosexual conduct has also prevented gays and lesbians from adopting children in some jurisdictions. By statute, some states categorically bar adoptions by homosexuals or by unmarried individuals or couples. *See, e.g.* Arkansas ballot referendum of November 4, 2008, not yet codified (citizen-initiated ballot initiative requiring adoptive parents to be married). These statutes and challenges to them are discussed below, as are the legal issues relating to second-parent adoption and claims by a same-sex partner for custody of or parental rights to their partner's child. See Chapter 6 for a discussion of the law affecting custody claims by gay or lesbian parents following marital dissolution.

Based on 2000 Census data, there were approximately 600,000 same-sex couples living together in the United States at the turn of the millennium. Tavia Simmons & Martin O'Connell, Census 2000 Special Reports: Married-Couple and Unmarried-Partner Households: 2000 4 (2003), *available at* http://www.census.gov/prod/2003pubs/censr-5.pdf; *see also* Letitia Anne Peplau & Adam W. Fingerhut, *The Close Relationships of Lesbians and Gay Men*, 58 Ann. Psychol. Rev. 405, 406–07 (2007). Of those between the ages of 22 and 55, 34% of lesbian couples and 22% of gay couples were raising children, comprising a total of approximately 250,000 children under eighteen that same-sex couples were raising in their homes. Peplau, *supra*, at 406–07; *see also* Simmons, *supra*, at 4. It is expected that these numbers will rise significantly with the release of the 2010 census data. *See also* Jay Weiser, *Forword: The Next Normal — Developments Since Marriage Rights for Same-Sex Couples in New York*, 13 Colum. J. Gender & L. 48, 48–49 (2004).

Charlotte J. Patterson, *Children of Lesbian and Gay Parents*
15 Current Directions Psychol. Sci. 241–44 (2006)

Does parental sexual orientation affect child development, and if so, how? This question has often been raised in the context of legal and policy proceedings relevant to children, such as those involving adoption, child custody, or visitation. Divergent views have been offered by professionals from the fields of psychology, sociology, medicine, and law. . . . [D]oes healthy human development require that a child grow up with parents of each gender? And if not, what would that mean for our theoretical understanding of parent — child relations? . . .

. . . .

[In 2005, a survey was conducted based on clientele from the Sperm Bank of California.] Over the more than 15 years of its existence, the Sperm Bank of California's clientele . . . included many lesbian as well as heterosexual women. . . . The Sperm Bank of California . . . allowed a sample in which, both for lesbian and for heterosexual groups, one parent was biologically related to the child and one was not.

We invited all clients who had conceived children using the resources of the Sperm Bank of California and who had children 5 years old or older to participate in our research. The resulting sample was composed of 80 families, 55 headed by lesbian and 25 headed by heterosexual parents. . . .

Results replicated and expanded upon those from earlier research. Children of lesbian and heterosexual parents showed similar, relatively high levels of social competence, as well as similar, relatively low levels of behavior problems on the parent form of the CBCL [Child Behavior Check List]. We also asked the children's teachers to provide evaluations of children's adjustment on the Teacher Report Form of the CBCL, and their reports agreed with those of parents. Parental sexual orientation was not related to children's adaptation. Quite apart from parental sexual orientation, however, and consistent with findings from years of research on children of heterosexual parents, when parent — child relationships were marked by warmth and affection, children were more likely to be developing well. Thus, in this sample drawn from a known population, measures of children's adjustment were unrelated to parental sexual orientation.

Even as they provided information about children born to lesbian mothers, however, these new results also raised additional questions. Women who conceive children at sperm banks are generally both well educated and financially comfortable. . . . What if a more diverse group of families were to be studied? In addition, the children in this sample averaged 7 years of age, and some concerns focus on older children and adolescents. What if an older group of youngsters were to be studied? Would problems masked by youth and privilege in earlier studies emerge in an older, more diverse sample?

[The 2006 National Longitudinal Study of Adolescent Health ("Add Health") study surveyed over 12,000 adolescents and their parents, both at home and at school.] Parents were not queried directly about their sexual orientation but were asked if they were involved in a "marriage, or marriage-like relationship." If parents acknowledged such a relationship, they were also asked the gender of their partner. Thus, we identified a group of 44 12- to 18-year-olds who lived with parents involved in marriage or marriage-like relationships with same-sex partners. We compared them with a matched group of adolescents living with other-sex couples. Data from the archives of the Add Health study allowed us to address many questions about adolescent development.

Consistent with earlier findings, results of this work revealed few differences in adjustment between adolescents living with same-sex parents and those living with opposite-sex parents. There were no significant differences between teenagers living with same-sex parents and those living with other-sex parents on self-reported assessments of psychological well-being, such as self-esteem and anxiety; measures of school outcomes, such as grade point averages and trouble in school; or measures of family relationships, such as parental warmth and care from adults and peers. Adolescents in the two groups were equally likely to say that they had been involved in a romantic relationship in the last 18 months, and they were equally likely to report having engaged in sexual intercourse. The only statistically reliable difference between the two groups — that those with same-sex parents felt a greater sense of connection to people at school — favored the youngsters living with same-sex couples. There were no significant differences in self-reported substance use, delinquency, or peer victimization between those reared by same- or other-sex couples.

Although the gender of parents' partners was not an important predictor of adolescent well-being, other aspects of family relationships were significantly associated with teenagers' adjustment. Consistent with other findings about adolescent development, the qualities of family relationships rather than the gender of parents' partners were consistently related to adolescent outcomes. . . .

These findings have been supported by results from many other studies, both in the United States and abroad. Susan Golombok and her colleagues have reported similar results with a near-representative sample of children in the United Kingdom. [Susan Golombok et al, *Children with Lesbian Parents: A Community Study*, 39 DEVELOPMENTAL PSYCHOL. 20 (2003)]. Others, both in Europe and in the United States, have described similar findings. [*E.g.*, A. Brewaeys et al, *Donor Insemination: Child Development and Family Functioning in Lesbian Mother Families*, 12 HUM. REPROD. 1349 (1997)]. The fact that children of lesbian mothers generally develop in healthy ways should not be taken to suggest that they encounter no challenges. Many investigators have remarked upon the fact that children of lesbian and gay parents may encounter anti-gay sentiments in their daily lives. For example, in a study of 10-year-old children born to lesbian mothers, Gartrell, Deck, Rodas, Peyser, and Banks reported that a substantial minority had encountered anti-gay sentiments among their peers. [N. Gartrell et al, *The National Lesbian Family Study: 4. Interviews with the 10-year-old Children*, 75 AM. J. ORTHOPSYCHIATRY 518 (2005).]

Those who had had such encounters were likely to report having felt angry, upset, or sad about these experiences. Children of lesbian and gay parents may be exposed to prejudice against their parents in some settings, and this may be painful for them, but evidence for the idea that such encounters affect children's overall adjustment is lacking.

. . . .

Conclusions

Does parental sexual orientation have an important impact on child or adolescent development? Results of recent research provide no evidence that it does.

. . . .

[T]he clarity of findings in this area has been acknowledged by a number of major professional organizations. For instance, the governing body of the American Psychological Association (APA) voted unanimously in favor of a statement that said, "Research has shown that the adjustment, development, and psychological well-being of children is unrelated to parental sexual orientation and that children of lesbian and gay parents are as likely as those of heterosexual parents to flourish." The American Bar Association, the American Medical Association, the American Academy of Pediatrics, the American Psychiatric Association, and other mainstream professional groups have issued similar statements.

In addition to the organizations Patterson notes have supported gay and lesbian parenting, several national organizations have published their own statements about their support generally of such familial arrangements. *See, e.g.*, American Psychological Association, *Policy Statement: Legal Benefits for Same-Sex Couples*, http://www.apa.org/pi/lgbc/policy/archive.html#legal (1998); American Psychoanalytic Society, *Position Statement: Gay and Lesbian Parenting*, http://www.apsa.org/aboutapsaa/positionstatements/gayandlesbianparenting/tabid/471/Default.aspx (2002).

For additional discussion of psychological research on gay and lesbian parenting, see SUZANNE M. JOHNSON & ELIZABETH O'CONNOR, THE GAY BABY BOOM: THE PSYCHOLOGY OF GAY PARENTHOOD (2002); Charlotte J. Patterson, *Lesbian and Gay Family Issues in the Context of Changing Legal and Social Policy Environments*, *in* HANDBOOK OF COUNSELING AND PSYCHOTHERAPY WITH LESBIAN, GAY, BISEXUAL AND TRANSGENDER CLIENTS 359 (K.J. Bieschke et al eds. 2d ed. 2007); Fiona Tasker & Charlotte J. Patterson, *Research on Gay and Lesbian Parenting: Retrospect and Prospect*, *in* GAY AND LESBIAN PARENTING: NEW DIRECTIONS 9-34 (Fiona Tasker & Jerry J. Bigner eds. 2007); Scott Ryan, *Parent-Child Interaction Styles Between Gay and Lesbian Parents and Their Adopted Children*, *in* GAY AND LESBIAN PARENTING, *supra*, at 105-32; Sean G. Massey, *Sexism, Heterosexism, and Attributions About Undesirable Behavior in Children of Gay, Lesbian, and Heterosexual Parents*, *in* GAY AND LESBIAN PARENTING, *supra*, at 457–84.

For application of these scientific findings to legal policy questions *see* Todd Brower, *It's Not Just Shopping, Urban Lofts, and the Lesbian Gay-by Boom: How Sexual Orientation Demographics Can Inform Family Courts*, 17 AM. U. J. GENDER, SOC. POL'Y & L. 1 (2009); Deborah L. Forman, *Interstate Recognition of Same-Sex Parents in the Wake of Gay Marriage, Civil Unions, and Domestic Partnerships*, 46 B.C. L. REV. 1, 22 (2004) (arguing that in spite of mini-Defense of Marriage Acts in some states, same-sex parenthood should be upheld in the best interest of the child); Lynn D. Wardle, *The Biological Causes and Consequences of Homosexual Behavior and Their Relevance for Family Law Policies*, 56 DEPAUL L. REV. 997, 1031 (2007)(arguing, *inter alia*, that it is not in the best interests of children to be parented by gays or lesbians).

[a] Adoptions by Same-Sex Couples and Gay or Lesbian Individuals

[i] Second-Parent Adoption

SHARON S. v. SUPERIOR COURT
California Supreme Court
73 P.3d 554 (2003)

WERDEGAR, J.

This dispute arises in independent adoption proceedings commenced by a birth mother, Sharon S. . . . and her former domestic partner Annette F. . . . to effect Annette's adoption of Joshua (now three and a half years old) who, like his older brother Zachary (now six years old and previously adopted by Annette), was conceived by artificial insemination of Sharon and born during the partnership.[1] The question presented is whether an independent adoption in which the birth parent does not agree to termination of her parental rights is legislatively authorized and, if so, whether the statutes are constitutional. . . .

Sharon and Annette attended Harvard Business School together and were in a committed relationship from 1989 through mid 2000. In 1996, after being artificially inseminated with sperm from an anonymous donor, Sharon gave birth to Zachary. With Sharon's consent and approval, Annette petitioned to adopt Zachary in a "second parent" adoption, using official forms and procedures that expressly provided that Sharon consented to Zachary's adoption by Annette, but intended to retain her own parental rights..[2] The trial court approved Annette's adoption petition, and Annette has since been one of Zachary's two parents.

Three years later, in 1999, Sharon was inseminated again with sperm from the same anonymous donor and gave birth to Joshua. On August 30 of that year, Sharon signed an Independent Adoption Placement Agreement (Agreement), which begins: "Note to birth parent: This form will become a permanent and irrevocable consent to adoption. Do not sign this form unless you want the adopting parents named below to adopt your child." The Agreement goes on to recite Sharon's "permanent and irrevocable consent to the adoption on the 91st day after I sign" the Agreement.

The Agreement also recites that, upon the court's approval of the Agreement, Sharon will "give up all rights of custody, services, and earning" with respect to Joshua. However, a written Addendum to Independent Adoption Placement

---

[1] Independent adoptions are those in which no agency, state or private, joins in the adoption petition, although the state does have a role in investigating, evaluating and commenting upon the petition.

[2] "The phrase 'second-parent adoption' refers to an independent adoption whereby a child born to [or legally adopted by] one partner is adopted by his or her non-biological or non-legal second parent, with the consent of the legal parent, and without changing the latter's rights and responsibilities." . . . As a result of the adoption, the child has two legal parents who have equal legal status in terms of their relationship with the child.

Agreement (Addendum), a form developed by the California Department of Social Services (CDSS), was signed by Sharon and Annette on the same date as they signed the Agreement. The Addendum stated Sharon's intent, as Joshua's birth parent, to retain parental rights and control of Joshua while placing him with Annette for the purpose of independent adoption. These were essentially the same procedures and forms Sharon and Annette had used for Zachary's adoption.[3]

Subsequently, Annette filed a petition to adopt Joshua as a second parent with Sharon. The petition stated that Sharon, as "birth mother of the children [Zachary and Joshua,] consents to this adoption and will execute a limited written consent to the child's [Joshua's] adoption in the manner required by law." The petition also stated that Sharon "intends to retain all her rights to custody and control as to said child." In April 2000, the San Diego County Department of Health and Human Services (HHS), acting in its capacity as an agency licensed by CDSS under the Family Code to investigate and report upon proposed independent adoptions, recommended that the court grant Annette's adoption petition.

[In mid-2000, the couple terminated their relationship.] . . .

On October 23, 2000, Annette filed a motion for an order of adoption respecting Joshua, contending . . . that Sharon's consent had become irrevocable pursuant to section 8814.5 and that the adoption was in Joshua's best interest.

After a family court mediator recommended that Sharon and Annette share custody and that Annette have specified visitation, Sharon moved for court approval to withdraw her consent to the adoption. She contended there was no legal basis for the adoption. . . . HHS subsequently filed a supplemental report with the court, noting that Sharon had moved to withdraw her consent but had not done so within the statutorily specified period for revocation. HHS further reported that Annette had shared in Joshua's medical expenses and in the planning and handling of his daily care since birth, that Annette had a close and loving relationship with Joshua as his second parent, and that Annette's relationship with Joshua was similar to her relationship with Zachary. Finding that adoption continued to be in Joshua's best interest, HHS again recommended that Annette's petition to adopt Joshua be granted.

. . . .

"The right to adopt a child, and the right of a person to be adopted as the child of another, are wholly statutory." . . .

. . . Pursuant to the current statutory scheme, birth parents can consent to an independent adoption by entering into an adoption placement agreement with a prospective adoptive parent. The birth parent(s) have 30 days in which to revoke this consent. If they fail to do so, their consent becomes permanent and irrevocable.

---

[3] CDSS forms and procedures for second parent adoptions have been developed over the past decade and presently are maintained in accordance with a policy announced by CDSS on November 15, 1999. . . .

Once the adoption placement agreement has been signed, the prospective adoptive parent may petition for adoption. The court clerk must give CDSS notice of the petition and the petitioner must file a copy of the petition with CDSS.

Subsequently, it is incumbent on CDSS to "investigate the proposed independent adoption" and "ascertain whether the child is a proper subject for adoption and whether the proposed home is suitable for the child" [and submit a report to the court with a recommendation regarding the granting of the petition]. Assuming other statutory prerequisites are met, if the court is "satisfied that the interest of the child will be promoted by the adoption, the court may make and enter an order of adoption of the child by the prospective adoptive parent or parents."

Annette argues that these statutes authorize the superior court to finalize her adoption of Joshua, because she has complied with the substantive and procedural prerequisites for an independent adoption. Sharon contends that the adoption is not authorized, because section 8617 mandates full termination of birth parental rights in every independent adoption.

Section 8617 provides: "The birth parents of an adopted child are, from the time of the adoption, relieved of all parental duties towards, and all responsibility for, the adopted child, and have no right over the child." The section does not appear in the chapter devoted to independent adoptions, but is, rather, one of the general provisions. . . .

"The rule is that the adoption statutes are to be liberally construed with a view to effect their objects and to promote justice. Such a construction should be given as will sustain, rather than defeat, the object they have in view." *Dept. Soc. Welfare v. Super. Ct.*, 459 P.2d 897 (Cal. 1969) (en banc). Consistently with these principles, we previously have concluded that the Legislature did not intend section 8617's nearly identical precursor to bar an adoption when the parties clearly intended to waive the operation of that statute and agreed to preserve the birth parent's rights and responsibilities. *Marshall v. Marshall*[,] 239 P. 36 ([Cal.] 1925). Nothing in section 8617's text, context, history, or function justifies departure in this case from "the established rule that rights conferred by statute may be waived unless specific statutory provisions prohibit waiver." *Bickel v. City of Piedmont*, 946 P.2d 427 (Cal. 1997).

. . . .

Since section 8617's provisions are for the benefit of the parties to an adoption petition and the section contains no language prohibiting a waiver, we conclude that section 8617 declares a legal consequence of the usual adoption, waivable by the parties thereto, rather than a mandatory prerequisite to every valid adoption.[6]

---

[6] In so holding, we do not decide, contrary to what our concurring and dissenting colleagues suggest, whether there exists an overriding legislative policy limiting a child to two parents. This case involves only a second parent adoption, so we have no occasion to address that point. Justice Baxter errs, therefore, in asserting that our decision today frees a family court to assign at will "as many legal parents as the lone judge deems in the child's best interest." While the Family Code contains in several sections language suggesting the Legislature may harbor a two-parent policy, those statutes are not in issue. Section 8617, which is in issue, does not speak to parental numerosity, except incidentally to recognize

. . . .

While California's adoption statutes nowhere concisely define "adoption," they do state the essential elements of a valid adoption. . . . "The proceeding is essentially one of contract between the parties whose consent is required." . . .

[T]he essential elements of every valid adoption are: a voluntary and informed parental consent to the adoption except where the parent has surrendered or has been judicially deprived of parental control, CAL. FAM. CODE §§ 8604–8606; a suitable adoptive parent at least 10 years older than, or in a specified preexisting family relationship with, the child, CAL. FAM. CODE §§ 8601, 8717, 8801, 8811–8811.5; and a judicial determination that "the interest of the child will be promoted by the adoption," CAL. FAM. CODE § 8612. When these essential elements are present, "the objective of the adoption statutes to protect the interests of both the natural or legal parent(s) and the child through the consent and best interests requirements" is not frustrated when statutory provisions like section 8617 are treated as nonmandatory. [Emily] Patt, *Second Parent Adoption: When Crossing the Marital Barrier is in a Child's Best Interests*, 3 BERKELEY WOMEN'S L.J. 96, 117 (1987–88) (discussing [CAL.] CIV. CODE former § 229).

. . . .

" 'Independent Adoption' means the adoption of a child in which neither the department nor an agency licensed by the department is a party to, or joins in, the adoption petition." CAL. FAM. CODE § 8524. In addition to the essential elements of all adoptions set out above, the independent adoption statutes require parental consent after notice and advisement, opportunities under specified conditions timely to revoke consent, or with court approval to withdraw it, selection of the adoptive parent or parents by the birth parent or parents personally, advice to the birth parent of his or her rights by an adoption service provider or licensed out-of-state agency, execution of an adoption placement agreement satisfying specified requirements on a form prescribed by CDSS, CAL. FAM. CODE § 8801.3, administrative investigation by CDSS or its delegate, an appropriate petition filed with the superior court, usually in the county in which the petitioner resides, and an appearance before the court by the prospective adoptive parents and the child. Nowhere does any mandate or requirement of relinquishment of a birth parent's rights and responsibilities appear.

. . . [S]ection 8617 neither prohibits a birth parent and another qualified adult from jointly waiving application of the statute in order to coparent an adoptable child, nor prohibits a court under such circumstances from ordering an otherwise valid adoption.

Decades ago, we held [the predecessor statute to] section 8617 . . . was no bar to second parent adoption of a type — stepparent adoption — that was then not expressly provided for by statute. . . .

In *Marshall*, the second husband of a widowed mother adopted her two minor children. . . .

---

in its use of the plural, "birth parents," that a child ordinarily has two of these.

. . . .

[W]e held in *Marshall* that "although no express authority therefor is to be found in the code, nevertheless a husband and wife may jointly adopt a child pursuant to the procedure therein prescribed, the result of which is to make the child, in law, the child of both spouses." . . .

In *Marshall*, we thus effectively read second parent adoption into the statutory scheme. . . . In so doing, we necessarily determined that relinquishment of the birth parent's rights was not essential to adoption and that section 8617's predecessor was not mandatory.

. . . .

California's adoption statutes have always permitted adoption without regard to the marital status of prospective adoptive parents. . . . [N]o justification appears for treating section 8617 differently in this case than we did its predecessor in *Marshall*.

. . . .

Several important considerations of public policy also buttress our conclusion. Precisely how many second parent adoptions have been granted in California over the years is difficult to know, partly because adoption proceedings are generally confidential, but published materials suggest they number 10,000 to 20,000. That the second parent adoption procedures promulgated by CDSS under the independent adoption statutes have received such widespread acceptance and have been so extensively used speaks not only to their utility in the modern context, but to their effectiveness in promoting the fundamental purposes that adoption has always served.

The basic purpose of an adoption is the "welfare, protection and betterment of the child," and adoption courts ultimately must rule on that basis. While the child's "best interest" is "an elusive guideline that belies rigid definition," obviously overall "[i]ts purpose is to maximize a child's opportunity to develop into a stable, well-adjusted adult." *Adoption of Michelle T.*, [117 Cal. Rptr. 856, 858] ([Ct. App.] 1975). That there are a variety of "costs . . . if a legal relationship with a second parent is not established — costs that can be both financial and emotional" is well recognized. [Emily] Doskow, *The Second Parent Trap[: Parenting for Same-Sex Couples in a Brave New World]*, 20 J. Juv. L. 1, 9 (1999). Second parent adoption can secure the salutary incidents of legally recognized parentage for a child of a nonbiological parent who otherwise must remain a legal stranger.

Second parent adoptions also benefit children by providing a clear legal framework for resolving any disputes that may arise over custody and visitation. Our explicitly recognizing their validity will prevent uncertainty, conflict, and protracted litigation in this area, all of which plainly are harmful to children caught in the middle. Unmarried couples who have brought a child into the world with the expectation that they will raise it together, and who have jointly petitioned for adoption, should be on notice that if they separate the same rules concerning custody and visitation as apply to all other parents will apply to them.

In addition, second parent adoptions offer the possibility of obtaining the security and advantages of two parents for some of California's neediest children, including many with "special needs" for whom a second parent adoption may constitute the "closest conceivable counterpart of the relationship of parent and child" available. The same is true as regards thousands of others in foster care for whom it is state policy to seek permanent adoptive placement.

. . . .

In sum, adherence to the Court of Appeal's construction of section 8617 as precluding second parent adoption would unnecessarily eliminate access to a duly promulgated, well-tested adoption process that has become "routine in California" and that is fully consistent with the main purpose of the adoption statutes to promote "the welfare of children 'by the legal recognition and regulation of the consummation of the closest conceivable counterpart of the relationship of parent and child[.]' " *Dept. Soc. Welfare v. Super. Ct.*, *supra.*

. . . .

Although second parent adoptions may involve children conceived, as in this case, by artificial insemination, others involve children placed directly by their birth parents or private agencies with two unmarried adoptive parents. Others involve dependent children, often with special needs because of prior abuse or neglect, who were placed by public agencies with an unmarried "fost-adopt" parent whose partner later became a second adoptive parent. Still others are "kinship" adoptions, in which a grandparent or other relative became a second legal parent of a child whose very young mother was unable to raise the child on her own. Such adoptions also have involved children born in other countries and adopted either in their country of origin or in California by an unmarried adult whose partner later became a second adoptive parent. Established practice in California thus has created settled expectations among many different types of adoptive families. Affirmance would unnecessarily risk disturbing these.

. . . .

For the foregoing reasons, we reverse the judgment of the Court of Appeal and remand the cause for further proceedings consistent with this opinion.

Concurring and Dissenting Opinion by BROWN, J.

This case raises questions concerning the past, present and future of California adoption law. Regarding the past, I agree that we should not disturb settled familial relationships. Regarding the present, Annette may deserve partial custody based on estoppel. The most important question, however, is whether the California Department of Social Services ought to continue authorizing these second parent adoptions in the thousands of cases that will arise in the future. The Legislature has heretofore required a legal relationship [of domestic partner] between the birth and second parent, and I would defer to this rule and bar second parent adoptions that violate the statutory scheme. [Justice Brown argues that by enacting statutes that permitted stepparent adoptions, and more recently, second-parent adoptions for domestic partners of the prospective adoptee's legal parent, the Legislature intended to limit the circumstances in which the natural parents need not sever parental rights in the adoption context to those two situations only.]

NOTES

1. *Case Law and Second-Parent Adoptions.* Most appellate courts in other states that have approved of second-parent adoptions have grounded their decisions on a different legal theory than the waiver theory used in *Sharon S.* Courts construing adoption statutes broadly to authorize second-parent adoptions have concluded that doing so furthers the underlying purposes of the state's adoption statutes in promoting the child's best interests, and therefore comports with legislative intent. For example, in *Adoptions of B.L.V.B. and E.L.V.B.*, 628 A.2d 1271, 1273–74 (Vt. 1993), the Vermont Supreme Court stated:

> In interpreting [our] statutes, we are mindful that the state's primary concern is to promote the welfare of children, and that application of the statutes should implement that purpose. In doing so, we must avoid results that are irrational, unreasonable or absurd. We must look "not only at the letter of a statute but also its reason and spirit."

> . . . .

> . . . [In enacting the step-parent adoption provision, the] legislature recognized that it would be against common sense to terminate the biological parent's rights when that parent will continue to raise and be responsible for the child, albeit in a family unit with a partner who is biologically unrelated to the child.

> . . . Despite the narrow wording of the step-parent exception, we cannot conclude that the legislature ever meant to terminate the parental rights of a biological parent who intended to continue raising a child with the help of a partner. Such a narrow construction would produce the unreasonable and irrational result of defeating adoptions that are otherwise indisputably in the best interests of children. . . .

Courts have also focused on the particular benefits to children of an adoption by their legal parent's same-sex partner:

> [The child's interests are] advanced . . . by allowing the two adults who actually function as a child's parents to become the child's legal parents. The advantages which would result from such an adoption include Social Security and life insurance benefits in the event of a parent's death or disability, the right to sue for the wrongful death of a parent, the right to inherit under rules of intestacy, and eligibility for coverage under both parents' health insurance policies. In addition, granting a second parent adoption further ensures that two adults are legally entitled to make medical decisions for the child in case of emergency and are under a legal obligation for the child's economic support.

> Even more important, however, is the emotional security of knowing that in the event of the biological parent's death or disability, the other parent will have presumptive custody, and the children's relationship with their parents, siblings and other relatives will continue should the co-parents

separate. Indeed, viewed from the children's perspective, permitting the adoptions allows the children to achieve a measure of permanency with both parent figures. . . .

In re Jacob, 660 N.E.2d 397, 398–99 (N.Y. 1995).

The number of state courts interpreting adoption statutes to permit second-parent adoption has increased annually, although the number is still small. As of this writing, a liberal estimate is that only one-third of the states allow second-parent adoption outside of the stepparent context in some form. High court decisions authorizing second-parent adoptions include California, *Sharon S., supra*; New York, *In re Jacob, supra*; Vermont, *Adoptions of B.L.V.B. and E.L.V.B., supra*; Massachusetts, *In re Adoption of Tammy*, 619 N.E.2d 315 (Mass. 1993); and Pennsylvania, *In re Adoption of R.B.F.*, 803 A.2d 1195 (Pa. 2002). *See also In re M.M.D. & B.H.M.*, 662 A.2d 837 (D.C. App. 1995). State courts of appeal have approved second-parent adoptions in several other jurisdictions. *See, e.g., In re Adoption of M.M.G.C., H.H.C, & K.E.A.C.*, 785 N.E.2d 267 (Ind. Ct. App. 2003); *Petition of K.M. and D.M.*, 653 N.E.2d 888 (Ill. App. At. 1995); *Adoption of Two Children by H.N.R.*, 666 A.2d 535 (N.J. App. Div. 1995). In several other states, trial courts (and even some appeals courts) have approved second-parent adoptions in individual cases, sometimes pursuant to a state department of family services policy of recommending such adoptions as in the best interests of the children, absent extenuating circumstances, but no published opinion has been filed explicitly authorizing such adoptions. A recent survey indicates that the following states fall within this category, based in part on "anecdotal evidence": Alabama, Alaska, Delaware, Hawaii, Iowa, Kentucky, Louisiana, Maryland, Michigan, Minnesota, Nevada, New Hampshire, New Mexico, Ohio, Oregon, Rhode Island, Texas, and Washington. Human Rights Campaign, *Second-Parent Adoption*, http://www.hrc.org/issues/2385.htm.

Some courts have rejected second-parent adoption petitions, awaiting explicit statutory authorization. Six of seven justices of the Connecticut Supreme Court took this position in *In re Adoption of Baby Z.*, 724 A.2d 1035 (Conn. 1999). *See also In re Adoption of Luke*, 640 N.W.2d 374 (Neb. 2002) (same-sex companion of mother ineligible to adopt child under adoption statute absent termination of mother's parental rights); *In Matter of Adoption of T.K.J. and K.A.K*, 931 P.2d 488 (Colo. Ct. App. 1996) (liberal construction of adoption statute does not permit court to "rewrite" statute in granting second-parent adoption without explicit legislative authorization); *Interest of Angel Lace M.*, 516 N.W.2d 678 (Wis. 1994) (statutory provision requiring termination of mother's rights is mandatory and applies to adoption by her lesbian partner); *In re Adoption of Jane Doe*, 719 N.E.2d 1071 (Ohio Ct. App. 1998); *S.J.L.S. v. T.L.S.*, 265 S.W.3d 804 (Ky. Ct. App. 2008) (holding legislature only contemplated stepparent adoption when passing the statute, and therefore unmarried same-sex partner was not authorized to adopt; nevertheless, challenge to adoption was time barred due to public policy concerns of disrupting adoption decree for procedural irregularity). For a general compilation of state policies, see William C. Duncan, *Marital Status and Adoption Values*, 6 J. L. & Fam. Stud. 1, 2–6 (2004); Hayden Curry, Denis Clifford, & Frederick Hertz, A Legal Guide for Lesbian and Gay Couples (13th ed. 2005).

2. *Statutory Second-Parent Adoption Provisions.* Several state statutes explicitly authorize second-parent adoptions outside the context of marital relationships. California enacted Family Code § 9000(b), effective 2001, providing that a "domestic partner . . . desiring to adopt a child of his or her domestic partner may for that purpose file a petition in the county in which the petitioner resides." CAL. FAM. CODE § 9000(b). Immediately following the Connecticut Supreme Court's decision in *In re Baby Z., supra* note 1, the Connecticut legislature enacted a statute permitting a person who shares parental responsibility with the child's parent to adopt, or join in an adoption, even if the two adults are not married. CONN. GEN. STAT. § 45a-724(a)(3). Vermont enacted a similar provision as part of its civil union legislation, making second-parent adoptions by partners to a civil union analogous to step-parent adoptions by spouses. VT. STAT. ANN. tit. 15, § 1204(e)(4). In those states where either the supreme court or the legislature has approved same-sex marriage, stepparent adoption statutes will apply in place of second-parent adoption. *See, e.g.*, IOWA CODE § 600.4(3)(a). A bill permitting second-parent adoptions outside of the step-parent context was introduced in the Wisconsin legislature following *Angel Lace M., supra* note 1, but was not enacted.

3. *Policy Positions of National Professional Associations.* In the past several years, several national professional groups have formally encouraged legal ratification of second-parent adoptions in the context of same-sex couples. *See, e.g.*, Committee on Psychosocial Aspects of Child and Family Health, American Academy of Pediatrics, *Coparent or Second-Parent Adoption by Same-Sex Parents*, 109 PEDIATRICS 339 (2002)(asserting that psychosocial research supports allowing second-parent adoption); Ellen C. Perrin & Committee on Psychosocial Aspects of Child and Family Health, American Academy of Pediatrics, *Technical Report: Coparent or Second-Parent Adoption by Same-Sex Parents*, 109 PEDIATRICS 341 (2002) (concluding relevant developmental research supports legal extension of second-parent adoption policies); American Psychiatric Association, *Adoption and Co-parenting of Children by Same-sex Couples*, http://www.psych.org/Departments/EDU/Library/APAOfficialDocumentsandRelated/PositionStatements/200214.aspx (2002) (contending that while some states are recognizing second parent adoptions, all same-sex couples should be allowed to legally co-parent their children);

4. *Scholarly Commentary.* Most scholarly commentary on the subject of second-parent adoption has recommended expansion of this procedure, arguing that it protects children's best interests for the reasons articulated by the state supreme courts above. *See, e.g.*, Patricia M. Logue, *The Rights of Gays and Lesbians and Their Children*, 18 J. AM. ACAD. MATRIMONIAL L. 95 (2002); Todd Brower, *It's Not Just Shopping, Urban Lofts, and the Lesbian Gay-by Boom: How Sexual Orientation Demographics Can Inform Family Courts*, 17 AM. U. J. GENDER, SOC. POL'Y & L. 1, 28 (2009); Patricia J. Falk, *Second-Parent Adoption*, 48 CLEV. ST. L. REV. 93 (2000); Richard E. Redding, *It's Really About Sex: Same-Sex Marriage, Lesbigay Parenting, and the Psychology of Disgust*, 15 DUKE J. GENDER L. & POL'Y 127 (2008). *But see* Lynn D. Wardle, *The Potential Impact of Homosexual Parenting on Children*, 1997 U. ILL. L. REV. 833 (arguing adoption by homosexuals is not in children's best interests).

5. *Second-Parent Adoption Outside of the United States.* Certain Scandinavian and European countries that preceded American states in recognizing same-sex partnerships (*see* Note on Formal Registration Schemes Outside of the United States, *supra*, Section A[4]), have been slower than many American states to permit same-sex couples to adopt. *See Developments in the Law — The Law of Marriage and Family*, 116 HARV. L. REV. 1999, 2010–12 (2003) (hereinafter *"Developments"*); *see also* WILLIAM N. ESKRIDGE, JR., EQUALITY PRACTICE: CIVIL UNIONS AND THE PRACTICE OF GAY RIGHTS 89–117 & Table 3.2 (2001); YUVAL MERIN, EQUALITY FOR SAME-SEX COUPLES 253–262 (2002). The Scandinavian and European resistance to extending parental rights to same-sex couples demonstrates that "popular acceptance of economic rights for same-sex couples does not necessarily imply a willingness to infringe on more established religious and cultural traditions." *Developments, supra*, at 1011. According to one commentator, the traditional belief that a child is best off with two parents of different genders has been more tenaciously held in these countries than in the United States. Merin, *supra* at 254. Yet, the resistance is eroding. The Netherlands, Denmark, and Iceland now permit second-parent adoptions. *Developments*, at 1011. Furthermore, in 2008, the European Court of Human Rights found "unlawful" France's denial of an adoption to a lesbian mother. The prospective mother in that case was involved in a long-term lesbian relationship but filed singly for adoption. A binding precedent in all forty-five member-countries of the Council of Europe, it is still unclear how this decision will change adoptions for same-sex couples in Europe. For further discussion of this landmark case, *see* Kathleen A. Doty, *From* Frette *to* E.B.: *The European Court of Human Rights on Gay and Lesbian Adoption*, 18 L. & SEXUALITY 121 (2009).

6. *An Alternative to Adoption?* *K.M. v. E.G.*, reprinted, *infra*, Section B[4][b][2], provides an alternative avenue through which lesbian partners may be able to establish concurrent legal maternity. If one woman contributes the genetic material for a child, and the other gives birth to the child, with the intent to raise the child jointly, both might be judged to be the legal parents of the child. This technology, known as "egg-sharing," "co-mothering" and "lesbian partner assisted reproduction" is now widely recommended for lesbian mothers who wish to both be considered the child's biological mother. *See, e.g.*, Sanja Zgonjanin, *What Does It Take to Be a (Lesbian) Parent? On Intent and Genetics*, 16 HASTINGS WOMEN'S L.J. 251 (2005).

7. *Effect of Same-Sex Couple Adoption Decrees in Other States.* Chapter 2 examined the debate over the application of the Full Faith and Credit Clause to same-sex marriages, including the impact of the Defense of Marriage Act. An adoption by a same-sex couple, however, stands on a different footing. Unlike a marriage, an adoption is completed only when a court issues a decree. The application of the Full Faith and Credit Clause to judicial decrees is clear, and applies to decrees of adoption as much as to any other judicial decree. Several recent cases illustrate this point. For example, the Tenth Circuit Court of Appeals recently held that an Oklahoma statute that barred recognition of an adoption by a same-sex couple that is finalized in another state violated the Full Faith and Credit Clause. *See Finstuen v. Crutcher*, 496 F.3d 1130 (10th Cir. 2007). *Accord Russell v. Bridgens*, 647 N.W.2d 56 (Neb. 2002); *Davenport v. Little-Bowser*, 611 S.E.2d 366

(Va. 2005); *Embry v. Ryan*, 2009 Fla. App. LEXIS 4633. For scholarly discussions of this issue, see Joanna L. Grossman, *When Same-Sex Couples Adopt: Problems of Interstate Recognition*, FINDLAW, http://writ.news.findlaw.com/grossman/20090609.html (2009); Deborah L. Forman, *Interstate Recognition of Same-Sex Parents in the Wake of Gay Marriage, Civil Unions, and Domestic Partnerships*, 46 B.C. L. REV 1 (2004); Lisa S. Chen, Comment: *Second-Parent Adoptions: Are They Entitled to Full Faith and Credit?* 46 SANTA CLARA L. REV. 171, 190–91 (2005); Rhonda Wasserman, *Are You Still My Mother?: Interstate Recognition of Adoptions by Gays and Lesbian*, 58 AM. U. L. REV. 1 (2008).

[ii] Statutory Bars to Adoptions by Gay and Lesbian Couples and Individuals

LOFTON v. DEPARTMENT OF CHILDREN AND FAMILY SERVICES
United States Court of Appeals, Eleventh Circuit
358 F.3d 804 (2004)

BIRCH, CIRCUIT JUDGE.

In this appeal, we decide . . . whether Florida Statute § 63.042(3), which prevents adoption by practicing homosexuals, is constitutional as enacted by the Florida legislature and as subsequently enforced. The district court granted summary judgment to Florida over an equal protection and due process challenge by homosexual persons desiring to adopt. We affirm.

I.

Since 1977, Florida's adoption law has contained a codified prohibition on adoption by any "homosexual" person.[1] For purposes of this statute, Florida courts have defined the term "homosexual" as being "limited to applicants who are known to engage in current, voluntary homosexual activity," thus drawing "a distinction between homosexual orientation and homosexual activity." During the past twelve years, several legislative bills have attempted to repeal the statute, and three separate legal challenges to it have been filed in the Florida courts. To date, no attempt to overturn the provision has succeeded. . . .

Six plaintiffs-appellants bring this case. The first, Steven Lofton, is a registered pediatric nurse who has raised from infancy three Florida foster children, each of whom tested positive for HIV at birth. By all accounts, Lofton's efforts in caring for these children have been exemplary, and his story has been chronicled in dozens of news stories and editorials as well as on national television. . . . John Doe, also named as a plaintiff-appellant in this litigation, was born on 29 April 1991. Testing positive at birth for HIV and cocaine, Doe immediately entered the Florida foster care system. Shortly thereafter, Children's Home Society, a private agency,

---

[1] Fla. Stat. § 63.042(3) provides: "No person eligible to adopt under this statute may adopt if that person is a homosexual."

placed Doe in foster care with Lofton, who has extensive experience treating HIV patients. At eighteen months, Doe sero-reverted and has since tested HIV negative. In September of 1994, Lofton filed an application to adopt Doe but refused to answer the application's inquiry about his sexual preference and also failed to disclose Roger Croteau, his cohabitating partner, as a member of his household. After Lofton refused requests from the Department of Children and Families ("DCF") to supply the missing information, his application was rejected pursuant to the homosexual adoption provision. . . .

Plaintiff-appellant Douglas E. Houghton, Jr., is a clinical nurse specialist and legal guardian of plaintiff-appellant John Roe, who is eleven years old. Houghton has been Roe's caretaker since 1996 when Roe's biological father, suffering from alcohol abuse and frequent unemployment, voluntarily left Roe, then four years old, with Houghton. That same year, Houghton was appointed co-guardian of Roe. . . . After Roe's biological father consented to termination of his parental rights, Houghton attempted to adopt Roe. Because of Houghton's homosexuality, however, he did not receive a favorable preliminary home study evaluation, which precluded him from filing the necessary adoption petition in state circuit court.

. . . .

Appellants. . . . alleged that the statute violates [their] fundamental rights and the principles of equal protection. Jointly, [they] asked the district court to declare Fla. Stat. § 63.042(3) unconstitutional and to enjoin its enforcement. . . . The district court . . . granted summary judgment in favor of the state on all counts. . . .

Appellants assert three constitutional arguments on appeal. First, appellants argue that the statute violates [their] rights to familial privacy, intimate association, and family integrity under the Due Process Clause of the Fourteenth Amendment. Second, appellants argue that the Supreme Court's recent decision in *Lawrence v. Texas*, 539 U.S. [558] (2003) recognized a fundamental right to private sexual intimacy and that the Florida statute, by disallowing adoption by individuals who engage in homosexual activity, impermissibly burdens the exercise of this right. Third, appellants allege that, by categorically prohibiting only homosexual persons from adopting children, the statute violates the Equal Protection Clause of the Fourteenth Amendment. Each of these challenges raises questions of first impression in this circuit.

II.

. . . .

. . . Under Florida law, "adoption is not a right; it is a statutory privilege." *Dept. of Health & Rehabilitative Servs. v. Cox*, 627 So.2d 1210 (Fla. Dist. Ct. App. 1993). Unlike biological parentage, which precedes and transcends formal recognition by the state, adoption is wholly a creature of the state.

In formulating its adoption policies and procedures, the State of Florida acts in the protective and provisional role of *in loco parentis* for those children who, because of various circumstances, have become wards of the state. Thus, adoption law is unlike criminal law, for example, where the paramount substantive concern is not intruding on individuals' liberty interests, *see, e.g., Lawrence,* [539 U.S. 558] (2003); Roe v. Wade, 410 U.S. 113 (1973), and the paramount procedural imperative is ensuring due process and fairness. Adoption is also distinct from such contexts as government-benefit eligibility schemes or access to a public forum, where equality of treatment is the primary concern. By contrast, in the adoption context, the state's overriding interest is the best interests of the children whom it is seeking to place with adoptive families. Florida, acting *parens patriae* for children who have lost their natural parents, bears the high duty of determining what adoptive home environments will best serve all aspects of the child's growth and development.

Because of the primacy of the welfare of the child, the state can make classifications for adoption purposes that would be constitutionally suspect in many other arenas. . . . In screening adoption applicants, Florida considers such factors as physical and mental health, income and financial status, duration of marriage, housing, and neighborhood, among others. Similarly, Florida gives preference to candidates who demonstrate a commitment to "value, respect, appreciate, and educate the child regarding his or her racial and ethnic heritage." FLA. ADMIN. CODE ANN. r. 65C-16.005(3) (2003). Moreover, prospective adoptive parents are required to sign an affidavit of good moral character. Many of these preferences and requirements, if employed outside the adoption arena, would be unlikely to withstand constitutional scrutiny. *See, e.g., Troxel v. Granville,* 530 U.S. 57, 68 (2000) (recognizing that, absent neglect or abuse, the state may not "inject itself into the private realm of the family to further question the ability of that parent to make the best decisions concerning the rearing of that parent's children").

The decision to adopt a child is not a private one, but a public act. At a minimum, would-be adoptive parents are asking the state to confer official recognition — and, consequently, the highest level of constitutional insulation from subsequent state interference, on a relationship where there exists no natural filial bond. In many cases, they also are asking the state to entrust into their permanent care a child for whom the state is currently serving as *in loco parentis.* In doing so, these prospective adoptive parents are electing to open their homes and their private lives to close scrutiny by the state. . . .

In short, a person who seeks to adopt is asking the state to conduct an examination into his or her background and to make a determination as to the best interests of a child in need of adoption. In doing so, the state's overriding interest is not providing individuals the opportunity to become parents, but rather identifying those individuals whom it deems most capable of parenting adoptive children and providing them with a secure family environment. Indicative of the strength of the state's interest — indeed duty — in this context is the fact that appellants have not cited to us, nor have we found, a single precedent in which the Supreme Court or one of our sister circuits has sustained a constitutional challenge to an adoption scheme or practice by any individual other than a natural parent. . . .

Neither party disputes that there is no fundamental right to adopt, nor any fundamental right to be adopted. . . .

Nevertheless, appellants argue that, by prohibiting homosexual adoption, the state is refusing to recognize and protect constitutionally protected parent-child relationships between Lofton and Doe and between Houghton and Roe. . . . Only by being given the opportunity to adopt, appellants assert, will they be able to protect their alleged right to "family integrity."

. . . .

. . . Here, we find that under Florida law neither a foster parent nor a legal guardian could have a justifiable expectation of a permanent relationship with his or her child free from state oversight or intervention. Under Florida law, foster care is designed to be a short-term arrangement while the state attempts to find a permanent adoptive home. . . .

. . . .

Laws that burden the exercise of a fundamental right require strict scrutiny and are sustained only if narrowly tailored to further a compelling government interest. See, e.g., Zablocki v. Redhail, 434 U.S. 374, 388 (1978); Shapiro v. Thompson, 394 U.S. 618, 634 (1969). Appellants argue that the Supreme Court's recent decision in Lawrence v. Texas, which struck down Texas's sodomy statute, identified a hitherto unarticulated fundamental right to private sexual intimacy. They contend that the Florida statute, by disallowing adoption to any individual who chooses to engage in homosexual conduct, impermissibly burdens the exercise of this right.

We begin with the threshold question of whether Lawrence identified a new fundamental right to private sexual intimacy. Lawrence's holding was that substantive due process does not permit a state to impose a criminal prohibition on private consensual homosexual conduct. The effect of this holding was to establish a greater respect than previously existed in the law for the right of consenting adults to engage in private sexual conduct. Nowhere, however, did the Court characterize this right as "fundamental." (Scalia, J., dissenting). . . .

We are particularly hesitant to infer a new fundamental liberty interest from an opinion whose language and reasoning are inconsistent with standard fundamental-rights analysis. . . .

We conclude that it is a strained and ultimately incorrect reading of Lawrence to interpret it to announce a new fundamental right. . . .

Moreover, the holding of Lawrence does not control the present case. Apart from the shared homosexuality component, there are marked differences in the facts of the two cases. The Court itself stressed the limited factual situation it was addressing in Lawrence:

> The present case does not involve minors. It does not involve persons who might be injured or coerced or who are situated in relationships where consent might not easily be refused. It does not involve public conduct or prostitution. It does not involve whether the government must give formal recognition to any relationship that homosexual persons seek to enter. The case does involve two adults who, with full and mutual consent from each other, engaged in sexual practices common to a homosexual lifestyle.

Lawrence, supra, [at 525]. Here, the involved actors are not only consenting adults, but minors as well. The relevant state action is not criminal prohibition, but grant of a statutory privilege. And the asserted liberty interest is not the negative right to engage in private conduct without facing criminal sanctions, but the affirmative right to receive official and public recognition. Hence, we conclude that the *Lawrence* decision cannot be extrapolated to create a right to adopt for homosexual persons.

. . . As we have explained, Florida's statute burdens no fundamental rights. Moreover, all of our sister circuits that have considered the question have declined to treat homosexuals as a suspect class. Because the present case involves neither a fundamental right nor a suspect class, we review the Florida statute under the rational-basis standard.

Rational-basis review, "a paradigm of judicial restraint," does not provide "a license for courts to judge the wisdom, fairness, or logic of legislative choices." *F.C.C. v. Beach Communications, Inc.*, 508 U.S. 307, 313–14 (1993). The question is simply whether the challenged legislation is rationally related to a legitimate state interest. *Heller v. Doe*, 509 U.S. 312, 320 (1993). Under this deferential standard, a legislative classification "is accorded a strong presumption of validity," *id.* at 319, and "must be upheld against equal protection challenge if there is any reasonably conceivable state of facts that could provide a rational basis for the classification." *Id* at 320. This holds true "even if the law seems unwise or works to the disadvantage of a particular group, or if the rationale for it seems tenuous." *Romer v. Evans*, 517 U.S. at 632. . . . "[T]he burden is on the one attacking the legislative arrangement to negative every conceivable basis which might support it, whether or not the basis has a foundation in the record." *Heller, supra,* at 320–21.

. . . Florida argues that the statute is rationally related to Florida's interest in furthering the best interests of adopted children by placing them in families with married mothers and fathers. Such homes, Florida asserts, provide the stability that marriage affords and the presence of both male and female authority figures, which it considers critical to optimal childhood development and socialization. In particular, Florida emphasizes a vital role that dual-gender parenting plays in shaping sexual and gender identity and in providing heterosexual role modeling. Florida argues that disallowing adoption into homosexual households, which are necessarily motherless or fatherless and lack the stability that comes with marriage, is a rational means of furthering Florida's interest in promoting adoption by marital families.

Florida clearly has a legitimate interest in encouraging a stable and nurturing environment for the education and socialization of its adopted children. . . . It is hard to conceive an interest more legitimate and more paramount for the state than promoting an optimal social structure for educating, socializing, and preparing its future citizens to become productive participants in civil society — particularly when those future citizens are displaced children for whom the state is standing *in loco parentis.*

More importantly for present purposes, the state has a legitimate interest in encouraging this optimal family structure by seeking to place adoptive children in homes that have both a mother and father. Florida argues that its preference for adoptive marital families is based on the premise that the marital family structure is more stable than other household arrangements and that children benefit from the presence of both a father and mother in the home. Given that appellants have offered no competent evidence to the contrary, we find this premise to be one of those "unprovable assumptions" that nevertheless can provide a legitimate basis for legislative action. Although social theorists from Plato to Simone de Beauvoir have proposed alternative child-rearing arrangements, none has proven as enduring as the marital family structure, nor has the accumulated wisdom of several millennia of human experience discovered a superior model. *See, e.g.*, Plato, *The Republic*, Bk. V, 459d–461e; Simone de Beauvoir, *The Second Sex* (H.M. Parshley trans., Vintage Books 1989) (1949). Against this "sum of experience," it is rational for Florida to conclude that it is in the best interests of adoptive children, many of whom come from troubled and unstable backgrounds, to be placed in a home anchored by both a father and a mother.

Appellants. . . . maintain that the statute is not rationally related to this interest[, that the statute] is both overinclusive and underinclusive, [and] that the real motivation behind the statute cannot be the best interest of adoptive children.

Appellants note that Florida law permits adoption by unmarried individuals and that, among children coming out [sic] the Florida foster care system, 25% of adoptions are to parents who are currently single. Their argument is that homosexual persons are similarly situated to unmarried persons with regard to Florida's asserted interest in promoting married-couple adoption. According to appellants, this disparate treatment lacks a rational basis and, therefore, disproves any rational connection between the statute and Florida's asserted interest in promoting adoption into married homes. . . .

. . . .

. . . The Florida legislature could rationally conclude that homosexuals and heterosexual singles are not "similarly situated in relevant respects." It is not irrational to think that heterosexual singles have a markedly greater probability of eventually establishing a married household and, thus, providing their adopted children with a stable, dual-gender parenting environment. Moreover, as the state noted, the legislature could rationally act on the theory that heterosexual singles, even if they never marry, are better positioned than homosexual individuals to provide adopted children with education and guidance relative to their sexual development throughout pubescence and adolescence. . . .

The possibility, raised by appellants, that some homosexual households, including those of appellants, would provide a better environment than would some heterosexual single-parent households does not alter our analysis. The Supreme Court repeatedly has instructed that neither the fact that a classification may be overinclusive or underinclusive nor the fact that a generalization underlying a classification is subject to exceptions renders the classification irrational. . . . We conclude that there are plausible rational reasons for the disparate treatment of homosexuals and heterosexual singles under Florida adoption law and that, to the extent that the classification may be imperfect, that imperfection does not rise to the level of a constitutional infraction. Appellants make much of the fact that Florida has over three thousand children who are currently in foster care and, consequently, have not been placed with permanent adoptive families. According to appellants, because excluding homosexuals from the pool of prospective adoptive parents will not create more eligible married couples to reduce the backlog, it is impossible for the legislature to believe that the statute advances the state's interest in placing children with married couples.

We do not agree that the statute does not further the state's interest in promoting nuclear-family adoption because it may delay the adoption of some children. Appellants misconstrue Florida's interest, which is not simply to place children in a permanent home as quickly as possible, but, when placing them, to do so in an optimal home, i.e., one in which there is a heterosexual couple or the potential for one. According to appellants' logic, every restriction on adoptive-parent candidates, such as income, in-state residency, and criminal record — none of which creates more available married couples — are likewise constitutionally suspect as long as Florida has a backlog of unadopted foster children. The best interests of children, however, are not automatically served by adoption into *any* available home merely because it is permanent. Moreover, the legislature could rationally act on the theory that not placing adoptees in homosexual households increases the probability that these children eventually will be placed with married-couple families, thus furthering the state's goal of optimal placement. Therefore, we conclude that Florida's current foster care backlog does not render the statute irrational.

Noting that Florida law permits homosexuals to become foster parents and permanent guardians, appellants contend that this fact demonstrates that Florida must not truly believe that placement in a homosexual household is not in a child's best interests. . . . We have not located and appellants have not cited any precedent indicating that a disparity between a law and its enforcement is a relevant consideration on rational-basis review, which only asks whether the legislature could have reasonably thought that the challenged law would further a legitimate state interest. Thus, to the extent that foster care and guardianship placements with homosexuals are the handiwork of Florida's executive branch, they are irrelevant to the question of the *legislative* rationale for Florida's adoption scheme. To the extent that these placements are the product of an intentional legislative choice to treat foster care and guardianships differently than adoption, the distinction is not an irrational one. Indeed, it bears a rational relationship to Florida's interest in promoting the nuclear-family model of adoption since foster care and guardianship have neither the permanence nor the societal, cultural, and legal significance as does adoptive parenthood, which is the legal equivalent of natural parenthood.

Appellants cite recent social science research and the opinion of mental health professionals and child welfare organizations as evidence that there is no child welfare basis for excluding homosexuals from adopting. They argue that the cited studies show that the parenting skills of homosexual parents are at least equivalent to those of heterosexual parents and that children raised by homosexual parents suffer no adverse outcomes. Appellants also point to the policies and practices of numerous adoption agencies that permit homosexual persons to adopt.

In considering appellants' argument, we must ask not whether the latest in social science research and professional opinion *support* the decision of the Florida legislature, but whether that evidence is so well established and so far beyond dispute that it would be irrational for the Florida legislature to believe that the interests of its children are best served by not permitting homosexual adoption. Also, we must credit any conceivable rational reason that the legislature might have for choosing not to alter its statutory scheme in response to this recent social science research. We must assume, for example, that the legislature might be aware of the critiques of the studies cited by appellants — critiques that have highlighted significant flaws in the studies' methodologies and conclusions, such as the use of small, self-selected samples; reliance on self-report instruments; politically driven hypotheses; and the use of unrepresentative study populations consisting of disproportionately affluent, educated parents. Alternatively, the legislature might consider and credit other studies that have found that children raised in homosexual households fare differently on a number of measures, doing worse on some of them, than children raised in similarly situated heterosexual households. Or the legislature might consider, and even credit, the research cited by appellants, but find it premature to rely on a very recent and still developing body of research, particularly in light of the absence of longitudinal studies following child subjects into adulthood and of studies of adopted, rather than natural, children of homosexual parents.

We do not find any of these possible legislative responses to be irrational. . . . Nor is it irrational for the legislature to proceed with deliberate caution before placing adoptive children in an alternative, but unproven, family structure that has not yet been conclusively demonstrated to be equivalent to the marital family structure that has established a proven track record spanning centuries. Accordingly, we conclude that appellants' proffered social science evidence does not disprove the rational basis of the Florida statute.

Finally, we disagree with appellants' contention that *Romer* requires us to strike down the Florida statute. In *Romer*, the Supreme Court invalidated Amendment 2 to the Colorado state constitution, which prohibited all legislative, executive, or judicial action designed to protect homosexual persons from discrimination. The constitutional defect in Amendment 2 was the disjunction between the "[s]weeping and comprehensive" classification it imposed on homosexuals and the state's asserted bases for the classification — respect for freedom of association and conservation of resources to fight race and gender discrimination. The Court concluded that the Amendment's "sheer breadth is so discontinuous with the reasons offered for it that the amendment seems inexplicable by anything but animus toward the class it affects."

Unlike Colorado's Amendment 2, Florida's statute is not so "[s]weeping and comprehensive" as to render Florida's rationales for the statute "inexplicable by anything but animus" toward its homosexual residents. . . . Thus, we conclude that *Romer*'s unique factual situation and narrow holding are inapposite to this case.

NOTES

1. ***Background on the* Lofton *case.*** Florida's ban on gays and lesbians adopting, codified in Section 63.042(3), was passed in 1977, as a result of strong lobbying by anti-gay activist Anita Bryant. Bryant had been successful throughout

the 1970s in overturning anti-discrimination statutes and ordinances that protected homosexuals in a variety of states and municipalities. Although Florida's ban on adoption by homosexuals was not unique in the country, the *Lofton* case quickly garnered national media attention. The plaintiffs' challenge to the statute received substantial publicity, due in part to the support of then-television talk show host Rosie O'Donnell, who reportedly "came out" for the purpose of assisting the plaintiffs. *See* Michael T. Morley, Richard Albert, Jennie L. Kneedler, & Chrystiane Pereira, *Developments in Law and Policy: Emerging Issues in Family Law*, 21 YALE L. & POL'Y REV. 169, 198 (2003).

2. ***Examining the Decision in* Lofton.** The Eleventh Circuit flatly rejected the petitioners' claims that the United States Supreme Court identified a fundamental right of private sexual intimacy in *Lawrence v. Texas*, reprinted in Section C[2] above, which the Florida infringed upon. As Note 2 in Chapter 1, Section C[2], suggests, the standard of review used by the Supreme Court in *Lawrence* was not clearly articulated in Justice Kennedy's majority opinion. Since the Supreme Court announced its opinion in *Lawrence* in 2003, no court has found that that case announced a fundamental right. Note, however, that two circuit courts have decided that *Lawrence* applied intermediate scrutiny. *See Witt v. Dep't of the Air Force*, 527 F.3d 806, 816–17, 818 (9th Cir. 2008); *Cook v. Gates*, 528 F.3d 42 (1st Cir. 2008). Further, several courts have begun to consider homosexuality a quasi-suspect class for equal protection purposes under state constitutions. *See, e.g., Kerrigan v. Comm'r of Pub. Health*, 957 A.2d 407, 461 (Conn. 2008) (quasi-suspect class); *Varnum v. Brien*, 763 N.W.2d 862, 896 (Iowa 2009) (determining that homosexuality is a class entitled to heightened scrutiny, but without settling the question of whether that scrutiny is intermediate or strict).

While the *Lofton* court discussed *Romer*, it does not appear to have scrutinized the rationale for singling out homosexuals as stringently as the Supreme Court scrutinized Colorado Amendment 2 in *Romer*. Thus, in effect, the *Lofton* and *Romer* courts applied distinctly different standards of review, despite the "rational basis" label. Can this differential treatment be justified?

Note that the *Lofton* court differed markedly from the court in *Goodridge v. Department of Public Health*, 798 N.E.2d 941 (Mass. 2004), in its interpretation of the body of social science research that examines the effects on children of parenting by gays or lesbians as contrasted with heterosexuals. Social scientists have concluded that the relevant empirical research thus far reveals no significant or relevant differences between children raised by gay or lesbian parents and those raised by heterosexual parents on a host of measures of psychological and social adjustment. *See, e.g.,* Charlotte J. Patterson, *Children of Lesbian and Gay Parents*, 15 CURRENT DIRECTIONS PSYCHOL. SCI. 241–44 (2006), reprinted in Section B[4] above. Despite these appraisals of the literature, the *Lofton* court deferred to the possibility that the legislature "might find it premature to rely on a very recent and still developing body of research." One might observe, however, that this body of research, like most others, will always be "developing." Professor Michael Wald noted, "as a practical matter, there may never be sufficient research to convince the skeptics." *Same-Sex Couple Marriage: A Family Policy Perspective*, 9 VA. J. SOC. POL'Y & L. 291, 328 (2001). Arguably, the burden *Lofton* places on the law's challengers is so heavy that the scientific method will always be an inadequate tool.

3. *State Prohibitions on Adoptions by Gay and Lesbian Individuals and Couples.* Most state statutes are silent on the eligibility of gay or lesbian couples or individuals to adopt children. A small minority of states have statutes that create categorical bars to adoptions by gay and lesbian or unmarried individuals or couples, which have the same effect. Mississippi and Alaska both have an outright prohibition on adoption by same-sex couples. *See* MISS. CODE § 93-17-3(2) (2003) ("Adoption by couples of the same gender is prohibited");1998 Alaska Legis. Serv. 439 (House Joint Resolution stating "that we hereby express our intent to prohibit child adoption by homosexual couples"). In a well-publicized 2008 election, fifty-seven percent of the voters of Arkansas approved a ban on adoptions by unmarried couples, thus barring all homosexual couples from adopting in that state. *See* Arkansas, ballot referendum of Nov. 4, 2008 (not yet codified); Robbie Brown, *Antipathy Toward Obama Seen as Helping Arkansas Limit Adoption*, THE NEW YORK TIMES, Nov. 9, 2008, at A26. Interestingly, Connecticut allows both private adoption agencies and the state itself to take sexual orientation into account when placing a child in an adoptive home and allows, but does not require, sexual orientation of the prospective adoptive parent to be a bar to an individual adoption. CONN. GEN. STAT. § 45a-726a.

Several states have repealed bans on gays and lesbians adopting in recent years. New Jersey was the first state formally to lift a ban against unmarried-couple adoptions as part of a consent decree in litigation brought by the American Civil Liberties Union on behalf of a gay couple. *Holden v. New Jersey Dept. of Hum. Svcs.*, Sup. Ct. N.J., No. C-203-97 (1996). The state's administrative code was revised to provide a general non-discrimination clause that included sexual orientation as a protected status in seeking adoptive homes for children of that state. *See* N.J. Admin. Code § 10:121C-2.6, 4.1 (New Jersey "shall not discriminate in a child's adoptive placement based on the child's or the adoptive parent's race, color, national origin, age, gender, disability, marital status, sexual orientation, state of residence, or religion"). New Hampshire followed in 1999, when the legislature repealed a statute precluding homosexuals from adopting. N.H. REV. STAT. ANN. § 170-B:4. In addition, the Oklahoma state legislature repealed a similar provision in 2004, likely in response to the Supreme Court's holding in *Lawrence*. *See former* OKLA. ST. ANN. § 7007-1.4.A.6.f. (2003) (indicating that among the duties and responsibilities of the child welfare system is "prohibiting homosexuals from adopting children").

4. *Judicial Approval of Joint Adoptions.* Some state courts that in the past only allowed married persons to adopt jointly are now allowing unmarried same-sex couples to adopt jointly. For example, a New York appellate court recently approved a lesbian couple's joint adoption of a child who was biologically related to neither party in *In re Adoption of Carolyn B.*, 774 N.Y.S.2d 227 (N.Y. App. Div. 2004). Although New York's adoption statute provided that "[a]n adult married person or an adult husband and his adult wife may adopt another person," the appellate court held the provision to be no bar to the adoption by two women of a child with whom neither had a preexisting relationship. The appellate court stated that its decision was consistent with "both the letter and the spirit of the statute as it has developed: 'encouraging the adoption of as many children as possible regardless of the sexual orientation or marital status of the individuals seeking to adopt them.' " *Id.* at 229.

For a summary of state adoption and foster care policies with respect to gay and lesbian adoption and fostering as of 2007, *see* GARY J. GATES, M.V. LEE BADGETT, KATE CHAMBERS, & JENNIFER MACOMBER, WILLIAMS INSTITUTE, ADOPTION AND FOSTER CARE BY LESBIANS & GAY MEN IN THE UNITED STATES (2007), available at http://www.law.ucla.edu/williamsinstitute/publications/FinalAdoptionReport.pdf.

5. Lofton *superseded?* In 2007, the Florida ACLU brought another constitutional challenge to Florida's ban on adoption by gays on behalf of a same-sex couple whose petition for adoption was denied. After an extensive trial in the Dade County Circuit Court with numerous experts testifying to similar social science data and studies as cited in *Lofton*, Circuit Court Judge Lederman ruled that the statute violated the children's and prospective parents' equal protection rights under the Florida Constitution. To reach this conclusion, the court held that the statute's ban on homosexuals adopting did not withstand even rational basis review. In examining *Lofton*, the trial court judge determined that, "based on the developments in the fields of social science," the constitutionality of the Florida statute was again ripe for examination. *Adoption of Doe*, 2008 WL 5006172, *27 (Fla. Cir. Ct. Nov. 25, 2008). Based on the social science discussed *supra*, the court found no rational basis in upholding the statute to promote the well-being of the children or based on any social stigma or requirement for dual gender roles in the home. *Id.* at *28 ("[T]his Court rejects the Department's attempt to justify the statute by reference to a supposed dark cloud hovering over homes of homosexuals and their children."). Furthermore, applying *Lawrence*, the *Doe* Court found, contrary to *Lofton*, that public morality was not a legitimate state interest for this statute to withstand even rational basis review. *Id.*, at *29. As of this writing, an appeal is pending in the Florida District Court of Appeals.

[b] Parenting Disputes Between Former Same-Sex Partners

In the past several decades, increasing numbers of lesbian couples have jointly planned the conception and parenting of children, effecting those plans through the artificial insemination of one of the women. If the couple happens to live in a state that either authorizes same-sex marriage or recognizes same-sex marriages celebrated in other states and they marry before the birth, the marital presumption will generally apply to ensure that the partner without the biological tie to the child has parental status. However, if the partners are not validly married and no second-parent adoption follows the conception and birth of the child, the legal status of the biological mother's ex-partner is uncertain. In a number of jurisdictions, after the same-sex partnership dissolves, the partner who is not biologically related to the child has sued to obtain legal recognition of her relationship with the child. As the cases below reveal, sometimes this quest for recognition is presented as an issue of parentage, and sometimes it is presented as an issue of custody or visitation.

[1]   Custody Disputes Between Same-Sex Partners

V.C. v. M.J.B.
New Jersey Supreme Court
748 A.2d 539 (2000)

[*V.C. v. M.J.B.* is reprinted in Chapter 6, Section F[2].]

[2]   Parentage Disputes Between Same-Sex Partners

Two California cases decided in 2005, which are reproduced below, develop the claims of former lesbian partners who are not biologically related to their ex-partners' children as parentage issues.[7] The legal prelude to these decisions in California law came twelve years earlier, in *Johnson v. Calvert*, 851 P.2d 776 (Cal. 1993). *Johnson* involved a dispute over parentage rights between a surrogate and the heterosexual married couple who had hired her. Although the surrogate had gestated the child, the husband and wife had contributed the genetic material from which the child was conceived. The California Supreme Court held that in cases such as this one, in which each of two women had a legally valid claim to maternity, under the Uniform Parentage Act of 1973, which governed parentage in California, "intent" to be the child's parent should break the tie between the two claimants. While the court did not elaborate substantially on the concept of "intent," it was clear from the court's application of this test that it meant intention to set in motion the reproductive process *in order to* conceive a child that *she would raise as her own.* The court distinguished the situation before it from "a true 'egg donation' situation, where a woman gestates and gives birth to a child formed from the egg of another woman with the intent to raise the child as her own." 851 P.2d at 782, n.10. In such a case, the *Johnson* court stated, the birth mother would be the natural mother under California law. (For a more detailed discussion of *Johnson v. Calvert*, see Chapter 11.)

ELISA B. v. SUPERIOR COURT OF EL DORADO COUNTY
California Supreme Court
117 P.3d 660 (2005)

We granted review in this case, as well as in *K.M. v. E.G*, and *Kristine H. v. Lisa R.*, to consider the parental rights and obligations, if any, of a woman with regard to a child born to her partner in a lesbian relationship.

. . . .

On June 7, 2001, the El Dorado County District Attorney filed a complaint in superior court to establish that Elisa B. is a parent of two-year-old twins Kaia B. and Ry B., who were born to Emily B., and to order Elisa to pay child support.

---

[7] A third case, *Kristine H. v. Lisa R.*, 117 P.3d 690 (Cal. 2005), not reproduced here, considered whether the biological mother of a child could contest the validity of a judgment to which she and her ex-partner had previously stipulated, declaring her partner to be the second parent of the child. The court held that the biological mother was estopped to contest the judgment.

Elisa filed an answer in which she denied being the children's parent.

A hearing was held at which Elisa testified that she entered into a lesbian relationship with Emily in 1993. They began living together six months later. . . .

Elisa and Emily discussed having children and decided that they both wished to give birth. Because Elisa earned more than twice as much money as Emily, they decided that Emily "would be the stay-at-home mother" and Elisa "would be the primary breadwinner for the family." At a sperm bank, they chose a donor they both would use so the children would "be biological brothers and sisters."

After several unsuccessful attempts, Elisa became pregnant in February 1997. Emily was present when Elisa was inseminated. Emily began the insemination process in June of 1997 and became pregnant in August 1997. Elisa was present when Emily was inseminated and, the next day, Elisa picked up additional sperm at the sperm bank and again inseminated Emily at their home to "make sure she got pregnant." They went to each other's medical appointments during pregnancy and attended childbirth classes together so that each could act as a "coach" for the other during birth, including cutting the children's umbilical cords.

Elisa gave birth to Chance in November 1997, and Emily gave birth to Ry and Kaia prematurely in March 1998. Ry had medical problems; he suffered from Down's syndrome, and required heart surgery.

They jointly selected the children's names, joining their surnames with a hyphen to form the children's surname. They each breast-fed all of the children. Elisa claimed all three children as her dependents on her tax returns and obtained a life insurance policy on herself naming Emily as the beneficiary so that if "anything happened" to her, all three children would be "cared for." Elisa believed the children would be considered both of their children.

Elisa's parents referred to the twins as their grandchildren, and her sister referred to the twins as part of their family and referred to Elisa as the twins' mother. Elisa treated all of the children as hers and told a prospective employer that she had triplets. Elisa and Emily identified themselves as coparents of Ry at an organization arranging care for his Down's syndrome.

Elisa supported the household financially. Emily was not working. Emily testified that she would not have become pregnant if Elisa had not promised to support her financially, but Elisa denied that any financial arrangements were discussed before the birth of the children. Elisa later acknowledged in her testimony, however, that Emily "was going to be an at-home mom for maybe a couple of years and then the kids were going to go into day care and she was going to return to work."

They consulted an attorney regarding adopting "each other's child," but never did so. Nor did they register as domestic partners or execute a written agreement concerning the children. Elisa stated she later reconsidered adoption because she had misgivings about Emily adopting Chance.

Elisa and Emily separated in November 1999. Elisa promised to support Emily and the twins "as much as I possibly could" and initially paid the mortgage payments of approximately $1,500 per month on the house in which Emily and the twins continued to live, as well as other expenses. Emily applied for aid. When they sold the house and Emily and the twins moved into an apartment in November 2000, Elisa paid Emily $1,000 a month. In early 2001, Elisa stated she lost her position as a full-time employee and told Emily she no longer could support her and the twins. At the time of trial, Elisa was earning $95,000 a year.

The superior court rendered a written decision on July 11, 2002, finding that Elisa and Emily had rejected the option of using a private sperm donor because "[t]hey wanted the child to be raised exclusively by them as a couple." The court further found that they intended to create a child and "acted in all respects as a family," adding "that a person who uses reproductive technology is accountable as a de facto legal parent for the support of that child. Legal parentage is not determined exclusively by biology."

. . . .

[The Court of Appeals reversed the trial court, instead holding that Elisa was not a parent of the twins and was therefore not required to pay child support, and the Supreme Court accepted review.]

We must determine whether the Court of Appeal erred in ruling that Elisa could not be a parent of the twins born to her lesbian partner, and thus had no obligation to support them. This question is governed by the [1973] Uniform Parentage Act (UPA). [CAL. FAM. CODE §§ 7600–7730]. The UPA defines the " '[p]arent and child relationship' " as "the legal relationship existing between a child and the child's natural or adoptive parents.". . . . [T]he UPA provides that the parentage of a child does not depend upon " 'the marital status of the parents' " stating: "The parent and child relationship extends equally to every child and to every parent, regardless of the marital status of the parents." [CAL. FAM. CODE § 7602].

The UPA contains separate provisions defining who is a "mother" and who is a "father." Section 7610 provides that "[t]he parent and child relationship may be established . . . : [¶] (a) Between a child and the natural mother . . . by proof of her having given birth to the child, or under this part." [§ 7610(b)] states that the parental relationship "[b]etween a child and the natural father . . . may be established under this part."

Section 7611 provides several circumstances in which "[a] man is presumed to be the natural father of a child," including: if he is the husband of the child's mother, is not impotent or sterile, and was cohabiting with her, [CAL FAM. CODE § 7540]; if he signs a voluntary declaration of paternity stating he is the "biological father of the child," [CAL. FAM. CODE § 7574 (b)(6)]; and if "[h]e receives the child into his home and openly holds out the child as his natural child." [Cal. Fam. Code § 7611(d)].

Although, as noted above, the UPA contains separate provisions defining who is a mother and who is a father, it expressly provides that in determining the existence of a mother and child relationship, "[i]nsofar as practicable, the provisions of this part applicable to the father and child relationship apply." [CAL. FAM. CODE § 7650].

The Court of Appeal correctly recognized that, under the UPA, Emily has a parent and child relationship with each of the twins because she gave birth to them. CAL. FAM. CODE § 7610(a). Thus, the Court of Appeal concluded, Emily is the twins' natural mother. Relying upon our statement in *Johnson v. Calvert*, [19 Cal. Rptr. 2d 494, 499 (Cal. 1993)], that "for any child California law recognizes only one natural mother," the Court of Appeal reasoned that Elisa, therefore, could not also be the natural mother of the twins and thus "has no legal maternal relationship with the children under the UPA."

. . . .

[W]hat we considered and rejected in *Johnson* was the argument that a child could have three parents: a father and two mothers. We did not address the question presented in this case of whether a child could have two parents, both of whom are women. The Court of Appeal in the present case erred, therefore, in concluding that our statement in *Johnson* that a child can have only one mother under California law resolved the issue presented in this case. . . .

We perceive no reason why both parents of a child cannot be women. That result now is possible under the current version of the domestic partnership statutes, which took effect this year. [CAL. FAM. CODE §§ 297–299.6]. Two women "who have chosen to share one another's lives in an intimate and committed relationship of mutual caring" and have a common residence [CAL. FAM. CODE] § 297[,] can file with the Secretary of State a "Declaration of Domestic Partnership" [CAL FAM. CODE] § 298. Section 297.5[(d)] provides, in pertinent part: "The rights and obligations of registered domestic partners with respect to a child of either of them shall be the same as those of spouses."

Prior to the effective date of the current domestic partnership statutes, we recognized in an adoption case that a child can have two parents, both of whom are women. In *Sharon S. v. Superior Court*, [73 P.3d 554 (2003), reproduced above at Section B[4][a][i]], we upheld a "second parent" adoption in which the mother of a child that had been conceived by means of artificial insemination consented to adoption of the child by the mother's lesbian partner. If both parents of an adopted child can be women, we see no reason why the twins in the present case cannot have two parents, both of whom are women.

Having determined that our decision in *Johnson* does not preclude a child from having two parents both of whom are women and that no reason appears that a child's two parents cannot both be women, we proceed to examine the UPA to determine whether Elisa is a parent to the twins in addition to Emily. As noted above, section 7650 provides that provisions applicable to determining a father and child relationship shall be used to determine a mother and child relationship "insofar as practicable." . . .

[Section 7611(d)] states that a man is presumed to be the natural father of a child if "[h]e receives the child into his home and openly holds out the child as his natural child." . . .

Applying [§ 7611(d)] we must determine whether Elisa received the twins into her home and openly held them out as her natural children. There is no doubt that Elisa satisfied the first part of this test; it is undisputed that Elisa received the twins into her home. Our inquiry focuses, therefore, on whether she openly held out the twins as her natural children.

The circumstance that Elisa has no genetic connection to the twins does not necessarily mean that she did not hold out the twins as her "natural" children under § 7611. We held in *In re Nicholas H.*[, 46 P.3d 932 (2005),] that the presumption under [§ 7611(d)], that a man who receives a child into his home and openly holds the child out as his natural child is not necessarily rebutted when he admits he is not the child's biological father.

. . . .

We conclude that the present case . . . is not "an appropriate action" in which to rebut the presumption of presumed parenthood with proof that Elisa is not the twins' biological parent. This is generally a matter within the discretion of the superior court, but we need not remand the matter to permit the superior court to exercise its discretion because it would be an abuse of discretion to conclude that the presumption may be rebutted in the present case. It is undisputed that Elisa actively consented to, and participated in, the artificial insemination of her partner with the understanding that the resulting child or children would be raised by Emily and her as coparents, and they did act as coparents for a substantial period of time. Elisa received the twins into her home and held them out to the world as her natural children. She gave the twins and the child to whom she had given birth the same surname, which was formed by joining her surname to her partner's. The twins were half siblings to the child to whom Elisa had given birth. She breast-fed all three children, claimed all three children as her dependents on her tax returns, and told a prospective employer that she had triplets. Even at the hearing before the superior court, Elisa candidly testified that she considered herself to be the twins' mother.

Declaring that Elisa cannot be the twins' parent and, thus, has no obligation to support them because she is not biologically related to them would produce a result similar to the situation we sought to avoid in *Nicholas H.* of leaving the child fatherless. The twins in the present case have no father because they were conceived by means of artificial insemination using an anonymous semen donor. Rebutting the presumption that Elisa is the twin's [sic] parent would leave them with only one parent and would deprive them of the support of their second parent. Because Emily is financially unable to support the twins, the financial burden of supporting the twins would be borne by the county, rather than Elisa.

. . . .

In the present case, Elisa did not meet Emily after she was pregnant, but rather was in a committed relationship with her when they decided to have children together. Elisa actively assisted Emily in becoming pregnant, with the understanding that they would raise the resulting children together. Having helped cause the children to be born, and having raised them as her own, Elisa should not be permitted to later abandon the twins simply because her relationship with Emily dissolved.

As we noted in the context of a husband who consented to the artificial insemination of his wife using an anonymous sperm donor, but later denied responsibility for the resulting child: "One who consents to the production of a child cannot create a temporary relation to be assumed and disclaimed at will, but the arrangement must be of such character as to impose an obligation of supporting those for whose existence he is directly responsible." *People v. Sorensen*[, 437 P.2d 495 (Cal. 1968)]; *see Dunkin v. Boskey*[, 98 Cal. Rptr. 2d 44 (Ct. App. 2000)]. We observed that the "intent of the Legislature obviously was to include every child, legitimate or illegitimate, born or unborn, and enforce the obligation of support against the person who could be determined to be the lawful parent." *Sorensen*[, 437 P.2d at 499]. Further: "a reasonable man who, because of his inability to procreate, actively participates and consents to his wife's artificial insemination in the hope that a child will be produced whom they will treat as their own, knows that such behavior carries with it the legal responsibilities of fatherhood and criminal responsibility for nonsupport. . . . [I]t is safe to assume that without defendant's active participation and consent the child would not have been procreated." *Id.*; *see Dunkin v. Boskey*, [98 Cal. Rptr. 2d at 56–57].

We were careful in *Nicholas H.*, therefore, not to suggest that every man who begins living with a woman when she is pregnant and continues to do so after the child is born necessarily becomes a presumed father of the child, even against his wishes. The Legislature surely did not intend to punish a man like the one in *Nicholas H.* who voluntarily provides support for a child who was conceived before he met the mother, by transforming that act of kindness into a legal obligation.

But our observation in *Nicholas H.* loses its force in a case like the one at bar in which the presumed mother under [§ 7611(d)], acted together with the birth mother to cause the child to be conceived. In such circumstances, unlike the situation before us in *Nicholas H.*, we believe the Legislature would have intended to impose upon the presumed father or mother the legal obligation to support the child whom she caused to be born. As stated by amicus curiae the California State Association of Counties, representing all 58 counties in California: "A person who actively participates in bringing children into the world, takes the children into her home and holds them out as her own, and receives and enjoys the benefits of parenthood, should be responsible for the support of those children — regardless of her gender or sexual orientation."

We conclude, therefore, that Elisa is a presumed mother of the twins under [§ 7611(d)], because she received the children into her home and openly held them out as her natural children, and that this is not an appropriate action in which to rebut the presumption that Elisa is the twins' parent with proof that she is not the children's biological mother because she actively participated in causing the children to be conceived with the understanding that she would raise the children as her own together with the birth mother, she voluntarily accepted the rights and obligations of parenthood after the children were born, and there are no competing claims to her being the children's second parent.

. . . .

The judgment of the Court of Appeal is reversed.

K.M. v. E.G.
California Supreme Court
117 P.3d 673 (2005)

MORENO, JUSTICE.

We granted review in this case, as well as in *Elisa B. v. Superior Court*, and *Kristine H. v. Lisa R.*, to consider the parental rights and obligations, if any, of a woman with regard to a child born to her partner in a lesbian relationship.

In the present case, we must decide whether a woman who provided ova to her lesbian partner so that the partner could bear children by means of in vitro fertilization is a parent of those children. For the reasons that follow, we conclude that Family Code [§ 7613(b)], which provides that a man is not a father if he provides semen to a physician to inseminate a woman who is not his wife, does not apply when a woman provides her ova to impregnate her partner in a lesbian relationship in order to produce children who will be raised in their joint home. Accordingly, when partners in a lesbian relationship decide to produce children in this manner, both the woman who provides her ova and her partner who bears the children are the children's parents.

On March 6, 2001, petitioner K.M. filed a petition to establish a parental relationship with twin five-year-old girls born to respondent E.G., her former lesbian partner. K.M. alleged that she "is the biological parent of the minor children" because "[s]he donated her egg to respondent, the gestational mother of the children." E.G. moved to dismiss the petition on the grounds that, although K.M. and E.G. "were lesbian partners who lived together until this action was filed," K.M. "explicitly donated her ovum under a clear written agreement by which she relinquished any claim to offspring born of her donation."

On April 18, 2001, K.M. filed a motion for custody of and visitation with the twins.

A hearing was held at which E.G. testified that she first considered raising a child before she met K.M., at a time when she did not have a partner. She met K.M. in October 1992 and they became romantically involved in June 1993. E.G. told K.M. that she planned to adopt a baby as a single mother. E.G. applied for adoption in November 1993. K.M. and E.G. began living together in March 1994 and registered as domestic partners in San Francisco.

E.G. visited several fertility clinics in March 1993 to inquire about artificial insemination and she attempted artificial insemination, without success, on 13 occasions from July 1993 through November 1994. K.M. accompanied her to most of these appointments. K.M. testified that she and E.G. planned to raise the child together, while E.G. insisted that, although K.M. was very supportive, E.G. made it clear that her intention was to become "a single parent."

In December 1994, E.G. consulted with Dr. Mary Martin at the fertility practice of the University of California at San Francisco Medical Center (UCSF). E.G.'s first attempts at in vitro fertilization failed because she was unable to produce sufficient ova. In January 1995, Dr. Martin suggested using K.M.'s ova. E.G. then asked K.M. to donate her ova, explaining that she would accept the ova only if K.M. "would really be a donor" and E.G. would "be the mother of any child," adding that she would not even consider permitting K.M. to adopt the child "for at least five years until [she] felt the relationship was stable and would endure." E.G. told K.M. that she "had seen too many lesbian relationships end quickly, and [she] did not want to be in a custody battle." E.G. and K.M. agreed they would not tell anyone that K.M. was the ova donor.

K.M. acknowledged that she agreed not to disclose to anyone that she was the ova donor, but insisted that she only agreed to provide her ova because she and E.G. had agreed to raise the child together. K.M. and E.G. selected the sperm donor together. K.M. denied that E.G. had said she wanted to be a single parent and insisted that she would not have donated her ova had she known E.G. intended to be the sole parent.

On March 8, 1995, K.M. signed a four-page form on UCSF letterhead entitled "Consent Form for Ovum Donor (Known)." The form states that K.M. agrees "to have eggs taken from my ovaries, in order that they may be donated to another woman." After explaining the medical procedures involved, the form states on the third page: "It is understood that I waive any right and relinquish any claim to the donated eggs or any pregnancy or offspring that might result from them. I agree that the recipient may regard the donated eggs and any offspring resulting therefrom as her own children." The following appears on page 4 of the form, above K.M.'s signature and the signature of a witness: "I specifically disclaim and waive any right in or any child that may be conceived as a result of the use of any ovum or egg of mine, and I agree not to attempt to discover the identity of the recipient thereof." E.G. signed a form entitled "Consent Form for Ovum Recipient" that stated, in part: "I acknowledge that the child or children produced by the IVF procedure is and shall be my own legitimate child or children and the heir or heirs of my body with all rights and privileges accompanying such status."

E.G. testified she received these two forms in a letter from UCSF dated February 2, 1995, and discussed the consent forms with K.M. during February and March. E.G. stated she would not have accepted K.M.'s ova if K.M. had not signed the consent form, because E.G. wanted to have a child on her own and believed the consent form "protected" her in this regard.

K.M. testified to the contrary that she first saw the ovum donation consent form 10 minutes before she signed it on March 8, 1995. K.M. admitted reading the form, but thought parts of the form were "odd" and did not pertain to her, such as the part stating that the donor promised not to discover the identity of the recipient. She did not intend to relinquish her rights and only signed the form so that "we could have children." Despite having signed the form, K.M. "thought [she] was going to be a parent."

Ova were withdrawn from K.M. on April 11, 1995, and embryos were implanted in E.G. on April 13, 1995. K.M. and E.G. told K.M.'s father about the resulting pregnancy by announcing that he was going to be a grandfather. The twins were born on December 7, 1995. The twins' birth certificates listed E.G. as their mother and did not reflect a father's name. As they had agreed, neither E.G. nor K.M. told anyone K.M. had donated the ova, including their friends, family and the twins' pediatrician. Soon after the twins were born, E.G. asked K.M. to marry her, and on Christmas Day, the couple exchanged rings.

Within a month of their birth, E.G. added the twins to her health insurance policy, named them as her beneficiary for all employment benefits, and increased her life insurance with the twins as the beneficiary. K.M. did not do the same.

E.G. referred to her mother, as well as K.M.'s parents, as the twins' grandparents and referred to K.M.'s sister and brother as the twins' aunt and uncle, and K.M.'s nieces as their cousins. Two school forms listed both K.M. and respondent as the twins' parents. The children's nanny testified that both K.M. and E.G. "were the babies' mother."

The relationship between K.M. and E.G. ended in March 2001 and K.M. filed the present action. In September 2001, E.G. and the twins moved to Massachusetts to live with E.G.'s mother.

The superior court granted E.G.'s motion to dismiss finding, in a statement of decision, "that [K.M.] . . . knowingly, voluntarily and intelligently executed the ovum donor form, thereby acknowledging her understanding that, by the donation of her ova, she was relinquishing and waiving all rights to claim legal parentage of any children who might result from the *in vitro* fertilization and implantation of her ova in a recipient (in this case, a known recipient, her domestic partner [E.G.]). . . .

. . . .

". . . By voluntarily signing the ovum donation form, [K.M.] was donating genetic material. Her position was analogous to that of a sperm donor, who is treated as a legal stranger to a child if he donates sperm through a licensed physician and surgeon under [California Family Code § 7613(b)]. The Court finds no reason to treat ovum donors as having greater claims to parentage than sperm donors. . . .

"The Court accepts the proposition that a child may have two legal mothers and assumed it to be the law in its analysis of the evidence herein."

. . . .

[The Court of Appeals affirmed the judgment.]

K.M. asserts that she is a parent of the twins because she supplied the ova that were fertilized in vitro and implanted in her lesbian partner, resulting in the birth of the twins. As we will explain, we agree that K.M. is a parent of the twins because she supplied the ova that produced the children, and [California] Family Code § 7613(b) (hereafter § 7613(b), which provides that a man is not a father if he provides semen to a physician to inseminate a woman who is not his wife, does not apply because K.M. supplied her ova to impregnate her lesbian partner in order to produce children who would be raised in their joint home.

The determination of parentage is governed by the Uniform Parentage Act (UPA). As we observe in the companion case of *Elisa B. v. Superior Court*, the UPA defines the " 'parent and child relationship[, which] extends equally to every child and to every parent, regardless of the marital status of the parents.' " [CAL. FAM. CODE § 7602].

In *Johnson v. Calvert*, [19 Cal. Rptr. 2d 494, (Cal. 1993)], we determined that a wife whose ovum was fertilized in vitro by her husband's sperm and implanted in a surrogate mother was the "natural mother" of the child thus produced. We noted that the UPA states that provisions applicable to determining a father and child relationship shall be used to determine a mother and child relationship "insofar as practicable." We relied, therefore, on the provisions in the UPA regarding presumptions of paternity and concluded that "genetic consanguinity" could be the basis for a finding of maternity just as it is for paternity. Under this authority, K.M.'s genetic relationship to the children in the present case constitutes "evidence of a mother and child relationship as contemplated by the Act."

The Court of Appeal in the present case concluded, however, that K.M. was not a parent of the twins, despite her genetic relationship to them, because she had the same status as a sperm donor. § 7613(b) states: "The donor of semen provided to a licensed physician and surgeon for use in artificial insemination of a woman other than the donor's wife is treated in law as if he were not the natural father of a child thereby conceived.". . . . We held that the statute did not apply under the circumstances in *Johnson*, because the husband and wife in *Johnson* did not intend to "donate" their sperm and ova to the surrogate mother, but rather "intended to procreate a child genetically related to them by the only available means."

The circumstances of the present case are not identical to those in *Johnson*, but they are similar in a crucial respect[:] both the couple in *Johnson* and the couple in the present case intended to produce a child that would be raised in their own home. In *Johnson*, it was clear that the married couple did not intend to "donate" their semen and ova to the surrogate mother, but rather permitted their semen and ova to be used to impregnate the surrogate mother in order to produce a child to be raised by them. In the present case, K.M. contends that she did not intend to donate her ova, but rather provided her ova so that E.G. could give birth to a child to be raised jointly by K.M. and E.G. E.G. hotly contests this, asserting that K.M. donated her ova to E.G., agreeing that E.G. would be the sole parent. It is undisputed, however, that the couple lived together and that they both intended to bring the child into their joint home. Thus, even accepting as true E.G.'s version of the facts (which the superior court did), the present case, like *Johnson*, does not present a "true 'egg donation' " situation. K.M. did not intend to simply donate her ova to E.G., but rather provided her ova to her lesbian partner with whom she was living so that E.G. could give birth to a child that would be raised in their joint home. Even if we assume that the provisions of § 7613(b) apply to women who donate ova, the statute does not apply under the circumstances of the present case. . . .

As noted above, K.M.'s genetic relationship with the twins constitutes evidence of a mother and child relationship under the UPA, *Johnson v. Calvert*, and, as explained above, § 7613(b) does not apply to exclude K.M. as a parent of the twins. The circumstance that E.G. gave birth to the twins also constitutes evidence of a mother and child relationship. Thus, both K.M. and E.G. are mothers of the twins under the UPA.

It is true we said in *Johnson* that "for any child California law recognizes only one natural mother." But as we explain in the companion case of *Elisa B. v. Superior Court*, this statement in *Johnson* must be understood in light of the issue presented in that case; "our decision in *Johnson* does not preclude a child from having two parents both of whom are women. . . ."

Justice Werdegar's dissent argues that we should determine whether K.M. is a parent using the "intent test" we developed in *Johnson v. Calvert*. In *Johnson*, an embryo created using the sperm and egg of a married couple was implanted in a surrogate mother. It was undisputed that the husband was the father of the resulting child, but the wife and the surrogate both claimed to be the mother. . . . In order to determine which woman was the child's sole mother under the UPA, we looked to their respective intents: "Because two women each have presented acceptable proof of maternity, we do not believe this case can be decided without enquiring into the parties' intentions. . . ."

As the dissent acknowledges, a child can have two mothers. Thus, this case differs from *Johnson* in that both K.M. and E.G. can be the children's mothers. Unlike in *Johnson*, their parental claims are not mutually exclusive. K.M. acknowledges that E.G. is the twins' mother. K.M. does not claim to be the twins' mother *instead of* E.G., but *in addition to* E.G., so we need not consider their intent in order to decide between them. Rather, the parentage of the twins is determined by application of the UPA. E.G. is the twins' mother because she gave birth to them and K.M. also is the twins' mother because she provided the ova from which they were produced.

. . . We simply hold that § 7613(b), which creates an exception to the usual rules governing parentage that applies when a man donates semen to inseminate a woman who is not his wife, does not apply under the circumstances of this case in which K.M. supplied ova to impregnate her lesbian partner in order to produce children who would be raised in their joint home. Because the exception provided in § 7613(b) does not apply, K.M.'s parentage is determined by the usual provisions of the UPA. As noted above, under the UPA, K.M.'s genetic relationship to the twins constitutes "evidence of a mother and child relationship."

The judgment of the Court of Appeal is reversed.

JUSTICE KENNARD dissenting.

Unlike the majority, I would apply the controlling statutes as written. The statutory scheme for determining parentage contains two provisions that resolve K.M.'s claim to be a parent of the twins born to E.G. Under one provision, a man who donates sperm for physician-assisted artificial insemination of a woman to whom he is not married is not the father of the resulting child. [CAL. FAM. CODE] § 7613(b). Under the other provision, rules for determining fatherhood are to be used for determining motherhood "[i]nsofar as practicable." [CAL. FAM. CODE] § 7650. Because K.M. donated her ova for physician-assisted artificial insemination and implantation in another woman, and knowingly and voluntarily signed a document declaring her intention *not* to become a parent of any resulting children, she is not a parent of the twins.

. . . .

The majority's desire to give the twins a second parent is understandable and laudable. To achieve that worthy goal, however, the majority must rewrite a statute and disregard the intentions that the parties expressed when the twins were conceived. The majority amends the sperm-donor statute by inserting a new provision making a sperm donor the legal father of a child born to a woman artificially inseminated with his sperm whenever the sperm donor and the birth mother *"intended that the resulting child would be raised in their joint home,"* even though both the donor and birth mother also intended that the donor *not* be the child's father.

JUSTICE WERDEGAR dissenting.

The majority determines that the twins who developed from the ova K.M. donated to E.G. have two mothers rather than one. While I disagree, as I shall explain, with that ultimate conclusion, I agree with the majority's premise that a child can have two mothers. Our previous holding that "for any child California law recognizes only one natural mother" (*Johnson*) must be understood in the context in which it arose — a married couple who intended to become parents and provided their fertilized ova to a gestational surrogate who did not intend to become a parent — and, thus understood, may properly be limited to cases in which to recognize a second mother would inject an unwanted third parent into an existing family. When, in contrast to *Johnson*, no natural or adoptive father exists, two women who intend to become mothers of the same child may do so either through adoption or because both qualify as natural mothers under the Uniform Parentage Act (*Fam. Code, § 7600 et seq.*) (UPA), one having donated the ovum and the other having given birth.

While scientific advances in reproductive technology now afford individuals previously unimagined opportunities to become parents, the same advances have also created novel, sometimes heartbreaking issues concerning the identification of the resulting children's legal parents. Declarations of parentage in this context implicate complex and delicate biological, personal, legal and social policy considerations. For these reasons, courts have sought above all to avoid foreseeable disputes over parentage with rules that provide predictability by permitting the various persons who must cooperate to bring children into the world through assisted reproduction to determine in advance who will and will not be parents, based on their expressed and voluntarily chosen intentions.

Precisely because predictability in this area is so important, I cannot agree with the majority that the children in this case do in fact have two mothers. Until today, when one woman has provided the ova and another has given birth, the established rule for determining disputed claims to motherhood was clear: we looked to the intent of the parties. "[I]n a true 'egg donation' situation, where a woman gestates and gives birth to a child formed from the egg of another woman with the intent to raise the child as her own, the birth mother is the natural mother under California law." Contrary to the majority's apparent assumption, to limit *Johnson*'s holding that a child can have only one mother to cases involving existing two-parent families does not require us to abandon *Johnson*'s intent test as the method for determining disputed claims of motherhood arising from the use of reproductive technology. Indeed, we have no other test sufficient to the task.

Furthermore, to apply *Johnson*'s intent test to the facts of this case necessarily leads to the conclusion that E.G. is a mother and K.M. is not. That E.G. intended to become the mother — and the only mother — of the children to whom she gave birth is unquestioned. . . .

The new rule the majority substitutes for the intent test entails serious problems. First, the rule inappropriately confers rights and imposes disabilities on persons because of their sexual orientation. In a standard ovum donation agreement, such as the agreement between K.M. and E.G., the donor confirms her intention to assist another woman to become a parent without the donor becoming a parent herself. The majority's rule vitiates such agreements when its conditions are satisfied — conditions that include the fact the parties to the agreement are lesbian. Although the majority denies that its rule depends on sexual orientation, the opinion speaks for itself. . . .

Perhaps the most serious problem with the majority's new rule is that it threatens to destabilize ovum donation and gestational surrogacy agreements. One important function of *Johnson*'s intent test was to permit persons who made use of reproductive technology to create, before conception, settled and enforceable expectations about who would and would not become parents. *Johnson* thus gave E.G. a right at the time she conceived to expect that she alone would be the parent of her children — a right the majority now retrospectively abrogates. E.G.'s expectation has a constitutional dimension. (See *Troxel v. Granville (2000) 530 U.S. 57, 65*.) We cannot recognize K.M. as a parent without diminishing E.G.'s existing parental rights. In light of the majority's abrogation of *Johnson* and apparent willingness to ignore preconception manifestations of intent, at least in some cases, women who wish to donate ova without becoming mothers, serve as gestational surrogates without becoming mothers, or accept ovum donations without also accepting the donor as a coparent would be well advised to proceed with the most extreme caution. While the majority purports to limit its holding to cohabiting lesbians, and possibly only to those cohabiting lesbians who are also domestic partners, these limitations, as I have explained, rest on questionable legal grounds and may well not stand the test of time.

The majority seems to believe that, having concluded the sperm donation statute (*Fam. Code, § 7613, subd. (b)*) does not apply, one must necessarily conclude that K.M. is the mother of the children who developed from the ova she donated to E.G. This reasoning entails a non sequitur. The statute, when it applies, merely *excludes* someone as a possible parent; it does not *establish* parentage. In order to reach the further conclusion that K.M. is a parent, the majority must entertain a string of questionable assumptions: first, that we would refuse to apply the sperm donation statute (*Fam. Code, § 7613, subd. (b)*), despite its plain language, to cut off the parental rights and responsibilities of a man who donates his sperm through a physician to a woman who is not his wife but with whom he lives, and, second, that two women who live together and divide between themselves the genetic and gestational aspects of pregnancy must be treated in exactly the same way as the man and woman just posited. The latter assumption, in turn, embodies additional, unstated assumptions about the effect of the equal protection clause. But ovum donation, which requires substantial medical and scientific assistance, is not sufficiently like sperm donation, which can easily be accomplished by unassisted laypersons, to require equal treatment under the law for all purposes. Accordingly, to recognize the sperm donation statute's inapplicability does not dispose of this case; it merely leaves us with the same question with which we began, namely, whether K.M. is a second mother of E.G.'s children. Until today, the *Johnson* intent test would have required us to answer the question in the negative. In my view, it still should.

Perhaps the best way to understand today's decision is that we appear to be moving in cases of assisted reproduction from a categorical determination of parentage based on formal, preconception manifestations of intent to a case-by-case approach implicitly motivated at least in part by our intuitions about the children's best interests. We expressly eschewed a best interests approach in *Johnson*, explaining that it "raises the repugnant specter of governmental interference in matters implicating our most fundamental notions of privacy, and confuses concepts of parentage and custody." This case, in which the majority compels E.G. to accept K.M. as an unintended parent to E.G.'s children, in part because of E.G.'s and K.M.'s sexual orientation and the character of their private relationship, shows that *Johnson*'s warning was prescient. Only legislation defining parentage in the context of assisted reproduction is likely to restore predictability and prevent further lapses into the disorder of ad hoc adjudication.

NOTES

1. ***Multiple Legal Theories.*** As you can see from the two cases reproduced here, and the *V. C. v. M.J.B.* case reproduced in Chapter 6 as well as the notes that follow it, ex-partners in lesbian parenting cases have presented a variety of theories to assert their right to a relationship with their partner's children. Some assert that they are a parent under the UPA, as in *Elisa B.* and *K.M. v. E.G.*. Others assert that they have a right to custody or visitation as a *de facto* or psychological parent, as in *V.C. v. M.J.B.* In other cases, they have invoked the doctrine of equitable estoppel to prevent their ex-partner from denying them either parentage or custody rights. This was the case in the third companion case to *Elisa B.* and *K.M. v. E.G., Kristine H. v. Lisa R.*, 117 P.3d 690 (Cal. 2005), in which the California Supreme Court held that the biological mother was estopped to contest the validity of a judgment to which she and her ex-partner had previously stipulated, declaring her partner to be the second parent of the child. Finally, plaintiffs have argued that insofar as the biological mother has fostered a parental relationship between them and the child, she has abrogated her constitutional parental rights to sole custody of the child, and therefore must be considered on a par with her ex-partner for purposes of custody. *See Mason v. Dwinnell*, 660 S.E.2d 58 (N.C. App. 2008). Note that while a court's declaration of parentage puts the plaintiff on a par with the biological mother for purposes of custody, a declaration that the plaintiff is a *de facto* or psychological parent usually means that the plaintiff, although not considered a stranger to the child, does not attain rights on par with the biological parent and will be entitled only to visitation. *See V.C. v. M.J.B., supra; Holtzman v. Knott (In re H.S.H-K)*, 193 Wis. 2d 649 (1995).

In an Oregon Court of Appeals case issued as this casebook went to press, *Shineovich v. Kemp*, 2009 Ore. App. LEXIS 1017 (July 15, 2009), the court awarded parenting rights to the ex-partner of a biological mother who conceived through insemination of donor semen to which the partner consented. In contrast to California, which still relies on the UPA 1973, Oregon has a provision similar to the UPA 2002, which declares a husband to be the father of a child if it was born to his wife using donor insemination to which he consented. The *Shineovich* court held that equal protection under the Oregon Constitution required recognition of the plaintiff as a parent because the statute would have granted her parenting rights if she was a married, heterosexual male, but, as a lesbian, she could not marry under Oregon law. Under the Oregon Constitution, according to prior law, homosexuals are a suspect class on whose behalf heightened scrutiny is applied. In the court's words:

> Because same-sex couples may not marry in Oregon, that privilege is not available to the same-sex domestic partner of a woman who gives birth to a child conceived by artificial insemination, where the partner consented to the procedure with the intent of being the child's second parent. We can see no justification for denying that privilege on the basis of sexual orientation, particularly given that same-sex couples may become legal coparents by other means — namely, adoption. There appears to be no reason for permitting heterosexual couples to bypass adoption proceedings by conceiving a child through mutually consensual artificial insemination, but not permitting same-sex couples to do so.

A still more recent decision by the New York Court of Appeals, *Debra H. v. Janice R.*, 2010 N.Y. LEXIS 620 (May 4, 2010), denied a visitation claim by the partner of the child's biological mother on the ground that she had no standing as a parent under New York's custody statute based on her relationship with the child. According to the court, New York's refusal to recognize de facto relationships as giving standing in such cases, in concert with its permitting second-parent adoptions for same sex couples, "creates a bright-line rule that promotes certainty in the wake of domestic breakups. . . ." *Id.* at *7.

2. *The Implications of* Troxel v. Granville *on Lesbian Co-parenting Cases.* To what extent does *Troxel v. Granville*, 530 U.S. 57 (2000) (reproduced in Chapter 6, Section F[1]), which states that that parents have a constitutional right to determine issues of custody and visitation, limit the claims of persons who do not have traditional legal parental relationships with children? Is recent constitutional precedent likely to affect current law defining the rights of biological mothers and their same-sex partners in such contests? This issue is just beginning to be explored in judicial opinions.

Professor June Carbone asserts that the California Supreme Court treated the line of cases that culminated in *Elisa B.* and *K.M. v. E.G.* as involving parental status rather than custody in order to avoid the U.S. Supreme Court's ruling in *Troxel.* She asserts that the California courts could have held non-biological partners to fit into some intermediate category between parents and strangers, such as that which used to be filled by stepparents. Shoehorning non-biological partners into such a quasi-parent role, however, she contends, requires fitting them into some exception to *Troxel*, since parents have the right to determine their children's custody and visitation. California, however, avoided this issue by simply declaring these non-biological partners to be parents. June Carbone, *From Partners to Parents Revisited: How Will Ideas of Partnership Influence the Emerging Definition of California Parenthood?*, 7 WHITTIER J. CHILD & FAM. ADVOC. 3, 32–33 (2007).

Carbone argues that in granting equal parental status to non-biological partners whose relationship with the child is not grounded in an agreement with the existing legal parents, the California courts are skating on thin constitutional ice. While the U.S. Supreme Court has been loath to intervene in family law cases generally, and does so only rarely, Carbone suggests that the California decisions may violate constitutional boundaries insofar as they allow a nontraditional caregiver custody over a traditional parent, and insofar as they do not allow some parents sufficient notice that they are engaging in conduct that may divest them of parental rights. In this respect, she is less sanguine about the future of the California precedent than Emily Buss, who has argued that:

> [t]he Constitution should be read to afford strong protection to parents' exercise of child-rearing authority but considerably weaker protection to any individual's claim to parental identity. This means that a state has broad authority to identify nontraditional caregivers as parents, and, if it does so, it must afford their child-rearing decisions the same strong protection afforded more traditional parental figures.

Emily Buss, *"Parental" Rights*, 88 VA. L. REV. 635, 636 (2002). Buss' view seems buttressed by *Michael H.*, Section B[2][b] above, in which the court held California could constitutionally deny parental status to a child's biological father in favor of the mother's husband who knew of the other man's biological paternity. *Michael H.* necessarily means that a state may constitutionally assign parental status on the basis of social realities. Of course, the social reality in *Michael H* itself, marriage, may present a stronger case than the *de facto* family relationships at issue in *Elisa* and *K.M.*. On the other hand, recognizing the husband's paternity in *Michael H.* required displacing entirely the parental status claim of his wife's lover, a far greater burden on him than is the burden placed on the biological mother in *Elisa* and *K.M.* by recognizing her partner as an *additional*, second parent.

The California Court of Appeals recently addressed this issue in a dispute between two former same-sex partners, *Charisma R. v. Kristina S.*, 175 Cal. App. 4th 361 (2009). In that case, the biological mother of the disputed child argued that her rights under *Troxel* were violated by granting parentage rights to her ex-partner. The court rejected that argument:

> *Troxel* is inapposite. There, the court considered a nonparental visitation statute; at issue here is a statute determining the identity of Amalia's parents. Unlike the order in *Troxel*, the order declaring Charisma a parent of Amalia by definition did not extend rights to a nonparent. Moreover, as in *K.M. v. E.G.*, neither Charisma's nor Kristina's "claim to parentage preceded the other's." In that case, the California Supreme Court rejected an analogy to *Troxel*, reasoning "K.M.'s claim to be the twins' mother because the twins were produced from her ova is equal to, and arose at the

same time as, E.G.'s claim to be the twins' mother because she gave birth to them." In this case, Kristina and Charisma decided to have a child together, they jointly pursued the goal of Kristina becoming pregnant, and Charisma was present at the birth and cut the umbilical cord. Kristina's parentage claim arises from the fact that she gave birth to Amalia. And, at the time of the birth, Charisma had an inchoate parentage claim because she "actively consented to, and participated in, the artificial insemination of her partner with the understanding that the resulting child . . . would be raised by [Kristina] and her as coparents." Charisma's parentage claim was not legally complete until she accepted Amalia into her home, but it arose at the same time as Kristina's claim. Because Charisma ultimately satisfied the legal standards for presumed parent status and her showing was not rebutted, declaring her a parent is not giving parental rights to an unrelated individual; it is recognizing the parental role that existed from birth. (See *Sharon S. v. Superior Court* (2003) 31 Cal. 4th 417, 422, 445 [2 Cal. Rptr. 3d 699, 73 P.3d 554] [rejecting analogy to *Troxel* in second-parent-adoption context and stating that former same-sex partner with no biological connection to child is not "just 'any person'; she is a prospective adoptive mother"].)

Although Kristina fails to frame the issue in this fashion, her true complaint is that the state has seen fit to declare a person without a biological connection to Amalia a parent. This involves a different liberty interest than those at issue in *Troxel* and other cases cited by Kristina; in those cases, the identity of the parents was not in dispute. (*Troxel, supra,* 530 U.S. 57; *Stanley v. Illinois* (1972) 405 U.S. 645 [92 S. Ct. 1208, 31 L. Ed. 2d 551]; *Prince v. Massachusetts* (1944) 321 U.S. 158 [64 S. Ct. 438, 88 L. Ed. 645].) The distinction is critical because the courts "have required in substantive-due-process cases a 'careful description' of the asserted fundamental liberty interest." . . . Kristina's claim is essentially that as the biological mother, and in the effective absence of a biological father, she has a fundamental right to decide whether Amalia has a second parent. However, she presents no authority or reasoned argument that a state infringes on a biological parent's substantive due process rights by extending parental status to a nonbiological parent in the circumstances of this case. (See *Michael H. v. Gerald D.* (1989) 491 U.S. 110, 129–130 [109 S. Ct. 2333, 105 L. Ed. 2d 91] (plur. opn. of Scalia, J.) [state did not violate biological father's constitutional rights by denying him an opportunity to rebut a presumption that husband of mother was father; "[i]t is a question of legislative policy and not constitutional law whether California will allow the presumed parenthood of a couple desiring to retain a child conceived within and born into their marriage to be rebutted"].) It may be that there are different circumstances in which such an order would be unconstitutional, but any such determination would require a careful analysis of the specific facts and interests involved in the case.

Not only has Kristina failed to present relevant authorities and analysis regarding the actual asserted liberty interest at issue, but she fails to address the "complex balancing of competing interests" * * * necessary to resolution of substantive due process claims, despite the fact that this court identified some of the potential competing interests in *Charisma I*. There, we pointed out that "a rule that allowed the biological mother to unilaterally deny presumed parent status would potentially implicate the constitutional rights of the person seeking such status and the constitutional rights of the child in the establishment of the parent-child relationship." (*Charisma I*, [140 Cal. App. 4th 301 (2006)], at p. 308. * * * We also pointed out that "[s]uch a rule would be contrary to the 'public policy favoring that a child has two parents rather than one.' " (*Charisma I*, at p. 308.) Finally, an assessment of the weight of Kristina's interest in denying parental status to Charisma would need to take into account Kristina's own conduct prior to and immediately after Amalia's birth, which led Charisma to understand that she would be a parent.

We point out these competing interests and considerations to elucidate the fallacy of Kristina's simplistic analogy to *Troxel*, and to demonstrate the complexity of a substantive due process claim based on the actual liberty interest affected by the trial court's order. However, because Kristina has failed to provide citations to authority and reasoned argument regarding the balancing of interests necessary to resolve that due process claim, we deem the argument waived.

175 Cal. App. 4. For further discussion of *Troxel*, as well as its implications for de facto parent claims by same-sex partners, see Chapter 6.

3. *The Biological Mother's Intent.* Most cases allowing some rights to the nonbiological partner, under whatever theory, require that the parent who already has parenting rights (because of the biological connection) must *intend* to allow the developmental of a parental relationship between her partner and the child. *See, e.g., V.C. v. M.J.B, supra, Holtzman v. Knott (In re H.S.H-K)*, 193 Wis. 2d 649, 696 (1995); *Mason v. Dwinnell*, 660 S.E.2d 58 (N.C. Ct. App. 2008); *E.N.O. v. L.M.M.*, 429 Mass. 824, 829; *see also ALI* § 2.03(1) (requiring the acquiescence of the legal parent to the development of the parent-child relationship between the *de facto* parent and the child). The *K.M. v. E.G.* case, however, contains no such requirement, and the *Charisma R. v. Kristina S.* case, discussed in note 2, rejects this logic in arguing that neither the biological nor non-biological parent's rights precede the other. In the article discussed *supra* note 2, Professor Carbone argues that this absence infringes on the constitutional right of parents. *See also* E. Gary Spitko, The *Constitutional Function of Biological Paternity: Evidence of the Biological Mother's Consent to the Biological Father's Co-parenting of Her Child*, 48 Ariz. L. Rev. 97, 111 (2006) ("As part of the constitutional parent's right to impart a set of moral principles or values to her child, the constitutional parent enjoys the right to determine who else shall be allowed to interact with and influence the moral development of her child. . . . Such a right of inclusion and exclusion necessarily should include the power of the constitutional parent to decide whether one who is not a constitutional parent shall become a second parent to her child.").

4. *Incorporating the Child's Perspective?* For arguments that the law should incorporate the child's perspective when determining the legal status of parent-like figures under certain circumstances, see, e.g., Katharine T. Bartlett, *Rethinking Parenthood as an Exclusive Status: The Need for Legal Alternatives When the Premise of the Nuclear Family Has Failed*, 70 VA. L. REV. 879 (1984). Professor Barbara Bennett Woodhouse urges that "[a] child who has formed a parent-child relationship with a nonbiological co-parent or de facto parent has a right to legal recognition and protection of this relationship . . ." *Children's Rights in Gay and Lesbian Families: A Child-Centered Perspective*, *in* CHILD, FAMILY, AND STATE 273, 285 (S. Macedo & I.M. Young eds. 2003).

The drafters of Section 2.03 of the ALI *Principles of the Law of Family Dissolution* included within the definition of "parent," for purposes of custody and visitation decisions, categories referred to as *parents-by-estoppel* and *de facto parents*. In so doing, they sought to create predictability, to protect expectations, and to recognize functional parent-child relationships in order to protect the interests of children. *See ALI Principles*, Chapter 2; *see also* Katharine T. Bartlett, *U.S. Custody Law and Trends in the Context of the ALI Principles of the Law of Family Dissolution*, 10 VA. J. SOC. POL'Y & L. 5, 44–47 (2002); discussion of the *ALI Principles* § 2.03 in Chapter 6, Section F[2], Note 4. The *Principles* have engendered much scholarly commentary, and some writers argue that the *Principles* extend the notion of parent too broadly, *see, e.g.*, Gregory A. Loken, *The New "Extended Family" — "De Facto" Parenthood and Standing Under Chapter 2*, 2001 BYU L. REV. 1045 (criticizing the Principles for potentially authorizing parental rights in multiple parties and promoting increased indeterminacy in and interference with parent-child relationships), while others question whether the outlook is sufficiently child-centered. *See, e.g.*, Barbara Bennett Woodhouse, *Horton Looks at the ALI Principles*, 4 J.L. & FAM. STUD. 151 (2002) (arguing the *ALI Principles* retain vestiges of legal emphasis on adults' rights over children's needs).

5. *Further Reading.* For a discussion of the increasingly complex issues in determining parenthood, see June Carbone, *The Legal Definition of Parenthood: Uncertainty at the Core of Family Identity*, 65 LA. L. REV. 1295 (2005); David D. Meyer, *Parenthood in a Time of Transition: Tensions Between Legal, Biological, and Social Conceptions of Parenthood*, 54 AM. J. COMP. L. 125 (2006); Susan Frelich Appleton, *Presuming Women: Revisiting the Presumption of Legitimacy in the Same-Sex Couples Era*, 86 B.U. L. REV. 227 (2006); Laura Oren, *Honor Thy Mother?: The Supreme Court's Jurisprudence of Motherhood*, 17 HASTINGS WOMEN'S L.J. 187 (2006). Mary Patricia Byrn, *From Right To Wrong: A Critique Of The 2000 Uniform Parentage Act*, 16 UCLA WOMEN'S L.J. 163 (2007) (critiquing 2000 UPA for not recognizing both members of a same-sex couple who have a child through ART as parents).

PROBLEMS

Problem 9-23. Two women, Beth and Amy, lived together as intimate partners for seven years. They planned that Beth would become pregnant by artificial insemination so that the two of them could raise a child together. During these seven years, the women shared all of those aspects of their lives as a married couple would typically share. The two participated together in selecting a physician and an anonymous donor of the sperm (based on nonidentifying information provided by the fertility clinic). They also discussed names for the not-yet-conceived child, and agreed that the child's last name would be a hyphenated version of Beth and Amy's last names.

It took two years of artificial insemination attempts before Beth became pregnant. The two women shared the financial cost of the procedures. Beth and Amy learned that Beth was pregnant, and jointly made preparations for the birth of twin boys. They shared the financial costs of the prenatal care, participated jointly in prenatal classes, and set up a nursery in their home. Amy was Beth's "coach" during labor and delivery. They named one boy after Amy's father and the other after Beth's grandfather, giving both boys the hyphenated last name. They shared typical parenting functions during the first six months of the boys' lives, both providing for the boys' care and support relatively equally during that period. Yet, when the boys were six months old, the women decided to end their partnership. At Beth's request, Amy moved out and took an apartment a few blocks away from the home where they had lived together. For the next three months, the women cooperated amicably in the care of the twins. Although the boys' primary residence was with Beth, the boys spent about 30% of their time with Amy. Amy voluntarily paid Beth $1,000 a month to help with the boys' support. Beth, however, curtailed Amy's contact with the boys gradually thereafter. By the time the boys were one year old, Beth refused Amy any further contact with the boys. At that point in time, Amy stopped making support payments.

Address each of the following questions, and indicate whether you think the result would differ depending upon the jurisdiction in which the women lived. Also note whether there are any particular facts not provided above that would assist the claims of either party.

(A) Is Amy likely to succeed in a claim for joint custody of the twins?

(B) Is Amy likely to succeed in a claim for visitation with the twins?

(C) Is Beth likely to succeed in a claim for child support from Amy?

(D) Is Amy likely to succeed in an attempt to adopt the twins?

Problem 9-24. Assume the same facts as Problem 9-24 except here the women separated just before learning that Beth was pregnant. They attended counseling to see if they could resolve their differences and reconcile, but the counseling was not successful in achieving this goal. Amy offered to assist Beth with support for the twins, and made voluntary payments of approximately $1,000 per month for the first eight months after the twins' birth. Although Beth initially permitted Amy to take the boys for an overnight visit every other week, Beth curtailed the overnight visits after two months, allowing Amy to take the twins for a few hours on alternate Saturday afternoons only. When the twins became one year old, Beth refused to allow Amy further visitation. Amy then stopped making support payments. Address the same four questions set forth in Problem 9-23 above and indicate whether you think the result would differ depending upon the jurisdiction in which the women lived. Also note whether there are any particular facts not provided above that would assist the claims of either party.

Problem 9-25.   Assume the same facts as Problem 9-24 except the women separated before Beth learned she was pregnant, but Beth never informed Amy of the pregnancy. Amy learned Beth was pregnant from a mutual friend a few weeks before the twins were born. Amy contacted Beth, and offered to provide whatever assistance Beth needed, including financial support for the boys. She also requested the opportunity to have a relationship with the twins. Beth rebuffed all of Amy's overtures, and refused to allow Amy to see the twins. Address the same four questions set forth in Problem 9-24 above and indicate whether you think the result would differ depending upon the jurisdiction in which the women lived. Also note whether there are any particular facts not provided above that would assist the claims of either party.

Part IV

PARENT AND CHILD

Chapter 10

STATE REGULATION OF THE PARENT-CHILD RELATIONSHIP

This chapter examines the central ways in which the law regulates parent-child relationships. Like the marital relationship, the parent-child relationship is viewed as one of the essential building blocks in our society. As philosopher John Rawls observed:

> [O]ne of [the family's] main roles is to be the basis of the orderly production and reproduction of society and its culture from one generation to the next. . . . [A] central role of the family is to arrange in a reasonable and effective way the raising of and caring for children, ensuring their moral development and education into the wider culture. Citizens must have a sense of justice and the political virtues that support political and social institutions. The family must ensure the nurturing and development of such citizens in appropriate numbers to maintain an enduring society.

John Rawls, *The Idea of Public Reason Revisited*, 64 U. CHI. L. REV. 765, 788 (1997).

Generally, the state allows parents substantial discretion in deciding how to raise their children. At the same time, however, the state monitors the parent-child relationship and may intervene when such intervention is deemed necessary to the state's *parens patriae* interests in protecting and promoting the welfare of children. The state may also restrict parental autonomy in order to promote societal interests (i.e., its police power goals), such as helping children grow into well-educated and productive citizens.

At times, parental choices undermine state interests. And, at times, state policies interfere with parental authority in childrearing. Section A addresses the key tensions in the relationship between parents and the state regarding the upbringing of children. As demonstrated below, federal constitutional law has played a major role in delineating the proper roles and authority of parents versus the state in the lives of children. Section B explores the circumstances in which parental authority or state regulation may conflict with children's claims of autonomy interests. Federal constitutional law has been influential in this area as well, guiding the balance of the respective interests of parents, children, and the state.

Section C focuses on the role of the state in protecting children who may be endangered because of parental conduct or omissions. It examines the goals, standards, and procedures characterizing the states' child protection systems, and the ways in which federal statutory and constitutional law have shaped modern child protection efforts. It also examines some of the special issues confronted in the criminal prosecution of alleged abuse, particularly alleged sexual abuse, of children.

A. PARENTAL AUTONOMY AND STATE AUTHORITY: THE CONSTITUTIONAL BOUNDARIES

Parental autonomy refers to parental control over the many aspects of a child's upbringing, such as education, health care, and inculcation of values. The traditional explanation for parental autonomy is that parental *rights* are the natural and logical *quid pro quo* of parental obligations. That is, because parents are responsible for meeting their children's needs, they are given some measure of discretion in how they execute those duties. In addition, given that children are typically viewed as incapable of meeting their own needs (see Section B below), parents are well-situated to act on their children's behalf, promoting their children's best interests. Professors Elizabeth and Robert Scott have reasoned that allowing parents substantial autonomy in raising their children enhances parental motivation and ability to act in their children's interests, and protects parental investment in the rearing of their children. *See* Elizabeth S. Scott & Robert Scott, *Parents as Fiduciaries*, 81 VA. L. REV. 2401(1995); Elizabeth S. Scott, *Parental Autonomy and Children's Welfare*, 11 WM. & MARY BILL OF RTS. J. 1071(2003). In general, parental autonomy also dovetails with state interests, in that it promotes society's interests in diversity and cultural pluralism.

As the cases in this section demonstrate, parental authority over children was elevated to the status of a "fundamental" constitutional right during the last century. This relatively recent development can be understood not as an enhancement of parental autonomy but as a response to state policies limiting parental authority. Until the late nineteenth century, parental authority was almost absolute and state involvement in the family was minimal. Parental decisions about education, discipline, and the employment of children received little state supervision. The late nineteenth and early twentieth centuries, however, brought the Progressive Movement, which introduced far more state involvement in the rearing of children. Laws prohibiting child labor appeared, as did compulsory education policies. The juvenile court allowed the state unparalleled authority to intervene in families and remove children whose upbringing did not mesh with prevailing standards. Professor Lois Weithorn observes:

> [The Progressive Movement introduced] increasingly aggressive policies of intervention in the lives of children viewed as needing rescue from their [allegedly] unfortunate lots in life. . . . Middle- and upper-class Americans were alarmed at the plight of inner-city, lower-class, and immigrant children, and a breed of Progressive reformers or "child savers" gained growing influence and legitimacy in social policy formation. Professor Michael Grossberg characterizes social reforms of this era as propelled by a kind of "moral panic" — that is, fear "that urbanization, industrial capitalism, and massive immigration were undermining the nation's homes and thus, the republic itself." Historian Ronald Cohen notes that "[a]dults worried about children — everyone's children, not just their own — for their own sake and also out of fear for the country's future." Whereas some observers emphasize the humanitarian underpinnings of the Progressive ideology, others argue that the primary motive for this focus on children was the desire for social control over growing population subgroups viewed

as dependent, different, or deviant. [¶] These efforts culminated in the creation of the juvenile justice system, which authorized state involvement in children's lives as a "superparent" that substituted itself in the rearing of those children whose parents were viewed as harmful or inadequate.

Lois A. Weithorn, *Protecting Children from Exposure to Domestic Violence: The Use and Abuse of Child Maltreatment Statutes*, 53 HASTINGS L.J. 1, 47–48 (2001). In response to the trend of expanded state involvement in the family, the U.S. Supreme Court clarified that parental autonomy in childrearing is protected by the Due Process Clause of the Fourteenth Amendment. The cases that follow demonstrate how the Court has attempted to define the parameters of parental versus state authority.

MEYER v. NEBRASKA
United States Supreme Court
262 U.S. 390 (1923)

[Nebraska made it a crime for teachers to provide instruction to students in eighth grade and below in any language other than English. A teacher in the Zion Parochial School was tried and convicted of violating that statute by "unlawfully taught the subject of reading in the German language to . . . a child of 10 years, who had not attained and successfully passed the eighth grade." The state supreme court affirmed the conviction. Review was granted by the United States Supreme Court.]

MR. JUSTICE McREYNOLDS delivered the opinion of the Court.

[In summarizing the opinion of the Nebraska Supreme Court, Justice McReynolds quotes from that court's opinion the "reasons advanced to support the conclusion:"]

> The salutary purpose of the statute is clear. The Legislature had seen the baneful effects of permitting foreigners, who had taken residence in this country, to rear and educate their children in the language of their native land. The result of that condition was found to be inimical to our own safety. To allow the children of foreigners, who had emigrated here, to be taught from early childhood the language of the country of their parents was to rear them with that language as their mother tongue. It was to educate them so that they must always think in that language, and, as a consequence, naturally inculcate in them the ideas and sentiments foreign to the best interests of this country. The statute, therefore, was intended not only to require that the education of all children be conducted in the English language, but that, until they had grown into that language and until it had become a part of them, they should not in the schools be taught any other language. The obvious purpose of this statute was that the English language should be and become the mother tongue of all children reared in this state. The enactment of such a statute comes reasonably within the police power of the state.

The problem for our determination is whether the statute as construed and applied unreasonably infringes the liberty guaranteed to the plaintiff in error by the Fourteenth Amendment [which reads] "No state * * * shall deprive any person of life, liberty or property without due process of law."

While this court has not attempted to define with exactness the liberty thus guaranteed, the term has received much consideration and some of the included things have been definitely stated. Without doubt, it denotes not merely freedom from bodily restraint but also the right of the individual to contract, to engage in any of the common occupations of life, to acquire useful knowledge, to marry, establish a home and bring up children, to worship God according to the dictates of his own conscience, and generally to enjoy those privileges long recognized at common law as essential to the orderly pursuit of happiness by free men.

The established doctrine is that this liberty may not be interfered with, under the guise of protecting the public interest. . . . Determination by the Legislature of what constitutes proper exercise of police power is not final or conclusive but is subject to supervision by the courts.

[¶] . . . Corresponding to the right of control, it is the natural duty of the parent to give his children education suitable to their station in life; and nearly all the states, including Nebraska, enforce this obligation by compulsory laws.

. . . . Mere knowledge of the German language cannot reasonably be regarded as harmful. Heretofore it has been commonly looked upon as helpful and desirable. [The Court asserted that the teacher had a right to teach German and that the parents of the children had the right] to engage him so to instruct their children, [and that these rights] are within the liberty of the [fourteenth] amendment.

. . . Evidently the Legislature has attempted materially to interfere with the calling of modern language teachers, with the opportunities of pupils to acquire knowledge, and with the power of parents to control the education of their own.

[The Court acknowledges the state's purpose in passing the statute to require immigrant children to learn English and to inculcate them in American ways and values, and continues:] That the state may do much, go very far, indeed, in order to improve the quality of its citizens, physically, mentally and morally, is clear; but the individual has certain fundamental rights which must be respected. The protection of the Constitution extends to all, to those who speak other languages as well as to those born with English on the tongue. Perhaps it would be highly advantageous if all had ready understanding of our ordinary speech, but this cannot be coerced by methods which conflict with the Constitution-a desirable end cannot be promoted by prohibited means.

[The Court cites Plato and Sparta, whose political theories would "submerge the individual" in order to "develop ideal citizens," and indicates that these philosophies are inconsistent with the "ideas touching the relation between individual and state . . . upon which our institutions rest" and that no legislature in the U.S. could adopt their views "without doing violence to both letter and spirit of the Constitution."]

The desire of the Legislature to foster a homogeneous people with American ideals prepared readily to understand current discussions of civic matters is easy to appreciate. . . . But the means adopted . . . exceed the limitations upon the power of the state. . . . [¶] The power of the state to compel attendance at some school and to make reasonable regulations for all schools, including a requirement that they shall give instructions in English, is not questioned. Nor has challenge been made of the state's power to prescribe a curriculum for institutions which it supports. Those matters are not within the present controversy. . . . No emergency has arisen which renders knowledge by a child of some language other than English so clearly harmful as to justify its inhibition with the consequent infringement of rights long freely enjoyed. We are constrained to conclude that the statute as applied is arbitrary and without reasonable relation to any end within the competency of the state.

[The Court reversed the decision of the court below and remanded for further proceedings consistent with this opinion.]

Mr. Justice Holmes and Mr. Justice Sutherland, dissent.

PIERCE v. SOCIETY OF SISTERS
United States Supreme Court
268 U.S. 510 (1925)

Mr. Justice McReynolds delivered the opinion of the Court.

[Oregon law required every child between 8 and 16 years of age to attend public schools, with certain limited exceptions. Certain private schools obtained an injunction against the statute's enforcement. Among other claims, the schools challenged the statute on the basis that it conflicted with the constitutional rights of parents to choose where their children would be educated. The Court asserted that there was no question] concerning the power of the state reasonably to regulate all schools, to inspect, supervise and examine them, their teachers and pupils; to require that all children of proper age attend some school, that teachers shall be of good moral character and patriotic disposition, that certain studies plainly essential to good citizenship must be taught, and that nothing be taught which is manifestly inimical to the public welfare.

. . . .

Under the doctrine of Meyer v. Nebraska, . . . the Act . . . unreasonably interferes with the liberty of parents and guardians to direct the upbringing and education of children under their control. . . . The fundamental theory of liberty [under the U.S. Constitution] excludes any general power of the state to standardize its children by forcing them to accept instruction from public teachers only. The child is not the mere creature of the state; those who nurture him and direct his destiny have the right, coupled with the high duty, to recognize and prepare him for additional obligations.

. . . .

NOTE

In *Meyer* and *Pierce*, the Supreme Court announced a right of parents to rear their children as they see fit without undue interference from the government. The Court subsequently used these opinions as the basis for constitutionally protected privacy rights in the 1960s and 1970s. *Griswold v. Connecticut*, 381 U.S. 479 (1965); *Eisenstadt v. Baird*, 405 U.S. 438 (1972); *Roe v. Wade*, 410 U.S. 959 (1973). Professor Barbara Bennett Woodhouse has challenged the standing of *Meyer* and *Pierce* as liberal landmarks, arguing that *Meyer* and *Pierce* are grounded in traditional views that parents have property-like rights in their children. She argues further that the opinions effectively "constitutionaliz[e] a patriarchal notion of parental rights. Barbara Bennett Woodhouse, *"Who Owns the Child?"* Meyer *and* Pierce *and the Child as Property,*" 33 Wm. & Mary L. Rev. 995 (1992).

PRINCE v. MASSACHUSETTS
United States Supreme Court
321 U.S. 158 (1944)

[Sarah Prince, a Jehovah's Witness, appealed her conviction of an offense involving her 9-year-old niece and ward, Betty Simmons, under a Massachusetts statute regulating child labor. Ms. Prince had allowed Betty to accompany her when she went out in the evening to preach in the streets. Betty, who testified that she was also an ordained minister of the Jehovah's Witness sect, offered Watchtower and Consolation magazines to passers-by for 5 cents a copy. Betty later testified that "it was her religious duty to perform this work" and that failure would bring condemnation "to everlasting destruction at Armageddon."

Ms. Prince was charged and convicted under a Massachusetts statute that provided in part:. "No boy under twelve and no girl under eighteen shall sell, expose or offer for sale any newspapers, magazines in any street or public place.' . . . . [¶] Any parent [or] guardian . . . who compels or permits such minor to work in violation" of the statute was also guilty of an offense.]

Mr. Justice Rutledge delivered the opinion of the Court.

The case brings for review another episode in the conflict between Jehovah's Witnesses and state authority.

. . .

Appellant . . . rests squarely on freedom of religion under the First Amendment, applied by the Fourteenth to the states. She buttresses this foundation, however, with a claim of parental right as secured by the due process clause of the latter Amendment. *Cf. Meyer v. Nebraska* . . . These guaranties, she thinks, guard alike herself and the child in what they have done. Thus, two claimed liberties are at stake. One is the parent's, to bring up the child in the way he should go, which for appellant means to teach him the tenets and the practices of their faith. The other freedom is the child's, to observe these; and among them is "to preach the gospel . . . by public distribution" of "Watchtower" and "Consolation," in conformity with the scripture: "A little child shall lead them."

. . .

. . . Against these sacred private interests, basic in a democracy, stand the interests of society to protect the welfare of children, and the state's assertion of authority to that end, made here in a manner conceded valid if only secular things were involved.

The rights of children to exercise their religion, and of parents to give them religious training and to encourage them in the practice of religious belief, as against preponderant sentiment and assertion of state power voicing it, have had recognition here . . . [Citing to *Pierce* and *Meyer*, the Court states:] It is cardinal with us that the custody, care and nurture of the child reside first in the parents, whose primary function and freedom include preparation for obligations the state can neither supply nor hinder. And it is in recognition of this that these decisions have respected the private realm of family life which the state cannot enter.

But the family itself is not beyond regulation in the public interest, as against a claim of religious liberty. . . . And neither rights of religion nor rights of parenthood are beyond limitation. Acting to guard the general interest in youth's well being, the state as parens patriae may restrict the parent's control by requiring school attendance, regulating or prohibiting the child's labor, and in many other ways. Its authority is not nullified merely because the parent grounds his claim to control the child's course of conduct on religion or conscience. Thus, he cannot claim freedom from compulsory vaccination for the child more than for himself on religious grounds. The right to practice religion freely does not include liberty to expose the community or the child to communicable disease or the latter to ill health or death. . . . [T]he state has a wide range of power for limiting parental freedom and authority in things affecting the child's welfare; and that this includes, to some extent, matters of conscience and religious conviction.

But it is said the state cannot do so here. This, first, because when state action impinges upon a claimed religious freedom, it must fall unless shown to be necessary for or conducive to the child's protection against some clear and present danger, . . . and, it is added, there was no such showing here. The child's presence on the street, with her guardian, distributing or offering to distribute the magazines, it is urged, was in no way harmful to her, nor in any event more so than the presence of many other children at the same time and place, engaged in shopping and other activities not prohibited. . . .

[The Court acknowledges that a statute such as this could not be constitutionally applied to prohibit adults from engaging in this activity. But, it asserts:] The state's authority over children's activities is broader than over like actions of adults. This is peculiarly true of public activities and in matters of employment. A democratic society rests, for its continuance, upon the healthy, well-rounded growth of young people into full maturity as citizens, with all that implies. It may secure this against impeding restraints and dangers, within a broad range of selection. Among evils most appropriate for such action are the crippling effects of child employment, more especially in public places, and the possible harms arising from other activities subject to all the diverse influences of the street. It is too late now to doubt that legislation appropriately designed to reach such evils is within the state's police power, whether against the parent's claim to control of the child or one that religious scruples dictate contrary action.

[The] streets afford dangers for [children] not affecting adults. . . . What may be wholly permissible for adults therefore may not be so for children, either with or without their parents' presence.

. . . The zealous though lawful exercise of the right to engage in propagandizing the community, whether in religious, political or other matters, may and at times does create situations difficult enough for adults to cope with and wholly inappropriate for children, especially of tender years, to face. Other harmful possibilities could be stated, of emotional excitement and psychological or physical injury. Parents may be free to become martyrs themselves. But it does not follow they are free, in identical circumstances, to make martyrs of their children before they have reached the age of full and legal discretion when they can make that choice for themselves. Massachusetts has determined that an absolute prohibition, though one limited to streets and public places and to the incidental uses proscribed, is necessary to accomplish its legitimate objectives. Its power to attain them is broad enough to reach these peripheral instances in which the parent's supervision may reduce but cannot eliminate entirely the ill effects of the prohibited conduct. We think that with reference to the public proclaiming of religion, upon the streets and in other similar public places, the power of the state to control the conduct of children reaches beyond the scope of its authority over adults, as is true in the case of other freedoms, and the rightful boundary of its power has not been crossed in this case.

. . .

The judgment is affirmed.

[Four justices dissented. JUSTICE JACKSON filed a dissent, joined JUSTICES ROBERTS and FRANKFURTER. The dissent challenged the application of a child labor law to the instant case. Justice Jackson asserted that "the mere fact that the religious literature is 'sold' by itinerant preachers rather than 'donated' does not transform evangelism into a commercial enterprise. If it did, then the passing of the collection plate in church would make the church service a commercial project. The constitutional rights of those spreading their religious beliefs through the spoken and printed word are not to be gauged by standards governing retailers or wholesalers of books.'"

[JUSTICE MURPHY also filed a dissent. He argued that the religious nature of the activities should warrant a different analysis than if there was no religious claim involved. Furthermore, he stated: "If the right of a child to practice its religion in that manner is to be forbidden by constitutional means, there must be convincing proof that such a practice constitutes a grave and immediate danger to the state or to the health, morals or welfare of the child. The vital freedom of religion. . . . cannot be erased by slender references to the state's power to restrict the more secular activities of children. [¶] The state, in my opinion, has completely failed to sustain its burden of proving the existence of any grave or immediate danger to any interest which it may lawfully protect.]

WISCONSIN v. YODER
United States Supreme Court
406 U.S. 205 (1971)

MR. CHIEF JUSTICE BURGER delivered the opinion of the Court.

On petition of the State of Wisconsin, we . . . review a decision of the Wisconsin Supreme Court holding that respondents' convictions of violating the State's compulsory school-attendance law were invalid under the Free Exercise Clause of the First Amendment to the United States Constitution . . . [W]e affirm . . .

[The Wisconsin statute required attendance at school for all children until the age of 16. Respondents were three Amish parents who refused to send their children (aged 14 and 15) to school beyond the eighth grade.]

On complaint of the school district administrator for the public schools, respondents were. . . . convicted of violating the compulsory-attendance law in Green County Court and were fined the sum of $5 each. [¶] Respondents defended on the ground that the application of the compulsory-attendance law violated their rights under the First and Fourteenth Amendments.

. . . . As a result of their common heritage, Old Order Amish communities today are characterized by a fundamental belief that salvation requires life in a church community separate and apart from the world and worldly influence. [¶]. . . . Amish beliefs [also] require members of the community to make their living by farming or closely related activities. Broadly speaking, the Old Order Amish religion pervades and determines the entire mode of life of its adherents. . . .

Amish objection to formal education beyond the eighth grade is firmly grounded in these central religious concepts. They object to the high school, and higher education generally, because the values they teach are in marked variance with Amish values and the Amish way of life; they view secondary school education as an impermissible exposure of their children to a "worldly" influence in conflict with their beliefs. The high school tends to emphasize intellectual and scientific accomplishments, self-distinction, competitiveness, worldly success, and social life with other students. Amish society emphasizes informal learning-through-doing; a life of "goodness," rather than a life of intellect; wisdom, rather than technical knowledge; community welfare, rather than competition; and separation from, rather than integration with, contemporary worldly society. Formal high school education beyond the eighth grade is contrary to Amish beliefs, not only because it places Amish children in an environment hostile to Amish beliefs with increasing emphasis on competition in class work and sports and with pressure to conform to the styles, manners, and ways of the peer group, but also because it takes them away from their community, physically and emotionally, during the crucial and formative adolescent period of life. During this period, the children must acquire Amish attitudes favoring manual work and self-reliance and the specific skills needed to perform the adult role of an Amish farmer or housewife. They must learn to enjoy physical labor. Once a child has learned basic reading, writing, and elementary mathematics, these traits, skills, and attitudes admittedly fall within the category of those best learned through example and "doing" rather than in a classroom. And, at this time in life, the Amish child must also grow in his faith and his relationship to the Amish community if he is to be prepared to accept the heavy obligations imposed by adult baptism. In short, high school attendance with teachers who are not of the Amish faith — and may even be hostile to it — interposes a serious barrier to the integration of the Amish child into the Amish religious community. . . .

The Amish do not object to elementary education through the first eight grades as a general proposition because they agree that their children must have basic skills in the "three R's" in order to read the Bible, to be good farmers and citizens, and to be able to deal with non-Amish people when necessary in the course of daily affairs. They view such a basic education as acceptable because it does not significantly expose their children to worldly values or interfere with their development in the Amish community during the crucial adolescent period. In the Amish belief higher learning tends to develop values they reject as influences that alienate man from God.

On the basis of such considerations, Dr. Hostetler [an expert on Amish society] testified that compulsory high school attendance could not only result in great psychological harm to Amish children, because of the conflicts it would produce, but would also, in his opinion, ultimately result in the destruction of the Old Order Amish church community as it exists in the United States today. The testimony of Dr. Donald A. Erickson, an expert witness on education, also showed that the Amish succeed in preparing their high school age children to be productive members of the Amish community. He described their system of learning through doing the skills directly relevant to their adult roles in the Amish community as "ideal" and perhaps superior to ordinary high school education. The evidence also showed that the Amish have an excellent record as law-abiding and generally self-sufficient members of society.

Although the trial court in its careful findings determined that the Wisconsin compulsory school-attendance law "does interfere with the freedom of the Defendants to act in accordance with their sincere religious belief" it also concluded that the requirement of high school attendance until age 16 was a "reasonable and constitutional" exercise of governmental power, and therefore denied the motion to dismiss the charges. The Wisconsin Circuit Court affirmed the convictions. The Wisconsin Supreme Court, however, sustained respondents' claim under the Free Exercise Clause of the First Amendment and reversed. . . .

I

There is no doubt as to the power of a State, having a high responsibility for education of its citizens, to impose reasonable regulations for the control and duration of basic education. Providing public schools ranks at the very apex of the function of a State. Yet even this paramount responsibility was, in *Pierce*, made to yield to the right of parents to provide an equivalent education in a privately operated system. . . . As that case suggests, the values of parental direction of the religious upbringing and education of their children in their early and formative years have a high place in our society. Thus, a State's interest in universal education, however highly we rank it, is not totally free from a balancing process when it impinges on fundamental rights and interests, such as those specifically protected by the Free Exercise Clause of the First Amendment, and the traditional interest of parents with respect to the religious upbringing of their children so long as they, in the words of *Pierce*, "prepare [them] for additional obligations." 268 U.S. at 535. . . .

II

. . . A way of life, however virtuous and admirable, may not be interposed as a barrier to reasonable state regulation of education if it is based on purely secular considerations; to have the protection of the Religion Clauses, the claims must be rooted in religious belief . . .

III

Neither the findings of the trial court nor the Amish claims as to the nature of their faith are challenged in this Court by the State. . . . Its position is that the State's interest in universal compulsory formal secondary education to age 16 is so great that it is paramount to the undisputed claims of respondents. . . .

The State advances two primary arguments [in support of its contention that its interest in its system of compulsory education outweighs the established religious practices of the Amish] . . . It notes, as Thomas Jefferson pointed out early in our history, that some degree of education is necessary to prepare citizens to participate effectively and intelligently in our open political system if we are to preserve freedom and independence. Further, education prepares individuals to be self-reliant and self-sufficient participants in society. We accept these propositions.

However, the evidence adduced . . . is persuasively to the effect that an additional one or two years of formal high school for Amish children in place of their long-established program of informal vocational education would do little to serve those interests. Respondents' experts testified at trial, without challenge, that the value of all education must be assessed in terms of its capacity to prepare the child for life. It is one thing to say that compulsory education for a year or two beyond the eighth grade may be necessary when its goal is the preparation of the child for life in modern society as the majority live, but it is quite another if the goal of education be viewed as the preparation of the child for life in the separated agrarian community that is the keystone of the Amish faith.

The State attacks respondents' position as one fostering "ignorance" from which the child must be protected by the State. No one can question the State's duty to protect children from ignorance but this argument does not square with the facts disclosed in the record. Whatever their idiosyncrasies as seen by the majority, this record strongly shows that the Amish community has been a highly successful social unit within our society, even if apart from the conventional "mainstream." Its members are productive and very law-abiding members of society; they reject public welfare in any of its usual modern forms. The Congress itself recognized their self-sufficiency by authorizing exemption of such groups as the Amish from the obligation to pay social security taxes. . . .

. . . . There can be no assumption that today's majority is "right" and the Amish and others like them are "wrong." A way of life that is odd or even erratic but interferes with no rights or interests of others is not to be condemned because it is different.

The State, however, supports its interest in providing an additional one or two years of compulsory high school education to Amish children because of the possibility that some such children will choose to leave the Amish community, and that if this occurs they will be ill-equipped for life. . . . However, on this record, that argument is highly speculative. There is no specific evidence of the loss of Amish adherents by attrition, nor is there any showing that upon leaving the Amish community Amish children, with their practical agricultural training and habits of industry and self-reliance, would become burdens on society because of educational short-comings. Indeed, this argument of the State appears to rest primarily on the State's mistaken assumption, already noted, that the Amish do not provide any education for their children beyond the eighth grade, but allow them to grow in "ignorance." . . .

There is nothing in this record to suggest that the Amish qualities of reliability, self-reliance, and dedication to work would fail to find ready markets in today's society. Absent some contrary evidence supporting the State's position, we are unwilling to assume that persons possessing such valuable vocational skills and habits are doomed to become burdens on society should they determine to leave the Amish faith, nor is there any basis in the record to warrant a finding that an additional one or two years of formal school education beyond the eighth grade would serve to eliminate any such problem that might exist. . . .

IV

Finally, the State, on authority of *Prince v. Massachusetts*, argues that a decision exempting Amish children from the State's requirement fails to recognize the substantive right of the Amish child to a secondary education, and fails to give due regard to the power of the State as *parens patriae* to extend the benefit of secondary education to children regardless of the wishes of their parents. Taken at its broadest sweep, the Court's language in *Prince*, might be read to give support to the State's position. However, the Court was not confronted in *Prince* with a situation comparable to that of the Amish. . . . ; this is shown by the Court's severe characterization of the evils that it thought the legislature could legitimately associate with child labor, even when performed in the company of an adult. . . . [¶ By contrast, this case] is not one in which any harm to the physical or mental health of the child or to the public safety, peace, order, or welfare has been demonstrated or may be properly inferred. . . .

Contrary to the suggestion of the dissenting opinion of Mr. Justice Douglas, our holding today in no degree depends on the assertion of the religious interest of the child as contrasted with that of the parents. It is the parents who are subject to prosecution here for failing to cause their children to attend school, and it is their right of free exercise, not that of their children, that must determine Wisconsin's power to impose criminal penalties on the parent. . . . The children are not parties to this litigation. The State has at no point tried this case on the theory that respondents were preventing their children from attending school against their expressed desires, and indeed the record is to the contrary. The State's position from the outset has been that it is empowered to apply its compulsory-attendance law to Amish parents in the same manner as to other parents — that is, without regard to the wishes of the child. That is the claim we reject today.

Our holding in no way determines the proper resolution of possible competing interests of parents, children, and the State in an appropriate state court proceeding in which the power of the State is asserted on the theory that Amish parents are preventing their minor children from attending high school despite their expressed desires to the contrary. Recognition of the claim of the State in such a proceeding would, of course, call into question traditional concepts of parental control over the religious upbringing and education of their minor children recognized in this Court's past decisions. It is clear that such an intrusion by a State into family decisions in the area of religious training would give rise to grave questions of religious freedom comparable to those raised here and those presented in *Pierce*. On this record we neither reach nor decide those issues. The State's argument proceeds without reliance on any actual conflict between the wishes of parents and children. It appears to rest on the potential that exemption of Amish parents from the requirements of the compulsory-education law might allow some parents to act contrary to the best interests of their children by foreclosing their opportunity to make an intelligent choice between the Amish way of life and that of the outside world. The same argument could, of course, be made with respect to all church schools short of college. There is nothing in the record or in the ordinary course of human experience to suggest that non-Amish parents generally consult with children of ages 14–16 if they are placed in a church school of the parents' faith.

Indeed it seems clear that if the State is empowered, as parens patriae, to "save" a child from himself or his Amish parents by requiring an additional two years of compulsory formal high school education, the State will in large measure influence, if not determine, the religious future of the child. Even more markedly than in *Prince*, therefore, this case involves the fundamental interest of parents, as contrasted with that of the State, to guide the religious future and education of their children. The history and culture of Western civilization reflect a strong tradition of parental concern for the nurture and upbringing of their children. This primary role of the parents in the upbringing of their children is now established beyond debate as an enduring American tradition. . . .

. . . *Pierce* stands as a charter of the rights of parents to direct the religious upbringing of their children. And, when the interests of parenthood are combined with a free exercise claim of the nature revealed by this record, more than merely a "reasonable relation to some purpose within the competency of the State" is required to sustain the validity of the State's requirement under the First Amendment. To be sure, the power of the parent, even when linked to a free exercise claim, may be subject to limitation under *Prince* if it appears that parental decisions will jeopardize the health or safety of the child, or have a potential for significant social burdens . . .

V

. . . . [W]e hold . . . that the First and Fourteenth Amendments prevent the State from compelling respondents to cause their children to attend formal high school to age 16 . . . [¶] Aided by a history of three centuries as an identifiable religious sect and a long history as a successful and self-sufficient segment of American society, the Amish in this case have convincingly demonstrated the sincerity of their religious beliefs, the interrelationship of belief with their mode of life, the vital role that belief and daily conduct play in the continued survival of Old Order Amish communities and their religious organization, and the hazards presented by the State's enforcement of a statute generally valid as to others . . . In light of this convincing showing . . . and weighing the minimal difference between what the State would require and what the Amish already accept, it was incumbent on the State to show with more particularity how its admittedly strong interest in compulsory education would be adversely affected by granting an exemption to the Amish. . . .

Affirmed.

Mr. Justice Powell and Mr. Justice Rehnquist took no part in the consideration or decision of this case.

Mr. Justice Stewart, with whom Mr. Justice Brennan joins, concurring. . . .

. . . . [T]here is no suggestion whatever in the record that the religious beliefs of the children here concerned differ in any way from those of their parents. Only one of the children testified. The last two questions and answers on her cross-examination accurately sum up her testimony:

Q. So I take it then, Frieda, the only reason you are not going to school, and did not go to school since last September, is because of *your* religion?

A. Yes.

Q. That is the only reason?

A. Yes. (Emphasis supplied.)

It is clear to me, therefore, that this record simply does not present the interesting and important issue discussed in Part II of the dissenting opinion of Mr. Justice Douglas. With this observation, I join the opinion and the judgment of the Court.

Mr. Justice White, with whom Mr. Justice Brennan and Mr. Justice Stewart join, concurring.

. . . It is possible that most Amish children will wish to continue living the rural life of their parents, in which case their training at home will adequately equip them for their future role. Others, however, may wish to become nuclear physicists, ballet dancers, computer programmers, or historians, and for these occupations, formal training will be necessary. . . . [A]lthough the question is close, I am unable to say that the State has demonstrated that Amish children who leave school in the eighth grade will be intellectually stultified or unable to acquire new academic skills later. . . .

. . . I join the Court because the sincerity of the Amish religious policy here is uncontested, because the potentially adverse impact of the state requirement is great, and because the State's valid interest in education has already been largely satisfied by the eight years the children have already spent in school.

Mr. Justice Douglas, dissenting in part.

. . . The Court's analysis assumes that the only interests at stake in the case are those of the Amish parents . . . and those of the State. . . . The difficulty with this approach is that, despite the Court's claim, the parents are seeking to vindicate not only their own free exercise claims, but also those of their high-school-age children.

It is argued that the right of the Amish children to religious freedom is not presented by the facts of the case, as the issue before the Court involves only the Amish parents' religious freedom to defy a state criminal statute imposing upon them an affirmative duty to cause their children to attend high school.

. . . .

. . . . [I]t is essential to reach the question to decide the case. . . . If the parents in this case are allowed a religious exemption, the inevitable effect is to impose the parents' notions of religious duty upon their children. Where the child is mature enough to express potentially conflicting desires, it would be an invasion of the child's rights to permit such an imposition without canvassing his views. . . . And, if an Amish child desires to attend high school, and is mature enough to have that desire respected, the State may well be able to override the parents' religiously motivated objections.

Religion is an individual experience. It is not necessary, nor even appropriate, for every Amish child to express his views on the subject in a prosecution of a single adult. Crucial, however, are the views of the child whose parent is the subject of the suit. Frieda Yoder has in fact testified that her own religious views are opposed to high-school education. I therefore join the judgment of the Court as to respondent Jonas Yoder. But Frieda Yoder's views may not be those of Vernon Yutzy or Barbara Miller. I must dissent, therefore, as to respondents Adin Yutzy and Wallace Miller as their motion to dismiss also raised the question of their children's religious liberty. . . .

This issue has never been squarely presented before today. . . . [W]e have in the past analyzed similar conflicts between parent and State with little regard for the views of the child. Recent cases, however, have clearly held that the children themselves have constitutionally protectible interests. [¶] These children are "persons" within the meaning of the Bill of Rights. We have so held over and over again. . . .

On this important and vital matter of education, I think the children should be entitled to be heard. While the parents, absent dissent, normally speak for the entire family, the education of the child is a matter on which the child will often have decided views. He may want to be a pianist or an astronaut or an oceanographer. To do so he will have to break from the Amish tradition.

It is the future of the student, not the future of the parents, that is imperiled by today's decision. If a parent keeps his child out of school beyond the grade school, then the child will be forever barred from entry into the new and amazing world of diversity that we have today. The child may decide that that is the preferred course, or he may rebel. It is the student's judgment, not his parents', that is essential if we are to give full meaning to what we have said about the Bill of Rights and of the right of students to be masters of their own destiny.[3]

If he is harnessed to the Amish way of life by those in authority over him and if his education is truncated, his entire life may be stunted and deformed. The child, therefore, should be given an opportunity to be heard before the State gives the exemption which we honor today.

The views of the two children in question were not canvassed by the Wisconsin courts. The matter should be explicitly reserved so that new hearings can be held on remand of the case. . . .

NOTES

1. ***Religious Free Exercise, Parental Autonomy or Both?*** Is *Yoder* a First Amendment free exercise case, a Fourteenth Amendment parental autonomy case, or a "hybrid" case grounded in both sets of rights? The short answer is that both sets of protections worked together in this case, strengthening the parents' claims. As we know from *Meyer* and *Pierce*, parents have a right to direct their children's education. Thus, respect for parental autonomy was essential to the success of this claim, in that such autonomy is what empowers parents to direct their children's lives in the first place. *Prince* tells us that there are limits to all facets of parental discretion, in light of the state's *parens patriae* and police power concerns. Thus, *Yoder* focused on a balancing of parental rights and state interests. What role did the parents' claim of religious freedom play in strengthening the parents' claims? The Court relied heavily on the religious nature of the beliefs underlying the Amish "way of life" and on the parental assertion that, without an accommodation to their religious views, their ability to raise their children in their religious tradition would be seriously compromised. With that in mind, the right vindicated here might best be characterized as the right of parents to raise their children in their religious tradition, a right grounded in the convergence of parental autonomy and religious

---

[3] The court below brushed aside the students' interests with the offhand comment that "[w]hen a child reaches the age of judgment, he can choose for himself his religion." *Wisconsin v. Yoder*, 182 N.W.2d 539, 543 (Wis. 1971). But there is nothing in this record to indicate that the moral and intellectual judgment demanded of the student by the question in this case is beyond his capacity. Children far younger than the 14- and 15-year-olds involved here are regularly permitted to testify in custody and other proceedings. . . . Moreover, there is substantial agreement among child psychologists and sociologists that the moral and intellectual maturity of the 14-year-old approaches that of the adult. *See, e.g.*, J. Piaget, THE MORAL JUDGMENT OF THE CHILD (1948); D. Elkind, CHILDREN AND ADOLESCENTS 75–80 (1970); Kohlberg, *Moral Education in the Schools: A Development View*, in R. Muuss, ADOLESCENT BEHAVIOR AND SOCIETY 193, 199–200 (1971); W. Kay, MORAL DEVELOPMENT 172–183 (1968); A. Gesell & F. Ilg, YOUTH: THE YEARS FROM TEN TO SIXTEEN 175–182 (1956). . . .

freedom. What we do not know, however, is whether the religious freedom claims were essential to the result. In other words, might parental claims grounded in secular reasons entitle parents to exemptions from certain compulsory education regulations?

There are no precedents precisely on this point. In *In re McMillan*, 226 S.E.2d 693 (N.C. App. 1976), a court rejected claims by parents that beliefs arising out of their Native American cultural traditions deserve the same protection as religious beliefs in the context of children's nonattendance at public school. But, the case can be distinguished from *Yoder* because the family was not providing an alternative educational program for the children, and there was "no showing that the Indian heritage or culture of these children will be endangered or threatened in any way by their attending school." There are no useful precedents that can resolve this question satisfactorily, although recent developments in constitutional jurisprudence of the Free Exercise Clause suggest that the "hybrid" nature of the rights claimed (that is, deriving from both the First Amendment and Fourteenth Amendment) may have contributed to the success. *See* Note 2 below.

2. *Recent Developments in the Law Affecting Constitutional Interpretation of the Free Exercise Clause.* Beginning with the Supreme Court's decision in *Employment Division v. Smith*, 494 U.S 872 (1990), the law governing free exercise of religion has undergone several transitions. Prior to *Smith*, claims of entitlement to religious exemptions under the First Amendment were analyzed under a test set forth in *Sherbert v. Verner*, 374 U.S. 398 (1963). The *Sherbert* test required strict scrutiny of laws alleged to violate the Free Exercise Clause. The inquiry focused on whether such laws substantially burden a religious practice and if so, whether the laws are justified by a compelling state interest. As such, the balance was tipped in favor of Free Exercise claims. In 1990, in *Smith*, the Court applied a different test. It held that "the right of free exercise does not relieve an individual of the obligation to comply with a 'valid and neutral law of general applicability on the ground that the law proscribes (or prescribes) conduct that his religious prescribes (or proscribes).'" *Smith, supra* at 879. This test shifted the balance in favor of laws that may burden religious exercise. The Court in *Smith* asserted that it was not changing the law. Rather, according to the majority in *Smith*: "The only decisions in which [this Court has] held that the First Amendment bars application of a neutral, generally applicable law to religiously motivated action have involved not the Free Exercise Clause alone, but the Free Exercise Clause in conjunction with other constitutional protections, such as freedom of speech and of the press." *Id.* at 881. *Yoder* is among those cases cited as support for this proposition. Referred to as "hybrid" cases, disputes involving two constitutional claims still require strict scrutiny. Thus, the convergence of claims of First and Fourteenth Amendment rights appears, at least in retrospect, to have strengthened the Amish parents' case for exemption of their children from the state's policy mandating compulsory school attendance up to age 16.

In the years following *Smith*, the law governing religious exemptions from governmental policies has undergone much change. In 1993, Congress passed the Religious Freedom Restoration Act (RFRA), 42 U.S.C. § 2000bb, to reinstate the *Sherbert* test. Several years later, however, in *City of Boerne v. Flores*, 521 U.S. 507 (1997), the Court held that Congress did not have the authority to apply RFRA to the states, but upheld RFRA's validity with respect to federal laws burdening religious exercise. Following *Boerne*, however, many states passed their own RFRAs. And, Congress passed the Religious Land Use and Institutionalized Persons Act of 2000 (RLUIPA), 42 U.S.C. § 2000cc *et seq.* (2009), under the authority of its spending and commerce powers. RLUIPA governs a smaller subset of free exercise challenges to state laws than did RFRA.

Thus, at the time of this writing, the *Smith* test governs analysis of many claims for exemptions from state laws burdening religious exercise. Three types of claims against state laws are analyzed according to the strict scrutiny standard: (1) "hybrid" claims, grounded in the Free Exercise Clause together with another constitutional guarantee (such as a valid Fourteenth Amendment claim of parental autonomy); (2) claims governed by a state RFRA; and (3) claims under RLUIPA (concerning the use of land for religious purposes or affecting persons in institutions, such as prisons). Finally, RFRA and the strict scrutiny test apply to federal legislation that is challenged as infringing religious freedom. Many observers disagree with the Court's assertion that *Smith* did not change the law as it affects non-hybrid Free Exercise claims. For further discussion of these issues, see Benjamin I. Siminou, Student Author, *Making Sense of Hybrid Rights: An Analysis of the Nebraska Supreme Court's Approach to the Hybrid-Rights Exception in Douglas County v. Anaya*, 85 NEB. L. REV. 311 (2006); Michael E. Lechliter, Student Author, *The Free Exercise of Religion and Public Schools: The Implications of Hybrid Rights on the Religious Upbringing of Children*, 103 MICH. L. REV. 2209 (2005). *See also* Nicholas Nugent, *Toward a RFRA that Works*, 61 VAND. L. REV. 1027 (2008); W. Cole Durham, Jr., *State RFRAs and the Scope of Free Exercise Protection*, 32 U.C. DAVIS L. REV. 665, 712 (1999); LESLIE C. GRIFFIN, LAW AND RELIGION 165–236 (2007).

The *Yoder* Court notes that the requested exemption is important to the survival of the Amish community. Should the court be concerned with the Amish *community's* interests, and if so, what role should those interests play when balanced against the rights of parents and/or children, or the interests of the state, where these interests conflict? Today, a case like *Yoder* might have involved application of the state's home-schooling policy. *See* Note 7, below, and consider how the Amish parents might have fared under the provisions of various home-schooling laws.

3. *Reconciling* Yoder *and* Prince. In *Yoder*, the Supreme Court struggled to distinguish *Prince* on the ground that the religiously-motivated conduct in *Prince* dealt with the "evil" of child labor, while the relevant conduct in *Yoder* involved no threat of harm to the child or to public welfare. Are you persuaded? The different outcomes in the two cases may be due to the Court's view that the *state's* interest in *Yoder* was less substantial than that asserted in *Prince*. In *Yoder*, the Court did not seem to take very seriously the claim that the state's interest in a productive and educated citizenry was negatively affected by the exemption sought by the Amish parents. It observed that the Amish community was very productive and self-sustaining, imposing no burden on the rest of society. On the other hand, does *Prince* really implicate the state's interest in prohibiting child labor?

4. *The Competing Interests of Parent and the State.* Professor Maxine Eichner underscores the challenges of reconciling the competing interests of parents and the state in the education of children in our society. She asks:

> So who, ultimately, should control students' education in public schools? And, in the event of disagreement about what this task entails and how it should be accomplished, whose views should trump? In a liberal democracy, it is inevitable that there will be conflicts among parents, children, and the state's interests with respect to education. . . . [¶] The issue of children's *civic* education is a particularly thorny one for a liberal democracy like the United States. As democratic theorists have long recognized, preparing children for democratic citizenship is an important and demanding responsibility. The collective self-rule required of democracy means that, among other things, citizens must be committed to political equality, to listening to other points of view, to resolving issues through deliberation rather than force, and to the rule of law. These qualities do not simply arise in citizens spontaneously, but require nurture. To add to the complexity of the issue, however, the United States is not merely a democracy, it is a liberal democracy, whose commitment to majoritarian rule is tempered by the understanding that some personal rights and liberties should not be subject to the majority's preferences. The deliberate promotion of the qualities that make for good citizens therefore stands in tension with the great weight that liberalism places on respecting citizens' own views of the good life, including how to rear their children.

Maxine Eichner, *Who Should Control Children's Education?: Parents, Children, and the State*, 75 U. CIN. L. REV. 1339, 1340–41 (2007) (emphasis added).

In *Yoder*, the Court does not address the implications of its decision in light of the state's interest in educating citizens to become participants in democratic government with the ability to participate in the "marketplace of ideas." *See Tinker v. Des Moines Community Sch. Dist.*, 393 U.S. 503, 512 (1966) (observing that "[t]he vigilant protection of constitutional freedoms is nowhere more vital than in the community of American schools, [that the] classroom is peculiarly the 'marketplace of ideas,'[and that the] Nation's future depends upon leaders trained through wide exposure to that robust exchange of ideas . . ."). Our society would not function well if the Old Order Amish traditions of withdrawal and isolation were widespread. On the other hand, central to our nation's core values is respect for cultural, religious and ethnic diversity and a belief that groups in our society should be permitted to maintain their identity and to resist pressures to be submerged in or assimilated into the mainstream of society. This tension between state interests and the autonomy rights of parents arises frequently in a range of areas relating to socialization of children.

5. *What About the Children's Interests?* Justice Douglas' dissent in *Yoder* is well known, perhaps because it was the first suggestion in a Supreme Court opinion (albeit a dissent) that children might have a legally protected interest in participating in important decisions affecting their welfare separate from (and possibly in opposition to) that of their parents. This dissent provided authority (and inspiration) for advocates seeking expanded minors' rights of self-determination and influenced the arguments supporting reproductive rights of minors. *See* Section B. Justice Douglas would require confirmation from the child before honoring the parents' claim. But, what if the child's views differ from that of the parents? Which views prevail? And, is a child in this situation likely to disagree openly with her parent(s), even if her preferences are at odds with theirs? Justice Douglas' dissent does not answer these questions. Scholars have considered the question of how children's preferences should be considered in such contexts, if at all. *See, e.g.*, Margaret F. Brinig, *Children's Beliefs and Family Law*, 58 EMORY L.J. 55 (2008); Emily Buss, *What Does Frieda Yoder Believe*? 2 U. PA. J. CONST. L. 53 (1999). *See also* Eichner, *supra* Note 4. See also Section B, which considers what role should play in making decisions affecting their own welfare.

Over the years, jurists, scholars, and others have debated what is meant by the term "children's rights." Some have focused, as did Justice Douglas, on the importance of promoting children's autonomy interests. Others have focused on protecting children from their own immaturity and vulnerability. In the past several decades, commentators have offered increasingly sophisticated analyses of these and other competing or converging perspectives. *See, e.g.*, Lee E. Teitelbaum, *Children's Rights and the Problem of Equal Respect*, 2006 UTAH L. REV. 173; David S. Tanenhaus, *Between Dependency and Liberty: The Conundrum of Children's Rights in the Gilded Age*, 23 L. & HISTORY REV. 351 (2005); William Galston, *When Well-Being Trumps Liberty: Political Theory, Jurisprudence, and Children's Rights*, 79 CHI.-KENT L. REV. 279 (2004). In a relatively recent and provocative book, Professor Martin Guggenheim challenges the concept of children's rights, asserting that it "is both deeper and more shallow than is often recognized." MARTIN GUGGENHEIM, WHAT'S WRONG WITH CHILDREN'S RIGHTS xii (2005). He criticizes the concept's application in a range of contexts, providing new interpretations of classic cases and scenarios. For responses to Professor Guggenheim's book, see, *e.g.*, Justine Dunlap, *A Review of* What's Wrong with Children's Rights*: Still a "Slogan in Search of a Definition,"* 11 U.C. DAVIS J. JUV. L. & POL'Y 181 (2007); Howard Davidson, *Children's Rights and American Law: A Response to* What's Wrong with Children's Rights, 20 EMORY INT'L L. REV. 69 (2006). For a dramatically different characterization and analysis of children's rights, see JAMES G. DWYER, THE RELATIONSHIP RIGHTS OF CHILDREN (2006) (arguing for increasing attention to children's rights in various circumstances involving children's relationships with adults). For classic expositions of children's rights, see, *e.g.*, THE RIGHTS OF CHILDREN, HARV. EDUC. REV., Reprint Ser. 9 (1974). For an excellent collection of more recent essays, see *Symposium: Existing and Emerging Constitutional Rights of Children* 2 U. PA. J. CONST. L. 1 (1999–2000).

6. *Special Accommodations and the "Clash" between the Free Exercise and Establishment Clauses.* The First Amendment contains the Free Exercise Clause and the Establishment Clause which, at times, may conflict with one another. The Free Exercise Clause protects the rights of individuals to practice their religious beliefs, exempting individuals from the reach of a state or federal law in some instances. *See, e.g., Prince, supra.* In contrast to the Free Exercise Clause, the Establishment Clause requires that the government be neutral in its treatment of religion. The government may not adopt a state religion, favor one religion over another, or favor religion over the absence of religious beliefs. *See,* *e.g.*, *McCreary County, Ky. v. Am. Civil Liberties Union of Ky.*, 545 U.S. 844, 860 (2005) ("When the government acts with the ostensible and predominant purpose of advancing religion, it violates that central Establishment Clause value of official religious neutrality"). The Court has recognized that there is often a "tension" between these two clauses. *See, e.g.*, *Cutter v. Wilkinson*, 544 U.S. 709, 719 (2005) (observing that "[w]hile the two Clauses express complementary values, they often exert conflicting pressures" and at times "clash" or are "in tension" with one another). Thus, while "the Free Exercise Clause is said to require, or at least permit, exceptions from generally applicable laws that conflict with religious exercise[,] some say that such exceptions are an unconstitutional benefit to religion, forbidden under the Establishment Clause." MICHAEL W. MCCONNELL ET AL. (EDS.), RELIGION AND THE CONSTITUTION (2d 2006).

The Supreme Court has decided many cases regarding whether government funds can be used to assist children in religious schools with purportedly secular aspects of their education (such as bus transportation to school, textbooks for secular subjects, or special education services). Many observers characterize this body of cases as fraught with inconsistencies. For further discussion of the complex evolution of Establishment Clause jurisprudence as it relates to school funding, see Stephen Feldman, *Divided We Fall: Religion, Politics, and the Lemon Entanglements Prong*, 7 FIRST AMENDMENT L. REV. 253 (2009); Richard D. Garnett, *Religion, Division, and the First Amendment*, 94 GEO. REV. 1667 (2006).

7. *Home Schooling.* Most states provide an exception to compulsory school attendance for children receiving adequate instruction at home. In recent years, the number of home-schooled children has increased. Statistics tracked by the U.S. Department of Education indicate that in 2007, 1.5 million children (or 2.9 % of the school-aged population) were home-schooled, up 74% from 1999, the first year in which these data were collected. According to the Department, most home-schooled children's parents cite "concern about the school environment, [the desire] to provide religious or moral instruction [to their children], and dissatisfaction with the academic instruction available at other schools" as the reasons underlying the decision to home-school their children. U.S. Dep't Educ., *1.5 Million Home-Schooled Students in the United States*, Issue Brief, Dec. 2008, http://nces.ed.gov/pubs2009/2009030.pdf.

States vary in their approaches to home schooling and state policies have been in flux in some jurisdictions. For example, Florida had required home school teachers to be state-certified, but the relevant statute was repealed in 2002. The current statute, which became effective in 2007, does not require that the person teaching at home have an educational certificate or training as an educator. FLA. STAT. ANN. §§ 1001.21; 1002.41 (2009). The statute retained requirements that parents must maintain an academic portfolio with the student's work products and that the student would be evaluated annually by a credentialed teacher selected by the school district. In contrast to the recent statutory changes in Florida, California continues to maintain a requirement that home-schooling teachers have state-granted teaching credentials appropriate to the grade in which the student is instructed. CAL. EDUC. CODE § 48224 (2009). The qualifications of parents providing home-schooling in Virginia are fairly easy to meet. *See* VA. CODE ANN. § 22.1–254.1 (2009) (acquisition of a high school diploma by a parent can qualify parent as a teacher for purposes of home-schooling her child). While Virginia, like Florida, requires that the family demonstrate the student's proficiency in subjects on the state curriculum, it provides parents with many ways of satisfying this requirement, and does not require, like Florida, that a credentialed state educator conduct the assessment. *Id.*

In 1988, the Eighth Circuit Court of Appeals decided a challenge to Arkansas's statutory provisions mandating state monitoring of the academic progress of home-schooled students. *Murphy v. State*, 852 F.2d 1039 (1988). While recognizing parents' First and Fourteenth Amendment rights to guide their children's education in a manner consistent with their religious beliefs, the court held that the state had a compelling interest in insuring that the child achieves a basic level of competence in the subject matter contained in its state educational curriculum. *Id.* at 1042. It further held that "Arkansas has created the least restrictive system possible to assure its goal. By providing the option of home schooling, Arkansas allows parents vast responsibility and accountability in terms of their children's education — control far in excess" of what is constitutionally required. *Id.* at 1042–43. Consistent with this position is the decision of a California Court of Appeal case, *Jonathan L. v. Superior Court*, 81 Cal. Rptr.3d 571 (2008). The court stated: "No . . . absolute right to home school exists. Instead, . . . parents possess a constitutional liberty interest in directing the education of their children, but the right must yield to state interests in certain circumstances." *Id.* at 592. The court cited *Meyer, Pierce, Prince,* and *Yoder*, as well as other precedents, and concluded that, in some instances, the state's compelling interest in the welfare and education of minors may limit parental autonomy.

In general, legal challenges to state regulation of home schooling have found the regulations to be constitutional. *See, e.g., Care and Protection of Charles*, 504 N.E.2d 592 (Mass. 1987) (sustaining state's requirements as constitutional). Not inconsistent with these decisions is *Delconte v. North Carolina*, 329 S.E.2d 636 (N.C. 1985) (interpreting state's education statutes as permitting home schooling that meets certain requirements and deferring question of whether an absolute state prohibition of home schooling would be unconstitutional). For further discussion of these issues, see Donald D. Dorman, Student Author, *Michigan's Teacher Certification Requirement as Applied to Religiously Motivated Home Schools*, 23 U. MICH. J.L. REF. 733, 738–45 (1990); Ralph D. Mawdsley, *Parent's Rights to Direct Their Children's Education: Changing Perspectives*, 162 EDUC. L. REP. 659 (2002). For an elucidation of the position for strong parental authority to make educational choices for their children, see Stephen Gilles, *On Educating Children: A Parentalist Manifesto*, 63 U. CHI. L. REV. 937 (1996). For contrasting views, see James Dwyer, *Parents' Religion and Children's Welfare: Debunking the Doctrine of Children's Rights*, 82 CAL. L. REV. 1371 (1994); Emily Buss, *The Adolescents' Stake in the Allocation of Educational Control Between Parent and State*, 67 U. CHI. L. REV. 1233 (2000) (criticizing home schooling on the basis that exposure to peers of different backgrounds is critically important to adolescent development). For a perspective that seeks to reconcile competing interests "in a manner most consistent with the ideals that underlie the liberal democratic project," see Maxine Eichner, *Who Should Control Children's Education?: Parents, Children, and the State*, 75 U. CIN. L. REV. 1339 (2007).

8. *School Vouchers.* In recent years, legislatures have initiated voucher programs aimed at offering low-income parents a choice of educational alternatives for their children attending inferior inner city schools. The Supreme Court upheld an Ohio program that provided tuition aid to children attending participating public or private schools against an Establishment Clause challenge. *Zelman v. Simmons-Harris*, 536 U.S. 639 (2002). In this case, 96% of the children receiving vouchers attended religious schools. In an opinion by Justice Rehnquist, a divided Court rejected the argument that the program provided benefits to religious schools. The Court emphasized that the program was enacted for a secular purpose, to provide educational aid to poor children in a failing school system, and that the assistance was provided directly to parents (who then used the aid to pay religious school tuition). The Court held the program was neutral toward religion and could not be interpreted as endorsement of a religious message. Justice Souter argued in dissent that the program had the impermissible effect of advancing religious education. School voucher programs and other policies to improve the quality of education for poor urban children have attracted considerable academic interest. For a series of scholarly perspectives on a range of issues relating to vouchers specifically, and school choice more generally, see *Symposium: Educational Choice: Emerging Legal and Policy Issues*, 2008 B.Y.U. L. Rev. 227. *See also* James Dwyer, Religious Schools Verses Children' Rights (1998); James E. Ryan, *Schools, Race, and Money*, 109 Yale L.J. 249 (1999). For an analysis of *Zelman*, see Charles Fried, *Five to Four: Reflections on the School Voucher Case*, 116 Harv. L. Rev. 163 (2002).

PARKER v. HURLEY
United States Court of Appeals, First Circuit
514 F.3d 87 (2008), *cert. denied* 129 S. Ct. 56 (2008)

Lynch, Circuit Judge.

Two sets of parents . . . sued the Lexington, Massachusetts school district in which their young children are enrolled. They assert that they must be given prior notice by the school and the opportunity to exempt their young children from exposure to books they find religiously repugnant. Plaintiffs assert violations of their own and their children's rights under the Free Exercise Clause and their substantive parental and privacy due process rights under the U.S. Constitution.

The Parkers object to their child being presented in kindergarten and first grade with two books that portray diverse families, including families in which both parents are of the same gender. The Wirthlins object to a second-grade teacher's reading to their son's class a book that depicts and celebrates a gay marriage. The parents do not challenge the use of these books as part of a nondiscrimination curriculum in the public schools, but challenge the school district's refusal to provide them with prior notice and to allow for exemption from such instruction. They ask for relief until their children are in seventh grade.

Massachusetts does have a statute that requires parents be given notice and the opportunity to exempt their children from curriculum which primarily involves human sexual education or human sexuality issues. The school system has declined to apply this statutory exemption to these plaintiffs on the basis that the materials do not primarily involve human sexual education or human sexuality issues.

The U.S. District Court dismissed plaintiffs' complaint for failure to state a federal constitutional claim upon which relief could be granted. Plaintiffs appeal. [¶] Because plaintiffs appeal the dismissal of their complaint under Rule 12(b)(6), we take the allegations in their complaint as true and draw all reasonable inferences in plaintiffs' favor . . .

[We start by taking notice] of the statewide curricular standards of [Massachusetts]. . . . Massachusetts enacted a comprehensive education reform bill in 1993, [which] mandates that the [academic standards for core subjects] "be designed to inculcate respect for the cultural, ethnic and racial diversity of the commonwealth[, and] avoid perpetuating gender, cultural, ethnic or racial stereotypes." [One goal set forth by the state standards] states: "Students will gain knowledge about the significance of the family on individuals and society, and will learn skills to support the family, balance work and family life, be an effective parent, and nurture the development of children." ¶ [In elementary school, a goal of the curriculum is] that children should be able to "[d]escribe different types of families [and] learn that [healthy interpersonal] relationships with others are an integral part of the human life experience. . . . [¶] [An] associated [s]tandard for pre-kindergarten through grade 5 recommends that children be able to "[d]escribe the concepts of prejudice and discrimination." [¶] It is not until grades 6-8 that the [standards call for education of students regarding] "the detrimental effect of prejudice (such as prejudice on the basis of race, gender, sexual orientation, class, or religion) on individual relationships and society as a whole." [Another component of the curriculum provides] that by grade 5, students should be able to "[d]efine sexual orientation using the correct terminology (such as heterosexual, and gay and lesbian)."

These statewide academic standards do not purport to select particular instructional materials. . . . [¶] By statute, the actual selection of books is the responsibility of a school's principal, with the approval of the superintendent of schools . . . Plaintiffs allege in their complaint that Lexington school officials began integrating books like these into their elementary school's curriculum at the behest of gay rights advocates.

[The relevant Massachusetts statute] requires school districts to provide parents with notice of and an opportunity to exempt their children from "curriculum which primarily involves human sexual education or human sexuality issues.". . . . Schools must make the relevant curricular materials available for parents to review . . . though they do not necessarily have to allow parents to observe the classes. . . .

On November 18, 2003, a divided Supreme Judicial Court of Massachusetts held, in *Goodridge v. Department of Public Health* . . . that the state constitution mandates the recognition of same-sex marriage. A later effort to reverse this decision through the mechanism of a constitutional convention and a popular vote failed.

David and Tonia Parker's sons, Jacob and Joshua Parker, and Joseph and Robin Wirthlin's son, Joseph Robert Wirthlin, Jr., are students at Estabrook Elementary School in Lexington, Massachusetts. Both families assert that they are devout Judeo-Christians and that a core belief of their religion is that homosexual behavior and gay marriage are immoral and violate God's law. [¶] In January 2005, when Jacob . . . was in kindergarten, he brought home a "Diversity Book Bag." This included a picture book, *Who's in a Family?*, which depicted different families, including single-parent families, an extended family, interracial families, animal families, a family without children, and — to the concern of the Parkers — a family with two dads and a family with two moms. The book concludes by answering the question, "Who's in a family?": "The people who love you the most!" The book says nothing about marriage.

The Parkers were concerned that this book was part of an effort by the public schools "to indoctrinate young children into the concept that homosexuality and homosexual relationships or marriage are moral and acceptable behavior." Such an effort, they feared, would require their sons to affirm a belief inconsistent with their religion. [The Parkers expressed this position to Estabrook's Principal Jay, and requested] that Jacob not be exposed to any further discussions of homosexuality. Principal Jay disagreed that the school had any obligation under [the governing statute] to notify parents in advance of such class discussions. [The Parkers' assertions were also rejected by the Superintendent of the county's schools and two other district administrators.] A further meeting to discuss these issues was held at Estabrook on April 27, 2005, which resulted in Mr. Parker's arrest when he refused to leave the school until his demands were met. [At the beginning of the 2005-06 school year, the district Superintendent] released a public statement explaining the school district's position that it would not provide parental notification for "discussions, activities, or materials that simply reference same-gender parents or that otherwise recognize the existence of differences in sexual orientation." When Jacob entered first grade that fall, his classroom's book collection included *Who's in a Family?* as well as *Molly's Family*, a picture book about a girl who is at first made to feel embarrassed by a classmate because she has both a mommy and a mama but then learns that families can come in many different varieties. In December 2005, the Parkers repeated their request for advance notice, which Superintendent Ash again denied.

. . . In March 2006, an Estabrook teacher read aloud *King and King* to her second grade class, which included [Joey Wirthlin]. This picture book tells the story of a prince, ordered by his mother to get married, who [falls] in love with another prince. A wedding scene between the two princes is depicted. The last page of the book shows the two princes kissing, but with a red heart superimposed over their mouths. . . . That evening, Joey told his parents about the book; his parents described him as "agitated" and remembered him calling the book "so silly." Eventually the Wirthlins were able to secure a meeting with the teacher and [Principal] Jay on April 6, 2006, to object to what they considered to be indoctrination of their son about gay marriage in contravention of their religious beliefs. [Principal] Jay reiterated the school district's position that no prior notice or exemption would be given.

[After all of their objections to school officials failed, the families filed this action.] The complaint alleges that the public schools are systematically indoctrinating the [their] young children contrary to the parents' religious beliefs and that the defendants held "a specific intention to denigrate the [families'] sincere and deeply-held faith." They claim, under 42 U.S.C. § 1983, violations of their and their children's First Amendment right to the free exercise of religion and of their Fourteenth Amendment due process right to parental autonomy in the upbringing of their children, as well as of their concomitant state rights.[3] They also assert a violation of the Massachusetts "opt out" statute. The plaintiffs argue that their ability to influence their young children toward their family religious views has been undercut in several respects. First, they believe their children are too young to be introduced to the topic of gay marriage. They also point to the important influence teachers have on this age group. They fear their own inability as parents to counter the school's approval of gay marriage, particularly if parents are given no notice that such curricular materials are in use. As for the children, the parents fear that they are "essentially" required "to affirm a belief inconsistent with and prohibited by their religion." The parents assert it is ironic, and unconstitutional under the Free Exercise Clause, for a public school system to show such intolerance towards their own religious beliefs in the name of tolerance.

For relief, the plaintiffs seek a declaration of their constitutional rights; damages; and an injunction requiring the school (1) to provide an opportunity to exempt their children from "classroom presentations or discussions the intent of which is to have children accept the validity of, embrace, affirm, or celebrate views of human sexuality, gender identity, and marriage constructs," (2) to allow the parents to observe any such classroom discussions, and (3) to not present any "materials graphically depicting homosexual physical contact" to students before the seventh grade.

[The lower court granted defendants motion to dismiss for failure to state a claim upon which relief could be granted. This court reviews, at some length, the relevant constitutional jurisprudence addressing parental requests for religious exemptions from public school curricular and other policies. It concludes] that parental rights and the free exercise of religion by parents are interests that overlap and inform each other, and thus are sensibly considered together. [It noted that, in this case, the threshold] question is "whether the plaintiff's free exercise is interfered with at all." . . . In this case there is no pleading of a constitutionally significant burden on plaintiffs' rights.

In *Yoder*, the Court found unconstitutional Wisconsin's application of its compulsory school attendance law to Amish parents who believed that any education beyond eighth grade undermined their entire, religiously focused way of life. The heart of the *Yoder* opinion is a lengthy consideration of "the interrelationship of belief with [the Amish] mode of life, the vital role that belief

---

[3] The plaintiffs also claim that defendants violated § 1983 by conspiring to deprive them of these constitutional rights. They do not assert an Establishment Clause claim. We note that the Supreme Judicial Court has held that the Massachusetts state constitution provides greater protection for free exercise claims then does the federal constitution. Plaintiffs brought their suit in federal court and have chosen not to request certification of any state law issues to the Supreme Judicial Court.

and daily conduct play in the continued survival of Old Order Amish communities and their religious organization," and how as a result compulsory high school education would "substantially interfer[e] with the religious development of the Amish child and his integration into the way of life of the Amish faith community." *Id.* The Court thus found Wisconsin's compulsory attendance law to be flatly incompatible with the plaintiffs' free exercise rights and parental liberty interests, which it considered in tandem. That is, compulsory attendance at any school-whether public, private, or home-based-prevented these Amish parents from making fundamental decisions regarding their children's religious upbringing and effectively overrode their ability to pass their religion on to their children, as their faith required. Further, the parents in *Yoder* were able to demonstrate that their alternative informal vocational training of their older children still met the state's professed interest behind its compulsory attendance requirement.

To the extent that *Yoder* embodies judicial protection for social and religious "sub-groups from the public cultivation of liberal tolerance," plaintiffs are correct to rely on it. But there are substantial differences between the plaintiffs' claims in *Yoder* and the claims raised in this case. One ground of distinction is that the plaintiffs have chosen to place their children in public schools and do not live, as the Amish do, in a largely separate culture. There are others. While plaintiffs do invoke *Yoder's* language that the state is threatening their very "way of life," they use this language to refer to the centrality of these beliefs to their faith, in contrast to its use in *Yoder* to refer to a distinct community and life style. Exposure to the materials in dispute here will not automatically and irreversibly prevent the parents from raising Jacob and Joey in the religious belief that gay marriage is immoral. Nor is there a criminal statute involved, or any other punishment imposed on the parents if they choose to educate their children in other ways. They retain options, unlike the parents in *Yoder*. Tellingly, *Yoder* emphasized that its holding was essentially *sui generis*, as few sects could make a similar showing of a unique and demanding religious way of life that is fundamentally incompatible with any schooling system. Plaintiffs' case is not *Yoder.*

. . . .

. . . . Plaintiffs' opening premise is that their rights of parental control are fundamental rights. They rely on a Supreme Court decision recognizing a substantive due process right of parents "to make decisions concerning the care, custody, and control of their children." *Troxel v. Granville*, 530 U.S. 57 (2000) (plurality opinion). *Troxel* is not so broad as plaintiffs assert. The cases cited by the Court in *Troxel* as establishing this parental right pertain either to the custody of children, which was also the issue in dispute in *Troxel*, or to the fundamental control of children's schooling, as in *Yoder*.[15] . . .

The schooling cases cited in *Troxel* "evince the principle that the state cannot prevent parents from choosing a specific educational program." In *Meyer v.*

---

[15] In slight variations on these themes, the Court also cited Parham v. J.R., 442 U.S. 584 (1979), which pertained to the power of parents to commit their children to mental institutions, and Prince v. Massachusetts, 321 U.S. 158 (1944), in which the Court determined that the parent's liberty interest was outweighed in that instance by the state's interest in enforcing child labor and compulsory attendance laws.

Nebraska, 262 U.S. 390 (1923), the Supreme Court found unconstitutional a prohibition on the teaching of foreign languages to young children in part because it interfered with "the power of parents to control the education of their own." Two years later, *in Pierce v. Society of Sisters*, the Court overturned an Oregon statute compelling children to attend public schools on the grounds that the statute "unreasonably interfere[d] with the liberty of parents and guardians to direct the upbringing of children under their control." Plaintiffs argue their request for notice and exemption is simply a logical extension of their parental rights under *Meyer* and *Pierce*, as reinforced by their free exercise rights.

Defendants respond that plaintiffs' argument runs afoul of the general proposition that, while parents can choose between public and private schools, they do not have a constitutional right to "direct how a public school teaches their child." That proposition is well recognized . . . Indeed, *Meyer* and *Pierce* specified that the parental interests they recognized would not interfere with the general power of the state to regulate education, including "the state's power to prescribe a curriculum for institutions which it supports."

Plaintiffs say, in response, that they are not attempting to control the school's power to prescribe a curriculum. . . . They do not seek to change the choice of books available to others but only to require notice of the books and an exemption, and even then only up to the seventh grade. Nonetheless, we have found no federal case under the Due Process Clause which has permitted parents to demand an exemption for their children from exposure to certain books used in public schools. . . . In sum, the substantive due process clause by itself . . . does not give plaintiffs the degree of control over their children's education that their requested relief seeks. We turn then to whether the combination of substantive due process and free exercise interests give the parents a cause of action.

The First Amendment's prohibition on laws "respecting an establishment of religion, or prohibiting the free exercise thereof" applies to the states through the Fourteenth Amendment. In *Smith*, the Supreme Court noted that the "free exercise of religion means, first and foremost, the right to believe and profess whatever religious doctrine one desires." As a result, the government may not, for example, (1) compel affirmation of religious beliefs; (2) punish the expression of religious doctrines it believes to be false; (3) impose special disabilities on the basis of religious views or religious status; or (4) lend its power to one side or the other in controversies over religious authorities or dogma. [¶] The Free Exercise Clause, importantly, is not a general protection of religion or religious belief. It has a more limited reach of protecting the free exercise of religion. . . . Specifically, "it is necessary in a free exercise case for one to show the coercive effect of the enactment as it operates against him in the practice of his religion."

Preliminarily, we mark the distinction between the alleged burden on the parents' free exercise rights and the alleged burden on their children's. The right of parents "to direct the religious upbringing of their children," see *Yoder*, is distinct from (although related to) any right their children might have regarding the content of their school curriculum. . . . This is not a new distinction. In *Prince v. Massachusetts*, the Court explained that "two claimed liberties are at stake. One is the parent's, to bring up the child in the way [the parent desires], which for appellant means to teach him the tenets and the practices of their faith. The other freedom is the child's, to observe these [tenets and practices]." We start with the parents' claim.

In *Mozert v. Hawkins County Board of Education*, 827 F.2d 1058 (6th Cir.1987), which is more factually similar to this case, the Sixth Circuit rejected a broader claim for an exemption from a school district's use of an entire series of texts. The parents in that case asserted that the books in question taught values contrary to their religious beliefs and that, as a result, the school violated the parents' religious beliefs by allowing their children to read the books and violated their children's religious beliefs by requiring the children to read them. The court, however, found that exposure to ideas through the required reading of books did not constitute a constitutionally significant burden on the plaintiffs' free exercise of religion. In so holding, the court emphasized that "the evil prohibited by the Free Exercise Clause" is "governmental compulsion either to do or refrain from doing an act forbidden or required by one's religion, or to affirm or disavow a belief forbidden or required by one's religion," and reading or even discussing the books did not compel such action or affirmation.

In the present case, the plaintiffs claim that the exposure of their children . . . to ways of life contrary to the parents' religious beliefs violates [the parents'] ability to direct the religious upbringing of their children. . . . The parents do not allege coercion in the form of a direct interference with their religious beliefs, nor of compulsion in the form of punishment for their beliefs, as in *Yoder*. Nor do they allege the denial of benefits. Further, plaintiffs do not allege that the mere listening to a book being read violated any religious duty on the part of the child. There is no claim that as a condition of attendance at the public schools, the defendants have forced plaintiffs-either the parents or the children-to violate their religious beliefs. In sum there is no claim of direct coercion.

The heart of the plaintiffs' free exercise claim is a claim of "indoctrination": that the state has put pressure on their children to endorse an affirmative view of gay marriage and has thus undercut the parents' efforts to inculcate their children with their own opposing religious views.[1] The Supreme Court, we believe, has never

---

[1] [In a different segment of this opinion, the court addressed the law's recognition of the "impressionability of children of different ages." It observed:

The impressionability of young school children has been noted as a relevant factor in the Establishment Clause context. *See, e.g., Lee v. Weisman*, 505 U.S. 577 (1992) (identifying concerns about the "subtle coercive pressure [of state endorsement of religion] in the elementary and secondary public schools"); *Sch. Dist. of Abington Twp. v. Schempp*, 374 U.S. 203 (1963) (Goldberg, J., concurring) (expressing concern about the impact of school prayer and Bible reading on "young impressionable children") . . . Just as university students "are less impressionable than younger students" when it comes to school policies regarding religion, . . . so also are high school students less impressionable than the very youngest children. . . . The relevance of the age of school children has been noted in a free speech case involving religious expression [and] in the context of parental due process rights. [Citations to federal circuit court decisions omitted.]

We see no principled reason why the age of students should be irrelevant in Free Exercise Clause cases. *See, e.g.*, M. Eichner, *Who Should Control Children's Education?: Parents, Children, and the State*, 75 U. CIN. L. REV. 1339 (2007) (age of children should be taken into account when considering parental due process or free exercise claims in the public school context) . . .

utilized an indoctrination test under the Free Exercise Clause, much less in the public school context. The closest it has come is *Barnette*, a free speech case that implicated free exercise interests and which *Smith* included in its hybrid case discussion. In *Barnette*, the Court held that the state could not coerce acquiescence through compelled statements of belief, such as the mandatory recital of the pledge of allegiance in public schools. It did not hold that the state could not attempt to inculcate values by instruction, and in fact carefully distinguished the two approaches. We do not address whether or not an indoctrination theory under the Free Exercise Clause is sound. Plaintiffs' pleadings do not establish a viable case of indoctrination, even assuming that extreme indoctrination can be a form of coercion.

First, as to the parents' free exercise rights, the mere fact that a child is exposed on occasion in public school to a concept offensive to a parent's religious belief does not inhibit the parent from instructing the child differently. A parent whose "child is exposed to sensitive topics or information [at school] remains free to discuss these matters and to place them in the family's moral or religious context, or to supplement the information with more appropriate materials." The parents here did in fact have notice, if not prior notice, of the books and of the school's overall intent to promote toleration of same-sex marriage, and they retained their ability to discuss the material and subject matter with their children. Our outcome does not turn, however, on whether the parents had notice.

Turning to the children's free exercise rights, we cannot see how Jacob's free exercise right was burdened at all: two books were made available to him, but he was never required to read them or have them read to him. Further, these books do not endorse gay marriage or homosexuality, or even address these topics explicitly, but merely describe how other children might come from families that look different from one's own. There is no free exercise right to be free from any reference in public elementary schools to the existence of families in which the parents are of different gender combinations.

Joey has a more significant claim, both because he was required to sit through a classroom reading of *King and King* and because that book affirmatively endorses homosexuality and gay marriage. It is a fair inference that the reading of *King and King* was precisely *intended* to influence the listening children toward tolerance of gay marriage. That was the point of why that book was chosen and used. Even assuming there is a continuum along which an intent to influence could become an attempt to indoctrinate, however, this case is firmly on the influence-toward-tolerance end. There is no evidence of systemic indoctrination. There is no allegation that Joey was asked to affirm gay marriage. Requiring a student to read a particular book is generally not coercive of free exercise rights.

Public schools are not obliged to shield individual students from ideas which potentially are religiously offensive, particularly when the school imposes no requirement that the student agree with or affirm those ideas, or even participate in discussions about them. The reading of *King and King* was not instruction in religion or religious beliefs. [¶] On the facts, there is no viable claim of

---

514 F.3d at 100–01. Eds.].

"indoctrination" here. Without suggesting that such showings would suffice to establish a claim of indoctrination, we note the plaintiffs' children were not forced to read the books on pain of suspension. Nor were they subject to a constant stream of like materials. There is no allegation here of a formalized curriculum requiring students to read many books affirming gay marriage. The reading by a teacher of one book, or even three, and even if to a young and impressionable child, does not constitute "indoctrination." [¶] Because plaintiffs do not allege facts that give rise to claims of constitutional magnitude, the district court did not err in granting defendants' motion to dismiss the claims under the U.S. Constitution.

Public schools often walk a tightrope between the many competing constitutional demands made by parents, students, teachers, and the schools' other constituents. The balance the school struck here does not offend the Free Exercise or Due Process Clauses of the U.S. Constitution. [¶] We do not suggest that the school's choice of books for young students has not deeply offended the plaintiffs' sincerely held religious beliefs. If the school system has been insufficiently sensitive to such religious beliefs, the plaintiffs may seek recourse to the normal political processes for change in the town and state. They are not entitled to a federal judicial remedy under the U.S. Constitution. [¶] We affirm the district court's dismissal with prejudice of plaintiffs' federal claims. . . .

NOTE

1. *School Curriculum and Parents' Constitutional Rights.* The *Parker* court distinguishes the instant case from *Yoder*, and therefore holds that parental authority to guide their children's education has important limits, even when parents claim that aspects of the public school's curriculum offends their religious beliefs. Since *Yoder*, federal and state courts have had to consider whether parents should be able to shield their children from exposure to material in the public school curriculum by demanding (1) that certain topics, lessons, or teaching materials should not be included in the public school curriculum; (2) that, if those topics, lessons, or teaching materials remain part of the curriculum, the district should provide accompanying materials or lessons promulgating "alternative perspectives," or (3) that the children should be able to "opt-out" of exposure to the offending topics, lessons, or teaching.

Parental challenges of sexuality or family life education programs were common in the 1970s and 1980s. Since the 1960s, school districts have offered these programs, largely in response to concerns about teenage sexual activity, teen pregnancy, and venereal disease. Parents' objections to these programs have been based on claims that the state interferes with parents' authority to instruct their children on moral issues according to their religious beliefs when it seeks to educate children about sexuality. Most commonly, parents have claimed that sexuality education programs (and regulations authorizing such programs) violate the Free Exercise and Establishment Clauses and parental rights under the Fourteenth Amendment. Programs with policies allowing parents to opt out of the program have been upheld, *e.g. Smith v. Ricci*, 446 A.2d 501 (N.J. 1982), as have most compulsory programs, such as one promoting AIDS awareness, in spite of inclusion of allegedly sexually-suggestive skits as part of the program. *See Brown v. Hot, Sexy, and Safer Productions*, 68 F.3d 525 (1st Cir. 1995). In the latter case, the court rejected parents' claim that their rights to rear their children under *Meyer* and *Pierce* "encompasses a . . . right to dictate the curriculum at the public school to which they have chosen to send their children." *Id.* at 533. Such a right, in the court's view, would require the school to customize the curriculum for every child whose parents raised moral objections. The court also rejected the Free Exercise claim, finding the burden to religious expression far less substantial than that experienced by the parents in *Yoder*.

The 2005 decision of a federal district court in Pennsylvania in *Kitzmiller v. Dover Area School District*, 400 F. Supp. 2d 707 (M.D. Pa. 2005), attracted national attention. In this case, the court struck down a school board resolution requiring teachers to make students aware of alternative perspectives on evolution such as "intelligent design." *Id.* at 708–09. In its careful examination of the notion of "intelligent design" ("ID"), the court noted that ID relied on a belief in the existence of God as a "supernatural designer" of human beings and other species. *Id.* at 720. As such, the court characterized ID as "religious" in nature, despite its proponents' careful avoidance of the terms "creation" or "creationism." *Id.* at 720–23, 728–29, 734–35. The court noted that "every major scientific association that has taken a position on the issue" had concluded that ID is not *science*. *Id.* at 737. It therefore held that the inclusion of ID in the public school classroom was an official endorsement of religion, thereby violating the First Amendment. *Id.* at 765–66.

Parents have also challenged textbooks used in public schools on religious grounds. *Mozert v. Hawkins County Bd. of Educ.*, 827 F.2d 1058 (6th Cir. 1987). The parents objected, in particular, to descriptions in the textbooks of magic, witchcraft, situational ethics, humanistic values, and the theory of evolution. They argued that material in the texts might influence a child to become "a feminist, a humanist, a pacifist, an anti-Christian, a vegetarian or an advocate of a 'one-world government.' " The federal circuit court held that the textbooks did not burden the parents' Free Exercise rights. The opinion stressed the importance of the state's secular purposes in teaching independent thinking, critical judgment, logical decisionmaking, and tolerance. It emphasized that the students were not required to affirm or deny any belief or engage in any practice that contradicted their religious beliefs.

Another recent debate concerns what role discussions about sexual orientation or same-sex marriage should play in the public school curriculum, as demonstrated by *Parker v. Hurley*. Scholars have lined up on both sides of the fence. Some have argued that discussions of same-sex marriage in public schools violates parents' Due Process and Free Exercise rights. *See, e.g.*, Charles J. Russo, *Same-Sex Marriage and Public School Curricula: Parental Rights To Direct the Education of their Children*, 32 U. Dayton L. Rev. 361 (2007). Others assert that inclusion of such subject matter in the public schools does not violate parents' constitutional rights. *See, e.g.*, Carolyn Depoian, *Homosexuality, The Public School Curriculum and the First Amendment: Issues of Religion and Speech*, 18 L. & Sexuality 163 (2009). Depoian argues that open discussions of sexual orientation promote the traditional virtues of public education, such as preparing students for participation in a democracy. Such preparation, she asserts, entails development of tolerance and respect for the varying viewpoints and lifestyles that characterize our pluralistic society.

For further discussion of the more general issues raised in this note, see, *e.g.* Eric A. DeGroff, *Parental Rights and Public School Curricula: Revisiting* Mozert *after Twenty Years*, 38 J. Educ. & L. 83 (2009); Maxine Eichner, *School Surveys and Children's Education: The Argument for Shared Authority Between Parents and the State*, 38 J. L. & Educ. 459 (2009); Maxine Eichner, *Who Should Control Children's Education?: Parents, Children, and the State*, 75 U. Cin. L. Rev. 1339 (2007); Nomi Maya Stolzenberg, *"He Drew a Circle that Shut Me Out": Assimilation, Indoctrination and the Paradox of a Liberal Education*, 106 Harv. L. Rev. 581 (1993); Ira Lupu, *Where Rights Begin: The Problem of Burdens on the Free Exercise of Religion*, 102 Harv. L. Rev. 933 (1989).

2. *The Pledge of Allegiance.* In his dissent in *Prince v. Massachusetts*, Justice Murphy cited *West Virginia Board of Education v. Barnette*, 319 U.S. 624, the 1943 case in which the Court held that First Amendment's speech and religion clauses precluded the states from compelling school children to salute the flag. In Justice Murphy's view, the Court's decision in *Barnette* requires a state to demonstrate that intervention in the family — particularly in matters relating to the free exercise of religion — is justified by "convincing proof that such a practice constitutes a grave and immediate danger to the state or to the health, morals, or welfare of the child." That burden, according to Justice Murphy, was not met by Massachusetts in *Prince*.

In recent years, there have been several challenges to state-mandated recitation of the Pledge of Allegiance in schools, typically grounded in various First and Fourteenth Amendment claims. In 2004, in *Elk Grove Unified School District v. Newdow*, the U.S. Supreme Court considered a challenge to a California school district's policy of beginning the elementary school day with the Pledge of Allegiance. *Newdow*, 542 U.S. at 6. In this case, however, the Court did not reach the merits, because it concluded that the petitioner, the child's noncustodial father, did not have the legal authority to represent his daughter's interests in this case. The custodial parent, the mother, indicated that neither she or her daughter objected to the pledge.

Are minors' decisions to abstain from reciting the Pledge constitutionally protected? In his dissent in *Yoder*, Justice Douglas argued that the preferences of adolescents should be solicited in the context of important educational decisions, such as the decision to exit school. The question of the relative roles that parents versus children are entitled to play in exercising constitutional protections in the educational context has been raised in other contexts as well. For example, two federal courts have disagreed as to the constitutionality of parental permission or notification requirements concerning children's abstention from participation in the Pledge of Allegiance. In 2009, an *en banc* panel of the Eleventh Circuit Court of Appeal overturned the decision of a three-judge panel that had sustained a Florida statute requiring public high school students to secure parental permission in order to abstain from reciting the Pledge. *Frazier v. Alexandre*, 555 F.3d 1292 (11th Cir. 2009). The court held that students' basic rights to freedom of expression and belief are invoked in compulsory pledge policies, and there is no countervailing parental right that would justify restricting students' free choice in this context. The Third Circuit arrived at a similar conclusion in *Circle School v. Pappert*, 381 F.3d 172 (3rd Cir. 2004). For further discussion of the constitutional issues raised by school policies on the recitation of the Pledge, see David A. Toy, *The Pledge: The Constitutionality of an American Icon*, 34 J.L. & EDUC. 25 (2005); Luke Meier, *Constitutional Structure, Individual Rights, and the Pledge of Allegiance*, 5 FIRST AMENDMENT L. REV. 162 (2006).

PROBLEM

Problem 10-1.   The Johnsons are members of a religious sect that teaches, among other things, that the body is fundamentally sinful, with urges and pleasures that must be fought and overcome through an allegiance to God. They object strongly to the instruction which their daughter Mary is scheduled to receive in her high school physical education class, which teaches that certain bodily urges are "healthy," and stresses the importance of having a positive self-image. The Johnsons consider these teachings heretical and likely to lead Mary to question her religious training. When they object to the high school principal, he seeks your advice on how to respond. The principal has no doubt about the sincerity of the Johnsons' objections. What do you advise him to do?

B.   THE CHILD'S CLAIMS AGAINST PARENTAL AND STATE AUTHORITY

The threshold decision for the state to make when presented with a parent-child conflict is whether to intervene at all. If courts were generally available as a forum of appeal from parental authority, considerable time could be consumed deciding such issues as how late teenagers can stay out, whether they should be required to eat their vegetables, and whether they can use the car. In addition to the judicial resources this would involve, such intervention would constitute a level of intrusion in family life, and thus parental autonomy, that most would consider unacceptable. Therefore, courts typically deny relief to children challenging parental authority, and generally avoid second-guessing parental decisions if there is no evidence of abuse or neglect. In some instances, however, a minor's challenge to parental authority is heard by the courts. These cases reveal a legal tension among three sets of interests: the child's interests in liberty or autonomy, the parents' interests in family privacy and parental autonomy, and the state's *parens patriae* and police power interests in the child's welfare. Three contexts in which such claims by minors are given special treatment by the law are examined below: (1) claims by minors for independence from parental authority; (2) minors' objection to parental medical decisions (with particular attention to psychiatric hospitalization decisions); and (3) minors' autonomy interests in the context of reproductive health (that is, independent and confidential access to contraception, sexuality education, and abortion).

[1]   Claims of Independence by the Child from Parental Authority

[a]   Legal Emancipation

There are some circumstances in which an individual younger than age 18 is treated by law as if she is an adult. Generally, in these cases, minors are living independent of their parents or guardians and are shouldering adult responsibilities, such as supporting themselves financially. In this situation, most states provide a mechanism by which a minor child can become "emancipated" from her parents. The legal consequence of emancipation is that the child acquires some rights and privileges of adulthood and that the minor's parents no longer have custody of or the obligation to support the child. At common law and, in many jurisdictions by statute, legal emancipation occurs automatically upon entry into the military or upon marrying. *See, e.g.,* CAL. FAM. CODE § 7002 (2009). *See also, e.g., La Voice v. La Voice,* 214 A.2d 53 (Vt. 1965) (military service); *Meyer v. Meyer,* 493 S.W.2d 42 (Mo. App. 1973) (marriage). Prior to the shift in the age of majority from age 21 to age 18, all minors under the age 21 in the military were thereby emancipated. Presently, in the United States, minors can enter the military once they turn age 17, if they have parental consent. See Military.Com, Website for United States Military Services, http://www.military.com/Recruiting/Content/0,13898,rec_step02_eligibility,,00.html. Minors can also become emancipated by judicial declaration if, for example, the minor is willingly living separate and apart from parents and supporting him- or herself financially. *See, e.g.,* CAL. FAM. CODE § 7020 (2009); *Holt v. Holt,* 633 S.W.2d 171 (Mo. App. 1982) (19-year-old son who had left home to live with others, retaining his monthly earnings of $900 was emancipated). Generally, pregnancy and parenthood are not bases for full legal emancipation in that the minor's parents remain financially responsible for them. Stacey Amodio, *Emancipation through Pregnancy,* 11 J. CONTEMP. LEGAL. ISSUES 648 (2000). However, from a practical standpoint, some minors may become "socially" emancipated during or following the birth of a child, and may move away from home, thus creating the circumstances that satisfy the legal requirements for emancipation. *See, e.g., Town v. Anonymous,* 467 A.2d 687 (Conn. Super. Ct. 1983 (16-year-old girl voluntarily left parents' home to live with putative father of her baby). Minors who are pregnant or who have become parents are generally authorized to consent to their own health care and to that of their children, and therefore may become *medically emancipated* while remaining legally dependent on their parents for other purposes. *See* Subsection [3] below; *see also* Sharon Smith, *The Medical Emancipation of Minors: A California History,* 11 J. CONTEMP. LEGAL ISSUES 637 (2000). Despite such medical emancipation, as noted below in Section 3, minors' access to abortion is subject to separate legal regulation. Emancipated minors are not treated as adults for purposes such as voting or drinking alcohol.

Although a child seeking to escape parental authority can bring an emancipation action, it is far more typical for the issue to be litigated when a parent seeks to avoid a child support obligation in response to a claim brought by a third party who provided services (such as medical treatment) to the child. See Chapter 5, Section A[1][d], for a discussion of emancipation in connection with child support.

Professors Carol Sanger and Eleanor Willemsen studied the emancipation process under the California statute. *See* Carol Sanger & Eleanor Willemsen, *Minor Changes: Emancipating Children in Modern Times*, 25 U. MICH. J. L. REFORM 239 (1992). The authors found that the statute, enacted as a reform measure to assist mature minors living independently, is often urged upon the minor by parents in situations of family conflict. They noted that the process is simple and quick, requiring no waiting period, counseling, or investigation, and no real best interests assessment by the court. The authors concluded that emancipation under the California statute operates as an unsupervised out-of-home placement for children in dysfunctional families and that it may serve parents' interests rather than the interests of the affected children. *See also* S. Elise Kert, *Should Emancipation be for Adolescents or for Parents?* 16 J. CONTEMP. LEGAL ISSUES 307 (2000) (citing commentary contending that emancipation statutes help create a class of minors referred as "throwaways," that is, children ejected from the home by parents). For an interesting interview with a superior court judge in California regarding his views about the proper application of the law, see Austin Sung, *Interview: Emancipating Minors from a Judicial Perspective*, 11 J. CONTEMP. LEGAL ISSUES 666 (2000).

[b]   Other Claims By Minors Against Parental Authority

Some parents cannot exercise control or discipline over their children. In most states, the juvenile court has authority to intervene where children are "incorrigible," "beyond parental control" or "in need of supervision." These cases usually involve children who run away from home, are truant, violate parental or legal curfews or other rules, or engage in drug or alcohol use. VA. CODE ANN. §§ 16.1-278.4 to 16.1-278.5 (2009) (stating criteria for court intervention in situations where the child is either in need of supervision or services). Minors who come to the juvenile court's attention for these types of conduct are frequently referred to as "status offenders." "Status offenses [constitute] a family of noncriminal infractions so named because the acts that underlie them would not be considered offenses but for the perpetrator's minority status." *See* Lois A. Weithorn, *Envisioning Second-Order Change in America's Responses to Troubled and Troublesome Youth*, 33 HOFSTRA L. REV. 1305, 1327–28 (2005). In most states, the juvenile court has jurisdiction over three primary, and sometimes overlapping, populations: dependency cases (i.e., child abuse or neglect cases, as discussed in Section C below); delinquency cases (in which minors have allegedly committed acts that constitute crimes); and status offense cases.

When the juvenile court takes jurisdiction over the minor, it substitutes its authority over the child for that of the parent and has considerable leeway to impose a range of dispositions or restrictions. Parents may initiate these actions, frustrated by the child's resistance to their authority. Or, police or others in the community may trigger such a case, if they find the child engaged in some type of disapproved conduct. In *In re Welfare of Snyder*, 532 P.2d 278 (Wash. 1975), a teen's parents initiated the court's intervention but then reversed their position. The minor, however, wanted the court to proceed and substitute its jurisdiction for that of her parents. In this case, the court supported the child's position, overriding parental authority. For a criticism of *Snyder* as being out of step with the law's traditional deference to the authority of fit parents, see Bruce C. Hafen, *Children's Liberation and the New Egalitarianism: Some Reservations About Abandoning Youth to Their Rights*, 1976 B.Y.U. L. REV. 605.

Can a minor initiate an action to terminate parental rights? If so, in what circumstances? In a Florida case that received a great deal of media attention, 11-year-old Gregory Kingsley brought an action to terminate the parental rights of his biological mother. Gregory's foster parents were eager to adopt him, but the state did not terminate his mother's parental rights. With the encouragement of his foster father, who later became the boy's attorney of record, Gregory petitioned to terminate his mother's parental rights and filed an adoption petition. Gregory claimed a fundamental liberty interest in freedom from abuse and neglect. Other petitions to terminate his mother's parental rights were later filed by his guardian *ad litem*, the state, and his foster parents. The trial court ruled that Gregory had standing to bring an action to terminate parental rights on his own behalf. The appellate court, *Kingsley v. Kingsley*, 623 So. 2d 780 (Fla. App. 1993), held that unemancipated minors lack the capacity to initiate legal proceedings in their own names, but upheld the termination of parental rights on the basis of abandonment. Dissenting in part, Chief Judge Harris emphasized, "Florida recognizes no cause of action that permits a child to divorce his parents . . . [T]here is no right to change parents simply because the child finds substitutes he . . . likes better or who can provide a better standard of living." *Id.* at 790.

Consider the following case, which attracted significant media attention in the early 1980s.

POLOVCHAK v. MEESE
United States Court of Appeals, Seventh Circuit
774 F.2d 731 (1985)

Michael and Anna Polovchak, citizens of the U.S.S.R., left that country with their three children and came to the United States in January 1980. They settled in Chicago, but after several months, they decided to return to the Soviet Union. Their two older children, Nataly, then seventeen years old, and Walter, then twelve, decided that they wished to stay in the United States. Michael and Anna Polovchak did not agree with Walter's decision,[2] and on July 13, 1980, Walter and Nataly left their parents' home and went to live with a cousin . . . On July 18 Michael Polovchak sought the assistance of the Chicago police to bring Walter home. The police took Walter from his cousin's apartment and brought him to the police station, where Walter informed them that he had left home because he did not wish to return to the Soviet Union. Upon the advice of the Immigration and Naturalization Service (INS) and the State Department, the police did not take Walter home but instead instituted custody proceedings in the Circuit Court of Cook County. On July 19 the trial judge temporarily placed Walter in the State's custody, as a minor in need of supervision, pursuant to Ill. Ann. Stat. ch. 37, § 702-3. Walter's parents had notice of and attended this hearing.

---

[2] Apparently, the elder Polovchaks did not dispute Nataly's choice, although she was not yet eighteen at that time.

Later that same day Walter, with his attorney but without his parents, filed an application for asylum with the regional INS office. His application stated that his religion was Baptist and that he did not want to return to the Soviet Union because he would be "persecuted . . . prevented from higher education, considered suspect [and] restricted in mobility." The application further stated that the government of the Soviet Union had knowledge of his asylum application through the media. Walter's application for asylum was granted . . . In October 1981 Walter's status was changed to that of permanent resident alien, which is the status he enjoys today.

On July 30 the state trial court held a hearing on Walter's wardship, at which the elder Polovchaks were present and represented by counsel. On August 4 the court adjudicated both Walter and Nataly as wards of the court, thereby removing them from the custody of their parents. In December 1981 the Illinois Appellate Court reversed the decision of the trial court, determining that the Polovchaks should not have been deprived of parental custody and releasing Walter to his parents. *In re Polovchak*, 432 N.E.2d 873 (1981). Michael and Anna Polovchak had, however, returned to the Soviet Union in the interim, where they reside today. The Illinois Supreme Court affirmed the appellate court's decision in May 1983. 454 N.E.2d 258 (1983), *cert. denied*, [465 U.S. 1065 (1984)].

. . . .

In October 1980, shortly after Walter was granted asylum, the Polovchaks filed this action in federal district court. The Polovchaks asserted that the grant of asylum to Walter violated their rights of procedural due process because they were not notified of Walter's application for asylum nor afforded an opportunity to be heard. They also alleged that the grant of asylum violated substantive constitutional rights protecting their privacy and the integrity of their family, as well as their right to raise and control their son and to participate in his major life decisions . . . In September 1983 the Polovchaks amended the complaint to allege that the same substantive and procedural constitutional rights were violated as a result both of the issuance of the departure control order and of the adjustment of Walter's immigration status to that of permanent resident alien. In November 1983 Walter's motion to intervene was granted and he filed a counterclaim against his parents, alleging that their attempts to return him to the U.S.S.R. violated his rights under the U.S. and Illinois Constitutions. The counterclaim was dismissed as meritless in August 1984.

On July 17, 1985 the district court entered summary judgment for Michael and Anna Polovchak on the issue whether the procedure followed in issuing the departure control order denied due process and granted an injunction against enforcement of the departure control order. It is from this judgment that the government appealed . . . It is important to our disposition that Walter becomes eighteen, and an adult under both Illinois and Soviet law, on October 3, 1985.

This case raises issues in an unusual and sensitive area of the administration of federal immigration law. When a minor seeks political asylum over the objections of his family, his interest in choosing his own residence for political purposes is pitted against the right of parents to raise their child in the environment they deem proper. Family disputes are usually handled at the state level because of the special expertise of local agencies in matters of domestic relations. But here, because of the federal government's obligation to provide refuge to those threatened with political persecution, Refugee Act of 1980, the role of mediation falls to the INS, an agency without any such special expertise. The primary question before us concerns what action the government must take to ensure that both parties, the parents and the child, receive an adequate opportunity to assert their interests.

Free personal choice in matters involving family life is a fundamental liberty interest of a parent because "the parents' claim to authority in their own household to direct the rearing of their children is basic in the structure of our society," *Ginsberg v. New York*, 390 U.S. 629 (1968). [ ] State intervention that results in the termination of that close parent-child relationship must adhere strictly to the requirements of procedural due process. *Santosky v. Kramer*, 455 U.S. 745, (1981). . . . This case does not present quite so stark a scenario as the total severing of that relationship by the government: the departure control order merely prevented Walter from leaving the country; it did not prevent his parents from returning to Chicago and living with him there. But when the order was issued, the parents had already returned to their native country, and to condition their right to regain Walter on leaving it nonetheless significantly undercuts their liberty interest of family association. As for the grant of asylum, it too did not work a complete termination of parental rights; nonetheless, such an action has a divisive impact on family relations, especially (as here) if it is the predicate for further government action, such as the grant of resident alien status or the issuance of a departure control order. In any event, we agree with the district court that Michael and Anna Polovchak have a "very strong interest," which was implicated in the matters of both the asylum and the departure control order and which has been treated rather cavalierly by the INS. . . .

Neither the notice nor the opportunity to be heard afforded the parents in regard to both the grant of asylum and the departure control order were of a sort consonant with the fundamental importance of the parents' interest in the residence, nurture and education of a minor child, then twelve or thirteen. The Polovchaks were never notified that Walter was applying for asylum, and obviously no provision was made for a hearing. [The court concluded that the parents' due process rights were violated and it affirmed the district court's entry of summary judgment on this issue].

Although we agree with the district court that Walter's parents have been injured and must be afforded a remedy, we do not agree with the remedy that has been provided by the district court . . . [A]n equitable remedy should be fashioned with the interests of *all* potentially affected persons in mind, and where we think the judge stepped over the bounds of his discretion was in failing to give any but the most perfunctory attention to Walter's rights.

The subject of the departure control order is a person who, though a minor, has constitutional rights that the government must respect. *Tinker v. Des Moines Independent Community School District*, 393 U.S. 503, 511 (1969); *In re Gault*, 387 U.S. 1 (1967); *West Virginia State Board of Education v. Barnette*, 319 U.S. 624 (1943). Thus, we do not necessarily agree with the district court that the "private interest of . . . Walter . . . is by its very nature considerably less than that of his parents." Even if this were true in 1980 when Walter sought political asylum, Walter's rights have evolved over the past five years, and facts and circumstances relevant to such a balancing have changed.

At the age of twelve, Walter was presumably near the lower end of an age range in which a minor may be mature enough to assert certain individual rights that equal or override those of his parents; at age seventeen (indeed, on the eve of his eighteenth·birthday), Walter is certainly at the high end of such a scale, and the question whether he should have to subordinate his own political commitments to his parents' wishes looks very different. The minor's rights grow more compelling with age, particularly in the factual context of this case.

The ability of a young person to decide to which political system he professes allegiance necessarily increases with age. We do not suggest that every twelve year old entertains serious political views (although some may); we would, however, suggest that many seventeen year olds do. Similarly, as the child grows, his parents' influence over him weakens, and the time his parents have in which to guide him grows shorter. The district court may be correct that parents "have the right to bring up their children as atheists or Communists," but it is surely relevant that Walter has decided that he does not want to be a communist or an atheist and that his parents have only the few remaining days of his minority to try to change his mind. This consideration is of great importance here because, were Walter's parents to take him back to the Soviet Union before October 3, there is no evidence that he would be allowed to return to the United States as an adult on October 4 should his parents' influence fail.[10]

The district court also did not adequately weigh Walter's interest in avoiding the sanctions often imposed by the Soviets upon those who leave their country, refuse to return to it and publicly criticize it . . . Soviet citizens who refuse to return to the Soviet Union and publicly derogate that country are at risk of seriously adverse government action if they should involuntarily return to the U.S.S.R. . . .

. . .

---

[10] It is this factor — the finality of the decision and its grave and potentially irreversible consequences — that makes this case analogous to the Supreme Court decisions in which a minor's right to obtain an abortion over the objections of her parents was affirmed. In *Bellotti v. Baird*, 443 U.S. 622 (1978), the Court stressed that although "[l]egal restrictions on minors, especially those supportive of the parents' role, may be important to the child's chances for the full growth and maturity that make eventual participation in a free society meaningful and rewarding," such "deference to parents" makes less sense in the face of a decision with such a "unique nature and consequences" as the abortion decision. "In sum, there are few situations in which denying a minor the right to make an important decision will have consequences so grave and indelible."

Like the decision facing the minors in the abortion cases, Walter's decision is grave and unique. A minor seeking political asylum, if sufficiently mature, should have his wishes heard and taken into account. . . .

NOTE

If we assume that there was no abuse or neglect by his parents underlying Walter's desire to remain in the U.S., it is highly unlikely that Walter would have prevailed if the INS had not become embroiled in this family dispute. For example, consider the result if a 12-year-old wished to stay in Chicago instead of moving to Dallas with his parents. Even if a child articulated understandable reasons for this preference (e.g., that during his previous years living in Dallas, he was severely bullied by other children), parental autonomy would still have prevailed. In addition, a court adjudicating such a parent-child dispute would probably hold that the minor's preferences were not material to the court's decision, in light of traditional deference to parental autonomy. One must reflect, therefore, on what made this case one in which the interests of a 12-year-old were given so much weight in the balance?

What role, if any, should the *reasons* underlying a child's preferences play in cases such as this? For example, does Walter's claim that he wished to stay in the U.S. in order to practice his religion and avoid persecution strengthen his claim? Consider whether this case would have had a different outcome if Walter had asserted that he wished to remain in the United States because of the excellent school system and the opportunities that would be afforded him to attend college and to have a more productive life in the U.S. Or, what if he asserted that the U.S. offered him a greater choice of television programs and movies? While some reasons appear weightier than others, it is not at all clear how Walter's reasons should be weighed in the type of analysis held to be constitutionally required in *Polovchak*. Consider, as well, whether there is any basis for analogizing this case to *Bellotti*, which appears in Subsection [3][c] below.

The Eleventh Circuit reached a very different result in the highly-publicized case concerning Elian Gonzalez, a 6-year-old whose mother had died as the two of them made their way by boat as refugees from Cuba to Florida. *Gonzalez v. Reno*, 212 F.3d 1338 (11th Cir. 2000). The mother and father were estranged. The child's father, who still resided in Cuba, sought the child's return to Cuba. Relatives of Elian living in Florida filed asylum petitions on Elian's behalf. The INS "after, among other things, consulting with Plaintiff's father and considering [Elian's] age — decided that [Elian's] asylum applications were legally void and refused to consider their merit. [Elian] then filed this suit in federal district court, seeking on several grounds to compel the INS to consider and to determine the merit of his asylum applications."

Elian's asylum applications stated that he:

> "is afraid to return to Cuba." The applications claimed that [he] had a well-founded fear of persecution because many members of Plaintiff's family had been persecuted by the Castro government in Cuba. In particular, according to the applications, [Elian's] stepfather had been imprisoned for several months because of opposition to the Cuban government [as had two of his great-uncles. Elian's] mother had also been harassed and intimidated by communist authorities in Cuba. The applications also alleged that, if [Elian] were returned to Cuba, he would be used

as a propaganda tool for the Castro government and would be subjected to involuntary indoctrination in the tenets of communism.

The Eleventh Circuit said of the INS decision:

> In this case, because the law . . . is silent about the validity of Plaintiff's purported asylum applications, it fell to the INS to make a discretionary policy choice. The INS, exercising its gap-filling discretion, determined these things: (1) six-year-old children lack the capacity to sign and to submit personally an application for asylum; (2) instead, six-year-old children must be represented by an adult in immigration matters; (3) absent special circumstances, the only proper adult to represent a six-year-old child is the child's parent, even when the parent is not in this country; and, (4) that the parent lives in a communist-totalitarian state (such as Cuba), in and of itself, does not constitute a special circumstance requiring the selection of a non-parental representative. Our duty is to decide whether this policy might be a reasonable one in the light of the statutory scheme.
>
> . . .
>
> The INS determination that ordinarily a parent (even one outside of this country) and, more important, *only* a parent — can act for his six-year-old child (who is in this country) in immigration matters also comes within the range of reasonable choices. In making that determination, INS officials seem to have taken account of the relevant, competing policy interests: the interest of a child in asserting a non-frivolous asylum claim; the interest of a parent in raising his child as he sees fit; and the interest of the public in the prompt but fair disposition of asylum claims. The INS policy — by presuming that the parent is the sole, appropriate representative for a child — gives paramount consideration to the primary role of parents in the upbringing of their children. But we cannot conclude that the policy's stress on the parent-child relationship is unreasonable. *See Ginsberg v. New York*, 390 U.S. 629, (1968) ("[T]he parents' claim to authority in their own household to direct the rearing of their children is basic in the structure of our society.").

Id. at 1352. The court distinguished *Polovchak*, noting that a child would have an "independent and separate interest . . . apart from his parents, in applying for asylum," due to "special circumstances . . . that [may] render a parent an inappropriate representative for the child." In a footnote, the court indicated what it meant by "special circumstances":

> Under the INS policy, a substantial conflict of interest between the parent and the child may require or allow another adult to speak for the child on immigration matters. In considering whether a substantial conflict of interest exists, the INS considers the potential merits of a child's asylum claim. If the child would have an exceedingly strong case for asylum, the parent's unwillingness to seek asylum on that child's behalf may indicate, under the INS policy, that the parent is not representing adequately the child's interests.

Id. at 1352, n.21. It continued that "[w]here such circumstances do exist, the INS policy appears to permit other persons, besides a parent, to speak for the child in immigration matters. So, to some extent, the policy does protect a child's own right to apply for asylum . . . despite the contrary wishes of his parents." *Id.* The court indicated some sympathy for Elian's plight, but that its hands were tied by the standards guiding the deference that it must give to agency decisions of this type:

> We recognize that, in some instances, the INS policy of deferring to parents — especially those residing outside of this country — might hinder some six-year-olds with non-frivolous asylum claims and prevent them from invoking their statutory right to seek asylum. But, considering the well-established principles of judicial deference to executive agencies, we cannot disturb the INS policy in this case just because it might be imperfect . . .

Id. at 1352–53. In conclusion, the court asserted:

> The final aspect of the INS policy also worries us some. According to the INS policy, that a parent lives in a communist-totalitarian state is no special circumstance, sufficient in and of itself, to justify the consideration of a six-year-old child's asylum claim (presented by a relative in this country) against the wishes of the non-resident parent. We acknowledge, as a widely-accepted truth, that Cuba does violate human rights and fundamental freedoms and does not guarantee the rule of law to people living in Cuba. *See generally* U.S. Dept. of State, 1999 Country Reports on Human Rights Practices: Cuba (2000) ("[The Cuban Government] continue[s] systematically to violate fundamental civil and political rights of its citizens."). Persons living in such a totalitarian state may be unable to assert freely their own legal rights, much less the legal rights of others. Moreover, some reasonable people might say that a child in the United States inherently has a substantial conflict of interest with a parent residing in a totalitarian state when that parent — even when he is not coerced — demands that the child leave this country to return to a country with little respect for human rights and basic freedoms.

Id. at 1353. The court noted that it was indeed possible that Elian's father was insisting that Elian be returned to Cuba because the Cuban government was coercing him to do so. Despite that possibility, it indicated that it must defer to the INS decision.

What distinguished the INS response to the asylum applications made by Walter and Elian? The Eleventh Circuit cites the difference in the ages of the two boys and implies that in Walter's case, there existed a parent-child conflict that made the parents inappropriate representatives of the child's interest. Yet, it is unclear what factors the INS or a reviewing court should consider in determining whether there is such a conflict of interest. For further discussion of the INS policies affecting the disposition of both *Polovchak* and *Gonzalez*, see Cynthia R. Mabry, *Coming to America: The Child's Voice in Asylum Proceedings*, 11 TEMP. POL. & CIV. RTS. L. REV. 63 (2001) (examining INS policies governing who can file asylum claims for minors); Peter Margulies, *Children, Parents & Asylum*, 15 GEO. IMMIGR. L.J. 289 (2001) (critiquing the Eleventh Circuit decision in *Gonzalez*); Amity R. Boye, Student Author, *Making Sure Children Find Their Way Home: Obligating States*

Under International Law To Return Dependent Children To Family Members Abroad, 69 BROOK. L. REV. 1515 (2004) (discussing relevant laws governing international child abduction). *See also* Karen Syma Czapanskiy, *Musing About Community, or Why is it Better to be an American Grandparent Than a Cuban Father?*, 102 W. VA. L. REV. 729 (2000) (examining the challenges Elian's father faced in seeking his son's return to Cuba).

PROBLEMS

Problem 10-2.   Ozzie and Harriet seek your advice on controlling their 14-year-old son, Bruno. Although he has never gotten into legal trouble, they consider him somewhat unruly and undisciplined, and therefore decided to send him to a private military academy instead of the public school. For the second time now, however, Bruno has stayed away from home in order to avoid going to the school. On the last occasion, he stayed with his Aunt Happy for five days and attempted to attend public school again, but the aunt sent him home when the parents insisted. This time, he has been with Aunt Happy for two days, and she seems reluctant to force him out. She keeps urging Ozzie and Harriet to come talk to him and work out some compromise. They are confident that they have made the correct decision about schooling, however, and have no interest in negotiating with their son. They want to know whether the law might be of any assistance to them. You've known Ozzie and Harriet for some time now, and they seem to you like concerned, caring people, although strict and somewhat rigid. What do you advise?

Problem 10-3.   Bob and Anna Westfield have come to you for advice about their options for responding what they view as a crisis involving their 22-year-old daughter Elizabeth. Elizabeth, who has always had emotional problems, graduated from college and was at loose ends about what to do with her life when she became involved with what the Westfields feel is a religious cult. The leader, who calls himself "the Holy One," demands extraordinary discipline and absolute obedience to his commands by his followers. The group lives together in an ashram and follows a rigid schedule of programmed communal mediation, lectures, rituals, meals and work from early morning until late night. Elizabeth has hardly seen her parents since she moved into the ashram. They saw her last week and were shocked by the transformation. Their daughter told them that she had renounced all her former relationships and that they were no longer her parents. She had dedicated her life to achieving purity by following the Holy One. The Westfields believe that Elizabeth has been brainwashed. They have consulted a de-programmer who has promised them that he can assist them to "bring back" their daughter, through an intervention that requires that she be confined for a week in a treatment center. What do you advise the Westfields?

[2]   Minors' Objection to Parental Medical Decisions — The Case of Psychiatric Hospitalization

PARHAM v. J. R.
United States Supreme Court
442 U.S. 584 (1979)

MR. CHIEF JUSTICE BURGER delivered the opinion of the Court.

The question presented in this appeal is what process is constitutionally due a minor child whose parents or guardian seek state administered institutional mental health care for the child and specifically whether an adversary proceeding is required prior to or after the commitment.

I

[J. R.], a child being treated in a Georgia state mental hospital, ... sought a declaratory judgment that Georgia's voluntary commitment procedures for children under the age of 18 . . . violated the Due Process Clause of the Fourteenth Amendment and requested an injunction against their future enforcement. . . . [¶] A three-judge District Court [considered] expert and lay testimony and extensive exhibits[. After] visiting two of the State's regional mental health hospitals, the District Court held that Georgia's statutory scheme was unconstitutional because it failed to protect adequately the appellees' due process rights. [¶] To remedy this violation, the court enjoined future commitments based on the procedures in the Georgia statute. It also commanded Georgia to . . . provide [community-based mental health] facilities . . . to be the most appropriate for the treatment of [children in the state hospital] who could be treated in a less drastic, nonhospital environment.

J. L., a plaintiff before the District Court who is now deceased, was admitted in 1970 at the age of 6 years to [the state hospital]. J. L.'s mother then requested the hospital to admit him indefinitely. [¶] The admitting physician interviewed J. L. and his parents. . . . He . . . learned that J. L. had been expelled from school because he was uncontrollable. He accepted the parents' representation that the boy had been extremely aggressive and diagnosed the child as having a "hyperkinetic reaction of childhood."

. . .

In 1972, the child was returned to his mother and stepfather [to] live at home but go to school at the hospital. The parents found they were unable to control J. L. to their satisfaction, and this created family stress. Within two months, they requested his readmission to [the state hospital]. J. L.'s parents relinquished their parental rights to the county in 1974. [¶] Although several hospital employees recommended that J. L. should be placed in a special foster home with "a warm, supported, truly involved couple," the Department of Family and Children Services was unable to place him in such a setting. On October 24, 1975, J. L. (with J. R.)

filed this suit requesting [that he be placed] in a less drastic environment suitable to his needs.

Appellee J. R. was declared a neglected child by the county and removed from his natural parents when he was three months old. He was placed in seven different foster homes in succession prior to his admission to [the state hospital] at the age of 7. [¶] Immediately preceding his hospitalization, J. R. received outpatient treatment at a county mental health center for several months. He then began attending school where he was so disruptive and incorrigible that he could not conform to normal behavior patterns. Because of his abnormal behavior, J. R.'s seventh set of foster parents requested his removal from their home. The Department of Family and Children Services then sought his admission [to the state hospital]. The agency provided the hospital with a complete sociomedical history at the time of his admission. In addition, three separate interviews were conducted with J. R. by the admission team of the hospital.

It was determined that he was borderline retarded, and suffered an "unsocialized, aggressive reaction of childhood." It was recommended unanimously that he would "benefit from the structured environment" of the hospital and would "enjoy living and playing with boys of the same age." [¶] J. R.'s progress was re-examined periodically. In addition, unsuccessful efforts were made by the Department of Family and Children Services during his stay at the hospital to place J. R. in various foster homes. On October 24, 1975, J. R. (with J. L.) filed this suit requesting an order of the court placing him in a less drastic environment suitable to his needs.

Georgia Code § 88-503.1 (1975) provides for the voluntary admission to a state regional hospital of children such as J. L. and J. R. Under that provision, admission begins with an application for hospitalization signed by a "parent or guardian." Upon application, the superintendent of each hospital is given the power to admit temporarily any child for "observation and diagnosis." If, after observation, the superintendent finds "evidence of mental illness" and that the child is "suitable for treatment" in the hospital, then the child may be admitted "for such period and under such conditions as may be authorized by law."

Georgia's mental health statute also provides for the discharge of voluntary patients. Any child who has been hospitalized for more than five days may be discharged at the request of a parent or guardian. Even without a request for discharge, however, the superintendent of each regional hospital has an affirmative duty to release any child "who has recovered from his mental illness or who has sufficiently improved that the superintendent determines that hospitalization of the patient is no longer desirable." Georgia's Mental Health Director has not published any statewide regulations defining what specific procedures each superintendent must employ when admitting a child under 18. Instead, each regional hospital's superintendent is responsible for the procedures in his or her facility. There is substantial variation among the institutions with regard to their admission procedures and their procedures for review of patients after they have been admitted.

. . . .

II

In holding unconstitutional Georgia's statutory procedure for voluntary commitment of juveniles, the District Court first determined that commitment to any [state mental hospital] constitutes a severe deprivation of a child's liberty. The court defined this liberty interest in terms of both freedom from bodily restraint and freedom from the "emotional and psychic harm" caused by the institutionalization. Having determined that a liberty interest is implicated by a child's admission to a mental hospital, the court considered what process is required to protect that interest. It held that the process due "includes at least the right after notice to be heard before an impartial tribunal."

In requiring the prescribed hearing, the court rejected Georgia's argument that no adversary-type hearing was required since the State was merely assisting parents who could not afford private care by making available treatment similar to that offered in private hospitals and by private physicians. The court acknowledged that most parents who seek to have their children admitted to a state mental hospital do so in good faith. It, however, relied on one of appellees' witnesses who expressed an opinion that "some still look upon mental hospitals as a 'dumping ground.' " . . .

The District Court also rejected the argument that review by the superintendents of the hospitals and their staffs was sufficient to protect the child's liberty interest. The court held that the inexactness of psychiatry, coupled with the possibility that the sources of information used to make the commitment decision may not always be reliable, made the superintendent's decision too arbitrary to satisfy due process . . .

III

In an earlier day, the problems inherent in coping with children afflicted with mental or emotional abnormalities were dealt with largely within the family. Sometimes parents were aided by teachers or a family doctor. While some parents no doubt were able to deal with their disturbed children without specialized assistance, others especially those of limited means and education, were not. Increasingly, they turned for assistance to local, public sources or private charities. Until recently, most of the states did little more than provide custodial institutions for the confinement of persons who were considered dangerous. . . . [¶] As medical knowledge about the mentally ill and public concern for their condition expanded, the states, aided substantially by federal grants, have sought to ameliorate the human tragedies of seriously disturbed children. Ironically, as most states have expanded their efforts to assist the mentally ill, their actions have been subjected to increasing litigation and heightened constitutional scrutiny. . . . In this case, appellees have challenged Georgia's procedural and substantive balance of the individual, family, and social interests at stake in the voluntary commitment of a child to one of its regional mental hospitals.

The parties agree that our prior holdings have set out a general approach for testing challenged state procedures under a due process claim. Assuming the existence of a protectible property or liberty interest, the Court [in Mathews v.

Eldridge, 424 U.S. 319 (1976)] has required a balancing of a number of factors. . . .

In applying these criteria, we must consider first the child's interest in not being committed. . . . [¶] It is not disputed that a child, in common with adults, has a substantial liberty interest in not being confined unnecessarily for medical treatment and that the state's involvement in the commitment decision constitutes state action under the Fourteenth Amendment. We also recognize that commitment sometimes produces adverse social consequences for the child because of the reaction of some to the discovery that the child has received psychiatric care. . . . [¶] For purposes of this decision, we assume that a child has a protectible interest not only in being free of unnecessary bodily restraints but also in not being labeled erroneously by some persons because of an improper decision by the state hospital superintendent.

We next deal with the interests of the parents who have decided, on the basis of their observations and independent professional recommendations, that their child needs institutional care. Appellees argue that the constitutional rights of the child are of such magnitude and the likelihood of parental abuse is so great that the parents' traditional interests in and responsibility for the upbringing of their child must be subordinated at least to the extent of providing a formal adversary hearing prior to a voluntary commitment.

Our jurisprudence historically has reflected Western civilization concepts of the family as a unit with broad parental authority over minor children. Our cases have consistently followed that course; our constitutional system long ago rejected any notion that a child is "the mere creature of the State" and, on the contrary, asserted that parents generally "have the right, coupled with the high duty, to recognize and prepare [their children] for additional obligations." [citing *Meyer, Pierce, Prince* and *Yoder*]. Surely, this includes a "high duty" to recognize symptoms of illness and to seek and follow medical advice. The law's concept of the family rests on a presumption that parents possess what a child lacks in maturity, experience, and capacity for judgment required for making life's difficult decisions. More important, historically it has recognized that natural bonds of affection lead parents to act in the best interests of their children.

As with so many other legal presumptions, experience and reality may rebut what the law accepts as a starting point; the incidence of child neglect and abuse cases attests to this. That some parents "may at times be acting against the interests of their children" . . . creates a basis for caution, but is hardly a reason to discard wholesale those pages of human experience that teach that parents generally do act in the child's best interests. The statist notion that governmental power should supersede parental authority in all cases because some parents abuse and neglect children is repugnant to American tradition.

Nonetheless, we have recognized that a state is not without constitutional control over parental discretion in dealing with children when their physical or mental health is jeopardized . . . Appellees urge that [our] precedents . . . require us to hold that the parents' decision to have a child admitted to a mental hospital must be subjected to an exacting constitutional scrutiny, including a formal, adversary, pre-admission hearing.

Appellees' argument, however, sweeps too broadly. Simply because the decision of a parent is not agreeable to a child or because it involves risks does not automatically transfer the power to make that decision from the parents to some agency or officer of the state. The same characterizations can be made for a tonsillectomy, appendectomy, or other medical procedure. Most children, even in adolescence, simply are not able to make sound judgments concerning many decisions, including their need for medical care or treatment. Parents can and must make those judgments. . . . We cannot assume that the result in [*Meyer* and *Pierce*] would have been different if the children there had announced a preference to learn only English or a preference to go to a public, rather than a church, school. The fact that a child may balk at hospitalization or complain about a parental refusal to provide cosmetic surgery does not diminish the parents' authority to decide what is best for the child. Neither state officials nor federal courts are equipped to review such parental decisions.

. . .

In defining the respective rights and prerogatives of the child and parent in the voluntary commitment setting, we conclude that our precedents permit the parents to retain a substantial, if not the dominant, role in the decision, absent a finding of neglect or abuse, and that the traditional presumption that the parents act in the best interests of their child should apply. We also conclude, however, that the child's rights and the nature of the commitment decision are such that parents cannot always have absolute and unreviewable discretion to decide whether to have a child institutionalized. They, of course, retain plenary authority to seek such care for their children, subject to a physician's independent examination and medical judgment.

The State obviously has a significant interest in confining the use of its costly mental health facilities to cases of genuine need. The Georgia program seeks first to determine whether the patient seeking admission has an illness that calls for inpatient treatment[, and therefore charges the supervising physician at each hospital to determine] before authorizing an admission, whether a prospective patient is mentally ill and whether the patient will likely benefit from hospital care. In addition, the State has imposed a continuing duty on hospital superintendents to release any patient who has recovered to the point where hospitalization is no longer needed.

The State in performing its voluntarily assumed mission also has a significant interest in not imposing unnecessary procedural obstacles that may discourage the mentally ill or their families from seeking needed psychiatric assistance. The parens patriae interest in helping parents care for the mental health of their children cannot be fulfilled if the parents are unwilling to take advantage of the opportunities because the admission process is too onerous, too embarrassing, or too contentious. It is surely not idle to speculate as to how many parents who believe they are acting in good faith would forgo state-provided hospital care if such care is contingent on participation in an adversary proceeding designed to probe their motives and other private family matters in seeking the voluntary admission.

The State also has a genuine interest in allocating priority to the diagnosis and treatment of patients as soon as they are admitted to a hospital rather than to time-consuming procedural minuets before the admission. . . .

[With respect to] what process protects adequately the child's constitutional rights by reducing risks of error without unduly trenching on traditional parental authority [or undercutting the state's efforts to provide treatment, we] conclude that . . . some kind of inquiry should be made by a "neutral factfinder" to determine whether the statutory requirements for admission are satisfied. . . . [¶] Due process has never been thought to require that the neutral and detached trier of fact be law trained or a judicial or administrative officer. Surely, this is the case as to medical decisions, for "neither judges nor administrative hearing officers are better qualified than psychiatrists to render psychiatric judgments." Thus, a staff physician will suffice, so long as he or she is free to evaluate independently the child's mental and emotional condition and need for treatment.

It is not necessary that the deciding physician conduct a formal or quasi-formal, hearing. A state is free to require such a hearing, but due process is not violated by use of informal traditional medical investigative techniques . . . What is best for a child is an individual medical decision that must be left to the judgment of physicians in each case. We do no more than emphasize that the decision should represent an independent judgment of what the child requires and that all sources of information that are traditionally relied on by physicians and behavioral specialists should be consulted.

. . . .

Although we acknowledge the fallibility of medical and psychiatric diagnosis, [adversary proceedings do not necessarily ameliorate this problem. The] supposed protections of an adversary proceeding to determine the appropriateness of medical decisions for the commitment and treatment of mental and emotional illness may well be more illusory than real. [¶] Another problem with requiring a formalized, factfinding hearing lies in the danger it poses for significant intrusion into the parent-child relationship. Pitting the parents and child as adversaries often will be at odds with the presumption that parents act in the best interests of their child. It is one thing to require a neutral physician to make a careful review of the parents' decision in order to make sure it is proper from a medical standpoint; it is a wholly different matter to employ an adversary contest to ascertain whether the parents' motivation is consistent with the child's interests.

. . .

MR. JUSTICE BRENNAN, with whom MR. JUSTICE MARSHALL and MR. JUSTICE STEVENS join, concurring in part and dissenting in part.

. . .

. . . . Commitment to a mental institution necessarily entails a "massive curtailment of liberty," and inevitably affects "fundamental rights." Persons incarcerated in mental hospitals are not only deprived of their physical liberty, they are also deprived of friends, family, and community. Institutionalized mental patients must live in unnatural surroundings under the continuous and detailed control of strangers. They are subject to intrusive treatment which, especially if unwarranted, may violate their right to bodily integrity . . . [¶] Because of these considerations, our cases have made clear that commitment to a mental hospital "is a deprivation of liberty which the State cannot accomplish without due process of law." O'Connor v. Donaldson, 422 U.S. 563, 580 (1975) (BURGER, C. J., concurring). In the absence of a voluntary, knowing, and intelligent waiver, adults facing commitment to mental institutions are entitled to full and fair adversary hearings in which the necessity for their commitment is established to the satisfaction of a neutral tribunal. At such hearings they must be accorded the right to "be present with counsel, have an opportunity to be heard, be confronted with witnesses against [them], have the right to cross-examine, and to offer evidence of [their] own."

These principles also govern the commitment of children. "Constitutional rights do not mature and come into being magically only when one attains the state-defined age of majority. Minors as well as adults are protected by the Constitution and possess constitutional rights . . . [¶] Indeed, it may well be argued that children are entitled to more protection than are adults. The consequences of an erroneous commitment decision are more tragic where children are involved. Children, on the average, are confined for longer periods than are adults. Moreover, childhood is a particularly vulnerable time of life and children erroneously institutionalized during their formative years may bear the scars for the rest of their lives. Furthermore, the provision of satisfactory institutionalized mental care for children generally requires a substantial financial commitment that too often has not been forthcoming. Decisions of the lower courts have chronicled the inadequacies of existing mental health facilities for children.

In addition, the chances of an erroneous commitment decision are particularly great where children are involved. Even under the best of circumstances psychiatric diagnosis and therapy decisions are fraught with uncertainties. These uncertainties are aggravated when, as under the Georgia practice, the psychiatrist interviews the child during a period of abnormal stress in connection with the commitment, and without adequate time or opportunity to become acquainted with the patient. These uncertainties may be further aggravated when economic and social class separate doctor and child, thereby frustrating the accurate diagnosis of pathology.

These compounded uncertainties often lead to erroneous commitments since psychiatrists tend to err on the side of medical caution and therefore hospitalize patients for whom other dispositions would be more beneficial. The National Institute of Mental Health recently found that only 36% of patients below age 20 who were confined at St. Elizabeth's Hospital actually required such hospitalization. Of particular relevance to this case, a Georgia study Commission on Mental Health Services for Children and Youth concluded that more than half of the State's institutionalized children were not in need of confinement if other forms of care were made available or used.

Notwithstanding all this, Georgia denies hearings to juveniles institutionalized at the behest of their parents. Georgia rationalizes this practice on the theory that parents act in their children's best interests and therefore may waive their children's due process rights . . . [¶] In our society, parental rights are limited by the legitimate rights and interests of their children. "Parents may be free to be become martyrs themselves. But it does not follow they are free, in identical circumstances, to make martyrs of their children before they have reached the age of full and legal discretion when they can make that choice for themselves." Prince v. Massachusetts, 321 U.S. 158 (1944). This principle is reflected in the variety of statutes and cases that authorize state intervention on behalf of neglected or abused children and that, inter alia, curtail parental authority to alienate their children's property, to withhold necessary medical treatment, and to deny children exposure to ideas and experiences they may later need as independent and autonomous adults. [¶] Similarly, more recent legal disputes involving the sterilization of children had led to the conclusion that parents are not permitted to authorize operations with such far-reaching consequences.

This principle is also reflected in constitutional jurisprudence. Notions of parental authority and family autonomy cannot stand as absolute and invariable barriers to the assertion of constitutional rights by children. States, for example, may not condition a minor's right to secure an abortion on attaining her parents' consent since the right to an abortion is an important personal right and since disputes between parents and children on this question would fracture family autonomy . . .

. . . The right to be free from wrongful incarceration, physical intrusion, and stigmatization has significance for the individual surely as great as the right to an abortion. Moreover, . . . the parent-child dispute at issue here cannot be characterized as involving only a routine child-rearing decision made within the context of an ongoing family relationship. . . . [H]ere a break in family autonomy has actually resulted in the parents' decision to surrender custody of their child to a state mental institution. In my view, a child who has been ousted from his family has even greater need for an independent advocate.

Additional considerations counsel against allowing parents unfettered power to institutionalize their children without cause or without any hearing to ascertain that cause. The presumption that parents act in their children's best interests, while applicable to most child-rearing decisions, is not applicable in the commitment context. Numerous studies reveal that parental decisions to institutionalize their children often are the results of dislocation in the family unrelated to the children's mental condition. Moreover, even well-meaning parents lack the expertise necessary to evaluate the relative advantages and disadvantages of inpatient as opposed to outpatient psychiatric treatment. Parental decisions to waive hearings in which such questions could be explored, therefore, cannot be conclusively deemed either informed or intelligent. In these circumstances, I respectfully suggest, it ignores reality to assume blindly that parents act in their children's best interests when making commitment decisions and when waiving their children's due process rights.

. . . .

The informal postadmission procedures that Georgia now follows are simply not enough to qualify as hearings-let alone reasonably prompt hearings. The procedures lack all the traditional due process safeguards. . . .

. . . .

NOTES

1. *The General Rule of Parental Authority to Consent to and Refuse Health Care for Minor Children.* As the *Parham* majority makes clear, parents are legally authorized to make most medical decisions for their children, regardless of those children's preferences. This authority is grounded in the constitutional protection of parental autonomy. Children are presumed to be incapable of making important decisions about their own welfare, and parents, by contrast, are presumed to have the capacity that children lack. Furthermore, the Court continues, the "natural bonds of affection" lead parents to make decisions in their children's best interests. In other words, the interests of children and their parents are generally presumed to be aligned.

There are exceptions to the general rule of parental consent for children's health care. The Court mentions one such exception: the state can intervene when parental care is so poor that it constitutes abuse or neglect. We will examine this exception in some depth in Section C of this Chapter. In addition, however, the following exceptions to the doctrine of parental consent exist in most jurisdictions:

a. Emergency exception. The requirement for parental consent is typically waived if there is an emergency requiring immediate medical care for the child, no parent is available, and delaying treatment would cause harm to the minor. *See, e.g.*, Jennifer L. Rosato, *The Ultimate Test of Autonomy: Should Minors Have A Right to Make Decisions Regarding Life-Sustaining Treatment?* 49 RUTGERS L. REV. 1, 18–34 (1996); Lois A. Weithorn, *Consent to Medical Care and Procedures*, CHIC. COMPANION TO THE CHILD (forthcoming). Pain that can be easily alleviated is typically characterized as one form of such "harm."

b. Emancipated minor exception. Minors who are legally emancipated, as discussed in Section B[1][a] above, have authority to make their own medical decision. Minors who are pregnant or who are parents are also legally authorized to consent to their own health care, even though they are not fully legally emancipated. *See* Nancy Batterman, *Under Age: A Minor's Right to Consent to Health Care*, 10 TOURO L. REV. 637, 660–63 (1994); Weithorn, *supra*. Access to abortion, however, is governed by separate policies. *See* Subsection [3] below.

c. "Mature minor" exception. Under certain circumstances, a state may permit a minor to consent independently to treatment, if the minor demonstrates the psychological maturity necessary to make a competent treatment decision. In some jurisdictions, a statutory provision may allow minors who meet this criterion make decisions in certain situations (e.g., gaining access to contraception or abortion). The authority to consent to treatment more generally may also fall within this exception. *See, e.g., In re E.G.*, 549 N.E.2d 322, 327–28 (Ill. 1990) (holding that clear and convincing evidence that "a minor [who] is mature enough to appreciate the consequences of her actions, and . . . exercise the judgment of an adult" can refuse life-saving medical treatment). This exception is recognized at common law, and thus, a judge may confer decisionmaking authority on a minor if the facts warrant it. *Id.*; *see* Rosato, *supra* at 21–34; Batterman, *supra* at 663–68; Weithorn, *supra*.

d. Statutes conferring on minors' authority to consent to specific types of treatment. Most states have adopted statutes that allow minors to provide independent consent for certain specific types of treatment. All states allow minors to consent to testing and treatment for sexually transmitted diseases (STDs). Almost all states permit minors to access contraception independent of parental consent and knowledge. *See* Subsection [3][b], below. Minors' access to abortion, which is discussed in depth below, is another area that receives special treatment in state statutes. *See* Subsection [3][c] below. Statutes may also authorize minors to access substance abuse and mental health treatment independently. These exceptions have several things in common. First, each of these categories of treatment falls into areas we might think of as "sensitive," in that minors will be less likely to discuss their need for such services with parents than they would be for a sore throat or painful knee. Second, the state's *parens patriae* interests in the welfare of minors is implicated because minors might forego these treatments if required to obtain parental consent. Third, the state's police power interests also come into play, because failure to receive needed treatment for sexually-transmitted diseases, substance abuse, or mental health problems creates risks to others. Even an unintended and unwanted pregnancy has implications for another in that a child might be born as a result of the pregnancy. Fourth, some of these types of treatment have constitutional dimensions (*e.g.*, decisions involving childbearing or liberty) that further justify legal policies creating exceptions to the doctrine of parental consent. *See* Rhonda Gay Hartman, *Adolescent Decisional Autonomy For Medical Care: Physician Perceptions And Practices*, 8 U. CHIC. L. SCH. ROUNDTABLE 87 (2001); Weithorn, *supra*. For a classic analysis of these issues, see ANGELA RODDEY HOLDER, LEGAL ISSUES IN PEDIATRICS AND ADOLESCENT MEDICINE (2d ed. 1985). For an excellent collection of classic works, see MICHAEL FREEMAN (ED.), CHILDREN, MEDICINE AND THE LAW (2005).

2. Criticism of the Court's Reliance on Parents to Safeguard Children's Liberty Interests. The Court in *Parham* held: "It is not disputed that a child, in common with adults, has a substantial liberty interest in not being confined unnecessarily for medical treatment . . ." The Court concluded however, that formal judicial hearings were not necessary to protect those interests. Justice Burger placed substantial reliance on parental judgment and the parent-child relationship as the mechanism to protect minors from unnecessary hospitalization. Justice Brennan, in his dissent, challenged the majority's presumption that the interests of a parent and child are necessarily aligned when a parent chooses to surrender custody of the child to a mental hospital. At that point, he observes, there has already been a break in family autonomy. A description of the *Parham* plaintiffs provides some support. J.L. was admitted to the hospital at age 6 by his mother and stepfather after expulsion from school because he was aggressive and uncontrollable. Efforts to return him to his family were unsuccessful and stressful for the family, and ultimately his parents relinquished parental rights. J.R. was in state custody at the time he was admitted to the hospital (and had not lived with his parents for many years). Thus no parent was available to look out for his interest, even if the Court's assumptions about parents as decisionmakers in this context were accurate. Despite that, the Court held that no additional due process protections were necessary, even where the legal decisionmaker was a caseworker employed by the state.

Taking Justice Brennan's critique one step further, there is evidence that, even if parents mean well, the challenges they face handling troubled youth may lead them to take steps out of desperation. For example, investigations by the U.S. Government Accountability Office and two congressional committees revealed that tens of thousands of parents across the nation have *relinquished custody* of children diagnosed with mental health problems to the child welfare or juvenile justice systems. In the absence of available mental health service, and feeling helpless, parents followed the recommendations of police, doctors, or others, who told them (inaccurately), that if custody was relinquished to the state, the children would receive the needed mental health treatment. Lois A. Weithorn, *Envisioning Second-Order Change in Americas Response to Troubled and Troublesome Youth*, 33 Hofstra L. Rev. 1305, 1308, 1375–78 (2005).

Furthermore, there is evidence that due process protections prior to psychiatric hospitalization of minors may be welcomed by some parents. Professor Michael Perlin found that when the mental health advocate's office in New Jersey obtained independent clinical evaluations of minors for whom psychiatric hospitalization was sought, they were able to avoid a large proportion of hospitalizations. Michael Perlin, *An Invitation to the Dance: An Empirical Response to Chief Justice Warren Burger's 'Time-Consuming Procedural Minuets' Theory in* Parham v. J.R., 9 Bull. Am. Acad. Psychiatry & L. 149, 156–62 (1981). The governing statute did not permit non-emergency hospitalization (of minors or adults) unless less restrictive alternatives had been considered and deemed inappropriate. The advocate's office found, through its investigation of each child's needs, more appropriate interventions for many children. In contrast to the picture painted by Justice Burger, Professor Perlin found that parents were grateful for the assistance provided.

3. *Criticism of the Court's Reliance on the Hospital Superintendent as a "Neutral Factfinder."* The Court concluded that a review of the child's need for hospitalization by "neutral factfinder" would provide the additional safeguard needed to protect children's liberty interests. The Georgia statute required the hospital superintendent to determine if the treatment was necessary, and if so, to approve the admission. Unfortunately, however, at the time *Parham* was decided, and for a decade or so thereafter, financial and other incentives led to significant overuse of mental health institutions, many of which were private, for-profit entities in which treating physicians had a financial stake. *See* Lois A. Weithorn, *Mental Hospitalization of Troublesome Youth: An Analysis of Skyrocketing Admission Rates*, 40 Stanford L. Rev. 773, 788–91 (1988). In addition, research revealed that a large proportion of the minors hospitalized in psychiatric facilities did not suffer from severe mental disorders. Professor Weithorn reported that:

> Fewer than one-third of those juveniles admitted for inpatient mental health treatment.. were diagnosed as having severe or acute mental disorders of the type typically associated with such admissions (such as psychotic, serious depressive, or organic disorders)[, compared with] one-half to two-thirds of adults admitted for inpatient mental health

treatment . . . Yet, once hospitalized, juvenile psychiatric patients remain in the hospital approximately twice as long as do adults. And, children hospitalized in private facilities are both more likely to have longer stays and less likely to be severely disturbed than are children in public facilities. [¶] About two-thirds of juvenile inpatients receive initial diagnoses of conduct disorder, personality or childhood disorder, or transitional disorder. An examination of the various "symptoms" that characterize each type of disorder reveals that, in general, [hospitalized youth are] troublemakers, children with relatively mild psychological problems, and children who do not appear to suffer from anything more serious than normal developmental changes.

Id. at 788–89.

In a 2005 study, Professor Weithorn found that admission patterns have changed in the past two decades. Lois A. Weithorn, *Envisioning Second-Order Change in Americas Response to Troubled and Troublesome Youth*, 33 HOFSTRA L. REV. 1305 (2005). In response to dramatic reductions in private and public funds for adolescent mental health services, seriously emotionally disturbed youth are ending up in juvenile justice facilities. In addition, many youth end up on the streets, having run away or been ejected from their homes because of difficulties not adequately addressed by available intervention programs. *Id.* Ironically, there exists a range of highly-successful, evidence-based interventions that can provide assistance to these children and their families in the community. Yet, despite evidence of cost-effectiveness, these interventions are not typically employed on a wide scale as alternatives to institutionalization. *Id.* at 1487–1504. For further discussion of issues relating to psychiatric hospitalization and alternative options for troubled youth and their families, see also GARY B. MELTON ET AL., NO PLACE TO GO: THE CIVIL COMMITMENT OF MINORS (1988); Barbara Kahn et al., *Making the Connection: Legal Advocacy and Mental Health Services*, 45 FAM. CT. REV. 486 (2007); Susan Stefan, *Accommodating Families: Using the Americans With Disabilities Act to Keep Families Together*, 2 ST. LOUIS U. J. HEALTH L. & POL'Y 135 (2008); Justin Keller, Student Author, *Pieces of the Puzzle: Examining the Problem of Mental Health Coverage for Homeless Children*, 45 CAL. WEST. L. REV. 235 (2008); Jan C. Costello, *"The Trouble Is They're Growing, The Trouble Is They're Grown": Therapeutic Jurisprudence And Adolescents' Participation In Mental Health Care Decisions*, 36 J. LEG. MED. 311 (2005). For updated information about problems and solutions relevant to this population of youth, see the Children's Issues webpage of the Bazelon Center for Mental Health Law, http://www.bazelon.org/issues/children/index.htm.

4. *Statutory and Judicial Regulation of Psychiatric Hospitalization.* Beginning in the 1970s, states changed their statutes governing adult involuntary psychiatric hospitalization to provide greater procedural due process protections, including a judicial hearing. In addition, states adopted more specific substantive standards to be applied at the required hearings. In most jurisdictions, it must be proven with clear and convincing evidence that the individual for whom admission is sought is either imminently dangerous to himself, imminently dangerous to others, or unable to care for himself. These protections do not kick in, however, if the individual chooses hospitalization voluntarily.

Because parents generally make the health care decisions for their children, if a parent willingly seeks to admit her child to a psychiatric hospital, that admission was typically treated as a voluntary admission. Critics have argued that an admission of an unwilling minor to a hospital by a parent is more similar to an *involuntary* admission of an adult than it is to a voluntary admission. Those critics urge greater oversight of such admissions than would accompany the voluntary admission of an adult. James W. Ellis, *Volunteering Children: Parental Commitment of Minors to Mental Institutions*, 62 CAL. L. REV. 840 (1974).

Even though the U.S. Supreme Court held that the Georgia procedure was constitutional, states can provide *greater* protections for minors than the constitutional minimum. For example, in Virginia, admissions of minors ages 14 and older are subject to similar procedures and standards as are admissions of adults. "Voluntary" admission of juveniles age 14 and older can only occur if the parent *and* minor jointly consent. Minors younger than 14 can be admitted on parental consent alone. However, in all cases, a minor cannot be admitted to a psychiatric hospital unless less restrictive alternatives to hospitalization have been explored. VA. CODE ANN. § 16.1-338 (2009). If the minor refuses treatment and the parents wish to pursue hospitalization, an involuntary commitment may be sought, applying the following standards:

> (1) Because of mental illness, the minor (i) presents a serious danger to himself or others to the extent that severe or irremediable injury is likely to result, as evidenced by recent acts or threats or (ii) is experiencing a serious deterioration of his ability to care for himself in a developmentally age-appropriate manner, as evidenced by delusionary thinking or by a significant impairment of functioning in hydration, nutrition, self-protection, or self-control; (2) The minor is in need of inpatient treatment for a mental illness and is reasonably likely to benefit from the proposed treatment; *and* (3) Inpatient treatment is the least restrictive alternative that meets the minor's needs.

VA. CODE ANN. § 16.1-339 (2009) (emphasis added). Ohio requires judicial oversight of admissions of minors to psychiatric facilities, but unlike Virginia, the substantive standard in Ohio allows parental admission of a minor when it is in the minor's "best interests." OHIO REV. CODE § 5122.02 (2009). State courts have likewise varied in their responses to *Parham*-like challenges under state constitutions. In 1977, the California Supreme Court held that California's statutes empowering parents to admit their children "voluntarily" to psychiatric hospitals were unconstitutional. While the court required a range of due process protections and more rigorous admission standards, it stopped short of requiring procedures identical to those available to adults. Thus, for example, it held that the application of the preponderance of evidence standard of proof was constitutionally adequate. *In re Roger S.*, 569 P.2d 1286 (1977). By contrast, the New Jersey Supreme Court, in *Commitment of N.N.*, 679 A.2d 1174 (1996), sustained as constitutional an involuntary admission statute that required the state to prove only that the minor needs treatment.

PROBLEM

Problem 10-4.   Jessica and Harrison are the parents of 14-year-old Laura, who lately has been causing them a great deal of concern. She no longer sees her old friends, her grades have plummeted, and she spends a lot of time lying on her bed listening to music. When she emerges from her room, Laura, who was a very cheerful pleasant child until recently, snarls at her parents and starts fights with Sam, her brother. The few friends who come by to see Laura seem to be fringe types who she would not have associated with a year ago. Lately, Laura has stayed out all night a couple of times, and refused to tell her parents where she was. The household has been in a continuous uproar for months, and Jessica and Harrison are desperate. Jessica took Laura to a psychiatrist, who after talking to Laura for an hour, told Jessica that her daughter was very depressed, and needed to be hospitalized. Laura is vehemently opposed and refuses to consent to hospitalization. Jessica and Harrison consult you seeking legal advice.

[3]   Minors' Autonomy Interests in the Context of Reproductive Health

[a]   Trends in Adolescent Sexual Activity, Pregnancy, Childbearing, and Abortion

According to a study conducted by the Centers for Disease Control ("CDC") in 2003, 48% of boys and 45% of girls in grades 9 through 12 reported having had sexual intercourse. Most of these students (that is, 62%) were 12th graders. CDC, *Youth Risk Behavior Surveillance Summary — United States, 2003*, 53 MORBIDITY & MORT. WEEKLY RPT. May 21, 2004, http://www.cdc.gov/mmwr/PDF/SS/SS5302 .pdf. The trends in adolescent sexual activity reveal some dramatic fluctuations over time. According to national surveys, rates of sexual intercourse for female adolescents (ages 15–19) increased through the 1960s and 1970s. Sandra L. Hofferth et al., *Premarital Sexual Activity Among U.S. Teenage Women Over the Past Three Decades*, 19 FAM. PLANNING PERSPECTIVES 46 (1987). The rates continued to increase through the 1980s. In the 1990s however, sexual activity for teenagers began to decrease, and that decline continued through the 1990s. John S. Santelli et al., *Adolescent Sexual Behavior: Estimates and Trends from Four Nationally Representative Surveys*, 32 FAM. PLANNING PERSP. 156 (2000). It appears that the decline continued up through 2002, the last year for which comprehensive data are available. *See* Guttmacher Institute, *Facts on American Teens' Sexual and Reproductive Health*, http://www.guttmacher.org/pubs/fb_ATSRH.html. These declines are welcome news to public health experts, who observe that sexually-active adolescents have higher rates than do adults of sexually transmitted diseases (STDs) and unintended pregnancies. Santelli et al. *supra* at 156.

The teen *pregnancy* rate also dropped substantially in the 1990s. While peaking in 1991, the rate declined precipitously — 35% — between 1991 and 2002 (from 115.3 to 75.4 per 1,000 females in the 15–19 year age bracket). As one might expect, when pregnancy rates rise or fall, rates of either births or abortions follow a similar path. And indeed, while the rate of *births* to adolescent mothers rose during the 1980s, it dropped steeply through the 1990s and early 2000s. CDC, *Births:*

Preliminary Data for 2007, 57(12) NATIONAL VITAL STATISTICS REPORTS (Mar. 2009), www.cdc.gov/nchs/data/nvsr/nvsr57/nvsr57_12.pdf. The CDC calculates a 50% decrease in nonmarital births to teenagers between 1970 and 2007. CDC, *Changing Patterns of Nonmarital Childbearing in the United States*, 18 NCHS DATA BRIEF (May 2009), www.cdc.gov/nchs/data/databriefs/db18.htm. This statistic is all the more dramatic when contrasted with the steep rise in births to unmarried women more generally: an 80% increase between 1980 and 2007. *Id.*

Between 2005 and 2007, however, the rate of childbearing by teen mothers increased. CDC, *Births: Preliminary Data for 2007 supra.* An initial analysis suggests that the increase is due to a reduction in use of contraceptives among sexually-active teens, rather than an increase in the rate of sexual activity. *See* Santini et al, *Changing Behavior Risk for Pregnancy Among High School Students in the United States, 1991–2007*, J. ADOL. HEALTH (forthcoming). In response to this trend, public health experts recommend intensified efforts to encourage contraceptive use among sexually-active teens. A recent CDC report has expressed concern about this rise and about the particularly high rate among minority-group youth (particularly African-American and Hispanic teens) in the teen childbearing group. CDC, *Preventing Teen Pregnancy: An Update in 2009* (Apr. 2009), www.cdc.gov/reproductivehealth/AdolescentReproHealth/About TP.htm. In addition, despite the decreases in adolescent childbearing in the prior decades, the United States confronts substantially higher rates than do other industrialized nations. *See* Jacqueline E. Darroch et al., *Differences in Teenage Pregnancy Rates Among Five Developed Countries: The Roles of Sexual Activity and Contraceptive Use*, 33 FAM. PLANNING PERSPECTIVES 244 (2001) (22% of women surveyed in the U.S. report having a child before age 20, compared with 15% in Great Britain, 11% in Canada, 6% in France and 4% in Sweden).

Research reveals that there are many negative consequences of teen births to the young mothers and their children. Teen mothers are less likely than their peers to complete high school and to avoid or escape economic disadvantage. NATIONAL RESEARCH COUNCIL, RISKING THE FUTURE (1987). While some observed differences in economic circumstances are related to pre-pregnancy factors, teen childbearing clearly creates challenges for male and female teen parents. SAUL D. HOFFMAN & REBECCA A. MAYNARD (EDS.), KIDS HAVING KIDS: ECONOMIC COSTS AND SOCIAL CONSEQUENCES OF TEEN PREGNANCY (2d ed. 2008). Furthermore, studies demonstrate that children born to teen mothers are far more likely than children born to older mothers to be victims of abuse or neglect, to be in poor health, and to exhibit a range of academic and behavioral problems. Daughters of teen mothers are more likely to become teen parents themselves. Sons of adolescent mothers have a higher risk of eventual incarceration in juvenile or criminal justice facilities. *See, e.g., id.*; CDC, *Preventing Teen Pregnancy: An Update in 2009, supra*; Judith A. Levine et al., *Academic and Behavioral Outcomes Among Children of Young Mothers*, 63 J. MARR. & FAM. 355 (2001).

National statistics reveal that the rate of teen *abortion* increased during the 1970s, and stabilized in the early 1980s at approximately 43 per 1,000 females under age 20. By 2000, the rate had declined to 24 abortions per 1,000 females in this age group. Child Trends Data Bank, *Teen Abortions* (2003), http://www.childtrendsdatabank.org/indicators/27TeenAbortions.cfm. One report estimates that the teen abortion rates dropped 50% between 1988 and 2002. *See* Guttmacher Institute, *U.S. Teen Pregnancy Statistics: National and State Trends by Race and Ethnicity* (Sept. 2006). Between 2000 and 2005, the teen abortion rate remained relatively stable. *See* CDC, *Abortion Surveillance—2005* (2008), http://www.cdc.gov/mmwr/preview/mmwrhtml/ss5713a1.htm?s_cid=ss5713a1_e.

Various interpretations have been offered for the declines in teen pregnancy, birth, and/or abortion rates. The CDC attributes the decreases in pregnancies, births, and abortions between 1976 to 1996 to the availability of "easier-to-use, effective birth control methods by sexually-active teenagers" as well as educational programs focusing teens on "responsible [sexual] behavior." *See* CDC, *Trends in Pregnancies and Pregnancy Rates by Outcome: Estimates for the United States, 1976–1996* (2000), http://www.cdc.gov/nchs/data/series/sr_21/sr21_056.pdf. In a statistical analysis of the bases for the declines, the Guttmacher Institute attributed approximately 75% of the reduction in teen pregnancy between 1988 and 1995 to increased use of contraceptives, particularly long-acting hormonal methods such as implants or injectible types. Heather Boonstra, *Teen Pregnancy: Trends and Lessons Learned*, THE GUTTMACHER REPORT ON PUBLIC POLICY 8 (Feb. 2002). The Institute attributed another quarter of the 1988–1995 decline to an increase in the numbers of teens who chose to abstain from sexual intercourse. *Id.* A study in the *American Journal of Public Health* estimates that 86% of the drop in teen pregnancy between 1995 to 2002 was due to increased contraceptive use, while 14% was attributed to decreases in teens' sexual activity. John S. Santelli et al., *Explaining Recent Declines in Adolescent Pregnancy in the United States: The Contribution of Abstinence and Improved Contraceptive Use*, 97 AM. J. PUB. HEALTH 1 (2007).

[b]   Regulation of Adolescent Access to Contraception

CAREY v. POPULATION SERVICES INTERNATIONAL
United States Supreme Court
431 U.S. 678 (1977)

MR. JUSTICE BRENNAN delivered the opinion of the Court.

Under New York Educ. Law § 6811 (8) . . . it is a crime for any person to sell or distribute any contraceptive of any kind to a minor under the age of 16 years . . . [The federal district court held §] 6811 (8) unconstitutional in its entirety under the First and Fourteenth Amendments of the Federal Constitution insofar as it applies to nonprescription contraceptives, and enjoined its enforcement as so applied. We affirm.

. . . .

[T]he extent of state power to regulate conduct of minors not constitutionally regulable when committed by adults is a vexing one, perhaps not susceptible of precise answer. . . . "Minors, as well as adults, are protected by the Constitution and possess constitutional rights." *Planned Parenthood of Central Missouri v. Danforth*, 428 U.S. 52 (1976). . . . On the other hand, we have held in a variety of contexts that "the power of the state to control the conduct of children reaches beyond the scope of its authority over adults." *Prince v. Massachusetts*, 321 U.S. 158, 170 (1944). Of particular significance to the decision of this case, the right to privacy in connection with decisions affecting procreation, extends to minors as well as to adults. [*Danforth*] held that a State may not impose a blanket provision . . . requiring the consent of a parent or person *in loco parentis* as a condition for abortion of an unmarried minor during the first 12 weeks of her pregnancy. . . .

Since the State may not impose a blanket prohibition, or even a blanket requirement of parental consent, on the choice of a minor to terminate her pregnancy, the constitutionality of a blanket prohibition of the distribution of contraceptives to minors is *a fortiori* foreclosed. The State's interests in protection of the mental and physical health of the pregnant minor, and in protection of potential life are clearly more implicated by the abortion decision than by the decision to use a nonhazardous contraceptive.

Appellants argue, however, that significant state interests are served by restricting minors' access to contraceptives, because free availability to minors of contraceptives would lead to increased sexual activity among the young, in violation of the policy of New York to discourage such behavior. The argument is that minors' sexual activity may be deterred by increasing the hazards attendant on it. . . . [Yet, as we stated in] *Eisenstadt:* "It would be plainly unreasonable to assume that [the State] has prescribed pregnancy and the birth of an unwanted child [or the physical and psychological dangers of an abortion] as punishment for fornication." We remain reluctant to attribute any such "scheme of values" to the State.

[The Court rejects the assertion by the state that access to contraceptives increases teen sexual behavior, noting that no research was offered in support. The Court concludes that, since the statute] burdens the exercise of a fundamental right, [the state must produce more than a] bare assertion, based on a conceded complete absence of supporting evidence [in order to justify that burden.]

[MR. JUSTICE POWELL concurred in finding the New York's prohibition to be unconstitutional, but rejected the rationale that the statute in restricting minors' access to contraceptives violated a fundamental right of minors to make reproductive decisions. His primary concern about the statute was that it interfered impermissibly with parental autonomy, limiting the authority of parents to distribute contraception to their children.]

MR. JUSTICE STEVENS, concurring in part and concurring in the judgment. . . .

. . . I would not leave open the question whether there is a significant state interest in discouraging sexual activity among unmarried persons under 16 years of age. Indeed, I would describe as "frivolous" appellees' argument that a minor has the constitutional right to put contraceptives to their intended use, notwithstanding the combined objection of both parents and the State.

. . .

[Our precedent] that a minor's decision to abort her pregnancy may not be conditioned on parental consent, is not dispositive here. The options available to the already pregnant minor are fundamentally different from those available to nonpregnant minors. The former must bear a child unless she aborts; but persons in the latter category can and generally will avoid childbearing by abstention. [I do] not agree that the Constitution provides the same measure of protection to the minor's right to use contraceptives as to the pregnant female's right to abort.

. . . .

Common sense indicates that many young people will engage in sexual activity regardless of what the New York Legislature does; and further, that the incidence of venereal disease and premarital pregnancy is affected by the availability or unavailability of contraceptives. Although young persons theoretically may avoid those harms by practicing total abstention, inevitably many will not. The statutory prohibition denies them and their parents a choice which, if available, would reduce their exposure to disease or unwanted pregnancy.

. . . .

Although the State may properly perform a teaching function, it seems to me that an attempt to persuade by inflicting harm on the listener is an unacceptable means of conveying a message that is otherwise legitimate. The propaganda technique used in this case significantly increases the risk of unwanted pregnancy and venereal disease. It is as though a State decided to dramatize its disapproval of motorcycles by forbidding the use of safety helmets. One need not posit a constitutional right to ride a motorcycle to characterize such a restriction as irrational and perverse.

Even as a regulation of behavior, such a statute would be defective. Assuming that the State could impose a uniform sanction upon young persons who risk self-inflicted harm by operating motorcycles, or by engaging in sexual activity, surely that sanction could not take the form of deliberately injuring the cyclist or infecting the promiscuous child. . . . This kind of government-mandated harm, is, in my judgment, appropriately characterized as a deprivation of liberty without due process of law.

NOTES

1. **What is the Central Holding of** Carey? *Carey* struck down a statute that criminalized the sale of contraceptives to minors under the age of 16. It did not, however, address the contours of permissible state policies other than holding *criminalization* unconstitutional. The emphasis in *Carey* on the right that underlies its decision suggests that, even absent criminal penalties, minors have a right of access to contraceptives, even if that access is more heavily regulated than it would be for adults. And indeed, as Note 2 reveals, most states' policies are consistent with such a reading.

2. **The Current Status of Laws Governing Minors' Access to Contraceptives.** In most states, minors can obtain contraceptives without parental consent, consultation, or notification. Twenty-one states have passed statutes that explicitly grant minors the same access to contraceptives as adults. *See* Guttmacher Institute, *Minors' Access to Contraceptive Services*, State Policies in Brief, July 1, 2009; Rachel K. Jones & Heather Boonstra, *Confidential*

Reproductive Health Services for Minors: The Impact of Mandated Parental Involvement for Contraception, 36 PERSP. ON SEXUAL & REPROD. HEALTH 182 (2004). The Maryland and Virginia statutes provide that "A minor has the same capacity as an adult to consent to [treatment] for or advice about contraception other than sterilization." MD. CODE ANN., HEALTH GEN. § 20-102(C)(5)(2009). *See also* VA. CODE § 54.1-2969 (2009) (accord). Some statutes impose conditions on minors' access to contraceptives. For example, a Colorado statute permits minors to obtain birth control information or supplies when referred by a "physician, a clergyman, a family planning clinic, a school. . . ." COLO. REV. STAT. § 13-22-105 (2009). Statutes of this type are unlikely to impede access by most adolescents, who may easily find someone in one of these categories to provide a referral, such as the family planning clinic that dispenses the information or supplies. Hawaii, like several other states, authorizes adolescents age 14 and above to consent independently to family planning services, including access to contraceptives. *See, e.g.*, HAW. REV. ST. § 577A-1 (2009). Some statutes restrict access to pregnancy prevention services to minors who meet one of the following requirements: they are married, they are already parents, they are pregnant, they have parental consent, or they "may, in the opinion of the physician, suffer probably health hazards if such services are not provided." *See* FLA. ST. ANN. § 381.0051 (5) (2009); ILL. ST. Ch. 325 § 10/1 (2009). This latter provision does not specify the nature of the hazards, leaving the door open for physicians to conclude that unprotected exposure to STDs and the risk of adolescent pregnancy constitute probable "health hazards" within the purview of the statute. Other states permit "mature minors," that is, minors who demonstrate a capacity to make treatment decisions, to provide independent consent for contraception. For complete list of statutory provisions, see Guttmacher Institute, *Minors' Access to Contraceptive Services*, STATE POLICIES IN BRIEF, July 1, 2009; Jones & Boonstra *supra*.

While some states do not have explicit statutes authorizing minors' consent to family planning services, minors' access to most forms of birth control is substantially less controversial than their access to abortion. Policies allowing minors access to contraception are justified not only by the autonomy interests expressed in *Carey*, but also by the state's interests in preventing teen pregnancy. This interest is a substantial one in light of the deleterious social and public health consequences of high rates of teen pregnancy. For an argument against requiring parental consent for minors' access to contraception, see Jessica R. Arons, *Misconceived Laws: The Irrationality of Parental Involvement Requirements for Contraception*, 41 WM. & MARY L. REV. 1093 (2000). For an opposing view, see Lynn Wardle, *Parents' Rights vs. Minors' Rights Regarding the Provision of Contraceptives to Teenagers*, 68 NEB. L. REV. 216 (1989).

3. *Minors Access to "Emergency Contraception."* In the 1990s, a form of "emergency contraception" called "Plan B" became available by prescription. Plan B contains a concentrated dose of hormones contained in regular birth control pills. While most effective at preventing pregnancy if taken 24 hours after sexual intercourse, Plan B is still fairly effective up to 72 hours after intercourse. Substantial controversy has accompanied Plan B's availability. Many states have sought to restrict access, see Samantha Harper, *The "Morning After": How Far Can States Go to Restrict Access to Emergency Contraception?* 38 COLUM. HUM.

RTS. L. REV. 221 (2006), and some pharmacists claim that dispensing it offends their right of free religious exercise. Jessica D. Yoder, *Pharmacists' Right of Conscience: Strategies for Showing Respect for Pharmacists' Beliefs While Maintaining Adequate Care for Patients*, 41 VAL. U.L. REV. 975 (2006).

In 2006, after much dissension within the FDA, that agency approved over-the-counter dispensing of Plan B to women age 18 and older, while retaining the requirement that minors obtain a prescription in order to access the drug. In a challenge to this latter policy, a group of minors represented by advocacy organizations filed suit in federal district court to compel the FDA to make Plan B available without a prescription to minors. *Tummino v. Torti*, 603 F. Supp. 2d 519 (E.D.N.Y. 2009). In March 2009, the court chastised the FDA's handling of the Plan B policymaking, concluding that the FDA had "repeatedly and unreasonably delayed" its decisions regarding the non-prescriptive availability of Plan B "for suspect reasons." The court concluded that there was substantial "evidence of a lack of good faith and reasoned agency decision-making" on the part of the FDA. *Id.* at 523. It ordered the FDA to make Plan B available to minors age 17 without a prescription, based on documents setting forth the FDA's own conclusions about the safety of the drug for women ages 17 and older. The FDA decided not to appeal the ruling. *See Updated FDA Action on Plan B (levonorgestrel) Tablets* (Apr. 22, 2009), http://www.fda.gov/NewsEvents/Newsroom/PressAnnouncements/ucm 149568.htm. Plan B is now available to 17 year olds without a prescription. The court also ordered the FDA to reconsider its decision regarding the nonprescriptive availability of Plan B to minors under the age of 17. *Tummino*, 603 F. Supp. 2d at 549.

4. *The Confidentiality of Minors' Access to Contraception and Pregnancy Prevention Services.* In general, confidentiality has accompanied minors' receipt of pregnancy prevention services. The promise of confidentiality flows from state laws, federal policies accompanying certain forms of funding, or from professional practice obligations of the health care personnel providing the services. *See* Jones & Boonstra, *supra*; Cynthia Dailard & Chinue Turner Richardson, *Teenagers' Access to Confidential Reproductive Health Services*, GUTTMACHER RPT. ON PUB. POL'Y (Nov. 2005), www.guttmacher.org/pubs/spib_MACS.pdf. In recent years, however, there have been several initiatives at the federal, state, and even county level — some successful and some not — aimed at requiring or promoting parental notification of such services. *See* Jones & Boonstra *supra*; Dailard & Richardson, *supra*. Empirical studies indicate that, in the face of a parental notification requirement, 6.4% or 92 of 1526 adolescents presently seeking family planning services would engage in unprotected sexual relations rather than seek services. Another 13.3% or 196 in 1526 adolescents indicated they would use the "rhythm" or withdrawal method in the hope of preventing pregnancy. *See* Rachel K. Jones et al, *Adolescents' Reports of Parental Knowledge of Adolescents' Use of Sexual Health Services and Their Reactions to Mandated Parental Notification for Prescription Contraception*, 293 J.A.M.A. 340 (2005). These latter methods are not regarded by health care professionals as effective ways of preventing pregnancy, and they do not prevent transmission of STDs. The findings suggest that parental notification requirements would likely increase the numbers of sexually-active teenagers at risk for pregnancy and STD infection. The majority of surveyed adolescents (approximately 60%) indicated that a parental notification provision would not affect their willingness to seek services. The same percentage of surveyed adolescents reported that they had already voluntarily informed a parent or guardian of their use of family planning services, or that they had sought these services at the suggestion of a parent or guardian. *Id.*

5. *Sexuality Education Programs and Pregnancy/STD Prevention Programs in the Schools.* There has been substantial debate over the content of sexuality education programs in the public schools. The federal government and some private groups have promoted "abstinence-only" programs in place of more "comprehensive" curricula that encourage abstinence but also include information about birth control and prevention of STDs. Studies have revealed substantial scientific inaccuracies (and content that perpetuates numerous gender-role stereotypes) in the information conveyed in federally-funded abstinence-only programs. *See* U.S. House of Rep. Comm. on Gov't Reform, *The Content of Federally-Funded Abstinence-Only Education Programs* (2004), http:// oversight.house.gov/documents/20041201102153-50247.pdf.   A   Congressional committee report concluded that "moral judgments" and religious beliefs are misleadingly presented to students as scientific facts. *Id. See also* Alison Jeanne Lin & John S. Santelli, *The Accuracy of Condom Information in Three Selected Abstinence-Only Education Curricula,* 5 SEXUALITY RES. & SOC. POL'Y 56 (2008) (finding scientifically-inaccurate information dispensed in these programs); Michael Darflinger, Student Author, *Honesty is the Best Policy,* 29 J. LEG. MED. 81 (2008) (arguing for legal liability for schools that convey medically-inaccurate information, which expose students to greater risks of becoming pregnant or contracting STDs).

The President of the Institute of Medicine of the National Academy of Sciences summarized his conclusions regarding the evidence for the efficacy of these two approaches in his testimony before a congressional committee:

> Studies indicate that abstinence-only programs do not result in a delay in the initiation of sexual activity, a reduction in the frequency of unprotected vaginal sex, or a reduction in the number of sexual partners. Among sexually active teens, abstinence-only programs have not been shown to increase the return to sexual abstinence nor to affect condom use.
>
> [By contrast, in evaluating comprehensive sex-education programs several] studies found a positive effect on a number of behavioral outcomes. Comprehensive programs have reduced the self-reported incidence and frequency of unprotected sex and the number of sex partners. These programs have also been demonstrated to increase reported condom use and to delay initiation of sexual activity.

Harvey V. Fineberg, *Domestic Abstinence-Only Programs: Assessing the Evidence,* Testimony Before U.S. House of Representatives Oversight and Government Reform Committee, 100th Congress (Apr. 23, 2008), http://oversight.house.gov/ documents/20080423115949.pdf; *see also* GOVERNMENT ACCOUNTABILITY OFFICE, ABSTI-NENCE EDUCATION: EFFORTS TO ASSESS THE ACCURACY AND EFFECTIVENESS OF FEDERALLY-FUNDED PROGRAMS, Oct. 2006, http://www.gao.gov/new.items/d0787.pdf.

Contrary to the claims of opponents of the comprehensive programs, there is no evidence that programs informing teens about contraception increase the likelihood that teens will engage in sexual intercourse. Douglas Kirby, *Promoting Sexual Health and Responsible Sexual Behavior* 39 J. SEX RES. 51 (2002). Some of the features of the most effective programs include provision of "basic, accurate information about the risks of teen sexual activity and about methods of avoiding intercourse or using protection against pregnancy and STDs"; encouragement of abstinence during adolescence and; incorporation of "activities [addressing the] social pressures that influence sexual behavior [while providing] modeling and practice of communication, negotiation, and refusal skills." Kirby *supra* at 53. The few studies comparing comprehensive versus abstinence-only programs reveal that students in the latter programs are less likely to use protection when engaging in sexual intercourse. *See also* Douglas B. Kirby, *The Impact of Abstinence and Comprehensive Sex and STD-HIV Education Programs on Adolescent Sexual Behavior*, 5 SEXUALITY RES. & SOC. POL'Y 18 (2008). In 2009, the CDC indicated that its approach to stemming the tide of future increases in the teen pregnancy and birth rates is a "science-based approach to teen pregnancy prevention." *See* CDC, *Preventing Teen Pregnancy: An Update in 2009* (2009). For recent commentary about legal regulation of school sexuality education programs see Keith Brough, Student Author, *Sex Education Left at the Threshold of the School Door: Stricter Requirements for Parental Opt-Out Provisions*, 22 FAM. CT. REV. 409 (2008); Stacy Stockard, Student Author, *Is Abstinence Still the Best Policy? Modernizing Human Sexuality Instruction in Texas Public Schools*, 10 TEX. TECH ADMIN. L.J. 315 (2008).

School systems in many cities have initiated efforts to provide teenagers with direct access to contraceptives in public high schools, sometimes encountering resistance from community and religious groups. Courts have generally rejected challenges to condom distribution programs in schools. A federal appellate court concluded that a Philadelphia program did not interfere with fundamental parental rights where the program was voluntary and parents could refuse to allow their children to participate. *Parents United for Better Sch. Inc. v. Philadelphia Bd. of Educ.* 148 F.3d 260 (3rd Cir. 1998). *See also Curtis v. Sch. Comm. of Falmouth*, 652 N.E.2d 580 (Mass. 1995) (rejecting claim by students and parents that school sponsored condom program violated their right to familial privacy, parental liberty, and free exercise of religion); Karl S. Sanders, *Kids and Condoms: Constitutional Challenges to the Distribution of Condoms in Public Schools*, 61 U. CIN. L. REV. 1479 (1993). A study comparing Massachusetts schools with and without condom programs found no higher rates of sexual intercourse in the schools in which condoms were available. Susan M. Blake, et al., *Condom Availability Use in Massachusetts High Schools: Relationships with Condom Use and Sexual Behavior*, 93 AM. J. PUB. HEALTH 955 (2003). The researchers found, however, that twice as many sexually-active teens in these schools used condoms as compared to teens in the schools without programs. *Id.* For further discussion of public school contraception distribution programs, see Joshua A. Douglas, *When Is a "Minor" Also an "Adult"?: An Adolescent's Liberty Interest in Accessing Contraceptives from Public School Distribution Programs*, 43 WILLAMETTE L. REV. 545 (2007). For a comprehensive discussion of topics relating to adolescent sexuality and the law, see ROGER J. R. LEVESQUE, ADOLESCENTS, SEX, AND THE LAW: PREPARING ADOLESCENTS FOR RESPONSIBLE CITIZENSHIP 3 (2000).

[c]   State Regulation of Adolescent Abortion

States also regulate minors' access to abortion. Not surprisingly, the "default" regarding such access in most states is that a minor requires parental consent in order to obtain an abortion. Yet not all teenage girls feel they can discuss a pregnancy and its possible termination with their parents and some parents, if asked, might refuse consent. Given the life-changing consequences of decisions to carry a child to term or terminate a pregnancy, there has been substantial debate as to whether and under what circumstances mechanisms should be in place so that pregnant females under the age of 18 can access an abortion without parental consent. Massachusetts had enacted a statute with a parental consent requirement. If one or both of the minor's parents refused consent, the statute allowed access to an abortion if a superior court judge determined that there existed "good cause" for the abortion to be ordered. The Massachusetts Supreme Judicial Court interpreted the phrase "good cause" to mean that a judge could overrule a parental refusal upon a finding that the abortion was in the minor's best interests. Even if a minor was deemed capable of making an informed and reasonable decision to have an abortion, the judge could deny the request if he or she concluded that such denial was in the best interests of the minor. The Massachusetts court also held that a minor could not obtain a judicial hearing unless she had already sought parental consent or there existed an "emergency" requiring an immediate abortion. In the latter instance, parents would be notified of the abortion. After this statute was held unconstitutional by a lower federal court, the U.S. Supreme Court agreed to hear the case.

BELLOTTI v. BAIRD (II)
United States Supreme Court
443 U.S. 622 (1979)

MR. JUSTICE POWELL announced the judgment of the Court and delivered an opinion, in which THE CHIEF JUSTICE, MR. JUSTICE STEWART, and MR. JUSTICE REHNQUIST joined. . . .

. . . .

II

A child, merely on account of his minority, is not beyond the protection of the Constitution. . . . This observation, of course, is but the beginning of the analysis. . . . We have recognized three reasons justifying the conclusion that the constitutional rights of children cannot be equated with those of adults: the peculiar vulnerability of children; their inability to make critical decisions in an informed, mature manner; and the importance of the parental role in child rearing. . . .

The Court's concern for the vulnerability of children is demonstrated in its decisions dealing with minors' claims to constitutional protection against deprivations of liberty or property interests by the State. With respect to many of these claims, we have concluded that the child's right is virtually coextensive with that of an adult. For example, the Court has held that the Fourteenth Amendment's guarantee against the deprivation of liberty without due process of law is applicable to children in juvenile delinquency proceedings. . . .

These rulings have not been made on the uncritical assumption that the constitutional rights of children are indistinguishable from those of adults. . . . Viewed together, our cases show that although children generally are protected by the same constitutional guarantees against governmental deprivations as are adults, the State is entitled to adjust its legal system to account for children's vulnerability and their needs for "concern, . . . sympathy, and . . . paternal attention."

Second, the Court has held that the States validly may limit the freedom of children to choose for themselves in the making of important, affirmative choices with potentially serious consequences. These rulings have been grounded in the recognition that, during the formative years of childhood and adolescence, minors often lack the experience, perspective, and judgment to recognize and avoid choices that could be detrimental to them. . . .

Third, the guiding role of parents in the upbringing of their children justifies limitations on the freedoms of minors. The State commonly protects its youth from adverse governmental action and from their own immaturity by requiring parental consent to or involvement in important decisions by minors. But an additional and more important justification for state deference to parental control over children is that "[t]he child is not the mere creature of the State; those who nurture him and direct his destiny have the right, coupled with the high duty, to recognize and prepare him for additional obligations." *Pierce v. Society of Sisters*, 268 U.S. 510 (1925). . . . Thus, "[i]t is cardinal with us that the custody, care and nurture of the child reside first in the parents, whose primary function and freedom include *preparation for obligations the state can neither supply nor hinder.*" *Prince v. Massachusetts, supra,* 321 U.S. at 166, (emphasis added). . . .

Properly understood, then, the tradition of parental authority is not inconsistent with our tradition of individual liberty; rather, the former is one of the basic presuppositions of the latter. Legal restrictions on minors, especially those supportive of the parental role, may be important to the child's chances for the full growth and maturity that make eventual participation in a free society meaningful and rewarding. Under the Constitution, the State can "properly conclude that parents and others, teachers for example, who have [the] primary responsibility for children's well-being are entitled to the support of laws designed to aid discharge of that responsibility." *Ginsberg v. New York*, 390 U.S. at 639.

III

The question before us . . . is whether [the statute], as authoritatively interpreted by the Supreme Judicial Court, provides for parental notice and consent in a manner that does not unduly burden the right to seek an abortion. . . . [P]arental notice and consent are qualifications that typically may be imposed by the State on a minor's right to make important decisions. As immature minors often lack the ability to make fully informed choices that take account of both immediate and long-range consequences, a State reasonably may determine that parental consultation often is desirable and in the best interest of the minor. It may further determine, as a general proposition, that such consultation is particularly desirable with respect to the abortion decision — one that for some people raises profound moral and religious concerns. . . .

But we are concerned here with a constitutional right to seek an abortion. The abortion decision differs in important ways from other decisions that may be made during minority. The need to preserve the constitutional right and the unique nature of the abortion decision, especially when made by a minor, require a State to act with particular sensitivity when it legislates to foster parental involvement in this matter.

A

The pregnant minor's options are much different from those facing a minor in other situations, such as deciding whether to marry. A minor not permitted to marry before the age of majority is required simply to postpone her decision. She and her intended spouse may preserve the opportunity for later marriage should they continue to desire it. A pregnant adolescent, however, cannot preserve for long the possibility of aborting, which effectively expires in a matter of weeks from the onset of pregnancy.

Moreover, the potentially severe detriment facing a pregnant woman . . . is not mitigated by her minority. Indeed, considering her probable education, employment skills, financial resources, and emotional maturity, unwanted motherhood may be exceptionally burdensome for a minor. In addition, the fact of having a child brings with it adult legal responsibility, for parenthood, like attainment of the age of majority, is one of the traditional criteria for the termination of the legal disabilities of minority. In sum, there are few situations in which denying a minor the right to make an important decision will have consequences so grave and indelible. . . .

For these reasons, as we held in[*Planned Parenthood of Central Missouri v. Danforth*, 428 U.S. 52 (1976)],"the State may not impose a blanket provision . . . requiring the consent of a parent or person *in loco parentis* as a condition for abortion of an unmarried minor during the first 12 weeks of her pregnancy. Although such deference to parents may be permissible with respect to other choices facing a minor, the unique nature and consequences of the abortion decision make it inappropriate "to give a third party an absolute, and possibly arbitrary, veto over the decision of the physician and his patient to terminate the patient's pregnancy, regardless of the reason for withholding the consent." We therefore conclude that if the State decides to require a pregnant minor to obtain one or both parents' consent to an abortion, it also must provide an alternative procedure whereby authorization for the abortion can be obtained.

A pregnant minor is entitled in such a proceeding to show either: (1) that she is mature enough and well enough informed to make her abortion decision, in consultation with her physician, independently of her parents' wishes; or (2) that even if she is not able to make this decision independently, the desired abortion would be in her best interests. The proceeding in which this showing is made must assure that a resolution of the issue, and any appeals that may follow, will be completed with anonymity and sufficient expedition to provide an effective opportunity for an abortion to be obtained. In sum, the procedure must ensure that the provision requiring parental consent does not in fact amount to the "absolute; and possibly arbitrary, veto" that was found impermissible in *Danforth*.

[The Court also held unconstitutional the requirement that minors must consult with a parent or parents before seeking judicial authorization for an abortion. The Court held that this requirement] would impose an undue burden upon the exercise by minors of the right to seek an abortion. As the District Court recognized, "there are parents who would obstruct, and perhaps altogether prevent, the minor's right to go to court." There is no reason to believe that this would be so in the majority of cases where consent is withheld. But many parents hold strong views on the subject of abortion, and young pregnant minors, especially those living at home, are particularly vulnerable to their parents' efforts to obstruct both an abortion and their access to court. It would be unrealistic, therefore, to assume that the mere existence of a legal right to seek relief in superior court provides an effective avenue of relief for some of those who need it the most.

We conclude, therefore, that under state regulation such as that undertaken by Massachusetts, every minor must have the opportunity — if she so desires — to go directly to a court without first consulting or notifying her parents. If she satisfies the court that she is mature and well enough informed to make intelligently the abortion decision on her own, the court must authorize her to act without parental consultation or consent. If she fails to satisfy the court that she is competent to make this decision independently, she must be permitted to show that an abortion nevertheless would be in her best interests. If the court is persuaded that it is, the court must authorize the abortion. If, however, the court is not persuaded by the minor that she is mature or that the abortion would be in her best interests, it may decline to sanction the operation.

There is, however, an important state interest in encouraging a family rather than a judicial resolution of a minor's abortion decision. Also, as we have observed above, parents naturally take an interest in the welfare of their children — an interest that is particularly strong where a normal family relationship exists and where the child is living with one or both parents. These factors properly may be taken into account by a court called upon to determine whether an abortion in fact is in a minor's best interests. If, all things considered, the court determines that an abortion is in the minor's best interests, she is entitled to court authorization without any parental involvement. On the other hand, the court may deny the abortion request of an immature minor in the absence of parental consultation if it concludes that her best interests would be served thereby, or the court may in such a case defer decision until there is parental consultation in which the court may participate. But this is the full extent to which parental involvement may be required. For the reasons stated above, the constitutional right to seek an abortion may not be unduly burdened by state-imposed conditions upon initial access to court. . . .

[The Court affirmed the judgment of the District Court insofar as it invalidated this statute and enjoined its enforcement.]

[Justice Stevens, joined by Justices Brennan, Marshall, and Blackmun, concurred in the judgment, but differed with the plurality that anyone, even a judge, should retain absolute veto power over an abortion decision. Stating that pregnant minors have a privacy interest in making an independent abortion decision.]

In Massachusetts . . . every minor who cannot secure the consent of both her parents . . . is required to secure the consent of the sovereign. As a practical matter, . . . the need to commence judicial proceedings in order to obtain a legal abortion would impose a burden at least as great as, and probably greater than, that imposed on the minor child by the need to obtain the consent of a parent. Moreover, [the best interests] standard provides little real guidance to the judge, and his decision must necessarily reflect personal and societal values and mores whose enforcement upon the minor-particularly when contrary to her own informed and reasonable decision-is fundamentally at odds with privacy interests underlying the constitutional protection afforded to her decision.

NOTES

1. ***Parental Consent Provisions in State Laws After*** Bellotti ***and Constitutional Challenges.*** *Bellotti* sets forth the minimum constitutional requirements with which states must comply. States can choose to allow minors access to abortion without a parental consent requirement. A recent survey of state statutes, see Guttmacher Institute, *An Overview of Abortion Laws*, STATE POLICIES IN BRIEF (July 1, 2009), www.guttmacher.org/pubs/spib.html, indicates that nine states and the District of Columbia require neither parental consent or parental notice. For example, the Connecticut statute requires a physician or counselor to discuss with the minor "the possibility of involving the minor's parents, guardian or other adult family members in the minor's decision-making concerning the pregnancy and whether the minor believes that involvement would be in the minor's best interests." CT. GEN. ST. ANN. § 19a-601(a)(5) (2009). The statute also indicates that the discussion of all of the factors set forth in this section "is not intended to coerce, persuade, or induce the minor to choose to have an abortion or to carry the pregnancy to term." CT. GEN. ST. ANN. § 19a-601(a)(1) (2009). *See also* MAINE REV. STAT. ANN. tit. 22 § 1597-A (2009) (allowing minor to provide independent consent for abortion if she "is mentally and physically competent to give consent").

The statutes of another seven states with parental consent or parental notification provisions have been enjoined and cannot be enforced. Thus, for example, in 1989, California's statute, CAL. HEALTH & SAFETY CODE § 123450 (2009), which required the written consent of a minor's parent or guardian prior to an abortion and provided a judicial bypass procedure in apparent compliance with *Bellotti*, was temporarily enjoined by a California appellate court. *Am. Acad. of*

Pediatrics v. Van de Kamp, 263 Cal. Rptr. 46 (Cal. App. 1989). Eight years later, those provisions were held unconstitutional under the state constitution's privacy protections. *Am. Acad. of Pediatrics v. Lungren*, 940 P.2d 797 (Cal. 1997). Twenty-four states have statutes that require parental consent that have not been challenged or have been found to comply with constitutional requirements. *See* Guttmacher Institute, *An Overview of Abortion Laws, supra.* An additional seven states require parental notification but not parental consent.

Some states interpret their state constitutions as providing greater protection for minors' autonomy interests than the federal Constitution. *See, e.g., Lungren, supra* (state constitution provides broader protection of privacy than federal Constitution); *In re T.W.*, 551 So.2d 1186 (Fla. 1989) (same); *State v. Planned Parenthood of Alaska*, 171 P.3d 577 (Alaska 2007). In contrast, Massachusetts, although finding a two-parent consent requirement unduly burdensome, upheld the other provisions of the state's judicial bypass procedure as not violating the state constitution. *Planned Parenthood of Mass. v. Attorney Gen.*, 677 N.E.2d 101 (Mass. 1997).

2. *Parental Notification Provisions and Constitutional Challenges.* Some states have not required parental consent when minors seek abortion, but have established parental notification requirements. The first Supreme Court opinion confronting the issue was *H.L. v. Matheson*, 450 U.S. 398 (1981). At issue in *Matheson* was a Utah statute requiring a physician to "notify, if possible" the parents of a "dependent, unmarried, minor girl" prior to performing an abortion. In an opinion by Chief Justice Burger, the Supreme Court upheld the statute against constitutional attack. The Court emphasized that it was not deciding the constitutionality of the statute as applied to *mature* minors, because the girl had not placed the question of her maturity into evidence:

> As applied to immature and dependent minors, the statute plainly serves the important considerations of family integrity and protecting adolescents . . . In addition, as applied to that class, the statute serves a significant state interest by providing an opportunity for parents to supply essential medical and other information to a physician and enhancing the potential for parental consultation concerning a decision that has potentially traumatic and permanent consequences. [¶] . . . If the pregnant girl elects to carry her child to term, the *medical* decisions to be made entail few — perhaps none — of the potentially grave emotional and psychological consequences of the decision to abort.

Id. at 412–13. Justice Marshall, in dissent, concluded that the notice requirement burdened the young woman's abortion decision. Although, in the ideal family, a pregnant minor may seek the advice and support of her parents, he asserted that "'many families do not conform to this ideal." *Id.* at 438–41 (Marshall, J., dissenting). He continued:

> Many minor women will encounter interference from their parents after the state-imposed notification. In addition to parental disappointment and disapproval, the minor may confront physical or emotional abuse, withdrawal of financial support, or actual obstruction of the abortion decision. Furthermore, the threat of parental notice may cause some minor women

to delay past the first trimester of pregnancy, after which the health risks increase significantly. Other pregnant minors may attempt to self-abort or to obtain an illegal abortion rather than risk parental notification. Still others may forsake an abortion and bear an unwanted child. . . .

The Court has not resolved whether notification statutes, like consent statutes, must include a judicial bypass procedure to evaluate maturity and best interest. The statutes that have been reviewed since *H.L. v. Matheson* include such procedures, and legislatures and courts assume that they are required. In *Hodgson v. Minnesota*, 497 U.S. 417 (1990), in a splintered (and confusing) 5-4 decision, the Court upheld a Minnesota statute requiring that a minor wait forty-eight hours after both parents have been notified before obtaining an abortion. The Court concluded that the waiting period "would reasonably further the legitimate state interest in ensuring that the minor's decision is knowing and intelligent." The Court recognized that the statute's requirement that *both* parents be notified could inflict harm on a pregnant minor if the parents are divorced or the family is otherwise dysfunctional. However, even this requirement was upheld. Justice O'Connor, who held the "swing vote," determined that her constitutional objection to the two-parent notice requirement was adequately addressed by the judicial by-pass procedure, which allowed the minor to avoid notifying any parent. *See also Lambert v. Wicklund*, 520 U.S. 292 (1997) (upholding parental notice requirement given that it could be waived by a reviewing court if notice was not in minor's best interest). More recently, in *Ayotte v. Planned Parenthood*, 546 U.S. 320 (2006), the Court held that the New Hampshire parental notification statute was constitutionally flawed, in that it did not contain an exception to notification if necessary to protect the minor's health in an emergency. Yet, Justice O'Connor, writing for the Court, did not enjoin enforcement of the statute. Rather, the Court remanded the case, ordering the lower court to craft an exception to the statute to insure that it is not applied in the face of such an emergency.

Since *Hodgson*, lower federal appellate courts have evaluated parental notification procedures. *See, e.g., Planned Parenthood of the Rocky Mountains Services Corp. v. Owens*, 287 F.3d 910 (10th Cir. 2002) (striking Colorado notification statute with no exception for protecting health of minor in non-imminently life-threatening situations); *Planned Parenthood of the Blue Ridge v. Camblos* 116 F.3d. 707 (4th Cir. 1997) (holding unconstitutional Virginia notification statute giving judges discretion to require parental notice even if minor is mature); *Nova Health Sys. v. Edmondson*, 460 F.3d 1295 (10th Cir. 2006) (upholding denial of injunction against enforcement of challenged Oklahoma parental notification statute on the grounds it did not provide for sufficiently expeditious process). Two recent variations of parental notification statutes have surfaced. A federal district court struck Idaho's post-abortion notification requirement, holding that, among other infirmities, the statute failed to protect minors at risk of abuse or neglect if parents were so informed, and did not contain an exception for mature minors. *Planned Parenthood of Idaho, Inc. v. Wasden*, 376 F. Supp. 2d 1012 (D. Idaho 2005). Another federal district court distinguished a school board policy requiring school personnel to notify parents of a positive pregnancy test from parental notification statutes in the abortion context. Although ultimately holding that the suit was not ripe, the court rejected the plaintiff's argument that the policy was unconstitutional without a bypass procedure. For discussion of this case, see Melissa Prober, Student Author, *Please Don't Tell My Parents: The Validity of School Policies Mandating Parental Notification of a Student's Pregnancy*, 71 BROOK. L. REV. 557 (2005). Challenges to notice requirements have also been brought on state constitutional grounds. The New Jersey Supreme Court struck down that state's parental notification statute under the equal protection provision in that state's constitution because of the differential treatment of pregnant teens who continue the pregnancy (and make a myriad of medical decisions for themselves and their offspring) versus pregnant teens who seek to terminate the pregnancy. *Planned Parenthood of Central N.J. v. Farmer*, 762 A.2d 620 (N.J. 2000). Presently, a challenge to Florida's parental notice requirement on state constitutional grounds is proceeding through that state's courts. *See In re Doe*, 5 So.3d 721 (Fla. Ct. App. 2009).

Studies indicate that about 60% of pregnant minors who seek an abortion in states without parental consent or notification requirements inform or consult with their parents voluntarily once their pregnancy is confirmed. *See, e.g.*, Michael D. Resnick et al, *Patterns of Consultation Among Adolescent Minors Obtaining an Abortion*, 64 AM. J. ORTHOPSYCHIATRY 310, 312 (1994) (56% of minors in sample consulted with their parents); Stanley K. Henshaw & Kathryn Kost, *Parental Involvement in Minors' Abortion Decisions*, 21 FAM. PLANNING PERSP. 85 (1992) (finding that 60% of minors informed their parents). Seventy-five percent, however, consult with at least one trusted adult, although that person may not be a parent. Resnick et al., *supra*. Studies also suggest that many of those minors who do not inform their parents fear punitive or angry parental reactions, and in some cases physical violence or expulsion from the home, if one or both parents learned of the abortion. *See, e.g.*, Nancy E. Adler et al, *Abortion Among Adolescents*, 58 AM. PSYCHOL. 211–214 (2003); Henshaw & Kost, *supra*. For this subset of minors, a parental consent or notification requirement could substantially burden their access to abortion. For further analysis of parental notification requirements, see Amanda M. Lanham, Student Author, *Parental Notification Under the Undue Burden Standard: Is a Bypass Mechanism Required?* 37 RUTGERS L.J. 551 (2006).

3. The Meaning of "Maturity." Justice Powell's opinion in *Bellotti v. Baird* emphasized that a minor who establishes that she is "mature enough and well enough informed" has the right to decide whether to terminate her pregnancy without involvement of her parents. But, what is maturity? What must a minor show to demonstrate that she is sufficiently mature to make her own decision? In her examination of legal conceptions of adolescence, Professor Elizabeth Scott observes that the law has not fared particularly well in moving beyond the traditional "binary classification" of individuals as either adults or children, with the first group perceived to be fully capable of mature decisions, and the second group, completely incapable. Elizabeth S. Scott, *The Legal Construction of Adolescence*, 29 HOFSTRA L. REV. 547 (2000). In particular, she notes, "[t]he picture is complicated further by the fact that policy makers have no clear image of adolescence. Generally, they ignore this transitional developmental stage, classifying adolescents legally either as children or as adults, depending on the issue at hand." *Id.* at 547–48. Thus, it is not surprising that courts employ a haphazard and non-systematic approach to determining whether a minor is "mature enough" to make an abortion decision.

One sensible approach to evaluating the maturity of minors to make abortion decisions is to apply the legal standard for competence to make medical decisions developed under informed consent doctrine. *See, e.g.*, Lois A. Weithorn & Susan B. Campbell, *The Competency of Children and Adolescents to Make Informed Treatment Decisions*, 53 CHILD DEV. 1589 (1982). Although legal tests for competence in this context vary, the focus is on capacity for understanding relevant information and for reasoning about the choice. Thus, a judge applying an informed consent standard would examine the minor's understanding of disclosed information about the procedure, its risks and benefits, and available alternatives. Empirical research suggests that teenagers ages 14 and older are not significantly different from adults in their decisionmaking skills in treatment contexts generally, *see id.*, or when considering decisions to continue or terminate a pregnancy more specifically. *See* Bruce Ambuel & Julian Rappaport, *Developmental Trends in Adolescents' Psychological and Legal Competence to Consent to Abortion*, 16 L. & HUM. BEHAV. 129 (1991). A policy statement by an American Psychological Association (APA) Committee is in accord with this conclusion, based on the body of empirical research on adolescent decisionmaking. APA Interdivisional Committee on Adolescent Abortion, *Adolescent Abortion: Psychological and Legal Issues*, 42 AMER. PSYCHOL. 73 (1987).

Unfortunately, no consistent standard for evaluating maturity has emerged from jurisprudence. Substantial interstate and intrastate variability characterizes courts' approaches. For example, Professor Robert Mnookin reported that data regarding the 1,300 bypass hearings held in Massachusetts after *Bellotti* between April 1981 and February 1983 indicated that the minor was found "mature" by the court in about 90 percent of these cases. Robert H. Mnookin, *Bellotti v. Baird: A Hard Case*, in IN THE INTEREST OF CHILDREN 239–40 (R. Mnookin ed. 1985). Professor Mnookin concluded that the judicial overview operated more like a "rubber stamp" than an assessment of maturity, and suggested that "the superior court judges realize that it would be impossible . . . to justify a finding that a pregnant minor was too immature to decide whether to have an abortion for herself, but that it was in her best interests to bear the child." *Id.* Unfortunately, there are no data to indicate whether this high rate of successful petitions still prevails today in Massachusetts.

Some other jurisdictions set a very high standard under which few minors are likely to qualify. In *H.B. v. Wilkinson*, 639 F. Supp. 952 (D. Utah 1986), a federal district court analyzed the meaning of maturity under *Bellotti:*

> [A]s related to a minor's abortion decision, maturity is not solely a matter of social skills, level of intelligence or verbal skills. More importantly, it calls for experience, perspective and judgment. As to experience, the minor's prior work experience, experience in living away from home, and handling personal finances are some of the pertinent inquiries. Perspective calls for appreciation and understanding of the relative gravity and possible detrimental impact of each available option, as well as realistic perception and assessment of possible short term and long term consequences of each of those options, particularly the abortion option. Judgment is of very great importance in determining maturity. The exercise of good judgment requires being fully informed so as to be able to weigh

alternatives independently and realistically. Among other things, the minor's conduct is a measure of good judgment. Factors such as stress and ignorance of alternatives have been recognized as impediments to the exercise of proper judgment by minors, who because of those factors "may not be able intelligently to decide whether to have an abortion."

The court concluded that the 17 year old pregnant minor before the court was "immature," and thus subject to a statutory requirement of parental notification. It described several factors central to this conclusion: the young woman lived at home, was not regularly employed and was financially dependent on her parents (and expected this to continue through college); she engaged in sexual activity several times without using contraceptives, believing that if she became pregnant she could obtain an abortion and deal with any complications without her parents' knowledge; she sought counsel from friends, rather than from family members or church or school officials; she did not consider marriage to be a viable option as a response to the pregnancy; her demeanor as a witness was initially characterized by nervousness and stress; and she failed to give due consideration to the possibility of post-abortion depression. Based on these facts, the court found the young woman to be "immature, lacking the experience, perspective and judgment to recognize and avoid choice that could be detrimental to herself." 639 F. Supp. at 958. *See also In re Jane Doe*, 566 N.E.2d 1181 (Ohio 1990) (trial court decision that a 17-year-old failed to establish maturity upheld despite minor's superior academic performance and physician's testimony that she understood the risks of the procedure; the court noted the minor's previous abortion and discontinuance of birth control as evidence of immaturity). Many courts hold that minors must provide clear and convincing evidence of maturity, making the burden all the more difficult for a teenager to satisfy. *See, e.g., In re Doe*, 932 So. 2d 278 (Fla. Ct. App. 2005); *In re B.S.*, 74 P.3d 285 (Ariz. Ct. App. 2003). Alabama sets a particularly high threshold for findings of maturity. *See, e.g., Ex Parte Anonymous*, 803 So. 2d 542 (Ala. 2001); *Ex Parte Anonymous*, 808 So. 2d 1030 (Ala. 2001); *Ex Parte Anonymous*, 806 So. 2d 1269 (Ala. 2001). *See* Elizabeth S. Scott, *The Legal Construction of Adolescence*, 29 HOFSTRA U. L. REV. 547 (2000) (arguing that judge's attitudes toward abortion affect their judgments of maturity in this context).

In a 1989 decision, the Florida Supreme Court observed that Florida law authorizes pregnant minors to make their own medical decisions if they continue with a pregnancy, as well as medical decisions for their children if they give birth, and decisions whether to place their children for adoption. *In re T.W.*, 551 So. 2d 1186 (Fla. 1989). The court held that, in light of the state's confidence in minors' decisionmaking skills in these latter situations, there was no compelling interest justifying restrictions on minors' decisional autonomy under Florida's abortion statutes. Along similar lines, Professor Shoshanna Ehrlich has argued that "it is difficult to grasp the logic of a statutory scheme that treats young women differently based on their intended pregnancy outcomes. If a young woman is capable of deciding to become a mother, with all of the responsibility this decision entails, she is similarly capable of deciding not to become a mother." J. Shoshanna Ehrlich, *Grounded in the Reality of their Lives: Listening to Teens Who Make the Abortion Decision Without Involving their Parents*, 18 BERK. WOMEN'S L.J. 61, 146 (2003).

4. *Empirical Research on the Operation of State Provisions in Practice.* Unfortunately, there is a dearth of methodologically-sophisticated research examining the operation of state policies governing minors' access to abortion. There are some findings, however, that provide initial insights. Two studies (one in Pennsylvania and one in Alabama) investigated how courts respond when a female calls for information on "how a minor who wants an abortion can get a judge's permission to avoid involving her parents." Helena Silverstein, *Road Closed: Evaluating the Judicial Bypass Provision of the Pennsylvania Abortion Control Act*, 24 L. & Soc. Inquiry 73, 80 (1999). In Pennsylvania, personnel in only 8 of 60 judicial districts provided fully accurate information. In Alabama, the researchers found that approximately half of Alabama's 67 counties provided callers with information that would allow them to proceed effectively. Helena Silverstein & Leanne Speitel, *"Honey, I Have No Idea": Court Readiness to Handle Petitions to Waive Parental Consent for Abortion*, 88 Iowa L. Rev. 75 (2002). Contacts with courts in 25 Alabama counties "reveal[ed] widespread lack of familiarity with a statute the state legislature adopted fourteen years ago." *Id.* at 101. Personnel in six Alabama jurisdictions stated their county does not perform bypass hearings. *Id.* at 102. Based on these findings, teenagers without additional knowledge or assistance would have difficulty determining how to proceed.

Some commentators have observed that there are very few judges to hear these cases in some jurisdictions because many have recused themselves from hearing minors' abortion petitions. Thus, in some counties, it may not be possible to get a hearing. In others, a "dramatically increased workload," may result in substantial delays. *See* Lauren Treadwell, *Informal Closing of the Bypass: Minors' Petitions to Bypass Parental Consent for Abortion in an Age of Increasing Judicial Recusals*, 38 Hast. L. J. 869, 870–71 (2007). One researcher investigating the operation of bypass procedures in Minnesota found that, although 87 counties in that state have jurisdiction to hear bypass petitions, almost all of the petitions are heard in three locations because judges in the remaining counties have refused to hear these cases on "moral or political" grounds. Patricia Donovan, *Judging Teenagers: How Minors Fare When They Seek Court-Authorized Abortions*, 15 Fam. Planning Persp. 259, 259 (1983).

A detailed analysis of the empirical literature on the impact of parental consent and notification requirements reported the following conclusions:

> The clearest impact documented is the increase in the number of minors who travel outside their home states [e.g., Massachusetts, Mississippi, Missouri] to obtain services in state that do not have such laws or that have less restrictive ones . . . For example, in Massachusetts, 29% of minors who had abortions did so in neighboring states . . . In South Carolina, on the other hand, where the law applied only to minors younger than 17 and a grandparent could satisfy the consent requirement, no out-of-state travel was detected.

Amanda Dennis et al., *The Impact of Laws Requiring Parental Involvement for Abortion: A Literature Review*, Guttmacher Inst., Mar. 2009 at 27. A Massachusetts study revealed similar results and found no evidence that the state's parental consent requirement promoted family unity, enhanced parent-child communication, or reduced the rates of teenage abortion or parenthood. Virginia G. Cartoof & Lorraine V. Klerman, *Parental Consent for Abortion: Impact of the Massachusetts Law*, 76 AM. J. PUB. HEALTH 397, 400 (1986).

PROBLEM

Problem 10-5. Sarah Johnson, age 15, has petitioned your court for permission to abort without notifying her parents. Sarah is a 10th grade honor student who has become pregnant by her boyfriend. She testifies that she does not want to tell her parents about her decision because they will be upset with her; they do not know that she is sexually active and they do not like her boyfriend. She also thinks they will be angry because her mother talked to her last year about using contraceptives if she became sexually active. Sarah wants the abortion because everyone at school will laugh at her when her pregnancy starts to show and she will not be able to be a cheerleader. She hates the way she would look if she were pregnant — "like a blimp." She also thinks that, if she has the baby, she will have to drop out of school for a while and will lose a grade, which she really does not want to do. The psychologist who evaluated Sarah testifies that she understands the medical procedure, including its risks and benefits. She also understands the alternatives available to her, and is firm about choosing abortion. You are the judge hearing Sara's petition. What is your response?

C. OVERRIDING PARENTAL AUTHORITY IN ORDER TO PROTECT ENDANGERED CHILDREN

It is virtually impossible to estimate accurately the frequency of child abuse and neglect in this country today because so many cases are shielded from view. The findings of studies intended to demonstrate the incidence of abuse and neglect, one expert writes, "are a direct consequence of the definition used. Thus, estimates of the number of children abused and neglected each year range from 60,000 to 4.5 million. Comparing these findings is indeed like comparing apples and oranges." Donald Besharov, *Improved Research on Child Abuse and Neglect through Better Definitions*, in FAM. VIOLENCE 42, 43 (D. BESHAROV ED., 1990). In 2007, there were 3.2 million reports to child protection agencies in the United States (that, together, concerned the welfare of 5.8 million children). Of the 3.2 million reports, child protection agencies determined that 61.7% or 1.97 million, were appropriate for investigation. In 25.2% or approximately 496,400 of those cases, the investigations determined that at least one child was a victim of abuse or neglect. CHILD MALTREATMENT 2007, U.S. DEP'T HEALTH & HUMAN SVCS. (2009), http://www.acf.hhs.gov/programs/cb/pubs/cm07/cm07.pdf. Of those 496,400 cases, the categories of maltreatment were represented in the following approximate percentages: neglect (59%); multiple maltreatments (13.1%); physical abuse (10.8%); sexual abuse (7.6%); psychological maltreatment (4.2%); medical neglect (.9%). *Id.* at 26. DHHS indicates that another 4.2% of the cases fell into "other" categories, and that data were not available for .1%. *Id.*

The number of *reported* cases was 500,000 in 1977. U.S. Dep't of Health, Education and Welfare, Children's Bureau, *National Analysis of Official Child Abuse and Neglect Reporting 1977*, 3, 5–6 (1979), as contrasted with 3.2 million in

2007. Does this apparent increase reflect a true increase in the incidence of abuse and neglect? Does it reflect an increase in the proportion of cases coming to the attention of authorities because of mandatory abuse reporting laws, discussed, below? Does it relate to different methods of data collection? While many experts share opinions to these questions, the short answer is that it is impossible to know.

Some cases of suspected child abuse and neglect trigger civil actions brought by the state for the purpose of intervening in a parent-child relationship to protect a child. In these cases, referred to as "dependency" cases, the court ultimately determines whether there is sufficient evidence to find that parental conduct satisfies one or more of the statutory grounds defining abuse or neglect. If so, a variety of dispositions are possible, such as monitoring the child in the home while requiring the parent(s) to participate in various interventions. Or, the court can order the temporary removal of the child from the home. Many children found to be neglected or abused are placed in foster care, the focus of Section 4. Section 5 addresses questions raised when the state seeks to terminate parental rights. The state may also bring a criminal action against a parent, guardian or other party for child abuse or neglect. Criminal defendants are constitutionally entitled to certain protections not required in civil proceedings. The challenges that arise in proving child maltreatment under a state's criminal statutes are the focus of Section 6.

[1]   Standards for State Intervention in Child Abuse and Neglect Cases

MINNESOTA STATUTES (2009)

§ 260C.007. Definitions

Subdivision 6. "Child in need of protection or services" means a child who is in need of protection or services because the child:

(1) is abandoned or without parent, guardian, or custodian;

(2) (i) has been a victim of physical or sexual abuse, (ii) resides with or has resided with a victim of domestic child abuse . . . , (iii) resides with or would reside with a perpetrator of domestic child abuse or child abuse . . . or (iv) is a victim of emotional maltreatment as defined in subdivision 15,

(3) is without necessary food, clothing, shelter, education, or other required care for the child's physical or mental health or morals because the child's parent, guardian, or custodian is unable or unwilling to provide that care;

(4) is without the special care made necessary by a physical, mental, or emotional condition because the child's parent, guardian, or custodian is unable or unwilling to provide that care;

(5) is medically neglected, which includes, but is not limited to, the withholding of medically indicated treatment from a disabled infant with a life-threatening condition. . . .

(6) is one whose parent, guardian, or other custodian for good cause desires to be relieved of the child's care and custody . . . ;

(7) has been placed for adoption or care in violation of law;

(8) is without proper parental care because of the emotional, mental, or physical disability, or state of immaturity of the child's parent, guardian, or other custodian. . . .

Subdivision 13. "Domestic child abuse" means:

(1) any physical injury to a minor family or household member inflicted by an adult family or household member other than by accidental means. . . .

Subdivision 15. "Emotional maltreatment" means the consistent, deliberate infliction of mental harm on a child by a person responsible for the child's care, that has an observable, sustained, and adverse effect on the child's physical, mental, or emotional development. "Emotional maltreatment" does not include reasonable training or discipline administered by the person responsible for the child's care or the reasonable exercise of authority by that person.

. . . .

IN RE TEXAS DEPARTMENT OF FAMILY AND PROTECTIVE SERVICES
Texas Supreme Court
255 S.W.3d 613 (2008)

PER CURIAM.

The Yearning for Zion Ranch is a 1,700-acre complex near Eldorado, Texas, that is home to a large community associated with the Fundamentalist Church of Jesus Christ of Latter Day Saints. On March 29, 2008, the Texas Department of Family Protective Services received a telephone call reporting that a sixteen-year-old girl named Sarah was being physically and sexually abused at the Ranch. On April 3, about 9:00 p.m., Department investigators and law enforcement officials entered the Ranch, and throughout the night they interviewed adults and children and searched for documents. Concerned that the community had a culture of polygamy and of directing girls younger than eighteen to enter spiritual unions with older men and have children, the Department took possession of all 468 children at the Ranch without a court order.[1] The Department calls this "the largest child

---

[1] See TEX. FAM. CODE § 262.104(a) ("If there is no time to obtain a temporary restraining order or attachment before taking possession of a child consistent with the health and safety of that child, an authorized representative of the Department of Family and Protective Services . . . may take possession of a child without a court order under the following conditions, only: (1) on personal knowledge of facts that would lead a person of ordinary prudence and caution to believe that there is an immediate danger to the physical health or safety of the child; (2) on information furnished by another that has been corroborated by personal knowledge of facts and all of which taken together would lead a person of ordinary prudence and caution to believe that there is an immediate danger to the physical health or safety of the child; (3) on personal knowledge of facts that would lead a person of ordinary prudence and caution to believe that the child has been the victim of sexual abuse; (4) on information furnished by another that has been corroborated by personal knowledge of facts and all of which taken together would lead a person of ordinary prudence and caution to believe that the child has been the victim of sexual abuse. . . .").

protection case documented in the history of the United States." It never located the girl Sarah who was the subject of the March 29 call.

The Department then filed several suits affecting the parent-child relationship ("SAPCRs")[2] requesting emergency orders removing the children from their parents and limiting the parents' access to the children. The Department also requested appointment as temporary sole managing conservator of the children, genetic testing, and permanent relief. On April 17–18, the district court conducted the adversary hearing required by section 262.201(a) of the Texas Family Code.[3] Subsections (b) and (c) state in relevant part:

> (b) At the conclusion of the full adversary hearing, the court shall order the return of the child to the parent . . . entitled to possession unless the court finds sufficient evidence to satisfy a person of ordinary prudence and caution that:
>
> > (1) there was a danger to the physical health or safety of the child which was caused by an act or failure to act of the person entitled to possession and for the child to remain in the home is contrary to the welfare of the child;
> >
> > (2) the urgent need for protection required the immediate removal of the child and reasonable efforts, consistent with the circumstances and providing for the safety of the child, were made to eliminate or prevent the child's removal; and
> >
> > (3) reasonable efforts have been made to enable the child to return home, but there is a substantial risk of a continuing danger if the child is returned home.
>
> (c) If the court finds sufficient evidence to satisfy a person of ordinary prudence and caution that there is a continuing danger to the physical health or safety of the child and for the child to remain in the home is contrary to the welfare of the child, the court shall issue an appropriate temporary order under Chapter 105.

The hearing was attended by scores of attorneys for the parties, attorneys ad litem, guardians ad litem, Texas Court Appointed Special Advocates (CASA), and many others. . . . At the conclusion of the hearing, the district court issued temporary orders continuing the Department's custody of the children and allowing for visitation by the parents only with the Department's agreement.

---

[2] *See* Tex. Fam. Code § 262.105(a) ("When a child is taken into possession without a court order, the person taking the child into possession, without unnecessary delay, shall: (1) file a suit affecting the parent-child relationship; (2) request the court to appoint an attorney ad litem for the child; and (3) request an initial hearing to be held by no later than the first working day after the date the child is taken into possession.").

[3] Section 262.201(a) provides: "Unless the child has already been returned to the parent, managing conservator, possessory conservator, guardian, caretaker, or custodian entitled to possession and the temporary order, if any, has been dissolved, a full adversary hearing shall be held not later than the 14th day after the date the child was taken into possession by the governmental entity."

Thirty-eight mothers petitioned the court of appeals for review by mandamus, seeking return of their 126 children. The record reflects that at least 117 of the children are under 13 and that two boys are 13 and 17. The ages of the other seven, at least two of whom are boys, are not shown. Concluding that the Department had failed to meet its burden of proof under section 262.201(b)(1), the court of appeals directed the district to vacate its temporary orders granting the Department custody . . .

The Department petitioned this Court for review by mandamus. Having carefully examined the testimony at the adversary hearing and the other evidence before us, we are not inclined to disturb the court of appeals' decision. On the record before us, removal of the children was not warranted. The Department argues without explanation that the court of appeals' decision leaves the Department unable to protect the children's safety, but the Family Code gives the district court broad authority to protect children short of separating them from their parents and placing them in foster care. The court may make and modify temporary orders "for the safety and welfare of the child," [*id.* § 105.001(a); *see id.* § 262.205], including an order "restraining a party from removing the child beyond a geographical area identified by the court." [*Id.* § 105.001(a)(4)]. The court may also order the removal of an alleged perpetrator from the child's home [*id.* § 262.1015] and may issue orders to assist the Department in its investigation. [*Id.* § 261.303(b)–(c).] The Code prohibits interference with an investigation, [*id.* § 261.303(a)], and a person who relocates a residence or conceals a child with the intent to interfere with an investigation commits an offense. [*Id.* § 261.3032.]

While the district court must vacate the current temporary custody orders as directed by the court of appeals, it need not do so without granting other appropriate relief to protect the children, as the mothers involved in this proceeding concede in response to the Department's motion for emergency relief. The court of appeals' decision does not conclude the SAPCR proceedings.

Although the SAPCRs involve important, fundamental issues concerning parental rights and the State's interest in protecting children, it is premature for us to address those issues. The Department's petition for mandamus is denied.

JUSTICE O'NEILL, joined by JUSTICE JOHNSON and JUSTICE WILLETT, concurring in part and dissenting in part.

In this case, the Department of Family and Protective Services presented evidence that "there was a danger to the physical health or safety" of pubescent girls on the Yearning for Zion (YFZ) Ranch from a pattern or practice of sexual abuse, that "the urgent need for protection required the immediate removal" of those girls, and that the Department made reasonable efforts, considering the obstacles to information-gathering that were presented, to prevent removal and return those children home. TEX. FAM. CODE § 262.201(b)(1)–(3). As to this endangered population, I do not agree with the Court that the trial court abused its discretion in allowing the Department to retain temporary conservatorship until such time as a permanency plan designed to ensure each girl's physical health and safety could be approved. *See id.* §§ 263.101–.102. On this record, however, I agree that there was no evidence of imminent "danger to the physical health or safety" of boys and pre-pubescent girls to justify their removal from the YFZ Ranch, and to this extent I join the Court's opinion. *Id.* § 262.201(b)(1).

Evidence presented in the trial court indicated that the Department began its investigation of the YFZ Ranch on March 29th, when it received a report of sexual abuse of a sixteen-year-old girl on the property. On April 3rd, the Department entered the Ranch along with law-enforcement personnel and conducted nineteen interviews of girls aged seventeen or under, as well as fifteen to twenty interviews of adults. In the course of these interviews, the Department learned there were many polygamist families living on the Ranch; a number of girls under the age of eighteen living on the Ranch were pregnant or had given birth; both interviewed girls and adults considered no age too young for a girl to be "spiritually" married; and the Ranch's religious leader, "Uncle Merrill," had the unilateral power to decide when and to whom they would be married. Additionally, in the trial court, the Department presented "Bishop's Records" — documents seized from the Ranch-indicating the presence of several extremely young mothers or pregnant "wives"[1] on the Ranch: a sixteen-year-old "wife" with a child, a sixteen-year-old pregnant "wife," two pregnant fifteen-year-old "wives," and a thirteen-year-old who had conceived a child. The testimony of Dr. William John Walsh, the families' expert witness, confirmed that the Fundamentalist Church of Jesus Christ of Latter Day Saints accepts the age of "physical development" (that is, first menstruation) as the age of eligibility for "marriage." Finally, child psychologist Dr. Bruce Duncan Perry testified that the pregnancy of the underage children on the Ranch was the result of sexual abuse because children of the age of fourteen, fifteen, or sixteen are not sufficiently emotionally mature to enter a healthy consensual sexual relationship or a "marriage."

Evidence presented thus indicated a pattern or practice of sexual abuse of pubescent girls, and the condoning of such sexual abuse, on the Ranch[2] evidence sufficient to satisfy a "person of ordinary prudence and caution" that other such girls were at risk of sexual abuse as well. *Id.* § 262.201(b). This evidence supports the trial court's finding that "there was a danger to the physical health or safety" of pubescent girls on the Ranch. *Id.* § 262.201(b)(1); *see id.* § 101.009 (" 'Danger to the physical health or safety of a child' includes exposure of the child to loss or injury that jeopardizes the physical health or safety of the child without regard to whether there has been an actual prior injury to the child."); *cf. Tex. Dep't of Human Servs. v. Boyd*, 727 S.W.2d 531, 533 (Tex.1987) (affirming the termination of parental rights

---

[1] Although referred to as "wives" in the Bishop's Records, these underage girls are not legally married; rather, the girls are "spiritually" married to their husbands, typically in polygamous households with multiple other "spiritual" wives. Subject to limited defenses, a person who "engages in sexual contact" with a child younger than seventeen who is not his *legal* spouse is guilty of a sexual offense under the Texas Penal Code. *See* Tex. Penal Code § 21.11(a)–(b). Those who promote or assist such sexual contact, *see id.* § 7.02(a)(2), or cause the child to engage in sexual contact, *see id.* § 21.11(a)(1), may also be criminally liable.

[2] The Family Code defines "abuse" to include "sexual conduct harmful to a child's mental, emotional, or physical welfare" — including offenses under section 21.11 of the Penal Code-as well as "failure to make a reasonable effort to prevent sexual conduct harmful to a child." Tex. Fam. Code § 261.001(1)(E)–(F). In determining whether there is a "continuing danger to the health or safety" of a child, the Family Code explicitly permits a court to consider "whether the household to which the child would be returned includes a person who . . . has sexually abused another child." *Id.* § 262.201(d).

for "endanger[ing] . . . the physical well-being of [a] child," and holding: "While we agree that 'endanger' means more than a threat of metaphysical injury or the possible ill effects of a less-than-ideal family environment, it is not necessary that the conduct be directed at the child or that the child actually suffers injury. Rather, 'endanger' means to expose to loss or injury; to jeopardize."). Thus, the trial court did not abuse its discretion in finding that the Department met section 262.201(b)(1)'s requirements.

Notwithstanding this evidence of a pattern or practice of sexual abuse of pubescent girls on the Ranch, the court of appeals held-and the Court agrees today-that the trial court abused its discretion in awarding temporary conservatorship to the Department because the Department failed to attempt legal steps, short of taking custody, to protect the children. Based on the language of section 262.201 of the Family Code, I disagree. Subsections (b)(2) and (b)(3) of section 262.201 require the Department to demonstrate that "reasonable efforts, consistent with the circumstances and providing for the safety of the child, were made to eliminate or prevent the child's removal," TEX. FAM. CODE § 262.201(b)(2), and that "reasonable efforts have been made to enable the child to return home," *id.* § 262.201(b)(3). The Court suggests, consistent with the mothers' arguments in the court of appeals below, that the Department failed to adequately justify its failure to seek less-intrusive alternatives to taking custody of the children: namely, seeking restraining orders against alleged perpetrators under section 262.1015 of the Family Code, or other temporary orders under section 105.001 of the Family Code. *Id.* §§ 262.1015, 105.001.

However, the Family Code requires only that the Department make "reasonable efforts, consistent with the circumstances" to avoid taking custody of endangered children. *Id.* § 262.201(b)(2). Evidence presented in the trial court indicated that the actions of the children and mothers precluded the Department from pursuing other legal options. When the Department arrived at the YFZ Ranch, it was treated cordially and allowed access to children, but those children repeatedly pled "the Fifth" in response to questions about their identity, would not identify their birth-dates or parentage, refused to answer questions about who lived in their homes, and lied about their names-sometimes several times. Answers from parents were similarly inconsistent: one mother first claimed that four children were hers, and then later avowed that they were not. Furthermore, the Department arrived to discover that a shredder had been used to destroy documents just before its arrival.

Thwarted by the resistant behavior of both children and parents on the Ranch, the Department had limited options. Without knowing the identities of family members or of particular alleged perpetrators, the Department could not have sought restraining orders under section 262.1015 as it did not know whom to restrain. *See id.* § 262.1015. Likewise, it could not have barred any family member from access to a child without filing a verified pleading or affidavit, which must identify clearly the parent and the child to be separated. *See id.* § 105.001(c)(3) ("Except on a verified pleading or an affidavit . . . an order may not be rendered . . . excluding a parent from possession of or access to a child."). Furthermore, the trial court heard evidence that the mothers themselves believed that the practice of underage "marriage" and procreation was not harmful for young girls; the Department's witnesses testified that although the Department "always wants kids to be with their parents," they will only reunify children with their parents after "it's determined that [their parents] know and can express what it was in the first place that caused harm to their children." This is some evidence that the Department could not have reasonably sought to maintain custody with the mothers. Thus, evidence presented to the trial court demonstrated that the Department took reasonable efforts, consistent with extraordinarily difficult circumstances, to protect the children without taking them into custody. *Id.*

The record demonstrates that there was evidence to support the trial court's order as it relates to pubescent female children. Although I agree with the Court that the trial court abused its discretion by awarding custody of male children and pre-pubescent female children to the Department as temporary conservator, I would hold that the trial court did not abuse its discretion as to the demonstrably endangered population of pubescent girls, and to this extent would grant the Department's petition for mandamus. Because the Court does not, I respectfully dissent.

NOTES

1. ***Events Following the Texas Supreme Court's Decision in* In Re Texas Department of Family and Protective Services ("T.D.F.P.S.").** Several days after the Texas Supreme Court's decision was announced, the return of most of the children to their parents commenced. Kirk Johnson & Gretel C. Kovach, *Sect's Children Returned to Parents, But Inquiry Continues*, N.Y. TIMES, June 3, 2008. In a news conference, one member of the sect, Willie Jessop, stated that "his sect would now formally forbid any girl to marry if she was under the legal consent age in the state where she lives." *Id.* The investigation continued, however, to determine whether any underage girls had been "married" to, and required to engage in sexual relations with, men in the sect. In the ensuing months, the Texas Department of Family and Protective Services (FPS) obtained an order to remove several of the children who had returned home in May on the basis that these children had indeed been involved in underage marriages. Gretel C. Kovach, *Texas Seeking Custody of 8 Children From Sect*, N.Y. TIMES, Aug. 6, 2008. In December 2008, FPS released the findings of its investigation, indicating that twelve girls ages 12 to 15 had been involved in "spiritual marriages" to older men. Dan Frosch, *Texas Report Says 12 Girls at Sect Ranch Were Married*, N.Y. TIMES, Dec. 24, 2008. Twelve men from the sect were indicted on criminal charges pertaining to sexual relations with underage females and bigamy. Hilary Hylton, *Texas Polygamists Prep for Criminal Trial*, TIME MAG., July 26, 2009, http://www.time.com/time/nation/article/0,8599,1912477,00.html. One defendant was sentenced to 75 years in prison in 2010 for violation of laws prohibiting bigamy and sexual assault of a minor. AP WORLDSTREAM, Mar. 20, 2010. Two other defendants pled guilty, receiving sentences up to 8 years in prison. AP ALERT-TEXAS, Apr. 15, 2010. The legal proceedings against some of the defendants have not been resolved at the time of this writing. Elsewhere, sect leader Warren S. Jeffs was convicted and sentenced to ten years in prison as an accomplice to rape for his role in forcing a 14-year-old girl in Utah to marry and have sex with an older man. John Dougherty, *Polygamist Is Indicted in Assault of Child*, N.Y. TIMES, July 23, 2008. While Jeffs awaited trial in Arizona for arranging underage marriages there,

he was indicted in Texas for sexually assaulting a 17-year-old girl. *Id.*

2. *Stages of a Legal Action for Child Abuse or Neglect.* An abuse and neglect case may proceed through several stages. Once a report has been received by the state, if the information provided leads authorities to believe there is a case warranting further investigation, that investigation begins. The emergency proceedings at issue in *In re T.D.F.P.S.* allow state intervention (*e.g.,* temporary state custody of the child) in emergency circumstances, without notice and a hearing. In most states, emergency custody without a hearing may continue for only a few days, or in some instances, even less than a day. *See, e.g.,* North Carolina, N.C. GEN. STAT. § 7B-501 (2009) (allowing detention of the child for only 12 hours). In most jurisdictions, this emergency custody period may be extended after a hearing on temporary custody. For the state to justify intervention beyond the short periods of time allowed under the emergency hearing procedures, regular child protection hearings must be held. These hearings are often divided into two stages: the jurisdictional or adjudicatory stage, and the dispositional stage. In the first stage, the state must show that one of the grounds for state intervention exists *See* MINN. STAT. § 260C.007 (6), *supra* (defining child in need of protection services). If grounds for intervention are established, the court then proceeds to determine the appropriate disposition of the case (*e.g.,* supervision in the home or foster care). The state is obliged, in all but the most egregious cases, to make "reasonable efforts" to help the family remedy the problems leading to the state intervention. Thus, if the parents are abusing drugs or alcohol, they may be required to participate in appropriate treatment programs. If the parents do not understand, for example, that it is not appropriate to use corporal punishment on an infant, they may be required to attend parenting classes. If these "reasonable efforts" are unsuccessful, the state may petition for permanent severing of parental rights. The evidentiary requirements necessary for a termination of parental rights is addressed in greater depth in Subsection [5] below.

3. *The Tension Between Overly-Aggressive and Inadequate Intervention.* The goal of child protection policy is to avoid unnecessary intervention in and disruption to the family, while at the same time, intervening quickly and effectively when children are in danger. Some commentators have faith in the abilities of courts and state social workers to recognize and repair the damage caused by inadequate homes. Others express concern that unnecessary intervention in the family undermines parental authority, separating family members and traumatizing children. In *Before The Best Interests of the Child*, a team of authors argued that the state should refrain from coercive intervention except in cases where: a parent has violated immunization, education or labor laws; a parent has been convicted of a sexual offense against the child; a parent has inflicted or attempted to inflict serious bodily injury to the child; or a parent has refused to authorize non-experimental medical care, the denial of which will result in the child's death. JOSEPH GOLDSTEIN, ANNA FREUD & ALBERT SOLNIT, BEFORE THE BEST INTERESTS OF THE CHILD 193–94 (1979). Under these standards, no intervention is allowed in the following cases: sexual abuse not established in a criminal conviction; emotional maltreatment; failure to provide medical care where a child's health, but not life, is endangered; and severe neglect based upon "inadequate parenting" where no serious injury to the child has yet occurred. For a critical

analysis of this view, see Michael S. Wald, *Thinking About Public Policy Toward Abuse and Neglect of Children: A Review of "Before the Best Interests of the Child,"* 78 MICH. L. REV. 645 (1980).

A more moderate approach is represented by the *Model Standards Relating to Abuse and Neglect* (Tentative Draft 1981), drafted as part of the Juvenile Justice Standards Project, a major juvenile law reform project of the Institute of Judicial Administration (IJA) and the American Bar Association (ABA) in the 1970s. These standards allow intervention when "the child is suffering serious emotional damage" for which parents are unwilling to get treatment; the child has been sexually abused or allowed to be sexually abused by the parent; the parent's failure to supervise the child creates a substantial risk of imminent serious bodily injury; or the parent does not provide medical treatment which may "cure, alleviate, or prevent him/her from suffering serious physical harm which may result in death, disfigurement, or substantial impairment of bodily functions." Because these proposed standards would restrict state intervention to a greater extent than do the statutes of most states, the standards were never adopted by the sponsoring organizations, although 20 volumes of Juvenile Justice Standards were adopted by the ABA and IJA. For analysis of these matters by Michael S. Wald, see *State Intervention on Behalf of Neglected Children: A Search for Realistic Standards,* 27 STAN. L. REV. 985 (1975); Michael S. Wald, *State Intervention on Behalf of "Neglected" Children: Standards for Removal of Children From Their Homes, Monitoring the Status of Children in Foster Care, and Termination of Parental Rights,* 28 STAN. L. REV. 623 (1976). *See also* Robert H. Mnookin, *Foster Care — In Whose Best Interest?,* 43 HARV. EDUC. REV. 599 (1973). Professor Marsha Garrison, by contrast, argues that minimum intervention advocates have: (1) not adequately supported the claim that state intervention poses serious risks to children; (2) overlooked the importance of state intervention in cases where assistance is voluntarily sought (about one-half of child welfare caseloads); (3) proposed standards that are vague and obscure; and (4) been overly optimistic about the consequences of non-interventionist reforms. *See* Marsha Garrison, *Child Welfare Decisionmaking: In Search of the Least Drastic Alternative,* 75 GEO. L.J. 1745 (1987).

4. *The Constitutionality of Child Abuse and Neglect Legislation.* As noted above, in our discussions of *Meyer, Pierce, Prince, Yoder, Parham,* and *Bellotti,* the federal Constitution recognizes a fundamental liberty interest of parents in directing the lives of their children free from state inference. As these cases reveal, however, parental autonomy is not absolute, but is subject to limitation if state intervention is determined to be necessary either to protect the welfare (*see, e.g., Prince*) or the constitutional interests of a minor (*see, e.g., Bellotti*). How are these principles applied to abuse and neglect cases? A federal district court's opinion in a 1976 challenge to Alabama's neglect statute illustrates the proper analysis.

> [T]he Constitution includes the right to family integrity among the fundamental rights secured to all persons. This right is applied to the States through the Fourteenth Amendment and is accorded strong protection from state interference. States, in the exercise of their inherent police powers, may abrogate such rights only to advance a compelling state interest and pursuant to a narrowly-drawn statute restricted to achieve

only the legitimate objective. It is not disputed that the State of Alabama has a legitimate interest in the welfare of children. . . .

See Roe v. Conn, 417 F. Supp. 769, 779 (D.C. Ala. 1976). What types of statutory language satisfy these constitutional principles? In this class action in Alabama, the lead plaintiffs, Margaret Wambles and her son, Richard Roe, had been separated when the state forcibly removed Richard from his home. He and his mother were white and living with the mother's boyfriend, who was African-American. The apartment in which they lived was located in a black neighborhood. The boy's father, who was white, contacted child protection services, informing them that he wanted custody of the child because the boy's mother was "now living with a black man and entertaining other black men . . ." The boy's forcible removal followed, even though there existed no evidence that the child was in danger or that the care his mother provided was inadequate in any way. A judge subsequently approved the removal, giving permanent custody to the boy's father, indicating that "this habitation in a black neighborhood could be dangerous for a child," because "it was not a healthy thing for a white child to be the only (white) child in a black neighborhood." *Id.* at 775.

In reviewing this case, the federal court struck down the governing statutes as unconstitutional. It held that the Alabama statute that "authorize[d] summary seizure of a child 'if it appears that * * * the child is in such condition that its welfare requires [removal],' " violated parents' due process rights because it permits removal of a child "[w]ithout danger of immediate harm or threatened harm to the child . . ." *Id.* at 777. The court held that, without imminent harm, "the State's interest in protecting the child is not sufficient to justify a removal of the child prior to notice and a hearing." *Id.* at 778. However, in *Roe*, one a hearing took place, the judge terminated the mother's parental rights under the authority of a statute that "defines a 'neglected child' as 'any child, who, while under sixteen years of age has no proper parental care or guardianship or whose home . . . is an *unfit* or *improper* place for such child.' " *Id.* at 773 (emphasis added). Considering the constitutionality of that statute, the federal district court held:

> The Alabama statute defining "neglected" children sweeps far past the constitutionally permissible range of interference into the sanctity of the family unit. The fact that a home is "improper" in the eyes of the state officials does not necessarily mean that a child in that home is subject to physical or emotional harm. [T]he state's burden is not only to show that the child is being disadvantaged but also to show that the child is being harmed in a real and substantial way. Accordingly, this Court declares Alabama Code, Title 13, §§ 350 and 352 unconstitutional, because it violates the family integrity of Margaret Wambles and all other mothers in the class represented by her and the family integrity of Richard Roe and all other children in the class represented by him. This Court holds, as an alternative ground, that the challenged statutory provisions are unconstitutionally vague. . . . "[D]ue Process requires the state to clearly identify and define the evil from which the child needs protection and to specify what parental conduct so contributes to that evil that the state is justified in terminating the parent-child relationship." In the present case, not only is the statutory definition of neglect circular (a neglected child is any child who has no

proper parental care by reason of neglect), but it is couched in terms that have no common meaning. When is a home an "unfit" or "improper" place for a child? Obviously, this is a question about which men and women of ordinary intelligence would greatly disagree. Their answers would vary in large measure in relation to their differing social, ethical, and religious views. Because these terms are too subjective to denote a sufficient warning to those individuals who might be affected by their proscription, the statute is unconstitutionally vague.

Id. at 780. These constitutional principles presently guide legislative drafting, and constitutional scrutiny, of child abuse and neglect statutes.

Compare the statutes struck down in *Roe v. Conn* to the operative statutes in *In re T.D.F.P.S.* The Texas statutes are far more explicit in defining what harms justify state intervention and summary seizure. The Alabama statutes were held to be facially invalid. By contrast, the challenge in Texas concerned the *application* of the governing statutes. In *Roe*, the only allegation asserted by the state in justification of Richard's removal was that he was a white child living in a black neighborhood, sharing a residence with his white mother and her black boyfriend. There were no facts alleged to suggest that Richard was in danger or that his mother did not provide adequate care for him. By contrast, in *In re T.D.F.P.S.*, the allegation that underage girls were forced to "marry," and engage in sexual relations with, adult men, would, if proven, fall squarely within a category of child maltreatment known to cause substantial harm to its victims. This conduct is also prohibited under criminal statutes. (See discussion of sexual abuse in Note 6, below.) The court's concern in the Texas case was the *scope* of the removal (i.e., removing *all* children at the ranch, rather than only the teenage girls at risk of sexual abuse) and whether evidence indicated that the children were at *imminent* risk of harm, as required for emergency removal. For further commentary on the Texas case, see Catherine J. Ross, *Legal Constraints on Child-Saving: The Strange Case of the Fundamentalist Latter-Day Saints at Yearning for Zion Ranch*, 37 Cap. U.L. Rev. 361 (2008) (arguing that the state overstepped its authority in removing any children other than the pubescent girls).

5. ***Mandatory Reporting Laws.*** In 1974, Congress passed the Child Abuse Prevention and Treatment Act (CAPTA), which required states to adopt mandatory reporting statutes in order to qualify for certain categories of federal funds. Seth C. Kalichman, Mandatory Reporting of Suspected Child Abuse (2d ed. 1999). The purpose of these laws is to enable information about child maltreatment to come to the attention of state authorities. Children are unlikely to report such maltreatment. Younger children, of course, do not have the verbal skills to do so. Even older children, however, may not know how to obtain help. In addition, loyalty to family members, fear of reprisal, feelings of shame (i.e., a belief that the abuse they experienced must have been warranted by their own flaws) and other feelings and thoughts may prevent older children from disclosing what goes on behind closed doors in their families. See Myrna S. Raeder, *Enhancing the Legal Profession's Response to Victims of Child Abuse*, 24 (Spr.) Crim. Just. 12 (2009). In addition, given our society's traditional respect for family autonomy, there may not be much opportunity for others to learn about maltreatment within a particular household.

Mandatory reporting laws seek to counter these difficulties. Beginning in 1974, in compliance with the Child Abuse Prevention and Treatment Act, states could receive funding for certain services if they adopted statutes consistent with federal guidelines. The guidelines required states to develop mandatory reporting statutes. Since that time, with ongoing guidance from Congress, all states passed mandatory reporting statutes. *See* Margaret H. Meriwether, *Child Abuse Reporting Laws: Time for a Change*, 20 FAM. L.Q. 141 (1986). These statutes typically require certain classes of persons, mostly professionals, to make a report to an appropriate state agency (generally law enforcement or child protection services) when they have "reason to believe" that a child has been abused or neglected. While reporting laws initially focused on physicians, today most jurisdictions require reports from all health and mental health care personnel, social service workers, teachers and other school personnel, law enforcement officers, child care workers, and even commercial photograph developers. *See, e.g.,* CAL. PENAL CODE § 11166(e) (2009) ("Any commercial film and photographic print processor who has knowledge of or observes, within the scope of his or her professional capacity or employment, any film, photograph, videotape, negative, or slide depicting a child under the age of 16 years engaged in an act of sexual conduct . . .). California's statute lists 38 different categories of professionals mandated to report their "reasonable suspicions" that a child may be experiencing abuse or neglect. *See* CAL. PENAL CODE § 11166.7 (2009). A few states, such as New Jersey and North Carolina, impose a duty upon "any person" who has reason to suspect that abuse or neglect has occurred. *See* N.J. STAT. ANN. § 9:6-8.10 (2009); N.C. GEN. STAT. § 7B-301 (2009).

Typically, reporting statutes confer immunity upon persons who make reports, even when the reports are based on questionable information. For example, in *L.A.R. v. Ludwig*, 821 P.2d 291 (Ariz. App. 1991), a counselor who was aware of the couple's marital problems was found to be immune from tort liability for a report to child protective services alleging the father's sexual abuse of his daughter that was based entirely upon the mother's report. *See also, e.g., Storch v. Silverman*, 231 Cal. Rptr. 27 (1986) (interpreting reporting statute to confer absolute immunity upon those required to report child abuse and qualified immunity for those reporting voluntarily). For mandated reporters who do not report, however, criminal sanctions may follow. *See, e.g., Kimberley S.M. v. Bradford Central Sch.*, 649 N.Y.S.2d 588 (1996) (teacher who failed to report that she was told by student that her uncle sexually abused her could be held liable, even though report was not substantiated). *But see Wilson v. Darr*, 553 N.W.2d 579 (Iowa 1996) (priest counselor exempt from reporting duty); *Childers v. A.S.*, 909 S.W.2d 282 (Tex. App. 1995) (parents not required to report child's inappropriate sexual conduct with friend). The problem of false reporting (and statutes designed to deal with the problem) is covered in Section 6.

In most jurisdictions, the one professional *not* identified on most statutorily enumerated-lists of mandatory reporters is the attorney. A mandatory obligation for attorneys to report suspected child abuse or neglect creates a conflict between the attorney-client privilege and the policy of protecting children. This conflict could ostensibly be resolved by carving out exceptions in relevant state laws and in ethical guidelines, allowing attorneys to make reports. But, the question of whether such exceptions *should* exist is at the heart of much spirited debate. *Compare, e.g.,* Adrienne Jennings Lockie, *Salt in the Wounds: Why Attorneys Should Not Be Mandated Reporters of Child Abuse,* 36 N.M. L. Rev. 125 (2006) *with* Robin A. Rosencrantz, Student Author, *Rejecting "Hear No Evil, Speak No Evil:" Expanding the Attorney's Role in Child Abuse Reporting,* 8 Geo. J. Legal Ethics 327 (1994). In the handful of jurisdictions that do not enumerate mandatory reporters, but require that "any person" with cause to suspect that a child has been abused or neglected, an attorney may be obligated to report unless the statute indicates otherwise. *See, e.g.,* 23 Pa. Stat. § 6311 (2009) (stating that any person who has reasonable cause to suspect, based on information obtained in the course of her employment, that a child is a victim of abuse must report *except* where the information derived from "confidential communications" to a member of the clergy or an attorney).; Or. Rev. Stat. § 419B.010 (2009) (same). Some jurisdictions, however, specifically include attorneys among designated mandatory reporters. *See, e.g.,* Miss. Code Ann. § 43-21-353 (2009); Tex. Fam. Code Ann. § 261.101(c) (2009). Some statutes specify that those in particular roles, such as guardians ad litem, are required to report. *See, e.g.,* Mont. Code Ann. § 41-3-201 (2009). For additional commentary see Robert J. Lukens, *The Impact of Mandatory Reporting Requirements on the Child Welfare System,* 5 Rutgers L. Rev. 177 (2007); Robert P. Hosteller, *Child Abuse Reporting Laws and Attorney-Client Confidences: The Reality and the Specter of the Lawyer as Informant,* 42 Duke L.J. 203 (1992).

6. *Sexual Abuse.* *Civil* sexual abuse statutes apply primarily to the actions or failure to act on the part of parents and guardians. State intervention under these statutes seeks to insure that the child is safe (i.e., not in a setting where the abuse can continue to be perpetrated), and that interventions are provided to the family that, where possible, will remediate the family situation. *Criminal* sexual abuse statutes can apply to any adults who violate them. Thus, the criminal statutes reach not only to parents and guardians, but also to other family members, strangers, neighbors, teachers, clergy, or others. Frequently, in sexual abuse cases in which a family member is the perpetrator, the child protection system and law enforcement pursue parallel courses of action. In other cases, if the abuse is deemed to be less serious and the family situation remediable, the state may decide to defer criminal prosecution, attempting instead to help the family deal with its problems with therapeutic and other interventions. The civil statutes, however, frequently borrow from the state's criminal statutes in defining what types of conduct are characterized as sexual abuse. *See, e.g.,* N.C. Gen. Stat. §§ 14-27.2, 14-27.3 (2009) (all degrees of rape and crimes against nature with a juvenile); §§ 14-202.1 & 14-202.2 (2009) (taking indecent liberties with a juvenile); § 14-190.5 (2009) (preparation of obscene photographs involving a juvenile, promoting prostitution of a juvenile, and sexual exploitation).

In the context of sexual abuse, many statutes also create liability for a parent or guardian who has "failed to protect" a child from the abuse perpetrated by another. Thus, the governing statute in California defines liability as follows:

> The child has been sexually abused, or there is a substantial risk that the child will be sexually abused, as defined in Section 11165.1 of the Penal Code, by his or her parent or guardian or a member of his or her household,

or the parent or guardian has failed to adequately protect the child from sexual abuse when the parent or guardian knew or reasonably should have known that the child was in danger of sexual abuse.

CAL. WELF. & INST. CODE § 300(d) (2009).

What types of harms follow from sexual victimization of children? Empirical research demonstrates that children who have been sexually abused manifest a range of psychological symptoms such as "fear, nightmares, general post-traumatic stress disorder, withdrawn behavior. . . , cruelty, delinquency, sexually inappropriate behavior, regressive behavior, running away, general problem behaviors, and self-injurious behavior." *See* NAT'L RESEARCH COUNCIL, UNDERSTANDING CHILD ABUSE AND NEGLECT 215 (1993). Studies also reveal that some proportion of sexually-abused children experience "high levels of dissociation, a process that produces a disturbance in the normally integrative functions of memory and identity . . . Many abused children are able to self-hypnotize themselves, space out, and dissociate themselves from abusive experiences." *Id.* More recent findings indicate that a substantial proportion of sexually-abused children meet the diagnostic criteria for post-traumatic stress disorder (PTSD). *See* Regina Schuller & Patricia A. Hastings, *The Battered Child Syndrome and Other Psychological Effects of Sexual and Physical Abuse of Children: Scientific Status,* in 2 MOD. SCI. EVID. § 14:8 (David L. Faigman et al. eds. 2005-06). Other sexually-abused children, while not meeting all of the disorder's criteria, exhibit many of the symptoms. *Id.* The researchers found that children experiencing sexual abuse or more than one type of abuse (both sexual abuse and physical abuse) experienced more psychological difficulties than did children who were physically abused. A recent survey of empirical research on the impact of sexual abuse on children indicated that " 'the variables most consistently associated with more adverse impact are longer duration of abuse, force or violence accompanying the abuse, and father or father-figure as the perpetrator.' " *Id.* (quoting Penelope K. Trickett & Frank W. Putman, *Developmental Consequences of Child Sexual Abuse,* in VIOLENCE AGAINST CHILDREN IN THE FAMILY AND THE COMMUNITY 49 (Penelope K. Trickett & Cynthia J. Schellenbach eds. 1998)).

7. *Corporal Punishment and Physical Abuse.*   State statutes define physical abuse in terms of actual physical injury or risk of injury. *See, e.g.,* IND. STAT. ANN. § 31-34-1-2 (2009) (a child in need of services is one whose "physical or mental health is seriously endangered due to injury by the act or omission of the child's parent . . ."). There is wide societal disagreement about where the boundary between physical abuse and permissible corporal punishment should be drawn. Some statutes describe "excessive corporal punishment" as abuse. On the other hand, "reasonable" corporal punishment used for disciplinary purposes is generally treated as a parental privilege. *See, e.g.* COLO. REV. STAT. ANN. § 18-1-703 (2002); *State v. Jones* 747 N.E.2d. 891 (Ohio App. 2000) (criminal child abuse statute not meant to punish "reasonable . . . discipline," but only corporal punishment that causes substantial injury). Courts in civil abuse proceedings also are called upon to determine whether corporal punishment constitutes abuse.

Do switch marks and bruises qualify as excessive punishment? In *In re Ethan H.,* 609 A.2d 1222 (N.H. 1992), a trial court finding of abuse was reversed in a case involving a physician mother, who struck her seven-year-old with a belt six times when he ignored her admonition at dinner not to throw food. The court noted that the child, who had bruises still visible after five days, suffered no lasting harm. Furthermore, the doctor who evaluated the injury reported that he did not believe that the injury constituted child abuse. The mother testified that she believed in corporal punishment "done judiciously" and that such punishment was appropriate in this case. She introduced testimony that the child bruised easily and that he was playing happily outside shortly after being punished. The trial court decided that Ethan was an abused child, because "a bruise . . . by its plain meaning is an injury." It expressed concern that the mother intended to discipline him through "strappings" in the future. The appellate court rejected this reasoning, finding no evidence that the bruises constituted "harm or threatened harm to his health or welfare," the statutory requirement for a finding of abuse. *See also In the Interest of J.P.*, 692 N.E.2d 338 (Ill. App. 1998) (reversing trial court decision that mother's use of wooden spoon to paddle child as discipline was abuse).

Acceptance of corporal punishment has declined over the past generation. In recent years, critics have argued that corporal punishment by parents should be banned in this country as it has been in many European countries. There is a strong trend toward prohibiting physical punishment in schools and day care centers. Many critics point to research that indicates that physical punishment is ineffective and has detrimental effects on children. *See* Deana A. Pollard, *Banning Child Corporal Punishment*, 77 Tul. L. Rev. 575 (2003); Kandace K. Johnson, *The Parental Corporal Punishment Defense — Reasonable and Necessary or Excused Abuse?* 1998 U. Ill. L. Rev. 413.

8. *Emotional Maltreatment.* One of the most controversial areas in child abuse and neglect law is that of emotional abuse and neglect. While in the past, open-ended abuse and neglect statutes typically allowed state intervention where the family circumstances presented the risk of emotional damage to a child, see Wald (1976), *supra*, at 628–29, the trend has been in favor of limiting intervention for emotional neglect. Subdivision 15 of Minn. Stat. § 260C.007, set forth above, like many statutes today, provides that emotional neglect or "maltreatment" cannot be found absent "consistent, deliberate infliction of mental harm" that has some "observable, sustained, and adverse" effects on the child's development. State intervention would not be warranted under this statute merely on the grounds that a parent is engaged in conduct *likely* to cause emotional damage to the child; some actual symptoms of neglect or maltreatment must be shown to already exist.

There are several reasons why state statutes require particularly strong evidence of a causal link between the allegedly-damaging parental conduct and "observable, sustained, and adverse" effects of such conduct on the child in the context of emotional harm. First, the realm of parent-child emotional interactions is one in which a wide range of variation exists. Views as to what practices constitute good, adequate, or bad parenting abound, are quite subjective, and are frequently the focus of debate in our society. Given disagreement in society as to what constitutes better versus worse emotional interactions between parents and children, and in light of the degree to which personal and cultural values influence such judgments, it makes sense to restrict state intervention in families on grounds of emotional maltreatment to the clearest and most extreme cases. Second, without the limitations present in current statutory language, the concept of "emotional maltreatment" would be somewhat vague, thereby failing to give parents fair warning of societal criteria for intervention. GOLDSTEIN, FREUD & SOLNIT, *supra*, at 75; *see also* Wald (1975), *supra*, at 1000-04 (detailing harmful nature of intervention based upon vague standards more generally). Third, even when a child manifests emotional problems, it is often not possible to determine with certainty whether those problems stem from hereditary or other innate predispositions, pernicious parental conduct, environmental factors unrelated to parental conduct (e.g., victimization by bullies at school or sexual molestation perpetrated by a clergyman or teacher), or some combination of factors. Goldstein, Freud & Solnit, *supra*, at 75–77. Finally, even if the parents' treatment of the child is reprehensible, it is often unclear whether intervention will make things better or worse. Some authors, nonetheless, advocate more aggressive proactive intervention in cases of emotional maltreatment. *See, e.g.*, Judith Gorske McMullen, *The Inherent Limitations of After-the-Fact Statutes Dealing with Emotional and Sexual Maltreatment of Children*, 41 DRAKE L. REV. 483 (1992).

9. *Failure to Supervise.* A parent's failure to supervise his child is a common basis for an abuse or neglect report. *See In re JA*, 962 P.2d 173 (Alaska 1998); *In re Esmerelda B.*, 14 Cal. Rptr. 2d 179 (Cal. Ct. App. 1992). In many of these cases, there is no demonstrable harm to the child. Should harm be required before state intervention is authorized on grounds of failure to supervise? A "harm" requirement limits potentially undesirable intervention and also reduces the chance of intervention based upon personal or cultural differences between the parent and the judge or social worker. On the other hand, if actual harm is required, more children may be left in dangerous circumstances without assistance or protection.

Courts vary in response to deaths of children due to parental failure to supervise. Surrounding circumstances play an important role in the outcomes. In one Virginia case, a 21-month old child died of hyperthermia when her father left her in the family van for seven hours on a sweltering day. Kevin Kelly, father of 12 children, was responsible for the children while his wife was in Ireland. He received a token jail sentence despite the jury's recommendation that he serve a year in jail. *See* Josh White, *Father Gets Scant Jail Time in Death*, Wash. Post, Feb. 22, 2003, at A01. Kelly told the police that he thought that the child had been removed from the van by an older child. Although members of the Kellys' church testified that the family was close knit and the children were hard-working and well-behaved, neighbors reported that other children had been left in the van before. Josh White, *Inquiry Expands in Death of Girl*, WASH. POST, Jun. 1, 2003, at B1. In contrast, consider *State v. Goff*, 686 P.2d 1023 (Ore. 1984), in which a mother left her two children, ages eight and 22 months, at home alone at 9:30 p.m. while she attended a Halloween party at a local tavern. She left the older child watching television, with the telephone numbers of the tavern and a friend's residence directly across the street. Both children died in a fire that started before the mother returned at 2 a.m. An appellate court reversed the mother's conviction of child neglect, on the grounds that there was "no evidence of a substantial and unjustifiable risk that defendant should have recognized would be likely to endanger her children." The Oregon Supreme Court reversed, reinstating the criminal conviction.

10. *Exposure to Domestic Violence as Child Maltreatment.*　In recent years, empirical research has revealed that children who are living in a home in which one adult perpetrates domestic violence against another adult are harmed by exposure to that violence, even if they are not direct victims of physical abuse. *See* Lois A. Weithorn, *Protecting Children from Exposure to Domestic Violence: The Use and Abuse of Child Maltreatment Statutes*, 53 HASTINGS L.J. 1, 6–8 (2001). "Exposed children may develop a range of social, emotional, and academic problems, including aggressive conduct, anxiety symptoms, emotional withdrawal, and serious difficulties in school." *Id.* at 6. Research also reveals that in families where there is evidence of either domestic violence against an adult or child abuse, there is a high likelihood that the other form of violence will also occur. *Id.* Initial responses to this problem, unfortunately, focused on the adult victim of the violence, typically the mother, finding her liable for failing to protect the child from exposure to the violence against her. Courts frequently removed the child from the domestic violence victim's custody. In a federal case originating in New York, a court of appeals held unconstitutional the protective services agency's policy of removing children from their mothers, if their mothers were victims of domestic violence, in the absence of evidence that doing so was necessary to their welfare. *See Nicholson v. Scoppetta*, 344 F.3d 154 (2d Cir. 2003).

In situations in which a child is physically abused at the hands of the same adult perpetrating the domestic violence, a domestic violence victim might be found liable for failing to protect the child from the direct physical or sexual abuse he suffered. Gradually, states are changing their approaches to this problem, increasingly adopting the model advanced by the National Council of Juvenile and Family Court Judges in a 1999 report entitled *Effective Intervention in Domestic Violence and Child Maltreatment Cases: Guidelines for Policy and Practice.* This approach focuses on removing the *perpetrator* from the home and holding him accountable under criminal statutes while providing a range of supportive and ameliorative services to the domestic violence victim and child. For a discussion of the varying approach to these issues, see Weithorn, *supra.* For additional commentary regarding emerging approaches to this problem, see Clare Dalton & Nancy Ver Steegh, *Report from the Wingspread Conference on Domestic Violence and Family Courts*, 46 FAM. CT. REV. 454 (2008); NANCY E. DOWD ET AL. (EDS.), HANDBOOK OF CHILDREN, CULTURE, AND VIOLENCE (2006); Susan A. Kim, *Reconstructing Family Privacy*, 57 HASTINGS L.J. 557 (2006).

11. *Abuse of One Child as Evidence of Risk of Abuse of Another Child.*　Should a parent's abuse of a child constitute grounds for state intervention as to other children in the same family? Many courts have held that abuse or neglect of one child may not be established based upon facts constituting abuse or neglect of another. *See, e.g., In re Appeal in Cochise County Juvenile Action No. 5666-J*, 650 P.2d 459 (Ariz. 1982). Some courts have concluded that abuse of another child in the household is relevant, but that the judge has discretion to weigh the evidence. *See, e.g. Matter of Nicholson*, 440 S.E.2d 852 (N.C. App. 1994) (no mandate to remove child whose half-brother died at hands of mother and stepfather, victim of shaken baby syndrome). Other courts, in severe enough circumstances, find that abuse of one child establishes that other children are in "imminent danger." *See, e.g., In re S.G.*, 581 A.2d 771 (D.C. Ct. App. 1990) (sexual abuse of 12-year-old girl by stepfather since she was seven years old warranted finding of neglect as to stepfather's younger three children); *In re Christina Maria C.*, 453 N.Y.S.2d 33 (App. Div. 1982) (physical brutalizing of seven-year-old boy warranted finding that one-year-old half-sister was in imminent danger of excessive physical punishment).

12. *Federal Child Protection Legislation.* Since 1974, state child protection statutes have incorporated provisions dictated by federal legislation. Federal funds are available if states adopted prescribed standards for intervention in abuse and neglect cases. Among the provisions guiding child welfare practice for several decades are those requiring the state to make reasonable efforts to prevent removal of children from their homes as well as to reunify the family once removal occurs. Furthermore, a case plan must be developed that is designed to achieve placement in the least restrictive setting available. If the child cannot be returned home, a plan must be made for the child's adoption, legal guardianship or other permanent placement.

In 1997, Congress enacted the Adoption and Safe Families Act (AFSA) to facilitate adoption of children in foster care. The new statute amended the requirements of prior law to provide that the state may place the child in foster care without making reasonable efforts to retain her in the home in the following cases: cases involving "aggravated circumstances" (abandonment, chronic abuse, sexual abuse); cases in which the parent has committed murder or voluntary manslaughter of another child, or; cases involving felony assault resulting in serious bodily injury to any child. The new statute also directs states to initiate termination of parental rights for children who have been in foster care for 15 of the preceding 22 months.

13. *The State's Obligation to Make "Reasonable Efforts" to Remediate the Problems Leading to the Court's Finding of Abuse or Neglect.* If the court finds that one of the statutory grounds defining abuse or neglect is satisfied, and the child becomes a dependent of the court, the state takes on the obligation to provide services to the parents to assist them in ameliorating the conditions that led to the abuse or neglect finding. Minnesota's statutes set forth that obligation as follows:

> (a) Once a child alleged to be in need of protection or services is under the court's jurisdiction, the court shall ensure that reasonable efforts including culturally appropriate services by the social service agency are made to prevent placement or to eliminate the need for removal and to reunite the child with the child's family at the earliest possible time, consistent with the best interests, safety, and protection of the child. . . .

> (b) "Reasonable efforts" means the exercise of due diligence by the responsible social service agency to use appropriate and available services to meet the needs of the child and the child's family in order to prevent removal of the child from the child's family; or upon removal, services to eliminate the need for removal and reunite the family. . . . The social service agency has the burden of demonstrating that it has made reasonable efforts.

MINN. ST. ANN. § 260.012 (2009). As illustrated in Subsection [5] below, with the case of *In re Adoption/Guardianship No. J9610436*, 796 A.2d 778 (Md. 2002), in most cases, the state cannot terminate parental rights unless it has made "reasonable efforts" to help the parents ameliorate the underlying problems. There are exceptions, however, in the case of egregious abuse or neglect that does not appear susceptible to intervention. *See, e.g., In Interest of T.M.*, 641 So.2d 410 (Fla. 1994) (holding that case of severe, continuing, or egregious abuse or neglect, a state may petition for termination of parental rights, bypassing the usual attempt to remediate the problems); *Carr v. Prader*, 725 A.2d 291 (R.I. 1999) (same).

PROBLEM

Problem 10-6. The police in Eucalyptus County received a call from a 16 year old girl. She called to say that she lived in the Smithtown "Compound" in the western portion of Eucalyptus County. She said her 16 year old twin brother had just been "expelled" from the Compound, and that she was worried about him and that he might end up living on the streets. For fear of what would happen if it was learned she had made this call, the girl abruptly hung up, and the police were unable to learn of her identity.

The police contacted Child Protective Services (CPS) and together the police and CPS began to investigate the situation at the Smithtown Compound. Over 500 members of a religious sect lived in the Compound. They had their own schools and doctors and the members rarely came into contact with people outside of the Compound. The investigation revealed that the sect members engaged in polygamy, but unlike the Texas case, there was no evidence that any minor girls were encouraged or even permitted to engage in sexual relations with adult men. To the contrary, girls were taught to refrain from any sexual contact until they were over 18 years of age.

Police did find, however, that many boys aged 16 or older were "expelled" from the Compound in order to reduce the number of adult men ultimately competing for "wives." It was not clear precisely how the sect members made the decision as to which boys would stay and which would be expelled, but evidence revealed that many were expelled. Some expelled boys went to live in group housing units in local towns. The group housing units were "funded" by the Smithtown sect, which paid for rent, food, clothing and other necessities for the boys, as well as an adult supervisor who lived on the premises of each unit. There was a modest budget for other essentials for the boys (e.g., medical care). Because the boys were aged 16 or older, they were not legally mandated to attend school. Some boys managed to find menial jobs in the community to supplement the expenses paid by the sect. Once the boys were aged 18, however, they were on their own in that neither the sect or their parents provided any financial or other support for them. Once boys were "expelled" from the Compound, they no longer were permitted to have contact with anyone in the Compound. Thus, their relationships with their parents, siblings, friends, and others from the Compound were severed.

The conditions in the various group housing units varied. In some units, the supervisor took a parental interest in the boys, encouraged them to enroll in local schools, and helped them to bridge the gap between the sheltered and restrictive environment of the Smithtown Compound and the relatively unrestricted environment of the outside world. In other units, however, the supervisors did little more than insure that the boys' basic material needs were met. In still other group housing units, however, the supervisors kept for themselves some of the funds intended for the boys. In those units, the premises were often dilapidated and below standard, with inadequate heating and plumbing, for example. Even worse, in some locations, the supervisors abused the boys physically or sexually, introduced them to illegal drugs, or acted as "pimps," involving the boys in prostitution. In one unit, on 10th Avenue, six teenage boys had developed HIV infections as a result of such drug use and prostitution. They were also found to be addicted to drugs or alcohol, and to be suffering from other health problems as well. The six boys were also found to have developed a range of psychological symptoms consistent with a serious psychiatric disorder called Post-Traumatic Stress Disorder ("PTSD") as a result of those experiences. It was also found that many boys who were expelled from the Smithtown Compound ran away from the group housing units in which they were placed. They lived in varying situations on the streets or elsewhere.

If you were working for the child protection services in Eucalyptus County, would you file a petition alleging abuse or neglect of any of these boys? If so, which boys, on which statutory grounds, and which adults would you allege were liable for that abuse or neglect? Would you file any petitions against adults for abuse or neglect of any of the children still remaining at the Compound? If so, which children, which statutory grounds, and which adults would you allege were liable? What about 15 year old boys still living there? What about the 16 year old girl at the Compound who was worried about her brother?

[2]   Failure to Provide Medical Treatment for the Child

[a]   The Minor Child

NEWMARK v. WILLIAMS
Delaware Supreme Court
588 A.2d 1108 (1991)

MOORE, JUSTICE.

Colin Newmark, a three year old child, faced death from a deadly aggressive and advanced form of pediatric cancer known as Burkitt's Lymphoma . . . The Delaware Division of Child Protective Services ("DCPS") petitioned the Family Court for temporary custody of Colin to authorize the Alfred I. duPont Institute ("duPont Institute"), a nationally recognized children's hospital, to treat Colin's condition with chemotherapy. His parents, Morris and Kara Newmark, are well educated and economically prosperous. As members of the First Church of Christ, Scientist ("Christian Science") they rejected medical treatment proposed for Colin, preferring instead a course of spiritual aid and prayer. The parents rely upon provisions of Delaware law, which exempt those who treat their children's illnesses "*solely* by spiritual means" from the abuse and neglect statutes. Thus, they opposed the State's petition. *See* 10 *Del.C.* § 901(11) & 16 *Del.C.* § 907 (emphasis added). The Newmarks also claimed that removing Colin from their custody would violate their First Amendment right . . . to freely exercise their religion. . . .

The Family Court rejected both of these arguments and awarded custody of Colin to DCPS. . . . [¶] We heard this appeal on an emergency basis. . . .

. . . . In late August, 1990, the Newmarks noticed that [Colin] had lost most of his appetite and was experiencing frequent vomiting. The symptoms at first appeared occasionally but soon worsened. [¶] The Newmarks reluctantly took Colin to the duPont Institute for examination. The parties stipulated that this violated the Newmarks' Christian Science beliefs in the effectiveness of spiritual healing. The parties further stipulated that the Newmarks acted out of concern for their potential criminal liability, citing a Massachusetts case which held parents liable for manslaughter for foregoing medical treatment and treating their minor child only in accordance with Christian Science tenets.

Dr. Meek [a pediatric oncologist] . . . diagnosed Colin's condition as Burkitt's Lymphoma,[and] recommended . . . a heavy regimen of chemotherapy. [¶] Dr. Meek opined that the chemotherapy offered a 40% chance of "curing" Colin's illness. She concluded that he would die within six to eight months without treatment. The Newmarks, learning of Colin's condition only after the surgery, advised Dr. Meek that they would place him under the care of a Christian Science practitioner and reject all medical treatment for their son. . . . There was no doubt that the Newmarks sincerely believed . . . that the tenets of their faith provided an effective treatment. . . .

. . . . [W]e turn to the novel legal question whether, under any circumstances, Colin was a neglected child when his parents refused to accede to medical demands that he receive a radical form of chemotherapy having only a forty percent chance of success . . . Other jurisdictions differ in their approaches to this important and intensely personal issue. Some courts resolved the question on an *ad hoc* basis, without a formal test. . . . [Others, such as t]he California Court of Appeals in *In re Eric B. v. Ted B.*, 189 Cal. App. 3d 996, 235 Cal. Rptr. 22 (1987), employed the best interests test to determine if a child was neglected when his parents refused to permit treatment of his cancer with "mild" chemotherapy following more intense treatment. *Eric B.* weighed the gravity, or potential gravity of the child's illness, the treating physician's medical evaluation of the course of care, the riskiness of the treatment and the child's "expressed preferences" to ultimately judge whether his parents' decision to withhold chemotherapy served his "best interests." Finally, the Supreme Judicial Court of Massachusetts, in *Custody of a Minor*, 375 Mass. 733, 379 N.E.2d 1053 (1978), utilized a tripartite balancing test which weighed the interests of the parents, their child and the State to determine whether a child was neglected when his parents refused to treat his leukemia with non-invasive chemotherapy. . . .

While we do not recognize the primacy of any one of the tests employed in other jurisdictions, we find that the trial court erred in not explicitly considering the competing interests at stake. The Family Court failed to consider the special importance and primacy of the familial relationship, including the autonomy of parental decision making authority over minor children. The trial court also did not consider the gravity of Colin's illness in conjunction with the invasiveness of the proposed chemotherapy and the considerable likelihood of failure. . . .

Any balancing test must begin with the parental interest. . . . The primacy of the familial unit is a bedrock principle of law. . . . We have repeatedly emphasized that the parental right is sacred which can be invaded for only the most compelling reasons. . . .

[T]he essential element of preserving the integrity of the family is maintaining the autonomy of the parent-child relationship. . . .

Parental autonomy to care for children free from government interference therefore satisfies a child's need for continuity and thus ensures his or her psychological and physical well-being. . . . [¶] Parental authority to make fundamental decisions for minor children is also a recognized common law principle. . . . [T]he common law recognizes that the only party capable of authorizing medical treatment for a minor in "normal" circumstances is usually his parent or guardian.

Courts, therefore, give great deference to parental decisions involving minor children. . . . [¶] We also recognize that parental autonomy over minor children is not an absolute right. Clearly, the State can intervene . . . where the health and safety of the child and the public at large are in jeopardy. *See Prince[v. Mass.]*, 321 U.S. at 166–67.

. . . . [C]ourts have accepted the doctrine of *parens patriae* to justify State intervention in cases of parental religious objections to medical treatment of minor children's life threatening conditions. . . . [I]n *Prince*, 321 U.S. at 170, . . . [t]he Court found that parental autonomy, under the guise of the parents' religious freedom, was not unlimited. . . .

Parents may be free to become martyrs themselves. But it does not follow they are free, in identical circumstances, to make martyrs of their children before they have reached the age of full and legal discretion when they can make that choice for themselves. *Id.*

The basic principle underlying the *parens patriae* doctrine is the State's interest in preserving human life. . . . In its recent *Cruzan* opinion, the Supreme Court announced that the state's interest in preserving life must "be weighed against the constitutionally protected interests of the individual." 497 U.S. 261 (1990). . . .

The individual interests at stake here include both the Newmarks' right to decide what is best for Colin and Colin's own right to life. . . .

. . . .

All children indisputably have the right to enjoy a full and healthy life. Colin, a three year old boy, unfortunately lacked the ability to reach a detached, informed decision regarding his own medical care. This Court must therefore substitute its own objective judgment to determine what is in Colin's [best interests]. There are two basic inquiries when a dispute involves chemotherapy treatment over parents' religious objections. The court must first consider the effectiveness of the treatment and determine the child's chances of survival with and without medical care. . . . The court must then consider the nature of the treatments and their effect on the child. . . .

The "best interests" analysis is hardly unique or novel. Federal and State courts have unhesitatingly authorized medical treatment over a parent's religious objection when the treatment is relatively innocuous in comparison to the dangers of withholding medical care. . . . [C]ourts are reluctant to authorize medical care over parental objection when the child is not suffering a life threatening or potential life threatening illness. *See In re Green*, 292 A.2d 387, 392 (1972) (court refused to authorize corrective spine surgery on minor). . . .

The linchpin in all cases discussing the "best interests of a child" . . . is an evaluation of the risk of the procedure compared to its potential success. This analysis is consistent with the principle that State intervention in the parent-child relationship is only justifiable under compelling conditions. The State's interest in forcing a minor to undergo medical care diminishes as the risks of treatment increase and its benefits decrease. . . .

[M]ost courts which have authorized medical treatment on a minor over parental objection have . . . noted that a different situation exists when the treatment is inherently dangerous and invasive. . . . *Muhlenberg Hospital*, 128 N.J. Super. at 503, 320 A.2d at 521 ("if the disputed procedure involved a significant danger to the infant, the parents' wishes would be respected.").

Applying the foregoing considerations to the "best interests standard" here, the State's petition must be denied. . . . Colin's proposed medical treatment was highly invasive, painful, involved terrible temporary and potentially permanent side effects, posed an unacceptably low chance of success, and a high risk that the treatment itself would cause his death. The State's authority to intervene in this case, therefore, cannot outweigh the Newmarks' parental prerogative and Colin's inherent right to enjoy at least a modicum of human dignity in the short time that was left to him. . . .

Dr. Meek . . . testified that the cancer was "a very bad tumor" in an advanced disseminated state. . . . She accordingly recommended that the hospital begin an "extremely intensive" chemotherapy program scheduled to extend for at least six months. . . .

Dr. Meek prescribed "maximum" doses of at least six different types of cancer-fighting drugs during Colin's chemotherapy. This proposed "maximum" treatment represented the most aggressive form of cancer therapy short of a bone marrow transplant. The side effects would include hair loss, reduced immunological function creating a high risk of infection in the patient, and certain neurological problems. The drugs also are toxic to bone marrow.

[T]his form of chemotherapy also would adversely affect other parts of Colin's body. . . . The chemotherapy would reduce Colin's white blood count, and it would be extremely likely that he would suffer numerous infections. Colin would require multiple blood transfusions with a resultant additional risk of infection. . . .

The physicians planned to administer the chemotherapy in cycles, each of which would bring Colin near death. Then they would wait until Colin's body recovered sufficiently before introducing more drugs. . . . The doctor noted that it would then be necessary to radiate Colin's testicles if drugs alone were unsuccessful. Presumably, this would have rendered him sterile.

Dr. Meek also wanted the State to place Colin in a foster home after the initial phases of hospital treatment. Children require intensive home monitoring during chemotherapy. . . . She believed that the Newmarks, although well educated and financially responsible, were incapable of providing this intensive care because of their firm religious objections to medical treatment.

Dr. Meek ultimately admitted that there was a real possibility that the chemotherapy could kill Colin. In fact, assuming the treatment did not itself prove fatal, she offered Colin at "best" a 40% chance that he would "survive." [Dr. Meek . . . stated that the term "survival", as applied to victims of leukemia or lymphoma, refers only to the probability that the patient will live two years after chemotherapy without a recurrence of cancer.] Dr. Meek additionally could not accurately predict whether, if Colin completed the therapy, he would subsequently suffer additional tumors. . . .

No American court, even in the most egregious case, has ever authorized the State to remove a child from the loving, nurturing care of his parents and subject him, over parental objection, to an invasive regimen of treatment which offered, as Dr. Meek defined the term, only a forty percent chance of "survival". . . ."

[The court cites several cases in which the disputed treatment was ordered, but was less invasive or the prospect of success greater than in the case before it, including a New York case in which the prospect for a "cure" with treatment was 25–30%. The court distinguished this case on the ground that the Jehovah's Witness parents were not per se opposed to the prescribed chemotherapy, but to the blood transfusion that accompanied it. The court also cites an Ohio case in which the child was placed in state custody because the parents refused to consent to the amputation of the child's shoulder and arm. *In re Willmann*, 493 N.E.2d at 1383 (Ohio App.) The court acknowledges that the mandated treatment was invasive, but notes that the child had a 60% chance of survival with the surgery.]"

The aggressive form of chemotherapy that Dr. Meek prescribed for Colin was more likely to fail than succeed. [I]t was also highly invasive and could have independently caused Colin's death. Dr. Meek also wanted to take Colin away from his parents and family during the treatment phase and place the boy in a foster home. This certainly would have caused Colin severe emotional difficulties given his medical condition, tender age, and the unquestioned close bond between Colin and his family.

In sum, Colin's best interests were served by permitting the Newmarks to retain custody. . . . Parents must have the right at some point to reject medical treatment for their child. Under all of the circumstances here, this clearly is such a case. The State's important and legitimate role in safeguarding the interests of minor children diminishes in the face of this egregious record.

Parents undertake an awesome responsibility in raising and caring for their children. No doubt a parent's decision to withhold medical care is both deeply personal and soul wrenching. It need not be made worse by the invasions which both the State and medical profession sought on this record. Colin's ultimate fate therefore rested with his parents and their faith.

[Tragically, Colin died shortly after we announced our oral decision.]

NOTES

1. *Overriding Parents' Refusal of Medical Treatment.* As *Newmark* suggests, courts are generally deferential toward parents' decisions not to seek conventional medical treatment for their children. Many courts will not override parents' refusal of treatment unless the decision poses a serious threat of the child's death or permanent impairment. In *Custody of a Minor*, 379 N.E.2d 1053 (Mass. 1978); *Custody of a Minor*, 393 N.E.2d 836 (Mass. 1979), the court ordered treatment in the case of a boy named Chad Green who was diagnosed with lymphocytic leukemia. This form of childhood leukemia responds well to chemotherapy, with a very high rate of success. With the leukemia in remission, Chad's parents discontinued treatment and refused to resume treatment until ordered by the court. The court declined to allow them to supplement chemotherapy with "metabolic therapy" that included laetrile (a substance made from apricot pits) and vitamins, persuaded by the state's physicians that the laetrile would actually harm the child by causing cyanide poisoning. Rather than comply with the court's order, the parents fled with the child to Mexico, where he received laetrile treatment and died at age three. When his parents later returned to Massachusetts, they were held in contempt for having violated the court order, but were not fined or imprisoned because, in the judge's view, they had already been punished enough. *Judge Declines to Punish Parents in Laetrile Case; Father Apologizes to Judge over Couple's Actions*, N.Y. TIMES, Dec. 9, 1980, at B21.

One may contrast Chad's case with Colin's, noting the differential likelihood of success of the two forms of intervention, as well as the invasive and painful nature of the treatment in *Newmark*. In general, when asked to order treatment over a parental refusal, courts will consider: (1) the nature and potential benefits of the proposed treatment and the likelihood that those benefits will occur; (2) the potential risks, side effects, and discomforts of the proposed treatment and their likelihood of occurring; (3) the nature, potential benefits, risks, side effects, or discomforts of alternative forms of treatment, and their likelihood; and (4) the outcome for the child without treatment. The courts may also consider the reasons offered by the parents for rejecting treatment. Courts are less likely to intervene in circumstances in which loving and responsible parents object to treatment that does not have a high likelihood of success, or in which the risks may, in the view of some reasonable persons, outweigh the possible benefits. By contrast, parents who reject treatment based on obviously irrational beliefs do not fare as well. Thus, in *A.D.H. v. State Department of Human Resources*, 640 So. 2d. 969 (Ala. Civ. App. 1994), the court ordered AZT treatment for an HIV-positive child where the mother objected to treatment on the grounds that her child was not HIV-infected.

Court authority to override parental decisions in these cases derives from the states' medical neglect provisions. For example, the pertinent California statute reads:

Any child who comes within any of the following descriptions is within the jurisdiction of the juvenile court which may adjudge that person to be a dependent child of the court:

. . .

(b) The child has suffered, or there is a substantial risk that the child will suffer, serious physical harm or illness . . . by the willful or negligent failure of the parent or guardian to provide the child with adequate food, clothing, shelter, or *medical treatment* . . .

CAL. WELF. & INST. CODE § 300(b) (2009) (emphasis added). As in California, most state statutes do not provide specific guidelines for courts regarding when intervention is appropriate versus not, other than noting that, in order to justify overriding parental autonomy, the *risk* of harm (if the harm has not already occurred) must be "substantial" and the harm itself must be "serious." This, of course, leaves much room for judicial interpretation. If the court determines that the parents have failed to provide adequate medical treatment for their child, the court will find the parents neglectful, declare the child a dependent of the court, and order treatment. As in all cases in which the court takes jurisdiction over the child's welfare under the abuse and neglect statutes, it must also determine the appropriate disposition. In *Newmark*, the judge paid particular attention to the fact that if treatment was ordered, Colin would be placed in a foster home, separated from his parents in what might be his last days, weeks, or months of life.

2. *Parental Objections to Treatment on Religious Grounds.* What role do you think the Newmarks' religious beliefs played in the result? Would a court be likely to refrain from mandating treatment against parental wishes in an identical situation, with no religious claims? The California code section cited above continues with the following language:

Whenever it is alleged that a child comes within the jurisdiction of the court on the basis of the parent's or guardian's willful failure to provide adequate medical treatment or specific decision to provide spiritual treatment through prayer, the court shall give deference to the parent's or guardian's medical treatment, nontreatment, or spiritual treatment through prayer alone in accordance with the tenets and practices of a recognized church or religious denomination, by an accredited practitioner thereof, and shall not assume jurisdiction unless necessary to protect the child from suffering serious physical harm or illness. In making its determination, the court shall consider (1) the nature of the treatment proposed by the parent or guardian, (2) the risks to the child posed by the course of treatment or nontreatment proposed by the parent or guardian, (3) the risk, if any, of the course of treatment being proposed by the petitioning agency, and (4) the likely success of the courses of treatment or nontreatment proposed by the parent or guardian and agency. The child shall continue to be a dependent child pursuant to this subdivision only so long as is necessary to protect the child from risk of suffering serious physical harm or illness.

CAL. WELF. & INST. CODE § 300(b) (2009). If Colin and his family resided in California, how might the case have turned out? What role, if any, do you think the religious objections of the parents would play?

Many state statutes include an exemption to the application of abuse and neglect statutes in cases where the objection is grounded in religious beliefs. There is substantial variability from state to state with respect to such exemptions. For example, in California, the statute notes that the court "shall not assume jurisdiction unless necessary to protect the child from suffering serious physical harm or illness," indicating that if the physical harm or illness the child will suffer without treatment is not "serious," the court will not intervene. And, even if the illness or harm is serious, the consideration of the four factors enumerated in the statute may lead the court to defer to parental discretion when, for example, the proposed treatment has an extremely low likelihood of success. The relevant Arizona statute reads: "A child who in good faith is being furnished Christian Science treatment by a duly accredited practitioner shall not, for that reason *alone*, be considered to be an abused, neglected or dependent child." ARIZ. REV. STAT. ANN. § 8-201.01 (2009) (emphasis added). Thus, according to this formulation, if a parent's failure to accept medical treatment for their child does not in itself pose a risk to the child's health and well-being, the parents cannot be found to be neglectful solely because they elected not to pursue conventional treatment. However, if the child's condition becomes life-threatening or creates the risk of serious harm, disability, or suffering which the refused treatment could likely ameliorate, a court may determine that a neglect finding is appropriate. As stated by the Colorado Supreme Court in interpreting its statute:

> We believe that [section 19-1-114] does not provide an absolute defense to a finding of dependency and neglect when the child's life is in imminent danger as a result of a failure to comply with a program of medical treatment on religious grounds. . . . In our view, the meaning of the statutory language, "for that reason alone," is quite clear. It allows a finding of dependency and neglect for other "reasons," such as where the child's life is in imminent danger, despite any treatment by spiritual means. In other words, a child who is treated solely by spiritual means is not, for that reason alone, dependent or neglected, but if there is an additional reason, such as where the child is deprived of medical care necessary to prevent a life-endangering condition, the child may be adjudicated dependent and neglected under the statutory scheme.

People In Interest of D.L.E., 645 P.2d 271 (Colo. 1982). Because the provisions in the Arizona and Colorado statutes were influenced by federal regulations, many states have similar provisions.

The language of these statutes may also provide the benefit of the exemption to one or more specific religious groups. Most of these statutes were enacted in response to lobbying efforts by Christian Scientists. Consider the Delaware statute, which exempts from the definition of "neglected child" children who receive treatment by spiritual means "in accordance with the tenets and practices of a recognized church . . . by a duly accredited practitioner thereof." 16 DEL. CODE 913 (2009). In a part of the *Newmark* opinion not included above, the court suggests that this provision may violate the Establishment Clause. The court concluded that the statute was designed to benefit Christian Scientists, noting that the language (typical of many statutes) reflects the belief that only approved Christian Science practitioners can conduct spiritual healing. The court declined to resolve the constitutional question, which had not been raised by the parties, but it invited a future challenge. *See also State v. Miskimens, supra* (finding exemption to violate the Establishment Clause and Equal Protection Clause).

The American Academy of Pediatrics asserts that children should receive effective treatment despite parents' religiously-based objections "when such treatment is likely to prevent substantial harm or suffering or death." Committee on Bioethics, American Academy of Pediatrics, *Religious Objections to Medical Care,* 99 PEDIATRICS 279 (1997). For discussion of religious exemptions from the medical neglect statutes, see, e.g., Kent Greenawalt, *Objections in Conscience to Medical Procedures: Does Religion Make A Difference?* 2006 U. ILL. L. REV. 799; James G. Dwyer, *Spiritual Treatment Exemptions to Child Medical Neglect Laws: What We Outsiders Should Think,* 76 NOTRE DAME L. REV. 147 (2000); James G. Dwyer, *The Children We Abandon: Religious Exemptions to Child Welfare and Education Laws as Denials of Equal Protection to Children of Religious Objectors,* 74 N.C.L. REV. 1321 (1996); Eric W. Treene, Student Author, *Prayer-Treatment Exemptions to Child Abuse and Neglect Statutes, Manslaughter Prosecutions, and Due Process of Law,* 30 HARV. J. LEGIS. 135 (1993).

3. *Parental Liability under Criminal Child Maltreatment or Homicide Statutes.* What if the child dies as a result of the failure of parents to consent to life-saving treatment? Can the parents be held liable under the state's criminal child abuse or homicide statutes? While the religious exemption statutes described above concern the application of the civil child protection statutes, which allow courts to order treatment over parental objection, there is also language in the statutes of some states that relieves parents of *criminal* liability for failure to provide treatment to their child. For example, California's Penal Code contains an exemption from misdemeanor child abuse or neglect liability if "a parent provides a minor with treatment by spiritual means through prayer alone in accordance with the tenets and practices of a recognized church or religious denomination, by a duly accredited practitioner thereof." CAL. PENAL CODE § 270 (2009). The California Supreme Court, however, held that this section did not shield the parents from manslaughter liability under the state's felony statutes when their four year old daughter died as a result of meningitis for which the parents obtained spiritual treatment only. *Walker v. Superior Court,* 763 P.2d 852 (Cal. 1988). California is not alone in its refusal to extend its statutory exemption to shield parents from homicide liability when a child dies as a result of their refusal of conventional treatment. *See, e.g., Hall v. State,* 493 N.E.2d 433 (Ind. 1986); *see also Commonwealth v. Twitchell,* 617 N.E.2d. 609 (Mass. 1993) (holding that statutory spiritual treatment exemption did not bar prosecution of parents for manslaughter when child died, although parents could offer as affirmative defense that Attorney General had issued an opinion to the contrary on which they relied).

Other courts have held that criminal conviction under similar circumstances is unconstitutional. In *Hermanson v. State,* 604 So. 2d 775 (Fla. 1992), the Supreme Court of Florida held that the existence of a religious accommodation provision in the state's child abuse statute barred prosecution of the parents for manslaughter. Specifically, the court held that the parents did not have constitutionally adequate notice that they might be subject to criminal liability. As such, the prosecution violated the Due Process Clause. The court did not ground its decision on the Free Exercise Clause of the First Amendment. Thus, presumably, clear statutory delineation of potential criminal liability would allow prosecution of parents under similar facts. *See also State v. McKown*, 461 N.W.2d 720 (Minn. App. 1990), *aff'd* 475 N.W.2d. 63 (Minn. 1991), *cert. denied*, 502 U.S. 1036 (1992) (same result on similar facts).

Is it possible to give parents "fair notice" that their conduct of consulting a faith healer does not trigger civil or criminal liability under the child abuse statute, but may lead to liability for homicide if the child dies? One court suggested that the child's deteriorating condition should lead parents to take affirmative steps when prayer has failed to heal. In this case, the child's "common" untreated "bacterial infection which responds to the most basic of modern antibiotics," developed into "a more serious illness" that ultimately weakened the child's heart and lungs, causing death. *State v. Miskimens*, 490 N.E.2d 931, 938 (Ohio Misc. 1984).

4. *Treatment Refusals for Mature Minors.* Is parental refusal to consent to life-saving treatment for a child more readily justified if the child is an adolescent who agrees with the parents' decision on the basis of her own religious belief? In this situation, the minor may be competent to make the decision herself, and, indeed, a few courts have held that mature minors can refuse life-saving treatment. In *In re E.G.*, 549 N.E.2d. 322 (Ill. 1989), the Illinois Supreme Court reversed a trial court decision ordering blood transfusions for a 17-year-old suffering from leukemia over the objection of the minor and her mother, both Jehovah's Witnesses. Applying the state's mature minor doctrine, the court concluded that a minor who is mature enough to "exercise the judgment of an adult" has a right to refuse treatment, unless her interest is overridden by other interests. In this case, the parental interest aligned with that of the child, leading the court to conclude that treatment should not be ordered. Was the case correctly decided? One concern might be that a dependent minor is not well situated to make an autonomous medical decision, and that intervention is appropriate where her life is at stake.

Should the fact that a mature child concurred with her parents' decision to refuse treatment be available as a defense to a manslaughter charge after the child's death? One court rejected this claim brought by parents of a 16-year-old who died of untreated diabetes. *Commonwealth v. Nixon*, 761 A.2d 1151 (Pa. 2000). The parents and the child belonged to the Faith Tabernacle Church, a sect which rejected medical treatment in favor of spiritual treatment. The court rejected the parents' argument that the mature minor doctrine provided them with an affirmative defense to the manslaughter charge. For a discussion of the role that minors might play in decisions regarding the conflict between religious beliefs and recommended treatment see Jennifer E. Chen, Student Author, *Family Conflicts: The Role of Religion in Refusing Medical Treatment for Minors*, 58 Hastings L.J. 643 (2007).

PROBLEMS

Problem 10-7. As hospital legal counsel, you are told that physicians have concluded that the only real prospect for saving the life of an eight-year-old girl is a kidney transplant, and that the only potentially successful donor of likely success is her healthy twin sister. The attending physicians are confident that the children's parents will consent to such an operation if so advised by the physicians. Although it is a major operation with some risk, the healthy sister should be able to recover and live a normal life, apart from any speculative problems she might encounter if her remaining kidney were to become diseased. Should the hospital go forward with the operation on the basis of the parents' consent? If judicial authority is sought, is it likely to be granted?

Problem 10-8. Assume the same facts as Problem 10-7 except that the parents refuse to consent. The ill sister will die shortly if the operation is not performed. Should the hospital seek judicial authority for the operation? If it does, should the court grant it?

[b]   The Infant

MINNESOTA STATUTES (2009)

§ 260C.007

Subd. 6 (5) "Child in need of protection or services" means a child who is in need of protection or services because the child: . . . is medically neglected, which includes, but is not limited to, the withholding of medically indicated treatment from a disabled infant with a life-threatening condition. The term "withholding of medically indicated treatment" means the failure to respond to the infant's life-threatening conditions by providing treatment, including appropriate nutrition, hydration, and medication which, in the treating physician's or physicians' reasonable medical judgment, will be most likely to be effective in ameliorating or correcting all conditions, except that the term does not include the failure to provide treatment other than appropriate nutrition, hydration, or medication to an infant when, in the treating physician's or physicians' reasonable medical judgment: (i) the infant is chronically and irreversibly comatose; (ii) the provision of the treatment would merely prolong dying, not be effective in ameliorating or correcting all of the infant's life-threatening conditions, or otherwise be futile in terms of the survival of the infant; or (iii) the provision of the treatment would be virtually futile in terms of the survival of the infant and the treatment itself under the circumstances would be inhumane . . .

NOTES

1. *The "Baby Doe" Regulations.* Both federal and state law regulate decisions to withhold medical treatment from critically ill infants. The Minnesota statute set forth above is patterned after the Child Abuse Amendments of 1984, (amending The Child Abuse Prevention and Treatment Act of 1974 (CAPTA)). This law conditions federal financial assistance to states for programs relating to child

abuse and neglect on the incorporation of many child protection standards into state law. The federal rules relating to withholding of medically-indicated treatment apply only to infants.

Federal intervention in this area began in 1982 in the wake of public controversy over the death of a Down's Syndrome baby ("Baby Doe") whose Bloomington, Indiana parents refused to consent to necessary but routine, life-saving surgery. *In re Guardianship of Infant Doe*, No. 1-782 A157 (Ind. 1982). The Reagan Administration enacted regulations under Section 504 of the Rehabilitation Act of 1973, 29 U.S.C. § 794 (1982), which prohibits recipients of federal funds from discriminating against an "otherwise qualified" individual "on the basis of his handicap." The government claimed that by denying a handicapped newborn medical treatment that other children would receive, the hospital violated the statutory nondiscrimination provision. The Supreme Court eventually held that Congress had not intended the Rehabilitation Act to apply to such cases, thus voiding the regulations. *Bowen v. Am. Hosp. Ass'n*, 476 U.S. 610 (1986). Congress subsequently enacted the Child Abuse Amendments, grounding the mandated response to critically-ill newborns in the law of child maltreatment rather than disability law. The Minnesota statute represents typical state legislation based on the federal requirements.

There is wide variation among the conditions to which these restrictions may apply. Down's Syndrome yields a range of mental disabilities, and it is difficult to tell at birth how severe a particular child's mental disability will be. As newborns, Down's Syndrome babies suffer disproportionately from intestinal blockages (experienced by the Bloomington Baby Doe). An infant with an intestinal blockage will shortly die of starvation without corrective surgery, since he cannot ingest food — which was what happened to the Bloomington baby. Surgery to repair the intestinal blockage is relatively minor, involves little risk, and would be performed without question on an otherwise healthy baby. For children with spina bifida, surgery early in life to close the lesion to prevent infection is often indicated. Today, few would argue against performing those surgeries over the parents' objections for children with these conditions.

Other conditions where the outcome is very unpredictable present more difficulty. For example, some infants are born so prematurely that their prognosis and prospects for survival are highly uncertain. Because of advances in neonatal technology, infants whose birth weight is very low and whose respiratory and other bodily systems are not developed at birth can receive sophisticated treatment that greatly improves their chances for survival, compared to those that such infants faced a generation ago. Often, however, both the likelihood of survival and the extent of physical or mental impairment if the child survives are very uncertain. Moreover, in some cases, the treatment itself will cause great pain and discomfort for the child. In evaluating the burdens of the treatment and its uncertain outcome, people will vary in the decisions that they reach for their children. Should the law impose a particular choice?

Finally there are cases in which the prognosis is grim and the child's prospects for a minimally satisfying life are slim. The child may face a life which predictably will be very brief; or which, whatever its duration, will be filled with pain and discomfort; or the child's impairment may be so profound that she will have little ability to function mentally or physically — she may be unable to see, hear, sit, walk, understand language or relate to other people. Where the child does not face imminent death, many observers believe that the decision about treatment is not straightforward or simple. If the child cannot look forward to "a life worth living," the question becomes whether medical efforts should be made to sustain the child's life. The federal regulations reflect the view that society, or parents, should not make judgments about whether a child should receive medical treatment based upon the quality of life that the child can expect. On the other hand, adults, at least in practice, are able to (and do) make this decision for themselves. Should newborn cases be treated differently from those involving treatment of older children?

2. *The Debate About Non-Treatment.* Recent years have seen considerable efforts to ensure through advanced directives that adult patients can decline additional medical care in appropriate circumstances. Indeed, the Supreme Court has suggested that it is their right, at least where they express their wishes clearly enough. *Cruzan v. Missouri Dep't Health*, 497 U.S. 261 (1990). The extension of this principle to newborns is challenging. The right to refuse life-saving treatment is grounded in the principle of autonomy. In that newborns cannot express their own views, and do not have a record of competence and expressed preferences to use as a guidepost for what they may have wanted in a given situation, autonomy-based decision theories cannot decide decisionmaking. *See* Ira Ellman, *Can Others Exercise an Incapacitated Patient's Right to Die?*, 20 Hastings Center Rep., Jan./Feb. 1990, at 47.

The exclusion of "quality of life" considerations under federal law does not reflect the norms of the medical profession. A study in a neonatal intensive care unit over a 3-year period in the 1990s suggested that medical care is withdrawn or withheld resulting in death only in the most extreme cases, but that quality-of-life concerns affect the decisions in many cases. Stephen N. Wall & John Colin Partridge, *Death in the Intensive Care Nursery: Physician Practice of Withdrawing or Withholding Life Support*, 99 Pediatrics 64 (1997). A large percentage of the decisions were based on a conclusion that treatment was "futile" based on imminent death — which is a basis of withholding treatment under the regulations. The American Medical Association Code of Medical Ethics, § 217 (1994), also provides that the quality of life of a severely disabled newborn is a factor to be considered in treatment decisions. Scholarly commentary has also been critical of the federal law, in large part because of its failure to allow adequate consideration of quality of life factors. *See, e.g.*, Nancy K. Rhoden, *Treatment Dilemmas for Imperiled Newborns: Why Quality of Life Counts*, 58 S. Cal. L. Rev. 1283 (1985). *See also*, Martha Minow, *Beyond State Intervention in the Family: For Baby Jane Doe*, 18 U. Mich. J.L. Ref. 933 (1985) (criticizing adversarial structure promoted by state intervention mechanisms and suggesting strategies for building more trust in medical decisionmaking).

What happens if parents choose to treat a child who meets the criteria for withdrawal? Ordinarily a parent's decision controls, but under some circumstances courts will override a parental decision to treat. In *In re K.I.*, 735 A.2d 448 (D.C. Ct. 1999), a District of Columbia appellate court upheld an order not to aggressively resuscitate a neglected two-year-old over the mother's objection. For some, non-treatment decisions are intertwined with political, ideological, and religious views, with some arguing that non-treatment violates the infant's right to life. In a highly publicized case in Virginia, a mother insisted on continuing aggressive treatment for her anencephalic infant. *Matter of Baby "K"*, 16 F.3d 590 (4th Cir. 1994). This child had a sufficiently developed brainstem that her basic respiratory functions could continue unassisted for some time. The court held that the hospital was obliged to place the child on a ventilator when needed, under the federal Emergency Medical Treatment and Active Labor Act, a statute that had been passed to deal with a very specific problem: hospital "dumping" of patients with no medical insurance. It requires covered hospitals to provide stabilizing treatment in emergency medical situations, to ensure that they do not turn away uninsured patients. The language of the act can nonetheless be read as requiring the hospital to provide any person with an "emergency" medical condition with either stabilizing treatment or appropriate transfer to another institution. By considering the child's episodic bouts with respiratory distress, rather than the anencephaly, as the relevant medical condition, the court concluded that the Act required repeated treatment by the hospital. *See* Flannery, *One Advocate's Viewpoint: Conflicts and Tensions in the Baby K Case*, 23 J.L. MED. & ETHICS 7 (1995) (discussion by attorney for Baby K's mother).

The article that initially focused attention on the Baby Doe issue is Raymond S. Duff & A.G.M. Campbell, *Moral and Ethical Dilemmas in the Special-Care Nursery*, 289 N.E.J. MED. 890 (1973). Other influential works include: ARTHUR CAPLAN ET AL., COMPELLED COMPASSION: GOVERNMENT INTERVENTION IN THE TREATMENT OF CRITICALLY ILL NEWBORNS (1992); PRESIDENT'S COMMISSION FOR THE STUDY OF ETHICAL PROBLEMS IN MEDICINE AND BIOMEDICAL AND BEHAVIORAL RESEARCH, DECIDING TO FOREGO LIFE SUSTAINING TREATMENT (1983) (containing section specifically on newborns); PAUL RAMSEY, ETHICS AT THE EDGES OF LIFE (1978) (rejecting assessments of the baby's probable quality of life as a basis for treatment decisions); John Robertson, *Involuntary Euthanasia of Defective Newborns: A Legal Analysis*, 27 STAN. L. REV. 213 (1975).

PROBLEM

Problem 10-9. Baby Jane is born on Nov. 1, and her parents come to consult you shortly thereafter. The child has a number of severe congenital defects. The parents and their doctors have agreed not to perform surgery on her, but the doctors are nervous because of a recent call to the hospital from county welfare department officials who are aware of the baby as a result of a complaint filed with them by a nurse on the hospital staff. The parents anticipate a neglect proceeding may be brought.

Consultations with the attending physicians reveal that the child was born with a lesion high on her back, exposing the spinal cord (spina bifida). There is also an abnormality on the spine above the lesion. She has massive hydrocephalus (fluid on the brain) and very little brain tissue as a result of the damage caused by the hydrocephalus. Regardless of what care is provided, the physicians believe the child will be so severely retarded she will never talk or understand speech. They are not certain that she will ultimately be able to recognize people or be able to smile. As a result of spinal cord damage, she will never be able to walk, sit up or become continent. Another physician with experience treating such children, however, gives a more optimistic prognosis regarding her intellectual development, saying that some similar babies he had cared for ultimately developed I.Q.s of 60 or 70. He is not confident that this child will be so fortunate, however.

Aggressive treatment would ultimately involve 30 to 45 surgeries to deal with problems such as curvature of the spine and urinary problems, as well as shunts to drain the fluid from the brain. The immediate question is whether to perform surgery to close the opening on the back, to prevent infection which could be fatal, and to drain the fluid on the brain, to make the baby easier to handle and prevent further damage. The attending physicians estimate that with aggressive treatment, the child would still probably not survive more than a year, although survival up to 20 years is conceivable. Without aggressive treatment, her life span will probably be between six weeks and six months.

As a result of their discussions with physicians, the parents have concluded that the child would be better off without treatment. On the other hand, if they will be compelled ultimately to authorize surgery, they would prefer to begin immediately, so as to give their daughter the best chance of success. They want to know their prospects for resisting legal challenges to their right to decide their daughter's treatment. What do you advise under the federal standards adopted by Minnesota?

[3]   Abuse or Neglect of the Fetus

[a]   Court-Ordered Caesareans and Other Mandated Treatment of Mothers

Can medical treatment of a parent be ordered to save the life of her child? The issue sometimes arises when a pregnant woman refuses medical treatment (often a caesarean section) when that procedure is necessary for the child to survive. Although trial courts have occasionally ordered caesareans against the wishes of the mother, appellate courts typically reject efforts to override the decisions of competent women refusing invasive medical procedures. In explaining this position, an Illinois court held: "a woman's competent choice in refusing medical treatment as invasive as a caesarean section during her pregnancy must be honored, even in circumstances where the choice may be harmful to her fetus." *In re Baby Boy Doe*, 632 N.E.2d 326, 326 (Ill. App. Ct. 1994). The court recognized that the right to refuse unwanted treatment was a protected liberty interest under the Due Process clause and "is not diminished during pregnancy." While "the fetus has the legal right to begin life with a sound mind and body, assertable against third parties after it has been born alive," the court held, this right "is not assertable against its mother" who "cannot be compelled to do or not do anything merely for the benefit of her unborn child." *Id.* at 332. The *Doe* court emphasized that one person cannot be forced to undergo medical procedures for the purpose of benefitting another person "even where the two persons share a blood relationship, and even where the risk to the first person is perceived to be minimal and the benefit to the second person may be great." *Id.* at 332. It also rejected the argument that the viable fetus had rights under *Roe v. Wade*, 410 U.S. 113 (1973), that supported mandatory treatment. *See also In re A.C.*, 573 A.2d 1235 (D.C. Ct. App. 1990) (overturning lower court's order of Cesarean section where mother heavily sedated and dying of cancer). *But see Jefferson v. Griffin-Spalding Cty. Hosp. Auth.*, 274 S.E.2d 457 (Ga. 1981) (compelling caesarian procedure).

The Committee on Ethics of the American College of Obstetricians and Gynecologists has issued an opinion on Maternal-Fetal Conflict, which concludes in part:

> The use of courts to resolve . . . conflict [between maternal and fetal interests] is almost never warranted. Obstetricians should refrain from performing procedures that are unwanted by pregnant women. The use of judicial authority to implement treatment regimens in order to protect the fetus violates the pregnant woman's autonomy. Furthermore, inappropriate reliance on judicial authority may lead to undesirable societal consequences, such as the criminalization of noncompliance with medical recommendations.

ACOG Committee Op. No. 55, Patient Choice: Maternal-Fetal Conflict (Oct. 1987). *See also* American Medical Association Board of Trustees Report, *Legal Interventions During Pregnancy: Court-Ordered Medical Treatments and Legal Penalties for Potentially Harmful Behavior by Pregnant Women*, 264 JAMA 2663 (1990) (allowing physicians to seek judicial intervention where the invasion of bodily integrity and health risk to the mother is minimal and the harm to the fetus without surgery is great). For commentary on the issues, see Nancy Rhoden, *The Judge in the Delivery Room: The Emergence of Court-Ordered Caesarians*, 74 CAL. L. REV. 1951 (1986); Martha Field, *Controlling the Woman to Protect the Fetus*, 17 L. MED. & HEALTH CARE 114 (1989); John Robertson, *Procreative Liberty and the Control of Conception, Pregnancy, and Childbirth*, 69 VA. L. REV. 405 (1983).

The issue of court-ordered treatment for pregnant women can arise in other contexts as well. For example, some courts have ordered blood transfusions over the mother's objections. *See, e.g., Raleigh Fitkin-Paul Moran Mem. Hosp. v. Anderson*, 201 A.2d 537 (N.J.), *cert. denied*, 377 U.S. 985 (1964); *In re Jamaica Hosp.*, 491 N.Y.S.2d 898 (Sup. Ct. 1985); *Crouse Irving Mem. Hosp. v. Paddock*, 485 N.Y.S.2d 443 (Sup. Ct. 1985). Many courts see no difference between transfusions and caesarean sections and decline to override the mother's refusal of blood transfusion, which is usually based on religious beliefs. *See In re Fetus Brown*, 689 N.E.2d 397 (Ill. App. 1997) (reversing trial court order of blood transfusion holding that competent woman had virtually absolute right to refuse.) Should HIV-positive pregnant women be ordered to submit to perinatal administration of AZT, which can substantially reduce the risk of HIV infection in the child? Most commentators argue against mandatory treatment, in part because of the risks of AZT treatment to the mother. *See, e.g.,* Michael A. Grizzi, *Compelled Antiviral Treatment of HIV Positive Pregnant Women*, 5 UCLA WOMEN'S L. J. 473 (1995); *see also* April A. Cherry, *The Free Exercise Rights of Pregnant Women Who Refuse Medical Treatment*, 69 TENN. L. REV. 563 (2002) (arguing that pregnant women have a constitutional right to refuse treatment which trumps any state interest in the viable fetus).

[b]   Drug Abuse by Pregnant Women

ANGELA M.W. v KRUZICKI
Wisconsin Supreme Court
561 N.W. 2d. 729 (1997)

BRADLEY, JUSTICE.

[Blood test performed on a woman pregnant with a viable fetus confirmed her obstetrician's suspicion that she was using cocaine or other drugs. The physician reported his concerns to county authorities. The county filed a petition in the juvenile court, alleging that the woman's fetus was in need of protection or services because of neglect that seriously endangered the physical health of the child, pursuant to Section 48.13(10) of the Wisconsin Statutes, ordering the detention of the child, which necessarily required the detention of the woman. The juvenile court rejected the mother's claims that it lacked jurisdiction over her and her viable fetus and that the court's authority would violate the constitutional guarantees of procedural and substantive due process, as well as equal protection. The court of appeals determined that the juvenile court did not exceed its jurisdiction in this case, reasoning that the U. Supreme Court, the Wisconsin legislature, and this court have each articulated public policy considerations supporting the conclusion that a viable fetus is a "child" under the Children in Need of Protection or Services [CHIPS] statute. The court also held that application of the CHIPS statute to the petitioner did not deprive her of equal protection or due process, since the statute was a properly tailored means of vindicating the State's compelling interest in the health, safety, and welfare of a viable fetus.]

We stress at the outset [that] this case is one of statutory construction. The issue presented is whether a viable fetus is included in the definition of "child" provided in Wis. Stat. § 48.02(2) . . . [¶] The [statute] confers on the juvenile court "exclusive original jurisdiction over a child alleged to be in need of protection or services which can be ordered by the court. . . ." § 48.13. A "child" is defined . . . as "a person who is less than 18 years of age." § 48.02(2). The [pregnant woman, Angela M.W.] contends that the Chapter 48 definition of "child" [means] a person born alive. . . . In contrast, the County asserts that courts . . . have determined that "child" and "person" are ambiguous terms. [T]he County contends that we [must] to look beyond the [statutory language] for the meaning of "child." . . .

[The court note that it had] previously held that a viable fetus is a "person" for purposes of Wisconsin's wrongful death statute[, but that the U.S. Supreme Court, in Roe, has concluded that a fetus is not a "person" under the Fourteenth Amendment. It noted that, in construing language to identical to that in § 48.02(2), Ohio and South Carolina have arrived at conflicting conclusions as to whether a fetus is "child" under the statute.].

[The court looks to the legislative history, and observes that the "heated dialogue and intense debate" that would expected it if intended to "include fetus within the definition of "child," did not occur. It looked next at the meaning of "child" in conjunction with other relevant sections of the Code. In so doing, it found] a compelling basis for concluding that the legislature intended a "child" to mean a human being born alive. Code provisions dealing with taking a child into custody, providing parental notification, and releasing a child from custody would require absurd results if the § 48.02(2) definition of "child" included a fetus. Each of the provisions addresses a critical juncture in a CHIPS proceeding. Yet, each also anticipates that the "child" can at some point be removed from the presence of the parent. It is manifest that the separation envisioned by the statute cannot be achieved in the context of a pregnant woman and her fetus.

. . . [W]e agree with the United States Supreme Court that declaring a fetus a person for purposes of the wrongful death statute does no more than vindicate the interest of parents in the potential life that a fetus represents. Indeed, we have recognized that until born, a fetus has no cause of action for fetal injury . . . [¶] Similarly, we reject the County's argument that the protections accorded fetuses by property law have a bearing on the . . . definition of "child." . . . "[P]roperty law does not confer the full rights of personhood upon the fetus. Instead, it creates a means of fulfilling the intentions of testators by protecting the right of a fetus to inherit property upon live birth". . . .

[The legislature referred specifically to an "unborn child" in Wis. St. § 940.04(2)(a), which criminalizes the intentional destruction of an unborn child", thereby demonstrating] the ease and clarity with which the legislature may, if it so chooses, apply a statute to the unborn. In its several amendments to the Children's Code, the legislature has had ample opportunity to state in similarly clear and unambiguous terms that a fetus is a child. Yet, [it] has failed to take such action. . . .

. . . [¶] . . . [W]e conclude that the legislature did not intend to equate a fetus with a child . . . [¶] Finally, the confinement of a pregnant woman for the benefit of her fetus is a decision bristling with important social policy issues. [T]he legislature is in a better position than the courts to gather, weigh, and reconcile the competing policy proposals addressed to this sensitive area of the law. . . .

NOTES

1. Prenatal Substance Abuse.   The problem of substance abuse by pregnant women has generated a great deal of legal and policy interest in recent years. The risks to the child of maternal drug use are serious. Research reveals risks to the pregnancy (e.g., spontaneous abortion, premature delivery or other serious complications of delivery), to the fetus (e.g., abnormalities in organ development, inadequate oxygen to the brain), to the newborn (e.g., low birth weight, birth defects, abnormalities of heart and brain; breathing difficulties, drug withdrawal symptoms); and to the child in infancy (e.g., higher rates of Sudden Infant Death Syndrome). Lee M. Robins & James L. Mills eds., *Effects of In Utero Exposure to Street Drugs* 83 Am. J. Pub. Health 9 (Supp. 1993) (report funded by National Inst. of Child Health and Human Development in response to request by U.S. Sen. Comm. on Appropriations). For updated research findings, see the website of National Institute of Drug Abuse on prenatal effects of use of cocaine, heroin, inhalants, marijuana, MDMA (i.e., "ecstasy"), methamphetamine, and nicotine at http://www.nida.nih.gov/consequences/prenatal/.

Should civil or criminal child abuse laws extend to prenatal drug abuse? Often, as in *Angela M.W.*, the issue is framed as a jurisdictional question of whether harm done to a fetus is injury to a "child" under the statute. Most courts interpret statutes that are silent about prenatal abuse consistent with the Wisconsin court, holding that a fetus is not a "child" in the absence of evidence that the legislature intended this meaning. In an Oklahoma case somewhat similar to *Angela M.W.*, the trial court took temporary emergency custody of a seven month fetus as a "deprived child," after the mother was arrested for the manufacture and possession of methamphetamine. The court ordered the mother to submit to random drug tests, inspections of her living quarters, and weekly pre-natal medical visits and removed the child from her custody shortly after birth, based on the arrest evidence. The Oklahoma Supreme Court reversed the order, concluding that neither the language of the statute nor legislative intent supported defining a viable fetus as a "child" under the Children's Code. *Starks v. Oklahoma*, 18 P.3d 342 (Okla. 2001). *See also People ex rel. H.*, 74 P.3d 494 (Colo. App. 2003) (holding fetus is not a "child" under civil child abuse and neglect statute); *Reinesto v. Superior Court*, 894 P.2d 733 (Ariz. App. 1995) (fetus is not a "child" under criminal child abuse statute); *Commonwealth v. Welch*, 864 S.W.2d 280 (Ky. 1993) (same). South Carolina is the notable exception in its holdings on this question. *See Whitner v. State*, 492 S.E.2d 777 (S.C. 1996) (viable fetus is a "person under the age of eighteen," under child abuse statute).

Some courts decline to frame the issue in this way, focusing instead on whether a positive drug toxicology test on the mother and newborn can be the basis of an abuse finding. In *In re Baby Boy Blackshear*, 736 N.E.2d 462 (Ohio 2000), the Ohio Supreme Court concluded that the plain language of the statute applied to the case of a mother and infant who tested positive for cocaine. Under Ohio's abuse statute, an abused child was a child who "because of the acts of his parents . . . suffers physical or mental injury." The court determined that this provision justified finding the drug-exposed infant to be abused on the basis of the mother's conduct before his birth. New York's highest court concluded that a post-birth positive toxicology test alone was not sufficient to support a finding of abuse. *In re Matter of Dante M.*, 661 N.E. 2d. 138 (N.Y. 1995). However, toxicology results could be considered along with other evidence (in the case, the child's low birth weight, the mother's history of drug use, and testimonial evidence from relatives) to support an abuse finding. Some state legislatures have enacted special laws addressing the subject. See, e.g., FLA. STAT. ANN. § 39.01(32)(g)(1) (2009) (dependency jurisdiction can be grounded in child's exposure to a controlled substance or alcohol found at birth in "child's blood, urine, or meconium" not resulting from medical treatment administered to the mother or the newborn infant"); MASS. GEN. LAWS ANN. ch. 119, § 51A (2009) (child who has a "physical dependence upon an addictive drug at birth" can be determined to be abused under statute). In some states, standards for the termination of parental rights have been expanded to specifically include drug dependency which the parent has failed to have treated successfully. *See* MINN. STAT. § 260C.301 (2009), Section C[5], *infra.*

Efforts by prosecutors to use existing criminal child abuse statutes in prenatal drug use cases have generally not been successful. Some prosecutors have charged mothers under criminal statutes prohibiting the delivery of a controlled substance to a minor. The Supreme Court of Florida reversed the conviction of Jennifer Johnson, whose child was born with traces of cocaine in its blood. *Johnson v. State*, 602 So. 2d 1288 (Fla. 1992). The Court held that such a statute does not apply to the "delivery" of cocaine through the umbilical cord after birth but before the severing of the cord. This conclusion was supported by the provisions of the Florida child abuse statute quoted above, in which the purpose to treat maternal drug use as a public health issue and not as a crime is clear. *See also State v. Hardy*, 469 N.W.2d 50 (Mich. 1991) (same theory, same result). However, the South Carolina Supreme Court (which earlier found a fetus to be a child under the state's child abuse statute) upheld the homicide conviction of a mother whose child was stillborn where the prosecution demonstrated that the death was caused by the effect of the mother's ingestion of cocaine during pregnancy. *State v. McKnight*, 576 S.E.2d 168 (S.C. 2003). The Court concluded that the mother's use of cocaine with the knowledge she was pregnant was sufficient to constitute extreme indifference to human life.

A few academic commentators have argued for increased regulation of pregnancy. *See, e.g.*, Janet Stepherson, *Stopping Fetal Abuse with No-Pregnancy and Drug Treatment Conditions*, 34 Santa Clara L. Rev. 295 (1994) (urging criminal prosecution of those pregnant women who abuse substances during pregnancy). Others argue against punitive measures, in favor of better treatment programs. *See, e.g.*, Ellen M. Weber, *Child Welfare Interventions for Drug-Dependent Pregnant Women: Limitations of a Non-Public Health Response*, 75 U.M.K.C. L. Rev. 789 (2007) (examining the disconnect between child welfare intervention with drug-dependent pregnant women and the current state of scientific knowledge about how to ameliorate the problem and best protect the fetus); Linda Fentiman, *The New "Fetal Protection": The Wrong Answer to the Crisis of Inadequate Health Care for Women and Children*, 84 Denv. U. L. Rev. 537, 551–68 (2006) (critiquing a range of approaches to pregnant women's use of drugs or alcohol during pregnancy, including criminal prosecution and civil commitment).

2. *Maternal Liability for Other Conduct Potentially Injurious to a Fetus.* Medical experts have estimated that alcohol consumption by pregnant women causes a range of serious problems including mental retardation. *See* Am. Acad. Child & Adol. Psychiatry, *Drinking Alcohol in Pregnancy: Fetal Alcohol Effects*, http://www.aacap.org/cs/root/facts_for_families/drinking_alcohol_in_pregnancy_fetal_alcohol_effects. Pregnant women who smoke are also potential targets of regulations. What about pregnant women who maintain poor nutrition? Should a line be drawn between behavior that threatens harm to the fetus and is itself illegal (drug use) and behavior which may harm the fetus but is generally allowed (smoking and drinking)?

3. *Detection of Maternal Drug Use and the Fourth Amendment.* Does the state's role as protector of children justify policies of detecting prenatal drug use by mothers through involuntary testing? The Supreme Court struck down a public hospital policy of testing pregnant patients suspected of using drugs on Fourth Amendment grounds. *Ferguson v. City of Charleston*, 532 U.S. 67 (2001). The policy was created by the hospital in cooperation with the police and public officials. Women were tested without their knowledge or consent and positive results were reported to the police. Several women who were arrested after testing positive for cocaine challenged the policy, arguing that the warrantless and nonconsensual drug tests were unconstitutional searches. The Supreme Court agreed.

4. *Alternative Approaches to Maternal Substance Use During Pregnancy.*   Many authors have argued for an approach that views pregnant women's substance abuse as a public health problem, for which a therapeutic approach is most likely to be successful in protecting the health of the children born to these women. Elizabeth E. Coleman & Monica K. Miller, *Assessing Legal Responses to Prenatal Drug Use: Can Therapeutic Responses Produce More Positive Outcomes than Punitive Responses?*, 20 J. L. & HEALTH 35, 62 (2007); Janet W. Steverson & Traci Rieckmann, *Legislating For The Provision Of Comprehensive Substance Abuse Treatment Programs For Pregnant and Mothering Women*, 16 DUKE J. GENDER L. & POL'Y 315 (2009). Currently, there are few options for those pregnant women who wish to treat their drug and alcohol problems. Good programs are few, most have waiting lists, and few will accept pregnant women. Costs can be prohibitive for those without good health insurance. Some authors argue that punitive responses, such as bringing the weight of the criminal justice system to bear, drives these women underground, away from any prenatal health care services because they fear detection. For a summary of key issues and draft policy, see Rommel P. Cruz, *The Greatest Source of Wealth: Washington State's Response to Prenatal Substance Abuse*, 41 GONZAGA L. REV. 1 (2005-06).

PROBLEM

Problem 10-10.   Jennifer has been found guilty of child abuse for taking heroin while pregnant. The maximum sentence possible is a 30-year jail term. The judge, however, sentences her to 15 years' probation. One of the terms of her probation is that she submit to random drug testing, for one year, and that if she becomes pregnant again, she will submit to a supervised prenatal program. Is the sentence constitutional? Is it wise?

[4]   State Duties Arising from its Child Protection System

DESHANEY v. WINNEBAGO COUNTY DEPARTMENT OF SOCIAL SERVICES
United States Supreme Court
489 U.S. 189 (1989)

CHIEF JUSTICE REHNQUIST delivered the opinion of the Court.

Petitioner is a boy who was beaten and permanently injured by his father, with whom he lived. The respondents are social workers and other local officials who received complaints that petitioner was being abused by his father and had reason to believe that this was the case, but nonetheless did not act to remove petitioner from his father's custody. Petitioner sued respondents claiming that their failure to act deprived him of his liberty in violation of the Due Process Clause of the Fourteenth Amendment to the United States Constitution. We hold that it did not.

I

The facts of this case are undeniably tragic. Petitioner Joshua DeShaney was born in 1979. In 1980, a Wyoming court granted his parents a divorce and awarded custody of Joshua to his father, Randy DeShaney. The father shortly thereafter moved to . . . Winnebago County, Wisconsin, taking the infant Joshua with him. There he entered into a second marriage, which also ended in divorce.

The Winnebago County authorities first learned that [Joshua] might be a victim of child abuse in January 1982, when his father's second wife complained to the police, at the time of their divorce, that he had previously "hit the boy causing marks and [was] a prime case for child abuse." . . . The Winnebago County Department of Social Services (DSS) interviewed the father, but he denied the accusations, and DSS did not pursue them further. In January 1983, Joshua was admitted to a local hospital with multiple bruises and abrasions. The examining physician suspected child abuse and notified DSS, which immediately obtained an order from a Wisconsin juvenile court placing Joshua in temporary custody of the hospital. Three days later, the county convened an ad hoc "Child Protection Team" — consisting of a pediatrician, a psychologist, a police detective, the county's lawyer, several DSS caseworkers, and various hospital personnel — to consider Joshua's situation. At this meeting, the Team decided that there was insufficient evidence of child abuse to retain Joshua in the custody of the court. The Team did, however, decide to recommend several measures to protect Joshua, including enrolling him in a preschool program, providing his father with certain counseling services, and encouraging his father's girlfriend to move out of the home. Randy DeShaney entered into a voluntary agreement with DSS in which he promised to cooperate with them in accomplishing these goals.

Based on the recommendation of the Child Protection Team, the juvenile court dismissed the child protection case and returned Joshua to the custody of his father. A month later, emergency room personnel called the DSS caseworker handling Joshua's case to report that he had once again been treated for suspicious injuries. The caseworker concluded that there was no basis for action. For the next six months, the caseworker made monthly visits to the DeShaney home, during which she observed a number of suspicious injuries on Joshua's head; she also noticed that he had not been enrolled in school and that the girlfriend had not moved out. The caseworker dutifully recorded these incidents in her files, along with her continuing suspicions that someone in the DeShaney household was physically abusing Joshua, but she did nothing more. In November 1983, the emergency room notified DSS that Joshua had been treated once again for injuries that they believed to be caused by child abuse. On the caseworker's next two visits to the DeShaney home, she was told that Joshua was too ill to see her. Still DSS took no action.

In March 1984, Randy DeShaney beat 4-year-old Joshua so severely that he fell into a life-threatening coma. Emergency brain surgery revealed a series of hemorrhages caused by traumatic injuries to the head inflicted over a long period of time. Joshua did not die, but he suffered brain damage so severe that he is expected to spend the rest of his life confined to an institution for the profoundly retarded. Randy DeShaney was subsequently tried and convicted of child abuse.

Joshua and his mother brought this action under [§ 1983] in the United States District Court for the Eastern District of Wisconsin against respondents Winnebago County, its Department of Social Services, and various individual employees of the Department. The complaint alleged that respondents had deprived Joshua of his liberty without due process of law, in violation of his rights under the Fourteenth Amendment, by failing to intervene to protect him against a risk of violence at his father's hands of which they knew or should have known. The District Court granted summary judgment for respondents.

The Court of Appeals for the Seventh Circuit affirmed . . . holding that petitioners had not made out an actionable § 1983 claim. . . .

. . . We now affirm.

II

. . . Petitioners contend that the State deprived Joshua of his liberty interest in "free[dom] from . . . unjustified intrusions on personal security," . . . by failing to provide him with adequate protection against his father's violence. The claim is one invoking the substantive rather than procedural component of the Due Process Clause. . . .

But nothing in the language of the Due Process Clause itself requires the State to protect the life, liberty, and property of its citizens against invasion by private actors. The Clause is phrased as a limitation on the State's power to act, not as a guarantee of certain minimal levels of safety and security. It forbids the State itself to deprive individuals of life, liberty, or property without "due process of law," but its language cannot fairly be extended to impose an affirmative obligation on the State to ensure that those interests do not come to harm through other means. Nor does history support such an expansive reading of the constitutional text. . . . Its purpose was to protect the people from the State, not to ensure that the State protected them from each other. The Framers were content to leave the extent of governmental obligation in the latter area to the democratic political processes.

Consistent with these principles, our cases have recognized that the Due Process Clauses generally confer no affirmative right to governmental aid, even where such aid may be necessary to secure life, liberty, or property interests of which the government itself may not deprive the individual. *See, e.g., Harris v. McRae*, 448 U. S. 297, 317–318 (1980) (no obligation to fund abortions or other medical services) . . . If the Due Process Clause does not require the State to provide its citizens with particular protective services, it follows that the State cannot be held liable under the Clause for injuries that could have been averted had it chosen to provide them. . . .

Petitioners contend, however, that even if the Due Process Clause imposes no affirmative obligation on the State to provide the general public with adequate protective services, such a duty may arise out of certain "special relationships" created or assumed by the State with respect to particular individuals. . . . Petitioners argue that such a "special relationship" existed here because the State knew that Joshua faced a special danger of abuse at his father's hands, and specifically proclaimed, by word and by deed, its intention to protect him against that danger. . . . Having actually undertaken to protect Joshua from this danger — which petitioners concede the State played no part in creating — the State acquired an affirmative "duty," enforceable through the Due Process Clause, to do so in a reasonably competent fashion. Its failure to discharge that duty, so the argument goes, was an abuse of governmental power that so "shocks the conscience" . . . as to constitute a substantive due process violation. . . .

We reject this argument. It is true that in certain limited circumstances the Constitution imposes upon the State affirmative duties of care and protection with respect to particular individuals. . . . [But our prior cases stand only] for the proposition that when the State takes a person into its custody and holds him there against his will, the Constitution imposes upon it a corresponding duty to assume some responsibility for his safety and general well-being. *See Youngberg v. Romeo*, [457 U.S. 307, 317 (1982)] ("When a person is institutionalized and wholly dependent on the State[,] . . . a duty to provide certain services and care does exist"). . . . The affirmative duty to protect arises not from the State's knowledge of the individual's predicament or from its expressions of intent to help him, but from the limitation which it has imposed on his freedom to act on his own behalf. . . .

. . . Petitioners concede that the harms Joshua suffered did not occur while he was in the State's custody, but while he was in the custody of his natural father, who was in no sense a state actor. While the State may have been aware of the dangers that Joshua faced in the free world, it played no part in their creation, nor did it do anything to render him any more vulnerable to them. That the State once took temporary custody of Joshua does not alter the analysis, for when it returned him to his father's custody, it placed him in no worse position than that in which he would have been had it not acted at all; the State does not become the permanent guarantor of an individual's safety by having once offered him shelter. . . .

It may well be that, by voluntarily undertaking to protect Joshua against a danger it concededly played no part in creating, the State acquired a duty under state tort law to provide him with adequate protection against that danger. *See* Restatement (Second) of Torts § 323 (1965). . . . But the claim here is based on the Due Process Clause of the Fourteenth Amendment, which, as we have said many times, does not transform every tort committed by a state actor into a constitutional violation. . . .

Judges and lawyers, like other humans, are moved by natural sympathy in a case like this to find a way for Joshua and his mother to receive adequate compensation for the grievous harm inflicted upon them. But before yielding to that impulse, it is well to remember once again that the harm was inflicted not by the State of Wisconsin, but by Joshua's father. The most that can be said of the state functionaries in this case is that they stood by and did nothing when suspicious circumstances dictated a more active role for them. In defense of them it must also be said that had they moved too soon to take custody of the son away from the father, they would likely have been met with charges of improperly intruding into the parent-child relationship, charges based on the same Due Process Clause that forms the basis for the present charge of failure to provide adequate protection.

The people of Wisconsin may well prefer a system of liability which would place upon the State and its officials the responsibility for failure to act in situations as the present one. They may create such a system, if they do not have it already, by changing the tort law of the State in accordance with the regular law-making process. But they should not have it thrust upon them by this Court's expansion of the Due Process Clause of the Fourteenth Amendment.

Affirmed.

Justice Brennan, with whom Justice Marshall and Justice Blackmun join, dissenting.

The Court's baseline is the absence of positive rights in the Constitution and a concomitant suspicion of any claim that seems to depend on such rights. From this perspective, the DeShaneys' claim is first and foremost about inaction (the failure, here, of respondents to take steps to protect Joshua), and only tangentially about action (the establishment of a state program specifically designed to help children like Joshua). And from this perspective, holding these Wisconsin officials liable — where the only difference between this case and one involving a general claim to protective services is Wisconsin's establishment and operation of a program to protect children — would seem to punish an effort that we should seek to promote.

I would begin from the opposite direction. I would focus first on the action that Wisconsin has taken with respect to Joshua and children like him, rather than on the actions that the State failed to take. Such a method is not new to this Court. . . .

[T]o the Court, the only fact that seems to count as an "affirmative act of restraining the individual's freedom to act on his own behalf" is direct physical control. . . . I would recognize, as the Court apparently cannot, that "the State's knowledge of [an] individual's predicament [and] its expressions of intent to help him" can amount to a "limitation of his freedom to act on his own behalf" or to obtain help from others. . . .

Wisconsin has established a child-welfare system specifically designed to help children like Joshua. Wisconsin law places upon the local departments of social services such as respondent (DSS or Department) a duty to investigate reported instances of child abuse. . . . While other governmental bodies and private persons are largely responsible for the reporting of possible cases of child abuse . . . Wisconsin law channels all such reports to the local departments of social services for evaluation and, if necessary, further action. . . . Wisconsin law invites — indeed, directs — citizens and other governmental entities to depend on local departments of social services such as respondent to protect children from abuse.

The specific facts before us bear out this view of Wisconsin's system of protecting children. Each time someone voiced a suspicion that Joshua was being abused, that information was relayed to the Department for investigation and possible action. When Randy DeShaney's second wife told the police that he had "hit the boy causing marks and [was] a prime case for child abuse," the police referred her complaint to DSS. . . . When, on three separate occasions, emergency room personnel noticed suspicious injuries on Joshua's body, they went to DSS with this information. . . . When neighbors informed the police that they had seen or heard Joshua's father or his father's lover beating or otherwise abusing Joshua, the police brought these reports to the attention of DSS. . . . And when respondent Kemmeter, through these reports and through her own observations in the course of nearly 20 visits to the DeShaney home . . . compiled growing evidence that Joshua was being abused, that information stayed within the Department — chronicled by the social worker in detail that seems almost eerie in light of her failure to act upon it. (As to the extent of the social worker's involvement in and knowledge of Joshua's predicament, her reaction to the news of Joshua's last and most devastating injuries is illuminating: "I just knew the phone would ring some day and Joshua would be dead." 812 F.2d 298, 300 [(7th Cir. 1987)].)

Even more telling than these examples is the Department's control over the decision whether to take steps to protect a particular child from suspected abuse. While many different people contributed information and advice to this decision, it was up to the people at DSS to make the ultimate decision . . . whether to disturb the family's current arrangements. . . . Unfortunately for Joshua DeShaney, the buck effectively stopped with the Department.

In these circumstances, a private citizen, or even a person working in a government agency other than DSS, would doubtless feel that her job was done as soon as she had reported her suspicions of child abuse to DSS. Through its child-welfare program, in other words, the State of Wisconsin has relieved ordinary citizens and governmental bodies other than the Department of any sense of obligation to do anything more than report their suspicions of child abuse to DSS. If DSS ignores or dismisses these suspicions, no one will step in to fill the gap. Wisconsin's child-protection program thus effectively confined Joshua DeShaney within the walls of Randy DeShaney's violent home until such time as DSS took action to remove him. Conceivably, then, children like Joshua are made worse off by the existence of this program when the persons and entities charged with carrying it out fail to do their jobs.

It . . . simply belies reality, therefore, to contend that the State "stood by and did nothing" with respect to Joshua. . . . Through its child-protection program, the State actively intervened in Joshua's life and, by virtue of this intervention, acquired ever more certain knowledge that Joshua was in grave danger. . . .

. . . My disagreement with the Court arises from its failure to see that inaction can be every bit as abusive of power as action, that oppression can result when a State undertakes a vital duty and then ignores it. Today's opinion construes the Due Process Clause to permit a State to displace private sources of protection and then, at the critical moment, to shrug its shoulders and turn away from the harm that it has promised to try to prevent. Because I cannot agree that our Constitution is indifferent to such indifference, I respectfully dissent.

[JUSTICE BLACKMUN wrote a separate dissent.]

NOTES

1. *Section 1983 Liability for Failure to Protect After Social Agency Intervention.* A question left open by *DeShaney* was whether the state has a duty to protect children in state custody, such that a child who is wrongfully injured can recover in a § 1983 action against the government. Justice Rehnquist distinguished the situation in *DeShaney*, in which the child was in his father's custody, from the institutional contexts of *Youngberg v. Romeo*, in which the plaintiff was in state custody, indicating that the outcome in *DeShaney* might be different if Joshua was harmed while in the state's custody. Is foster care sufficiently analogous to institutionalization to support state liability for failure to protect the child?

Most post-*DeShaney* courts concur that the child who is placed in foster care by the state is in custody and has a substantive due process right to reasonable safety, although the liability standard has varied. Many lower federal courts have applied a *deliberate indifference* standard of liability to the government's conduct. One court, for example, found that the state could be liable for harm to children in foster care under § 1983 only if it had knowledge or suspicion that the foster parents were child abusers. *Lewis v. Anderson*, 308 F.3d 768 (7th Cir. 2002); *see also Lintz v. Skipski*, 25 F.3d 304 (6th Cir. 1994) (no deliberate indifference because social worker made some effort to protect children's safety upon suspecting they might be sexually abused in foster home); *Norfleet v. Ark. Dep't of Human Servs.*, 796 F. Supp. 1194 (E.D. Ark. 1992), *aff'd*, 989 F.2d 289 (8th Cir. 1993) (deliberate indifference to serious medical needs of child who died in foster care violated due process). A few courts have applied a *professional judgment* standard to liability in the foster care context, expanding the potential for state liability. *See, e.g., Yvonne L. v. N.M. Dep't of Human Servs.*, 959 F.2d 883, 894 (10th Cir.1992) (applying the professional judgment standard in a foster care case); *Brian A. ex rel. Brooks v. Sundquist*, 149 F. Supp. 2d 941, 952–954 (M.D. Tenn. 2000) (same); *LaShawn A. v. Dixon*, 762 F. Supp. 959 (D.D.C.1991)(same). *See also Olivia ex rel. Johnson v. Barbour*, 351 F. Supp. 2d 543 (S.D. Miss. 2004) (holding that children harmed in unsuitable foster care placements stated claim, regardless of whether the deliberate indifference or professional judgment standard is ultimately applied).

Some courts reject any state duty to protect children in foster care. The Fourth Circuit Court of Appeals in *Milburn v. Anne Arundel County Department of Social Services*, 871 F.2d 474 (4th Cir. 1989), *cert. denied*, 110 S. Ct. 148 (1989), for example, found *DeShaney* applicable even to agency negligence in supervising a child who had been placed in voluntary foster care. Emphasizing that the placement of the child was voluntary, the court concluded that the agency had no duty to protect the child and was not liable for gross negligence in failing to remove the child when he was physically abused in foster care. The court also concluded that foster parents were private rather than state actors and that the foster parents, rather than the state, retained custody. The Eleventh Circuit also rejected a claim by siblings in state custody against their foster parents, claiming they were molested by other foster children in the home. *Rayburn v. Hogue*, 241 F.3d 1341 (11th Cir. 2001). The court concluded that the foster parents were not subject to § 1983 actions, because they were private individuals contracting with the state, and not state actors. The appellate court rejected the district court's conclusion that the foster parents became state actors, under a test that looked to whether "the state had so far insinuated itself into a position of interdependence with private parties that it was a joint participant in the enterprise." 241 F.3d at 1347.

Where a child in state custody is placed with a *parent* and then injured, courts have varied in their responses to § 1983 claims. The Eighth Circuit Court of Appeals upheld the dismissal of a § 1983 complaint in a case in which Family Services returned the child to her father, from whose custody she had earlier been taken, despite the fact that the agency had notice that the father allowed her to have contact with a known pedophile (who later abused her). *S.S. v. McMullen*, 225 F.3d 960 (8th Cir. 2000). The court rejected the child's claim that the state had placed her in a dangerous environment, reasoning that the case was similar to *DeShaney.* The court concluded that the two-year interval of state custody did not increase the risk that she faced. A federal district court reached a different result where a child, placed by the state in his father's custody, was killed when his father poured boiling water on him. *Currier v. Doran*, 23 F. Supp. 2d 1277 (D.N.M. 1998), *aff'd in part and rev'd in part*, 242 F.3d 905 (10th Cir. 2001). *DeShaney* was distinguished because the state, having removed the child from his mother's custody, assumed control over the child. At that point, the court concluded, the state had a duty to avoid creating a dangerous condition for the child by knowingly or recklessly relinquishing control to an abusive person, even if that person is a family member. Thus, the defendants, a social worker and supervisor, could be held liable for the acts of the third party father if the officials created the danger that caused the harm. For discussion of claims by children in foster care, see Kimberly A. Sackmann, *What Happened to Protecting the Children? An Argument Against Parental Immunity For Foster Parents*, 19 DCBA Brief 32 (2007); Laura A. Harper, Student Author, *The State's Duty to Children in Foster Care-Bearing the Burden of Protecting Children*, 51 Drake L. Rev. 793 (2003); Brendan P. Kearse, *Competing Constitutional Standards for the State's Duty to Protect Foster Children*, 29 Colum. J. L. & Soc. Probs. 385 (1996).

2. *Section 1983 Liability for Intervention.* Can social workers be liable under § 1983 for their actions in intervening to protect children? Some courts conclude that social workers must be immune from § 1983 actions for wrongfully bringing dependency actions that result in removal of the child from the home. A federal appellate court concluded that absolute immunity was as important here as in the prosecutorial context. "Like a prosecutor, a child welfare worker must exercise independent judgment in deciding whether or not to bring a child dependency proceeding, and such judgment would likely be compromised if that worker faced the threat of personal liability for every mistake in judgment." *Ernst v. Child and Youth Servs.*, 108 F.3d 486, 496 (3d Cir. 1997); *see also Rippy v. Hattaway*, 270 F.3d 416 (6th Cir. 2001) (social workers' investigation and recommendation regarding return of child in state custody entitled to absolute immunity comparable to that of probation officer making sentencing recommendation).

Some courts have permitted § 1983 actions against social workers and against city governments for policies that violate constitutional rights of parents and children. Many of the cases involve aggressive investigations of child sexual abuse that include medical examinations without court orders. In a bizarre California case, city police officers seized two young children from their home on the basis of a "tip" from the children's mentally ill and institutionalized aunt, who claimed that the father and grandparents were involved in Satanic ritual abuse and planned to sacrifice the children. *Wallis v. Spencer*, 202 F.3d 1126 (9th Cir. 1999). The officers took the children at 1 a.m. and subjected them to intrusive genital examinations. The children were not returned to their parents until two months later. The parents and children brought a § 1983 claim against the officers and the city on the basis of the unreasonable seizure without a court order and the medical evaluations without parents' consent or presence. The Ninth Circuit Court of Appeals held that the city could be liable if the officers acted pursuant to a city custom or operating procedure of removing children and of subjecting them to medical exams without court orders. Similarly, New York parents and their daughter were allowed to bring a § 1983 claim against the city and social workers who removed the child from school and had her examined for sexual abuse in a nearby hospital without a court order. *Tenenbaum v. Williams*, 193 F.3d 581 (2d Cir. 1999), *cert. denied*, 529 U.S. 1098 (2000). The court concluded that the medical examination without parental consent or court order violated the parents' and child's procedural due process rights and protection against unreasonable seizure if a jury determined that there was sufficient time to safely secure judicial authorization. Here, the removal occurred more than a day after the decision by state officials was made. Since the emergency removal was undertaken pursuant to city policy, the city was liable, although the individual caseworkers were entitled to qualified immunity if it was reasonable for them to believe that they did not violate clearly established rights. *See also Jordan v. Jackson*, 15 F.3d 333 (4th Cir. 1994) (holding the county's failure to train its employees regarding appropriate circumstances for emergency removal under state statute could support a § 1983 action if it demonstrated deliberate indifference). Note that if social workers face the possibility of liability if intervening to protect a child, but face no prospect of liability if they fail to protect, there is an asymmetry that may reinforce nonintervention.

3. *State Tort Actions and Social Worker Immunity.* In many states, state tort law may provide a remedy for harms caused by social worker or agency actions or omissions. *See, e.g., Newton v. County of Napa*, 266 Cal. Rptr. 682 (Cal. App. 1990) (immunity recognized for decision to investigate and for actions necessary to conduct meaningful investigation in emergency situations, but not for tortious conduct in connection with certain aspects of investigation (such as strip search); *Dep't of Rehab. Servs. v. Yamuni*, 529 So. 2d 258 (Fla. 1988) (upholding finding of liability against caseworker, although reducing $3.1 million jury verdict for failure of agency to protect child from abuse). In many states, however, social worker actions and omissions are protected by qualified or even absolute immunity. *See, e.g., Marshall v. Montgomery County Children's Serv. Bd.*, 750 N.E.2d 549 (Ohio 2001) (sovereign immunity bars wrongful death claim even if agency failed to investigate reported abuse); *Williams v. State*, 376 N.W.2d 117 (Mich. App. 1985) (upholding immunity for failure to act upon reports of abuse to protect child, who died at age two from starvation).

State law varies, as well, as to whether foster parents have immunity for harm caused while they have custody of a child. If they are not state actors, they cannot be sued under § 1983, but they could still be liable under state tort law. *Compare Nichol v. Stass*, 735 N.E. 2d 582 (Ill. 2000) (foster parents protected by qualified parental immunity against negligence claim), *and* TENN. CODE ANN. § 8-42-101(3)(A), (2008) (foster parents covered by rule giving immunity to state officials), *with Mayberry v. Pryor*, 374 N.W.2d 683 (Mich. 1985) (foster parents not protected by defense of parental immunity).

4. *Evaluating* DeShaney *and Liability Policy.* Much of the scholarly commentary on *DeShaney* has been extremely critical, especially of the Court's formalistic distinctions used to justify the failure of public agency responsibility. *See, e.g.*, Akhil Reed Amar, *Remember the Thirteenth*, 10 CONST. COMMENTARY 403 (1993); Louis Michael Seidman, *The State Action Paradox*, 10 CONST. COMMENTARY 379 (1993); Laura E. Oren, *The State's Failure to Protect Children and Substantive Due Process: DeShaney in Context*, 68 N.C. L. REV. 659 (1990); Patricia Wald, *Government Benefits: A New Look at an Old Gifthorse*, 65 N.Y.U. L. REV. 247 (1990); David A. Strauss, *Due Process, Government Inaction, and Private Wrongs*, 1989 SUP. CT. REV. 53; Aviam Soifer, *Moral Ambition, Formalism, and the "Free World" of DeShaney*, 57 GEO. WASH. L. REV. 1513 (1989). For a rare, but interesting, defense of *DeShaney*, see Barbara E. Armacost, *Affirmative Duties, Systemic Harms, and the Due Process Clause*, 94 MICH. L. REV. 982 (1996). Armacost argues that the Court's refusal to find an affirmative state duty to protect children can be understood as judicial reluctance to second-guess legislative decisions about allocating resources for public services.

Putting aside the constitutional issue, would expansive social worker liability necessarily be good policy? When it appears that a child's injury or death could have been avoided through state intervention, public outrage is understandable. On the other hand, social workers perform stressful jobs with inadequate resources. Burnout is common; in most large city departments, turnover rates are high. Douglas Besharov, former director of the National Center on Child Abuse and Neglect, expressed concern about expansion of social worker liability: "They can be blamed if they report suspected child abuse, and they can be blamed if they don't. They can be blamed if they remove a child from parental custody, and they can be blamed if they don't. They can be blamed if they return a child to the home, and they can be blamed if they don't." DONALD BESHAROV, THE VULNERABLE SOCIAL WORKER: LIABILITY FOR SERVING CHILDREN AND FAMILIES (1985). While preferring agency liability to liability for individuals, Besharov opposes liability for agencies and individuals, because it deflects public attention away from the real issues of inadequate financial and political support for child protection. *Id.* at 157–59.

NOTE ON FOSTER CARE

Most children who are removed from their parents' custody due to abuse or neglect enter the foster care system, typically in foster homes rather than institutions. Of the 51,000 children in foster care in 2006, about 24% were placed with relatives in "kinship" care, 46% in non-relative foster homes and 18% in group homes or institutions. *See* Child Welfare Info. Gateway, Dep't of Health & Human Servs., http://www.childwelfare.gov/pubs/factsheets/foster.cfm#place.

Foster parents are typically paid and supervised by a state agency, though the supervision may be fairly loose. Under the typical court order, parents lose custody to the state agency, which chooses a foster parent but retains authority to change the child's placement as it deems necessary to serve the child's interest. At the same time, the rights of the child's natural parents are suspended and not permanently severed. The agency lacks power to make any permanent adoptive placement for the child, although it may petition the court to terminate the parents' rights permanently, thus freeing the child for adoption. Children also come into the foster care system through voluntary placements by parents seeking state help in dealing with family crises. Voluntary placement usually requires an entrustment agreement which defines the rights and duties of each party, including when the child is to be returned to the parent. *But see* Kenneth L. Karst, *Law, Cultural Conflict, and the Socialization of Children*, 91 CAL. L. REV 967 (2003) (arguing that "voluntary placements" of children into state custody is rarely voluntary, in that parents may act under the threat of involuntary removal and termination of parental rights).

State-run foster care has been heavily criticized. Ideally, a foster care system works to provide a short term home for children whose parents will soon be able to reclaim them and a temporary way station for children who will soon be placed for adoption. In practice, however, children remain in foster care for extended periods, often moving among foster homes for much of their childhood. Foster care "drift" occurs, in part, because agencies and courts are reluctant both to terminate the rights of biological parents and to return the children home. The children affected are most often from poor, minority group families. In response to this problem, federal and state law reform efforts have focused on permanency planning for children. Permanency planning has multiple dimensions: avoiding unnecessary removal of children from their families; promoting speedy and safe reunification with their families of children in foster care; and finding a new permanent home in a reasonable time when children cannot be reunified with their families. The emphasis has varied at different times; federal legislation, for example, has shifted its focus from reunification to facilitating adoption.

The Adoption Assistance and Child Welfare Act of 1980 sought to deter unnecessary removal of children from their families and to encourage remediation and return to parental custody. *See generally* THE ADOPTION ASSISTANCE AND CHILD WELFARE ACT OF 1980: TEN YEARS LATER (North American Council on Adoptable Children 1990). In contrast, the more recent Adoption and Safe Families Act (AFSA) of 1997, deemphasizes the goal of reunification with parents and focuses on facilitating permanent placement with a new family. AFSA mandates that the state petition for termination of parental rights (*see* Subsection [5] below) if a child spends 15 of a period of 22 consecutive months in foster care. If the court grants the petition, the child will become free for adoption. Some observers critique AFSA, indicating that parents may not have sufficient time to correct the problems that led to their child's placement in foster care. *See, e.g.*, Kristen R. Humphrey et al., *Impact of the Adoption and Safe Families Act on Youth and their Families: Perspectives of Foster Care Providers, Youth with Emotional Disorders, Service Providers, and Judges*, 28 CHILDREN & YOUTH SVCS. REV. 113 (2006). One critic argues that AFSA "lumps parents who have engaged in unspeakable acts of child abuse together with parents whose only failing is being too poor to maintain children at home without subsidies — which have been declared no longer available to families." Martin Guggenheim, *Issues Surrounding Initial Intervention*," 3 CARDOZO PUB. L., POL'Y, & ETHICS J. 359, 361–62 (2005). Others argued that AFSA would increase the numbers of "legal orphans" whose parents' rights have been terminated, without also increasing the number of children adopted. Richard Barth, et al., *From Anticipation to Evidence: Research on the Adoption and Safe Families Act*, 12 VA. J. SOC. POL'Y & L. 371 (2005). See further discussion of AFSA in Subsection [5] below, including a summary of empirical evidence as to its impact.

Some argue that the problem lies with the absence of adequate interventions to help children from entering foster care in the first place, rather than with the difficulty promoting adoptions out of foster care. *See, e.g.*, Martin Guggenheim, *The Foster Care Dilemma and What to Do About it: Is the Problem That Too Many Children are Not Being Adopted out of Foster Care or that Too Many Children are Entering Foster Care?* 2 U. PA. J. CONST. LAW 150 (1999). For analysis of the past thirty years of federal policymaking in the area of child abuse and neglect, see the papers presented at the symposium *Advocating for Change: the Status & Future of America's Child Welfare System 30 Years After CAPTA* at 3 CARDOZO PUB. L., POL'Y & ETHICS J. 353 (2005). *See also* ROGER J.R. LEVESQUE, CHILD MALTREATMENT AND THE LAW: RETURNING TO FIRST PRINCIPLES (2008).

Periodically, a high profile incident brings the problems with a state's foster care system to public attention. In 2003, New Jersey officials were ordered to release 1300 confidential files of children in state custody, following the death of a 7-year-old Newark boy who was imprisoned with his 4-year-old twin brothers in the basement of his aunt's home, while his mother (who had been subject to abuse petitions) served a prison term. Richard Lezin Jones & Leslie Kaufman, *New Jersey Opens Files Showing Failures of Child Welfare System*, N.Y. TIMES, Apr. 15, 2003 at A1. The files revealed some cases of horrendous abuse and neglect in foster care, and instances of ineptitude and indifference of agency personnel. One child died of AIDS after receiving no medical care for a year. A drug exposed-infant died in foster care, after agency workers placed the child without explaining his medical condition to the foster mother. Numerous children were found to have been beaten and sexually abused, although agency review found the allegations to have been unsubstantiated. Evidence that children in foster care often do not get the protection that justified removal from their parents fuels criticism of broad intervention policies.

Of course, many children receive nurturing care while in state custody, and some children in long term placements develop deep emotional ties with their foster parents. In a sense, these ties are incompatible with the premise of foster care as a temporary arrangement. Should foster parents have any rights when the agency seeks to remove a foster child from his "psychological family"?

SMITH v. ORGANIZATION OF FOSTER FAMILIES FOR EQUALITY & REFORM
United States Supreme Court
431 U.S. 816 (1977)

[In this case, an organization of foster parents (OFFER) claimed that removing children whom they had had in their care for a substantial period of time without a hearing violated their liberty interests under the Due Process Clause. The Supreme Court avoided the constitutional issue, holding that even if such a liberty interest existed, New York's hearing procedures satisfied any due process rights the foster parents might have. The Court's opinion by Justice Brennan, however, provided *dicta* both supportive and disparaging of foster parent claims.]

[T]he usual understanding of "family" implies biological relationships, and most decisions treating the relation between parent and child have stressed this element. . . .

. . . But biological relationships are not [the] exclusive determination of the existence of a family. . . .

[T]he importance of the familial relationship, to the individuals involved and [to society], stems from the emotional attachments that derive from the intimacy of daily association . . . as well as from the fact of blood relationship. No one would seriously dispute that a deeply loving and interdependent relationship between an adult and a child in his or her care may exist even in the absence of blood relationship. At least where a child has been placed in foster care as an infant, has never known his natural parents, and has remained continuously for several years in the care of the same foster parents, it is natural that the foster family should hold the same place in the emotional life of the foster child, and fulfill the same socializing functions, as a natural family. For this reason, we cannot dismiss the foster family as a mere collection of unrelated individuals.

But there are also important distinctions between the foster family and the natural family. First, unlike the earlier cases recognizing a right to family privacy, the State here seeks to interfere, not with a relationship having its origins entirely apart from the power of the State, but rather with a foster family which has its source in state law and contractual arrangements. The individual's freedom to marry and reproduce is "older than the Bill of Rights," *Griswold v. Connecticut,* *supra*, 381 U.S., at 486. Accordingly, . . . the liberty interest in family privacy has its source, and its contours are ordinarily to be sought, not in state law, but in intrinsic human rights, as they have been understood in "this Nation's history and tradition." *Moore v. City of East Cleveland*, 431 U.S., at 503. Here, however, whatever emotional ties may develop between foster parent and foster child have their origins in an arrangement in which the State has been a partner from the outset. While the Court has recognized that liberty interests may in some cases arise from positive-law sources, where, as here, the claimed interest derives from a knowingly assumed contractual relation with the State, it is appropriate to ascertain from state law the expectations and entitlements of the parties. In this case, the limited recognition accorded to the foster family by the New York statutes and the contracts executed by the foster parents argue against any but the most limited constitutional "liberty" in the foster family.

A second consideration . . . is that ordinarily procedural protection may be afforded to a liberty interest of one person without derogating from the substantive liberty of another. Here, however, such a tension is virtually unavoidable. Under New York law, the natural parent of a foster child in voluntary placement has an absolute right to the return of his child in the absence of a court order obtainable only upon compliance with rigorous substantive and procedural standards, which reflect the constitutional protection accorded the natural family. Moreover, the natural parent initially gave up his child to the State only on the express understanding that the child would be returned in those circumstances. These rights are difficult to reconcile with the liberty interest in the foster family relationship claimed by appellees. It is one thing to say that individuals may acquire a liberty interest against arbitrary governmental interference in the family-like associations into which they have freely entered, even in the absence of biological connection or state-law recognition of the relationship. It is quite another to say that one may acquire such an interest in the face of another's constitutionally recognized liberty interest that derives from blood relationship, state-law sanction, and basic human right — an interest the foster parent has recognized by contract from the outset. Whatever liberty interest might otherwise exist in the foster family as an institution, that interest must be substantially attenuated where the proposed removal from the foster family is to return the child to his natural parents.

NOTES

1. ***Foster Parents' Constitutional Claims.***   Claims that foster parents have a Fourteenth Amendment "liberty" interest in the relationship with their foster children have generally been unsuccessful. *See Procopio v. Johnson*, 785 F. Supp. 1317 (N.D. Ill. 1992); *In re Dependency of J.H.* 815 P.2d 1380 (Wash. 1991) (foster parents have no standing to challenge removal). Some courts have reached results more supportive of the claim. Delaware's highest court found that foster parents have standing to petition for guardianship without the consent of the Department of Family Services. *Div. of Family Serv. v. Harrison*, 741 A.2d 1016 (Del. 1999). The court held that the foster parents had a legally protected interest because they had cared for the child for most of his life. *See also In re Jonathan G.*, 482 S.E.2d 893 (W. Va. 1996) (foster parents who had care and custody of abused child for more than two years were entitled to hearing in termination of parental rights proceedings, to determine whether it was in the child's best interests to have a continuing association with them); *Rivera v. Marcus*, 696 F.2d 1016 (2d Cir. 1982) (foster mother who was half-sister of children has protected "liberty" interest in their custody). In *Smith v. O.F.F.E.R.*, the Court emphasized that recognizing a protectable interest in foster parents was in tension with natural parents' rights. However, courts sometimes dismiss foster parents' claims where no biological parent is in the picture. *See, e.g., In re G.C.*, 735 A.2d 1226 (Pa. 1999) (holding that foster parents lacked standing against grandfather to seek custody of a child who

had lived with them since he was an infant).

2. *Children's   Interests   in   Maintaining   Relationship   with   Foster Parents.*   What of the *children's* liberty interests in remaining with foster parents who have provided them with the only stable home they know? Such a claim was not considered by *Smith*, which framed the inquiry solely in terms of the foster parents' rights. A few courts have denied children's claims. *See, e.g., Del A. v. Roemer*, 777 F. Supp. 1297 (E.D. La. 1991) (Adoption Assistance and Child Welfare Act of 1980 did not create a private right of action enforceable by foster children under § 1983). Some have argued for legal recognition of the child's interest in a relationship with psychological parents (including foster parents). *See* Gilbert A. Holmes, *The Tie That Binds: The Constitutional Right of Children to Maintain Relationship with Parent-like Individuals*, 53 MD. L. REV. 358 (1994).

3. *Foster Parents as Adoptive Parents.*   Traditionally, foster parents fared poorly in claiming the right to adopt the foster children for whom they care if the biological parents' rights are terminated. *See, e.g., Nye v. Marcus*, 502 A.2d 869 (Conn. 1985). Agencies viewed foster parents as temporary custodians who should maintain an emotional distance from the children to facilitate the children's reunification with their natural parents. In addition, some foster parents may not qualify for adoption under age criteria sometimes employed by the agencies. *See, e.g., In re Adoption of K.M.*, 668 So. 2d 862 (Ala. Ct. App. 1995); *Bledsoe v. Dep't of Human Resources*, 241 S.E.2d 304 (Ga. Ct. App. 1977).

Gradually, in some jurisdictions, this policy is changing, as policymakers appreciate that stability, consistency, and preservation of bonded emotional relationships is essential to children's well-being. Thus, increasingly, if a child becomes eligible for adoption, foster parents are permitted to petition for adoption and may, in some jurisdictions, be favored as adoptive parents. Recent legislation at the state and federal levels facilitates adoption by foster parents. Many state codes today clarify that foster parents are eligible to adopt children in their care and they may be preferred. *See, e.g., In re Adoption of C.D.*, 729 N.E.2d 553, 560 (Ill. Ct. App. 2000) (citing the Illinois Adoption Act as creating a preference for adoption to foster parents who have cared for child one year or more); N.Y. SOC. SERVICES LAW § 383 (2003) (giving preference in adoption proceedings to foster parents who have had continuous custody of child for more than 12 months). Some courts have become more receptive to adoption petitions by foster parents. *See, e.g., In the Interest of C.F.*, 796 So.2d 922 (La. Ct. App. 2001) (foster parents can petition for termination of parental rights to adopt child where state does not act); *Adoption of Gwendolyn*, 558 N.E.2d 10 (Mass. App. Ct. 1990) (clear and convincing evidence of biological parents' unfitness supported finding that child would benefit from adoption by foster parents in whose care she had been for four years).

For further discussion of the role of foster parents as permanent caregivers of the children for whom they care, either as adoptive parents, or long-term custodians, see, e.g., Pamela Laufer-Ukeles, *Money, Caregiving, and Kinship: Should Paid Caregivers Be Allowed to Obtain De Facto Parental Status?*,74 MO. L. REV. 25, 55–69 (2009); Elizabeth A. Neary, *In the Best Interest of Children: When Foster Parents May Keep Placement*, 80-SEP. WIS. 10 (2007); Alice Bussiere, *Permanence for Older Foster Youth*, 44 FAM. CT. REV. 231 (2006); Teresa Lazo-

Miller, *Foster Parents, Children and Youth Services, and the Court: Can Foster Children Escape the Bermuda Triangle?*, 6 WIDENER J. PUB. L. 181 (1996).

[5]   Termination of Parental Rights

MINNESOTA STATUTES (2009)

§ 260C.301. Grounds for Termination of Parental Rights

Subd. 1. Voluntary and Involuntary. The juvenile court may, upon petition, terminate all rights of a parent to a child:

(a) with the written consent of a parent who for good cause desires to terminate his parental rights; or

(b) if it finds that one or more of the following conditions exist:

(1) that the parent has abandoned the child;

(2) that the parent had substantially, continuously, or repeatedly refused or neglected to comply with the duties imposed upon that parent by the parent and child relationship, including but not limited to providing the child with necessary food, clothing, shelter, education, and other care and control necessary for the child's physical, mental, or emotional health and development, if the parent is physically and financially able, and either reasonable efforts by the social service agency have failed to correct the conditions that formed the basis of the petition or reasonable efforts would be futile.;

(3) that a parent has been ordered to contribute to the support of the child or financially aid in the child's birth and has continuously failed to do so without good cause . . . ;

(4) that a parent is palpably unfit to [to parent the child] because of a consistent pattern of specific conduct . . . determined by the court to be of a duration or nature that renders the parent unable, for the reasonably foreseeable future, to care appropriately for the ongoing physical, mental, or emotional needs of the child . . . ;

(5) that following the child's placement out of the home, reasonable efforts, under the direction of the court, have failed to correct the conditions leading to the child's placement. It is presumed that reasonable efforts under this clause have failed upon a showing that:

(i) a child has resided out of the parental home under court order for cumulative period of 12 months within the preceding 22 months. . . . ;

(ii) the court has approved the out of home placement plan required [by statute];

(iii) conditions leading to the out of home placement have not been corrected. . . . upon a showing that the parents have not substantially complied with the court's orders and reasonable case plan; and

(iv) reasonable efforts have been made by the social service agency to rehabilitate the parent and reunite the family.

This clause does not prohibit the termination of parental rights prior to one year . . .

It is also presumed that reasonable efforts have failed under this clause upon a showing that:

(A) the parent has been diagnosed as chemically dependent by a professional certified to make the diagnosis;

(B) the parent has been required by a case plan to participate in a chemical dependency treatment program;

. . . .

(D) the parent has either failed two or more times to successfully complete a treatment program or has refused at two or more separate meetings with a caseworker to participate in a treatment program; and

(E) the parent continues to abuse chemicals.

(6) that a child has experienced egregious harm in the parent's care which is of a nature, duration, or chronicity that indicates a lack of regard for the child's well-being, such that a reasonable person would believe it contrary to the best interest of the child or of any child to be in the parent's care; [or]

. . . .

(8) That the child is neglected and in foster care. . . .

IN RE ADOPTION/GUARDIANSHIP NO. J9610436
Maryland Supreme Court
796 A.2d 778 (2002)

CATHELL, JUDGE.

Prior to a termination of parental rights, the parent and perhaps the child have fundamental federal and state constitutional rights to the maintenance of the parent/child relationship. This relationship, absent constitutional amendments, cannot be unreasonably abrogated. . . . These rights are the same where parents or children are alleged to be disabled. Under our Constitutions, the poor and the disabled are no less citizens entitled to the full range of constitutional protections. The Constitutions apply in the social welfare area as fully as in any other area of American life. There is a strong presumption in matters relating to termination of parental rights cases, that the "best interests" of a child, generally, are met by not terminating the parental rights of natural parents. In termination of parental rights cases, it is this presumption that most insures the proper deference to a parent's fundamental and constitutional right to parent. It is from this perspective that we commence our review of this case . . .

I. Parenting as a Fundamental Right

In *Santosky v. Kramer*, 455 U.S. 745 (1982), the [U.S.] Supreme Court reaffirmed the rights of parents when there are allegations of neglect and they are involved in a proceeding to terminate their parental rights. . . . In *Santosky*, the . . . Court concluded that in order to terminate a parent-child relationship, a "clear and convincing evidence" standard of proof was needed. . . .

The applicable State laws, in order to meet the requirements of the Federal Constitution and Article 24 of the Maryland Declaration of Rights, contain certain protections for parents. First, Maryland law presumes that reunification with the natural parent is in the child's "best interest." Additionally, Maryland's law requires that the court must consider the nature and extent of services offered by the child placement agency to facilitate reunion of the child with the natural parent prior to a termination of parental rights . . .

. . .

Cases that involve poverty as neglect are perhaps the most compelling candidates for family preservation and reunification services. Unfortunately, poverty is also a deeply-rooted problem and, thus, one that cannot be alleviated quickly. As such, [AFSA's] new time lines for child protective cases may actually work to tear apart families who would otherwise have succeeded in rebuilding their lives.

Finally, charges of neglect effectively render poor parents powerless. The strain of having one's children taken away is extremely distressing for parents in poverty, who are often undereducated and unworldly. This stressful situation weakens parents and, therefore, further exacerbates the imbalance of power that already favors the state in child protection proceedings. The state is clearly in control in neglect proceedings, for not only does it present the case to the court, but its 'adversary,' the parent, is unfamiliar with the intricacies of the legal proceedings. As such, parents are often unable to effectively assert their rights . . .

. . .

III. Statement of Facts

. . . . The oldest of the two sons, Tristynn, was born on June 18, 1995 to petitioner and Ms. H. who were never married. . . . Petitioner testified that he has permanently terminated his relationship with Ms. H. . . . Ms. H. ultimately abandoned the children and consented to termination of her parental rights.

. . . . Tristynn . . . came into the care of CCDSS [Carroll County Department of Social Services] on December 28, 1995, at the age of six months, when petitioner went to CCDSS and asked for help in caring for his child. Petitioner testified that there was no electricity in the apartment where the family had been living at the time he brought Tristynn to CCDSS and that he had no food to feed Tristynn. There was no other evidence bearing on the issue of neglect and no evidence of abuse. Petitioner stated that "[I] thought [I] was going to get [my] kids back once [I] got [my] electricity turned back on". . . .

[Petitioner's second son, Edward, tested positive at birth for drugs, and entered the care of CCDSS on June 18, 1996 when he was three weeks old. He was immediately placed in foster care with Mr. and Mrs. M. (with whom he continues to reside)].

The initial permanency plan for both children was to return them to the home of either parent. On May 13, 1997, petitioner was informed that CCDSS's permanency plan had changed from a plan of reunification to guardianship with the right to consent to adoption. That plan was adopted by the court on June 10, 1997.

The adequacy of the reunification services provided to petitioner by CCDSS are disputed. CCDSS claims that the services provided to petitioner were adequate and ultimately unsuccessful. . . . Specifically, CCDSS states that shortly after Tristynn entered foster care, CCDSS began arranging for him to have supervised visits with petitioner. . . . CCDSS claims that they had scheduling problems with petitioner from the beginning of the visitation [and] the initial visitation schedule had to be changed frequently to accommodate petitioner's work schedule. . . . Further, CCDSS claims that during his early visits with the children, petitioner demonstrated trouble in caring for the children, was unable to remember child care techniques repeatedly shown to him by the social worker, had difficulty in choosing age-appropriate toys for the children, and was not able to help Tristynn with his beginning verbal skills. Moreover, CCDSS states that in later supervised visits when petitioner started seeing Tristynn and Edward together, petitioner needed supervision and direction to understand how to properly care for the two children, how to give them both proper attention when the children are together, and to understand the special medical and dietary needs of Edward.

. . . . CCDSS states that other than visitation, petitioner did not request additional services from CCDSS, and [denied] his need for services. The social worker assigned to assist petitioner claimed petitioner was not cooperative, was not truthful, and provided inadequate information.

Finally, unlike CCDSS's usual practice of entering into a new service agreement every six months with those seeking assistance, CCDSS entered into only one Social Services Agreement with petitioner (on July 3, 1996) that had the goal of reunification. The agreement required petitioner to obtain electricity in his apartment, attend parenting classes, complete a domestic violence program, complete an alcohol and drug evaluation, submit to random urine analysis, confirm in advance his intent to keep scheduled visits, be completely truthful with the CCDSS, and remain drug and alcohol free.

Petitioner attended parenting classes, as well as a parents anonymous group, but the social worker believed that petitioner made very little progress. Petitioner finished the first phase of a domestic violence program, but allegedly could not complete the second phase due to his alleged cognitive limitations. Also petitioner completed a drug and alcohol evaluation . . . the evaluator concluding that he did not need treatment.

A social worker also noted that petitioner never prepared a household budget, presumably for when reunification occurred, or came up with a plan for child care. . . . According to CCDSS, petitioner has a reduced mental capacity that renders him incapable of parenting the children on his own.

Insofar as we have been able to discern from the record, CCDSS never offered any specialized services designed to be particularly helpful to a parent with the intellectual and cognitive skill levels CCDSS alleges are possessed by petitioner. We are informed by the amicus brief that such services are available. . . . [F]inancial advising services, family support services, and other programs were available from . . . various Association Retarded Citizens (ARC) entities, and numerous other entities, private and public. None of these services were utilized by CCDSS. . . .

Petitioner. . . . [claims] that the services offered by CCDSS to him were minimal, inadequate, and inappropriate for his particular situation. Moreover, petitioner proffers that he has completed his education, obtained a driver's license, has secured employment, and maintains his own residence, indicating that he can, in fact, parent his own children.

. . . . Petitioner asserts that CCDSS did not fulfill its role as a social service department by seeking out programs specific to petitioner's parenting deficiencies, programs that would aid in the primary and ultimate goal of reunification. The failure, it is argued, of CCDSS to address its services to his specific need has a discriminatory impact. . . . [¶]. . . . CCDSS apparently did not even offer petitioner services to assist him with literacy. . . .

. . . . [A]t CCDSS's request, Neil Blumberg, M.D., conducted a psychiatric evaluation of petitioner. Dr. Blumberg reported that petitioner suffered from a serious intellectual impairment and categorized petitioner as disabled and unfit to parent. Dr. Blumberg noted that standard testing was not and could not be completed because of petitioner's inability to read well. . . .

. . . . Dr. Blumberg testified: "Well I would *probably* categorize his intellectual impairment as-a disability. I mean, it really does hamper him; he's — he — he cannot read. . . ." (Emphasis added). . . .

. . . . The extent to which Dr. Blumberg relies on a person's inability to read in order to find mental "impairment" or "retardation" is troubling, especially when it is used in proceedings to determine whether to terminate parental rights. . . .

. . . . C. Michael Hardesty, an expert in developmental disabilities, who was petitioner's employment supervisor . . . testified to petitioner's strong work ethic, and to petitioner's duties as a house counselor for United Cerebral Palsy . . . including providing assistance like toileting, dressing, and feeding to persons with profound disabilities, such as quadriplegia.

Some CCDSS caseworkers . . . testified that . . . in their view, unsupervised visitation would endanger the safety of the children. The caseworkers, however, did recognize that petitioner . . . demonstrated an ability to learn and improve his parenting skills through his progress in paying attention to and caring for the children. . . . Also, the caseworkers testified that Tristynn called petitioner "Dada" and was happy to see petitioner, and while the visits with Edward were more difficult for petitioner, Edward would at times seek petitioner for comfort. Finally, a social worker observing some of the visits testified that when petitioner needed assistance with the children during the visits he knew to ask for help, and that . . . given the opportunity, petitioner could learn the necessary skills. In essence, even CCDSS testified to a certain degree that reunification in the future was reasonably possible, if not probable.

Petitioner is a thirty-eight-year-old African-American male. He graduated from high school in 1982 and has maintained steady employment as a maintenance/cleaning person, a cook, and for six years as a house counselor. . . . Petitioner . . . has enrolled, voluntarily and without prompting from CCDSS, in remedial reading classes to improve his reading ability. He has attended parenting classes two times per week for approximately three and a half years and he has attended Parents Anonymous. Petitioner has little history of drug or alcohol abuse, and no history of child abuse or willful neglect. He now lives in a two bedroom townhouse, which includes a bedroom for himself and one which would be shared by the boys were they to be allowed to live with him. He testified that his parents live close to his home and that if he were to encounter problems with the children while in his care, he would know to call his parents or CCDSS for help. Finally, petitioner contends that the short visits under supervised conditions, which is all that CCDSS now permits, render it nearly impossible to establish any regularity with the children. . . .

[T]he children are both adjusting well to, and doing well in, their foster homes. . . . Tristynn is happy and is comfortable with his foster parents, but shows affection for petitioner and displays no negative reactions after visits. Mr. and Mrs. F. wish to adopt Tristynn, but expect Tristynn to continue his relationship with petitioner.

. . . . Mr. and Mrs. M. want Edward to know his father, but stated that Edward has had difficulty in visiting with petitioner. . . . Mr. and Mrs. M. wish to adopt Edward at the end of this litigation.

. . . .

IV. Discussion

[The Court reviews the relevant provisions of the Maryland statute regulating adoption/guardianship without parental consent]

[§ 5-313] (c) In determining whether it is in the best interest of the child to terminate a natural parent's rights as to the child . . . , the court shall give:

(1) primary consideration to the safety and health of the child; and

(2) consideration to:

(i) the timeliness, nature, and extent of the services offered by the child placement agency to facilitate reunion of the child with the natural parent;

(ii) any social service agreement between the natural parent and the child placement agency, and the extent to which all parties have fulfilled their obligations under the agreement;

(iii) the child's feelings toward and emotional ties with the child's natural parents, the child's siblings, and any other individuals who may significantly affect the child's best interest; . . .

(v) the result of the effort the natural parent has made to adjust the natural parent's circumstances, conduct, or conditions to make it in the best interest of the child to be returned to the natural parent's home, including:

> 1. the extent to which the natural parent has maintained regular contact with the child under a plan to reunite the child with the natural parent. . . .

> 4. whether additional services would be likely to bring about a lasting parental adjustment so that the child could be returned to the natural parent within an ascertainable time, not exceeding 18 months from the time of placement. . . .

(d) *Considerations following juvenile adjudication.* —

(1) In determining whether it is in the best interest of the child to terminate a natural parent's rights as to the child in a case involving a child who has been adjudicated to be a child in need of assistance, a neglected child, an abused child, or a dependent child, the court shall consider the factors in subsection (c) of this section and whether any of the following continuing or serious conditions or acts exist:

> (i) the natural parent has a disability that renders the natural parent consistently unable to care for the immediate and ongoing physical or psychological needs of the child for long periods of time;

> (ii) the natural parent has committed acts of abuse or neglect toward any child in the family;

. . . ."

In cases where the termination of parental rights is involved, there is . . . a strong presumption that the child's best interests are served by maintaining parental rights. It is only when clear and convincing evidence exists that the child's best interests are served by termination, may a parent's constitutional right to parent his child be permanently foreclosed. In our view, in the instant case, considering the allegations made by CCDSS as to petitioner's mental capacity, the parenting and reunification services offered to petitioner were not sufficient and not sufficiently tailored to his alleged specific situation to support a finding that, with sufficient and properly tailored services, he could not maintain a parental relationship with his children. . . . There was evidence of only one reunification agreement between the natural parent and CCDSS. . . . While there may be no easily ascertainable levels of assistance that must be offered when the termination of parental rights of a "disabled" parent is involved, that level is far above the minimal services CCDSS offered [here]. . . .

There was uncontradicted evidence that petitioner had made extensive and extraordinary efforts to further reunification with his children. He had, to the best of his ability, attempted to do almost everything asked of him, and more, in order to become a capable parent. . . . In so far as the record reflects, he maintained as regular a contact with his children as CCDSS would permit. . . . [T]here is little evidence, as opposed to conjecture, that petitioner was inherently disabled to such an extent that he would be unable to care for the needs of the children for considerable periods of time. . . . He had, in fact, cared for the needs of other disabled persons as a part of his steady employment. He could not adequately read, but was taking classes to address that deficiency. He was a high school graduate. He had adequate living facilities. There was no scientific evidence that he was mentally impaired — that was an assumption that was made by CCDSS and Dr. Blumberg, who apparently presumed that he was, but undertook no tests to establish the extent, if any, of such impairment. . . . There was no evidence that petitioner had ever committed acts of abuse or willful neglect in respect to the children. In fact, when he was unable to care for Tristynn for a temporary period he approached CCDSS seeking assistance. . . .

. . . . Upon our review of the record . . . it is evident that there was not clear and convincing evidence . . . sufficient to overcome the presumption that the "best interests" of the children rest in the retention, generally, of petitioner's parental rights, *although at the present time actual custody may not be appropriate.* . . .

[The Court rejected the claim that the children's long relationship with the foster parents was relevant.]. . . . In cases such as this, parents who . . . love their children . . . and seek assistance [from CCDSS] . . . are placed at great risk of losing their children altogether. If . . . the Department places their children . . . with foster parents with whom they bond (and that is the type of foster parents one hopes are found), the natural parent runs the very real risk of later having that bonding in the foster home, created, in part, by CCDSS and court forced inaccessibility to his own children, be a major factor used to later terminate his parental rights . . .

. . . . Our holding today reflects the idea that fundamental constitutional rights, *i.e.,* the child rearing rights at issue here, can only be completely terminated upon the clearest and most convincing evidence that the parent, however poor, uneducated, or disabled, cannot and will not, even with proper assistance, be able to sufficiently parent his children in the reasonable future. . . .

The judgment of the Court of Special Appeals is reversed, and the case shall be remanded to that court for it to reverse the judgment of the Circuit Court. . . .

Dissenting Opinion by WILNER, J.

. . . . This case does *not* involve discrimination against disabled parents or poor parents. It does *not* involve any trampling upon the legitimate parental rights of Mr.

F. . . . It is simply a case in which (1) nearly six years ago, two children were found to be in need of assistance by the juvenile court, (2) no appeal from or attack on those decisions has ever been made, (3) efforts were made to reunify the children with their father, but (4) the conclusion was drawn, based on evidence that the trial court found persuasive, that Mr. F. was not in a position, and was not likely to be in a position in the foreseeable future, to be able to care properly for the children, who have special needs, and (5) there *are* prospective adoptive parents willing and able to care for the children on a permanent basis. Everyone seemed to agree that if an adoption proceeds, it should be an open one, in which Mr. F. may maintain contact with the children.

Although parents do have a Constitutional right to raise their children, if they are able to do so, the law allows a court to terminate parental rights, under specified circumstances, when the welfare of the children would best be served by that course of action. . . . It is for the trial judge, not for us, to weigh and consider the evidence. . . . The Court has thrown appellate restraint to the wind, and, in doing so, has not only subordinated the welfare of these two children to its incorrect view of how far the parent's rights extend but has also injected considerable uncertainty into termination proceedings generally.

NOTES

1. ***Burden of Proof and Procedural Considerations in Termination Proceedings.*** Both the burden and standard of proof are procedural devices that reflect particular policy choices as to how to weigh the interests at stake in termination proceedings. The state has the burden of proof in termination hearings, and under *Santosky v. Kramer*, 455 U.S. 745 (1982), it must meet its burden with "clear and convincing evidence." The Court focused on the need to protect parental rights by avoiding mistaken terminations — a risk aggravated in termination cases by such factors as (1) the imprecision of the substantive termination standards, (2) the "vast array" of resources which the state could command to prove its case, (3) the trial court's "unusual" discretion, and (4) the vulnerability of poor, uneducated or minority parents to cultural or class bias.

While the *Santosky* rule reflects the Court's emphasis on parental interests, it shows less recognition of the other interests at stake, such as the child's. A normal preponderance of the evidence standard yields the fewest errors in total, and gives equal priority to avoiding errors on either side. *See* David H. Kaye, *The Limits of the Preponderance of the Evidence Standard: Justifiably Naked Statistical Evidence and Multiple Causation*, 1982 Am. B. Found. J. 487. The more demanding standard of proof *Santosky* requires reduces the frequency of mistaken terminations, but *increases* the frequency of mistaken *failures* to terminate by an even larger amount, thus increasing the total number of mistaken adjudications. *Santosky* concludes that the parents' interests are particularly strong, and assumes that until grounds for termination are established, there is no equally weighty interest on the part of the child. In his *Santosky* dissent, Justice Rehnquist, joined by Chief Justice Burger and Justices White and O'Connor, emphasized the numerous protections already afforded by the New York statutory schemes relating to abuse, neglect and termination proceedings; parental rights had been terminated in *Santosky* only "after four and one-half years of involvement . . . more than seven complete hearings, and additional periodic supervision of the State's rehabilitative efforts. . . ." *Id.* at 783. The *Santosky* result has been criticized for encouraging "a disproportionately large number" of parental appeals in termination cases, on technical procedural grounds. One judge commented that, "Every right accorded to the parents, every reunification service ordered, every continuance, and especially every appeal taken is purchased at the expense of the person who is in law and morality their primary object of judicial solicitude, namely the child." *In re Micah*, 243 Cal. Rptr. 756 (1988) (Brauer, J., concurring).

Do indigent parents have a constitutional right to court-appointed counsel at termination proceedings? This claim was rejected by the Supreme Court in *Lassiter v. Department of Social Services of Durham County*, 452 U.S. 18 (1981). In *Lassiter*, the Court by a 5-4 vote held that the Due Process Clause does not require appointment of counsel for indigent parents in every termination case, but that the issue should be considered on a case-by-case basis, taking into account the complexity of the case and the parent's capacity to proceed without counsel. The Court affirmed termination of the mother's parental rights without benefit of counsel, because the issues were not sufficiently complicated to require counsel. The Supreme Court held that a parent whose parental rights have been terminated cannot be denied a right to an appeal of the decision because she lacks the means to pay for the record preparation fees. *M.L.B. v. S.L.J.*, 519 U.S. 102 (1996). The Court concluded that a Mississippi statute conditioning the parent's right to appeal on advance payment of the fees violated the parent's equal protection and due process rights. In the case, the mother's parental rights were terminated in an action brought by the custodial father and his wife, who sought to adopt the children. The mother filed a timely appeal, but was unable to pay the $2350 filing fee to reproduce the transcript and other court records. The Court emphasized the importance to the parent of a decision to sever the parent-child relationship in aligning appeals in this category of cases with other types of cases in which indigent parties have a right to appeal — criminal appeals and appeals in cases involving the right to participate in the political process.

Several courts have held that in a termination action, a claim of ineffectiveness of counsel — a claim generally available only in criminal appeals — can provide a basis for appeal. *See, e.g., State ex rel. Juvenile Dep't v. Geist*, 799 P.2d 674 (Or. App. 1990); *Johnson v. J.K.C.*, 781 S.W.2d 226 (Mo. App. 1989) (citing cases from other jurisdictions, including Arizona, California, Colorado, Illinois, Iowa, Kansas, Massachusetts, Michigan, New York, North Carolina and Washington). In *Guardianship of S.A.W. v. Torres*, 856 P.2d 286 (Okla. 1993), the Supreme Court of Oklahoma held that a minor child who was the subject of an action to terminate parental rights is entitled to independent representation. In Oklahoma, parents have a right to counsel in a termination proceeding, and, the Court reasoned, the child has an equally important interest at stake.

2. The Substantive Standards for Termination of Parental Rights. While all states have separate statutes which set forth grounds and procedures for termination of parental rights, typically the grounds overlap with the substantive standards for abuse and neglect. When termination grounds relate to a prior finding of child abuse or neglect, usually the conditions resulting in removal of the child must have continued for a minimum period without sufficient improvement, despite reunification efforts by the state in the form of remedial services. If abuse is severe, however, or if the parent is found to be unfit and unlikely to be capable of caring for the child in a reasonable time, parental rights can be terminated without providing an opportunity to remediate. Under recent federal legislation that reflects a policy of promoting permanency planning for children in foster care, termination is facilitated in cases of severe abuse; in other cases, the time period for remediation is limited.

a. *Is unfitness required?* The Maryland statute applied in *Adoption No. J9610436* provides that parental rights can only be terminated in abuse or neglect cases when termination is in the best interests of the child. As the court's analysis indicates, however, this is a necessary but not sufficient condition. Many statutes are interpreted to require that a parent's rights cannot be terminated without some showing of unfitness, even if the child's interests might be furthered by termination. *See, e.g., In re Kristina L.*, 520 A.2d 574 (R.I. 1987). If a state could override parental rights merely because it believes a child could be made better off as a result, it could remove children from their parents' custody to place them in better homes.

Does the Constitution prohibit the termination of a parent's rights without a showing of unfitness? As the Supreme Court opinions that begin this chapter make clear, parents have a fundamental right to rear their children under the Due Process Clause of the Fourteenth Amendment. Although the issue of whether parental unfitness is required for termination has never been directly addressed, a number of Supreme Court decisions have suggested that the termination of parental rights on grounds of the child's interests alone, without any showing of unfitness, is unconstitutional. *See, e.g., Smith v. Org. of Foster Families*, 431 U.S. 816, 862–63 (1977) (Stewart, J. concurring) ("If a State were to attempt to force the breakup of a natural family, over the objections of the parents and their children, without some showing of unfitness and for the sole reason that to do so was thought to be in the children's best interest, I should have little doubt that the State would have intruded impermissibly on the 'private realm of family life which the state cannot enter.' "). The Court has also held, in *Santosky v. Kramer*, that due process requires that termination on statutory unfitness grounds must be proved by clear and convincing evidence. *See* Note 1, *supra*. In 2000, the Court reiterated that parents' right to control the upbringing of their children is a fundamental right, in rejecting the application of the best interest of the child standard to grandparent visitation decisions and requiring courts to give substantial weight to the objection of a fit parent. *Troxel v. Granville*, 530 U.S. 57 (2000). *See* Chapter 6, Section F. Most lower courts assume that unfitness is a constitutional requirement. *See, e.g., In the Interest of Jane Doe*, 20 P.3d 616 (Haw. 2001) (interpreting statute to require a finding of parental unfitness and therefore, holding it to be constitutional).

Because a showing of parental unfitness is required, termination cases can present a tension between protecting the child's interests and respecting parental rights. For example, as the principal case illustrates, the protection of parents' rights may undermine children's relationships with psychological parents. Would the interest of Tristynn and Edward be promoted if their foster parents were allowed to adopt, especially since an open adoption (and a continued relationship with their father) was contemplated? The lower appellate court suggested that an important consideration in the decision was protection of the children's long-term relationships with their foster parents, a consideration that the Court of Appeals rejected out of hand as unfair to the father in this case, and perhaps in general. Some courts allow consideration of the bonds between children and foster parents in the termination decision if separation from foster parents would cause "serious psychological and emotional harm." *See Matter of the Guardianship of J.C.*, 608 A.2d 1312 (N.J. 1992) (announcing this standard).

b. *Is parental "fault" required for termination?* Should parental rights be terminated even if the parent has done all that he or she can to remediate the conditions that led to removal of the child, but has been unable to assume parental responsibilities because of conditions beyond her control? This question is at the center of *Adoption No. J9610436*; the father's sincere efforts to become a competent parent and the agency's failure to tailor its remedial efforts to his needs are the basis of the court's determination that termination was wrongly ordered. But was the case correctly decided? From the child's perspective, parental "innocence" may not be relevant to the decision of whether termination promotes her welfare. Perhaps children receive benefits from ongoing relationships with inadequate parents who are sincerely trying to fulfill their duties, benefits that do not exist where the parent has culpably harmed the child or has not tried to remediate. *See* Elizabeth S. Scott & Robert E. Scott, *Parents as Fiduciaries*, 81 VA. L. REV. 2401 (1995).

c. *Mental disability.* Perhaps the best example of a "no-fault" ground for termination is the one at issue in *Adoption No. J9610436*: the parent's inability to care adequately for the child because of limited mental capacity. Even when mental disability does not render a parent unable to care for a child, it may seriously affect the degree of supervision and guidance the parent can offer. Courts have consistently upheld this ground of termination if its effect is to severely impair parenting ability. *See Tennessee v. Smith*, 785 S.W.2d 336 (Tenn. 1990) ("mental disability" can form the basis for termination of parental rights, even though the acts of mentally disabled parent are not willful). Modern courts emphasize that mental disability alone is not a sufficient basis for termination of parental rights; it must also be shown that the disability renders the parent unable to fulfill parental responsibilities. *See, e.g., In re R.C., a Minor*, 745 N.E.2d 1233 (Ill. 2001).

A question that frequently arises in cases involving mentally disabled parents is whether, in fulfilling its obligation to undertake "reasonable efforts" to reunify the family, the agency has a heightened obligation to provide appropriate services and support. *See* Note 4, *infra*. Although the court in *Adoption No. J9610436* faulted the state for not tailoring its efforts to Mr. F.'s needs, many courts would find standard programs adequate to satisfy "reasonable efforts." *See, e.g., In Interest of D.L.S.*, 432 N.W.2d 31 (Neb. 1988) (where mother's "mental deficiency" was not improved, although she was trying to comply with rehabilitation plan, agency is not required to wait for some indeterminate period, "on the speculative hope that [her] deficiency would be remedied"); *Interest of J.A.L.*, 432 N.W.2d 876 (N.D. 1988) (agency is not required to provide constant, round-the-clock supervision in order to keep the family together).

Where emotional bonds between the mentally disabled parent and child are significant, the "reasonable efforts" requirement may be more strictly interpreted. *See, e.g., In re E.M.*, 620 A.2d 481 (Pa. 1993) (termination order set aside where trial court failed to sufficiently consider the emotional bond between the children and their mentally impaired mother). In *P.A.B.*, 570 A.2d 522 (Pa. Super. 1990), a termination order was reversed even though reunification was deemed totally unrealistic, because of the positive emotional relationship enjoyed by the parties.

Response to mentally disabled parents has become more complicated with the enactment of the Americans with Disabilities Act (ADA) in 1990. This statute embodies a policy of protection of disabled individuals from discrimination and has been invoked in support of mentally disabled individuals facing termination of parental rights. The ADA provides that "no qualified individual with a disability shall, by reason of such disability, be excluded from participation, or denied the benefits of, the services, programs, or activities of a public entity, or be subject to discrimination by any such entity." 42 U.S.C. § 12132. In a part of the opinion not reprinted here, the court in *Adoption No. J9610436* suggested that the ADA constitutes part of the interpretive framework for applying Maryland's statutory termination provisions (although the court declined to decide whether the ADA directly applied to termination decisions). 796 A.2d at 783.

A few courts have concluded that the ADA applies to termination proceedings. *See In re C.M.*, 996 S.W.2d 269 (Tex. App. 1999) (ADA creates defense in termination proceeding, but parent waived defense in this case). Other courts have found ADA inapplicable to this context. For example, Massachusetts' highest court rejected an appeal by a father who argued that the trial court in terminating his parental rights had failed to reasonably accommodate his cognitive disorder and attention deficit disorder, as required under the ADA. *Adoption of Gregory*, 747 N.E.2d 120 (Mass. 2001). The court concluded that proceedings to terminate parental rights do not constitute "services, programs, or activities" under the ADA. Even without the ADA, the court noted, Massachusetts law directed that the parents' special needs be accommodated, and that parents with children in state custody be offered services that were responsive to handicapping conditions. Most other courts have reached the same conclusion. *See In re Antony B.*, 735 A.2d 893 (Conn. App. 1999) (termination proceedings not subject to ADA, and thus federal statute neither provides a defense nor creates special obligations). For a discussion of this topic, see Chris Watkins, *Beyond Status: The Americans with Disabilities Act and the Parental Rights of People Labeled Developmentally Disabled or Mentally Retarded*, 83 CAL. L. REV. 1415, 1469 (1995); Robert L. Hayman, *Presumptions of Justice: Law, Politics, and the Mentally Retarded Parent*, 103 HARV. L. REV. 1202, 1269 (1990).

d. *Mental illness*. Similar issues are raised with respect to parents who are mentally ill, although some of these conditions can be ameliorated with treatment, and may change over time. When the social services agency attempts to terminate a parent's rights based upon mental illness, ordinarily it must show that the illness is permanent, or that there is no reasonable likelihood that the parent will be able to take care of the child in the future. *See, e.g.*, COLO. REV. STAT. § 19-5-105(3.1)(a)(I) (2008) (disability of such duration or nature as to render the parent unlikely within a reasonable time to care for the needs of the child); N.Y. SOC. SERV. LAW § 384-

b(4)(c) (2009) (disability will continue for the foreseeable future). Outcomes in termination actions involving mentally ill parents vary. Some courts require special efforts on the part of the state. In *In Matter of Star A.*, 435 N.E.2d 1080 (N.Y. 1982), the mother who suffered from mental illness was receiving treatment from independent sources, and the social workers monitored her treatment, but "apparently did little to channel her toward appropriate psychiatric care when she strayed from her treatments." In the termination proceedings, the court rejected the agency claim that further services would have been duplicative of the services the mother was receiving, holding that the agency's duty to provide services could not be excused by its predetermination that further efforts would be "futile." In *In re Interest of Brown*, 736 P.2d 1355 (Idaho App. 1987), on the other hand, the court concluded that "any course of psychotherapeutic treatment would have been unproductive." because the mother had declined to take advantage of other services offered by the agency, such as help with family budgeting and home maintenance. *Id.* at 1358.

    e. *Imprisonment.* Parents who cannot fulfill their parental obligations because they are incarcerated present another challenging case. Can imprisonment *per se* be a ground for termination? Illinois recently added a statutory unfitness ground for termination on the basis of "repeated incarceration" which prevented the discharge of parental duties. Illinois Adoption Act, 750 ILL. COMP. STAT 50/1(D)(S) (2009). Illinois' highest court determined that the termination decision under this ground could include evidence of imprisonment before the child's birth. *In re D.D.*, 752 N.E.2d 1112 (Ill. 2001). Thus, the criminal record of the father, who began serving a 10 year term for aggravated assault shortly after the child's birth, was appropriately considered in the termination decision. Having been imprisoned almost all of his adult life, he had no parenting abilities or interest in meeting the child's needs. The Arizona Supreme Court examined the meaning of unfitness based on abandonment, as applied to an imprisoned father. *Michael J. v. Ariz. Dep't of Econ. Sec.*, 995 P.2d 682 (Ariz. 2000). The court concluded that, although the father's incarceration alone did not constitute abandonment, the father's failure to make more than minimal efforts to support and communicate with the child, the finding of abandonment was justified.

    Some courts have been sympathetic toward prisoner parents. A Florida court held that a four-and-a-half year sentence did not support termination of the father's rights, under a statute that allowed termination in response to an expected sentence that would constitute a substantial portion of the child's minority. *W.W. v. Dep't of Children and Families*, 811 So. 2d 791 (Fla. App. 2002). As no other ground existed, termination was not warranted. A termination decision based on the imprisoned father's failure to visit or support the children was reversed by one court, where the Department of Social Services would not permit visits requested by the father and he was not permitted to earn money in prison. *Dep't of Soc. Serv. v. Wilson*, 543 S.E.2d 580 (S.C. App. 2000). The evidence indicated that prior to his imprisonment, the father had fulfilled his parental responsibilities.

    3. *The Limits of the State's "Reasonable Efforts" Obligation.* In most cases, the state is obliged to use "reasonable efforts" to rehabilitate the parents or the conditions that lead to the child's removal before it can initiate termination proceedings. Thus, where the agency has failed to offer appropriate services that would assist the parent in resuming his parental responsibilities, the court may decline to terminate parental rights on that ground. However, although successful remedial efforts can lead to reunification, extensive efforts to reunite the family can mean long periods of foster care for the child. Thus, the trend is to puts limits on the state's obligation to undertake reunification efforts and the parent's opportunity to remediate. Some courts attach far less importance to the state's remedial obligation than did the Maryland court in *Adoption No. J9610436*.

The Connecticut Supreme Court interpreted that state's statute to provide that termination of parental rights could be ordered without proof by the state that reasonable efforts at reunification had been made. *In re Eden F.*, 741 A.2d 873 (Conn. 1999). The case involved a mother suffering from chronic schizophrenia, which had seriously hampered her ability to care for her child. The court upheld termination on the statutory ground that, in response to an earlier neglect finding, she had failed to achieve rehabilitation sufficient to encourage the belief that she would, in a reasonable period of time, be able to resume a "responsible position in the child's life." The statute (which is quite similar to the Maryland statute) directed that, once the termination ground was established by clear and convincing evidence, the court should consider the state's reunification efforts and the services provided to the parent to determine if termination was in the child's best interest. The court concluded that the statute did not require an explicit demonstration by the state that it had made reasonable reunification efforts, and that such a finding was not constitutionally required. If a parent is simply incapable of parenting, regardless of the services provided or if the necessary services would virtually amount to full-time substitute care (see, *In Interest of J.A.L., supra*), the agency may be excused from providing them. Other circumstances in which courts may excuse the agency's failure to provide further services include parental failure to make use of previously offered services, see *In re Kathaleen*, 460 A.2d 12 (R.I. 1983), or parental failure to keep in touch with the agency. *See In re Katina Valencia H.*, 119 A.D.2d 821 (N.Y. App. 1986).

4. *Promoting Children's Adoption from Foster Care.* As noted above, the Adoption and Safe Families Act of 1997 (ASFA) seeks to promote the adoption of children from foster care by requiring states to petition for termination of parental rights of children. In general, pressure has been building in recent years to promote the adoption of children in foster care. A study conducted by the National Center for Policy Analysis and the Institute for Children revealed that states vary widely in the percent of children in foster care who are ultimately adopted, from 10 % in Hawaii to 96 % in North Dakota. Some observers argue that the current system of Federal payments to the states for foster care services encourage states to keep children in foster care. *See* Irvin Molotsky, *Adoption Rate in Foster Care Varies Widely among States*, N.Y. Times, Aug. 8, 1997, A12. ASFA encourages states to increase and expedite adoption of abused and neglected children. The statute offers financial incentives to states to move children from foster care to permanent adoptive homes by awarding substantial payments for each adoption. The new law also directs states to initiate termination of parental rights of children who have been in foster care for 15 of the preceding 22 months. 42 U.S.C. § 675 (5)(E) (2009). The statute further provides that reasonable efforts are not required where the parent has subjected the child to "aggravated circumstances," as defined by state law, including abandonment, torture, chronic abuse, sexual abuse or has committed a felony assault on the child resulting in serious bodily injury. 42 U.S.C. § 671(a)(15) (2009).

It is not yet clear whether ASFA achieves its goal of expediting termination of parental rights in the interest of permanency planning for children. Although some states amended their termination statutes to conform to this requirement, there is evidence of judicial resistance. The court in *Adoption No. J9610436* did not seem to feel constrained by the federal statute — and, indeed, criticizes it in a part of the opinion not reprinted here. The Illinois Supreme Court recently reviewed a new statutory provision (enacted in response to ASFA) creating a presumption of parental unfitness when a child has been in foster care for the congressionally-prescribed time period. *In re H.G.*, 757 N.E.2d 864 (Ill. 2001). The court concluded that the statute represented an unconstitutional violation of parents' liberty interest in their relationship with their children. Although the state has a compelling state interest in protecting children, in the court's view, the statutory provision failed strict scrutiny review. It was not narrowly tailored to achieve the state's goal because it defines unfitness solely on the basis of passage of time, and not on parents' inability to care for their children. The court noted that the length of a child's stay in foster care sometimes is due to circumstances beyond the parents' control. In the case under review, delays of many months were caused by continuances and other problems in bringing the case to trial. The use of time periods was appropriate, in the court's view, only when it was linked to the parent's conduct (*i.e.* addiction or habitual drunkenness for at least a year.) The fact that under the statute the parent could rebut the presumption by showing that termination was not in the child's best interest did not correct the constitutional defect, because a parent able to care for her child (but who satisfied the presumption) should not have her rights determined by a best interest inquiry.

ASFA has been subject to much academic commentary, often quite critical. *See* David J. Herring, *The Adoption and Safe Families Act: Hope and its Subversion*, 34 FAM. L. Q. 329 (2000). Herring argues that ASFA's goal of permanency will be undermined because judges view the statute as unfair, especially where participation in programs is delayed due to lack of resources. *See also* Libby S. Adler, *The Meaning of Permanence: A Critical Analysis of the Adoption and Safe Families Act of 1997*, 38 HARV. J. LEGIS. 1 (2001). Adler criticizes the ASFA goal of permanence as embodying "the ideology of the ideal family." A more neutral analysis is offered by Stephanie Jill Gendell, *In Search of Permanency: A Reflection on the First Three Years of the Adoption and Safe Families Act*, 39 FAM. & COUNCIL CTS. REV. 25 (2001). Some commentators criticize an approach to permanency planning which focuses on efficient termination of parental rights. Children may have meaningful relationships with parents who are unable to provide care by taking custody. *See* Elizabeth S. Scott & Robert E. Scott, *Parents as Fiduciaries*, 81 VA. L. REV. 585 (1995). Moreover, many children are not, in fact, adopted after their parents' rights are terminated. Marsha Garrison, *Parents' Rights vs. Children's Interests: The Case of the Foster Child*, 22 N.Y.U. REV. L. & SOC. CHANGE 371 (1996). A federal report indicated that in 2000, 75,000 children whose parents' rights had been terminated were in foster care. *See* Children's Bureau AFCARS Report, *supra*.

In an analysis of existing research on the impact of AFSA, three social scientists summarize empirical findings:

Richard Barth, Fred Wulczyn & Tom Crea, *From Anticipation To Evidence: Research on the Adoption and Safe Families Act*
12 Va. J. Soc. Pol'y & L. 371, 392–98 (2005)

. . . Preliminary research . . . suggests that policy changes that ASFA instigated have combined with other ongoing trends to generate a meaningful increase in the rate of adoption of young children. The impact of ASFA is less clear regarding older children. The number of children awaiting adoption has not declined with the growth in adoptions. The U.S. Department of Health and Human Services identified more than 125,000 children as waiting for adoption in 2001, up from 122,000 just a few years before. Children over the age of six comprise nearly all of this increase. The numbers of children who are in this waiting status include a substantial proportion who have had parental rights terminated, but do not even have a record of an active adoption case.

. . .

Despite progress in increasing exits from foster care, ... there may be a shift of children from reunification to adoption, indicating a change in the composition of reasons for exiting foster care. The simultaneous increase in the rate of adoption and decrease in the rate of children leaving to foster care leaves open the possibility that adoption is preempting some reunifications. This was clearly not the objective of ASFA, which was intended to increase the use of adoption to preempt long-term foster care. This trend could also reflect a shift in priorities away from encouraging opportunities for families to remain intact following child welfare service involvement.

. . .

. . . ASFA may have its most adverse impact on reunifications that would have taken many years to achieve. . . . [¶] . . . Reunifications often result after quite a long time, well beyond what the law has now set as the time for the first permanency review (i.e., twelve months). Prior investigations have shown that about half of reunifications that occur do so in the first six to eighteen months, but that the remaining half will require an additional two or more years to do so. . . . African American children, in particular, [have] the longest reunification periods . . . Children living with relatives also [have] prolonged reunification periods. Thus, ASFA may intercede in more cases that might have resulted in reunification, instead terminating parental rights and finding adoptive homes.

[A]lthough the law holds the expectation that [terminations of parental rights] will be guided by the statutory timeframes, it offers the agency and the courts the option of identifying compelling reasons why such action should not be taken in any given case. . . . Thus, if adoptions are displacing reunifications, this result stems from decisions made in implementing the law and not from the law per se.

When [terminations of parental rights] are followed by adoption into a lifetime family, it contributes to the goal of having children move into legally permanent homes. But if it fails, it may result in children who have no legal relationship to any parents or guardians. . . . The development of legal and practical options to increase the likelihood of adoption without first terminating parental rights should be among the highest priorities of child welfare research.

More generally, reunification policy and practice needs an intensive review to ensure that a high proportion of the reunifications that can occur do, in fact, occur. Financing for family reunification services is very limited and inflexible . . . The inflexibility of . . . funding works against innovation in foster care and adoption. . . . There is almost no mechanism to develop new innovations in child welfare services. . . .

. . .

ASFA may be creating "a system that encourages speedy resolution of children's legal status but lacks the resources to assure permanency once children are legally free.". . . . [¶] . . . The failure of ASFA to account for developmental issues may result in some imprudent decisions to terminate the parental rights of older youth, even though they have little chance of being adopted and a substantial chance of disrupting important family relationships in the process. . . .

PROBLEMS

Problem 10-11.   Shortly after the birth of their child, Edward M. killed his wife, Julie M., in a violent domestic dispute. Edward received a 10-year jail sentence. Can Edward M.'s parental rights be terminated under the Minnesota statute set forth above? What are the best statutory and policy arguments that can be made on each side of this question?

Problem 10-12.   Six-year-old Darla J. was removed from the home on an emergency petition after several suspicious bruises were reported by her teacher to the welfare department. Physical abuse was never confirmed, but upon investigation of the family situation, the welfare department found that the living conditions at the J's home were unacceptable; Mr. & Mrs. J were living with their two other children in a small and somewhat run-down one-bedroom apartment. Neither parent was regularly employed. Because of the home situation, the Juvenile Court found Darla neglected, although her siblings were not removed. For the next four years, the parents visited with Darla only on five occasions. The reason for the lack of visits is unclear, although during this period, the parents have moved frequently without leaving a forwarding address; they themselves seldom initiated contact with Darla. The welfare department has not really attempted to assist the parents in locating better housing and employment, claiming they have been very hard to track down because of the frequent moves.

Darla is now 10 and has emotionally bonded with her foster parents, the S family. Under the Minnesota statute set forth above, are there grounds for termination of parental rights? If so, what about the other two children?

Problem 10-13.   Gershon and Golda Jonisz were Polish Jews. Shortly after their daughter Shifra was born in April, 1941, the Germans confined all Jews in the most miserable section of their town surrounded by a wall. In October 1942, Gershon and Golda escaped with 18-month-old Shifra. They soon became persuaded that they ensured Shifra's death as well as their own if they kept her with them. In desperation, they left her on the edge of the forest, near a Polish town, where she was found and taken in by Leokadia, a 34-year-old Polish Catholic woman whose husband had been arrested by the Gestapo two years earlier. She named the child Bogusia and cared for her for the remaining three years of the war. Leokadia worked in a German factory to support them, and was without family to care for the child while she was at work. She could not obtain a food ration for the child because that would have raised suspicions among the Germans. Despite a number of close calls, somehow she and the child survived the war.

Golda died in the extermination camp near Maidanek, but Gershon survived and searched for Shifra. In September 1945, he succeeded. When he appeared at Leokadia's apartment to claim the child, she said, "I am not giving up this child to anyone. God sent her to me and means for her to have me." She asked Bogusia if she wanted to go with the stranger who said he was her father. The child held tightly to Leokadia and said, "You are my mother. I love only you and we will always be together."

Who should have custody of Shifra-Bogusia? If you believe Leokadia should have custody, should Gershon's parental rights be terminated? If you believe Gershon should have custody, should Leokadia retain any rights? (The facts are borrowed from a true story told in P. HELLMAN, AVENUE OF THE RIGHTEOUS 167–264 (1980)).

[6]   Proving Child Abuse and Neglect in Criminal Court

Most of the discussion in this Chapter has thus far focused on the policies governing the operation of the *civil* child maltreatment laws. Child abuse and neglect can also be prosecuted through the criminal justice system. While the two systems can function in tandem, there are certain important differences between them. The civil system responds to child maltreatment perpetrated by a child's parents or guardians or in response to a parent or guardian's failure to protect a child from abuse perpetrated by others. In all but the most severe cases, it attempts to remediate the problematic conduct or conditions that led to the maltreatment, with a goal of keeping a family together if possible, while it seeks to protect the child from further harm. By contrast, the criminal justice system's reach is not limited by the existence of a parent-child relationship between the adult perpetrator and child victim. In fact, the criminal justice system provides the only formal avenue for state intervention in cases of child maltreatment where the perpetrator is not the child's legal parent or guardian. Included within this category, therefore, are cases of sexual abuse perpetrated by extended family members, neighbors, clergy, teachers and others.

The state may also file criminal charges against parents or guardians, most typically in cases characterized by circumstances in which one of the goals of the criminal justice system is deemed an appropriate response to the adults' conduct. For example, removal of the perpetrator from the community may appear necessary because of a continuing danger to the abused child or others; the nature (and/or consequences) of the maltreatment is sufficiently serious to trigger a punitive response from the community; the nature (and/or consequences) of the maltreatment are sufficiently serious to render remediation of the perpetrator and reunification of the family unlikely; or prosecutors determine that it is important to "send a message" to the perpetrator and others in the community regarding the seriousness of this offense. Indeed, law students may recognize among these factors some of the underlying goals of criminal justice system intervention: incapacitation, retribution, deterrence, and denunciation. Prosecuting child abuse cases through the criminal justice system has its own challenges, however, because of the myriad of constitutional protections available to defendants in such trials.

[a]   Testimony by the Alleged Child Victim

MARYLAND v. CRAIG
United States Supreme Court
497 U.S. 836 (1990)

O' CONNOR, J.,

I

[Defendant was charged with various sexual offenses against a child who had attended defendant's child care center.]

[B]efore . . . trial, the State sought to invoke a Maryland statutory procedure that permits a judge to receive, by one-way closed circuit television, the testimony of a child witness who is alleged to be a victim of child abuse. To invoke the procedure, the trial judge must first "determin[e] that testimony by the child victim in the courtroom will result in the child suffering serious emotional distress such that the child cannot reasonably communicate." MD. CTS. & JUD. PROC. CODE ANN. § 9-102(a)(1)(ii) (1989). Once the procedure is invoked, the child witness, prosecutor, and defense counsel withdraw to a separate room; the judge, jury, and defendant remain in the courtroom. The [child] is then examined and cross-examined in the separate room, while a video monitor records and displays the witness' testimony to those in the courtroom. During this time the witness cannot see the defendant. The defendant remains in electronic communication with defense counsel, and objections may be made and ruled on as if the witness were testifying in the courtroom.

In support of its motion invoking the one-way closed circuit television procedure, the State presented expert testimony that Brooke, as well as a number of other children who were alleged to have been sexually abused by Craig, would suffer "serious emotional distress such that [they could not] reasonably communicate," § 9-102(a)(1)(ii), if required to testify in the courtroom. . . .

II

The Confrontation Clause of the Sixth Amendment . . . provides: "In all criminal prosecutions, the accused shall enjoy the right . . . to be confronted with the witnesses against him."

. . . .

We have never held . . . that the Confrontation Clause guarantees criminal defendants the absolute right to a face-to-face meeting with witnesses against them at trial. . . . *Coy* [*v. Iowa*, 487 U.S., at 1012 (1988)] involved the placement of a screen that prevented two child witnesses in a child abuse case from seeing the defendant as they testified against him at trial. . . . In holding that the use of this procedure violated the defendant's right to confront witnesses against him, we suggested that any exception to the right "would surely be allowed only when necessary to further an important public policy" — *i.e.*, only upon a showing of something more than the generalized, "legislatively imposed presumption of trauma" underlying the statute at issue in that case. . . . We concluded that "[s]ince there ha[d] been no individualized findings that these particular witnesses needed special protection, the judgment [in the case before us] could not be sustained by any conceivable exception." . . . Because the trial court in this case made individualized findings that each of the child witnesses needed special protection, this case requires us to decide the question reserved in *Coy*.

The central concern of the Confrontation Clause is to ensure the reliability of the evidence against a criminal defendant by subjecting it to rigorous testing in the context of an adversary proceeding before the trier of fact. The word "confront," after all, also means a clashing of forces or ideas, thus carrying with it the notion of adversariness. . . .

[T]he right guaranteed . . . includes not only a "personal examination," *id.*, at 242, but also "(1) insures that the witness will give his statements under oath — thus impressing him with the seriousness of the matter and guarding against the lie by the possibility of a penalty for perjury; (2) forces the witness to submit to cross-examination, the 'greatest legal engine ever invented for the discovery of truth'; [and] (3) permits the jury that is to decide the defendant's fate to observe the demeanor of the witness in making his statement, thus aiding the jury in assessing his credibility." [*California v. Green*, 399 U.S. 149, 158]. . . .

The combined effect of these elements of confrontation — physical presence, oath, cross-examination, and observation of demeanor by the trier of fact — serves the purposes of the Confrontation Clause by ensuring that evidence admitted against an accused is reliable and subject to the rigorous adversarial testing that is the norm of Anglo-American criminal proceedings.

. . . .

Although face-to-face confrontation forms "the core of the values furthered by the Confrontation Clause," *Green, supra*, at 157, we have nevertheless recognized that it is not the sine qua non of the confrontation right . . . [¶] Instead, we have repeatedly held that the Clause permits, where necessary, the admission of certain hearsay statements against a defendant despite the defendant's inability to confront the declarant at trial. . . . We have accordingly stated that a literal reading of the Confrontation Clause would "abrogate virtually every hearsay exception, a result long rejected as unintended and too extreme." [*Ohio v. Roberts*, 448 U.S. 56, 63]. Thus, in certain narrow circumstances, "competing interests, if 'closely examined,' may warrant dispensing with confrontation at trial." *Id.*, at 64. . . .

That the face-to-face confrontation requirement is not absolute does not, of course, mean that it may easily be dispensed with. . . . [O]ur precedents confirm that a defendant's right to confront accusatory witnesses may be satisfied absent a physical, face-to-face confrontation at trial only where denial of such confrontation is necessary to further an important public policy and only where the reliability of the testimony is otherwise assured. . . .

III

Maryland's statutory procedure, when invoked, prevents a child witness from seeing the defendant as he or she testifies. . . . We find it significant, however, that Maryland's procedure preserves all of the other elements of the confrontation right: the child witness must be competent to testify and must testify under oath; the defendant retains full opportunity for contemporaneous cross-examination; and the judge, jury, and defendant are able to view (albeit by video monitor) the demeanor (and body) of the witness as he or she testifies. Although we are mindful of the many subtle effects face-to-face confrontation may have on an adversary criminal proceeding, the presence of these other elements of confrontation — oath, cross-examination, and observation of the witness' demeanor — adequately ensures that the testimony is both reliable and subject to rigorous adversarial testing in a manner functionally equivalent to that accorded live, in-person testimony. [W]e think these elements . . . not only permit a defendant to "confound and undo the false accuser, or reveal the child coached by a malevolent adult," *Coy,* . . . but may well aid a defendant in eliciting favorable testimony from the child witness. Indeed, to the extent the child witness' testimony may be said to be technically given out-of-court (though we do not so hold), these assurances of reliability and adversariness are far greater than those required for admission of hearsay testimony under the Confrontation Clause. We are therefore confident that use of the one-way closed-circuit television procedure, where necessary to further an important state interest, does not impinge upon the truth-seeking or symbolic purposes of the Confrontation Clause.

The critical inquiry in this case, therefore, is whether use of the procedure is necessary to further an important state interest. The State contends that it has a substantial interest in protecting children who are allegedly victims of child abuse from the trauma of testifying against the alleged perpetrator and that its statutory procedure for receiving testimony from such witnesses is necessary to further that interest.

We . . . conclude today that a State's interest in the physical and psychological well-being of child abuse victims may be sufficiently important to outweigh, at least in some cases, a defendant's right to face his or her accusers in court. That a significant majority of States has enacted statutes to protect child witnesses from the trauma of giving testimony in child abuse cases attests to the widespread belief in the importance of such a public policy.

. . . . [W]e will not second-guess the considered judgment of the Maryland Legislature regarding the importance of its interest in protecting child abuse victims from the emotional trauma of testifying. Accordingly, we hold that, if the State makes an adequate showing of necessity, the state interest in protecting child witnesses from the trauma of testifying in a child abuse case is sufficiently important to justify the use of a special procedure that permits a child witness in such cases to testify at trial against a defendant in the absence of face-to-face confrontation with the defendant.

The requisite finding of necessity must of course be a case-specific one: the trial court must hear evidence and determine whether use of the one-way closed circuit television procedure is necessary to protect the welfare of the particular child witness who seeks to testify. . . . The trial court must also find that the child witness would be traumatized, not by the courtroom generally, but by the presence of the defendant. Denial of face-to-face confrontation is not needed to further the state interest in protecting the child witness from trauma unless it is the presence of the defendant that causes the trauma. . . . Finally, the trial court must find that the emotional distress suffered by the child witness in the presence of the defendant is more than de minimis, ... [T]he Maryland statute, which requires a determination that the child witness will suffer "serious emotional distress such that the child cannot reasonably communicate," § 9-102(a)(1)(ii), clearly suffices to meet constitutional standards.

To be sure, face-to-face confrontation may be said to cause trauma for the very purpose of eliciting truth, cf. Coy, but we think that the use of Maryland's special procedure . . . adequately ensures the accuracy of the testimony and preserves the adversary nature of the trial. . . . Indeed, where face-to-face confrontation causes significant emotional distress in a child witness, there is evidence that such confrontation would in fact [disserve] the Confrontation Clause's truth-seeking goal. . . . Brief for American Psychological Association as Amicus Curiae 18–24. . . .

IV

[The Court vacated the judgment of the Maryland Court of Appeals, because that court had imposed too high a standard in requiring that the determination of necessity be made through questioning of the child in the defendant's presence and requiring that the trial court consider less burdensome alternatives, such as two-way television testimony.]

JUSTICE SCALIA, with whom JUSTICE BRENNAN, JUSTICE MARSHALL, and JUSTICE STEVENS join, dissenting.

Seldom has this Court failed so conspicuously to sustain a categorical guarantee of the Constitution against the tide of prevailing current opinion. The Sixth Amendment provides, with unmistakable clarity, that "[i]n all criminal prosecutions, the accused shall enjoy the right . . . to be confronted with the witnesses against him". . . .

Because of [the] subordination of explicit constitutional text to currently favored public policy, the following scene can be played out in an American courtroom for the first time in two centuries: A father whose young daughter has been given over to the exclusive custody of his estranged wife, or a mother whose young son has been taken into custody by the State's child welfare department, is sentenced to prison for sexual abuse on the basis of testimony by a child the parent has not seen or spoken to for many months; and the guilty verdict is rendered without giving the parent so much as the opportunity to sit in the presence of the child, and to ask, personally or through counsel, "it is really not true, is it, that I — your father (or mother) whom you see before you — did these terrible things?" Perhaps that is a procedure today's society desires; perhaps (though I doubt it) it is even a fair procedure; but it is assuredly not a procedure permitted by the Constitution. . . .

II

Much of the Court's opinion consists of applying to this case the mode of analysis we have used in the admission of hearsay evidence. . . .

Some of the Court's analysis seems to suggest that the children's testimony here was itself hearsay of the sort permissible under our Confrontation Clause cases. . . . That cannot be. Our Confrontation Clause conditions for the admission of hearsay have long included a "general requirement of unavailability" of the declarant. . . . "Live" closed-circuit television testimony, however — if it can be called hearsay at all — is surely an example of hearsay as "a weaker substitute for live testimony," . . . which can be employed only when the genuine article is unavailable. . . .

The Court's test today requires unavailability only in the sense that the child is unable to testify in the presence of the defendant. That cannot possibly be the relevant sense. . . .

III

The Court characterizes the State's interest which "outweigh[s]" the explicit text of the Constitution as an "interest in the physical and psychological well-being of child abuse victims," an "interest in protecting" such victims "from the emotional trauma of testifying." That is not so. A child who meets the Maryland statute's requirement of suffering such "serious emotional distress" from confrontation that he "cannot reasonably communicate" would seem entirely safe. Why would a prosecutor want to call a witness who cannot reasonably communicate?. . . . The State's interest here is . . . what the State's interest always is when it seeks to get a class of evidence admitted in criminal proceedings: more convictions of guilty defendants.

And the interest on the other side is also what it usually is when the State seeks to get a new class of evidence admitted: fewer convictions of innocent defendants — specifically, in the present context, innocent defendants accused of particularly heinous crimes. The "special" reasons that exist for suspending one of the usual guarantees of reliability in the case of children's testimony are perhaps matched by "special" reasons for being particularly insistent upon it in the case of children's testimony. Some studies show that children are substantially more vulnerable to suggestion than adults, and often unable to separate recollected fantasy (or suggestion) from reality. . . ."

[As evidence of the injustice of erroneous testimony by children in sexual abuse cases, Justice Scalia describes the charges of sexual abuse brought against 24 adults in Jordan, Minnesota, on the basis allegations by children obtained through questionable investigational techniques. Most of the charges were later dropped. [This case is discussed in the Note on Child Abuse Reform, below. *Eds.*]]"

In the last analysis, however, this debate is not an appropriate one. . . . For good or bad, the Sixth Amendment requires confrontation, and we are not at liberty to ignore it. To quote the document one last time . . . : "In *all* criminal prosecutions, the accused shall enjoy the right . . . to be confronted with the witnesses against him" (emphasis added). . . .

NOTES

1. ***Two-Fold Concerns Regarding Courtroom Testimony of Alleged Child Abuse Victims.*** The plan to place an alleged victim of child abuse on the stand in a criminal trial invokes two sets of concerns: those relating to the trustworthiness of the testimony and those relating to the potentially traumatic psychological effects of testifying on the child. At common law, young children were typically presumed incapable of testifying in court, although there is ample evidence of some courts in England and the United States questioning this categorical exclusion of children from the witness stand. *See, e.g.*, John E.B. Myers, *New Era of Skepticism Regarding Children's Credibility*, 1 PSYCHOL. PUB. POL'Y & L. 387, 387–88 (1995). State and federal law formally shifted the presumption of incompetence to one of competence in the 1970s. Rule 601 of the Federal Rules of Evidence, adopted in 1975, state that "[e]very person is competent to be a witness except as otherwise provided in these rules . . ." FED. RULE EVID. 601, 28 U.S.C.A. (2009). Eighty years earlier, the U.S. Supreme Court asserted that age alone was an inadequate determinant of one's capacity to testify.

> While no one should think of calling as a witness an infant only two or three years old, there is no precise age which determines the question of competency. This depends on the capacity and intelligence of the child, his appreciation of the difference between truth and falsehood, as well as of his duty to tell the former. The decision of this question rests primarily with the trial judge, who sees the proposed witness, notices his manner, his apparent possession or lack of intelligence, and may resort to any examination which will tend to disclose his capacity and intelligence, as well as his understanding of the obligations of an oath.

Wheeler v. U.S., 159 U.S. 523, 525 (1895). While some states preceded the Federal Rules in formally recognizing children as capable to testify, other states followed. The standards for competency to testify are generally recognized as fairly low, and encompass the following skills or abilities: the capacity to attend to, observe, remember, and report the events about which the individual will testify and, importantly, the ability to distinguish what is true from what is not and to appreciate that courtroom testimony must be truthful. *See, e.g.*, Lois A. Weithorn, *Children's Competencies in Legal Contexts* in CHILDREN, MENTAL HEALTH & THE LAW (N. Dickon Reppucci, Lois A. Weithorn, Edward Mulvey & John Monahan eds. 1984). *See also Ryan v. State*, 988 P.2d 46, 57 (Wyo. 1999).

Today, in response to challenges to a child witness' capacity, judges make individualized assessments. Depending upon the events that are the subject of testimony and a range of associated factors (e.g., how much time elapsed between the events in question and the testimony), children of various ages may meet the standard. In recent years, there has been substantial empirical research examining children's testimonial capacities. *See, e.g.*, STEPHEN J. CECIL & MAGGIE BRUCK, JEOPARDY IN THE COURTROOM: A SCIENTIFIC ANALYSIS OF CHILDREN'S TESTIMONY (1995); John E.B. Myers et al., *Psychological Research on Children as Witnesses: Practical Implications for Forensic Interviews and Courtroom Testimony*, 28 PAC. L.J. 3 (1996). Among the myriad of empirical findings, research indicates that the mode of questioning children about events, prior to and during courtroom testimony, can affect the accuracy of children's recall. Thus, it is extremely important that adults exercise caution in the manner in which they question and talk with children who may ultimately testify about their experiences as victims of abuse or neglect.

Even if there are no questions about a child's capacity to testify, there may still be concern that abused children will be traumatized further by the obligation to recount their experiences in the open courtroom and in the presence the alleged abuser. There is concern that the child may, under these circumstances, be unable to testify because of ongoing fear of the perpetrator or because the physical and psychological reactions to the situation incapacitate him. It is this latter concern that has motivated state and federal policies allowing for the type of modification held constitutional in *Maryland v. Craig*.

2. *The Right of Confrontation and the* Craig *Exception.* The critical difference between what the Court allows in *Craig* and what it did not allow in *Coy v. Iowa*, discussed by the Court in *Craig*, lies in the Maryland requirement of a case-by-case determination of the emotional trauma that face-to-face testimony might cause, as opposed to a general rule for all children based upon a general belief about the need to protect them. Under the Iowa rule, struck down in *Coy*, a screen was placed between the child witness and the defendant in all cases. Consider, however, whether this distinction between *Craig* and *Coy* effectively serves to protect defendant's rights. Might it not be less prejudicial for the jury to be told that children's testimony categorically is taken out-of-court, rather than to allow the inference that this child has particular reason to fear this defendant? Moreover, it may not be possible to escape reliance on general findings, even under a *Craig* standard, because courts will likely rely on psychological evidence based upon the usual reactions of children of the same age and circumstances as the proposed witness. In *Lomholt v. Iowa*, 327 F.3d 748 (8th Cir. 2003), for example, a federal appellate court accepted the testimony of the children's sexual abuse counselor about the trauma to children of testifying with their abuser present as sufficient to support the more particularized finding regarding the impact of such testimony on the children in the case.

3. *The Child Victims' and Witnesses' Rights Act.* In 1990, Congress enacted the Child Victims' and Child Witnesses' Protection Law, 18 U.S.C.A. § 3509 (2009), in response to *Maryland v. Craig.* The statute was designed to protect alleged child victims as witnesses in federal courts, while conforming to the requirements that the Supreme Court suggested were necessary to protect criminal defendants' confrontation rights under the Sixth Amendment. The statute provides that, in a proceeding involving an alleged offense against a child, the court may order that a child's testimony be taken in a room outside the courtroom and televised by two-way closed circuit television. This modification may be ordered if (1)"The child is unable to testify because of fear; (2) There is substantial likelihood, established by expert testimony, the child is likely to suffer emotional trauma from testifying; (3) The child suffers a mental or other infirmity[; or] (4) Conduct of the defendant or defense counsel causes the child to be unable to testify." *Id* at § 3509(b)(1)(B).

Under the statute, the prosecutor and the defense attorney must be present in the room with the child, and the child is subject to direct and cross-examination. The testimony is transmitted to the courtroom for viewing by all present, including the defendant. The defendant must be provided with a means of private contemporaneous communication with his attorney. The guardian ad litem and an adult attendant (to offer support to the child, but not to assist in answering questions) may also be present in the room with the child. The statute further provides for videotaped depositions of alleged child victims, which may be introduced later at trial if the child is altogether unable to testify for one of the above reasons.

Most federal circuit courts have upheld the use of out-of courtroom closed circuit television testimony by children under this statute against Sixth Amendment challenges. In *United States v. Garcia,* 7 F.3d 885 (9th Cir. 1993), the Ninth Circuit Court of Appeals interpreted provisions of the statute as codifying *Maryland v. Craig.* In that case, the fact that the child's counselor (who testified that the child would experience emotional trauma) was not an expert in child testimony was held to go to the weight and not the admissibility of her expert testimony. In *United States v. Etimani,* 328 F.3d 493 (9th Cir. 2003), the same court held that the statutory requirement that the defendant's television image be transmitted into the room where the child is testifying is satisfied if the monitor is called to the child's attention and is visible from where she is seated, but that it does "not have to be in her direct field of vision while she is facing forward."

The Eighth Circuit, however, has interpreted Section 3509 and *Craig* more narrowly. In *U.S. v. Bordeaux,* it held that Section 3509 was unconstitutional as applied, where the district court had permitted the child to testify from a separate room by two-way closed-circuit television because it "found that [the child] was afraid of the defendant and of testifying in front of the jury in the large courtroom." 400 F.3d 548, 552 (8th Cir. 2005). It chastised the lower court for failing to determine whether the fear related primarily to the presence of the defendant, in which case the use of the closed-circuit television would have been warranted, or whether the fear related more generally to the prospect of testifying in a courtroom. *Id.* at 553. The court held as well that *Craig* did not control because the procedure approved in *Craig* was a one-way closed-circuit television rather than the two-way process used in the instant case. This particular conclusion is puzzling because the two-way procedure arguably provides better protection of the defendant's Sixth Amendment rights because the view of the courtroom and defendant are accessible to the child via the monitor located in the room in which the child is questioned. The court demonstrated its distrust of children's credibility as witnesses when emphasizing the insufficiency of "virtual" as contrasted with face-to-face confrontation, particularly concerning the possibility that the circumstances of out-of-courtroom testimony" will not have the same truth-inducing effect as the "unmediated gaze [of the defendant] across the courtroom." *Id.* at 554. For further discussion of Section 3509, see Scott M. Smith, *Validity, Construction and Application of the Child Victims' and Child Witnesses' Rights Statute*, 121 A.L.R. FED. 631 (2008).

4. State Law Responses.   Some states have experimented with closed circuit television and other devices to avoid face-to-face confrontation between the child witness and the defendant. In child sexual abuse prosecutions, for example, a California statute allows both one-way and two-way closed-circuit television testimony if the child victim is age thirteen or younger, if one of the following is found by clear and convincing evidence: that testimony by the minor in the presence of the defendant would cause the child serious emotional distress; that a deadly weapon was used during the commission of the crime; that great bodily harm was inflicted on the child during the crime; that the defendant or that the child or the child's family was threatened with serious bodily harm if the child testifies; that the defendant inflicted great bodily injury upon the child in the commission of the offense; or that the defendant or defense counsel acted in a way during the trial that caused the child to discontinue giving testimony. CAL. PENAL CODE § 1347 (2009). *See also* WIS. STAT. ANN. § 967.04(7) (2008), upheld in *State v. Thomas*, 442 N.W.2d 10 (Wis. 1989).

The Illinois Supreme Court found that state's Child Shield Act in violation of its state constitution in *People v. Fitzpatrick*, 633 N.E.2d 685 (Ill. 1994), after which Illinois amended its constitution. The statutory procedure was very similar to the one upheld by the U.S. Supreme Court in *Craig*, but the court held that the use of closed circuit television violated the defendant's right to *face-to-face* confrontation, because the Illinois Constitution stated that criminal defendants have the right to "meet witnesses face to face." ILL. CONST. ART. I § 8. The Illinois legislature amended the relevant provision to track the language of the Confrontation Clause in the U.S. Constitution, deleting the words "face to face." The amendment was quickly ratified by the voters. These developments are discussed in Timothy R. Gilleran-Johnson & Barbara Evans, *The Criminal Courtroom — Is it Childproof?* 26 LOY. U. CHI. L. J. 681 (1995).

Some courts have been rather relaxed in applying the statutory procedures regulating the use of closed circuit television. In *Iowa v. Shearon*, 660 N.W.2d 52 (Iowa 2003), for example, the defendant's conviction was upheld, although the child was not instructed that the defendant would be viewing the televised testimony, as the statute required, and the defendant had no means to consult with his attorney during the testimony. The court emphasized the attorney's vigorous cross-examination. *But see Etimani, supra*. In competency hearings, during which it is determined whether a child is competent to testify, the Supreme Court has held that the defendant, but not his attorney, may be excluded. *Kentucky v. Stincer*, 482

U.S. 730 (1987). A recent survey found that the statutes or case law of 46 states allow children to testify via some form of closed-circuit television procedures. *See* Margaret Brancatelli, *Facilitating Children's Testimony: Closed Circuit Television*, 43-Jun Prosecutor 40 (2009).

5. *Special Exceptions to the Hearsay Rule in Child Abuse Prosecutions.*

The Supreme Court has considered whether evidentiary rules that allow easier admissibility of certain forms of hearsay in child abuse cases comply with the Sixth Amendment Confrontation Clause. Until very recently, statements by a child about alleged abuse could be admitted into evidence through the testimony of a third party if the evidence met the requirements established for admissibility of hearsay evidence as set forth in *Ohio v. Roberts*, 448 U.S. 56, 66 (1980). *Roberts* held that hearsay statements could be admitted if the declarant was unavailable and the evidence bore "particular guarantees of trustworthiness." The Court in *Idaho v. Wright*, 497 U.S. 805 (1990), applied this test to testimony by a pediatrician describing statements made to him by a 2 1/2-year-old child about her abuse. In *Wright*, the Court upheld an Idaho Supreme Court determination that the hearsay statements did not have sufficient "indicia of reliability" to satisfy the defendant's Confrontation Clause rights under *Roberts*. In so doing, the Court emphasized that "particularized guarantees of trustworthiness" must be established from the circumstances surrounding the making of the statement, not from corroboration of the statement offered at trial.

In *Crawford v. Washington*, 541 U.S. 36 (2004), the Court overruled *Ohio v. Roberts*. It held that testimonial hearsay evidence was barred under the Confrontation Clause unless the witness was unavailable and the defendant had a prior opportunity to cross-examine the witness. Writing for the majority, Justice Scalia discussed the history of the Confrontation Clause. He emphasized that cross-examination was the means through which the Framers sought to achieve reliability of testimony. He rejected the notion that a judicial determination of reliability adequately protected defendants' Confrontation Clause rights. In *Crawford*, the Court noted that evidence based on a child's statements may sometimes be admitted through a third party witness where the evidence is not "testimonial." The Court explicitly left for "another day any effort to spell out a comprehensive definition of 'testimonial.' "

Two years later, in *Davis v. Washington*, 547 U.S. 813 (2006), the Court provided a bit more clarification, while still leaving many questions unanswered. Specifically, in the context of domestic violence, the Court held that the statements made by a domestic violence victim in her 9-1-1 call for help were not testimonial. The Court, in a decision authored by Justice Scalia, concluded that: "the circumstances of [the victim's 9-1-1 call] objectively indicate its primary purpose was to enable police assistance to meet an ongoing emergency. She simply was not acting as a *witness;* she was not *testifying*." *Id.* at 828. As such, evidence of the 9-1-1 call was admissible. In a second case, however, where the police interviewed a domestic violence victim after the assault had occurred, the Court found her statements to be testimonial: "It is entirely clear from the circumstances that the interrogation was part of an investigation into possible criminal past conduct — as, indeed, the testifying officer expressly acknowledged . . . There was no emergency in progress. . . ." *Id.* at 829.

Scholars have sharply criticized *Crawford* and *Davis* because of their impact on state prosecution of child abuse cases, as well as the challenges they raise for defendants. For example, as Professor Myrna Raeder observes:

> Child abuse cases are difficult for prosecutors to win because the abuse takes place in secret, and no physical evidence of molestation may be present either because of the nature of the abuse or because children heal quickly and the crime is often reported well after it occurred. [Children's] statements are viewed skeptically by jurors because of concerns about their susceptibility to suggestion, manipulation, coaching, or confusing fact with fantasy, whether or not they testify. In practice, hearsay is a dominant feature of child abuse litigation, primarily introduced in the context of excited utterances, statements for medical diagnosis or treatment, forensic interviews, or via ad hoc exceptions. Even pre-*Crawford v. Washington*, reversals based on the admission of child hearsay were more frequent than hearsay reversals in other types of cases. However, *Crawford* and *Davis v. Washington* up the ante for prosecutors who are trying to protect vulnerable young children who are unable or unwilling to testify at trial, because they defeat the admission of testimonial statements, including the highly regarded best practice of videotaping multidisciplinary forensic interviews. . . .

> Generally, the testimonial approach appears to exalt cross-examination for a limited category of statements, while viewing it as constitutionally unnecessary for everything else, which in a world of expansive modern statutory hearsay exceptions seems to promote the wrong message. In other words, cross-examination and live witnesses are not essential for a fair trial, unless the defendant has the good luck of facing a testimonial statement . . .

> The testimonial approach not only disadvantages defendants facing nontestimonial hearsay, but also the government, which has no way of overcoming a testimonial statement when the declarant is unavailable to testify, despite any lack of negligence or wrongdoing on its part, or its inability to duplicate the statement through other witnesses, even when the statement is critical to its case.

Myrna S. Raeder *Comments on Child Abuse Litigation in a "Testimonial" World: The Intersection of Competency, Hearsay, and Confrontation*, 82 IND. L. REV. 1009, 1009–11 (2007).

Case law interpreting these precedents in the context of child abuse cases reveals that evidence that would previously have been admissible is now routinely excluded. For example, in *State v. Henderson*, 160 P.3d 776 (Kansas 2007), the diagnosis of gonorrhea in a three-year-old girl set in motion the prosecution of her mother's boyfriend. The girl had been interviewed by a social worker and detective who were members of the Exploited and Missing Children Unit. In that interview, the child had identified her abuser and provided information about the encounter. The prosecution introduced the videotaped statement because the child was unable to testify in light of her inability to fully understand the duty to tell the truth in a courtroom. The evidence was introduced and the defendant was convicted. His conviction was overturned on appeal. Because the interviews were conducted as part of the process of collecting evidence for the prosecution, they were "testimonial" and therefore inadmissible. In *State v. Blue*, 717 N.W.2d 558 (N.D. 2006), the conviction of a defendant was overturned because a videotaped interview of four-year-old girl by a forensic interviewer at a medical center was determined on appeal to be "testimonial." In *Rangel v. State*, 199 S.W.3d 523 (Tex. App. 2006), a defendant's conviction on aggravated sexual assault and other offenses were overturned in part because a videotaped interview of the child by a child protective services worker was introduced. The appellate court held that this evidence was "testimonial" in character and therefore inadmissible. It is possible that some of these interviews would have been excluded under the prior test. In evaluating prosecution efforts to use hearsay evidence in sexual abuse prosecutions, many courts strictly construe the protections of the Confrontation Clause. For example, the Washington Supreme Court reversed a conviction, concluding that, before the trial court admitted hearsay evidence on the ground that the child was unavailable to testify, it should have considered whether she could testify by closed circuit television. *Washington v. Smith*, 59 P.3d 74 (Wash. 2002).

For further discussion of the impact of *Crawford* and *Davis* on child abuse prosecutions, see Robert P. Mosteller, *Testing the Testimonial Concept and Exceptions to Confrontation: "A Little Child Shall Lead Them,"* 82 IND. L. REV. 917 (2007); Myrna Raeder, *Remember the Ladies and the Children Too:* Crawford's *Impact on Domestic Violence and Child Abuse Cases*, 71 BROOK. L. REV. 311 (2005); Eileen A. Scallen, *Coping with* Crawford: *Confrontation of Children and Other Challenging Witnesses*, 35 WM. MITCHELL L. REV. 1558 (2009); Jonathan Scher, Student Author, *Out-of-Court Statements by Victims of Child Sexual Abuse to Multidisciplinary Teams: A Confrontation Clause Analysis*, 47 FAM. CT. REV. 167 (2009).

[b]   Expert Testimony in Child Sexual Abuse Cases

SANDERSON v. COMMONWEALTH
Kentucky Supreme Court
291 S.W.3d 610 (2009)[2]

Opinion of the Court by JUSTICE NOBLE.

After a jury trial, [Sanderson] was convicted of two counts of Second-Degree Sodomy and three counts of First-Degree Sexual Abuse, and was sentenced to thirty-five years in prison and five years of conditional discharge. He raises five claims of error on appeal. Because [Sanderson]'s Child Sexual Abuse Accommodation Syndrome claim constitutes reversible error, his conviction is reversed and the case is remanded for a new trial. . . .

---

[2] This decision was promulgated by the Kentucky Supreme Court on May 21, 2009, and was modified on denial of rehearing on October 1, 2009. At the time of this writing, the court has noted that the language in the opinion is not final. Thus, some changes in language may appear in the final opinion after the publication of this book.

[The court relates the facts of the case. Sanderson met and ultimately married Mendy Terrell. Although it appeared that Sanderson and Mendy's daughter B.T. had a good relationship, B.T. ultimately testified that Sanderson sexually abused her on a weekly basis for six years, as much as two to three times per week while Mendy was at work or sleeping. She said he told B.T. that he would hurt her if she ever said anything about the abuse. The abuse came to light after a friend of B.T., who spent the night at B.T.'s house reported that Sanderson showed a pornographic movie to the girls. Initially, B.T. denied this when Mendy questioned her. Ultimately, however, B.T. "later confessed to having watched the movie and told Mendy about the abuse that had taken place.

[Sanderson was indicted, convicted by a jury, and sentenced to thirty-five years in prison.]

. . . .

[Sanderson] claims the trial court improperly admitted testimony about Child Sexual Abuse Accommodation Syndrome (CSAAS) from . . . Lori Brown, a clinical psychologist. . . . who counseled B.T. and gave testimony that B. T.'s addition of new allegations of sexual abuse is normal. [Sanderson objected to Brown's testimony at trial. The court concurred that testimony by Brown as to the diagnosis of CSAAS was inadmissible,] but still allowed Brown to give propensity testimony . . .

In *Kurtz v. Commonwealth*, 172 S.W.3d 409 (Ky.2005), this Court quoted the basic rule against CSAAS testimony: [¶] "[W]here a victim had delayed reporting of abuse, we held improper the testimony of a seasoned child sex abuse investigator stating that it was common, in her experience, for sexually abused victims to delay reporting of the abuse. [Such testimony seeks to use the] habit of a class of individuals either to prove that another member of the class acted the same way under similar circumstances or to prove that the person was a member of that class *because* he/she acted the same way under similar circumstances." *Id.* at 414 (quoting *Miller v. Commonwealth*, 77 S.W.3d 566, 571–72 (Ky.2002)).

In *Hellstrom v. Commonwealth*, 825 S.W.2d 612 (Ky.1992), this Court reversed a conviction based on testimony [by the] director of the Child Abuse Center at the University of Kentucky Medical Center (who had a Masters degree in clinical social work) testified that " 'delayed disclosure' is common in these types of cases." *Id.* at 613. The Court noted that . . . "it does not matter that the social worker listed the symptoms but refrained from classifying them directly as the 'child sexual abuse syndrome.' Avoiding the term 'syndrome' does not transform inadmissible hearsay into reliable scientific evidence." *Id.* at 614.

In *Newkirk v. Commonwealth*, 937 S.W.2d 690 (Ky.1996), this Court applied the rule against CSAAS testimony to experts. *Newkirk* first noted that "[i]n an unbroken line of decisions . . . this Court has repeatedly expressed its distrust of expert testimony which purported to determine criminal conduct based on a perceived psychological syndrome." *Id.* at 690–91. The multiple rationales for the specific rule against CSAAS testimony include "the lack of diagnostic reliability, the lack of general acceptance within the discipline from which such testimony emanates, and the overwhelmingly persuasive nature of such testimony effectively dominating the decision-making process, uniquely the function of the jury." *Id.* at 691. *Newkirk* contains a lengthy discussion of CSAAS cases, and it concludes:

> [T]he cases demonstrate unmistakably that this Court has not accepted the view that the CSAAS or any of its components has attained general acceptance in the scientific community justifying its admission into evidence to prove sexual abuse or the identity of the perpetrator. Moreover, such evidence has been rejected on grounds that it lacks relevancy for failure to make the existence of any fact of consequence more probable or less probable than it would have been without the evidence.

Id. at 693.

This Court further noted that even if it were to " 'become accepted by the scientific community that a child who had been sexually abused is likely to develop certain symptoms or personality traits, there would remain the question of whether other children who had not been similarly abused might also develop the same symptoms or traits.' " *Id.* . . . And finally, this Court "expressed grave concern that the expert may invade the province of the jury by unduly influencing its assessment of credibility." *Id.* "This Court has previously stated there is no such thing as expertise in the credibility of children." *Id.* at 694. This Court has "embraced the view that mental health professionals are not experts at discerning the truth; they are trained to accept facts provided by their patients without critical examination of those facts." *Id.*

In this case, Brown testified that it is normal for child victims of sexual abuse, like B. T., to add details about their abuse after they have been in counseling for an extended period of time, and to appear happy in their outward life and be able to excel in their extracurricular activities and make good grades. The Commonwealth even asked whether what Brown described as a child's attempt to disconnect from such abuse is the reason sexually abused girls become prostitutes.

Here, the testimony in the Commonwealth's case-in-chief that sexually abused children, like B. T., commonly add details over time through counseling is analogous to the situation in *Miller*, where this Court held testimony that sexually abused victims commonly delay reporting of their abuse to be reversible error. In essence, victims are delaying their reporting of some of their abuse when they later add details. In addition, when Brown was recalled in the Commonwealth's rebuttal, she went even further in identifying generic characteristics of child sex abuse victims by describing them as outwardly appearing happy. This is the type of testimony this Court feared in *Newkirk*; this was testimony where there ' "remain[s] the question of whether other children who had not been similarly abused might also develop the same symptoms or traits.' *Newkirk*, 937 S.W.2d at 691–92. Finally, the Commonwealth even went so far as to ask whether these "symptoms" are what cause sexually abused children to become prostitutes. . . . [¶] Brown's "expert" testimony in this case, coupled with the Commonwealth's speculation about the creation of prostitutes, are the exact type of generic and unreliable evidence this Court has repeatedly held to be reversible error. Therefore, this case must be reversed for a new trial because of the admission of CSAAS testimony against [Sanderson].

[The court addresses certain other claims by Sanderson, not related to CSAAS, to guide the lower court on remand.] In conclusion, the trial court committed reversible error by admitting propensity testimony, a key reason for the rule against Child Sexual Abuse Accommodation Syndrome testimony . . . [¶] . . . Therefore, the conviction and judgment . . . is reversed, and the case is remanded for a new trial.

[Justices Minton, Cunningham, Schroder & Venters concurred in this opinion. Justice Scott concurred and dissented in part — dissenting on that portion of the decision that addressed CSAAS [reprinted immediately below]. Justice Abramson concurred with the majority as to the result only, and stated: "Justice Scott raises an important question. The time is ripe to reconsider our position on CSAAS and whether any refinement is appropriate."

JUSTICE SCOTT, [concurring and dissenting in part.]

Although I concur with the majority's analysis and resolution of the other issues, I respectfully dissent from its view of certain elements of evidence often referred to as the Child Sexual Abuse Accommodation Syndrome (CSAAS), which provide explanations for the otherwise inconsistent conduct of abused children, and thus properly assists the jury in making determinations as to whether such inconsistent conduct is an indicator of untruthfulness or is conduct commonly experienced with abused children. I speak, here, of delayed reporting and recantation, as well as, their presentment with demeanors that, at first blush, appear inconsistent with their allegations of abuse.

Like the overwhelming majority of other states, I believe that such evidence, when not used to impermissibly establish the abuse, but rather as a viable tool to explain the sometimes confusing and commonly misunderstood behavioral patterns of children who may have been subjected to abuse, should be admissible.

CSAAS "first came to light in an article published in 1983 which described five (5) characteristics commonly observed in sexually abused children: (1) secrecy; (2) helplessness; (3) entrapment and accommodation; (4) delayed, conflicted, and unconvincing disclosure; and (5) retraction [or recantation]." Elisabeth Trainor, J.D., *Admissibility of Expert Testimony on Child Sexual Abuse Accommodation Syndrome (CSAAS) In Criminal Case*, 85 A.L.R. 5th 595 (2001).

> There are six (6) categories of social science expert testimony that have developed and have regularly been proffered to support child witnesses in sexual abuse cases. The first category is "rehabilitative" testimony offered to explain the puzzling conduct of the child victim to meet a defense attack on the child's credibility. These behaviors have been termed as CSAAS. The second category is syndrome evidence, including CSAAS evidence, of supposed typical child victim behavior proffered, not to explain unusual conduct of the child, but to prove affirmatively that sexual abuse has occurred. The third category is a spin-off of the second with the expert testifying to typical behaviors of a child victim specifically related to the child victim in the case. The fourth is expert testimony that the child has in

fact been abused, and the fifth is testimony that the child is credible. The final category involves profile testimony on the actual sexual offender or alleged perpetrator of the abuse.

[*Id.*] *citing State v. J.Q.*, 617 A.2d 1196 (N.J.1993)).

This Court has dealt with all categories in one form or another, with a multitude of reasons for their rejection. *See Kurtz v. Commonwealth*, 172 S.W.3d 409, 413, 414 (Ky.2005) (habit and profile characteristics of perpetrators); *Miller v. Commonwealth*, 77 S.W.3d 566, 571, 572 (Ky.2002) (delayed reporting denied as habit evidence); *Newkirk v. Commonwealth*, 937 S.W.2d 690, 691–696 (Ky.1997) (considered psychiatric rebuttal evidence explaining in general terms child victims' recantation); *Hall v. Commonwealth*, 862 S.W.2d 321, 322, 323 (Ky.1993) (psychiatric testimony that child was sexually abused and was telling the truth); *Hellstrom v. Commonwealth*, 825 S.W.2d 612, 613, 614 (Ky.1992) (testimony on abuse and delayed disclosure invaded province of jury); . . . *Mitchell v. Commonwealth*, 777 S.W.2d 930, 932, 933 (Ky.1989) (use of CSAAS for determination of guilt and perpetrator profile); *Hester v. Commonwealth*, 734 S.W.2d 457, 458 (Ky.1987) (recantation); *Lantrip v. Commonwealth*, 713 S.W.2d 816, 817 (Ky.1986) (use of CSAAS to prove abuse); *Bussey v. Commonwealth*, 697 S.W.2d 139, 140, 141 (Ky.1985) (use of CSAAS as proof of abuse and perpetrator profile). Although we have come close, *see Newkirk*, 937 S.W.2d at 690, we have yet to recognize the validity of CSAAS evidence of the first category of use (rehabilitation) when only offered "to explain the puzzling conduct of the child victim to meet a defense attack on the child's credibility." Trainor, *Admissibility of Expert Testimony on Child Sexual Abuse Accommodation Syndrome (CSAAS) In Criminal Case*, *supra*. I believe it's time we did.

"In general our reasons have been the lack of diagnostic reliability, the lack of general acceptance within the discipline from which such testimony emanates, and the overwhelmingly persuasive nature of such testimony effectively dominating the decision-making process, uniquely the function of the jury." *Newkirk*, 937 S.W.2d at 691. Interestingly. . . , the closest we have come was our consideration of the commonality of recantation by abuse victims as analyzed in *Newkirk*, where the Court split 4-3. *Id.* at 696.

In *Newkirk*, the trial court allowed expert testimony regarding recantation "for the limited purpose of rebutting any attack on [the victim's] credibility based upon the recantation of her allegations of her abuse, by explaining in general terms why an alleged victim might recant." *Id.* at 697. Moreover, the evidence was admitted subject to a limiting admonition by the court; "[t]his witness is being called to testify for the limited purpose of explaining the psychological dynamics surrounding a recantation following an accusation of the sexual abuse. This evidence is not offered for the purpose of proving whether [the victim] was or was not sexually abused." *Id.* Recantation, delayed reporting, and inconsistent demeanors of child victims, all involve puzzling conduct of the child and therefore support a defense attack on the child's credibility. As was noted by the dissent in *Newkirk:*

> Kentucky remains as one of the few jurisdictions that still rejects all testimony regarding the phenomenon clinically identified and demonstrated as the Child Sexual Abuse Accommodation Syndrome which

provides jurors a psychological explanation for certain behavior in small children following sexual abuse. Such testimony is necessary because these children often exhibit conduct that is inconsistent with the jurors' life experiences or understanding of human nature in children.

Id. at 696 (Graves, J., dissenting). As the dissent also pointed out, "the recantation symptom is widely accepted and confirmed by credible studies at renowned research institutions by well credentialed experts." *Id.* [Special Justice Barry Willett, in *Newkirk* indicated that the "alleged perpetrator [attains] an unfair advantage to exploit the process of how some child sexual abuse victims respond to abuse" if the defense can "impeach the child victim's credibility on the basis of a previous recantation", . . . delayed reporting of the incident, or, his demeanor "without also allowing the Commonwealth to present testimony explaining" these behaviors. . . . Special Justice Willett noted further that "a jury of lay adults, hearing the horrible details in a typical child sexual abuse case, is confronted with a child victim recanting his or her previous allegations of sexual abuse," they would likely apply an adult standard to the child victim's behavior, concluding that the testimony is not trustworthy.] "The reality of child sexual abuse is that children respond differently than do adults to both the abuse and the process of disclosing the abuse to the proper authorities." *Id.* at 698–99 . . .

For these reasons, most states allow CSAAS "rehabilitative" testimony offered to explain the puzzling conduct of the victim in order to meet the defense's attack on the victim's credibility. [Justice Scott cites to cases supporting "rehabilitative" use of such testimony in two federal courts of appeal, *see, e.g., Mindombe v. United States*, 795 A.2d 39, 46 (D.C.Cir.2002) ("[E]xpert testimony is admissible in cases where the government successfully proffers that the facts and evidence to be presented at trial are likely to be inconsistent with a lay juror's expectations as to how a child sexual abuse victim should respond to such a traumatizing event.");] *United States v. Bighead*, 128 F.3d 1329, 1331 (9th Cir.1997) ("[T]estimony had significant probative value in that it rehabilitated (without vouching for) the victim's credibility after she was cross-examined about the reasons she delayed reporting and about the inconsistencies in her testimony."). . . . [Justice Scott cites supporting admissibility for "rehabilitative" purposes in Alabama, Alaska. Arizona. California, Colorado, Connecticut Delaware, Florida, Georgia, Hawaii, Illinois, Indiana, Iowa, Kansas, Louisiana, Massachusetts, Minnesota, Mississippi, Montana, Nebraska, Nevada, New York, North Carolina, Ohio, Oklahoma, Pennsylvania, South Dakota, Texas, Vermont, Wisconsin, and Wyoming. Representative holdings include:] *State v. Spigarolo*, 556 A.2d 112, 122 (Conn.2003) ("[T]he overwhelming majority of courts have held that, where the defendant has sought to impeach the testimony of the minor victim based on inconsistencies, partial disclosures, or recantations relating to the alleged incidents, the state may present expert opinion evidence that such behavior by minor sexual abuse victims is common."); . . . *State v. Batangan*, 799 P.2d 48, 49 (Haw.1990) ("Thus, while expert testimony explaining 'seemingly bizarre' behavior of child sex abuse victims is helpful to the jury and should be admitted, conclusory opinions that abuse did occur and that the child victim's report of abuse is truthful and believable is of no assistance to the jury, and therefore, should not be admitted."); . . . *Steward v. State*, 652 N.E.2d 490, 499 (Ind.1995) (Rehabilitative aspects of CSAAS "merely informs jurors that commonly held assumptions are not necessarily accurate and allows [the jury] to fairly judge credibility."); . . . . [*State v. Foret*, 628 So.2d 1116, 1130 (La.1993)] ("So long as the expert limits the testimony to general characteristics that would explain delays in reporting, recantations, and omission of details, the testimony will not substitute [the expert's] estimation of credibility for that of the jury [but provides] a scientific perspective for the jury according to which it can evaluate the complainant's testimony for itself."). . . .

[Justice Scott cites with approval the dissent of Special Justice Willett in *Newkirk*:] "Expert testimony explaining the phenomenon of recantation [, delayed reporting and omission of details] by some victims of child sexual abuse should be admissible for the limited purpose of rebutting an attack on the child victim's credibility [accompanied by a limiting instruction directing the jury not to use such testimony] to determine whether the victim's sexual abuse allegation is true." [Justice Scott then applies this standard to the instant case, and concludes that the testimony of Ms. Brown, Director of Clinical Service for the Purchase Area Sexual Assault Center, should have been admitted to rebut the defense's implication that the "child victim's demeanor, initial omission of details and delayed reporting" revealed that the child's testimony was fabricated. Testimony such as Ms. Brown's, consistent with "established and acceptable scientific studies" assists "the trier fact to understand the evidence [and] to determine a fact in issue, a witness qualified as an expert by knowledge, skill, experience, training, or education, [should be able to] testify thereto"].

For these reasons, we should now break with precedent, joining the majority of jurisdictions in allowing the introduction of such evidence for rehabilitation purposes only and with an accompanying admonition limiting the use to such purpose. It is for this reason that I dissent from the majority's opinion on this issue.

NOTES

1. ***Psychological Testimony About Sexually Abused Children.*** Consistent with Justice Scott's opinion, most courts allow experts to testify about research findings indicating certain patterns of response by children who are sexually abused are incomplete, inconsistent, and at times, recanted. As such, Justice Scott's opinion in *Sanderson* is in line with current trends. In addition, as noted by Justice Scott, there is less consensus on whether evidence of CSAAS can be introduced by the prosecution to establish that sexual abuse occurred than on its use to rehabilitate a child's testimony. In other words, some prosecutors have sought to introduce the CSAAS diagnosis as evidence from which the jury can infer or extrapolate that the child was indeed abused, as long as the expert does not give an explicit opinion on whether abuse occurred. *See United States v. St. Pierre*, 812 F.2d 417 (8th Cir. 1987); *State v. Reser*, 767 P.2d 1277 (Kan. 1989); *State v. Bachman*, 446 N.W.2d 271(S.D. 1989). Other courts have held such evidence inadmissible. *See State v. Moran*, 728 P.2d 248, 255 (Ariz. 1986); *People v. Jeff*, 204 Cal. App. 3d 309 (1988). Courts have typically rejected testimony by an expert who concludes that, because the child meets CSAAS criteria, the child has been abused. *See, e.g., Mindombe v. United States*, 795 A.2d 39 (D.C. Ct. App. 2002), *cert. denied*, 537 U.S. 1234 (2003) (expert cannot give opinion on whether sexual abuse

occurred); *Louisiana v. Chauvin*, 846 So. 2d 697 (La. 2003) (same); *People v. Duell*, 163 A.D.2d 866 (N.Y. App. Div. 1990). Critiquing the use of CSAAS as evidence of abuse, a New Jersey court asserts that most decisions allowing such a use

> failed to distinguish between the rehabilitative and affirmative use of syndrome evidence; a number misread the cases which approved the rehabilitative use of such evidence as support for the more expansive use, and several incorrectly analogized child sexual abuse accommodation syndrome evidence to battered child and battered wife syndrome evidence. [The court cites an article by John E.B. Myers explaining] how this misuse of syndrome evidence came about: "[Roland Summit, the scholar who introduced the concept of CSAAS] did not intend the accommodation syndrome as a diagnostic device. The syndrome does not detect sexual abuse. Rather, it . . . explains the child's reactions to it."

State v. J.Q., 599 A.2d 172, 185–86, 185–86

   2. *Current Scientific Support for CSAAS.* Psychiatrist Rolland Summit, in his 1983 article setting forth the features of CSAAS, contended that the following five key factors typically characterize the context of and child's reactions to sexual abuse: "(1) secrecy; (2) helplessness; (3) entrapment and accommodation; (4) delayed, conflicted and inconsistent disclosure; (5) recantation." Rolland C. Summit, *The Child Sexual Abuse Accommodation Syndrome*, 7 CHILD ABUSE & NEGLECT 177, 181 (1983). The first two factors, according to Summit, explain children's special vulnerability to sexual abuse. Threats made by the perpetrator, feelings of shame, fear one will not be believed, and other factors contribute to the maintenance of secrecy about the abuse. Children may not know that the perpetrator's conduct is socially disapproved and legally prohibited. According to Summit, these factors — together with the child's dependency and unfamiliarity with, or inability to exercise, modes of self-protection used by adults — contribute to children's helplessness with respect to the abuse. He states further that, given the experience of entrapment, that is, the belief that there is no escape from recurrent sexual abuse, the child uses a range of psychological strategies to help him or her accept this reality and to deal with the ongoing trauma. He notes that much sexual abuse experienced by children is never disclosed because of the factors noted above (fear, shame, acceptance of the abuse, etc.). When it is disclosed, its disclosure may be delayed, incomplete, and inconsistent in light of the conflict the child experiences regarding disclosure, and may be recanted because of such conflict, as well as in response to the reactions of those in the child's life.

   While Summit referred to his clinical observations in developing this model, he did not support his analysis with empirical research. The use of "syndrome" evidence more generally as a way of describing "a cluster or pattern of [primarily psychological or behavioral] symptoms that appear together in a way that is considered clinically meaningful" has been the subject of criticism in recent years, most frequently with respect to the absence of scientific evidence underlying them. Veronica B. Dahir et al., *Judicial Application of* Daubert *to Psychological Syndrome and Profile Evidence*, 11 PSYCHOL. PUB. POL'Y & L. 62, 63 (2005); David Faigman, *The Law's Scientific Revolution: Reflections and Ruminations on the Law's Use of Experts in Year Seven of the Revolution*, 57 WASH. & LEE L. REV. 661

(2000). Referring to most behavioral "syndromes" about which experts currently testify (including CSAAS) as "pseudoscience," Professor David Faigman argues that, without a basis in rigorous and systematic empirical research, such evidence should not be admissible. David L. Faigman, *The Syndromic Lawyer Syndrome: A Psychological Theory of Evidentiary Munificence*, 67 U. Colo. L. Rev. 817 (1996).

Empirical investigations of sexually-abused children support some of the clinical observations Summit incorporated into his theory of CSAAS, but have not borne out others. Research suggests that most child sexual abuse is not disclosed during childhood. Kamala London et al., *Disclosure of Child Sexual Abuse: What Does the Research Tell Us About the Ways That Children Tell?*, 11 Psychol. Pub. Pol'y & L. 194 (2005) (summarizing several dozen empirical studies). Research has revealed a range of factors that help predict which children are likely to disclose (e.g., children abused by family members are less likely to disclose than are children abused by others). *Id.* Existing research does not support the conclusion that most children who disclose abuse subsequently deny or recant that allegation, although "there does exist a minority of children who fit the behavioral pattern that is put forth by the CSAAS model." *Id.* at 217–18. The authors underscore that more research is required to better understand the factors associated with the different behavioral patterns and developmental trends characterizing sexually-abused children.

As reported in Note 6, Section C[1], above, there is strong evidence that many child sexual abuse victims meet all or some of the criteria for post-traumatic stress disorder (PTSD). One researcher studying patterns of expert testimony in child sexual abuse cases observed that experts testifying about children's reticence to disclose the abuse are increasingly explaining such conduct with references to PTSD rather than CSAAS. *See* Mary Ann Mason, *Expert Testimony Regarding the Characteristics of Sexually Abused Children: A Controversy on Both Sides of the Bench*, in Expert Witnesses in Child Abuse Cases: What Can and Should be Said in Court? 217, 223 (Stephen J. Ceci et al. eds. 1998). PTSD is regarded by the mental health professions as a mental disorder (which can be found in the American Psychiatric Association's *Diagnostic and Statistical Manual of Mental Disorders*), with scientific evidence of its existence.

3. *Legal Responses to Allegations of Child Sexual Abuse by Adults.* In recent decades, many adults claiming that they were sexually abused as children have sought redress under tort or criminal law. Statutes of limitations have barred many of these actions. Even though statutes of limitations are typically tolled during childhood, the actions involving adult plaintiffs alleging childhood sexual abuse may still be time-barred. In 2003, the U.S. Supreme Court held that a 1993 California statute, enacted after the expiration of a previously applicable limitations period, violated the Ex Post Facto Clause of Article I of the Constitution when applied to revive a previously time-barred prosecution. *Stogner v. California*, 539 U.S. 607 (2003). The statute permitted prosecution of child sexual abuse charges even after the prior limitations period expired. The petitioner was indicted in 1998 for child sexual abuse committed between 1955 and 1973. At the time of the abuse, the statute of limitations was three years. Application of this 1993 statute to permit prosecution of the defendant in 1998 was held to be unconstitutional.

Many adults claiming to be victims of child sexual abuse seek redress through a tort action. In most states, the statute of limitations begins to accrue at the time the plaintiff knew or should have known of the tort. A number of cases have allowed such actions to go forward under a "delayed discovery" theory, on the basis of the plaintiffs' claims that the psychological stress associated with childhood sexual abuse caused them to repress their memory of it until recently. *See, e.g., Hearndon v. Graham*, 767 So. 2d 1179 (Fla. 2000) (delayed discovery doctrine applies to accrual of action based on claim of childhood abuse and traumatic amnesia); *J.L. v. J.F.*, 722 A.2d 558 (N.J. Super. Ct. App. Div. 1999) (court must hold plenary hearing to "determine plaintiffs' state of mind regarding the date they reasonably discovered the injury and causal connection"). In response to such claims, some states have extended the ordinary statute of limitations for a specified period in childhood sexual abuse claims. *See Johnson v. Johnson*, 766 F. Supp. 662 (N.D. Ill. 1991) (12 years). *See also D.M.S. v. Barber*, 645 N.W.2d 383 (Minn. 2002) (6 year statute of limitation period under the delayed discovery statute began to run when the victim reached the age of majority).

Other courts have declined to extend the statute of limitations in these cases. *See Moriarty v. Garden Sanctuary Church of God*, 534 S.E.2d 672 (S.C. 2000) (statute of limitations extended only where there is independent evidence corroborating repressed memory); *Clay v. Kuhl*, 727 N.E.2d 217 (Ill. 2000) (statute of limitations not tolled until plaintiff learns the "full extent of the injuries she allegedly sustained as a result of childhood occurrences" where she does not contend that she was not aware or did not recall that the alleged sexual abuse had harmed her); *M.H.D. v. Westminster Schs.*, 172 F.3d 797 (11th Cir. 1999) (delayed discovery rule does not apply to personal injury claims); *Dalrymple v. Brown*, 701 A.2d 164 (Pa. 1997) (discovery rule does not toll statute of limitations in repressed memory cases due to the inability to determine time of memory as objective fact); *Lemmerman v. Fealk*, 534 N.W.2d 695 (Mich. 1995) (discovery rule does not apply to extend statute of limitations). Some states require plaintiffs relying on memory repression to toll the statute to produce corroborating evidence of the alleged abuse, such as contemporaneous physical manifestations or evidence that there were other victims.

At the time of this writing, the California Supreme Court is reviewing a challenge to statutes extending the time period during which such tort actions can be filed. *K.J. v. Roman Catholic Bishop of Stockton*, 92 Cal. Rptr. 3d 673 (Cal. Ct. App. 2009), *rev. granted* 211 P.3d 1061 (Cal. 2009). One provision allows plaintiffs who allege sexual abuse as children to "revive" a third-party claim that has otherwise lapsed (*i.e.*, against a church for failure to protect plaintiff from continuing sexual abuse by its clergy) by filing it within a one-year statutory window. In this case, the victim did not file the claim within this one year window, but alleged that he was hampered by his repression of the memories of the abuse. The California Court of Appeals held that the one-year window was the legislature's remedy to the effects of such repressed memories, and that by not filing within that window, he forfeited the opportunity to bring his claim. The court also held that a more recent provision added to the statutes in 2002 could not be applied retroactively, thereby barring a claim under that provision. For further commentary, see William A. Gray, Student Author, *A Proposal for Change in*

Statutes of Limitations in Childhood Sexual Abuse Cases, 43 BRANDEIS L.J. 493 (2005); Jodi Leibowitz, *Criminal Statutes of Limitations: An Obstacle to the Prosecution and Punishment of Child Sexual Abuse*, 25 CARDOZO L. REV. 907 (2003).

4. *The Scientific Status of Claims of "Repressed" or "Recovered" Memories of Child Sexual Abuse by Adults.* The notion that memories of sexual abuse in childhood may be altered by protective psychological processes has led many to focus on "repressed" or "recovered" memories by adults regarding sexual abuse they allegedly experienced as children. There is substantial debate about whether such memories are trustworthy in the field of psychology and in the mental health professions more generally. At one end of the continuum are therapists who specialize in memory "recovery" and assume that most people who seek therapy were likely sexually abused as children. Their techniques and theories are not generally well-regarded among mainstream psychologists, and their former patients have at times later recanted their accusations. *See* Leon Jaroff & Jeanne McDowell, *Lies of the Mind*, TIME, Nov. 29, 1993, at 52 (describing therapists who routinely inform patients that problems for which they seek help arise from sexual abuse they have repressed). Much of the recovered memory "industry" has been inspired by a best seller, THE COURAGE TO HEAL (1988), whose authors, Ellen Bass and Laura Davis, have no formal training in psychology or psychiatry. Other therapists accept the validity of repressed memories of sexual abuse, but are concerned about the possibility of contamination through aggressive therapy interventions.

The American Psychological Association convened a Working Group to evaluate the scientific evidence on repressed memory. The members disagreed sharply on this topic, and two subgroups filed competing statements. One group asserted: "[T]here is no compelling biological or social evidence to support the view that once-viable memories of traumatic experiences can be submerged and then recovered after intervals that extend many years." Peter A. Ornstein et al., *Reply to the Albert, Brown, and Curtois Document: The Science of Memory and the Practice of Psychotherapy*, in AMER. PSYCHOLOGICAL ASSN. WORKING GROUP OF THE INVESTIGATION OF MEMORIES OF CHILDHOOD ABUSE: FINAL REPORT 93 (1996), http://www.apa.org/pi/memories_report/homepage.html. Furthermore, the researchers express concern about accounts of recovered memories because of the extensive evidence that memories can be manipulated and false or inaccurate "memories" created. *See* Elizabeth F. Loftus, *The Reality of Repressed Memories*, 48 AMER. PSYCHOLOGIST 518 (1993); Elizabeth Loftus & Katherine Ketcham, THE MYTH OF REPRESSED MEMORY: FALSE MEMORIES AND ALLEGATIONS OF SEXUAL ABUSE (1996). In the conclusory section of the Working Group report, the two sides joined in the following statements:

1. Controversies regarding adult recollections should not be allowed to obscure the fact that child sexual abuse is a complex and pervasive problem in American that has historically gone unacknowledged.

2. Most people who were sexually abused as children remember all or part of what happened to them.

3. It is possible for memories of abuse that have been forgotten for a long time to be remembered.

4. It is also possible to construct convincing pseudomemories for events that never occurred.

5. There are gaps in our knowledge about the processes that lead to accurate and inaccurate recollections of childhood memories.

Final Conclusions of the APA Working Group on Investigation of Memories of Childhood Abuse, supra APA WORKING GROUP at 227.

In a twist to the conventional fact pattern, the Wisconsin Supreme Court recognized an action by parents against therapists who negligently "implanted" false memories of abuse in their adult children. *Sawyer v. Midelfort*, 595 N.W.2d 423 (Wis. 1999). For an analysis of therapist liability for "false memory syndrome," see Kathleen A. Biesterveld, *False Memories and the Public Policy Debate: Toward a Heightened Standard of Care for Psychotherapy*, 2002 WIS. L. REV. 169. In 1994, a California jury awarded $500,000 to Gary Ramona against a therapist who he claimed used hypnotic drugs to con his bulimic daughter into "remembering" false incidents of incest. The daughter herself had testified in the defendant therapists' behalf. *Dad Wins $500,000 in 'False Memory' Case of Sex Abuse*, SEATTLE TIMES, May 14, 1994.

For further discussion of the debate regarding these issues, see Laurence Alison, *Considerations for Experts in Assessing the Credibility of Recovered Memories of Child Sexual Abuse*, 12 PSYCHOL. PUB. POL'Y & L 419 (2006); Elizabeth A. Wilson, *Suing for Lost Childhood: Child Sexual Abuse: The Delayed Discovery Rule, and the Problem of Finding Justice for Adult-Survivors of Child Abuse*, 12 U.C.L.A. WOMEN's L.J. 145 (2003); Richard A. Leo, *The Social and Legal Construction of Repressed Memory*, 22 LAW & SOC. INQUIRY 653 (1997).

5. *Sexual Abuse in the Catholic Church.* In the past few years much media attention and litigation has centered on sexual abuse allegations against Roman Catholic priests. In a scandal that has shaken the Church and threatens to result in substantial direct and indirect economic loss, allegations have been brought against hundreds of priests in Catholic dioceses across the country. Among the most publicized cases are those within the Boston Archdiocese. There were numerous criminal prosecutions of priests and civil suits against the Archdiocese, which apparently engaged in a cover-up, relocating abusive priests to unsuspecting churches where the abuse often continued. Cardinal Bernard Law of Boston and many other high officials resigned in the wake of the scandal. In 2003, the Archdiocese settled 542 claims for $85 million. *Boston Archdiocese Settles Sex Abuse Cases for $85 million.* American Catholic.org, Sept. 11, 2003, http://www.americancatholic.org/News/ClergySexAbuse. In 2005, the California Diocese settled claims against it for $100 million in response to the claims of 90 alleged victims. *See* Nick Madigan, *California Diocese Settles Sexual Abuse Case $100 Million*, N.Y. TIMES, Jan. 5, 2005, http://www.nytimes.com/2005/01/05/national/05settle.html.

In response to the scandals and lawsuits, the Catholic Bishops of the United States adopted the *Charter for the Protection of Children and Young People.* On its website, the U.S. Conference of Catholic Bishops indicates that the *"Charter* created a National Review Board, which was assigned responsibility to commission a descriptive study, with the full cooperation of the dioceses/eparchies, of the nature and scope of the problem of sexual abuse of minors by clergy." *See* U.S. Conference of Catholic Bishops Website, http://www.usccb.org/nrb/johnjaystudy/index.htm. The study, conducted by the John Jay College of Criminal Justice of the City University of New York, was made public in 2004. Using one database, the study found allegations by 10,667 individuals of sexual abuse against 4,127 (or 4.36%) of priests serving between 1960 and 2002. In 17.2% of these cases, more than one child in a family alleged abuse. According to the findings, very few *(i.e.,* 13% of) allegations were made at the time the abuse occurred. Most allegations were made years later, with over 25% of the allegations made 30 years after the alleged abuse began. For further discussion of the liability of the church for sexual abuse perpetrated by its priests, see Marjorie A. Shields, *Liability of Church or Religious Organization for Negligent Hiring, Retention, or Supervision of Priest, Minister, or Other Clergy Based on Sexual Misconduct,* 101 ALR 5th 530 (2008) (summarizing the state and federal cases involving liability of religious organization for negligent hiring, retention, or supervision of a clergy member based on sexual conduct).

6. *Medical Evidence About Physical Abuse.* Courts are much more open to the use of expert testimony in proving physical abuse than sexual abuse. An important issue in these cases is whether the child's injury was intentionally inflicted or accidental. Most courts allow expert testimony by physicians that the child's injuries conform to a pattern that is consistent with "battered child syndrome" or "child maltreatment syndrome." *See, e.g., State v. Wilkerson,* 247 S.E.2d. 905 (1978) (citing numerous opinions upholding admissibility of expert testimony on battered child syndrome.) Battered child syndrome was first described by Dr. Harry Kempe and associates, in Harry C. Kempe et. al. *The Battered Child Syndrome,* 181 JAMA 17 (1962), and denotes both the general health and condition of the child and a pattern of injuries that are consistent with abuse and inconsistent with natural and accidental causes. Bruising over the body is common and radiological evidence often indicates multiple fractures inflicted over an extended period of time. Abdominal injuries and spiral fractures of limbs (caused by twisting) are common. *See also* THE BATTERED CHILD (RAY E. HELFER & HENRY C. KEMPE EDS. 1968). This syndrome has become so well recognized, that in 1976, a California court held that a physician who failed to report under the child abuse reporting laws a case which presented the symptoms characteristic of this syndrome could be held civilly liable to the child for medical malpractice. *See Landeros v. Flood,* 551 P.2d 389 (Cal. 1976). The diagnosis is admissible only to show there was a non-accidental injury; it cannot identify the perpetrator of the violence. *See State v. Loss,* 204 N.W.2d 404 (Minn. 1973); *People v. Henson,* 304 N.E.2d 358 (N.Y. 1973).

NOTE ON CHILD ABUSE LAW REFORM

The facts underlying the case of Joshua DeShaney, Section C[4] above, are not unique. Newspaper reports from around the nation tell the stories of children subjected to horrifying abuse and neglect, some of whom die, while the child protection system fails to intervene in a timely and effective manner. For example:

> There was Sierra Roberts, 7, who died after her father kicked her in the stomach and beat her with a belt over two torturous days. And there was Nixzmary Brown, 7, whose beating death last year spurred an eruption of outrage and scrutiny upon the agency meant to protect children like these from abuse.

> In each of those cases, and others like them, [New York City's] child welfare agency received warnings that the children were in danger but never fully acted on them, according to a . . . report released . . . by city investigators. The report says that caseworkers often accepted parents' word that there was nothing wrong, then failed to interview witnesses or examine records that would have revealed patterns of abuse.

> . . . .

> The report . . . said that caseworkers frequently dismissed abuse allegations as "unfounded" with little or no investigation, . . . that caseworkers repeatedly failed to obtain . . . school and medical records; and that caseworkers often carried heavy caseloads and seldom had prior investigatory experience or training, yet were expected to conduct complex investigations. . . . Many of the missteps and failings detailed in the report have been chronicled before as the agency has sought remedies. But the compilation of problems outlined in the new report reveals a level of deep failings that continued to occur. Six months after Nixzmary's death, for example, another girl, Sharllene Morillo, 2, was beaten to death. That attack came just a few weeks after the agency received an anonymous complaint that her mother's companion was abusing her.

Ray Rivera, *Agency Lags in Protecting Children, Report Says*, N.Y. TIMES, Aug. 10, 2007. This report is consistent with many across the nation. *See, e.g., Child Welfare Reform: Will Recent Changes Make At-Risk Children Safer?* 15 CONG. Q. RES. 345, Apr. 22, 2005 (citing the failures of the U.S. child welfare system, noting that "more than 900,000 children were maltreated in 2003 — and . . . 1,300 died").

Perhaps most disturbing is that, despite decades of concerns about the failure of the system to reach many of the children it was created to protect, the problems continue. For example, as a 2009 *New York Times* article indicates, substantial systemic change remains but an aspiration.

> A new report shows that more children in families said to be known to the New York City child welfare system died in 2008 than in any of the previous 20 years. There were 49 fatalities, according to Child Welfare Watch, a policy journal, including 14 homicides; the other children died in accidents or of natural causes, and, in some cases, the cause was not determined.

Julie Bosman, *Study Reports More Deaths of Children Linked to Child-Welfare System*, N.Y. TIMES, Mar. 25, 2009.

At the same time, there are questions as to whether, in some instances, child welfare system interventions cause more harm than good. Reports like the one published in a Milwaukee newspaper in 2007 appear across the country as well:

"Over the last year, three Milwaukee foster children with serious medical or behavioral problems have died at state-licensed facilities. [S]taff members at the facilities were cited for child neglect by the child welfare system . . ." Sarah Carr, *Foster Care Deaths Raise Concerns*, JOURNAL SENTINEL, June 24, 2007.

Special needs children are particularly poorly served. The child welfare system frequently fails to provide them with the medical, psychiatric, or educational services they need, and does not typically provide adequate training to foster families or the staff at residential facilities in whose care these children are placed. Sandra Stukes Chipungu & Tricia B. Bent-Goodley, *Meeting the Challenges of Contemporary Foster Care*, 14 FUTURE OF CHILDREN: CHILDREN, FAMILIES & FOSTER CARE 76 (2004):

> Living within the foster care system can be trying for both children and foster parents. From a child's perspective, the foster care experience can be emotionally traumatic, and it is associated with detrimental developmental outcomes and lower educational achievement. Foster parents are often expected to care for children, many with special needs, with inadequate financial support, minimal training, and limited access to respite care.

Id. at 84–85. For an update on the status of class action litigation for the benefit of children in the welfare system, including children with special needs, see the website of the National Center for Youth Law, at http://www.youthlaw.org/ child_welfare/. This problem is quite serious, because studies suggest that the *majority* of children in the foster care children have special needs.

> Children who are removed from their homes and placed in foster care often experience detrimental short and long-term effects. Researchers estimate that 30% to 80% of children in foster care exhibit emotional and/or behavioral problems, either from their experiences before entering foster care or from the foster care experience itself. Children entering foster care may experience grief at the separation from or loss of relationship with their natural parents. Children in care also face emotional and psychological challenges as they try to adjust to new and often changeable environments. Within three months of placement, many children exhibit signs of depression, aggression, or withdrawal. Some children with severe attachment disorders may exhibit signs of sleep disturbance, hoarding food, excessive eating, self-stimulation, rocking, or failure to thrive.

Chipungu & Bent-Goodley, *supra* at 85. Many critics argue, however, that public concern about extreme cases has generated an over-zealous response to child abuse that causes harm to many innocent people. These criticisms have targeted many different problems. In 1990, the New York State Department of Social Services estimated that 60% of the 130,000 reports of child abuse in 1989 were unsubstantiated, and 15% were intentionally false. Complaints of child abuse by divorcing parents against one another are said to be a particular problem. The law in many states criminalize false reporting. *See, e.g.*, N.Y. PENAL LAW § 240.55 (2009). In addition, mistakes may occur. Intrusive investigations of allegations of sexual abuse have been the subject of numerous civil suits against government officials. In one particularly egregious case, social workers removed a developmentally delayed 5-year old from school, on the basis of mistaken information about parental sex abuse, and required her to submit to a pelvic examination. *Tenenbaum v. Williams*, 193 F.3d. 581 (2d Cir. 1999), *cert. denied*, 529 U.S. 1098 (2000).

Parents who are erroneously accused of abusing their children may experience costs that persist after the case is investigated. Their names may be kept in a child abuse information registry for years, even though the complaint is determined to be unfounded. Practices used in child abuse investigations have also been the subject of intense criticism for their intrusiveness and potential to produce distorted information. Several highly publicized cases have focused this complaint. One, involving 24 adults who were charged with molesting 37 children in the small town of Jordan, Minnesota, is described in Justice Scalia's *Craig* dissent as evidence of the potential for convictions to be based on erroneous testimony.

Clearly, there are many problems haunting child protection efforts in this nation. Is there any consensus on whether, and if so how, the child welfare system can be reformed so as to succeed more effectively in its goals and in a manner that causes less harm to the children and adults in whose lives it intervenes? One problem with the system is the inadequacy of funding. In one publicized 2002 case, in which a 7-year-old New Jersey boy was found dead in the basement of his aunt's Newark home, where he had been kept with his twin 4-year-old brothers who were severely malnourished, the investigation that followed revealed that the social worker who closed the most recent investigation was working on more than 100 other investigations. *See* Richard Lezin Jones & Leslie Kaufman, *Worker in Abuse Case in Newark Juggled 107 Child Care Inquiries*, N.Y. TIMES, Jan. 8, 2003. Most observers and experts agree that the funding provided for child protection efforts is one cause for the system's problems. *See, e.g.*, JOHN E.B. MYERS, CHILD PROTECTION IN AMERICA: PAST, PRESENT AND FUTURE (2006); U.S. ADVISORY BOARD ON CHILD ABUSE & NEGLECT, DEP'T OF HEALTH AND HUMAN SERVS., ADMIN. FOR CHILDREN AND FAMILIES, THE CONTINUING CHILD PROTECTION EMERGENCY: A CHALLENGE TO THE NATION (1993).

Yet, many argue that adequate funding will only partially address the many problems plaguing the child welfare system in America. Dramatic reforms in policies and practices are, in the view of many experts and observers, absolutely necessary in order to meet the needs of America's children and families. The U.S. Advisory Board on Child Abuse and Neglect observed that child protection policy in the United States is "largely unplanned; it has consisted primarily of ad hoc responses to crises." U.S. ADVISORY BD. ON CHILD ABUSE & NEGLECT, U.S. DEP'T OF HEALTH & HUMAN SERVS., CREATING CARING COMMUNITIES: BLUEPRINT FOR AN EFFECTIVE FEDERAL POLICY ON CHILD ABUSE AND NEGLECT xi (1991). Ironically, while much effort has been expended to create policies that bring increasing numbers of maltreated children to the attention of authorities, very little emphasis has been placed on how to intervene effectively with affected families. *See, e.g.*, DUNCAN LINDSEY, THE WELFARE OF CHILDREN 96-126 (1994). The limited empirical research conducted on the efficacy of traditional child welfare interventions has been mixed, at best, leaving scientific observers uncertain as to whether such intervention makes a difference in the lives of children and families. *See, e.g.*, Gary B. Melton et al., *Empirical Research on Child Maltreatment and the Law*, 24 J. CLINICAL CHILD PSYCHOL. 47 (1995); Ross A. Thompson & Brian L. Wilcox, *Child Maltreatment Research: Federal Support and Policy Issues*, 50 AM. PSYCHOL. 789 (1995).

There have been many shifts in philosophy characterizing the child protection movement. An emphasis on family reunification gave way to family preservation, and then to timely termination of parental rights and adoption. Howard Davidson, *Child Protection Policy and Practice at Century's End*, 33 FAM. L.Q. 765 (1999). More recently, community-based approaches toward prevention and intervention have emerged. *See, e.g., id.*; GARY B. MELTON ET AL. (EDS.), TOWARD A CHILD-CENTERED, NEIGHBORHOOD-BASED CHILD PROTECTION SYSTEM (2001); GARY B. MELTON & FRANK D. BARRY (EDS.), PROTECTING CHILDREN FROM ABUSE AND NEGLECT: FOUNDATIONS FOR A NEW NATIONAL STRATEGY (1994). Some authors suggest that a critical flaw in the current child welfare system is the timing of its involvement with families: that is, intervention occurs only after suspicions of abuse or neglect surface. At that point in time, children have already been exposed to harm. Professor Howard Eisenberg proposes that the state act preemptively, requiring training and licensing of parents. According to this proposal children would be removed from homes far earlier in the chronology than occurs under the current system. *See* Howard B. Eisenberg, *A "Modest" Proposal: State Licensing of Parents*, 26 CONN. L. REV. 1416 (1994). Others propose that greater state involvement in the family consist of supportive services. Professor Maxine Eichner suggests that such assistance "would reduce, at the very least, some of the most tragic costs incurred [by children] under the current approach to child welfare." Maxine Eichner, *Children, Parents, and the State: Rethinking Relationships in the Child Welfare System*, 12 VA. J. SOC. POL'Y & L. 448 (2005). She states further that our society's view of "parenting as an activity that can and should be performed autonomously, without aid from those outside the family; which treats the child's welfare as solely the parents' responsibility in the normal course of events, without considering how systems outside of the parent-child relationship affect the child's welfare; and which views the state's intervention in families as a sign of the failure of parents, imposes significant costs on the state, parents, and most particularly, children." *Id.* at 448–49. Professor of History and Family Studies Stephanie Coontz argues that our society "should adopt standards of childrearing that do not confine responsibility to parents . . ." STEPHANIE COONTZ, THE WAY WE NEVER WERE: AMERICAN FAMILIES AND THE NOSTALGIA TRAP 210 (1994). She observes:

> If there is any pattern to be found in the variety of families that have succeeded and failed over the course of history, it is that children do best in societies where childrearing is considered too important to be left entirely to parents. In modern America as well, a growing body of research demonstrates that the crucial difference between functional and dysfunctional families lies not in the form of the family but in the quality of support networks outside the family, including the presence of nonkin in those networks.

Id. at 230.

Some critics focus on the overrepresentation of minority-group children in the child welfare system. For example, Professor Sarah Ramsey notes that some "believe that children of color should be kept out of a racist foster care system by directing more assistance to low-income families. Proponents want to fix foster care by rescuing foster children who have been abused and neglected by their parents and placing them in homes that are separated from their troubled kin and communities." Sarah Ramsey, *Fixing Foster Care or Reducing Child Poverty: The Pew Commission Recommendations and the Transracial Adoption Debate*, 66 MONT. LA. REV. 21, 47–48 (2005). Professor Dorothy Roberts states "disproportionate intervention in black families reinforces the continued political subordination of blacks as a group," and criticizes those who "believe child protective services must intervene immediately to save black children from their current crisis." Dorothy L. Roberts, *Child Welfare & Civil Rights*, 2003 U. ILL. L. REV. 171, 181. *See also* DOROTHY L. ROBERTS, SHATTERED BONDS: THE COLOR OF CHILD WELFARE (2001).

In recent years, there has been increasing recognition of the importance of children's continuing ties with their families, resulting in greater acceptance of the notion of "kinship care" as a substitute for the traditional model of foster care by strangers to the child's family. *See, e.g.*, Fostering Connections to Success and Increasing Adoptions Act of 2008, PL 100–351, 22 Stat. 3949 (2008) (federal legislation containing several provisions that facilitate involvement of relatives in the lives of children in child welfare system); A.B.A., *Kinship Care Legal Research Center, Summary Memo on Statutory Preferences for Relative Placement*, http://www.abanet.org/child/summary-memo.pdf; Am. Bar Assoc., Kinship Care Legal Research Center, *State Policies at a Glance*, http://www.abanet.org/child/placement.pdf (providing 50-state survey). *See generally*, A.B.A., Kinship Care Legal Research Ctr., http://www.abanet.org/child/kinshipcare.shtml. For thoughtful discussions of potential reforms *see, e.g.*, CENTER FOR THE STUDY OF SOCIAL POLICY, CHILD WELFARE SUMMIT: LOOKING TO THE FUTURE (2003); OLIVIA GOLDEN, REFORMING CHILD WELFARE (2009); Annie C. Casey Foundation, *Rebuild the Nation's Child Welfare System: Issue Brief* (Jan. 2009); National Coalition for Child Protection Reform, *Twelve Ways to Do Child Protection Right: Successful Alternatives to Taking Children from their Parents*, http://www.nccpr.org/index_files/page0005.html.

Yet, as policymakers consider newer philosophies and evaluate the efficacy of various approaches, children remain at risk. "[B]ecause children's lives are at stake, [the child protection system] cannot stop its work while the public debates its mission, or while researchers discover which interventions might help which families. This plane must be fixed while it flies through the air." Mary B. Larner et al., *Protecting Children from Abuse and Neglect: Analysis and Recommendations*, 8 FUTURE OF CHILDREN: PROTECTING CHILDREN FROM ABUSE AND NEGLECT 5 (1998) (citing the NAT'L COMM'N ON CHILDREN, BEYOND RHETORIC: A NEW AMERICAN AGENDA FOR CHILDREN AND FAMILIES 293 (1991)). The feat of repairing and reforming the child protection system while the metaphorical plane is in flight is, to say the least, a daunting task. Lois A. Weithorn, *Protecting Children from Exposure to Domestic Violence: The Use and Abuse of Child Maltreatment Statutes*, 53 HASTINGS L.J. 1 (2001).

Chapter 11

ADOPTION AND ASSISTED REPRODUCTIVE TECHNOLOGIES

INTRODUCTION

While most children in the United States are the biological children of their legal parents, adoption laws create the mechanism by which adults without the biological parent-child link can assume the role of legal parent. Once a legally-valid adoption is finalized, the relationship between the adopted child and adoptive parent(s) is identical — for all legal purposes — to the relationship a child has with his or her birth parents. This Chapter addresses a range of issues related to adoption law and practice in the United States. It also examines critical issues raised by the increasing use of Assisted Reproductive Technologies (ARTs) as alternatives to adoption for those adults for whom because sexual procreation is not a viable route to parentage. While the law regulating certain ARTs is settled and non-controversial, the law governing other ARTs is anything but.

Section A provides a general overview of the history and current trends characterizing adoptions in the U.S. Section B addresses the first legal step in the adoption process: freeing the child for adoption. Traditionally, in order for a child to be adopted, the child's legal relationship with his or her existing parents — typically the biological parents — must be severed. There are several legal scenarios that can lead to a child's availability for adoption, some of which require the consent of one or both birth parents, and some of which occur without that consent. In Section B, we examine whose consent is required under what circumstances and what constitutes a valid consent.

Before a new parent-child relationship can be created through the adoption process, the prospective adoptive parent(s) and prospective adoptive child must somehow be brought together. In some types of adoptions, such as adoptions by stepparents, "second parents," other family members, or foster parents, the goal of adoption is to create a formal and binding legal relationship between a specific adult and a specific child who already have functional parent-child or other familial or family-like relationship. Therefore, the question of who will be adopted by whom if the adoption goes forward is already determined. By contrast, in other forms of adoption, prospective adoptive parents and children must, in some way, be identified, selected, or otherwise "introduced," typically by a third party. Public and private adoption agencies frequently perform this third-party function, although there are other parties or organizations that may serve the role of intermediary as well. Adoptions not arranged by state or state-licensed agencies are referred to as "independent" adoptions. Regulatory attention ordinarily focuses on independent adoptions by persons unrelated to the child. Section C discusses the traditional and modern mechanisms that facilitate the linking of prospective adoptive parents to children eligible for adoption, discussing the roles of agencies and independent intermediaries in the process. In addition, it examines some of the themes, challenges, and controversies that have characterized the "selection" or "matching" processes, including examination of the roles of religion and race can permissibly play. It also considers the trends regarding intercountry adoptions by adults in the United States.

Section D examines the legal effects of the final adoption decree, including the impact of the decree on prior legal relationships. In recent years, the secrecy that traditionally surrounded information about an adoptees birth family has begun to give way to two trends: (1) increasing receptiveness in some jurisdictions to adult adoptees' interest in learning about their "roots," and (2) a continuum of "openness" of information flow and contact that characterizes some adoptions. Section D also considers the circumstances under which an adoption can be nullified. Section E explores the legal challenges posed by the increasing reliance on ARTs as a path to parenthood. It examines legal treatment of artificial insemination, donations of eggs and sperm, surrogacy arrangements, and human embryos.

A. ADOPTION TRENDS IN THE UNITED STATES: PAST, PRESENT, AND FUTURE

Adopted children constitute approximately 2.5% of all minor children living in U.S. households (or approximately 1.6 million children), according to the 2000 U.S. Census. Rose M. Kreider, *Adopted Children and Stepchildren: 2000*, 3 (2003).[1] The U.S. Department of Health and Human Services (DHHS) reports that 127,407 adoptions were finalized in the United States in 2001 (the most recent year for which comprehensive governmental statistics are available). DHHS, *How Many Children Were Adopted in 2000 and 2001?*, at 1 (2004) http://www.childwelfare.gov/pubs/s_adopted/s_adopted.pdf. Between 1992 and 2001, the number of adoptions in the U.S. remained relatively stable at approximately 127,000 annually. *Id.* at 3. As noted in Section [2] below, however, over time there have been some shifts in the relative proportions of particular subtypes of adoptions in the U.S. Most notably, the numbers of children adopted from the child welfare system and from other countries have increased, while the numbers of children born to unmarried women in the U.S. who are voluntarily relinquished for adoption have decreased.

---

[1] The Census questionnaire inquired about the relationship between the child and the person identified as the "householder," that is, the "person in whose name the housing unit is owned, being bought, or rented." Rose M. Kreider, *Adopted Children and Stepchildren:2000*, at 1 & n.1 (2003). It is not uncommon, however, for a child to be adopted by one adult in a household and related biologically, or not related at all, to another adult in that household. The data therefore, are limited, in that they do not permit a more nuanced analysis of the relationships in the household. They also rely on the respondents' designation of which adult is the "householder" in situations where two adults may share that status. Despite those limitations, however, the data still reveal some interesting findings and are thus reported here.

[1] Adoption in Historical Perspective

Formal legal adoption first appeared in America during the mid-nineteenth century. It had not been a part of the common law the U.S. inherited from England. Prior to the creation of formal adoption laws, a range of informal practices were employed to provide for children who were orphaned or whose parents were unable to care for them because of illness or financial hardship. Some such children were taken in by family members or by others in the community who assumed a functional parent-like role. David Ray Papke, *Pondering Past Purposes: A Critical History of American Adoption Law*, 102 W. VA. L. REV. 459, 460–61 (1999). "Fictive kinship" arrangements (that is, functional familial relationships among individuals who are not related by blood or marriage) were particularly prevalent in African-American families as a way to cope with the destruction of biological family ties engendered by slavery. *See* Barbara Bennett Woodhouse, *"It All Depends On What You Mean By Home": Toward A Communitarian Theory Of The "Nontraditional" Family*, 1996 UTAH L. REV. 561, 591–92; Gilbert Holmes, *The Extended Family System in the black Community: A Child-Centered Model for Adoption Policy*, 68 TEMPLE L. REV. 1649, 1658–1667 (1995).

Some children were placed with families with the understanding that the children would provide labor in exchange for food, clothing, and shelter. CYNTHIA MABRY & LISA KELLY, ADOPTION LAW: THEORY, POLICY, & PRACTICE 1–2 (2006). The circumstances of such placements varied greatly. While some children were fortunate enough to be treated like a member of the new family, others were treated merely as laborers, functioning like indentured servants. Still other children benefitted from an apprenticeship arrangement with tradesmen, craftsmen, or professionals, who provided training to the children in addition to room and board in exchange for labor. Not surprisingly, exploitation and abuse of these children characterized some of these arrangements. David Ray Papke, *Pondering Past Purposes: A Critical History of American Adoption Law*, 102 W. VA. L. REV. 459, 461 (1999).

Charitable organizations developed in the nineteenth century with the goal of assisting not only orphans, but children whose parents were poor, immigrant, or otherwise viewed as providing less than ideal home environments. Propelled by fear "that urbanization, industrial capitalism, and massive immigration were undermining the nation's homes and thus, the republic itself," tens of thousands of inner-city, immigrant, and/or impoverished children were removed from their homes and placed with other families in informal foster care or adoption-like situations. Michael Grossberg, *Balancing Acts: Crisis, Change, and Continuity in American Family Law, 1890–1990*, 28 IND. L. REV. 273, 275 (1995). Whereas some observers emphasize the humanitarian underpinnings of these efforts, others argue that the primary motive for this focus on children was the desire for social control over growing population subgroups viewed as dependent or deviant.

Early adoption statutes were passed in Mississippi (1846) and Texas (1850), permitting adults to adopt a child by recording a "deed" much like that required for ownership of land. See MABRY & KELLY, *supra*, at 2. In addition, petitions could be filed with state legislatures to authorize individual adoptions. Most legal historians, however, point to the 1851 Massachusetts adoption act as the first "modern" adoption statute.

> The Statute, called "An Act to Provide for the Adoption of Children," was revolutionary because it transformed adoption from a parent-centered process to a child-centered process. An older child's consent and his or her biological parents' or guardian's consent to the adoption were required. Prospective parents had to be certified before they could adopt a child. Prospective parents rights and responsibilities toward the adoptee were described. Furthermore, judges had to be persuaded that the adoption was in the child's best interests.

MABRY & KELLY at 3. Beliefs that adoption was not a natural way of creating families and popular notions of eugenics contributed to a relatively low rate of adoption (compared with modern trends) until the mid-1920s. It had been widely assumed that the children available for adoption would inherit mental disabilities and other unfavorable traits from their parents. *Id.* at 6. Attitudes changed, however. Adoption gained increasing legitimacy as a mode of family formation.

National estimates reveal that there were approximately 50,000 formal adoptions in the U.S. in 1944. Kathy Stolley, *Statistics on Adoption in the United States*, 3 THE FUTURE OF CHILDREN 26, 30 (1993). The annual numbers grew steadily, peaking at 175,000 adoptions in 1970. During the 1950s, prospective adoptive parents began to outnumber the adoptable children. As discussed below, would-be adoptive parents, who were mostly white and middle class, turned to children of other races (e.g., Indian children and African-American children) and foreign-born children in order to adopt. At the same time, the goals of adoption law gradually shifted in the view of some, "from promoting the welfare of children in need of parents — traditionally and unproblematically a 'public' function — to fulfilling the needs and desires of couples who want children." Jana B. Singer, *The Privatization of Family Law*, 1992 WIS. L. REV. 1443, 1478. The tensions between these two sets of goals provides the backdrop to many of the issues discussed in this Chapter.

The history of adoption policy and practice in the United States is paved with missteps and controversies as well as achievements, some of which are addressed in subsequent sections of this Chapter. Despite continuing challenges, the legal institution of adoption serves over 100,000 children annually, most of whom are placed in loving homes where they have the opportunity to develop into healthy, well-adjusted, and productive adults. For more on the history of American adoption policy and practice, see CYNTHIA MABRY & LISA KELLY, ADOPTION LAW: THEORY, POLICY, & PRACTICE 1–14 (2006); Naomi Cahn, *Perfect Substitutes or the Real Thing?* 52 DUKE L.J. 1077 (2003); NAOMI R. CAHN & JOAN HEIFETZ HOLLINGER (EDS.), FAMILIES BY LAW: AN ADOPTION READER 7–32 (2004); David Ray Papke, *Pondering Past Purposes: A Critical History of American Adoption Law*, 102 W. VA. L. REV. 459 (1999). For an alternative view of the history of adoption in the U.S., Amanda C. Pustilnik, Student Author, *Private Ordering, Legal Ordering, and the Getting of Children: A Counterhistory of Adoption Law*, YALE L. & POL'Y REV. 263 (2002).

[2]   Modern Adoption Trends

[a]   Relinquishment of Newborns by Unmarried Women

The legal and social circumstances that lead to adoption in the U.S. fall into several categories.[2] The scenario that is most commonly associated with adoption in the eyes of the public is the voluntary relinquishment of parental rights by an unwed mother alone or, in recent years, together with the baby's father. Yet, in recent years, this scenario accounts for only about 11% of adoptions in the United States. While some unmarried birth parents in the U.S. still consent to the adoption of their infant children, the frequency with which this occurs has decreased dramatically in the past several decades. For example, data analyzed by the Center for Disease Control and Prevention (CDC) reveal that prior to 1973, approximately 8.7% of children born to unmarried women were voluntarily placed for adoption shortly after birth. *Adoption Experiences of Women and Men and Demand for Children to Adopt by Women 18–44 Years of Age in the United States, 2002*, VITAL AND HEALTH STATISTICS SERIES 23, No. 27 at 34 (2008). After decreasing steadily, the percentage ultimately stabilized at approximately 1% during the mid-1990s. *Id.* at 16. This drop has occurred at the same time as the number of births to unmarried women has *increased*. Nonmarital births accounted for over one-third of births in 2003. Brady E. Hamilton et al., *Births: Preliminary Data for 2003, National Vital Statistics Reports*, Vol. 53, No. 9, at 5.

The decrease in voluntary relinquishments is likely attributable to the increasing social acceptance of single parenting by unmarried women and nonmarital parenting by couples. Some of the unmarried women giving birth may procreate intentionally in order to raise the resulting offspring as single parent or with a nonmarital opposite-sex or same-sex partner. *Adoption Experiences of Women and Men and Demand for Children to Adopt by Women 18–44 Years of Age in the United States, 2002*, VITAL AND HEALTH STATISTICS, Series 23, No. 27 at 2 (2008). In addition, the overall teen birth rate has declined since 1970, from 68.3 births per thousand women ages 15–19 years to 41.9 births per thousand in 2006. The availability of contraception and abortion most likely account for this decrease in teen pregnancies. Because teenage mothers were far more likely to relinquish children than were unmarried women in other age groups, this shift has likely contributed to the shrinking of the pool of children available for adoption. Demographers estimate that fewer than 14,000 children were voluntarily

---

[2] There is no single comprehensive database providing reliable data on the numbers and types of adoptions in the United States. Mary F. McFarland, *Adoption Trends in 2003: A Deficiency of Information*, National Center for State Courts (2003). The data presented in this section are culled from a range of sources, using a range of methodologies, some more accurate than others. *See also* DHHS, *How Many Children Were Adopted in 2000 and 2001?* 4–6 (2006), http://www.childwelfare.gov/pubs/s_adopted/s_adopteda.cfm (revealing the various sources of data used to compile national statistics). Therefore, the figures presented in this Section are only approximate. As a result, the percentages of children identified as adopted in the different adoption scenarios does not add up to an even 100 percent. In addition, the adoption subtypes discussed in this Section are not all mutually exclusive. About one quarter of children adopted out of foster care are adopted by relatives. These children are thus "double counted" in the figures for these two categories.

relinquished by unmarried women shortly after birth in 2003, or 11% of annual adoptions. *Id.*

[b]   Children in the Child Welfare System

Children whose parents' rights were terminated because of abuse, neglect, or abandonment comprise another group of prospective adopted children in the U.S. (See Chapter 10 for discussion of the state's dependency jurisdiction, foster care, and the substantive and procedural requirements for termination of parental rights.) This group accounts for approximately 40% of children adopted in a given recent calendar year. In recent years, approximately one-half million children in the child welfare system can be found in foster care placements on a given day. *See* Administration for Children & Families (AFCARS), *Trends in Foster Care and Adoption — FY 2002–FY 2007* (2008), http://www.acf.hhs.gov/programs/cb/stats_ research/afcars/trends.htm. These numbers have remained fairly constant between 2002 and 2007.[3] In 2007, by the end of the fiscal year, of 181,000 children eligible for adoption, only 28% or 51,000 had been adopted. *Id.* Therefore, 72% of the children eligible for adoption in 2007, or 130,000, remained in foster care at the end of the year. *Id. Thus, the number of children waiting for adoption in the child welfare system at the end of each recent calendar year through 2007 exceeds the number of children adopted annually across all categories of adoption in the United States.* In other words, if all of these children were adopted in a given year, the adoption rate would effectively *double* for that year.[4] Do the children who are adopted from the child welfare system differ in any systematic way from the children in that system who are not adopted? The children who were adopted were generally younger than those children still waiting for an adoptive family. The median age of the children adopted during the twelve months preceding September 2006 was 5.4 years compared to 7.7 for children still waiting. Twenty-three percent of the waiting group were adolescents (ages 13–17), compared with 11% of the adopted group. While the percentages of Hispanic children in the two groups was approximately the same (20% in the waiting group versus 19% in the adopted group), the percentages of white and black children in the two groups differed. Black children comprised 34% of the waiting group compared with 27% of the adopted group. By contrast, white children comprised 38% of the waiting group as

---

[3] Based on these statistics, children are counted once yearly. Thus, the half million children counted in 2007 may include some subgroup of the children already counted in 2006, because the children in this subgroup remain in foster care from one year to the next.

[4] The data do not reveal how many of the waiting children counted in consecutive years reappear in the tabulations in successive years. Given that only 51,000 children are adopted from this group annually, many of the children counted in a prior year remain in foster care, still waiting, unless they "age out" of the system. AFCARS data reveal that almost 40% of children who had been waiting for adoption in continuous foster care have waited over three years, and half of those children had been waiting *over five years*. DHHS, AFCARS Report: Preliminary FY 2006 Estimates as of January 2008 (14) (2008), http://www.acf.hhs.gov/programs/cb/stats_research/afcars/tar/report14.htm. Of the 51,000 children adopted from the child welfare system in Fiscal Year 2006, most (57%) were adopted *within the year* that their parents' rights were legally terminated, and 85% were adopted within two years after becoming free for adoption. Thus, it is reasonable to conclude that those children who have been in the system the longest are less likely to be adopted than those children whose parents' rights were most recently terminated.

compared with 45% of the adopted group. DHHS, AFCARS Report: Preliminary FY 2006 Estimates as of January 2008 (2008), http://www.acf.hhs.gov/programs/cb/stats_research/afcars/tar/report14.htm.

What trends characterize adoptions of children with "special needs"? Children with "special needs" constitute a disproportionately high percentage of children eligible for adoption from the child welfare system. States vary in their definitions of "special needs." While all states include illnesses, behavioral problems, and physical, psychological, or educational disabilities, some states also include many factors that make placement more challenging, including the child's age or minority-group race. *See* V. Gaylord et al. (eds.), *Understanding Adoption Subsidies: An Analysis of AFCARS Data*, IMPACT NEWSLETTER: FEATURE ISSUE ON CHILDREN WITH DISABILITIES IN THE CHILD WELFARE SYSTEM (U. Minn. Coll. Educ. & Hum. Dev.) Vol. 19 at 16 (2006). With respect to those special needs children with disabilities, research reveals that children with disabilities are more likely to be abused or neglected than are non-disabled children. Sheryl A. Larson & Lynda Anderson, *Children with Disabilities and the Child Welfare System: Prevalence Data*, in V. Gaylord et al. (eds.), IMPACT NEWSLETTER: FEATURE ISSUE ON CHILDREN WITH DISABILITIES IN THE CHILD WELFARE SYSTEM (U. Minn. Coll. Educ. & Hum. Dev.) Vol. 19 at 6 (2006), http://ici.umn.edu/products/impact/191/191.pdf. Furthermore, studies indicate that a subset of special needs children in the child welfare system develop disabilities as a result of the maltreatment they experienced prior to removal by the state. *Id.* While data as to the percentage of children in the child welfare system with special needs who are waiting for adoption are not available, the percentage of children with special needs who are adopted is extraordinarily high: 88% during Fiscal Year 2001. *Id.*

What are the attitudes of prospective adoptive parents regarding adoption of children from the child welfare system? Many prospective adoptive parents indicate a reluctance to adopt children from the foster care system. A 2002 Harris survey revealed that prospective adoptive parents are particularly hesitant to adopt children with medical or psychological problems. *Persons Seeking to Adopt*, CHILD WELFARE INFORMATION GATEWAY, DHHS (2005). Given that many prospective adoptive parents seek younger children who are healthy and without known disabilities, children in the child welfare system are at a distinct disadvantage regarding their prospects for adoption. There are some hopeful signs, however. A very high percentage of the children adopted out of foster care are adopted by their foster parents (59% in Fiscal Year 2006). DHHS, AFCARS Report: Preliminary FY 2006 Estimates as of January 2008 (14) (2008), http://www.acf.hhs.gov/programs/cb/stats_research/afcars/tar/report14.htm.   In addition, relatives adopted another 26% of the children from the foster care pool in 2006. These statistics are promising because, in recent years, the child welfare system has increasingly encouraged foster parent and kinship adoptions. In fact, only in recent decades have foster parents been *permitted* to adopt the children for whom they care once the children become available for adoption. Urban Institute, *Who Will Adopt the Foster Care Children Left Behind?* Caring for Children, Brief No. 2 (2003). Some recent child welfare policies favor and create incentives for kinship foster care, which can of course, lead to kinship adoptions. Thus, if policymakers actively promote, and create incentives for, these two types of adoptions, higher rates of adoption from the child welfare system may result. For information about current pilot projects designed to encourage kinship adoption see the Child Welfare Information Website at http://www.childwelfare.gov/adoption/types/domestic/kinship.cfm.

[c]   Adoptions by Relatives

Across all categories of adoption in the U.S., relatives comprise the single largest group of individuals who adopt. Approximately half of all children adopted in the United States are adopted by family members.[5] Rose M. Kreider, *Adopted Children and Stepchildren: 2000*, 2 & n.4 (2003). Based on a 1992 study, "stepparent adoptions" constituted 42% of all adoptions in the U.S. See *How Many Children Were Adopted*, *supra* at 1. In a stepparent adoption, a child's custodial parent retains his or her legal status as one of the child's parents. That parent provides consent for his or her spouse to adopt the child and become the child's second legal parent. In that no jurisdiction in the United States formally recognizes a family in which a child has three legal parents, a stepparent adoption can only go forward if one of several conditions exists: the child does not have a second parent (e.g., if one the child's birth parents has died); the child's noncustodial parent consents to the stepparent adoption, thereby voluntarily relinquishing parental rights in favor of the custodial parent's spouse; the parental rights of the noncustodial parent have already been terminated by the state on the basis of abuse, neglect, or abandonment; or it is determined by the judge acting on the adoption petition that the noncustodial biological parent's consent is not necessary as a prerequisite to the stepparent's adoption.

As noted in Chapter 9, until the 1970s, unwed biological fathers' consent was not required, although a series of U.S. Supreme Court cases has established that states must create some avenue by which these men have an opportunity to express their interest in developing a parent-child relationship, such as registering with the state's putative father's registry. The consent of divorced noncustodial fathers to their biological children's adoption by a stepfather is discussed in Section B[2][a][i] below. This discussion reveals variations from state to state in the legal standards applied to determine whether a noncustodial divorced father can block an adoption by the mother's husband.

[d]   Intercountry Adoptions

One of the most significant trends in U.S. adoptions is the increase of foreign-born children adopted by American families. Data reveal that intercountry adoptions increased from 5% to 15% of total adoptions in the U.S. between 1992 and 2001. *How Many Children Were Adopted? supra*, at 1. In 2001, approximately 19,000 children entered the United States for the purpose of adoption by an American family or individual. The most recent data posted on the U.S. Department of State's Office of Children's Issues website indicates that the numbers of foreign-born children adopted in the U.S. continued to rise after 2001,

---

[5] Because some proportion of the children adopted by relatives are adopted from the child welfare system and thus appear in more than one subtype of adoption discussed here, the percentages attributed to each subgroup will exceed 100.

reaching a high of 22,884 in 2004. *See* Total Adoptions to the United States, Office of Children's Issues, U.S. Dept. of State, http://adoption.state.gov/news/total_chart.html. The numbers then dipped slightly, with a total of 17,438 foreign-born children adopted in the U.S. in 2008.

There has been fluctuation in the numbers of children adopted from various countries. China ranked first for several years. Only in 2008 did Guatemala overtake China as the birthplace of a greater number of foreign-born children adopted by Americans. *Id.* Other nations at the top of the list in recent years are Russia, South Korea, and Ethiopia.

The statistics just cited tell us about the numbers of children who are adopted from other nations annually. We can also examine the numbers of foreign-born adopted children who lived in American households at the time of the 2000 Census., See *Adopted Children and Stepchildren 2000*, supra, at 12. Of the 1.586 million adopted children in U.S. households at the time of the 2000 census, 1.387 million or 87.4% were born in the U.S, while the remaining 199,000 adopted children living in American households were born in other countries. The 2000 Census reveals that the foreign-born adopted children in America's households were most likely to have immigrated from the following nations: Korea (23.9%); China (10.5%); Russia (9.9%); and Mexico (9.1%). The 2010 census data will, of course, incorporate the trends characterizing intercountry adoptions for the prior ten years, by which time more than half of the adopted children sampled in 2000 will no longer be minors, and will therefore not appear in tabulations of minor adopted children living in American households. Intercountry adoptions and the legal challenges they present will be discussed in greater detail in Section C[2][e] below.

[e] Adoptions by Gays and Lesbians

No discussion of trends in U.S. adoptions would be complete without considering the increase in recent years of adoptions by gays and lesbians. A recent survey indicated that 41.4% of surveyed lesbian women and 51.8% of surveyed gay men hoped to have children, and a large percentage of those surveyed are considering adoption as an option. Gary J. Gates et al., *Adoption and Foster Care by Gay and Lesbian Parents in the United States* 5 (2007), http://www.urban.org/UploadedPDF/411437_Adoption_Foster_Care.pdf.
Researchers estimate that gay or lesbian parents are now raising approximately 65,500 or 4 percent of adopted children in the United States. The circumstances leading to adoptions by gays and lesbians are quite varied, touching on all of the subtypes of adoption discussed above. In those states that permit gays and lesbians to marry, stepparent adoption is a viable option in the appropriate circumstances. As noted in Chapter 9, several states that do not allow same-sex partners to marry do authorize second-parent adoptions, and many same-sex couples have taken advantage of this method of creating binding legal ties between an unrelated adult and child. Some of the children adopted by a legal parent's same-sex partner may have been born prior to the partners' relationship. Other children may be conceived by one of two female partners with the benefit of artificial insemination or other ART. In most jurisdictions, in this type of situation, the woman who gives birth will be the only adult recognized as that child's legal parent. Thus, where permitted, the mother's same-sex partner adopts the child. Two same-sex partners may, in

most states, jointly adopt a child unrelated to both of them. In addition, Gates and colleagues report that approximately 14% of the children adopted by same-sex couples are foreign-born, *id.* at 12–13, a statistic that parallels the percentage of foreign-born children adopted by all Americans.

Finally, and importantly, some gay or lesbian adults become foster parents to, and subsequently adopt, foster children. As the statistics cited above reveal, there are more children in the foster care system waiting for adoptive families than there are families willing to adopt them. Gay and lesbian adults like several of the plaintiffs in *Lofton v. Kearny, see* Chapter 9, volunteer to raise children from the pool within the child welfare system. Many of these children are identified as "hard-to-place" because of their age, race, or disabilities. One study revealed that adoption agencies serving special needs children have, in recent years, been making outreach efforts to gays and lesbians. *See* Evan B. Donaldson, Adoption Institute, *Adoption by Lesbians and Gays: A National Survey of Adoption Agency Policies, Practices, and Attitudes* (2003), http://www.adoptioninstitute.org/whowe/Gay%20and%20Lesbian%20Adoption1.html. Many of the children potentially adoptable by these individuals or couples might otherwise spend the remainder of their minority in temporary foster care, "aging out" of the system without the permanent family supports and connections that can make the difference in how one copes with the demands of young adulthood. Thus, adoptions of these children by gays and lesbians, like adoptions by foster parents and relatives, hold promise for children stuck in foster care, who need a loving and stable family. For a series of relevant reports, see Evan B. Donaldson, Adoption Institute's publications webpage, http://www.adoptioninstitute.org/publications/#gaylesbianadoption (last visited June 29, 2009).

For a discussion of the legal issues relating to adoptions by gays and lesbians, see Chapter 9.

[3]   The Psychological Adjustment of Adopted Children

Are adopted children at greater risk for development of psychological problems than are children raised in their biological family, either because they are adopted, or because of experiences they may have had prior to adoption? Contrary to stereotypes, adopted children are no more likely to have emotional or adjustment difficulties than are non-adopted children. *See, e.g.*, DAVID BRODZINSKY & DANIEL W. SMITH; CHILDREN'S ADJUSTMENT TO ADOPTION (1998); Jeffrey Haugaard, *Is Adoption a Risk Factor for the Development of Adjustment Problems?* 18 CLINICAL PSYCHOL. REV. 47 (1998); DiAnne Borders et al., *Are Adopted Children and their Parents at Risk for Negative Outcomes?*, 47 FAM. RELATIONS 237 (1998); Michael A. Snyder et al., *Childhood Adoption: Long-Term Effects in Adulthood*, 61 PSYCHIATRY 191 (1998). The research reveals that *some* adopted children may be particularly vulnerable to the development of emotional, behavioral, or academic problems, findings attributable to children's preadoption experiences (such as exposure to maltreatment, institutionalization, or multiple foster placements), their ages at adoption (children adopted older are more likely to have psychological difficulties), or special needs. BRODZINSKY & SMITH, *supra*. In a sophisticated analysis of the research on children's adjustment and adoption, the investigators point out that the observed differences between adopted and nonadopted children found in some studies are relatively small. BRODZINSKY & SMITH, *supra*. Some groups of adopted children who might be expected to experience problems given early deprivation, traumatic experiences, or developmental disabilities, seem to adjust well within their adoptive families. *See, e.g.,* W. Monique van Londen, et al., *Attachment, Cognitive, and Motor Development in Adopted Children: Short-Term Outcomes after International Adoption,* 2007 J. PED. PSYCHOL. 1; Laraine Masters Glidden, *Adopting Children with Developmental Disabilities: A Long-Term Perspective,* 40 FAM. RELATIONS 397 (2000). Researchers are investigating what factors create vulnerabilities among adopted children that might manifest as problems and, importantly, what factors and interventions create more positive functioning for adopted children. In recent years, there has been greater emphasis on the importance of providing professional post-adoption services to adoptive families, particularly where the children have special needs. *See, e.g.,* Evan B. Donaldson Adoption Institute, *What's Working for Children: A Policy Study of Adoption Stability and Termination* (2004).

B. "FREEING" THE CHILD FOR ADOPTION

[1] Involuntary Termination of Parental Rights

Chapter 10 addresses the substantive standards and procedural requirements of involuntary termination of parental rights. As noted above, approximately 40% of children adopted in the U.S. today are adopted from the child welfare system after the children's parents' rights have been terminated. While a large proportion of those children are freed for adoption through a court's involuntary termination of their parents' rights, some children's parents voluntarily relinquish their rights to the state. In some of these cases, the parents relinquish their rights because child welfare personnel advise them that involuntary termination proceedings will be commenced, are likely to be successful, and that therefore it is in the interest of the parent and the child that the termination be accomplished without adversarial litigation. Other parents make the decision to voluntarily relinquish their rights without this impetus, because they have concluded that the child (or they) would be better off if their parental rights are terminated. This decision might be motivated by a desire to free the child for adoption, perhaps by a relative or the child's foster parents. In some instances, a parent may simply come to terms with his or her difficulty adequately fulfilling the parental role.

The 1997 Federal Adoption and Safe Families Act, Pub. L. 105-89, 111 Stat. 2115 *codified at* 42 U.S.C.A.§ 1305 et seq. (2008) seeks to move children out of foster care more quickly, either returning them to their parents or creating a more permanent placement. As such, states are required to petition for termination of parental rights of children who have been in foster care for 15 of the prior 22 months. One author addresses the role that voluntary relinquishment might play in achieving permanency goals.

> The federal mandates do not specifically address the role that voluntary relinquishment may play as an alternative for exploration before the agency is mandated to [petition for] involuntarily terminate parental rights.

[This] does not preclude such a consideration in the context of concurrent planning and/or mediation with families whose children are in foster care. Particularly in those cases in which reasonable efforts are required and termination of parental rights may be sought on time-based grounds, there are potential benefits in providing parents with an opportunity to consider voluntarily a range of options prior to positioning the matter in an adversarial mode. In addition to savings in time and money that nonadversarial approaches may make possible, alternatives such as mediation and voluntary relinquishment may provide a stronger foundation for permanency for children. Research suggests that adoption practice involving involuntary termination of parental rights may create serious problems for many children. One study, which compared outcomes for children in foster care freed for adoption through involuntary termination of parental rights with outcomes for children in foster care freed through voluntary relinquishment, found that "the adversary nature of the [involuntary] proceedings and their length left the child[ren] in a limbo of anxiety and heightened loyalty conflicts in relation to the parents, grief about losing them, and hostility toward the agency seeking termination." A significant number of children in this study who were freed for adoption through involuntary termination successfully resisted their adoptions and returned to foster care after their adoptions disrupted. By contrast, the more stable adoptions were associated with voluntary relinquishment of parental rights which parents and children alike seemed to view in a positive light.

Madelyn Freundlich, *Expediting Termination of Parental Rights: Solving a Problem or Sowing the Seeds of a New Predicament?* 28 CAP. U. L. REV. 97, 106–07 (1999) (quoting Robert Borgman, *Antecedents and Consequences of Parental Rights Termination for Abused and Neglected Children*, 60 CHILD WELFARE 391, 402–03 (1991)).

[2]   Consent to Adoption

[a]   Whose Consent is Necessary?

[i]   Stepparent Adoption

The biological parents' consent is ordinarily required before a child can be adopted. Despite this general rule, unwed fathers historically had no legally-enforceable parental claims (or responsibilities), and therefore, their consent to an adoption was not required. Beginning in the 1970s, with *Stanley v. Illinois*, 405 U.S. 645 (1972), the U.S. Supreme Court extended to unwed fathers constitutional protection for their relationships with "the children [they have] sired and raised . . . absent a powerful countervailing interest. . . ." In subsequent years, a line of Supreme Court cases (*see* Chapter 9), considered specifically what procedural and substantive constitutional protections are due unmarried fathers before their parental rights can be severed by adoption. According to the U.S. Supreme Court, states may constitutionally require that unwed fathers take certain affirmative steps to demonstrate their commitment to parenthood before the parental authority to block (or even be notified of) an adoption "vests." Thus, some adoptions still take place without the involvement of a child's unmarried biological father.

In contrast to unwed fathers, a man who was married to a child's mother when the child was conceived, gestated, or born has had far greater constitutional protection. Even when separated or divorced from the mother and no longer living with the child, a noncustodial father had been empowered to block an adoption. In recent years, however, some jurisdictions have set forth more "modern" standards that make it easier to go forward with an adoption over the objection of a noncustodial marital father. In reading *In re J.J.J.* below, consider how the standard used by the court compares to the standard required to terminate parental rights under the dependency statutes discussed in Chapter 10.

In a stepparent adoption, at some time after the birth of a child, the custodial parent marries someone other than the child's other biological parent. At some point thereafter, the custodial parent and his or her spouse (the child's stepparent) file a petition for the stepparent to adopt the child. This scenario can present in circumstances in which the biological parents were not married (as in *Lehr v. Robertson* and related cases in Chapter 9) or were married and divorced. In both types of cases, however, the stepparent may be the *de facto* second parent by virtue of his or her daily presence, assumption of parental responsibilities, and establishment of an emotional bond with the child. If the noncustodial biological parent opposes the adoption petition, the custodial parent and spouse may ask the court to approve the adoption petition without the noncustodial parent's consent. States vary somewhat in their approach to such requests. Some are fairly deferential to the parental rights of the child's noncustodial parent, while others much less so.

IN THE MATTER OF J.J.J.
Alaska Supreme Court
718 P.2d 948 (1986)

MOORE, JUSTICE.

This is an expedited appeal from an adoption decree whereby a 7-year-old boy was adopted by his stepfather over the objections of the boy's biological father. Because of the biological father's history of nonsupport, his consent was deemed unnecessary.

The primary issue in this case is whether the master erred in finding that for at least a 12-month period, the biological father failed significantly without justifiable cause to provide support required by judicial decree. This finding was sustained by the superior court. . . .

We conclude that the superior court correctly affirmed the master's finding with respect to support and correctly reversed her best interests determination. . . .

On May 25, 1982 the boy's biological parents were divorced. B.J., the biological mother, was awarded custody of the boy and J.B., the biological father, was ordered to pay $200 per month as child support. J.B. made no payments until August 1982, when he made a single $200 payment after being contacted by the

Child Support Enforcement Agency (C.S.E.A.).

Thereafter, from September 1982 through March 1983, J.B. made no payments toward the support of the boy. In April and May of 1983 the C.S.E.A. garnished a total of $1,000 of J.B.'s wages to apply toward his child support arrearages. Thereafter, from May through October 1983, J.B. continued to pay nothing toward the boy's support.[2]

In August 1983 the boy's mother and his stepfather, S.J., decided that S.J. should seek to adopt the boy and so advised J.B. In November 1983, shortly before the filing of the adoption petition, J.B. and his new wife paid $1,800 against part of his child support arrearages, after again being contacted by the C.S.E.A.

From December 1981 until the filing of the adoption petition, on December 19, 1983, J.B. had almost no contact with the boy. Twice during the last six months of this period J.B. reportedly informed the boy's mother, B.J., that he now wanted to visit the boy. However, B.J. resisted J.B.'s request for unsupervised visitation with the boy, stating that she believed that J.B. should slowly develop a relationship with the boy after having had no contact with him for such a long period. It does appear that, beginning well before the divorce, J.B. virtually ignored the boy.

During the period since his marriage to B.J., the boy's stepfather evidently established a close parental relationship with the boy.

In December 1983 the boy's stepfather, S.J., filed the petition to adopt him. The biological father, J.B., refused to consent to the adoption. The stepfather contended that J.B.'s consent was unnecessary pursuant to AS 25.23.050(a)(2)(B), because J.B. had "failed significantly, without justifiable cause . . . to provide for the care and support of the child as required by law or judicial decree."

The probate master found that J.B. had, for at least a year, significantly and unjustifiably failed to provide court-ordered support and had lost his right to withhold consent to the adoption. However, the master also found that the adoption decree would not be in the boy's best interests because he was curious about his biological father and seemed interested in knowing him (notwithstanding the boy's attachment to his stepfather). By law an adoption decree would terminate J.B.'s parental rights regarding the boy. . . .

. . . .

As commentators have noted, the very problem now before us is an increasingly common occurrence, given the increase in divorce and remarriage in our society. Nevertheless, despite voluntarily assumed obligations and the existence of a strong bond between stepparent and stepchild, such a relationship lacks legal protection in the event of the desertion or death of the stepparent's spouse (the custodial "natural" parent). In such an event the noncustodial "natural" parent, even a parent who has rarely paid child support or merely made an occasional gesture of communication, may automatically assert primary rights to take legal custody of the child, despite the child's need for a stable and continuous family relationship.

---

[2] J.B.'s earnings in 1982 appear to have been $22,518; his earnings during three quarters of 1983 appear to have been $18,750. . . .

Stepparent adoption assures that the child may remain with his existing family. However, adoption has seemed a harsh remedy when the biological parent refuses consent. . . .

Alaska has adopted a modified version of the Uniform Adoption Act [which] sets forth the circumstances under which an adoption should be granted without a natural parent's consent. . . . Alaska's version of the Act focuses on a noncustodial parent's failure to meaningfully communicate with a child, significant failure to pay child support, and other acts of abandonment.

In this court's prior decisions in this area we have declined to dispense with a noncustodial parent's right to withhold consent to a stepparent adoption as long as the noncustodial parent had made a few perfunctory communications or an occasional gesture of support. In *Matter of Adoption of K.M.M.*, 611 P.2d 84 (Alaska 1980), we found that the biological father's unwillingness to visit his children for over one year was justified by "the mere fact that it was emotionally traumatic for the natural father to see his children and former wife living with a man who had been the father's closest friend." . . . In *R.N.T. v. J.R.G.*, 666 P.2d 1036 (Alaska 1983) this court reversed a superior court's decision to allow a stepfather to adopt the children of R.N.T. because R.N.T. had not maintained meaningful communication with his young children during the 14-month period that he was in prison. We emphasized that parental conduct that causes the loss of a parent's right to consent must be willful . . . Upon reflection, however, we now find that the *R.N.T.* dissent actually presented the better approach:"

> R.N.T. states that the terms of his imprisonment and parole effectively prevented him from having contact with his children. This should not be the end of the analysis, as it is for this court, but only the beginning. Not all parents who are incarcerated or on parole are precluded from communicating with their children; it simply is not an automatic condition of imprisonment or parole. The issue that must be addressed is whether the constraints imposed on R.N.T. were the result of his own conduct, in which case his failure to communicate would not be justifiable, or were instead the result of circumstances over which he had no control . . ."

We take this opportunity to clarify that, in order for a noncustodial parent to block a stepparent adoption, he or she must have maintained meaningful contact with a child, and must have provided regular payments of child support, unless prevented from doing so by circumstances beyond the noncustodial parent's control. Circumstances resulting from the noncustodial parent's own conduct cannot excuse such a parent's significant failure to provide support or maintain meaningful communication. Moreover, failure to support or to maintain contact with a child should not be excused by the emotional antagonism or awkwardness that may exist between former spouses. . . .

AS 25.23.050(a) specifies: "Persons as to whom consent and notice not required" in adoption cases. This provision provides that consent is not required of . . ."

> (2) a parent of a child in the custody of another, if the parent for a period of at least one year has failed significantly without justifiable cause, including but not limited to indigency,

(A) to communicate meaningfully with the child, or

(B) to provide for the care and support of the child as required by law or judicial decree . . .

J.B. contends that the "period of at least one year" of significant nonsupport must immediately precede the adoption petition. We disagree, as do other courts. J.B. also suggests that his occasional payment should suffice to preserve his right to withhold consent to any adoption of J.J.J.

The statute does not say that the period of "at least one year" must immediately precede the filing of an adoption petition. One year is the minimum period which may be considered. Thus the superior court correctly considered the entire 17-month period during which J.B. made only one voluntary payment of $200 on his court-ordered obligation to contribute to J.J.J.'s support.

Sporadic partial payments do not preclude a finding of significant failure to provide child support. . . . Child support payments should be substantial or "regular" and constitute a "material factor" in the support of a child. . . .

The dissent insists that "no rule of law or principle of logic" requires that child support must be "uncompelled." However, the purpose of the waiver-of-consent statute was to provide an objective measure (at least one year) of when a parent has, in the practical sense, forsaken a child. It would make no sense at all to infer parental concern from payments that a government agency has to garnish from the income of a parent who has refused to provide support. Nevertheless, the dissent suggests that payments garnished from a recalcitrant parent's income should signify the same parental concern that voluntary support payments signify, because all court-ordered child support is "compelled" and "there is no certainty what the terms 'compulsion' or 'voluntary' mean" in this context. [Yet, we note that g]arnishment occurs only as a last resort, when a parent has refused to meet this important obligation. . . .

As for J.B.'s 11th-hour (or 19th-month) payment to partially pay off his arrearages a few weeks before the adoption petition was filed, it would be absurd to believe that the legislature meant for a last-minute balloon payment to cancel out the import of a substantial period of nonsupport and noninvolvement. Other courts have expressed similar views: After the required period of one year has passed, resumption of payment of support for a brief period, particularly after the commencement of the adoption proceeding or just prior thereto, is not sufficient to bar an adoption without the consent of the delinquent father by starting a new one year period of non-support under the statute. . . .

We hold that courts shall consider a parent's entire history of support or nonsupport to determine whether that parent has waived his or her right to block a child's adoption by a stepparent[20]. . . .

---

[20] If, for instance, four years ago a parent significantly failed to support a child for a year, but thereafter (for the next three years) fully supported the child until the filing of an adoption petition, a court should find that that parent had not waived his or her right to withhold consent to the child's adoption. Although the dissent labels our position "harsh," this opinion actually considers the broader picture of the problems posed and recognizes that a child needs regular support (and meaningful

. . . .

J.B. also argues that his significant failure to support the boy was the excusable result of his ex-wife's resistance to his belated interest in having the boy visit him, in August 1983, after more than a year of no communication at all with him. This, however, is no justification at all. . . . [¶] Nor does his contention counter the fact that he made virtually no effort to communicate with the boy from April 1982 to August 1983, despite his ex-wife's requests that he do so.

MATTHEWS, Justice, joined by RABINOWITZ, Chief Justice, dissenting.

. . . [T]he father had paid $3,250 of the total support due of $3,800 and was less than three months behind in child support when the petition for adoption was filed.

Two questions of statutory interpretation . . . are presented."

(1) Does the period of at least one year referred to in the statute mean any period of one year or that period which immediately precedes the filing of the petition for adoption?

(2) Should the amounts obtained by the Child Support Enforcement Agency from the father's employer be taken into account as part of the provision of support by the father?"

Only if one concludes that the statute refers to any year rather than the year which precedes the filing of the petition for adoption and that the withheld wages cannot be counted as the provision of support, can the conclusion be drawn that the father in this case has waived his right to withhold consent to the adoption of his son . . .

. . . In interpreting AS 20.15.050(a)(2), we have required that it be strictly construed in favor of a natural parent. *In re Adoption of K.M.M.*, 611 P.2d 84, 87 (Alaska 1980). . . . [P]arents should not be deprived of the fundamental rights and duties inherent in the parent-child relationship except for "grave and weighty reasons." This policy of strict construction means that where two interpretations of the statute are reasonably possible, that interpretation which is most protective of the rights of the natural parent is to be selected. Since interpreting this statute to refer to the one year period immediately preceding the petition is reasonable, and since that interpretation is more protective of the rights of the natural parent than construing the statute to refer to any one year period, the former interpretation should be adopted.

. . . . Under a strict "any year" interpretation, if a parent did not support his children for one year long before the filing of a petition for adoption, but since that year had been faithful in supporting them and had made up all arrearages, his consent would nonetheless not be required under the statute. Such a result would be extremely unjust in many cases. This harshness may be tempered to some extent by the majority's declaration that "courts shall consider a parent's entire history of support" in determining waiver. The trouble with this is that it cuts us completely

---

communication) in the here-and-now. A young child's needs cannot be put on hold for years until a parent might have a "change of heart."

adrift from the statute. The purpose of the statute was to provide a relatively simple means by which waiver could be determined. . . .

B. Provision of Support

The majority concludes that only payments which are made without compulsion should count as provision of support by the parent. There are several reasons why this construction should not be adopted.

First, the requirement of non-compulsion is not expressed in the statute, nor may it reasonably be implied. . . . All that the statute calls for is support. . . .

Second, the rule of construction that the statute be interpreted in the manner most protective of the rights of parents indicates that a requirement of non-compulsion should not be read into the statute.

Third, there is no certainty what the terms "compulsion" or "voluntary" mean in the context of court ordered child support. All payments of support under such an order are compelled. . . .

The majority tells us that "the purpose of the waiver of consent statute was to provide an objective measure of when a parent has, in the practical sense, forsaken a child." I agree. It does not follow, however, that coerced payments necessarily indicate abandonment or lack of parental concern. An aggressive former spouse can garnish wages after only a slight delay in payment, and a non-custodial parent may be passively content to provide support in that way. . . . So long as the non-custodial parent visits with his children it cannot be said that, in a practical sense, he has forsaken them.

NOTES

1. *Alaska's Policies After* **J.J.J.** The Alaska Supreme Court's decision in *J.J.J.* also reflects the modern trend requiring the objecting biological parent to demonstrate that he or she has earned the right to continued parental status by fulfilling parental responsibilities and maintaining a relationship with the child. As such, the subsequent events in Alaska provide further evidence of shifting perspectives. The two dissenting Justices in *J.J.J.*, argue that the statute should be construed in favor of the biological father's rights, giving him every benefit of the doubt that is reasonable in close cases. In 1990, however, the Alaska Legislature amended Section 25.23.005 by adding the following language: "This chapter shall be liberally construed to the end that the best interests of adopted children are promoted. Due regard shall be given to the rights of all persons affected by a child's adoption." This amendment made clear that the Legislature viewed the majority's interpretation of the statute in *J.J.J.* to be the correct one.

Subsequent decisions by the Alaska Supreme Court in cases where a biological marital father seeks to block a stepparent adoption reveal a fact-intensive mode of analysis. For example, in *In the Matter of K.L.J.*, 813 P.2d 276 (Alaska 1991), the court unanimously held that a biological father who was disabled and indigent and without legal representation had a right to receive such representation prior to severance of his parental rights in favor of a stepparent adoption. In this case, the father maintained regular contact with his daughter and paid child support following the parents' separation. He testified that, after a certain date, his letters to his daughter were returned with no forwarding address and he could not locate his ex-wife and child. In addition, his former wife had moved with the child from Washington to Alaska, in violation of the divorce decree's mandate that neither party remove the child from the state of Washington. The court emphasized the language in Section 25.23.005(a)(2) restricting an override of a parent's consent to an adoption to situations where the parent fails to communicate or support the child "without justifiable cause." In light of the multiple obstacles confronting the biological father, the court reversed the lower court's granting of the adoption and remanded the case for proceedings below in which the father was to be assisted by an appointed counsel.

In a 1993 case, *In the Matter of the Adoption of J.B.K*, 865 P.2d 737, the same court held that the consent of a biological marital father who had remarried his former wife several years after their divorce could not be dispensed with, based on the man's conduct in the interim period between the two marriages. Viewing the remarriage as "a renewal of their rights and obligations as parents [nullifying] the custody and support provisions of the previous divorce decree," the court held that the focus of the court's inquiry must be the period of time following the second divorce. The court was satisfied that the father had met his obligations during that period. These decisions, together with the 1990 statutory amendment, reveal that Alaska's approach to these cases is highly dependent on the facts. While the court does not appear to accord substantial deference to the claims of the noncustodial parents, as would the dissenters in *J.J.J.*, it does not disregard their rights either, in favor of a straightforward "best interests of the child" test. Rather, in scrutinizing the facts of the case, the court seeks to balance the child's best interests with clear evidence that the language of the statute has been satisfied.

2. *Uniform Adoption Act.* The 1994 Uniform Adoption Act is a comprehensive proposal for reform of adoption law. An express goal of the Act is to facilitate adoption and to promote its benefits, not only for children, but also for the adults involved. Although the Act seeks to accommodate the interests of birth parents and adoptive parents in a coherent regulatory scheme, its primary goal is not preservation of the ties between the child and her biological parent. As Professor Joan Hollinger, the principal architect of the Act put it:

> [The Act] rejects the view that adoption is a "last resort," to be invoked only after multiple public efforts to preserve or establish a child's ties to biological parents have failed. Instead the Act is premised on the belief that children's ties to the individuals who actually parent them — or who are committed to parenting them deserve legal protection — even if those ties are psychologically and socially constructed and not biologically rooted[.]"

Hollinger, *Adoption and Aspiration: The Uniform Adoption Act, The DeBoer-Schmidt Case, and the American Quest for the Ideal Family*, 2 DUKE J. GENDER L. & POL. 15, 17–18 (1995). The Uniform Adoption Act § 3-504(c) emphasizes the distinctions between stepparent adoptions and placement of the child with a new family. In stepparent adoptions, the child does not enter a new home and family. Rather, she remains in a family setting with which he is familiar. A stepparent adoption often ratifies an existing functional parent-child relationship by providing formal legal acknowledgement of that relationship. In addition, whether the adoption goes forward or not, the custodial arrangement of the child is not likely to change. Furthermore, because the custodial parent has "chosen" the prospective adoptive parent, evaluation of the suitability of the stepparent as a parent requires less scrutiny. Under the Uniform Act, evaluation of the stepparent is discretionary; the child's inheritance rights from the biological parent are preserved; and continued post-adoption visitation by the biological parent is facilitated. U.A.A. § 4-113. (*See* discussion of post-adoption visitation in Section D below).

3. *Shifting Standards: Reconsidering the Level of Deference Accorded to Noncustodial Marital Fathers Who Refuse Consent for Stepparent Adoption.* Until recently, marital noncustodial biological parents were generally accorded great deference when stepparents sought to adopt over their objection. Increasingly, states have revised their policies, placing the burden on the objecting biological parent to demonstrate that he or she has earned the right to continued parental status by fulfilling parental responsibilities and maintaining a relationship with the child. States may accomplish this goal by requiring a court to consider the child's "best interests" in deciding whether a noncustodial marital father can block a stepparent adoption, rather than needing to demonstrate that the noncustodial parent is "unfit" or that failure to grant the adoption would be detrimental to the child. In light of the constitutional concerns attending reduced deference to the biological parents' rights in these cases, many statutes now delineate precisely what types of conduct place that parent's right to block the adoption in jeopardy, such as failure to remain in continued contact with the child, or provide consistent financial support for a specific period of time (ranging from six months proposed by the U.A.A. to two years, see Kan. Stat. § 59-2136(d) (2009)).

In examining the trends in state policies, consider whether these changes accord sufficient weight to the noncustodial marital father's constitutional rights. To what extent do these policy reforms facilitate an adoption when there is strong evidence that the noncustodial biological parent has shown little or no interest in the child and when granting an adoption legally ratifies the factual absence of any meaningful functional parent-child relationship? By contrast, to what extent do these policy changes erase *all* deference to the noncustodial father's parental rights — an approach facially inconsistent with the constitutional protections typically accorded parent-child relationships? Ideally, the policy reforms primarily instruct a judge to consider the child's "best interests" in addition to the range of findings regarding the noncustodial parent's efforts to create and sustain a relationship with the child. To illustrate these themes, we examine the policy changes that have occurred in Virginia and New Jersey.

For some time, the state of Virginia was one of the more traditional jurisdictions, steadfast in its support of the parental rights of marital biological fathers. In *Ward v. Faw*, 253 S.E.2d 658 (Va. 1979), the father had almost no contact with the child for more than three years (in part because of military service in Germany). He had made child support payments and sent greeting cards and occasional gifts. In response to the question of why he refused to consent to the adoption, Ward replied that the boy was his only son and that he wanted his name to be "carried on." In reversing the trial court's grant of the adoption, the Virginia Supreme Court cited the heavy burden on the party seeking to adopt the child over the objections of a fit biological parent. The court held that where "there is no question of the fitness of the non-consenting parent and he has not by conduct or previous legal action lost his rights to the child, it must be shown that continuance of the relationship between the two would be detrimental to the child's welfare." 192 S.E.2d at 799.

In 1997, a court of appeal in Virginia took an even stronger stance in favor of leaving the biological father's rights undisturbed, stating that "even when the parent proved unfit, the unfitness ha[s] to make the continuance of the relationship detrimental to the child's welfare." *See Hickman v. Futty*, 498 S.E.2d 232, 236 (Va. App. 1997). That court held that the standard required not only a finding of benefit to the child in a parent-child relationship with the prospective adoptive parent, but also that "the continued relationship between [birth] parent and child would be detrimental to the child's welfare . . ." *Id.*

The Virginia Legislature modified the statute, effective July 1, 2006, to read as follows:

> In determining whether the valid consent of any person whose consent is required is withheld contrary to the best interests of the child . . . , the [court] shall consider whether granting the petition pending before it would be in the best interest of the child. The [court] shall consider all relevant factors, including the birth parent(s)' efforts to obtain or maintain legal and physical custody of the child; whether the birth parent(s) are currently willing and able to assume full custody of the child; whether the birth parent(s)' efforts to assert parental rights were thwarted by other people; the birth parent(s)' ability to care for the child; the age of the child; the quality of any previous relationship between the birth parent(s) and the child and between the birth parent(s) and any other minor children; the duration and suitability of the child's present custodial environment; and the effect of a change of physical custody on the child.

VA. CODE § 63.2-1205 (2009). In *Gooch v. Harris*, 662 S.E.2d 95 (Ct. App. 2008), a Virginia appellate court discussed the legislative purpose motivating this revision and its impact on Virginia law. It indicated that, after a study of the then-existing policies by a joint subcommittee, the General Assembly removed "all mention of the detriment-to-the-child standard," eliminating the requirement that a court make a "specific finding that the failure to grant the adoption petition would be detrimental to the child." A reading of the statutory language above, however, indicates that the term "best interests of the child" here is shorthand for a multi-factor test. Most of the factors focus on whether the parent has maintained contact with the child, has provided support, is willing to assume custody, and so on. However, the last two factors focus on the child's current custodial environment and the predicted effect of a change in physical custody on the child. Thus, while it appears that the primary focus remains on the adequacy of the parental efforts and capabilities of the nonconsenting parent, the inquiry is broadened to take into account the child's current custodial situation and needs. Because the Virginia legislature appears to grant judges discretion in how to apply the statute and prioritize the enumerated factors, it is difficult to predict what impact this change will have on the disposition of cases.

Very few cases applying the new standard have resulted in appellate decisions, but a review of those that have indicate that, at least thus far, Virginia courts are still resting their decisions to grant adoptions on strong evidence of the legal parent's inadequacy. *Gooch v. Harris*, the one published appellate case, did not focus on objections of a marital father. Rather, it involved the petition by a 7-year-old boy's aunt and uncle — his custodians for the prior five years — to adopt him over the objection of the boy's mother. The case is still helpful in evaluating how judges are applying the new standard, however. In *Gooch*, the child had initially been removed from the mother's custody because she had left him alone sleeping in a car while she was inside a bar. She was described as an alcoholic who also abused drugs and had not successfully overcome her addictions. The mother had reportedly shown little interest in the child in the prior five years, only visiting him four times during that period. In this case, in applying the statutory standard, the court noted that there was "overwhelming" evidence that the adoption would be in the child's best interests, grounded in its concerns about the mother's conduct, as well as the benefits to the child of finding stability in the permanence of a life in the home of his aunt and uncle. The court below chose to apply a clear and convincing evidence standard, finding that the mother was "either unwilling or unable to care for the child." *Id.* at 160–61.

Crabb v. Jara, 2009 Va. App. LEXIS 42 (Feb. 3, 2009), is an unpublished case involving a petition for adoption of a child by the mother's husband over the objection of the child's biological father. In that case the appellate court indicated that, "although [the trial court] was not required by the statute to do so, that court made a finding from the bench that failing to grant the petition would 'in fact be detrimental to the child.' Furthermore, this finding was supported by clear and convincing evidence." *Id.* While these two cases do not reveal how the new standard has been applied in cases not appealed, they do suggest that trial court judges in Virginia may interpret the new standard as still requiring strong evidence of parental inadequacy or disinterest prior to the granting of these adoptions.

New Jersey amended its statutes in 1998 to eliminate the need to prove that an adoption by a non-parent could only go forward if there was evidence of a danger or serious harm to the child if the parent's rights were not terminated. Rather, the new standard asserts that:

> The best interest of a child requires that a parent affirmatively assume the duties encompassed by the role of being a parent. In determining whether a parent has affirmatively assumed the duties of a parent, the court shall consider, but is not limited to consideration of, the fulfillment of financial obligations for the birth and care of the child, demonstration of continued interest in the child, demonstration of a genuine effort to maintain communication with the child, and demonstration of the establishment and maintenance of a place of importance in the child's life.
>
> . . .
>
> The regular and expected functions of care and support of a child shall include the following:

(a) the maintenance of a relationship with the child such that the child perceives the person as his parent;

(b) communicating with the child or person having legal custody of the child and parenting time rights, or unless prevented from so doing by the custodial parent or other custodian of the child or a social service agency over the birth parent's objection; or

(c) providing financial support for the child unless prevented from doing so by the custodial parent or other custodian of the child or a social service agency.

. . . .

N.J. STAT. ANN. § 9:3-46 (2009). In *In re Adoption of Children by G.P.B., Jr.*, 736 A.2d 1277 (N.J. 1999), the New Jersey Supreme Court reversed a lower court's decision that an adoption should not go forward in the absence of evidence there was a danger of serious harm to the children if their father's parental rights were not terminated. In reversing and remanding the case for consideration in light of the new statute, the New Jersey Supreme Court wrote:

> Generally, courts do not terminate parental rights when the parent has maintained a relationship with a child. Conversely, when an adoptive parent has provided the child with a permanent home, courts often protect the child from interference by a biological parent with whom the child has no relationship. In recent years, increasing concern has arisen for the best interests of children whose parents have forsaken their parental duties. The child's right to a permanent home has gained increasing prominence. . . .
>
>   . . . . Fairly read, the amendment reflects decreasing legislative tolerance for biological parents who engage in the act of procreation, but do not assume the responsibilities of parenthood. First, when determining the best interests of the child in an action to terminate parental rights, the statute expressly states that "[t]he best interest of the child requires that a parent affirmatively assume the duties encompassed by the role of being a parent."

In re Adoption of Children by G.P.B., Jr., 736 A.2d 1277, 1281, 1284 (N.J. 1999). In this case, which involved a marital father's attempt to block his children's adoption by their stepfather, it appears that the court impliedly interpreted the governing statute to create parity in the obligations that marital and nonmarital noncustodial parents have towards their children. California recently raised the burden on noncustodial parents by adding the last sentence of Subsection (c) below to its stepparent adoption statute:

> (a) Except as provided in subdivision (b), a child having a presumed father under Section 7611 may not be adopted without the consent of the child's birth parents, if living. . . . (b) If one birth parent has been awarded custody by judicial order, or has custody by agreement of both parents, and the other birth parent for a period of one year willfully fails to communicate with and to pay for the care, support, and education of the child when able

to do so, then the birth parent having sole custody may consent to the adoption [after providing formal notice to the other birth parent]; (c) Failure of a birth parent to pay for the care, support, and education of the child for the period of one year or failure of a birth parent to communicate with the child for the period of one year is prima facie evidence that the failure was willful and without lawful excuse. *If the birth parent or parents have made only token efforts to support or communicate with the child, the court may disregard those token efforts.*

CAL. FAM. CODE § 8604 (2009) (emphasis added). Perhaps reflecting a "get tough on deadbeat dads" attitude, some courts have responded unsympathetically to excuses for non-support offered by parents. *See, e.g., In re Serre*, 665 N.E.2d 1185 (Ohio Com. Pl. 1996); *Dusseau v. Martyn*, 411 N.W.2d 743 (Mich. Ct. App. 1987).

Even though the term "best interests" has become more prominent in cases and statutes delineating when the consent of a marital biological father can be overridden, the published cases do not necessarily dispense with the requirement of strong evidence that the noncustodial parent has failed to meet parental obligations. The conduct of the father in fulfilling or attempting to fulfill his parental responsibilities remains a critical aspect in the analysis. *See, e.g., In the Matter of the Adoption of G.L.V. and M.J.V.*, 190 P.3d 245 (Kan. 2008) (interpreting 2007 statutory revisions to have added consideration of "the best interests of the child," as a companion to the inquiry as to whether the nonconsenting parent has assumed and adequately fulfilled his parental responsibilities to the child). Furthermore, some states explicitly treat the overriding of a parent's nonconsent for adoption as analogous to terminations of parental rights that occur in the dependency context. As such, consideration of the child's best interests in the adoption going forward do not arise unless the parent has been found to be "unfit" consistent with that term's meaning in dependency proceedings. *See, e.g., In re Adoption of C.A.P.*, 869 N.E.2d 214 (Ill. Ct. App. 2007) (indicating that the inquiry requires two steps: first it is determined whether it has been proven by clear and convincing evidence that the parent refusing consent for the adoption is "unfit," which can be shown by "failure to maintain a reasonable degree of interest, concern or responsibility as to the child's welfare," and only if this test is satisfied does the court inquire as to whether the adoption would be in the child's best interests").

4. Marital   Status,   Gender,   and   Constitutional Considerations.   Traditionally, marital fathers like the one in *J.J.J.* had a right to block an adoption while unwed fathers did not. Should the same standard apply irrespective of whether the parents had been married? The governing Alaska statutes explicitly indicate that "consent to adoption is not required of . . . the father of the minor [unless] the father was married to the mother at the time the minor was conceived or any time after conception, or the father has otherwise legitimated the minor under the laws of the state." *See* ALASKA ST. ANN. §§ 25.23.050 & 25.23.040(a)(2) (2009). The Alaska statute notwithstanding, some states now treat the marital and nonmarital fathers in a similar manner, dispensing with the requirement for the noncustodial father's consent only if he has seriously defaulted on his responsibilities. *See, e.g.,* CAL. FAM. CODE § 8604, *supra* note 3 (making no distinction between marital and nonmarital fathers). In addition, California's statute, is *gender-neutral*, as is the Uniform Adoption Act. In other words, birth mothers and birth fathers are subject to the same standards.

PROBLEM

Problem 11-1. Alice and Bob come to you to ask about arranging for Bob to adopt Alice's son from her former marriage, Tim. The boy is six. Alice left Tim's father, Ed, five years ago, in part, she says, because he abused the child. The uncontested divorce decree was entered four years ago, awarding Alice custody and modest child support. Since then Ed has paid support and visited the child sporadically. After Bob and Alice married two years ago, the support payments gradually ended, as did the visits. It has now been six months since Alice has heard from Ed or received support, and she is not even certain where he is. She has never attempted to enforce her support rights and is content to leave things as they are, except that she and Bob would like to complete an adoption. What do you do?

[ii]   Adoption into a New Family

In some instances, a biological parent seeks to place a child for adoption with a couple or individual who will assume exclusive parental responsibilities. These cases typically involve unwed, and often teenage, mothers relinquishing parental rights to an infant. Under what circumstances is the biological father's consent necessary? Consistent with the materials just discussed concerning stepparent adoption, unwed fathers were typically not involved in decisions regarding a child's adoption by a new family. In fact, the nonmarital father was not even entitled to notice of the prospective adoption. This approach assumed that most men were not interested in taking responsibility for the children they had fathered by unmarried women. In addition, some observed that a consent requirement would impose a costly administrative burden on the adoption process, delaying adoptions and possibly denying children the permanence and security that an adoptive home can provide. *See e.g.* Mary Shanley, *Unwed Fathers' Rights, Adoption, and Sex Equality: Gender Equality and the Perpetuation of Patriarchy*, 95 COLUM. L. REV. 60 (1994). Yet, in *Stanley v. Illinois*, 405 U.S. 645 (1972), the Supreme Court implied that unmarried fathers have a constitutional right to a hearing to demonstrate that they are fit parents before adoption can proceed without their consent. State adoption law changed to provide such an opportunity in ways that would avoid undue cost and delay to adoption.

The first issue is to determine which fathers are entitled to notice of the adoption proceedings. Consistent with *Lehr v. Robertson*, (see Chapter 9), the Court concluded that a state's maintenance of a putative father registry satisfied the constitutional requirement that states notify an unmarried father of any adoption proceedings. *See, e.g.*, 750 ILL. COMP. STAT. ANN. § 50/12-1 (2009); MINN. ST. ANN. § 259.49 (2009).

Where the father's identity or location is unknown, efforts must be made to discover his whereabouts or identity under various statutory provisions. Some states provide that an investigation be undertaken to locate the father. *See, e.g., Adoption of Hugh*, 619 N.E. 2d 979 (1993). Many states provide for notice by publication of the adoption proceeding (sometimes called "John Doe" notice) when personal notice is not feasible, a method that is generally sufficient to satisfy due process requirements in terminating parental rights. However, a South Carolina court reversed an adoption order in a case where the father challenged the sufficiency of notice published in a newspaper in a county near his residence, where the father had tried to demonstrate his commitment but was thwarted from doing so by the mother. *Brown v. Malloy*, 546 S.E.2d 195 (S.C. Ct. App. 2001). Generally, adoption agencies are expected to make "good faith" or "diligent" efforts to locate the biological father. Thus, for example, if information about his whereabouts or how to contact him is known, but not used to give him notice, publication may be determined insufficient to preserve his paternal rights. *See, e.g.*, OKLA. ST. ANN. 10 § 7505-4.3 (2009) (requiring a court to pursue an inquiry into a range of factors that may help identify the biological father so that he can be served with actual notice of the proposed adoption).

Requirements of notice by publication vary in the extent to which the birth mother's privacy is compromised. A 2001 Florida law, repealed in 2003, required a birth mother to publish her name and physical description and the name or description of recent sexual partners who might conceivably be the child's father. FLA. STAT. §§ 63.087, 63.088 (2009). An appellate court held that this statutory requirement violated Florida's constitutional right of privacy, interfering with the woman's rights to choose adoption and not disclose intimate personal information. *G.P. v. State*, 842 So. 2d 1059 (Fla. App. 4th Dist. 2003). *See also S. C. Dep't of Soc. Serv. v. Doe*, 527 S.E.2d 771 (S.C. App. 2000) (holding that publication of a mother's name violates her right to confidentiality and privacy protected by the adoption statutes). The amended statute provides that the unmarried father, by virtue of the fact that he has had a sexual relationship with a woman, will be deemed to have notice that a pregnancy and adoption proceeding may occur and he has a duty to protect his interests. § 60.088(1) (2009). The new provisions also created an adoption registry for this purpose. For further discussion of the Florida statute in particular and the issues raised by a biological father's right to notice prior to the child's adoption, see Jeffrey A. Parness, *Adoption Notices to Genetic Fathers: No To Scarlett Letters, Yes to Good-Faith Cooperation*, 26 CUMB. L. REV. 63 (2005-06).

The notice requirement does not necessarily result in a man's ability to block the adoption. Determining if the father's parental rights can be terminated over his objection requires a separate legal inquiry. In general, in order to prevent the adoption, biological fathers must be willing and able to demonstrate that he is ready to step in to assume full parental responsibility. *See, e.g., Matter of T.M.K.*, 617 N.W. 2d 925 (Mich. App. 2000). Accord, Uniform Adoption Act § 3-504(c) (for child *under six months of age*, father's consent to adoption not necessary where it is proven that: (1) he has failed to pay the mother's pre and post-birth medical expenses in accordance with his means; (2) he has failed to provide financial support or visit regularly with the minor; or (3) he is unable or unwilling to assume full custody of the child).

Fathers have a limited period during which to object to the adoption because of the disruption that delayed claims by a biological father can cause to the child and adoptive family. The problem is exacerbated by an often time-consuming appeals process. Thus, for example, in *Robert O. v. Russell K.*, 604 N.E.2d 99 (N.Y. 1992), the court rejected the petition of a biological father who sought to set aside the adoption of his 18-month-old son, ten months after the adoption had been finalized, because he was unaware of the child's existence. (*See* discussion of this case in Chapter 9.) The court emphasized the importance of "promptness and finality" in adoption proceedings, and stated that "[p]romptness is measured in terms of the baby's life, not by the onset of the father's awareness." The demand for prompt action by the father at the child's birth is neither arbitrary nor punitive, but instead a "logical and necessary outgrowth of the child's need for the early permanence and stability." *Id.* at 103–04. Courts vary, however, with respect to how strictly they apply statutory time limits and other requirements.

The highly publicized dispute over "Baby Jessica" Claussen, *In the Interest of B.G.C.* 496 N.W.2d 239 (Iowa 1992), is a case in point. The biological mother had identified a man named Scott as the baby's father. Scott accompanied her to the office of the lawyer representing the prospective adoptive parents, and consented to the adoption. Three weeks after Daniel Schmidt, the true biological father, learned of the baby's existence, he filed an affidavit of paternity and a petition for custody in an Iowa court. However, the litigation and appeals process dragged on for more than two years. When Schmidt finally prevailed in his custody claim, a sobbing Jessica was removed from the home of the de Boers, who had raised her almost from birth. The case was finally resolved when the United States Supreme Court denied the De Boers' application for a stay of an order of the Michigan Supreme Court and directed them to return the child to her biological parents. *DeBoer v. DeBoer*, 509 U.S. 1301 (1993). In its opinion, a unanimous court quoted the Iowa Supreme Court with approval and held:

> Neither Iowa law, nor Michigan law, nor federal law authorizes unrelated persons to retain custody of a child whose natural parents have not been found to be unfit simply because they may be better able to provide for her future and her education. As the Iowa Supreme Court stated: "[C]ourts are not free to take children from parents simply by deciding another home offers more advantages." *In re B.G.C.*, 496 N.W.2d 239, 241 (1992).

In a supplemental opinion upon denial of rehearing of an Illinois case, a justice of that state's supreme court cautioned that if a straightforward best interests test is applied in cases with such facts:

> [P]ersons seeking babies to adopt might profitably frequent grocery stores and snatch babies from carts when the parent is looking the other way. Then, if custody proceedings can be delayed long enough, they can assert that they have a nicer home, a superior education, a better job or whatever, and that the best interests of the child are with the baby snatchers. Children of parents living in public housing . . . and children of single parents might be considered particularly fair game. The law, thankfully, is otherwise.

Petition of Doe, 638 N.E.2d 181, 188 (Ill. 1994). On the other hand, many observers are concerned about the psychological impact on children who are removed from the home they have known. For example, Professor David Meyer hauntingly describes the disturbing experience of the boy referred to as "Baby Richard," *In re Kirchner*, 649 N.E.2d 324 (Ill.), *cert. denied*, 515 U.S. 1152 (1995), a case similar to that of "Baby Jessica":

Though his parents had told him a few hours earlier that he would be going on a "sleep over" at the home of a family he did not know, even at four years old he plainly sensed that something more life-altering was about to take place. . . . Inside the house, crying convulsively, oblivious to his national fame . . . young Richard Warburton pleaded with each member of his [adoptive] family to protect him. When his mother, wracked with tears, was unable to answer, Richard turned next to his father, and finally to his seven-year-old brother, begging each of them in turn to come with him. . . . As he sobbed and clung to his adoptive mother, his heart racing and pounding against her chest, a family friend gently pried his fingers from her neck and shoulders so that he could be wrested into the hands of his biological father. With that, he was whisked away from all he had known to join a new home and family.

David D. Meyer, *Family Ties: Solving the Constitutional Dilemma of the Faultless Father*, 41 ARIZ. L. REV. 753, 753–54 (1999). It is not known how such dislocations affect children in the long-term. Most likely, the long-term effects will vary with the particular children and their biological families. Regardless of the long-term impact, the distress children experience surrounding the separation is heart-wrenching. Clearly, the best response to these issues would be to prevent such traumatic events from occurring in the first place. Revisiting the DeBoer-Schmidt case, Professor Joan Hollinger examines how the problems in this case might have been avoided if the U.A.A. governed the jurisdictions in which the case took place. She identifies a range of procedural and substantive requirements that might have better protected Jessica from the heart-breaking result. U.A.A. provisions, she asserts, would have required that someone who did not have a conflict of interest would supervise the consent process, would have insured that the birth mother was adequately informed of the "meaning and consequences of consenting to an adoption" as well as the irrevocability of consent after the relevant statutory date. Furthermore, she indicates that the U.A.A. also "requires that the birth mother be warned of the risks to her own decision and to the child's well being if she does not name the father, but does not penalize her if she refuses to name him. Nonetheless, a parent who intentionally misidentifies the other parent, as Cara appears to have done, in order to deceive the other parent or the adoptive parents is subject to a civil penalty and may also be liable for common law fraud." Joan Heifetz Hollinger, *Adoption and Aspiration: The Uniform Adoption Act, the DeBoer-Schmidt Case, and the American Quest for the Ideal Family*, 2 DUKE J. GENDER L. & POL'Y 15 (1995). In addition, Professor Hollinger suggests that if the U.A.A. had governed "the initial adoptive placement would probably not have occurred. Even if it had, the status of the biological father and his ability or inability to block the adoption would have been established within a much shorter period of time." *Id.* at 20.

For further discussion of these issues, see Chapter 9, Section B; David D. Meyer, *Family Ties: Solving the Constitutional Dilemma of the Faultless Father*, 41 ARIZ. L. REV. 753, 753–54 (1999); Laura Oren, *Thwarted Fathers or Pop-Up Pops?: How to Determine When Putative Fathers Can Block the Adoption of their Newborn Children*, 40 FAM. L.Q 46 (2006); Carol A. Gorenberg, *Fathers' Rights vs. Children's Best Interests: Establishing a Predictable Standard for California Adoption Disputes*, 31 FAM. L.Q 169 (1997). For two analyses reaching contrasting conclusions, see Robbin Pott Gonzalez, *The Rights of Putative Fathers to their Infant Children In Contested Adoption: Strengthening State Laws that Currently Deny Adequate Protection*, 13 MICH. J. GENDER & L. 39 (2006) (arguing that current state policies reflect a *de facto* presumption that unwed fathers are unfit, and that registries and other protections do not give putative fathers adequate opportunities to assert their parental rights); Michelle Kaminsky, Student Author, *Excessive Rights For Putative Fathers:* Heart of Adoptions *Jeopardizes Rights of Mother and Child*, 57 CATH. U. L. REV. 917 (2008) (arguing that some courts weigh putative fathers' rights too heavily in the balance, unduly interfering in the child's opportunity for a stable adoptive home). For a comparison of policies in the U.S. and other nations, see, e.g., Margaret Ryznar, *Two To Tango, One In Limbo: A Comparative Analysis of Fathers' Rights In Infant Adoption Cases*, 47 DUQUESNE L. REV. 89 (2009); Allen E. Schoenberger, *Alternative Visions of the Family: The European Constitutional Perception of Family Law: Comparison with American Jurisprudence*, 18 TRANSNATIONAL L. & CONTEMP. PROBS. 419, 445–48 (2009); Cynthia Mabry, *Looking Beyond the United States: How Other Countries Handle Issues Related to Unwed Fathers in the Adoption Process*, 36 Cap. U. L. Rev. 363 (2007).

PROBLEM

Problem 11-2. Oscar lived with Daniella and supported her during her pregnancy. About a month before the baby was born, they became estranged and Oscar moved out. When their son was born, Daniella consented to his adoption shortly after his birth, telling the adoptive parents and their attorney that she knew who the father was but that she would not reveal his name. When Oscar returned from visiting his ill mother in Europe two weeks after the baby's birth, Daniella told him that the baby had died. Right away, Oscar began to investigate, and learned (57 days after the baby's birth) that he was alive. He immediately contested his son's adoption. Under the applicable statute, the father was required to show "a reasonable degree of interest in the child as to the welfare of a newborn child during the first 30 days of life." Should Oscar have standing to challenge the adoption?

[b]   What Constitutes Valid Consent?

If the birth parents' rights are not involuntarily terminated, adoption can proceed only if they consent or "relinquish" their rights. A relinquishment is a voluntary termination of parental rights, often to an agency, which then places the child for adoption. In recent years, however, many birth parents provide more limited consent for their child to be adopted by particular persons. In some instances, the birth parents meet and select the adoptive parents. The reporters are full of cases in which birth mothers seek to reclaim children after releasing them for adoption. While most claims of this sort do not succeed, in some instances, they do. Consider the following:

VELA v. MARYWOOD
Texas Court of Appeals
17 S.W.3d 750 (2000)

YEAKEL, JUSTICE.

This case presents the question of how forthright a licensed child-placing agency must be with an unmarried, expectant mother who seeks its counsel prior to the birth of her child. . . .

In September 1997, Corina, then nineteen years of age and unmarried, learned she was pregnant. . . . Corina, still living with her parents, [had] completed two years at Austin Community College where she had earned high grades and was planning to attend Southwest Texas State University. [She] is a member of a strong, stable, and supportive family . . .

In February 1998, this pregnant young woman sought counseling services from Marywood, a licensed child-placing agency. . . . She met with a Marywood counselor, Aundra Moore several times [and] informed Moore that she wanted to place her child for adoption. . . . Moore told Corina that. . . . Corina's "wishes and requests" as to what type of family she would place her child with and what type of relationship she would have with her child after adoption would be "considered." . . .

On March 25, Corina and Moore discussed what Marywood terms an "open adoption," a process by which the birth mother expresses her criteria for adoptive parents. Corina requested a Mexican-American, Catholic couple who had no other children. She also told Moore that "she wanted to visit with the child after the adoption.". . . .

Moore first showed Corina an "Affidavit of Voluntary Relinquishment of Parental Rights" (the "relinquishment affidavit") on March 30. Moore did not discuss the relinquishment affidavit with Corina and did not explain the meaning of the term "irrevocable"; rather, Moore simply "showed her the form" but did not give her a copy to take with her to study. . . .

Corina selected an adoptive couple at her next counseling session with Moore and had a face-to-face meeting with them on April 8. . . . The prospective adoptive parents met all of Corina's criteria and indicated their willingness to comply with post-adoption visits. Throughout Corina's counseling sessions, she and Moore discussed a "sharing plan," a standard practice of Marywood. A sharing plan ostensibly allows the birth mother to select the adoptive family, visit her child on a regular basis after the adoption, and exchange letters and pictures. The adoptive parents. . . . agree in writing with Marywood to conform to this arrangement. [N]either Marywood nor the adoptive parents enter into any agreement with the birth mother. Marywood admits that aside from advocating that the adoptive parents abide by the plan, Marywood can do nothing if the adoptive parents decide, post-adoption, to disregard it. In fact, the executive director of Marywood admits that the sharing plan is an "empty promise" Clearly, the birth mother has no power to enforce such an agreement. Marywood never discussed the unenforceability of the sharing plan with Corina.

    . . . .

Corina gave birth to a son on April 24. . . . Moore met with Corina on April 26 [and] told Corina that she "would always be able to visit her baby" and that her baby would always know that Corina was his mother. Corina cried throughout the one-and-one-half-hour visit. . . . The child was placed in foster care on April 27. [¶] On April 28, Corina and her parents visited Marywood. Before the meeting, Corina was not aware that she was to sign the relinquishment affidavit then and was undecided as to whether she wanted to sign it. [After a two hour meeting,] Corina signed the affidavit. During the meeting, and before Corina signed the relinquishment affidavit, Moore told Corina that she would "always be that child's birth mother and that with her sharing plan that she had with the adoptive family that she would have an opportunity to be in that child's life forever"; . . . that the baby would have "two mothers," "both of whom would have input into his life"; that Corina "would be able to see her son grow up". . . . According to Corina and her mother, these promises are what convinced Corina to sign the relinquishment affidavit. . . .

Before the April 28 meeting, Corina did not have a copy of the relinquishment affidavit and did not review it with her parents. Corina was crying when she signed the affidavit, but Moore testified that "it's very common to have tears." Moore asked Corina if signing the relinquishment affidavit "was what she wanted to do" and informed Corina that once she signed it, she "couldn't undo or take it back." Moore never told Corina that signing the relinquishment affidavit meant that she would "never have any legal rights to see [her] child." According to Corina, Moore told her that she would only be "giving up [her] guardianship of [the child]." . . . Corina was not aware and no one informed her that she could have signed a second foster-care agreement to allow herself more time to make the final decision [or] that she could seek legal counsel or another person's opinion. Marywood never revealed to Corina that the relinquishment affidavit could nullify the sharing plan that she believed would allow her a continuing role in her child's life. It is significant that the relinquishment affidavit was never mentioned to Corina until after she and Marywood had devised a sharing plan satisfactory to her. From that point forward, all of Corina's actions and decisions were founded on her belief in and reliance on the sharing plan.

The following day, ... Marywood filed a petition to terminate Corina's parental rights. On May 1, Corina was allowed to visit her son for one hour at Marywood. Later that day, Corina called Marywood. Exactly what was said in that phone call is disputed. Moore claims. . . . Corina never indicated that she wanted to terminate the adoption process. Corina claims that she told Moore that she "wanted [her] baby back" and that she "changed [her] mind." She asked if there was anything she could do, including hiring an attorney. Moore responded that there was nothing that could be done. . . . Moore [also] told Corina's mother that the relinquishment was "irrevocable and that it is signed and that there is no way to undo the document." . . .

On May 12, an associate judge recommended termination of Corina's parental rights. . . . Although Corina had that day retained counsel to contest the termination and adoption, the termination occurred before she could intervene. . . . Corina brings this appeal, arguing that [she did not] knowingly and voluntarily execute[ ] the relinquishment affidavit. . . . [¶] To set aside the affidavit, Corina had the burden to prove by a preponderance of the evidence that the relinquishment affidavit was executed as a result of some nature of wrongdoing, such as coercion, duress, misrepresentation, fraud, deception, undue influence, or overreaching . . .

. . . .

Corina argues that "no rational trier of fact could find . . . that the Affidavit of Relinquishment was executed voluntarily and knowingly, rather than as the result of misrepresentation, fraud, overreaching, and coercion." . . . [¶] [She also] argues that Marywood affirmatively misrepresented to her facts that induced her to sign the relinquishment affidavit. Specifically, Corina claims that the only reason she signed the relinquishment affidavit was that Marywood led her to believe that she had the right and would continue to play a significant role in her child's life after the adoption, would continue to have contact with her child, and was only giving up guardianship of her child. At the time they were made, these representations were either false or misleading because Marywood knew that Corina would have no legal right to enforce the sharing plan against the adoptive parents. And, because Marywood was in a close relationship with Corina as her counselor, it had a duty to fully disclose that the open-adoption arrangement had no legal effect. Corina also emphasizes that she was never given a copy of the relinquishment affidavit to bring home with her; Marywood never suggested she seek legal advice; and Moore was the only person who ever explained the relinquishment affidavit to her. Thus, Corina insists that she did not voluntarily and knowingly execute the relinquishment affidavit and that she signed only as the result of coercion, misrepresentation, fraud, and overreaching.

In general, coercion is "[c]ompulsion by physical force or threat," or "the improper use of economic power." Misrepresentation is a falsehood or untruth with the intent and purpose to deceive. In the context of fraud, courts have stated that misrepresentation is making a false statement of fact or a false expression of opinion by one claiming or implying special knowledge. Silence can constitute a misrepresentation: "When the particular circumstances impose on a person a duty to speak and he deliberately remains silent, his silence is equivalent to a false representation.

Fraud "is an elusive and shadowy term which has been defined in some cases as any cunning or artifice used to cheat or deceive another." Fraud may consist of both active misrepresentation and passive silence. At common law, the word "fraud" refers to an act, omission, or concealment in breach of a legal duty, trust, or confidence justly imposed, when the breach causes injury to another or the taking of an undue and unconscientious advantage.' [T]his "legal duty" may exist if it is established that one has placed special confidence in another where the latter is bound, in equity and good conscience, to act in good faith and with due regard for the interests of the other; it can arise when special confidence is placed in someone thereby giving that person a position of superiority and influence. In general, once a party undertakes to speak, that party assumes a duty to tell the whole truth. [¶]

Overreaching is "tricking, outwitting, or cheating a person into doing an act which he would not otherwise have done." Overreaching is generally synonymous with fraud.

Marywood, by its own admission, is more than an adoption agency. It provides extensive parental-counseling services and advertises these services to the public. . . . Corina, in seeking counseling from Marywood, was reasonably entitled to rely fully and unconditionally on Marywood's representations. We hold that Marywood owed Corina a duty of complete disclosure when discussing adoption procedures, including any proposed post-adoption plan. Complete disclosure encompassed the obligation to tell Corina the entire truth about the ramifications of the sharing plan she had chosen with Marywood's help and to make her fully aware that it lacked legally binding effect. Marywood's duty springs from two sources. First, when Marywood made a partial disclosure to Corina about the post-adoption plan, it assumed the duty to tell the whole truth. Second, the evidence conclusively establishes that Corina placed special confidence in Moore, who by virtue of the counseling relationship occupied a position of superiority and influence on behalf of Marywood; thus, Moore and Marywood became bound, in equity and good conscience, to act in good faith and with due regard to Corina's interests. This Court has recognized that a "higher obligation is owed to certain groups because of their vulnerabilities." A young unmarried mother considering placement of her child for adoption is clearly vulnerable and is owed that "higher obligation" when she confides in a maternity counselor.

To determine whether Corina has met her burden of conclusively proving that she did not sign the relinquishment affidavit voluntarily, we must first ascertain if the record contains any evidence to support the district court's finding to the contrary. . . . [¶] Although the face of the affidavit reflects it was signed knowingly and voluntarily, we must consider the surrounding circumstances to determine if Corina's signature on the document was procured by misrepresentation, fraud, or the like. . . . Corina neither signed nor understood the relinquishment affidavit in a vacuum. She signed and understood it in the context of and in reliance on the post-adoption plan that she and Marywood created, a plan that Marywood now admits is an "empty promise." The evidence conclusively establishes that Corina wanted to proceed with the adoption *only* if she could have post-adoption visits with her child; there is no evidence to the contrary. . . .

There is no evidence . . . that Corina was ever told that the post-adoption plan could not be legally enforced. Marywood's words to Corina were at worst deceptive and at best vague. . . . Marywood was obligated to answer Corina's question directly and tell her that the agency could not guarantee post-adoption visits. Instead, in counseling Corina, Moore carefully selected her words and minced her explanation of the sharing plan with the result that Corina understood one thing while Moore meant another. Whether the incomplete disclosure was deliberate or inadvertent, it does not satisfy the duty of full disclosure that Marywood owed Corina.

. . . .

We turn our attention now to [the] second hurdle: Has Corina established as a matter of law that the relinquishment affidavit was procured by fraud, coercion, overreaching, or misrepresentation? [¶] We find no evidence in the record that Corina was compelled by force or threat to sign the relinquishment affidavit. We overrule Corina's issue to the extent that it complains that the affidavit was procured by coercion. [¶] However, we find conclusive evidence in the record that the relinquishment affidavit was wrongfully procured. Considering only Marywood's version of events, we conclude as a matter of law that its statements and omissions to Corina constituted misrepresentation, fraud, or overreaching. Marywood admits that it told Corina that . . . she would "always have a relationship with [the adoptive] family and with [her] child" [and that it] never told Corina that she would not have any legal right to see her child after she signed the relinquishment affidavit, and even when Corina directly asked if Marywood could guarantee post-adoption visits, Marywood failed to give her a complete answer. Marywood's statements are misleading and stop short of complete disclosure. They are half-truths that would lead a reasonable person in Corina's circumstance to believe that she had a continuing right to see her child according to the terms of the sharing plan. . . . It is undisputed that Corina sought counseling from Marywood to aid her in the difficult decision of whether to keep her child. She was a young woman faced with a life-changing situation. She found comfort in and placed reliance on Marywood's counseling. We need not and do not determine whether Marywood deliberately misled Corina. At a minimum, Marywood's advice and counsel was incomplete. We hold that Corina conclusively established that the relinquishment affidavit was procured by misrepresentation, fraud, or overreaching and therefore was not voluntarily signed . . .

NOTES

1. *Revocation Rules and Conflicting Policy Objectives.* Like the issue of waiver of parental consent, rules about revocation of consent by the birth parent raise difficult policy (and political) questions. Professor Elizabeth Samuels characterizes these issues as follows:

> Two principal and widely accepted goals of domestic infant adoption are (1) preventing the unnecessary separation of family members by ensuring that birth parents make informed and deliberate decisions and (2) protecting the finality of adoptive placements. Ideally, these goals are complementary and can be balanced. There is, however, a danger of the second goal eclipsing the first. Many state laws appear to value an increase in infant adoptions over the goal of encouraging careful deliberation.

Elizabeth J. Samuels, *Time To Decide? The Laws Governing Mothers' Consents to the Adoption of their Newborn Infants*, 72 Tenn. L. Rev. 509 (2005). The danger cited by Professor Samuels appears to have influenced the approach taken by the Marywood agency in securing Corina's relinquishment.

States typically prescribe some period of time during which a birth parent can change her mind as a matter of right and deal separately with revocations grounded in allegations, such as those in *Vela v. Marywood*, that the consent was improperly obtained. Thus, for example, in Georgia, once a birth parent signs the relinquishment documents, she has ten days to revoke the consent, and is not required to make any showing to exercise that right. Ga. Code Ann. § 19-8-9 (2009). Maryland allows revocation within thirty days of giving consent. MD. CODE § 5-3B-21(b)(1)(i) (2009). Some states, like California, establish different revocation periods for agency and independent adoptions. This policy reflects the concern that without the regulation and oversight generally attending agency adoptions, birth parents may feel pressured to consent or may not fully understand their rights and the implications of their actions. While California had, for some years, treated a birth parent's relinquishment in the context of an agency adoption as irrevocable (unless it is set aside by mutual consent of the parties), recent statutory amendments create a 10 day revocation period. *See* CAL. FAM. CODE § 8700 (2009). By contrast, birth parents can revoke consent within 30 days of an independent adoption. CAL. FAM. CODE § 8814.5 (2009). The 1994 Uniform Adoption Act allows a birth parent to revoke consent within 8 days of the child's birth. § 2-404. According to the U.A.A., if consent is given before a judge it is immediately irrevocable. § 2-409. For additional detail as to the range of state policies, see Samuels, *supra.*

Most states have shortened their revocation periods with the goal of providing the child with stability and finality as early as possible. The traditional approach allowed revocation at any time prior to the adoption decree's finalization. *See* Gary D. Spivey, Annot., *Right of Natural Parent to Withdraw Valid Consent to Adoption of Child*, 74 A.L.R.3d 421 (1976, updated 2009). In a famous case that led to a change in New York law, an educated, 32-year-old Columbian woman was allowed to revoke her consent to the adoption of her nonmarital child, after discovering that her affluent family would help her raise the child. *Scarpetta v. Spence-Chapin Adoption Serv.*, 269 N.E.2d 787 (N.Y. 1971). The court held that the biological mother must be allowed to revoke her consent "unless it is clearly established that she is unfit to assume the duties and privileges of parenthood." The adoptive parents then fled with the child to Florida, whose courts refused to enforce the New York decree. *Scarpetta v. De Martino*, 254 So. 2d 813 (Fla. App. 1971), *cert. denied*, 262 So. 2d 442 (Fla.), 409 U.S. 1011 (1972). The traditional rule is rare today, but it is not extinct, and still governs in some jurisdictions. *See, e.g.*, TENN. CODE ANN. § 36-1-118(a) (2009). The Indian Child Welfare Act, discussed below, also gives a birth parent the right to revoke consent until the adoption is judicially finalized. 25 U.S.C.A. § 1913(c) (2009).

The modern approach, although applauded by some, has been criticized by others. Critics express concerns about disparities between biological and prospective adoptive parents in educational background, legal sophistication, and financial resources, creating an uneven playing field. Such imbalance could render birth parents particularly vulnerable to influence, overreaching, and other pressures. Some critics argue that additional procedural and substantive protections are needed to insure that birth parents' decisions are voluntary, informed, and otherwise respectful of the birth parents' rights and interests. Samuels, *supra* at 548–72; Karen D. Laverdiere, Student Author, *Content Over Form: The Shifting Adoption Consent Laws*, 25 WHITTIER L. REV. 599, 611–16 (2004). Others critique modern adoption law's failure to integrate the continuing importance that biological bonds have for children, even in the context of healthy relationships with adoptive parents. The reality that many adopted children seek connection with their biological parents and struggle with issues of personal identity is taken as evidence by some that the complete severing of the biological parent-child relationship, as is typically required by adoption law, may not always serve child's best interests. For discussion of the feminist perspective and criticism of the contemporary approach, see Annette R. Appell, *The Endurance of Biological Connection: Heteronormativity, Same-Sex Parenting and the Lessons of Adoption*, 22 BYU J. PUB. L. 289 (2008); Nancy Dowd, *A Feminist Analysis of Adoption*, 107 HARV. L. REV. 913 (1994) (reviewing ELIZABETH BARTHOLET, FAMILY BONDS: ADOPTION AND THE POLITICS OF PARENTING (1993)).

2. *Pre-Birth Consent.* In general, a birth parent's pre-birth consent to adoption is not valid, and statutes frequently set forth how much time after the birth of the child must pass before consent will be binding. *See, e.g.*, MASS. GEN. LAWS ANN. § 210.2 (2009) (four days); ARIZ. REV. STAT. ANN. § 8-107(B) (2009) (72 hours); KY. REV. STAT. ANN. § 199.500 (2009) (same). The one exception to this rule is that some states permit a mother to consent to the adoption before the child's birth, but provide a post-birth period of revocation. What explains this rule restricting the pregnant woman's freedom to commit to an adoption contract before the birth? A common concern is that pregnant women cannot make informed competent decisions about adoption because they cannot predict how they will feel about the baby until the baby's birth. Similar arguments are raised by some objections to surrogacy contracts entered into before birth (and conception). *See* Section E below.

3. *What Constitutes Fraud, Duress or Coercion?* States permit birth parents to revoke consent to adoption for cause, as illustrated in *Vela v. Marywood*. These challenges to the validity of the consent, grounded in claims of duress, coercion, fraud, misrepresentation or other factors allegedly rendering the agreement invalid, can be filed after the time period otherwise set forth for revocation. *See, e.g.*, U.A.A. § 2-408(b); 2-409(b). Most states do place some time limits on when such claims can be filed, and those time periods range from 90 days after the date when the allegedly invalid consent was provided to two years. *See* DHHS, *Consent to Adoption*, at 5 & n.16 (2007), http://www.childwelfare.gov/systemwide/laws_policies/statutes/consent.pdf. Courts typically construe defenses of fraud, duress, or coercion fairly narrowly. The birth mother's consent is likely to be considered valid unless there is fairly strong evidence that it was obtained improperly. The ordinary pressures and stresses experienced by unwed or teenage mothers, including family and financial pressures, do not reach the threshold necessary to invalidate a consent. *See, e.g.*, *In re Baby Boy L.*, 534 N.Y.S.2d 706 (1988) (rejecting claim by 17 year old birth mother that her mother's refusal to allow her to live in the family home if she kept the baby constituted coercion).

The court in *Vela* emphasized that the adoption counselor had a special disclosure duty in light of her relationship to the birth mother and the young woman's vulnerable position. Under general contract doctrine, a duty to disclose arises where the parties have a relationship of trust. *See* RESTATEMENT (SECOND) OF CONTRACTS § 161(D). The Restatement of Contracts (Second) also recognizes, as a basis for recission, undue influence of a weaker party in a relationship of trust, who may be subject to unfair persuasion by the dominant party. § 177. See also *Adventist Adoption & Family Servs. v. Perry*, 641 P.2d 178 (Wash. App. 1982) (mother was in unfamiliar environment with no independent counsel, and subject to pressure from adoption agency); *In re Dunn*, 656 N.E.2d 1341 (Ohio App. 1995) (mother relinquished child under the mistaken belief that only her cousin could adopt the child and that she would have visitation rights, where the agency was aware of the mother's misconception). For general consideration of this topic, see Susan Yates Ely, *Natural Parents' Right to Withdraw Consent to Adoption: How Far Should the Right Extend?*, 31 J. FAM. L. 685 (1992/93); Mindy Schulman Roman, Student Author, *Rethinking Revocation: Adoption from A New Perspective*, 23 HOFSTRA L. REV. 733 (1995).

4. *Other Bases for Revocation of Consent.* There are some jurisdictions in which a birth parent is permitted to revoke consent within a brief window of time (ranging from 10 to 180 days, depending on the state) if the court determines that the withdrawal is in the best interests of the child. *See, e.g.*, R.I. GEN. LAWS 1956 § 15-7-21.1(b) (2009) (permitting a challenge to a termination of parental rights or adoption within 180 days of the decree only if it is proven by clear and convincing evidence that the adoption is not in the best interests of the adoptee). Some states permit revocation of voluntary relinquishment if a petition for adoption is not filed within a given period of time. *See, e.g.*, 10 OKLA. STAT. ANN. § 7503-2.7B(1) (2009) (allowing revocation if birth parent can show, by a preponderance of the evidence that, without good cause, a petition to adopt was not filed within nine months after consent was provided and that setting aside the consent is also in the best interests of the child). *See also* DHHS, *Consent to Adoption*, at 6 & nn. 19–20 2(2007), http://www.childwelfare.gov/systemwide/laws_policies/statutes/consent.pdf.

5. *Validity of the Minor Birth Parent's Consent.* In most states, a minor parent's consent to her child's adoption is binding despite the ordinary contract rule allowing minors to avoid their agreements. Thus, for example, in *Baby Boy L*, *supra* note 3, the mother's youth was not an issue. *See, e.g.*, *Norfolk Div. of Social Servs. v. Unknown Father*, 345 S.E.2d 533 (Va. App. 1986) (sustaining adoption order under statute validating minor mother's consent absent proof of "fraud and duress"). Increasingly, states have added provisions to their adoption statutes explicitly addressing minors' capacity to consent to their children's adoptions. The Florida, Louisiana, and Kentucky statutory provisions reflect varying approaches. Most states follow the approach set forth in Florida.

> (b) A minor parent has the power to consent to the adoption of his or her child and has the power to relinquish his or her control or custody of the child to an adoption entity. . . . A minor parent, having executed a consent or relinquishment, may not revoke that consent upon reaching the age of majority or otherwise becoming emancipated.
>
> (c) A consent or an affidavit of nonpaternity executed by a minor parent who is 14 years of age or younger must be witnessed by a parent, legal guardian, or court-appointed guardian ad litem.

FLA. ANN. ST. §§ 63.082(1)((b) & (c) (2009). A handful of states (e.g., Michigan, Minnesota, New Hampshire, Rhode Island) require the consent of the minor's parents in addition to the minor, as set forth in Louisiana's code.

> A. Except as otherwise provided herein, if a parent executing a surrender in a private adoption is a minor, the parents . . . of the minor must join in

the surrender unless the minor parent has been judicially emancipated . . . or emancipated by marriage . . .

C. When the minor's parents . . . refuse to join in the act or cannot be located, the court may authorize the minor to surrender without the required consent if it finds that the minor is sufficiently mature and well-informed to surrender his child for adoption or that the surrender is otherwise in the child's best interest.

. . . .

E. A minor may surrender to an agency without the consent of the parents or tutor of the minor.

LA. ST. ANN. Ch. 4, Art. 1113 (2009). Finally, several states, such as Kentucky, Maryland, Montana and Vermont require appointment of a guardian ad litem or attorney to assist and represent the minor's interests in the process. *See, e.g.*, KY. STAT. ANN. §§ 199.500(2) & (3) (2009) (authorizing a minor to provide consent for adoption only after the appointment of a guardian ad litem, and requiring that the consent of a minor be given before the court). In most jurisdictions, consent of minor's parents may be sought, even if not legally required, in order to provide additional protection and support for the minor, and to reduce the likelihood of a subsequent successful challenge to the validity of the consent.

PROBLEMS

Problem 11-3. Alice, an 18-year-old unmarried woman, living on her own, gave birth in early February. In August, she decided to give the child up for adoption. The procedure was explained to her, including the fact that the adoption itself is not final until six months after the adoption petition is filed. Alice thought this meant that she could get her baby back within six months, but did not express this belief to the agency's counselor. The counselor gave her the agency consent form, which she read. When asked, she responded that she understood the form, and then proceeded to sign it. The form contained no reference to the six-month period, and stated clearly that she surrendered all parental rights to the agency, "voluntarily and unconditionally," conferring upon the agency "absolute and unrestricted power . . . to consent to the adoption of the child without further notice to me."

The surrender took place on Aug. 15. On Sept. 1, the baby was placed in an adoptive home. On Sept. 4, Alice sought the baby's return. She was told that it was too late, and she then brought a habeas corpus action. What result?

Problem 11-4. Fred consults you about his 16-year-old daughter, Vicki, who recently gave birth to a baby girl. Fred is determined that Vicki give the child up for adoption, but in the six months since the birth, she has resisted. To put pressure on Vicki, he has refused to allow her to bring the child into their home. Vicki's cousin has been keeping the baby, and Vicki has spent time with the child there. Two months ago, Fred went to the cousin's house while Vicki was there and told Vicki that if she did not give the child up for adoption, she would have to leave home. Shortly thereafter, Vicki left home, but after a month of living by herself and caring for the baby, she concluded she could not cope on her own, and moved back in with her family. In the last month, Vicki has finally yielded, and Fred wants to start adoption proceedings now, before she changes her mind again.

The baby's father is an 18-year-old high school student of a different race than Vicki and you believe that Fred's intransigence is related to the child's bi-racial identity. You think it is possible Fred might never become reconciled to bringing this baby into the family. Since Vicki moved back home, the baby has been with the father's family. Fred believes the father will go along with whatever Vicki wants to do. What do you advise?

C. THE ADOPTION PROCESS

[1]   Agency vs. Independent Adoptions

[a]   The Role of the Agency

Before a new parent-child relationship can be created through the adoption process, the prospective adoptive parent(s) and prospective adoptive child must somehow be brought together if there is no pre-existing relationship. Public and private (state-licensed) adoption agencies have traditionally played the role of intermediary. Adoption agencies perform many critical functions in the adoption process. Agency personnel act under state authority and must promote a process that complies fully with the jurisdiction's legal requirements As the discussion of *Vela v. Marywood* reveals, among the agency's responsibilities is to insure that the birth parents and prospective adoptive parents are fully informed about all aspects of adoption law that are material to the decisions they make with regard to the adoption. They are also expected to create an atmosphere where those decisions are rendered without pressure, coercion, or overreaching. As non-profit entities, state-licensed adoption agencies are "neutral," in that they do not owe loyalty to one party over another. Rather, their paramount concerns are the welfare of the child, and the safeguarding of the rights and interests of the birth and prospective adoptive parents. Agencies also certify the suitability of the adoptive parents to the court that confirms the adoption. The court typically relies upon the agency's investigation of the family to satisfy the requirement that a "social study" of the adoptive family be confirmed. Traditionally, the birth parents relinquish the child to the agency, which also handles arrangements for the care of the child until placement in the adoptive home.

Traditionally, the agencies handle the selection of the adoptive parents and the "matching" of a particular child with the would-be parents. It is not controversial for agency workers, in exercising discretion, to eliminate from consideration families with histories of abuse, alcoholism, or instability. By contrast, because there are many more adults seeking to adopt healthy (usually white) infants than there are available infants, the criteria by which placement decisions are made become very important. In Section C[2][a] below, agency practices relating to selection and matching are discussed. Increasingly, the preferences of the birth parents have come to influence agency choices among prospective adoptive homes. This change in practice flows from the shortage of available infants, which has led to competition among agencies to gain placement authority over available infants. By deferring to the birth parents' preferences, agencies can also better compete with independent adoption arrangements which allow birth parents to play a key role in the selection process.

An agency's placement of a child in the intended adoptive home ordinarily occurs before the adoption is final. During this probationary period, the agency retains legal custody and may withdraw the child from the adoptive home if it concludes that the child's interests so require. Adoptive parents have had some success in challenging agency decisions to withdraw a placement once the child has been living with them. Yet even here, if the agency offers evidence casting serious doubt on the suitability of the adoptive home, its decision will rarely be upset.

In recent years, state courts have recognized a cause of action against adoption agencies for misrepresentation of information about the child or the child's background material to the adoptive family's decision whether to adopt a particular child. The courts have generally held that there exists a common law and/or statutory duty (arising out of adoption statutes), to provide accurate and complete information to prospective adoptive parents. In some respects, this obligation complements the duty agencies owe birth parents, as discussed in *Vela v. Marywood*. The birth parents and prospective adoptive parents are both entitled to complete and accurate information about those factors material to their decisions to go ahead with a particular adoption arrangement (or perhaps whether to go through with an adoption at all).

JACKSON v. JACKSON
Montana Supreme Court
956 P.2d 35 (1998)

REGINIER, JUSTICE.

[Aaron, the adoptee, was born on November 8, 1983, to Deborah Russell. Based on a psychological evaluation undertaken while she was incarcerated during her pregnancy, Russell was found to have a full Scale I.Q. of 73. The evaluation also strongly suggested that Russell had an "organic or psychiatric impairment, with 'disorganized, unconventional, diffused, [and] possibly . . . delusional' thinking." In January, 1984, Russell "fed her infant son soda pop, meat, and vegetables, which caused him to aspirate and led to his hospitalization." The State intervened on the basis of this incident, and in a social study prepared in February, Russell was described as retarded and "quite disturbed." A psychological evaluation in June, 1984 described her diagnosis as "paranoid disorder and mild mental retardation." Aaron's putative father Roger Stevens was diagnosed with "schizophrenic disorder, paranoid type," in a report that the State acquired before the adoption. Parental rights for both parents were terminated in December, 1984.]

The Jacksons had applied with the State to become adoptive parents just one week after Aaron's birth, in November 1983. . . . During the course of this application process, the Jacksons advised [adoption agency resource worker Betty] Petek that they could not provide care for a child that had, or might be at risk for, developing a mental disorder [although they indicated] that they would consider adopting a child with "a minor correctable handicap." [¶] [In] January 1985 . . .

they were contacted by Petek about Aaron's availability. [The Jacksons subsequently] met with Petek and [Dave] Wallace [another state worker] to discuss Aaron's family background, and the possibility of initiating visits with Aaron. During this visit, the Jacksons specifically asked Wallace and Petek whether there was any history of mental illness in Aaron's family. [Petek and Wallace did not disclose the contents of the psychological evaluations to the Jacksons in response to their inquiry. Instead, they told the Jacksons that the child's parents were not capable of caring for him, and described the feeding incident. They mentioned the possibility of some drug use by the mother, but thought it was minimal. They also suggested that the mother was unable to care for Aaron because she moved around a lot, and lacked sufficient interest to learn the skills she needed to care for her child, but that she was physically healthy. T]he State never disclosed the content of these evaluations to the Jacksons prior to the finalization of Aaron's adoption in January 1986.

Aaron began to exhibit behavioral problems, [leading the Jacksons to have him evaluated [at] Child Study Center at the Children's Clinic in Billings, Montana. . . . [Aaron was diagnosed as having] psychotic disorder, history of attention deficit hyperactivity disorder, and pervasive developmental disorder [which led to hospitalization for psychiatric treatment.] On April 6, 1994, the Jacksons filed a negligence action in District Court [asserting] claims against the State for breach of contract, negligent misrepresentation, negligent disclosure, and negligent supervision . . .

. . .

The crux of the Jacksons' "wrongful adoption" suit is their allegation that the State negligently misrepresented, and failed to disclose to them, certain material facts regarding the psychological background of their adoptive son's birth mother and putative father. To determine whether Montana law recognizes a cause of action for "wrongful adoption," such as the one initiated in the present case, we must simply determine "whether long-standing common law causes of action should be applied to the adoption context."

. . . .

Courts have commonly recognized that a duty on the part of the adoption agency to use due care may arise only when the agency "begin[s] volunteering information to potential adopting parents". . . . Thus, courts will, under certain circumstances, impose upon adoption agencies a duty to use due care and to refrain from making negligent misrepresentations where the agencies undertake to volunteer information to potential adoptive parents. [¶] [W]e conclude, as has the recent majority of courts addressing this issue, that recognizing a cause of action for negligent misrepresentation in the adoption context will, in fact, promote public policy and ensure that "adoptive parents assume the awesome responsibility of raising a child with their eyes wide open.". . . .

In the instant case, the Jacksons argue the State, in fact, disclosed certain background information regarding Aaron's birth parents, and in doing so, assumed a duty to use due care and to completely and accurately disclose that information. . . . The State asserts [it did not assume that duty and] that, although it did provide the Jacksons with a great deal of information about Aaron's background prior to the adoption, it did not provide them with any inaccurate or misleading information regarding the psychological background of his birth parents. Specifically, the State argues its employees knew of no familial predisposition for mental illness, made no attempts to conceal information from the Jacksons, and did not assure them that Aaron would be free from mental illness.

As the State concedes, review of the record indicates that Wallace and Petek did indeed provide the Jacksons with certain information regarding Aaron's background[, such as] the possibility that Aaron's birth mother had used drugs or alcohol early in her pregnancy, that Aaron had been removed from the custody of his birth mother due to her inability to care for him, and that his birth mother had caused him to aspirate on solid food and soda pop when he was a young infant. . . . We conclude that the State, when it began volunteering such background information to the Jacksons, assumed a duty to do so with due care. Whether the State breached that duty and negligently misrepresented information to the Jacksons is a question of material fact precluding summary judgment in the State's favor.

. . . .

[T]o require anything less from the State than the exercise of due care in the dissemination of information in its possession to prospective adoptive parents would be simply unacceptable. We recognize that the imposition of such a duty indeed places a slight burden on the State, but conclude that burden is justified in light of the compelling need for adoptive parents to receive all available information regarding a child who may soon become a permanent part of their family. Full disclosure of a child's medical and familial background is warranted not only to enable adoptive parents to obtain timely and appropriate medical care for the child, but also to enable them to make an intelligent and informed decision to adopt. Furthermore, we note the imposition of such a duty will increase public trust in our State agencies, and will give potential parents more confidence in the adoption process and in the accuracy of the information they receive. . . . [P]ublic policy considerations justify the imposition of a duty upon the State in the present case."

[The court then concluded that the district court erred in deciding that the risk of injury to the Jacksons was not foreseeable.] [T]he Jacksons need only demonstrate that the State could reasonably have foreseen that Aaron was at risk for later manifesting an array of psychological and emotional problems, not that the psychological impairments suffered by Aaron's birth mother and putative father have definitively caused Aaron's present difficulties. . . .

[T]he District Court also rejected the Jacksons' claim that the State was negligent in violating a *statutorily* imposed duty.] On appeal, the Jacksons argue that the Uniform Adoption Act of Montana . . . imposed upon the State a duty to disclose all available non-identifying information regarding Aaron's familial background, sufficient to support their negligence-based claims. . . . [T]he State concedes that it had a limited duty of disclosure pursuant to § 40-8-122(1)(c) . . . but argues it fulfilled that duty by disclosing a variety of background information to the Jacksons. . . . Although [the Montana Code Ann.] § 40-8-122(1) . . . does not specifically describe that information which the State must include in the medical and social histories it provides to adoptive parents, the State's own policies and procedures manual provides additional detail. The Department of Social and Rehabilitation Services Policies and Procedures Manual (Manual) § CSD-SS 602-1 specifically provides that. . . . the child and his adoptive family need to have "*all* available information on the child and his birth family." This language, coupled with that portion of § 40-8-122(1)(c) . . . which mandates that the State provide adoptive parents with "medical and social histories" clearly evidences a statutory duty on the part of the State to fully and accurately disclose all relevant information, including psychological reports, regarding an adoptee and his or her family.

The State next argues, however, that the imposition of such a duty to disclose . . . would conflict with its statutory duties to maintain the confidentiality of the birth parents' medical records. . . . [¶] Although § 41-3-205 . . . generally prohibited the State from disclosing information contained in child protective services files, it provided an exception permitting such dissemination if authorized by court order. Had it obtained such an order from the court in this case, the State could have complied [with all of the governing policies.] Had the State sought, but failed to obtain, such a court order, the State could still have complied with the confidentiality requirements of § 41-3-205 . . . and its own policy by simply informing the Jacksons that Aaron would not have been an appropriate child for them to adopt in light of their concerns regarding a possible history of mental illness.

Thus, [we] conclude that § 40-8-122(1)(c) . . . construed in conjunction with the State's own policy and procedures manual, gives rise to a statutorily imposed duty on the part of the State to fully and accurately disclose to the Jacksons all relevant background information in its possession, including any reports regarding the psychological health of Aaron's birth parents. Whether the State breached that duty is a genuine issue of material fact precluding summary judgment in the State's favor on the Jacksons' claims for negligent nondisclosure and negligence based upon a lack of informed consent. . . .

. . . .

[T]he Jacksons will ultimately need to demonstrate that the State's conduct in allegedly withholding or misrepresenting information regarding Aaron's background led to their decision to adopt Aaron and thereby helped produce the injury in this case. Moreover, we hold the Jacksons will have to demonstrate that, but for the fact that the State withheld and misrepresented certain background information, they would not have adopted Aaron, would not have been injured, and would not have incurred the damages they now claim.

NOTES

1. *Liability for Agency Misrepresentations About the Child.* The tort of wrongful adoption is relatively new, first recognized in the 1980s. Yet, most states now recognize wrongful adoption claims based on intentional or negligent misrepresentation. *See Wolford v. Children's Home Soc'y of W. Va.*, 17 F. Supp. 2d 577 (S.D. W. Va. 1998) (holding that adoptive parents of child with fetal alcohol syndrome stated actionable claim against adoption agency for its intentional misrepresentation of facts regarding alcohol abuse by child's birth mother). *See also Moore v. Commonwealth*, 653 N.E.2d 1104 (Mass. 1995) (holding that adoptive parents may recover in "wrongful adoption" action based on adoption agency's material misrepresentations of fact regarding child's history prior to adoption); *Mallette v. Children's Friend & Serv.*, 491 N.E.2d 1101 (R.I. 1995) (holding that liability for negligent misrepresentation can be extended to the context of adoption and is not contrary to public policy); *M.H. & J.L.H. v. Caritas Adoption Servs.*, 488 N.W. 2d 282 (Minn. 1992) (holding that agency that failed to provide prospective adoptive parents with complete information about the incest in the child's family can be found liable for negligent misrepresentation, even if it had not intended to mislead the parents). *See also Gibbs v. Ernst*, 647 A.2d 882 (Pa. 1994) (recognizing liability theories of intentional misrepresentation, negligent misrepresentation and failure to disclose, but making clear that there is no duty to investigate). As in *Jackson*, the *Caritas* court emphasized that once the agency undertakes voluntary disclosures, due care must be exercised so as not to mislead the adoptive parents. This point was also emphasized in *Meracle v. Children's Serv. Soc'y of Wis.*, 437 N.W.2d 532 (Wis. 1989), in which the adoptive parents were told, inaccurately, that the child was not at risk for developing Huntington's Disease, even though there was a family history of the condition. While the court held that such affirmative misrepresentations by the agency would support an action for the extraordinary medical expenses, it concluded that the adoptive parents could not recover for emotional distress in the absence of a physical injury. The court stated that "to avoid liability, agencies must simply refrain from making affirmative misrepresentations about a child's health." In cases such as *Jackson* and others cited in this Note and Note 2, adoptive parents seek monetary damages which, in many cases, help defray the cost of raising a child who suffers from serious medical or emotional problems. A successful result in such a tort action does not alter the legal status of the adoptive parent-adoptive child relationship. In many cases, the adoptive parents do not seek to rescind the adoption. In some instances, however, the adoptive parents do wish to reverse or annul the adoption. Section D[5] below examines the policies governing actions by adoptive parents to abrogate an adoption.

2. *Liability Based on Failure to Disclose Information.*   Can an agency avoid liability by disclosing as little information as possible? Many states like Montana now impose on the agency a statutory duty to disclose information to adoptive parents about the birth parents' and child's medical history. This represents a significant change from the traditional approach. One author summarizes the changes in law as follows:

> [A]doptive parents are seeking remedies for an assortment of "wrongful adoption" tort claims ranging from intentional misrepresentation and fraud to negligent misrepresentation, and on to intentional and negligent infliction of emotional distress. Courts diverge in the treatment of these tort claims arising from misinformation or failure to disclose in the adoption process.

> The most successful of the[se] actions . . . allege deliberate acts of misconduct such as fraud and intentional misinformation. The common law fraud claim requires that adoptive parents allege and prove (1) a material

misrepresentation or omission was made to them in the course of the adoption, (2) made either with the intent of misleading them or with reckless disregard for the truth, (3) upon which they justifiably relied, and (4) in relying they were injured. . . .

But what of the duties of adoption agencies to disclose all known information? Increasingly the torts of negligent misrepresentation, negligent nondisclosure, and failure to investigate are finding application in the adoption context. . . . In holding an agency has a duty to disclose all known information about prospective adoptees, the Massachusetts Supreme Court reasoned that the duty is demanded by the notion of good faith and fair dealing. The court found that the burden on adoption agencies to disclose was substantially outweighed by the adoptive parents' need to for full disclosure. Other courts have shown reluctance to extend liability in negligence beyond this point. For example, no court as yet has held that an adoption agency has a duty to investigate, and several have specifically rejected such a claim.

Most wrongful adoption cases include claims for intentional or negligent infliction of emotional distress. Few courts have recognized the claim in the adoption context; and those that have set a difficult standard to meet, requiring that the adoptive parents show the defendant's reckless conduct was "outrageous and extreme."

Amanda Trefethen, *The Emerging Tort of Wrongful Adoption*, 11 J. CONTEMP. LEGAL ISSUES 620, 622–23 (2000). *See also* D. Marianne Brower Blair, *Lifting the Genealogical Veil: A Blueprint for Legislative Reform of the Disclosure of Health Related Information in Adoption*, 70 N.C. L. REV. 681 (1992) (citing state statutes). Under the 1994 Uniform Adoption Act § 2-106, the person placing the child for adoption must supply a report to the prospective adoptive parents that includes a medical and psychological history of the child, including prenatal care and exposure to drugs, history of abuse, and relevant information concerning the medical and psychological history of the parents and relatives, including predisposition to disease, drug or alcohol addiction, and information about the mother's prenatal health. Clearly, prospective parents have an interest in information about the child's genetic heritage and health background that might affect the child's future development in important ways. However, an onerous burden on agencies to collect information, together with the broad risk of potential liability, would impose significant costs on adoption.

3. *Further Reading.* For scholarly commentary on agency liability for misrepresentation, nondisclosure and other tort claims collectively referred to as "wrongful adoption," see Steve Mulligan, *Inconsistency in Illinois Adoption Law: Adoption Agencies' Uncertain Duty to Disclose, Investigate, and Inquire*, 39 LOY. U. CHI. L.J. 1 (2008) (summarizing developments in the various states); Student Author, *When Love Is Not Enough: Toward A Unified Wrongful Adoption Tort*, 105 HARV. L. REV. 1761 (1992) (arguing that disclosure statutes are ambiguous and allow too much agency discretion, thereby not insuring sufficient protection for adoptive parents); Jennifer Emmaneel, Student Author, *Beyond Wrongful Adoption: Expanding Adoption Agency Liability to Include A Duty To*

Investigate and A Duty to Warn, 29 GOLDEN GATE U. L. REV. 181 (1999).

[b]   Regulating Independent Adoptions

Independent adoptions are, by definition, not arranged through public or private state-licensed nonprofit agencies. The category includes, however, adoptions that occur without an intermediary (i.e., "direct adoptions"), the overwhelming majority of which are stepparent or other adoptions by family or friends of one of the birth parents. "Private placement" adoptions may be arranged more informally, by persons in the community, such as health care professionals and clergypersons, who do not arrange adoptions professionally, but help to "introduce" the parties, typically without expecting payment. Potential adoptive parents might place advertisements in newspapers, magazines, or on the internet, hoping that a pregnant woman considering adoption will contact them. Other independent adoptions are facilitated by professionals, often attorneys, who serve as intermediaries and do so for fees that are typically paid by the adoptive parents. Professionals specializing in private adoptions may also direct advertising at young pregnant women, targeting also college campuses and making contacts with health care professionals.

There are two primary concerns that drive the regulation of independent adoptions. One concern focuses on the competence of the persons serving as intermediaries. Are those persons sufficiently knowledgeable about adoption and the myriad of attendant legal, psychological, and social issues to insure that the child's best interests are served and that the rights and interests of all of the parties are adequately protected? A second concern is that some intermediaries may have loyalty to one party or another, may be influenced by financial compensation (that is, wanting an adoption to go forward because compensation is based, in part, on achieving that result), or other vested interests, and that these factors compromise their neutrality and ability to prioritize the welfare of the child and of the more vulnerable participants in the process. *See, e.g.*, Susan A. Munson, *Independent Adoption: In Whose Best Interest?* 26 SETON HALL L. REV. 803, 809–16 (1996); Jana B. Singer, *The Privatization of Family Law*, 1992 WIS. L. REV. 1443, 1481–1486; Sharon Fast Gustafson, Student Author, *Regulating Adoption Intermediaries Ensuring that the Solutions are No Worse than the Problem*, 3 GEO. J. LEGAL ETHICS 837, 844–45 (1990).

While most states legally permit non-relative independent adoptions, many prohibit most forms of independent adoption in which the parties do not have a preexisting family relationship. For example, Massachusetts statutes specify that no one other than a "duly authorized agent or employee of the department of children and families or a child care or placement agency licensed [by the state can publish an] advertisement or notice of children offered or wanted for adoption." Furthermore, such persons may not offer "to place, locate or dispose of children offered or wanted for adoption." Any unauthorized person engaging in these practices is subject to a fine of $100–$1,000. If the individual accepts payment, he may be fined between $5,000–$30,000, or subject to a prison term of up to five years. MASS. GEN. LAWS ANN. ch. 210, § 11A (2009). As this statutory language indicates, the Massachusetts legislature targets the conduct of persons who attempt to serve as private intermediaries or adoption brokers. Its language, however, appears also to prohibit birth parents from advertising the availability of their child for adoption. The statute does not appear to affect adoption arrangements that may flow from relationships between unrelated person in the community or from informal social networks. *See also, e.g.,* CONN. GEN. STAT. ANN. § 45a-727 (2009); MICH. COMP. LAWS § 710.55 (2009). The remaining states, while allowing non-agency intermediaries to arrange adoptions, generally still regulate their activities in some way, with particular attention to the concerns noted above regarding independent adoptions. For example, California requires that in non-agency adoptions, the birth parent(s) must select the prospective adoptive parents based on "personal knowledge" of those persons, including information about their full legal names, ages, religion, employment, etc. *See, e.g.,* CAL. FAM. CODE § 8801 (2009). It further sets forth the information that must be disclosed to the birth parent(s), mandates face-to-face counseling with an adoption counselor, and sets forth a duty of due care owed by the adoption counselor to the birth parent(s). CAL. FAM. CODE § 8801.3 *et seq.* (2009). In addition, California grants birth parent(s) a 30-day period within which the consent may be revoked for independent adoptions, while consents for agency adoptions can only be revoked within 10 days. *See also, e.g.,* LA. CHILD CODE ANN. art 1113 (2009) (allowing minor birth parents to provide consent for an adoption to an agency without additional requirements, while requiring the parents of a minor birth parent or the court to play a role in the provision of consent for independent adoptions.) The 1994 Uniform Adoption Act allows placement only directly by the child's parents or through a licensed agency. § 2-101. In direct placement, the parent herself must select the adoptive parents, and is limited to parties with a favorable pre-placement evaluation. Agents may assist in the adoption, but they may not charge brokerage fees or engage in any advertising. § 7-101.

Despite the potential drawbacks of independent adoption, they have become increasingly popular in recent decades. Adoptive parents often choose independent adoption as a way to avoid the agency process and long waiting periods. Some prospective adoptive parents may be unable to adopt through an agency because they fail to meet age, or marital status criteria, or have health problems. Independent adoptions often allow prospective adoptive parents and birth parents greater access to information about each other. Birth parents may be able to play a greater role in the selection of the parents. Furthermore, the child can be placed directly into the custody of the adoptive parents and not into foster care, as is sometimes required through traditional agency adoption processes. *See generally* Erika Lynn Kleiman, *Caring for Our Own: Why American Adoption Law and Policy Must Change,* 30 COLUM. J.L. & SOC. PROBS. 327 (1997); Carol Sanger, *Separating From Children,* 96 COLUM. L. REV. 375, 442 (1996).

Most states require a "home study" of the prospective adoptive parents before a court issues the final decree in an independent adoption. Thus, independent adoption does not go unscrutinized. In an agency adoption, the agency itself performs the evaluation, and its results are made available to the court. However, agency personnel who also perform home studies in independent adoptions may view their task differently than when evaluating agency applicants. In independent adoptions, they are certifying that the home meets minimal standards, but when the agency makes the placement decision, it is looking for the best possible home for the child. Thus, home studies done in connection with independent adoptions are less thorough, even though they are often conducted by the same people, in part because they are typically done after the child has already been placed in the home, making it less likely that the court would turn down the adoption petition. The 1994 Uniform Adoption Act requires a pre-placement evaluation in independent as well as agency adoptions (§ 2-102). In independent adoptions, the pre-placement evaluation "certifies" the prospective adoptive parents. A favorable pre-placement evaluation is a prerequisite for direct placement by the parent.

[i]   The Role of the Attorney

Many of the intermediaries arranging non-agency adoptions (that is, matching available babies with adoptive homes) are lawyers. The small group of attorneys who handle many adoptions have received considerable scrutiny. Attorneys can face ethical challenges in the adoption setting. Usually they represent the adoptive parents, while dealing also with birth parents who often do not have legal counsel. The birth mother typically looks to the adoptive parents to cover many of her expenses, and will rarely have funds to hire her own lawyer. In this situation, can the attorney inform the birth mother about legal matters? In general, attorneys are prohibited from representing two clients whose interests are adverse, although exceptions are sometimes made in situations of full disclosure and consent by both parties. The ABA Standing Committee on Ethics and Professional Responsibility has found that under both the Model Rules of Professional Conduct and the older Code of Professional Responsibility, an attorney may not ethically represent both the adoptive and birth parents in a private adoption, *Informal Opinion 87-1523*, Feb. 14, 1987 (discussed in Pamela K. Strom Amlung, *Conflicts of Interest in Independent Adoptions: Pitfalls for the Unwary*, 59 U. CIN. L. REV. 169, 176–77 (1990)). Dual representation is explicitly prohibited by statute in adoption cases in several states. *See, e.g.*, KY. REV. STAT. ANN. § 199.492 (2009) (an "attorney shall not represent both the biological parents and the prospective adoptive parents"); WIS. STAT. ANN. § 48.837(8) (2009) (same). But, avoiding violation of the rule against dual representation may be tricky in a somewhat complex legal context in which only one party is represented.

Even without the intent to engage in dual representation, an attorney for the prospective adoptive parents will inevitably meet with unrepresented birth parents, present them with documents to sign, explain the meaning of those documents, and perhaps relay funds to cover, for example, the medical expenses of pregnancy and childbirth. Do such activities cross the line to joint representation? The official comment to Rule 4.3 of the A.B.A.'s *Model Rules of Professional Conduct* states that the "lawyer should not give advice to an unrepresented person other than the advice to obtain counsel." AM. BAR. ASS'N MODEL RULES OF PROFESSIONAL CONDUCT, Rule 4.3, http://www.abanet.org/cpr/mrpc/rule_4_3.html. Consistent with this position, some courts indicate that advising the birth parent that the lawyer only represents the adoptive parents is insufficient to avoid an ethical violation. "If counsel for adoptive parents reviews the consent agreement or other legal documents with the natural mother, assists her in locating a place to live and obtains reimbursement of expenses and advises which expenses are reimbursable, a[n improper] conflict exists." *See Adoption of Anonymous*, 501

N.Y.S.2d 240 (Surr. 1986). Some state statutes address this potential problem directly, providing alternatives to insure that birth parents have access to their own counsel, if needed. *See, e.g.,* ME. REV. STAT. ANN. tit. 18-A, § 9-106(a) (2009) (attorney precluded from representing biological and prospective adoptive parents and "the biological parents are entitled to an attorney for any hearing held pursuant to this article" and may request the court to appoint an attorney if they cannot afford one); MINN. STAT. ANN. § 259.47 (2009) (attorney precluded from representing biological and prospective adoptive parents and prospective adoptive parents are required to pay for an independent attorney for the birth parent(s) if the birth parent(s) so request). Although a handful of additional states set forth requirements for separate representation for all birth parents or birth parents who are minors, in most cases, biological parents are not represented by legal counsel in independent adoptions. *See* Elizabeth J. Samuels, *Time to Decide? The Laws Governing Mothers' Consent to the Adoption of their Newborn Infants,* 72 TENN. L. REV. 509, 535–59 (2005).

In addition, attorneys may risk a conflict of interest when they assist more than one set of prospective adoptive parents who "compete" to adopt the same child. In *In re Petrie,* 742 P.2d 796 (Ariz. 1987), attorney Robert Petrie challenged his censure by the Arizona State Bar for "representing clients with adverse interests in violation of Disciplinary Rule 5-105(A) and (B)," and some additional charges. In this case, Petrie had initially met with a couple, the Pietzes, who indicated that they wished to adopt an infant. Petrie did not know of any available children at that time. Approximately 18 months later, the Pietzes learned from a friend about a child who might be available for adoption. They asked the friend to contact Petrie, connect him with the birth mother, and tell him that the woman was referred by the Pietzes. Petrie met with the birth mother and her sister, and advised them that he had a set of adoptive parents in mind. He exchanged written communications with Pietzes in which he told them about the availability of the child and they indicated their interest adopting the child. Shortly thereafter, Petrie received a phone call from another couple, the Buckmasters, who expressed an interest in adopting a second child. For various reasons unrelated to the welfare of the child (e.g., the geographical proximity of the Buckmasters), Petrie decided that the baby should be placed with the Buckmasters, and the birth mother followed that recommendation. When the Pietzes learned that the child was going to another couple, Mr. Pietz protested, reminding Petrie that the Pietzes had referred the child and they wanted the child placed with them. When Petrie did not comply, the Pietzes complained to the State Bar.

The court held that, in a situation involving two sets of parents and one child, an "attorney cannot simultaneously represent both sets of adoptive parents without compromising his representation of one of them." In addition, it held that, because the interests of the adoptive parents and the natural parents may be adverse, and the same attorney cannot represent both parties. The court cited an exception to these rules. It held that the relevant Disciplinary Rule allows a lawyer to represent multiple clients " 'if it is obvious that he can adequately represent the interests of each and if each consents to the representation after full disclosure of the possible effect of such representation on the exercise of his independent professional judgment on behalf of each.' Under this exception, then, it may be possible for an attorney to represent multiple parties to an adoption, but only after full disclosure and upon consent of the parties. This exception has no application to the current case, however, because there is no evidence that respondent complied with its provisions." It went on to determine, based on the facts, whether Petrie indeed had an attorney-client relationship with the Pietzes, the Buckmasters, and the birth mother. It concluded that he had.

Does the exception cited above adequately protect the parties from the harms that attend an attorney's potential conflict of interest? Given the facts of this case, would Petrie's actions have been ethically acceptable if he had informed them that he would be representing multiple parties? Professor Samuels asserts that

> [t]he ability of parties to knowingly consent to dual representation is doubted, given the emotional and stressful nature of their situations: "It is difficult to believe [that they] can really grasp the essential point: that the same lawyer is advising the biological mother and the couple who desperately want to obtain her child." Also, consent cannot be obtained from two [of the many] interested parties: that is, the child being adopted and the state. . . . [¶] Does any expression of doubt or ambivalence by a mother mean that the attorney must cease dual representation? Will a mother's interests be compromised if a conflict arises and dual representation ceases when a revocation period is about to expire? If there has been dual representation, will adoptive parents be vulnerable to a challenge to the adoption based on a claim of undue influence or duress? If a conflict arises, is it permissible for the attorney to continue to represent the adoptive parents who are paying for the legal services, even though the dual representation has "removed the communications of the parties to one another and to the attorney from the privileged category? If it is not permissible for the attorney to continue to represent one of the parties, [what of the increased costs borne by the prospective adoptive parents] in situations in which dual representation has been undertaken and terminated?

Elizabeth J. Samuels, *Time to Decide? The Laws Governing Mothers' Consent to the Adoption of their Newborn Infants*, 72 TENN. L. REV. 509, 537–38 (2005) (quoting Katherine G. Thompson & Douglas H. Reiniger, *Private-Placement Adoptions in New York; Separate Representation Required*, in 2 ADOPTION L. & PRAC. § 6.01(3)(a) (Joan Heifetz Hollinger et al. eds., 2004). The 1994 Uniform Adoption Act requires birth parents, adoptive parents and adoption agencies to have separate representation. U.A.A § 2-405(a)(4). When the birth parent is a minor, she must be expressly advised of her right to independent counsel. U.A.A § 2-405(d)(5). If a minor parent does not have independent counsel, her consent is presumed to be incompetent. U.A.A § 2-405(c). U.A.A § 3-201(a) authorizes court appointment of a lawyer for any indigent minor or incompetent individual who appears in the adoption proceedings and whose parental rights may be terminated, unless the court finds that the individual possesses adequate means to hire her own lawyer or waives the right to counsel. U.A.A § 3-201(b) requires the appointment of a guardian ad litem for any minor adoptee in a contested proceeding.

[ii]   Regulation of Fees

Most states regulate by statute the fees and expenses paid by prospective adoptive parents as part of the independent domestic adoption process. *See* DHHS, Regulation of Private Domestic Adoption Expenses: Summary of State Laws (2008), http://www.childwelfare.gov/systemwide/laws_policies/statutes/expensesall .pdf (finding such regulatory statutes in 47 states and the District of Columbia). It is prohibited — typically criminalized — for anyone to exchange money as payment for a child in every state. Approximately half of the states also explicitly bar anyone from receiving a fee for obtaining a birth mother's consent to an adoption, or for connecting the prospective adoptive parents and birth mother. Statutes typically indicate that some expenses are permissible such as: maternity-related medical and hospital costs; temporary living expenses of the mother during pregnancy; counseling fees; attorney and legal fees, including any guardian ad litem fees; travel costs, meals, and lodging when necessary for court appearances, foster care for the child, when necessary. Most states also require submission of an accounting so that it can police all payments to the birth mother in order to ensure that they are proper For a case in which the court carefully analyzed the different payments and fees, allowing some and disallowing others, *see In re Adoption of Baby Boy P.*, 700 N.Y.S.2d 792 (N.Y. Fam. Ct. 1999). *See also In re Adoption of Baby Boy M.*, 18 P.3d 304, 306 (Ks. Ct. App. 2001) (indicating that the Kansas statute regulating what payments may be made to birth mothers was passed by legislature to "prevent babies from being treated as a commodity"). The Arizona statutes below are illustrative of the approach taken by many states.

ARIZONA REVISED STATUTES (2009)

§ 8-114. Monies paid to or for parent; court approval; attorney fees; accounting; disallowance; exception

A. The court may approve any monies paid to a parent of a child placed for adoption or another person for the benefit of the parent or adopted child for reasonable and necessary expenses incurred in connection with the adoption. These expenses may include costs for medical and hospital care and examinations for the mother and child, counseling fees, legal fees, agency fees, living expenses and any other costs the court finds reasonable and necessary.

B. A person who wishes to pay the living expenses of a birth parent that exceed one thousand dollars shall file a motion with the court to permit that payment. . . . The court shall approve living expenses that the person has paid, unless found unreasonable. The person who wishes to pay . . . living expenses of a birth mother shall file an affidavit with the court signed by the birth mother verifying that the birth mother . . . understands that the payment of these expenses . . . does not obligate [her] to place the child for adoption . . . A maximum of one thousand dollars may be advanced for birth parent living expenses without a motion. In determining what living expenses are reasonable and necessary, the court shall consider but not be limited to . . . . : (1) The current standard of living of the birth parent; (2) The standard of living necessary to preserve the health and welfare of the birth parent and the unborn child . . .

C. Except as provided in subsection A, a person shall not be directly or indirectly compensated for giving or obtaining consent to place a child for adoption.

D. An attorney may be paid for the attorney's services in connection with adoption, paternity and severance proceedings only the amount the court approves as being reasonable and necessary.

E. [T]he prospective adoptive parent shall file with the court a verified accounting . . . of all fees, payments, disbursements or commitments of anything of value made or agreed to be made by the prospective adoptive parent or for the benefit of the prospective adoptive parent in connection with the adoption. The accounting shall include . . . an affidavit that is signed by the birth mother . . . that verifies that . . . she understands that the payment of these expenses does not obligate her to place her child for adoption. . . .

. . .

H. All adoption cases shall be reviewed by the juvenile court for reasonableness and necessity of expenses.

I. This section does not apply to an adoption by a stepparent whose spouse is a natural or adoptive parent of the child.

§ 8-128. Violation; classification

A person who knowingly violates any provision of this article is guilty of a class 6 felony.

The 1994 Uniform Adoption Act (§ 7-203) permits payment by the adoptive parent of medical and counseling expenses of the mother and living expenses during pregnancy and for up to 6 weeks after birth. The Act provides that the mother is not required to reimburse the birth parents if the adoption does not go through, but that the adoptive parents are not required to make additional payments unless they have agreed to do so regardless of the outcome. Is such regulation socially beneficial? Is there any rationale for the distinction drawn by some courts between medical expenses during the pregnancy (which are generally permitted) and living expenses (which sometimes are not)? Might a birth mother whose expenses have been paid may feel compelled to consent to adoption after the child is born, or to choose the adoptive parents who paid those expenses?

For example, in *Galison v. District of Columbia*, 402 A.2d 1263 (D.C. App. 1979), an attorney, Edward Galison, pressured an ambivalent 16 year old pregnant girl to go forward with an adoption. He "persuaded her that adoption was 'the right thing to do.' After he informed her that her medical and living expenses in the District would be paid for and that she would receive $2,000 in addition to her medical and living expenses, she executed documents by which she consented to the proposed adoption" and authorized the hospital to release her yet-unborn child to [Galison]. The girl repeatedly continued to express reservations. Each time, Galison reminded her of the money that had already been "invested" in her. Finally, at the birth of the child, "the mother once again decided that she wanted to keep the baby, but she was 'afraid of the money I owed and the money that he had invested in me. I was afraid to back out. I didn't know what to do.'. . . Galison, meanwhile, once again attempted to persuade the mother to continue with the planned placement by arguing that it was in everyone's best interest and by reminding her that there was already $6,000 'invested' in her." The girl's grandmother contacted a social worker and a police "sting" was arranged. After the child's birth, the "grandmother . . . received approximately $2,200 from Galison, and gave the baby to Galison. Upon leaving the hospital with the baby, Galison was arrested." *Id.*

Some states prohibit "baby brokerage" services, even where no payment is exchanged. For example, in *Galison*, the defendant was also convicted under the District of Columbia's "placing out" statute, which precludes anyone not acting under the auspices of a state or state-licensed agency from "plac[ing" or "arrang-[ing]" or "assist[ing] in placing or arranging for the placement of a child under sixteen years of age in a family home for adoption." D.C. Code § 14-1405 (2009) *as amended* (formerly § 32-785). For a more recent example of a conviction under a "placing out" statute, see *Balouch v. State*, 938 So.2d 253 (Miss. 2006). In the absence of any payment to the intermediary, many courts will decline to find a violation. *See In re Adoption of Baby Girl B.*, 544 N.Y.S.2d 963 (Surr. Ct. 1989) (court finds no violation where attending physician who found adoptive parents received no fee).

[iii]   White, Gray, and Black "Markets": Why Not Legalize Baby-Selling?

Some observers categorize the different methods by which children in the U.S. are placed for adoption as constituting "three general adoption markets: (1) 'white market' adoptions are those performed by agencies, either public or private; (2) 'gray market,' or independent, adoptions are those performed by the birth parents, often with the assistance of an intermediary; and (3) 'black market' adoptions are those illegal transfers in which children are sold for profit." Melinda Lucas, *Adoption: Distinguishing Between Grey Market and black Market Activities*, 34 FAM. L.Q. 553 (2000). Is the line between the "black market' and the "gray market" always discernable? Some argue that, while babies are not bought and sold outright in the "gray market," legally permissible compensation for a range of other expenses and services does influence the process. But, precisely what it takes to "cross the line" is not always clear.

While line-drawing is never easy in areas of law such as this, figuring out approximately where some of the lines should be drawn may be facilitated by thinking about *why* "baby-selling" is prohibited, and in particular, criminalized. In general, acts that are criminalized are those that our society views as "morally blameworthy" and that offend society's norms and values. If we can identify whether, *and for what reasons*, baby-selling offends our norms and values, we can better assess whether particular types or features of "gray market" transactions cross the line. In theory, the characteristics that distinguish "gray market" transactions (which are legally permissible to various degrees in most states) from the "black market" transactions (which are not legally permissible) should correlate to some extent with generally-accepted social values.

Legal scholars and policymakers were initially forced to confront their opposition to baby-selling in response to the publication of a now-famous article in 1978. In that article, Elisabeth Landes and Richard Posner argue that the legal restrictions on fees in private adoption have created a baby shortage with many unfortunate consequences. They suggest that a free market in which adoptive parents and birth mothers could freely negotiate for the transfer of babies offers a solution that should be considered. Elisabeth M. Landes & Richard A. Posner, *The Economics of the Baby Shortage*, 7 J. LEGAL STUD. 323 (1978). Under current law, these authors point out, many of the costs of producing and transferring a baby cannot be recovered, including the opportunity costs of the birth mother's time when she is unable to work; the pain or other disutility of the pregnancy and delivery; the subjective value of the child to her; and the costs of search by a middleman in locating and bringing buyer and seller together.

According to Landes and Posner, these constraints reduce the incentives that pregnant women have to place their children for adoption, rather than keeping or aborting them. At the same time, the authors argue, "constraints on payment discourage the emergence of an effective middleman function," which is a serious problem in a market in which buyers and sellers may have a hard time finding one another. They note that, as economists would predict, a clandestine black market in babies has emerged, characterized by high prices and fraud. Moreover, because abusive or neglectful parents have no incentive to choose adoption, they will place their children in foster care instead, even when they do not seriously plan to reacquire the child. This decision may "render the child unadoptable, for by the time the parents relinquish their parental rights the child may be too old to be placed for adoption." *Id.* at 338.

Landes and Posner review the objections to their position. Many criticisms, they believe, are more aptly directed at a black market than at a legal free market. For example, they challenge the claim that high prices favoring the wealthy would pervade a free market. Prices are high on the black market, they argue, because they include punishment costs. In a free market, prices for children of *equivalent quality* would be much lower. Fraud would also not be a significant problem in a legal market because sellers could give legally enforceable warranties about genealogy, health, etc. The authors describe the effect of a legal market:

> The current illegality of baby selling reduces the benefits of transacting to the buyer by depriving him of the contractual protections that buyers in legal markets normally receive. Prospective adoptive parents would presumably be willing to pay more for a child whose health and genealogy were warranted in a legally enforceable instrument than they are willing to pay under the present system where the entire risk of any deviation from expected quality falls on them. Thus the effect of legalizing the baby market would be not only to shift the marginal cost of baby production and sale downward but to move the demand curve for adoptive children upward. Conceivably these movements could cancel each other out, resulting in no change from the current black-market prices, but even if they did consumer satisfaction would be increased. The same price would buy a higher-quality package of rights.

Id. at 341.

The authors then address objections to baby selling in a legal market. In response to the criticism that a free market will not promote the best interests of the children, they acknowledge that "free exchange will maximize the satisfaction of the people trading, [and not] . . . the thing traded." *Id.* at 342. However, they question whether adoption agencies do any better "in finding homes for children that would maximize their satisfactions in life." *Id.* at 342–3. Moreover, in their view, criminal prohibitions of child abuse, together with background checks, would effectively screen out prospective parents who are likely to abuse their children. Further, they point out that most people do not adopt with such motives, and their willingness to pay is added assurance.

> Few people buy a car or a television set in order to smash it. In general, the more costly a purchase, the more care the purchaser will lavish on it. Recent studies suggest that the more costly it is for parents to obtain a child, the greater will be their investment in the child's quality attributes, such as health and education.

Id. at 343. Landes and Posner express skepticism that adoptive and birth parents will be vulnerable to overreaching by middlemen because the decisions involved have such a strong emotional component. They point out that this is true of "other goods and services, such as medical care, that are subject to market exchange." *Id.* at 344.

Finally, the authors address the objection that baby selling will lead to baby breeding, particularly the breeding of babies with "desirable" qualities and specified characteristics that could be matched with those characteristics sought by prospective adoptive parents. The authors acknowledge that "any market will generate incentives and improve the product." They rebut concerns that this proposal might lead to various eugenic efforts, stating that, as long as only "infertile couples and those with serious genetic disorders" take advantage of the baby market, "the impact of a free baby market on the genetic composition and distribution of the human race at large would be small." *Id.* at 345. According to Landes and Posner, the greatest long-run effect of legalizing the baby market is that it would induce "women who have unintentionally become pregnant to put up the child for adoption rather than raise it themselves or have an abortion." *Id.* at 345.

The Landes and Posner article certainly provoked a great deal of debate. Perhaps the most central critique comes from Professor Margaret Radin, whose broad-based theory of market-inalienability has applications for a range of legal and moral questions, including baby-selling. Margaret Jane Radin, *Market Inalienability*, 100 HARV. L. REV. 1849 (1987). "Something that is market-inalienable" she asserts, "is not to be sold, which in our economic system means it is not to be traded in a market." *Id.* at 1850. She explains:

> By making something nonsalable we proclaim that it should not be conceived of or treated as a commodity. When something is noncommodifiable, market trading is a disallowed form of social organization and allocation. We place that thing beyond supply and demand pricing, broker-

age and arbitrage, advertising and marketing, stockpiling, speculation, and valuation in terms of the opportunity cost of production.

Market-inalienability poses for us more than the binary choice of whether something should be wholly inside or outside the market, completely commodified or completely noncommodified. Some things are completely commodified — deemed suitable for trade in a laissez-faire market. Others are completely noncommodified — removed from the market altogether. But many things can be described as incompletely commodified — neither fully commodified nor fully removed from the market. Thus, we may decide that some things should be market — inalienable only to a degree, or only in some aspects.

. . .

Broadly construed, commodification includes not only actual buying and selling, but also market rhetoric, the practice of thinking about interactions as if they were sale transactions, and market methodology, the use of monetary cost-benefit analysis to judge these interactions. Universal commodification embraces this broad construction in its most expansive form, limiting actual buying and selling only by the dictates of market methodology, and solving problems of contested commodification by making everything in principle a commodity . . . .

Id. at 1858. She argues that one of the problems with conceiving of certain things, such as one's body (consider selling kidneys), one's reproductive capacity (consider surrogacy), one's children (consider baby-selling) as commodities is that doing so is an assault on our sense of "personhood," and our sense that certain attributes or capacities of human beings are inherently different from goods and services ordinarily sold on the market. Specifically focusing on baby-selling, Professor Radin continues:

[P]arent-child relationships are closely connected with personhood, particularly with personal identity. . . . Moreover, poor women caught in the double bind raise the issue of freedom: they may wish to sell a baby on the black market . . . perhaps to try to provide adequately for other children or family members. But the double bind is not the only problem of freedom implicated in baby-selling. . . . If we permit babies to be sold, we commodify not only the mother's (and father's) baby-making capacities . . . but we also conceive of the baby itself in market rhetoric. When the baby becomes a commodity, all of its personal attributes — sex, eye color, predicted I.Q., predicted height, and the like — become commodified as well. This is to conceive of potentially all personal attributes in market rhetoric, not merely those of sexuality. Moreover, to conceive of infants in market rhetoric is likewise to conceive of the people they will become in market rhetoric, and to create in those people a commodified self-conception.

. . . . If a capitalist baby industry were to come into being, with all of its accompanying paraphernalia, how could any of us, even these who did not produce infants for sale, avoid subconsciously measuring the dollar value of our children? How could our children avoid being preoccupied with measuring their own dollar value? This makes our discourse about ourselves (when we are children) and about our children (when we are parents) like our discourse about cars. Seeing commodification of babies as an inevitable and grave injury to personhood appears rather easy. In the worst case, market rhetoric could create a commodified self-conception in everyone, as the result of commodifying every attribute that differentiates us and that other people value in us, and could destroy personhood as we know it.

. . . .

Conceiving of any child in market rhetoric wrongs personhood. In addition, we fear, based on our assessment of current social norms, that the market value of babies would be decided in ways injurious to their personhood and to the personhood of those who buy and sell on this basis, exacerbating class, race, and gender divisions . . . . Conceiving of children in market rhetoric would foster an inferior conception of human flourishing, one that commodifies every personal attribute that might be valued by people in other people. In spite of the double bind, our aversion to commodification of babies has a basis strong enough to recommend that market-inalienability be maintained.

Id. at 1925–28. Echoing and adding to these themes, Professor J. Robert S. Prichard, *A Market for Babies?*, 34 U. Toronto L.J. 341 (1984), argues that a baby market would also be "oppressive." "Put bluntly, the proposal . . . smacks of slavery. [S]uch a scheme would oppressively and involuntarily relegate poor women to an occupation [of baby-making]." Id. at 352–354. In addition, he claims, it is problematic that the people who can pay the highest prices are not necessarily those who will be the best parent for a particular child, but in a market, the highest bidder may prevail. Can you think of any other factors that might make a market for babies problematic? Can you think of safeguards that might make a market for babies might be acceptable in our society? For additional critiques of the Landes-Posner proposal see Melinda Lucas, *Adoption: Distinguishing Between Grey Market and black Market Activities*, 34 Fam. L. Q. 553 (2000); Patricia Williams, *Spare Parts, Family Values, Old Children, Cheap*, 28 N.E. L. Rev. 913 (1994); Jane Maslow Cohen, *Posnerism, Pluralism, and Pessimism*, 67 B.U. L. Rev. 105 (1987). For defense of Landes and Posner's views, see Ronald A. Cass, *Coping with Life, Law and Market: A Comment on Posner and the Law and Economics Debate* 67 B.U. L. Rev. 73 (1987). For Posner's own response, see Richard A. Posner, *The Regulation of the Market in Adoptions*, 67 B.U. L. Rev. 59 (1987). For responses that are neither wholly supportive or wholly critical, see Martha E. Ertman, *What's Wrong with a Parenthood Market: A New and Improved Theory of Commodification*, 82 N.C. L. Rev. 1 (2003) (attempting to integrate the views of Landes-Posner with those of Radin); Jana Singer, *The Privatization of Family Law*, 1992 Wis. L. Rev. 1443, 1478–89 (stating that Judge Posner's proposal is not really very different from what is currently legally permissible, observing that the proposal would make "explicit what has largely been implicit in the growing acceptance of private-placement adoption: that the primary purpose of adoption reform should be the satisfaction of 'consumer' demand for more (and better) adoptable babies").

Do the points made by various authors above help with the line-drawing between black and gray markets? For example, which features, if any, of the current "gray" market (1) risk impairing the personhood or dignity of children, specifically, and human beings, more generally, (2) risk oppressing economically-disadvantaged women who give birth to the babies; (3) risk the child's welfare by allowing ability to pay high fees to substitute for a consideration of which home is best for a particular, or any, child? One's answers to these questions can perhaps guide policy decisions as to where the exchange of money in relation to adoption should or should not be permissible.

Focusing now on the current white and gray markets, should advertising be permissible? About half of the states have addressed the legality of advertisements in their statutes. Some states permit the birth parent(s) and/or the prospective adoptive parents to advertise, *see, e.g.*, CONN. GEN. STAT. ANN. § 45a-728d (2009), and some jurisdictions allow prospective adoptive parents to advertise only after they have received favorable preplacement evaluations through a home study. *See, e.g.*, WIS. STAT. ANN. 48.825 (2009) (also allowing birth parents and state licensed agencies to advertise). Other jurisdictions permit advertising by state-licensed agencies only, *see, e.g.*, DEL. CODE ANN. tit. 13 § 930 (2009); GA. CODE ANN., § 19-8-24 (2009). Other states, such as Alabama, categorically prohibit advertising by anyone offering to play any role in the adoption process. See ALA. CODE § 26-10A-36 (2009) ("It shall be unlawful for any person or persons, organizations, corporation, partnership, hospital, association, or any agency to advertise verbally, through print, electronic media, or otherwise that they will" (1) Adopt children or assist in the adoption of children. . . .). Some states specifically address what is permissible for an attorney to place in an advertisement. For example, while Wisconsin does not permit attorneys to advertise services as one who can find or place children for adoption, it does allow attorneys to advertise the availability of their *legal* services relating to adoption cases. See, e.g., WIS. ST. ANN. § 48.825(4) (2009) ("Nothing in this section prohibits an attorney licensed to practice in this state from advertising his or her availability to practice or provide services relating to the adoption of a child"). Indeed, in a case brought by attorneys in Arizona, the U.S. Supreme Court held that lawyers have a First Amendment right to place advertisements of their *legal* services. *See Bates v. O'Steen*, 433 U.S. 350 (1977).

Some attorneys are accused of coming dangerously close to "baby-selling." *See* Michele Galen, *Baby Brokers: How Far Can a Lawyer Go?* NAT'L. L.J. 1 (Feb. 9, 1987). Galen describes Seymour Kurtz, who ran four adoption agencies in four states and placed hundreds of mostly white babies each year. He spent $700,000 on national advertising to attract birth mothers, who (according to charges of the Arizona attorney general, who sought to deny his agency a license) were then offered lavish accommodations, vacations and other inducements to agree to adoption. Other attorneys, according to Galen, receive substantial fees for guiding their clients through the process, assisting them in placing ads that will appeal to pregnant women, screening candidates, etc. There are even reports of brokerage fees as high as $100,000 in states in which regulation is lax. *See* Laura Mansnerus, *Market Puts Price Tag on the Priceless*, N.Y. TIMES, Oct. 26, 1998, at A1, which offers an interesting account of the operation of the adoption market.

Internet baby-brokers have received attention as a result of a high-publicity case in which an internet broker assisted the mother in placing her twins with a California couple, the Allens, and then with a couple in England the Kilshaws, after the mother became dissatisfied with the Allens. After a highly publicized exchange between the claimants, Mr. Allen was arrested for sexual abuse of another child and it was revealed that Internet adoptions are illegal in England. The mother changed her mind and claimed custody and both couples withdrew. The Internet broker was charged with mail fraud for mishandling at least a dozen adoptions. *See* David Crary, *Manipulative Brokers Prey on Vulnerable, Anxious Couples: Beware Net Adoption Pitfalls*, PITTSBURGH POST GAZETTE, Jan. 24, 2001; Jeffrey McDonald, *Woman Pleads not Guilty to Fraud in Adoption Case*, COPLEY NEWS SERV., March 12, 2003.

[2]   Choosing Adoptive Parents and Children

[a]   Agency Selection Criteria and Matching Procedures

The number of "suitable" prospective adoptive parents seeking children through agencies has, in the last several decades, exceeded the number of available infants. Agencies have often relied on certain standard criteria in determining which families should be favored. Generally, agencies prefer couples who correspond to the model of the conventional nuclear family, that is, healthy, well-adjusted, heterosexual, and happily-married couples under age 40, in a middle or higher income bracket, with stable employment and economic prospects, whose life-styles and homes appear appropriate for childrearing. Erika Lynn Kleiman, *Caring for Our Own: Why American Adoption Law and Policy Must Change*, 30 COLUM. J. LAW & SOC. PROBS. 327, 344 (1997). These restrictions have arguably fueled the interest of many prospective adoptive parents in independent adoptions. Those couples or individuals who do not fit squarely within agency criteria realize that the likelihood of finding the type of child they seek through agencies is not great.

Recent cases and changing social attitudes regarding the suitability of a broader range of family forms as good environments in which to raise children have led to greater flexibility in the "suitability" determination. Thus, for example, several courts have determined that the existence of a health problem or disability per se is not relevant to suitability to adopt if that problem or disability does not affect that individual's ability to parent. *See, e.g., In re Hart*, 806 A.2d 1179 (Del. Fam. Ct. 2001). As noted below, increasingly, adoption agencies are accepting applications from gay and lesbian individuals and couples, and some agencies are reaching out to this pool of prospective adoptive parents. Some opportunities have opened up for single individuals as well. In addition, agencies are far more receptive to input from birth parents regarding the type of family they prefer.

While agencies will not recommend a prospective adoptive home to the court if the home does not meet certain minimum standards, they may allow birth parents to choose or rank order families according to their personal preferences. While some of the criteria listed above can be objectively assessed (e.g., age, marital status, income level), others rely on more subjective assessments. Thus, unquestionably, the personal values of the agency personnel evaluating the candidates will enter the calculus, a factor that contributes to criticism of agency procedures. In addition, critics have also assailed these criteria as excluding (or placing low on the list) many suitable black families, because the income levels of African-American families in the U.S. are typically lower than that of white families. *See, e.g.*, Elizabeth Bartholet, *Where do black Children Belong? The Politics of Race Matching in Adoption*, 139 U. Pa. L. Rev. 1163, 1198–2000 (1991).

Sometimes agencies attempt to "match" children with applicant families of similar physical stock and educational attainment as the child's birth parents, on the premise that the maturing child will fit in better with the family. While in the abstract, this approach may make some sense, particular concerns have emerged regarding agency policies as they relate to the religion, race, and national origin of prospective adoptive parents and the children who are eligible for adoption. "Matching" per se is only one of a plethora of controversial issues that have arisen in relation to the roles played in adoption policy and practice of factors such as religion, race, national origin, and sexual orientation. As noted below the discussion of some of these issues, some challenges have raised constitutional questions and some have triggered state and federal legislation.

[b]   The Role of Religion in Adoption Placement Decisions

The use of religious practice or affiliation of the prospective parents as an adoption selection criterion has generated considerable litigation, including constitutional challenges. A California court of appeal considered this factor in a famous case involving orphans brought from Cambodia by an evangelical Christian relief organization. *Scott v. Family Ministries*, 135 Cal. Rptr. 430 (1976). This group, World Vision, transferred the children to a licensed California agency, Family Ministries, with instructions that they be placed in Christian homes. After providing medical and recuperative care to one child, Dr. Scott, together with his wife, sought to adopt him. Their application was turned down, on the ground that, as Episcopalians, they were not members of an evangelical Protestant church and thus were not qualified to adopt. The Scotts challenged this decision. Relying on its interpretation of California's own statutes and of the Establishment Clause of the U.S. Constitution, the court held that private adoption agencies operating under state license are subject to the same constitutional restrictions that circumscribe other forms of state action. The court concluded, therefore, that the agency could not use religion as a factor in selecting adoptive parents except where the birth parents specifically indicated that they desire their children to be raised in their own religion. *Id.* at 437–40. This exception, the court noted, "preserves constitutionality by placing the state in a neutral position in which parentage or parents and not the state determines the religion of the home into which the child is to be adopted." *Id.* at 437. Deferring to birth parents' preferences in this context, it observed, is consistent with the "common law right of a natural parent to control the religious upbringing of his child." *Id.* In this case, there were no parental preferences expressed, and thus, the religious criterion was unconstitutional.

The analysis set forth by the *Scott* court reflects the general approach taken by those courts that have addressed this issue. *See generally* Don F. Vaccaro,

Religions as a Factor in Adoption Proceedings, 48 A.L.R.3d 383 (rev. 2009). The state and its agents must maintain a position of neutrality as it relates to the use of religion in adoption placement decisions. That said, the religion of the prospective adoptive parents, of the birth parents or, in the case of older children, the child can play a role in certain limited situations. The first exception, as noted in *Scott*, is that the state may consider religion if it is doing so in deference to the preferences of the birth parents. Thus, for example, a Delaware statute reads: "If either natural parent . . . specifies the religion in which he or she desires the child to be raised, the Department or licensed agency shall make placement in accordance with such statement." DEL. CODE § 911(a) (2009). The statute indicates further that religion will not otherwise be a factor in choosing an adoptive placement. In some jurisdictions this exception is somewhat broader, justifying a preference for a placement in which the adoptive parents practice the same religion as the birth parent(s), even if the absence of an expressed parental preference. *See, e.g.*, N.Y. SOC. SERV. LAW § 373(7) (2009) (noting deference to parental preference regarding religion of adoptive family; providing that, in the absence of an expressed preference for a particular religion or an expression of indifference, "it shall be *presumed* [unless there is evidence to the contrary] that the birth parent wishes the child to be reared in the religion of the birth parent") (emphasis added). This statute was upheld as constitutional in *Dickens v. Ernesto*, 281 N.E.2d 153, *appeal dismissed*, 407 U.S. 917 (1972), where the court determined that this policy did not violate the Establishment Clauses because it serves the secular and neutral governmental goal of promoting the child's best interests).

The second major exception relates to the court's mandate to serve the best interests of the child in making an adoption placement. Where consideration of the religious affiliation or practices of the prospective adoptive parents appear to be important to serving the child's best interests, the state is not precluded from considering religious as one among many factors influencing choice of placement. *See, e.g.*, N.J. ST. ANN. § 9:3-40 (2009) (state may not discriminate with respect to age, sex, race, national origin, or marital status of adoptive parents, but "these factors may be considered in determining whether the best interests of a child would be served by a particular placement.") However, even where the children in question have been raised previously in a particular religious tradition, a court may determine that other factors in favor of a particular placement outweigh the advantages of a religious match. *See, e.g.*, *Cooper v. Hinrichs*, 140 N.E.2d 293 (Ill. 1957) (holding that the match between the religion of the children and the adoptive family is not a dispositive factor, but one of a range of factors considered in choosing an optimal placement). Notably, another New York court held that a Catholic couple did state a claim in alleging that a placement grounded solely or predominantly on religious matching would be unconstitutional, even where the child's parents had specified a preference for such a placement. *Orzechowski v. Perales*, 582 N.Y.S.2d 341 (Sup. Ct. 1992).

The third exception, appearing only occasionally in modern state policies, allows consideration of whether prospective adoptive parents are religious as one of many factors indicating parental fitness. *See, e.g.*, MONT. STAT. § 42-4-201 (2009) (religion may be considered "as it relates to the ability to provide the child with an opportunity for religious or spiritual and ethical development"). While this statute has not been challenged, a New Jersey court held that the absence of a religious affiliation or beliefs cannot be used to exclude prospective adoptive parents. *See, e.g., In re Adoption of "E.",* 279 A.2d 785 (N.J. 1971) (otherwise qualified parents cannot be excluded solely because they do not believe in a "Supreme Being").

For further commentary on the role of religion in selecting adoptive placements see, e.g., Martha Minow, *All in the Family and in All Families: Membership, Loving and Owing,* 95 W. VA. L. REV. 275 (1993); Laura J. Schwartz, *Religious Matching for Adoption: Unraveling the Interests Behind the "Best Interests" Standard,* 25 FAM. L.Q. 171 (1991); Gregory A. Horwitz, *Accommodation and Neutrality under the Establishment Clause: The Foster Care Challenge,* 98 YALE L.J. 617 (1989).

PROBLEM

Problem 11-5.   Peggy O'Connor relinquishes her one-year-old son, Sean, to a public adoption agency in New York. While seeking an adoptive home, the agency places Sean in foster care with the Goldbergs, who become very fond of him. They apply to adopt, but are told that they will not be considered under an agency policy of placing children with adoptive parents who share the birth mother's religion, unless the birth mother instructs them otherwise. On the basis of this policy, the agency is considering only Catholic homes for Sean, and expects to place him in one shortly. In fact, no one at the agency has ever raised the question of the adoptive parents' religion with Peggy.

The agency tells the Goldbergs that they will be happy to consider them for the next Jewish child who becomes available for adoption, since the Goldbergs appear to be well qualified. The Goldbergs will also be eligible to adopt a non-Jewish child if the birth parents have expressly indicated indifference as to the religion of the adoptive home. In the past five years, the agency has had one Jewish child available for adoption.

The Goldbergs come to you for help in adopting Sean. What do you advise?

[c]   The Role of Race in Adoption Placement Decisions

The phenomenon referred to as "transracial adoption," that is, the adoption of children of one race by a parent or parents of another race, has been controversial since the practice began several decades ago. According to a 2000 U.S. Census report, 17.1% of adopted children are of a different race than the adoptive parent who is the primary householder. *Adopted Children and Stepchildren: 2000,* U.S. Census Bureau at 14–15 (2003), http://www.census.gov/prod/2003pubs/censr-6.pdf.[6] Transracial adoption in the U.S. prior to the 1960s consisted primarily of adoption of children from other countries. Asian children displaced during and after wartime accounted for most of these adoptions: from Japan (after World War II), Korea (during and after the Korean War), and a smaller number from China. Arnold R. Silverman, *Outcomes of Transracial Adoption,* 3 THE FUTURE OF CHILDREN:

---

[6] As noted in Section A above, the Census focuses only on the relationship between the primary householder and the children. Therefore, it is possible some of these households are led by interracial couple, and that the child is of the same race as one of the parents.

ADOPTION 104, 104–05 (1993). Consistent with this pattern, in the 1960s and 1970s, the numbers of children adopted from Vietnam increased. In smaller numbers that gradually increased, Americans also adopted children from various Latin American nations: Columbia, El Salvador, Mexico, and most recently, Guatemala. *Id.* at 106.

Beginning in the late 1950s, interest in adopting Native American children increased and continued to rise until the passage of the Indian Child Welfare Act in 1978, discussed below. Adoption of African-American children by white families was rare prior to the 1960s. But, once the civil rights movement took hold, transracial placement was viewed by many as an expression of commitment to racial integration and a "colorblind" society. The growing importance of racial identity to black Americans, however, was reflected in opposition to transracial adoption. In 1972, the National Association of Black Social Workers (NABSW) strongly opposed this phenomenon which it characterized as injurious to the children as well as to the preservation of the heritage of African-Americans. (*See* Note 1 below.) This policy was very influential. The number of transracial adoptions of black children by white families in the U.S. dropped substantially from its peak of 2,574 in 1971. CYNTHIA MABRY & LISA KELLY, ADOPTION LAW: THEORY, POLICY, AND PRACTICE 407 (2006). Estimates of the numbers of such adoptions thereafter varies, depending on the source, with one source reporting that black-white adoptions dropped to 1,076 by 1976, rising slightly to 1,169 by 1987. Silverman, *supra*, at 106. Other sources cite a figure closer to 800 adoptions of black children by white parents by 1975. Regardless, there is no question that there was a dramatic drop in the 1970s. Unfortunately, no national figures are available after 1987, although it does appear that there has been an increase in the percentage of transracial adoptions of black children in foster care by parents who are not black between 1999 and 2004. See *Adopting Children of a Different Race*, N.Y. TIMES, Aug. 17, 2006.

The case below illustrates a not uncommon scenario, that of white foster parents who seek to adopt their black or biracial foster child. The issues raised coincide with some of the central issues in the debate about transracial adoption in the U.S.

DEWEES v. STEVENSON
United States District Court, Eastern District of Pennsylvania
779 F. Supp. 25 (1991)

WALDMAN, DISTRICT JUDGE.

[Mr. and Mrs. DeWees] seek to enjoin [the Chester County Children and Youth Services, referred to hereinafter as CCCYS] from refusing to consider [them] as adoptive parents for their foster child . . . [They] allege that [CCCYS] refused to [allow them] to adopt Dante because of their race [in violation of] the equal protection and due process guarantees of the Fourteenth Amendment. . . .

Plaintiffs are a white couple . . . married for 27 years and who reside in Royersford, Pennsylvania in an almost exclusively white area. Mrs. DeWees is a high school graduate and housewife. Mr. DeWees is the maintenance manager for a trucking company. Plaintiffs have three natural children, ages 26, 23 and 21 years, and five grandchildren for whom they have cared. [¶] . . . In January of

1988, plaintiffs applied to CCCYS to be foster parents. During the ensuing review and evaluation process, Mrs. DeWees stated that she did not want to take any black foster children because "[she] did not want people to think that [she] or her daughter were sleeping with a black man." According to Mrs. DeWees, she gave this reason because she was reluctant to give her real reason which was her concern that she would not know how to take care of a black child. Plaintiffs requested for placement children under three years of age because they felt they "couldn't deal with children after three years old." CCCYS approved plaintiffs as foster parents and entered into a foster parents agreement with them on May 9, 1988. The agreement provides, inter alia, that CCCYS shall have all responsibility for planning for any foster child.

Pursuant to the agreement, CCCYS variously placed seven foster children with plaintiffs. They were from two to twenty months in age. Three were black and two were bi-racial. Plaintiffs never received any complaints from CCCYS about their care of any foster child. Plaintiffs' attitude about black children changed and they came "to accept them as any other child."

On November 10, 1989, CCCYS placed Dante Kirby, then two months old, with plaintiffs. Since August 20, 1991, Dante is [the DeWees'] only remaining foster child. Plaintiffs understood that Dante's placement with them was not permanent. On three different occasions Dante was to be returned to his parents, but it did not work out as planned.

Dante's mother is white and his father is black. On November 12, 1991, with their consent, their parental rights were terminated by the Chester County Court of Common Pleas.

[Mr. and Mrs. DeWees] have cared well for Dante. They provide him with his own room and interact frequently with him. He plays and interacts well with [the DeWees] grandchildren. They have supplemented the amounts provided by CCCYS for clothing and toys, and have provided Dante with medical care for his respiratory problems. There clearly is a bond of mutual affection between plaintiffs and Dante.

On June 13, 1991, after being advised by Dante's caseworker that Dante's mother and father intended to relinquish their parental rights, [Mr. and Mrs. DeWees] wrote to [CCCYS] to express an interest in adopting Dante. [In response, CCCYS proceeded with a full home study, including evaluation by a family therapist and a social worker. The social worker, who has] 20 years of experience in the field of adoption[,] has placed bi-racial children with white, black and bi-racial adoptive parents respectively. She is white. Dr. Crumbley is a family therapist and consultant with a Ph.D. in social work. He is a consultant to three adoption agencies and among his areas of specialization are child abuse, foster care and adoption. He has experience with trans-racial adoptions. He is black.

Dr. Crumbley forwarded an evaluation and recommendation to [CCCYS] on September 11, 1991. He concluded that although Dante was emotionally attached to plaintiffs, they would not be appropriate adoptive parents. . . . Dr. Crumbley was concerned about plaintiffs' responses that race had "no impact" on developing a child's identity and self-esteem, that addressing racial issues was not important in raising a minority child; and, that they would not prepare Dante to deal with racial discrimination but rather would address the problem if and when it occurred. He was also concerned about plaintiffs' lack of friends in and contact with the minority community, and Mrs. DeWees' statement that she would "not manufacture black friends." Dr. Crumbley concluded that plaintiffs lacked the ability to: be sufficiently sensitive to the needs of a bi-racial child during the critical period of socialization, self-identification and personality development of age two through six years; educate a minority child about prejudice and provide him with the skills effectively to respond to it; and, provide positive bi-racial and minority role models through interaction with the minority community.

[CCCYS ultimately] concluded that [Mr. and Mrs. DeWees] lacked the sensitivity to racial issues and inter-racial network of community resources needed properly to raise Dante [and denied their request to adopt Dante]. Since [learning of that decision,] plaintiffs have a greater realization of the importance of the issues identified by Dr. Crumbley and are willing to undertake any course of action recommended by defendants to prepare to address the needs of a bi-racial child. They are willing to "grow and learn." They have located and are prepared to participate in a support group of trans-racial adoptive families.

[Dr. Crumbley expressed concern that, while the DeWees may be able to learn to meet] Dante's race-related psychological and social needs with appropriate counseling, education and training[, this process would take too long to meet Dante's current needs.] The court has no expertise in the area of cross-racial adoption. Nevertheless, the court cannot accept Dr. Crumbley's view that generally only whites with extensive specialized training or who have experienced discrimination themselves will be able adequately to address the needs of a minority child in his or her formative years. The court does find that particular sensitivity, awareness and skills are necessary for a successful trans-racial adoption of a young child, and that Dr. Crumbley based his recommendation on his conclusion that plaintiffs had not demonstrated those qualities and could acquire them only over a long period.

CCCYS [is prepared] to place Dante for adoption with any suitable couple, regardless of race, who appear to her to have the awareness, sensitivity and skills to address adequately the needs of a bi-racial child in his formative years. Her decision was based on the perceived best interests of the child, and not on the color of plaintiffs' skins.

To sustain their due process claim, plaintiffs must show that they are being deprived of a federally secured right by persons acting under color of state law. . . . Foster parents do not have a cognizable liberty interest in maintaining a relationship with a foster child vis-a-vis prospective adoptive parents, particularly where the relationship is based on a contract under which the state retains responsibility for the child and places him in a foster home on a temporary basis. . . .

The essence of the equal protection clause is a requirement that similarly situated people be treated alike. . . . Racial classifications are inherently suspect and can survive an equal protection challenge only if they are necessary to achieve a compelling state interest. The state's responsibility to protect the best interests of a child in its custody is a compelling interest for purposes of the equal protection clause. . . . Because of the potential difficulties inherent in a trans-racial adoption, a state agency may consider race and racial attitudes in assessing prospective adoptive parents.

While the degree of plaintiffs' sensitivity and attitudes about racial issues may be related to their race and experience as whites in a white majority society, [CCCYS] refused their request to adopt a minority child because of perceptions about their attitudes and not their race. To the extent that perceived attitudes about race and coping with race-related problems motivated [the CCCYS] decision, this was Constitutionally permissible in determining the best interests of a young child eligible for adoption.

Plaintiffs have failed to establish on the record adduced and under applicable legal precedent and principles that their due process or equal protection rights have been violated. The court has not found that plaintiffs are in any way unfit or could not acquire the knowledge and skills necessary to provide for Dante's future needs. . . . This court is not empowered to sit as a super adoption agency review board. The court thus is not passing upon the wisdom of [CCCYS'] actions but only on whether they were motivated by Constitutionally impermissible considerations of race. The court has found that defendants made a considered judgment based on professional input and Constitutionally permissible factors.

This finding turns on the importance of awareness of and sensitivity to issues of race in the context of a trans-racial adoption. These factors, in turn, are important largely because of the realities of the larger society in which we live. . . . In making adoption decisions, state agencies cannot ignore the realities of the society in which children entrusted to them for placement will be raised, or the effect on children of those realities as documented by professional studies. The court would hope, however, that these agencies also will be mindful of the possibility that an overemphasis on racial issues may retard efforts to achieve a color blind society, and of the need to avoid even the appearance that an adoption decision may have been based on race per se.

NOTES

1. *Opposition to Transracial Adoptions and Alternative Viewpoints.* As noted above, in 1972, the National Association of Black Social Workers (NABSW) issued a position statement opposing transracial adoption of African-American children. The NABSW policy has been repeatedly reaffirmed by that organization. The original statement emphasized that, in order to function effectively in a society still characterized by racism, black children must learn sophisticated coping strategies that cannot be effectively taught if they are not raised by black parents. In addition, NABSW emphasized the importance to African-American children of a socialization process that includes in-depth exposure to their cultural heritage. NABSW, "Position Statement on Trans-Racial Adoption," September 1972, reprinted by The Adoption History Project, http://www.uoregon.edu/~adoption/archive/NabswTRA.htm (citing CHILDREN AND YOUTH IN AMERICA: A DOCUMENTARY HISTORY, Vol. 3, 777 (Robert H. Bremner, ed. 1974)). In 1994, NABSW elaborated substantially on its concerns and proposals.

While it is true that a key theme in the NABSW position is its concern that transracial adoptions do not serve the best interests of the adopted children, the organization seeks to focus attention on what it sees as the root *causes* of the disproportionate representation of black children in the child welfare system. It emphasizes that current state policies create the racial imbalance in that system. It further recommends changes to: (1) stop unnecessary out-of-home placements of children by the child welfare system; (2) reunify removed children with their parents; (3) favor placements of African-American children with relatives or others of the same race and culture; (4) reduce barriers to adoptions by African-American families; (5) promote culturally-relevant child welfare practices; and (6) consider transracial adoption as a last resort, when attempts to place children with families of similar race and culture have been unsuccessful. *See* NABSW, *Preserving Families of African Ancestry*, NABSW website at: http://www.nabsw.org/mserver/ PreservingFamilies.aspx. Thus, the crux of the NABSW view is that the problem of a disproportionate number of black children waiting for adoption in foster care lies not in the unavailability of permanent homes for these children. Rather, the real problem is *the failure of child welfare system policies to respond appropriately to the needs of African American children and their families well before a child is freed for adoption.* In other words, it asserts that reforms in the child welfare system can substantially reduce the numbers of African American children who end up in that system. And, even for those children for whom state intervention is appropriate, NABSW proposes less intrusive and more culturally-sensitive intervention, which makes effective use of existing family and other resources in the African-American community. These changes in approach, they argue, will substantially reduce the numbers of black children waiting for adoption in foster care. Professor Dorothy Roberts articulates similar views. In a recent article, she asserts:

> [D]isproportionate [child welfare system] intervention in black families reinforces the continued political subordination of blacks as a group. . . . [¶] Many well-meaning people think that the best way to help the thousands of black children in foster care is to terminate their parents' rights and place them in better adoptive homes. They do not see themselves as racists who are bent on destroying black families. They may even endorse stronger programs to provide social supports for America's struggling families. But they believe child protective services must intervene immediately to save black children from their current crisis.

Dorothy L. Roberts, *Child Welfare & Civil Rights*, 2003 U. ILL. L. REV. 171, 181; *see also*, DOROTHY L. ROBERTS, SHATTERED BONDS: THE COLOR OF CHILD WELFARE (2001); Sarah Ramsey, *Fixing Foster Care or Reducing Child Poverty: The Pew Commission Recommendations and the Transracial Adoption Debate*, 66 MONT. LA. REV. 21, 47–48 (2005) ("Opponents believe that children of color should be kept out of a racist foster care system by directing more assistance to low-income families. Proponents want to fix foster care by rescuing foster children who have been abused and neglected by their parents and placing them in homes that are separated from their troubled kin and communities").

Both the NABSW and Professor Roberts focus on two interrelated sources of harm attributable to transracial adoption of black children by white families: harms to the child and harms to the race. Various arguments have been raised, addressing the first question, which relates, of course, to the primary articulated goal of adoption policy: Does adoption of African-American children by white parents hinder or promote the best interests of the child? Some commentators argue that African-American parents are better able to inculcate racial identity and pride than are white parents. Placing black children with adoptive parents of the same race is also important, advocates argue, to help black children develop coping skills to deal with the racial discrimination that is unavoidable in American society. White parents arguably, will not understand the experience of being black in America, and cannot teach the necessary coping skills. Moreover, removed from the security of the black community, African American children growing up in a white home and neighborhood may experience even more discrimination than she would in a black family. Twila Perry, *The Transracial Adoption Controversy: An Analysis of Discourse and Subordination*, 21 N.Y.U. Rev. of L. & Soc. Change 33 (1993–94) (describing the importance of "survivor skills" from the "color and community conscious" perspective of opponents of transracial adoption). Consider what influence these views might have had on the social service workers and the judge in the *DeWees* case.

Race matching policies in adoption are also justified under a collective "group rights" theory. If a substantial number of African American children are adopted by white families (and therefore not developing an appropriate sense of cultural and racial identity), the African American community will be diminished and its future will be threatened. This theme of minority group rights is powerfully endorsed by the Supreme Court as applied to Native Americans, in its interpretation of the Indian Child Welfare Act in *Mississippi Band of Choctow Indians v. Holyfield*, 490 U.S. 30 (1989) (*see* discussion *infra*). It also received recognition in *Yoder v. Wisconsin* (*see* Chapter 10). *See* Perry, *supra* (describing the stake of the black community in transracial adoption); Jacinda T. Townsend, *Reclaiming Self Determination: A Call for Intraracial Adoption*, 2 Duke J Gender L. & Pol'y 173 (1995) (describing transracial adoption as the black community's loss of its children).

At the other end of the spectrum of views on transracial adoption, there are those who advocate for "color blind" adoption placements. One of the most vocal critics of race-matching policies is Professor Elizabeth Bartholet, who asserts that race-matching policies "represent a coming together of powerful and related ideologies — old-fashioned white racism, modern-day black nationalism, and what I will call 'biologism' [which is the view that] adoption in this country [should be] structured . . . in imitation of biology." *Where Do Black Children Belong? The Politics of Race Matching in Adoption*, 139 U. Pa. L. Rev. 1163, 1172–73 (1991). She points to the negative repercussions children experience remaining in foster care, either bonding with foster parents from whom they will eventually become separated, or without the opportunity to experience "the kind of bonding that is generally thought crucial to healthy development." *Id.* at 1255. Indeed, this argument is probably the one most often cited to support transracial adoption. Black children wait on average twice as long as white children for permanent homes, in part because the pool of African American prospective adoptive parents is not large enough to absorb the black children who need adoptive homes (and it is proportionately far smaller than the pool of white prospective parents). David S. Rosettenstein, *Trans-Racial Adoption and the Statutory Preference Scheme: Before the "Best Interests" and*

After the "Melting Pot," 68 ST. JOHN'S L. REV. 137, 142 (1994). Some authors point out that: "While we are pondering the efficacy of transracial adoptions, . . . tens of thousands of children are waiting for a home. . . . [They] do not have racial preferences. They just want their own family, a 'forever family' — quickly." Cynthia R. Mabry, *"Love Alone Is Not Enough" in Transracial Adoptions — Scrutinizing Recent Statutes, Agency Policies, and Prospective Adoptive Parents*, 42 WAYNE. L. REV. 1347, 1423 (1996). Can more black adoptive parents be found for these children? Because of lower income levels and lower proportions of two-parent families, fewer black applicants than whites qualify under traditional agency standards. However, many agencies now relax those standards in order to place black children in African American homes, and financially subsidies are available for some of these adoptions. Consider whether these arguments may have influenced the court in *DeWees*, or how the outcome might have differed if these perspectives prevailed. Note that, at the time the agency concluded that Mr. and Mrs. DeWees were not satisfactory adoptive parents for Dante, there were no other families ready to adopt Dante. The DeWees were the only consistent caregivers in Dante's life, and no one disputed that Dante had established an emotionally-bonded relationship with his foster parents. How should the existence of such a bond figure into the decisionmaking process?

Countering the claims that black children need black parents in order to establish a healthy identity and sense of belonging, one author argues that the dissimilarity in appearance between a child and adoptive parents can help the child to accept her racial *and* adoptive identities, giving her the freedom to develop as an individual. Jennifer Swize, Student Author, *Transracial Adoption and the Unlikable Difference: Racial Dissimilarity Serving the Interests of Adopted Children*, 88 VA. L. REV. 1079 (2002). Another author argues that a positive racial identity need not be a strong racial identity and that white parents can teach their children to value their racial identity and inculcate black culture, although probably not as capably as black parents. Kim Forde-Mazrui, *Black Identity and Child Placement: The Best Interests of the Child and Biracial Children*, 92 MICH. L. REV. 925 (1994). In a provocative challenge to racial separationism in sex, marriage and adoption, Randall Kennedy advocates that individuals should be allowed to determine their own racial identities and opposes race matching for "assign[ing] children a permanent racial identity." RANDALL KENNEDY, INTERRACIAL INTIMACIES: SEX, MARRIAGE, IDENTITY AND ADOPTION (2003). All of these arguments pro and con transracial adoption become even more challenging when one acknowledges that many of the children waiting for adoption are biracial. How should they be regarded in a regime that favors or disfavors race matching? See Julie C. Lythcott-Haims, Student Author, *Where do Mixed Babies Belong? Racial Classification in America and its Implications for Transracial Adoption*, 29 HARV. CIV. RTS-CIV. LIBERTIES L. REV. 531 (1994).

2. *The Psychological Adjustment of Transracially-Adopted Children.* In the last few decades, researchers have studied how children who were transracially adopted have fared psychologically. The findings reveal that the policies and practices that will best serve African American children waiting for adoption are most likely those that strike a balance between the policies and practices advocated respectively by the two groups. As two authors aptly convey in the title of their article: "The answer is neither simply black or white . . ." *See* Cynthia G. Hawkins-León & Carla Bradley, *Race And Transracial Adoption: The Answer Is Neither Simply Black or White Nor Right or Wrong*, 51 CATH. U. L. REV. 1227 (2002). Numerous studies indicate that transracial adoption in itself does not produce psychological or social maladjustment in children.

In other words, most transracially adopted children manifest healthy psychological and social adjustment. Approximately 70–80% of children adopted transracially showed few adjustment problems, consistent with the percentages experienced by children adopted by parents of the same race, and nonadopted children. *See, e.g.*, Richard M. Lee, *The Transracial Adoption Paradox: History, Research, and Counseling Implications of Cultural Socialization*, 31 COUNSEL. PSYCHOL. 711 (2003); Susan Smith et al., Evan B. Donaldson Adoption Institute, *Finding Families for African American Children: The Role of Race & Law in Adoption from Foster Care: Policy and Practice Perspective* (May 2008), http://www.adoptioninstitute.org/publications/MEPApaper20080527.pdf; Arnold R. Silverman, *Outcomes of Transracial Adoption*, 3 FUTURE OF CHILDREN 104 (1993). In one study, investigators compiled data over 17 years on the psychological adjustment of black, white, and Asian children adopted by Caucasian parents. The investigators found that male adoptees in the sample had a greater likelihood of manifesting adjustment problems than did female adoptees, regardless of whether their adoption was transracial or inracial. There were some differences among the racial groups within the male portion of the sample: Asian male adoptees experienced the fewest academic and behavioral difficulties. White and black male adoptees experienced the highest level of adjustment problems. Devon Brooks & Richard P. Barth, *Adult Transracial and Inracial Adoptees: Effects of Race, Gender, Adoptive Family Structure, and Placement History on Adjustment Outcomes*, 69 J. ORTHOPSYCHIATRY 87 (1999). In addition, while the girls in all three racial categories manifested higher levels of adjustment than did the boys, where differences among the girls were evident, the white girls appeared less well-adjusted than the transracially adopted Asian and black girls. The authors conclude that these results do not support the proposition that transracial adoptions necessarily place children at risk for maladjustment. In another study, Richard Weinberg and colleagues found that transracial adoptees manifested more behavioral difficulties than did the white or Asian adoptees, but the finding was explained by *the later age* at which the black adoptees were placed for adoption. Richard A. Weinberg et al., *The Minnesota Transracial Adoption Study: Parent Reports of Psychological Adjustment in Late Adolescence*, 8 ADOPTION Q. 27 (2004). For a more extensive review of the research, see Lee, *supra*; Smith, *supra*.

Studies reveal that some transracially-adopted children find it challenging to deal with the differences in physical appearances between them and the rest of their adoptive family. This challenge is exacerbated if their family lives in a predominantly white, rather than integrated, neighborhood. Smith, *supra* at 24–25. Transracial adoptees were also less likely than children adopted intraracially to incorporate a clear and strong sense of racial identity. *Id. See also* Kim DeBerry et al., *Family Socialization and Ecological Competence: Longitudinal Assessments of African-American Transracial Adoptees*, 67 CHILD DEV. 2375 (1996). Some transraciallly-adopted children and young adults reported feeling at times like outsiders of both black and white cultures, not quite feeling as if they belong to either. Smith, *supra*. While the studies do not demonstrate any overall impact on the adoptees' self-esteem, Smith *supra*, or general psychological adjustment, *see*, *e.g.*, Amanda L. Baden et al., *The Psychological Adjustment of Transracial Adoptees: An Application of the Cultural-Racial Identity Model*, 11 J. Soc. DISTRESS & THE HOMELESS, 167 (2002), it is nonetheless of concern that some of these children experience these feelings. On the positive side, studies reveal that when adoptive parents "facilitate their children's understanding of and comfort with their own ethnicities, the children show more positive adjustment in terms of higher levels of self-esteem, lower feelings of marginality, greater ethnic pride, less distress, and better psychological adjustment." Smith, *supra* at 27 (summarizing studies).

There is not much empirical research addressing the question of whether or not black children adopted by white families have greater difficulty coping with racial discrimination than do children adopted by same-race parents. There are some self-reports provided by transracial adoptees indicating that preparation for dealing with discrimination is important for African-American children. *See* Smith, *supra*, at 26. It makes sense that adoptive parents should be sensitive to the challenges or racial prejudice their adopted children may experience. Open discussion with parents about these issues may be helpful. Furthermore, parents can facilitate other learning opportunities, such as conversations about these issues with African-American family friends, teachers, coaches, or mentors. Reading materials, movies, and formal or informal support groups might also help transracially-adopted children deal with the challenges that racial prejudice may present as they make their way into the larger community.

In light of the research findings reported above, do you think that the decision in *DeWees* was correct?

3. *Legal Policies Regarding Race and Adoption Placements.* In 1972, a federal court struck down a Louisiana statute that categorically prohibited transracial placement decisions. *See, e.g., Compos v. McKeithen*, 341 F. Supp. 264 (D.C. La. 1972) (holding that while difficulties inherent in interracial adoption justify consideration of race as relevant factor in adoption, Louisiana statute prohibiting any interracial adoption is a violation of at the Equal Protection Clause). At that time, according to the court, Louisiana was the only state with such a statute still on the books; a similar Texas statute had been struck down by a court in 1967. *See Compos, id.* at 264 n.1; *In re Adoption of Gomez*, 424 S.W.2d 656 (Tex. Ct. App. 1967).

In the 1970s, 1980s, and early 1990s, many agencies applied a *preference* for placing a child in a home where the parents share the child's racial identity. *Where Do Black Children Belong? The Politics of Race Matching in Adoption*, 139 PA. L. REV. 1163 (1991). Sometimes the racial preference was set forth in the state's statutes, and if challenged, these statutes were typically struck down as unconstitutional. *See, e.g., In re D.L.*, 479 N.W.2d 408 (Minn. Ct. App. 1991); *aff'd* 486 N.W.2d 375 (Minn. 1992); *In re Moorhead*, 600 N.E.2d 778 (Ohio Ct. App. 1991). In contrast to categorical prohibitions on transracial adoptions or preferences for same-race placements, courts were more willing to allow agencies to consider race as one of several factors in individualized best interests determinations on a case-by-case basis. *See, e.g., In re Adoption No. 2633*, 646 A.2d 1036 (Md. Ct. Spec. App. 1994) (consideration of race not unconstitutional if one of several factors in best interests determination); *Tallman v. Tabor*, 859 F. Supp. 1078 (E.D. Mich. 1994) (same); *In Petition of R.M.G.*, 454 A.2d 776 (D.C. App. 1982) (same); *Drummond v. Fulton City Dep't of Family & Children's Servs.*, 563 F.2d 1200 (5th Cir. 1977) (en banc) (same).

Congress was concerned by the thousands of minority-group children who languished in foster care, waiting for adoption. It observed that the length of time African-American and Latino children waited in foster care was substantially longer than white children. Also of concern to Congress was the phenomenon discussed in Chapter 10, of "foster care drift," that is, the movement of children from one foster home to another, robbing them of the consistency, stability, and bonded emotional relationships that all children need. Viewing race-based placement decisions as partially to blame for these discrepancies in placement patterns for children of different races, Congress passed the Multi-Ethnic Placement Act (MEPA) in 1994. Congress indicated that the purpose of the legislation was to encourage "child welfare agencies [to] work to eliminate racial, ethnic, and national origin discrimination and bias in adoption and foster care recruitment, selection, and placement procedures. 42 U.S.C.A. § 5115a (1994), *repealed* Aug. 20, 1996 by Pub. L. 104-188, 110 Stat. 1904. Its provisions precluded any child welfare agency receiving federal assistance from basing foster care and adoption decisions *solely* on race, color, or national origin, and further discouraged delay or denial of adoptive placements for children *solely* on the basis of race, color, or national origin. It also contained a section with a "permissible consideration," indicating that agencies could *consider* the "cultural, ethnic, or racial background of the child and the capacity of the prospective foster or adoptive parents to meet the needs of a child of his background as one of a number of factors used to determine the best interests of the child." *Id.*

Critics of race-based placement decisions argued that MEPA did not change practices, leaving the door still open to a continuation of former agency practices. Two years later, Congress repealed the original MEPA language, replacing it with provisions that further limited the use of race in placement decisions. The 1996 provisions (referred to as the Interethnic Provisions Act) categorically prohibited — on the basis of race, color, or national origin of the adult or the child involved — the denial to anyone of the opportunity to become an adoptive or foster parent and the delay or denial of a child's placement for adoption or foster care. 42 U.S.C.A. § 1996b(1) (2009). The penalty for noncompliance was the loss of federal funding.

While Congress removed the "permissible consideration" language from the statute in 1996, it stopped short of prohibiting such considerations. Thus, for example, can agencies legitimately continue with a practice employed by some, of considering, for example, prospective adoptive parents' racial and cultural sensitivity, and their capacity to help the child develop a positive racial identity? For example, would *DeWees* be decided differently in light of the federal statute, given the concerns about the couple's racial attitudes? One court, in a contest between white foster parents and relatives of the African American child, held that race could be considered in evaluating the child's interest in "development, . . .

continuity and stability." *In re Shying B.*, 752 A.2d 1139 (Conn. App. Ct. 2000). *See also In re Infant Child J.*, 994 P.2d 279 (Wash. Ct. App. 1999) (upholding consideration of race as factor in adoption choice between two sets of parents; delay in adoption was not caused by race). A Massachusetts court held that MEPA restricts agencies, but not courts, in considering race as a factor in adoption. *Adoption of Vito*, 712 N.E.2d 1188 (Mass. App. 1999). For a discussion of the statute, see JOAN HOLLINGER, A GUIDE TO THE MULTI-ETHNIC PLACEMENT ACT OF 1994, AS AMENDED BY INTERETHNIC ADOPTION PROVISIONS OF 1996 (1998); Suzanne Brannen Campbell, *Taking Race Out of the Equation: Transracial Adoption in 2000*, 53 S.M.U. L. REV. 1599, 1617–19 (2000) (arguing that the statute has many loopholes that Congress had intended to render impermissible); *Recent Legislation — Transracial Adoption — Congress Forbids Use of Race as a Factor in Adoptive Placement Decisions*, 110 HARV. L. REV. 1352 (1997).

Can consideration of race as one of the factors in a placement decision be reconciled with *Palmore v. Sidoti*, 426 U.S. 429 (1984) (reprinted in Chapter 6)? *Palmore* held it unconstitutional for a trial court to take race into account in modifying a custody order when a Caucasian custodial mother married a black man. The Court suggested that even if the child might suffer because of the reactions of others, race could not be considered. "[T]he problems racially mixed households may pose for children . . . can[not] support a denial of constitutional rights." For a provocative argument that adoptive parents' racial preferences for children of the *same* race should be excluded, see Richard Banks, *The Color of Desire: Fulfilling Adoptive Parents' Racial Preferences Through Discriminatory State Action*, 107 YALE L.J. 875 (1998).

4. *Hard-to-Place Children.* Many who are concerned with the high numbers of children who remain in foster care, particularly older children, with a history of abuse or neglect focus on the need for agencies to expand their outreach and eligibility criteria so that more families can become adoptive parents. This approach dovetails with the goal of finding prospective adoptive parents from a wider range of racial and ethnic segments of society. For many families, finances make the prospect of adoption challenging.

The Adoption Assistance and Child Welfare Act of 1980, 42 U.S.C. § 1305, which amended Title IV of the Social Security Act, established federal involvement in monitoring, delivery and financing of state-subsidized foster care and adoption programs. The nation-wide adoption assistance program, permanently authorized under Title IV-E of the Social Security Act, 42 U.S.C. § 673 (2009), is an open-ended entitlement system contributing federal matching funds to states that provide adoption assistance payments to parents who adopt children with special needs. See Mary Eschelbach Hansen, *Raising the Cut-Off: The Empirical Case for Extending Adoption and Guardianship Subsidies from Age 18 to 21*, 13 U.C. DAVIS J. JUV. L. & POL'Y 1, 8–10 (2009) (discussing relevant federal statutes and regulations and how they interface with state policies). Parents adopting both special needs and other children receive a $10,0000 federal income tax credit to help them defray the costs of the adoption process. Public Law 107-16 (Sect. 202) (HR 1836)(2001). Another federal law intended to facilitate adoption is the 1997 Adoption and Safe Families Act, Pub. L. 105-89, 111 Stat. 2115 *codified at* 42 U.S.C. § 1305 et seq. (2008) which provides payments to states for special needs adoptions.

In a 2005 report, DHHS states that "Adoption subsidies are perhaps the single most powerful tool by which the child welfare system can encourage adoption and support adoptive families." DHHS, Understanding Adoption Subsidies: An Analysis of AFCARS Data (2005), http://aspe.hhs.gov/hsp/05/adoption-subsidies/research summary.htm. The federal Adoption Assistance Program was created by Congress in 1980 to create incentives for families who might otherwise be unable to adopt foster children with special needs to do so. The report reveals that 88% of the children adopted in 2001 were identified as "special needs," and all of those families received subsidies. The subsidies ranged from $171 to $876 per month, with a median amount of $444. Most notably, the statistical comparisons of data from the various states revealed "a significant correlation between subsidy receipt and the percentage of a state's eligible children who are adopted." *Id.* at 6. This finding is consistent with prior research indicating that the availability of subsidies is extremely influential in the decision of a family to adopt. *See* North American Council on Adoptable Children, *The Value of Adoption Subsidies: Helping Children Find Permanent Families* (2008), http://www.nacac.org/adoptionsubsidy/valueofsubsidies.pdf (summarizing empirical research findings). Not only do subsidies encourage adoption, but in the long-run, they save the state money because the cost of the subsidy is less than the cost of maintaining the child in foster care or an institution. See *Value of Adoption Subsidies*, supra at 4. Unfortunately, the subsidy rates are generally too low to cover the true costs of raising a special needs child, and often the rates are lower than those received by foster parents. Judith Rycus et al., *Confronting Barriers to Adoption Success*, 44 Fam. Ct. Rev. 210 (2006). Given the relationship that economists have observed between the availability of subsidies and adoption rates, they predict that if subsidy amounts were raised so that they truly cover the costs of children's special needs, the rate of adoption for these children would increase. Value of Adoption Subsidies, *supra*, at 7.

Beyond the economics of adoption, there are other services that would greatly enhance the likelihood that special needs children might be able to move from the foster care system to appropriate permanent homes. The most emotionally-troubled children in the foster care system may be too challenging for most families, unless additional assistance is provided. In her examination of "troubled and troublesome youth" who fall within the jurisdictions of the child welfare, juvenile justice and mental health systems, Professor Lois Weithorn examines the types of interventions that have been shown to reduce the need for institutional placements. Lois A. Weithorn, *Envisioning Second-Order Change in America's Responses to Troubled and Troublesome Youth*, 33 Hofstra L. Rev. 1305 (2005). She reviews the empirical literature revealing that certain intensive home-based interventions demonstrate a high level of success with some of the most difficult youth. *Id.* at 1491–1500. The interventions provide intensive skilled support and training to parents, whether the parents are birth parents, adoptive parents, or foster parents. In addition, these interventions are cost-effective and are likely to save the state funds as well as improving the adoption prospects for some of the most difficult "hard-to-place" children.

[d]   The Indian Child Welfare Act of 1978

In 1978 Congress enacted the Indian Child Welfare Act (ICWA), which was designed specifically to reduce the incidence of transracial adoption of Native American children. During much of the 1960s, many Indian children were placed in white homes, partly as a result of the Indian Adoption Project. The events leading to the passage of the ICWA are described by Professor Barbara Atwood:

> State child welfare officials . . . worked to "protect" Indian children by removing them from their families and tribes and placing them with non-Indian care-givers. The bias and cultural myopia of state child welfare authorities surfaced in a variety of ways: in particular, they too readily concluded that children who were being cared for by extended family were the victims of neglect, and they too often characterized impoverished parents as unfit. At the same time, the Indian Adoption Project mobilized state authorities to identify Indian children for adoption by white couples. As a result of the confluence of these factors, by the second half of the twentieth century a disturbingly high proportion of Indian children lived in out-of-home care.

Barbara Ann Atwood, *Achieving Permanency for American Indian and Alaskan Children: Lessons from Tribal Traditions*, 37 CAP. U. L. REV. 239, 243 (2008). Indeed, "Congress found that in some states more than one-fourth of all Indian children were living in out-of-home placements." *Id.* at 243 n.16. The parental rights of large numbers of Native American children were quickly terminated by state courts, leading to these children's adoption by non-Indian families. Advocates argued that white social workers and judges were contemptuous of Indian culture or, at best, misunderstood Indian traditions as reflected in domestic life and child rearing. These removal and adoption practices threatened the survival of the tribes themselves.

The Indian Child Welfare Act of 1978, 92 Stat. 3069, codified in large part at 25 U.S.C. § 1901 et seq. (1983), sought to remedy this problem through both jurisdictional and substantive reforms. The Act overrides conflicting state adoption laws insofar as Indian children are concerned. In pursuit of its express objective of both promoting the welfare of Indian children and preserving the stability of Indian tribes, the statute gives tribal courts exclusive jurisdiction over the adoption of Indian children living on a reservation, displacing the jurisdiction of state courts. § 1911. For Indian children not domiciled on a reservation, tribal and state courts have concurrent jurisdiction. In foster care placement or termination of parental rights cases, either the tribe or the Indian parent can petition and have the case transferred to tribal court. In placing Indian children for adoption, the Act creates a statutory preference for (1) members of the child's extended family, (2) members of the tribe, or (3) other Indian families. § 1915. The Act also creates a statutory rule allowing an Indian parent to revoke consent to adoption at any time prior to the entry of the final adoption decree, thus overriding contrary state law limiting the birth mother's right to revoke. *See, e.g., Appeal in Pima Cty. Juvenile Action No. 5-903*, 635 P.2d 187 (Ariz. App. 1981); *Adoption of K.L.R.F.*, 515 A.2d 33 (Pa. Super. 1986), *appeal dismissed as moot*, 533 A.2d 708 (Pa. 1987). Parental consent can be set aside for up to two years after entry of the adoption decree where fraud or duress can be shown. § 1913. Finally, the Act contains many provisions applicable to foster care placements and the termination of parental rights, making terminations more difficult, and establishing preferences in placements favoring Indian families. For example, termination of parental rights requires a determination, proved *beyond a reasonable doubt*, and supported by qualified expert witnesses, that the parent's continued custody is likely to result in serious emotional or physical damage. § 1912 (f). There has been some debate over whether the Act's displacement of state law is constitutional, although in general the Act has been sustained. *See, e.g., Guardianship of D.L.L. & C.L.L.*, 291 N.W.2d 278 (S.D. 1980).

For some time, there was also doubt about the extent to which the Act in fact displaced state court jurisdiction in favor of tribal courts, but these doubts were largely resolved in *Mississippi Band of Choctaw Indians v. Holyfield*, 490 U.S. 30 (1989), *rev'g* 511 So. 2d 918 (Miss. 1987). Under the Act, tribal courts have exclusive jurisdiction over Indian children "domiciled" on the reservation. When an Indian mother domiciled on the reservation gives birth to a child off a reservation, does the child assume the mother's reservation domicile, or the off-reservation domicile of the place where she is born? Most courts held that the Act required them to yield jurisdiction to tribal courts, even if the mother had left the reservation for the purpose of relinquishing the child to non-Indian adoptive parents. *See In re Halloway*, 732 P.2d 962 (Utah 1987). Some courts, such as the Mississippi Supreme Court in *Holyfield*, concluded otherwise.

Holyfield involved twin Native American babies who were born to an unmarried Indian mother. Both parents were members of the Mississippi band of Choctaw Indians and were domiciled on a reservation. The children were born 200 miles from the reservation because the mother sought to have the children adopted by a non-Indian family, the Holyfields. Both parents signed a consent-to-adoption form within two weeks of the birth. The Holyfields quickly petitioned for adoption, which was finalized shortly thereafter. Two months later the Tribe petitioned to set the adoption decree aside on the ground that the children were domiciliaries of the reservation, giving the tribal court had exclusive jurisdiction. The Mississippi Supreme Court concluded that these children were not domiciled on the reservation and that state courts therefore retain jurisdiction.

In reversing the Mississippi Supreme Court, the U.S. Supreme Court concluded that Congress intended a uniform national rule of jurisdiction in these cases, rather than to allow the definition of domicile to depend on state law. The use of state law to determine the key jurisdictional provision would undercut the Act's purpose to protect Indian families and tribes from state authority. The Court instead applied a common law rule that a child assumed the domicile of its parents (or, in the case of a nonmarital child, its mother). It noted that application of that rule here was particularly appropriate since it is consistent with the Congressional purpose of expanding exclusive tribal court jurisdiction. The Court did not consider persuasive that the parents had voluntarily relinquished their parental rights, and indeed, had gone to great lengths to give birth to the twins off the reservation so that the Holyfields could adopt them. The Court concluded that Congress's purpose was to protect tribal sovereignty over children born to reservation domiciliaries, even where the child's parents seek to avoid tribal authority to facilitate a non-Indian placement of their child. In short, tribal authority trumps the interests of Indian families where the two are in conflict. It quoted the 1977 Final Report of the congressionally established American Indian Policy Review Commission in articulating its dual concerns that "[r]emoval of Indian children from their cultural setting seriously impacts long-term tribal survival and has damaging social and psychological impact on many individual Indian children.: *Id.* at 1608–09.

In dissent, Justice Stevens, joined by Justices Rehnquist and Kennedy, focused on the conflict of the majority decision with constitutional protection of parental autonomy. He would have protected the choice of individual Indian parents by allowing them to choose an off-reservation domicile for their children for the purpose of facilitating an adoption by non-Indian persons. For a criticism of *Holyfield's* emphasis on domicile, see Wendy Lewis, Student Author, *The Role of Domicile in Adopting Indian Children: Mississippi Band of Choctaw Indians v. Holyfield*, 1990 UTAH L. REV. 899.

One issue that has been the subject of controversy (and litigation) since *Holyfield* is whether the ICWA only applies to children who are part of an "existing Indian family," from which they are being removed. The argument for the "existing Indian family" rule is that Congress' purpose in enacting the ICWA was to preserve American Indian culture by preventing the removal of children from Indian families and tribes. This purpose arguably is only relevant if the child's parents have significant social, cultural or political ties to the tribe. Thus, if the Indian parent has never lived on the reservation and has no connection with the tribe except membership, or if the child lives with a non-Indian parent before the placement issue arises, tribal jurisdiction under the ICWA may depend on whether the "existing Indian family" rule is applied. In the case of *In re Santos Y*, a California Court of Appeal took notice of the "split of authority [that] has developed between state courts adopting the doctrine, and those declining to do so." 112 Cal. Rptr. 2d 692, 716 (2001). It recognized that "[a]t present, nine states have adopted the doctrine, nine states have rejected it, and the position of the remaining states is unclear." *Id.* It noted also that "Congress considered amending the ICWA to preclude application of the 'existing Indian family doctrine' but did not do so." *Id.* at 717. Furthermore, the U.S. Supreme Court has denied certiorari. In *Santos*, the child had lived with foster parents off the reservation since birth (2-1/2 years), and had minimal contact with his birth parents, neither of whom lived on a reservation, and both of which the court described as "assimilated." *Id.* at 726. While acknowledging that preserving Native American culture is a significant, perhaps even compelling, governmental interest, the Court held that interest is not served by applying the ICWA in this case. It concluded that "[t]here is no Indian family here to preserve," and held that application of the ICWA to remove a child who is genetically one-quarter Indian, and who has lived all of his life with non-Indian foster parents would violate the child's Due Process and Equal Protection rights to continue his relationship with the only family he has ever known: his foster parents. *Id.* at 726. For other courts adopting the existing Indian family rule, see, e.g., *Rye v. Weasel*, 934 S.W.2d 257 (Ky. 1996); *In re Adoption of Crews*, 825 P.2d 305 (Wash. 1992); *In re Adoption of T.R.M.*, 525 N.E.2d 298 (Ind. 1988). For courts that have rejected this doctrine on the grounds that it undermines the purpose the ICWA, *see, e.g., In re Adoption of Baby Boy L.*, 103 P.3d 1099 (Okla.

2004); *A.B. v. K.B.*, 663 N.W.2d 625 (N.D. 2003); *Adoption of Riffle*, 922 P.2d 510 (Mont. 1996); *A.B.M. v. M.H.*, 651 P.2d 1170, 1173 (Alaska 1982).

How did Native American children fare, growing up in white families? In a study of Native American children adopted transracially published in 1972, David Fanschel found that most (78%) of the 97 children studied were well-adjusted. FAR FROM THE RESERVATION (1972). He also indicated, however, that this result does not necessarily support the removal of children from Indian communities for adoption by whites. Rather, he noted that other important concerns are prominent, such as Indians' rights of self-determination regarding the upbringing of their children, and their rights to sustain their heritage.

For additional discussion of the ICWA, see Barbara Ann Atwood, *The Voice of the Indian Child: Strengthening the Indian Child Welfare Act through Children's Participation*, 59 ARIZ. L. REV. 127 (2008) (arguing that children whose interest are at stake in child welfare proceedings under the ICWA should play a role in these proceedings); Barbara Ann Atwood, *Achieving Permanency for American Indian and Alaska Native Children: Lessons from Tribal Traditions*, 37 CAP. U. L. REV. 239 (2008) (proposing a model grounded in tribal values, to promote permanent placements for children under the ICWA); Christine D. Bakeis, *The Indian Child Welfare Act of 1978: Violating Personal Rights for the Sake of the Tribe*, 10 NOTRE DAME J. L., ETH. & PUB. POL'Y 543 (1996) (critiquing the ICWA); Lorie M. Graham, *"The Past Never Vanishes": A Contextual Critique of the Existing Indian Family Doctrine*, 23 AM. INDIAN L. REV. 1 (1998); Joan Heifetz Hollinger, *Beyond the Best Interests of the Tribe: The Indian Child Welfare Act and the Adoption of Indian Children*, 63 U. DET. L. REV. 451 (1989). Randall Kennedy challenges the ICWA as part of a broader critique of race matching policies in adoption. RANDALL KENNEDY, INTERRACIAL INTIMACIES: SEX, MARRIAGE, IDENTITY AND ADOPTION (2003).

[e]   Intercountry Adoption

As described in Section A, intercountry adoptions have increased in recent years, and constitute approximately 15% of adoptions by Americans. Many children adopted from other nations are of a different race from their adoptive parents. Thus, many of these adoptions invoke some of the same concerns raised above with respect to transracial adoptions. Children adopted from other nations are likely to benefit from parental guidance and support in learning about their ancestry and the nation and culture into which they were born. At least 70% of these adoptions are handled by agencies; the remainder are transacted privately. Generally, the agencies that handle intercountry adoptions specialize in these types of adoptions, and usually focus on a particular region of the world.

There are a range of issues and controversies surrounding intercountry adoption by Americans. First, some oppose such adoption, believing instead that Americans who wish to adopt should focus on children in the U.S. who are waiting for adoptive homes. In response, however, proponents of intercountry adoption point out that "[h]undreds of thousands of parentless children die each year from neglect, poverty, malnutrition and disease." Lisa Myers, *Preserving the Best Interests of the World's Children: Implementing the Hague Treaty on Intercountry Adoption Through Public-Private Partnerships*, 6 RUTGERS J. L. & PUB. POL'Y 780,

780 (2009) (observing that while 600,000 children in the U.S. are in the foster care system, there are "1.5 million children in Central and Eastern Europe forced to live in orphanages"). *See also* Rebecca Worthington, *The Road to Parentless Children is Paved with Good Intentions: How the Hague Convention and Recent Intercountry Adoption Rule are Affecting Potential Parents and the Best Interests of Children*, 19 DUKE J. COMP. & INT'L L. 559 (2009) (citing 2003 estimates that there are approximately 15 million orphans "in 93 countries in sub-Saharan Africa, Asia, Latin American, and the Caribbean"). While it is true that thousands of American children remain in foster care, the plight of orphaned children in other parts of the world is also compelling.

A second concern about intercountry adoption converges with those raised above regarding transracial adoption. Worthington, *supra* at 563–64. That is, will children of different races and ethnic backgrounds adjust well here in the U.S., given the differences between their backgrounds and those of their adoptive parents? Applying the research findings regarding transracial adoption above, we might predict that these children will face some challenges regarding their racial/ethnic identities, but that parental support and exposure to people and traditions connecting them to their biological, cultural, and national roots can help children to cope with these challenges.

A third, and very important concern, is that demand by Americans has created a black market in which babies are sold by parents or procured through theft, fraud, or force, and in which vulnerable birth parents and children are exploited. *See, e.g.*, Worthington, *supra*, at 562–63; Jonathan G. Stein, *A Call to End Baby Selling: Why the Hague Convention on Intercountry Adoption Should be Modified to Include the Consent Provisions of the Uniform Adoption Act*, 24 THOM. JEFFERSON L. REV. 39 (2001–02). Adoptive parents may be disadvantaged as well, in that there may be inadequate or inaccurate information about the children's health and well-being.

The Hague Conference on Private International Law adopted the Hague Convention on Cooperation in Respect to Intercountry Adoption on May 29, 1993. The Hague Convention seeks to regulate intercountry adoptions so as to reduce or eliminate the abuses cited above, while maximizing the mutual opportunities for prospective adoptive parents and needy children to find each other. *See, e.g.*, Gabriela Marquez, *Transnational Adoption: The Creation and Ill Effects of an International Black Market Baby Trade*, 21 J. JUV. L. 25 (2000). The United States was relatively late in ratifying the Convention, adopting it fifteen years after the first nations did so. Congress passed the Intercountry Adoption Act in 2000. The federal regulations implementing the Act were not finalized until 2007, however. The Convention became effective in the United States on April 1, 2008. For additional information about the United States' participation as provided by the U.S. Dept of State, see http://travel.state.gov/family/adoption/convention/convention_462.html. Several scholars, however, have predicted that the Convention, as implemented by the U.S., will have limited success in protecting prospective adoptive children from international adoption abuses. *See, e.g.*, Trish Maskew, *The Failure of Promise: The U.S. Regulations on Intercountry Adoption Under the Hague Convention*, 60 ADMIN. L. REV. 487 (2008); Kate O'Keeffe, *The Intercountry Adoption Act of 2000: The United States' Ratification of the Hague*

Convention on the Protection Of Children, and its Meager Effect on International Adoption, 40 Vand. J. Transnat'l L. 1611 (2007). For a discussion of the problems that continue to characterize international adoptions from Africa, as illustrated by several high-profile cases, see Benyam D. Mezmur, *From Angelina (to Madonna) to Zoe's Ark: What Are the 'A-Z' Lessons for Intercountry Adoptions in Africa?*, 23 INT'L J. L. POL'Y & FAM. 145 (2009). *See also* Stacie I. Strong, *Children's Rights in Intercountry Adoption: Towards a New Goal*, 13 B.U. INT'L L.J. 163 (1995); Richard R. Carlson, *The Emerging Law of Intercountry Adoptions: An Analysis of the Hague Conference on Intercountry Adoption*, 30 TULSA L.J. 243 (1994); Jorge L. Carro, *Regulation of Intercountry Adoption: Can the Abuses Come to an End?*, 18 HAST. INT. & COMP. L. REV. 121 (1994).

[f]   Gays and Lesbians as Adoptive Parents

Discussion of the range of legal issues relevant to adoption by gay and lesbian individuals and couples can be found in Chapter 9.

D.   THE LEGAL EFFECTS OF ADOPTION

Once an adoption in the U.S. is finalized, the adoptive parents become the child's legal parents and acquire the parental rights and obligations of birth parents. The birth parents' rights are fully and permanently severed and all of the rights and obligations of parenthood are transferred to the adoptive parents. There are some limited exceptions to this general rule, which will be discussed below. One of the most dramatic shifts in adoption policies and practices in recent years concerns a greater acceptance of "openness" relating to information flow, and at times, contact, between birth families and adoptive families and/or the child after adoption. That openness has resulted from several trends. On one hand, as noted below, the social stigma accompanying adoption and nonmarital pregnancy have dissipated substantially in our society, leading to greater comfort with openness between parties. In addition, because of the more limited availability of healthy infants for adoption in the U.S., as noted in Section A above, birth parents placing such children for adoption can bargain for greater control over and input into the process of their children's adoption. Thus, they may play a role in selecting the adoptive parents and in setting forth post-adoption conditions, such as access to updates on the child's development. As noted below, states vary in the degree to which they will enforce any agreements that limit the post-adoption autonomy of the adoptive parents. Subsection [1] briefly discusses the various facets of the adoption process and post-adoption arrangements that are sometimes referred to as "open adoptions." Subsection [2] examines challenges to traditional policies mandating secrecy and confidentiality regarding adoption records and information. As noted below, many states have revisited policies regarding confidentiality of records, and litigation has challenged certain changes in state policies. Subsection [3] addresses legal policies affecting post-adoption *contact* between the adopted child and members of his biological family. Subsection [4] addresses policies regarding residual inheritance rights adoptive children may be able to claim in relation to their birth parents. Subsection [5] considers the circumstances under which a legally-final adoption can be abrogated by the adoptive parents.

[1]   What is An "Open Adoption"?

The term "open adoption" is used to describe the situation where there is no confidentiality between the natural parents (or siblings) and the adoptive parents *or* where there is some degree of contact between the child and birth family following the adoption. While the adoptive parents are still the sole legal parents, the natural parents and/or siblings may have ongoing contact with the child, ranging from an exchange of photographs and letters up to visitation rights.

In Matter of Adoption of S.K.L.H., 204 P.3d 320, 322 n.1 (Alaska 2009). An "open adoption," therefore, may be one in which the birth parents and prospective adoptive parents exchange identifying information, perhaps meet, and/or spend extended time together as part of the selection process. Alternatively, the term may refer to post-adoption exchanges of information and/or contact between the birth family and adoptive family. The parties may even agree, informally or through a formal contract, to the nature and frequency of any post-adoption communications or contact. Openness can be best conceptualized as a continuum. Thus, as the diagram below illustrates the openness of information exchanges, the adoption selection process and/or post-adoption relations may be fully confidential, fully open, or somewhere in between. (Diagram reprinted from DHHS, Openness in Adoption (2003), http://www.childwelfare.gov/pubs/f_openadoptbulletin.cfm.)

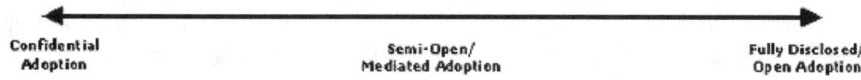

Confidential   Semi-Open/   Fully Disclosed/
Adoption   Mediated Adoption   Open Adoption

Because the term "open adoption" encompasses so many different types of arrangements, some of which involve the exchange of information only, and some of which occur only during the selection process, we will avoid using this term without additional clarification as to precisely what facet of openness we are referring.

[2]   Confidentiality of Adoption Records

Beginning in the 1940s and until the late 20th Century, most identifying adoption information in the U.S. was enshrouded in secrecy. Unless the adoption was arranged informally by parties who knew of or about each other, the identities of the birth and adoptive parents was maintained in confidence by the agency arranging the adoption. Typically, while these parties learned some basic nonidentifying facts about each other, identifying information was not shared, and there was no ongoing information flow once the adoption was finalized. The policy was reinforced by state laws sealing adoption records once the decree was granted. *See* Shannon Clark Kief, *Restricting Access to Judicial Records of Concluded Adoption Proceedings*, 103 A.L.R.5th 255 (2002 & Supp. 2009).

Recent scholarship, in tracing the history of confidentiality in adoption records, rebuts the common assumption that adoption records in the United States have *always* been sealed. Elizabeth J. Samuels, *The Idea of Adoption: An Inquiry into the History of Adult Adoptee Access to Birth Records*, 53 Rutgers L. Rev. 367 (2001); Heidi Hildebrand, *Because They Want to Know: An Examination of the Legal Rights of Adoptees and Their Parents*, 24 S. Ill. U. L.J. 515 (2000). During the 1930s and 1940s, all states moved to seal their adoption records. The confidentiality policies were viewed as serving the best interests of adopted children, adoptive parents, and birth parents. Public attitudes viewed adoption as a "second-rate" way of creating parent-child relationships. Adoptive families feared that the stigma of illegitimacy would somehow harm their adopted children (since so many were born out of wedlock). That stigma was also a concern for the birth mothers who, in principle, wanted to "move on" with their lives, forgetting the "mistake" that led to the relinquished child. The state supported the adoptive parents and children by joining with them in a "fiction" that the family was a biological one, allowing them to represent their family to the community as such. The policies also "protected" the adoptive family from the involvement of biological parents. There was concern that knowledge of or interaction with biological parents could confuse and disorient adoptive children, interfering with children's ability to bond with their adoptive parents.

Today, however, the stigma of adoption and illegitimacy are greatly reduced, and few adoptive parents seek to maintain the fiction of non-adoption. Views that it is best to hide the fact of adoption from adopted children have given way to recognition that frank and open discussion promotes healthier psychological adjustment of adopted children. The interest of adoptees in learning more about their biological families is no longer interpreted as a threat to adoptive parent-child relations or as a sign of family dysfunction. Rather, it is now seen as a natural manifestation of adoptees' curiosity about their biological heritage. Thus, there has been increasing interest in recent years by adoptees (and to a lesser extent, by birth parents) in opening up adoption records.

A recent report by the Evan B. Donaldson Adoption Institute summarizes the key arguments raised in support and in opposition of claims for adult adoptees' access. Among the arguments in favor of open access to records by adoptees, the Institute cites: (1) adult adoptees have a "right to know" personal information about themselves, and such information will aid them psychologically, medically, and legally (e.g., absent such information, adoptees are unable to claim their legal right to inheritance from their birth parents, consistent with the statutes of some states); (2) withholding birth and/or adoption information from adult adoptees conflicts with the states' primary interests in regulating adoption, that is, promoting the best interests of the adoptees; (3) withholding birth and/or adoption information violates equal protection rights because it treats adoptees differently from non-adopted persons relative to access to information about them maintained by the state, and that they are significantly disadvantaged by this differential treatment; (3) the presumption that most birth parents would object to disclosure is inaccurate; and (4) no deleterious consequences have followed in those states that have opened records to adult adoptees. Evan B. Donaldson Adoption Institute, For the Records: Restoring a Legal Right for Adult Adoptees 12-17 (2007). The Institute cites opponents of open access as arguing that such a change in policy (1) violates promises of confidentiality made to birth parents; (2) imposes unwanted relationships on some of the parties; (3) may lead future birth parents to choose abortion instead of adoption; and (4) undercuts the integrity of the adoptive family. *Id.* at 17–26. For in depth analysis of the various positions, including citations to the available empirical research, see FOR THE RECORDS, *supra.* The Institute ultimately concludes that greater access by adult adoptees is legally, socially, and psychologically appropriate, and sets forth a series of recommendations to achieve that result.

There are variations among the states in current policies. Some of the key themes are summarized below.

[a]   Access to Nonidentifying Information

All states allow adult adoptees to obtain "nonidentifying" information about their adoption. Generally, this information includes: date, place and circumstances of their adoption; the age and physical features of their birth parents; age of the birth parents and general physical description, such as eye and hair color; race, ethnicity, religion, and medical history of the birth parents; and educational level of the birth parents and their occupation at the time of the adoption. *See* DHHS, Access to Adoption Records: Summary of State Laws (2006), http://www.childwelfare.gov/systemwide/laws_policies/statutes/infoaccessapall.pdf; CYNTHIA R. MABRY & LISA KELLY, ADOPTION LAW: THEORY, POLICY, AND PRACTICE 620–21 (2006). About half of the states allow birth parents access to nonidentifying information about the child; and a handful of states permit adult biological siblings of an adopted child access to such information about the adopted sibling. DHHS, *supra.*

[b]   Access to Identifying Information

[i]   Registries and Intermediaries

Increasingly, adult adoptees have sought access to identifying information about their birth families. State legislatures and courts have tried to balance the competing interests of those who seek information against those who prefer for continued anonymity. A range of different approaches characterize state responses. In the absence of an objection to disclosure of confidential information by either the birth parents or adult adoptees, there is no generally no state interest justifying continued shielding of that information. Therefore, states have established a range of mechanisms allowing the parties to *consent* to disclosure. Increasingly popular are state and private "reunion registries." These registries allow biological parents and adult adoptees to indicate their willingness to be contacted by the other. If both involved parties sign up, the registry shares the information each has authorized with the other. *See, e.g.,* IDAHO CODE ANN. § 39-259A (2009); Nev. Rev. Stat. § 127.007 (2009); CAL. FAM. CODE §§ 9203–9205 (2009); ARK. CODE ANN. § 9-9-504 (2009). Other states have "search and consent" provisions: upon petition of the adult adoptee (usually), a search for the biological parent will be undertaken. If found, the parent's consent for contact or the release of information is solicited. Because "search and consent" policies do not require both parties to take the initiative to register, these laws offer a more proactive means of establishing contact than registries. *See, e.g.,* COLO. REV. STAT. ANN. § 19-

5-304 (2009). Some states achieve the same result with the use of confidential intermediaries to obtain the consent of the other parties prior to release. *See, e.g.*, OKLA. ST. ANN. § 7508-1.3 (2009). And, sensibly, planning prospectively, states now commonly allow the parties to new adoptions to indicate their preferences regarding future information sharing and contact. About two-thirds of the states provide some mechanism by which biological siblings who have been adopted can express a willingness to be contacted or exchange identifying information. *See* DHHS, *supra*, at 3–4.

[ii]   Exceptions for "Good Cause"

Traditionally, there have been, and continue to be, exceptions to confidentiality permissible in most states for "good cause." *See, e.g.*, FLA. ST. ANN. § 63-162(4)(d) (2009). Convincing a court that "good cause" exists typically requires a substantial reason. As articulated by the Iowa Supreme Court: "Under our statute, we think good cause to invade the privacy of biological parents by revealing their identities without their consent should include no less than a showing of a medical need to save the life of or prevent irreparable physical or mental harm to an adult adopted person requesting the identifying information." *In re Adoption of S.J.D.*, 641 N.W.2d 794, 801 (Iowa 2002). In *S.J.D.*, the court rejected the following reasons, articulated by an adult adoptee, as rising to that level: (1) satisfaction of his curiosity about his background, (2) thanking his biological parents for what they did, and (3) obtaining medical information. *Id. See also In re Philip S.*, 881 A.2d 931, 933 (R.I. 2005) (rejecting adult adoptee's assertion that he needed information about his birth family to better follow the dictates of his religion; citing the "*heavy burden*" borne by one who seeks to establish "good cause").

The classic application of this exception relates to the exchange of information deemed important to the health of the adoptee. For example, in a 2003 case, the South Carolina Supreme Court held that in order to demonstrate "good cause," an individual must "show a compelling need to remove the veil of privacy from the biological parents. The compelling need [can be] demonstrated by a variety of factors including the medical or mental health of the adopted child and whether not having the information impaired the child's ability to lead a stable, productive life." *Doe v. Ward Law Firm*, 359 S.E.2d 303, 305 (S.C. 2003). In this particular case, the court determined that the appointment by the court of a confidential intermediary would provide the adoptive parents and child with the necessary medical information, while still safeguarding the birth parents' privacy. Proponents of open records, however, assert that "good cause" exceptions do not go far enough. Arguably, with complete health and genetic information, adoptees could better prevent health problems for which they might be at risk, taking the precautions that are generally recommended by physicians when there is a "family history" of a particular condition. While states have allowed access to some of this data as non-identifying information, commentators argue that there remain serious deficiencies in the information yielded through these methods. *See* D. Marianne Brower Blair, *Lifting the Genealogical Veil: A Blueprint for Legislative Reform of the Disclosure of Health Related Information in Adoption*, 70 N.C. L. REV. 681 (1992); R. Scott Smith, *Disclosure Of Post-Adoption Family Medical Information: A Continuing Birth Parent Duty*, 35 FAM. L.Q. 553 (2001). In principle, courts recognize the prevention of serious psychological harm as a basis for a claim of "good cause" disclosure. *See, e.g., In re Matter of Wilson*, 544 N.Y.S.2d 886 (Sup. Ct. App. Div. 1989). However, in practice, psychological damage claims are seldom successful. *See, e.g., In re Dixon*, 323 N.W.2d 549 (Mich. App. 1982) (rejecting claim of severely depressed woman who had attempted suicide, whose condition was attributed in part to her lack of knowledge about her birth family).

[iii]   Modern Statutes Permitting Access to Birth Records

In the past decade, several states have done an "about face," and passed statutes opening birth records to adult adoptees. Maine is the most recent state to join the small, but expanding, group that includes Alabama, Alaska, Delaware, Kansas, New Hampshire, Oregon, and Tennessee. The policies in Alaska and Kansas are longstanding, whereas the other states passed their direct access statutes more recently. The Maine statute, effective January 1, 2009, provides that: "An adopted person [at least 18 years of age or that person's] descendants may obtain a copy of that person's original certificate of birth from the State Registrar of Vital Statistics . . ." upon providing satisfactory proof of identification. Me. Rev. St. Ann. § 2768 (2009). The Tennessee statute gives adoptees, age 21 and older, the right to any information that the state has about their birth parents. TENN. CODE ANN. §§ 36-1-127 et seq. (2009). The Tennessee statute includes a unique mechanism to protect the privacy of birth parents, however. The parent can file a "contact veto," conditioning the release of information on the adoptee's promise not to make contact. Violation results in civil and criminal penalties. In the view of supporters, this approach, borrowed from a law in New South Wales, Australia, satisfies the adoptee's need to know about her birth family without resulting in unwanted intrusion. *See also* ALA. CODE § 22-9A-12(c) (2009) (access to the original, unaltered birth certificate is available upon written request by the adult adoptee, along with accompanying adoption records). The Alabama statute also permits birth parents to file a "contact preference form" which would be given to the adoptee along with the birth certificate.

In 1999, Oregon voters enacted Measure 58, under which any adopted person over the age of 21 can apply to the state registrar for a copy of his or her original birth certificate. OR. REV. STAT. § 432.240(2009). Unlike the Tennessee statute, the measure includes no contact veto. The Tennessee and Oregon enactments have withstood state and federal constitutional challenges brought by classes of adoptive and birth parents. *Doe v. Sundquist*, 2 S.W.3d 919 (Tenn. 1999); *Doe 1 v. State*, 993 P.2d 822 (Or. Ct. App. 1999). Both courts rejected claims that the state opening of previously confidential records was a government intrusion into parental decisions about whether to bear children or that it infringed on birth mothers' constitutional rights of privacy. The Oregon court noted that the adoption decision, unlike those involving contraception and abortion, is not made unilaterally by the mother; it involves active oversight by the state. The Tennessee court emphasized that the parents' privacy was protected by the contact veto under that statute. Equally unsuccessful was the argument that the enactments impaired the obligation of contract. Both courts found that the prior adoption statutes offered no guarantee of confidentiality. Nor was there legislative intent to contract with birth mothers to prevent disclosure of their identities to their children. *See also Doe v. Sundquist,* 106 F.3d 702 (6th Cir. 1997) (rejecting federal constitutional challenge of Tennessee statute).

For further discussion of policies governing adoptees' access to birth records, see, e.g., Naomi Cahn & Jana Singer, *Adoption, Identity and the Constitution: The Case for Opening Closed Records,* 2 U. Pa. J. Const. L. 150 (1999); Lauren M. Fair, *Shame on U.S.: The Need for Uniform Open Adoption Records Legislation in the United States,* 48 Santa Clara L. Rev. 1039 (2008).

PROBLEM

Problem 11-6.   Michael and Alice adopted John at four weeks. He is now 17, and wants to track down his birth parents. He seeks your assistance because his adoptive parents have told him you were the attorney who handled the adoption. John tells you that he is interested in learning more about his biological heritage, but has no intention of making demands upon his birth parents. His curiosity about his birth parents seems sincere, although he has no special reason, such as medical necessity, to seek them out. He says his relationship with his adoptive parents is good. You call them and they urge you to provide him with any assistance you can, and offer to pay you any appropriate fees. They have full confidence in their son and are happy to support his quest in any way they can.

You have little independent recollection of this particular adoption, but your office records contain enough information about the mother to give someone a pretty good chance at finding her. She was unmarried at the time, but the records also provide some information about the man she identified as the father. As best as you can recall now, you never actually met or dealt with him. Your standard practice at the time in non-family adoptions was to maintain confidentiality. Often, either adoptive parents or birth mothers requested assurances on this point, which you always gave. Your records do not indicate whether such assurances were sought in this particular adoption. John's parents, however, recall the promise of confidentiality which you had made to them 17 years earlier, and say they were now prepared to waive it. Your records do not indicate any separate counsel for the birth mother in this case.

The only relevant state statute provides: "Except upon order of the court for good cause shown in exceptional cases, no person shall disclose from the court records the name or identity of either an adoptive parent or an adoptive child."

What do you do?

[3] Post-Adoption Contact Agreements and "Cooperative Adoption"

MICHAUD v. WAWRUCK
Connecticut Supreme Court
551 A.2d 738 (1986)

The sole issue in this case is whether a written visitation agreement between a genetic mother and adoptive parents violates the public policy of this state. The plaintiff, Jacqueline Michaud, filed a complaint seeking specific enforcement of an "Open Adoption and Visitation Agreement" between herself and the defendants, James Wawruck and Cynthia Wawruck. [The trial court granted the defendants' motion to strike and rendered judgment in their favor.] We find error and remand the case for further proceedings.

. . . . The Probate Court, on August 31, 1981, terminated the plaintiff's parental rights with respect to her child born on February 5, 1979. . . . [I]n 1982, the plaintiff filed a Superior Court action against the commissioner of children and youth services to set aside the Probate Court's decree terminating her parental rights, on the ground that her consent to that proceeding had been fraudulently procured by the child's father. . . . The plaintiff agreed to withdraw her lawsuit, and to allow the adoption to go forward, in exchange for the [foster parents'] agreement to permit regular visitation between the plaintiff and the child during the child's minor years.

[The agreement states that the] adopting parents will cooperate fully with the natural-mother in the natural mother's visits with the child both now and after the adoption takes place until the child's 18th birthday. . . . Each of the parties shall at all times in good faith endeavor to maintain in the child respect and affection for the other parties. . . . Visitation shall be twice a month for three (3) hours each visit at the Wawrucks' home. [¶] The agreement . . . was placed on record in the Superior Court on September 16, 1983. Acquiescence in the agreement was noted, in open court, by counsel for the plaintiff, for the defendants, for the commissioner, and for the minor child. The agreement was not, however, made part of the subsequent decree of the Probate Court permitting the defendants to adopt the child, although the parties to that proceeding, . . . were fully aware of its terms. After the adoption had been finalized, the defendants terminated all visitation between the plaintiff and the child.

The trial court, after reviewing these facts, granted the defendants' motion to strike the plaintiff's complaint because, in its view, enforcement of the "Open Adoption and Visitation Agreement" would violate Connecticut's adoption statutes. According to the trial court, adoption, as a creature of statute, must comply strictly with statutory requirements, and the existing statutes governing adoption preclude private "side agreements" that would serve to perpetuate a relationship, after adoption, between a genetic parent and an adopted child. The court noted that termination of parental rights, under General Statutes § 45-61b(g), operates as a "complete severance by court order of the legal relationship . . . between the child and his parent. . . ." Furthermore, under General Statutes § 45-64a, adoption creates new legal relationships in which the adopting parents are completely substituted for the genetic parents of an adopted person. . . . Relying on these statutory provisions, and a number of out-of-state cases, the court concluded that the contract between the parties could not confer upon the plaintiff a specifically enforceable right to visitation after completion of the adoption process.

[T]here is really only one question that we must resolve: did the trial court err in concluding that this agreement violated the public policy reflected in our adoption statutes? We disagree with the trial court's ruling.

The validity of an "open adoption" agreement is a matter of first impression for this court. Before we address the merits of this question, we should note that the title "open adoption," which has apparently become the standard characterization of such agreements, conveys a misleading impression of what such agreements intend to accomplish. The plaintiff does not seek to "open," to set aside or to diminish in any way the adoptive process that has substituted the defendants as the legal parents of the child. The plaintiff's rights are not premised on an ongoing genetic relationship that somehow survives a termination of parental rights and an adoption. Instead, the plaintiff is asking us to decide whether, as an adult who has had an ongoing personal relationship with the child, she may contract with the adopting parents, prior to adoption, for the continued right to visit with the child, so long as that visitation continues to be in the best interest of the child.

Our statutes recognize that visitation encompasses considerations that differ from those that govern custody, guardianship or parental status. . . . [T]he adoption statutes do not expressly make a visitation agreement void as against public policy.

[O]ur visitation statute, General Statutes § 46b-59, permits the Superior Court, upon a proper application, to "grant the right of visitation with respect to any minor child . . . to any person. . . . In making, modifying or terminating such an order, the court shall be guided by the best interest of the child. . . . Visitation rights granted in accordance with this section shall not be deemed to have created parental rights in the person . . . to whom such visitation rights are granted. The grant of visitation rights shall not prevent any court of competent jurisdiction from thereafter acting upon the custody of such child, the parental rights with respect to such child or the adoption of such child and any such court may include in its decree an order terminating such visitation rights". . . . All this plaintiff seeks is a court order consistent with the statutory constraints imposed on visitation by § 46b-59.

[W]e are [therefore] unpersuaded that the agreement between the parties in this case violates the public policy of Connecticut. It would be elevating form over substance to allow the plaintiff to obtain visitation rights by filing an appropriate "application" in the Superior Court, but to deny her the opportunity to seek such rights under a contractual umbrella. . . .

Traditional models of the nuclear family have come, in recent years, to be replaced by various configurations of parents, stepparents, adoptive parents and grandparents. . . . We are not prepared to assume that the welfare of children is best served by a narrow definition of those whom we permit to continue to manifest their deep concern for a child's growth and development. . . . In the present case, the "Open Adoption and Visitation Agreement" was openly and lovingly negotiated, in good faith, in order to promote the best interest of the child. The attorney for the child reported that the child thought the agreement between her mother and her soon-to-be adoptive parents would be "the best world that she could imagine." This agreement did not violate public policy, either ab initio or upon the subsequent entry of a decree of adoption.

We therefore remand this case to the trial court for a hearing on the merits of the plaintiff's claim that visitation would now be in the best interest of the child. . . .

NOTES

1. *Post-Adoption Contact Arrangements (i.e., "Cooperative Adoption") — A Response to the Complexity of Modern Families.* The rule that an adoption can only be finalized if the rights of the birth parents are severed is subject to the very narrow exceptions set forth in this Chapter (i.e., no severance required of custodial parent in a stepparent or second parent adoption). Traditionally, once the transfer of parental rights occurs, birth parents can no longer claim a right even to limited visitation. In recent years, courts have been increasingly willing to enforce agreements such as the one in *Michaud* that allow biological parent visitation rights. This trend, referred to by some as "cooperative adoption" recognizes that modern family relationships are complex, and that the child's interest may be promoted by maintaining important relationships beyond the two-parent nuclear family. As the court in *Michaud* suggests, post-adoption contact can be regarded as a category of nonparent visitation, discussed in Chapter 6, and reflects many of the same policy objectives. However, many of these arrangements, unlike other nonparent visitation, are created as a condition of the biological parents' consent to an adoption.

The most important benefit claimed by advocates of post-adoption contact is that the bond between the biological parent and child is not severed. Even if the parent has been deficient in fulfilling parental responsibilities, it may be beneficial to both the parent and child to continue an established relationship. *See* Elizabeth S. Scott & Robert E. Scott, *Parents as Fiduciaries*, 81 VA. L. REV. 2401 (1995) (arguing continued contact after adoption rewards parents who have invested in relationship with child, to the benefit of child); Katharine Bartlett, *Rethinking Parenthood as an Exclusive Status: The Need for Legal Alternatives When the Premise of the Nuclear Family Has Failed*, 70 VA. L. REV. 879 (1984) (arguing that once the premise of the nuclear family as failed, exceptions to the otherwise exclusive rights of parents, such as continued contact with a non-parent, might be appropriate in order to protect a child's established and bonded relationships). Moreover, when a family is dissolved because parents can no longer care for their children, post-adoption contact permits siblings to maintain ties. By encouraging birth parents to give consent to adoption which they might otherwise withhold, post-adoption contact also promotes permanent placement of the child with responsible adults eager to assume the parental role. Post-adoption contact may also have some costs, however. Prospective adoptive parents may feel pressured to agree to an arrangement, fearing that the adoption will not go forward otherwise. As time passes, conflicts may develop between the adoptive and biological parents which create stress for the child. *But see* Note 7 *infra*.

Post-adoption contact is commonly sought in two kinds of cases: adoptions by foster parents or other adults in the context of abuse or neglect, and stepparent adoptions. Post-adoption contact agreements could facilitate stepparent adoption in a broader range of cases. A biological parent might be more willing to consent to adoption, knowing that he will not lose all contact with his child. Would *J.J.J.*, *see* Section B[2] above, have been a good case for a post-adoption contact arrangement, given the child's curiosity about his father? This issue was raised in the case (in a part of the opinion not reprinted above), but the court concluded that it had no statutory authority to order continued visitation rights for the father. The court criticized this "all-or-nothing approach" to adoption as "unrealistic," often producing "an unfair result." 718 P.2d at 951. In addition, some courts continue to adhere to the traditional view that, absent statutory authority, post-adoption visitation agreements cannot be enforced because adoption terminates all parental rights. *See Matter of Adoption of Child by D.M.H.*, 641 A.2d 235 (N.J. 1994) (new adoption statute did not authorize the enforcement of visitation agreements). Without a statute or clear precedent, biological parents who consent to adoption on the condition that the they have continued visitation may find courts unwilling to enforce the agreement.

2. State Policies Regarding Post-Adoption Contact Agreements. In the past two decades, states have been increasingly receptive to the concept of post-adoption contact between children and their birth parents (and/or other members of the child's biological family). The statutes of about half of the states now authorize judicial enforcement of written post-adoption contact agreements between biological and adoptive parents. *See, e.g.*, MASS. GEN. LAWS ANN. ch. 210, § 6(C) (2009); MINN. STAT. § 259.58 (2009). Virginia joined these states in February 2009. *See, e.g.*, VA. ST. ANN. § 63.1228.1; 63.1228.2 (2009). Most statutes indicate that the court will not approve the agreement unless its terms serve the best interests of the child. *See, e.g.*, IND. CODE. ANN. § 31-19-16-2 (2009). Some codes require that the agreement be incorporated into the adoption decree in order to render it enforceable. *See, e.g.*, N.Y. DOM. REL. L. § 112(b)(2) (2009). Most statutes clarify that if a party does not comply with the agreement, the adoption will remain valid, but the aggrieved party may commence a civil action to compel specific performance. *See, e.g.*, MASS. GEN. LAWS ANN. ch. 210, § 6(D) (2009). In some instances, the statute requires that the parties attempt mediation before commencing a lawsuit to enforce compliance. *See, e.g.*, MINN. ST. ANN. § 259.58 (2009). The statutes generally limit the discretion of the court to refuse enforcement or to modify the terms of the agreement restricting such actions to circumstances in which continued enforcement is not in the best interests of the child, the parties agree to the modification, or where "exceptional circumstances have arisen since the agreement was entered into that justify modification . . ." *See, e.g.*, MINN. ST. ANN. § 259.58(c) (2009). *See also* CONN. GEN. ST. § 17-112(b) (2009); IND. CODE ANN. § 31-19-16-2 through § 31-19-16-4 (2009); MD. CODE ANN. FAM. L. § 5-308 (2009); NEB. REV. STAT. § 43-155 through § 43-162 (2009); N.M. STAT. ANN. § 32A-5-35 (2009); WASH. REV. CODE ANN. § 26.33.295 (2009). *But see Adoption* *of Edgar*, 853 N.E.2d 1068 (Mass. Ct. App. 2006) (modification of post-adoption visitation agreement permissible where agreement had not been judicially approved and modification was in the best interests of the child).

3. *Post-Adoption Contact by Court Order.* Should courts order post-adoption visitation by birth parents in the absence of agreement? Most courts find no authority to order post-adoption visitation without a judicially-approved agreement between the parties. The Illinois Supreme Court held that a juvenile court exceeded its authority when, after terminating parental rights of the biological parents, it gave appointed guardians the power to consent to adoption on the condition that the adoptive parents agree to continue contact between the children and their parents. *In re M.M.*, 619 N.E.2d 702 (1993). Some courts have concluded that their general equitable powers grant them discretion to mandate post-adoption contact. For example, the Alaska Supreme Court, in *In Matter of S.K.L.H.*, 204 P.3d 320 (Alaska 2009), held that nothing in the adoption statutes "prohibits an adoption that allows visitation between the adopted person and that person's natural parents or other relatives [and] allows the court to fashion open adoption decrees securing visitation rights to a biological parent if it is in the child's best interests to do so, *with or without an agreement* between the biological and adopting parents." *Id.* at 327. Similarly, the Supreme Judicial Court of Massachusetts held, in 2000, that the statute authorizing enforcement of post-adoption visitation agreements between biological and adoptive parents does not affect the previously-recognized equitable powers of the probate court to order post-adoption contact absent agreement. *In re Adoption of Vito*, 728 N.E.2d 292 (Mass. 2000) (declining to order visitation in the instant case because of the absence of evidence of a "significant existing bond between the child and a biological parent, such that a court order abruptly disrupting that relationship would run counter to the child's best interests").

4. *Post-Adoption Contact with Infants.* Are post-adoption contact arrangements appropriate when mothers place infants for adoption? There is no pre-existing established relationship between the birth parents and child. Nonetheless, this practice has increased in recent years and some observers advocate post-adoption contact with infants as part of a healthy trend away from secrecy in adoption — a trend that is also reflected in greater access to adoption records by adult adoptees and birth parents. *See e.g.* Annette Ruth Appell, *Blending Families Through Adoption: Implications for Collaborative Adoption Law and Practice*, 75 B.U. L. REV. 997 (1995); Baron & Pannor, *Open Adoption*, in BRODZINSKY & SCHECTER (EDS.), THE PSYCHOLOGY OF ADOPTION 316 (1990). One study found that contact was more likely to be sustained in infant post-adoption contact than when older children are involved. Berry, et. al., *The Role of Open Adoption in the Role of Adopted Children*, 20 CHILD & YOUTH SERV. REV. 151 (1998). The Uniform Adoption Act directs the court in stepparent adoptions to determine whether the visitation with the biological parent is in the best interest of the child. If so, visitation can be ordered over the objection of the adoptive stepparent and the custodial parent. The decision is based on several factors, including the child's preference; the length and quality of the child's relationship with the parent; the likely effect on the child of allowing the relationship to continue; and the likelihood that the parties will be able cooperate. U.A.A. § 4-113 (c).

5. *Post-Adoption Contact Agreements, including Grandparent Visitation Agreements, After* Troxel v. Granville. The nonparent visitation statute applied by the judge in *Michaud v. Wawruck*, CONN. GEN STAT. § 46b-59, has been subjected to constitutional scrutiny in recent years. In a 2002 case concerning grandparent visitation (which did not arise the adoption context), *Crockett v. Pastore*, 789 A.2d 453, the Connecticut Supreme Court held that the lower courts had unconstitutionally applied § 46b-59 in crafting their visitation orders, failing to give sufficient deference to the objections of the children's parents, consistent with the U.S. Supreme Court's decision in *Troxel v. Granville* (*see* Chapter 6, Section F). In 2008, in *Fish v. Fish*, 939 A.2d 1040 (Conn. 2008), the Connecticut Supreme Court held that Connecticut's custody and visitation statutes "are overly broad [in that they] fail to define with particularity those persons who may seek visitation and custody other than parents. . . . Accordingly, we conclude that, to avoid constitutional infirmity, the standing requirement that a third party allege a parent-like relationship with the child should be applied" to third parties seeking custody or visitation. *Id.* at 1053. The biological mother in *Michaud* might still have succeed under the new rule if she could claim provide that she had served as the child's functional mother.

Because an adoption severs the legal relationship between the child and her biological parents, it likewise severs the child's relationships with extended family members, such as grandparents. Prior to the Supreme Court's opinion in *Troxel*, many courts ordered post-adoption visitation with grandparents and other relatives. After *Troxel*, some courts have recognized constitutional constraints on ordering visitation over the objections of the adoptive parents. *See, e.g., Hede v. Gilstrap*, 107 P.3d 158 (Wyo. 2005) (declining to order post-adoption visitation between child and biological grandparents father in the absence of statutory authority); *Popwell v. State*, 998 So. 2d 841 (La. 2008) (same). What if a statute authorizes post-adoption visitation between the child and extended family members, such as grandparents? Will such a statute survive constitutional scrutiny after *Troxel*? According to the Alabama Supreme Court, the answer is "yes." In *Ex Parte D.W.*, 835 So. 2d 186 (Ala. 2002), the court held that the legislature had the power to restrict the adoptive parents' rights by enacting a provision that authorized courts to order reasonable post-adoption grandparent visitation if doing so was in the best interests of the child.

6. *Empirical Research on the Effects of Post-Adoption Contact.* What do we know about how information exchange and/or contact between birth and adoptive families affects those families and, importantly, the adopted child? In general, the empirical research reveals that openness has positive effects. Indeed, as one researcher observed: "the dire outcomes predicted by some opponents of open adoption did not emerge. In fact, many parents said they felt more enthusiasm for and comfort with [the contact with the adopted child's birth family] after seven years of successful experience with it." Deborah H. Siegel, *Open Adoption of Infants: Adoptive Parents' Feelings Seven Years Later*, 48 SOC. WORK 409 (2003). Siegel also found that the type and amount of contact changed over time to meet the needs of the parties. No adoptive families that had promised contact with birth families refused to honor their agreements. *Id.* at 417. Another group of researchers evaluated the feelings of adopted adolescents about post-adoption contact with their biological parent(s). Jerica M. Berge et al., *Adolescents' Feelings about Openness in Adoption: Implications for Adoption Agencies*, 83 CHILD WELFARE 1011 (2006). For most, the experience was positive, did not interfere with their relationships with their adoptive parents, and according to the adolescents' reports, "contributed to their understanding of who they are . . ." *Id.* at 1034. The researchers conclude that: "Adolescents can be happy and content with their adoptive families and also have positive feelings for their birthmothers." *Id.* at 1035. *See also* Judith S. Lee & James A. Twaite, *Open Adoption and Adoptive Mothers: Attitudes Toward Birthmothers, Adopted Children, and Parenting*, 67 AM. J. ORTHOPSYCHIATRY 576 (1997); Jeffrey Haugaard, *Open Adoptions: Attitudes and Experiences*, 4 ADOPTION Q. 89 (2000) (reviewing studies showing that most adoptive families found post-adoption contact arrangements to have substantial benefits and did not regret choice).

7. *Further Reading.* For a review and discussion of the legal status of post-adoption visitation agreements, see DHHS, *Postadoption Contact Agreements Between Birth and Adoptive Families* (2005), http://www.childwelfare.gov/systemwide/laws_policies/statutes/cooperative.pdf.
For further analysis of the relevant issues, see Danny R. Veilleux, *Postadoption Visitation by a Natural Parent*, 78 A.L.R.4th 218 (2009); Kirsten Widner, *Continuing the Evolution: Why California should Amend Family Code Section 8616.5 to Allow Visitation in All PostAdoption Contact Agreements*, 44 SAN DIEGO L. REV. 355 (2007); Joan Heifetz Hollinger, *Overview of Legal Status of Post-Adoption Contact Agreements*, in FAMILIES BY LAW 159 (NAOMI R. CAHN & JOAN HEIFETZ HOLLINGER EDS., 2004); Lucy S. McGough & Annette Peltier-Falahahwazi, *Secrets and Lies: A Model Statute for Cooperative Adoption*, 60 LA. L. REV. 13 (1999); Annette Ruth Appell, *The Move Toward Legally-Sanctioned Cooperative Adoption: Can it Survive the Uniform Adoption Act?*, 30 FAM. L.Q. 483 (1996).

[4]   Inheritance Rights after Adoption

The modern rule treating the adopted child exactly as if she were the birth child of the adopted parents is reflected in many statutes. Some statutes contain language stating that a persons' "issue" includes an adoptive child. Other statutes indicate that adoption terminates the right to inherit intestate from a blood relative. *See, e.g., Estate of Carlson*, 457 N.W.2d 789 (Minn. Ct. App. 1990). However, many statutes permit the adopted child to take by intestate succession from both adoptive and biological parents, particularly in stepparent adoptions. A California court held that the decedent's biological children, who had been adopted by their stepfather, were entitled to share his estate with his adopted son, under the California stepparent adoption statute. *In re Estate of Dye*, 112 Cal. Rptr. 2d 362 (Ct. App. 2001). The court pointed out that the decedent, who had had no contact with his birth children in the forty years since the adoption, could have avoided the outcome through a will provision. *Accord Raley v. Spikes*, 614 So. 2d 1017 (Ala. 1993). For an argument that intestate succession rights of adoptees should be contingent on a continued family relationship between the natural family and the adoptee, see Lisa A. Fuller, Student Author, *Intestate Succession Rights of Adopted Children: Should the Stepparent Exception be Extended?*, 77 CORN. L. REV. 1188 (1992). For more on adoption and inheritance, see E. Gary Spitko, *Open*

Adoption, Inheritance, and the "Uncleing" Principle, 48 SANTA CLARA L. REV. 765 (2008) (proposing reform of intestacy statutes to allow an adopted child and her birth parent who have maintained a "qualifying functional relationship" to inherit from and through each other as would an aunt or uncle and a niece or nephew); Jan Ellen Reim, *Relatives by Blood, Adoption and Association: Who Should Get What and Why,* 37 VAND. L. REV. 711 (1984).

On occasion, courts recognize a claim to an intestate estate under a doctrine called "equitable adoption." In these cases, there is no formal adoption judgment, but an individual lived with the decedent in a functional parent-child relationship, and there is evidence of an agreement to enter into a formal adoption which never took place. Ordinarily, the sole effect of this doctrine is to permit the alleged adoptee to inherit as if she were a child of the decedent. In most states, the doctrine has no effect outside of the probate context in which it was developed. Some courts have extended this doctrine, as did a Michigan Court of Appeal in *Atkinson v. Atkinson,* 408 N.W.2d 516 (Mich. Ct. App. 1987), which applied it to grant a man divorce visitation rights, where his wife revealed on divorce that he was not the biological father of her 5-year-old son. Most jurisdictions have rejected such expansion of the doctrine's application. *See, e.g., Randy A.J. v. Norma I.J.,* 677 N.W.2d 630 (Wis. 2004) (holding that Wisconsin does not follow the equitable adoption doctrine in paternity determinations); *Petition of Ash,* 507 N.W.2d 400 (Iowa 1993) (same regarding Iowa policy). Even in the probate context, courts do not apply the equitable adoption doctrine expansively. For more on equitable adoption, see Michael J. Higdon, *When Informal Adoption Meets Intestate Succession: the Cultural Myopia of the Equitable Adoption Doctrine,* 43 WAKE FOREST L. REV. 223 (2008); James R. Robinson, *Untangling the "Loose Threads": Equitable Adoption, Equitable Legitimation, and Inheritance in Extralegal Family Arrangements,* 48 EMORY L.J. 943 (1999).

[5]   Abrogation of Adoption by Adoptive Parents

As discussed in Section C[1][a] above, adoptive parents may bring a tort action against an adoption agency for misrepresentation or failure to disclose material information about the adoptive child's background. If parents succeed in such actions, they recover monetary damages which, in many cases, help defray the cost of raising a child who suffers from serious medical or emotional problems. "Wrongful adoption" actions, however, do not alter the legal status of the adoptive parent-adoptive child relationship. Very different legal issues are raised in cases where the adoptive parents seek termination of their legal obligations to the adoptive child through invalidation of the adoption itself, an action sometimes referred to as "abrogation" or "annulment" of the adoption. As one might expect, such actions are strongly disfavored. A New York Family Court explained the public policy goals underlying recent legislative repeal of a statute providing "a procedure for the abrogation of adoptions by reason of subsequent events." The repeal served the legislative goal of promoting "stability and permanency in the lives of the [adopted] children . . ." *Matter of Kane,* 427 N.Y.S.2d 575, 578 (N.Y. Fam. Ct. 1980). As such, the court noted, "final orders of adoption should not be lightly set aside." *Id.*

Some courts have held that an adoption decree cannot be vacated in the absence of an authorizing statute, while others have recognized equitable powers to vacate an adoption decree based on "the classical grounds that entitle such courts to vacate any other decree, such as judgments procured by fraud or to prevent injustice." *See In re McDuffee*, 352 S.W.2d 23, 26–27 (Mo. 1961) (discussing various state policies). Often, however, even where such "classical grounds" exist, state statutes or case law may require the court to find also that the abrogation of the adoption is in the best interests of the child. *Id.* If reversal of the adoption decree will leave the child parentless, a court may be reluctant to act. In the case before it, the Missouri Supreme Court refused to grant the adoptive parents' request based on evidence that the child was "mentally disturbed and in need of institutional care," where such information was not known to the adoptive parents prior to the adoption. The court observed: "Countless parents find themselves confronted with similar situations [and respond by] procuring the treatment needed . . ." *Id.* at 27–28. The court continued that "the natural parents abandoned their child. It cannot now be in the best interest of that child that a court of equity, on petition of its adoptive parents, decree it a similar fate." *Id.*

At one time, many states allowed adoptive parents to seek annulment of the adoption decree upon discovery of a previously unknown illness or other physical abnormality in the child, but very few states retain such provisions. Ann Harland Howard, Student Author, *Annulment of Adoption Decrees on Petition of Adoptive Parents*, 22 J. Fam. L. 549 (1983). California's Family Code 9100 (2009) provides:

> If any child adopted . . . shows evidence of a developmental disability or mental illness as a result of conditions existing before the adoption to an extent that the child cannot be relinquished to an adoption agency on the grounds that the child is considered unadoptable, and of which conditions the adopting parents or parent had no knowledge or notice before the entry of the . . . adoption [decree], a petition setting forth those facts may be filed by the adopting parents or parent with the court which granted the petition for adoption. If these facts are proved to the satisfaction of the court, it may make an order setting aside the order of adoption.

In *Adoption of Kay C.*, 228 Cal. Rptr. 209 (Ct. App. 1991), an appellate court upheld an order setting aside an adoption of a mentally ill child, aged 9 at the time of adoption. Although the prospective parents expressed concern and inquired about the possibility of emotional problems, the agency did not disclose psychiatric and other mental health evaluation reports diagnosing the child as having a borderline personality disorder and expressing doubts about the success of adoption. The child subsequently was hospitalized and diagnosed with schizophrenia and depression. After efforts at family therapy failed, the adoptive parents petitioned to set aside the adoption. In upholding the order, the appellate court rejected the child's claim that she had a liberty interest in the adoptive family relationship. It also rejected her equal protection claim that the statutory classification based on her developmental disability was suspect. The court held that the classification was rationally calculated to achieve the legitimate state interest of promoting adoption.

Should adoptive parents receive such a "warranty" regarding the child's health? Which state has the better approach: Missouri in *McDuffie* or California in *Kay C.*?

The gradual disappearance of provisions like California's indicates that most legislatures have come to believe that the risks as well as the joys of parenthood pass to the adoptive parents, who should be prepared to cope with whatever their newly undertaken responsibilities require. As noted by the Missouri court's language, courts occasionally permit revocations in the absence of a specific statute where a child's serious problems were *concealed* rather than *unknown*. *See In re Lisa Diane G.*, 537 A.2d 131 (R.I. 1988) (family court can revoke adoption and allow adoptive parents reimbursement for child-rearing expenses because of agency's failure to disclose physicians' advice against adoption based on eight-year-old girl's serious behavioral problems).

Many of the abrogation claims involve stepparent adoption, and courts are generally not sympathetic to the stepparent who seeks to reverse an adoption after his marriage to the biological parent ends in divorce. An Ohio court rejected a stepfather's petition to vacate the adoption order, where the mother (his now-former wife) allegedly had coerced him through misrepresentations to adopt her children, for the sole purpose of providing them with financial security. *Joslyn v. Reynolds*, 761 N.E.2d 48 (Ohio 2001). The marriage ended shortly after the end of the one-year time period of the statute of limitations for abrogation applied to stepparent adoptions. The court declined to extend the definition of fraud to allow the stepfather to qualify for an exception to the limitations period.

Courts are more receptive to these actions where the facts are not only compelling but the child's interests are not endangered by rescinding the adoption order, and may even be promoted by it. A stepfather's adoption was abrogated in a case in which the couple, who lived together only a year, separated three weeks after the adoption decree was issued. *Adoption of Children by O.*, 359 A.2d 513 (N.J. Super. Ct. Ch. Div. 1976). The mother had sufficient funds to provide for the children on her own, and neither she, the children nor the adoptive father wanted the adoption to be effective. The court concluded that the children's interest supported vacating this adoption decree. For further discussion of annulment of adoption actions, see Elizabeth N. Carroll, *Abrogation of Adoption by Adoptive Parents*, 19 FAM. L.Q. 155 (1985); Anne Harland Howard, *supra*.

PROBLEM

Problem 11-7. Debra was adopted by the Allens at age 3, after having been in state custody for two years. By the time Debra was 5 years old, she had severe behavior problems and was adjudged mentally deficient. Although she was committed to a public institution, two years later she still had not actually gained admission due to overcrowded conditions. The Allens have continued to care for her at home, but they are concerned over the disturbing effect she has on their family life and their other children. They are also anxious to be relieved of the heavy financial burden of caring for Debra, which will continue even after her ultimate institutionalization, since the state charges the parents of children committed to the institution. The Allens have recently learned that the agency had significant information about Debra's child's psychological condition in its possession at the time of the adoption, and did not communicate it to the Allens, although they inquired about potential problems.

The Allens seek your advice about their legal options. They would like to annul the adoption decree, to make the agency responsible for Debra. Advise them on this matter. What other remedies might be available? *See* B3, *supra*.

E. ALTERNATIVES TO ADOPTION: ASSISTED REPRODUCTIVE TECHNOLOGIES

[1] Insemination by Donor

Insemination by donor, often referred to as "artificial insemination" or AID, has long been used to assist couples who wish to procreate, where the husband's sperm cannot be used, either because they are not viable or because the couple risks passing on a genetic disorder with use of his sperm. In a simple procedure first reported in 1799, the woman is medically inseminated with sperm obtained from a donor, who is typically anonymous. According to a report in the early 1990s, about 30,000 American babies are born via AID each year. *See generally* Gibson, *Artificial Insemination by Donor: Information, Communication and Regulation*, 30 J. FAM. L. 1, 1 (1991–92); ROBERTSON, CHILDREN OF CHOICE: FREEDOM AND THE NEW REPRODUCTIVE TECHNOLOGIES 119 (1994). AID is facilitated by statutes, many of which were based on the 1973 Uniform Parentage Act, treating a man who consents to his wife's insemination with donor sperm as the child's legal father. The child is therefore the legitimate child of the husband and wife, and that the sperm donor has no legally recognized relationship with the child. The statutes typically require the husband's written consent to trigger the automatic recognition of his paternal status (and termination of any paternal claims by the sperm donor). Some statutes require that the implantation be performed by a physician for the legal effect of severing the sperm donor's relationship to occur. CAL. FAM. CODE § 7613 (2009). *See, e.g., Jhordan C. v. Mary K.*, 224 CAL. RPTR. 530 (App. 1986) (father's rights were not severed where child was conceived through informal AID performed at home); Michael J. Yaworsky, *Rights and Obligations Resulting from Human Artificial Insemination*, 83 A.L.R.4th 295 (1991 & Supp. 2009) (reviewing cases).

Courts have also addressed the applicability of these doctrines in nonmarital relationships. In a recent California case, the cohabiting partner of a woman whose child was conceived through AID was held to be the legal father. *Dunkin v. Boskey*, 98 Cal. Rptr. 2d 44 (Ct. App. 2000). The couple had executed a written contract, in which each promised never to allege that the child was not the couple's. Later the mother left and denied her partner custody or visitation. The court held the contract to grant paternity rights was binding between the parties. The partner had achieved parental status by virtue of his consent to insemination and assumption of parental duties. A Texas appeals court held that a sperm donor did not have standing to bring a claim to establish parentage in *In the Interest of H.C.S.*, 219 S.W.3d 33 (Tex. App. 2006). *See also In re Parentage of M.J.*, 759 N.E.2d 121 (Ill. App. Ct. 2001) (no support liability by cohabitation partner, absent written consent to AID).

Aside from statutes automatically conferring parental status on the woman's husband, AID has been relatively unregulated until recently. All states require tissue banks, including sperm banks, to screen donors for the HIV virus. But only a few states legislatively mandate more extensive screening. CAL. HEALTH & SAFETY CODE § 1644.5 (2009); IND. CODE ANN. § 16-41-14-5 (2009). Nonetheless, a study by the Office of Technology Assessment in the 1980s found that all sperm banks surveyed screened for HIV antibodies, and most screened for other sexually transmitted diseases and for genetic disorders. *See* U.S. Congress, Office of Technology Assessment, *Artificial Insemination Practice in the United States: Artificial Insemination Report*, at 68–70 (USGPO, Aug. 1988). However, the same survey found that only 44% of physicians who obtained sperm outside of sperm banks even tested donors for the HIV virus. *Id.* at 34–35. For an analysis of donor screening procedures, see Hodgson, *The Warranty of Sperm: A Modest Proposal to Increase the Accountability of Sperm Banks and Physicians in the Performance of Artificial Insemination Procedures*, 26 IND. L. REV. 357 (1993).

The lack of legal attention to AID, in part, reflects the fact that it has been relatively uncontroversial. There have been some issues, however, that have received attention in the popular press as well as in the scholarly literature. In the early 1980s, a sperm bank called the Repository for Germinal Choice offered customers the sperm of Nobel Prize winners. Nothing in current law would seem to bar or regulate eugenic selection of this kind. *See* Note, *Eugenic Artificial Insemination: A Cure for Mediocrity?*, 94 HARV. L. REV. 1850 (1981). The lack of records about sperm donors and the very strong tradition of anonymity have been questioned in recent years. In a trend parallel to that of adopted children seeking information about their biological parentage, some children procreated with the use of donor sperm have also been seeking information about their genetic fathers. Curiosity and a desire to know more about one's background underlies some of this interest, as does an interest in obtaining complete medical information, including about developments in the biological father's health in the years since the initial file on the donor was created.

In response to this quest for knowledge by AID offspring, Great Britain changed its laws in 2005, allowing children created with donor sperm to obtain information about the identities of their genetic fathers once they turned 18 years of age. The law operates only prospectively, and would therefore protect the anonymity of men who donated sperm prior to the law's passage. *Sperm Donor Anonymity Ends*, BBC News, Mar. 31, 2005, http://news.bbc.co.uk/2/hi/health/4397249.stm; Denise Grady, *Shortage of Sperm Prompts Calls for Change*, New York Times, Nov. 11, 2008. Despite some research in the U.S. indicating that 60% of sperm donors would be comfortable with their genetic offspring learning their identity once turning age 18, see P.P. Mahlstedt & K. I. Probasco, *Sperm Donors: Their Attitudes Toward Providing Medical and Psychological Information for Recipient Couples and Donor Offspring*, 56 FERTILITY & STERILITY 747, 749–752 (1991), the new British law created a severe shortage of sperm donors in England. Grady, *supra*.

A second concern regarding sperm donation is the possibility that, if multiple children are procreated from the same donor's sperm without the knowledge of the identity of the donor, some of the offspring may engage in what is called "inadvertent consanguinity," Grady, *supra*, or "accidental incest." *See* Naomi Cahn, *Accidental Incest: Drawing the Line — or Curtain? For Reproductive Technology,*

32 HARV. J. L. & GENDER 59 (2009). In such cases, unsuspecting half-siblings genetically fathered by the same man could end up producing children together. In 2008, the press reported that a man in South Australia provided sperm used to conceive 30 children. *See, e.g.*, Tory Shepherd, *30 South Australian Lesbian Mums "Impregnated by Same Man'"* Adelaide Now, Oct. 8, 2008, http://www.news.com.au/adelaidenow/story/0,22606,24465265-5006301,00.html). It is likely that there are other such cases that have not been publicized. In order to address this problem, some jurisdictions are limiting the number of offspring that can be created from the same man's sperm. Grady, *supra.*

[2]   In Vitro Fertilization and Egg Donation

Beginning with the birth of Louise Brown, the first "test tube" baby, in 1978, in vitro fertilization (IVF) became available to couples (and eventually also individuals) who experience difficulty conceiving a child. If a married couple uses IVF to conceive a child genetically related to both of them, eggs surgically removed from the woman are fertilized in the laboratory with the husband's sperm, and (one or more of) the resulting embryos are implanted in the woman's uterus. In some instances, donor sperm or donor eggs may be used if the parties do not have viable genetic material or are concerned about passing on a genetically-transmitted disorder or condition. Lyria Bennett Moses, *Understanding Legal Responses to Technological Change: The Example of In Vitro Fertilization*, 6 MINN. J. L. SCIENCE & TECH. 505 (2005). Another variation occurs when nonmarital heterosexual couples make use of IVF, either with their own, or donated, genetic material. In addition, the process can be used to assist same-sex partners or single individuals to procreate as well.

The Center for Disease Control and Prevention (CDC) tracks the use of ARTs in the U.S. *See, e.g.*, CDC, Assisted Reproductive Technology Success Rates: National Summary and Clinic Reports 2006 (2008), http://www.cdc.gov/art/ART2006/index.htm. The rates of ART use more than doubled between 1996 and 2006. *Id.* at 61. The report on IVF procedures performed in 2006 reveals that depending upon the specific technologies used, the success rates of IVF (i.e., leading to a live birth) range from approximately 22 to 35%. *Id.* at 19. While most children procreated through IVF are perfectly healthy, recent research indicates that children conceived through IVF are at greater risk for certain birth defects than are children not conceived in this manner. *See, e.g.*, J. Reefhuis et al., *Assisted Reproductive Technology and Major Structural Birth Defects in the United States*, 2008 HUMAN REPRODUCTION 1. *See also* Jaime S. King, *Predicting Probability: Regulating the Future of Preimplantation Genetic Screening*, 8 YALE J. HEALTH POL'Y L. & ETHICS 304–09 (summarizing empirical findings).

The IVF technology creates the option for procreation with donor eggs, and therefore raises questions as to whether parentage determinations in the context of egg donation are analogous to those established for sperm donation. There is surprisingly little law setting forth the legal rules to determine parentage of children conceived with eggs that are not the genetic material of the intended mother. A handful of states have modified their statutes concerning parentage of children resulting from artificial insemination so as to encompass egg donation and treating the two types of donations similarly for that purpose. *See, e.g.*, Ala. Code § 26-17-702 (2009):

> A donor who donates to a licensed physician for use by a married woman is not a parent of a child conceived by means of assisted reproduction. A married couple who, under the supervision of a licensed physician, engage in assisted reproduction through use of donated eggs, sperm, or both, will be treated at law as if they are the sole natural and legal parents of a child conceived thereby.

The following states are among the handful of jurisdictions that formally address parentage in the context of donated eggs, and are in accord with Alabama's approach. COLO. REV. ST. ANN. § 19-4-106 (2009); FLA. REV. ST. ANN. § 742.11, § 742.14 (2009); 10 OKLA. ST. ANN. § 554 & 555 (2009). All of these statutes use the terms "husband" and "wife," thereby leaving uncertain their application with nonmarital couples (which might include same-sex partners). The Uniform Parentage Act (2002) provides for analogous treatment of sperm and egg donors, stating that donors of eggs or sperm are not the legal parents of a resulting child, but the man and woman who engage the assisted reproduction process with the intent to be the parent of the resulting child are the legal parents. *See* UPA §§ 702–04 (2002). While the 2000 version of the UPA restricted application to married couples, the 2002 revisions changed the terminology so that the provisions apply to nonmarital couples as well as married couples. The use of gendered terms (i.e., "woman" and "man"), however, leaves the application to same-sex couples uncertain. All of the above statutes provide that *intent* and *consent* are the elements most relevant to the determination of parentage with donated genetic material. In other words, the individuals or couples who *consent* to the use of donated genetic material to substitute for the genetic material they or their spouse (or nonmarital partner in some jurisdictions) would use for conception, and do so with the *intent* of becoming the resulting offsprings' parents, *are* the legal parents (presuming that they properly execute documents testifying to their intent and consent). Those who donate the genetic material, by contrast, do so in order to facilitate *someone else's* procreative goals. Assuming all of the documentation is in order, the donors are not the legal parents.

What about regulation of the fees paid to egg donors? A search of the internet reveals that egg donors may be paid between $5,000 and $10,000 per cycle. *See, e.g.*, Egg Donation, Inc. at: http://eggdonor.com/?section=recipient&page=financial. One reporter observed advertisements on college campuses, one of which read: " 'Egg Donors Needed. $10,000,' " and specified that donors should be " 'attractive, under the age of 29' and have SAT scores above 1300." *See* Jim Hopkins, USA TODAY, March 15, 2006. A notorious website that brags $39.2 million in sales of genetic material "auctions off" eggs and sperm provided by donors identified as particularly attractive. *See* Ron's Angels Website at http://www.ronsangels.com/. Does this type of advertising and commercialization of genetic material raise the same issues articulated by Professor Radin (*see* Section C[1][b]) regarding "commodification"? And, if so, is that problematic? Women who donate eggs must receive hormone injections and permit ova to be harvested surgically. Does $5,000 to $10,000 appear appropriate, given the physical and psychological cost to the donor? The Ethics Committee of the American Society for Reproductive Medicine, in a balanced analysis of concerns and justifications for offering financial remuneration to women who donate oocytes, concluded that "[t]otal payments to donors in excess of $5,000 require justification and sums above $10,000 are not appropriate." *Financial Compensation of Oocyte Donors*, 88 FERTILITY & STERILITY 305 (2007). For a discussion of the medical risks of oocyte donation, see the National Institute of Medicine analysis. COMMITTEE ON ASSESSING THE MEDICAL RISKS OF HUMAN OOCYTE DONATION FOR STEM CELL RESEARCH, NATIONAL RESEARCH COUNCIL, ASSESSING THE MEDICAL RISKS OF HUMAN OOCYTE DONATION FOR STEM CELL RESEARCH: WORKSHOP REPORT (2007).

Florida addresses the financial compensation permitted for use of genetic material for assisted reproduction by providing that: "Only reasonable compensation directly related to the donation of eggs, sperm, and preembryos shall be permitted." FLA. REV. ST. ANN. § 742.14 (2009). Thus, presumably, the cost of the necessary hormone injections and surgical procedure required for egg donation could be covered, but payments that are substantially greater than the costs incurred are impermissible, although it is not clear precisely when the statute's restriction would be triggered. Section [3] addresses surrogacy contracts, and Section [4] addresses the legal status of human embryos and the emerging technology to perform preimplantation genetic diagnosis.

[3]   Surrogacy Contracts

IN RE BABY M
New Jersey Supreme Court
537 A.2d 1227 (1988)

WILENTZ, C.J.

In this matter the Court is asked to determine the validity of a contract that purports to provide a new way of bringing children into a family. For a fee of $10,000, a woman agrees to be artificially inseminated with the semen of another woman's husband; she is to conceive a child, carry it to term, and after its birth surrender it to the natural father and his wife. The intent of the contract is that the child's natural mother will thereafter be forever separated from her child. The wife is to adopt the child, and she and the natural father are to be regarded as its parents for all purposes. The contract providing for this is called a "surrogacy contract," the natural mother inappropriately called the "surrogate mother."

We invalidate the surrogacy contract because it conflicts with the law and public policy of this State. While we recognize the depth of the yearning of infertile couples to have their own children, we find the payment of money to a "surrogate" mother illegal, perhaps criminal, and potentially degrading to women. Although in this case we grant custody to the natural father, the evidence having clearly proved such custody to be in the best interests of the infant, we void both the termination of the surrogate mother's parental rights and the adoption of the child by the wife/stepparent. We thus restore the "surrogate" as the mother of the child. We remand the issue of the natural mother's visitation rights to the trial court.

We find no offense to our present laws where a woman voluntarily and without payment agrees to act as a "surrogate" mother, provided that she is not subject to a binding agreement to surrender her child. . . . Under current law, however, the surrogacy agreement before us is illegal and invalid.

I.

In February 1985, William Stern and Mary Beth Whitehead entered into a surrogacy contract. . . . [¶] The contract provided that through artificial insemination using Mr. Stern's sperm, Mrs. Whitehead would become pregnant, carry the child to term, bear it, deliver it to the Sterns, and thereafter do whatever was necessary to terminate her maternal rights so that Mrs. Stern could thereafter adopt the child. Mrs. Whitehead's husband, Richard, was also a party to the contract; Mrs. [Elizabeth] Stern was not. Mr. Whitehead promised to do all acts necessary to rebut the presumption of paternity under the Parentage Act. Although Mrs. Stern was not a party to the surrogacy agreement, the contract gave her sole custody of the child in the event of Mr. Stern's death. Mrs. Stern's status as a nonparty to the surrogate parenting agreement presumably was to avoid the application of the baby-selling statute to this arrangement.

Mr. Stern . . . agreed to attempt the artificial insemination and to pay Mrs. Whitehead $10,000 after the child's birth, on its delivery to him. In a separate contract, Mr. Stern agreed to pay $7,500 to the Infertility Center of New York ("ICNY"). . . .

The history of the parties' involvement in this arrangement suggests their good faith. William and Elizabeth Stern were married in July 1974, having met at the University of Michigan, where both were Ph.D. candidates. [Before they decided to start a family,] Mrs. Stern learned that she might have multiple sclerosis and that the disease in some cases renders pregnancy a serious health risk. Her anxiety appears to have exceeded the actual risk, which current medical authorities assess as minimal. Nonetheless that anxiety was evidently quite real. . . . Based on the perceived risk, the Sterns decided to forego having their own children. The decision had special significance for Mr. Stern. Most of his family had been destroyed in the Holocaust. As the family's only survivor, he very much wanted to continue his bloodline.

Initially the Sterns considered adoption, but were discouraged by the substantial delay apparently involved and by the potential problem they saw arising from their age and their differing religious backgrounds. . . .

The paths of Mrs. Whitehead and the Sterns to surrogacy were similar. Both responded to advertising by ICNY. . . . Mrs. Whitehead's response apparently resulted from her sympathy with family members and others who could have no children; she also wanted the $10,000 to help her family.

. . . . On February 6, 1985, Mr. Stern and Mr. and Mrs. Whitehead executed the surrogate parenting agreement. After several artificial inseminations over a period of months, Mrs. Whitehead became pregnant. The pregnancy was uneventful and on March 27, 1986, Baby M was born . . .

Mrs. Whitehead realized, almost from the moment of birth, that she could not part with this child. She had felt a bond with it even during pregnancy. Some indication of the attachment was conveyed to the Sterns at the hospital when they told Mrs. Whitehead what they were going to name the baby. She apparently broke into tears and indicated that she did not know if she could give up the child. . . .

Nonetheless, Mrs. Whitehead was, for the moment, true to her word. Despite powerful inclinations to the contrary, she turned her child over to the Sterns on March 30 at the Whiteheads' home. . . . [¶] Later in the evening of March 30, Mrs. Whitehead became deeply disturbed, disconsolate, stricken with unbearable sadness. . . . The next day she went to the Sterns' home and told them how much she was suffering.

. . . . She told them that she could not live without her baby, that she must have her, even if only for one week, that thereafter she would surrender her child. The Sterns, concerned that Mrs. Whitehead might indeed commit suicide, not wanting under any circumstances to risk that, and in any event believing that Mrs. Whitehead would keep her word, turned the child over to her. . . .

The struggle over Baby M began when it became apparent that Mrs. Whitehead could not return the child to Mr. Stern. Due to Mrs. Whitehead's refusal to relinquish the baby, Mr. Stern filed a complaint seeking enforcement of the surrogacy contract. . . .

The Whiteheads . . . fled to Florida with Baby M. . . . For the next three months, the Whiteheads and Melissa lived at roughly twenty different hotels, motels, and homes in order to avoid apprehension. From time to time Mrs. Whitehead would call Mr. Stern to discuss the matter; the conversations, recorded by Mr. Stern on advice of counsel, show an escalating dispute about rights, morality, and power, accompanied by threats of Mrs. Whitehead to kill herself, to kill the child, and falsely to accuse Mr. Stern of sexually molesting Mrs. Whitehead's other daughter.

Eventually the Sterns discovered where the Whiteheads were staying, . . . and obtained [a Florida] order requiring the Whiteheads to turn over the child. Police in Florida enforced the order, forcibly removing the child from her grandparents' home. She was soon thereafter brought to New Jersey and turned over to the Sterns. The prior order of the court, issued *ex parte*, awarding custody of the child to the Sterns *pendente lite*, was reaffirmed by the trial court. . . . Pending final judgment, Mrs. Whitehead was awarded limited visitation with Baby M. The Sterns' complaint, in addition to seeking possession and ultimately custody of the child, sought enforcement of the surrogacy contract. Pursuant to the contract, it asked that the child be permanently placed in their custody, that Mrs. Whitehead's parental rights be terminated, and that Mrs. Stern be allowed to adopt the child, i.e., that, for all purposes, Melissa become the Sterns' child. . . .

. . . . The trial court concluded that the various statutes governing this matter, including those concerning adoption, termination of parental rights, and payment of money in connection with adoptions, do not apply to surrogacy contracts. It reasoned that because the Legislature did not have surrogacy contracts in mind when it passed those laws, those laws were therefore irrelevant. . . . It then held that surrogacy contracts are valid and should be enforced, and furthermore that Mr. Stern's rights under the surrogacy contract were constitutionally protected. Mrs. Whitehead appealed. . . .

Mrs. Whitehead contends that the surrogacy contract . . . is invalid. . . . With the contract thus void, Mrs. Whitehead claims primary custody (with visitation rights in Mr. Stern) both on a best interests basis (stressing the "tender years" doctrine) as well as on the policy basis of discouraging surrogacy contracts. . . . [¶] . . . The Sterns claim that the surrogacy contract is valid and should be enforced . . . As for the child's best interests, their position is factual: given all of the circumstances, the child is better off in their custody with no residual parental rights reserved for Mrs. Whitehead.

II.

Invalidity and Unenforceability of Surrogacy Contract

We have concluded that this surrogacy contract is invalid. Our conclusion has two bases: direct conflict with existing statutes and conflict with the public policies of this State, as expressed in its statutory and decisional law.

One of the surrogacy contract's basic purposes, to achieve the adoption of a child through private placement, though permitted in New Jersey "is very much disfavored." Its use of money for this purpose . . . is illegal and perhaps criminal. In addition to the inducement of money, there is the coercion of contract: the natural mother's irrevocable agreement, prior to birth, even prior to conception, to surrender the child to the adoptive couple. Such an agreement is totally unenforceable in private placement adoption. Even where the adoption is through an approved agency, the formal agreement to surrender occurs only after birth (as we read N.J.S.A. 9:2-16 and -17, and similar statutes), and then, by regulation, only after the birth mother has been offered counseling. Integral to these invalid provisions of the surrogacy contract is the related agreement, equally invalid, on the part of the natural mother to cooperate with, and not to contest, proceedings to terminate her parental rights, as well as her contractual concession, in aid of the adoption, that the child's best interests would be served by awarding custody to the natural father and his wife — all of this before she has even conceived, and, in some cases, before she has the slightest idea of what the natural father and adoptive mother are like. . . .

A. Conflict with Statutory Provisions

The surrogacy contract conflicts with: (1) laws prohibiting the use of money in connection with adoptions; (2) laws requiring proof of parental unfitness or abandonment before termination of parental rights is ordered or an adoption is granted; and (3) laws that make surrender of custody and consent to adoption revocable in private placement adoptions.

(1) Our law prohibits paying or accepting money in connection with any placement of a child for adoption. [¶] . . . Considerable care was taken in this case

to structure the surrogacy arrangement so as not to violate this prohibition. . . . [T]he adopting parent, Mrs. Stern, was not a party to the surrogacy contract; the money paid to Mrs. Whitehead was stated to be for her services — not for the adoption; the sole purpose of the contract was stated as being that "of giving a child to William Stern, its natural and biological father"; the money was purported to be "compensation for services and expenses and in no way . . . a fee for termination of parental rights or a payment in exchange for consent to surrender a child for adoption"; the fee to the Infertility Center ($7,500) was stated to be for legal representation, advice, administrative work, and other "services." Nevertheless, it seems clear that the money was paid and accepted in connection with an adoption.

. . . The payment of the $10,000 [to Mrs. Whitehead] occurs only on surrender of custody of the child and "completion of the duties and obligations" of Mrs. Whitehead, including termination of her parental rights to facilitate adoption by Mrs. Stern. . . .

(2) The termination of Mrs. Whitehead's parental rights, called for by the surrogacy contract and actually ordered by the court, fails to comply with the stringent requirements of New Jersey law. . . .

. . . .

. . . As the trial court recognized, without a valid termination there can be no adoption. . . . [¶] [A] "best interests" determination is never sufficient to terminate parental rights. . . . [¶] In this case a termination . . . was obtained not by proving the statutory prerequisites but by claiming the benefit of contractual provisions . . . The Legislature would not have so carefully, so consistently, and so substantially restricted termination of parental rights if it had intended to allow termination to be achieved by one short sentence in a contract. [¶] Since the termination was invalid, it follows . . . that adoption of Melissa by Mrs. Stern could not properly be granted. (3) The provision in the surrogacy contract stating that Mary Beth Whitehead agrees to "surrender custody . . . and terminate all parental rights" . . . is intended to be an . . . irrevocable commitment by Mrs. Whitehead to . . . allow termination of her parental rights. . . .

. . . .

[S]trict prerequisites to irrevocability [set in New Jersey statutes] constitute a recognition of the most serious consequences that flow from such consents: termination of parental rights. . . . Because of those consequences, the Legislature severely limited the circumstances under which such consent would be irrevocable. . . .

. . . .

. . . . The provision in the surrogacy contract, agreed to before conception, requiring the natural mother to surrender custody of the child without any right of revocation [creates] a contractual system of termination and adoption designed to circumvent our statutes.

B. *Public Policy Considerations*

The surrogacy contract's invalidity . . . is further underlined [by] New Jersey's public policy. The contract's basic premise, that the natural parents can decide in advance of birth which one is to have custody of the child, bears no relationship to the settled law that the child's best interests shall determine custody. . . .

The surrogacy contract guarantees permanent separation of the child from one of its natural parents. Our policy, however, has long been that to the extent possible, children should remain with and be brought up by both of their natural parents. [As a result of this surrogacy contract] a child, instead of starting off its life with as much peace and security as possible, finds itself immediately in a tug-of-war between contending mother and father.

. . . .

Under the contract, the natural mother is irrevocably committed before she knows the strength of her bond with her child. She never makes a totally voluntary, informed decision, for quite clearly any decision prior to the baby's birth is, in the most important sense, uninformed, and any decision after that, compelled by a pre-existing contractual commitment, the threat of a lawsuit, and the inducement of a $10,000 payment, is less than totally voluntary. Her interests are of little concern to those who controlled this transaction.

Although the interest of the natural father and adoptive mother is certainly the predominant interest, realistically the only interest served, even they are left with less than what public policy requires. They know little about the natural mother, her genetic makeup, and her psychological and medical history. . . .

Worst of all, however, is the contract's total disregard of the best interests of the child. There is not the slightest suggestion that any inquiry will be made at any time to determine the fitness of the Sterns as custodial parents, of Mrs. Stern as an adoptive parent, their superiority to Mrs. Whitehead, or the effect on the child of not living with her natural mother.

This is the sale of a child, or, at the very least, the sale of a mother's right to her child, the only mitigating factor being that one of the purchasers is the father. Almost every evil that prompted the prohibition on the payment of money in connection with adoptions exists here.

The differences between an adoption and a surrogacy contract should be noted. . . . [¶] First, . . . [d]espite the alleged selfless motivation of surrogate mothers, if there is no payment, there will be no surrogates, or very few. That . . . contrasts with adoption; for obvious reasons, there remains a steady supply, albeit insufficient, despite the prohibitions against payment. . . .

Second, the use of money in adoptions does not produce the problem — conception occurs, and usually the birth itself, before illicit funds are offered. With surrogacy, the "problem," if one views it as such, consisting of the purchase of a woman's procreative capacity, at the risk of her life, is caused by and originates with the offer of money.

. . . .

The main difference, that the unwanted pregnancy is unintended while the situation of the surrogate mother is voluntary and intended, is really not significant. . . . On reflection, however, it appears that the essential evil is the same, taking advantage of a woman's circumstances (the unwanted pregnancy or the need for money) in order to take away her child, the difference being one of degree.

. . . .

Intimated, but disputed, is the assertion that surrogacy will be used for the benefit of the rich at the expense of the poor. . . . In response it is noted that the Sterns are not rich and the Whiteheads not poor. Nevertheless, . . . we doubt that infertile couples in the low-income bracket will find upper income surrogates.

In any event, even in this case . . . wealth . . . play[ed] a part . . . [The Whiteheads'] income derived from Mr. Whitehead's labors. Mrs. Whitehead is a homemaker, having previously held part-time jobs. The Sterns are both professionals, she a medical doctor, he a biochemist. Their combined income when both were working was about $89,500 a year and their assets sufficient to pay for the surrogacy contract arrangements.

. . . . There are, in a civilized society, some things that money cannot buy . . .

. . . . In New Jersey the surrogate mother's agreement to sell her child is void. Its irrevocability infects the entire contract, as does the money that purports to buy it.

III.

Termination

[The court found no basis for involuntary termination of Mary Beth Whitehead's parental rights because she was neither unfit nor has she abandoned her child under the applicable statutory standards.]

IV.

Constitutional Issues

[The court held that constitutional protection of the right to procreate had no bearing on this case because it cannot provide a basis for favoring the claim of either Mr. Stern or Mrs. Whitehead as against the other parent.] Mr. Stern also contends that he has been denied equal protection of the laws by the . . . statute granting full parental rights to a husband in relation to the child produced, with his consent, by the union of his wife with a sperm donor. N.J.S.A. 9:17-44. The claim really is that of Mrs. Stern [because] she is in precisely the same position as the husband in the statute: she is presumably infertile, as is the husband in the statute; her spouse by agreement with a third party procreates with the understanding that the child will be the couple's child. The alleged unequal protection is that the understanding is honored in the statute when the husband is the infertile party, but no similar understanding is honored when it is the wife who is infertile.

It is quite obvious that the situations are not parallel. A sperm donor simply cannot be equated with a surrogate mother. The State has more than a sufficient basis to distinguish the two situations — even if the only difference is between the time it takes to provide sperm for artificial insemination and the time invested in a nine-month pregnancy — so as to justify automatically divesting the sperm donor of his parental rights without automatically divesting a surrogate mother. Some basis for an equal protection argument might exist if Mary Beth Whitehead had contributed her egg to be implanted, fertilized or otherwise, in Mrs. Stern, resulting in the latter's pregnancy. That is not the case here, however.

[The court declined to rule on Mrs. Whitehead's claim that her constitutional right to companionship of her child was violated.]

V.

Custody

[The Court then resolved the custody dispute between the parents under the best interest of the child standard.]

[T]he trial court's decision awarding custody to the Sterns (technically to Mr. Stern) should be affirmed since "its findings . . . could reasonably have been reached on sufficient credible evidence present in the record." [¶] Our . . . conclusion is based on strongly persuasive testimony contrasting both the family life of the Whiteheads and the Sterns and the personalities and characters of the individuals. The stability of the Whitehead family life was doubtful at the time of trial. Their finances were in serious trouble . . . Mr. Whitehead's employment, though relatively steady, was always at risk because of his alcoholism. . . . The expert testimony contained criticism of Mrs. Whitehead's handling of her son's educational difficulties. [E]xperts noted that Mrs. Whitehead perceived herself as omnipotent and omniscient concerning her children. . . . As to Melissa, Mrs. Whitehead expressed the view that she alone knew what that child's cries and sounds meant. . . . In short, while love and affection there would be, Baby M's life with the Whiteheads promised to be too closely controlled by Mrs. Whitehead. The prospects for wholesome, independent psychological growth and development would be at serious risk.

The Sterns have no other children, but all indications are that their household and their personalities promise a much more likely foundation for Melissa to grow and thrive. There *is* a track record of sorts — during the one-and-a-half years of custody Baby M has done very well, and the relationship between both Mr. and Mrs. Stern and the baby has become very strong. The household is stable, and likely to remain so. Their finances are more than adequate, their circle of friends supportive, and their marriage happy. Most important, they are loving, giving, nurturing, and open-minded people. . . . All in all, Melissa's future appears solid, happy, and promising with them.

Based on all of this we have concluded, independent of the trial court's identical conclusion, that Melissa's best interests call for custody in the Sterns. . . .

[The Court then directed that in the future the mother should be awarded custody *pendente lite* because of "the probable bond between mother and child." Only where the mother is unfit should the natural father in a surrogacy dispute get temporary custody. The Court remanded the case to determine visitation for Ms. Whitehead.]

NOTES

1. *The Epilogue to the Case of* **Baby M.** On remand, the trial court granted Mary Beth Whitehead eight hours of unsupervised visitation a week, to increase over the course of the year to two days every two weeks, including an overnight. While observing that "William and Elizabeth Stern are extraordinarily good parents . . . and their daughter is firmly bonded to them," it also concluded that "Melissa is a resilient child who is no less capable than thousands of children of broken marriages who successfully adjust to complex family relationships when their parents remarry." It observed that Melissa had developed a warm and close relationship with her mother.

Mary Beth Whitehead subsequently divorced her husband and remarried. In a 1997 interview, she expressed continuing resentment of the Sterns, although she acknowledged being worried that her visitation might hurt Melissa. Under the visitation agreement, she saw Melissa on a regular basis, although their time together had been reduced since the child started school. Melissa, according to the interviewer, seemed comfortable with her mother and half-siblings, but expressed some anxiety, "It's weird having two moms." *See* Puzzanghera, *Unhappy Surrogate L.I. Mom Wants to Live Closer to Baby M.* NEWSDAY, Dec. 13, 1997, at 19. In 2008, the *New York Post* printed an article entitled "Tug O' Love Baby All Grown Up," accompanied by a photo of Melissa Stern, 22 years old and a college senior at George Washington University. It quotes Melissa as saying about the Sterns: "I'm very happy I ended up with them." Susannah Cahalan, *Tug O' Love Baby All Grown Up*, NEW YORK POST, Apr. 13, 2008, *available at* http://www.nypost.com/seven/04132008/news/nationalnews/tug_o_love_baby_m_all _grown_up_106337.htm.

2. *Distinguishing "Gestational" from "Traditional" Surrogates.* In resolving a dispute regarding parentage of a child procreated with the assistance of a surrogate, should it matter whether the child is also the *genetic* child of the surrogate, or if the ovum creating the child is that of the intended mother or of a donor? Given the advent of IVF, it is now possible for the woman who is the intended mother to use her own ova or that of a donor, fertilized by her husband's (or a donor's) sperm, to create the embryo that is ultimately implanted in the uterus of a "gestational surrogate." Women, like Mrs. Whitehead, who contribute genetic material and gestate the child, are now referred to by some writers as "traditional surrogates." Suppose that Mrs. Stern's ovum, rather than Mrs. Whitehead's, created Melissa. Would or should the legal result differ? A case with these facts was decided by the California Supreme Court.

In *Johnson v. Calvert*, 851 P.2d 776 (Cal. 1993), Mark and Crispina Calvert wished to have a child. Crispina had had surgery several years earlier which left her with the capacity to produce eggs. But, she could not gestate a pregnancy. The couple ultimately entered into a contract with Anna Johnson, who agreed to allow implantation of an embryo created from Mark and Crispina's genetic material in her uterus so that she could gestate a child for them. The Calverts promised to pay Anna $10,000 in a series of installments, the last to be paid six weeks after the child's birth. Mark and Crispina were also to pay for a $200,000 life insurance policy on Anna's life for the benefit her already-existing child. At some point during the pregnancy, Anna changed her mind and indicated that she would not surrender the child as planned to the Calverts. Anna and Crispina each claimed to be the child's legal mother. Anna's claim was grounded on the fact that she gave birth to the child while Crispina based her claim on her genetic relationship to the child.

In resolving the dispute, the California Supreme Court looked to the various California statutes that govern determinations of maternity. It noted that provisions of the Uniform Parentage Act (1973) adopted by California indicate that the mother-child relationship "*may* be established by proof of her having given birth to the child." On the other hand, California's Evidence Code indicated that parentage can be determined by means of blood testing (i.e., genetics). The court concluded that either of these two methods can be used to establish maternity in California. It therefore held:

> Because two women each have presented acceptable proof of maternity, we do not believe this case can be decided without enquiring into the parties' intentions as manifested in the surrogacy agreement. Mark and Crispina are a couple who desired to have a child of their own genetic stock but are physically unable to do so without the help of reproductive technology. They affirmatively intended the birth of the child, and took the steps necessary to effect in vitro fertilization. But for their acted-on intention, the child would not exist. Anna agreed to facilitate the procreation of Mark's and Crispina's child. The parties' aim was to bring Mark's and Crispina's child into the world, not for Mark and Crispina to donate a zygote to Anna. Crispina from the outset intended to be the child's mother. Although the gestative function Anna performed was necessary to bring about the child's birth, it is safe to say that Anna would not have been given the opportunity to gestate or deliver the child had she, prior to implantation of the zygote, manifested her own intent to be the child's mother. No reason appears why Anna's later change of heart should vitiate the determination that Crispina is the child's natural mother.

> We conclude that although the Act recognizes both genetic consanguinity and giving birth as means of establishing a mother and child relationship, when the two means do not coincide in one woman, she who intended to procreate the child — that is, she who intended to bring about the birth of a child that she intended to raise as her own — is the natural mother under California law.

851 P.2d at 782. In reaching its decision, the court relied heavily on scholarship arguing that, in assisted reproduction cases, parentage should be grounded on

intentionality (i.e., the purpose of bringing the child into the world with the intent of becoming that child's legal parent). As the court's language above reveals, however, it did not hold that intentionality is dispositive. It considered intentionality to be a "tie-breaker" of sorts in a situation where two women had split between them the two different biological functions that can establish maternity. The court did not address whether intentionality would play a role in assisted reproduction cases that did not split these two biological functions between the surrogate and intended mother.

How might the California Supreme Court have decided *Johnson v. Calvert* if Anna was the genetic *and* gestational mother? The California Supreme Court has not had the opportunity to answer that question. There are two very interesting circuit court decisions that point in different directions. In *Moschetta v. Moschetta*, 30 Cal. Rptr. 2d 893 (Ct. App. 1994), a court of appeal held that *Johnson v. Calvert's* holding did not govern the case before it, in which the surrogate was also the genetic mother. It held that intent only becomes relevant when the gestational mother is not also the genetic mother. Yet, the facts of this case were quite unusual and may have played some role in the result. In this case, the surrogate had planned to surrender the child to the married couple for whom she had served as a surrogate. However, while the surrogate was in labor, the couple informed her that they had decided to get a divorce. Feeling strongly that it was not in the child's best interests to be parented by a divorcing couple, the surrogate changed her mind, deciding to claim the child. The most unusual aspect of this case is that, although the husband claimed that his (soon-to-be-ex) wife was the lawful mother, the wife herself disclaimed maternity in favor of the surrogate. She even filed a brief on behalf of the surrogate. Thus, there was no other woman claiming maternity in a contest with the surrogate.

In another California case, *Buzzanca v. Buzzanca*, 72 Cal. Rptr. 2d 280 (Ct. App. 1998), a husband and wife decided to divorce while a surrogate was carrying their intended child. The husband, trying to avoid child support obligations, disclaimed any responsibility for the child. The facts of this case were rather extraordinary because five parties were involved in bringing about the child's birth. The embryo was created with donor sperm and a donor egg. A gestational surrogate (who was not the same woman that donated the eggs), carried the child to term. Neither the intended mother or intended father had any biological relationship to the child. Stumped by the facts, the trial court judged concluded that the child had *no* lawful parents, and held that the intended mother, could adopt the child, Jaycee. The court of appeal overturned that decision and held that the intended parents were the child's lawful parents. The reasoning used by the court was relatively straightforward. It regarded the donation of sperm in this case as analogous to the treatment of donor sperm in AID cases when a man's wife is inseminated. Here the court treated the husband's *consent* for the fertilization of an egg with donor sperm, with the *intent* to become the legal father of the resulting child as it would treat such consent if the intended mother had been directly inseminated. Therefore, consent in the context of IVF was treated as analogous to consent in the traditional AID scenario. Likewise, the court treated the egg donation in the instant case as analogous to AID in that the intended parents accepted donated genetic for the purpose of creating a child they intended to raise as their legal child. The court determined that the *intent* to bring about the conception and birth of a child controls, as it does in sperm and egg donation cases. That the embryo was implanted in a surrogate rather than the intended mother did not change the analysis. Thus, in *Buzzanca*, intentionality was dispositive. In *Buzzanca*, like *Moschetta*, only one woman claimed maternity. Yet in *Moschetta*, the *surrogate* claimed maternity while in *Buzzanca* the intended mother claimed maternity. How might *Buzzanca* have been decided if the egg donor or the surrogate claimed maternity? What if the surrogate was also the genetic mother? We don't know if and how these variations on the facts might have changed the analysis or the result. If intentionality always prevails, then the intended parents would be the parents regardless of who else competes with them. On the other hand, would the *Buzzanca* court have adhered to that rule if a gestational surrogate who was also the genetic mother contested Mrs. Buzzanca's maternity of the child?

It seems clear that, for those couples who can afford to do so, using IVF and the intended mother's eggs or those of a donor increase the chances that a court will enforce a surrogacy agreement in the event there is a dispute between the surrogate and the intended parents. Is it fair that the difference in legal enforcement might hinge on whether the parties can afford IVF, which costs between $10,000–$15,000 per cycle, compared with $300–$500 per cycle for artificial insemination?

3. ***Considerations of Public Policy.***   In 2000, relying on the New Jersey Supreme Court's decision in Baby M., a lower New Jersey court rejected the joint petition of a gestational surrogate and the intended and genetic parents of a not-yet-born baby for a pre-birth declaration that the intended/genetic parents are the legal parents. *A.H.W. v. G.H.B.*, 772 A.2d 948 (N.J. Super. Ct. 2000). While we don't know for certain how the New Jersey Supreme Court would have decided this case, or how it would have decided *Baby M.* if Mary Beth Whitehead was not Melissa's genetic mother, the court's objection's to surrogacy on public policy grounds suggest a generally hostile reception to surrogacy contracts, regardless of the specific facts. In *Baby M.*, the New Jersey Supreme Court cited conflicts between the law governing adoption and the enforcement of surrogacy contracts. Among other concerns, it expressed disapproval of the introduction of monetary compensation and prebirth agreements affecting parental rights.

The California Supreme Court saw the issues quite differently, however. In *Johnson v. Calvert*, it rejected the adoption analogy:

> Anna urges that surrogacy contracts violate several social policies. Relying on her contention that she is the child's legal, natural mother, she cites the public policy embodied in Penal Code section 273, prohibiting the payment for consent to adoption of a child. She argues further that the policies underlying the adoption laws of this state are violated by the surrogacy contract because it in effect constitutes a prebirth waiver of her parental rights.

> We disagree. Gestational surrogacy differs in crucial respects from adoption and so is not subject to the adoption statutes. The parties voluntarily agreed to participate in in vitro fertilization and related medical procedures before the child was conceived; at the time when Anna entered into the contract, therefore, she was not vulnerable to financial induce-

ments to part with her own expected offspring. . . . The payments to Anna under the contract were meant to compensate her for her services in gestating the fetus and undergoing labor, rather than for giving up "parental" rights to the child. Payments were due both during the pregnancy and after the child's birth. We are, accordingly, unpersuaded that the contract used in this case violates the public policies embodied in Penal Code section 273 and the adoption statutes. For the same reasons, we conclude these contracts do not implicate the policies underlying the statutes governing termination of parental rights.

851 P.2d at 783–84. In fact, the California and New Jersey Supreme Courts disagreed on just about every public policy issue they addressed.

4. *Cases Addressing Surrogacy in the States.* The initial legal responses to surrogacy have taken place in the courts, since most states have been slow to pass statutes dealing specifically with surrogacy arrangements. In *Baby M.* and *Johnson v. Calvert*, the courts were faced with questions of how to apply law that never anticipated surrogacy. Judges have, at times, bemoaned the lack of legislative guidance. In *Culliton v. Beth Israel Deaconess Medical Center*, 756 N.E.2d 1133 (Mass. 2001), the Massachusetts Supreme Judicial Court was called upon to settle a dispute between the intended parents and the hospital which was about to deliver twin babies that had been carried by a gestational surrogate. In this case, the intended mother and father both contributed the genetic material to create the embryos. The intended parents sought declaratory and injunctive relief in order to compel the hospital to name the intended mother and intended father as the parents on the birth certificates. (There was no dispute between the intended parents and the gestational surrogate.) The Massachusetts court observed that the state's statutes provided no guidance in the determination of whether, at birth (and without the need for adoption proceedings), the twins were the legal children of the intended parents. Speaking for a unanimous court, Chief Justice Greany noted that the statutes that govern establishment of parentage for married and nonmarital couples, and those governing adoption and artificial insemination were not helpful. He strongly encouraged the legislature to enact laws to govern these cases, rather than leaving the lawmaking to the courts. In resolving the instant case, however, the court held that where the intended parents were also the genetic parents, and there is no challenge by the surrogate, it was proper for the court below to enter a judgment declaring the intended parents to be the legal parents. The court distinguished this case from *R.R. v. M.H.*, 689 N.E.2d 790, which it had decided in 1998, because the surrogate in *R.R.* was both the genetic and gestational mother, and therefore, it held, had acquired parental rights.

The surrogate in *R.R.* changed her mind about giving up the baby in the sixth month of pregnancy. In that case, the Massachusetts Supreme Judicial Court indicated that its public policy objections to enforcing the surrogacy contract would be overcome if no compensation was paid beyond pregnancy-related expenses, and if the surrogate was not bound by her consent until a suitable period after the child's birth.

Some state courts have either enforced surrogacy contracts or held that the contracts do not violate the state's adoption statutes. In *Doe v. Roe*, 717 A.2d 706

(Conn. 1998), the Connecticut Supreme Court rejected the gestational mother's challenge of the trial court's jurisdiction to terminate her parental rights. The supreme court concluded that the trial court was not terminating her rights per se, but was issuing an order based on the parties' agreement, which it had reviewed for voluntariness. In *McDonald v. McDonald*, 608 N.Y.S.2d 477 (App. Div. 1994), a husband in a divorce action claimed custodial rights on the ground that he was the only natural parent. The court held that the wife was the natural mother of the children. She had arranged to give birth to children produced by her husband's sperm and a donor's eggs, and did so with her husband's consent.

5. ***Statutes Addressing Surrogacy in the States.***   Although a few states had statutes dealing with gestational contracts before *Baby M.*, there has been considerable legislative activity since the New Jersey opinion. In an attempt to guide the states, the National Conference of Commissioners on Uniform State Laws drafted the Uniform Status of Children of Assisted Conception Act (USCACA) in 1988. The USCACA created two options for states. One alternative provided that surrogacy agreements were prohibited and void. The second alternative provided that such agreements were permissible, but included provisions for heavy state regulation of such agreements with careful judicial supervision. The new Uniform Parentage Act (2002) replaced the 1988 USCACA with a new formulation regulating gestational agreements. Section 8 of the UPA (2002) grants the court discretionary authority to validate a gestational agreement before conception upon finding that a number of requirements are met. These include findings that the gestational mother has had a prior pregnancy; a home study has been conducted; and the consideration paid the gestational mother is reasonable. Under the UPA, the gestational agreement may not limit the right of the gestational mother to "make decisions to safeguard her health or that of the embryos or fetus." Any party can terminate the agreement before a pregnancy occurs and the court can terminate for "good cause" thereafter. Otherwise the agreement is enforceable and the intended parents become the child's legal parents on birth. There is no opportunity for the surrogate to revoke the agreement. An unvalidated agreement is unenforceable. The birth mother and her husband are the legal parents, but the agreement may give rise to child support obligations for the intended parents. It is noteworthy that the provisions of the UPA (2002) treat surrogacy arrangements in which the surrogate is the genetic mother *and* gestational mother as fully enforceable. In light of the reluctance many courts have had to enforce the agreements in such situations, the UPA's provisions reflect a departure. While a handful of states have adopted much of the UPA (2002) (e.g., Alabama, Delaware, North Dakota, Oklahoma, Texas, Utah, Wyoming), not one has adopted the provision of Section 8 that renders all surrogacy agreements that are judicially approved fully enforceable.

Some states criminalize the agreements, although most such statutes prohibit only those contracts that involve monetary compensation. Typically, they reserve the stiffest penalties for intermediaries. *See, e.g.*, MICH. COMP. LAWS § 722.859 (2009) (providing that no "person shall not enter into, induce, arrange, procure, or otherwise assist in the formation of a surrogate parentage contract for compensation" and that a person other than a participating party who induces, arranges, procures, or otherwise assists in the formation of a surrogate parentage contract for compensation is guilty of a felony punishable by a fine of not more than $50,000.00 or imprisonment for not more than five years, or both). Some states prohibit involvement in surrogacy arrangements, and create civil penalties. *See, e.g.*, N.Y. Dom. Rel. Law §§ 121 to 124 (2009) (providing for civil penalties up to $500 for participants in commercial surrogacy contracts and up to $10,000 for the intermediaries arranging surrogacy contracts for compensation).

One group of statutes declares these contracts void, without imposing criminal penalties on the parties, although pre-existing penalties for baby-selling might apply. *See, e.g.*, N.D. Code Ann. § 14-18-05 (2009) (providing that agreements in which "a woman agrees to become a surrogate or to relinquish [parental rights] of a child conceived through assisted conception is void," and that the surrogate will be the legal mother). As in this North Dakota statute, some codes specify how parentage will be determined. Two state statutes providing that the surrogate is conclusively determined to be the legal mother have been held unconstitutional. *Soos v. Superior Court*, 897 P.2d 1356 (Ariz. Ct. App. 1994) (holding Ariz. Stat. Rev. Ann. § 25.218 unconstitutional because it allows the genetic father in a surrogacy arrangement an opportunity to rebut the presumption that the surrogate's husband is the legal father, but does not allow the genetic mother any way to rebut the presumption that the surrogate is the legal mother); *J.R. v. Utah*, 261 F. Supp. 2d 1268 (U.S. Dist. Ct. D. Utah 2002) (holding that Utah Code Ann. § 76-7-204 is unconstitutional as a violation of the genetic/biological mother's fundamental right to procreate by conclusively presuming that the surrogate is the legal mother).

Other statutes recognize the contract as enforceable, although payments are restricted and the gestational mother has a right of recission for a limited period after birth. *See, e.g.*, Fla. Stat. Ann. § 63.213 (2009) ("pre-planned adoption agreements" permitted but gestational mother allowed only reimbursement for medical, legal and "reasonable living" expenses; may decide to keep baby up to 48 hours after birth; all brokerage fees barred).

Some states permit surrogacy arrangements and supervise them very carefully. For example, New Hampshire recognizes gestational contracts that have been judicially approved in advance of the child's birth. N.H. Stat. Ann. §§ 168-B:1 to B:32 (2009). The statute limits payments to pregnancy-related medical expenses; actual lost wages related to pregnancy, delivery and postpartum recovery; health, disability and life insurance during the pregnancy and recovery; reasonable attorney's fees; counseling fees; and costs associated with nonmedical evaluations of the gestational mother and her husband. New Hampshire also provides explicitly that the gestational mother may rescind her agreement to surrender the child within 72 hours of birth. The Virginia statute, based on one alternative of the now supplanted Uniform Status of Children of Assisted Conception Act (1988) (USCACA),is the most comprehensive effort to authorize enforceable gestational agreements, through regulation that seeks to mitigate the problems that have generated opposition to these contracts. Va. Code Ann. § 20-156 et. seq. (2009). The statute sets out a complex set of requirements which, if fulfilled, can result in an enforceable gestational agreement under which the child automatically becomes the child of the intended parents. The intended parents must be married and the wife must be unable to bear a child without unreasonable risk; the child must be the genetic child of one of the intended parents; psychological and physical evaluations and a home study are required of both the intended parents and the gestational mother; the gestational mother must be married and must have had at least one pregnancy and delivery; and all parties must receive mental health counseling. If these requirements are met, the parties can get advance judicial approval of the contract. Upon her birth, the child is the legal child of the intended parents and is not the child of the gestational mother and her husband. However, the gestational mother can terminate the contract by giving written notice to the court within 180 days of conception. § 20-161. If she terminates in a timely manner, the gestational mother and her husband (if any) are the parents. If prior judicial approval is not obtained, the Virginia statute permits the gestational mother, for 25 days after the birth of the child, to relinquish her parental rights. § 20-162. Thus, without judicial approval, the parties are subject to the standard prohibition of pre-birth consent to adoption. Is the statute effective at reducing the risks of gestational surrogacy?

6. *Empirical Research on the Effects of Surrogacy Arrangements on the Intended Parents, the Surrogates, and the Resulting Children.* Researchers have begun to study the effects of surrogacy arrangements on the parties and the resulting offspring. A team of researchers at the London Family and Child Psychology Research Centre in England report generally positive reactions and adjustment to surrogacy arrangements on the part of the commissioning couples and the surrogates. One study of 42 couples who commissioned a surrogacy arrangement revealed that the relationships between the couples and surrogates were generally quite good, with no reported difficulties in the transfer of the newborn from the surrogate to the intended parents. *See* Fiona McCallum et al., *Surrogacy: The Experience of Commissioning Couples*, 18 HUMAN REPRODUCTION 1334 (2003). In an examination of the experiences of 34 surrogate mothers, the same team again found no problems with respect to the relinquishment of the children, and found generally positive relationships with the intended parents. *See* Vasanti Jadva et al, *Surrogacy: The Experiences of Surrogate Mothers*, 18 HUM. REPRODUCTION 2196 (2003). The study did find that some of the surrogates experienced some depressive feelings after relinquishing the child, although those reactions did not rise to the level of a clinical depression, and did remit within a few weeks. The study did not find any differences between surrogates who were the genetic mother and those who were not in terms of their reactions to and feelings about the experience.

The researchers are also following the psychological development of the children, the parent-child relationships, and the parents' adjustment. *See, e.g.,* Susan Golombok et al., *Families Created Through Surrogacy Arrangements: Parent-Child Relationships in the 1st Year of Life*, 40 DEVELOPMENTAL PSYCHOL. 400 (2004); Susan Golombok et al., *Surrogacy Families: Parental Functioning, Parent-Child Relationships and Children's Psychological Development at Age 2*, 47 J. CHILD PSYCHOL. & PSYCHIATRY 213 (2006). Studying the children and families at the end of the child's first year of life, and then again at the two-year marker, the investigators found no differences in the developmental status and functioning of the children between families whose children were procreated through surrogacy arrangements and families whose children were conceived through traditional reproduction. The investigators found greater "psychological well-being and adaptation to parenthood" in the families created by surrogacy. The investigators offer some hypotheses to explain this unexpected finding. Of course, these findings involve a very small sample, and it is difficult to know whether they can be generalized to the larger population of participants in surrogacy arrangements. It does, however, suggest that some of the worst fears of observers may not materialize in most surrogacy arrangements.

7. *Complications Arising From Surrogacy Arrangements.* What happens if the child born to the surrogate is born with a disability or serious medical condition, and the contracting couple does not want to accept the child? In 1983, Judy Stiver, pregnant under a gestational agreement, gave birth to a severely retarded baby boy. Neither she nor the intended adoptive couple, the Malahoffs, wanted the child, and Mr. Malahoff claimed he was not the father. Blood tests established that Stiver's husband fathered the child, apparently before the insemination. Three lawsuits then resulted. Malahoff sued the Stivers for not producing the child consistent with the terms of their agreement; the Stivers sued the doctor, lawyer and psychiatrist involved in the gestational mother program for not advising them about the timing of intercourse; and the Stivers sued Malahoff for violating their privacy by making the incident public. The Stivers also alleged that the child's illness was not genetic but was caused by a virus transmitted by Malahoff's sperm. Andrews, *The Stork Market*, A.B.A. J. 50, 56, Aug. 1984.

8. *Feminist Views of Surrogacy Contracts.* Feminists have been divided in their views on surrogacy arrangements. For example, Professor Lori Andrews presents the liberal feminist case against restriction of women's freedom of choice in making reproductive decisions, drawing parallels to reproductive autonomy in the context of abortion decisions. *See* Lori B. Andrews, *Surrogate Motherhood: The Challenge for Feminists*, 16 LAW MED. & HEALTH CARE 72 (1988); Lori B. Andrews, *Beyond Doctrinal Boundaries: A Legal Framework for Surrogate Motherhood*, 81 VA. L. REV. 2343 (1995). Others characterize surrogacy as a form of baby-selling (i.e., a "commissioned adoption"), thereby raising some concerns similar to those articulated earlier in this chapter regarding the sale of children in the context of adoption. *See, e.g.,* MARGARET JANE RADIN, CONTESTED COMMODITIES 140–144 (1996); *see also* Margaret Brinig, *A Materialistic Approach to Surrogacy: Comment on Richard Epstein's Surrogacy: The Case for Full Contractual Enforcement*, 81 VA. L. REV. 2377 (1995). Alternatively, surrogacy has been conceptualized as commodification of women's reproductive capacities. *Id.* Some have expressed the view, like the New Jersey Supreme Court in *Baby M.*, that surrogacy contracts exploit women, by subordinating women's autonomy "to the independent interests of the contracting parents." Elizabeth S. Anderson, *Is Women's Labor A Commodity?* 19 PHILOSOPHY & PUBLIC AFFAIRS 71 (1988). The financial inducements inherent in monetary agreements, some argue, create powerful incentives for economically-disadvantaged women, leading them to enter into agreements that are neither in their best interests or those of the resulting children. For example, one article summarizes the debate:

> To some, payment . . . to a surrogate devalues the contributor and the sanctity of human life. However, others argue that it is not uncommon for money to be paid for things of value. . . . [I]t may be even more devaluing

of women [in the context of surrogacy] to not pay them and only allow their participation out of altruism. . . . [¶] . . . The surrogate may [derive] a significant benefit from the arrangement. . . . Some commentators argue that it is paternalistic to assume that individuals choosing to be donors or surrogates are incapable of making rational, informed choices. Such paternalism and elitism may do more to devalue, degrade, and exploit women than would payment for their reproductive products and services.

Lori B. Andrews & Nanette Elster, *Regulating Reproductive Technologies*, 21 J. LEG. MED. 35, 40–42 (2000).

In a recent article, Professor Elizabeth Scott examines how the views about surrogacy have changed over the past several decades. *Surrogacy and the Politics of Commodification*, 72 L. & CONTEMP. PROBS. 109 (2009). In particular, she observes that the publicity surrounding the *Baby M.* case stirred up a "moral panic," reflecting society's and some feminists' worst fears as to the social consequences of permitting surrogacy arrangements to flourish. Certain uneasy political alliances were formed in the process. Professor Scott concludes that today's legal responses to surrogacy are more pragmatic, focusing on regulating such arrangements so as protect and promote the welfare of the various participants. *Id.*

9. *Additional Commentary.*   Surrogacy contracts have been a subject of great academic interest. The most enthusiastic defense of the practice comes from those who view public policy issues from an economic perspective. *See* Richard A. Epstein, *Surrogacy: The Case for Full Contractual Enforcement*, 81 VA. L. REV. 2305 (1995); Richard Posner, *The Ethics and Economics of Enforcing Contracts of Surrogate Motherhood*, 5 J. CONTEMP. HEALTH L. & POL'Y 21 (1989). John Robertson defends gestational contracts on constitutional grounds. In his view the right of procreative liberty of both the intended parents and gestational mothers are promoted by enforcement. Moreover, the infertile couple's fundamental right to form a family through noncoital means should include enforcement of gestational agreements. *See* John A. Robertson, *Assisting Reproduction, Choosing Genes, and the Scope of Reproductive Freedom*, 76 GEORGE WASH. L. REV. 1490 (2008); JOHN A. ROBERTSON, CHILDREN OF CHOICE (1994). *See Symposium on John A. Robertson's CHILDREN OF CHOICE*, 52 WASH. & LEE L. REV. 133 (1995). An excellent discussion of state policies can be found at Steven H. Snyder & Mary Patricia Byrn, *The Use of Prebirth Parentage Orders in Surrogacy Proceedings*, 39 FAM. L.Q. 633 (2005). Marsha Garrison has offered a comprehensive legal framework for analyzing technologically assisted conception of all types, including conventional and "pure" gestational arrangements as well as artificial insemination by donor and in vitro fertilization. Marsha Garrison, *Law Making for Baby Making: An Interpretive Approach to the Determination of Legal Parentage*, 113 HARV. L. REV. 835 (2000). For additional analyses of the ethical, legal, and social dimensions of surrogacy, see, e.g., DEBORA L. SPAR, THE BABY BUSINESS: HOW MONEY, SCIENCE, AND POLITICS DRIVE THE COMMERCE OF CONCEPTION 69–96 (2006) (critically analyzing assisted reproductive technology markets, and arguing for regulation); SUSAN MARKENS, SURROGATE MOTHERHOOD AND THE POLITICS OF REPRODUCTION (2007) (presenting a sociological perspective); RACHEL COOK ET AL., (EDS.) SURROGATE MOTHERHOOD: INTERNATIONAL PERSPECTIVES (2003) (presenting a range of interdisciplinary and comparative analyses of surrogacy); RUTH MACKLIN, SURROGATES, MOTHERS, AND

OTHERS: THE DEBATES OVER ASSISTED REPRODUCTION (1994) (examining bioethical perspectives). For a compilation of the "stories" of many families in which parenthood was the product of surrogacy contracts, see ZARA GRISWOLD, SURROGACY WAS THE WAY: TWENTY INTENDED MOTHERS TELL THEIR STORIES (2006). For the stories of several surrogates, see Lorraine Ali & Raina Kelley, *The Curious Lives of Surrogates*, NEWSWEEK, April 7, 2008, http://www.newsweek.com/id/129594; Claudia Wallace & Ruth Mehrtens Galvin, *Medicine: A Surrogate's Story*, TIME MAGAZINE, Sept. 10, 1984, *available at* http://www.time.com/time/magazine/article/0,9171,952516,00.html.

PROBLEMS

Problem 11-8. Alice signs a surrogate mothering contract with Sally and Tom, under which she will bear a child conceived through artificial insemination and turn it over to Tom and Sally for adoption by Sally. She in fact relinquishes the child after birth, as planned, but Sally and Tom never complete a formal adoption. A year later, they break up. On divorce, Tom and Sally each file custody petitions. Alice, having a change of heart when she hears of the divorce, files her own action seeking custody of the child. What result? Suppose that because early attempts at insemination using Tom's sperm were unsuccessful, Alice was actually impregnated with sperm Tom obtained from a friend, who makes no claim on the child?

Problem 11-9. Your jurisdiction has adopted Section 8 of the UPA. You represent Jack and Jill, who have executed an agreement with Mary to bear Jack's child. The court approved the gestational agreement after a hearing in which an adoption agency home study was presented. What would you do in the following circumstances?

(A) In the week following birth, Mary refuses to relinquish the child in accordance with their agreement. She tells Jack and Jill that if the child is not returned, she will suffer grievous psychological injury.

(B) The child is born with Down's syndrome and Jack and Jill do not want it.

(C) When Mary is five months pregnant, an amniocentesis shows that the child has Down's syndrome. Jack and Jill want Mary to have an abortion. If she declines, they do not want the child.

(D) Jill unexpectedly becomes pregnant after Mary is already two months pregnant, and Jack and Jill no longer want Mary's child.

(E) During the pregnancy, Jack and Jill learn that Mary is drinking and using drugs.

(F) Mary requires an emergency Caesarian section at delivery, and the child spends a week in the intensive care nursery. This drives the medical costs associated with the pregnancy and birth from $3,000 to $20,000. The child is now well. Jack and Jill had not contemplated this possibility when they agreed to pay Mary $8,000 plus her medical costs. The additional expenses will be difficult, if not impossible, for them to bear.

[4]   The Legal Status of Embryos and Resolution of Disputes Over their Disposition

DAVIS v. DAVIS
Tennessee Supreme Court
842 S.W.2d 588 (1992)

DAUGHTREY, JUSTICE.

This appeal presents a question of first impression, involving the disposition of the cryogenically-preserved product of *in vitro* fertilization (IVF), commonly referred to in the popular press and the legal journals as "frozen embryos." The case began as a divorce action, filed by . . . Junior Lewis Davis, against his then wife, . . . Mary Sue Davis. The parties were able to agree upon all terms of dissolution, except one: who was to have "custody" of the seven "frozen embryos" stored in a Knoxville fertility clinic that had attempted to assist the Davises in achieving a much-wanted pregnancy during a happier period in their relationship.

I. *Introduction*

Mary Sue Davis originally asked for control of the "frozen embryos" with the intent to have them transferred to her own uterus, in a post-divorce effort to become pregnant. Junior Davis objected, saying that he preferred to leave the embryos in their frozen state until he decided whether or not he wanted to become a parent outside the bounds of marriage.

Based on its determination that the embryos were "human beings" from the moment of fertilization, the trial court awarded "custody" to Mary Sue Davis and directed that she "be permitted the opportunity to bring these children to term through implantation." The Court of Appeals reversed, finding that Junior Davis has a "constitutionally protected right not to beget a child where no pregnancy has taken place" and holding that "there is no compelling state interest to justify [ ] ordering implantation against the will of either party." The Court of Appeals further held that "the parties share an interest in the seven fertilized ova" and remanded the case to the trial court for entry of an order vesting them with "joint control . . . and equal voice over their disposition."

Mary Sue Davis then sought review in this Court, contesting the validity of the constitutional basis for the Court of Appeals decision. We granted review, not because we disagree with the basic legal analysis utilized by the intermediate court, but because of the obvious importance of the case in terms of the development of law regarding the new reproductive technologies, and because the decision of the Court of Appeals does not give adequate guidance to the trial court in the event the parties cannot agree.

[In the intervening years since the initiation of this suit] both [parties] have remarried and Mary Sue Davis (now Mary Sue Stowe) has moved out of state. She no longer wishes to utilize the "frozen embryos" herself, but wants authority to donate them to a childless couple. Junior Davis is adamantly opposed to such donation and would prefer to see the "frozen embryos" discarded. The result is, once again, an impasse, but the parties' current legal position does have an effect on the probable outcome of the case, as discussed below.

At the outset, it is important to note the absence of two critical factors that might otherwise influence or control the result of this litigation: When the Davises signed up for the IVF program at the Knoxville clinic, they did not execute a written agreement specifying what disposition should be made of any unused embryos that might result from the cryopreservation process. Moreover, there was at that time no Tennessee statute governing such disposition, nor has one been enacted in the meantime.[1]

In addition, because of the uniqueness of the question before us, we have no case law to guide us to a decision in this case. Despite the fact that over 5,000 IVF babies have been born in this country and the fact that some 20,000 or more "frozen embryos" remain in storage, there are apparently very few other litigated cases involving the disputed disposition of untransferred "frozen embryos," and none is on point with the facts in this case.

But, if we have no statutory authority or common law precedents to guide us, we do have the benefit of extensive comment and analysis in the legal journals. In those articles, medical-legal scholars and ethicists have proposed various models for the disposition of "frozen embryos" when unanticipated contingencies arise, such as divorce, death of one or both of the parties, financial reversals, or simple disenchantment with the IVF process. Those models range from a rule requiring, at one extreme, that all embryos be used by the gamete-providers or donated for uterine transfer, and, at the other extreme, that any unused embryos be automatically discarded.[3] Other formulations would vest control in the female gamete-provider-in every case, because of her greater physical and emotional contribution to the IVF process,[4] or perhaps only in the event that she wishes to use them herself.[5] There are also two "implied contract" models: one would infer from enrollment in an IVF program that the IVF clinic has authority to decide in the event of an impasse whether to donate, discard, or use the "frozen embryos" for research; the other would infer from the parties' participation in the creation of the embryos that they had made an irrevocable commitment to reproduction and would require transfer either to the female provider or to a donee. There are also the so-called "equity models": one would avoid the conflict altogether by dividing the "frozen embryos" equally between the parties, to do with as they wish;[6] the

---

[1] At the time of trial, only one state had enacted pertinent legislation. A Louisiana statute entitled "Human Embryos," among other things, forbids the intentional destruction of a cryopreserved IVF embryo and declares that disputes between parties should be resolved in the "best interest" of the embryo. 1986 La. Acts R.S. 9:121 *et seq.* Under the Louisiana statute, unwanted embryos must be made available for "adoptive implantation."

[3] Note, *The Legal Status of Frozen Embryos: Analysis and Proposed Guidelines for a Uniform Law,* 17 J. Legis. 97 (1990).

[4] This is the so-called "sweat-equity" model. Robertson, *Resolving Disputes over Frozen Embryos,* Hastings Center Report, Nov./Dec. 1989, at 7.

[5] Andrews, *The Legal Status of the Embryo,* 32 Loyola L.Rev. 357 (1986).

[6] Assuming that the parties do not change their current positions, in this case the result would be

other would award veto power to the party wishing to avoid parenthood, whether it be the female or the male progenitor.[7]

Each of these possible models has the virtue of ease of application. Adoption of any of them would establish a bright-line test that would dispose of disputes like the one we have before us in a clear and predictable manner. As appealing as that possibility might seem, we conclude that given the relevant principles of constitutional law, the existing public policy of Tennessee with regard to unborn life, the current state of scientific knowledge giving rise to the emerging reproductive technologies, and the ethical considerations that have developed in response to that scientific knowledge, there can be no easy answer to the question we now face. We conclude, instead, that we must weigh the interests of each party to the dispute, in terms of the facts and analysis set out below, in order to resolve that dispute in a fair and responsible manner.

II. *The Facts*

Mary Sue Davis and Junior Lewis Davis. . . . were married on April 26, 1980 . . . . Mary Sue became pregnant but unfortunately suffered [several tubal pregnancies. She ultimately agreed to surgery that left her] without functional fallopian tubes by which to conceive naturally. The Davises attempted to adopt a child but, at the last minute, the child's birth-mother changed her mind about putting the child up for adoption. Other paths to adoption turned out to be prohibitively expensive. *In vitro* fertilization became essentially the only option for the Davises to pursue in their attempt to become parents.

. . . .

Beginning in 1985, the Davises went through six attempts at IVF, at a total cost of $35,000, but the hoped-for pregnancy never occurred . . . [¶] There is . . . no indication that they ever considered the implications of storage beyond the few months it would take to transfer the remaining "frozen embryos," if necessary. There was no discussion, let alone an agreement, concerning disposition in the event of a contingency such as divorce. [They also were not asked to sign any consent forms. Apparently the clinic was in the process of moving its location when the Davises underwent this last round and, because timing of each step of IVF is crucial, it was impossible to postpone the procedure until the appropriate forms were located.] [¶] . . . Junior Davis filed for divorce in February 1989.

III. *The Scientific Testimony*

In the record, and especially in the trial court's opinion, there is a great deal of discussion about the proper descriptive terminology to be used in this case. Although this discussion appears at first glance to be a matter simply of semantics,

---

"the worst of both worlds": some of the frozen embryos would likely be destroyed, contrary to Mary Sue Davis's devout wish that they be implanted and given the opportunity to come to term; at the same time, the others would likely be implanted and might come to term, thus forcing Junior Davis into unwanted parenthood.

[7] Poole, *Allocation of Decision-Making Rights to Frozen Embryos*, 4 Am. J. of Fam. L. 67 (1990).

semantical distinctions are significant in this context, because language defines legal status and can limit legal rights. Obviously, an "adult" has a different legal status than does a "child." Likewise, "child" means something other than "fetus." A "fetus" differs from an "embryo." There was much dispute at trial about whether the four- to eight-cell entities in this case should properly be referred to as "embryos" or as "preembryos," with resulting differences in legal analysis.

One expert, a French geneticist named Dr. Jerome Lejeune, insisted that there was no recognized scientific distinction between the two terms. He referred to the four to eight-cell entities at issue here as "early human beings," as "tiny persons," and as his "kin. . . . [¶] Dr. LeJeune's opinion was disputed by Dr. Irving Ray King, the gynecologist who performed the IVF procedures in this case. Dr. King testified that the currently accepted term for the zygote immediately after division is "preembryo" and that this term applies up until 14 days after fertilization. He testified that this 14-day period defines the accepted period for preembryo research. At about 14 days, he testified, the group of cells begins to differentiate in a process that permits the eventual development of the different body parts which will become an individual.

Dr. King's testimony was corroborated by the other experts who testified at trial, with the exception of Dr. Lejeune. It is further supported by the American Fertility Society, an organization of 10,000 physicians and scientists who specialize in problems of human infertility. The Society's June 1990 report on *Ethical Considerations of the New Reproductive Technologies* [53. J. Amer. Fertility Soc'y (1990)] indicates that from the point of fertilization, the resulting one-cell zygote contains "a new hereditary constitution (genome) contributed to by both parents through the union of sperm and egg." *Id* . . . . [¶] For a . . . description of the biologic difference between a preembryo and an embryo, *see* Robertson, *In the Beginning: The Legal Status of Early Embryos*, 76 Va. L. Rev. 437 (1990), in which the author summarizes the findings of Clifford Grobstein in *The Early Development of Human Embryos*, 10 J. Med. & Phil. 213 (1984).

[T]he trial judge[, influenced by Dr. Lejeune's testimony,] concluded that the eight-cell entities at issue were not preembryos but were "children in vitro." He then invoked the doctrine of *parens patriae* and held that it was "in the best interest of the children" to be born rather than destroyed. Finding that Mary Sue Davis was willing to provide such an opportunity, but that Junior Davis was not, the trial judge awarded her "custody" of the "children in vitro." [¶] The Court of Appeals explicitly rejected the trial judge's reasoning, as well as the result. Indeed, the argument that "human life begins at the moment of conception" and that these four- to eight-cell entities therefore have a legal right to be born has apparently been abandoned by the appellant, despite her success with it in the trial court. We have nevertheless been asked by the American Fertility Society, joined by 19 other national organizations allied in this case as amici curiae, to respond to this issue because of its far-reaching implications in other cases of this kind. We find the request meritorious.

IV. *The "Person" vs. "Property" Dichotomy*

One of the fundamental issues the inquiry poses is whether the preembryos in this case should be considered "persons" or "property" in the contemplation of the law. The Court of Appeals held, correctly, that they cannot be considered "persons" under Tennessee law [citing statutes and case law indicating that a fetus is not considered a person for a range of purposes in Tennessee's civil and criminal law.] [¶] Nor do preembryos enjoy protection as "persons" under federal law. [See, e.g., *Roe v. Wade*, 410 U.S. 113, (1973).]

Left undisturbed, the trial court's ruling would have afforded preembryos the legal status of "persons" and vested them with legally cognizable interests separate from those of their progenitors. Such a decision would doubtless have had the effect of outlawing IVF programs in the state of Tennessee. But in setting aside the trial court's judgment, the Court of Appeals, at least by implication, may have swung too far in the opposite direction.

The intermediate court, without explicitly holding that the preembryos in this case were "property," nevertheless awarded "joint custody" of them to Mary Sue Davis and Junior Davis, citing T.C.A. §§ 68-30-101 and 39-15-208, and *York v. Jones*, 717 F. Supp. 421 (E.D.Va.1989), for the proposition that "the parties share an interest in the seven fertilized ova." The intermediate court did not otherwise define this interest.

The provisions of T.C.A. §§ 68-30-101 *et seq.*, on which the intermediate appellate court relied, codify the Uniform Anatomical Gift Act. T.C.A. § 39-15-208 prohibits experimentation or research using an aborted fetus in the absence of the woman's consent. These statutes address the question of who controls disposition of human organs and tissue with no further potential for autonomous human life; they are not precisely controlling on the question before us, because the "tissue" involved here *does* have the potential for developing into independent human life, even if it is not yet legally recognizable as human life itself. [¶] [¶] In this case, by citing to *York v. Jones* but failing to define precisely the "interest" that Mary Sue Davis and Junior Davis have in the preembryos, the Court of Appeals has left the implication that it is in the nature of a property interest . . .

To our way of thinking, the most helpful discussion on this point is found not in the minuscule number of legal opinions that have involved "frozen embryos," but in the ethical standards set by The American Fertility Society, as follows:

> Three major ethical positions have been articulated in the debate over preembryo status. At one extreme is the view of the preembryo as a human subject after fertilization, which requires that it be accorded the rights of a person. This position entails an obligation to provide an opportunity for implantation to occur and tends to ban any action before transfer that might harm the preembryo or that is not immediately therapeutic, such as freezing and some preembryo research.

> At the opposite extreme is the view that the preembryo has a status no different from any other human tissue. With the consent of those who have decision-making authority over the preembryo, no limits should be imposed on actions taken with preembryos.

A third view-one that is most widely held-takes an intermediate position between the other two. It holds that the preembryo deserves respect greater than that accorded to human tissue but not the respect accorded to actual persons. The preembryo is due greater respect than other human tissue because of its potential to become a person and because of its symbolic meaning for many people. Yet, it should not be treated as a person, because it has not yet developed the features of personhood, is not yet established as developmentally individual, and may never realize its biologic potential.

Although the report alludes to the role of "special respect" in the context of research on preembryos not intended for transfer, it is clear that the Ethics Committee's principal concern was with the treatment accorded the transferred embryo. Thus, the Ethics Committee concludes that "special respect is necessary to protect the welfare of potential offspring . . . [and] creates obligations not to hurt or injure the offspring who might be born after transfer [by research or intervention with a preembryo]." *Id.* at 35S.

In its report, the Ethics Committee then calls upon those in charge of IVF programs to establish policies in keeping with the "special respect" due preembryos and suggests:

> Within the limits set by institutional policies, decision-making authority regarding preembryos should reside with the persons who have provided the gametes. . . . As a matter of law, it is reasonable to assume that the gamete providers have primary decision-making authority regarding preembryos in the absence of specific legislation on the subject. A person's liberty to procreate or to avoid procreation is directly involved in most decisions involving preembryos.

We conclude that preembryos are not, strictly speaking, either "persons" or "property," but occupy an interim category that entitles them to special respect because of their potential for human life. It follows that any interest that Mary Sue Davis and Junior Davis have in the preembryos in this case is not a true property interest. However, they do have an interest in the nature of ownership, to the extent that they have decision-making authority concerning disposition of the preembryos, within the scope of policy set by law.

. . . .

VI. *The Right of Procreational Autonomy*

Although an understanding of the legal status of preembryos is necessary in order to determine the enforceability of agreements about their disposition, asking whether or not they constitute "property" is not an altogether helpful question. As the appellee points out in his brief, "[as] two or eight cell tiny lumps of complex protein, the embryos have no [intrinsic] value to either party." Their value lies in the "potential to become, after implantation, growth and birth, *children.*" Thus, the essential dispute here is not where or how or how long to store the preembryos, but whether the parties will become parents. The Court of Appeals held in effect that they will become parents if they both agree to become parents. The Court did not say what will happen if they fail to agree. We conclude that the answer to this dilemma turns on the parties' exercise of their constitutional right to privacy.

The right to privacy is not specifically mentioned in either the federal or the Tennessee state constitution, and yet there can be little doubt about its grounding in the concept of liberty reflected in those two documents. In particular, the Fourteenth Amendment to the United States Constitution provides that "[n]o state shall . . . deprive any person of life, liberty, or property, without due process of law." . . . [¶] [The court cites to key U.S. Supreme Court cases discussing the right of privacy. It further recognizes relevant provisions in the Tennessee Constitution.]

Obviously, the drafters of the Tennessee Constitution of 1796 could not have anticipated the need to construe the liberty clauses of that document in terms of the choices flowing from *in vitro* fertilization procedures. But there can be little doubt that they foresaw the need to protect individuals from unwarranted governmental intrusion into matters such as the one now before us, involving intimate questions of personal and family concern. Based on both the language and the development of our state constitution, we have no hesitation in drawing the conclusion that there is a right of individual privacy guaranteed under and protected by the liberty clauses of the Tennessee Declaration of Rights. [¶] . . . Here, the specific individual freedom in dispute is the right to procreate. In terms of the Tennessee state constitution, we hold that the right of procreation is a vital part of an individual's right to privacy. Federal law is to the same effect.

In construing the reach of the federal constitution, the United States Supreme Court has addressed the affirmative right to procreate in only two cases. In *Buck v. Bell*, 274 U.S. 200 (1927), the Court upheld the sterilization of a "feebleminded white woman." However, in *Skinner v. Oklahoma*, 316 U.S. 535 (1942), the Supreme Court struck down a statute that authorized the sterilization of certain categories of criminals. The Court described the right to procreate as "one of the basic civil rights of man [sic]," and stated that "[m]arriage and procreation are fundamental to the very existence and survival of the race." *Id.*

In the same vein, the United States Supreme Court has said:

> If the right of privacy means anything, it is the right of the *individual*, married or single, to be free from unwarranted governmental intrusion into matters so fundamentally affecting a person as the decision whether to bear or beget a child.

Eisenstadt v. Baird, 405 U.S. 438 (1972) (emphasis in original) . . . [The court cites additional U.S. Supreme Court opinions in support of the fundamental nature of rights of procreative autonomy, while noting some erosion of that right in the context of abortion in the most recent decisions.]

For the purposes of this litigation it is sufficient to note that, whatever its ultimate constitutional boundaries, the right of procreational autonomy is composed of two rights of equal significance-the right to procreate and the right to avoid procreation. . . . [¶] The equivalence of and inherent tension between these two interests are nowhere more evident than in the context of *in vitro* fertilization. None of the concerns about a woman's bodily integrity that have previously precluded men from controlling abortion decisions is applicable here. We are not unmindful of the fact that the trauma (including both emotional stress and physical discomfort) to which women are subjected in the IVF process is more severe than is the impact of the procedure on men. In this sense, it is fair to say that women contribute more to the IVF process than men. Their experience, however, must be viewed in light of the joys of parenthood that is desired or the relative anguish of a lifetime of unwanted parenthood. As they stand on the brink of potential parenthood, Mary Sue Davis and Junior Lewis Davis must be seen as entirely equivalent gamete-providers.

It is further evident that, however far the protection of procreational autonomy extends, the existence of the right itself dictates that decisional authority rests in the gamete-providers alone, at least to the extent that their decisions have an impact upon their individual reproductive status. [N]no other person or entity has an interest sufficient to permit interference with the gamete-providers' decision to continue or terminate the IVF process, because no one else bears the consequences of these decisions in the way that the gamete-providers do.

Further, at least with respect to Tennessee's public policy and its constitutional right of privacy, the state's interest in potential human life is insufficient to justify an infringement on the gamete-providers' procreational autonomy. The United States Supreme Court has indicated . . . that the state's interest in potential human life may justify statutes or regulations that have an impact upon a person's exercise of procreational autonomy. This potential for sufficiently weighty state's interests is not, however, at issue here, because Tennessee's statutes contain no statement of public policy which reveals an interest that could justify infringing on gamete-providers' decisional authority over the preembryos to which they have contributed. . . . [¶] Tennessee's abortion statute reveals a public policy decision weighing the interests of living persons against the state's interest in potential life. At least during certain stages of a pregnancy, the personal interests of the pregnant woman outweigh the state's interests and the pregnancy may be terminated.

Taken collectively, our statutes reflect the policy decision that, at least in some circumstances, the interest of living individuals in avoiding procreation is sufficient to justify taking steps to terminate the procreational process, despite the state's interest in potential life. [¶] The abortion statute reveals that the increase in the state's interest is marked by each successive developmental stage such that, toward the end of a pregnancy, this interest is so compelling that abortion is almost strictly forbidden. This scheme supports the conclusion that the state's interest in the potential life embodied by these four- to eight-cell preembryos (which may or may not be able to achieve implantation in a uterine wall and which, if implanted, may or may not begin to develop into fetuses, subject to possible miscarriage) is at best slight . . .

. . .

VII. *Balancing the Parties' Interests*

Resolving disputes over conflicting interests of constitutional import is a task familiar to the courts. One way of resolving these disputes is to consider the positions of the parties, the significance of their interests, and the relative burdens that will be imposed by differing resolutions. In this case, the issue centers on the two aspects of procreational autonomy-the right to procreate and the right to avoid procreation. We start by considering the burdens imposed on the parties by solutions that would have the effect of disallowing the exercise of individual procreational autonomy with respect to these particular preembryos.

Beginning with the burden imposed on Junior Davis, we note that the consequences are obvious. Any disposition which results in the gestation of the preembryos would impose unwanted parenthood on him, with all of its possible financial and psychological consequences. The impact that this unwanted parenthood would have on Junior Davis can only be understood by considering his particular circumstances, as revealed in the record. [The court recounts Junior's childhood experiences which include living in a church-run home for boys, and the absence and unavailability of his parents.]

In light of his boyhood experiences, Junior Davis is vehemently opposed to fathering a child that would not live with both parents. Regardless of whether he or Mary Sue had custody, he feels that the child's bond with the non-custodial parent would not be satisfactory. He testified very clearly that his concern was for the psychological obstacles a child in such a situation would face, as well as the burdens it would impose on him. Likewise, he is opposed to donation because the recipient couple might divorce, leaving the child (which he definitely would consider his own) in a single-parent setting.

Balanced against Junior Davis's interest in avoiding parenthood is Mary Sue Davis's interest in donating the preembryos to another couple for implantation. Refusal to permit donation of the preembryos would impose on her the burden of knowing that the lengthy IVF procedures she underwent were futile, and that the preembryos to which she contributed genetic material would never become children. While this is not an insubstantial emotional burden, we can only conclude that Mary Sue Davis's interest in donation is not as significant as the interest Junior Davis has in avoiding parenthood. If she were allowed to donate these preembryos, he would face a lifetime of either wondering about his parental status or knowing about his parental status but having no control over it. He testified quite clearly that if these preembryos were brought to term he would fight for custody of his child or children. Donation, if a child came of it, would rob him twice-his procreational autonomy would be defeated and his relationship with his offspring would be prohibited.

The case would be closer if Mary Sue Davis were seeking to use the preembryos herself, but only if she could not achieve parenthood by any other reasonable means. We recognize the trauma that Mary Sue has already experienced and the additional discomfort to which she would be subjected if she opts to attempt IVF again. Still, she would have a reasonable opportunity, through IVF, to try once again to achieve parenthood in all its aspects-genetic, gestational, bearing, and rearing.

Further, we note that if Mary Sue Davis were unable to undergo another round of IVF, or opted not to try, she could still achieve the child-rearing aspects of parenthood through adoption. The fact that she and Junior Davis pursued adoption indicates that, at least at one time, she was willing to forego genetic parenthood and would have been satisfied by the child-rearing aspects of parenthood alone.

VIII. *Conclusion*

In summary, we hold that disputes involving the disposition of preembryos produced by *in vitro* fertilization should be resolved, first, by looking to the preferences of the progenitors. If their wishes cannot be ascertained, or if there is dispute, then their prior agreement concerning disposition should be carried out. If no prior agreement exists, then the relative interests of the parties in using or not using the preembryos must be weighed. Ordinarily, the party wishing to avoid procreation should prevail, assuming that the other party has a reasonable possibility of achieving parenthood by means other than use of the preembryos in question. If no other reasonable alternatives exist, then the argument in favor of using the preembryos to achieve pregnancy should be considered. However, if the party seeking control of the preembryos intends merely to donate them to another couple, the objecting party obviously has the greater interest and should prevail.

But the rule does not contemplate the creation of an automatic veto, and in affirming the judgment of the Court of Appeals, we would not wish to be interpreted as so holding.

NOTES

1. *What Does it Mean to Accord Preembryos or Embryos[7] "Special Respect"?* The court in *Davis* concluded that preembryos are neither "persons" or "property." Rather, the court stated, preembryos "occupy an interim category that entitles them to special respect because of their potential for human life." It rejected the idea that the parties' interests in the preembryos was a "true property interest," but opined that the parties "do have an interest in the nature of ownership, to the extent that they have decision-making authority concerning disposition of the preembryos, within the scope of policy set by law." The court's rejection of either a purely "property" or purely "personhood" formulation has important implications for the disposition of the preembryos in the face of a dispute between divorcing parties. If the preembryos were treated wholly as property, they could be divided between the parties in a manner akin to a couple's cars or bank accounts. Depending upon the jurisdiction, the division might result in an equal or an equitable split of the preembryos between the parties. (For further discussion of modern regimes for division of property at divorce, see Chapter 4.) If the preembryos were viewed as persons, the court would arguably need to apply the "best interests" standard, an endeavor which ultimately leads to a debate about whether implantation is *per se* in the best interests of embryos. (For further discussion of the application of the best interests of the child standard in child custody disputes, see Chapter 6). The court chooses neither route. Yet, does the resolution of the case — a balance of the two parties' interests in procreating and not procreating — really entail characterization of the preembryos' nature? Or, does the method of resolution simply shift the entire inquiry to the privacy rights

---

[7] We use the terms preembryos and embryo interchangeably in this chapter because the distinctions between them are not pertinent to the legal or bioethical issues addressed here, and most of the sources cited in this chapter typically use the term embryo to encompass what is clarified in *Davis* **to mean preembryo.**

of the adults, thus avoiding clarification of what is meant by "special respect"? Or, perhaps the concept of "special respect" incorporates the unique relationship each progenitor has to the preembryos, thus requiring that any decision regarding the preembryos' disposition take that relationship into account. These questions are not resolved by existing law. There have been, however, many thought-provoking articles seeking to further develop the concepts discussed in *Davis*. *See, e.g.*, Bridget M. Fuselier *The Trouble with Putting All of Your Eggs in One Basket: Using A Property Rights Model to Resolve Disputes Over Cryopreserved Pre-Embryos*, 14 Tex. J. Civ. Lib. & Civ. Rts. 143 (2009) (arguing that modern concepts of property can encompass preembryos, imbuing those who contribute the genetic material with some, but not all, of the rights associated with the traditional "bundle" of rights).

2. *Can Embryos be Sold?* In most jurisdictions, there are no absolute barriers to the sale of sperm and ova. But, what about fertilized embryos? John Robertson, in a classic article, observes the nature of asserted objections to allowing a market for embryos:

> A deeper source of concern is a view of the corrupting effects of markets on altruism and the symbolic meaning of buying and selling embryos. [A]market tends to drive out the possibility of altruism, and increase costs for everyone. Just as money payment to organ donors is deemed unethical and illegal, payment to reproductive collaborators for gametes and embryos could be viewed as unethical and also be prohibited in order to give the community an opportunity to show social solidarity through voluntary donations.
>
> Objections to the sale of embryos is closely tied to the symbolic meaning that attaches to human embryos. Since the embryo is a genetically unique, potential person, payment seems to signify the buying and selling of potential persons, and conjures up dehumanizing images of slavery or trading of embryos like commodities in the marketplace. A fee to give up the embryo — relinquish the right to discard, transfer, or otherwise control the potential person-is deemed unacceptable because of the attitude it conveys or symbolizes about human life generally . . . .

John Robertson, *Embryos, Families, and Procreative Liberty: The Legal Structure of the New Reproduction*, 59 S. Cal. L. Rev. 939, 1019–20 (1986).

The permissibility of sales of human embryos has not been addressed by most jurisdictions. For example, a recent survey of state laws reveals few provisions expressly addressing such transactions. Nat'l Couns. State Legis., *Embryonic and Fetal Research Laws* (Jan. 2008), http://www.ncsl.org/programs/health/Genetics/embfet.htm. Of those states that regulate or prohibit such sales, some categorically prohibit embryo sales. *See, e.g.*, Fla. St. Ann. § 873.05(1) (2009) ("No person shall knowingly advertise or offer to purchase or sell, or purchase, sell, or otherwise transfer, any human embryo for valuable consideration"); Ind. St. Ann. § 35-46-5-3(a) (2009) ("A person who knowingly or intentionally purchases or sells a human . . . embryo . . . commits unlawful transfer of a human organism, a Class C felony"); La. Stat. Ann § 122 (2009) ("The sale of a human ovum, fertilized human ovum, or human embryo is expressly prohibited."). Others focus primarily on restricting the use of embryos for stem cell research, *see, e.g.*, CONN. ST. ANN. § 19a-32d (2009) ("A person who elects to donate for stem cell research purposes any human embryos . . . remaining after receiving infertility treatment . . . shall not receive direct or indirect payment for such human embryos . . ."), or research more generally, *see, e.g.*, MASS. GEN. LAWS ANN. § 111L-8 (2009) ("No person shall knowingly and for valuable consideration purchase, sell, transfer or otherwise obtain human embryos . . . for research purposes"). Authors have proposed a range of justifications for either prohibiting or permitting embryos sales. *See, e.g.*, Ann Bindu Thomas, *Avoiding Embryos "R" Us: Toward a Regulated Fertility Industry*, 7 WASH. U. J.L. & POL'Y 247 (2008) (analogizing embryo sales to organ sales, and proposing regulation of embryo procurement employing organ procurement models); Charles P. Kindregan, Jr., *Embryo Donation: Unresolved Legal Issues in the Transfer of Surplus Cryopreserved Embryos*, 49 VILLANOVA L. REV. 169 (2004) (distinguishing sales of ova — for which payment compensates donors for the inconvenience, risk, and discomfort inherent in extraction process — from sales of unused embryos following IVF, where the medical procedure is undertaken solely for the purpose of transfer to the recipients); John Robertson, *Embryos, Families, and Procreative Liberty: The Legal Structure of the New Reproduction*, 59 S. CAL. L. REV. 939, 1019–20 (1986) (arguing that the reproductive rights of persons who cannot procreate without donated embryos outweigh state interests in prohibiting embryo sales, to the extent that the supply of unused embryos created for IVF is insufficient to meet demand by prospective parents, concluding that embryos sales should be permitted in those circumstances).

3. *Can Embryos be "Adopted"?* While the permissible role of monetary exchanges in the transfer of embryos from progenitors to would-be parents for the purpose of implantation is not adequately resolved, there is generally no dispute that couples who have created more embryos than they ultimately need for the purpose IVF can donate the embryos to other persons for the purpose of implantation without financial compensation. In recent years, several groups have used the term "embryo adoption" to refer to a process that they intend to be analogous to adoptions of children. As Karen Moore, legislative counsel to a California Congressman explains:

> . . . Nightlight Christian Adoptions was the first to mix embryo donation with traditional adoption procedures. Up until Nightlight entered the embryo adoption scene, embryo donation in the IVF clinic setting had been treated as a medical procedure rather than a legal transaction of rights. Nightlight Christian Adoptions set up the Snowflakes Program specifically . . . to deal with the growing number of frozen embryos by emulating traditional adoption practices, and matching donors of surplus frozen embryos with recipients who are unable to have children. [¶] . . . The Snowflake program is unequivocally Christian and prolife in their view of the status of the embryo [as a child who is] unique, beautiful, and a creation of God. . . .

Karen Moore, *Embryo Adoption: The Legal and Moral Challenges*, 1 U. ST. THOMAS J.L. & PUB. POL'Y 100 (2007). The embryo adoption model, therefore, incorporates into the transfer process a program to evaluate the suitability of prospective parents in a manner analogous to those employed in the adoption context. "The adopting families participate in a home study, and are required to reveal medical, psychological, and other background information. The agency also provides counseling and education on common problems arising from adoption such as integrating the child into the home." *Id.* The contract Snowflakes presents to the parties "includes adoption language terminating parental rights, and transferring parental responsibility." *Id.*

The concept of encouraging the progenitors to transfer their unused embryos to couples who wish to procreate but otherwise cannot is certainly a positive goal. And, to the extent that the progenitors are more likely to donate their embryos if reassured that recipients will be "good" parents, or if they choose the recipients themselves, the impact of scrutiny of the prospective parents may be positive. On the other hand, informal agency practices could accomplish these goals without assigning the appellation "adoption" to the process. And, it is important to note that Snowflakes and other proponents of "embryo adoption," by using the term "adoption," are taking sides in the larger social and political discourse debating at what point which life begins. If one believes that life begins at conception, embryos arguably are entitled to the same moral and legal treatment as are persons. Following from these propositions is, of course, the notion that embryos cannot be transferred from the biological to the intended parents without a formal adoption. It is not surprising that groups opposing abortion and the use of embryos in stem cell research promote the concept of embryo adoption, while groups on the other side of these debates oppose the characterization of embryo donation as analogous to adoption of a child.

To date, only Georgia has approved legislation that uses the adoption terminology in regulating embryo donation. GA. STAT. ANN. §§ 19-8-40 to 19-8-43 (2009) (passed in 2009). Interestingly, other than the use of terms such as "adoption" and its reference to the embryo in a manner that is akin to a child, the statute is not that dissimilar from generic statutory provisions governing the transfer of sperm, eggs, or embryos. In other words, donors relinquish all legal rights and responsibilities to a child that may result from that genetic material and the intended parents accept those rights and responsibilities. This transfer of parentage accompanying the transfer of the genetic material therefore does not substantially alter the law governing embryo transfer, with one exception. Section § 19-8-43 allows the intended parents to "petition the court for an expedited order of adoption parentage" prior to the birth of a child. Yet, the well-established law governing artificial insemination by donor, and more recently governing donations of eggs and embryos, treats documents providing for transfer of parental rights and responsibilities from donors to intended parents as dispositive and self-executing. Thus, the Georgia statute actually complicates the embryo donation process by requiring intended parents to obtain a judicial order of adoption in circumstances that would otherwise have imbued the intended parents with legal parentage of resulting children at those children's birth *without* resort to the courts. While the symbolic treatment of embryo donation as an adoption might be a political victory for the proponents, Georgia's regulations appear to burden couples or individuals who avail themselves of assisted reproductive technology involving embryo donation by requiring them to file "a petition for adoption or parentage." GA. STAT. ANN.

§ 19-8-43 (2009). The courts are also burdened with obligations to evaluate and rule on these petitions.

For further analysis of the concept of "embryo adoption" and its legal implications, see Moore, *supra*; Brandon S. Mercer, Student Author, *Embryo Adoption: Where are the Laws?* 26 J. Juv. L. 73 (2006); Jaime E. Conde, *Embryo Donation: The Government Adopts a Cause*, 13 Wm. & Mary J. Women & L. 273 (2006).

4. *Enforcement of Agreements Regarding the Disposition of Preembryos.* The court in *Davis* points out that there was no formal contract between the parties or with the fertility clinic regarding the disposition of the preembryos. What if there had been such an agreement? In *Kass v. Kass*, New York's highest court upheld an agreement between marital partners. In this case, the couple had created and frozen multiple preembryos and could not agree on the disposition of the preembryos at divorce. Mrs. Kass petitioned for sole custody of the preembryos. She claimed that they provided her with "her only chance for genetic motherhood." Mr. Kass, by contrast, objected to "the burdens of unwanted fatherhood." He claimed that "the parties agreed at the time they embarked on the effort that in the present circumstances the pre-zygotes would be donated to the IVF program for approved research purposes." The language in a consent form signed by the parties read:

> In the event that we no longer wish to initiate a pregnancy or are unable to make a decision regarding the disposition of our stored, frozen pre-zygotes, [o]ur frozen pre-zygotes may be examined by the IVF Program for biological studies and be disposed of by the IVF Program for approved research investigation as determined by the IVF Program.

The *Kass* court held that the agreement between the parties dictated the result in this case, allowing the court to side-step some of the issues addressed in *Davis*. The court held:

> Agreements between progenitors, or gamete donors, regarding disposition of their pre-zygotes should generally be presumed valid and binding, and enforced in any dispute between them. Indeed, parties should be encouraged in advance, before embarking on IVF and cryopreservation, to think through possible contingencies and carefully specify their wishes in writing. Explicit agreements avoid costly litigation in business transactions. They are all the more necessary and desirable in personal matters of reproductive choice, where the intangible costs of any litigation are simply incalculable. Advance directives, subject to mutual change of mind that must be jointly expressed, both minimize misunderstandings and maximize procreative liberty by reserving to the progenitors the authority to make what is in the first instance a quintessentially personal, private decision. Written agreements also provide the certainty needed for effective operation of IVF programs. . . .

The court emphasized that, in light of the sensitive and personal nature of disposition of one's reproductive material, parties should decide and contract regarding the disposition of the preembryos before commencing their creation. The court noted that while "[t]he subject of this dispute may be novel[,] the common-law principles governing contract interpretation are not." It concluded that the documents signed by the parties "unequivocally manifest their mutual intention that in the present circumstances the pre-zygotes be donated for research to the IVF program." It concluded that "[t]hese parties having clearly manifested their intention, the law will honor it."

Courts in a handful of other jurisdictions faced with disputes over embryos created previously by divorcing couples have likewise decided to enforce agreements entered into by the parties prior to the creation of the embryos. Most recently, in *Roman v. Roman*, 193 S.W.3d 40 (Tex. Ct. App. 2006), a Texas court of appeals held that "allowing the parties voluntarily to decide the disposition of frozen embryos in advance of cryopreservation, subject to mutual change of mind, jointly expressed, best serves the existing public policy of this State and the interests of the parties. We hold, therefore, that an embryo agreement that satisfies these criteria does not violate the public policy of the State of Texas." In the case before it, the wife wished to implant the embryos and the husband wished to discard them. The court focused on the following language in their agreement: "If we are divorced or either of us files for divorce while any of our frozen embryos are still in the program, we hereby authorize and direct, jointly and individually, that one of the following actions be taken: The frozen embryo(s) shall be . . . Discarded." The court noted that the couple declined "the option of releasing the frozen embryos to either of the spouses," which was one of the choices offered in the document. The agreement also stipulated that, if the parties "are not able to agree on disposition of the remaining embryos for any reason," the clinic is authorized to discard them. Finding this language to be clear and unambiguous, it reversed the lower court's decision to award the embryos to the wife in its division of the community property.

In the Matter of Marriage of Litowitz, 48 P.3d 261 (Wash. 2002), *corrected as noted in* 53 P.3d 516 (Wash. 2002), the Washington Supreme Court approved a contractual agreement between a couple, signed prior to creation of preembryos, requiring the parties to petition a court to resolve any dispute between them regarding disposition of frozen preembryos. The *Litowitz* court noted that, given the passage of time, another contractual provision governed. This provision authorized the fertility clinic to "thaw" the embryos and to prevent their further development if, after five years, the embryos had not been used or disposed of otherwise. The court observed that the contract permitted the couple to request an extension of this period, but that no such requests had been made, and the five-year period had expired. *See also Vitakis v. Valchine*, 987 So.2d 171 (Fla. App. 2008) (upholding a mediated agreement between former spouses regarding disposition of frozen embryos).

Unlike the courts in New York, Washington and Florida, the supreme courts of New Jersey, Massachusetts, and Iowa have refused to enforce disposition agreements between progenitors who dissolve their marriage prior to implantation. *In J.B. v. M.B.*, 783 A.2d 707 (N.J. 2001), the New Jersey Supreme Court declined to allow the divorcing husband to offer proof of an oral agreement that he said existed between the parties. The agreement, he claimed, was that they would donate any unused preembryos to other prospective parents for implantation. By contrast, his ex-wife argued that the preembryos should be destroyed. The court held that an agreement of the type cited was unenforceable as a matter of public policy. In deciding about the disposition of the pre-embryos, the court adopted the *Davis* balancing test. It noted that destruction of the preembryos did little to burden the man's procreative rights, since he was free to procreate through some other means. In addition, as in *Davis*, the court was sympathetic to the asserted right of the party seeking to avoid procreation.

In *A.Z. v. B.Z.*, 725 N.E.2d 1051 (Mass. 2000), the Massachusetts Supreme Judicial Court reviewed an agreement between the prospective parents (executed as part of the consent agreement to the *in vitro* procedures) giving control of the preembryos to the woman in the event of the parties' separation. After raising questions about whether this agreement truly reflected the parties' intentions, the court held that any agreement that would compel one donor to become a parent against his will would be unenforceable (even though at the time of the agreement, he apparently assented). The court cited a strong policy against enforcement of agreements that bind parties to future family relationships. Such a policy enhances freedom of personal choice in these matters.

In 2003, the Supreme Court of Iowa rendered a similar decision in *In re Marriage of Witten*, 672 N.W.2d 768 (Iowa 2003). In this case, the court held that the state's child custody statutes did not apply to the disposition of frozen human embryos, and thus the case would not be resolved by determining what is the in the "best interests" of the embryos. As to the enforceability of a prior agreement regarding disposition, the court noted that the couple whose genetic material created the embryos has "primary, and equal, decision-making authority with respect to the use or disposition of their embryos." In the face of a dispute between these individuals, however, the court would balance the interests of the parties rather than enforce an agreement which one of the parties indicates does not reflect his or her current preferences. The court noted that Iowa's "statutes and case law evidence an understanding that decisions involving marital and family relationships are emotional and subject to change." It provided examples, such as the state's imposition of a 72-hour waiting period after a child's birth, before which the parents may not consent to relinquishment of their parental rights.

For commentary on the issue of frozen embryos and disputes regarding their disposition, see, e.g., Susan L. Crockin, *The "Embryo" Wars: At the Epicenter of Science, Law, Religion, and Politics*, 39 FAM. L.Q. 599 (2005); Susan B. Apel, *Cryopreserved Embryos: A Response to "Forced Parenthood" and the Role of Intent*, 39 FAM. L.Q. 663 (2005); Helene S. Shapo, *Frozen Pre-embryos and the Right to Change One's Mind*, 12 DUKE J. COMP.& INT'L L. 75 (2002); Christina C. Lawrence, Student Author, *Procreative Liberty and the Preembryo Problem: Developing a Medical and Legal Framework to Settle the Disposition of Frozen Embryos*, 52 CASE W. RES. L. REV. 721 (2001). For the "backstory" of the case of *Davis v. Davis*, 842 S.W.2d 588 (Tenn. 1992), see Margaret F. Brinig, *The Story of Mary Sue and Junior Davis*, FAMILY LAW STORIES 195 (Carol Sanger ed. 2008).

5. *Statutory Provisions Governing Disputes over the Disposition of Embryos.* Only a handful of states have created statutory provisions governing the resolution of disputes such as those in cases like *Davis* and *Kass*. Effective in 2004, California Health & Safety Code § 125315 (2009) reads:

(a) A physician and surgeon or other health care provider delivering fertility treatment shall provide his or her patient with timely, relevant, and appropriate information to allow the individual to make an informed and voluntary choice regarding the disposition of any human embryos remaining following the fertility treatment. The failure to provide to a patient this information constitutes unprofessional conduct . . .

(b) Any individual to whom information is provided . . . shall be presented with the option of storing any unused embryos donating them to another individual, discarding the embryos or donating the remaining embryos for research. When providing fertility treatment, [the] health care provider shall [present the progenitors with] a form . . . that sets forth advanced written directives regarding the disposition of the embryos [that] indicates the time limit on storage . . . at the clinic . . . and shall provide, at a minimum, the following choices . . . :

(1) In the event of the death of either the male or female partner, the embryos shall be . . . (A) Made available to the living partner. (B) Donat[ed] for research . . . (C) Thawed with no further action taken. (D) Donat[ed] to another couple or individual. (E) Other disposition that is clearly stated.

. . .

(3) In the event of separation or divorce of the partners, the embryos shall be disposed of by one of the following actions: (A) Made available to the female partner. (B) Made available to the male partner. (C) Donat[ed] for research purposes. (D) Thawed with no further action taken. (E) Donat[ed] to another couple or individual. (F) Other disposition that is clearly stated.

. . . .

Id. In its silence as to the impact of a change of heart by one of the partners at the point of separation or divorce, it appears that the agreements of the parties at the time they commenced fertility treatment is binding. By contrast, a Texas statute, effective in 2007, allows a prospective parent to withdraw his or her consent for implantation of an embryo in the case of marital dissolution:

(a) If a marriage is dissolved before the placement of eggs, sperm, or embryos, the former spouse is not a parent of the resulting child unless the former spouse consented in a record kept by a licensed physician that if assisted reproduction were to occur after a divorce the former spouse would be a parent of the child.

(b) The consent of a former spouse to assisted reproduction may be withdrawn by that individual in a record kept by a licensed physician at any time before the placement of eggs, sperm, or embryos.

TEX. FAM. CODE § 160.706 (2009). Florida requires couples to execute written agreements setting forth the disposition of frozen embryos in the event of death, separation or divorce prior to commencing the IVF process. FLA. STAT. ANN. § 742.17 (2009). The New Hampshire provision avoids the possibility of a dispute about the disposition of frozen embryos stored long after the couple has ceased attempts to have a common child by indicating that embryos may be stored outside of the body for no more than 14 days. N.H. REV. STAT. ANN. § 168-B:15 (2009).

In 2008, the *American Bar Association Model Act Governing Assisted Reproductive Technology, February 2008*, 42 FAM. L.Q. 171 (2008), was published. In Article 5 of the Model Act, the document addresses "Embryo Transfer and Disposition of Embryos not Transferred." While the ABA Model Act would allow intended parents to enter into agreements regarding many facets of the embryos' use and disposition, it would not allow embryos to be implanted for reproduction after one of the intended parents asserts his or desire not to procreate: "In the event of a subsequent disagreement between intended parents, wherein one intended parent no longer wishes to use stored embryos as previously agreed, after notice in a record of that person's intent to avoid conception to the other party and the clinic or storage facility, an intended parent may not transfer the embryos into the body of any woman with the intent to create a child. No agreement to the contrary will be enforceable." *See* Section 3(c), *id.* at 184–85. *See also* P. Kindregan, Jr. & Steven H. Snyder, *Clarifying the Law of ART: The New American Bar Association Model Act Governing Assisted Reproductive Technology*, 42 FAM. L.Q. 203 (2008).

6. *Regulation of Fertility Clinics.* A scandal at a fertility clinic at the University of California at Irvine illustrates the need for regulation. Three doctors were accused of taking embryos produced by couples for the couples' own procreation and implanting the embryos in other women who had been unsuccessful in producing healthy embryos. About 80 patients were involved and the genetic parentage of at least seven children was in question. Two of the doctors left the country. The third was indicted on mail fraud for allegedly falsely billing insurance companies through the mail, the only charge available in the absence of any more direct regulation of the process. The California legislature quickly enacted a statute making it a felony to transfer or implant human gametes without the informed written consent of both donor and recipient, and setting forth as possible penalties up to five years in prison and a fine no greater than $50,000 CAL. PENAL CODE § 367g (2009). More than 80 civil law suits were brought. *See* Miller, *Key Issue Absent on Eve of O.C. Fertility Trial Set to Open*, LOS ANGELES TIMES, Apr. 8, 1997, at A1. In 2002, a California court ruled that the request for paternity tests by a couple who believed that another couple receiving fertility treatments from the clinic were raising their now 14-year-old twins was properly denied. *Prato-Morrison v. Doe*, 126 Cal. Rptr. 2d 509 (Cal. App. 2002). Even if a genetic link could be proven, the court held, the child's best interest trumped any rights of the embryo's progenitors.

For discussion of the range of issues arguing for greater regulation of fertility clinics and service providers, see, *e.g.*, Ann Bindu Thomas, *Avoiding Embryos "R" Us: Toward a Regulated Fertility Industry*, 7 WASH. U. J.L. & POL'Y 247 (2008); June Carbone & Paige Gottheim, *Markets, Subsidies, Regulation and Trust: Building Ethical Understandings into the Market for Fertility Services*, 9 J. GENDER, RACE & JUST. 509 (2006); Student Author, *Guiding Regulatory Reform in Reproduction and Genetics*, 120 HARV. L. REV. 574 (2006).

TABLE OF CASES

[References are to pages.]

[References are to pages.]

[References are to pages.]

J

[References are to pages.]

K

[References are to pages.]

[References are to pages.]

M

[References are to pages.]

[References are to pages.]

N

O

P

[References are to pages.]

[References are to pages.]

[References are to pages.]

[References are to pages.]

[References are to pages.]

[References are to pages.]

E

[References are to pages.]

F

[References are to pages.]

[References are to pages.]

H

[References are to pages.]

I

[References are to pages.]

[References are to pages.]

[References are to pages.]

[References are to pages.]

INDEX

[References are to page numbers.]

[References are to page numbers.]

[References are to page numbers.]

[References are to page numbers.]

[References are to page numbers.]

[References are to page numbers.]